AMERICAN WRITERS

AMERICAN WRITERS

JAY PARINI
Editor

RETROSPECTIVE SUPPLEMENT III

CHARLES SCRIBNER'S SONS
A part of Gale, a Cengage Company

GALE
A Cengage Company

Farmington Hills, Mich • San Francisco • New York • Waterville, Maine
Meriden, Conn • Mason, Ohio • Chicago

GALE
A Cengage Company

American Writers Retrospective Supplement III

Editor in Chief: Jay Parini

Project Editor: Lisa Kumar

Permissions: Carissa Poweleit

Composition and Electronic Capture: Amy Darga

Manufacturing: Rita Wimberley

For product information and technology assistance, contact us at **Gale Customer Support, 1-800-877-4253.**
For permission to use material from this text or product, submit all requests online at **www.cengage.com/permissions**
Further permissions questions can be emailed to **permissionrequest@cengage.com**

LIBRARY OF CONGRESS CATALOGING-IN-PUBLICATION DATA

American writers: a collection of literary biographies / Leonard Unger editor in chief.
p. cm.
The 4-vol. main set consists of 97 of the pamphlets originally published as the University of Minnesota pamphlets on American writers; some have been rev. and updated. The supplements cover writers not included in the original series.
Supplement 2, has editor in chief, A. Walton Litz; Retrospective suppl. 1, c1998, was edited by A. Walton Litz & Molly Weigel; Suppl. 5–27 and Retrospective suppl. 2–3 have as editor in chief, Jay Parini.
Includes bibliographies and index.
Contents: v. 1. Henry Adams to T.S. Eliot — v. 2. Ralph Waldo Emerson to Carson McCullers — v. 3. Archibald MacLeish to George Santayana — v. 4. Isaac Bashevis Singer to Richard Wright — Supplement: 1, pt. 1. Jane Addams to Sidney Lanier. 1, pt. 2. Vachel Lindsay to Elinor Wylie. 2, pt. 1. W.H. Auden to O. Henry. 2, pt. 2. Robinson Jeffers to Yvor Winters. — 4, pt. 1. Maya Angelou to Linda Hogan. 4, pt. 2. Susan Howe to Gore Vidal — Suppl. 5. Russell Banks to Charles Wright — Suppl. 6. Don DeLillo to W.D. Snodgrass — Suppl. 7. Julia Alvarez to Tobias Wolff — Suppl. 8. T.C. Boyle to August Wilson.
ISBN 978-0-684-32550-7
1. American literature—History and criticism. 2. American literature—Bio-bibliography. 3. Authors, American—Biography. I. Unger, Leonard. II. Litz, A. Walton. III. Weigel, Molly. IV. Parini, Jay. V. University of Minnesota pamphlets on American writers.

PS129 .A55
810'.9

73-001759

ISBN-13: 978-0-684-32550-7

This title is also available as an e-book.
ISBN-13: 978-0-684-32551-4
Contact your Gale, A Cengage Company sales representative for ordering information.

Charles Scribner's Sons an imprint of Gale, A Cengage Company
27500 Drake Rd.
Farmington Hills, MI 48331-3535

Printed in Mexico
1 2 3 4 5 6 7 21 20 19 18 17

Acknowledgments

The editors wish to thank the copyright holders of the excerpted criticism included in this volume and the permissions managers of many book and magazine publishing companies for assisting us in securing reproduction rights. Following is a list of the copyright holders who have granted us permission to reproduce material in this volume of *American Writers.* Every effort has been made to trace copyright, but if omissions have been made, please let us know.

COPYRIGHTED EXCERPTS IN *AMERICAN WRITERS* RETROSPECTIVE SUPPLEMENT 3, WERE REPRODUCED FROM THE FOLLOWING SOURCES:

BRADSTREET, ANNE. "The Prologue," in *The Works of Anne Bradstreet,* edited by Jeannine Hensley, Belknap Press, 2010, pp. 15-17. Courtesy of Belknap Press. / "To My Dear and Loving Husband," in *The Works of Anne Bradstreet,* edited by Jeannine Hensley, Belknap Press, 2010, p. 245. Courtesy of Belknap Press. / "To Her Most Honoured Father," in *The Works of Anne Bradstreet,* edited by Jeannine Hensley, Belknap Press, 2010, p. 14. Courtesy of Belknap Press. / "The Four Elements," in *The Works of Anne Bradstreet,* edited by Jeannine Hensley, Belknap Press, 2010, pp. 18, 19, 23, 30, 31. Courtesy of Belknap Press. / "Of the Four Humours in Man's Constitution," in *The Works of Anne Bradstreet,* edited by Jeannine Hensley, Belknap Press, 2010, p. 35. Courtesy of Belknap Press. / "Of the Four Ages of Man," in *The Works of Anne Bradstreet,* edited by Jeannine Hensley, Belknap Press, 2010, pp. 54-55. Courtesy of Belknap Press. / "The Four Seasons," in *The Works of Anne Bradstreet,* edited by Jeannine Hensley, Belknap Press, 2010, p. 72. Courtesy of Belknap Press. / "Semiramis," in *The Works of Anne Bradstreet,* edited by Jeannine Hensley, Belknap Press, 2010, p. 81. Courtesy of Belknap Press. / "A Dialogue between Old England and New: Concerning Their Present Troubles, Anno, 1642," in *The Works of Anne Bradstreet,* edited by Jeannine Hensley, Belknap Press, 2010, pp. 191-200. Courtesy of Belknap Press. / "An Elegy Upon That Honorable and Renowned Knight Sir Philip Sidney, Who Was Untimely Slain at the Seige of Zutphen, Anno 1586," in *The Works of Anne Bradstreet,* edited by Jeannine Hensley, Belknap Press, 2010, pp. 201, 202, 204. Courtesy of Belknap Press. / "In Honour of Du Bartas, 1641," in *The Works of Anne Bradstreet,* edited by Jeannine Hensley, Belknap Press, 2010, pp. 205, 207, 208. Courtesy of Belknap Press. / "In Honour of That High and Mighty Princess queen Elizabeth of Happy Memory," in *The Works of Anne Bradstreet,* edited by Jeannine Hensley, Belknap Press, 2010, pp. 209, 212. Courtesy of Belknap Press. / "Contemplations," in *The Works of Anne Bradstreet,* edited by Jeannine Hensley, Belknap Press, 2010, pp. 220-230. Courtesy of Belknap Press. / "The Flesh and the Spirit," in *The Works of Anne Bradstreet,* edited by Jeannine Hensley, Belknap Press, 2010, pp. 231, 233, 234. Courtesy of

Belknap Press. / "The Vanity of All Worldly Things," in *The Works of Anne Bradstreet,* edited by Jeannine Hensley, Belknap Press, 2010, pp. 235, 237. Courtesy of Belknap Press. / "Here Follows Some Verses Upon the Burning of Our House July 10, 1666. Copied Out a a Loose Paper," in *The Works of Anne Bradstreet,* edited by Jeannine Hensley, Belknap Press, 2010, pp. 318-319. Courtesy of Belknap Press. / "An Epitaph on My Dear and Ever-Honoured Mother Mrs. Dorothy Dudley, Who Deceased December 27, 1643, and of Her Age, 61," in *The Works of Anne Bradstreet,* edited by Jeannine Hensley, Belknap Press, 2010, p. 219. Courtesy of Belknap Press. / "A Letter to Her Husband Absent Upon Public Employment," in *The Works of Anne Bradstreet,* edited by Jeannine Hensley, Belknap Press, 2010, pp. 246-247. Courtesy of Belknap Press. / "Another," in *The Works of Anne Bradstreet,* edited by Jeannine Hensley, Belknap Press, 2010, p. 248. Courtesy of Belknap Press. / "Another (different one)," in *The Works of Anne Bradstreet,* edited by Jeannine Hensley, Belknap Press, 2010, p. 251. Courtesy of Belknap Press. / "Upon a Fit of Sickness, Anno 1632 Aetatis Suae, 19," in *The Works of Anne Bradstreet,* edited by Jeannine Hensley, Belknap Press, 2010, p. 241. Courtesy of Belknap Press. / "Upon Some Distemper of Body," in *The Works of Anne Bradstreet,* edited by Jeannine Hensley, Belknap Press, 2010, p. 242. Courtesy of Belknap Press. / "In Memory of My Dear Grandchild Elizabeth Bradstreet, Who Deceased August, 1665, Being a Year and Half Old," in *The Works of Anne Bradstreet,* edited by Jeannine Hensley, Belknap Press, 2010, p. 257. Courtesy of Belknap Press. / "On My Dear Grandchild Simon Bradstreet, Who Dies on 16 November, 1669, Being but a Month, and One Day Old," in *The Works of Anne Bradstreet,* edited by Jeannine Hensley, Belknap Press, 2010, p. 259. Courtesy of Belknap Press. / "As Weary Pilgrim," in *The Works of Anne Bradstreet,* edited by Jeannine Hensley, Belknap Press, 2010, p. 322. Courtesy of Belknap Press. / John Woodridge, "To My Dear Sister, the Author of These Poems," in *The Works of Anne Bradstreet,* edited by Jeannine Hensley, Belknap Press, 2010, p. 5. Courtesy of Belknap Press.

CRANE, HART. "Indiana," in *The Complete Poems and Selected Letter and Prose of Hart Crane,* edited by Brom Weber, W.W. Norton & Company, 1966, p. 78. Courtesy of W.W. Norton & Company.

ELIOT, T.S. "East Coker," in *The Poems of T.S. Eliot Vol. I: Collected and Uncollected Poems,* edited by Christopher Ricks and Jim McCue, Johns Hopkins University Press, 2015, pp. 185, 188, 192. Courtesy of Johns Hopkins University Press. / "Preludes," in *The Poems of T.S. Eliot Vol. I: Collected and Uncollected Poems,* edited by Christopher Ricks and Jim McCue, Johns Hopkins University Press, 2015, pp. 15-17. Courtesy of Johns Hopkins University Press. / "Portrait of a Lady," in *The Poems of T.S. Eliot Vol. I: Collected and Uncollected Poems,* edited by Christopher Ricks and Jim McCue, Johns Hopkins University Press, 2015, p. 14. Courtesy of Johns Hopkins University Press. / "The Love Song of J. Alfred Prufrock," in *The Poems of T.S. Eliot Vol. I: Collected and Uncollected Poems,* edited by Christopher Ricks and Jim McCue, Johns Hopkins University Press, 2015, pp. 5, 6, 8, 9. Courtesy of Johns Hopkins University Press. / "The Fire Sermon," in *The Poems of T.S. Eliot Vol. I: Collected and Uncollected Poems,* edited by Christopher Ricks and Jim McCue, Johns Hopkins University Press, 2015, pp. 62, 66. Courtesy of Johns Hopkins University Press. / "What Thunder Said," in *The Poems of T.S. Eliot Vol. I: Collected and Uncollected Poems,* edited by Christopher Ricks and Jim McCue, Johns Hopkins University Press, 2015, pp. 69, 71. Courtesy of Johns Hopkins University Press. / "The Hollow Men," in *The Poems of T.S. Eliot Vol. I: Collected and Uncollected Poems,* edited by Christopher Ricks and Jim McCue, Johns Hopkins University Press, 2015, p. 82. Courtesy of Johns Hopkins University Press. / "Ash-Wednesday," in *The Poems of T.S. Eliot Vol. I: Collected and Uncollected Poems,* edited by Christopher Ricks and Jim McCue, Johns Hopkins University Press, 2015, pp. 87, 90, 94. Courtesy of Johns Hopkins University Press. / "Burnt Norton," in *The Poems of T.S. Eliot Vol. I: Collected and Uncollected Poems,* edited by Christopher Ricks and Jim McCue, Johns Hopkins University Press,

2015, pp. 179, 180, 181, 184, . Courtesy of Johns Hopkins University Press. / "The Dry Salvages," in *The Poems of T.S. Eliot Vol. I: Collected and Uncollected Poems,* edited by Christopher Ricks and Jim McCue, Johns Hopkins University Press, 2015, pp. 193, 197, 198, 200. Courtesy of Johns Hopkins University Press. / "Little Gidding," in *The Poems of T.S. Eliot Vol. I: Collected and Uncollected Poems,* edited by Christopher Ricks and Jim McCue, Johns Hopkins University Press, 2015, pp. 201, 202, 207, 208, 209. Courtesy of Johns Hopkins University Press.

FROST, ROBERT. "It Takes All Sorts," in *The Poetry of Robert Frost,* edited by Edward Connery Lathem, Henry Holt and Company, 1979, p. 470. Courtesy of Henry Holt and Company. / "The Trial by Exisitence," in *The Poetry of Robert Frost,* edited by Edward Connery Lathem, Henry Holt and Company, 1979, p. 21. Courtesy of Henry Holt and Company. / "The Tuft of Flowers," in *The Poetry of Robert Frost,* edited by Edward Connery Lathem, Henry Holt and Company, 1979, pp. 22-23. Courtesy of Henry Holt and Company. / "Into My Own," in *The Poetry of Robert Frost,* edited by Edward Connery Lathem, Henry Holt and Company, 1979, p. 5. Courtesy of Henry Holt and Company. / "The Pasture," in *The Poetry of Robert Frost,* edited by Edward Connery Lathem, Henry Holt and Company, 1979, p. 1. Courtesy of Henry Holt and Company. / "After Apple-Picking," in *The Poetry of Robert Frost,* edited by Edward Connery Lathem, Henry Holt and Company, 1979, p. 68. Courtesy of Henry Holt and Company. / "Death of a Hired Man," in *The Poetry of Robert Frost,* edited by Edward Connery Lathem, Henry Holt and Company, 1979, p. 38. Courtesy of Henry Holt and Company. / "Mending Wall," in *The Poetry of Robert Frost,* edited by Edward Connery Lathem, Henry Holt and Company, 1979, p. 33. Courtesy of Henry Holt and Company. / "The Road Not Taken," in *The Poetry of Robert Frost,* edited by Edward Connery Lathem, Henry Holt and Company, 1979, p. 105. Courtesy of Henry Holt and Company. / "The Bonfire," in *The Poetry of Robert Frost,* edited by Edward Connery Lathem, Henry Holt and Company, 1979, p. 133. Courtesy of Henry Holt and Company. / "Birches," in *The Poetry of Robert Frost,* edited by Edward Connery Lathem, Henry Holt and Company, 1979, p. 121. Courtesy of Henry Holt and Company. / "New Hampshire," in *The Poetry of Robert Frost,* edited by Edward Connery Lathem, Henry Holt and Company, 1979, pp. 161, 172. Courtesy of Henry Holt and Company.

MELVILLE, HERMAN. "Venice," in *Published Poems,* edited by Robert C. Ryan, Harrison Hayford, Alma MacDougall Reising and G. Thomas Tanselle, Northwestern University Press, 2009, p. 291. Courtesy of Northwestern University Press.

POE, EDGAR ALLEN. "The Haunted Palace," in *Collected Works,* edited by Thomas Ollive Mabbott, Belknap Press, 1969, p. 407. Courtesy of Belknap Press. / "The Lake," in *Collected Works,* edited by Thomas Ollive Mabbott, Belknap Press, 1969, p. 85. Courtesy of Belknap Press. / "Sonnet–To Science," in *Collected Works,* edited by Thomas Ollive Mabbott, Belknap Press, 1969, p. 91. Courtesy of Belknap Press. / "The Sleeper," in *Collected Works,* edited by Thomas Ollive Mabbott, Belknap Press, 1969, p. 188. Courtesy of Belknap Press. / "To Helen," in *Collected Works,* edited by Thomas Ollive Mabbott, Belknap Press, 1969, pp. 164, 166. Courtesy of Belknap Press. / "The Raven," in *Collected Works,* edited by Thomas Ollive Mabbott, Belknap Press, 1969, pp. 365-369. Courtesy of Belknap Press.

RICH, ADRIENNE. "The Knight," in *Collected Poems: 1950-2012,* W.W. Norton & Company, 2016, p. 112. Courtesy of W.W. Norton & Company. / "Orion," in *Collected Poems: 1950-2012,* W.W. Norton & Company, 2016, p. 231. Courtesy of W.W. Norton & Company. / "The Burning of Paper Instead of Children," in *Collected Poems: 1950-2012,* W.W. Norton & Company, 2016, p. 306. Courtesy of W.W. Norton & Company. / "The Blue Ghazals," in *Collected Poems: 1950-2012,* W.W. Norton & Company, 2016, p. 312. Courtesy of W.W. Norton & Company. / "The Will to Change," in

Collected Poems: 1950-2012, W.W. Norton & Company, 2016, p. 330. Courtesy of W.W. Norton & Company. / "Incipience," in *Collected Poems: 1950-2012,* W.W. Norton & Company, 2016, p. 362. Courtesy of W.W. Norton & Company. / "The Stranger," in *Collected Poems: 1950-2012,* W.W. Norton & Company, 2016, p. 368. Courtesy of W.W. Norton & Company. / "Trying to Talk With a Man," in *Collected Poems: 1950-2012,* W.W. Norton & Company, 2016, p. 355. Courtesy of W.W. Norton & Company. / "Love Poem XIII," in *Collected Poems: 1950-2012,* W.W. Norton & Company, 2016, p. 471. Courtesy of W.W. Norton & Company. / "Love Poem VI," in *Collected Poems: 1950-2012,* W.W. Norton & Company, 2016, p. 468. Courtesy of W.W. Norton & Company. / "Integrity," in *Collected Poems: 1950-2012,* W.W. Norton & Company, 2016, pp. 523-24. Courtesy of W.W. Norton & Company. / "Culture and Anarchy," in *Collected Poems: 1950-2012,* W.W. Norton & Company, 2016, p. 530. Courtesy of W.W. Norton & Company. / "Delta," in *Collected Poems: 1950-2012,* W.W. Norton & Company, 2016, p. 683. Courtesy of W.W. Norton & Company. / "Terza Rima," in *Collected Poems: 1950-2012,* W.W. Norton & Company, 2016, p. 878. Courtesy of W.W. Norton & Company. / "Powers of Recouperation," in *Collected Poems: 1950-2012,* W.W. Norton & Company, 2016, pp. 1095, 1099. Courtesy of W.W. Norton & Company.

WHITMAN, WALT. "Song of Myself," in *Complete Poetry and Selected Prose,* edited by James E. Miller, Houghton Mifflin Harcourt, 1959, pp. 44, 68. Courtesy of Houghton Mifflin Harcourt. / "That Music Always Round Me," in *Complete Poetry and Selected Prose,* edited by James E. Miller, Houghton Mifflin Harcourt, 1959, p. 313. Courtesy of Houghton Mifflin Harcourt. / "There Was A Child Went Forth," in *Complete Poetry and Selected Prose,* edited by James E. Miller, Houghton Mifflin Harcourt, 1959, pp. 258, 259. Courtesy of Houghton Mifflin Harcourt. / "Out of the Cradle Endlessly Rocking," in *Complete Poetry and Selected Prose,* edited by James E. Miller, Houghton Mifflin Harcourt, 1959, pp. 182, 183, 180, 181, 184. Courtesy of Houghton Mifflin Harcourt. / "Crossing Brooklyn Ferry," in *Complete Poetry and Selected Prose,* edited by James E. Miller, Houghton Mifflin Harcourt, 1959, pp. 116-120. Courtesy of Houghton Mifflin Harcourt.

WILSON, AUGUST. "The Play ," in *Ma Rainey's Black Bottom,* New American Library, 1985, p. vxvi. Courtesy of New American Library.

List of Subjects

Introduction *xi*

List of Contributors *xiii*

ANNE BRADSTREET 1
Sarah Gilbreath Ford

WILLA CATHER 17
Joshua Grasso

HART CRANE 41
Neil W. Browne

T. S. ELIOT 57
Julia E. Daniel

WILLIAM FAULKNER 73
Patrick A. Smith

ROBERT FROST 91
Jonathan N. Barron

NATHANIEL HAWTHORNE 109
Nancy L. Bunge

ZORA NEALE HURSTON 125
Windy Counsell Petrie

HERMAN MELVILLE 147
Nicholas Spengler

ARTHUR MILLER 165
Philip Parry

TONI MORRISON 183
Tracie Church Guzzio

FLANNERY O'CONNOR 207
Laurie Champion

EDGAR ALLAN POE 223
Jonas Prida

ADRIENNE RICH 241
Brett C. Millier

MARK TWAIN 255
Joe B. Fulton

EDITH WHARTON 275
Kathleen Pfeiffer

WALT WHITMAN 295
Joseph Dewey

AUGUST WILSON 313
L. Bailey McDaniel

Cumulative Index *331*

Introduction

F. Scott Fitzgerald, author of *The Great Gatsby* and other major works of fiction, once mused with a touch of cynicism: "A classic is a successful book that has survived the reaction of the next period or generation." If one thinks about *Gatsy*: here is a book that nearly vanished, almost lost in its own liftetime, selling few copies; but succcessive generations of readers found glory and pathos in its pages, as well as exquisitely beautiful prose, and the novel has become "a classic," a work that survives from era to era, and which lives on any important shelf of American literature. It's a book that young people "find" again and again, and it changes their view of the world. It's a book for re-reading, and one that keeps shifting as we grow older.

In this supplement of *American Writers,* we circle back to some of the key figures in our literature, writers who have drawn the interest of generation after generation of readers and attracted the attention of countless critics. We've already discussed their work in these pages; yet their work is so important that no single take is sufficient, as fresh scholarship alters our view of the work, if not the life. There are always fresh angles, deeper contexts, to consider. When Ezra Pound defined literature as "news that stays news," he was thinking of the writing of these writers, who had their fingers on the pulse of their own times, of course, but who also had an awareness of eternal truths, truths that do not fade as the decades fall.

This series began with a sequence of critical and biographical monographs that were published between 1959 and 1972. *The Minnesota Pamphlets on American Writers* were incisively written and informative, treating ninety-seven American writers in a format and style that found a devoted following of readers over the years. The series proved useful and informative to a generation of students and teachers, who could depend on these reliable, thoughtful, often incisive critiques of major figures. The idea of reprinting these essays occurred to Charles Scribner, Jr. (1921-1995), the well-known publisher. The series appeared in four volumes titled *American Writers: A Collection of Literary Biographies* (1974).

Since then, numerous supplements have appeared, treating well over four hundred American writers in any number of genres. The idea has been consistent with the original series: to provide clear, informative essays aimed at the general reader, which includes students in high school and college. As anyone looking through this volume will notice, these essays often rise to a high level of craft and critical vision, yet they aim to introduce a writer of note in the history of American literature, offering a sense of the scope and nature of the career under review. The relevant biographical and historical backgrounds are also provided, thus placing the work itself in a living context.

In this volume, we return to six of our finest poets: Anne Bradstreet, Walt Whitman, Hart Crane, T. S. Eliot, Robert Frost, and Adrienne Rich. Their work has defined the genre of American poetry, and these fresh articles reexamine their major works and consider this timeless poetry in the context of their lives and eras. The same is true of the articles here on nine major writers of fiction. We look at the work of several classic authors of the nineteenth century, Herman Melville, Nathaniel Hawthorne, Edgar Allan Poe, and Mark Twain, the latter perhaps the most widely known and beloved author of all time. We examine the work of early modernist writers Edith Wharton, Willa Cather, William Faulkner and (from the next generation) Flannery O'Connor. We also dig into the novels of our most celebrated living author, Toni Morrison, who won the Nobel Prize for Literature in 1993. Zora Neale Hurston, a novelist, short story writer, and anthopologist seems in a category by herself, a classic author perhaps best known for *Their Eyes Were Watching God* (1937), which compels generation after generation of readers. Among our playwrights, we take on two of our most produced and widely admired authors: Arthur Miller and August Wilson.

As noted above, every effort has been made to locate these authors in time and place: writing always emerges from a particular context, and this is deeply true of the authors at hand in this volume. But their work survives the time of its making, and speaks to further generations, continuing to inspire, terrify, encourage, and inform readers over the decades. Our hope is that this retrospective sequence of articles performs a valuable service by offering substantial reflections on eighteen classic writers who have had a significant impact on our culture.

—Jay Parini

Contributors

Jonathan N. Barron. Jonathan N. Barron is Professor of English at the University of Southern Mississippi. He is Director of the Robert Frost Society and editor of *The Robert Frost Review.* His scholarship on Robert Frost includes the book *How Robert Frost Made Realism Matter* (University of Missouri 2016). ROBERT FROST

Neil W. Browne. Neil W. Browne is an Associate Professor of English at Oregon State University Cascades, where he teaches in and directs the American Studies program. He is the author of *The World in Which We Occur: John Dewey, Pragmatist Ecology, and American Ecological Writing in the Twentieth Century.* His research and writing interests are in pragmatism, American literature, and the environmental humanities. Browne's work for Scribner's *Writers* series includes essays on Margaret Laurence, Robert Kroetsch, John Haines, Rachel Carson, and Isabella Bird. HART CRANE

Nancy L. Bunge. Nancy L. Bunge is the author of five books, including *Nathaniel Hawthorne: A Study of the Short Fiction.* Her most recent book is *The Midwestern Novel: Literary Populism from Huckleberry Finn to the Present.* A professor at Michigan State University, she has also taught as a Senior Fulbright Lecturer at the University of Vienna, the Free University of Brussels, the University of Ghent and the University of Siegen. NATHANIEL HAWTHORNE

Laurie Champion. A native Texan, Laurie Champion currently lives in San Diego, where she is Professor of English at San Diego State University. She has edited or co-edited ten books, including *Texas 5 X 5: Twenty-Five Stories by Five Texas Writers, Texas Told'em: Gambling Stories, American Women Writers, 1900-1945: A Bio-Bibliographical Critical Sourcebook, Texas Short Stories II,* and *Contemporary American Women Fiction Writers: An A-to-Z Guide.* Additionally, she has published numerous scholarly essays and short stories in distinguished magazines, literary journals, and anthologies. FLANNERY O'CONNOR

Julia E. Daniel. Julia E. Daniel is an Assistant Professor of modern American poetry at Baylor University. Her research interests include modern poetry and drama, urban studies, and environmental humanities. She has published on the role of urbanism in modernist literature, popular culture in *The Waste Land,* sonic depictions of traffic in American poetry, and T. S. Eliot's verse drama, *Sweeney Agonistes.* T. S. ELIOT

Joseph Dewey. Joseph Dewey, Professor of Literature and Composition at Broward College, has published eight books on American literature and culture, including *In a Dark Time: The Apocalyptic Temper in American Literature of the Nuclear Age, Beyond Grief and Loneliness: A Reading of the Don Delillo,* and *Understanding Michael Chabon.* WALT WHITMAN

Sarah Gilbreath Ford. Sarah Gilbreath Ford is Professor of American Literature at Baylor University, where she teaches early American literature, African American literature, and literature of the American South. She is author of *Tracing Southern Storytelling in Black and White,* published in 2014 by the University of Alabama Press. She has also published articles on Eudora Welty, Zora Neale Hurston, Sarah Pogson, and Ebenezer Cook. ANNE BRADSTREET

Joe B. Fulton. Joe B. Fulton is Professor of English at Baylor University in Waco, Texas, where he has been honored as a Baylor University Class of 1945 Centennial Professor. He has published five books on Mark Twain, most recently *Mark Twain Under Fire: Reception and Reputation, Criticism and Controversy, 1851-2015* (Camden House 2016). MARK TWAIN

Joshua Grasso. Joshua Grasso is an Associate Professor of English at East Central University (OK). He has a Ph.D. in English from Miami University specializing in the long eighteenth century. He has published articles on wide variety of eighteenth-century authors and topics, most recently in MLA's *Approaches to Teaching the Novels of Henry Fielding* (2016). His current research focuses on depictions of music and art in eighteenth-century century novels. WILLA CATHER

Tracie Church Guzzio. Tracie Church Guzzio is Professor of English at the State University of New York at Plattsburgh. She is the author of *All Stories Are True: History, Memory, and Trauma in the Work of John Edgar Wideman,* as well as several other short articles on African-American literature. TONI MORRISON

L. Bailey McDaniel. L. Bailey McDaniel is an Associate Professor of English at Oakland University, where she teaches undergraduate and graduate courses on U.S. and postcolonial drama, race and gender, and ethnic American fiction. She has published works on Tennessee Williams, Arthur Miller, Cherríe Moraga, and David Henry Hwang. Her latest book, *(Re)Constructing Maternal Performance in Twentieth-Century American Drama,* published by Palgrave Macmillan, explores racially-informed constructs of motherhood as they emerge in U.S. drama. She is the recipient of the 2014 Oakland University Educator of the Year award. AUGUST WILSON

Brett Millier. Brett Millier is the Reginald L. Cook Professor of American Literature at Middlebury College. She is the author of *Elizabeth Bishop: Life and the Memory of It,* and *Flawed Light: American Women Poets and Alcohol.* She is associate editor of *The Columbia History of American Poetry,* and co-editor of *Adrienne Rich: Poetry and Prose,* forthcoming from W.W. Norton in 2017. ADRIENNE RICH

Philip Parry. Philip Parry has recently retired from the University of St. Andrews in Scotland, where for forty years he specialised in the teaching of drama, in particular Shakespeare and twentieth-century British and American theater history. ARTHUR MILLER

Windy Counsell Petrie. Windy Counsell Petrie, Ph.D., received her B.A. in English from Pepperdine University, and her M.A. and Ph.D. from the University of Delaware. Her areas of specialization include literary autobiography, transatlantic authorship and readership in the long nineteenth century, the representation of faith in eighteenth-century and Victorian novels, and late nineteenth- and early twentieth-century female kunstlerroman. In 2006, she was selected as a Fulbright Scholar to Lithuania, where she lectured on tropes of exile in nineteenth- and twentieth-century novels, as well as on the roles of women and minorities in American literary history. She has published essays and reviews in *a/b: Autobiography Studies, Christianity and Literature, Literatura, American Writers* and *American Writers Retrospective* series and in the collections *American Writers in Europe* (Palgrave Macmillan), and *Postmodernism and Beyond* (Cambridge Scholars Press). Her book manuscript, *Professions of Authorship: American Women's Literary Autobiography in the 1930s,* is nearing completion. ZORA NEALE HURSTON

Kathleen Pfeiffer. Kathleen Pfeiffer, Ph.D., is professor of English at Oakland University in Rochester, Michigan. Her books include *Brother Mine: The Correspondence of Jean Toomer and Waldo Frank* (2010) and *Race Passing and American Individualism* (2003). She has edited and written the introductions to the re-issues of two Harlem Renaissance novels, Carl Van Vechten's *Nigger Heaven* (2000) and Waldo Frank's *Holiday* (2003). In 2012, she was awarded the Kresge Artist Fellowship in Literary Arts. EDITH WHARTON

Jonas Prida. Jonas Prida received his Ph.D. in English from Tulane University in 2006. He is an Associate Professor of English and interim Vice President for Academic Affairs at the College of St. Joseph, located in Rutland, VT. He has published on *Weird Tales* contributors H. P. Lovecraft and Robert Howard, as well as antebellum American author George Lippard. In addition to his work on *Weird Tales,* he has explored literary modernism in 1920s pulp fiction, as well as in *Conan the Barbarian.* EDGAR ALLAN POE

Patrick Smith. Patrick A. Smith is Professor of English at Bainbridge State College in Bainbridge, Georgia. His books include *Conversations with Tim O'Brien, Tim O'Brien: A Critical Companion,* and *"The true bones of my life": Essays on the Fiction of Jim Harrison.* Smith has been a frequent contributor to the *American* and *British Writers* Supplements since 2001. WILLIAM FAULKNER

Nicholas Spengler. Nicholas Spengler is a Ph.D. candidate in English Literature at the University of Edinburgh. His doctoral dissertation interprets Herman Melville's representation of Spanish America in the context of nineteenth-century hemispheric American politics and through the discourses of sympathy and natural law. He is the recipient of a Wolfson Foundation Postgraduate Scholarship in the Humanities. HERMAN MELVILLE

ANNE BRADSTREET

(1612—1672)

Sarah Gilbreath Ford

ANNE BRADSTREET WAS the first English poet in the New World. She immigrated to Massachusetts with fellow Puritans in 1630 and had her first collection of poetry, *The Tenth Muse,* published in 1650. Her poetry ranges from public topics conventional for her time, such as "The Four Ages of Man," to intimate portraits of her life as wife and mother. These works give a modern reader views of life in the seventeenth century, the world of Puritan New England, and the experience of a woman living on the frontier. Three and a half centuries later, her work is still being read and discussed. In 1997 as part of a "Celebration of Women at Harvard College," Harvard dedicated a gate to Anne Bradstreet. Not only was Bradstreet the poet being recognized for her work, Bradstreet the woman was in a sense returning home, as she and her family had lived on the land that later became Harvard Square. The gate has a plaque bearing her words: "I came into this country, where I found a new world and new manners at which my heart rose." That Bradstreet's heart originally "rose" in resistance to the prospect of living in the New World is not surprising, given that the Massachusetts colony was a barely settled community a long ocean's voyage away from the life she knew growing up in England. Anne Bradstreet, however, eventually made the colony her home and turned the hardship of living in America into poetry.

Her poems about her life and surroundings give readers insight into Puritan society. Through her poetry, she expresses her worry when her husband is away on business, her anxiety about the possibility of dying during childbirth, her distress at being ill for long periods of time, and her grief at the loss of grandchildren. These very human reactions to life's difficulties are then answered by Bradstreet's faith in a God that has a hand in every detail of daily earthly existence. In essence her poetry is a primer for how faith worked for Puritans. Bradstreet also exhibits the challenge Puritans faced of living an earthly, material existence while trying to keep focus on a heavenly outcome. This conversation between "flesh and spirit," as Bradstreet categorizes it in one poem, led the critic Ann Stanford to label her "worldly" in her book *Anne Bradstreet: The Worldly Puritan.* As a Puritan, Bradstreet sees that worldliness as a fault and chides herself for it. Even when her house with all of her belongings is destroyed in a fire, she is concerned that her feelings of loss constitute vanity. This struggle between earth and heaven is at the heart of many of her poems.

Her poetry also shows us how a woman in her time period negotiated her gender role; in fact most of the criticism written on Bradstreet since the 1960s has focused on gender, as Bradstreet's dual positions as female Puritan and female poet elicit interesting tensions and conjectures. Bradstreet was certainly aware that women in her day were not supposed to be poets, and in the poem titled "The Prologue," she announces,

> I am obnoxious to each carping tongue
> Who says my hand a needle better fits
> A poet's pen all scorn I should thus wrong,
> For such despite they cast on female wits....
>
> (p. 16)

Although she softens her harangue a bit by admitting "men can do best," she still insists on women's ability to write poetry: "Yet grant some small acknowledgement of ours" (p. 16). That "small acknowledgement" has become much larger with time. The prominent modern American poet Adrienne Rich says of Bradstreet: "To have written poems, the first good poems in America, while rearing eight children, lying frequently sick, keeping house at the edge of wilderness, was to have managed a poet's range and extension within confines as severe as any American poet has confronted" (p. xx). The range Bradstreet imagines she managed is rather small. At the end of "The Prologue," Bradstreet asks for a "thyme or parsley wreath" (p. 17). She does not ask for the bay wreath of a true classical poet, but something more domestic and better suited to a Puritan mother. Writing poetry was perhaps initially Bradstreet's way in a strange land to keep connected to the culture of her previous home, but those "good poems" ended up forging her identity in the New World both as "the tenth muse" and as America's first poet.

LIFE

Anne Dudley Bradstreet was born in England in 1612 to Thomas and Dorothy Yorke Dudley. Little is known of Bradstreet's mother, other than the short elegy Bradstreet penned upon her death, depicting her mother clearly if succinctly as a loving and pious Christian woman. Her father, however, was a large force both in her life and in Massachusetts politics, becoming the colony's second governor after John Winthrop. His influence on Bradstreet is evident in the three extant poems she wrote to him: a dedication of her original collection of poetry to him, an elegy upon his death, and the poem "To Her Father with Some Verses" that uses her debt to him as an extended metaphor. In England, Thomas Dudley served as steward to the earl of Lincoln, which allowed Bradstreet to spend her childhood at the earl's estates. Both Dudley and the earl of Lincoln were Nonconformists, and Bradstreet grew up surrounded by fervent Puritans. She explains in a letter written late in life to her children that she began around the age of six to feel guilty about sinful behavior and would often turn to scripture as comfort. At age sixteen Bradstreet was infected with smallpox, leading to a confession where she "besought the Lord and confessed my pride and vanity" (p. 263). Following her illness, she married Simon Bradstreet, her father's assistant and a Cambridge graduate who also eventually became a powerful figure in New England, serving as a governor as well.

In 1630, two years after her marriage, Bradstreet's family immigrated to Massachusetts on the *Arbella* with a group of Puritans led by John Winthrop. This small community of pilgrims envisioned themselves on a great mission to establish a church in the New World glorious enough to influence and reform the Church of England. Winthrop's sermon "A Model of Christian Charity," delivered either just before the group sailed or while on their journey, details both the promises and pitfalls of their covenant with God to complete this mission. If they succeed, he says, they will be a "city on a hill" with the "eyes of all people" on their deeds, but if they fail, the "Lord will surely break out in wrath against [them]" in what Winthrop describes as a "shipwreck" (pp. 157, 158). This frightening description surely made an impact on Bradstreet and her fellow passengers, whose journey on a crowded ship for more than nine weeks entailed difficult living conditions, seasickness, and scurvy. That Bradstreet did not forget the hardships of the sea voyage is evident in her use of the image of a ship tossed at sea to describe an illness in her poem "Upon Some Distemper of Body" and in the two poems written later in life expressing great anxiety about the safety of her husband and son when they each needed to travel to England. When Winthrop's group arrived in America, the Salem that greeted them was an overcrowded settlement with primitive buildings and scarce provisions. It is little wonder that Bradstreet's reaction to the migration was dismay, so that her "heart rose" (p. 163).

After this challenging beginning, Anne Bradstreet and her husband established their life in America, eventually settling in Andover, Massachusetts. Her "great grief" early in the marriage was her desire for children, which, she explains, "cost me many prayers and tears," but after five years Bradstreet's son Samuel was born, followed by seven more children (p. 264). That she survived eight births was fortunate in a time when many women died in childbirth, and her poem "Before the Birth of One of Her Children," which imagines that her death might be imminent, expresses her understandable fear. Her glory in her children and her enjoyment of her role as mother is abundantly clear in her poem "In Reference to Her Children, 23 June 1659," in which she depicts the children as eight birds who had hatched in her nest and herself as loving caretaker, teaching them to fly but sorry to see them go. The image of her marriage in her poetry is likewise positive. No fewer than nine poems are devoted to Simon Bradstreet. Several of these poems express her anxiety when he is away. In one poem she even gets a bit competitive: "If ever wife was happy in a man / Compare with me, ye women, if you can" (p. 245). These glimpses into Bradstreet's happy domestic life are tempered by several poems written while she was ill, as she seems to have had reoccurring bouts of sickness, and the poignant poems on the deaths of three grandchildren and a daughter-in-law.

Establishing a household in what was basically still a wilderness, albeit a "city on a hill," and raising eight children surely kept Anne Bradstreet more than occupied. But somehow in the midst of all that she had to do, she wrote poetry. Writing poems was certainly not unusual for a Puritan. The Puritans valued literacy and were interested in writing for edification if not solely for entertainment. It was, however, unusual for women to write poetry, both in Puritan circles and in English culture (at least as far as we know by what is left in the written record). Important colonial men such as Roger Williams, Will Bradford, John Cotton, and Cotton Mather all wrote poetry (Walker, p. 257). The other well-known Puritan poet from the seventeenth century, Edward Taylor, left behind poetry that shows the usefulness of poetic verse as "meditations" on scripture and life in general, an outlet Bradstreet certainly shared in her more personal poems. Bradstreet also had family members who at least dabbled in poetry. Her sister Mercy wrote a poem to Bradstreet about her book; Bradstreet's son wrote poems for an almanac; and her father wrote three poems that we are aware of, including one, "On the Four Parts of the World," that inspired the quaternions in Bradstreet's work (Hensley, p. xxvi).

Thus models existed for Bradstreet's poetic occupations, but many men in her time were openly hostile to women writing. Even John Winthrop expressed his doubts in his notations in his journal about another literary Puritan, Anne Yale Hopkins. Hopkins was apparently exhibiting signs of a mental disorder, which Winthrop attributed to her "giving herself wholly to reading and writing," activities "proper for men, whose minds are stronger" (quoted in Stanford 1983, p. 77). The anxiety that Bradstreet may be overstepping in adopting the role of the poet is evident in the "Epistle to the Reader" written by her brother-in-law John Woodbridge and prefacing the first edition of her poetry. Woodridge is adamant that Bradstreet is "honoured, and esteemed where she lives, for her gracious demeanour, her eminent parts, her pious conversation; her courteous disposition, her exact diligence in her place, and discrete managing of her family occasions," and he assures the reader the time for poetry writing was not taken from her motherly duties but was "curtailed from her sleep" (p. 2). Like the mother she depicts in her elegy, Bradstreet is a pious Christian woman.

Her ability, then, to be both a poet and a woman worthy of existing in the Puritan model community was a careful balancing act, which was made possible in part by that force of a father who allowed and perhaps even encouraged her good education. Anne Bradstreet's breadth of reading and knowledge was remarkable for her time. Bradstreet's biographer Elizabeth Wade White argues that "among the few English women writers before her none displayed so encyclopaedic a mind" (p. 60). Bradstreet probably had at her disposal in her youth the library of the earl of Lincoln and certainly later her father's extensive library. When Anne and Simon Bradstreet's own house burned in 1666, they reportedly lost eight hundred books, showing that Bradstreet and her husband not only flourished in America but had invested in a large library of their own. What Bradstreet read is reflected in her poetry. Her elegies to Sir Philip Sidney and Guillaume de Salluste Du Bartas, a French poet read widely in translation in seventeenth-century England, highlights their influence. Her work "The Four Monarchies" also shows the specific influence of Sir Walter Raleigh's *History of the World* (1614). And throughout all of her poems, she uses classical references that reflect her broad education.

Even with poetic influences and scholarly encouragement in her life, all indications are that Bradstreet wrote her poetry initially for herself and a small group of family and friends. It was common to circulate writing, such as letters and personal narratives, among intimates, but women did not usually publish their work for wider public consumption. The key event, then, in the literary biography of Anne Bradstreet and the reason centuries of readers have had access to her poetry was one out of her control and apparently even without her foreknowledge. Bradstreet had at some point prepared a collection of poems as a gift to her father with a dedicatory poem apologizing for their "ragged lines" and urging him to "Accept my best, my worst vouchsafe a grave" (p. 14). Bradstreet's brother-in-law John Woodbridge took this manuscript with him to England and had it published in 1650 as *The Tenth Muse Lately Sprung Up in America; or, Severall Poems, compiled with great variety of Wit and Learning, full of delight.* He claims in the preface that he is putting forth the poems without the author's knowledge and "contrary to her expectation" in order to "pleasure those that earnestly desired the view of the whole" of her poetic works (p. 2). That Woodbridge was in collusion with others is evident in the prefatory poems written by Woodbridge, Nathaniel Ward (who had published *The Simple Cobbler of Agawam* in 1647), and several other friends. In his poem Woodbridge anticipates Bradstreet's reaction: "If you shall think it will be to your shame / To be in print, then I must bear the blame" (p. 5). Here, however, Woodbridge is assuming Bradstreet's female modesty. Bradstreet did indeed express embarrassment but not because of her gender. Her poem "The Author to Her Book" suggests that the book, as a child with "blemishes," was not ready to be sent out into the world dressed in "homespun" (pp. 238, 239). How much of this demurral is candor and how much convention is anyone's guess. Bradstreet, however, did then edit the poems and add others including "The Author to Her Book" in preparation for a second edition, which was published six years after her death. This work suggests that she did not mind so much the publication of her poetry, but simply wanted to put her best efforts forward.

The Tenth Muse was popular in its time, and later Cotton Mather would praise Bradstreet in his *Magnalia Christi Americana* (1702), a work detailing the religious history of New England, by putting her in the company of the mathematician and philosopher Hipatia of Alexandria, the Renaissance polymath Margherita Sarrocchi, the Byzantine empress Eudocia, and other learned women in history. Bradstreet died in 1672 at the age of sixty, certainly unaware of the poetic legacy she had left behind. Her legacy as a mother, though, was surely evident, as her eight children had more than fifty children of their own.

THE TENTH MUSE: *"FOUR TIMES FOUR"*

The contents of the original 1650 edition of *The Tenth Muse* consisted of Woodbridge's preface, the poems by "friends" attesting to Bradstreet's ability, and thirteen of Bradstreet's poems. These include the dedication to her father; "The Prologue"; her "four times four" poems, which are four poems on the four elements, humors, ages of man, and seasons; a long historical poem titled "The Four Monarchies"; a poem on contemporary political troubles titled "A Dialogue Between Old England and New"; elegies to Sidney, Du Bartas, and Queen Elizabeth I; and two poems that speak to her Puritan background, "David's Lamentation for Saul and Jonathan" and "Of the Vanity of All Worldly Creatures." The poetry in this first edition is imitative and conventional, written almost entirely in heroic couplets. Most critics see these poems as ambitious but less appealing than Bradstreet's later, personal poems. Since the 1980s, however, critics have mined the public poems to find evidence of Bradstreet's feminism and the seeds of her particular interests, such as negotiating the balance between earthly concerns and faith. Though conventional, Bradstreet's poetry in this volume clearly shows off her vast education. In addition to Raleigh and Du Bartas, Bradstreet notes the British physician Helkiah Crooke as a source for the descriptions of physiology in "The Four Humours." Bradstreet's classical allusions, which are far more frequent than her biblical ones, speak to her reading and background. When, for example, she wants to defend her ability to write poetry in "The Prologue," she refers to the Greeks, who made their nine muses female. That her brother-in-law designated her, then, as the "tenth muse" situates the text within a particular context and audience: educated Englishmen. Even though Bradstreet probably did not imagine her poetry would end up being published and read by an English audience, the poems are nevertheless pitched for their current tastes and literary level.

"The Prologue," the opening poem, performs the conventional function of an apology to the reader for any deficits in the work to follow, showing a stance of humility on the part of the author. Bradstreet, however, offers both the standard apology and a defense of a woman writing in a man's genre. From the outset, then, she negotiates a very clever compromise between herself and her audience and begins by seemingly limiting her audience's expectations:

To sing of wars, of captains, and of kings,
Of cities founded, commonwealths begun,
For my mean pen are too superior things....

(p. 15)

Ironically, she will later discuss these very things in her long poem on the four monarchies of the world. After stanzas claiming that she cannot write as well as Du Bartas, that her muse is "foolish, broken, blemished," and that her "wounded brain admits no cure," she then transitions to complain about the "carping tongues" who do not acknowledge that women can write poetry (pp. 15–16). Some critics see this fifth stanza as a shift in the poem from appeasing her audience to critiquing them, while others see her employing an ironic tone throughout. Jane Donahue Eberwein argues that we should read the poem as "an argument: an attempt to articulate and reconcile opposition by emphasizing discrepancies while hinting at unity" (p. 219). Bradstreet attempts this reconciliation with those "carping tongues" by appealing to classical authority: the Greeks and those nine female muses. But in case this authority does not suffice, she then seems to cede the argument in stanza 7:

Men have precedency and still excel,
It is but vain unjustly to wage war;
Men can do best, and women know it well.

(p. 17)

The subtle irony in the last word "well" here suggests how much the tongues have to "carp" to keep the superiority in place. Bradstreet ends with the unity that Eberwein describes, as she asks the "high flown quills that soar the skies" to "give thyme or parsley wreath" to her attempts. She is then able to appeal to their vanity in a turn of mock humility: "This mean and unrefined ore of mine / Will make your glist'ring gold but more to shine" (p. 17).

"The Prologue" is followed by Bradstreet's poems on the four elements, humors, ages of man, and seasons. Although much of this poetry is simply reiterating the order of the world as seen by seventeenth-century society, Bradstreet chooses a dramatic approach for doing so, in writing the first two poems as dialogues between sisters who play the various parts, such as "Fire" and "Blood." The different aspects in each examination thus are contrasted as each sister tries to outdo the others, either by boasting of her own importance or by criticizing the others. Bradstreet herself was the eldest of five sisters, so surely some of her own experience finds its way into the personifications. Although this dialogue form does not originate with Bradstreet, it is useful to her in these poems because it allows her to draw on the power of oratory as each sister takes the stage and presents her case to the reader, and it allows her to insert human reactions, such as humor or anger. She will return to the dialogue between sisters in later poetry as well, suggesting that the early poems that rely heavily on other sources prepared her for the later, more personal poems.

The opening poem is "The Four Elements," which begins with the sisters arguing over who should speak first, an argument that is dramatized by their various aspects:

> the quaking earth did groan, the sky looked black,
> The fire, the forced air, in sunder crack;
> The sea did threat the heavens, the heavens the earth,
> All looked like a chaos or new birth....
>
> (p. 18)

Fire wins the battle to begin as "the noblest and most active element" and puts forth answers to the question of her worth (p. 19). The wide-ranging discussion pulls from classical astrology, as the planets are judged to be in Fire's purview, as well as from the Bible, as Sodom was consumed by fire. Earth answers with "I am th' original of man and beast," claiming not just the creation of life but the countries and cities that house that life (p. 23). Water is angry at Earth's description, and the drama is heightened here, as Water directly answers that Earth should have praised her because Water is the "Cause of your fruitfulness" (p. 26). Air speaks last but is able to answer them all: "I am the breath of every living soul" (p. 30). She claims that she is superior to the other elements because "when I'm thoroughly rarified turn Fire: / So when I am condense, I turn to Water" (p. 31). While this is questionable science, the poem focuses on the interconnected nature of the elements and the order of the universe. "The Four Humours," which appears as the next poem, is linked to the first in that each humor acknowledges an element as her mother, further portraying the unity of the universe. Carrie Galloway Blackstock argues that while "Bradstreet's fascination with the idea of wholeness" is evident in the structure of these poems, so too is her comment on gender (p. 223). In "The Four Humours," Choler explains that she and her mother, Fire, were "both once masculines / the world doth know" but are playing females because of the necessity of being sisters with the other elements and humors. This causes Blackstock to posit a "deconstruction of gendered identity" in these early poems, when most critics focus on "The Prologue" or Bradstreet's later personal poems to investigate concerns about gender (p. 226).

When Bradstreet turns to the poem "Of the Four Ages of Man," however, the gender is shifted as each age is depicted as masculine, although still in familial terms: Childhood is the son of Phlegm and grandson of Water, Youth descends from Blood and Air, Manly comes from Fire and Choler, and Old Age is aligned with Earth and Melancholy. In this poem Bradstreet again plays up the dramatic angle by dressing each age in the appropriate costume. Childhood is "clothed in white and green to show / His spring was intermixed with some snow," while Youth is in "gorgeous attire" with "his suit of crimson and his scarf of green" (pp. 54, 55). Manly appropriately wears a sword, while Old Age carries a cane. Bradstreet departs from her structure a bit in the section on Old Age, when the character begins rehearsing a history of everything he has seen, perhaps anticipating Bradstreet's later poem detailing the history of the world. "The Four Seasons" returns to depicting female characters but continues the staging of the different personas. Many critics note that it is clear the landscapes Bradstreet is describing in the seasons are not American but conventional English pastoral settings. In the section on summer, for example, she describes the "frolic swains, the shepherd lads" going to "wash the thick clothed flocks with pipes full glad," a description that owes more to Edmund Spenser than to New England (p. 72).

After the "four times four," Bradstreet includes one more poem similarly structured, "The Four Monarchies." This is her most ambitious poem in *The Tenth Muse,* running 3,572 lines and covering the Assyrian, Persian, Grecian, and Roman empires. Besides versifying Raleigh's *History of the World,* Bradstreet also retains some of his portrayals of the disputes about how to present specific historical events. She uses asides, such as "(but that I doubt)" and "(as we are told)" to give her readers a sense of the tenuous nature of the history that has been passed down (p. 80). She seems especially keen to defend the Assyrian queen Semiramis (Sammuramat), suggesting that "some think" the Greeks slandered "her name and fame / By their aspersions" when actually "Her wealth she showed in building Babylon / Admired of all, but equalized of none" (p. 81). This defense of a female leader will find an echo in the collection in Bradstreet's elegy to Queen Elizabeth. The poem ends with an "apology" because it is, despite its length, unfinished.

Bradstreet addresses a more courageous public topic in choosing to write on the contemporary empire of Britain in the next poem, "A Dialogue Between Old England and New; Concerning Their Present Troubles, Anno 1642." The events in this poem are current and the Puritan community directly implicated as the "New England" of the poem. She again uses the technique of personification in casting Old England as mother and New England as daughter. The poem is a conversation between the two on the mother's troubles. Bradstreet's lasting connection to her homeland is evident in her depiction of the daughter's distress at the mother's problems: "What means this wailing tone, this mournful guise? / Ah, tell thy daughter, she may sympathize" (p. 191). Written in 1642 when civil war had broken out in England, the poem also indicates the distance Bradstreet and perhaps her fellow colonists felt from the turmoil, when Old England answers, "Art ignorant indeed of these my woes? / Or must my forced tongue these griefs disclose?" (p. 191). Robert Boschman explains that the civil war not only made the colonists feel isolated, it made them question their very identity. With an exodus of Puritans back to England and the rise in Puritan power there, the colony in America seemed less crucial (p. 39). After a rehearsal of various historical possibilities for England's problems, Old England admits that the root causes are "my sins, / the breach of sacred laws," specifically religious persecution. Bradstreet's Puritan sentiments about the danger of Catholicism are quite strong when New England urges her mother to "root out Popelings head, tail, branch, and rush" because "We hate Rome's whore with all her trumpery" (p. 199). Although riskier than previous poems in its attention to current political concerns, Bradstreet affirms her community's beliefs while picturing the relationship of the colony to England as that of a caring and dutiful daughter who will not only speak the truth to the mother but will pray for her redemption.

THE TENTH MUSE: *ELEGIES*

In addition to the "four times four" poems and Bradstreet's exploration into politics and history, the original *Tenth Muse* also included elegies on Sir Philip Sidney, the French poet Du Bartas, and Queen Elizabeth. In the first two poems, about poets, Bradstreet continues the deprecating strain displayed in "The Prologue," ever mindful that she is an unknown poet writing about well-known and beloved poets. These poems also continue the careful attention to gender from "The Prologue," with Bradstreet often speaking in specifically feminine terms about her deficiencies in accurately lauding these male poets. In her elegy on Queen Elizabeth, though, Bradstreet does not hide her delight that such a powerful figure was female.

In "An Elegy upon That Honorable and Renowned Knight Sir Philip Sidney," Bradstreet begins by giving Sidney the bay wreath she denied herself earlier: "When England did enjoy her halcyon days, / Her noble Sidney wore the crown of bays" (p. 201). She then imagines how his poetry interacts with the muses; instead of the muses inspiring him, his art affects them, as, for example, when "His rhetoric struck Polymnia dead" or when "More worth was his than Clio could set down" (p. 201). The title of Bradstreet's collection, which was presumably given by her brother-in-law Woodbridge, nevertheless becomes quite interesting in that Bradstreet then becomes the tenth muse also affected by Sidney's poetry and also attempting to sing his praises. After detailing in seventy lines Sidney's importance as a British poet, Bradstreet's muse runs out of steam; she writes, "How to persist my Muse is more in doubt" (p. 203). Although she asks the nine muses to come to her aid, "Sidney had exhausted all their store" (p. 203). The muses then take her pen, seemingly injured by her weak attempt to elegize Sidney, but then "Errata through their leave [throws] me my pen," allowing her to write two more lines. Alice Henton points out that "Errata" is a feminized version of "Erato," the muse of lyric poetry, so Bradstreet plays with the gender in her bid to write a bit more, which ends up being six lines instead of the two she was allotted (p. 307). Much like "The Prologue" when Bradstreet asks for a "small acknowledgement," she is here asking for a few lines next to Sidney's brilliance.

Bradstreet also claims another connection with the great poet, one of nationality and perhaps even of blood. The poem's third line extols Sidney as "an honour to our British land" and later as "the brave refiner of our British tongue" (pp. 201, 202). Coming right after "A Dialogue Between Old England and New," this poem elides the differences and distance highlighted by the previous poem concerning the current civil war and instead portrays the common cultural heritage in Sidney's poetry. The generational metaphor of the previous poem continues as well when Bradstreet announces, "Then let none disallow of these my strains / Whilst English blood yet runs within my veins," suggesting a kinship by blood (p. 202). In the last ten years, scholars influenced by the surge in Atlantic studies have explored the focus on colonial versus national identity in Bradstreet's poetry, which has contributed to the renewed attention to Bradstreet's earlier nondomestic poetry such as the elegies.

In elegizing the French poet Du Bartas, Bradstreet is not claiming a national inheritance, but still perhaps an artistic one. Her language in this poem is almost fawning. Du Bartas is "matchless" and Bradstreet's sight is "dazzled" (p. 205). She again uses the imagery of the muse to convey her deference to the superior ability of a well-known poet by imagining her muse as a mere child who can only sit and watch. The conception of her work as a child connects this poem to "The Author to Her Book," in which she bemoans the fact that her work went into the world rather like a poorly dressed child. Bradstreet's experience of mothering eight children surely figures into how she perceives her poetry. What she admires about Du Bartas becomes clear when Bradstreet details all of the different fields his poetry engages with, from natural philosophy to anatomy. Her admiration of his style is also clear: "Pardon if I adore, when I admire" (p. 207). Bradstreet may, however, again be requesting some "small acknowledgement" in this poem. Louisa Hall points out that at the beginning, Du Bartas is pictured as the powerful sun and Bradstreet as bringing only a daisy, a "homely flower," to honor him because she is "barren," but by the end of the poem Du Bartas is in his grave, only being "revived" through his fame, which perhaps her poem has helped (pp. 205, 208).

Queen Elizabeth's fame does not need Anne Bradstreet's assistance, but Bradstreet adds her praise in "In Honor of That High and Mighty Princess Queen Elizabeth of Happy Memory," a laudatory title if there ever was one. That we hear more from Anne Bradstreet the Englishwoman than from Anne Bradstreet the Puritan is evident in the opening lines, when she claims that Elizabeth's glory is so great "That men account it no impiety / To say thou wert a fleshly deity" (p. 209). While this may not be exactly blasphemous, it is strong language. Unlike Sidney and Du Bartas, whose praises can just be captured by Bradstreet's elegies, Bradstreet claims that "No Phoenix pen, nor Spenser's poetry" can capture "Eliza's works[,] wars, praise" (p. 210). Elizabeth's acceptance of the larger Protestant cause would have made her an acceptable model of praise for Puritans, but Bradstreet's elegy focuses on gender: "She hath wiped off th' aspersion of her sex, / That women wisdom lack to play the rex" (p. 210). Elizabeth even becomes here a "Phoenix," the sun image used in other Bradstreet poems to refer to a powerful male figure, such as her husband, or to God. Bradstreet then rehearses Queen Elizabeth's many successes, from conquering the Spanish Armada to defeating the "rude untamed Irish." She compares Elizabeth to other powerful female figures in history, such as Semiramis, Dido, and Cleopatra, but finds that no one compares to the "Phoenix queen" (p. 212). After building up Elizabeth's honors, Bradstreet then returns to the question of gender, directing challenging males: "Now say, have women worth? Or have they none?" (p. 212). In elegizing Elizabeth, Bradstreet not only shows her continuing connection to her native land, referring to Elizabeth as "our Queen," she also enlists the queen's image and fame to suggest further that women do have worth and perhaps even the ability to write poetry.

"CONTEMPLATIONS": *EARTH AND HEAVEN*

"Contemplations" is Bradstreet's best work. In planning the second edition of her works, Bradstreet added this poem as well as five others. These poems show Bradstreet stretching beyond the earlier conventional forms, with the result that "Contemplations" is technically more sophisticated than the earlier published work. Instead of heroic couplets, the poem consists of seven-line stanzas, rhymed *ababccc,* with six lines of iambic pentameter, followed by the seventh in hexameter. The classical allusions that filled earlier poems are largely absent, as is the dramatic personification. In this poem, the poet speaks directly to the reader, sharing her thoughts as she goes for a walk in nature. The anxieties expressed in earlier poems about her ability to write well persist, but they are not tied to her gender because she is not comparing herself to famous and skilled male poets. The challenge presented to Bradstreet the poet in "Contemplations" is trying to write the glory of God with the problems of sin, mortality, and human frailty intervening. The difficulty is not that Anne Bradstreet herself as woman or novice is lacking skill but that humanity does not have the simple access to the creator that creatures in nature seem to have.

The poem's focus is this relationship between creation and creator, or between earth and heaven, a theme that will carry into other poems, including "The Flesh and the Spirit" and "Upon the Burning of Our House." Bradstreet was clearly interested in the tension between living a material earthly existence and trying to keep a faith focused on heavenly or spiritual matters. That earthly existence can take the form of the vanity of cherishing material belongings, as it does when her house burns down, or communion with nature, as it does in "Contemplations." Nature in this poem is no longer described according to the pattern of the English pastoral with shepherds and sheep seen earlier in "The Four Seasons." Here the natural world is more clearly a description of Bradstreet's own environs in New England. Her musings on the pleasures and pitfalls of the material world, then, are prompted not by an attempt to work in a literary genre through its accepted tropes but by her own experience in her immediate surroundings.

Those surroundings are rendered in beautiful detail, one of the principal reasons readers have been drawn to this particular poem. She clearly delights in the natural world around her, which makes this poem a kind of turning point in the relationship of the Puritans to the natural world. The earlier Puritan community saw the natural world around them as something they needed to civilize and tame. William Bradford, for example, in writing about the New World during the first half of the seventeenth century, in *Of Plymouth Plantation,* famously comments that all the pilgrims could see was a "hideous and desolate wilderness, full of wild beasts and wild men" (p. 116). The famed Puritan preacher of the eighteenth century Jonathan Edwards, however, describes in his "Personal Narrative" (1740) his "very secret and retired place" in the woods he used "for a place of prayer" (p. 356). Bradstreet's wandering through the woods to contemplate her relationship to God reveals a shift in Puritan thinking from the seventeenth century to the eighteenth century about the use of the natural world. Critics disagree about whether Bradstreet's stance toward nature in the poem puts her squarely within the Puritan theology of her day or whether it makes her a rebel. Some critics have connected her relationship to nature in this poem to that of the later Romantics. Josephine Piercy even wonders if Romantics such as Ralph Waldo Emerson or William Wordsworth read Bradstreet's poetry (p. 101). Ann Stanford argues, however, that Bradstreet differs from the later Romantics because nature is not the end in itself but the means to understanding God (Stanford 1974, p. 103). Despite disagreement about the implications of her portrayal of nature, critics all agree that Bradstreet is successful in writing a meditative poem set not just in the natural world but also clearly in the New World.

"Contemplations" opens with an autumn setting. That we are in a real setting and not a theater set piece is indicated early when Bradstreet comments that the trees' "leaves and fruits seemed painted, but was true," and so, "Rapt were my senses at this delectable view" (p. 220). This is not the formal presentation of the persona of Autumn in "The Four Seasons," but a personal experience and intimate reaction to nature; "delectable" suggests that the poet finds the view worthy of consumption. We are only in the second stanza when the poet begins to connect the natural world to a contemplation on God: "If so much excellence abide below, / How excellent is He that dwells on high" (p. 220). An oak tree that seems to have existed for a hundred years or perhaps a thousand causes Bradstreet to muse on eternity. Her vision then scans from the trees up to the sky, and she writes the next four stanzas on the sun. This is one of the places discussed by critics who argue she is rebelling against Puritan doctrine, as she writes, "Soul of this world, this universe's eye, / No wonder some made thee a deity" (p. 221). Her interest in nature borders on worship here, although in the next line she explains that she knows better. She then romanticizes the sun, picturing it as a "bridegroom" greeting the morning with "smiles and blushes" (p. 221). At the end of the fourth stanza she again connects nature to the creator, pondering that if the sun is so glorious, "How full of glory then must thy Creator be" (p. 222).

The poem shifts in stanza 8 to the problem of her inability to capture this glory, as she tries to "sing some song" to the "great Creator" but her "mazed Muse" fails her (p. 222). Her diagnosis of her "imbecility" echoes the "foolish, broken, blemished Muse" of "The Prologue," but the underlying issue has changed. She is not hampered because of her gender but because of her humanity (p. 223). She hears a grasshopper and a cricket who seem to sing and chirp quite easily, contrasting her muteness. The difference between these "creatures abject" and herself, she will discover, is the history of humanity. The next seven stanzas narrate the story of Genesis: the creation of Adam and Eve, their fall, their children Cain and Abel, and the first murder. The contrast running through these depictions is the potential for humanity to be "sovereign" and live in "Paradise" versus the penalty of sin, ending with "How Adam sighed to see his progeny, / Clothed all in his black sinful livery" (p. 225). Her resulting contemplation is on the mortality of humanity: "Living so little while we are alive" (p. 225).

The poet continues her walk and her musings as she comes to a river. Throughout the poem she depicts herself as alone. Here the river is a "lonely place" while earlier she was "silent alone": "In pathless paths I lead my wand'ring feet" (p. 222). The play on feet shows the connections of the journey into nature and the composition of the poem. The portrayal of a writer gaining insight while alone in nature foreshadows later American writers, such as Emerson, Henry David Thoreau, Walt Whitman, and even Emily Dickinson when she "started early" and "took my dog." This is perhaps another reason why this poem resonates with critics, who are familiar with the theme in subsequent American literature. If Bradstreet becomes "American" by describing a New England setting of autumn trees, dense woods, and the river heading to the ocean, she perhaps becomes more American in retrospect as later writers also combine sojourns in nature with meditations on larger ideas. At the river, Bradstreet expresses a kind of jealousy for the smooth trip the water makes to the ocean, as she imagines her own journey to heaven and expresses envy of the fish who follow instinct without having to know why.

Bradstreet is then again confronted with another creature who can sing, when a "sweet-tongued Philomel" lands nearby (p. 228). This is one of the poem's few classical references. Not only are nightingales not native to North America, Bradstreet references the mythic Philomela, whose tongue was cut out because she dared to expose her rapist and was eventually turned into a bird. In Bradstreet's poem, the one who could not speak then begins to sing "forth a most melodious train," causing Bradstreet, who has lamented her own inability to speak adequately, to wish for "wings with her a while to take my flight" (p. 228). In ruminating on the difference between the "merry Bird" who does not worry about the past or the future and "Man at the best a creature frail and vain," Bradstreet finds that only humans have the possibility of immortality. Although people are like the mariner who "sings merrily" and thinks himself "Master of the seas" until a sudden storm makes him "long for a more quiet port," she finds hope in an image of redemption in the ending couplet: "But he whose name is graved in the white stone / Shall last and shine when all of these are gone" (p. 230). Despite her misgivings about her ability to put her musings into verse and to articulate her praise for her creator, she, like the Philomel, finds a way to sing.

The theme of the materiality of earthly things versus the immortality of heaven is continued in three of Bradstreet's other poems: "The Flesh and the Spirit," "The Vanity of All Worldly Things," and "Here Follows Some Verses upon the Burning of Our House, July 10th, 1666." It is clear from the outset that in a battle between flesh/earth/material and spirit/heaven/faith, the Puritan Bradstreet will show the latter of these as the victors. In these poems, however, the earthly side of the struggle is shown sympathetically, and heaven is depicted in a way to appease the desire for material possessions. Bradstreet returns to personification in "The Flesh and the Spirit" by depicting an exchange between sisters. The familial paradigm makes the conversation competitive. Flesh begins by baiting her sister: "Doth contemplation feed thee so / Regardlessly to let earth go?," words that point the reader back to Bradstreet's desire in "Contemplations" to consume the "delectable" nature around her. Flesh argues her point by making her sister Spirit sound inconsequential and flighty: "Dost dream of things beyond the moon / And dost thou hope to dwell there soon?" (p. 231). In contrast to the ethereal, Flesh can offer the pleasures of the earth including pearls and gold. Spirit then answers by claiming that she is thinking of heavenly rewards, but her tone is haughty. She wants to be "victor" over her sister because of her "ambition" (p. 233). Spirit claims not to be tempted by the "trash which earth does hold," although her subsequent description of heaven is full of the same earthly goods that she rejects, as she imagines walls of "jasper stone," "gates of pearl," and streets of "transparent gold" (p. 234).

The other two poems on earth and heaven follow a similar pattern. "The Vanity of All Worldly Things" clearly depicts the folly of depending on earthly treasure: "He heaps up riches, and he heaps up sorrow" (p. 235). Even the wisest of men is tempted by vanity, but the alternative path to seek treasure in heaven is offered in the appealing terms of earthly treasure as the "pearl of price, this tree of life, this spring" (p. 237). Both this poem and "The Flesh and the Spirit" speak to the larger philosophical tension between earthly existence and faith, and even "Contemplations," which takes a more personal point of view, treats the subject as a kind of theological struggle. When Bradstreet's house burned down and she lost her earthly possessions, however, the struggle became immediate and real. As in "Contemplations," the poet speaks to the reader and leads us through her thought process. When the house burns, she first cries to God for strength and then has the appropriate response: "I blest His name that gave and took" (p. 318). If the poem ended here, we would have the correct view of worldly goods, but by extending the poem and showing us her subsequent reactions, Bradstreet gives her reader a glimpse into the process of her faith. She admits that after the fire she missed her "pleasant things" and mourned that her house would no longer be there to host a "pleasant tale" or a "bridegroom's voice" (p. 319). After these admissions, she chides herself for her dependence on earthly things. She appeases herself with the knowledge that she has treasure in heaven, but she pictures that heaven as a better house than the one she lost: "Thou hast an house on high erect, / Framed by that mighty Architect, / With glory richly furnished" (p. 319). Thus in all of the poems where Bradstreet contemplates the competing pulls of this world and the next, she gives the reader a dialogue. Heaven always wins, but earth in its beautiful autumn dress or its warm house gives her a way to imagine that heaven.

PERSONAL POEMS: FAMILY, ILLNESS, AND DEATH

None of Anne Bradstreet's personal poems written about her family members or herself were published in the first edition of her poetry. Only in the third edition published in 1678, which was probably assembled by Bradstreet's nephew-in-law, do the poems about herself and her family become public (Hensley, p. xxix). These poems, however, next to "Contemplations," are what critics have valued most (until the recent interest by several critics in the earlier work). That critics value what was not even published in Bradstreet's lifetime could show that the purpose of Bradstreet's poetry and the taste of her seventeenth-century audience was simply different from modern preferences for looser forms and more self-revelatory poems. For Adrienne Rich, these are the poems "which rescue Anne Bradstreet from the Women's Archives and place her conclusively in literature" (p. xvii). These are also the poems that provide insight into the daily life triumphs and struggles of a Puritan woman in seventeenth-century New England. Rich comments that Bradstreet's voice in these works is "direct and touching" (p. xix). Abram Van Engen argues that the domestic focus in Bradstreet's later verse even anticipates the sentimental literature popular in the eighteenth and nineteenth centuries. Bradstreet certainly talks about love, loss, marriage, and death in ways that focus attention on the value on the domestic realm.

As a daughter, a wife, and the mother of eight children, Bradstreet's numerous poems on her family reflect the time and care she devoted to her familial role. She gives every indication that she delighted in this role. Her poem about her mother, "An Epitaph on My Dear and Ever-Honoured Mother Mrs. Dorothy Dudley," is a brief but positive depiction of a "loving," "friendly," and "religious" woman who left "a blessed memory" (p. 219). Her poems about her father are more complex but appreciative nonetheless. In "To the Memory of My Dear and Ever Honoured Father Thomas Dudley," Bradstreet presents Dudley as her "father, guide, instructor too" (p. 216). She emphasizes his devotion to the community as a founder of New England and a "true patriot" to the colony (p. 217). In "To Her Father with Some Verses," Bradstreet's relationship to Dudley is depicted through the conceit of a debt she owes. She explains that any worth in her is due to his principal, a debt she will not be able to discharge but will pay until she dies. The positive influence of both of her parents is clear in the homage she pays them.

Bradstreet's poems about her husband likewise paint a picture of a happy relationship. She focuses on the unity in her marriage; in "To My Dear and Loving Husband" she begins, "If ever two were one, then surely we" (p. 245). She borrows the language from earlier poems expressing the richness of earth to emphasize the depth of her love, such as when she writes, "I prize thy love more than whole mines of gold" (p. 245). What makes this love poem interesting in terms of Bradstreet's specific experience is the way she combines the earthly attachment she has to her husband to her religious beliefs. Since she cannot repay him for his love, much as she cannot repay her father, she hopes that "the heavens reward thee" (p. 245). She then connects their persistence in maintaining their marriage to their spiritual lives: "Then while we live, in love let's so persevere / That when we live no more, we may live ever" (p. 245). Bradstreet continues to play with ideas of earth and heaven in "A Letter to Her Husband, Absent upon Public Employment," one of several poems written about her anxiety when he is gone from home. This poem echoes the natural imagery from the earlier poems "The Four Seasons" and "Contemplations" to describe their relationship. Here she is Earth, who is in mourning because "My Sun is gone" (p. 246). She extends this metaphor to portray her limbs as "chilled" without the heat of the sun, although she ends with another picture of unity: "I here, thou there, yet both but one" (p. 247). In the subsequent poem titled "Another," the sun again makes an appearance but here as "Phoebus," who is summoned as a messenger to "Commend me to the man more loved than life, / Show him the sorrows of his widowed wife" (p. 248). In a third poem also titled "Another," as if Bradstreet's sorrow at her husband's absence cannot be contained in just one poem, she writes that without him she leads "a joyless life" and emphasizes again the unity: "Let's still remain but one, till death divide" (p. 251). All together the poems to her husband are passionate; she does not seem to be speaking from the duty of a prescribed role but from her love for her husband and her distress at his absence.

Bradstreet's children are the subject of "In Reference to Her Children, 23 June 1659." She uses the metaphor of eight birds hatching in her nest as the basis of the poem. Each bird learns to fly and to sing. The image of the singing Philomela in "Contemplations" connects singing to both writing poetry and praising the creator. In this poem, singing is expressing joy. After detailing the life, direction, and mating of each of the eight birds, Bradstreet claims she will not "lament" in old age but will "sing" (p. 255). She only hopes that her children remember she loved them, echoing the feeling she expresses in her earlier poem about her mother.

The remainder of Bradstreet's personal poems center around two subjects: her multiple bouts of illness and her grief at the death of family members. The focus throughout her poetry on an earthly existence with a heavenly faith continues in these poems as she faces hardships, but while her poems on the deaths of grandchildren show that sometimes her loss was indeed inconsolable, she is able to negotiate this tension in dealing with her illnesses. In a letter written "To My Dear Children," which Bradstreet intended them to read after she died, she explains that throughout her life she would occasionally "sit loose from" God, but that "by one affliction or other [God] hath made me look home," and that this "correction" most often took the form of "sickness, weakness, pains" (p. 264). This belief in sickness as divine intervention affects her portrayal of illness in her poetry. Illness was part of the difficulty of earthly existence that led the sufferer to keep focusing on heaven. In her "Upon a Fit of Sickness, Anno 1632" she muses on mortality and the passage of time:

> O bubble blast, how long can'st last?
> that always art a breaking,
> No sooner blown, but dead and gone,
> ev'n as a word that's speaking.
>
> (p. 241)

The poem's tone changes, however, when Bradstreet references her salvation: "The race is run, the field is won, / the victory's mine I see" (p. 241). Her poem "Upon Some Distemper of Body" follows the same trajectory but this time by using the metaphor of a ship tossed at sea, probably drawn from Bradstreet's experience of the transatlantic voyage. She is "tossing" and "drenched with tears" until the one "who sendeth help" becomes her "anchor" (p. 242).

The hopeful tone ending these poems is likewise attempted in the poems about the deaths of three grandchildren, but whether she actually achieves peace or is being ironic is debated by critics. In any case these poems honestly and bluntly express Bradstreet's grief at their deaths and her struggle with God's hand in their early demise. In her poem "In Memory of My Dear Grandchild Elizabeth Bradstreet" she relies on the natural imagery that has helped her contemplate before. The child is a "fair flower that for a space was lent" (p. 257). As in her poem about her house burning, Bradstreet is mourning but chiding herself for her grief, asking, "why should I once bewail thy fate" when the girl is "settled in an everlasting state," but just as in the earlier poem, Bradstreet continues to process her grief (p. 257). In the second stanza she admits that it is natural for things to die, although fruit falls when it is ripe, whereas the flower of her granddaughter is more like a plant "new set" (p. 257). She can only point to God as the cause, because God guides both "nature and fate" (p. 257). When her second granddaughter, Anne, died, Bradstreet again turned to natural imagery to process the loss. The girl is a "withering flower" that was simply "lent" for a season (p. 258). Bradstreet attempts the turn toward faith in this poem by imagining she will eventually join the child in heaven. The third poem, on the death of a grandson, suggests the most difficulty for Bradstreet in reconciling her grief. He is the third flower gone. In this poem Bradstreet expresses faith, but perhaps only because she is supposed to: "Let's say He's merciful as well as just" (p.

259). It is unclear whether she is assured by this statement of faith and aware that "He will return and make up all our losses" or whether she says this in the ironic voice critics have found in other poems. What is clear is that when faced with loss, Bradstreet turned to poetry to process her pain and to contemplate her faith. She even crafts a kind of epitaph for herself in her poem "As Weary Pilgrim," written three years before her death. Here she is the "pilgrim" who has lived on earth but now is a "clay house mold'ring away" (p. 322). That she is suffering physically is quite clear when she writes, "Oh, how I long to be at rest" where there will be "no fainting fits" and no "grinding pains" (p. 322). She ends by beckoning: "Lord make me ready for that day, / Then come, dear Bridegroom, come away" (p. 322).

CONCLUSION: LEGACY

When we consider the remarkable breadth of Anne Bradstreet's subject matter and her honest portrayal of faith and doubt in the context of her life as Puritan pilgrim in colonial New England, we can only conclude that Bradstreet was a remarkable woman living in interesting times. The Irish poet Eavan Boland comments, "Anne Bradstreet is that rare thing: a poet who is inseparable from history. The proportions are not usually so equal and compelling. She can be located in the same way as a place name on a map, and we can judge the distance more accurately because of that" (p. 180). That place and history was harsh, as Adrienne Rich put it, with "confines as severe as any American poet has confronted" (p. xx). But given Bradstreet's portrayal of her many illnesses as interventions by God to shift her attention back to heavenly things, in addition to her tendency to write during these times of stress to process her doubts and her faith, it is possible that the hardships were not hurdles for the poetry but were the reason for the poetry. Her writing connects her to her English roots in the middle of a colonial wilderness and it displays her education as she versifies her readings, but it also allows her a place to gain understanding of the hardships of her life and even the history of her particularly interesting place on the map.

Whatever the impetus for the poetry, what she wrote endures for readers and for other poets. John Berryman's 1953 poem "Homage to Mistress Bradstreet" imagines her rebelling and submitting to her culture and her female role. Though controversial on a purely factual basis and because of Berryman's appropriation of Bradstreet's voice, the poem nonetheless shows the power of Bradstreet's seventeenth-century poetry for a modern audience. Part of that power derives from Bradstreet's different roles; as Boland remarks, "It is Anne Bradstreet's unique achievement that she could burrow into the cracks, discover the air of history, and find a breathing space to be Puritan, poet, and woman" (p. 185). Questions of who Bradstreet is—Puritan, rebel, worldly, feminist—remain part of the intrigue of her poetry, but one identity is clear: America's first poet.

Selected Bibliography

COLLECTED WORKS OF ANNE BRADSTREET

The Works of Anne Bradstreet in Prose and Verse. Edited by John Harvard Ellis. Charleston, Mass.: Abram E. Cutter, 1867.

The Poems of Mrs. Anne Bradstreet (1612–1672) Together with Her Prose Remains. Edited by Frank E. Hopkins. New York: Duodecimos, 1897.

The Works of Anne Bradstreet. Edited by Jeannine Hensley. Cambridge, Mass.: Belknap Press of Harvard University Press, 1967. (All citations to the works of Bradstreet in the text are to this edition.)

The Complete Works of Anne Bradstreet. Edited by Joseph R. McElrath, Jr., and Allan P. Robb. Boston: Twayne, 1981.

BIBLIOGRAPHIES

Piercy, Josephine K. "Selected Bibliography." In her *Anne Bradstreet.* New York: Twayne, 1965. Pp. 129–137.

Scheick, William J., and JoElla Doggett. *Seventeenth-Century American Poetry: A Reference Guide.* Boston: G. K. Hall, 1977. Pp. 34–54.

Stanford, Ann. "Anne Bradstreet: An Annotated Checklist." *Early American Literature* 3, no. 3:217–228 (1968–1969).

———. "Scholarship and Criticism Since 1930." In her *Anne Bradstreet: The Worldly Puritan.* New York: Burt Franklin, 1974. Pp. 129–137.

CRITICAL AND BIOGRAPHICAL STUDIES

Blackstock, Carrie Galloway. "Anne Bradstreet and Performativity: Self-Cultivation, Self-Deployment." *Early American Literature* 32, no. 3:222–248 (1997).

Boland, Eavan. "Finding Anne Bradstreet." In *Green Thoughts, Green Shades: Essays by Contemporary Poets on the Early Modern Lyric.* Edited by Jonathan F. S. Post. Oakland: University of California Press, 2002. Pp. 176–190.

Boschman, Robert. *In the Way of Nature: Ecology and Westward Expansion in the Poetry of Anne Bradstreet, Elizabeth Bishop, and Amy Clampitt.* Jefferson, N.C.: McFarland, 2009.

Eberwein, Jane Donahue. "'No Rhet'ric We Expect': Argumentation in Bradstreet's 'The Prologue.'" In *Critical Essays on Anne Bradstreet.* Edited by Pattie Cowell and Ann Stanford. Boston: G. K. Hall, 1983. Pp. 218–225.

Gordon, Charlotte. *Mistress Bradstreet: The Untold Life of America's First Poet.* New York: Little, Brown, 2005.

Hall, Louisa. "The Influence of Anne Bradstreet's Innovative Errors." *Early American Literature* 48, no. 1:1–27 (2013).

Hensley, Jeannine. "Anne Bradstreet's Wreath of Thyme." Introduction to *The Works of Anne Bradstreet.* Edited by Jeannine Hensley. Cambridge, Mass.: Belknap Press of Harvard University Press, 1967. Pp. xxiii–xxix.

Henton, Alice. "'Once Masculines ... Now Feminines Awhile': Gendered Imagery and the Significance of Anne Bradstreet's *The Tenth Muse.*" *New England Quarterly* 85, no. 2:302–325 (2012).

Martin, Wendy. *An American Triptych: Anne Bradstreet, Emily Dickinson, Adrienne Rich.* Chapel Hill: University of North Carolina Press, 1984.

Piercy, Josephine K. *Anne Bradstreet.* New York: Twayne, 1965.

Rich, Adrienne. "Anne Bradstreet and Her Poetry." Foreword to *The Works of Anne Bradstreet.* Edited by Jeannine Hensley. Cambridge, Mass.: Belknap Press of Harvard University Press, 1967. Pp. ix–xxii.

Stanford, Ann. *Anne Bradstreet: The Worldly Puritan.* New York: Burt Franklin, 1974.

———. "Anne Bradstreet: Dogmatist and Rebel." In *Critical Essays on Anne Bradstreet.* Edited by Pattie Cowell and Ann Stanford. Boston: G. K. Hall, 1983. Pp. 76–88.

Van Engen, Abram. "Advertising the Domestic: Anne Bradstreet's Sentimental Poetics." *Legacy* 28, no. 1:47–68 (2011).

Walker, Cheryl. "Anne Bradstreet: A Woman Poet." In *Critical Essays on Anne Bradstreet.* Edited by Pattie Cowell and Ann Stanford. Boston: G. K. Hall, 1983. Pp. 254–261.

White, Elizabeth Wade. *Anne Bradstreet: "The Tenth Muse."* New York: Oxford University Press, 1971.

OTHER SOURCES

Bradford, William. *Of Plymouth Plantation.* In *The Norton Anthology of American Literature.* 7th ed. Edited by Nina Baym. New York: Norton, 2007. Pp. 105–137.

Edwards, Jonathan. "Personal Narrative." In *The Norton Anthology of American Literature.* 7th ed. Edited by Nina Baym. New York: Norton, 2007. Pp. 386–395.

Winthrop, John. "A Model of Christian Charity." In *The Norton Anthology of American Literature.* 7th ed. Edited by Nina Baym. New York: Norton, 2007. Pp. 147–157.

WILLA CATHER

(1873—1947)

Joshua Grasso

IN 1936 WILLA CATHER published a book she hoped the greater mass of readers (or at least those younger than she was) would entirely ignore. The book, a series of essays titled *Not Under Forty,* contains a much-anthologized piece about the art of novel writing, "The Novel Démeublé." At this time she had reached the height of her powers, becoming successful enough to be widely appreciated and widely misunderstood. Her novels were lumped together with the "local color" writers and the "realists," though Cather would always look askance at these terms. She feared that the novel had become a collection of documentary details, more a technical manual than a work of art. As she explains,

> The higher processes of art are all processes of simplification. The novelist must learn to write, and then he must unlearn it.... In this direction only, it seems to me, can the novel develop into anything more varied and perfect than all the many novels that have gone before.
>
> (*Not Under Forty,* p. 49)

By "simplification" she means the stripping away of extraneous details to arrive at that alchemic combination of story and suggestion. The story should be clear to the reader without being explained; it should, like a sudden idea, occur naturally to the reader without knowing how or why it came about. In other words, it should read like "art," something that can only be felt, not explained.

Going a bit further, she writes,

> Whatever is felt upon the page without being specifically named there—that, one might say, is created. It is the inexplicable presence of the thing not named, of the overtone divined by the ear but not heard by it, the verbal mood, the emotional aural of the fact or the thing or the deed, that gives high quality to the novel or the drama, as well as to poetry itself.
>
> (p. 50)

These were increasingly unpopular ideas in the 1930s, and even more so as the century went on: speaking of "things not named," and "emotional auras" and "high quality" would make modernists raid the medicine cabinet. Yet she was quite sincere, since her stories, like a piece of music, utilized silence as much as notes. Within the silences lie the story, which the reader half-creates as he or she imagines the details a writer can only approximate. Music without pauses is just busyness, a stream of notes; so too, novels need the poetry of suggestion rather than ham-fisted propaganda. Cather maintained the belief that an artist creates art, not a product for mass consumption. However, she also believed—quite prophetically—that works of literature never find their ideal audience; they continue to be read and pondered over, the "things not named" adapting to each reader's inner world. Otherwise, literature would be consumed and discarded in an instant. Like a verse from the *Tao te Ching,* to read Cather once is not to read her at all. Her books continue to evolve and mature, though they paradoxically remain rooted in their historical moment. For Cather, the particular opened the door to the universal, which was the "highest quality" of the writer's art.

WESTWARD HO

Readers of Cather's work are often surprised to learn that she hailed not from the plains of Nebraska but instead from Winchester, Virginia (in the northwestern part of the state), in the village of Back Creek. Of Irish, Scottish, and Welsh descent, her ancestors had come to Virginia in the early 1800s, cultivating the land and becoming relatively well-to-do. Indeed, her mother's side of the family, the Boaks, owned slaves and were ardent Confederates, with three sons in the Confederate Army. The Cather side of the family had a more mixed response to the war: her paternal grandfather supported the Union, and her own father, though equally opposed to slavery, believed more in states' rights and joined the Confederacy. Yet unlike many families with divided loyalties, the Cathers and Boaks weathered the storm and were reunited after the war. As Mildred Bennet explains in *The World of Willa Cather,* "As a Unionist, [William Cather] was the only man in the community left with enough money to hire a Baptist minister to conduct a school at Willow Shade. All the children—Southern sympathizers included—were invited to attend" (p. 9). Here his son Charles met Mary Virginia Boak, something of a Southern belle, and they married in December 1872, with Willa following a year later, on December 7, 1873. Six siblings, four boys and two girls, would follow in the years 1877 to 1892.

Though Cather would draw on this Southern past for her final novel, *Sapphira and the Slave Girl* (1940), Virginia played little role in her formative years. An uncle had already migrated to Nebraska looking for new land and a new lease on life (the family was afflicted with tuberculosis), and by 1877 most of the clan decided to relocate to what must have seemed like the end of the earth. Cather clearly felt this way, as she was only nine when she first reached Nebraska in 1883, roughly the same age as Jim Burden, her alter ego in *My Ántonia* (1918). As Jim recalls of his arrival on the plains,

> There was nothing but land: not a country at all, but the material out of which countries are made. No, there was nothing but land.... I had the feeling that the world was left behind, that we had got over the edge of it, and were outside man's jurisdiction. I had never before looked up at the sky when there was not a familiar mountain ridge against it.... Between that earth and that sky I felt erased, blotted out.
>
> (p. 37)

Cather would later tell her dear friend Elizabeth Sergeant that she most of all feared "dying in a cornfield." When asked to explain this remark (particularly from someone who specialized in writing about cornfields), Cather said, "You could not understand. You have not seen those miles of fields. There is no place to hide in Nebraska. You can't hide under a windmill" (Sergeant, p. 49). The vastness of the untamed landscape would indeed "blot out" the young Southerner and leave something quite different in its place: William Cather, the "boy" who would one day conquer the East and become a famous novelist.

About a year after arriving in Nebraska, the family moved to Red Cloud, a bustling frontier town recognizable from the fictional worlds of *O Pioneers!* (1913), *The Song of the Lark* (1915), and many others. Far from being the end of the earth, Red Cloud boasted an opera house, traveling theater troupes, and immigrants from every corner of Europe. Cather's education here was twofold, as she eagerly listened to the stories of Czech, Scandinavian, and German immigrants, even to the extent that her mother feared they had become surrogate parents. Equally important was the opera house, where she had her first taste of European culture. Touring companies from the East would regularly perform the classics of nineteenth-century theater, such as Shakespeare, adaptations of *Uncle Tom's Cabin* and *The Count of Monte Cristo,* and Michael William Balfe's opera *The Bohemian Girl,* which shares the title of Cather's breakthrough story of 1912. A fascination with acting seemingly inspired her to perform in her daily life as well: in 1888 she adopted the name "William Cather, Jr." (or sometimes "M.D.," reflecting her early interest in medicine) and cut her hair short, often adopting men's clothing and accessories. More importantly, she aspired to male pursuits and interests, assiduously studying Greek and Latin and considering the "male" professions of becoming a doctor or a writer. As Sharon O'Brien suggests in *Willa*

Cather: The Emerging Voice, "male impersonation was her first major work of fiction, a text in which she was both author and character" (p. 97).

THE "MAN" OF LETTERS

This role may have been partially a response to her mother, known for being an elegant, sophisticated Southern woman and, like many such women, given to spells of sickness and ennui. Cather instinctively rebelled from the weakness inherent in such a role, gravitating toward the strong immigrant women she observed around her, as well as their tough, taciturn husbands. However, in later years Cather claimed to take most after her mother, and her use of male fashion was perhaps no different than her mother's use of feminine costume. Indeed, her mother seemed strangely supportive of Cather's experimentation, even allocating her own room, which she "kept locked when she left for college, not assigning it to one of the younger children as might have been expected in such a crowded household" (O'Brien, p. 85). This suggests a certain appreciation for her daughter's predicament, a young woman of intellectual aspirations in a backwater western town. Perhaps realizing Willa could never use her feminine charms to get ahead, meeting men on their own terms seemed the likeliest plan of attack. While Willa quickly became the talk of Red Cloud, she pursued her own path, becoming the private pupil of the local classics scholar, Will Ducker. In this way, she gained an initiation into the male world of letters and scholarship closed to many of her peers.

At sixteen she enrolled in the Latin school at Lincoln, and a year later began studies at the University of Nebraska, while still receiving lessons with Ducker on the side. Her writing career truly began at college, since Lincoln, though no New York City, teemed with artistic possibility. She contributed to numerous publications, such as the *Lasso,* the *Hesperian,* and even the *Nebraska State Journal,* ultimately creating a column for the newspaper called "The Passing Show." As if to distance herself from her Red Cloud provincialism, Cather became an exacting critic, not only of plays and operas but of her fellow students—particularly her fellow women. She gleefully lampooned sororities, literary clubs (often run by and for female students), and high society culture, which she often found insufferably feminine. Cather kept up her "William Cather" pose for her first few years, shocking her classmates, one of whom recalled, "She was the first girl that I ever saw in suspenders." Others noted her brazen, "egotistical ... boy-like" personality and her preference for the name "Billy" (quoted in O'Brien, p. 121). To the young Cather, the one thing holding her back from success, either as a journalist or a doctor, was her gender; yet gender could be performed in any number of ways, and the more convincing the performance, the less society seemed to question it. In this manner Will Cather flourished at the university.

Though Cather kept her love life very private, and certainly never spoke of being a lesbian (a term that lacked wide currency at that time), college constituted a sort of "coming out" for her. In her columns, she warmly praised the work of Sappho (the only woman writer she unequivocally supported), writing of her, "Those broken fragments have burned themselves in the consciousness of the world like fire. All great poets have wondered at them, all inferior poets have imitated them. Twenty centuries have not cooled the passion in them" (quoted in O'Brien, p. 175). As she wrote this, Cather had formed a deep friendship with a fellow student, Louise Pound, a musician, athlete, and scholar of distinct promise (who would go on to earn a doctorate and teach at the University of Nebraska). Cather became infatuated with Louise, and the two were inseparable for the short time they spent together—Louise was three years ahead of her at the university. When Cather returned to Red Cloud on breaks, she wrote quasi-Romantic letters entreating Louise to visit, and signed them "William." She even sent Louise one of her favorite books of poetry, Edward FitzGerald's *The Rubaiyat of Omar Khayyam,* a work in the sensual mold of Sappho, either as a memento of shared feelings or a way to instigate them. Louise, however, never visited her after college, and the relationship quickly cooled. Even so,

Louise became the first of many close female relationships throughout Cather's life, each one allowing her to write more openly and passionately of women. Seen in this way, novels like *O Pioneers!* and *My Ántonia* are the love letters Cather destroyed or suppressed from this time, and women such as Alexandria and Ántonia are her loving portraits of former and current companions.

BECOMING AN AUTHOR

Upon graduation Cather spent a lonely year back in Red Cloud, listlessly pursuing local journalism and planning her next move. At this point in her life, Nebraska and the plains were far from inspiring: her university education made her look east, to the true centers of American culture—Boston and New York. Even Lincoln had become too provincial for her taste. Escape came through an offer to assume editorial duties for *Home Monthly,* a new women's magazine based in far-off Pittsburgh. This seems a strange first job for a woman who preferred men's slacks to dresses and who had only recently dropped the signature "William," but she took it for what it was worth. Moving to Pittsburgh in 1896, she plunged herself into editorial work, often writing the majority of the articles for each issue under a host of pseudonyms—many of them male. Indeed, this work allowed her to adopt different authorial masks and styles while protecting her artistic integrity. However, she managed to slip in a few stories she felt worthy of her name, and began experimenting with the Jamesian voice that would dominate her first collection of stories, *The Troll Garden* (1905). Editorial work was often at odds with serious creative work, a frustration that would haunt Cather for years to come. She left her job at *Home Monthly* in 1897, and for the next few years she worked at the *Pittsburgh Leader*, contributed to various journals and magazines, and even flirted with government jobs in Washington, D.C. In her most unprecedented move, in 1901 Cather accepted a position teaching Latin and English at Central High School in Pittsburgh, followed by a job at nearby Allegheny High School. Though Cather might not have had the ideal temperament for a teacher—she reportedly preferred advanced students to the common core—the job undoubtedly gave her more time to think, write, and be surrounded by the raw material of literature.

Whatever the imaginative constraints her working life may have placed upon her, Cather had found an unexpected source of inspiration in 1899 when she met Isabelle McClung, perhaps the greatest love of her life. The wealthy daughter of a Pittsburgh judge, Isabelle represented the East Coast elite that Cather hoped to emulate. Yet far from mere social climbing, the relationship was a true meeting of the minds, as Isabelle enjoyed slumming with the bohemian elements of Pittsburgh society and had a keen appreciation of books and theater. After their first meeting, the pair became inseparable to the extent that McClung established Cather in her parents' home, not as a guest but as a live-in companion. Clearly this caused some dismay in the McClung household, as Isabelle's father felt that Cather's questionable social status might raise a few eyebrows; his daughter was a woman of marriageable age, so she had to think of potential suitors, many of whom would question this bohemian living arrangement. Of course, Isabelle typically got her way, and Cather suddenly had a fashionable address among the Pittsburgh upper crust. As an added attraction, Isabelle set up an attic for her friend's exclusive use, a room where she could spend the summers devoted to her craft. This arrangement proved beneficial for many years, and the works poured forth: a collection of poems titled *April Twilights* (1903) and, soon after, her first collected stories.

Her collection of lyric verse was well received, though something of a false start for Cather, whose gift lay elsewhere. However, the stories that eventually became *The Troll Garden* represented an important step forward. While many of these are under the spell of Henry James (notably "Flavia and Her Artists" and "The Marriage of Phaedra"), a few show her grappling with western themes, even if they lack the nostalgia and grit of her later stories. Four stories—"The Sculptor's Funeral," "Paul's Case," "A Wagner Matinée," and "A Death in the

Desert"—escaped her censure and were revised and republished in later collections, almost indistinguishable from the mature Cather. Whereas "Flavia and Her Artists" seems a sterile attempt to record drawing room banter, a story like "A Wagner Matinée" allows a real woman to speak, a woman Cather might have carved straight out of memory (and did, as she herself admitted). These stories didn't make Cather an overnight success, but they did catch the attention of someone in a position to change her life, even if this change seemed to offer her the proverbial two steps backward rather than a strident foot forward.

In 1903 Cather was officially discovered by S. S. McClure, founder of the McClure Newspaper Syndicate and editor of *McClure's Magazine.* As Cather's biographer James Woodress details, Cather had submitted stories to *McClure's,* whose manuscript readers had recommended rejection each time. But in 1903 McClure's cousin H. H. McClure, who was looking for new writers on behalf of the syndicate, contacted Will Owen Jones, Cather's former editor at the *Nebraska State Journal.* Jones recommended Cather's work to H. H., who in turn passed it on to S. S. He wrote to Cather inviting her to resubmit her work and, after reading it, summoned the Pittsburgh schoolteacher to New York for a meeting, where he enthusiastically told her he wanted to publish all of her future work. Though he didn't publish enough to allow her to quit her teaching job, he did release the collection *The Troll Garden* in 1905. A year later Cather's relationship with McClure would deepen when, with a staffing crisis looming at the magazine, he traveled to Pittsburgh to ask Cather to join the editorial staff of his magazine. Thus in 1906 she left Pittsburgh for New York and a job as associate editor at *McClure's,* rising to the position of managing editor in 1908.

Even though Cather was now a published book author, she had little time to enjoy her brief flirtation with literary success: the editorial work at *McClure*'s proved all-consuming, made no easier by an assignment to write (uncredited) a biography of the religious leader Mary Baker Eddy. (Cather would also later write what was billed as an "autobiography" of S. S. McClure himself—which at least gave her a chance to mimic his speech, a useful task for a novelist.) These projects gave her precious little time to write and even less time to be with friends such as Isabelle. Yet for all her misgivings, Cather became a force to be reckoned with in New York, and many a younger writer looked up to her with a sufficient amount of respect—and dread. Elizabeth Sergeant recalls their first meeting in McClure's offices in January 1910. Expecting a "tall, grave, imposing" woman, she saw instead someone

> youngish, buoyant, not tall, rather square. No trace of the reforming feminist in this vital being who smiled at me, her face open, direct, honest, blooming with warmth and kindness.... Her boyish, enthusiastic manner was disarming, and as she led me through the jostle of the outer office, I was affected by the resonance of her Western voice, and by the informality of her clothes—it was as if she rebelled against urban comformities.
>
> (p. 33)

Clearly something of her "Will Cather" remained in the "boyish" character of her appearance and manners. However, Cather proceeded to grill Sergeant, whose article on the Italian tenements did not meet with her approval—she felt it was too liberal, too "welfare state." She may have been a progressive woman, but she had decidedly old-fashioned tastes, and cultivated these for *McClure's.*

FINDING A VOICE

For all the professional prestige that came with being an editor for a major national magazine, Sergeant (and many others) wondered what kept Cather in a rather thankless editorial position when stories remained to be written, books to be published. Partly it was the relationship between Cather and McClure, which was one of deep mutual respect. As Cather confided to Sergeant: "He reveres genius.... He's lost more money on Joseph Conrad than any editor alive!" (p. 40). McClure wanted the best, not just what sold, which meant that Cather's job was itself a profound validation. The cross-dressing girl from Red Cloud had triumphed on the grandest stage in America, an achievement that Sergeant, born in Massachusetts and a graduate of Bryn Mawr, couldn't fully appreciate. However, as her friendship with McClure deepened, Cather admitted that "nobody in the publishing world could let an artist *be* an artist—some other motive seeped in" (Sergeant, p. 50). She longed to be a Henry James or an Edith Wharton, writing for the love of art, and not to pad her bank account. Sooner or later, a break was inevitable.

The seeds of the rupture had been sown several years earlier, in 1908. At the literary salon of Mrs. Fields, a grande dame of Boston society, Cather met Sarah Orne Jewett, author of the famous collection of stories about rural Maine, *The Country of the Pointed Firs* (1896). Though Cather knew these stories in passing, before actually meeting Jewett she tended to lump all women writers in the same category—as peddlers of ineffectual, overly romantic potboilers. Jewett changed all this, as she proved that working on a small canvas—much like Jane Austen's famous "two-inch bit of ivory"—could still result in great art. Cather's previous use of Nebraska had been fleeting, usually seen as a negative force to run away from; Jewett urged her to inhabit her own literary landscape, which could prove just as fertile as a Boston drawing room. As their acquaintance deepened, Jewett became more forthright in her advice to Cather, singling out specific stories in *The Troll Garden* as the way forward: "the Sculptor's Funeral stands alone a head higher than the rest, and it is to that level you must hold and take for a starting-point.... if you don't keep and guard and mature your force, and above all, have time and quiet to perfect your work, you will be writing things not much better than you did five years ago" (quoted in O'Brien, p. 345). Such advice flew in the face of her previous mentors, such as McClure and Mrs. Fields, who wanted high society stories and polished wit. Cather knew she either had to strike off on her own and attempt something new, or else remain in McClure's shadow for the rest of her life.

With McClure's blessing, she took a leave of absence in the fall of 1911 and retired to Cherry Valley, New York, with her dearest companion, Isabelle McClung, in tow. There, she prepared her first novel, *Alexander's Bridge* (1912), a work still haunted by James's presence, for serial publication in *McClure's* (it appeared the next year under the title "Alexander's Masquerade"). However, at the same time, she experimented with something in the vein of "The Sculptor's Funeral," a story of life back home called "The Bohemian Girl." In some ways a trial run for *O Pioneers!,* it vividly paints the world of immigrants and farmers on the Nebraska plains, complete with a powerful, alluring heroine who is herself a trial run for Marie Shabata. While *Alexander's Bridge* was hardly a failure—garnering many positive reviews and pleasing the Mrs. Fieldses of the world—it represented a leave-taking for Cather. Having succeeded in the great literary metropolis, she may have felt validated in returning home, at least in print. As Cather's mentor, Jewett, had written, "You must know the world before you can know the village" (quoted in Sergeant, p. 89). By following Jewett's lead in *The Country of the Pointed Firs,* Cather could use Nebraska as her "Maine," yet at the same time fulfill her ambition to become a serious novelist. Why not write a grand epic about the pioneers and immigrants of the West? The only significant obstacle was public taste, and many a Mrs. Fields would find the subject matter of Nebraska an unsuitable theme for "great" literature.

A new generation of readers, however, begged to differ. Upon reading "The Bohemian Girl," Sergeant felt that "this was it," and Cameron McKenzie, McClure's son-in-law and an editor at the magazine, immediately accepted the story, offering her a whopping $750. For all her self-assurance, Cather balked and refused to accept so much for a mere story (the usual rate was $500). Yet publication swiftly followed, as did great enthusiasm for this unusual tale. She had no more excuses, and after Jewett's death in 1909, Cather was ready to find her own way. In 1912 she decided to visit her brother Douglass in Arizona; there she began her love affair with the

Southwest, touring the Grand Canyon and the Pueblo cliff dwellings, all of which would figure in her later fiction. She also reportedly was entranced by a handsome young Mexican guitar player, Julio, which further awakened her artistic sensibilities. Before returning east, she stopped in Nebraska to share the wheat harvest with her family; inspired by her surroundings, she sent Sergeant a poem called "Prairie Spring," which signaled the beginning of a new project, one that would fulfill the promise of "The Bohemian Girl." She returned to Pittsburgh and Isabelle—having finally left her job at *McClure's*—and set to serious work on the novel.

INDIAN SUMMER

In 1913 Sergeant received the manuscript of *O Pioneers!,* a novel that would definitively begin Cather's career. Cather had serious doubts about the book, largely because she felt it so deeply, more than any of her previous work. She instructed Sergeant to "hand her the unvarnished truth. She was given to emotional writing—if I found any, come down on it hard. She was not one who took offense—she could be detached from something she had created" (Sergeant, p. 92). Needless to say Sergeant found the book a revelation, writing that "the only flaw I could find in *O Pioneers!* was that it had no sharp skeleton." Cather hastily agreed, remarking that, true enough, Sergeant had named a weakness. But, she said, "the land has no sculptured lines or features. The soil is soft, light, fluent, black, for the grass of the plains creates this type of soil as it decays. This influences the mind and the memory of the author and so the composition of the story" (p. 97). Here was a new credo for Cather, an attempt to mimic the land in prose, to capture its soil and features not merely in description but in the very contour of the narrative. The novel proved to be her greatest success to date, and while the *Bookman* dismissed it as an "ordinary local color novel" (much as some critics had dismissed Jewett's work), the *New York Times* hailed it as "[an] expansion of the very essence of femininity.... American in the best sense of the word" (quoted in O'Brien, p. 446).

A brief Indian summer followed this period of happiness and success, as Cather basked in the warm acceptance of *O Pioneers!* and wrote her next novel, *The Song of the Lark* (1915). She had established herself as a successful novelist and independent woman, making pilgrimages—often with Isabelle—to the West to collect new material. However, when Isabelle's father died in 1915 the house had to be sold, and with it, Cather's beloved writing space. She suffered an even worse blow the following year when Isabelle married Jan Hambourg, a famous violinist. It was the end of an era, as Sergeant recalls: "Her face—I saw how bleak it was, how vacant her eyes. All her natural exuberance had drained away" (p. 140). The couple did their utmost to include Cather in their new life, offering her a writing study in their Toronto home as well as at their estate in France. But Cather found herself uninspired in these locales and hopelessly out of place in her companion's marriage. As the dark days of World War I closed in on the country, Cather nursed her wounds in the only way she knew how: through work. As Sergeant recalls, "She had not been able to forget that, in these war days, the youth of Europe, its finest flower, was dying" (p. 138). Though her next work, *My Ántonia* (1918), had nothing to do with the present, it stood as a monument to the past that was gone forever—much like the Europe buried under the smoke and debris of war.

Though Cather had found her way in fiction, she seemed less sure of her place in the world. As she told Sergeant during the war years, "Our present is ruined—but we had a beautiful past" (p. 121). All her subsequent fiction seems to affirm this, as she never allied herself with current trends or authors but doggedly spent her life exploring the past and the people left behind in history's wake. She did attempt to respond to the Great War in her next novel, *One of Ours* (1922), which told the story of an idealistic young Nebraskan dying in World War I. Sergeant, who had been a war correspondent and had even been injured in France, found it disappointing. She wrote that the book seemed "middle aged" and somewhat clinical: indeed, Cather began noting the sales of her book for the first time, as if maintaining her perch was a prime consideration (she was reportedly pleased to be outselling Sinclair Lewis' *Babbitt*). Despite a lack of critical acceptance, Cather stood by her book, and this confidence paid off in 1923 when it won the Pulitzer Prize. Sergeant felt that the public, devastated by the brutal reality of war, warmed to a story that treated war in an old-fashioned way, where violence and sexuality cast shadows over the work but never had to be seen.

THE PRIVATE PERSONA

Cather became increasingly private in her later years, notoriously disinterested in giving interviews or holding court; she had no circle, no followers, and never attended literary salons. She was also very protective of her work, especially after she allowed a motion picture adaptation of her next novel, *A Lost Lady* (1923), to go forward. The 1924 movie (remade as a talkie in 1934) distressed her to such an extent that "she not only refused all future movie commitments in her lifetime but saw to it, in her will, that her works should not be given on radio, television, or any other scientific invention of the future" (Sergeant, p. 272). Though she continued her rounds of travel and writing, her private life was largely spent with her live-in assistant, Edith Lewis, who selflessly made the author's life as comfortable and convenient as possible. Though the true nature of their relationship remains unclear, to her acquaintances it was a marriage in all but name. Lewis, who once worked at *McClure's* with Cather, also proved a canny editor, helping to shape many of her novels and stories through countless drafts. The two continued to live together until the end of Cather's life, and upon her death, Lewis became her literary executor and ruthlessly protected her legacy.

Though Cather often shocked her friends by her intolerance for anything modern, Cather continued to evolve as a writer, responding in her own way to the zeitgeist of the twenties and thirties. The beauty and mystery of the Southwest assumes center stage in two important novels, *The Professor's House* (1925) and *Death Comes for the Archbishop* (1927). Indeed, Cather seemed to go beyond her own nostalgic past and into history itself, trying to see through other times and voices. Works such as *Shadows on the Rock* (1931) and *Sapphira and the Slave Girl* (1940) would be considered historical fiction today, and the latter work explores her own family in the era of slavery. In this, she was inspired by the Norwegian author Sigrid Undset, who wrote beautiful evocations of the Icelandic sagas from the perspective of voiceless women. Cather followed her example by reaching into the distant past for her final novel, a work set in medieval Avignon to be called "Hard Punishments." Unfortunately, the work remained unfinished, and according to her will, all drafts and sketches were to be destroyed (a task which Edith Lewis dutifully fulfilled).

Cather retreated even further in her last decade, drawing away from old friends both physically and intellectually. As Sergeant explains,

> The world we lived in had now moved on, with the Second World War, into a menacing period of change. Willa feared and hated the psychological repercussions of change, even in peacetime, and was increasingly troubled by the heroic and tragic disasters of the war.... Her seeming withdrawal from vital participation into a mold of almost rigid quietness resulted. She is saving herself for her work, I thought ... [but] no other new books appeared in her lifetime.
>
> (p. 271)

Nevertheless, she did leave some important thoughts to future generations in one of her final books, *Not Under Forty* (1936), which contains the much anthologized essay "The Novel Démeublé." Though she had withdrawn her presence and much of her voice, she remained a careful observer and clearly still had much to say—and the ability to say it. Cather died suddenly from a cerebral hemorrhage at age seventy-three on April 24, 1947, in the midst of writing a novel and a collection of short stories (later published as "The Old Beauty and Others"). Fittingly, the following words from *My Ántonia* were carved on her gravestone: "... that is happiness; to be dissolved into something complete and great."

THE TROLL GARDEN *AND OTHER SHORT FICTION*

Cather had a natural gift for short stories, a talent she shares with her near contemporary, Anton Chekhov. Both could make the smallest canvas seem large and create vivid characters with a mere brushstroke; additionally, both were masters of dialogue and dialect, capturing the various social classes and backgrounds that existed in the western plains and Imperial Russia. However, unlike Chekhov, Cather made a number of false starts and had trouble matching her ability to her audience. Whereas Chekhov started out in humor magazines and gradually evolved these sketches into more humane, nuanced comedies, Cather often started too large and had trouble allowing her material to "grow up." Her first stories were written in the shadow of Gustave Flaubert, one of her favorite writers; her story "A Tale of the White Pyramid" (1892) attempts to delve into the orientalist mania of the late nineteenth century with disastrous results. As Sharon O'Brien notes, "The story's flaws are so glaring that it has not attracted attention even among critics interested in Cather's apprenticeship fiction. Its derivativeness is obvious: What did a girl from Nebraska know about pyramids and pharaohs?" (p. 199). Clearly she knew too much, though all of it derived from operas such as Giuseppe Verdi's *Aida* (1871), with its melodrama and picture-postcard orientalism. In general, her early stories suffered from hero worship, and she had a difficult time writing stories that couldn't have been written twenty or thirty years before by any number of writers.

She made a surprising leap forward in 1900, while working for the *Pittsburgh Leader*—a long, ambitious story titled "Eric Hermannson's Soul." The story explores a relationship similar to that in D. H. Lawrence's *Lady Chatterley's Lover* (1928), though of course, as the dates reveal, Cather thought it up first—and she famously detested Lawrence. Set in the Nebraska plains among the Scandinavian immigrant community, the story concerns a joyless farm worker, Eric Hermannson, who has given up music and dancing (his only true love) to follow the Lord. His dreary existence is disturbed when Margaret Elliot, a woman of society and polish, passes through on a western "tour" for amusement. He sees in her a feminine ideal far removed from the brutality and lifelessness of his world, while she is stirred by his rugged manhood, so different from the suitor who awaits her at home in New York City. Unlike many of the stories in *The Troll Garden,* Cather deftly avoids melodrama in this romance and makes the hapless farmer come alive in her suggestive prose. Eric is akin to Cather's later heroines such as Alexandra and Maria, though he also prefigures Aunt Georgiana in "A Wagner Matinée" (1904); all of these characters find themselves surrounded by "little men" in a world devoid of art and understanding. In each story, a man is responsible for this exile—in Eric's case, Asa Skinner, the Free Gospeller who forces him to abandon his artistic gods and live in mute subjection.

In a telling passage, Margaret tries to explain Eric's fascination to her brother, Wyllis: "I played the intermezzo from *Cavalleria Rusticana* for him ... He shuffled his feet and twisted his big hands up into knots and blurted out that he didn't know there was any music like that in the world. Why, there were tears in his voice, Wyllis!... it dawned upon me that it was probably the first good music he had ever heard in all his life. Think of it, to care for music as he does and never to hear it, never to know that it exists on earth!" (p. 10). This was Cather's fear her entire life, that her love of art and beauty would be stifled in Nebraska, where only the table scraps from touring companies and second-rate schools would provide it (or so she thought at that time). In Eric's life the only beauty he knows comes from the scriptures, which are preached to him in a compassionless fire-and-brimstone manner. Music is his first true god, one unafraid to speak of peace and consolation. Yet it proves only a momentary glimpse, for Margaret knows that his charm is part and parcel with the Nebraska landscape and would be completely out of place in New York: "*There he would be altogether sordid; impossible—a machine who would carry one's trunks upstairs, perhaps. Here he is every inch a man, rather picturesque; why is it?*" (p. 17). Though Margaret is bold enough to dance with a "servant," she could never abandon her position nor the approbation of her peers. She goes home to the East and leaves him unrepentant, having seen a glimpse of beauty that will sustain him for the rest of his life, despite the pastor's eternal shame: "And it is for things like this that you set your soul back a thousand years from God" (p. 29).

Though Cather sold "Eric Hermannson's Soul" to *Cosmopolitan* and even left the *Pittsburgh Leader* to work on her fiction, she seems to have second guessed its direction. Instead, she wrote many of the stories which, thanks to S. S. McClure, would be published as *The Troll Garden.* These stories are a curious mix of what Cather assumed readers wanted to read and what she thought she could get away with. In later years, only a few of these stories satisfied her, and she concocted the myth—only partially true—that her stylistic revelation came after the composition of "The Bohemian Girl." Yet both "Eric Hermannson's Soul" and at least three of the *Troll Garden* stories are recognizable to anyone familiar with the prairie novels, and at least one of them is worthy to stand with her greatest fiction. Sadly, the collection opens with one of the weakest stories in the collection, "Flavia and Her Artists," which tells of an artistic social gathering arranged by a wealthy patroness. While some of the characters were undoubtedly captured from life, the story reads like an unfinished sketch, the characters dressed for a party at which they never seem to arrive. A colleague of Cather's, Witter Bynner, noticed the debt this story and others had to Henry James and decided to send the great author the book (he had a passing acquaintance with James). However, James's only comment on the book was a lame apology made to Bynner for *not* reading it: "The sacred truth is that, being now almost in my 100th year, with a long and weary experience of such matters behind me, promiscuous fiction has become abhorrent to me, and I find it the hardest thing in the world to read almost *any* new novel" (Sergeant, p. 68). Indeed, "Flavia and Her Artists" does read like "promiscuous fiction" and might send any world-weary author running for the hills.

Much more promising is the second story, "The Sculptor's Funeral," which follows the artist's body back to the sleepy western town he hailed from. The mood is controlled and the characters spare and full of life, much more like a story of Chekhov's. Indeed, the style of the piece is curiously Russian, reminding one as much of Chekhov as Leo Tolstoy (one of Cather's favorite writers). Jewett singled out this particular story for praise and more or less proclaimed "this is it" even before the writing of "The Bohemian Girl." Yet this story is quickly buried in the Jamesian mode of the next three stories, "The Garden Lodge," "A Death in the Desert," and "The Marriage of Phaedra." Of these, "A Death in the Desert" shows the most promise and initially returns to the spare yet pregnant atmosphere of "The Sculptor's Funeral" (both open in train stations). As soon as Cather returns to a western setting her prose crackles with life and small details that elude her society yarns. The story also contains the germ of a familiar theme—a woman of art and beauty swallowed up by the wasteland of the endless "desert" (in this case, somewhere outside Cheyenne, Wyoming). Everett Hilgarde steps off the train and is mistaken for his brother, a composer who is known worldwide for his salon compositions. The woman who "recognized" him turns out to be a famous protégé and lover of Adriance (his brother), and she is slowly wasting away from an illness. Everett agrees to return home with her as a proxy for his brother, and she, in turns, tells him her history and regrets. At this point the story—quite unlike "Eric Hermannson's Soul"—becomes melodramatic, bogged down with too much nineteenth-century Romantic cliché: "This is the tragedy of effort and failure, the thing Keats called hell. This is my tragedy, as I lie here spent by the racecourse, listening to the feet of the runners as they pass me. Ah, God! The swift feet of the runners!" (p. 81).

In general, these early stories suffer whenever Cather tries to write of art and artists (again, a favorite Jamesian theme). Perhaps her own art was too personal to explore, so she felt compelled to borrow from others, using not only their hackneyed turns of phrase but their stock characters—the eccentric German archeologist, the doomed opera singer, and so on. Only in the last two stories does Cather hit her stride, saved largely by their protagonists, a young boy and an old woman. "Paul's Case" is one of her most forward-looking stories, as it examines a malcontent teenager on the verge of being expelled from school. But far from being a narcissistic thug, Paul spends every spare moment working as an usher at the symphony hall, drinking in the music, operas, and famous people who pass between its walls. Yet Paul's tragedy is similar to Eric Hermannson's: he weeps to hear the music but scarcely knows what it is—only that it is rarer, and purer, than anything in life: "in Paul's world, the natural nearly always wore the guise of ugliness, [so] ... a certain element of artificiality seemed to him necessary in beauty" (p. 71). For this reason, he bristles when he sees one of his workaday teachers at the symphony hall, looking far shabbier than the usual patrons of the arts. On the same hand, he reveres the singers and actors as rarified beings, though most of them are broken, cynical souls who hold him in contempt. Paul is ultimately crushed by this rebuff, as music is not a thing unto itself but merely an escape, a way to separate and raise himself above his teachers and peers. This story may have been Cather's own way of working out her disappointment in her own heroes, figures like James and A. E. Housman, the latter of whom she had met in England in 1902. During their visit he had dismissed his own poetry (which she worshipped) and had merely droned on about philology to Cather's friend Dorothy Canfield (O'Brien, p. 251).

The crowning achievement of *The Troll Garden,* however, is the brilliant story "A Wagner Matinée," which is worlds away from the superfluous "Flavia and Her Artists." The story concerns the arrival of the narrator's aunt to Boston to arrange her late husband's estate. His aunt had once been a teacher at the conservatory in Boston, a woman of great culture and sophistication. However, like many women in Cather's stories, she became smitten with a shiftless young man who follows opportunity to Nebraska. Together, they emigrated to Red Willow County where "For thirty years, my aunt had not been farther than fifty miles from the homestead" (p. 50). Now she arrives in Boston to reimagine her life as it was, though she seems terrified to confront it. As she once told her nephew, practicing the piano back in Nebraska, "Don't love it so well, Clark, or it may be taken from you. Oh! dear boy, pray that whatever your sacrifice may be, it be not that" (p. 51). This is one of the first stories where Cather is mindful of the sacrifices made by women of the plains. They all had lives and dreams that were slowly whittled away by the Nebraska wind, leaving only a dim reminder of their civilized past.

At the end of the story, the narrator takes her to a Boston Symphony concert, which he fears will either embarrass her or go over her head. However, once she enters the concert hall a change comes over her: "She sat looking about her with eyes as impersonal, almost as stony, as those which the granite Ramses in a museum watches the froth and fret that ebbs and flows about his pedestal—separated from it by the lonely stretch of centuries" (p. 53). Though many of her early stories lay on the classical learning with a trowel, here the allusion to Ramses is poignant: Aunt Georgiana is indeed something of a mummy, preserved in state on her humble homestead, her identity swallowed up by the vastness of the plains. Cather then adds an authentic touch that speaks to her future fiction:

> I have seen the same aloofness in old miners who drift into the Brown Hotel at Denver, their pockets full of bullion, their linen soiled, their haggard faces unshaven; standing in the thronged corridors as solitary as though they were still in a frozen camp on the Yukon, conscious that certain experiences have isolated them from their fellows by a gulf no haberdasher could bridge.
>
> (p. 53)

While the comparison seems unflattering, it suggests how place marks identity: the miner can never "unsee" the horrors of a Yukon winter. In the same way, Aunt Georgiana now carries the toils of Nebraska with her; its rituals and rhythms are carved on her skin, as her nephew notices: "Poor old hands! They had been stretched and twisted into mere tentacles to hold and lift and knead with" (p. 55). She may have returned to civilization with money to spend, but she has nothing to buy and nowhere to take it.

Throughout the concert, Aunt Georgiana maintains her composure despite the overflow of emotion and memory. Only when a famous song is intoned by a tenor—a song an old German once sang to her in Nebraska—does she finally break down. Contemplating his aunt, Clark has a revelation similar to that in "Eric Hermannson's Soul": "I was still perplexed as to what measure of musical comprehension was left to her, she who had heard nothing but the singing of Gospel Hymns at Methodist services in the square frame schoolhouse on Section Thirteen for so many years" (p. 57). How could a woman so sensitive to art retain her humanity for years and decades without it? Could a spark remain buried deep down, like a plant waiting to burst through the soil for spring? As the story ends, his aunt makes an uncharacteristic plea to her nephew: "I don't want to go, Clark. I don't want to go!" (p. 58). By now, he finally understands that her Indian summer will soon be swallowed up by an eternal winter, a complete whiteout of Western civilization. This had been Cather's greatest fear of returning home, to leave the sumptuous hall of art for a famine of culture. The story ends here, with the narrator contemplating the life he, himself, has escaped with a shudder: "the tall, unpainted house, with weather-curled boards; naked as a tower, the crook-backed ash seedlings where the dish-cloths hung to dry; the gaunt, moulting turkeys picking up refuse about the kitchen door" (p. 58). It was a world that still terrified Cather but would soon bring about her artistic liberation, since like Aunt Georgiana she had become one of the miners herself, looking at the wonders of New York through the gaze of a Yukon-haunted survivor.

The Troll Garden, for all its false starts, pointed the way forward to the mature novels. Throughout her career, stories served as touchstones for her larger work, a way to experiment and refine her material. The two most important stories following on the heels of *The Troll Garden* are "The Enchanted Bluff" (1909) and "The Bohemian Girl" (1912). The former story is more of a sketch, recalling the dreams of a group of boys to explore "the Enchanted Bluff," where the Cliff Dwellers of New Mexico built their fantastic cities carved into rock. The boys make a pact to be the first one there, but twenty years later, the narrator discovers that none of them have—himself included. Instead, they've passed down the legend to their children, who have their own dreams of discovering the Enchanted Bluff. This theme spills into many of her later works, featuring older, world-weary men learning that their heroes were only human and their dreams merely cloud puffs. Similarly, "The Bohemian Girl" is Cather's first attempt to create a strong female protagonist in Clara Vavrika, who would resurface more or less as Marie in *O Pioneers!* Married into a family of immigrants who have been shaped by the landscape into solemn respectability, Clara laments, "I'd like something to happen to stir them all up, just for once. There never was such a family for having nothing ever happen to them but dinner and threshing. I'd almost be willing to die, just to have a funeral" (p. 117). Clara finally runs off with Nils, a man who has gone abroad and come back to find her, and unlike Marie, she escapes to happiness and prosperity. The only solemn note is sounded by Nils's younger brother, Eric, who similarly longs for adventure. But when he is given money to reunite with Nils in far-off Bergen, the young boy falters, ultimately returning home. Like Clark in "A Wagner Matinée," young Eric realizes the fate of a lonely woman on the plains, a woman whose sacrifices are doomed to be forgotten. When he rushes back to her side, the woman receives him with an unexpected gesture—a familiar stroke of his head. This, to him, is ultimately greater than the ticket to Bergen. By now Cather realized that not everyone can escape to the East; someone has to stay home, otherwise the sacrifices will blow away in the wind, like so many ghost towns that dot the western landscape.

TWO MAJOR NOVELS: O PIONEERS! *AND* MY ÁNTONIA

O Pioneers! is the story of an America happening behind the scenes of Gilded Age excess and colonial largesse. No one in Boston or New York could have glimpsed it, as it ran against East Coast snobbery and ethnic prejudice. The throngs of immigrants who had settled the West from Germany, Scandinavia, Bohemia, and Russia were little more than a vaudeville theme and hardly a subject for serious literature. Yet, as Sergeant remarked,

> The story of the pioneer Puritans, "our over-rated progenitors" (after all they were middle-class malcontents, chock-full of narrow prejudice) had been a hundred times told ... But this fiercely untamed, untrammelled, sweeping natural world of the Divide, of which the author gave such rare and measured visual images, had new, almost cosmic vistas, overtones, and undertones.... The author seemed to be looking through objective lenses at something new God had made.
>
> (pp. 95–96)

Few Americans would have looked twice as the fields of Nebraska rushed past their train windows. Yet Cather knew that among each featureless, eternal vista was a vision of hope, perhaps the seeds of a future generation. As she writes in chapter 5 of part 1 of the novel, titled "The Wild Land," "The history of every country begins in the heart of a man or a woman" (p. 46). Though the stories of these simple folk would never be told, even by themselves, they planted more than seeds on the plains: their cultures, religions, languages, and dreams all went into the soil. Though their names and even countries of origin might be forgotten, their sacrifice would give birth to "something new God had made."

Cather's earlier stories about the plains carried a dark edge: it was a place to escape from, and those who didn't were slowly smothered to death, losing all sense of culture and identity (as Cather feared she would lose herself). By *O Pioneers!* she had come to a deeper understanding of the land, yet she also realized the cost of working it. Many of those who toiled all their lives on the plains were destroyed in body and spirit. Indeed, the very first sentence of the novel reads, "One January day, thirty years ago, the little town of Hanover, anchored on a windy Nebraska tableland, was trying not to be blown away" (p. 11). The sentence bubbles over with meaning: a story of a forgotten past, told of a town which tries to keep the past alive in its name—"Hanover." Yet the town is like a ship buffeted to and fro by the waves of a storm, being held in place by a tenuous anchor, the hopes and faith of the immigrant settlers. Yet hope and faith often failed, and so many little towns were rubbed out, despite years of selfless dedication. Alexandra's father, on his deathbed, realizes the terrible cost of settling the plains: "He felt [Alexandria's] youth and strength.... But he would not have had it again if he could, not he! He knew the end too well to wish to begin again. He knew where it all went to, what it all became" (p. 23). He kindled a vague hope that children like Alexandra could tame the land, but to what end he could no longer remember. He had seen "the end" too many times to doubt the result—an accruing of debt that could never be paid, only passed on to the next generation. Against such a sum, death seemed a reasonable payment.

Even for the younger men, the land is either terrifying or inscrutable. As their father is dying, Alexandra's brothers are ready to pull up stakes and flee to Chicago. Only Alexandra retains an almost spiritual belief in the land, as if she can already see the life busting forth: "When you drive about over the country you can feel it's coming" (p. 48). This deep conviction is echoed in a recurring dream she has throughout the novel, where a mysterious man "like no man she knew" carried her across the fields like "a sheaf of wheat." The man was "yellow like the sunlight, and there was the smell of ripe cornfields about him" (p. 127). As she ages, the dream comes to her after an exhausting day of work, when fatigue challenges her wide-awake ideals. Whether this figure is the land itself, or death, or a muted sexual fantasy, the images are always of sun and fields and wheat. Alexandra never looks for salvation elsewhere or plans a hasty escape; she pledges herself to the land like a bride, and it willingly accepts her on her own terms, as a woman.

Notably, her brothers refuse to see her as anything but a sister, and a singularly androgynous one at that. Her sex is effectively erased in this society, since she cannot run a farm and manage the business and be a woman; only a *man* can do these things (successfully, at any rate). When she contemplates marrying her longtime love, Carl, at forty, her brothers rebel; even the youngest and most sensible, Emil, responds, "Alexandra's never been in love, you crazy!... She wouldn't know how to go about it. The idea!" (p. 98). She is expected to sacrifice herself for their well-being, since men are the true saviors of the family: "That's the woman of it; if she tells you to put in a crop, she thinks she's put it in. It makes women conceited to meddle in business" (p. 107). Yet even Carl abandons her when she insists on being a woman on a man's terms. When he tells her "It is your fate to be always surrounded by little men" (p. 113), he is also talking about himself. She cannot hope for a true partnership, as even the best men—Emil and Carl—are too "small" to share her vision. She is just "Alexandra," much as Cather herself was just "Willa," a woman who had to wear pants and become an editor to see the world.

Even a "smaller" woman, such as Marie Shabata, ends up sacrificed to the gods; in this case, the gods of greed and disappointment. As the beautiful daughter of a happy-go-lucky Bohemian, she commands high value among the male farmers. Yet she falls for a sour dandy, Frank Shabata, who abandons his pretensions to work the land—and then blames her for it. As he admits to himself much later,

> For three years he had been trying to break her spirit.... He wanted his wife to resent that he was wasting his best years among these stupid and unappreciated people; but she had seemed to find the people quite good enough.... he wanted her to feel that life was as ugly and unjust as he felt it. He had tried to make her life ugly.
>
> (p. 162)

Like Alexandra's love of the land, Marie loves the people: she smiles too readily, forgives too easily, and pays far too little deference to her husband. Yet she too is trapped and squandered in a foolish marriage and longs for the simple pleasures of life—which she ultimately finds with Emil, another trapped would-be man of the world. Throughout the novel—and in much of her other fiction—men are lured by the beauty of the natural world, only to harm it cruelly when they find themselves "wasted." Marie seems to embody Cather's own belief, as told to Elizabeth Sergeant: "What could be more beautiful, if you had it in you, than to be the wife of a farmer and raise a big family in Nebraska?" (Sergeant, pp. 115–116). For Cather, and for all her women, "work was all" (p. 115), and in work they found a higher calling and a freedom from the oppressive smallness of men.

Sergeant writes, "Robert Frost once said to me that the word 'escape' is ambiguous; is one escaping *from* something or *to* something? It seems to me that Willa, if possible, and certainly quite without shame or repentance, escaped both *from* and *to*" (p. 197). Cather's next novel, *The Song of the Lark,* was very much about escaping from something—the story of an artist escaping her cage and finding success on the grandest stage, much as Cather had herself. *My Ántonia,* however, captures more of this sense of escaping "from and to." Though Ántonia is the spiritual center of the book, Cather cleverly frames her tale in a story within a story: an unnamed editor has published Jim Burden's account of his experiences with Ántonia and the "hired girls." In the first edition published in 1918, Cather opened the book with more of Jim's life as an unhappy railroad lawyer with a failing marriage, but she cut this in her revised version of 1926, since it makes Jim a character to be observed rather than a perspective. For Jim's eyes are very much Cather's own, and choosing a male protagonist for this most personal of novels seems akin to her early impersonation as Will Cather. Jim is driven to find success away from the small-town life of the plains, yet success for him (like Cather) only taught him to love the village and the people he left behind.

In book 2, chapter 6, of *My Ántonia,* Jim is fighting against the cold winter wind that has just overtaken the land. As he reflects,

> The pale, cold light of the winter sunset did not beautify—it was like the light of truth itself. When the smoky clouds hung low in the west and the red sun went down behind them, leaving a pink flush on the snowy roofs and the blue drifts, then the wind sprang up afresh, with a kind of bitter song, as if it said: "This is reality, whether you like it or not. All those frivolities of summer, the light and

> shadow, the living mask of green that trembled over everything, they were lies, and this is what was underneath. This is the truth." It was as if we were being punished for loving the loveliness of summer. (p. 156)

This passage embodies so much of the book itself, where the stark, cold truth of existence casts long shadows over the beautiful reverie of the author's "summer." *My Ántonia* is a book suffused with longing and regret, as the narrator looks back on the most fascinating woman he has ever known, the Czech immigrant Ántonia Shimerda, and his bucolic prairie upbringing in Nebraska.

As the story begins, his life is in the grips of winter—a man of the city, with a rather cold marriage, though we learn nothing further about this. He runs into a friend who also knew Ántonia (the actual author/editor of the book, establishing a clever frame story). His life explodes into one final spring, prompting him to write the story of his life with Ántonia, though she fades in and out of his reminiscences. He offers the book to his friend as a hastily written draft, though he claims "I didn't arrange or rearrange. I simply wrote down what of herself and myself and other people Ántonia's name recalls to me." (p. 30). This suggests that what follows is not a novel per se, but a beautiful poem of the plains. It is also a kind of innocence/experience story much as William Blake might have written had he been a woman and raised in Nebraska. The novel's epigram from Virgil, *"optima dies ... prima fugit"* (the best days are the first to flee), carries through the novel, as the author's hopes and dreams are all realized, yet his best days were those of his childhood, when he and Ántonia were young, watching thunderheads on the horizon and listening to tales of the old country.

The novel opens with Jim moving from Virginia to Nebraska after his parents die, so he can live with his grandparents (slightly autobiographical, since Cather made the same move, but *with* her parents). As he arrives in town, he notices a family of immigrants, whom he later learns are the Shimerda family, come to make a life on the plains. Jim's kindhearted grandmother takes pity on the Shimerdas, who have purchased a miserable hovel from a fellow countryman and struggle to eke out an existence. Indeed, the father is a nostalgia-plagued musician who has no head for farming and no love for the New World; this leaves his wife, a somewhat vain, grasping woman, to keep their three children fed and their farm in some sort of working order. Jim befriends the children, particularly Ántonia, the middle child, who longs to learn English and go to school. With the father's blessing—but much less the mother's—Jim tutors Ántonia in English and brings her into the family fold.

Together, the two children go off on adventures, meet the other immigrants in town—including two Russians who have a terrible past—and learn that not everyone finds the life they're looking for in America. As Ántonia tells Jim, "If I live here, like you, that is different. Things will be easy for you. But they will be hard for us" (p. 131). This strikes a surprisingly modern note, as few in the community welcome the new immigrants, though they work themselves to the bone to prosper—and become the true inheritors of the prairie (as future chapters reveal). However, Ántonia is also speaking of her own father, who cannot find peace away from home, dreaming of old friends and old lands. Eventually, he kills himself, despite the love he has for his children. As Jim reflects, "I remembered the account of Dives in torment, and shuddered. But Mr. Shimerda had not been rich and selfish; he had only been so unhappy that he could not live any longer" (p. 104). For so many people in the book, the winter always threatens to eat up the promise of spring as punishment for past joys. In his old age, Jim can perhaps relate even more to poor Mr. Shimerda, as he finds himself stranded in his own foreign country: the future, where he has success and stability but only memories of the ones he loved.

Each chapter can almost stand alone as a short story, haunting in its evocation of landscape, character, and memory. Some are mere vignettes, as when Jim and the immigrant girls (all teenagers now) witness the sun set behind a distant tractor: "Magnified across the distance by the horizontal light, it stood out against the sun, was exactly contained within the circle of the disc;

the handles, the tongue, the share—black against the molten red. There it was, heroic in size, a picture writing on the sun" (p. 204). Others are dramatic narratives, as when Russian Peter recounts a fateful trip across the wolf-haunted plains of Russia with a wedding party. Each "book" of the novel roughly traces Jim's development, with the longest being the first book, documenting his childhood relationship with Ántonia and her family. "The Hired Girls" is the second book, which recounts the immigrant girls migrating to town to become servants and setting the polite, hypocritical society aflame with dancing and intrigue. Here Jim becomes smitten not only with Ántonia but also the Norwegian Lena Lingard, with whom he embarks upon a tenuous relationship. Ántonia watches from afar and remains his distant admirer and protector, as their childhood bond is stronger than blood or marriage. In one of the most touching scenes of the book, Jim gives a graduation speech which the entire town attends, including all the "hired girls." At the end, Ántonia rushes over to him and says his speech reminded her of her father, now long dead. Jim admits he thought of her father the entire time. Then, says Jim, "she threw her arms around me, and her dear face was all wet with tears. I stood watching their white dresses glimmer smaller and smaller down the sidewalk as they went away. I have had no other success that pulled at my heartstrings like that one" (p. 195). His speech was for Ántonia, the one gift he could offer her in a world where her father was just a memory, lost in an unmarked grave at the corner of a forgotten country road.

The last two books of the novel are brief, and Ántonia scarcely makes an appearance until the end. In "Lina Lingard," Jim is at college in Lincoln and takes up with Lina, who has opened up her own business making clothes for the prairie elite. The two take in the local theater and embark upon a romance of high culture, though remain otherwise chaste. These chapters crackle with understated passion, as Jim can never quite bring himself to settle down with Lina, and Lina herself worries that she isn't good enough for Jim. In the end, he leaves her forever, going off to follow his mentor to Harvard. The final book, "Cuzak's Boys," is some twenty years later, when Jim finally decides to track down Ántonia, who has settled down in the country with a husband and nearly a dozen children. Terrified to encounter an aged, worn-out wife, he instead finds her brimming with life and laughter. Her children are like Ántonia herself—full of cleverness and curiosity—and immediately take to Jim, whom they have heard endless stories about. It's a bittersweet ending, as Jim learns that not everyone has given up hope and become snowed in by the storms of old age.

As part of the earth herself, Ántonia is reborn every spring, her youth shining through her gray hairs and failing limbs, quite unlike the women of the towns and cities—or even Jim himself, who only looks to the past for comfort. Reflecting on Tiny, one of the "hired girls" who traveled to Alaska and became a canny businesswoman, he writes, "She was satisfied with her success, but not elated. She was like some one in whom the faculty of becoming interested is worn out" (p. 242). The same, sadly, was true for Jim as well, until he heard the casual mention of Ántonia's name. His manuscript is a final flicker of spring, or perhaps an autumnal burst of color before the flame goes out forever. Yet out on the plains, Ántonia and her children will live and laugh in the language of the old country, still remembering how to be interested in life and not terribly concerned with modern notions of success.

TWO LATE NOVELS: A LOST LADY *AND* THE PROFESSOR'S HOUSE

In 1925 the *Saturday Review of Literature* published a review of Cather's recent book, *The Professor's House,* which addressed the stylistic change in the author's work:

> Miss Cather, I suspect, is wearying of broad pioneer movements and sharp contrasts between flaming emotion and commonplace environment. She is going deeper, and is prepared to defend the thesis that a new country may have old souls in it.... An old soul, as the philosophers say, is driven toward recognition. Life ... is a progress in self-realization, a series of discoveries as to what experience means

> for *him* when stripped of illusion and in its ultimate reality. Such a soul is most likely to fall away from his closest associates: success may be a burden, an admired wife a growing problem, children who become the hard worldlings that most of us are in our thirties, a depression rather than a comfort.... This, more than *O Pioneers!,* is a pioneering book.
>
> (quoted in Murphy, p. 198)

Many of the books that followed *My Ántonia* capture this sense of moving away, much as Cather herself was withdrawing from her friends and society. The characters are more private, more disillusioned, and less sure of their place in the world. Fittingly, these novels are the last to deal explicitly with Nebraska and her childhood memories; after this, she moves farther afield, both in geography and imagination. Indeed, her last completed novel *(Sapphira and the Slave Girl)* went back in time and space to her childhood home of Virginia, long before she had any true memories to conjure up. Yet in these late novels, considered problematic by some, she challenges the notion that her works are mere elegies of the plains, or even a reactionary defense of the past. They remain her most "modernist" works—if not in form, then in her response to the ideas rapidly shaping twentieth-century American life.

A Lost Lady (1923) is most explicitly about the world that vanished after the First World War, as symbolized in the alluring, tragic portrait of Mrs. Forrester. As Cather told Flora Merrill of the *New York World* shortly after its publication, "*A Lost Lady* was a beautiful ghost in my mind for twenty years before it came together.... All the lovely emotions that one has had some day appear with bodies, and it isn't as if one found ideas suddenly. Before this, the memories of these experiences and emotions have been like perfumes" (April 19, 1925; Willa Cather Archive). The words "a beautiful ghost" capture not only Mrs. Forrester's character, but the elegiac tone of the work itself, as something half-remembered, half-dreamed. The story follows Niel Herbert, a young man who grows up in the Colorado town of Sweet Water, and his fascination with the most important people in town, the Forresters. For Niel, Mrs. Forrester represents the beauty and grace of a vanished ideal, both of aristocracy and femininity. Mrs. Forrester is always on hand to indulge the village children, have fresh-baked cookies delivered to them in a basket, and tend their wounds when they tumble out of a tree. Niel also notes how men from all over the country stop to greet her, feeling it an incredible honor to receive her smiles—even when, occasionally, she playfully mimics them in good-natured sport.

However, as Niel grows up he realizes that the idyllic world of the Forresters hides a dark secret: Mrs. Forrester is having a long-standing affair with a local cad, Frank Ellinger, who doesn't respect her or deserve her affection. Niel overhears one of their trysts through an open window, his idol's voice full of coy sensuality. The realization strikes Niel with all the self-righteousness of adolescence, as he remarks, "In that instant between stooping to the window-still and rising, he had lost one of the most beautiful things in his life.... Beautiful women, whose beauty meant more than it said ... was their brilliancy always fed by something coarse and concealed? Was that their secret?" (pp. 71–71). How could the woman so many people adored, and who commanded the respect of the upright, virtuous Captain Forrester, nurse a snake in her bosom? As the novel continues, Mrs. Forrester becomes more and more sordid, with only fleeting glimpses of her former dignity and grace. Indeed, after the captain is confined to a wheelchair, she clings to the support of the most hated man in town, Ivy Peters. For Niel, this stings the worse, since Ivy (like all the boys in town) once felt it an honor to be recognized by her; now he treats her like a servant and ignores her husband. Worse still, when taking his final leave of Mrs. Forrester, Niel catches Ivy "unconcerningly [putting] both arms around her, his hands meeting over her breast. She did not move, did not look up, but went on rolling out pastry" (p. 144). The sentence reveals a broken woman, forced to endure Ivy's leering advances to preserve some semblance of social status. Sadly, the very men who should protect her—Niel, Captain Forrester, and even the Judge (Niel's uncle)—all sit by in silence, waiting for her to become irrecoverably lost to society.

As a young man, Niel cannot appreciate the vulnerable position Mrs. Forrester finds herself in, particularly after her husband loses his fortune and then his health in a single blow. Alone in a small town, with the world of class and privilege dwindling around them, she is left with a single coin to purchase her freedom—though at an exorbitant rate. Even Niel abandons her the moment she ceases to be lovely and artistic: he has no use for a real woman, preferring the shallow artifice of smiles and swishing skirts (similar to the boy in "Paul's Case"). As he reflects toward the end of the novel, when he postpones his study in architecture to nurse the ailing Captain, "He liked being alone with the old things that had seemed so beautiful to him in his childhood.... No other house could take the place of this one in his life" (p. 121). The word "seemed" is important here, as he knows better now—but prefers the presence of ghosts. Even Mrs. Forrester can be who she once was with the proper stagecraft and lightning. Yet new characters insist on intruding, and Ivy Peters' presence effectively exorcises his childhood bliss. Not coincidentally, Peters finally buys the house and evicts Mrs. Forrester, installing his own "Wyoming bride" in her place, who will undoubtedly become some other boy's "Mrs. Forrester."

Something of Cather's own life bleeds through this passage, since Cather also tried to be "alone with the old things" when Isabelle McClung married her beloved violinist. Having lost her writing study when Isabelle's house was sold, she attempted to install herself in a new McClung property—first in Toronto, then in France. In neither one could she find the proper "light." Interestingly, Cather dedicated *A Lost Lady* to Isabelle's husband, Jan Hambourg, only to remove it some years later. The multiple portraits of seedy, enterprising men who seduce Mrs. Forrester may be a sour reflection of the worldly Hambourg, particularly that of Frank Ellinger. Though their friendship endured, Isabelle shifted much of her attention to her husband, another artist in need of a muse. To a writer, this was the ultimate betrayal, particularly as Cather once claimed all her novels were written for (and through) Isabelle. Niel expresses Mrs. Forrester's betrayal in no uncertain terms: "she was not willing to immolate herself, like the widow of all these great men, and die with the pioneer period to which she belonged" (p. 145). Instead, she "preferred life on any terms," and Cather might have laid the same crime at Isabelle's feet—a woman who obstinately clung to vanity and wealth rather than living (and dying) for art.

This notion of choosing between wealth and art is also at the heart of *The Professor's House,* perhaps one of her most original novels. It also boasts an innovative structure, two linked short stories framing a novella, "Tom Outland's Story," which was indeed a self-contained work. Though the characters of St. Peter and Tom (and their stories) might initially seem disparate, Cather had a strict plan from the beginning. As she explained to the College English Association,

> I tried to make Professor St. Peter's house rather overcrowded and stuffy with new things; American properties, clothes, furs, petty ambitions, quivering jealousies—until one got rather stifled. Then I wanted to open the square window and let in the fresh air that blew off the Blue Mesa, and the fine disregard of trivialities which was in Tom Outland's face and in his behaviour.
>
> ("On *The Professor's House,*" p. 31)

As this passage suggests, Cather is at war with the products and advertisements of a selfish world, a world that had become "feminine" in the most commercial sense. In *A Lost Lady,* Ivy Peters polluted the simple beauty of Mrs. Forrester's house, converting it to yet another joyless mansion. For Cather, both society and literature were being similarly overcrowded by expensive tastes and up-to-the-minute fads. As she wrote in "The Novel Démeublé," "The higher processes of art are all processes of simplification. ... In this direction only, it seems to me, can the novel develop into anything more varied and perfect than all of the many novels that have gone before" (*Not Under Forty,* p. 49). Her late novels were an attempt to achieve this simplicity, even at the expense of Cather being thought old fashioned or "past her prime."

In *The Professor's House,* Tom Outland, as his allegorical name suggests, is a young man looking for something beyond the cramped boundaries of civilization, a promised land to complement his artistic vision. Not surprisingly, he finds it much where Cather found it herself, in the sublime remains of the cliff dwellers. This hearkens back to her brief short story, "The Enchanted Bluff," where the boys all bet they would be the first to penetrate the secret of the cliffs; in this story, Tom really *does* go, and finds an exotic, primeval beauty that has never been bought or sold. As he explains it, "I see them here, isolated, cut off from other tribes, working out their destiny, making their mesa more and more worthy to be a home for man, purifying life by religious ceremonies and observances.... They were, perhaps, too far advanced for their time and environment" (p. 198). Their demise, he feels, came from a horde of uncivilized tribes who couldn't appreciate their great experiment; they simply "killed and went their way" (p. 199). Anxious to protect this land from vulgar commercialism, he goes to the Smithsonian and navigates through the endless streams of red tape, only to find disinterest and disappointment. Finally, after weeks and weeks of waiting, an office assistant tells him that "the only thing Dr. Ripley really cared about was getting a free trip to Europe and acting on a jury, and maybe getting a decoration. 'And that's what the Director wants, too,' she said. 'They don't care much about dead and gone Indians'" (p. 212).

This is the fear of every artist, and of Cather most of all: can anything pure and artistic remain so for long? Can the "world" as a commercial entity truly understand art that has no market value other than timeless beauty? Tom Outland finds his El Dorado in the desert, but ultimately no one is interested; he can only share his story with the professor of history, Godfrey St. Peter, another "explorer" in the realm of art. Yet he too has become obsolete in his own country, as his magnum opus on Spanish explorers in the New World has brought him fortune and a degree of fame—all of which is taken by his wife and daughters to buy a new house with new responsibilities. Meanwhile, St. Peter refuses to leave his modest study, the one place where he can work and dream among the ancient monuments of civilization. Fittingly, his family despairs over his foolish condition, and his wife even laments, "I wonder what it is that makes you draw away from your family.... I'd much rather see you foolish about some woman than becoming lonely and inhuman" (p. 141). Interestingly, his pursuit of art is seen as "inhuman" because it draws him away from the conventional world of houses, clothing, and "sensible" adultery. The artistic crises of both men draw them away from the world—and especially from the world of women, who increasingly represent convention and commercialism.

The absence of strong women in the book is surprising and perhaps suggests Cather's despair about not finding suitable woman among the ranks of authors. Perhaps they were being lured into more commercial fiction, writing the kind of romantic potboilers—or worse, modernist claptrap—she always detested as an editor. Cather instinctively sides with St. Peter and Outland, both of them iconoclastic explorers and worshippers of the past. St. Peter is also a teacher, much as Cather once was, and the novel shows Cather keenly aware of the pressures being brought upon higher education. Like Tom's concern for the cliffs, St. Peter is protective of his university, which threatens to be overrun by an uncivilized bureaucracy:

> [St. Peter] had resisted the new commercialism, the aim to "show results" that was undermining and vulgarizing education. The State Legislature and the board of regents seemed determined to make a trade school of the university. Candidates for the degree of Bachelor of Arts were allowed credits for commercial studies; courses in book-keeping, experimental farming, domestic science, dress-making, and what not. Every year the regents tried to diminish the number of credits required in science and the humanities.
>
> (p. 120)

Just like the director of the Smithsonian, the professors are left scrambling for honors rather than cultivating young minds, with the prizes handed out to those professors willing "to give the taxpayers what they wanted" (p. 121). It is a grim and prophetic passage, as Cather contrasts the noble but devastated ruins of Blue Mesa with the eventual fate of the Western university—and by extension, the Western mind.

CRITICAL FORTUNES

Writing in an afterword to *The Troll Garden* in 1961, the writer Katherine Anne Porter admitted that "[Cather] was not, in the popular crutch-word to describe almost any kind of sensation, 'exciting'; so far as I know, no body, not even one of the Freudian school of critics, ever sat up at nights with a textbook in one hand and her works in the other, reading between the lines to discover how much sexual autobiography could be mined out of her stories" (quoted in Murphy, "Critical Essays on Willa Cather," p. 31). Though that situation has dramatically changed, it does capture the state of Cather studies in the decades following her death. Despite the enormous commercial success of her stories, she quickly faded from view even in her own lifetime, becoming more a respected writer than an important one. In the 1910s she had been adopted by the naturalists, who saw works like *O Pioneers!* and *My Ántonia* as a remedy against the formulaic drawing-room banter of so many fashionable novels. Unfortunately, this praise tended to typecast her as a "local color" writer, or a "writer of the plains," which didn't allow much room for growth. Critical assessment quickly soured upon the 1922 publication of *One of Ours,* which even good friends like Elizabeth Sergeant found naive and sentimental; the new generation of artists, including Ernest Hemingway, were outright contemptuous of it. Hemingway joked that in *One of Ours,* she had taken the theme of war and "Catherized" it, instead of protesting against the senseless waste of human life. Whatever the merits of that work, the young Turks of the modernist movement—most of them men—had little use for a middle-aged woman of the previous generation. She didn't write like them, didn't think like them, and held to old-fashioned ideas of war and nationalism (almost like Rudyard Kipling, another detested idol). Winning the Pulitzer Prize in 1923 for *One of Ours* was the final nail in the coffin.

As Cather entered her darker period, starting with the publication of *A Lost Lady,* the critical establishment had gone further left politically. Her works seemed either completely apolitical or tastelessly reactionary. Cather declined to help matters in her interviews and nonfiction, including her final book of essays, *Not Under Forty* (1936), which she suggested no one under forty should even bother reading. All the while, her books sold out, universities gave her honorary doctorates, and publications such as *Catholic World* showered her with praise. She became, much like Kipling in England, an establishment writer, which removed her completely from the vanguard of critical thought. Upon her death, the critics had a chance to establish her legacy, calling her a minor novelist and fixing on her "charm" rather than her art. In short, she was filed away as a successful—if gauche—female novelist, suitable for polite reading but little else. Throughout the 1940s and 1950s, most surveys of American literature barely mentioned her at all or offered the indulgent gesture of a footnote. It seemed she had gone the way of an Ann Radcliffe or a Mary Corelli, contemporary success fading into posthumous obscurity.

Though a small band of admirers kept her flame alive, Cather's true literary rehabilitation came in the 1970s, when feminists found a way "in" to her works. For many years, Cather had been the elephant in the room, a woman who preferred writing of men and, worse still, even adopted a male persona in her youth. Yet few could deny her originality and artistic voice, particularly when writers such as Eudora Welty, Katherine Anne Porter, and Joanna Russ were devoted fans. A new way of thinking about Cather emerged when scholars considered the role of her male narrators: did she intend them to be unreliable narrators? An example of this approach is found in Jean Schwind's essay "The Benda Illustrations to *My Ántonia*: Cather's 'Silent' Supplement to Jim Burden's Narrative" (1985): here, Schwind suggests the Benda illustrations that Cather added to the text (against the expressed wishes of her publishers) "correct" Jim's authority as a narrator and expose him as not only unreliable but biased and sexist. After all, we never truly get Ántonia's story in the novel—it is simply "*my* Ántonia," which Schwind sees as being an ironic title and perspective. Once scholars realized one actually could "[read] between the lines to discover how much sexual autobiography could be mined out of her stories" (to quote Porter once more), Cather became a hot commodity in academia as never before.

Feminist and psychoanalytical studies of Cather's novels made the next step somewhat inevitable: the queering of Willa Cather. Scholars had already suggested that she might have been a lesbian, but this was difficult to "prove" in any definitive way. Cather had burned all of her correspondence with Isabelle McClung, for example, and had her companion, Edith Lewis, destroy other documents. Moreover, Cather's will embargoed the publication of her remaining personal letters, and for many years Cather scholars who did gain access to them were legally allowed only to paraphrase them in their published studies. The embargo eased in 2011, and in 2013, five hundred of Cather's original letters were finally published in *The Selected Letters of Willa Cather.* Though the letters shed light on a great variety of subjects, they contained little in the way of revelations about her sexual life, beyond some candid words written at age nineteen to her college crush, Louise Pound.

Aside from letters, however, what has remained for scholars since the 1980s are the books themselves, which still have the power to speak of things hidden and forgotten. Perhaps the most important work to establish this approach was Sharon O'Brien's 1984 essay "'The Thing Not Named': Willa Cather as a Lesbian Writer," which paraphrased the abovementioned letter to Louise Pound to prove Cather's same-sex inclinations. O'Brien went on to produce one of the best autobiographical studies of the early Cather, *Willa Cather: The Emerging Voice* (1987), which examined not only the "Will Cather" years but also Cather's ambivalent relationship with her mother. The book's strength is its documentation of Cather's male literary models and of how consciously she envisioned herself in this tradition—at least until encountering her most important female mentor, Sarah Orne Jewett. While some have criticized O'Brien's rather limited focus (she stops at *O Pioneers!*), it still remains a compelling and often persuasive account of the inner struggle that led to Cather's breakthrough as a writer.

More recently, multicultural studies have examined—and at times, tried to rehabilitate—an author who often expressed racist and nationalist views in line with her times (she *was* born in the nineteenth century, after all). Yet for many scholars, she remains something of an anomaly: a woman who had male role models, who expressed conservative politics, who ignored Native Americans and trivialized Mexicans, who espoused an almost Victorian sense of religion. The best artists, it seems, can never be reduced to aesthetic propaganda; they doggedly resist having words put in their mouths, forcing scholars to examine her works piecemeal or out of context. Yet, like Shakespeare or Jane Austen, Cather's works not only continue but also lend themselves to new times and readers, even those blissfully unaware of theoretical trends. In many ways, her inability to come out for any one cause, or to espouse a specific political system or agenda, is what makes her universal (a term many twenty-first-century scholars detest). As Joanna Russ, author of *The Female Man* (1975), explains, "It was possible for Cather, in masquerade, to speak more completely, more clearly, and less self-consciously than could, for example, Djuna Barnes in *Nightwood*" (quoted in Acocella, p. 73). Had Cather been born in the twentieth century, she might have identified as lesbian and been forced to write more doctrinal texts. Luckily for us, she wrote of half-lights and shadowy truths, obscuring her own beliefs and leaving readers and scholars to find what meaning they can. This might be the despair of the biographer, but it assures that each new generation can encounter Cather anew, without baggage, and simply accept the works as they are. As Porter herself admitted, "I am not much given to reading about authors, or not until I have read what they have to say for themselves. I found Willa Cather's books for myself, early, and felt no need for intermediaries between me and them" (quoted in Murphy, p. 34). Here, then, is the beauty and frustration of Cather's art: anyone can read her books, and they speak gloriously, artistically, for themselves.

Selected Bibliography

WORKS OF WILLA CATHER

NOVELS

Alexander's Bridge. Boston: Houghton Mifflin, 1912.

O Pioneers! Boston: Houghton Mifflin, 1913; New York: Everyman's Library, 2011.

The Song of the Lark. Boston: Houghton Mifflin, 1915.

My Ántonia. Boston: Houghton Mifflin, 1918. Revised, 1926; New York: Signet, 1994.

One of Ours. New York: Knopf, 1922.

A Lost Lady. New York: Knopf, 1923; New York: Vintage, 1990.

The Professor's House. New York: Knopf, 1925.

My Mortal Enemy. New York: Knopf, 1926.

Death Comes for the Archbishop. New York: Knopf, 1927.

Shadows on the Rock. New York: Knopf, 1931.

Lucy Gayheart. New York: Knopf, 1935.

Sapphira and the Slave Girl. New York: Knopf, 1940.

The Professor's House. New York: Vintage, 1990.

SHORT STORY AND POETRY COLLECTIONS

April Twilights. Boston: R. G. Badger, 1903.(Poetry.)

The Troll Garden. New York: McClure, Phillips, 1905; New York: Signet, 1961.

Youth and the Bright Medusa. New York: Knopf, 1920.

Obscure Destinies. New York: Knopf, 1932.

The Old Beauty, and Others. New York: Knopf, 1948.

Great Short Works of Willa Cather. Edited by Robert K. Miller. New York: Harper Perennial, 1993.

ESSAYS, JOURNALISM, AND LETTERS

Not Under Forty. New York: Knopf, 1936.

"On *The Professor's House*." In Cather's *On Writing: Critical Studies on Writing as an Art*. New York: Knopf, 1949. Pp. 30–32.

Willa Cather in Europe: Her Own Story of the First Journey. Edited by George N. Kates. New York: Knopf, 1956.

The Kingdom of Art: Willa Cather's First Principles and Critical Statements, 1893–1896. Edited by Bernice Slote. Lincoln: University of Nebraska Press, 1966.

The World and the Parish: Willa Cather's Articles and Reviews, 1893–1902. 2 vols. Edited by William M. Curtin. Lincoln: University of Nebraska Press, 1970.

The Selected Letters of Willa Cather. Edited by Andrew Jewell and Janis Stout. New York: Knopf, 2013.

PAPERS AND ARCHIVES

Willa Cather Archive, University of Nebraska–Lincoln, is a digital archive of her books and writings, also featuring interviews, letters, scholarly studies, maps, and images. http://cather.unl.edu/ The Cather Collection at the Newberry, Chicago, contains first editions, translations, personal books of Cather's, and magazines featuring her work.

BIOGRAPHICAL STUDIES AND MEMOIRS

Bennet, Mildred R. *The World of Willa Cather*. New York: Dodd, Mead, 1951.

Lewis, Edith. *Willa Cather Living: A Personal Record*. Athens: Ohio University Press, 1989.

O'Brien, Sharon. *Willa Cather: The Emerging Voice*. New York: Oxford University Press, 1987.

Sergeant, Elizabeth Shepley. *Willa Cather: A Memoir*. Lincoln: University of Nebraska Press, 1953.

Stout, Janis P. *Willa Cather: The Writer and Her World*. Charlottesville: University Press of Virginia, 2000.

Woodress, James. *Willa Cather: A Literary Life*. Lincoln: University of Nebraska Press, 1987.

CRITICAL STUDIES

Acocella, Joan. *Willa Cather and the Politics of Criticism*. Lincoln: University of Nebraska Press, 2000.

Ammons, Elizabeth. "Cather and the New Canon: 'The Old Beauty' and the Issue of Empire." *Cather Studies*. Vol. 3. Edited by Susan J. Rosowski. Lincoln: University of Nebraska Press, 1996. Pp. 256–266.

Arnold, Marilyn. "The Allusive Cather." *Cather Studies*. Vol. 3. Edited by Susan J. Rosowski. Lincoln: University of Nebraska Press, 1996. Pp. 137–148.

Edel, Leon. "The Man in the Woman." *New Republic*, November 14, 1983, pp. 34–36.

Lindemann, Marilee. *The Cambridge Companion to Willa Cather*. Cambridge, U.K., and New York: Cambridge University Press, 2005.

March, John. *A Reader's Companion to the Fiction of Willa Cather*. Edited by Marilyn Arnold and Debra Lynn Thornton. Westport, Conn.: Greenwood, 1993.

Murphy, John J. *Critical Essays on Willa Cather*. Boston: G. K. Hall, 1984.

Rosowski, Susan J., ed. *Approaches to Teaching Cather's "My Ántonia."* New York: MLA, 1989.

Russ, Joanna. "To Write 'Like a Woman': Transformations of Identity in the Work of Willa Cather." In *Historical, Literary, and Erotic Aspects of Lesbianism*. Edited by Monika Kehoe. New York: Harrington Park Press, 1986. Pp. 77–87.

Schwind, Jean. "The Benda Illustrations to *My Ántonia*: Cather's 'Silent' Supplement to Jim Burden's Narrative." *PMLA* 100, no. 1:51–67 (1985).

FILMS BASED ON THE WORKS OF WILLA CATHER

A Lost Lady. Screen adaptation by Dorothy Farnum. Directed by Harry Beaumont. Warner Bros., 1924. Rereleased 1934, with a screenplay by Gene Markey and Kathryn Scola and directed by Alfred E. Green and Phil Rosen. (Silent film.)

O Pioneers! Teleplay by Robert W. Lenski. Directed by Glenn Jordan. Hallmark Hall of Fame, CBS, 1992.

My Antonia. Teleplay by Victoria Riskin. Directed by Joseph Sargent. Gideon/Wilshire Court, USA Network, 1995.

Song of the Lark. Teleplay by Joseph Maurer. Directed by Karen Arthur. Paramount Pictures, PBS, 2001.

HART CRANE

(1899—1932)

Neil W. Browne

THE ESSENTIAL QUALITY of Hart Crane's poetry is his ongoing effort to transform the real into the ideal, the actual into the possible, the quotidian into the universal. While remaining deeply rooted in his Romantic forebears, Crane sought to modify that romanticism, insisting upon its centrality, even its necessity, to the modernist literary landscape. Robert Lowell clearly recognized this lineage in Crane. In 1959 Lowell published one of his most important collections, *Life Studies,* which included a modified sonnet titled "Words for Hart Crane," in which Hart Crane, by then twenty-seven years dead, claims to know his Walt Whitman by heart and to be the embodiment of a twentieth-century Percy Bysshe Shelley (p. 61). Lowell rightly aligns Crane with these two foremost Romantic poets, both claiming a voice for their time, with Shelley laying a claim to prophecy itself—"Be through my lips to unawakened Earth // The trumpet of a prophecy! O Wind, / If Winter comes, can Spring be far behind? ("Ode to the West Wind," (p. 223)—and Walt Whitman claiming to sound an American "barbaric yawp" around the world. Shelley writes further in "A Defence of Poetry"that "poets are the hierophants of an unapprehended inspiration, the mirrors of the gigantic shadows which futurity casts upon the present" (p. 508). It seems Crane took to heart Shelley's claims for a hierophantic poetry, and, following Whitman, he then relocates unapprehended inspiration and gigantic shadows of futurity from Britain to the landscapes, cityscapes, and everyday voices of North America, most particularly of the now fully industrialized United States. He grounds the ideal in concrete places. He also attempts to merge his internalized romanticism with the meticulous modernism of his time, a modernism most often a bit embarrassed by its Romantic and Victorian forebears. In this, as throughout his life, Crane often found himself in uncomfortable positions and in skeptical company.

BACKGROUNDS AND BEGINNINGS

Harold Hart Crane was born on July 21, 1899, in Garrettsville, Ohio. He was the only child of Clarence A. Crane and Grace Hart Crane. On his father's side, Crane's ancestors in North America date back to 1646 when the Beardsley family sailed from England to the New World aboard the ship *Planter.* They settled in Connecticut, where the line continued until Simeon Crane emigrated to Ohio in 1801. On his paternal side, Crane's forebears include Revolutionary War soldiers, legislators, and Civil War heroes. Hart Crane's grandfather, Arthur Edward Crane, was born to Edward and Sylvia Crane and outlived his grandson by seven years, dying in 1939. Arthur Crane became a highly successful businessman in Garrettsville, Ohio, and he married Ella Beardsley in 1870; the poet's father, Clarence Arthur Crane, known as C.A., was born in April 1875. C.A. attended public schools and Allegheny College, though he left Allegheny without taking a degree, and upon leaving college, he worked for Nabisco as a traveling salesman. He was an adamant American midwestern booster in the style of his time—he believed in hard work and hard play and was solidly grounded in the notion of the American Dream. At the end of the nineteenth century he fell in love with a visiting beauty from Chicago, Grace Hart, and courted her intensely; she finally relented and married him in Chicago on June 1, 1898. C.A. became a wealthy confectioner, restaurateur, businessman, and innkeeper. However, in one of his more ill-advised business deals he sold one of his creations—Life Savers candy—for $2,900.

Crane's family lineage reads like a list of early Protestant settlers. Grace Hart too came from a pedigreed American family. Her forebears on the maternal side, the Beldens, like the Beardsleys, arrived in America in the seventeenth century. By the mid-nineteenth century they had drifted to California, where they amassed a considerable fortune, built in the booming economic environment of the gold rush. The paternal side of Grace's family, the Harts, also arrived in the colonies in the seventeenth century, settling eventually in Ohio. Hart Crane's maternal grandfather, Clinton Orestes Hart, was born in 1839 and became a schoolmaster in Pennsylvania after attending Western Reserve Seminary. Following service in the Civil War, he opened a clothing business and later became a partner in a lucrative steel roofing business, eventually retiring to East 115th Street in Cleveland. In 1865 he married Elizabeth Belden, who, like Hart, had attended Western Reserve Seminary. They were prosperous citizens of Cleveland throughout their lives. Hart Crane's grandmother Elizabeth became an essential figure in his life, probably the one and only person who showed him a constant and unconditional love.

In 1901 the Clarence Cranes moved from Garretsville to Warren, Ohio, where C.A. expanded his business and became an innovator in packaging American confections. (He seems to be one of the first to use decorative cellophane as wrapping.) He also laid plans to build a large new factory in Warren. While C.A. was successful as a businessman, he was far less skilled as a marriage partner. The marriage between C.A. and Grace proved disastrous from the outset. They quarreled regularly, often loudly and violently, and their sexual reconciliations were equally loud and violent, causing young Harold intense embarrassment, frequently manifested physically in hives and fever. At the conclusion of intense arguing, C.A. would leave the house, claiming an obligation to be away on business and leaving Harold alone with his mother, who often regaled the young boy with detailed stories of his father's perfidy. In 1908 the couple separated, C.A. moving to Chicago and Grace entering a sanatorium in the East, leaving Harold alone. At this point he moved in with his grandparents at 1709 East 115th Street in Cleveland.

The house was a large Victorian structure, dominated by two cylindrical towers. Throughout his life, it housed Crane's memory. The future poet resided in a room in the northern tower, and this place remained his until the house was sold in 1925. Here Harold Hart Crane began to write poetry, and here he formed his first conception of his greatest work, *The Bridge* (1930), which he understood as a mystical "synthesis of America and its structural identity" (*Letters 1916–1932,* p. 127). In a sense, this room is the symbolic center of Crane's work. When Crane talks about *The Bridge* as a great synthesis of America, its imaginative center is right here in this house. His youth, his experience of both the rural and industrial Midwest, and the notion that the ideal is rooted in a very real place—in American towns, cities, and landscapes—were perceived and centered in both the image and the reality of this place. In the "Van Winkle" section of *The Bridge,* Crane writes: "The grind-organ says ... Remember, remember / The cinder pile at the end of the backyard," centering the poem firmly in Crane's memory of his Cleveland home, where the cinder pile is anything but a bucolic landscape. Here is where Crane "stoned the family of young / Garter snakes under ..."—and then breaks the train of memory and the syntax of the poem with elipses and evokes the balsa wood model airplanes "We launched—with paper wings and twisted / Rubber bands ... Recall—recall" (p. 55). While slaughtering garter snakes is a bit grim, the poem is firmly centered in Crane's memory of his Cleveland home. The opening line of the stanza repeats "Remember, remember," the first term capitalized and preceded by an ellipsis. The final line of the stanza parallels this structure exactly, using the synonymous term, "... Recall, recall." Crane's childhood place is literally bracketed by references to memory, suggesting that it is centrally ensconced there. In this key section of *The Bridge* emerges a clear imperative for the poem to remember. Shortly following the above passage is a chilling recollection of his childhood relationship with his parents. First comes his father: "Is it the whip stripped from the lilac tree / One day in the spring my father took to me," and then his mother, "Or is it the Sabbatical, unconscious smile / My mother almost brought me once from church." As if this reflection of his mother were not icy enough, he closes the stanza, "And once only, as I recall—?" (p. 56) The two parental vignettes in this stanza too are framed by terms of memory and recall. A more chilling and telling memory than the father's whip is the point that his mother "almost" brought him an "unconscious smile," and almost brought it "once only." In Crane's poetry, as perhaps in most literature, the poem works with and recasts memory as a kind of recompense for something lost or perceived and felt to have been lost. Crane's lyric gift is often a condensation of the feelings experienced in the retrieval of that loss, and the house at 1709 East 115th Street in Cleveland is a key locus of Crane's aesthetics, an aesthetics in part built upon poetic rendering of the ideal rooted in the real, and upon the imperative to remember.

When his mother returned in 1909, they continued to live on East 115th Street. Beginning in 1913 Harold Crane attended East High School, one of the most highly regarded schools in Cleveland. He was a run-of-the-mill student whose attendance was erratic, like his home life. Much like her husband, Grace found relief from domestic tensions through travel, and she often pulled Harold out of school and dragged him behind her for companionship when she left town. One can only imagine the acute embarrassment of her sixteen-year-old son on one such trip when she insisted that he share her berth in a sleeping car. Also in 1909, C.A. returned to Cleveland in an attempt to save the marriage, which ran smoothly for a time, perhaps because C.A. was deeply involved in new business ventures and because Grace had become deeply entwined with Mary Baker Eddy's Christian Science, attempting to convert the entire household. C.A. seems to have been moderately interested until he understood that Christian Science placed severe restrictions on sexual activity, and his was not a personality with much proclivity toward sexual restraint. Harold, even though his own sexual activities were at odds with the teachings at that time, practiced Christian Science into his early manhood. With his parents either distracted or traveling, Harold was largely raised by his grandparents, who introduced him to the booming cultural scene in Cleveland—one of the most powerful cities in the country in the first half of the twentieth century. He took piano lessons from his Aunt Alice, a cultured woman who also made available to him her own extensive poetry collection.

Just as Cleveland grew in power during the first half of the twentieth century, the United States at the turn of the century was stepping forward as a world power. Although the 1823 Monroe Doctrine claimed any interference in the Western Hemisphere to be an act of aggression toward the United States, this does not seem to have precluded the American urge to intervene in the affairs of countries in Latin America, the Caribbean, and the Pacific. Around the time of Hart Crane's birth, the United States asserted itself as an imperial power. After the Spanish-American War, the United States gained control of Cuba, Puerto Rico, Guam, and the Philippines. Well-heeled Americans began investing and buying property in the Caribbean, and Crane's grandparents were among them, purchasing a small estate, Villa Casas, on the Isle of Pines, which would remain in his mother's family and become another important sanctuary for Hart Crane. In "O Carib Isle!" he writes: "Under the poinciana, of a noon or afternoon / Let fiery blossoms clot the light, render my ghost." The poet, lingering under the poinciana tree, dissolves into a black-and-white ghost, "Sieved upward, white and black along the air / Until it meets the blue's comedian host" (p. 111). Rising through the intense red of the tree's blossoms suggests resurection, and the verb "clot" aligns the red flowers with blood, and the blood, along with "ghost," rhymed with "host," suggests a sacrifice of some sort. Thus the poem takes on strong religious overtones, with images of sacrifice and resurrection dominating the passage. The "host," of angels presumably, are referred to as "comedians," and the phrasing tempers the religiosity of the passages and lightens the ghost's passage into the heavens. However, the reference to the ghost as black-and-white suggests something of Crane's feeling about this place and his role, perhaps, in the family dynamic. All around him are startling colors, yet he sees his ghost as black-and-white. C.A. and Grace continued to squabble, and in 1915 the family took a trip to the Isle of Pines hoping a change of scene would help things, but the problems only escalated, ending as usual in loud arguments and loud sexual reconciliation. At some point during the trip, Harold tried to commit suicide by slashing his wrists. He also ingested a large amount of Grace's sleeping powders at one point of his stay in the Caribbean.

Crane never graduated from high school. Instead, he studied the works of Percy Bysshe Shelley, Samuel Taylor Coleridge, Lord Byron, Edgar Allan Poe, Nathaniel Hawthorne, Algernon Charles Swinburne, and Oscar Wilde. In preparation for composing his own poems, he smoked cigars and sprinkled his mother's perfume about his room. All his writing life, Crane used music and, later, alcohol in preparation for writing, once claiming to have envisioned the ideal world while he was under anesthetic in a dentist's chair. Outside stimulus aside, Crane believed that the poet could approach an ideal world, locating him in a long tradition of European and American romanticism. Although the Romantic tradition often roots the ideal in nature, Crane, expanding on Whitman, often locates the ideal in the urban and suburban landscapes of the United States. Crane's brief, frequently tormented life kept pace with the cultural tendencies of the first part of the twentieth century. His youth and early adulthood correspond with the burgeoning wealth, excess, celebration, and sexual indulgences of the Jazz Age. The end of his life in the early 1930s tracks with the fall of the U.S. economy and his perceived failure to achieve his dream for a poetic synthesis of American culture and history. While the literary criticism of his time largely affirmed his perception of failure, over the years a reevaluation of Crane's work has proved both those critics and Crane wrong. His life is the arc of a great creative gift that rises to ecstasy then falls through dissipation, progressive alcoholism, and psychological deterioration to despair and suicide, when, a few minutes before noon on April 26, 1932, Crane walked to the stern of S.S. *Orizaba,* removed his overcoat, folded it neatly over the rail, and dropped into the Caribbean Sea.

EARLY WORK AND INFLUENCE

Richard Laukhuff opened a bookstore in Cleveland in 1916 that specialized in works and periodicals at the modernist edge of contemporary literature. On the shelves, Crane discovered many of the little magazines essential to the dissemination of modernist literature: *Poetry, Soil, Seven Arts,* the *Pagan,* and *Bruno's Monthly.* Oscar Wilde was celebrated in a series of essays in *Bruno's Weekly* in the winter of 1916, and after reading the issue Crane composed his first published poem, "C33," whose title is the number of Wilde's prison cell in Reading Gaol. The poem contains a hint of the later hierophantic nature of Crane's poetry, but at this stage the work is still quite bound to traditional forms—the easily scanned lines and the obvious regular rhyme scheme, along with several instances of inverted syntax, mark the poem's roots solidly in the nineteenth century, and the phrasing reaches back even further. But certainly Crane felt some affinity with Wilde, who died in the year Crane was born and who was jailed from 1895 to 1897 for homosexual activity. Crane on some level intuited his own "paths tear-wet," even as he romanticizes those paths in the poem.

Concurrent with his public debut as a poet came the further deterioration of his parents' marriage. Divorce proceedings began in 1916, and Harold, who had already formed ideas of moving to New York to be near the center of literary America, convinced his distracted parents to allow him to move to New York. Right after Christmas 1916, Harold Crane climbed aboard a New York–bound train, embarking on a journey that would attempt to bridge the Midwest of his youth and urban America and lead to a poetic re-envisioning of the United States.

Crane had difficulty finding gainful employment in New York, and he was forced to appeal to his affluent father for money—certainly more often than either Harold or C.A. would have liked. C.A. believed in the American work ethic as strongly as his son held faith in the power of art and literature, and the growing tension between them abated only toward the end of both men's lives. C.A. was not one to give something for nothing, and Crane often traveled back to the Midwest to work for his father for periods of time, especially when he was destitute. The correspondence from this time between Harold and his family rehearses the marital battle in print, and much of the pain, intentionally or not, was visited on the son—the eighteen-year-old poet, who, despite himself and them, deeply loved both his parents. Following one such letter from Grace in which she admonished him to acknowledge her side of the family, Harold, when "Echoes" was published in 1917, for the first time signed his name as Hart Crane, much to his father's irritation. Following the publication of "Echoes," Crane published "In Shadow" in the *Little Review,* a primary vehicle for introducing the work of Ezra Pound, T. S. Eliot, W. B. Yeats, and other prominent modernists to an American reading public. The magazine was also the first to introduce James Joyce's *Ulysses* to the United States in serial form, resulting in the U.S. Postal Service burning several issues of the *Little Review* as obscene.

"In Shadow" retains much of the traditional prosody of Crane's early work. He sees, "Out in the late amber afternoon, / Confused among chrysanthemums," a woman, "Her parasol, a pale balloon, / Like a waiting moon, in shadow swims" (p. 13). Yet, while the rhyme scheme is obvious, on the sonic level the poem is more sophisticated than his prior work. The poem evidences a subtle assonance, the use of which Crane will perfect in his later work: the "a" sounds in "late," "amber," and "afternoon," for example; or the "m" and "n" sounds coupled with "o" and "u" in "among chrysanthemums"; or "a," "o," the bilabials "p" and "b," and the liquid "l" in "parasol," "pale," and "balloon," which rhymes internally with "moon." In fact, the poem is held together by these internal sonic characteristics more fully than it is by the end rhymes. In this poem, we can see Crane moving away from more traditional forms into a more modernist aesthetic, laced with the musicality that becomes a formidable power in Crane's later work.

He continued to publish poems—"North Labrador," "Legend," and "Interior" were published in the *Modernist*—and after enthusiastically reading several stories from *Winesburg, Ohio* in the *Little Review,* Crane reviewed Sherwood Anderson's work for the *Pagan,* instigating a short-lived friendship between the two Ohioans. Finally, broke again, Crane returned to Ohio to work for C.A. in one of his Akron stores. One evening, following a quarrel with his father, Crane went to the movies and experienced a watershed event in his creative life—the arrival of Charlie Chaplin's *The Kid* in Cleveland. Crane wrote to his friend Gorham Munson that "Comedy ... has never reached a higher level in this country before. We have ... in Chaplin a dramatic genius that truly approaches the fabulous sort. I could write pages on the overtones and brilliant subtleties of this picture" (*Letters 1916–1932,* p. 65). Though he did not write pages, he did compose a poem, "Chaplinesque," in which the poet is aligned with the Chaplin character, who can still love by showing compassion for a stray and finding "Recesses for it from the fury of the street, / Or warm torn elbow coverts" (p. 11). In a letter to his childhood friend William Wright, who had difficulty grasping the poem's meaning, Crane explained:

> I am moved to put Chaplin with the poets (of today); hence the "we." In other words, he, especially in *The Kid,* made me feel myself, as a poet, as being "in the same boat" with him. Poetry, the human feelings, "the kitten," is so crowded out of the humdrum, rushing, mechanical scramble of today that the man who would preserve them must duck and camouflage for dear life to keep them or keep himself from annihilation.
>
> (p. 68)

In his quest to articulate this poetry, these human feelings, Crane looked inward to his own sense of alienation. On many levels, from his family relationships to his sexual orientation to his need to find recognition on his poetry, Crane must have felt the need to keep himself incognito for fear of psychic annihilation.

However, Crane, as his aesthetic evolved, realized both the need and the difficulty of moving out beyond himself. When he returned to Ohio from New York, he brought along the kernel of a poem, "My Grandmother's Love Letters." While many of the poems preceding "Love Letters" were imagistic in their conception, this poem represents an advance in Crane's early poetics. The poem more explicitly engages his personal milieu, but beyond that, it effectively engages memory for the first time. His willingness to pry open and imagine the intimate memories of his grandmother in an era under the dominance of T. S. Eliot, who insisted upon the impersonality of poetry, represents an early glimpse of Crane's attempt to revise modernist aesthetics in order to create his own idiom within modernism. Crane for most of his life was haunted by Eliot, and although he aspired to Eliot's technical virtuosity, he fought to deny within himself and his work the pessimism that permeated Eliot's work.

"Love Letters" opens quietly with a night sky in which only stars of memory shine. The poet considers, "Yet how much room for memory there is / In the loose girdle of soft rain" (p. 6), attempting to walk a thin line between his respect and love for his grandmother (whose first name, Elizabeth, is given in the poem) and his desire to reach into her past, subtly eroticized by the evocation of a loosened girdle and the soft rain. Found bundled in an attic corner, her letters are "brown and soft, / And liable to melt as snow" (p. 6). The delicacy and whiteness of the snow are echoed by an old woman's white hair: "It is all hung by an invisible white hair. / It trembles as birch limbs webbing the air" (p. 6). Moving gently along, this poem is again guided by subtle internal rhymes and assonance along with occasional end rhymes. The poet poses himself a question that ramifies into a query about the efficacy of poetry itself, though he never loses sight of the actual person who inspired the poem: "Are your fingers long enough to play / Old keys that are but echoes"; and he extends the question, "Is the silence strong enough / To carry back the music to its source"? It is then reflected back to the poet himself, "And back to you again / As though to her?" (p. 6). The question becomes one that wonders whether the music of poetry is able to retrieve a particular experience and, if so, whether it can provide a song that is as true to the poetry as it was to the poet's grandmother. The silence must be powerful enough to enable the poetry; the silence provides a space for the poem. The query is of course unanswerable, but it provides the impetus to a poetry that evokes great love, intense sensuality, and a concern for how a poem can create a bridge between the past and the present, between a real life already lived and the poetic evocation of certain heightened moments in that life.

"Love Letters" becomes even more poignant when it is taken into consideration that Crane is coming to understand and embrace his homosexuality. In Akron, Crane was befriended by Harry Candee, a member of an established gay community, and Crane began to feel more at ease with his sexuality. Crane, however, had also developed a taste for seeking out strangers for short and sometimes dangerous sexual liaisons. With Candee, also, his taste for Prohibition liquor increased. Late in the summer of 1920, Crane was sent as a sales representative to Washington, D.C., where he met another member of the gay community, Wilbur Underwood, who enabled Crane to feel a part of a vibrant group of marginalized people. Crane experienced a strong attraction to the dangerous and potentially violent aspects of physical love, and though he often found it necessary to cloak his sexual adventures for practical reasons, especially from his family, he was not ashamed of them. Quite to the contrary, he seems to have enjoyed them greatly, and, difficult as it must have been to sustain, he exerted a stiff determination to see his sexuality as natural, not aberrant or diseased as his culture most often termed it. He created some of the most beautiful love lyrics in the English language, particularly the sequence "Voyages," inspired by his love affair with the sailor Emil Opffer.

AESTHETIC ADVANCES

By the end of 1922, Crane's focus had matured and shifted to an attempt to incorporate American culture in all its bleakness, brutality, and beauty into poetry. This would demand the inclusion of jazz, bridges, subways, acetylene torches, airplanes, and elevators. The year 1922 was a modernist watershed. Eliot's *The Waste Land* appeared, as did James Joyce's *Ulysses,* Willa Cather's *One of Ours,* Virginia Woolf's *Jacob's Room,* F. Scott Fitzgerald's *The Beautiful and the Dammed,* Hermann Hesse's *Siddhartha,* Claude McKay's *Harlem Shadows,* Eugene O'Neill's *The Hairy Ape,* and James Weldon Johnson's *The Book of American Negro Poetry.* Oswald Spengler published *The Decline of the West,* and Albert Einstein's *The Meaning of Relativity* appeared. The USSR was created and construction on Yankee Stadium begun. Walt Disney's first film company was formed, the Lincoln Memorial was opened, and Johnny Weissmuller became the first human to swim the 100-meter freestyle in under a minute. Out of this cultural milieu, Eliot's *The Waste Land* provided one model for Crane, but Crane sensed a thorough morbidity running through the great work. William Carlos Williams wrote: "There was heat in us, a core and a drive that was gathering headway upon the theme of a rediscovery of a primary impetus, the elementary principle of all art, in the local conditions. Our work staggered to a halt for a moment under the blast of Eliot's genius which gave the poem back to the academics" (*Autobiography,* p. 146). Crane, like Williams, knew that Eliot demanded a response; in fact, he rather petulantly wrote to Waldo Frank that "Eliot and others of that kidney have whimpered fastidiously" (*Letters 1916–1932,* p. 261), and a rejoinder, for Crane, would, while retaining the complexity demanded to represent the modern world, transcend any kind of fastidious, academic, poetry. And although it was fine to accuse Eliot of whimpering, Crane also realized Eliot's key influence on his own work:

> There is no one writing in English who can command so much respect, to my mind, as Eliot. However, I take Eliot as a point of departure toward an almost complete reverse of direction. His pessimism is amply justified, in his own case. But I would apply as much of his erudition and technique as I can absorb and assemble toward a more positive, or (if [I] must put it so in a skeptical age) ecstatic goal.
>
> (pp. 114–115)

Already working along these lines on his most ambitious poem to date, "For the Marriage of Faustus and Helen," Crane was gaining increased notice in widely circulated periodicals. In the December 6, 1922, issue of the *New Republic,* Crane's name was included among those of E. E. Cummings, Edmund Wilson, Kenneth Burke, Malcolm Cowley, and John Dos Passos in an article by the influential critic Louis Untermeyer called "The New Patricians." Part of what distinguished these writers was a sense of strangeness in their work and, notably, a heightened complexity.

"For the Marriage of Faustus and Helen," Crane's first foray into the long poem, is an attempt at the kind of poetic synthesis Crane would enact on a much larger scale in his masterwork, *The Bridge.* "Marriage" weds the hectic present of urban, commercial America to classical culture. Crane wrote to the critic Waldo Frank that "The whole poem is a kind of fusion of our own time with the past" (p. 120). The poet—the Faust figure—encounters Helen of Troy on a trolley car. Helen symbolizes beauty, and Crane explicitly states that Faust symbolizes not only a generalized poet but also Crane himself. On a deeper level, "The street car device is the most concrete symbol I could find for the transition of the imagination from the quotidian details to the universal consideration of beauty" (p. 120). This sense that universals emerge from the everyday is thematized in most of his mature work. However, within this grand sense of beauty lodged in the quotidian resides a certain danger, especially for *"Those untwisted by the love of things / Irreconcilable ..."* (p. 26). Clearly, for a poet like Crane—twisted by love of irreconcilable things—the dimensional world is a difficult place.

Crane, like millions of urban Americans, commuted by trolley to and from work in the "world dimensional," and "Marriage" pivots on an evening trolley ride: "And yet, suppose some evening I forgot / The fare and transfer, yet got by that way. / Without recall,—lost yet poised in traffic" (p. 26). The poem continues, "Then I might find your eyes across an aisle, / Still flickering with those prefigurations—" (p. 27), and the poet encounters Helen half-smiling, framed in the streetcar window as the evening lights of the city flicker in her eyes. This first section of the poem evokes beauty, and the second section brings the poet and Helen to a hypnotic, glittering rooftop party: "Glee shifts from foot to foot, / Magnetic to their tremolo" (p. 29). The dance crescendos into a strange mixture of ecstasy and grotesquerie, joined to a concise imaging of the American economic citizen, "Striated with nuances, nervosities / That we are heir to" (p. 30). The closing lines of the poem then transcend the typical American urge to link bargains and prayer, the economic and the spiritual: "The imagination spans beyond despair, / Outpacing bargain, vocable and prayer" (p. 32).

While working on "Marriage," Crane generated an idea for a poem that would use the Brooklyn Bridge as a central symbol. In a 1923 letter written to Gorham Munson from the tower room on East 115th Street, Crane makes the first written reference to *The Bridge* that we know of. He confides, "I am ruminating on a new longish poem under the title of *The Bridge* which carries on further the tendencies manifest in 'F and H.' It will be exceedingly difficult to accomplish it as I see it now, so much time will be wasted in thinking about it" (p. 118). It was exceedingly difficult. Though many parts of *The Bridge* were published separately, the poem as a whole was not published until 1930, and its composition would shuttle Crane between ecstasy and despair through this entire range of years.

In 1923 Crane moved back to New York, where he met the novelist Jean Toomer, the poet E. E. Cummings, the playwright Eugene O'Neill, the critic Kenneth Burke, and the writer William Slater Brown. Typically, Crane worked at advertising for a while and then resigned. He then moved to Woodstock, New York, to live with Slater Brown and Susan Jenkins. The following year he returned to the city, met the poet Allen Tate, and worked with Malcolm Cowley at a catalog service, finally moving to a room at 110 Columbia Heights in Brooklyn. This is the second room that would exert a powerful influence on Crane. It had a view of the Manhattan towers across the East River, framed by the Brooklyn Bridge. Amazingly, decades earlier the engineer Washington Roebling had inhabited this room while overseeing construction of the Brooklyn Bridge. About this place, Crane wrote to his mother:

> Everytime one looks at the harbor and NY skyline across the river it is quite different, and the range of atmospheric effects is endless. But at twilight on a foggy evening, such as it was at this time, it is beyond description. Gradually the lights in the enormously tall buildings begin to flicker through the mist. There was a great cloud enveloping the top of the Woolworth tower, while below, in the river, were streaming reflections of myriad lights, continually being crossed by the twinkling mast and deck lights of little tugs scudding along, freight rafts, and occasional liners starting outward. Look far to your left toward Staten Island and there is the statue of Liberty, with that remarkable lamp of hers that makes her seen for miles. And up at the right Brooklyn Bridge, the most superb piece of construction in the modern world, I'm sure, with strings of light crossing it like glowing worms as the Ls and surface cars pass each other going and coming. It is particularly fine to feel the greatest city in the world from enough distance, as I do here, to see its larger proportions. When you are actually in it you are often too distracted to realize its better and more imposing aspects. Yes, this location is the best one on all counts for me. For the first time in many weeks I am beginning to further elaborate my plans for my Bridge poem. Since the publication of my Faustus and Helen poem I have had considerable satisfaction in the respect accorded me....
>
> (*Letters of Hart Crane and His Family,* pp. 312–313)

Clearly, this residence was another place central to Crane's evolving poetics, and the lines of the letter describing New York Harbor anticipate lines later composed for *The Bridge.* Also living in the house in Columbia Heights was Emil Opffer, with whom Crane engaged in the most meaningful, though tempestuous, love affair of his life.

Throughout the winter of 1926, Crane lived in Patterson, New York, and worked on *The Bridge,* beginning with "Atlantis," which would eventually become the final poem of the book. Still desperate for the means to support himself while he worked on *The Bridge,* Crane asked for a $1,000 loan from the New York financier and philanthropist Otto Kahn, who presented Crane with a gift outright of $2,000. Thus far he had a rough outline of the ideas and dramatis personae of the poem. Some of the characters, such as John Brown, would fall away before the poem was completed, but the most important figures in the poem—Christopher Columbus, Pocahontas, Walt Whitman, the New York subway, and the Brooklyn Bridge—were firmly in Crane's design. But although he was making progress on his poem, he bickered with his friends in Patterson, who eventually and understandably tired of late-night tapping on the keyboard, loud music, and drunken rampages that sometimes sent typewriters sailing through second-story windows.

WHITE BUILDINGS

Crane needed someplace to write. A portion of the money from Kahn remained, so he appealed to his mother for the use of her family's house on the Isle of Pines, Villa Casas. Accompanied by Waldo Frank, Crane set sail on May 1, 1926, aboard SS *Orizaba*; in an eerie twist, this was the same ship from which Crane would jump to his death in 1932. Crane was difficult company, and Frank shortly returned home. Crane shared the house with the caretaker, Sally Simpson (who has a cameo appearance in "The River" section of *The Bridge*), undergoing a splendid ten-week period of creativity, during which he completed much of *The Bridge*. Never again would he experience such productivity.

Good news arrived in July, in the form of a contract with Liveright for *White Buildings*, his first collection of poems, for which Allen Tate had agreed to write the introduction. *White Buildings* selects the finest poems Crane had written to date, and concluding the 1926 collection is the masterful cycle "Voyages," among the most accomplished love lyrics in the English language. "Voyages" was written with Emil Opffer in mind, but the poem is also a powerful paean to the sea. "Voyages" is more properly a cycle of six love lyrics; each stands alone, but together the poems sing. "Voyages I" opens with images of young boys playing on the beach, but quickly voices a warning about the transience of such happiness: "O brilliant kids, frisk with your dog, / Fondle your shells and sticks, bleached / By time and the elements; but there is a line," as Crane well knows, "You must not cross nor ever trust beyond it / Spry cordage of your bodies to caresses" (p. 54). The poet warns against crossing a line too far, warns against the young body's urge to caress beyond limits, and the rest of the sequence provides a meditation on this warning. "Voyages II" picks up where "Voyages I" left off, with a dash that seems to shift the stress to "And," creating the spondee "And yet." The emphasis falls on this phrase, demanding that the preceding warning be questioned and modified: "And yet this great wink of eternity, / Of rimless floods, unfettered leewardings" (p. 35). Though the seafloor may be cruel, the surface of the ocean arches toward the moon in a metaphor that links the natural phenomenon—the pull of the moon creating the tides—to the imagined act of the sea offering herself to the lovers, and laughing with them in a sensuous embrace, "Her undinal vast belly moonward bends, / Laughing the wrapt inflections of our love" (p. 35). The lines also evoke Crane's connection to Whitman, particularly Whitman's homoeroticism in section 11 of "Song of Myself": "The young men float on their backs, their white bellies bulge to the sun, they do not ask who seizes fast to them, / They do not know who puffs and declines with pendant and bending arch, / They do not think whom they souse with spray" (p. 34). In "Voyages II," the waves become "scrolls of silver snowy sentences" (p. 35), and the Caribbean, "these poinsettia meadows of her tides,— / Adagios of islands" (p. 35). The sea becomes poetry and music, "The imaged Word, it is, that holds / Hushed willows anchored in its glow," and Crane utters the power of poetry with the final lines of "Voyages VI": "It is the unbetrayable reply / Whose accent no farewell can know" (p. 40).

And it seems as if the best reply to the warning issued in " Voyages I" is the "imaged word"; poetic language itself shores one up, just as Crane suggested in "Chaplinesque." But if the sea and the weather are excellent material for poetry, in the tropics they are also a violent threat. On October 18, 1926, a hurricane nearly flattened the Isle of Pines and heavily damaged Villa

Casas. With the house in ruins, Crane returned to New York, and shortly thereafter *White Buildings* was published. Though the book received harsh reviews in the *Dial* and in the *New York Herald Tribune,* Ivor Winters, Allen Tate, and Waldo Frank publicly praised the book, ranking Crane among the country's most important poets. Ironically, Winters and Tate—later, powerful New Critics—were instrumental in the later dismissal of Crane's work.

In 1927 Crane worked sporadically on *The Bridge.* Through a friend, he was introduced to Herbert Wise, a neurotic millionaire who had recently suffered a nervous breakdown and wanted a literary traveling companion to accompany him to Southern California. Crane's only responsibility would be to keep Wise amused. As Crane wrote, "about all I have to do is to be agreeable, talk about Aristotle, Einstein, T. S. Eliot, Gertrude Stein, etc., etc., (in other words, my boss is really a very cultured man and didn't want to take too much of a chance on running into a vacuum as regards companionship out here)" (*Letters 1916–1932,* p. 311). This relationship lasted about as long as could have been expected—not long. Crane found both his job and Southern California oppressive, and as if that were not enough, his mother, after the breakup of her second marriage, had also moved to the Los Angeles area. Crane disliked the culture of Southern California, and tension arose in his relationship with his employer. Crane left Wise's mansion and moved in with his mother and his sick grandmother, but his heavy drinking, cruising, and dockside brawls exacerbated his already pathological relationship with his mother. During an argument, Crane divulged his homosexuality to his mother, which resulted in a dramatic confrontation that ended with Crane sneaking out of the house on the night of May 15, 1928, leaving only a note. He never saw his mother again. The following autumn, Crane learned that his grandmother had finally succumbed to a long illness. Elizabeth Hart left a bequest of $5,000 to be paid upon her death to her grandson, but Grace used all her wiles to withhold the money until he returned to live with her in Los Angeles. Crane threatened suit, and when he received the money, he experienced a desperate need to put the greatest distance possible between his mother and him, finally sailing for Europe at the end of November.

THE BRIDGE

Crane spent seven months in Europe, first London, then Paris, where he fell in with a fast-moving crowd dominated by Harry and Caresse Crosby, rich, flamboyant people who surrounded themselves with members of the cultural avant-garde. (Caresse claimed to have invented the bra.) They also owned a small publishing company called the Black Sun Press. They were enticed by the work Crane showed them—drafts of *The Bridge.* The Crosbys agreed to publish *The Bridge* in a deluxe edition upon the poem's completion; instead of finishing the poem, Crane embarked on an extended debauch. His drinking spiraling beyond control, Crane exceeded even his limits and spent the last week of his stay in a Paris prison for assaulting police officers following a fight in a café.

Returning to New York in July 1929, he worked strenuously on *The Bridge* to meet a January 1 deadline for the Black Sun edition. In the meantime, Harry Crosby had invited his wife to join him in a double suicide by jumping from a New York hotel room, but she had declined. So on December 10, Harry instead shot himself and his twenty-two-year-old mistress to death, further destabilizing Crane's already chaotic life. In January 1930 Caresse Crosby brought out the Black Sun Press edition of *The Bridge* in Paris, followed in April by the Boni & Liveright edition in the United States. Crane's masterpiece received mixed reviews: some critics were enthusiastic, but many were dismayed by the book's complexity, its Shelleyan idealism, or its unfashionable Whitmanian echoes. Most devastating to Crane were the harsh reviews of his erstwhile friends Allen Tate and Ivor Winters.

The Bridge is Crane's contribution to the modernist urge to compose a lyric epic, an epic poem built not on classical forms but from the modernist lyric poem. William Carlos Williams' *Paterson,* Ezra Pound's *Cantos,* Eliot's *The Waste*

Land, Wallace Stevens' *Notes Toward a Supreme Fiction,* and H.D.'s *Helen in Egypt* are formidable examples contemporary with Crane's work. Both Crane and Williams sought to write a modernist epic of America, resulting in two of the finest poems in the English language. *The Bridge* consists of a proem and eight sections that themselves contain in total fourteen lyrics, so fifteen in all. The proem, "To Brooklyn Bridge," introduces the overarching metaphor of the entire work. The Brooklyn Bridge is transformed from a material object into a metaphorical structure that stands for the act of bridging and all its accompanying potentiality. "To Brooklyn Bridge" opens at dawn and puts us in flight with seagulls over New York Harbor, a clearly idealistic image akin to Shelley's skylark: "How many dawns, chill from his rippling rest / The seagull's wings shall dip and pivot him" (p. 43). The bird's wings dip and pivot like the cables of the bridge that chain the waters of New York Harbor and its famous statue: "Over the chained waters Liberty—" (p. 43).

The gulls, like the bridge, trace an "inviolate curve." The traditional symbol of the bird rises out of sight, beyond our reach. Here the lines are enjambed, and as we drop down a line to complete the syntax, "Some page of figures to be filed away; /—Till elevators drop us from our day" (p. 43), we find ourselves no longer looking up to the heavens but at pages of figures and filing cabinets. Admittedly these lines seem a deflation of the ideal but also a welcome sense of the material environment emerges. The elevator drops us to the city floor, just as the prosody of the lines connects the apparition (the ideal) to the page (the material). In this poem, the ideal exists in an inextricable relation to the material—the actual in light of the possible.

Later, the poet—haunting the Brooklyn piers that may have moored Whitman's Brooklyn Ferry—awaits his inspiration in the night: "Under thy shadow by the piers I waited; / Only in darkness is thy shadow clear" (p. 44).

The poem begins at dawn and ends at night, encompassing the course of a day, but the metaphorical valence of the poem transforms the day into a divine mythology. In these last quatrains is a sense of foreboding, of the fleetingness of a lyrical vision—"The city's fiery parcels all undone, / Already the snow submerges an iron year" (p. 44). But the river and the bridge are sleepless, alive. And at this point, the lines are as much addressed to *The Bridge* as they are to the Brooklyn Bridge.

The Bridge does indeed vault the oceans and the prairies in its attempt to create a myth of America from first contact to the physical and cultural landscape of Crane's United States, hovering on the brink of the Great Depression. The poem travels time and space. The first section, "Ave Maria," takes the reader back in time to the deck of Columbus' ship on its return voyage to Spain. "Powhatan's Daughter," the second section, echoes Columbus' voyage with the contemporary "Far strum of fog horns," and trucks rumble past wharves. The bridge and ship are replaced by highways: "Macadam, gun-grey as the tunny's belt, / Leaps from Far Rockaway to Golden Gate" and Crane calls the reader to "Listen! the miles a hurdy-gurdy grinds— / Down gold arpeggios mile on mile unwinds" (p. 55). All arteries of travel become intensely metaphorical, traverse the body of the continent, and encompass the music of the American landscape before the focus of the poem turns back to memory, this time the memory of the poet walking to school, an image that links the past to the present: "Times earlier, when you hurried off to school, / —It is the same hour though a later day" (p. 55).

Characters shift identities. An Indian princess is exchanged for a pioneer woman. Roles are strangely juxtaposed, the pioneer woman heading east, and the Indian woman walking west. Pocahontas becomes a dispossessed person, "A homeless squaw." By the penultimate poem, "The Tunnel," the explorer from Genoa—Columbus—has morphed into a "Wop washerwoman," and Crane addresses her, "O Genoese, do you bring mother eyes and hands / Back home to children and to golden hair?" (p. 100). Columbus ("O Genoese"), who sailed to the Americas and, in Crane's vision at least, perceived the wondrous potential of the New World, has become a scrubwoman riding the subway home from Manhattan to Brooklyn, traveling beneath the East River, not above it on the bridge.

In *The Bridge,* and in all of Crane's mature work, the physical environment is not a stage, it enters into all that we do. It comprises the natural world and the environment of manmade things. Extending this idea, aesthetic experience, including the relation of the material to the ideal, is rooted in physical environments—often, for Crane, suburban and urban landscapes. If we exist in a potential aesthetic relation to these landscapes, as is clearly the case in *The Bridge,* then it is possible to see not only our bodies and our deeds and our landfills as participating in these ecologies, but also our art, literature, music, and dance. All of these things move in relation to the landscapes with which they participate. "The River" opens with a hawker's voice: "Stick your patent name on a signboard / brother—all over—going west—young man" (p. 57). The poem evokes places and memories in the American landscape, from a trinity of hoboes ("So the 20th Century—so / whizzed the Limited—roared by and left / three men, still hungry on the tracks") to the backyards of Crane's childhood homes in the towns and suburbs of Garrettsville, Warren, and Cleveland, Ohio ("Behind / my father's cannery works I used to see / Rail-squatters ranged in nomad raillery" (p. 58). The poem moves down the Mississippi, and at its close the great river slows: "The Passion spreads in wide tongues, choked and slow, / Meeting the Gulf, hosannas silently below" (p. 61). Diffused in the river, the everyday landscapes of the early twentieth-century United States are released into "the Passion" and "hosannas," into suffering, sacrifice, prayer, and praise. The material place exists in relation to the ideal implied in hosannas and prayers, the actual exists terms of the possible. In "The Tunnel," the poet takes a nightmarish subway ride under the East River from Manhattan to Brooklyn during which he sees the severed head of Poe swinging from the hand strap and imagines love as "A burnt match skating in a urinal" (p. 99), a juxtaposition of an apparition and a very concrete image. Then, once again, the penultimate stanza of the poem moves from material to ideal: "A tugboat, wheezing wreaths of steam, / Lunged past, with one galvanic blare stove up the River. / I counted the echoes assembling, one after one" (p. 101). The real sounds of the city accumulate and begin to move the poem toward the ideal, and "The Tunnel" ends with an appeal to a "hand of Fire" (p. 101), implored to bless our agony and at the same time gather together, just as the sounds of the tugboat whistle gather around Crane and set in motion the relation between the material city and an abstract power, the power of art, a hand of fire.

And finally, *The Bridge* ends where it began, at the Brooklyn Bridge. The bridge is transformed into an enormous aeolian harp, recalling a dominant Romantic symbol. The music is tied to the material thing, the cables of the bridge, and just as Joseph Stella's paintings abstracted an ideal image from the material bridge, so Crane abstracts possibility from the actual. In *The Bridge,* the forces that sustain the human imagination—in the conception and creation of a bridge or a poem—are released via figurative language and conducted upward via arching steel cables, "Through the bound cable strands, the arching path / Upward, veering with light, the flight of strings" (p. 105). Through the work of the poem, cables, granite, and steel—material things—release the abstract, the music of the bridge, the flight of strings like unwinding gold arpeggios, the ragtime syncopation of moonlit jazz. Finally, the bridge becomes poetry itself, high art, a "multitudinous Verb": "And synergy of waters ever fuse, recast / In myriad syllables" (p. 106).

Rock, wire, and iron create a material structure that literally creates a relation between the physical shores of the East River. The bridge itself enables us to perceive the relation between those two shores in a different way. Enter *The Bridge* to the equation and we include another cultural artifact of the human being. Without the geography, the city, and the bridge that connects them, the poem, the work of art, does not exist. As William Carlos Williams insisted, all art emerges out of "the local conditions." No work of art exists without the physical environment, both built and natural, entering into it. *The*

Bridge, and much of Crane's work, is worth revisiting in the context of its participation in urban and suburban ecologies. How we perceive our environments and our relations to them is a prior step to living more ecologically in them. Crane's version of modernist idealism allows us to glimpse the ideal rooted in the urban and suburban landscapes that have seemed to obscure it. Crane roots it out, locates an ecstatic ideal grounded in material places. Crane understands humans and our suburban and urban ecologies as participants in aesthetic experience—as environments able to contribute more fully to aesthetic experience, more able to sustain our lives and our art.

Finally, time and space, symbolized in this poem by the recurring images of, respectively, the serpent and the eagle, come to roost: "The serpent with the eagle in the leaves ... ? / Whispers antiphonal in azure swing" (p. 108). The reader leaves the poem both exhilarated and with Crane's question mark lingering in the mind. How is such a vision sustained in America, then or now? Crane, though he believed that the poem is its own experience, suffered great difficulty sustaining whatever optimism he found in *The Bridge,* and, exhausted after his massive effort, he feared for his creative gift. He had worked himself half to death and drank himself into near oblivion at the same time. He was physically and psychically spent.

To recuperate, in 1931 Crane visited his father, who had opened an inn near Chagrin Falls, Ohio. The two finally reconciled, and both were tolerant of the other's worldviews, though they must have chafed a bit. This was, perhaps, the calmest, happiest time in Crane's life. But he was never cut out for a sedate life away from books, art, and the company of creative people. He applied for a Guggenheim Fellowship, which he was awarded in March, and he opted for travel to Mexico, with vague ideas toward a poem encompassing the conquest of Latin America. While living in Mixcoac, on the outskirts of Mexico City, Crane associated with the writer Katherine Anne Porter, also a Guggenheim fellow, and other members of the art community, including the Mexican artist David Alfaro Siqueiros, who painted a portrait of Crane. In a fit of drunken despair, Crane sliced the portrait to ribbons with a razor, beginning with the eyes.

While Crane was in Mexico City, the estranged wife of his friend Malcolm Cowley, Peggy, arrived in pursuit of a divorce. Both needed company, so Crane and Peggy were often together exploring the Mexican countryside, especially around Taxco, where Peggy was living. On Christmas night 1931, with the sound of cathedral bells ringing through the town, Crane and Peggy became lovers. Certainly, Peggy helped to kindle his last burst of creativity, but Crane's first and only heterosexual affair was anything but subdued. Crane's final poem, "The Broken Tower," dates from this period, and in it Crane uttered what now can be seen as his famous parting words: "And so it was I entered the broken world / To trace the visionary company of love, its voice," and once again the enjambed lines force the eye down the page to, "An instant in the wind (I know not whither hurled) / But not for long to hold each desperate choice" (p. 160). He was indeed desperate. He spent a year as a Guggenheim fellow with only one poem to show for it. He drank suicidally, mourned the recent death of his father, made a spectacle of himself chasing Indian boys, and had too many run-ins with the local police. He had to leave. Crane borrowed the money for passage home from his father's widow and cash for the train fare to the port of Vera Cruz from the Guggenheim Foundation. Crane and Peggy Cowley boarded the *Orizaba* on April 24, 1932, bound for Havana and New York, and around noon on the 26th, Crane walked to the stern, folded his coat over the rail, and dropped into the sea.

Crane's poetry is among the most vital American work of the twentieth century. His *Collected Poems* was published posthumously in 1933, and though his reputation suffered during the reign of the New Critics, it has seen great renewed attention since the 1950s. Because the literary community has outgrown its reticence about homosexuality, solid critical attention has been paid to the relationship between Crane's sexuality and his art. We can now understand his alcohol abuse as an addiction, left tragically untreated. At the close of the "Cape Hatteras" section of *The Bridge,* Crane wrote: "yes, Walt, / Afoot again, and onward without halt," vowing to grasp forever,

> My hand
> in yours,
> Walt Whitman—so—
>
> (p. 84)

It is not until Allen Ginsberg runs into Whitman in "A Supermarket in California" that we see another American poet encounter the bearded old gay American poet with such tenderness. And Robert Lowell, in "Words for Hart Crane," put these lines in Crane's mouth:

> Who asks for me, the Shelley of my age,
> Must lay his heart out for my bed and board.
>
> (p. 61)

Though Crane did not live to experience it, many hearts have laid themselves out reading his poems. Like Shelley, a great poet passed too soon from life into the sea.

Selected Bibliography

WORKS OF HART CRANE

Poetry

White Buildings. New York: Boni & Liveright, 1926.

The Bridge: A Poem. With Three Photographs by Walker Evans. Paris: Black Sun Press, 1930.

The Bridge. New York: Liveright, 1930.

The Collected Poems of Hart Crane. Edited by Waldo Frank. New York: Liveright, 1933.

Complete Poems and Selected Letters and Prose. Edited by Brom Weber. New York: Liveright, 1966.

Complete Poems of Hart Crane. Edited by Marc Simon. New York: Liveright, 1986.

Letters

The Letters of Hart Crane 1916–1932. Edited by Brom Weber. Berkeley: University of California Press, 1965.

Robber Rocks: Letters and Memories of Hart Crane, 1923–1932. Edited by Susan Jenkins Brown. Middletown, Conn.: Wesleyan University Press, 1968.

Letters of Hart Crane and His Family. Edited by Thomas S. W. Lewis. New York: Columbia University Press, 1974.

O My Land, My Friends: The Selected Letters of Hart Crane. Edited by Langdon Hammer and Brom Weber. New York: Four Walls Eight Windows, 1997.

Papers

Hart Crane Collection. Beinecke Rare Book and Manuscript Library, Yale University, New Haven, Conn.

Hart Crane Collection. Harry Ransom Center, University of Texas, Austin.

Hart Crane Collection. Kelvin Smith Library, Special Collections Research Center, Case Western Reserve University, Cleveland, Ohio.

Hart Crane and Family Papers. Special Collections and Archives, Kent State University Libraries, Kent, Ohio.

Hart Crane Papers, ca. 1909–1937. Archival Collections, Columbia University Libraries, New York.

Papers of Hart Crane 1926, 1932. Special Collections, University of Virginia Library, Charlottesville.

BIOGRAPHICAL STUDIES

Fisher, Clive. *Hart Crane: A Life.* New Haven, Conn.: Yale University Press, 2002.

Horton, Philip. *Hart Crane: The Life of an American Poet.* New York: Norton, 1937.

Mariani, Paul. *The Broken Tower: A Life of Hart Crane.* New York: Norton, 1999.

Unterecker, John. *Voyager: A Life of Hart Crane.* New York: Farrar, Straus and Giroux, 1969.

CRITICAL STUDIES

Albernaz, Joseph. "'Looking for the God in Brooklyn': The Romantic Affinities of Thomas Wolfe and Hart Crane." *Thomas Wolfe Review* 36, nos. 1–2:45–53 (2012).

Bellew, Paul Bradley. "'My Trespass Vision': Disability, Sexuality, and Nationality in Hart Crane's Versions of 'The Idiot.'" *Twentieth Century Literature* 62, no. 1:56–74 (2016).

Bloom Harold, ed. *Modern Critical Views: Hart Crane.* New York: Chelsea House, 1986.

Butterfield, R. W. *The Broken Arc: A Study of Hart Crane.* Edinburgh: Oliver & Boyd, 1969.

Clark, David R. *Critical Essays on Hart Crane.* Boston: G. K. Hall, 1982.

Combs, Robert Long. *Vision of the Voyage: Hart Crane and the Psychology of Romanticism.* Memphis, Tenn.: Memphis State University Press, 1978.

Djos, Matts G. "The Contaminated Vision: The Alcoholic Perspective in Hart Crane's 'The Wine Menagerie.'" *Popular Culture Review* 17, no. 1:59–66 (2006).

Gabriel, Daniel. *Hart Crane and the Modernist Epic: Canon and Genre Formation in Crane, Pound, Eliot, and Williams.* New York: Palgrave Macmillan, 2007.

Guiguet, Jean. *The Poetic Universe of Hart Crane.* Orono, Maine: Puckerbrush, 1993.

Hall, Susanne E. "Hart Crane in Mexico: The End of a New World Poetics." *Mosaic* 46, no. 1:135–149 (2013).

Irwin, John T. *Hart Crane's Poetry: "Appollinaire Lived in Paris, I Live in Cleveland, Ohio."* Baltimore: Johns Hopkins University Press, 2011.

Lewis, R. W. B. *The Poetry of Hart Crane: A Critical Study.* Westport, Conn.: Greenwood Press, 1978.

Liberman, Laurence. "Hart Crane's Monsoon: A Reading of White Buildings, Part Two." *American Poetry Review* 39, no. 2:9–17 (2010).

Liebowitz, Herbert A. *Hart Crane, An Introduction to the Poetry.* New York: Columbia University Press, 1968.

Lohf, Kenneth A. "The Library of Hart Crane." *Proof: Yearbook of American Bibliographical and Textual Studies* 3:283–334 (1973).

Lurie, Peter. "Querying the Modernist Canon: Historical Consciousness and the Sexuality of Suffering in Faulkner and Hart Crane." *Faulkner Journal* 20, nos. 1–2:149–176 (2004–2005).

Martin, Robert K. *The Homosexual Tradition in American Poetry.* Austin: University of Texas Press, 1979.

Monacell, Peter. "In the American Grid: Modern Poetry and the Suburbs." *Journal of Modern Literature* 35, no. 1:122–142 (2011).

Munro, Niall. *Hart Crane's Queer Modernist Aesthetic.* New York: Palgrave Macmillan, 2015.

Neubauer, Paul. "Brooklyn Bridge: Sign and Symbol in the Works of Hart Crane and Joseph Stella." In *Space in America: Theory, History, Culture.* Edited by Klaus Benesch and Kerstin Schmidt. Amsterdam: Rodopi, 2005. Pp. 541–555.

O'Neill, Michael. "'Altered Forms': Romanticism and the Poetry of Hart Crane." In *Romantic Presences in the Twentieth Century.* Edited by Mark Sandy. Farnham, U.K.: Ashgate, 2012. Pp. 57–72.

Paul, Sherman. *Hart's Bridge.* Urbana: University of Illinois Press, 1972.

Smith, Ernest. "Spending Out the Self: Homosexuality and the Poetry of Hart Crane." *Literature and Homosexuality.* Edited by Michael J. Meyer. Amsterdam: Rodopi, 2000. Pp. 161–181.

Stalter, Sunny. "Subway Ride and Subway System in Hart Crane's 'The Tunnel.'" *Journal of Modern Literature* 33, no. 2:70–91 (2010).

Taylor, Julie. "On Holding and Being Held: Hart Crane's Queer Intimacy." *Twentieth Century Literature* 60, no. 3:305–335 (2014).

Trachtenberg, Alan, ed. *Hart Crane: A Collection of Critical Essays.* Englewood Cliffs, N.J.: Prentice Hall, 1982.

Uroff, Margaret Dickie. *Hart Crane: The Patterns of His Poetry.* Urbana: University of Illinois Press, 1976.

Wargacki, John P. "The 'Logic of Metaphor' at Work: Hart Crane's Marian Metaphor in *The Bridge.*" *Religion and the Arts* 10, no. 3:329–354 (2006).

Weber, Brom. *Hart Crane: A Biographical and Critical Study.* New York: Bodley Press, 1948.

Yaffe, David. "Special Pleading and Counter-Intuition: Hart Crane's Swinging Muse." *Antioch Review* 57, no. 3:327–332 (1999).

Yingling, Thomas E. *Hart Crane and the Homosexual Text: New Thresholds, New Anatomies.* Chicago: University of Chicago Press, 1990.

OTHER SOURCES

Lowell, Robert. "Words for Hart Crane." *Life Studies and For the Union Dead.* New York: Farrar, Straus and Giroux, 1967. Reprinted, 2007.

Shelley, Percy Bysshe. "In Defence of Poetry." In *Shelley's Poetry and Prose.* Edited by Donald H. Reiman and Sharon B. Powers. New York: Norton, 1977.

Whitman, Walt. *Leaves of Grass.* New York: Norton, 2002.

Williams, William Carlos. *The Autobiography of William Carlos Williams.* New York: New Directions, 1967.

T. S. ELIOT

(1888—1965)

Julia E. Daniel

WHILE T. S. ELIOT rightfully enjoys a prominent seat in the pantheon of American literature, he is a strangely difficult poet to place. While he eventually became more English than the English, down to the umbrella and tailored suit, he always felt ties to his American homeland, as he affirmed several times during his visits back to the States toward the end of his career. And while his poetry dwells upon dry plains, lush gardens, riverbanks, seasides, and country manors, Eliot began in a midwestern city and settled in the metropolis of London, and his poetry would return to cityscapes, either washed in a decadent fog or crammed with commuters and the dead. Eliot's writing often voices the experience of dislocation, both in his personal life and in the wider cultural milieu, but it also turns to images of pilgrimage and homecoming later in his life. These paradoxes of locale are perhaps nowhere better felt than before the resting place of Eliot's ashes. Although he was interred more than four thousand miles from his birthplace in St. Louis, his memorial plaque in St. Michael's Church at East Coker strikes a note of homecoming in lines from *Four Quartets*: "In my beginning is my end. In my end is my beginning." While there are countless scholarly entry points into Eliot's oeuvre, whether an accounting of influences, a study of form, or a biographical or contextual reconstruction, we may approach Eliot through "another gate," into the places, both real and imagined, that define, elude, torture, or redeem his several speakers and, in some senses, the poet himself. Making sense of Eliot is an invitation to tease out the logic of his epigraph, a task that sends readers voyaging in order to understand how the ground of Eliot's end and beginning are, mysteriously, one.

Thomas Stearns Eliot was born on September 26, 1888, in St. Louis, Missouri, a burgeoning midwestern city that had been little more than a frontier outpost on the banks of the Mississippi only a generation prior. Robert Crawford's 2015 biography takes us back to these formative years, drawing a portrait of the big-eared, mischievous, shy, and trussed young man (a treatment for his hernia) who would eventually grow into the tweed-clad man of letters. Eliot's father, Henry Ware Eliot, president of the Hydraulic-Press Brick Company, was one of many who benefited from the rapidly growing and industrializing city. Eliot's mother, born Charlotte Champe Stearns, a writer and educator, impressed the importance of art and literature upon her children, as well as emphasizing propriety and the family's Bostonian pedigree. Eliot's paternal grandfather, William Greenleaf Eliot, moved from Boston to St. Louis in 1834 to found the first Unitarian church west of the Mississippi and, eventually, Washington University. During these early years, Eliot spent summers sailing with his brother off the coast of Gloucester, Massachusetts, where the family kept a summer cottage. To understand Eliot as an American is thus to see him as a writer situated at the nexus of not only East and West, Boston and St. Louis, but also the urban and the organic: city streets and parlor rooms, windblown coasts and muddy river banks. He entered Harvard in 1906, where he served as editor for the *Advocate* and first encountered Arthur Symons' *The Symbolist Movement in Literature* (1899). Symons introduced the young poet to Jules Laforgue, as well as to Charles Baudelaire and Stéphane Mallarmé, all of whom cast a prominent, purple shadow over Eliot's early works. He spent a formative year abroad (1910–1911) at the Sorbonne, during which time he was exposed to modern French art and philosophy, particularly the lectures of Henri Bergson. When he returned to Harvard in 1911, Eliot went on to study philosophy as a graduate student, during which time his expansive studies ranged from Eastern philosophy to histories of primitive ritual.

However, he would never defend his dissertation of the idealist philosopher F. H. Bradley and take up the family mantle of a Harvard-educated intellectual. Rather, the advent of the war caused Eliot to change his plans for studying abroad as he hastily made his way from Germany to Oxford. What was supposed to be a brief academic sojourn became an official expatriation as Eliot settled into his English environs and the Bloomsbury scene. In 1914 he met Ezra Pound, who not only brought Eliot into the London literary fold, but served as a mentor and collaborator, as can be seen in the facsimile draft of *The Waste Land.* Another important voice from the draft is that of Eliot's first wife, Vivien Haigh-Wood, whom he married on June 26, 1916, only a few months after they met each other. The vivacious spirits that so enchanted Eliot during their courtship soon gave way to physical and mental illness, along with crushing infidelities. Letters reveal Eliot's mental anguish over the decision to institutionalize Vivien, who would eventually die in a convalescent home in 1947. Caring for Vivien and eking out a meager salary teaching continuing education classes took a toll on the young poet. He found some pecuniary stability in 1917 when he joined Lloyds Bank. His literary star seemed to be rising with the publication of *Prufrock and Other Observations* (1917) and his editorial work for an avant-garde journal, the *Egoist.* Yet his personal life continued to deteriorate and Eliot suffered a mental breakdown in 1921. He took an extended leave from the bank to recuperate in the seaside town of Margate and then Lausanne, Switzerland. From this experience *The Waste Land* was born, and many readers have noted the personal parallels embedded in this modernist masterpiece, from nods to Margate's sands to the tortured romance of Dante Alighieri's Paolo and Francesca.

In 1922, the annus mirabilis of modernism, *The Waste Land,* was published in the *Dial.* That same year, Eliot founded the *Criterion,* a periodical that featured some of the most intensely debated issues of literary and cultural modernism during its run. By the next year, he was experimenting with verse drama in his drafts of *Sweeney Agonistes,* the first of what would later be his major attempts to find a new public life for poetry on the stage. His acceptance of the position of literary editor at Faber & Gwyer (later Faber & Faber) in 1925 uniquely situated Eliot as a major curator of literary modernism. It was soon after accepting this position that, in 1926, Eliot startled his traveling companions by suddenly genuflecting before Michelangelo's *Pietà* at St. Peter's in Rome. Shortly thereafter, he was quietly baptized and confirmed into the Church of England, famously (or infamously) professing himself a "classicist in literature, royalist in politics, and anglo-catholic in religion" in his essay collection *For Lancelot Andrewes* in 1928 (p. vii). The news hit the literary world like a thunderbolt, as Eliot knew it would. Readers and many of Eliot's own friends still regarded him as the iconoclastic poet of "Prufrock" and *The Waste Land,* even though the stirrings of his conversion had quietly been at work for some time.

Eliot's postconversion pieces, such as *Ash-Wednesday* (1930) and *Four Quartets* (1943), retain the density, high allusiveness, and experimentation with form that had long been a hallmark of his work. But now Eliot turned increasingly and earnestly to Christian rituals and medieval sources. As the *Complete Prose of T. S. Eliot* (2014) shows, his critical prose output skyrocketed and turned more frequently to pressing issues of the public good and the role of the church in everyday life. He also renewed contact with Emily Hale, an old flame from his Harvard days. While little is known for certain about their relationship (as we await the release of Eliot's letters to Hale, sealed until 2020), it was founded on an intense, though unconsummated, love. Biographers have likened her to Dante's Beatrice, with *Ash-Wednesday* and "Burnt Norton" (from *Four Quartets*) standing as Eliot's *La Vita Nuova.* But Hale and Eliot were never to marry, even after Vivien's death. Eliot seemed intent on fulfilling his role as the solitary man of letters and following a nearly monastic spiritual path in his later years. He gave the prestigious Norton Lectures back at Harvard in 1932–1933 and was awarded the Nobel Prize and the British Order of Merit in 1948. But Eliot again shocked the public (and his coworkers) with news of his marriage to Valerie Fletcher, his secretary from the Faber offices, on January 10, 1957. This union brought the extraordinary joy of ordinary married life into the poet's final years, from nights at the theater holding hands to card games by the fire. Eliot died at home from emphysema on January 4, 1965, and his ashes were interred at St. Michael's. In 1967 a memorial stone for Eliot was added to Poet's Corner in Westminster Abbey.

When tasked with eulogizing Eliot in the *Sewanee Review* in 1966, Pound ended with exhortation rather than mourning: "I can only repeat, but with the urgency of 50 years ago: READ HIM" (p. 109). The history of how critics have read Eliot in the years after his death attests to the inexhaustible nuance of the poet's compositions. During his lifetime, Eliot's poetry, particularly *The Waste Land,* was regarded as a high-water mark for modernism. He was often read through the lens of his own theories: concrete and impersonal, drawing from literary tradition while, in turn, transforming it. The upstart craftsman of "Prufrock" was then rebranded as the elder statesman in the 1960s, during which time his works were deemed too academic and conservative. By the 1990s Eliot scholarship witnessed a new bloom in activity as critics reconsidered his use and depictions of popular culture, politics and economics, philosophy and religion, and gender and sexuality. Eliot's assumed place of veneration, the classroom and the academy, also expanded when his light verse found a popular audience with the debut of Andrew Lloyd Webber's musical *Cats* in 1981. In 1996 the publication of Eliot's early poetry journal, *Inventions of the March Hare,* turned us back to his apprenticeship years. *Inventions* provided new insights into the composition of "Prufrock" but also made public previously unavailable minor pieces, many of which are now receiving well-deserved attention. As of this writing, Eliot studies are undergoing another sea change, thanks to the publication of *The Complete Prose,* several volumes of which have been published with more on the way. Prior to this, only about 10 percent of Eliot's critical prose was available in print. The dedicated work of the poet's widow and the editor Ronald Schuchard in readying this simply voluminous body of writing will keep the poet's readers busy for decades to come. The extant new material challenges some of our preconceptions about the stolid writer (who once taught baseball at London's Highgate School) and broadens our understanding of his public engagements. In the *Complete Prose,* we find his comments on a host of social issues ranging from copyright reform to urban infrastructure in London slums. *The Complete Prose* also confirms some long-held beliefs about Eliot as writer and editor, most notably the depth of his erudition, his widely expansive reading habits, and his intellectual largesse, whether mentoring and publicizing new poets or delivering lectures for schoolchildren.

The time is therefore both ripe and inopportune for any summation of Eliot's career, as we are only beginning to discover how this new material will inflect the way we read his poetry. Our present study will approach Eliot via the real landscapes that influenced him, the imaginative locations that he alludes to and builds, and the backdrops that constrain or elude his speakers. One of the benefits of entering through the garden gate, as it were, is that a place-based reading models diverse kinds of scholarly approaches to the poetry along the way, including studies of allusion and influence, recurring themes and structures, appropriations of popular culture, and biographical and cultural contextualization.

FROM PRUFROCK AND OTHER OBSERVATIONS *TO* THE WASTE LAND

While 1917 found Eliot entrenched in his adoptive London home toward the end of World War I, most of the major works in *Prufrock and Other Observations* (1917) were first penned by a twenty-three-year-old in the United States four years before the war. This early poetry testifies to Eliot's Laforgian influences as well as his abhorrence of the stifling drawing rooms of the Boston Brahmin class. From Laforgue, Eliot would discover the possibilities of free verse and the aesthetic elevation of prosaic modern subjects, such as the muttering electric street lamps of "Rhapsody on a Windy Night." As the title of his collection suggests, many of his speakers assume a detached Laforgian observatory stance laced with irony. At the same time, some of those speakers display more robust characterization than typically found in symbolist verse, drawing in part from Eliot's Victorian influences, such as the dramatic monologue. They also suffer from the endless performance of New England middle-class rituals that prevent genuine human connection, usually figured as failed romances and thwarted erotic desires. The combination of these influences, Bostonian high culture and Laforgian detachment, results in two major stages for Eliot's early speakers and subjects: the street and the parlor. The phantasmagoric and seedy street scenes owe much to Charles Baudelaire's *flâneur*, a strolling urban explorer and man of leisure who possesses a keen eye and a poetic temperament. In contrast, the confining domestic interiors restrict the literal movements and metaphorical social theater played out therein.

In the maze of twilight streets, Eliot's speakers play the game of attached detachment typical of the flâneur while occasionally catching glimpses of the transcendent. At times omniscient, at others merely impersonal, they voice the value, beauty, and luminous terror of city. The after-midnight wanderings in "Rhapsody" offer glimpses of sex workers in grinning doorways and feral cats licking garbage in the gutters. The speakers assume a kinship with these spatially improper places while maintaining the aloofness required to regard them as art objects. In "Preludes," for example, Eliot's characteristic fragmentation results in a landscape where both place and people lack coherence. Just as the city becomes a nigh-cubist arrangement of little more than a few empty lots, cracked chimneys, and a thousand furnished rooms, people are similarly disassembled into stubby fingers, yellowed feet, and curls of hair. "I," "you," "he," and "one" enter and exit with a sense of urban anonymity as the rhythms of daily life, from the raising of shades to the lighting of lamps, provide a structure that endlessly withholds some unaccomplished event. The speaker is nonetheless moved by "fancies that are curled / About these images" (p. 16). This intimate clinging prefaces his sudden apprehension of "some infinitely gentle / Infinitely suffering thing" that emanates out of his disjointed impressions. However, this minor epiphany is hastily wiped away with a laugh either embarrassed or ironic. Rather than linger with the piteous gentleness, the poem concludes by looping back again to refuse-laden lots. The divine dance of the spheres atrophies into "ancient" women gathering garbage to burn. It is a waste land in miniature (p. 15).

While the bourgeois zones in *Prufrock* appear less sinister, they are also less enchanted and are far more anxiety provoking, like the purgatorial stoop of Cousin Harriet's house in "The Boston Evening Transcript" or the formal garden of "La Figlia Che Piange." In "Portrait of a Lady," the lady traps the speaker in the carefully arranged stage of her drawing room. "Portrait," as the title suggests, draws heavily from Henry James's novel of the same name but also hearkens to a literary tradition of female portraiture practiced by Alfred, Lord Tennyson, Robert Browning, and Algernon Charles Swinburne. It is also dramatic monologue parading as dialogue: the lady keeps addressing her visitor while he slips deeper into critical deliberations about both the lady and himself. This failed romantic performance plays out in different theaters: her highly Victorian and feminized interior and his retreats to out-of-doors male safe havens, extended in the end to his travel "abroad." As director, she dutifully arranges her room as if staging the final moments of *Romeo and Juliet.* As actress, she hits her marks, twirling the lilac in her hand at the right moment. Her speech is similarly scripted, and the speaker struggles to reconcile its high artifice with the intimacy of the feelings conveyed by the lady.

But for all the points of contrast between the two—her age and his youth, her Victorian pretense and his modernist hyperawareness—his outdoor retreats are just as middle-class, proper, and staged as is her parlor. He reads uninteresting news in the park, smokes and drinks his beer at the open-air café with the rest of the crowd, and even keeps time with the public clocks. There is no outside to the performance, and the deceptively open spaces provide no real answer to his inner turmoil, nor do they offer escape. He maintains his reserved mask in the park until the tune of a street piano brings him back to memories of the lady, just as he knows his time abroad will never resolve his guilt and muddled emotions when he receives news of her death. A crepuscular atmosphere descends on that imagined moment. As the "grey and smoky" atmosphere associated with the modern, symbolist city meets with the Victorian palate of a "yellow and rose" sunset, both lady and speaker are folded in a darkening obscurity where neither has truly known the other, nor has the speaker known himself (p. 14).

In "The Love Song of J. Alfred Prufrock," modern *flânerie* and bourgeois anxiety collide in the twisting alleyways of the speaker's mind. From the very title, Eliot builds irreconcilable tensions into the piece, as the pathos of a love song smashes into the terribly ordinary name of one J. Alfred. Scholars have linked the name to several possible sources, including a St. Louis furniture purveyor and Eliot himself, who once went by the name T. Stearns. Just as Prufrock cannot say what he means, it is nearly impossible to pin down exactly where the poem takes place, as locations and bodies hopelessly fragment across the jagged edges of the speaker's neurotic monologue. Before Prufrock begins with his invitation, the epigraph lands reader and speaker in the eighth circle of Dante's hell before the war criminal Guido da Montefeltro. Guido offers to tell his story only after reassuring himself that Dante cannot possibly be a mortal who would bring word of his sins back to the living. The epigraph situates this love song as more of a confessional, and, like Guido, Prufrock suffers from an overweening concern about his appearance to others. Even more uncannily, like the Dantean soul whose body has been torturously reduced to a flickering flame, Prufrock's anxieties over the public reception of his body are cast in terms of painful dislocations or metamorphoses: a severed, balding head, a pinned-down specimen insect, the shuttling claws of a crab. The major landscape of the poem, Prufrock's mind, is full of impotent evasions and self-recriminations that he returns to again and again, without hope of real outward action or interior resolution, much as Dante's damned symbolically reenact their sins for eternity.

Prufrock's invocation, "Let us go, then, you and I" (p. 5), gestures to a proffered act of flânerie through the nighttime "muttering retreats" of the city, a location Eliot described as "St. Louis, upon which that of Paris and London have been superimposed" ("Influence," p. 422). While the other city poems largely use pronouns in an absolute or impersonal fashion, here the use of "us" and "you" places the reader in an assumed intimacy with Prufrock, in contrast with the faceless ladies who float throughout the piece. Somewhere between the impersonal and the intimate, Prufrock's object of love is captured as the remote "one" who wraps herself in a shawl or settles into a pillow. She is the "One" of all love songs but also the unreal "one" of a hypothetical proposition. Appropriately, the surreal city becomes like a forestalled philosophical rumination, as the streets "follow like a tedious argument" that abruptly dead-ends (p. 5). His repeated invitation to go is met with a stanza break, followed by two lines where women drift through a room while discussing Michelangelo, after which he again shuttles back outside to consider a feral fog nuzzling against the windows. These breaks and interruptions make it unclear if we have ever accepted his invitation, let alone where he, and we, are. As with the insidious streets in the first stanza, Eliot invites questions of spatiality only to stifle them. Just as he cannot bring himself to speak, the solipsistic Prufrock cannot place himself, either literally or metaphorically, in his environs. He is mired so completely in his own mind that the exterior world is little more than the screen on which the magic-lantern show of his thoughts play out, just as the night sky becomes the unconscious, sprawling patient, a massive astral projection of Prufrock's own malaise.

Despite his early insistence that we go with him, Prufrock then switches to a conciliatory tone as he insists, again and again, that "indeed there will be time" (p. 6). Part of the illusion of endless time for equally endless ruminations is the routine of life in polite society, specifically tea and mealtimes that break days into mornings, afternoons, and evenings, to the point that Prufrock can conceive of his life as little more than a devastating progression of coffee spoons. His misguided belief that all can be done before "the taking of a toast and tea" (p. 6) is met with blocked images of chewing later in the piece: he cannot bite the matter off, nor does he ultimately dare to eat a peach. Questions, the likes of which terrify Prufrock, are lifted and dropped on plates like slices of cake, ones he cannot consume. The ladies even whisper, in a parenthetical aside, that he's growing thin, and he likens his mental anguish to a form of penitential, if ineffectual, fasting. Eliot quietly parallels Prufrock's frustrated longings in a world full of unobtainable women with his inability to find real nourishment at any of the well-appointed parlor tables, complete with marmalades and ices, which shape his days.

Scholars have long noted the subtle play of verbs that keep Prufrock locked in endless inaction and repetition. His "shoulds" slide into "woulds" as the moment of self-revelation almost imperceptibly passes him by. His excuses after the fact involve raising mythic and literary parallels only to demote them. He is more Polonius than Hamlet, and even when decapitated like John the Baptist he fails to be the prophet, all of which is "no great matter" (p. 8) before what he assumes will be the casual disinterestedness of the "one." However, Prufrock is not so capable of shaking off his final mythic parallel. The women who speak of Michelangelo morph into the mermaids of the poem's last stanza. Eliot contrasts the "Let us go" of the beginning with a last vision of going, as the mermaids swim "seaward" (p. 9), away from the man on the beach. The lure of absent voices disturbs Prufrock's fantasy of a solitary old age spent walking on the strand, as he frets that the mermaids will not sing to him. And yet, the actual danger is not their music but is rather the human voice of banal life, the real siren that wakes him into death by water. And if Prufrock suffers, he does not do so alone: the voices "wake *us,* and *we* drown" (p. 9). We wake from reading the poem at the moment Prufrock is roused by the all too mundane whispering in another room. We have, we discover, accompanied Prufrock on his imagined and remembered visits, only to arrive, suffocating, on the ocean bed of a disenchanted modernity.

It was on another beach, the sands of Margate, that Eliot would search for much-needed rest following his bout of severe mental and physical exhaustion in 1921, before going on to Switzerland for psychiatric treatment. If the writer of "Prufrock" was still steeped in an American milieu, a fresh expat before his marriage and the onset of war, the poet of *The Waste Land* (1922) is now firmly settled on British soil and has weathered much in the interim. Yet the shoreline lament in *The Waste Land,* "On Margate Sands. / I can connect / Nothing with nothing" (p. 66), resonates beyond personal turmoil to a whole generation's sense of dislocation. While such assertions have become something of a truism in the near-century since its publication, and *The Waste Land* now justly stands as a monument of modernism, it is hard to recuperate exactly how radical the poem appeared to its early readership in 1922. It was, at the time, a poetic animal the likes of which the public had yet not seen. Its experimental nature still invites the question of what, exactly, one ought to *do* with *The Waste Land.* Early scholarship expertly explicated the hyper-abundance of allusions that breed like lilacs throughout the lines, while more recent studies have foregrounded the high importance of lowbrow entertainments and modern material cultures throughout the poem, from ragtime rhythm to the rise of the automobile. Just as past and present, high and low, harmonize or jar discordantly in the polyphony of voices, so too do ancient and modern, real and unreal landscapes merge, melt, burst, and burn. The title raises questions of grounding. Where and what is the wasted land that confines these voices? Why has it been laid to waste and is there any hope of rejuvenation? In the year after the publication of *The Waste Land,* Eliot expounded on the "mythical method" in his essay "Ulysses, Order and Myth," a method by which allusions to myths create a "continuous parallel between contemporaneity and antiquity" (*Selected Prose,* p. 177) in lieu of narrative. This method has been broadly used to understand *The Waste Land* as a whole, and it aptly describes Eliot's multivalent landscapes that trap and define their speakers, such as the recurring city and waterscapes throughout the poem.

The shoring up of fragments against ruins has long been read as an analog to the poem and to the modern project as a whole: a ready-made bulwark constructed from broken cultural remnants. Provocatively, the referents for this image are the eternally crumbling, burning, and falling city structures that stand for a modern experience of urbanism as well as the entire history of Western culture, imagined around its city centers. In the London Bridge scene in "The Burial of the Dead," the here and the hereafter touch as the crowds of London urbanites thoughtlessly trudging down King William Street overlap with the throngs of the dead in Dante's *Inferno.* Like the self-absorbed souls in hell, the London commuters fix their eyes on their feet as they go. Despite its density, the London scene keeps its citizens hopelessly isolated even in their shared rounds of commuting. Even when the speaker hails the familiar ghost in the crowd, identified as anyone from Pound to a St. Louis hatmaker, there is no reply given to his many questions. Unlike the talkative damned in the *Inferno,* the ghost keeps its silence. Here, Eliot diverges from his Dantean parallel; London is much worse. In hell, Dante, with Virgil's aid, successfully identifies his interlocutors, but Eliot leaves his reader with no sure guide, inducing in his reader the same feelings of dislocation endemic to life in the modern city.

And yet, while hellishly crowded, the city is also tragically vacant, as the lack of trash by the banks of the Thames in "The Fire Sermon" signals that "the nymphs are departed," along with their beaus, the "loitering heirs of City directors" (p. 62). The departure of the nymphs strikes a note of alarm, as these minor fertility figures were always closely tied to a specific natural place. Eliot condemns the rootlessness of the young ruling class, who "have left no addresses," as a tragedy parallel to the abandonment of the nymphs from their sacred springs. In an unexpected twist, the lack of literal waste signals how the riverside has been wasted in an asocial world that lacks even the detritus of leisure, let alone signs of amorous retreats and their ritualized precedents as signaled by the mention of nymphs. Where elsewhere pollution suggests a sullied city, here the lack of sandwich wrappers and "other testimony of summer nights" (p. 62) makes present the nymph's absence. Through the speaker's tears, this loveless, empty Thames flows into the ancient rivers of the Babylonian exile, where the Psalmist sat and remembered a lost Jerusalem, as the allusion adds yet another layer of displacement. But this is now an exile in situ, as if the speaker of this passage mourns an exile within the homeland—or an inability to locate a homeland at all, for, as we are told later in the poem, London and Jerusalem are equally unreal. One can read Eliot-as-expat into this moment, but it also recalls the many Europeans who found themselves scattered, displaced, or simply restless in the interwar period, like the French-speaking Greek merchant in "The Fire Sermon" or the countess who endlessly flees the coming of winter in the poem's first lines.

Even as the oily Thames runs through it, Eliot's London burns like Dante's *città del foco,* city of fire. This combustion also unites London with Carthage toward the end of "The Fire Sermon," the poem's nadir, as both lands testify to the waste of human passions and the inevitable downfall of empires. London overlaps with an ancient Carthage that is "Burning burning burning burning" (p. 66). The notes send us to St. Augustine's late-fourth-century *Confessions,* in which Carthage is a cauldron of steaming concupiscence. Like Carthage, the wasted London is also a bubbling pot of unholy loves, seen in the many episodes of twisted, tepid, or violent desires, like the encounter in the typist's flat. There is no escaping this fire. Eliot interrupts a scrap of a prayer from the *Confessions,* "O Lord Thou pluckest me out," with yet another repetition of "burning" to conclude the fire sermon.

Speaker, city, and civilization slip out of God's grasp and back into the blaze. But Carthage burns beyond the Augustinian reference to the burning of London by association as well, including a fire that consumed part of London Bridge in the early 1630s and the Great Fire of London in 1666. Carthage was also destroyed by fire at end of the Third Punic War, which ultimately reduced the entire empire to ash. Burning London as Burning Carthage, and vice versa, creates a smoldering vision of civilization in which empires keep collapsing back into conflagrations that punctuate the end of an era, a vision that captures the modernist preoccupation with the as-yet uncertain character of the epoch to come.

Part of the unreality of the cities in the poem is this sense of their perpetuity in the midst of their perpetual downfall, as seen in the list of unreal cities in "What the Thunder Said." London becomes trapped in the same historical cycles of destruction, reconstruction, and destruction that characterize Jerusalem and Alexandria, as the imagined ur-city "Cracks and reforms and bursts" (p. 69) in a violet atmosphere redolent of the end of an era. A similar note is struck with a last glance back at London Bridge, "London Bridge is falling down falling down falling down" (p. 71), in the final lines. Tone seeps strangely in all directions. The repetition of "falling down" in the popular child's ditty becomes disturbingly morbid, infecting the innocence of the source with the reader's sudden awareness of its referent within the context of the poem. The burning of the bridge, and the masses of ghostly city dwellers upon it, return again to fall again, much like the children who play the game over and over. At the same time, the historical fact of one of London's many tragedies is brutally reduced to a few bars of a nursery rhyme.

From the beginning, readers have grappled with the essential tone of the piece and therefore the potential success of shoring up these fragments against the ruins. Is *The Waste Land* an ode to modern disillusionment, where one can at best rearrange the rubble of blasted personal and cultural experience only for it to fall apart again? Or is there a hard-won promise of hope in this creative act of construction in the midst of a warlike world? These questions come to a head in the final, cryptic lines of the poem and its penultimate landscape, one that returns us to the wasted land of the Fisher King myth. Like "Prufrock," we finally arrive neither quite at land nor wholly at sea, as the king sits fishing, facing the water, with the parched land to his back. Despite the promise of rain offered by the voice of the thunder in the lines before this tableau, the land remains "arid" (p. 71). Worse, the hints of progress, like the present tense of the singing grass around the chapel, fall backward into recollection, as the king "sat" in a past that keeps asserting its presentness. The fruitless land signals that the king still suffers from his wound, even at this late moment in the poem. However, his physical situation at the shore is an apt analog for the modern poet caught between past and present, a wounded modernity and an unfathomable expanse of history, trying draw some nourishment from the depths of history to be consumed in the present. Unlike the heirs who abandon their city, the king wishes to "at least set my lands in order" (p. 71).

And yet the ground shifts again, as Eliot couches the king's call to emplacement and imperial responsibility as question that precedes a last group of lines that feel eminently disordered. They offer no immediate logic in relation to one another, cry out from no one coherent voice, and are situated in a placeless void. We jump from the London Bridge nursery rhyme, back to a hint of Philomel's cry, to Hieronymo's feigned act of madness, back to an echo of thunder, before the unexpected assertion of peace, "Shantih." The crisis here is largely one of place: the reader's attempt to place the quotes in their original sources, to make sense of their physical placement on the page in that particular order, and the groping for a place from which this utterance, or these utterances, comes. If the nymphs have departed from their lands, so too has Eliot exiled the reader from any stabilizing location. The landlessness of the lines makes it impossible to tell if *shantih* is a proffered reality. It may embody a hopeless aspiration as the reader lands in the vacuum of a rootless modernity where water and dust never meet. In such a landscape, a no-where, neither

London nor hell, we are left alone with only the drifting voices of an indecipherable tradition. Then again, perhaps peace comes to freshen the earth with rain, but we cannot see or feel this blessing as the land remains to our backs, situating the reader as a healed Fisher King who is just on the cusp of his revitalization as we continue to pull decontextualized fragments out of the depths of history. We, like the king, are left wondering how to set these lands in order, while the shards of the final lines offer themselves as both the ruins and the building material that might yet salvage a deteriorating culture.

FROM "THE HOLLOW MEN" *TO* THE ELDER STATESMAN

"The Hollow Men" (1925) stand as Janus figures in Eliot's corpus: they look backward to the wastes of *The Waste Land* while looking ahead to the austere styles and contemplative concerns of "Ash-Wednesday" (1930) and *Four Quartets* (1943). Their landscape, a "dead land" and a "cactus land" (p. 82), owes much to the arid plains that precede them, but the locations in "The Hollow Men" feel emphatically more abstract, as the particular contours of London are stripped away into bare, hollow valleys. The hollow men, little more than an effigy of themselves like the Guy Fawkes dummies they evoke, are trapped in a kind of nowhere. Unlike the violent souls who cross into hell, their spiritual tepidness keeps them tethered to the shore of the Acheron. Fittingly, here there is no burning, unlike *The Waste Land*: there is no ritual bonfire, as is typical on Guy Fawkes Day, and unlike the flaming cities, this world ends not with a bang but with a weak whimper, rendered again in the devastating diminutive of a children's rhyme. Eliot captures the trial of this spiritual paralysis in the sparse, repetitive lines that do mount, for a moment, to an attempted prayer, though a failed one, before falling back into dry mutterings. A divine reality does seem to exist beyond the hollow men's ambit, though they cannot bring themselves to address it.

In contrast, the repetitiveness and halting struggle to pray in *Ash-Wednesday* testifies to a slow and arduous spiritual progression. Between the publication of "The Hollow Men" in 1925 and *Ash-Wednesday* in 1930, Eliot was formally baptized into the Church of England. *Ash-Wednesday* portrays the process of conversion, literally "turning around," in a succession of turning movements and twisting stairs that owes much to Dante's *Purgatorio* and *La Vita Nuova* as well to as medieval iconography. Like Prufrock's "Let us go" and the muted note of failed pilgrimage that begins *The Waste Land, Ash-Wednesday* opens with an arrested movement: "Because I do not hope to turn again," a statement that the speaker enacts by reiterating the same phrase in minor variants over the next lines (p. 87). By the poem's conclusion, however, "Because" will be replaced by "Although" (p. 96), as grace breaks through despite the speaker's recalcitrance. The path from "Because" to "Although" is one of renunciation, rendered as a stripping away of the flesh down to praying bones, as well as an ascent up the turning stair where the speaker must battle the temptations of sensual life. The lady who appears in several forms throughout functions as intercessor, whether as the Blessed Virgin, Dante's Beatrice, or a lightly veiled Emily Hale. Unlike the vapid hollow men, both lady and, eventually, speaker can lift up their voices in prayer. The land, too, carries the promise of redemption, as the rocks of *The Waste Land* become cool blue stones from whence prayer is utterable. The world as a whole becomes a creation where meaningful speech is possible because of the incarnation of God as Word: "The Word within / The world and for the world" (p. 94). This sanctified vision of the world fulfills the lines of Ezekiel from the second section: "This is the land. We have our inheritance" (p. 90). While the land is to be divided by lot among the tribes of Israel, a portion is to be set aside for the Lord. In the end, the divine territory expands to encompass all things, redeeming too even the rocks, gardens, and shores the speaker passed by on the path to his conversion.

Eliot returns to the theme of conversion and pilgrimage in *Four Quartets,* where the stroll of the flâneur and the wandering of *The Waste Land* are transfigured into journeys both physical and spiritual that lead closer to the divine. That road, as captured in *Four Quartets,* is a *via negativa* in which the speaker must attempt, again and again, to subsume ego in acts of endless humility. This way is also the path of the poet late in his career. In "Tradition and the Individual Talent," published in *The Sacred Wood* in 1920, Eliot described the progress of the writer as "a continual self-sacrifice, a continual extinction of personality" (*Selected Prose,* p. 40). Like *Ash-Wednesday, Four Quartets* addresses the problem of articulation, this time in relation to voicing a sacred reality that constantly outstrips language. The self-sacrifice attempted throughout is therefore the practice of both the poet and the saint. At the same time, *Four Quartets* remains a work born of deeply personal circumstance in which Eliot returns to landscapes of acute importance in his own life. Each quartet takes a specific location as its grounding principle, and every ground is a personal shrine to which the speaker travels in search of purgation and salvation. The poems were composed during a long period between 1935 and 1942, beginning with some repurposed lines from Eliot's play *Murder in the Cathedral* (1935). The first quartet in the sequence, "Burnt Norton," refers to a country estate in Gloucestershire whose name retains the singed memory of a fire that destroyed one of the structures in the 1740s. Eliot visited the estate's gardens in the summer of 1934 with Emily Hale. Given this personal connection, "Burnt Norton" unsurprisingly dwells on choices not made, paths not taken, while it also moves toward a consideration of a refinement of love beyond individual passion. The next quartet and pilgrimage site moves to East Coker in Somerset, which Eliot visited in August 1937. This visit served as a kind of homecoming and point of departure, as it was from East Coker that the poet's ancestor, Andrew Eliot, emigrated to New England in 1669. The quartet "The Dry Salvages," then, brings us back to the beaches of the New World. The title refers to a cluster of rocks off Pigeon Cove, close to Cape Ann in Gloucester, Massachusetts, where Eliot summered as a child. He would pass this rocky outcropping during his boyhood sailing excursions. But these American waters provide no terra firma, and the last quartet moves to the chapel of Little Gidding in Cambridgeshire, where a small Anglican community founded by Nicholas Ferrar gave refuge to King Charles I during English Civil War in 1625. Here, Eliot also returns to the threatened rooftops of London during the blitz, during which time he served as a night warden on the roof of Faber's offices.

Whereas the persistence of cities in *The Waste Land* bodied forth eternal decay and decline, the persistence of landscapes in *Four Quartets* exerts pressure in a different direction. The crumbling, flooding, or burning locations in *Four Quartets* transcend their own destruction. Their temporal cycles surpass bare history by partaking in kairos, divine time, while also testifying to the rhythms of liturgical cycles and the seasonal flow of death and birth in a world of chronos. Because of the underlying stability of kairos, these seasons, and the death they proffer, need not be a cause of anxiety, though it is no small act for the speaker to move into that sacred assurance. By extension, if in the early poetry dislocated people become like dissolute places, in *Four Quartets* the human person becomes whole in its relation to places: the soul is like a tree with quivering sap; the river is within us. The body is materially entangled in place as well. While Stetson's corpse has yet to bloom, here bodies branch endlessly out of the soil, which is composed of decaying houses and dancers. If "Only through time time is conquered" (p. 181), as the speaker avers in "Burnt Norton," so too are the rose garden, the house, the shore, the chapel, and even the city, necessary places through which creation is redeemed.

Like "Prufrock," "Burnt Norton" begins with an invitation to join the speaker on a journey into a surreal landscape. Rather than reflecting the tortured contours of Prufrock's mind, this locale exists as a numinous possibility returned to, though never taken: a rose garden behind the door never opened. And whereas Prufrock presumes to "go" as a kind of evasion, the reflective garden stroll here happens as a response to a call: echoes and birdsong draw speaker and reader onward. Rather than foreclosing conversation, the speaker of "Burnt Norton" invites and seeks out communication with possible pasts and, ultimately, presents and futures. This is "our first world," which suggests the early world of childhood, replete with hidden, giggly children in the trees, and a partial vision of Eden, in which godlike presences still stroll with humanity in our first garden. While a hypothetical space, this green world is emphatically concrete, down to the actual concrete of a drained pool on the estate's grounds. This miniature waste land, brown and dry, unexpectedly bursts forth in "water out of sunlight" (p. 180) in which a radiant "lotos-rose" is reflected. The lotus recurs as a symbol of purity and enlightenment throughout the Upanishads, and Eliot will layer the Eastern valences of this blossom with Christian ones, such as the roses and gardens from "The Spiritual Canticle" of Saint John of the Cross and the roses associated with Marian devotions. Waste becomes "ridiculous" (p. 184) rather than inevitable when considered against this epiphanic moment. However, it is yet just a moment, and the speaker has only a brief flash of apprehension, as "human kind / Cannot bear very much reality" (p. 180). In the face of this limitation, the bird exiles us from the garden to begin the long process of purgation. That process immediately involves a recognition of paradoxes, as the rest of "Burnt Norton" places us in the living tension between a host of oppositions: time and timelessness, flesh and fleshlessness, movement and stillness, unbeing and being.

"East Coker" and "The Dry Salvages" explore the living out of these contradictions, and the spiritual path through them, in greater detail. In lieu of the constantly burning cities of *The Waste Land,* "East Coker" begins with a more domestic and human-scale vision of houses as they "rise and fall, crumble, are extended" (p. 185). One need not shore fragments against these ruins, as falling into ruin becomes an organic reclamation of the house back into its fundamental elements rather than a terrifying dissolution. This optimism, for now, is achieved through consideration of material existence, paired with the wisdom of Ecclesiasticus. The life-giving earth that gives up old stones for new buildings is composed of ash, flesh, fur, and leaf, each of which has its fit season for death or birth. But this sense of seasonal fitness is threatened in the disorder of the middle sections, where winter smashes into spring, covering the roses in snow, and the stars themselves are at war. And whereas the formal marriage dance of the first section, a pattern symbolic of well-ordered life-in-time, quietly and appropriately concludes in death, the thought of these same dancers buried under the hill sparks a morbid, fearful litany of the dead in section 3. Scholars, soldiers, and statesmen all "go into the dark" (p. 188). In this Good Friday piece, the solution is to enter farther into that graveyard blackness rather than flee it, while calling on one's soul to wait patiently in a state of spiritual abstention. Such renunciation leads not away from houses, earth, and flesh, but back to them, just as the bleeding Eucharistic sacrifice in section 4 proffers life from death. And so "East Coker" begins with houses and ends with a return home, one that mirrors Eliot's return to this ancestral homestead. But just as the end is the beginning, home is the place one starts from, and it is from this place that the speaker will go forth again, as did his forebears, to a new shore.

"The Dry Salvages" returns us to America and opens with a primitivist critique of modernity's technological dislocation in a world of natural forces. Thanks to civil engineering, the "dwellers in cities" (p. 193) can ignore the primal powers of the river god beneath their bridges. This fluvial power, the muddy Mississippi, refuses to be reduced to a mere topographical inconvenience by "worshippers of the machine." Denying the river is simultaneously a denial of our place in those rhythms, as "the river is within us, the sea is all about us." Eliot washes us out into deeper waters, where the god-saturated ocean acts as an undulant reliquary of a sunken culture and the terrifying embodiment of time as an endless flux. So too will the Mississippi strand our sins, both corporate and particularly American, on his banks, as the bitter apple from the Fall floats beside the "cargo" of dead black men (p. 197). This tidal chronology is yet another waste land, here presented as unending lamentation on impossibly vast, churning waters, far more violent and overwhelming than the seasonal cycles of "Burnt Norton." Yet the solution, or at least, the path through, is similar. In "Burnt Norton," the *via negativa* moves downward into deeper dark, and the spiritual sailor in "The Dry Salvages" must "fare forward" (p. 198), if not well, farther out into the threatening expanse. But how is one to determine the direction of such forward-faring in the midst of chaos? Section 4 raises a prayer to the Blessed Virgin as Stella Maris, star of the sea, asking her intercession for all such struggling voyagers. "Stella Maris" also refers to Polaris, the motionless North Star used as a fixed point for navigation at night. Like the still point of the turning world, or the still center of the dance, the arrival of Stella Maris signals a locus or orientation beyond this mutable sphere that can order the journey. Once this beacon, like the beacon light on the rocks of the dry salvages, breaks into the poem, section 5 returns to shore. As with the homecoming of "East Coker," the conclusion of "The Dry Salvages" brings us back to solid ground, the "life of significant soil" (p. 200).

"Little Gidding" explicitly returns to the movement of pilgrimage, conjured in section 1 through the description of Eliot's own approach to the chapel paralleled with that of the fugitive King Charles making his way to Little Gidding. Seasonal and elemental chaos asserts itself again during "Midwinter spring" (p. 201), but the rite of the journey transcends the situational specifics of any one way of going. This is not an elevation beyond place, though there are "other places ... in a desert or a city" (p. 202) where the same spiritual practice could be pursued. Rather, "Now and in England" takes on new urgency as the pilgrim's contact point with the timeless moment and still center of being: it is the ground where the pilgrim comes to kneel, "Where prayer has been valid" (p. 202). Section 2 expands on the hints of material chaos in the opening by detailing the death of air, earth, water, and fire in their turn. Yet this is purgation rather than dissolution, captured in well-ordered stanzas that glance backward at each location with the calm of spiritual indifference. The speaker is now ready to receive another image of eternal fire, once promised in the garden, in a Pentecostal vision experienced in the heart of London. At once the biblical "dove descending" (p. 207) with tongues of flame and a German bomber threatening the city's rooftops, this compound figure welds together contexts, as London becomes Jerusalem and a foretaste of Heaven. Or, at least the speaker and reader are presented with such a possibility, as the choice between death by fire, understood as secular, unredeemed time and the disordered loves suffered therein, and *fire,* its divine, eternal, refining opposite, remains open. At the poem's conclusion, the apprehension of the burning rose, where "the fire and the rose are one" (p. 209), suggest the latter, as does the allusion to Saint Julian of Norwich's *Revelations of Divine Love,* in which the English mystic wrote "all shall be well" (p. 209).

If the spatial logic of *Four Quartets* draws heavily from pilgrimage, it is also a homecoming. Appropriately so, as the Anglo-Catholic tradition that Eliot draws from codes each pilgrimage as a modest reenactment of the return of the soul to its divine end. The return of the pronoun "we" at the poem's end also emphasizes that this homecoming is the corporate end, or purpose, of the Church, a voyage undertaken in community, while gesturing toward the intimate hope of sharing this mystical path with "you," the poet's beloved. The speaker's recurrent journey is a return to where we started with a fresh knowledge of this beginning, whether humanity's Eden or Eliot's personal moment in the garden. In *Four Quartets,* home indwells within the poetic line as well. This metapoetics, "where every word is at home, / Taking its place to support the others" (p. 208), resolves the crisis of articulation that has plagued the speaker throughout the piece, making prayer and poetry hospitable again.

Many biographies of the poet take *Four Quartets* as a stopping point, a place after which Eliot's artistic works tapered off almost completely as he spent the last of his days on critical prose and lectures, his editorial work at Faber, and enjoying the company of his radiant new wife, Valerie, before his death in 1965. But Eliot's creative career hardly concluded after "Little Gidding." Rather, he shifted the literal placement of his poetry off of the page and onto the stage. If we tend to overlook this fresh aesthetic venture during the twilight of Eliot's career, it may be because the poet seems to succeed far more surely on the safe side of the footlights. While the dramas are arguably more skillful than we often acknowledge, even the ways they fail demonstrate Eliot's evolving attempts to place poetry in the ears and lives of a wider public. Nor is Eliot's move to drama a clean break from what precedes it. His began work on his first dramatic piece, *Sweeney Agonistes,* in the early 1920s, and saw it performed by the Group Theatre in 1934. (He distanced himself from this first, jazz-inflected experiment by demoting it to the status of a poetic fragment later in life.) He wrote about dramatic theory and performance extensively, particularly Renaissance drama, the staging of poetry, the ritual structures of drama, and the communal character of theatergoing. Eliot regarded the theater as the space where an antisocial, secular public could come together as a group and actively participate in a repurposed ritual form that had the benefit of entertaining while echoing the lost rhythms of pagan rites and Christian worship. Moreover, theater was an extension of his ongoing work in verse. In his Norton Lectures, he argued that poetry finds its perfection in dramatic presentation: "The ideal medium for poetry ... is the theatre" (*The Use of Poetry and the Use of Criticism,* pp. 152–153). Unsurprisingly, many of the images, themes, and landscapes that recur in his nondramatic verse appear in his later plays, while the role of the family, and of human community more broadly, comes to the fore. On Eliot's stage, we find again chapels and gardens, crumbling towers, claustrophobic drawing rooms, and hints of deadly oceans beyond the walls. Pilgrimage and homecoming also assert themselves as modes of spiritual progression, with some provocative variants.

Eliot's plays of the mid-1930s foreground ritual and dramatic structure and tend to be more metatheatrical and experimental as a result. They also feature more surely identifiable choric groups or figures as audiences within the play and as a technique for exploring issues of community. His first two explicitly Christian dramas take the church as their place, in one as an edifice that must be built in the world of the play and in the other as the site of performance and pilgrimage. *The Rock,* a pageant play for a London church reconstruction fund-raiser in 1934, describes the construction and repair of a church through a series of vignettes, from the Israelites rebuilding the Temple to the completion of St. Paul's Cathedral. Cockney construction workers punctuate these scenes as they discuss the spiritual worth of their labor. The chorus provides a similar lesson through far more restrained, chantlike lines that Eliot would later reprint in his *Collected Poems, 1909–1962* (1963). Unfortunately, this was an unwieldy theatrical undertaking, especially for the relatively untested playwright, involving more than three hundred amateur performers and twenty-plus scene changes. Reviews of the performance at Sadler's Wells Theatre were underwhelming—the production was labeled sententious and heavy-handed in its Christian appeal—and might have signaled the end of Eliot's barely begun dramatic career. But his fortunes changed with *Murder in the Cathedral,* the tale of the martyrdom of Saint Thomas Beckett, which was performed as part of the Canterbury Festival in the chapterhouse of the cathedral in 1935, only a few yards from where Beckett was actually killed. The play was far more simple and ritualistic in its presentation than *The Rock.* Eliot and longtime collaborator and director E. Martin Browne used the location to great effect, down to a formal procession of Beckett's body out of the chapterhouse while the "Dies irae" was sung at the play's conclusion. The chorus, the women of Canterbury, theatrically double as another audience within the play, as they watch, wait, and try to make sense of the saint's murder alongside the trials of their own mundane lives. Many of their lines presage *Four Quartets* and focus on the journey out of daily suffering in human time into a spiritual awareness grounded in seasons and places, like Beckett's shrine, now imbued with divine presence. The play was a success beyond the festival, enjoying a West End run through 1937 and Broadway productions in 1936 and 1938. But it found even more humble locations for staging, from church basements to air-raid shelters.

The Family Reunion (1939) bridges the experimental, ritualized, and pronouncedly Christian character of his early plays and Eliot's attempt to wrap the same concerns and structures in the palatable guise of family dramas for a popular audience. It also marks a halfway point between the emphatically poetic diction and cadences of prior scripts and the far more conventional conversations in his later plays. But the chorus would continue to lurk in different costumes throughout *The Family Reunion,* even as the seat of community moved from the church and into the family parlor. The play presents a homecoming of a different sort as Harry's overbearing mother tries to force him into taking over management of the family manor. The leaderless estate is in terrible disrepair, with the aristocratic rock gardens tumbling to ruin. Provocatively, unlike the rebuilding in *The Rock* or Beckett's return to Canterbury in *Murder,* Harry's destiny is not to shore up these ruins. His spiritual purgation requires that he break free of the upper-class banalities of his patrimony, an echo of similar concerns in Eliot's early verse, and venture out again. The chorus of attendant family members help him move toward this realization while commenting on their own role as actors in a family farce. Removing the explicitly Christian tone of the piece led Eliot to heavily foreground its Aeschylean inspiration, resulting in the awkward appearance of the Eumenides as the avenging ghosts who haunt Harry and ultimately release him. The staging of the specters was never quite right, in Eliot's mind, and mixed poorly with the realist gestures he was attempting in a more conventional drama.

Eliot's last three dramatic works, *The Cocktail Party, The Confidential Clerk,* and *The Elder Statesman,* first performed in 1949, 1953, and 1958, respectively, move more surely into realist and popular genres, like the family drawing-room drama and the comedy of manners. They also feature some of his best work integrating ritual structure and poetic language into popular entertainment, such as the well-timed patter and comedic exchanges in *The Cocktail Party.* All three involve families and lovers who must come to a recognition of their self-delusions and sins before reconciling with their community and following their proper paths to redemption. In *The Cocktail Party* and *The Confidential Clerk,* Eliot explores two major paths to sanctification: an active life led in the world where marriage becomes the means of conquering one's ego; and a contemplative life of worldly renunciation. In *The Cocktail Party,* Edward's mistress, Celia, will end her days as a religious sister in Africa before she is crucified on an anthill (which horrified many critics), and Colby in *The Confidential Clerk* seems destined for holy orders and parish life. And all three plays include choric guardian figures, at times charmingly bumbling and others mysteriously wise, who providentially aid the main characters. It is *The Elder Statesman,* the last of Eliot's plays, that reconciles the apparent gulf between the two paths. In this family comedy, patterned on Sophocles's *Oedipus at Colonus,* the penitence and self-renunciation of the aging father brings about not only a union between two lovers but a unification of an entire family that had been fractured by his pride. Eliot dedicated this play to his wife Valerie, and it contains some of his most tender and romantic lines. In the character of Lord Claverton, he also presents an aging public figure struggling with past sins who comes to unexpected joy at the end of his life, a biographical parallel that was not lost on audiences. Ultimately, as a playwright, Eliot fared forward more often than he fared well. While he hardly achieved his lofty goal of inspiring a mass revival of verse drama, his later pieces enjoyed robust runs on both sides of the Atlantic. And if we read *The Elder Statesman* as Eliot's valedictory piece, both love song and swan song, it leaves us with a picture of the poet one hardly could have anticipated during his *Prufrock* years: earnest, pious, happily married, looking peacefully toward death.

True to his epigraph, Eliot's end was in many ways just a beginning, as his poetry profoundly influenced generations of readers and writers long after his death. And in his beginning, much of his end was prefigured. Techniques, figures, allusions, and landscapes from his Laforgian years found new uses in his postconversion verse, just as his American upbringing continued to color his later work. For these reasons, and countless others, he has earned and held his place of honor in the history of American letters. But the epigraph is not meant as literary commentary. It captures the poet's personal quest back to a homeland and a faith that would redeem, rather than annul, his past. The flesh that began by the banks of the Mississippi comes to rest as ash in the stones of an English country church. Such is a felicitous resting place for the modernist voice of both St. Louis and London, the city and the country, the land and the sea. Ultimately, Eliot remained grounded in the places that shaped him while transcending the boundaries of each.

Selected Bibliography

WORKS OF T. S. ELIOT

POETRY AND PLAYS

Prufrock and Other Observations. London: Egoist, 1917.

Poems. Richmond, U.K.: L. and V. Woolf at the Hogarth Press, 1919.

The Waste Land. New York: Boni & Liveright, 1922; Richmond, U.K.: L. and V. Woolf at the Hogarth Press, 1923.

Ash-Wednesday. London: Faber & Faber, 1930; New York: Putnam, 1930.

Sweeney Agonistes. London: Faber & Faber, 1932.

The Rock: A Pageant Play. London: Faber & Faber, 1934.

Murder in the Cathedral. London: Faber & Faber, 1935; New York: Harcourt, Brace, 1935.

The Family Reunion. London: Faber & Faber, 1939; New York: Harcourt, Brace, 1939.

Old Possum's Book of Practical Cats. London: Faber & Faber, 1939; New York: Harcourt, Brace, 1939.

Four Quartets. New York: Harcourt, Brace, 1943; London: Faber & Faber, 1944.

The Cocktail Party. London: Faber & Faber, 1950; New York: Harcourt, Brace, 1950.

The Confidential Clerk. London: Faber & Faber, 1954; New York: Harcourt, Brace, 1954.

The Elder Statesman. London: Faber & Faber, 1959; New York, Farrar, Straus and Cudahy, 1959.

The Waste Land: A Facsimile and Transcript of the Original Drafts Including the Annotations of Ezra Pound. Edited by Valerie Eliot. New York: Harcourt Brace Jovanovich, 1971.

Inventions of the March Hare: Poems, 1909–1917. Edited by Christopher Ricks. New York: Harcourt, Brace, 1996.

EDITIONS AND COLLECTIONS: POETRY AND PLAYS

Ara Vos Prec. London: Ovid Press, 1919.

Poems. New York: Knopf, 1920.

Poems 1909—1925. London: Faber & Gwyer, 1925; New York, Harcourt, Brace, 1932.

Collected Poems 1909—1935. London: Faber & Faber, 1936; New York: Harcourt, Brace, 1936.

The Complete Poems and Plays. New York: Harcourt, Brace, 1952.

Selected Poems. London: Faber & Faber, 1961; New York: Harcourt, Brace & World, 1967.

Collected Poems 1909—1962. New York: Harcourt, Brace & World, 1963.

Poems Written in Early Youth. New York: Farrar, Straus and Giroux, 1967.

The Poems of T. S. Eliot. Vol. 1, *Collected and Uncollected Poems.* Vol. 2, *Practical Cats and Further Verses.* Baltimore: Johns Hopkins University Press, 2015. (This is now used as the main scholarly edition of the poetry and is the one cited throughout.)

PROSE

The Sacred Wood: Essays on Poetry and Criticism. London: Methuen, 1920.

For Lancelot Andrewes. London: Faber & Gwyer, 1928; published as *For Lancelot Andrews,* Garden City, N.Y.: Doubleday, Doran, 1929.

The Use of Poetry and the Use of Criticism. London: Faber & Faber, 1933; Cambridge, Mass.: Harvard University Press, 1933.

After Strange Gods: A Primer of Modern Heresy. London: Faber & Faber, 1934; New York: Harcourt, Brace, 1934.

Elizabethan Essays. London: Faber & Faber, 1934.

The Idea of a Christian Society. London: Faber & Faber, 1939; New York: Harcourt, Brace, 1940.

Notes Towards the Definition of Culture. London: Faber & Faber, 1948; New York: Harcourt, Brace, 1949.

"The Influence of Landscape upon the Poet." *Daedalus* 89, no. 2:419–422 (spring 1960).

EDITIONS AND COLLECTIONS: PROSE AND LETTERS

Selected Essays 1917–1932. London: Faber & Faber, 1932; New York: Harcourt, Brace, 1932. (Expanded editions of *Selected Essays* followed in 1950 and 1951.)

On Poetry and Poets. London: Faber & Faber, 1936; New York: Harcourt, Brace, 1936.

To Criticize the Critic and Other Writings. New York: Farrar, Straus and Giroux, 1965.

Selected Prose of T. S. Eliot. Edited by Frank Kermode. London: Faber & Faber; New York: Harcourt Brace Jovanovich, 1975.

The Letters of T. S. Eliot. 6 vols. Edited by Valerie Eliot, Hugh Haughton, and John Haffenden. New Haven, Conn.: Yale University Press, 1988–2016.

The Complete Prose of T. S. Eliot: The Critical Edition. 4 vols. Edited by Ronald Schuchard et al. Baltimore: Johns Hopkins University Press, 2014. Digital.

BIBLIOGRAPHIES

"Annual Bibliography of Eliot Criticism." *Time Present: Newsletter of the T. S. Eliot Society.* Summer 2016. (The Eliot Society has published an annual bibliography of criticism or a "books received" section in the spring or summer edition of the newsletter since 1992. The archive of these newsletters is available online: www.luc.edu/eliot/newsletter.htm)

Behr, Caroline. *T. S. Eliot: A Chronology of His Life and Works.* New York: Macmillan, 1982.

Gallup, Donald. *T. S. Eliot: A Bibliography.* Revised and expanded ed., London: Faber & Faber, 1969.

Knowles, Sebastian, David Guy, and Scott A. Leonard. *T. S. Eliot: Man and Poet.* Vol. 2, *An Annotated Bibliography of a Decade of Eliot Criticism* 1977–1986. Orono, Maine: National Poetry Foundation, 1992.

CRITICAL AND BIOGRAPHICAL STUDIES

Ackroyd, Peter. *T. S. Eliot: A Life.* New York: Simon & Schuster, 1984.

Bloom, Harold. *T. S. Eliot.* Philadelphia: Chelsea House, 2003.

Browne, E. Martin. *The Making of T. S. Eliot's Plays.* New York: Cambridge University Press, 1969.

Chinitz, David E. *T. S. Eliot and the Cultural Divide.* Chicago: University of Chicago Press, 2005.

———, ed. *A Companion to T. S. Eliot.* Chichester, U.K.: Wiley-Blackwell, 2009.

Crawford, Robert. *Young Eliot: From St. Louis to the Waste Land.* New York: Farrar, Straus and Giroux, 2015.

Cuda, Anthony. *The Passions of Modernism: Eliot, Yeats, Woolfe, and Mann.* Columbia: University of South Carolina Press, 2011.

Gardner, Helen. *The Art of T. S. Eliot.* London: Cresset Press, 1949.

Gordon, Lyndall. *T. S. Eliot: An Imperfect Life.* New York: Norton, 1999.

Harding, Jason. *T. S. Eliot in Context.* New York: Cambridge University Press, 2011.

Hughes, Ted. *T. S. Eliot: A Tribute.* London: Privately printed by Faber & Faber, 1987.

Kenner, Hugh. *The Invisible Poet: T. S. Eliot.* New York: McDowell, Obolensky, 1959.

Kirk, Russell. *Eliot and His Age: T. S. Eliot's Moral Imagination in the Twentieth Century.* New York: Random House, 1971.

Laity, Cassandra, and Nancy K. Gish, eds. *Gender, Desire, and Sexuality in T. S. Eliot.* Cambridge, U.K.: Cambridge University Press, 2007.

Lockerd, Benjamin, ed. *T. S. Eliot and Christian Tradition.* Madison, N.J.: Fairleigh Dickinson University Press, 2016.

Moody, A. David. *The Cambridge Companion to T. S. Eliot.* Cambridge, U.K.: Cambridge University Press, 2005.

Pound, Ezra. "For T. S. E." *Sewanee Review* 74, no. 1:109 (winter 1966).

Raine, Craig. *T. S. Eliot.* New York: Oxford University Press, 2006.

Schuchard, Ronald. *Eliot's Dark Angel: Intersections of Life and Art.* New York: Oxford University Press, 1999.

Spender, Stephen. *Eliot.* London: Fontana, 1975.

Unger, Leonard. *T. S. Eliot: Moments and Patterns.* Minneapolis: University of Minnesota, 1966.

WILLIAM FAULKNER

(1897—1962)

Patrick A. Smith

William Cuthbert Falkner (the "u" came later) was born on September 25, 1897, in New Albany, Mississippi, a small town thirty miles northeast of his eventual home in Oxford. The first of four sons (Murry, John, and Dean followed) of Murry Falkner and Maud Butler Falkner, William—or "Billy" as he was known as a boy and even into adulthood by the locals and in his letters home to his mother and his wife, Estelle—had a lukewarm relationship with his father, instead living in deference to Maud (who occasionally chastised her famous son for the salaciousness of his novels) until her death in 1960. Steeped in history and the mythos of a people's relationship to the land, especially a small-town America still coming to grips with Reconstruction, mechanization, and the changing cultural and social attitudes of the Old South, Faulkner took early to "shaping and reshaping his persona to suit himself and the needs of his career and personal life," Jay Parini writes in his biography *One Matchless Time: A Life of William Faulkner.* "The characters in his fiction, and the nature of his own character, enthralled him, and he worked busily at inventing and deepening both, looking for reality through the lens of art in both instances" (p. 5). Historical events, including the Civil War and World War I—one of which he lived vicariously and the other on the periphery, as a cadet in Canada—and the Great Depression also influenced the author's artistic vision.

Along the way, Faulkner became a—arguably *the*—most important figure in American literary modernism, borrowing from and making his own the European modernists' experimentation with language, time, history, and identity, aided by a preternatural understanding of his characters' psyches in the context of their ancestral pasts. Or, as Faulkner portentously intoned in his 1951 novel *Requiem for a Nun,* "The past is never dead. It's not even past" (p. 85). Indeed, Billy grew up to soaring, likely apocryphal tales of the derring-do and doggedness of his own successful forebears: a great-grandfather, the Old Colonel (William Clark Falkner), railroad entrepreneur, the family's first novelist (*The White Rose of Memphis,* published in 1881), and Civil War hero, was shot to death in 1889 in the Oxford town square by Richard J. Thurmond, a disgruntled business partner, in what Faulkner described charitably as a "duel"; an equally formidable grandfather, the Young Colonel (John Wesley Thompson Falkner), shouldered the family's reputation in Oxford into the twentieth century. Faulkner's own less memorable father, Murry, a feckless fixture in the town who seemed not to be able to get out of his own way in business dealings, little influenced his eldest son, who regarded him "as a phantom, a weak man who depended heavily on the Young Colonel for his very existence and thus resented (as well as pitied) him" (Parini, p. 18). To the chagrin of those remaining from previous generations, Murry oversaw the family's relegation to the second tier of Oxford society.

The ignominy rubbed off on Billy, who became known as "Count No 'Count" around town. Even after being elevated to the highest echelons in literature decades later when awarded the 1949 Nobel Prize, Faulkner fought the perception that he was putting on airs or that he had outgrown once-sleepy Oxford, which benefited economically and culturally from the reputation of its most popular—and for some who knew him from the time he was "Billy Falkner," perhaps its most unexpected—literary son. Still, although a source of continued embarrassment for the young William, the family's diminution provided a wealth of grist for the fictional mill in *Sartoris* (1929), *The Sound and the Fury* (1929), *Light in August* (1932), *Absalom, Absalom!* (1936), and other of the author's most important novels and short fiction.

At times an indifferent student, Billy cultivated an ear for reading and writing as a way of impressing his classmates. Of particular interest was Estelle Oldham, the daughter of one of the most powerful men in Lafayette County, what later became the fictive Yoknapatawpha County, an elaborately conceived analogue to the land and people he thought of as his birthright. Faulkner kept a torch burning for Estelle throughout his adolescence, even after she left Oxford for Mary Baldwin College in Virginia; upon returning, she married Cornell Franklin, president of the class of 1919 at the University of Mississippi and a graduate of the Ole Miss law school, at her family's behest. The failed relationship affected Faulkner profoundly, though the unrequited love seems to have fueled a romantic impulse, resulting in the early poetry and a few tentative fictional sketches. William and Estelle eventually reconciled after the disintegration of her marriage. Together, the two raised her children, Malcolm and Victoria (Cho-Cho), buried an infant child of their own, Alabama, and celebrated a daughter, Jill, in a relationship that ran the emotional gamut from 1929 until Faulkner's death in 1962.

But Faulkner's personal life, tempestuous as it could be, always took a back seat to his writing. One of his early supporters, Phil Stone, was a fixture in Oxford society, and the great friends often spoke of literary matters when Stone returned from his studies at Yale. Faulkner studied the popular poets of the time—among others, W. B. Yeats, T. S. Eliot, Ezra Pound, John Keats, A. E. Housman, and Algernon Charles Swinburne, whose worked inspired many a budding romantic—and Stone introduced Faulkner to Stark Young, a poet of some note who graduated from Ole Miss in 1901. Beginning with a position in a bank, Faulkner worked a string of jobs he loathed (save for a stint as the town's scoutmaster, a role he embraced but from which he was let go for his apparent bohemian manners) so long as they afforded him time to read and write. Famously, he was fired from a position in the post office at Oxford for gross negligence, as he spent far more time reading and writing than sorting mail.

As a young man intrigued by the goings-on in the wider world, Faulkner tirelessly followed the war in Europe, particularly descriptions of air battles, and envied the soldiers who received accolades for their battlefield heroics. "I had seen an aeroplane and my mind was filled with names: Ball, and Immelman and Boelcke, and Guynemer and Bishop, and I was waiting, biding, until I would be old enough or free enough or anyway could get to France and become glorious and beribboned too," Faulkner writes of that early, naive yearning to join the war (*The Faulkner Reader,* p. viii). At loose ends in Oxford, Faulkner followed Stone to Yale for a brief stay. Pretending to be an Englishman, he managed to enlist in the Royal Air Force in June 1918 and reported for training in Toronto, Canada, in July. Despite the tales Faulkner told later of his being injured in battle, none of them had much basis in truth. Although his brother Murry (known as "Jack") was wounded in trench fighting on the western front, Faulkner never left North America during the remaining four months of the war. Instead, he returned to Oxford, wrote poetry derivative of the French Symbolists, pined over Estelle's marriage, drank, walked with a pronounced limp, and affected a British accent to distinguish his speech from the Southern drawl that, for reasons known only to Faulkner, he longed to scrape off his boot.

He also explored in earnest "my own little postage stamp of native soil" (Stein, p. 52), excursions that ignited a newfound artistic energy and led him to the fecund cultural scene of New Orleans that provided the creative spark for his first novel. Along the way, he continued to experiment with poetry and, with Stone's help (without whom the poems likely never would have seen the light of day), published the collection *The Marble Faun* in 1924. In the book's autobiographical note, Faulkner gives short shrift to his parents, instead aligning himself with the family's more illustrious past. It was also, the story goes, the first time he used the familiar "u," an homage to his great-grandfather the Old Colonel (whose name he spelled similarly in the note). In doing so, Faulkner "claimed the Old Colonel for himself. Now it was the two of them against Murry Falkner and the hostile masculine world of Oxford, which Faulkner gave as only his 'present temporary address'" (Oates, p. 37).

As Faulkner's biographers Parini, Stephen B. Oates, Joseph Blotner, and others point out, the stories that he told and retold of his own life—the spelling of his surname in *The Marble Faun* being the first of many examples of his playing with the truth, either in broad brushstrokes or ever so slightly—were inextricable from fiction. "Of course he was bragging, inventing, distorting," Parini writes. "But he was also carving masks for himself, taking the act of self-creation quite a few steps further than is usual for young men" (p. 43). None of that self-invention would be remarkable had Faulkner not had the genius to channel the zeitgeist and the raw human spirit coursing through the South into a writing style that changed the way readers thought of literature. Indeed, one of the most important contributions Faulkner made to American literature, in addition to crediting a new generation of American writers and readers with the ability to decipher increasingly complex narratives, was his application of the interior monologue and stream-of-consciousness to a distinctly Southern literature that owed its sweeping scope, existential enquiry, and psychological insight to the rise of modernism, which at its root questioned the individual's role in a changing society. As Bruce Kawin writes in his essay "Sharecropping in the Golden Land,"

> If the modernists' key insights were that the conventionally known world—the world before Cézanne, Freud, Einstein, and mustard gas—had ceased to exist, both in itself and for the purposes of art; that its false notions of order confirmed themselves in the structures of false art; that the world not only lay busted into exciting fragments but was also inherently and almost unanalyzably multiple, so that the look might well become many looks as attention passed through the prism of consciousness ... then [the modernists'] key determination was to ensure that those systems of fragments were themselves coherent, projecting an underlying unity and declaring their own completeness.
>
> (p. 196)

The primary themes in modernism are not statements, but rather questions: What are the limits of language to convey meaning? Why is the "I," the individual, suddenly so alienated from society? Why is society fragmenting? Why is the impermanence of life and our obsessive dwelling on that fact displacing many other (perhaps more important and immediate) concerns?

In his Nobel Prize speech in Stockholm on December 10, 1950, toward the end of a writing career during which he published at least a half-dozen novels and a score of short stories that became canon, Faulkner said that the writer's task was "to create out of the materials of the human spirit something which did not exist before" (*Essays, Speeches,* p. 119). He posited fear—of change, of incessant and audacious questioning, of annihilation—as the greatest obstacles for future generations of writers and, indeed, humanity itself. The difficulty in making successful art, he continued, was that "the young man or woman writing today has forgotten the problems of the human heart in conflict with itself which alone can make good writing because only that is worth writing about, worth the agony and the sweat" (p. 119). That speech, no more than five hundred words, is still one of the most read and quoted of Faulkner's nonfiction.

THE EARLY FICTION

Nicholas Fargnoli's *William Faulkner: A Literary Companion,* which surveys literary criticism of the author over his career, includes a comment from the influential critic and longtime Faulkner friend and correspondent Malcolm Cowley. "Among all the empty and witless tags attached to living American authors perhaps the most misleading is that of Southern Realist as applied to William Faulkner," writes Cowley, in comparing the author's work to the "single effect" sought by Edgar Allan Poe, Faulkner's innovative fellow traveler, particularly in the short form. "But Faulkner's daemon does not often permit him to be broadly humorous or to echo the mild confusions of daily life. The daemon forces him to be always intense, to write in a wildly lyrical style, to omit almost every detail that does not contribute to a single effect of somber violence and horror" (*Literary Companion,* p. 229). Although

Faulkner's first literary yawps were made in fealty to romantic poetry, he published a novel before turning thirty. Written in a two-room apartment in Pirates Alley off Jackson Square in New Orleans (the site houses Faulkner House Books, a bookstore that stocks many first editions of Faulkner's work), *Soldiers' Pay* (1926) "is a remarkable first novel," Cleanth Brooks writes. "But [Faulkner] definitely went through a period of growth and development which shows, among other things, a movement from a rather decadent Swinburnian romanticism to a robust acceptance of reality and tough-minded appraisal of it" (*First Encounters,* p. 5). While the novel serves in part as a young writer's apprenticeship, the range of its characters and the complexity of their relationships signal the approach of a major talent.

In New Orleans, Faulkner had the great fortune of meeting and befriending Sherwood Anderson, one of the leading writers of the time. Anderson's *Winesburg, Ohio,* published in 1919, brought modern fiction to America (arguably, modern poetry arrived somewhat earlier thanks to Ezra Pound and the short-lived imagist movement) and influenced such notable writers as Ernest Hemingway, John Steinbeck, Thomas Wolfe. After numerous dinners and extended drinking sessions with Anderson in New Orleans, Faulkner seems to have absorbed a great deal of his friend's knowledge of the workings of literature, not least the shifting narrative perspectives that became the author's stock-in-trade.

In letters home, Faulkner reported selling a few of his "sketches" to local newspapers and journals, including the *Double Dealer,* which published the period's most influential modern writers. Those sketches became short stories, and Faulkner would often heavily edit them and repurpose their structures, particularly in the later work, to fit into the vision he had for his novels. But Faulkner wrote his debut novel, *Soldiers' Pay,* from scratch. While not as stylistically pyrotechnic as the work of his remarkable middle period, *Soldiers' Pay* fit the genre of literature that had sprung up in the aftermath of World War I in the form of the disillusioned—and in many cases, as with Faulkner's protagonist Donald Mahon, profoundly disabled—war veteran returning home to salvage the remains of his life.

Faulkner explores his own frustration at not fighting in the war through his character Cadet Julian Lowe, whose flight training is interrupted by the war's end in November 1918. On the other hand, Mahon's disfigurement and blindness is a cautionary tale for the cast of characters who befriend him on the train back home to Charlestown, Georgia, including Lowe, fellow veteran Joe Gilligan, and Margaret Powers, a former aid worker and now a war widow and "the only character in *Soldiers' Pay* who seems to intuit the brutal, unromantic nature of war" (Parini, p. 81). Mahon's return to Charlestown, unexpected and met with ambivalence by his father, an Episcopal rector, and his fiancée, Cecily Saunders, causes a stir in the small community.

Faulkner's deft handling of the relationships between Cecily and George Farr (the two elope when Cecily, who thought Mahon dead, sees the extent of his wounds and knows that she can never marry him), and a second betrothal for Mahon to Emmy, the rector's servant and Mahon's former lover, ends in a tryst with the satyr-like Januarius Jones, a precursor to the intricate social dynamics that drive the later, mature novels. As has been foreshadowed since the novel's outset, Mahon dies of his injuries, while Lowe's facile fantasies of a similar, romanticized death remain unfulfilled. The juxtaposition of Lowe and Mahon hints at Faulkner's burgeoning realization of the horrors of war and a tipping of the experiential scale from innocence to experience, romanticism to brutal reality. In a 1925 essay titled "Literature and War," Faulkner writes, "Mankind's emotional gamut is like his auricular gamut: there are some things which he cannot feel, as there are sounds he cannot hear. And war, taken as a whole, is one of these things" (*Essays, Speeches,* p. 255). Of course, at the same time that Faulkner relates Mahon's horrific story, he must reconcile himself as Lowe does to his own role as noncombatant. The novel explores and explodes quixotic notions of war, even though Faulkner embellished his own role for years in a "process of revision that occurs when the imagination confronts reality. *Soldiers' Pay* is only a beginning, with characters and situations drawn from life but changed as the author conducts a highly personal seminar in autobiographical transmutation" (Parini, p. 82).

The follow-up to *Soldiers' Pay, Mosquitoes* (1927), is a roman à clef based in part on the author's relationship with Sherwood Anderson before inertia and professional jealousy weakened the friendship. Describing the goings-on of a circle of artists on the yacht *Nausikaa* on New Orleans' Lake Pontchartrain, the novel highlights Faulkner's sly, probing humor for the first time, hinting at the author's insecurity at the caprices of the writing life when some in his hometown still treated him with amused indulgence, an intelligent if ungrounded man-child trying to find his way in the world. At the time, Faulkner was deeply infatuated with Helen Baird, who in the novel becomes Patricia Robyn, the lover of the *Nausikaa*'s steward, David West. Faulkner's extravagant efforts at wooing Helen included a visit to her aunt in Pascagoula, where he professed his undying love for her niece. "A bold and explicit tale for 1926 America," Oates writes, "*Mosquitoes* contained references to constipation, masturbation, incest, lesbianism, perversion, and syphilis, and words in dialogue like 'bastard' and 'whore.' Despite its flaws as a work of art, Faulkner did think of himself as a novelist now" (p. 59). In terms of its place in the body of Faulkner's work, *Mosquitoes* is most similar to the later *Pylon* (1935), which also has its roots in the author's autobiography and a place in the second rank of his work.

Having written two novels set in places that Faulkner had come to know only as a young man searching for a literary voice and vision, his third, *Sartoris* (1929; later republished in an authoritative text edited by Douglas Day as *Flags in the Dust* in 1973), returned to his ancestral past, examining the lives of his most memorable and important characters, many patterned on those in his own family tree. "More than ever now," Oates writes, "[Faulkner] sought refuge in his imagination, in a cherished inner sanctum in which he could escape the vicissitudes of the outside world and record what his voices said to him" (p. 64). Within a year after publishing *Mosquitoes,* he brought to life, fully formed, the Yoknapatawpha County upon which his reputation would be built. "I would never live long enough to exhaust it, and by sublimating the actual into the apocryphal I would have complete liberty to use whatever I might have to its absolute top," Faulkner recalled to Jean Stein in a *Paris Review* interview. "It opened up a goldmine of other peoples, so I created a cosmos of my own" (p. 52).

That cosmos included Bayard Sartoris, a pilot returning from World War I without his twin brother, Johnny, who was killed in combat after jumping from his Sopwith Camel. Facing the prospect of a long life with the agonizing guilt of his brother's death haunting him, Bayard succumbs to his own death wish. While driving recklessly, he unwittingly brings about his grandfather's fatal heart attack. Later, having married Narcissa Benbow for murky reasons, Bayard manages to kill himself in an airplane crash—recalling, of course, the death of his own brother—on the day Narcissa gives birth to a son. Narcissa's brother Horace, a veteran of the war who never saw battle, carries on an affair with Belle Mitchell, a married woman. The two end up together despite Narcissa's disdain for Belle, a union that suggests the favoring of the contemplative intellectual over the impetuous man of action.

Perhaps as important as a glimpse into his maturing vision as an artist and the genesis of Yoknapatawpha was Faulkner's dogged persistence in seeing the novel through to publication. Certain that the manuscript he sent to Boni & Liveright, who published both *Soldiers' Pay* and *Mosquitoes,* was his best work yet, Faulkner was surprised and hurt by the response from the house's editorial team: an unequivocal rejection, with few kind words for the possibility of its ever seeing the light of day. Eventually, the author saw fit to edit the manuscript substantively so it could find an audience; upon further analysis, decades after its publication, perhaps Faulkner was correct in his initial assessment. In his perceptive review of *Sartoris,* a novel that bridges the transition from the merely observational to the transcendent style and multifarious characters for which the author became known,

Henry Nash Smith observed, "[Faulkner's] books are simply not the thing that could have been expected from postwar Mississippi.... When you get to the heart of what almost any of the men called great in literature you find something a little chill and disturbing; they leave you with a sobering suspicion that perhaps life is like that. Mr. Faulkner's disillusion is of this sort" (in Fargnoli, *Literary Companion,* p. 3). Indeed, for many critics, *Sartoris* marked the end of Faulkner's apprenticeship, even if they—and perhaps the author himself—could not have imagined what he had in store for the next decade.

TOURS DE FORCE

Despite what reviewers thought of *The Sound and the Fury* (1929)—early criticism acknowledged that Faulkner's latest effort broke new literary ground, though some seemed hard-pressed to articulate just *how*—they agreed that the author and his work deserved serious attention at a time when the European modernists still held sway in the country's university literature departments. Lionel Trilling, while recognizing the depth of Faulkner's talent, asserted that the novel "seems somehow hidden in itself, relevant only to itself" (*A Literary Companion,* p. 49). Smith, taking the long view, drew parallels between Faulkner's work and that coming out of Europe, insisting that the author's borrowing "the stream-of-consciousness technique from Europe seems to me of minor importance; to say the least, [Faulkner] has modified it to his own use and has refused to be tyrannized by conventions, even the conventions of revolt" (*Literary Companion,* p. 30). Faulkner, in an interview with Smith three years after the novel's publication, claimed not to have read James Joyce's *Ulysses* (1922), a book often recognized as the progenitor of the stream-of-consciousness narrative. The assertion seems improbable, given Faulkner's penchant for dissimulation and diversion in his interviews and references to Joyce in other published profiles and criticism, as well as the obvious stylistic similarities between the writers' novels.

The novel's title comes from Macbeth's soliloquy in act 5, scene 5, of Shakespeare's play upon news of Lady Macbeth's death: "it is a tale / Told by an idiot, full of sound and fury, / Signifying nothing." Those lines resonate on multiple levels, not least Faulkner's continued fascination with epistemology and time (the soliloquy famously begins, "Tomorrow, and tomorrow, and tomorrow, / Creeps in this petty pace ..."). In the decade since the war's end in November 1918, the author had searched for ways to articulate the horrors of trench warfare and the return of a generation of soldiers to the United States, Britain, France, and Canada who wholesale suffered from "shell shock," a useful euphemism, if a great disservice to the soldiers' subsequent diagnosis and treatment. Even from his cloistered vantage point in rural Mississippi, Faulkner felt the pressure of a rapidly changing world, the inexorable shift away from a quiet, dignified agrarianism to the impersonal efficiency of a machine society. So when it came to juxtaposing Macbeth's existential terror with the characters who populated the fictional Yoknapatawpha County, he had a vast supply of material from which to draw.

The Sound and the Fury is made up of four sections, the first three narrated by each of three Compson brothers and the fourth by the author. In 1957 Faulkner recalled the novel's origin:

> It began with a picture of the little girl's muddy drawers, climbing that tree to look in the parlor window with her brothers that didn't have the courage to climb the tree waiting to see what she saw. And I tried first to tell it with one brother, and that wasn't enough. That was Section One. I tried with another brother, and that wasn't enough. That was Section Two. I tried the third brother, because Caddy was still to me too beautiful and too moving to reduce her to telling what was going on, that it would be more passionate to see her through somebody else's eyes, I thought. And that failed and I tried myself—the fourth section—to tell what happened, and I still failed.
>
> (*Faulkner in the University,* p. 1)

Faulkner's self-deprecation, the preposterous (at least in hindsight) opinion that the novel is somehow merely a string of failures, might be attributable to his intensely guarded privacy and the incessant misdirection that kept interlopers at bay. In any case, a great deal of his fiction reads as a refashioning and evolution of his thoughts on modern narrative structure and style, issues always under consideration and protean in the author's work up to his last novels. Faulkner's playing with time throughout *The Sound and the Fury*—only the sections involving Jason Compson and the concluding section are organized in anything approaching "traditional" narrative and chronological order—begins with Benjy Compson's futile attempts at making sense of his world and his intense sexual feelings for his sister, Caddy.

An analogue to the "idiot" in Macbeth's soliloquy, the thirty-three-year-old, castrated Benjy has often been described as Christlike by critics. Benjy's greater significance, however, is as an unreliable, free-associative observer. Spanning the period from 1898 and the death of his grandmother, Damuddy, to the narrative present on April 7, 1928, the day before Easter, the edifice of "jumbled time sequences and confusingly ambiguous references" in Benjy's section "stands like a great dragon folded in the gate of the novel" (Parini, p. 116), introducing themes and images fleshed out in the following sections. Most of Benjy's recollections come full circle to his obsessive love for Caddy (a fixation shared by his brother, Quentin), though a number of deaths—Damuddy, Mr. Compson, Quentin, and Roskus, the husband of the Compsons' servant Dilsey—also act as signposts for readers in parsing the book's convoluted time line and action.

Quentin's section takes place on June 2, 1910, the day of his suicide in Cambridge, Massachusetts, as he prepares to leap from a bridge. Even more fixated than Benjy with Caddy and hyperaware of her sexuality, Quentin spends a great deal of time in his mind countering the arguments of his father, who insists that life is neither complicated nor worthy of deep introspection. Added to Quentin's inability to accept his father's simplistic philosophy is his inability to understand the workings of time, always in flux in Faulkner's fiction and a source of existential angst for so many of his characters—Quentin pulls the hands off a watch in an effort to control time, to cease its forward slog. These struggles contribute to his decision to end his life.

Caddy's sexual promiscuity, which sin (as Quentin sees it) her brother takes upon himself, going so far as contemplating incest with Caddy and a double suicide, is a repudiation of the benighted views of the men in her family. "Purity is a negative state and therefore contrary to nature," the elder Compson maintains. "It's nature is hurting you not Caddy and I said That's just words and he said So is virginity and I said you dont know. You cant know and he said Yes. On the instant when we come to realise that tragedy is second-hand" (p. 116). Even Mrs. Compson turns on her daughter, forbidding the speaking of her name in the house after she becomes pregnant out of wedlock. In a torrent of language, Quentin fashions in his mind one last time the inchoate, elusive ideas that can never transcend the mean attitudes of his father and brother, Jason:

> if i could tell you we did it would have been so and then the others wouldnt be so and then the world would roar away and he and now this other you are not lying now either but you are still blind to what is in yourself to that part of general truth the sequence of natural events and their causes which shadows every mans brow even benjys you are not thinking of finitude you are contemplating an apotheosis in which a temporary state of mind will become symmetrical above the flesh and aware both of itself and of the flesh it will not quite discard you will not even be dead.
>
> (p. 177)

Instead of acting on his own philosophy, Quentin brushes his teeth and grabs his hat on his way out the door to commit suicide.

In sharp contrast to Quentin's torment, his brother Jason's attitude toward his much younger sister, women generally, and anyone not like him is crude, misogynistic, and virulently racist: "Once a bitch always a bitch, what I say" (p. 180). In a letter to Malcolm Cowley, Faulkner confirms his own dislike for the character, asserting that "Jason is the new South ... [and] would have chopped up a Georgian Manse and sold it off in shotgun bungalows as quick as any man" (*Selected Letters,* p. 197). The sociopathic Jason, who devises a complicated pyramid scheme involving his mother and his sister to pad his own bank account, lays the blame for his lack of accomplishment on Caddy, whose promiscuity only fuels her brother's misplaced disdain. Jason has a similar all-consuming scorn for his brother Benjy and his mother, who still claims, gravid as always with an unwavering martyr complex, "You are the only one of [my children] that isn't a reproach to me" (p. 181).

The three Compson brothers signify, each in his own way, the dissolution of a once-proud Southern family and, by extension, the weakening of the Old South, issues that Faulkner explores repeatedly in both his novels and short fiction. By contrast, the Compsons' black cook, Dilsey, who figures prominently in the book's final section, comports herself with self-assured dignity and insists on maintaining an order within the household that seems to be beyond the ken of the Compson family. As Dilsey arrives for work on Easter Sunday, April 8, 1928, she steps into the aftermath of Jason's realization that Caddy's daughter, Miss Quentin, stole several thousand dollars of ill-begotten money from him. In fact, according to Jason, his entire life has been one betrayal after the next. Dilsey handles his puerile anger with typical aplomb, defusing Jason's anger and whisking Benjy off to church, where she listens to a sermon on death with great interest and connects the preacher's Easter message to the Compson clan's downward spiral. Despite Dilsey's insistence afterward that Luster, Dilsey's grandson and Benjy's caretaker, follow the usual route on a surrey ride through town, he deviates, immediately setting Benjy to bellowing. Only after getting back to the accustomed route does Benjy calm, "his eyes ... empty and blue and serene again as cornice and façade flowed smoothly once more from left to right, post and tree, window and doorway and signboard each in its ordered place" (p. 321).

As I Lay Dying (1930), though similar to *The Sound and the Fury* in its narrative intricacy and psychological intensity, breaks from the author's previous work with fifty-nine clearly attributed vignettes delivered by fifteen different narrators. These include the moribund heroine and her children—one of whom, Darl, is gifted with "second sight"—as well as characters ancillary to the narrative's action whose observations give the story an imagistic, filmic perspective mirroring the relentless forward progress of the machine age. Faulkner claimed in a 1931 profile that the novel "was written in a coal bunker at Oxford, Mississippi when he was working on the night shift of a power plant. The hum of the dynamo fascinated Faulkner and his book seemed to fairly build itself; it was completed in six weeks. He says he never rewrote a line" (collected in Meriwether and Millgate, eds., *Lion in the Garden,* p. 13). Only taken together do these snapshots provide a picture of the whole. An apt analogy here, one illustrating Faulkner's debt to a nascent European modernism and the visual arts of the late nineteenth century, might be the work of the pointillist painter Georges Seurat, whose meticulously crafted *Sunday Afternoon on the Island of La Grande Jatte* (1884–1886) consists of myriad discrete dots of color suggesting pent-up energy and the immanence of motion.

The brevity of each section and the shifting narration in *As I Lay Dying,* which often exposes discrepancies in the story through multiple tellings, exposes the narrators' tenuous relation to the "truth." The speakers, confined to their own limited perceptions, have limited knowledge of the world at large (with the exception of Darl, perhaps, and one wonders if anybody *really* wants to know what goes on in his head) and thus must rely on other equally unreliable narrators to complete the picture. For instance, the child Vardaman's guileless, unintentionally ironic and darkly humorous acceptance of the world—after all, who can disclaim him for making a series of specious connections that ends with "My mother is a fish" (p. 84) as he drills holes into Addie's pine coffin to allow her to breathe—is but one piece of Faulkner's vast Yoknopatawpha that, taken out of its quite specific context within the novel, has become a punch line regarding the difficulty of reading Faulkner's prose. But a close reading of that consistently fragmented perspective offers a Rosetta stone of sorts to both the later work, including *Light in August* and *Absalom! Absalom!,* and the earlier *Sound and the Fury,* which many readers find more difficult than *As I Lay Dying.*

The novel centers on the Bundren family's attempts at burying its dead matron, Addie, in her family's plot in Jefferson, despite the ham-handed incompetence and ulterior motives of Anse, her husband, the root of the family's many problems. What should be a relatively simple trip becomes instead a ten-day horror show: Addie's body, wet from falling in a rain-swollen river on the way to Jefferson and subjected to unseasonable heat, decomposes rapidly; Cash, the level-headed son, a carpenter who fashions Addie's coffin for her as she listens to the pounding and sawing from her deathbed, breaks a leg and nearly dies; Vardaman, the youngest child, cannot conceive that his mother has died; the pregnant naïf and Addie's only daughter, Dewey Dell, seeks a remedy for her condition from an unscrupulous pharmacist's assistant; and Jewel and Darl, both mercurial outcasts for their own reasons, threaten to sabotage the journey.

As Mary Jane Dickerson points out in "*As I Lay Dying* and *The Waste Land*: Some Relationships," one of the novel's

> most distinctive features is its revelation of William Faulkner's mythopoeic imagination at work: "I took this family and subjected them to the two greatest catastrophes which a man can suffer—flood and fire, that's all." These elemental and primal forces, the resonances of myth and ritual present in the journey motif and the landscape of the South itself create a visible world of relentless motion that affects us with the power we generally attribute to poetry.
>
> (p. 189)

If the sweeping Narrative—capital "N"—articulates the modern condition, then the event of Addie Bundren's death is a powerful and fitting synecdoche of Faulkner's South. Addie, beholden all her life to the men in a society for which she feels only contempt, understands her fate better than any other of Faulkner's characters. Her understanding of language's essential inadequacy to communicate meaning is evident in her deathbed remembrance—related in a first-person account in section 40 *after* her death—as she listens to Cash's macabre work outside her bedroom window and muses, with equanimity and hard-earned bitterness, "My father said that the reason for living is getting ready to stay dead" (pp. 175–176).

In a matter-of-fact statement of her relationship with Anse, Addie juxtaposes the drudgery of everyday life and even the banal finality of death itself to the mulelike actions and thoughts of the Bundren men: "And when I knew that I had Cash, I knew that living was terrible and that this was the answer to it. That was when I learned that words are no good; that words don't ever fit even what they are trying to say at" (p. 171). The characters' alienation from one another and from society at large is reinforced by the novel's fragmented structure, the vignettes a chorus of discordant voices woven into the narrative's cacophonous symphony, what "Faulkner called ... nailing a henhouse together in a hurricane" (Kawin, p. 197). That alienation and fragmentation, indicative of literary modernism, blurs the boundary between the modern and the postmodern in its early form, hinting at the important experimental work to come.

A cause célèbre when published in 1931 because of the scandalous rape scene involving the seventeen-year-old ingénue Temple Drake, Faulkner's sixth novel, *Sanctuary,* nonetheless drew a great deal of critical attention to the author, perhaps even leading some readers to revisit his more auspicious literary accomplishments. Faulkner's reasons for writing the book, though, were apparently more prosaic. "The basic reason was that I needed money. I had already written two or three books that had not sold. I wrote *Sanctuary* to sell," Faulkner recalled of the novel's raison d'être. "After I sent if off, the publisher told me, 'Good God! We can't print this. We would both be put in jail!' The blood and guts period hadn't arrived yet" (*Lion in the Garden,* p. 54). If the blood-and-guts period hadn't arrived yet, Faulkner was ahead of the game, introducing Popeye, an impotent bootlegger prone to extravagant violence, and Temple Drake, whose brutal defilement and subsequent hypersexuality and absolute corruption, Faulkner suggests, are somehow connected.

Ironically, two men, including Popeye, are convicted of crimes of which they are innocent. Temple, after a stint in a Memphis brothel, perjures herself in court and accuses a man other than Popeye of raping her before returning, as a profoundly damaged woman, to her previous life. An anonymous review in the *Times Literary Supplement* asserted that Temple, despite her ordeal, is "unworthy of pity," and further questioned the motives of the author, who "has a remarkable power of presentation, but it is unfortunate this power is not at its height unless he is describing terrors and brutalities, giving flesh and circumstantiality to nightmare doings perpetrated by creatures almost too sick or too depraved to be called human" (*Literary Companion,* p. 119). Although not all notices were negative by any means, time has been kinder to the novel than to the early critics. "Faulkner in *Sanctuary* taught modern and contemporary writers exactly how to embody this dark world of violence and corruption, of moral failure and intellectual waste," Parini writes. "The novel anticipates much of what was to come in the latter half of the twentieth century" (p. 136).

Published the same year as *Sanctuary,* the collection *These 13* (1931), including "All the Dead Pilots," "A Rose for Emily," "That Evening Sun," and "Dry September," showcased Faulkner's consistent attention to short fiction, but his indefatigable work in the longer form secured his literary fame. Focusing on four characters who all share a quest for identity and represent Faulkner's growing discontentment with Southern society's rejection of its history and culture, *Light in August* (1932) was a new high-water mark for Faulkner, who was "still indebted ... to James Joyce and the earlier followers of Joyce," according to Floyd Van Buren in an early review of the novel: "His Joycean heritage is still apparent, but now it does not get in the way of the story Faulkner has to tell and his style and mannerisms seem more an integral part of his novel" (*Literary Companion,* p. 169).

With renewed vigor, *Light in August* explores identity and the myriad ways that culture cleaves to outmoded notions of race and miscegenation (among other of its deeply held prejudices), embodied here in four characters: Joe Christmas, a thirty-three-year-old man convinced that he is of mixed blood and driven to madness by the possibility; Lena Grove, a pregnant young woman wandering the dusty roads toward Jefferson, Mississippi, in search of the baby's father; Joanna Burden, a white woman who advocates for the rights of black residents of Jefferson and eventually carries on a lengthy affair with Christmas; and Gail Hightower, a local minister, "a figure antic as a showman" (p. 488), who spends his life fighting any connection to society after an ostensible incident involving his grandfather's death in a henhouse during the Civil War and, later, the stain of his wife's infidelity and her death while with her lover in a Memphis hotel.

As with Benjy Compson in *The Sound and the Fury,* Faulkner draws on obvious Christ-imagery to flesh out Joe's character, including his name, his age, the manner in which he is treated upon arriving in Jefferson, and so on. Joe's story works on a deeper level, though, with the revelation of a heavy-handed adoptive father, Simon McEachern, and Joe's unwitting observation from a closet at age five of a woman having sex and the inevitable punishment that followed. The episode indelibly taints Joe's view of all women and leads, at least in part, to the death of Joanna Burden and his own lynching and emasculation in the novel's climax at the hands of the young, sadistic Mississippi National Guard captain Percy Grimm. One of the novel's great ironies is that Joe, adopted by McEachern and his wife from a Memphis orphanage, can never be sure of his mixed blood. Rather, he only *feels* the black blood coursing through his veins and supposes that he will be treated poorly by both black people and white people because of it. To emphasize Joe's fatalistic opposition to his heritage, he "seems almost to delight in telling whites that he is black and telling blacks that he is white. In this, Faulkner offers a subtle critique of the deeply arbitrary quality of racial prejudice in the South" (Parini, p. 181).

Joe and his plight are at the novel's center, with the narrative structure resembling a wagon wheel with Joe at the hub, but the novel opens and closes with a close-up of Lena Grove and her journey to and from Jefferson. In a touchstone to later events, Lena and Armstid, a local farmer who stops to help her, look "across the valley toward the town on the opposite ridge. Following his pointing whip, she sees two columns of smoke: the one the heavy density of burning coal above a tall stack, the other a tall yellow column standing apparently from among a clump of trees some distance beyond the town" (p. 30). It is the house of Joanna Burden, and she has just been murdered and nearly immolated by Joe Christmas. The novel's redeeming character, Lena represents the most desirable characteristics of Faulkner's ideal South: optimism, perseverance, and, despite her preparing to give birth out of wedlock, an innocent spirit that engenders empathy in those who befriend her. Despite becoming pregnant by Lucas Burch (whose alias is "Joe Brown"), a man who obviously wants nothing to do with her, Lena continues her ingenuous search for him, never succumbing to the cynicism and hatred toward which many of Faulkner's characters are inclined. Her intrinsic goodness can be seen in the book's first section as Armstid approaches in his wagon, intending to take her to his farm so that he and his wife, Martha, can board her for the night: "From beneath a sunbonnet of faded blue, weathered now by other than formal soap and water, she looks up at him quietly and pleasantly: young, pleasantfaced, candid, friendly, and alert" (p. 11). While seeking Brown to make an honest man of him, Lena, in a case of mistaken identity, befriends the similarly forthright, if single-minded, Byron Bunch (Lena supposed "Bunch" to be "Burch"), a devout Calvinist set in stark opposition to Joe's atavistic menace. Bunch falls in love with Lena and, in the novel's final pages, leaves Jefferson with her and her three-week-old child.

In a spasm of creativity in the last two months of 1934, frustrated with his progress on *Absalom, Absalom!*, an epic, sweeping novel that stands as one of his masterpieces, Faulkner drew on his own and his brother Dean's barnstorming experience (sadly, Dean died in a plane crash the same year the novel appeared, an event that understandably devastated Faulkner) for the relatively minor novel *Pylon* (1935). The primary relationship in the novel is among a husband-and-wife barnstorming team, Roger and Laverne Shumann, and their open relationship with Jack Holmes, a parachutist. Set outside Yoknapatawpha County, the book examines the wider world that fascinated Faulkner as a younger man with its shabby romanticism and the frisson of unexplored possibility.

Just a year after the publication of *Pylon*—"One can hardly judge *Pylon* as anything less than a failure, though an interesting failure," Parini asserts (p. 190)—*Absalom, Absalom!* (1936) appeared, and with it the accolades, hand-wringing, scoff, and confusion that accompanied all of the author's rigorously modern novels. A young Wallace Stegner, who knew Faulkner's work well and would become one of America's finest twentieth-century novelists in his own right, observed the evolution of a major literary figure and his transformation of the traditional narrative structure with great interest. "This novel, despite its shadowy, nightmarish quality, is in one respect the most realistic thing Faulkner has done," Stegner writes. "It reconstructs historical materials as any individual in reality has to reconstruct them—piece-meal, eked out with surmise and guess, the characters ghostly shades except in brief isolated passages" (*Literary Companion*, p. 232). It was Faulkner's fifth major effort in seven years, an output unmatched in serious literature before or since. Any trepidation from New York publishing houses that Faulkner was not a force in contemporary literature abated, though even at the height of his career, many of the author's novels had gone out of print. To be sure, his private life, including a persistent drinking problem, a souring marriage and his own infidelity, and too many unpaid bills still gave him cause for concern, but no one who knew literature could claim other than that Faulkner was one of his generation's most influential writers.

In *Absalom, Absalom!*, the full weight of history comes crashing down on Quentin Compson, who receives the story from Miss Rosa Coldfield in 1909, a year before his suicide in Boston (the epicenter of the earlier *Sound and the Fury*). Rosa is the erstwhile sister-in-law of Thomas Sutpen, one of Faulkner's more unlikeable characters and the patriarch of a family whose penchant for violence is remarkable even in Faulkner's conception. Sutpen, the story goes, settled in Jefferson in 1833 and insinuated himself into the community through shadowy land deals and his marriage to Ellen Coldfield, a local girl. The couple have two children, Judith and the volatile Henry ("the provincial, the clown almost, given to instinctive and violent action rather than to thinking, ratiocination" [p. 76]), whose lives are interrupted by the Civil War. Judith wants nothing more than to marry Charles Bon, a college friend of Henry's with whom she is smitten, though she is forbidden to do so. The reasons for the book's many violent actions, including the deaths of Bon at the hands of Henry in 1865 and Thomas Sutpen four years later after seducing the granddaughter of Wash Jones, a squatter, become clear only later, gradually, when Rosa and the elder Jason Compson, Quentin's father, flesh out the pathological details of the Sutpens' rise in Jefferson. (Perhaps Faulkner and his editors understood how difficult the narrative might be for his readers: appendices include a chronology, a genealogy, and a map of Yoknapatawpha County.)

Once again, Faulkner draws on a structure similar to that in *The Sound and the Fury* and *As I Lay Dying,* introducing the novel's plot in a first section untethered from context, instead focusing on themes common to Faulkner's fiction: the past's inexorable encroachment on the present, race, the elusive comfort of community, the lasting legacy of wanton violence, and incest. Those themes are engendered in Miss Rosa's abiding hatred for Thomas Sutpen and the spectral image of Sutpen's Hundred, the manse raised out of the Mississippi wilderness in the 1830s. The Sutpens are symbolic of the dissipated South, not unlike a similar image of death and degeneracy implied in "A Rose for Emily" (1930), Faulkner's first published and still widely read short story that details Emily Grierson's fall from grace in a small Southern town and the sensational death of her lover, Homer Barron. The critic Bernard De Voto, who asserted in the *Saturday Review of Literature* that *Absalom, Absalom!* marked Faulkner's surpassing of noted American modern writer John Dos Passos with its "magnificent technical dexterity," nonetheless took issue with Faulkner's "obsession with pathology, this parade of Grand Guignol tricks and sensations" whose characters "remain wraiths blown at random through fog by winds of myth" (*Literary Companion,* pp. 211, 217). Irving Howe, a consistent advocate of the author's work, deemed the novel "Faulkner's greatest risk [and] never likely to be read widely; it is for aficionados willing to satisfy the large and sometimes excessive demands it makes upon attention.... Wild, twisted and occasionally absurd, the novel has, nonetheless, the fearful impressiveness which comes when a writer has driven his vision to an extreme" (p. 231).

THE LATE NOVELS

While finishing *Light in August* in December of 1931, Faulkner was approached by Sam Marx of MGM Studios in Hollywood to write screenplays and treatments for feature films. Always in need of money—Faulkner's letters were often obsessive about the author's well-founded concerns for his finances—he continued to write short fiction while working with the acclaimed director Howard Hawks on a film treatment. In successive years after the publication of *Light in August,* Faulkner brought out *A Green Bough* (1933), a book of poems, and *Doctor Martino and Other Stories* (1934), most of whose stories had appeared in slick magazines, including the eponymous piece, "Death-Drag," "Pennsylvania Station," and "Wash."

But the idea of writing for the big screen was appealing to the author. His story "Turnabout"—a tale first published in the *Saturday Evening Post* in 1932 and brimming with the sorts of war adventures Faulkner only wished he had experienced (replete with, in the end, the strong antiwar ethos common in the author's later war stories)—caught the attention of Hawks and Irving Thalberg, a producer known for identifying up-and-coming writing talent. Hawks turned the story into the film *Today We Live* (1933), starring Gary Cooper, Joan Crawford, and Robert Young. The money was good, and Faulkner was grateful, after some characteristic hemming and hawing, for the opportunity. In Faulkner, Thalberg got more than he bargained for. With a glass of whiskey by his side, a pastime shared by Estelle and eventually one of several sticking points in their marriage, Faulkner sedated himself when his professional or personal self-confidence took a hit, an occurrence not as uncommon as one might think of a celebrated writer. Also, although not particularly close to Murry after reaching adulthood, Faulkner was blindsided by his father's death in August 1932. He returned to Oxford to put affairs in order; even though he continued to write while there, his absence did nothing to bolster his exposure and reputation in Hollywood. In 1935, after working for the industry in fits and starts, Faulkner met Meta Carpenter, Hawks's secretary. The two carried on a long affair, prompting Faulkner to request a divorce from Estelle, which she categorically refused. Subsequent affairs included aspiring writers Joan Williams and Jean Stein, both much younger women. Those events, in and of themselves likely manageable, in their totality became the author's bête noire, giving his handlers in Hollywood pause when considering whether to bring Faulkner on full time to write for the big screen. He worked in the industry for more than two decades and had a handful of his screenplays produced, including *To Have and Have Not* (1944) and *The Big Sleep* (1946), both starring Humphrey Bogart and Lauren Bacall, though predictably, Faulkner's passion for the long form remained undiminished by what he thought of as well-paid piecework.

Published in 1938, *The Unvanquished,* a prequel of sorts to *Sartoris,* comprises seven related stories, six of which came out as early as 1934 (five of those in the immensely popular *Saturday Evening Post*), with Bayard Sartoris narrating. "An Odor of Verbena," the volume's capstone piece, ties the stories together by exploring the inevitable end of the Civil War and its aftermath as tribulation for the Sartoris family. Critics were generally favorable to the book, which combined Faulkner's typically expansive vision with the tightly focused and more comprehensible style of his short stories. "In the series of pictures he has penned of the Sartoris family in Mississippi during the latter days of the Civil War and the first days of the Reconstruction period he has not merely tried to perpetuate the spirit of a past age but also to indicate that the spirit is inherently alive to this day," John Cournos writes. "[The sketches] have been skillfully rewritten and linked together to form one continuous narrative, which is episodic and atmospheric at the same time" (*Literary Companion,* p. 263). Because of the necessarily episodic nature of stories published as separate entities, plot takes a backseat as Faulkner's humor and closely observed characters come to the fore, even if the book's organization suggests (for the pedant) something between a short-story cycle and a novel.

In "Ambuscade," the opening story, which takes places shortly after the fall of Vicksburg in 1863, the adolescent Bayard and his black friend Ringo Strother fire at a Yankee officer and hide under the skirts of Granny Millard to avoid capture. Other of the book's stories feature war and adventure, hidden treasure, and acts of heroism against the Union. But, as Irving Howe points out, "When so much of the action is presented in a slick and jolly manner, no adequate treatment is possible of such themes as civil war, the disruption of a society, and the cost of immoral behavior in behalf of urgent human needs" (Howe, p. 44). The later stories take a dark turn, with the death of Granny and Bayard's and Ringo's gruesome act of revenge on the killer, Grumby, and the demise of the patriarch John Sartoris in a scene that recalls the similar death of Faulkner's own great-grandfather, the Old Colonel, which concludes with Bayard's feeling the weight of responsibility as he considers his father's legacy.

Published in 1939 as *The Wild Palms* and later reissued with Faulkner's preferred title, *If I Forget Thee, Jerusalem,* Faulkner's eleventh novel paired two novellas, "The Wild Palms" and "The Old Man" (with little success, according to critics, though Irving Howe gave the book a solid notice), and received relatively little notice after the creative whirlwind of the preceding decade. Continuing what had become the author's modus operandi, Faulkner opened the more significant Snopes trilogy by repurposing previously published stories for *The Hamlet* (1940)—"Spotted Horses," "Lizards in Jamshyd's Courtyard," and "Barn Burning" among them. Nearly two decades passed before *The Town* (1957) and *The Mansion* (1959) rounded out the epic.

The Hamlet and later works illustrate a humor not always apparent until the author had made peace in his middle and late periods with his own indisputable status as a writer of the first water. Set in 1907, *The Hamlet* introduces Ab Snopes and his son Flem in Frenchman's Bend, a small town in Yoknapatawpha County. The Snopes' unvarnished quest for control of the village upsets Will Varner, its current powerbroker. The novel's first section delves into the history of Frenchman's Bend, the reign of Will Varner, and his eventual end at the hands of Flem Snopes. The second section, "Eula," describes the title character's sexual hold from an early age over the men in her life, "her entire appearance suggest[ing] some symbology out of the old Dionysic time—honey in sunlight and bursting grapes, the writhen bleeding of the crushed fecundated vine beneath the hard rapacious trampling goat-hoof" (p. 107). "The Long Summer" details Ike Snopes's romantic affection for a cow and the complications that follow. And in "The Peasants," Flem Snopes returns to Frenchman's Bend from Texas with an ill-fated scheme to sell wild ponies to the locals and an even more audacious plan to unload the worthless Old Frenchman place onto Henry Armstid by tricking him and eventually driving him mad.

The second volume in the Snopes trilogy, *The Town* (1957), focuses on the venality of Flem Snopes from his arrival in Jefferson in 1909 with his wife, Eula, and their child, Linda, up to Eula's death by her own hand in 1927. Several different narrators and contributors to the story, including the young Charles Mallison, his cousin Gowan Stevens (who figures in the earlier *Sanctuary* and later in *Requiem for a Nun*), his uncle Gavin, and Ratliff, give a communal feel and voice to the novel, which was taken to task by some critics for its lack of a coherent structure and thematic unity across narratives. Flem Snopes's success in Jefferson hinges on his allowing himself to be cuckolded by the town's mayor, Manfred de Spain, which indiscretion offers Flem an opportunity for blackmail. Gavin Stevens, who harbors a barely concealed love for Eula, will not allow himself to become part of the ménage; instead, he pursues a graduate degree in Heidelberg and returns to Jefferson several years later to practice law and to mentor Eula's daughter. Eula's death shifts the social dynamic, compelling de Spain to disappear, leaving the odious Flem to scheme his way to respectability in Jefferson. Linda, in what Faulkner must have seen as a rejection of her Southern heritage and the agrarian ethos, moves to New York City.

Based in part on the short story "By the People," *The Mansion* (1959) completes the Snopes trilogy. The first of the novel's three sections revisits the incarceration of Mink Snopes for the murder of Jack Houston in 1907. "Linda" takes up a decade after *The Town* left off, with Linda Snopes returning to Jefferson after losing her husband, the Greenwich Village sculptor Barton Kohl, in the Spanish Civil War (Linda herself lost her hearing while driving an ambulance in the war). The concluding section focuses on Mink Snopes' release from the Mississippi State Penitentiary at Parchman in 1946 and his revenge on Flem for turning his back on Mink during the trial for Houston's death, which resulted in his four-decade stint in prison. Few of the trilogy's characters are innocent of collusion in the death of Flem Snopes, save perhaps Gavin Stevens, whose loyalty to Linda juxtaposes the romantic and the pragmatic without offering any real answers to the existential questions that vex Faulkner and, by extension, his characters. The trilogy marks the strongest work of Faulkner's late period, prompting David L. Stevenson to posit, "It may be that Faulkner will, finally, be judged as the great American novelist 'Manque,' as Maxwell Geismar thinks. I wish to assert quite bluntly, however, that in reading *The Mansion,* I have been in the presence of the best in Faulkner—that is to say, in the presence of magnificent writing" (*A Literary Companion,* pp. 403–404).

Between volumes of the Snopes trilogy, Faulkner busied himself with multiple projects, including *Go Down, Moses* (1942), *Intruder in the Dust* (1948), and *Requiem for a Nun* (1951), a sequel to his controversial *Sanctuary* two decades before. Importantly, the *Collected Stories of William Faulkner* appeared in 1950, bringing forty-two of Faulkner's stories to a wide audience. Not surprisingly, history and race are key in the works, expanding on and revising themes from the earlier novels and continuing the author's stylistic experimentation. *Go Down, Moses,* a series of novellas and short fiction (significantly, "Was," "The Bear," "Delta Autumn," and the title story), examines the history of the McCaslin family. *Intruder in the Dust* is a straightforward murder mystery that explores race when Lucas Beauchamp (who also figures in *Go Down, Moses*) is falsely accused of shooting Vinson Gowrie, a business associate. *Requiem for a Nun* incorporates aspects of drama and fiction into a broad overview of Yoknapatawpha County's political and social dynamic and, specifically, the sordid story of Temple Drake, now married to Gowan Stevens (whose drunk driving in *Sanctuary* precipitated the events that led to Temple's rape and indenture in a Memphis brothel), and the trial of Nancy Mannigoe, the nanny accused of killing one of Temple's two children.

All three works, each with its own particular strengths and flaws, have an aspect of opportunism about them. Despite Faulkner's extraordinary success as a literary writer, that success rarely translated into the sort of monetary windfall that could make the Faulkners comfortable in their lives at Oxford and in the Big Woods. Concern for the family's finances was eased by an offer of $50,000 for the film rights to *Intruder in the Dust.* But money as a symbol was as important to the author as its buying power, and "the obsession with money that seems to dog Faulkner throughout his life must, I think, be regarded as a measure of his waxing and waning feelings of stability, value, purchase on the world," Parini writes. "It was simply a barometer of his spirits, a way of attempting to control his fate in the world, a means of calculating his reputation, his power, his reality" (p. 296).

If Faulkner indeed still questioned his place in the literary pantheon, the late-period effort that served as testament to his literary stamina and innate genius was *A Fable* (1954). Stark witness to the author's devotion to the project are notes in Faulkner's hand still visible on the four walls of his writing room at Rowan Oak, where one can imagine Faulkner working in fits and starts of manic energy through another of his intricately structured, flawed, wise, and utterly remarkable novels. Although some critics relegate *A Fable* to the second rank of Faulkner's work—often while praising its stunning ambition—the book won both the Pulitzer Prize and the National Book Award.

Returning to his fascination with World War I, Faulkner takes as his plot a French regiment's orders to attack a German stronghold near the end of the war and the soldiers' refusal to engage in an action that would have been tantamount to suicide. When the French stop firing, the Germans withhold their own attack, in effect bringing about a spontaneous peace to the hell of the trenches (a reality that Faulkner's brother, Jack, understood too well). An investigation into the mutiny reveals a cadre of soldiers who advocate peace with troops on both sides. A corporal, the son of the marshal who hands down the punishment, and Major General Gragnon are executed for their role in the incident. Not for the first time, Faulkner grounds his story in religious symbolism and allegory—the corporal's disciple-like followers, his ostensibly having died more than once during the war, and his betrayal at the hands of a fellow soldier, Polchek, among other plot points—while driving home the more immediate antiwar message reinforced by Faulkner's own observations on two world wars and the passing of four decades since his romantic, misguided dreams of fighting in World War I.

Eight years passed between the publication of *A Fable* and the arrival of Faulkner's last novel, *The Reivers,* just a month before the author's death from a heart attack on July 6, 1962. Taking place around the turn of the last century but narrated in 1960 by Lucius Priest, the novel flashes back to the exploits of eleven-year-old Lucius and his great friends Boon Hogganbeck and Ned McCaslin. Together they borrow a Winton Flyer belonging to Boon's grandfather, drive to Memphis, visit a brothel, and bet on Coppermine, a horse that the boys exchanged for the car. Surprisingly, perhaps, things turn out reasonably well for the boys, whose knack for subterfuge makes the best of a dicey situation.

George Plimpton compared *The Reivers* to Robert Louis Stevenson's *Treasure Island* (1883) and Mark Twain's *Adventures of Huckleberry Finn* (1884). Faulkner's break from the thoroughgoing gravity of the earlier work signals the author's acceptance, finally, of his lot: a spectacular literary career by any measure, despite the inevitable intrusion of tragedy, uncertainty, and self-questioning that go hand in hand with a life fully lived. "The author was willing himself toward closure, recasting his own past in a rosy glow," Parini writes. "He didn't require anything of the outside world now, not even recognition. Indeed, when President John F. Kennedy invited him (and other Nobel laureates) to the White House, he said offhandedly: 'I'm too old at my age to travel that far to eat with strangers'" (p. 415).

Selected Bibliography

WORKS OF WILLIAM FAULKNER

Novels

Soldiers' Pay. New York: Boni & Liveright, 1926.

Mosquitoes. New York: Boni & Liveright, 1927.

Sartoris. New York: Harcourt, Brace, 1929. Unabridged version, published as *Flags in the Dust.* Edited by Douglas Day. New York: Random House, 1973.

The Sound and the Fury. New York: Cape & Smith, 1929. New York: Vintage International, 1990.

As I Lay Dying. New York: Cape & Smith, 1930. New York: Vintage International, 1990.

Sanctuary. New York: Cape & Smith, 1931.

Light in August. New York: Smith & Haas, 1932. New York: Vintage International, 1990.

Pylon. New York: Smith & Haas, 1935.

Absalom, Absalom! New York: Random House, 1936. New York: Vintage International, 1990.

The Unvanquished. New York: Random House, 1938.

The Wild Palms. New York: Random House, 1939. Released as *If I Forget Thee, Jerusalem* in *Novels: 1936–1940.* New York: Library of America, 1990.

The Hamlet. New York: Random House, 1940.

Intruder in the Dust. New York: Random House, 1948.

Requiem for a Nun. New York: Random House, 1951.

A Fable. New York: Random House, 1954.

Big Woods. New York: Random House, 1955.

The Town. New York: Random House, 1957.

The Mansion. New York: Random House, 1959. New York: Vintage International, 2011.

The Reivers. New York: Random House, 1962.

Short Fiction

These 13. New York: Cape & Smith, 1931.

Doctor Martino and Other Stories. New York: Smith & Haas, 1934.

Go Down, Moses, and Other Stories. New York: Random House, 1942.

Knight's Gambit. New York: Random House, 1949.

Collected Stories of William Faulkner. New York: Random House, 1950.

Notes on a Horsethief. Greenville, Miss.: Levee Press, 1950.

The Faulkner Reader: Selections from the Work of William Faulkner. New York: Random House, 1954.

Uncollected Stories of William Faulkner. Edited by Joseph Blotner. New York: Vintage, 1979.

Poetry

The Marble Faun. Boston: Four Seas, 1924.

A Green Bough. New York: Smith & Haas, 1933.

Produced Screenplays

Today We Live. Written with Edith Fitzgerald and Dwight Taylor. Directed by Howard Hawks. MGM, 1933.

The Road to Glory. Written with Joel Sayre. Directed by Howard Hawks. Twentieth-Century Fox, 1936.

Slave Ship. Written with Sam Hellman, Lamar Trotti, and Gladys Lehman. Directed by Tay Garnett. Twentieth-Century Fox, 1937.

To Have and Have Not. Written with Jules Furthman. Directed by Howard Hawks. Warner Bros., 1944.

The Big Sleep. Written with Leigh Brackett and Jules Furthman. Directed by Howard Hawks. Warner Bros., 1946.

Land of the Pharaohs. Written with Harry Kurnitz and Harold Jack Bloom. Directed by Howard Hawks. Warner Bros., 1955.

Essays and Lectures

William Faulkner: Essays, Speeches & Public Letters. Edited by James B. Meriwether. New York: Random House, 1966.

Faulkner in the University: Class Conferences at the University of Virginia, 1957–1958. Edited by Frederick

L. Gwynn and Joseph Blotner. Charlottesville: University of Virginia Press, 1959.

LETTERS

Selected Letters of William Faulkner. Edited by Joseph Blotner. New York: Random House, 1977.

The Faulkner-Cowley File: Letters and Memories, 1944–1963. Edited by Malcolm Cowley. New York: Viking Press, 1966.

Thinking of Home: William Faulkner's Letters to His Mother and Father, 1918–1925. Edited by James G. Watson. New York: Norton, 1992.

MAJOR LIBRARY HOLDINGS AND MANUSCRIPT COLLECTIONS

Louis Daniel Brodsky William Faulkner Collection. Kent Library, Southeastern Missouri State University, Cape Girardeau. One of the largest collections in the world of material on Faulkner, his life, and his work. Includes manuscripts, letters, and an extensive chronicle of his time in Hollywood.

William B. Wisdom Collection on William Faulkner. Howard-Tilton Memorial Library, Tulane University, New Orleans. Strong collection of Faulkner's work in translation, as well as items from the author's own library, many of them with Faulkner's handwritten notes.

William Faulkner Collection. Albert and Shirley Small Special Collections Library, University of Virginia, Charlottesville. The largest manuscript collection of Faulkner's work and a treasure trove of the author's personal papers.

William Faulkner Archives and Special Collections. John Davis Williams Library, University of Mississippi, Oxford. Manuscripts and ephemera, as well as a substantial collection of secondary material on Faulkner's life and work.

William Faulkner Collection. Department of Rare Books and Special Collections, Princeton University Library, Princeton, N.J. Manuscripts and letters, including the manuscripts of four novels Maurice Coindreau translated into French (*As I Lay Dying, Requiem for a Nun, The Sound and the Fury,* and *The Wild Palms*) and correspondence between Faulkner and Coindreau.

William Faulkner Collection. Harry Ransom Center, University of Texas, Austin. Manuscripts and correspondence, with a wealth of letters from Faulkner to his mother, his great friend Phil Stone, and his mistress Meta Carpenter Rebner.

CRITICAL AND BIOGRAPHICAL STUDIES

Blotner, Joseph L. *Faulkner: A Biography.* New York: Random House, 1974.

Brodsky, Louis Daniel. *William Faulkner: Life Glimpses.* Austin: University of Texas Press, 1990.

Brooks, Cleanth. *William Faulkner: The Yoknapatawpha Country.* New Haven, Conn.: Yale University Press, 1966.

———. *William Faulkner: Toward Yoknapatawpha and Beyond.* New Haven, Conn.: Yale University Press, 1978.

———. *William Faulkner: First Encounters.* New Haven, Conn.: Yale University Press, 1983.

Dickerson, Mary Jane. "*As I Lay Dying* and *The Waste Land*: Some Relationships." In *William Faulkner's "As I Lay Dying": A Critical Casebook.* Edited by Dianne L. Cox. New York: Garland, 1985. Pp. 189–197.

Fargnoli, A. Nicholas, ed. *William Faulkner: A Literary Companion.* New York: Pegasus Books, 2008.

Fargnoli, A. Nicholas, and Michael Goley. *William Faulkner A to Z: The Essential Reference to His Life and Work.* New York: Facts on File, 2002.

Fowler, Doreen, and Ann J. Abadie, eds. *Faulkner and Popular Culture.* Jackson: University Press of Mississippi, 1990.

Gray, Richard J. *The Life of William Faulkner: A Critical Biography.* Oxford: Blackwell, 1994.

Gresset, Michel. *Fascination: Faulkner's Fiction, 1919–1936.* Durham, N.C.: Duke University Press, 1989.

Harrington, Evans, and Ann J. Abadie, eds. *The South and Faulkner's Yoknapatawpha: The Actual and the Apocryphal.* Jackson: University Press of Mississippi, 1976.

———. *The Maker and the Myth: Faulkner and Yoknapatawpha.* Jackson: University Press of Mississippi, 1978.

———. *Faulkner, Modernism, and Film: Faulkner and Yoknapatawpha.* Jackson: University Press of Mississippi, 1979.

Howe, Irving. *William Faulkner: A Critical Study.* New York: Random House, 1962.

Karl, Frederick. *William Faulkner: American Writer: A Biography.* New York: Weidenfield & Nicolson, 1989.

Kawin, Bruce. "Sharecropping in the Golden Land." In *Faulkner and Popular Culture.* Edited by Doreen Fowler and Ann J. Abadie. Jackson: University Press of Mississippi, 1990. Pp. 196–206.

Meriwether, James B. *The Literary Career of William Faulkner: A Bibliographical Study.* Columbia: University of South Carolina Press, 1972.

Millgate, Michael. *William Faulkner.* New York: Grove Press, 1961.

Minter, David L. *William Faulkner: His Life and Work.* Baltimore: John Hopkins University Press, 1980.

Moreland, Richard C. *Faulkner and Modernism: Rereading and Rewriting.* Madison: University of Wisconsin Press, 1990.

Morris, Willie. *Faulkner's Mississippi.* Birmingham, Ala.: Oxmore House, 1990.

Oates, Stephen B. *William Faulkner: The Man and the Artist: A Biography.* New York: Harper & Row, 1987.

Parini, Jay. *One Matchless Time: A Life of William Faulkner.* New York: HarperCollins, 2004.

Polk, Noel. *Children of the Dark House: Text and Context in Faulkner.* Jackson: University Press of Mississippi, 1996.

Warren, Robert Penn, ed. *Faulkner: A Collection of Critical Essays.* Englewood Cliffs, N.J.: Prentice-Hall, 1966.

Wilde, Meta Carpenter, and Orin Borsten. *A Loving Gentleman: The Love Story of William Faulkner and Meta Carpenter.* New York: Simon & Schuster, 1976.

Williamson, Joel. *William Faulkner and Southern History.* New York: Oxford University Press, 1993.

INTERVIEWS

Inge, M. Thomas, ed. *Conversations with William Faulkner.* Jackson: University Press of Mississippi, 1999.

Meriwether, James B., and Michael Millgate, eds. *Lion in the Garden: Interviews with William Faulkner, 1926–1962.* New York: Random House, 1968.

Stein, Jean. "William Faulkner: The Art of Fiction No. 12." *Paris Review* 12:28–52 (spring 1956).

FILMS BASED ON THE NOVELS OF WILLIAM FAULKNER

Intruder in the Dust. Screenplay by Ben Maddow. Directed by Clarence Brown. MGM, 1949.

The Sound and the Fury. Screenplay by Irving Ravetch and Harriet Frank, Jr. Directed by Martin Ritt. Twentieth-Century Fox, 1959.

Sanctuary. Screenplay by Ruth Ford and James Poe. Directed by Tony Richardson. Twentieth-Century Fox, 1961.

The Reivers. Screenplay by Irving Ravetch and Harriet Frank, Jr. Directed by Mark Rydell. National General Pictures, 1969.

As I Lay Dying. Screenplay by James Franco and Matt Rager. Directed by James Franco. Picture Entertainment/RabbitBandini, 2013.

The Sound and the Fury. Screenplay by Matt Rager. Directed by James Franco. New Films International et al., 2014.

ROBERT FROST

(1874—1963)

Jonathan N. Barron

ROBERT FROST MAY be the least understood popular poet the United States ever produced. He is also the most paradoxical. Known as the New England Yankee bard of nature, he actually spent his first eleven years in the city of San Francisco. And while he did have a brief career in poultry and apple farming, beginning in 1911 he made the substantial part of his living teaching in colleges and universities, even creating the very concept of a poet in residence. He ultimately would receive more than forty honorary degrees yet he himself never graduated from college (though he did attend both Dartmouth and Harvard). Throughout, he remained dedicated to poetry and believed in poetry's public role. He often said, "I am a teacher, and I like to be understood" (Francis, 2015, p. 202). Beloved for poetry often considered optimistic, simple, and homiletic, Frost encouraged that view of his work. But in fact, posing as a beloved Yankee bard, he brought challenging and difficult ideas to a general public that would otherwise not discover them. Fascinated equally by scientific, philosophical, and religious questions, Frost's poetry is, in fact, surprisingly intellectual and not nearly as optimistic as a first reading often suggests. Through a conviction that the best poetry is always metaphorical, that good poetry says one thing and means another, Frost managed to sneak his intellectualism into the public arena just as the Greeks used the famous Trojan horse to sneak their civilization into the city of Troy. His American audience typically made his books best sellers, and his ability to court the unsuspecting reader is also evidenced from the publication of his first poetic success, "My Butterfly" (1894), in a leading national magazine, to the last years of his life, when he read "The Gift Outright" at President John F. Kennedy's inauguration and engaged in a series of quasi-diplomatic missions on behalf of the United States to such varied countries as Brazil, Israel, Greece, and the Soviet Union. As he wrote in his last volume of poetry in 1962, "It takes all sorts of in- and out-door schooling / To get adapted to my kind of fooling" (*Poems,* p. 478).

EARLY YEARS

Boy gangs, streetcars, late-night visits from the social reformer Henry George, political campaigns conducted in saloons—these were the backdrop to Robert Frost's childhood. Robert Lee Frost was born in San Francisco on March 26, 1874, the child of Robert Prescott Frost, Jr., and Isabelle Moodie Frost. In an era when newspapers belonged to political parties, Frost's father, a journalist, had come with his new wife to San Francisco, where he wrote for the San Francisco *Bulletin* and then the *Evening Post,* where Henry George was editor. Frost's mother, born in Scotland, was a mystical woman devoted to the religious philosophy of Emanuel Swedenborg; she wrote and published her own poems in addition to raising Frost and his younger sister, Jeanie. Of his childhood, then, one can say that Frost was reared under the double influence of hard-edged machine politics and ethereal spiritual reform, an influence that can be found in the poetry he would later write.

Frost's lifelong familiarity with tragedy began in 1885, when he was eleven. His father, despondent after losing a campaign for a plumb political job with the city, and having quit his position at the *Evening Post,* died from a combination of alcoholism and tuberculosis. His death left his widow and two children with nothing; he had never taken out a life insurance policy and had no savings. With no relatives of her own in the United States, Frost's mother turned to her in-laws for help. They, fortunately, were relatively wealthy. Frost's grandfather, William Prescott Frost, was a manager in one of the largest woolen mills in the world, located in Lawrence, Massachusetts (it would later be the site of the great Lawrence Textile Strike of 1912). Able if not necessarily enthusiastic to host their relatives, the stern New England Frosts settled their son's widow and children in a modest home among the factory workers. While nothing like San Francisco, Lawrence in 1886 was also not the New England of Currier and Ives or Norman Rockwell. An immigrant-filled, bustling city dominated by woolen mills, Lawrence had two daily newspapers and an unusually intellectually rigorous public high school. Seeking to support her children and free herself from dependence on the Frosts, Isabelle Frost found work teaching in various elementary schools in a small New Hampshire town, Salem Depot, just ten miles north. In 1888, a few years after arriving in Lawrence, both Frost and his sister were admitted to the competitive and rigorous Lawrence public high school, after passing their entrance exams.

If poets and intellectuals can be said to have beginnings, then Frost's beginning came when he entered Lawrence High School. His experience there was nothing short of a revelation, introducing him to serious intellectual life. As with many New England public high schools of the era, the school had devised a tracking system: a classical curriculum meant to prepare one for college and life as a good professional citizen and a general curriculum meant mostly for the girls who were not expected to enter professions, as well as for boys who for one reason or another knew they would never pass classes in either Greek or Latin. Frost elected the classical track and excelled beyond all expectation—even his own. He would go on to graduate at the top of his class, known particularly for his skill with Latin. Editor of the *Lawrence High School Bulletin,* he also published his first poems there. Not all his activity was intellectual. At Lawrence High School, Frost also fell in love with Elinor White, the woman he would eventually marry and with whom he shared the honor of valedictorian of the class of 1892. There, too, he befriended an older student, Carl Burell, who introduced him, as his teachers did not, to the philosophical challenges posed by contemporary science, especially astronomy and biology—a conundrum that would interest Frost for the rest of his life and influence his best poetry.

Frost's intellectual acumen, coupled with his success in high school, succeeded in winning him an almost full scholarship to Dartmouth, a college he entered in the fall of 1892. But within a few months Frost dropped out and returned to Lawrence. In the course of his one semester at Dartmouth, however, he discovered three things that would change the course of his poetic career. First, he discovered that poetry mattered as a public art; second, he learned that there was a public place for poetry in the various print media of his era; and third, he discovered the heritage behind the art he so admired, in Francis Turner Palgrave's anthology *The Golden Treasury of the Best Songs and Lyrical Poems in the English Language,* first published in 1861.

Frost left Dartmouth ostensibly to help his mother in her classroom, where she had a group of violently unruly students. Upon his return to Lawrence, Frost took over her class, according to Jay Parini, actually beating the young miscreants with a cane (Parini, 1999, p. 38). Frost went on to take various jobs such as working in his grandfather's mill and trying his hand as a young impresario managing a Shakespearean actor. All the while, though, he determined to be a poet in the mode he had come to admire most. Frost had already begun to develop a theory of poetry as action. Poetry, he once said, is "doing something that means something" (*Robert Frost Speaking on Campus: Excerpts from His Talks,* p. 94). Fascinated by the sound and form of language, he discovered that poetry could at once satisfy what he described as "the craving I have for form" and allow him to explore the beliefs, ideas, and emotions he found most compelling (*Talks,* p. 82). At Dartmouth, he had discovered that the serious media of his time cared enough about poetry to put it on the front page.

Eventually, in 1894, Frost gathered up enough courage to send one of his poems, "My

Butterfly," to the *Independent* in New York. Later, he recalled what a leap of faith this act took: "I didn't know where to send things. I didn't go to summer schools where they teach people where to send their manuscripts. I didn't know how to make a manuscript out" (*Talks,* p. 57). Remarkably, the editors accepted this poem from an unknown nineteen-year-old. In so doing, the *Independent*'s literary editor, Susan Hayes Ward, also became the poet's mentor and would guide his subsequent work (much of which he sent to her) until the publication of his first book in 1913.

Even as he continued to write, between 1892 and 1897 Frost did his best to make a living, working blue-collar jobs, teaching, and becoming a newspaperman. Despite his best efforts, in this period very few of his poems saw print. Yet if he was unsuccessful in poetry, he was successful in love. On December 19, 1895, after a rocky courtship, Robert Frost and Elinor White wed. Within a year, they had a little boy, Elliott. The economic realities of a young family becoming pressing, Frost determined to return to college and complete the plan he had originated when he graduated high school: in 1897, Robert Frost, at age twenty-three, became a student at Harvard.

As he had in high school, Frost triumphed at Harvard, receiving a scholarship and honors after his first year. And, as in high school, the young poet underwent an intellectual revolution at Harvard. There, for instance, he learned the context, the larger implications and nuances, of what he had been teaching himself about the natural sciences and literature. This was the golden age of philosophy at Harvard, where William James, Josiah Royce, George Santayana, and Hugo Munsterberg were forwarding the American philosophy soon to be known as pragmatism. In his first two years at Harvard, Frost systematized, contextualized, and studied on a formal basis the many ideas that were already informing his youthful poetry. After the conclusion of his second year, however, Frost suffered a serious bout of depression. Living apart from his wife and child itself was difficult, and the workload was crushing, since, to cover expenses, Frost had taken a job running a private night school. Whatever the cause, in the spring of 1899 Frost suffered from a profound nervous collapse and wrote to the dean that he would be withdrawing from Harvard.

FARMING AND POETRY: THE DERRY YEARS

On his return to Lawrence, Frost was in dire straits. A doctor friend of the family, however, gave what Frost's biographer calls "the best piece of advice he ever got": he recommended that Frost take up farming (Parini, 1999, p. 66). Frost began to raise poultry and sell the eggs. The resulting mess, however, resulted in expulsion from the family's rented property and yet further depression. And while the joy of a daughter, Lesley, mitigated the hardship, Frost's mother, Belle, was diagnosed with cancer and moved to a sanatorium. That loss was followed by the nadir of Frost's life to that point: on July 28, 1900, his son, Elliott, age three, died of typhoid fever. It seemed little worse could befall the Frost family.

Taking matters into her own hands, however, Frost's mother-in-law determined to save the family from itself. She told Elinor about a thirty-acre farm in nearby Derry, New Hampshire, that was for sale. Without telling her husband, Elinor appealed to Frost's grandfather, who agreed to purchase the farm. Before the year was out, the family had found what would be the making of a poet and the savior of the family: the Derry farm, complete with apple orchard and barn. Now the Robert Frost Farm State Historic Site, the Derry farm witnessed the birth of the poet we know today. Robert Frost's granddaughter, Lesley Lee Francis, puts it best: "It would be difficult to overstate the importance of the Derry years not only in the development of the poet's idiom but also in the formation of a close-knit family.... The years spent on the Derry farm in New Hampshire, farming and writing, then teaching and writing, would establish the foundation and provide the confidence for RF to move forward as a poet" (2015, pp. 3–4).

Once in Derry, Frost began to write poetry that reveals most of the major themes that would subsequently occupy him. In the poems he wrote during these years, one finds Frost exploring the relationship between Darwinian biology and faith, and between the need for isolated personal independence and the facts of society and community. One finds as well his intense interest in botany, nature, and astronomy and in a wide array of complex moral problems and dilemmas. Among the poems to reflect such themes are the first major poem he ever published, "My Butterfly" (1894), as well as "Trial by Existence" (1906), "Tuft of Flowers" (1906), and "Into My Own" (1909).

"Trial by Existence" had actually been written while Frost was still in high school and was influenced by Frost's encounter with the philosopher Arthur Schopenhauer's view that, in Frost's words, "our world, my world, your world, everybody's world—was a product of our will.... I had one of these things occur to me: that probably I had volunteered to exist—that my own existence was an act of my own will" (*Talks,* p. 62). In a nutshell, the poem depicts a story told in Plato's *Republic* concerning the myth of Er. There, souls gather before God, who informs them of a life they will live on earth and they select it, celebrating those who select the most difficult of lives. Three familiar elements of all Frost's great poetry can be found in this poem: first, its fundamentally intellectual and philosophical interest; second, its interest in education, in this case one's own education from experience; and finally, its double-edged ambiguity, which can be read either as heroic and comic or as despondent and tragic. The poem ends ambiguously, saying that only after death do we realize our life had been a choice. At the time of death, all seems meaningless, as Frost says: "Thus are we wholly stripped of pride / In the pain that but one close, / Bearing it crushed and mystified" (*Collected Poems, Prose, and Plays,* p. 30). From the outset, then, Frost proves himself to be a poet of profound questions rather than a poet of easy answers. In this case, he raises questions about the very idea of free will and individuality itself.

Like "Trial by Existence," "The Tuft of Flowers" had been written earlier, composed while Frost attended Harvard. Frost had actually submitted a version of the poem to his English composition teacher in 1897, only to be insulted for "pretending" to be a poet. The poem itself depicts a simple and typical farm scene: the narrator comes in the afternoon, after the grass, wet with morning dew, had been mown, "to toss the grass to dry" in the sun so that it can become hay. The poem's plot, however, concerns a "tuft of flowers" that the initial mower had let live. Reveling in the fact that the flowers were not cut, Frost writes a few lines that summarize his take on both poetry and people. First, he wonders why the mower let the tuft of flowers survive. It must have been, he reckons, "from sheer morning gladness at the brim." The poem ends with a now famous couplet where the narrator imagines a conversation with the mower: "'Men work together,' I told him from the heart, 'Whether they work together or apart'" (*Poems,* p. 31). Not only does this poem meditate on the meaning of human solidarity and individuality, it also wonders just what place beauty and aesthetics have in anyone's life. Here, too, Frost makes a subtle but important point: read as a metaphor, even a parable for an aesthetic sensibility, for the love of beauty for its own sake, the poem challenges those who associate such considerations only with the elite, the educated, and the urban.

This poem also played a significant part in Frost's life. By 1906 the Frosts had had three more children—daughters Irma and Marjorie, and a son, Carol (a fourth daughter, Elinor, would die a few days after her birth in 1907). Contacts from Lawrence paved the way for Frost to interview as a teacher at a prestigious local preparatory school, the Pinkerton Academy in Derry. Asked to read "Tuft of Flowers" during a kind of tryout before the town elders, Frost proved too shy to perform, and someone else read for him. Nonetheless, the poem struck those in attendance as masterful. It was duly published in the local newspaper and secured him a position, despite his lack of a college degree, as an English teacher at Pinkerton Academy. From 1906 to 1911 Frost would make his living there.

In the midst of these years at Derry, Frost published "Into My Own," a sonnet that, like the other two published poems discussed, had been composed much earlier. (It is notable that Frost destroyed most of his early drafts and manuscripts, and it is nearly impossible to tell what revisions, if any, he made to poems he sometimes kept from publication for as much as thirty or forty years.) "Into My Own" manages in its small sonnet frame to bring together the themes of nature, intellectual inquiry, and education that are found in all of Frost's best work. Imagining that someone might seek him out if he were to walk far away from all those he knew, he concludes the sonnet with this couplet: "They would not find me changed from him they knew— / Only more sure of all I thought was true" (*Poems,* p. 15). The couplet expresses the contradiction that defined Frost throughout his life, a contradiction best summarized by the literary scholar Priscilla Paton: "on a farm in Derry New Hampshire, Frost became an insider and outsider—a New Englander with a 'mood apart'" (p. 47). Like "Tuft of Flowers," this poem meditates on the meaning of individuality and solitude. Unlike the other poem, however, in this one, Frost learns to accept what he would later term his own "inner weather."

Frost is not typically read as a student of psychology, yet his poetry manifests a powerful understanding of it through his charting of this "inner weather." "Into My Own," then, can be read as one of his first experiments in psychological investigation. The poem, from that perspective, contrasts one's inner sensibility to the "front" one puts on in social situations, which he terms "outer weather." The disconnect between the two, one's inner psychological condition and the outer social demands, would be most famously set in opposition in his poem "Stopping by Woods on a Snowy Evening," a poem that, though written later, has its seeds in the Derry years.

Frost continued to juggle teaching and poetry. He designed Pinkerton's English curriculum, lectured on teaching throughout New Hampshire, and, in 1911, he was invited to join the faculty of Plymouth Normal School (now Plymouth State University), the state teacher's college. All the while, he had been writing poetry. By 1911 he had enough poems for a book, but he was also unknown and had published fewer than twenty poems over the course of fifteen years. In short, even as his success as a teacher increased, he had little reason to think he would be able to make his mark as a poet. In the end, ironically, this great American poet would come into his own and find fame and publication in England.

ENGLAND AND THE MAKING OF A POET

Life in Plymouth, New Hampshire, proved daunting, and within a year, Frost had given notice to the head of school, Ernest Silver. Having sold the Derry Farm, he and Elinor determined to live as long as they could on the proceeds along with a small legacy his grandfather had left as an annual trust. Deciding between moving to Vancouver, Canada, and England, the family tossed a coin and, as Lesley Lee Francis tells it, "the toss of a coin came up England" (2015, p. 16). In September 1912, Robert and Elinor Frost and their four children arrived at Euston Station in London and shortly thereafter settled in a little town, Beaconsfield, just outside the city limits. Altogether Frost's English years would be second only to his Derry years in having a lasting impact on his future life as a poet. Admirably chronicled by John Evangelist Walsh in *Into My Own: The English Years of Robert Frost* (1988), Frost's time in England gave him the public notice he had so long sought. Less than a month after his arrival, he took a book manuscript of poems to the well-regarded poetry publisher David Nutt, run by the founder's widow. Amazingly for an unknown American in England, by December, Frost had signed a contract for his first book, to be called *A Boy's Will.*

Publication was arranged for April 1913. Meanwhile, Frost discovered that a young English poet, Harold Monro, had just opened his Poetry Bookshop not far from the offices of David Nutt in London. Monro advertised an official grand opening for January 8, 1913. Frost made sure to be there and soon found himself among a crowd of well-known writers, including the English poets F. S. Flint, Wilfrid Gibson, and John Drinkwater and Americans such as John Gould Fletcher and Ezra Pound. Having fallen into easy conversation with Frost, Flint, as John Evangelist Walsh puts it, "performed his first important service for Frost" by "volunteering to arrange a meeting between Frost and his countryman" Pound (p. 84). Flint also said he would review Frost's forthcoming book in the magazines to which he had access. These were not idle promises. Flint did review Frost's book, and Frost did meet Pound, in a now legendary meeting between two important writers. Pound proved so enamored of Frost's book that he no sooner finished reading his copy of it than he fired off a review for the new and soon to be profoundly influential American magazine *Poetry: A Magazine of Verse.* It proved an auspicious beginning for a book not yet officially published.

When Nutt published *A Boy's Will* (1913), it had thirty-two poems, including those already mentioned ("Tuft of Flowers," "Trial by Existence," "Into My Own," and "My Butterfly") and other well-known lyrics such as "My November Guest," "Mowing," "October," and "Reluctance." In an age when few foreign poets received any attention for their first books, Frost's *A Boy's Will* struck a happy chord with British reviewers. Widely reviewed in the literary and the mainstream magazines and newspapers, the book was singled out for praise. Most significant, however, is the role the book played in helping Frost identify his poetic stance. By this point, he was fully immersed in a debate between two distinct poetic camps, the Georgians and the imagists, both of which sought to disrupt and challenge the nineteenth-century tradition of specialized poetic diction, artificial-sounding syntax, and excessively idealist or emotional subject matter. Favoring realism instead, the two groups mostly differed on method and technique. The imagists, centered around Ezra Pound and F. S. Flint, preferred free verse and a classically based, stripped-down diction, while the Georgians, centered around Edward Marsh and Wilfred Gibson, preferred both narrative and meter in their work. Never before had Frost spent extended time with literary men and women. As a result, ideas about poetry that he had come to on his own now met the test of argument among peers. Debating the merits of meter, diction, and even his preferred subject matter of rural New England life, Frost found himself formulating a set of principles that would subsequently guide his best poetry, much of it written in these English years.

Corresponding throughout his English years with John Bartlett (a former student, now friend, who was then living in Vancouver), Frost made his new principles clear. In a famous letter to Bartlett (July 4, 1913), he defined his first poetic principle, "the sound of sense":

> To be perfectly frank with you I am one of the most notable craftsmen of my time. That will transpire presently. I am possibly the only person going who works on any but a worn out theory of versification. ... I alone of English writers have consciously set myself to make music out of what I may call the sound of sense ... It is the abstract vitality of our speech. It is pure sound—pure form. One who concerns himself with it more than the subject is an artist.
>
> (*The Letters of Robert Frost,* pp. 122–123)

Here Frost means that, "properly done, a written record of spoken language would also incorporate the spoken tones of voice that accompanied any conversation. Those tones, he said, reveal the psychological and ethical essence of both character and situation" (Barron, p. 183). A true artist of language would know how to replicate the tone, not just the words, and would be able to do so *even while using meter.* As far as Frost was concerned (and in this he agreed with the free-verse poets), a poet did not prove talent by mastery of meter and rhyme. The art was in the ability to capture the tone of speech. For all that, though, Frost insisted on retaining meter as the fundamental frame against which he would experiment. And experimentation was the artistic order of the day. By 1913 composers had begun to experiment with music that had no melody; painters had begun to favor the abstract over the mimetic image; novelists no longer told stories in logical sequence; poets had forsaken meter.

As an artist, Frost would attempt to capture living speech tones in the frozen silence of written poetry. As an educator and public communicator, however, he did not wish to challenge readers to such a degree as to defy their expectations of poetry. Developing a new idea of poetry as a kind of Trojan horse of subversive unexpected ideas, Frost determined to hide a modern sensibility, one influenced by his reading in biology (Charles Darwin), philosophy (Henri Bergson), and psychology (William James), in seemingly innocent narratives set in apparently conventional iambs.

When, in the letter to Bartlett, Frost says his experimentalism and craft will "transpire presently," he had in mind his second book—*North of Boston* (1914), also published by David Nutt in England. Unlike anything he had yet published, *North of Boston* contained lengthy narrative poems and only a few lyrics. About the same size as his first book, it had half as many poems, almost all of which are well known today. Among the lyrics are "The Pasture," "After Apple-Picking," and "The Wood-Pile." Among the narratives are such famous and important poems as "Mending Wall," "Death of a Hired Man," and "Home Burial." What had been latent social and psychological themes in his first book now became even clearer. Described on the title page as "This Book of People," this collection, unlike the first book, does not purport to be autobiography or the sustained lyric expression of a single speaker. Instead, multiple residents of rural New Hampshire are given equal time. Always an educator, Frost in each of his narrative poems dramatizes a moment of profound and often surprising discovery, an education. His Trojan horse method, then, comes precisely from the surprise readers receive when they, like the person gaining insight for the first time in the poem's narrative, realize that a truism or premise that had been taken for granted is in fact suddenly questioned. This questioning occurs through Frost's mastery of poetic metaphor. For instance, the book's first poem, "The Pasture," set in italics, acts as a prelude to the sort of "schooling" that will follow. A mere eight lines in two quatrains, this is the poem in full:

I'm going out to clean the pasture spring;
I'll only stop to rake the leaves away
(And wait to watch the water clear, I may):
I sha'n't be gone long.—You come too.

I'm going out to fetch the little calf
That's standing by the mother. It's so young,
It totters when she licks it with her tongue.
I sha'n't be gone long.—You come too.

(*Poems,* p. 3)

The poem insists on talking to its readers. It does not ask to be read or to appear as anything other than speech, as the contractions alone make clear. It is as if Frost has put his arm around his readers and begun to explain to them what to expect when they turn his pages. On one level it is a simple narrative of a farmer inviting readers to his pasture. On another level it is also a metaphor following a familiar classical image of the pastoral, where the shepherd and farmer stands for everyman and the pasture stands for the world of the book, of poetry, of literature itself, which we are invited to enter. On both levels, the story is tricky. The farmer's invitation is potentially grim. The only reason a dairy farmer would remove a calf from the mother is to preserve the milk for some other purpose. The calf's fate is unclear—is it going to the slaughterhouse or will it be sold to someone else? In either case, we see that the world of the farm is not the pastoral ideal of Victorian myth but rather the hard fact of calves ripped mercilessly from their mothers.

The book's other lyrics are equally complicated and just as intriguing. For instance, in "After Apple-Picking" the narrator describes a dream where every blossom on every apple tree in his orchard bears fruit. It proves a kind of curse because in the dream it becomes impossible to pick all of the apples for sale before they fall on the ground—and every farmer knows that a fallen apple cannot be sold. Like "The Pasture," the poem also has its double meaning, its ulterior reference in this case to the Bible and Genesis—both the story of Eve, the apple, and the Garden of Eden, and the story of Jacob wrestling with the angel. Whether on that deeper level or as a simple description of a dream, one of the poem's lines has today entered the realm of familiar quotations: "But I am done with apple-picking now." On the one hand, he is giving up on his dream of economic success, on dreams themselves, perhaps even on hope. On the other hand, if read in terms of the biblical allusion, he is done with courting sin and will live a righteous life. Which is it? Optimistic or pessimistic? Even today, among scholars of Frost the jury is still out. As we have seen, in much of his early poetry Frost hides the metaphorical potential, the ulterior meaning of his poetry. In this case, however, the clear presence of a metaphor suggested by the many biblical allusions does nothing to resolve the ambiguity of the larger questions raised.

In addition to the lyrics, the book's narratives portray characters from the farms of New Hampshire, which biographers have traced to numerous people Frost knew in and around Derry itself. In these poems, Frost the student of human psychology, of the tension between "inner" and "outer" weather, reveals himself again and again. For instance, in "Death of a Hired Man," a husband and wife debate how to deal with a hired man who, now that he is old and decrepit, has come to their farmhouse apparently to die. "Home," says the acerbic farmer, Warren, "is the place where, when you have to go there, / They have to take you in." His wife, Mary, responds with equally famous lines, "I should have called it / Something you somehow haven't to deserve" (p. 43). In "Mending Wall," two men set about in spring repairing the stone wall that, as is typical of New England, has been ruined by a harsh winter. "Something there is that doesn't love a wall," the narrator famously declares, even though he is the one to initiate its repair. The other famously says, "Good fences make good neighbors" (p. 40). One wonders, would he have repaired that fence had his neighbor not reminded him? Finally, with regard to a poetry of psychological depth, few are more harrowing than the poem "Home Burial," which describes the death of a couple's only child and the conversation they have shortly after the husband finishes digging the child's grave in the family plot outside.

Stylistically, the lyrics and narratives of this book proved Frost's mastery of tones of speech even as he also demonstrated an uncanny familiarity with the principles of meter. Mostly in blank verse (though a few of the poems rhyme), the book's meter is subverted by the sound of sense. To read these poems aloud is to say them, not to chant or even intone them. In the media, the reviewers made their awe of both theme and technique clear. In so doing, they made Frost a poet to watch and read.

North of Boston was published in May 1914. Several months before, Frost and his family had moved from Beaconsfield to the rural hamlet of Leddington in Gloucestershire's Dymock Valley. The Frost family moved there after Frost had befriended a group of English poets, the Georgians, who wrote narrative metrical verse charting the lives of everyday people in rural England. Ultimately, Frost would call one of these poets, Edward Thomas, "the only brother I ever had" (*Letters,* p. 552). During their time together, Frost further refined his poetic theories. As John Evangelist Walsh reports, "What the two certainly did talk about, and at considerable length, was Frost's sound-of-sense theories of versification" (pp. 192–193). In many respects, this was the most bucolic time of Frost's life. He lived among fellow writers in the rural environment he preferred. But World War I put an end to all that. With his friends volunteering or drafted, and the seas, due to the German threat of torpedoes, becoming ever more hazardous, the family returned to the United States, departing England in February 1915 and settling on a farm in Franconia, New Hampshire.

RETURN TO THE UNITED STATES AND FAME

Henry Holt had just published American editions of Frost's work when he returned to the United States. On disembarking in New York, he found to his great delight that one of the leading anthologists and poets of the American branch of imagist poets, Amy Lowell, had given *North of Boston* a glowing review in the recently launched *New Republic.* That review sparked more, and soon Frost found himself the subject of a full-page profile in the leading newspaper in Boston, the *Boston Evening Transcript,* and a full-blown study of his poetry by one of the leading English critics of the day, Edward Garnett, in the leading U.S. literary magazine, the *Atlantic Monthly.* The latter study, published in August 1915, was followed by the first publication of two poems that would soon become among Frost's best known, "The Road Not Taken" and "Birches." Suddenly Frost found himself in demand; he was asked to speak to colleges and book groups, and his American publisher wanted to know if he had another book. Frost was ready indeed. Comprising lyrics and narratives written at the Derry farm and in England, his third book, *Mountain Interval,* would be published in December 1916. It contained not only "The Road Not Taken" and "Birches" but also such other well-known poems as "The Oven Bird," "'Out, Out—,'" and "The Hill Wife." This book combined the poetic talents he had already exhibited in his first two books. Whereas *A Boy's Will* had almost entirely comprised lyrics and *North of Boston* almost entirely comprised narratives, this third book contained a balance of the two. By demonstrating a mastery of both modes, Frost proved his stylistic acumen. As with his previous two books, this one depicted the rural world of contemporary New Hampshire and demonstrated Frost's interest in psychological, moral, and ethical themes with an eye toward secretly educating his readers, as a look at "The Road Not Taken"—the most famous poem Frost ever wrote—demonstrates. This poem is typically read as a celebration of nonconformity. Read as a parable with an understanding that the road refers to choices in life, the poem is often invoked as proof of Frost's simplicity and homiletic imagination. Such readings, however, as David Orr declares in *The Road Not Taken: Finding America in the Poem Everyone Loves and Almost Everyone Gets Wrong* (2015), are incorrect. If, for instance, one looks only at the last two lines of the poem, "I took the one less traveled by, / And that has made all the difference" (*Poems,* p. 103), one finds Frost's Trojan horse technique. The intellectual steeped in the philosophy of William James's pragmatism understood that given a situation's limits in real time, one must make the best of unknowables. If the roads are metaphors of the future, the future is unknowable, and any choice one makes is itself going to lead to more unexpected choices since, "knowing how way leads on to way," one will not likely be able to revisit the first choice in the chain. In sum, both roads *are* untaken. The speaker has not yet lived his future. Whichever road, left or right, he might choose will be the one less traveled. Despite David Orr's book, then, the ending is ironic precisely because it is as correct as it is misleading.

While "The Road Not Taken" is optimistic, but not for the reasons many suspect it to be, this third collection also had its share of bleak poetry that probed the darker psychological states of being. For instance, the lyric sequence of five poems, "The Hill Wife," describes the loneliness and paranoia of a farm woman far out in the hills of New England, while "'Out, Out—'" depicts the death of a child who lost his hand working on a saw mill. "The Vanishing Red" describes the murder of the last Native American resident in a small New England town, and "The Bonfire," a narrative poem, alludes to the current war and carries the striking line, in italics for emphasis, "*War is for everyone, for children too*" (*Poems,* p. 127).

By contrast with these bleak psychological studies, Frost also provides readers with optimism in such poems as "Birches," which seems to be a description of trees in a wood that have been bent and damaged by an ice storm but which soon becomes a paean to the poetic imagination itself. Like his praise of the aesthetic imagination in "Tuft of Flowers," in "Birches" Frost makes a case for the imagination over bare bland necessity. He does this through the power of metaphor because the poem is itself a description of an imagined act. The speaker knows he is looking at the results of an ice storm, but he says, "I like to think some boy's been swinging them." Unlike "Tuft of Flowers," however, the poem takes another step in metaphor making. The poetic imagination itself becomes the occasion for a deep meditation on the human capacity to think. Jonathan Levin explains that "'Birches' describes a boy's game, but as Frost's metaphors and analogies suggest, the stakes are considerably greater than a mere game would imply. For one thing, swinging birches can be regarded as a metaphor for poetry. More broadly, swinging birches serves as a metaphor for our natural instinct for philosophical and spiritual thinking" (p. 140). It is in that deeper philosophical terrain that the poem's most famous lines have their fullest resonance. On the one hand, the poem has the famous lines, "Earth's the right place for love: / I don't know where it is likely to go better." And, on the other hand, it has the famous line, "One could do worse than be a swinger of birches" (*Poems,* p. 118). Earth, as a metaphor for everyday practical life without imaginative color, becomes worthy of praise. However, as a metaphor for a life *with* imagination, "swingers of birches" seem far better than "ice-storms," themselves metaphors of mere reality.

In *Mountain Interval,* Frost advanced his view that poetry, above all else, is the art of metaphor. He would eventually make his views on metaphor public in a talk called "Education by Poetry" (1931), where he asserted that "poetry provides the one permissible way of saying one thing and meaning another" (*The Collected Prose of Robert Frost,* p. 104). The need for this, he believed, had to do with making sense of what would otherwise be the chaos of experience and information. Punning on the word "materialist," Frost says in this same talk that "the only materialist—be he poet, teacher, scientist, politician, or statesman—is the man who gets lost in his material without a gathering metaphor to throw it into shape and order. He is the lost soul" (p. 107). He reminds his audience that a word like "event," used to name a collection of experiences in a single instant of time, is a metaphor, as are such words as "atom" and "evolution." As he says, "I have wanted in late years to go further and further in making metaphor the whole of thinking" (p. 104). To think, for Frost, is to arrange an analogy that can encapsulate the random information one absorbs and make sense of it. For him, a literary artist does this when he or she makes stories or poems, and in his third book he came as close as ever to asserting that view.

Certainly, Frost had arrived as a poet. This fame led to invitations for the sorts of readings and talks from which he would, throughout his life, earn a substantial part of his livelihood. Fame also led to his appointment to the faculty of Amherst College in Amherst, Massachusetts, where the family moved in 1917. There Frost taught three courses, including a class in pre-Shakespearean drama, which no doubt inspired him to take a turn at playwriting himself. Published in the poet and anthologist Louis Untermeyer's new *Seven Arts* magazine in 1917, *A Way Out* was Frost's first attempt at a play. A one-act expressionist drama, it depicts the desperate attempt of a murderer to escape the police by hiding in an old hermit's cabin. He eventually kills the hermit and adopts his nondescript, retiring demeanor. Offering a subtle meditation on the problems of identity, solitude, and the need for community, the play has yet to receive the critical attention it deserves.

In January 1920, after three years at Amherst, Frost, disillusioned with the school's politics, resigned. The family returned to the farm in Franconia, where tragedy again struck the family, as Frost's sister, from whom he had grown estranged, had to be committed to a mental hospital in New Hampshire, for which Frost had to sign the papers. Also the family began a search for a more suitable farm because Frost's son, Carol, was interested in full-time farming. Eventually Frost sold the Franconia farm and moved to a stone cottage in South Shaftsbury, Vermont. There, Frost set about once more as an apple farmer, adding pine lumber and syrup to the enterprise and putting his son in charge. Like the Frost homes in Derry and Franconia, New Hampshire, this home in Vermont has been preserved and is now known as the Robert Frost Stone House Museum.

NEW HAMPSHIRE *(1923) AND A PULITZER PRIZE*

It had been four years since Frost had published a book. Despite his many readings and the numerous articles about him, including a chapter in Amy Lowell's book of critical essays, *Tendencies in Modern American Poetry* (1917), and inclusion in Louis Untermeyer's anthology *Modern American Poetry: An Introduction* (1919), Frost was in danger of becoming a "fading star." He had never stopped writing poetry and expected to have a complete collection soon. In fact, in

1920 two of the most prestigious literary magazines in America published groups of his new poems. *Harper's* published a number of poems, including the now famous "For Once, Then, Something" and "Fire and Ice." The strictly literary *Yale Review,* meanwhile, also published four poems, including "Dust of Snow" and "Star in a Stoneboat." As he gathered those and other poems for his next collection, he discovered that his friend and editor Alfred Harcourt was unhappy at Holt and was about to form his own company, taking such writers as Carl Sandburg and Walter Lippmann with him. He asked Frost to follow. Frost would have agreed had not Holt's copyright on his first three books prevented him from keeping control. Frost was unexpectedly rewarded for his loyalty when Harcourt's replacement, Lincoln MacVeagh, offered Frost a consulting editor position with an annual salary of $1,200. The deal proved that Frost, on the strength of his first three books, was already an important poet, worth keeping at any cost.

As he worked on his fourth collection, Frost, still in need of money to make up for the loss of salary following from quitting Amherst, embarked on a relentless speaking schedule that took him from Ontario to Philadelphia, Princeton to Chicago. It was an exhausting way to make a living, and Frost had begun to doubt its wisdom when he received an offer from the president of the University of Michigan to join the faculty for a one-year poet-in-residence position. He agreed. Moving with his family to Ann Arbor in the fall of 1921, he quickly became a legendary teacher. He also made the campus a hub for the newest American poets, bringing in such luminaries as Amy Lowell, Vachel Lindsay, and Carl Sandburg for a wildly popular speaking series. The result was an invitation for a second year as poet in residence beginning in the fall of 1922. In his two years at Michigan, even while continuing to deliver public talks all over the country, Frost put the finishing touches on his fourth book, *New Hampshire,* which was published in November 1923.

Unlike his first three books, this volume was clearly the work of a public poet. While it did contain lyrics and narratives, its title poem, the collection's first and longest, is clearly in the voice of a public bard. Aware of his new public position, Frost adopts a form used by the Roman poet Horace to make his case as a poet to his newfound public. The poem is ostensibly a disquisition on economics and the virtues of New Hampshire compared with other states. Describing what he has been told about the South, Arkansas, California, and elsewhere, he writes: "Just specimens is all New Hampshire has, / One each of everything as in a show-case / Which naturally she doesn't care to sell" (*Poems,* p. 152). In keeping with his love of metaphor, the poem uses New Hampshire as a vehicle to convey the problem of value in a materialist age and culture. The poem proceeds to praise New Hampshire only, ironically, to end with this line: "At present I am living in Vermont" (p. 162). That was no joke, either. The poem in fact *was* written in his new home in South Shaftsbury.

Given the poetry he had published, then, why did Frost so radically change his tone, his very persona? Among Frost scholars, the book is understood to be a way for him to wrestle with the gender implications of his newfound success and fame as a poet when poetry was increasingly understood as a feminine art. As Karen Kilcup puts it, "The title poem of *New Hampshire* ... makes explicit his concern—revealed in the letters as an obsession—with popularity and sales, which measured his ability to support his family, and hence, his masculinity" (p. 105). She and others find a change in Frost's gender politics here as he embraces the role of the bard speaking to his public. In addition to the gender issues, the problem of literary value in a materialist culture also becomes central in this poem. Frost meditates on the meaning of poetry, even of beauty and other intangibles in a culture as materialist as America. When people speak of economy and work, he wonders, what do they mean to imply about art, about literature and the imagination?

In the early 1920s other poets were also wrestling with the problem of literary value and materialism. Most famously, T. S. Eliot, in his poem *The Waste Land* (1922), made difficulty and complexity a hallmark of serious poetry and argued that only through such complexity could poetry prove its intellectual and emotional worth. As if to parody that view, Frost, as Eliot notoriously had done with his *Waste Land,* also included notes in his long poem "New Hampshire." The notes, however, refer to other poems in the collection. For instance, the title poem makes up the book's first section. Its notes then refer to poems in the book's second section, called, appropriately, "Notes." The final section of the book subtly makes the case for beauty as something desired but not essential. Called "Grace Notes," the third section, ironically given its title, contains some of the most important poems Frost ever wrote, including "Stopping by Woods on a Snowy Evening."

Even as he appeared to wrestle with the idea of poetic vocation, in "Stopping by Woods" and other now famous poems such as "Fire and Ice," "Dust of Snow," "Nothing Gold Can Stay," and "For Once, Then, Something," Frost was once more able to strike a chord with the public. Indeed, "Stopping by Woods" achieved immediate (and enduring) fame. That poem, like all of Frost's best work, offers a seemingly simple story of a man stopping in the middle of the woods to contemplate a late-night snowfall, behind which exists a powerful exploration of value. It does this by putting the very idea of ownership and property into the context of value and meaning. The first stanza famously reads:

> Whose woods these are I think I know.
> His house is in the village though [...]
>
> (*Poems,* p. 207)

In a masterful reading by Richard Poirier, for instance, the poem is explained as "concerned with ownership and also with someone who cannot be or does not choose to be very emphatic even about owning himself" (p. 182). Given that the poem's narrator is on someone else's land, says Poirier, the meaning of ownership, and therefore also of value, is raised. Additionally, the poem suggests that, regardless of ownership, sometimes the most human thing one can do is simply contemplate the beauty and wonder of falling snow in the woods. Contemplation and appreciation of such beauty mystifies the horse, and in the contrast between beast and human Frost makes a case for transcendent value beyond materialism.

Combined, the poetry in Frost's fourth collection revealed a poet who welcomed his newfound role as a public bard. More than ever willing to assert his views, he still managed to bury under what appeared to be simple anecdotes an ulterior motive rich in nuance and philosophical ambiguity. Once again, too, the critics agreed. *New Hampshire* won for Frost the first of what would become four Pulitzer Prizes, a record still unsurpassed. Also in 1923, Holt revived interest in his earlier books, and published his *Selected Poems.*

1920S AND 1930S: POET, EDUCATOR, PHILOSOPHER

It would be another five years before Robert Frost published another book. In the interim, his two-year stint at Michigan concluded, and a bidding war erupted for Frost between that university and Amherst. Ultimately choosing Amherst, Frost returned to New England and began teaching there again in 1926. When not teaching or pursuing his speaking tours, he lived and wrote on the South Shaftsbury farm where his son, Carol, now married, also lived.

His fifth book, *West-Running Brook* (1928), made as much of an impression as his previous one. It too had a highly organized structure, with thirty-nine poems divided into six parts. As Frost biographer Lawrance Thompson was the first to argue, the book revolved around the theme of "different ways of looking at 'contraries'" (p. 308). The title poem, placed in the middle by itself as the third section, is one of Frost's most famous narratives. In it, a newly married couple, surveying a brook on their property, decide that it, and a little wave created by a rock in its midst, are apt metaphors for their relationship. Out of this metaphor, then, Frost returns to the drama of psychological revelation. Aside from psychological narratives, this collection also has such famous lyrics as "Once by the Pacific" and "Acquainted with the Night," both of which explore the autobiographical consequences of inner and outer weather. Meanwhile, in 1928, Holt also released a second expanded edition of his *Selected Poems* and began preparations for a volume to include all five of his previous collections.

From 1928 to 1936, meanwhile, Frost did not publish another book. As the country plunged into the Great Depression, Frost followed suit. He and Elinor had been living about a mile away from the stone cottage in South Shaftsbury in order to leave his son and daughter-in-law to themselves. Their daughter Marjorie, who lived with them, had long been in ill health. Believing that travel would help, in 1928 Elinor, Frost, and Marjorie left for France, where Marjorie would stay with family friends. Marjorie did seem to recover, but five years later, she died after the birth of her first child. Adding to the woe, in 1929, Frost's sister, Jeanie, died while still institutionalized. As a result of the stress brought about by these deaths, Elinor developed a heart condition that, on doctor's orders, sent the Frosts south. Beginning in 1935, they began wintering in Florida, first in a rented house in the Coconut Grove area of Miami.

Meanwhile, Frost continued to write poetry and eventually published two books in the 1930s, including, at the decade's outset, his *Collected Poems* (1930), containing his first five books. This volume won enormous praise and garnered Frost his second Pulitzer Prize. The second book of this decade, *A Further Range* (1936), is Frost's most overtly political. As much a switch in tone as *New Hampshire* had been compared to the books that preceded it, this book made Frost a more public voice than ever before. Altogether, in fifty-one poems divided into six sections, Frost made his views concerning social welfare and the obligations of the state to its citizens more stark than ever before. Although the book garnered Frost his third Pulitzer Prize, Tyler Hoffman, in his scholarly assessment of the book, writes, "it drew scathing attacks from leftist critics at the time of its publication for its conservative political cast" (p. 128). In addition to such overtly political poems as "Build Soil" and "Departmental," the collection also contained such important lyrics as "Design," "Desert Places," "Two Tramps in Mudtime," and "Neither Out Far nor In Deep." Meanwhile, to counter whatever negative attention that various attacks from the left might have achieved, Holt rushed into print a homage to Robert Frost in the form of a volume of essays, *Recognition of Robert Frost: Twenty-Fifth Anniversary* (1937), edited by Richard Thornton, his editor at Holt.

In addition to the Pulitzer, Frost received another distinction when Harvard College invited him to deliver the Charles Eliot Norton Lectures for the academic year 1935–1936. The series, which began in 1926, was so recent that Frost was only the eighth person so honored and, given that T. S. Eliot, who delivered the 1932–1933 lectures, had renounced his U.S. citizenship in favor of Britain, Frost was also the first U.S. citizen so honored. In these six lectures delivered in the spring of 1936 he made public his views concerning what, five years earlier, he had called "education by poetry." He explained again what he meant by the importance of metaphor, and to that device he also added that all good poetry needed form. As he said, everything had pattern and form. The job of the poet, then, as he wrote in a letter published in the 1935 student newspaper of Amherst College (the *Amherst Student*), "When in doubt there is always form for us to go on with" (*Prose,* p. 115).

With the exception of the winter of 1936–1937, when he and Elinor went to south Texas, Frost continued a pattern of migrating from Amherst, where he taught, to Florida for the winter and lecturing throughout the country. Elinor's death in 1938 nearly destroyed him. Plunged into the worst depression of his life, Frost changed course following her death, quitting his teaching position at Amherst College. Two years later he had a home built on a five-acre property in Coconut Grove neighborhood of Miami, Florida, which he named Pencil Pines.

His absence from the classroom only lasted a year. At decade's end, Frost's friends lobbied Harvard to hire the poet, and he was appointed to a two-year term as Ralph Waldo Emerson Fellow in Poetry. He returned to poetry as well. Meanwhile, his publisher released a *Collected Poems* (1939) that included each of his six books along with an introductory essay, "The Figure a Poem Makes." In that essay, Frost made clear to readers just how necessary poetry could be, even in the darkest of times. No doubt thinking of Elinor, he explained that poetry "begins in delight and ends in wisdom. The figure is the same as for love" (*Prose,* p. 132). Famously, he also added that poetry was itself "a momentary stay against confusion" (*Prose,* p. 132). For the first time, and for the general readers to whom his collected poems were marketed, Frost made his philosophical inclination overt.

1940S: A TURN TO PHILOSOPHY

The 1940s began with new tragedy. That year Frost's adult son, Carol, married and with teenage son of his own, shot himself and died. Somehow in the midst of that tragedy the poet put together a seventh collection, *A Witness Tree* (1942). In this collection, a latent philosophical theme in all of Frost's work concerning the meaning of love and its implications for one's sense of identity now became overt. Specifically, *A Witness Tree* refers to the name given to a tree used to demarcate a property's boundary. The book not only came with a cover drawing of such a tree but also a preface of two poems, "Beech" and "Sycamore," that between them act as a cipher, a hidden set of clues. The scholar Timothy O'Brien goes so far as to say these opening two poems gave readers "a clarifying proverb and ... [a] riddle to be decoded" (p. 153). He discovers, for instance, that the volume's first poem, "Beech" "also picks up on the last poem in Frost's previous volume, ... in *A Further Range,* called 'A Missive Missile'" (p. 157), where the speaker tries to understand an image on a beach. By connecting the beach image to its homonym, "beech," Frost calls attention to the peculiarities of language and, in so doing, tells his readers to attend to the distinction between the speaking voice and the material imagery of poetry. Where his previous poetry distinguished between the inner psychological weather of people and the outer facts of social necessity, he now calls attention to an even more fundamental distinction: between form and content, material body and essence or soul.

A meditation on love, the ten poems that follow "Beech" and "Sycamore" constitute a sequence of poems about love that William Pritchard (2001) was the first to recognize. His reading of these poems as a meditation on love is still unsurpassed. For instance, Pritchard shows that the first ten poems, which include "The Silken Tent," "The Most of It," and "Never Again Would Birds' Song Be the Same," each express the profundity of love as never before in Frost's published poetry. Nor were all the poems in this collection new. That same section of love poems, for instance, also contains "The Quest of the Purple-Fringed," a poem he had first published in a magazine (under a slightly different title) in 1901. These poems alone proved that Frost still had surprises left for his readers, few of whom associated him with love poetry. In a preface to a book of poetry by Edwin Arlington Robinson, Frost had famously defined poetic success as follows: "The utmost of ambition is to lodge a few poems where they will be hard to get rid of" (*Prose,* p. 118). In each of his collections so far, Frost had managed to do precisely this.

Following the publication of *A Witness Tree,* which earned him his fourth Pulitzer Prize, Frost left Harvard in 1943 for a permanent teaching position at Dartmouth College. Ever the public poet, and always an educator at heart, he determined to give voice to what had become the most profound of spiritual doubts. Although he had met a woman, Kay Morrison (to whom he had dedicated *A Witness Tree*), who would be an amanuensis and one of his closest friends, her love for him and his for her did not eradicate the world of woe that had beset him. He exorcised his deepest religious and moral questions through a dramatic form used by the religious poet he most admired, John Milton. Milton had written a masque, "Comus," which Frost had his students perform when he taught at Pinkerton Academy. With Milton's model in mind, Frost wrote *A Masque of Reason* (1945), which was published as a book and concerns Job in a contemporary setting. In 1947 Frost published *A Masque of Mercy.* This second masque puts both a contemporary Noah and a contemporary Saint Paul into conversation. Both masques bore the stamp of

Victor Reichert, a rabbi whom Frost had befriended. Indeed, it appears that Frost's conversations with Reichert led to his poetic meditations on the new and shocking events of Hiroshima and Nagasaki. Frost was arguably the first major American poet to address America's use of nuclear weapons.

Also in 1946, the Modern Library imprint of Random House gathered Frost's seven collections of poetry for publication. The preface to that collection came from an essay Frost had just written for the *Atlantic Monthly,* an essay that is one of his most important statements of poetic art: "The Constant Symbol." There, for instance, he expressed his view that poetry and metaphor were symbiotically linked: "Every poem is a new metaphor inside or it is nothing" (*Prose,* p. 147).

Metaphor was much on Frost's mind in these years as he continued his religious explorations of evil, design, and moral purpose. Through Rabbi Reichert, for instance, Frost was invited to deliver a Succoth sermon to Reichert's congregation in Cincinnati. There, Frost meditated again on the meaning of wisdom, saying, "religion always seems to me to come round to something beyond wisdom. It's a straining of the spirit forward to a wisdom beyond wisdom" (*Poems,* p. 792).

Not long after that sermon, in May 1947 Frost published his eighth collection, *Steeple Bush,* which had forty-three poems. Sadly, the joy of this newest volume was tempered by another family disaster. His daughter Irma, who had long exhibited signs of mental illness, finally had to be committed to a mental institution in New Hampshire. Given that her husband had divorced her in 1946, Frost had to sign the papers, as he had done for his sister so many years before. Many of the poems in this collection had been written in the midst of the turmoil provoked by Irma's illness, as well as by the news of the Holocaust and the onset of the cold war. Perhaps that is why, of all his volumes, this one is Frost's least personal and most public, reminiscent in its bardic pronouncements of *New Hampshire.* On the other hand, the book does contain one acknowledged masterpiece, "Directive," called by Jay Parini "one of the strongest poems written in the twentieth century by an American poet" (2014, p. 65). Another Frost scholar, Robert Faggen, explains that, in "Directive," "the narrator seems to direct or order us 'back out' of the present confusion and then 'back in a time made simple.' The goal of this 'directive' would seem for us to become so lost as to restore our belief" (p. 147). Faggen summarizes the gist of the poem as follows: "Looking deep into the past for simplicity, one finds divergence, competition, and destruction" (p. 148). In so doing, it causes one to ask, according to Faggen, such questions as "was Frost poking fun at the obscurity of Eliot's Christian modernism? Or was he making more of a suggestion that one need become 'as little children' in order to understand?" (pp. 148–149).

In the 1940s, then, Frost published *Steeple Bush, A Masque of Reason,* and *A Masque of Mercy.* In 1949 Holt decided it was time to release what it deemed *The Complete Poems of Robert Frost,* a volume that, in addition to his eight collections and two masques, also included three new poems ("Choose Something Like a Star," "Closed for Good," and "From Plane to Plane") in a section called "An Afterword." Introduced by the same preface he had first penned for his 1939 collected poems, "The Figure a Poem Makes," the *Complete Poems* proved the lasting impact of Robert Frost. As William Pritchard says, he had become "a public figure, a pundit, an institution" (p. 241). In the 1950s, he would add to that exalted triad the title, to use Pritchard's phrase, of "cultural emissary."

1950–1963: ROBERT FROST AS INSTITUTION AND CULTURAL EMISSARY

The 1950s opened with perhaps the single greatest honor Frost had yet received. On March 26, 1950, the U.S. Senate adopted a resolution to honor the poet for his seventy-fifth birthday. Far from retired and resting on his laurels, however, Frost in this decade was as active as ever. In late 1948, for instance, he had resigned his teaching position at Dartmouth in order to return to teaching at Amherst College. He continued to travel the country, "barding around," as he put it, giving poetry readings and talks, and divided his time between homes in Ripton, Vermont; Coconut Grove, Florida; and Cambridge, Massachusetts.

Meanwhile, his poems had struck deep into the national culture. In 1954, through his friend Sherman Adams (former governor of New Hampshire, now President Dwight Eisenhower's chief of staff), Frost was invited to the White House to read his poems. In the midst of the cold war, it became apparent to Adams and other literary figures in the government that the best argument for an "American" way of life would come from writers. To that end, when the World Congress of Writers convened later that year in São Paulo, Brazil, and the organizers asked the United States to delegate a poet and a prose writer, it was Adams who made sure the poet would be Robert Frost (the prose writer was William Faulkner). It was Frost's first trip as an official representative of the United States and proved such a success that he would soon become a major figure in the cold war cultural effort. For instance, that trip to Brazil was followed in 1957 by an invitation from the U.S. embassy in London for Frost to travel to England, where the embassy was putting on an exhibit to honor his life and work. Traveling to England, Frost also became the only American writer after Henry Wadsworth Longfellow and James Russell Lowell to receive honorary degrees from both Oxford and Cambridge universities. That trip also took Frost to Ireland, where he received an honorary degree from University College, Dublin.

Brazil, Great Britain, and Ireland were not the only stops in this diplomatic conclusion to a life in poetry. In 1958 he was appointed consultant in poetry to the Library of Congress, a position renamed in 1986 to United States poet laureate. In an interview to a journalist following his appointment, Frost said, "I would rather perish as Athens than prevail as Sparta. The tone is Athens" (Thompson and Winnick, p. 264). He was referring to the great debate between science and the humanities; to his mind the militarism and materialism of Sparta could never produce what he believed to be the core values of genuine civilization, something that went back to the ancient Greeks, to Plato and Athens, a point he reiterated in his official speech on accepting the Library of Congress position.

In 1959 Frost's secret as a Trojan horse of intellectual critique was discovered. In what is now referred to as a famous "cultural episode," the eminent cultural critic Lionel Trilling delivered a speech at Frost's eighty-fifth birthday celebration, describing the poet not as a benevolent rustic bard but rather as an existential prophet: "The universe that he [Frost] conceives is a terrifying universe." Trilling went on: "Read the poem called 'Design' and see if you sleep better for it. Read 'Neither Out Far nor In Deep,' which seems to me the most perfect poem of our time, and see if you are warmed by anything in it except the energy with which emptiness is perceived" (Thompson and Winnick, pp. 267–268). Widely reported in newspapers, the speech exposed the dark ulterior meaning in many of Frost's poems and in so doing provoked a public controversy. Many were upset that the grand old man was, as Trilling implied, a prophet of doom. In response to the controversy, Frost quipped: "No sweeter music can come to my ears than the clash of arms over my dead body when I am down ..." (Thompson and Winnick, pp. 269–270).

Also in 1959, Frost gave an interview in which he appeared to endorse John F. Kennedy for president in the forthcoming election. This praise elicited a letter to Frost from then Senator Kennedy and initiated one of the few instances in American history when a poet and a president collaborated. Ultimately, as is well known, the new president selected Robert Frost to be the first poet in American history to read a poem for the inaugural ceremony. On January 20, 1961, Frost read "The Gift Outright" at the U.S. Capitol.

The reading had been the idea of a former congressman from Arizona, Stewart L. Udall, who, like Sherman Adams, had grown up with and been deeply affected by Frost's poetry. As a congressman, he had sought the poet out and befriended him. When Udall was selected to be Kennedy's secretary of the interior he suggested that Kennedy have Frost read a poem as part of the inaugural ceremony. The success of that reading led to yet another diplomatic call.

Following the inauguration Frost was asked

to represent the United States on a whirlwind tour on behalf of the U.S. Information Agency to the three places that Frost most associated with the deep history of American culture: Israel, Greece, and England. Carefully charted in books by Sholom Jacob Kahn and Lesley Lee Francis, these trips only added to Frost's singular importance as an American institution. They did not, however, have anything like the political implication of his final diplomatic mission. In 1962, as F. D. Reeve explains, "Frost was certain that an accord between Russia and the United States could be achieved at the highest, personal level.... Kennedy drew the connection closer, allowing Frost to go see [Soviet Premier Nikita] Khrushchev to participate in achieving an accord" (p. 10). As part of a cultural exchange of writers between the USSR and the United States, Frost went to Russia with the intention of meeting Khrushchev and easing the increased tensions wrought by the erection in 1961 of the Berlin Wall. He did meet with the Soviet premier for an hour and a half, and on his return to the United States he declared that the premier had said the United States was too liberal to fight. It turned out that Khrushchev had said no such thing. But the phrase "too liberal to fight" became a massive political controversy in the midst of increasing tension during the run-up to the Cuban missile crisis. When Kennedy learned that the phrase had been Frost's spin and that the controversy need never have happened, he cut off Frost from all communication. Still, as F. D. Reeve, says, "I like to think that Frost's talk with Khrushchev and Khrushchev's pledge to stop the name calling and the propaganda helped improve the conditions of our world" (p. 146). And conditions for writers in the USSR did improve under Khrushchev following Frost's visit.

At age eighty-eight, Frost knew he had mismanaged the one most important diplomatic adventure of his life. Nonetheless, he also knew that his legacy would rest on his poetry. To that end, he put the finishing touches on his final volume of poetry, *In the Clearing* (1962), which, despite his advanced age, contains some of his most impressive work. The familiar themes are still present in these poems. So too is the now no-longer-secret darker side of Frost. The volume saw the first publication of a poem he had written in 1920, "The Draft Horse." This terrifying and bizarre poem tells the story of a man on a horse riding through the woods who is suddenly forced to dismount as a random stranger kills the horse. As a parable for spiritual and political hubris it leaves one wondering where one is to go once one has been left without means to go anywhere. Frost's interest in spirituality and politics is more directly evidenced by such poems as "Kitty Hawk" (about spirituality) and "How Hard It Is to Keep from Being King When It's in You and in the Situation" (about political power).

On January 29, 1963, Robert Frost died of complications from prostate surgery. As if to apologize for his own anger, Kennedy himself attended a ceremony to dedicate the Robert Frost Library at Amherst College, nine months after the poet's death and less than a month before his own. There, he said, "A nation reveals itself not only by the men it produces but also by the men it honors, the men it remembers." His words are as fitting a tribute as any to the legacy and importance of the great educator and poet Robert Frost.

Selected Bibliography

WORKS OF ROBERT FROST

Poetry and Prose

Collected Poems, Prose, and Plays. Edited by Richard Poirier and Mark Richardson. New York: Library of America, 1997.

The Collected Prose of Robert Frost. Edited by Mark Richardson. Cambridge, Mass.: Belknap Press of Harvard University Press, 2007.

Lectures and Letters

Robert Frost Speaking on Campus: Excerpts from His Talks, 1949–1962. Edited by Edward Connery Lathem. New York: Norton, 2009.

The Letters of Robert Frost. Vol. 1, *1886–1920.* Edited by Donald Sheehy, Mark Richardson, and Robert Faggen. Cambridge, Mass.: Belknap Press of Harvard University Press, 2014.

PAPERS

Amherst College, Amherst, Mass. Robert Frost Collection, http://asteria.fivecolleges.edu/findaids/amherst/ma181_main.html

Dartmouth College, Hanover, N.H. Rainer Special Collections Library, Robert Frost Papers, https://ead.dartmouth.edu/html/ms1178_fullguide.html

Jones Library, Amherst, Mass. Special Collections, http://www.joneslibrary.org/315/Frost-Robert

Plymouth State University, Plymouth, N.H. Lampson Library, Robert Frost Collection, http://library.plymouth.edu/archives/collections

State University of New York at Buffalo, Buffalo, N.Y. Victor E. Reichert Robert Frost Collection, http://libweb1.lib.buffalo.edu/poetry/detail.asp?ID=43

University of New Hampshire, Durham, N.H. Special Collections, https://www.library.unh.edu/find/archives/collections/robert-frost-papers-1909-1987

University of Virginia. Clifton Barrett Special Collections, http://ead.lib.virginia.edu/vivaxtf/view?docId=uva-sc/viu00639.xml

CRITICAL AND BIOGRAPHICAL STUDIES

Barron, Jonathan N. *How Robert Frost Made Realism Matter.* Columbia: University of Missouri Press, 2015.

Cramer, Jeffrey S. *Robert Frost Among His Poems: A Literary Companion to the Poet's Own Biographical Contexts and Associations.* Jefferson, N.C.: McFarland, 1996.

Faggen, Robert. *The Cambridge Introduction to Robert Frost.* Cambridge, U.K., and New York: Cambridge University Press, 2008.

Francis, Lesley Lee. *The Frost Family's Adventure in Poetry: Sheer Morning Gladness at the Brim.* Columbia: University of Missouri Press, 1994.

———. *You Come Too: My Journey with Robert Frost.* Charlottesville: University of Virginia Press, 2015.

Hoffman, Tyler. "A Further Range." In *The Robert Frost Encyclopedia.* Edited by Nancy Lewis Tuten and John Zubizarreta. Westport, Conn.: Greenwood Press, 2001. Pp. 128–130.

Kahn, Sholom Jacob. *Robert Frost and Jerusalem: The Hidden Scenario.* Jerusalem: Academon, 1997.

Kilcup, Karen L. *Robert Frost and Feminine Literary Tradition.* Ann Arbor: University of Michigan Press, 1998.

Levin, Jonathan. "Robert Frost and Pragmatism." In *Robert Frost in Context.* Edited by Mark Richardson. New York: Cambridge University Press, 2014.

O'Brien, Timothy D. *Names, Proverbs, Riddles, and Material Text in Robert Frost.* New York: Palgrave Macmillan, 2010.

Orr, David. *The Road Not Taken: Finding America in the Poem Everyone Loves and Almost Everyone Gets Wrong.* New York: Penguin, 2015.

Parini, Jay. *Robert Frost: A Life.* New York: Holt, 1999.

———. "The Lay of the Land in Frost's *Steeple Bush.*" In *Robert Frost in Context.* Edited by Mark Richardson. New York: Cambridge University Presss, 2014. Pp. 62–71.

Paton, Priscilla. *Abandoned New England: Landscape in the Works of Homer, Frost, Hopper, Wyeth, and Bishop.* Hanover, N.H.: University Press of New England, 2003.

Poirier, Richard. *Robert Frost: The Work of Knowing; With a New Afterword.* Stanford, Calif.: Stanford University Press, 1990.

Pritchard, William H. *Frost: A Literary Life Reconsidered.* New York: Oxford University Press, 1984.

———. "Frost Biography and *A Witness Tree.*" In *The Cambridge Companion to Robert Frost.* Edited by Robert Faggen. Cambridge, U.K.: Cambridge University Press, 2001. Pp. 35–47.

Reeve, F. D. *Robert Frost in Russia.* Rev. ed. Brookline, Mass.: Zephyr, 2001.

Thompson, Lawrance. *Robert Frost: The Years of Triumph, 1915–1938.* New York: Holt, Rinehart and Winston, 1970.

Thompson, Lawrance, and R. H. Winnick. *Robert Frost: The Later Years, 1938–1963.* New York: Holt, Rinehart and Winston, 1976.

Walsh, John Evangelist. *Into My Own: The English Years of Robert Frost.* New York: Grove Weidenfeld, 1988.

NATHANIEL HAWTHORNE

(1804—1864)

Nancy L. Bunge

NATHANIEL HAWTHORNE WAS born July 4, 1804, in Salem, Massachusetts, to Elizabeth Clarke Manning and Nathaniel Hathorne, a sailor. (The younger Nathaniel later added the "w" to the surname.) He had an older sister, Elizabeth Manning, born two years before him on March 7, 1802, and a younger sister, Maria Louisa, born a little over three years after him on January 9, 1908. In April 1808 his father died at sea and his mother moved the family into her parents' home, where they joined her eight single brothers and sisters, who happily welcomed them all, especially the children. On November 10, 1813, Hawthorne hurt his leg playing ball and did not attend school until January 1816. He spent this time reading voraciously and later claimed this period established his propensity for solitude. In June 1816 Hawthorne and his family moved in with his uncle Robert Manning in Raymond, Maine. Hawthorne loved country life and resisted returning to school in Salem, but he had no choice. The whole family moved back to Maine in 1818, and the following year Hawthorne attended various boarding schools, first in Maine, then back in Salem.

In September 1821 Hawthorne entered Bowdoin College in Maine. He had a mediocre college career, but his colleagues at Bowdoin included people who became remarkably distinguished later in life, including Franklin Pierce, the future president of the United States, and the poet Henry Wadsworth Longfellow. Hawthorne graduated in the middle of his class, eighteenth in a class of thirty-eight. When he got into trouble for gambling, the college president tried to attribute his misbehavior to the influence of others. This outraged Hawthorne, who threatened to do it again just to prove that he made his own choices.

At age sixteen, Hawthorne had announced to his mother that he intended to become an author, even though he knew this would create financial challenges for him. This proclamation proved prophetic, for he not only became an accomplished fiction writer, he struggled with finances for much of his career. When he graduated from Bowdoin on September 7, 1825, he moved into his mother's house in Salem and began writing. The twelve years between this move and the appearance of Hawthorne's first commercially published book, *Twice-Told Tales,* in 1837, typically get linked to the stereotype of the solitary artist, a view of this period Hawthorne himself encouraged in his letters to Longfellow and to his future wife, Sophia Peabody. He did take some trips, but as far as anyone can discover, he spent most of this time writing in his room until his 1836 move to Boston, where he edited the *American Magazine of Useful and Entertaining Knowledge* and the book *Peter Parley's Universal History, on the Basis of Geography* (1837), the latter with his sister Elizabeth. And, in fact, the impressive quantity and quality of the work that emerged from this period in Salem suggests that he invested most of his time and energy in his literary efforts.

At the Salem library, Hawthorne checked out books on the New England history that played a large role in his work, but he also withdrew many volumes of Jonathan Swift's work, suggesting that despite his protestations that a didactic purpose undermines good literature, the idea of writing political satire interested him. He also read Voltaire, Jean-Jacques Rousseau, and Samuel Taylor Coleridge, authors whose works included philosophy as well as literature. These choices, along with other philosophical books he withdrew from the Salem library, indicate that he spent his time reflecting as well as writing. Hawthorne argued that intellectual exercise provides the foundation for all greatness and that the quality of people's minds determines the quality of their lives. As he wrote in the *American Magazine*: "Whatever knowledge they have acquired, it must all have been gained by the vigorous toil of their own intellects; and such toil never fails of its reward, in the increase of mental aliment, and of the mind's capacity to digest it" (*Hawthorne as Editor,* p. 195).

EARLY TALES

Hawthorne self-published his first work to appear in print, a gothic novel titled *Fanshawe* (1828). He came to regret it so profoundly that he retrieved all the copies he could and burned them. He even failed to mention the existence of this book to his wife. And he claimed to have set other unsatisfactory literary efforts on fire. If one has access to an author's writings over a period of time, generally one can observe a pattern of change in his or her work, but Hawthorne's withdrawal from the world and disposal of fiction he considered unsatisfactory make it difficult to get a sense of his evolution as a writer. Some of the first tales he published in magazines, like "Young Goodman Brown" and "My Kinsman, Major Molineux," include those generally considered his finest. But he withheld some strong tales, including these, from *Twice-Told Tales,* saving them for later collections. So one cannot even assume that the sequence in which the collected tales appear reflect his literary development. Still, that the central concerns in an early tale, "The Wives of the Dead," coordinate so well with early pronouncements he made, both in his notebook and in an essay, suggests that looking at this story can help define Hawthorne's central concerns as an author. That these concerns remained important to him seems verified by his decision to collect "The Wives of the Dead," for the first time, in his last compilation of his short stories, *The Snow-Image* (1851).

Hawthorne declared in an early letter that he sought to realize as much as possible the full range of his capacities without ever violating his character. In a notebook entry he added that taking a fresh angle on the world helpfully disrupts one's habitual ways of seeing. And in an essay, he commented that the capacity to grow wiser with time distinguishes people from beasts. All these comments suggest that he saw it as eminently desirable to expose oneself to fresh ways of seeing the world. This gives "The Wives of the Dead" special import, since it deals almost exclusively with the central role imagination plays in the ability to adapt to changes in one's reality or, more simply, to learn.

In this tale, both wives are told that their husbands have died. One of them, Mary, turns to religious consolation as she attempts to accept her husband's passing. She also has enough imaginative vitality to lose her sorrow temporarily in dreams. When someone knocks at the door, she has to struggle to coax herself back into reality. When she does, her grief returns, but after she answers the door, she is told her husband lives. Since she has begun the work of moving beyond her sorrow, she has trouble believing this but eventually does.

Her sister-in-law Margaret reacts to the news of her own husband's death much more passionately. Mary attempts to share the religious stance that has consoled her, but this infuriates Margaret, who refuses to pray since she has no reason for gratitude. She cannot sleep, let alone dream. She cannot begin to move into a new reality, so she uses her imagination to hover over the past, intensifying her pain. When someone arrives and tells her that her husband lives, she accepts it immediately because she remains completely unreconciled to his death. Only after she learns that her husband lives can she sleep and dream.

The tale also considers the impact of their husbands' supposed deaths on the relationship between these two women and the townspeople. Well-meaning friends attempt to console them, but the knowledge that Mary and Margaret struggle with creates a chasm between them and others. Similarly, when Mary learns that her husband is in fact alive while Margaret remains locked in grief, the sympathy between them weakens. So this tale seems to be a complex meditation on the powerful impact of individual temperament and imaginative capacities on a person's view of the world as well as on the extent to which sympathy requires a shared situation. Some critics argue the tale suggests that one or the other of these women may imagine a visitor who arrives with good news, but this simply adds another layer to this argument, stressing further the role imagination plays in one's definition of reality.

Perhaps Hawthorne wrote in part to fulfill his vow to live out his personality as fully as possible by expanding his own imaginative capacities, for his tales and novels not only manifest a persistent fascination with issues of perspective, they allow him to explore a multitude of angles on reality. Hawthorne scholarship certifies the complexity and intelligence of his work, for proponents of every critical fashion discover something useful in it. Those interested in moralistic truths can find plenty in Hawthorne, as can the New Critics in search of ambiguity and complexity, as can biographical critics looking for evidence of Hawthorne's psychological quirks, as can historical critics interested in seeing his work as a reflection of his own time or as a comment on the early American history that it discusses. Presumably because of the psychological complexity of Hawthorne's work, Freudian analyses have proved particularly persistent. And for decades critics have debated Hawthorne's attitude toward women, sometimes focusing on his work and sometimes concentrating on his biography and the women who shared his life. Some more recent Hawthorne critics have focused their attention on his portrayals of science and scientists. Childhood has also received particular attention in contemporary literary criticism; Hawthorne offers his critics bountiful material on this subject, for he wrote many short stories specifically for children. The growing interest in transnational literature coordinates well with Hawthorne's attachment to European writers as well as his sojourn abroad and its impact on his fiction. Similarly, those who come to literature with an interest in ecology, or in law, find something relevant in Hawthorne's writing. Hawthorne even wrote a tale that explains all these changing approaches, "Old News." In it, the narrator studies a series of newspapers published twenty years apart and attempts to empathize with the original readers of each period. He discovers not only that people's interests shift with time but that his engagement changes too, further complicating any attempt to define reality objectively. Samuel Coale, who surveys Hawthorne criticism in his book *The Entanglements of Nathaniel Hawthorne,* points out that behind all these shifting theories rests one body of literature: "The prominence of certain veils comes and goes as the critical terrain shifts and shivers, but the work remains" (p. 90). All these exegeses of his fiction would probably please Hawthorne because they not only reflect the energetic intellectual activity he valued, but they also help expose the depth and complexity of his writing. But given a choice between focusing on these various representations of Hawthorne's work and the writing itself, one must choose the latter.

After the disappointment of *Fanshawe,* Hawthorne hoped to publish collections of short stories focusing on the history of New England, under titles like "Seven Tales of My Native Land" and "Provincial Tales," but he failed to attract a publisher. So he began to publish his tales individually in periodicals, and his third story to see print, "An Old Woman's Tale" (1830), perhaps reveals why Hawthorne turned to the history of New England for much of his earliest published work. The story's narrator notes that by including the past, the old woman's stories achieve exceptional richness. So do Hawthorne's history tales. Certainly one of the finest stories Hawthorne wrote using Puritan history is "Young Goodman Brown." Hawthorne read Puritan history extensively, perhaps partly motivated by his lineage, for he descended from Judge John Hathorne, who participated in the Salem witch trials. Some suggest that Hawthorne added the "w" to his name to distinguish himself from his ancestor, and perhaps he did, but even though "Young Goodman Brown" grounds itself in Salem history by including characters with the same names as condemned witches, and who convene in the same pasture where the witches' meetings supposedly took place, the story implicates virtually all human beings in the self-righteousness at the heart of these tragic events in Salem. So here, and in many of his tales about New England, Hawthorne uses the events from a specific historical moment to address universal issues.

In this tale, Goodman Brown leaves his wife, Faith, whose pink ribbons testify to her innocence, to complete an evil errand in the woods. Soon after entering the untamed wilderness the Puritans loathed, Brown meets a man who resembles him while having many characteristics of the devil, like a walking stick that sometimes turns into a snake. Brown informs this man that he has decided not to join him in the unidentified errand they had planned because it would disgrace Brown's ancestors and village. Brown's devilish double finds this reasoning hilarious, assuring Brown that he has known many distinguished members of Brown's community, past and present. Brown still hesitates, but as evidence accumulates that other people he had revered are heading for the meeting in the woods, including Goody Cloyse, the woman who taught Brown his catechism, Brown's reluctance weakens. When Brown thinks he hears Faith's voice and catches a glimpse of her pink ribbons, he charges into the woods, impelled, the narrator explains, by the evil in his heart. Brown arrives at a witches' sabbath conducted by a dark figure who maintains that all people are evil. Seeing Faith there, Brown urges her to resist the call to give in to sinfulness. But before she can respond, the scene disappears and a shaken Brown finds himself alone in the forest.

Hawthorne uses ambivalent descriptions throughout the story to underline the unreliability of Brown's conclusions, leaving open the possibility that Brown may have dreamed the tale's events. But Brown has complete confidence that his entire society, including his wife, has given itself over to the sin that he has successfully resisted. Brown's disgust with those he regards as morally weak makes him hate everyone in his community, including his wife, until his death. Unable to accept his own frailty, Brown sees and condemns it in everyone else. His righteousness emotionally isolates him, but, ironically, the townspeople fail to notice, perhaps because they too nourish an isolating arrogance. Despite his contempt for everyone else, he dies an honored citizen. Brown's experience, whether it occurred in reality or in a dream, gives him an opportunity to move beyond the sanctimonious stereotypes of his community, but instead, he embraces self-righteous illusion and freezes himself intellectually and emotionally. So although Hawthorne ostensibly writes about the Puritans, the tale in fact describes anyone inclined to project his or her flaws on others instead of owning them.

In "My Kinsman, Major Molineux," Hawthorne writes about the beginnings of the American Revolution, another event he describes as being shaped by people inclined to imagine evil in others. The tale opens as Robin Molineux arrives in a town where his uncle serves as the representative of the British Crown, hoping that his distinguished relative will help him achieve success. Many critics see traces of Benjamin Franklin's ascent from lowly origins in this story, and, in fact, Hawthorne checked out books about Franklin from the Salem library. But when Robin asks directions to his uncle's home, he encounters strange hostility. Finally, a man tells Robin to stand still and he will see his uncle. And, indeed, Major Molineux does appear in a cart, tarred and feathered by rabid revolutionaries whom the narrator describes as guilty of destroying a kind man who did all he could to soften the instructions he received from England: "On they went, like fiends that throng in mockery round some dead potentate, mighty no more, but majestic still in his agony. On they went, in counterfeited pomp, in senseless uproar, in frenzied merriment, trampling all on an old man's heart" (*Centenary Edition,* vol. 11, p. 230; hereafter *CE*). The community Robin hoped to join cruelly humiliates his uncle, and Robin finds himself swept up into the hysteria. After his uncle passes, Robin tells the man who has stood by him during this spectacle that he plans to return to his village, but Robin's new friend urges him to stay in town and see if he can rise on his own. The tale closes before revealing whether Robin's experience has complicated his view of society and, especially, his notions of success.

TWICE-TOLD TALES

One can only guess why Hawthorne excluded the early tales described above from *Twice-Told Tales,* instead including stories that make the destructive impact of ideological positions obvious, such as "The Maypole of Merry Mount," where the Puritans encounter the Merry Mounters, a group of people as determinedly cheerful as they are negative. A young couple, Edith and Edgar, learn through experiencing love for one another that the truth necessarily combines and transcends the perspectives of both the Puritans and the Merry Mounters. Another tale, "The Gentle Boy," depicts a clash between Puritans and Quakers, both convinced of their absolute rectitude, who harm both themselves and the young boy they claim to care for so passionately.

Several other stories in this first collection focus on the power of perspective, including "Sunday at Home," "Sights from a Steeple," "Peter Goldthwaite's Treasure," and "Edgar Fane's Rosebud." In all these stories the narrator or the central character has a limited point of view. Even an apparently light tale about the somber narrator taking the hand of a little girl and imagining her delight at what they encounter as they walk becomes a story about the need to round out one's perspective. "Little Annie's Ramble" concludes with a testimonial to the child's reinvigorating impact on the narrator's point of view; he reports that he will resume his life "with a kinder and purer heart, and a spirit more lightly wise. All this by thy sweet magic, dear little Annie!" (*CE* 9, p. 129)

Twice-Told Tales also includes musings on ambition that seem to warn against it. In "The Ambitious Guest" a young man who wants to achieve greatness, but has no idea how, appears at a remote cottage near a mountain and finds himself welcomed by a warm and happy family spending the evening around the fireplace. The young man's desperation contrasts with the contentment of the people he joins. When he starts talking about his grand but vague aspirations, the family members begin discussing their own secret yearnings. What began as a comfortable family becomes a group pulled into isolation and discontentment by their longings. When they hear the rumblings of an avalanche, they flee their cabin. Ironically, the collapsing snow goes around the place they have left, but overwhelms the family and the young man in the shed where they seek shelter. That staying put would have saved them all seems to be a comment on ambition's futility and further underlines the irony that everyone knows and grieves the family's passing because of their connections with others, but no one even knows that the young man had joined them. So the story presents a rather clear argument that ties with other people have far more value than vague ambitions. In "Mr. Higginbotham's Catastrophe," Hawthorne examines the destructive impact of ambition on literary efforts. In this tale, a peddler who reports events to the towns he visits begins inventing facts to satisfy his demanding audiences and, as a result, finds himself exposed and dismissed when his fictions come to life, suggesting that authors who allow the desire for fame to corrupt their productions will find their work undermined by their lack of integrity.

The publication of *Twice-Told Tales* thrust Hawthorne into the world, and this made him happy. His letter thanking Longfellow for his favorable review of the book reveals Hawthorne's faith that a return to society will enrich his work along with his life: "I have seen so little of the world, that I have nothing but thin air to concoct my stories of, and it is not easy to give a lifelike semblance to such shadowy stuff. Sometimes, through a peep-hole, I have caught a glimpse of the real world; and the two or three articles, in which I have portrayed such glimpses, please me better than the others." He tells Longfellow, "I have not lived, but only dreamed about living" (*CE* 15, pp. 251–252).

When Hawthorne met Sophia Peabody, his future wife, he found himself irretrievably drawn into the world. Sophia's sister, Elizabeth Peabody, an early admirer of Hawthorne's fiction, advocated for him, and their families became close. When Hawthorne's interest in Mary Silsbee ended with her decision to marry someone else, it was assumed that he would marry Elizabeth. Instead, he fell in love with Elizabeth's sister, Sophia. Hawthorne documents his attachment to Sophia in a collection of adoring love letters that identify Sophia as his muse. They became engaged in 1838, but the courtship was lengthened by Hawthorne's struggles to find a way to write and make enough money to support a family.

Hawthorne was thrilled when he landed a job at the U.S. customhouse in Boston in 1839, hoping that he would collect not only a salary but also a more vivid sense of the world, which he could use to enrich his fiction. But, instead, he could not write at all. He reported in his love letters to Sophia that while she nourished his higher insights, the world's business dulled his imagination. Then Hawthorne went to Brook Farm, a colony established precisely to provide a way for people to support themselves and their families while sustaining their intellectual lives. Although the residents did not have to spend many hours at manual labor, Hawthorne still found his imagination dulled so badly that he wrote even less than when he was at the customhouse.

MOSSES FROM AN OLD MANSE

When he and Sophia married on July 9, 1842, they moved to the Old Manse, a house in Concord, Massachusetts, that they rented from Ralph Waldo Emerson, who lived just down the road, as did Bronson Alcott's family. There the Hawthornes enjoyed a garden laid out for them as a wedding present by Henry David Thoreau. But given Hawthorne's suspicion of those who consider themselves in possession of the truth, he never grew close to these Transcendentalists.

In the essay that introduces his next collection of short stories, *Mosses from an Old Manse* (1846), Hawthorne talks of arriving at the Manse determined to take stronger control of his life. He says he had hoped that reading the sermons left there by ministers who inhabited it earlier would inspire him to shape his present more energetically than he had in the past. In other words, he continues to ponder ambition here, claiming to see it as an unambiguous good. But he goes on to explain, instead, that he found himself functioning passively, spending his time in aimless wandering, mimicking the river that ran past his house. He claims that the somnambulant air at the Manse even put his visitors to sleep.

Indeed, many of the stories that he wrote at the Old Manse concern themselves with resisting the arrogance that nourishes ambition in order to cultivate the humility that facilitates ties to others. For instance, in "Egotism; or, The Bosom Serpent," Roderick Elliston believes he has a snake growing in him. This spectacularly unusual event makes him proud and self-absorbed. The tale consists of various attempts, sometimes by Roderick, sometimes by others, to rid him of this snake. But they all fail until Rosina, the woman who becomes his wife, reaches out to him and he responds. When Roderick loses his narcissism, his snake slithers away.

"The Birth-mark," written during Sophia's first pregnancy, links the self-absorption that plagues Roderick to the focus on achievement Hawthorne claims he sought while inhabiting the Old Manse. In this tale, Aylmer, its scientist protagonist, takes an uncharacteristic break from working in his lab and meets and marries the beautiful Georgiana. With time, he becomes obsessed with a birthmark that he believes diminishes his wife's great beauty. He determines to remove it, certain that this trivial act rests within his abilities. As he tries various solutions and fails, Georgiana whiles away the time reading his scientific journals, and she realizes, as Aylmer apparently has not, that failure has played a large role in his career. Finally, Aylmer manages to remove the birthmark but at the cost of his wife's life. As she leaves this earth, Georgiana congratulates Aylmer on his noble aspirations: "You have aimed loftily!—you have done nobly! Do not repent, that, with so high and pure a feeling, you have rejected the best that earth could offer. Aylmer—dearest Aylmer—I am dying!" (*CE* 10, p. 55). As early as 1831, Hawthorne had published a tale titled "The Haunted Quack" about a doctor who has no idea what he is doing, a theme picked up again in "Dr. Heidegger's Experiment," included in *Twice-Told Tales*. In "The Birth-mark," Hawthorne makes this arrogance appear even more repugnant by having it destroy a marital relationship.

In "Rappaccini's Daughter," a story also written at the Old Manse, this pride manifests itself in even more malignant form with Dr. Rappaccini making his daughter Beatrice poisonous as part of an experiment. Rappaccini is clearly the villain of this story, raising his poisonous daughter in an isolated garden and observing her as he contaminates her. But in this tale, Hawthorne finally blames everyone, including Beatrice, for their confidence in their limited perspectives. Rappaccini's experiment becomes exposed when a young man named Giovanni falls in love with the lovely Beatrice and seeks her out. Giovanni continues this relationship even though he sees flowers wither in her hands and insects perish from her breath, so his adoration requires that he cultivate remarkable blindness. When he discovers that his exposure to Beatrice has left him poisonous too, he condemns her, and she accuses him of coldness. But, in fact, Beatrice also has remained remarkably unaware of her destructive impact on her environment. Professor Baglioni, who has orchestrated Giovanni's attack on Beatrice, enjoys the denouement, admitting that he sought to destroy Dr. Rappaccini because he refused to follow scientific convention. When Beatrice asks her father how he could do this to her, he finds her anger astonishing because he has given her power: "Wouldst thou, then, have preferred the condition of a weak woman, exposed to all evil, and capable of none?" (*CE* 10, p. 127). All these tales about scientists portray arrogance and power hunger run amuck, but "Rappaccini's Daughter" extends the blame to everyone. No one has any idea what they are doing, and yet they all have total confidence in their perceptions and decisions and blame everyone else for the difficulties their lack of awareness produces. That arrogance has spread to the whole society also serves as the central theme of another tale, "The Celestial Rail-road." The fashionable people believe that technological advances make it possible for them to skip the unpleasant process of facing their sins and travel directly to heaven on a comfortable train. At story's end, they find they have taken a trip to hell.

Hawthorne also implicates artists in this arrogance. In "The Artist of the Beautiful," Owen Warland tries to make a mechanical butterfly, inspired in part by his love for Annie Hovenden. As he works at this task, he invites her to view it, convinced that she empathizes with him. Instead, she touches the butterfly in a way that damages it, requiring Owen to redo his work. By the time Owen completes his project, Annie has married someone considerably more earthly than Owen and produced a child. Still, Owen invites Annie and her child to see his final triumph. As the butterfly flies, the child grabs it and destroys it. But the narrator, like Georgiana as she dies, praises Owen's lofty aspirations, explaining that Owen still cherishes even more magnificent butterflies in his imagination: "When the artist rose high enough to achieve the Beautiful, the symbol by which he made it perceptible to mortal senses became of little value in his eyes, while his spirit possessed itself in the enjoyment of the Reality" (*CE* 10, p. 475). Owen's aesthetic standards alienate him from his common sense, but the tale's judgment of this choice finally remains ambiguous. The story makes clear that the artist's perspective can disconnect him or her from reality and that artists, like scientists, often consider their eccentric points of view superior. At the same time, ordinary mortals also remain enmeshed in points of view that are limited in ways they do not acknowledge. Annie may be more tied to common sense than Owen, and she may rightly value her son more than a mechanical butterfly, but her perspective is no more balanced than Owen's, and she shows little sign of believing that she needs to expand it.

This notion of everyone's limited perspective rests at the center of "The Hall of Fantasy," another tale composed at the Old Manse. The narrator, who claims to be a realist, wanders through a hall and discovers that a wide variety of people live in fantasy: politicians, religious figures, scientists—all of them see the world through their private windows and all of them consider themselves, as he does, realists. At the end, he claims he has escaped the Hall of Fantasy, but the tale makes clear that is impossible.

When Hawthorne published the short-story collection *Mosses from an Old Manse,* he included a number of stories written earlier. But the stories he actually composed at a writing table facing a wall in the Old Manse focus on the importance of relationships that can only be nurtured by having the humility to let go of the arrogant notion that one has possession of the truth. In Hawthorne's fictional universe, no one knows the truth, least of all those certain that they do.

THE SCARLET LETTER

In the fall of 1845 the Hawthornes left the Old Manse and returned to Salem. Shortly before the birth of their second child, Julian, in June 1846, Hawthorne took a job again, this time at the customhouse in Salem. Once again, he found himself too entrenched in the real world to write. He explains much of this in "The Custom-House," his introduction to *The Scarlet Letter,* written after losing his political appointment in 1848 and returning to writing full time. Although his customhouse work interfered with his literary career, losing the job made Hawthorne furious. In a letter to Longfellow, he calls his dismissal an insult to all authors. But when he turned to composing *The Scarlet Letter* (1850), the novel completely consumed him: the process of writing it exhilarated him. He had intended to write something more cheerful and apologized to his friend and literary booster Horatio Bridge because he suspected a more positive book would sell better. It seems obvious why Hawthorne's fascination with the book overwhelmed his commercial aspirations: the novel explores in one place issues that reverberate through his earlier work.

Its setting in Puritan New England recalls his early tales, and here again, the Puritans appear stolid, fervent, confident, and mindlessly conventional. They have no doubt that Hester Prynne deserves their contempt for her sexual activities. The cold-hearted scientist appears in the person of Roger Chillingworth, the husband Hester betrayed. Hester's child, Pearl, plays the role of an innocent who rightfully attempts to coax Hester to accept her guilt. But the novel's extended length allows Hawthorne to examine whether his central characters, Hester Prynne and Arthur Dimmesdale, have the humility to accept the flaws in their perspectives and alter them. Hawthorne has portrayed multiple people with mistaken points of view, and a few of them, like Roderick in "Egotism; or, The Bosom Serpent," actually learn to understand and correct their mistakes. But *The Scarlet Letter* offers Hawthorne his first opportunity to explore at length whether his two central characters can achieve intellectual and emotional evolution and to portray exactly how this might happen.

Paradoxically, Hester has the easier task, for the community has forced her to accept her sinfulness. The opening description of her looking like "that sacred image of sinless motherhood, whose infant was to redeem the world" (*CE* 1, p. 56) while the Puritans pillory her suggests that Hester's punishment may offer her salvation. But later in the novel, when she urges Dimmesdale to flee with her, throwing off the letter and disclosing the sensual beauty that has rested just beneath her marble exterior through all the intervening years, it becomes clear that Hester does not repent her actions. She has not learned the letter's lesson, and as a result, the narrator describes her as cold and lost: "Hester Prynne, whose heart had lost its regular and healthy throb, wandered without a clew in the dark labyrinth of mind" (*CE* 1, p. 166). She gathers women about her and talks with them about society's oppression, hoping that one day a society will evolve and accept women like her. But in reality, her action betrayed her husband, her child, and her own integrity. While Hester never really accepts her sin, wandering instead through an amoral universe, the townspeople consider her particularly humble and wise. They welcome her at their deathbeds because they believe she has special knowledge of how to deal with life's limits. They come to believe that her "A" stands for "Angel." Meanwhile, Pearl reminds Hester of her sin, persistently asking questions about the letter's meaning and insisting Hester replace it when she throws it aside.

Dimmesdale, on the other hand, not only violates community norms, he successfully evades confession for much of the novel. Chillingworth goads him so persistently that Dimmesdale eventually proclaims that Chillingworth saved him by reminding him of his sin. After Dimmesdale and Hester discuss fleeing, his corrupt nature temporarily surfaces and he says something shocking to a parishioner, but he soon returns to beating himself for his misdeeds in private. He needs to make a public admission to save himself, and at the novel's end, he does. This acknowledgment of his sinfulness constitutes the most powerful sermon of his life. Consistent with Hawthorne's suggestion that those who want to connect with others need to embrace humility, the power of Dimmesdale's final sermon makes it legendary. But his goodness shines through so powerfully that his speech leaves many listeners unaware that Dimmesdale has confessed. They assume he is discussing sin abstractly rather than personally, perhaps because they believe so fervently in the public persona he has sustained for decades. So their community remains blind to the psychological realities that shape the lives of Hester and Dimmesdale.

THE SNOW-IMAGE

The year after *The Scarlet Letter* appeared, Hawthorne published another collection of short stories, *The Snow-Image* (1851). Once again, he republished a lot of earlier work in this volume, along with three important recent compositions: "Ethan Brand," "The Snow-Image," and "The Great Stone Face."

In "Ethan Brand," the eponymous protagonist, like many Hawthorne characters, develops an obsession: the discovery of the unpardonable sin. Before his search, he had been a kind man, but his new focus has alienated him from the tenderness and humility that once linked him to others. Now, as he returns to the place where his search began, he understands that the unpardonable sin rests in himself. The cold stance he has trained himself to take toward others as he pursues his psychological research makes him irredeemably evil. But as townspeople gather around to insult and judge Ethan Brand, he begins to doubt whether he has in fact discovered the unpardonable sin and discovered it in himself. For most of them have little obvious sympathy for others and certainly manifest none toward Brand. The lime-burner takes a particular dislike to Brand, whose talk reminds him of his own sins. Others urge Brand to have a drink, suggesting that he needs to evade rather than accept self-awareness. Only the unspoiled child, Joe, manifests the appropriate emotions: sympathy and fear.

After the townspeople leave, Brand commits suicide by throwing himself into the lime kiln. Some critics argue he resorts to this to avoid facing that he failed in his quest and that the enormous sin he believed he had committed is actually common: most people regard other human beings as objects. As if to certify the universality of the crime Brand proudly claimed he had committed, when the lime burner happens upon Brand's incinerated skeleton the next morning, he smashes it to bits while calculating his potential profit on the lime market. This tale offers a slightly different angle on Hawthorne's stories about obsession and pride, since Hawthorne focuses here on the destructive result of this behavior: distance from other people. As in "Rappaccini's Daughter," he suggests that that the narrow, righteous perspective that causes scientists to go astray is shared by everyone; in this story, so is the unkindness that results.

The optimism about children's rectitude that surfaces in Pearl's insisting that Hester replace the letter and Joe's terror of Ethan Brand shows up again in the title story of *The Snow-Image.* Here two children function as artists, each supplementing the other as they produce a snow girl. The intuitive Violet guides her more practical brother, Peony, and he realizes her vision. They must work together to create this work of art, which comes to life and runs around the yard with them. Their loving mother not only understands their enthusiasm, she shares it: it charms her when the snow maiden plays with her children. But the children's commonsensical father sees the dancing snow image as a cold child and drags her into the house to warm by the stove. She melts. But the persistently blind father so successfully disowns any event challenging his rectitude that he explains the puddle left by the snow maiden as the remnant of snow his children dragged into the house, forgetting the child he sought to rescue. In this tale, Hawthorne suggests the optimistic faith that the artistic impulse develops naturally in all human beings. But convention too often stifles it, either by an inability to comprehend the work of art or by training people to repress it.

In "The Great Stone Face," apparently composed about the same time as "The Snow-Image," Hawthorne suggests that despite art's power and importance, decent behavior deserves even more admiration. The Great Stone Face is a kindly-looking visage that appears on the side of a mountain. The people it overlooks believe that one day a human version of the Great Stone Face will appear among them. Ernest, the tale's protagonist, grows up studying it and fervently looks for someone who realizes in the world the kindly character this rock formation suggests to him. Ernest watches as one supposedly heroic personage after another arrives at his town, hopeful that one of them will embody the Great Stone Face. But when Ernest sees Mr. Gathergold, who has collected great wealth, or Old Blood-and-Thunder, the military hero, or the politician Old Stony Phiz, he instantly sees that these men, although praised by society, bear no resemblance to the benevolent face on the mountain.

Ernest has hopes for a poet whose work he admires because reading it helps Ernest see the celestial aspect of nature. And when the poet arrives in town, he and Ernest have open conversations that launch both of them into the heavens. All the same, Ernest has to admit that the poet does not manifest the kindness of the Great Stone Face. The poet explains why. He points out that while he can articulate celestial thoughts and convey them to others, his actions do not realize these ideas in the world: "But my life, dear Ernest, has not corresponded with my thought. I have had grand dreams, but they have been only dreams" (*CE* 11, p. 46).

Disappointed, Ernest returns to his normal activities and preaches to the townspeople. As the poet watches, he sees that Ernest, with his generosity and hopefulness, has come to resemble the Great Stone Face. Those who hear the poet's comment agree. Ernest responds by continuing to hope that the Great Stone Face will appear, underlining the modesty and unselfishness that undergird his achievement. In this late tale, Hawthorne not only stresses once more the tie between art and nature, he sees generous behavior as superior to anything the artist can produce.

THE HOUSE OF THE SEVEN GABLES

The focus on real-world activity seen in stories like "The Great Stone Face" may help explain why Hawthorne grounded his next two novels in actualities, as opposed to the hallucinatory universe of *The Scarlet Letter.* Hawthorne's next novel, *The House of the Seven Gables* (1851), has as its heroine a woman who differs strikingly from both Dimmesdale and Hester. While Hester ignores community mores when possible, Phoebe embraces them. While Dimmesdale struggles with his conscience, Phoebe's is completely clear. While both Hester and Dimmesdale rest miserably in the shadows, Phoebe not only possesses a sunny disposition, she passes it on to others. Rather than struggling with complicated thoughts and tensions, she produces healing actions. Perhaps not incidentally, Hawthorne called his wife, Sophia, "Phoebe."

The novel focuses on a feud between two families, the Pyncheons, who have received society's approval, and the rebellious Maules. Both like domination, but because of their different abilities, they seek it in different ways. The objects used to symbolize these families connect them to disease: a scrawny collection of inbred chickens represents the Pyncheons and a well filled with rancid water, the Maules. The modern representative of the Maules is Holgrave, an artist who shares his family's moody withdrawal from the world. Judge Pyncheon, with his cold self-assurance born of unthinking acceptance of social norms and bottomless greed, is the quintessential Pyncheon. When his elderly uncle dies of a stroke, he frames his cousin Clifford for murder, resulting in a jail sentence of thirty years. Meanwhile, Clifford's sister, the timid Hepzibah Pyncheon, hides in the ancestral home waiting for his return. When Clifford arrives home, Phoebe Pyncheon joins them. Hepzibah repeatedly maintains that Phoebe's mother helps explain her daughter's character, perhaps because Phoebe lacks the sense of innate superiority that seems to infect all the other Pyncheons. Instead, she accommodates to and feels with the world. She also accepts conventional norms, bewildered by any suggestion that the authorities could make a mistake.

Phoebe learns from interacting with her relatives, but she also educates them. In Phoebe's presence, Hepzibah allows her feelings to break through her scowling exterior and sometimes even expresses warmth. Clifford comes to see that beauty and kindness do not exist solely in his imagination. And Phoebe brings to life the haunted, withdrawn world where Clifford and Hepzibah live by helping them feel connected to the rest of humanity. Meanwhile, Judge Pyncheon chokes to death on his own blood. Phoebe also corrects Holgrave's cold attitude toward her relatives, telling him in an uncharacteristically angry outburst that he needs to soften his distanced perspective with empathy.

She changes all of them. She resurrects in Clifford and Hepzibah a sense of the world's richness that moves them to try to follow her to church, but they cannot find the courage. Later, when she leaves the house briefly, they go outdoors and nervously enjoy a train ride. But Clifford and Hepzibah are too entrapped in their dusty lives for Phoebe to give them more than moments of joy. Nevertheless, by marrying Holgrave, she undermines the limited perspectives that have made the Pynchons and Maules enemies for generations and narrowed all their lives.

Phoebe and Holgrave know they are opposites. She is as conventional as he is unconventional and as warm as he is cold. But they will learn from each other and develop through their union; delight in growth and change unites them, as reflected by their shared interest in the garden. Holgrave declares at the novel's end that Phoebe has begun to transform him. And the sadness that surrounds her alters Phoebe. Tragically, as Holgrave explains to her, she must lose the unquestioning joy that she brought to her ancestral home. The marriage of their two lines represents the synthesis of two attitudes toward reality that enriches the individuals involved as well as their world. So this novel argues that although character has a clear and predictable influence on understanding and behavior, the limits of family, national, and personal history can be outgrown. *The House of the Seven Gables* suggests that genuine revolutions begin with one person loving another person intensely enough to prod both into questioning and then complicating their habitual stances toward the world. Those who find the courage to face all of reality, including their own flaws, will mature rather than crumble.

THE BLITHEDALE ROMANCE

With *The Blithedale Romance* (1852), Hawthorne not only moved his fiction into the present, he wrote a novel about a colony set apart for artists to work—a version of Brook Farm, where Hawthorne tried unsuccessfully to live and write as he searched for a mode of living that would allow him to both nourish his writing and raise a family. One group of Hawthorne's short stories consists of tales told by unreliable narrators whose productions reflect their intellectual and emotional shortcomings. He began writing these early, publishing "Wakefield," the most discussed of these tales, in 1835. Critics tend to gloss over these stories, if they comment on them at all. But in his creation of Coverdale, the protagonist of *The Blithedale Romance,* Hawthorne brings together a number of these narrators' faults.

Like the narrator of the earlier "Earth's Holocaust," who watches people frantically incinerate various cultural symbols because he likes fires, Coverdale has no strong motivation for joining the Blithedale experience: he just gives it a try. This passivity, like that of the earlier narrator, invites Coverdale to attach himself to others, appropriating their points of view. Since the narrator of "Earth's Holocaust" fails to notice that the judgments he adopts contradict, that tale, like most of those narrated by unreliable authors, lacks coherence. Similarly, Coverdale pries into the lives of Zenobia, Hollingsworth, and Priscilla, justifying his nosiness by claiming God has sent him these companions so he can serve as their chorus. Despite this divine basis, Coverdale takes a cavalier attitude toward his assignment, leaving Blithedale to go into town and laugh with his friends there about the fools he left behind. But then he decides he cares deeply about the people he just abandoned, so he returns to spy on them further, arriving just after an important confrontation between the three of them to which neither Coverdale nor his readers are privy. So this novel, like several of the stories with unreliable narrators, bounces from one event and perspective to another, rather than moving coherently toward a denouement.

Coverdale also manifests the spiritual arrogance possessed by other detached narrators, like the one in "Sights from a Steeple" who delivers a series of condescending judgments of the activities of the people below him, and the narrator of "Chippings with a Chisel," who observes a tombstone maker whom he judges as shallow. Like these authors, Coverdale congratulates himself on his superiority, condemning the superficiality of the society he has left behind, but he also criticizes those with whom he shares the idealistic universe of Blithedale. He constantly judges his companions, almost always negatively but rarely consistently. For instance, after linking Zenobia's beauty to her intensity and claiming that love would best fulfill her character, he later sees her as tasteless and frivolous and finally finds it bewildering that a woman with her abilities would kill herself simply because she failed at love.

Like the narrator of "The Christmas Banquet," or Roderick, the character saved by his wife's love in "Egotism," Coverdale often provides details without explaining their significance. Roderick describes three banquets where miserable people get together and only those who suffer because of attachments to others profit from these interactions. But in order to understand what he has in mind, it helps a great deal to have read the tale Hawthorne has written about him. Roderick worries that his story has fallen short, and his wife, Rosina, tells him she can understand him only because she knows him so well. So Roderick has begun to overcome his egotism but not enough to put himself in the place of his potential audience. Lacking both Roderick's self-doubt and a companion who can help him understand his limits, Coverdale unapologetically fills his novel with apparently random events. Zenobia and Priscilla appear in town shortly after Coverdale; no explanation is offered. A character named Westervelt shows up from time to time for no discernible reason. Coverdale insinuates that Westervelt has satanic qualities but does not bother to justify this conclusion. Coverdale's final proclamation that he loves Priscilla constitutes perhaps the most perplexing event of all. His interactions with her throughout the novel have provoked no deep response. On the rare occasions when he praises her, he does so ambiguously. For instance, he calls her graceful but attributes it partly to her questionable health, describing her as one "whose impalpable grace lay so singularly between disease and beauty" (*CE* 3, p. 101). And yet somehow the whole meaning of the novel supposedly rests on the reality that she is the love of his life.

This conclusion recalls "Wakefield." That narrator sets out by saying that he has no idea what moral his tale will culminate in, but he assures the reader it will appear, even if his story does not lead him to it, because "thought has always its efficacy, and every striking incident its moral" (*CE* 9, p. 131). Then he begins a rambling tale about a man named Wakefield who leaves his wife, lives nearby for twenty years, and then goes back home. The narrator makes himself very present during the telling of the tale, manipulating events, even proclaiming, "Now for a scene!" (*CE* 9, p. 137). He has little respect for Wakefield, whom he describes as a "crafty nincompoop," or even for his story, which he declares "a long whim-wham" (*CE* 9, p. 135). When Wakefield goes back into his house, the narrator suggests the reunion goes well, calling it "this happy event." But his promised moral declares that one who steps out of normal patterns is forever lost: "like Wakefield, he may become, as it were, the Outcast of the Universe" (*CE* 9, p. 140).

Like many of these narrators, including those of "Wakefield" and "Chippings with a Chisel,"

Coverdale has an emotional emptiness that makes it impossible for him to commit to Blithedale or anything else. The world exists to amuse him. As long as he finds Blithedale entertaining, he stays; when he gets bored, he goes to the city and stays there until ennui sends him back to Blithedale. Sometimes he makes things happen by pestering others. Since he dislikes the role Zenobia has adopted, he vows to prod her out of it. Suspecting Priscilla has been wounded by a moment of intimacy between Zenobia and Hollingsworth, he rubs her wound to get a reaction. Afterward he realizes his cruelty, but this recognition does not make him change. Instead, thinking that Hollingsworth must be a sad, defeated man, Coverdale arranges to see for himself as the book closes and he confronts Hollingsworth with his failure. He has a fleeting recognition that unkindness shapes much of his behavior, but he rationalizes it away, replacing it with the "truth" that he cares too much about people.

Coverdale cannot begin to accept his flaws because he has shaky self-esteem. Indeed, he has no self or integrity, the quality Hawthorne suggests is most important to producing good work. Instead, he has a miscellaneous collection of unintegrated capacities, including dependency, arrogance, coldness, and even sadism. Hollingsworth tells him he needs a purpose and, indeed, a passionate commitment to something beyond aggrandizing himself would give Coverdale's life direction, making him less interested in comforting himself by hurting others. Coverdale says he would adopt a goal if he could think of anything worthy of his efforts, as long as it didn't require too much energy. All his personal defects infect the novel until it becomes a manifestation of his emptiness. The book lacks conceptual and plot coherence. It shifts between apparently pointless details and unsupported judgments, But, most of all, the narrator's unkindness and shallowness shape the entire volume.

CONSUL IN LIVERPOOL

Despite writing and publishing *The Scarlet Letter, The House of the Seven Gables, The Snow-Image,* and *The Blithedale Romance*—as well as the anthology *True Stories of History and Biography* and a book of mythology titled *A Wonder-Book for Girls and Boys* (both in 1851)—in a period of three years, Hawthorne found himself, again, struggling to support his family. When his friend Franklin Pierce sought the presidency of the United States, he asked Hawthorne to write his campaign biography. Hawthorne obliged and, after his election, Pierce helped him out in 1853 with a consulship to Liverpool. The introverted Hawthorne found himself thrust wholesale into the world: consoling the families of sailors who perished, rescuing stranded Americans, and, worst of all, giving vacuous speeches at banquets. Although external circumstances produced this change, and although Hawthorne commented afterward that he felt as though someone else had served as consul, his move seems consistent with his work's increasing focus on actualities and the praise of those who not only think brilliantly but also function kindly in the world. In any case, given his work history, Hawthorne knew that this position would interfere with his writing. And it did.

He performed his job conscientiously. In response to a set of ninety-seven inquiries about his job, Hawthorne produced a 107-page report. Most of the others who received the same request ignored it. This performance certifies his judgment in a letter to a friend that writers, unlike politicians, deserve to be trusted. The writing he produced for the journals he kept during his time there suggests that he changed in a way that made writing well difficult: his entries lack life and depth. They read like an attempt to record his environment in the hope that eventually his descriptions will take flight. Hawthorne, unfortunately, remained sharply aware that he could not write. Presumably this happened because, like those unreliable narrators who produce bad tales, by playing a diplomatic role he lost his integrity.

He especially detested speaking at banquets, suggesting that he found this activity about as pleasant going to the gallows. He reported his gratitude to S. C. Hall for suggesting empty-headed material he could use for a speech: "I could not have found a better artist in whip-syllabub and flummery; and, without an instant's hesitation, he suggested a whole rivulet of lukewarm stuff, which I saw would be sufficiently to the purpose, if I could but remember it" (*CE* 21, p. 484). Also, after criticizing Margaret Fuller for training herself to become a certain kind of person instead of cultivating qualities that came naturally to her, Hawthorne restrained his impulse to flee all art museums and became an art connoisseur, recording many of his insights in his notebooks. He found it bewildering that he had a recurrent dream of failure when he had never enjoyed so much success, but his achievement rested on dishonesty. He vowed when a child to do nothing against his genius; he broke that pledge and lost his writing.

THE MARBLE FAUN

When he finished his work in England, Hawthorne went to France and Italy and kept more notebooks full of flat, detailed descriptions of his travels as well as of artworks he encountered. He imported some of this material directly into *The Marble Faun* (1860), his next novel, which he began in Italy and completed in England. In *The Marble Faun* he returned once more to the subject of art, but this time his discussion was totally free of irony, arguing directly for aesthetic ideals implied by his other work.

In this novel, Hawthorne links sin, maturity, and the work of art. It presents Hawthorne's only sympathetic portrait of a materialist in its characterization of Donatello, an Italian uncontaminated by American moralism. His antithesis, the religious Hilda, is repeatedly linked to the Puritans. Both live in a sin-free world, but Donatello's consists of pleasant, almost animalistic sensations while an otherworldly spiritualism pervades Hilda's. Donatello becomes associated with the hedonism of the Faun, while Hilda's pristine life links her to the Virgin.

The novel's denouement focuses on shifts in these two characters when sin disrupts their worlds, enriching them. Both surrender the easy pleasure of their earlier lives: Donatello can no longer empathize with forest animals and Hilda's capacity for losing herself in the religious works of the great masters deteriorates. Their encounters with sin shock them both, but Donatello acquires new depths, and Hilda comes to understand the value of losing her simplistic worldview. Both of them acquire a greater capacity to connect with and understand others.

Their friends and lovers, Miriam and Kenyon, contrast with Hilda and Donatello in their acceptance of human complication as well as in their willingness to reach out to their friends. They associate purity with superficiality and seek confrontation with their opposites because they believe disruption will complicate and improve them. Moreover, in this novel, Hawthorne ties the collapse of a narrow point of view and the construction of a truer, broader perspective not only to increased tolerance for others but also to a more discriminating artistic sense. Miriam and Kenyon are both artists, and while they sympathize with Hilda and Donatello, they consider Donatello's and Hilda's transformations positive.

The novel says little about the relationship between Kenyon's art and his perspective, but Miriam's troubled life has supplied her with a background that allows her to produce beautifully balanced works of art. Her paintings reflect a delicate blend of the physical and spiritual, of conformity and independence, and of reason and emotion in their portrait of an idealized domesticity pervaded by deep feeling and rich imagination. Hawthorne finally produces a picture of artistic success, but in the novel generally considered his weakest. Hawthorne had become so disconnected from his former self that in 1854, when *Mosses from an Old Manse* was republished, he reread it and found it bewildering. In the introduction to *Our Old Home* (1863), a book about England, Hawthorne says it embarrasses him to publish journal entries he had hoped to use as background for his fiction, but he finds himself shut out of the imaginative world: "The Present, the Immediate, the Actual, has proven too potent for me" (*CE* 5, p. 4).

After Hawthorne returned to the United States, free to produce whatever he liked, he wrote extensively: massive manuscripts survive from these years. But he did not publish any of them, and critics rarely speak of them. Although some critics believe Hawthorne's rendition of himself as fundamentally isolated was a pose, it does seem that moving completely into the world interfered fatally with his ability to enter into the imaginative worlds that dominated his earlier fiction. Others suggest that his depression over the Civil War resulted in physical problems that impeded his writing. Still others suggest that he had developed into a fine nonfiction writer but refused to accept the change and continued to cling, fruitlessly, to his fictional work. In any case, that he never attempted to publish the long manuscripts left behind at his death suggests that no one understood better than Hawthorne that even though he continued to write, his creative life had stagnated. But his persistence suggests a faith that if he just kept working, the complicated, subtle awareness that enriched his best work would return. Be that as it may, he passed away on May 19, 1864, from mysterious physical causes undoubtedly nourished by his writing frustrations, leaving behind a large collection of unpublished material.

Given his repeated discovery that mundane work obstructed his fiction writing, Hawthorne knew that he put his literary career at serious risk when he accepted the consulship in Liverpool. But his making this choice shows he embraced the claim his works assert repeatedly: that one's connections to other human beings matter far more than anything else, even artistic achievement. His family needed money, so he provided it. And that choice seems to have slowly undermined the imaginative richness that had produced such a wide variety of wonderful work. But, finally, it seems a condemnation of Hawthorne's society that it rewarded him so generously for functioning well as a bureaucrat but made it so difficult for him to survive on the earnings resulting from one of the most successful literary careers the United States has ever seen.

Selected Bibliography

WORKS OF NATHANIEL HAWTHORNE

The Centenary Edition of the Works of Nathaniel Hawthorne. Edited by William Charval, Roy Harvey Pearce, Claude M. Simpson, and Thomas Woodson. 23 vols. Columbus: Ohio State University Press, 1962–1994.

Hawthorne as Editor: Selections from His Writings in rhe "American Magazine of Useful and Entertaining Knowledge." Edited by Arlin Turner. University: Louisiana University Press, 1941.

BIBLIOGRAPHIES AND CONCORDANCES

Boswell, Jeanetta. *Nathaniel Hawthorne and the Critics: A Checklist of Criticism, 1900–1978.* Metuchen, N.J.: Scarecrow Press, 1982.

Browne, Nina E. *A Bibliography of Nathaniel Hawthorne.* Boston: Houghton, Mifflin, 1905.

Byers, John R., and James Jarratt Owen. *A Concordance to the Five Novels of Nathaniel Hawthorne.* 2 vols. New York: Garland, 1979.

Clark, C. E. Frazer. *The Merrill Checklist of Nathaniel Hawthorne.* Columbus, Ohio: C. E. Merrill, 1970.

———. *Nathaniel Hawthorne: A Descriptive Bibliography.* Pittsburgh, Pa.: University of Pittsburgh Press, 1978. bibcit.composed>

Gross, Theodore L., and Stanley Wertheim. *Hawthorne, Melville, Stephen Crane: A Critical Bibliography.* New York: Free Press, 1971.

Jones, Buford. *A Checklist of Hawthorne Criticism, 1951–1966.* Hartford, Conn.: Transcendental Books, 1967.

Martin, Terrence. *Nathaniel Hawthorne.* Boston: Twayne, 1983.

Newman, Lea Bertani Vozar. *A Reader's Guide to the Short Stories of Nathaniel Hawthorne.* Boston: G. K. Hall, 1979.

Scharnhorst, Gary. *Nathaniel Hawthorne: An Annotated Bibliography of Comment and Criticism Before 1900.* Metuchen, N.J.: Scarecrow Press, 1988.

Wilson, James C. "The Hawthorne--&Melville Relationship: An Annotated Bibliography." *ATQ (American Transcendental Quarterly)* 45–48:5–79 (1980).

CRITICAL AND BIOGRAPHICAL STUDIES

Argersinger, Jana L., and Leland S. Person. *Hawthorne and Melville: Writing a Relationship.* Athens: University of Georgia Press, 2008.

Baym, Nina. *The Shape of Hawthorne's Career.* Ithaca, N.Y.: Cornell University Press, 1976.

Bell, Millicent, ed. *Hawthorne and the Real: Bicentennial Essays.* Columbus: Ohio University Press, 2005.

Bosco, Ronald A., and Jillmarie Murphy. *Hawthorne in His Own Time.* Iowa City: University of Iowa Press, 2007.

Bridge, Horatio. *Personal Recollections of Nathaniel Hawthorne.* New York: Haskell House, 1968.

Brodhead, Richard H. *The School of Hawthorne.* New York: Oxford University Press, 1986.

Coale, Samuel Chase. *The Entanglements of Nathaniel Hawthorne: Haunted Minds and Ambiguous Approaches.* Rochester, N.Y.: Camden House, 2011.

Colacurcio, Michael J. *The Province of Piety: Moral History in Hawthorne's Early Tales.* Cambridge, Mass.: Harvard University Press, 1984.

Crews, Frederick C. *The Sins of the Fathers: Hawthorne's Psychological Themes.* Berkeley: University of California Press, 1989.

Dolis, John. *The Style of Hawthorne's Gaze.* Tuscaloosa: University of Alabama Press, 1993.

Fogle, Richard H. *Hawthorne's Fiction: The Light & the Dark.* Norman: University of Oklahoma Press, 1964.

Folsom, James K. *Man's Accidents and God's Purposes: Multiplicity in Hawthorne's Fiction.* New Haven, Conn.: College and University Press, 1963.

Gilmore, Michael T. *American Romanticism and the Marketplace.* Chicago: University of Chicago Press, 1985.

Greven, David. *The Fragility of Manhood: Hawthorne, Freud, and the Politics of Gender.* Columbus: Ohio State University Press, 2012.

Hawthorne, Julian. *Nathaniel Hawthorne and His Wife.* 2 vols. Boston: James R. Osgood, 1889.

James, Henry. *Hawthorne.* New York: Harper, 1879.

Male, Roy R. *Hawthorne's Tragic Vision.* Austin: University of Texas Press, 1957.

Marshall, Meagan. *The Peabody Sisters: Three Women Who Ignited American Romanticism.* Boston: Houghton Mifflin, 2005.

McPherson, Hugo. *Hawthorne as Myth-Maker: A Study in Imagination.* Toronto: University of Toronto Press, 1969.

Milder, Robert. *Hawthorne's Habitations: A Literary Life.* Oxford: Oxford University Press, 2013.

Millington, Richard H. *Practicing Romance: Narrative Form and Cultural Engagement in Hawthorne's Fiction.* Princeton, N.J.: Princeton University Press, 2014.

Reynolds, Larry J. *A Historical Guide to Nathaniel Hawthorne.* Oxford, U.K.: Oxford University Press, 2001.

———. *Devils and Rebels: The Making of Hawthorne's Damned Politics.* Ann Arbor: University of Michigan Press, 2010.

Stewart, Randall. *Nathaniel Hawthorne: A Biography.* New Haven, Conn.: Yale University Press, 1961.

Turner, Arlin. *Nathaniel Hawthorne: A Biography.* New York: Oxford University Press, 1980.

West, Peter. *The Arbiters of Reality: Hawthorne, Melville, and the Rise of Mass Information Culture.* Columbus: Ohio State University Press, 2008.

Wineapple, Brenda. *Hawthorne: A Life.* New York: Random House, 2003.

Wright, Sarah Bird. *Critical Companion to Nathaniel Hawthorne: A Literary Reference to His Life and Work.* New York: Facts on File, 2006.

FILMS, PLAYS, AND OPERAS BASED ON THE WORKS OF NATHANIEL HAWTHORNE

The Scarecrow. Play by Percy MacKaye. Garrick Theatre, New York City, 1911. (Adaptation of "Feathertop.")

Puritan Passions. Silent film. Screenplay by Frank Tuttle. Directed by Frank Tuttle. W. W. Hodkinson, 1923. (Adaptation of Percy MacKaye's play.)

The Scarlet Letter. Silent film. Screenplay by Frances Marion. Directed by Victor Seastrom. MGM, 1926.

Merry Mount. Opera. Music by Howard Hanson; libretto by Richard Stokes. May Festival, University of Michigan, May 20, 1933. (Adaptation of "The Maypole of Merry Mount.")

The Scarlet Letter. Screenplay by Leonard Fields and David Silverstein. Directed by Robert G. Vignola. Majestic Pictures, 1934.

The House of the Seven Gables. Screenplay by Lester Cole. Directed by Joe May. Universal Pictures, 1940.

Twice-Told Tales. Screenplay by Robert E. Kent. Directed by Sidney Salkow. United Artists, 1963. (Adaptations of "Dr. Heidegger's Experiment," "Rappaccini's Daughter," and *The House of the Seven Gables.*)

The Old Glory. Play by Robert Lowell. American Place Theatre, New York, 1964. (Adaptations of "Endicott and the Red Cross" and "My Kinsman, Major Molineux.")

The Scarecrow. Television adaptation of the play by Percy MacKaye. Directed by Boris Sagal. PBS, 1972.

The Scarlet Letter. Screenplay by Tankred Dorst, Ursula Ehler, Bernardo Fernández, and Wim Wenders. Directed by Wim Wenders. Westdeutscher Rundfunk, 1973.

The Scarlet Letter. Play by Phyllis Nagy. Classic Stage Company, New York City, 1994.

The Scarlet Letter. Screenplay by Douglas Day Stewart. Directed by Roland Joffé. Buena Vista, 1995.

The Scarecrow. Opera. Music by Joseph Turrin; libretto by Bernard Stambler. University of Texas at Austin, 2006. (Adaptation of Percy MacKaye's play.)

shAme. Rock opera by Mark Governor. Directed and choreographed by Janet Roston. Los Angeles Rock Opera Company, 2008.

Easy A. Screenplay by Bert V. Royal. Directed by Will Gluck. Screen Gems, 2010.

The Scarlet Letter. Opera. Music and libretto by Margaret Garwood. Academy of Local Arts, Philadelphia, 2010.

The Scarlet Letter. Opera. Music by Lori Laitman; libretto by David Mason. Opera Colorado, May 7, 2013.

ZORA NEALE HURSTON

(1891—1960)

Windy Counsell Petrie

LIKE THE LEGENDARY Mule Bone for which her ill-fated 1930 stage collaboration with Langston Hughes was named, Zora Neale Hurston's life, work, and reputation have been disputed, picked over, and wielded in ideological debates from the 1920s to the present day. A complex woman, about whom scholars are still discovering biographical facts more than fifty years after her death, Hurston wrote, researched, created, and performed in many modes and genres, often overlapping forms to create hybrids for multiple purposes and for multiple audiences. Her works proffer ample room for divergent, sometimes opposite, interpretations of the same material, depending on the critical lens through which they are read. Ranging from classical mythology to African oral tradition, holiness rituals of the Christian Sanctified Church to Haitian voodoo practice, the folk of rural Florida to the sophisticated denizens of New York, Hurston herself utilized just as many sources of inspiration in her lifetime as there are critical lenses through which to read her now. Her continual travels, via means as prestigious as Guggenheim fellowships and as humble as domestic service, provided her with a steady stream of new material, material that she always used to reflect back on her roots. Everywhere she went, and in everything she wrote, her indefatigable spirit and insistent individuality could equally charm and frustrate those who encountered her in person or on the page.

ROOTS

Zora Neale Hurston was born on January 15, 1891, in Nostulga, Alabama. The date and the place were only confirmed more than five decades after her death, as Hurston altered both of them in a number of official and unofficial ways—and for multiple reasons—over the course of her lifetime. Hurston always claimed to have been born in the all-black town of Eatonville, Florida, perhaps because it was the first community she consciously remembered being a part of, or perhaps because she loved the idea of hailing from an entirely independent African American community. The sixth child of John and Lucy Hurston, Hurston was named Zora Neal Lee Hurston, according to the family Bible. It's not clear when and why she eliminated the Lee and added the "e" to Neal, but we do know that she came into the world as dramatically as she would traverse it later. On a day when the entire community was out participating in the annual hog-killing, working together to preserve the meat for the rest of the year, Hurston was born with no doctor or midwife present, according to her autobiography. Her umbilical cord was cut by a white neighbor who had come to bring some of the meat from his hogs and produce from his garden to the Hurstons. This "robust, gray-haired white man," whose name Hurston could not recall, apparently saw this happenstance as a call to take the little girl under his wing as she grew (*Dust Tracks on a Road,* p. 30). Hurston spent many hours fishing with him while he listened to her endless childish ruminations and gave her advice about life in return.

Once the family moved to Eatonville, Hurston would lurk under the general store's porch, listening to the content and the cadence of the town gossip, running away when she was caught hearing things not meant for young ears. Obsessed with listening to and telling stories, she would then perch on the fencepost at the edge of the highway, often trading a mile's worth of stories and tall tales for rides in white folks' automobiles—a practice that deeply worried her parents. These liminal positions would prefigure a career of border-crossing. Ultimately, Hurston would spend her life investigating and translating cultural and regional wisdom, folly, and practice, always in motion, making the best of whatever resources, financial, natural, or human, she could muster.

Little Zora's bold adventurousness was a source of distress to both of her parents. John Hurston feared she would meet a violent end, too spunky for white society to tolerate in the turn-of-the-twentieth-century South. For instance, when Zora asked for a fine white horse for Christmas, he threatened to beat her for such insouciant ambition (Boyd, p. 14). And while Lucy Hurston indulged her youngest daughter's dream of riding around on that same imaginary horse, she also wondered if a local enemy had cursed her child via "hoodoo" (the term for the form of syncretic voodoo in the American South), by sprinkling "traveling dust" on her doorstep when Zora was born (p. 25). Lucy protected her youngest daughter's big dreams and wild imagination from John's frequent frustrations with them, often encouraging her child to "jump at de sun" (*Dust Tracks,* p. 13).

Perhaps the difference in Hurston's parents' backgrounds explains the difference in their reactions to their bold, fearless, daughter. John came from a family of poor sharecroppers, while Lucy's family were successful landowners and quite wealthy for an African American family in the postbellum South. Lucy's family had objected strenuously to her daughter's marriage to a poor boy from an undistinguished family, despite his charming manners and skill at carpentry, even refusing to attend the wedding. John Hurston was definitely marrying up, and the community often referred to him as a "wife-made man" (Boyd, p. 25). Whatever the reason for it, John Hurston did significantly increase his social status after his marriage to Lucy. He eventually became a landowner in his own right, served as mayor of Eatonville from 1912–1916, and was a well-known pastor in Sanford, Florida. Valued for his powerful, engaging preaching, John Hurston's success provided an example of how to employ the power of words that would inspire Zora's own career and sustain her throughout her life.

But John Hurston's success, and the charm that helped engender it, would contribute to a rocky marriage between him and Lucy, one that would inspire Hurston's lifelong interest in and exploration of gender roles and politics in relationships, a topic around which most of her fiction revolves. A jealous and proud husband, John Hurston continually cheated on his wife but threatened to kill her if she so much as teased him about finding a man who would appreciate her. Perhaps his sense of being the lesser in status coming into the marriage, the sting of being known as "wife-made," or merely the chauvinistic attitudes that his daughter would repeatedly dissect in her long and short fiction contributed to these inappropriate demonstrations of power that so hurt his wife and children. To his children, the most painful choice he made was remarrying, less than five months after Lucy Hurston died in 1904, a woman close to the same age as his oldest son. The marriage caused the whole town to speculate that he'd been having an affair with this woman, Mattie Moge, before his wife died. Moge's disinterest in caring for Lucy and John's children would inspire Zora not only to base an evil character on her, in her first novel, *Jonah's Gourd Vine* (1934)but also to engage in a violent physical confrontation with her years later.

The pain, anger, and rejection that came to a boil in that confrontation reveals the depth of the tragedy that her mother's early death was for young Zora. She always described herself as her "mama's child," while her docile older sister Sarah was clearly John Hurston's favorite. Losing her mother in the middle of puberty, Zora not only lost her primary source of female guidance, but she also lost her home in her beloved Eatonville, which meant leaving its highly effective school. The Hungerford School was a strict, Booker T. Washington–inspired institution in which Zora had impressed visitors with her intellect and oratory, so much so that they mailed her gifts of clothes and, more importantly, books, which would become models for her own future writing. Still in the early stages of grieving for her mother, Zora was sent away to another school, only to have her father quit paying her tuition within a year. As a result she was publicly shamed at the new school.

Unwelcome at both home and school, the teenaged Zora became essentially homeless, wandering to live with one sibling and then another for about ten years, helping out in their homes and businesses, possibly cohabiting with an unknown, abusive man around 1914–1915, and then working as a ladies' maid for a traveling Gilbert and Sullivan theater troupe. All the while, she yearned to continue her education, but she was unable to. However, she persevered, until she finally conceived the idea of erasing ten years from her age on an application to qualify for free public education in Baltimore, where Hurston finished high school at age twenty-six. Her craving for knowledge, her unique perspective, and her notable spunk would get her noticed by influential people again, and lead her northward to prestigious colleges: Howard, Barnard, and Columbia, in that order. While she attended Howard, a historically black college in Washington, D.C., Hurston balanced the social and academic expectations of the college with her work schedule, listening to stories of power-brokering from Washington insiders as she manicured their hands at her off-campus job. At school, she attained her first literary successes, writing poems and her first published short story, "John Redding goes to Sea," for the campus literary magazine, the *Stylus*. Always bestriding at least two worlds at once, she recognized the grand scope of her curiosity and ambition and openly wished for her own pair of "seven-league boots" to make it easier (Boyd, p. 111).

THE HARLEM RENAISSANCE

Having left Howard, most likely because of a combination of illness and impecuniosity, Hurston moved to New York in 1924, where one of her brothers was living. She found quick success as a creative writer, winning awards for her play "Color Struck" and her short story "Spunk" in *Opportunity* magazine in 1925. Her Harlem friends and acquaintances included the best-selling authors Carl Van Vechten and Fannie Hurst as well as the Harlem Renaissance luminaries Langston Hughes, Countee Cullen, James Weldon Johnson, Wallace Thurman, Dorothy West, Jesse Fauset, and Alain Locke. Gaining in reputation, she began attending Barnard College—an all-women college run in association with the all-male Columbia College—in September 1925, supporting herself by her work as Hurst's secretary until she was awarded a scholarship in February 1926. Taking courses at Columbia University to round out her studies, Hurston met Franz Boas, the prominent anthropologist, and impressed him enough that he helped get her a fellowship in 1927. Because of her training in Boas's participant-observer method, Hurston is now studied almost as frequently by anthropologists as by literature scholars. The scholar Lynda Hoffman-Jeep has compared Hurston to ethnographers such as Lydia Cabrera, Anzia Yezierska, and Hungarian Roma narrators, paralleling their use of "creative ethnographic strategies as part of their response to scholarly tradition" (p. 337).

In the twenty-first century, a handful of short stories that Hurston wrote and set in Harlem in the period 1927–1933 were discovered in microfilm copies of the *Pittsburgh Courier* and given critical attention by various scholars. Including the titles "She Rock" (1927), "Monkey Junk: A Satire on Modern Divorce," and "The Country in the Woman" (1933), these stories seem to critique both the Great Migration (the concentrated movement of rural, southern blacks to the urban north in the early twentieth century) and the fabled "New Negro" of the northern city by satirizing urban sophistication, sympathizing with characters who fall victim to urban philandering, freeloading, and gold-digging and by celebrating characters who overcome such things. M. Genevieve West argues that Hurston's early impressions of Harlem model a "folk-based, alternative ... identity" to the prevalent urban ethos of the era (p. 478).

Hurston graduated from Barnard in 1928—in absentia, because she was already on the road studying African American folk culture in Florida. She had met Charlotte Osgood Mason, a prominent philanthropist, before she left New York, and Mason would pick up the financial slack when Hurston's first research grant ran out. Mason, who also served as a patron to Langston Hughes and Alain Locke, among others, would fund Hurston's research trips, dramatic productions, and domestic expenses intermittently for most of Hurston's career. Though Mason could be difficult and controlling, and insisted that whatever material Hurston found was legally Mason's property—a dictate that Hurston found creative ways to circumvent when need be—Mason nearly always came through with assistance whenever Hurston needed it, and her funding allowed Hurston to travel, research, and write intermittently during the period 1927–1932.

These early research trips provided Hurston with the material for *Mules and Men* (1935), a loose blend of folklore, autobiography, and anthropological scholarship, along with several scholarly articles for the *Journal of American Folklore* and numerous plays and stage productions. Having met up with and traveled from the South to New York with Langston Hughes in 1927, then having corresponded with him in 1928 and 1929, she and Hughes set about adapting some of Hurston's Eatonville material into a play, titled *Mule Bone,* in 1930. The play was originally about two friends whose dispute over a wild turkey expands into a town-wide dispute over theological differences, but Hughes felt that it would be more attractive as a Broadway production if the men fought over a woman instead. This, among other creative and personal differences, ended their collaboration, but Hurston continued writing for the theater for financial reasons, including rewriting *Mule Bone* on her own, an action that led to a public dispute eerily similar to the dispute in the play, as each sought to defend their own actions to their mutual friends.

Moving on to other projects, Hurston created and produced her own stage concert, *The Great Day,* based on her observations of life in the Florida lumber camps. It was a great artistic success (if not a financial one) when first staged at the John Golden Theatre in New York in 1932, and she would reprise it a number of times in a number of places—not only in New York but also in the cities of Chicago and St. Louis, and in venues in North Carolina and Florida—throughout the 1930s and 1940s, sometimes transporting her dancers to performances in her own car, when she was lucky enough to have one. Not only did the production serve to provide advance publicity for her forthcoming books, but Hurston believed it to be a more authentic correction and counterbalance to other popular "Negro" musicals of the time, such as the Broadway hits *Showboat* (1927) or *Porgy and Bess* (1935), which she considered "not true to our lives" (*Zora Neale Hurston: A Life in Letters,* p. 499).

In May 1932, Hurston convinced Mason to fund her move to Florida, where she could live and work much more cheaply than in New York. This established a recognizable pattern in Hurston's life: she repeatedly returned home to Florida to warm up from northern winters and cool off from northern pressures. Wherever she found to roost on her numerous returns to Florida, she would immediately plant a garden with vegetables and flowers and get back to a writing routine.

JONAH'S GOURD VINE

Although *Mules and Men* was really written first, Hurston's first published work was *Jonah's Gourd Vine* (1934), a loosely autobiographical novel set in Eatonville in which Hurston laid the ghosts of her parents to rest in a fashion not dissimilar to the way that Virginia Woolf invoked her parents in 1927's *To the Lighthouse.* The original title of *Jonah's Gourd Vine* was "Big Nigger," a name John Hurston's children were known to have called him behind his back. The deathbed scene of Lucy Pearson, the strong, virtuous, long-suffering wife of this "wife-made man," reads as an almost exact parallel to the description of Lucy Hurston's death in Hurston's autobiography *Dust Tracks on a Road* (1942), the one exception being that the novel adds a violent slap from John Pearson, when he can no longer stand his wife's bold, fearless, truth-telling about his sins. Their child, Isis, experiences her mother's death the way Zora describes she did in *Dust Tracks.* Isis was a name Hurston also used to portray her semiautobiographical self in other early texts, particularly the 1924 short story "Drenched in Light."

The novel is dedicated to African American preachers, to whom she refers as "the first and only real Negro poets in America." Its title also has a rich allusive spiritual history. In the Bible (Jonah 4:6–10), Jonah's gourd vine provided him with protective shade and was given to him by God, but the vine withered and died because of his disobedience. The book's protagonist, the preacher John Pearson, is, like Jonah, a man called by God whose selfishness ultimately precludes him from fulfilling his purpose. In African American folklore, the gourd vine was a mythic symbol of bringing on one's own downfall; in the same folklore, preachers were the butt of many jokes about Sunday anointing and weekday cupidity. Interestingly enough, Hurston notes in her autobiography that she was referred to as a gourd vine as a child; perhaps a hint that her boldness would also contribute to her father's downfall (Lowe, p. 88). Indeed, John Hurston's spirit was broken when he witnessed the horrible fight between his daughter and his second wife, and Zora never saw him again after that, not even returning for his funeral.

In the novel, the gourd vine signifies the blight that rots the vine of John Pearson's success in the text. Critics speculate that it is Pearson's charisma that leads to both his rise and his downfall. It helps him woo his first wife, the one who helps him rise in social status and become a preacher. But his success with women also leads to affairs, especially one with the evil character, Hattie, his second wife, the one clearly inspired by Mattie Moge. Critics speculate that Hattie herself might be the worm that withers John Pearson's gourd vine and leads to his downfall.

When the book came out, Hurston had the sense and foresight to send advance copies of the book to key black intellectuals, such as W. E. B. Du Bois—something her publisher, Lippincott, had not thought to do. Named a Book-of-the-Month Club title, the novel was almost universally well-reviewed, giving an excellent start to Hurston's career as a novelist and folklorist. Reviewers lauded her "authenticity," and her "superb" use of dialogue, praising "the beauty of the Negro dialect," declaring Hurston a source of "double authority ... as a Negro and a student of folklore" (quoted in West, p. 484). Such praise gave her an authoritative platform for her observations in Nancy Cunard's *Negro* anthology of the same year. In her groundbreaking essay "Characteristics of Negro Expression," her outspoken *American Mercury* essay titled "You Don't Know Us Negroes," and her December 1934 *Washington Tribune* piece, "Race Cannot Become Great Until It Recognizes Its Talent," she spoke boldly, the last essay indicting fellow black writers for "emulating whites" and exhorting them to create something "which is our own." (n.p.). The authentic characteristics she found in "Negro Expression" included "drama," "asymmetry," and the "will to adorn," by which she meant linguistic improvisation. By these means, she contends that both secular and sacred language become unique works of art, including not only polished and striking metaphor and simile, but double-layered adjectives, and verbal nouns (Moylan, p. 27). Another Hurston essay from 1934, "Spirituals and Neo-Spirituals," also focuses on the need for improvisation within traditional forms, explaining that there are "definite forms" to religious expressions, ranging from "sermons, prayers, moans, and testimonies," but that individuality is also prized, with each individual innovating within the form to create "new ornaments" (Krasner, p. 83).

Her fiction, folklore, and scholarly essays had vaulted Hurston into the national spotlight, and, influenced by her successful Chicago production of *The Great Day* in 1935, the Rosenwald Fund awarded her a fellowship to conduct doctoral study in anthropology at Columbia. When the amount was reduced from three thousand to seven hundred dollars until she could prove she was a steady, dedicated student, Hurston had the last laugh by dropping her coursework and taking the reduced grant on the road instead. Her travel would maximize the reduced amount's effectiveness in gathering anthropological knowledge, as she facilely explained in a letter to the foundation. Before she left Columbia, Hurston had become involved with a fellow graduate student, Percival Punter. However, he wanted her to give up her career for marriage, a dispute they never resolved, once coming to blows in their mutual anger (Boyd, p. 275). Though their marriage (the first of three short-lived marriages for Hurston, always to much younger men) would not last, she considered Punter the love of her life and they stayed in contact until near the end of Hurston's life, by which time they could write friendly letters about his work as a doctor and hers as a writer. Hurston ended what she felt was becoming a toxic relationship in 1935 by fleeing back to the South, using the Rosenwald grant to research and awaiting the release of *Mules and Men.*

MULES AND MEN

Published in October 1935 as a more accessible version of the material she had collected for the *Journal of American Folklore, Mules and Men* is a fascinating blend of autobiography, anthology, folklore, and fiction, with no clear demarcations between any of these modes. Hurston convinced Franz Boas to write a foreword for the book by arguing that it would spread her expert observations more broadly than scholarly journal articles and claiming that the editors at Lippincott favored the autobiographical narrative style for its easy readability. Critics have claimed that the book itself, as well as the story of how it came to be, is a "trickster's bible" (Washington, p. 263), showcasing folktales, songs, tall tales, and "signifying." "Signifying" is a broad term inclusive of multiple types of wordplay in which one can say one thing but mean another, or say one thing that means multiple things to different listeners. A traditionally African folkloric practice that has become a strong component of African American literature as well, it and the other oral-traditional practices in African American culture were used as "everyday acts of resistance ... in the Jim Crow South" (Nicholls, p. 467). The book interpolates tales of everyday life in the lumber camps with classic folktales of Brer Rabbit, John Henry, and folkloric explanations for the existence of the soul, the origins of the battle of the sexes, or the rivalry between cats and dogs. Of particular note is the legend of God's giving women "three keys"—to the kitchen, to the bedroom, and to the cradle—which would help them balance out of the physical and socioeconomic power of men (p. 33).

The last section of *Mules and Men* focuses on hoodoo, describing curses and "recipes" for their invocation and offering anthropological explanations for the existence and true nature of hoodoo, including recollections of her own tutelage by Louisiana practitioners who were often also Christian pastors, and a description of the ceremony by which Hurston became a "Boss of candles" (p. 217). Henry Louis Gates, Jr., and Teresa Washington have also traced some elements of the material in *Mules and Men* back to African sources, particularly Yoruban divination verses, and folklore. Overall, the text is like a maze in the twists and turns of which one becomes happily lost until suddenly jettisoned out into the familiar world at the end.

America's deepening economic depression found Hurston, along with many other writers, on government relief, working for the federal theater project of the Works Progress Administration (WPA) in 1935 along with writers such as Orson Welles. Always indefatigably translating narratives into different cultural contexts, Hurston staged a version of Macbeth set in Haiti with voodoo at its center for the WPA project, and then landed a prestigious Guggenheim Flowship—for two thousand dollars—to study voodoo in Jamaica and Haiti in 1936. Also preoccupying her mind was an idea for another project of cultural translation and intercultural exploration: researching the prevalence of the Moses myth in the Caribbean. She successfully renewed the Guggenheim in 1937, and these combined trips would ultimately yield three new books: *Their Eyes Were Watching God* (1937), *Tell My Horse* (1938), and *Moses, Man of the Mountain* (1939).

THEIR EYES WERE WATCHING GOD

Having arrived in Haiti to conduct research, Hurston holed in up her hotel room for the first seven weeks, frenetically writing the book that encapsulated her feelings about her doomed marriage to Punter. Finished by December 1936, *Their Eyes Were Watching God* (1937) follows its protagonist, Janie Crawford, through her three marriages and continual search for the "horizon," a trope also echoed and emphasized in Hurston's 1942 autobiography, *Dust Tracks on a Road.* First married, at her grandmother's behest, to Logan Killicks, an older man with sixty acres and the only organ in town, then to Joe Starks, a successful man of the type that the Eatonville folks would have called a "big nigger," who often belittles Janie to make himself feel as big as he looks, Janie finally finds the "sweet" love about which she had always dreamed with her third husband, the young, playful, laborer and musician called "Tea Cake." However, when Tea Cake is bitten by a rabid dog in the aftermath of a Florida hurricane, Janie ends up on trial for shooting him to save her own life. Acquitted at the trial, she returns to her hometown to acquit herself to the community as a self-determined, fully realized, independent woman.

This novel was well-reviewed by everyone except for the black intelligentsia, primarily Alain Locke and Richard Wright, who both objected to its lack of focus on racial injustice. Writing her own scathing, sarcastic counterattack, Hurston instead panned Wright's *Uncle Tom's Children* (1938), labeling it "a book about hatreds" with "tone-deaf" dialect and "not one act of understanding or sympathy" (quoted in Carpio and Sollors, p. B6).

TELL MY HORSE

Hurston herself manifested more a significant, though imperfect, effort to acquire a sympathetic understanding of the cultural practices of Jamaica and Haiti in 1938's *Tell My Horse,* a volume that has a feeling similar to *Mules and Men* but from a less intimate perspective than the earlier volume. Early reviewers seemed less enthusiastic about Hurston's usual mélange of genres, with Harold Courlander musing, "Here is a curious mixture of remembrances, travelogue, sensationalism, and anthropology" and that "the material was not completely digested" ("Witchcraft in the Caribbean Island," reprinted in Cronin, pp. 141–142). Other reviewers valued the text for its informativeness: one noting that Hurston took the first-ever-known photo of a Haitian "zombie" and that the volume was "an important chapter in the conflict and fusion of cultures" (C. G. Woodson, reprinted in Cronin, p. 146) and another calling it a "harvest unbelievably rich" (Carl Carmer, "In Haiti and Jamaica," reprinted in Cronin, p. 144). Hurston's biographer Robert Hemenway regarded it as her least successful work. More recent critics have noted that the prevailing narrative uncertainty in *Tell My Horse* replaces the authority present in *Mules and Men.*

The book, a loose collection of topically arranged chapters, has three essential foci: voodoo practice, the role of women in Caribbean cultures, and the American occupation of Haiti (1915–1934). However, one could conclude that all three primary topics are really about the machinations of power. Hurston contemplatively concludes that the Haitians she met took the risks involved in voodoo out of desperation. Many critics have highlighted this idea in the text, labeling voodoo a means of leveling the playing field or creating cultural resistance to imperialist occupation. The volume is titled in reference to a voodoo practice wherein a spirit, called a *loa,* "mounts" a "horse," the term for a person in an induced trance. The "horse" then speaks—not, ostensibly, for him- or herself but for the possessing spirit (p. 221). Depending on what a reader/observor believes is actually happening—which Hurston does not commit to in the text, adding taglines such as "if you want to look at it like that" (p. 329)—either the "horse" is being silenced, or he or she is speaking for themselves but cannot be held responsible for their words because of their ostensible possession.

Tell My Horse also focuses on the subjugation of women in Jamaica, their reduction to well-trained sex objects, and the resistance of Haiti's Celestina Simon, whom Hurston calls the Black Joan of Arc, through secret voodoo rituals. Indeed, the book claims that female sexuality serves as a primary motivation and power in voodoo practice. Other embedded texts in the book suggest voodoo might be mostly a show designed to gain power, particularly in its conclusion, which relates a folktale called "God and the Pintards." The story goes that God was angry with the "pintards," or guinea fowl, and intended to destroy them. However, they charm those sent to exterminate them by a continual show of song and dance, and they eventually charm God himself in the same way, thus saving their own lives. As Emery observes, "The pintards' cannily strategic performance of primitivism demonstrates once again that the vulnerable and powerless have the ability ... to subvert authority from below" (p. 334). Emery connects this observation not only to the coded tales in *Mules and Men* but potentially to voodoo itself as a distracting, subversive, performance that aims to appropriate power. But Hurston also seems to feel uneasy about the voiceless suffering of the victims of voodoo, both animal and human, describing the bloody ritualistic torture of animals and specifically noting that the zombie she photographed was trying to hide her face from the camera and was physically forced to submit to Hurston's visual documentation. Hurston herself fled Haiti in 1937 after becoming violently, terrifyingly ill; she was nearly certain she had been either poisoned or cursed for her investigations of voodoo secrets. As Amy Fass Emery has observed, Hurston herself was abruptly silenced by her mysterious illness, possibly an object of voodoo rather than just the practicing subject she intended to be.

Having fled to New York after her brush with death in Haiti, Hurston promoted *Their Eyes Were Watching God,* which had recently been released, and then found herself more work with the WPA, this time on the Florida Writers' Project, in May 1938. Somehow, while investigating the Sanctified Church and staging her own concerts for the project, she also finished writing *Moses, Man of the Mountain,* living happily in Eatonville with one of her nieces, writing in the yard in her overalls, enjoying one of those intermittent times at peace with nature and with herself that Hurston so cherished, the same kind she allows Janie Crawford to find at the end of *Their Eyes Were Watching God.*

MOSES, MAN OF THE MOUNTAIN

In her 1939 novel, Hurston shocked even those who knew her well with her irrepressible audacity. While her first novel had taken on the powerful figure of the Southern black preacher, *Moses, Man of the Mountain* seemed to take on not only her entire race but also God himself. While African American oral and literary tradition had often equated itself with the beleaguered Israelites, a people who suffered in slavery but were also chosen by God, Hurston transforms Moses into an ethnic Egyptian, which many critics read as an assertion that racial identity is a choice, a social construct rather than a biologically determined fact. The narrator also spends much of the text emphasizing not only the external oppression ancient Israelites and modern African Americans faced but also the internal problems of factionalism, leadership, jealousy, irresponsibility, and selfishness. Written entirely in black vernacular, and with hoodoo assigned as one of Moses' gifts, this novel makes one understand why God becomes so frustrated with his chosen people in the book, but it also reinscribes their chosen-ness, showing their unique facility with words and understanding of the sacredness of life. There are many rivalries in the text: of especial note is the one between Zipporah, Moses' wife, and Miriam, Moses' sister, which satirizes female rivalry and gossip, color prejudice, bourgeois pretense, and vanity.

Ultimately, many have argued, the novel examines the quest for freedom on multiple levels: between groups, genders, and generations, including exploring the tensions between individual and communal identity.

Moses himself, and his myth within the African diaspora, had long been a topic of particular interest to Hurston. *Mules and Men* indicates why quite clearly: "Moses was the first man who ever learned God's power-compelling words.... God let Moses make" (p. 184). She also refers to Moses as "the greatest hoodoo man dat God ever made" in *Jonah's Gourd Vine* (p. 147). Finally, in her introduction to *Moses,* she reiterates that it is the "power" Moses held that makes him "worshipped as a god" in Africa (p. xxi). One could, in fact, argue that an examination of the power of words and of "making" is at the heart of everything Hurston wrote. Of critical importance is the fact that Moses chooses his own ethnicity, essentially *making* himself Hebrew although both his parents are not. Not only does Hurston signify on the idea of race, Lowe points out, but she is "obviously signifying on God" by rewriting the Bible, essentially making herself a Moses figure by specifically reauthoring the Pentateuch (p. 212). The workings of power in relation to words is a crucial part of the book, with Jethro, Moses' adoptive father, instructing him in how to talk to God, and the Hebrew people mocking Aaron's "stiff" speeches (p. 251). Lowe observes that "Hurston presents Moses as a kind of deconstructionist who penetrates through layers of mystery to the underlying truth" (p. 234).

Moses received mixed reviews, some critics complaining that there was too much comedy and not enough serious content. For instance, Philip Slomovitz complained that the work was "weak in its interpretation of the ethical contributions of the prophet" ("The Negro's Moses," reprinted in Cronin, p. 152). Others worried that the book seemed ultimately unresolved, with the reviewer Percy Hutchison bemusedly wondering about Hurston's intent in portraying a Moses who seems "almost to be greater than God" ("Led His People Free," reprinted in Cronin, p. 149). About a decade earlier, Louis Untermeyer had written a similar novel, simply titled *Moses,* and his review of Hurston's text reveals that he felt she had "borrowed from him" (p. 215). Lowe also notes that more than forty films based in Bible lore had been made in Hurston's lifetime and that Hurston was clearly interested in selling *Moses* for a screenplay (p. 217). She pursued this option, and the book was reviewed but ultimately rejected by Warner Bros. in 1941 (Binggelli, p. 5).

While awaiting the release of *Moses,* Hurston had married Albert Price in June 1939, possibly because he reminded her of Punter, but the union lasted only six weeks (the divorce would not be final until months later). Still hustling to find work and finance her writing, she had also taken a faculty position at the North Carolina College for Negroes to start a drama department. The department never materialized, but she staged several successful reprises of *The Great Day* at nearby white colleges before conflicts with the college president led to her resignation before the academic year was out.

By March 1940, Hurston had attached herself to a research expedition to South Carolina with Margaret Mead and was off to record and preserve more of the music and rituals of the Sanctified Church. Her articles on the subject, especially "The Sanctified Church," reveal how well her work there dovetailed with her lifelong quest to observe, translate, celebrate, and preserve the modes of speaking, singing, and just plain being in the African American communities of the South. She clearly admires the drama, intensity, and improvisations around a central musical and thematic core of each song, the preaching, and the shouting, which can either be an audience response to the first two or an individual or divine inspiration. Each rendition of them is a "new creation," Hurston enthuses (p. 80).

DUST TRACKS ON A ROAD

The next year, 1941, found Hurston finally acquiescing to her publisher's repeated requests to write her autobiography, which she also was hoping to turn into a film, as she was working for Paramount studios in Hollywood that year. Read in conjunction with the other texts she wrote during her lifetime, including the visual, oral, and essay forms, *Dust Tracks on a Road* can be viewed as one component of Hurston's nearly kaleidoscopic auto-ethnography. As her "official" print autobiography, it has met with dubious reviews and assessments since its publication in 1942. Many critics have pointed out how fictionalized it is, how evasive it seems, how disjointed it feels. W. Edward Farrison, reviewing the book in the *Journal of Negro History* in 1943, noted that it read a bit like a fairytale—specifically, a "Cinderella story"—but also that Hurston did a bit of "hash-warming," or reusing material from her other books (reprinted in Cronin, pp. 170–171). The 1991 HarperPerennial edition includes a chronology as an appendix, one that reveals all the factual discrepancies in the book itself. Since the 1990s, critical focus has rested on how heavily edited the volume was and how Hurston's long-standing, complex relationships to her white patrons may have been another reason for its awkwardness. Perhaps the best way to view the text as Hurston may have viewed it is through the lens Phillip A. Snyder suggests in his analysis, "Zora Neale Hurston's *Dust Tracks*: Autobiography and Artist Novel" (in Cronin, pp. 173–189). When one reads *Dust Tracks* as a narrative about an artist's development into maturity, and in the context of all the other American women's literary autobiographies published in that era—most of which are also formed in the *Künstlerroman* tradition—Hurston's evasions, omissions, shaving, and shaping of her autobiography is not as odd as all the outrage over them would suggest. She would have to return again to the North to promote the book and reconnect with her old Harlem Renaissance friends by the end of 1942, the year the book came out.

SERAPH ON THE SUWANEE

After her stay in New York, Hurston returned once more to her beloved Florida, where she got a temporary job teaching at the Florida Normal and Industrial College. She also befriended Marjorie Rawlings, a white author whose depictions of black life Hurston had judged to be authentic. As their friendship grew, it may have partially inspired Hurston to try her own hand at depicting white characters, which she did in her 1948 novel, *Seraph on the Suwanee.* Rawlings then introduced Hurston to her own editor at Charles Scribner's Sons, who arranged an advance for the book that was big enough for Hurston to head for Honduras—a country about which she had long been curious—to write and mail drafts from her hotel in 1947.

Seraph, like *Dust Tracks,* has been a controversial text in Hurston's oeuvre from its publication until today, largely because its main characters are white. Hurston had written to her lifelong friend, Carl Van Vechten, years before, saying that she had "hopes of breaking that old, silly rule about Negroes writing about white people" (quoted in Binggelli, p. 6). Some have said the book is a black novel in "whiteface," due to the folk-dialect all the characters use, but other criticism has revealed Hurston's own research into "poor white" speech while she worked with the Florida Writers' Project and the relationship of that speech to black vernacular (Lowe, p. 282). Others argue that Hurston was merely mocking white folk, revealing racial exploitation through the ubiquitous "pet Negro system," a phrase Hurston coined in an essay of the same title. Another group of critics focuses on the novel's depiction of marriage, sexual violence, and the objectification of women. The novel certainly offers food for thought in all those areas, but it is much bigger than any of them, and it reveals more of Hurston's authorial abilities than it has been credited with.

The novel begins with Arvay Henson, an angelic-looking (read "seraph") Southern "cracker"—which is a slang term for poor, unsophisticated, white folk in the South—being courted by the man she would later marry, Jim Meserve. But Arvay has a secret: she's madly in love with her sister's husband, a local pastor who courted her first. Ashamed of her sexual dreams about him, Arvay has committed herself to the church, rejecting suitors for a supposedly sacral life of service. When Jim Meserve shows his determination to woo Arvay, the whole town is watching and laughing at her, and Arvay knows it. Arvay's volatile psychology—her repression, guilt, and denial when she experiences sexual desire, her inability to rid herself of an inferiority complex linked to her "cracker" roots, and her masochistic obsession that her disabled firstborn child is some sort of punishment—is reflected in the title of Frank G. Slaughter's early review of the book: "Freud in Turpentine" (collected in Cronin, pp. 193–194). More recently, John Lowe has carefully traced Arvay's psychological condition as possible "melancholia" and scrupulously outlined Hurston's own probable awareness of this Freudian theory and its relevance to her own life (p. 271): Lowe points out that Hurston herself may have always battled a similar feeling, one stemming from early emotional rejection.

The plot is a multigenerational, multifamily saga of the kind that Edna Ferber or Gertrude Atherton were also publishing in the 1940s. It traces Arvay's marriage to Jim and focuses on her feelings of inadequacy as he rises in socioeconomic status, her resistance to their children's marriages and careers (one of them becomes a successful blues musician, which she also has trouble accepting, because that's "darky music"), and finally, the sad plunge of Arvay's side of the family into such degradation that one of the best moments in Arvay's life is setting her old family home on fire and watching it burn. In another plot twist, Arvay's disabled son attacks a neighbor and is killed trying to escape. Beyond the tragic double-loss Arvay experiences at that event, it also reveals her racism. She was never friendly with those neighbors anyway, viewing them as inferior since they were Italian, and she is bewildered and horrified when her surviving son falls in love with one of the Corregio girls, especially since the rest of society seems to approve the match. Arvay also has a strained relationship with her husband's right-hand man and his family, who are black and who are clearly wiser and more stable than she is. It is possible that Hurston may also have been examining race and racism as social constructs through Arvay's many prejudices, demonstrating how Arvay's own interminable sense of inadequacy causes her continual quest to find someone to whom she can feel superior.

Likely inspired by Hurston's time working and researching for the Florida Writers' Project, the novel can also be read as a "love song to Florida" (Lowe, p. 261), a pastoral idyll, or even a work of ecocriticism as it investigates the numerous landscapes and industries Florida's topography offers, as Jim works his way up from poor, itinerant worker to wealthy businessman. The book ends with Arvay's reconciliation with her husband on one of his shrimping boats and her final awakening to the beauty of living, aided by the time she has spent observing his love of the sea. A number of critics, between 1948 and 1988, interpreted the book as a tale of a woman who takes nearly three decades to learn how to love, laugh, and accept both others and herself, which clearly ties *Seraph on the Suwanee* back to *Their Eyes Were Watching God* as well.

"THE CONSCIENCE OF THE COURT"

While Hurston was back in New York to promote *Seraph,* a disaster occurred that shook her oft-expressed belief "that the world would treat you alright if you are alright" (quoted in Moylan, p. 45). Falsely accused of molesting a young boy, she was arrested in September 1948. Several newspapers convicted her in the press and even excerpted parts of *Seraph* in an attempt to pillory her and sensationalize the case. Scribners leaped to hire her a good lawyer, and old and new friends such as Rawlings and Fannie Hurst also leaped to her defense. The case was eventually dismissed, but it had been shamefully mishandled in the early stages, including the suppression of incontrovertible exonerating evidence: Hurston had been in Honduras when she was allegedly molesting the boy, and the charges could and should have been dismissed by a simple check of her passport. Hurston was so shaken by the potential miscarriage of justice that she practically lost the will to live. She was deeply offended that the accusations had come from her former landlady, since she had worked indefatigably on behalf of the black community—particularly the mothers in the neighborhood, organizing a child care co-op—while she lived there. Once she was exonerated, she again retreated to the sunshine, flora, and waters of Florida to heal her wounded soul, living on a friend's boat in Biscayne Bay, picking local fruits in the morning and watching the sun set in the evening until she felt "that I have come to myself at last" (Moylan, p. 51).

While she recuperated, Hurston had started work on another novel about Southern whites, to be titled "The Lives of Barney Turk." The book was never published, but a worthwhile short story came out of this period nonetheless. Published in the *Saturday Evening Post* in March 1950, "The Conscience of the Court," now collected in *The Complete Stories,* is a fascinating, difficult-to-decipher tale about an African American domestic servant facing—and acquitted for—charges for assaulting a white bill-collector on behalf of her mistress. Since Hurston's books were all out of print at the time, when the story was published she was temporarily earning her living cooking and cleaning for a white family ignorant of her status as an author and scholar. The story vaulted her to fame again when a splashy newspaper article revealed her identity to her employers and her current work situation to the world.

This renewal of fame resulted in several ghostwriting jobs for Hurston, including political op-eds analyzing the racial-political controversies of the early to mid-1950s, and other journalistic assignments. Hurston opposed both enforced desegregation and the promotion of communism as a socioeconomic solution for African Americans. She felt that the former was patronizing and disingenuous and the latter was exploitative and suppressed the ingenuity, initiative, and independence she so valued. Her national coverage of a famous 1953 murder trial of a black woman who had shot her white lover, most likely because of his greed, corruption, and continual attempts at extorting her, rather than the sexual jealousy motive that the prosecution emphasized, is notable as well. Her journalistic and personal work on Ruby McCollum's behalf, including bringing the story to the attention of another writer who published a full book on the trial, may have helped save McCollum from the electric chair. Hurston had also committed herself to a number of cooperative and solitary projects, including the creation, production, and marketing of an authentic black baby doll; a biography-based fiction about the first black female millionaire in America (whose daughter she had known in Harlem in the 1920s), titled "The Golden Bench of God" (sadly rejected and then lost in manuscript); and a grand revisionary biography of the biblical King Herod, which she had hoped would eventually receive a grand Cecil B. DeMille–style treatment in Hollywood but which was rejected by publishers.

She remained in Florida for her last decade, renting cottages or apartments—her favorite rental was a tiny cottage in Eau Gallie, where she had found solace and productive work decades earlier—sometimes living on boats, always dreaming of owning her own plot of land, large or small, on which to grow citrus, vegetable, and flowers. For Hurston, gardening was both a solace and a means of survival from her childhood onward: as she often noted, it's both cheaper and healthier to grow your own food.

Sadly, her dream of owning her own piece of Florida never materialized, and she spent her last four years in Fort Pierce working as a librarian, teacher, speaker, and writer until her deteriorating health prevented her from earning her own living. Her friends in the town chipped in to help care for her in her final illness, visited her at her rest home, and mourned at her death, many contributing to her funeral in 1960. That her final community understood how valuable a contribution she had made was long denied in literary biography and criticism: her original biographers declared that she was forgotten, neglected, and died a pauper, until Valerie Boyd and Virginia Lynn Moylan's newer biographies (2004 and 2011, respectively) demonstrated otherwise. The locals must have known that Hurston's work was important, otherwise why would local sheriff's deputy Patrick Duval intervene when he found her neighbors starting to burn her personal papers, a traditional practice when someone died in that county? Duval put out the fire and carefully preserved the surviving material, to the great benefit of Hurston scholars today. Some of Hurston's manuscripts and materials now reside in the George A. Smathers library at Florida State University. Others are in the Library of Congress.

LEGACY

Biographers and critics agree that by 1940, Zora Neale Hurston was the most published, the most famous, and the most highly regarded black woman writer in the United States. How, then, were most of her works out of print a decade later and lost to literary criticism for almost forty years? It has been theorized that Hurston "got sandwiched in between the exotic primitivism of the Harlem Renaissance and the protest mood of the forties," resulting in her critical neglect from around 1950 until Alice Walker's dramatic rediscovery and "search" for her (Bloom, p. 127).

Robert Hemenway concluded Hurston was an "autonomous imagination" (Bloom, p. 137), which made her difficult to interpret and therefore to teach.

Hurston was also one of the earliest African American writers to openly expose the tragedy of internalized racism, particularly based on skin color, in her early, award-winning play "Color Struck" (1925), which came out before Wallace Thurman's more well-known *The Blacker the Berry* (1929). Alice Walker has famously praised Hurston for her "racial health—a sense of black people as complete, complex, and undiminished human beings" (quoted in Bloom, p. 64) and expressed gratitude for Zora Hurston's preservation of and admiration for Southern, African American folklore, which was in danger of being lost after the Great Migration. Hurston was eminently quotable; one of her most famous sayings was "I love myself when I am laughing ... and then again when I am looking mean and impressive"—her famous response to seeing the results of her photo shoot with Carl Van Vechten.

The wonderful collection of photos we now have of Hurston, including the famous ones taken by Carl Van Vechten, show an irrepressible, multifaceted, adaptable woman who could play many roles. Langston Hughes recalled "she could make you laugh one minute and cry the next" (quoted in Bloom, p. 14) and claimed that he knew no one else who could freely and without repercussions go around measuring the foreheads of strangers in Harlem or borrowing money for the subway from a blind beggar's cup (Bloom, p. 14). Fannie Hurst, for whom Hurston worked briefly, but whose friendship endured long after, confirmed Hurston's inextinguishable verve, recalling how Hurston added her own comments to Hurst's letters when she disagreed with the dictated comments, and Hurston's habit of quoting canonical works, folk sayings, sacred and "bawdy songs" in one continuous stream (Bloom, p. 22).

Just as Hurst best recalled Hurston for her performative genius—including Zora's famous impersonation of an African princess to circumvent Jim Crow laws when the two traveled together—much of the twenty-first-century criticism of Hurston's work has focused on her performativity. Since 2001, studies of Hurston's stage work have proliferated. But although the critical interest in Hurston and performance is new, Hurston's own performativity was old news to her family and friends. Her biographers note that she was widely known in 1920s Harlem as a highly entertaining "raconteur" and that most of her friends had heard her published material at parties long before they read it (Frydman, p. 103).

Another newly appreciated aspect of the performative nature of Hurston's work is her use of gesture. In a 2015 article published in *Modern Drama,* Elin Diamond points to a crucial moment in the draft of "Characteristics of Negro Expression" where Hurston writes "note gesture [in] place of words" (p. 114). Diamond's essay queries "what Hurston means by gesture" and concludes it "comprise[s] both the body's 'unconscious' cultural sign system and the communal pleasures of skillful mimicry" (p. 114). Both aspects of gesture are employed, in endless combinations, in Hurston's plays "Color Struck" (1925), "Cold Keener" (1930), "Woofing" (1931), and "The Great Day"(1932), exemplifying Hurston's own assertion that "everyday life" was a form of drama, a "condition of being that permeates the Negro's entire self" (p. 114). One finds this technique and perspective not only in her plays but in all of Hurston's works. For instance, she declares a dice game to be a form of art in both *Mules and Men* and *Their Eyes Were Watching God.* She also emphasizes the ritual dance/play between Joe and Missy May in "The Gilded Six-Bits" when he comes home with his wages and makes that same ritual a gestural sign that their marriage is all right again near the story's end.

This "communal choreography" that Hurston intended to use to create a new, authentic black theater in the 1920s and 1930s is, as Diamond suggests, "both expressive and habitually withholding" (p. 117). Hurston's essay "Characteristics of Negro Expression" explains it this way: "[the speaker] is restrained ... [forcing] the beholder ... to finish the action the performance suggests" (quoted in Diamond, p. 117). In addition to studies of performativity that examine the plays she wrote, others apply performance studies or speech act theory to her work as an ethnographer and creative writer. Parker English, writing in the *Journal of Pragmatics,* uses the conventionalist/intentionalist debate to try to decipher the nature of Hurston's communication, specifically asserting that "Hurston's ethnography shows that communicative success need not require our identifying a speaker's communicative intention" (p. 1626). This dovetails neatly with Hurston's own astute observation in *Mules and Men* about giving the white listener "something to play with and handle" rather than the keys to all her secrets. "He can read my writing, but he sho' can't read my mind," she explains (p. 3). In other words, communication can still occur, even without full disclosure of her intentions. Even 1930s reviewers wrote of her works in terms of speech and performance: H. I. Brock's 1935 *New York Times* review declared that *Mules and Men* invited outsiders to "listen in" to a side of African American culture usually closed to them ("The Full, True Flavor of Life in a Negro Community," reprinted in Cronin, p. 39). Brock's comment further reflects African American oral tradition both in Negro spirituals and in its canon of "Ole Massa" stories, wherein that character never quite sees the entire significance of what "John"—the usual character outsmarting Ole Massa in the stories—is saying. However, English also notes the way some speech acts in Hurston's texts reveal that "a sincere speaker's communicative success can involve an intentionalistic interpretation," where the listener understands, through context and subtext, more than has actually been said (p. 1634). What English does not emphasize is that this second type of performative speech act in Hurston's works generally occurs between two African American characters, who understand both the context and subtext of the speech act.

Hurston's almost acrobatic flexibility in her own use of performative speech acts—through her own voice or those of her characters—further underscores the necessity of audience awareness in reading her work. It can be argued that she was always speaking to at least two audiences at once, usually three, even in her private letters, much less in her stage performances. For instance, Cynthia Ward has picked up on the multiple texts incipient in each of Hurston's works. Ward highlights Hurston's use of vernacular as a rhetorical strategy that "not only tolerates but thrives on multiple loyalities, multiplicities of address, and contradiction" (p. 302). Hurston's roots in oral tradition, both that of the Eatonville general store porch and the gospel church, demand that every act be engendered by, and demanding of, audience participation and that the flexibility or indecipherability of meaning critics often encounter trying to read her work is a natural outgrowth of those roots. Laura Dubek refers to this as the "gospel impulse" in Hurston's works (p. 109). The gospel is a word that demands a response, Dubek argues, reading *Their Eyes* as a combination of gospel, jazz, and blues—two more performative forms whose use of evolutionary improvisation demands audience participation. We do know that Hurston admired blues, jazz, and spirituals, particularly when they were sung by Ethel Waters, to whom she devotes half a chapter of her autobiography. Since multiple audiences and multiple contexts were always present for Hurston, perhaps multiple reactions were always anticipated—or even intended—when she spoke or wrote.

Finally, understanding the use of humor within African American folklore and performative tradition is crucial to cracking the complex codes within Hurston's texts. Reflecting the influence of the theorist Mikhail Bakhtin, John Lowe's excellent study of Hurston's work elucidates many roles that comedy plays in her writing: correction of vice or injustice by mockery; making a "safe" complaint; indirectly courting to test the waters (called "woofing"); defusing tensions by substituting a battle of witty verbal escalations (that is, "playing the dozens") for a physical confrontation; creating hierarchies of wit; and using "leveling jokes" to overturn false or oppressive hierarchies (pp. 146–148). It would probably behoove Hurston scholars to reexamine her letters, collected in Carla Kaplan's 2002 volume, with these same rhetorical theories and cultural codes in mind. Such an activity might help resolve the consternation that the varying, and sometimes uncomfortably obsequious, tones that her letters to people like Mason, Boas, and Hurst utilize.

GENDER POLITICS

Hurston's work has perhaps been most widely used in classrooms and interpreted in scholarship for its investigation of gender politics in familial and sexual relationships. Her most famous anthologized stories, "The Gilded Six-Bits" (1933) and "Sweat" (1926), involve complex negotiations between married couples: one marriage happy until an outsider tempts the wife with a show of wealth, and the other marriage abusive. Other stories, like "Spunk" (1925), show the tragedies that can ensue when female sexual power is wielded carelessly. Hurston's unpublished 1947 essay "The Lost Keys of Glory" examines the struggles of women in the workplace, while the unpublished (and subsequently lost) manuscript "The Golden Bench of God" examined the life of the first black female millionaire in the United States. Diana Miles, in her 2003 volume, *Women, Violence, and Testimony in the Works of Zora Neale Hurston,* reexamines Hurston's depiction of gender politics through another performative form of speech and gesture: testimony. Testimony usually occurs either in a courthouse, wherein listeners judge it as evidence, or in a church when one individual's personal story is related to a group, whose members will interpret it as indicative of a greater, universal truth and then employ it in understanding their own spiritual journey and making their own personal decisions. Miles focuses on the use of testimony around the question of violence toward and by women in Hurston's short fiction and in several of her novels.

SOURCES

It might be fair to say, in paraphrase of a tagline from another famously charming American, Will Rogers, that Hurston never met a source she didn't like. She used a wide swath of sources, garnered from the porch and from the classroom, from Southern folklore and African oral tradition, to classical, Norse, and Egyptian mythology. Given Jonathan Swift's *Gulliver's Travels* (1726) in fifth grade, and having found John Milton's *Paradise Lost* (1667) in the garbage as a teenager—and loved it—(Boyd, p. 65), Hurston reveled in British poetry as much as she did the Brer Rabbit tales she would hear at the Eatonville general store, and she might well have claimed all literature for her ancestry, as Ralph Ellison would publicly do later. She also clearly associated herself with the fairy-tale character Cinderella, in her designation of her patron, Charlotte Osgood Mason, as "godmother." If one can imagine Hurston chuckling at the idea of Cinderella being freed from her housework and sent to the ball, while also contemplating whether "godmother" was acting more like a wicked stepmother in demanding possession of all Hurston's labor and—on one occasion—hesitating to buy her a pair of shoes without holes in them, then surely all the potential jokes and word play in that comparison were not lost on Hurston herself. Hurston loved comedy, and her work has been compared productively to Jonathan Swift, Nikolai Gogol, and Charles Dickens, among others. This multivocal type of comedy may well prove another fruitful area of future Hurston studies, when read through the lenses of both Bakhtinian theory and Brer Rabbit tradition.

Perhaps the two most dominant sources to which Hurston returned time after time were Judeo-Christian scripture and mythology, with Shakespeare's plays coming in as an interesting third. *Jonah's Gourd Vine* and *Moses, Man of the Mountain* are Hurston's most overt uses of the Bible, but scriptural references appear in nearly every long work she wrote, perhaps coming easily and naturally to the former preacher's daughter. Glenda Weathers' article "Biblical Trees, Biblical Deliverance" explores the use of Edenic metaphors, specifically imagery related to the tree of the knowledge of good and evil, in Hurston's *Their Eyes Were Watching God.* The tree imagery may also have been influenced by Milton's *Paradise Lost,* another favorite of Hurston's, but Weathers also notes the play on the Old Testament trope of the Promised Land in the text, specifically when Janie's grandmother, Nanny, announces that in arranging her first marriage she hoped to "throw up a highway in the wilderness" (p. 15), a clear invocation of Isaiah 40:3. Possibly playing on both the text of Genesis and the gospel of John, Weathers investigates how Hurston allows Janie, like God and Moses in the Bible, to speak herself and her world into being.

In his persuasive book-length study of Hurston, *Jump at the Sun: Zora Neale Hurston's Cosmic Comedy,* John Lowe has effectively demonstrated the author's repeated use of other biblical tropes popular in African American literature as well, particularly the figure of Hagar, handmaid to Abraham's wife, Sarah—who bears Abraham's son, becomes an outcast through Sarah's jealousy, and becomes the source of a nation that will always be a rival to Israel. Lowe also insightfully reads Hurston's repeated invocation of the Bible stories of the woman at the well and of Jacob and Esau, wherein a younger brother cons his older brother out of his birthright.

Her use of sources has been problematic in some aspects. Hurston has posthumously suffered from charges of plagiarism, possibly more well-founded than the other charges she suffered in her lifetime. The scholar Jon Woodson has speculated that *Their Eyes Were Watching God* may have been a retelling (or perhaps a cultural retranslation) of Jens Peter Jacobsen's *Marie Grubbe,* a Danish novel about a woman's three marriages, which was translated into English for Americans in 1917 and to which Nella Larsen, who ran in the same Harlem circles as did Hurston, had referred in print, as had periodicals like the *Nation,* the *Dial,* and the *New York Times.* Many similarities exist, Woodson claims, such as the motifs of traveling and of trial, and the type of narrator, but most disconcerting is the striking similarity of Hurston's language and imagery in her final paragraph, as compared to a key paragraph in Jacobsen's novel. There has also been some serious speculation that Hurston plagiarized some of her material in *The Journal of Negro History* on Cudjo Lewis, the last surviving African American slave.

Her intentions or her motivations are unknowable in respect to these instances: was she struggling under the ultrastrict parameters of "godmother's" patronage, or did she resent the expectations and restrictions of some of the foundations who granted her research funds to do one thing when she really wished to do something else? Perhaps, since she clearly considered mimicry a fine art, and a type of "signifying" unique to authentic "Negro expression," these instances were intended as play along those lines? Hurston herself once wrote "what we mean by originality is the modification of ideas. The most ardent admirer of the great Shakespeare cannot claim the first source even for him. It is his treatment of borrowed material" ("Characteristics," p. 838). Over the course of her career, Hurston successfully rewrote and utilized several Shakespearean tragedies and comedies to structure her work. Perhaps she also considered her gifts, technique, and place in literature to be like Shakespeare's: use borrowed material, but make it fresh and accessible to a new audience.

NEW DIRECTIONS

Some twenty-first-century critics have been considering Hurston "beyond black/white binaries" as a means "to study the common denominators of human psychodynamics" (Kanthak, p. 113), particularly in the areas of violence against women and dysfunctional marriages and families. These studies seem to align with Hurston's own desire to be considered a sage observer of the entire human race, not merely one branch of it. The critic Nick Aaron Ford recalled a conversation he had with Hurston in which she explained why her novels did not focus on "the race problem," which had endlessly frustrated famous acquaintances like Richard Wright and Alain Locke. Smiling, she claimed, "I think only in terms of individuals ... I am not interested in the *race* problem, but I am interested in the problems of *individuals,* white ones and black ones" (quoted in Bloom, p. 8). New articles comparing Hurston to her contemporaries of all ethnicities reveal the promise of this critical direction. Additionally, Hurston's work is now being used in college composition courses as an example of a successful "code switcher" (an individual who has mastered the use of more than one verbal or written form of a single language) and as an example of a brilliant rhetorician handling multiple audiences (Heard, p. 129). Her authentic portrayal of both Southern American English and African American vernacular English have also become of increasing interest in linguistics since the turn of the twenty-first century.

Whether one reads her to relish the joy and sophistication of her word play, to understand the anguish of power struggle and violence between races and genders, or within families, to experience the complexity of her many rhetorical and performative modes, or to see the world through her unique, individual perspective, American literature has been deeply enriched by Hurston and her work. More than once, Hurston herself, or one of her characters, shared this pearl of African-American folk wisdom "Don't say no more with your mouth than your back can stand." Thus far, Hurston's metaphorical back has been broad and strong enough to bear everything that has been said or written in response to her; doubtlessly, she will continue to endure.

Selected Bibliography

WORKS BY ZORA NEALE HURSTON

Books

Jonah's Gourd Vine. Philadelphia: J. B. Lippincott, 1934. Reprint, with an introduction by Larry Neal, 1971. Reprint, with a foreword by Rita Dove, New York: HarperCollins, 1990.

Mules and Men. Preface by Franz Boas. Philadelphia: J. B. Lippincott, 1935. Reprint, with a foreword by Arnold Rampersand, New York: HarperCollins, 1990.

Their Eyes Were Watching God. Philadelphia: J. B. Lippincott, 1937. Reprint, with a foreword by Sherley Anne Williams, Urbana: University of Illinois Press, 1978.

Tell My Horse: Voodoo and Life in Haiti and Jamaica. Philadelphia: J. B. Lippincott, 1938. Reprint, with a foreword by Ishmael Reed, New York: HarperCollins, 1990.

Moses, Man of the Mountain. Philadelphia: J. B. Lippincott, 1939. Reprint, with a foreword by Deborah E. McDowell, New York: HarperCollins, 1991.

Dust Tracks on a Road. Philadelphia: J. B. Lippincott, 1942. Reprint, with a foreword by Maya Angelou, New York: HarperCollins, 1991.

Seraph on the Suwanee: A Novel. New York: Charles Scribner's Sons, 1948. Reprint, with a foreword by Hazel V. Carby, New York: HarperCollins, 1991.

I Love Myself When I Am Laughing ... and Then Again When I Am Looking Mean and Impressive: A Zora Neale Hurston Reader. Edited by Alice Walker, with an introduction by Mary Helen Washington. Old Westbury, N.Y.: Feminist Press, 1979.

The Sanctified Church. Edited and with a foreword by Toni Cade Bambara. Berkeley, Calif.: Turtle Island, 1981.

Spunk: The Selected Short Stories of Zora Neale Hurston. Edited and foreword by Bob Callahan. Berkeley, Calif.: Turtle Island, 1985.

The Complete Stories. Edited and with a foreword by Henry Louis Gates, Jr., and Sieglinde Lemke; afterword by Henry Louis Gates, Jr. New York: HarperCollins, 1995.

Zora Neale Hurston: Folklore, Memoirs, and Other Writings. Compiled by Cheryl A. Wall. New York: Library of America, 1995.

Zora Neale Hurston: A Life in Letters. Edited by Carla Kaplan. New York: Doubleday, 2002.

Zora Neale Hurston: Collected Plays. New Brunswick, N.J.: Rutgers University Press, 2008.

Short Fiction

"John Redding Goes to Sea." *Stylus* 1 (May 1921):1–22. Reprinted in *Opportunity* 4:16–21 (January 1926). Reprinted in *The Complete Stories,* pp. 1–16.

"Drenched in Light." *Opportunity* 2:371–374 (December 1924). Reprinted in *The Complete Stories,* pp. 17–25.

"Spunk." *Opportunity* 3:171–173 (June 1925). Reprinted in *The New Negro.* Edited by Alain Locke. New York: Albert and Charles Boni, 1925. Pp. 105–111. Reprinted in *The Complete Stories,* pp. 26–32.

"Magnolia Flower." *Spokesman,* July 1925, pp. 26–29. Reprinted in *The Complete Stories,* pp. 33–40.

"Muttsy." *Opportunity* 4:246–250 (August 1926). Reprinted in *The Complete Stories,* pp. 41–36.

"'Possum or Pig." *Forum* 76:465 (September 1926). Reprinted in *The Complete Stories,* pp. 57–58.

"Sweat." *Fire!!* 1:40–45 (November 1926). Reprinted in *I Love Myself When I Am Laughing,* pp. 197–207. Reprinted in *The Complete Stories,* pp. 73–85.

"The Gilded Six-Bits." *Story* 3:60–70 (August 1933). Reprinted in *I Love Myself When I Am Laughing,* pp. 208–218.

"Uncle Monday." In *Negro: An Anthology.* Edited by Nancy Cunard. London: Wishart, 1934. Pp. 57–61. Reprinted in

The Sanctified Church, pp. 30–40. Reprinted in *The Complete Stories,* pp. 106–116.

"Now Take Noses." In *Cordially Yours: A Collection of Original Short Stories and Essays by America's Leading Authors.* Edited by Thomas Page Smith. Philadelphia: L. B. Lippincott, 1939. Pp. 25–27.

"Cock Robin, Beale Street." *Southern Literary Messenger* 3: 321–323 (July 1941). Reprinted in *The Complete Stories,* pp. 122–126.

"Story in Harlem Slang." *American Mercury* 55:84–96 (July 1942). Reprinted in *The Complete Stories,* pp. 127–138.

"Lawrence of the River." *Saturday Evening Post,* September 5, 1942, pp. 18, 55–57. Condensed in *Negro Digest,* March 1943, pp. 47–49.

"High John de Conquer." *American Mercury* 57:450–458 (October 1943). Reprinted in *The Sanctified Church,* pp. 69–78. Reprinted in *The Complete Stories,* pp. 139–148.

"Conscience of the Court." *Saturday Evening Post,* March 18, 1950, pp. 22–23, 112–122. Reprinted in *The Complete Stories,* pp. 162–177.

"Book of Harlem." First printed in *Spunk: The Selected Short Stories of Zora Neale Hurston,* 1985, pp. 75–81. Reprinted in *The Complete Stories,* pp. 22–26.

"Isis." First printed in *Spunk: The Selected Short Stories of Zora Neale Hurston,* 1985, pp. 9–18.

"Black Death." Short story submitted to 1925 *Opportunity* contest. First printed in *The Complete Stories,* 1995, pp. 202–208.

"The Bone of Contention." First printed in *The Complete Stories,* 1995, pp. 209–220.

"Harlem Slanguage." First printed in *The Complete Stories,* 1995, pp. 227–232.

"Now You Cookin' with Gas." In *The Complete Stories,* 1995, pp. 233–241.

"The Seventh Veil." In *The Complete Stories,* 1995, pp. 242–260.

"The Woman in Gaul." In *The Complete Stories,* 1995, pp. 261–283.

POEMS

"O Night." *Stylus* 1:42 (May 1921).

"Poem." *Howard University Record* 16:236 (February 1922).

PLAYS

"Color Struck: A Play." *Fire!!* 1:7–15 (November 1926).

"The First One: A Play." In *Ebony and Topaz.* Edited by Charles S. Johnson. New York: National Urban League, 1927. Pp. 53–57.

ARTICLES

"The Hue and Cry About Howard University." *Messenger* 7:315–319, 338 (September 1925).

"The Eatonville Anthology." *Messenger* 8:261–62, 297, 319, 332 (September–November 1926). Reprinted in *I Love Myself When I Am Laughing,* pp. 177–188. Reprinted in *The Complete Stories,* pp. 59–72.

"Cudjo's Own Story of the Last American Slaver." *Journal of Negro History* 12:648–663 (October 1927).

"Communication." *Journal of Negro History* 12:664–667 (October 1927). (About the Fort Moosa settlement and Negro colony in Florida.)

"How It Feels to Be Colored Me." *World Tomorrow* 11: 215–216 (May 1928). Reprinted in *I Love Myself When I Am Laughing,* pp. 152–155.

"Dance Songs and Tales from the Bahamas." *Journal of American Folklore* 43:294–312 (July–September 1930).

"Hoodoo in *America." Journal of American Folklore* 44: 317–418 (October–December 1931).

"Characteristics of Negro Expression." In *Negro: An Anthology.* Edited by Nancy Cunard. London: Wishart, 1934. Pp. 39–46. Reprinted in *The Sanctified Church,* pp. 41–68.

"Conversions and Visions." In *Negro: An Anthology.* Edited by Nancy Cunard. London: Wishart, 1934. Pp. 47–49.

"Mother Catharine." In *Negro: An Anthology.* Edited by Nancy Cunard. London: Wishart, 1934. Pp. 54–57. Reprinted in *The Sanctified Church,* pp. 23–29. Reprinted in *The Complete Stories,* pp. 99–105.

"The Sermon." In *Negro: An Anthology.* Edited by Nancy Cunard. London: Wishart, 1934. Pp. 50–54.

"Shouting." In *Negro: An Anthology.* Edited by Nancy Cunard. London: Wishart, 1934. Pp. 49–50.

"Spirituals and Neo-Spirituals." In *Negro: An Anthology.* Edited by Nancy Cunard. London: Wishart, 1934. Pp. 359–361.

"The Fire and the Cloud." *Challenge* 1:10–14 (September 1934). Reprinted in *The Complete Stories,* pp. 117–121.

"Race Cannot Become Great Until It Recognizes Its Talent." *Washington Tribune,* December 29, 1934, n.p.

"Full of Mud, Sweat, and Blood." *New York Herald Tribune Books,* November 3, 1935, p. 8. (Review of *God Shakes Creation* by David M. Cohn.)

"Fannie Hurst." *Saturday Review,* October 9 1937, pp. 15–16.

"Star-Wrassling Sons-of-the-Universe." *New York Herald Tribune Books,* December 26, 1937, p. 4. (Review of *The Hurricane's Children* by Carl Carmer.)

"Rural Schools for Negroes." *New York Herald Tribune Books,* February 20, 1938, p. 24. (Review of *The Jeanes Teacher in the United States* by Lance G. E. Jones.)

"Stories of Conflict." *Saturday Review,* April 2, 1938, p. 32. (Review of *Uncle Tom's Children* by Richard Wright.)

"The 'Pet Negro' System." *American Mercury* 56 (May 1943): 593–600. Condensed in *Negro Digest,* June 1943, pp. 37–40. Reprinted in *I Love Myself When I Am Laughing,* pp. 156–162.

"Negroes Without Self-Pity." *American Mercury* 57:601–603 (November 1943).

"The Last Slave Ship." *American Mercury* 58:351–358 (March 1944). Condensed in *Negro Digest,* May 1944, pp. 11–16.

"My Most Humiliating Jim Crow Experience." *Negro Digest,* June 1944, pp. 25–26. Reprinted in *I Love Myself When I Am Laughing,* pp. 163–164.

"Beware the Begging Jones." *American Mercury* 60:288–294 (March 1945). Condensed in *Negro Digest,* May 1945, pp. 27–32.

"Crazy for This Democracy." *Negro Digest,* December 1945, pp. 45–48. Reprinted in *I Love Myself When I Am Laughing,* pp. 165–168.

"Bible, Played by Ear in America" *New York Herald Tribune Weekly Book Review,* November 24, 1946, p. 5. (Review of *How God Fix Jonah* by Lorenz Graham.)

"Jazz Regarded as Social Achievement." *New York Herald Tribune Weekly Book Review,* December 22, 1946, p. 8. (Review of *Shining Trumpet* by Rudi Blesh.)

"Thirty Days Among Maroons." *New York Herald Tribune Weekly Book Review,* January 12, 1947, p. 8. (Review of *Journey to Accompong* by Katharine Dunham.)

"The Transplanted Negro." *New York Herald Tribune Weekly Book Review,* March 9 1947, p. 20. (Review of *Trinidad Village* by Melville Herskovits and Frances Herskovits.)

"At the Sound of the Conch Shell." *New York Herald Tribune Weekly Book Review,* March 20, 1949, p. 4. (Review of *New Day* by Victor Stafford Reid.)

"What White Publishers Won't Print." *Negro Digest,* April 1950, pp. 85–89. Reprinted in *I Love Myself When I Am Laughing,* pp. 169–173.

"I Saw Negro Votes Peddled." *American Legion Magazine,* November 1950, pp. 12–13, 54–57, 59–60. Condensed in *Negro Digest,* September 1951, pp. 77–85.

"Some Fabulous Caribbean Riches Revealed." *New York Herald Tribune Weekly Book Review,* February 4, 1951, p. 5. (Review of *The Pencil of God* by Pierre Marcelin and Philippe Thoby Marcelin.)

"Mourner's Bench, Communist Line: Why the Negro Won't Buy Communism." *American Legion Magazine,* June 1951, pp. 14–15, 55–60.

"A Negro Voter Sizes Up Taft." *Saturday Evening Post,* December 8, 1951, pp. 29, 150.

"Victim of Fate." *Pittsburgh Courier,* October 11, 1952.

"Zora's Revealing Story of Ruby's First Day in Court." *Pittsburgh Courier,* October 11, 1952.

"Ruby Sane." *Pittsburgh Courier,* October 18, 1952.

"Ruby McCollum Fights for Life." *Pittsburgh Courier,* November 22, 1952.

"Bare Plot Against Ruby." *Pittsburgh Courier,* November 29, 1952.

"Trial Highlights." *Pittsburgh Courier,* November 29, 1952.

"McCallum-Adams Trial Highlights." *Pittsburgh Courier,* December 27, 1952.

"Ruby Bares Her Love." *Pittsburgh Courier,* January 3, 1953.

"Doctor's Threats, Tussle over Gun Led to Slaying." *Pittsburgh Courier,* January 10, 1953.

"Ruby's Troubles Mount." *Pittsburgh Courier,* January 17, 1953.

"The Life Story of Mrs. Ruby J. McCollum." *Pittsburgh Courier,* weekly from February 28 through May 2, 1953.

"The Trial of Ruby McCollum." In William Bradford Huie, *Ruby McCollum: Woman in the Suwanee Jail.* New York: E. P. Dutton, 1956. Pp. 89–101.

"This Juvenile Delinquency." *Fort Pierce Chronicle,* December 12, 1958.

"The Tripson Story." *Fort Pierce Chronicle,* February 6, 1959.

"The Farm Laborer at Home." *Fort Pierce Chronicle,* February 27, 1959.

"Hoodoo and Black Magic." Column for the *Fort Pierce Chronicle,* July 11, 1958, to August 7, 1959.

Unpublished Materials

"Barracoon." 1931. Biography of Cudjo Lewis, 117 pp.

"The Chick with One Hen." Character sketch, 2 pp.

"The Elusive Goal-Brotherhood of Mankind." Essay.

"The Emperor Effaces Himsel£" Character sketch, 7 pp.

"The Enemy." Personal experience, 10 pp.

"The Fiery Chariot." Play in one act, 7 pp.

"The Florida Negro." Manuscript (183 pp.) prepared by Zora Neale Hurston and others for the Florida Federal Writers' Project; includes "Eatonville When You Look at It" (2 pp.), "Maitland" (2 pp.), "Negro Mythical Places" (3 pp.), "New Children's Games" (9 pp.), "Turpentine" (3 pp.), and "Uncle Monday" (2 pp.).

"Herod the Great." Biography, 269 pp.

"Joe Wiley of Magazine Point." Folklore, 5 pp.

"The Lost Keys of Glory." 1947. Essay.

"The Migrant Worker in Florida." Journalism, 7 pp.

"Mule Bone: A Comedy of Negro Life." 1930. Play in three acts written with Langston Hughes. Act 3 was published in *Drama Critique* 7:103–107 (spring 1964).

"Negro Folk Tales." Folklore, 2 pp.

"Negro Legends." Folklore, 7 pp.

"Negro Work Songs." Folklore, 5 pp.

"Polk County: A Comedy of Negro Life on a Sawmill Camp, with Authentic Negro Music." 1944. Play in three acts written with Dorothy Waring.

"The South Was Had." Essay, 7 pp.

"Spear." Play. In possession of Wyatt Houscon Day.

"Take for Instance." Spessard Holland. Essay, 11 pp.

"The Ten Commandments of Charm." 1930. Essay.

"Under the Bridge." 1925. Short story.

"Unique Personal Experience." 11 pp.

"Which Way the NAACP." Essay, 14 pp. In possession of Marjorie Silver, Fort Pierce, Fla.

ARCHIVES

Hurston materials are included in the Folklore Collection at the Library of Congress, in Special Collections at the Florida State University, and in the online archives available at the University of Central Florida. A small amount of additional material is housed in the Zora Neale Hurston collection, Schomburg Center for Research in Black Culture, the New York Public Library.

CRITICAL AND BIOGRAPHICAL STUDIES

Bloom, Harold, ed. *Zora Neale Hurston.* New York: Bloom's Literary Criticism, 2008.

Boyd, Valerie. *Wrapped in Rainbows: The Life of Zora Neale Hurston.* New York: Scribner, 2004.

Akins, Adrienne. "'Just like Mister Jim': Class Transformation from Cracker to Aristocrat in Hurston's *Seraph on the Suwanee.*" *Mississippi Quarterly* 63, nos. 1–2:31–43.

Barry, Betsy. "'It's hard fuh me to understand what you mean, de way you tell it': Representing Language in Zora Neale Hurston's *Their Eyes Were Watching God.*" *Language and Literature* 10, no. 2:171–186 (2001).

Batker, Carol. "'Love Me Like I Like to Be': The Sexual Politics of Hurston's *Their Eyes Were Watching God,* the Classic Blues, and the Black Women's Club Movement." *African American Review* 32, no. 2:199–213 (1998).

Bealer, Tracy L. "'The Kiss of Memory': The Problem of Love in Hurston's *Their Eyes Were Watching God.*" *African American Review* 43, nos. 2–3:311–327 (2009).

Cappetti, Carla, and Zoral Neale Hurston. "Defending Against Her Legend: Two Previously Unpublished Letters." *Amerikastudien/American Studies* 55, no. 4: 602–614 (2010).

Carpio, Glenda R., and Werner Sollors. "The Newly Complicated Zora Neale Hurston." *Chronicle of Higher Education* 57, no. 18:B6–B10 (January 2, 2011). http://www.chronicle.com/article/The-Newly-Complicated-Zora/125753/

Cartwright, Keith. "'To Walk with the Storm': Oya as the Transformative 'I' of Zora Neale Hurston's Afro-Atlantic Callings." *American Literature* 78, no. 4:741–467 (2006).

Cronin, Gloria L., ed. *Critical Essays on Zora Neale Hurston.* New York: Prentice Hall, 1998.

Davis, Cynthia, and Verner D. Mitchell, eds. *Zora Neale Hurston: An Annotated Bibliography of Works and Criticism.* London: Scarecrow Press, 2013.

Deck, Alice A. "Autoenthnography: Zora Neale Hurston, Noni Jabavu, and Cross-Disciplinary Discourse." *Black American Literature Forum* 24, no. 2:237–256 (1990).

Diamond, Elin. "Folk Modernism: Zora Neale Hurston's Gestural Drama." *Modern Drama* 58, no. 1:112–134 (2015).

Dilbeck, Keiko. "Symbolic Representation of Identity in Hurston's *Their Eyes Were Watching God.*" *Explicator* 66, no. 2:102–104 (2008).

Dubek, Laura. "'[J]us' Listenin' tuh You': Zora Neale Hurston's *Their Eyes Were Watching God* and the Gospel Impulse." *Southern Literary Journal* 41, no. 1:109–130 (2008).

Binggeli, Elizabeth. "The Unadapted: Warner Bros. Reads Zora Neale Hurston." *Cinema Journal* 48, no. 3:1–15 (2009).

Emery, Amy Fass. "The Zombie in/as the Text: Zora Neale Hurston's *Tell My Horse.*" *African American Review* 39, no. 3:327–336 (2005).

English, Parker. "Performative Speech Acts, Ethnography, and Fiction.*Journal of Pragmatics* 39:1624–1637 (2007).

Fischer-Hornung, Dorothea. "'Keep Alive the Powers of Africa': Katherine Dunham, Zora Neale Hurston, Maya Deren, and the Circum-Caribbean culture of Vodoun." *Atlantic Studies* 5, no. 3:347–362 (2008).

Frydman, Jason. "Zora Neale Hurston, Biographical Criticism, and African Diasporic Vernacular Culture." *MELUS* 34, no. 4:100–118 (2009).

Gates, Henry Louis, Jr. "Why the *Mule Bone* Debate Goes On." In *Critical Essays on Zora Neale Hurston.* Edited by Gloria L. Cronin. New York: Prentice Hall, 1998. Pp. 225–228.

Haas, Robert. "The Story of Louis Pasteur and the Making of *Their Eyes Were Watching God:* A Famous Film Influencing a Famous Novel?" *Literature-Film Quarterly* 32, no. 1:12–19 (January 2004).

Hardison, Ayesha K. "Crossing the Threshold: Zora Neale Hurston, Racial Performance, and *Seraph on the Suwanee.*" *African American Review* 46, no. 2–3:271–235 (2013).

Harney, Daniel. "Scholarship and the Modernist Public: Zora Neale Hurston and the Limitations of Art and Disciplinary Anthropology." *Modernism/modernity* 22, no. 3:471–492 (2015).

Heard, Matthew. "'Dancing Is Dancing No Matter Who Is Doing It': Zora Neale Hurston, Literacy, and Contemporary Writing Pedagogy." *College Literature* 34, no. 1: 129–155 (2007).

Hoefel, Roseanne. "'Different by Degree': Ella Cara Deloria, Zora Neale Hurston, and Frank Boas Contend with Race and Ethnicity." *American Indian Quarterly* 25, no. 2:181–202 (2001).

Hoeller, Hildegard. "Racial Currency: Zora Neale Hurston's 'The Gilded Six-Bits' and the Gold-Standard Debate." *American Literature* 77, no. 4:761–785 (2005).

Hoffman-Jeep, Lynda. "Creating Ethnography: Zora Neale Hurston and Lydia Cabrera." *African American Review* 39, no. 3:337–353 (2005).

Hood, Judy. "Born with a Skillet in Her Hands." *Southern Quarterly* 44, no. 2:74–87 (2007).

Jirousek, Lori. "Ethnics and Ethnographers: Zora Neale Hurston and Anzia Yezierska." *Journal of Modern Literature* 29, no. 2:19–32 (2006).

Johnson, Maria V. "'The World in a Jug and the Stopper in [Her] Hand': *Their Eyes* as Blues Performance." *African American Review* 32, no. 3:401–413 (2006).

Kam, Tanya Y. "Velvet Coats and Manicured Nails: The Body Speaks Resistance in *Dust Tracks on a Road.*" *Southern Literary Journal* 42, no. 1:73–87 (2009).

Kanthak, John F. "Legacy of Dysfunction: Family Systems in Zora Neale Hurston's *Jonah's Gourd Vine.*" *Journal of Modern Literature* 28, no. 2:113–129 (2005).

Krasner, David. "Dark Tower and the Saturday Nighters: Salons as Themes in African American Drama." *American Studies* 49, nos. 1–2:81–95 (2008).

Lawless, Elaine J. "What Zora Knew: A Crossroads, a Bargain with the Devil, and a Late Witness." *Journal of American Folklore* 126, no. 500:152–173 (2013).

Lee, Jid. "Teachin Zora." *Teaching American Literature* 8, no. 1:80–90 (2015).

Lowe, John. *Jump at the Sun: Zora Neale Hurston's Cosmic Comedy.* Urbana: University of Illinois Press, 1994.

Marino, Mark. "Multimedia Hurston: Zora Neale Hurston's Auto-Ethnographic Projects of Sound, Image, Movement, and Text." *Explorations: The Twentieth Century,* December 14, 2011. https://explorations20th.wordpress.com/2011/12/14/multimedia-hurston-zora-neale-hurstons-auto-ethnographic-projects-of-sound-image-movement-and-text/

Maroto, Ines Casas. "'So This Was a Marriage!': Intersections of Natural Imagery and the Semiotics of Space in Zora Neale Hurston's *Their Eyes Were Watching God.*" *Journal of English Studies* 11:69–82 (2013).

Meaey, Shealeen. "'In My American Fashion': National Identity, Race, and Gender Tourism in Select Works by Zora Neale Hurston, Grace Seton-Thompson, and Zatella Turner." *Women's Studies* 38:765–790 (2009).

Miles, Diana. *Women, Violence, and Testimony in the Works of Zora Neale Hurston.* New York: P. Lang, 2003.

Moylan, Virginia Lynn. *Zora Neale Hurston's Final Decade.* Gainesville: University of Florida Press, 2011.

Newell, Carol E. "Folk Culture in Women's Narratives: Literary Strategies for Diversity in Nationalist Climates." *Mississippi Quarterly* 57, no. 1:124–134 (winter 2003–2004).

Newman, Judie. "'Dis Ain't Gimme, Florida': Zora Neale Hurston's *Their Eyes Were Watching God.*" *Modern Language Review* 98, no. 4:817–825 (2003).

Nicholls, David G. "Migrant Labor, Folklore, and Resistance in Hurston's Polk County: Reframing *Mules and Men.*" *African American Review* 33, no. 3:467–479 (1999).

Noyes, Roger L. "Narrative Frames: The Poetics of Rhetorical Transformation in Charles Chestnutt and Zora Neale Hurston." *Obsidian* 8, no. 1:92–125 (2007).

Nwankwo, Ifeoma C. "Insider and Outsider, Black and American: Rethinking Zora Neale Hurston's Caribbean Enthography." *Radical History Review* 87:49–77 (2003).

Obourn, Megan. "Early Civil Rights 'Voice Work' in Richard Wright and Zora Neale Hurston." *Twentieth-Century Literature* 58, no. 2:238–265 (2012).

Pederson, Joshua. "Letting Moses Go: Hurston ad Reed, Disowning Exodus." *Twentieth-Century Literature* 58, no. 3:439–460 (2012).

Roberts, Brian Russell. "Archipelagic Diaspora, Geographical Form, and Hurston's *Their Eyes Were Watching God.*" *American Literature* 85, no. 1:122–149 (2013).

Ryan, Barbara. "'Rubbed and Polished': Reflecting on Zora Neale Hurston's 'The Conscience of the Court.'" *American Literature* 79, no. 3:554–575 (2007).

Sanchez-Pardo, Esther. "Decline and Regeneration in Modernist (Hi)stories: How to Be Modern in the Tropics." *European Journal of English Studies* 12, no. 3:291–305 (2008).

Schmidt, Amy. "Horses Chomping at the Global Bit: Ideology, Systemic Injustice, and Resistance in Zora Neale Hurston's *Tell My Horse.*" *Southern Literary Journal* 46, no. 2:173–192 (2014).

Sorenson, Leif. "Modernity on a Global Stage: Hurston's Alternative Modernism." *MELUS* 30, no. 4:3–24 (2005).

Staple, Jennifer. "Zora Neale Hurston's Construction of Authenticity Through Ethnographic Innovation." *Western Journal of Black Studies* 30, no. 1:62–68 (2006).

Stuelke, Patricia. "'Times When Greater Disciplines Are Born': The Zora Neale Hurston Revival and the Neoliberal Transformation of the Caribbean." *American Literature* 86, no. 1:117–145 (2014).

Thomas, Marion A. "Reflections on the Sanctified Church as Portrayed by Zora Neale Hurston." *Black American Literature Forum* 25, no. 1:35–41 (1991).

Tones, Emilie M. "Walking on the Rim Bones of Nothingness: Scholarship and Activism." *Journal of the American Academy of Religion* 77, no. 1:1–15 (2009).

Trefzer, Annette. "Possessing the Self: Caribbean Identities in Zora Neale Hurston's *Tell My Horse.*" *African American Review* 34, no. 2:299–312 (2000).

Wagers, Kelley. "'How come you ain't got it?': Dislocation as Historical Act in Hurston's Documentary Texts." *African American Literature* 46, nos. 2–3:201–216 (2013).

Ward, Cynthia. "Truths, Lies, Mules and Men: Through the 'Spyglass of Anthropology' and What Zora Saw There." *Western Journal of Black Studies* 36, no. 4:301–313 (2012).

Ward, Jerry W., Jr. "*Uncle Tom's Children* Revisited." *Papers on Language and Literature* 44, no. 4:343–353 (2008).

Washington, Terea N. "*Mules and Men* and Messiahs: Continuity in Yoruba Divination Verses and African American Folktales." *Journal of American Folklore* 125, no. 497:263–285 (2012).

Weathers, Glenda B. "Biblical Trees, Biblical Deliverance: Literary Landscapes of Zora Neale Hurston and Toni Morrison." *African American Review* 39, nos. 1–2:201–212 (2005).

West, M. Genevieve. "'Youse in New Yawk': The Gender Politics of Zora Neale Hurston's 'Lost' Caroline Stories." *African American Review* 47, no. 4:477–493 (2014).

Williams, Susan Millar. "'Something to Feel About': Zora Neale Hurston and Julia Peterkin in African Town." *Mississippi Quarterly* 63, nos. 1–2:294–298 (2010).

Woodson, Jon. "Zora Neale Hurston's *Their Eyes Were Watching God* and the Influence of Jens Peter Jacobsen's Marie Grubbe." *African American Review* 26, no. 4:619–635 (1992).

Yitah, Helen. "Rethinking the African American Great Migration Narrative: Reading Zora Neale Hurston's *Jonah's Gourd Vine*." *Southern Quarterly* 49, no. 1:11–29 (fall 2011).

HERMAN MELVILLE

(1819—1891)

Nicholas Spengler

The story of Herman Melville's emergence as one of the most iconic American writers of the nineteenth century might begin in 1819, the year of his birth into an aristocratic but ill-fated family in Manhattan. But it could just as easily begin a century later, when his centenary occasioned a flurry of studies and new editions of his works that brought the relatively obscure author into the literary spotlight. The centerpiece of the so-called Melville revival was *Moby-Dick* (1851), a novel that had enjoyed limited success in his own lifetime. Melville started to attract renewed attention near the end of his life, but with the revival beginning in the 1920s came his rapid canonization on both sides of the Atlantic, setting off an explosion of interest that has continued unabated to the present day.

Aside from the complexity of the texts themselves, one of the challenges of reading Melville is to parse the many versions of him that have proliferated since the revival. To the early revivalists, he was a genius ahead of his time who was finally getting his due as a protomodernist—or "a futurist long before futurism," as D. H. Lawrence put it (*Studies in Classic American Literature,* p. 138)—in a post-Victorian and postwar world that better understood him. During the Second World War and the cold war, he became a prophet warning of totalitarianism and mass violence, a characterization that continues to resonate in the twenty-first century. Poststructuralist critics have perceived in Melville's work an anticipation of postmodern aesthetics and epistemology. Other studies have identified a "transnational" Melville, a gay or "queer" Melville, and an eco-critical Melville, to name just a few interpretations. Herman Melville as he is known and read today is as much a product of the revival and subsequent scholarship as he is of the nineteenth century.

At the same time, as historically minded studies have shown, Melville fully inhabited the literary landscape of his own age. Melville's first novels of island-hopping adventure in the South Pacific, *Typee* (1846) and *Omoo* (1847), profited from their place within the popular travel literature genre of the day and made him a literary celebrity. The stylistically hybrid novels that followed, including *Mardi* (1849), challenged the tastes and expectations of his readers and met with a less-enthusiastic reception, but they nonetheless engaged with a wide range of literary genres and debates. Melville's artistic ambition often suffered from an inverse relation to critical and commercial success, but they were not mutually exclusive. *Redburn* (1849) and *White-Jacket* (1850) were popular novels, but they also prepared Melville for two more ambitious (though less profitable) ones: *Moby-Dick,* a whaling adventure turned cosmic epic, and *Pierre* (1852), a darkly subversive gothic romance. Melville struck a finer balance between artistry and the literary marketplace with his turn to magazine fiction, earning wide readership and critical acclaim for masterful stories such as "Bartleby, the Scrivener" (1853) and "Benito Cereno" (1855). This period was short-lived, however, and the fiction career that began auspiciously with *Typee* ended ominously just over a decade later with *The Confidence-Man* (1857), a mordant portrait of a divided and distrustful nation. Melville then turned to poetry, a vocation that occupied him for the rest of his life as he all but disappeared from the public eye. When he died in 1891, he left a final work of fiction, *Billy Budd: Sailor* (1924), unpublished in manuscript. Early scholars of the revival portrayed Melville as a writer who turned increasingly away from the world around him, but historicist criticism has balanced this portrait by demonstrating the significance of Melville's cultural contexts to an understanding of the range and complexity of his work.

However prophetic he appeared to later readers, Melville mapped in his writings the contours and crises of his nation and world. His early novels were published against the backdrop of rapid national expansion: both at sea, with U.S. whaleships and warships cruising around the world's oceans, and on land, with the 1845 annexation of Texas and the seizure of vast territories during the Mexican-American War (1846–1848). Many Americans perceived national expansion as part of what John L. O'Sullivan, an influential magazine editor, famously called "our manifest destiny to overspread the continent allotted by Providence" (p. 5). From this perspective, U.S. expansion was not only inevitable but beneficial, realizing the promise of what Thomas Jefferson had decades earlier called "an empire for liberty" (p. 1586). In practice, however, expansion threatened the stability of the United States. Critics of manifest destiny feared that the young republic was becoming an old-fashioned empire of conquest, spreading violence instead of liberty. Even more worryingly, expansion was pulling the nation apart from within, as debates raged about whether new states and territories would allow slavery. Disunion and disaster loomed.

Melville's novels replicate the expansive (and often inflated) rhetoric of manifest destiny and American exceptionalism, but they also reveal its inconsistencies and anxieties. In his stridently nationalistic passages, it is difficult to distinguish enthusiasm from parody. Moreover, Melville's tone evolved from the playful irony and jokiness of his early novels to the sardonic humor and bleakness of his mature fiction and poetry. Scholars have ascribed this shift to Melville's career frustrations as well as his growing disenchantment with the national destiny that was becoming manifest in the years leading up to the Civil War. For Melville, the exuberance of Jacksonian democracy lost its persuasiveness in the divisive decade before the war. Ishmael, Melville's sailor-narrator in *Moby-Dick,* states his democratic ambition to elevate "meanest mariners, renegades and castaways" to "the exalted mounts" of literature, and to accomplish the task he invokes "thou great democratic God ... who didst pick up Andrew Jackson from the pebbles; who didst hurl him upon a war-horse; who didst thunder him higher than a throne!" (1988 ed., p. 117). The hero of the novel is not a common sailor, however, but the demagogic captain Ahab, suggesting that for all its merits, democracy can become a vehicle for tyranny. More grimly, *The Confidence-Man* insinuates that the rhetoric of democratic equality and national confidence may be nothing but a swindler's device for popular manipulation.

At the same time, Melville looked beyond the nation's borders to create a highly comparative body of work. His sea fictions depict a diverse but profoundly interconnected world, in which people of many nations, races, and classes are brought together in the close quarters of the sailing ship, the port city, and the island. On one hand, this closeness has an equalizing effect; the hero of *Redburn,* though "the son-of-a-gentleman" (as the novel's subtitle establishes), learns to dispense with his elitism among sailors to whom he is nothing but a "green-hand, a landsman on his first voyage" (p. 60). On the other hand, these close encounters reveal conflicts and disparities of power: between captains and crews, between black sailors and white sailors, between "civilized" nations and "savage" ones. Melville's writings play at the boundaries of these conflicts, making his cosmopolitan vision a challenging rather than blithely reassuring one.

A sense of camaraderie, as well as an erotic charge, is evident in many of these intimate encounters, but they also reveal underlying anxieties. In the whaling port of New Bedford in *Moby-Dick,* Ishmael must share a bed with Queequeg, a tattooed Pacific Islander and reputed cannibal. Terrified at first, Ishmael nonetheless sleeps soundly and wakes to find "Queequeg's arm thrown over me in the most loving and affectionate manner" (p. 25). They become "bosom friends" (p. 51), and Queequeg no longer appears threatening. A subtler threat emerges, however, as this bond compromises Ishmael's sense of self. In a later passage, after the pair has shipped out aboard the whaleship *Pequod,* Queequeg has the perilous task of standing on the carcass of a slain whale and inserting a "blubber-hook" (p. 319). Ishmael, on deck, is attached to his friend by a "monkey-rope" joining them at the waist, soberly aware of "the dangerous liabilities which the hempen bond entailed" (p. 320); if Queequeg slips, Ishmael will go down with him. This "bond" leads him "to perceive that my own individuality was now merged in a joint stock company of two" (p. 320). No longer is his identity based entirely on "self-reliance," to borrow the title of Ralph Waldo Emerson's 1841 essay. Moreover, Ishmael realizes that everyone, "one way or other, has this Siamese connexion with a plurality of other mortals" (p. 320). Melville thus casts doubt on the practicability of radical individualism; in an increasingly linked world, we benefit from our connections, but we are also bound and may suffer by their "dangerous liabilities." In such a world, it becomes impossible to think of any individual as completely self-reliant or of any nation as completely exceptional.

Destabilizing encounters and binding connections appear throughout Melville's works. Tommo, the sailor-narrator of *Typee,* living in "captivity" among purported cannibals (Queequeg's literary predecessors), at once delights in the seductions of their island life and anxiously considers "a fate marked by the most frightful contingencies" (p. 141). Amasa Delano, the protagonist of a far different work of fiction, "Benito Cereno," finds himself in a similar bind; having boarded a Spanish slave ship in distress, the North American captain Delano is caught in the "juggling play" (p. 87) between the Spanish American captain Cereno and his attentive slave, neither of who is what he seems. If the emblem of Ishmael's contingency is the monkey-rope, the symbol of Delano's intricate connection to master and slave is the "Gordian knot" that captivates him, "his mind ... passing from its own entanglements to those of the hemp" (p. 76). Melville's tale suggests the ethical implications of U.S. involvement in slavery and empire building, entangling its American hero—"a man of ... native simplicity" (p. 63)—in complex networks of trade, exploitation, and violence.

Nor are such encounters unique to Melville's sea fictions. *Pierre,* though a domestic romance, draws upon gothic motifs of foreignness and racial difference to convey the uncanny allure of Pierre's dark-featured half-sister, Isabel. Her unknown provenance ensnares him: "he lost himself trying to follow out this tangle" (p. 49). Similarly, the lawyer-narrator of "Bartleby, the Scrivener" describes Bartleby, his former clerk, as "one of those beings of whom nothing is ascertainable" (p. 13). When Bartleby refuses—or rather, "prefer[s] not" (p. 20)—to complete his duties as a copyist, his obscurity makes it impossible for the lawyer to be rid of him: "he seemed alone, absolutely alone in the universe. A bit of wreck in the mid Atlantic" (p. 32). Like Isabel, Bartleby unsettles the boundary between the domestic and the foreign, and between the self and the inscrutable other.

Despite differences of style and subject, Melville's works share a commitment to complicating the perceived autonomy of the self. Melville's true heroes are those who struggle to reorient themselves after the dislocation of travel, contact, and exchange. Melville's poetry, while associated with his withdrawal from public life, is no exception. His epic poem *Clarel* (1876), chronicling an American theology student's pilgrimage in the Holy Land, is at once his most introspective work and among his most worldly, concerned with both the spiritual and the material conditions of existence. A similar dynamic animates *Billy Budd*; subtitled *An Inside Narrative,* the novella is about the struggle of good and evil, but it is also about the inner workings of a warship in which law and order override morality. From the cosmic to the mundane, Melville's writing demonstrates his persistent grappling with a restless world.

EARLY LIFE: FROM SON OF A GENTLEMAN TO SAILOR

Herman Melville was born on August 1, 1819, into a world that appeared relatively small and secure. His father, Allan Melvill (without the final "e"), considered himself a member of an American "aristocracy," as he wrote to his friend (and Melville's future father-in-law) Lemuel Shaw (quoted in Rogin, p. 52). Allan's father, Major Thomas Melvill, was a hero of the Boston Tea Party and the Revolutionary War and subsequently enjoyed a lucrative career at the Boston customhouse. Melville's mother, Maria Gansevoort, belonged to another American "aristocracy," a deep-seated Dutch family from Albany, New York. Her father, General Peter Gansevoort, was an even more distinguished revolutionary hero and patriarch than Major Melvill. The novel *Pierre* opens with an idyllic description of its young hero's rural family seat, an amalgam of the Melvill and Gansevoort estates. The familiar landscape that surrounds Pierre is inscribed with the colonial exploits of his great-grandfather and the revolutionary ones of his grandfather: "Thus loftily, in the days of his circumscribed youth, did Pierre glance along the background of his race" (p. 6). In his own "circumscribed youth," with frequent visits to the Melvill homes in Boston and the Berkshires, and to the Gansevoort homes in Albany and the hamlet of Gansevoort (named for his grandfather), Herman Melville was encouraged to do the same.

Unlike Pierre, however, Melville spent the first years of his life in New York City. After marriage, his parents moved to Manhattan so that Allan could pursue a career as an importer of luxury dry goods. Allan financed his enterprise with large loans from his and his wife's families, as well as from other creditors, promising a windfall that never arrived; his small firm could not keep up with the burgeoning wholesale market, and he fell deeper into debt. To make matters worse, he periodically moved his growing family—Melville was the third of eight children—into grander houses in wealthier neighborhoods. Finally, in October 1830, Allan was forced to abandon his career and life in Manhattan, fleeing with his family to Albany. Pressure from his New York creditors mounted, and in January 1832, having caught pneumonia on his return from an attempt to appease them, Allan Melvill died in a delirious fit. In *Pierre,* Melville contrasts the stability of his hero's country home with "the democratic element [that] operates as a subtile acid" in America's urban centers, "forever producing new things by corroding the old." "In our cities," Melville writes, "families rise and burst like bubbles in a vat" (p. 9).

After Allan's death, Maria changed the family name to "Melville." The Melville scholar Michael Paul Rogin speculates that Maria wished "to replace the name of a bankrupt with that of an aristocrat" (p. 32); "Melville" was the name of her husband's noble Scottish ancestors. Likewise, the flight to Albany was less a new beginning than a retreat into the security of family. As Melville suggests in *Pierre,* however, such security often proves illusory: "Now Pierre stands on this noble pedestal; we shall see if he keeps that fine footing" (p. 12). Maria and her children had already lost their footing, and family connections did little to help them regain it. Melville's schooling became sporadic as he worked a number of jobs, though he dabbled in debating and writing. He took a surveying course in 1838 in the hopes of working in the construction of the Erie Canal, but when those plans failed he went to sea instead. In June 1839, he left New York as a "green-hand" on a merchant ship bound for Liverpool.

Melville's family had its share of sailors, and the decision to "to sail about a little and see the watery part of the world" (p. 3), as he writes in *Moby-Dick,* did not necessarily contradict his genteel background or his budding literary ambitions. In 1834, Richard Henry Dana, Jr., another son of a prominent Boston family, had taken a break from Harvard to sail on a merchant ship, the literary fruit of which was his memoir *Two Years Before the Mast* (1840). Melville's first experience as a sailor would provide the basis for his fourth novel, *Redburn.* Melville became a sailor not just for worldly experience, however, but also because, unlike Dana, he had few prospects at home; he had no college or career to return to. Redburn is introduced to his captain as the son of "a gentleman of one of the first families in America" (p. 16), but he accepts a low salary with no advance, too ashamed to admit that his father, like Allan Melvill, "died a bankrupt" (p. 155). Like Redburn, Melville left New York with the dubious honor of his family reputation, but he returned from Liverpool several months later as a sailor. After another failed attempt at finding work as a surveyor, traveling as far west as the prairies, Melville shipped out again, in January 1841, this time aboard the whaleship *Achushnet,* bound for the whaling grounds of the Pacific. What Ishmael says of his education in *Moby-Dick* reflects Melville's own experience: "a whale-ship was my Yale College and my Harvard" (p. 112).

Unlike merchant voyages, whaling cruises typically lasted for multiple years, and whaleships often sailed for months without visiting any harbor, doggedly pursuing their colossal quarry. Melville communicates these circumstances in the opening lines of *Typee*: "Six months at sea! Yes, reader, as I live, six months out of sight of land; cruising after the sperm-whale beneath the scorching sun of the Line" (p. 3). When they did drop anchor, many sailors seized the opportunity to escape the dreary and exhausting conditions through desertion. Melville would not return home until nearly four years later, but he spent only the first year and a half on the *Achushnet.* In that time, the ship made brief stops at Rio de Janeiro in Brazil, the northern coast of Peru, and the Galápagos Islands. More frequent were the "gams," or visits between passing whaleships, when captains and crews could share stories and news—or even exchange letters from or bound for home, since many of the ships hailed from the same handful of ports. Indeed, the world of whaling ships could seem almost as small as the communities its sailors had left behind.

In June 1842, the *Acushnet* arrived at Nuku Hiva in the Marquesas Islands, which promised the exotic thrills Melville describes in *Typee*: "The Marquesas! What strange visions of outlandish things does the very name spirit up! Naked houris—cannibal banquets—groves of cocoa-nut—coral reefs—tattooed chiefs—and bamboo temples" (p. 5). When Melville arrived, however, France had just seized the islands, marring these imaginative associations of a savage paradise. Tommo describes entering the sweeping bay of Nuku Hiva, "but that beauty was lost to me then, and I saw nothing but the tri-colored flag of France trailing over the stern of six vessels, whose black hulls and bristling broadsides proclaimed their warlike character" (p. 12). (On a lighter note, Tommo relates the uninhibited pleasures that await them when naked indigenous women swim out to the ship like "so many mermaids"; p. 14.) Despite the uncertainty of what they would find beyond the shore, Melville and a fellow sailor, Toby Greene, took their chances and deserted at Nuku Hiva, hoping to hide out long enough to evade a search party and then sign on with another ship.

Typee relates Melville's experience on the island, albeit through the fictional guise of Tommo. Having scaled the island's mountainous interior, Tommo and Toby find themselves in the valley of the "Typee" (Taipi) people, reputed to be the most cannibalistic of the island's inhabitants. They are relieved to find that the Typees are generous hosts, though Tommo is effectively trapped in their company by a leg injury. He is parted from Toby when the latter goes to investigate reports of ships in the Typees' bay and fails to return. Now alone, Tommo gradually adjusts to his circumstances, befriending his personal attendant, Kory-Kory, and "the beauteous nymph Fayaway" (p. 85). He also observes a variety of indigenous practices, fulfilling the subtitle's promise of *A Peep at Polynesian Life*: tattooing, the mystifying social codes of the "taboo," religious rites, and feasts. Tommo's tone blends anthropological curiosity with frantic concern; notwithstanding his good terms with the Typees, he fears that he might end up being eaten or, perhaps even worse, branded for life with a facial tattoo. These worries prompt his escape at the novel's conclusion, hobbling to the bay when another whaling ship approaches.

It is impossible to know to what degree Melville's experiences on Nuku Hiva corresponded with Tommo's. What is certain is that after one month on the island—the "captivity" that he would extend to four months in the novel—Melville signed aboard an Australian whaler bound for Tahiti. Tensions among the officers and crew were already running high, and once they reached Tahiti, Melville joined other sailors in refusing to work. The British consul sent the rebels to the island's prison, but discipline was erratic and Melville was soon set loose to wander the island and neighboring Eimeo, before shipping out on a Nantucket whaleship. The eventful period between his departure from Nuku Hiva in August 1842 and his departure from Eimeo in November provided the basic plot for *Omoo.*

After a six-month cruise on his third whaler, Melville disembarked in the Sandwich Islands (now Hawaii), working odd jobs until August 1843, when he joined the crew of the USS *United States.* Compared with whaling, life in a naval frigate—or *The World in a Man-of-War,* as the subtitle to *White-Jacket* puts it—featured more discipline but also more free time, with long spells in port. Melville received a shore leave while anchored in Callao, Peru, and traveled inland to Lima, the old colonial capital that would figure in several of his fictions. The frigate also had a well-stocked library, containing many travel accounts and histories. When the *United States* finally reached Boston in October 1844, Melville returned to his family and friends with his own well-rehearsed adventures and those of other sailors, ready to embellish and to modify, depending on his audience.

A YOUNG WRITER IN YOUNG AMERICA: TYPEE, OMOO, MARDI, REDBURN, *AND* WHITE-JACKET

Beyond a rough trajectory sketched in ships' logs and other records, what we know of Melville's experiences as a sailor is based on his fictionalized accounts of them in *Typee* (1846), *Omoo* (1847), *Redburn* (1849), and *White-Jacket* (1850). From the 1930s, however, scholars began to discover that Melville was not only a crafty embellisher but also a prolific pilferer of other material. Biographies such as those by Andrew Delbanco and Hershel Parker balance inferences drawn from Melville's fictions with a wealth of contextual material, including his creative use of sources. Mary Bercaw-Edwards, Geoffrey Sanborn, John Samson, and other scholars have used Melville's widespread borrowings to illuminate his development and strategies as a young writer. From his breezily conversational tone to his references to cannibalism and other racy topics guaranteed to attract readers, Melville copied, adapted, and tested a host of written and spoken narrative traditions.

Typee and *Omoo* were published as travel narratives, though his readers (and publishers) suspected Melville of at least some fictional license. Many critics praised *Typee*'s literary merit and thrilling plot but on the same grounds expressed doubt that it could be the work of a sailor. Another strain on the U.S. reception of *Typee* was its acerbic treatment of American missionaries in the Pacific; in Honolulu, Melville relates, "the small remnant of the natives had been civilized into draught horses, and evangelized into beasts of burden" (p. 196). Melville revised *Typee* for a second U.S. edition that expurgated the most contentious material. Meanwhile, *Typee*'s credibility received a boost from Toby Greene, who had parted ways with Melville sometime during their stay on Nuku Hiva—perhaps under circumstances similar to those in the novel—and found his own way home. Greene publicly corroborated *Typee,* and Melville prepared "The Story of Toby" as a postscript.

Typee is more than a travel book, however. Melville drew upon other travel narratives not only to lend credibility to his own but also as a subject meriting as much scrutiny as the exotic cultures they purported to lay bare. Melville describes one author's "accounts" as "calculated to leave upon the reader's mind an impression that human victims are daily cooked and served up upon the altars": "Be it observed, however, that all this information is given by a man who ... was only at one of the islands and remained there but two weeks, sleeping every night on board his ship, and taking little kid-glove excursions ashore in the day-time, attended by an armed party" (p. 170). On one hand, this passage reflects the competition between travel writers; Melville (or Tommo) claims to be a closer and more reliable eyewitness than this fussy tourist. On the other hand, it calls into question the reliability of any account of the island's inhabitants. Despite Tommo's privileged insights into Typee culture, he never resolves the question of whether they practice cannibalism. Melville provides enough hints to fuel Tommo's and his readers' excited imaginations, but he never allows them to draw firm conclusions. *Typee* is as much a study of how travelers construct "savage" cultures, often (as in Melville's case) for the sake of making a profit and a name for oneself. There is a hint of wry self-portraiture in Melville's description of an "old chief" who advertises himself as "the living tomb of Captain Cook's big toe," "giving very profitable audiences to all curious travellers who were desirous of beholding the man who had eaten the great navigator's great toe" (p. 234). In the era of P. T. Barnum's "American Museum" in New York, which exhibited curiosities for visitors to gawk at, *Typee* made Melville a literary spectacle: the "man who lived among the cannibals" (*Correspondence,* p. 193), as he later self-mockingly wrote to Nathaniel Hawthorne.

Typee also suggests Melville's awareness of his place within the travel genre's promotion of exploration and settlement. Tommo hopes that the "yet uncontaminated" Typees may be spared from "foreign inflictions," but his rousing narrative of discovery makes that preservation unlikely. If *Typee* holds out some hope that they may "remain the happy and innocent heathens and barbarians that they now are" (p. 181), *Omoo* offers no such vision. The peoples of Tahiti and Eimeo, overrun with missionaries, warships, and foreign diseases, are now "less civilized than formerly" (p. 189), having abandoned their native industries and dramatically declined in population. Melville blunts his critique, however, by suggesting that no civilizing mission can succeed among "an indolent people like the Polynesians," who are "calculated for a state of nature" (p. 190). Melville thus perpetuates the notion, held by both promoters and critics of "civilization," that indigenous peoples were frozen in an earlier stage of human development, doomed to perish through increasing contact with outsiders likc Melville himself.

In *Omoo,* Melville also turns his ethnographic eye on the culture of the sailing ship. The first part of *Omoo* takes place aboard the Australian whaler, describing the political vacuum caused by the ineffectual Captain Guy, "more like a sickly counting-house clerk than a bluff sea-captain" (p. 6). Tommo (known in this novel as "Typee" and later as "Omoo," meaning "rover") sympathizes with his fellow sailors, but he also urges caution, "impressing upon them that a little patience and management would ... accomplish all that their violence could ... without making a serious matter of it" (p. 73). He writes out a list of grievances to present to the British consul, at the bottom of which the sailors sign "in a ring" so that "no man can be picked out as the leader of it" (p. 74)—at once a practical measure and a symbol of the signers' equality and solidarity. The crew here resembles a republic in miniature; "Typee" and his fellow signers create a document like the Declaration of Independence, an act of democratic authority and foundation.

Unfortunately, that action lands them in jail, but even that is no "serious matter" in *Omoo,* which defuses political tensions with humor. As Christopher Sten points out, in its comic episodes, *Omoo* fits within the tradition of the "picaresque" novel, using humor as a safe platform for social critique. Melville portrays both the ship and the islands, Sten writes, "in such advanced states of disorder and decay as to abound in subjects fit for satire ... the picaresque writer's stock in trade" (p. 53). Melville's early experiments with genre and form allowed him to write in a way that was entertaining but also critical of a world in which injustice and corruption prevail and in which people must rely on their wits and on each other to survive.

Typee and *Omoo* may portray a distant world, but while writing them Melville was swept up in activity at home. His older brother, Gansevoort, had made a name for himself as a Democratic speechmaker, helping usher James K. Polk to the presidency in 1844 on an aggressively expansionist platform. Gansevoort then went to London as a diplomat, but he died of illness there shortly after *Typee*'s publication. Before learning of Gansevoort's death, Melville sent his brother a letter reacting to Polk's belated declaration of war on Mexico; "something great is impending" (*Correspondence,* p. 41), Melville wrote, with a mixture of excitement and foreboding. Melville's own future looked promising: in short order, he published two successful novels; married Elizabeth Shaw, who was the daughter of his father's friend Lemuel Shaw, now chief justice of the Supreme Court of Massachusetts; and (with a loan from his father-in-law) bought a house with his brother Allan in Manhattan. When he started writing *Mardi* in 1847, however, Melville was growing ambivalent about the national destiny his older brother had championed. *Mardi* (1849) began as another Pacific adventure, but it wandered into uncharted waters, becoming a sprawlingly philosophical work as well as an allegorical satire in the style of Jonathan Swift's *Gulliver's Travels* (1726).

Mardi's narrator deserts with a fellow sailor, navigating in a whaleboat to a fictional archipelago ("Mardi"), with islands representing the United States ("Vivenza") and various European powers. Most of the novel is spent pursuing the beautiful and elusive Polynesian girl Yillah—a metaphysical as well as romantic quest—but Melville also uses this wandering plot to comment upon current events, from the war in Mexico to the republican revolutions (and subsequent restorations of monarchy) that rocked Europe in 1848. The prophetic scroll addressed to the "sovereign-kings" of Vivenza compares the island unfavorably to "Dominora" (Britain) and its tyrant king; therein, Melville condemns U.S. foreign policy ("your great chieftain"—a reference to Polk—has done "a still more imperial thing," having "gone to war without declaring intentions") and the gross inequality of the supposed land of liberty ("your federal temple of freedom ... was the handiwork of slaves") (p. 528). Nevertheless, Melville tacitly accepts the idea of manifest destiny, suggesting that expansion could happen naturally without bloodshed: "Time, but Time only, may enable you to cross the equator; and give you the Arctic Circles for your boundaries" (p. 530). *Mardi* evinces, among other things, the struggle to maintain faith in the American "empire for liberty," given the "imperial thing[s]" that U.S. leaders were doing in liberty's name.

In literary as well as political terms, *Mardi* was Melville's first attempt to write an "American" book. Alongside calls for national expansion were calls for a national form of writing, distinct from Old World models. Literary nationalists did not always agree with political nationalists, but they shared many values (and central figures, like O'Sullivan), and they even bore the same name: "Young America." At the forefront of literary Young America was the New York editor and tastemaker Evert Duyckinck, whom Melville befriended in 1846. Like O'Sullivan, Duyckinck called for a national literature, and with *Mardi,* Melville aimed to answer that call. Duyckinck reviewed the novel favorably in his magazine, the *Literary World,* but *Mardi* exhausted the patience of other critics; twice as long and far more "roving" than *Omoo, Mardi* struck some readers as a new and exciting book but most as a hodge-podge of borrowed styles and rhapsodic ramblings.

Melville's first child, Malcolm, was born in February 1849, shortly before *Mardi* was published. Hoping to turn a quick profit after his lengthy investment in *Mardi,* Melville rapidly wrote *Redburn* and *White-Jacket* that spring and summer. He later dismissed them as "two *jobs,* which I have done for money" (*Correspondence,* p. 138) in a letter to Lemuel Shaw, but they nevertheless represent the consolidation and maturation of his narrative voice. Compared to Melville's earlier sea fictions, *Redburn* offers a fuller portrait of its sailor-hero. Redburn recalls his late merchant father, whose memory is associated with a glass ship he had brought back from France. The ship is at once a symbol of Redburn's youthful fascination with the sea, of his adolescent frustration with his family's sinking fortunes, and of his adult retrospection. "I had learned to think much and bitterly before my time," the narrator says of his younger self. No longer bitter about the "hardhearted world" (p. 10), the experienced Redburn is almost cheerfully resigned to it. He has inherited the glass ship. The warrior figurehead has snapped off, "but I will not have him put on his legs again, till I get on my own; for between him and me there is a secret sympathy; and my sisters tell me

... that he fell ... the very day I left home to go to sea on this *my first voyage*" (p. 9). In the novel's first pages, Melville conveys the sweeping scope of a life, and a depth of perspective he had not achieved before.

Like *Omoo,* Redburn also relates a series of adventures at sea and on land. Among the ship's crew, he is no longer Wellingborough Redburn, named after a distinguished great-uncle, but "Buttons," derisively named for the large buttons on his shooting jacket. A hand-me-down from his older brother, the jacket is a symbol of Redburn's struggle to fit in, both with the crew and with new acquaintances ashore in England, among whom "that miserable shooting-jacket of mine was a perpetual drawback to my claims to gentility" (p. 214). At the same time, his loneliness endows him with sympathy for society's overlooked margins. In Liverpool, equipped with his father's old guidebook, he traces the path his father had taken decades before, "performing a filial pilgrimage" (p. 154) that leads him to a square where a monument to Horatio Nelson has since been erected. At the base of the monument are "four naked figures in chains," "emblematic of Nelson's principal victories" (p. 155), but they remind Redburn of slaves and of the commerce of human suffering that once linked the Atlantic world. Further suffering confronts him when he hears "the low, hopeless, endless wail of some one forever lost" (p. 180) and finds a woman and her infant children dying in a cellar. Rather than connecting him to his dead father, Liverpool only reinforces the world's hard-heartedness.

White-Jacket's narrator is similarly ostracized for his unsuitable coat, "an outlandish garment of my own devising" (p. 3) that sets him apart within the crew of the naval frigate. When he falls overboard, he is forced to cut himself out of it to survive. Rogin calls these jackets "instruments of anxious self-dramatization" (p. 89); Redburn and White-Jacket must break free of that stuffy sense of self to be reborn into the democratic fraternity of the crew. Indeed, both novels, like *Omoo,* use the ship as a stage for playing out democratic politics in miniature. Multiple versions of popular (and populist) authority emerge: in *Redburn,* the crew's leader is Jackson, "a great bully" (p. 57) who commands both respect and fear; and in *White-Jacket,* the natural leaders are Jack Chase, who wins loyalty through charm and bravado, and Mad Jack, who leads by capability and cunning. These characters represent alternatives to the autocratic rule of captains. In *White-Jacket,* Mad Jack intervenes twice to save the ship: first countermanding the captain in a violent storm and later preventing a mutiny against the captain's tyranny. Nevertheless, the very leadership qualities that keep the ship afloat in *White-Jacket* anticipate the destructiveness of authority in *Moby-Dick.*

After finishing *White-Jacket,* Melville traveled to London to negotiate the terms for its publication. This was also an opportunity for him to gather inspiration and materials for future writings: first and foremost, the story of his white whale.

WHALES AND KRAKENS: MOBY-DICK *AND* PIERRE

Melville began *Moby-Dick* early in 1850, while he was still living in New York; the novel, published in 1851, opens with its affable narrator ("Call me Ishmael," he insists) in the "insular city of the Manhattoes" (p. 3). Like Ishmael, however, Melville escaped the city—not for the sea but for a summer in the Berkshires. He soon decided to move there permanently, purchasing (with the help of another loan from Lemuel Shaw) a homestead neighboring the old Melvill estate. Events conspired not only to slow down Melville's writing but also to push it in a new direction. In August, he met Nathaniel Hawthorne, who had recently moved to the Berkshires. They became, as Ishmael says, "bosom friends"—though Hawthorne was relatively reserved compared to his effusive younger friend—and Melville ultimately dedicated *Moby-Dick* to him. With Hawthorne, Melville experienced "an infinite fraternity of feeling" (*Correspondence,* p. 212), as he would write to his friend in November 1851, after Hawthorne had read and praised the finished novel.

Melville also found in Hawthorne an example of the darkly Romantic but distinctly "American" writing he had attempted in *Mardi* and would weave into the developing form of *Moby-Dick.* Around the time of their meeting, Melville reviewed Hawthorne's *Mosses from an Old Manse* (1846) for the *Literary World,* admiring the "mystical blackness" (*The Piazza Tales and Other Prose Pieces,* p. 243) beneath the surface of his stories and comparing him to William Shakespeare. At the same time, Melville dismissed criticism of U.S. writers as cheap imitators of their British and Continental counterparts, noting that "in his own life-time," Shakespeare "was hooted at, as an 'upstart crow' beautified 'with other birds' feathers' [for] imitation is often the first charge brought against real originality" (p. 246). Using Shakespeare to make the case for American literary novelty might seem odd, but it conveys Melville's sense that "real originality" emerges through engagement with past forms and ideas. Indeed, Melville drew deeply on Shakespeare and many other writers in composing *Moby-Dick.*

Scholars have debated his process, but all agree that Melville finished a markedly different novel from the one he started. As with most of his writings, no manuscript survives, but traces of Melville's radical revisions made it into the final book. Early in the novel, Ishmael describes a sailor "held somewhat aloof" (p. 15) from the rest: "He stood full six feet in height, with noble shoulders, and a chest like a coffer-dam" (p. 16). Melville seems to have big plans for this sailor, Bulkington, but he disappears from the narrative, resurfacing only in a "six-inch chapter" that marks his "stoneless grave" (p. 106). Temperamentally and physically, Bulkington resembles Jack Chase, the "noble," "tall and well-knit" sailor in *White-Jacket* (p. 13). It is likely that Melville intended to make Bulkington a similar sailor-hero in *Moby-Dick.* (Another hint is an isolated chapter, "The Town-Ho's Story," which recounts a "tall and noble" [p. 246] sailor's revolt against an overbearing captain and malicious mate; Melville may have had such a plot in mind for the novel as a whole, but instead he reduces it to a yarn that Ishmael spins for the amusement of aristocratic Peruvians in Lima.) Aboard the *Pequod,* Bulkington is scrapped in favor of the pragmatic Starbuck, whose "bravery ... while generally abiding firm in the conflict with seas, or winds, or whales ... yet cannot withstand those more terrific, because more spiritual terrors, which sometimes menace you from the concentrating brow of an enraged and mighty man" (p. 117). That mighty man is Ahab, the novel's darkly attractive hero, like Satan in John Milton's seventeenth-century epic poem, *Paradise Lost.* No one is a match for him—except for Moby-Dick, the "White Whale [that] swam before him as the monomaniac incarnation of all those malicious agencies which some deep men feel eating in them" (p. 184). Ahab seeks revenge on the albino whale that "dismasted" (p. 124) him, taking off his leg. (Many critics also interpret this as a sexual wound.)

In Ahab, Melville unites the legal authority of the captain with the popular authority of the crew, and the combination is deadly. In a theatrical speech, Ahab convinces the crew to adopt his vendetta as their collective mission. In the meantime, the crew gets on with the business of whaling; the "chase" as Melville depicts it is thrilling and dangerous, while the aftermath converts the ship into a smoking factory, rendering blubber into oil. Melville finds poetry and communion in both aspects of the job: he evokes the whispered encouragement to sailors rowing in unison after a whale ("Pull, pull, my good boys," says Starbuck [p. 222]); and he describes the men squeezing lumps of sperm-whale oil to break them up, inadvertently catching each others' hands ("Come; let us squeeze hands all round; nay, let us all squeeze ourselves into each other; let us squeeze ourselves universally into the very milk and sperm of kindness" [p. 416]). Melville's language is at once erotic and transcendental; as in his intense attraction to Hawthorne, the boundary between the sensual and the spiritual is never clear. Wherever it lies, Melville emphasizes the fellowship of men united in work, which makes Ahab's appropriation of them as "tools" in "accomplish[ing] his object" (p. 211) all the more tragic. Starbuck comes close to rebellion, prompting the crew to raise "a half mutinous cry," but Ahab stifles it by reminding them, "All your oaths to hunt the White Whale are as binding as mine" (p. 508).

In *Moby-Dick,* Melville expands the political allegory of captain and crew. Scholars have identified models for Ahab in leaders from across the political spectrum of antebellum America, from the expansionist Polk, to the proslavery senator John C. Calhoun, to the abolitionist senator Charles Sumner. Unlike *Mardi*'s satire, in which the allegorical referents are clear, however, Melville makes Ahab irreducible to any single figure. Ahab expresses Melville's sense that, regardless of rhetoric, the United States had sacrificed the promise of democracy to the practice of empire. The *Pequod* is a "cannibal of a craft" (p. 70), and its fatal trajectory portends a nation wrecked by its insatiable appetite.

At the same time, Ahab's "monomaniac" ambition is a metaphysical one; like the search for Yillah in *Mardi,* the quest for the white whale represents the desire for ultimate knowledge. At the end of his infamous speech, Ahab tells a wary Starbuck, "All visible objects, man, are but as pasteboard masks.... If man will strike, strike through the mask!" (p. 164). For Ahab, harpooning the white whale is equivalent to penetrating the secrets of the universe. Subscribers to this reading align Ahab with Melville himself, as an ambitious artist pursuing "the ungraspable phantom of life" (p. 5). Others have read Ahab as a sort of mad scientist, with an uncanny aptitude for making compass needles twitch and lightning strike. The text supports an astonishing range of readings, as Melville blends metaphysics with materiality. Ishmael extols the whale's blubber as evidence of "the rare virtue of a strong individual vitality," paraphrasing the Gospel when he exclaims, "Oh, man! admire and model thyself after the whale! ... Do thou, too, live in the world without being of it" (p. 307). Yet the whale in question is being stripped of its blubber, converted into oil as well as a symbol of integrity. As Samuel Otter argues, the technical and anatomical aspects of *Moby-Dick* "do not simply form the documentary base that moors Melville's speculation" (p. 133); rather, they are integral to the novel's meaning, cutting across fields of knowledge and experience to articulate the manifold ways in which people represent and relate to the world around them.

This cutting across of fields and mixing of forms met with a variable response from readers. Hawthorne lauded *Moby-Dick,* but many reviewers, including Duyckinck, complained that the characters were too literary to be credible as sailors. Duyckinck also objected to Melville's "piratical running down of creeds and opinions" (quoted in 1988 ed., p. 722), fusing scripture with blubber and commerce with cannibalism. Accusations of blasphemy were not as prevalent in Britain, where Melville's publisher, Richard Bentley, toned down his gleeful irreverence to avoid offending the sensibilities of the middle-class reading public. Nor did the novel's literariness bother British reviewers, though many had reservations about its jarring shuffle of genres. (Another much-remarked flaw was not Melville's own; his British publisher had declined to print the "Epilogue" in which Ishmael explains how he alone "survive[d] the wreck" [p. 573], so to British readers it appeared that Ishmael narrates from beyond the grave.) Despite enthusiasm from some readers, *Moby-Dick* fell short of Melville's critical and commercial expectations.

In a November 1851 letter to Hawthorne, buoyed by his friend's praise, Melville hinted at his next monstrous ambition: "Leviathan is not the biggest fish;—I have heard of Krakens" (*Correspondence,* p. 213). With *Moby-Dick* finished, Melville immediately began *Pierre* (1852). He later wrote gratefully to Hawthorne's wife, Sophia, for her own praise of *Moby-Dick,* before promising something different with *Pierre*: "But, My Dear Lady, I shall not again send you a bowl of salt water. The next chalice I shall commend, will be a rural bowl of milk" (p. 219). It is difficult to square these contrasting images of *Pierre*—the giant squid versus the bucolic bowl—but its subtitle, *The Ambiguities,* indicates its capacity for both. *Pierre* is a gothic romance, a genre designed to appeal mainly to female readers, full of sentiment and intrigue set against a domestic backdrop. Like other examples of the genre, such as Hawthorne's *The House of the Seven Gables* (1851), *Pierre* also tests the limits of familial and social relationships and identities. Melville was less subtle than Hawthorne about his subversion of those relationships, however, and the question of identity becomes a riddle murkier than any in *Moby-Dick.*

From "the embowered and high-gabled old home of his fathers" (p. 3), Pierre falls precipitously, ending up in "The Tombs," the Manhattan prison where he dies in Isabel's arms, "her long hair ... arbor[ing] him in ebon vines" (p. 362). Isabel is the dark, mysterious creature that drags Pierre to his death. "Pierre's great life revolution," Melville writes, is "the receipt of Isabel's letter" (p. 225)—a common gothic trope—revealing her identity as the product of his late father's youthful affair with an unknown woman. Pierre's knowledge of Isabel has a strange effect on him: "his very blood seem[ing] to flow through all his arteries with unwonted subtileness, when he thought that the same tide flowed through the mystic veins of Isabel" (p. 139). *Pierre* is about the inextricability of blood ties, but it is also about the fear of racial mixture embodied by Isabel, who casts a "black shadow" (p. 190) on Pierre. The incest plot reinforces this anxiety. In order to care for Isabel without revealing her identity and tarnishing his father's image (represented in the novel by two contrasting portraits), Pierre marries her, forsaking his engagement to his respectable and fair-featured fiancée. Reeling at the news, Pierre's mother feels "as though I had borne the last of a swiftly to be extinguished race" (p. 131). She dies of despair, but not before disinheriting him.

As Christopher Freeburg argues, the "blackness" in *Pierre* is both racial and metaphysical. Having taken the moral high ground, Pierre feels liberated, declaring that he has "no paternity, and no past" but only "his ever-present self" (p. 199). He moves with Isabel to New York, that city of democratic possibility. Yet his course of action is not a product of "self-will" (p. 199) but of "a silent and tyrannic call" (p. 49), and Pierre begins to doubt the substance of his attachment to Isabel. Is she really his sister? He has penetrated "the first superficiality of the world," but as he continues to puzzle over his sister's and his own identity, he finds, like a "geologist," that the world "consist[s] of nothing but surface stratified on surface" (p. 285).

Melville's novel of ambiguities was a complete flop upon publication in July 1852. Compounding its failure was his decision, after accepting a poor deal from his American publishers (Harper & Brothers) and falling out with Duyckinck, to expand the manuscript with chapters detailing Pierre's career as a struggling writer, allowing for a bitter satire not only of himself but also of his publishers and Duyckinck. Melville thus almost ensured that his novel would fail, at a moment when he needed it to succeed; his flagging career could not pay off his debts or support a growing family—with four children by 1855 in addition to his wife, mother, and sisters.

PERIODICALS AND POP CULTURE: MAGAZINE FICTION AND THE CONFIDENCE-MAN

Early Melville scholars considered *Pierre* the beginning of the end of Melville's career, viewing *Moby-Dick* as the cresting of his wave just before it collapsed. In fact, in *Pierre*'s wake came a productive and successful period, from 1853 to 1856, when Melville wrote for popular magazines. Sheila Post-Lauria observes that "for the first time in his career, he discovered large audiences receptive to his literary interests" (p. 163). Melville wrote pieces for two periodicals: *Harper's New Monthly Magazine,* a Harper & Brothers venture with a massive circulation; and the recently inaugurated *Putnam's Monthly Magazine,* with a smaller (though still substantial) circulation and a mission to promote American literature. Melville became one of *Putnam's* best writers, and his contributions were later collected in *The Piazza Tales* (1856). Among his most celebrated *Putnam's* pieces was "The Encantadas, or Enchanted Isles" (1854), a series of "sketches" depicting the natural and human history of the Galápagos Islands. Critics hailed it as a welcome return to his early travel writing, drawing from other accounts (such as Charles Darwin's 1839 survey of the islands) to construct his own captivating episodes and philosophical meditations. In 1854–1855 *Putnam's* also serialized a well-liked novel, *Israel Potter: His Fifty Years of Exile* (1855), based on the memoir of a Revolutionary War hero who was captured by the British Navy and spent most of his adult life impoverished in London. Melville fictionalized Israel Potter as a comically naive but sympathetic hero.

Melville's pieces for *Harper's* are shorter and less known today, but like the *Putnam's* fictions they demonstrate Melville's engagement with popular culture and popular forms to express his perennial concerns. Among the *Harper's* pieces are two "diptychs," or paired stories, juxtaposing an American scene with a corresponding British one. "The Paradise of Bachelors and the Tartarus of Maids" (1855), for example, first depicts a convivial feast among "bachelors" in the privileged confines of the Temple in London, and next it describes a snowbound paper mill in the Berkshires, where the laborers, all unmarried women, are as blank-faced as the sheets they produce. These isolated worlds have little in common, but Melville relates them by an "inverted similitude" (*The Piazza Tales,* 1987 ed., p. 327), suggesting the impossibility of considering anything in isolation.

Melville's first *Putnam's* contribution, "Bartleby, the Scrivener" (1853), is another tale of the deadening effects of repetitive labor—in this case, copying legal documents. Bartleby copies well, but when asked to complete any other task he responds, "I would prefer not to" (p. 20). Finally, like a worn-out part, he ceases working altogether, becoming simply "a fixture" (p. 32) in the law office. Bartleby is evicted only after his exasperated employer moves his office to another building, and Bartleby ends his days, like Pierre, in the "Tombs." Admired when it was first published, "Bartleby" continues to attract readers and interpretations. The poststructuralist critic Gilles Deleuze identifies Bartleby as a recurrent type in Melville's works, whose repeated "formula" ("I would prefer not to") unsettles the conventions on which social relationships and identities are based.

Two gothic tales appeared in *Putnam's* in 1855: "The Bell-Tower" and "Benito Cereno." In the former, the architect Bannadonna designs a grand tower with an elaborate mechanism using an automaton to strike its giant bell, but his "creature" (*The Piazza Tales,* p. 186) ultimately kills him. Melville's epigraphs to "The Bell-Tower" indicate how he wanted readers to interpret this baroque allegory. The first reads, "Like negroes, these powers own man sullenly; mindful of their higher master; while serving, plot revenge" (p. 174). Melville's story of failed mastery was therefore well matched for the antislavery editorial position of *Putnam's.* The last epigraph goes beyond the slavery question, however, to challenge the broader premise of Jefferson's "empire for liberty": "Seeking to conquer a larger liberty, man but extends the empire of necessity" (p. 174).

These epigraphs serve just as well to introduce "Benito Cereno," which deals directly and more extensively with slavery. Like *Israel Potter,* Melville adapted it from an autobiographical account, but in this case the naïveté of his hero is not charming but disturbing. Set in 1799 off the coast of Chile, Melville's story relates Captain Delano's encounter with Benito Cereno and his disorderly ship full of slaves. (Melville names the ship the *San Dominick,* suggestive of the contemporary revolution in Saint-Domingue, or Haiti.) Delano vacillates between sympathizing with the sickly Spaniard and suspecting him of a darker plot. On the other hand, Delano is beguiled by Cereno's personal slave, Babo, who presents the very picture of docility: "As master and man stood before him ... Captain Delano could not but bethink him of the beauty of that relationship which could present such a spectacle of fidelity on the one hand and confidence on the other" (p. 57). The bitter irony of this "spectacle" is that Babo has led the slaves in rebellion, and he now orchestrates an elaborate masquerade to conceal it. When Delano finally discovers the plot, he calls on his crew to suppress the mutiny, and the story concludes in Lima with Babo's execution and Cereno's death from illness. Like Pierre, Cereno's contact with blackness has "cast ... a shadow upon [him]" (p. 116) from which he cannot recover. Of the three, Delano is the only survivor, but he is hardly a triumphant hero. The tale indicates the hollowness of Delano's self-professed "good nature, compassion, and charity" (p. 115).

"Benito Cereno" has generated a vast amount of scholarship and debate. Some scholars demonstrate its reliance on racial and ethnic stereotypes, while others show how it subverts them. Some accuse Melville of failing to offer more than an opaque criticism of Delano's naïveté and paternalism, while others argue that the process of reading the text is itself a morally and politically challenging exercise. The allegorical scope of the tale is another subject of debate. Many have read "Benito Cereno" as a national allegory, with Delano representing the industrious North and Cereno the aristocratic, slave-owning South. Others have argued for a broader reading that considers the place of the United States within the larger hemisphere and the world. The widespread interest and interpretation it has attracted places "Benito Cereno" in the company of *Moby-Dick* and *Billy Budd* as one of Melville's most enduring fictions.

Melville's final novel, *The Confidence-Man: His Masquerade,* describes an even more elaborate charade than Babo's. Unlike Melville's magazine fictions, *The Confidence-Man* was not popular with readers, but in its representation of a motley crew of American characters, it grew out of his close engagement with periodical and popular culture. Post-Lauria argues that *The Confidence-Man* represents Melville's answer to *Putnam's* call for "a truly *American* novel," taking "the popular folk type of the confidence man" (p. 214) as both his main character and his narrative structure. The novel, set on a Mississippi River steamboat, consists almost entirely of dialogue between this shape-shifting swindler and his fellow passengers, suggesting that identity is a function of social correspondence and performance. These exchanges range in subject from theology and philosophy to etiquette and economics, with many amusing anecdotes and parables along the way, but taken together they become repetitive and labyrinthine. Indeed, contemporary critics were baffled by this disjointed series of conversations between characters who appear and disappear seemingly at random. Melville's novel is an intricate puzzle for the committed reader: to approach its central character, one must track his method as he changes guises multiple times, from a stockbroker to an herb doctor to a self-avowed "cosmopolitan" who praises the "geniality" of "our age ... of joint-stock companies and free-and-easies" (1984 ed., p. 175). By winning the confidence of his fellows, he robs them not only of money and trust but also of integrity, as their own characters shift in response to his verbal ploys.

The Confidence-Man portrays a world so corrupt that "geniality" and "confidence" in one's fellows are not qualities to be praised but weaknesses to be exploited. The safest stance in such a world is skepticism, embodied in the novel by various misanthropes. But such an attitude suggests a degree of mutual suspicion that makes sympathy impossible and society unbearable. The novel shows the gullibility of certain trusting individuals, but it also signals the prevalence of distrust and hatred in antebellum America.

The novel's open ending—"Something further may follow of this Masquerade" (p. 251)—serves as the ambiguous capstone to Melville's public career in fiction. Available evidence indicates that he was exhausted and that his health and family life were strained at best. Elizabeth Melville's letters reflect a fear for—and often of—her husband. In the fall of 1856, after finishing *The Confidence-Man,* Melville began a solitary pilgrimage to the Holy Land, with stops in Europe along the way. When he returned the following May, he tried his hand at delivering public lectures, but that career did not stick. Instead, he turned to poetry.

"THE LITTLE CRAFTSMAN": THE POETRY AND BILLY BUDD

With Pantheist energy of will
The little craftsman of the Coral Sea
Strenuous in the blue abyss,
Up-builds his marvellous gallery
And long arcade,
Erections freaked with many a fringe
Of marble garlandry,
Evincing what a worm can do.

—from "Venice," *Timoleon* (1891)

One point that Melville's critics, past and present, generally agree upon is that Melville was, first and foremost, a fiction writer. Nonetheless, Melville wrote poetry for more than three decades, from the late 1850s to his death in 1891, far outstripping his twelve-year career in prose. Unlike the rapid composition of most of his fiction, Melville's process as a poet was gradual and painstaking, as surviving manuscripts and journals indicate. He spent ten years writing *Clarel* (1876). Even his end-of-life return to fiction began as a poem, "Billy in the Darbies," the seed for the novella that he continued to write and rewrite until his death. In this sense, there is a touch of self-description in his ode to the "little craftsman of the Coral Sea," which creates its wonders by accretion, like the city of Venice, which "rose in reefs of palaces" (*Timoleon,* p. 291). Melville had visited that city during his pilgrimage, and "Venice" was likely among the poems that Melville intended for his first collection in 1860, but he failed to find a publisher.

Meanwhile, as Melville embarked on trying to publish his poetry, the Civil War was on the verge of breaking out. That conflict would inspire Melville's next poetic output, culminating in *Battle-Pieces and Aspects of the War* (1866). That collection expresses the scope of the war's devastation as well as its fraught allegiances and animosities. In his two "Stonewall Jackson" poems, for example, Melville balances a Northern perspective on the Confederate general in the first with the assumed voice of "a Virginian" (p. 60) in the second. He also draws parallels between Jackson and John Brown, the radical abolitionist who was executed for his failed 1859 raid on the arsenal at Harper's Ferry, Virginia. Melville refers to Brown as "The meteor of the war" (p. 5), and Jackson is the "stormer of the war" who "followed his star" (p. 60). Stonewall Jackson, he writes, was "True to the thing he deemed was due, / True as John Brown or steel" (p. 59). Melville conveys both admiration for and fascinated horror with these men of Ahab-like resolve and conviction. Unfortunately, Melville's circumspection did not win him many friends among reviewers. They also ridiculed Melville's unorthodox rhyming—a criticism he did not take to heart in later poems.

In 1863, Melville had moved back to New York, unable to maintain his farm in the Berkshires any longer, and after the publication of *Battle-Pieces* he found a reasonably respectable job as a customs inspector, a post he would keep for two decades. Working by day, he composed *Clarel* by night, until it swelled to over eighteen thousand lines. In the process of writing that soul-searching work, Melville suffered an immense personal loss: in September 1867, his son Malcolm, who had been spared by age from the war, shot himself dead. Delbanco considers *Clarel* "in part, a work of mourning" (p. 279). It is a tortured and tortuous poem, an older man's vision of a young man's struggle for faith amid the mute relics of the world's religions, in the company of other pilgrims. His party includes, among others, the gregarious adventurer Rolfe; the reclusive genius Vine (whom critics interpret as a figure for Hawthorne's reserve in his rejection of "the soul's caress" [p. 227] between men); and Margoth, a geologist who views the world through the narrow prism of his science. *Clarel* derides those who accept physical science, or any regulated system of thought, as a universal "umpire," but Melville does not reject it entirely; rather, he treats science as one pilgrim among many in the quest for meaning. Spirituality in *Clarel* emerges through the constellation of characters and their lengthy discourses. A couplet from the "Epilogue" reads: "The running battle of the star and clod / Shall run forever—if there be no God" (p. 498). As in *Moby-Dick,* faith in *Clarel* is caught up in the inextricable bond between the mystical and the material.

Melville published two final poetry collections in the last years of his life: *John Marr and Other Sailors* (1888) and *Timoleon* (1891). The former is a maritime collection, including several sailor-sketches and a number of "Sea-Pieces," while the latter focuses on Old World monuments and civilizations, divided between meditations on antiquity and a number of poems, such as "Venice," likely intended for the unpublished 1860 collection and gathered here under the heading "Fruit of Travel Long Ago." Many of the poems in these last collections are wistful and elegiac in tone, anticipating the nostalgic opening line of Melville's last work, the novella *Billy Budd: Sailor*: "In the time before steamships ..."

Melville's novella (not published until 1924) is set in a hazy, "less prosaic" past that he associates with "the 'Handsome Sailor'"—a figure of "natural regality" like Jack Chase (p. 43). Billy Budd fits the type, almost. He is the embodiment of male beauty and of uncorrupted purity—"in the nude [he] might have posed for a statue of young Adam before the Fall" (p. 94)—but his absolute innocence makes him unfit for a world defined by what Melville calls "sinister dexterity" (p. 49). (Delbanco and others perceive in Billy's tragic innocence a portrait of Melville's lost sons; his second son, Stanwix, had died in 1886, around the time that Melville began *Billy Budd.*) Aboard the merchant ship *Rights-of-Man,* Billy is the "peacemaker" (p. 47), universally admired by his fellows. When he is impressed into the British Navy aboard the warship *Bellipotent,* however, he attracts the wrong kind of attention from the malicious master-at-arms, Claggart. At this point, the nostalgic mood of the story falls away, replaced by the specificity of a historical moment marked by discipline and fear; the year is 1797, Britain is at war with France, and the *Bellipotent* sails in the wake of two major mutinies in the British Navy. In this tense atmosphere, Claggart falsely accuses Billy of a mutinous plot. Shocked and incapable of speech, Billy strikes Claggart dead. The captain sympathizes with Billy and believes his innocence of the first crime but punishes him for the second: "Struck dead by an angel of God! Yet the angel must hang!" (p. 101). *Billy Budd* is a tale of the great gulf between law and morality. It is also about the spectacle of power and authority. Captain Vere is no "monomaniac" like Ahab, but he is among the darkest characters in Melville's fiction, precisely because his execution of Billy is perfectly executed—justifiable but fundamentally unjust.

Like "Benito Cereno," another compressed narrative of psychological and political tension, *Billy Budd* is set in a distant past that nevertheless has the immediacy and urgency of a current crisis. Alongside *Moby-Dick,* it has become Melville's most well-known and discussed work, inviting critical approaches from legal theory to queer theory.

AFTERMATH

Melville died on September 28, 1891, leaving behind his wife, two daughters, and several grandchildren—one of whom, Eleanor Melville Metcalf, would become instrumental in the Melville revival, granting access to his papers (including the manuscript of *Billy Budd*) to Melville's first biographer, Raymond Weaver. Since then, Melville scholarship has moved through many cycles, and it has its own historiographies, tracking the ways in which Melville has been interpreted through the grain of his scholars' worlds as well as his own. In 1952, the Trinidadian writer C. L. R. James wrote that Melville "painted a picture of the world in which we live" (p. 3). James's immediate world was a detention center on Ellis Island, where he was held as a suspected Communist, and his study of Melville reflects his experience. James also understood, however, that Melville's prescience was attributable to his keen and persistent awareness of the world in which he lived. The double-edged features of Melville's world—democracy and demagoguery, patriotism and violence, cosmopolitanism and globalization—anticipate and in many ways resemble the world of his modern audience. His writings continue to attract readers for their uniqueness and insights into the past but also for their uncanny ability to speak to us in the present.

Selected Bibliography

WORKS OF HERMAN MELVILLE

NOVELS AND STORIES

Typee: A Peep at Polynesian Life. London: John Murray, 1846. New York: Wiley & Putnam, 1846. [Authoritative edition: Edited by Harrison Hayford, Hershel Parker, and G. Thomas Tanselle. Evanston, Ill.: Northwestern University Press/Newberry Library, 1968. (All quotations in text are from this edition.)]

Omoo: A Narrative of Adventures in the South Seas. London: John Murray, 1847. New York: Harper & Brothers, 1847. [Authoritative edition: Edited by Harrison Hayford,

Hershel Parker, and G. Thomas Tanselle. Evanston, Ill.: Northwestern University Press/Newberry Library, 1968. (All quotations in text are from this edition.)]

Mardi; and a Voyage Thither. London: Richard Bentley, 1849. New York: Harper & Brothers, 1849. [Authoritative edition: Edited by Harrison Hayford, Hershel Parker, and G. Thomas Tanselle. Evanston, Ill.: Northwestern University Press/Newberry Library, 1970. (All quotations in text are from this edition.)]

Redburn: His First Voyage (Being the Sailor-Boy Confessions and Reminiscences of the Son-of-a-Gentleman, in the Merchant Service). London: Richard Bentley, 1849. New York: Harper & Brothers, 1849. [Authoritative edition: Edited by Harrison Hayford, Hershel Parker, and G. Thomas Tanselle. Evanston, Ill.: Northwestern University Press/Newberry Library, 1969. (All quotations in text are from this edition.)]

White-Jacket; or, The World in a Man-of-War. London: Richard Bentley, 1850. New York: Harper & Brothers, 1850. [Authoritative edition: Edited by Harrison Hayford, Hershel Parker, and G. Thomas Tanselle. Evanston, Ill.: Northwestern University Press/Newberry Library, 1970. (All quotations in text are from this edition.)]

Moby-Dick; or, The Whale. London (published as *The Whale*): Richard Bentley, 1851. New York: Harper & Brothers, 1851. [Authoritative edition: Edited by Harrison Hayford, Hershel Parker, and G. Thomas Tanselle. Evanston, Ill.: Northwestern University Press/Newberry Library, 1988. (All quotations in text are from this edition.)]

Pierre; or, The Ambiguities. New York: Harper & Brothers, 1852. [Authoritative edition: Edited by Harrison Hayford, Hershel Parker, and G. Thomas Tanselle. Evanston, Ill.: Northwestern University Press/Newberry Library, 1971. (All quotations in text are from this edition.)]

Israel Potter: His Fifty Years of Exile. New York: G. P. Putnam, 1855. (Authoritative edition: Edited by Harrison Hayford, Hershel Parker, and G. Thomas Tanselle. Evanston, Ill.: Northwestern University Press/Newberry Library, 1982.)

The Piazza Tales. New York: Dix & Edwards, 1856. (Contains "Bartleby, the Scrivener," "Benito Cereno," "The Encantadas," and "The Bell-Tower.") [Authoritative edition also including uncollected stories, such as "The Paradise of Bachelors and the Tartarus of Maids": *The Piazza Tales and Other Prose Pieces, 1839–1860.* Edited by Harrison Hayford, Alma A. MacDougall, and G. Thomas Tanselle. Evanston, Ill.: Northwestern University Press/Newberry Library, 1987. (All quotations in text are from this edition.)]

The Confidence-Man: His Masquerade. New York: Dix & Edwards, 1857. [Authoritative edition: Edited by Harrison Hayford, Hershel Parker, and G. Thomas Tanselle. Evanston, Ill.: Northwestern University Press/Newberry Library, 1984. (All quotations in text are from this edition.)]

Billy Budd: Sailor (An Inside Narrative). Edited by Raymond Weaver. London: Constable, 1924. [Authoritative edition: Edited by Harrison Hayford and Merton M. Sealts. Chicago: University of Chicago Press, 1962. (All quotations in text are from this edition.)]

POETRY

Battle-Pieces and Aspects of the War. New York: Harper & Brothers, 1866. [Authoritative edition in *Published Poems.* Edited by Robert C. Ryan, Harrison Hayford, Alma MacDougall Reising, and G. Thomas Tanselle. Evanston, Ill.: Northwestern University Press/Newberry Library, 2009. (All quotations in text are from this edition.)]

Clarel: A Poem and Pilgrimage in the Holy Land. New York: G. P. Putnam's Sons, 1876. [Authoritative edition: Edited by Harrison Hayford, Alma A. MacDougall, Hershel Parker, and G. Thomas Tanselle. Evanston, Ill.: Northwestern University Press/Newberry Library, 1991. (All quotations in text are from this edition.)]

John Marr and Other Sailors, with Some Sea-Pieces. New York: De Vinne Press, 1888. (Authoritative edition in *Published Poems.* Edited by Robert C. Ryan, Harrison Hayford, Alma MacDougall Reising, and G. Thomas Tanselle. Evanston, Ill.: Northwestern University Press/Newberry Library, 2009.)

Timoleon, Etc. New York: Caxton Press, 1891. [Authoritative edition in *Published Poems.* Edited by Robert C. Ryan, Harrison Hayford, Alma MacDougall Reising, and G. Thomas Tanselle. Evanston, Ill.: Northwestern University Press/Newberry Library, 2009. (All quotations in text are from this edition.)]

OTHER WRITINGS

The Piazza Tales and Other Prose Pieces, 1839–1860. Edited by Harrison Hayford, Alma A. MacDougall, and G. Thomas Tanselle. Evanston, Ill.: Northwestern University Press/Newberry Library, 1987. (Collects reviews, lectures, and attributed pieces.)

Journals. Edited by Howard C. Horsford and Lynn Horth. Evanston, Ill.: Northwestern University Press/Newberry Library, 1989.

Correspondence. Edited by Lynn Horth. Evanston, Ill.: Northwestern University Press/Newberry Library, 1993.

CRITICAL AND BIOGRAPHICAL STUDIES

Barnum, Jill, Wyn Kelley, and Christopher Sten, eds. *"Whole Oceans Away": Melville and the Pacific.* Kent, Ohio: Kent State University Press, 2007.

Bercaw-Edwards, Mary K. *Cannibal Old Me: Spoken Sources in Melville's Early Works.* Kent, Ohio: Kent State University Press, 2009.

Bryant, John, Mary Bercaw-Edwards, and Timothy Marr, eds. *"Ungraspable Phantom": Essays on "Moby-Dick."* Kent, Ohio: Kent State University Press, 2006.

Delbanco, Andrew. *Herman Melville: His World and Work.* New York: Knopf, 2005.

Deleuze, Gilles. "Bartleby; or, The Formula." *Essays Critical and Clinical.* Translated by Daniel W. Smith and Michael A. Greco. New York: Verso, 1998. (Originally published in French as *Critique et Clinique.* Paris: Editions de Minuit, 1993.)

Dimock, Wai-chee. *Empire for Liberty: Melville and the Poetics of Individualism.* Princeton, N.J.: Princeton University Press, 1991.

Freeburg, Christopher. *Melville and the Idea of Blackness: Race and Imperialism in Nineteenth-Century America.* Cambridge, U.K.: Cambridge University Press, 2015.

James, C. L. R. *Mariners, Renegades, and Castaways.* New York: C. L. R. James, 1953. Reprint, Hanover, N.H.: University Press of New England, 2001.

Karcher, Carolyn L. *Shadow over the Promised Land: Slavery, Race, and Violence in Melville's America.* Baton Rouge: Louisiana State University Press, 1980.

Kelley, Wyn, ed. *A Companion to Herman Melville.* Oxford: Blackwell, 2006.

Levine, Robert S, ed. *The New Cambridge Companion to Herman Melville.* Cambridge, U.K.: Cambridge University Press, 2013.

Otter, Samuel. *Melville's Anatomies.* Berkeley: University of California Press, 1999.

Otter, Samuel, and Geoffrey Sanborn, eds. *Melville and Aesthetics.* New York: Palgrave Macmillan, 2001.

Parker, Hershel. *Herman Melville: A Biography.* Vol. 1, *1819–1851.* Baltimore: John Hopkins University Press, 1996.

———. *Herman Melville: A Biography.* Vol. 2, *1851–1891.* Baltimore, Md.: John Hopkins University Press, 2002.

Post-Lauria, Sheila. *Correspondent Colorings: Melville and the Marketplace.* Amherst: University of Massachusetts, 1996.

Rogin, Michael Paul. *Subversive Genealogy: The Politics and Art of Herman Melville.* Berkeley: University of California Press, 1985.

Samson, John. *White Lies: Melville's Narratives of Facts.* Ithaca, N.Y.: Cornell University Press, 1989.

Sanborn, Geoffrey. *The Sign of the Cannibal: Melville and the Making of a Postcolonial Reader.* Durham, N.C.: Duke University Press, 1998.

Spanos, William V. *Herman Melville and the American Calling: The Fiction after "Moby-Dick," 1851–1857.* Albany: State University of New York Press, 2008.

Sten, Christopher. *The Weaver-God, He Weaves: Melville and the Poetics of the Novel.* Kent, Ohio: Kent State University Press, 1996.

Weaver, Raymond M. *Herman Melville, Mariner and Mystic.* New York: Doran, 1921.

OTHER CITED SOURCES

Jefferson, Thomas. *The Republic of Letters: The Correspondence Between Thomas Jefferson and James Madison, 1776–1826.* Vol. 3. Edited by James Morton Smith. New York: W. W. Norton, 1995. Pg. 1586.

Lawrence, D. H. *Studies in Classic American Literature.* 1923. London: Heinemann, 1964.

O'Sullivan, John L. "Annexation." *U.S. Magazine and Democratic Review* 17, no. 1:5–10 (July–August 1845).

ARTHUR MILLER

(1915—2005)

Philip Parry

ARTHUR MILLER'S LONG career as a dramatist began in earnest in the 1940s and concluded just six months before his death with the world premiere of his final play. His reputation, however, rests largely on four works written and first performed between 1947 and 1956. *All My Sons* (1947), *Death of a Salesman* (1949), *The Crucible* (1953), and the two-act version of *A View from the Bridge* (1956) were gathered together in 1957 into a volume, grandly and prematurely titled *Collected Plays,* which in the eyes of many admirers established Miller as America's greatest dramatist. However, mainly because of his left-wing political opinions, he had been from as early as the mid-1940s a controversial figure in the United States. There was soon to be added anger in the face of his disastrous marriage to Marilyn Monroe; and more recently his high-profile opposition to Israel's treatment of Palestinian Arabs brought him both quiet admirers and vocal detractors. Elsewhere in the English-speaking world, where political and personal issues have counted for less, his position as one of the twentieth century's leading playwrights has scarcely been questioned. But friend and foe alike agree that this first volume of *Collected Plays* is where Miller's principal achievement rests; the part played in that achievement by the plays that he released subsequently is a far less settled matter.

Miller is best thought of in relation to two informal trinities of American playwrights. Together with Eugene O'Neill (1888–1953) and Tennessee Williams (1911–1983) he helped to shape and define the drama of the United States in the twentieth century. O'Neill, much the oldest of the three, received a Nobel Prize in Literature in 1936, when Miller was twenty-one years of age and Williams was twenty-five. Neither Williams nor Miller became Nobel laureates, but Miller's productive career in the theater has been of an unequaled duration and distinction. At the same time, being Jewish, he invites comparison with David Mamet (born in 1947) and Tony Kushner (born in 1956). Much of the story of modern American theater can be told in terms of these five playwrights. In Miller's case, moreover, part of that story derives from his own very extensive comments on his dramaturgical practices. Among playwrights only Bernard Shaw (1856–1950) has been more intent on supplying readers with his own views of his work and of its social significance.

EARLY YEARS

Arthur Asher Miller was born in New York City in 1915 into a prosperous Jewish family that ran a thriving clothing business. This business collapsed in 1929, because his father invested too much money in the stock market. This collapse, and the consequent loss of a sense of self-worth that financial failure brought in its wake, lies at the root of many of Miller's plays. In a version of *The American Clock* (used as the basis of a production in Birmingham in the English Midlands in 1983) the play's principal narrator (Lee Baum) addresses the audience in a speech that foregrounds Miller's own abiding concerns:

> There have been only two American disasters that were truly national. Not the first or second World Wars, not Vietnam or even the Revolution. Only the Civil War and the Great Depression touched nearly everyone wherever they lived and whatever their social class. (*Slight pause.*) Personally, I believe that deep down we are still afraid that, suddenly without warning, it may all fall apart again.
>
> (*Plays: Three,* p. 5)

With the voicing of a single word—*personally*—the opinions both of Baum and of his creator perfectly coincide. It is the loss of name, face, and status within the narrow realm of family and of neighborhood that drives Joe Keller, Willy Loman, John Procter, and Eddie Carbone forward toward their tragic end.

The newly impoverished Miller took several temporary jobs in order to raise money to study at the University of Michigan, which he entered in 1934. Once there he began to write plays in an attempt to boost his funds, and in 1936 and 1937 he won two lucrative awards sponsored by the Avery Hopwood Foundation. After graduation he continued to write, both for live performance and for radio, and for a short time he was on the payroll of the Federal Theatre Project. The Library of America edition of Miller's *Collected Plays* (completed in 2015) provides in its third volume a small corpus of early works for stage and radio that twenty years ago were unknown to all save specialist scholars.

Two of Miller's early plays, however, are much better-known. *The Man Who Had All the Luck* became in 1944 his first play to be staged on Broadway, where it closed after four performances. In 1989 it reemerged in a revised version alongside another early play, *The Golden Years,* written between 1939 and 1941 but not performed until a British Broadcasting Corporation radio production in 1987. By the time of its BBC transmission, *The Golden Years,* a "New World tragedy" about the defeat of the Aztec empire, was a mere historical curiosity, but when first planned it had been meant to encourage reflection upon serious contemporary issues. Its large cast anticipated some of Miller's later plays, *The American Clock* in particular, but has discouraged modern productions. By contrast *The Man Who Had All the Luck* has had since its reemergence a modest success on both professional and amateur stages. David Beeves, a young man who prospers whatever he does, superstitiously offers up the life and health of his unborn child as a propitiatory sacrifice against impending failure. Paralyzed by shame and guilt, he becomes the passive victim of his own fears and is thus typical of many of Miller's later heroes. What all of them need to learn is that a positive response to circumstances, whether those circumstances are good or bad, is what indicates the truly active man. The particular moral that Miller was highlighting in the 1940s, through the characters of Montezuma and Beeves, was that America needed to avoid the brutally self-punishing urges that were to entice so many on the European mainland to embrace fascism.

In 1936 Miller met in university, and in 1940 he married, Mary Grace Slattery, a young woman of Irish Catholic descent, whose political views matched his own. The marriage, which produced two children, coincided with the most productive and successful period in Miller's theatrical career, but it ended in divorce in 1956. In an insensitive move he dedicated the 1957 *Collected Plays* to Marilyn Monroe (1926–1962), whom he married in 1956 but who divorced him in 1961. Two broken marriages in rapid succession were not, however, the only problems facing Miller in these troubled years, for he was already under political disapproval. In 1952 Elia Kazan (1909–2003), who had directed *All My Sons* and *Death of a Salesman,* gave a list of names of Communists and their sympathizers to the House Un-American Activities Committee. Miller's name was not on this list, but he was angered by Kazan's actions and responded by arranging for his 1953 play *The Crucible*—a work that is very much about the naming of names—to be directed by Jed Harris (1900–1979) instead. Then Miller's application for a passport was denied. Summoned to give evidence to HUAC he was found to be in contempt of Congress in 1957 for refusing to add to Kazan's list of names, but he was vindicated in the following year when this ruling was overturned.

COLLECTED PLAYS *(1957)*

Readers who in 1957 purchased the "collected" plays of a playwright who seemed to be near the beginning of his career might well have puzzled over the book they now owned. A statement on the dust jacket (perhaps scripted by Miller himself) addressed them with admirable terseness:

> Arthur Miller's place in the very forefront of American playwrights is already secure. Though he has known enormous success, he has never compromised his art nor has he pilfered his own talent by repeating the pattern of any of his plays; always his work has shown change and growth. Now, for the first time, his complete dramatic works to date have been gathered together into one volume—a volume that offers wonderfully various fare.

But the words "complete dramatic works to date" are seriously misleading: a one-act version of *A View from the Bridge* (complete in itself and first performed in 1955) was excluded—as were, we now know, many earlier plays.

Collected Plays, however, consists of more than plays. The essay "on dramatic technique" with which it begins has near-classic status in the canon of American theater criticism, though both its clarity and its usefulness have from time to time been questioned, perhaps on the back of Miller's admission that he lacked both the patience and the scholarly industry to define terms in a way that would satisfy all of his readers. One of these very basic terms is the word "actor," by which he means (a shade carelessly) not the actor per se but the character whom the actor bodies forth on stage. It is of this character and not of the actor in real life that we are to ask the following questions:

> Who is he? What is he doing here? How does he live or make his living? Who is he related to? Is he rich or poor? What does he think of himself? What do other people think of him, and why? What are his hopes and fears; and what does he say they are? What does he claim to want, and what does he really want?
>
> (*Collected Essays,* p. 108)

These questions suggest, Miller says, that a play is realistic, whereas a different question—about whether performers are wearing masks, for instance—would suggest that we are dealing with a more obviously symbolic production. But at this point Miller's defense of his own "wonderfully various fare" runs into difficulties, since none of the plays in *Collected Plays* makes use of masks; all of them are naturalistically costumed; and the characters' ordinary clothing might lead readers and playgoers to expect a realistic treatment of them. Yet, and this is where Miller's argument clouds over, "when the career of a person rather than the details of his motives stands to the forefront of the play, we move closer to non-naturalistic styles" (p. 108). What he is seeking to establish here is a distinction between, on the one hand, *All My Sons* and *Death of a Salesman* (which are realistic) and, on the other, *The Crucible* and *A View from the Bridge* (which are symbolic). The basis of this distinction is that the principal characters in the first two plays are individuals sketched out in detail in and for themselves, whereas in the latter two plays the principal characters are representative instances of more general cases, in which we see what they do and understand their symbolic import without ever needing fully to understand why they act. John Proctor's adultery, for example, is part of the story that *The Crucible* tells and is relevant to that story, but it is a mere peripheral detail in our more general understanding of the symbolic import of Proctor's conflict with Governor Danforth, which is what the play truly exists to reveal.

In itself Miller's distinction is intelligible and interesting but is not easily applied to these four plays. Willy Loman's death is indeed the death of one salesman in particular; *Death of a Salesman* is not a manual showing us how salesmen commonly die. But Willy is an individual instance of a widespread case of which Eddie Carbone in *A View from the Bridge* is another instance; they are a salesman and a longshoreman who fail in the way they live their lives because they have not adjusted to the reality of the demands that surround them. Might that not also be Joe Keller's plight in *All My Sons*? He is a man who sees the family in very simple terms—"A father is a father"—without ever recognizing the revaluation of familial responsibility that both of his sons instinctively adopt once they have had to lead others into the near-certainty of death. As a result, a father and his sons are torn apart: "Where do you live?" Chris asks him. "Where have you come from?" (*Collected Plays,* vol. 1, p. 146; except where otherwise noted, quotations are from the Library of America *Collected Plays,* with numbers indicating volume and page). And Proctor's, too, is a failure of a similar kind. Unlike Joe, he is not trying to deny the past (he *has* committed adultery); unlike Willy he is not misremembering it (he *knows* he has committed adultery). But he is still allowing the past, imaged almost as a person, to restrict his freedom in the present. And if we can say, with a high degree of credibility, that this broken relationship between past and present is the common situation in which all four men fail, then what becomes of the distinction between realistic and symbolic plays? Perhaps some symbolic plays are not realistic, but there are no realistic plays that are not symbolic.

At this stage in his career, despite a few questionable remarks about theater's underlying poetry, Miller knows that drama is a matter of action and of actions. In *All My Sons,* for instance, a tiny slip of the mind ends up costing Joe Keller everything. That slip is the date of the (bogus) illness that keeps him from work on the very day that his company ships out defective airplane parts. It is captured for us, as the earth opens up to swallow him, in a brief passage of dialogue that is typical both of Miller's artfulness and of his interest in mapping battles between competing egos. The self-important Keller, his attitude a measure of his lack of inward self-confidence, boasts once too often: "I ain't got time to get sick." Then his wife's seemingly automatic support of him ("He hasn't been laid up for fifteen years") sends him spinning, and her dropping of the conversational baton ("Huhh?") as he tries to save himself speeds his fall from grace into deadly sin:

> KELLER: Say, I ain't got time to get sick.
>
> MOTHER: He hasn't been laid up in fifteen years.
>
> KELLER: Except my flu during the war.
>
> MOTHER: Huhh?
>
> KELLER: My flu, when I was sick during ... the war.
>
> MOTHER: Well, sure ... *To George*: I mean apart from that flu.
>
> *George stands perfectly still.*
>
> (1.141–142)

The word that matters most here—more often spelled "huh?" than "huhh?"—is scarcely a word at all. And the action that signals that the dropped baton has been spotted is no action at all: "*George stands perfectly still.*" What makes this brief episode a brilliant playlet in itself are the questions that it prompts. Is Kate's stumbling brought about by her *inability* to keep up with the speed of her husband's duplicity? Or is she *refusing* to keep up with him? Our being in doubt here (both answers resting upon ground prepared by Miller) is an example of what links mythos (plot) and ethos (character) in this play, and links them moreover in a way that Aristotle, from whom the terms derive, would certainly have understood.

Again a single word and a simple action speak out loud in the fine ending of the first act of the two-act version of *A View from the Bridge.* Here Marco questions Eddie's ownership of Catherine by challenging him to lift a chair above his head by grasping with one hand just one of its legs. Eddie tries and fails. Uttering just a single word ("Here") Marco humiliates him: "*Marco is face to face with Eddie, a strained tension gripping his eyes and jaws, his neck stiff, the chair raised like a weapon over Eddie's head—and he transforms what might appear like a glare of warning into a smile of triumph, and Eddie's grin vanishes as he absorbs his look*" (1.612).

Ivo van Hove's London production (2014), which, like the first version of the play, was performed without an interval, did this scene magnificently, but, because there was no interval, missed Miller's crucial trick. In van Hove's staging, Eddie and Marco and those surrounding them end the play in a dense huddle covered with blood poured down over them to the accompaniment of Gabriel Fauré's "Requiem." (Perhaps it was the subtitle of *Death of a Salesman—Certain Private Conversations in Two Acts and a Requiem*—that prompted the Fauré.) Undoubtedly a brilliant climax, but who sets out to stab whom? Lost sight of in all of that blood is our knowledge that it is Eddie who brings the dagger to his own death scene; who wrestles with Marco; and, in an echo of the earlier chair scene, has the dagger forced back upon himself by an opponent whose forearms are massively stronger than his own. What makes this the right reading? The nephew of the local butcher has been picked up by the immigration officers because of Eddie's act of community betrayal, and Miller brings Lipari (a butcher both literally and symbolically) on stage to witness his nephew's arrest and Eddie's shame. Thus Eddie, having no escape, is forced to contrive an honorable suicide.

Alfieri's puzzling last words—Alfieri is Eddie's legal adviser and confidante and the play's onstage narrator—are that Eddie was lovable because "he allowed himself be wholly known" (1.636). Yet all four heroes of these tragedies of the common man are largely opaque to themselves, and all of them (more or less) kill themselves. Why then are their actions felt to be moral? Aristotle, not the inventor of tragedy but certainly the inventor of the principal ways in which we now talk about it, allows that it is possible for a tragedy to end without the death of its hero, but he nonetheless assumes that most tragic heroes will die a death that has the nature of a sacrifice. At the end of *The Crucible,* Proctor is urged to confess to what he knows not to be true and is promised a retraction of the death sentence if he does so. He signs a confession but then (in what is the essential tragic act) snatches it back when he realizes that this is a ruse that will be used to justify the execution of his neighbors. Danforth asks him why he was willing to sign a private document that he is unwilling to have made public. Proctor "with a cry of his whole soul" replies: "Because it is my name! Because I cannot have another in my life! Because I lie and sign myself to lies! Because I am not worth the dust on the feet of them that hang! How may I live without my name? I have given you my soul; leave me my name!" (1.453).

The differences between soul and name and reputation, and the values—of humble pride and proud humility—upon which these distinctions rest, lie at the root of Miller's interests in all four of these plays. The most famous of them is *Death of a Salesman,* a play that since its first performance has been a controversial and much misunderstood piece of work. Does Miller's introductory essay clarify it for us, by showing us whether it operates within a broadly naturalistic tradition or as a symbolist or expressionist work? His argument so far has enlisted *Salesman* on the side of realism, but a different argument enlists it differently, for Miller's conception and manipulation of time is not easily reconciled with naturalism: "*All My Sons* attempts to account for time in terms of months, days, and hours. *Death of a Salesman* explodes the watch and the calendar. *The Crucible* is bound by natural time—or strives to appear so" (*Collected Essays,* p. 109).

Since *A View from the Bridge* lines up in its treatment of time behind *All My Sons* and *The Crucible,* this is an argument that drives a division between *Death of a Salesman* and the other three plays: the compacting of time [in *Death of a Salesman*] destroys the realistic style not only because it violates our sense of reality but also because collapsing time inevitably emphasizes an element of existence that in life is not visible or ordinarily felt with equivalent power, and this is its symbolic meaning (p. 109).

Viewed one way *Salesman* is realistic while viewed another way it is not. (But one can say that of every play, surely.) The original stage designs for its first production, worked out in close consultation between Jo Mielziner (1901–1976) and Miller, showed the Loman house as an open wooden framework that the play's performers had to negotiate in a fixed but meaningful fashion: "*Whenever the action is in the present the actors observe the imaginary wall-lines, entering the house only through its door at the left. But in the scenes of the past these boundaries are broken, and characters enter or leave a room by stepping 'through' a wall onto the forestage*" (1.161).

But how does Miller register in the theater events that in real life we are confident have happened *in the past* even though we remember them *here and now*? There is no law of art or nature that requires that the past be re-created on stage merely as a present-day memory, since a playwright is free to shift chronology from one scene to the next, and his doing so will be what we think of as flashes backward or forward. But does Miller shift our focus in the scenes where Willy confronts Uncle Ben by taking us back into

Willy's past independently of Willy himself? Or are we always the prisoners of Willy's editorial memory? These are questions that Miller worries over inordinately in his introductory essay but that he tries to settle by answering a slightly different question. He does so, moreover, in order to deflect attention away from his play and onto László Benedek's 1950 film version of it, which he strongly disliked. The film's cinematic flashbacks, Miller insists, are dislocations within its chronological reporting of time, unlike the play's "mobile concurrency of past and present," which expresses how Willy's present-day needs impose themselves upon the past by means of a present-tense act of remembering. But we cannot measure the distortions of memory if our only access to the past is through the distorting agency of memory itself. Indeed the play's original title—"The Inside of His Head"—abolishes the past. Yet Miller believes that "friction, collision and tension between past and present" are at the heart of his play's "particular construction" (p. 123). Evidence, though, does not wholly support him, whether we think of the investor who withdrew financial support when he grew to believe that the play was about Willy's mental disruption or we think of those observers who saw it as a training session on how to weed out ineffective employees.

Is *Death of a Salesman* a "condition of America" play or a moving depiction of one man's mental breakdown? It might, of course, be both; that the world is driving us mad is a possibility that Miller certainly raises in *The Last Yankee* (1993). But there is nonetheless a failure of relationship between theory and practice in *Death of a Salesman,* which causes further trouble whenever it crops up later in the canon. *After the Fall* (1964) is not Miller's greatest play but it is by some considerable margin his most ambitious, and it "takes place in the mind, thought and memory of Quentin," where (as in Mielziner's stage settings for both *Salesman* and *After the Fall*) "there are no walls or substantial boundaries" (2.3). Equally troublesome, though on a much smaller scale, is *Mr Peters' Connections,* a late play (1998) that dramatizes again what are essentially mental activities (3.869). This late return to the basic dramaturgy of *Death of a Salesman* clarifies what is at issue without resolving the problem. When Harry Peters says in explanation of his growing confusion that "it's not Alzheimer's, I've been examined" (3.425), Miller is trying, surely, to safeguard himself against a criticism leveled against *Salesman* from the very beginning. Similarly, in a brief preface to *Mr Peters' Connections* (3.869), Miller tells us things that the play itself can neither confirm nor disconfirm: some of its characters are dead; some are imaginary; one of them is Peters' long-dead brother. But no amount of exposure to the play in performance can confirm this last point, for its truth depends upon an authorial intervention that lies beyond the reach of whatever can be seen or heard on stage.

THE MARILYN PLAYS

The most glamorous of Miller's three marriages but much the shortest ran into difficulties almost from the start. *The Misfits* (1961) was a film project put together so that Marilyn Monroe might star in it, but, by the time that Miller and she had reached Nevada to begin location-shooting, they were well on the way to a divorce. Indeed Miller was soon to meet Inge Morath (1923–2002), a professional photographer whom he married in 1962 and to whom he remained married until her death forty years later. The situation was awkward for all concerned, and Monroe, whose talent was real though fragile, became seriously unstable during filming. Nevertheless the film's director—John Huston (1906–1987)—managed to get commanding performances out of an immensely distinguished but variously damaged cast. Indeed, if one judges *The Misfits* simply by watching it, one might wonder what all the fuss was about, for it remains a far more moving piece of work than *Finishing the Picture* (2004), the last of three plays in which, however misguidedly, Miller tried to bring Marilyn back to life.

The first and most substantial of these "Marilyn" plays was *After the Fall,* the great enigma in the Miller canon. Meant to help Miller to recover a reputation that had been badly bruised by personal and political conflicts, the new play was a major commission with which New York City's Lincoln Center Repertory Company was to be inaugurated. It was to be directed by Elia Kazan, who, though Miller had not requested him, was a much more congenial interpreter of his work than Jed Harris had been. And, reassembling the team that had launched *Salesman,* Jo Mielziner was to design the set. But Miller's script trod heavily on delicate ground by requiring Kazan to direct a dramatized version of his own conduct during the HUAC hearings. This step-too-far perhaps prompted Kazan to dress his future wife, Barbara Loden, who played Maggie, in a platinum-blond wig that did nothing to ease a difficult situation, which had been made more extreme by Monroe's death in August 1962. Perhaps Miller hoped that sympathy for Marilyn and for Maggie would have faded by the production's opening date in January 1964, but if so he seriously miscalculated. For instance, Nöel Coward (1899–1973), the British playwright and cabaret entertainer, knew Miller and liked him, but Coward's *Diaries* reflect growing sympathy for Monroe and waning sympathy for Miller, and when he saw the play early in its run he vigorously expressed his disapproval. The play was too long, and immature, and self-pitying. Worst of all, the part of the play that dealt with Monroe was vulgar beyond belief.

Coward's reaction was typical of widespread revulsion at the way in which Miller portrayed both the wife he had recently lost and the one he had recently acquired, yet the failures identified by Coward are a breach of taste rather than a failure of art, and they are intermittent. Maggie is by a considerable margin the liveliest character in the play and the one who is most interestingly presented, which suggests that the problems with *After the Fall* are not matters of characterization or the product of its author's personal bias but lie far more deeply hidden within its structure. Maggie's decline and fall, Stella Adler (1901–1992), the preeminent acting-coach, would later point out to students in her acting classes, is not so much of a character in her own right as it is one more staging post in the endless process of displaying Quentin's introspection. Adler's insight is easily confirmed: when Quentin and Maggie first meet and begin to flirt, his treatment of her (she says) shows that he values her and wants her to value herself; other men in the same situation would have been patronizing and predatory. Instantly Quentin turns to the audience, conceived of as a single invisible listener in an empty chair, and reveals that he would have behaved as badly as other men did had he not feared Maggie's rejection. Part of that program of self-discovery and self-cleansing that he has set himself requires him to disown her praise of him by capturing her comments in order to give himself the last word:

> [*To Listener*:] Yes! It's all so clear: the honor! The first honor ... was that I hadn't tried to go to bed with her! God, the hypocrisy! ... Because, I was only afraid, and she took it for a tribute to her ... "value"! No wonder I can't find myself here! (*He has gotten to his feet in agony.*)
>
> (2.81)

The play's listener, represented by the empty chair, is a device designed to make Quentin's innermost thoughts available to an audience. In short it is another solution to the problem, resolved differently in *Death of a Salesman,* of getting an audience inside a character's head, but it is a solution that forces Miller to force Quentin into repeated and public acts of self-investigation. It is the repetitiveness of these acts that is intolerable. Quentin's never-ending attempt to build himself up by every verbal means at his disposal, even by cutting himself down to size from time to time, is ego-ridden because, like all self-centred monsters, he supposes that his hapless listener is there just to hear about him.

An empty chair cannot be bored, but real audiences who have paid for their seats may surely ask themselves what Miller's formal innovations amount to. The structure of *Death of a Salesman* still has the power to confuse readers and audiences, but its real weakness comes up to the surface ready to trip us up afresh when Miller reuses the idea much more thoroughly in *After the Fall,* whose action takes place inside Quentin's head but also *upon* a stage that

> *consists of three levels rising to the highest at the back, crossing in a curve from one side of the stage to another.* [...] *On the two lower levels are sculpted areas; indeed the whole effect is neolithic, a lava-*

> *like, supple geography, in which, like pits and hollows found in lava, the scenes take place.* [...] *People appear and disappear instantaneously, as in the mind; but it is not necessary that they walk off the stage.* [...] *The effect, therefore, will be the surging, flitting, instantaneousness of a mind questing over its own surfaces and into its depths.*
>
> (2.3)

The calculations of right and wrong that Quentin spends the entire play making are not untrue to life. What is galling is the way in which they are presented to an audience; for *After the Fall* is little more than a giant soliloquy with speeches given to others only as Quentin dictates. In real life, confronted with garrulous self-justification on this massive scale, most people would avoid him in the conviction that he has not even tried to acquire balance or poise or a sense of proportion.

Oddly, the account of *After the Fall* that Miller gives in his memoir *Timebends* (1987) is remarkably distant from the play that those who have seen it think they have seen. Maggie (originally named Lorraine) is said to represent the self-destructive fragility of modern insecure and ill-conducted lives that fall prey to dependence upon drugs or bad politics, and Miller contends that "the play [is] about how we—nations and individuals—destroy ourselves by denying that this is precisely what we are doing" (*Timebends,* p. 527). But this yoking together of the political, the personal, the national, and the individual is deeply unconvincing. *After the Fall* invests too much symbolically in Maggie and in Marilyn, an excess that anticipates aspects both of *The Price* (1968) and of *The Last Yankee* (1993)—plays where domestic narratives have imposed upon them a symbolic significance that the stories they tell are not strong enough to sustain. By a happy contrast, the next time that Monroe appears in a Miller play his investment in her is altogether more modest. Cathy-May, described as Peters' dead lover in the list of characters that prefaces *Mr Peters' Connections,* makes several dream-like appearances in the play but in doing so brings with her little more than a strong feeling of an eroticism locked up in the past of an old man who is trying to make sense of his life before he dies.

Finishing the Picture, Miller's last play and also his final Marilyn play, is a lightly disguised rerunning of issues that arose and adversely affected the progress of *The Misfits.* The disguise is minimal, as is the plot, in which various characters, prompted by self-interest, try to get the exploited, disorganized, and drug-dependent Kitty back on set in order to finish a picture before its financiers pull the funding. This simple play was one that some of the reviewers of the original production in the Goodman Theatre in Chicago thought too simple and too little dramatized. The play's opening act, they pointed out, is just a series of conversations between characters who have something to gain or something to lose if Kitty gets back on set. But what we see of Kitty herself (in Robert Falls's production: Miller's stage directions are less explicit) is the briefest possible glimpse of her naked back as she wanders nude and helpless round her apartment. Things have improved only slightly by the time we reach the third act, where she lies, intermittently conscious and in near total darkness, in a bedroom lit fitfully only when its door is opened to admit other characters. They speak copiously, but Kitty, having rushed from the bedroom to the bathroom, says just one word—"Yes!"—before reemerging, poorly lit from behind, in a bathrobe, a bandana, and a pair of sunglasses. What does she amount to then? In total sixteen words, all spoken within or offstage; a few mumbled utterances from which distinct words do not emerge; some screams and a hysterical burst of laughter. Kitty—never heard, scarcely seen, and never seen and heard at the same time—is one of the least glamorous roles in modern theater. Miller's final balancing of the reckoning between himself and Monroe is not a generous one.

THE JEWISH PLAYS

Miller's Jewish identity, very much a matter of fact, has nonetheless generated controversy, especially among a small number of critics and dramatists who are themselves American and Jewish. *Death of a Salesman,* according to David Mamet, fails to be the greatest of all American Jewish plays precisely because it never explicitly enough acknowledges its Jewish origins. But is the Loman household Jewish? The most surprising feature of Miller's short essay "*Salesman* at Fifty" (first published in 1999) is his seemingly casual characterization of Willy Loman and his family as "Jews light-years away from religion or a community that might have fostered Jewish identity" (*Collected Essays,* pp. 465–467). Thirty years earlier, in an interview with Robert Martin, he had gone no further than to admit that Loman, Keller, and indeed Miller itself were surnames borne by both Jewish and Gentile families. At the same time he had also insisted that the social, ethnic, or cultural classification of family-names is significant only where history and geography allow it to be so. In *A View from the Bridge,* Eddie's Sicilian origins are relevant because the play is based upon patterns of revenge common in Italy; the Jewish characters in *Incident at Vichy* (1964) have to be Jewish because this is a play that deals with the imposition of Nazi race laws in the Auvergne region of central France. By contrast, the evidence within *Death of a Salesman* that the Lomans are a highly assimilated Jewish family is vanishingly slight, for what makes Willy truly representative of working-class Americans in early postwar New York is neither race, nor ethnicity, nor faith but his distance from secure economic well-being.

Although he was raised in a Jewish family, the adult Miller was an atheist and not an observant Jew—but he was Jewish enough to be the victim of anti-Semitic prejudice. The origins of his 1945 novel *Focus,* his exposure of American anti-Semitism, lie in the months in 1942 and 1943 when he worked the night shift at the Brooklyn Navy Yard. Here he encountered high levels of intolerance toward Jews and a casual acceptance of the racial myths that underpinned Nazism. It was a time and an experience that made clear to him how much his Jewish identity had shaped him both as a Jew (secular and assimilated though he was) and as a twentieth-century American citizen. This perhaps helps to make sense of *The Ride down Mt Morgan*—an otherwise confusing and difficult play (first staged in 1991)—within which questions about specifically Jewish identity lie deeply embedded. Lyman Felt, the child of a Jewish mother and a Gentile father, is married to a Gentile (Theo), by whom he has a daughter (Bessie), and is bigamously married to Leah, by whom he has a son (Benjamin). The significance of the contrasted names is stressed in a scene where Lyman's wives compare their culinary achievements. "My gefilte fish," Leah says, "is feather-light." Lyman's imagining of Theo's response stresses how far he has departed from Jewish dietary observances: "He does love my glazed ham" (3.241). Since the real Lyman is both Theo's Lyman and Leah's Lyman, a conclusion that might be drawn is that American Jews must be free to live out their lives both within the local and the larger community. But the play is problematic, not least because once again Miller lodges it firmly inside the head of its principal protagonist, who is torn between two women in a society where the grammar of acceptable conduct will not let him be faithful to *both* while being unfaithful to *either.*

Probably the most widely admired of Miller's Jewish plays is *The Price* (first performed in 1968), which rejoices in the verbal and physical eccentricities of Gregory Solomon, an eighty-nine-year-old Jewish furniture dealer who is called in to value furniture that two brothers wish to sell. *The Price* was widely seen as a return to form after Miller's recent misfortunes, but does Solomon's being in it make it a Jewish play? The question is not easily answered. Walter and Victor, the antagonistic and competitive brothers at the center of its plot are not (at least not obviously) Jewish but their interactions with each other (whether they are Jewish or not) and with Solomon (who is most definitely Jewish) are clearly important.

Miller, because he had so much riding on the play's success, was anxious to direct his audiences' understanding of it but he does so by other than strictly dramatic means. These include a production note (2.760–761) in which he insists, as he did every time he discussed *The Price,* that the play must not be seen as an unequal struggle between a good brother (Victor) and a bad one (Walter). Instead, both brothers have made decisions—whether right or wrong, generous or mean-spirited—and both have paid the price of doing so. But is there anything within the dialogue that Miller supplies that convinces us that Walter is doing other than purchase at small cost to himself forgiveness from a brother whom he has duped once and is about to dupe again? On this reading, heightening the play's underlying irony, is the fact that *Victor* is the *loser* who truly pays "the price."

One moment likely to guide interpretation is embodied in some highly controversial stage directions. Esther is Victor's wife but is at this point siding with Walter, which partly explains the tension of the moment. Will Walter and Esther acting in tandem be strong enough to overcome Victor's unwillingness to accept Walter's advice? Walter is joking about Solomon's claim to have ethically regulated the furniture appraiser's trade:

> *Esther bursts out laughing, and Walter with her, and Victor manages to join. As it begins to subside, Walter turns to him.*
>
> WALTER: What do you say, Vic? Will you come by?
>
> *The laughter is gone. The smile is just fading on Victor's face. He looks at nothing, as though deciding. The pause lengthens, and lengthens still. Now it begins to seem he may not speak at all. No one knows how to break into his puzzling silence. At last he turns to Walter with a rather quick movement of his head as though he had made up his mind to take the step.*
>
> VICTOR: I'm not sure I know what you want, Walter.
>
> *Walter looks shocked, astonished, almost unbelieving. But Victor's gaze is steady on him.*
>
> ESTHER, *with a tone of the conciliator shrouding her shock and protest*: I don't think that's being very fair, is it?
>
> (2.245–246)

Here are 27 words of dialogue and an additional 119 words of commentary, without which the dialogue would scarcely register. In context "shrouding," for example, effectively means "failing to shroud." Heavy dependence upon the printed rather than the spoken word is not unknown in the Miller canon; it is something that both Williams and he borrowed from Eugene O'Neill. But Miller is rarely as intrusive in other plays as he is throughout *The Price* and whenever commenting on it. The play, he says, in a brief essay—"*The Price*: The Power of the Past" (first published in 2000; reprinted in *Collected Essays,* pp. 484–486)—was prompted by his desire to show that a realistic play engages better than does an absurdist one with the failure of those who led the United States into the Vietnam War. It does so by suggesting (symbolically) that the origins of that war lay in a misunderstanding of past events: just as—and this is what completes the analogy—the fraternal hostilities in *The Price* draw their strength from a long-term misunderstanding between the brothers. But at this low level of analogy, anything can recall anything.

What, then, of Gregory Solomon's Jewishness? He is said to be yards ahead of Victor, Walter, and Esther in his understanding of their family's situation as he tries to steer them away from a precipice toward which they are headed. The argument of the play seems to run thus: Gregory, like King Solomon, is a wise Jew; the Jewish nation is the product of its history; Gregory, despite his vast age, looks always in hope and joy to the future; the Jews, with the establishment of the state of Israel, now have a future as well as a past; Victor, Esther, and Walter (whether they are Jewish or not) should learn to move forward also. Gregory has to be Jewish, Miller told Robert Martin, because the theme of survival "seemed to me to point directly to the Jewish experience through centuries of oppression" (quoted in Roudané, p. 183).

The Jew, for Miller, then, is both a symbolic and a real victim of suffering throughout history, and specifically at the hands of the Nazis. But it is notable that only a small handful of his plays directly address issues of the Holocaust, and of these only *Playing for Time* (first broadcast on television in 1980), an adaptation of someone else's work and a film rather than a play, is set within a death camp. Miller's Holocaust plays form a small group of ambiguous works that have divided audiences and critics, in part no doubt because they prompt uncomfortable questions about innocence, guilt, and victimhood. When Lawrence Newman, the initially anti-Semitic hero of *Focus,* buys a pair of dark-rimmed spectacles he begins to see the world differently not because of their lenses but because of their frames. Since these make him look Jewish and affect the way people treat him, he begins to see the world from a previously despised point of view. At the end of the novel, with persecution ramped up to dangerous levels, he accepts a sort of honorary Jewishness when he chooses to stand beside Mr. Finkelstein, whose name proclaims his Jewish origins and identity but whom we are specifically told is not a religious man.

The boldest of the plays that takes up the central insight of *Focus*—that there is no physical sign that uniquely identifies the Jew—is *Incident at Vichy,* performed at the Washington Square Theatre in December 1964, at the end of a year that had opened with *After the Fall.* Perhaps it suffered from guilt by association with the earlier play; at any rate in an essay—titled "Guilt and *Incident at Vichy*" (*Collected Essays,* pp. 179–181) and written just a year after it was first performed—Miller sought to protect it from misunderstanding by claiming that most of those who had seen it fully understood that it was not a play about how the Nazis behaved in World War II. Those who thought it was had simply mixed up its story (which was one thing) and its theme (which is another). Whoever supplied the cover notes for the Penguin American edition of the play, which say that it is set up to recall Dante's Hell, was already well on the way to converting a Jewish story into a Christian myth. That story (a true one, Miller says) is set in a detention center in Vichy in 1942, where six men and an adolescent boy are to have their papers checked, in an attempt, everyone fears, to see whether they are Jewish. Several of them, including a character identified simply as an Old Jew, are obviously Jewish, others may or may not be, but all are to be physically examined to see if they are circumcised, which suggests that this is no mere exercise in checking paperwork. Indeed a collaborationist professor admits that circumcision is not an infallible identifier of Jewishness, which is crucial to Miller's point and which should have been obvious to a New York audience in 1964, granted the very high incidence of secular, rather than religious, circumcision in the United States. As one prisoner, the psychiatrist Leduc, says (acting as Miller's spokesman), "Jews are not a race you know. They can look like anybody else" (2.151). This, however, is irrelevant to the professor's purpose, which is to ease his task by dismissing from further investigation anyone who is not circumcised. But for Miller's very different purposes—since in this play Jews are not Jews in themselves so much as symbols of the oppressed Other within any community—anyone oppressed because he is the member of a minority may be said to be symbolically Jewish. Another prisoner, Monceau, driven desperate by fear of deportation to a death camp, converts the victim into the villain when he blames Leduc for bringing down persecution upon himself and other Jews: "I think it's people like you who brought this on us. People who give Jews a reputation for subversion, and this Talmudic analysis, and this everlasting, niggling discontent" (2.169).

Monceau, who is (symbolically as well as by actual profession) a stage actor, believes that so long as he performs his role as a Gentile onstage and offstage well enough he can redefine himself sufficiently to deceive his interrogators. But what can he do, Leduc asks, when they make him unbutton his fly? Because Monceau has adopted the viewpoint of his oppressors, Leduc tells him, his heart is already conquered territory. Even those who are genuinely Jewish need Jews, conceived of as symbolic entities, to direct their destructive urges against. This is uneasy stuff, but it is an extension of a point, equally uneasy, that had already been made in *After the Fall,* a play that is staged under the shadow cast down upon it by the tower of a concentration camp. At the end of *After the Fall,* when Maggie is dead and Quentin is simultaneously blaming and exonerating himself, "*he turns toward the tower, moves toward it as toward a terrible God,*" and says:

> Or is it possible ... that this is not bizarre ... to anyone? And [possible that] I am not alone, and [that] no man lives who would not rather be the sole survivor of this place than all its finest victims? What is the cure? Who can be innocent again on this mountain of skulls? I tell you what I know! My brothers died here ... [*He looks down at the fallen*

> *Maggie.*] ... but my brothers built this place; our hearts have cut these stones! And what's the cure!
> (2.128–129)

What Miller is saying, with Quentin as his mouthpiece, is complex and daring: in a world that is universally a prison and a torture chamber, all of us are oppressors (Nazis) and all of us are victims of oppression (Jews). It is a point reinforced in *Homely Girl* (1995), a very short novel whose Jewish heroine, Janice Sessions, decides to split with her Jewish boyfriend when he boasts of having raped a German woman ("I don't know if you'd call it rape") who supports Hitler.

This is the context in which to interpret *Broken Glass* (1994), set in Brooklyn in 1938, a place and a date within which the play does not sit comfortably. Phillip Gellburg is a Jew who is ill at ease with his Jewish identity and who has been impotent for twenty years. How, if at all, are these two facts to be related? His wife, Sylvia, distressed by newspaper reports of Nazi mistreatment of elderly Jews who have been forced to clean pavements with toothbrushes, loses all powers of locomotion and takes permanently to her bed. Phillip, perhaps sharing her distress but unwilling to acknowledge it, tells her that events in Berlin need not impact upon life in Brooklyn, adding that German Jews are in any case needlessly provoking the German authorities. In short, he shares Monceau's point of view—but inexcusably, since he is not in the immediate physical danger that faces Monceau.

There is, however, some confusion in the plot here, as there often is in Miller's later plays when he seeks to relate the personal and the societal. Sylvia's retreat to bed, a place where she knows that her impotent husband will never disturb her, is a symbolic protest at his lack of sexual threat, but the larger symbolism is clear enough, too. Phillip and Sylvia are American Jews, whose very desire to succeed as Americans leaves them impotent and paralyzed in the face of rising anti-Semitism. "God, I always thought there'd be time to get to the bottom of myself!" the dying Phillip Gellburg calls out just in time (3.379). And for him, "getting to the bottom" of himself means establishing a right relationship to his own Jewishness, by accepting and acknowledging (while not apologizing for) its distinctiveness while at the same time accepting that Jewishness is not a unique affliction with a unique call upon the world's sympathy: "*Everybody's* persecuted," his Jewish doctor (Harry Hyman) tells him (3.384), and that is what Miller, in his own way another Jewish doctor, is telling all of us. But Hyman (a name that contrasts with Loman) provides us with a problem that depends upon whether we read his last major speech in the play as coming from him in 1938 or from Miller more than fifty years later: "*Everybody's* persecuted. The poor by the rich, the rich by the poor, the black by the white, the white by the black, the men by the women, the women by the men, the Catholics by the Protestants, the Protestants by the Catholics—and of course all of them by the Jews" (3.384).

But Sylvia's fear of the extremity of what the Nazis were doing during the night of November 9, 1938—"They're smashing up the Jewish stores [...] The streets are covered with broken glass" (3. 339)—and of what the *Kristallnacht* did lead to in Germany and might have led to elsewhere is entirely legitimate. With the benefit of the hindsight that fifty years brings in its wake, we should surely accept that she, rather than her husband or her doctor, is the prescient one, even though her defensive paralysis is plainly the worst possible response to the threat that she correctly identifies. The play's original title was "Gellburg," but when Miller took the advice of the theater director David Thacker and chose the more resonant title *Broken Glass* he seems, as have too many modern critics, not sufficiently to have allowed for the far-reaching implications of the change.

LAST THINGS

Plays: Six (2009), the final volume in Methuen's British edition of Miller's *Plays,* was put together posthumously by printing in a single volume the four last plays that Miller had composed. Three of these—*Broken Glass, Mr Peters' Connections,* and *Finishing the Picture*—clearly recall earlier plays and revisit earlier theatrical practices. Only *Resurrection Blues,* written and premiered in

2002, and the next-to-last play that Miller wrote, is radically different and quite unsettling. It begins with a stage direction: "*Dark stage. Light from* JEANINE *in wheelchair; she is wrapped in bandages, one leg straight out. She addresses the audience*" (3.439).

It is not, of course, unusual for a Miller character to address an audience. Sometimes, indeed, as has been already noted, two modes of speaking cohere, when his characters speak so that we listen to them and overhear them at one and the same time. This is what people mean when they say, often disapprovingly, that Miller's characters do not just speak but speak also on Miller's behalf. *Resurrection Blues,* a satire on ways of making money from public executions, is in its entirety a work of this divided kind. Satire, Miller once noted—borrowing a witticism from the comic playwright George S. Kaufman (1889–1961)—is what closes a theatrical run on its first Saturday. On its American debut *Resurrection Blues* secured a middling response from reviewers who, even while approving of it, invoked earlier plays (generally *The Crucible*) against which to find it lacking in seriousness. When, a year after Miller's death, the play crossed the Atlantic to London's Old Vic in a production by Robert Altman, opinions both of the new production and of the play itself were unfavorable, there being a widespread acknowledgment that satire was not Miller's strongest suit. Perhaps this is no more than the story of two productions of radically different quality or of a play that nobody has yet had quite enough time to assess. There need be no surprise: in a life as long as Miller's, a life whose productivity ran right through to the end without running out, there are bound to be some questions left unresolved.

Miller died on February 10, 2005, still a forceful presence intellectually but physically worn out by the spread of cancer. He is survived by four children, two of whom have followed with some distinction in their father's creative footsteps: Robert Miller (born in 1947) is a film producer who has produced film versions of *The Crucible* (1996) and *Focus* (2001); Rebecca Miller (born in 1962) is a filmmaker, screenwriter, novelist, and playwright and is married to the actor Sir Daniel Day-Lewis. Miller's robust and contentious personality has inevitably made him difficult to be sentimental about: obituarists, forgetting the honorable hypocrisy of their calling, picked away gracelessly at his later failures. But everyone with a genuine interest in drama sensed that with Miller's death an era had ended, and those with foresight sensed that another was beginning. The best of Miller's plays, we can say with confidence, will survive him: the years since his death have seen many distinguished revivals across the world and a more confident acceptance of his merits within the United States. His place beside Eugene O'Neill and Tennessee Williams is assured not merely on bookshelves but on the stage.

Selected Bibliography

WORKS OF ARTHUR MILLER

PLAYS PRODUCED AND PUBLISHED

The Man Who Had All the Luck. First produced November 1944, Fortune Theatre, New York. Directed by Joseph Fields. Published in *Cross-Section: A Collection of New American Writing.* Edited by Edwin Seaver. New York: Fischer, 1944.

All My Sons. First produced January 1947, Coronet Theatre, New York. Directed by Elia Kazan. New York: Reynal and Hitchcock, 1947.

Death of a Salesman. First produced February 1949, Morosco Theatre, New York. Directed by Elia Kazan. New York: Viking, 1949.

An Enemy of the People. First produced December 1950, Broadhurst Theatre, New York. Directed by Robert Lewis. New York: Viking, 1951.

The Crucible. First produced January 1953, Martin Beck Theatre, New York. Directed by Jed Harris. New York: Viking, 1953.

A Memory of Two Mondays. First produced September 1955, Coronet Theatre, New York. Directed by Martin Ritt. New York: Viking, 1955.

A View from the Bridge. (One-act version.) First produced September 1955, Coronet Theatre, New York. Directed by Martin Ritt. New York: Viking, 1955.

A View from the Bridge. (Two-act version.) First produced October 1956, Comedy Theatre, London. Directed by Peter Brook. New York: Compass, 1960.

After the Fall. First produced January 1964, ANTA-Washington Square Theater, New York. Directed by Elia Kazan. New York: Viking, 1964.

Incident at Vichy. First produced December 1964, ANTA-Washington Square Theater, New York. Directed by Harold Clurman. New York: Viking, 1965.

The Price. First produced February 1968, Morosco Theatre, New York. Directed by Ulu Grosbard. New York: Viking, 1968.

The Creation of the World and Other Business. First produced November 1972, Shubert Theater, New York. Directed by Gerald Freeman. New York: Viking, 1973.

Up from Paradise. First produced April 1974, Power Center for the Performing Arts, Ann Arbor. Directed by Arthur Miller.

The Archbishop's Ceiling. First produced April 1977, Eisenhower Theater, Washington, D.C. Directed by Arvin Brown. Published with *The American Clock,* New York: Grove Press, 1989.

The American Clock. (1) First produced May 1980. Dock-side Theater. Charleston, South Carolina. Directed by Vivian Matalon. (2) First produced November 1980. Biltmore Theatre. New York. Directed by Dan Sullivan; New York: Dramatists Play Service, 1982; also published with *The Archbishop's Ceiling,* New York: Grove Press, 1989.

Playing for Time. Screenplay directed by Daniel Mann and broadcast by CBS on September 30, 1980. New York: Bantam, 1981; Woodstock, Ill.: Dramatic Publishing, 1985. (This is the text of Miller's stage adaptation of his 1981 screenplay.)

Elegy for a Lady. First produced October 1982, Long Wharf Theatre, New Haven, Conn. Directed by Arthur Miller. New York: Dramatists Play Service, 1982.

Some Kind of Love Story. First produced October 1982, Long Wharf Theatre, New Haven, Conn. Directed by Arthur Miller. New York: Dramatists Play Service, 1982.

Clara. First produced February 1987, Lincoln Center, New York. Directed by Gregory Mosher.

I Can't Remember Anything. First produced February 1987, Lincoln Center, New York. Directed by Gregory Mosher.

The Golden Years. Broadcast as a radio play on BBC Radio 3 on November 6, 1987. Directed by Martin Jenkins.

Almost Everybody Wins: A Screenplay. Directed by Karel Reisz and given its first showing on January 19, 1990.

The Ride down Mt Morgan. First produced October 1991, Wyndham's Theatre, London. Directed by Michael Blakemore. New York: Dramatists Play Service, 1999. (A revised text of the play as emended for performance in 1998.)

The Last Yankee. First produced January 1993, Manhattan Theatre Club, New York. Directed by John Tillinger.

Broken Glass. First produced March 1994, Long Wharf Theatre, New Haven, Conn. Directed by John Tillinger. Moved one month later to the Booth Theatre, New York. New York: Penguin, 1994.

The Ryan Interview. First produced May 1995, Ensemble Studio Theatre, New York. Directed by Curt Dempster.

Mr Peter's Connections. First produced April 1998, Signature Theatre, New York. Directed by Gary Hynes. New York: Penguin, 1999.

Resurrection Blues. First produced August 2002, Guthrie Theater, Minneapolis. Directed by David Esbjornson.

Finishing the Picture. First produced September 2004, Goodman Theatre, Chicago. Directed by Robert Falls.

PLAYS PUBLISHED

Collected Plays. Vol. 1. New York: Viking, 1957. London: Cresset Press, 1958. Vol. 2. New York: Viking, 1981.

Danger: Memory! New York: Grove Press, 1987.

METHUEN EDITIONS, *PLAYS: ONE* TO *PLAYS: SIX*

Plays: One. London: Methuen Drama, 1988. (This reissue of Miller's 1957 *Collected Plays,* contains Miller's substantial introductory essay, the texts of *All My Sons, Death of a Salesman, The Crucible, A Memory of Two Mondays,* and the revised two-act version of *A View from the Bridge.*)

Plays: Two. London: Methuen Drama, 1988. (This reissue of the second volume of Miller's *Collected Plays* (1981) contains *The Misfits, After the Fall, Incident at Vichy, The Price, The Creation of the World and Other Business,* and *Playing for Time.*)

Plays: Three. London: Methuen Drama, 1990. (Contains *The American Clock, The Archbishop's Ceiling, Elegy for a Lady,* and *Some Kind of Love Story.*)

Plays: Four. London: Methuen Drama, 1994. (Contains *The Golden Years, The Man Who Had All the Luck, I Can't Remember Anything,* and *Clara.*)

Plays: Five. London: Methuen Drama, 1995. (Contains *The Last Yankee, The Ride down Mt Morgan,* and *Almost Everybody Wins: A Screenplay.*)

Plays: Six. London: Methuen Drama, 2009. (Published posthumously. Contains *Broken Glass, Mr Peters' Connections, Resurrection Blues,* and *Finishing the Picture.*)

LIBRARY OF AMERICA SERIES, EDITED BY TONY KUSHNER

The three volumes of collected plays released by the Library of America, prepared by the Tony Award– and Pulitzer Prize–winning playwright Tony Kushner, includes texts of forty-two plays, rather than the twenty-four collected in the Methuen editions. The second and third volumes in this series contain generous extracts from Miller's own notes and essays to his plays. Wherever possible quotations from Miller's plays, notes, and critical essays are taken from this edition and are referenced parenthetically by volume and page number.

Collected Plays: 1944–1961. New York: Library of America, 2006. (Contains *The Man Who Had All the Luck: A Fable, All My Sons, Death of a Salesman, An Enemy of the*

People, The Crucible, A Memory of Two Mondays, A View from the Bridge (one-act version), *A View from the Bridge* (two-act version), and *The Misfits.*)

Collected Plays: 1964–1982. New York: Library of America, 2012. (Contains *After the Fall, Incident at Vichy, The Price, Fame, The Reason Why, The Creation of the World and Other Business, Up from Paradise, The American Clock, The Poosidin's Resignation, The Archbishop's Ceiling, Playing for Time, I Think About You a Great Deal, Elegy for a Lady,* and the 1982 version of *Some Kind of a Love Story.*)

Collected Plays: 1987–2004: With Stage and Radio Plays of the 1930s and 1940s. New York: Library of America, 2015. (Contains two early plays: *The Grass Still Grows* [1939] and *The Half-Bridge* [1942]. Also includes six radio-plays: *Captain Paul* [1941], *Buffalo Bill Disremembers* [1941], *The Battle of the Ovens* [1942], *Thunder from the Mountains* [1942], *Glider Doctor* [1944], and *Mare Island and Back* [1945]. Rejoining the main chronological sequence are *Danger: Memory!* [consisting of *I Can't Remember Anything* and *Clara*], *The Golden Years, Almost Everybody Wins, The Ride down Mt Morgan, The Last Yankee, Broken Glass, The Ryan Interview, Mr Peters' Connections, Resurrection Blues,* and *Finishing the Picture.*)

CRITICAL ESSAYS

Quotations from Miller's critical essays that are not included in Kushner's Library of America editions are taken wherever possible from *The Collected Essays of Arthur Miller.* Edited and introduced by Matthew Roudané. London and New York: Bloomsbury Methuen, 2015. This is the fullest edition currently in print, but Roudané selected the contents of the 2015 *Collected Essays* from two other volumes: *The Theater Essays of Arthur Miller.* Edited by Robert A. Martin and Steven R. Centola. New York, 1996; and *Echoes down the Corridor: Collected Essays, 1944–2000.* Edited by Steven R. Centola. London: Methuen, 2000. Miller's "Introduction to the Collected Plays" is printed in *Collected Plays* (1957), pp. 3–55, and in *Collected Essays* (2015), pp. 107–141.

INTERVIEWS

Bigsby, Christopher, ed. *Arthur Miller and Company: Arthur Miller Talks About His Work in the Company of Actors, Designers, Directors, and Writers.* London: Methuen, 1990. (This seventy-fifth birthday tribute to Miller consists of a long interview with him that Bigsby has pieced together from conversations held between 1979 and 1989. The interview has then been divided into thirteen parts that are interspersed with comments supplied by eighty friends and associates. The interview includes substantial sections that are also available in Miller's 1987 memoir, *Timebends.*)

Gussow, Mel, ed. *Conversations with Miller.* London: Nick Hern Books, 2002.

Hayman, Ronald. *Arthur Miller.* 2nd ed. London: Heinemann, 1973. (Contains, at pp. 1–14, an interview with Miller that is reprinted in Roudané, *Conversations with Arthur Miller* [1987], pp. 187–199.)

Martin, Robert A. "The Creative Experience of Arthur Miller: An Interview." *Educational Theatre Journal* 21, no. 3:310–317 (1969). (Reprinted in Roudané, *Conversations with Arthur Miller* [1987], pp. 177–186.)

Moss, Leonard. *Arthur Miller.* Rev. ed. Boston: G. K. Hall, 1980 (Includes, at pp. 107–122, an interview where Miller describes *The Price* as an investigation of "the architecture of sacrifice." In effect he gives an early version of the argument developed further in "*The Price*: The Power of the Past," reprinted in the 2015 *Collected Essays,* pp. 484–485.)

Roudané, Matthew, ed. *Conversations with Arthur Miller.* Jackson and London: University Press of Mississippi, 1987.

Toubiana, Serge, et al. *The Misfits: Story of a Shoot.* London: Phaidon, 2000. (Chiefly a book of photographs, but it also contains a valuable interview with Miller.)

OTHER WORKS

Situation Normal. New York: Reynal and Hitchcock. 1944.

Focus. New York: Reynal and Hitchcock, 1945. (Also London: Methuen, 1992. The Methuen edition includes a brief essay, "The Face in the Mirror: Anti-Semitism Then and Now," written by Miller in 1984 and reprinted in the 2015 *Collected Essays,* pp. 346–348.)

The Misfits. (Film version.) Directed by John Huston. Produced by Frank E. Taylor. Screenplay by Arthur Miller. Seven Arts Productions, 1961.

I Don't Need You Anymore: Stories. New York: Viking, 1967. (Includes a text of the short story that was to become *The Misfits.*)

In Russia. With Inge Morath. New York: Viking, 1969.

"Salesman" in Beijing. New York: Viking, 1984. (An account, based on a log that Miller kept of his 1983 Beijing production of *Death of a Salesman,* in which he ranges widely over many aspects of his drama and of drama generally.)

Timebends: A Life. New York: Grove Press, 1987. (An autobiography that is also a detailed account of individual plays.)

Homely Girl: A Life. New York: Peter Blum, 1995. (Published in the United Kingdom as *Plain Girl.* London: Methuen. 1995.)

The Crucible. (Film version.) Directed by Nicholas Hytner. Produced by Robert A. Miller and David V. Picker. Screenplay by Arthur Miller. Twentieth Century Fox, 1996.

The Crucible: A Screenplay. London: Methuen Film. 1996. (Not just a screenplay but a revision of the text that editors and critics need to take into account.)

Death of a Salesman. (Film version.) Directed by Laslo Benedek. Produced by Stanley Kramer. Screenplay by Stanley Roberts. Columbia Pictures, 1950.

Focus. (Film version.) Directed by Neal Slavin. Produced by Robert A. Miller, Michael R. Bloomberg, and Neal Slavin. Screenplay by Kendrew Lascelles. Paramount Classics, 2001.

On Politics and the Art of Acting. New York: Viking Adult, 2001.

"His Jewish Question." *Vanity Fair,* September 24, 2009. (An essay on *Focus* in advance of the 2009 movie release.) http://www.vanityfair.com/culture/2001/10/arthur-miller-200110

BIOGRAPHICAL AND CRITICAL STUDIES

Biographies

Bigsby, Christopher. *Arthur Miller, 1915–1962.* London: Weidenfeld & Nicolson, 2008.

———. *Arthur Miller, 1962–2005.* London: Weidenfeld & Nicolson, 2011.

Gottfried, Martin. *Arthur Miller: A Life.* London: Faber & Faber, 2003.

Secondary Reading

Adler, Stella. *Stella Adler on America's Master Playwrights.* Edited by Barry Paris. New York: Knopf, 2012. (Contains essays on *Death of a Salesman* and *After the Fall,* pp. 225–235.)

Arbanel, Jonathan. "*Finishing the Picture.*" *Theatermania,* October 11, 2004. (Review of the 2004 production directed by Robert Falls at the Goodman Theater, Chicago.) http://www.theatermania.com/chicago-theat/reviews/10-2004/finishing-the-picture_5212.html

"Arthur Miller, Moral Voice of American Stage, Dies at 89." *New York Times,* February 11, 2005. http://www.nytimes.com/2005/02/11/theater/newsandfeatures/arthur-miller-moral-voice-of-american-stage-dies-at.html

Bigsby, Christopher. *Confrontation and Commitment: A Study of Contemporary American Drama, 1959–66.* London: MacGibbon & Kee, 1967.

———. *A Critical Introduction to Twentieth-Century American Drama.* Vol. 2: *Tennessee Williams, Arthur Miller, and Edward Albee.* Cambridge, U.K.: Cambridge University Press, 1984. (Miller is discussed at pp. 135–248.)

———, ed. *The Cambridge Companion to Arthur Miller.* Cambridge, U.K.: Cambridge University Press, 1997.

———. *Arthur Miller: A Critical Study.* Cambridge, U.K.: Cambridge University Press, 2005.

———. *Remembering and Imagining the Holocaust: The Chain of Memory.* Cambridge, U.K.: Cambridge University Press, 2006. (The discussion of Miller's work, heavily weighted toward *Playing for Time,* is at pp. 176–218.)

Billington, Michael. "The Crucifixion Will Be Televised." *Guardian,* August 22, 2002. https://www.theguardian.com/stage/2002/aug/21/theatre.artsfeatures (Review of the American premiere of *Resurrection Blues,* seen at the Guthrie Theater in Minneapolis.)

———. "*Resurrection Blues.*" *Guardian,* March 3, 2006. http://www.theguardian.com/stage/2006/mar/03/theatre3 (A noticeably less friendly review of Robert Altman's Old Vic production of *Resurrection Blues.*)

Brater, Enoch. *Arthur Miller: A Playwright's Life and Works.* London: Thames & Hudson, 2005.

———, ed. *Arthur Miller's America: Theater and Culture in a Time of Change.* Ann Arbor: University of Michigan Press, 2005.

Carson, Neil. *Arthur Miller.* 2nd ed. Basingstoke, U.K.: Palgrave Macmillan, 2008.

Centola, Steven, ed. *The Achievement of Arthur Miller.* Dallas, Tex.: Contemporary Research Press, 1995.

Christiansen, Richard. "Miller's Tale." *Guardian,* October 29, 2004. http://www.theguardian.com/stage/2004/oct/30/theatre.stage1 (Review of *Finishing the Picture.*)

Coward, Noël. *The Noël Coward Diaries.* Edited by Graham Payn and Sheridan Morley. London: Weidenfeld & Nicolson, 1982.

Cox, Brian. *Salem to Moscow: An Actor's Odyssey.* London: Methuen, 1991. (Cox's account of directing *The Crucible* at the Moscow Art Theatre School in 1988.)

Dickson, Andrew. "'My aim is the ultimate production': Ivo van Hove on directing Arthur Miller." *Guardian,* April 2, 2014. https://www.theguardian.com/stage/2014/apr/02/ultimate-production-ivo-van-hove-arthur-miller-theatre (Van Hove discusses his 2014 production of *A View from the Bridge* at the Young Vic, London.)

Dukore, Bernard F. *"Death of a Salesman" and "The Crucible": Text and Performance.* London: Macmillan Education, 1989.

Eyre, Peter. *National Service: Diary of a Decade at the National Theatre.* London: Bloomsbury, 2003. (Eyre was director of the United Kingdom's national theater in 1987–1997. The two references to Miller here are fleeting but revealing.)

Foulkes, A. P. *Literature and Propaganda.* London: Methuen, 1983. ("Demystifying the Witch Hunt," pp. 83–104, is a detailed discussion of early critical reaction to *The Crucible.*)

Goldstein, Laurence. "Finishing the Picture: Arthur Miller, 1915–2005." *Michigan Quarterly Review* 64, no. 2 (spring 2005). http://hdl.handle.net/2027/spo.act2080.0044.201 (Includes an obituary tribute to Miller and a detailed discussion of *Finishing the Picture.*)

Goode, James. *The Story of "The Misfits."* Indianapolis, Ind.: Bobbs-Merrill, 1963.

Griggin, Alice. *Understanding Arthur Miller.* Columbia: University of South Carolina Press, 1996.

Kalb, Jonathan. *Play by Play: Theater Essays and Reviews, 1993–2002.* New York: Limelight, 2003. (Contains an essay, "Arthur Miller and the Barbecue Grill," pp. 217–232, in which Kalb reviews three American productions from the late 1990s of *Death of a Salesman, A Ride down Mt Morgan,* and *The Price.*)

Kazan, Elia. *Elia Kazan: A Life.* New York: Knopf, 1988.

———. *Kazan on Directing.* Edited by Robert Cornfield. New York: Knopf, 2009. (Skillfully recovered by the editor from Kazan's unpublished notebooks. The section on *Death of a Salesman,* pp. 69–86, is highly informative.)

Kushner, Tony. "Kushner on Miller." In *The American Stage: Writing on Theater from Washington Irving to Tony Kushner.* Edited by Laurence Senelick. New York: Library of America, 2010. Pp. 822–828. (Originally appeared in the *Nation,* June 13, 2005.)

Livesay, Lewis. "*The Ride down Mt Morgan*: Miller's Critique of Libido Through Ibsen's Method of Causation." *Arthur Miller Journal* 10, no. 2: 110–134 (autumn 2015).

Martine, James J. *"The Crucible": Politics, Property, and Pretense.* New York: Twayne, 1993.

Murphy, Brenda. *Miller: "Death of a Salesman."* Cambridge, U.K.: Cambridge University Press, 1995.

———. *Congressional Theatre: Dramatizing McCarthyism on Stage, Film, and Television.* Cambridge, U.K.: Cambridge University Press, 1999. (Discussion of Miller's plays on pp. 133–161, 206–225, and 232–240.)

Nelson, Benjamin. *Arthur Miller: Portrait of a Playwright.* London: Owen, 1970.

Németh, Lenke. "Arthur Miller's *The Ride down Mt Morgan* and the Family Play Tradition." *Hungarian Journal of English and American Studies* 11, no. 2: 77–88 (fall 2005).

Phillips, Michael. "Where's the Wit in Miller's Latest?" *Los Angeles Times,* August 12, 2002. http://articles.latimes.com/2002/aug/12/entertainment/et-philllips12 (Review of *Resurrection Blues* at the Guthrie Theater, Minneapolis.)

Ponto, Sarah. "*Death of a Salesman* Set Designer Jo Mielziner: Design Awareness Case Study Group Project." *Prezi,* February 11, 2013. https://prezi.com/48rojnm-hzyh/death-of-a-salesman-set-designer-jo-mielziner/

Poore, Charles. "Books of the Times." *New York Times,* November 24, 1945. https://www.nytimes.com/books/00/11/12/specials/miller-focus.html (Review of the novel *Focus.*)

Radavich, David. "Arthur Miller's Sojourn in the Heartland." *American Drama* 16, no. 2: 28–45 (summer 2007).

Savran, David. *Breaking the Rules: The Wooster Group.* New York: Theatre Communications Group, 1988. (Chronicles the attempt by America's leading performance group to stage its own radical and controversial reworking of *The Crucible.*)

———. *Communists, Cowboys, and Queers: The Politics of Masculinity in the Work of Arthur Miller and Tennessee Williams.* Minneapolis and London: University of Minnesota Press, 1992.

Schlueter, Jane, and James K. Flanagan. *Arthur Miller.* New York: Unger, 1987.

Sharrar, Jack F. *Avery Hopwood: His Life and Plays.* Ann Arbor: University of Michigan Press, 1989.

Spencer, Charles. "A Miller's Tale That's Beyond Resurrection." *Telegraph,* March 3, 2006. http://www.telegraph.co.uk/culture/theatre/3650636/A-Millers-tale-thats-beyond-resurrection.html (A remorselessly hostile review of *Resurrection Blues.*)

Weatherby, W. J. *Conversations with Marilyn.* 1976. Reprint, New York: Paragon, 1992. (Consists of a narrative by Weatherby incorporated into which are extensive extracts from interviews with Marilyn Monroe. Especially interesting, inevitably, on *The Misfits.*)

Selected Websites

"A View from the Bridge." Young Vic Theatre. http://www.youngvic.org/whats-on/a-view-from-the-bridge (Discussion of Ivo van Hove's 2014 production).

Arthur Miller Society Official Website. http://www.ibiblio.org/miller/

Arthur Miller Journal. Biannual publication by the Pennsylvania State University Press, the Arthur Miller Society, and the Arthur Miller Centre of the University of East Anglia (U.K.). Lists contents of all issues published since its inauguration in 2006. http://www.ibiblio.org/miller/journal.html

TONI MORRISON

(1931—)

Tracie Church Guzzio

FEW SCHOLARS AND literary critics would disagree that Toni Morrison is one of the most important writers of her era. Not only has she received every notable writing award, including a Nobel Prize, she has achieved immense mainstream popularity, due in some part to the support of the television star and producer Oprah Winfrey, who introduced millions of viewers to Morrison by choosing several of Morrison's novels for the "Oprah's Book Club" section of her talk show. Besides the fame, the best-selling status, and the accolades Morrison has achieved, her fiction, her essays, and her life have been the subject of thousands of doctoral dissertations and literary criticism, further cementing her status as both author and cultural icon. Her prominence is not only in American arts and letters; she is globally recognized by fellow writers, activists, historians, and even world leaders as possessing a voice that travels far beyond the page.

LIFE AND CAREER

Given her modest beginnings, Morrison's meteoric achievements are all the more impressive. Born in 1931 in Lorain, a small "plant" town in Ohio, to George and Ella Ramah Willis Wofford, Chloe Ardelia Wofford was taught early that hard work was important to success. Her parents took on extra work during and after the years of the Great Depression in order to take care of their four children and to help send Morrison and her older sister, Lois, to college. During her secondary school years, Morrison excelled in writing, producing essays that were often read aloud to the school. She also fed her passion for reading while working in the school library. In addition to her diligent and successful performance in school, Morrison occasionally worked as a maid after school—starting at age twelve—to help her family make ends meet. Despite the challenging times, Morrison was very close to her parents and siblings as well as to her maternal grandparents and great-grandmother. Within this transgenerational dynamic, Morrison's family would share ancestor stories, folktales, and history. In an interview with the scholar Karla F. C. Holloway, she described her childhood home as a "spoken library" (quoted in Wagner-Martin, *Toni Morrison,* pp. 4–5). Morrison's maternal grandfather, John Solomon Willis, was a violinist. And her mother was a piano player at the local church who also sang throughout the house almost every day. The interplay of music, storytelling, and the past would provide the fertile environment for Morrison's imagination and inimitable style to take root and grow.

Morrison attended Howard University in 1949–1953, majoring in English and minoring in classical languages. Washington, D.C., was still a segregated city when Morrison went to Howard, a historically black college, and as a member of the university's dramatic troupe she often traveled throughout parts of the South. During these years, she directly experienced, for the first time, Jim Crow racism. After receiving her bachelor's degree, Morrison entered the masters program at Cornell University in Ithaca, New York. Her thesis on alienation in the work of Virginia Woolf and William Faulkner would later influence her first work, *The Bluest Eye* (1970), which she began while in college. When she completed her master's degree in 1955, Morrison accepted a job teaching at Texas Southern University in Houston. She returned to Howard as an instructor in 1957. The following year she married Harold Morrison, an architect from Jamaica. Their son Harold Ford was born in 1961. Morrison continued to teach at

Howard until 1963. Some of her students there who went on to national and global importance included the politician and human rights activist Andrew Young; the civil rights leader Stokely Carmichael; the literary critic Houston Baker, Jr.; and the writer Claude Brown, Jr. In 1964, while she was pregnant with her second son, Slade, Morrison divorced her husband and moved back home to Lorain.

Her new career began soon after that move, when she accepted a position as associate editor in Syracuse, New York, at a Random House subsidiary in 1965. Within two years, she was a senior editor at Random House in New York City, a position she held for seventeen more years. She guided the work of the writers Gayl Jones and Toni Cade Bambara, and she edited works by Muhammad Ali and Angela Davis. Through her efforts, the writing of Henry Dumas was posthumously published after he was fatally shot by a transit officer. It was also during this time that she began to edit a collection of transcripts, images, and other historical artifacts eventually published as *The Black Book* in 1974. Here she discovered the story of the slave Margaret Garner that would inspire her 1987 novel, *Beloved,* and an eponymous libretto. Besides her life as a busy, single mother of two young boys and her editorial work, every evening after her children went to bed, she revised the manuscript that would later become *The Bluest Eye.* When she signed the contract for the novel, she mistakenly used her nickname, "Toni" (which she had gone by since college), and her writing pseudonym was established. During this same period, she began meeting with several other prominent African American women writers, including Alice Walker and June Jordan, to form a "sisterhood" to promote collaboration and support for black female writers.

Her second novel, *Sula,* published in 1973, ushered in a lifetime of writing nominations and awards when it gained recognition as a National Book Award nominee. In 1975, she began lecturing at Yale University in New Haven, Connecticut. Her third book, *Song of Solomon* (1977), won the National Book Critics' Circle Award in 1978, and that same year Morrison received the American Academy of Arts and Letters Award. She took other teaching positions near New York City, at Bard College in Annandale-on-Hudson and at the State University of New York at Purchase, before accepting the Albert Schweitzer Professor of the Humanities position at SUNY Albany in 1984 (the same year she left Random House). She was appointed to several boards, including the National Council on the Arts. In 1986 her play *Dreaming Emmett,* was performed in Albany and received the New York State Governors' Award. In 1987, her fifth novel, *Beloved,* received numerous major writing awards, but not the National Book Award, which prompted forty-eight African American writers to publish a letter of protest—and praise for Morrison's work—in the *New York Times Book Review. Beloved* did go on to win the Pulitzer Prize for Fiction in 1988, and the following year Morrison left Albany for the Robert Goheen Chair in the Council in the Humanities at Princeton University, where she remained until her retirement in 2006. In 1990 she also presented the William E. Massey, Sr., Lectures in the History of American Civilization at Harvard University, which she later published as the book of literary criticism, *Playing in the Dark: Whiteness and the Literary Imagination* (1992). Her sixth novel, *Jazz,* appeared in the same year.

Morrison was the first African American to win the Nobel Prize for Literature and only the second American woman when she received the award in 1993. But only two weeks after she returned home from delivering her Nobel address, fire almost completely destroyed Morrison's home in Grand-View-on-Hudson, New York. Most of her manuscripts were either at Princeton or spared by the fire, but Morrison did lose almost everything else.

For the next five years, Morrison garnered several international awards, including the National Book Foundation Award in 1996 (the occasion was marked by her acceptance speech, "The Dancing Mind"), while working on the novel *Paradise,* writing lyrics for several musical compositions performed by Kathleen Battle and Jessye Norman at Carnegie Hall, editing several collections of critical essays, and lecturing throughout the United States and the world. At the same time, her mainstream success was elevated by the incorporation of the Toni Morrison Society (a nonprofit organization devoted to scholarship on Morrison's work), by the promotion of her work through the Oprah Book Club, and by the release of a film version of *Beloved,* directed by Jonathan Demme, in 1998. And in 1999, she published her first coauthored work with her son Slade Morrison, an artist and musician. The work, *The Big Box,* would be the first of numerous collaborations on children's books between the two.

Since the year 2000, Morrison has been constantly at work—publishing more novels as well as other works—and has won more honors and awards than are possible to recount here. At a time when most writers are winding down in their career, Morrison released four novels—*Love* (2003), *A Mercy* (2008), *Home* (2012), and *God Help the Child* (2015)—in the space of a dozen years, and all to critical acclaim. During this time, she received the National Humanities Medal as well as the Pell Award for Lifetime Achievement in the Arts. She was named Harvard's Radcliffe Medalist in 2007 and was awarded a doctor of letters degree from Oxford University and also an honorary doctorate from the Sorbonne. For her work in literature and in social justice, she was invited to give the United Nations Secretary General's Lecture and the Amnesty International Lecture. Also in this period, she developed the range of her art even further by completing an opera based on the life of Margaret Garner (2004), curating an exhibit at the Louvre (2006), and collaborating on the play *Desdemona,* which premiered in Vienna, Austria, in 2011. Her life and work were celebrated in a Lincoln Center event in 2006, and her contributions to world and American literature were further commemorated in 2012 when President Barack Obama presented her with the Presidential Medal of Freedom.

In 2006, Toni Morrison retired from Princeton University after seventeen years as a member of the teaching faculty, and while her later years have been filled with dozens of tributes to her contributions to literature, she has also suffered immense pain and loss. Her son Slade died of pancreatic cancer in 2010 while Morrison was working on *Home.* Their last work together, *Please, Louise,* was published in 2014. She currently lives in Manhattan and is the grandmother to the two daughters of her son Harold Ford Morrison, who is an attorney.

THE BLUEST EYE *(1970)*

Morrison's first novel, published in 1970, continues to be one of her most controversial. Regularly challenged in school libraries for its frank portrayal of the tragic life of the main character, Pecola Breedlove, the novel directly critiques white middle-class values and culturally reinforced racism. Morrison began the work while at Howard University. She initially conceived it as a short story, and she revised it for years, sending it to various publishers during the process. The manuscript was rejected numerous times, even during the period when Morrison was working as an editor at Random House. Eventually published by a rival house, the book initially received lukewarm to negative reviews. Critics who measured it against other books by black authors complained that it had little of the optimism of the movement—and not enough white characters. As Morrison notes in her afterword to the 1993 (Oprah's Book Club) edition of the novel, "*The Bluest Eye* was like Pecola's life: dismissed, trivialized, misread" (p. 216).

It was only after black critics, journalists, and writers championed the work and its novelist that the book gained more support. Morrison's afterword, as well several interviews she has given over the years, suggests that *The Bluest Eye* grew from some of her own experiences growing up in Lorain. But the work also grew out of the absences she felt in American literature and in the mainstream culture:

> I wrote the first book because I wanted to read it. I thought that kind of book, with that subject—those most vulnerable, most undescribed, not taken seriously little black girls—had never existed seriously in literature. No one had ever written about them except as props. Since I couldn't find a book that did that, I thought, "Well, I'll write it and then I'll read it."
>
> (Gross, NEA interview online)

The story examines, through Pecola's self-loathing and desire for blue eyes, an insistent racism that sees the Pecolas of the world as less than human. The racist attitudes that damage Pecola's self-image are not directly verbalized by white characters. Instead American culture pervades Pecola's home, school, neighborhood, community, and consciousness like a toxic cloud. The black community in the work is unwittingly complicit in participating in the same society and culture that is guilty of poisoning them. The novel opens with echoes of shame and trauma: "quiet as it's kept" (p. 1). The narration reports that the flower seeds that Claudia McTeer and her sister, Frieda, planted, in an act of empathy and hope, have not transformed into marigolds. The community lacks self-sustenance and the ability to nurture its "seedlings"—the children, like Pecola, who cannot grow in this hostile land and climate.

The Dick-and-Jane narrative that follows emphasizes the vulnerability of children to hegemonic cultural standards—this will be a consistent theme in Morrison's writing. The reading primer, which was a ubiquitous sign of middle-class conformity and success, educates children and the community to accepted norms of race, sex, and gender. It is the narrative of the American Dream—Dick and Jane, because of their privilege, enjoy a safe neighborhood, loving family, and warm home. This image is quickly juxtaposed with the Breedlove's storefront dwelling. Their "home" is little more than a roof and four walls. Its lack of individual décor, empty and open space, and color signal the family's alienation from the concept of "homeliness" and from each other. They fight, hide, cower, and dream of various forms of flight from one another. Sammy and Pecola call their mother Mrs. Breedlove—a sign of her distance from them. No one visits or helps them in securing a better dwelling. Instead their life is contrasted to everything Dick and Jane represent. Because they stand "as the epitome of everything that white culture rejects—the darkest skin and the direst economic situation—the Breedloves embody trauma" (Schreiber, p. 73). This pain turns inward, so that each member of the family judges the others' and their own worth based on how their community sees them.

This is clearly expressed in several prominent scenes of the book. The women in town make fun of Pauline because she doesn't straighten her hair. And Claudia feels forced to love the white baby doll that her parents give her as a gift, even though she would prefer to "dismember" it (p. 22). The girls buy Mary Jane candy wrapped in Mary Jane's blond image. Pecola finds the picture beautiful: "to eat the candy is somehow to eat the eyes, eat Mary Jane, Love Mary Jane. Be Mary Jane" (*The Bluest Eye,* p. 50). Pecola also becomes fascinated with the McTeers' "Shirley Temple" cup. She drinks quarts of milk just so she can gaze at the picture of the happy, cute, white child on the outside of the cup. Her desire for whiteness is further emphasized by the whiteness of the milk itself. The scene foreshadows Pecola's attempt to acquire blue eyes to attain the happiness she believes comes with whiteness. The proliferation of white imagery is accelerated in the novel's time period through film and popular culture. Morrison's focus on Pecola's tragedy within this time frame illustrates the roots of media's power to shape perceptions of beauty and conformity.

Pecola is not the only victim of this influence. Her mother, Pauline, becomes enraptured by the images of happiness and white beauty she sees in films from the 1930s. She goes to the cinema almost every day imagining a happier life:

> There in the dark her memory was refreshed, and she succumbed to her earlier dreams. Along with the idea of romantic love, she was introduced to another—physical beauty. Probably the most destructive ideas in the history of human thought. Both originated in envy, thrived in insecurity, and ended in disillusion. In equating physical beauty with virtue, she stripped her mind, bound it and collected self-contempt by the heap.
>
> (p. 122)

She tries to emulate the physical appearance of the actress, Jean Harlow, and like her daughter, attempts to transform her unhappiness by adopting a white mask. But her pregnancy and the loss of a front tooth keep her from attaining her goal, and so she accepts "just being ugly" (p. 123). After this, she gives up on her marriage and her family. When Pecola is born, Pauline admits to having imagined a girl that looked like her mother, but following the dehumanizing treatment she receives from the white doctors at the hospital, Pauline sees her daughter through their eyes: "I knowed she was ugly. Head full of pretty hair, but Lord she was ugly" (p. 126).

Pauline's rejection of her daughter—and by extension herself, her mother, and all black women—has a profound effect on how Pecola views herself and how the community will see her as well. Unable to find beauty at home, Pauline seeks it in her work as a housekeeper for a white family who have a blond little girl. In this space, Pauline can find "beauty, order, cleanliness, and praise," and she can be a "proper" mother to a beautiful child (p. 99). This is clear when she protects and soothes the surrogate white child, who's upset over losing her dessert, rather than soothing Pecola—who has actually been burned by the spilled, boiling-hot cobbler. The novel suggests the "central role mothering plays" in determining self-worth (Wagner-Martin, p. 6), but it also indicts the community for embracing values that diminish the lives of black Americans. No one steps forth to mother Pecola or to befriend her—instead she is bullied by her schoolmates and cast aside by other adults. The older Claudia explains: "All of our waste which we dumped on her and which she absorbed. And all of our beauty, which was hers first and which she gave to us. All of us—all who knew her—felt so wholesome after we cleaned ourselves on her. We were so beautiful when we stood astride her ugliness" (p. 205).

It is unclear if this critique comes from Claudia or from an omniscient narrator that seems to emerge at the end of the work. Employing such a narrator would suggest that Morrison is leveling a charge against society rather than against the fictional characters in this book.

Pecola's desire for love and wholeness intensifies following the rape by her father that leaves her pregnant and plunges Pecola into a tragic, psychic break with reality. Pecola's wish for blue eyes, perverted by Soaphead Church's own selfish actions, is a search for love, and even in this section, she is unable to tell her own story. The narrative is fragmented, reflecting a split in Pecola's consciousness where she can only see the image of white beauty that will guarantee her acceptance in this community. It is only in the midst of this hallucinatory breakdown that Pecola is able to free herself from "blackness" and thus her "stigmatized racial identity" (Bouson, p. 32). Pecola's rejection by her mother, family, and community reveal the vulnerability of African American children to violence, to predators, and to damaging external and internal racism.

SULA *(1973)*

Morrison's follow-up work, *Sula,* appeared in 1973, three years after *The Bluest Eye,* and for many critics it signaled the arrival of a major new talent in American literature. The novel was nominated for a National Book Award in 1974. Developing many of the themes she introduced in *The Bluest Eye,* Morrison presents a work that Jan Furman describes as, "without a doubt, a manifesto of freedom" (*Toni Morrison's Fiction,* 2014, p. 26). The work follows three generations of women living in the "Bottom," an African American neighborhood in the small Ohio town of Medallion. Set in the years between the beginning of World War I and the civil rights era, the novel opens with a brief history of the Bottom and its legendary beginnings. It was a tight-knit and tenacious community. Its members helped one another survive the horrors of the past and move on. Unlike the characters of *The Bluest Eye,* this novel portrays strong family and communal ties; nurturing, yet complex, mother-daughter relationships; and confident and self-possessed women. Nevertheless, this portrait also reveals the lasting historical issues that black Americans must face and its negative impact on personal relations. In their yearly celebration of National Suicide Day, the inhabitants of the Bottom are able to exorcize their demons through ritual and through shared communal grief and support.

But as the story continues into the civil rights era, the reader begins to realize that life in the Bottom is changing. This change is reflected in the lives and personalities of the women in the Peace family. Eva is the matriarch, as her name suggests. Her freedom as an African American woman is one withheld from many others that came before—to love her children as powerfully as she wishes and to be bound to them throughout their entire lives. She is the first of her family to have such freedom as a mother.

Even though she has little to offer her children in terms of material possessions, other than the basic necessities, she loves her children, Hannah and Plum, fiercely. It is possible that she has purposely thrown herself under a train to collect insurance money so she can sustain the family. She recalls how she nearly lost Plum when he was born: "it was such a carrying on to get him born and to keep him alive. Just to keep his little heart beating" (*Sula,* p. 71). And later, when she sees Hannah on fire, she knows there was "time for nothing in this world other than the time it took to get there and cover her daughter's body with her own" (p. 75).

However, her protection of her children has complicated their lives. In contrast to Pauline's negligence in *The Bluest Eye,* Eva has been a committed mother, but her commitment has made her children overly dependent on her. Hannah lives a carefree, dreamy, childlike existence. When Plum suffers from heroin addiction, he is even more dependent on his mother's intervention. She slowly understands what her mothering has cost her children, and when Plum is beyond hope, she decides to set him on fire to end his suffering. She understands the limit of what she can do as a mother: "I had room enough in my heart, but not in my womb, not no more. I birthed him once" (p. 71).

Eva's granddaughter, Sula, has been raised by both Hannah and Eva. Sula's confidence, individuality, and willfulness set her apart from the community and her own family. Her best friend, Nel, has had a very different upbringing. Her family life has been more secure, which leads her to accept the white middle-class gender roles ascribed to women in this era. She sees herself as a wife and mother, and in assuming this self-image so completely, she loses her own identity. Her love for her children is even more controlling than Eva's; "it was a love that, like a pan of syrup kept too long on the stove, had cooked out, leaving only its odor and a hard, sweet sludge, impossible to scrape off" (p. 145). When she discovers her husband, Jude, in bed with Sula, Nel loses everything that she had embraced as her identity.

Sula, on the other hand, is bound to no one in the formation of her identity. This absolute freedom makes her a unique, attractive, and dangerous individual. She notes that "I got my mind. And what goes on in it. Which is to say, I got me" (p. 143). Because she feels little deference to the opinion of others (until she meets Ajax), she is unable to connect to her family and most of the community; some call her evil and others merely selfish. She seems to feel no remorse over Hannah's horrible death, and when Nel confronts her about Jude, Sula is angry that Nel's marriage takes precedence over their friendship. Sula's behavior is a reflection of a society that does not provide opportunities for strong women to flourish or to forge an identity separate from marriage and motherhood. "Had she paints, or clay, or knew the discipline of the dance, or strings; had she anything to engage her tremendous curiosity and her gift for metaphor, she might have exchanged the restlessness and preoccupation with whim for an activity that provided her with all she yearned for. And like any artist with no art form, she became dangerous" (p. 121). The community turns on Sula over the years because of her freedom and her strength. And though she becomes a scapegoat for the Bottom, as Pecola was for her community, Sula does not wither under their condemnation. Many years later, after Sula has died, Nel comes to visit the grave; it is here that Nel realizes that she has been the one who violated their unique bond: "'All that time, all that time, I thought I was missing Jude.' And the loss pressed down on her chest and came up into her throat. 'We was girls together,' she said, as though explaining something. 'O, Lord, Sula,' she cried, 'girl, girl, girlgirlgirl.'" (p. 174).

After Sula's death, the Bottom suffers because the inhabitants lose their sense of community and of connection. Families no longer stay together as they once had; generations move into the middle class or away from the Bottom. Writing in the post–civil rights era, Morrison signals a concern about what will happen to black community in the wake of recent political progress—will communities, families, and friends lose the ties that once sustained them through years of slavery and segregation? What will be the cost of freedom? For Sula it has meant independence, but it is has also meant isolation and a lack of empathy for anyone but herself.

SONG OF SOLOMON *(1977)*

Morrison's third novel, *Song of Solomon,* won the National Book Critics Circle Award in 1977, the year of its publication. Critics who had praised her portraits of black women as protagonists reacted against her focus on a male hero in this work, Milkman Dead. In numerous interviews, Morrison has been questioned about her reasons for her emphasis on a "typical" male-centered quest story and about Milkman's treatment of women—especially Hagar, who dies after he abandons her. Some readers, however, defend Morrison's focus on Milkman's initiation story as a critique of Western narratives and their embedded racist and sexist overtones. *Song of Solomon* as a "male epic does not represent a break with female-centered concerns of *The Bluest Eye* and *Sula,* but is a bold extension of these concerns in a confrontation with the tenets of Western literature and most 'sacred narrative' forms," one scholar has suggested (Awkward, p. 496). And as Morrison pointed out in a 1994 interview with Nellie McKay, Pilate, Milkman's aunt, represents the true moral force in the work. By learning to love her, "Milkman's hope, almost a conviction, has to be that he can be like her" (p. 146). It is through Milkman's interactions with women that he learns about the past and regains his humanity. Without black women, he would be trapped by the same desire as his father's—to live a white middle-class existence, to be "dead" to his roots and his African American heritage, as his chosen last name suggests.

The importance of naming figures prominently in the novel. Biblical and mythic allusions are found in almost every character's name, emphasizing many of Morrison's themes. But names also figure as points in the plot and are clues to the "treasure" that Milkman is seeking. Pilate's father chooses her name from the Bible even though he cannot read the text itself. She acknowledges that her name is a gift from her father, which is why she carries it in an earring fashioned from her mother's snuff box. Milkman understands this significance near the end of the novel, when he is learning about his family's past: "under the recorded names were other names ... names that had meaning. No wonder Pilate put hers in her ear. When you know your name, you should hang on to it, for unless it is noted down and remembered it will die when you do" (*Song of Solomon,* p. 329). Milkman's real last name is Solomon—the name of his great-grandfather who had escaped slavery. Solomon's name has become a myth—a legend, and a literal song. Naming one's children in the period after slavery ended was an act of freedom and agency. Names that come from outside of the family disrupt the connection to the past and reveal the disruptions caused by slavery.

Pilate's name, carried on "her ear," also illustrates the novel's celebration of African American orality and storytelling. As the quote from the Morrison interview supports, Pilate and her stories and songs educate Milkman about his past and his family—and his humanity is saved through his understanding of these connections. Pilate literally saves Milkman even before he is born, when she protects his mother from the anger of Pilate's brother, Macon. Her singing of the "Solomon song" at Milkman's birth connects him to the mythic tale of the "flying Africans." The story in its various iterations has been passed down from slavery, and in each version it includes an old man—who possesses special knowledge or "words"—who helps slaves fly back to Africa. The story calls upon African Americans to remember their past and their culture because those memories offer a way of escaping the painful legacy of slavery and racism. Because flight back to Africa is a metaphor throughout the book, and because the story is delivered initially to him by Pilate, the myth is "the key to Milkman's quest and illustrates the function of the African American woman in passing on stories to future generations," and it also demonstrates his readiness to embrace "African values and cultural heritage" (Wilentz, pp. 63, 65).

Throughout most of the novel, Milkman could care little about his past or his connection to the community. The only relationship he values is his friendship with Guitar. He misuses Hagar, his sisters, his mother, and even Pilate. When he hears the locals talking about a boy named Emmett Till being lynched, he becomes disinterested in the conversation because he doesn't see what it has to do with him. Despite the cultural and social changes happening around him, he does not get involved, and he teases Guitar about sounding like Malcolm X even though he has decided to hold onto his "slave name." Milkman, like his father, travels through life directed by self-interest. Even his trip to Shalimar, Virginia, to look for the family's buried treasure is motivated by selfish desire. Morrison makes clear, however, that this "quest" has more a profound meaning for Milkman. His travel south is an inversion of the flight of his family north during the Great Migration. He must travel south to the site of his family's suffering and slave history, but he must also discover his roots, his family stories, and his traditions, all of which are embodied in finding out his family's true name. Once he arrives in Shalimar he finds himself "walking the earth like he belonged on it" (p. 284). In searching for clues to find the place where the "gold" is buried, he begins to reassemble the pieces of his familial past. When he understands that the treasure is really his grandfather's bones, he realizes what the most valuable elements of his life are: his history and his family. It is at this moment he takes responsibility for Hagar's suffering, and he fathoms the depth of his appreciation for Pilate: "now he knew why he loved her so. Without ever leaving the ground, she could fly" (p. 336).

The final lines of the book are widely debated. Does Milkman fly? Does Guitar kill him? They both appear to leap toward one another off the cliff and into the air. Clearly the end represents Milkman's acceptance of the past and the conclusion of the quest for self-knowledge. But as the book ends, with Milkman suspended with Guitar, waiting to see if he can fly, the reader might also feel like Morrison: that "the promise of freedom for blacks has gone unfulfilled" (Dubek, p. 93).

TAR BABY *(1981)*

Like many of Morrison's other characters, the protagonist of her 1981 novel, *Tar Baby,* has suffered from a traumatic childhood. Orphaned at a young age, Jadine has been raised by her aunt and uncle who are employed by a wealthy businessman, Valerian Street. Although Jadine has benefited from Street's generosity in terms of opportunities, education, and lifestyle, she finds only material comfort in her life. Her world appears on the surface to be perfect—she is a high-fashion model and is completing her doctoral dissertation. She has choices ahead of her that her aunt and uncle could never have had. But Jadine is disconnected from her culture and from her blackness. While on a trip to Paris, she is unsettled by seeing a woman dressed in yellow, an African, who has "skin like tar" (*Tar Baby,* p. 45). Jadine is transfixed by the woman's beauty, but she is also taken by the woman's ease with her own identity and confidence. Despite all of her successes, Jadine does not inhabit her body or her consciousness in the same way the stranger does.

Jadine visits her aunt and uncle and the Street family during their stay at a Caribbean island. The fictional geography sets the stage for a narrative that "recasts the Genesis story" (Lepow, p. 167). The island is certainly Edenic, but it also is reminiscent of Prospero's island in William Shakespeare's *The Tempest.* Nature itself, as seen in the description of a river that has been rerouted for Street's factory, reflects the colonial transformation that has also affected cultures and people:

> Evicted from the place where it had lived and forced into unknown turf, it could not form its pools or waterfalls, and ran every which way. The clouds gathered together, stood still and watched the river scuttle around the forest floor, crash headlong into

> the haunches of hills with no notion of where it was going, until exhausted, ill and grieving, it slowed to a stop.
>
> (p. 9)

Further along the river is described as if it is heartbroken. The island's new contours and "emotions" resemble those Africans of the diaspora spread out across the new world.

Characters in the text also inhabit roles from *The Tempest.* Valerian is a Prospero figure, controlling the island, nature, his servants and workers, his wife, and child. He has also shaped Jadine's life, viewing himself as creator of the woman she has become—and he is threatened by the appearance of Son Green. Green is drawn in a manner that closely resembles Caliban. His hair is wild and untamed; and he is continually referred to in animalistic terms. He has come to the island to discover his heritage, reclaim his roots, and stage revolutions. Morrison revises the Caliban narrative, however, by empowering Son with his own poetic power. He causes upheaval in the Street home. And for a time, he convinces Jadine to leave behind Valerian and the island. Unlike his Shakespearean counterpart, he is able to steal Jadine (a Miranda and Ariel figure combined) away in order to disrupt the power structures on the island. For Jadine, Son "unorphaned her completely. Gave her a new childhood" (p. 197).

After a while, however, Jadine realizes that Son, like Valerian, wishes to create and shape Jadine's identity. She is a tool, an object, in the historical drama that Son and Valerian represent. It is a story that continues to be acted out over and over again. Until Jadine can uncover her own identity, she will continue to be "stuck" in others' presentations of her in their narratives.

BELOVED *(1987)*

Beloved is the most discussed and analyzed text in Morrison's canon. Its critical and popular success firmly established Morrison as one of America's most notable authors. Both its subject matter and style have shaped the conversations about African American literature in the decades since its publication in 1987, and it has inspired legions of readers, scholars, and teachers to learn more about African American history. Morrison experienced this desire herself while working on *The Black Book* in 1974 for Random House. *The Black Book* was a collection of artifacts and little-known stories from African American history. In the midst of the project, she discovered references to Margaret Garner, a slave who had escaped to Ohio with her children in 1850. During her recapture by federal authorities, she murdered one of her children. Even though the story did not appear in *The Black Book,* Morrison continued to be interested in the psychology of the slave mother and what would compel her to make this choice. Over the next few years, Morrison did more research and considered how little was known about the inner lives of slaves and how many personal stories of the estimated sixty million African slaves in the Americas were lost and unknown. No matter how much archaeology and historical research could be done, most of these slaves would never be known to future generations, and even less would be understood about their psyches. In her essay "The Site of Memory" (2008), Morrison explains that in writing *Beloved,* which is loosely based on the Garner story, she sought to "fill in the blanks that slave narratives" were forced to leave open (p. 72).

The novel's structure attempts to embrace the multiple narratives of the countless people who cannot tell their story; the resurrected Beloved is the gothic embodiment of all the dead who would like to speak. This "speakerly text" (Rushdy, 1999, p. 55) attempts to recover these voices from the past in a manner that resists and confronts the traditional historiography that has silenced African American lives at the same time that it celebrates the "resiliency of black people" (Bell, p. 14). Remembering the strength of African American ancestors and the painful past, no matter how "unspeakable" it might be (*Beloved* p. 58), was an urgent concern of Morrison's at the time she was writing the novel. Its publication followed renewed attacks on African American mothers and the welfare state. The policies of the Ronald Reagan administration and the media analysis of black families and crime all harkened back to the Moynihan Report (1965), which argued that the problems of the African American family were based on the inherent relationships between the husband and wife and the husband's inability to be a stable and powerful figure in the household because the woman, in her role as mother, was too much in command of the family. Morrison's novel sought to counter the continued mainstream belief that race was not a "continuing, traumatic, and structural problem in contemporary America" (Berger, p. 408). *Beloved* commanded readers to see that the psychological trauma suffered by African American families under the institution of slavery continued to haunt American society.

The work opens after the end of slavery, nearly two decades after the novel's protagonist Sethe escaped to the North and after she murdered her daughter, Beloved—whom she calls "her best thing" (p. 320). Sethe lives with her daughter, Denver (named for the woman who helped her during labor). Her two sons have left the house frightened of their mother's "monstrous" love and of the poltergeist that disrupts the home (Wester, p. 201). Paul D, a former slave on the same plantation as Sethe, arrives at the house in Ohio and soon realizes that it is haunted by a sad and envious spirit. Denver accepts the "child" poltergeist as her older sister, but she does not accept Paul D's intrusion into the family. Once Paul D wins over Denver and establishes himself as a member of the household, the poltergeist is exorcised—but soon returns in the rebirth scene at the river, where a flesh-and-blood twenty-year-old woman emerges as the grown Beloved. The scene suggests an "uncanny return of the dead to haunt the living, the return of the past to shadow the present" (Henderson, p. 91).

Initially, Paul D does not know the story of Beloved's death. He is wary of Sethe's mothering almost immediately, sensing that the trauma enveloping the house is connected: "for a used-to-be slave woman to love anything that much was dangerous, especially if it was her children she had settled on to love" (*Beloved,* p. 45). In revealing to Paul D how Beloved died, Sethe describes the murder and how it was spurred on by the appearance of the four men on horseback who had come to return her and her children to slavery. The allusion to the apocalypse suggests the catastrophic nature of Sethe's act and its eternal impact on this family—a sign that the institution of slavery and its traumatic aftereffects will also be a sin that will burden America forever (Berger, p. 410). This was the warning that Amy Denver, the runaway indentured servant who helped her give birth to her last child, imparted to Sethe—and by extension to us—"anything dead coming back to life hurts" (*Beloved,* p. 35). This pain will never go away as long as the dead haunt us.

It is not until Sethe's life is endangered by the spirit that the black community intervenes. The town has shunned Sethe since the murder, but once they know that Beloved has taken bodily form, they are concerned that the dead no longer understand the boundaries. Ella, one of the townspeople, notes that the past is "something to leave behind" (p. 256). Every survivor has to live with their painful choices—clearly Ella's history of loss is also traumatic—and in order to move forward the past must be appreciated, but it cannot be consistently present in your house. Beloved embodies both the necessity to remember and to the need to forget. She "acts as insurance against the death of Sethe's memories, as a repository for stories too difficult for Sethe to carry around by herself" (Yeates, p. 520). The novel acts in the same way for the reader. Morrison "makes the writing of history a resurrection of ancestral spirits, the spirit of the long buried past, so that Beloved—and the novel—will live to haunt us" (Krumholz, p. 41). Sethe's most salient description of "rememory" (a word that recurs throughout the book) could also be used to characterize the novel's lasting effect on readers and scholars: "even though it's all over—over and done with—it's always going to be there waiting for you" (*Beloved,* p. 36). The novel also asks us to consider that "this was not a story to pass on" (p. 322). The dual meaning of "pass on" is explicit to readers: we must not pass over this story nor should we continue being overwhelmed by the past—although it is unclear whether or not society is capable of the latter.

JAZZ *(1992)*

Morrison told the interviewer Ann Hostetler that her next novel, *Jazz* (1992), was an "attempt to reclaim the era from F. Scott Fitzgerald, but it also uses the techniques of jazz—improvisation, listening" (quoted in Denard, p. 204). The novel's style and structure also share much in common with *Beloved* as texts that attempt to hear all the voices and stories of a community. The novel presents multiple variations of a theme—in this case, the same event: the death of Dorcas. In layering these various narratives or modes, the novel, like jazz music, "resists the traditional" form (Jewett, p. 445). Music has a thematic significance here as well. It drives the movement of black Americans to the North, especially Harlem, during the Great Migration. And it connects the immigrants as they navigate the harsh realities of life in the North once they discover it's not the Promised Land they had believed it would be.

Morrison's desire to recover the Jazz Age from white modernists like Fitzgerald reminds readers that jazz—and even modernism itself—was a unique African American cultural product that captured the contradictions of the black experience in America in the North in the 1920s. The sound of jazz reverberates with dislocation, possibility, confusion, joy, sadness, optimism, and monotonous work—everything that defined that generation of African Americans who left home hoping for a paradise. The immigrants exclaim "history is over, you all, and everything is ahead at last" (*Jazz* p. 7). And New York City "danced with them, proving already how much it loved them. Like a million more they could hardly wait to get there and love it back" (p. 32). Despite believing that the world would soon be better because slavery was over and they had escaped from the South, most black Americans felt isolated and disconnected.

This is the case for Violet and Joe Trace, who have both experienced childhood traumas before they are wed. Each has had difficult relationships with their mothers. Violet's grandmother was forced to abandon her daughter, Rose Dear, who commits suicide when Violet is still a child. Because of this, Violet never wants to have children, for fear of being a bad mother or for fear of possibly losing something that she loves too much. Joe condemns his own mother for abandoning him and for her vulgarity; he says she couldn't even do "what the meanest sow managed; nurse what she birthed" (p. 179). When he kills his mistress, Dorcas, he claims it is because he "didn't know how to love anybody" (p. 213). Both Joe and Violet's past suffering has kept them from ever developing strong emotional bonds with one another. And because they did not have the language to share their suffering, their marriage was a distant and mundane relationship. Their attempts at being a family include having a home and a pet bird. The bird requires little care, but when Violet discovers Joe's betrayal after the death of Dorcas, she releases the parrot outside where it freezes to death.

Like Violet and Joe, Dorcas has also had a traumatic childhood. In a later chapter, after Dorcas is already dead, the reader sees the moment when her parents die during the riots in St. Louis in 1917. She is unable to ever share the tragedies of her past and is equally disconnected from others and unable to experience emotional love. Beautiful, mysterious, and chaotic, she embodies both Harlem and jazz. She inspires passion in both Joe and Violet (who attempts to slash her face at her funeral), because of her unconventional and risky lifestyle.

Joe and Violet attempt to rebuild their lives after Dorcas' death. They take in her friend, Felice, as a ward, and they buy a new bird. But until they are able to understand and express their suffering, they will remain isolated from one another. Their relationship signifies the hundreds of thousands of southern immigrants who never really acclimated to Harlem. Like others they "cannot solve this dilemma by abandoning their southern roots and traditions for northern ones" (Barnes, p. 286). By escaping north, they have attempted to flee from their traumatic pasts. It will only be through shared cultural practices such as storytelling and music that they will be able to heal. Jazz as trope in the work illustrates the necessity of understanding the painful, blues history of African Americans, which must be "excavated through acts of rememory" (Scheiber, p. 472).

PLAYING IN THE DARK: WHITENESS AND THE LITERARY IMAGINATION *(1992)*

Morrison's achievements as a novelist should not overshadow her fine work as a literary critic. Her master's thesis on the work of William Faulkner prepared her for later examinations of writers, criticism, and literary history. As a novelist and editor, she has analyzed the works of many of her peers and inspirations, including Gayl Jones, Toni Cade Bambara, Henry Dumas, and James Baldwin. She has also examined the relationship between the slave narrative and the development of the African American novel, in "The Site of Memory." Many of her own novels include critical forewords, and she has written forewords for other writers' works including August Wilson and Mark Twain.

One of her critical essays, "Unspeakable Things Unspoken: The Afro-American Presence in American Literature," suggests that the relationship between "blackness" and the American experience is a significant trope in American literature. Published in 1989, the essay lays the groundwork for the series of lectures that she gave at Harvard in 1990, published as *Playing in the Dark: Whiteness and the Literary Imagination* (1992). In this study. Morrison analyzes more deeply the idea that the African presence is a fundamental characteristic of American literary consciousness. She argues that this presence surrounds and penetrates the American literary canon, concluding that our most notable writers—almost exclusively white and primarily male—have responded to "blackness" either implicitly or explicitly in their work. While not an exhaustive study, *Playing in the Dark* is nevertheless a revolutionary reading of the literature that has been integral to American cultural identity.

Beginning with an exploration of canonical nineteenth-century American literature, Morrison discovers a deep fascination with darkness: a symbolic presentation of blackness or what she calls "American Africanism." This presence in nineteenth-century American literature allowed some of that literature's most iconic writers—Nathaniel Hawthorne, Herman Melville, and Edgar Allan Poe among them—to use blackness as a method of constructing American identity and engaging with their own cultural anxieties about slavery, nationhood, and civil strife. She is struck by how prevalent "darkness" is as an idea in this period: "For a people who made much of their 'newness'—their potential, freedom, and innocence—it is striking how dour, how troubled, how frightened and haunted our early and founding literature truly is" (*Playing,* p. 35). Morrison spends considerable time with the work of Poe, anointing him as the most important writer of American Africanism. Poe, like his contemporaries, was able to forge an American identity based on the juxtaposition of the American "free" man and the black "Other."

Morrison also analyzes the African presence in the work of writers such as Mark Twain, Willa Cather, Flannery O'Connor, Henry James, Ernest Hemingway, and, of course, the subject of her graduate thesis, William Faulkner. In the late-nineteenth- and early-twentieth-century American writers she considers, Morrison traces the ways that many of them continued to use the African presence to construct their own troubled American identity—even though slavery had ended. One of her most salient arguments in this section of the study is the way writers like Hemingway and Gertrude Stein project animalism, sexuality and sexual freedom, and savagery onto the African body in order to explore their own desires, fears, and isolation. Morrison's examination follows the work of many postcolonial critics, including Franz Fanon and Edward Said, but her emphasis on the African presence in American literature led the way in reconsidering the significance of invisible African Americans—except as metaphors—in American literary history.

PARADISE *(1998)*

With the publication of *Paradise* in 1998, Morrison completed her trilogy of novels dedicated to the history of African Americans following the end of slavery. *Beloved, Jazz,* and *Paradise* each consider how the traumatic past continues to be a burden on the lives of black Americans. *Beloved* opens with an epigraph alluding to the Middle Passage, and *Paradise* closes with an image of "another ship, perhaps, but different, heading to port, crew and passengers, lost and saved, atremble, for they have been disconsolate for some time. Now they will rest before shouldering the endless work they were created to do down here" (p. 318). This could be a reference to the pilgrims aboard the *Mayflower,* but within the context of this novel and within the trilogy, it is more likely a sign of African Americans adrift in the diaspora still waiting and looking for a safe harbor. After Reconstruction, after the Great Migration, and after the civil rights era, the promise of paradise is still unfulfilled.

Some former slaves believe they have found paradise when they head out west in the 1890s. Turned away from towns numerous times, they finally settle the community of Haven. The men of Haven refer to this history as the time of "the Disallowing." Based on several all-black communities in Oklahoma, Haven is formed to protect its inhabitants against "out there where your children were sport, your women quarry, and where your very person can be annulled" (p. 16). The town is also created to affirm racial solidarity. But when Haven begins to fail economically in 1950, the town elders migrate to a new area. Their hardships, including the death of Ruby Morgan, for whom they name their new town, engender a deeper mistrust of whites and strangers. In Ruby, the strongest families (and most racially pure) are led by the descendants of the eight founding fathers, who will try to ensure a renewed adherence to the color line. Because the original inhabitants of Haven were originally shut out of Fairly, Oklahoma (a town largely populated by fair-skinned former slaves) because of their "blackness," the bitterness about their past has evolved from a devotion to community spirit to pernicious and violent isolationism. As was clear in *Beloved* and in *Jazz,* when groups become too insular after attempting to create safe havens for African Americans, they can devolve into intolerant and nativistic communities and do damage to the individuals who feel disconnected and isolated. In each of the works, Morrison points out the hypocrisy of such social formations given the history of racial exclusion in America. But she also contends, especially in the case of *Paradise,* that this structure "emulates official United States culture" and its racism, patriarchal dominance, and misogyny (Osucha, p. 258).

The original "founding fathers" of Haven had strong family and communal ties, no matter how racially "black" the members were. They also had compassion for other outsiders. But the new evolution of fathers in Ruby controls the bloodlines and includes no "founding mothers." Women are defined by their husbands, and in an allusion to the caste system in slavery and the miscegenation of post-Reconstruction South, they are celebrated for their ability to present dark children. Men are not allowed to marry light-skinned women or outsiders, and fewer and fewer children exhibit any signs of white bloodlines. Delia Best dies in childbirth when she is refused medical treatment based on her lighter skin.

When hard times befall the town, the elders (especially the Morgan brothers) began to look for evidence outside of themselves for why paradise is failing; "the proof they had been collecting since the terrible discovery in the spring could not be denied: the one thing that connected all these catastrophes was in the Convent. And in the Convent were those women" (*Paradise,* p. 11). The "women" include survivors of abuse, the discarded, orphaned, and unloved in Ruby. The Convent is a safe space for battered and vilified women. The men of Ruby scapegoat the women in a manner similar to the seventeenth-century Salem witch trials. Because these women live outside the power of the men they are dangerous to the patriarchal order. The delight with which the men massacre the women in the Convent suggests that they enjoy their power over women's bodies and identities as much as Europeans did over African female slaves. Their idea of a protected "paradise" is doubly ironic because the "founding fathers" of Ruby have become like their white counterparts, withholding utopia from creatures they regard as less human than themselves. The fathers' "pride is arrogance, isolation is exclusivity, and those who had inscribed the narrative of disallowance are disallowers themselves" (Furman, p. 97).

The Convent has provided women with a nurturing environment based on healthy models of sisterhood and motherhood. The various women who seek shelter at the Convent heal their trauma by sharing their stories with one another and by working together for the good of the community. The leader, Consolata, was once known as Connie; she was abandoned by her lover, Deacon Morgan, one of the town elders. Consolata establishes the Convent because she believes that a matriarchal community will balance the society of men that control Ruby. She also has a religious conversion that helps her marry a "reverence for the way of the spirit with respect for the carnal life of the body" (Grewal, p. 48). Her vision for the Convent is to eradicate the segregation of women based on sexual and gender differences and to reconcile men and women, white and black. The women at the Convent find safety, but they also discover their own voice and their "authentic self" (*Paradise,* p. 177). After Consolata, Pallas, Seneca, Gigi, and women from the Convent are killed in the massacre, Deacon Morgan understands what the men of Ruby have become—a reflection of all they have hated in white men and in American society. The racism that their forefathers faced should have inspired them to be more moral and more ethical; instead they have let unlimited power and control over others debase them and disgrace their ancestors and their past.

LOVE *(2003)*

After the completion of her historical trilogy, Morrison returns to a contemporary setting in the 2003 novel *Love.* The story considers the lives of two elderly women, Christine and Heed, and their complicated relationship over the course of their lifetimes. The novel is narrated by a character, L. (which stands for Love), who died almost twenty years earlier. L. was a cook in the resort hotel on the "Up-Beach" section of a fictional coastal town called Silk. The resort was once owned by Bill Cosey, a powerful and controlling figure who was both the grandfather of Christine and the husband of Heed. His dominance in the lives of all of these women also controls the structure of the novel itself—all of the section headings are titles and roles occupied by Cosey in his relationships with the female characters and the town. As such, the male history and narrative eclipses the stories of the women in the novel. Cosey still overpowers them all.

Cosey's manipulation of the female characters in the story is quickly apparent. Christine and Heed are inseparable as children. They are happy and almost spiritually united in the way they share space, intimacy, and private language. Their "idagay" lets them communicate in a secure and secret world where their identities are developed in a supportive and loving atmosphere. But as they approach adolescence, their Eden becomes vulnerable. As is true in the relationship between Sula and Nel, Christine and Heed's "passionate female friendship presents a radical challenge to patriarchal norms" (Li, p. 33). This is a common problem in female friendships as a forced patriarchal ideal will inevitably separate them, but in the novel this is exacerbated by Cosey's sexualization of Heed and thus also of his own granddaughter. His objectification of the girls, and of other female characters in the novel, destroys the natural bonds of women.

During an afternoon of playing when they are eleven, Heed and Christine are separated for a few moments. In this interim, Cosey fondles Heed, and moments later Christine sees her grandfather masturbating. Both girls blame themselves for these events and develop unhealthy attitudes toward each other, toward their bodies, and toward sexuality. Cosey chooses Heed soon after this as his new bride (his second wife), and he takes on the role of father and then lover. At one point, upset with Heed's behavior, he gives her a public spanking. There is a little evidence that he loves Heed as much as he wants to control her; it appears that he has only married her so he "could educate [her] to his taste" (*Love,* p. 110). The damage to Christine and Heed's relationship is irrevocable. Christine vilifies Heed's "choice": "You a slave! He bought you with a year's rent and a candy bar" (p. 129). Cosey's daughter-in-law, May, manipulates the rift between the girls to drive them further apart. Afraid that Heed will now inherit the family fortune, she is happy that her daughter is no longer friends with the competition for Cosey's affections and finances.

Other women in the community are equally harsh in their judgment of Heed. Sandler Gibbons, a townsperson, points out to his wife, Vida, that she "acted as though Heed had chased and seduced a fifty-two-year-old man, older than her father. That she had chosen to marry him rather than being told to ... [Most people] forgave Cosey. Everything. Even to the point of blaming a child for a grown man's interest in her" (p. 147). Christine and others do not understand the financial hardship Heed and her family were suffering nor how Heed's own low self-opinion further created an environment where Heed had no choice but do as Cosey commanded. This is the case throughout their marriage.

But it is Love's voice that narrates the work. As a defining trope of the work, the voice represents love in all of its forms, joys, and complications. Love can create and it can destroy in the novel, and as a servant in the Cosey household, the character represents all of these aspects of how "love" operates in this family. The character is also the agent of transformation and reconciliation. She has tried to protect Christine and Heed, and eventually she poisons Cosey to rid the home of his influence; she also places a false will leaving everything to "the sweet Cosey child" (p. 79) in hopes that it will renew the women's friendship. Initially, this is not the case, as they fight over the interpretation of "legal" language instead of seeing how the words should connect them. At the end of their lives, they forgive themselves for believing the stories of others over their own shared language, as Christine laments to Heed: "we could have been living our lives hand in hand instead of looking for Big Daddy everywhere" (p. 189). It is Love's voice that closes the work, reminding the reader of the necessity of our own stories in defining our choices: "My menu worked just fine. Gave them a reason to stay connected and maybe figure out how precious the tongue is. If properly used it can save you" (p. 210).

A MERCY *(2008)*

Set in colonial America in the 1680s and 1690s, *A Mercy* (2008) reexamines some of the themes found in *Beloved,* Morrison's previous historical novel cast as a slave narrative. At the emotional center of the novel is another slave girl and her relationship to her mother. But Morrison intertwines this story with other marginalized actors in the American narrative. She includes indentured servants, free Africans, homosexual men, and Native Americans. Though slavery and its destructive influence on motherhood is still a significant thread of the narrative, Morrison equally wants readers to reconsider early, shared cultural relationships between disparate groups in America. Many of the characters who have different legal statuses in the colonial period are connected, nonetheless, by their shared outsider status and by their suffering. At one point, the Dutch colonist Jacob Vaark recalls a recent time in the region when "blacks, natives, whites, mulattoes—freedmen, slave and indentured—had waged war against the local gentry" (*A Mercy,* p. 11). One critic suggests that Morrison revisits her own definition of "rememory" from *Beloved* in *A Mercy* to illustrate a "re-thinking of the past as not the history of *either* the dominating *or* the dominated, but rather the shared history of both" (Tedder, p. 147).

Even the trader Vaark is outlier in this community at the beginning of the book. He sees his friend, an African blacksmith, as his equal in this new world. Despite wanting no part of slavery, he takes Florens, a slave girl, as repayment of a debt owed to him by a wealthy Spanish Catholic landowner. It is only after Vaark is exposed to the power and possessions of the slave owner that he sees what his privilege can offer him. His position in the text signifies the historical alignment of race with power and legal standing. At this time in America, the law did not recognize race as the sole characteristic in determining slave status. Servants, slaves, and indentured servants all shared the same legal status no matter what their race was. Morrison draws attention to the roots of the alteration that significantly disrupted the class connections between groups. Morrison's "imbrications of legal statutes and novelistic language inserts *A Mercy* into early American discourses that enforced the conception that the emerging United States was to be a free, white nation" (Babb, p. 152). These ensuing legal distinctions alter the landscape of the community at Vaark's farm. What once had been a peaceful, shared space with different people who viewed each other as a family changes when Vaark enacts his power as a white man. Vaark's wife, Rebekka, and Lina, his Native American servant, had worked together on the farm making it a home and being surrogate mothers to Florens, but after Vaark becomes obsessed with turning the farm into an extravagant house the women are in violent opposition to each other. By the novel's conclusion, Rebekka, who has barely escaped the smallpox that kills Vaark, is contemplating the sale of Florens, and the community that once thrived on the farm has become a microcosm of the new hierarchy in America.

The novel ends with Florens' mother describing the moment she observes Vaark on the D'Ortega plantation and the painful yet necessary decision she makes when she offers Florens to him when her master needs to repay Vaark. She perceives that Florens will be safe with a man like Vaark, who has "no animal in his heart" (p. 191); he will never rape Florens or use her as a breeder. She will escape the fate her mother has suffered. Florens has never understood the reason behind her mother's choice—and she has felt unloved and abandoned her entire life. But her mother's decision, "a mercy," is made to save her daughter from a place where to be a woman is an "open wound that cannot heal" (p. 191). The act is an echo of Sethe's murder of Beloved, and a "replayed traumatic separation ... the primal scene of slavery; the separation of mother and child" (Morgenstern, p. 15). The interruption of mother love ultimately damages the lives of everyone on Vaark's farm, and it signals the roots of the disease that would continue to plague American society centuries later.

HOME *(2012)*

The 2012 novel *Home* reflects many of Morrison's assertions for the necessity of healthy African American intrarelationships in order to combat racism. Set in the 1940s and 1950s, the work follows a brother and sister, Frank and Cee Money, as they try to navigate the violent American racial attitudes pervading the landscape before the civil rights era. Morrison places that violence front and center through the characters' last name, which may be an allusion to Money, Mississippi, where Emmett Till was murdered (discussed in Wagner-Martin, p. 165). Frank is a veteran of the Korean War and Cee is the victim of a doctor's eugenics experiments. Each is physically and emotionally wounded by these experiences; and even though Frank was in Korea and Cee was at home in the United States, their trauma is the result of society's racist practices and attitudes toward the value of black American lives. Morrison illuminates the way external racism has affected Frank and Cee's view of themselves when the women of the community ask Cee during her convalescence, "who told you you was trash?" (*Home,* p. 122). The answer is both implicitly and explicitly American society.

Frank understands this as well, when he returns to America after the war. Despite his service, he does not feel welcomed and "everything reminded him of something loaded with pain" (p. 8). When he sees a couple on the street fending off a racially motivated attack, he knows that the couple will internalize this moment:

> He will beat her when they get home, thought Frank. And who wouldn't? It's one thing to be publicly humiliated. A man could move on from that. What was intolerable was the witness of a woman, a wife, who not only saw it, but had dared to try to rescue—rescue!—him. He couldn't protect himself and he couldn't protect her either, as the rock in her face proved. She would have to pay for that broken nose. Over and over again.
>
> (p. 26)

Frank's killing of a Korean child during the war deeply troubles him, and, as he comes to realize in the course of the novel, the death and his guilt stem from his own inability to uphold the heroic masculine ideal denied to him by American society. Even though he served in an integrated military, society still does not grant him his full citizenship or manhood. The Korean War and his experience there is echoed in the scenes of racism and violence that he finds when he returns home, suggesting that what the war symbolizes in the novel is "neither over nor remote" (Darda, p. 98).

Cee has always been protected by her brother, but when Frank leaves for Korea she is vulnerable to people who would prey on her innocence and low self-esteem. When the doctor she works for, who is clearly interested in eugenics, begins to violate her body through his experiments, Cee cannot seem to summon the strength to leave his house or ask for help. Her passivity is not only the result of Frank's overprotectiveness but also of her troubled childhood, which left her emotionally scarred in ways similar to Pecola Breedlove. Her mother, Ida, never truly loved her. Like Pauline Breedlove, Ida seemed more concerned with white definitions of beauty and love. Ida never tells Cee that she is beautiful and loved, and this has a lasting and devastating impact on her; she realizes after her ordeal: "if not her mother, somebody somewhere should have said those words and meant them" (*Home,* p. 129). Only Frank loved her, but as a child himself, he could not really give her the support she needed to find her voice. Without self-love, she believes that she deserves the pain and torture she is experiencing. It is only through the intervention of others that she is rescued and physically healed. Ethel, one of the leaders of the women in the community, tells her to never let someone else, including the "devil doctor decide who you are. That's slavery" (p. 126).

Frank and Cee's traumatic experiences originate in their childhood and each share a history of abandonment, isolation, and loneliness. Much of what has happened to them as adults has roots in a moment from their past where they saw a black body being buried by white men in a field. That evening, they learn that the man who owned some horses they had been watching in the field has been murdered, and much later, Frank discovers that those strong and beautiful horses, which "stood like men" (p. 7), were sent to the slaughterhouse. This incident and Cee's relationship to her mother orphan them from their home. It is only after they have experienced more trauma that Frank brings Cee home to heal and that they understand "the pleasure of being among those who do not want to degrade or destroy you" (p. 118). The women of the community bring Cee back to life and remind Frank that "home," despite its challenges, can be a place to resist pain and confront trauma. This is illustrated by Ethel's garden that was "not Eden; it was so much more than that. For her the whole predatory world threatened her garden, competing with its nourishment, its beauty, its benefits, and its demands. And she loved it" (p. 130). Cee and Frank revisit the field where their first realization about the ugly brutality of society took place to find the fences broken and the space overgrown. In remembering their past, they are able to survive with grace and dignity like the bay tree: "so strong / So beautiful. / Hurt right down the middle / But alive and well" (p. 147).

GOD HELP THE CHILD *(2015)*

Morrison's 2015 novel explores many of the same issues and themes that are found in her earliest work and includes some recognizable tones, characters, and voices—in particular, the novel has echoes of Pecola and Pauline Breedlove from Morrison's first work, *The Bluest Eye. God Help the Child* again forefronts an unloved child, a neglectful and distant mother, and a pain so immense it stretches across all relationships, a lifetime, and the future.

Unlike her double, Pecola, the little girl in *God Help the Child,* Lula Ann, reclaims her life: she becomes known as a great beauty and a successful businesswoman; she renames herself Bride; and she experiences moments of triumph and perhaps even deep transformation. Nevertheless, Bride has made poor choices because she desired her mother's love. As she confronts those choices, Bride is "erased" and "the scared little black girl" Lula Ann returns (*God Help the Child,* p. 143). Like every other character in the work, her childhood innocence has been betrayed.

What has brought Morrison back to this familiar environment? Morrison has situated a vast amount of her writing examining the past, trying to comprehend the ways history has left lasting scars on individual black American lives. If *The Bluest Eye* illustrates Morrison's post–civil rights era concerns that black American families and children will still be internally traumatized by racism despite the political and cultural changes of her time, then *God Help the Child* is the reflection of those same concerns more than forty years later despite living in the ostensibly "postracial" world of the Barack Obama presidency. The novel also displays the current cultural anxiety about child safety at the same time it notes that the lives of African American and poor children, invisible to the media and to law enforcement, are even more at risk.

The challenges facing the African American parent within this racist society have also clearly not been resolved. Morrison's canon is filled with equally damaged parents: the Breedloves, Florens' mother, Eva Peace, Margaret Street, Sethe, and finally, in *God Help the Child,* Sweetness. Sweetness, certainly a double for Pauline, considers for a moment whether it wouldn't be better to suffocate her daughter with a blanket. She sees the child's blackness as ugly, as a curse. In her sections, Sweetness attempts to explain how her mothering was meant to prepare Lula Ann for the world: she says the child "needed to learn how to behave, how to keep her head down and not to make trouble, I don't care how many times she changes her name. Her color is a cross she will always carry" (p. 7). Sweetness also suggests that Bride does not understand "how her black skin would scare" white people (p. 41). But she also understands that "what you do to children matters. And they never forget" (p. 43). This sentiment is an assertion that Morrison clearly wants to emphasize to her readers in this work and in others.

Morrison's novels are full of abandoned, abused, and murdered children, and *God Help the Child* is no exception. Every character, minor and incidental characters included, has suffered some abuse or torture as a child, or has abandoned or killed a child, or has raped or been accused of molestation of a child. And African American children are especially vulnerable, even within their own family and community. When Booker's brother Anthony is reported missing, the police ask a few questions, and "then they dropped it. Another little black boy gone. So?" (p. 114). When he is finally found in culvert, raped and murdered, its several years before the killer is apprehended. Booker's anger spurs him to vigilantism and violence, but it is clear that Booker's wounds are compounded by his awareness that the men responsible for protecting society fail to see his brother's innocence and humanity. In a work completed and published after the highly publicized death of Trayvon Martin in Florida, the novel resonates with concerns that young lives, but especially young black lives, are more endangered than ever before. It is noteworthy that this is one of the very few of Morrison's novels set primarily in the present day.

The hope promised by Booker and Bride's unborn child, a possible salve to heal their traumatic childhoods, is negated in three final words in the conclusion of their sections: "a child. New life. Immune to evil or illness, protected from kidnap, beatings, rape, racism, insult, hurt, self-loathing, abandonment. Error-free. All goodness. Minus wrath.—So they believe" (p. 175). The chilling warning here illustrates that not much has changed for black American lives—children or parents—and if anything, things may be worse. But these are the words of the grandmother-to-be, Sweetness, who has made mistakes but who also knows the past and has seen the present. Her lines are plea, prayer, and commandment: "Listen to me. You are about to find out what it takes, how the world is, how it works and how it changes when you are a parent. Good luck and God help the child" (p. 178). These lines stretch across Morrison's literary canon to all of her readers committed to confronting racism and promoting social justice. Her legacy as an intellectual and artist will be marked by its commitment to protecting and loving all children as an antidote to the continuing disease of racial and ethnic prejudice.

Selected Bibliography

WORKS OF TONI MORRISON

NOVELS

The Bluest Eye. New York: Holt, Rinehart & Winston, 1970. Oprah's Book Club edition, New York: Knopf, 1993, with an afterword by Morrison (all quotations in the essay are taken from this edition).

Sula. New York: Knopf, 1973.

Song of Solomon. New York: Knopf, 1977.

Tar Baby. New York: Knopf, 1981.

Beloved. New York: Knopf, 1987.

Jazz. New York: Knopf, 1992.

Paradise. New York: Knopf, 1998.

Love. New York: Knopf, 2003.

A Mercy. New York: Knopf, 2008.

Home. New York: Knopf, 2012.

God Help the Child. Knopf, 2015.

Selected Essays, Criticism, and Other Nonfiction

"Afterword." In *The Bluest Eye.* New York: Knopf, 1993. Pp. 209–216.

"Unspeakable Things Unspoken: The Afro-American Presence in American Literature." *Michigan Quarterly Review* 28 (winter 1989): 1–34.

Playing in the Dark: Whiteness and the Literary Imagination. Cambridge, Mass.: Harvard University Press, 1992.

"Introduction." In *Adventures of Huckleberry Finn,* by Mark Twain. Edited by Shelley Fisher Fishkin. New York: Oxford University Press, 1996.

The Dancing Mind. New York: Knopf, 1997.

"Home." In *The House That Race Built: Black Americans, U.S. Terrain.* Edited by Waneema Lubiano. New York: Pantheon Books, 1997. Pp. 3–12.

"Foreword." In *Love.* New York: Vintage, 2005. Pp. ix–xii.

"The Nobel Lecture." In *Toni Morrison: What Moves at the Margin: Selected Nonfiction.* Edited by Carolyn Denard. Jackson: University Press of Mississippi, 2008. Pp. 198–208.

"Rootedness: The Ancestor as Foundation." In *Toni Morrison: What Moves at the Margin: Selected Nonfiction.* Edited by Carolyn Denard. Jackson: University Press of Mississippi, 2008. Pp. 56–64.

"The Site of Memory." In *Toni Morrison: What Moves at the Margin: Selected Nonfiction.* Edited by Carolyn Denard. Jackson: University Press of Mississippi, 2008. Pp. 65–80.

Toni Morrison: What Moves at the Margin: Selected Nonfiction. Edited by Carolyn Denard. Jackson: University Press of Mississippi, 2008.

Children's Books

The Big Box. With Slade Morrison. New York: Jump at the Sun, 1999.

The Book of Mean People. With Slade Morrison. New York: Hyperion, 2002.

Who's Got Game? The Ant or the Grasshopper? With Slade Morrison. New York: Scribner, 2003.

Who's Got Game? The Lion or the Mouse? With Slade Morrison. New York: Scribner, 2003.

Remember: The Journey to School Integration. New York: Houghton Mifflin, 2004.

Who's Got Game? The Mirror or the Glass? With Slade Morrison. New York: Scribner, 2004.

Who's Got Game? Poppy or the Snake? With Slade Morrison. New York: Scribner, 2004.

Who's Got Game? Three Fables. With Slade Morrison. New York: Scribner, 2007.

Peeny Butter Fudge. With Slade Morrison. New York: Simon & Schuster, 2009.

Little Cloud and Lady Wind. With Slade Morrison. New York: Simon & Schuster, 2010.

Please, Louise. With Slade Morrison. New York: Simon & Schuster, 2014.

Other Work

"Recitatif." In *Conformation: An Anthology of African American Women.* Edited by Amiri Baraka. New York: William Morrow, 1983. Pp. 243–262. (Short story.)

Dreaming Emmett. Directed by Gilbert Moses. Performed on January, 5, 1986, at the Market Theater in Albany, N.Y. (Drama; never published.)

Five Poems. Illustrated by Kara Walker. Las Vegas: Rainmaker Editions, 2002.

Margaret Garner: An Opera in Two Acts. Rev. ed. New York: Associated Music, 2004. (Libretto.)

Desdemona. London: Oberon, 2012. (Play; directed by Peter Sellars; premiered in May 2011 at the Theater Akzent in Vienna, Austria.)

Collections as Editor

The Black Book. With Middleton Harris, et al. New York: Random House, 1974. (With a preface by Morrison.) Repring, 2009. (With a foreword by Morrison.)

Burn This Book: PEN Writers Speak Out on the Power of the Word. New York: Harper, 2009. (With an introduction by Morrison at pp. 1–4).

Race-ing Justice, En-gendering Power: Essays on Anita Hill, Clarence Thomas, and the Construction of Social Reality. New York: Pantheon, 1992. (With an introduction by Morrison, "Friday on the Potomac," at pp. vii–xxx.)

Birth of a Nation'hood: Gaze, Script, and Spectacle in the O. J. Simpson Case. With Claudia Brodsky Lacour. New York: Pantheon, 1997. (With an introduction by Morrison, "The Official Story: Dead Man Golfing," pp. vii–xxviii.)

Interviews

Denard, Carolyn. ed. *Toni Morrison: Conversations.* Jackson: University Press of Mississippi, 2008.

Ghansah, Rachel Kaadzi. "The Radical Vision of Toni Morrison." *New York Times Magazine* April 8, 2015. http://www.nytimes.com/2015/04/12/magazine/the-radical-vision-of-toni-morrison

Gross, Rebecca. "Toni Morrison: Write, Erase, Do It Over." *NEA Arts Magazine,* no. 4 (2014). https://www.arts.gov/NEARTS/2014v4-art-failure-importance-risk-and-experimentation/toni-morrison

Hostetler, Ann. "The Art of Teaching: An Interview with Toni Morrison." In *Toni Morrison: Conversations.* Edited by Carolyn Denard. Jackson: University Press of Mississippi, 2008. Pp. 196–205.

LeClair, Thomas. "The Language Must Not Sweat: An Interview with Toni Morrison." In *Conversations with Toni Morrison.* Edited by Danielle Taylor-Guthrie. Jackson: University Press of Mississippi, 1994. Pp. 119–128.

McKay, Nellie. "An Interview with Toni Morrison." In *Conversations with Toni Morrison.* Edited by Danielle Taylor-Guthrie. Jackson: University Press of Mississippi, 1994. Pp. 138–155.

Schappell, Elissa, and Claudia Brodsky Lacour. "Interviews: Toni Morrison: The Art of Fiction No. 134." *Paris Review,* no. 128:83–125 (fall 1993).

Taylor-Guthrie, Danielle. *Conversations with Toni Morrison.* Jackson: University Press of Mississippi, 1994.

ARCHIVE

Toni Morrison's manuscripts, drafts, proofs, and other working materials, along with correspondence, diaries and appointment books, photographs, audiobooks, videotapes, juvenilia, memorabilia, and other files are held in collection as the Papers of Toni Morrison in the Manuscripts Division, Department of Rare Books and Special Collections, at the Firestone Library of Princeton University, Princeton, N.J.

CRITICAL AND BIOGRAPHICAL STUDIES

Aguir, Sarah Appleton. "'Passing on' Death: Stealing Life in Toni Morrison's *Paradise.*" *African American Review* 38, no. 3:513–519 (2004).

Akhtar, Jaleel. *Dismemberment in the Fiction of Toni Morrison.* Cambridge, U.K.: Cambridge Scholars, 2014.

Anderson, Melanie. *Spectrality in the Novels of Toni Morrison.* Knoxville: University of Tennessee Press, 2013.

Andrews, William L. and Nellie McKay, eds. *Toni Morrison's "Beloved": A Casebook.* New York: Oxford University Press, 1999.

Awkward, Michael. "'Unruly and Let Loose:' Myth, Ideology, and Gender in *Song of Solomon.*" *Callaloo* 13, no. 3:482–498 (1990).

Babb, Valerie. "*E Pluribus Unum?* The American Origins Narrative in Toni Morrison's *A Mercy.*" *MELUS* 36, no. 2:147–164 (2011).

Baillie, Justine Jenny. *Toni Morrison and the Literary Tradition: The Invention of an Aesthetic.* London: Bloomsbury, 2013.

Barnes, Deborah. "'Movin' on Up': The Madness of Migration in Toni Morrison's *Jazz.*" In *Toni Morrison's Fiction: Contemporary Criticism.* Edited by David Middleton. New York: Routledge, 1999. Pp. 283–296.

Beaulieu, Elizabeth Ann, ed. *Toni Morrison Encyclopedia.* Westport, Conn.: Greenwood, 2003.

Bell, Bernard W. "*Beloved:* A Womanist Neo-Slave Narrative; or Multivocal Rememberances of Things Past." *African American Review* 26, no. 1:7–15 (1992).

Bennett, Juda. *Toni Morrison and the Queer Pleasure of Ghosts.* Albany: State University of New York Press, 2014.

Berger, James. "Ghosts of Liberalism: Morrison's *Beloved* and the Moynihan Report." *PMLA* 111:408–420 (1996).

Bloom, Harold, ed. *Toni Morrison: Bloom's Critical Views.* Rev. ed. New York: Infobase Publishing, 2014.

———. *Toni Morrison's "The Bluest Eye": Bloom's Modern Critical Interpretations.* Rev. ed. New York: Infobase Publishing, 2007.

Bouson, J. Brooks. *Quiet as It's Kept: Shame, Trauma, and Race in the Novels of Toni Morrison.* Albany: State University of New York Press, 2000.

Branch, Eleanor. "Through the Maze of the Oedipal: Milkman's Search for Self in the *Song of Solomon.*" *Literature and Psychology* 41, nos. 1–2:52–84 (1995).

Bump, Gerome. "Racism and Appearance in *The Bluest Eye:* A Template for an Ethical Emotive Criticism." *College Literature* 37, no. 2:147–170 (2010).

Caesar, Terry Paul. "Slavery and Motherhood in Toni Morrison's *Beloved.*" *Revista de Letras* 34:111–120 (1994).

Cantiello, Jessica Wells. "From Pre-Racial to Post-Racial? Reading and Reviewing *A Mercy* in the Age of Obama." *MELUS* 36, no. 2:165–183 (2011).

Childs, Dennis. "'You Ain't Seen Nothin' Yet': *Beloved,* the American Chain Gang, and the Middle Passage Redux." *American Quarterly* 61:271–297 (2009).

Christian, Barbara. "Beloved, She's Ours." *Narrative* 5:36–49 (1997).

Christianse, Yvette. *Toni Morrison: An Ethical Poetics.* New York: Fordham University Press, 2013.

Coonradt, Nicole M. "To Be Loved: Amy Denver and Human Need—Bridges to Understanding in Toni Morrison's *Beloved.*" *College English* 32, no. 4:168–187 (2005).

Cutter, Martha J. "The Story Must Go On and On: The Fantastic, Narration, and Intertextuality in Toni Morrison's *Beloved* and *Jazz.*" *African American Review* 34:61–75 (2000).

Dalsgard, Katrine. "The One All-Black Town Worth the Pain: (African) American Exceptionalism, Historical Narration, and the Critique of Nationhood in Toni Morrison's *Paradise.*" *African American Review* 35, no. 2:233–248 (2001).

Darda, Joseph. "The Literary Afterlife of the Korean War." *American Literature* 87, no. 1:79–105 (2015).

David, Ron. *Toni Morrison Explained: A Reader's Road Map to the Novels.* New York: Random House, 2000.

Davis, Kimberly Chabot. "'Postmodern Blackness': Toni Morrison's *Beloved* and the End of History." *Twentieth-Century Literature* 44:242–260 (1998).

Dubek, Laura. "'Pass It On!' Legacy and the Freedom Struggle in Toni Morrison's *Song of Solomon.*" *Southern Quarterly* 52, no. 2:90–109 (2015).

Dubey, Madhu. "The Politics of Genre in *Beloved.*" *Novel: A Forum on Fiction* 32, no. 2:187–206 (1999).

Duvall, John. *The Identifying Fictions of Toni Morrison: Modernist Authenticity and Postmodern Blackness.* New York: Palgrave, 2010.

Fallon, Robert. "Music and the Allegory of Memory in *Margaret Garner.*" *Modern Fiction Studies* 52, no. 2:524–541 (summer 2006).

Flint, Holly. "Toni Morrison's *Paradise:* Black Cultural Citizenship in the American Empire." *American Literature* 78, no. 3:585–612 (2008).

Fultz, Lucille P. *Toni Morrison: Playing with Difference.* Urbana: University of Illinois Press, 2003.

———, ed. *Toni Morrison: "Paradise," "Love," "A Mercy."* New York: Continuum, 2013.

———. "*Love*: An Elegy for the African American Community, or the Unintended Consequences of Desegregation/Integration." In *Toni Morrison: Memory and Meaning.* Edited by Adrienne Lanier Seward and Justine Tally. Jackson: University Press of Mississippi, 2014. Pp. 93–104.

Furman, Jan. "Telling Stories: Evolving Narrative Identity in Toni Morrison's *Home.*" In *Toni Morrison: Memory and Meaning.* Edited by Adrienne Lanier Seward and Justine Tally. Jackson: University Press of Mississippi, 2014. Pp. 231–242.

———. *Toni Morrison's Fiction.* 1996. Rev. ed. Columbia: University of South Carolina Press, 2014.

Gates, Henry Louis, Jr., and Kwame Anthony Appiah, eds. *Toni Morrison: Critical Perspectives Past and Present.* New York: Amistad, 1993.

Gillespie, Carmen. *Critical Companion to Toni Morrison: A Literary Reference to Her Life and Work.* New York: Facts on File, 2008.

Gillespie, Carmen, ed. *Toni Morrison: Forty Years in the Clearing.* Lewisburg, Pa.: Bucknell University Press, 2012.

Goulimari, Pelagia. *Toni Morrison.* New York: Routledge, 2011.

Grewal, Gurleen. *Circles of Sorrow: The Novels of Toni Morrison.* Baton Rouge: Louisiana University Press, 1998.

———. "The Working Through the Disconsolate: Transformative Spirituality in *Paradise.*" In *Toni Morrison: "Paradise," "Love," "A Mercy."* Edited by Lucille Fultz. New York: Continuum, 2013. Pp. 40–54.

Guarracino, Serena. "Africa as Voices and Vibes: Musical Routes in Toni Morrison's *Margaret Garner* and *Desdemona.*" *Research in African Literatures* 46, no. 4:56–71 (2015).

Harris, Trudier. *Fiction and Folklore: The Novels of Toni Morrison.* Knoxville: University of Tennessee Press, 1991.

Heinert, Jennifer Lee Jordan. *Narrative Conventions and Race in the Novels of Toni Morrison.* New York: Routledge, 2009.

Heinze, Denise. *The Dilemma of "Double Consciousness": Toni Morrison's Novels.* Athens: University of Georgia Press, 1993.

Henderson, Mae G. "Toni Morrison's *Beloved:* Remembering the Body as Historical Text." In *Toni Morrison's "Beloved": A Casebook.* Edited by William L. Andrews and Nellie McKay. New York: Oxford University Press, 1999. Pp. 79–106.

Higgins, Therese E. *Religiosity, Cosmology, and Folklore: The African Influences in the Novels of Toni Morrison.* New York: Routledge, 2001.

Holloway, Karla F. C., and Stephanie Demetrakapoulos. *New Dimensions of Spirituality: A Biracial and Bicultural Reading of the Novels of Toni Morrison.* Westport, Conn.: Greenwood, 1987.

Hostetler, Ann. "Resurrecting the Dead Girl: Modernism and the Problem of the History in *Beloved, Jazz,* and *Paradise.*" In *Toni Morrison: Memory and Meaning.* Edited by Adrienne Lanier Seward and Justine Tally. Jackson: University Press of Mississippi, 2014. Pp. 33–41.

Jennings, LaVinia Delois. *Toni Morrison and the Idea of Africa.* Cambridge, U.K.: Cambridge University Press, 2008.

Jewett, Chad. "The Modality of Toni Morrison's *Jazz.*" *African American Review* 48, no. 4:445–456 (2015).

Joyner, Louise, Margaret Reynold, and Jonathan Noakes. *Toni Morrison: "Beloved," "Jazz," "Paradise."* Essential Guides to Contemporary Literature. London: Vintage, 2003.

King, Lovalerie, and Lynn Orilla Scott, eds. *James Baldwin and Toni Morrison: Comparative and Theoretical Essays.* New York: Palgrave Macmillan, 2006.

Kitts, Lenore. "The Sound of Change: A Musical Transit Through the Wounded Modernity of *Desdemona.*" In *Toni Morrison: Memory and Meaning.* Edited by Adrienne Lanier Seward and Justine Tally. Jackson: University Press of Mississippi, 2014. Pp. 255–268.

Kolmerten, Carol A., Stephen M. Ross, and Judith Bryant Wittenberg. *Unflinching Gaze: Morrison and Faulkner Re-Envisioned.* Jackson: University Press of Mississippi, 1997.

Krumholz, Linda. "Ghosts of Slavery: Historical Recovery in Toni Morrison's *Beloved.*" *African American Review* 26, no. 3: 395–408 (1992).

———. "Dead Teachers: Rituals of Manhood and Rituals of Reading in *Song of Solomon.*" *Modern Fiction Studies* 39, no. 3: 551–574 (1993).

———. "Reading and Insight in Toni Morrison's *Paradise.*" *African American Review* 36, no. 1: 21–34 (2002).

———. "Blackness and Art in Toni Morrison's *Tar Baby.*" *Contemporary Literature* 49, no. 2: 263–292 (2008).

Lepow, Lauren. "Paradise Lost and Found: Dualism and Edenic Myth in Toni Morrison's *Tar Baby.*" In *Toni Morrison's Fiction: Contemporary Criticism.* Edited by David Middleton. Garland: New York, 1997. Pp. 165–181.

Li, Stephanie. "Paradise Lost: Reconciling the Semiotic and Symbolic in Toni Morrison's *Love.*" *Studies in the Literary Imagination* 47, no. 1: 27–47 (2014).

Lubiano, Wahneema. "The Postmodern Rag: Political Identity and the Vernacular in *Song of Solomon.*" In *New Essays on "Song of Solomon."* Edited by Valerie Smith. Cambridge, U.K.: Cambridge University Press, 1995. Pp. 93–116.

McDowell, Deborah. E. "'The Self and the Other': Reading Toni Morrison's *Sula* and the Black Female Text." In *Critical Essays on Toni Morrison.* Edited by Nellie McKay. Boston: G. K. Hall, 1988. Pp. 77–90.

McKay, Nellie Y., and Kathryn Earle. *Approaches to Teaching the Novels of Toni Morrison.* New York: Modern Language Association, 1997.

Middleton, David. *Toni Morrison's Fiction: Contemporary Criticism.* New York: Routledge, 1999.

Montgomery, Maxine L., ed. *Contested Boundaries: New Critical Essays on the Fiction of Toni Morrison.* Newcastle upon Tyne, U.K.: Cambridge Scholars, 2013.

Morgenstern, Naomi. "Maternal Love/Maternal Violence: Inventing Ethics in Toni Morrison's *A Mercy.*" *MELUS* 29, no. 1: 7–29 (2014).

O'Reilly, Andrea. *Toni Morrison and Motherhood: Politics of the Heart.* Albany: State University of New York Press, 2004.

Osucha, Eden. "Race and the Regulation of Intimacy in the Moynihan Report, the Griswold Decision, and Morrison's *Paradise.*" *American Literary History* 27, no. 2: 256–284 (2015).

Otten, Terry. *The Crime of Innocence in the Fiction of Toni Morrison.* Columbia: University of Missouri Press, 1989.

Page, Philip. *Dangerous Freedom: Fusion and Fragmentation in Toni Morrison's Novels.* Jackson: University Press of Mississippi, 1995.

Parker, Emma. "A New Hystery: History and Hysteria in Toni Morrison's *Beloved.*" *Twentieth-Century Literature* 47: 1–19 (2001).

Peach, Linden. *Toni Morrison.* New York: St. Martin's Press, 2000.

Peterson, Christopher. "Beloved's Claim." *Modern Fiction Studies* 52, no. 3: 548–567 (2006).

Peterson, Nancy J. *Toni Morrison: Critical and Theoretical Approaches.* Baltimore: Johns Hopkins University Press, 1997.

Roynon, Tessa. *The Cambridge Introduction to Toni Morrison.* New York: Cambridge University Press, 2013.

Rushdy, Ashraf. "'Rememory': Primal Scenes and Constructions in Toni Morrison's Novels." *Contemporary Literature* 31, no. 3:300–323 (1990).

———. "Daughters Signifyin(g) History: The Example of Toni Morrison's *Beloved.*" In *Toni Morrison's "Beloved": A Casebook.* Edited by William L. Andrews and Nellie McKay. New York: Oxford University Press, 1999. Pp. 37–66.

Samuels, Wilfred, and Clenora Hudson Weems. *Toni Morrison.* Boston: Twayne, 1990.

Scheiber, Andrew. "Jazz and the Future Blues: Toni Morrison's Urban Folk Zone." *Modern Fiction Studies* 52, no. 2: 470–494 (2006).

Schreiber, Evelyn Jaffe. *Race, Trauma, and Home in the Novels of Toni Morrison.* Baton Rouge: Louisiana University State Press, 2010.

Scott, Joyce Hope. "*Song of Solomon* and *Tar Baby:* The Subversive Role of Language and the Carnivalesque." In *The Cambridge Companion to Toni Morrison.* Edited by Justine Tally. Cambridge, U.K.: Cambridge University Press, 2007. Pp. 26–42.

Seward, Adrienne Lanier, and Justine Tally, eds. *Toni Morrison: Memory and Meaning.* Jackson: University Press of Mississippi, 2014.

Stave, Shirley A. "*Jazz* and *Paradise:* Pivotal Moments in Black History." In *The Cambridge Companion to Toni Morrison.* Edited by Justine Tally. Cambridge, U.K.: Cambridge University Press, 2007. Pp. 59–74.

Stave, Shirley A., and Justine Tally, eds. *Toni Morrison's "A Mercy": Critical Approaches.* Newcastle upon Tyne, U.K.: Cambridge Scholars, 2011.

Tally, Justine, ed. *The Cambridge Companion to Toni Morrison.* Cambridge, U.K.: Cambridge University Press, 2007.

Tedder, Charles. "Post-Racialism and Its Discontents: The Pre-National Scene in Toni Morrison's *A Mercy.*" In *Contested Boundaries: New Critical Essays on the Fiction of Toni Morrison.* Edited by Maxine L. Montgomery. Newcastle upon Tyne, U.K.: Cambridge Scholars, 2013. Pp. 144–159.

Wagner-Martin, Linda. *Toni Morrison and a Literary Life.* New York: Palgrave Macmillan, 2015.

———. *Toni Morrison and the Maternal: From "The Bluest Eye" to "Home."* New York: Peter Lang, 2014.

Werrlein, Deborah. "Not So Fast, Dick and Jane: Reimagining Childhood and Nation in *The Bluest Eye.*" *MELUS* 30, no. 4: 53–72 (2005).

Wester, Maisha. "'Murdered by Piece-Meal:' The Destruction of African American Family in *Beloved.*" In her *African American Gothic: Screams from Shadowed Places.* New York: Palgrave, 2012. Pp. 185–214.

Wilentz, Gay. "Civilizations Underneath: African Heritage as Cultural Discourse in Toni Morrison's *Song of Solomon.*" *African American Review* 26, no. 1: 61–76 (1992).

Wyatt, Jean. "Failed Messages, Maternal Loss, and Narrative Form in Toni Morrison's *A Mercy.*" *Modern Fiction Studies* 58, no. 1: 128–151 (2012).

Yeates, Robert. "'The Unshriven Dead, Zombies on the Loose:' African and Caribbean Religious Heritage in Toni Morrison's *Beloved.*" *Modern Fiction Studies* 61, no. 3: 515–537 (2015).

Zauditu-Selassie, K. *African Spiritual Traditions in the Novels of Toni Morrison.* Gainesville: University Press of Florida, 2009.

FLANNERY O'CONNOR

(1925—1964)

Laurie Champion

FLANNERY O'CONNOR IS one of America's finest short story writers. Because the short story is the only genre considered uniquely American, her short fiction has also helped shape the American literary canon. Her body of work includes over thirty short stories, as well as two novels, many essays, reviews, and personal and professional letters. Although not among her highest achievements, her nonfiction essays and letters are important to understanding her life and her fiction. Her Catholicism is also an important means of understanding her writings, for her faith underscores almost all of her work. Illustrating ethical, moral, and religious ideology, her work raises philosophical questions in which lines between good and evil are not so clear. In the midst of such thought-provoking prose, her work reveals an extraordinary sense of humor in which she uses comedy and satire to tell stories that often convey violence and personal suffering.

Born March 25, 1925, in Savannah, Georgia, Mary Flannery O'Connor was the only child of Edward Francis and Regina Cline O'Connor. Her father, who expressed an interest in writing and doted on Flannery throughout her childhood, died of lupus in 1941, when O'Connor was a teenager. In 1931, O'Connor started first grade at St. Vincent's Grammar School, in Savannah, then transferred to Sacred Heart Academy in 1936 after the fifth grade. O'Connor had a peculiar childhood: she referred to her parents by their first names, had a strange affinity for birds, particularly fowl, and did not welcome friendships.

When she was six years old, she garnered local notoriety for having trained a chicken to walk backward—attracting the interest of Pathé News, which sent a photographer from New York to Savannah to film the chicken with its young owner. To meet a home economics assignment to create an outfit for a toddler, she brought a chicken dressed in a white piqué coat to school. She wrote three books about geese when in high school, and her later, distinguished writings are sprinkled with references to all sorts of fowl.

O'Connor was reserved as a child. Her mother tried to establish and maintain a social life for her daughter, but the young O'Connor resisted. Her mother forced her to enroll in dancing lessons, but she detested social groups and didn't appreciate frilly dresses or the strong sense of femininity the dancing lessons encouraged. Even as a child, she was more interested in artistic endeavors than in socializing. When she was twelve, she enrolled in a summer reading course at the Atlanta Public Library.

When her father took a position with the Federal Housing Administration in 1938, O'Connor and her mother moved to Atlanta with him, and O'Connor finished seventh grade at St. Joseph's Church, a parochial school. After the school year ended, her father stayed in Atlanta, while she and her mother moved to Milledgeville, Georgia, where they resided with two of O'Connor's maternal aunts in the historically renowned Cline family residence. Here, O'Connor spent her teenage years, where she remained reclusive, kept her interest in reading and writing, and maintained a fondness for fowl. O'Connor never developed a connection with Milledgeville, and she developed an ability to view it somewhat objectively, an attribute that no doubt influenced her ability to write realistically about the South.

O'Connor attended Peabody High School, which offered an experimental curriculum monitored by the government. The school was noted for its nontraditional curriculum that taught critical thinking and brought lessons outside the classroom, but O'Connor thought the education was poor quality. While a student at Peabody, O'Connor drew cartoons and wrote for the school paper. During her senior year, she won a state essay contest, for which she was awarded a scholarship to any Georgia college. During a high school interview, O'Connor announced she had written three books about a goose and said she strived to continue writing.

After graduating from Peabody High School, O'Connor remained in Milledgeville to attend Georgia State College for Women, where she began her studies in 1942. In 1945, she completed a degree in sociology, then she attended the prestigious Writer's Workshop at the State University of Iowa (now the University of Iowa), where she received her M.F.A. in 1947. In 1946, O'Connor's story "The Geranium" was published in *Accent.* This was her first published short story.

In the summer of 1948, O'Connor began a residence at Yaddo, the well-known artists' colony in Saratoga Springs, New York. In February 1949 she met Sally and Robert Fitzgerald, who became extremely influential in her writing. Later that year, the Fitzgeralds invited her to stay with them in Connecticut, an arrangement that led to a lifelong friendship. Robert later became O'Connor's literary executor, and he and Sally edited and collected manuscripts of her essays, magazine articles, and lectures and published them in *Mystery and Manners: Occasional Prose* (1969). After Robert died, Sally collected O'Connor's letters in *The Habit of Being,* which appeared in 1979.

In 1951, O'Connor was diagnosed with lupus, the disease that had killed her father. In 1951, she returned to Milledgeville to live with her mother, where they maintained a dairy farm they called Andalusia. She continued to write and also continued her passionate interest in barnyard fowl, raising peacocks until she had a flock of over forty. She was at Andalusia in 1952 when her first novel, *Wise Blood,* was published. During the 1950s and 1960s, her writing career continued to flourish. During the mid-1950s, she began to lecture occasionally at colleges and universities, and she received two honorary doctor of letters degrees: one from St. Mary's College, Notre Dame (1962), and the other from Smith College (1963). She received the Kenyon Review Fellowship in 1953, reappointed in 1954, and a National Institute of Arts and Letters grant in 1957. In 1959, she received a Ford Foundation grant. Her short story "The Life You Save May Be Your Own" received the O. Henry Award second prize in 1955. "Greenleaf" won the O. Henry Award first prize in 1957, and "Revelation" took first prize in 1964. Her first collection of short stories, *A Good Man Is Hard to Find,* was published in 1955, followed by her second collection, *Everything That Rises Must Converge,* in 1965. Her second novel, *The Violent Bear It Away,* was published in 1960.

Flannery O'Connor died on August 3, 1964, in Atlanta, Georgia, at the Baldwin County Hospital. She was thirty-nine years old. *Everything That Rises Must Converge* appeared posthumously in 1965, and *The Complete Stories,* published in 1971, received that year's National Book Award. She has since secured a solid place in the American literary canon and is considered a master of the short story; scholarly interest in her work and her life has remained high.

Although untangling various themes, subjects, and writing techniques that recur throughout O'Connor's work poses challenges because these components overlap, a thematic approach yields a richer understanding of her oeuvre than a text-by-text, story-by-story analysis. O'Connor's signature subjects include Christianity, violence, the notion of grace, the journey motif, a character's spiritual awakening or epiphany, race relations, and social class hierarchies.

RELIGIOUS THEMES

In a letter to a friend in 1955, O'Connor offered some thoughts about the religious nature of her writing:

> I write the way I do because (not though) I am a Catholic. This is a fact and nothing covers it like the bald statement. However, I am a Catholic peculiarly possessed of the modern consciousness, that thing Jung describes as unhistorical, solitary,

> and guilty. To possess this *within* the Church is to bear a burden, the necessary burden for the conscious Catholic. It's to feel the contemporary situation at the ultimate level. I think that the Church is the only thing that is going to make the terrible world we are coming to endurable; the only thing that makes the Church endurable is that it is somehow the body of Christ and that on this we are fed. It seems to be a fact that you have to suffer as much from the Church as for it but if you believe in the divinity of Christ, you have to cherish the world at the same time that you struggle to endure it. This may explain the lack of bitterness in the stories.
>
> (*The Habit of Being* [hereafter cited as HB], p. 90)

One of the most defining elements of Flannery O'Connor's life and of her writings, both fiction and nonfiction, is her Christian identity, and her affiliation with Catholicism in particular. Excerpts from lectures and correspondence demonstrate her lifelong commitment to Catholicism, and her fiction is often interpreted as it relates to Christian concepts and ideology. In a paper titled "Novelist and Believer," presented by O'Connor during a symposium at Sweet Briar College (Virginia) in 1963, she explains how religion enhances the power of a story:

> The serious writer has always taken the flaw in human nature for his starting point, usually the flaw in an otherwise admirable character. Drama usually bases itself on the bedrock of original sin, whether the writer thinks in theological terms or not. Then, too, any character in a serious novel is supposed to carry a burden of meaning larger than himself. The novelist doesn't write about people in a vacuum; he writes about people in a world where something is obviously lacking, where there is the general mystery of incompleteness and the particular tragedy of our own times to be demonstrated, and the novelist tries to give you, within the form of the book, the total experience of human nature at any time. For this reason, the greatest dramas naturally involve the salvation or loss of the soul. Where there is no belief in the soul, there is very little drama.
>
> (from *Mystery and Manners* [hereafter cited as MM], p. 167)

Throughout O'Connor's work, Christianity appears as an overt subject as well as a subtle one. In the novel *Wise Blood,* for instance, the protagonist Hazel (Haze) Motes is a young Southern Baptist man whose circuit-preacher grandfather "had ridden over three counties with Jesus hidden in his head like a stinger" (*Flannery O'Connor: Collected Works* [hereafter cited as CW], pp. 9–10). The novel opens as Haze travels to Taulkinham, where he sits on a train across from Mrs. Hitchcock, who says, "I guess you're going home" (p. 3). When he ignores her, she says "there's no place like home," then asks him again: "Are you going home?" (pp. 4–5). From the opening, the novel reflects the journey motif, as Haze is clearly on both a physical and a spiritual journey. References to home suggest in the Christian sense that he is headed home to Christ.

Yet *Wise Blood* immediately contradicts Christian notions of home, as Haze, a World War II vet returning from a four-year enlistment, announces that he is not headed home but to Taulkinham "to do some things I never have done before" (p. 5). Since he was a young boy, Haze has believed he was destined to be a preacher, but now he is confused about his religious upbringing and seeks to avoid sin as a means to evade Jesus. He grew up hearing evangelical sermons with messages such as Jesus died to redeem our sins and Jesus died "one death for all, but He would have died every soul's death for one!" (p. 11). Haze remembers his grandfather standing atop the hood of his car and asking the audience if it understood him as he shouted to them: Jesus "would have died ten million deaths, had His arms and legs stretched on the cross and nailed ten million times for one of them" (p. 11).

Once in Taulkinham, Haze's journey begins. In addition to representing both a physical and a spiritual journey, Haze's meanderings exemplify the mythical journey illustrated by the quest motif in classic literature. He meets a variety of people, falls into various adventures, and ultimately ends his journey with a newfound knowledge, even if it is not the wisdom he originally sought. He first meets a prostitute and is quick to assure her that he is no preacher, then he encounters Enoch Emery, along with Asa Hawks, a false prophet who pretends to be blind, and Hawk's daughter, Sabbath Lily. Haze distinguishes himself from Hawks by announcing to crowds that he teaches "a new church—the church of truth without Jesus

Christ Crucified. It won't cost you nothing to join my church" (p. 31). His teachings include sermons such as this one: "I want to tell you people something. Maybe you think you're not clean because you don't believe. Well you are clean, let me tell you that. Every one of you people are clean and let me tell you why if you think it's because of Jesus Christ Crucified you're wrong. I don't say he wasn't crucified but I say it wasn't for you. Listenhere [sic], I'm a preacher myself and I preach the truth" (p. 30). Haze's street preaching, more blasphemy than gospel from a Christian point of view, fails to attract followers.

While preaching outside movie theaters, he encounters another false prophet, Onnie Jay Holy, who tells the crowd that Haze helped him through his Holy Church of Christ Without Christ ministry that brought out his sweet nature. Haze tells the crowd he's never met Onnie Jay, but Onnie Jay nevertheless publicly endorses Haze's teachings, confirming that while the church bases its messages on the Bible, it also allows for personal interpretations. Haze again calls Onnie Jay a liar, and Onnie Jay persists in claiming that he knows Haze. When Onnie Jay asks the crowd for a dollar to join the Church of Christ Without Christ, Haze retorts that it doesn't cost money for the truth. Onnie Jay finally admits that his name is Hoover Shoats and threatens to run Haze out of business: "I can get my own new jesus [sic] and I can get Prophets for peanuts, you hear?" (p. 91).

Hoover and Haze become rivals, and Hoover hires Solace Layfield to disguise himself as Haze and act as a prophet. A confrontation leads to Haze running over Solace as he begs Jesus to help him. On his way out of town, Haze passes a sign that says, "Jesus Died for YOU" (p. 117), then he hears a siren. A police officer pushes his car over an embankment, where it lands on its top. The officer asks Haze where he's going and Haze shakes his head. Haze goes home with a sack of quicklime and tin bucket and informs his landlady that he's planning to blind himself.

The blind Haze continues to live in his rented room, where he refuses to wear dark glasses to cover his damaged eyes, puts rocks and glass chips in his shoes, and wraps barbed wire around his chest for self-punishment. One night, as Haze is suffering and weak from influenza, the landlady suggests they get married, but he walks out into the cold night. Two days later, two police officers find him lying in a ditch. He dies in the squad car on the way home.

In addition to the obvious Christian subjects, the novel demonstrates subtle religious ideas such as the notion of the blind prophet who sees spiritually and the sighted prophet who cannot see spiritually. Haze's last name, Motes, refers to his figurative blindness. The Bible teaches that Jesus tells the hypocritical Pharisees that they criticize the motes in other's eyes while ignoring the logs in their own. Also, as Connie Kirk points out in her 2007 study *Critical Companion to Flannery O'Connor,* blood imagery recurs throughout the novel, such as when Haze checks his car for blood after running over Solace Layfield. Especially for Catholic doctrine, but also for Christianity in general, blood symbolizes the blood of Christ. Catholics commemorate the Last Supper during Holy Communion, or the Eucharist, where they eat bread and drink wine, symbolic of the body and blood of Christ. As Kirk elaborates, "To a writer working from a Catholic sensibility, it is reasonable to make the connection between wise blood and this special blood, the blood of Christ" (p. 176). O'Connor explains that since her characters are Protestants and not Catholic, "Haze is saved by virtue of having wise blood; it's too wise for him ultimately to deny Christ. Wise blood has to be these people's means of grace—they have no sacraments" (HB, p. 350). One could also argue that both the literal and the symbolic blood on his hands from running over Solace is the wise blood that leads to Haze's repentance. Kirk points out that the wise blood of the title refers to Emery's comment that he inherited from his father wise blood, a kind of intuition. Likewise, in a Christian sense, faith is dependent on a sort of intuitive, unexplainable trust.

The title of O'Connor's 1960 novel, *The Violent Bear It Away,* is taken directly from the New Testament. Like *Wise Blood, The Violent Bear It Away* represents both obvious and more subtle Christian subjects and themes. The novel's protagonist is fourteen-year-old Francis Marion Tarwater, who has been raised by his great-uncle, Mason Tarwater, to become a prophet. He rejects his great-uncle's teachings, even finds them repulsive. When his great-uncle dies, he knows that as a prophet he must give his uncle a proper burial and baptize Bishop, his great-uncle's mentally challenged great-nephew, who is young Tarwater's first cousin. Deliberately rebelling against these two obligations, he burns down his great-uncle's house, where he thinks the dead body lies.

He then goes to visit his Uncle Rayber, not to baptize Rayber's son, Bishop, as his great-uncle expected of him, but to experience city life in order to dissociate himself from his religious calling. During the drive, Tarwater recalls that Mason had "kidnapped" the young Rayber from his parents when he was a young boy, kept him for four days, and baptized and preached the gospel to him. Rayber later rejected Mason's lessons. After Tarwater's mother and father died, he went to live with his Uncle Rayber. Trying to ensure that Rayber did not spiritually corrupt Tarwater, Mason baptized Tarwater, claiming that a voice had come to him and commanded, "HERE IS THE PROPHET TO TAKE YOUR PLACE BAPTIZE HIM" (CW, p. 376), then stole him from Rayber and left a note in the empty crib: "THE PROPHET I RAISE UP OUT OF THIS BOY WILL BURN YOUR EYES CLEAN" (p. 379).

When Tarwater arrives at Rayber's house in the city, Rayber seizes the opportunity to undo Mason's teachings. When Tarwater sees Bishop, he has a vision that he needs to baptize him and become a prophet, but he rejects and resists these urges. Rayber, ringing Bishop, sets off with Tarwater to take him back to his old home at Powderhead, Tennessee, to expunge Mason's teaching; along the way, they stop at a lodge near a lake and Tarwater again feels the urge to baptize Bishop. Rayber offers to allow Tarwater to baptize Bishop in a restaurant, but Tarwater instead takes Bishop out on the lake and drowns him. However, as he is drowning the boy, Tarwater begins to recite a baptism ceremony, although he believes he has purged himself of his great-uncle's influence. When a man picks up Tarwater on his way back to Powderhead, Tarwater tells the driver that he drowned the boy and the baptism was an accident. The driver takes him to the woods and rapes him. When Tarwater makes it back to Powderhead, he discovers that his great-uncle has been buried. He has a vision of Christ and sees loaves of bread and fish. After all these events, he leaves Powderhead a changed man, vowing to live the life of a prophet.

The novel juxtaposes action against thoughts, a notion that Mason had explained to Tarwater when he stated that he was a man of action whereas Rayber kept thoughts in his head. This need to act motivates Tarwater throughout the novel. However, the more Tarwater attempts to shed his great-uncle's influence, the more compelled he feels to baptize Bishop. He finally realizes he cannot escape God merely by running. As he tells the clerk at the Cherokee Lodge, "You can't just say NO.... You got to do NO. You got to show it. You got to show you mean it by doing it. You got to show you're not going to do one thing by doing another. You got to make an end of it. One way or another" (p. 427). Ironically, Tarwater's attempt to drown Bishop fulfills the prophecy that he will baptize the boy. His willingness to act leads him to the very redemption he seeks to avoid.

EPIPHANIES

O'Connor's portrayals of Christian concepts often involve a character's moment of awareness, a specific point in which he or she experiences a spiritual epiphany that depends on grace in the Christian sense. In O'Connor's fiction, the spiritual awareness exemplifies the Christian sense of redemption and leads to the character's personal and spiritual transformation, a notion central to Christianity, for it is only through grace received through the death of Christ that a believer is redeemed. O'Connor believes this central concept, for she acknowledges, "our return [to innocence] is through the Redemption which was brought about by Christ's death and by our slow participation in it" (MM, p. 148).

Although this sort of spiritual awakening occurs in most of her short stories, two stories serve as good examples: "A Good Man Is Hard to Find" and "Revelation." The plot of "A Good Man Is Hard to Find" involves a Southern family that embarks on a journey from Georgia to Florida. The grandmother has warned her son about going to Florida because she read a newspaper article that said "The Misfit," an escaped convict, was headed there. The grandmother hides her cat in the car and makes comments about the scenery along the way. When the cat jumps on her son's shoulder, an accident ensues in which the car flips over. When the grandmother hails another car for help, she thinks she recognizes the man who approaches. She tells everyone that he is The Misfit, and he tells her it would have been better for all of them had she not recognized him.

The Misfit asks his companion to take the other victims to the woods, while he stays with the grandmother. She utters, "Jesus, Jesus," to which he responds, "Jesus thrown everything off balance" (*The Complete Stories* [hereafter cited as CS], p. 131). A conversation about whether or not Jesus raised the dead ensues. When The Misfit says, "I wasn't there so I can't say He didn't.... [if] I had of been there I would of known and I wouldn't be like I am now," she answers, "Why you're one of my babies. You're one of my own children!" (p. 132). He immediately kills her with three shots to the chest.

Although the grandmother uses preaching discourse to The Misfit, she does not fully recognize or accept him as a human until her epiphany just before she is shot. She has compassion toward him, even referring to him as one of her own. Because she arrives at this insight, she dies in a state of grace. Moreover, The Misfit also experiences an epiphany as a result of these events. During his discussion with the grandmother about Jesus, he instructs her to "enjoy the few minutes you got left the best way you can—by killing somebody or burning down his house or doing some other meanness to him. No pleasure but meanness" (p. 132), but at the very end of the story he claims that there's "no real pleasure in life" (p. 133). He seems to have changed from one who seeks pleasure through violence to one who understands that violence, particularly murder, does not bring about pleasure.

Similar to the transformation of the grandmother in "A Good Man Is Hard to Find," Mrs. Turpin, the protagonist of "The Revelation" experiences an epiphany, or spiritual awareness, that leads to redemption. Mrs. Turpin considers herself above all blacks and most whites. She spends a good deal of energy classifying people in a hierarchical scale:

> Sometimes Mrs. Turpin occupied herself at night by naming the classes of people. On the bottom of the heap were most colored people, not the kind she would have been if she had been one, but most of them; then next to them—not above, just away from—were the white-trash; then above them were the home-owners, and above them the home-and-land owners, to which she and Claud belonged.
>
> (CS, p. 491)

In a doctor's waiting room, Mrs. Turpin begins to chat with another woman, whom she has deemed "white trash," and soon their conversation reeks of racist attitudes. Mrs. Turpin tries to start a conversation with the woman's daughter, Mary Grace, who sits reading a college textbook, but the young woman ignores her. When Mrs. Turpin goes so far as to thank Jesus out loud for her lot in life, the girl whirls the book at her—thus, literally "tossing the book" at her. Mary Grace gazes at her and says, "Go back to hell where you came from, you old wart hog" (p. 500).

Near the end of the story, Mrs. Turpin tells a group of African Americans who have come to work on her farm about Mary Grace, and they express sympathy, telling her she is "the sweetest white lady" they know. Another tells her she is "pretty" and that "Jesus [is] satisfied with her!" (p. 505). Mrs. Turpin seems to invite the (insincere) compliments, yet she resents herself for it, thinking they are "idiots" and that she couldn't "say anything intelligent to a nigger. You could talk at them but not with them" (p. 505). She then approaches Claud, who is busy spraying the hogs with a water hose, to take "them niggers" home, and she takes the water hose from him and sprays the hogs. The conversation with the black farmhands and the act of hosing the hogs mirrors the comment the "white trash" woman told Mrs. Turpin in the doctor's waiting room: "Two thangs I ain't going to do: love no niggers or scoot down no hog with no hose" (p. 494). Mrs. Turpin understands that she has just engaged in the two activities the "white trash" woman said she'd never do. Not only does Mrs. Turpin think she's crossed racial boundaries, she also thinks she has crossed social class boundaries by engaging in activities even the "white trash" consider beneath them.

Furthermore, Mrs. Turpin accepts that what Mary Grace said to her may have been a personal message, for she asks God, "What do you send me a message like that for? ... How am I a hog and me both? How am I saved and from hell too?" (p. 506). Still spraying the hogs, Mrs. Turpin looks back at the pasture as Claud's truck rolls beyond the hill. She observes the scenery, contemplating the events that have unfolded throughout the story, then sees Claud's tiny truck returning on the highway. She watches until it reappears on the return home and turns toward the road leading to the farm: "Then like a monumental statue coming to life, she bent her head slowly and gazed, as if through the very heart of mystery, down into the pig parlor at the hogs.... A red glow suffused them. They appeared to pant with a secret life." She continues to stare at the pasture "until the sun slipped finally behind the tree line" (p. 508). She

> remained there with her gaze bent to them as if she were absorbing some abysmal life-giving knowledge. At last she lifted her head. There was only a purple streak in the sky, cutting through a field of crimson and leading, like an extension of the highway, into the descending dusk. She raised her hands from the side of the pen in a gesture hieratic and profound. A visionary light settled in her eyes. She saw the streak as a vast swinging bridge extending upward from the earth through a field of living fire. Upon it a vast horde of souls were rumbling toward heaven. There were whole companies of white-trash, clean for the first time in their lives, and bands of black niggers in white robes, and battalions of freaks and lunatics shouting and clapping and leaping like frogs. And bringing up the end of the procession was a tribe of people whom she recognized at once as those who, like herself and Claud, had always had a little of everything and the God-given wit to use it right.... They were marching behind the others with great dignity, accountable as they had always been for good order and common sense and respectable behavior. They alone were on key. Yet she could see by their shocked and altered faces that even their virtues were being burned away.... In a moment the vision faded but she remained where she was, immobile.
>
> (pp. 508–509)

Her epiphany contradicts her classist and sexist hierarchies. She grasps the notion that Christians receive grace because of God's mercy, not because of ethnicity or social class. She absorbs this sense of grace, "her eyes small but fixed unblinkingly on what lay ahead" (pp. 508–509). The vision demonstrates that she understands that she is like those she has snubbed and mocked and those to whom she has condescended. They are all in the same group as far as God is concerned, and Jesus loves and saves them all. Her deeds and attitudes do not get her to heaven; God's grace does. Interestingly, it is Mary "Grace" who hurls the book at her, as though God's message is symbolically tossed to her in a gesture that offers grace.

Ranging from gestures such as Mary Grace hurling the book at Mrs. Turpin in "Revelation" to The Misfit's execution-style shooting of the grandmother in "A Good Man Is Hard to Find," acts of violence appear in almost every one of O'Connor's novels and short stories. In many, violence is directly related to the state of grace the characters experience: O'Connor once mused that "violence is strangely capable of returning my characters to reality and preparing them to accept their moment of grace" (MM, p. 112).

Other works of fiction in which characters experience epiphanies that lead to change and to forms of spiritual grace include *Wise Blood, The Violent Bear It Away,* "Good Country People," "Everything That Rises Must Converge," "The Artificial Nigger," "Parker's Back," "Greenleaf," "The Enduring Chill," and "The River." O'Connor talked about the importance of such transformation in her fiction in a 1958 letter, writing, "It seems to me that all good stories are about conversion, about a character's changing. ...The action of grace changes a character.... All my stories are about the action of grace on a character who is not very willing to support it." (HB, p. 275).

Although in a typical O'Connor story a character experiences an epiphany that leads to spiritual grace, in "Judgement Day," the protagonist is left in a purgatory state, neither redeemed nor damned. "Judgement Day" concerns T. C. Tanner, who lives in New York City with his daughter but plans to get home to Georgia by walking as far as he can, then trusting "the Almighty to get him the rest of the way" (CS, p. 531). He conserves his energy in preparation for the trip and pins a note to his pocket: "IF FOUND DEAD SHIP EXPRESS COLLECT TO COLEMAN PARRUM, CORINTH, GEORGIA" (p. 531). Getting home is what matters, whether "dead or alive did not" (p. 532). When his daughter says she plans to bury him in New York, he retorts, "Bury me here and burn in hell!" (p. 533).

Throughout the story, Tanner shuns others and considers himself superior to other people in a race-conscious hierarchy in which he looks down on African Americans. When his daughter scolds him, he warns, "The Judgment is coming.... The sheep'll be separated from the goats" (p. 541). He refers to a black man who moves into his daughter's apartment complex as a preacher from South Alabama, and even though the man corrects him, explaining that he's an actor from New York City, Tanner continues to refer to the man as Preacher. Finally, the man shouts, "I'm not no preacher! I'm not even no Christian. I don't believe that crap. There ain't no Jesus and there ain't no God" (p. 545), then he slams Tanner against the wall and shoves him inside his door.

When Tanner's daughter goes to the grocery store one afternoon, he attempts to leave on his homeward journey, but soon his body sways and he feels scared. He realizes he will never get home, "dead or alive," and begins to say a prayer. He makes it to the hall but falls down the stairs and grabs the banister post. He hangs down, gazing at "unlighted steps" (p. 548). Amid visions that his body is being delivered to Georgia, he sees the black actor, who tells him, "Judgement day.... Maybe this here judgement day for you" (p. 549). When Tanner asks for help, he again refers to the actor as Preacher: "Hep me up, Preacher. I'm on my way home!" (p. 549). The police come and cut Tanner's dangling body from the stairwell. They tell his daughter he's been dead for about an hour. She first buries him in New York then moves the body to Corinth.

In "Judgement Day" the protagonist does not experience an epiphany; he continues to refer to the actor as "Preacher," suggesting he clings to his racist ideology in which he is superior to the black actor. O'Connor physically situates the dying man between floor levels, in a symbolic purgatory. Just as he wishes to be taken home dead or alive, he is between states of being. He experiences God's grace neither when he is alive nor when he is dead. In Catholicism, purgatory is a state of waiting for grace after death, a spiritual space between heaven and hell. In a similar vein, Tanner says he is going home, but he is first buried in New York and then later sent home, further suggesting he has been in a state of waiting before returning home. Although "home" sometimes refers to a spiritual home, in this story it does not, for Tanner is still in a state of spiritual purgatory even after his daughter ships his body to Georgia.

THE GROTESQUE

O'Connor's fiction is known for its use of the grotesque, particularly the Southern grotesque, which is an element of the literary tradition known as the "Southern gothic." Southern gothic fiction is set in the South and portrays Southern culture with all its idiosyncratic values, habits, and customs. Sometimes social outcasts and misfits, characters in Southern gothic fiction frequently speak in dialect, express racist beliefs, and preach Christian "virtue." Some of the characters are helpless victims of mental disorders or physical ailments or deformities.

In its literary sense, the "grotesque" refers to portrayals of distortions and exaggerations of the human body that simultaneously elicit compassion and loathing from readers. The grotesque in fiction blends the familiar with the unfamiliar, sometimes illustrating distorted variations of the familiar. It jolts readers with the unexpected, challenging them to look at the familiar in unusual ways or to see the unfamiliar in usual ways: "I find that any fiction that comes out of the south is going to be called 'grotesque' by the Northern reader unless it is grotesque, in which case it is going to be called 'photographic realism.'" O'Connor says in her essay "The Catholic Novelist in the Protestant South":

> The word "grotesque" should not necessarily be used as a pejorative term. There is the grotesque of the animated cartoon. But there is also that grotesque which is a constant in literature when any considerable depth of reality has been penetrated. In Southern fiction there is a growing tradition of the grotesque... [O]ur present grotesque heroes are not comic, or at least not primarily so. They seem to carry an invisible burden and to fix us with eyes that remind us that we all bear some heavy responsibility whose nature we have forgotten....
>
> Whenever I am asked why Southern writers particularly have this penchant for writing about freaks, I say it is because we are still able to recognize one. To be able to recognize a freak, you have to have some conception of the whole man. And in the South, the general conception of man is still, in the main, theological.... But approaching the subject from the standpoint of the writer, I think it is safe to say that while the South is hardly Christ-centered, it is most certainly Christ-haunted.
>
> (CW, pp. 860–861)

In O'Connor's fiction, portrayals of the grotesque include "idiots," such as the daughter in "The Life You Save May Be Your Own" and Bishop in *The Violent Bear It Away*; Hulga Hopewell's artificial leg in "Good Country People"; the club-footed Rufus Johnson in "The Lame Shall Enter First"; Tom Shiftlet, the unscrupulous carpenter who is missing half an arm, in "The Life You Save May Be Your Own"; and an array of elements including the shrunken mummy, the human gorilla, and Haze's forms of self-mutilation, including blinding himself, in *Wise Blood*.

One of the most notable examples of the use of the grotesque in O'Connor's fiction occurs in "A Temple of the Holy Ghost." "A Temple of the Holy Ghost" concerns a twelve-year-old, unnamed protagonist who is visited by her second cousins, two fourteen-year-old sisters who attend Mount St. Scholastica convent school. Near the beginning of the story, references to people being temples of the Holy Ghost abound: The cousins call themselves Temple One and Temple Two, because a nun had instructed them that if a boy made sexual advances toward them, they should say, "Stop sir! I am a Temple of the Holy Ghost!" (*A Good Man Is Hard to Find and Other Stories* [hereafter cited as GM], p. 61). Responding to this explanation, the protagonist's mother says, "After all, that's what you are—Temples of the Holy Ghost" (p. 61). The schoolteacher who boards with the protagonist's family feels as though she's been given a gift when she contemplates, "I am a Temple of the Holy Ghost" (p. 61), and the protagonist thinks that in addition to being a poor, lonesome soul, the teacher is "a Temple of the Holy Ghost" (p. 61).

Seeking entertainment for the cousins, the protagonist's mother arranges for them to be escorted to the fair. Upon their return, they tell the protagonist, they saw "All kinds of freaks" (p. 67). (The circuses, carnivals, and fairs that were popular in the United States from the turn of the twentieth century until the late 1970s often included "freak" shows—sideshows in which attendees could pay extra to gawk at the human anomalies presented as "freaks.") At first they don't elaborate, until the protagonist says she once witnessed a rabbit give birth. They then explain that they saw someone who is "a man and a woman both" (p. 68). Before showing himself to the audience, he had warned, "God made me this away and if you laugh He may strike you the same way. This is the way He wanted me to be and I ain't disputing His way" and said, "God done this to me and I praise Him" (p. 68). He then began to preach, instructing the audience to "Raise yourself up. A temple of the Holy Ghost. You! You are God's temple don't you know? Don't you know? God's Spirit has a dwelling in you, don't you know?" (p. 69). He continued to make references to the temple of the Holy Ghost, then announced, "I am a temple of the Holy Ghost!" (p. 69).

The cousins and the protagonist are jolted when exposed to the unfamiliar. For the protagonist, this jolting leads to a spiritual awareness, and in this way O'Connor's use of the grotesque blends with her portrayal of a spiritual epiphany. After the protagonist listens attentively to the cousins describe seeing the "freak," she feel confused that the hermaphrodite praises God for his body. Since the "freak" is able to praise his body as the temple of the Holy Ghost, the protagonist is prompted to do so as well. At the end of the cousins' visit, a driver takes them back to the convent, and the protagonist and her mother go along. They arrive just as benediction is beginning in the chapel, and the protagonist feels the presence of God. She prays for God to help her be less mean and not so sassy. As the priest raises the "host"—the Communion wafer—her mind turns to the hermaphrodite who has acknowledged that God made him the way he wanted him to be.

At the end of the story, during the drive home, the protagonist observes how the red sun looks "like an elevated Host drenched in blood" (p. 71). In Catholicism, the Communion wafer is understood to be the literal (not symbolic) body of Christ—that is, when the host (or wafer) is swallowed in the sacrament of the Eucharist, Christ virtually becomes part of the partaker. The image of the blood-drenched host represents Catholic doctrine regarding the Communion wafer consumed during the Eucharist, which is a serious matter for O'Connor. A well-known anecdote involves an evening she spent at a dinner party among intellectuals. Someone remarked that the host was a symbol, to which O'Connor retorted, "Well, if it's a symbol, to hell with it" (HB, p. 125).

The grotesque embodied by a carnival or circus "freak" is a staple in the Southern grotesque, or Southern gothic, tradition, and it arises again in O'Connor's story "Parker's Back." Told from the title character's point of view, the story relates that when Parker was fourteen, he'd seen a man at a fair who was "tattooed from head to foot" (CS, p. 512). Reacting to the unfamiliar sight, Parker "was filled with emotion" and after the show, he stood "staring where the tattooed man had been, until the tent was almost empty" (p. 513). He felt sensations and thoughts he'd never before imagined, sensations that led to feelings of disorientation:

> Parker had never before felt the least notion of wonder in himself. Until he saw the man at the fair, it did not enter his head that there was anything out of the ordinary about the fact that he existed. Even then it did not enter his head, but a peculiar unease settled in him. It was as if a blind boy had been turned so gently in a different direction that he did not know his destination had been changed.
>
> (p. 513)

Soon after he saw the tattooed man, he got his first tattoo, then continued to get them, noting that they attracted girls. He joined the navy and "everywhere he went he picked up more tattoos" (p. 514). After being discharged from the navy, he got married but remained unhappy. Whenever he reached a point in which he felt life was unbearable, he'd get another tattoo, until the only spot without a tattoo was on his back.

He now visualizes a tattoo on his back and decides that a tattoo of a religious image might make his wife more accepting of the idea. After he is in an accident while baling hay, he experiences "a great change in his life" and is inspired to follow through with the religious tattoo he had earlier considered (p. 521). After perusing a tattoo book with religious icons, he decides on "a flat stern Byzantine Christ with all-demanding eyes" (p. 522). When he shows it to his wife, she accuses him of idolatry and beats him with a broom. Although she never approves of Parker's tattoos, referring to them as "vanity of vanities" (p. 515), she has never reacted as strongly as she does when she sees the one of a Christ figure. This suggests that her disapproval of the tattoos is not because of their grotesque nature but because she sees them as a form of idolatry. However, his wife's rejection leads Parker to an epiphany, a moment of grace, and at the end of the story, he leans against a tree and cries "like a baby" (p. 132). Earlier resisting his name, Parker now calls himself Obadiah Elihue, Hebrew for "servant of the Lord."

In both "A Temple of the Holy Ghost" and "Parker's Back," a reaction to the grotesque ultimately leads the protagonist, directly or indirectly, to a redemption. In the latter story, Parker's reaction to the tattoo man at the fair leads him to getting tattoos of his own, which leads to his wife's rejection. Thrown off balance both physically and spiritually, Parker has reached a state of grace at the end of the story, where he is physically balanced by a tree, symbolic of the tree of life.

JOURNEYS

Throughout O'Connor's fiction, characters embark upon literal journeys—sometimes just short bus rides, other times cross-country road trips—and these geographical journeys take on mythical implications at times, suggesting the journey motif in the classical sense. At other times, the journeys symbolize spiritual journeys, as in finding one's way to Christ. Sometimes in O'Connor's stories a stranger comes to town; in other stories, the protagonist embarks on some sort of trip—arguably, these two types of journeys are at the center of most great literature.

The notion of the stranger who comes to town is illustrated in "Good Country People." From the beginning of the story, references to motion abound. The narrator refers to Mrs. Freeman's expressions, noting that in addition to "neutral," she expresses "forward and reverse" (GM, p. 122)—details that could just as easily describe automobile gears as they do facial expressions. In "Good Country People," the Freemans work for Mrs. Hopewell, who has hired them because "they were good country people" (p. 123). Mrs. Hopewell has a thirty-two-year-old daughter, Joy, who has a Ph.D. and has an artificial leg due to a hunting accident that occurred when she was ten. Bitter and grumpy, Joy changed her name to Hulga, a name her mother suspects she chose because it's the ugliest she could think of.

As the story opens, Mrs. Hopewell sits wondering what sort of conversation her daughter might have had with a Bible salesman who had visited the day before. Descriptions of his visit reflect the notion of mystery often portrayed in the plot structure of the stranger-comes-to-town storyline: "He had appeared at the door, carrying a large black suitcase that weighed him so heavily on one side that he had to brace himself against the door facing" (p. 128). He calls the Hopewells by the wrong last name, makes a bad joke, then says he's "come to speak of serious things" (p. 128). When he says he's selling Bibles, Mrs. Hopewell explains that her atheist daughter doesn't allow Bibles to be set in the parlor. He says, "People like you don't like to fool with country people like me!" (p. 129), and she says "there aren't enough good country people in the world" (p. 129). This description sets the salesman apart from the general population and highlights the notion that someone unique has come to visit.

The salesman introduces himself as "Manley Pointer from out in the country around Willohobie, not even from a place, just from near a place" (p. 129). This description adds mystery, as he seems to be a man from nowhere. His name embeds "man" and "point," alluding to a common man and to a direction, as though one would "point" to a place. When he returns the next day, he and Hulga go on a picnic, and they end up in the loft of a barn. He entices her to remove her leg, then takes it from her and won't return it. She pleads, asking, "Aren't you just good country people?" (p. 140). She accuses him of being a hypocritical Christian, to which he responds that he hopes she doesn't think he believes "that crap!" He continues, "I may sell Bibles but I know which end is up and I wasn't born yesterday and I know where I'm going" (p. 140). He stuffs the leg in his suitcase, then tells Hulga he has a lot of interesting things he acquired this way: "One time I got a woman's glass eye this way. And you needn't to think you'll catch me because Pointer ain't really my name. I use a different name at every house I call at and don't stay nowhere long" (p. 141). Manley the anonymous, transient "Bible salesman" is a typical con man, gaining the victim's confidence, then executing a swindle before quickly leaving town again before he is exposed, disappearing to move on to a new victim.

In "Good Country People," the protagonist, Hulga, is the person who changes as a result of a visitor, of the classic "stranger who comes to town." The Bible salesman forces her to confront her intellectual pride and her condescending attitude: "And I'll tell you another thing, Hulga," he says, "you ain't so smart. I been believing in nothing ever since I was born!" (p. 141). He challenges the intellectual snobbery of her atheism, which she presents as a superior belief that comes from being highly educated, and he also uses her name "as if he didn't think much of it," thus challenging—or refusing to acknowledge—the rebellious nature of her changing her name from the beautiful Joy to the ugly Hulga. By the end of the story, Hulga-Joy comes to realize that she has been outwitted and thus must face the reality that she is not as wise as she once thought she was.

Whereas a stranger comes to town in "Good Country People," in "The Artificial Nigger," characters go on a journey. Mr. Head, a blatant racist, takes his grandson, Nelson, to Atlanta, Georgia (where Nelson was born), with the intention of teaching him that the city is not such a wonderful place to live—he wants Nelson (who has never been to the city but likes to boast about having been born there) to appreciate living with him in the country. Mr. Head warns his grandson that the city is "full of niggers" and reminds him that he's never "seen a nigger," adding that "there hasn't been a nigger in this country since we run that one out twelve years ago and that was before you were born" (GM, p. 74). When they see a black man on the train, Mr. Head asks Nelson to label the man and he can't, so he defines the man as "a nigger," then tells the man across from them, "That's his first nigger" (p. 78). To demonstrate the uncleanliness of the city, Mr. Head instructs Nelson to squat down and look inside a sewer, then warns him to stay away from holes.

Although Mr. Head is full of confidence about knowing his way around the city, they soon get lost and find themselves in an African American section of town, surrounded by "niggers." Nelson nervously asks for directions from a black woman who is standing in a doorway. Following the streetcar tracks in an effort to get back to the train station, they come to a white neighborhood and Nelson falls asleep when they stop there to rest. Mr. Head hides around the corner, with the idea that when Nelson wakes up to find himself alone and lost he will appreciate his grandfather more. When Nelson gets scared, Mr. Head feels bad for hiding from him. Finally, Mr. Head admits he is lost and seeks directions, then he and Nelson walk toward the nearest train station (they have mistakenly ended up out in the suburbs). Along the way, Mr. Head sees a battered plaster statue of a black man eating a watermelon, set as an ornament on a fence that surrounds a residential yard. He exclaims, "An artificial nigger!" Nelson uses the same tone when he repeats the phrase. However, staring at the statue seems to humble Mr. Head and Nelson:

> They stood gazing at the artificial Negro as if they were faced with some great mystery, some monument to another's victory that brought them together in their common defeat. They could both feel it dissolving their differences like an action of mercy. Mr. Head had never known before what mercy felt like because he had been too good to deserve any, but he felt he knew now.
>
> (p. 91)

Recognizing Nelson's need for an explanation, Mr. Head says, "They ain't got enough real ones here. They got to have an artificial one" (p. 91). Nelson nods, then says: "Let's go home before we get ourselves lost again" (p. 91). It's as though the young Nelson intuitively wants to go home on a positive note—he doesn't want to "get lost," a state in which he will be shown his unclean city full of "niggers." On a spiritual level, the boy's desire not to get lost symbolically suggests he doesn't want to be a lost soul—damned, unsaved by God's grace. Once home, as they depart the train, Mr. Head contemplates his epiphany:

> Mr. Head stood very still and felt the action of mercy touch him again but this time he knew that there were no words in the world that could name it. He understood that it grew out of agony, which is not denied to any man and which is given in strange ways to children. He understood it was all a man could carry into death to give his Maker and he suddenly burned with shame that he had so little of it to take with him. He stood appalled, judging himself with the thoroughness of God, while the action of mercy covered his pride like a flame and

> consumed it. He had never thought himself a great sinner before but he saw now that his true depravity had been hidden from him lest it cause him despair. He realized that he was forgiven for sins from the beginning of time, when he had conceived his own heart the sin of Adam, until the present, when he had denied poor Nelson. He saw that no sin was too monstrous for him to claim as his own, and since God loved in proportion as HE forgave, he felt ready at that instant to enter Paradise.
>
> (pp. 91–92)

Mr. Head's moment of awareness reveals that although he sought to teach his grandson a lesson and cut down the boy's pride, it was the grandfather who learned the greatest lesson. Mr. Head's ultimate purpose in taking Nelson to the city was so Nelson would be exposed to "niggers" and thus be content to stay home for the rest of his life. But Nelson does not learn racism from his grandfather. However, the trip to the city indeed inspires Nelson to stay home, which was his grandfather's goal all along. So his grandfather's goal is met but in a way different from his original plan.The last line of the story details Nelson's comment as the train that has brought them home disappears down the tracks: "I'm glad I've went once, but I'll never go back again!" he says (p. 92).

"The Life You Save May Be Your Own" illustrates both the notion of a character going on a journey and that of a stranger who comes to town, as events are told both from the visitor's point of view and from the point of view of the person being visited. "The Life You Save May Be Your Own" opens with Mrs. Crater and her daughter, Lucynell, "sitting on their porch" in a "desolate spot," watching the sun balance on a mountain (CW, p. 172). A desolate spot in which the setting sun balances on a mountain represents a static state; moreover, they own a car that hasn't run in fifteen years. Against this background of immobility, a stranger appears, and only then does Mrs. Crater "change her position" (p. 172). She tells the man that the sun sets like this "every evening," further suggesting immobility. He immediately introduces himself: "Name Tom T. Shiftlet" (p. 173). When asked where he's from, he at first doesn't answer, then after Lucynell shakes her finger at him, he says,

> I can tell you my name is Tom T. Shiftlet and I come from Tarwater, Tennessee, but you never have seen me before: how you know I ain't lying? How you know my name ain't Aaron Sparks, lady, and I come from Singleberry, Georgia, or how you know it's not George Speeds and I come from Lucy, Alabama, or how you know I ain't Thompson Bright from Toolafalls, Mississippi?
>
> (p. 174)

Mrs. Crater answers, "I don't know nothing about you" (p. 174). The story thus begins with the journey formula in which a mysterious stranger arrives in town, coming out of nowhere; he arouses the lifeless setting and hides his identity.

Mrs. Crater agrees to let Mr. Shiftlet stay if he works on the property and as long as he is willing to sleep in the car. He convinces her to pay him and give him the car if he'll marry Lucynell, which he does. However, under the pretense of taking Lucynell on a vacation, he dumps her at a diner and continues his journey. Here, the story turns from being about Lucynell and her mother to being about Mr. Shiftlet, who is no longer the "stranger in town" but rather a character who goes on a journey. This shift is indicated by the sign Mr. Shiftlet sees immediately after he drops off Lucynell at the diner: "Drive carefully. The life you save may be your own" (p. 182). He picks up a hitchhiker, an act that ultimately leads to his epiphany: "Mr. Shiftlet felt that the rottenness of the world was about to engulf him" (p. 183). While the major characters all witness unusual events as the result of Mr. Shiftlet's journey, ultimately, Mr. Shiftlet is the character whose life needs saving.

CONCLUSION

Scholars from all schools of literary criticism have analyzed Flannery O'Connor's works, exploring, among other observations, the distinct writing techniques, unique characters, and recurring patterns in her seemingly simple yet complex plots that carry meaning both on and beneath the surface. Additionally, they address O'Connor's themes of Christian grace, as well as her depictions of Southern culture, her images of freaks and the grotesque, her use of humor and satire, and her portrayals of epiphanies, class hierarchies, violence, and race relations. Her fiction is included in almost every volume of American short stories and her stories are commonly studied in university classes. The massive volume of critical attention given to O'Connor reflects her importance as an American writer and solidifies her position in the American literary canon.

One of American's finest short story writers, Flannery O'Connor built her work on a solid tradition and provided groundwork for future writers. Recognized both for her contributions to the short story as well as for her influence on the evolution of the short story, she is among only a handful of authors acclaimed more as short story writers than as novelists.

Selected Bibliography

WORKS OF FLANNERY O'CONNOR

NOVELS

Wise Blood. New York: Harcourt, Brace, 1952.

The Violent Bear It Away. New York: Farrar, Straus and Giroux, 1960.

SHORT STORY COLLECTIONS

A Good Man Is Hard to Find and Other Stories. New York: Harcourt, Brace, 1955.

Everything That Rises Must Converge. New York: Farrar, Straus and Giroux, 1965.

The Complete Stories. New York: Farrar, Straus and Giroux, 1971.

OTHER WORKS

Mystery and Manners: Occasional Prose. Edited by Sally Fitzgerald and Robert Fitzgerald. New York: Farrar, Straus and Giroux, 1969.

The Habit of Being: The Letters of Flannery O'Connor. Edited by Sally Fitzgerald. New York: Farrar, Straus and Giroux, 1979.

The Presence of Grace and Other Book Reviews. Compiled by Leo J. Zuber. Athens: University of Georgia Press, 1983.

Conversations with Flannery O'Connor. With Rosemary M. Magee. Jackson: University Press of Mississippi, 1987.

Flannery O'Connor: Collected Works. New York: Library of America, 1988.

Flannery O'Connor: The Cartoons. With Barry Moser and Kelly Gerald. Seattle: Fantagraphics, 2012.

A Prayer Journal. Edited by William A. Sessions. New York: Farrar, Straus and Giroux, 2013.

CRITICAL AND BIOGRAPHICAL STUDIES

Basselin, Timothy J. *Flannery O'Connor: Writing a Theology of Disabled Humanity.* Waco, Tex.: Baylor University Press, 2013.

Boyagoda, Randy. "A Patriotic Deus ex Machina in Flannery O'Connor's 'The Displaced Person.'" *Southern Literary Journal* 43, no. 1:59–74 (2010).

Brinkmeyer, Robert H. *The Art & Vision of Flannery O'Connor.* Baton Rouge: Louisiana State University Press, 1993.

Cash, Jean W. *Flannery O'Connor: A Life.* Knoxville: University of Tennessee Press, 2002.

Coles, Robert. *Flannery O'Connor's South.* Baton Rouge: Louisiana State University Press, 1980.

Coulthard, A. R. "From Sermon to Parable: Four Conversion Stories by Flannery O'Connor." *American Literature* 55:55–71 (1983).

Eggenschwiler, David. *The Christian Humanism of Flannery O'Connor.* Detroit: Wayne State University Press, 1972.

Farmer, David R. *Flannery O'Connor: A Descriptive Bibliography.* New York: Garland, 1981.

Fickett, Harold, and Douglas R. Gilbert. *Flannery O'Connor: Images of Grace.* Grand Rapids, Mich.: Eerdmans, 1986.

Flora, Joseph M. "Desire, Faith, and Flannery O'Connor." *Mississippi Quarterly* 67:327–333 (2014).

Friedman, Melvin J., and Beverly Lyon Clark. *Critical Essays on Flannery O'Connor.* Boston: G. K. Hall, 1985.

Gentry, Marshall Bruce. *Flannery O'Connor's Religion of the Grotesque.* Jackson: University Press of Mississippi, 1986.

Giannone, Richard. *Flannery O'Connor and the Mystery of Love.* Urbana: University of Illinois Press, 1989.

Gooch, Brad. *Flannery: A Life of Flannery O'Connor.* New York: Little, Brown, 2009.

Gretlund, Jan Nordby, and Karl-Heinz Westarp. *Flannery O'Connor's Radical Reality.* Columbia: University of South Carolina Press, 2006.

Grimshaw, James A. *The Flannery O'Connor Companion.* Westport, Conn.: Greenwood Press, 1981.

Hardy, Donald E. *Narrating Knowledge in Flannery O'Connor's Fiction.* Columbia: University of South Carolina Press, 2003.

Kirk, Connie Ann. *Critical Companion to Flannery O'Connor.* New York: Facts on File, 2007.

Kreyling, Michael. *New Essays on "Wise Blood."* Cambridge, U.K.: Cambridge University Press, 1995.

Morel, Lucas E. "Bound for Glory: The Gospel of Racial Reconciliation in Flannery O'Connor's 'The Artificial Nigger.'" *Perspectives on Political Science* 34, no. 4:202–210 (2005).

Park, Clara Claiborne. "Crippled Laughter: Toward Understanding Flannery O'Connor." *American Scholar* 51:249–257 (1982).

Paulson, Suzanne Morrow. *Flannery O'Connor: A Study of the Short Fiction.* Boston: Twayne, 1988.

Pinkerton, Steve. "Profaning the American Religion: Flannery O'Connor's *Wise Blood.*" *Studies in the Novel* 43: 449–469 (2011).

Pollack, Eileen. "Flannery O'Connor and the New Criticism: A Response to Mark McGurl." *American Literary History* 19:546–556 (2007).

Prown, Katherine Hemple. *Revising Flannery O'Connor: Southern Literary Culture and the Problem of Female Authorship.* Charlottesville: University Press of Virginia, 2001.

Rath, Sura Prasad, and Mary Neff Shaw. *Flannery O'Connor: New Perspectives.* Athens: University of Georgia Press, 1996.

Robillard, Douglas. *The Critical Response to Flannery O'Connor.* Westport, Conn.: Praeger, 2004.

Scott, R. Neil. *Flannery O'Connor: An Annotated Reference Guide to Criticism.* Milledgeville, Ga.: Timberlane, 2002.

Srigley, Susan. *Dark Faith: New Essays on Flannery O'Connor's "The Violent Bear It Away."* Notre Dame, Ind.: University of Notre Dame Press, 2012.

Walters, Dorothy. *Flannery O'Connor.* New York: Twayne, 1973.

Whitt, Margaret Earley. *Understanding Flannery O'Connor.* Columbia: University of South Carolina Press, 1995.

Williams, Melvin G. "Black and White: A Study in Flannery O'Connor's Characters." *Black American Literature Forum* 10, no. 4:130–132 (1976).

FILMS BASED ON THE WORKS OF FLANNERY O'CONNOR

The Life You Save May Be Your Own. Screenplay by Nelson Gidding. Directed by Herschel Daugherty. Schlitz Playhouse of Stars, 1957.

Good Country People. Screenplay by Jeffrey F. Jackson. Directed by Jeffrey F. Jackson. Taos Land & Film, 1976.

Wise Blood. Screenplay by Benedict Fitzgerald. Directed by John Huston. Anthea Films, 1980.

EDGAR ALLAN POE

(1809—1849)

Jonas Prida

MORE THAN TWO centuries after his birth, Edgar Allan Poe remains one of America's most celebrated authors. Poems such as "The Raven" and short stories such as "The Fall of the House of Usher" and "The Tell-Tale Heart" are embedded in American popular culture. His life of poverty, drink, and sadness mixed with his own hopes of editorial success and artistic attainment. His marriage to a sickly younger cousin, while not unusual for the time, became a template for many literary romances. Circumstances around his death remain mysterious, and misinformation and outright fabrications about his life still circulate. Skilled enough as an author to create the detective story and bring an American flair to the gothic, he was also his own worst enemy, picking fights with successful editors and foolishly befriending the American literary critic and editor Rufus Griswold, whose is most responsible for propagating the image of Poe as a drunken, drug-using deviant.

Poe's writing career coincides with the dynamic growth of American cities and American publishing in the first half of the nineteenth century. In his stays in Boston, New York, and Philadelphia, Poe was at the center of a sweeping print revolution. Magazines, journals, and newspapers mushroomed as the demand for information and entertainment grew. Some periodicals lasted for one issue, some for decades, but all needed content and editors; Poe fulfilled both roles, ably in some cases but not in others. He had a sensitivity for giving the public what it wanted, often using his knowledge to participate in hoaxes at these same readers' expense.

Poe's reputation with other writers of the period was mixed: Ralph Waldo Emerson (1803–1882) called him "the jingle-man," and James Russell Lowell (1819–1891) coined the memorable "There comes Poe, with his raven, like Barnaby Rudge, Three fifths of him genius and two fifths sheer fudge." Poe's readership, however, never waned, even during periods of critical dismissal. Collected edition of his works began soon after his death and continue to this day. Fellow antebellum luminaries like Nathaniel Hawthorne (1804–1864) and Herman Melville (1819–1891) remain in academic circulation, but Poe's grip on the popular imagination has never wavered.

BIOGRAPHY

Edgar Poe was born in Boston on January 19, 1809, to parents who were involved in the acting profession. His mother, Elizabeth Arnold Hopkins Poe, was an actress of some note, and his father, David Poe, Jr., while less successful on stage, managed to gather small roles. In an almost literary foreshadowing of Poe's extremely literary life, his mother's first dramatic performance was in a gothic melodrama, *The Mysteries of the Castle*. David Poe's father, David Poe, Sr., was well known in Baltimore because of his Revolutionary War service, earning him the honorary nickname "General." David Poe, Jr., abandoned his wife and infant son by 1810, and in Richmond, Virginia, on December 8, 1811, Elizabeth Poe died, leaving Edgar; his older brother, William Henry Leonard (known as Henry); and a younger sister, Rosalie. William was taken in by David Poe, Sr.; Rosalie went to live with a Richmond family, and Edgar joined the household of John Allan, a well-to-do but childless merchant.

The Allans had business interests in England, and the family lived in Scotland and the area surrounding London until returning to the United

States in 1820. While in boarding school near London, Poe learned French, studied history and literature, and began writing. According to his headmaster, "'Edgar Allan was a quick and clever boy and would have been a very good boy if he had not been spoilt by his parents" (Quinn, pp. 71–72). Difficult economic circumstances and the poor health of Mrs. Allan forced the 1820 return of the family to the United States, and Poe enrolled in private schools to continue his education. Poe's place in the household was a tentative one; he was never officially adopted by the Allans, and, as Poe moved through adolescence, his relationship with John Allan became strained. In 1826, Poe enrolled at the University of Virginia; in less than a year, however, he left the university because of money problems that included gambling debts and unpaid tuition. This combination led to a near complete estrangement between Poe and John Allan, with Poe writing in a letter that "it was wholly and entirely your own mistaken parsimony that caused all the difficulties" (Quinn, p. 110).

After briefly working in Boston, Poe took the step of joining the U.S. Army, enlisting under the assumed name of Edgar A. Perry, as well as changing his birth year to appear older. In that same year, 1827, Poe also published his first work, *Tamerlane and Other Poems.* The volume passed with little notice, and meanwhile Poe discovered that regular army life was not to his liking. The 1829 death of Mrs. Allan gave Poe a reason to recontact John Allan, and the combination of Allan's political connections and money opened a place at the U.S. Military Academy at West Point for Poe. Poe also published his second poetry collection in 1829: *Al Aaraaf, Tamerlane, and Minor Poems.* In 1830, Poe enrolled at West Point, but by 1831, he was already planning on leaving, eventually being court-martialed for missing roll calls and classes. His dismissal led to his final break with John Allan. In April 1831, he published his third collection, *Poems,* which contained an early version of the later classic, "To Helen."

In 1831, Poe moved to Baltimore and into the Clemm household, relations on his father's side, where he would meet young Virginia Clemm, who eventually became his wife. His older brother, Henry, died in early August of the same year. Poe's falling out with his father, and his inability to find steady work, led to the first of many struggles with poverty. By 1832, however, he was placing short pieces in the *Philadelphia Saturday Courier,* and over the course of the next two years, he published frequently in literary magazines and mass-circulation papers. In October 1833, his story "The Manuscript Found in a Bottle" won first place in a Baltimore writing contest, and Poe became acquainted with the influential writer and editor John Pendleton Kennedy, who helped Poe land later editorial positions. In 1834, John Allan died; Allan's will left nothing to Poe and made no mention of his foster son.

Poe gained his first professional post in 1835, as assistant editor at the *Southern Literary Messenger* in Richmond. On September 22 of the same year, he took out a marriage license with Virginia Clemm, his thirteen-year-old cousin. While much has been made about the age difference in the marriage, all the surviving correspondence between Poe and Virginia or Poe and Virginia's mother (Maria Poe Clemm, his aunt) showed a loving, dutiful relationship that lasted until Virginia's death in 1847. However, Poe's self-destructive streak appeared during his time at the *Messenger,* and he was temporarily fired for drinking on the job. He was later rehired, and he remained editor until early 1837, helping boost the *Messenger*'s circulation, as well as enhancing his own reputation as a writer and a critic.

Poe moved Virginia and Mrs. Clemm to New York City, hoping for more permanent work, but the Panic of 1837 made getting any employment difficult. Poe used this time to work on his only novel, *The Narrative of Arthur Gordon Pym,* published in 1838 to mixed reviews. By 1839, Poe and his family were living in Philadelphia, with Poe working as an assistant editor at *Burton's Gentleman's Magazine.* While at *Burton's,* Poe published his classic "The Fall of the House of Usher," and "William Wilson" appeared in a Baltimore periodical, *The Gift.* By 1840, he had fallen out of favor with *Burton's,* but Poe's first collection of short stories, the two-volume *Tales of the Grotesque and Arabesque* (which included "Wilson" and "Usher," as well as less-well-known pieces such as "The Man Who Was Used Up") was published in that year. Poe was criticized for his allegiance to the German school of writing, to which he responded in the introduction, "If in many of my productions terror has been the thesis, I maintain that terror is not of Germany, but of the soul." Poe was hired by another Philadelphia magazine, *Graham's,* where he started work in 1841. *Graham's* published Poe's "The Murders in the Rue Morgue" in April 1841, arguably the first modern detective story. During the two years he worked at *Graham's,* Poe published "Masque of the Red Death," among other short stories, as well as his most famous piece of literary criticism, a review of Nathaniel Hawthorne's *Twice-Told Tales* (which had been published in two volumes, the first in 1837 and the second in 1842), outlining Poe's conception of artistic unity and effect.

In January 1842, Virginia Clemm broke a blood vessel while singing, leading Poe to fear for her life. His drinking habit became worse. Much of the year was spent looking for permanent work, worrying about Virginia's declining health, and publishing. The same year, angling for a government job, he used his connections to obtain an interview with members of the John Tyler administration. On the day of the meeting, Poe was ill, either from an actual sickness or a hangover, and nothing came of the arrangement. Poe also met Rufus Griswold in 1842, an encounter that would affect Poe's legacy for more than a hundred years.

Over the next three years, Poe would move to New York City again, editing and owning the *Broadway Journal*; he would publish "The Purloined Letter" in 1844 and "The Raven" in 1845; and engage in a pointless literary feud with the eminent American poet Henry Wadsworth Longfellow (1807–1882). In 1845, Poe published another short story collection, *Tales,* which included many of his best works and generated enough sales to have publishers interested in another poetry collection. Despite this success, Poe was desperately poor, consistently asking editors, friends, and other writers for money. Of greater personal note was the health of Virginia, problems exacerbated by a poverty so ingrained that she was only kept warm by Poe's greatcoat and a cat. One contemporary account said of Virginia that "her pale face, her brilliant eyes, and her raven hair gave her an unearthly look. One felt that she was almost a disrobed spirit, and when she coughed it was made certain that she was rapidly passing away" (Quinn, p. 508). Virginia Clemm Poe died on January 30, 1847, in the Poe house in what is now the Bronx.

After Virginia's death, Poe continued working on *Eureka,* his prose poem on creativity published in 1848, and traveling to meet various literary women who were interested in him. It is difficult to evaluate these later relationships. Some, like his relationship with the poet Sarah Helen Whitman, which nearly ended in marriage, were legitimate; others were of a more mercenary quality. In an effort to revive his career, he returned to Richmond, where he gave lectures from his essay "The Poetic Principle" and tried to drum up interest for his own magazine.

Poe's last days remain largely a mystery, despite 150 years of investigation. Leaving Richmond to go to Baltimore on September 27, 1849, Poe was not seen again until October 3, when he was found, according to a letter to his friend Dr. J. E. Snodgrass, "rather the worse for wear" (Quinn, p. 638). Snodgrass took Poe to the Washington College Hospital, where he slipped in and out of delirium. On Sunday, October 7, Poe died, silencing a seminal American voice. Medical records from the period are nonexistent, as is Poe's death certificate. Theories surrounding Poe's death abound, ranging from alcohol poisoning to rabies and diabetes to "cooping," an antebellum voting fraud method where citizens were kidnapped, moved from precinct to precinct, and kept in line with liquor and physical violence. Barring the uncovering of heretofore unknown evidence, the mystery of Poe's death is unlikely to be solved.

Despite the untimely end to his life and career, Poe's importance in American literature is inarguable. His detective tale "The Murders in the Rue Morgue," with his amateur sleuth C. Auguste Dupin, created a template followed by Arthur Conan Doyle in creating Sherlock Holmes. His "Cask of Amontillado" and "The Fall of the House of Usher" helped give gothic fiction an American face. His "The Balloon Hoax" and "The Gold Bug" took advantage of expanding newspaper readership to "humbug" his audience, creating hoaxes that infuriated and at the same time delighted his readers. In his more than sixty short pieces—the exact number depends on how rewrites and resubmissions are calculated—Poe shaped the American literary landscape. Since 1951, the Mystery Writers of America have given the annual Edgar Allan Poe award to honor works deemed the year's best short mystery or detective fiction, and calling a writer "Poe-like" is understood to denote a mixture of psychological torment and gothic trappings. Poe's short fiction remains central the American literary canon, both reflecting the antebellum culture that produced it and enchanting the twenty-first-century world that continues to read it.

DETECTIVE TALES

Although Poe only wrote three pure detective stories—and one other, "The Man of the Crowd" that closely resembles one—these stories' influence was immediate and long-lasting. Poe's use of a highly analytic, but imaginative, amateur detective together with a less-brilliant sidekick, investigating a case that seems unsolvable, only to have the case turn on one clue, is the model for 150 years of detective and mystery fiction. Poe's urban mysteries, brilliant dilettantes, and well-meaning but hapless police are the parts to an American original subgenre.

Poe was not the first American writer to place solving a crime at the center of a text—that honor that might go to Charles Brockden Brown's *Wieland; or, The Transformation* (1798) or Brown's short story "Somnambulism" (1805)—but Poe is undoubtedly the author who popularized "tales of ratiocination," as he called them. Starting with "The Murders in the Rue Morgue" in April 1841, Poe's detective uses his powers of analysis, deduction, and ingenuity to solve crimes ranging from stolen letters to double murders.

While working as an assistant editor for Philadelphia's *Graham's Magazine,* Poe published his short story "The Murders in the Rue Morgue," introducing C. Auguste Dupin, Poe's protagonist through his three most famous detective stories. Told from the point of view of an unnamed narrator, Dupin is first described as a young man "of an excellent—indeed of an illustrious family, but, by a variety of untoward events, had been reduced to such poverty that the energy of his character succumbed beneath it, and he ceased to bestir himself in the world, or to care for the retrieval of his fortunes" (*Collected Works of Edgar Allan Poe,* vol. 2, 1978, p. 531). Quickly becoming friends with the narrator through a shared love of books and solitude, Dupin displays "a peculiar analytic ability" and claims "most men, in respect to himself, wore windows in their bosom" (p. 533).

The narrator and Dupin find that their talents are needed after they read about a hideous double murder on Rue Morgue. Madame L'Espanaye and her daughter are found dead, with the mother's body shoved feet first up a chimney and the daughter nearly decapitated. The newspaper gives contradictory accounts from witnesses, who each heard a different language during the time of the crime. Intrigued by the mystery, and confident that "truth is not always in a well. In fact, as regards the more important knowledge, I do believe that she is invariably superficial" (p. 544), Dupin uses his combination of imagination and analysis to find the superficial clues—a ribbon, a broken nail, an outsized handprint—that the police have missed. From these he pieces together the crime. After planting a notice about the capture of an ape in a maritime paper and confronting a sailor who comes to retrieve it, Dupin solves the mystery. The murderer was not human; instead, it is an escaped "ourang-outang," capable of mimicking a variety of languages because of its time spent on a merchant ship. Gaining entrance to the apartment by swinging from a lightning rod into an open window, the animal surprised and killed the mother-daughter pair.

Despite the story's popularity, Poe remained somewhat mystified by the response to it. In a letter to his friend Philip Pendleton Cooke, he wrote, "Where is the ingenuity of unravelling a web which you yourself (the author) have woven for the express purpose of unravelling?" (p. 521). Filled with graphic violence along with philosophic speculation—including his famous pronouncement that "the ingenious are always fanciful, and the *truly* imaginative never otherwise than analytic" (p. 531)—"Murders" brought together various cultural anxieties about urban anonymity and growing cities, as well as the rise of the popular press. The information of the crime is circulated through various newspapers, and Dupin sets the trap for the orangutan's owner in the paper. Additionally, Poe's story itself circulated in similar papers to the fictional ones in "Murder."

Papers and letters also feature prominently in "The Purloined Letter," published in the September 1844 issue of *The Gift.* Again featuring Dupin and the unnamed narrator, "The Purloined Letter" focuses on the theft of "a certain document of the last importance" (*Collected Works,* vol. 3, 1978, p. 976) that threatens the personal reputation of the powerful original owner. Brought into the case by the Parisian police, and not disinterested in the reward of fifty thousand francs, Dupin uses his powers of ingenuity and analysis to find the stolen letter. Little action takes place; most of the text explores how the police spent their time looking for the letter in intricate hiding places of the suspect's apartment. They look for it in table legs, under floorboards, and behind mirrors. But Dupin's method is similar to his method in "Murders"; he knows that the truth is more likely to hide in plain sight than in any hidden place. Upon gaining entry into the same apartment that the police have scrutinized, Dupin focuses his attention on the most commonplace articles. He notices a smudged letter thrown casually into a rack, a disarray unlike the rest of the apartment. After orchestrating a return visit, complete with the distraction of a gunshot in the street, he retrieves the purloined letter, leaving in its place a duplicate containing a classical insult.

Poe said of this story that "'The Purloined Letter' ... is perhaps the best of my tales of ratiocination" (*The Collected Letters of Edgar Allan Poe,* vol. 1, p. 258), and, although lacking in the action of his other detective tales, it crystallizes Poe's analytic methodology and powers of identification. In the text's most famous passage, Poe uses the example of boys playing "odds or evens," where one player guesses if the other player has an odd or even amount of marbles in hand. The most successful players are those who have "an identification of the reasoner's intellect with that of his opponent" (*Collected Works,* vol. 3, p. 984). Dupin uses this same tactic to find the stolen letter. The problem with the police's search was that they looked in places where they would have hidden the letter, instead of thinking where the thief would have hidden the letter. Identifying with the criminal leads one to think like a criminal, increasing the chance of solving the crime. With Dupin, Poe creates the figure of the criminal profiler, a figure that features prominently in the contemporary imagination.

Since the time of Poe's pioneering tales, hundreds of Dupin clones have found their way into popular detective fiction, and the identification with the criminal mind has become central to the modern recasting of sleuthing. Directly engaging sensational (actual) crimes of the early 1840s, at a time that coincided with the expansion of the reading public, Poe shaped this raw material into narratives that rise above the true crime stories of the period. His detective stories would have secured his place in American letters even if he had written nothing else. But detective material is not the only genre he helped define.

TALES OF HORROR, THE GROTESQUE, AND THE ARABESQUE

Even more than Poe's detective stories, his tales of horror and terror cemented his place in the American imagination. His one-eyed vengeful cat ("The Black Cat"), ax murderer ("The Tell-Tale Heart"), and deranged, teeth-collecting lover ("Berenice") maintain their place in high school curriculums, as well as providing material for countless movies, television shows, and comic books. Growing out of his love for the "German school" (as it was called by critics of the period),

Poe's gothic stories that mix psychological nuance with otherworldly experiences shaped the American literary scene.

Poe's "The Fall of the House of Usher," for example, uses dreary landscapes, crumbling houses, and an unstable cast of characters. Published in the September 1839 issue of *Burton's,* it opens with "I had been passing alone, on horseback, through a singularly dreary tract of country; and at length found myself, as the shades of the evening drew on, within view of the melancholy House of Usher" (*Collected Works,* vol. 2, p. 397). This dreary tract of land, dominated by the hereditary house of the Usher family, reflects the later distressed psychological state of the owners, as does the "barely perceptible fissure, which, extending from the roof of the building in front, made its way down the wall in a zigzag direction" (p. 400). The first-person narrator, a childhood friend of Roderick Usher, finds that Usher suffers from "a morbid acuteness" (p. 403) of the senses, eating only the blandest food and wearing the most comfortable clothes. Even worse, his twin sister, Madeline, suffers from bouts of catalepsy, a disorder where sleep is deep enough to mimic death, as well as a wasting disease.

During his visit, the narrator finds that Roderick is also given to philosophical speculations about the sentience of all matter, and the creation of wild art, at one point observing that "if ever mortal painted an idea, that mortal was Roderick Usher" (p. 405). As disturbing for the narrator is the sudden death and entombment of Madeline, which leads to the story's conclusion. In the middle of a wild storm, Roderick and the narrator hear banging at the door; when it swings open, they are faced with "the lofty and enshrouded figure of the lady Madeline of Usher" with "blood upon her white robes, and the evidence of some bitter struggle upon every portion of her emaciated frame" (p. 416). Madeline and Roderick collapse in an embrace of death, and the narrator escapes the "mighty halls rushing asunder—there was a long tumultuous shouting sound like the voice of a thousand waters—and the deep and dank tarn at my feet closed sullenly and silently over the fragments of the '*House of Usher*'" (p. 417).

"The Fall of the House of Usher" is a nearly perfect piece of gothic literature, displaying a unity of form and theme seldom equaled. Details such as the line from the embedded poem, "The Haunted Palace," reading "But evil things, in robes of sorrow, // Assailed the monarch's high estate" echo Usher's shaky mental condition (p. 407). The opening description of the "barely perceptible fissure" (p. 400) returns as the fissure widens and the house collapses into the tarn. Both Roderick and Madeline are childless, and their deaths are the literal fall of the house of Usher. Even the tarn that reflects the house acts as a mirror to the twinning of Roderick and Madeline, and the house's eventual submersion beneath the surface of the lake mirrors the final burial of the Usher line. Praise for, and reprinting of, this story started almost immediately; for example, "The Fall of the House of Usher" is found in *Bentley's Miscellany,* edited by Charles Dickens in 1840.

"Ligeia," published in the September 1838 issue of *American Museum* and included in the 1840 *Tales of the Grotesque and Arabesque,* was Poe's choice for his best work. Writing to the editor Evert Duyckink in early 1846, Poe says the tale is "undoubtedly the best story I have written" (*The Collected Letters of Edgar Allan Poe,* vol. 2, p. 309), and it is not surprising he felt that way. Mixing several of his favorite themes—a beautiful woman's death, the potential for souls to exist after death, fragile psychological states—with the artistic unity that Poe considered the goal of all successful fiction, "Ligeia" deserves Poe's pride in the tale.

"Ligeia" follows the meeting, wooing, and marriage of a man—another of Poe's unnamed narrators—to the Lady Ligeia, a tall, slender, pale woman with startlingly white teeth and eyes "the most brilliant of black" (*Collected Works,* vol. 2, p. 313). In addition to her physical charms, she possesses a powerful intellect: "I have spoken of the learning of Ligeia: it was immense—such as I have never known in woman" (p. 315). Speaking almost all European languages and many ancient ones, Ligeia quickly entrances the narrator and the two are married.

But as is the case in Poe's gothic tales, the marriage does not last. Ligeia is sickened by an unknown disease. Before she dies, her last words are "man doth not yield him to the angels, nor unto death utterly, save only through the weakness of his feeble will" (p. 319). Crushed by his love's death, the narrator buys a decaying abbey in a deserted part of England and, "in a moment of mental alienation" (pp. 320–321), he marries the decidedly un-Ligeia-like Lady Rowena Trevanion. The second marriage is doomed from the start: the narrator, addicted to opium, wanders the halls of the abbey, calling out Ligeia's name. Lady Rowena sickens and by the end of the second month of marriage is nearly dead. At this point the narrator suspects supernatural forces at work. He sees a shadow in Rowena's chamber as she is dying, and later, when looking at Rowena's corpse, he notices that her teeth are whiter, she has grown taller, and her hair is a different color. In the final lines, he is forced to admit what he has thought to be true: "'Here then, at least,' I shrieked aloud, 'can I never—can I never be mistaken—these are the full, and the black, and the wild eyes of my lost love—of the lady—of the LADY LIGEIA!'" (p. 330).

"Ligeia" is a masterwork of misdirection, subtle horror, mystical allusions, and brooding romance. Neither narrator nor reader knows much about Ligeia's background; Poe focuses on her appearance, using various parts of her anatomy to hint at her past. The narrator cannot even remember where he met Ligeia, stating in the opening lines, "I cannot, for my soul, remember how, when, or even precisely where, I first became acquainted with the lady Ligeia" (p. 310). Her expansive knowledge covers "studies but little sought—but less known" (p. 316), and her final words about the human will's power to cheat death set up the story's second half. The abbey's wedding chamber is steeped in mystical trappings: the room is a pentangle, and each of its angles is occupied by a "gigantic sarcophagus of black granite," looted from Luxor (p. 322). Readers can never be sure of what the narrator is recounting; his opium addiction colors everything he sees, hears, and remembers. It is not until the tale's final lines that any definite change is stated. It is only through the eyes, the same eyes that first bewitched the narrator, that he knows for sure that Ligeia's will has triumphed over death, a triumph at the cost of another life.

Another brilliantly executed and oft-anthologized Poe story is "The Cask of Amontillado," published by *Godey's Magazine and Lady's Book* in November 1846. A tale of revenge and its aftereffects, "The Cask" ironically combines the setting of carnival with the meticulously planned murder of the unfortunately named Fortunado. Montresor, the murderous narrator, opens the story vowing revenge for an unnamed insult; however, to complete his plan, "I must not only punish, but punish with impunity" (*Collected Works,* vol. 3, p. 1256). Knowing Fortunado's knowledge of wine, Montresor sets the trap. Claiming to have purchased a pipe of the rare wine Amontillado, he asks Fortunado to confirm its authenticity by joining him in his wine cellar, located in the catacombs beneath Montresor's house. Leading the unsuspecting Fortunado deep into the vaults, Montresor eventually chains Fortunado in a niche in the wall. But chaining is not enough of a vengeance; Montressor then walls Fortunado into the niche, hearing only the weakening cries of "For the love of God, Montresor" (p. 1263). The story ends with another powerful irony: "Against the new masonry I re-erected the old rampart of bones. For the half of a century no mortal has disturbed them. *In páce requiescat!*" (p. 1263). While Fortunado has been resting in death, Montresor's conscience is the one that clearly cannot rest.

"The Cask" is filled with a wide range of ironies—one of the reasons it continues to be studied and taught. Fortunado, whose name roughly translates into "fortunate," is anything but. As the two men descend into the vaults, Fortunado starts coughing, but in response to Montresor's feigned concern, he states, "The cough is a mere nothing; it will not kill me. I shall not die of a cough" (p. 1259). The two exchange jokes around Freemasonry, prefiguring Montresor's later use of a trowel in walling Fortunado up. Even the name of a wine they share, De Grâve, plays on the later fate of Fortunado. Of course, it is the final lines of "The Cask" that carry the most ironic weight. There is no resting in peace for Montresor; fifty years after the murder, he still dwells on it. His desire to punish with impunity has been thwarted, and Montresor's guilt around the murder undermines his family's motto, *Nemo me impune lacessit,* which translates into "No one provokes me with impunity."

HOAXES AND DARK HUMOR

To see Poe only as a writer of gothic tales or detective stories is to ignore a large part of his total work. Befitting a writer deeply involved in the cultural conversations of antebellum America, many of Poe's other texts use contemporary touchstones, fads, and events as the raw material for dark humor and satire.

For example, Poe's "Hop-Frog; or, The Eight Chained Ourang-Outangs" mixes anxieties about slave revolts with ludicrous situations occurring in a far-off country, allowing Poe, and his readership, to displace these same concerns. Published in the March 1849 issue of the *Flag of Our Union,* "Hop-Frog" centers around the revenge of the titular character, who works as a jester in an unnamed court. But Hop-Frog is not an ordinary jester: "His value was trebled in the eyes of the king, by the fact of his being also a dwarf and a cripple" (*Collected Works,* vol. 3, p. 1345). Sporting a pair of deformed legs, which cause him to walk with an "interjectional gait—something between a leap and a wriggle" (p. 1346), and endowed with tremendous upper-body strength, Hop-Frog is a figure of ridicule and jest. His only friend in the court is the equally small, but beautiful, Trippetta, who uses her position to protect Hop-Frog from the worst of the king's japes.

The opportunity for revenge comes in the form of a masquerade. Hop-Frog and Trippetta are called before the king, who wants ideas for the party. He forces Hop-Frog to drink and, as a final insult, pushes Tippetta to the floor, throwing wine in her face. Hop-Frog regains his wits, convincing the king and his seven ministers to dress as orangutans, complete with chains on their wrists, so "the resemblance shall be so striking, that the company of masqueraders will take you for real beasts" (p. 1350). Creating their costumes out of flammable flax and tar, Hop-Frog leads the unsuspecting eight to a grisly end. Linking their chains to a chandelier in the middle of courtroom, he uses his prodigious strength to pull the costumed king and his ministers high above the floor. After lighting them on fire, Hop-Frog announces to the crowd, "I am simply Hop-Frog, the jester—and *this is my last jest*" (p. 1354). As flax and tar burn, leaving a "fetid, blackened, hideous, and indistinguishable mass," Hop-Frog and Trippetta escape through the roof.

Written, according to a letter of Poe's, "to get out of my pecuniary difficulties" (p. 1344), "Hop-Frog" is a bizarre mixture of grotesque characters, gruesome vengeance, and social anxiety. Trippetta and Hop-Frog are sideshow characters: Trippetta's skill as a ballerina and Hop-Frog's strongman act could be in one of the itinerant shows touring America. The king is equally grotesque, both reveling in a good jest and willing to laugh at a crippled man and throw wine in a woman's face. Poe tars and feathers the king and his ministers, a tactic used against both antislavery activists and slaves themselves. The cultural commonplace linking African Americans to apes is at play as well; the faux orangutans are chained together and their ferocity frightens the rest of the masquerade goers.

Poe also loved to tweak and deceive his audiences, as seen in his stories like "The Gold Bug" and "The Balloon Hoax." The latter, published in April 1844, used the growing interest in balloon flight to posit an intercontinental flight from England to South Carolina. Opening with a false account from Charleston, South Carolina, about a balloon landing, and including a technical section explaining the workings of the balloon itself, complete with discussions of the screw powering the craft and details on the construction material, the story is the supposed journal entry of the flight. Originally the balloon's path was to Europe, but prevailing winds and occasional accidents shifted the craft's direction toward America. After seventy-five hours of flight, the balloon dropped its grappling hook on the sandy beaches of South Carolina.

"The Balloon Hoax" was presented to New York audiences as an actual event, and previously circulating plans to cross the Atlantic by balloon made the publication less outrageous. The *Extra Sun,* which published the article, had also published "The Moon Hoax" in 1835, creating a sensation that added thousands of readers, and it hoped that Poe's story would do the same. However, Poe's story was not as successful, with Poe himself commenting in his column "Doings from Gotham" that "the more intelligent believed, while the rabble, for the most part, rejected the whole with disdain," and by April 15, the *Sun* printed a retraction, stating "We are inclined to believe that the intelligence is erroneous" (*Collected Works,* vol. 3, p. 1067). Poe's interest in playing against his readership's expectations, and his willingness to alienate an audience as a gamble to gather a larger one, would follow him throughout his career.

POETRY

Like many American writers of his era, Poe's first interest was poetry. Conversant in the classical poets, as well as writers such as the seventeenth-century author John Milton, Poe saw verse as embodying aesthetic principles of balance, unity, and effect. Starting with his first piece, written when he was fifteen years old and consisting of two lines, Poe wrote more than ninety poems during his lifetime, alternating his usual themes of unrequited love, early death, and psychological torment with more philosophical explorations of science, history, and existence.

In 1827, a forty-page collection, *Tamerlane and Other Poems,* was published, with the author simply named as "A Bostonian." The volume attracted almost no notice, simply listed as a publication in the *North American Review,* and only twelve copies are known to exist. Yet *Tamerlane* contains the seeds of later, more acclaimed work. For example, "The Lake," considered by the Poe scholar Thomas Mabbott as "the best of Poe's early poems" (*Collected Works,* vol. 1, 1969, p. 82), has the narrator visiting a wild lake where "So lovely was the loneliness" (p. 85). As with much of Poe's poetry, "The Lake" works through a series of associations and subtleties, and the twice-removed nature of the tale—the narrator imagines the death of the others—makes the poem as much about the narrator's psychological state as the fate of the imagined drowned couple.

Roughly two years later, Poe released a second collection, *Al Aaraaf, Tamerlane, and Minor Poems* (1829). Although many critics and readers were baffled by the title poem, with one calling it "pile of brick bats" (Quinn, p. 165), a few, including the influential editor Sarah Josepha Hale, wrote that the author "is evidently a fine genius, but he wants judgment, experience, tact" (p. 165). Of the poems in *Al Aaraaf,* the later-named "Sonnet—To Science" displays Poe's mixed feelings toward science and the practical arts animating much of antebellum America. Opening with the declaration that "Science! true daughter of Old Time thou art! Who alterest all things with thy peering eyes" (*Collected Works,* vol. 1, p. 91), and observing that science has "dragged Diana from her car" (p. 91), the providence of the poet allows for ignoring these facts when imagination and beauty are served. This interest in beauty over truth, as well as Poe's realization that long poems—"Al Aaraaf" runs 422 lines—work against his aesthetic principles, makes the collection of *Al Aaraaf* an important development for Poe's poetry.

Although Poe continued to produce poetry throughout the 1830s, including a collection simply titled *Poems* in 1831, his poetic output was embedded within his short stories such as "The Fall of the House of Usher" (with "The Haunted Palace") or appeared as individual poems in various literary magazines. In 1841, the Philadelphia *Saturday Chronicle* published "The Sleeper," a rewrite of the poem "Irene," first published in 1831. Poe thought highly of his piece, later writing, "In the higher qualities of poetry, it is better than 'The Raven'—but there is not one man in a million who could be brought to agree with me in this opinion" (*Collected Works,* vol. 1, p. 179). Poe is not wrong in his second phrase: although "The Sleeper" contains memorable lines such as "My love, she sleeps! Oh, may her sleep, / As it is lasting, so be deep! /

Soft may the worms about her creep!" (p. 188), neither the plot of a dead woman's beauty nor the poem's execution merit Poe's high praise of it.

The 1843 publication of "To Helen" in the Philadelphia *Saturday Museum* was the fruition of more than a decade's worth of revisions. Originally published in 1831, again in 1836, and again in 1841, this frequently anthologized poem, as published in its 1843 version, includes the famous lines "To the glory that was Greece, / And the grandeur that was Rome" (*Collected Works,* vol. 1, p. 166), revising a similar line found in all the other versions. James Russell Lowell, a frequent Poe commentator, saw the poem as being "like a Greek column, because of its perfection" (p. 164); "To Helen" links the beauty of Poe's own idealized Helen with the classical Helen, and both of these to past grandeurs. The Helen to whom the title refers is identified in an 1848 letter to another Helen, Helen Whitman, with whom Poe carried on an intellectual relationship. Poe writes, "the lines I had written, in my passionate boyhood, to the first, purely ideal love of my soul—to the Helen Stannard of whom I told you" (p. 164).

None of these poems had the impact of "The Raven," easily his most popular poem. As is the case with many of Poe's works, "The Raven" has a complex publication history. He first offered it to *Graham's* in Philadelphia, where it was refused, although his old employer charitably gave Poe fifteen dollars. He then successfully offered the piece to the New York City–based *American Review: A Whig Journal,* which bought it for less than twenty dollars (sources differ on the exact amount), and the poem was published in the journal's February 1845 issue under the pseudonym "Quarles." However, the first appearance of "The Raven" was in the January 29 issue of another New York periodical, N. P. Willis' *Evening Mirror,* printed from advance sheets of the *American Review.* Poe is named as the author, and Willis' praise of the piece is unqualified, calling it "unsurpassed in English poetry for subtle conception, masterly ingenuity of versification, and consistent, sustaining of imaginative lift and 'pokerishness'" (*Collected Works,* vol. 1, p. 361). Success was immediate; the poem was reprinted across the country, and, in another indication of its popularity, more than a dozen imitations and parodies of it circulated even before Poe's death.

"The Raven" starts with another of Poe's first-person narrators lamenting the death of "the rare and radiant maiden" Lenore (p. 365). Hearing a rapping on his door, the narrator is surprised when a raven enters his room, perching "upon a bust of Pallas" (p. 366), where it waits, silent except for occasionally croaking the word "nevermore." At first, the narrator assumes the bird's singular response is the result of "some unhappy master whom unmerciful Disaster / Followed fast and followed faster" (p. 367). Growing frustrated with the bird's oracular pronouncement concerning forgetfulness of Lenore's memory, the narrator accuses the raven of being a demon from "the Night's Plutonian shore," begging him to "Take thy beak from out my heart" (p. 369). The work ends with the raven sitting on its perch, "And his eyes have all the seeming of a demon's that is dreaming" as the narrator realizes the shadow on his soul caused by the death of Lenore "shall be lifted—nevermore" (p. 369).

One reason for the popularity of "The Raven" is its encapsulation of Poe's recurring themes: a despondent first-person narrator yearning for a lost love; the natural world reflecting the psychological state of the narrator; ambiguity about good and evil; an emotionally resonant, climactic ending line. The poem's formal qualities are a second reason for its popularity. An easily remembered rhyming pattern and repetition of some version of "nevermore" ending the last eight stanzas work together to make the poem accessible, both in the nineteenth century and now. To return to N. P. Willis' editorial upon printing the poem, "It will stick to the memory of everybody who reads it" (p. 361).

Poe's poetry resists categorization. Pieces such as "Annabel Lee," which Mabbott claimed "is widely recognized as one of the great lyric poems of the English language" (*Collected Works,* vol. 1, p. 468), mix with "Dream Within a Dream," Poe's questioning of external realities. From his first poetic stumblings as an unnamed Bostonian to his later fame in "The Raven," Poe grappled with the craft of poetics, in some cases rewriting his poems for more than a decade. Constantly searching for an organic mixture of form and content, Poe's poems, filled with longing and regret, remain some of American literature's best remembered and most insightful popular works.

ESSAYS AND CRITICISM

In addition to his contributions to poetry and short stories, Poe is one of nineteenth-century America's most insightful literary critics, if not also the most divisive. Known for starting literary feuds with some of the country's most successful writers and for a critical edge that earned him the nickname "The Tomahawk Man," Poe's newspaper articles, essays, and reviews placed him in the center of a rapidly changing publishing landscape. As the new country struggled to develop its own literary identity, Poe saw himself as a voice that would shape this identity. Despite his futile quest to start his own journal, Poe's writings on writing are important landmarks.

In April 1835, while at *Southern Literary Messenger,* Poe reviewed *Confessions of a Poet,* a book of poems by Laughton Osborn, a New York writer who claimed that he had loaded a pistol with the intention of killing himself after completing his collection. Unimpressed by the collection, Poe wrote, "A flash in the pan"—that is, were the pistol to misfire, and the suicide not succeed—"were a thing to be lamented. Indeed, there would be no answering for the consequences. We might even have a second series of the *Confessions*" (*Collected Works,* vol. 1, p. 459). In another issue, he savagely reviewed a novel by another New Yorker, Theodore S. Fay, claiming the work was the "most inestimable piece of balderdash with which the common sense of the good people of America was ever so openly or villainously insulted" (*Southern Literary Messenger,* December 1835, p. 56). These reviews did Poe no favors, since New York City was rapidly becoming America's publishing center and those insulted had long memories.

As Poe continued his itinerant career as an editor in the second half of the 1830s, he slowly developed his own aesthetic principles. Following on the English poet Samuel Taylor Coleridge's psychological discussions of art, Poe focused on questions of beauty in art, art's need to be divorced from moral values, and the importance of unity of artistic experience. Early in 1842, Poe published two reviews that brought together his ideas. The first appeared in the April issue of *Graham's,* where, in his discussion of the American poets Henry Wadsworth Longfellow and James Russell Lowell, Poe wrote "Beyond the limits of Beauty its [poetry's] province does not extend. Its sole arbiter is Taste. With the Intellect or with the Conscience it has only collateral relations. It has no dependence, unless incidentally, upon either Duty or *Truth*" (Quinn, p. 334). Breaking from traditional American critical thought that placed moral uplift at the center of literature, Poe argued that beauty and the appreciation of beauty through taste should provide the judgment for artistic worth.

Another review, of Nathaniel Hawthorne's collection *Twice-Told Tales,* has become a landmark in American criticism. Published in *Graham's* in May 1842, Poe outlined the unity of effect he saw as essential to effective writing: "We allude to the short prose narrative, requiring from a half-hour to one or two hours in its perusal" (Quinn, p. 335). Longer works require the readers to take breaks, destroying the suspension of disbelief, a concept Poe had taken from Coleridge. A careful writer, according to Poe, "fashioned his thoughts to accommodate his incidents; but having conceived, with deliberate care, a certain unique or single *effect* to be wrought out, he then invents such incidents—he then combines such events as may best aid him in establishing this preconceived effect" (Quinn, p. 335). The quest for the single effect should animate all decisions in writing; for Poe, every word and line should be chosen with this outcome in mind. As seen in Poe's own obsessive rewriting of his short fiction and poetry, the choices needed for singularity of effect were not simply theoretical.

Poe expanded this line of thinking in his essay "Philosophy of Composition" (1846), written for the April issue of *Graham's* after the success of "The Raven." Ostensibly outlining Poe's construction of his most famous poem, the piece works as a frame through which Poe discusses his ideas of singular effect and artistic unity. The essay begins with Poe stating the importance of knowing where a piece ends before the author starts: "it is only with the *dénouement* constantly in view that we can give a plot its indispensable air of consequence." A few lines later, Poe continues, "I prefer commencing with the consideration of an *effect*." Constantly focusing on the effect of the piece forces the writer to realize every word, rhyme, or pattern matters, reiterating the point Poe made in his Hawthorne essay. Another idea developed in this essay is the importance of brevity: "If any literary work is too long to be read at one sitting, we must be content to dispense with the immensely important effect derivable from unity of impression—for, if two sittings be required, the affairs of the world interfere, and every thing like totality is at once destroyed." Poe gives exceptions to this rule: long poems such as Milton's *Paradise Lost* (1667), which he claims are essentially smaller poems put together, or formless narratives such as Daniel Defoe's *Robinson Crusoe* (1719). Later, Poe returns to his argument that poetry has one transcendent aim: "Beauty is the sole legitimate province of the poem." Aimed at the soul, instead of the intellect or the heart, beauty's contemplation excites the soul; a poem with beauty as its effect will strike the reader in a way that truth or passion will not. The rest of the essay recounts, in almost a self-parodying way, the nearly mathematical construction of "The Raven." At times a burlesque of critical writing, and at other times the most original American literary analysis to date, "The Philosophy of Composition" embodies the split of late-period Poe.

The last iteration of Poe's aesthetics is his "The Poetic Principle," first given as a lecture in late 1848 in Providence, Rhode Island, and printed in *Sartain's Union Magazine* in 1850, after Poe's death. In it, he returns to his three major concepts. The first is the length of effective poetry: "I maintain that the phrase, 'a long poem,' is simply a flat contradiction in terms." Second is the importance of unity of effect: "If, to preserve its Unity—its totality of effect or impression—we read it (as would be necessary) at a single sitting, the result is but a constant alternation of excitement and depression." As he outlined in earlier essays, for Poe a totality of impression is at the heart of all successful poetry. Anything breaking the unity, whether too many lines or a misplaced word, threatens artistic integrity. Last, he returns to the primacy of beauty in art, railing against "the heresy of *The Didactic*" present in American arts. True art, art that elevates the soul through beauty, cannot be written with the purpose of dictating a truth; instead it strikes and engages the soul.

Much like his contributions to short stories and poetry, Poe's writings on aesthetics have shaped American literary criticism for more than a hundred years. His emphasis on artistic unity, along with his disavowal of didactic works, prefigure the writings of T. S. Eliot and the New Critics. His analysis of Hawthorne's *Twice-Told Tales* made the case that writing by Americans was worth studying under its own merits and that his at times harsh criticism of fellow writers meant that these writers should be taken seriously.

THE NARRATIVE OF ARTHUR GORDON PYM *AND OTHER WRITINGS*

In addition to the stories and poems for which he is remembered, Poe also wrote one novel, an unfinished dramatic piece, *Politian* (composed in 1835); an epic prose poem, *Eureka* (1848), exploring cosmology and the creative impulse; and a textbook (1839) that subjected him to charges of plagiarism, in addition to essays on furniture, gardening, and architecture, to name a few. Most of the latter writings are slight pieces, of interest only to Poe enthusiasts and scholars, but his novel, *The Narrative of Arthur Gordon Pym of Nantucket* (1838), influenced later weird fiction writers such as H. P. Lovecraft and its ending remains one of American literature's most cryptic.

Poe began working on *The Conchologist's First Book; or, A System of Testaceous Malacology, Arranged Expressly for the Use of Schools* in late 1838, seeing it as an easy payday.

However, by 1839, Poe was accused of using a previously published work on shells and simply putting his name on the cover page—as he put it, "as best known and most likely to aid its circulation" (Quinn, p. 277). Poe certainly wrote the preface and the introduction for the 1839 version, as well as using his knowledge of French and skills as an editor to heavily revise an 1833 text, *The Conchologist's Text Book.* However, certain chapters are almost verbatim from the earlier piece, giving birth to the plagiarism accusation, which Poe would later call, in an 1847 letter "infamous" (p. 277). The almost literary irony of Poe's contribution to *Conchologist* is that it was the only Poe work that went through a second American edition during his life.

More literary, but less successful, is Poe's *Narrative of Arthur Gordon Pym.* Originally conceived as a serialized novel for the *Southern Literary Messenger,* Poe gave up on the serial after leaving the *Messenger* in early 1837. Hoping to capitalize on the popular interest in polar exploration, Poe's *Pym* is a fictional account of the supposed true adventures of Arthur Gordon Pym, who, with his friend Augustus Barnard and his dog, Tiger, stows away on a whaler. Unfortunately for the stowaways, the whaler's crew has mutinied; on the fortunate side, Augustus made friends with the muscular and violent Dirk Peters, who leads a mutinous faction. Through a combination of trickery—Pym dresses in a dead sailor's clothes to imitate a ghost—and force, Peters, Pym, and Barnard kill the remaining mutineers, with the exception of one needed to work the ship.

Although the men now have their freedom, they find themselves in increasing peril. A storm breaks off the sails and overturns the boat, and the four survive by strapping themselves to the hull. Assailed by thirst and hunger, the group draws straws to determine who is to be cannibalized. Parker draws the short one and is eaten, a scene that Quinn claims, "leads from interest to disgust" (p. 264). Barnard dies of his wounds soon after, but Pym and Peters are saved by the timely arrival of the *Jane Guy,* a ship hunting in the southern oceans.

The *Jane Guy* continues sailing south, eventually crossing a barrier of ice and then entering into warm water and discovering the island of Tsalal, inhabited by natives having "complexion a jet black, with thick and long woolly hair" (p. 150). The natives act as though "they had never before seen any of the white race" (p. 151). Everything about Tsalal is unusual: the water is multicolored, animals are slightly misshapen and usually black, and the natives seldom wear clothing. While all seems fine on the surface, Pym consistently feels a sense of menace, and his intuition is correct. The night before the *Guy* sets sail, the Tsalal massacre the crew, leaving only Peters and Pym, who hide in a labyrinth on the village outskirts. Again facing starvation, the two steal a small boat, kidnapping one of the locals. With no other direction to go but south, the three sail into a warm sea of "milky consistency and hue" (p. 196). The narrative ends with the Pym and Peters facing a giant waterfall, but before they go over, they see "a shrouded human figure, very far larger in its proportions than any dweller among men. And the hue of the skin of the figure was of the perfect whiteness of the snow" (p. 197).

In Poe's effort to exploit the public's interest in exploration, one of the chapters in *Pym* contains a long excerpt from the noted explorer Jeremiah Reynolds, whose travel narrative Poe reviewed early in 1837. *Pym* is written as an accurate journal, complete with dates and an editorial afterword explaining the labyrinth's hieroglyphs. As pointed out by later commentators, Poe's efforts to add verisimilitude to the narrative works against the novel's success. Since the text is supposed to be an accurate account of Pym's voyage, details that have little to do with the larger narrative are recounted with the same detail as arguably more important events.

Despite *Pym*'s flaws, its imaginative writing influenced generations of other writers of the fantastic. The Argentine writer Jorge Luis Borges, who cites Poe as a major influence, called *Pym* Poe's greatest work. The French writer Jules Verne wrote a sequel to the novel in 1897, where another ship tries to find Pym. The American horror writer H. P. Lovecraft's *At the Mountains of Madness* (1936) uses the theme of Antarctic exploration and incorporates the Tsalal's cry of "tekeli-li." More recently, the American author Mat Johnson published *Pym* (2011), a comically satirical novel that uses the Pym narrative to explore questions of race and empire in early twenty-first-century America.

Pym's racial implications, its strange mixture of whiteness, blackness, savagery, and civilization, are central to the novel's continued critical interest. Dirk Peters, whose skills and strength keep Pym alive, is mixed race, having a fur trapper father and a Native American mother. The leader of the mutiny, an African American cook, chops off the heads of thirty-two crewmen. The Tsalal, with teeth that are as dark as their skins, are passive and helpful on the surface but hide murderous intent. Antebellum race relations contribute to Poe's description of the Tsalal's uprising, as well as his description of the Tsalal's houses being "of the most miserable description imaginable" (*Collected Works,* vol. 1, p. 172). The writings found in the labyrinth outside of the Tsalal village are later connected with Egyptian hieroglyphics, complicating the seemingly primitive nature of the Tsalal. Sailing into a world where even the sea is white, the giant white figure at the novel's end remains one of the most enigmatic figures in Poe's works. His arrival coincides with the Tsalal captive's death, but it is never made explicit that one directly causes the other. In the end, *Pym*'s strange concoction of adventure novel, racism, and imperialism make it one of Poe's most fraught and complex narratives.

CRITICAL TRADITION

In addition to his inability to maintain cordial relationships with other editors, Poe's biggest literary mistake was, indisputably, his relationship with Rufus Griswold, who altered and forged Poe letters, lied about Poe's personal life, and led a defamation crusade against Poe. When Poe first met Griswold in 1841, the relationship was friendly, with Griswold publishing three poems in his 1842 anthology *The Poets and Poetry of America.* The relationship soon grew colder, with Poe calling Griswold's anthology "humbug" and questioning his skill as an editor. However, Griswold managed to connive his way into becoming Poe's literary executor. Griswold's feelings toward Poe's legacy could be seen less than a week after Poe's death, when Griswold's obituary claimed, "This announcement will startle many, but few will be grieved by it" (Quinn, p. 646). A longer version followed, with Griswold lifting verbatim passages from a novel by the English writer Edward Bulwer-Lytton and applying them to Poe. These articles circulated quickly throughout America, solidifying Poe's reputation as a sneering, social climbing ingrate.

Griswold, along with two more-sympathetic editors—Nathaniel Parker Willis and James Russell Lowell—published a three-volume collection, *Works of the Late Edgar Allan Poe: With Notices of His Life and Genius,* in 1850 (with a fourth volume appearing in 1856), with Griswold writing a biographical sketch that used forged letters and innuendo to further destroy Poe's legacy. According to Griswold, Poe deserted his army service and "was known as the wildest and most reckless student" at the University of Virginia (Quinn, p. 671). Griswold's memoir became the source for many Poe falsehoods, falsehoods repeated enough times to replace the truth. Although figures who knew Poe, such as Sarah Whitman, tried to defend his reputation, they were ultimately drowned out by sensational accounts of drinking and opium use. However, the French poet Charles Baudelaire, who by 1848 was already translating Poe, published his own reviews of Poe's writings and life in 1852 and later called Griswold a "pedagogue vampire" for his defamations (Quinn, p. 684). The early adoption of Poe in France did much to solidify his continental reputation as an artistic sophisticate ruined by chattering rubes.

Biographies and sketches, usually repeating many Griswold lies, were published throughout the late 1800s, and by the 1920s multiple collections of Poe texts, letters, and life were available. In 1941, the Poe scholar Arthur Hobson Quinn's *Edgar Allan Poe: A Critical Biography* appeared, one of the landmarks in Poe criticism. Exhaustively researched and documented, Quinn talked with remaining living Poe acquaintances, found

Griswold's changed passages in letters, and provided sympathetically insightful readings of Poe's work. It is a testament to Quinn's work that it is still considered one of the most useful examinations of Poe's life. Thomas Ollive Mabbott, another Poe scholar, made it his life's goal to compile all of Poe's work. Mabbott originally conceived the project in 1923 when he was a Ph.D. candidate at Columbia University, and he worked on the *Collected Works of Edgar Allan Poe* until his death in 1968; volume 1, *Poems,* appeared in 1969. After Mabbott's death, his wife, Maureen Cobb Mabbott, worked from notes to prepare two further volumes: *Tales and Sketches, 1831–1842,* and *Tales and Sketches, 1843–1849.* These final two volumes were published in 1978, and Mabbott's collections remain central to Poe criticism.

The arrival of deconstruction, Marxism, and other literary theories in the 1960s and 1970s offered Poe scholars new examination tools. The French psychoanalyst Jacques Lacan and the French philosopher Jacques Derrida's ongoing exchange concerning "The Purloined Letter" is one of the landmarks in Poe studies. Dwight Thomas and David Kelly Jackson's research represented in *The Poe Log: A Documentary Life, 1809–1849* (1987) is another critical milestone, providing a heavily documented account of Poe's daily movements and activities. Poe's involvement with the popular press was the focus of two 1990s monographs: Jonathan Elmers' 1995 *Reading at the Social Limit,* which explores the tension between Poe's artistic elitism and his involvement in mass culture, and Terence Whalen's *Edgar Allan Poe and the Masses* (1999), which analyzes Poe's work in the juncture of politics and economics. The collection *Romancing the Shadow: Poe and Race* (2001), edited by J. Gerald Kennedy and Liliane Weissberg, contains nine essays analyzing the racial tensions in a variety of Poe's works, and *The Cambridge Companion to Poe* (2002), edited by Kevin Hayes, examines Poe's work from multiple perspectives. The W. W. Norton company's *Selected Writings of Edgar Allan Poe: Authoritative Texts, Backgrounds and Contexts, Criticism* (2004) provides annotated versions of Poe's best-known tales, in addition to the cultural context of the 1830s and 1840s. Two academic journals are dedicated to Poe studies, and the Edgar Allan Poe Society maintains an active web presence, with its site containing annotated texts, comparisons of revisions, and full-text versions of the Quinn and Mabbott volumes.

Poe's troubled life and mysterious death have helped to keep him in the public consciousness, but seeing him only as a morose, cousin-marrying indigent is unfair to his enormous skills as a writer and editor. He was one of the first American writers to demand that American writers be judged on their own merits, instead of their American-ness. He helped popularize detective fiction, and his horror short stories shocked and mesmerized readers. "The Raven" was one of the most popular poems of the nineteenth century. His ideas of artistic unity and the importance of effect helped shape literary judgment for two centuries. In many ways, Edgar Allan Poe encapsulates the central tension of American letters: that of commerce and art.

Selected Bibliography

WORKS OF EDGAR ALLAN POE

SHORT FICTION

"Ligeia." *American Museum* (Baltimore), September 1838, pp. 25–37. Reprinted in *Tales of the Grotesque and Arabesque* (1840). A slightly edited 1848 version by Sarah Whitman is used by Mabbott in *Collected Works of Edgar Allan Poe,* vol. 2 (see "Collected Works").

"The Fall of the House of Usher." *Burton's Gentleman's Magazine,* September 1839, pp. 145–152. Reprinted in *Tales of the Grotesque and Arabesque* (1840) and in *Tales* (1845) with slight differences. Mabbott used the version from *Tales* in *Collected Works of Edgar Allan Poe,* vol. 2 (see "Collected Works").

"The Murders at the Rue Morgue." *Graham's,* April 1841, pp. 166–179. Reprinted in *The Prose Romances of Edgar Allan Poe* (1843) and *Tales* (1845) with minor revisions. Mabbott used the version from *Tales* in *Collected Works of Edgar Allan Poe,* vol. 2 (see "Collected Works").

"The Balloon-Hoax." *Extra Sun,* April 13, 1844, p. 1. Reprinted in Griswold's *Works of the Late Edgar Allan*

Poe (1850), and this version is used in Mabbott's *Collected Works of Edgar Allan Poe,* vol. 3 (see "Collected Works").

"The Purloined Letter." *The Gift,* September 1844, pp. 41–61. Reprinted in *Tales* (1845). Mabbott used this version for *Collected Works of Edgar Allan Poe,* vol. 2 (see "Collected Works").

"The Cask of Amontillado." *Godey's Magazine and Lady's Book,* November 1846, pp. 216–218. Slightly revised by Griswold in *The Works of the Late Edgar Allan Poe* (1850), and Mabbott used this version for *Collected Works of Edgar Allan Poe,* vol. 3 (see "Collected Works").

"Hop-Frog; or, The Eight Chained Ourang-Outangs." *Flag of Our Union* (Boston), March 17, 1849, p 2. Reprinted in Griswold's *Works of the Late Edgar Allan Poe* (1850) as "Hop-Frog," with minor corrections, and this version is used by Mabbott in *Collected Works of Edgar Allan Poe,* vol. 3 (see "Collected Works").

POETRY

"The Lake." In *Tamerlane and Other Poems* (1827). Reprinted several times, including in Poe's *Al Aaraaf, Tamerlane, and Minor Poems* (1829) and *The Raven and Other Poems* (1845). Mabbott used the version from *The Raven* in *Collected Works of Edgar Allan Poe,* vol. 1 (see "Collected Works").

"Sonnet—To Science." In *Al Aaraaf, Tamerlane, and Minor Poems* (1829). Repeatedly reprinted, with Mabbott using the version from Poe's *The Raven and Other Poems* (1845) in *Collected Works of Edgar Allan Poe,* vol. 1 (see "Collected Works").

"To Helen." In *Poems* (1831). Reprinted and revised consistently throughout Poe's lifetime. The most well-known version is from *The Raven and Other Poems* (1845); Mabbott used this version in *Collected Works of Edgar Allan Poe,* vol. 1 (see "Collected Works").

"The Sleeper." *Saturday Chronicle* (Philadelphia), May 22, 1841, p. 1. "The Sleeper" is a rewrite of Poe's earlier "Irene," published in *Poems* (1831). "The Sleeper" was reprinted frequently, including in *The Raven and Other Poems* (1845). Mabbott used a slightly revised 1849 version for *Collected Works of Edgar Allan Poe,* vol. 1 (see "Collected Works").

"The Raven." *Evening Mirror* (New York), January 29, 1845, p. 4 (advance publication of the first printing); *American Review,* February 1845, pp. 143–145. The version from the *Semi-Weekly Examiner* (Richmond), September 25, 1849, p. 2, which Poe authorized, is used by Mabbott in *Collected Works of Edgar Allan Poe,* vol. 1 (see "Collected Works").

ESSAYS, REVIEWS, AND CRITICISM

"Review of Laughton Osborn, *Confessions of a Poet.*" *Southern Literary Messenger,* April 1835.

"Critical Notices, *Norman Leslie: A Tale of the Present Time.*" *Southern Literary Messenger,* December 1835, pp 57–59.

"Review of *Ballads and Other Poems.*" *Graham's,* April 1842, pp. 248–251. This review is reprinted in Quinn's *Critical Biography* (1941) (see "Critical and Biographical Studies").

"Review of *Twice-Told Tales.*" *Graham's,* May 1842, pp. 298–300. This review is reprinted in Quinn's *Critical Biography* (1941) (see "Critical and Biographical Studies").

"Doings in Gotham [Letter II]." *Columbia Spy* (Columbia, Pa.), May 25, 1844, p. 3, col 2.

"The Philosophy of Composition." *Graham's,* April 1846, pp. 163–167. Reprinted in Griswold's *The Works of the Late Edgar Allan Poe* (1850) (see "Collected Works").

"The Poetic Principle." First given as a lecture at the Franklin Lyceum in Providence, Rhode Island, December 1848. Poe's manuscript was lost when his valise was stolen in Philadelphia in 1849. He rewrote the lecture for a Virginia talk, and this version is subsequently printed in *Sartain's Union Magazine,* October 1850, p. 231, and Griswold's 1850 *Works of the Late Edgar Allan Poe.* (See "Collected Works.")

OTHER WRITINGS

Politian. Southern Literary Messenger, December 1835 (scenes 4, 6, and 7) and January 1836 (scenes 3 and 9). Revisions to these scenes were added in Poe's *The Raven and Other Writing* (1845), and then reprinted in Griswold's *Works of the Late Edgar Allan Poe* (1850), where scene 2 was also added. Although the play was never completed, Mabbott's *Collected Works of Edgar Allan Poe,* vol. 1, includes the most complete text (see "Collected Works").

The Narrative of Arthur Gordon Pym of Nantucket. New York: Harper & Brothers, 1838. This novel has gone through many reprints and is included in *The Selected Writings of Edgar Allan Poe.* Edited by Gary Richard Thompson. New York: W. W. Norton, 2004. (Norton Critical Edition.)

The Conchologist's First Book; or, A System of Testaceous Malacology, Arranged Expressly for the Use of Schools. Philadelphia: Haswell, Barrington, and Haswell, 1839. (This textbook is the only Poe work to see a second printing in his lifetime.)

Eureka: A Prose Poem. New York: George Putnam, 1848. (The original print run of this volume was five hundred. Like much of Poe's work, it is available through a variety of reprints and electronically.)

COLLECTIONS

Tamerlane and Other Poems. Boston: Calvin F. S. Thomas, 1827. (Fewer than fifteen copies of this collection are known.)

EDGAR ALLAN POE

Al Aaraaf, Tamerlane, and Minor Poems. Baltimore: Hatch & Dunning, 1829. (Fewer than thirty copies of this collection are known.)

Poems. New York: Elam Bliss, 1831.

Tales of the Grotesque and Arabesque. 2 vols. Philadelphia: Lea and Blanchard, 1840. (This collection of previously written pieces includes "The Fall of the House of Usher," "Ligeia," and "William Wilson," in addition to lesser-known works.)

The Prose Romances of Edgar Allan Poe. Philadelphia: William Graham, 1843. (Produced as a pamphlet that included "The Murders at the Rue Morgue" and "The Man That Was Used Up." It was the first of a planned series of Poe pamphlets, but the series was cancelled because of poor sales. Fewer than twenty original copies exist.)

The Raven and Other Poems. New York: Wiley and Putnam, 1845. (In addition to "The Raven," this collection includes scenes from Poe's unfinished *Politian.*)

Tales. New York: Wiley and Putnam, 1845. (Poe did not approve of the selections for this collection, claiming in a letter to Philip Pendleton Cooke that the stories did not represent "my mind in it [sic] various phases.")

COLLECTED WORKS

Starting with Rufus Griswold's 1850 *Works* (see below), there have been numerous collections of Poe's writings. Many have claimed to be complete, but given the amount of minor criticism and essays Poe wrote, much of it anonymously, no collection is likely to actually contain all of Poe's writing.

The Works of the Late Edgar Allan Poe: With Notices of His Life and Genius. 4 vols. Edited by Nathaniel Parker Willis, James Russell Lowell, and Rufus Griswold. Vols. 1–3, New York: J. S. Redfield, 1850; vol. 4, 1856. (This collection was the first systematic effort to collect Poe's work. Griswold's biographical sketch in volume 3, however, is full of untruths and was the start of many misconceptions about Poe.)

The Complete Works of Edgar Allan Poe. 17 vols. Edited by James Albert Thompson. New York: J. D. Morris, 1902. (This collection includes Poe's literary criticism, marginalia, and letters.)

The Collected Letters of Edgar Allan Poe. 2 vols. Edited by John Ostrom. Cambridge, Mass.: Harvard University Press, 1948. Rev., 2nd ed., 1966. Rev., 3rd corrected ed., edited by Ostrom, Burton Pollin, and Jeffrey Savoye, 2008. (This collection is available electronically through the Edgar Allan Poe Society.)

Collected Works of Edgar Allan Poe. 3 vols. Edited by Thomas Mabbott with assistance from Eleanor D. Kewer and Maureen C. Mabbott. Vol. 1, Cambridge, Mass.: Belknap Press of Harvard University Press, 1969; vols. 2–3, 1978. (Heavily annotated with introductory material, this collection remains central to Poe scholarship. It is available electronically through the Edgar Allan Poe Society.)

The Selected Writings of Edgar Allan Poe: Authoritative Texts, Backgrounds and Contexts, Criticism. Edited by Gary Richard Thompson. New York: W. W. Norton, 2004. (In addition to selected writings, this collection is also annotated and gives cultural context and criticism to Poe's material.)

CRITICAL AND BIOGRAPHICAL STUDIES

Elmer, Jonathan. *Reading at the Social Limit: Affect, Mass Culture, and Edgar Allan Poe.* Stanford, Calif.: Stanford University Press, 1995.

Hayes, Kevin J. *The Cambridge Companion to Poe.* New York: Cambridge University Press, 2002.

Kennedy, J. Gerald, and Liliane Weissberg. *Romancing the Shadow: Poe and Race.* Oxford and New York: Oxford University Press, 2001.

Muller, John P., and William J. Richardson. *The Purloined Poe: Lacan, Derrida, and Psychoanalytic Reading.* Baltimore: Johns Hopkins University Press, 1988. (This collection includes essays on Poe by Jacques Lacan and Jacques Derrida as well as several other critical essays on psychology and Poe.)

Quinn, Arthur Hobson. *Edgar Allan Poe: A Critical Biography.* New York: D. Appleton-Century, 1941. (This critical biography remains an important piece of Poe scholarship. It is available electronically through the Edgar Allan Poe Society.)

Thomas, Dwight, and David Kelly Jackson. *The Poe Log: A Documentary Life of Edgar Allan Poe, 1809–1849.* Boston: G. K. Hall, 1987. (This log of dates and locations is available electronically through the Edgar Allan Poe Society.)

Whalen, Terence. *Edgar Allan Poe and the Masses: The Political Economy of Literature in Antebellum America.* Princeton, N.J.: Princeton University Press, 1999.

ADRIENNE RICH

(1929—2012)

Brett C. Millier

ADRIENNE RICH WAS a major American poet, thinker, and witness for social justice in the second half of the twentieth century and well into the twenty-first. She put to rest the (primarily American) notions that poetry could not contend with politics and remain poetry and that the poet should be solitary and isolated at the margins of the culture. She forged a "political lyric" voice in which the poet is at once meditative and reflective and also socially engaged and in dialogue with both reader and culture. "To say that a poet is responsive, responsible—what can that mean?" she wrote in the essay "The Muralist," collected in her 2003 volume *What Is Found There*: "To me it means that she or he is free to become artistically most complex, serious, and integrated when most aware of the great questions of her, of his, own time" (p. 52). In nearly two dozen volumes of verse and seven collections of prose, Rich forged an enduring and influential ethical poetics.

BIOGRAPHY

Adrienne Cecile Rich was born on May 16, 1929, in Baltimore, Maryland, the elder of two sisters (Cynthia was born in 1933). Her father, Arnold Rice Rich, was an Alabama-born, secular Jewish physician and educator who encouraged the precociously talented Adrienne in her literary ambitions and gave her access to his extensive library of canonical nineteenth-century poets. Her mother, Helen Jones Rich, was a Southern Protestant concert pianist who ended her performing career with her marriage. Adrienne was educated at home until the fourth grade, and eventually she attended the Roland Park Country School, an Episcopal girls' preparatory school. In 1947, she entered Radcliffe College, graduating in 1951, noting later that in her English and writing coursework, she had encountered no female teachers. Her poetry career was launched in 1951, when her first collection, *A Change of World,* won the Yale Younger Poet's Prize, chosen and introduced by the distinguished Anglo-American poet W. H. Auden. She received her first Guggenheim Fellowship in 1952, which she spent in England and Italy. While abroad, she fell ill and was diagnosed with acute rheumatoid arthritis, which she suffered from—enduring many surgeries and nearly continuous pain—for the rest of her life.

On June 26, 1953, against her parents' wishes, she married Alfred Haskell Conrad, a Harvard economics professor of Jewish origin whom she had met in college, and she settled into the role of a faculty wife in Cambridge, Massachusetts. In the early years of her marriage, Rich continued to write, and her second volume of poetry, *The Diamond Cutters,* appeared in 1955, in the same month she gave birth to David, the first of three sons. Pablo was born in 1957, and Jacob in 1959. "The experience of motherhood was eventually to radicalize me," Rich said in a 1982 essay titled "Split at the Root: An Essay on Jewish Identity" (collected in *Blood, Bread, and Poetry,* 1986, p. 117). She continued to receive honors and fellowships—including a National Institute of Arts and Letters Award (1960) and her second Guggenheim (1961)—and her poetry began to change. In 1963, the volume *Snapshots of a Daughter-in-Law,* with its trenchant title poem, announced the arrival of Rich's major subject of the 1960s and 1970s: the experience and condition of women. Together with Betty Friedan's *The Feminine Mystique,* also published in 1963, *Snapshots* provided a founding discourse for the women's liberation movement, later known to historians as second-wave feminism.

When Alfred Conrad joined the faculty of the City University of New York in 1966, Rich and her family left Cambridge and joined the political and social foment of New York City in the era of the civil rights and anti–Vietnam War movements. Rich became increasingly politically active in this era, even as she explored new poetic forms and modes of expression. Her volumes *Necessities of Life* (1966), *Leaflets* (1969), and *The Will to Change* (1971) show her engagement with and exploration of the relationship between poetry and civic and political life. Rich separated from her husband in 1970, and later that year Alfred Conrad committed suicide. In 1976, with the publication of her lyric sequence *Twenty-One Love Poems,* Rich made public her lesbian identity and began a relationship with the writer Michelle Cliff that lasted until Rich's death. Her volumes *Diving into the Wreck* (1973) and *The Dream of a Common Language* (1978), which included the love-poem sequence, marked the culmination of this phase of her career. The prose volumes *Of Woman Born* (1976), a political examination of the institution of motherhood, and *On Lies, Secrets, and Silence* (1979), a collection of essays, announced Rich as a major feminist thinker and cultural critic as well.

Rich taught English and writing at several colleges and universities, including Columbia, Rutgers, and Stanford, and she was a visiting writer or fellowship holder at several more. She continued to publish both poetry and prose and continued to receive prizes and awards, including a National Endowment for the Arts Fellowship in 1970, the National Book Award (1974) for *Diving into the Wreck,* and a MacArthur Fellowship (the "genius grant") in 1994. Other awards include honorary degrees from several colleges, as well as Brandeis University and Harvard University, the Ruth Lilly Poetry Prize (1986), election to the American Academy of Arts and Sciences (1991), the Lenore Marshall Poetry Prize (1992), the Frost Medal (1992), the Wallace Stevens Award (1996), the National Medal for the Arts (refused) (1997), a Lifetime Achievement Award from the Lannan Foundation (1999), the Bollingen Prize (2003), the National Book Foundation Medal for Distinguished Contribution to American Letters (2006), and a Lifetime Recognition Award from the Griffin Poetry Prize (2010).

Rich and Cliff lived for many years in Santa Cruz, California, where Rich died of complications from rheumatoid arthritis on March 27, 2012.

EARLY CAREER

Albert Gelpi has written that the word "change" should be the banner stretching across all of Rich's work, and indeed evolution was fundamental to her understanding of herself as a poet. She meticulously dated nearly every poem and every volume, and one recurring subject in her work is the ongoing changes in her understanding of herself, her art, and the world. The first Adrienne Rich we know was a senior at Radcliffe, well trained in the techniques and values of high modernism, already an accomplished poet. When her first volume, *A Change of World,* was chosen for the Yale Younger Poets Prize, the prize judge W. H. Auden caught this dutiful tendency in the poems in his introduction to the volume. These poems, he said, were "neatly and modestly dressed, speak quietly but do not mumble, respect their elders but are not cowed by them, and do not tell fibs" (quoted in *Adrienne Rich's Poetry and Prose,* 1993, p. 279). Readers with the benefit of hindsight have seen in these early poems the seeds of Rich's later political engagement and forthrightness. "Storm Warnings," the first poem in that volume (and in all subsequent volumes in which it appears, including the 2016 *Collected Poems*), suggests that political awareness was disciplined by the conservatism of Rich's modernist poetic training, rather than unacknowledged. The poem's speaker secures a substantial and well-appointed house against a coming storm. The final lines offer a prescient metaphor: "These are the things that we have learned to do / Who live in troubled regions" (*Collected Poems,* p. 3; hereafter cited as *CP*).

"Aunt Jennifer's Tigers" also represents, in a disciplined and objective yet musical form, a nascent understanding of the situation of women in postwar American culture. Aunt Jennifer works at a needlepoint tapestry depicting prancing tigers. Images of such "female labor"—knitting, needlework, weaving—appear frequently throughout Rich's work, often valuing that work despite its origins in patriarchal institutions like marriage. "The massive weight of Uncle's wedding band" weighs down Aunt Jennifer's work, and "When Aunt is dead, her terrified hands will lie / Still ringed with ordeals she was mastered by" (p. 4). The modernist value of impersonality is reflected in Rich's choice of a gender-neutral, "universal" poetic voice in these early poems. In "The Diamond Cutters," the title poem from her second volume (1955), the poet admonished herself to avoid both the personal and political, to create poetry from intellect rather than feeling. "Be hard of heart" she insists, and "Keep your desire apart" (*CP*, p. 105).

Rich said later, "In those years formalism was part of the strategy—like asbestos gloves, it allowed me to handle materials I couldn't pick up bare-handed" (*On Lies, Secrets, and Silence,* pp. 40–41). And in her foreword to *The Fact of a Doorframe* (1984), her "selected poems" volume, Rich acknowledged that the young writer of these poems did not yet understand "that she was neither unique nor universal, but a person in history, a woman and not a man, a white and also Jewish inheritor of a particular Western consciousness" (p. xv). As her attention turned toward raising a family in the late 1950s, Rich suffered for several years from the exhausting intensity of caring for young children, and when she began to emerge, she shed the formalism and especially the gender-neutrality of her earlier work; she began experimenting with looser meters, irregular stanza forms, the use of white space within lines, and other strategies to convey nontraditional content. This emergence began the second phase of Rich's career.

MIDDLE PHASE

Rich reemerged as a writer into the heady poetic atmosphere of Boston and Cambridge and, later, New York City. The late 1950s and 1960s represent a pinnacle of popular interest in serious American poetry. Readings by Robert Lowell, John Berryman, and Anne Sexton in the east (and Allen Ginsberg, Gary Snyder, and others in the west) drew large audiences and the attention of local and national media. Thus Rich saw firsthand that contemporary poets had both audiences and readers and a responsibility to communicate with them. While Rich resisted what she saw as the solipsism and self-involvement of the so-called confessional poets, including Lowell, Berryman, Sexton, and Sylvia Plath, she nonetheless had persuasive models in these poets who wrote frankly of personal experience.

Composed between 1958 and 1960, "jotted in fragments during children's naps, brief hours in a library, or at 3:00 a.m. after rising with a wakeful child," the ten sections of "Snapshots of a Daughter-in-Law" each reflect on women living under the limiting terms of long-standing patriarchy (*On Lies, Secrets, and Silence,* p. 44). Rich had been reading Simone de Beauvoir's study of women in Western culture, *The Second Sex* (1953), and that influence is apparent in the poem. The second section presents a woman, perhaps a mother of young children, who fears that the voices in her head mean that she is going mad: "Only a week since They said: *Have no patience. //* The next time it was: *Be insatiable*" (*CP*, p. 117). The third section laments, "A thinking woman sleeps with monsters. / The beak that grips her, she becomes" (p. 118). And the ninth section acknowledges the crippling intellectual distortions patriarchy imposed upon women: "Bemused by gallantry, we hear / our mediocrities over-praised" (p. 121). The poem's final section looks forward to the arrival of a female savior, "at least as beautiful as any boy / or helicopter," an image from Beauvoir, who will free women from these bonds, or show them a new way to live.

Rich had found the great subject of this middle phase of her career—the condition of women under patriarchy, the realization that not only was she "inheritor of a particular Western consciousness" but also one "from the making of which most women have been excluded" (*The Fact of a Doorframe* [1984], p. xv). Other poems in her 1963 volume *Snapshots of a Daughter-in-*

Law look closely at the institution of heterosexual marriage ("A Marriage in the 'Sixties") and gender differences ("Ghost of a Chance"). Many readers and critics and even friends were shocked by Rich's turn toward looser forms and political subject matter, but the volume caught the attention of the W. W. Norton publishing company, which picked up her next volume (and reissued *Snapshots of a Daughter-in-Law*), and remained the publisher, through all the changes in her poetry and her politics, for all of Rich's work.

During the 1960s and under the influence of the struggle for civil rights for African Americans and against the Vietnam War, Rich grew increasingly radical in her embrace of antiestablishment politics. Understanding that the poet's only tool is a language controlled by the forces of oppression and designed to fix binaries and boundaries between races, genders, and social classes, she worked toward the inclusive political-lyric voice that remains her distinctive contribution to Anglo-American poetry. Maintaining lyric poetry's inward focus and reflective mode, this voice engages with both culture and reader in a way not seen in American poetry since Walt Whitman, whom Rich acknowledged as an important influence. At the same time, she argued forcefully—and would continue to argue—for poetry's place in the civic and political realm, maintaining that a culture is imaginatively impoverished without poetry's insistent disruption and renewal of that captured language.

The three collections that followed *Snapshots of a Daughter in Law* reveal Rich's refinement of that voice; the poems of *Necessities of Life* (1966), *Leaflets* (1969), and *The Will to Change* (1971) develop the political-lyric form of Rich's best mature work—which understands that personal experience always takes place in a cultural and historical context—and continue to experiment with a variety of formal innovations. The title poem of *Necessities of Life* acknowledges this new beginning, speaking in a frank first-person, easily identified with the poet herself: "Piece by piece I seem / to re-enter the world" (*CP,* p. 167). "Nightbreak," from *Leaflets,* demonstrates the union of personal feeling with the political and cultural despair of 1968 (the year of the assassinations of Martin Luther King, Jr., and Robert Kennedy, and of a significant escalation of the Vietnam War, and also the year of the death of Rich's father), expressed in both diction and form. "Something broken," the poem ominously begins, "By someone / I love." The images flow through the poem like newsreel footage of "a village // blown open by planes // that did not finish the job" (*CP,* pp. 265–266).

Also developing in several poems in *Leaflets* is Rich's identification of the costs of patriarchy for men, and she began to give voice to a tentative androgynous ideal. Earlier, in "The Knight," from *Snapshots of a Daughter-in-Law,* she had offered the image of the knight's armor as representing the soul-crushing restrictions patriarchy inflicts on masculinity and men. "Who will unhorse this rider," the poem asks, "and free him from between / the walls of iron, the emblems / crushing his chest with their weight?" (*CP,* p. 112). The opening poem in *Leaflets,* "Orion," is the fullest expression of the poet's identification with a masculine principle or ideal represented in the constellation of stars of that name. The poem remembers a childhood identification with Orion, "my genius," "my cast-iron Viking, my helmed / lion-heart king in prison." But now, years on into the poet's adulthood, Orion is "my fierce half-brother." "[Y]ou burn, and I know it," she says, while "Indoors I bruise and blunder, / break faith, leave ill enough / alone" (p. 231). This desire to break the binaries of gender identification, to free both women and men from the definitions and restrictions that patriarchy (and patriarchal language) imposes, appears in nearly all of Rich's work of this period, and identification with the figure of Orion is presented and examined in several later poems.

Rich's poems of the late 1960s also show her refining her use of images from the natural world in her poems and reflect her developing consciousness of the link between environmental devastation and social oppression. Rich never became a "nature poet" as such, but her work is remarkable for the detailed and deep knowledge and understanding reflected in the nature images she deploys, which range from large geographical and geological structures, to meteorological phenomena of sun and moon and rain, to the characteristics of seasonal changes, to the familiar and Latin names of trees and plants. She learned from Whitman and William Carlos Williams, and from poets in other traditions, not the Romantic belief in nature's analogies or correspondences with human feeling but rather the understanding that human beings live their lives in a compelling natural context, as well as a cultural and historical one. Says the critic Rachel Stein, "her work illuminates the ecofeminist assertion that our relations to the natural world are deeply intertwined with social patterns and that improving our treatment of nature requires that we also redress social inequities" (p. 198).

The Will to Change: Poems 1968–1970 (1971), its title taken from a poem by Charles Olson, articulates explicitly the central paradox for a poet determined to change the world: that language itself must be transformed, that the language formed and shaped in the Western patriarchal tradition can only get in the way of attempts to transform that tradition. The volume contains poems in a variety of forms, including the long, multisectioned "Shooting Script," nearly all of which explore the possibilities and impediments to forging a new language. "Planetarium" Rich saw as a kind of companion poem to the earlier "Orion," and it was dedicated to the eighteenth-century female astronomer Caroline Herschel. At the end of the poem, she images herself not as a terrestrial "blunder" but as a cosmic translator of messages from beyond: "I am an instrument in the shape / of a woman trying to translate pulsations / into images" (*CP,* p. 302).

This revision of the Romantic idea of the poet as an Aeolian harp—waiting for the winds of inspiration to blow across the passive strings—casts the poet as active in the vital task of reinterpreting the world in order to remake it. The following poem in the volume, "The Burning of Paper Instead of Children," contemplates the history of book-burning as a form of oppression and meditates on the confining history of language itself. In the end, however, the poet has no other medium, and admits: "this is the oppressor's language // yet I need it to talk to you" (*CP,* p. 304). "A language is a map of our failures," she says later in the poem, and it is the poet's task to address those failures (p. 306). One way to remake the language is to acknowledge that, indeed, "the personal is political." That phrase, later taken up as a feminist rallying cry, is not Rich's, but the idea dominates this volume: *"The moment when a feeling enters the body /* is political. This touch is political" ("The Blue Ghazals," p. 312), and "We're living through a time / that needs to be lived through us" ("The Will to Change," p. 330).

Not all readers and critics were happy with Rich's forceful turn toward the political, or with her radical feminism, and she regularly endured negative reviews attacking her political positions and expressing disappointment at the fall of this promising inheritor of the modernist tradition into worldly affairs. The critic and editor Robert Boyers, an admirer of Rich's earlier work, lamented in 1973 that she had become "charged ... with the nauseous propaganda of the advance-guard cultural radicals" (p. 144). "A point has been passed beyond which the poet has ceased to be herself," he concluded (p. 148). (Similar criticism accompanied Robert Lowell's turn toward "confessional" poetry in the late 1950s.) The broader cultural backlash against women's liberation produced, on the one hand, direct attacks and parodies of Rich (the satirist Robert Peters, in his 1983 volume, *The Great American Poetry Bake-Off,* referred to her as "Adrienne Poor," for example) and, on the other hand, omission (beyond her early work) from academic studies of developments in postwar American poetry. It is perhaps difficult to see now how controversial Rich's feminist, antiwar, and pro-equality positions were in the 1960s and 1970s, and how closely defended was the idea that "serious" poetry could not be political.

Rich's personal life was changing as the poems of *The Will to Change* were being composed as well. Her political activities and increasingly feminist understanding of how patriarchy distorts personal lives influenced Rich's decision to separate from her husband; the call for cultural and political transformation is equally a call to remake one's own life. "A Valediction Forbidding Mourning" (the title echoes a poem by the seventeenth-century poet John Donne, which asks his wife not to mourn his absence) presents the conflict in terms of language and states the poet's modest ambition to be understood: "At last attempt," she says, "To do something very common, in my own way" (*CP,* p. 338). Shortly after their formal separation began, in the fall of 1970, Alfred Conrad killed himself, and Rich's new life went forward in that shadow of grief and sorrow.

In 1971, Rich was asked to participate in a Modern Language Association convention panel on "The Woman Writer in the Twentieth Century," the first such panel in the history of that organization of professors and teachers of literature. Rich's paper for the occasion became her influential essay "When We Dead Awaken: Writing as Re-Vision" (published in the journal *College English* in 1972 and included in her collection of essays *On Lies, Secrets, and Silence* in 1979). In the essay, Rich reflects on the story of her own coming of age as a writer, offers readings of several of her early poems, and, in particular, identifies the impediments nearly all women artists face: the problem of caring for children and household chores, the problem of "all those poems about women, written by men: it seemed to be a given that men wrote poems and women frequently inhabited them."

> I think it has been a peculiar confusion to the girl or woman who tries to write because she is peculiarly susceptible to language. She goes to poetry or fiction looking for *her* way of being in the world, since she too has been putting words and images together...[and] she comes up against something that negates everything she is about: she meets the image of Woman in books written by men....[P]recisely what she does not find is that absorbed, drudging, puzzled, sometimes inspired creature, herself, who sits at a desk trying to put words together.
>
> (*On Lies, Secrets, and Silence,* p. 39)

In the end, she says, despite the real restrictions on women's creativity, which are endemic in "society, language, the structures of thought," it is both possible and time for a revolution by women, who must first seize the language and make it their own (p. 49). The essay launched Rich's parallel career as an essayist and thinker about women, culture, and language and the role of the artist in the political and social world. Many of her essays begin with a reinterpretation of her own upbringing and education, as does her controversial book-length study of motherhood, *Of Woman Born: Motherhood as Experience and Institution,* which appeared in 1976. Taking on perhaps the most sacred idea in the culture—the idea of the unconditional and unambivalent "natural" love of a mother for her children—Rich insisted that even motherhood itself is the product of centuries of shaping by patriarchal laws and institutions.

Diving into the Wreck: Poems 1971–1972 (1973) suggested that this period of Rich's self-transformation was nearing its climax. The volume's central motif is of exploration and excavation, of seeking origins and foundational myths and ideas. The poem titled "When We Dead Awaken" figures the quest in terms of knitting and sewing, traditional woman's work, imagining a two women, sisters, "working ...to remake // this trailing knitted thing, this cloth of darkness, ... trying to save the skein" (*CP,* p. 357).

"Incipience" "imagin[es] the existence / of something uncreated / this poem / our lives" (p. 362). And the title poem of the volume, nearly universally acknowledged to be one of Rich's best, develops the metaphor fully. The speaker is a diver, equipped to explore, alone, a sunken shipwreck. As the speaker descends the ship's ladder and then the depths of the sea, she enters an unfamiliar and disorienting element, "bluer and then green and then / black... // you breathe differently down here" (pp. 371–372). The wreck the speaker sets out to explore has been read by critics in several ways. Perhaps it is the wreck of Western civilization itself, or American civilization in aftermath of the 1960s, or perhaps it is the distorting prison of gender binaries that patriarchal civilization has imposed on both women and men. "I came to explore the wreck," is the first of three consecutive declarative sentences in the middle of the poem. The following lines (and much of the poem's earlier imagery) identify this exploration with the whole of Rich's poetic and political evolution: "The words are purposes. / The words are maps" (p.

372). The quest is for original understanding, before the language itself was appropriated: "the thing I came for: / the wreck and not the story of the wreck / the thing itself and not the myth" (p. 372). The speaker/diver arrives at a place prior to rigidly defined gender ("I am here, the mermaid whose dark hair / streams black, the merman in his armored body"; p. 373) and yet stops short of defining what that discovery might mean. The poem leaves the androgynous (or ungendered, perhaps) speaker in the hold of the sunken ship, inviting others to join in the exploration: "We are, I am, you are... / the one who find our way" to the book of stories and misconceptions, "in which / our names do not appear" (p. 373). "We are" "the one" "who find our way." Rich's transformations of the first-person pronoun identifies the speaker with all—men and women—who seek to remake the world by rebuilding its language. "The Stranger," also from *Diving into the Wreck,* makes a similar claim more succinctly: "I am the androgyne / I am the living mind you fail to describe / in your dead language" (*CP,* p. 368).

Rich would later disavow the idealized image of androgyny that poems in this and earlier volumes put forth, in favor of a distinctly woman-centered vision also being developed in *Diving into the Wreck.* "Trying to Talk with a Man" opens the volume: "Out in this desert we are testing bombs" (*CP,* p. 355). "Rape" caused a stir of controversy among even Rich's admirers for its supposed gender-essentialized depiction of a female rape victim's interactions with a masculine and uncomprehending criminal justice system. (Poems like Rich's and first-person accounts of women doubly victimized by the rapist and the police and courts led to substantial changes in this period in the way rape cases were processed in the United States.) "The Phenomenology of Anger," a poem in ten sections, takes on the social and political products of patriarchy—war, poverty, racism—in specifically gendered terms. The fifth section identifies the object of the poet's anger as unmistakably male, the most "destructive" being, "gunning down the babies at My Lai... / computing body counts, masturbating / in the factory / of facts" (p. 378). "I hate you," "I hate your words," says the seventh section (p. 379). But "I would have loved to live in a world / of women and men gaily / in collusion with green leaves," she says in the eighth, "a conspiracy to coexist" (p. 380). The poem's final line observes sadly that "Every act of becoming conscious / (it says here in this book) / is an unnatural act" (p. 381).

Diving into the Wreck won the National Book Award in 1974, shared with the poet Allen Ginsberg's *The Fall of America.* At the ceremony in New York, Rich refused to accept the award for herself, and she called from the audience two other nominated female writers, Audre Lord and Alice Walker (both African American), and together they accepted the award on behalf of all women writers, especially those who had been silenced. By the time *Diving into the Wreck* was published in 1973, Rich knew herself to be lesbian. "The suppressed lesbian I had been carrying in me since adolescence began to stretch her limbs," she wrote (*Blood, Bread, and Poetry,* p. 121). She identified her own political stance in the mid-1970s as "lesbian-feminist."

After the National Book Award, and due in part to the continuing support of her publishers (W. W. Norton issued Rich's first selected poems volume—*Poems: Selected and New, 1950–1974*—as well as a Norton Critical Edition of her work, in 1975), Rich achieved a level of national celebrity rare among living poets. In this period, she was invited frequently to review books, give lectures, write essays for collections, and judge prize competitions. Much of this work is collected in the volume *On Lies, Secrets, and Silence: Selected Prose 1966–1978* (1979). Here one sees Rich developing a deeply woman-centered philosophy and politics, both influenced by and influential in the broad cultural shift taking place as second-wave feminism roared through the decade. Many of her lectures and essays argue passionately in favor of women's primary connections to one another and against the way patriarchal institutions and norms consign women to destructive competition. In "Women and Honor: Some Notes on Lying," Rich urged women to escape the pervasive (since Adam and Eve, at least) idea that women are fundamentally less honest than men, by practicing a radical truthfulness among themselves. "Women have been forced to lie, for survival, to men. How to unlearn this among other women?" (p. 189). Her essay on Emily Dickinson, "Vesuvius at Home" is a major reconsideration of Dickinson's work that rescues the earlier poet from the persistent charge of insanity or extreme neurosis, by claiming her idiosyncratic genius and by examining Dickinson's relationships with the women who surrounded her as being particularly fertile for her poetry. "It Is the Lesbian in Us ...," which Rich first delivered as a paper for the Modern Language Association conference in 1976, caused considerable controversy, as even the most sympathetic heterosexual women in the audience were uncomfortable with the label "lesbian" as a metaphor for solidarity among women. "I believe it is the lesbian in every woman who is compelled by female energy. ... It is the lesbian in us who is creative, for the dutiful daughter of the fathers in us is only a hack" (pp. 200–201). Rich later regretted many of this essay's claims and her expansion of the word "lesbian." "Toward a Woman-Centered University," "Conditions for Work: The Common World of Women," and "Disloyal to Civilization: Feminism, Racism, and Gynephobia" all seek to bring the needs of women to the attention of government and social institutions and to encourage women to speak for themselves. Her essay on the poet Judy Grahn ("Power and Danger: Works of a Common Woman") produced Rich's first defining statement on what constitutes legitimate political poetry:

> No true political poetry can be written with propaganda as an aim, to persuade others "out there" of some atrocity or injustice (hence the failure, as poetry, of so much anti-Vietnam poetry of the sixties). *As poetry,* it can come only from the poet's need to identify her relationship to atrocities and injustice, the sources of her pain, fear, and anger, the meaning of her resistance.
>
> (p. 251)

Rich's strongest poems are characterized by this origin in individual experience, engagement with the wider world, and an acceptance of personal, social, and political complexity rather than its reduction.

In 1976, Rich published a chapbook collection of short poems, in the manner of a traditional sonnet sequence, under the title *Twenty-One Love Poems,* with the small, lesbian-run Effie Press of Emeryville, California. The sequence presents the first explicitly lesbian love poetry by a major American poet, and it also represented Rich's effective "coming out" to the literary and publishing world. Effie Press printed two editions of the chapbook before the sequence was incorporated as the middle section of Rich's next W. W. Norton volume, *The Dream of a Common Language: Poems 1974–1977* (1978). Rich insisted that the *Twenty-One Love Poems* were not meant to be universal; they were meant to both celebrate and defend the legitimacy of two women in love hoping to make a life together, though the sequence has achieved wide popularity among heterosexual readers as well. These poems demonstrate the effectiveness of Rich's melding of the personal and the political into powerful lyric expression, and her mastery of what the critic Kevin McGuirk calls her "relational, not unitary [poetic] subjectivity—social, gendered, historical: a politicized lyric self" (p. 61). "The rules break like a thermometer," she says in the thirteenth section, "quicksilver spills across the charted systems, / we're out in a country that has no language / no laws" (*CP,* p. 471). The sequence traces a love affair from the pleasures of companionship ("Your small hands, precisely equal to my own— / only the thumb is larger, longer," p. 468) to sexual ecstasy ("[THE FLOATING POEM, UNNUMBERED]," pp. 472–473) to the relationship's end, victim in part of the pressures exerted by social and legal condemnation of their love: "and these are the forces they had ranged against us / and these are the forces we had ranged within us, / within us and against us, against us and within us" (p. 474).

The Dream of a Common Language makes reference in its title not to hope for better communication between women and men but, rather, for a language of understanding and identification between women. The poems in the volume insistently explore the possibility for female connection: among contemporary women and with nearly forgotten women from the personal and historical past. The book opens with the poet thinking about the Nobel prize–winning physicist Marie Curie (the first woman so honored), whose discoveries of radium and plutonium helped to usher in the nuclear age. Curie died in 1934 of radiation sickness,

> She died a famous woman denying
> her wounds
> denying
> her wounds came from the same source as her power
> (*CP*, p. 443)

The second poem imagines the experiences of a Russian women's climbing team killed in a storm on Lenin's Peak in 1974. "The Phantasia for Elvira Shatayev" imagines the diary of Shatayev reflecting on the bond between the women on the team: "*We have dreamed of this / all of our lives*" (pp. 445–446).

Several poems in the volume present the poet's fear and resolve about the new life she has undertaken, her determination to live and love in the open as a lesbian ("Origins and History of Consciousness," "Splittings"), consider questions of social justice from a feminist point of view ("Hunger," "Mother-Right," "Natural Resources"), and attempt to make connections with women from the past ("Power," "Paula Becker to Clara Westhoff," "A Woman Dead in Her Forties"). Taken together the poems present a rich panorama of female experience, expressed less with anger toward men than admiration for the resourcefulness of women. "I have to cast my lot with those" women and mothers, who, "with no extraordinary power, / reconstitute the world" ("Natural Resources," p. 506).

The Dream of a Common Language ends with "Transcendental Etude," which the critic Jane Hedley identifies as a "greater ode" such as the Romantic poets wrote, and its reference to "transcendental" as evoking specifically the nineteenth-century American Romantics, the transcendentalists—Ralph Waldo Emerson and Henry David Thoreau, in particular ("Re-Forming the Cradle: Adrienne Rich's 'Transcendental Etude,'" p. 344). The poem is perhaps the best example of Rich's characteristic deployment of images from the natural world, as it contemplates a northern Vermont landscape familiar to one that might have been observed by Thoreau ("a green so dense with life, / minute, momentary life—slugs, moles, pheasants, gnats, / spiders, moths, hummingbirds, groundhogs, butterflies"; *CP*, p. 511) as well as a twentieth-century culture he would probably not recognize. All this is context for the poet's consideration of the conduct of her own life relative to geological time, "the huge / rockshelves that underlie all that life" (p. 511). Musical metaphors dominate the poem's interior reflections. Life is not like music lessons, that begin with "simple exercises." No, "we're forced to begin / in the midst of the hardest movement, / the one already sounding as we are born" (pp. 511–512). The poem is dedicated to Michelle Cliff, and it also celebrates Rich's pleasure and happiness in the relationship, "*I am the lover and the loved,*" she says, "a whole new poetry beginning here" (p. 514).

Rich's next volume of poetry, *A Wild Patience Has Taken Me This Far: Poems 1978–1981,* generally reflects the poet's settled personal happiness, and readers and critics expressed some disappointment at the volume's relatively inward focus. "Integrity," the first line of which provides the volume's title, expresses the poet's satisfaction at having successfully brought "to shore / a boat with a spasmodic outboard motor"—the boat, that is, of the poet's life—"this / long-dreamed involuntary landing / on the arm of an inland sea" (*CP*, pp. 523–524). Even "Culture and Anarchy," which contemplates the frustrated careers of earlier female thinkers, artists, and activists, finally expresses gratitude for love: "How you have given back to me / my dream of a common language / my solitude of self" (p. 530). "Frame" tells the story of a young black woman arrested for taking brief shelter from a storm in a university building in Boston, and "Heroines" recalls legal restrictions women faced in the past—but the poems return again and again to the joy and wonder of finding love.

LATER CAREER

In the 1980s and 1990s, Rich taught at Cornell and Stanford Universities, as well as for briefer periods as a visiting professor at Scripps College and San Jose State University, and she continued to garner prizes and awards along with increasing public recognition. She also continued to suffer from rheumatoid arthritis and had several surgeries related to the disease; she nonetheless continued to lecture and write both poetry and prose. But after the publication of *A Wild Patience Has Taken Me This Far* in 1981, Rich's political concerns began to widen beyond the specific concerns of women. She began to engage deeply with more broadly defined injustice in the United States and in the world. She demonstrated, in a dozen subsequent volumes of verse and three essay collections, that a major poet with deep political commitments could have a voice in the culture. Her later subjects range among social and economic inequality, racial injustice, American imperialism, globalization, environmental devastation, the rights of disabled and displaced persons, and media saturation, as well as the development of her own thought and understanding. While she never ceased being a feminist and writing about and on behalf of women, Rich grew increasingly concerned with the political, economic, and social structures that supported systems of oppression and alienated many individuals from their own perceptions and experience. Like other thinkers, Rich found the post-1970s world confusing and disorienting but she never lost her faith in the capacity of language to explain ourselves to ourselves. "I am both a poet and one of the 'everybodies' in my country," she said (*Poetry and Commitment,* p. 15). And being a poet always involved for Rich a special responsibility to use intentional language to push back against the social and economic forces of injustice and their false and deceptive language. "If there is a line to be drawn," she said, "it's not so much between secularism and belief as between those for whom language has metaphoric density and those for whom it is merely formulaic—to be used for repression, manipulation, empty certitudes to ensure obedience" (*Poetry and Commitment,* p. 33). She saw as her task to reform language made tired, less now by patriarchy itself but rather by its cynical manipulation in advertising and political rhetoric.

Albert Gelpi has said that Rich's rhetorical position in her later poems is that of prophetic witness, and he has identified Rich as the first female American poet to claim the role, occupied by the likes of Alfred Lord Tennyson and Henry Wadsworth Longfellow in the nineteenth century, and W. H. Auden and T. S. Eliot in the twentieth, of moral spokesperson for a nation and culture. Having arrived at a position of considerable literary authority, and of enduring personal happiness, writing, "from the center of her culture, speaking to and from and for the people of her time and place—women and men, dark-skinned and white, gay and straight" (Gelpi, 2001, p. 8), Rich continued to feel that poetry could play a role in a national discussion of human rights. The volumes of her later career have titles that reflect this civic focus and responsibility: *Your Native Land, Your Life: Poems* (1986), *Time's Power: Poems 1985–1988* (1989), *An Atlas of the Difficult World: Poems 1988–1991* (1991), and *Dark Fields of the Republic: Poems 1991–1995* (1995). And all through this period, Rich had to contend with readers and critics who wanted to fix her politics and thought in the mid-1970s. In "North American Time," from *Your Native Land Your Life,* she lamented, "Everything we write / will be used against us... / We move but our words stand" (*CP,* p. 595). "Delta," from *Time's Power,* expresses a similar lament: "If you have taken this rubble for my past / raking through it for fragments you could sell / know that I long ago moved on" (p. 683).

Rich's expanding vision is also reflected in her poetic forms. Longer lines, more discursive diction, and more frequent very long poems composed of multiple sections characterize her later work. The first poem she published after *A Wild Patience Has Taken Me This Far* is the searching and deeply reflective sequence "Sources"—a poem of twenty-three sections, which contemplates the many places and influences in the poet's life, including her Jewish inheritance from her father. "Yom Kippur 1984," included, like "Sources," in *Your Native Land, Your Life,* features long, prose-like lines, evoking the darkly prophetic poems of Robinson Jeffers, exploring nature, solitude, and atonement partly in the language of Jewish scripture.

Rich's later poems also make freer use of her own bodily suffering as analogy or metaphor for the world's increasing violence and the suffering of millions. She gives words to both the victims of violence and the otherwise physically disabled and laments their invisibility to the culture at large. In the long sequence "Contradictions: Tracking Poems," also from *Your Native Land, Your Life,* Rich explored explicitly for the first time what it had meant and would mean for her to live on with her disease. "The problem, / unstated till now, is how / to live in a damaged body" (*CP,* p. 650). "I feel signified by pain" she said earlier in the poem, "I'm already living the rest of my life / not under conditions of my choosing / wired into pain" (p. 644). Several later poems take this analogy between the pain of one's body and the world's pain as a starting point.

The many sections of the title poem of *An Atlas of the Difficult World* explore that difficulty in landscapes from Vermont to the poet's new home in California (Rich and her partner moved to Santa Cruz in 1984). The second section establishes the moral geography, "Here is a map of our country: / here is the Sea of Indifference" (*CP,* p. 711). The poem's final section, "XIII (Dedications)," turns decisively to imagine its readers, young and old, male and female, American and immigrant. The refrain "I know you are reading this poem" introduces a dozen scenarios: "late, before leaving your office," "standing up in a bookstore far from the ocean," "in a room where too much has happened for you to bear" (p. 728).

Rich carried this mode of authoritative address and cultural criticism into her prose writing as well. Her second collection of essays, *Blood, Bread, and Poetry: Selected Prose 1979–1985,* contains influential reflections on the negative influence of cultural norms on individual lives, as in "Compulsory Heterosexuality and Lesbian Experience," on the growing influence of feminist scholarship in academia, essays on other female poets ("The Eye of the Outsider" on Elizabeth Bishop, for example), as well as personal essays on her identification with her Jewish inheritance ("Split at the Root") and on what it means to be an engaged political poet. The title essay, as well as "Notes Toward a Politics of Location," are major statements on the subject. "Blood, Bread, and Poetry" begins as an autobiographical account of how the young Adrienne Rich came to connect the art of poetry with a sense of the world's injustice. "Notes Toward a Politics of Location" reflects Rich's renewed interest in the writings of Karl Marx, as well as her own sense of her Western, American identity. "I need to understand how a place on the map is also a place in history within which as a woman, a Jew, a lesbian, a feminist I am created and trying to create" (p. 212). "These notes are the marks of a struggle to keep moving, a struggle for accountability" (p. 211).

Beginning in the late 1980s, Rich also began to collect brief essays and reflections under the title "Notebooks on Poetry and Politics." The notebook was published in 1993 as *What Is Found There* (reissued with some additions in 2003). In this part anthology, part set of contemplations, Rich considers poets with whom she and her work have been in dialogue—including the modernists Wallace Stevens, T. S. Eliot, Robert Frost, and William Carlos Williams, as well as Walt Whitman and Emily Dickinson from the nineteenth century, and Elizabeth Bishop, Muriel Rukeyser, and many others from around the world in the twentieth century. In the section titled "Someone Is Writing a Poem," Rich claims that "every poem breaks a silence that had to be overcome," and succeeds when it arises from a symbiosis between the poet, the readers, and the world.

> [M]ost often someone writing a poem believes in, depends on, a delicate, vibrating range of difference, that an "I" can become a "we" without extinguishing others, that a partly common language exists to which strangers can bring their own heartbeat, memories, images. A language that itself has learned from the heartbeat, memories, images of strangers.
>
> (2003, p. 86)

Each of the last volumes of Rich's poetic career contains at least one long, multisectioned meditation on the political and spiritual condition of the world and of the poet. After the mid-1990s, Rich saw the United States turn away from poetry and art more generally, in favor of an overwhelming materialism, nearly every gesture arising from the profit motive. As her American readership began to disappear (Rich was and continues to be a widely read poet elsewhere in the world), she continued to write and publish but with an increasing sense of alienation from the culture. When she was awarded the National Medal for the Arts, the United States's highest award for artists, in 1997, she refused to accept it, saying in a letter to Jane Alexander, then director of the National Endowment for the Arts, that "the very meaning of art, as I understand it, is incompatible with the cynical politics of this [Bill Clinton] administration." She went on to say, "In my lifetime I have seen the space for the arts opened by movements for social justice, the power of art to break despair. Over the past two decades I have witnessed the increasingly brutal impact of racial and economic injustice in our country." Art, Rich continued, "means nothing if it simply decorates the dinner table of power that holds it hostage" (*Arts of the Possible,* p. 99). This "political culture of managed spectacles and passive spectators" nevertheless continues to need the "rift, a peculiar lapse, in the prevailing mode" that poetry can provide (*What Is Found There,* p. 84). The long poems of Rich's late career seek, over and over, to provide that rift. "Calle Visión," from *The Dark Fields of the Republic*—the Spanish translates literally as "vision street"), plays that refrain through ten sections, its central meaning the prophetic vision born of extreme suffering. Her own physical pain, "wounded knee / wounded spine wounded eye" is the starting point: "Calle Visión / never forget / the body's pain" (*CP,* pp. 760–762). The analogy to her own pain in the poem is that suffered by laborers in difficult, repetitive jobs, and the poet is their witness: "I wear my triple eye as I walk along the road / past, present, future all are at my side" (p. 765).

The title poem of *Midnight Salvage: Poems 1995–1998* (1999) recalls the exploration/excavation metaphors of "Diving into the Wreck," but what is to be salvaged is the poet's struggling sense of her own vocation. The poem announces the dispirited end of her teaching career and reflects on the faded goals of her political and poetic work: "Had never expected hope would form itself / completely in my time... // But neither was expecting in my time / to witness this" (*CP,* p. 809). "This" is both the state of the culture and the state of the poet's own body.

"Terza Rima," from *Fox: Poems 1998–2000* (2001), contemplates through thirteen sections of three-line stanzas the turn of the twentieth-century to the twenty-first, in the world and in the poet's life. (At the time, many predicted mass confusion when computer software would fail to recognize dates beginning 20- rather than 19-, a non-crisis known as "Y2K.") "At the end of the beaten path we're sold free / tickets for the celebration / of the death of history" (*CP,* p. 878). The title poem of *The School Among the Ruins: Poems 2000–2004* (2004) was written just after the terrorist attacks in the United States on September 11, 2001, and the start of the war in Afghanistan launched in response to those attacks. The poem's epigraph recalls with some bitterness the world's recent wars: "*Beirut. Baghdad.Sarajevo.Bethlehem.Kabul. Not of course here,*" and the poem itself imagines a school in an unspecified war zone that becomes a makeshift shelter when the bombs start to fall. The juxtaposition between the setting and norms of a school day and the desperate situation of the teacher and students gives the poem its pathos.

"Powers of Recuperation," from Rich's final volume, *Tonight No Poetry Will Serve: Poems 2007–2010* (2011), shares a distinctly valedictory feeling with many other late poems, and it also illustrates once again the connection that animated and inspired all of Rich's best work, the analogy between the experience of the self and the history of the world. "A woman of the citizen party—*what's that*— / is writing history backward // her body the chair she sits in / to be abandoned repossessed" (*CP,* p. 1095), but "her documentary alphabet [is] still evolving" (p. 1099). In "Endpapers," the last poem Rich chose to publish, the poet provides her own postscript, "the signature to a life": "rejection of posturing / trust in the witnesses" (p. 1119).

ADRIENNE RICH

The poetry, prose, and cultural influence of Adrienne Rich helped to transform the critical understanding of what poetry could be, of the relationship between poetry and politics, of the shape and trajectory of the American poetic tradition, and of the value of poetry to culture and society. And along the way, she gave compelling voice to the pressing cultural and human rights movements of her time. In 1978, the poet and novelist Margaret Atwood memorably reviewed *The Dream of a Common Language,* saying, "Rich's poems do not demand the willing suspension of disbelief. They demand belief, and it is a measure of her success as a poet that most of the time they get it" (p. 2).

Selected Bibliography

WORKS OF ADRIENNE CECILE RICH

POETRY

A Change of World. New Haven, Conn.: Yale University Press, 1951.

The Diamond Cutters and Other Poems. New York: Harper & Brothers, 1955.

Snapshots of a Daughter-in-Law: Poems 1954–1962. New York: Harper & Row, 1963. New York: W. W. Norton, 1967. London: Chatto & Windus, 1970.

Necessities of Life: Poems 1962–1965. New York: W. W. Norton, 1966.

Selected Poems. London: Chatto & Windus, 1967.

Leaflets: Poems 1965–1968. New York: W. W. Norton, 1969. London: Chatto & Windus, 1973.

The Will to Change: Poems 1968–1970. New York: W. W. Norton, 1971. London: Chatto & Windus, 1973.

Diving into the Wreck: Poems 1971–1972. New York: W. W. Norton, 1973.

Poems: Selected and New, 1950–1974. New York: W. W. Norton, 1975.

Twenty-One Love Poems. Emeryville, Calif.: Effie's Press, 1976.

The Dream of a Common Language: Poems 1974–1977. New York: W. W. Norton, 1978.

A Wild Patience Has Taken Me This Far: Poems 1978–1981. New York: W. W. Norton, 1981.

Sources. Woodside, Calif.: Heyeck Press, 1983.

The Fact of a Doorframe: Poems Selected and New 1950–1984. New York: W. W. Norton, 1984.

Your Native Land, Your Life: Poems. New York: W. W. Norton, 1986.

Time's Power: Poems 1985–1988. New York: W. W. Norton, 1989.

An Atlas of the Difficult World: Poems 1988–1991. New York: W. W. Norton, 1991.

Collected Early Poems 1950–1970. New York: W. W. Norton, 1993.

Dark Fields of the Republic: Poems 1991–1995. New York: W. W. Norton, 1995.

Midnight Salvage: Poems 1995–1998. New York: W. W. Norton, 1999.

Fox: Poems 1998–2000. New York: W. W. Norton, 2001.

The Fact of a Doorframe: Poems 1950–2001. New York: W. W. Norton, 2002.

The School Among the Ruins: Poems 2000–2004. New York: W. W. Norton, 2004.

Telephone Ringing in the Labyrinth: Poems 2004–2006. New York: W. W. Norton, 2007.

Tonight No Poetry Will Serve: Poems 2007–2010. New York: W. W. Norton, 2011.

Later Poems: Selected and New 1971–2012. New York: W. W. Norton, 2012.

PROSE

Of Woman Born: Motherhood as Experience and Institution. New York: W. W. Norton, 1976. Tenth anniversary edition, with new foreword, 1986.

On Lies, Secrets, and Silence: Selected Prose 1966–1978. New York: W. W. Norton, 1979.

Blood, Bread, and Poetry: Selected Prose 1979–1985. New York: W. W. Norton, 1986.

What Is Found There: Notebooks on Poetry and Politics. New York: W. W. Norton, 1993. Revised and expanded, 2003.

Poetry and Commitment: An Essay. New York: W. W. Norton, 2007.

The Human Eye: Essays on Art in Society, 1997–2008. New York: W. W. Norton, 2009.

Arts of the Possible: Essays and Conversations. New York: W. W. Norton, 2013.

MANUSCRIPTS

Adrienne Rich's papers are housed at the Schlesinger Library, Radcliffe College, Cambridge, Massachusetts.

COLLECTED WORKS

Adrienne Rich's Poetry. Edited by Barbara Charlesworth Gelpi and Albert Gelpi. New York: W. W. Norton, 1975. (Revised and enlarged as *Adrienne Rich's Poetry and Prose,* 1993.)

Collected Poems: 1950–2012. New York: W. W. Norton, 2016.

ADRIENNE RICH

CRITICAL AND BIOGRAPHICAL STUDIES

BOOKS ABOUT ADRIENNE RICH

Cooper, Jane Roberta, ed. *Reading Adrienne Rich: Reviews and ReVisions, 1951–1981.* Ann Arbor: University of Michigan Press, 1984.

Keyes, Claire. *The Aesthetics of Power: The Poetry of Adrienne Rich.* Athens: University of Georgia Press, 1986.

Templeton, Alice. *The Dream and the Dialogue: Adrienne Rich's Feminist Poetics.* Knoxville: University of Tennessee Press, 1994.

Werner, Craig. *Adrienne Rich: The Poet and Her Critics.* Chicago: American Library Association, 1988.

BOOKS WITH CHAPTERS ON ADRIENNE RICH

Altieri, Charles. *Self and Sensibility in Contemporary American Poetry.* Cambridge, U.K.: Cambridge University. Press, 1984.

Bennett, Paula. *My Life a Loaded Gun: Feminist Creativity and Feminist Poetics.* Boston: Beacon Press, 1986.

Dickie, Margaret. *Stein, Bishop, and Rich: Lyrics of Love, War and Place.* Chapel Hill: University of North Carolina Press, 1997.

Hedley, Jane. *I Made You to Find Me: The Coming of Age of the Woman Poet and the Politics of Poetic Address.* Columbus: Ohio State University Press, 2009.

Juhasz, Suzanne. *Naked and Fiery Forms: Modern American Poetry by Women, a New Tradition.* New York: Harper, 1976.

Kalaidjian, David. *Languages of Liberation: The Social Text on Contemporary American Poetry.* New York: Columbia University Press, 1989.

Kalstone, David. *Five Temperaments: Elizabeth Bishop, Robert Lowell, James Merrill, Adrienne Rich, John Ashbery.* New York: Oxford University Press, 1989.

Martin, Wendy. *An American Triptych: Anne Bradstreet, Emily Dickinson, Adrienne Rich.* Chapel Hill: University of North Carolina Press, 1984.

Ostriker, Alicia. *Writing Like a Woman.* Ann Arbor: University of Michigan Press, 1986.

Speigelman, Willard. *The Didactic Muse.* Princeton, N.J.: Princeton University Press, 1989.

ARTICLES

Atwood, Margaret. "Unfinished Women." *New York Times Book Review,* June 11, 1978, p. 2.

Boyers, Robert. "On Adrienne Rich: Intelligence and Will." *Salmagundi* 22–23:132–148 (spring–summer 1973).

Clark, Miriam Marty. "Human Rights and the Work of the Lyric in Adrienne Rich." *Cambridge Quarterly* 38, no. 1:45–65 (2009).

Erickson, Peter. "Singing America: From Walt Whitman to Adrienne Rich." *Kenyon Review* 17, no. 1:103–119 (winter 1995).

Estrin, Barbara L. "Re-Versing the Past: Adrienne Rich's Postmodern Inquietude." *Tulsa Studies in Women's Literature* 16, no. 2:345–371 (autumn 1997).

Gelpi, Albert. "Adrienne Rich: The Poetics of Change." *American Poetry Since 1960.* Edited by R. B. Shaw. Cheadle, Cheshire, U.K.: Carcanet Press, 1973.

———. "The Transfiguration of the Body: Adrienne Rich's Witness." *Wallace Stevens Journal.* 23, no. 1:7–18 (spring 2001).

Hedley, Jane. "Re-Forming the Cradle": Adrienne Rich's "Transcendental Etude." *Genre* 28, no. 3:339–370 (fall 1995).

Hogue, Cynthia. "The 'Possible Poet': Pain, Form, and the Embodied Poetics of Adrienne Rich in Wallace Stevens' Wake." *Wallace Stevens Journal* 25, no. 1:40–51 (spring 2001).

McGuirk, Kevin. "Philoctetes Radicalized: 'Twenty-One Love Poems' and the Lyric Career of Adrienne Rich." *Contemporary Literature* 34, no. 1:61–87 (spring 1993).

Stein, Rachel. "'To Make the Visible World Your Conscience': Adrienne Rich as Revolutionary Nature Writer." In *Reading Under the Sign of Nature: New Essays in Ecocriticism.* Edited by John Tallmadge and Henry Harringon, 199–207. Salt Lake City: University of Utah Press, 2000.

INTERVIEWS

Gelpi, Barbara Charlesworth, and Albert Gelpi. "Three Conversations with Adrienne Rich." In Rich, *Adrienne Rich's Poetry.* Edited by Gelpi and Gelpi, 105–122. New York: W. W. Norton, 1975.

Montenegro, David. "An Interview with Adrienne Rich." *American Poetry Review* 20, no. 1:7–14 (January–February 1991). Reprinted in Rich, *Adrienne Rich's Poetry and Prose.* Edited by Gelpi and Gelpi. New York: W. W. Norton, 1993, pp. 258–272.

Rothschild, Matthew. "Adrienne Rich: 'I Happen to Think That Poetry Makes a Huge Difference.'" *Progressive,* January 1994, p. 31. Reprinted at http://www.english.illinois.edu/maps/poets/m_r/rich/progressive.htm

MARK TWAIN

(1835—1910)

Joe B. Fulton

MARK TWAIN DESCRIBED himself as America's "special ambassador to the world" (*Mark Twain Speaking,* 1976, p. 440), and certainly no American writer has ever matched his level of international fame, popular affection, or critical acclaim. A revered figure at home and abroad, Twain wrote works that have been translated into French, Spanish, Italian, German, Russian, Japanese, Chinese, and Hindi. His characters Tom Sawyer and Huckleberry Finn are among the most recognized and beloved literary figures ever created, and through his characters and writing style Twain has continued to influence generations of writers in the decades since his death.

Twain's importance to literary history owes something to the quality of his best work as well as to the quantity and diversity of his secondary work. Twain patterned his most memorable characters on people he knew during his Hannibal, Missouri, boyhood—so much so that his sister Pamela exclaimed when hearing the description of Huck in *The Adventures of Tom Sawyer* (1876), "Why, that's Tom Blankenship!" (Webster, p. 265). At the same time, Twain wrote brilliant stories in dialect such as "Jim Smiley and His Jumping Frog" (1865), delightful tall tales like "Jim Baker's Blue-Jay Yarn" (collected in *A Tramp Abroad,* 1880), and the historical romance *The Prince and the Pauper* (1882), which established a plot line now so common that many, perhaps most, people do not realize it was written by Twain. Or consider the genre of dystopian or even science fiction with *A Connecticut Yankee in King Arthur's Court* (1889), in which the mechanic Hank Morgan is hit over the head with a crowbar and travels back in time to Arthurian England. Twain coined many sayings and proverbs, too, placing him in a pantheon of most-quoted Americans along with Benjamin Franklin, Henry Wadsworth Longfellow, and Ralph Waldo Emerson. Many of Twain's apothegms were designed to be comic proverbs and were used for chapter epigraphs, like these examples from *Following the Equator* (1897): "When in doubt, tell the truth," "'*Classic.*' A book which people praise and don't read," and "Man is the only animal that blushes. Or needs to" (pp. 35, 241, 256). As a further measure of Twain's importance, one might also note that people frequently ascribe to Mark Twain any witticism anyone has ever said.

Twain's impact extends far beyond memorable characters, plots, and proverbs, however, for his greatness is also measured by his influence on writers who came after him. With his dialect writing, sense of humor, and humanity, Mark Twain turned regional writing into a viable universal aesthetic. Ernest Hemingway famously said in *Green Hills of Africa* (1935) that "all modern American literature comes from one book by Mark Twain called *Huckleberry Finn*" (p. 22). In a 1953 address titled "American Literature and the American Language," the poet T. S. Eliot identified Twain as one of the writers who "purified the dialect of the tribe" and "discovered a new way of writing" that others could use as well (pp. 16–17). Twain truly changed the way stories are written; just as Dante embraced Italian over Latin, Twain embraced the American dialect over formal English, except for Twain this was a comic device. When Twain finished writing *Tom Sawyer,* he felt that he had made a mistake in not writing it in the first person, and he began writing the sequel almost immediately. By adopting as his narrator Huck Finn, Twain expanded the writer's ability to convey irony in all its forms, to reveal the world through the ingenuous eyes of a naive youth, and to embrace an American picaresque that has generated countless road stories. That the opening line of *Adventures of Huckleberry Finn* (1884)—"You don't know about me, without you have read a book by the name of *The Adventures of Tom Sawyer*"—and Huck's statement at the end of the book—"I reckon I got to light out for the Territory"—are two of the most famous lines in world literature illustrates the supreme importance of that book and its author (2003 edition, pp. 1, 362).

LIFE

The writer known to the world as Mark Twain was born Samuel Langhorne Clemens on November 30, 1835, in Florida, Missouri, to John Marshall Clemens and Jane Lampton Clemens. Sam Clemens had six siblings, two of whom survived into adulthood: his brother Orion and his sister Pamela. Sam's family had emigrated to Missouri from Virginia, and the southern influence remained strong throughout his life, from his pronounced drawl that he often exaggerated for comic or theatrical effect to the lasting legacy of slavery on his writing. Born into a slaveholding family in a slave state, Sam wrote in the 1890 eulogy "Jane Lampton Clemens" that his mother and everyone in the community were taught, even from the pulpit, that slavery was "right, righteous, sacred" (*Mark Twain's Hannibal, Huck, and Tom,* pp. 48–49). Only later did Sam question the slave system that prevailed in Missouri. While Sam's family had few slaves at any given time, he spent a lot of time at his Uncle John Quarles's plantation, where there were many more slaves. In later years, Mark Twain often wrote with a sense of nostalgia of his boyhood, but his happy memories were haunted by a sense of injustice as he realized that his own happy childhood was not happy for the slaves he remembered fondly.

Sam's father, an elected judge, died in 1847, greatly impoverishing the family. The next year, at twelve years old, Sam began working as a printer's devil (a person who set the metal type in a print shop), for Joseph P. Ament at the *Hannibal Gazette.* In 1851, Sam went to work for his brother Orion's newspaper, which changed names several times before becoming the *Hannibal Journal.* Although Sam did not adopt the pseudonym Mark Twain until 1863, he actually became a writer at a much younger age. Scholars do not know for certain when Sam first wrote for the newspapers, but it was perhaps as early as 1848. His first known piece is "A Gallant Fireman" (1851) and his first story is "The Dandy Frightening the Squatter" (1852). Like another important American writer, Benjamin Franklin, Twain became a writer in great measure due to his early experiences writing for his brother's newspaper. Setting into type what other writers had written also helped him learn effective writing style.

Another great influence on the young author was the Mississippi River itself. Sam's family moved from Florida, Missouri, to the river town of Hannibal, Missouri, in 1839. As Twain chronicles in *Life on the Mississippi* (1883), when he was growing up on the river, with two packet boats arriving each day, one from the north and one from the south, it was natural that "there was but one permanent ambition among my comrades in our village on the bank of the Mississippi River. That was, to be a steamboatman" (p. 32). Twain became a cub pilot with Horace Bixby as his teacher, experiences he lovingly described in "Old Times on the Mississippi" (1875), later included in *Life on the Mississippi.*

Twain had not long to serve as a pilot, however, for with the onset of the Civil War, river traffic was closed as a result of the federal blockade. The Civil War was a crisis in Twain's life, for Missouri was a border state and the northernmost outpost of slavery, making it difficult for him to choose sides. As he wrote in "The Private History of a Campaign That Failed" (1885), "Out West there was a good deal of confusion in men's minds during the first months of the great trouble" (*Collected Tales, Sketches, Speeches, and Essays, 1852–1890,* p. 863). Northern Missouri was culturally the most southern part of the state, with the highest population of slaves living in the cotton-growing region along the Missouri River, a region referred to as "Little Dixie" (Rafferty, p. 42). Samuel Clemens enlisted in a state militia called the Marion Rangers, named for the county where Hannibal is located. Although the Marion Rangers was ostensibly a state militia, it was Confederate in its very bones and sinews, a part of the Missouri State Guard proposed by the secessionist governor Claiborne Fox Jackson for the repelling of "invaders," coded language referring to federal forces; the secessionist nature of the militia was obvious to people at the time, and Union General William Harney denounced the legislation that brought the guard into existence as "an indirect secession ordinance" (Root, p. 261). The adjutant-general of the Missouri State Guard, Colonel Thomas L. Snead, went on to become the Confederacy's chief of staff of the Army of the West, while Sam Clemens' own commander in the guard, General Thomas A. Harris, likewise had a distinguished military career on the Southern side and served in the Confederate Congress. The guard fought against federal troops at Boonville, Carthage, and Wilson's Creek (McReynolds, pp. 224–230). In 1862, the Confederate Congress provided one million Confederate dollars "for the defense of the State of Missouri," much of it funding Missouri State Guard units, and by 1863, the Missouri State Guard was largely subsumed into the Confederate Army; the United States War Department classed the Missouri State Guard with "Confederate Organizations" (Root, pp. 281–282, 5).

According to Sam's niece, Annie Moffett, he had intended to move south with the militia to join with Confederate General Sterling Price's army (Webster, p. 60). Prevented by the quick action of Union forces, which had divided the state, Sam found himself marooned, a member of a Confederate militia prevented from going south to join General Sterling Price. His brother Orion had been appointed by the Abraham Lincoln administration to serve as secretary for the Nevada Territory, and Sam went with him as an assistant mainly to get out of Missouri. Sam thus left "the states" that were then at war—like Huck Finn, lighting out for the territory.

It was in the Nevada Territory that Sam Clemens became Mark Twain. Silver and gold had brought many prospectors to the territory, and Sam himself had hopes of striking it rich. While in the mining fields, he continued his practice of lampooning people, politicians in particular. A burlesque of a Fourth of July speech came to the attention of Joseph Goodman, the editor of the Virginia City (Nevada) *Territorial Enterprise.* Clemens began writing for the *Enterprise* in 1862 with such works as the hoaxes "Petrified Man," "A Bloody Massacre near Carson," and comic reports on the territorial legislature. Twain began to establish a name for himself as a comic and satirical writer, but his wit and pro-Southern views led to a scandal when he published an article insulting the Republican ladies of Carson City, who had been raising money for the Sanitary Fund, a forerunner of the American Red Cross (recounted in Fulton, 2010, pp. 71–87). The resulting ruckus led to Twain's rapid departure from the territory in 1864, as he hoped to avoid a duel.

Twain landed on his feet in San Francisco, where he wrote burlesques of popular fiction and continued his wildly humorous reportage on events as diverse as police scandals, earthquakes, and boxing matches. His pieces were frequently reprinted in the West, and by 1865 he had achieved considerable regional fame. It was a visit to a California mining camp, however, that first made his national, even international, reputation, for it was at "Angel's Camp" that Twain heard a story that he crafted into "Jim Smiley and His Jumping Frog," the dialect tale of a man who loses a bet when a stranger tips his jumping frog full of quail shot. This sketch, first published in the New York *Saturday Press* in November 1865, made readers hop with laughter. In 1867, the sketch became the title story of Twain's first book, *The Celebrated Jumping Frog of Calaveras County, and Other Sketches.*

Twain also conceived of the scheme of booking passage on the charter steamship *Quaker City* during its cruise to Europe and the Holy Land in 1867. Twain contrived to have himself introduced as the "Reverend Mark Twain" to trick the ship's committee on character into allowing him aboard. Twain then wrote humorous sketches about the journey, many of them poking satirical fun at the other members on the trip. Those *Quaker City* sketches, revised and expanded, were published as *The Innocents Abroad* two years later. One of the passengers on the trip was a young Charles

Langdon, whose sister had presented him with a cameo before his departure. Twain fell in love with the woman depicted on the cameo and asked Charles to introduce them when they returned to New York. Twain and the young woman, Olivia ("Livy") Langdon, were married in 1869; over the next eleven years they had a son and three daughters. The family was as different from Twain's as one could imagine: Northern, abolitionist Republican, and wealthy. Twain's first full-length books *The Innocents Abroad* (1869) and *Roughing It* (1872) solidified his reputation as a writer but led readers to see him only as a comic writer. One exception was the influential author and critic William Dean Howells, who discerned in Twain a genius for capturing American speech and folkways in his writing.

Twain's popularity expanded with the publication of his travel books and novels. Much of Mark Twain's best work owes an obvious debt to his early life. The "Matter of the River" and the "Matter of Hannibal," as Henry Nash Smith has called it in *Mark Twain: The Development of a Writer* (1962), played a tremendous role in providing many characters, story ideas, and many of the lifelong preoccupations with race (p. 72). It is as hard to imagine Twain's writing without the presence of the Mississippi River as it is to imagine Herman Melville's without the ocean. Likewise, his formative experiences as a writer in the West left a lasting imprint on Twain's writing. One sees it especially in *Tom Sawyer* and *Huckleberry Finn,* both of which contain moments of charm and lyricism as well as elements of serious social commentary. From an early point in his career, Twain took an active role in the publication of his books, certainly from *The Innocents Abroad* on, frequently blurring the line between author and publisher, ultimately purchasing the Charles L. Webster publishing company. Twain's increasing involvement in the business of publishing was paralleled by his increasing involvement in investments of all sorts, usually with negative consequences. By far the most disastrous investment was in the Paige typesetting machine. The former printer's devil must have been fascinated by the dream of a machine that would automatically set type, but the invention was ill-conceived and never worked properly. Meanwhile, the publishing house was doing poorly. When the depression of 1893 struck, Twain's business and personal creditors demanded payments he could not make. Twain was rescued by a businessman who knew what he was doing: Henry Huttleston Rogers, of Standard Oil fame. Under Rogers' guidance, Twain was able to declare bankruptcy to gain time to pay his debts honorably, a feat he completed in 1898.

Personal tragedies likewise marred Twain's later years. Twain felt responsible for the death of his nineteen-month-old son, Langdon, who died of diphtheria in 1872, blaming himself for allowing the child to catch chill, but the death of his oldest daughter, Susy, from meningitis in 1896 was a blow from which he never really recovered. Twenty-four-year-old Susy and her sister Jean had remained in America while the rest of the family was in Europe as Twain lectured and wrote to recover the family finances. After receiving word by telegraph that Susy was ill, Livy left with their daughter Clara for America; Twain departed a short time later. The child perished before they arrived. Susy's death has often been identified as a cause of the bitterness visible in Twain's later writings, and if Twain never recovered from the blow, neither did his wife, whose health declined over the next years. Livy died in 1904. A controversy surrounding Twain's private secretary Isabell Lyon and business manager Ralph Ashcroft also soured his later years. Lyon and Ashcroft gained power of attorney over the author and used it to misappropriate funds. Lyon also alienated Twain from his daughters Clara and Jean. After recriminations and lawsuits, Twain disentangled himself from the pair, reunited with his daughters, and enjoyed something of a renaissance in his outlook. With the death of Jean on Christmas Eve 1909, all of his children except for Clara had preceded him in death.

Although Twain's last years were marked by business disaster and personal tragedy, many scholars have demonstrated that he produced many minor masterpieces during this era. William Macnaughton has pointed out that the period between July 1904 and October 1906 was "one of the most remarkable and creative periods in Clemens's long career" (p. 202). Harold K. Bush has suggested that the death of Susy Clemens contributed to Twain's anti-imperialist writings and other polemical work by providing a better angel of his nature—Susy became a person whose ideals he fought for (pp. 155, 162). When Mark Twain died, there was an outpouring of affection rarely seen for a literary figure. Fans, fellow writers, and politicians issued statements about his death. At his funeral, his friend William Dean Howells famously said, "Emerson, Longfellow, Lowell, Holmes—I knew them all and all the rest of our sages, poets, seers, critics, humorists; they were like one another and like other literary men; but Clemens was sole, incomparable, the Lincoln of our literature" (p. 101).

When Twain was born, Halley's Comet was visible in the sky. When Mark Twain passed away in 1910, Halley's Comet was again streaking through the heavens, having returned on its seventy-six-year orbit. The celestial fire was a fitting tribute to a writer whose work changed the literary world.

EARLY WORK AND THE FROG THAT MADE AMERICA JUMP WITH LAUGHTER

Twain was profoundly influenced by newspaper and magazine culture, and many of his earliest writings burlesqued the literary models he was familiar with as a typesetter in the 1850s. Burlesques, humorous imitations of literary genres, comprised a large portion of his early literary output, both in Hannibal and in the West. Considering his writings from the 1850s, mainly in Missouri, and from the 1860s in the Nevada Territory and California, one is struck by the variety of genres Twain experimented with as he burlesqued letters to the editor, advice columns, boxing reviews, fashion columns, romantic and sentimental fiction, political biography and reporting, crime reporting, advertisements, and social criticism.

At the same time, Twain was influenced by the southwestern humorists and dialect writers—"southwestern" at this time denoting writers from Georgia, Alabama, Tennessee, Arkansas, and Mississippi. (In more recent times this region has been referred to as the "Old Southwest.") The writing of the southwestern humorists was characterized by a gentleman narrator describing frontier life with heavy use of dialect and frequently coarse or violent plots. Writers in the genre include Joseph G. Baldwin, Augustus Baldwin Longstreet, and Thomas Bangs Thorpe, and their influence is visible in Twain's earliest known story, "The Dandy Frightening the Squatter" (1852). The Missouri squatter, or pioneer, is a man of few words who makes short work of the bragging dandy.

Kenneth Lynn's book *Mark Twain and Southwestern Humor* (1959) is one of the most useful books for understanding Twain's literary antecedents. Impatient with the view of Twain as a naive writer composing solely from his own experience, Lynn explores Twain's literary predecessors, making the important point that Twain adopted from southwestern humor the frame structure of the story with an educated gentleman as narrator who introduces the dialect speaker (pp. 64, 167). David E. E. Sloane has argued in *Mark Twain as a Literary Comedian* (1979) that Twain's true literary ancestors were not the southwestern humorists but were in fact "the literary comedians of the 1850s and the Civil War era" (p. 1). Both scholars reveal that behind Twain's writing are deep traditions of literary humor that he exploited as he created his own brilliant work.

On February 3, 1863, Twain's "Letter from Carson City" was published in the *Territorial Enterprise.* In this comic letter, Twain ranged freely from the Nevada weather to politics and dancing. The publication is remembered today for the simple reason that it is thought to be the first time Samuel Clemens used the pseudonym Mark Twain, but it is notable that even with that first work known to have been signed with his pseudonym, the writer went well beyond the bounds of the typical newspaper humorist. In many instances, he tested what was and was not acceptable. In 1863, he published "The Great Prize Fight," a raucous reporting of the Republican gubernatorial conflict between the California governor Leland Stanford and Stanford's successor, Frederick Ferdinand Low. Twain reported the infighting within the Republican party as if it were a bare-knuckled brawl, depicting Low's fans as yelling "Bully for the fat Boy!" when their candidate landed a punch on Stanford and "split him in the mug" (in *Collected Tales, Sketches, Speeches, and Essays, 1852–1890,* p. 52). The sketch featured exaggerated, grotesque depictions of physical violence to comically depict a no-holds-barred political fight during the Civil War. In "Lucretia Smith's Soldier," Twain burlesqued the sentimental Civil War stories about lovers who had been separated by war but were reunited with the young woman nursing the wounded soldier back to health. In Twain's story, however, the protagonist, Lucretia Borgia Smith, nurses the wrong soldier back to health—a fact only apparent when she unwraps the bandages from his face. If such works tested the bounds of the acceptable, consider that Twain even wrote a burlesque about John Wilkes Booth's assassination of President Lincoln less than two months after the tragedy (Fulton, 2010, pp. 99–102). Twain's earliest writings in Missouri and the West are typified by a wild, even reckless, sense of the comic.

Twain first achieved national fame when he published "Jim Smiley and His Jumping Frog" in New York's *Saturday Press* in November 1865. The story is the perfect example of Twain's dialect writing. Using the convention of a frame narrator drawn from southwestern humorists, Twain introduces a narrator named Simon Wheeler who tells the story of an acquaintance named Jim Smiley who would bet on anything from dog fights, to which bird would fly off a fence first, to whose frog could jump farthest. Like many dialect sketches, the plot is rather skeletal, with the fun all in the telling of the story, the comical diction, the descriptions, and the characterizations. The story was republished throughout the country and became the basis for Twain's first book, *The Celebrated Jumping Frog of Calaveras County, and Other Sketches* (1867). The line repeated in the story became a byword, with many quoting it, "Well—I don't see no points about that frog that's better'n any other frog" (*Early Tales and Sketches,* vol. 2, p. 286).

THE INNOCENTS ABROAD *AND* ROUGHING IT

The publication of *The Innocents Abroad* (1869) widened and extended Twain's popularity. Many of the letters Twain wrote as a traveling correspondent for the *Alta California,* a San Francisco daily paper, had already been reprinted, but rather than dampening sales this fact seemed to expand the market for the book. The book was a standard book—that is, a book that would have a defined number of pages, be profusely illustrated, and would provide humor as well as information. Twain published his book through the subscription method, by which canvassers would take a prospectus, or mock-up, of the book along with sample pages of both the writing and the illustrations. By this method, subscription publishers could reach many people outside of the large cities. Sales were brisk and amounted to nearly 70,000 copies in the first year, but the book continued to sell respectably and reached around 125,000 on its ten-year anniversary (Hill, p. 39).

Hamlin Hill has noted that subscription publishing favored books that were "patently subliterary" (p. 10), and that was a reputation that transferred to Twain's work. The means by which his book was published, together with its popular success, saddled Twain with a "lowbrow" reputation that he fought for many years. The humor of *The Innocents Abroad* also contributed to this reputation, of course. In his "Preface" to the book, Twain wrote that his purpose was "to suggest to the reader how *he* would be likely to see Europe and the East if he looked at them with his own eyes instead of the eyes of those who travelled in those countries before him" and that his method was to present how he himself saw with "impartial eyes" (1869 edition, p. v). The significance of his statement is twofold. From the outset, he would write by distancing himself from those learned commentators who had visited Europe and the Holy Land before him, and in doing so he identified with his audience, as a representative American. Frequently, the result was a humor that was also pragmatic, providing an honest assessment of what he saw with his own eyes, distinct from any authorities that, however revered, might be spurious. So, for instance, he joked about relics, shrines, and saints that many writers treated reverentially; among many other examples, he joked that he had seen the ashes of St. John in two different churches, had seen so many nails purportedly used at the crucifixion that it amounted to an entire "keg of these nails," and "as for the bones of St. Denis, I feel certain we have seen enough of them to duplicate him, if necessary" (p. 165).

He also joked about his fellow "pilgrims," giving them names like "The Oracle," "The Poet," and "The Pilgrim," often satirizing them mercilessly. These aspects of Twain's work appealed to many people, who found his work refreshing, as it slashed through sham and fakery. For others, it revealed Twain's fundamental irreverence, coarseness, and mean-spiritedness. Among those who criticized Twain were Matthew Arnold, who classed him with the philistines, and the Dartmouth College professor Charles F. Richardson, whose *American Literature, 1607–1885,* is considered the first full-length history of American literature. Richardson specifically cited Twain's *Innocents Abroad* as showing that the author was merely a humorist rather than a serious writer. Richardson famously chided that Twain had better "make hay while the sun shines," with the folk proverb expressing his disdain for a writer who had too much "flavor of the soil" and whose works did not actually constitute literature (1886, pp. 521–522).

Twain's second book, *Roughing It* (1872), was based on his experiences in the Nevada Territory, California, and Hawaii. The structure of *The Innocents Abroad* was based on the itinerary of the *Quaker City,* but *Roughing It* was more arbitrary, recording what Twain called in the "Prefatory" his "variegated vagabondizing" of the 1860s. Twain did rely on many of his publications from that era, but he also included sections written specifically for the book. Many of Twain's chapters have achieved an existence apart from the larger narrative: the description of the jackrabbit in chapter 3 and the coyote in chapter 5, the tall tale of the buffalo that climbed a tree in chapter 7, the story of the "genuine Mexican plug" in chapter 24, the mutually incomprehensible dialects in the story of Scotty Briggs and the Parson in chapter 47, and the comic meandering of "The Story of the Old Ram" in chapter 53, among many others. At the same time, Twain does achieve a unity amid variety in his story, and the book also offers the sense of beginning as a naive traveler going West and becoming less of a tenderfoot greenhorn as the work progresses. The biographer Justin Kaplan called Twain's *Roughing It* the author's attempt to join the eastern literary establishment, and the book was generally well-received (p. 81). Harriet Smith's introduction to a 1993 edition of the book notes that sales in the first year surpassed sales of *The Innocents Abroad,* topping 75,000 copies. The reviews of Twain's book were largely positive, but nearly all employed the word "grotesque" when characterizing it—an emphasis that suggests Twain was viewed as something new and unexpected but perhaps unliterary. The book was a solid hit in every respect other than as a bid to join the literary world.

TWAIN BECOMES A "LITTERY" MAN AND WRITES THE ADVENTURES OF TOM SAWYER

Those who rejected Twain's work as inartistic did not comprehend how much work went into refining what he published. As Daniel Morley McKeithan has pointed out in *Traveling with the Innocents Abroad* (1958), "Twain did not reprint a single letter verbatim" (p. xii); he revised the *Alta California* letters extensively to craft a book from the disparate sketches. With *Roughing It,* he also carefully attended to the book as a whole, writing to his wife, Olivia, that "I admire the book more & more, the more I cut & slash & lick & trim & revamp it" (*Mark Twain's Letters,* vol. 4, p. 443). Likewise, an important attribute of Twain was that he helped to change attitudes toward certain things felt to be outside the realm of art, such as humor itself, the use of dialect, and the depiction of characters from lower classes. Twain's persona required the projection of artlessness, but it annoyed him when people accepted that image as reality. He explained and defended his aesthetic ideas in many works, most effectively in "How to Tell a Story" (1895), in which he argued that "the humorous story is strictly a work of art,—high and delicate art—, and only an artist can tell it" (*Collected Tales, Sketches, Speeches, and Essays, 1891–1910,* p. 201). In the 1870s and 1880s, Twain strove to become part of the literary establishment, yet works from that era contain a volatile mixture of defiance and accommodation. Twain wrote the hilariously bawdy works "[Date, 1601.] Conversation, as it Was by the Social Fireside, in the Time of the Tudors" (1876) and "Some Thoughts on the Science of Onanism" (1879), works that still offend the fastidious and delight the lighthearted. Yet he also coauthored *The Gilded Age* (1874, with his friend and neighbor Charles Dudley Warner) and wrote *The Prince and the Pauper* (1882), which were viewed even at the time as attempts to be accepted as a serious author. Perhaps the piece that most captures the poles of Twain's practice in the years leading up to *Huckleberry Finn* was the infamous "Whittier Birthday Speech" (1877), in which he lampooned the most famous "littery swells" of the day: Ralph Waldo Emerson, Henry Wadsworth Longfellow, and Oliver Wendell Holmes (*Mark Twain: Collected Tales, Sketches, Speeches, and Essays, 1852–1890,* p. 696). Twain depicted them as drunken, thieving, cardsharps who quote poetry while cheating at cards and making off with a miner's boots. The dinner was to honor John Greenleaf Whittier on his seventieth birthday, and Twain's rollicking deflation of many of the eastern literary figures in attendance caused a stir inside and outside the banquet hall. Twain himself had many conflicting responses to his performance and its reception, feeling at times it was a mistake and that at other times the problem was with the audience, not with him. In the 1910 reminiscence *My Mark Twain,* Twain's friend William Dean Howells, who had served as the master of ceremonies, described the reception Twain's speech received: "There fell a silence, weighing many tons to the square inch" (p. 60). The speech is quite entertaining, but it does seem to express some aggression toward the eastern literary establishment in attendance. The story features three poetry-spouting cardsharps who are described as impersonating Emerson, Longfellow, and Holmes, but the clear intimation is that those actual representatives of the literary establishment are, in a sense, imposters. Their writing is less connected to the common American life and not as authentic as Twain's.

Twain wrote some of his most brilliant work in this era, from his masterpiece in miniature, "A True Story" (1874), a work in dialect that lifts the southwestern frame story to its artistic apex, to his Poe-esque "The Facts Concerning the Recent Carnival of Crime in Connecticut" (1876), a story that combines comedy with insightful psychological speculation. It was appropriate, too, that in the American centennial year 1876, Twain published one of his most popular and enduring works, *The Adventures of Tom Sawyer.* Featuring a third-person narrator with an adult perspective, the book was designed to appeal to two audiences, children and adults. Twain later explained that the formula for writing "a story for boys" was to compose one for "any man *who has ever been a boy*" (quoted in Gribben, p. 151). The narrator plays in many scenes a very minor role, so much so that if one removes all the narratorial description, what is left is as entirely comprehensible as a playscript, which is essentially what Twain did with many sections of the dramatic version of *Tom Sawyer.* The young people provide the main focus of the story save for those places when they collide with adult characters. When the narrator does engage, it is frequently charming and compelling. Consider the last line of chapter 4, for example, when Tom has been asked to name the first two disciples and he blurts out, "David and Goliah!"; the chapter could have ended effectively at that point, but Twain ends the passage with a final brilliant stroke from the narrator: "Let us draw the curtain of charity over the rest of the scene" (1980 ed., p. 65).

The plot of *Tom Sawyer* has been the subject of a great deal of study, with scholars connecting the book to the genre of Sunday school books, which were intended to educate young readers into the precepts of the Christian religion. The basic structure is a burlesque of the Sunday school book, a genre that Twain satirized early in his career. In the genre, it was most typical for the good to be rewarded and the bad to be punished. Twain wrote his own versions, however, with such classic burlesques as "The Story of the Bad Little Boy That Bore a Charmed Life" (1865) and "The Story of the Good Little Boy Who Did Not Prosper" (1870), the latter being a work that adopts "all the Sunday-school books" as the pattern, but in this particular story "there was a screw loose somewhere, and it all happened just the other way" (*Collected Tales, Sketches, Speeches, and Essays, 1852–1890,* pp. 374, 376). Tom Sawyer is the bad boy who lives a charmed life. In episode after episode, he converts punishment to praise, and by the end of the book he has wealth and respect.

Because *Huckleberry Finn* looms so large in American culture, *Tom Sawyer* has been subjected to less criticism than the later volume. While this may have allowed some readers to enjoy the story apart from political controversy, it has also tended to obscure the serious issues posed by the novel: religious hypocrisy, social conformity, classism, and racism. At the same time, these issues are handled with a considerably lighter touch in *Tom Sawyer* than in *Huckleberry Finn.* One sees a moribund Christianity in the character of Aunt Polly, whose formulaic religion lacks vitality. One sees the degraded Calvinism in the community in chapter 5's sermon which is "so prosy" it puts people to sleep, "yet it was an argument that dealt in limitless fire and brimstone and thinned the predestined elect down to a company so small as to be hardly worth the saving" (1980 edition, p. 68). Undeniably comic, the scene reveals that the people are so accustomed to hearing this sermon they pay no attention to it and, in fact, do not actually believe it.

Southern class structure is also fully at play, with all of the gradations of village life, such as in chapter 4, when Judge Thatcher visits the Sunday school and everyone, from top to bottom, shows off for each other. The children reproduce the class awareness they see among adults. The replication of class structures among the children is seen most importantly in a pair of scenes that connects classism with racism, chapters 27 and 28. In the first of these, Tom and Huck, hunting for Injun Joe's treasure, agree to separate and the narrator states of Tom, "He did not care to have Huck's company in public places" (p. 189). Tom has clearly imbibed the class prejudices of society even when they concern his friend. If anyone would escape the class boundaries, one would think it might be Huck, for he is practically an outlaw anyway. Yet in the very next chapter, Huck tells Tom he has been sleeping in a barn, courtesy of a slave named Uncle Jake, who also gives him food. "That's a mighty good nigger, Tom. He likes me, becuz I don't ever act as if I was above him. Sometimes I've set right down and eat *with* him. But you needn't tell that. A body's got to do things when he's awful hungry he wouldn't want to do as a steady thing" (p. 193). Huck the pariah, Huck the outlaw, Huck the son of the town drunk, still recognizes that in a white supremacist culture, he is by definition always above a slave. Even Huck does not want it mentioned that he has "set right down" and eaten with Uncle Jake. Huck seems to genuinely appreciate and even like Uncle Jake; Jake may be "a mighty good nigger," but he is still a "nigger." The irony is plainly intended in this juxtaposition of the two scenes, for Twain was conveying the important fact that even the outlaw Huck has his inhumanities taught to him by a hypocritical society.

Even as Twain depicts society through this village on the Mississippi River, nature plays a central role as well, often as a purifying force. In chapter 4, for example, Twain juxtaposes the way the sun "beamed down upon the peaceful village like a benediction" in the first sentence with the much harder work of the Mosaic law as expressed through Aunt Polly's religion in the second sentence (p. 57). Perhaps the greatest example of the purifying aspect of nature occurs in chapter 14, with Tom, Huck, and Joe Harper having run off to the woods on Jackson's Island on the Mississippi River. Their raft having drifted away, the boys feel that "its going was something like burning the bridge between them and civilization" (p. 122). The lengthy description in the first paragraphs of how the natural world wakes up, and Tom's reaction to it, is a classic description of the power of nature to restore one's soul. Tellingly, Twain's narrator notes that on the island, the boys "found plenty of things to be delighted with but nothing to be astonished at" (p. 123). A manifesto of realism as well as a more general call to paying attention to the everyday realities of the natural world, this line captures many of the charms of the book as a whole.

ADVENTURES OF HUCKLEBERRY FINN

On July 5, 1875, Twain wrote to his friend William Dean Howells announcing that he had finished writing *The Adventures of Tom Sawyer* and also commenting that "I perhaps made a mistake in not writing it in the first person" (*Mark Twain–Howells Letters,* vol. 1, p. 91). With that thought, Twain's work on *Adventures of Huckleberry Finn* (1884) began. Twain composed the sequel with numerous starts and stops. During the protracted composition of the novel, Twain completed other projects as well as engaging in a kind of research by writing about his childhood in "Old Times on the Mississippi," which began as a series of articles for the *Atlantic Monthly* in 1875; he returned to the river in 1882 and traveled by steamboat to New Orleans to aid with the expanding of that series of articles into the larger book *Life on the Mississippi* (1883). Twain's reminiscences are priceless in their own right, and *Life on the Mississippi* contains peerless examples of Twain's descriptive power—for instance in the kinetic depiction of Hannibal as a "white town drowsing" waking suddenly to the cry, "S-t-e-a-m-boat a-comin'!" as well as the reflective "Two Views of the River" in chapter 9 (1883 ed., p. 33). Writing these works was invaluable in sparking Twain's memories and genius as he completed his masterpiece, *Huckleberry Finn.*

Twain's most influential book, *Huckleberry Finn,* was from the outset one of his most controversial. When first published, the book was controversial primarily because it was judged inappropriate for children because of its crude language and vulgar characters and actions. After all, the book's narrator is the son of the town drunkard, smokes a pipe, uses questionable language, kills a pig and uses the blood to fake his own death, and justifies stealing whatever he needs to survive, whether chickens or watermelons. Since the 1950s, however, the book has more frequently received criticism because of its use of the word "nigger," with some readers considering the use of the word offensive, even in the historical context of the story, and also excessive, given that it is used more than two hundred times in the book. The depiction of Jim, too, has drawn criticism, with some suggesting that he becomes a mere object of fun, particularly after Tom Sawyer shows up and indulges in what seem mere pranks in an otherwise serious story. Even Ernest Hemingway, who identified the book as the origin of all modern American literature and stated that nothing before or since was as good, declared also in *Green Hills of Africa* that "if you read it you must stop where the Nigger Jim is stolen from the boys. That is the real end. The rest is just cheating" (p. 22).

The book has always had its defenders, with some praising the work as an example of the old Twain they had adored rather than the one who had written *The Prince and the Pauper.* Others saw the work as great art. The influential critic and Columbia University professor Brander Matthews lauded *Huckleberry Finn* as an "Odyssey of the Mississippi" in his introduction to the 1899 "Uniform Edition" of the author's complete works, an honorific title many critics would repeat (p. xiii). The scholar Bernadette Lear has documented that despite criticisms of the book's morality such as that by the board of the public library of Concord, Massachusetts, which had banned *Huckleberry Finn,* Twain was well represented in libraries of the day, more so than many other classic authors.

It was precisely the moral honesty of *Huckleberry Finn,* in fact, that brought it much praise, especially in the post–Civil War era when audiences hungered for art that offered candid depictions of the world and refused to lie about life. A great deal of the honesty in the book comes from the use of irony, as when Huck complains that the Widow Douglass will not let him smoke, though she herself took snuff: "of course that was all right, because she done it herself" (p. 3). Huck, the innocent, unschooled narrator of the story may not know the word "hypocrite," but he clearly knows one when he sees one. Situational irony is also important at many points in the book—for example, when Huck attends church, where the feuding Grangerfords and Shepherdsons keep their guns handy during the sermon on "brotherly love and such-like tiresomeness" (p. 147). Dramatic irony is most visible in chapter 31, when Huck decides not to turn the runaway slave Jim in to the authorities, declaring, "All right, then, I'll *go* to hell" (p. 271). One sees in that moment the ironic climax of Huck's character development, as he has been so indoctrinated into white supremacist ideology that he believes he will go to hell for helping his friend. Attentive readers will understand that Huck arrived at a moral decision despite his miseducation by an immoral society. Some early reviewers of *Huckleberry Finn* endorsed the book because of its progressive view of race; the writer of "Ruling Out Humor" (1885) in the San Francisco *Chronicle* praised it as "the sharpest satire on the ante-bellum estimate of the slave" (p. 274).

Language is also a major source of any reader's delight in the work. In *Writing Huck Finn: Mark Twain's Creative Process* (1991), Victor Doyno has revealed how carefully Twain revised the manuscript for dialect and diction, striving to use the most descriptive words possible. Perhaps because he wrote in dialect, Twain's craftsmanship has often been slighted, yet he wrote many essays on artistic concerns: "A Couple of Sad Experiences" (1870), "Reply to the Editor of 'The Art of Authorship'" (1890), "Fenimore Cooper's Literary Offences" (1895), and "How to Tell a Story" (1895), to name a few notable examples. Indeed, Twain's descriptive power is evident throughout *Huckleberry Finn,* as Huck describes the world around him using the language he knows. Huck describes Pap's white face behind the stringy black vines of his hair as "a tree-toad white, a fish-belly white" (p. 23). After running away from his drunkard father, Huck wakes up at night in the canoe he has stolen, disoriented, and says, "It looked late, and *smelt* late. You know what I mean—I don't know the words to put it in" (p. 42). It is this ingenuous Huck, alive to the impressions the world has to offer, that has captivated generations of readers. We *do* know what Huck means, and Twain has given us exactly the right words to express the impact of the world on a narrator not yet inured to the wonder of the everyday. Likewise, Twain was a brilliant dialectician, and his use of archaisms, malapropisms, and, above all, Americanisms has contributed to his enormous cultural status. Twain's works actually provided a significant source for the researchers compiling the four-volume *Dictionary of American English* (1938–1944), and the editors, William A. Craigie and James R. Hulbert, credited a series of language studies that had been made of Twain's works (vol. 4, pp. xi–xi). In the "Explanatory" prefacing *Huckleberry Finn,* Twain cautioned his readers that he had carefully delineated the many dialects heard in the regions visited in the book. "I make this explanation," he wrote, "for the reason that without it many readers would suppose that all these characters were trying to talk alike and not succeeding" (p. xxxiii). The Missouri-born linguist David Carkeet has studied the obvious care Twain took with dialectal differences, noting the nuance between Huck's dialect and that of other white characters but also the difference between Huck's dialect and that of all the story's black characters (p. 317). Jim's voice is authentic, and it is a powerful moment when he converts the racist valuation that has been imposed upon him into a declaration of self-worth: "Yes—en I's rich now, come to look at it. I owns mysef, en I's wuth eight hund'd dollars" (p. 57).

Huckleberry Finn remains both a lightning rod for current racial tensions and a much beloved book, with many readers agreeing with Huck and Jim that "there warn't no home like a raft, after all" (p. 155).

A CONNECTICUT YANKEE IN KING ARTHUR'S COURT

The composition of *A Connecticut Yankee in King Arthur's Court* (1889) began with a rainstorm in Rochester, New York, in November 1884. Twain and the writer George Washington Cable were traveling together on a lecture tour, modestly billing themselves as the "Twins of Genius." A sudden rainstorm caused them to seek shelter in a bookshop. There, Twain happened upon an edition of Sir Thomas Malory's *Le Morte d'Arthur* (1485), which Cable advised him to purchase. Always attracted to language, Twain began conversing with Cable in archaic English, the two dubbing one another "Sir Mark" and "Sir George." Twain wrote in his notebook, "X Dream of being a knight errant in armor in the middle ages" and proceeded to outline the philosophical and humorous possibilities of such a book (*Mark Twain's Notebooks and Journals,* vol. 3, p. 78). The basic plot also set up the possibility of a dual satire, whereby Twain could subject to criticism British versus American values and the relative merits of the past versus the present. The story in some ways features American nineteenth-century fealty to progress colliding with medieval notions of fealty to church and king. Henry Nash Smith has called *A Connecticut Yankee* "Mark Twain's fable of progress" (in his 1964 book with that title)—an apt expression of the folkloric aspects of the work as well as its mixed attitude toward the idea of progress. Smith makes much of the final battle scene that destroys both chivalry and Hank Morgan's attempt to institute reforms in a feudal society, arguing that Twain was converted to a negative view of American progress. Joe B. Fulton argues in his study of the composition of the book, *Mark Twain in the Margins* (2000), that Twain created a book whose hidden theme was really historical change: the idea of change itself and the disruption this engenders. With his rapid and radical industrialization of Camelot, Hank Morgan attempts to concentrate a thousand years of human progress into a few short years. While Mallory's work provided language, incidents, and even whole pages of text, most of Twain's sources dealt with centuries other than the sixth century or the nineteenth century, the two ostensible subjects of the book. From his sources in history, most notably Thomas Carlyle's *History of the French Revolution* (1837), Twain gleaned many examples of violent historical change that he included in his work.

Philosophical concerns aside, much of the book's enduring comedy resides in the incongruity of modern American technology, values, and language in an Arthurian world. Memorable examples include the use of a lariat and a six-shooter when Hank jousts with Arthurian knights, the establishment of military academies and soap factories next to castles, and absurd language such as Hank's title—"The Boss" or "Sir Boss"—and vivid descriptions such as characterizing knight-errantry as "just a corner in pork" (1979 ed., p. 223). The comedic collision of nineteenth-century values with sixth-century or medieval values creates a dual satire of the past and present. Likewise, the book satirizes contemporary attitudes, targeting both England and the United States. Twain published *A Connecticut Yankee* during a tremendous resurgence of interest in the Arthurian age, sparked in part by Alfred, Lord Tennyson's *Idylls of the King,* which was published in installments from the 1840s through the 1880s. *A Connecticut Yankee* has a pronounced, pervasive strain of social criticism of the two countries. The illustrations by Dan Beard were all approved by Twain and support the social criticism directed at both England and America. One might instance Beard's depiction of Tennyson as Merlin in chapter 2 and his depiction of the American industrialist and robber baron Jay Gould as the "Slave Driver" at the end of chapter 35. The book is thus both "a Yankee's say against monarchy and its several natural props" (Stein, p. 591), as Twain called it, and a critique of American history and democracy, with Hank explicitly referring to Arthurian England as the antebellum American South (p. 343). He likewise frequently compares the inhabitants of Camelot to Indians at numerous points, and he even describes the final battle as "the last stand of the chivalry of England" (p. 478). Comparing the inhabitants of Camelot to Southerners or Indians suggests that this "Yankee of Yankees" (p. 50) makes war on the inhabitants as a type of Reconstruction or Manifest Destiny. The final "Battle of the Sand-Belt" is a symbolic re-creation of the American Civil War and the Indian Wars, with Hank Morgan—the eponymous Yankee—bringing to bear all manner of modern weaponry against a foe perceived as both morally and technologically inferior. The ending is one of literature's most trenchant critiques of the presumed moral superiority of a technologically superior people.

THE TRAGEDY OF PUDD'NHEAD WILSON

Just as Hank Morgan enjoyed a technological advantage over the inhabitants of Camelot but was defeated by Merlin's magic, David "Pudd'nhead" Wilson experiences an odd sort of victory that seems much like a satirical joke on the racist community of Dawson's Landing, a small town on the Mississippi River. Although often thought of as a comedy, *Pudd'nhead Wilson* (1894) was labeled a tragedy by the author and was first published with that title, though most later editions have been published simply as *Pudd'nhead Wilson.* The original full title gave a slightly different tone to the book than it would otherwise have. The story is a satire of miscegenation and post-Reconstruction Jim Crow laws, though its events take place before the abolition of slavery. Roxy, one of the most powerful female characters Twain ever created, is a nursemaid to her white master's infant son, and she has an infant son of her own, by another white man. The skin of both children is so white they can hardly be told apart, so Roxy switches her own child, who is one-thirty-second black, with the white child, to enable her own son to lead a privileged life.

Predictably, the children grow up to be thoroughly identified with the race they are treated as, satirically demonstrating the absurdity of Southern laws that defined a person with one drop of "black blood" as black. The character Pudd'nhead Wilson's part in this tragedy is that he had taken fingerprints of the children before they were switched. This evidence became the basis for revealing the identity of a murderer but also that the "black" baby had been switched with the "white" one. The book's ultimate satire is that the child who had been raised as a slave is welcomed into the local version of high society, while the child who had been raised as a master was sold "down the river," into the Deep South, as a slave. Twain's satire demonstrated that cherished definitions such as race are more socially determined than scientifically fixed.

Pudd'nhead Wilson occupies an unusual position in the Twain canon. One the one hand, it is marred by some aesthetic issues that resulted from the way Twain wrote it. Originally, two of the characters, Angelo and Luigi, were conjoined twins. Twain later separated that element out, creating the novella *Those Extraordinary Twins,* which he called a "comedy" to accompany the tragedy of the other book. They were published in the same volume in 1894, though as separate works. However, Twain left a number of elements in *Pudd'nhead Wilson* that do not make sense without that original plot. These defects have been most cogently discussed by Hershel Parker in *Flawed Texts and Verbal Icons: Literary Authority in American Fiction* (1984).

Despite those plot oddities, *Pudd'nhead Wilson* has been the subject of an increasing number of books and articles, is often taught in courses on the American novel, and is considered by many to be among Twain's most relevant and provocative works. The rise of New Historicist criticism in the 1980s and 1990s, which was less concerned about aesthetics than the New Critical school had been, supported a focus on the many "tensions" in the work and the interesting things it has to say about race in the post-Reconstruction era of Jim Crow laws. The New Historicist approach has helped increase the book's profile in American literary studies.

TWAIN AND TRAVEL NARRATIVES

Mark Twain frequently wrote in the travel genre. His first full-length books, *The Innocents Abroad* and *Roughing It,* were both in this genre, and so too were *Life on the Mississippi, A Tramp Abroad* (1880), *Following the Equator* (1897), and many individual essays and sketches. Among these, in the broadest sense, one might include the many "Letters from Washington" he wrote in 1866–1867 for the Chicago *Republican* and other newspapers and his later series of articles for the New York *Sun* in 1891–1892. Among the letters for the latter group was "Aix-les-Bains" (1891), a classic philosophical essay that ruminates on time, history, and eternity.

Travel books, more than the essays, allowed Twain to include a variety of material, frequently drawn from American experiences. Perhaps the best example of this is *A Tramp Abroad*; in addition to providing Twain's unique perspective on Germany, Switzerland, France, and Italy, the work includes his classic tall tale "Jim Baker's Blue-Jay Yarn." Included, too, is Twain's essay "The Awful German Language," a bumptious expression of love masquerading as hate for Twain's favorite second language, a comic screed that has endeared him to generations of Germans—and to generations of students of the German language. Twain was a world traveler who developed an international reputation not just by his writings about the Mississippi River and the American West, but by going abroad, lecturing abroad, and by writing about his experiences abroad.

TWAIN AS A LECTURER AND SPEAKER

For a writer as involved with dialect as Mark Twain, it should be no surprise that performance played a significant role in his career. In 1874, Twain wrote to William Dean Howells, "I amend dialect stuff by talking & talking & *talking* it till it sounds right" (*Mark Twain–Howells Letters,* vol. 1, p. 26). Twain's spoof of a Fourth of July speech while mining in the Nevada Territory, his mock orations as the "governor" of the Third House, a faux legislature consisting mainly of drunken newspapermen, and his propensity for telling stories in dialect to friends illustrate his early interest in performance.

In the nineteenth century, the lecture circuit, the lyceum, was an influential cultural phenomenon—and an important source of income for writers, reformers, and politicians. Twain's first real foray into this world was his 1866 humorous lecture on Hawaii, later given the title "Our Fellow Savages of the Sandwich Islands." Fred Lorch has credited Twain's early lectures as virtually creating Mark Twain the author, for lecturing publicly required him to respond to audience tastes beyond his immediate region (p. x). As any stand-up comic could attest, there is no more reliable way of seeing if a joke works than to test it out on an audience. The lectures Twain gave on the lyceum circuit throughout his career remain a vital part of his oeuvre, as do the public speeches he gave.

As Twain became an increasingly prominent man of letters, he was often invited to banquets, dinners, and public celebrations by those hoping that his speeches would enliven the program. Some of these speeches have become significant subjects of study, such as his "Whittier Birthday Dinner" speech and his speech in response to a toast to "The Babies" at a reunion of the Army of the Tennessee at Chicago's famed Palmer House on November 13, 1879, an event honoring Ulysses S. Grant. The most comprehensive collection is the edition edited by Paul Fatout, *Mark Twain Speaking* (1976), and Fatout's introduction provides an admirable description of Twain's speaking style, which he calculated to seem haphazard and even unprepared. As Fatout discusses, Twain carefully wrote, memorized, and practiced his speeches "so skillfully that they sounded like improvisations" (p. xxiv). Similarly, Twain was a highly sought after interview subject. Gary Scharnhorst's *Mark Twain: The Complete Interviews* (2006) collects the vast majority of these. Perusing Twain's speeches and interviews restores to the contemporary reader something of the personality and public role Twain played during his lifetime.

REFORMIST WORKS AND LATER CLASSICS

While a reformist strain existed in Twain's satire from the very beginning, many of his later works become more overtly reformist, with his attack on anti-Semitism in "Concerning the Jews" (1899); anger at lynching in "The United States of Lyncherdom" (1901); advocacy of animal rights in "A Dog's Tale" (1903; published as an article and as a pamphlet for England's National Anti-Vivisection Society); hectoring of Mary Baker Eddy in a series of articles beginning in 1899, followed by the book *Christian Science* in 1907; criticism of American missionaries in China and of President William McKinley's policies in Cuba and the Philippines in "To the Person Sitting in Darkness" (1901), "To My Missionary Critics" (1901), and "A Defence of General Funston" (1902); membership in the Anti-Imperialist League and consequent attacks on international imperialism in works like "King Leopold's Soliloquy: A Defense of His Congo Rule" (1905); appearances before Congress to lobby for copyright reform, resplendent in his white flannel suit, along with the publication of "Concerning Copyright" (1905); and with his activism against tsarist oppression in "The Czar's Soliloquy" (1905). Even as he became more famous, he seemed intent on using that fame for the purposes of social and political advocacy.

Twain left many interesting works unfinished, such as the manuscripts that his literary executor Albert Bigelow Paine added to and subtracted from to create the spurious work *The Mysterious Stranger* (1916). Nevertheless, during the last fifteen years of his life he published many gems in the short story and essay genres. Chief among the stories is "The Man That Corrupted Hadleyburg" (1899), the classic tale of a misanthrope out to prove that the pious people of Hadleyburg are no better than the rest of the world. Other late classics in other genres include his essay "Corn-Pone Opinions" (1901), the moving "Eve's Diary" (1905), and the dialogue "What Is Man?" (1906). Each a classic of a particular genre, these works show how vital remained Twain's creativity even in the last years of his life. Indeed, it is the rare writer of any age who publishes classic works in so many genres.

CONCLUSION

A writer of considerable inspiration, talent, and versatility, Mark Twain chronicled America with great affection for its freshness and vitality as well as an understanding of its deepest ironies and injustices. One of the most prolific American writers, Mark Twain became even before his death *the* American writer, one of the most identifiable figures at home and abroad, unmistakable with his white suit and drawling delivery. By attending to the life and language of American folkways, he created an impressive body of literature that continues to influence writers around the world.

Selected Bibliography

WORKS OF MARK TWAIN

EDITIONS PUBLISHED IN TWAIN'S LIFETIME

The Celebrated Jumping Frog of Calaveras County, and Other Sketches. New York: C. H. Webb, 1867. (This was Twain's first book and reprinted the title story as well as "The Story of the Bad Little Boy Who Didn't Come to Grief" and "Lucretia Smith's Soldier.")

The Innocents Abroad. Hartford, Conn.: American, 1869.

Roughing It. Hartford, Conn.: American, 1872.

The Gilded Age. With Charles Dudley Warner. Hartford, Conn.: American, 1874.

Mark Twain's Sketches, New and Old. Hartford, Conn.: American, 1875.

The Adventures of Tom Sawyer. Hartford, Conn.: American, 1876.

A True Story and The Recent Carnival of Crime. Boston: James R. Osgood, 1877. (It is a sign of Twain's importance and the importance of these two stories that they were reprinted in this separate volume. Both had appeared in the *Atlantic Monthly,* the first in 1874 and the second in 1876.)

A Tramp Abroad. Hartford, Conn.: American, 1880.

The Prince and the Pauper. Boston: James R. Osgood, 1882.

Life on the Mississippi. Boston: James R. Osgood, 1883.

Adventures of Huckleberry Finn. New York: Charles L. Webster, 1885.

A Connecticut Yankee in King Arthur's Court. New York: Charles L. Webster, 1889.

Tom Sawyer Abroad. New York: Charles L. Webster, 1894.

The Tragedy of Pudd'nhead Wilson and the Comedy Those Extraordinary Twins. Hartford, Conn.: American, 1894.

Personal Recollections of Joan of Arc. New York: Harper and Brothers, 1896.

Following the Equator. Hartford, Conn.: American, 1897.

The Man That Corrupted Hadleyburg and Other Stories and Essays. New York: Harper and Brothers, 1900.

To the Person Sitting in Darkness. New York: Anti-Imperialist League of New York, 1901. (Originally published in the *North American Review* in February 1901, this work was given royalty free by Twain to the Anti-Imperialist League for publication in pamphlet form.)

A Dog's Tale. New York: National Anti-Vivisection Society, 1903. ("A Dog's Tale" was first published in *Harper's* magazine and later the same year reprinted in pamphlet form for use by the National Anti-Vivisection Society.)

King Leopold's Soliloquy. Boston: P. R. Warren, 1905. (Rejected by the *North American Review,* this scorching essay first appeared in pamphlet form, with all of the proceeds supporting the Congo Reform Association.)

What Is Man? New York: De Vinne, 1906. (Twain referred to this philosophical dialogue as his "gospel" and first published it anonymously.)

Christian Science. New York: Harper and Brothers, 1907.

Mark Twain's Speeches. New York: Harper and Brothers, 1910. (With an introduction by William Dean Howells.)

POSTHUMOUS AND MODERN EDITIONS

The Mysterious Stranger: A Romance. New York: Harper and Brothers, 1916. (Published posthumously, this work did much to solidify the view that Twain's last years were given over to despair. The volume was discredited in 1963 when John Sutton Tuckey revealed, in his monograph *Mark Twain and Little Satan,* that the book was a fraud perpetrated by Twain's literary executor, Albert B. Paine. Paine, together with Frederick Duneka, an editor for Harper's, conflated three different manuscripts by Twain into one. This spurious 1916 edition is usually referred to as the Paine-Duneka text.)

Mark Twain's Works. 37 vols. New York: Gabriel Wells, 1923–1925.

Mark Twain's Satires and Burlesques. Edited by Franklin Rogers. Berkeley: University of California Press, 1967.

Mark Twain's "Which Was the Dream" and Other Symbolic Writings of the Later Years. Edited by John S. Tuckey. Berkeley: University of California Press, 1967.

What Is Man? In *What Is Man? and Other Philosophical Writings.* Edited by Paul Baender. Berkeley: University of California Press, 1973. Pp. 124–214.

What Is Man? and Other Philosophical Writings. Edited by Paul Baender. Berkeley: University of California Press, 1973.

A Connecticut Yankee in King Arthur's Court. Edited by Bernard L. Stein. Berkeley: University of California Press, 1979.

Early Tales and Sketches. Vol. 1, *1851–1864.* Edited by Edgar M. Branch. Berkeley: University of California Press, 1979.

The Prince and the Pauper. Edited by Victor Fischer and Lin Salamo. Berkeley and Los Angeles: University of California Press, 1979.

The Adventures of Tom Sawyer. In *The Adventures of Tom Sawyer; Tom Sawyer Abroad; Tom Sawyer, Detective.* Edited by John Gerber, Paul Baender, and Terry Firkins. Berkeley: University of California Press, 1980. Pp. 31–237.

Early Tales and Sketches. Vol. 2, *1864–1865.* Edited by Edgar M. Branch. Berkeley: University of California Press, 1981.

Life on the Mississippi. In *Mark Twain: Mississippi Writings.* New York: Library of America, 1982. Pp. 217–616.

Pudd'nhead Wilson. In *Mark Twain: Mississippi Writings.* New York: Library of America, 1982. Pp. 913–1056.

Mark Twain: Collected Tales, Sketches, Speeches, and Essays, 1852–1890. New York: Library of America, 1992.

Mark Twain: Collected Tales, Sketches, Speeches, and Essays, 1891–1910. New York: Library of America, 1992.

Roughing It. Edited by Harriet Elinor Smith and Edgar Marquess Branch. Berkeley: University of California Press, 1993.

Personal Recollections of Joan of Arc. In *Historical Romances.* Edited by Susan K. Harris. New York: Literary Classics of the United States, 1994. Pp. 541–970.

Adventures of Huckleberry Finn. Edited by Victor Fischer, Lin Salamo, and Walter Blair. Berkeley: University of California Press, 2003.

CORRESPONDENCE, PAPERS, AND AUTOBIOGRAPHICAL WRITING

Mark Twain's Letters. 2 vols. Edited by Albert Bigelow Paine. New York: Harper and Brothers, 1917.

Mark Twain's Notebook. Edited by A. B. Paine. New York: Harper, 1935.

Mark Twain's Travels with Mr. Brown. Edited by Franklin Walker and G. Ezra Dane. New York: Alfred A. Knopf, 1940.

Mark Twain, Businessman. Edited by Samuel Charles Webster. Boston: Little, Brown, 1946.

Mark Twain–Howells Letters: The Correspondence of Samuel Langhorne Clemens and William D. Howells, 1869–1910. 2 vols. Edited by Henry Nash Smith and William M. Gibson. Cambridge, Mass.: Belknap Press of the Harvard University Press, 1960.

Mark Twain's San Francisco. Edited by Bernard Taper. New York: McGraw-Hill, 1963.

Mark Twain's Letters to His Publishers, 1867–1894. Edited by Hamlin Hill. Berkeley: University of California Press, 1967.

Mark Twain's Hannibal, Huck, and Tom. Edited by Walter Blair. Berkeley: University of California Press, 1969.

Mark Twain's "Mysterious Stranger" Manuscripts. Edited by William M. Gibson. Berkeley: University of California Press, 1969. Pp. 35–174.

Mark Twain Speaking. Edited by Paul Fatout. Iowa City: University of Iowa Press, 1976.

Mark Twain's Notebooks and Journals. Vol. 3, *1883–1891.* Edited by Robert Pack Browning, Michael B. Frank, and Lin Salamo. Berkeley: University of California Press, 1979.

Mark Twain's Letters. Vol. 1, *1853–1866.* Edited by Edgar Marquess Branch, Michael B. Frank, and Kenneth M. Sanderson. Berkeley: University of California Press, 1988.

Mark Twain's Letters. Vol. 2, *1867–1868.* Edited by Harriet Elinor Smith and Richard Bucci. Berkeley: University of California Press, 1990.

Mark Twain's Letters. Vol. 3, *1869.* Edited by Victor Fischer and Michael B. Frank. Berkeley: University of California Press, 1992.

Mark Twain's Letters. Vol. 4, *1870–1871.* Edited by Victor Fischer and Michael B. Frank. Berkeley: University of California Press, 1995.

Mark Twain's Letters. Vol. 5, *1872–1873.* Edited by Lin Salamo and Harriet Elinor Smith. Berkeley: University of California Press, 1997.

Mark Twain's Letters. Vol. 6, *1874–1875.* Edited by Michael B. Frank and Harriet Elinor Smith. Berkeley: University of California Press, 2002.

Autobiography of Mark Twain. Vol. 1. Edited by Harriet Elinor Smith et al. Oakland: University of California Press, 2010. (Published posthumously, the *Autobiography* was Twain's final masterpiece. The author left instructions that the work not be published until a century after his death. Although some sections were published during Twain's life, and some extracts were published in the decades since his death, the complete *Autobiography* was not published until this three-volume set was completed in 2015.)

Autobiography of Mark Twain. Vol. 2. Edited by Benjamin Griffin and Harriet Elinor Smith. Oakland: University of California Press, 2013.

Autobiography of Mark Twain. Vol. 3. Edited by Benjamin Griffin and Harriet Elinor Smith. Oakland: University of California Press, 2015.

Individual Works Mentioned (Alphabetical)

"Aix-les-Bains." 1891. In *Collected Tales, Sketches, Speeches, and Essays, 1891–1910.* New York: Library of America, 1992. Pp. 1–14.

"The Babies." 1879. In *Mark Twain Speaking.* Edited by Paul Fatout. Iowa City: University of Iowa Press, 1976. Pp. 131–134.

"A Bloody Massacre near Carson." 1862. In *Early Tales and Sketches.* Vol. 1, *1851—1864.* Edited by Edgar M. Branch et al. Berkeley: University of California Press, 1979. Pp. 324–326.

"Concerning Copyright." 1905. In *Collected Tales, Sketches, Speeches, and Essays, 1891–1910.* New York: Library of America, 1992. Pp. 627–634.

"Concerning the Jews." 1899. In *Collected Tales, Sketches, Speeches, and Essays, 1891–1910.* New York: Library of America, 1992. Pp. 354–370.

"Corn-Pone Opinions." 1901. In *Collected Tales, Sketches, Speeches, and Essays, 1891–1910.* New York: Library of America, 1992. Pp. 507–511.

"The Czar's Soliloquy." 1905. In *Collected Tales, Sketches, Speeches, and Essays, 1891–1910.* New York: Library of America, 1992. Pp. 642–647.

"A Couple of Sad Experiences." 1870. In *Mark Twain: Collected Tales, Sketches, Speeches, and Essays, 1852–1890.* New York: Library of America, 1992. Pp. 388–395.

"[Date, 1601.] Conversation as It Was by the Social Fireside, in the Time of the Tudors." 1876. In *Mark Twain: Collected Tales, Sketches, Speeches, and Essays, 1852–1890.* New York: Library of America, 1992. Pp. 661–666.

"A Defense of General Funston." *North American Review* 174:613–624 (May 1902).

"A Dog's Tale." 1903. In *Mark Twain: Collected Tales, Sketches, Speeches, and Essays, 1891–1910.* New York: Library of America, 1992.

"Eve's Diary." 1905. In *Mark Twain: Collected Tales, Sketches, Speeches, and Essays, 1891–1910.* New York: Library of America, 1992. Pp. 695–709.

"The Facts Concerning the Recent Carnival of Crime in Connecticut." 1876. In *Mark Twain: Collected Tales, Sketches, Speeches, and Essays, 1852–1890.* New York: Library of America, 1992. Pp. 644–660.

"Fenimore Cooper's Literary Offences." 1895. In *Mark Twain: Collected Tales, Sketches, Speeches, and Essays, 1891–1910.* New York: Library of America, 1992. Pp. 180–192.

"A Gallant Fireman." 1851. In *Early Tales and Sketches.* Vol. 1, *1851–1864.* Edited by Edgar M. Branch et al. Berkeley: University of California Press, 1979. P. 62.

"The Great Prize Fight." 1863. In *Mark Twain: Collected Tales, Sketches, Speeches, and Essays, 1852–1890.* New York: Library of America, 1992. Pp. 49–56.

"How to Tell a Story." 1895. In *Collected Tales, Sketches, Speeches, and Essays, 1891–1910.* New York: Library of America, 1992. Pp. 201–206.

"Jane Lampton Clemens." 1890. In *Mark Twain's Hannibal, Huck, and Tom.* Edited by Walter Blair. Berkeley: University of California Press, 1969. Pp. 41–53.

"Jim Smiley and His Jumping Frog." 1865. In *Early Tales and Sketches.* Vol. 2, *1864–1865.* Edited by Edgar M. Branch. Berkeley: University of California Press, 1981. Pp. 282–288.

"King Leopold's Soliloquy." 1905. In *Collected Tales, Sketches, Speeches, and Essays, 1891–1910.* New York: Library of America, 1992. Pp. 661–686.

"Letter from Carson City." 1863. In *Early Tales and Sketches.* Vol. 1, *1851–1864.* Edited by Edgar M. Branch et al. Berkeley: University of California Press, 1979. Pp. 192–198.

"Lucretia Smith's Soldier." 1864. In *Early Tales and Sketches.* Vol. 2, *1864–1865.* Edited by Edgar M. Branch. Berkeley: University of California Press, 1981. Pp. 128–133.

"Old Times on the Mississippi." Serilaized in seven parts in the *Atlantic Monthly*: January 1875, pp. 69–74; February 1875, pp. 217–224; March 1875, pp. 283–290, April 1875, pp. 446–452; May 1875, pp. 567–575; June 1875, pp. 721–730; and August 1875, pp. 190–196.

"Our Fellow Savages of the Sandwich Islands." 1866. *Mark Twain Speaking.* Edited by Paul Fatout. Iowa City: University of Iowa Press, 1976. Pp. 4–15.

"Petrified Man." 1862. In *Early Tales and Sketches.* Vol. 1, *1851–1864.* Edited by Edgar M. Branch et al. Berkeley: University of California Press, 1979. P. 159.

"The Private History of a Campaign That Failed." 1885. In *Mark Twain. Collected Tales, Sketches, Speeches, and Essays, 1852–1890.* New York: Library of America, 1992. Pp. 863–882.

"Reply to the Editor of the 'The Art of Authorship.'" 1890. In *Mark Twain: Collected Tales, Sketches, Speeches, and Essays, 1852–1890.* New York: Library of America, 1992. Pp. 945–946.

"Some Thoughts on the Science of Onanism." 1879. In *Mark Twain: Collected Tales, Sketches, Speeches, and Essays, 1852–1890.* New York: Library of America, 1992. Pp. 722–724.

"The Story of the Bad Little Boy That Bore a Charmed Life." 1865. In *Early Tales and Sketches.* Vol. 2, *1864–1865.* Edited by Edgar M. Branch. Berkeley: University of California Press, 1981. Pp. 407–410.

"The Story of the Good Little Boy Who Did Not Prosper." 1870. In *Mark Twain: Collected Tales, Sketches, Speeches, and Essays, 1852–1890.* New York: Library of America, 1992. Pp. 374–378.

"To My Missionary Critics." *North American Review* 172:520–534 (April 1901).

"To the Person Sitting in Darkness." 1901. In *Mark Twain: Collected Tales, Sketches, Speeches, and Essays, 1891–1910.* New York: Library of America, 1992. Pp. 457–473.

"A True Story." 1874. In *Mark Twain: Collected Tales, Sketches, Speeches, and Essays, 1852–1890.* New York: Library of America, 1992. Pp. 578–582.

"The United States of Lyncherdom." 1901. In *Mark Twain: Collected Tales, Sketches, Speeches, and Essays, 1891–1910.* New York: Library of America, 1992. Pp. 479–486.

"Whittier Birthday Speech." 1877. In *Mark Twain: Collected Tales, Sketches, Speeches, and Essays, 1852–1890.* New York: Library of America, 1992. Pp. 695–699.

Writings of Mark Twain (Uniform Edition). 25 vols. New York: Harper, 1899-1907.

BIBLIOGRAPHIES AND CONCORDANCE

American Literary Scholarship. Durham, N.C.: Duke University Press. (Published annually, this work features a chapter on Twain scholarship.)

Budd, Louis J. *Mark Twain: The Contemporary Reviews.* New York: Cambridge University Press, 1999.

Fulton, Joe B. *Mark Twain Under Fire: Reception and Reputation, Criticism and Controversy, 1851–2015.* Rochester, N.Y.: Camden House, 2016.

Gohdes, Clarence. *American Literature in Nineteenth-Century England.* Carbondale: Southern Illinois University Press, 1944.

———. *Bibliographical Guide to the Study of the Literature of the USA.* 4th ed., revised and enlarged. Durham, N.C.: Duke University Press, 1976.

Horn, Jason G. *Mark Twain: A Descriptive Guide to Biographical Sources.* Lanham, Md.: Scarecrow Press, 1999.

Johnson, Merle. *A Bibliography of the Works of Mark Twain: A List of First Editions in Book Form and of First Printings in Periodicals and Occasional Publications of His Varied Literary Activities.* New York: Harper, 1935.

Tenney, Thomas A. *Mark Twain: A Reference Guide.* Boston: G. K. Hall, 1977. (This is the most important bibliography of criticism on Mark Twain. See also the annual supplements from 1977–1983 in *American Literary Realism,* the *Mark Twain Circular* after that and, since 1997, in the *Mark Twain Journal.*)

CRITICAL AND BIOGRAPHICAL STUDIES

Arnold, Matthew. "Civilization in the United States." *Civilization in the United States: First and Last Impressions of America.* Boston: Cupples and Hurd, 1888. Budd, Louis J. *Our Mark Twain: The Making of His Public Personality.* Philadelphia: University of Pennsylvania Press, 1983.

Bush, Harold K. *Continuing Bonds with the Dead: Parental Grief and Nineteenth-Century American Authors.* Tuscaloosa: University of Alabama Press, 2016.

Carkeet, David. "The Dialects in *Huckleberry Finn.*" *American Literature* 51:315–332 (1979).

Craigie, William A., and James R. Hulbert, eds. *A Dictionary of American English on Historical Principles.* 4 vols. Chicago: University of Chicago Press, 1938–1944.

Doyno, Victor A. *Writing Huck Finn: Mark Twain's Creative Process.* Philadelphia: University of Pennsylvania Press, 1991.

Eliot, T. S. "American Literature and the American Language: An Address Delivered at Washington University on June 9, 1953." St. Louis, Mo.: Washington University, 1953.

Fulton, Joe B. *Mark Twain in the Margins: The Quarry Farm Marginalia and "A Connecticut Yankee in King Arthur's Court.* " Studies in American Literary Realism and Naturalism. Tuscaloosa: University of Alabama Press, 2000.

———. *The Reverend Mark Twain: Theological Burlesque, Form, and Content in Mark Twain's Works.* Columbus: Ohio State University Press, 2006.

———. *The Reconstruction of Mark Twain: How a Confederate Bushwhacker Became the Lincoln of Our Literature.* Baton Rouge: Louisiana State University Press, 2010.

Gribben, Alan. "'I Did Wish Tom Sawyer Was There': Boy-Book Elements in *Tom Sawyer* and *Huckleberry Finn.*" *One Hundred Years of Huckleberry Finn: The Boy, His Book, and American Culture.* Edited by Robert Sattelmeyer and J. Donald Crowley. Columbia: University of Missouri Press, 1985. Pp. 149–70.

Hemingway, Ernest. *Green Hills of Africa.* New York: Scribner, 1935.

Hill, Hamlin. *Mark Twain and Elisha Bliss.* Columbia: University of Missouri Press, 1964.

Howells, William Dean. *My Mark Twain.* New York: Harper, 1910.

Kaplan, Justin. *Mr. Clemens and Mark Twain.* New York: Simon & Schuster, 1966.

Lear, Bernadette A. "Were Tom and Huck On-Shelf? Public Libraries, Mark Twain, and the Formation of Accessible Canons, 1869–1910." *Nineteenth-Century Literature* 64:189–224 (2009).

Lorch, Fred W. *The Trouble Begins at Eight: Mark Twain's Lecture Tours.* Ames: Iowa State University Press, 1966.

Lynn, Kenneth S. *Mark Twain and Southwestern Humor.* Boston: Little, Brown, 1959.

Lystra, Karen. *Dangerous Intimacy: The Untold Story of Mark Twain's Final Years.* Berkeley: University of California Press, 2004.

Macnaughton, William R. *Mark Twain's Last Years as a Writer.* Columbia: University of Missouri Press, 1979.

McKeithan, Daniel Morley. *Traveling with the Innocents Abroad: Mark Twain's Original Reports from Europe and the Holy Land.* Norman: University of Oklahoma Press, 1958.

McReynolds, Edwin C. *Missouri: A History of the Crossroads State.* Norman: University of Oklahoma Press, 1962.

Parker, Hershel. *Flawed Texts and Verbal Icons: Literary Authority in American Fiction.* Evanston, Ill.: Northwestern University Press, 1984.

Rafferty, Milton D. *Historical Atlas of Missouri.* Norman: University of Oklahoma Press, 1982.

Richardson, Charles F. *American Literature, 1607–1885.* 2 vols. New York: G. P. Putnam's Sons, 1886, 1889.

Rodney, Robert M. *Mark Twain International: A Bibliography and Interpretation of His Worldwide Popularity.* Westport, Conn.: Greenwood Press, 1982.

Root, Elihu. *Missouri Troops in Service During the Civil War.* Washington: Government Printing Office, 1902. (57th Congress, 1st session, document no. 412.)

"Ruling Out Humor." *Mark Twain: The Contemporary Reviews.* Edited by Louis J. Budd. New York: Cambridge University Press, 1999. Pp. 274–275.

Scharnhorst, Gary. *Mark Twain: The Complete Interviews.* Tuscaloosa: University of Alabama Press, 2006.

Sloane, David E. E. *Mark Twain as a Literary Comedian.* Baton Rouge: Louisiana State University Press, 1979.

Smith, Harriet Elinor. "Introduction." In *Roughing It.* Edited by Harriet Elinor Smith and Edgar Marquess Branch. Berkeley: University of California Press, 1993. Pp. 797–911.

Smith, Henry Nash. *Mark Twain: The Development of a Writer.* Cambridge, Mass.: Harvard University Press, 1962.

———. *Mark Twain's Fable of Progress: Political and Economic Ideas in "A Connecticut Yankee."* New Brunswick, N.J.: Rutgers University Press, 1964.

Stein, Bernard L. "Textual Introduction." In *A Connecticut Yankee in King Arthur's Court.* Berkeley: University of California Press, 1979. 571–619.

Tuckey, John Sutton. *Mark Twain and Little Satan.* West Lafayette, Ind.: Purdue Univeristy Studies, 1963.

Webster, Samuel Charles. *Mark Twain, Businessman.* Boston: Little, Brown: 1946.

EDITH WHARTON

(1862—1937)

Kathleen Pfeiffer

THOUGH RAISED TO be a society matron in Old New York, Edith Newbold Jones Wharton developed her extraordinary intellectual and artistic sensibility to become a prolific writer whose work mastered several genres. She was a dignified, mannered, and highly private woman, and she maintained close friendships with a network of influential writers and intellectuals, including Henry James, Walter Berry, Bernard Berenson, Robert and Sara Norton, Paul Bourget, and André Gide. Born in New York City during the American Civil War, she died in France at the dawn of the Second World War, thereby cultivating a life that spanned two centuries and two continents; moreover, she explored European and American themes with equal felicity. Wharton didn't publish her first fiction until age thirty-six, but once she launched as a creative writer, she published consistently, often producing a book per year and sometimes more. Her novels and stories were psychologically sophisticated, offering nuanced insights into the possibilities and limits of selfhood. Wharton is best known for devastatingly satirical realist fiction, particularly in tales that examine marriage, individualism, and the stultifying effect of social convention, especially for women. Though she jokingly derided her writing as "littery" efforts, Wharton clearly took herself and her writing seriously, acting as her own best and strongest advocate, agent, business manager, and marketer.

CHILDHOOD

Born at home in New York City on January 24, 1862, Edith Newbold Jones was the only daughter and pampered youngest child of George Frederick and Lucretia Stevens Rhinelander Jones. Though younger than her twelve- and sixteen-year-old brothers Frederic "Freddy" Rhinelander and Henry "Harry" Edward, she grew up accompanied socially by their circle of friends and supported by their appreciation for her tremendous imagination and intellect. The family was sufficiently comfortable financially that George Jones never had to work for a living, and they were socially prominent enough to be included in the crème de la crème of Manhattan society referred to as the "New York Four Hundred," a class whose size was popularly thought to be determined by the number of people who could fit in the ballroom where "*the* Mrs. Astor" hosted the New York elite at her mansion in Newport, Rhode Island. "Pussy," as Edith was known, was an awkward child, often teased by her brothers for her red hair and her large hands and feet. Wharton recalls her desire to emulate her mother as a small child, when her chief ambition was to be "the best dressed woman in New York!" Lucretia Jones was fashion conscious and socially ambitious; the phrase "keeping up with the Joneses" was attributed to two of Edith's great aunts on her father's side. Raised to be a debutante, Edith was drawn instead to her father's library where she learned to value literature. "I cannot remember the time when I did not want to 'make up' stories," she writes (*A Backward Glance,* p. 33).

The Jones family traveled to Europe for an extended stay when Edith was four. They were wealthy, but not extravagantly so (particularly following a postwar economic loss), and their journey was motivated by economy, since Europe offered a much better cost of living than New York. "Happy misfortune, which gave me, for the rest of my life, that background of beauty and old-established order!" (*A Backward Glance,* p. 44). In Spain, Italy, and France, young "Puss" was deeply impressed by gorgeous landscapes and noble relics; she imbibed an intense appreciation for Europe's architecture and its established cultural traditions. Life abroad was not without challenges, however; at age eight, while in Germany, Edith was stricken with a near-fatal case of typhoid fever. Though she recovered, the severity of this illness marked her with anxiety for several years afterward, and it proved to be the first instance of serious illness in a lifetime plagued with health challenges.

Edith was ten when the Joneses returned to the United States to resume their lives in the social order, but she found New York a drab disappointment after the splendors of Europe. She read and spoke French, Italian, and German by twelve years old, the year she undertook tutoring with Anna Bahlmann, who "finished" her extraordinary education. Under Bahlmann's guidance, Edith "read German literature and mythology in the original ... and also, in translation, Norse, Greek, and Roman mythology and Arthurian legend, as well as English and American literature" (Goldman-Price, p. 5). Edith was just sixteen when her mother arranged for and financed the publication of *Verses* (1878), her first collection of poetry.

For many years, Wharton's 1934 autobiography *A Backward Glance* was the primary source of information about her childhood and upbringing. This account, written when she was in her early seventies, was particularly harsh toward her mother, depicting Lucretia Jones not only as highly critical, icy, and exacting but as fundamentally opposed to cultivating young Edith's fertile imagination. In one oft-cited anecdote, the writer recounts how, at age eleven, she showed her mother a first effort at novel writing. "Timorously I submitted this to my mother, and never shall I forget the sudden drop of my creative frenzy when she returned it with [an] icy comment" (p. 73). Of her childhood, Wharton wrote, "I was never free from the oppressive sense that I had two absolutely inscrutable beings to please God & my mother and my mother was the most inscrutable of the two" (*Life and I,* in *Novellas and Other Writings,* p. 1074). Wharton's autobiographical reminiscences of her father were far more tender and affectionate, and she depicts him as sharing and encouraging her academic curiosity and love of reading. In *Life and I,* another unfinished autobiography (published in 1990 as part of *Novellas and Other Writings*), Wharton similarly portrays herself as something of a spiritual orphan in childhood, raised in "complete mental isolation" in a home where "no one else ever *told* me a story or gave a personal interpretation to the narrative," always separated and alienated from her family by her vivid imagination and intellectual ambition (*Novellas and Other Writings,* p. 1077).

When a collection of Wharton's letters to her governess Anna Bahlmann came to light in 2009 and was published in 2012, however, this autobiographical narrative of isolation was revealed to be highly fashioned. "The romantic notion that Edith Wharton was a solitary autodidact," writes Irene Goldman-Price of this discovery, "is one of her most successful fictions" (*My Dear Governess: The Letters of Edith Wharton to Anna Bahlmann,* p. 7).

Wharton's correspondence provides an evidence-based corrective to the life narrative offered in *A Backward Glance* and *Life and I,* providing richly illustrative details about her childhood and coming of age. In fact, Wharton's parents and her brother Harry encouraged and supported her intellectual development, her voracious reading, and her literary aspirations. Harry Jones cultivated a literary contact that led to the first appearance of Edith's poetry in the *Atlantic Monthly.* She was not only free to read fiction, but she received novels as gifts and apparently collected numerous books even as a teenager.

She made her society debut just before her seventeenth birthday, in December 1879; a budding romance with a young man named Harry Stevens soon followed. In 1880, her poetry appeared, anonymously, in the *Atlantic Monthly* and the *New York World.* Around this time, however, her father's health was failing, and upon his doctor's recommendation, the family returned to Europe for restful recuperation. Edith and her father were close, and they apparently enjoyed a connection that was deeply sympathetic. It was a blow to the family, and particularly to Edith, when he died in 1882.

Following George Jones's death, the family returned to New York, and on August 19 of that year the New York City society journal (and scandal sheet) *Town Topics* announced Edith's engagement to Harry Stevens. Although the romance was apparently sincere and happy, the engagement was short-lived. Mrs. Paran Stevens, Harry's mother, was a difficult, socially ambitious woman, and she is believed to have orchestrated their breakup, which was reported in a late October issue of *Town Topics.* The published account seemed designed to humiliate Edith by noting that the cause was "an alleged preponderance of intellectuality on the part of the intended bride." Edith's letters to her governess at this time make it clear that the engagement did not, in fact, end in October, but rather it continued until at least March of 1883; indeed, she was then still fully expecting to be married that summer. She writes from Cannes that "Mama & Harry & I drove to La Verriere Church" (*My Dear Governess,* p. 59) for Easter and that "Mr. Stevens gave me such a pretty ring for Easter." Whether the engagement ended in the fall of 1882 or later on, in the spring of 1883, it ended painfully for Edith nevertheless.

MARRIAGE

The lingering sorrow of her broken engagement to Harry Stevens was evident in her appreciation for her next beau. Edward "Teddy" Wharton, who was a friend of her brother Harry, met Edith in 1883. Teddy's disposition suited her very well. She wrote about him to Anna Bahlmann, joyful in her "present happiness," noting wryly that, "coming to me after Certain Experiences of which you know, it seems almost incredible that a man can be so devoted, so generous, so sweet-tempered & unselfish" (*My Dear Governess,* p. 62). Teddy won Edith's hand in marriage, and their quiet wedding took place on April 29, 1885, in the Trinity Chapel in New York City. The marriage began amiably enough, with her letters from the time indicating what Goldman-Price describes as "an atmosphere of cheerful comradeship in travel, homemaking, and sport" (*My Dear Governess,* p. 64). In the early years, they were companionable and affectionate partners.

As befits an upbringing that taught her to be a hostess and socially adept "True Woman," Edith Wharton took home decoration, gardening, and entertaining seriously. She and Teddy lived for the first years of their marriage in Pencraig Cottage, across the street from her family's Newport summer residence. In 1893, they purchased their first home in Newport, a house called "Land's End," which she decorated and designed with the assistance of the Boston architect Ogden Codman, Jr. "Wharton was equally interested in the ethics of style," explains Hermione Lee, "whether in the production values of her books, in her house and garden designs, in her appreciation of Europe or in her theorizing of interior decoration" (*Edith Wharton,* p. 125). Wharton's collaboration with "Coddy," as she called her architect, suited her personally and professionally: her writing career launched in 1897 with the publication of *The Decoration of Houses,* coauthored with Codman. Though *Decoration* ostensibly addresses the practical matters of interior design, home decoration, and architecture, in scope, aesthetic vision, and philosophy its argument anticipates the central concerns in Wharton's creative writing. When she and Codman insist that the "interior of a house is as much a part of its organic structure as the outside," they are also making a claim about the interdependence of public and private spheres, a concern that runs throughout her writing and her life.

Early in her writing life, Wharton established a routine that would pattern many of her days: she would write in the mornings, propped up in bed and equipped with a tea service nearby. Her handwritten pages would be collected by her personal secretary and typed. Wharton maintained an extensive collection of servants throughout her life, and yet it is a testament to her household management and her personality that her closest servants demonstrated extraordinary loyalty. Her housekeeper Catherine Gross, for example, served Wharton for nearly fifty years. Anna Bahlmann, who began as governess when Edith was twelve years old, remained in the employ of the Jones family and then in Edith Wharton's own household, intermittently, as tutor, chaperone, companion, household manager, and personal secretary for the rest of her life.

A few years into Edith and Teddy's marriage, the Jones family faced a difficult conflict when the marriage of Edith's older brother Frederic ended; Frederic's infidelity and divorce led to deep disagreement between them. Edith had grown very close to Freddy's wife, Mary ("Minnie"), and her daughter, Beatrix ("Trix"); she was deeply distressed by the cruelty of her brother's betrayal and the humiliation of a paltry financial settlement that left the two women disadvantaged economically. Edith and her brother Harry supported Minnie and Trix, while Lucretia Jones seems to have sided with her other son. This family fracture—with Lucretia and Freddy, citing family loyalty, pitted against Edith and Harry, citing compassion for the betrayed Minnie and Trix—may be at the root of the harsh depiction Wharton left of her mother later in life. Irene Goldman-Price notes that Wharton experienced

> the shocking disloyalty and rejection by her oldest brother, Frederic, when he chose to divorce Minnie and persuaded their mother to take his side against [Edith] Wharton in the long financial struggle that ensued. Lucretia all but broke off relations with her only daughter and died unreconciled to Wharton, who had devoted her first thirty years to caring for her mother.
>
> (p. 274)

Numerous critics have noted the connection between Wharton's conflicted relationship with her own mother and the notable absence of nurturing or supportive mother figures throughout Wharton's fiction. Gloria C. Erlich, for example, posits that "flaws in the mother-daughter relationship ... derailed [Wharton's] emotional development and caused a massive sexual repression" (p. ix). In Wharton's fiction, mothers are often absent, dead, or ineffectual; many wives are childless, as was Edith herself.

The absence of children in the Wharton marriage is understood to reflect an absence of intimacy between husband and wife. While Teddy and Edith shared similar upbringings, social circles, and family histories, they were temperamentally quite different, with Teddy drawn to sporty, outdoor activities like hunting and fishing and disinclined to intellectual or literary life. These differences created tension over time, and they traveled separately on many occasions, as each pursued their individual lives and interests. Further stressing the marriage, both Whartons suffered from a number of ailments, including neuralgia, allergies, neurasthenia, chronic fatigue, and, for Edith, nearly twelve years of constant nausea "nervous dyspepsia," as she describes it (*My Dear Governess,* p. 131).

As numerous biographers and critics have noted, as time went on, the marriage fractured under the strain of these differences, a tension that was exacerbated in later years by Teddy's deteriorating mental health, as symptoms of what would now be known as bipolar disorder manifested themselves. Edith Wharton's own mental and emotional well-being was strained by Teddy's deteriorating mental and physical health in the later years of their marriage. "I heard the key turn in my prison-lock," Wharton wrote in her diary in 1908, upon returning to Teddy after some time apart. "Oh, Gods of derisions! And you've given me over twenty years of it. Je n'en peux plus ["I can't take any more of it"]" (quoted in Wolff, p. 51). Yet even in these difficulties, Edith remained a committed wife, managing his medical appointments and treatments, patiently offering guidance and counsel, and encouraging Teddy to develop a peaceful and productive routine.

EARLY FICTION

Wharton's writing career began with the ambitious and prolific production of short fiction. In a five-year span between 1899 and 1904, she published three collections of stories (totaling twenty-four stories altogether)—*The Greater Inclination* (1899), *Crucial Instances* (1901), and *The Descent of Man, and Other Stories* (1904)—as well as two novellas, *The Touchstone* (1900) and *Sanctuary* (1903), among other books. Wharton labored over the crafting of her stories and paid close attention to structure. She considered a successful story to be "a shaft driven straight into the heart of human experience" (*The Writing of Fiction,* p. 29). In "Souls Belated," an oft-anthologized social satire, this careful plot development is particularly evident. The story highlights Wharton's interest in women's lives. As the story opens, Lydia Tillotson has just received her divorce papers; she has finally escaped her oppressive marriage, and she finds herself free to plan a future with her lover, Ralph Gannett. But what is the meaning of freedom for a divorced woman in a society organized around the fiction that marriage is sacred? As Lydia and Ralph struggle to move beyond the constricting categories of their social order, they cannot help becoming further entrapped by convention, continually seduced by the protective rituals of society. "Do you know, I begin to see what marriage is for," Lydia realizes in the end. She explains to Gannett,

> It's to keep people away from each other. Sometimes I think that two people who love each other can be saved from madness only by the things that come between them—children, duties, visits, bores, relations—the things that protect married people from each other. We've been too close together—that has been our sin. We've seen the nakedness of each other's souls.
>
> (*The Greater Inclination,* p. 121)

The lack of options available to Lydia proves too damning for her to overcome. The story concludes with the clear implication that Lydia and Gannett will marry, but this seems like both a loss and a tragedy.

"The Muse's Tragedy," also included in *The Greater Inclination,* first appeared separately in *Scribner's* magazine. A structurally nuanced story, it employs indirect narration and multiple points of view to examine unrequited love and missed opportunities. The title pays homage to Wharton's friend Henry James (whose novel *The Tragic Muse* had appeared in 1890), but its themes also inform *The Touchstone,* published the following year. "The two belong together," notes Hermione Lee. "They are both about a woman's unrequited love, the publishing of private letters and the cost of literary fame" (*Edith Wharton,* p. 190). In *The Touchstone,* Stephen Glennard betrays the woman who loved him, a famous writer named Margaret Aubyn, when, after her death and against her wishes, he sells her love letters for publication. While his exploitation of Margaret's private feelings for his personal profit does net him a tidy sum, it also puts *his* behavior up for public discussion; Glennard fares poorly in the court of public opinion when his own limitations are on such glaring display. In the end, he bitterly regrets his betrayal.

Wharton's early fiction revealed a keen interest in the personal privacy of public people (such as authors), and this interest remained steadfast throughout her life. Like Henry James, who famously burned numerous personal letters in a 1909 bonfire, Wharton expected loyalty and privacy from her friends and insisted that they destroy all of her correspondence. Large gaps in her personal papers indicate that she seems to have destroyed many of the letters in her possession (no letters remain, for example, from her parents or her brothers). In another illustrative example, upon the death of her dear friend Walter Berry in 1927, she entered his apartment and collected all documentation of their relationship; just two letters survive from their lifelong correspondence. Not everyone respected her wishes, and she surely would have been distressed at the posthumous publication of her own private papers, particularly those documenting her relationships with her governess and tutor—and later, personal secretary and friend—Anna Bahlmann (mentioned above) and her lover Morton Fullerton (discussed in more detail below).

The Valley of Decision (1902), Wharton's first full-length novel, draws heavily on her extensive travels in Europe. The tale chronicles the emerging leadership of Odo Valsecca, an Italian nobleman of the mid-eighteenth century. A consciously literary historical romance, the novel not only draws on Wharton's childhood memories of Italian life, but it both contributes to and benefits from her research for *Italian Villas and Their Gardens* (1904) and *Italian Backgrounds* (1905). In the latter book, Wharton encourages her readers to avoid mere tourism and become, instead, "the dawdler, the dreamer and the serious student of Italy" (p. 177); she develops a critically astute, deeply informed and detail-oriented depiction of Italy its landscape, architecture, culture, and people. The *Century* magazine editor Richard

Watson Gilder commissioned *Italian Villas and Their Gardens* to supplement a series of watercolors by Maxfield Parrish as well as other artists. Wharton's contribution is impressively researched and filled with historical references and literary allusions.

THE MOUNT AND THE HOUSE OF MIRTH

In the midst of this multigenre literary productivity, Edith and Teddy Wharton purchased 113 acres near the Berkshire Mountains of western Massachusetts in 1901. Wharton's interest in architecture continued to develop following *The Decoration of Houses,* and during the next year, she consulted closely on the design and construction of their "spacious and dignified house," a grand estate that came to be called "The Mount" (*A Backward Glance,* p. 125). The architects Ogden Codman, Jr., and Francis L. V. Hoppin based the main house structure on a seventeenth-century English country home. Wharton and Codman designed the interior spaces according to the principles adumbrated in *The Decoration of Houses,* with classical Italian and French influences. Within the home and without, Wharton's aesthetic emphasizes harmony and balance. Other buildings included a gatehouse and stable (both in the style of Georgian revival) and a greenhouse with potting shed. Wharton's dedication to gardening was evident in several distinguished formal flower gardens: not only an Italian walled garden but also a rock garden, the pathway of linden trees known as a lime walk, and numerous grass terraces. "Decidedly, I'm a better landscape gardener than novelist," she wrote to Morton Fullerton, "and this place, every line of which is my own work, far surpasses *The House of Mirth*" (Lewis and Lewis, p. 242).

Designed and built according to Wharton's well-honed aesthetic principles, The Mount offered her private space for work and intimate friendship as well as formal spaces for entertaining. "I liked New York well enough, [though] it was only at The Mount that I was really happy," she wrote.

> The Mount was to give me country cares and joys, long happy rides and drives through the wooded lanes of that loveliest region, the companionship of a few dear friends, and the freedom from trivial obligations which was necessary if I was to go on writing. The Mount was my first real home ... its blessed influence still lives in me.
>
> (*A Backward Glance,* p. 125)

Wharton's passion for gardening was evident in The Mount's design as well. Horticulture, according to her design philosophy, functions on numerous levels beyond the merely ornamental, and it influenced her writing as well as her imagination. In discussing her creative process, she uses gardening metaphors, explaining, "I shall try to depict the growth and unfolding of the plants in my secret garden, from the seed to the shrub-top for I have no intention of magnifying my vegetation into trees!" (*A Backward Glance,* p. 198). A lifetime study of gardening also made Wharton well acquainted with the "language of flowers," that Victorian tradition in which floral arrangements communicated fairly detailed secret messages that would have been socially prohibited from direct expression. In the opening scene of her first best seller, *The House of Mirth* (1905), for example, the protagonist Lily Bart proclaims her wish for daily deliveries of lilies of the valley, an expensive fantasy that soon proves brutally ironic, as Lily's father experiences financial ruin that will catapult her into a tragic downward spiral. The irony of Lily's desire is underscored by the flower's meaning, "a return to happiness," since such a return will elude Lily to her death.

Taking its title from the biblical passage in Ecclesiastics (7:4), which notes, "The heart of the wise is in the house of mourning; but the heart of fools is in the house of mirth," Wharton's first critically and financially successful novel provided a biting satire on the moral decay of "Old New York." Lily Bart is raised in the socially conscious wealth of old New York but finds herself orphaned and penniless when her father's catastrophic business failure leads to his untimely death, followed soon by that of her mother. Though Lily possesses extraordinary beauty and a vivacious spirit, she must navigate the marriage market while living under the strict and exacting household run by her maiden aunt. The navigation proves treacherous, as she confides to Laurence Selden, noting that "the other women—my best friends—well, they use me or abuse me; but they don't care a straw what happens to me" (p. 13). Without parents to guide or protect her, Lily unwittingly becomes her own worst enemy as she repeatedly, and unintentionally, sabotages advantageous putative marriage proposals. Though it is Selden alone who gives voice to her deep desire for freedom when he sketches his vision for "a kind of republic of the spirit" (p. 108), he fails to understand the inaccessibility of such freedom for a woman. Lily's fall from grace comes with tragic rapidity when she naively makes several fatal social missteps. Impoverished and socially outcast in the end, she dies from an accidental overdose of the sedative chloral.

Wharton intended Lily's tragedy as an ironic commentary on the peculiarly American materialism of "a society of irresponsible pleasure-seekers" (*A Backward Glance,* p. 207). She notes that "a frivolous society can acquire dramatic significance only through what its frivolity destroys. Its tragic implication lies in its power of debasing people and ideals" (*A Backward Glance,* p. 207). While Wharton's goals were high minded and literary (and, by some reviewers, recognized and lauded as such), some readers were drawn to the novel by Scribner's gossipy advertising campaign, which promised that "the veil has been lifted from New York society." The novel's success led to adaptation for the stage, which played in New York and Detroit during the summer of 1906. While the play was not well received, the novel itself brought Wharton astonishing success: it sold 30,000 copies in its first three weeks, and totaled 140,000 at the end of its first year in print. *The House of Mirth*'s reception signaled a shift in her status: Edith Wharton became a major American author.

MORTON FULLERTON AND "L'AME CLOSE"

Their love for The Mount notwithstanding, Edith and Teddy Wharton lived for extended periods in Paris beginning in 1906, in an apartment on the Rue de Varenne. There was much about French cultural life that suited Edith in particular, and she reveled in the intellectual stimulation provided by French literary salons. Just as her extensive travels through, and immersion in, Italian life had influenced her choice of Italian themes in the previous few years, living in Paris led Wharton to write about American expatriates in France. Her novella *Madame de Treymes,* which first appeared in Scribner's magazine in August 1906, offers a good example of her ability to weave French and American themes into timeless, resonant fiction. Her American characters' naive good intentions are often contrasted against the corrupt manipulations of the French. The bitter tale considered how adultery and divorce pose peculiar challenges to Americans living in France. While the novella introduces what will be an ongoing interest in the subtle French "ways" that blind so many Americans, it also offers an eerily prescient treatment of the themes that would soon inform her personal life, when she fell in love with another man.

Wharton first met Morton Fullerton in 1907. A charismatic writer who worked as the Paris correspondent of the London *Times,* Fullerton was also a friend of Henry James. Wharton was forty-five at the time of their meeting, three years his senior, and she and Fullerton began a friendship that developed into a romantic flirtation and, eventually, a sexual relationship. Beginning around the spring of 1908, their sexual affair was, from all accounts, erotically intense and deeply passionate. From October 29, 1907, to June 12, 1908, Wharton documented the emotional chaos of this liaison in a private diary she titled "The Life Apart: L'Ame Close." The diary functions as an extended epistolary of sorts to the absent, and imagined, Fullerton. She writes, "now I shall have the illusion that I am talking to you" (Price and McBride, p. 21). The loneliness and disappointment from her marriage to Teddy is manifestly evident in contrast to the joy she finds with Fullerton:

> I said to myself all the week: "I have never in my life known what it was to be happy (as a woman understands happiness) even for a single hour—

> now at last I shall be happy for a whole day, talking à Coeur ouvert [with an open heart], saying for once what I feel and *all that I feel* as other women do."
>
> (Price and McBride, p. 672)

She is frank about her sexual desire: "the mortal weakness the blind cry: 'I want you! I want you!' that bears down on everything else" (Price and McBride, p. 674). For a woman whose life had been carefully shaped according to principles of dignity and propriety, these personal writings revealed extraordinary vulnerability.

Apart from this private diary, Wharton expresses her emotions freely in her correspondence with Fullerton himself. "I am mad about you Dear Heart," she writes,

> and sick at the thought of our parting and the days of separation and longing that are to follow. It is a wonderful world that you have created for me, Morton dear, but how I am to adjust it to the *other* world is difficult to conceive. Perhaps when I am once more on land my mental vision may be clearer at present, in the whole universe I see but one thing, am conscious of but one thing, you, our love for each other.
>
> (Lewis and Lewis, p. 145)

After Wharton left Fullerton in Paris for a planned return to The Mount in the summer of 1908, many of her love letters to him went unanswered. In fact, Morton Fullerton was a cad, and he was managing and hiding several other ongoing romantic entanglements, including an engagement to his younger cousin Katharine Fullerton, who had been raised as his sister.

Wharton knew none of this at the time, and she became desperate, anxious, and confused. Months of silence drove her to distraction. "Anything on earth wd be better ... than to sit here and wonder: *What was I to him,* then?" (Lewis and Lewis, p. 156), she writes in despair. In spite of her repeated request that Fullerton either return or destroy all of her letters—"I beg instant cremation for this" she writes at one point (Lewis and Lewis, p. 139)—many of the letters were preserved. Eventually he wrote to her, a brief line in late December, 1908, after nearly six full months of silence. Though Wharton was deeply pained by his inattention, she continued in the affair. Their time together was certainly limited by the demands of her deteriorating marriage, her time-consuming work, her extensive social life, and the logistical challenges of finding privacy in which to conduct an extramarital affair in early-twentieth-century Paris. Their correspondence makes it clear that the emotional intensity took a toll on Wharton over time. She requested and gradually achieved a transition in their relationship from lovers to friends. Though they drifted apart around 1912, Fullerton reappeared later in her life, with a friendly exchange of letters in the early 1930s. They were both writers—though she was clearly the better and more successful of the two, and this fact, along with some mutual friends and their shared intellectual interests, dominated their friendship in the end.

For many years, this affair was unknown. In 1980, however, approximately three hundred of Wharton's letters to Fullerton, written between 1907 and 1915, appeared unexpectedly, offered for sale by a Parisian bookseller. While they are invaluable, significant historical documents that offer detailed information about this time in Wharton's life, they are also extraordinarily intimate, and they have since been published, quoted, analyzed, and reprinted, in publications ranging from the *New York Times* to *Vogue* magazine. Edith Wharton, who had repeatedly, insistently requested the return or destruction of these letters, would surely have been horrified about such an affront to her privacy, not to mention the betrayal by her former lover. Yet as R. W. B. Lewis and Nancy Lewis remind us, the vulnerability presented in these epistles render Wharton "quite remarkably human." They explain, "This woman, whose public image was that of the austerely self-contained (and who could be exactly that in her formal correspondence), was in fact extraordinarily open to experience, immediately responsive to the here-and-now of life" (*The Letters of Edith Wharton,* p. 17).

Wharton's erotic life was surely nourished by her affair, and her writing gained a corresponding depth and nuance. If the "love diary" (as "L'Ame Close" is often referred to by scholars) offered her one outlet for the intense emotions associated with this affair, poetry offered her another. While Wharton is known primarily for her fiction, her first published book was verse, and she wrote poetry throughout her life. Moreover, she read poetry seriously, having studied it closely since childhood. A disciplined student of poetic form, Wharton memorized poems and scanned the poetry of English, American, Italian, German, French, Chinese, and Japanese writers. "Edith used poetry to focus her intense emotional responses," writes her biographer Shari Benstock, when she was "unable to concentrate on novel-writing" (p. 191). Hermione Lee agrees, arguing that "the love affair turned her into more of a poet" (*Edith Wharton,* p. 344). In the 1909 *Artemis to Actaeon and Other Verses,* Wharton's first mature collection of poetry (*Verses,* her previous publication, was written during her teens), love poems abound, and they evince a passionate lyricism and romantic intention that rarely appears so directly in her fiction. Indeed, Wharton's fiction often grinds its romantic characters and poets in the mill of realism. "Terminus," now perhaps best known among her love poems, was included in the "love diary" and therefore unpublished during Wharton's life. Addressed to a lover, presumably Fullerton, the poem commemorates a night of lovemaking at London's Charing Cross Hotel. "Wonderful was the long secret night you gave me, my Lover," the opening line reads, "Palm to palm, breast to breast in the gloom." The poem's title, which refers to the tryst's inevitable end, pays homage to a poem by Ralph Waldo Emerson, yet in form it evokes Walt Whitman, with frank eroticism and free-verse style.

MAJOR FICTION

Wharton's writing life remained highly productive during these years of personal tumult; indeed, some of her most enduring fiction emerged from this period, and it seems clear that the emotional complexity of this work grew from her personal suffering. *Ethan Frome,* one of her best known and most oft-taught works, appeared in 1911. That the tale's grim depiction of marital frustration, thwarted love, and spiritual poverty is situated in the Berkshire Mountains (near The Mount, where Fullerton had visited her) suggests that some autobiographical concerns informed the writing. Ethan's tragic story is told through flashback, narrated by a visitor to Starkfield who learns the details of Ethan's "smash up" more than a quarter century after it occurred. His destruction has been multifaceted, encompassing his academic promise and intellectual curiosity as well as any potential for financial prosperity. From the start, Ethan is presented as an organic product of New England life. "He seemed a part of the mute melancholy landscape, an incarnation of its frozen woe, with all that was warm and sentient in him fast bound below the surface; but there was nothing unfriendly in his silence" (pp. 14–15). Ethan's life seems like something that happened to him rather than a trajectory over which he had any control: family obligation keeps him bound to a bleak farm, and a sense of duty leads him into a loveless marriage with the querulous hypochondriac, Zeena. When Zeena's cousin Mattie arrives to care for her, Ethan is irresistibly drawn to the younger woman's vivacious ebullience; he falls in love with her, glimpsing a life of potential happiness.

The fantasy of a life with Mattie turns less on erotic or sexual desire and more on the "intoxicating" (p. 91) effect of her smiling kindness, and the pleasure of talking "easily and simply" (p. 90). In marked contrast to the anxiety produced by Zeena's grumbling sarcasm, with Mattie, "Ethan was suffocated with the sense of well-being" (p. 82). When Zeena conspires to have her cousin sent away, Mattie and Ethan plan a suicide pact in the form of a sleigh ride, an escapade that proves more tragic than suicide would have been when it leaves them both horribly crippled rather than mercifully dead. The three are left miserably bound together for life, with Mattie's pessimistic bitterness surpassing even Zeena's.

Wharton understood that the novella marked a transition in her control over structure after continual effort. "I wrote two or three novels without feeling that I had made much progress," she explains (*A Backward Glance,* p. 209). "It was not until I wrote 'Ethan Frome' that I suddenly felt the artisan's full control of his implements." In pursuit of increased technical mastery, she wrote the first draft in French, part of "an exercise in improving her style" (Lee, p. 280). While the story was based on an actual 1904 sledding crash that took place in Lenox (Wharton was acquainted with one of the survivors), its larger truth echoes beyond the historical facts and into the more resonant emotional experience of imprisonment in a deeply unhappy marriage.

The Reef, published in 1912, engages the central themes in Wharton's private life through its uncompromising focus on duplicity, sexual jealousy, desire, and shame. The emotional legacy of her love affair is everywhere evident in the novel's subtle, Jamesian plot. "*The Reef* was an extraordinarily candid expression of private feelings about her own desires and sexual knowledge," explains Hermione Lee, "immaculately disguised by the novel's formal control and careful, dramatic design" (*Edith Wharton,* p. 354). As it opens, the American diplomat George Darrow is detained in Paris at the request of his putative fiancée, a wealthy widow named Anna Leath. He has traveled to France to see Anna, in the hopes that she has decided to accept his earlier proposal of marriage. Yet while awaiting Anna's summons to join her at Givre, her late husband's French estate, Darrow falls into what he believes is an inconsequential but charming romance with Sophy Viner, a naive young American. He is, however, tragically and awkwardly wrong about the consequences of his fling: upon arrival at Givres, he discovers that Sophy Viner has been hired as the governess for Anna's daughter Effie. Worse yet, Sophy becomes engaged to Anna's stepson Owen.

Anna Leath's carefully controlled emotional life is shattered by her sexual desire for Darrow, and she is deeply unsettled by "the flood of her pent-up anguish" (p. 284) upon learning of Darrow's affair. The novel's conclusion remains ambivalent about Anna and Darrow's destiny, leaving unstated whether they will reunite. About Sophy Viner, however, the novel is clear: she breaks with Owen and faces a bleak life as the companion of a London woman traveling to India. The cruelty of Sophy's fate—she renounces Owen Leath's sincere love—offers a bitter commentary on the sexual double standard, which leaves Darrow socially and professionally unscathed. Wharton called on Morton Fullerton to advise her on the novel; she read him several chapters and asked for his help. "So the ex-lover was summoned to give literary advice about the novel whose emotions he had inspired," remarks Hermione Lee (*Edith Wharton,* p. 343). This was one of her final appeals to Fullerton's friendship.

The Custom of the Country, which appeared in 1913, most specifically reveals influences from Wharton's personal challenges at this time in its harsh and satirical view of marriage and divorce. Undine Spragg, the compelling, vexing, and extraordinary character at the center of the novel, is aligned with American identity by her very initials. Vain, shallow, materialistic, and exquisitely manipulative, Undine operates with total impunity, in a moral vacuum. As a child, her "chief delight was to 'dress up' in her mother's Sunday skirt and 'play lady' before the wardrobe mirror" and as an adult, "she could yield without afterthought to the joy of dramatizing her beauty" (p. 22). She has been indulged by doting, nouveau riche parents who remove her from her native Apex City after her impulsive, secret marriage (which is hastily dissolved) to the brash Elmer Moffatt. The Spraggs land in New York, where Undine hopes to launch socially. She succeeds in marrying the aristocratic Old New Yorker Ralph Marvell, only to grow quickly dissatisfied with his family's conservative modesty. Ralph realizes the mistake of his marriage when confronted with Undine's cavalier flippancy about divorce. She seduces, and uses, a string of men—from Ralph, to the wealthy and dashing Peter Van Degen, to the French nobleman the Comte Raymond de Chelles, to Elmer Moffatt, her girlhood lover and secret first husband.

At the novel's end, Undine's manipulations have left a path of destruction that includes divorce, suicide, abandonment, and heartbreak. Yet even through all of her triumphs, Undine remains unfulfilled, the personification of acquisitive desire. Charles Bowen, an ostensibly minor character, gives voice to the novel's harshest critique, castigating a society of material pleasures and surface appearances, where "Nothing ever goes on! Nothing that ever happens here is real" (p. 275). *The Custom of the Country* decries a world of such promiscuous wealth and concomitant spiritual poverty.

Undine's casual attitude toward divorce did not reflect her author's: Wharton was a product of her conservative social upbringing and had no desire for the publicity of scandal. Still, Teddy's behavior caused just that. His manic moods made him unpredictable and publicly embarrassing, his numerous adulterous affairs shamed her socially, and his reckless behavior extended to gambling and dangerous financial mismanagement. In 1909, he confessed that he lost nearly $50,000 of her money. In 1911, he finalized the sale of The Mount without Edith's knowledge after promising her that he would not. The stress of his disorder was compounded by his family's unwillingness to recognize the depth of his illness, even though—or perhaps, because—his father had died from suicide after a lifetime struggle with mental illness. Wharton found it untenable to remain in the marriage, and she filed for divorce. In Paris courts, she was better able to protect her privacy, since reporters there did not have access to court proceedings, as they did in New York. The divorce was granted in April 1913.

Formidable and detail oriented in her personal legal affairs, Edith Wharton also kept close watch over the business end of her writing career. As was the custom in nineteenth-century publishing, many of her novels were serialized before appearing as individual books. Charles Scribner's Sons began publishing her poems and stories in 1889, and Wharton developed a productive relationship with the company—the firm published her fiction, nonfiction, translations, poetry, and criticism. Around 1911, however, Wharton's correspondence revealed a growing dissatisfaction with some Scribner business practices: she objected to the company's advertising and marketing philosophy, and she quibbled over copyediting practices and design decisions. In 1912, as she was negotiating divorce from her husband, she also "divorced" Charles Scribner's Sons, signing a contract with the rival D. Appleton and Company publishing firm, which offered her more money and promised her more control. *The Reef* was her first Appleton book. She did honor earlier agreements with Scribner's, and published several stories, essays, and books with the firm even after signing with Appleton.

THE GREAT WAR

Once The Mount was sold in 1911, Wharton established her homestead in France permanently; beginning in 1914, she became active in relief efforts for World War I. Like many Parisian women seeking to contribute to the war effort, she established an *ouvroir,* "a 'workroom,' or, more specifically, 'a needlework school for indigent young women'" (Lee, p. 463). There, women left unemployed by the war could earn a nominal salary and hot meals in exchange for their labor in various sewing projects, producing not only war supplies but civilian attire as well. Regarding the latter, Wharton's New York network of affluent socialites proved quite valuable, as she pressured her wealthy American friends to order clothing in support of her *ouvroir.* She also became deeply involved in the "Children of Flanders Rescue Committee," not only in fundraising but in organizing and development: it was Wharton who suggested incorporating a lacemaking school into the refugee housing effort, an endeavor for which she also sought support from her New York friends. She also, and simultaneously, raised funds for and then opened several fresh-air sanatoriums for tuberculosis patients. Endlessly energetic, Wharton was also adamantly pro-Allies and so furious about U.S. neutrality that she vetted publishers to determine their political sympathies, resisting the placement of her work in any outlet that did not share her loyalty.

Wharton's wealth aided her relief work in several ways: her possession of a Mercedes (named "Her") proved a valuable asset to the war effort. At the request of the French government, she took supplies to the front, expeditions that gave her remarkable access to the trenches. She was not only one of the first women to be allowed front-line access but also one of the first writers; this was possible in part because of her fame and in part because she became involved so early, before restrictions for journalists were in place. In writing to Charles Scribner after one of her five journeys into battle zones, she remarked, "We were given opportunities *no one else* has had of seeing things at the front" (Lee, p. 485). Wharton's extraordinary service was well recognized by the French government, which awarded her the Chevalier de l'Ordre National de la Légion d'Honneur in 1916 and then promoted her from Chevalier to Officier in 1923.

Much of her writing from this time, both fiction and nonfiction, was propagandist in nature, reflecting the fullness of her commitment to the cause. Her trips to the front resulted in several pieces of wartime journalism that appeared first in *Scribner's Magazine* and then were collected as *Fighting France from Dunkerque to Belfort,* published in 1915. These articles, which often focus on images or human-interest angles, reveal a tension between "hard" and "soft" wartime news. Being a woman precluded her from writing gritty accounts of violence and carnage; instead, she developed aesthetic impressions through which to present the war. Luminous bombs and flares appear as "a white light [which] opened like a tropical flower, spread to full bloom ... those infernal flowers continued to open and shut along the curve of death" (pp. 148–149). Such imagery allowed her to convey a sense of the war's destruction, but in sublimated terms. Her political sympathies are often clear, nevertheless, as she contrasts "the feathery drift of French gunsmoke" against "the red lightnings ... of the German artillery" (p. 64). Note the differing implications of the "feathery" French weaponry versus the harsher "red lightnings" produced by the Germans.

Wharton's war novels from this period, *The Marne* (1918) and *A Son at the Front* (begun in 1918 but not published until 1923), idealize American young men who join the war cause, celebrating the heroism that comes through wartime self-sacrifice. In *The Marne,* Wharton's sympathies are channeled through Troy Belknap. The privileged young American's love for France is inspired by annual summer visits and then cultivated by Paul Gantier, his beloved French tutor who is killed in the first Battle of the Marne. Troy's horror at the war's outbreak matches Wharton's own: "France, his France, attacked, invaded, outraged; and he, a poor helpless American boy, who adored her, and could do nothing for her ... It was bitter" (p. 10). Troy returns to France and joins the ambulance corps a few years later; in the chaos of frontline action, he takes up a rifle and joins the new battle of the Marne. While *The Marne*'s denouement turns on spectral intervention (we are led to believe that Troy's life is saved by the ghost of Paul Gantier), in *A Son at the Front,* Paris's wealthy expatriate Americans stand at the center of action. The group provides fodder for Wharton's satire, and she coolly examines the whole lot of them, "the quarrelling relief-workers, the society ladies with their charity concerts, the heroic French parents, the foolish pacifists and 'subversive' modern Bohemians" (Lee, p. 458), while celebrating the superiority of French culture and civilization.

In the 1917 novella *Summer,* which unfolds within the same New England landscape as *Ethan Frome* (The Mount's Massachusetts backyard), the reader can still see vestiges of the war's impact on Wharton. The grim realist tale of Charity Royall's thwarted romance leaves her imprisoned by her provincial life. Charity's destiny turns on a gruesome scene where she encounters her mother's corpse, a moment of graphic description that was surely informed by front-line carnage. As Charity looks at the dead body, her mother

> seemed to have fallen across her bed in a drunken sleep, and to have been left lying where she fell, in her ragged, disordered clothes. One arm was flung above her head, one leg drawn up under a torn skirt that left the other bare to the knee: a swollen glistening leg with a ragged stocking rolled down about the ankle.
>
> (p. 250)

In contrast to this grisly imagery, *Summer* also vibrates with intense sexual passion; Wharton referred to it as her "hot Ethan" (Lee, p. 508). Charity seems predestined to engage in an affair with Lucius Harney, given her sensual characterization and deep sense of yearning. In a richly descriptive erotic scene, Charity presses her body into a slope of grass until "the fingering of the wind in her hair and through her cotton blouse" leaves her "immersed in an inarticulate well-being" (p. 21). She is trapped in small-town North Dormer, simultaneously connected to and repulsed by her guardian, Lawyer Royall, and she is hungry for change. "How I hate everything!" she states in the book's opening dialogue (p. 9). Like many of Wharton's yearning young women, Charity's fate has been sealed by her disadvantaged social class, her insufficient education, her lack of a mother to guide her.

Wharton left Paris and was living in the south of France when she wrote *The Age of Innocence* in 1919; it was published a year later, and won her the Pulitzer Prize—the first awarded to a woman writer—in 1921. Set in the Old New York of Wharton's youth, the novel's nostalgia seems highly autobiographical. Mrs. Manson Mingott's character evokes her father's aunt, Mrs. Mary Mason Jones, for example, and the purple and yellow satin curtains of the fictional Welland drawing room match those of the Jones's New York home during Edith's childhood. This nostalgia also seems stylistically anachronistic, however—a realist account of the highly mannered nineteenth century, written at a time when experimental and avant-garde literary modernism had influenced literary traditions on both sides of the Atlantic. Nevertheless, though set in the past, *The Age of Innocence,* like *Summer,* deals with sexual desire and erotic longing far more directly than any of her previous fiction; in this regard, the writings of Wharton's later life are influenced by the sexual freedom expressed throughout the modernist era.

The novel's irony begins with its merciless title, for Wharton depicts an age that is hardly innocent, and the narrator draws us into a world of secrets and lies, codes and hieroglyphics. As the novel opens, Newland Archer impulsively announces his engagement to May Welland earlier than planned, in order to enhance family solidarity and provide more substantial social "backing" for May's cousin, the Countess Ellen Olenska. Ellen has recently returned to New York from Europe, where she's lived an eclectic, unconventional life; she is also escaping a brutal husband whom she wishes to divorce. While Newland is drafted by the family to advise Ellen against the divorce (these are people who "dreaded scandal more than disease"; p. 338), he finds himself falling in love with her bohemian individuality. Newland and Ellen are drawn to each other because they share a desire to escape the social codes that bind them, yet they realize—like Gannett and Lydia in "Souls Belated"—how much they depend on those very codes for their own identity. Even after marrying May, Newland pursues Ellen. He explains to her, "I want—I want somehow to get away with you into a world where words like that—categories like that—won't exist. Where we shall be simply two human beings who love each other, who are the whole of life to each other; and nothing else on earth will matter." Ellen's response highlights the impossibility of his vision, telling him, "there's no *us* in that sense! We're near each other only if we can stay far from each other" (pp. 293–294). Manners, Wharton reminds us, not only preserve the social order, they also protect us from the devastating consequences of our desires.

Wharton's major fiction engages issues of erotic desire and sexual longing repeatedly during these years. From *Ethan Frome*'s sexual repression to the harsh punishment Charity Royall receives for her carnal indulgence, from Anna Leath's simmering unexpressed sexuality to Newland Archer's inability to act on his passion—these are tales that ask whether the better path is to follow indulgence or repression. In an uncompleted and unpublished story fragment written (as many scholars believe) around the same time as *The Age of Innocence,* Wharton examined taboo sexual desire even more explicitly: in "Beatrice Palmato," the sexually graphic story of father-daughter incest is sufficiently explicit that many readers might call it pornographic. Wharton's biographer Hermione Lee notes that the story, which was hidden in a collection of documents marked "For My Biographer," "is loaded with what obsessed her: double lives, repression, sexual hypocrisy, hidden longings" (Lee, p. 589). An erotic two-page scene describes the moment when Beatrice and her father consummate their affair. It is clear that while they have been lovers for an indeterminate number of years, they have withheld from intercourse to protect her virginity. But as the scene opens, she is newly married and no longer needs to abstain. "'And now, darling,' Mr. Palmato said, drawing her to the deep divan, 'let me show you what only you and I have the right to show each other'" (Lewis, p. 547). Though the number of pages is few, they are powerful. The Palmatos are a family haunted by the suicide of an older daughter, the subsequent suicide attempt and breakdown of the mother, and the eventual suicide of Beatrice, the incest victim herself. No evidence exists to suggest that the incest was in any way an autobiographical theme for Wharton, but the materials themselves are as shocking as the fact that she preserved them and called her biographer's attention to them. Their presence indicates her willingness to face the hard facts of life directly, without flinching.

Edith Wharton turned sixty in 1922, the year that *The Glimpses of the Moon* was published. The successful novel reconfirmed Wharton's status as a popular author, with sales rivaling those of *The House of Mirth.* Indeed, many critics have noted thematic similarities between the two novels, suggesting that *Glimpses* might be best understood as a reconsideration of *Mirth.* As Laura K. Johnson notes, both works share an interest in marriage that is surely autobiographical: "By the time Wharton published *The House of Mirth,* she had endured an often unhappy marriage for twenty years, and by the time she published *The Glimpses of the Moon,* she had successfully sued her husband for divorce" (p. 948). Susy Branch and Nick Lansing, the socially ambitious but underfunded protagonists in *Glimpses,* take advantage of the increasingly liberal social attitudes toward marriage and divorce of the 1920s by designing a short-term companionate marriage. Deeply in love, they are also both attached to lavish lifestyles that neither can afford. They agree to marry and to stay together and "wing it"—relying on their wealthy friends' goodwill (loans of vacant houses, vacation invitations and the like) until or unless one of them gets a better, more lucrative option—for example, in the form of a wealthy lover. The agreement seems practical in theory but soon proves deeply unsettling in practice, as secrecy, jealousy, and uncertainty set them against each other. The novel's setting is deliberately, if unspecifically, modern—Nick and Susy's unconventional marriage agreement is supported by their friends' Jazz Age sensibilities, glib conversation, and social freedom. Yet they find themselves romantically conservative at heart, distressed and disconcerted about the tentative nature of their commitment when the going gets tough. In *Glimpses,* we see how the themes of Wharton's personal life had resonance beyond her own experience. What is the cost of love, and what is the value of money? Her repeated, multifaceted examination of marriage's impact on the social order, on individual identity, and on women specifically spoke to a central tension in American culture.

LATER YEARS

In the spring of 1923, Wharton crossed the Atlantic for her final visit to the United States in order to receive an honorary doctor of letters degree from Yale University. She was the first woman to be offered this honor. As recognition of her work expanded, honors mounted. Among the more distinguished merits were a gold medal from the National Institute of Arts and Letters in 1925 (she was the first woman to receive this) and the Gold Medal of the American Academy of Arts and Letters in 1929; she joined the American Academy the following year.

Old New York, a themed series of four stories, appeared in 1924, As its title suggests, the collection continues the "backward glance" so evident in *The Age of Innocence,* with each story examining characters whose lives were shaped by the social conventions of the early and mid-nineteenth century. Writing from the perspective of her early sixties, having suffered the loss of many of her close friends in previous years, Wharton offers "painful treatments of individuals crushed by their 'age'" (Lee, p. 601). *The Mother's Recompense,* serialized in 1924 and published as a book a year later, offers a similarly bitter examination of the limited choices a woman faces when her identity is socially bound by the roles of wife and mother. Wharton continually challenges the hypocrisy of a social order that allows men so much more freedom professionally, creatively, and romantically than women can ever obtain.

Wharton's productivity was consistent and prodigious during the 1920s and 1930s: she continued publishing about a book a year, sometimes more, even as she had to manage the increasing health challenges of her advancing age. Wharton faced numerous illnesses throughout her life, beginning with her childhood affliction of typhoid fever; continuing with the neuralgia, respiratory illness, and digestive ailments of her young adulthood; and developing vertigo, high blood pressure, and cardiac episodes in her later years. She was struck ill with a serious fever in 1929, requiring a four-month break from writing. More seriously, she suffered a stroke in 1935. Elisina Tyler, one of her dearest and most loyal friends of her later years, provided incomparable companionship during these difficult times. Wharton had a heart attack in 1937, which proved to be the final year of her life. She was taken to the hospital by ambulance following the heart attack on June 1, and her health deteriorated from there. By July, Wharton's doctors "told Elisina there was no hope, and she noted 'twitching in left side, sudden drooping of the eyelid, weakness in walking a few steps'—suggesting that a stroke may have followed on from the heart attack" (Lee, p. 748). Another stroke followed in early August, and she died at home on the evening August 11. Her last words, as recorded by Tyler, were "I want to go home" (Lee, p. 749).

POSTHUMOUS PUBLICATION AND FILMS

Wharton left *The Buccaneers,* an unfinished novel, at her death. Its title refers to a group of spirited, newly wealthy, and socially ambitious American girls who, at the suggestion of their British-Italian governess, break into the London social scene. Their recklessness is rewarded when it leads to advantageous marriages; but the deep-seated cultural disconnect by which free-spirited, romantic American girls find themselves trapped in a harsh and demanding aristocratic order proves overwhelming. The trope of wealthy Americans marrying cash-poor but landed British nobles recalls the highly publicized and bitterly unhappy marriage of Consuelo Vanderbilt to the Duke of Marlborough in 1895. Unlike Vanderbilt, who reportedly wept beneath her wedding veil throughout the ceremony, Wharton's brides—the sisters Virginia and Nan St. George, South American beauty Conchita Closson, and Lizzie Elmsworth—enter into marriages that begin somewhat happily. But the stultifying grind of tradition wears them down—particularly Nan, whose marriage is at once the most brilliant (she becomes the Duchess of Tintagel) and the most disappointing.

Wharton's idea for the novel dates to the late 1920s, and she began working on it in 1933; however, the British monarchal crisis of 1936, when King Edward VIII abdicated the throne to marry the American divorcée Wallis Simpson, made it especially timely. Still, the novel was left uncompleted, and its evolution since Wharton's death has been controversial. It's not clear, for example, if Wharton never finished the novel because her poor health prevented her or whether she faced irresolvable challenges with the plot itself (she had, after all, been working on it since 1933). *The Buccaneers*' initial posthumous (1938) appearance, edited by Gaillard Lapsley, was a partial manuscript derived from her final typescripts; it included Wharton's synopsis to give readers a sense of her intended conclusion. It was still an incomplete tale, however, lacking the planned denouement in which Nan leaves her husband the Duke to pursue happiness and freedom with her lover. Another, scholarly edition appeared in 1993, published together with *Fast and Loose,* an unpublished novel Wharton had written as a teenager. This version, edited by Viola Hopkins Winner, included explanatory notes, a contextualizing introduction, and a list of all changes and deviations, including corrections and revisions. Also in 1993 an ostensibly "completed" version of *The Buccaneers* appeared, edited by Marion Mainwaring, who also made untold adjustments in silently editing Wharton's text, adding twelve new chapters of her own without noting what is hers and what is Wharton's. As the critic Gabriele Annan noted in the *New York Review of Books,* "Wharton's own chapters read like a parody of Wharton, and Mainwaring's like a parody of that—except for mistakes that Wharton would never have made" (November 4, 1993).

Marion Mainwaring took many liberties with Wharton's text, but not nearly as many as a 1995 BBC/Masterpiece Theater adaptation, a four-part miniseries based on Mainwaring's version of *The Buccaneers.* In the BBC version, Nan's husband the Duke is both homosexual and a rapist. Examining how the politics of revisionary nostalgia have informed what John Updike calls the "bastardization" of Wharton's vision, Eleanor Hersey notes, "Although the number of revisions of this particular text may be unusual, the process of reinscribing our own cultural fears and denials onto older texts as part of a nostalgic appeal has become increasingly common" (p. 190).

The Buccaneers, in its many iterations, was an element of a "Wharton revival" launched by Martin Scorsese's 1993 high-budget adaptation of *The Age of Innocence.* A costume drama assiduously faithful to the historical details of fashion, design, architecture, and setting, the film won an Academy Award for Best Costume Design. Yet while lush scenery, voluptuous meals, and lavish period sets illustrate the wealth of Old New York, the story itself depends on Joanne Woodward's voice-over. "The voice overs remind us that Wharton's writing throughout *The Age of Innocence* is masterful, and, that while the novel is about restraint, Wharton's prose never approaches a repressed writing style," explains Linda Costanzo Cahir (p. 120). Scorsese's *The Age of Innocence* was often viewed in relation to the film adaptation of *Ethan Frome,* which also appeared in 1993. Under John Madden's direction, the Hollywood version of *Ethan Frome* was seen as "a distant reflection of the Wharton work," unable to successfully translate the nuanced sophistication of Wharton's structure while capturing the tale's subtleties. "The delicate, mysterious Wharton precision is gone," wrote the *New York Times* critic Vincent Canby. "In the place of a nearly perfect novella is a sad and solemn little film that never has a life of its own" (p. C8).

Terrence Davies' 2000 adaptation of *The House of Mirth* was made with a far more limited budget than *The Age of Innocence,* thereby precluding the lavish period details that distinguished Scorsese's film. Unable to replicate the novel's material artifacts, Davies' film was thus more psychological in nature, exploring Lily Bart's relevance to contemporary life and themes. The *New York Times* critic Stephen Holden noted how the film "anticipates today's postfeminist climate of *Sex and the City,* prenuptial agreements and trophy wives" (p. A26). Without the narrative voice-over that kept *The Age of Innocence* film connected to the novel, *The House of Mirth* develops its own vision and stands apart as a creative production independent of Wharton's text. In this way, in Davies' film—as in so much of Wharton's writing—the "depiction of social mores and their influence gives it universal resonance" (Gemma Kappala-Ramsamy, *Guardian,* December 18, 2010).

CONCLUSION

Many readers and scholars are familiar with Edith Wharton's realist fiction and readily compliment her exquisite prose and deft social commentary. Fewer are aware of the extraordinary range of her oeuvre: readers unacquainted with Wharton's rigorously researched travel writing, or her aesthetic philosophy, her writings on design (in homes, gardening, and writing), her poetry, and her war writing are left with an incomplete understanding of her accomplishments. This lacuna will presumably be filled by the forthcoming *Complete Works of Edith Wharton,* a twenty-nine volume Oxford University Press project comprising print volumes and an online component. Scholarly print editions will include authoritative text with variants, editorial notes, a critical introduction to each text, and chronology. The companion Digital Wharton will be an open-access, digitally searchable site providing contextual information about Wharton's life, her craft, and her world. While this is a massive, long-term undertaking, the collaborative effort on the part of numerous dedicated Edith Wharton scholars will surely offer a new narrative about Edith Wharton's significance, illuminating the remarkable range, depth, and variety of her life's work.

Selected Bibliography

WORKS OF EDITH WHARTON

Novels, Novellas, and Short Stories

The Greater Inclination. New York: Charles Scribner's Sons, 1899. (Stories.)

The Touchstone. New York: Charles Scribner's Sons, 1900.

Crucial Instances. New York: Charles Scribner's Sons, 1901. (Stories.)

The Valley of Decision. New York: Charles Scribner's Sons, 1902.

Sanctuary. New York: Charles Scribner's Sons, 1903.

The Descent of Man and Other Stories. New York: Charles Scribner's Sons, 1904.

The House of Mirth. New York: Charles Scribner's Sons, 1905.

Madame de Treymes. New York: Charles Scribner's Sons, 1906.

The Fruit of the Tree. New York: Charles Scribner's Sons, 1907.

The Hermit and the Wild Woman and Other Stories. New York: Charles Scribner's Sons, 1908.

Tales of Men and Ghosts. New York: Charles Scribner's Sons, 1910.

Ethan Frome. New York: Charles Scribner's Sons, 1911.

The Reef. New York: D. Appleton, 1912.

The Custom of the Country. New York: Charles Scribner's Sons, 1913.

Xingu and Other Stories. New York: Charles Scribner's Sons, 1916.

Summer. New York: D. Appleton, 1917.

The Marne. New York: D. Appleton, 1918.

The Age of Innocence. New York: D. Appleton, 1920.

The Glimpses of the Moon. New York: D. Appleton, 1922.

A Son at the Front. New York: Charles Scribner's Sons, 1923.

Old New York. New York: D. Appleton, 1924.

The Mother's Recompense. New York: D. Appleton, 1925.

Here and Beyond. New York: D. Appleton, 1926. (Stories.)

Twilight Sleep. New York: D. Appleton, 1927.

The Children. New York: D. Appleton, 1928.

Hudson River Bracketed. New York: D. Appleton, 1929.

Certain People. New York: D. Appleton, 1930. (Stories.)

The Gods Arrive. New York: D. Appleton, 1932.

Human Nature. New York: D. Appleton, 1933. (Stories.)

The World Over. New York: D. Appleton, 1936. (Stories.)

Ghosts. New York: D. Appleton, 1937. (Stories.)

The Buccaneers (unfinished novel published posthumously). Edited by Thomas Gaillard. New York: Appleton Century, 1938.

Edith Wharton: The Collected Short Stories. Edited by R. W. B. Lewis. New York: Charles Scribner's Sons, 1968.

Fast and Loose: A Novelette. Edited by Viola Hopkins Winner. Charlottesville: University Press of Virginia, 1977.

The Buccaneers. Edited and "completed" by Marion Mainwaring. New York: Viking, 1993.

"Fast and Loose" and "The Buccaneers." Edited and with notes by Viola Hopkins Winner. Charlottesville: University Press of Virginia, 1993. (Annotated editions in one volume.)

Nonfiction

The Decoration of Houses. With Odgen Codman. New York: Charles Scribner's Sons, 1897.

Italian Villas and Their Gardens. New York: Charles Scribner's Sons, 1904.

Italian Backgrounds. New York: Charles Scribner's Sons, 1905.

A Motor-Flight Through France. New York: Charles Scribner's Sons, 1908.

Fighting France from Dunquerque to Belforte. New York: Charles Scribner's Sons, 1915.

The Book of the Homeless (as editor). New York: Charles Scribner's Sons, 1916.

French Ways and Their Meaning. New York: D. Appleton, 1919.

In Morocco. New York: Charles Scribner's Sons, 1920.

The Writing of Fiction. New York: Charles Scribner's Sons, 1925.

A Backward Glance. New York: Appleton Century, 1934.

Novellas and Other Writings. New York: Library of America, 1990. (Includes *Life and I.*)

The Cruise of the Vanadis. Edited by Claudine Lesage Sterne. Amiens, France: Presses de l'UFR Clerc Université Picardie, 1991.

The Uncollected Critical Writings of Edith Wharton. Edited by Frederick Wegener. Princeton, N.J.: Princeton University Press, 1996.

The Unpublished Writings of Edith Wharton. Edited by Laura Rattray. 2 vols. London: Pickering & Chatto, 2009.

POETRY

Verses. Privately printed by C. E. Hammett, Jr., Newport R.I., 1878.

Artemis to Actaeon and Other Verses. New York: Charles Scribner's Sons, 1909.

Twelve Poems. London: Medici Society, 1926.

Eternal Passion in English Poetry. Selected by Wharton and Robert Norton with the collaboration of Gaillard Lapsley. New York: Appleton Century, 1939.

CORRESPONDENCE

Goldman-Price, Irene. *My Dear Governess: The Letters of Edith Wharton to Anna Bahlmann.* New Haven, Conn.: Yale University Press, 2012.

Lewis, R. W. B., and Nancy Lewis. *The Letters of Edith Wharton.* New York: Scribner, 1988.

Powers, Lyall H. *Henry James and Edith Wharton, Letters 1900–1915.* London: Weidenfeld & Nicolson, 1990.

Towheed, Shafquat. *The Correspondence of Edith Wharton and Macmillan, 1901–1930.* Basingstoke, U.K.: Palgrave Macmillan, 2007.

Tuttleton, James, Kristin O. Lauer, and Margaret P. Murray, eds. *Edith Wharton: The Contemporary Reviews.* Cambridge, U.K.: Cambridge University Press, 1992.

BIBLIOGRAPHIES AND CONCORDANCE

Garrison, Stephen. *Edith Wharton: A Descriptive Bibliography.* Pittsburgh, Pa.: University of Pittsburgh Press, 1990.

Ramsden, George. With an introduction by Hermione Lee. *Edith Wharton's Library.* Settrington, U.K.: Stone Trough Books, 1999.

Wright, Sarah Bird. *Edith Wharton A to Z: The Essential Guide to the Life and Work.* New York: Facts on File, 1988.

CRITICAL AND BIOGRAPHICAL STUDIES

Ammons, Elizabeth. *Edith Wharton's Argument with America.* Athens: University of Georgia Press, 1980.

Annan, Gabriele. "A Night at the Opera." *New York Review of Books,* November 4, 1993, pp. 3–4. (Review of *"Fast and Loose" and "The Buccaneers"* by Edith Wharton, edited by Viola Hopkins Winner; *"The Buccaneers"* by Edith Wharton, completed by Marion Mainwaring; *The Age of Innocence,* directed by Martin Scorsese; *The Age of Innocence: A Portrait of the Film Based on the Novel by Edith Wharton* by Martin Scorsese and Jay Cocks; and *The Age of Innocence* by Edith Wharton with an introduction by R. W. B. Lewis.)

Auchincloss, Louis. *Edith Wharton: A Woman in Her Time.* New York: Viking, 1971.

Bauer, Dale. *Edith Wharton's Brave New Politics.* Madison: University of Wisconsin Press, 1994.

Bell, Millicent. *Edith Wharton and Henry James: The Story of Their Friendship.* New York: Braziller, 1965.

———, ed. *The Cambridge Companion to Edith Wharton.* Cambridge, U.K.: Cambridge University Press, 1995.

Benstock, Shari. *No Gifts from Chance: A Biography of Edith Wharton.* Austin: University of Texas Press, 2004.

Canby, Vincent. "Liam Neeson in Lead of Wharton Classic." *New York Times,* March 12, 1993, p. C8.

Colquitt, Clare, Susan Goodman, and Candace Waid, eds. *A Forward Glance: New Essays on Edith Wharton.* Newark: University of Delaware Press, 1999.

Costanzo Cahir, Linda. *Literature into Film: Theory and Practical Approaches.* Jefferson, N.C., and London: McFarland, 2006.

Dwight, Eleanor. *Edith Wharton: An Extraordinary Life.* New York: Abrams, 1994.

Erlich, Gloria C. *The Sexual Education of Edith Wharton.* Berkeley: University of California Press, 1992.

Goodman, Susan. *Edith Wharton's Inner Circle.* Austin: University of Texas Press, 1994.

Harden, Edgar F. *An Edith Wharton Chronology.* Basingstoke, U.K.: Palgrave Macmillan, 2005.

Hersey, Eleanor. "'I am not a Monster': Homophobia, Nostalgia, and Edith Wharton's *The Buccaneers.*" *Legacy* 16, no. 2: 177–192 (1999).

Holden, Stephen. "The Not So Discreet Evil of the 1905 Upper Crust." *New York Times,* September 23, 2000, p. A26.

Horner, Avril, and Janet Beer. *Edith Wharton: Sex, Satire, and the Older Woman.* New York: Palgrave, 2011.

Johnson, Laura K. "Edith Wharton and the Fiction of Marital Unity." *Modern Fiction Studies* 47, no. 4:947–976 (2001).

Joslin, Katherine. *Edith Wharton and the Making of Fashion.* Durham: University of New Hampshire Press, 2009.

Lee, Hermione. "The Unknown Edith Wharton." *New York Review of Books,* October 4, 2001, pp. 19–23. (Review of *Edith Wharton: Collected Stories, 1891–1910* and *Edith Wharton: Collected Stories, 1911–1937.*)

———. *Edith Wharton.* New York: Knopf, 2007.

Lewis, R. W. B. *Edith Wharton: A Biography.* New York: Harper & Row, 1975.

Lubbock, Percy. *Portrait of Edith Wharton.* New York: Appleton Century, 1947.

Mainwaring, Marion. *Mysteries of Paris: The Quest for Morton Fullerton.* Lebanon, N.H.: University Press of New England, 2000.

Marshall, Scott, et al. *The Mount: Home of Edith Wharton.* Lenox, Mass.: Edith Wharton Restoration, 1997.

Price, Alan. *The End of the Age of Innocence: Edith Wharton and the First World War.* New York: St. Martin's Press, 1996.

Price, Alan, and Katherine Joslin, eds. *Wretched Exotic: Essays on Edith Wharton in Europe*. New York: Peter Lang, 1993.

Price, Kenneth, and Phyllis McBride, "'The Life Apart': Text and Contexts of Edith Wharton's Love Diary." *American Literature* 66, no. 4: 663–688 (December 1994).

Rattray, Laura, ed. *Edith Wharton in Context*. Cambridge, U.K.: Cambridge University Press. 2012.

Singley, Carol J. *Edith Wharton: Matters of Mind and Spirit*. Boston: Houghton Mifflin, 2000.

———. *A Historical Guide to Edith Wharton*. Oxford: Oxford University Press, 2003.

Waid, Candace. *Edith Wharton's Letters from the Underworld: Fictions of Woman and Writing*. Chapel Hill: University of North Carolina Press, 1991.

Wolff, Cynthia Griffin. *A Feast of Words: The Triumph of Edith Wharton*. Oxford: Oxford University Press, 1977.

FILMS AND TELEVISION MINISERIES BASED ON THE WORKS OF EDITH WHARTON

The Age of Innocence. Screenplay by Jay Cocks and Martin Scorsese. Directed by Martin Scorsese. Columbia, 1993.

Ethan Frome. Screenplay by Richard Nelson. Directed by John Madden. Miramax, 1993.

The Buccaneers. Screenplay by Maggie Wadey. Directed by Philip Saville. BBC, 1995.

The House of Mirth. Written and directed by Terence Davies. Sony Pictures Classics, 2000.

WALT WHITMAN

(1819—1892)

Joseph Dewey

Adrift in midlife, estranged from a decrepit father he has warehoused in a convenient rest home, clinging to a wife he more needs than loves, distant from his own three children (he must constantly be reminded, in fact, that he has a third child), an incompetent underachiever stuck in a dead-end job for which he is not qualified, anesthetizing himself with cycles of self-destructive eating and binge drinking, Homer Simpson, more bored than desperate, decides to stage his own death. Not surprisingly, he botches it. In an uncharacteristic moment of self-reflection and bald vulnerability, however, he decides to visit the grave of his long-dead mother, which is adjacent to his own freshly dug burial plot. Hoping for some emotional dimension to his life, some redemptive epiphany, he slowly approaches his mother's tomb, itself guarded by a forbidding stone angel. As he gently moves aside the tangle of weeds that obscures the inscription, he is stunned to find that the grave is in fact the grave of Walt Whitman. In a life defined by mute passivity and dumb acceptance, in an awkward moment of genuine emotion and sudden vulnerability, Homer vents, kicks violently at the tomb: "Damn you, Walt Whitman ... *Leaves of Grass,* my ass." Overwhelmed, he reels and tumbles clumsily into his own open grave. The moment pitches toward existential tragedy when suddenly a shadow appears at the lip of the grave—it is Homer's mother, not dead at all, come home to bury her son. There, under the gentle aegis of Walt Whitman, the two affect a most heartfelt reunion.

Adrift in midlife, estranged from his family (his only child crippled by cerebral palsy; his wife carrying their second child, conceived by accident), stuck in a dead-end job (once a promising grad student working in cutting-edge chemistry research, he now teaches general science in a public high school in Albuquerque, a job that pays so poorly he must hold down a second job washing cars), his childhood love of the sheer magic and transformative power of chemistry long since cashiered, the nerdy Walter White (another W.W.) receives with curious indifference the diagnosis that he has terminal lung cancer. Concerned over his family's financial well-being after he is dead, he sets about, using his considerable gifts in chemistry, to fashion a remarkably potent variant of crystal meth that, when it hits the New Mexico streets, transforms him (according to the laws of chemistry itself); he morphs into a most unlikely drug lord, a chilling, predatory killer, ruling over an underground empire sustained by fear, paranoia, and violence. At the direction of the regional drug overlord, who improbably enough moonlights as the manager of a fast-food joint, Walter is introduced to a lab assistant to expedite the meth production: Gale Boetticher, a man half Walter's age but with considerable gifts in the field and still aglow with the magic of science and the wonder of the laboratory. To thank Walter for agreeing to become his mentor in the lab, Gale tenders to Walt an unexpected gift, an inscribed copy of *Leaves of Grass.* In presenting it, Gale recites from memory "When I Heard the Learn'd Astronomer," Whitman's buoyant hymn to the power of nature untamable by science. It is a spellbinding moment. Thanks to Whitman, their brief partnership finds its way to an awkward moment of authentic emotion, vulnerability, and intimacy—weeks later, Walter will arrange Gale's execution, point blank in the face. But for that moment, in the half light of the underground meth lab, under the gentle aegis of Walt Whitman, the two affect a most emotional moment.

That same inscribed book later will lead to Walter White's undoing and, finally, to his hard-earned redemption.

Adrift in midlife, after decades spent rising with Jimmy Gatz–like efficiency from a backwater Arkansas upbringing to the corridors of the White House, distracted, like Alexander the Great, with no worlds left to conquer, a very married Bill Clinton careens into near political suicide midway through his second term by relishing an unseemly game of calculated seduction played out with a Rubenesque White House intern half his age, a woman-child dazzled by Clinton's easy charms. Even as he manipulates the trappings of his office for quick gratifications—the sordid details of which would become sworn, all-too-public congressional testimony within months—even amid those tacky narratives of clandestine oral sex-capades, dildo-cigars (cigar-dildos?), sophomoric late-night Oval Office rendezvous over pizza, and queasily graphic phone sex, on the very evening that leads to the infamous semen-splashed Gap dress, there improbably enough is Walt Whitman. The two lovers are wedged into a phone booth–sized White House side office. Clinton proffers his starry-eyed paramour an inscribed copy of *Leaves of Grass* (apparently a staple in his courtship protocol since his days courting a wonky Yale law student named Hillary Rodham). Under the gentle aegis of Whitman, what is an otherwise tacky liaison touches an awkward moment of authentic emotion, vulnerability, and intimacy that boldly, unapologetically celebrates the spiritual dazzle and emotional vitality of physical love, a reminder between these clandestine lovers that this ... whatever it is ... has to be more than what it seems to be: shabby assignations, careless frictions, spasms of relief, and unwashable stains on a blue cocktail dress.

Again and again, it seems, there is Whitman. Whitman asserted more than a century ago he would always be there. "Failing to fetch me at first keep encouraged / Missing me one place search another / I stop somewhere waiting for you" ("Song of Myself," ll. 1344–1346, p. 68; all quotations from *Leaves of Grass* in this essay are from the 1891 edition collected in *Complete Poetry and Selected Prose by Walt Whitman,* 1959). Ironically, he felt largely forgotten at the time of his death, save for a devoted coterie of homegrown disciples and a reverent following overseas. By then, although his mind was still alert, his much celebrated body had been wracked by two decades of ignoble infirmities. He lived modestly in a clapboard house in Camden, New Jersey, just across the river from the cradle of American independence. Whitman died convinced that he had failed in his deepest ambition, that he had never quite become the national poet he fervently believed his infant country demanded. Today, Whitman is everywhere—in films, music, television, advertising, the Internet—robust, vital, rendering the unexpected confirmation of the vibrant heart to those mired in emotional crises, bringing awkward reclamation to the lost and lonely misfits of the twenty-first century. Like the sardonic writers of *The Simpsons*; like Vince Gilligan, the architect of *Breaking Bad*'s darkling vision; and, yes, like Bill Clinton, we evoke Walt Whitman to assert the viability of the American heart against and amid the steadily accumulating evidence, often sordid and tacky, of its irrelevancy. It would be difficult (really impossible) to see any other poet in the nearly 350 years of the American literary experiment who could be so readily available to celebrate so unironically the American heart. Anne Bradstreet? Too judgmental. Emily Dickinson? Too wounded. Robert Frost? Too prickly. William Carlos Williams? Too precious. Wallace Stevens? Too erudite. Edgar Allan Poe? Too ironic. Ralph Waldo Emerson? Too obscure. There is a spacious, inviting intimacy about Walt Whitman (imagine calling Frost, Bob, or Stevens, Wally), a fetching welcome despite the odd reality that after composing thousands of the most unconventional and formally extravagant poetic lines ever penned, a prolific rate of composition that went on for nearly five decades, for most Americans, Whitman is most associated with one of his least successful (and most conventional) poems, a tear-jerking elegy, propelled by heavy-handed rhymes, written, according to urban legend, in a single sitting, giving voice to the national anguish over Abraham Lincoln's assassination: "O Captain! My Captain!," a terribly serious Big Theme poem, has been force-fed to generations of schoolchildren largely because its insistent rhythms and obvious rhymes accommodated memorization and dramatic recitation.

More than America's national poet (although he is most certainly that), Whitman is our most thoroughly American poet. His verse was unkempt, a declaration of formal independence that so uncompromisingly altered the very perception of what a line of poetry could do that it would take his native culture more than seventy-five years just to develop the ear to hear his poems. Whitman's poems embodied the American will to individuality even as the American political experiment itself was coming apart at every nail; his verse asserted America's celebrated refusal to kowtow to authority, its willful rebelliousness, its fathomless arrogance. A line of poetry, he showed, is not like a line of music—rather it *is* a line of music, a concept so obvious today that it is difficult to appreciate Whitman's daring use of language, his total reinvention of poetry. Free verse just looks too easy—in fact, Whitman's exemplum has licensed a century of earnest, if clumsy imitators.

Yet, approaching the bicentennial of Whitman's birth, his poetry still demanded to be experienced: it is too restless to be read in the respectful silence of contemplative study; it cannot bear to be lacerated by the yellow highlighters of dull-eyed undergraduates in hushed libraries. It is spontaneous, bursting, urgent. It demands even now to be declaimed from rooftops, chanted in the streets. It is poetry that brings out the ham in its proclaimers (YouTube archives legions of Whitman's present-day acolytes who joyously give voice to Whitman's verse). The tight orchestration, the rolling texture of the words, demands extravagant intonation (after all, Whitman shaped his concept of poetry listening in rapt wonder to the newest European operas, not knowing the languages themselves but enthralled by how sounds, sonorous vowels and hatchet consonants, could create and sustain complex moods). His verse even today startles—after all, as a poet, he consciously turned to face more than seven centuries of careful poetic evolution and defiantly proffered that tradition his middle finger, which is, after all, far more the national bird of America than John Adams' eagle or even Dr. Franklin's turkey.

OVERVIEW

Few dispute Whitman's status as America's premier poet. He is a fixture in high school anthologies, on college syllabi, in the animated discourse of grad school roundtables, and in doctorates in disciplines ranging from queer studies to economics, from theology to media studies. However, hailing Whitman as America's premier poet may be damning with faint praise, rather like dubbing someone America's premier butter churner. America, after all, has never much trusted poetry; poems are not stories that entertain, they are not parables that teach, they are not newspapers or textbooks and certainly not manuals of instruction. What exactly is the reward for reading a poem? As a system of communication, poetry is impractical, inefficient, inexact, indirect, burdened deliberately with layers of suggestion and fogged by obscure wordplay, a frivolous (and vaguely effeminate) pastime, a narrow enthusiasm for the bored elite and the hyper-educated, inevitably irrelevant in an aggressive culture of Builders, Do-ers, Designers, and Inventors. Americans fix things, solve problems, invent gadgets. Poems that teach lessons, well, OK. After all, "Casey at the Bat" and "A Visit from St. Nicholas" are more America's poetic epics than "The Idea of Order at Key West" or "The Sphinx." For most Americans, their own long tradition of poets divides handily into two broad groups: the Goobers, luminous philosophers gifted with easy wisdom and conventional platitudes, and the Creeps, morbid misfits haunted by gothic anxieties and dark longings. Bradstreet? Goober. Philip Freneau? Creep. Joel Barlow? Goober. The Fireside Poets—Henry Wadsworth Longfellow, William Cullen Bryant, John Greenleaf Whittier, James Russell Lowell, Oliver Wendell Holmes, Sr.? An exultation of Goobers. Poe? Creep. Emerson? Goober. Dickinson? Creep. Hart Crane? Who? E. E. Cummings? Goober. Sylvia Plath? Creep. Robert Lowell?

Creep. Anne Sexton? Creep. Maya Angelou? Goober. Robert Frost? Something different, a Creepy Goober.

Whitman, gloriously, is neither. And unlike the unwashed Beats, who so neatly, so completely mimicked Whitman's cosmic vision and his unconventional form, Whitman achieved his beatific energy without the crippling reliance on recreational pharmaceuticals or hard liquor. More to the point, Whitman's poetry does not need the incessant blather of learn'd academics to thin it into explanation. Although his verse has generated, at best count, more than fifteen thousand separate exegeses, the poetry itself exists within an energy field of untutored call and response; his poems are dialogues, conducted between reader and poet, a call to a vision at once cosmic and immediate, elemental and complex, transcendental and realistic, organic and spiritual. His vision is remarkably simple, erected as it is on three premises: embrace the self in all its (im)perfect parts; embrace nature in all its (im)perfect elements; and embrace each and all, the (im)perfect others. Nevertheless, his vision is edged by a baffling, if persistent question: what part of this is not clear? Make the join, Whitman counsels. Yet, we resist; and we are left empty and aching, and we don't know why. Whitman does. In *Leaves of Grass,* Whitman's ambitious epic that effloresced from an initial gathering of twelve poems into more than four hundred interconnected poems during forty years of Whitman's own revisions through eight separate editions, he offers candid explanations for such reluctance: we are all too willing to be sad, we hide our heart like a hostage, too willing to be lonely, too intractably carnal, too given to the easy logic of violence, too complacent, too accepting of the clean logic of damnation, too enthralled by surfaces, too in love with pain, too hypnotized by our narrow moment to ever grasp its widest dimensions, both vertical and horizontal. Whitman does not seek merely to change how his reader lives—after all, that is cosmetic and can be done by just changing jobs or getting married or losing weight; rather Whitman dares his reader to change the very perception of that masquerade life of smooth mediocrity and squalid contentment, an act of will more demanding but far more rewarding.

Nevertheless, there is a refreshing there-ness to Whitman and his verse, an invitation to step into any of his poems and initiate the call-and-response process he conceived operating between his own poet-persona, fast-talking and open-hearted, and his reader, blind-hearted and needful, a binding that he envisioned could defy even time and space. In a contemporary too-cool post-everything era when poetry in America has become a distinctly minority enthusiasm (in 2014, the IRS reported that more than twenty-one thousand Americans listed "poet" as their principal occupation, although most Americans would be hard pressed to name two), in an era when poetry is kept relevant largely within the hothouse of the classroom (save for moments that seem to demand poetry: say, weddings or memorial services or presidential inaugurations), there is Whitman. He has been embraced as the harbinger of virtually every defining cultural movement of modern America. Whitman, it seems, was always there first. He was the fountainhead of gay liberation and gay pride; the harbinger of the sexual revolution; the augur of militant environmentalism; the pre-visionary of Eastern-tinged New Age mysticism; the godfather of civil rights; the presager of drum-beating xenophobic patriotism; the unabashed prophet of feminism; the vaticinator of the propaganda of self-promotion, the celebration of the selfie, and the cult of manufactured celebrity; the grandfather of the catapult exploration into the astral horizons of space; the John the Baptist of uncompromising pacifism; the herald of modern science and technology (at least their metaphors), anticipating both quantum physics and molecular genetics as well as the reach of the Internet, the barbaric yawp of social media, and strike-force of image technologies; he is our earliest confidence-man, selling the gospel of self-empowerment and the white-hot rage against the machine; an unapologetic Communist who out-Marxed Marx as well as a misty-eyed disciple of democracy who out-Jeffersoned Jefferson; and, of course, he has been invoked as the father of virtually every modern musical expression from minimalist symphonies to punk rock, from blues to folk protest, from gospel to alt country, from rock to hard-bop jazz.

Ultimately, Whitman is America's own Rorschach test; all horizon, all outline, at once there and here, then and now, theirs and ours, yours and mine, effortlessly protean, pliable, elastic, wonderfully, maddeningly contradictory. If his great body of verse (now archived online) is still largely unread (most readers content to engage a handful of titles), he is somehow still familiar. For Homer Simpson, for Walter White, for Bill Clinton, for all of us, there is the grand and towering metaphor of Whitman, a self-willed matrix of staggering contradictions—"Do I contradict myself? / Very well I contradict myself / (I am large, I contain multitudes)" ("Song of Myself," ll. 1324–1326, p. 68): Whitman is at once defiantly less than a conventional poet and so much more; he is a vigor, an attitude, a posture, an urgency, a rage, an innocence, a hunger; in short, he is the very heart of American identity and the very identity of American heart.

BIOGRAPHY

Of course, the abiding mystery of American literature is where exactly did Walt Whitman come from? Generations of Americanists have sifted through Whitman's biography for some episode, some influence, some epiphany that might account for how the son of a career failure, a father prone to violence and drink, and a smothering, overly possessive, barely literate mother, a boy raised amid poverty in a large dysfunctional family, a part-time carpenter, a failed house painter, a disillusioned schoolteacher, a journeyman printer who, with only a sixth-grade education, scratched out a living as a journalist, went, in his late thirties (at a time when life expectancy was barely forty years), from writing doggerel wisdom verses and didactic parables intended largely as newspaper filler to writing the stunning opening thirteen lines of "Song of Myself." How did a newspaper columnist known for bombast and caustic derision intuit that conventional (read: British) poetry—tightly metered, richly allusive, formally conservative—had become entirely unworkable and wildly irrelevant within the bracing environment of the new that was antebellum America? Where did this blue-collar journalist find the nerve to dismiss the most accomplished poet-practitioners in his America, most notably the revered New England Fireside Poets, as fussy tea-drinkers and unimaginative upholsterers? How, indeed, did that same journalist—single-handedly and against a chorus of establishment naysayers who dismissed his experimental line as inchoate and blasphemous—dare to return poetry to its most ancient roots: poetry, Whitman's every crude and undisciplined line testified, happens in the ear.

Where did Whitman's verse come from? Maybe from a childhood in rural Long Island spent listening to the rich cadences of the Bible read to him by his doting Quaker mother. Maybe from an adolescence joyfully entombed in Brooklyn public libraries amid stacks of classical literature—Dante, *The Arabian Nights,* Shakespeare, Aeschylus, Homer. Perhaps from a decade spent happily immersed in the cacophonous blab of Manhattan's crowded sidewalks. Could it have come from countless nights Whitman spent listening enthralled to repertory opera? Could it have come from Whitman reading Emerson's clarion call for a truly American poet, the polished Emerson playing a buttoned-down Sinatra to Whitman's crazy Elvis? Or, more tantalizing, did it originate in that mysterious three-month interlude in New Orleans in 1848 when Whitman at last tapped a justification for dedicating his considerable energies to poetry? What happened there? No one is entirely sure. Either Whitman confronted the barbaric realities of slavery or he found expression for his manic sexual energy (homosexuality? bisexuality? insatiable heterosexuality? something called omnisexuality?).

How, then, did Walt Whitman happen?

Walter Elias Whitman was born in West Hills just outside the hamlet of Huntington on New York's Long Island on May 31, 1819, the second of eight surviving children born to Walter Whitman (1789–1855), a struggling farmer and part-time carpenter, and Louisa Van Velsor Whitman (1795–1873), a strong-willed woman who despite the family's difficult economic straits maintained a buoyant optimism and who, despite a minimum education, was a voracious reader. Whitman's was by any measure a hardscrabble childhood. After the father spiraled into debt following a disastrous attempt to speculate in real estate development, the family relocated to take advantage of the employment opportunities for unskilled blue-collar work in the burgeoning neighborhoods of New York City, specifically the village of Brooklyn, just across the East River from the tip of Manhattan. Whitman's father still struggled (and began turning to the escape of alcohol), and the large family was forced to relocate often; to help his family's finances, Whitman left school at eleven (although neither parent had completed even that much education). He worked first as office help for a law office and then as an apprentice typesetter in a printing firm, thankless and grimy work, certainly, but the young Whitman relished the work, loved the touch, the physical feel of words as he set line after line of inky type. When his family returned to Long Island, the boy, self-reliant and confident, remained in the city. He was all of fourteen.

At the age of seventeen, amid the economic catastrophe of the 1837 Panic and after a fire ravaged the newspaper offices where he worked, Whitman returned to his family home. Despite his limited formal schooling, he was something of an accomplished autodidact, and over the next several years he managed to secure a number of positions as a schoolteacher; but he loathed the classroom—the discipline, the rote memorization, the students' evident boredom and complacency, and, of course, the poor pay. And he missed the hustle and hum of the city—he abandoned teaching in 1841. After a brief stint as a printer in New York City, at the age of twenty-two, he returned to Brooklyn, becoming the editor of the *Brooklyn Daily Eagle.* He began to write his own pieces (although he fashioned a character, The Schoolteacher, to serve as his public persona) and quickly found a readership for his often incendiary stands on education, women's rights, workers' rights, prison reform, immigrant policy, and, supremely, slavery. In addition, he began to write short fictional pieces that dramatized the moral implications of hot-button issues of the day. Caught up in the rhetoric of possibility that animated America's assorted visionary moral reform movements of the era, Whitman wrote in just three days his first (and only) novel, *Franklin Evans; or, The Inebriate.* Published in 1842, the melodramatic novel traced the sorry decline of a young man who comes to the big city only to be led into the precipitous spiral of alcoholism but who ends reformed, swearing never to imbibe again. The novel, with its tidy moral resolution, its two-dimensional characters, and its reader-friendly journalistic prose, sold well (although Whitman himself would later contemptuously dismiss the novel and claim he had been drunk when he had written most of it)—it sold more than twenty thousand copies, far more than all of Whitman's later volumes of poetry combined.

Over the next several years, Whitman worked at a number of newspapers around Manhattan—in 1848, he, along with his brother Jeff, accepted an invitation to serve as editor for the *New Orleans Crescent,* one of the newest and most successful dailies in that city. The two stayed in the city for only three months, but in that time Whitman had his first exposure to the hard brutalities of the slave business, which in Manhattan had largely been an abstract sort of evil. (Other accounts of his time in New Orleans suggest that Whitman may have had an incendiary affair with a married woman or perhaps may have accepted the reality of his homosexuality or perhaps both.) When he returned to New York, Whitman became an outspoken opponent of slavery, starting a newspaper, the *Brooklyn Freeman,* which became the vehicle for some of Whitman's most passionate abolitionist editorials—slavery, he believed, destroyed the entire concept of America as a New World, a democracy designed to elevate and sustain every individual. It was during these next several years that, moving between part-time newspaper gigs, Whitman began composing what would become the cycle of twelve poems that would make up the first edition of *Leaves of Grass.* It was published in 1855. Whitman himself paid for the initial printing and even set most of the type—optimistically, he printed 795 copies. The poetry was heavily influenced by

Emerson. Whitman had attended a lecture Emerson delivered in New York in 1842. He had been deeply moved by Emerson's radical essay titled simply "The Poet," which called for a new kind of poet for a new kind of nation. Whitman's volume, published unironically on Independence Day, celebrated the unbounded energy of the American imagination—its more than two thousand lines were irregular, its rhymes and rhythms subtle and unforced, but its temperament was undeniably bold and inviting, its themes accessible and clarion-clear, its optimism palpable. The poems worked diligently to appear not to be poems. The poems had no individual titles, were not even numbered. Structural unity emerged only from recurring imagery, from phrases repeated like chants, and from gorgeously indulgent lists that swept the willing reader along, often for pages. No author was listed—only an engraving of this bearded Everyman Poet, Whitman himself dressed like a blue-collar laborer, his shirt opened, his hat cocked confidently, his zipper menacingly long, his eyes looking straight at the reader.

Although sales were disappointing (the critical response was tepid—save for the glowing reviews Whitman himself wrote and published, anonymously, in Manhattan newspapers), Whitman now relished playing the New American Poet—amid the theaters, oyster bars, and cellar taverns along Broadway, he quickly became a presence, a self-conceived and self-sustaining celebrity. Developing a shameless sense of self-promotion, Whitman sent a copy to Emerson himself, who responded with a surprisingly laudatory letter, more than five pages, the best lines of which Whitman unabashedly quoted on the cover of the volume's second edition one year later (although Emerson himself would publicly temper his praise). That second edition had grown to more than double the original's length. Whitman was now confident in his voice, uncompromising in his upbeat argument, and daringly expansive in his themes—the self, he trumpeted, belonged not merely to an ever-expanding natural world but as well to a thriving and vital organic cosmos, the universe itself a single pulsating organism that defied boundaries and made death itself ironic.

Two years later, Whitman published yet a newer edition of the volume (this time through publishers in Boston who saw in a collection that so trumpeted unity an inspirational counterargument to the nation's rapid-spiral into dissolution); now that there were more than 140 new or revised poems, Whitman began organizing the poems under broad thematic headings, such as America, love, nature, and the soul. The outbreak of the Civil War, however, shook Whitman emotionally and psychically. At first, as a journalist he wrote compassionate prose sketches about conditions in Manhattan hospitals struggling to provide adequate care for the sudden flood of wounded Union soldiers (Whitman had become a familiar figure in Manhattan hospitals a decade earlier when he had volunteered during a cholera outbreak). Whitman observed how these young men, initially entranced by the hot rhetoric of patriotism, now struggled ingloriously against a messy death. Whitman would hold their trembling hands, speak compassionate words of encouragement, distribute candies and fruit slices. In December 1862, news of his younger brother's wounding at Fredericksburg reported in a newspaper account compelled a frantic Whitman to head to Washington to find his brother (the report turned out to be in error). But after touring the understaffed hospital facilities in the nation's capital, Whitman decided to remain.

He lived on the meager salary as a part-time clerk in the army paymaster's office but spent most of his time in the army hospitals, volunteering to nurse both Union and Confederate soldiers amid the primitive conditions of understaffed hospitals unable to handle the sheer volume of casualties. He sat with the sick and the dying, wrote out letters to their families, read to them, prayed with them—on occasion he even changed wound dressings and assisted in amputations. Whitman's 1865 volume *Drum-Taps,* a cycle of seventy-two poems, recorded, with unblinking realism, his observations of the war's devastation, juxtaposing the idealism of the young soldiers and the hard realities of the battlefield. In January 1865, thanks largely to the intervention of friends who knew of his poetry, Whitman was given a better-paying job as a clerk in the Bureau of Indian Affairs in the Department of the

Interior. Still, it was a most sobering time for Whitman—the pressing realities of the war sorely tested the very integrity of his compelling vision of cosmic unity and spiritual transcendence. He found inspiration only in the towering figure of Abraham Lincoln, himself a kind of prairie-born Everyman, a deeply spiritual leader imbued with the vision for unity among even a people so divided. As the bloody war finally ground toward its conclusion in late spring 1865, however, Whitman (along with the battered nation) reeled within the trauma and shock of Lincoln's assassination.

A month later, Whitman was summarily dismissed from his government post by James Harlan, an ultraconservative former senator from Iowa, who as President Andrew Johnson's secretary of the interior undertook a crusade to rid the department of un-Christian undesirables, among them, of course, the scraggly-bearded "poet" of that "obscene" *Leaves of Grass* (although Harlan, just after Whitman's death, would aver that the position—not Whitman—had been terminated as a budgetary move). Friends again intervened, now proclaiming Whitman (largely on the strength of his war poems) as America's Good Gray Poet, a national asset, a democratic visionary—Whitman was reassigned within a month to a clerical position in the attorney general's office. The office work was mind-numbing and routine, but Whitman returned to writing poetry with a new vigor, releasing two new editions of *Leaves of Grass* between 1868 and 1872; biographers have conjectured the revival of Whitman's artistic energies might be tied to a lengthy (and evidently quite intense) relationship he maintained with Peter Doyle, a Confederate veteran half his age who worked for the city's transit company. The relationship is often marked as the first substantive indication of Whitman's sexual orientation, although there is copious evidence in Whitman's prewar poetry of his attraction for men, which he had celebrated, at least metaphorically, in the twelve-poem cycle "Calamus," which talked so passionately about "adhesion" and the powerful bond between men as brothers and then, more directly, in the cycle of poems known as "The Children of Adam," which fearlessly hymned the glories of the body and the tonic magic of sexual love and particularly the enchantment of the swelled, aching man-root. *Leaves of Grass* enjoyed a resurgence of interest. In addition to new editions released in America, Whitman's verse appeared in England, where its manic creative energy, formal inventiveness, and risqué themes found an enthusiastic welcome among daring young poets rebelling against the stifling conventions of Victorian life.

Beyond revisiting *Leaves of Grass,* Whitman published *Democratic Vistas* (1871), a collection of scathing essays that harshly criticized the growing materialism of what Mark Twain would caustically dub "The Gilded Age." Whitman castigated this America as cankered, spiritually enervated, materialistic and shallow, increasingly obsessed by economic competitiveness, its arts bankrupt of passion and authenticity—he counseled reclaiming a grand vision of oneness as the country's last, best hope. Then, in January 1873, Whitman suffered a catastrophic stroke that rendered his left side largely paralyzed (a second stroke four years later would similarly impair his right side). He had to quit his job in Washington. Whitman opted to move in with his brother George, now a successful engineer, back in the family home in Camden. In short order, Whitman's mother died. Her influence on her son had been profound, and Whitman spiraled into depression. When the country celebrated its centennial in 1876, however, Whitman was hailed as America's greatest living poet, the poet of democracy—a new edition of *Leaves of Grass* became part of the nation's year-long celebration. When his brother retired in 1884, Whitman took his modest cache of royalties (a little over twelve hundred dollars) and, at the age of sixty-five, finally bought his first home, an unprepossessing two-story clapboard home along the railroad tracks on Mickle Street in Camden. Whitman traveled as far as the Mississippi River, giving lectures to packed houses, often on Lincoln and reciting his own essays and poetry about the martyred president with dramatic flair. Although his confidence and optimism lapsed as he grew increasingly weaker, Whitman continued to play Walt Whitman, America's Good Gray Poet (with his carelessly flowing white beard, he became, save for Mark Twain, America's most photographed and most recognized celebrity). Whitman's celebrity continued to rise, helped in part by a kerfuffle in 1882 when the Boston district attorney's office threatened to ban the newest edition of *Leaves of Grass* unless Whitman removed some of the more obviously sexual passages. Whitman, of course, refused.

Over the next several years, even as his health deteriorated, Whitman found himself the center of a kind of cultlike following among America's younger poets, who discovered in Whitman's unconventional poetry—with its celebration of the spiritual dimension of the organic world—a clear rejection of the staid middle-class values of Gilded Age America and a welcome tonic to the burgeoning school of dreary dishwater realism. Trips to Camden by young writers became more like pilgrimages. Whitman societies sprang up, mystic clubs with elaborate initiation rites, illustrated psalm books, and complex secret handshakes: Whitman less a poet and more a kind of American saint, or saint-enough. Just past his seventieth birthday, in the closing months of 1891, Whitman felt a disquieting urgency to conclude what had been a nearly forty-year-long revision of the poems in *Leaves of Grass*. In short order, he finished what he dramatically termed the "deathbed edition." He published as well a much smaller volume of valedictory verse and short meditative prose pieces, titled simply *Good-Bye My Fancy,* that looked with unflinching honesty into the unsettling reality of illness and his own mortality.

After years of heroic resistance to a host of physical debilities (Whitman's autopsy would read like one of his own massive catalogs), in the gloaming of dusk on March 26, 1892, Whitman, nearly paralyzed, died in the company of only Horace Traubel (1858–1919), a would-be poet who fancied himself Whitman's most ardent disciple and who would later write a sprawling nine-volume hagiography of Whitman. But when the word of Whitman's death spread, the public reaction was unprecedented for an American poet. In the three hours set aside for public viewing, an estimated two thousand admirers braved a chilly spring rain to view Whitman's body on display in the front room of his Camden house. Four days later, thousands more took the day off work to line the streets of Camden just to get a glimpse of Whitman's hearse heading to nearby Harleigh Cemetery. Crowds packed the shallow hillside in the cemetery as Whitman's body was interred in a 650-square foot mausoleum he had designed (and paid for) himself, a stately edifice that resembled nothing so much as a stone house. It bore no elaborate inscription, no verse, no dates—it read simply "Walt Whitman."

LEAVES OF GRASS: *AN OVERVIEW*

Leaves of Grass is at once inviting and intimidating. Yes, it beckons, begs, seduces, coaxes, lures, even taunts, but its sheer scale, its ferocious eccentricities, its unrelenting brio, its bald emotionalism, its unironic seriousness, its evident disdain for conventional structure frustrates, confuses, un-eases, overwhelms—even bores. For more than a century and a half now, readers and scholars alike have worked to answer how to approach this behemoth work. It does not seem enough to simply read it—so much appears to happen beyond what the words themselves say. It has an emotional energy, at once surging, primal, intense, that is somehow greater than the lines or words themselves, an energy that some readers get, and others simply don't. In that way, *Leaves of Grass* may be more like music, really, than poetry. After all, from his twenties onward, Whitman was fascinated by the emotional impact of music. Discovering music was for him a critical rite of passage. "Music always round me, unceasing, unbeginning, yet long untaught I did not hear / But now the chorus I hear and am elated" ("That Music Always Round Me," ll. 1–2, p. 313). Shortly before his death, Whitman acknowledged to the novelist John Townsend Trowbridge (1827–1916) that but for opera, *Leaves of Grass* could never have been written at all. Whitman would often describe his ideal reader as a "philosopher-musician," hyphenated as inseparable roles, able to intuit, to feel rather than merely understand the gospel message in the poems and in turn to respond to its music, not merely to its words. Whitman's titles reflected his fascination with the dynamics of music—they are songs, carols, hymns, chants, ballads, chansons. He does not merely celebrate himself—he sings himself. Not surprisingly, more than twelve hundred different musical settings have drawn on Whitman's deftly cadenced poems. And, in 2015, Whitman himself become the focal character of a stunning new opera, *Crossing,* by the Los Angeles Opera Company wunderkind Matthew Aucoin, centering on a brief (and largely fabricated) affair between Whitman and a wounded Confederate soldier in a Washington hospital at the height of the Civil War.

In the late 1840s, when Whitman began to draft the first volume's poems, he himself had become enthralled by opera. Initially he had found opera inaccessible, pretentious, even un-American; but over time he understood at last what he was hearing and became one of the genre's most ardent fans, writing extravagantly generous reviews of stage performances in Manhattan, the operas of Gaetano Donizetti, Guiseppi Verdi, Gioachino Rossini, Charles Gounod, Vincenzo Bellini, Wolfgang Amadeus Mozart. Night after night he would listen enraptured by the voluptuous music, the purity of the spellbinding voices, swept up in a complex spectacle of sound that, though (or perhaps because) he did not know the language, inexplicably uncaged in him ardors and ecstasies, joys and sorrows. For Whitman—inveterate reader, licensed typesetter, professional journalist, and apprentice poet—opera was a glorious release, a surrender, as meaning soared beyond words, emotion catapulted beyond language. Whitman never actually played a musical instrument, had no talent for singing, could not even read music, but he taught himself the elements of opera: recitatives, bel canto arias, grand choruses. To Whitman, the world itself—urban and rural—was composed not of words but rather of sounds, living and vital and expressive. "I hear the chorus, it is a grand opera, / Ah this indeed is music—this suits me" ("Song of Myself," ll. 599–600, p. 44). Whitman, not surprisingly, works the ear; as poet he is a consummate musician, intoxicated by sounds, selecting words not only for their meaning but for their vowels and consonants, their syllable crispness, their pronunciation, their meter; his lines are ear-gasms with sonic texture and acoustic appeal. As with an opera score, poetry on the page, Whitman asserted, must be performed into life.

With its extravagant development; its ambition; its massive scale; its near mystical rapport with the willing auditor/reader; its tightly organized individual sections, each with its own lyricism, its own meter, its own aural integrity, its own complex of sounds, *Leaves of Grass* is less America's first epic poem and more its first grand opera, the novice reader like Whitman in his twenties in the back row of New York opera houses, initially resistant but ultimately swept up, sonically assaulted, and quietly blown away. Like a grand opera, *Leaves of Grass* is at once welcoming and formidable, at once familiar and inaccessible, its truest achievement beyond explanation, beyond commentary, beyond words, its most profound exhilaration stirred by its music, its rhythmic and sonic impact. Like an opera, the individual poems of *Leaves of Grass* work a single overarching theme—nothing less than the heroic redemption of the reader through spiritual union with the powerful narrator-poet—but to accomplish this, the poet-composer crafts a sumptuous multipart opera: there are busy recitatives such as "There Was a Child Went Forth," matter of fact, journalistic, sung speeches that advance the rich storyline of the reader's pilgrimage toward transcendence; there are gorgeous bel canto arias such as "Out of the Cradle Endlessly Rocking," intense interludes of grand emotion, at once lyrical and richly melodious, in turn joyful and aching, that lay bare both the frustrations and triumphs of Whitman himself; and ultimately there are the grand choruses, perhaps most boldly "Crossing Brooklyn Ferry," sweeping, magisterial, thundering moments when the poet triumphantly transcends the limits of space and time, indeed bursts the frame of the poem itself, and defiantly bonds with the reader/audience.

THE RECITATIVE: "THERE WAS A CHILD WENT FORTH"

The aesthetic achievement and sonic impact of Whitman's recitatives are perhaps easiest to miss. Recitatives after all have long held as the opera's decidedly unflashy narrative interlude, necessary for moving along the plot but without showy musical stylings or extraordinary melody. Indeed, often the recitative relies on the manipulation of one or two notes. It can seem plainsong and even dull. Much like recitatives in opera, they can seem merely busy—lacking the grandeur of his more expressive musical moments. For Whitman, his hectic recitatives—among them, the middle sections (7–16) of "Song of Myself," "I Sing the Body Electric," "Proud Music of the Storms," "Song of the Open Road," "A Song for Occupations," "By Blue Ontario's Shore," "Starting from Paumanok," "A Broadway Pageant"—seem more conversational than poetic, more journalistic than artistic; after all, entire sections of "Song of Myself" appear given over to simply cataloguing the poet's restless observations, pages of lists that the uninitiated reader might be tempted to hurry through, even skip over. Whitman here does not appear to be trying for poetry—he simply relishes the things in the world; he appears to employ the accessibility of common speech, the chiseled rhythms and forced rhymes of formal poetry conceding to the carefree ad lib of the colloquial. If this is poetry, the word surely requires air quotes—these are too immediate, too familiar, too much the plainsong of the everyday. But Whitman listened to opera. In opera, the recitative is a most demanding challenge for the composer—after all, the recitative can leave the uninitiated decidedly unimpressed, waiting for the bang and awe of the opera's grander moments. How then is the composer, ever aware of the complicated tension of the ear, to make musical what seems so obviously, indeed so deliberately, nonmusical? Here is the subtlety, the quiet acoustics of Whitman's prosody.

Consider "There Was a Child Went Forth." One of the untitled twelve poems in the original 1855 edition, the apparently uncomplicated thirty-nine-line poem has become a staple in the Whitman oeuvre, known as perhaps his most uncompromising mandate to engage the world, every day, and to become a part of everything here; his eponymous child, with his yearning and swelling heart, absorbs a remarkable catalog of natural phenomena, forever expanding the limited self beyond space, beyond time, until the child big-bangs into the energy of the cosmos itself. This, Whitman challenges, is how each of us is to live everyday—not in expectation of wonder but in wonder itself. That invitation is evident, clear—do not lose the gaudy confidence, the extravagant wonder, the glorious selfishness, the unapologetic cockiness of the child who without question demands every moment, every day that the world present itself anew. For critics of Whitman's lack of mathematical form, here is poetry at its worst, an unrefined catalog, rendered in uneven and irregular lines, less a poem and more a careless accretion of stuff in support of the simple narrative imperative: go forth, Whitman demands, and feel the (un)complicated ecstasy of being part of the world. The poem achieves whatever organizational structure it has by the increasingly complex organic structures that the child engages, going from simple spears of grass to birds in flight to farm animals to humans to families to neighborhoods and ultimately to entire cities as the poem itself moves fearlessly from daybreak to sunset, from birth to death.

The poem itself, however, is rendered in a most challenging recitative. Listen to—not simply read—the most apparently mundane line and anatomize its musicality—say, "And the Third-month lambs and the sow's pink-faint litter, and the mare's foal and the cow's calf" (l. 7, p. 258). Imagine one of the Fireside Poets cringing over the line—its lack of studied diction, its reckless abandonment of meter and rhyme, its eccentric punctuation, its clunky reportorial style, its lack of stylized ornamentation. Nothing happens. But Whitman was schooled in opera—something is indeed happening. It is a long and careless line, certainly, but its apparent excess and casual proliferation mimics exactly the springtime with its carefree fertility; it is a line of ceaseless and unlicensed expansion. How could spring be contained in a tidy couplet? But why not just say March—why "Third-month"? The Quaker calendar is nicely exotic, of course, helping to make the spring more intriguing, but to use the word "March," with its military cadence and its abrupt hard one-syllable chop, would create an untenable break in a line that must perforce flow, liquid-y and unstoppable (by comparison, "Third-month," with its long drop vowels and its complex *th*'s, begs to linger, begs to be rolled around the mouth)—after all, Whitman permits only a single comma. The line itself is a complex weave of delightful consonants—gentle sibilant *S*'s, languorous *L*'s that tickle the mouth and lips erotically, and forceful *F*'s and hard *K* sounds that push outward in hard exhale—countered by the exquisite luxury of multiple long *A*'s and long *O*'s, a push-and-pull acoustic effect that re-creates in sound the hesitant struggle of nature itself lurching as it does clumsily into spring. Pink-faint? Why not "faint pink," why not the adjective before the noun? That would make far more grammatical sense. Whitman's unusual backward arrangement is sonically challenging, compels a different reading, a syncopation. The construct slows the reader down, creates in a line otherwise hurrying about the business of procreation a respite, compelling the reader to slow down, to marvel as it were at the stumbling rush into spring.

Each of the thirty-nine lines in the poem demands (and rewards) a reader willing to listen to the play of careful phrasing—assonance, consonance, alliteration, sight rhymes, slant rhymes, internal rhymes, repetition, onomatopoeia, pauses, stressed and unstressed syllables, long and short vowel sounds, word selection (even word invention), convoluted syntax—each line of poetry constructed to re-create the effect of that line's theme. Every word, as it turns out, has a melody. The effect is not forced. Whitman never studied prosody; rather with his extraordinary untutored ear, he heard words into music. Take line 14: "And the old drunkard staggering home from the out-house of the tavern whence he had lately risen" (p. 258)—read aloud, it is an ugly, unseemly line, an awkward line clumsily constructed (too many prepositional phrases bumping gracelessly into each other), a line, of course, that mimics exactly the staggering and uncertain walk of the town drunkard. Take line 9: "And the fish suspending themselves so curiously below there, and the beautiful curious liquid" (p. 258)—a subtle delight of suspended animation realized in exaggerated open vowels that demand the reader slow down, the line defies quick reading. Take line 34: "Shadows, aureola and mist, the light falling on roofs and gables of white or brown two miles off" (p. 259)—the subject matter itself blurs into irrelevancy, the line a stunning recitative of sonorous vowels and lazy *S*'s. The line begs to be lingered over, a slowing down, even as the poem ushers in the forbidding reality of nightfall, that is death itself. Line after line of Whitman's recitatives, the willing reader can hear the meaning of the poem in the sounds the words create. Sound here is action, sound here is theme. Whitman creates a narrative experience within his recitative poems that is at once creative and interactive and supremely democratic—readers do not need footnotes or explanatory notes (any more than they require translated lines during an opera); Whitman beams, just unstop your ears.

THE ARIA: "OUT OF THE CRADLE ENDLESSLY ROCKING"

The aria is surely any opera's showpiece, that riveting stand-apart moment when the main character, whether tragic or comic, whether hero or villain, stops the action to define their character. The aria creates dramatic revelation; for that spellbinding moment, the character is vulnerable, emotional, sumptuously commanding. The action, the narrative, is suspended. In melodies that are at once voluptuous, bold, and soaring, opera characters use the aria to define their essence, from Mozart's Queen of the Night to Bellini's Norma, from Gounod's Marguerite to Donizetti's Lucia di Lammermoor—and each of these arias moved Whitman profoundly. Whitman responded to the self-reflective dynamic of the aria. In the confessional arias of *Leaves of Grass,* Whitman himself steps forward, not some crafted persona like that voracious Child who goes forth daily, but rather Walter Whitman, a nondescript journalist from the streets of Brooklyn, summoned to be simply, grandly what he is: a poet. As with opera, Whitman's arias are moments of tremendous emotional revelation. For Whitman, the arias can be moments of heart-stuttering sadness, such as his war poems, when Whitman acknowledges the depths of the barbarity he cannot hope to redeem or he mourns a noble president ingloriously shot dead; they are moments of painful longing (and ecstatic union), when Whitman speaks of his own complicated and often contradictory sexual identity; they can be moments of doubt and despair, when Whitman senses that maybe the vaunting power of the transcendental soul able to join the weak and terrified I to the very cosmos itself might be, after all, an enticing chimera; they can be moments of difficult honesty, when an aging Whitman confronts the absolute horizon of his own death. These arias soar with some of Whitman's finest lyrical expressiveness, lines that ache to be declaimed lovingly and grandly, poetic arias whose very music lifts and buries.

There is perhaps no better example of Whitman's use of arias than "Out of the Cradle Endlessly Rocking." Written, appropriately, as a stand-apart and published on Christmas Eve, 1859, in the *Saturday Press,* a short-lived underground literary weekly for New York's bohemian crowd, "Out of the Cradle Endlessly Rocking" is a most exquisitely realized aria-within-an-aria that records the tectonic moment when little Walter Whitman, an innocent child happily sporting along the beaches of Long Island, first intuits the power and responsibility of the poet—that is, first conceives Walt Whitman. Whitman juxtaposes two expressive arias, one from a mockingbird pining the loss of his lover-bird, the other from a joyous Whitman looking back on the experience from the perspective of adulthood; these arias define each character, and Whitman, ever the student of opera, uses a full repertoire of acoustic devices to render beyond the words themselves the powerful emotions of each—for the mockingbird, sorrow, and for the nascent poet, exultation.

The poem's narrative premise is simple: Whitman, as adult, recalls an experience while growing up on the beaches of Long Island and listening to the song of a lonely mockingbird. The opening twenty-two lines, a gorgeous recitative, introduce the primary character—Whitman himself—in direct address. It is a single sweeping sentence that uses a sequence of prepositional phrases that builds, rises and surges sonically like the ocean itself that surrounds the action, all moving toward the basic narrative premise: I "[a] reminiscence sing" (l. 22, p. 180). Whitman then thinks back to a lilac-scented May when he was nine, when, each day, he would listen, mesmerized, to the playful call and response of two mockingbirds that had migrated from the south. They would call to each other as they guarded their nest. The bird offers the first soaring aria, this to the sun. which Whitman as poet translates:

Shine! shine! shine!
Pour down your warmth, great sun!
While we bask—we two together.
Two together!

(ll. 32–35, pp. 180–181)

This is clearly no recitative—there is no hurrying action, no reportorial directness, no busy-ness. Here is a gorgeous showcase aria, its emotional drama accentuated by the italics: the rich apostrophe, the rolling long vowels, the generous use of exclamation points, the repetition, the stunning immediacy uncomplicated by metaphor, the phrasing that compels the lines to be delivered with full voice.

Later in the spring, however, the boy hears only the he-bird and intuits within its plaintive call—another aria—a compelling sense of loss. Now a solitary singer whose throat trembles from desolation, the melancholic bird sings of his impossible hope of his mate's return in the longer, second aria, gently pleading with the sea to return his love.

Loud! loud! loud!
Loud I call to you, my love!
High and clear I shoot my voice over the waves,
Surely you must know who is here, is here,
You must know who I am, my love.

(ll. 82–86, p. 182)

However, this shattering aria, which covers nearly sixty lines, does not serve as Whitman's final word. Rather, the condition of love lost, the reality of loneliness, the cataclysmic collapse of emotion into irony becomes the jolting epiphany that first reveals to Whitman even as a boy the glorious ministry of the poet. The boy is moved, tears burst not from his eyes but rather from his heart. "Now in a moment I know what I am for—I awake" (l. 150, p. 183). His heart opens, his tongue stirs awake, he hears thousands upon thousands of heart-wrenching arias pouring from thousands of shattered hearts. And here Whitman offers his own confident aria—he sings as an adult familiar with love lost in a way a boy could not be; he celebrates the poet's privileged status, the power of art to conquer loss by elevating it into art. The sea, however, rises to make the most profound challenge—its ceaseless rise and fall lisps menacingly to Whitman the "low and delicious word death / And again death—ever death, death, death" (ll. 178–179, p. 184). The repetition—as much in anxiety as in panic—accentuates death's ominous reality. But the poet no longer fears it. "My own songs awaked from that hour / And with them the key, the word up from the waves / The word of the sweetest song, and all songs" (ll. 188–190, p. 184). It is Whitman awakened to his destiny. Against the aria of the mockingbird that wallows within the desolate claustrophobia of self-pity and loss, the poet's counter-aria celebrates art itself. It is as if just as the tempestuous and doomed high priestess Norma, praying desperately to the Goddess of the Moon for peace to avoid war that would most certainly claim her Roman lover, who has already betrayed her, completes her wrenching aria "Casta Diva," Bellini himself steps out on stage to celebrate in a glorious aria of his own the gift of elevating such devastating fears, such crippling love, to soaring art. For Whitman, understanding the role of the poet is, of course, a bittersweet triumph—as his aria acknowledges, once he has intuited the power of the poet, he must turn away forever from the uncomplicated joys of his childhood; he has learned the ephemera of love and has heard the lurking whisper of death. Only the poem, his aria affirms triumphantly, is manifestly greater.

THE GRAND CHORUS: "CROSSING BROOKLYN FERRY"

But ultimately there is the grand chorus. If the recitative makes musical the narrative action, if the aria defines character, the grand chorus bonds the audience to the action, defies the very stage itself. The chorus is opera's bold moment of immodest—read Whitmanesque—fusion; characters, music, orchestra, and audience at last make the join. Typically, a formidable choral grouping gathers on stage (high priests or slaves, soldiers or pilgrims) and with the full orchestra often beginning quietly, subtly, the grand chorus builds, swells with delicious deliberateness to booming, majestic chords compelled by an imminently hummable melody. The opera, for that transcendent moment, catapults beyond the limits of theater into a gaudy community spectacle, shattering the neat artifice of the stage itself. The audience happily capitulates to the spectacle. It is a moment of supreme invitation to the audience to defy the pedestrian limits of real time and private space.

Whitman, with his faith in the democratic gospel of union, with his intuitive sense of poetry as an intimacy with the reader that defied time and space, understood the majestic implications of the grand chorus. His grand choruses—among them sections 42–52 of "Song of Myself," "The Children of Adam," "The Sleepers," "Passage to India"—use broad and sweeping lines of stately and uncomplicated emphasis (often set in the commanding invitation of the imperative) to reach out to the listener/reader, to command/demand, to un-ease and upend their comfortable and quiet complacency, to get them swept up even for a moment in the clarion energy of language itself. They are choruses of splendid bonding. "I am with you, you men and women of a generation, or ever so many generations hence" (l. 21, p. 116)—so says Whitman in the grandest of his choruses: "Crossing Brooklyn Ferry," his epochal celebration of hundreds of commuters packed onto the Fulton Ferry crossing the East River at sunset from Brooklyn to Manhattan. The poet finds himself surrounded by these complacent drones—the poem is a sort of Chorus of the Commuters—the slaves of the city grinding out their lives in day-to-day routine, their eyes closed, their hearts stilled, more like cargo being shuttled across the river. The river, with its powerful current and its unstoppable eddies, becomes Whitman's grand metaphor for the journey of life itself and the opportunity at every moment to take in the grandeur of the Now—the "glories strung like beads on [his] smallest sights and hearings" (l. 9, p. 116). Whitman feels an intuitive bond to those metaphoric river crossers all around him as well as to the earlier generations of river-crossers and those river-crossers of generations to come, an expansive energy that of course includes the reader. I, the poet says, am part of this splendor, the commuters all about me are part of this splendor, and so most assuredly are you. It is a triumphant moment of choral union—for Whitman, that soul-deadening commute explodes into an expansive vision that triumphantly defies time, dismisses death as a sorry hobgoblin, and, in the glorious chorus that closes the poem in stanza 9, catapults the willing reader into nothing less than eternity itself.

Like all opera choruses, "Crossing Brooklyn Ferry" begins quietly—the poet, himself crowded among the nameless, faceless commuters, happens to peer over the railing of the ferry into the river and sees there his own reflection bedazzled by radiant centrifugal spokes of light from the setting sun, a dazzling unexpected reminder of the self-canonization that belongs as well, he trumpets, to everyone crowded on the deck of the ferry, this evening, yesterday, and tomorrow, if only they would open their eyes wide, if only they would look on what is so obviously there—at the haze on the hills, the ships at anchor in the river, the dropping gulls, the sailors working their riggings, the scallop waves in the twilight. These are not objects—they are invitations. "These and all else were to me the same as they are to you" (l. 49, p. 117). These inconsequential objects carry consequence only when generation to generation, the poet argues, we see them into dazzle. So, then, what is really between us? "Whatever it is, it avails not" (l. 56, p. 118). That consanguinity, that linkage, the poet celebrates: "I too have been struck from the float forever held in solution" (l. 62, p. 118). I am not perfect, Whitman admits, nor are you—we are as much saint as sinner, as great as we are small (he embraces rather than despairs of that "old knot of contrariety" [l. 71, p. 118]). Indeed, stanza 6 catalogs the darker impulses, the animal energies in everyone—the wolf of lust, the snake of envy, the hog of gluttony—in a sweeping gesture of inclusiveness. For Whitman, they are part of us. Emboldened by this confederacy, Whitman pulls nearer. "Closer yet I approach you" (l. 86, p. 119). What need, he argues, does he have for a Christian soul—Christianity uses the soul to create enslavement, division, and competition. "What is more subtle than this which ties me to the woman or man that looks at my face?" (l. 96, p. 119).

Whitman is ready now for the centrifugal expansion, the *con spirito* of his chorus. Stanza 9 indeed stirs, leaps, and then explodes into Whitman's grand chorus—flow on, river, the poet sings out, in a sweeping cadence of building imperatives, irresistible verbs that command the physical world itself to affirm its own spiritual dimension. Be what is, he intones, be glorious—you commuters passing between birth and death cannot be content with what simply is or what might be in some myth-y afterlife. For the first time in the poem, Whitman thunders into the imperial first-person plural—"we." We say to the earth, "we fathom you not" (l. 130, p. 120), but we love you as perfection enough. With grand expression and double-forte emphasis, Whitman moves to his ringing peroration: "You furnish your parts toward eternity / Great or small, you furnish your parts toward the soul" (ll. 131–132, p. 120). The "you," of course, can refer to the earth as much to the commuters as much to the reader. Each, Whitman celebrates, can be catapulted into the mystery of the eternal. The dead-eyed commuters, the poet-herald, the elemental earth, and at last the willing reader, swept up by Whitman's irresistible exclamatory energy, merge into a radiant moment of supra-theater. It is the grandest of Whitman's grand choruses.

CONCLUSION

In a sprawling essay he titled simply "The Opera," published in *Life Illustrated* in November 1855, just after the release of the first edition of *Leaves of Grass,* Whitman articulated as best he could the life-changing impact when at last a person actually hears opera. "You listen to this music, and the songs, and choruses—all of the highest range of composition known to the world of melody ... A new world opens up—a liquid world—rushes like a torrent through you" (quoted in Faner, p. 80). Surely there are few better descriptions of the impact of *Leaves of Grass* itself. *Leaves of Grass* offers a stunning invitation that, like opera, is as clear as it is undefinable. After all, the themes of *Leaves of Grass,* detached from their crafted musical settings, can seem like metaphysical mumbo-jumbo, frustratingly imprecise nineteenth-century Ur-drafts of contemporary New Age clichés. Revere the world, Whitman demands, as both substance and revelation. Observe, share, and participate in the world, but affirm nothing less than its spiritual reality—it is there, the poet trumpets, believe me. Wake from your lifelong slumber. Every dawn, be Adam new to the Garden; live rebellious, wary of any artificial construct—religion, the state, communities, families, race, economic class, gender, sexual orientation—that distracts from the organic unity of the cosmos itself. It sounds so perfect. But contemporary readers know that even Whitman could not sustain that faith, overwhelmed finally by the immemorial evidence of humanity's shabby failures—violence, greed, selfishness, pride, hate, lust. Can the cosmos be simply talked into glory? Is not a thing simply and entirely what it is, not what it is called?

But set to the music of Whitman's gorgeous prosody, Whitman convinces. The themes register, like music itself, in the spontaneous immediacy of consent, more emotional than rational, more mystical than understood. In the end, Whitman understands it is not what a reader believes but rather what a reader wants to believe. If *Leaves of Grass* is not, really could not be, a blueprint for a New Eden; if, there are finally too many Homer Simpsons, too many Walter Whites, too many Bill Clintons; if (as Whitman's own late-career despair testifies) optimism succumbs to irony, promise fades into betrayal, and expectation stales into disappointment, Whitman generously gifts the modern reader the only way a philosopher-musician could: with the sheer aural persuasion of the lines themselves, the invitation to be engaged by the subtle, resilient acoustic play. *Leaves of Grass* is grand opera at its most American—at once elegantly designed and wildly spontaneous, at once tightly conceived and recklessly ad-libbed, at once terrifyingly transparent yet vitally mysterious, at once abidingly spiritual yet insistently sensuous. Like the score of an opera, the poems of *Leaves of Grass* are necessarily revitalized, entirely reinvented, passionately reconceived each time they are recited, each time they are interpreted anew through the instrument of a human voice. If the plot points of *Leaves of Grass* are childlike in their simplicity—embrace friendship, courage, gratitude, love, nature—its music is anything but. Whitman's music is complex, layered, emphatic, and supremely original. Like all opera, *Leaves of Grass* testifies to the paucity of language and the sheer magnitude of what lies beyond those moments when language, at last, gloriously fails.

Selected Bibliography

WORKS OF WALT WHITMAN

Poetry

Leaves of Grass (self-published), 1855.

Drum-Taps. New York: William E. Chapin, 1865.

Sequel to Drum-Taps. New York: William E. Chapin, 1865.

Passage to India. New York: J. S. Redfield, 1870.

Good-Bye, My Fancy. Philadelphia: David McKay, 1891.

Leaves of Grass: Death-Bed Edition. Philadelphia: David McKay, 1891.

Prose

Franklin Evans; or, The Inebriate. New York: New World, 1842.

Democratic Vistas. Philadelphia: David McKay, 1871.

Memoranda During the War (self-published) 1875.

November Boughs. Philadelphia: David McKay, 1888.

Complete Prose Works. Philadelphia: David McKay, 1892.

Complete Poetry and Selected Prose by Walt Whitman. Edited by James E. Miller, Jr. Boston: Houghton Mifflin, 1959.

Archives

Available in the following collections: Walt Whitman Papers, 1837–1957, Library of Congress, Washington, D.C. (also available on the Library of Congress website, http://hdl.loc.gov/loc.mss/collmss.ms000040); Walt Whitman Papers, 1842–1969, Columbia University Libraries, New York, NY.

CRITICAL AND BIOGRAPHICAL STUDIES

Aspiz, Harold. *So Long! Walt Whitman's Poetry of Death.* Tuscaloosa: University of Alabama Press, 2004.

Assilineau, Roger. *The Evolution of Walt Whitman: An Expanded Version.* 1962. Iowa City, University of Iowa Press, 1999.

Blake, David Haven. *Walt Whitman and the Culture of American Celebrity.* New Haven, Conn.: Yale University Press, 2006.

Bloom, Harold. *The Daemon Knows: Literary Greatness and the American Sublime.* New York: Random House/ Spiegel and Grau, 2015.

Brasas, Juan A. Herrero. *Walt Whitman's Mystical Ethics of Comradeship: Homosexuality and the Marginality of Friendship at the Crossroads of Modernity.* Albany: State University of New York Press, 2010.

Erkkila, Betsy, and Jay Grossman, eds. *Breaking Bounds: Whitman and American Cultural Studies.* New York: Oxford University Press, 1996.

Faner, Robert D. *Walt Whitman and Opera.* Carbondale: Southern Illinois Press, 1951.

Gerhardt, Christine. *A Place for Humility: Whitman, Dickinson, and the Natural World.* Iowa City: University of Iowa Press, 2014.

Hollis, C. Carroll. *Language and Style in Leaves of Grass.* Baton Rouge: Louisiana State University Press, 1983.

Kaplan, Justin. *Walt Whitman: A Life.* New York: Simon & Schuster, 1980.

Klammer, Martin. *Whitman, Slavery, and the Emergence of Leaves of Grass.* University Park: Pennsylvania State University Press, 1995.

Kummings, Donald, ed. *A Companion to Walt Whitman.* Malden, Mass.: Blackwell, 2006.

LeMaster, J. R., and Donald D. Kummings, eds. *The Routledge Encyclopedia of Walt Whitman.* 1998. Reprint, New York: Routledge, 2011.

Loving, Jerome. *Walt Whitman: The Song of Himself.* Berkeley: University of California Press, 1999.

Miller, James E., Jr. *"Leaves of Grass": America's Lyric-Epic of Self and Democracy.* New York: Twayne, 1992.

Perlman, Jim, Ed Folsom, and Dan Campion, eds. *Walt Whitman: The Measure of His Song.* 1981. Minneapolis: Holy Cow! Press, 1998.

Pollak, Vivian R. *The Erotic Whitman.* Berkeley: University of California Press, 2000.

Reynolds, David S. *Walt Whitman's America: A Cultural Biography.* New York: Knopf, 1995.

Skaggs, Carmen Trammell. *Overtones of Opera in American Literature from Whitman to Wharton.* Baton Rouge: Louisiana State University, 2010. Pp. 13–33.

Thomas, M. Wynn. *The Lunar Light of Whitman's Poetry.* Cambridge, Mass.: Harvard University Press, 1987.

Trowbridge, John Townsend. "Reminiscences of Walt Whitman." *Atlantic Monthly,* February 1902, pp. 163–175. http://www.theatlantic.com/past/docs/unbound/poetry/whitman/walt.htm

MEDIA WORKS ON WALT WHITMAN

Crossing. Opera and libretto by Matthew Aucoin. First production: American Repertory Theater, Cambridge, Mass., 2015.

"Walt Whitman." Directed by Mark Zwonitzer. *American Experience,* PBS Television, 2008.

AUGUST WILSON

(1945—2005)

L. Bailey McDaniel

UNTIL THE THIRD decade of the twentieth century, American dramatic literature and the cultural institution of its theater was something of a bastard child in the artistic and scholarly landscape outside U.S. borders. Before the arrival of Eugene O'Neill's plays in the 1910s and 1920s, most universities and professional stages around the world considered serious theater only that which emerged from Western Europe or ancient Greece. While American theater certainly existed before this, it wasn't until O'Neill's consistent successes that drama written by and about Americans was considered academically and aesthetically important. Along with the twentieth-century playwrights Tennessee Williams and Arthur Miller, O'Neill belongs to that very small group of individuals who are considered the greatest national playwrights of the United States—playwrights whose dramatic work put a still-young country on the map alongside the so-called legitimate works of, among others, Sophocles, William Shakespeare, Molière, and William Butler Yeats.

Sometimes referred to as "America's Shakespeare," August Wilson is without a doubt included in this seminal club along with O'Neill, Miller, and Williams. In fact, it would be difficult (arguably, impossible) to find a modern playwright whose critical achievements have been as consistent and whose commercial successes have been so long-standing. That Wilson is the only face of color in this prestigiously small group of "great American playwrights" is no trivial matter. For the man who permanently left high school after only one year because of the consistent and overt racism he experienced from his white peers and teachers, producing an internationally revered body of work would involve a lifelong journey of reconciling two identities: writing as both an American and African American. Because Wilson writes from a simultaneously native and diasporic perspective (what the writer Sherman Alexie calls the subject position of the "indigenous immigrant"), his plays and his politics repeatedly inform each other in often explicit, frequently brilliant ways that no other American playwright has yet to equal.

In *August Wilson: The Ground on Which I Stand,* a 2015 PBS television documentary on Wilson's life directed by Sam Pollard, former colleagues, scholars, theater practitioners, and cultural critics use words such as "visionary," "genius," "truth teller," and "prophet" to describe the man who created something no other playwright in the world has ever done. With his *Century Cycle* (sometimes referred to as the Pittsburgh Cycle), written between 1982 and 2005 and published in one volume in 2007, Wilson wrote ten individual plays about a specific group of people and a specific human experience for every decade of the twentieth century. Although he wrote and staged other works, Wilson is best known by audiences and scholars for the *Century Cycle* and the impact those plays continue to have on contemporary drama and letters. In this sense, those who describe him as the American Shakespeare are not far off. Wilson has few if any peers with this collection of ten plays that repeatedly succeeded both commercially, with live audiences, and critically, with scholarly attention and awards—including multiple Pulitzer Prizes and Tony Awards for Best Play. Along with a body of work that greatly influenced the theater of his lifetime and generations of playwrights to come, however, Wilson is also one of contemporary drama's most important voices for the questions he repeatedly raised about American theater and its (non)engagement with issues of race, diversity, and (mis)representations of America's history.

BIOGRAPHY

When he dropped out of Pittsburgh's Central Catholic High School after only one year, August Wilson might have had difficulty imagining the critical and commercial triumphs that would define his more-than-five-decade professional career. Indeed, as the poor grandson of an African American woman who (literally) walked from North Carolina to Pennsylvania in search of freedom and opportunity, Wilson's astronomical successes paradoxically imply the possibility of an American dream narrative that his larger body of work challenges.

Born Frederick August Kittel, Jr., on April 27, 1945, August Wilson was the fourth of six children born to Frederick August Kittel, Sr., a white Eastern European immigrant and baker who dealt with frequent unemployment and alcoholism, and Daisy Wilson, an African American woman who, mostly on her own, raised the young Wilson and his five siblings in a two-room apartment while also working as a maid. Wilson's childhood was marked by poverty and his father's absence. When his mother divorced his father and eventually remarried, Wilson moved with his family from Pittsburgh's ethnically diverse Hill District to the mostly white working-class neighborhood of Hazelwood, where racial tensions directed at Wilson's family reached such dangerous levels that the family was forced to move to another home. In addition to his father's absence, the culturally rich seeds of history and language planted in the Hill District (the location of most of his plays), and his experiences surviving white hostilities in his community and schools, had an immeasurable impact on Wilson's art and politics.

After he left the consistently overt racism he faced as one of the few faces of color at Central Catholic High School, Wilson endured a brief stint of intellectual boredom at a vocational school, and finally, after receiving a false accusation of plagiarism by an instructor at Gladstone High School, he left formal education for good in favor of a self-designed curriculum at the Carnegie Library of Pittsburgh. Freed from the racial hostilities and intellectual boredom of his previous institutions, the avid reader who had begun to enjoy books at the age of four read widely and voraciously and, perhaps most significantly, was able to explore deeply the literature of American authors of color—an opportunity his public education did not afford.

In addition to a rigorous engagement with important American writers of the twentieth century such as Langston Hughes, Richard Wright, and Ralph Ellison, it was at the Carnegie Library that Wilson first began to encounter the poetics and the politics of black nationalism and its artistic arm, the Black Arts movement. Indeed, artists such as Amiri Baraka and Ed Bullins would be extremely influential in Wilson's artistic endeavors and his political identity, and these writers most definitely would not have been made available to him in a public or parochial school curriculum. Although he received other honorary degrees in his lifetime, when the Carnegie Library awarded Wilson an honorary diploma in 1989, he became the only individual to be so honored.

Wilson's discovery of the music of the early-twentieth-century blues singer Bessie Smith in his youth also had an inestimable influence on his plays. Describing how he felt upon first hearing the stacks of used 78s he purchased for five cents each, he explained, "I somehow knew intuitively that this person, this music was mine." More than a just genre of music, for Wilson the blues was, as he described, "an encapsulation of black American cultural ideas" (Pollard documentary). In his discussion of the 1984 play *Ma Rainey's Black Bottom,* the scholar Harry Elam explains that "the blues is something that suffuses all of [Wilson's plays] ... that spirit. The musicality of Wilson is not just in the sense of it, or the frame of the blues, but also in the content and in the language and the rhythms that he creates within his drama" (Pollard). For Wilson, then, the blues was a way to *express* but also *make sense of* a sometimes fractured, often misrepresented history defined by power and beauty, as much as it was racism and suffering. As Wilson's Ma Rainey says of the blues quite explicitly, "You don't sing to feel better. You sing because that's a way of understanding life."

At the age of twenty Frederick August Kittel took his father's middle name and his mother's maiden name and became August Wilson. When he left Pittsburgh and arrived in St. Paul, Minnesota, in 1978, although he'd already written a handful of plays, Wilson nevertheless considered himself a poet. Among other jobs, he earned money writing "scripts" for the educational programming at the Science Museum of Minnesota. Following early successes with St. Paul's Penumbra Theatre Company, the move to playwright was complete and his Midwest achievements were soon supplanted by more prestigious attention from the Eugene O'Neill Theater Center and its National Playwrights Conference. In particular, he benefited from the mentorship of the conference director Lloyd Richards, whose presence in Wilson's personal and professional life would change the course of American theater. With Richards' guidance and collaboration, August Wilson's body of work would reach heights that few could dare to imagine, earning numerous awards and redefining the term "American drama" for the institution of theater worldwide.

Since Wilson's death in 2005, his plays have continued to enjoy enormous critical and commercial success on Broadway and worldwide, not to mention consistent attention and praise from scholars in the fields of drama, theater studies, critical race studies, and gender. But Wilson's impact is also political. Through his tireless work to stage the experiences and histories of Americans whose stories were either misrepresented or erased altogether, through his controversial and important disagreements with the critic Robert Brustein over the funding of black theater in the United States, and through the countless playwrights, actors, directors, and audiences his plays have influenced, August Wilson changed the world in which he lived.

On October 16, 2005, just fourteen days after Wilson lost his battle with cancer, Broadway's Virginia Theatre made history when it officially changed its name to the August Wilson Theatre. Located at 245 West 52nd Street in New York City's Theater District, the building became the first Broadway house to be named after a black American. (A prestigious and rare honor, only eight of the current forty Broadway venues bear the name of a playwright or musical composer or lyricist.) The August Wilson Theatre is not the only building or landmark to publicly reflect Wilson's important position in American literature and culture. At 980 Liberty Avenue in the heart of Pittsburgh's Cultural District, the August Wilson Center for African American Culture opened in 2009 and stages plays in a 472-seat theater, houses a museum, and offers space for the visual and performing arts, classes, and public lectures. In Seattle, Washington, which became Wilson's home base with his wife Constanza Romera beginning in 1990, the street on which the Seattle Repertory Theatre sits has been renamed August Wilson Way. And while the state of Pennsylvania already declared Wilson's Hill District childhood home at 1727 Bedford Avenue an historical monument in 2007, in 2016 the Daisy Wilson Artist Community (a group named after Wilson's mother) began work on restoring and memorializing the location. When the project is completed, the restored home will serve as a public commemoration of Wilson's powerful influence on the community and on American drama, as well as house meeting and performance spaces for visiting scholars and artists.

CAREER OVERVIEW

With several years of a self-taught education from the Carnegie Library already behind him, August Wilson spent a good part of the mid-1960s sitting with his notebook and pen at Hill District diners such as Pat's Place and Eddie's Restaurant. In this way, he spent countless hours writing and, by his own account, finely honing a sensibility and sensitivity to the black voices whose history, pain, humor, and strength would come to characterize his plays. While Wilson continued to sharpen his skills with language and dialogue as he listened to what he described as "community elders" (Pollard), something else was occurring that would shape his theater and his politics in seminal ways. As Wilson continued to live and write in the Hill District, the Black Power movement and its artistic arm, the Black Arts movement, was quickly gaining traction as black Americans tired of the too-slow, too-small changes from unkept promises of the more assimilationist-oriented civil rights movement. Whereas the peaceful resistance and compromising tenor of the early civil rights agenda had initially captured the hope of black Americans forced to live second-class lives defined by economic, legislated, often violent marginalization, that moment was coming to a close in the mid-1960s. Increasingly, black Americans found less value in the quiet, patient, assimilating model of racial harmony offered by figures such as Martin Luther King, Jr., and demanded equality that was immediate and not tied to pleasing whites in power who still refused to offer the equality the early civil rights movement had promised. Along with the inspiring promise (and unapologetic demands) of uncompromising equality and due process offered by figures such as Malcolm X, helping fuel the engine of consciousness was an increase in the awareness of police brutality against black Americans in cities across the United States. No longer willing to politely *ask* for freedom (or protection from violence), many black Americans began to *demand* change and, more significantly, create entirely separate avenues of opportunity, protection, and consciousness that did not (1) model itself in an aesthetic or politics that coalesced with white America and (2) did not require (or care about) white America's approval.

James Brown's 1968 hit "Say It Loud—I'm Black and I'm Proud" perfectly illustrated this new consciousness, one based in ethnic pride and a celebration of black identity and culture (and for some, a burgeoning Pan-African consciousness). Without apology and with communal and individual pride, for many the Black Power movement coincided with a shift whereby one defined oneself as a black American before one identified as American. In Brown's "I'm Black and I'm Proud"; in the iconic maxim of "Black is beautiful"; in the choice to wear Kente cloth or African iconography on one's clothing or around one's neck; and even in the choice to wear one's hair naturally rather than chemically straightened (presumably to emulate white standards of beauty), the Black Power movement had cultural and artistic manifestations that bespoke a new, celebratory refusal to assimilate to white culture, aesthetics, or politics and instead moved to a nonapologetic joy and pride in all things African American.

The Black Power movement was an historically rich moment in U.S. history, and one that was of course not homogenous or uncontested in its agenda or its followers. But one generalization that can be made about this significant moment in American history is that the Black Power movement rested on a pride and celebration of the specifically black experience. This more than anything else spoke to Wilson. For him and countless others, black nationalism's attitude of self-love, community empowerment, and ethnically specific pride carried over into how people aspired to govern themselves, educate their children, protect one's self against violence, and certainly carried into the cultural landscape of how one created and shared art purported to represent a people and a country.

No other artistic movement in U.S. history has seen such a direct link between politics and art. The position of black nationalism in the mid-1960s through the early 1970s was that one's aesthetic and political sensibilities were two equally important components of social, cultural, economic revolution. Or as Larry Neal and other writers of the Black Arts movement would posit, one's aesthetics and one's politics were one and the same. This proposal of art—and theater in particular—existing *for* political or ideological reasons rather than, for example, escapism or "art of for art's sake" is one that would inform Wilson's entire body of work. Wilson was deeply inspired, both artistically and politically, by Black Arts movement playwrights such as Ed Bullins, Amiri Baraka, and Sonia Sanchez, to name a few. For these important American writers, a play was more than an artistic object to provide enjoyment. And despite what some conservative twenty-first-century writers and critics would continue to argue, a play was also more than the Aristotelian model of raising humanity's engagement with so-called higher truths. Following in the critical footsteps that would be firmly planted (and widely accepted) in academia by the end of his lifetime, Wilson held the position that a play (or a novel or a poem or a film) is an ideologically rich instrument which (1) relies on and also (2) expostulates specific sets of values.

Like his Black Arts movement predecessors, Wilson felt strongly that an artistic object, especially something like a play that has the power to offer a version of "reality" with real human bodies on a stage, unavoidably offers a specific morality vis-à-vis the fictional world it creates on the stage and page. Perhaps more insidiously, but also more significantly (as the Black Arts movement and followers such as Wilson argued), a cultural product such as a play in effect represents (or misrepresents) history—whether it be a people's or a nation's. This perspective—held by the Black Arts movement, Wilson, and now widely accepted by scholars in literary, history, and cinema studies, to name a few—maintains that when only one group of people is allowed to "tell the society's stories" decade after decade, or even century after century (in this case, stories told from the positon of the generally white, Western, Judeo-Christian, liberal humanist perspectives that define most of the canon of Western literature), not only do those values and ideologies become presented as "truthful" or "universal," but their versions of history—and their (mis)representations of entire groups of people and *their* histories—become normalized as "truth." For groups of people such as black Americans who have been disenfranchised (or whose history has been erased completely), what the literature is about and who gets to write it becomes a very serious question, indeed.

While by the end of the twentieth century, literary, cultural, and aesthetic theorists had come to acknowledge art's inherent (unavoidable) political and social subjectivities, it was still fairly new ground being made when Wilson and the playwrights, artists, and poets of the Black Arts movement argued that the *what* (what stories get told) and the *how* (how those stories are told) of one's art influences the way people think of themselves—what pride or shame a community has in itself, what economic, political, and social freedoms a community might imagine it deserves or, eventually, demand. In other words, the Black-Arts-movement-inspired idea that one's art not only represented one's community but had the power—the *responsibility*—to speak and fight for that community, shaped Wilson's work immediately in Pittsburgh. And as the Hill District's diners would eventually be replaced by Pittsburgh theaters, followed by St. Paul, and then finally to the stages of New York, his plays and persona would increasingly operate from that specific position of "responsibility."

In 1968, Wilson followed the call heard by many black Americans at the time—to employ art as a tool to realize what activism alone was not yet accomplishing—and together with the writer and critic Rob Penney, he started a small theater company in his hometown. Following in the philosophical footsteps of Amiri Baraka's Black Arts Repertory Theatre in Harlem, Wilson's Black Horizons Theatre in Pittsburgh's Hill District was a response to what he described as his personal "duty and honor to participate in altering the relationship of blacks to the society in which we live" (Pollard). Although at this time he still identified primarily as a poet, Wilson and his partner Penney started Black Horizons as a theater company that would have, as he described it, "the particular purpose of raising the consciousness of the people and politicizing the community so that we could all better understand the situation ... that we found ourselves in in America, and how this related to our historical situation" (Pollard). To be sure, while the poetry in Wilson's drama is seen easily in his characters' speech and in the moving, expressive front matter he provides in his plays, by the time he moved to St. Paul in 1978 he increasingly found drama as the best vehicle for both his aesthetic and political sensibilities.

With his move to St. Paul and his growing relationship with that city's Penumbra Theatre, Wilson began stretching his artistic legs as a dramatist more seriously. His first play that resulted from the new relationship with the

Penumbra Theatre, *Black Bart and the Sacred Hills* (1977), is set in the Old West and riffs on the theme of Aristophones' *Lysistrata,* in which women withhold sex until their male counterparts agree to end war. Wilson would later say that only with the absence and insight afforded by his life in St. Paul could he fully articulate the power of the language he heard in Pittsburgh diners and billiard halls. Wilson's next project with Penumbra, *Jitney* (1982), was a play that would eventually be included in the *Century Cycle* and marked the beginning of his plays set in his beloved Hill District, a locale whose history and flavor would as associated with Wilson as strongly as William Faulkner and his Yoknapatawpha County.

With the Broadway success of *Ma Rainey's Black Bottom* (in 1984) and *Fences* (in 1985) under his belt, Wilson began work in earnest on what he would now define as the *Century Cycle* with his next play, the elegiac *Joe Turner's Come and Gone,* reaching Broadway in 1988. At the end of the 1980s Wilson left St. Paul for Seattle following a divorce, but the late 1980s were also a time when he solidified his professional and personal relationships with the Eugene O'Neill Theatre Center and with the National Playwrights Conference director, Lloyd Richards—relationships that would change the face of American drama.

Wilson's early relationship with the Eugene O'Neill Theatre Center in Waterford, Connecticut, is pivotal to understanding the monumental mark his plays leave on American drama. Through support provided by its National Playwrights Conference, the O'Neill center gave Wilson's play *Ma Rainey's Black Bottom* an audience in 1982 and, just as crucially, a public platform from which to receive national critical attention. This was the first of many collaborative relationships the conference facilitated with Wilson's work. Following *Ma Rainey,* other plays by Wilson, such as *Fences* (in 1983), *Joe Turner's Come and Gone* (in 1984), and *The Piano Lesson* (in 1986), were successfully staged as part of the National Playwrights Conference.

The conference also facilitated Wilson's most significant professional relationship. In addition to the years of mentorship Wilson received from conference director Lloyd Richards, many of Wilson's most successful plays would be a product of the writing, directing, and producing collaboration he shared with Richards. (In his role as head of the conference, Richards, also a former dean of the Yale School of Drama, supported a number of playwrights who rose to prominence, including Wendy Wasserstein, John Guare, David Henry Hwang, John Patrick Shanley, Athol Fugard, and Derek Wolcott.)

Richards' work with Wilson earned countless awards for Richards, including the 1987 Drama Desk and Tony Awards for Best Play for *Fences*; a Tony Award as Best Director for *Fences*; the 1990 Drama Desk Award (Outstanding New Play) for *The Piano Lesson*; and countless nominations in his roles as producer and director of Wilson's work. And certainly the 1991 Regional Theatre Tony Award presented to Richards' Yale Repertory Theatre and the National Medal of Arts Award he received in 1993 was in no small part informed by his professional achievements with Wilson. Until the cooling in their professional relationship, which transpired with the Broadway staging of *Seven Guitars* in 1995 (the last August Wilson play to be directed by Richards), the two retained a personal and creative partnership whose successes had few peers in contemporary drama.

The painter Romare Bearden was a direct inspiration to Wilson's work on more than one occasion. Bearden's 1978 painting *Mill Hand's Lunch Bucket,* for example, not only provided what was the original title of *Joe Turner,* but the painting itself is what moved Wilson to the idea for the play. In an interview with the *Paris Review,* Wilson explained that in looking at Bearden's work, "I learned that the fullness and richness of everyday life can be rendered without compromise or sentimentality." Also a direct inspiration from what he appreciated in Bearden's paintings, Wilson would continue to write with the grammar and sensibility of collage, using what he described as "the image of a stewing pot in which I toss various things that I'm going to make use of—a black cat, a garden, a bicycle, a man with a scar on his face, a pregnant woman, a man with a gun" (Lyons and Plimpton, 1999).

But Wilson also shares with Bearden a powerful specificity of black American experience whose truthfulness in the telling also manages to become, paradoxically, universal to the human experience. These seemingly incongruent ambitions, to be at once culturally and politically particular while also speaking to a universality of the human condition, is something few artists ever achieve. In the PBS documentary on Wilson's life and work, former colleagues and scholars all speak to this paradox, a feat that reveals technical mastery as much as it does creative genius. Indeed, while the film's narrator posits that Wilson's work is "uncompromisingly grounded in the belief that ordinary black life was ennobled with gifts of blood, memory, and history," the Pulitzer Prize–winning playwright Suzan Lori-Parks also contends, "August Wilson helps us remember who we are, *all of us,* as an American people" (Pollard). Perhaps no other modern playwright, and certainly no American playwright, has been able to document a specific group of people's experiences and histories so powerfully while also speaking to what many audiences and critics celebrate as universal human truths.

Wilson's achievements on the Broadway stage were as consistent as they were critically recognized. But his successes in no way quelled his passion to increase the visibility and cultural significance of African American lives and experiences. To be sure, his determination arguably expanded in tandem with the increasing space he occupied in the contemporary theater. One of the most famous manifestations of Wilson's professional decision to "walk the walk" as well as "talk the talk" of a more diverse and equitable American canon is in his public debate with the conservative theater critic and *New Republic* writer Robert Brustein.

On January 27, 1997, when New York City's famous Town Hall hosted the public discussion "On Cultural Power: The August Wilson–Robert Brustein Discussion," a sold-out crowd was treated to a crucial, at times heated debate from two of American theater's most influential voices. As the author of more than one unflattering review of Wilson's plays, Brustein had already carved out an antagonistic role for himself concerning Wilson's professional aesthetic and personal politics. Because his credits included, among other things, founding the American Repertory Theater and the Yale Repertory Theatre, Brustein's views as a critic (positions that were as much artistic as they were political in nature) packed as much of a punch as did his live opinions shared on the Town Hall stage that January.

Among the key differences in the two men's positions at the Town Hall debate was the role of drama and perhaps art itself. Although each man's stance contained nuances and complexities, a perhaps unfair reduction of each perspective could be the question, "What should a play do?" Wilson had first publicly expressed his position on this question (and others) at the 1996 Theatre Communication Group's annual conference, when he delivered what would be his infamous keynote address: "The Ground on Which I Stand." (As a testament to the importance of this now-published address to American theater and the issues of diversity and race, the McCarter Theatre Center and Princeton University hosted an additional conference on April 18, 2016, to recognize and revisit Wilson's seminal speech on its twenty-year anniversary.) In his 1996 speech, Wilson outlined his contention that the current state of American drama was one defined by unequal critical (scholarly) attention and financial resources paid to any theater or drama that was not white. Arguing with passion and compelling evidence for an increase in funding for plays written by and about black Americans, Wilson went on to argue that implicit racism was the de facto result (and perhaps cause) of the current, imbalanced state of American theater—a "national" institution did not and still does not represent all of America.

As a result of the attention that Wilson's keynote address had garnered, as well as the hostilities that continued to grow between the two men as Brustein continued to take public potshots at Wilson (as well as potshots at what Brustein found to be an increasingly problematic "multicultural" theater), by the time the Town Hall event took place, the low embers of hostility between the two resembled more of an angry brushfire. More important than the tenor of the disagreements, however, the Town Hall debate seemed to ride on stakes higher than merely who was right or wrong, who was a cultural imperialist (of which Wilson accused Brustein), or who had "fallen into a monotonous tone of victimization" (an insult hailed at Wilson by Brustein). Indeed, in paraphrasing Brustein's opening comments, the *New York Times* described the event's debate as a "tension between two ideas of the theater as old as Plato and Aristotle." The Platonic ideal understands theater (or more broadly, art) as a mechanism for political change and the elevation of humanity, while the Aristotelian perspective conceives art and theater as a means through which "the workings of the human soul, which has no color'" can be explored.

Brustein's contention of a colorless human soul is already one that many writers of color would find potentially problematic. That is not to say that Brustein or other American theater practitioners and critics believe that a human soul (and thus the art that speaks for it) have an ethnic specificity in and of themselves, but rather there is a danger and slippery universalizing tendency, one that liberal humanism and Western culture is often guilty of, in asserting a universality or colorlessness to human experience (or souls). The danger and slipperiness come from the unspoken assumption that what is considered "the universal" is right or correct, and anything deviating from that is wrong or less human. The problem with this more Aristotelian (and Western) understanding of art—a problem that has been recognized and criticized by Wilson as well as writers such as Toni Morrison, Salmon Rushdie, Sherman Alexie, Derek Walcott, and countless other seminal writers who fall outside of the Western, white, Christian ideology of much of the canon—is that stories and histories that are *not* considered part of the "universal" palette get left out (at best) or misrepresented and caricatured (at worst).

Brustein's position, although admittedly more nuanced than the following allows for, assumes from the outset that art, human experience, and history are *universal* and that they can facilitate an objective, honest, "lens-free" experiencing and telling—whether on the stage or the page. Among the many problems with this position—problems that have been pointed out by literary and dramatic theorists since early-twentieth-century New Criticism went out of favor—is the underlying assumption that one, true, "good" or "best" way of staging a play (or writing a poem, novel, or the like) exists at all. This assumption contends, in other words, that it is possible to determine—free from all subjectivity, bias, or politically informed opinions—which stories, or storytelling style, is best.

As Wilson and countless others would point out repeatedly, this potentially dangerous assumption bypasses the reality that those in power are the ones who get to define what the rules of "good" and "bad" theater, poetry, and fiction are (and in American theater, it is overwhelmingly the tradition of Western, humanist realism that is purported to be "good"—an aesthetic choice which itself comes with a host of ideological arguments). Further, and more importantly, the values of those who get to tell (stage) the stories are presented as "right" or "universal." And worst of all, the histories, values, and experiences of those *not* in power never get told or are misrepresented by those who do have the power. This is the crux of an argument for a diversified canon of literature and drama.

Trying to support his side of the debate at Town Hall, Brustein took inspiration from the novelist Milan Kundera and, as William Grimes of the *New York Times* reported, he "rejected what he called 'ideological art,' proposing instead that the artist's function was to 'speak truth to power' rather than to seek power" (Grimes, online). Wilson was quick to point out that Brustein's position does not acknowledge what the majority of literary, cinema, and theater scholars take as fact: all art is already ideological, whether it intends to be or not. Akin to claiming "not to be political," Brustein's positon, according to Wilson and others, dangerously fails to account for the (historical) reality that one of the most political statements an artist or art object can make is to be "not political" or worse, to be "objective." To claim universality, objectivity, or a freedom from political perspective implies that what is presented in the piece or art, or the play in this case, is ideologically neutral and is presenting mere "truth." Unfortunately—and this is especially relevant when only one group of people, one set of beliefs, or one people's culture gets represented in what is supposed to be a national body of work—that perspective is implied to be correct, right, objectively true, and normal, while anything outside of it is deemed wrong (or uncivilized, savage, backward, unqualified, immoral, and so on). Operating from an assumption that "art is not necessarily or should not be ideological" generates more than marginalization; it results in actual exclusion and erasure (of a people's theater, paying jobs for its practitioners, and the stories and histories that get told). As Wilson argued repeatedly that night, many would describe convincingly so, only by increasing funding for black theater in America would those marginalized voices get the opportunity to be heard.

While neither the feud with Brustein nor the issue of insufficiently staged and funded black theater disappeared, Wilson's prodigious writing continued with more plays, more critical acclaim, and more audiences. Completing the last two plays of the ten-play *Century Cycle* with *Gem of the Ocean* in 2003 and *Radio Golf* in 2005, he not only represented African American life in the 1900s and 1990s, respectively, but he also continued earning profitable box office numbers and prestigious awards. Indeed, the critical and commercial attention paid to Wilson's body of work and legacy only increased with time. A Paramount Pictures film adaptation of *Fences,* directed by the film's star Denzel Washington, was released in December 2016; in the film version, Washington and the award-winning actor Viola Davis reprise their roles from the 2010 Tony Award–winning revival of the play. Wilson's 1982 play *Jitney* (the only play in the *Century Cycle* not previously staged on Broadway), had its Broadway premiere in January 2017 at the Manhattan Theatre Club under the direction of the frequent Wilson collaborator Ruben Santiago-Hudson.

Whether in film adaptations or staged revivals, in academic conferences organized around his plays and ideas, or in the plethora of scholarship that continues to examine his work, August Wilson's drama will certainly persist in influencing and inspiring artists, audiences, and readers in their experience with one of the twentieth-century's most influential writers.

SELECTED MAJOR PLAYS

While the four plays explored below represent what some might describe as Wilson's major plays, the list should not be confused with an all-inclusive inventory of Wilson's most significant (or "major") works. For scholars, theater practitioners, and artists alike, coming up with a circumscribed catalog of plays from Wilson's oeuvre that deserve singular attention would be a difficult if not impossible task.

MA RAINEY';S BLACK BOTTOM

As the only play in Wilson's *Century Cycle* not set in Pittsburgh's Hill District, *Ma Rainey's Black Bottom* explores the lives and the struggles of African Americans in a Chicago recording studio. Dealing with the decade of the 1920s, this powerful two-act play earned Wilson the 1985 New York Drama Critics' Circle Award for Best American Play, as well as nominations for the Drama Desk Award (Outstanding New Play) and the Tony Award (Best Play).

After being presented as a staged reading in 1982 at the Eugene O'Neill Theater Center, *Ma Rainey's Black Bottom* opened on April 6, 1984, in New Haven, Connecticut, at the Yale Repertory Theater. It made its Broadway debut at New York City's Cort Theater on October 11, 1984. On Broadway the play ran for 276 performances, and in 2003, it was revived at the Royale Theatre (later renamed the Bernard B. Jacobs Theatre), this time running for 68 performances.

Set in 1927, the play explores, among other things, the mercurial and imbalanced fight for power and profits between the white businessmen running the music industry and the black talent who were often on the losing side of both. While American blues is a consistent character in its own right in Wilson's oeuvre, the music industry specifically becomes a focus of *Ma Rainey's* meditation on the lives of African Americans in the 1920s. Wilson uses the historically accurate realities of the white-run music business and the black Americans whose voices, instruments, and songwriting generated wealth that never found its way back to them.

Most obviously, the play underscores the harsh realities African Americans experienced personally and professionally from unethical business practices, racist record producers, and an explicitly segregated Chicago landscape that placed black Americans in perennially vulnerable circumstances. But *Ma Rainey* also underscores African Americans' struggles within their own community, how the fight for self-determination often gets perverted into a shift away from an empowering solidarity and toward destructive self-interest and pride. Indeed, many of the play's most dramatic conflicts emerge between black characters who, although explicitly oppressed by a racist white power structure, find their ultimate demise at the actions of another African American character who has given in to the rage, resentment, or shame elicited by life in 1920s America.

The character named in the play's title is based on the real life Gertrude "Ma Rainey" Pridgett (1886–1939). A Columbus, Georgia, native, Pridgett was often billed as "the mother of the blues," and among her other credits, she performed and recorded with Louis Armstrong and Tommy Dorsey; she is reputed to have taught Bessie Smith how to sing the blues when she put Smith in her Rabbit's Foot Minstrels. She was also among the first American blues singers to record professionally. As is the case with Wilson's fictional Ma Rainey, Pridgett was also openly bisexual and an overtly sexual performer whose lyrics were often as suggestive as their delivery.

As the play opens, Ma's band is waiting for her to show up for a scheduled recording session and the audience learns quickly that her occasional tardiness and her consistent refusal to submit (in attitude or actions) to the racist attitudes of the white studio owner Sturdyvant has set the stage for an angry confrontation between the two upon her arrival. As band members Toledo, Levee, Cutler, and Slow Drag interact with each other and with Ma's white manager, Irvin, audiences also see that not all of the ribbing and mocking between the band members is good-natured. Performing a role that Wilson would engage in so many other plays—that of the African American man who craves self-determination, nurtures dreams of greatness, but seethes with a shame and rage toward a racist America that prevents both—the character of Levee sets himself apart from his bandmates with his constant talk of recording with his own style and his own songs. At once bombastic and vulnerable, Levee also deems himself worthy to go after Ma's girlfriend, Dussie Mae, and eventually, he takes himself out of the band completely, believing his would-be solo career promises more success than anything he might accomplish with the men he sees as bringing him down.

When Ma eventually arrives with her nephew Sylvester and her girlfriend Dussie Mae, conflict emerges not just over the petty hagglings and disrespect Sturdyvant hails in Ma's direction but, more importantly, from Ma's refusal to record the songs or styles Irvin and Sturdyvant prefer her to sing. In particular, Ma's insistence that her nephew Sylvester speak/sing the introduction to her signature song, "Ma Rainey's Black Bottom," meets with opposition not just from the whites in the control booth but from her band members as well. Sylvester's noticeable stutter makes his first attempts at the introduction uncomfortable to hear. As precious time continues to pass and studio dollars are spent, tensions palpably increase as Ma maintains her proud refusal to deviate from her own choices on the recording, Levee persists in his flirting and boastful swaggering, and Sturdyvant continues his overtly racist attitudes and speech while fighting for control of the recording.

The play's final climax occurs when recording has completed and, after Levee's threats and peacocking have finally gone too far, Ma has fired him. When a rejected Levee discovers that Sturdyvant's promise to record the trumpeter's songs was an empty one, a physical altercation erupts between the older, quieter Cutler and Levee. The violence turns fatal when Levee stabs the introspective Toledo and, along with the piano player's life, ends any chance he himself may have had to play or live freely and on his own terms.

In addition to exploring the personal and cultural dangers of self-interest and individual hubris (especially when in the place of communal needs and identity), *Ma Rainey's Black Bottom* stages Wilson's fascination with the blues as a language of cultural memory and a grammar of emotional and spiritual transformation. Like Wilson's drama, the blues is specific to black experience but at the same time seemingly universal in its emotional truth. Describing the music that would serve as a kind of character itself in the play, Wilson writes in a preface to the play:

> It is hard to define the music. Suffice it to say that it is music that breathes and touches. That connects. That is in itself a way of being separate and distinct from any other. This music is called the blues ... The men and women who make this music have learned it from the narrow cooked streets of East St. Louis, or the streets of the city's South Side, and the Alabama or Mississippi roots have been strangled by the northern manners and customs of free men of definite and sincere worth, men for whom this music often lies at the forefront of their conscience and concerns. Thus, they are laid open to be consumed by it; its warmth and redress, its braggadocio and roughly poignant comments, its vision and prayer, which would instruct and allow them to reconnect, to reassemble and gird up for the next battle in which they would be both victim and the ten thousand slain.
>
> (p. 16)

For Wilson and the characters of *Ma Rainey,* the blues has the ability to help a person and a people endure life's hardship and celebrate life's joy, but it is also a means of making sense of those things. It is both the leftover result of battles fought and the weapons that might help in surviving the next one. It is that which is "most separate and distinct" in its experience, but also that which sanctifyingly "connects"—very much like the plays Wilson offered audiences and readers for decades to come.

FENCES

Like many of Wilson's plays, after a staged reading at the Eugene O'Neill Theater Center (1983), *Fences* was first professionally staged at the Yale Repertory Theatre in New Haven, Connecticut. After opening in New Haven on April 30, 1985, the play moved to Broadway on March 26, 1987, and ran for 525 performances at the 46th Street Theatre (now the Richard Rogers Theatre). *Fences* was revived in 2010 at the Cort Theatre, running for a limited 88 performances with Denzel Washington and Viola Davis playing the roles originated by James Earl Jones and Mary Alice, respectively.

With Lloyd Richards as director, in 1987 the play earned the Drama Desk Award for Outstanding Play, the Tony Award for Best Play, and the Pulitzer Prize for Drama. Its 2010 revival similarly won the Drama Desk Award (Outstanding Revival of a Play) and Tony Award (Best Revival of a Play).

In its part of the *Century Cycle, Fences* explores the experience of African Americans in the 1950s, a decade that delivered economic success to countless white Americans in what was to be known as the "postwar boom." The jump in economic mobility that was enabled by a healthy postwar economy and also thousands of American veterans taking advantage of the GI Bill was typically not enjoyed by African Americans, however. As with many of Wilson's plays, *Fences* features at its center a man who faces more than just social racism and interpersonal conflicts; he faces an entire economic system that has two separate sets of rules for white Americans and everyone else. With the protagonist Troy Maxson, a garbage man and former baseball player who never quite made it out of the Negro leagues, *Fences* revisits a frequent theme in Wilson's oeuvre: African Americans' struggle to carve out a piece of the American dream for themselves in country that does not play anything close to fair. A wounded, angry, passionate man who lives with the daily awareness that he's been a victim of the cultural and economic systems of his own country, Troy exerts power and control in the only place he can: with various family members and in a house he claims as his own. The home he "owns" and wants to protect with a soon-to-be-built fence comes with baggage, however, since its purchase was enabled by a veteran's settlement from Troy's younger brother, Gabriel. Gabriel's war injuries involve brain trauma that sometimes manifests as madness, sometimes mere eccentricity. As a result, Troy's decision years ago to keep Gabriel out of a hospital and with him—thus freeing Gabriel's settlement money to buy Troy's home—is one marked by ethical ambiguity throughout the play.

Underscoring the nebulous nature of Troy's motives regarding his vulnerable brother as well as his relationships to his sons, Lyons and Cory, is the emotional reward he seems to enjoy in having small moments of power over family members, particularly when that power emerges from his qualified role as breadwinner. For example, Lyons, his older son from a previous marriage, repeatedly shows up asking for short-term loans; Troy is then hesitant to allow Lyons to pay him back, seeming to enjoy the guilt-throwing martyrdom of the man whose (small degree of) power comes only from his ability to spare a dollar or two to those even poorer than he is.

Fences' complicated, heartbreaking, sometimes cruel patriarch is perhaps most flawed in his relationship with his younger son, Cory, who, like his father, has been blessed with athletic talent but who, unlike his father, enjoys the real possibility of professional and economic success in a more integrated American sports culture. As a high school football star, Troy's youngest son is being courted by a college recruiter who sees a scholarship and eventual professional career in Cory's future, but none of this can happen without Troy's permission. While Cory juggles part-time work and his classes, it is clear that football is his passion and priority; when Cory tries to temporarily reduce his work hours to facilitate his new athletic responsibilities and ensure his scholarship, Troy's reaction is one of rage and resentment.

When Troy explicitly refuses to provide permission for Cory to continue his football aspirations (and secretly informs Cory's coach to take him off the team), Wilson reveals a complex protagonist who, on the one hand, seemingly fears that his son will experience the same racism that crushed his own dreams. But, on the other hand, Wilson also suggests a bitter paternal resentment of a son's talent and opportunities: resentment of opportunities that escaped Troy and a future that if pursued could eclipse Troy's own dreams by leaps and bounds.

As a wounded and furious Cory leaves his father's house for good, audiences also learn that Alberta, the woman Troy has had an open affair with and who is pregnant with his child, has given birth and subsequently died. Cory's mother Rose, dutiful and steady, agrees to raise the baby as her own. When the play concludes, it is seven years later and the family—including Troy's seven-year-old daughter, Raynell, and his son Cory, returned from military service—gather for Troy's funeral.

With *Fences,* Wilson explores the painful and unjust reality faced by those systematically precluded from an American dream that claimed to promise economic rewards for hard work and merit—a promise that *was* kept for many white Americans after the war. As he fights to move from garbage collector to garbage truck driver, and fights to fence off his private property and publicly display his economic independence via home ownership, Troy's attempts at success or even modest advancement are as empty as his early dreams of professional baseball. But the fences of the play's title function as more than metaphorically keeping others out and keeping others trapped in. When in the play's preface Wilson describes "the descendants of African slaves" who lived in "quiet desperation and vengeful pride," he could have easily been describing his play's protagonist. The desperate, resentful pride of Troy—as well as other characters in the play—emerge not just from living in an unjust landscape but also from broader existential realities of life, such as its impermanence. While Troy eventually reveals that his emotional investment in the titular fence largely involves the idea of keeping death out, the loyal and long-suffering Rose explains that her conception of the fence involved a living metaphor to keep her straying husband at home.

As is the case with all of Wilson's work, *Fences*' powerful language is simultaneously stylized and real; the characters' speech is defined by an elegiac rhythm that never veers from emotional truth. Together, these rhythms and truths reveal the emotional (and sometimes physical) violence endured by characters whose fight for survival is not always successful.

JOE TURNER'S COME AND GONE

When *Joe Turner's Come and Gone* was staged at the National Playwrights Conference at the Eugene O'Neill Theater Center in 1984, Wilson was already following back-to-back hits with *Ma Rainey* and *Fences*. Part of what makes *Joe Turner* noteworthy is not merely its individual testament to Wilson's prowess as a playwright but also his ability to create important and powerful work with a consistency few playwrights in the world can boast. After premiering under Lloyd Richards' direction at the Yale Repertory Theatre on April 29, 1986, *Joe Turner* was later staged at the Arena Stage with a slightly different cast and Richards still directing on October 2, 1987. The play made its Broadway debut on March 26, 1988, at the Ethel Barrymore Theatre, where it ran for 105 performances. Its 2009 revival on Broadway opened on March 19 and ran for 69 performances at the Belasco Theatre. The original Broadway production won the 1988 New York Drama Critics' Circle Award (Best Play) and was nominated for the Drama Desk Award (Best Play) and Tony Award (Best Play).

Exploring the 1910s, the often mystical, beautifully poetic *Joe Turner's Come and Gone* takes place in a 1911 Pittsburgh boardinghouse run by Seth Holly and his wife, Bertha. As with *Fences*' Troy Maxson, *Ma Rainey's* Levee, and *The Piano Lesson*'s Boy Willie, *Joe Turner*'s Seth is a man driven by dreams of economic success, personal freedom and expression, and self-determination. Seth's unquenchable entrepreneurial spirit does not end with his role as landlord of the rooming house he runs with Bertha; part of his income comes from the metal kitchen paraphernalia he makes from the raw materials he buys from a white man: Rutherford Selig, a "people finder" who then takes Seth's finished products and sells them door-to-door. Seth is certain that riches are there to be made if only he could secure the funds to buy more raw material and hire workers to help him create more product.

The rooming house's boarders reflect the loneliness and cruelty faced by African Americans who are desperate to make meaning and connections in lives that have all too recently been freed from slavery. Indeed, the play suggests that the pseudo-kin connection—the makeshift family—that the boardinghouse literally and metaphorically affords is the only hope for many of its occupants. Wilson describes these men and women in the play's front matter: "Foreigners in a strange land, they carry as part and parcel of their baggage a long line of separation and dispersement which informs their sensibilities and marks their conduct as they search for ways to reconnect, to reassemble, to give clear and luminous meaning to the song which is both a wail and a whelp of joy" (p. xii). The "baggage" to which Wilson refers is of course more than literal. Each character who resides in the "temporary" home of the rooming house is searching for some connection—to each other or to a shared cultural past—after the pain and loss that has fueled their travels.

Through the plays' engagement with "migration," a concept imbued in the very definition of a rooming house and its transient occupants, Wilson also speaks to the often painful challenges of the Great Migration—a real-world phenomenon that shows up in several *Century Cycle* plays. But for Wilson, the theme of migration—of transient family units, parents searching for children, spouses separated from spouses—most poignantly harkens to the painful reality of slavery. With family members sold away from each other forever, and makeshift kin networks sometimes providing the only connections available to a human being, the legacy of painful migration and the consequent "searching for one's people" became a painful reality.

Perhaps the most dramatic characters who are in search of connection in *Joe Turner* are the brooding and mysterious Loomis, a sometimes intimidating but also heartbroken man whose stint in prison helped put miles and years between him and his wife, and Loomis' eleven-year-old daughter, Zonia. The two are desperately searching for Zonia's mother, Martha. With periodic tips provided by the rooming house's "conjure man," Bynum Walker, and the sporadically successful "people finder," Selig, Martha finally appears in the play's climactic final scene. While it is revealed that the social and legal forces that kept the family apart were typically cruel, out of their control, and racially motivated, Martha also confesses to Loomis that she gave up waiting for him and has moved on.

Loomis' rage that follows is significant not just for the immediate violence that results. With a campaign of self-destruction that mirrors *Ma Rainey*'s Levee, Loomis' lifetime of oppression and rage culminate in physical aggression as he slashes his own chest. Loomis' fury is equally relevant for *what* he expresses as he engages in self-harm. "Having found his song, the song of self-sufficiency, fully resurrected, cleansed and given breath," Wilson writes in parenthetical stage direction, "having accepted the responsibility for his own presence in the world, [Loomis] is free to soar about the environs that weighed and pushed his spirit into terrifying contractions" (pp. 93–94). Accompanying Wilson's telling description are Loomis' words themselves, in which he condemns the Christian ideology, which, not unlike the passive resistance of the early civil rights movement, preached peace and accommodation in the face of injustice (not to mention the promise of redemption and reward only after death). Refusing Christian "salvation" and the empty promises that come with being "baptized with the blood of the lamb and the fire of the Holy Ghost" (p. 93), Loomis takes matters (and his destiny) into his own hands and literally and figuratively baptizes himself in his own blood, perhaps also his people's blood, and in a pseudo-baptismal rite, is reborn.

This critical interrogation of Western spiritual practice (or outright dismissal of Christianity) is also seen in one of the play's most important scenes, when in the first act the rooming-house residents engage in a Bynum-led *juba*. Part celebration, part spiritual calling out, part ancestral tribute, and part possession, the juba is, as Williams writes, "reminiscent of the ring shouts of the African slaves. It is a call and response dance ... It should be as African as possible, with the performers working themselves up into a near frenzy. The words can be improvised, but should include some mention of the Holy Ghost" (p. 52).

As is true of the play itself—arguably true of the entire *Century Cycle*—the juba, like Loomis' final dramatic exit, is an affirmation of black spiritual life and experience that, while dismissing the Western traditions which often misrepresent or erase it, also speaks to a universality of human suffering and triumph, no doubt due to the emotional truth that supports its telling.

THE PIANO LESSON

When Lloyd Richards and the Eugene O'Neill Theater Center selected *The Piano Lesson* for its 1987 National Playwrights Conference, it was the fourth Wilson play to be staged at the center and, like its predecessors, it went on to triumphant success. After its 1987 professional premiere at the Yale Repertory Theatre, *The Piano Lesson* opened on April 16, 1990, at Broadway's Walter Kerr Theatre, where it ran for 328 performances.

Under Lloyd Richards' direction, this fifth play in Wilson's *Century Cycle* earned numerous awards in 1990, including the Drama Desk Award (Outstanding New Play), the New York Drama Critics' Circle Award (Best Play), and the Pulitzer Prize for Drama. *The Piano Lesson*'s 2013 revival off Broadway was similarly recognized, winning the Lucille Lortel Award for Outstanding Revival. The play was adapted into a made-for-television film, which aired on CBS in 1995 and, like the original stage production, was directed by Lloyd Richards.

As the play in Wilson's *Century Cycle* that explores the 1930s, *The Piano Lesson* interrogates, among other things, the experiences of African Americans living in northern cities and the varied (dis)connections they experience as a result of the Great Migration. One of the greatest shifts of human population in the world and certainly in U.S. history, the Great Migration occurred from the 1910s through the 1970s as approximately six million African Americans (such as Wilson's maternal grandmother) left the rural American south in search of jobs and the promise of a safer life. The disconnection the play's characters face is literal, as they no longer live in the geographic landscape their family called home, but the emotional and spiritual disconnection the characters endure is far costlier. With *The Piano Lesson,* Wilson articulates most explicitly a theme his plays (and his politics) revisited for the rest of his career: the complicated and painful dilemma of how to claim or make peace with your legacy when your history has been erased, misrepresented, or, in the case of the play's titular piano, literally stolen.

When the play begins, several Charles family members are about to be reunited, so to speak. Berniece, her uncle Doaker, and her daughter Maretha have been living in Doaker's Hill District home since leaving their family in Mississippi. Berniece's brother Boy Willie, a sharecropper who has himself worked the land their family has lived on for generations, has just shown up with his friend Lymon, announcing at first that his trip is motivated by the truckload of watermelons that he and Lymon have brought with them to sell. It is eventually revealed that Boy Willie's plans actually involve selling the priceless family piano that belongs to him and his sister and that currently resides with Berniece. If sold, the piano could garner enough funds to enable Boy Willie to finally buy the piece of Mississippi land that his family has worked for generations, sometimes as slaves, and that carries the literal and figurative blood of the Charles family in its soil.

The piano is not merely a musical instrument. As both a figurative and a literal documentation of the family's history, its pain, and its enduring strength, the piano is a historical document in every sense of the word. The piano's beautiful carvings—initially created by and then painstakingly polished with the blood of Charles family ancestors—details not just family members' individual likenesses but entire scenes that form a kind of narrative of the family's past under the ownership and then the financial power of the landowning, formerly slave-owning Sutters. Adding to the piano's relevance to the Charles family's legacy, the one-of-a-kind instrument was initially purchased by a Sutter ancestor with money he accumulated by selling off and separating a Charles mother and son. Indeed, the carvings that made the piano priceless were done by an abandoned son hoping to keep the memory of his separated family alive. When Boy Willie and Berniece's father later attempted to steal the piano back from Sutter, the father was captured and killed. The piano, quite literally, bears the blood, tears, and soul of a family and its legacy.

In many ways, *The Piano Lesson* pulls at two threads that much of Wilson's work explores in depth: the presence of a (frequently non-Western, non-Christian, African) spirituality as a force in his characters' lives, and the role of music (and the blues in particular) as means to document and communicate one's life, history, and pain—but also as a mechanism to understand all of those things in the first place.

The spiritual components of the play are informed by a celebration of African belief systems and spiritual practice (including music) as a way of understanding and preserving cultural legacy. In the play's first scene, in fact, Berniece suspects that Boy Willie has actually pushed the landowner Sutter down a well to facilitate his death (and the hoped-for purchase of his land), and she is convinced that Sutter's ghost is now appearing in the Hill District home. In the play's second act, it is Doaker who believes he has seen Sutter's ghost, while elsewhere—and perhaps more significantly—Berniece fears the rising anger of her late family members' spirits as Boy Willie pushes for a sale of the piano. Berniece's friend Avery—tellingly, a Christian preacher—fails in his attempt to appease both Berniece's fears and the rage of the ancestors with practices and discourse rooted in Western faith traditions. It is not until the play's conclusion, as the brother and sister's fight over what to do with the piano comes to a powerful climax, that the anguish of the ancestors' spirits and the pain of the present seem to collide and reconcile.

Not accidentally, the climactic final scene takes place with and around the piano, and Berniece's playing specifically. Although she used to play frequently, especially for her late mother, the loss and bitterness of Berniece's life have resulted in her steady refusal to make music and, metaphorically, face her pain. Amid an intense confrontation fueled by Boy Willie's attempt to remove the piano from the home after he has sold it without his sister's permission, Berniece uses her late husband's gun to try to force her brother to back down. Sutter's ghost is again dramatically revived, this time explicitly, and despite Avery's failed Christianity-informed attempts to remove the angry spirit, it is only Berniece's at-times-frenzied piano playing that acts as a legitimate (and eventually successful) plea to her ancestors. Wilson describes her actions in a manner that befits spiritual rebirth as much as emotional breakthrough:

> It is in this moment, from somewhere old, that Berniece realizes what she must do. She crosses to the piano. She begins to play. The song is found piece by piece. It is an old urge to sing that is both a commandment and a plea. With each repetition it gains in strength. It is intended as an exorcism and a dressing for battle. A rustle of wind blowing across two continents.
>
> (p. 106)

This climactic reconciliation of past and present, using music as the language of healing and legacy, is not unlike a moment earlier in the play when Doaker's musician brother, Wining Boy, bursts into a joyous boogie-woogie and blues. As another of the play's musical interludes, Wining Boy's music functions as an instructional moment of cultural history as well as celebration. A wandering musician and a gambler whose most consistent connection in life is his relationship with the blues, Wining Boy himself emerges in the play as a kind of griot, or West African storyteller. Similar to the role of "priestess" that Berniece fulfills in the play's final scene as she attempts to lead her family and ancestors out of the painful past using the only thing she can, music, Wining Boy performs the role of storyteller, using the blues as a language of joy and misery alike—a description that fits Wilson's play as well.

Selected Bibliography

WORKS OF AUGUST WILSON

The Coldest Day of the Year. First produced at the Black Horizons Theater, Pittsburgh, Pa., 1976.

The Homecoming. First produced at the Kuntu Repertory Theatre, Pittsburgh, Pa., 1976.

Black Bart and the Sacred Hills. First produced at the Penumbra Theatre, St. Paul, Minn., 1977.

Fullerton Street. First produced at the Allegheny Repertory Theatre in Pittsburgh, Pa., 1980.

Ma Rainey's Black Bottom: A Play in Two Acts. New York: New American Library, 1985.

Fences: A Play. New York: Plume/Penguin, 1986.

Joe Turner's Come and Gone: A Play in Two Acts. New York: New American Library, 1988.

The Piano Lesson. New York: Plume, 1990.

Two Trains Running. New York: Plume, 1991.

Seven Guitars. New York: Dutton, 1996.

Jitney. Woodstock, N.Y.: Overlook Press, 2000.

The Ground on Which I Stand. New York: Theatre Communications Group, 2001.

How I Learned What I Learned. First produced at the Seattle Repertory Theatre, 2003.

King Hedley II. New York: Theatre Communications Group, 2005.

Gem of the Ocean. New York: Theatre Communications Group, 2006.

August Wilson Century Cycle. New York: Theatre Communications Group, 2007. (With a series introduction by John Lahr; individual volumes introduced by Laurence Fishburne, Samuel G. Freedman, Tony Kushner, Romulus Linney, Marion McClinton, Toni Morrison, Suzan-Lori Parks, Phylicia Rashad, Ishmael Reed, and Frank Rich.)

Radio Golf. New York: Theatre Communications Group, 2007.

ELECTRONIC MEDIA AND FILM ADAPTATIONS

Ma Rainey's Black Bottom: Original Cast Album. Manhattan Records, 1985. (LP record.)

"A World of Ideas: August Wilson." *Bill Moyers Journal.* PBS Television, 1989. http://www.pbs.org/moyers/journal/archives/wilsonwoi_flash.html

August Wilson: The American Dream, in Black and White. Directed by Tony Knox. Films Media Group, 1990. (DVD.)

The Piano Lesson. Directed by Lloyd Richards. Performed by Charles S. Dutton, Alfre Woodard, Carl Gordon, Tommy Hollis, Lou Myers, Courtney B. Vance. Hallmark Home Entertainment, 2006. (Television movie.)

August Wilson: The Ground on Which I Stand. Directed by Sam Pollard. PBS, 2015. (Television documentary.)

Fences. Directed by Denzel Washington. Performed by Denzel Washington, Viola Davis, Mykelti Williamson, Stephen Henderson, Russel Hornsby. Paramount Pictures, 2016. (Major motion picture.)

CRITICAL AND BIOGRAPHICAL STUDIES

Bigsby, C. W. E. *The Cambridge Companion to August Wilson.* New York: Cambridge University Press, 2007.

Bloom, Harlold. *August Wilson.* Broomhall, Pa.: Chelsea House, 2002.

Bogumil, Mary L. *Understanding August Wilson.* Columbia: University of South Carolina Press, 1999.

Booker, Margaret. *Lillian Hellman and August Wilson: Dramatizing a New American Identity.* New York: Peter Lang, 2003.

Bryer, Jackson R., and Mary C. Hartig. *Conversations with August Wilson.* Jackson: University Press of Mississippi, 2006.

Clark, Keith. *Black Manhood in James Baldwin, Ernest J. Gaines, and August Wilson.* Urbana: University of Illinois Press, 2002.

Elam, Harry Justin. "August Wilson, Doubling, Madness, and Modern African American Drama." *Modern Drama* 43, no. 4:611–632 (2000).

———. *The Past as Present in the Drama of August Wilson.* Ann Arbor: University of Michigan Press, 2004.

———. "Teaching *Joe Turner's Come and Gone.*" *Modern Drama* 50, no. 4:582–600 (2007).

Elkins, Marilyn Roberson. *August Wilson: A Casebook.* New York: Garland, 1994.

Grimes, William. "Face-to-Face Encounter on Race in the Theater." *New York Times,* January 29, 1997. http://www.nytimes.com/1997/01/29/theater/face-to-face-encounter-on-race-in-the-theater.html

Hanlon, John J. "'Nig*ers Got a Right to be Dissatisfied': Postmodernism, Race, and Class in *Ma Rainey's Black Bottom.*" *Modern Drama* 45, no. 1:95–124 (2002).

Harrison, Paul Carter. "August Wilson's Blues Poetics." In *August Wilson: Three Plays.* Pittsburgh, Pa.: University of Pittsburgh Press, 1991. Pp. 291–318.

———, moderator. "August Wilson and Derek Walcott: A Conversation." *Black Renaissance/Renaissance Noire* 9, nos. 2–3:24ff (2009).

Heard, Elisabeth J. "August Wilson on Playwriting: An Interview." *African American Review* 35, no. 1:93 (2001).

Lyons, Bonnie. "An Interview with August Wilson." *Contemporary Literature* 40, no. 1:1–21 (1999).

Lyons, Bonnie, and George Plimpton. "Interviews: August Wilson, the Art of Theater No. 14." *Paris Review,* no. 153 (winter 1999). http://www.theparisreview.org/interviews/839/the-art-of-theater-no-14-august-wilson

Mills, Alice. "The Walking Blues: An Anthropological Approach to the Theater of August Wilson." *Black Scholar* 25, no. 2:30–35 (1995).

Nadel, Alan. *May All Your Fences Have Gates: Essays on the Drama of August Wilson.* Iowa City: University of Iowa Press, 1994.

———. "August Wilson and the (Color Blind) Whiteness of Public Space." *Theater* 27, nos. 2–3:38–41 (1998).

———. *August Wilson: Completing the Twentieth-Century Cycle.* Iowa City: University of Iowa Press, 2010.

Pease, Donald E. "August Wilson's Lazarus Complex." *Criticism* 51, no. 1:1–28 (2009).

Pereira, Kim. *August Wilson and the African-American Odyssey.* Urbana: University of Illinois Press, 1995.

Plum, Jay. "Blues, History, and the Dramaturgy of August Wilson." *African American Review* 27, no. 4:561–567 (1993).

Roberts, Jackie M. "Healing Myths from the Ethnic Community; or, Why I Don't Teach August Wilson." *Theatre Topics* 20, no. 2:147–156 (2010).

Shafer, Yvonne. *August Wilson: A Research and Production Sourcebook.* Westport, Conn.: Greenwood Press, 1998.

Shannon, Sandra Garrett. "The Good Christian's Come and Gone: The Shifting Role of Christianity in August Wilson Plays." *MELUS* 16, no. 3:127–142 (1989).

———. *The Dramatic Vision of August Wilson.* Washington, D.C.: Howard University Press, 1995.

Shannon, Sandra Garrett, and Dana A. Williams. *August Wilson and Black Aesthetics.* New York: Palgrave Macmillan, 2004.

Snodgrass, Mary Ellen. *August Wilson: A Literary Companion.* Jefferson, N.C.: McFarland, 2004.

Cumulative Index

All references include volume numbers in boldface roman numerals followed by page numbers within that volume. Subjects of articles are indicated by boldface type.

"A" (Zukofsky), **Supp. III Part 2:** 611, 612, 614, 617, 619, 620, 621, 622, 623, 624, 626, 627, 628, 629, 630, 631; **Supp. IV Part 1:** 154; **Supp. XVI:** 287, 287
Aal, Katharyn Machan, **Supp. IV Part 1:** 332; **Supp. XXIII:** 54
Aaron, Daniel, **IV:** 429; **Supp. I Part 2:** 647, 650
Aaron's Rod (Lawrence), **Supp. I Part 1:** 255
Abacus (Karr), **Supp. XI: 240–242,** 248, 254
Abádi-Nagy, Zoltán, **Supp. IV Part 1:** 280, 289, 291
"Abandoned Farmhouse" (Kooser), **Supp. XIX:** 117, 119
"Abandoned House, The" (L. Michaels), **Supp. XVI:** 214
"Abandoned Newborn, The" (Olds), **Supp. X:** 207
"Abandoned Stone Schoolhouse in the Nebraska Sandhills, An" (Kooser), **Supp. XIX:** 124–125
"Abba Jacob" (Nelson), **Supp. XVIII:** 177
"Abbé François Picquet"(Kenny), **Supp. XXIII:** 153
Abbey, Edward, **Supp. VIII:** 42; **Supp. X:** 24, 29, 30, 31, 36; **Supp. XIII: 1–18; Supp. XIV:** 179; **Supp. XXV:** 208; **Supp. XXVI:** 31, 37
Abbey's Road (Abbey), **Supp. XIII:** 12
Abbott, Carl, **Supp. XVIII:** 142
Abbott, Clifford F., **Supp. XXVI:** 89
Abbott, Edith, **Supp. I Part 1:** 5
Abbott, Jack Henry, **Retro. Supp. II:** 210
Abbott, Jacob, **Supp. I Part 1:** 38, 39
Abbott, Lyman, **III:** 293
Abbott, Sean, **Retro. Supp. II:** 213
ABC of Color, An: Selections from Over a Half Century of Writings (Du Bois), **Supp. II Part 1:** 186
ABC of Reading (Pound), **III:** 468, 474–475
"Abdication, An" (Merrill), **Supp. III Part 1:** 326
'Abdu'l-Bahá, **Supp. XX: 117, 122**
Abel, Lionel, **Supp. XIII:** 98
Abel, Sam, **Supp. XIII:** 199
Abelard, Peter, **I:** 14, 22
Abeles, Sigmund, **Supp. VIII:** 272
Abeng (Cliff), **Supp. XXII:** 66, 69–71
Abercrombie, Joe, **Supp. XXV:** 74
Abercrombie, Lascelles, **III:** 471; **Retro. Supp. I:** 127, 128
Abernathy, Milton, **Supp. III Part 2:** 616
Abernon, Edgar Vincent, Viscount d', **Supp. XVI:** 191
Aberration of Starlight (Sorrentino), **Supp. XXI:** 234–235
Abhau, Anna. See Mencken, Mrs. August (Anna Abhau)
"Abide with Me" (Hoffman), **Supp. XVIII:** 86
Abide with Me (Strout), **Supp. XXIII:** 273, 275, **278–280,** 285
"Ability" (Emerson), **II:** 6
Abingdon, Alexander, **Supp. XVI:** 99
Abish, Walter, **Supp. V:** 44
"Abishag" (Glück), **Supp. V:** 82
"Abnegation, The" (Bronk), **Supp. XXI:** 32
Abney, Lisa, **Supp. XXII:** 9
Abood, Maureen, **Supp. XXII:** 90
"Abortion, The" (Sexton), **Supp. II Part 2:** 682
"Abortions" (Dixon), **Supp. XII:** 153
"About C. D. Wright" (Colburn), **Supp. XV:** 341
"About Effie" (Findley), **Supp. XX: 50**
"About Hospitality" (Jewett), **Retro. Supp. II:** 131
"About Kathryn" (Dubus), **Supp. VII:** 91
"About Language" (Wrigley), **Supp. XVIII:** 300–301
"About Looking Alone at a Place: Arles" (M. F. K. Fisher), **Supp. XVII:** 89, 91
About the House (Auden), **Supp. II Part 1:** 24
About These Stories: Fiction for Fiction Writers and Readers (Huddle, ed.), **Supp. XXVI:** 160
About Town: "The New Yorker" and the World It Made (Yagoda), **Supp. VIII:** 151
"About Zhivago and His Poems"(O'Hara), **Supp. XXIII:** 214
"Above Pate Valley" (Snyder), **Supp. VIII:** 293
Above the River (Wright), **Supp. III Part 2:** 589, 606
Above the Waterfall (Rash), **Supp. XXVII:** 221, 225, 226–227, 228
"Abraham" (Schwartz), **Supp. II Part 2:** 663
Abraham, Nelson Algren. See Algren, Nelson
Abraham, Pearl, **Supp. XVII:** 49; **Supp. XX: 177; Supp. XXIV: 1–15**
"Abraham Davenport" (Whittier), **Supp. I Part 2:** 699
"Abraham Lincoln" (Emerson), **II:** 13
Abraham Lincoln: The Prairie Years (Sandburg), **III:** 580, 587–589, 590
Abraham Lincoln: The Prairie Years and the War Years (Sandburg), **III:** 588, 590
Abraham Lincoln: The War Years (Sandburg), **III:** 588, 589–590; **Supp. XVII:** 105
"Abraham Lincoln Walks at Midnight" (Lindsay), **Supp. I Part 2:** 390–391
"Abram Morrison" (Whittier), **Supp. I Part 2:** 699
Abramovich, Alex, **Supp. X:** 302, 309
Abrams, David, **Supp. XXII:** 61
Abrams, M. H., **Supp. XVI:** 19; **Supp. XXIII:** 42
Abridgment of Universal Geography,

An: Together with Sketches of History (Rowson), **Supp. XV:** 243
"Absalom" (Rukeyser), **Supp. VI:** 278–279
Absalom, Absalom! (Faulkner), **II:** 64, 65–67, 72, 223; **IV:** 207; **Retro. Supp. I:** 75, 81, 82, 84, 85, 86, 87, 88, 89, 90, 92, 382; **Retro. Supp. III:** 74, 80, 83–84; **Supp. V:** 261; **Supp. X:** 51; **Supp. XIV:** 12–13; **Supp. XXVI:** 8, 12
"Absence"(J. Schoolcraft), **Supp. XXIII:** 228, 231
"Absence of Mercy" (Stone), **Supp. V:** 295
"Absentee, The" (Levertov), **Supp. III Part 1:** 284
Absentee Ownership (Veblen), **Supp. I Part 2:** 642
"Absent-Minded Bartender" (X. J. Kennedy), **Supp. XV:** 159
"Absent Thee from Felicity Awhile" (Wylie), **Supp. I Part 2:** 727, 729
Absolutely True Diary of a Part-Time Indian, The (Alexie), **Supp. XXVI:** 108
"Absolution" (Fitzgerald), **Retro. Supp. I:** 108
"Absolution" (Sobin), **Supp. XVI:** 289
"Abuelita's Ache" (Mora), **Supp. XIII:** 218
Abysmal Brute, The (London), **II:** 467
Abyssinia and the Imperialists (C. L. R. James), **Supp. XXI:** 166
Abyss of Human Illusion, The (Sorrentino), **Supp. XXI:** 225, 227, 237–238
"Academic Story, An" (Simpson), **Supp. IX:** 279–280
"Academic Zoo, The: Theory—in Practice" (Epstein), **Supp. XIV:** 107–108, 109
"A Capella" (Wrigley), **Supp. XVIII:** 300
"Accident" (Minot), **Supp. VI: 208–209**
"Accident" (Munro), **Supp. XXVII:** 188
"Accident, The" (Southern), **Supp. XI:** 295
"Accident, The" (Strand), **Supp. IV Part 2:** 624
Accident/A Day's News (Wolf), **Supp. IV Part 1:** 310
Accidental Tourist, The (Tyler), **Supp. IV Part 2:** 657, 668–669; **Supp. V:** 227
Accordion Crimes (Proulx), **Supp. VII:** 259–261
"Accountability" (Dunbar), **Supp. II Part 1:** 197, 204
"Account of the Method of Drawing Birds" (Audubon), **Supp. XVI:** 12
"Accusation, The" (Wright), **Supp. III Part 2:** 595
"Accusation of the Inward Man, The" (Taylor), **IV:** 156
"Accusing Message from Dead Father" (Karr), **Supp. XI:** 244
Ace, Goodman, **Supp. IV Part 2:** 574
Ache of Appetite, The (Hadas), **Supp. XXIII: 120–121**
Achievement in American Poetry (Bogan), **Supp. III Part 1:** 63–64
Acker, Kathy, **Supp. XII:1–20; Supp. XXI:** 236
Ackerley, J. R., **Supp. XX: 237**
Ackerman, Diane, **Supp. XIII:** 154
"Acknowledgment" (Lanier), **Supp. I Part 1:** 364
"Acknowledgment, Adaptation, and Shakespeare in Ron Rash's Serena" (Morrow), **Supp. XXVII:** 216
Ackroyd, Peter, **Supp. V:** 233; **Supp. XVII:** 180
"Acquaintance in the Heavens, An" (Dillard), **Supp. VI:** 34
"Acquainted with the Night" (Frost), **II:** 155; **Retro. Supp. I:** 137; **Retro. Supp. III:** 102; **Supp. XXI:** 26
Across Spoon River (Masters), **Supp. I Part 2:** 455, 457, 459, 460, 466, 474–475, 476
Across the Layers: Poems Old and New (Goldbarth), **Supp. XII:** 181, **187–189**
Across the River and into the Trees (Hemingway), **I:** 491; **II:** 255–256, 261; **Retro. Supp. I:** 172, **184–185; Supp. XIX:** 248
"Acteon" (Stallings), **Supp. XXV:** 231–232
"Actfive" (MacLeish), **III:** 18–19, 22
Actfive and Other Poems (MacLeish), **III:** 3, 17–19, 21
Action (Shepard), **Supp. III Part 2:** 446
Active Anthology (Pound, ed.), **Supp. III Part 2:** 617; **Supp. XXVI:** 224
Active Service (Crane), **I:** 409
"Act of Creation and Its Artifact, The" (Sorrentino), **Supp. XXI:** 229, 235
Act of Love (film), **Supp. XXVI:** 136
Act of Love, An (Wolfert), **Supp. XXI:** 270**, 275–277**
Act of Love, An: A Completely Retold Version of the Novel (Wolfert), **Supp. XXI:** 276
Acton, Patricia Nassif, **Supp. X:** 233
Actors and Sin (film), **Supp. XXVII:** 94
"Actor's Blood" (Hecht), **Supp. XXVII:** 94
Actor's Nightmare, The (Durang), **Supp. XXIV:** 116, 119
Acts and Monuments of These Latter and Perilous Days (Fox), **Supp. XXII:** 36
Acts of Faith (Caputo), **Supp. XIX: 29–30**
"Acts of the Apostles, The" (Bronk), **Supp. XXI:** 28
Actual, The (Bellow), **Retro. Supp. II:** 33
"Actual Experience, Preferred Narratives" (Julier), **Supp. IV Part 1:** 211
Acuff, Roy, **Supp. V:** 335
Ada (Nabokov), **Retro. Supp. I:** 265, 266, 270, 276–277, 278, 279
"Ada" (Stein), **IV:** 43
"Adagia" (Stevens), **IV:** 78, 80, 88, 92
"Adagio" (Hull), **Supp. XXI:** 136–137
"Adam" (Hecht), **Supp. X:** 62
"Adam" (W. C. Williams), **Retro. Supp. I:** 422, 423
"Adam and Eve" (Eugene), **Supp. X:** 204
"Adam and Eve" (Shapiro), **Supp. II Part 2:** 708, 712
"Adamantine Practice of Poetry, The" (Wright), **Supp. XV:** 341–342, 343–344
Adam Bede (G. Eliot), **II:** 181
Adamé, Leonard, **Supp. XIII:** 316
Adam & Eve & the City (W. C. Williams), **Retro. Supp. I:** 423
Adamic, Louis, **Supp. XXIII:** 166
"Adamic Purity as Double Agent" (Whalen-Bridge), **Retro. Supp. II:** 211–212
"Adam Robinson Acquires Grandparents and a Little Sister" (P. E. Jones), **Supp. XXII:** 151
"Adams" (Saunders), **Supp. XIX:** 232
Adams, Althea. See Thurber, Mrs. James (Althea Adams)
Adams, Annie. See Fields, Annie Adams
Adams, Brooks, **Supp. I Part 2:** 484
Adams, Charles, **Supp. I Part 2:** 644
Adams, Charles Francis, **I:** 1, 4; **Supp. I Part 2:** 484
Adams, Franklin P., **Supp. I Part 2:** 653; **Supp. IX:** 190; **Supp. XV:** 294, 297
Adams, Henry, **I: 1–24,** 111, 243, 258; **II:** 278, 542; **III:** 396, 504; **IV:** 191, 349; **Retro. Supp. I:** 53, 59; **Retro. Supp. II:** 207; **Supp. I Part 1:** 299–

300, 301, 314; **Supp. I Part 2:** 417, 492, 543, 644; **Supp. II Part 1:** 93–94, 105; **Supp. III Part 2:** 613; **Supp. IV Part 1:** 31, 208; **Supp. XXIV:** 224
Adams, Mrs. Henry (Marian Hooper), **I:** 1, 5, 10, 17–18
Adams, Henry B., **Supp. I Part 1:** 369
Adams, James Truslow, **Supp. I Part 2:** 481, 484, 486
Adams, J. Donald, **IV:** 438
Adams, John, **I:** 1; **II:** 103, 301; **III:** 17, 473; **Supp. I Part 2:** 483, 506, 507, 509, 510, 511, 517, 518, 520, 524
Adams, John Luther, **Supp. XII:** 209
Adams, John Quincy, **I:** 1, 3, 16–17; **Supp. I Part 2:** 685, 686
Adams, Léonie, **Supp. I Part 2:** 707; **Supp. IX:** 229; **Supp. V:** 79; **Supp. XVII:** 75
Adams, Luella, **Supp. I Part 2:** 652
Adams, Noah, **Supp. XVII:** 218
Adams, Phineas, **Supp. XXV:** 37
Adams, Phoebe, **Supp. IV Part 1:** 203; **Supp. VIII:** 124
Adams, Samuel, **Supp. I Part 2:** 516, 525
Adams, Tim, **Supp. XXVII:** 269
Adams, Timothy Dow, **Supp. XVI:** 67, 69
Ada; or Ardor (Nabokov), **III:** 247
Adaptation (film), **Supp. XXV:** 160
"Ad Castitatem" (Bogan), **Supp. III Part 1:** 50
Adcock, Betty, **Supp. XVIII:** 181–182, 182
Addams, Jane, **Supp. I Part 1: 1–26; Supp. XI:** 200, 202
Addams, John Huy, **Supp. I Part 1:** 2
"Add Blue to Make White Whiter" (Vaz), **Supp. XXVI:** 263
"Addendum" (Wright), **Supp. V:** 339
Addiego, John, **Supp. XII:** 182
Adding Machine, The (Rice), **I:** 479
Adding Machine, The: Selected Essays (Burroughs), **Supp. III Part 1:** 93, 97
"Adding to the Unhappiness: Those Poems You Are Writing" (Gallagher), **Supp. XXIV:** 172
Addison, Joseph, **I:** 8, 105, 106–107, 108, 114, 131, 300, 304; **III:** 430
"Address Delivered at Lenox, An" (Channing), **Supp. XXIV: 79–80**
"Addressed to a Political Shrimp, or, Fly upon the Wheel" (Freneau), **Supp. II Part 1:** 267
"Address to My Soul" (Wylie), **Supp. I Part 2:** 729
"Address to the Deist, An" (Wheatley), **Supp. XX: 287**
"Address to the Devil" (Jarman), **Supp. XVII:** 114
Address to the Government of the United States on the Cession of Louisiana to the French, An (Brown), **Supp. I Part 1:** 146
"Address to the Scholars of New England" (Ransom), **III:** 491
"Address with Exclamation Points, A" (Simic), **Supp. VIII:** 283
"Adieu to Norman, Bon Jour to Joan and Jean-Paul"(O'Hara), **Supp. XXIII:** 219
Adisa, Opal Palmer, **Supp. XXII:** 66, 74, 78
"Adjutant Bird, The" (Banks), **Supp. V:** 5
Adkins, Nelson F., **II:** 20
Adler, Alfred, **I:** 248
Adler, Betty, **III:** 103
Adler, George J., **III:** 81
Adler, Renata, **Supp. X:** 171
Adler, Stella, **Retro. Supp. III:** 171
Admiral of the Ocean Sea: A Life of Christopher Columbus (Morison), **Supp. I Part 2:** 486–488
"Admirals" (Chabon), **Supp. XI:** 72
"Admonition, An" (Brodsky), **Supp. VIII:** 33
"Adolescence" (Bidart), **Supp. XV:** 32
"Adolescence" (Dove), **Supp. IV Part 1:** 245
"Adolescence" (Olds), **Supp. X:** 211
"Adolescence II" (Dove), **Supp. IV Part 1:** 242, 244–245
Adolescent's Christmas, An: 1944 (C. Bly), **Supp. XVI:** 31–32
"Adolf Eichmann" (Carruth), **Supp. XVI:** 47
"Adonais" (Shelley), **II:** 516, 540
Adonai: The Pilgrim of Eternity (Lippard), **Supp. XXIII:** 180, 189, 190
Adorno, Theodor, **Supp. I Part 2:** 645, 650; **Supp. IV Part 1:** 301
"Adrienne Rich: The Poetics of Change" (Gelpi), **Supp. I Part 2:** 554
Adrift in Macao (Durang), **Supp. XXIV:** 125
"Adultery" (Banks), **Supp. V:** 15
"Adultery" (Dubus), **Supp. VII:** 85
Adultery and Other Choices (Dubus), **Supp. VII:** 83–85
Adulthood Rites (O. Butler), **Supp. XIII:** 63, **64–65**
Adult Life of Toulouse Lautrec by Henri Toulouse Lautrec, The (Acker), **Supp. XII:** 5, 6, **8–9**
Adventure (London), **II:** 466
Adventures in Ancient Egypt (Goldbarth), **Supp. XII:** 191
Adventures in Value (Cummings), **I:** 430
"Adventures of a Book Reviewer" (Cowley), **Supp. II Part 1:** 137, 142
Adventures of a Novelist (Atherton), **Supp. XXIV:** 17–18, 19–20, 21
Adventures of Augie March, The (Bellow), **I:** 144, 147, 149, 150, 151, 152–153, 154, 155, 157, 158–159, 164; **Retro. Supp. II:** 19, 20, **22–23,** 24, 30; **Supp. VIII:** 234, 236–237; **Supp. XXIV:** 220
Adventures of a Young Man (Dos Passos), **I:** 488, 489, 492
Adventures of Captain Bonneville (Irving), **II:** 312
Adventures of Harry Franco, The: A Tale of the Great Panic (Briggs), **Supp. XVIII:** 1, 2, 5–8
Adventures of Harry Richmond, The (Meredith), **Supp. XX: 234**
Adventures of Huckleberry Finn, The (Twain), **I:** 307, 506; **II:** 26, 72, 262, 266–268, 290, 418, 430; **III:** 101, 112–113, 357, 554, 558, 577; **IV:** 198, 201–204, 207; **Retro. Supp. I:** 188; **Retro. Supp. II:** 121; **Retro. Supp. III:** 88, 256, 258, 263, 264–265; **Supp. I Part 1:** 247; **Supp. IV Part 1:** 247, 257; **Supp. IV Part 2:** 502; **Supp. V:** 131; **Supp. VIII:** 198; **Supp. X:** 230; **Supp. XII:** 16; **Supp. XVI:** 222; **Supp. XX: 171; Supp. XXII:** 81; **Supp. XXVII:** 104
Adventures of Jimmy (Broughton), **Supp. XV:** 146
Adventures of Roderick Random, The (Smollett), **I:** 134
Adventures of the Letter I (Simpson), **Supp. IX:** 266, **273–274**
Adventures of Tom Sawyer, The (Twain), **II:** 26; **III:** 223, 572, 577; **IV:** 199–200, 203, 204; **Retro. Supp. III:** 255, 258, 262–264; **Supp. I Part 2:** 456, 470; **Supp. XVI:** 66
Adventures While Preaching the Gospel of Beauty (Lindsay), **Supp. I Part 2:** 374, 376, 381, 382–384, 389, 399
Adventures with Ed (Loeffler), **Supp. XIII:** 1
Advertisements for Myself (Mailer), **III:** 27, 35–38, 41–42, 45, 46; **Retro. Supp. II:** 196, 199, 200, 202, 203, 212; **Supp. IV Part 1:** 90, 284;

Supp. XIV: 157; **Supp. XXIV:** 281
"Advertisements for Myself on the Way Out" (Mailer), **III:** 37
Advice (Bodenheim), **Supp. XXV:** 22
"Advice to a Prophet" (Wilbur), **Supp. III Part 2:** 555–557
Advice to a Prophet and Other Poems (Wilbur), **Supp. III Part 2:** 554–558
"Advice to a Raven in Russia" (Barlow), **Supp. II Part 1:** 65, 74, 80, 83
"Advice to Players" (Bidart), **Supp. XV:** 35
Advice to the Lovelorn (film), **Retro. Supp. II:** 328
Advice to the Privileged Orders, Part I (Barlow), **Supp. II Part 1:** 80
Aegerter, Lindsay Pentolfe, **Supp. XXII:** 69
"Aeneas and Dido" (Brodsky), **Supp. VIII:** 24–25
"Aeneas at Washington" (Tate), **IV:** 129
Aeneid (Virgil), **I:** 396; **II:** 542; **III:** 124; **Supp. XV:** 23; **Supp. XXIV:** 162–163
Aeneus Tacticus, **I:** 136
Aerial View (Barabtarlo), **Retro. Supp. I:** 278
"Aeria the Evanescent" (Sobin), **Supp. XVI:** 292
Aeschylus, **I:** 274, 433; **III:** 398; **IV:** 358, 368, 370; **Retro. Supp. I:** 65; **Supp. I Part 2:** 458, 494
Aesop, **I:** 387; **II:** 154, 169, 302; **III:** 587
Aesthetic (Croce), **III:** 610
"Aesthetics" (Mumford), **Supp. II Part 2:** 476
"Aesthetics of Silence, The" (Sontag), **Supp. III Part 2:** 459
"Aesthetics of the Shah" (Olds), **Supp. X:** 205
"Affair at Coulter's Notch, The" (Bierce), **I:** 202
Affaire de viol, Une (C. Himes). See Case of Rape, A (C. Himes)
"Affair of Outposts, An" (Bierce), **I:** 202
Affliction (Banks), **Supp. V:** 15, 16
Affluent Society, The (Galbraith), **Supp. I Part 2:** 648
Afghanistan Picture Show, An: or, How I Saved the World (Vollmann), **Supp. XVII:** 226, **228–229,** 233
"Aficionados, The" (Carver), **Supp. III Part 1:** 137
"Afloat" (Beattie), **Supp. V:** 29
Afloat and Ashore (Cooper), **I:** 351, 355
"Afoot" (P. N. Warren as Kilina), **Supp. XX: 261–262**
Africa, Its Geography, People, and Products (Du Bois), **Supp. II Part 1:** 179
Africa, Its Place in Modern History (Du Bois), **Supp. II Part 1:** 179
"Africa, to My Mother" (D. Diop), **Supp. IV Part 1:** 16
Africana (H. L. Gates, ed.), **Supp. XX: 99**
African American Century, The : How Black Americans Have Shaped Our Country (H. L. Gates), **Supp. XX: 102**
African American Lives (television production), **Supp. XX: 99**
African American Lives 2 (television production), **Supp. XX: 99**
African American National Biography (H. L. Gates, ed.), **Supp. XX: 99**
African American Writers (Smith, ed.), **Supp. XIII:** 115, 127
"African Book" (Hemingway), **II:** 259
"African Chief, The" (Bryant), **Supp. I Part 1:** 168
"African Fragment" (Brooks), **Supp. III Part 1:** 85
African Queen, The (film), **Supp. XI:** 17
"African Roots of War, The" (Du Bois), **Supp. II Part 1:** 174
African Silences (Matthiessen), **Supp. V:** 203
African Treasury, An (Hughes, ed.), **Supp. I Part 1:** 344
"Afrika Revolution" (Baraka), **Supp. II Part 1:** 53
"AFRO-AMERICAN LYRIC" (Baraka), **Supp. II Part 1:** 59
After (Bukiet), **Supp. XVII:** 43, **44–45**
After (Hirshfield), **Supp. XXIII:** 133–135, 139
"After a Greek Proverb" (Stallings), **Supp. XXV:** 225
After All: Last Poems (Matthews), **Supp. IX:** 155, **167–169**
After and Before the Lightning (Ortiz), **Supp. IV Part 2:** 513
"After a Nightmare" (Davison), **Supp. XXVI:** 69
"After a Party" (Salinas), **Supp. XIII:** 327
"After Apple-Picking" (Frost), **Retro. Supp. I:** 126, 128; **Retro. Supp. III:** 97–98
"After Arguing against the Contention That Art Must Come from Discontent" (Stafford), **Supp. XI:** 327
After Confession: Poetry as Autobiography (Harris), **Supp. XIV:** 269
After Confession: Poetry as Autobiography (K. Sontag and D. Graham), **Supp. XV:** 104
"After Cowboy Chicken Came to Town" (Jin), **Supp. XVIII:** 97–98
"After Disappointment" (Jarman), **Supp. XVII:** 118–119
After Disillusion: Poems (Wolf), **Supp. XXII:** 275
"After Edward Hopper: Somebody in a Bar" (Ferry), **Supp. XXIV:** 162
After Experience (Snodgrass), **Supp. VI:** 314–316, 317
"After great pain, a formal feeling comes" (Dickinson), **Retro. Supp. I:** 37
"After Hearing a Waltz by Bartók" (A. Lowell), **II:** 522
After Henry (Didion), **Supp. IV Part 1:** 195, 196, 199, 207, 208, 211
"After Henry" (Didion), **Supp. IV Part 1:** 211
"After Holbein" (Wharton), **IV:** 325; **Retro. Supp. I:** 382
After House, The (Rinehart), **Supp. XXV:** 193
After Ikkyu and Other Poems (Harrison), **Supp. VIII:** 42
"After-Image" (Bierds), **Supp. XVII:** 31–32
"After-Image" (Caldwell), **I:** 309
After-Images: Autobiographical Sketches (Snodgrass), **Supp. VI:** 314, **319–323,** 324, 326–327
After I's (Zukofsky), **Supp. III Part 2:** 628, 629
Afterlife (Monette), **Supp. X:** 153
Afterlife (Updike), **Retro. Supp. I:** 322
Afterlife, The (Levis), **Supp. XI:** 259, **260–264**
"After Magritte" (McClatchy), **Supp. XII:** 264
"After Making Love" (Dunn), **Supp. XI:** 153
Aftermath (Longfellow), **II:** 490
"Aftermath" (Longfellow), **II:** 498
After New Formalism (A. Finch, ed.), **Supp. XVII:** 74
"Afternoon" (Ellison), **Supp. II Part 1:** 238
"Afternoon at MacDowell" (Kenyon), **Supp. VII:** 159
"Afternoon Miracle, An" (O. Henry), **Supp. II Part 1:** 390
Afternoon of a Faun (Hearon), **Supp. VIII: 63–64**
Afternoon of an Author: A Selection of

Uncollected Stories and Essays (Fitzgerald), **II:** 94
"Afternoon of a Playwright" (Thurber), **Supp. I Part 2:** 620
Afternoon of the Unreal (Salinas), **Supp. XIII:** 311, **316–318**
"Afternoon with the Old Man, An" (Dubus), **Supp. VII:** 84
"After Parting" (Teasdale), **Supp. XXVII:** 283
"After Punishment Was Done with Me" (Olds), **Supp. X:** 213
"After Reading Barely and Widely," (Zukofsky), **Supp. III Part 2:** 625, 631
"After Reading 'In the Clearing' for the Author, Robert Frost" (Corso), **Supp. XII:** 130
"After Reading Mickey in the Night Kitchen for the Third Time before Bed" (Dove), **Supp. IV Part 1:** 249
"After Reading the Greek Poet"(Kenny), **Supp. XXIII:** 150
"After Reading Tu Fu, I Go Outside to the Dwarf Orchard" (Wright), **Supp. V:** 343
"After Reading Wang Wei, I Go Outside to the Full Moon" (Wright), **Supp. V:** 343
Aftershocks (Stallings), **Supp. XXV:** 222
"Aftershocks" (Stallings), **Supp. XXV:** 222, 231
After Shocks, Near Escapes (Dobyns), **Supp. XIII: 80–82**
"After Song, An" (W. C. Williams), **Retro. Supp. I:** 413
After Strange Gods (T. S. Eliot), **I:** 588
After Such Knowledge: Memory, History, and the Legacy of the Holocaust (E. Hoffman), **Supp. XVI:** 152–153, **158–161**
"After the Alphabets" (Merwin), **Supp. III Part 1:** 356
"After the Argument" (Dunn), **Supp. XI:** 149
"After the Baptism" (C. Bly), **Supp. XVI:** 40
"After the Burial" (J. R. Lowell), **Supp. I Part 2:** 409
"After the Curfew" (Holmes), **Supp. I Part 1:** 308
"After the Death of John Brown" (Thoreau), **IV:** 185
"After the Denim" (Carver), **Supp. III Part 1:** 144
"After the Dentist" (Swenson), **Supp. IV Part 2:** 645
After the Fall (A. Miller), **III:** 148, 149, 156, 161, 162, 163–165, 166; **Retro. Supp. III:** 170–172, 175–176
"After the Fire" (Merrill), **Supp. III Part 1:** 328
"After the Flood" (Sanders), **Supp. XVI:** 274–275
After the Fox (film), **Supp. IV Part 2:** 575
After the Genteel Tradition (Cowley), **Supp. II Part 1:** 143
"After the Heart's Interrogation" (Komunyakaa), **Supp. XIII:** 120
After the Lost Generation: A Critical Study of the Writers of Two Wars (Aldridge), **Supp. IV Part 2:** 680; **Supp. XIX:** 250
"After the Night Office—Gethsemani Abbey" (Merton), **Supp. VIII:** 195–196
After the Others (Weigl), **Supp. XIX:** 282, 283–284
"After the Persian" (Bogan), **Supp. III Part 1:** 64
After the Plague (Boyle), **Supp. XX: 20**
"After the Plague" (Boyle), **Supp. XX: 20**
"After the Pleasure Party" (Melville), **III:** 93
"After the Rain" (Halliday), **Supp. XIX:** 91
"After the Resolution" (Dunn), **Supp. XI:** 151
After the Stroke (Sarton), **Supp. VIII:** 264
"After the Surprising Conversions" (R. Lowell), **I:** 544, 545; **II:** 550; **Retro. Supp. II:** 187
"After 37 Years My Mother Apologizes for My Childhood" (Olds), **Supp. X:** 208
After This (McDermott), **Supp. XVIII:** 155, **166–167**
Afterthoughts (L. P. Smith), **Supp. XIV:** 339, 345
"Afterthoughts on the Rosenbergs" (Fiedler), **Supp. XIII:** 99
"After Twenty Years" (Rich), **Supp. I Part 2:** 559–560
"Afterwake, The" (Rich), **Supp. I Part 2:** 553
"Afterward" (Wharton), **Retro. Supp. I:** 372
"Afterword"(Hadas), **Supp. XXIII:** 113
"After Working Long" (Kenyon), **Supp. VII:** 170
"After Yitzl" (Goldbarth), **Supp. XII:** 186
"After You, My Dear Alphonse" (Jackson), **Supp. IX:** 119
"After Your Death" (Trethewey), **Supp. XXI:** 255
"After Your Nap" (B. Kelly), **Supp. XVII:** 124
"Again" (Dixon), **Supp. XII:** 157
"Again, Kapowsin" (Hugo), **Supp. VI:** 141
"Again Just Now" (Budbill), **Supp. XIX:** 11
"Against" (Goldbarth), **Supp. XII:** 193
"Against Decoration" (Karr), **Supp. XI:** 248
"Against Epiphanies" (C. Baxter), **Supp. XVII:** 20
Against Interpretation (Sontag), **Supp. III Part 2:** 451, 455; **Supp. XIV:** 15
"Against Interpretation" (Sontag), **Supp. III Part 2:** 456–458, 463
"Against Modernity" (Ozick), **Supp. V:** 272
"Against Nature" (Karr), **Supp. XI:** 243
Against Nature (Updike), **Retro. Supp. I:** 323
Against Our Vanishing: Winter Conversations with Allen Grossman on the Theory and Practice of Poetry (Halliday), **Supp. XIX: 82–84,** 88
"Against Realism" (Halliday), **Supp. XIX:** 93
Against the Cold (Bynner), **Supp. XV:** 51
"Against the Crusades" (Stern), **Supp. IX:** 300
Against the Current: As I Remember F. Scott Fitzgerald (Kroll Ring), **Supp. IX:** 63
Agamben, Giorgio, **Supp. XVI:** 289
Agapida, Fray Antonio (pseudonym). See Irving, Washington
"Agassiz" (J. R. Lowell), **Supp. I Part 2:** 414, 416
Agassiz, Louis, **II:** 343; **Supp. I Part 1:** 312; **Supp. IX:** 180
ge cassant, L' (Char; Sobin, trans.), **Supp. XVI:** 282
"Aged Wino's Counsel to a Young Man on the Brink of Marriage, The" (X. J. Kennedy), **Supp. XV:** 156
Agee, Emma, **I:** 26
Agee, James, **I: 25–47,** 293; **IV:** 215; **Supp. IX:** 109; **Supp. XIV:** 92; **Supp. XV:** 143
"Agency Without Mastery: Chronic Pain and Posthuman Life Writing" (Gilmore), **Supp. XXVI:** 53
"Agent, The" (Wilbur), **Supp. III Part 2:** 557–561

Age of Anxiety, The (Auden), **Supp. II Part 1:** 2, 19, 21
"Age of Conformity, The" (Howe), **Supp. VI:** 117
Age of Grief, The: A Novella and Stories (Smiley), **Supp. VI:** 292, **299–301**
Age of Innocence, The (film, Scorsese), **Retro. Supp. III:** 290
Age of Innocence, The (Wharton), **IV:** 320–322, 327–328; **Retro. Supp. I:** 372, 374, **380–381; Retro. Supp. III:** 287; **Supp. IV Part 1:** 23
Age of Longing, The (Koestler), **I:** 258
Age of Reason, The (Paine), **Supp. I Part 2:** 503, 515–517, 520
"Age of Strolling, The" (Stern), **Supp. IX:** 297
"Ages, The" (Bryant), **Supp. I Part 1:** 152, 155, 166, 167
"Ages of the Women, The" (Gibran), **Supp. XX: 115**
"Aggrandizement, The" (Bronk), **Supp. XXI:** 32
"Aging" (Jarrell), **II:** 388
Aging and Gender in Literature (George), **Supp. IV Part 2:** 450
"Agio Neró" (Mora), **Supp. XIII:** 224
"Agitato ma non Troppo" (Ransom), **III:** 493
"Agnes of Iowa" (Moore), **Supp. X:** 165, 178
Agnes of Sorrento (Stowe), **Supp. I Part 2:** 592, 595–596
Agnon, S. Y., **Supp. V:** 266; **Supp. XXV:** 267
Agony & the Agony, The (Silver), **Supp. XXIV:** 265, **274–275**
"Agosta the Winged Man and Rasha the Black Dove" (Dove), **Supp. IV Part 1:** 246–247
Agrarian Justice (Paine), **Supp. I Part 2:** 517–518
"Agricultural Show, The" (McKay), **Supp. X:** 139
Agrippa: A Book of the Dead (W. Gibson), **Supp. XVI:** 125
Agua de dos ríos/Water from Two Rivers (Espaillat), **Supp. XXI:** 104, 112–113
Agua Fresca: An Anthology of Raza Poetry (Rodríguez, ed.), **Supp. IV Part 2:** 540
Agua Santa/Holy Water (Mora), **Supp. XIII: 222–225**
Agüero Sisters, The (García), **Supp. XI: 185–190**
Aguiar, Marian, **Supp. XXII:** 68
Aguiar, Sarah Appleton, **Supp. XIII:** 30
Aguilar, Carmen, **Supp. XXIII:** 200
Ah, Wilderness! (O'Neill), **III:** 400–401; **Supp. IV Part 2:** 587
Ah, Wilderness!: The Frontier in American Literature (Humphrey), **Supp. IX:** 104
Ahearn, Barry, **Retro. Supp. I:** 415
Ahearn, Frederick L., Jr., **Supp. XI:** 184
Ahearn, Kerry, **Supp. IV Part 2:** 604
Ahmed Arabi Pasha, **I:** 453
Ahnebrink, Lars, **III:** 328
Ahrens, Sylvia, **Supp. XX: 162**
Ah Sin (Harte), **Supp. II Part 1:** 354–355
"Ah! Sun-flower" (Blake), **III:** 19
Ai, **Supp. XXVI:** 66
Aida (rock musical), **Supp. XXI:** 148
Aidoo, Ama Ato, **Supp. XXII:** 68
AIDS and Its Metaphors (Sontag), **Supp. III Part 2:** 452, 466–468
Aids to Reflection (Coleridge), **II:** 10
Aiieeeee! An Anthology of Asian-American Writers (The Combined Asian Resources Project), **Supp. X:** 292
Aiken, Conrad, **I: 48–70,** 190, 211, 243; **II:** 55, 530, 542; **III:** 458, 460; **Retro. Supp. I:** 55, 56, 57, 58, 60, 62; **Supp. X:** 50, 115; **Supp. XV:** 144, 297, 298, 302, 306, 309; **Supp. XVII:** 135; **Supp. XXIV:** 36; **Supp. XXV:** 19; **Supp. XXVI:** 225
"Aimless Love" (Collins), **Supp. XXI:** 61
"Aim Was Song, The" (Frost), **Retro. Supp. I:** 133
Ainger, Arthur Campbell, **Supp. XX: 230**
Ainsworth, Linda, **Supp. IV Part 1:** 274
Ainsworth, William, **III:** 423
Air-Conditioned Nightmare, The (H. Miller), **III:** 186
Airing Dirty Laundry (Reed), **Supp. X:** 241
"Air Is Full of Little Holes, The" (Brockmeier), **Supp. XXII:** 60
"Airmail from Mother" (Kooser), **Supp. XIX:** 120
"Air Plant, The" (Crane), **I:** 401
Air Raid: A Verse Play for Radio (MacLeish), **III:** 21
"Airs above the Ground" (Sarton), **Supp. VIII:** 261
Air Tight: A Novel of Red Russia. See We the Living (Rand)
Air Up There, The (film, Glaser), **Supp. XVII:** 9
"Airwaves" (Mason), **Supp. VIII:** 146
Airways, Inc. (Dos Passos), **I:** 482
A Is for Anne: Mistress Hutchinson Disturbs the Commonwealth (Schott), **Supp. XXIII:** 240, **246–247**
"A is for Dining Alone" (M. F. K. Fisher), **Supp. XVII:** 86
Aitken, Robert, **Supp. I Part 2:** 504
"Aix-les-Bains" (Twain), **Retro. Supp. III:** 267
Aizenberg, Susan, **Supp. XXI:** 131
Akhmadulina, Bella, **Supp. III Part 1:** 268
Akhmatova, Anna, **Supp. III Part 1:** 268, 269; **Supp. VIII:** 20, 21, 25, 27, 30; **Supp. XXI:** 132
Akhmatova Translations, The (Kenyon), **Supp. VII:** 160
"Akhnilo" (Salter), **Supp. IX:** 260
Akins, Zoë, **Supp. XVI:** 187; **Supp. XXVII:** 285
Aksenev, Vasily P., **Retro. Supp. I:** 278
"Al Aaraaf" (Poe), **III:** 426–427
Al Aaraaf, Tamerlane, and Minor Poems (Poe), **III:** 410
"Alabama Jones" (Mosher), **Supp. XXII:** 204, 211
"Alain Locke and Cultural Pluralism" (Kallen), **Supp. XIV:** 197
"Alain Locke: Bahá'í Philosopher" (Buck), **Supp. XIV:** 199
Alain Locke: Faith and Philosophy (Buck), **Supp. XIV:** 200
"Al Araaf" (Poe), **Retro. Supp. III:** 231
Al Araaf, Tamerlane, and Minor Poems (Poe), **Retro. Supp. III:** 224, 231
Alarçon, **Supp. XVII:** 74
Alarcón, Justo, **Supp. IV Part 2:** 538, 539, 540
Alarcón, Norma, **Supp. XXIII:** 194, 204–205
À la Recherche du Temps Perdu (Proust), **IV:** 428
"Alarm" (X. J. Kennedy), **Supp. XV:** 163
"Alastor" (Shelley), **Supp. I Part 2:** 728
"Alatus" (Wilbur), **Supp. III Part 2:** 563
Alaya (Hirshfield), **Supp. XXIII:** 131
"Alba" (Creeley), **Supp. IV Part 1:** 150
Alba, Richard D., **Supp. XX: 43**
Albee, Edward, **I: 71–96,** 113; **II:** 558, 591; **III:** 281, 387; **IV:** 4, 230; **Retro. Supp. II:** 104; **Supp. VIII:** 331; **Supp. XIII:** 196, 197; **Supp. XXIV:** 113, 263, 270

Albers, Joseph, **Supp. IV Part 2:** 621
Alberti, Rafael, **Supp. XV:** 75
Albright, Margery, **Supp. I Part 2:** 613
"Album, The" (Morris), **III:** 220
Album, The (Rinehart), **Supp. XXV:** 197, 200
Alcestiad, The (Wilder), **IV:** 357, 374
"Alchemist, The" (Bogan), **Supp. III Part 1:** 50
"Alchemist in the City, The" (Hopkins), **Supp. IV Part 2:** 639
Alchymist's Journal, The (Connell), **Supp. XIV:** 80
"Alcmena" (Winters), **Supp. II Part 2:** 801
Alcott, Abba. See Alcott, Mrs. Amos Bronson (Abigail May)
Alcott, Amos Bronson, **II:** 7, 225; **IV:** 172, 173, 184; **Retro. Supp. I:** 217; **Supp. I Part 1:** 28, 29–32, 35, 39, 41, 45; **Supp. II Part 1:** 290; **Supp. XVI:** 84, 89; **Supp. XXV:** 250
Alcott, Mrs. Amos Bronson (Abigail May), **IV:** 184; **Supp. I Part 1:** 29, 30, 31, 32, 35
Alcott, Anna. See Pratt, Anna
Alcott, Louisa May, **IV:** 172; **Supp. I Part 1: 28–46; Supp. IX:** 128; **Supp. XV:** 338; **Supp. XVI:** 84
Alcott, May, **Supp. I Part 1:** 41
Alcuin: A Dialogue (Brown), **Supp. I Part 1:** 126–127, 133
Alden, Hortense. See Farrell, Mrs. James T. (Hortense Alden)
Alden, John, **I:** 471; **II:** 502–503
"Alder Fork, The" (Leopold), **Supp. XIV:** 186
Aldington, Perdita, **Supp. I Part 1:** 258
Aldington, Richard, **II:** 517; **III:** 458, 459, 465, 472; **Retro. Supp. I:** 63, 127; **Supp. I Part 1:** 257–262, 270
Aldington, Mrs. Richard. See Doolittle, Hilda
Aldo Leopold: His Life and Work (Meine), **Supp. XIV:** 179
"Aldo Leopold's Intellectual Heritage" (Nash), **Supp. XIV:** 191–192
Aldon, Raymond, **Supp. XV:** 297
Aldrich, Thomas Bailey, **II:** 400; **Supp. II Part 1:** 192; **Supp. XIV:** 45; **Supp. XVIII:** 4
Aldrich, Tom, **Supp. I Part 2:** 415
Aldridge, John W., **Supp. I Part 1:** 196; **Supp. IV Part 1:** 286; **Supp. IV Part 2:** 680, 681; **Supp. VIII:** 189; **Supp. XI:** 228; **Supp. XIX:** 250
Aleck Maury Sportsman (Gordon), **II:** 197, 200, 203–204
Alegría, Claribel, **Supp. IV Part 1:** 208
Aleichem, Sholem, **Supp. XXIII:** 4, 7
Aleichem, Sholom, **IV:** 3, 10; **Supp. IV Part 2:** 585
"Alert Lovers, Hidden Sides, and Ice Travelers: Notes on Poetic Form and Energy" (Dunn), **Supp. XI:** 153
"Ale&sacaron; Debeljak" (Simic), **Supp. VIII:** 279
"Alex" (Oliver), **Supp. VII:** 232
Alexander, Doris, **Supp. XVII:** 99
Alexander, Elizabeth, **Supp. XVIII:** 171, 185, 186; **Supp. XXI:** 246, 257
Alexander, George, **II:** 331
Alexander, Michael, **Retro. Supp. I:** 293
Alexander, Paul, **Supp. XXV:** 84
Alexander, Will, **Supp. XXVII:** 163
"Alexander Crummell Dead" (Dunbar), **Supp. II Part 1:** 207, 208–209
Alexander's Bridge (Cather), **I:** 313, 314, 316–317, 326; **Retro. Supp. I:** 1, 6, 7, 8; **Retro. Supp. III:** 22
Alexander the Great, **IV:** 322
"Alexandra" (Cather), **Retro. Supp. I:** 7, 9, 17
Alexandrov, V. E., **Retro. Supp. I:** 270
Alexie, Sherman, **Retro. Supp. III:** 313; **Supp. XVIII:** 58; **Supp. XXVI:** 103, 108
Alger, Horatio, **Supp. XXVII:** 84
Algic Researches (H. Schoolcraft), **Supp. XXIII:** 227
Algonquin Round Table, **Supp. IX:** 190, 191, 197
Algren, Nelson, **I:** 211; **Supp. IX: 1–18; Supp. V:** 4; **Supp. XII:** 126; **Supp. XIII:** 173; **Supp. XIV:** 3; **Supp. XVII:** 161; **Supp. XXI:** 264; **Supp. XXIII:** 165; **Supp. XXV:** 185; **Supp. XXVII:** 87, 134
Alhambra, The (Irving), **II:** 310–311
Ali, Agha Shahid, **Supp. XVII:** 74
Ali, Ayaan Hirsi, **Supp. XXIV:** 15
Alias Grace (Atwood), **Supp. XIII:** 20, **31–32**
Alice (film; Allen), **Supp. XV:** 2, 11
"Alice Doane's Appeal" (Hawthorne), **II:** 227
"Alice Drops Her Cigarette on the Floor ... " (Findley), **Supp. XX: 50–51**
"Alice in the Looking Glass" (Stallings), **Supp. XXV:** 234
Alice in Wonderland (Carroll), **Supp. I Part 2:** 622
Alice Ordered Me to Be Made (Notley), **Supp. XXII:** 224, 227, 228
"Alice Ordered Me to Be Made" (Notley), **Supp. XXII:** 227
Alice's Adventures in Wonderland (Carroll), **Supp. XVI:** 261
"Alicia and I Talking on Edna's Steps" (Cisneros), **Supp. VII:** 64
"Alicia Who Sees Mice" (Cisneros), **Supp. VII:** 60
Alien 3 (screenplay, W. Gibson), **Supp. XVI:** 120, 124
"Ali in Havana" (Talese), **Supp. XVII:** 207, 208
Alison, Archibald, **Supp. I Part 1:** 151, 159
Alison's House (Glaspell), **Supp. III Part 1:** 182, 188, 189
Alive (screenplay, Shanley), **Supp. XIV:** 316
Alive and Writing: Interviews with American Authors of the 1980s (McCaffery and Gregory), **Supp. X:** 260
"Alki Beach" (Hugo), **Supp. VI:** 135
Alla Breve Loving (Wright), **Supp. XV:** 339, 340
"Alla Breve Loving" (Wright), **Supp. XV:** 340
"All Apologies" (Biss), **Supp. XXVI:** 56
"All Around the Town" (Benét), **Supp. XI:** 48, 58
"All Around the Town" (Taggard), **Supp. XXVI:** 144
All at Sea (Lardner), **II:** 427
All Aunt Hagar's Children (E. P. Jones), **Supp. XXII:** 140, 143, **150–153**
"All Aunt Hagar's Children" (E. P. Jones), **Supp. XXII:** 151
"All Boy" (Rawlings), **Supp. X:** 222
Allegiances (Stafford), **Supp. XI: 322–323,** 329
"Allegory of the Cave" (Dunn), **Supp. XI:** 150
"Allegory Unlimited" (Cassill), **Supp. XIX:** 266
Allegro, Johnny (film, Tetzloff), **Supp. XVII:** 62
"Allegro, L' " (Milton), **Supp. XIV:** 8
Allen, Brooke, **Supp. VIII:** 153
Allen, Bruce, **Supp. XXII:** 205, 212; **Supp. XXIII:** 106, 300
Allen, Claudia, **Supp. XXIII:** 79
Allen, Dick, **Supp. IX:** 279
Allen, Donald, **Supp. VIII:** 291; **Supp. XIII:** 112; **Supp. XXIII:** 215, 220; **Supp. XXVI:** 223; **Supp. XXVII:** 25
Allen, Frank, **Supp. XI:** 126; **Supp. XII:** 186; **Supp. XXVI:** 150

Allen, Fred, **Supp. XXV:** 255
Allen, Frederick Lewis, **Supp. I Part 2:** 655
Allen, Gay Wilson, **IV:** 352; **Supp. I Part 2:** 418
Allen, Ivan, **Supp. XXII:** 245
Allen, Paula Gunn. See Gunn Allen, Paula
Allen, Robert Moore, **Supp. XX: 164**
Allen, Walter, **I:** 505; **III:** 352; **Supp. IV Part 2:** 685; **Supp. IX:** 231
Allen, Woody, **Supp. I Part 2:** 607, 623; **Supp. IV Part 1:** 205; **Supp. X:** 164; **Supp. XI:** 307; **Supp. XV: 1–18; Supp. XVII:** 48
"Aller et Retour" (Barnes), **Supp. III Part 1:** 36
Aller Retour New York (H. Miller), **III:** 178, 182, 183
Allerton, Isaac, **Supp. XXII:** 44
Allessandrini, Goffredo, **Supp. IV Part 2:** 520
Alleys of Eden, The (R. O. Butler), **Supp. XII:** 62, **62–64,** 68
All God's Children Need Traveling Shoes (Angelou), **Supp. IV Part 1:** 2, 9–10, 12–13, 17
All God's Chillun Got Wings (O'Neill), **III:** 387, 391, 393–394
All Gone (Dixon), **Supp. XII:** 148, 149
"All Hallows" (Glück), **Supp. V:** 82
"All I Can Remember" (Jackson), **Supp. IX:** 115
"Alligators, The" (Updike), **IV:** 219
Allingham, John Till, **Supp. XV:** 243
All in the Family (Boyce), **Supp. XXI:** 8
"ALL IN THE STREET" (Baraka), **Supp. II Part 1:** 53
"All in Time" (Stone), **Supp. XXVII:** 251
Allison, Dorothy, **Supp. XVIII:** 195
"All I Want" (Tapahonso), **Supp. IV Part 2:** 508
"All Little Colored Children Should Play the Harmonica" (Patchett), **Supp. XII:** 309
"All Mountains" (Doolittle), **Supp. I Part 1:** 271
All My Friends Are Going to Be Strangers (McMurtry), **Supp. V:** 224, 228, 229
All My Pretty Ones (Sexton), **Supp. II Part 2:** 678, 679–683
"All My Pretty Ones" (Sexton), **Supp. II Part 2:** 681–682
"All My Sad Captains" (Jewett), **Retro. Supp. II:** 134
All My Sons (A. Miller), **III:** 148, 149, 150, 151–153, 154, 155, 156, 158, 159, 160, 164, 166; **Retro. Supp. III:** 165, 167, 168
All New People (Lamott), **Supp. XX: 135–136**
"All Night, All Night" (Schwartz), **Supp. II Part 2:** 665
All Night Long (Caldwell), **I:** 297
"All-Night Melodies" (Nelson), **Supp. XVIII:** 185
All-Night Visitors (Major), **Supp. XXII: 173–174**
"All of Us" (Major), **Supp. XXII:** 185
All of Us: The Collected Poems (Carver), **Supp. XXIV:** 167
All of What We Loved (Bronk), **Supp. XXI:** 32
"All Our Lost Children: Trauma and Testimony in the Performance of Childhood" (Pace), **Supp. XI:** 245
All Our Yesterdays (Parker), **Supp. XIX: 187–188**
"All Out" (Hecht), **Supp. X:** 72
All Over (Albee), **I:** 91–94
"Allowance" (Minot), **Supp. VI:** 206, 207–208
"Alloy" (Rukeyser), **Supp. VI:** 279
"All Parrots Speak" (Bowles), **Supp. IV Part 1:** 89
Allport, Gordon, **II:** 363–364
All Quiet on the Western Front (Remarque), **Supp. IV Part 1:** 380, 381
"ALL REACTION IS DOOMED-!-!-!" (Baraka), **Supp. II Part 1:** 59
"All Revelation" (Frost), **II:** 160–162
"All Riptides Roar with Sand from Opposing Shores" (Vaz), **Supp. XXVI:** 264–265
Allsburg, Christ Van, **Supp. XXV:** 83, 87
"All Shall Love Me and Despair"(Thompson), **Supp. XXIII:** 295
All Shot Up (C. Himes), **Supp. XVI:** 143, 144
"All Souls" (Gioia), **Supp. XV:** 117
"All Souls" (Wharton), **IV:** 315–316; **Retro. Supp. I:** 382
"All Souls' Night" (Yeats), **Supp. X:** 69
All Souls' Rising (Bell), **Supp. X:** 12, **13–16,** 17
"All-Star Literary Vaudeville" (Wilson), **IV:** 434–435
Allston, Washington, **II:** 298
All Stories Are True (Wideman), **Supp. X:** 320
"All That Is" (Wilbur), **Supp. III Part 2:** 563
All That Was Possible (Sturgis), **Supp. XX: 227, 232, 235–237**
"All the Bearded Irises of Life: Confessions of a Homospiritual" (Walker), **Supp. III Part 2:** 527
"All the Beautiful Are Blameless" (Wright), **Supp. III Part 2:** 597
ALL: The Collected Poems, 1956–1964 (Zukofsky), **Supp. III Part 2:** 630
ALL: The Collected Short Poems, 1923–1958 (Zukofsky), **Supp. III Part 2:** 629
All the Conspirators (Isherwood), **Supp. XIV:** 156, 159, 160
All the Dark and Beautiful Warriors (Hansberry), **Supp. IV Part 1:** 360, 374
All the Days and Nights: The Collected Stories (Maxwell), **Supp. VIII:** 151, 158, 169
"All the Dead Dears" (Plath), **Retro. Supp. II:** 246; **Supp. I Part 2:** 537
"All the Dead"(P. Benedict), **Supp. XXIII:** 37
"All the Dead Pilots" (Faulkner), **Retro. Supp. III:** 82
All the Good People I've Left Behind (Oates), **Supp. II Part 2:** 510, 522, 523
"All the Hippos Were Boiled in Their Tanks" (Burroughs and Kerouac), **Supp. III Part 1:** 94
All the King's Men (Warren), **I:** 489; **IV:** 243, 248–249, 252; **Supp. V:** 261; **Supp. VIII:** 126; **Supp. X:** 1; **Supp. XVIII:** 77, 79; **Supp. XXIV:** 226
All the Little Live Things (Stegner), **Supp. IV Part 2:** 599, 604, 605, 606, 609–610, 611, 613
All the Pretty Horses (film), **Supp. VIII:** 175
All the Pretty Horses (McCarthy), **Supp. VIII:** 175, **182–183,** 188
All the Sad Young Men (Fitzgerald), **II:** 94; **Retro. Supp. I:** 108
"All the Time in the World" (Dubus), **Supp. VII:** 91
"All the Way to Flagstaff, Arizona" (Bausch), **Supp. VII:** 47, 49
"All This and More" (Karr), **Supp. XI:** 243
All Thy Conquests (Hayes), **Supp. XXVI:** 134,135–136
All Tomorrow's Parties (W. Gibson), **Supp. XVI:** 119, 121, 123, 124, **130**
"All Too Real" (Vendler), **Supp. V:** 189
All Trivia: Triva, More Trivia, After-

thoughts, Last Words (L. P. Smith), **Supp. XIV:** 339
All-True Travels and Adventures of Lidie Newton (Smiley), **Supp. VI:** 292, **305–307**
All We Need of Hell (Crews), **Supp. XI: 114**
Almack, Edward, **Supp. IV Part 2:** 435
al-Maghut, Muhammad, **Supp. XIII:** 278
"Almanac" (Swenson), **Supp. IV Part 2:** 641
Almanac of the Dead (Silko), **Supp. IV Part 2:** 558–559, 560, 561, 570–571
Alma: or, The Dead Women (Notley), **Supp. XXII:** 223, 224, 231, 236
Almon, Bert, **Supp. IX:** 93
"Almost" (Untermeyer), **Supp. XV:** 304
Almost Learning to Live in This World (Schott), **Supp. XXIII: 247–248**
Almost Revolution, The (Priaulx and Ungar), **Supp. XI:** 228
Alnilam (Dickey), **Supp. IV Part 1:** 176, 186, 188–189
"Alone" (Caputo), **Supp. XIX:** 29
"Alone" (Levine), **Supp. V:** 184, 185, 186
"Alone" (Pickering), **Supp. XXI:** 204
"Alone" (Poe), **Retro. Supp. II:** 266
"Alone" (Singer), **IV:** 15
"Alone" (Winters), **Supp. II Part 2:** 786, 811
"Alone and Lonely" (Budbill), **Supp. XIX:** 10
Aloneness (Brooks), **Supp. III Part 1:** 85, 86
Alone with America (Corso), **Supp. XII:** 131
Alone with America (Howard), **Supp. IX:** 326
"Along America's Edges" (Sobin), **Supp. XVI:** 288
"Along the Color Line" (Du Bois), **Supp. II Part 1:** 173
Along the Illinois (Masters), **Supp. I Part 2:** 472
Alouette, L' (Anouilh), **Supp. I Part 1:** 286–288
"Alphabet" (Nye), **Supp. XIII:** 283
Alphabet, An (Doty), **Supp. XI:** 120
Alphabet for Gourmets, An (M. F. K. Fisher), **Supp. XVII:** 86, 87, 92
Alphabet of Grace, The (Buechner), **Supp. XII:** 52
"Alphabet of My Dead, An" (Pinsky), **Supp. VI:** 235, 250
"Alphabet of Subjects, An" (Zukofsky), **Supp. III Part 2:** 624
"Alpine Christ, The" (Jeffers), **Supp. II Part 2:** 415, 419
Alpine Christ and Other Poems, The (Jeffers), **Supp. II Part 2:** 419
"Alpine Idyll, An" (Hemingway), **II:** 249; **Retro. Supp. I:** 176
Al Que Quiere! (W. C. Williams), **Retro. Supp. I:** 414, 416, **417,** 428
Alraune (Ewers; Endore, trans.), **Supp. XVII:** 54
Alsop, Joseph, **II:** 579
"Altar, The" (Herbert), **Supp. IV Part 2:** 646
"Altar, The" (MacLeish), **III:** 4
"Altar Boy" (Fante), **Supp. XI:** 160, 164
"Altar of the Dead, The" (James), **Retro. Supp. I:** 229
"Altars in the Street, The" (Levertov), **Supp. III Part 1:** 280
Alter, Robert, **Supp. XII:** 167
Altgeld, John Peter, **Supp. I Part 2:** 382, 455
Althea (Masters), **Supp. I Part 2:** 455, 459
Altick, Richard, **Supp. I Part 2:** 423
Altieri, Charles, **Supp. VIII:** 297, 303; **Supp. XXIII:** 220
Altman, Robert, **Supp. IX:** 143; **Supp. XXIV:** 166, 172
"Alto" (C. Frost), **Supp. XV:** 101
"Altra Ego" (Brodsky), **Supp. VIII:** 31–32
Altruists, The (Silver), **Supp. XXIV: 273**
A Lume Spento (Pound), **Retro. Supp. I:** 283, 285
"Aluminum House" (F. Barthelme), **Supp. XI:** 26
Alvares, Mosseh, **Supp. V:** 11
Alvarez, A., **Supp. I Part 2:** 526, 527; **Supp. II Part 1:** 99; **Supp. IX:** 248
Alvarez, Joseph A., **Supp. XXII:** 13–14
Alvarez, Julia, **Supp. VII: 1–21; Supp. XI:** 177; **Supp. XVII:** 71, 112; **Supp. XXIV:** 86, 89
"Always a Rose" (L.-Y. Lee), **Supp. XV:** 215, 216
"Always in Good Humor" (Adams), **Supp. XV:** 294
Always Outnumbered, Always Outgunned (Mosley), **Supp. XIII:** 242
"Always the Stories" (Ortiz), **Supp. IV Part 2:** 499, 500, 502, 504, 512
Always the Young Strangers (Sandburg), **III:** 577–578, 579
Always Young and Fair (Richter), **Supp. XVIII: 215–216**
Amadeus (Shaffer), **Supp. XIV:** 330
"Amahl and the Night Visitors: A Guide to the Tenor of Love" (Moore), **Supp. X:** 167
"Am and Am Not" (Olds), **Supp. X:** 212
"Amanita, The" (Francis), **Supp. IX:** 81
Amaranth (Robinson), **III:** 509, 510, 512, 513, 522, 523
"Amateur Iconography: Resurrection" (Stallings), **Supp. XXV:** 233
"Amateurs, The" (Swados), **Supp. XIX:** 256
Amazing Adele, The (Barillet and Grédy; Loos, trans.), **Supp. XVI:** 194
Amazing Adventures of Kavalier and Clay, The (Chabon), **Supp. XI:** 68, 76, **77–80; Supp. XXII:** 49
Amazing Adventures of Leticia Carberry (Rinehart), **Supp. XXV:** 194
Amazing Adventures of the Escapist, The (Chabon, ed.), **Supp. XIX:** 174
Amazing Interlude, The (Rinehart), **Supp. XXV:** 194
Amazing Science Fiction Stories, **Supp. XVI:** 121
Amazons: An Intimate Memoir by the First Woman to Play in the National Hockey League (DeLillo), **Supp. VI:** 2
Ambassador Morgenthau's Story (Morgenthau), **Supp. XXIII:** 21, 22
Ambassador of Peace, An (Abernon), **Supp. XVI:** 191
Ambassadors, The (H. James), **II:** 320, 333–334, 600; **III:** 517; **IV:** 322; **Retro. Supp. I:** 215, 218, 219, 220, 221, **232–233**
Ambassador's Son, The (Hickam), **Supp. XXVII:** 111
Ambelain, Robert, **Supp. I Part 1:** 260, 273, 274
"Amber" (Gansworth), **Supp. XXVI:** 114
"Ambition Bird, The" (Sexton), **Supp. II Part 2:** 693
Ambition: The Secret Passion (Epstein), **Supp. XIV:** 113–114
"Ambitious Guest, The" (Hawthorne), **Retro. Supp. III:** 113
Ambler, Eric, **III:** 57
Ambrose Holt and Family (Glaspell), **Supp. III Part 1:** 175, 181, 184, 187, 188
"Ambrose Seyffert" (Masters), **Supp. I Part 2:** 464
"Ambuscade" (Faulkner), **Retro. Supp. III:** 85

"Ambush" (Komunyakaa), **Supp. XIII:** 122
Amen Corner, The (Baldwin), **Retro. Supp. II:** 5, 7; **Supp. I Part 1:** 48, 51, 54, 55, 56
America (Benét), **Supp. XI:** 46, 47, 51
"America" (Ginsberg), **Supp. II Part 1:** 58–59, 317
"America" (song), **IV:** 410
"America, America!" (poem) (Schwartz), **Supp. II Part 2:** 665
"America, Commerce, and Freedom" (Rowson and Reinagle), **Supp. XV:** 240
"America, Home of the Red Man" (Zitkala-Ša), **Supp. XXV:** 281
"America, Seen Through Photographs, Darkly" (Sontag), **Supp. III Part 2:** 464
"America! America!" (story) (Schwartz), **Supp. II Part 2:** 640, 658–659, 660
America and Americans (Steinbeck), **IV:** 52
"America and the Vidal Chronicles" (Pease), **Supp. IV Part 2:** 687
America as a Civilization (Lerner), **III:** 60
America Behind the Color Line (H. L. Gates), **Supp. XX: 102, 105**
America Beyond the Color Line (television program), **Supp. XX: 99**
America Hispana: A Portrait and a Prospect (W. Frank), **Supp. XX: 76**
"America Independent" (Freneau), **Supp. II Part 1:** 261
America Is Worth Saving (Dreiser), **Retro. Supp. II:** 96
American, The (James), **I:** 226; **II:** 326–327, 328, 331, 334; **IV:** 318; **Retro. Supp. I:** 220, **221,** 228, 376, 381
Americana (DeLillo), **Supp. VI:** 2, **3,** 5, 6, 8, 13, 14
American Adam, The (R. W. B. Lewis), **II:** 457–458; **Supp. XIII:** 93
American Almanac (Leeds), **II:** 110
American Anthem (Doctorow and Suares), **Supp. IV Part 1:** 234
"American Apocalypse" (Gunn Allen), **Supp. IV Part 1:** 325
American Aristocracy (film), **Supp. XVI:** 185–186
American Blood, (Nichols), **Supp. XIII:** 268
American Blues (T. Williams), **IV:** 381, 383
American Buffalo (Mamet), **Supp. XIV:** 239, 241, 242, 244–245, 246, 254, 255
American Caravan: A Yearbook of American Literature (Mumford, ed.), **Supp. II Part 2:** 482
American Cause, The (MacLeish), **III:** 3
American Childhood, An (Dillard), **Supp. VI: 19–21,** 23, 24, 25, 26, 30, 31
"American Childhood in the Dominican Republic, An" (Alvarez), **Supp. VII:** 2, 5
American Child Supreme, An: The Education of a Liberation Ecologist (Nichols), **Supp. XIII:** 256, 257, 258, 264, 265, 266, 267, 268, 269
American Civilization (C. L. R. James), **Supp. XXI:** 169
American Claimant, The (Twain), **IV:** 194, 198–199
American Clock, The (A. Miller), **Retro. Supp. III:** 165–166
American Crisis I (Paine), **Supp. I Part 2:** 508
American Crisis II (Paine), **Supp. I Part 2:** 508
American Crisis XIII (Paine), **Supp. I Part 2:** 509
"American Critic, The" (J. Spingarn), **I:** 266
American Culture, Canons, and the Case of Elizabeth Stoddard (Smith and Weinauer), **Supp. XV:** 270
American Daughter, An (Wasserstein), **Supp. XV: 330–332,** 333
American Democrat, The (Cooper), **I:** 343, 346, 347, 353
American Desert (Everett), **Supp. XVIII: 62–63**
American Diary (Webb), **Supp. I Part 1:** 5
American Drama since World War II (Weales), **IV:** 385
American Dream, An (Mailer), **III:** 27, 33–34, 35, 39, 41, 43, 44; **Retro. Supp. II:** 203, **204–205**
American Dream, The (Albee), **I:** 74–76, 77, 89, 94; **Supp. XXIV:** 113
"American Dreams" (Simpson), **Supp. IX:** 274
American Earth (Caldwell), **I:** 290, 308
"American Emperors" (Poirier), **Supp. IV Part 2:** 690
American English (Marckwardt), **Supp. XXIV:** 255
American Exodus, An (Lange and Taylor), **I:** 293
American Experience, The (Parkes), **Supp. I Part 2:** 617–618
American Express (Corso), **Supp. XII:** 129
"American Express" (Salter), **Supp. IX:** 260–261
"American Fear of Literature, The" (Lewis), **II:** 451
American Female Patriotism (S. Warner as Wetherell), **Supp. XVIII: 260–261,** 262, 263
American Fictions (Hardwick), **Supp. X:** 171
American Fictions, 1940–1980 (Karl), **Supp. IV Part 1:** 384; **Supp. XXI:** 234
"American Financier, The" (Dreiser), **II:** 428
American Folkways (book series), **I:** 290
American Guerilla in the Philippines (Wolfert), **Supp. XXI:** 267
"American Heart of Darkness: The Moral Vision of Five Novels of the Vietnam War" (Palm), **Supp. XXII:** 103
"American Heritage" (Gansworth), **Supp. XXVI:** 114
American Heroine: The Life and Legend of Jane Addams (A. F. Davis), **Supp. I Part 1:** 1
American Historical Novel, The (Leisy), **Supp. II Part 1:** 125
"American Horse" (Erdrich), **Supp. IV Part 1:** 333
American Humor: A Study of the National Character (Rourke), **IV:** 339, 352; **Supp. XIX:** 147
American Hunger (Wright), **Supp. IV Part 1:** 11
"American Husband, The" (Atherton), **Supp. XXIV:** 24
American Indian Anthology, An (Tvedten, ed.), **Supp. IV Part 2:** 505
American Indian Stories (Zitkala-Ša), **Supp. XXV:** 272–273, 282–283, 284–285
"American Indian Women: At the Center of Indigenous Resistance in Contemporary North America" (Jaimes and Halsey), **Supp. IV Part 1:** 331
"American in England, An" (Wylie), **Supp. I Part 2:** 707
Americanize the First American (Zitkala-Ša), **Supp. XXV:** 283
American Jitters, The: A Year of the Slump (Wilson), **IV:** 427, 428
American Journal (Hayden), **Supp. II Part 1:** 367
American Journey: The Times of Robert F. Kennedy (Plimpton, ed.), **Supp. XVI:** 245

"American Land Ethic, An" (Momaday), **Supp. IV Part 2:** 488
American Landscape, The, **Supp. I Part 1:** 157
American Language, The (Mencken), **II:** 289, 430; **III:** 100, 104, 105, 108, 111, 119–120
American Language, The: Supplement One (Mencken), **III:** 111
American Language, The: Supplement Two (Mencken), **III:** 111
"American Letter" (MacLeish), **III:** 13
"American Liberty" (Freneau), **Supp. II Part 1:** 257
"American Life in Poetry" (column, Kooser), **Supp. XIX:** 116, 127
American Linden (Zapruder), **Supp. XXVI:** 54
American Literary History (Harrison), **Supp. VIII:** 37
American Literature, 1607–1885 (Richardson), **Retro. Supp. III:** 261
"American Literature and the American Language" (T. S. Eliot), **Retro. Supp. III:** 255
American Mercury, **Supp. XI:** 163, 164
American Milk (Stone), **Supp. XXVII:** 257
American Mind, The (Commager), **Supp. I Part 2:** 650
American Moderns: Bohemian New York and the Creation of a New Century (Stansell), **Supp. XVII:** 106
American Moderns: From Rebellion to Conformity (Geismar), **Supp. IX:** 15; **Supp. XI:** 223
"American Names" (Benét), **Supp. XI:** 47
American Nature Writers (Elder, ed.), **Supp. IX:** 25
American Nature Writers (Winter), **Supp. X:** 104
American Negro, The (W. H. Thomas), **Supp. II Part 1:** 168
American Notebooks, The (Hawthorne), **II:** 226
American Novel Since World War II, The (Klein, ed.), **Supp. XI:** 233
Americano, The (film), **Supp. XVI:** 185
"American Original, An: Learning from a Literary Master" (Wilkinson), **Supp. VIII:** 164, 165, 168
American Ornithology (Wilson), **Supp. XVI:** 4, 6
American Pastoral (P. Roth), **Retro. Supp. II:** 279, 289, **292–293; Supp. XI:** 68
American Pictures: A Personal Journey Through the American Underclass (Holdt), **Supp. XXVI:** 26
American Places (Porter, Stegner and Stegner), **Supp. IV Part 2:** 599
"American Poet" (Shapiro), **Supp. II Part 2:** 701
"American Poetry" (Simpson), **Supp. IX:** 272
American Poetry, 1922: A Miscellany (Untermeyer, ed.), **Supp. XV:** 306
"American Poetry and American Life" (Pinsky), **Supp. VI:** 239–240
American Poetry from the Beginning to Whitman (Untermeyer, ed.), **Supp. XV:** 310
American Poetry since 1900 (Untermeyer, ed.), **Supp. XV:** 306
American Poetry since 1945: A Critical Survey (Stepanchev), **Supp. XI:** 312
American Poetry since 1960 (Mesic), **Supp. IV Part 1:** 175
American Poets since World War II Dictionary of Literary Biography (Gwynn, ed.), **Supp. XV:** 343
American Popular Song (Wilder), **Supp. XXVII:** 42
American Primer, An (Boorstin), **I:** 253
American Primer, An (Whitman), **IV:** 348
"American Primitive" (W. J. Smith), **Supp. XIII:** 333
American Primitive: Poems (Oliver), **Supp. VII:** 234–237, 238
American Procession, An: The Major American Writers from 1830–1930—-the Crucial Century (Kazin), **Supp. VIII: 105–106,** 108
"American Prose Writers" articles (Briggs), **Supp. XVIII:** 11
American Psycho (Ellis), **Supp. XXVII:** 67, 71–74, 75, 76
American Psycho (film), **Supp. XXVII:** 68, 79
American Psycho 2 (film), **Supp. XXVII:** 68
American Psycho: The Musical, **Supp. XXVII:** 68
American Radio Company, The (radio show, Keillor), **Supp. XVI:** 176–177
"American Realist Playwrights, The" (McCarthy), **II:** 562
American Register, or General Repository of History, Politics, and Science, The (Brown, ed.), **Supp. I Part 1:** 146
American Renaissance (Matthiessen), **I:** 259–260; **III:** 310; **Supp. XIII:** 93
"American Rendezvous, An" (Beauvoir), **Supp. IX:** 4
American Scene, The (James), **II:** 336; **III:** 460; **Retro. Supp. I:** 232, 235
American Scenes (Kozlenko, ed.), **IV:** 378
"American Scholar, The" (Emerson), **I:** 239; **II:** 8, 12–13; **Retro. Supp. I:** 62, 74–75, 149, 298; **Retro. Supp. II:** 155; **Supp. I Part 2:** 420; **Supp. IX:** 227, 271; **Supp. XIV:** 104
"American Scholar, The" (Pickering), **Supp. XXI:** 196
Americans in England; or, Lessons for Daughters (Rowson), **Supp. XV:** 240
"American Soldier, The" (Freneau), **Supp. II Part 1:** 269
American Songbag, The (Sandburg), **III:** 583
"American Student in Paris, An" (Farrell), **II:** 45
"American Sublime, The" (Stevens), **IV:** 74
American Taliban (Abraham), **Supp. XXIV:** 2, **12–14**
"American Tar, The; or, The Press Gang Defeated" (Rowson and Taylor), **Supp. XV:** 238
"American Temperament, The" (Locke), **Supp. XIV:** 211
American Tragedy, An (Dreiser), **I:** 497, 498, 499, 501, 502, 503, 511–515, 517, 518, 519; **III:** 251; **IV:** 35, 484; **Retro. Supp. II:** 93, 95, **104–108; Supp. XVII:** 155
"American Triptych" (Kenyon), **Supp. VII:** 165
"American Use for German Ideals" (Bourne), **I:** 228
American Village, The (Freneau), **Supp. II Part 1:** 256, 257
"American Village, The" (Freneau), **Supp. II Part 1:** 256
American Wives and English Husbands (Atherton), **Supp. XXIV:** 18, 22
America's Coming-of-Age (Brooks), **I:** 228, 230, 240, 245, 258; **IV:** 427
America's Humor: From Poor Richard to Doonesbury (Blair and Hill), **Retro. Supp. II:** 286
"America's Indian Problem" (Zitkala-Ša), **Supp. XXV:** 282
"America's Part in World Peace" (Locke), **Supp. XIV:** 208
America's Rome (Vance), **Supp. IV Part 2:** 684
America: The Story of a Free People (Commager and Nevins), **I:** 253

America Was Promises (MacLeish), **III:** 16, 17
"Amerika" (Snyder), **Supp. VIII:** 301
Ames, Christopher, **Supp. XVIII:** 242–243
Ames, Fisher, **Supp. I Part 2:** 486
Ames, Lois, **Supp. I Part 2:** 541, 547
Ames, William, **IV:** 158
Ames Stewart, Beatrice, **Supp. IX:** 200
Amichai, Yehuda, **Supp. XI:** 267
Amick, Steve, **Supp. XXII:** 205, 216
Amidon, Stephen, **Supp. XI:** 333
Amiel, Henri F., **I:** 241, 243, 250
Amis, Kingsley, **IV:** 430; **Supp. IV Part 2:** 688; **Supp. VIII:** 167; **Supp. XIII:** 93; **Supp. XV:** 117
Amis, Martin, **Retro. Supp. I:** 278
"Amish, The"(Thompson), **Supp. XXIII:** 295–296
"Amity Hills" (Skloot), **Supp. XX: 204**
Ammons, A. R., **Supp. III Part 2:** 541; **Supp. IX:** 41, 42, 46; **Supp. VII: 23–38; Supp. XII:** 121; **Supp. XIX:** 83; **Supp. XV:** 115; **Supp. XVII:** 242; **Supp. XXVI:** 67
Ammons, Elizabeth, **Retro. Supp. I:** 364, 369; **Retro. Supp. II:** 140
Amnesia Moon (Lethem), **Supp. XVIII:** 136, **138–139**
"Among Children" (Levine), **Supp. V:** 192
Among Friends (M. F. K. Fisher), **Supp. XVII:** 89, 90–91, 92
Among My Books (J. R. Lowell), **Supp. I Part 2:** 407
"Among School Children" (Yeats), **III:** 249; **Supp. IX:** 52; **Supp. XIV:** 8
Among the Believers (Rash), **Supp. XXVII:** 218–220, 221
"Among the Hills" (Whittier), **Supp. I Part 2:** 703
Among the Isles of Shoals (Thaxter), **Supp. XIII:** 152
"Among Those Present" (Benét), **Supp. XI:** 53
"Amoral Moralist" (White), **Supp. I Part 2:** 648
Amory, Cleveland, **Supp. I Part 1:** 316
Amory, Fred, **Supp. III Part 1:** 2
Amos (biblical book), **II:** 166
Amos and Andy (television program), **Supp. XX: 103**
Amplitude (Gallagher), **Supp. XXIV:** 166, 170
Amran, David, **Supp. XIV:** 150
"Am Strand von Tanger" (Salter), **Supp. IX:** 257
"AMTRAK" (Baraka), **Supp. II Part 1:** 60
"Amulet, The" (Antin), **Supp. XX: 10**
"Amulets" (Hull), **Supp. XXI:** 139
Amy and Isabelle (film), **Supp. XXIII:** 275–276
Amy and Isabelle (Strout), **Supp. X:** 86; **Supp. XXIII:** 273, 274–275, **276–278,** 285
"Amy Lowell of Brookline, Mass." (Scott), **II:** 512
Amy Lowell: Portrait of the Poet in Her Time (Gregory), **II:** 512
"Amy Wentworth" (Whittier), **Supp. I Part 2:** 694, 696
Anabase (Perse), **III:** 12
"Anabasis (I)" (Merwin), **Supp. III Part 1:** 342, 346
"Anabasis (II)" (Merwin), **Supp. III Part 1:** 342, 346
Anagrams: A Novel (Moore), **Supp. X:** 163, 164, 167, **169–171,** 172
Analects (Confucius), **Supp. IV Part 1:** 14
Analects, The (Pound, trans.), **III:** 472
Analogy (J. Butler), **II:** 8
"Analysis of a Theme" (Stevens), **IV:** 81
Anarchiad, The, A Poem on the Restoration of Chaos and Substantial Night, in Twenty Four Books (Barlow), **Supp. II Part 1:** 70
Anarchist Woman, An (Hapgood), **Supp. XVII:** 102–103; **Supp. XXI:** 5
Anatomy Lesson, and Other Stories, The (Connell), **Supp. XIV:** 84, 87, 89
"Anatomy Lesson, The" (Connell), **Supp. XIV:** 84, 86, 87
Anatomy Lesson, The (P. Roth), **Retro. Supp. II:** 286, 290; **Supp. III Part 2:** 422–423, 425
"Anatomy Lesson of Dr. Nicholaas Tulp, Amsterdam, 1632, The" (Bierds), **Supp. XVII:** 27–28
Anatomy of Criticism (Frye), **Supp. XIII:** 19; **Supp. XIV:** 15
Anatomy of Melancholy (Burton), **III:** 78; **Supp. XVII:** 229
Anatomy of Nonsense, The (Winters), **Supp. II Part 2:** 811, 812
Anaya, Rudolfo A., **Supp. IV Part 2:** 502; **Supp. XIII:** 213, 220; **Supp. XIX:** 97
"Ancestor" (A. Finch), **Supp. XVII:** 72
Ancestors (Atherton), **Supp. XXIV:** 23, 25
Ancestors (Maxwell), **Supp. VIII:** 152, 168
"Ancestors, The" (Tate), **IV:** 128
Ancestral Voice: Conversations with N. Scott Momaday (Woodard), **Supp. IV Part 2:** 484, 485, 486, 489, 493
"Anchorage" (Harjo), **Supp. XII:** 220–221
Ancient Child, The: A Novel (Momaday), **Supp. IV Part 2:** 488, 489–491, 492, 493
"Ancient Dog Grave, Unearthed During Construction of the Athens Metro, An" (Stallings), **Supp. XXV:** 232
"Ancient Egypt/Fannie Goldbarth" (Goldbarth), **Supp. XII:** 191–192
Ancient Evenings (Mailer), **Retro. Supp. II:** 206, 210, 213
Ancient Law, The (Glasgow), **II:** 179–180, 192
Ancient Musics (Goldbarth), **Supp. XII:** 191–192
"Ancient Semitic Rituals for the Dead" (Goldbarth), **Supp. XII:** 191–192
Ancient Track, The (Lovecraft), **Supp. XXV:** 120
"Ancient World, The" (Doty), **Supp. XI:** 122
& (And) (Cummings), **I:** 429, 431, 432, 437, 445, 446, 448
Andersen, Hans Christian, **I:** 441; **Supp. I Part 2:** 622
Andersen, Hendrik Christian, **Supp. XX: 232**
Anderson, Charles R., **Supp. I Part 1:** 356, 360, 368, 371, 372
Anderson, Frances, **I:** 231
Anderson, Guy, **Supp. X:** 264, 265
Anderson, Henry J., **Supp. I Part 1:** 156
Anderson, Irwin M., **I:** 98–99
Anderson, Mrs. Irwin M., **I:** 98–99
Anderson, Jon, **Supp. V:** 338
Anderson, Judith, **III:** 399
Anderson, Karl, **I:** 99, 103
Anderson, Lorraine, **Supp. XVIII:** 189
Anderson, Margaret, **I:** 103; **III:** 171, 471; **Supp. XXV:** 18; **Supp. XXVII:** 86
Anderson, Marian, **Supp. XXII:** 283
Anderson, Mary Jane. See Lanier, Mrs. Robert Sampson (Mary Jane Anderson)
Anderson, Maxwell, **III:** 159
Anderson, Quentin, **Retro. Supp. I:** 392
Anderson, Robert, **Supp. I Part 1:** 277; **Supp. V:** 108
Anderson, Sally, **Supp. XIII:** 95
Anderson, Sherwood, **I: 97–120,** 211, 374, 375, 384, 405, 423, 445, 480,

487, 495, 506, 518; **II:** 27, 38, 44, 55, 56, 68, 250–251, 263, 271, 289, 451, 456–457; **III:** 220, 224, 382–383, 453, 483, 545, 576, 579; **IV:** 27, 40, 46, 190, 207, 433, 451, 482; **Retro. Supp. I:** 79, 80, 177; **Retro. Supp. III:** 45, 76; **Supp. I Part 2:** 378, 430, 459, 472, 613; **Supp. IV Part 2:** 502; **Supp. IX:** 14, 309; **Supp. V:** 12, 250; **Supp. VIII:** 39, 152; **Supp. XI:** 159, 164; **Supp. XII:** 343; **Supp. XV:** 298; **Supp. XVI:** 17, 20; **Supp. XVII:** 105; **Supp. XX: 69, 75; Supp. XXIII:** 68, 162, 164; **Supp. XXIV:** 136; **Supp. XXV:** 18; **Supp. XXVII:** 83, 86
Anderson, Mrs. Sherwood (Tennessee Mitchell), **I:** 100; **Supp. I Part 2:** 459, 460
Anderson, T. J., **Supp. XIII:** 132
Anderson, Wendy, **Supp. XXI:** 255
Anderssen, A., **III:** 252
"And Hickman Arrives" (Ellison), **Retro. Supp. II:** 118, 126; **Supp. II Part 1:** 248
And in the Hanging Gardens (Aiken), **I:** 63
"And It Came to Pass" (Wright), **Supp. XV:** 348
And I Worked at the Writer's Trade (Cowley), **Supp. II Part 1:** 137, 139, 141, 143, 147, 148
"...And Ladies of the Club" (J. W. Miller), **Supp. XX: 161**
And Live Apart (Peacock), **Supp. XIX: 196–197**
Andorra (Cameron), **Supp. XII:** 79, 81, **88–91**
"—and Other Poets" (column; Untermeyer), **Supp. XV:** 294
"—and Other Poets" (Untermeyer), **Supp. XV:** 297
"Andoumboulous Brush" (Mackey), **Supp. XXVII:** 156
Andracki, Thaddeus, **Supp. XXVI:** 108
Andral, Gabriel, **Supp. I Part 1:** 302
Andre, Michael, **Supp. XII:** 117–118, 129, 132, 133–134
"Andrea Is Changing Her Name" (Brockmeier), **Supp. XXII:** 61
Andre's Mother (McNally), **Supp. XIII:** 206
Andress, Ursula, **Supp. XI:** 307
"Andrew Jackson" (Masters), **Supp. I Part 2:** 472
Andrews, Bruce, **Supp. IV Part 2:** 426
Andrews, Peter, **Supp. XX: 87**
Andrews, Raymond, **Supp. XXVI: 1–16**
Andrews, Roy Chapman, **Supp. X:** 172
Andrews, Tom, **Supp. XI:** 317
Andrews, Wayne, **IV:** 310
Andrews, William L., **Supp. IV Part 1:** 13; **Supp. XIX:** 72; **Supp. XX: 105**
Andrews, William P., **Supp. XXV:** 250
Andreyev, Leonid Nikolaevich, **I:** 53; **II:** 425
Andria (Terence), **IV:** 363
"Androgynous Kiss" (Gallagher), **Supp. XXIV:** 170
"Andromache" (Dubus), **Supp. VII:** 84
"And Summer Will Not Come Again" (Plath), **Retro. Supp. II:** 242
"And That Night Clifford Died" (Levine), **Supp. V:** 195
And the Band Played On (Shilts), **Supp. X:** 145
"And the Moon Be Still as Bright" (Bradbury), **Supp. IV Part 1:** 106
"And the Sea Shall Give up Its Dead" (Wilder), **IV:** 358
And Things That Go Bump in the Night (McNally), **Supp. XIII: 196–197,** 205, 208
And to Think That I Saw It on Mulberry Street (Geisel), **Supp. XVI:** 100, 101, 104
"And Ut Pictura Poesis Is Her Name" (Ashbery), **Supp. III Part 1:** 19
And We Are Millions (Ryan), **Supp. XVIII:** 225
"And Winter" (Boyle), **Supp. XXIV:** 63
"Andy Warhol: Andy Do It" (Brainard), **Supp. XXVII:** 25
"Anecdote and Storyteller" (Howe), **Supp. VI:** 127
"Anecdote of the Jar" (Stevens), **IV:** 83–84
"Anemone" (Rukeyser), **Supp. VI:** 281, 285
"Angel, The" (Buck), **Supp. II Part 1:** 127
"Angel and Unicorn and Butterfly" (Everwine), **Supp. XV:** 76
Angela's Ashes (McCourt), **Supp. XII: 271–279,** 283, 285; **Supp. XXII:** 94
"Angel at the Grave, The" (Wharton), **IV:** 310; **Retro. Supp. I:** 365
"Angel Butcher" (Levine), **Supp. V:** 181
Angel City (Shepard), **Supp. III Part 2:** 432, 445
Angelica (Holding), **Supp. XXII: 120–121**
"Angel Is My Watermark!, The" (H. Miller), **III:** 180
Angell, Carol, **Supp. I Part 2:** 655
Angell, Katharine Sergeant. See White, Katharine
Angell, Roger, **Supp. I Part 2:** 655; **Supp. V:** 22; **Supp. VIII:** 139
Angel Landing (Hoffman), **Supp. X: 82–83**
"Angel Levine" (Malamud), **Supp. I Part 2:** 431, 432, 433–434, 437
Angel of Bethesda, The (Mather), **Supp. II Part 2:** 464
"Angel of the Bridge, The" (Cheever), **Supp. I Part 1:** 186–187
"Angel of the Odd, The" (Poe), **III:** 425
Angelo Herndon Jones (Hughes), **Retro. Supp. I:** 203
"Angel on the Porch, An" (Wolfe), **IV:** 451
Angelou, Maya, **Supp. IV Part 1: 1–19; Supp. XI:** 20, 245; **Supp. XIII:** 185; **Supp. XVI:** 259; **Supp. XXI:** 172
"Angel Poem, The" (Stern), **Supp. IX:** 292
Angels and Earthly Creatures (Wylie), **Supp. I Part 2:** 709, 713, 724–730
Angels Flight (Connelly), **Supp. XXI:** 72, **72–73,** 75, 80
"Angels for Djuna Barnes" (Boyle), **Supp. XXIV:** 63
Angels in America: A Gay Fantasia on National Themes (Kushner), **Supp. IX:** 131, 134, **141–146; Supp. XXIV:** 272
"Angels of the Love Affair" (Sexton), **Supp. II Part 2:** 692
Angels over Broadway (screenplay, Hecht), **Supp. XXVII:** 93
"Angel's Trumpet, The"(P. Benedict), **Supp. XXIII:** 48
"Angel Surrounded by Paysans" (Stevens), **IV:** 93
Angel That Troubled the Waters, The (Wilder), **IV:** 356, 357–358
"Anger" (Creeley), **Supp. IV Part 1:** 150–152
Anger (Sarton), **Supp. VIII: 256**
"Anger against Children" (R. Bly), **Supp. IV Part 1:** 73
Angle of Ascent (Hayden), **Supp. II Part 1:** 363, 367, 370
"Angle of Geese" (Momaday), **Supp. IV Part 2:** 485
Angle of Geese and Other Poems (Momaday), **Supp. IV Part 2:** 487, 491
Angle of Repose (Stegner), **Supp. IV**

Part 2: 599, 605, 606, 610–611
"Angle of Repose and the Writings of Mary Hallock Foote: A Source Study" (Williams-Walsh), **Supp. IV Part 2:** 611
"Anglo-Mongrels and the Rose" (Loy), **Supp. XXII:** 156, 159, 166–167
Anglo-Saxon Century, The (Dos Passos), **I:** 474–475, 483
Angoff, Charles, **III:** 107
"Angola Question Mark" (Hughes), **Supp. I Part 1:** 344
Angry Hills, The (Uris), **Supp. XX: 246, 250**
Angry Wife, The (Sedges), **Supp. II Part 1:** 125
"Angry Women Are Building: Issues and Struggles Facing American Indian Women Today" (Gunn Allen), **Supp. IV Part 1:** 324
"Animal, Vegetable, and Mineral" (Bogan), **Supp. III Part 1:** 66
"Animal Acts" (Simic), **Supp. VIII:** 278
Animal and Vegetable Physiology Considered with Reference to Natural Theology (Roget), **Supp. I Part 1:** 312
"Animal Bodies: Corporeality, Class, and Subject Formation in The Wide, Wide World" (Mason), **Supp. XVIII:** 263
Animal Dreams (Kingsolver), **Supp. VII:** 199, 204–207
Animal Magnetism (Prose), **Supp. XVI:** 251, 260
"Animals, The" (Merwin), **Supp. III Part 1:** 348
"Animals Are Passing from Our Lives" (Levine), **Supp. V:** 181, 182
Animals in That Country, The (Atwood), **Supp. XIII:** 20, 33
Animals of the Soul: Sacred Animals of the Oglala Sioux (Brown), **Supp. IV Part 2:** 487
"Animals You Eat, The" (X. J. Kennedy), **Supp. XV:** 169
"Animula" (Eliot), **Retro. Supp. I:** 64
Anita Loos Rediscovered (M. A. Loos), **Supp. XVI:** 196
Ankor Wat (Ginsberg), **Supp. II Part 1:** 323
Ann, Leslee, **Supp. XXIV:** 264
"Annabelle" (Komunyakaa), **Supp. XIII:** 117
"Annabel Lee" (Poe), **Retro. Supp. I:** 273; **Retro. Supp. II:** 266; **Retro. Supp. III:** 232
Anna Christie (O'Neill), **III:** 386, 389, 390; **Supp. XXII:** 24
"Anna Grasa" (Weigl), **Supp. XIX:** 278
"Anna in Mourning" (Weigl), **Supp. XIX:** 288
Anna Karenina (Tolstoy), **I:** 10; **II:** 290; **Retro. Supp. I:** 225; **Supp. V:** 323
"Anna Karenina" (Trilling), **Supp. III Part 2:** 508
Annan, Gabriele, **Retro. Supp. III:** 290
Annan, Noel, **Supp. XX: 240**
"Anna's Grace" (Weigl), **Supp. XIX:** 282–283
"Anna Who Was Mad" (Sexton), **Supp. II Part 2:** 692
"Ann Burlak" (Rukeyser), **Supp. VI:** 280
"Anne" (Oliver), **Supp. VII:** 232
"Anne" (R. H. Davis), **Supp. XVI:** 91, 92
"Anne at the Symphony" (Shields), **Supp. VII:** 310
"Anne Bradstreet's Poetic Voices" (Requa), **Supp. I Part 1:** 107
Anne Bradstreet: The Worldly Puritan (Stanford), **Retro. Supp. III:** 1
Anne of Geierstein: or, The Maiden of the Mist (Scott), **Supp. XX: 234**
Anne Sexton: The Artist and Her Critics (McClatchy), **Supp. XII:** 253
"Ann from the Street" (Dixon), **Supp. XII:** 146–147
"Ann Garner" (Agee), **I:** 27
"Anniad, The" (Brooks), **Supp. III Part 1:** 77, 78
Annie (musical), **Supp. IV Part 2:** 577
Annie Allen (Brooks), **Supp. III Part 1:** 76–79
Annie Dillard Reader, The (Dillard), **Supp. VI:** 23
Annie Hall (film; Allen), **Supp. IV Part 1:** 205; **Supp. XV:** 1, 2, 4, 5, **6–7,** 14
Annie John (Kincaid), **Supp. VII:** 184–186, 193
Annie Kilburn, a Novel (Howells), **II:** 275, 286, 287
"Annihilation" (X. J. Kennedy), **Supp. XV:** 168
"Annihilation of Matter, The" (Bronk), **Supp. XXI:** 30
Anniversary (Shields), **Supp. VII:** 320, 322, 323, 324
"Anniversary Poem" (Oppen), **Supp. XXVI:** 237
"Annunciation" (Nelson), **Supp. XVIII:** 174
"Annunciation, The" (Le Sueur), **Supp. V:** 130
Ann Vickers (Lewis), **II:** 453
"A No-Account Creole, A" (Chopin), **Retro. Supp. II:** 64
"Anodyne" (Komunyakaa), **Supp. XIII:** 130
"Another" (Bradstreet), **Retro. Supp. III:** 12–13
Another America/Otra America (Kingsolver), **Supp. VII:** 207–209
"Another Animal" (Swenson), **Supp. IV Part 2:** 639
Another Animal: Poems (Swenson), **Supp. IV Part 2:** 639–641, 649
Another Antigone (Gurney), **Supp. V:** 97, 98, 100, 101, 102, 105
"Another August" (Merrill), **Supp. III Part 1:** 326
"Another Beer" (Matthews), **Supp. IX:** 158
Another Country (Baldwin), **Retro. Supp. II: 9–11,** 14; **Supp. I Part 1:** 51, 52, 56–58, 63, 67, 337; **Supp. II Part 1:** 40; **Supp. VIII:** 349
"Another Language" (Jong), **Supp. V:** 131
Another Mother Tongue: Gay Words, Gay Worlds (Grahn), **Supp. IV Part 1:** 330
"Another Night in the Ruins" (Kinnell), **Supp. III Part 1:** 239, 251
"Another Night with Snow" (W. V. Davis), **Supp. XXI:** 90, 91
"Another Old Woman" (W. C. Williams), **Retro. Supp. I:** 423
Another Part of the Forest (Hellman), **Supp. I Part 1:** 282–283, 297
Another Republic: 17 European and South American Writers (Strand, trans.), **Supp. IV Part 2:** 630
Another Roadside Attraction (Robbins), **Supp. X:** 259, 261, 262, 263, 264, 265–266, **267–269,** 274, 275, 277, 284
Another Side of Bob Dylan (album, Dylan), **Supp. XVIII:** 25
"Another Spring Uncovered" (Swenson), **Supp. IV Part 2:** 644
Another Thin Man (film), **Supp. IV Part 1:** 355
Another Time (Auden), **Supp. II Part 1:** 15
Another Turn of the Crank (Berry), **Supp. X:** 25, 35
"Another upon the Same" (Taylor), **IV:** 161
"Another Voice" (Wilbur), **Supp. III Part 2:** 557
"Another Wife" (Anderson), **I:** 114
"Another Winter Night" (Budbill), **Supp. XIX:** 10

This World" (J. W. Miller), **Supp. XX: 165**
"Appalachian Values/American Values" (J. W. Miller), **Supp. XX: 165**
Appaloosa (Parker), **Supp. XIX:** 187
"Appeal to H. G. Wells" (Sturgis), **Supp. XX: 233, 240**
"Appeal to Progressives, An" (Wilson), **IV:** 429
Appeal to Reason (Paine), **I:** 490
Appeal to the World, An (Du Bois), **Supp. II Part 1:** 184
Appearance and Reality (Bradley), **I:** 572
Appel, Richard, **Supp. XXVII:** 233
"Appendix to 'The Anniad' " (Brooks), **Supp. III Part 1:** 77
"Applause, Applause"(Thompson), **Supp. XXIII:** 289, 291, 301
Apple, Max, **Supp. VIII:** 14; **Supp. XVII: 1–11,** 49–50
Apple, Sam, **Supp. XVII:** 8
"Apple, The" (Kinnell), **Supp. III Part 1:** 250
Applebaum, Anne, **Supp. XVI:** 153
Applebome, Peter, **Supp. XXI:** 38
Applegarth, Mabel, **II:** 465, 478
"Apple-Maggot Fly, The" (Major), **Supp. XXII:** 182
"Apple of Discord, The" (Humphrey), **Supp. IX:** 109
"Apple Peeler" (Francis), **Supp. IX:** 82
"Apple Rind" (C. Frost), **Supp. XV:** 102
"Apples" (Brockmeier), **Supp. XXII:** 51, 53
"Apples, The" (Di Piero), **Supp. XIX:** 46
Appleseed, Johnny (pseudonym). See Chapman, John (Johnny Appleseed)
Apple That Astonished Paris, The (Collins), **Supp. XXI:** 53, 57
Appleton, Nathan, **II:** 488
Appleton, Thomas Gold, **Supp. I Part 1:** 306; **Supp. I Part 2:** 415
"Apple Tree, The" (McCarriston), **Supp. XIV:** 263, 268
"Applicant, The" (Plath), **Retro. Supp. II:** 252; **Supp. I Part 2:** 535, 544, 545
"Application, The" (Neugeboren), **Supp. XVI:** 219, 220, 225
"Applications of the Doctrine" (Hass), **Supp. VI: 100–101**
Appointment, The (film), **Supp. IX:** 253
Appointment in Samarra (O'Hara), **III:** 361, 363–364, 365–367, 371, 374, 375, 383
Appreciation of Sarah Orne Jewett (Cary), **Retro. Supp. II:** 132
"Apprentice, The"(Dybek), **Supp. XXIII:** 71
"Approaches, The" (Merwin), **Supp. III Part 1:** 350
"Approaching Artaud" (Sontag), **Supp. III Part 2:** 470–471
"Approaching Prayer" (Dickey), **Supp. IV Part 1:** 175
"Approaching the Mohawk Village: Jogues' Journal"(Kenny), **Supp. XXIII:** 152
Approach to Literature, An: A Collection of Prose and Verse with Analyses and Discussions (Brooks, Warren, and Purser), **Su pp. XIV:**4
"Approach to Thebes, The" (Kunitz), **Supp. III Part 1:** 265–267
Approach to Vedanta, An (Isherwood), **Supp. XIV:** 157, 163, 164
"Appropriation of Cultures, The" (Everett), **Supp. XVIII:** 66
Approximately Paradise (Skloot), **Supp. XX: 196, 202, 203–204**
"Après-midi d'un faune, L' " (Mallarmé), **III:** 8
"April" (Bierds), **Supp. XVII:** 29
"April" (W. C. Williams), **Retro. Supp. I:** 422
"April" (Winters), **Supp. II Part 2:** 788
April, Steve. See Lacy, Ed
April Galleons (Ashbery), **Supp. III Part 1:** 26
"April Galleons" (Ashbery), **Supp. III Part 1:** 26
April Hopes (Howells), **II:** 285, 289
"April Lovers" (Ransom), **III:** 489–490
"April Saturday 1960" (Huddle), **Supp. XXVI:** 150
"April Showers" (Wharton), **Retro. Supp. I:** 361
"April Today Main Street" (Olson), **Supp. II Part 2:** 581
April Twilights (Cather), **I:** 313; **Retro. Supp. I:** 5; **Retro. Supp. III:** 20
"Apt Pupil" (King), **Supp. V:** 152
Arabian Nights, **I:** 204; **II:** 8; **Supp. I Part 2:** 584, 599; **Supp. IV Part 1:** 1
"Arabic Coffee" (Nye), **Supp. XIII:** 276
"Araby" (Joyce), **I:** 174; **Supp. VIII:** 15
Aragon, Louis, **I:** 429; **III:** 471; **Retro. Supp. II:** 85, 321
Arana-Ward, Marie, **Supp. VIII:** 84
Ararat (Glück), **Supp. V:** 79, 86–87
Aratani, Mariko, **Supp. XXIII:** 136
"Arbiter, The" (Toole), **Supp. XXVI:** 243
Arbre du voyageur, L' (W. J. Smith; Haussmann, trans.), **Supp. XIII:** 347
Arbus, Diane, **Supp. XII:** 188
Arbuthnott, John (pseudonym). See Henry, O.
"Arc, The" (Bidart), **Supp. XV:** 25–26, 27
Archaeologist of Morning (Olson), **Supp. II Part 2:** 557
Archaeology of the Circle: New and Selected Poems (Weigl), **Supp. XIX:** 282
"Archaic Maker, The" (Merwin), **Supp. III Part 1:** 357
Archaic Smile (Stallings), **Supp. XXV:** 221, 222, 223, 224, 228–231, 233
"Archaic Torso of Apollo" (Rilke), **Supp. XV:** 148
"Archaischer Torso Apollos" (Rilke), **Supp. XVII:** 244
"Archbishop, The" (Gioia), **Supp. XV:** 126, 127
Archer (television show), **Supp. IV Part 2:** 474
Archer, William, **IV:** 131; **Retro. Supp. I:** 228
Archer at Large (Macdonald), **Supp. IV Part 2:** 473
Archer in Hollywood (Macdonald), **Supp. IV Part 2:** 474
"Archetype and Signature: The Relationship of Poet and Poem" (Fiedler), **Supp. XIII:** 101
"Archibald Higbie" (Masters), **Supp. I Part 2:** 461
"Architect, The" (Bourne), **I:** 223
Architect, The (Briggs and Ranlett), **Supp. XVIII:** 3
Architect, The (Levin), **Supp. XXVII:** 133
Archuleta, Elizabeth, **Supp. XXVI:** 106
Arctic Dreams (Lopez), **Supp. V:** 211
Arctic Refuge: A Circle of Testimony (Haines), **Supp. XII:** 205
"Arcturus" (Connell), **Supp. XIV:** 88
À rebours (Huysmans), **Supp. XX: 239**
Arendt, Hannah, **II:** 544; **Retro. Supp. I:** 87; **Retro. Supp. II:** 28, 117; **Supp. I Part 2:** 570; **Supp. IV Part 1:** 386; **Supp. VIII:** 98, 99, 100, 243; **Supp. XII:** 166–167
Arensberg, Louise, **Supp. XXII:** 162
Arensberg, Walter, **IV:** 408; **Retro. Supp. I:** 416; **Supp. XXII:** 162
Aren't You Happy for Me? (Bausch),

Supp. VII: 42, 51, 54
Areopagitica (Milton), **Supp. I Part 2:** 422
"Are You a Doctor?" (Carver), **Supp. III Part 1:** 139–141
"Are You Mr. William Stafford? (Stafford), **Supp. XI:** 317
Are You My Mother? A Comic Drama (Bechdel), **Supp. XXV:** 1, 2, 9–14
"Are You Okay?" (video, Ellis), **Supp. XXVII:** 80
Argall: The True Story of Pocahontas and Captain John Smith (Vollmann), **Supp. XVII:** 225, 226, 231, 232, 233
"Argonauts of 49, California's Golden Age" (Harte), **Supp. II Part 1:** 353, 355
"Arguantando" (Díaz), **Supp. XXIV:** 88–89
"Arguments of Everlasting" (B. Kelly), **Supp. XVII:** 129
"Arguments with the Gestapo Continued: II" (Wright), **Supp. XV:** 344
"Arguments with the Gestapo Continued: Literary Resistance" (Wright), **Supp. XV:** 344
Ari (musical, Uris), **Supp. XX: 247**
Aria da Capo (Millay), **III:** 137–138
"Ariadne and the Rest" (Stallings), **Supp. XXV:** 223, 229
Ariadne's Thread: A Collection of Contemporary Women's Journals (Lifshin, ed.), **Supp. XVI:** 37–38
"Arias, 1971" (Hull), **Supp. XXI:** 135
Ariel (Plath), **Retro. Supp. II: 250–255; Supp. I Part 2:** 526, 539, 541; **Supp. V:** 79; **Supp. XXI:** 58; **Supp. XXII:** 93; **Supp. XXVII:** 296
"Ariel" (Plath), **Supp. I Part 2:** 542, 546
"Ariel Poems" (Eliot), **I:** 579
Ariosto, Ludovico, **Supp. XV:** 175
"Ariosto: Critical Notice of His Life and Genius" (Hunt), **Supp. XV:** 175
Arise, Arise (Zukofsky), **Supp. III Part 2:** 619, 629
Aristides. See Epstein, Joseph
"Aristocracy" (Emerson), **II:** 6
Aristocracy and Justice (More), **I:** 223
Aristocrat, The (Richter), **Supp. XVIII:** 220
Aristophanes, **I:** 436; **II:** 577; **Supp. I Part 2:** 406
Aristotle, **I:** 58, 265, 280, 527; **II:** 9, 12, 198, 536; **III:** 20, 115, 145, 157, 362, 422, 423; **IV:** 10, 18, 74–75, 89; **Supp. I Part 1:** 104, 296; **Supp. I Part 2:** 423; **Supp. IV Part 1:** 391; **Supp. IV Part 2:** 526, 530; **Supp. X:** 78; **Supp. XI:** 249; **Supp. XII:** 106; **Supp. XIV:** 242–243
Aristotle Contemplating the Bust of Homer (Rembrandt), **Supp. IV Part 1:** 390, 391
"Arkansas Traveller" (Wright), **Supp. V:** 334
"Arkham" (Howard), **Supp. XXVII:** 118
Arlen, Harold, **Supp. XXII:** 6
"Arm, The" (X. J. Kennedy), **Supp. XV:** 169
"Armadillo, The" (Bishop), **Supp. I Part 1:** 93
Armadillo in the Grass (Hearon), **Supp. VIII: 58–59**
"Armageddon" (Ransom), **III:** 489, 492
Armageddon (Uris), **Supp. XX: 243, 247, 248, 252–253**
Armah, Aiy Kwei, **Supp. IV Part 1:** 373
Armenian Golgotha: A Memoir of the Armenian Genocide, 1915– 1918 (Grigoris Balakian; trans. Peter Balakian and Sevag), **Supp. XXIII:** 28, **29–32**
Armies of the Night, The (Mailer), **III:** 39–40, 41, 42, 44, 45, 46; **Retro. Supp. II:** 205, 206–207, 208; **Supp. IV Part 1:** 207; **Supp. XIV:** 49, 162
"Arm in Arm" (Simpson), **Supp. IX:** 267–268
Arminius, Jacobus, **I:** 557
Armitage, Shelley, **Supp. IV Part 2:** 439
Arm of Flesh, The (Salter), **Supp. IX:** 251
"Armor" (Dickey), **Supp. IV Part 1:** 179
Armored Attack (film), **Supp. I Part 1:** 281
Arms, George W., **Supp. I Part 2:** 416–417
Armstrong, George, **Supp. I Part 2:** 386
Armstrong, Louis, **Retro. Supp. II:** 114
"'Arm the Paper Arm': Kenneth Koch's Postmodern Comedy" (Chinitz), **Supp. XV:** 180, 185
"Army" (Corso), **Supp. XII:** 117, 127
Army Brat (W. J. Smith), **Supp. XIII:** 331, 347
"Army Recruiting Methods" (Bodenheim), **Supp. XXV:** 19
Arna Bontemps Langston Hughes: Letters 1925–1967 (Nichols), **Retro. Supp. I:** 194
"Arna Bontemps Talks About the Renaissance" (Collins), **Supp. XXII:** 7
Arner, Robert D., **Retro. Supp. II:** 62
"Arnie" (Budbill), **Supp. XIX:** 6
Arnold, Edwin T., **Supp. VIII:** 189
Arnold, George W., **Supp. I Part 2:** 411
Arnold, Marilyn, **Supp. IV Part 1:** 220
Arnold, Matthew, **I:** 222, 228, 275; **II:** 20, 110, 338, 541; **III:** 604; **IV:** 349; **Retro. Supp. I:** 56, 325; **Retro. Supp. III:** 261; **Supp. I Part 2:** 416, 417, 419, 529, 552, 602; **Supp. IX:** 298; **Supp. XIV:** 11, 335; **Supp. XIX:** 41; **Supp. XXI:** 90
Arnold, Thurman, **Supp. I Part 2:** 645
Aronson, Steven M. L., **Supp. V:** 4
Around about America (Caldwell), **I:** 290
"Arrangement in Black and White" (Parker), **Supp. IX:** 198
Arregoces, Christina, **Supp. XXVI:** 148, 158
"Arrival at Santos" (Bishop), **Retro. Supp. II:** 46; **Supp. IX:** 45–46
"Arrival of the Bee Box, The" (Plath), **Retro. Supp. II:** 255
Arrivistes, The: Poem 1940–1949 (Simpson), **Supp. IX:** 265, **267–268**
Arrogance (J. Scott), **Supp. XVII: 186–188,** 189, **191, 192, 194**
"Arrow" (Dove), **Supp. IV Part 1:** 250
"Arrowhead Hunting" (Stallings), **Supp. XXV:** 232
Arrow mystery series (Myers), **Supp. XXVII:** 212
Arrowsmith (Lewis), **I:** 362; **II:** 445–446, 449
"Arsenal at Springfield, The" (Longfellow), **Retro. Supp. II:** 168
"Arson at Midnight" (Nelson), **Supp. XVIII:** 186
"Arson Plus" (Hammett), **Supp. IV Part 1:** 343; **Supp. XXI:** 68
"Ars Poetica" (Dove), **Supp. IV Part 1:** 250
"Ars Poetica" (Dunn), **Supp. XI:** 154
"Ars Poetica" (MacLeish), **III:** 9–10
"Ars Poetica" (X. J. Kennedy), **Supp. XV:** 154
"Ars Poetica: A Found Poem" (Kumin), **Supp. IV Part 2:** 455
"Ars Poetica; or, Who Lives in the Ivory Tower" (McGrath), **Supp. X:** 117
"Ars Poetica: Some Recent Criticism" (Wright), **Supp. III Part 2:** 603
"Art" (Emerson), **II:** 13
Art (Reza), **Supp. XXI:** 148
"Art and Architecture of the Double Ending, The"(Painter), **Supp.**

XXIII: 295
"Art and Neurosis" (Trilling), **Supp. III Part 2:** 502
Art and Technics (Mumford), **Supp. II Part 2:** 483
Art & Ardor: Essays (Ozick), **Supp. V:** 258, 272
Art as Experience (Dewey), **I:** 266
Art by Subtraction (Reid), **IV:** 41
Art Chronicles 1954–1966 (O'Hara), **Supp. XXIII:** 220
Art de toucher le clavecin, L' (Couperin), **III:** 464
"Artemis" (Davison), **Supp. XXVI:** 69
Artemis to Actaeon and Other Verse (Wharton), **Retro. Supp. I:** 372; **Retro. Supp. III:** 283
Arte of English Poesie (Puttenham), **Supp. I Part 1:** 113
"Art"(Hadas), **Supp. XXIII:** 115–116
"Art History" (Cliff), **Supp. XXII:** 75–76
Arthur, Anthony, **Supp. IV Part 2:** 606
Arthur Mervyn; or, Memoirs of the Year 1793 (Brown), **Supp. I Part 1:** 137–140, 144
"Article of Faith" (Sobin), **Supp. XVI:** 291
Articles of Light & Elation (Sobin), **Supp. XVI:** 291
Articulation of Sound Forms in Time (Howe), **Supp. IV Part 2:** 419, 431–433
"Artifical Nigger, The" (O'Connor), **Retro. Supp. III:** 213, 218–219
"Artificer" (X. J. Kennedy), **Supp. XV:** 160
"Artificial Nigger, The" (O'Connor), **III:** 343, 351, 356, 358; **Retro. Supp. II:** 229, 232
Artist, The: A Drama without Words (Mencken), **III:** 104
Artist as Revolutionary, The (Buhle), **Supp. XXI:** 172
"Artist of the Beautiful, The" (Hawthorne), **Retro. Supp. I:** 149; **Retro. Supp. III:** 115
Artistry of Grief (Torsney), **Retro. Supp. I:** 224
Artists and Concubines (Silver), **Supp. XXIV:** 265
"Artists' and Models' Ball, The" (Brooks), **Supp. III Part 1:** 72
Art of Detective Fiction, The (Swales), **Supp. XIX:** 183
"Art of Disappearing, The" (Nye), **Supp. XIII:** 287
Art of Drowning, The (Collins), **Supp. XXI:** 54, 60, 64
Art of Eating, The (M. F. K. Fisher), **Supp. XVII:** 87, 90, 91
Art of Fiction, The (Gardner), **Supp. VI:** 73
"Art of Fiction, The" (H. James), **Retro. Supp. I:** 226; **Retro. Supp. II:** 223
Art of Hunger, The (Auster), **Supp. XII:** 22
"Art of Keeping Your Mouth Shut, The" (Heller), **Supp. IV Part 1:** 383
"Art of Literature and Commonsense, The" (Nabokov), **Retro. Supp. I:** 271
Art of Living and Other Stories, The (Gardner), **Supp. VI:** 72
Art of Love, The (Koch), **Supp. XV:** 182
"Art of Love, The" (Koch), **Supp. XV:** 182
Art of Poetry, The (Koch), **Supp. XV:** 175–176, 178, 188
"Art of Poetry, The" (Koch), **Supp. XV:** 182
"Art of Poetry, The" (McClatchy), **Supp. XII:** 262
Art of Political Murder, The (Goldman), **Supp. XXV:** 49, 57–59
"Art of Romare Bearden, The" (Ellison), **Retro. Supp. II:** 123
"Art of Storytelling, The" (Simpson), **Supp. IX:** 277
Art of Sylvia Plath, The (Newman), **Supp. I Part 2:** 527
Art of the Moving Picture, The (Lindsay), **Supp. I Part 2:** 376, 391–392, 394; **Supp. XVI:** 185
Art of the Novel (H. James), **Retro. Supp. I:** 227
"Art of Theodore Dreiser, The" (Bourne), **I:** 235
Art of the Personal Essay, The (Lopate, comp.), **Supp. XIII:** 280–281; **Supp. XVI:** 266
Art of the Self, The: Essays a Propos "Steps" (Kosinski), **Supp. VII:** 222
Art of the Wasted Day, The (Hampl), **Supp. XXII:** 85
Arts and Sciences (Goldbarth), **Supp. XII: 184–186**
Arts and Sciences: A Seventies Seduction (Mallon), **Supp. XIX:** 132, 135
"Art's Bread and Butter" (Benét), **Retro. Supp. I:** 108
Artsybashev, Mikhail, **Supp. XXIII:** 1
Arvin, Newton, **I:** 259; **II:** 508; **Retro. Supp. I:** 19, 137
Asali, Muna, **Supp. XIII:** 121, 126
"As a Little Child" (Taggard), **Supp. XXII:** 272
"As a Young Man" (Hayes), **Supp. XXVI:** 134–135
Asbury, Herbert, **Supp. IV Part 1:** 353
"Ascent, The" (Rash), **Supp. XXVII:** 228–229
Ascent of F6, The (Auden), **Supp. II Part 1:** 11, 13
Ascent to Truth, The (Merton), **Supp. VIII:** 208
Asch, Nathan, **Supp. XV:** 133, 134; **Supp. XXIII:** 4; **Supp. XXVI: 17–29**
Asch, Sholem, **IV:** 1, 9, 11, 14; **Retro. Supp. II:** 299; **Supp. XXIII: 1–18; Supp. XXVI:** 18
Ascherson, Neal, **Supp. XII:** 167
Ascher-Walsh, Rebecca, **Supp. XIX:** 54
"As Close as Breathing" (Jarman), **Supp. XVII:** 120
As David Danced (Bronk), **Supp. XXI:** 24
"As David Danced" (Bronk), **Supp. XXI:** 26
As Does New Hampshire and Other Poems (Sarton), **Supp. VIII:** 259
"As Evening Lays Dying" (Salinas), **Supp. XIII:** 319
"As Flowers Are" (Kunitz), **Supp. III Part 1:** 265
"Ash" (Sobin), **Supp. XVI:** 284–285
Ash, Nathan, **Supp. XXII:** 277
Ashbery, John, **Retro. Supp. I:** 313; **Supp. I Part 1:** 96; **Supp. III Part 1: 1–29; Supp. III Part 2:** 541; **Supp. IV Part 2:** 620; **Supp. IX:** 52; **Supp. VIII:** 272; **Supp. XI:** 139; **Supp. XIII:** 85; **Supp. XIX:** 40, 83; **Supp. XV:** 176, 177, 178, 188, 250; **Supp. XXI:** 227; **Supp. XXIII:** 207, 209, 210, 211, 215, 217, 220; **Supp. XXIV:** 33, 37, 44; **Supp. XXVI:** 70; **Supp. XXVII:** 17, 18, 22, 23
"Ashes" (Lamott), **Supp. XX: 141**
"Ashes" (Levine), **Supp. V:** 188
"Ashes of the Beacon" (Bierce), **I:** 209
Ashes: Poems Old and New (Levine), **Supp. V:** 178, 188–189
Ashford, Margaret Mary (Daisy), **II:** 426
Ashman, Angela, **Supp. XXIV:** 200
"Ash Wednesday" (Garrett), **Supp. VII:** 109–110
"Ash Wednesday" (Merton), **Supp. VIII:** 199
Ash Wednesday (T. S. Eliot), **I:** 570, 574–575, 578–579, 580, 582, 584, 585; **Retro. Supp. I:** 64; **Retro. Supp. III:** 58, 65
"Ash Wednesday" (T. S. Eliot), **Supp.**

IV Part 2: 436
Asian American Authors (Hsu and Palubinskas, eds.), **Supp. X:** 292
Asian American Heritage: An Anthology of Prose and Poetry (Wand), **Supp. X:** 292
Asian Figures (Mervin), **Supp. III Part 1:** 341
Asian Journal of Thomas Merton, The (Merton), **Supp. VIII:** 196, 206, 208
"Asian Peace Offers Rejected without Publication" (R. Bly), **Supp. IV Part 1:** 61
"Asides on the Oboe" (Stevens), **Retro. Supp. I:** 305
"As I Ebb'd with the Ocean of Life" (Whitman), **IV:** 342, 345–346; **Retro. Supp. I:** 404, 405
As I Lay Dying (Faulkner), **II:** 60–61, 69, 73, 74; **IV:** 100; **Retro. Supp. I:** 75, 82, 84, 85, 86, 88, 89, 91, 92; **Retro. Supp. III:** 80–81, 84; **Supp. IV Part 1:** 47; **Supp. IX:** 99, 103, 251; **Supp. VIII:** 37, 178; **Supp. XIV:** 24
"As I Lay Dying and The Waste Land: Some Relationships" (Dickerson), **Retro. Supp. III:** 81
"As I Lay with My Head in Your Lap, Camerado" (Whitman), **IV:** 347
Asimov, Isaac, **Supp. IV Part 1:** 116; **Supp. XVI:** 122
Asinof, Eliot, **II:** 424
As I Remember It (PBS documentary), **Supp. XVIII:** 277
Asirvatham, Sandy, **Supp. XVI:** 249
"As Is the Daughter, So Is Her Mother" (Patchett), **Supp. XII:** 310
"As It Was in the Beginning" (Benét), **Supp. XI:** 56
"As I Walked Out One Evening" (Auden), **Supp. II Part 1:** 13; **Supp. XV:** 126; **Supp. XX: 138**
"As I Went Down by Havre de Grace" (Wylie), **Supp. I Part 2:** 723
Ask a Policeman (Hinojosa), **Supp. XIX: 110–111**
"Ask Me" (Stafford), **Supp. XI:** 326–327
Ask Me Tomorrow (Cozzens), **I:** 365–367, 379
Ask the Dust (Fante), **Supp. XI:** 159, 160, 166, **167–169,** 172, 173, 174
"Ask the Optimist!" (Saunders), **Supp. XIX:** 235
Ask Your Mama (Hughes), **Supp. I Part 1:** 339, 341–342
Ask Your Mama: 12 Moods for Jazz (Hughes), **Retro. Supp. I:** 210, 211
As Little Children (R. P. Smith), **Supp. XIV:** 333
"As One Put Drunk into the Packet Boat" (Ashbery), **Supp. III Part 1:** 18
"Asparagus" (Nelson), **Supp. XVIII:** 178
"Aspects of Robinson" (Kees), **Supp. XV:** 134
Aspects of the Novel (Forster), **Retro. Supp. I:** 232; **Supp. VIII:** 155; **Supp. XXI:** 233
"Aspen and the Stream, The" (Wilbur), **Supp. III Part 2:** 555, 556
Aspern Papers, The (James), **Supp. V:** 101, 102
"Aspern Papers, The" (James), **Retro. Supp. I:** 219, 227, 228
Asphalt Georgics (Carruth), **Supp. XVI:** 54
Asphalt Jungle (film, Huston), **Supp. XIII:** 174
"Asphodel" (Welty), **IV:** 265, 271
"Asphodel, That Greeny Flower" (W. C. Williams), **Retro. Supp. I:** 429
"Aspic and Buttermilk" (Olds), **Supp. X:** 213
Asquith, Herbert Henry, **Retro. Supp. I:** 59
"Ass" (Cisneros), **Supp. VII:** 67
Assante, Armand, **Supp. VIII:** 74
Assassin, The: A Play in Three Acts (Shaw), **Supp. XIX:** 248
Assassins, The (Oates), **Supp. II Part 2:** 512, 517–519
"Assault" (Millay), **III:** 130–131
"Assemblage of Husbands and Wives, An" (Lewis), **II:** 455–456
"Assembloir" (Monson), **Supp. XXIV:** 237
Assembly (O'Hara), **III:** 361
As She Climbed Across the Table (Lethem), **Supp. XVIII: 140–141,** 148
Assignment, Wildlife (LaBastille), **Supp. X: 99,** 104
"Assimiliation in Recent American Jewish Autobiographies" (Krupnick), **Supp. XVI:** 153
Assistant, The (Malamud), **Supp. I Part 2:** 427, 428, 429, 431, 435, 441–445, 451; **Supp. XVI:** 220
Assommoir, L' (Zola), **II:** 291; **III:** 318
Assorted Prose (Updike), **IV:** 215–216, 218; **Retro. Supp. I:** 317, 319, 327
Astaire, Adele, **Supp. XVI:** 187
"As the Mist Leaves No Scar" (Cohen), **Supp. XXVII:** 56
As They Were (M. F. K. Fisher), **Supp. XVII:** 88
As They Were (M. F. K. Fisher), **Supp. XVII:** 89, 91
Astor, Mary, **Supp. IV Part 1:** 356; **Supp. XII:** 173
Astoria, or, Anecdotes of an Enterprise beyond the Rocky Mountains (Irving), **II:** 312
"Astounding News by Electric Express via Norfolk! The Atlantic Crossed in Three Days Signal Triumph of Mr. Monck's Flying-Machine . . ." (Poe), **III:** 413, 420
Astraea (Holmes), **III:** 82
Astro, Richard, **Supp. I Part 2:** 429, 445
"Astrological Fricassee" (H. Miller), **III:** 187
"Astronomer's Wife" (Boyle), **Supp. XXIV:** 58
Astrophil and Stella (Sidney), **Supp. XIV:** 128
Asturias, Miguel Ángel, **Supp. XXIV:** 89
"As Weary Pilgrim" (Bradstreet), **Retro. Supp. III:** 14; **Supp. I Part 1:** 103, 109, 122
As We Know (Ashbery), **Supp. III Part 1:** 9, 21–25
"As We Know" (Ashbery), **Supp. III Part 1:** 21–22
Aswell, Edward C., **IV:** 458, 459, 461
"Asylum, The" (Carruth), **Supp. XVI:** 48–49
"As You Like It" (Chopin), **Supp. I Part 1:** 217
As You Like It (Shakespeare), **Supp. I Part 1:** 308
"At a Bar" (Ferry), **Supp. XXIV:** 162
"At a Bar in Charlotte Amalie" (Updike), **IV:** 214
"At a Lecture" (Brodsky), **Supp. VIII:** 33
"At a Low Bar" (Ferry), **Supp. XXIV:** 149
"At a March against the Vietnam War" (R. Bly), **Supp. IV Part 1:** 61
"At a Reading" (McClatchy), **Supp. XII:** 256–257
"Atavism of John Tom Little Bear, The" (O. Henry), **Supp. II Part 1:** 410
"At Chênière Caminada" (Chopin), **Supp. I Part 1:** 220
"At Chinese Checkers" (Berryman), **I:** 182
Atchity, Kenneth John, **Supp. XI:** 227
"At Death's Window" (Lamott), **Supp. XX: 144**
At Eighty-Two (Sarton), **Supp. VIII:** 264

Atet A.D. (Mackey), **Supp. XXVII:** 158–159
"At Every Gas Station There Are Mechanics" (Dunn), **Supp. XI:** 144
At Fault (Chopin), **Retro. Supp. II:** 57, 60, **62–63; Supp. I Part 1:** 207, 209–211, 220
"At Fifty" (Bronk), **Supp. XXI:** 31
At Heaven's Gate (Warren), **IV:** 243, 247–248, 251
Atheism Refuted: in a Discourse to Prove the Existence of God (Paine), **Supp. I Part 2:** 517
"Athénaïse" (Chopin), **Retro. Supp. II:** 66, 67; **Supp. I Part 1:** 219–220
At Her Majesty's Request: An African Princess in Victorian England (Myers), **Supp. XXVII:** 209
Atherton, Gertrude, **I:** 199, 207–208; **Supp. XXIV: 17–32; Supp. XXVI:** 276
Athey, Jean L., **Supp. XI:** 184
At Home: Essays, 1982–1988 (Vidal), **Supp. IV Part 2:** 682, 687, 688
"At Home With" (column; Leland), **Supp. XV:** 69
"At Kino Viejo, Mexico" (Ríos), **Supp. IV Part 2:** 541
Atkinson, Brooks, **IV:** 288; **Supp. IV Part 2:** 683; **Supp. XIX:** 244; **Supp. XXVII:** 90
Atlanta (film, July), **Supp. XXIV:** 201, 209–210
Atlantis (Doty), **Supp. XI:** 121, **126–129**
"Atlantis" (Doty), **Supp. XI:** 127–128
"Atlantis" (H. Crane), **Retro. Supp. III:** 48
Atlas, James, **Supp. V:** 233; **Supp. XV:** 25; **Supp. XXIV:** 172
Atlas, The (Vollmann), **Supp. XVII:** 226, 227
"Atlas of the Difficult World, An" (Rich), **Retro. Supp. III:** 251
Atlas of the Difficult World, An: Poems 1988–1991 (Rich), **Retro. Supp. III:** 250
Atlas Shrugged (Rand), **Supp. IV Part 2:** 517, 521, 523, 524–526, 528, 531
At Liberty (T. Williams), **IV:** 378
"At Melville's Tomb" (H. Crane), **I:** 393; **Retro. Supp. II:** 76, 78, 80, 82
"At Mother Teresa's" (Nye), **Supp. XIII:** 276
"At Nightfall" (Kooser), **Supp. XIX:** 122–123
At Night the Salmon Move (Carver), **Supp. III Part 1:** 142
At Night the States (Notley), **Supp. XXII:** 224, 231–232
"At night the states" (Notley), **Supp. XXII:** 232
"At North Farm" (Ashbery), **Supp. III Part 1:** 1–2
At Paradise Gate (Smiley), **Supp. VI:** 292, **293–294**
"At Paso Rojo" (Bowles), **Supp. IV Part 1:** 87
At Play in the Fields of the Lord (Matthiessen), **Supp. V:** 199, 202, 204–206, 212
"At Play in the Paradise of Bombs" (Sanders), **Supp. XVI:** 272–273, 274, 277
"At Pleasure By" (Pinsky), **Supp. VI:** 245
"A-Train / Ziggurat / Elegy"(Balakian), **Supp. XXIII:** 32
At Risk (Hoffman), **Supp. X:** 87
"At Sea" (Hemingway), **II:** 258
"At Shaft 11" (Dunbar), **Supp. II Part 1:** 212
"At Sixty" (Davison), **Supp. XXVI:** 77
"At Slim's River" (Haines), **Supp. XII:** 208–209
"At St. Croix" (Dubus), **Supp. VII:** 83, 87
At Sundown (Whittier), **Supp. I Part 2:** 704
"At Sunset" (Simic), **Supp. VIII:** 282
At Swim-Two-Birds (O'Brien), **Supp. XXV:** 65
Attaway, William, **Supp. XXI:** 264
Attebery, Brian, **Supp. IV Part 1:** 101
Attendant, The (Bronk), **Supp. XXI:** 24
"Attendant, The" (Bronk), **Supp. XXI:** 26
"Attention"(Hadas), **Supp. XXIII:** 121
"At That Time, or The History of a Joke" (Paley), **Supp. VI:** 229–230
"At the Alhambra"(P. Benedict), **Supp. XXIII:** 40
At the Back of the North Wind (Macdonald), **Supp. XIII:** 75
"At the Birth of an Age" (Jeffers), **Supp. II Part 2:** 432
"At the Bomb Testing Site" (Stafford), **Supp. XI:** 317–318, 321, 323
At the Bottom of the River (Kincaid), **Supp. VII:** 182–184, 185
"At the 'Cadian Ball" (Chopin), **Retro. Supp. II:** 64, 65, 68
"At the Cancer Clinic" (Kooser), **Supp. XIX:** 127
"At the Chelton-Pulver Game" (Auchincloss), **Supp. IV Part 1:** 27
"At the Drugstore" (Taylor), **Supp. V:** 323
At the Edge of the Body (Jong), **Supp. V:** 115, 130
"At the End of the Curse, a Blessing" (Verducci), **Supp. XXII:** 209
At the End of the Open Road (Simpson), **Supp. IX:** 265, 269, **271–273,** 277
At the End of This Summer: Poems 1948–1954, **Supp. XII:** 211
"At the End of War" (Eberhart), **I:** 522–523
"At the Executed Murderer's Grave" (Wright), **Supp. III Part 2:** 595, 597
"At the Fishhouses" (Bishop), **Retro. Supp. II:** 45; **Supp. I Part 1:** 90, 92
At the Gates of the Animal Kingdom (Hempel), **Supp. XXI:** 115, **122–124**
"At the Grave of My Guardian Angel: St. Louis Cemetery, New Orleans" (Levis), **Supp. XI:** 268–269
"At the Gym" (Doty), **Supp. XI:** 135
"At the Indian Store" (McCarriston), **Supp. XIV:** 271
"At the Lake" (Oliver), **Supp. VII:** 244
"At the Landing" (Welty), **IV:** 265–266; **Retro. Supp. I:** 348
"At the Last" (Bynner), **Supp. XV:** 44
"At the Last Rites for Two Hot Rodders" (X. J. Kennedy), **Supp. XV:** 166
At the Mountains of Madness (Lovecraft), **Retro. Supp. III:** 235–236; **Supp. XXII:** 58; **Supp. XXV:** 109, 111, 114
"At the Owl Club, North Gulfport, Mississippi, 1950" (Trethewey), **Supp. XXI:** 249
At the Owl Woman Saloon (Gallagher), **Supp. XXIV:** 166, 172, 173, 174, 175–177
"At the Premiere" (Keillor), **Supp. XVI:** 167
At the Rendezvous of Victory (C. L. R. James), **Supp. XXI:** 172
At the Root of Stars (Barnes), **Supp. III Part 1:** 34
At the Sign of the Sphinx (Wells), **Supp. XXVI:** 274
"At the Site of Last Night's Fire" (Davison), **Supp. XXVI:** 69
"At the Slackening of the Tide" (Wright), **Supp. III Part 2:** 597
"At the Street Corner" (Ferry), **Supp. XXIV:** 162
"At the Tomb of Walt Whitman" (Kunitz), **Supp. III Part 1:** 262
"At the Tourist Centre in Boston"

(Atwood), **Supp. XIII:** 33
"At the Town Dump" (Kenyon), **Supp. VII:** 167
"At the Worcester Museum" (Pinsky), **Supp. VI:** 251
"At the Zoo in Spain" (Major), **Supp. XXII:** 182
"Atticus Finch and the Mad Dog: Harper Lee's To Kill a Mockingbird" (Jones), **Supp. VIII:** 128
"Atticus Finch—Right and Wrong" (Freedman), **Supp. VIII:** 127–128
"Attic Which Is Desire, The" (W. C. Williams), **Retro. Supp. I:** 422
"At Tikal" (Bronk), **Supp. XXI: 28–29**
"At Times in Flight: A Parable" (H. Roth), **Supp. IX:** 234
Attitudes toward History (Burke), **I:** 274
Atwan, Robert, **Supp. XVI:** 273, 277
At Weddings and Wakes (McDermott), **Supp. XVIII:** 155, **160–162,** 166
"At White River" (Haines), **Supp. XII:** 208–209
Atwood, Margaret, **Retro. Supp. III:** 253; **Supp. IV Part 1:** 252; **Supp. V:** 119; **Supp. XI:** 317; **Supp. XIII: 19–39,** 291, 306; **Supp. XXI:** 39, 42
"Atwood's Gorgon Touch" (Davey), **Supp. XIII:** 33
"Aubade" (McCarriston), **Supp. XIV:** 271
"Aubade: November" (McCarriston), **Supp. XIV:** 261–262
"Aubade of an Early Homo Sapiens" (C. Frost), **Supp. XV:** 97–98
"Aubade: Opal and Silver" (Doty), **Supp. XI:** 129
"Au Bal Musette" (Van Vechten), **Supp. II Part 2:** 735
Auchincloss, Hugh D., **Supp. IV Part 2:** 679
Auchincloss, Louis, **I:** 375; **III:** 66; **Retro. Supp. I:** 370, 373; **Supp. IV Part 1: 21–38**
"Auction" (Simic), **Supp. VIII:** 278
"Auction, The" (Crane), **I:** 411
"Auction Model 1934" (Z. Fitzgerald), **Supp. IX:** 61
Auden, W. H., **I:** 71, 381, 539; **II:** 367, 368, 371, 376, 586; **III:** 17, 134, 269, 271, 292, 476–477, 504, 527, 530, 542, 615; **IV:** 136, 138, 240, 430; **Retro. Supp. I:** 430; **Retro. Supp. II:** 183, 242, 244, 323; **Retro. Supp. III:** 241, 242; **Supp. I Part 1:** 270; **Supp. I Part 2:** 552, 610; **Supp. II Part 1: 1–28; Supp. III Part 1:** 2, 3, 14, 26, 60, 61, 64, 341; **Supp. III Part 2:** 591, 595; **Supp. IV Part 1:** 79, 84, 136, 225, 302, 313; **Supp. IV Part 2:** 440, 465; **Supp. IX:** 94, 287, 288; **Supp. V:** 337; **Supp. VIII:** 19, 21, 22, 23, 30, 32, 155, 190; **Supp. X:** 35, 57, 59, 115–116, 117, 118–119; **Supp. XI:** 243, 244; **Supp. XII:** 253, 264–265, 266, 269–270; **Supp. XIV:** 156, 158, 160, 162, 163; **Supp. XIX:** 147, 151; **Supp. XV:** 74, 117–118, 139, 144, 186; **Supp. XX: 138; Supp. XXI:** 60, 98; **Supp. XXIII:** 117, 207
"Auden's OED" (McClatchy), **Supp. XII:** 264–265
"Audition" (Alvarez), **Supp. VII:** 10
Audubon, John James, **III:** 210; **IV:** 265; **Supp. IX:** 171; **Supp. XVI: 1–14**
Audubon, John Woodhouse, **Supp. XVI:** 10
Audubon, Maria Rebecca, **Supp. XVI:** 11
Audubon, Victor Gifford, **Supp. XVI:** 10
Audubon and His Journals (M. Audubon, ed.), **Supp. XVI:** 11, 12
Audubon Reader, The: The Best Writings of John James Audubon (Sanders, ed.), **Supp. XVI:** 269
Auer, Jane. See Bowles, Jane
Auerbach, Eric, **III:** 453
Auerbach, Nina, **Supp. I Part 1:** 40
"August" (Oliver), **Supp. VII:** 235
"August" (Rich), **Supp. I Part 2:** 564
August, Timothy K., **Supp. XXVI:** 210, 211
"August 1968" (Auden), **Supp. II Part 1:** 25
"August 2026: There Will Come Soft Rains" (Bradbury), **Supp. XXVII:** 295
"August Darks, The" (Clampitt), **Supp. IX:** 43, **50–51,** 52
Augustine, Saint, **I:** 279, 290; **II:** 537; **III:** 259, 270, 292, 300; **IV:** 69, 126; **Retro. Supp. I:** 247; **Supp. VIII:** 203; **Supp. XI:** 245; **Supp. XIII:** 89; **Supp. XXI:** 83; **Supp. XXII:** 92–93
August Snow (Price), **Supp. VI:** 264
August Wilson: The Ground on Which I Stand (television documentary), **Retro. Supp. III:** 313, 319
"Au Jardin" (Pound), **III:** 465–466
Aunt Carmen's Book of Practical Saints (Mora), **Supp. XIII: 227–229**
"Aunt Cynthy Dallett" (Jewett), **II:** 393
"Aunt Gladys" (Karr), **Supp. XI:** 241
"Aunt Granny Lith" (Offutt), **Supp. XIX:** 165, 166
"Aunties, The" (Lamott), **Supp. XX: 141**
"Aunt Imogen" (Robinson), **III:** 521
"Aunt Jemima of the Ocean Waves" (Hayden), **Supp. II Part 1:** 368, 379
"Aunt Jennifer's Tigers" (Rich), **Retro. Supp. III:** 242–243; **Supp. XV:** 252
Aunt Jo's Scrapbooks (Alcott), **Supp. I Part 1:** 43
"Aunt Mary" (Oliver), **Supp. VII:** 232
"Aunt Mary" (Stowe), **Supp. I Part 2:** 587
"Aunt Moon's Young Man" (Hogan), **Supp. IV Part 1:** 400
"Aunt Rectita's Good Friday" (X. J. Kennedy), **Supp. XV:** 166
"Aunt Sarah" (R. Lowell), **II:** 554
"Aunt Sue's Stories" (Hughes), **Retro. Supp. I:** 197, 199
"Aunt Violet's Canadian Honeymoon/ 1932" (Shields), **Supp. VII:** 311
"Aunt Violet's Things" (Shields), **Supp. VII:** 311–312
"Aurelia: Moon Jellies" (Mora), **Supp. XIII:** 224
"Aurelio" (Di Piero), **Supp. XIX:** 38
Au revoir les enfants (film, Malle), **Supp. XXIII:** 122
Aurora 7 (Mallon), **Supp. XIX:** 132, **135–136**
Aurora Dawn (Wouk), **Supp. XXV:** 255, 258
Aurora Leigh (E. Browning), **Retro. Supp. I:** 33; **Supp. XI:** 197
Aurora Means Dawn (Sanders), **Supp. XVI:** 268
Auroras of Autumn, The (Stevens), **Retro. Supp. I:** 297, 300, **309–312**
"Auroras of Autumn, The" (Stevens), **Retro. Supp. I:** 311, 312; **Supp. III Part 1:** 12
Auschwitz: the Nazis and the "Final Solution" (television documentary), **Supp. XVII:** 40
Auslander, Joseph, **Supp. XIV:** 120
"Auspex" (Frost), **Retro. Supp. I:** 122
"Auspex" (J. R. Lowell), **Supp. I Part 2:** 424
Austen, Jane, **I:** 130, 339, 375, 378; **II:** 272, 278, 287, 568–569, 577; **IV:** 8; **Retro. Supp. I:** 354; **Supp. I Part 1:** 267; **Supp. I Part 2:** 656, 715; **Supp. IV Part 1:** 300; **Supp. IX:** 128; **Supp. VIII:** 125, 167; **Supp. XII:** 310; **Supp. XV:** 338; **Supp. XX: 108; Supp. XXII:** 206; **Supp. XXVI:** 130; **Supp. XXVII:** 187

Austenfeld, Thomas, **Supp. XXIV:** 64
Auster, Paul, **Supp. XII: 21–39; Supp. XIV:** 292; **Supp. XXI:** 20; **Supp. XXVII:** 26
Austerities (Simic), **Supp. VIII: 276–278,** 283
"Austerities" (Simic), **Supp. VIII:** 277
"Austerity Measures" (Stallings), **Supp. XXV:** 221
"Austerity Measures: A Letter from Greece" (Stallings), **Supp. XXV:** 221, 224, 225
Austin, Mary, **Supp. XXVI:** 31
Austin, Mary Hunter, **Retro. Supp. I:** 7; **Supp. IV Part 2:** 503; **Supp. X:** 29; **Supp. XIII:** 154
"Authentic Unconscious, The" (Trilling), **Supp. III Part 2:** 512
Author and Agent: Eudora Welty and Diarmuid Russell (Kreyling), **Retro. Supp. I:** 342, 345, 347, 349–350
"Author at Sixty, The" (Wilson), **IV:** 426
"Author of 'Beltraffio,' The" (James), **Retro. Supp. I:** 227
"Author's Explanation, The" (Larsen), **Supp. XVIII:** 131
"Author's House" (Fitzgerald), **Retro. Supp. I:** 98
"Author's Reflections, An: Willie Loman, Walter Younger, and He Who Must Live" (Hansberry), **Supp. IV Part 1:** 370
"Author to Her Book, The" (Bradstreet), **Retro. Supp. III:** 4, 8; **Supp. I Part 1:** 119; **Supp. V:** 117–118; **Supp. XV:** 125–126
"Autism Poem #20: The Knot Garden"(Crooker), **Supp. XXIII:** 56–57
"Autobiographical Note" (H. Miller), **III:** 174–175
"Autobiographical Notes" (Baldwin), **Supp. I Part 1:** 54
"Autobiographical Notes" (Holmes), **Supp. I Part 1:** 301
"Autobiographic Chapter, An" (Bourne), **I:** 236
Autobiography (Franklin), **II:** 102, 103, 108, 121–122, 302
Autobiography (James), **I:** 462
"Autobiography" (MacLeish), **III:** 20
Autobiography (Van Buren), **III:** 473
Autobiography (W. C. Williams), **Supp. I Part 1:** 254
Autobiography (Zukofsky), **Supp. III Part 2:** 627
Autobiography by Jesus of Nazareth (Pettis), **Supp. XXIII:** 189
"Autobiography"(Dybek), **Supp. XXIII:** 78
"Autobiography in the Shape of a Book Review" (Bynner), **Supp. XV:** 40
"Autobiography of a Confluence, The" (Gunn Allen), **Supp. IV Part 1:** 321
Autobiography of Alice B. Toklas, The (Stein), **IV:** 26, 30, 35, 43; **Supp. IV Part 1:** 11, 81
Autobiography of an Ex-Colored Man, The (J. W. Johnson), **Supp. II Part 1:** 33, 194; **Supp. XVIII:** 127; **Supp. XXII:** 7
Autobiography of a Schizophrenic Girl (Renée), **Supp. XVI:** 64, 66
Autobiography of a Thief, The (Hapgood), **Supp. XVII:** 96, 101–102
Autobiography of Benjamin Franklin (Franklin), **Supp. IV Part 1:** 5
Autobiography of LeRoi Jones, The (Baraka), **Retro. Supp. I:** 411
Autobiography of Malcolm X (Little), **Supp. I Part 1:** 66; **Supp. X:** 27; **Supp. XIII:** 264; **Supp. XXII:** 95
Autobiography of Mark Twain, The (Twain), **IV:** 209
Autobiography of My Dead Brother (Myers), **Supp. XXVII:** 204–205
Autobiography of My Mother, The (Kincaid), **Supp. VII:** 182, 188–190, 191, 192, 193
Autobiography of Red: A Novel in Verse (Carson), **Supp. XII:** 97, **106–110**
Autobiography of Upton Sinclair, The (Sinclair), **Supp. V:** 276, 282
Autobiography of W. E. B. Du Bois, The (Du Bois), **Supp. II Part 1:** 159, 186
Autobiography of William Carlos Williams, The (W. C. Williams), **Retro. Supp. I:** 51, 428
Autocrat of the Breakfast-Table, The (Holmes), **Supp. I Part 1:** 306–307
"Autographic Disclosures and Genealogies of Desire in Alison Bechdel's Fun Home" (Watson), **Supp. XXV:** 8
"Automatic Gate, The" (Southern), **Supp. XI:** 294
"Automotive Passacaglia" (H. Miller), **III:** 186
"Autopsy Room, The" (Carver), **Supp. III Part 1:** 137
"Auto Wreck" (Shapiro), **Supp. II Part 2:** 706
"Autre Temps" (Wharton), **IV:** 320, 324
"Autumn" (Berrigan), **Supp. XXIV:** 37
"Autumn, Mist" (Hull), **Supp. XXI:** 133
"Autumn Afternoon" (Farrell), **II:** 45
"Autumnal" (Eberhart), **I:** 540–541
"Autumn Begins in Martins Ferry, Ohio" (Wright), **Supp. III Part 2:** 599
"Autumn Courtship, An" (Caldwell), **I:** 309
"Autumn Equinox" (Skloot), **Supp. XX: 202**
Autumn Garden, The (Hellman), **Supp. I Part 1:** 285–286, 290
"Autumn Garden, The: Mechanics and Dialectics" (Felheim), **Supp. I Part 1:** 297
"Autumn Holiday, An" (Jewett), **II:** 391; **Retro. Supp. II:** 140–141
"Autumn Musings" (Harte), **Supp. II Part 1:** 336
"Autumn of the Revolutionary, The" (Goldman), **Supp. XXV:** 54–55
"Autumn's Day" (Rilke; Berrigan, trans.), **Supp. XXIV:** 37
Autumn Spring (Pickering), **Supp. XXI:** 204–205, 206
"Autumn Within" (Longfellow), **II:** 499
"Autumn Woods" (Bryant), **Supp. I Part 1:** 164
Autum of the Patriarch, The (García Márquez), **Supp. XXIV:** 89
"Au Vieux Jardin" (Aldington), **Supp. I Part 1:** 257
"Aux Imagistes" (W. C. Williams), **Supp. I Part 1:** 266
Available World, The (Monson), **Supp. XXIV:** 230, **239–240,** 241
Avakian, Aram, **Supp. XI:** 294, 295, 309
Avalanche (Boyle), **Supp. XXIV:** 62
Avalanche, The (Atherton), **Supp. XXIV:** 24–25
"Ave Atque Vale" (Bynner), **Supp. XV:** 49
Avedon, Richard, **Supp. I Part 1:** 58; **Supp. V:** 194; **Supp. X:** 15
Aveling, Edward, **Supp. XVI:** 85
"Avenue" (Pinsky), **Supp. VI:** 248
Avenue Bearing the Initial of Christ into the New World: Poems 1946–1964 (Kinnell), **Supp. III Part 1:** 235, 239–241
"Avenue of the Americas" (Simic), **Supp. VIII:** 278
"Average Torture" (Karr), **Supp. XI:** 243
Avery, George C., **Supp. XX: 84**
Avery, John, **Supp. I Part 1:** 153
"Avey" (Toomer), **Supp. IX:** 317

Avi, **Supp. XXVII:** 212
Avon's Harvest (Robinson), **III:** 510
Awake and Sing! (Odets), **Supp. II Part 2:** 530, 531, 536–538, 550; **Supp. IV Part 2:** 587
"Awake at Midnight"(Schott), **Supp. XXIII:** 246
Awake in Spain (O'Hara), **Supp. XXIII:** 216
Awakening, The (Chopin), **Retro. Supp. I:** 10; **Retro. Supp. II:** 57, 59, 60, 67, **68–71,** 73; **Supp. I Part 1:** 200, 201, 202, 211, 220–225; **Supp. V:** 304; **Supp. VIII:** 198; **Supp. XII:** 170
Awakening Land, The (Richter), **Supp. XVIII:** 207, 215
Away from Her (film), **Supp. XXVII:** 193
"Awful German Language, The" (Twain), **Retro. Supp. III:** 268
Awful Rowing Toward God, The (Sexton), **Supp. II Part 2:** 694–696
Awiakta, Marilou, **Supp. IV Part 1:** 319, 335
Awkward Age, The (James), **II:** 332; **Retro. Supp. I:** 229, **230–231**
Axe Handles (Snyder), **Supp. VIII: 303–305**
Axel's Castle: A Study in the Imaginative Literature of 1870 to 1930 (Wilson), **I:** 185; **II:** 577; **IV:** 428, 431, 438, 439, 443; **Supp. VIII:** 101
"Ax-Helve, The" (Frost), **Retro. Supp. I:** 133
Azikewe, Nnamdi, **Supp. IV Part 1:** 361
"Aztec Angel" (Salinas), **Supp. XIII:** 314
Aztec Treasure House, The: New and Selected Essays (Connell), **Supp. XIV:** 80, 97
"Bab, the Sub-Deb" (Rinehart), **Supp. XXV:** 195
Babbitt (Lewis), **II:** 442, 443–445, 446, 447, 449; **III:** 63–64, 394; **IV:** 326
Babbitt, Irving, **I:** 247; **II:** 456; **III:** 315, 461, 613; **IV:** 439; **Retro. Supp. I:** 55; **Supp. I Part 2:** 423
Babcock, Elisha, **Supp. II Part 1:** 69
Babel, Isaac, **IV:** 1; **Supp. IX:** 260; **Supp. XII:** 308–309; **Supp. XVII:** 41; **Supp. XXIII:** 68
Babel, Isaak, **Supp. XIV:** 83, 84
Babel to Byzantium (Dickey), **Supp. IV Part 1:** 177, 185
Baber, Asa, **Supp. XXIII:** 52
Baber, Bob Henry, **Supp. XXIII:** 39
Babeuf, François, **Supp. I Part 2:** 518
"Babies, The" (Strand), **Supp. IV Part 2:** 625
Babouk (Endore), **Supp. XVII: 56–57,** 61, 64
Baby, Come on Inside (Wagoner), **Supp. IX: 335**
"Baby, The" (Barthelme), **Supp. IV Part 1:** 49
Baby Doll (T. Williams), **IV:** 383, 386, 387, 389, 395
"Baby Face" (Sandburg), **III:** 584
"Babylon Revisited" (Fitzgerald), **II:** 95; **Retro. Supp. I:** 109
"Baby or the Botticelli, The" (Gass), **Supp. VI:** 92
"Baby Pictures of Famous Dictators" (Simic), **Supp. VIII:** 276
"Baby's Breath" (Bambara), **Supp. XI:** 15, 16
"Babysitter, The" (Coover), **Supp. V:** 43–44
Baby Sweet's (Andrews), **Supp. XXVI:** 7–9, 12, 14
"Baby Villon" (Levine), **Supp. V:** 182
Baby with the Bathwater (Durang), **Supp. XXIV: 121–122**
Bacall, Lauren, **Supp. IV Part 1:** 130
"Baccalaureate" (MacLeish), **III:** 4
Bacchae, The (Euripides), **Supp. VIII:** 182
Bach, Caleb, **Supp. XXV:** 53
Bach, Johann Sebastian, **Supp. I Part 1:** 363; **Supp. III Part 2:** 611, 612, 619
Bachardy, Don, **Supp. XIV:** 166, 170, 172, 173
Bache, Richard, **Supp. I Part 2:** 504
Bachelard, Gaston, **Supp. XIII:** 225; **Supp. XVI:** 292
"Bachelor Girl, The" (Boyce), **Supp. XXI:** 3
Bachelor Girls (Wasserstein), **Supp. XV: 327–328,** 332
Bachman, John, **Supp. XVI:** 10, 11
Bachmann, Ingeborg, **Supp. IV Part 1:** 310; **Supp. VIII:** 272
Bachofen, J. J., **Supp. I Part 2:** 560, 567
Back Bog Beast Bait (Shepard), **Supp. III Part 2:** 437, 438
Backbone (C. Bly), **Supp. XVI: 34–36,** 37, 40, 41
Back Country, The (Snyder), **Supp. VIII: 296–299**
"Back from the Argentine" (Leopold), **Supp. XIV:** 186
"Background with Revolutionaries" (MacLeish), **III:** 14–15
"Back in the Saddle Again" (Swados), **Supp. XIX:** 259
Back in the World (Wolff), **Supp. VII:** 344, 345
"Back in Tulsa Again" (Brainard), **Supp. XXVII:** 25
Backis, Charles, **Supp. XXI:** 195
"Backlash Blues, The" (Hughes), **Supp. I Part 1:** 343
"Backlash of Kindness, A" (Nye), **Supp. XIII:** 285, 286
"Backslider, The" (R. Fisher), **Supp. XIX:** 70, 71
"Back Street Guy" (Halliday), **Supp. XIX:** 88
Back to China (Fiedler), **Supp. XIII: 102–103**
Back to Methuselah (Shaw), **IV:** 64
"Backwacking: A Plea to the Senator" (Ellison), **Retro. Supp. II:** 126; **Supp. II Part 1:** 248
Backward Glance, A (Wharton), **Retro. Supp. I:** 360, 363, 366, 378, 380, 382; **Retro. Supp. III:** 276; **Supp. XX: 229; Supp. XXVI:** 271
"Backward Glance o'er Travel'd Roads, A" (Whitman), **IV:** 348
Bacon, Francis, **II:** 1, 8, 11, 15–16, 111; **III:** 284; **Retro. Supp. I:** 247; **Supp. I Part 1:** 310; **Supp. I Part 2:** 388; **Supp. IX:** 104; **Supp. XIV:** 22, 210
Bacon, Helen, **Supp. X:** 57
Bacon, Katie, **Supp. XXII:** 207; **Supp. XXIII:** 275
Bacon, Leonard, **II:** 530; **Supp. XXII:** 273
Bacon, Roger, **IV:** 69
"Bacterial War, The" (Nemerov), **III:** 272
Bad and the Beautiful, The (film), **Supp. XVIII:** 250
Bad Boy: A Memoir (Myers), **Supp. XXVII:** 209, 210
Bad Boy Brawly Brown (Mosley), **Supp. XIII:** 237, 239, 240–241
Bad Boys (Cisneros), **Supp. VII:** 58
"Bad Company" (Gallagher), **Supp. XXIV:** 174, 176
"Bad Dream" (Taylor), **Supp. V:** 320
Badè, William Frederic, **Supp. IX:** 178
"Badeye" (Rash), **Supp. XXVII:** 216–217
"Bad Fisherman, The" (Wagoner), **Supp. IX:** 328
Bad for Each Other (film), **Supp. XIII:** 174
"Badger" (Clare), **II:** 387
Badger, A. G., **Supp. I Part 1:** 356
"Badger and the Bear, The" (Zitkala-Ša), **Supp. XXV:** 275
Bad Government and Silly Literature

(C. Bly), **Supp. XVI:** 37, 38, 40
Badlands (film; Malick), **Supp. XV:** 351
"Bad Lay" (McCarriston), **Supp. XIV:** 267
Badley, Linda, **Supp. V:** 148
Bad Man, A (Elkin), **Supp. VI: 47**
Bad Man Ballad (Sanders), **Supp. XVI:** 268
Bad Man Blues: A Portable George Garrett (Garrett), **Supp. VII:** 111
"Bad Music, The" (Jarrell), **II:** 369
"Bad People" (Halliday), **Supp. XIX:** 90, 91
"Bad Summer on K2, A" (Krakauer and Child), **Supp. XVIII:** 107, 108
"Bad Woman, A" (Fante), **Supp. XI:** 165
Baeck, Leo, **Supp. V:** 260
Baecker, Diann L., **Supp. VIII:** 128
Baer, William, **Supp. XIII:** 112, 118, 129; **Supp. XXIII:** 124
Baez, Joan, **Supp. IV Part 1:** 200; **Supp. VIII:** 200, 202; **Supp. XVIII:** 24, 25–26, 27
Bag of Bones (King), **Supp. V:** 139, 148, 151
"Bagpipe Music" (MacNeice), **Supp. X:** 117
"Bahá'í Faith: Only Church in World That Does Not Discriminate" (Locke), **Supp. XIV:** 200
Bahá'u'lláh, **Supp. XX: 117, 121, 122**
"Bahá'u'lláh in the Garden of Ridwan" (Hayden), **Supp. II Part 1:** 370, 378
Bahr, David, **Supp. XV:** 66
Bahr, Thomas, **Supp. XXII:** 206, 214
"Bailbondsman, The" (Elkin), **Supp. VI:** 49, **50,** 58
Bailey, Gamaliel, **Supp. I Part 2:** 587, 590
Bailey, Peter, **Supp. XVI:** 69
Bailey, William, **Supp. IV Part 2:** 631, 634
Bailey's Café (Naylor), **Supp. VIII: 226–228**
Bailyn, Bernard, **Supp. I Part 2:** 484, 506
Bair, Deirdre, **Supp. X:** 181, 186, 187, 188, 192, 194, 195, 196, 197
Baird, Linnett, **Supp. XII:** 299
Baird, Peggy, **I:** 385, 401
Baiting the Void (Schott), **Supp. XXIII: 247–248**
Bakan, David, **I:** 59
Baker, Carlos, **II:** 259
Baker, Chet, **Supp. XXI:** 131
Baker, David, **Supp. IX:** 298; **Supp. XI:** 121, 142, 153; **Supp. XII:** 175, 191–192; **Supp. XIX:** 115
Baker, George Pierce, **III:** 387; **IV:** 453, 455
Baker, Gladys, **Supp. XIV:** 121
Baker, Houston, **Supp. XXII:** 6
Baker, Houston A., Jr., **Retro. Supp. II:** 121; **Retro. Supp. III:** 184; **Supp. IV Part 1:** 365; **Supp. X:** 324
Baker, Jeff, **Supp. XXIV:** 166, 178
Baker, Katherine, **Supp. XX: 69**
Baker, Kevin, **Supp. XIV:** 96
Baker, Mabel, **Supp. XVIII:** 259, 263, 266–267, 269
Baker, Nicholson, **Supp. XIII: 41–57**
Baker, Robert, **Supp. XVI:** 288, 290
Bakerman, Jane S., **Supp. IV Part 2:** 468
Bakhtin, Mikhail, **Retro. Supp. II:** 273; **Retro. Supp. III:** 138; **Supp. IV Part 1:** 301; **Supp. X:** 120, 239; **Supp. XXII:** 259
Bakst, Léon, **Supp. IX:** 66
Bakunin, Mikhail Aleksandrovich, **IV:** 429
Balaban, John, **Supp. XIX:** 281
Balakian, Anna, **Supp. XXIII:** 20
Balakian, Diran, **Supp. XXIII:** 28
Balakian, Grigoris, **Supp. XXIII:** 28, 29–32
Balakian, Jan, **Supp. XV:** 327
Balakian, Nona, **Supp. XXIII:** 20
Balakian, Peter, **Supp. XXIII: 19–34**
"Balance" (Bierds), **Supp. XVII:** 31
"Balance" (Nelson), **Supp. XVIII:** 174–175
Balbo, Ned, **Supp. XIX:** 161; **Supp. XVII:** 120
Balbuena, Bernado de, **Supp. V:** 11
Balch, Emily Greene, **Supp. I Part 1:** 25
Balcony, The (Genet), **I:** 84
Bald Soprano, The (Ionesco), **I:** 74
Baldwin, David, **Supp. I Part 1:** 47, 48, 49, 50, 51, 54, 65, 66
Baldwin, James, **Retro. Supp. II: 1–17; Retro. Supp. III:** 194; **Supp. I Part 1: 47–71,** 337, 341; **Supp. II Part 1:** 40; **Supp. III Part 1:** 125; **Supp. IV Part 1:** 1, 10, 11, 163, 369; **Supp. V:** 201; **Supp. VIII:** 88, 198, 235, 349; **Supp. X:** 136, 324; **Supp. XI:** 288, 294; **Supp. XIII:** 46, 111, 181, 186, 294; **Supp. XIV:** 54, 71, 73, 306; **Supp. XVI:** 135, 141, 143; **Supp. XVIII:** 25; **Supp. XX: 147; Supp. XXI:** 245; **Supp. XXIV:** 185; **Supp. XXVII:** 201
Baldwin, Joseph G., **Retro. Supp. III:** 259
Baldwin, Kara, **Supp. XXVII:** 216
Baldwin, Samuel, **Supp. I Part 1:** 48
Bales, Jack, **Supp. XXVII:** 100, 106
Balint, Benjamin, **Supp. XXVII:** 134
Balitas, Vincent D., **Supp. XVI:** 222; **Supp. XXVI:** 149
Balkian, Nona, **Supp. XI:** 230
Balkun, Mary McAleer, **Supp. XX: 281**
Ball, Gordon, **Supp. XIV:** 148
Ball, John, **Supp. XV:** 202
"Ballad: Between the Box Cars" (Warren), **IV:** 245
"Ballade" (MacLeish), **III:** 4
"Ballade at Thirty-Five" (Parker), **Supp. IX:** 192
"Ballade for the Duke of Orléans" (Wilbur), **Supp. III Part 2:** 556
"Ballade of Broken Flutes, The" (Robinson), **III:** 505
"Ballade of Meaty Inversions" (White), **Supp. I Part 2:** 676
"Ballad of a Thin Man" (song, Dylan), **Supp. XVIII:** 30, 31
"Ballad of Aunt Geneva, The" (Nelson), **Supp. XVIII:** 175
"Ballad of Billie Potts, The" (Warren), **IV:** 241–242, 243, 253
"Ballad of Carmilhan, The" (Longfellow), **II:** 505
"ballad of chocolate Mabbie, the" (Brooks), **Supp. IV Part 1:** 15
"Ballad of Dead Ladies, The" (Villon), **Retro. Supp. I:** 286
Ballad of Dingus Magee, The (Markson), **Supp. XVII:** 139, 141
"Ballad of East and West, The" (Kipling), **Supp. IX:** 246; **Supp. XX: 23**
"Ballad of Jesse Neighbours, The" (Humphrey), **Supp. IX:** 100
"Ballad of Jesus of Nazareth, A" (Masters), **Supp. I Part 2:** 459
"Ballad of John Cable and Three Gentlemen" (Merwin), **Supp. III Part 1:** 342
"Ballad of Larry and Club" (Jarman), **Supp. XVII:** 115
"Ballad of Nat Turner, The" (Hayden), **Supp. II Part 1:** 378
"Ballad of Pearl May Lee, The" (Brooks), **Supp. III Part 1:** 74, 75
"Ballad of Plastic Fred, The" (Gansworth), **Supp. XXVI:** 104
Ballad of Remembrance, A (Hayden), **Supp. II Part 1:** 367
"Ballad of Remembrance, A" (Hayden), **Supp. II Part 1:** 368, 372, 373
"Ballad of Ruby, The" (Sarton), **Supp. VIII:** 259–260

"Ballad of San Isidro, The" (Espaillat), **Supp. XXI:** 108
"Ballad of Sue Ellen Westerfield, The" (Hayden), **Supp. II Part 1:** 364
Ballad of the Brown Girl, The (Cullen), **Supp. IV Part 1:** 167, 168, 169–170, 173
"Ballad of the Brown Girl, The" (Cullen), **Supp. IV Part 1:** 168
"Ballad of the Children of the Czar, The" (Schwartz), **Supp. II Part 2:** 649
"Ballad of the Girl Whose Name Is Mud" (Hughes), **Retro. Supp. I:** 205
"Ballad of the Goodly Fere", **III:** 458
"Ballad of the Harp-Weaver" (Millay), **III:** 135
"Ballad of the Sad Cafe, The" (McCullers), **II:** 586, 587, 588, 592, 595, 596–600, 604, 605, 606
"Ballad of the Sixties" (Sarton), **Supp. VIII:** 259
"Ballad of Trees and the Master, A" (Lanier), **Supp. I Part 1:** 370
"Ballad of Typical Lovers" (Taggard), **Supp. XXII:** 277
"Ballad of William Sycamore, The" (Benét), **Supp. XI:** 44, 47
Ballads and Other Poems (Longfellow), **II:** 489; **III:** 412, 422; **Retro. Supp. II:** 157, 168
Ballads for Sale (A. Lowell), **II:** 527
"Ballads of Lenin" (Hughes), **Supp. I Part 1:** 331
Ballantyne, Sheila, **Supp. V:** 70
Ballard, J. G., **Supp. XVI:** 123, 124; **Supp. XVIII:** 136
Ballard, Josephine. See McMurtry, Josephine
"Ballena" (Mora), **Supp. XIII:** 224
"Ballet in Numbers for Mary Ellen, A" (Karr), **Supp. XI:** 241
"Ballet of a Buffoon, The" (Sexton), **Supp. II Part 2:** 693
"Ballet of Central Park, The" (Boyle), **Supp. XXIV:** 59
"Ballet of the Fifth Year, The" (Schwartz), **Supp. II Part 2:** 650
Ball Four (Bouton), **Supp. XX: 274**
"Ball Game, The" (Creeley), **Supp. IV Part 1:** 140
Ballistics (Collins), **Supp. XXI:** 57, 65
"Ballistics" (Collins), **Supp. XXI:** 65
"Balloon Hoax, The" (Poe), **III:** 413, 420; **Retro. Supp. III:** 226, 230–231
Balloonists, The (Biss), **Supp. XXVI:** 45, 48–50
"Balm of Recognition, The: Rectifying Wrongs through Generations" (E. Hoffman, lecture), **Supp. XVI:** 155
Balo (Toomer), **Supp. III Part 2:** 484
Balsan, Consuelo, **IV:** 313–314
Balthus, **Supp. IV Part 2:** 623
Balthus Poems, The (Dobyns), **Supp. XIII:** 87
Baltimore, Lord, **I:** 132
Balzac, Honoré de, **I:** 103, 123, 339, 376, 474, 485, 499, 509, 518; **II:** 307, 322, 324, 328, 336, 337; **III:** 61, 174, 184, 320, 382; **IV:** 192; **Retro. Supp. I:** 91, 217, 218, 235; **Retro. Supp. II:** 93; **Supp. I Part 2:** 647; **Supp. XVI:** 72
Bambara, Toni Cade, **Retro. Supp. III:** 184, 194; **Supp. XI: 1–23**
Bam opgrunt (At the abyss) (Asch), **Supp. XXIII:** 6
Banana Book, The (Brainard), **Supp. XXVII:** 20, 27–28
Banana Bottom (McKay), **Supp. X:** 132, **139–140**
Bananas (film; Allen), **Supp. XV:** 3, 4
Bancal, Jean, **Supp. I Part 2:** 514
Bancroft, George, **I:** 544; **Supp. I Part 2:** 479; **Supp. XXII:** 33
Band, Millen, **Supp. XVIII:** 238
Bandaged Nude, The (Ryan as Finnegan), **Supp. XVIII:** 233, **235–236**
"Bandages" (Davison), **Supp. XXVI:** 72
Bandbox (Mallon), **Supp. XIX:** 132, 143
Band of Angels (Warren), **IV:** 245, 254–255
Bandung Files (television series), **Supp. XXI:** 170
Bang the Drum Slowly (Harris), **II:** 424–425
Banjo: A Story without a Plot (McKay), **Supp. X:** 132, **138–139**
"Banjo Song, A" (Dunbar), **Supp. II Part 1:** 197
Bank Director's Son, The: A Real and Intensely Interesting Revelation of City Life (Lippard), **Supp. XXIII:** 184
Bankhead, Tallulah, **IV:** 357; **Supp. IV Part 2:** 574
"Banking Potatoes" (Komunyakaa), **Supp. XIII:** 126
"Bank of England Restriction, The" (Adams), **I:** 4
Banks, Carolyn, **Supp. XXVI:** 9
Banks, Joanne Trautmann, **Supp. XIII:** 297
Banks, Russell, **Supp. IX:** 153; **Supp. V: 1–19,** 227; **Supp. X:** 85; **Supp. XI:** 178; **Supp. XII:** 295, 309, 343; **Supp. XX: 90; Supp. XXIV:** 97
"Banned Poem" (Nye), **Supp. XIII:** 282
Bannon, Barbara, **Supp. XI:** 228
"Banyan" (Swenson), **Supp. IV Part 2:** 651, 652
"Baptism" (Olsen). See "O Yes" (Olsen)
"Baptism" (Trethewey), **Supp. XXI:** 246
Baptism, The (Baraka), **Supp. II Part 1:** 40, 41–42, 43
Baptism of Desire (Erdrich), **Supp. IV Part 1:** 259
Barabtarlo, Gennady, **Retro. Supp. I:** 278
Baraka, Imamu Amiri (LeRoi Jones), **Retro. Supp. I:** 411; **Retro. Supp. II:** 280; **Retro. Supp. III:** 316, 317; **Supp. I Part 1:** 63; **Supp. II Part 1: 29–63,** 247, 250; **Supp. III Part 1:** 83; **Supp. IV Part 1:** 169, 244, 369; **Supp. VIII:** 295, 329, 330, 332; **Supp. X:** 324, 328; **Supp. XIII:** 94; **Supp. XIV:** 125, 144; **Supp. XXI:** 172, 227, 228; **Supp. XXIII:** 215; **Supp. XXIV:** 34, 183; **Supp. XXVII:** 18, 22, 160, 161, 166
"Bar at the Andover Inn, The" (Matthews), **Supp. IX:** 168
"Barbados" (Marshall), **Supp. XI:** 281
"Barbara Frietchie" (Whittier), **Supp. I Part 2:** 695–696
Barbarella (film), **Supp. XI:** 293, **307–308**
"Barbarian Status of Women, The" (Veblen), **Supp. I Part 2:** 636–637
Barbarous Coast, The (Macdonald), **Supp. IV Part 2:** 472, 474
Barbary Shore (Mailer), **III:** 27, 28, 30–31, 33, 35, 36, 40, 44; **Retro. Supp. II: 199–200,** 207; **Supp. XIV:** 162
Barber, Charles, **Supp. XXIII:** 125
Barber, David, **Supp. IV Part 2:** 550; **Supp. XII:** 188–189
Barber, Rowland, **Supp. IV Part 2:** 581
Barber, Samuel, **Supp. IV Part 1:** 84
"Barber's Unhappiness, The" (Saunders), **Supp. XIX:** 229
"Barclay of Ury" (Whittier), **Supp. I Part 2:** 693
Barcott, Bruce, **Supp. XVII:** 32
Bard of Savagery, The: Thorstein Veblen and Modern Social Theory (Diggins), **Supp. I Part 2:** 650
"Barefoot Boy, The" (Whittier), **Supp. I Part 2:** 691, 699–700

Barefoot in the Park (Simon), **Supp. IV Part 2:** 575, 578–579, 586, 590
Bare Hills, The (Winters), **Supp. II Part 2:** 786, 788
"Bare Hills, The" (Winters), **Supp. II Part 2:** 790
Barely and Widely (Zukofsky), **Supp. III Part 2:** 627, 628, 635
Barenblat, Rachel, **Supp. XIII:** 274
Barfield, Owen, **III:** 274, 279
"Bargain Lost, The" (Poe), **III:** 411
Barillas, William, **Supp. XIV:** 177
Barillet, Pierre, **Supp. XVI:** 194
Barker, Arthur, **Supp. XIII:** 167
Barker, Clive, **Supp. V:** 142
Barker, Wendy, **Supp. XXVII:** 261, 263
Barking Dog (Budbill), **Supp. XIX:** 1, 5
"Barking Man" (Bell), **Supp. X:** 9
Barking Man and Other Stories (Bell), **Supp. X: 9**
Barksdale, Richard, **Retro. Supp. I:** 202, 205; **Supp. I Part 1:** 341, 346
Barlow, Joel, **Supp. I Part 1:** 124; **Supp. I Part 2:** 511, 515, 521; **Supp. II Part 1: 65–86,** 268
Barlow, Judith, **Supp. XXI:** 6
Barlow, R. H., **Supp. XXV:** 122
Barlow, Ruth Baldwin (Mrs. Joel Barlow), **Supp. II Part 1:** 69
"B.A.R. Man, The" (Yates), **Supp. XI:** 341
Barnaby Rudge (Dickens), **III:** 421
Barnacle Soup and Other Stories of the West of Ireland (Gallagher and Gray), **Supp. XXIV:** 166, 172, 178
Barnard, Frederick, **Supp. I Part 2:** 684
Barnard, Rita, **Retro. Supp. II:** 324
Barn Blind (Smiley), **Supp. VI: 292–293**
"Barn Burning" (Faulkner), **II:** 72, 73; **Retro. Supp. III:** 85; **Supp. IV Part 2:** 682; **Supp. XX: 174**
Barnes, Djuna, **Supp. III Part 1: 31–46; Supp. IV Part 1:** 79, 80; **Supp. XVI:** 282; **Supp. XXII:** 165, 167
Barnes, Kate, **Supp. XXVI:** 36
Barnes, Kim, **Supp. XVIII:** 293
Barnet, Andrea, **Supp. XXII:** 159, 164
Barnett, Claudia, **Supp. XV:** 323, 330, 334
Barnett, Samuel, **Supp. I Part 1:** 2
Barn Fever (Davison), **Supp. XXVI:** 66, 75–76, 77
"Barn Fever" (Davison), **Supp. XXVI:** 75, 77
"Barn-Fox, The" (Rash), **Supp. XXVII:** 222
Barnhardt, Wilton, **Supp. XXII:** 266; **Supp. XXVII: 1–15**
"Barn Owl" (Kooser), **Supp. XIX:** 123
Barnstone, Tony, **Supp. XIII:** 115, 126
Barnstone, Willis, **Supp. I Part 2:** 458
Barnum, P. T., **Supp. I Part 2:** 703
Baro, Gene, **Supp. XXVII:** 253
Baroja, Pío, **I:** 478
Baron, Zach, **Supp. XVIII:** 150
"Baroque Comment" (Bogan), **Supp. III Part 1:** 56, 58
"Baroque Sunburst, A" (Clampitt), **Supp. IX:** 49
"Baroque Wall-Fountain in the Villa Sciarra, A" (Wilbur), **Supp. III Part 2:** 553
Barr, Robert, **I:** 409, 424
Barracks Thief, The (Wolff), **Supp. VII:** 344–345
"Barred Owl" (Offutt), **Supp. XIX:** 170
Barren Ground (Glasgow), **II:** 174, 175, 178, 179, 184–185, 186, 187, 188, 189, 191, 192, 193, 194; **Supp. X:** 228
Barrés, Auguste M., **I:** 228
Barresi, Dorothy, **Supp. XV:** 100, 102
Barrett, Amy, **Supp. XVIII:** 136
Barrett, E. B., **Supp. XV:** 309
Barrett, Elizabeth, **Supp. IV Part 2:** 430
Barrett, George, **Supp. IX:** 250
Barrett, Ralph, **Supp. I Part 2:** 462
Barrie, J. M., **Supp. XX: 234**
"Barrie Cooke Painting" (Gallagher), **Supp. XXIV:** 171
Barrier, Rober G., **Supp. XXI:** 48–49
Barrier of a Common Language: An American Looks at Contemporary British Poetry (Gioia), **Supp. XV:** 112, **116–117**
"Barroco: An Essay" (Sobin), **Supp. XVI:** 291
Barron, Jonathan, **Supp. IX:** 299
Barrow, John, **II:** 18
Barrus, Clara, **I:** 220
"Barry" (Biss), **Supp. XXVI:** 47
Barry, Iris, **Supp. XIII:** 170
Barry, Philip, **Retro. Supp. I:** 104; **Supp. IV Part 1:** 83; **Supp. V:** 95
Barstow, Elizabeth Drew. See Stoddard, Elizabeth
Bart, Lily, **Retro. Supp. III:** 290
Bartas, Seigneur du, **IV:** 157
"Barter" (Teasdale), **Supp. XXVII:** 290, 291
Barth, John, **I: 121–143; Supp. I Part 1:** 100; **Supp. III Part 1:** 217; **Supp. IV Part 1:** 48, 379; **Supp. IX:** 208; **Supp. V:** 39, 40; **Supp. X:** 263, 301, 302, 307; **Supp. XI:** 309; **Supp. XII:** 29, 289, 316; **Supp. XIII:** 41, 101, 104; **Supp. XVII:** 183; **Supp. XVIII:** 136, 140, 141; **Supp. XX: 21; Supp. XXII:** 259, 261; **Supp. XXIII:** 42; **Supp. XXVII:** 183
Barth, Karl, **III:** 40, 258, 291, 303, 309; **IV:** 225; **Retro. Supp. I:** 325, 326, 327
Barth, Robert C., **Supp. XV:** 169
Barthé, Richmond, **Retro. Supp. II:** 115
Barthelme, Donald, **Supp. IV Part 1: 39–58,** 227; **Supp. V:** 2, 39, 44; **Supp. VIII:** 75, 138; **Supp. X:** 263; **Supp. XI:** 25; **Supp. XII:** 29; **Supp. XIII:** 41, 46; **Supp. XIX:** 235; **Supp. XVI:** 206; **Supp. XXVII:** 183
Barthelme, Frederick, **Supp. XI: 25–41; Supp. XXI:** 38
Barthelme, Peter, **Supp. XI:** 25
Barthelme, Steven, **Supp. XI:** 25, 27, 37
Barthes, Roland, **Supp. IV Part 1:** 39, 119, 126; **Supp. XIII:** 83; **Supp. XVI:** 285, 294; **Supp. XVII:** 244
Bartholomew and the Oobleck (Geisel), **Supp. XVI:** 104
"Bar Time" (B. Collins), **Supp. XVII:** 245
"Bartleby, the Scrivener; A Story of Wall-Street" (Melville), **III:** 88–89; **Retro. Supp. I:** 255; **Retro. Supp. III:** 147, 149, 159
Bartleby in Manhattan and Other Essays (Hardwick), **Supp. III Part 1:** 204, 210
"Bartleby the Scrivener" (Melville), **Supp. XVIII:** 4
Bartlet, Phebe, **I:** 562
Bartlett, Lee, **Supp. VIII:** 291
Bartlett, Mary Dougherty, **Supp. IV Part 1:** 335
Bartlett, William Irving, **Supp. XXV:** 250–251
Barton, Bruce, **III:** 14; **Retro. Supp. I:** 179
Barton, Priscilla. See Morison, Mrs. Samuel Eliot (Priscilla Barton)
Barton, Ralph, **Supp. XVI:** 195
Barton, Rev. William E., **Retro. Supp. I:** 179
Bartov, Omer, **Supp. XVI:** 153–154
Bartram, John, **Supp. I Part 1:** 244
Bartram, William, **II:** 313; **Supp. IX:** 171; **Supp. X:** 223
Barzun, Jacques, **Supp. XIV:** 54
"Basement" (Bambara), **Supp. XI:** 5

Basement Tapes, The (album, Dylan), **Supp. XVIII:** 27, 30, 32
"Base of All Metaphysics, The" (Whitman), **IV:** 348
"Base Stealer, The" (Francis), **Supp. IX:** 82
Bashevis, Isaac. See Singer, Isaac Bashevis
Bashir, Antonious, **Supp. XX: 116, 120**
Basil Stories, The (Fitzgerald), **Retro. Supp. I:** 109
Basin and Range (McPhee), **Supp. III Part 1:** 309
"Basin of Eggs, A" (Swenson), **Supp. IV Part 2:** 645
"Basket" (Huddle), **Supp. XXVI:** 150
"Basket, The" (A. Lowell), **II:** 522
"Basketball and Beefeaters" (McPhee), **Supp. III Part 1:** 296
"Basketball and Poetry: The Two Richies" (Dunn), **Supp. XI:** 140
"Basketball Player" (L. Michaels), **Supp. XVI:** 209
"Basket of Trips"(Strout), **Supp. XXIII:** 283, 285
Baskin, Leonard, **Supp. X:** 58, 71; **Supp. XV:** 348
Bass, George, **Supp. XXII:** 6
Bass, Rick, **Supp. XIV:** 227; **Supp. XVI: 15–29; Supp. XXI:** 40, 45; **Supp. XXVI:** 31, 187
Bassard, Katherine Clay, **Supp. XXII:** 148
Bass Cathedral (Mackey), **Supp. XXVII:** 159
Basso, Hamilton, **Retro. Supp. I:** 80
Bastard, The (Caldwell), **I:** 291, 292, 308
"Bastille Day" (Lamott), **Supp. XX: 143**
"Bat, The" (Kenyon), **Supp. VII:** 168
Bat, The (Rinehart and Hopwood), **Supp. XXV:** 195, 200
Bataille, Georges, **Supp. VIII:** 4; **Supp. XII:** 1
"Batard" (London), **II:** 468–469
Batchelor, John Calvin, **Supp. XIX:** 142
Bate, Walter Jackson, **II:** 531; **Supp. XXVI:** 63
"Bateau ivre, Le" (Rimbaud; Berrigan, trans.), **Supp. XXIV:** 40
Bates, Arlo, **Retro. Supp. I:** 35
Bates, Blanche, **Supp. XVI:** 182
Bates, Kathy, **Supp. XIII:** 207
Bates, Lee, **Retro. Supp. II:** 46
Bates, Milton J., **Supp. XII:** 62
Bates, Sylvia Chatfield, **II:** 586
Bateson, Gregory, **Supp. XV:** 146
"Bath, The" (Carver), **Supp. III Part 1:** 144, 145
"Bath, The" (Snyder), **Supp. VIII:** 302
Bathwater Wine (Coleman), **Supp. XI:** 83, 90, **91**
Battaglia, J. F., **Supp. XXVII:** 256, 258, 263
"Batter my heart, three person'd God" (Donne), **Supp. I Part 2:** 726; **Supp. XVII:** 119
"Battle, The" (Simpson), **Supp. IX:** 268–269
Battle Cry (film), **Supp. XX: 246**
Battle Cry (Uris), **Supp. XX: 243, 246, 248–250, 255, 256**
Battlefield Where the Moon Says I Love You, The (Stanford), **Supp. XV:** 345
Battle for the Solomons (Wolfert), **Supp. XXI:** 267
Battle-Ground, The (Glasgow), **II:** 175, 176, 177, 178, 193
"Battle Hymn of the Republic" (Sandburg), **III:** 585
"Battle Hymn of the Republic, The" (Howe), **III:** 505
"Battle Hymn of the Republic, The" (Updike), **Retro. Supp. I:** 324
Battle of Angels (T. Williams), **IV:** 380, 381, 383, 385, 386, 387
"Battle of Aspen, The" (Thompson), **Supp. XXIV:** 286–287
"Battle of Lovell's Pond, The" (Longfellow), **II:** 493
Battle of the Atlantic, The (Morison), **Supp. I Part 2:** 490
"Battle of the Baltic, The" (Campbell), **Supp. I Part 1:** 309
"Battle of the Bunker, The" (Snodgrass), **Supp. VI:** 319–320
"***Battle of the Century!!!, The***" (Goldbarth), **Supp. XII:** 193
Battle of the Little Big Horn, The (Sandoz), **Supp. XXIII:** 146
Battle-Pieces and Aspects of the War (Melville), **II:** 538–539; **III:** 92; **IV:** 350; **Retro. Supp. I:** 257
Battle-Piecs and Aspects of the War (Melville), **Retro. Supp. III:** 161
"Battler, The" (Hemingway), **II:** 248; **Retro. Supp. I:** 175
"Battle That Ended the Century, The" (Lovecraft and Barlow), **Supp. XXV:** 122
Baubles (Wells), **Supp. XXVI:** 275
"Baubles after Bombs" (Peacock), **Supp. XIX:** 200
"Baudelaire" (Schwartz), **Supp. II Part 2:** 663
Baudelaire, Charles, **I:** 58, 63, 384, 389, 420, 569; **II:** 543, 544–545, 552; **III:** 137, 141–142, 143, 409, 417, 418, 421, 428, 448, 466, 474; **IV:** 74, 79, 80, 87, 211, 286; **Retro. Supp. I:** 56, 90; **Retro. Supp. II:** 261, 262, 322, 326; **Retro. Supp. III:** 57, 60, 236; **Supp. I Part 1:** 271; **Supp. III Part 1:** 4, 6, 105; **Supp. XIII:** 77, 284; **Supp. XV:** 165; **Supp. XXI:** 228; **Supp. XXIV:** 152; **Supp. XXVI:** 39
Baudrillard, Jean, **Supp. IV Part 1:** 45
Bauer, Dale, **Retro. Supp. I:** 381
Bauer, Douglas, **Supp. XII:** 290
Baum, L. Frank, **Supp. I Part 2:** 621; **Supp. IV Part 1:** 101, 113; **Supp. XII:** 42
Baumann, Walter, **III:** 478
Bausch, Richard, **Supp. VII: 39–56; Supp. XVII:** 21; **Supp. XXVI:** 13
Bawer, Bruce, **Supp. IX:** 135; **Supp. VIII:** 153; **Supp. X:** 187
Baxter, Charles, **Supp. XII:** 22; **Supp. XIV:** 89, 92; **Supp. XVII: 13–24; Supp. XXIII:** 289
Baxter, John, **Supp. XI:** 302
Baxter, Richard, **III:** 199; **IV:** 151, 153; **Supp. I Part 2:** 683
"Baxter's Procrustes" (Chesnutt), **Supp. XIV:** 76
"Bay City Blues" (Chandler), **Supp. IV Part 1:** 129
Baylies, William, **Supp. I Part 1:** 153
Baym, Nina, **Supp. IV Part 2:** 463; **Supp. X:** 229; **Supp. XVI:** 92; **Supp. XVIII:** 258, 259; **Supp. XXIV:** 28
"Bayou" (Di Piero), **Supp. XIX:** 37
Bayou Folk (Chopin), **Retro. Supp. II: 64–65,** 73; **Supp. I Part 1:** 200, 216, 218
Baziotes, William, **Supp. XV:** 144
"B.C." (Taggard), **Supp. XXII:** 278
Beach, Anna Hampstead, **Supp. XVII:** 75
Beach, Joseph Warren, **I:** 309, 500; **II:** 27; **III:** 319
Beach, Sylvia, **IV:** 404; **Retro. Supp. I:** 109, 422; **Supp. XXII:** 165
"Beaches in Winter" (Kriegel), **Supp. XXIV:** 220, 225
"Beach Women, The" (Pinsky), **Supp. VI:** 241
"Beaded Pear, The" (Simpson), **Supp. IX:** 276
Beagle, Peter, **Supp. X:** 24
Beam, Jeffrey, **Supp. XII:** 98
Beaman, E. O., **Supp. IV Part 2:** 604
Bean, Michael, **Supp. V:** 203
Bean, Robert Bennett, **Supp. II Part 1:** 170

Bean Eaters, The (Brooks), **Supp. III Part 1:** 79–81
Be Angry at the Sun (Jeffers), **Supp. II Part 2:** 434
Bean Spasms (Berrigan, Padgett, and Brainard), **Supp. XXIV:** 41–42
"Beanstalk Country, The" (T. Williams), **IV:** 383
Bean Trees, The (Kingsolver), **Supp. VII:** 197, 199–201, 202, 207, 209
"Bear" (Hogan), **Supp. IV Part 1:** 412
Bear, The (Faulkner), **Supp. VIII:** 184
"Bear, The" (Faulkner), **II:** 71–72, 73, 228; **IV:** 203; **Supp. IV Part 2:** 434; **Supp. IX:** 95; **Supp. X:** 30; **Supp. XIV:** 32; **Supp. XXI:** 37
"Bear, The" (Kinnell), **Supp. III Part 1:** 244
"Bear, The" (Momaday), **Supp. IV Part 2:** 480, 487
Bear and His Daughter: Stories (Stone), **Supp. V:** 295, 308
"Bear Came Over the Mountain, The" (Munro), **Supp. XXVII:** 193
Beard, Charles, **I:** 214; **IV:** 429; **Supp. I Part 2:** 481, 490, 492, 632, 640, 643, 647
Beard, Dan, **Retro. Supp. III:** 266
Beard, James, **I:** 341; **Supp. XVII:** 89, 90
Beard, Mary, **Supp. I Part 2:** 481
"Bearded Oaks" (Warren), **IV:** 240
Bearden, Romare, **Retro. Supp. I:** 209; **Retro. Supp. III:** 318–319; **Supp. VIII:** 337, 342; **Supp. XXI:** 249
"Beard of Bees, A" (X. J. Kennedy), **Supp. XV:** 171
Beardon, Romare, **Supp. XV:** 144
"Beards, The" (Lethem), **Supp. XVIII:** 148
Beardsley, Aubrey, **II:** 56; **IV:** 77
"Bearings" (Rash), **Supp. XXVII:** 218
Beaser, Robert, **Supp. XV:** 259
"Beast" (Swenson), **Supp. IV Part 2:** 639
"Beast & Burden, The: Seven Improvisations" (Komunyakaa), **Supp. XIII:** 120, 121
Beast God Forgot to Invent, The (Harrison), **Supp. VIII:** 37, 46, **51–52**
Beast in Me, The (Thurber), **Supp. I Part 2:** 615
"Beast in the Jungle, The" (H. James), **I:** 570; **II:** 335; **Retro. Supp. I:** 235; **Supp. V:** 103–104; **Supp. XXVI:** 141
Beast in View (Rukeyser), **Supp. VI:** 272, 273, 279, 280
Beasts of Bethlehem, The (X. J. Kennedy), **Supp. XV:** 163
"Beat! Beat! Drums!" (Whitman), **III:** 585
Beat Down to Your Soul: What Was the Beat Generation? (Charters, ed.), **Supp. XIV:** 152
"Beatific Effigies" (Bronk), **Supp. XXI:** 31
Beaton, Cecil, **Supp. XVI:** 191
"Beatrice Palmato" (Wharton), **Retro. Supp. I:** 379; **Retro. Supp. III:** 287–288
Beats, The (Krim, ed.), **Supp. XV:** 338
Beattie, Ann, **Supp. V: 21–37; Supp. XI:** 26; **Supp. XII:** 80, 139, 294; **Supp. XXI:** 118; **Supp. XXIII:** 289; **Supp. XXVII:** 269
Beattie, L. Elisabeth, **Supp. XX: 164, 165**
Beatty, General Sam, **I:** 193
Beaty, Jerome, **Supp. IV Part 1:** 331
"Beau Monde of Mrs. Bridge, The" (Connell), **Supp. XIV:** 88, 89
Beaumont, Francis, **Supp. I Part 2:** 422
"Beauties of Santa Cruz, The" (Freneau), **Supp. II Part 1:** 260
Beautiful and Damned, The (Fitzgerald), **II:** 88, 89–91, 93, 263; **Retro. Supp. I: 103–105,** 105, 106, 110; **Supp. IX:** 56, 57
Beautiful Changes, The (Wilbur), **Supp. III Part 2:** 544–550
"Beautiful Changes, The" (Wilbur), **Supp. III Part 2:** 549, 550
Beautiful Child (Silver), **Supp. XXIV: 273–274**
"Beautiful Child, A" (Capote), **Supp. III Part 1:** 113, 125
"Beautiful & Cruel" (Cisneros), **Supp. VII:** 63, 67
"Beautiful Gestures, The" (Huddle), **Supp. XXVI:** 154
Beautiful Losers (Cohen), **Supp. XXVII:** 51, 54, 57–58, 59
"Beautiful Wall, Machu Picchu, The" (Bronk), **Supp. XXI:** 31, 32
"Beautiful Woman Who Sings, The" (Gunn Allen), **Supp. IV Part 1:** 326
"Beauty" (Emerson), **II:** 2, 5
"Beauty" (Sanders), **Supp. XVI:** 277
"Beauty" (Wylie), **Supp. I Part 2:** 710
"Beauty and the Beast" (Dove), **Supp. IV Part 1:** 245
"Beauty and the Beast" (fairy tale), **IV:** 266; **Supp. X:** 88
"Beauty and the Shoe Sluts" (Karr), **Supp. XI:** 250
Beauty of the Husband, The: A Fictional Essay in Twenty-Nine Tangos (Carson), **Supp. XII: 113–114**
Beauty Queen, The (P. N. Warren), **Supp. XX: 268–269**
Beauty's Punishment (Rice), **Supp. VII:** 301
Beauty's Release: The Continued Erotic Adventures of Sleeping Beauty (Rice), **Supp. VII:** 301
Beauvoir, Simone de, **IV:** 477; **Retro. Supp. III:** 243; **Supp. I Part 1:** 51; **Supp. III Part 1:** 200–201, 208; **Supp. IV Part 1:** 360; **Supp. IX:** 4
Beaver Men: Spearheads of Empire (Sandoz), **Supp. XXIV:** 244, **246–247**
"Be Careful" (Zach; Everwine, trans.), **Supp. XV:** 86
Be Careful How You Live (Lacy), **Supp. XV:** 203–204
"Because I could not stop for Death—" (Dickinson), **Retro. Supp. I: 38–40,** 41, 43, 44
"Because It Happened" (Goldbarth), **Supp. XII:** 192
"Because of Libraries We Can Say These Things" (Nye), **Supp. XIII:** 283
"Because of the Waters of the Flood" (Helprin), **Supp. XXV:** 85
"Because the Body Is a Flower"(Crooker), **Supp. XXIII:** 55
"Because You Mentioned the Spiritual Life" (Dunn), **Supp. XI:** 154
Bech: A Book (Updike), **IV:** 214; **Retro. Supp. I:** 329, 335
Bechdel, Alison, **Supp. XXV: 1–15**
Beck, Dave, **I:** 493
Beck, Ervin, **Supp. XXIII:** 94, 95
Beck, Jack, **Supp. IV Part 2:** 560
Beck, Nicholas, **Supp. XVIII:** 252
Beck, Stefan, **Supp. XXII:** 268
Becker, Carl, **Supp. I Part 2:** 492, 493
Becker, Paula. See Modersohn, Mrs. Otto (Paula Becker)
Beckett, Samuel, **I:** 71, 91, 142, 298, 461; **III:** 387; **IV:** 95; **Retro. Supp. I:** 206; **Supp. IV Part 1:** 297, 368–369; **Supp. IV Part 2:** 424; **Supp. V:** 23, 53; **Supp. XI:** 104; **Supp. XII:** 21, 150–151; **Supp. XIII:** 74; **Supp. XIV:** 239; **Supp. XVII:** 185; **Supp. XX: 17; Supp. XXI:** 18; **Supp. XXII:** 263
Beckett, Tom, **Supp. IV Part 2:** 419
Beckford, William, **I:** 204
Beckonings (Brooks), **Supp. III Part 1:** 85
"Becky" (Toomer), **Supp. III Part 2:** 481, 483; **Supp. IX:** 312
Becky and Her Friends (Hinojosa),

Supp. XIX: 108–109
Becoming a Man: Half a Life Story (Monette), **Supp. X:** 146, 147, 149, 151, 152, **155–157**
"Becoming a Meadow" (Doty), **Supp. XI:** 124–125
"Becoming and Breaking: Poet and Poem" (Ríos), **Supp. IV Part 2:** 539
Becoming Canonical in American Poetry (Morris), **Retro. Supp. I:** 40
Becoming Light: New and Selected Poems (Jong), **Supp. V:** 115
Bécquer, Gustavo Adolfo, **Supp. XIII:** 312
"Bed, The" (Dixon), **Supp. XII:** 154
Beddoes, Thomas Lovell, **III:** 469; **Retro. Supp. I:** 285
Bedichek, Roy, **Supp. V:** 225
Bedient, Calvin, **Supp. IX:** 298; **Supp. XII:** 98
"Bed in the Sky, The" (Snyder), **Supp. VIII:** 300
Bednarik, Joseph, **Supp. VIII:** 39
Bedouin Hornbook (Mackey), **Supp. XXVII:** 157–158
"Bedrock" (Proulx), **Supp. VII:** 253
"Bed Time" (Davison), **Supp. XXVI:** 72
"Bee, The" (Lanier), **Supp. I Part 1:** 364
"Beech" (Frost), **Retro. Supp. III:** 104
Beecher, Catharine, **Supp. I Part 2:** 581, 582–583, 584, 586, 588, 589, 591, 599; **Supp. X:** 103; **Supp. XI:** 193
Beecher, Charles, **Supp. I Part 2:** 588, 589
Beecher, Edward, **Supp. I Part 2:** 581, 582, 583, 584, 588, 591
Beecher, Harriet. See Stowe, Harriet Beecher
Beecher, Henry Ward, **II:** 275; **Supp. I Part 2:** 581; **Supp. XI:** 193; **Supp. XVIII:** 4
Beecher, Lyman, **Supp. I Part 2:** 580–581, 582, 583, 587, 588, 599; **Supp. XI:** 193
Beecher, Mrs. Lyman (Roxanna Foote), **Supp. I Part 2:** 580–581, 582, 588, 599
Beeching, Jack, **Supp. X:** 114, 117, 118, 123, 125, 126
"Beehive" (Toomer), **Supp. IX:** 317
"Bee Hunt, The" (Irving), **II:** 313
"Beekeeper's Daughter, The" (Plath), **Retro. Supp. II:** 246–247
"Bee Meeting, The" (Plath), **Retro. Supp. II:** 254–255
Bee Poems (Plath), **Retro. Supp. II:** 254–255
Beer, John, **Supp. XVII:** 239
Beer, Thomas, **I:** 405
Beerbohm, Max, **III:** 472; **IV:** 436; **Supp. I Part 2:** 714
"Beer Bottle" (Kooser), **Supp. XIX:** 117
"Beer in the Sergeant Major's Hat, or The Sun Also Sneezes" (Chandler), **Supp. IV Part 1:** 121
Beers, Henry A., **Supp. XX: 68**
"Bees Bees Bees" (J. Scott), **Supp. XVII:** 188, 190
Beethoven, Ludwig van, **II:** 536; **III:** 118; **IV:** 274, 358; **Supp. I Part 1:** 363; **Supp. VIII:** 103
Beet Queen, The (Erdrich), **Supp. IV Part 1:** 259, 260, 264–265, 266, 273, 274, 275
Befo' de War: Echoes in Negro Dialect (Gordon), **Supp. II Part 1:** 201
"Before" (Goldbarth), **Supp. XII:** 175
"Before" (Snyder), **Supp. VIII:** 301
Before Adam (London), **II:** 466
Before Breakfast (O'Neill), **Supp. XXII:** 22
Before Disaster (Winters), **Supp. II Part 2:** 786, 800
"Before Disaster" (Winters), **Supp. II Part 2:** 801, 815
"Before I Knocked" (D. Thomas), **III:** 534
Beforelife, The (F. Wright), **Supp. XVII:** 240, 245–246
"Before March" (MacLeish), **III:** 15
Before My Life Began (Neugeboren), **Supp. XVI: 224–225**
"Before the Altar" (A. Lowell), **II:** 516
"Before the Birth of One of Her Children" (Bradstreet), **Retro. Supp. III:** 2; **Supp. I Part 1:** 118
Before the Gringo Came (Atherton), **Supp. XXIV:** 22
"Before the Sky Darkens" (Dunn), **Supp. XI:** 155
"Begat" (Sexton), **Supp. II Part 2: 693**
Beget, Philippe, **Supp. XXIII:** 74
"Beggar Maid, The" (Munro), **Supp. XXVII:** 187
Beggar Maid, The: Stories of Flo and Rose (Munro). See Who Do You Think You Are? (Munro)
Beggarman, Thief (Shaw), **Supp. XIX:** 251–252
Beggar on Horseback (Kaufman and Connelly), **III:** 394
"Beggar Said So, The" (Singer), **IV:** 12
Beggars in the House of Plenty (Shanley), **Supp. XIV:** 316, **327–328**
Beggar's Opera, The (Gay), **Supp. I Part 2:** 523
Begiebing, Robert, **Retro. Supp. II:** 210
Begin Again (Paley), **Supp. VI:** 221
Beginners (Carver), **Supp. XXIV:** 177
"Beginning and the End, The" (Jeffers), **Supp. II Part 2:** 420–421, 424
"Beginning of Decadence, The" (Jeffers), **Supp. II Part 2:** 420
"Beginning of Enthusiasm, The" (Salinas), **Supp. XIII:** 327–328
Beginning of Wisdom, The (Benét), **I:** 358; **Supp. XI:** 44
"Beginnings of Sorrow, The"(P. Benedict), **Supp. XXIII:** 48
Be Glad You're Neurotic (Bisch), **Supp. I Part 2:** 608
"Begotten of the Spleen" (Simic), **Supp. VIII:** 277
"Behaving Like a Jew" (Stern), **Supp. IX: 290–291,** 294
"Behavior" (Emerson), **II:** 2, 4
Behavior of Titans, The (Merton), **Supp. VIII:** 201
Behind a Mask (Alcott), **Supp. I Part 1:** 36–37, 43–44
"Behind a Wall" (A. Lowell), **II:** 516
Behind the Movie Camera (radio show), **Supp. XV:** 147
"Behold the Key" (Malamud), **Supp. I Part 2:** 437
Behrendt, Stephen, **Supp. X:** 204
Behrman, S. N., **Supp. V:** 95
Beichman, Arnold, **Supp. XXV:** 254, 258, 264
Beidler, Peter G., **Supp. IV Part 2:** 557
Beidler, Philip D., **Supp. XII:** 69
Beige Dolorosa (Harrison), **Supp. VIII:** 40, 51
Beiles, Sinclair, **Supp. XII:** 129
Beiliss, Mendel, **Supp. I Part 2:** 427, 446, 447, 448
"Being a Constellation" (A. Finch), **Supp. XVII:** 72
"Being a Lutheran Boy-God in Minnesota" (R. Bly), **Supp. IV Part 1:** 59, 67
Being and Race (C. Johnson), **Supp. VI:** 193, 199
Being and Time (Heidegger), **Supp. VIII:** 9
Being Busted (Fiedler), **Supp. XIII:** 95, 102, 104
Being Geniuses Together: 1920–1930 (Boyle), **Supp. XXIV:** 63, 64
Being John Malkovich (Kaufman), **Supp. XV:** 16

Being Perfect (Quindlen), **Supp. XVII:** 167, 179
Being There (Kosinski), **Supp. VII:** 215, 216, 222–223
Beiswanger, George, **Retro. Supp. II:** 220
Beka Lamb (Edgell), **Supp. XXIII:** 83, 85**, 86–88,** 93–94, 95
Belasco, David, **Supp. XVI:** 182; **Supp. XXI:** 151
Bel Canto (Patchett), **Supp. XII:** 307, 310, **320–322**
Belchamber (Sturgis), **Supp. XX: 227, 233, 238–240**
"Beleaguered City, The" (Longfellow), **II:** 498
Belfry of Bruges, The, and Other Poems (Longfellow), **II:** 489; **Retro. Supp. II:** 157, 168
"Belief" (Levine), **Supp. V:** 186, 190
"Belief in the Self Abandoned, The" (Bronk), **Supp. XXI:** 30
"Beliefs of Writers, The" (Doctorow), **Supp. IV Part 1:** 235–236
Believeniks! (Lethem and Sorrentino), **Supp. XVIII:** 148–149
Believers (C. Baxter), **Supp. XVII:** 20–21, 22
"Believers" (C. Baxter), **Supp. XVII:** 21
"Believers, The/Los Creyentes" (Kingsolver), **Supp. VII:** 208
Belinda (Rice), **Supp. VII:** 301–302
"Belinda's Petition" (Dove), **Supp. IV Part 1:** 245
"Belita" (Ríos), **Supp. IV Part 2:** 541
Belitt, Ben, **Supp. XII:** 260
Bell, Archibald, **Supp. XX: 284, 285**
Bell, Bernard, **Supp. XXII:** 182
Bell, Clive, **IV:** 87
Bell, Daniel, **Supp. I Part 2:** 648
Bell, George Kennedy Allen, **Retro. Supp. I:** 65
Bell, Madison Smartt, **Supp. X: 1–20;** **Supp. XIX:** 58–59, 60–61; **Supp. XVII:** 236; **Supp. XXI:** 48; **Supp. XXIII:** 43
Bell, Marvin, **Supp. IX:** 152; **Supp. V:** 337, 339; **Supp. XI:** 316; **Supp. XXIV:** 165
Bell, Michael, **Retro. Supp. II:** 139
Bell, Pearl K., **Supp. XI:** 233; **Supp. XXV:** 253; **Supp. XXVII:** 134
Bell, Quentin, **Supp. I Part 2:** 636
Bell, Whitfield J., Jr., **II:** 123
Bellafante, Gina, **Supp. VIII:** 85
Bellamy, Edward, **II:** 276; **Supp. I Part 2:** 641; **Supp. XI:** 200, 203
Bellarosa Connection, The (Bellow), **Retro. Supp. II:** 31, 32
"Belle Dollinger" (Masters), **Supp. I Part 2:** 463
Belleforest, François de, **IV:** 370
"Belle Zoraïde, La" (Chopin), **Supp. I Part 1:** 215–216
Bell in the Fog and Other Stories, The (Atherton), **Supp. XXIV:** 23
Bell Jar, The (Plath), **Retro. Supp. II:** 242, **249–250; Supp. I Part 2:** 526, 527, 529, 531–536, 539, 540, 541, 542, 544
Belloc, Hilary, **III:** 176; **IV:** 432
"Bellocq" (Trethewey), **Supp. XXI:** 253
Bellocq, E. J., **Supp. XXI:** 246, 251
Bellocq's Ophelia (Trethewey), **Supp. XXI:** 243, 246, **251–254**
"Bellocq's Ophelia" (Trethewey), **Supp. XXI:** 254
Bellow, Saul, **I:** 113, 138–139, **144–166,** 375, 517; **II:** 579; **III:** 40; **IV:** 3, 19, 217, 340; **Retro. Supp. II: 19–36,** 118, 279, 307, 324; **Supp. I Part 2:** 428, 451; **Supp. II Part 1:** 109; **Supp. IV Part 1:** 30; **Supp. IX:** 212, 227; **Supp. V:** 258; **Supp. VIII:** 98, 176, 234, 236–237, 245; **Supp. XI:** 64, 233; **Supp. XII:** 159, 165, 170, 310; **Supp. XIII:** 106; **Supp. XIX:** 157, 158, 261; **Supp. XV:** 143; **Supp. XVI:** 208; **Supp. XVIII:** 90; **Supp. XX: 244; Supp. XXII:** 268; **Supp. XXIII:** 166; **Supp. XXV:** 79; **Supp. XXVII:** 95
Bellows, George, **Supp. XV:** 295
"Bells, The" (Poe), **III:** 593; **Retro. Supp. II:** 266; **Supp. I Part 2:** 388
"Bells, The" (Sexton), **Supp. II Part 2:** 673
"Bells for John Whiteside's Daughter" (Ransom), **III:** 490
"Bells of Lynn, The" (Longfellow), **II:** 498
"Bells of San Blas, The" (Longfellow), **II:** 490–491, 493, 498
"Bell-Tower, The" (Melville), **III:** 91; **Retro. Supp. III:** 159
"Belly, The" (Dobyns), **Supp. XIII:** 87
'Bel of Prairie Eden (Lippard), **Supp. XXIII:** 178, 186
"Belonging" (Pickering), **Supp. XXI:** 202
"Belonging Kind, The" (W. Gibson and J. Shirley), **Supp. XVI:** 123
Beloved (film, Demme), **Retro. Supp. III:** 185
Beloved (Morrison), **Retro. Supp. III:** 184, 191–192, 193, 194–195, 197; **Supp. III Part 1:** 364, 372–379; **Supp. IV Part 1:** 13–14; **Supp. V:** 259; **Supp. VIII:** 343; **Supp. XIII:** 60; **Supp. XXII:** 78, 109; **Supp. XXIV:** 186
Beloved, The (Gibran), **Supp. XX: 125**
"Beloved, The" (Halliday), **Supp. XIX:** 92
Beloved Lady: A History of Jane Addams' Ideas on Reform and Peace (Farrell), **Supp. I Part 1:** 24
Beloved Stranger, The (Bynner), **Supp. XV:** 44, 50
Bemorse, John, **Supp. XX: 62**
Benchley, Robert, **I:** 48, 482; **II:** 435; **III:** 53; **Supp. IX:** 190, 195, 204
Benda, W. T., **Retro. Supp. I:** 13
"Benda Illustrations to My Ántonia, The: Cather's 'Silent' Supplement to Jim Burden's Narrative" (Schwind), **Retro. Supp. III:** 36–37
Bender, Aimee, **Supp. XXII:** 49
Bending of a Twig, The (Coke), **Supp. XX: 235**
Bend Sinister (Nabokov), **III:** 253–254; **Retro. Supp. I:** 265, 266, 270
"Beneath the Sidewalk" (Dunn), **Supp. XI:** 145
"Beneath the Smooth Skin of America" (Sanders), **Supp. XVI:** 275
Benedict, Elizabeth, **Supp. XVIII:** 289
Benedict, Laura, **Supp. XXIII:** 35, 36, 49
Benedict, Pinckney, **Supp. XXIII: 35–50**
Benedict, Ruth, **Supp. IX:** 229
Benefactor, The (Sontag), **Supp. III Part 2:** 451, 455, 468, 469
"Benefit Performance" (Malamud), **Supp. I Part 2:** 431
Benét, Laura, **Supp. XI:** 44
Benét, Rosemary, **Supp. XI:** 44, 51; **Supp. XXV:** 201
Benét, Stephen Vincent, **I:** 358; **II:** 177; **III:** 22; **IV:** 129; **Supp. XI: 43–61**
Benét, William Rose, **II:** 530; **Retro. Supp. I:** 108; **Supp. I Part 2:** 709; **Supp. XI:** 43, 44; **Supp. XIV:** 119, 122, 129
Ben Franklin's Wit and Wisdom (Franklin), **II:** 111
Ben-Gurion, David, **Supp. XX: 243**
Ben-Hur (film), **Supp. IV Part 2:** 683
Benigna Machiavelli (Gilman), **Supp. XI:** 201, 208
Benitez, R. Michael, **Retro. Supp. II:** 264
"Benito Cereno" (Melville), **III:** 91; **Retro. Supp. I:** 255; **Retro. Supp. II:** 188; **Retro. Supp. III:** 147, 149, 159–160, 162; **Supp. XVII:** 185

Benito Cereno (R. Lowell), **II:** 546; **Retro. Supp. II:** 181
Benito's Dream Bottle (Nye), **Supp. XIII:** 278
"Bênitou's Slave, The" (Chopin), **Retro. Supp. II:** 64
Benjamin, Walter, **Supp. IX:** 133; **Supp. XVI:** 290, 291; **Supp. XXIII:** 28, 29, 30, 31
Benjamin Franklin (Van Doren), **Supp. I Part 2:** 486
"Benjamin Pantier" (Masters), **Supp. I Part 2:** 461
Bennet, Mildred, **Retro. Supp. III:** 18
Bennett, Anne Virginia, **II:** 184
Bennett, Arnold, **I:** 103; **II:** 337; **Supp. XVI:** 190
Bennett, Elizabeth, **Supp. VIII:** 58
Bennett, Patrick, **Supp. V:** 225
Bennett, Paula, **Retro. Supp. I:** 29, 33, 42; **Supp. XX: 286**
Bennett, Reginald, **Supp. XXII:** 218
Bennett, William, **Supp. VIII:** 245
Benson, A. C., **Supp. XX: 238**
Benson, Arthur, **Supp. XX: 233**
Benson, E. F., **Supp. XX: 229**
Benson, Heidi, **Supp. XVIII:** 136
Benson, Jackson J., **Supp. IV Part 2:** 613
Benson, Martin, **Supp. XVIII:** 38
Benstock, Shari, **Retro. Supp. I:** 361, 368, 371, 382; **Retro. Supp. III:** 283; **Supp. XX: 240**
Bentham, Jeremy, **I:** 279; **Supp. I Part 2:** 635
Bentley, Anna, **Supp. XXI:** 5
Bentley, Arthur, **Supp. XXI:** 4, 5
Bentley, Eric R., **IV:** 396
Bentley, Nelson, **Supp. IX:** 324
Bentley, Richard, **III:** 79, 86; **Retro. Supp. III:** 157
Benton, Robert, **Supp. IV Part 1:** 236
"Bent Tones" (Wright), **Supp. XV:** 346
Benveniste, Emile, **Supp. XVI:** 292
Benzel, Jan, **Supp. XVI:** 112
Beowulf, **Supp. II Part 1:** 6; **Supp. XVII:** 70, 73
Beran, Carol, **Supp. XIII:** 25
Bercaw-Edwards, Mary, **Retro. Supp. III:** 152
"Berck-Plage" (Plath), **Retro. Supp. II:** 253–254
Bercovitch, Sacvan, **Retro. Supp. I:** 408; **Retro. Supp. II:** 325, 330; **Supp. I Part 1:** 99; **Supp. I Part 2:** 659
Berdyaev, Nikolai, **I:** 494; **III:** 292
"Bereaved Apartments" (Kingsolver), **Supp. VII:** 203
"Bereavement in their death to feel" (Dickinson), **Retro. Supp. I:** 43, 44
"Berenice" (Poe), **III:** 415, 416, 425; **Retro. Supp. II:** 270; **Retro. Supp. III:** 227
Bérénice (Racine), **II:** 573
Berenson, Bernard, **Retro. Supp. I:** 381; **Retro. Supp. III:** 275; **Supp. IV Part 1:** 314; **Supp. XIV:** 335, 336, 337; **Supp. XVII:** 99; **Supp. XXI:** 5
Berenson, Mary Smith, **Supp. XXI:** 4, 5, 6
Berg, James, **Supp. XIV:** 157, 159
Berg, Stephen, **Supp. IV Part 1:** 60
Berger, Alan, **Supp. XVII:** 39
Berger, Charles, **Retro. Supp. I:** 311
Berger, John, **Supp. XVI:** 284; **Supp. XXIII:** 167, 168–169; **Supp. XXIV:** 94
Berger, Roger, **Supp. XIII:** 237
Berger, Thomas, **III:** 258; **Supp. XII:** 171
Berghash, Rachel, **Supp. XXIV:** 172
Bergman, Ingmar, **I:** 291; **Supp. XV:** 7, 8, 12
Bergson, Henri, **I:** 224; **II:** 163, 165, 166, 359; **III:** 8, 9, 488, 619; **IV:** 86, 122, 466, 467; **Retro. Supp. I:** 55, 57, 80; **Retro. Supp. III:** 57; **Supp. IV Part 1:** 42; **Supp. XXII:** 158
Berkeley, Anthony, **Supp. IV Part 1:** 341
Berkeley, George, **II:** 10, 349, 357, 480, 554
Berkman, Alexander, **Supp. XXIII:** 161; **Supp. XXV:** 19
Berkman, Leonard, **Supp. XV:** 321
Berkow, Ira, **Supp. XXVII:** 139
Berkowitz, Gerald, **Supp. IV Part 2:** 590
Berkson, Bill, **Supp. XXIII:** 217, 218; **Supp. XXVII:** 22, 23
Berlin, Isaiah, **Supp. XXII:** 258
Berlin Alexanderplatz (Döblin), **Supp. XV:** 137
Berlin Stories (Isherwood), **Supp. IV Part 1:** 82; **Supp. XIV:** 155, 156, 161, 162, 164, 165
Berlioz, Hector, **Supp. XV:** 33
Berlyne, Daniel E., **Supp. I Part 2:** 672
Berman, Alexander, **Supp. XVII:** 103
Berman, Carolyn Vellenga, **Supp. XXII:** 147
Bernard Clare (Farrell), **II:** 38, 39
Bernardin, Susan, **Supp. XXVI:** 111
Bernard of Clairvaux, Saint, **I:** 22; **II:** 538
Bernays, Thekla, **Retro. Supp. II:** 65
Berne, Suzanne, **Supp. XII:** 320
Berne, Victoria (pseudonym). See Fisher, M. F. K.
Berneis, Peter, **IV:** 383
Bernhard, Brendan, **Supp. XIV:** 163
Bernhard, Thomas, **Supp. XX: 91**
Bernhardt, Sarah, **I:** 484; **Retro. Supp. I:** 377
Bernice (Glaspell), **Supp. III Part 1:** 179
"Bernice Bobs Her Hair" (Fitzgerald), **II:** 88; **Retro. Supp. I:** 103
Bernstein, Aline, **IV:** 455, 456
Bernstein, Andrea, **Supp. IX:** 146
Bernstein, Carl, **Supp. XXIV:** 293
Bernstein, Charles, **Supp. IV Part 2:** 421, 426; **Supp. XXIV:** 40, 41, 45–46
Bernstein, Elizabeth, **Supp. XII:** 318
Bernstein, Leonard, **I:** 28; **Supp. I Part 1:** 288, 289; **Supp. IV Part 1:** 83, 84
Bernstein, Melvin, **Supp. XIV:** 41, 46
Bernstein, Michael André, **Retro. Supp. I:** 427
Bernstein, Richard, **Supp. IX:** 253, 262; **Supp. XII:** 113; **Supp. XIV:** 33; **Supp. XXII:** 261
Berrett, Jesse, **Supp. XIII:** 241, 242
Berrigan, Ted, **Supp. XIV:** 150; **Supp. XXII:** 224, 225, 228, 231; **Supp. XXIII:** 218, 221; **Supp. XXIV: 33–47; Supp. XXVII:** 18, 22, 24
Berroa y Canelo, Quiterio, **Supp. XXI:** 104
"Berry" (Hughes), **Supp. I Part 1:** 329, 330
Berry, Eleanor, **Supp. XXIII:** 246
Berry, Faith, **Retro. Supp. I:** 194, 201
Berry, Walter, **IV:** 313–314, 326; **Retro. Supp. III:** 275, 279
Berry, Wendell, **Supp. VIII:** 304; **Supp. X: 21–39; Supp. XII:** 202; **Supp. XIII:** 1–2; **Supp. XIV:** 179; **Supp. XVI:** 39, 56; **Supp. XVIII:** 192; **Supp. XXI:** 90
"Berry Feast, A" (Snyder), **Supp. VIII:** 289, 297
Berryman, John, **I: 167–189,** 405, 441–442, 521; **II:** 554; **III:** 273; **IV:** 138, 430; **Retro. Supp. I:** 430; **Retro. Supp. II:** 175, 178; **Retro. Supp. III:** 14, 243; **Supp. I Part 2:** 546; **Supp. II Part 1:** 109; **Supp. III Part 2:** 541, 561, 595, 596, 603; **Supp. IV Part 2:** 620, 639; **Supp. IX:** 152; **Supp. V:** 179–180, 337; **Supp. XI:** 240; **Supp. XV:** 93; **Supp. XVII:** 111; **Supp. XXII:** 83
Berryman, Mrs. John, **I:** 168–169

Berryman's Sonnets (Berryman), **I:** 168, 175–178
"Berry Territory" (Snyder), **Supp. VIII:** 304
Berthoff, Warner, **Supp. I Part 1:** 133
Berthoff, Werner, **Supp. XXVI:** 23
Bertolucci, Bernardo, **Supp. IV Part 1:** 94
"Bertrand Hume" (Masters), **Supp. I Part 2:** 463–464
Besco, Glenn, **Supp. XXIII:** 125
"Be Serious" (Stone), **Supp. XXVII:** 263
Bessie, Alvah C., **Supp. XXVI:** 28
"Best, the Most, The" (Carruth), **Supp. XVI:** 59
Best American Essays 1987, The (G. Talese and R. Atwan, eds.), **Supp. XVI:** 273
Best American Essays 1988, The (Dillard, ed.), **Supp. VIII:** 272
Best American Essays 1989, The (Wolff, ed.), **Supp. XVII:** 208
Best American Essays 1993, The (J. Epstein, ed.), **Supp. XVI:** 275
Best American Essays 1997, The (Frazier, ed.), **Supp. VIII:** 272; **Supp. XVII:** 207
Best American Essays 1999, The (E. Hoagland and R. Atwan, eds.), **Supp. XVI:** 277
Best American Essays 2008, The, **Supp. XXIV:** 230
Best American Essays 2009, The, **Supp. XXIV:** 230
Best American Essays for College Students, The (R. Atwan, ed.), **Supp. XVI:** 273
Best American Fantasy, 2010 (Brockmeier, ed.), **Supp. XXII:** 49–50
Best American New Voices 2001 (C. Baxter, ed.), **Supp. XVII:** 22
Best American Poetry, The: 1988 (Ashbery, ed.), **Supp. III Part 1:** 26
Best American Poetry 2000, The (Dove and Lehman, eds.), **Supp. XXI:** 246
Best American Poetry 2006, The (Collins, ed.), **Supp. XXI:** 54
Best American Short Stories, **I:**174; **II:** 587; **III:** 443; **Supp. IV Part 1:** 102, 315; **Supp. IX:** 114; **Supp. X:** 301
Best American Short Stories, 1915–1050, The, **Supp. IX:** 4
Best American Short Stories 1965, The (Foley, ed.), **Supp. XVI:** 225
Best American Short Stories 1979, The, **Supp. XXIII:** 290
Best American Short Stories 1982, The (Gardner, ed.), **Supp. XVII:** 16
Best American Short Stories 1983, The (A. Tyler, ed.), **Supp. XVI:** 37
Best American Short Stories 1986, The (Carver, ed.), **Supp. XVII:** 17
Best American Short Stories 1988, The (Helprin, ed.), **Supp. XVI:** 16
Best American Short Stories 1989, The (Atwood, ed.), **Supp. XVII:** 18; **Supp. XXI:** 39, 42
Best American Short Stories 1991, The (Adams and Kenison, eds.), **Supp. XVI:** 256
Best American Short Stories 1996, The, **Supp. XXIII:** 295
Best American Short Stories 1997, **Supp. XXII:** 75
Best American Short Stories 2001, The (Kenison and Kingsover, eds.), **Supp. XVI:** 24
Best American Short Stories 2007, The, **Supp. XXIII:** 290
Best American Short Stories 2010, The (Russo and Pitlor, eds.), **Supp. XXVII:** 228
Best American Short Stories of 1942, The, **Supp. V:** 316
Best American Short Stories of 1944, The, **Supp. IX:** 119
Best American Short Stories of the Century (Updike, ed.), **Supp. X:** 163
Best American Short Stories of the Eighties, The (Ravenal, ed.), **Supp. IV Part 1:** 93
Best American Sports Writing of the Century, The (Halberstam, ed.), **Supp. XVII:** 204
"Best China Saucer, The" (Jewett), **Retro. Supp. II:** 145–146
Best Creative Nonfiction, Vol. 1, The (Gutkind, ed.), **Supp. XXVI:** 53
Best Creative Nonfiction, Vol. 2, The (Gutkind, ed.), **Supp. XXIV:** 230
Bester, Alfred, **Supp. XVI:** 123
Best Hour of the Night, The (Simpson), **Supp. IX: 277–279**
Bestiaire, Le (Apollinaire), **IV:** 80
Bestiary, A (Wilbur), **Supp. III Part 2:** 552
"Bestiary for the Fingers of My Right Hand" (Simic), **Supp. VIII:** 274, 275
Best Man, The: A Play About Politics (Vidal), **Supp. IV Part 2:** 683
Best Mystery Stories (Wells, ed.), **Supp. XXVI:** 277
"Best of Everything, The" (Yates), **Supp. XI:** 341
Best of Pickering, The (Pickering), **Supp. XXI:** 192, 198
Best of Plimpton (Plimpton), **Supp. XVI:** 238, 239, 240
Beston, Henry, **Supp. XXVI: 31–44**
Best Short Plays, The (Mayorga), **IV:** 381
Best Short Stories, The (O'Brien, ed.), **I:** 289
Best Short Stories by Negro Writers, The (Hughes, ed.), **Supp. I Part 1:** 345
Best Short Stories of 1926, The (O'Brien, ed.), **Supp. XVIII:** 279
Best Short Stories of 1934 (O'Brien, ed.), **Supp. XVIII:** 227
Best Short Stories of 1938 (O'Brien, ed.), **Supp. XIX:** 256; **Supp. XX: 34**
Best That Ever Did It, The (Lacy), **Supp. XV:** 201–202
Best Times, The: An Informal Memoir (Dos Passos), **I:** 475, 482
Best Words, Best Order: Essays on Poetry (Dobyns), **Supp. XIII:** 74, **76–78,** 87
Best Years of Our Lives, The (film; Wyler), **Supp. XV:** 195
"BETANCOURT" (Baraka), **Supp. II Part 1:** 33, 34
Bête humaine, La (Zola), **III:** 316, 318
"Beth Ann and Macrobioticism" (Christgau), **Supp. XXVII:** 37–39
"Bethe" (Hellman), **Supp. I Part 1:** 293
Bethea, David, **Supp. VIII:** 27
Bethel Merriday (Lewis), **II:** 455
Bethke, Bruce, **Supp. XVI:** 121
Bethlehem in Broad Daylight (Doty), **Supp. XI:** 121, **122–123**
Bethune, Jane, **Supp. XXVI:** 240, 245
Bethune, Mary McLeod, **Retro. Supp. I:** 197; **Supp. I Part 1:** 333
Bethurum, Dorothy, **IV:** 121
"Betrayal" (Lanier), **Supp. I Part 1:** 364
"Betrothed" (Bogan), **Supp. III Part 1:** 49–51
Bettelheim, Bruno, **Supp. I Part 2:** 622; **Supp. X:** 77, 84; **Supp. XIV:** 126; **Supp. XVI:** 33
Better Days (Price), **Supp. VI:** 264
Better Sort, The (James), **II:** 335
Better Than Sex (Thompson), **Supp. XXIV:** 283
"Better Things in Life, The" (Loos), **Supp. XVI:** 194
Betty Leicester (Jewett), **II:** 406
Betty Leicester's Christmas (Jewett), **II:** 406; **Retro. Supp. II:** 145
Betty's Summer Vacation (Durang), **Supp. XXIV: 125–126**

Between Angels (Dunn), **Supp. XI: 149–159**
"Between Angels" (Dunn), **Supp. XI:** 150
Between Fantoine and Agapa (Pinget), **Supp. V:** 39
"Between Memory and History: A Writer's Voice" (Kreisler), **Supp. XVI:** 155
"Between Queer Performances" (Hardin), **Supp. XXVI:** 242
Between Silences: A Voice from China (Jin), **Supp. XVIII:** 91, 92, 93
"Between the Porch and the Altar" (R. Lowell), **II:** 540–541
"Between the World and Me" (Wright), **Supp. II Part 1:** 228
Between Time and Timbuktu (Vonnegut), **Supp. II Part 2:** 753, 759
Between Two Rivers (Kenny), **Supp. XXIII:** 143
Beuka, Robert A., **Supp. XIX:** 263; **Supp. XXI:** 47
"Be Very Afraid—Of Loss of Liberty at Home" (P. N. Warren), **Supp. XX: 272–273**
Bevis, Howard L., **Supp. I Part 2:** 611
Bevis, John, **Supp. I Part 2:** 503
Bewilderment: New Poems and Translations (Ferry), **Supp. XXIV: 160–161**
"Bewitched" (Wharton), **IV:** 316
Bewley, Marius, **I:** 336
Beyer, Werner, **Supp. XXIII:** 145
Beyle, Marie Henri. See Stendhal
Beyond (Goldbarth), **Supp. XII:** 192
Beyond a Boundary (C. L. R. James), **Supp. XXI:** 159, 170–171
Beyond Black Bear Lake (LaBastille), **Supp. X:** 95, **99–102,** 108
"Beyond Charles River to the Acheron" (R. Lowell), **II:** 541
Beyond Criticism (Shapiro), **Supp. II Part 2:** 703, 711
Beyond Culture (Trilling), **Supp. III Part 2:** 508–512
Beyond Desire (Anderson), **I:** 111
Beyond Document: The Art of Nonfiction Film (Warren, ed.), **Supp. IV Part 2:** 434
Beyond Forgetting (Hughes, ed.; foreword by Gallagher), **Supp. XXIV:** 167, 171
Beyond Good and Evil (Nietzsche), **Supp. IV Part 2:** 519
"Beyond Harm" (Olds), **Supp. X:** 210
Beyond Katrina: A Meditation on the Mississippi Gulf Coast (Trethewey), **Supp. XXI:** 248
"Beyond My Solitude" (Gibran), **Supp. XX: 119**
"Beyond the Alps" (R. Lowell), **II:** 547, 550
"Beyond the Bayou" (Chopin), **Supp. I Part 1:** 215
"Beyond the Black River" (Howard), **Supp. XXVII:** 126
Beyond the Boom: New Voices on American Life, Culture and Politics (Teachout), **Supp. XIX:** 137
Beyond the Horizon (O'Neill), **III:** 389; **Supp. XXI:** 13; **Supp. XXII:** 22
Beyond the Hundredth Meridian: John Wesley Powell and the Second Opening of the West (Stegner), **Supp. IV Part 2:** 599, 603–604, 611
"Beyond the Kittery Bridge" (Hatlen), **Supp. V:** 138
Beyond the Law (film) (Mailer), **Retro. Supp. II:** 205
Beyond Therapy (Durang), **Supp. XXIV: 119–120**
"Beyond the Sea (at the sanatorium)" (Salinas), **Supp. XIII:** 325
Beyond the Wall: Essays from the Outside (Abbey), **Supp. XIII:** 13
Beyond the Wall of Sleep (Lovecraft), **Supp. XXV:** 113
Beyond the Writers' Workshop: New Ways to Write Creative Nonfiction (C. Bly), **Supp. XVI:** 41
Beyond Tragedy (Niebuhr), **III:** 300–303
Bezner, Kevin, **Supp. XII:** 202
B. F.'s Daughter (Marquand), **III:** 59, 65, 68, 69
Bhagavad Gita, **III:** 566; **IV:** 183
"Biafra: A People Betrayed" (Vonnegut), **Supp. II Part 2:** 760
Bianchi, Martha Dickinson, **I:** 470; **Retro. Supp. I:** 35, 37, 38
Bible, **I:** 191, 280, 414, 421, 490, 506; **II:** 6, 12, 15, 17, 108, 231, 237, 238, 252, 267, 302; **III:** 28, 199, 308–309, 341, 343, 350, 356, 402, 492, 519, 565, 577; **IV:** 11, 13, 42, 57, 60, 67, 152, 153, 154, 155, 164, 165, 296, 337, 341, 367, 369, 370, 371, 438; **Retro. Supp. I:** 91; **Supp. I Part 1:** 4, 6, 63, 101, 104, 105, 113, 193, 369; **Supp. I Part 2:** 388, 433, 494, 515, 516, 517, 583, 584, 587, 589, 653, 689, 690, 691; **Supp. IV Part 1:** 284; **Supp. IX:** 246; **Supp. VIII:** 20; **Supp. XIV:** 225. See also names of biblical books; New Testament; Old Testament
Biblia Americana (Mather), **Supp. II Part 2:** 442
Biblical Dialogues between a Father and His Family (Rowson), **Supp. XV:** 245–246
"Biblical Trees, Biblical Deliverance" (Weathers), **Retro. Supp. III:** 139–140
"Bibliography of the King's Book, A, or, Eikon Basilike" (Howe), **Supp. IV Part 2:** 435
Bibliography of the King's Book, A; or, Eikon Basilike (Almack), **Supp. IV Part 2:** 435
"Bicentennial" (Davison), **Supp. XXVI:** 73, 77
Bickel, Freddy. See March, Fredric
Bicycle Thieves (film, De Sica), **Supp. XXVI:** 134
Bidart, Frank, **Retro. Supp. II:** 48, 50, 52, 182, 183, 184; **Supp. XIX:** 82; **Supp. XV: 19–37; Supp. XVIII:** 91,92
Bid Me to Live (Doolittle), **Supp. I Part 1:** 258, 260, 268, 269, 270
"Bien Pretty" (Cisneros), **Supp. VII:** 70
"Bienvenidos" (Mora), **Supp. XIII:** 220
Bierce, Albert, **I:** 191, 209
Bierce, Ambrose, **I: 190–213,** 419; **II:** 74, 264, 271; **IV:** 350; **Retro. Supp. II:** 72; **Supp. XXV:** 26
Bierce, Mrs. Ambrose, **I:** 194–195, 199
Bierce, Day, **I:** 195, 199
Bierce, Helen, **I:** 210
Bierce, Leigh, **I:** 195, 198, 208
Bierce, General Lucius Verus, **I:** 191
Bierce, Marcus, **I:** 190, 191
Bierce, Mrs. Marcus, **I:** 190, 191
Bierds, Linda, **Supp. XVII: 25–37**
Biffle, Kent, **Supp. V:** 225
"Bi-Focal" (Stafford), **Supp. XI:** 318, 321
Bigamist's Daughter, A (McDermott), **Supp. XVIII:** 155, **156–158,** 160, 166
Big as Life (Doctorow), **Supp. IV Part 1:** 231, 234
Big Bad Love (film, Howard), **Supp. XXI:** 39
Big Bad Love (L. Brown), **Supp. XXI:** 40, 42, **44–45**
"Big Bite" (Mailer), **Retro. Supp. II:** 204
"Big Blonde" (Parker), **Supp. IX:** 189, 192, 193, 195, 196, 203
Big Box, The (Morrison and S. Morrison), **Retro. Supp. III:** 185
Big Bozo, The (Glaspell), **Supp. III Part 1:** 182

Bigelow, Gordon, **Supp. X:** 222, 227, 229
Bigelow, Jacob, **Supp. I Part 1:** 302
Bigelow Papers, Second Series, The (J. R. Lowell), **Supp. I Part 2:** 406, 415–416
Bigelow Papers, The (J. R. Lowell), **Supp. I Part 2:** 406, 407, 408, 410, 411–412, 415, 417, 424
"Big Fiddle" (Boyle), **Supp. XXIV:** 54
Big Fix, The (Lacy), **Supp. XV:** 204–205
Bigfoot Dreams (Prose), **Supp. XVI:** 253–254
Big Funk, The: A Casual Play (Shanley), **Supp. XIV:** 316, **327**
"Big Game" (Boyle), **Supp. XX: 20**
Big Game, The (film), **Supp. XIX:** 244
Big Gold Dream, The (C. Himes), **Supp. XVI:** 143, 144
"Bight, The" (Bishop), **Retro. Supp. II:** 38, 45
Big Hunger: Stories 1932–1959 (Fante), **Supp. XI:** 160
Big Knife, The (Odets), **Supp. II Part 2:** 546, 547, 548
Big Knockover, The (Hammett), **Supp. I Part 1:** 292; **Supp. IV Part 1:** 344, 345, 356
Big Laugh, The (O'Hara), **III:** 362, 373–375
Big Man (Neugeboren), **Supp. XVI:** 219, **220,** 221, 225
Big Money, The (Dos Passos), **I:** 482, 483, 486–487, 489; **Supp. I Part 2:** 646, 647
Big Picture (Everett), **Supp. XVIII:** 54, 66
"Big Picture" (Everett), **Supp. XVIII:** 66
"Big Picture" (Halliday), **Supp. XIX:** 93
"Big Rock Candy Figgy Pudding Pitfall, The" (Didion), **Supp. IV Part 1:** 195
Big Rock Candy Mountain, The (Stegner), **Supp. IV Part 2:** 596, 597, 598, 599, 600, 603, 604, 605, 606–607, 608, 610–611
Bigsby, C. W. E. (Christopher), **Supp. IX:** 137, 140; **Supp. XV:** 332
Big Sea, The (Hughes), **Retro. Supp. I:** 195, 197, 199, 201, 204; **Supp. I Part 1:** 322, 332, 333; **Supp. II Part 1:** 233–234; **Supp. XIX:** 77; **Supp. XXII:** 3
Big Sky, The (Mora), **Supp. XIII:** 221
Big Sleep, The (Chandler), **Supp. IV Part 1:** 122–125, 127, 128, 134
Big Sleep, The (film), **Retro. Supp. III:** 85; **Supp. IV Part 1:** 130; **Supp. XVIII:** 148
Big Strike, The (Ryan as Quin), **Supp. XVIII:** 226,**232–233**
Big Sur (Kerouac), **Supp. III Part 1:** 230
Big Sur and the Oranges of Hieronymous Bosch (H. Miller), **III:** 189–190
Big Time, The (Hayes), **Supp. XXVI:** 144
Big Town, The (Lardner), **II:** 426, 429
"Big Two-Hearted River" (Hemingway), **II:** 249; **Retro. Supp. I:** 170–171; **Supp. IX:** 106; **Supp. XIV:** 227, 235
"Big Wind" (Roethke), **III:** 531
"Big Winner Rises Late, The" (Dunn), **Supp. XI:** 146
"Bilingual/Bilingüe" (essay; Espaillat), **Supp. XXI:** 103
"Bilingual/Bilingüe" (poem; Espaillat), **Supp. XXI:** 104
"Bilingual Christmas" (Mora), **Supp. XIII:** 216–217
"Bilingual Sestina" (Alvarez), **Supp. VII:** 10
"Bill" (Winters), **Supp. II Part 2:** 792
"Bill, The" (Malamud), **Supp. I Part 2:** 427, 430, 434
"Bill Collector's Vacation, The" (Hampl), **Supp. XXII:** 83
"Billie Holiday" (Carruth), **Supp. XVI:** 50
Billings, Gladys. See Brooks, Mrs. Van Wyck
Billings, Josh, **Supp. XVIII:** 1, 4
Bill of Rites, a Bill of Wrongs, a Bill of Goods, A (Morris), **III:** 237
"Bill's Beans" (Nye), **Supp. XIII:** 283
"Billy" (Gordon), **Supp. IV Part 1:** 306
"Billy" (McCarriston), **Supp. XIV:** 265
Billy Bathgate (Doctorow), **Supp. IV Part 1:** 217, 219, 222, 224, 227, 229–231, 231, 232, 233, 238
Billy Bathgate (film), **Supp. IV Part 1:** 236
Billy Budd, Sailor (Melville), **III:** 40, 93–95; **IV:** 105; **Retro. Supp. I:** 249, **258–260; Retro. Supp. III:** 147, 149, 160, 161–162
Billy Collins Live: A Performance at the Peter Norton Symphony Space April 20, 2005 (CD, Collins), **Supp. XXI:** 51
"Billy Gardner's Ground Out" (Skloot), **Supp. XX: 205, 207**
Billy Phelan's Greatest Game (W. Kennedy), **Supp. VII:** 131, 132, 134, 135, 142–147, 149, 151, 153, 155
Billy Ray's Farm: Essays from a Place Called Tula (L. Brown), **Supp. XXI:** 48, 49
Billy's Boy (P. N. Warren), **Supp. XX: 261, 265–267**
Billy the Kid, **Supp. IV Part 2:** 489, 490, 492
Biloxi Blues (Simon), **Supp. IV Part 2:** 576, 577, 584, 586–587, 590
"Bimini" (Hemingway), **II:** 258
Bingham, Anne, **Supp. XV:** 239
Bingham, Millicent Todd, **I:** 470; **Retro. Supp. I:** 36
Bingham, Remica L., **Supp. XXI:** 256
Bingo Palace, The (Erdrich), **Supp. IV Part 1:** 259, 260, 261, 263–264, 265, 266–267, 268–269, 270, 271–273, 274, 275
"Binsey Poplars" (Hopkins), **Supp. I Part 1:** 94; **Supp. IV Part 2:** 639
Binswanger, Ludwig, **Supp. XV:** 26
Biographia Literaria (Coleridge), **II:** 10; **Retro. Supp. I:** 308
"Biography" (Francis), **Supp. IX:** 77
"Biography" (Pinsky), **Supp. VI:** 235, 236, 239, 241, **243,** 249, 250
Biography and Poetical Remains of the Late Margaret Miller Davidson (Irving), **II:** 314
"Biography in the First Person" (Dunn), **Supp. XI:** 144
"Biography of an Armenian Schoolgirl" (Nye), **Supp. XIII:** 275, 280
"Biography of a Story" (Jackson), **Supp. IX:** 113
Biondi, Joann, **Supp. XI:** 103
"Biopoetics Sketch for Greenfield Review" (Harjo), **Supp. XII:** 216
"Biotherm"(O'Hara), **Supp. XXIII:** 208, 218–219
"Birchbrook Mill" (Whittier), **Supp. I Part 2:** 699
"Birches" (Frost), **II:** 154; **Retro. Supp. I:** 132; **Retro. Supp. III:** 99–100; **Supp. XIII:** 147
Bird, Alan, **Supp. I Part 1:** 260
Bird, Gloria, **Supp. XII:** 216
Bird, Isabella, **Supp. X:** 103
Bird, Robert M., **III:** 423
"Bird, The" (Simpson), **Supp. IX:** 269–270
"Bird, the Bird, the Bird, The" (Creeley), **Supp. IV Part 1:** 149
"Bird, The"(Le Sueur), **Supp. XXIII:** 167
"Bird Banding with the Biologists" (Ray), **Supp. XVIII:** 194
Bird by Bird: Some Instructions on

Writing and Life (Lamott), **Supp. XX: 132, 137–138**
"Bird came down the Walk, A" (Dickinson), **Retro. Supp. I:** 37
"Bird Frau, The" (Dove), **Supp. IV Part 1:** 245
"Bird in Hand" (screen story) (West and Ingster), **Retro. Supp. II:** 330
Bird Kingdom of the Mayas (LaBastille), **Supp. X:** 96
"Bird on a Wire" (Cohen), **Supp. XXVII:** 51
Birds and Beasts (W. J. Smith), **Supp. XIII:** 346
"Birds for Christmas, The" (Richard), **Supp. XIX:** 221
Bird's Nest, The (Jackson), **Supp. IX: 124–125**
Birds of America (McCarthy), **II:** 579–583; **Supp. X:** 177
Birds of America (Moore), **Supp. X:** 163, 165, 167, 168, 171, **177–179**
Birds of America, The (Audubon), **Supp. XVI: 5–6,** 7, 9, 10, 12, 13
"Birds of Killingsworth, The" (Longfellow), **Retro. Supp. II:** 164
Birds of North America (Audubon Society), **Supp. X:** 177
"Birds of Vietnam, The" (Carruth), **Supp. XVI:** 55
"Bird-Window-Flying" (Gallagher), **Supp. XXIV:** 169
"Bird-Witted" (Moore), **III:** 214
Birkelo, Cheryl, **Supp. XX: 220–221**
Birkerts, Sven, **Supp. IV Part 2:** 650; **Supp. V:** 212; **Supp. VIII:** 85; **Supp. X:** 311; **Supp. XX: 92**
Birkhead, L. M., **III:** 116
"Birmingham Sunday" (Hughes), **Supp. I Part 1:** 343
Birnbaum, Henry, **Supp. XII:** 128
Birnbaum, Robert, **Supp. X:** 13; **Supp. XVI:** 75; **Supp. XXIII:** 73, 75, 275
Birney, James G., **Supp. I Part 2:** 587, 588
Birstein, Ann, **Supp. VIII:** 100
"Birthday, A" (Untermeyer), **Supp. XV:** 296
Birthday Basket for Tía, A (Mora), **Supp. XIII:** 221
"Birthday Cake" (Carruth), **Supp. XVI:** 59
"Birthday Cake for Lionel, A" (Wylie), **Supp. I Part 2:** 721
"Birthday Girl: 1950" (McCarriston), **Supp. XIV:** 261
"Birthday of Mrs. Pineda, The" (Ríos), **Supp. IV Part 2:** 542, 546
"Birthday Poem, A" (Hecht), **Supp. X:** 64
"Birthday Present, A" (Plath), **Supp. I Part 2:** 531
"Birthmark" (July), **Supp. XXIV:** 206
"Birthmark, The" (Ellison), **Retro. Supp. II:** 116; **Supp. II Part 1:** 237–238
"Birth-mark, The" (Hawthorne), **Retro. Supp. I:** 152; **Retro. Supp. III:** 114
Birth-mark, The: Unsettling the Wilderness in American Literary History (Howe), **Supp. IV Part 2:** 422, 431, 434
Birth of a Nation, The (film), **Supp. I Part 1:** 66
Birth of a World: Bolívar in Terms of His Peoples (W. Frank), **Supp. XX: 80**
Birth of the Poet, The (Gordon), **Supp. XII:** 7
Birth of Tragedy, The (Nietzsche), **Supp. IV Part 1:** 105, 110; **Supp. IV Part 2:** 519; **Supp. VIII:** 182
"Birth of Venus, The" (Botticelli), **IV:** 410
"Birth of Venus, The" (Rukeyser), **Supp. VI:** 281
"Birth of Water Stories, The" (Vaz), **Supp. XXVI:** 260
"Birthplace: New Rochelle" (Oppen), **Supp. XXVI:** 231
"Birthplace Revisited" (Corso), **Supp. XII:** 123
"Birthright" (McKay), **Supp. X:** 136
Bisch, Louis E., **Supp. I Part 2:** 608
Bisco, John, **Supp. XVIII:** 11
"B is for Bachelors" (M. F. K. Fisher), **Supp. XVII:** 86
Bishop, Elizabeth, **Retro. Supp. I:** 140, 296, 303; **Retro. Supp. II: 37–56,** 175, 178, 189, 233, 234, 235; **Retro. Supp. III:** 251; **Supp. I Part 1: 72–97,** 239, 320, 326; **Supp. III Part 1:** 6, 7, 10, 18, 64, 239, 320, 326; **Supp. III Part 2:** 541, 561; **Supp. IV Part 1:** 249, 257; **Supp. IV Part 2:** 439, 626, 639, 641, 644, 647, 651, 653; **Supp. IX:** 40, 41, 45, 47, 48; **Supp. V:** 337; **Supp. X:** 58; **Supp. XI:** 123, 136; **Supp. XIII:** 115, 348; **Supp. XV:** 20–21, 100, 101, 112, 119, 249, 251; **Supp. XVII:** 36, 76; **Supp. XXI:** 58, 84, 131; **Supp. XXIII:** 117; **Supp. XXV:** 222; **Supp. XXVI:** 67, 78; **Supp. XXVII:** 228
Bishop, James, Jr., **Supp. XIII:** 1, 5, 6, 7, 9, 11, 15
Bishop, John Peale, **I:** 432, 440; **II:** 81, 85, 86–87, 91, 209; **IV:** 35, 140, 427; **Retro. Supp. I:** 109; **Supp. I Part 2:** 709
Bishop, John W., **Supp. I Part 1:** 83
Bishop, Judith, **Supp. XVI:** 295
Bishop, Morris, **Supp. I Part 2:** 676
Bishop, Rudine Sims, **Supp. XXVII:** 203
Bishop, William Thomas, **Supp. I Part 1:** 83
"Bishop Orders His Tomb at St. Praxed's Church, The" (R. Browning), **Supp. XV:** 127
"Bishop's Beggar, The" (Benét), **Supp. XI:** 56
"Bismarck" (Chapman), **Supp. XIV:** 52, 53
Bismark, Otto von, **Supp. I Part 2:** 643
Biss, Eula, **Supp. XXVI: 45–60**
"Bistro Styx, The" (Dove), **Supp. IV Part 1:** 250–251
Bitov, Andrei, **Retro. Supp. I:** 278
Bits of Gossip (R. H. Davis), **Supp. XVI:** 82–83, 84, 85, 89
"Bitte Nehmen Sie Die Blumen" (Boyle), **Supp. XXIV:** 57
"Bitter Drink, The" (Dos Passos), **Supp. I Part 2:** 647
"Bitter Farce, A" (Schwartz), **Supp. II Part 2:** 640, 657–658
Bitter Medicine (Paretsky), **Supp. XXV:** 174, 179, 183
"Bitter Pills for the Dark Ladies" (Jong), **Supp. V:** 118
Bitterroot (Burke), **Supp. XIV:** 34, 35
"Bittersweet Nightshade" (Skloot), **Supp. XX: 202**
Bitter Victory (Hardy; Kinnell, trans.), **Supp. III Part 1:** 235
Bittner, William, **Supp. XX: 74,Supp. XX: 77, 76, 78, 80**
Bitzer, G. W. "Billy", **Supp. XVI:** 183
Bixby, Horace, **IV:** 194
Bjerre, Thomas Aervold, **Supp. XXI:** 41, 47; **Supp. XXVII:** 218
Bjorkman, Frances Maule, **Supp. V:** 285
Bjorkman, Stig, **Supp. XV:** 6
Björnson, Björnstjerne, **II:** 275
Black, Cheryl, **Supp. XXI:** 6
Black 100, The (Salley), **Supp. XIV:** 195
Blackamerican Literature, 1760-Present (R. Miller), **Supp. X:** 324
Black American Literature Forum, **Supp. XI:** 86, 92, 93
Black and Blue (Quindlen), **Supp. XVII:** 166, **176–178**
"Black and Tan" (Bell), **Supp. X:** 9
Black and White (Sorrentino), **Supp. XXI:** 228

Black Armour (Wylie), **Supp. I Part 2:** 708, 709, 712–714, 729
"Black Art" (Baraka), **Supp. II Part 1:** 49, 50–51, 59, 60
"Black Art, The" (Sexton), **Supp. II Part 2:** 682
"Black Aspen, The" (Davison), **Supp. XXVI:** 78
"Black Ball, The" (Ellison), **Retro. Supp. II:** 124
Black Bart and the Sacred Hills (Wilson), **Retro. Supp. III:** 318; **Supp. VIII:** 330, 331
Black Beetles in Amber (Bierce), **I:** 204, 209
"Blackberries" (Komunyakaa), **Supp. XIII:** 126
"Blackberry Eating" (Kinnell), **Supp. III Part 1:** 250
"Blackberrying" (D. West), **Supp. XVIII:** 283
Blackberry Winter (Warren), **IV:** 243, 251, 252
Black Betty (Mosley), **Supp. XIII:** 237, **Supp. XIII:** 240, 243
"Black Birch in Winter, A" (Wilbur), **Supp. III Part 2:** 561
Black Book, The (Morrison, ed.), **Retro. Supp. III:** 184, 191
"Black Boy" (Boyle), **Supp. XXIV:** 59
Black Boy (Wright), **IV:** 477, 478, 479, 480–482, 488, 489, 494; **Retro. Supp. II:** 117; **Supp. II Part 1:** 235–236; **Supp. IV Part 1:** 11; **Supp. XVIII:** 286
"Black Boys and Native Sons" (Howe), **Retro. Supp. II:** 112
Blackburn, Alex, **Supp. XIII:** 112
Blackburn, Paul, **Supp. XXII:** 164, 169; **Supp. XXIV:** 34, 37
Blackburn, William, **IV:** 100
"Black Buttercups" (Clampitt), **Supp. IX:** 42
Black Cargo, The (Marquand), **III:** 55, 60
Black Cargoes: A History of the Atlantic Slave Trade (Cowley), **Supp. II Part 1:** 140
"Black Cat, The" (Poe), **III:** 413, 414, 415; **Retro. Supp. II:** 264, 267, 269, 270; **Retro. Supp. III:** 227; **Supp. XXV:** 112
Black Cherry Blues (Burke), **Supp. XIV:** 30
"Black Christ, The" (Cullen), **Supp. IV Part 1:** 170, 171–172
Black Christ and Other Poems, The (Cullen), **Supp. IV Part 1:** 166, 170
"Black Clay Fish from Oaxaca, A" (Bronk), **Supp. XXI:** 31
"Black Colossus" (Howard), **Supp. XXVII:** 126
"Black Cottage, The" (Frost), **Retro. Supp. I:** 128
"BLACK DADA NIHILISMUS" (Baraka), **Supp. II Part 1:** 39, 41
"Black Death" (Hurston), **Supp. VI:** 153
Black Dog, Red Dog (Dobyns), **Supp. XIII:** 87, **88–89**
"Black Dog, Red Dog" (Dobyns), **Supp. XIII:** 89
Black Dog of Fate: A Memoir (Balakian), **Supp. XXIII:** 19, **20–24,** 24, 25
"Black Earth" (Moore), **III:** 197, 212
Black Echo, The (Connelly), **Supp. XXI:** 67, 68, 75, 80
Blacker the Berry, The (Thurman), **Retro. Supp. III:** 137
"Black Experience in Children's Books, The: One Step Forward, Two Steps Back" (Myers), **Supp. XXVII:** 200
Black Fire (Jones and Neal, eds.), **Supp. X:** 324, 328
Black Fire: An Anthology of Afro American Writing (Baraka, ed.), **Supp. II Part 1:** 53
Black Flame, The (Du Bois), **Supp. II Part 1:** 159, 185–186
Black Folk, Then and Now: An Essay in the History and Sociology of the Negro Race (Du Bois), **Supp. II Part 1:** 159, 178, 183, 185
Blackford, Holly, **Supp. XXII:** 300
"Black Fox, The" (Whittier), **Supp. I Part 2:** 692
Black Freckles (Levis), **Supp. XI:** 257, 271
"Black Gang", **IV:** 406, 407
Black Genius (Mosley, ed.), **Supp. XIII:** 246
Blackguard (Bodenheim), **Supp. XXV:** 17, 18, 22, 23–24
"Black Hood, The" (Francis), **Supp. IX:** 83, 91
Black House, The (Theroux), **Supp. VIII:** 319
Black Humor (C. Johnson), **Supp. VI:** 187, 199
Black Ice, The (Connelly), **Supp. XXI:** **70,** 75
Black Image in the White Mind, The (Fredrickson), **Supp. I Part 2:** 589
"Black Is My Favorite Color" (Malamud), **Supp. I Part 2:** 437
Black Jacobins, The (C. L. R. James), **Supp. XXI:** 159, 166–167
"Black Jewel, The" (Merwin), **Supp. III Part 1:** 355
Black Lamb and Grey Falcon (R. West), **Supp. XVI:** 152
"Black Laughter" (Taggard), **Supp. XXII:** 274
"Blacklegs" (B. Kelly), **Supp. XVII:** 131
Black Light (Kinnell), **Supp. III Part 1:** 235, 243
Black Like Me (Griffin), **Supp. XXV:** 51
Blacklist (Paretsky), **Supp. XXV:** 182, 184
"Blacklist and the Cold War, The" (Kramer), **Supp. I Part 1:** 295
Black Literature in America (Baker), **Supp. X:** 324
Black Magic, A Pictorial History of the Negro in American Entertainment (Hughes), **Supp. I Part 1:** 345
Black Magic: Collected Poetry 1961–1967 (Baraka), **Supp. II Part 1:** 45, 49–50
"Blackmailers Don't Shoot" (Chandler), **Supp. IV Part 1:** 121–122
Black Manhattan (J. W. Johnson), **Supp. IV Part 1:** 169
Black Mass, A (Baraka), **Supp. II Part 1:** 46, 48–49, 56, 57
"Black Mesa, The" (Merrill), **Supp. III Part 1:** 328
Black Metropolis (Cayton and Drake), **IV:** 475, 486, 488
Black Misery (Hughes), **Supp. I Part 1:** 336
Blackmur, Helen Dickson (Mrs. R. P. Blackmur), **Supp. II Part 1:** 90
Blackmur, Richard P., **I:** 50, 63, 67, 280, 282, 386, 455, 472; **II:** 320, 537; **III:** 194, 208, 462, 478, 497; **Supp. II Part 1: 87–112,** 136; **Supp. II Part 2:** 543, 643; **Supp. XII:** 45
Black Music (Baraka), **Supp. II Part 1:** 47, 51
Black Nativity (Hughes), **Retro. Supp. I:** 196
"Black News" (Biss), **Supp. XXVI:** 56
Black No More (Schuyler), **Supp. XIX:** 73; **Supp. XVI:** 142
Black on Black: "Baby Sister" and Selected Writings (C. Himes), **Supp. XVI:** 145
"Black or White" (Major), **Supp. XXII:** 185
"Blackout" (Hay), **Supp. XIV:** 121
Black Oxen (Atherton), **Supp. XXIV:** 25–26
Black Oxen (Atherton, Dawson, ed.),

Supp. XXIV: 31
"Black Panther" (Hughes), **Retro. Supp. I:** 211
"Black Petal" (L.-Y. Lee), **Supp. XV:** 224–225
Black Power (Wright), **IV:** 478, 488, 494
"Black Rainbow, A: Modern Afro-American Poetry" (Dove and Waniek), **Supp. IV Part 1:** 244
Black Reconstruction (Du Bois), **Supp. II Part 1:** 159, 162, 171, 182
Black Riders and Other Lines, The (Crane), **I:** 406, 419
Black Riviera, The (Jarman), **Supp. XVII:** 109, 110, **115–116**
Blackrobe: Isaac Jogues (Kenny), **Supp. XXIII:** 143, 147, **151–152,** 153, 154
"Black Rook in Rainy Weather" (Plath), **Supp. I Part 2:** 543, 544; **Supp. XXIII:** 63
Blacks (Brooks), **Supp. III Part 1:** 69, 72, 86, 87
Blacks, The (Genet), **Supp. IV Part 1:** 8
Black Skin, White Masks (Fanon), **Retro. Supp. II:** 118
Black Sleuth, The (J. Bruce), **Supp. XVI:** 143
Blacksnake at the Family Reunion (Huddle), **Supp. XXVI:** 147, 151
Black Spear, The (Hayden), **Supp. II Part 1:** 375
Black Spring (H. Miller), **III:** 170, 175, 178, 180–182, 183, 184; **Supp. X:** 187
Blackstock, Carrie Galloway, **Retro. Supp. III:** 6
"Black Stone, The" (Howard), **Supp. XXVII:** 119
"Black Stone Lying on a White Stone" (Vallejo), **Supp. XIII:** 324
Black Sun (Abbey), **Supp. XIII:** 4, **8–9,** 17
"Black Swan" (B. Kelly), **Supp. XVII:** 130–131
"Black Swan, The" (Jarrell), **II:** 382
Black Swan, The (Merrill), **Supp. III Part 1:** 319, 320
"Black Tambourine" (Crane), **I:** 387–388; **II:** 371
Black Thunder (Bontemps), **Supp. XXII:** 4, 9
"Black Tuesday" (Swenson), **Supp. IV Part 2:** 646
Black Virgin Mountain (Heinemann), **Supp. XXII:** 103, **114–116**
Black Voices (Chapman), **IV:** 485
"Blackwater Mountain" (Wright), **Supp. V:** 335, 340
"Black Wedding, The" (Singer), **IV:** 12–13
Blackwell, Alice Stone, **Supp. XI:** 195, 197
Blackwell, Elizabeth, **Retro. Supp. II:** 146
Black Woman, The (Bambara, ed.), **Supp. XI:** 1
"Black Workers" (Hughes), **Retro. Supp. I:** 202
"Black Writer and the Southern Experience, The" (Walker), **Supp. III Part 2:** 521
Black Zodiac (Wright), **Supp. V:** 333, 344, 345
Blade Runner (film), **Supp. XI:** 84
Blades, John, **Supp. XX: 87**
"Blades of Steel" (R. Fisher), **Supp. XIX:** 72
Blaine, Anita McCormick, **Supp. I Part 1:** 5
Blaine, Nell, **Supp. XV:** 179; **Supp. XXIII:** 217
Blair, Hugh, **II:** 8, 17; **Supp. I Part 2:** 422
Blair, Robert, **Supp. I Part 1:** 150
Blair, Walter, **II:** 20; **Retro. Supp. II:** 286
Blaisdell, Gus, **Supp. XIV:** 87
Blake, Casey Nelson, **Supp. XX: 69, 70, 78**
Blake, William, **I:** 381, 383, 389, 390, 398, 447, 476, 525, 526, 533; **II:** 321; **III:** 5, 19, 22, 195, 196, 197, 205, 485, 528, 540, 544–545, 567, 572; **IV:** 129; **Retro. Supp. II:** 76, 300; **Supp. I Part 1:** 80; **Supp. I Part 2:** 385, 514, 517, 539, 552, 708; **Supp. V:** 208, 257, 258; **Supp. VIII:** 26, 99, 103; **Supp. X:** 120; **Supp. XII:** 45; **Supp. XIV:** 344; **Supp. XVI:** 282; **Supp. XVII:** 119; **Supp. XX: 115, 116; Supp. XXII:** 225, 257; **Supp. XXIV:** 159; **Supp. XXV:** 248; **Supp. XXVI:** 235; **Supp. XXVII:** 292
Blakely, Barbara, **Supp. XIII:** 32
Blanc, Marie Thérèse, **Retro. Supp. II:** 135
Blanc-Bentzon, Mme. Thérèse, **II:** 405
Blanchard, Paula, **Retro. Supp. II:** 131, 133–134, 135
Blanche, Jacques-Émile, **Supp. XX: 232**
Blanche of Brandywine (Lippard), **Supp. XXIII:** 178, 185
Blanchot, Maurice, **Supp. XVI:** 288; **Supp. XXIV:** 40
Blancs, Les (Hansberry), **Supp. IV Part 1:** 359, 364, 365, 369, 372–374
Blancs, Les: The Collected Last Plays of Lorraine Hansberry (Nemiroff, ed.), **Supp. IV Part 1:** 365, 368, 374
"'Blandula, Tenulla, Vagula' " (Pound), **III:** 463; **Supp. V:** 336, 337, 345
Blankenship, Tom, **IV:** 193
"Blank Paper" (Peacock), **Supp. XIX:** 198–199
Blank Wall, The (Holding), **Supp. XXII:** 119, 120, 121, 130, **131–133,** 134
Blanshard, Rufus A., **I:** 67
Blassingame, John, **Supp. XX: 106**
Blauvelt, William Satake, **Supp. V:** 171, 173
Blavatsky, Elena Petrovna, **III:** 176
"Blazing in Gold and Quenching in Purple" (Dickinson), **Retro. Supp. I:** 30
Bleak House (Dickens), **II:** 291; **Supp. IV Part 1:** 293
Blechman, Burt, **Supp. I Part 1:** 290
"Bleeder" (Dobyns), **Supp. XIII:** 88
"Bleeding" (Swenson), **Supp. IV Part 2:** 646–647
Bleeding Kansas (Paretsky), **Supp. XXV:** 183
"Blessed Is the Man" (Moore), **III:** 215
"Blessed Man of Boston, My Grandmother's Thimble, and Fanning Island, The" (Updike), **IV:** 219
"Blessing, A" (Wright), **Supp. III Part 2:** 600, 606
Blessing on the Moon, A (Skibell), **Supp. XVII:** 48
Blessings (Quindlen), **Supp. XVII:** 167, **178–179**
"Blessing the Animals" (Komunyakaa), **Supp. XIII:** 129–130
"Blessing the Children" (Hogan), **Supp. IV Part 1:** 401
Bless Me, Ultima (Anya), **Supp. XIII:** 220
Blew, Mary Clearman, **Supp. XIV:** 227
Bligh, S. M., **I:** 226
"Blight"(Dybek), **Supp. XXIII:** 72
Blind Alleys (film), **Supp. XXI:** 146
Blind Assassin, The (Atwood), **Supp. XIII:** 20, **32**
Blind Bow-Boy, The (Van Vechten), **Supp. II Part 2:** 737, 740–742
"Blind Date" (Halliday), **Supp. XIX:** 85
Blind Date (Kosinski), **Supp. VII:** 215, 224–225
"Blinded by the Light" (Boyle), **Supp. XX: 20**

Blind Lion, The (Gunn Allen), **Supp. IV Part 1:** 324
"Blind Man's Holiday" (O. Henry), **Supp. II Part 1:** 401
Blind Man with a Pistol (C. Himes), **Supp. XVI:** 143, 144
Blindness and Insight (de Man), **Retro. Supp. I:** 67
"Blind Poet, The: Sidney Lanier" (Warren), **Supp. I Part 1:** 371, 373
"Blindsided" (E. P. Jones), **Supp. XXII:** 151–152
"Blind Tom" (R. H. Davis), **Supp. XVI:** 89, 90
Blithedale Romance, The (Hawthorne), **II:** 225, 231, 239, 241–242, 271, 282, 290; **IV:** 194; **Retro. Supp. I:** 63, 149, 152, 156–157, **162–163; Retro. Supp. III:** 119–121; **Supp. I Part 2:** 579; **Supp. II Part 1:** 280; **Supp. VIII:** 153, 201
Blitzstein, Marc, **Supp. I Part 1:** 277
Blix (Norris), **III:** 314, 322, 327, 328, 333
Blixen, Karen Denisen Baroness. See Dinesen, Isak
"Blizzard in Cambridge" (R. Lowell), **II:** 554
Blizzard Voices, The (Kooser), **Supp. XIX: 123**
Bloch, Ernest, **Supp. XX: 75**
Bloch, Robert, **Supp. XXV:** 111, 145; **Supp. XXVII:** 119
Block, Lawrence, **Supp. XXI:** 67
"Blocks"(O'Hara), **Supp. XXIII:** 214
Blok, Aleksandr Aleksandrovich, **IV:** 443; **Supp. XXVI:** 144
"Blond" (Trethewey), **Supp. XXI:** 244
Blonde Bait (Lacy), **Supp. XV:** 204
Blonde on Blonde (album, Dylan), **Supp. XVIII:** 20, 27, 30
Blondin, Antoine, **Supp. XVI:** 230
"Blood" (Hoffman), **Supp. XVIII:** 86
"Blood" (Singer), **IV:** 15, 19
"Blood, Bread, and Poetry" (Rich), **Retro. Supp. III:** 251
Blood, Bread, and Poetry: Selected Prose 1979–1985 (Rich), **Retro. Supp. III:** 251
Blood, Tin, Straw (Olds), **Supp. X: 212–215**
Blood and Guile (Hoffman), **Supp. XVIII: 83–84**
Blood and Guts in High School (Acker), **Supp. XII:** 5, 6, **11–12**
Blood and Thunder (Finn), **Supp. XXVII:** 128
"Blood Bay, The" (Proulx), **Supp. VII:** 262–263
"Blood-Burning Moon" (Toomer), **Supp. III Part 2:** 483; **Supp. IX:** 314–315
"Bloodchild" (O. Butler), **Supp. XIII:** 61, **69–70**
Bloodchild and Other Stories (O. Butler), **Supp. XIII:** 69
"Blood Donor" (Hay), **Supp. XIV:** 121
Blood for a Stranger (Jarrell), **II:** 367, 368–369, 370–371, 375, 377
"Blood from the Stone" (Oppen), **Supp. XXVI:** 230–231
Blood Issue (Crews), **Supp. XI:** 103
Bloodlines (Wright), **Supp. V:** 332, 335, 340
Blood Meridian (McCarthy), **Supp. XXIII:** 42
Blood Meridian; or, The Evening Redness in the West (McCarthy), **Supp. VIII:** 175, 177, **180–182,** 188, 190
Blood of My Blood (Gambino), **Supp. XX: 35**
"Blood of the Conquistadores, The" (Alvarez), **Supp. VII:** 7
"Blood of the Lamb, The" (hymn), **Supp. I Part 2:** 385
Blood of the Martyr (Crane), **I:** 422
"Blood of the Martyrs, The" (Benét), **Supp. XI:** 56, 58
Blood of the Prophets, The (Masters), **Supp. I Part 2:** 458, 459, 461
Blood on the Forge (Attaway), **Supp. II Part 1:** 234–235
Blood on the Tracks (album, Dylan), **Supp. XVIII:** 20, 27, 30
"Blood Relatives" (Apple), **Supp. XVII:** 6
"Blood Returns, The" (Kingsolver), **Supp. VII:** 209
"Bloodroot" (Rash), **Supp. XXVII:** 222
"Bloodshed" (C. Ozick), **Supp. XVII:** 43
Bloodshed and Three Novellas (Ozick), **Supp. V:** 259–260, 261, 266–268
"Blood Soup"(Dybek), **Supp. XXIII:** 71
"Blood Stains" (Francis), **Supp. IX:** 86
Blood Work (Connelly), **Supp. XXI: 72**
Blood Work (film, Eastwood), **Supp. XXI:** 74
Bloody Crossroads, The: Where Literature and Politics Meet (Podhoretz), **Supp. VIII: 241–242**
"Bloody Massacre near Carson, A" (Twain), **Retro. Supp. III:** 257
Bloody News from My Friend (Samianto, trans. Balakian), **Supp. XXIII:** 28
Bloom, Alice, **Supp. IV Part 1:** 308
Bloom, Allan, **Retro. Supp. II:** 19, 30, 31, 33–34
Bloom, Claire, **Retro. Supp. II:** 281; **Supp. IX:** 125
Bloom, Harold, **Retro. Supp. I:** 67, 193, 299; **Retro. Supp. II:** 81, 210, 262; **Supp. IV Part 2:** 620, 689; **Supp. IX:** 146, 259; **Supp. V:** 178, 272; **Supp. VIII:** 180; **Supp. XII:** 261; **Supp. XIII:** 46, 47; **Supp. XIV:** 14; **Supp. XV:** 134; **Supp. XVII:** 70, 141; **Supp. XXIII:** 42; **Supp. XXV:** 251
Bloom, Larry, **Supp. XIII:** 133
Bloom, Leopold, **I:** 27, 150; **III:** 10
Bloom, Lynn Z., **Supp. IV Part 1:** 6
Bloomfield, Leonard, **I:** 64
Bloomingdale Papers, The (Carruth), **Supp. XVI:** 48–50
"Blossom and Fruit" (Benét), **Supp. XI:** 52–53
Blotner, Joseph, **Retro. Supp. I:** 88; **Retro. Supp. III:** 75
Blouin, Lenora, **Supp. VIII:** 266
"Blouse, The"(Rudman), **Supp. XXIII:** 124
"Blowing Soap Bubbles"(Crooker), **Supp. XXIII:** 56
"Blowin' in the Wind" (song, Dylan), **Supp. XVIII:** 24, 25, 26, 29
Bluckled Bag, The (Rinehart), **Supp. XXV:** 197
Blue Angel (Prose), **Supp. XVI:** 249, 259–260
Blue Angel, The (film), **Supp. XVIII:** 243
Blue Arabesque: A Search for the Sublime (Hampl), **Supp. XXII:** 86, 98–99
"Blue Battalions, The" (Crane), **I:** 419–420
"Blue Bead, The"(Hadas), **Supp. XXIII:** 118, 119
"Bluebeard" (Barthelme), **Supp. IV Part 1:** 47
"Bluebeard" (Millay), **III:** 130
"Blueberries" (Frost), **Retro. Supp. I:** 121, 128
"Blue Boy"(Dybek), **Supp. XXIII:** 76
Blue Calhoun (Price), **Supp. VI:** 265–266
Blue Caterpillar, The (Pickering), **Supp. XXI:** 202–203
Blue City (Macdonald, as Millar), **Supp. IV Part 2:** 466–467
Blue Devils of Nada, The: A Contemporary American Approach to Aesthetics (Murray), **Supp. XIX: 159–160**

Blue Estuaries, The: Poems, 1923–1968 (Bogan), **Supp. III Part 1:** 48, 57, 66
Blue Hammer, The (Macdonald), **Supp. IV Part 2:** 462
"Blue Hotel, The" (Crane), **I:** 34, 415–416, 423
"Blue Hour, The" (Komunyakaa), **Supp. XIII:** 130
Blue in the Face (Auster), **Supp. XII:** 21
Blue Jay's Dance, The: A Birth Year (Erdrich), **Supp. IV Part 1:** 259–260, 265, 270, 272
"Blue Juniata" (Cowley), **Supp. II Part 1:** 144
Blue Juniata: Collected Poems (Cowley), **Supp. II Part 1:** 140
"Blue Lick" (Offutt), **Supp. XIX:** 164, 165
Blue Light (Mosley), **Supp. XIII: 245–247,** 248, 249
"Blue Light Lounge Sutra for the Performance Poets at Harold Park Hotel" (Komunyakaa), **Supp. XIII:** 125
"Blue Meridian" (Toomer), **Supp. III Part 2:** 476, 487; **Supp. IX:** 320
"Blue Moles" (Plath), **Supp. I Part 2:** 539
Blue Mountain Ballads (music) (Bowles), **Supp. IV Part 1:** 84
Blue Movie (Southern), **Supp. XI:** 309
"Blue Notes" (Matthews), **Supp. IX:** 169
Blue Pastoral (Sorrentino), **Supp. XXI:** 226, 235–236
Blue Pastures (Oliver), **Supp. VII:** 229–230, 245
"Blueprint for Negro Writing" (Wright), **Supp. XVIII:** 282–283
"Blueprints" (Kingsolver), **Supp. VII:** 203
Blue Religion, The (Connelly, ed.), **Supp. XXI:** 74–75, 79
Blue Rhine, Black Forest (Untermeyer), **Supp. XV:** 310
"Blue Ribbon at Amesbury, A" (Frost), **Retro. Supp. I:** 138
"Blues Ain't No Mockin Bird" (Bambara), **Supp. XI:** 3
"Blues and the Fable in the Flesh, The" (lecture, Murray), **Supp. XIX:** 153
Blues Baby: Early Poems (Mullen), **Supp. XXVII:** 174
"Blues Chant Hoodoo Rival" (Komunyakaa), **Supp. XIII:** 117, 118
Blue Screen (Parker), **Supp. XIX:** 186
"Blues for Another Time" (Dunn), **Supp. XI:** 148
"Blues for Jimmy" (McGrath), **Supp. X:** 116
"Blues for John Coltraine, Dead at 41" (Matthews), **Supp. IX:** 157
Blues for Mister Charlie (Baldwin), **Retro. Supp. II:** 8; **Supp. I Part 1:** 48, 61–62, 63
"Blues for Warren" (McGrath), **Supp. X:** 116
Blue Shoe (Lamott), **Supp. XX: 138–140**
Blues If You Want (Matthews), **Supp. IX:** 155, **163–165**
"Blues I'm Playing, The" (Hughes), **Retro. Supp. I:** 204; **Supp. XIX:** 75
Blues Journey (Myers), **Supp. XXVII:** 211
"Blue Sky, The" (Snyder), **Supp. VIII:** 306
Blues Legacies and Black Feminism (A. Davis), **Supp. XXVI:** 50
Bluesman (Dubus III), **Supp. XXIV: 102–104**
"Blues on a Box" (Hughes), **Retro. Supp. I:** 208
"Blues People" (Ellison), **Retro. Supp. II:** 124
Blues People: Negro Music in White America (Baraka), **Retro. Supp. II:** 124; **Supp. II Part 1:** 30, 31, 33–35, 37, 41, 42, 53
"Blue Spruces in Pairs, a Bird Bath Between": (Bronk), **Supp. XXI:** 30
Bluest Eye, The (Morrison), **Retro. Supp. III:** 183, 184, 185–187, 199–200; **Supp. III Part 1:** 362, 363–367, 379; **Supp. IV Part 1:** 2, 253; **Supp. VIII:** 213, 214, 227; **Supp. XI:** 4, 91
Bluestone, George, **Supp. IX:** 7, 15
Blue Swallows, The (Nemerov), **III:** 269, 270, 271, 274–275, 278, 284, 286–288
"Blue Tattoo" (Nelson and Espeland), **Supp. XVIII:** 181
Blue Voyage (Aiken), **I:** 53, 56
Bluhm, Norman, **Supp. XXIII:** 217
Blum, Gustav, **Supp. XV:** 194
Blum, Morgan, **I:** 169
Blum, W. C (pseudonym). See Watson, James Sibley, Jr.
Blumenthal, Nathaniel. See Branden, Nathaniel
Blumenthal, Sidney, **Supp. VIII:** 241
Blunden, Edmund, **Supp. XIX:** 133
Blunt, Wilfrid Scawen, **III:** 459
Bly, Carol, **Supp. XVI: 31–43**
Bly, Robert, **I:** 291; **Supp. III Part 2:** 599; **Supp. IV Part 1: 59–77,** 177; **Supp. IV Part 2:** 623; **Supp. IX:** 152, 155, 265, 271, 290; **Supp. V:** 332; **Supp. VIII:** 279; **Supp. X:** 127; **Supp. XI:** 142; **Supp. XIII:** 284; **Supp. XV:** 74, 176; **Supp. XVI:** 32, 36, 39, 177, 212, 230; **Supp. XVII:** 243, 244; **Supp. XXI:** 83, 84–86, 87, 91, 93, 94, 95; **Supp. XXII:** 83; **Supp. XXIII:** 136; **Supp. XXIV:** 219
"B Negative" (X. J. Kennedy), **Supp. XV: 156–157**
"Boarder, The" (Simpson), **Supp. IX:** 269
Boarding House Blues (Farrell), **II:** 30, 43, 45
Boarding School, The (Foster), **Supp. XXV:** 35, 36, 37, 45–47
Boas, Franz, **I:** 214; **Retro. Supp. III:** 127, 130; **Supp. I Part 2:** 641; **Supp. IX:** 329; **Supp. VIII:** 295; **Supp. XIV:** 199, 209, 210
"Boat, The" (Oliver), **Supp. VII:** 247
"Boat, The" (Sexton), **Supp. II Part 2:** 692
Boating Party, The (Renoir), **Supp. XII:** 188
"Boat Is Tethered to the Floor,' The: After the Harlem Renaissance" (H. Johnson), **Supp. XXVI:** 175
Boat of Quiet Hours, The (Kenyon), **Supp. VII:** 167–169, 171
"Boat of Quiet Hours, The" (Kenyon), **Supp. VII:** 168
"Boat Ride" (Gallagher), **Supp. XXIV:** 169
"Bob and Spike" (Wolfe), **Supp. III Part 2:** 580
Bobbed Hair (Wells, et al), **Supp. XXVI:** 275
"Bobby Shafter's Gone to Sea" (Swados), **Supp. XIX:** 267
"Bob Dylan's 115th Dream" (song, Dylan), **Supp. XVIII:** 25
Bobrowski, Johannes, **Supp. XV:** 78
Bob the Gambler (F. Barthelme), **Supp. XI:** 30, 31, 32, 34–35, 36–37
Boccaccio, Giovanni, **III:** 283, 411; **IV:** 230
"Bocca della Verità, La" (Davison), **Supp. XXVI:** 74
Bocock, Maclin, **Supp. X:** 79
Boddy, Kasia, **Supp. XXII:** 261
Bodelson, Anders, **Supp. XVI:** 33
Bodenheim, Maxwell, **II:** 42, 530; **Retro. Supp. I:** 417; **Supp. I Part 1:** 257; **Supp. XXV: 17–33; Supp. XXVII:** 86, 87, 139
"Bodies" (Oates), **Supp. II Part 2:** 520

"Bodies and Souls: The Haitian Revolution and Madison Smartt Bell's All Souls' Rising" (Trouillot), **Supp. X:** 14
Bodies of Water (Cliff), **Supp. XXII:** 66–67, 74–75
Bodies of Work: Essays (Acker), **Supp. XII:** 7
Bodily Harm (Atwood), **Supp. XIII:** **25–27**
Bodley Head Jack London (London), **II:** 483
Body (Crews), **Supp. XI:** **108–109**
"Body, The" (Heldreth), **Supp. V:** 151
Body and Soul (Conroy), **Supp. XVI:** 63, **72–74,** 77
"Body and Soul: A Meditation" (Kumin), **Supp. IV Part 2:** 442, 452
Body and Soul: Essays on Poetry (Jarman), **Supp. XVII:** 110, **111–112**
"Body and Soul: Parts of a Life" (Jarman), **Supp. XVII:** 112, 113
Body and the Song, The (Bishop), **Retro. Supp. II:** 40
"Body Bright" (Sanders), **Supp. XVI:** 276
Body of Martin Aquilera, The (Everett), **Supp. XVIII:** 57
Body of Poetry, The: Essays on Women, Form, and the Poetic Self (A. Finch), **Supp. XVII:** 69–70, **77–78**
Body of This Death: Poems (Bogan), **Supp. III Part 1:** 47, 49–52, 58
Body of Waking (Rukeyser), **Supp. VI:** 274, 281
"Body of Waking" (Rukeyser), **Supp. VI:** 279
"Body on Fire, the Soul in Flight, The" (Jarman), **Supp. XVII:** 111, 112
Body Rags (Kinnell), **Supp. III Part 1:** 235, 236, 243–245, 250, 253, 254
"Body's Curse, The" (Dobyns), **Supp. XIII:** 87
"Body's Weight" (Espaillat), **Supp. XXI:** 111
"Body's Weight, The" (Dobyns), **Supp. XIII:** 89
Body Traffic (Dobyns), **Supp. XIII:** 87, 89
"'Body with the Lamp Lit Inside, The' " (Mills), **Supp. IV Part 1:** 64
Body Work (Paretsky), **Supp. XXV:** 177, 178, 179, 181, 184–185
Boehm, David, **Supp. XVII:** 58
Boehme, Jakob, **I:** 10
Bogan, Louise, **I:** 169, 185; **Retro. Supp. I:** 36; **Supp. I Part 2:** 707, 726; **Supp. III Part 1:** **47–68;** **Supp. IX:** 229; **Supp. VIII:** 171, 265; **Supp. X:** 58, 102; **Supp. XIII:** 347; **Supp. XIV:** 129; **Supp. XVII:** 75; **Supp. XXIII:** 145; **Supp. XXVII:** 261
Bogan, Major Benjamin Lewis, **IV:** 120
Bogart, Humphrey, **Supp. I Part 2:** 623; **Supp. IV Part 1:** 130, 356
Bogdanovich, Peter, **Supp. V:** 226
Bogey Man, The (Plimpton), **Supp. XVI:** 241
Boggs, Francis W., **Supp. XVI:** 182
"Bogs" (Pickering), **Supp. XXI:** 198
"Bohemian, The" (Hapgood), **Supp. XVII:** 103
"Bohemian, The" (Harte), **Supp. II Part 1:** 339
"Bohemian Girl, The" (Cather), **Retro. Supp. I:** 7; **Retro. Supp. III:** 22, 26, 28
"Bohemian Hymn, The" (Emerson), **II:** 19
"Bohemians" (Saunders), **Supp. XIX:** 234
"Boids and Beasties" (Geisel), **Supp. XVI:** 100
Boissevain, Eugen, **III:** 124
Boissière, Ralph de, **Supp. XXI:** 160
Boit, Edward, **Retro. Supp. I:** 366
Bojorquez, Jennifer, **Supp. XII:** 318
"Boke, A" (Berrigan), **Supp. XXIV:** 42
Boker, George, **Supp. XV:** 269
Boland, Eavan, **Retro. Supp. III:** 14
Bolaño, Roberto, **Supp. XXV:** 49
"Bold Words at the Bridge" (Jewett), **II:** 394
Boleslavsky, Richard, **Supp. XIV:** 240, 243
Boleyn, Anne, **Supp. I Part 2:** 461
Bolick, Katie, **Supp. XVI:** 167; **Supp. XXIII:** 135, 137, 138; **Supp. XXIV:** 167, 173, 177
Bolinas Journal (Brainard), **Supp. XXVII:** 20, 27
Bolivar, Simon, **Supp. I Part 1:** 283, 284, 285
Bolonik, Kera, **Supp. XVIII:** 60
Bolton, Guy, **Supp. I Part 1:** 281
Bolts of Melody: New Poems of Emily Dickinson (Todd and Bingham, eds.), **I:** 470; **Retro. Supp. I:** 36
"Bomb" (Corso), **Supp. XII:** 117, 124, 125–126, 127
Bombeck, Erma, **Supp. XVII:** 168
Bombs Away (Steinbeck), **IV:** 51–52
"Bona and Paul" (Toomer), **Supp. IX:** 307, 318–319
Bonaparte, Darren, **Supp. XXVI:** 88
Bonaparte, Marie, **III:** 418; **Retro. Supp. II:** 264, 266
"Bon-Bon" (Poe), **III:** 425
Bond, The (Boyce), **Supp. XXI:** **5, 11–12**
Bond, The (N. Boyce), **Supp. XVII:** 99, 100
Bondage (Hwang), **Supp. XXI:** 147
Bondsman, The (Massinger), **Supp. XV:** 238
Bondwoman's Narrative, by Hannah Crafts, a Fugitive Slave, Recently Escaped from North Carolina, The, **Supp. XX:** **105**
Bone, Martyn, **Supp. XXII:** 247
Bone, Robert, **Supp. IX:** 318–319; **Supp. XI:** 283; **Supp. XVIII:** 285
Bone by Bone (Matthiessen), **Supp. V:** 199, 212, 213, 214
"Bone Deposit" (Ray), **Supp. XVIII:** 194
Boners (Abingdon). See Schoolboy Howlers (Abingdon)
"Bones" (Goldbarth), **Supp. XII:** **173–174**
"Bones and Jewels" (Monette), **Supp. X:** 159
"Bones and Shells" (Sanders), **Supp. XVI:** 271–272
"Bones of a House" (Cowley). See "Blue Juniata"
Bones on Black Spruce Mountain, The (Budbill), **Supp. XIX:** **11–12**
Bonetti, Kay, **Supp. VIII:** 47, 152, 159, 160, 165, 168, 170, 223; **Supp. XII:** 61; **Supp. XIV:** 232, 234; **Supp. XXI:** 36
"Bonfire" (Gallagher), **Supp. XXIV:** 170
"Bonfire, The" (Frost), **Retro. Supp. III:** 99
Bonfire of the Vanities, The (Wolfe), **Supp. III Part 2:** 584–586
Bonheur, Rosa, **Supp. XV:** 276
Bonhoeffer, Dietrich, **Supp. VIII:** 198
Boni, Charles, **Supp. XIV:** 288
Boni and Liveright, **Retro. Supp. I:** 59, 80, 178
Bonicelli, Vittorio, **Supp. XI:** 307
Bonifacius (Mather), **Supp. II Part 2:** 461, 464
Bonnefoy, Yves, **Supp. III Part 1:** 235, 243
Bonner, Robert, **Retro. Supp. I:** 246
Bonneville, Mme. Marguerite, **Supp. I Part 2:** 520, 521
Bonneville, Nicolas de, **Supp. I Part 2:** 511, 518, 519
Bonney, William. See Billy the Kid
Bontemps, Arna, **Retro. Supp. I:** 194,

196, 203; **Supp. I Part 1:** 325; **Supp. IV Part 1:** 170; **Supp. IX:** 306, 309; **Supp. XVIII:** 282; **Supp. XXII: 1–16**
Book, A (Barnes), **Supp. III Part 1:** 36, 39, 44
Book about Myself, A (Dreiser), **I:** 515; **Retro. Supp. II:** 104
"Book as a Container of Consciousness, The" (Gass), **Supp. VI:** 92
Booker, Keith, **Supp. XV:** 197
"Bookies, Beware!" (Heller), **Supp. IV Part 1:** 383
"Book Notes and News" (column, Boyce), **Supp. XXI:** 2
Book of American Negro Poetry, The (J. W. Johnson, ed.), **Supp. IV Part 1:** 165, 166; **Supp. XXII:** 11; **Supp. XXVI:** 165
Book of Americans, A (Benét), **Supp. XI:** 46, 47, 51
Book of Beb, The (Buechner), **Supp. XII:** 53
Book of Breeething, The (Burroughs), **Supp. III Part 1:** 97, 103
Book of Burlesques, A (Mencken), **III:** 104
Book of Common Prayer, A (Didion), **Supp. IV Part 1:** 196, 198, 203–205, 207, 208
Book of Daniel, The (Doctorow), **Supp. IV Part 1:** 218, 219, 220–222, 227, 231, 237–238, 238; **Supp. V:** 45
Book of Dreams (Kerouac), **Supp. III Part 1:** 225
"Book of Ephraim, The" (Merrill), **Supp. III Part 1:** 330–334
Book of Folly, The (Sexton), **Supp. II Part 2:** 691, 692–694
Book of Gallant Vagabonds, The (Beston), **Supp. XXVI:** 33
Book of Gods and Devils, The (Simic), **Supp. VIII: 281**
Book of Guys, The (Keillor), **Supp. XVI:** 177
"Book of Hours of Sister Clotilde, The" (A. Lowell), **II:** 522
Book of Jamaica, The (Banks), **Supp. V:** 11, 12, 16
"Book of Life" (Bidart), **Supp. XV:** 23
Book of Living Verse, The; English and American Poetry from the Thirteenth Century to the Present Day (Untermeyer, ed.), **Supp. XV:** 310
Book of Longing (Cohen), **Supp. XXVII:** 56
Book of Love, A (Vildrac; Bynner, trans.), **Supp. XV:** 50
Book of Lyrics (Bynner), **Supp. XV:** 51
Book of Martyrs (Fox). See Acts and Monuments of These Latter and Perilous Days (Fox)
Book of Medicines, The (Hogan), **Supp. IV Part 1:** 397, 410, 411–414
"Book of Medicines, The" (Hogan), **Supp. IV Part 1:** 412, 413
"Book of Memory, The" (Auster), **Supp. XII:** 21–22
Book of Mercy (Cohen), **Supp. XXVII:** 54
Book of My Nights (L.-Y. Lee), **Supp. XV: 215, 223–226**
Book of Negro Folklore, The (Hughes, ed.), **Supp. I Part 1:** 345; **Supp. XXII:** 11–12
Book of Nightmares, The (Kinnell), **Supp. III Part 1:** 235, 236, 243, 244, 246–254
Book of One's Own, A: People and Their Diaries (Mallon), **Supp. XIX:** 134
Book of Prefaces, A (Mencken), **III:** 99–100, 105
Book of Repulsive Women, The (Barnes), **Supp. III Part 1:** 33
Book of Revelation, **Supp. XXIII:** 44
Book of Roses, The (Parkman), **Supp. II Part 2:** 597, 598
Book of the Body, The (Bidart), **Supp. XV: 21, 25–27**
"Book of the Dead, The" (Rukeyser), **Supp. VI:** 272, 278, 279; **Supp. XV:** 349
"Book of the Grotesque, The" (Anderson), **I:** 106
Book of the Homeless, The (Wharton), **Retro. Supp. I:** 377
Book of the Hopi (Waters), **Supp. X:** 124
Book of Tobit (Bible), **Supp. XII:** 54
Book of Verses, A (Masters), **Supp. I Part 2:** 458
Book of Wonder (Dunsany), **Supp. XXV:** 113
Book of Yaak, The (Bass), **Supp. XVI: 18–19**
"Book of Yolek, The" (Hecht), **Supp. X:** 69, **70–71**
"Books" (Collins), **Supp. XXI:** 55
"Books Considered" (Bloom), **Supp. I Part 1:** 96
"Books I Left Behind, The" (Pickering), **Supp. XXI:** 196
Books in My Life, The (H. Miller), **II:** 176, 189
"Books/P,L,E, The" (Goldbarth), **Supp. XII:** 190
Bookviews, **Supp. XI:** 216
"Book World Live", **Supp. XVIII:** 143–144
"Boolean Algebra: X2=X" (Bronk), **Supp. XXI:** 30
"Boom" (Nemerov), **III:** 278
Boom! (T. Williams), **IV:** 383
Boomer Girls: Poems by Women of the Baby Boom Generation (Gemin and Sergi, eds.), **Supp. XXI:** 246
Boom Town (Wolfe), **IV:** 456
"Boom Town" (Wolfe), **IV:** 469
Boone, Daniel, **II:** 207; **III:** 444; **IV:** 192, 193
Boorstin, Daniel, **I:** 253
Booth, Charles, **Supp. I Part 1:** 13
Booth, John Wilkes, **III:** 588
Booth, Philip, **I:** 522; **Supp. IX:** 269; **Supp. XI:** 141; **Supp. XIII:** 277; **Supp. XV:** 92; **Supp. XXVI:** 68
Booth, General William, **Supp. I Part 2:** 384, 386
"Booze"(P. Benedict), **Supp. XXIII:** 36
Borah, William, **III:** 475
Borden, Lizzie, **II:** 5
Border and the Buffalo, The (J. Cook), **Supp. XXIV:** 248
"Border Crossings: An Interview with Eric Gansworth" (de la Paz and Purdy), **Supp. XXVI:** 101
Borderlands/La Frontera: The New Mestiza (Anzaldúa), **Supp. XIII:** 223
Border Matters (Saldívar), **Supp. XIX:** 112–113
Borders (Mora), **Supp. XIII:** 213, **215–217**
Border Trilogy (McCarthy), **Supp. VIII:** 175, 182
"Border View, Hot Springs, Texas" (W. V. Davis), **Supp. XXI:** 95
Borel, Pétrus, **III:** 320
Borges, Jorge Luis, **I:** 123, 135, 138, 140, 142; **Retro. Supp. III:** 235; **Supp. III Part 2:** 560; **Supp. IV Part 2:** 623, 626, 630; **Supp. V:** 238; **Supp. VIII:** 15, 348, 349; **Supp. XII:** 21, 147; **Supp. XIX:** 131; **Supp. XV:** 34; **Supp. XVI:** 201, 206; **Supp. XVII:** 47; **Supp. XXIII:** 68; **Supp. XXV:** 50, 69
"Borges and I" (Bidart), **Supp. XV:** 34, 35
"Borinken Blues" (Komunyakaa), **Supp. XIII:** 117
"Born, The" (Lamott), **Supp. XX: 143–144**

"Born a Square: The Westerner's Dilemma" (Stegner), **Supp. IV Part 2:** 595; **Supp. V:** 224
"Born Bad" (Cisneros), **Supp. VII:** 62
Born on the Fourth of July (Kovic), **Supp. XIX:** 17
"Borough of Cemeteries" (Shaw), **Supp. XIX:** 246
Borrowed Time: An AIDS Memoir (Monette), **Supp. X:** 145, 146, 147, 152, 154, 155
Boschman, Robert, **Retro. Supp. III:** 7
Bose, Sudip, **Supp. XXII:** 205, 206, 214
Bosmajian, Hamida, **Supp. XXII:** 290
"Bosque del Apache Wildlife Refuge" (Mora), **Supp. XIII:** 218
Boss Dog, The: A Story of Provence (M. F. K. Fisher), **Supp. XVII:** 91
Bossin, Gary, **Supp. XXVII:** 133, 143, 145
Bost, Suzanne, **Supp. XXII:** 66, 70, 75, 78
"Boston" (Hardwick), **Supp. III Part 1:** 201
Boston (Sinclair), **Supp. V:** 282, 288–289
Boston, B. H., **Supp. XIII:** 312
Boston Adventure (Stafford), **Retro. Supp. II:** 177, 178
"Boston Common" (Berryman), **I:** 172
"Boston Evening Transcript, The" (T. S. Eliot), **Retro. Supp. III:** 60
"Boston Hymn" (Emerson), **II:** 13, 19
Bostonians, The (H. James), **I:** 9; **II:** 282; **IV:** 202; **Retro. Supp. I:** 216, 225
Boston Marriage (Mamet), **Supp. XIV:** 247
"Boston Nativity, The" (R. Lowell), **II:** 538
Boswell, James, **IV:** 431; **Supp. I Part 2:** 656
Boswell: A Modern Comedy (Elkin), **Supp. VI:** 42, **44–45,** 57
Bosworth, Patricia, **Supp. IV Part 2:** 573, 591
"Bothersome Sex and O'Brien, The" (Ryan as Quin), **Supp. XVIII:** 238
Botticelli (McNally), **Supp. XIII:** 197
Botticelli, Sandro, **IV:** 410; **Retro. Supp. I:** 422
"Botticellian Trees, The" (W. C. Williams), **Retro. Supp. I:** 422
"Bottled" (H. Johnson), **Supp. XXVI:** 164, 165
"Bottle of Milk for Mother, A" (Algren), **Supp. IX:** 3
"Bottle of Perrier, A" (Wharton), **IV:** 316
"Bottles" (Kenyon), **Supp. VII:** 171
"Bottom Line, The" (Elkin), **Supp. VI:** 52, **53**
Bottom: On Shakespeare (Zukofsky), **Supp. III Part 2:** 622, 624, 625, 626, 627, 629
Boublil, Alain, **Supp. XXI:** 155
Boucher, Anthony, **Supp. IV Part 2:** 473; **Supp. XV:** 203, 205
Boucicault, Dion, **Supp. XXII:** 70
Boughton, Henrietta Breckenridge. See Young, Barbara
Boukreev, Anatoli, **Supp. XVIII:** 112
Boulanger, Nadia, **Supp. IV Part 1:** 81
"Boulot and Boulette" (Chopin), **Supp. I Part 1:** 211
Boulton, Agnes, **III:** 403; **Supp. XXII: 17–31**
Bound East for Cardiff (O'Neill), **III:** 388
Bound for Glory (Guthrie), **Supp. XVIII:** 23
"Bounty" (Saunders), **Supp. XIX:** 226, 227
"Bounty"(P. Benedict), **Supp. XXIII:** 41
"Bouquet, The" (Stevens), **IV:** 90
"Bouquet of Dark Red Mums, The" (Notley), **Supp. XXII:** 230
"Bouquet of Roses in Sunlight" (Stevens), **IV:** 93
Bourdin, Henri L., **Supp. I Part 1:** 251
Bourgeois, Monique, **Supp. XXII:** 99–100
Bourgeois Poet, The (Shapiro), **Supp. II Part 2:** 701, 703, 704, 713, 714–716
Bourget, James, **IV:** 319
Bourget, Paul, **II:** 325, 338; **IV:** 311, 315; **Retro. Supp. I:** 224, 359, 373; **Retro. Supp. III:** 275; **Supp. XX: 232; Supp. XXIV:** 23
Bourjaily, Vance, **III:** 43; **Supp. IX:** 260; **Supp. XXIV:** 225
Bourke-White, Margaret, **I:** 290, 293, 295, 297
Bourne, Charles Rogers, **I:** 215
Bourne, Mrs. Charles Rogers, **I:** 215
Bourne, Randolph, **I: 214–238,** 243, 245, 246–247, 251, 259; **Supp. I Part 2:** 524; **Supp. XV:** 141, 298, 301
Boursicot, Bernard, **Supp. XXI:** 152, 153, 154
Bouton, Jim "Bulldog", **Supp. XX: 274**
Bouton, John Bell, **Supp. XXIII:** 188, 189
Bowden, Charles, **Supp. XIII:** 17
Bowditch, Nathaniel, **Supp. I Part 2:** 482
Bowen, Barbara, **Supp. IX:** 311
Bowen, Elizabeth, **Retro. Supp. I:** 351; **Supp. IV Part 1:** 299; **Supp. IX:** 128; **Supp. VIII:** 65, 165, 251, 265
Bowen, Francis, **Supp. I Part 2:** 413
Bowen, Henry, **Supp. XVIII:** 4
Bowen, Louise de Koven, **Supp. I Part 1:** 5
Bowen, Michael, **Supp. VIII:** 73
Bowers, John, **Supp. XI:** 217–218
"Bowlers Anonymous" (Dobyns), **Supp. XIII:** 86
Bowles, Emily, **Supp. XVIII:** 200, 202
Bowles, Jane (Jane Auer), **II:** 586; **Supp. IV Part 1:** 89, 92
Bowles, Paul, **I:** 211; **II:** 586; **Supp. II Part 1:** 17; **Supp. IV Part 1: 79–99**
Bowles, Samuel, **I:** 454, 457; **Retro. Supp. I:** 30, 32, 33
"Bowl of Blood, The" (Jeffers), **Supp. II Part 2:** 434
"Bowls" (Moore), **III:** 196
Bowman, James, **I:** 193
"Bows to Drouth" (Snyder), **Supp. VIII:** 303
Box, Edgar (pseudonym). See Vidal, Gore
Box and Quotations from Chairman Mao Tse-tung (Albee), **I:** 89–91, 94
Boxer and the Spy, The (Parker), **Supp. XIX:** 190
Box Garden, The (Shields), **Supp. VII:** 314–315, 320
"Box of Pastels, A" (Kooser), **Supp. XIX:** 128
"Box of Rocks, A" (Gallagher), **Supp. XXIV:** 175
"Box Seat" (Toomer), **Supp. III Part 2:** 484; **Supp. IX:** 316, 318
Boy, A (Ashbery), **Supp. III Part 1:** 5
"Boy and Dog" (L. Brown), **Supp. XXI:** 38, 42, **43–44**
Boyce, Horace, **II:** 136
Boyce, Neith, **Supp. XVII:** 96, 97, 98–99, 100, 106; **Supp. XXI: 1–16**
Boyd, Brian, **Retro. Supp. I:** 270, 275
Boyd, Janet L., **Supp. X:** 229
Boyd, Kristen, **Supp. XXIII:** 246
Boyd, Nancy (pseudonym). See Millay, Edna St. Vincent
Boyd, Thomas, **I:** 99; **IV:** 427
Boyd, Valerie, **Retro. Supp. III:** 136
Boyelston, Matthew, **Supp. XXVII:** 216
Boyers, Robert, **Retro. Supp. III:** 245
Boyesen, H. H., **II:** 289

"Boy from Lam Kien, The" (July), **Supp. XXIV:** 200, 204
"Boyhood" (Collins), **Supp. XXI:** 64
"Boyhood" (Farrell), **II:** 28
"Boy in France, A" (Salinger), **III:** 552–553
"Boy in the Basement, The" (Inge), **Supp. XXV:** 105, 106
Boy in the Water (Dobyns), **Supp. XIII:** 75, **84**
Boyle, Kay, **IV:** 404; **Supp. XXIV:** **49–66**
Boyle, T. Coraghessan, **Supp. VIII:** **1–17; Supp. XX: 17–32; Supp. XXI:** 226; **Supp. XXII:** 262
Boyle, Thomas John. See Boyle, T. C.
Boynton, H. W., **Supp. IX:** 7
Boynton, Percy Holmes, **Supp. I Part 2:** 415
Boynton, Robert, **Supp. XVII:** 209; **Supp. XVIII:** 105, 107, 116
Boynton, Robert S., **Supp. XXV:** 158
"Boy on a Train" (Ellison), **Retro. Supp. II:** 124
"Boy Riding Forward Backward" (Francis), **Supp. IX:** 82
"Boys and Girls" (Cisneros), **Supp. VII:** 59–60
"Boys and Girls" (Munro), **Supp. XXVII:** 184
"Boy's Dream Ballad, The" (Very), **Supp. XXV:** 244
Boy's Froissart, The (Lanier), **Supp. I Part 1:** 361
"Boys"(Kenny), **Supp. XXIII:** 149
Boy's King Arthur, The (Lanier), **Supp. I Part 1:** 361
Boy's Mabinogion, The (Lanier), **Supp. I Part 1:** 361
"Boys of '29, The" (Holmes), **Supp. I Part 1:** 308
Boys of '76, The (Coffin), **III:** 577
Boy's Percy, The (Lanier), **Supp. I Part 1:** 361
"Boy Story" (Huddle), **Supp. XXVI:** 151
Boy's Town (Howells), **I:** 418
Boy's Will, A (Frost), **II:** 152, 153, 155–156, 159, 164, 166; **Retro. Supp. I:** 124, 127, 128, 131; **Retro. Supp. II:** 168; **Retro. Supp. III:** 95, 96
"Boy Up a Tree" (Hoffman), **Supp. XVIII:** 86
"Boy Who Wrestled with Angels, The" (Hoffman), **Supp. X:** 90
"Boy with One Shoe, The" (Jewett), **Retro. Supp. II:** 132
"Brace, The" (Bausch), **Supp. VII:** 48
Bracebridge Hall, or, The Humorists (Irving), **I:** 339, 341; **II:** 308–309, 313
Bracher, Frederick, **I:** 378, 380; **Supp. I Part 1:** 185
Brackenridge, Hugh Henry, **Supp. I Part 1:** 124, 127, 145; **Supp. II Part 1:** 65
Brackett, Leigh, **Supp. IV Part 1:** 130
Bradbury, John M., **I:** 288–289; **IV:** 130, 135
Bradbury, Malcolm, **Supp. VIII:** 124; **Supp. XVIII:** 140
Bradbury, Ray, **Supp. I Part 2:** 621–622; **Supp. IV Part 1: 101–118; Supp. XVI:** 122; **Supp. XVII:** 41; **Supp. XXIII:** 290; **Supp. XXV:** 141; **Supp. XXVII:** 295
"Brad Carrigan, American" (Saunders), **Supp. XIX:** 233
Braddon, Mary E., **Supp. I Part 1:** 35, 36
Bradfield, Scott, **Supp. VIII:** 88
Bradford, Gamaliel, **I:** 248, 250
Bradford, Roark, **Retro. Supp. I:** 80
Bradford, William, **Retro. Supp. II:** 161, 162; **Retro. Supp. III:** 9; **Supp. I Part 1:** 110, 112; **Supp. I Part 2:** 486, 494; **Supp. XXII:** **33–47**
Bradlee, Ben, **Supp. V:** 201
Bradley, Bill, **Supp. VIII:** 47
Bradley, F. H., **Retro. Supp. I:** 57, 58
Bradley, Francis Herbert, **I:** 59, 567–568, 572, 573
Bradshaw, Barbara, **Supp. XIII:** 313
Bradstreet, Anne, **I:** 178–179, 180, 181, 182, 184; **III:** 505; **Retro. Supp. I:** 40; **Retro. Supp. III:** **1–15; Supp. I Part 1: 98–123,** 300; **Supp. I Part 2:** 484, 485, 496, 546, 705; **Supp. V:** 113, 117–118; **Supp. XIII:** 152; **Supp. XIV:** 128; **Supp. XVIII:** 304; **Supp. XXII:** 46
Bradstreet, Elizabeth, **Supp. I Part 1:** 108, 122
Bradstreet, Simon, **I:** 178; **Supp. I Part 1:** 103, 110, 116
Bradstreet, Mrs. Simon. See Bradstreet, Anne
Brady, Alice, **III:** 399
Brady, Catherine, **Supp. XXIII:** 301
Brady, Matthew, **Supp. XVIII:** 4
Bragdon, Claude, **Supp. XX: 117**
"Bragdowdy and the Busybody, The" (Thurber), **Supp. I Part 2:** 617
Bragg, Rick, **Supp. XVIII:** 195
"Brahma" (Emerson), **II:** 19, 20
Brahms, Johannes, **III:** 118, 448
"Brahms in Delirium" (Skloot), **Supp. XX: 203**
Braided Creek (Kooser and Harrison), **Supp. XIX:** 126
"Braiding" (L.-Y. Lee), **Supp. XV:** 214
"Brain and the Mind, The" (James), **II:** 346
Brainard, Joe, **Supp. XV:** 33; **Supp. XXIII:** 217; **Supp. XXIV:** 33, 34, 35, 39, 41, 42, 43; **Supp. XXVII:** **17–31**
"Brain Damage" (Barthelme), **Supp. IV Part 1:** 44
"Braindead Megaphone, The" (Saunders), **Supp. XIX:** 235
Braindead Megaphone, The: Essays (Saunders), **Supp. XIX: 234–236**
"Brain Scan" (Skloot), **Supp. XX: 200**
"Brain to the Heart, The" (Komunyakaa), **Supp. XIII:** 120
Braithwaite, Chris, **Supp. XXII:** 212
Braithwaite, Edward Kamau, **Supp. XXVII:** 160
Braithwaite, William Stanley, **Retro. Supp. I:** 131; **Supp. IX:** 309; **Supp. XV:** 296–297, 301–302, 305, 306
Brakhage, Stan, **Supp. XII:** 2
Braly, Malcolm, **Supp. XVIII:** 147
"Bramble, The" (Wrigley), **Supp. XVIII:** 301
Brame, Gloria, **Supp. XV:** 113; **Supp. XXIII:** 122
Bramen, Carrie Tirado, **Supp. XXIV:** 192
Bramer, Monte, **Supp. X:** 152
Branch Will Not Break, The (Wright), **Supp. III Part 2:** 596, 598–601; **Supp. IV Part 1:** 60; **Supp. IX:** 159
Brancusi, Constantin, **III:** 201; **Retro. Supp. I:** 292
Brancusi, Constantine, **Supp. XXVI:** 224
Brande, Dorothea, **Supp. I Part 2:** 608
Brandel, Marc, **Supp. XXI:** 276
Branden, Nathaniel, **Supp. IV Part 2:** 526, 528
"Branding Cities" (Greenberg), **Supp. XXII:** 244
"Brand-Name Blues" (Kaufmann), **Supp. XI:** 39
Brand New Life, A (Farrell), **II:** 46, 48
Brando, Marlon, **II:** 588; **Supp. IV Part 2:** 560; **Supp. XVIII:** 251
Brandon, Henry, **Supp. I Part 2:** 604, 612, 618
Brandt, Alice, **Supp. I Part 1:** 92
Brandt, Carl, **Supp. XI:** 45
Brant, Sebastian, **III:** 447, 448
Brantley, Ben, **Supp. XXIV:** 268, 269–270, 271, 272, 274
Braque, Georges, **III:** 197; **Supp. IX:** 66; **Supp. XXVI:** 259

Brashford, Jake, **Supp. X:** 252
Brasil, Emanuel, **Supp. I Part 1:** 94
"Brasília" (Plath), **Supp. I Part 2:** 544, 545
"Brass Buttons" (McCoy), **Supp. XIII:** 161
"Brass Candlestick, The" (Francis), **Supp. IX:** 89
Brass Check, The (Sinclair), **Supp. V:** 276, 281, 282, 284–285
Brass Knuckles (Dybek), **Supp. XXIII: 68–69**
"Brass Ring, The" (Carver), **Supp. III Part 1:** 137
"Brass Spittoons" (Hughes), **Supp. I Part 1:** 326–327
Brass Verdict, The (Connelly), **Supp. XXI: 78–79**
Brats (X. J. Kennedy), **Supp. XV:** 163
Brautigan, Richard, **III:** 174; **Supp. VIII:** 42, 43; **Supp. XII:** 139; **Supp. XVI:** 172; **Supp. XXI:** 53
Brave Cowboy, The (Abbey), **Supp. XIII:** 4–5
Brave Men (Pyle), **Supp. XVII:** 61
Brave New World (Huxley), **II:** 454; **Supp. XIII:** 29; **Supp. XVIII:** 137
"Brave New World" (MacLeish), **III:** 18
Bravery of Earth, A (Eberhart), **I:** 522, 524, 525, 526, 530
"Brave Tailors of Maida, The" (Talese), **Supp. XVII:** 208
"Brave Words for a Startling Occasion" (Ellison), **Retro. Supp. II:** 118
Braving the Elements (Merrill), **Supp. III Part 1:** 320, 323, 325–327, 329
Bravo, The (Cooper), **I:** 345–346, 348
"Bravura" (Francis), **Supp. IX:** 90
Brawley, Benjamin, **Supp. I Part 1:** 327, 332
Brawl in a Tavern, A (Shaw), **Supp. XIX:** 241
Brawne, Fanny, **I:** 284; **II:** 531
Braxton, Joanne, **Supp. IV Part 1:** 12, 15
Brazil (Bishop), **Retro. Supp. II:** 45; **Supp. I Part 1:** 92
"Brazil" (Marshall), **Supp. XI:** 281
Brazil (Updike), **Retro. Supp. I:** 329, 330, 334
"Brazil, January 1, 1502" (Bishop), **Retro. Supp. II:** 47
Braziller, George, **Supp. X:** 24; **Supp. XXIII:** 214
Brazzi, Rossano, **Supp. IV Part 2:** 520
"Bread" (Dickey), **Supp. IV Part 1:** 182
"Bread" (Olds), **Supp. X:** 206
"Bread Alone" (Wylie), **Supp. I Part 2:** 727
Bread in the Wilderness (Merton), **Supp. VIII:** 197, 208
"Bread of Desire, The" (Nelson), **Supp. XVIII:** 177
Bread of Idleness, The (Masters), **Supp. I Part 2:** 460
"Bread of This World, The" (McGrath), **Supp. X:** 119, 127
Bread of Time, The (Levine), **Supp. V:** 180
Bread without Sugar (Stern), **Supp. IX: 297–298**
"Break, The" (Sexton), **Supp. II Part 2:** 689
"Breakaways, The" (Siddons), **Supp. XXII:** 244
Breakdown (Paretsky), **Supp. XXV:** 185
Breakfast at Tiffany's (Capote), **Supp. III Part 1:** 113, 117, 119–121, 124, 126
Breakfast of Champions (Vonnegut), **Supp. II Part 2:** 755, 759, 769, 770, 777–778
Breaking and a Death, A (Kees), **Supp. XV:** 145
Breaking and Entering (X. J. Kennedy), **Supp. XV:** 153, **160–162**
Breaking Hard Ground (D. Hunter), **Supp. XVI:** 38
Breaking Ice (McMillan, ed.), **Supp. XIII:** 182–183
Breaking of the Day, The (Davison), **Supp. XXVI:** 65, 68–70
"Breaking of the Day, The" (Davison), **Supp. XXVI:** 68, 69
Breaking Open (Rukeyser), **Supp. VI:** 274, 281
"Breaking Open" (Rukeyser), **Supp. VI:** 286
Breaking Point, The (Rinehart), **Supp. XXV:** 196
Breaking Ranks: A Political Memoir (Podhoretz), **Supp. VIII: 239–241,** 245
"Breaking the Code of Silence: Ideology and Women's Confessional Poetry" (Harris), **Supp. XIV:** 269
"Breaking the Whistle" (Rash), **Supp. XXVII:** 218
"Breaking Up of the Winships, The" (Thurber), **Supp. I Part 2:** 616
Brearton, Fran, **Supp. XXIV:** 167
Breast, The (P. Roth), **Retro. Supp. II:** 287–288; **Supp. III Part 2:** 416, 418
"Breast, The" (Sexton), **Supp. II Part 2:** 687
"Breasts" (Gallagher), **Supp. XXIV:** 168, 174
"Breasts" (Simic), **Supp. VIII:** 275
"Breasts"(Dybek), **Supp. XXIII:** 77
"Breath" (Espaillat), **Supp. XXI:** 109
"Breath" (Levine), **Supp. V:** 185
Breathe No More, My Lady (Lacy), **Supp. XV:** 203
Breathing Lessons (Tyler), **Supp. IV Part 2:** 669–670
Breathing Room (Davison), **Supp. XXVI:** 66, 78–79
"Breathing Room" (Davison), **Supp. XXVI:** 79
Breathing the Monster Alive (Gansworth), **Supp. XXVI:** 112–113
Breathing the Water (Levertov), **Supp. III Part 1:** 274, 283, 284
"Breath of Life, The" (C. Baxter), **Supp. XVII:** 23
Breath's Burials (Sobin), **Supp. XVI: 288–289**
Breaux, Zelia, **Retro. Supp. II:** 114
Brecht, Bertolt, **I:** 60, 301; **III:** 161, 162; **IV:** 394; **Supp. I Part 1:** 292; **Supp. II Part 1:** 10, 26, 56; **Supp. IV Part 1:** 359; **Supp. IX:** 131, 133, 140; **Supp. X:** 112; **Supp. XIII:** 206, 286; **Supp. XIV:** 162; **Supp. XVIII:** 33; **Supp. XXIV:** 267
Breen, Jon L., **Supp. XXVI:** 277, 281
Breen, Joseph I., **IV:** 390
Breines, Ron, **Supp. XVIII:** 97
Breit, Harvey, **I:** 433; **III:** 575; **Retro. Supp. II:** 230; **Supp. XVIII:** 254; **Supp. XXI:** 277
Breman, Paul, **Supp. XXII:** 8
Bremer, Anne, **Supp. XXII:** 277
Bremer, Fredrika, **Supp. I Part 1:** 407
Bremer, Richard, **Supp. XXIII:** 236
Brendan: A Novel (Buechner), **Supp. XII:** 53
Brennan, Matthew C., **Supp. XIX:** 121; **Supp. XV:** 113, 125
Brent, David, **Supp. XXII:** 259
Brent, Linda, **Supp. IV Part 1:** 12, 13
Brentano, Franz, **II:** 350; **Supp. XIV:** 198, 199
Brer Rabbit (tales), **Supp. IV Part 1:** 11, 13; **Supp. XIV:** 88
Breslin, James E. B., **Retro. Supp. I:** 430
Breslin, John B., **Supp. IV Part 1:** 308
Breslin, Paul, **Supp. VIII:** 283
Bresson, Robert, **Supp. IV Part 1:** 156
"Bresson's Movies" (Creeley), **Supp. IV Part 1:** 156–157
"Bret Easton Ellis Podcast, The", **Supp. XXVII:** 79
Breton, André, **III:** 425; **Supp. XIII:**

114; **Supp. XVII:** 244
Brett, George, **II:** 466; **Supp. V:** 286
Brett, Reginald Baliol, **Supp. XX: 230**
Brevoort, Henry, **II:** 298
Brew, Kwesi, **Supp. IV Part 1:** 10, 16
Brewer, Gaylord, **Supp. XV:** 330
"Brewing of Soma, The" (Whittier), **Supp. I Part 2:** 704
Brewsie and Willie (Stein), **IV:** 27
Brewster, Martha, **Supp. I Part 1:** 114
"Brewsterville Croesus, A" (Briggs), **Supp. XVIII:** 16
Brewsterville letters (Briggs), **Supp. XVIII:** 1, 5, **15–16**
"Brian Age 7" (Doty), **Supp. XI:** 136
Briand, Paul, **Supp. XVIII:** 155
"Briar Patch, The" (Warren), **IV:** 237
Briar Rose (Coover), **Supp. V:** 52
"Briar Rose (Sleeping Beauty)" (Sexton), **Supp. II Part 2:** 690
Brice, Fanny, **II:** 427
"Brick, The" (Nye), **Supp. XIII:** 276
"Bricklayer in the Snow" (Fante), **Supp. XI:** 164–165
"Brick Layer's Lunch Hour, The" (Ginsberg), **Supp. II Part 1:** 318
Brickman, Marshall, **Supp. XV:** 5
"Bricks, The" (Hogan), **Supp. IV Part 1:** 413
"Bridal Ballad, The" (Poe), **III:** 428
"Bridal Bed, The" (Gibran), **Supp. XX: 124**
Bridal Dinner, The (Gurney), **Supp. V:** 109, 110
Bridal Hunt (Silver), **Supp. XXIV:** 264
"Bride Comes to Yellow Sky, The" (Crane), **I:** 34, 415, 416, 423
Bridegroom, The (Jin), **Supp. XVIII: 97–98**
"Bridegroom, The" (Jin), **Supp. XVIII:** 98
Bridegroom Cometh, The (W. Frank), **Supp. XX: 77**
"Bridegroom's Body, The" (Boyle), **Supp. XXIV:** 54, **55–56**
"Bride in the 30's, A" (Auden), **Supp. II Part 1:** 9
Bride of Lammermoor (Scott), **II:** 291
Bride of Samoa (film), **Supp. IV Part 1:** 82
"Bride of the Innisfallen, The" (Welty), **IV:** 278–279; **Retro. Supp. I:** 353
Bride of the Innisfallen, The, and Other Stories (Welty), **IV:** 261, 275–279; **Retro. Supp. I:** 352–353, 355
Brides of the South Wind: Poems 1917–1922 (Jeffers), **Supp. II Part 2:** 419
Bridge, Horatio, **II:** 226; **Retro. Supp. III:** 116
"BRIDGE, THE" (Baraka), **Supp. II Part 1:** 32, 36
Bridge, The (H. Crane), **I:** 62, 109, 266, 385, 386, 387, 395–399, 400, 402; **IV:** 123, 341, 418, 419, 420; **Retro. Supp. I:** 427; **Retro. Supp. II:** 76, 77, 81, 83, **84–87; Retro. Supp. III:** 42–43, 47, 48–49, 50–53, 54; **Supp. IX:** 306; **Supp. V:** 342; **Supp. XXIII:** 146; **Supp. XXVI:** 21, 25, 28
Bridge, The (Talese), **Supp. XVII:** 202, 203, 208
Bridge at Remagen, The (film), **Supp. XI:** 343
"Bridge Burners, The" (Van Vechten), **Supp. II Part 2:** 733
Bridgehead: The Drama of Israel (W. Frank), **Supp. XX: 80**
Bridge of San Luis Rey, The (Wilder), **I:** 360; **IV:** 356, 357, 360–363, 365, 366
"Bridge of Sighs"(P. Benedict), **Supp. XXIII:** 47–48
Bridge of Years, The (Sarton), **Supp. VIII:** 253
"Bridges" (Kingsolver), **Supp. VII:** 208
Bridges, Harry, **I:** 493; **Supp. XIX:** 264; **Supp. XVIII:** 238
Bridges, Lloyd, **Supp. XV:** 202
Bridges, Robert, **II:** 537; **III:** 527; **Supp. I Part 2:** 721; **Supp. II Part 1:** 21; **Supp. XIV:** 336, 341, 342, 343
"Bridging" (Apple), **Supp. XVII:** 5
Bridgman, P. W., **I:** 278
"Bridle, The" (Carver), **Supp. III Part 1:** 138
"Brief and Blameless Outline of the Ontogeny of Crow, A" (Wright), **Supp. XV:** 347
Brief and Frightening Reign of Phil, The (Saunders), **Supp. XIX: 230–231,** 233
"Brief Début of Tildy, The" (O. Henry), **Supp. II Part 1:** 408
"Brief Encounters on the Inland Waterway" (Vonnegut), **Supp. II Part 2:** 760
"Brief History of My Mother's Temper, A" (Huddle), **Supp. XXVI:** 150
Brief History of the Dead, The (Brockmeier), **Supp. XXII: 57–59,** 61
Briefings (Ammons), **Supp. VII:** 29
Brief Interviews with Hideous Men (Wallace), **Supp. X: 308–310**
"Brief Interviews with Hideous Men" (Wallace), **Supp. X:** 309
"Briefly It Enters, and Briefly Speaks" (Kenyon), **Supp. VII:** 174
"Brief Study of the British, A" (Saunders), **Supp. XIX:** 235
Brief Wondrous Life of Oscar Wao, The (Díaz), **Supp. XXIV:** 83, 84, 85, 87, **89–92,** 93
Brier, His Book (J. W. Miller), **Supp. XX: 165, 168, 170**
"Brier Grows Wild, The" (J. W. Miller), **Supp. XX: 170**
"Brier Losing Touch with His Traditions, The" (J. W. Miller), **Supp. XX: 165, 169**
Brier Poems, The (J. W. Miller), **Supp. XX: 168**
"Brier Sermon, The—You Must Be Born Again" (J. W. Miller), **Supp. XX: 165, 169–170**
Briffault, Robert, **Supp. I Part 2:** 560, 567
"Brigade de Cuisine" (McPhee), **Supp. III Part 1:** 307–308
Brigadier and the Golf Widow, The (Cheever), **Supp. I Part 1:** 184–185, 192
Briggs, Charles Frederick, **Supp. I Part 2:** 411; **Supp. XVIII: 1–18**
brigham, besmilr, **Supp. XV:** 349
"Bright and Morning Star" (Wright), **IV:** 488
Bright Book of Life: American Novelists and Storytellers from Hemingway to Mailer (Kazin), **Supp. VIII:** 102, 104
Bright Center of Heaven (Maxwell), **Supp. VIII: 153–155,** 164
"Brightness from the North" (B. Kelly), **Supp. XVII:** 131
Brighton Beach Memoirs (Simon), **Supp. IV Part 2:** 576, 577, 584, 586–587, 590
Bright Procession (Sedges), **Supp. II Part 1:** 125
Bright Room Called Day, A (Kushner), **Supp. IX:** 133, **138–141,** 142
Brillat-Savarin, Jean Anthelme, **Supp. XVII:** 82, 86, 87
"Brilliance" (Doty), **Supp. XI:** 124, 128
"Brilliant California Novelist, A" (Forman), **Supp. XXIV:** 30
"Brilliant Leaves" (Gordon), **II:** 199
"Brilliant Sad Sun" (W. C. Williams), **Retro. Supp. I:** 422
"Bring Brang Brung" (Muñoz), **Supp. XXV:** 135–136
"Bringing Back the Trumpeter Swan" (Kumin), **Supp. IV Part 2:** 454
Bringing It All Back Home (album,

Dylan), **Supp. XVIII:** 20, 25, 26, 30
Bringing It All Back Home (McNally), **Supp. XIII:** 197–198
Bringing the Devil to His Knees (C. Baxter), **Supp. XVII:** 22
"Bringing the Strange Home" (Dunn), **Supp. XI:** 141
"Bring the Day!" (Roethke), **III:** 536
Brinkley, Douglas, **Supp. XIII:** 9; **Supp. XXIV:** 281, 293
Brinkmeyer, Robert H., Jr., **Supp. XI:** 38
Brinnin, John Malcolm, **IV:** 26, 27, 28, 42, 46; **Supp. XV:** 139
Brissot, Jacques Pierre, **Supp. I Part 2:** 511
"Britain's Negro Problem in Sierra Leone" (Du Bois), **Supp. I Part 1:** 176
"British Guiana" (Marshall), **Supp. XI:** 281–282
"British Poets, The" (Holmes), **Supp. I Part 1:** 306
"British Prison Ship, The" (Freneau), **Supp. II Part 1:** 261
Brittan, Gordon G., Jr., **Supp. XIV:** 234
Britten, Benjamin, **II:** 586; **Supp. II Part 1:** 17; **Supp. IV Part 1:** 84
Broadwater, Bowden, **II:** 562
Broadway, Broadway (McNally). See It's Only a Play (McNally)
Broadway, J. William, **Supp. V:** 316
Broadway Bound (Simon), **Supp. IV Part 2:** 576, 577, 584, 586–587, 590
Broadway Danny Rose (film; Allen), **Supp. XV:** 9
"Broadway Pageant, A" (Whitman), **Retro. Supp. III:** 305
"Broadway Sights" (Whitman), **IV:** 350
Broccoli, Albert R. "Cubby", **Supp. XI:** 307
Brock, H. I., **Retro. Supp. III:** 138
Bröck, Sabine, **Supp. XI:** 275, 277, 278
Brockmeier, Kevin, **Supp. XXII: 49–63**
Brodeur, Brian, **Supp. XXVI:** 150
Brodhead, Richard, **Retro. Supp. II:** 139; **Supp. XIV:** 61
Brodkey, Harold, **Supp. VIII:** 151; **Supp. X:** 160
Brodkin, Joel, **Supp. XXV:** 261
Brodskii, Iosif Alexsandrovich. See Brodsky, Joseph
Brodsky, Joseph, **Supp. VIII: 19–35; Supp. X:** 65, 73; **Supp. XV:** 134, 135, 256; **Supp. XXIII:** 122
Brody, Alter, **Supp. XV:** 302, 307
Brodyar, Anatole, **Supp. XIV:** 106
Brokeback Mountain (film), **Supp. XX: 273**
"Brokeback Mountain" (Proulx), **Supp. VII:** 264–265
"Broken Balance, The" (Jeffers), **Supp. II Part 2:** 426
"Broken Field, The" (Teasdale), **Supp. XXVII:** 294
"Broken Field Running" (Bambara), **Supp. XI:** 10, 11
Broken Frieze, The (Everwine), **Supp. XV:** 74, 75, 89
Broken Glass (A. Miller), **Retro. Supp. III:** 176
Broken Ground, The (Berry), **Supp. X:** 30
"Broken Home, The" (Merrill), **Supp. III Part 1:** 319, 325
"Broken Oar, The" (Longfellow), **Retro. Supp. II:** 169
"Broken Promise" (MacLeish), **III:** 15
Broken Span, The (W. C. Williams), **IV:** 419; **Retro. Supp. I:** 424
"Broken Tower, The" (H. Crane), **I:** 385, 386, 400, 401–402; **Retro. Supp. II:** 89, 90; **Retro. Supp. III:** 53
Broken Vessels (Dubus), **Supp. VII:** 90–91; **Supp. XI:** 347
"Broken Vessels" (Dubus), **Supp. VII:** 90
Broken Wings, The (al-Ajni&hudot;a al-Mutakassirah) (Gibran), **Supp. XX: 115, 124, 125**
"Broker" (H. Roth), **Supp. IX:** 234
Bromfield, Louis, **IV:** 380
"Brompton Cocktail" (Mamet), **Supp. XIV:** 252
Bromwich, David, **Retro. Supp. I:** 305; **Supp. XII:** 162
"Broncho That Would Not Be Broken, The" (Lindsay), **Supp. I Part 2:** 383
Bronk, William, **Supp. XV:** 115; **Supp. XXI: 17–34; Supp. XXVI:** 237
Brontë, Anne, **Supp. IV Part 2:** 430
Brontë, Branwell, **I:** 462
Brontë, Charlotte, **I:** 458; **II:** 175; **Supp. IV Part 2:** 430; **Supp. IX:** 128; **Supp. XII:** 104, 303; **Supp. XV:** 338; **Supp. XVI:** 158; **Supp. XX: 108**
Brontë, Emily, **I:** 458; **Retro. Supp. I:** 43; **Supp. IV Part 2:** 430; **Supp. IX:** 128; **Supp. X:** 78, 89; **Supp. XV:** 338
"Bronze" (Francis), **Supp. IX:** 76
"Bronze" (Merrill), **Supp. III Part 1:** 336
Bronze Booklets on the History, Problems, and Cultural Contributions of the Negro series, **Supp. XIV:** 202
"Bronze Buckaroo, The" (Baraka), **Supp. II Part 1:** 49
"Bronze Horses, The" (A. Lowell), **II:** 524
"Bronze Tablets" (A. Lowell), **II:** 523
Bronzeville Boys and Girls (Brooks), **Supp. III Part 1:** 79
"Bronzeville Mother Loiters in Mississippi, A. Meanwhile, a Mississippi Mother Burns Bacon" (Brooks), **Supp. III Part 1:** 80
"Brooch, The" (Singer), **IV:** 20
Brook, Peter, **Retro. Supp. II:** 182
Brooke, Rupert, **II:** 82; **III:** 3
Brook Evans (Glaspell), **Supp. III Part 1:** 182–185
"Brooking Likeness" (Glück), **Supp. V:** 85
"Brooklyn" (Marshall), **Supp. XI:** 281, 282
"Brooklyn" (Shaw), **Supp. XIX:** 239, 240
Brooklyn Noir (McLoughlin, ed.), **Supp. XXIV:** 14
Brooks, Albert (Al Pew), **Supp. XXI:** 22
Brooks, Carrellin, **Supp. XXV:** 8
Brooks, Cleanth, **I:** 280, 282; **III:** 517; **IV:** 236, 279; **Retro. Supp. I:** 40, 41, 90; **Retro. Supp. II:** 235; **Retro. Supp. III:** 76; **Supp. I Part 2:** 423; **Supp. III Part 2:** 542; **Supp. IX:** 153, 155; **Supp. V:** 316; **Supp. X:** 115, 123; **Supp. XIV: 1–20; Supp. XIX:** 246
Brooks, David, **Supp. IV Part 2:** 623, 626, 630; **Supp. VIII:** 232
Brooks, Gwendolyn, **Retro. Supp. I:** 208; **Supp. III Part 1: 69–90; Supp. IV Part 1:** 2, 15, 244, 251, 257; **Supp. XI:** 1, 278; **Supp. XIII:** 111, 112, 296; **Supp. XIV:** 73; **Supp. XVIII:** 175, 181, 185; **Supp. XXI:** 230
Brooks, Mel, **Supp. IV Part 1:** 390; **Supp. IV Part 2:** 591
Brooks, Paul, **Supp. IX:** 26, 31, 32
Brooks, Phillips, **II:** 542; **Retro. Supp. II:** 134; **Supp. XIII:** 142
Brooks, Van Wyck, **I:** 106, 117, 215, 222, 228, 230, 231, 233, 236, **239–263,** 266, 480; **II:** 30, 271, 285, 309, 337, 482; **III:** 394, 606; **IV:** 171, 312, 427, 433; **Retro. Supp. II:** 46, 137; **Supp. I Part 2:** 423, 424, 650; **Supp. II Part 1:** 137; **Supp. VIII:** 98, 101; **Supp. XIV:** 11; **Supp. XV:**

298, 301; **Supp. XX: 68**
Brooks, Mrs. Van Wyck (Eleanor Kenyon Stimson), **I:** 240, 245, 250, 252
Brooks, Mrs. Van Wyck (Gladys Billings), **I:** 258
Broom of the System, The (Wallace), **Supp. X:** 301, **302–305,** 310
"Brooms" (Simic), **Supp. VIII:** 275
Brosi, George, **Supp. XX: 166; Supp. XXIII:** 39
Brosnan, Jim, **II:** 424–425; **Supp. XX: 195**
Brossard, Chandler, **Supp. XXII:** 258
Brother Carl (Sontag), **Supp. III Part 2:** 452
"Brother Death" (Anderson), **I:** 114
Brother Fire (Di Piero), **Supp. XIX:** 35, 38, 45–47
Brotherhood of the Grape, The (Fante), **Supp. XI:** 160, **171–172**
Brother in Elysium, The: Ideas of Friendship and Society in the United States (Bronk), **Supp. XXI:** 21, 22, 25, 31
"Brothers" (Anderson), **I:** 114
"Brothers" (Huddle), **Supp. XXVI:** 154
"Brothers" (Stone), **Supp. XXVII:** 254
"Brothers" (W. Stone), **Supp. XXVII:** 255
Brothers, The (F. Barthelme), **Supp. XI:** 25, 28, 29, 30, 32–33
Brothers and Keepers (Wideman), **Supp. X:** 320, 321–322, 323, **325–327,** 328, 329–330, 331, 332
Brothers Ashkenazi, The (Singer), **IV:** 2
Brothers Karamazov, The (Dostoevsky), **II:** 60; **III:** 146, 150, 283; **Supp. IX:** 102, 106; **Supp. XI:** 172; **Supp. XII:** 322
Brothers of No Kin (Richter), **Supp. XVIII:** 209
"Brothers of No Kin" (Richter), **Supp. XVIII:** 208
Brother to Dragons: A Tale in Verse and Voices (Warren), **IV:** 243–244, 245, 246, 251, 252, 254, 257
Broughton, James, **Supp. XV:** 146
Broughton, Rhoda, **II:** 174; **IV:** 309, 310; **Supp. XX: 232**
Broun, Heywood, **I:** 478; **II:** 417; **IV:** 432; **Supp. IX:** 190; **Supp. XXII:** 277
Broussais, François, **Supp. I Part 1:** 302
Brouwer, Joel, **Supp. XXII:** 223, 237
Browder, Earl, **I:** 515; **Supp. XX: 76, 77**
Brower, David, **Supp. X:** 29
Brower, Reuben, **Supp. XV:** 20
Brown, Alice, **II:** 523; **Retro. Supp. II:** 136
Brown, Andrew, **Supp. XVI:** 150
Brown, Ashley, **Retro. Supp. II:** 48; **Supp. I Part 1:** 79, 80, 82, 84, 92
Brown, Charles Brockden, **I:** 54, 211, 335; **II:** 74, 267, 298; **III:** 415; **Retro. Supp. III:** 226; **Supp. I Part 1: 124–149; Supp. II Part 1:** 65, 292; **Supp. XXIII:** 178
Brown, Mrs. Charles Brockden (Elizabeth Linn), **Supp. I Part 1:** 145, 146
Brown, Claude, Jr., **Retro. Supp. III:** 184
Brown, Clifford, **Supp. V:** 195
Brown, Dan, **Supp. XXVII:** 5
Brown, Deborah, **Supp. XVII:** 75
Brown, Dee, **Supp. IV Part 2:** 504
Brown, Elijah, **Supp. I Part 1:** 125
Brown, Fleda, **Supp. XXIII:** 59
Brown, George Douglas, **III:** 473
Brown, Harry, **Supp. IV Part 2:** 560
Brown, Harvey, **Supp. XIV:** 148
Brown, Himan, **Supp. XIX:** 241, 242
Brown, H. Rap, **Supp. XXI:** 171
Brown, Jeffrey, **Supp. XXVII:** 205
Brown, John, **II:** 13; **IV:** 125, 126, 172, 237, 249, 254; **Supp. I Part 1:** 345; **Supp. VIII:** 204
Brown, Joseph Epes, **Supp. IV Part 2:** 487
Brown, Larry, **Supp. XVIII:** 195; **Supp. XXI: 35–50**
Brown, Leonard, **Supp. IX:** 117
Brown, Mary Armitt, **Supp. I Part 1:** 125
Brown, Mick, **Supp. XXVII:** 268, 270
Brown, Nell Porter, **Supp. XXV:** 130, 131, 138
Brown, Percy, **II:** 20
Brown, Robert (Anahalihs), **Supp. XXVI:** 89, 95
Brown, Robert E., **Supp. X:** 12
Brown, Scott, **Supp. XI:** 178
Brown, Slater, **IV:** 123; **Retro. Supp. II:** 79
Brown, Solyman, **Supp. I Part 1:** 156
Brown, Sterling, **Retro. Supp. I:** 198; **Supp. IV Part 1:** 169; **Supp. XIV:** 202; **Supp. XXII:** 1, 8, 12
Brown, Tina, **Supp. XVI:** 176–177
Brown, Wesley, **Supp. V:** 6
Brown, William Hill, **Supp. XXV:** 38
Brown, William Wells, **Supp. XXIII:** 184
Brown Angels (Myers), **Supp. XXVII:** 209
Brown Decades, The (Mumford), **Supp. II Part 2:** 475, 478, 491–492
Brown Dog (Harrison), **Supp. VIII:** 51
Brown Dog of the Yaak: Essays on Art and Activism (Bass), **Supp. XVI:** 22
"Brown Dwarf of Rügen, The" (Whittier), **Supp. I Part 2:** 696
Browne, Charles Farrar, **II:** 289; **IV:** 193, 196; **Supp. XVIII:** 1, 4
Browne, Roscoe Lee, **Supp. VIII:** 345
Browne, Thomas, **II:** 15–16, 304; **III:** 77, 78, 198, 487; **IV:** 147; **Supp. IX:** 136; **Supp. XII:** 45; **Supp. XVI:** 292
Browne, William, **Supp. I Part 1:** 98
Brownell, W. C., **II:** 14
Brownell, William Crary, **Retro. Supp. I:** 365, 366
Browner, Stephanie P., **Supp. XVIII:** 17
Brown Girl, Brownstones (Marshall), **Supp. XI:** 275, 276, **278–280,** 282
Brownies' Book, The (Hughes), **Supp. I Part 1:** 321
Browning, Dominique, **Supp. XXVI:** 131
Browning, Elizabeth Barrett, **I:** 458, 459; **Retro. Supp. I:** 33, 43; **Supp. XVIII:** 175–176; **Supp. XX: 108; Supp. XXVII:** 284
Browning, Oscar, **Supp. XX: 231**
Browning, Robert, **I:** 50, 66, 103, 458, 460, 468; **II:** 338, 478, 522; **III:** 5, 8, 467, 469, 484, 511, 521, 524, 606, 609; **IV:** 135, 245, 366, 416; **Retro. Supp. I:** 43, 55, 217; **Retro. Supp. II:** 188, 190; **Retro. Supp. III:** 60; **Supp. I Part 1:** 2, 6, 79, 311; **Supp. I Part 2:** 416, 468, 622; **Supp. III Part 1:** 5, 6; **Supp. IV Part 2:** 430; **Supp. X:** 65; **Supp. XV:** 92, 250, 275
Brownmiller, Susan, **Supp. X:** 252
Brownrigg, Sylvia, **Supp. XXV:** 59–60
"Brown River, Smile" (Toomer), **Supp. IV Part 1:** 16
Brownstone Eclogues and Other Poems (Aiken), **I:** 65, 67
Brown: The Last Discovery of America (Rodriguez), **Supp. XIV:** 297, 298, 300, **305–309,** 310, 311–312
Broyard, Anatole, **Supp. IV Part 1:** 39; **Supp. VIII:** 140; **Supp. X:** 186; **Supp. XI:** 348; **Supp. XVI:** 213
Broyles, Yolanda Julia, **Supp. XIX:** 112
Bruccoli, Matthew, **Retro. Supp. I:** 98, 102, 105, 114, 115, 359; **Supp. IV**

Part 2: 468, 470
Bruce, John Edward, **Supp. XVI:** 143
Bruce, Lenny, **Supp. VIII:** 198
Bruce, Virginia, **Supp. XII:** 173
Bruce-Novoa, Juan, **Supp. VIII:** 73, 74
Bruchac, Joseph, **Supp. IV Part 1:** 261, 319, 320, 321, 322, 323, 325, 328, 398, 399, 403, 408, 414; **Supp. IV Part 2:** 502, 506
Brueghel, Pieter, **I:** 174; **Supp. I Part 2:** 475
Brueghel, Pieter, the Elder, **Retro. Supp. I:** 430
Bruell, Edwin, **Supp. VIII:** 126
Brugh, Spangler Arlington. See Taylor, Robert
"Bruja: Witch" (Mora), **Supp. XIII:** 214, 220, 221, **Supp. XIII:** 222
Brulé, Claude, **Supp. XI:** 307
Brumer, Andy, **Supp. XIII:** 88
Brummels, J. V., **Supp. XIX:** 119
Brunner, Emil, **III:** 291, 303
"Brush Fire" (J. Wright), **Supp. XVII:** 241
Brustein, Robert, **Retro. Supp. III:** 315, 319–320; **Supp. VIII:** 331; **Supp. XXIV:** 116
Brutus, **IV:** 373, 374; **Supp. I Part 2:** 471
"Brutus and Antony" (Masters), **Supp. I Part 2:** 472
"Bryan, Bryan, Bryan, Bryan" (Lindsay), **Supp. I Part 2:** 394, 395, 398
Bryan, George, **Retro. Supp. II:** 76
Bryan, Sharon, **Supp. IX:** 154
Bryan, William Jennings, **I:** 483; **IV:** 124; **Supp. I Part 2:** 385, 395–396, 455, 456
Bryant, Austin, **Supp. I Part 1:** 152, 153
Bryant, Frances, **Supp. I Part 1:** 153
Bryant, Louise, **Supp. X:** 136
Bryant, Peter, **Supp. I Part 1:** 150, 151, 152, 153. See also George, Peter
Bryant, William Cullen, **I:** 335, 458; **II:** 311; **III:** 81; **IV:** 309; **Retro. Supp. I:** 217; **Retro. Supp. II:** 155; **Supp. I Part 1: 150–173,** 312, 362; **Supp. I Part 2:** 413, 416, 420; **Supp. IV Part 1:** 165; **Supp. XIII:** 145; **Supp. XIX:** 4; **Supp. XXV:** 250
Bryant, Mrs. William Cullen (Frances Fairchild), **Supp. I Part 1:** 153, 169
Bryer, Jackson R., **Supp. IV Part 2:** 575, 583, 585, 586, 589, 591; **Supp. XIII:** 200, **Supp. XIII:** 205
Bryher, Jackson R. (pseudonym). See Ellerman, Winifred
Brynner, Witter, **Supp. XXII:** 273
Bubber Goes to Heaven (Bontemps), **Supp. XXII:** 4
"Bubbs Creek Haircut" (Snyder), **Supp. VIII:** 306
Buber, Martin, **II:** 228; **III:** 45, 308, 528; **IV:** 11; **Supp. I Part 1:** 83, 88; **Supp. XVI:** 291
Buccaneers, The (television miniseries), **Retro. Supp. III:** 290
Buccaneers, The (Wharton), **IV:** 327; **Retro. Supp. I:** 382; **Retro. Supp. III:** 289–290
Buchanan Dying (Updike), **Retro. Supp. I:** 331, 335
Buchbinder, David, **Supp. XIII:** 32
Buchwald, Art, **Supp. XII:** 124–125; **Supp. XVI:** 110–111
Buchwald, Emilie, **Supp. XVI:** 35, 36
Buck, Dudley, **Supp. I Part 1:** 362
Buck, Gene, **II:** 427
Buck, John, Sr., **Supp. XXVI:** 89
Buck, Pearl S., **Supp. II Part 1: 113–134; Supp. XIV:** 274
Buckdancer's Choice (Dickey), **Supp. IV Part 1:** 176, 177, 178, 180
"Buckdancer's Choice" (Dickey), **Supp. IV Part 1:** 191
Bucke, Richard Maurice, **Retro. Supp. I:** 407
"Buckeyes"(P. Benedict), **Supp. XXIII:** 46
"Buck Fever" (Humphrey), **Supp. IX:** 109
"Buck in the Snow, The" (Millay), **III:** 135
Buckley, Christopher, **Supp. IX:** 169; **Supp. XI:** 257, 329; **Supp. XV:** 76–77, 86
Buckley, James, Jr., **Supp. XVII:** 220
Buckminster, Joseph, **Supp. II Part 1:** 66–67, 69
Bucknell, Katherine, **Supp. XIV:** 170
Bucolics (Auden), **Supp. II Part 1:** 21, 24
Budbill, David, **Supp. XIX: 1–16**
Budd, Louis J., **IV:** 210
Buddha, **I:** 136; **II:** 1; **III:** 173, 179, 239, 567; **Supp. I Part 1:** 363; **Supp. I Part 2:** 397
Buddha, The: The Story of Siddhartha (film, Grubin), **Supp. XXIII:** 138, 140
"Buddha Boy" (Saunders), **Supp. XIX:** 235
"Buddha's Last Instruction, The" (Oliver), **Supp. VII:** 239
"Buddies"(Kenny), **Supp. XXIII:** 150
Budding Prospects (Boyle), **Supp. VIII: 8–9; Supp. XX: 27–28**
Buechner, Frederick, **III:** 310; **Supp. XII: 41–59**
Buell, Lawrence, **Supp. IX:** 29; **Supp. V:** 209; **Supp. XV:** 269, 282
"Buffalo" (Peacock), **Supp. XIX:** 198
"Buffalo, The" (Moore), **III:** 215
"Buffalo Bill". See Cody, William
Buffalo Girls (McMurtry), **Supp. V:** 229
Buffalo Girls (screenplay) (McMurtry), **Supp. V:** 232
Buffalo Hunters, The: The Story of the Hide Men (Sandoz), **Supp. XXIV:** 244, **247–249,** 256
Buffett, Jimmy, **Supp. VIII:** 42
Buffon, Comte de, **II:** 101
Buford, Fanny McConnell, **Retro. Supp. II:** 117
Bugeja, Michael, **Supp. X:** 201
Bugged for Murder (Lacy), **Supp. XV:** 205
"Buglesong" (Stegner), **Supp. IV Part 2:** 606
Buhle, Paul, **Supp. XXI:** 172
"Buick" (Shapiro), **Supp. II Part 2:** 705
"Builders" (Yates), **Supp. XI: 342–343**
Builders, The (Glasgow), **II:** 183–184, 193
"Builders, The" (Hay), **Supp. XIV:** 125
Builders in Sand (W. Frank), **Supp. XX: 68**
Builders of the Bay Colony (Morison), **Supp. I Part 2:** 484–485
"Builders of the Bridge, The" (Mumford), **Supp. II Part 2:** 475
"Building" (Snyder), **Supp. VIII:** 305
"Building, Dwelling, Thinking" (Heidegger), **Retro. Supp. II:** 87
Building a Character (Stanislavsky), **Supp. XIV:** 243
" 'Building' Larry Brown(s) at Algonquin Books of Chapel Hill" (Perry), **Supp. XXI:** 42
"Building of the Ship, The" (Longfellow), **II:** 498; **Retro. Supp. II:** 159, 167, 168
"Build Soil" (Frost), **Retro. Supp. I:** 138, 139; **Retro. Supp. III:** 103
"Build Soil" (Snyder), **Supp. VIII:** 304
Build-Up, The (W. C. Williams), **Retro. Supp. I:** 423
Bukiet, Melvin Jules, **Supp. XVII: 39–51**
Bukowski, Charles, **Supp. III Part 1:** 147; **Supp. XI:** 159, 161, 172, 173; **Supp. XVII:** 245

Bulgakov, Mikhail, **Supp. XIV:** 97
"Bulgarian Poetess, The" (Updike), **IV:** 215, 227; **Retro. Supp. I:** 329
Bull, Ole, **II:** 504
"Bulldozer, The" (Francis), **Supp. IX:** 87
"Bullet in the Brain" (Wolff), **Supp. VII:** 342–343
Bullet Park (Cheever), **Supp. I Part 1:** 185, 187–193, 194, 195
Bullets over Broadway (film; Allen), **Supp. XV:** 12, **12–13**
Bullfight, The (Mailer), **Retro. Supp. II:** 205
Bullfighter Checks Her Makeup, The: My Encounters with Extraordinary People (Orlean), **Supp. XXV:** 159, 163–164
Bullins, Ed, **Retro. Supp. III:** 316; **Supp. II Part 1:** 34, 42
Bullock, Sandra, **Supp. X:** 80
"Bull-Roarer, The" (Stern), **Supp. IX:** 297
"Bully, The" (Dubus), **Supp. VII:** 84
"Bulsh" (X. J. Kennedy), **Supp. XV:** 161
Bultmann, Rudolf, **III:** 309
Bulwark, The (Dreiser), **I:** 497, 506, 516–517; **Retro. Supp. II:** 95, 96, 105, 108
Bulwer-Lytton, Edward George, **IV:** 350
"Bums in the Attic" (Cisneros), **Supp. VII:** 62
Bunche, Ralph, **Supp. I Part 1:** 343; **Supp. XIV:** 202; **Supp. XXII:** 12
"Bunchgrass Edge of the World, The" (Proulx), **Supp. VII:** 263
Bunge, Nancy, **Supp. XVII:** 218; **Supp. XXII:** 175, 177, 178, 180, 183; **Supp. XXVI:** 257
"Bunner Sisters, The" (Wharton), **IV:** 317
Bunting, Basil, **Retro. Supp. I:** 422; **Supp. III Part 2:** 616, 620, 624; **Supp. XIV:** 286
Buntline, Ned, **Supp. XXIII:** 182
Buñuel, Luis, **III:** 184; **Retro. Supp. II:** 337
Bunyan, John, **I:** 445; **II:** 15, 104, 228; **IV:** 80, 84, 156, 437; **Supp. I Part 1:** 32
Bunyan, Paul, **Supp. XXII:** 203
Burana, Lily, **Supp. XI:** 253
Burbank, Luther, **I:** 483
Burbank, Rex, **IV:** 363
Burch, Michael, **Supp. XXI:** 99
Burchfield, Alice, **Supp. I Part 2:** 652, 660
Burden of Proof, The (Turow), **Supp. XVII: 216–217,** 218
Burden of Southern History, The (Woodward), **Retro. Supp. I:** 75
Burdens of Formality, The (Lea, ed.), **Supp. X:** 58
Burger, Gottfried August, **II:** 306
Burgess, Anthony, **Supp. IV Part 1:** 227; **Supp. IV Part 2:** 685; **Supp. V:** 128; **Supp. XXIII:** 42
Burgh, James, **Supp. I Part 2:** 522
"Burglar of Babylon, The" (Bishop), **Retro. Supp. II:** 47; **Supp. I Part 1:** 93
Burgum, E. B., **IV:** 469, 470
Burham, Philip, **Supp. XX: 44**
"Burial of Jonathan Brown, The"(Hadas), **Supp. XXIII:** 115
Buried Child (Shepard), **Supp. III Part 2:** 433, 447, 448; **Supp. XIV:** 327
"Buried Lake, The" (Tate), **IV:** 136
Burkard, Michael, **Supp. XXIV:** 165
Burke, Carolyn, **Supp. XXII:** 156, 158, 162, 165, 167, 168
Burke, Edmund, **I:** 9; **III:** 310; **Supp. I Part 2:** 496, 511, 512, 513, 523; **Supp. II Part 1:** 80; **Supp. XVII:** 236
Burke, James Lee, **Supp. XIV: 21–38; Supp. XXI:** 67, 72, 80
Burke, Kenneth, **I: 264–287,** 291; **III:** 497, 499, 546; **IV:** 123, 408; **Retro. Supp. I:** 297; **Retro. Supp. II:** 117, 120; **Retro. Supp. III:** 48; **Supp. I Part 2:** 630; **Supp. II Part 1:** 136; **Supp. IX:** 229; **Supp. VIII:** 105; **Supp. XIV:** 3; **Supp. XXI:** 89
Burke, Rusty, **Supp. XXVII:** 128
Burke, William, **Supp. XXI:** 215
"Burl" (Mosher), **Supp. XXII:** 204, 211
Burley, Justin, **Supp. XVI:** 158
"Burly Fading One, The" (Hayden), **Supp. II Part 1:** 366
Burn, Stephen J., **Supp. XX: 85; Supp. XXII:** 266, 268
"Burned" (Levine), **Supp. V:** 186, 192
"Burned" (Stallings), **Supp. XXV:** 233
"Burned Diary, The" (Olds), **Supp. X:** 215
"Burned Man" (Huddle), **Supp. XXVI:** 148, 151
Burne-Jones, Edward, **Supp. XXII:** 156
Burnett, Allison, **Supp. XVII:** 22
Burnett, David, **Supp. XI:** 299
Burnett, Frances Hodgson, **Supp. I Part 1:** 44
Burnett, Whit, **III:** 551; **Supp. XI:** 294
Burnett, W. R., **Supp. XXVII:** 93
Burney, Fanny, **Supp. XV:** 232; **Supp. XX: 108**
Burnham, James, **Supp. I Part 2:** 648
Burnham, John Chynoweth, **I:** 59
"Burning, The" (Welty), **IV:** 277–278; **Retro. Supp. I:** 353
Burning Angel (Burke), **Supp. XIV:** 30, 32
Burning Bright (Rash), **Supp. XXVII:** 228–229
Burning Bright (Steinbeck), **IV:** 51, 61–62
Burning Bright: An Anthology of Sacred Poetry (Hampl, ed.), **Supp. XXII:** 87
"Burning Bush" (Cliff), **Supp. XXII:** 75
Burning Bush (Untermeyer), **Supp. XV: 309**
"Burning Bush" (Untermeyer), **Supp. XV:** 309
Burning Bush, The (Asch), **Supp. XXIII:** 7
Burning Bush, The (H. and G. Herczeg), **Supp. XVII:** 62
Burning Chrome (W. Gibson), **Supp. XVI:** 118, 122, **128**
"Burning Chrome" (W. Gibson), **Supp. XVI:** 117, 120, 123, 124, 128
Burning City (Benét), **Supp. XI:** 46, 58
Burning Daylight (London), **II:** 474, 481
Burning Down the House: Essays on Fiction (C. Baxter), **Supp. XVII:** 13, 20, 21
"Burning Down the Little House on the Prairie: Asian Pioneers in Contemporary North America" (Martín-Lucas), **Supp. XXVI:** 218
Burning House, The (Beattie), **Supp. V:** 29
"Burning Ladder, The" (Gioia), **Supp. XV:** 118
Burning Mystery of Anna in 1951, The (Koch), **Supp. XV:** 182–183
"Burning of Paper Instead of Children, The" (Rich), **Retro. Supp. III:** 245; **Supp. I Part 2:** 558
"Burning Shit at An Khe" (Weigl), **Supp. XIX:** 279–280
Burning the Days (Salter), **Supp. XIX:** 252
Burning the Days: Recollections (Salter), **Supp. IX:** 245, 246, 248, 260, **261–262**
"Burning the Small Dead" (Snyder), **Supp. VIII:** 298
Burning Tigris, The: The Armenian Genocide and America's Response

(Balakian), **Supp. XXIII:** 19, 21, 22**, 25–28,** 30
"Burning Tobacco Beds" (J. W. Miller), **Supp. XX: 167**
Burn Marks (Paretsky), **Supp. XXV:** 174–175, 178, 180
Burns, Carol, **Supp. XVIII:** 162
Burns, David, **III:** 165–166
Burns, Ken, **Supp. XIV:** 14
Burns, Michael, **Supp. XV:** 339
Burns, Robert, **II:** 150, 306; **III:** 592; **IV:** 453; **Supp. I Part 1:** 158; **Supp. I Part 2:** 410, 455, 683, 685, 691, 692; **Supp. IX:** 173; **Supp. XII:** 171; **Supp. XIII:** 3; **Supp. XVIII:** 82
Burnshaw, Stanley, **Retro. Supp. I:** 298, 303; **Supp. III Part 2:** 615
"Burn the Cities" (West), **Retro. Supp. II:** 338
Burnt Mountain (Siddons), **Supp. XXII:** 253
"Burnt Norton" (T. S. Eliot), **I:** 575, 580–581, 582, 584, 585; **III:** 10; **Retro. Supp. I:** 66; **Retro. Supp. III:** 66–67, 68; **Supp. XV:** 216
Burnt-Out Case, A (Greene), **Supp. VIII:** 4
"Burnt-out Spa, The" (Plath), **Retro. Supp. II:** 246
Burn Witch Burn (A. Merritt), **Supp. XVII:** 58
Burr, Aaron, **I:** 7, 549, 550; **II:** 300; **IV:** 264; **Supp. I Part 2:** 461, 483
Burr: A Novel (Vidal), **Supp. IV Part 2:** 677, 682, 684, 685, 687, 688, 689, 691
Burr Oaks (Eberhart), **I:** 533, 535
Burroughs, Edgar Rice, **Supp. IV Part 1:** 101
Burroughs, John, **I:** 220, 236, 506; **IV:** 346; **Supp. IX:** 171; **Supp. XXVI:** 37
Burroughs, William S., **III:** 45, 174, 258; **Supp. II Part 1:** 320, 328; **Supp. III Part 1: 91–110,** 217, 226; **Supp. IV Part 1:** 79, 87, 90; **Supp. XI:** 297, 308; **Supp. XII:** 1, 3, 118, 121, 124, 129, 131, 136; **Supp. XIV:** 137, 140–141, 143–144, 150; **Supp. XVI:** 123, 135; **Supp. XVII:** 225; **Supp. XVIII:** 137; **Supp. XXIII:** 213; **Supp. XXIV:** 42
Burrow, Trigant, **Supp. II Part 1:** 6
Burrows, Ken, **Supp. V:** 115
Bursey, Jeff, **Supp. XXII:** 257
Burson, Claudia, **Supp. XV:** 343
Burstein, Janet, **Supp. XVII:** 41, 44, 48
"Bursts of Light" (Bronk), **Supp. XXI:** 33
Burt, Stephen, **Supp. XV:** 341, 342, 345, 347, 351; **Supp. XVII:** 18, 246
Burt, Steve, **Supp. V:** 83
Burtis, Thomson, **Supp. XIII:** 163
Burton, Robert, **II:** 535; **III:** 77, 78; **Supp. I Part 1:** 349
Burton, Sue D., **Supp. XIX:** 90
Burton, William Evans, **III:** 412
"Burying Ground by the Ties" (MacLeish), **III:** 14
Bury My Heart at Wounded Knee (Brown), **Supp. IV Part 2:** 504
Bury the Dead (Shaw), **IV:** 381; **Supp. XIX: 242–244,** 249, 252
"Bus Along St. Clair: December, A" (Atwood), **Supp. XIII:** 33
Busch, Frederick, **Supp. X:** 78; **Supp. XII:** 343; **Supp. XVII:** 175; **Supp. XXVI:** 9
Bush, Barney, **Supp. XII:** 218, 222
Bush, Douglas, **Supp. I Part 1:** 268; **Supp. XIV:** 10
Bush, Harold K., **Retro. Supp. III:** 259
"Busher Comes Back, The" (Lardner), **II:** 422
"Busher's Letters Home, A" (Lardner), **II:** 418–419, 421
Bushmiller, Ernie, **Supp. XXVII:** 21
Bushrui, Suheil, **Supp. XX: 113, 117, 120, 122, 126–127**
"Business and Poetry" (Gioia), **Supp. XV:** 113, 115
"Business Deal" (West), **IV:** 287
"Business Man, A" (Jewett), **Retro. Supp. II:** 132
Business of Memory, The: The Art of Remembering in an Age of Forgetting (C. Baxter, ed.), **Supp. XVII:** 21
"Business Trip" (Hoffman), **Supp. XVIII:** 86
"Bus Riley's Back in Town" (Inge), **Supp. XXV:** 95
Buss, Helen M., **Supp. IV Part 1:** 12
Bus Stop (Inge), **Supp. XXV:** 93, 99–100
Butcher, Fanny, **Supp. XXV:** 199
Butcher, Margaret Just, **Supp. XIV:** 203
"Butcher, The" (Southern), **Supp. XI:** 294
"Butcher Cock, The"(P. Benedict), **Supp. XXIII:** 46–47
"Butcher Shop" (Simic), **Supp. VIII:** 273
But Gentlemen Marry Brunettes (Loos), **Supp. XVI:** 190–191
"But He Says I Misunderstood" (Notley), **Supp. XXII:** 227
Butler, Benjamin, **I:** 457
Butler, Dorothy. See Farrell, Mrs. James T. (Dorothy Butler)
Butler, Elizabeth, **Supp. I Part 1:** 260
Butler, Ethel, **Supp. XIV:** 125
Butler, Hugo, **Supp. XVII:** 63
Butler, James D., **Supp. IX:** 175
Butler, Joseph, **II:** 8, 9
Butler, Judith, **Supp. XII:** 6
Butler, Maud. See Falkner, Mrs. Murray C. (Maud Butler)
Butler, Nicholas Murray, **I:** 223; **Supp. I Part 1:** 23; **Supp. III Part 2:** 499
Butler, Octavia, **Supp. XIII: 59–72**
Butler, Robert Olen, **Supp. XII: 61–78,** 319
Butler, Samuel, **II:** 82, 86; **IV:** 121, 440; **Supp. VIII:** 171
Butler-Evans, Elliot, **Retro. Supp. II:** 121
"But Only Mine" (Wright), **Supp. III Part 2:** 595
Butscher, Edward, **Supp. I Part 2:** 526
Butter Battle Book, The (Geisel), **Supp. XVI:** 110
"Buttercups" (R. Lowell), **Retro. Supp. II:** 187
Butterfield, R. W., **I:** 386
Butterfield, Stephen, **Supp. IV Part 1:** 3, 11
Butterfield 8 (O'Hara), **III:** 361
"Butterflies Under Persimmon" (Jarman), **Supp. XVII:** 120
Butterfly (Harvey), **Supp. XIII:** 184
"Butterfly, The" (Brodksy), **Supp. VIII:** 26
"Butterfly and the Traffic Light, The" (Ozick), **Supp. V:** 263, 265
Butterfly in the Typewriter (MacLaughlin), **Supp. XXVI:** 241, 243, 252
Butterfly Plague, The (Findley), **Supp. XX: 50, 52, 53**
Butterfly Stories (Vollmann), **Supp. XVII:** 226
"Butterfly-toed Shoes" (Komunyakaa), **Supp. XIII:** 126
Butter Hill and Other Poems (Francis), **Supp. IX:** 88, 89
"Button-Down Builders, The" (Siddons), **Supp. XXII:** 243–244
Buttons, Red, **Supp. IV Part 2:** 574
Buttrick, George, **III:** 301; **Supp. XII:** 47–48
"But What Is the Reader to Make of This?" (Ashbery), **Supp. III Part 1:** 25
Butz, Earl, **Supp. X:** 35

"Buz" (Alcott), **Supp. I Part 1:** 43
Buzinski, Jim, **Supp. XX: 273**
"By an Objibwa Female Pen: Invitation to sisters to a walk in the Garden, after a shower"(J. Schoolcraft), **Supp. XXIII:** 230
Byatt, A. S., **Supp. XXI:** 147
By Avon River (Doolittle), **Supp. I Part 1:** 272
"By Blue Ontario's Shore" (Whitman), **Retro. Supp. I:** 399, 400; **Retro. Supp. III:** 305
"By Candlelight" (Major), **Supp. XXII:** 185
"By Disposition of Angels" (Moore), **III:** 214
"By Earth" (Olds), **Supp. X:** 214
"Bye for Now, Broadway, My New Friend" (Silver), **Supp. XXIV:** 276
"By Fire" (Olds), **Supp. X:** 214
Bygones (Untermeyer), **Supp. XV:** 304, **308–309,** 312, 313
By Land, By Sea (Hoffman), **Supp. XVIII:** 86
By Land and by Sea (Morison), **Supp. I Part 2:** 492
Byles, Mather, **Supp. XX: 279, 282**
By-Line: Ernest Hemingway (Hemingway), **II:** 257–258
By Love Possessed (Cozens), **I:** 358, 365, 372–374, 375, 376, 377, 378, 379
"By Morning" (Swenson), **Supp. IV Part 2:** 642
"By Night" (Francis), **Supp. IX:** 76
Bynner, Witter, **II:** 513, 527; **Supp. XIII:** 347; **Supp. XV: 39–54**
Byrd, William, **Supp. IV Part 2:** 425; **Supp. XXI:** 35; **Supp. XXII:** 193
Byrne, Donn, **IV:** 67
Byrne, Edward, **Supp. XXV:** 226, 227
Byron, George Gordon, Lord, **I:** 343, 568, 577; **II:** 135, 193, 296, 301, 303, 310, 315, 331, 566; **III:** 82, 137, 170, 409, 410, 412, 469; **IV:** 245, 435; **Retro. Supp. III:** 44; **Supp. I Part 1:** 150, 312, 349; **Supp. I Part 2:** 580, 591, 683, 685, 719; **Supp. XIII:** 139; **Supp. XVI:** 188, 203, 206, 210
"Byron's Cain" (L. Michaels), **Supp. XVI:** 203
"Bystanders" (Matthews), **Supp. IX:** 160
By the Bias of Sound (Sobin), **Supp. XVI:** 281
By the North Gate (Oates), **Supp. II Part 2:** 504
"By the People" (Faulkner), **Retro. Supp. III:** 86
"By the People" (Stratton-Porter), **Supp. XX: 221**
"By the Sea" (Teasdale), **Supp. XXVII:** 294
By the Shores of Silver Lake (L. I. Wilder), **Supp. XXII:** 294, 295, 299
"By the Time You Get There, by the Time You Get Back" (Muñoz), **Supp. XXV:** 134
"By the Waters of Babylon" (Benét), **Supp. XI:** 56, 58
By the Waters of Manhattan (Reznikoff), **Supp. XIV:** 288, 293, 294
By the Waters of Manhattan: An Annual (Reznikoff), **Supp. XIV:** 277, 280, 289
By the Waters of Manhattan: Selected Verse (Reznikoff), **Supp. XIV:** 281, 291
By the Well of Living and Seeing and the Fifth Book of the Maccabees (Reznikoff), **Supp. XIV:** 281
By the Well of Living and Seeing: New and Selected Poems 1918–1973 (Reznikoff), **Supp. XIV:** 281, 287–288, 295
By Way of Orbit (O'Neill), **III:** 405
Byzantine Parables (Notley), **Supp. XXII:** 235, 237
"C 33" (H. Crane), **I:** 384; **Retro. Supp. II:** 76; **Retro. Supp. III:** 44
Cabala, The (Wilder), **IV:** 356, 358–360, 369, 374
"Cabaret" (Boyle), **Supp. XXIV:** 61
Cabaret (film), **Supp. XIV:** 155, 162
Cabaret (play), **Supp. XIV:** 162; **Supp. XVII:** 45
Cabbages and Kings (O. Henry), **Supp. II Part 1:** 394, 409
Cabell, James Branch, **II:** 42; **III:** 394; **IV:** 67, 359, 360; **Retro. Supp. I:** 80; **Supp. I Part 2:** 613, 714, 718, 721; **Supp. X:** 223
"Cabin, The" (Carver), **Supp. III Part 1:** 137, 146
Cabin, The: Reminiscence and Diversions (Mamet), **Supp. XIV:** 240
Cabinet of Dr. Caligari, The (film), **Retro. Supp. I:** 268
Cable, George Washington, **II:** 289; **Retro. Supp. II:** 65; **Retro. Supp. III:** 265; **Supp. I Part 1:** 200; **Supp. II Part 1:** 198; **Supp. XIV:** 63
Cables to the Ace; or, Familiar Liturgies of Misunderstanding (Merton), **Supp. VIII:** 208
Cabot, James, **II:** 14; **IV:** 173
Cabot, John, **Supp. I Part 2:** 496, 497
Cachoeira Tales and Other Poems, The (Nelson), **Supp. XVIII: 178–179**
"Cachoiera Tales, The" (Nelson), **Supp. XVIII:** 179
Cactus Flower (Barillet and Grédy), **Supp. XVI:** 194
"Caddy's Diary, A" (Lardner), **II:** 421–422
"Cadence" (Dubus), **Supp. VII:** 84–85
Cadieux, Isabelle, **Supp. XIII:** 127
"Cadillac Flambé" (Ellison), **Retro. Supp. II:** 119, 126; **Supp. II Part 1:** 248
Cadillac Jack (McMurtry), **Supp. V:** 225
Cadillac Jukebox (Burke), **Supp. XIV:** 32
Cadle, Dean, **Supp. I Part 2:** 429
Cady, Edwin H., **II:** 272
"Caedmon" (Garrett), **Supp. VII:** 96–97
Caesar, Julius, **II:** 12, 502, 561–562; **IV:** 372, 373
Caesar, Sid, **Supp. IV Part 2:** 574, 591
"Cafeteria, The" (Singer), **Retro. Supp. II:** 316
Cage, John, **Supp. IV Part 1:** 84; **Supp. V:** 337, 341; **Supp. XXIII:** 211
"Cage and the Prairie: Two Notes on Symbolism, The" (Bewley), **Supp. I Part 1:** 251
Cage Keeper, The (Dubus III), **Supp. XXIV: 99–102**
"Cage Keeper, The" (Dubus III), **Supp. XXIV:** 101–102, 104
Cage of Age, The (Bronk), **Supp. XXI:** 32
Cage of Spines, A (Swenson), **Supp. IV Part 2:** 641–642, 647
"Cage of the Body, The"(Schott), **Supp. XXIII:** 243–244
Cagney, James, **Supp. IV Part 1:** 236; **Supp. XIII:** 174
Cagney, William, **Supp. XIII:** 174
Cahalan, James, **Supp. XIII:** 1, 2, 3, 4, 12
Cahan, Abraham, **Supp. IX:** 227; **Supp. XIII:** 106; **Supp. XXI:** 3, 14; **Supp. XXIII:** 1, 2, 9, 16; **Supp. XXVI:** 123
Cahill, Tim, **Supp. XIII:** 13
Cahir, Linda Costanzo, **Retro. Supp. III:** 290
Cain, James M., **III:** 99; **Supp. IV Part 1:** 130; **Supp. XI:** 160; **Supp. XIII:** 159, 165
Cain, Kathleen Shine, **Supp. XX: 247, 248**
Caine Mutiny, The (film), **Supp. XXV:** 260, 261

Caine Mutiny, The (Wouk), **Supp. XXV:** 253, 255, 256, 259–261
Caine Mutiny Court-Martial, The (Wouk), **Supp. XXV:** 253, 256
Caird, G. B., **Supp. XXI:** 91–92
Cairns, Huntington, **III:** 103, 108, 114, 119
Cairo! Shanghai! Bombay! (Williams and Shapiro), **IV:** 380
C: A Journal of Poetry, **Supp. XXVII:** 18, 24
Cake (Bynner), **Supp. XV:** 50
Cakes and Ale (Maugham), **III:** 64
Calabria, Frank, **Supp. XIII:** 164
Calamity Jane (Martha Jane Canary), **Supp. V:** 229–230; **Supp. X:** 103
"Calamus" (Whitman), **IV:** 342–343; **Retro. Supp. I:** 52, 403, 404, 407; **Retro. Supp. III:** 302
Calasso, Roberto, **Supp. IV Part 1:** 301
Calavito, Jason, **Supp. XXV:** 123
Calder, William M., III, **Supp. XXIII:** 112
Calderón, Hector, **Supp. IV Part 2:** 544
Caldwell, Christopher, **Supp. IV Part 1:** 211
Caldwell, Erskine, **I:** 97, 211, **288–311; IV:** 286; **Supp. IV Part 2:** 601; **Supp. XXI:** 35; **Supp. XXII:** 196
Caldwell, Mrs. Erskine (Helen Lannegan), **I:** 289
Caldwell, Mrs. Erskine (Margaret Bourke-White), **I:** 290, 293–295, 297
Caldwell, Mrs. Erskine (Virginia Fletcher), **I:** 290
Caldwell, Gail, **Supp. XXVI:** 158
Caldwell, Reverend Ira Sylvester, **I:** 289, 305
Caldwell, Zoe, **Supp. XIII:** 207
Caleb Williams (Godwin), **III:** 415
"Calendar" (Creeley), **Supp. IV Part 1:** 158
Calendar of Saints for Unbelievers, A (Wescott), **Supp. XIV:** 342
Calendars (A. Finch), **Supp. XVII: 76–77**
Calhoun, John C., **I:** 8; **III:** 309
"Caliban in the Coal Mines" (Untermeyer), **Supp. XV:** 296
"California" (Carruth), **Supp. XVI:** 56
"California" (Didion), **Supp. IV Part 1:** 195
"California, This Is Minnesota Speaking" (Dunn), **Supp. XI:** 146
California and Oregon Trail, The (Parkman), **Supp. I Part 2:** 486
California: An Intimate History (Atherton), **Supp. XXIV:** 27
California Daughter (Leider), **Supp. XXIV:** 30
"California Hills in August" (Gioia), **Supp. XV:** 118–119
"California Indians of Today, The" (Zitkala-Ša), **Supp. XXV:** 284
"California Indian Trails and Prayer Trees" (Zitkala-Ša), **Supp. XXV:** 284
Californians (Jeffers), **Supp. II Part 2:** 415, 418, 420
Californians, The (Atherton), **Supp. XXIV:** 18, 21, 22
"California Oaks, The" (Winters), **Supp. II Part 2:** 798
"California Plush" (Bidart), **Supp. XV:** 23
"California Republic" (Didion), **Supp. IV Part 1:** 205
"California Requiem, A" (Gioia), **Supp. XV:** 126
California Suite (film), **Supp. IV Part 2:** 589
California Suite (Simon), **Supp. IV Part 2:** 581, 582
"Caligula" (R. Lowell), **II:** 554
Callahan, John F., **Retro. Supp. II:** 119, 126, 127
"Call at Corazón" (Bowles), **Supp. IV Part 1:** 82, 87
Calle, Sophia, **Supp. XII:** 22
"Called Back" (Kazin), **Supp. VIII:** 104
"Calle Visión" (Rich), **Retro. Supp. III:** 252
Calley, Captain William, **II:** 579
Calley, John, **Supp. XI:** 305
Callicott, J. Baird, **Supp. XIV:** 184
Calligrammes (Apollinaire), **I:** 432
"Calling Jesus" (Toomer), **Supp. III Part 2:** 484
Calling Myself Home (Hogan), **Supp. IV Part 1:** 397, 399, 400, 401, 413
Calling the Wind: Twentieth Century African-American Short Stories (Major, ed.), **Supp. XXII:** 172
Calling Western Union (Taggard), **Supp. XXII:** 271–272, **281–283**
Call It Experience (Caldwell), **I:** 290–291, 297
"Call It Fear" (Harjo), **Supp. XII:** 220
Call It Sleep (H. Roth), **Supp. IX:** 227, 228, **229–231; Supp. VIII:** 233; **Supp. XIII:** 106
"Call Letters: Mrs. V. B." (Angelou), **Supp. IV Part 1:** 15
Call Me Ishmael (Olson), **Supp. II Part 2:** 556; **Supp. XXI:** 21
Call Me Shakespeare (Endore), **Supp. XVII:** 65
"Call of Cthulhu, The" (Lovecraft), **Supp. XXV:** 109, 114, 116–117, 118; **Supp. XXVII:** 123
Call of the Gospel, The (Mather), **Supp. II Part 2:** 448
Call of the Wild, The (London), **II:** 466, 470–471, 472, 481
"Call of the Wild, The" (Snyder), **Supp. VIII:** 301
"Calloway's Code" (O. Henry), **Supp. II Part 1:** 404
"Call to Arms" (Mumford), **Supp. II Part 2:** 479
Call to Arms, The (film), **Retro. Supp. I:** 325
Calmer, Ned, **Supp. XI:** 219
Calvert, George H., **Supp. I Part 1:** 361
Calverton, V. F., **Supp. VIII:** 96
Calvin, John, **II:** 342; **IV:** 160, 490
Calvino, Italo, **Supp. IV Part 2:** 623, 678; **Supp. XIX:** 34; **Supp. XXI:** 225; **Supp. XXII:** 263
Cambridge Companion to Native American Literature, The (Porter and Roemer, eds.), **Supp. XX: 270**
Cambridge Companion to Poe, The (Hayes, ed.), **Retro. Supp. III:** 237
Cambridge Edition of the Works of F. Scott Fitzgerald, The (Bruccoli, ed.), **Retro. Supp. I:** 115
Cambridge Film Handbook for On the Waterfront (Rapf), **Supp. XVIII:** 251
"Cambridge"(O'Hara), **Supp. XXIII:** 219
"Cambridge Thirty Years Ago" (J. R. Lowell), **Supp. I Part 2:** 419
Cambridge University Press, **Retro. Supp. I:** 115
"Camellia Sabina" (Moore), **III:** 208, 215
"Cameo" (Trethewey), **Supp. XXI:** 250
"Cameo Appearance" (Simic), **Supp. VIII:** 283
"Camera Notes" (column, Stratton-Porter), **Supp. XX: 217**
Camera Obscura (Nabokov), **III:** 255
Cameron, Angus, **Supp. XXI:** 268, 269, 275, 278
Cameron, Elizabeth, **I:** 10, 17
Cameron, Kenneth W., **II:** 16
Cameron, Peter, **Supp. XII: 79–95**
Cameron, Sharon, **Retro. Supp. I:** 43; **Retro. Supp. II:** 40
Camerson, Don, **I:** 10, 17
Camino, Léon Felipe, **Retro. Supp. II:** 89

Camino Real (T. Williams), **IV:** 382, 385, 386, 387, 388, 391, 392, 395, 398
Camões, Luiz Vaz de, **II:** 133; **Supp. I Part 1:** 94
"Camouflaging the Chimera" (Komunyakaa), **Supp. XIII: 122–123**
Camp, James, **Supp. XV:** 165
Camp, Walter, **II:** 423
Campana, Dino, **Supp. V:** 337
Campbell, Alan, **Supp. IV Part 1:** 353; **Supp. IX:** 196, 198, 201
Campbell, Alexander, **Supp. I Part 2:** 381, 395
Campbell, Donna, **Retro. Supp. II:** 139
Campbell, E. Simms, **Supp. XXII:** 12
Campbell, Helen, **Supp. XI:** 200, 206
Campbell, James, **Supp. XII:** 127
Campbell, James Edwin, **Supp. II Part 1:** 202
Campbell, Joanna (pseudonym). See Bly, Carol
Campbell, Joseph, **I:** 135; **IV:** 369, 370; **Supp. IX:** 245; **Supp. XXV:** 74
Campbell, Lewis, **III:** 476
Campbell, Thomas, **II:** 8, 303, 314; **III:** 410; **Supp. I Part 1:** 309, 310
Campbell, Virginia, **Supp. XIII:** 114
Campbell, Will D., **Supp. XXI:** 247
Campbell (Hale), Janet, **Supp. IV Part 2:** 503
"Campers Leaving: Summer 1981" (Kenyon), **Supp. VII:** 169
"Camp Evergreen" (Kenyon), **Supp. VII:** 168
"Camping in Madera Canyon" (Swenson), **Supp. IV Part 2:** 649
Campion, Jane, **Supp. XXIV:** 172
Campion, Peter, **Supp. XXV:** 227, 233
Campion, Thomas, **I:** 439; **Supp. VIII:** 272
"Campo" (Muñoz), **Supp. XXV:** 130
Campo, Rafael, **Supp. XVII:** 112
Camus, Albert, **I:** 53, 61, 292, 294, 494; **II:** 57, 244; **III:** 292, 306, 453; **IV:** 6, 211, 236, 442, 487; **Retro. Supp. I:** 73; **Retro. Supp. II:** 20; **Supp. I Part 2:** 621; **Supp. VIII:** 11, 195, 241; **Supp. XI:** 96; **Supp. XIII:** 74, 165, 233, 247; **Supp. XVII:** 137
Camuto, Christopher, **Supp. V:** 212–213
"Canada" (Di Piero), **Supp. XIX:** 39
Canada Fragrant with Resin, **Supp. XVI:** 149
Canadé, Eugene, **Supp. XXI:** 22, 23
"Canadian Mosaic, The" (Beran), **Supp. XIII:** 25
"Canadians and Pottawatomies" (Sandburg), **III:** 592–593
Canadian Short Stories (radio show), **Supp. XXVII:** 181
"Can a Good Wife Be a Good Sport?" (T. Williams), **IV:** 380
"Canal, The: A Poem on the Application of Physical Science to Political Economy" (Barlow), **Supp. II Part 1:** 73
Canan, Peter, **Supp. XXV:** 123
Canary, Martha Jane. See Calamity Jane (Martha Jane Canary)
"Canary for One, A" (Hemingway), **Retro. Supp. I:** 170, 189
Canary in a Cat House (Vonnegut), **Supp. II Part 2:** 758
"Canary in Bloom" (Dove), **Supp. IV Part 1:** 248
Canby, Henry Seidel, **IV:** 65, 363
Canby, Vincent, **Retro. Supp. III:** 290
"Cancer" (McClatchy), **Supp. XII:** 266
"Cancer Match, The" (Dickey), **Supp. IV Part 1:** 182
"Cancíon y Glosa" (Merwin), **Supp. III Part 1:** 342
Candide (Hellman), **I:** 28; **Supp. I Part 1:** 288–289, 292
Candide (Voltaire), **Supp. I Part 1:** 288–289; **Supp. XI:** 297; **Supp. XVI:** 189
Candide (Voltaire; Wilbur, trans.), **Supp. III Part 2:** 560
"Candle Hat" (Collins), **Supp. XXI:** 60
Candle in the Cabin, The (Lindsay), **Supp. I Part 2:** 398, 400
"Candles" (Plath), **Retro. Supp. II:** 248, 257
Candles in Babylon (Levertov), **Supp. III Part 1:** 283
Candles in the Sun (T. Williams), **IV:** 381
Candles of Your Eyes, The (Purdy), **Supp. VII:** 278
Candy (Southern), **Supp. XI:** 297, **298–299,** 305
"Candy-Man Beechum" (Caldwell), **I:** 309
Cane (Toomer), **Supp. III Part 2:** 475, 481–486, 488; **Supp. IV Part 1:** 164, 168; **Supp. IX:** 305, 306, 307, **308–320; Supp. XIX:** 73; **Supp. XX: 73**
"Cane in the Corridor, The" (Thurber), **Supp. I Part 2:** 616
Canfield, Cass, **Supp. I Part 2:** 668
Canfield, Dorothy, **Retro. Supp. I:** 4, 11, 14, 18; **Retro. Supp. III:** 27; **Supp. XX: 39**. See also Fisher, Dorothy Canfield
Canfield, William W., **Supp. XXVI:** 86
Can Grande's Castle (A. Lowell), **II:** 518, 524
"Canicula di Anna" (Carson), **Supp. XII: 101–102**
"Can I Get You Anything?" (Carver and Gallagher), **Supp. XXIV:** 178
"Canis Major" (Frost), **Retro. Supp. I:** 137
"Canned Stuff" (Pickering), **Supp. XXI:** 198
Cannery Row (Steinbeck), **IV:** 50, 51, 64–65, 66, 68
Cannibal Galaxy, The (Ozick), **Supp. V:** 270
Cannibals and Christians (Mailer), **III:** 38–39, 40, 42; **Retro. Supp. II:** 203, 204, 205; **Supp. XXIV:** 281
Canning, George, **I:** 7, 8
Canning, Richard, **Supp. X:** 147
Cannon, Jimmy, **II:** 424
Cannon, Steve, **Retro. Supp. II:** 111
Cannon between My Knees, A (Gunn Allen), **Supp. IV Part 1:** 324
Canolle, Jean, **Supp. XVI:** 194
"Canonization, The" (Donne), **Supp. XIV:** 8
"Can Poetry Matter?" (Gioia), **Supp. XV:** 113, 114
Can Poetry Matter?: Essays on Poetry and American Culture (Gioia), **Supp. XV:** 112, **113–115**
"Canso" (Merwin), **Supp. III Part 1:** 344
Can Such Things Be? (Bierce), **I:** 203, 204, 205, 209
Canterbury Tales (Chaucer), **II:** 504; **III:** 411; **IV:** 65
Canterbury Tales, The (Chaucer), **Supp. XIX:** 4
"Canticle of Her Coming and Going" (Espaillat), **Supp. XXI:** 106
"Canto Amor" (Berryman), **I:** 173
Canto I (Pound), **III:** 469, 470; **Retro. Supp. I:** 286
Canto II (Pound), **III:** 470
Canto III (Pound), **III:** 470
Canto IV (Pound), **III:** 470
Canto VIII (Pound), **III:** 472
Canto IX (Pound), **III:** 472
Canto X (Pound), **III:** 472
Canto XIII (Pound), **III:** 472
Canto XXXIX (Pound), **III:** 468
Canto LXV (Pound), **Retro. Supp. I:** 292
Canto LXXXI (Pound), **III:** 459;

Retro. Supp. I: 293
Cantor, Lois, **Supp. IV Part 1:** 285
Cantos (Pound), **I:** 482; **III:** 13–14, 17, 457, 462, 463, 466, 467, 469–470, 472–473, 474, 475, 476, 492; **Retro. Supp. I:** 284, 292, **292–293,** 293, 427; **Retro. Supp. III:** 50; **Supp. I Part 1:** 272; **Supp. II Part 1:** 5; **Supp. II Part 2:** 420, 557, 564, 644; **Supp. IV Part 1:** 153; **Supp. V:** 343, 345; **Supp. VIII:** 305; **Supp. XIV:** 55, 96; **Supp. XV:** 349
"Cantus Planis" (Pound), **III:** 466
Cantwell, Robert, **Retro. Supp. I:** 85; **Supp. VIII:** 96; **Supp. XIII:** 292
Can Women Be Gentlemen? (Atherton), **Supp. XXIV:** 20–21, 30
"Canyon de Chelly, Return, 1978"(Kenny), **Supp. XXIII:** 155
Canyons, The (film), **Supp. XXVII:** 79–80
"Can You Carry Me" (O'Hara), **III:** 369
Can You See Me Yet? (Findley), **Supp. XX: 52–53**
Canzoneri, Robert, **IV:** 114, 116
Canzoni (Pound), **Retro. Supp. I:** 286, 288, 413
"Cap" (Shaw), **Supp. IV Part 1:** 345
"Cape Breton" (Bishop), **Supp. I Part 1:** 92; **Supp. IX:** 45
Cape Cod (Thoreau), **II:** 540
"Cape Cod, Rome, and Jerusalem" (Chapman), **Supp. XIV:** 55
Capital City (Sandoz), **Supp. XXIV:** 244, **252–253,** 255
Capitalism: The Unknown Ideal (Rand), **Supp. IV Part 2:** 518, 527, 531, 532
Caponi, Gena Dagel, **Supp. IV Part 1:** 95
Capote, Truman, **Supp. I Part 1:** 291, 292; **Supp. III Part 1: 111–133; Supp. III Part 2:** 574; **Supp. IV Part 1:** 198, 220; **Supp. VIII:** 105; **Supp. XII:** 43, 249; **Supp. XV:** 146; **Supp. XVI:** 245–246; **Supp. XVII:** 236
Capouya, Emile, **Supp. I Part 1:** 50
Cappetti, Carla, **Supp. IX:** 4, 8
Capra, Frank, **Supp. XVI:** 102
Capra, Fritjof, **Supp. X:** 261
"Capricious Gardens" (Eugenides), **Supp. XXIV:** 133–134
"Capricorn Rising" (Mackey), **Supp. XXVII:** 153
Capron, Marion, **Supp. IX:** 193
"Capsule History of Conservation, A" (Stegner), **Supp. IV Part 2:** 600
"Captain Carpenter" (Ransom), **III:** 491
Captain Craig (Robinson), **III:** 508, 523; **Supp. II Part 1:** 192
"Captain Jim's Friend" (Harte), **Supp. II Part 1:** 337
"Captain Jones's Invitation" (Freneau), **Supp. II Part 1:** 261
"Captain's Son, The" (Taylor), **Supp. V:** 314, 325, 327
"Captain's Wife, The" (Salter), **Supp. IX:** 261
"Capt Christopher Levett (of York)" (Olson), **Supp. II Part 2:** 576, 577
Captive Israel (Reznikoff), **Supp. XIV:** 283
"Captivity and Restoration of Mrs. Mary Rowlandson, The" (Howe), **Supp. IV Part 2:** 419, 431, 434
"Captivity of the Fly" (MacLeish), **III:** 19
"Captured Goddess, The" (A. Lowell), **II:** 520
Caputi, Jane, **Supp. IV Part 1:** 334, 335
Caputo, Philip, **Supp. XI:** 234; **Supp. XIX: 17–31; Supp. XXII:** 104; **Supp. XXV:** 153
Capuzzo, Michael, **Supp. XIII:** 254
Car (Crews), **Supp. XI: 110–111**
Carabi, Angels, **Supp. VIII:** 223; **Supp. XII:** 215
"Caramels" (Zinberg), **Supp. XV:** 195
"Caravaggio: Swirl & Vortex" (Levis), **Supp. XI:** 258, 269
Caravan (Bynner), **Supp. XV:** 50
Carby, Hazel B., **Supp. IV Part 1:** 13; **Supp. XXI:** 171
"Carcassonne" (Faulkner), **Retro. Supp. I:** 81
Card, Antha E., **Supp. I Part 2:** 496
Cárdenas, Lupe, **Supp. IV Part 2:** 538, 539, 540
Cardinale, Anthony, **Supp. XVII:** 239
Cardinale, Ernesto, **Supp. XII:** 225
"Cardinal Ideograms" (Swenson), **Supp. IV Part 2:** 645
"Cards" (Beattie), **Supp. V:** 31
"Career Woman" (Hay), **Supp. XIV:** 131
Carefree (film, Sandrich), **Supp. XVII:** 59
"Careful" (Carver), **Supp. III Part 1:** 138
Careful and Strict Enquiry into the Modern Prevailing Notions of That Freedom of Will, Which Is Supposed to be Essential to Moral Agency, Vertue and Vice, Reward and Punishment, Praise and Blame, A (Edwards), **I:** 549, 557, 558, 562
Carel: A Poem and Pilgrimage in the Holy Land (Melville), **III:** 92–93
Careless Love and Its Apostrophes (Bronk), **Supp. XXI:** 32
"Carentan O Carentan" (Simpson), **Supp. IX:** 267
Carew, Thomas, **IV:** 453
Carey, Gary, **Supp. XVI:** 186
Carey, Lynn, **Supp. XXIII:** 273
Carey, Mathew, **Supp. XV:** 238
"Car Games" (Conroy), **Supp. XVI:** 72
Cargill, Oscar, **Supp. II Part 1:** 117
Caribbean as Columbus Saw It (Morison and Obregon), **Supp. I Part 2:** 488
"Caribou Kitchen" (A. Finch), **Supp. XVII:** 76–77
Caribou Rising: Defending the Porcupine Herd, Gwich-'in Culture, and the Arctic National Wildlife Refuge (Bass), **Supp. XVI:** 27–28, 28
Carillo, Donna, **Supp. XXVII:** 204
"Caring for the World"(Schott), **Supp. XXIII:** 249–250
Carkeet, David, **Retro. Supp. III:** 265
Carl, K. A., **III:** 475
Carleton, George W., **Supp. XVIII:** 4
Carlin, George, **Supp. XXI:** 51
Carlin, Terry, **Supp. XXI:** 4, 5, 14
Carlisle, Harry, **Supp. XVIII:** 223, 233
Carl Krinken: His Christmas Stocking (S. and A. Warner), **Supp. XVIII:** 264
"Carlos Who Died, and Left Only This, The" (Ríos), **Supp. IV Part 2:** 547
Carlotta (empress of Mexico), **Supp. I Part 2:** 457
Carl Sandburg (Golden), **III:** 579
Carlson, Susan L., **Supp. XV:** 323
Carlyle, Thomas, **I:** 103, 279; **II:** 5, 7, 11, 15–16, 17, 20, 145, 315; **III:** 82, 84, 85, 87; **IV:** 169, 182, 338, 350; **Retro. Supp. I:** 360, 408; **Retro. Supp. III:** 266; **Supp. I Part 1:** 2, 349; **Supp. I Part 2:** 410, 422, 482, 485, 552; **Supp. XXV:** 242
"Carma" (Toomer), **Supp. III Part 2:** 481–483; **Supp. IX:** 312–313
"Carmen de Boheme" (Crane), **I:** 384
Carmen Jones (film), **Supp. I Part 1:** 66
Carmina Burana, **Supp. X:** 63
Carmon, Walt, **Supp. XXII:** 277
Carnegie, Andrew, **I:** 483; **IV:** 192; **Supp. I Part 2:** 639, 644; **Supp. V:** 285
Carnegie, Dale, **Supp. I Part 2:** 608

"Carnegie Hall: Rescued" (Moore), **III:** 215
Carne-Ross, Donald S., **Supp. I Part 1:** 268, 269; **Supp. XXIV:** 153
Carnes, Mark C., **Supp. X:** 14
"Carnets" poems (Sobin), **Supp. XVI:** 286–287
Carnovsky, Morris, **III:** 154
"Carol for Carolyn, A" (A. Finch), **Supp. XVII:** 74, 75
"Carolina Parakeet" (Rash), **Supp. XXVII:** 220
Caroling Dusk: An Anthology of Verse by Negro Poets (Cullen, ed.), **Supp. IV Part 1:** 166, 169; **Supp. XXVI:** 165, 170
"Carol of Occupations" (Whitman), **I:** 486
"Carolyn Kizer and the Chain of Women" (A. Finch), **Supp. XVII:** 74–75
Carolyn Kizer: Perspectives on Her Life and Work (A. Finch), **Supp. XVII: 74–75**
"Carpe Diem" (Frost), **Supp. XII:** 303
"Carpe Noctem, if You Can" (Thurber), **Supp. I Part 2:** 620
Carpenter, Dan, **Supp. V:** 250
Carpenter, David, **Supp. VIII:** 297
Carpenter, Edward, **Supp. XX: 230**
Carpenter, Frederic I., **II:** 20
"Carpenter Bee" (Trethewey), **Supp. XXI:** 250
Carpentered Hen and Other Tame Creatures, The (Updike), **IV:** 214; **Retro. Supp. I:** 320
Carpenter's Gothic (Gaddis), **Supp. IV Part 1:** 288, 289–291, 293, 294
Carr, Dennis W., **Supp. IV Part 2:** 560
Carr, Elias, **Supp. XIV:** 57
Carr, Rosemary. See Benét, Rosemary
Carrall, Aaron, **Supp. IV Part 2:** 499
Carrel, Alexis, **IV:** 240
"Carrell/Klee/and Cosmos's Groom" (Goldbarth), **Supp. XII:** 183
"Carriage from Sweden, A" (Moore), **III:** 212
Carrie (King), **Supp. V:** 137
Carried Away (Harrison), **Supp. VIII:** 39
Carrier of Ladders (Merwin), **Supp. III Part 1:** 339, 346, 350–352, 356, 357
"Carriers of the Dream Wheel" (Momaday), **Supp. IV Part 2:** 481
Carriers of the Dream Wheel: Contemporary Native American Poetry (Niatum, ed.), **Supp. IV Part 2:** 484, 505
Carrington, Carroll, **I:** 199
"Carrion Spring" (Stegner), **Supp. IV Part 2:** 604
Carroll, Bart, **Supp. XXV:** 71
Carroll, Charles, **Supp. I Part 2:** 525
Carroll, Lewis, **I:** 432; **II:** 431; **III:** 181; **Supp. I Part 1:** 44; **Supp. I Part 2:** 622, 656; **Supp. XVI:** 103; **Supp. XXV:** 87; **Supp. XXVI:** 274
Carroll, Maureen P., **Supp. XXIV:** 177
"Carrots, Noses, Snow, Rose, Roses" (Gass), **Supp. VI:** 87
Carrouges, Michel, **Supp. IV Part 1:** 104
"Carrousel, The" (Rilke), **III:** 558
Carruth, Hayden, **Supp. IV Part 1:** 66; **Supp. IX:** 291; **Supp. VIII:** 39; **Supp. XIII:** 112; **Supp. XIV:** 273–274; **Supp. XIX:** 1; **Supp. XVI: 45–61; Supp. XXI:** 31; **Supp. XXIV:** 167
Carruth, Joe-Anne McLaughlin, **Supp. XVI:** 47
"Carry" (Hogan), **Supp. IV Part 1:** 412
Carrying Albert Home (Hickam), **Supp. XXVII:** 111
"Carrying On" (Dunn), **Supp. XI:** 145
Cars of Cuba (García), **Supp. XI:** 190
Carson, Anne, **Supp. XII: 97–116; Supp. XV:** 252; **Supp. XXV:** 222
Carson, Johnny, **Supp. IV Part 2:** 526
Carson, Rachel, **Supp. IX: 19–36; Supp. V:** 202; **Supp. X:** 99; **Supp. XVI:** 36; **Supp. XXVI:** 31
Carson, Tom, **Supp. XI:** 227
Cart, Michael, **Supp. X:** 12; **Supp. XXVII:** 205
"Car Tags" (Rash), **Supp. XXVII:** 222
Carter, Angela, **Supp. XXVII:** 190
Carter, Elliott, **Supp. III Part 1:** 21
Carter, Hodding, **Supp. XIV:** 2
Carter, Jared, **Supp. XVII:** 110
Carter, Jimmy, **Supp. I Part 2:** 638; **Supp. XIV:** 107
Carter, Lin, **Supp. XXVII:** 128
Carter, Marcia, **Supp. V:** 223
Carter, Mary, **Supp. IV Part 2:** 444
Carter, Paul, **Supp. XX: 77, 78**
Carter, Peter, **Supp. XVIII:** 267
Carter, Stephen, **Supp. XI:** 220
Cartesian Sonata and Other Novellas (Gass), **Supp. VI: 92–93**
Cartier, Jacques, **Supp. I Part 2:** 496, 497
Cartier-Bresson, Henri, **Supp. VIII:** 98
"Cartographies of Silence" (Rich), **Supp. I Part 2:** 571–572
"Cartography" (Espaillat), **Supp. XXI:** 107
Cartwright, Louis, **Supp. XIV:** 147, 149, 151
Carver, Raymond, **Supp. III Part 1: 135–151; Supp. IV Part 1:** 342; **Supp. V:** 22, 23, 220, 326; **Supp. VIII:** 15; **Supp. X:** 85, 167; **Supp. XI:** 26, 65, 116, 153; **Supp. XII:** 79, 139, 289, 294; **Supp. XIX:** 209; **Supp. XXI:** 36, 115, 116, 118, 119; **Supp. XXIII:** 289, 296; **Supp. XXIV:** 97, 166, 167, 173, 177–178; **Supp. XXVI:** 147, 180; **Supp. XXVII:** 269
Carver: A Life in Poems (Nelson), **Supp. XVIII:** 171, 172, **181–182,** 183
Carville, James, **Supp. XXIV:** 282
Carving Hawk (Kenny), **Supp. XXIII:** 143, 150
Cary, Alice, **Retro. Supp. II:** 145; **Supp. XV:** 273; **Supp. XXII:** 206
Cary, Phoebe, **Supp. XV:** 273
Cary, Richard, **Retro. Supp. II:** 132, 137
"Casabianca" (Bishop), **Retro. Supp. II:** 42; **Supp. I Part 1:** 86
Casablanca (film), **Supp. VIII:** 61; **Supp. XV:** 14
Casanova: His Known and Unknown Life (Endore), **Supp. XVII:** 54
"Casa solariega, La" ("The Family Mansion") (Espaillat), **Supp. XXI:** 107
"Case Against Mist, The" (Halliday), **Supp. XIX:** 91
Casebook (Simpson), **Supp. XXVII:** 234, 244–246
Case for West-Indian Self-Government, The (C. L. R. James), **Supp. XXI:** 159, 161
Case of Jennie Brice, The (Rinehart), **Supp. XXV:** 193, 200
Case of Rape, A (C. Himes), **Supp. XVI:** 143
Case of the Crushed Petunias, The (T. Williams), **IV:** 381
Case of the Officers of Excise (Paine), **Supp. I Part 2:** 503–504
Casey, Helen Marie, **Supp. XXIII:** 246
Casey, John, **Supp. X:** 164
Cash, Arthur, **Supp. IV Part 1:** 299
Cashman, Nellie, **Supp. X:** 103
Casiero, Robert, **Supp. XIV:** 167
Casino Royale (film), **Supp. XI: 306–307; Supp. XXVII:** 96
Caskey, William, **Supp. XIV:** 166
"Cask of Amontillado, The" (Poe), **II:** 475; **III:** 413; **Retro. Supp. II:** 268, 269, 270, 273; **Retro. Supp. III:** 226, 229–230

Caso, Frank, **Supp. XVIII:** 95
Caspary, Vera, **Supp. XIX:** 78
Casper, Robert N., **Supp. XV:** 339, 347
Casper and His Friends (S. and A. Warner), **Supp. XVIII:** 264
Cassada (Salter), **Supp. IX: 251–252**
Cassada, Jackie, **Supp. XXIII:** 291
Cassady, Carolyn, **Supp. XIV:** 150
Cassady, Neal, **Supp. II Part 1:** 309, 311; **Supp. XIV:** 137, 144
"Cassandra" (Stallings), **Supp. XXV:** 233
"Cassandra Southwick" (Whittier), **Supp. I Part 2:** 693
Cassell, Verlin, **Supp. XI:** 315
Cassill, Ronald Verlin, **Supp. V:** 323; **Supp. XIX:** 266; **Supp. XVIII:** 72
Cassirer, Ernst, **I:** 265; **IV:** 87, 89
Cass Timberlane (Lewis), **II:** 455–456
Cast a Cold Eye (McCarthy), **II:** 566
Castaway (Cozzens), **I:** 363, 370, 374, 375, 379
"Caste in America" (Du Bois), **Supp. II Part 1:** 169
Castiglione, Baldassare, **I:** 279; **III:** 282
"Castilian" (Wylie), **Supp. I Part 2:** 714
Castillo, Ana, **Supp. XI:** 177; **Supp. XXIII:** 194
"Castle in Lynn, A" (McCarriston), **Supp. XIV:** 265, 268
"Castles and Distances" (Wilbur), **Supp. III Part 2:** 550
Castle Sinister (Marquand), **III:** 58
Cast of Thousands (Loos), **Supp. XVI:** 192, 193, 195
Castro, Fidel, **II:** 261, 434; **Supp. XX: 80**
Cast the First Stone (C. Himes), **Supp. XVI:** 135, 137–138
"Casual Incident, A" (Hemingway), **II:** 44
Casualties (Rash), **Supp. XXVII:** 227
"Casualty Report" (Halliday), **Supp. XIX:** 85
Caswell, Michelle, **Supp. XXII:** 262
"Cat, The" (Matthews), **Supp. IX: 157–158**
Cat, You Better Come Home (Keillor), **Supp. XVI:** 177
"Catbird Seat, The" (Thurber), **Supp. I Part 2:** 623
"Catch" (Francis), **Supp. IX:** 82
Catch-22 (Heller), **III:** 558; **Supp. IV Part 1:** 379, 380, 381–382, 383, 384–386, 387, 390, 391, 392, 393, 394; **Supp. V:** 244, 248; **Supp. XII:** 167–168; **Supp. XXIII:** 100; **Supp. XXVII:** 207
Catcher in the Rye, The (Salinger), **I:** 493; **III:** 551, 552, 553–558, 567, 571; **Retro. Supp. I:** 102; **Retro. Supp. II:** 222, 249; **Supp. I Part 2:** 535; **Supp. V:** 119; **Supp. VIII:** 242; **Supp. XI:** 65; **Supp. XVII:** 2; **Supp. XXIII:** 100; **Supp. XXIV:** 133
"Catching Frogs" (Kenyon), **Supp. VII:** 170
Catching the Mermother (A. Finch), **Supp. XVII:** 72
catechism of d neoamerican hoodoo church (Reed), **Supp. X:** 240, 241
Catered Affair, The (film), **Supp. IV Part 2:** 683
"Cathay" (Goldbarth), **Supp. XII:** 185, 186
Cathay (Pound), **II:** 527; **Retro. Supp. I:** 289
Cathedral (Carver), **Supp. III Part 1:** 144–146; **Supp. XII:** 139
"Cathedral" (Carver), **Supp. III Part 1:** 144–145; **Supp. XXIV:** 177
Cathedral, The (J. R. Lowell), **Supp. I Part 2:** 407, 416–417
Cather, Willa, **I: 312–334,** 405; **II:** 51, 96, 177, 404, 412; **III:** 453; **IV:** 190; **Retro. Supp. I: 1–23,** 355, 382; **Retro. Supp. II:** 71, 136; **Retro. Supp. III: 17–39**; **Supp. I Part 2:** 609, 719; **Supp. IV Part 1:** 31; **Supp. VIII:** 101, 102, 263; **Supp. X:** 103; **Supp. XIII:** 253; **Supp. XIV:** 112; **Supp. XIX:** 131; **Supp. XV:** 40, 51; **Supp. XVI:** 226; **Supp. XVIII:** 207; **Supp. XXIII:** 290; **Supp. XXIV:** 29, 30, 244; **Supp. XXV:** 201
Catherine, Saint, **II:** 211
Catherine II, **Supp. I Part 2:** 433
Catholic Art and Culture (Watkin), **Retro. Supp. II:** 187
"Catholic Novelist in the Protestant South, The" (O'Connor), **Retro. Supp. II:** 223, 224; **Retro. Supp. III:** 215
"Cathy Queen of Cats" (Cisneros), **Supp. VII:** 59
Cat Inside, The (Burroughs), **Supp. III Part 1:** 105
Cat in the Hat, The (Geisel), **Supp. XVI:** 106–107, 112
Cat in the Hat Come Back, The (Geisel), **Supp. XVI:** 107
"Cat in the Hat for President, The" (Coover), **Supp. V:** 44, 46–47
Cat in The Hat Songbook, The (Geisel), **Supp. XVI:** 104
Cato, **II:** 114, 117
Cat on a Hot Tin Roof (T. Williams), **II:** 190; **IV:** 380, 382, 383, 386, 387, 389, 390, 391, 394, 395, 397–398; **Supp. XXV:** 93
"Cat People: What Dr. Seuss Really Taught Us" (Menand), **Supp. XVI:** 106
Cats and Dogs (Silver), **Supp. XXIV:** 265, 274
Cat's Cradle (Vonnegut), **Supp. II Part 2:** 758, 759, 767–768, 770, 771, 772; **Supp. V:** 1
Cat's Eye (Atwood), **Supp. XIII: 29–30**
Catskill Eagle, A (Parker), **Supp. XIX:** 185
"Cat's Meow, A" (Brodsky), **Supp. VIII:** 31
"Cats of Ulthar, The" (Lovecraft), **Supp. XXV:** 114
Cat's Quizzer, The (Geisel), **Supp. XVI:** 111
"Catterskill Falls" (Bryant), **Supp. I Part 1:** 160
"Cattle Car Complex" (T. Rosenbaum), **Supp. XVII:** 48
Cattlemen from the Rio Grande Across the Far Marias (Sandoz), **Supp. XXIV:** 244, **249–251,** 256
Catullus, **Supp. XII:** 2, 13, **112; Supp. XV:** 23, 27, 35, 36
Catullus, Gaius Valerius, **I:** 381; **Supp. I Part 1:** 261; **Supp. I Part 2:** 728
Catullus (Gai Catulli Veronensis Liber) (Zukofsky), **Supp. III Part 2:** 625, 627, 628, 629
"Catullus: Carmina" (Carson), **Supp. XII: 112**
"Catullus: Excrucior" (Bidart), **Supp. XV:** 32, 35
"Cat Walked Through the Casserole, The" (Nelson and Espeland), **Supp. XVIII: 181**
Cat Walked Through the Casserole and Other Poems for Children (Nelson and Espeland), **Supp. XVIII:** 181
"Cat Who Aspired to Higher Things, The" (X. J. Kennedy), **Supp. XV:** 163
Cat Who Went to Heaven, The (Coatsworth), **Supp. XXVI:** 33
"Caucasian Storms Harlem, The" (R. Fisher), **Supp. XIX:** 78
Caudwell, Christopher, **Supp. X:** 112; **Supp. XXII:** 284
"Caul, The" (Banks), **Supp. V:** 10–11
Cause for Wonder (Morris), **III:** 232–233
"Causerie" (Tate), **IV:** 129
Causes and Consequences (Chapman),

Supp. XIV: 41, 49, 51
"Causes of American Discontents before 1768, The" (Franklin), **II:** 120
Causley, Charles, **Supp. XV:** 117
Cavafy, Constantine P., **Supp. IX:** 275; **Supp. XI:** 119, 123; **Supp. XXI:** 131; **Supp. XXIII:** 150; **Supp. XXV:** 225, 233
Cavalcade of America, The (radio program), **III:** 146
Cavalcanti (Pound, opera), **Retro. Supp. I:** 287
Cavalcanti, Guido, **I:** 579; **III:** 467; **Supp. III Part 2:** 620, 621, 622, 623
Cavalieri, Grace, **Supp. IV Part 2:** 630, 631
"Cavalry Crossing the Ford" (Whitman), **IV:** 347
"Cave, The" (Bass), **Supp. XVI:** 23
Cave, The (Warren), **IV:** 255–256
Cavelieri, Grace, **Supp. XXIII:** 135
Cavell, Stanley, **Retro. Supp. I:** 306–307, 309
Cavender's House (Robinson), **III:** 510
Caver, Christine, **Supp. XXI:** 215
Caves of Death, The (Atherton; Joshi, ed.), **Supp. XXIV:** 23
"Caviar" (Boyle), **Supp. XX: 19**
Caviare at the Funeral (Simpson), **Supp. IX:** 266, **276–277**
"Cawdor" (Jeffers), **Supp. II Part 2:** 431
Caxton, William, **III:** 486
Cayton, Horace, **IV:** 475, 488
Cazamian, Louis, **II:** 529
C Comics, **Supp. XXVII:** 23
"Ceiling, The" (Brockmeier), **Supp. XXII:** 52–53
Celan, Paul, **Supp. X:** 149; **Supp. XII:** 21, 110–111; **Supp. XVI:** 284–285, 288; **Supp. XVII:** 241
"Celebrated Jumping Frog of Calaveras County, The" (Twain), **IV:** 196
Celebrated Jumping Frog of Calaveras County, The, and Other Sketches (Twain), **IV:** 197; **Retro. Supp. III:** 257, 260
Celebration (Crews), **Supp. XI:** 103, **108**
Celebration (Swados), **Supp. XIX: 269–270**
Celebration at Dark (W. J. Smith), **Supp. XIII:** 332
"Celebration for June 24th" (McGrath), **Supp. X:** 116
Celebration of the Sound Through (Sobin), **Supp. XVI:** 284–285
Celebrations after the Death of John Brennan (X. J. Kennedy), **Supp. XV:** 165
Celebrity (film; Allen), **Supp. XV:** 11
"Celebrity" (Pickering), **Supp. XXI:** 198
"Celery" (Stein), **IV:** 43
"Celestial Games" (Conroy), **Supp. XVI:** 72
"Celestial Globe" (Nemerov), **III:** 288
Celestial Navigation (Tyler), **Supp. IV Part 2:** 662–663, 671
"Celestial Railroad, The" (Hawthorne), **Retro. Supp. I:** 152; **Retro. Supp. III:** 115; **Supp. I Part 1:** 188
Celibate Season, A (Shields), **Supp. VII:** 323, 324
Cellini (Shanley), **Supp. XIV:** 316, **329–330**
"Cemetery at Academy, California" (Levine), **Supp. V:** 182
Cemetery Nights (Dobyns), **Supp. XIII:** 85, 87, 89
"Cenotaph, The" (Stallings), **Supp. XXV:** 225, 234
"Censors As Critics: To Kill a Mockingbird As a Case Study" (May), **Supp. VIII:** 126
"Census-Taker, The" (Frost), **Retro. Supp. I:** 129
"Centaur, The" (Swenson), **Supp. IV Part 2:** 641
Centaur, The (Updike), **IV:** 214, 216, 217, 218, 219–221, 222; **Retro. Supp. I:** 318, 322, 324, 331, 336
"Centennial Meditation of Columbia, The" (Lanier), **Supp. I Part 1:** 362
Centeno, Agusto, **IV:** 375
"Centipede" (Dove), **Supp. IV Part 1:** 246
"Cento: A Note on Philosophy" (Berrigan), **Supp. XXIV:** 42–43
"Central Man, The" (Bloom), **Supp. IV Part 2:** 689
"Central Park" (R. Lowell), **II:** 552
Central Park (Wasserstein and Drattel), **Supp. XV:** 333
"Central Park at Dusk" (Teasdale), **Supp. XXVII:** 286, 289
Central Park West (Allen), **Supp. XV:** 13
Century Cycle (Wilson), **Retro. Supp. III:** 313, 318, 321, 323, 325, 326
Century of Dishonor, A (Jackson), **Retro. Supp. I:** 31
"Cerebral Snapshot, The" (Theroux), **Supp. VIII:** 313
"Ceremonies" (Rukeyser), **Supp. VI:** 279
"Ceremony" (Monson), **Supp. XXIV:** 230
Ceremony (Silko), **Supp. IV Part 1:** 274, 333; **Supp. IV Part 2:** 557–558, 558–559, 559, 561–566, 570; **Supp. XVIII:** 59
Ceremony (Wilbur), **Supp. III Part 2:** 550–551
"Ceremony, The" (Harjo), **Supp. XII:** 230
"Ceremony, The—Anatomy of a Massacre" (E. Hoffman, play), **Supp. XVI:** 160
Ceremony in Lone Tree (Morris), **III:** 229–230, 232, 238, 558
Ceremony of Brotherhood, A (Anaya and Ortiz, eds.), **Supp. IV Part 2:** 502
Cerf, Bennett, **III:** 405; **IV:** 288; **Retro. Supp. II:** 330; **Supp. XIII:** 172; **Supp. XIX:** 244
"Certain Attention to the World, A" (Haines), **Supp. XII:** 201
"Certain Beasts, Like Cats" (Bronk), **Supp. XXI:** 30
Certain Distance, A (Francis), **Supp. IX:** 85
"Certain Music, A" (Rukeyser), **Supp. VI:** 273
Certain Noble Plays of Japan (Pound), **III:** 458
Certain People (Wharton), **Retro. Supp. I:** 382
"Certain Poets" (MacLeish), **III:** 4
Certain Slant of Sunlight, A (Berrigan), **Supp. XXIV:** 43
"Certain Testimony" (Bausch), **Supp. VII:** 48
Certificate, The (Singer), **IV:** 1; **Retro. Supp. II: 314–315**
"Cerulean" (Everett), **Supp. XVIII:** 66
Cervantes, Lorna Dee, **Supp. IV Part 2:** 545
Cervantes, Miguel de, **I:** 130, 134; **II:** 8, 272, 273, 276, 289, 302, 310, 315; **III:** 113, 614; **IV:** 367; **Retro. Supp. I:** 91; **Supp. I Part 2:** 406; **Supp. V:** 277; **Supp. XIII:** 17; **Supp. XXIII:** 4
Cervantes. Lorna Dee, **Supp. XXVII:** 168
Césaire, Aimé, **Supp. X:** 132, 139; **Supp. XIII:** 114
"Cesarean" (Kenyon), **Supp. VII:** 173
Cézanne, Paul, **II:** 576; **III:** 210; **IV:** 26, 31, 407; **Supp. V:** 333, 341–342; **Supp. XIX:** 36
Chabon, Michael, **Supp. XI: 63–81; Supp. XIX:** 135, 138, 174, 223; **Supp. XVI:** 259; **Supp. XX: 177; Supp. XXII:** 49; **Supp. XXIV:** 131
Chaboseau, Jean, **Supp. I Part 1:** 260

Chace, Bill, **Supp. XXI:** 256
Chagall, Marc, **Supp. XXIII:** 6
Chaikin, Joseph, **Supp. III Part 2:** 433, 436–437
"Chain, The" (Kumin), **Supp. IV Part 2:** 452
Chainbearer, The (Cooper), **I:** 351, 352–353
"Chain of Love, A" (Price), **Supp. VI: 258–259,** 260
Chain Saw Dance, The (Budbill), **Supp. XIX: 5–6**
Chains of Dew (Glaspell), **Supp. III Part 1:** 181
Chalk Face (W. Frank), **Supp. XX: 73–74**
Challacombe, Robert Hamilton, **III:** 176
Challenge (Untermeyer), **Supp. XV:** 296, 303
"Challenge" (Untermeyer), **Supp. XV:** 296
"Challenge from Beyond, The" (Lovecraft, Howard, Long, Merritt, and Moore), **Supp. XXV:** 122
Chalmers, George, **Supp. I Part 2:** 514, 521
"Chambered Nautilus, The" (Holmes), **Supp. I Part 1:** 254, 307, 312–313, 314
Chamberlain, John, **Supp. I Part 2:** 647; **Supp. IV Part 2:** 525
Chamberlain, Neville, **II:** 589; **Supp. I Part 2:** 664
Chamber Music (Joyce), **III:** 16
Chambers, Richard, **Supp. III Part 2:** 610, 611, 612
Chambers, Whittaker, **Supp. III Part 2:** 610; **Supp. IV Part 2:** 526; **Supp. XV:** 143
Chameleon (C. Baxter), **Supp. XVII:** 14–15
"Champ, The" (Zinberg), **Supp. XV:** 193
"Champagne Regions" (Ríos), **Supp. IV Part 2:** 553
"Champion" (Lardner), **II:** 420–421, 428, 430
Champion, Laurie, **Supp. VIII:** 128
"Champ of the Forecastle" (Howard), **Supp. XXVII:** 124
Champollion-Figeac, Jean Jacques, **IV:** 426
"Chance" (Doolittle), **Supp. I Part 1:** 271
"Chance" (Munro), **Supp. XXVII:** 193
Chance, Frank, **II:** 418
Chance Acquaintance, A (Howells), **II:** 278
"Chance Encounter, A" (Swados), **Supp. XIX:** 261, 262
"Chanclas" (Cisneros), **Supp. VII:** 61
Chandler, Raymond, **Supp. III Part 1:** 91; **Supp. IV Part 1: 119–138,** 341, 344, 345; **Supp. IV Part 2:** 461, 464, 469, 470, 471, 472, 473; **Supp. XI:** 160, 228; **Supp. XII:** 307; **Supp. XIII:** 159, 233; **Supp. XIV:** 21; **Supp. XIX:** 178, 189; **Supp. XV:** 119; **Supp. XVI:** 122; **Supp. XVII:** 137; **Supp. XVIII:** 136,137, 137–138; **Supp. XXI:** 67; **Supp. XXII:** 119; **Supp. XXIV:** 284; **Supp. XXV:** 180
Chandler, Sherry, **Supp. XXIII:** 247
Chaney, "Professor" W. H., **II:** 463–464
Chang, Leslie C., **Supp. IV Part 1:** 72
"Change, The: Kyoto-Tokyo Express" (Ginsberg), **Supp. II Part 1:** 313, 329
Changed Man, A (Prose), **Supp. XVI:** 261–262
"Changeling" (Espaillat), **Supp. XXI:** 100
Changeling (Middleton), **Retro. Supp. I:** 62
"Changeling, The" (J. R. Lowell), **Supp. I Part 2:** 409
"Changeling, The" (Whittier), **Supp. I Part 2:** 697
Change of World, A (Rich), **Retro. Supp. III:** 241, 242; **Supp. I Part 2:** 551, 552
"Changes of Mind" (Baker), **Supp. XIII:** 52
"Changes of the Soul" (Taggard), **Supp. XXII:** 280
"Change the Joke and Slip the Yoke" (Ellison), **Retro. Supp. II:** 118
Change Your Bedding! (O'Hara), **Supp. XXIII:** 210
Changing Light at Sandover, The (Merrill), **Supp. III Part 1:** 318, 319, 323, 327, 332, 335–336; **Supp. XII:** 269–270; **Supp. XV:** 264
"Changing Same, The" (Baraka), **Supp. II Part 1:** 47, 51, 53
Changing the Bully Who Rules the World: Reading and Thinking about Ethics (C. Bly), **Supp. XVI:** 32, **39–40,** 41
Chanler, Mrs. Winthrop, **I:** 22; **IV:** 325
Channing, Carol, **IV:** 357
Channing, Edward, **Supp. I Part 2:** 479–480
Channing, Edward Tyrrel, **Supp. I Part 1:** 155; **Supp. I Part 2:** 422; **Supp. XXV:** 240
Channing, William Ellery, **I:** 336; **II:** 224, 495; **IV:** 172, 173, 176, 177; **Retro. Supp. I:** 54; **Supp. I Part 1:** 103; **Supp. I Part 2:** 589; **Supp. XXIV: 67–81; Supp. XXV:** 250
Channing, William Henry, **IV:** 178; **Supp. II Part 1:** 280, 285; **Supp. XXIV:** 68
Channing: The Reluctant Radical (Mendelsohn), **Supp. XXIV:** 72
Chanson de Roland, La, **I:** 13
"Chanson un Peu Naïve" (Bogan), **Supp. III Part 1:** 50–51
"Chanteuse" (Doty), **Supp. XI:** 119
"Chant for May Day" (Hughes), **Supp. I Part 1:** 331
Chants (Mora), **Supp. XIII: 214–215**
Chaos (Dove), **Supp. IV Part 1:** 243
Chapelle, Howard I., **Supp. XXV:** 217
"Chaperone, The" (Van Vechten), **Supp. II Part 2:** 728
Chaplin, Charles Spencer "Charlie," **I:** 27, 32, 43, 386, 447; **III:** 403; **Supp. I Part 2:** 607; **Supp. IV Part 1:** 146; **Supp. IV Part 2:** 574; **Supp. XX: 75; Supp. XXI:** 170; **Supp. XXII:** 25, 26
"Chaplinesque" (H. Crane), **Retro. Supp. II:** 79; **Retro. Supp. III:** 45, 49
"Chapman" (Rukeyser), **Supp. VI:** 273
Chapman, Abraham, **IV:** 485
Chapman, George, **Supp. I Part 2:** 422
Chapman, Ian, **Supp. XXVII:** 212
Chapman, John, **Supp. XXV:** 105
Chapman, John (Johnny Appleseed), **Supp. I Part 2:** 397
Chapman, John Jay, **IV:** 436; **Supp. XIV: 39–56**
Chapman, Stephen, **Supp. XIII:** 12
Chappell, Fred, **Supp. IV Part 1:** 69; **Supp. XI:** 317; **Supp. XVIII:** 87
Chapters in a Mythology: The Poetry of Sylvia Plath (Kroll), **Supp. I Part 2:** 541–543
Chapters on Erie (Adams and Adams), **Supp. I Part 2:** 644
Chapter Two (Simon), **Supp. IV Part 2:** 575, 586
"Chapter VI" (Hemingway), **II:** 252
Char, René, **Supp. XVI:** 282; **Supp. XVII:** 244
"Character" (Emerson), **II:** 6
"Characteristics of Negro Expression" (Hurston), **Retro. Supp. III:** 129, 137
"Character of Aboriginal Historical Tradition"(J. Schoolcraft), **Supp. XXIII:** 228–229
"Character of Presidents, The" (Doctorow), **Supp. IV Part 1:** 224

"Character of Socrates, The" (Emerson), **II:** 8–9
Character of the Poet, The (Simpson), **Supp. IX:** 273, 275, 278
"Characters in Fiction" (McCarthy), **II:** 562
"Charades" (Moore), **Supp. X:** 178
"Charge It" (Fante), **Supp. XI:** 164–165
"Charioteer, The" (Stallings), **Supp. XXV:** 233
Chariot in the Sky: A Story of the Jubilee Singers (Bontemps), **Supp. XXII:** 6, 13
"Charity" (Peacock), **Supp. XIX:** 221–222
Charity (Richard), **Supp. XIX: 220–222**
Charlatan, The (Singer), **IV:** 1
"Charles" (Jackson), **Supp. IX:** 125
Charles, Abram, **Supp. XXVI:** 87
Charles, Larry, **Supp. XVIII:** 21
"Charles Baxter, August Kleinzahler, Adrienne Rich: Contemporary Stevensians and the Problem of 'Other Lives' " (S. Burt), **Supp. XVII:** 18–19
Charles Goodnight: Cowman and Plainsman (Haley), **Supp. V:** 226
Charles Simic: Essays on the Poetry (Weigl), **Supp. VIII:** 269
Charles the Bold, Duke of Burgundy, **III:** 487
Charleville, Victoria Verdon, **Supp. I Part 1:** 200–201, 205, 206, 210
Charley's Aunt (B. Thomas), **II:** 138
Charlie Chan Is Dead: An Anthology of Contemporary Asian American Fiction (Hagedorn), **Supp. X:** 292
"Charlie Christian Story, The" (Ellison), **Retro. Supp. II:** 121
"Charlie Howard's Descent" (Doty), **Supp. XI:** 122
Charlie: The Improbable Life and Times of Charles MacArthur (Hecht), **Supp. XXVII:** 95
Charlotte: A Tale of Truth (Rowson), **Supp. I Part 1:** 128; **Supp. XV: 234–235,** 238. See also Charlotte Temple (Rowson)
Charlotte's Daughter; or, The Three Orphans (Rowson), **Supp. XV: 246**
Charlotte's Web (White), **Supp. I Part 2:** 655, 656, 658, 667, 670
Charlotte Temple (Rowson), **Supp. XV:** 229, **238–239; Supp. XXV:** 35, 36. See also Charlotte: A Tale of Truth (Rowson)
Charm, The (Creeley), **Supp. IV Part 1:** 139, 141, 144, 149–150
Charmed Life, A (McCarthy), **II:** 571–574
Charming Billy (McDermott), **Supp. XVIII:** 155, **162–164,** 166
Charms for the Easy Life (Gibbons), **Supp. X:** 45, **47–48**
Charnel Rose, The (Aiken), **I:** 50, 57, 62
Charney, Samuel, **Supp. XXIII:** 6
Charon's Cosmology (Simic), **Supp. VIII: 276–278**
Charterhouse, The (Percy), **Supp. III Part 1:** 388
Chart for Rough Water (W. Frank), **Supp. XX: 78**
Charvat, William, **II:** 244
Charyn, Jerome, **Supp. XVII:** 5
Chase, Mary Ellen, **Retro. Supp. II:** 243, 245; **Supp. XXIV:** 30
Chase, Richard, **IV:** 202, 443; **Retro. Supp. I:** 40, 395
Chase, Salmon P., **Supp. I Part 2:** 584
Chase, Stuart, **Supp. I Part 2:** 609
Chase, The (Foote), **Supp. I Part 1:** 281
Chasing the Dime (Connelly), **Supp. XXI: 74**
"Chaste Land, The" (Tate), **IV:** 122
Château, The (Maxwell), **Supp. VIII:** 152, 160, **165–167,** 168, 169
Chatham, Russell, **Supp. VIII:** 40
"Chattanooga Nights" (L. Brown), **Supp. XXI:** 39
Chatterdon, The Black Death, and Meriwether Lewis (Reznikoff), **Supp. XIV:** 288
Chatterton, Thomas, **Supp. I Part 1:** 349; **Supp. I Part 2:** 410, 716
Chatterton, Wayne, **Supp. IX:** 2, 4, 11–12
"Chatty Letters During a Journey from Aruba to Rio" (Thompson), **Supp. XXIV:** 282
Chatwin, Bruce, **Supp. VIII:** 322
Chaucer, Geoffrey, **I:** 131; **II:** 11, 504, 516, 542, 543; **III:** 283, 411, 473, 492, 521; **Retro. Supp. I:** 135, 426; **Supp. I Part 1:** 356, 363; **Supp. I Part 2:** 422, 617; **Supp. V:** 259; **Supp. XII:** 197; **Supp. XIX:** 4; **Supp. XVII:** 70
Chauncy, Charles, **I:** 546–547; **IV:** 147
Chavez, César, **Supp. V:** 199
Chávez, Denise, **Supp. IV Part 2:** 544; **Supp. XI:** 316
Chavez, Lydia, **Supp. VIII:** 75
Chavkin, Allan, **Supp. IV Part 1:** 259
Chavkin, Nancy Feyl, **Supp. IV Part 1:** 259
Chawla, Louise, **Supp. XXI:** 24
Chayefsky, Paddy, **Supp. XI:** 306
Cheang, Shu Lea, **Supp. XI:** 20
Cheap: New Poems and Ballads (Stone), **Supp. XXVII:** 249, 250, 257, 262
"Cheater's Guide To Love, The" (Díaz), **Supp. XXIV:** 84, 92, 93
"Cheat Takes Over" (Leopold), **Supp. XIV:** 189
"Cheers" (Carver), **Supp. III Part 1:** 138
Cheetham, James, **Supp. I Part 2:** 521
Cheever, Benjamin Hale, **Supp. I Part 1:** 175; **Supp. XXIV:** 97
Cheever, David W., **Supp. I Part 1:** 304
Cheever, Ezekiel, **Supp. I Part 1:** 174, 193
Cheever, Federico, **Supp. I Part 1:** 175
Cheever, Fred, **Supp. I Part 1:** 174
Cheever, Frederick L., **Supp. I Part 1:** 174
Cheever, John, **Retro. Supp. I:** 116, 333, 335; **Supp. I Part 1: 174–199; Supp. IX:** 114, 208; **Supp. V:** 23, 95; **Supp. VIII:** 151; **Supp. XI:** 65, 66, 99; **Supp. XII:** 140; **Supp. XIV:** 93; **Supp. XV:** 119, 142; **Supp. XXIII:** 104, 109, 275; **Supp. XXV:** 79, 142; **Supp. XXVI:** 147
Cheever, Mrs. John (Mary Winternitz), **Supp. I Part 1:** 175
Cheever, Mary Liley, **Supp. I Part 1:** 174
Cheever, Susan. See Cowley, Susan Cheever (Susan Cheever)
Cheever Evening, A (Gurney), **Supp. V:** 95
Chekhov, Anton, **I:** 52, 90; **II:** 27, 38, 44, 49, 198, 542; **III:** 362, 467; **IV:** 17, 53, 359, 446; **Retro. Supp. I:** 5, 355; **Retro. Supp. II:** 299; **Retro. Supp. III:** 25; **Supp. I Part 1:** 196; **Supp. II Part 1:** 6; **Supp. IV Part 2:** 585; **Supp. IX:** 260, 265, 274; **Supp. V:** 265; **Supp. VIII:** 153, 332; **Supp. XI:** 66; **Supp. XII:** 94, 307; **Supp. XIII:** 79; **Supp. XIV:** 87, 242; **Supp. XIX:** 172, 241; **Supp. XV:** 320, 329; **Supp. XVIII:** 102; **Supp. XXII:** 60; **Supp. XXIII:** 162, 290; **Supp. XXVII:** 218
"Chekhov's Sense of Writing as Seen Through His Letters" (Dobyns), **Supp. XIII:** 77–78
"Chemin de Fer" (Bishop), **Retro. Supp. II:** 41; **Supp. I Part 1:** 80, 85, 86
"Chemistry" (Rash), **Supp. XXVII:** 227

Chemistry and Other Stories (Rash), **Supp. XXVII:** 222, 225, 227–228
Cheney, Brainard, **Retro. Supp. II:** 229
Cheney, Matthew, **Supp. XXII:** 50
Chenzira, Ayoka, **Supp. XI:** 19
Chéri (Colette; stage adaptation, Loos), **Supp. XVI:** 194
Cherkovski, Neeli, **Supp. XII:** 118, 132, 134
Chernyshevski, Nikolai, **III:** 261, 262, 263; **Retro. Supp. I:** 269
Cherokee Lottery, The: A Sequence of Poems (W. J. Smith), **Supp. XIII: 340–344**
"Cherríe Moraga's Radical Revision of Death of a Salesman"(Wiley), **Supp. XXIII:** 199
Cherry (Karr), **Supp. XI:** 239, **251–254**
"Cherrylog Road" (Dickey), **Supp. XVIII:** 191
Cherry Orchard, The (Chekhov), **IV:** 359, 426; **Supp. VIII:** 153
Cheslock, Louis, **III:** 99, 118, 119
Chesnutt, Charles Waddell, **Supp. II Part 1:** 174, 193, 211; **Supp. IV Part 1:** 257; **Supp. XIV: 57–78**
"Chess House, The" (Dixon), **Supp. XII:** 139
Chessman, Caryl, **Supp. I Part 2:** 446
Chester, Alfred, **Retro. Supp. II:** 111, 112; **Supp. X:** 192
Chesterfield, Lord, **II:** 36
Chesterton, Gilbert Keith, **I:** 226; **IV:** 432
Cheuse, Alan, **Supp. IV Part 2:** 570
Chevigny, Bell Gale, **Supp. XI:** 283
Cheyenne Autumn (Sandoz), **Supp. XXIII:** 146; **Supp. XXIV:** 244, 248, 256, **258–260**
"Chicago" (Sandburg), **III:** 581, 592, 596; **Supp. III Part 1:** 71
Chicago (Shepard), **Supp. III Part 2:** 439
Chicago: City on the Make (Algren), **Supp. IX:** 1, 3
"Chicago Defender Sends a Man to Little Rock, The" (Brooks), **Supp. III Part 1:** 80–81
"Chicago Hamlet, A" (Anderson), **I:** 112
Chicago Loop (Theroux), **Supp. VIII:** 324
"Chicago Picasso, The" (Brooks), **Supp. III Part 1:** 70–71, 84
Chicago Poems (Sandburg), **III:** 579, 581–583, 586
"Chicano/Borderlands Literature and Poetry" (Ríos), **Supp. IV Part 2:** 537, 538, 542, 545
Chicano! The History of the Mexican American Civil Rights Movement (Rosales), **Supp. XXV:** 133
Chick, Nancy, **Supp. IV Part 1:** 1
"Chickamauga" (Bierce), **I:** 201
"Chickamauga" (Wolfe), **IV:** 460
Chickamauga (Wright), **Supp. V:** 333, 343–344
"Chickamauga" (Wright), **Supp. V:** 334
"Chicken Market" (Skloot), **Supp. XX: 198, 200**
"Chiefly about War Matters" (Hawthorne), **II:** 227; **Retro. Supp. I:** 165
"Chiffon" (Hull), **Supp. XXI:** 138
"Child" (Plath), **Supp. I Part 2:** 544
Child, Greg, **Supp. XVIII:** 107
Child, Julia, **Supp. XVII:** 89, 90
Child, Lydia Maria, **Supp. XIII:** 141; **Supp. XVIII:** 11
"Child, The" (Ríos), **Supp. IV Part 2:** 543
"Child by Tiger, The" (Wolfe), **IV:** 451
"Childhood" (Wright), **Supp. V:** 341
Childhood, A: The Biography of a Place (Crews), **Supp. XI:** 102–103, 245
"Childhood, When You Are in It . . ." (Kenyon), **Supp. VII:** 160, 170
Childhood and Other Neighborhoods (Dybek), **Supp. XXIII:** 68, **69–70**
"Childhood Sketch" (Wright), **Supp. III Part 2:** 589
"Child Is Born, A" (Benét), **Supp. XI:** 46
"Child Is the Meaning of This Life, The" (Schwartz), **Supp. II Part 2:** 659–660
"Childlessness" (Merrill), **Supp. III Part 1:** 323
"Childless Woman" (Plath), **Supp. I Part 2:** 544
Child-Life (Whittier and Larcom, eds.), **Supp. XIII:** 142
Child-Life in Prose (Whittier and Larcom, eds.), **Supp. XIII:** 142
Childlike Life of the Black Tarantula, The (Acker), **Supp. XII:** 4, 6, **7–8**
"Child Margaret" (Sandburg), **III:** 584
"Child of Courts, The" (Jarrell), **II:** 378, 379, 381
Child of God (McCarthy), **Supp. VIII: 177–178**
Child of My Heart (McDermott), **Supp. XVIII:** 155, **164–166**
Child of the Century, A (Hecht), **Supp. XXV:** 29; **Supp. XXVII:** 83, 84, 91, 95, 96
"CHILD OF THE THIRTIES" (Baraka), **Supp. II Part 1:** 60
"Child on Top of a Greenhouse" (Roethke), **III:** 531
Children (Gurney), **Supp. V:** 95, 96
"Children" (Stowe), **Supp. I Part 2:** 587
"Children, The" (Jarman), **Supp. XVII:** 116
Children, The (Wharton), **IV:** 321, 326; **Retro. Supp. I:** 381
"Children, the Sandbar, That Summer" (Rukeyser), **Supp. VI:** 274
Children and Others (Cozzens), **I:** 374
Children Is All (Purdy), **Supp. VII:** 277, 278, 282
"Children of Adam" (Whitman), **IV:** 342; **Retro. Supp. I:** 403, 405; **Retro. Supp. III:** 302, 308
Children of Job, The: American Second-Generation Witnesses to the Holocaust (A. Berger), **Supp. XVII:** 39
Children of Light (Stone), **Supp. V:** 304–306
Children of Light and the Children of Darkness, The (Niebuhr), **III:** 292, 306, 310
"Children of the Dirty War" (Goldman), **Supp. XXV:** 52
Children of the Frost (London), **II:** 469, 483
Children of the Holocaust (H. Epstein), **Supp. XVII:** 48; **Supp. XXII:** 95
"Children of the Lord's Supper, The" (Tegnér), **Retro. Supp. II:** 155, 157
Children of the Market Place (Masters), **Supp. I Part 2:** 471
"Children on Their Birthdays" (Capote), **Supp. III Part 1:** 114, 115
Children Playing Before a Statue of Hercules (Sedaris, ed.), **Supp. XXIII:** 289
"Children Selecting Books in a Library" (Jarrell), **II:** 371
Children's Hour, The (Hellman), **Supp. I Part 1:** 276–277, 281, 286, 297
"Children's Rhymes" (Hughes), **Supp. I Part 1:** 340
Childress, Mark, **Supp. X:** 89
Child's Garden of Verses, A (Stevenson), **Supp. IV Part 1:** 298, 314; **Supp. XIII:** 75
"Child's Nature, A" (Jin), **Supp. XVIII:** 93
"Child's Reminiscence, A" (Whitman), **IV:** 344
Childwold (Oates), **Supp. II Part 2:** 519–520

Chile Woman (G. Jones), **Supp. XXIV:** 185
Chill, The (Macdonald), **Supp. IV Part 2:** 473
Chills and Fever (Ransom), **III:** 490, 491–492, 493
Chilly Scenes of Winter (Beattie), **Supp. V:** 21, 22, 23, 24, 26, 27
Chime of Words, A: The Letters of Logan Pearsall Smith (Tribble, ed.), **Supp. XIV:** 348–349
Chimera (C. Frost), **Supp. XV:** 94, 95, 100
"Chimes for Yahya" (Merrill), **Supp. III Part 1:** 329
Chin, Frank, **Supp. V:** 164, 172
Chin, Mei, **Supp. XVIII:** 95
"China" (C. Johnson), **Supp. VI: 193–194**
Chinaberry Tree, The (Fauset), **Supp. XIX:** 73
"Chinaman's Hat" (Kingston), **Supp. V:** 169
China Men (Kingston), **Supp. V:** 157, 158, 159, 160, 161, 164–169; **Supp. X:** 292; **Supp. XV:** 220
"China Poet, The" (Sturgis), **Supp. XX: 233, 240**
China Trace (Wright), **Supp. V:** 332, 340, 341, 342
"Chinese Apples" (Di Piero), **Supp. XIX:** 40
Chinese Apples: New and Selected Poems (Di Piero), **Supp. XIX:** 33, 36, 37, 38, 39, 40, 44, 45, 46, 47–48
Chinese Classics (Legge), **III:** 472
Chinese Materia Medica (P. Smith), **III:** 572
"Chinese New Year" (Hull), **Supp. XXI:** 135
"Chinese Nightingale, The" (Lindsay), **Supp. I Part 2:** 392–393, 394
Chinese Nightingale and Other Poems, The (Lindsay), **Supp. I Part 2:** 392
Chinese Siamese Cat, The (Tan), **Supp. X:** 289
Chinese Translations, The (Bynner), **Supp. XV:** 47, 52
Chinitz, David, **Supp. XV:** 180, 185
"Chinoiseries" (A. Lowell), **II:** 524–525
Chip (Untermeyer), **Supp. XV:** 310
"Chipeta, Widow of Chief Ouray with a Word About a Deal in Blankets" (Zitkala-Ša), **Supp. XXV:** 281
"Chippings with a Chisel" (Hawthorne), **Retro. Supp. III:** 120
Chirico, Giorgio de, **Supp. III Part 1:** 14
Chirico, Miriam M., **Supp. XV:** 323
"Chiron" (Winters), **Supp. II Part 2:** 801
"Chitlins at the Waldorf" (Crouch), **Supp. XIX:** 158
"Chloroform Jags" (J. Scott), **Supp. XVII:** 189
"Chocklit Geography: Raymond Andrews's Mythical South" (Harris), **Supp. XXVI:** 14
Chodorov, Jerome, **IV:** 274
"Choice, The" (Karr), **Supp. XI:** 251
"Choice of Accommodations, A" (Lahiri), **Supp. XXI:** 183
"Choice of Profession, A" (Malamud), **Supp. I Part 2:** 437
Choice of Wars, A (Shaw), **Supp. XIX:** 245
"Choices" (Gallagher), **Supp. XXIV:** 171
Chomei, Kamo No, **IV:** 170, 171, 184
Chomsky, Noam, **Supp. IV Part 2:** 679
"Choose Something Like a Star" (Frost), **Retro. Supp. III:** 105
Choosing not Choosing (Cameron), **Retro. Supp. I:** 43
Chopin, Felix, **Supp. I Part 1:** 202
Chopin, Frédéric, **Supp. I Part 1:** 363
Chopin, Jean, **Supp. I Part 1:** 206
Chopin, Kate, **II:** 276; **Retro. Supp. I:** 10, 215; **Retro. Supp. II: 57–74; Supp. I Part 1: 200–226; Supp. V:** 304; **Supp. X:** 227; **Supp. XVIII:** 194
"Chopin in Winter"(Dybek), **Supp. XXIII:** 72
"Choral: The Pink Church" (W. C. Williams), **Retro. Supp. I:** 428
"Chord" (Merwin), **Supp. III Part 1:** 356
"Chord"(Dybek), **Supp. XXIII:** 78
"Chords and Dischords" (column; Untermeyer), **Supp. XV:** 294
"Chorus, The"(Hadas), **Supp. XXIII:** 119–120
Choruses from Iphigenia in Aulis (Doolittle, trans.), **Supp. I Part 1:** 257, 268, 269
Chosen, The (Potok), **Supp. XXVI:** 125
"Chosen Blindness" (Karr), **Supp. XI:** 251
Chosen Country (Dos Passos), **I:** 475, 490–491
Chosen Place, The Timeless People, The (Marshall), **Supp. XI:** 275, 276, **282–284**
Chosön (P. Lowell), **II:** 513
Choukri, Mohamed, **Supp. IV Part 1:** 92
Chovteau, Mane Thérèse, **Supp. I Part 1:** 205
Chris Durang and Dawne (Durang), **Supp. XXIV:** 113, 124
"ChrisEaster" (Peacock), **Supp. XIX:** 198, 199
Chrisman, Robert, **Supp. IV Part 1:** 1
Christabel (Coleridge), **Supp. IV Part 2:** 465
"Christ for Sale" (R. Lowell), **II:** 538
Christgau, Robert, **Supp. XXVII: 33–47**
Christian, Graham, **Supp. XII:** 193
Christian Dictionary, A (Wilson), **IV:** 153
"Christian in World Crisis, The" (Merton), **Supp. VIII:** 203
Christianity and Power Politics (Niebuhr), **III:** 292, 303
"Christianity and the Survival of Creation" (Berry), **Supp. X:** 30
Christianity of Sholem Asch, The: An Appraisal from the Jewish Viewpoint (Lieberman), **Supp. XXIII:** 3, 7
"Christian Minister, The" (Emerson), **II:** 10
Christian Philosopher, The (Mather), **Supp. II Part 2:** 463–464
Christian Realism and Practical Problems (Niebuhr), **III:** 292, 308
"Christian Roommates, The" (Updike), **IV:** 226–227; **Retro. Supp. I:** 319, 323
Christian Science (Twain), **Retro. Supp. III:** 268
Christiansen, Carrie, **I:** 210
Christian's Secret of a Happy Life, The (H. W. Smith), **Supp. XIV:** 333–334
Christie, Agatha, **Supp. IV Part 1:** 341; **Supp. IV Part 2:** 469
Christ in Concrete (di Donato), **Supp. XX: 33, 34–40, 42, 43, 46**
"Christ in Concrete" (di Donato), **Supp. XX: 34**
Christine (King), **Supp. V:** 139, 148
"Christ Light, The" (Chopin), **Retro. Supp. II:** 61
"Christmas" (Saunders), **Supp. XIX:** 232
"Christmas, or the Good Fairy" (Stowe), **Supp. I Part 2:** 586
"Christmas 1944" (Levertov), **Supp. III Part 1:** 274
"Christmas Banquet, The" (Hawthorne), **II:** 227; **Retro. Supp. III:** 120
Christmas Card, A (Theroux), **Supp. VIII:** 322
Christmas Carol, A (Dickens), **Retro.**

Supp. I: 196; **Supp. I Part 2:** 409–410; **Supp. X:** 252, 253; **Supp. XXV:** 149, 152
Christmas Carollin' (Wells), **Supp. XXVI:** 275
"Christmas Eve at Johnson's Drugs N Goods" (Bambara), **Supp. XI:** 11–12
"Christmas Eve in the Time of War: A Capitalist Meditates by a Civil War Monument" (R. Lowell), **II:** 538
"Christmas Eve under Hooker's Statue" (R. Lowell), **II:** 539–540
"Christmas Gift" (Warren), **IV:** 252–253
"Christmas Greeting, A" (Wright), **Supp. III Part 2:** 601
"Christmas Hymn, A" (Wilbur), **Supp. III Part 2:** 557
Christmas Memory, A (Capote), **Supp. III Part 1:** 118, 119, 129
"Christmass Poem" (West), **Retro. Supp. II:** 338
Christmas Story (Mencken), **III:** 111
"Christmas to Me" (Lee), **Supp. VIII:** 113
Christographia (Taylor), **IV:** 164–165
Christ on a Clothesline (Loy), **Supp. XXII:** 168
"Christ on the Cross/Nuestro Señor Crucificado" (Mora), **Supp. XIII:** 229
Christopher, Mary (pseudonym). See West, Dorothy
Christopher and His Kind: 1929–1939 (Isherwood), **Supp. XIV:** 157, 163, 164, 171
"Christopher Cat" (Cullen), **Supp. IV Part 1:** 173
Christopher Columbus, Mariner (Morison), **Supp. I Part 2:** 488
Christopher Isherwood: A Critical Biography (Finney), **Supp. XIV:** 158
Christophersen, Bill, **Supp. IX:** 159, 167; **Supp. XI:** 155; **Supp. XIII:** 87; **Supp. XXI:** 103
"Christ's Passion" (Karr), **Supp. XI:** 251
Christus: A Mystery (Longfellow), **II:** 490, 493, 495, 505–507; **Retro. Supp. II:** 161, 165, 166
Chroma (F. Barthelme), **Supp. XI:** 30, 33, 34
"Chroma" (F. Barthelme), **Supp. XI:** 31
"Chronicle" (W. Stone), **Supp. XXVII:** 255
"Chronicle of Race Relations, A" (Du Bois), **Supp. II Part 1:** 182
Chronicle of the Conquest of Granada (Irving), **II:** 310
Chronicles: Volume One (Dylan), **Supp. XVIII:** 20, 21, 23, 24, 28, **32–33**
"Chronologues" (Goldbarth), **Supp. XII:** 183, 184
"Chrysanthemums, The" (Steinbeck), **IV:** 53
"Chrysaor" (Longfellow), **II:** 498
Chu, Louis, **Supp. X:** 291
Chuang, Hua, **Supp. X:** 291
Chuang-Tzu, **Supp. VIII:** 206
"Chunk of Amethyst, A" (R. Bly), **Supp. IV Part 1:** 72
Church, Margaret, **IV:** 466
"Church and the Fiction Writer, The" (O'Connor), **Retro. Supp. II:** 223, 233; **Supp. XVIII:** 161
"Church Going" (Larkin), **Supp. XXI:** 93
"Churchgoing" (Nelson), **Supp. XVIII:** 173
Churchill, Charles, **Supp. XV:** 232
Churchill, Winston, **I:** 9, 490; **Supp. I Part 2:** 491
Church of Dead Girls, The (Dobyns), **Supp. XIII:** 75, **83–84**
"Church of Omnivorous Light, The" (Wrigley), **Supp. XVIII:** 306–307
"Church of the Latter Day Saints, The" (Mosher), **Supp. XXII:** 208
"Church Porch, The" (Herbert), **IV:** 153
Church Psalmody, Selected from Dr. Watts and Other Authors (Mason and Greene, ed.), **I:** 458
Ciannic, Saint, **II:** 215
Ciano, Edda, **IV:** 249
Ciardi, John, **I:** 169, 179, 535; **III:** 268; **Supp. IV Part 1:** 243; **Supp. IV Part 2:** 639; **Supp. IX:** 269, 324; **Supp. XII:** 119
Cicada (Haines), **Supp. XII: 206–207**
"Cicadas" (Wilbur), **Supp. III Part 2:** 549
Cicero, **I:** 279; **II:** 8, 14–15; **III:** 23; **Supp. I Part 2:** 405
Cider House Rules, The (Irving), **Supp. VI:** 164, **173–175**
"Cigales" (Wilbur), **Supp. III Part 2:** 549
"Cigarette" (L. Michaels), **Supp. XVI:** 214
Cigarette Book, The (Brainard), **Supp. XXVII:** 20
Cimarron, Rose (Burke), **Supp. XIV:** 22, 35
"Cimetière Marin, Le" (Valéry), **IV:** 91–92
Cimino, Michael, **Supp. X:** 126
Cincinnati Kid, The (film), **Supp. XI: 306**
"Cinderella" (Jarrell), **II:** 386
"Cinderella" (Perrault), **IV:** 266, 267
"Cinderella" (Sexton), **Supp. II Part 2:** 691
"Cinema, The" (Salter), **Supp. IX:** 257
Cinema of Tony Richardson, The: Essays and Interviews (Phillips), **Supp. XI:** 306
Cinthio, **IV:** 370
Ciolkowski, Laura, **Supp. XVI:** 24
CIOPW (Cummings), **I:** 429
"Circe" (Welty), **Retro. Supp. I:** 353
Circle Game, The (Atwood), **Supp. XIII:** 20, 33
Circle in the Dirt (Moraga), **Supp. XXIII:** 195, 202
"Circle in the Fire, A" (O'Connor), **III:** 344–345, 349–350, 351, 353, 354; **Retro. Supp. II:** 229, 232
"Circle of Breath" (Stafford), **Supp. XI:** 318, 322
Circle of Hanh, The (Weigl), **Supp. XIX:** 273, 275, 282, **284–286**
"Circles" (Emerson), **I:** 455, 460
"Circles" (R. Lowell), **II:** 554
Circular Staircase, The (Rinehart), **Supp. XXV:** 189, 192, 200
Circumference: Varieties of Metaphysical Verse 1456–1928 (Taggard, ed.), **Supp. XXII:** 279
"Circus" (Huddle), **Supp. XXVI:** 150
"Circus, The" (Porter), **III:** 443, 445
"Circus Animals' Desertion" (Yeats), **I:** 389
Circus Fire, The (O'Nan), **Supp. XXV:** 153
"Circus in the Attic" (Warren), **IV:** 253
Circus in the Attic, The (Warren), **IV:** 243, 251–253
"Circus in Three Rings" (Plath), **Retro. Supp. II:** 243; **Supp. I Part 2:** 536
Circus of Needs, A (Dunn), **Supp. XI: 147–148**
"Cirque d'Hiver" (Bishop), **Supp. I Part 1:** 85
Cisneros, Sandra, **Supp. IV Part 2:** 544; **Supp. VII: 57–73; Supp. XI:** 177; **Supp. XVII:** 71; **Supp. XXII:** 177; **Supp. XXV:** 133
Cities of the Interior (Nin), **Supp. X:** 182
Cities of the Plain (McCarthy), **Supp. VIII:** 175, **186–187**
Cities of the Red Night (Burroughs), **Supp. III Part 1:** 106
"Citizen Cain" (Baraka), **Supp. II Part 1:** 49

Citizen Kane (film), **Retro. Supp. I:** 115; **Supp. V:** 251; **Supp. XI:** 169
"Citizen of the World" (Goldsmith), **II:** 299
Citizens (Levin), **Supp. XXVII:** 133, 134, 139, 142, 143–144
Citro, Joseph, **Supp. XXII:** 208, 218
"City" (Francis), **Supp. IX:** 87
"City, The" (Stallings), **Supp. XXV:** 233
"City and Country"(Hadas), **Supp. XXIII:** 115, 116
City and the Island, The (Davison), **Supp. XXVI:** 65, 70–71
City and the Pillar, The (Vidal), **Supp. IV Part 2:** 677, 680–681; **Supp. XIV:** 170
"City and the Pillar, The, as Gay Fiction" (Summers), **Supp. IV Part 2:** 680–681
"City Articles" series (Briggs), **Supp. XVIII:** 12
City Block (W. Frank), **Supp. XX: 71, 72, 76**
City Boy (L. Michaels), **Supp. XVI:** 212
"City Boy" (L. Michaels), **Supp. XVI:** 203–204
City Boy (Thompson), **Supp. XXIII:** 294**, 298–299**
City Boy, The (Wouk), **Supp. XXV:** 256, 259
City Dog (Di Piero), **Supp. XIX:** 33–34, 35, 38, 46, 48
"City Dog" (Di Piero), **Supp. XIX:** 47
City in History, The (Mumford), **Supp. II Part 2:** 495
"City in the Sea, The" (Poe), **III:** 411; **Retro. Supp. II:** 274
City in Which I Love You, The (L.-Y. Lee), **Supp. XV:** 212, **215–220**
"City in Which I Love You, The" (L.-Y. Lee), **Supp. XV:** 215, **217–218**
City in Winter, A (Helprin), **Supp. XXV:** 84, 87
City Life (Barthelme), **Supp. IV Part 1:** 44, 47
City of Bones (Connelly), **Supp. XXI: 74–75,** 77
"City of Change, A" (Bynner), **Supp. XV:** 45
City of Dreadful Night (Siegel), **Supp. XXII:** 258
City of Glass (Auster), **Supp. XII:** 22, **24–26**
City of God, The (St. Augustine), **IV:** 126
City of Names (Brockmeier), **Supp. XXII:** 55–56, 57
"City of Refuge, The" (R. Fisher), **Supp. XIX:** 65, 66, **67–68**
City of Refuge, The: The Collected Stories of Rudolph Fisher (McCluskey, ed.), **Supp. XIX:** 68–69
City of the Living and Other Stories, The (Stegner), **Supp. IV Part 2:** 599, 609, 613
City of Words: American Fiction 1950-1970 (T. Tanner), **Supp. XVI:** 69
City of Your Final Destination, The (Cameron), **Supp. XII:** 79, 82, **91–94**
"City on a Hill" (R. Lowell), **II: 552**
City on a Hill: Testing the American Dream at City College (Traub), **Supp. XXIV:** 221
"City Person Encountering Nature, A" (Kingston), **Supp. V:** 170
"City Planners, The" (Atwood), **Supp. XIII:** 33
"City Winter, A"(O'Hara), **Supp. XXIII:** 210
City Winter and Other Poems, A (O'Hara), **Supp. XXIII:** 210, 214
City Without Men (film), **Supp. XVIII:** 247
City Without Walls (Auden), **Supp. II Part 1:** 24
Civil Disobedience (Thoreau), **IV:** 185; **Supp. I Part 2:** 507
Civilization in the United States (Stearns), **I:** 245
"Civil Rights" (Lanier), **Supp. I Part 1:** 357
CivilWarLand in Bad Decline (Saunders), **Supp. XIX: 224–227**
"CivilWarLand in Bad Decline" (Saunders), **Supp. XIX:** 224–225, 227
Civitatis Anthology of African American Slave Narratives, The (H. L. Gates and Andrews, eds.), **Supp. XX: 105**
Cixous, Hélène, **Supp. X:** 102; **Supp. XIII:** 297; **Supp. XV:** 347
Clabough, Casey, **Supp. XXIV:** 194
Claiborne, Craig, **Supp. XVII:** 89
Claiborne, William, **I:** 132
"Claim, The"(Balakian), **Supp. XXIII:** 20
Claiming an Identity They Taught Me to Despise (Cliff), **Supp. XXII:** 66, 67–68, 70
Claiming of Sleeping Beauty, The (Rice), **Supp. VII:** 301
Claman, Emily Rosamund, **Supp. XXVI:** 175
Clampitt, Amy, **Supp. IX: 37–54; Supp. X:** 120; **Supp. XI:** 249; **Supp. XV:** 251, 256
Clancy's Wake, At (Crane), **I:** 422
"Clandeboye" (Leopold), **Supp. XIV:** 189
"Clara" (Hecht), **Supp. XXVII:** 95
Clara Howard; or, The Enthusiasm of Love (Brown), **Supp. I Part 1:** 145
Clara's Ole Man (Bullins), **Supp. II Part 1:** 42
Clara Wharton (Hayden), **Supp. XXV:** 38
Clare, John, **II:** 387; **III:** 528; **Supp. XVI:** 295
Clarel: A Poem and Pilgrimage in the Holy Land (Melville), **Retro. Supp. I:** 257; **Retro. Supp. III:** 149, 161
Clarence Major and His Art (Bell), **Supp. XXII:** 182
Clarissa (Richardson), **II:** 111; **Supp. I Part 2:** 714; **Supp. V:** 127; **Supp. XV:** 231; **Supp. XX: 236**
Clarissa Harlow (Richardson), **Supp. XXV:** 39
Clark, Alex, **Supp. XII:** 307
Clark, Charles, **I:** 470
Clark, Eleanor. See Warren, Mrs. Robert Penn (Eleanor Clark)
Clark, Francis Edward, **II:** 9
Clark, Geoffrey, **Supp. XI:** 342
Clark, Harry Hayden, **Supp. I Part 2:** 423
Clark, John Bates, **Supp. I Part 2:** 633
Clark, Kenneth, **Supp. XIV:** 342, 348; **Supp. XIX:** 151
Clark, Lewis Gaylord, **Supp. XVIII:** 4, 7, 8
Clark, Shirley, **Supp. XXI:** 22
Clark, Thomas, **Supp. III Part 2:** 629; **Supp. IV Part 1:** 140, 145, 147
Clark, Tom, **Supp. XXIV:** 36, 37, 41, 44
Clark, Walter, **Supp. XI:** 315
Clark, William, **III:** 14; **IV:** 179, 283
Clark, Willis Gaylord, **Supp. I Part 2:** 684
Clarke, Brock, **Supp. XXIII:** 109
Clarke, James Freeman, **Supp. II Part 1:** 280; **Supp. XXV:** 250
Clarke, John, **Supp. IV Part 1:** 8
Clarke, John J., **III:** 356
Clarke, Samuel, **II:** 108
Clark Lectures, **Retro. Supp. I:** 65
Claros varones de Belken (Hinojosa). See Fair Gentlemen of Belken County (Hinojosa)
Clash by Night (film), **Supp. XXVI:** 134
Clash by Night (Odets), **Supp. II Part 2:** 531, 538, 544–546, 550, 551

Classical Tradition, The (Highet), **Supp. I Part 1:** 268
Classic Ballroom Dances (Simic), **Supp. VIII:** 271, **276–278,** 283
Classics (Hadas), **Supp. XXIII: 124**
Classics and Commercials: A Literary Chronicle of the Forties (Wilson), **IV:** 433
"Classics"(Hadas), **Supp. XXIII:** 124
"CLASS STRUGGLE" (Baraka), **Supp. III Part 1:** 55
"Claude Glass, The: 1890" (Bierds), **Supp. XVII:** 27
Claudel, Paul, **I:** 60
Claudelle Inglish (Caldwell), **I:** 304
Clavel, Marcel, **I:** 343
"CLAY" (Baraka), **Supp. II Part 1:** 54
Clay, Henry, **I:** 8; **Supp. I Part 2:** 684, 686
Clay's Ark (O. Butler), **Supp. XIII:** 63
Clayton, John J., **Supp. IV Part 1:** 238
Clayton, Sarah Turner, **Supp. XXV:** 251
"Clean, Well Lighted Place, A" (Hemingway), **Retro. Supp. I:** 181
"Clear, with Light Variable Winds" (A. Lowell), **II:** 522
"Clear Days" (White), **Supp. I Part 2:** 664, 665
Clearing (Berry), **Supp. X:** 22
"Clearing, A" (Simpson), **Supp. IX:** 280
"Clearing, The" (Kenyon), **Supp. VII:** 174
"Clearing the Title" (Merrill), **Supp. III Part 1:** 336
"Clearing Up the Question of Stesichoros' Blinding by Helen" (Carson), **Supp. XII:** 107–108
"Clear Morning" (Glück), **Supp. V:** 88
"Clearness" (Wilbur), **Supp. III Part 2:** 544, 550
"Clear Night" (Wright), **Supp. V:** 341
Clear Pictures: First Loves, First Guides (Price), **Supp. VI:** 253, 254, 255, 256, 265
Clear Springs (Mason), **Supp. VIII:** 134–136, 137–138, 139, 147
Cleary, Rebecca Lauck, **Supp. XVIII:** 195
Cleaver, Eldridge, **Retro. Supp. II:** 12; **Supp. IV Part 1:** 206; **Supp. X:** 249
"Cleaving, The" (L.-Y. Lee), **Supp. XV:** 215, **218–220**
Cleland, John, **Supp. V:** 48, 127
Clemenceau, Georges, **I:** 490
"Clemency" (Wrigley), **Supp. XVIII:** 307–308
Clemens, Jane, **I:** 247
Clemens, Orion, **IV:** 193, 195
Clemens, Samuel Langhorne. See Twain, Mark
Clemens, Mrs. Samuel Langhorne (Olivia Langdon), **I:** 197, 208, 247; **Supp. I Part 2:** 457
Clemens, Susie, **IV:** 208
Clementine Recognitions (novel), **Supp. IV Part 1:** 280
Clements, Colin Campbell, **Supp. XVI:** 190
Clemons, Walter, **Supp. IV Part 1:** 305, 307
Cleopatra, **III:** 44; **IV:** 373; **Supp. I Part 1:** 114
"Clepsydra" (Ashbery), **Supp. III Part 1:** 10–15
"Clerks, The" (Robinson), **III:** 517–518
"Cleveland" (Halliday), **Supp. XIX:** 90
Cleveland, Carol, **Supp. IX:** 120, 125
Cleveland, Ceil, **Supp. V:** 222
Cleveland, Grover, **II:** 126, 128, 129, 130, 137, 138; **Supp. I Part 2:** 486
"Clever Magician Carrying My Heart, A" (Salinas), **Supp. XIII:** 323
Cliff, Michelle, **Retro. Supp. III:** 242; **Supp. XXII: 65–80**
"Cliff, The" (C. Baxter), **Supp. XVII:** 16–17
Clifford, Craig, **Supp. IX:** 99
Clift, Montgomery, **III:** 161
Clifton, Lucille, **Supp. XVIII:** 177
Climate of Monastic Prayer, The (Merton), **Supp. VIII:** 205, 207
Climb, The (Boukreev), **Supp. XVIII:** 112
"Climber, The" (Mason), **Supp. VIII:** 140–141
Climbing High: A Woman's Account of Surviving the Everest Tragedy (Gammelgaard), **Supp. XVIII:** 112
"Climbing the Tower" (Crews), **Supp. XI:** 102
Clinton, De Witt, **I:** 338
"Clipped Wings" (H. Miller), **III:** 176–177
Clippinger, David, **Supp. XXI:** 24
Clive, Robert, **Supp. I Part 2:** 505
Clock Winder, The (Tyler), **Supp. IV Part 2:** 661–662, 670
Clock Without Hands (McCullers), **II:** 587–588, 604–606
Clockwork Orange, A (Burgess), **Supp. XIII:** 29
Clorindy (Cook), **Supp. II Part 1:** 199
"Close, The" (Jarman), **Supp. XVII:** 113
"Close Calls" (Wolff), **Supp. VII:** 332–333
"Closed Book, A" (Mosley), **Supp. XIII:** 237
"Closed for Good" (Frost), **Retro. Supp. III:** 105
Close Quarters (Heinemann), **Supp. XXII:** 103, **104–109,** 111, 115
Close Range: Wyoming Stories (Proulx), **Supp. VII:** 261–265
"Close Reading: Windows"(Hirshfield), **Supp. XXIII:** 131
Closers, The (Connelly), **Supp. XXI: 76–77**
Closest Possible Union, The (J. Scott), **Supp. XVII: 185–186,** 188, 191
"Closet, The" (Goodman), **Supp. XXVI:** 121
Close the Book (Glaspell), **Supp. III Part 1:** 179
"Close the Book" (R. Lowell), **II:** 554
Close to Me & Closer ... (The Language of Heaven) and Désamère (Notley), **Supp. XXII:** 234
Close to Shore: A True Story of Terror in an Age of Innocence (Capuzzo), **Supp. XIII:** 254
Closet Writing & Gay Reading: The Case of Melville's Pierre (Creech), **Retro. Supp. I:** 254
Closing Circle, The (Commoner), **Supp. XIII:** 264
Closing of the American Mind, The (Bloom), **Retro. Supp. II:** 19, 30, 31
"Closing of the Rodeo, The" (W. J. Smith), **Supp. XIII:** 332
Closing Time (Heller), **Supp. IV Part 1:** 382, 386, 391–394
Closset, Marie, **Supp. VIII:** 251, 265
Clotel (Brown), **Supp. XXIII:** 184
"Cloud, The" (Shelley), **Supp. I Part 2:** 720
"Cloud and Fame" (Berryman), **I:** 173
Cloud Atlas (D. Mitchell), **Supp. XXIV:** 86
Cloud Forest, The: A Chronicle of the South American Wilderness (Matthiessen), **Supp. V:** 202, 204
"Cloud on the Way, The" (Bryant), **Supp. I Part 1:** 171
"Cloud River" (Wright), **Supp. V:** 341
"Clouds" (Levine), **Supp. V:** 184
Cloudsplitter (Banks), **Supp. V:** 16
"Clover" (Lanier), **Supp. I Part 1:** 362–364
Clover and Other Poems (Lanier), **Supp. I Part 1:** 362
"Clown" (Corso), **Supp. XII:** 127
Clown in the Belfry, The: Writings on

Faith and Fiction (Buechner), **Supp. XII:** 53
Cluck, Julia, **Supp. I Part 2:** 728
Clue, The (Wells), **Supp. XXVI:** 277
Clue of the Eyelash, The (Wells), **Supp. XXVI:** 280
Clum, John M., **Supp. XIII:** **200,** 201, 209
Cluny, Hugo, **IV:** 290
Clurman, Harold, **I:** 93; **IV:** 381, 385
Clytus, Radiclani, **Supp. XIII:** 128, **Supp. XIII:** 129, 132
"C.O." (Wrigley), **Supp. XVIII:** 298
"Coal: Beginning and End" (Winters), **Supp. II Part 2:** 791
Coale, Howard, **Supp. XIII:** 15
Coale, Samuel, **Retro. Supp. III:** 111
"Coals" (Hoffman), **Supp. XVIII:** 86
Coalwood Way, The (Hickam), **Supp. XXVII:** 106, 107–108
"Coast, The" (column), **Supp. IV Part 1:** 198
"Coast Guard's Cottage, The" (Wylie), **Supp. I Part 2:** 723
Coast of Chicago, The (Dybek), **Supp. XXIII:** **72–74,** 75
Coast of Trees, A (Ammons), **Supp. VII:** 24, 34
"Coast-Range Christ, The" (Jeffers), **Supp. II Part 2:** 414, 419
"Coast-Road, The" (Jeffers), **Supp. II Part 2:** 425
"Coat, The" (Everwine), **Supp. XV:** 80
Coates, Joseph, **Supp. VIII:** 80; **Supp. XXII:** 205
Coates, Robert, **I:** 54; **IV:** 298
"Coatlicue's Rules: Advice from an Aztec Goddess" (Mora), **Supp. XIII:** 223
"Coats" (Kenyon), **Supp. VII:** 172
Coatsworth, Elizabeth Jane, **Supp. XXVI:** 33
Cobb, Lee J., **III:** 153
Cobb, Ty, **III:** 227, 229
Cobbett, William, **Supp. I Part 2:** 517; **Supp. XV:** 237
"Cobbler Keezar's Vision" (Whittier), **Supp. I Part 2:** 699
"Cobweb, The" (Carver), **Supp. III Part 1:** 148
Cobwebs From an Empty Skull (Bierce), **I:** 195
Coccimiglio, Vic, **Supp. XIII:** 114
"Cock-a-Doodle-Doo!" (Melville), **III:** 89
"Cockayne" (Emerson), **II:** 6
"Cock-Crow" (Gordon), **II:** 219
Cock Pit (Cozzens), **I:** 359, 378, 379
Cockpit (Kosinski), **Supp. XII:** 21
Cockpit: A Novel (Kosinski), **Supp. VII:** 215, 223–224, 225
"Cock Robin Takes Refuge in the Storm House" (Snodgrass), **Supp. VI:** 319
Cocktail Hour, The (Gurney), **Supp. V:** 95, 96, 100, 101, 103, 105, 108
Cocktail Hour and Two Other Plays: Another Antigone and The Perfect Party (Gurney), **Supp. V:** 100
Cocktail Party, The (T. S. Eliot), **I:** 571, 582–583; **III:** 21; **Retro. Supp. I:** 65; **Retro. Supp. III:** 70; **Supp. V:** 101, 103
Cocteau, Jean, **III:** 471; **Retro. Supp. I:** 82, 378; **Supp. IV Part 1:** 82; **Supp. XVI:** 135; **Supp. XX:** **236**
"Coda: Wilderness Letter" (Stegner), **Supp. IV Part 2:** 595
"Code, The" (Frost), **Retro. Supp. I:** 121, 128
Codex (Grossman), **Supp. XXV:** 64, 66–68
Codman, Florence, **Supp. II Part 1:** 92, 93
Codman, Ogden, Jr., **Retro. Supp. I:** 362, 363; **Retro. Supp. III:** 277, 280
Codrescu, Andrei, **Supp. XXII:** 155
Cody, William ("Buffalo Bill"), **I:** 440; **III:** 584; **Supp. V:** 230
"Coffee and Sweet Rolls" (Stone), **Supp. XXVII:** 253
"Coffee Lips" (Ferry), **Supp. XXIV:** 153, 162
Coffey, Michael, **Supp. V:** 243; **Supp. XV:** 65; **Supp. XX:** **88**
Coffey, Warren, **III:** 358
Coffin, Charles, **III:** 577
Coffman, Frank, **Supp. XXVII:** 118
Cogan, David J., **Supp. IV Part 1:** 362
Cogan, Joshua, **Supp. XXI:** 247
Cogewea the Half-Blood: A Depiction of the Great Montana Cattle Range (Mourning Dove (Christal Quintasket)), **Supp. XXV:** 285
Coghill, Nevill, **Supp. II Part 1:** 4; **Supp. XIV:** 13
Cohan, George M., **II:** 427; **III:** 401
Cohen, Edward M., **Supp. XVI:** 212
Cohen, Esther, **Supp. XV:** 323
Cohen, Hettie, **Supp. II Part 1:** 30
Cohen, Joshua, **Supp. XXII:** 268
Cohen, Leonard, **Supp. XXVII:** **49–65**
Cohen, Marty, **Supp. X:** 112
Cohen, Norman J., **Supp. IX:** 132, 143
Cohen, Rosetta, **Supp. XV:** 257
Cohen, Sarah Blacher, **Supp. V:** 273
Cohen, Victor, **Supp. XVIII:** 235, 236
"Coherent Decentering: Towards a New Model of the Poetic Self" (A. Finch), **Supp. XVII:** 76
Cohn, Jan, **Supp. XXV:** 192, 200
"Coin" (Goldbarth), **Supp. XII:** 187
Coindreau, Maurice, **III:** 339
Coiner, Constance, **Supp. XIII:** 297, 302
Coit, Lille Hitchcock, **Supp. X:** 103
"Coitus" (Pound), **III:** 466
Coke, Desmond, **Supp. XX:** **235**
Colburn, Nadia Herman, **Supp. XV:** 339, 341, 347
"Cold, The" (Kenyon), **Supp. VII:** 164
"Cold, The" (Winters), **Supp. II Part 2:** 790–791, 809, 811
"Cold-blooded Creatures" (Wylie), **Supp. I Part 2:** 729
Colden, Cadwallader, **Supp. I Part 1:** 250
"Colder the Air, The" (Bishop), **Supp. I Part 1:** 86
Cold Feet (Harrison), **Supp. VIII:** 39
Cold Frame (C. Frost), **Supp. XV:** 93, 96
Cold Ground Was My Bed Last Night (Garrett), **Supp. VII:** 98
"Cold Ground Was My Bed Last Night" (Garrett), **Supp. VII:** 100
"Cold Hill Side, The"(Hadas), **Supp. XXIII:** 121
"Cold Keener" (Hurston), **Retro. Supp. III:** 137
"Cold Night, The" (W. C. Williams), **Retro. Supp. I:** 418
"Cold Plunge into Skin Diving, A" (Knowles), **Supp. XII:** 241
Cold Spring, A (Bishop), **Retro. Supp. II:** 45
Cold Springs Harbor (Yates), **Supp. XI:** 348
Cold War American Poetry, **Supp. V:** 182
Cold War and the Income Tax, The (Wilson), **IV:** 430
Cole, Bruce, **Supp. XX:** **106**
Cole, Goody, **Supp. I Part 2:** 696–697
Cole, Lester, **Retro. Supp. II:** 329
Cole, Nat King, **Retro. Supp. I:** 334; **Supp. X:** 255
Cole, Thomas, **Supp. I Part 1:** 156, 158, 171
Cole, William, **Supp. XIX:** 120
"Coleman" (Karr), **Supp. XI:** 244
Coleman, Wanda, **Supp. XI:** **83–98**
Coleridge, Samuel Taylor, **I:** 283, 284, 447, 522; **II:** 7, 10, 11, 19, 71, 169, 273, 301, 502, 516, 549; **III:** 77, 83–84, 424, 461, 488, 523; **IV:** 74, 173, 250, 349, 453; **Retro. Supp. I:** 65, 308; **Retro. Supp. III:** 44, 109, 233; **Supp. I Part 1:** 31, 311, 349;

Supp. I Part 2: 376, 393, 422; **Supp. IV Part 2:** 422, 465; **Supp. IX:** 38, 50; **Supp. V:** 258; **Supp. XIII:** 139; **Supp. XIV:** 21–22; **Supp. XV:** 250; **Supp. XXI:** 52, 55; **Supp. XXIII:** 231; **Supp. XXIV:** 74
Coles, Katharine, **Supp. IV Part 2:** 630
Coles, Robert, **Supp. XXIV:** 172, 265; **Supp. XXVI:** 250, 252
Colette, Sidonie-Gabrielle, **Supp. VIII:** 40, 171; **Supp. XVI:** 193–194
"Coliseum, The" (Poe), **III:** 411
Collage of Dreams (Spencer), **Supp. X:** 196
"Collapse of Tomorrow, The" (Mumford), **Supp. II Part 2:** 482
"Collected by a Valetudinarian" (E. Stoddard), **Supp. XV:** 286–287
Collected Earlier Poems (Hecht), **Supp. X:** 58, 59
Collected Earlier Poems (W. C. Williams), **Retro. Supp. I:** 414, 428
Collected Earlier Poems 1940–1960 (Levertov), **Supp. III Part 1:** 273, 275
Collected Essays (Tate), **IV:** 133–134
Collected Essays, Volume 2: Literary Criticism (Lovecraft), **Supp. XXV:** 121
Collected Essays of Ralph Ellison, The (Ellison), **Retro. Supp. II:** 119
Collected Essays of Robert Creeley, The (Creeley), **Supp. IV Part 1:** 153, 154
Collected Later Poems (W. C. Williams), **Retro. Supp. I:** 428
Collected Plays (A. Miller), **III:** 158; **Retro. Supp. III:** 165, 166–167
Collected Plays, 1974–1983 (Gurney), **Supp. V:** 99
Collected Poems (Aiken), **I:** 50
Collected Poems (Berrigan), **Supp. XXIV:** 39, 45, 46
Collected Poems (Burke), **I:** 269
Collected Poems (Cummings), **I:** 430, 439, 441
Collected Poems (Doolittle), **Supp. I Part 1:** 264–267, 269
Collected Poems (Frost), **Retro. Supp. I:** 136; **Retro. Supp. III:** 103
Collected Poems (H. Crane), **Retro. Supp. III:** 53
Collected Poems (Hull), **Supp. XXI:** 141
Collected Poems (Kees; Justice, ed.), **Supp. XV:** 134
Collected Poems (Lindsay), **Supp. I Part 2:** 380, 387, 392, 396–397, 400
Collected Poems (Markson), **Supp. XVII:** 143
Collected Poems (Moore), **III:** 194, 215
Collected Poems (O'Hara), **Supp. XXIII:** 207, 211, 220
Collected Poems (Price), **Supp. VI:** 267
Collected Poems (R. Lowell), **Supp. XV:** 20
Collected Poems (Simpson), **Supp. IX:** 279
Collected Poems (W. C. Williams), **IV:** 415; **Retro. Supp. I:** 430
Collected Poems (Winters), **Supp. II Part 2:** 791, 810
Collected Poems (Wright), **Supp. III Part 2:** 602
Collected Poems (Yeats), **Supp. XV:** 152
Collected Poems, 1909–1935 (T. S. Eliot), **I:** 580; **Retro. Supp. I:** 66
Collected Poems, 1909–1962 (T. S. Eliot), **I:** 583; **Retro. Supp. III:** 69
Collected Poems, 1918–1938 (Taggard), **Supp. XXII:** 283
Collected Poems, 1923–1953 (Bogan), **Supp. III Part 1:** 64
Collected Poems, 1936–1976 (Francis), **Supp. IX:** 77, 80, **87**
Collected Poems, The (Stevens), **III:** 273; **IV:** 75, 76, 87, 93; **Retro. Supp. I:** 296, 309
Collected Poems 1917–1952 (MacLeish), **III:** 3, 4, 19
Collected Poems 1921–1931 (W. C. Williams), **Retro. Supp. I:** 422; **Supp. XIV:** 285
Collected Poems 1930–1960 (Eberhart), **I:** 522, 525–526, 540, 541
Collected Poems: 1939–1989 (W. J. Smith), **Supp. XIII:** 332, 340, 343, 345
Collected Poems: 1940–1978 (Shapiro), **Supp. II Part 2:** 703, 717
Collected Poems: 1951–1971 (Ammons), **Supp. VII:** 24, 26–29, 32, 33
Collected Poems: 1956–1976 (Wagoner), **Supp. IX:** 323, **328–329**
Collected Poems of Amy Clampitt, The (Clampitt), **Supp. IX:** 37, 44, 53
Collected Poems of George Garrett (Garrett), **Supp. VII:** 109
Collected Poems of Hart Crane, The (Crane), **I:** 399–402
Collected Poems of James Agee, The (Fitzgerald, ed.), **I:** 27–28
Collected Poems of James T. Farrell, The (Farrell), **II:** 45
Collected Poems of Kay Boyle (Boyle), **Supp. XXIV:** 63
Collected Poems of Langston Hughes, The (Rampersad and Roessel, ed.), **Retro. Supp. I:** 194, 196, 212
Collected Poems of Muriel Rukeyser, The (Rukeyser), **Supp. VI:** 274
Collected Poems of Sara Teasdale, The (Teasdale), **Supp. XXVII:** 287, 294–295
Collected Poems of Thomas Merton, The, **Supp. VIII:** 207, 208
Collected Poetry (Auden), **Supp. II Part 1:** 18
Collected Prose (Wright), **Supp. III Part 2:** 596
Collected Prose, The (Bishop), **Retro. Supp. II:** 51
Collected Recordings (W. C. Williams), **Retro. Supp. I:** 431
Collected Shorter Poems, 1946-1991 (Carruth), **Supp. XVI:** 47
Collected Short Stories, The (Wharton), **Retro. Supp. I:** 362, 363, 366
Collected Sonnets (Millay), **III:** 136–137
Collected Stories (Carver), **Supp. XXIV:** 177
Collected Stories, 1939–1976 (Bowles), **Supp. IV Part 1:** 92
Collected Stories, The (Paley), **Supp. VI:** 218
Collected Stories, The (Price), **Supp. VI:** 266
Collected Stories, The (Theroux), **Supp. VIII:** 318
Collected Stories, The (Wharton), **Retro. Supp. I:** 361
Collected Stories of Amy Hempel, The (Hempel), **Supp. XXI:** 115, 117
Collected Stories of Eudora Welty, The (Welty), **Retro. Supp. I:** 355
Collected Stories of Isaac Bashevis Singer (Singer), **Retro. Supp. II: 307–308**
Collected Stories of Katherine Anne Porter (Porter), **III:** 454
Collected Stories of Peter Taylor (Taylor), **Supp. V:** 314, 320, 323–324, 325, 326
Collected Stories of Richard Yates, The, **Supp. XI:** 349
Collected Stories of Wallace Stegner (Stegner), **Supp. IV Part 2:** 599, 605
Collected Stories of William Faulkner (Faulkner), **II:** 72; **Retro. Supp. I:** 75; **Retro. Supp. III:** 86–87
Collected Stories of William Hum-

phrey, The (Humphrey), **Supp. IX:** 106
Collected Works (Bierce), **I:** 204, 208–210
Collected Works of Buck Rogers in the 25th Century, The (Bradbury), **Supp. IV Part 1:** 101
Collected Works of Edgar Allan Poe (Mabbott, ed.), **Retro. Supp. III:** 237
Collected Writings (Brainard), **Supp. XXVII:** 17, 26–27, 29
Collected Writings, The (Z. Fitzgerald; Bruccoli, ed.), **Supp. IX:** 65, 68
Collecting the Animals (Everwine), **Supp. XV:** 73, 75, **78–81,** 85, 88
Collection of Epigrams, **II:** 111
Collection of Poems, on American Affairs, and a Variety of Other Subjects . . . (Freneau), **Supp. II Part 1:** 274
Collection of Select Aphorisms and Maxims (Palmer), **II:** 111
"Collectors" (Carver), **Supp. III Part 1:** 141–142
Collette, **Supp. XVII:** 86
Collier, John, **Supp. XXI:** 8
Collier, Lucy Wood, **Supp. XXI:** 8
Collier, Michael, **Supp. XVII:** 23, 110
Collingwood, R. G., **I:** 278
Collins, Billy, **Supp. XI:** 143; **Supp. XIV:** 123; **Supp. XVII:** 245; **Supp. XXI: 51–66; Supp. XXIII:** 138
Collins, Brennan, **Supp. XXVI:** 12, 13
Collins, Doug, **Supp. V:** 5
Collins, Eddie, **II:** 416
Collins, L. M., **Supp. XXII:** 7
Collins, Richard, **Supp. XI:** 171
Collins, Ronald, **Supp. XXI:** 24
Collins, Wilkie, **Supp. I Part 1:** 35, 36; **Supp. IV Part 1:** 341; **Supp. XX: 236**
Collins, William, **Supp. I Part 2:** 714
Collinson, Peter , **II:** 114
Collinson, Peter (pseudonym). See Hammett, Dashiell
"Collision" (Huddle), **Supp. XXVI:** 155
Colloff, Pamela, **Supp. XIII:** 281
Colloque Sentimental (ballet), **Supp. IV Part 1:** 83
"Colloquy" (Kees), **Supp. XV:** 133
"Colloquy in Black Rock" (Lowell), **II:** 535
"Colloquy in Black Rock" (R. Lowell), **Retro. Supp. II:** 178
"Colloquy of Monos and Una, The" (Poe), **III:** 412
"Colloquy on a Bed" (Bronk), **Supp. XXI:** 31
Colonel's Dream, The (Chesnutt), **Supp. XIV:** 63, 75–76
Colônia, Regina, **Retro. Supp. II:** 53
Colony (Siddons), **Supp. XXII:** 239
Color (Cullen), **Supp. IV Part 1:** 164, 166, 167, 168
"Colorado" (Beattie), **Supp. V:** 27
Color and Democracy: Colonies and Peace (Du Bois), **Supp. II Part 1:** 184, 185
"Color-Blind Raspberry Picker, The"(Hadas), **Supp. XXIII:** 113
Color Curtain, The (Wright), **IV:** 478, 488
"Colored Americans" (Dunbar), **Supp. II Part 1:** 197
Colored People (H. L. Gates), **Supp. XX: 101, 103, 104–105, 109, 111**
"Color Line, The" (Douglass), **Supp. III Part 1:** 163–165
Color Line, The (W. B. Smith), **Supp. II Part 1:** 168
Color of a Great City, The (Dreiser), **Retro. Supp. II:** 104
Color of Darkness (Purdy), **Supp. VII:** 271
Color of Water, The (McBride), **Supp. XXVI:** 191
Color Purple, The (Walker), **Supp. III Part 2:** 517, 518, 520, 525–529, 532–537; **Supp. VIII:** 141; **Supp. X:** 252, 330; **Supp. XX: 107**
Color Schemes (Cheang; film), **Supp. XI:** 20
"Colors of Night, The" (Momaday), **Supp. IV Part 2:** 490
"Color Struck" (Hurston), **Retro. Supp. III:** 127, 137
"Colors without Objects" (Swenson), **Supp. IV Part 2:** 645
"Color: The Unfinished Business of Democracy" (Locke), **Supp. XIV:** 202, 207
Colossus, The (Plath), **Retro. Supp. II: 245–247; Supp. I Part 2:** 529, 531, 536, 538, 540; **Supp. V:** 79; **Supp. XI:** 317
"Colossus, The" (Plath), **Retro. Supp. II:** 250; **Supp. XXIII:** 113
Colossus of Maroussi, The (H. Miller), **III:** 178, 185–186
"Colour out of Space, The" (Lovecraft), **Supp. XXV:** 109, 111, 114–116, 118, 121
"Colt, The" (Stegner), **Supp. IV Part 2:** 600
Coltelli, Laura, **Supp. IV Part 1:** 323, 330, 335, 409; **Supp. IV Part 2:** 493, 497, 559
Colter: The True Story of the Best Dog I Ever Had (Bass), **Supp. XVI:** 23
Coltrane, John, **Supp. VIII:** 197; **Supp. XXII:** 172
Coltrane, John (pseud.). See O'Nan, Stewart
Colum, Mary, **I:** 246, 252, 256; **Supp. I Part 2:** 708, 709
"Columba" (Cliff), **Supp. XXII:** 74, 76
Columbia Anthology of American Poetry (Parini, ed.), **Supp. XXV:** 251
Columbiad, The (Barlow), **Supp. II Part 1:** 67, 72, 73, 74, 75–77, 79
Columbia History of the American Novel, **Supp. XV:** 270
Columbia Literary History of the United States, **Supp. XV:** 270
"Columbian Ode" (Dunbar), **Supp. II Part 1:** 199
"Columbia U Poesy Reading—1975" (Corso), **Supp. XII:** 134
"Columbine, The" (Very), **Supp. XXV:** 242, 244
Columbus, Christopher, **I:** 253; **II:** 6, 310; **III:** 8; **Supp. I Part 2:** 397, 479, 480, 483, 486–488, 491, 495, 497, 498
"Columbus to Ferdinand" (Freneau), **Supp. II Part 1:** 255
Comanche Moon (McMurtry), **Supp. V:** 232
"Come, Break With Time" (Bogan), **Supp. III Part 1:** 52
Come, Thief (Hirshfield), **Supp. XXIII:** 134, 138
Come Along with Me (Jackson), **Supp. IX:** 117, 118, 122
Come Back, Charleston Blue (film), **Supp. XVI:** 144
Come Back, Little Sheba (film), **Supp. XXV:** 95
Come Back, Little Sheba (Inge), **Supp. XXV:** 94–95, 96–97
Comeback, The (Gurney), **Supp. V:** 97
"Come Back to the Raft Ag'in, Huck Honey!" (Fiedler), **Supp. XIII:** 93, **96–97,** 101
Come Blow Your Horn (Simon), **Supp. IV Part 2:** 574, 575, 577, 578, 586, 587, 591
Come By Here (Major), **Supp. XXII:** 171, 182
"Come Dance with Me in Ireland" (Jackson), **Supp. IX:** 119
"Comedian as the Letter C, The" (Stevens), **IV:** 84–85, 88; **Retro. Supp. I:** 297, 301, 302
"Comedy Cop" (Farrell), **II:** 45
Comedy of a Country House (J. Sturgis), **Supp. XX: 238**

"Comedy's Greatest Era" (Agee), **I:** 31
"Come In" (Frost), **Retro. Supp. I:** 139
"Come On, Baby" (Zinberg), **Supp. XV:** 195
Come On All You Ghosts (Zapruder), **Supp. XXVI:** 54
"Come on Back" (Gardner), **Supp. VI:** 73
"Come Out into the Sun" (Francis), **Supp. IX:** 82
Come Out into the Sun: Poems New and Selected (Francis), **Supp. IX: 82–83**
"Come out the Wilderness" (Baldwin), **Supp. I Part 1:** 63
Comer, Anjanette, **Supp. XI:** 305
Comer, Cornelia, **I:** 214
"Come Rain or Come Shine" (song), **Supp. XXII:** 6
"Come Shining: The Spiritual South" (exhibition; Luster), **Supp. XV:** 350
Come with Me: Poems for a Journey (Nye), **Supp. XIII:** 279
"Comforts of Home, The" (O'Connor), **III:** 349, 351, 355; **Retro. Supp. II:** 237
Comic Artist, The (Glaspell and Matson), **Supp. III Part 1:** 182
"Comic Imagination of the Young Dickens, The" (Wright), **Supp. III Part 2:** 591
"Comic Textures and Female Communities 1937 and 1977: Clare Boothe and Wendy Wasserstein" (Carlson), **Supp. XV:** 323
Comic Tragedies (Alcott), **Supp. I Part 1:** 33
Coming After (Notley), **Supp. XXII:** 223, 227, 230, 232, 236
"Coming and Going" (Gallagher), **Supp. XXIV:** 175, 176–177
"Coming Close" (Levine), **Supp. V:** 192
Coming Forth by Day of Osiris Jones, The (Aiken), **I:** 59
"Coming Home" (Gordon), **Supp. IV Part 1:** 309
"Coming Home to Vermont" (McCarriston), **Supp. XIV:** 269
"Coming in From the Cold" (Walker), **Supp. III Part 2:** 526
Coming into Eighty (Sarton), **Supp. VIII:** 262
"Coming into Eighty" (Sarton), **Supp. VIII:** 262
Coming into the Country (McPhee), **Supp. III Part 1:** 298, 301–306, 309, 310
Coming Into Writing (Cixous), **Supp. X:** 102
Coming of Age in Mississippi (Moody), **Supp. IV Part 1:** 11
Comings Back (Goldbarth), **Supp. XII:** 180
"Coming to Canada--Age Twenty Two" (Shields), **Supp. VII:** 311
Coming to Canada: Poems (Shields), **Supp. VII:** 311–312
"Coming to Memoir as a Journalist" (Epstein), **Supp. XXII:** 95
"Coming to the Morning" (Merwin), **Supp. III Part 1:** 356
"Coming to This" (Strand), **Supp. IV Part 2:** 627
Comiskey, Charles, **II:** 422
Commager, Henry Steele, **I:** 253; **Supp. I Part 1:** 372; **Supp. I Part 2:** 484, 647, 650
Command the Morning (Buck), **Supp. II Part 1:** 125
"CommComm" (Saunders), **Supp. XIX:** 234
"Commencement Address, A" (Brodsky), **Supp. VIII:** 31
"Commencement Day Address, The" (Schwartz), **Supp. II Part 2:** 660
Commentaries (Caesar), **II:** 502, 561
"Commentary" (Auden), **Supp. II Part 1:** 13
"Comment on Curb" (Hughes), **Supp. I Part 1:** 340
"Comments/Questions" (Nelson), **Supp. XVIII:** 172
"Commerce" (Nye), **Supp. XIII:** 281
Commins, Saxe, **Retro. Supp. I:** 73; **Retro. Supp. II:** 337
Commodity of Dreams & Other Stories, A (Nemerov), **III:** 268–269, 285
Common Carnage (Dobyns), **Supp. XIII:** 87
"Common Ground, A" (Levertov), **Supp. III Part 1:** 277
"Common Life, The" (Auden), **Supp. IV Part 1:** 302, 313
"Common Meter" (R. Fisher), **Supp. XIX:** 71
Common Room, A: Essays 1954–1987 (Price), **Supp. VI:** 264–265, 267
Commons, John, **Supp. I Part 2:** 645
Common Sense (Paine), **II:** 117; **Supp. I Part 1:** 231; **Supp. I Part 2:** 505, 506–508, 509, 513, 516, 517, 521
Communal Cot (Loy), **Supp. XXII:** 168
"Communication" (Dobyns), **Supp. XIII:** 91
"Communion" (Dubus), **Supp. VII:** 91
Communion (Mora), **Supp. XIII: 217–219**
Communist Manifesto, The (Marx and Engels), **II:** 463; **Supp. XXI:** 162–163
"Community Life" (Moore), **Supp. X:** 178
"Community of Glaciers, The" (Bass), **Supp. XVI:** 23
Comnes, Gregory, **Supp. IV Part 1:** 283, 284, 291
"Companions, The" (Nemerov), **III:** 269, 278, 287
Company of Poets, A (Simpson), **Supp. IX:** 265, 275
Company of Women, The (Gordon), **Supp. IV Part 1:** 302–304, 304, 306, 313
Company She Keeps, The (McCarthy), **II:** 562, 563–566
"Comparisons of Wonder" (Jarman), **Supp. XVII:** 114
Compass Flower, The (Merwin), **Supp. III Part 1:** 353, 357
"Compassionate Friendship" (Doolittle), **Supp. I Part 1:** 257, 258, 259, 260, 271
"Compatibility" (C. Frost), **Supp. XV:** 103
"Compendium" (Dove), **Supp. IV Part 1:** 248
"Compensation" (Teasdale), **Supp. XXVII:** 293
"Complaint" (W. C. Williams), **Retro. Supp. I:** 418
"Complete Birth of the Cool, The" (Wright), **Supp. XV:** 343, 344
Complete Collected Poems of William Carlos Williams, 1906–1938, The (W. C. Williams), **Retro. Supp. I:** 424
"Complete Destruction" (W. C. Williams), **IV:** 413
"Complete Life of John Hopkins, The" (O. Henry), **Supp. II Part 1:** 405
Complete Poems (Frost), **II:** 155, 164
Complete Poems (Reznikoff), **Supp. XIV:** 281
Complete Poems (Sandburg), **III:** 590–592, 594, 596
Complete Poems, The (Bishop), **Retro. Supp. II:** 49; **Supp. I Part 1:** 72, 82, 94
Complete Poems, The (Bradbury), **Supp. IV Part 1:** 105
Complete Poems, The: 1927–1979 (Bishop), **Retro. Supp. II:** 51
Complete Poems of Emily Dickinson, The (Bianchi and Hampson, eds.), **Retro. Supp. I:** 35

Complete Poems of Emily Dickinson, The (T. H. Johnson, ed.), **I:** 470
Complete Poems of Frederick Goddard Tuckerman, The (Momaday), **Supp. IV Part 2:** 480
Complete Poems of Hart Crane, **Retro. Supp. II:** 81
Complete Poems of Robert Frost, The (Frost), **Retro. Supp. III:** 105
Complete Poems to Solve, The (Swenson), **Supp. IV Part 2:** 652
Complete Poetical Works (A. Lowell), **II:** 512, 516–517
Complete Poetical Works (Hulme), **III:** 464
Complete Poetical Works (Longfellow), **Retro. Supp. II:** 154
Complete Poetical Works of Amy Lowell, The (A. Lowell), **Supp. XV:** 295–296
Complete Prose of T. S. Eliot (T. S. Eliot), **Retro. Supp. III:** 58, 59
Complete Stories, The (O'Connor), **Retro. Supp. III:** 208; **Supp. X:** 1
Complete Tragedies, The: Euripedes II, **Supp. XV:** 50
"Complete with Starry Night and Bourbon Shots" (Goldbarth), **Supp. XII:** 192–193
Complete Works of Kate Chopin, The (Seyersted, ed.), **Supp. I Part 1:** 212, 225
Complete Works of the Gawain-Poet (Gardner), **Supp. VI:** 64, 65
"Complex Histories, Contested Memories: Some Reflections on Remembering Difficult Pasts" (E. Hoffman, lecture), **Supp. XVI:** 155
"Complicated Thoughts About a Small Son" (White), **Supp. I Part 2:** 678
"Compliments of the Season" (O. Henry), **Supp. II Part 1:** 392, 399
"Compline" (Auden), **Supp. II Part 1:** 23
"Composing a Life" (Pickering), **Supp. XXI:** 191, 196
Composition as Explanation (Stein), **IV:** 32, 33, 38
"Composition as Explanation" (Stein), **IV:** 27, 28
"Compound Eye, The" (Davison), **Supp. XXVI:** 74
"Compounding of Consciousness" (James), **II:** 358–359
Comprehensive Bibliography (Hanneman), **II:** 259
Compton-Burnett, Ivy, **I:** 93; **II:** 580; **Supp. XXIII:** 209
Compulsion (Levin), **Supp. XXVII:** 133, 139, 142, 144–145, 147
"Compulsory Heterosexuality and Lesbian Experience" (Rich), **Retro. Supp. III:** 251
"Comrade Laski, C.P.U.S.A. [M.L.]" (Didion), **Supp. IV Part 1:** 200
"Comrade Poets" (Hayes), **Supp. XXVI:** 144
Comstock, Anthony, **Retro. Supp. II:** 95
Comus (Milton), **II:** 12; **Supp. I Part 2:** 622
Conan Doyle, Arthur. See Doyle, Arthur Conan
Conan the Barbarian (comic), **Supp. XXVII:** 129
Conan the Barbarian (film), **Supp. XXVII:** 129
Conceptions of Reality in Modern American Poetry (Dembo), **Supp. I Part 1:** 272
"Concept of Character in Fiction, The" (Gass), **Supp. VI:** 85, **86**
Concept of Dread, The (Kierkegaard), **III:** 305
"Concerning a Woman of Sin" (Hecht), **Supp. XXVII:** 94
Concerning Children (Gilman), **Supp. XI:** 206
"Concerning Copyright" (Twain), **Retro. Supp. III:** 269
"Concerning Mold upon the Skin, Etc." (J. Scott), **Supp. XVII:** 188
"Concerning Necessity" (Carruth), **Supp. XVI:** 57
"Concerning Some Recent Criticism of His Work" (Doty), **Supp. XI:** 131
Concerning the End for Which God Created the World (Edwards), **I:** 549, 557, 559
"Concerning the Jews" (Twain), **Retro. Supp. III:** 268
Concerning the League (Woodbury, Henry, and Webster, trans.), **Supp. XXVI:** 81, 82, 87, 90
"Concerning Things That Can Be Doubled"(Crooker), **Supp. XXIII:** 64
Concerto for Two Pianos, Winds, and Percussion (Bowles), **Supp. IV Part 1:** 83
"Concert of Tenses, A" (Gallagher), **Supp. XXIV:** 172
Concert of Tenses, A: Essays on Poetry (Gallagher), **Supp. XXIV:** 166, 167, 171–172
Conchologist's First Book, The (Poe), **III:** 412; **Retro. Supp. III:** 234–235
Conclusive Evidence (Nabokov), **III:** 247–250, 252
"Concord Hymn" (Emerson), **II:** 19
Concrete Blonde, The (Connelly), **Supp. XXI: 70–71,** 78, 80
"Concrete Universal, The: Observations on the Understanding of Poetry" (Ransom), **III:** 480
Concurring Beasts (Dobyns), **Supp. XIII:** 76
Condé, Maryse, **Supp. XXIII:** 94
Condensed Novels and Other Papers (Harte), **Supp. II Part 1:** 342
"Condition, The" (Karmi; Everwine, trans.), **Supp. XV:** 78
Condition of Man, The (Mumford), **Supp. II Part 2:** 483, 484, 486, 495–496, 498
"Conditions for Work: The Common World of Women" (Rich), **Retro. Supp. III:** 248
"Condolence" (Parker), **Supp. IX:** 191
"Condominium, The" (Elkin), **Supp. VI:** 49, **50–51,** 55, 56
Condon, Charles R., **Supp. XIII:** 163
Condor and the Cows, The: A South American Travel Diary (Isherwood and Caskey), **Supp. XIV:** 166
"Condor and the Guests, The" (Connell), **Supp. XIV:** 86
Condorcet, Marquis de, **Supp. I Part 2:** 511
Conduct of Life, The (Emerson), **II:** 1–5, 8
Conduct of Life, The (Mumford), **Supp. II Part 2:** 485, 496–497
"Conductor of Nothing, The" (Levine), **Supp. V:** 189
"Coney Island" (Teasdale), **Supp. XXVII:** 289
Coney Island of the Mind, A (Ferlinghetti), **Supp. XIX:** 4; **Supp. XXI:** 53
Confederacy of Dunces, A (Toole), **Supp. XXVI:** 239, 240, 242, 243–244, 246, 250–253
"Conference Male, The" (Mora), **Supp. XIII:** 218
"Confession" (Peacock), **Supp. XIX:** 206
Confession, The (Rinehart), **Supp. XXV:** 200
"Confessional" (Bidart), **Supp. XV:** 29–30, 31
"Confessional Poem" (Nelson), **Supp. XVIII:** 174
Confession de Claude, La (Zola), **I:** 411
"Confession of a House-Breaker, The" (Jewett), **Retro. Supp. II:** 146–147
Confession of Jereboam O. Beauchamp, The (pamphlet), **IV:** 253
Confessions (Augustine), **I:** 279;

Retro. Supp. III: 63; **Supp. XVI:** 288; **Supp. XXII:** 93
"Confessions" (Huddle), **Supp. XXVI:** 150
Confessions (Rousseau), **I:** 226
Confessions of a Barbarian: Selections from the Journals of Edward Abbey, 1951–1989 (Abbey; Petersen, ed.), **Supp. XIII:** 2, 4
"Confessions of a Latina Author" (Mora), **Supp. XIII:** 221
"Confessions of a Wannabe Negro" (McKnight), **Supp. XX: 152–153, 158**
Confessions of Nat Turner, The (Styron), **IV:** 98, 99, 105, 113–117; **Supp. X:** 16, 250
Confetti (Mora), **Supp. XIII:** 221
Confidence (James), **II:** 327, 328
Confidence-Man, The (Melville), **III:** 91; **Retro. Supp. I:** 255–256, 257; **Retro. Supp. II:** 121; **Supp. XIV:** 49
Confidence Man, The (Van Vechten), **Supp. II Part 2:** 737
Confidence-Man, The: His Masquerade (Melville), **Retro. Supp. III:** 147, 148, 160
Confidential Clerk, The (T. S. Eliot), **I:** 570, 571–572, 583, 584; **Retro. Supp. I:** 65; **Retro. Supp. III:** 70
Confident Years, 1885–1915, The (Brooks), **I:** 257, 259; **Supp. I Part 2:** 650
"Configurations" (Ammons), **Supp. VII:** 28
Configurations: New and Selected Poems, 1958–1998 (Major), **Supp. XXII: 182**
Confronting the Horror: The Novels of Nelson Algren (Giles), **Supp. IX:** 11, 15
Confucius, **II:** 1; **III:** 456, 475; **Supp. IV Part 1:** 14
Confusion (Cozzens), **I:** 358, 359, 377, 378
"Confusion of Planes We Must Wander in Sleep, The" (Weigl), **Supp. XIX:** 283
Congdon, Don, **Supp. XXII:** 204
Congo (film), **Supp. IV Part 1:** 83
Congo (screenplay, Shanley), **Supp. XIV:** 316
"Congo, The" (Lindsay), **Supp. I Part 2:** 388–389, 392, 395
Congo and Other Poems, The (Lindsay), **Supp. I Part 2:** 379, 382, 389, 390, 391; **Supp. XXV:** 18
"Congregation" (Trethewey), **Supp. XXI:** 245, 247
"Congregation of Grackles, A"(Crooker), **Supp. XXIII:** 63
"Congress of the Insomniacs, The" (Simic), **Supp. VIII:** 281–282
Congreve, William, **III:** 195; **Supp. V:** 101; **Supp. XVIII:** 12
Coningsby (Disraeli), **II:** 127
"Conjectural Reading" (Bronk), **Supp. XXI:** 31
Conjectures of a Guilty Bystander (Merton), **Supp. VIII:** 197, 206, 207
Conjugal Bliss: A Comedy of Marital Arts (Nichols), **Supp. XIII:** 269
"Conjugation of the Paramecium, The" (Rukeyser), **Supp. VI:** 271
Conjugations and Reiterations (Murray), **Supp. XIX:** 161
"Conjuration" (Wilbur), **Supp. III Part 2:** 551
Conjure (recording), **Supp. X:** 241
Conjure (Reed), **Supp. X:** 240, 242
Conjure-Man Dies, The: A Mystery Tale of Dark Harlem (R. Fisher), **Supp. XIX:** 65, 71**, 77–78; Supp. XVI:** 143
Conjure Woman, The (Chesnutt), **Supp. II Part 1:** 193; **Supp. XIV:** 57, **58–61,** 62, 63
Conklin, Grof, **Supp. I Part 2:** 672
Conklin, Peggy, **Supp. XXII:** 27
Conkling, Hilda, **II:** 530
Conkling, Roscoe, **III:** 506
Conley, Robert J., **Supp. V:** 232
Conley, Susan, **Supp. XIII:** 111, 112
Connaroe, Joel, **Supp. IV Part 2:** 690
"Connecticut Lad, A" (White), **Supp. I Part 2:** 677
"Connecticut Valley" (Cowley), **Supp. II Part 1:** 141–142
Connecticut Yankee in King Arthur's Court, A (Twain), **I:** 209; **II:** 276; **IV:** 205; **Retro. Supp. III:** 255, 265–267
Connell, Evan S., **Supp. XIV: 79–100; Supp. XXIII:** 302
Connell, Norreys (pseudonym). See O'Riordan, Conal Holmes O'Connell
Connelly, Marc, **III:** 394; **Supp. I Part 2:** 679; **Supp. IX:** 190
Connelly, Michael, **Supp. XXI: 67–82**
Conner, Dan, **Supp. XXIII:** 125
Connery, Thomas B., **Supp. XVII:** 106
Connoisseur, The (Connell), **Supp. XIV:** 87
"Connoisseur of Chaos" (Stevens), **IV:** 89; **Retro. Supp. I:** 306
Connolly, Cyril, **Supp. XIV:** 158, 343, 348
Connors, Elizabeth. See Lindsay, Mrs. Vachel (Elizabeth Connors)
Connotations (Kenny), **Supp. XXIII:** 143, 144, 146, 150, 155
Conover, Roger, **Supp. I Part 1:** 95
Conover, Roger L., **Supp. XXII:** 155, 162
Conquering Horse (Manfred), **Supp. X:** 126
Conqueror, The (Atherton), **Supp. XXIV:** 23
"Conqueror Worm, The" (Poe), **Retro. Supp. II:** 261
Conquest of Canaan (Dwight), **Supp. I Part 1:** 124
Conquistador (MacLeish), **III:** 2, 3, 13–14, 15
Conrad, Alfred, **Retro. Supp. II:** 245
Conrad, Alfred H., **Supp. I Part 2:** 552
Conrad, C. A., **Supp. XXII:** 155
Conrad, David, **Supp. I Part 2:** 552
Conrad, Jacob, **Supp. I Part 2:** 552
Conrad, Joseph, **I:** 123, 343, 394, 405, 409, 415, 421, 485, 506, 575–576, 578; **II:** 58, 73, 74, 91, 92, 144, 263, 320, 338, 595; **III:** 28, 102, 106, 328, 464, 467, 491, 512; **IV:** 476; **Retro. Supp. I:** 80, 91, 106, 108, 231, 274, 377; **Retro. Supp. II:** 222; **Supp. I Part 1:** 292; **Supp. I Part 2:** 621, 622; **Supp. IV Part 1:** 197, 341; **Supp. IV Part 2:** 680; **Supp. V:** 249, 251, 262, 298, 307, 311; **Supp. VIII:** 4, 310; **Supp. XIV:** 112; **Supp. XIX:** 27; **Supp. XVI:** 158, 212; **Supp. XVIII:** 98, 102; **Supp. XX: 195; Supp. XXIV:** 286; **Supp. XXV:** 208
Conrad, Paul, **Supp. I Part 2:** 552
Conrad, Peter, **Supp. IV Part 2:** 688
"Conrad Aiken: From Savannah to Emerson" (Cowley), **Supp. II Part 1:** 43
Conrad Richter's Ohio Trilogy (Edwards), **Supp. XVIII:** 220
Conroy, Frank, **Supp. VIII:** 145; **Supp. XI:** 245; **Supp. XVI: 63–78; Supp. XXII:** 50
Conroy, Jack, **Supp. XXII:** 1, 5, 10
Conroy, Pat, **Supp. XVIII:** 193; **Supp. XXII:** 239
Cons, Scams, and Grifts (Gores), **Supp. XXI:** 70
"Conscience of the Court, The" (Hurston), **Retro. Supp. III:** 135–136
Conscience with the Power and Cases thereof (Ames), **IV:** 158
"Conscientious Objector, The" (Shapiro), **Supp. II Part 2:** 710
"Consciousness and Dining"

(Harrison), **Supp. VIII:** 46
"Conscript, The" (Lovecraft), **Supp. XXV:** 119
"Conscription Camp" (Shapiro), **Supp. II Part 2:** 705
"Consejos de Nuestra Señora de Guadalupe: Counsel from the Brown Virgin" (Mora), **Supp. XIII:** 224
"Conservation Esthetic" (Leopold), **Supp. XIV:** 179, 181, 186, 189–190
"Conserving Natural and Cultural Diversity: The Prose and Poetry of Pat Mora" (Murphy), **Supp. XIII:** 214
Considerable Town, A (M. F. K. Fisher), **Supp. XVII:** 90
"Considerations by the Way" (Emerson), **II:** 2, 5
Consider the Oyster (M. F. K. Fisher), **Supp. XVII:** 84, 87
Considine, Bob, **II:** 424
"Consolation" (Bausch), **Supp. VII:** 48
"Consolation for Tamar" (Stallings), **Supp. XXV:** 228
Consolation of Philosophy, The (Boethius), **Supp. XXVI:** 250
"Consolations" (Stafford), **Supp. XI:** 329
"Conspiracy of History, The: E. L. Doctorow's The Book of Daniel" (Levine), **Supp. IV Part 1:** 221
Conspiracy of Kings, The (Barlow), **Supp. II Part 1:** 80
Conspiracy of Pontiac, The (Parkman), **Supp. II Part 2:** 590, 595, 596, 599–600
Constab Ballads (McKay), **Supp. X:** 131, 133
Constance (Kenyon), **Supp. VII:** 170–172
Constancy (Boyce), **Supp. XVII:** 100; **Supp. XXI:** 6, 7, 12
"Constant Symbol, The" (Frost), **Retro. Supp. III:** 105
"Constellation Orion, The" (Kooser), **Supp. XIX:** 120
Constitution of the Confederacy by Dekanawidah: Collected and Translated from [the] Mohawk Text by Chief Seth Newhouse, **Supp. XXVI:** 90
Constitution of the Five Nations, The (Parker), **Supp. XXVI:** 87
Construction of Boston, The (Koch), **Supp. XV:** 187
"Constructive Work" (Du Bois), **Supp. II Part 1:** 172
"Consumer's Report" (X. J. Kennedy), **Supp. XV:** 161–162
"Consumption" (Bryant), **Supp. I Part 1:** 169–170
Contact Collection of Contemporary Writers (McAlmon), **Supp. XXII:** 166
"Contagiousness of Puerperal Fever, The" (Holmes), **Supp. I Part 1:** 303–304
"Contemplation in a World of Action" (Merton), **Supp. VIII:** 204
"Contemplation of Poussin" (Sarton), **Supp. VIII:** 261
"Contemplations" (Bradstreet), **Retro. Supp. III:** 9–11, 12, 13; **Supp. I Part 1:** 112, 113, 119–122
Contemporaries (Kazin), **Supp. VIII:** 102, **103–104**
Contemporary American Playwrights (Bigsby), **Supp. XV:** 332
Contemporary American Poetry (Poulin, ed.), **Supp. IX:** 272; **Supp. XI:** 259
Contemporary Authors Autobiography, **Supp. XXII:** 225
Contending Forces (Hopkins), **Supp. XVIII:** 284
"Contentment" (Holmes), **Supp. I Part 1:** 307
"Contents" (Halliday), **Supp. XIX:** 92
"Contest, The" (Paley), **Supp. VI:** 223, 230, 231
"Contest for Aaron Gold, The" (P. Roth), **Supp. III Part 2:** 403
Continental Drift (Banks), **Supp. V:** 13–14, 16, 227
Continental Op, The (Hammett), **Supp. IV Part 1:** 344
Continent's End: An Anthology of Contemporary California Poets (Taggard, Sterling, and Rorty, eds.), **Supp. XXII:** 276
Continuing Education, A (Pickering), **Supp. XXI:** 194, 195–196
Continuity of American Poetry, The (Pearce), **Supp. I Part 1:** 111; **Supp. I Part 2:** 475
Continuous Harmony, A: Essays Cultural and Agricultural (Berry), **Supp. X:** 33
Continuous Life, The (Strand), **Supp. IV Part 2:** 630, 631–633
Contoski, Victor, **Supp. XII:** 181
"Contract" (Lardner), **II:** 432
"Contradictions: Tracking Poems" (Rich), **Retro. Supp. III:** 251
"Contraption, The" (Swenson), **Supp. IV Part 2:** 643
"Contrariness of the Mad Farmer, The" (Berry), **Supp. X:** 35
"Contrast, a Spenetic Effusion, The" (J. Schoolcraft), **Supp. XXIII:** 231–232
"Contrition" (Dubus), **Supp. VII:** 84
"Control Burn" (Snyder), **Supp. VIII:** 301
"Control Is the Mainspring" (Komunyakaa), **Supp. XIII:** 122, 124
"Controlling the 'Sloppiness of Things' in Frank Conroy's Stop-Time" (Strychacz), **Supp. XVI:** 69–70
Control of Nature, The (McPhee), **Supp. III Part 1:** 310–313
Controversial Sholem Asch, The (Siegel), **Supp. XXIII:** 3
"Conventional Wisdom, The" (Elkin), **Supp. VI: 52–53**
"Convergence" (Ammons), **Supp. VII:** 28
"Convergence of the Twain, The" (Hardy), **Supp. VIII:** 31, 32
Conversation (Aiken), **I:** 54
Conversation at Midnight (Millay), **III:** 138
"Conversation of Eiros and Charmion, The" (Poe), **III:** 412
"Conversation on Conversation" (Stowe), **Supp. I Part 2:** 587
"Conversations in Moscow" (Levertov), **Supp. III Part 1:** 282
Conversations on Some of the Old Poets (J. R. Lowell), **Supp. I Part 2:** 405
Conversations with Albert Murray (Maguire, ed.), **Supp. XIX:** 160–161
Conversations with Byron (Blessington), **Retro. Supp. II:** 58
Conversations with Eudora Welty (Prenshaw, ed.), **Retro. Supp. I:** 339, 340, 341, 342, 343, 352, 354
"Conversations with Helmholtz" (Allen), **Supp. XV:** 15
Conversations with Ishmael Reed (Dick and Singh, eds.), **Supp. X:** 244
Conversations with James Baldwin (Standley and Pratt, eds.), **Retro. Supp. II:** 6
Conversations with Richard Wilbur (Wilbur), **Supp. III Part 2:** 542–543
"Conversation with a Fireman from Brooklyn" (Gallagher), **Supp. XXIV:** 169–170
"Conversation with My Father, A" (Paley), **Supp. VI:** 220
"Conversion of the Jews, The" (P. Roth), **Retro. Supp. II:** 281; **Supp.**

III Part 2: 404, 406; **Supp. XXVI:** 119
Convict, The: Stories (Burke), **Supp. XIV:** 25
"Convicta et Combusta" (J. Scott), **Supp. XVII:** 189
"Convolvulus" (Schott), **Supp. XXIII:** 248
"Convoy" (Weigl), **Supp. XIX:** 278
Conway, Jill, **Supp. I Part 1:** 19
Coode, John, **I:** 132
Cook, Bruce, **Supp. XII:** 130, 131, 133–134
Cook, Captain James, **I:** 2
Cook, Eleanor, **Retro. Supp. I:** 311
Cook, Elisha, **Supp. IV Part 1:** 356
Cook, Elizabeth Christine, **II:** 106
Cook, George Cram "Jig", **Supp. XXI:** 5, 6
Cook, Jessie W., **Supp. XXV:** 278
Cook, Johnny, **Supp. XXIV:** 248
Cook, Mercer, **Supp. IV Part 1:** 368
Cook, Richard, **Supp. XXII:** 158
Cookbook Collector, The (Goodman), **Supp. XXVI:** 130–131
Cooke, Alistair, **III:** 113, 119, 120
Cooke, Delmar G., **II:** 271
Cooke, Grace MacGowan, **Supp. V:** 285
Cooke, Philip Pendleton, **III:** 420; **Retro. Supp. III:** 227
Cooke, Rose Terry, **II:** 401; **Retro. Supp. II:** 51, 136, 138; **Supp. XIII:** 152
"Cookie" (Taylor), **Supp. V:** 320
"Cookies, The" (Nye), **Supp. XIII:** 281
Cooking of Provincial France, The (M. F. K. Fisher), **Supp. XVII:** 89
Cook-Lynn, Elizabeth, **Supp. IV Part 1:** 325
"Cool Air" (Lovecraft), **Supp. XXV:** 110
Coolbrith, Ina, **I:** 193, 196
"Coole Park" (Yeats), **Supp. VIII:** 155, 159
"Coole Park and Ballylee" (Yeats), **Supp. VIII:** 156
Cooler by the Lake (Heinemann), **Supp. XXII:** 103, **114**
Cooley, John, **Supp. V:** 214
Cooley, Peter, **Supp. XIII:** 76
Coolidge, Calvin, **I:** 498; **II:** 95; **Supp. I Part 2:** 647
Cooling Time: An American Poetry Vigil (Wright), **Supp. XV:** 353
Cool Million, A (West), **III:** 425; **IV:** 287, 288, 297–299, 300; **Retro. Supp. II:** 321, 322–323, 328, **335–337**
"Cool Million, A" (screen story) (West and Ingster), **Retro. Supp. II:** 330
"Cool Tombs" (Sandburg), **III:** 554
Coon, Ross, **IV:** 196
Cooney, Seamus, **Supp. XIV:** 289
"Coon Hunt" (White), **Supp. I Part 2:** 669
Co-op (Sinclair), **Supp. V:** 290
Cooper, Bernard, **Supp. XI:** 129
Cooper, Frederic Taber, **Supp. XX:** **219–220; Supp. XXIV:** 28–29
Cooper, Gary, **Supp. IV Part 2:** 524
Cooper, James Fenimore, **I:** 211, 257, **335–357; II:** 74, 277, 295–296, 302, 306, 309, 313, 314; **III:** 51; **IV:** 205, 333; **Retro. Supp. I:** 246; **Retro. Supp. II:** 160; **Supp. I Part 1:** 141, 155, 156, 158, 171, 372; **Supp. I Part 2:** 413, 495, 579, 585, 652, 660; **Supp. IV Part 1:** 80; **Supp. IV Part 2:** 463, 469; **Supp. V:** 209–210; **Supp. VIII:** 189; **Supp. XIV:** 227; **Supp. XVIII:** 4; **Supp. XXIII:** 178
Cooper, Mrs. James Fenimore (Susan A. De Lancey), **I:** 338, 351, 354
Cooper, Jane, **Supp. XV:** 259
Cooper, Rand Richards, **Supp. XVI:** 74
Cooper, Susan Fenimore, **I:** 337, 354
Cooper, William, **I:** 337–338, 351
Cooper, Mrs. William, **I:** 337
Cooperman, Robert, **Supp. XXIII:** 247
Coover, Robert, **Supp. IV Part 1:** 388; **Supp. V: 39–55; Supp. XII:** 152; **Supp. XIV:** 96; **Supp. XVII:** 6; **Supp. XXI:** 236; **Supp. XXII:** 259
Copacetic (Komunyakaa), **Supp. XIII:** **116–118,** 126
Cope, Wendy, **Supp. XV:** 117
Copelin, David, **Supp. XXIV:** 264
Copland, Aaron, **II:** 586; **Supp. I Part 1:** 281; **Supp. III Part 2:** 619; **Supp. IV Part 1:** 79, 80–81, 84; **Supp. XXII:** 283; **Supp. XXVI:** 134
Coplas de Don Jorge Manrique (Longfellow, trans.), **II:** 488, 492
Coppée, François Edouard Joachim, **II:** 325
Copperhead, The (Frederic), **II:** 134–135
Copperhead Cane (J. W. Miller), **Supp. XX: 163, 164, 166–167**
Copper Sun (Cullen), **Supp. IV Part 1:** 167, 168
Coppola, Francis Ford, **Supp. XI:** 171, 172; **Supp. XII:** 75
Coprolites (Goldbarth), **Supp. XII:** **177–178,** 180, 183
Coquette, The (Foster), **Supp. XXV:** 35, 36, 38–45
Coral and Captive Israel (Reznikoff), **Supp. XIV:** 288
"Coral Ring, The" (Stowe), **Supp. I Part 2:** 586
"Cora Unashamed" (Hughes), **Supp. I Part 1:** 329, 330
"Corazón del Corrido" (Mora), **Supp. XIII:** 225
Corban Ephphata (Li Lin Lee), **Supp. XV:** 225
Corbett, Gentlemen Jim, **II:** 416
Corbett, William, **Supp. XI:** 248; **Supp. XVI:** 286, 295; **Supp. XXIV:** 45
Corbière, Jean Antoine, **II:** 354–355, 528
Cordiall Water, A: A garland of Odd & Old Receipts to Assuage the Ills of Man and Beast (M. F. K. Fisher), **Supp. XVII:** 88, 90
Cording, Robert, **Supp. IX:** 328; **Supp. XII:** 184
Core, George, **Supp. XVIII:** 86; **Supp. XXI:** 193
Corelli, Marie, **III:** 579
Corey, Lewis, **Supp. I Part 2:** 645
"Corinna's Going a-Maying" (Herrick), **Supp. XIV:** 8, 9
"Coriolan" (Eliot), **I:** 580
"Coriolanus and His Mother" (Schwartz), **Supp. II Part 2:** 643, 644–645
"Corkscrew" (Hammett), **Supp. IV Part 1:** 345, 347
Corkum, Gerald, **I:** 37
Corky's Brother (Neugeboren), **Supp. XVI:** 225
"Corky's Brother" (Neugeboren), **Supp. XVI:** 225
Corliss, Richard, **Supp. VIII:** 73; **Supp. XXVII:** 96
Corman, Cid, **Supp. III Part 2:** 624, 625, 626, 627, 628; **Supp. IV Part 1:** 144; **Supp. VIII:** 292; **Supp. XV:** 74, 153; **Supp. XXI:** 23, 27
Corman, Roger, **Supp. XXV:** 154
"Corn" (Lanier), **Supp. I Part 1:** 352, 353, 354, 356–361, 364, 366
Corn, Alfred, **Supp. IX:** 156; **Supp. XV:** 250
Corneille, Pierre, **Supp. I Part 2:** 716; **Supp. IX:** 131
Cornelius, Randy, **Supp. XXVI:** 89
Cornell, Esther, **I:** 231
Cornell, Joseph, **Supp. XXI:** 131; **Supp. XXII:** 167, 168
Cornell, Katherine, **IV:** 356
Cornell, Valerie, **Supp. XX: 94–95**

"Corners" (Dunn), **Supp. XI:** 148
Cornhuskers (Sandburg), **III:** 583–585
"Corn-Planting, The" (Anderson), **I:** 114
"Corn-Pone Opinions" (Twain), **Retro. Supp. III:** 269
"Corn story (or the origin of corn)"(J. Schoolcraft), **Supp. XXIII:** 234–235
Cornucopia: New and Selected Poems, 1975–2002 (Peacock), **Supp. XIX: 203–204**
Corn Village (Le Sueur), **Supp. XXIII:** 167
Coronation Murder-Mystery, The (O'Hara, Ashbery, and Koch), **Supp. XXIII:** 217
"Coroner's Report" (Wrigley), **Supp. XVIII:** 295
"Corporal of Artillery" (Dubus), **Supp. VII:** 84, 85
"Corpse Bird, The" (Rash), **Supp. XXVII:** 219, 228
"Corpse Plant, The" (Rich), **Supp. I Part 2:** 555
Corpus Christi (McNally), **Supp. XIII: 205–206,** 209
Corradi, Juan, **Supp. IV Part 1:** 208
Corrections, The (Franzen), **Supp. XIX:** 54; **Supp. XX: 83, 84, 85, 90, 91, 91–93, 95**
Corregidora (G. Jones), **Supp. XXIV:** 183–184, **185–187,** 190, 193, 194, 195
"Correspondences" (Baudelaire), **I:** 63
"Corrido de Gregorio Cortez" (Mora), **Supp. XIII:** 225
"Corrigenda" (Komunyakaa), **Supp. XIII:** 115, 116
Corrosive Sublimate (Sorrentino), **Supp. XXI:** 226, 228
Corruption City (McCoy), **Supp. XIII:** 175
Corso, Gregory, **Supp. II Part 1:** 30; **Supp. IV Part 1:** 90; **Supp. XII: 117–138; Supp. XIV:** 150; **Supp. XVI:** 135; **Supp. XXI:** 53; **Supp. XXIII:** 215
Corsons Inlet (Ammons), **Supp. VII:** 25–26, 28–29, 36
"Corsons Inlet" (Ammons), **Supp. VII:** 25–26
Cortázar, Julio, **Retro. Supp. I:** 278; **Supp. XXII:** 265
"Cortège for Rosenbloom" (Stevens), **IV:** 81
Cortez, Hernando, **III:** 2
" 'Coruscating Glamour': Lynda Hull and the Movies" (Goldstein), **Supp. XXI:** 134
Cory, William Johnson, **Supp. XX: 230, 231**
Coser, Lewis, **Supp. I Part 2:** 650
Cosgrave, Patrick, **Retro. Supp. II:** 185
Cosmic Optimism: A Study of the Interpretation of Evolution by American Poets from Emerson to Robinson (Conner), **Supp. I Part 1:** 73
Cosmogony of the Iroquois Confederacy (Newhouse), **Supp. XXVI:** 87
Cosmological Eye, The (H. Miller), **III:** 174, 184
"Cosmological Eye, The" (H. Miller), **III:** 183
"Cosmos" (Beattie), **Supp. V:** 35
"Cost, The" (Hecht), **Supp. X:** 62–63
Costello, Bonnie, **Retro. Supp. II:** 40
Costello, Mark, **Supp. XXIII:** 290
Costner, Kevin, **Supp. VIII:** 45
"Cost of Living, The" (Malamud), **Supp. I Part 2:** 429, 437
"Costume as Metaphor" (Bronk), **Supp. XXI:** 26
Cott, Jonathan, **Supp. XVI:** 104, 106
"Cottagers' Corner" column (D. West), **Supp. XVIII:** 286
"Cottage Street, 1953" (Wilbur), **Supp. III Part 2:** 543, 561
"Cottagette, The" (Gilman), **Supp. XI:** 207
Cotten, Joseph, **Supp. IV Part 2:** 524
Cotter, James Finn, **Supp. X:** 202
Cotton, John, **Supp. I Part 1:** 98, 101, 110, 111, 116
Cotton, Joseph, **Supp. XII:** 160
Cotton, Seaborn, **Supp. I Part 1:** 101
Cotton Club, The (Major), **Supp. XXII:** 174
"Cotton Club Classics" (Halliday), **Supp. XIX:** 92, 93
Cotton Comes to Harlem (C. Himes), **Supp. XVI:** 143, 144
Cotton Comes to Harlem (film, O. Davis), **Supp. XVI:** 144
"Cotton Song" (Toomer), **Supp. IX:** 312
Couch, W. T., **Supp. X:** 46
Coughlin, Ruth Pollack, **Supp. VIII:** 45
Coulette, Henri, **Supp. V:** 180; **Supp. XIII:** 312; **Supp. XV:** 74, 75
Coultrap-McQuin, Susan, **Supp. XVI:** 85, 92
"Council of State, A" (Dunbar), **Supp. II Part 1:** 211, 213
Count Bruga (Hecht), **Supp. XXV:** 27; **Supp. XXVII:** 89
"Count Dracula" (Allen), **Supp. XV:** 15
"Countee Cullen at 'The Heights' " (Tuttleton), **Supp. IV Part 1:** 166
Counterfeiters, The (Gide), **Supp. IV Part 1:** 80; **Supp. IV Part 2:** 681
"Countering" (Ammons), **Supp. VII:** 28
Counterlife, The (P. Roth), **Retro. Supp. II:** 279, 280, 291; **Supp. III Part 2:** 424–426
Counter-Statement (Burke), **I:** 270–272; **IV:** 431
"Countess, The" (Whittier), **Supp. I Part 2:** 691, 694
Count Frontenac and New France Under Louis XIV (Parkman), **Supp. II Part 2:** 607, 609–610
"Counting Small-Boned Bodies" (R. Bly), **Supp. IV Part 1:** 62
"Counting the Body"(Schott), **Supp. XXIII:** 251–252
"Counting the Children" (Gioia), **Supp. XV: 122–123**
"Counting the Mad" (Justice), **Supp. VII:** 117
"Count Lothar's Heart" (Boyle), **Supp. XXIV:** 58
Count of Monte Cristo, The (Dumas), **III:** 386, 396; **Supp. XVII:** 64, 216
"Countries We Live In, The" (Zach; Everwine, trans.), **Supp. XV:** 87
"Country Boy in Boston, The" (Howells), **II:** 255
Country By-Ways (Jewett), **II:** 402
Country Doctor, A (Jewett), **II:** 391, 392, 396, 404–405; **Retro. Supp. II:** 131, 141, 146
"Country Full of Swedes" (Caldwell), **I:** 297, 309
Country Girl, The (Odets), **Supp. II Part 2:** 546, 547, 548–549
"Country House" (Kumin), **Supp. IV Part 2:** 446
"Country Husband, The" (Cheever), **Supp. I Part 1:** 184, 189
"Country in the Woman, The" (Hurston), **Retro. Supp. III:** 127
"Country Life" (Pickering), **Supp. XXI:** 197
"Country Marriage" (C. Frost), **Supp. XV:** 99
Countrymen of Bones (R. O. Butler), **Supp. XII:** 62, **65–66**
"Country Mouse, The" (Bishop), **Retro. Supp. II:** 37, 38, 51
Country Music: Selected Early Poems (Wright), **Supp. V:** 332, 335, 338, 342
Country of a Thousand Years of Peace,

The (Merrill), **Supp. III Part 1:** 321, 322, 331
"Country of Elusion, The" (O. Henry), **Supp. II Part 1:** 407
Country Of Language, The (Sanders), **Supp. XVI:** 277
Country of Marriage, The (Berry), **Supp. X:** 33
Country of Strangers, A (Richter), **Supp. XVIII:** 217
Country of Survivors (Di Piero), **Supp. XIX:** 36
Country of the Pointed Firs, The (Jewett), **II:** 392, 399, 405, 409–411; **Retro. Supp. I:** 6; **Retro. Supp. II:** 134, 136, 139, 140, 141, 145, 146, 147; **Retro. Supp. III:** 22; **Supp. VIII:** 126; **Supp. XIII:** 152; **Supp. XXIII:** 275, 278
"Country Printer, The" (Freneau), **Supp. II Part 1:** 269
"Country Song" (Stallings), **Supp. XXV:** 222, 234
"Country Wife, The" (Gioia), **Supp. XV:** 120
Count Your Bullets (film), **Supp. XVII:** 141
Count Zero (W. Gibson), **Supp. XVI:** 19, **126–127,** 129
Coup, The (Updike), **Retro. Supp. I:** 331, 334, 335
"Coup de Grâce, The" (Bierce), **I:** 202
Couperin, François, **III:** 464
"Couple, The" (Olds), **Supp. X:** 206
"Couple of Hamburgers, A" (Thurber), **Supp. I Part 2:** 616
"Couple of Nuts, A" (Z. Fitzgerald), **Supp. IX:** 58, 71, 72
"Couple of Sad Experiences, A" (Twain), **Retro. Supp. III:** 265
"Couples" (Halliday), **Supp. XIX:** 89
Couples (Updike), **IV:** 214, 215, 216, 217, 227, 229–230; **Retro. Supp. I:** 320, 327, 330; **Supp. XII:** 296
Courlander, harold, **Retro. Supp. III:** 131
Cournos, John, **III:** 465; **Retro. Supp. III:** 85; **Supp. I Part 1:** 258
"Course in Creative Writing, A" (Stafford), **Supp. XI:** 327
"Course of a Particular, The" (Stevens), **Retro. Supp. I:** 312
"Coursier de Jeanne d'Arc, Le" (McCarriston), **Supp. XIV:** 267–268
Courtier, The (Castiglione), **III:** 282
" 'Courtin,' The" (J. R. Lowell), **Supp. I Part 2:** 415
"Courting" (Huddle), **Supp. XXVI:** 151
"Courting of Sister Wisby, The" (Jewett), **Retro. Supp. II:** 134, 135, 146
"Courting the Famous Figures at the Grotto of Improbable Thought" (B. Kelly), **Supp. XVII:** 127–128
Courtney, W. L., **Supp. XXIV:** 29
"Courtship" (Dove), **Supp. IV Part 1:** 248
"Courtship, A"(Thompson), **Supp. XXIII:** 293
"Courtship, Diligence" (Dove), **Supp. IV Part 1:** 248
Courtship of Miles Standish, The (Longfellow), **II:** 489, 502–503; **Retro. Supp. II:** 155, **161–162,** 163, 166, 168
"Cousin Aubrey" (Taylor), **Supp. V:** 328
"Cousin Claire" (Andrews), **Supp. XXVI:** 11
Cousine Bette (Balzac), **Retro. Supp. II:** 98
Couturier, Maurice, **Supp. IV Part 1:** 44
Covarrubias, Miguel, **Supp. XVI:** 187
Cove, The (Rash), **Supp. XXVII:** 225–226
"Covered Bridges" (Kingsolver), **Supp. VII:** 203
"Cover Photograph" (Nelson), **Supp. XVIII:** 173
"Cover Stories" (Skloot), **Supp. XX: 195, 207**
"Cover Versions" (Halliday), **Supp. XIX:** 84
Cowan, Lester, **III:** 148
Cowan, Louise, **IV:** 120, 125
Coward, Noel, **Retro. Supp. I:** 65; **Retro. Supp. III:** 171; **Supp. I Part 1:** 332; **Supp. V:** 101; **Supp. XV:** 329; **Supp. XXIV:** 267
"Cowardice" (Theroux), **Supp. VIII:** 313
Cowboy Mouth (Shepard), **Supp. III Part 2:** 441–442
"Cowboys" (Salter). See "Dirt" (Salter)
Cowboys (Shepard), **Supp. III Part 2:** 432
Cowboys #2 (Shepard), **Supp. III Part 2:** 437, 438
Cowell, Henry, **Supp. IV Part 1:** 80, 82
Cowen, Philip, **Supp. XX: 2**
Cowen, Wilson Walker, **Supp. IV Part 2:** 435
Cowie, Alexander, **IV:** 70
"Cow in Apple Time, The" (Frost), **II:** 154; **Retro. Supp. I:** 131
Cowl, Jane, **IV:** 357
Cowley, Abraham, **III:** 508; **IV:** 158; **Supp. I Part 1:** 357
Cowley, Malcolm, **I:** 246, 253, 254, 255, 256, 257, 283, 385; **II:** 26, 57, 94, 456; **III:** 606; **IV:** 123; **Retro. Supp. I:** 73, 91, 97; **Retro. Supp. II:** 77, 83, 89, 221, 330; **Retro. Supp. III:** 48, 75, 79; **Supp. I Part 1:** 174; **Supp. I Part 2:** 609, 610, 620, 647, 654, 678; **Supp. II Part 1:** 103, **135–156; Supp. VIII:** 96; **Supp. XV:** 142; **Supp. XX: 76; Supp. XXVI:** 17
Cowley, Marguerite Frances Baird (Mrs. Malcolm Cowley), **Supp. I Part 2:** 615; **Supp. II Part 1:** 138, 139
Cowley, Muriel Maurer (Mrs. Malcolm Cowley), **Supp. II Part 1:** 139
Cowley, Susan Cheever (Susan Cheever), **Supp. I Part 1:** 175; **Supp. IX:** 133; **Supp. XXIV:** 97
Cowper, William, **II:** 17, 304; **III:** 508, 511; **Supp. I Part 1:** 150, 151, 152; **Supp. I Part 2:** 539
"Cow Wandering in the Bare Field, The" (Jarrell), **II:** 371, 388
Cox, Martha Heasley, **Supp. IX:** 2, 4, 11–12
Cox, Sidney, **Retro. Supp. I:** 131; **Supp. XXI:** 19, 21
Cox, Stephen, **Supp. IV Part 2:** 523, 524
Cox, Steve, **Supp. XIX:** 116, 128
Coxey, Jacob, **II:** 464
"Coxon Fund, The" (James), **Retro. Supp. I:** 228
"Coy Mistress" (A. Finch), **Supp. XVII:** 72
Coyne, Patricia, **Supp. V:** 123
"Coyote Ortiz: Canis latrans latrans in the Poetry of Simon Ortiz" (P. C. Smith), **Supp. IV Part 2:** 509
Coyote's Daylight Trip (Gunn Allen), **Supp. IV Part 1:** 320, 324
Coyote Was Here (Ortiz), **Supp. IV Part 2:** 499
Cozzens, James Gould, **I: 358–380; II:** 459
Crabbe, George, **II:** 304; **III:** 469, 508, 511, 521; **Supp. XXIV:** 159
"Crab-Boil" (Dove), **Supp. IV Part 1:** 249
"Cracked Looking-Glass, The" (Porter), **III:** 434, 435, 446
"Cracker Chidlings" (Rawlings), **Supp. X:** 224, 228
Cracks (Purdy), **Supp. VII:** 277–278
Cracks Between What We Are and What We Are Supposed to Be, The (Mullen), **Supp. XXVII:** 175

"Cracks in the Universe" (Davison), **Supp. XXVI:** 78
Crack-Up, The (Fitzgerald), **II:** 80; **III:** 35, 45; **Retro. Supp. I:** 113, 115; **Supp. IX:** 61; **Supp. V:** 276
"Crack-Up, The" (Fitzgerald), **I:** 509; **Retro. Supp. I:** 113, 114
"Crack-up of American Optimism, The: Vachel Lindsay, the Dante of the Fundamentalists" (Viereck), **Supp. I Part 2:** 403
"Cradle and the Bookcase, The"(Hadas), **Supp. XXIII:** 122
"Cradle Me" (Biss), **Supp. XXVI:** 48
Cradle Will Rock, The (Blitzstein), **Supp. I Part 1:** 277, 278
Craft of Fiction, The (Lubbock), **I:** 504; **Supp. VIII:** 165
Craft of Peter Taylor, The (McAlexander, ed.), **Supp. V:** 314
Craig, David M., **Supp. XXII:** 187, 191, 192
Craig, Gordon, **III:** 394; **Supp. XXI:** 6
Craigie, William A., **Retro. Supp. III:** 265
Crain, Jane Larkin, **Supp. V:** 123; **Supp. XII:** 167, 168
Crais, Robert, **Supp. XXI:** 70
Cram, Ralph Adams, **I:** 19
Cramer, Steven, **Supp. XI:** 139; **Supp. XV:** 26
"Cramped Quarters" (Davison), **Supp. XXVI:** 77
"Cranbrook Schools: Adventures in Bourgeois Topologies" (Monson), **Supp. XXIV:** 235
Crandall, Reuben, **Supp. I Part 2:** 686
Crane, Agnes, **I:** 406
Crane, Edmund, **I:** 407
Crane, Hart, **I:** 61, 62, 97, 109, 116, 266, **381–404; II:** 133, 215, 306, 368, 371, 536, 542; **III:** 260, 276, 453, 485, 521; **IV:** 122, 123–124, 127, 128, 129, 135, 139, 140, 141, 341, 380, 418, 419; **Retro. Supp. I:** 427; **Retro. Supp. II: 75–91; Retro. Supp. III: 41–55; Supp. I Part 1:** 86; **Supp. II Part 1:** 89, 152; **Supp. III Part 1:** 20, 63, 350; **Supp. IX:** 38, 229, 320; **Supp. V:** 342; **Supp. VIII:** 39; **Supp. X:** 115, 116, 120; **Supp. XI:** 123, 131; **Supp. XII:** 198; **Supp. XIX:** 35; **Supp. XV:** 138; **Supp. XX: 80; Supp. XXI:** 131, 132, 136, 230; **Supp. XXII:** 274; **Supp. XXIII:** 146, 174, 207; **Supp. XXV:** 19; **Supp. XXVI:** 21, 23–24, 25, 28, 143
Crane, Jonathan, Jr., **I:** 407
Crane, Jonathan Townley, **I:** 406
Crane, Mrs. Jonathan Townley, **I:** 406
Crane, Luther, **I:** 406
Crane, Milton, **Supp. XV:** 144
Crane, Nellie, **I:** 407
Crane, R. S., **Supp. I Part 2:** 423
Crane, Stephen, **I:** 34, 169–170, 201, 207, 211, **405–427,** 477, 506, 519; **II:** 58, 144, 198, 262, 263, 264, 276, 289, 290, 291; **III:** 314, 317, 334, 335, 454, 505, 585; **IV:** 207, 208, 256, 350, 475; **Retro. Supp. I:** 231, 325; **Retro. Supp. II:** 97, 123; **Supp. I Part 1:** 314; **Supp. III Part 2:** 412; **Supp. IV Part 1:** 350, 380; **Supp. IV Part 2:** 680, 689, 692; **Supp. IX:** 1, 14; **Supp. VIII:** 98, 105; **Supp. X:** 223; **Supp. XI:** 95; **Supp. XII:** 50; **Supp. XIV:** 21, 50, 51, 227; **Supp. XVII:** 71, 228; **Supp. XVIII:** 74, 75; **Supp. XXIII:** 26
Crane, William, **I:** 407
Cranford (Gaskell), **Supp. IX:** 79
Crash (film, Cronenberg), **Supp. XXVI:** 28
Crashaw, William, **IV:** 145, 150, 151, 165
"Crash Report" (McGrath), **Supp. X:** 116
Crater (Hickam), **Supp. XXVII:** 111
Crater, The (Cooper), **I:** 354, 355
Crater Trueblood and the Lunar Rescue Company (Hickam), **Supp. XXVII:** 111
Cratylus (Plato), **II:** 10
Cravan, Arthur, **Supp. XXII:** 164, 169
"Craven Street Gazette" (Franklin), **II:** 119
"Crawdad, The" (F. Wright), **Supp. XVII:** 244
Crawdad Creek (Sanders), **Supp. XVI:** 269
Crawford, Brad, **Supp. XI:** 133
Crawford, Eva, **I:** 199
Crawford, F. Marion, **III:** 320
Crawford, Joan, **Supp. I Part 1:** 67
Crawford, John E., **Supp. XXIII:** 165
Crawford, Kathleen, **I:** 289
Crawford, Neta C., **Supp. XXVI:** 85
Crawford, Robert, **Retro. Supp. III:** 57
"Crayon House" (Rukeyser), **Supp. VI:** 273
Crayon Miscellany, The (Irving), **II:** 312–313
Crazed, The (Jin), **Supp. XVIII: 99–100**
"Crazy about her Shrimp" (Simic), **Supp. VIII:** 282
"Crazy Cock" (H. Miller), **III:** 177
Crazy Gypsy (Salinas), **Supp. XIII:** 311, **313–315,** 316
"Crazy Gypsy" (Salinas), **Supp. XIII:** 313–314
Crazy Horse, **Supp. IV Part 2:** 488, 489
Crazy Horse (McMurtry), **Supp. V:** 233
Crazy Horse in Stillness (Heyen), **Supp. XIII:** 344
Crazy Horse: The Strange Man of the Oglaglas (Sandoz), **Supp. XXIV:** 244, 256, **257–258**
"Crazy Hunter, The" (Boyle), **Supp. XXIV: 54–55**
Crazy Hunter, The: Three Short Novels (Boyle), **Supp. XXIV: 54–56**
"Crazy in the Stir" (C. Himes), **Supp. XVI:** 137
Crazy Kill, The (C. Himes), **Supp. XVI:** 143
Crazy Man (Bodenheim), **Supp. XXV:** 22, 24
Creating a Role (Stanislavsky), **Supp. XIV:** 243
"Creation, According to Coyote, The" (Ortiz), **Supp. IV Part 2:** 505
Creation: A Novel (Vidal), **Supp. IV Part 2:** 677, 685, 688
"Creation of Anguish" (Nemerov), **III:** 269
"Creation Story" (Gunn Allen), **Supp. IV Part 1:** 325
"Creative and Cultural Lag" (Ellison), **Retro. Supp. II:** 116; **Supp. II Part 1:** 229; **Supp. XVIII:** 283
Creative Criticism (Spingarn), **I:** 266
"Creative Democracy" (Locke), **Supp. XIV:** 208
Creative Present, The (Balkian and Simmons, eds.), **Supp. XI:** 230
"Creatures" (Gallagher), **Supp. XXIV:** 176, 177
Creatures in an Alphabet (illus. Barnes), **Supp. III Part 1:** 43
"Creatures of the Genitive" (Davison), **Supp. XXVI:** 74
"Credences of Summer" (Stevens), **IV:** 93–94
"Credentials" (Halliday), **Supp. XIX:** 90
"Credo" (Bynner), **Supp. XV:** 50
"Credo" (Du Bois), **Supp. II Part 1:** 169
"Credo" (Jeffers), **Supp. II Part 2:** 424
"Credos and Curios" (Thurber), **Supp. I Part 2:** 606, 613
Creech, James, **Retro. Supp. I:** 254
"Creed for Americans, A" (Benét), **Supp. XI:** 52

"Creed of a Beggar, The" (Lindsay), **Supp. I Part 2:** 379
Creegan, Andy, **Supp. XIX:** 205
Creekmore, Hubert, **II:** 586
Creeley, Robert, **Retro. Supp. I:** 411; **Supp. II Part 1:** 30; **Supp. III Part 1:** 2; **Supp. III Part 2:** 622, 626, 629; **Supp. IV Part 1: 139–161,** 322, 325; **Supp. XI:** 317; **Supp. XIII:** 104, 112; **Supp. XIV:** 150; **Supp. XVI:** 283; **Supp. XXI:** 23, 27, 227, 230; **Supp. XXII:** 227; **Supp. XXIV:** 35, 37; **Supp. XXVII:** 18, 22, 160
Creelman, James Ashmore, **Supp. XVI:** 186–187
"Cremona Violin, The" (A. Lowell), **II:** 523
"Crêpe de Chine" (Doty), **Supp. XI:** 128
"Crêpes Flambeau" (Gallagher), **Supp. XXIV:** 170
Crescent (Hickam), **Supp. XXVII:** 111
"Cressy" (Harte), **Supp. II Part 1:** 354, 356
"Cretan Woman, The" (Jeffers), **Supp. II Part 2:** 435
Crèvecoeur, Michel-Guillaume Jean de, **I:** 229; **Supp. I Part 1: 227–252**
Crèvecoeur's Eighteenth-Century Travels in Pennsylvania and New York (Adams), **Supp. I Part 1:** 251
Crevel, René, **Supp. XIV:** 343
Crewe-Jones, Florence, **Supp. XVII:** 58
Crewe Train (Macaulay), **Supp. XII:** 88
Crews, Harry, **Supp. X:** 11, 12; **Supp. XI: 99–117,** 245; **Supp. XVIII:** 195; **Supp. XXI:** 35, 38, 40, 44
Crews, James, **Supp. XXIII:** 134–135
Crichton, Michael, **Supp. XIV:** 316
Crick, Philip, **Supp. XVI:** 289
Cricket (C. L. R. James; Grimshaw, ed.), **Supp. XXI:** 172
"Cricket" (C. Miller), **Supp. XXII:** 199
"Crickets" (R. O. Butler), **Supp. XII:** 71
Criers and Kibitzers, Kibitzers and Criers (Elkin), **Supp. VI: 45–46,** 57
Crime and Punishment (Dostoevsky), **II:** 60, 130; **IV:** 484; **Supp. IV Part 2:** 525; **Supp. VIII:** 282; **Supp. XII:** 281; **Supp. XIX:** 276; **Supp. XVII:** 155; **Supp. XVIII:** 278
Crime at Scottsboro, The (Endore), **Supp. XVII:** 59
Crime Beat (Connelly), **Supp. XXI:** 67, 79
Crimes and Misdemeanors (film; Allen), **Supp. XV:** 1, **2, 11,** 12
Crime Without Passion (film), **Supp. XXVII:** 90
"Criminal"(Strout), **Supp. XXIII:** 283, 285
Crisis papers (Paine), **Supp. I Part 2:** 508–509, 510
"Criteria of Negro Art" (Du Bois), **Supp. II Part 1:** 181; **Supp. XIX:** 66–67
"Critiad, The" (Winters), **Supp. II Part 2:** 794, 799
Critical Anthology A (Untermeyer), **Supp. XV:** 310
Critical Companion to Flannery O'Connor (Kirk), **Retro. Supp. III:** 210
Critical Essays on Charlotte Perkins Gilman (Karpinski, ed.), **Supp. XI:** 201
Critical Essays on Kay Boyle (Elkins, ed.), **Supp. XXIV:** 64
Critical Essays on Peter Taylor (McAlexander), **Supp. V:** 319, 320, 323–324
Critical Essays on Robert Bly (W. V. Davis), **Supp. IV Part 1:** 64, 69
Critical Essays on Wallace Stegner (Arthur), **Supp. IV Part 2:** 606
Critical Fable, A (A. Lowell), **II:** 511–512, 527, 529–530
Critical Guide to Leaves of Grass, A (J. Miller), **IV:** 352
Critical Mass (Paretsky), **Supp. XXV:** 185
Critical Response to Joan Didion, The (Felton), **Supp. IV Part 1:** 210
Critical Temper of Alain Locke, The: A Selection of His Essays on Art and Culture (Stewart, ed.), **Supp. XIV:** 196, **210–211,** 213
"Critic as Artist, The" (Wilde), **Supp. X:** 189
Criticism and Fiction (Howells), **II:** 288
Criticism and Ideology (Eagleton), **Retro. Supp. I:** 67
Criticism in the Borderlands (Calderón and Saldívar, eds.), **Supp. IV Part 2:** 544
"Critics, The" (Jong), **Supp. V:** 119
"Critics and Connoisseurs" (Moore), **III:** 209
Critic's Notebook, A (Howe), **Supp. VI:** 126–128
"Critic's Task, The" (Kazin), **Supp. VIII:** 103
"Critic Who Does Not Exist, The" (Wilson), **IV:** 431
"Critique de la Vie Quotidienne" (Barthelme), **Supp. IV Part 1:** 50
Critique of Pure Reason (Kant), **Supp. XVI:** 184
Croce, Benedetto, **I:** 58, 255, 265, 273, 281; **III:** 610
Crockett, Davy, **II:** 307; **III:** 227; **IV:** 266; **Supp. I Part 2:** 411
"Crocodilopolis" (Cliff), **Supp. XXII:** 76
Crofter and the Laird, The (McPhee), **Supp. III Part 1:** 301–302, 307
Croll, Nora Swan, **Supp. XXVII:** 262
Croly, Herbert, **I:** 229, 231, 235; **IV:** 436
Cromwell, Oliver, **IV:** 145, 146, 156; **Supp. I Part 1:** 111
Cronenberg, David, **Supp. XXI:** 152, 154
Cronin, A. J., **Supp. XVII:** 59
Cronin, Dr. Archibald, **III:** 578
Cronin, Gloria, **Supp. XXVI:** 123
Cronin, Justin, **Supp. X:** 10
Crooke, Dr. Helkiah, **Supp. I Part 1:** 98, 104
Crooked Little Heart (Lamott), **Supp. XX: 138**
Crooker, Barbara, **Supp. XXIII: 51–66,** 245, 246, 251
Crooks, Alan, **Supp. V:** 226
Crooks, Robert, **Supp. XIII:** 237
"Crop, The" (O'Connor), **Retro. Supp. II:** 223–225
Crosby, Caresse, **I:** 385; **III:** 473; **Retro. Supp. II:** 85; **Supp. XII:** 198
Crosby, Harry, **I:** 385; **Retro. Supp. II:** 85
"Cross" (Hughes), **Supp. I Part 1:** 325; **Supp. XVIII:** 124
Cross, Charles, **Supp. XXIV:** 173
Crossan, John Dominic, **Supp. V:** 251
"Cross Country Snow" (Hemingway), **II:** 249
Cross Creek (Rawlings), **Supp. X:** 223, 226, 228, **231–232,** 233, 234, 235
Cross Creek Cookery (Rawlings), **Supp. X:** 233
"Cross Cut" (Davison), **Supp. XXVI:** 74
"Crossing, The" (Huddle), **Supp. XXVI:** 154
Crossing, The (McCarthy), **Supp. VIII:** 175, **184–186**
"Crossing, The" (Swenson), **Supp. IV Part 2:** 644
"Crossing Brooklyn Ferry" (Whitman), **IV:** 333, 340, 341; **Retro. Supp. I:** 389, 396, 397, 400–401; **Retro. Supp. III:** 304, 308–309; **Supp.**

XXIII: 109
"Crossing into Poland" (Babel), **Supp. XIV:** 84
"Crossing New River" (Huddle), **Supp. XXVI:** 148, 150
Crossings (Chuang), **Supp. X:** 291
"Crossings" (Hogan), **Supp. IV Part 1:** 412
"Crossing the Void" (Davison), **Supp. XXVI:** 76
Crossing the Water (Plath), **Retro. Supp. II:** 248; **Supp. I Part 2:** 526, 538
Crossing to Safety (Stegner), **Supp. IV Part 2:** 599, 606, 612, 613–614
"Cross of Snow, The" (Longfellow), **II:** 490; **Retro. Supp. II:** 169–170
"Crossover" (O. Butler), **Supp. XIII:** 61
"Cross-PolliNation" (Gansworth), **Supp. XXVI:** 111
"Cross-Roads, The" (A. Lowell), **II:** 523
"Crossroads of the World Etc." (Merwin), **Supp. III Part 1:** 347, 348
Cross-Section (Seaver), **IV:** 485
Cross the Border, Close the Gap (Fiedler), **Supp. XIII:** 104
Cross Ties (X. J. Kennedy), **Supp. XV:** 165, **166–167**
"Cross Ties" (X. J. Kennedy), **Supp. XV:** 158
Crouch, Stanley, **Supp. XIX:** 158
"Croup" (Karr), **Supp. XI:** 243
Crouse, Russel, **III:** 284
"Crow" (Hogan), **Supp. IV Part 1:** 405
Crow (Hughes), **Supp. XV:** 347, 348
"Crow, The" (Creeley), **Supp. IV Part 1:** 148–149
Crow and the Heart,The (Carruth), **Supp. XVI:** 47–48
"Crowded Countries of the Bomb, The" (Oppen), **Supp. XXVI:** 232
"Crowded Street, The" (Bryant), **Supp. I Part 1:** 168
Crowder, A. B., **Supp. XI:** 107
"Crow Jane" (Baraka), **Supp. II Part 1:** 38
Crow Mercies (Schott), **Supp. XXIII: 252–254**
"Crow Mercies" (Schott), **Supp. XXIII:** 253
Crowninshield, Frank, **III:** 123; **Supp. IX:** 201
Crown of Columbus (Erdrich and Dorris), **Supp. IV Part 1:** 260
"Crows, The" (Bogan), **Supp. III Part 1:** 50, 51
Crucial Instances (Wharton), **Retro. Supp. I:** 365, 367; **Retro. Supp. III:** 278
Crucible, The (A. Miller), **III:** 147, 148, 155, 156–158, 159, 166; **Retro. Supp. III:** 165, 166, 167, 169; **Supp. XIII:** 206; **Supp. XXV:** 93
"Crucified" (Gibran), **Supp. XX: 119**
"Crucifix in the Filing Cabinet" (Shapiro), **Supp. II Part 2:** 712
"Crude Foyer" (Stevens), **Retro. Supp. I:** 310
"Cruel and Barbarous Treatment" (McCarthy), **II:** 562, 563
"Cruel Mother, The" (B. Kelly), **Supp. XVII:** 126
Cruise of the Dazzler, The (London), **II:** 465
Cruise of the Snark, The (London), **II:** 476–477; **Supp. XXV:** 217
Cruisers, The (Myers), **Supp. XXVII:** 212
"Cruising with the Beach Boys" (Gioia), **Supp. XV:** 118
" 'Crumbling Idols' by Hamlin Garland" (Chopin), **Supp. I Part 1:** 217
"Crusade of the Excelsior, The" (Harte), **Supp. II Part 1:** 336, 354
"Crusoe in England" (Bishop), **Retro. Supp. II:** 50; **Supp. I Part 1:** 93, 95, 96; **Supp. III Part 1:** 10, 18
Cruz, Angie, **Supp. XXVI:** 263–264
Cruz-Hacker, Alba, **Supp. XXI:** 107
Cry, the Beloved Country (Paton), **Supp. VIII:** 126
Cryer, Dan, **Supp. VIII:** 86, 88; **Supp. XII:** 164
Crying of Lot 49, The (Pynchon), **Supp. II Part 2:** 618, 619, 621, 630–633
"Crying Sisters, The" (Rand), **Supp. IV Part 2:** 524
"Crying Wolf" (C. Frost), **Supp. XV:** 101
"Cry of the Graves, The" (Gibran), **Supp. XX: 124**
Cryptogram, The (Mamet), **Supp. XIV:** 240, 247, 255
"Crystal, The" (Aiken), **I:** 60
"Crystal, The" (Lanier), **Supp. I Part 1:** 364, 370
"Crystal Cage, The" (Kunitz), **Supp. III Part 1:** 258
Crystal Cup, The (Atherton), **Supp. XXIV:** 26
"Crystal Cup, The" (Teasdale), **Supp. XXVII:** 287
"Crystal Gazer, The" (Teasdale), **Supp. XXVII:** 287, 296
Crystal Vision (Sorrentino), **Supp. XXI:** 235, 236
"Crytal" (Sobin), **Supp. XVI:** 283
Cry to Heaven (Rice), **Supp. VII:** 300–301
"Cuba" (Hemingway), **II:** 258
"Cuba Libre" (Baraka), **Supp. II Part 1:** 33
Cuba: Prophetic Island (W. Frank), **Supp. XX: 80, 81**
"Cubism, Barcelona" (Hull), **Supp. XXI:** 137
Cudjoe, Selwyn, **Supp. IV Part 1:** 6
"Cudjo's Own Story of the Last American Slaver" (Hurston), **Supp. VI:** 153
Cudlipp, Thelma, **I:** 501
Cudworth, Ralph, **II:** 9, 10
"Cuentista" (Mora), **Supp. XIII:** 224
"Cuento de agua santa, Un" (Mora), **Supp. XIII:** 224
"Cui Bono" (H. Johnson), **Supp. XXVI:** 167, 173
Cujo (King), **Supp. V:** 138–139, 143, 149, 152
Cukor, George, **Supp. XVI:** 192
Cullen, Countee, **Retro. Supp. I:** 207; **Retro. Supp. II:** 114; **Retro. Supp. III:** 127; **Supp. I Part 1:** 49, 325; **Supp. III Part 1:** 73, 75, 76; **Supp. IV Part 1: 163–174; Supp. IX:** 306, 309; **Supp. X:** 136, 140; **Supp. XIII:** 186; **Supp. XIX:** 78; **Supp. XVIII:** 122,131; **Supp. XVIII:** 185, 279, 280, 282, 284; **Supp. XXII:** 3, 6, 7, 8
"Cultivation of Christmas Trees, The" (Eliot), **I:** 579
Cult of Alien Gods, The: H. P. Lovecraft and Extraterrestrial Pop Culture (Calavito), **Supp. XXV:** 123
"Cult of Personality in American Letters, The" (Swados), **Supp. XIX:** 265
"Cult of the Best, The" (Arnold), **I:** 223
"Cultural Exchange" (Hughes), **Supp. I Part 1:** 341
"Cultural Pluralism: A New Americanism" (Locke), **Supp. XIV:** 195
"Cultural Relativism and Ideological Peace" (Locke), **Supp. XIV:** 202, 212
"Culture" (Emerson), **III:** 2, 4
"Culture, Self, and Style" (Gass), **Supp. VI:** 88
"Culture and Anarchy" (Rich), **Retro. Supp. III:** 249
"Culture and Religion" (Olds), **Supp. X:** 214
Culture of Cities, The (Mumford),

Supp. II Part 2: 492, 494–495
Cummings, E. E., **I:** 44, 48, 64, 105, 176, **428–450,** 475, 477, 482, 526; **III:** 20, 196, 476; **IV:** 384, 402, 415, 427, 433; **Retro. Supp. II:** 178, 328; **Retro. Supp. III:** 48; **Supp. I Part 2:** 622, 678; **Supp. III Part 1:** 73; **Supp. IV Part 2:** 637, 641; **Supp. IX:** 20; **Supp. XV:** 312, 338; **Supp. XXVI:** 32; **Supp. XXVII:** 261
Cummings, Robert, **Supp. IV Part 2:** 524
Cummins, Ann, **Supp. XXIII:** 280
Cummins, James, **Supp. XVII:** 74
Cunard, Lady, **III:** 459
Cunard, Nancy, **Retro. Supp. III:** 129
Cunningham, Brent, **Supp. XXVII:** 153
Cunningham, J. V., **Supp. XV:** 169
Cunningham, Merce, **Supp. IV Part 1:** 83; **Supp. XV:** 187
Cunningham, Michael, **Supp. XII:** 80; **Supp. XV: 55–71**
Cunningham, Rodger, **Supp. XXIII:** 38–39
Cup of Gold (Steinbeck), **IV:** 51, 53, 61–64, 67
"Cupola, The" (Bogan), **Supp. III Part 1:** 53
"Curandera" (Mora), **Supp. XIII:** 214, 222
Curé de Tours, Le (Balzac), **I:** 509
Cure for Dreams, A: A Novel (Gibbons), **Supp. X: 45–47,** 48, 50
Curie, Marie, **IV:** 420, 421; **Supp. I Part 2:** 569
Curie, Pierre, **IV:** 420
Curiosa Americana (Mather), **Supp. II Part 2:** 463
Curiosities (Matthews), **Supp. IX:** 151, 152
"Curious Case of Sidd Finch, The" (Plimpton), **Supp. XVI:** 244
"Curious Shifts of the Poor" (Dreiser), **Retro. Supp. II:** 97
"Current" (Espaillat), **Supp. XXI:** 106
"Currents and Counter-Currents in Medical Science" (Holmes), **Supp. I Part 1:** 305
"Curried Cow" (Bierce), **I:** 200
Curry, Professor W. C., **IV:** 122
Curse of Downers Grove, The (film), **Supp. XXVII:** 80
Curse of the Jade Scorpion, The (film; Allen), **Supp. XV:** 11
Curse of the Starving Class (Shepard), **Supp. III Part 2:** 433, 447–448
Curse of the Werewolf, The (film), **Supp. XVII:** 56
"Curse of Yig, The" (Lovecraft and Bishop), **Supp. XXV:** 122
"Curse on a Thief, A" (X. J. Kennedy), **Supp. XV:** 171
"Curtain, The" (Chandler), **Supp. IV Part 1:** 122
Curtain Calls: British and American Women and the Theater, 1660–1820 (Saar), **Supp. XV:** 237
Curtain of Green, A (Welty), **IV:** 261–264, 268, 283
"Curtain of Green, A" (Welty), **IV:** 263–264
Curtain of Green and Other Stories, A (Welty), **Retro. Supp. I:** 343, 344, 345, 346, 347, 355
Curtain of Trees (opera), **Supp. IV Part 2:** 552
"Curtain Raiser, A" (Stein), **IV:** 43, 44
"Curtains" (Cisneros), **Supp. VII:** 66
Curtin, John, **Supp. IX:** 184
Curtis, George William, **Supp. I Part 1:** 307; **Supp. XVIII:** 3, 14
Curve (Goldbarth), **Supp. XII:** 181
Curve of Binding Energy, The (McPhee), **Supp. III Part 1:** 301
Curzon, Mary, **III:** 52
Cushing, Caleb, **Supp. I Part 2:** 684, 686
Cushman, Howard, **Supp. I Part 2:** 652
Cushman, Stephen, **Retro. Supp. I:** 430
Cusick, Albert, **Supp. XXVI:** 87
"Custard Heart, The" (Parker), **Supp. IX:** 201
Custer, General George, **I:** 489, 491
Custer Died for Your Sins (Deloria), **Supp. IV Part 1:** 323; **Supp. IV Part 2:** 504
"Custody"(Schott), **Supp. XXIII:** 241
"Custom House, The" (Hawthorne), **II:** 223; **Retro. Supp. I:** 147–148, 157; **Retro. Supp. III:** 116; **Supp. XXI:** 181
Custom of the Country, The (Wharton), **IV:** 318; **Retro. Supp. I:** 374, **375–376; Retro. Supp. III:** 284–285; **Supp. XXIV:** 23
"Cut" (Plath), **Retro. Supp. II:** 253
"Cut-Glass Bowl, The" (Fitzgerald), **II:** 88
Cutting, Bronson, **III:** 600
Cutting Lisa (Everett), **Supp. XVIII: 56**
"Cuttings, later" (Roethke), **III:** 532
"Cyberpunk" (Bethke), **Supp. XVI:** 121
Cyberspace trilogy (W. Gibson). See Sprawl trilogy (W. Gibson)
"Cycles, The" (Pinsky), **Supp. VI:** 250–252
Cyclopedia of American Literature (Duyckinck and Duyckinck), **Supp. XXV:** 250
Cynic's Word Book, The (Bierce), **I:** 197, 205, 208, 209, 210
Cynthia Ozick (Lowin), **Supp. V:** 273
Cynthia Ozick's Comic Art (Cohen), **Supp. V:** 273
Cynthia Ozick's Fiction (Kauvar), **Supp. V:** 273
"Czar's Soliloquy, The" (Twain), **Retro. Supp. III:** 269
"Czeslaw Milosz and Memory" (Hampl), **Supp. XXII:** 92
Da Capo: Best Music Writing 2002 (Lethem, ed.), **Supp. XVIII:** 148
Dacey, Philip, **Supp. IV Part 1:** 70
Dacier, André, **II:** 10
"Dad" (Cullen), **Supp. IV Part 1:** 167
"Daddy" (Plath), **Retro. Supp. II:** 250–251; **Supp. I Part 2:** 529, 542, 545, 546; **Supp. II Part 2:** 688; **Supp. XXII:** 30; **Supp. XXIII:** 112, 113
"Daddy"(Hadas), **Supp. XXIII:** 112, 113
Daddy's Little Boy (Collins), **Supp. XXI:** 54
"Daemon, The" (Bogan), **Supp. III Part 1:** 58, 61
"Daemon Lover, The" (Jackson), **Supp. IX:** 116–117
"Daffodils" (Nelson and Espeland), **Supp. XVIII:** 181
"Daffodils" (Wordsworth), **Supp. XIII:** 284
"Daffy Duck in Hollywood" (Ashbery), **Supp. III Part 1:** 18
D'Agata, John, **Supp. XII:** 97, 98
"Dagon" (Lovecraft), **Supp. XXV:** 111, 121
Dago Red (Fante), **Supp. XI:** 160, 169
Dahl, Roald, **Supp. IX:** 114
Dahlberg, Edward, **I:** 231; **Retro. Supp. I:** 426; **Supp. III Part 2:** 624; **Supp. XIV:** 148; **Supp. XVIII:** 148; **Supp. XXII:** 257
Dahlberg, R'lene, **Supp. XIV:** 148
Daiches, David, **Retro. Supp. II:** 243; **Supp. I Part 2:** 536
Daily Horoscope (Gioia), **Supp. XV:** 112, **118–121,** 126
"Daily Horoscope" (Gioia), **Supp. XV:** 119
Daily Modernism (Podnieks), **Supp. X:** 189
Dain Curse, The (Hammett), **Supp. IV Part 1:** 348

"Daisies" (Glück), **Supp. V:** 88
"Daisy" (Oates), **Supp. II Part 2:** 523
Daisy (S. and A. Warner), **Supp. XVIII:** 268
Daisy-Head Mayzie (Geisel), **Supp. XVI:** 112
Daisy Miller (H. James), **Retro. Supp. I:** 216, 220, 222, 223, 228, 231; **Supp. XVIII:** 165; **Supp. XXIV:** 23
"Daisy Miller" (H. James), **II:** 325, 326, 327, 329; **IV:** 316
"Dakota (IV)" (Gansworth), **Supp. XXVI:** 111
Dale, Charlie, **Supp. IV Part 2:** 584
Daley, Yvonne, **Supp. XXII:** 216
Dali, Salvador, **II:** 586; **Supp. IV Part 1:** 83; **Supp. XIII:** 317
Dalibard, Thomas-François, **II:** 117
"Dallas-Fort Worth: Redband and Mistletoe" (Clampitt), **Supp. IX:** 45
"Dalliance of Eagles, The" (Whitman), **IV:** 348
Dalva (Harrison), **Supp. VIII:** 37, 45, 46, **48–49**
Daly, Carroll John, **Supp. IV Part 1:** 343, 345
Daly, John, **II:** 25, 26
Daly, Julia Brown, **II:** 25, 26
"Dalyrimple Goes Wrong" (Fitzgerald), **II:** 88
"Dam, The" (Rukeyser), **Supp. VI:** 283
Damas, Leon, **Supp. X:** 139
Damascus Gate (Stone), **Supp. V:** 308–311
Damballah (Wideman), **Supp. X:** 319, 320, 321, 322, 323, 326, 327, 331, 333–334
Dameshek, Brandon, **Supp. XIX:** 273, 277, 287
Damnation of Theron Ware, The (Frederic), **II:** 140–143, 144, 146, 147; **Retro. Supp. I:** 325
Damned If I Do (Everett), **Supp. XVIII:** 66
"Damned Thing, The" (Bierce), **I:** 206
Damon, Matt, **Supp. VIII:** 175
Damon, S. Foster, **I:** 26; **II:** 512, 514, 515
"Damon and Vandalia" (Dove), **Supp. IV Part 1:** 252
Dana, H. W. L., **I:** 225
Dana, Richard Henry, Jr., **III:** 81; **Retro. Supp. III:** 150; **Supp. XX: 227; Supp. XXV:** 208
Dana, Richard Henry, Sr., **I:** 339, 351; **Supp. I Part 1:** 103, 154, 155; **Supp. I Part 2:** 414, 420; **Supp. XXV:** 250
Dana, Robert, **Supp. V:** 178, 180
"Dana Gioia and Fine Press Printing" (Peich), **Supp. XV:** 117
"Dance" (Kenny), **Supp. XXIII:** 148
"Dance, The" (Crane), **I:** 109
"Dance, The" (Roethke), **III:** 541
"Dance, The" (W. C. Williams), **Supp. XVII:** 113
Dance and the Railroad, The (Hwang), **Supp. XXI:** 145, 146
"Dance in a Buffalo Skull" (Zitkala-Ša), **Supp. XXV:** 276
"Dance Me to the End of Love" (Cohen), **Supp. XXVII:** 61
Dance of Death, The (Auden), **Supp. II Part 1:** 10
Dance of Death, The (Bierce and Harcourt), **I:** 196
Dance of Life, The (Ellis), **Supp. XX: 117**
Dance of the Happy Shades (Munro), **Supp. XXVII:** 181, 182, 194
Dance of the Sleepwalkers (Calabria), **Supp. XIII:** 164
"Dance of the Solids, The" (Updike), **Retro. Supp. I:** 323
"Dancer" (Hoffman), **Supp. XVIII:** 86
Dancer (Myers), **Supp. XXVII:** 200
"Dancer, The" (Swados), **Supp. XIX:** 261, 263–264
Dancers, The (Myers), **Supp. XXVII:** 211
"Dancers Work by Forgetting" (Espaillat), **Supp. XXI:** 102
"Dances of Madness" (Schott), **Supp. XXIII:** 245
Dances with Wolves (film), **Supp. X:** 124
Dance to the Music of Time, A (Powell), **Supp. XVIII:** 146
Dancing After Hours (Dubus), **Supp. VII:** 91
Dancing Back Strong the Nation (Kenny), **Supp. XXIII:** 144, **148**
Dancing Bears, The (Merwin), **Supp. III Part 1:** 343–344
"Dancing Mind, The" (speech, Morrison), **Retro. Supp. III:** 184
Dancing on the Stones (Nichols), **Supp. XIII:** 256, 257, 259, 267, 269
"Dancing the Jig" (Sexton), **Supp. II Part 2:** 692
Dandelion Wine (Bradbury), **Supp. IV Part 1:** 101, 109–110
Dandurand, Karen, **Retro. Supp. I:** 30
"Dandy Frightening the Squatter, The" (Twain), **IV:** 193–194; **Retro. Supp. III:** 256, 259
Dangel, Mary Jo, **Supp. XVIII:** 156
Dangerous Crossroads (film), **Supp. XIII:** 163
Dangerous Day (Rinehart), **Supp. XXV:** 195
Dangerous Moonlight (Purdy), **Supp. VII:** 278
"Dangerous Road Before Martin Luther King" (Baldwin), **Supp. I Part 1:** 52
"Dangerous Summer, The" (Hemingway), **II:** 261
Dangerous Thoughts (Ryan as Quin), **Supp. XVIII:** 226
"Dangers of Authorship, The" (Blackmur), **Supp. II Part 1:** 147
Dangling Man (Bellow), **I:** 144, 145, 147, 148, 150–151, 153–154, 158, 160, 161, 162, 163; **Retro. Supp. II:** 19, 20–21, 22, 23; **Supp. VIII:** 234; **Supp. XIX:** 157
"Dang Little Squirt" (Bontemps), **Supp. XXII:** 4
Daniel (biblical book), **Supp. I Part 1:** 105
Daniel (film), **Supp. IV Part 1:** 236
Daniel, Arnaut, **III:** 467
Daniel, Robert W., **III:** 76
Daniel, Samuel, **Supp. I Part 1:** 369
Daniel Deronda (G. Eliot), **I:** 458
Daniels, Frank, **Supp. XXII:** 196
Daniels, Kate, **Supp. XVII:** 112
Danielson, Linda, **Supp. IV Part 2:** 569
D'Annunzio, Gabriele, **II:** 515
Danny and the Deep Blue Sea: An Apache Dance (Shanley), **Supp. XIV:** 315, **318–319,** 320, 321, 323, 324
Danny O'Neill pentalogy (Farrell), **II:** 35–41
Danse Macabre (King), **Supp. IV Part 1:** 102; **Supp. V:** 144; **Supp. XXV:** 123
"Danse Russe" (W. C. Williams), **IV:** 412–413
"Dans le Restaurant" (Eliot), **I:** 554, 578
Dans l'ombre des cathédrales (Ambelain), **Supp. I Part 1:** 273
Dante Alighieri, **I:** 103, 136, 138, 250, 384, 433, 445; **II:** 8, 274, 278, 289, 490, 492, 493, 494, 495, 504, 508, 524, 552; **III:** 13, 77, 124, 182, 259, 278, 448, 453, 467, 533, 607, 609, 610–612, 613; **IV:** 50, 134, 137, 138, 139, 247, 437, 438; **Retro. Supp. I:** 62, 63, 64, 66, 360; **Retro. Supp. II:** 330; **Supp. I Part 1:** 256, 363; **Supp. I Part 2:** 422, 454; **Supp. III Part 2:** 611, 618, 621; **Supp. IV Part 2:** 634; **Supp. V:** 277, 283, 331, 338, 345; **Supp.**

VIII: 27, 219–221; Supp. X: 120, 121, 125; Supp. XII: 98; Supp. XV: 254; Supp. XVII: 227, 241
Danvis Tales: Selected Stories (Robinson; Budbill, ed.), Supp. XIX: 6
Danziger, Adolphe, I: 199–200
Danziger, Jeff, Supp. XXII: 208
Dar (Nabokov), III: 246, 255
D'Arcy, Randall, Supp. XVII: 76
Dardis, Tom, Supp. XVIII: 249
"Dare's Gift" (Glasgow), II: 190
Darius & Twig (Myers), Supp. XXVII: 205
Dark and Feeling, The: Black American Writers and Their Work (Major), Supp. XXII: 180
Dark Angel, The (Bolton), Supp. I Part 1: 281
"Dark Angel Travels With Us to Canada and Blesses Our Vacation, The" (Dunn), Supp. XI: 146
Dark at the Top of the Stairs, The (film), Supp. XXV: 102
Dark at the Top of the Stairs, The (Inge), Supp. XXV: 93, 95, 100–102
Dark Barbarian, The (Howard, Herron ed.), Supp. XXVII: 118, 128
Dark Carnival (Bradbury), Supp. IV Part 1: 102
Darker (Strand), Supp. IV Part 2: 619, 626–628
Darker Face of the Earth, The (Dove), Supp. IV Part 1: 255–257
Dark Fields of the Republic: Poems 1991–1995 (Rich), Retro. Supp. III: 250, 252
"Dark Fire" (Hadas), Supp. XXIII: 126
Dark Green, Bright Red (Vidal), Supp. IV Part 2: 677
Dark Half, The (King), Supp. V: 141
Dark Harbor: A Poem (Strand), Supp. IV Part 2: 633–634
"Dark Hills, The" (Robinson), III: 523
Dark Horses (X. J. Kennedy), Supp. XV: 167–170
Dark Hours, The (W. V. Davis), Supp. XXI: 91–92, 93
"Dark Houses" (Davison), Supp. XXVI: 72
Dark Laughter (Anderson), I: 111, 116; II: 250–251
"Darkling Alphabet, A" (Snodgrass), Supp. VI: 323
Darkling Child (Merwin and Milroy), Supp. III Part 1: 346
"Darkling Summer, Ominous Dusk, Rumorous Rain" (Schwartz), Supp. II Part 2: 661
"Darkling Thrush" (Hardy), Supp. IX: 40
"Dark Man, The" (Howard), Supp. XXVII: 123
"Dark Men, The" (Dubus), Supp. VII: 86
Dark Mirrors (Sobin), Supp. XVI: 295
Dark Mother, The (W. Frank), Supp. XX: 70–71
Dark Mountains, The (Hoffman), Supp. XVIII: 76–77
Darkness and the Light, The (Hecht), Supp. X: 58
Darkness at Noon (Koestler), Supp. XXIII: 1
Darkness More Than Night, A (Connelly), Supp. XXI: 73–74, 80
"Darkness on the Edge of Town" (O'Brien), Supp. V: 246
Darkness Surrounding Us, The (Sorrentino), Supp. XXI: 227, 228
Darkness under the Trees/Walking behind the Spanish (Salinas), Supp. XIII: 311, 319–324
"Dark Night" (St. John of the Cross), Supp. XV: 30
Dark Night of the Soul, The (St. John of the Cross), I: 1, 585
Dark of the Moon (Teasdale), Supp. XXVII: 284, 286, 295–296
"Dark Ones" (Dickey), Supp. IV Part 1: 182
Dark Power (Holding), Supp. XXII: 122–123, 124
Dark Princess: A Romance (Du Bois), Supp. II Part 1: 179, 181–182
Dark Room, The (T. Williams), IV: 381
Dark Sacred Night (CD), Supp. XXI: 75
Dark Shadows (television show), Supp. XIX: 57
"Dark Summer" (Bogan), Supp. III Part 1: 51, 53
Dark Summer: Poems (Bogan), Supp. III Part 1: 52–53, 57
"Dark Tower, The" (column), Supp. IV Part 1: 168, 170
Dark Tower, The: The Gunslinger (King), Supp. V: 152
Dark Tower IV, The: Wizard and Glass (King), Supp. V: 139
Dark Tunnel, The (Macdonald as Millar), Supp. IV Part 2: 465, 466
"Dark TV Screen" (Simic), Supp. VIII: 282
Dark Valley Destiny (Sprague de Camp), Supp. XXVII: 115, 128
"Dark Voyage, The" (McLay), Supp. XIII: 21
"Dark Walk, The" (Taylor), Supp. V: 320–321, 322, 326
Darkwater: Voices from Within the Veil (Du Bois), Supp. II Part 1: 178, 180, 183
Dark Waves and Light Matter (Goldbarth), Supp. XII: 176, 193
Dark World (Carruth), Supp. XVI: 55
"Darling" (Nye), Supp. XIII: 283–284
"Darling, The" (Chekhov), Supp. IX: 202
Darling-Darling (Barillet and Grédy; Loos, trans.), Supp. XVI: 194
Darnell, Linda, Supp. XII: 173
Darragh, Tina, Supp. IV Part 2: 427
Darreu, Robert Donaldson, Supp. II Part 1: 89, 98, 102
Darrow, Clarence, Supp. I Part 1: 5; Supp. I Part 2: 455; Supp. XXVII: 88
Dartmouth, Earl of, Supp. XX: 284
Darwin, Charles, I: 457; II: 323, 462, 481; III: 226, 231; IV: 69, 304; Retro. Supp. I: 254; Retro. Supp. II: 60, 65; Supp. I Part 1: 368; Supp. IX: 180; Supp. XI: 203; Supp. XVI: 13; Supp. XX: 18; Supp. XXVII: 34, 126
"Darwin in 1881" (Schnackenberg), Supp. XV: 253, 254, 258
Daryush, Elizabeth, Supp. V: 180
Dasburg, Andrew, Supp. XXI: 6
Dash, Julie, Supp. XI: 17, 18, 20
Dash, Robert, Supp. XXVII: 23
Dashell, Alfred, Supp. X: 224
"DAS KAPITAL" (Baraka), Supp. II Part 1: 55
"[Date, 1601.] Conversation, as it Was by the Social Fireside, in the Time of the Tudors" (Twain), Retro. Supp. III: 262
Datlow, Ellen, Supp. XVI: 123
"Datum Centurio" (Wallace), Supp. X: 309
Daudet, Alphonse, II: 325, 338
"Daughter" (Caldwell), I: 309
"Daughter in the House" (X. J. Kennedy), Supp. XV: 160
Daughter of Earth (Smedly), Supp. XIII: 295
"Daughter of Erlik Khan, The" (Howard), Supp. XXVII: 121
Daughter of the Land, A (Stratton-Porter), Supp. XX: 222
Daughter of the Snows, A (London), II: 465, 469–470
Daughter of the Vine, A (Atherton), Supp. XXIV: 18, 22
"Daughters" (Anderson), I: 114
Daughters (Marshall), Supp. XI: 275,

276, 277, **286–288,** 289, 290
"Daughters, 1900" (Nelson), **Supp. XVIII:** 175
Daughters, I Love You (Hogan), **Supp. IV Part 1:** 397, 399, 401
"Daughters of Invention" (Alvarez), **Supp. VII:** 9
Daughters of the Dust (Dash; film), **Supp. XI:** 17, 18; **Supp. XX: 154**
Daughters of Valor: Contemporary Jewish American Women Writers (Halio and Siegel, eds.), **Supp. XXVI:** 123
Daumier, Honoré, **IV:** 412
Dave, R. A., **Supp. VIII:** 126
Davenport, Abraham, **Supp. I Part 2:** 699
Davenport, Basil, **Supp. XXV:** 27
Davenport, Gary, **Supp. IX:** 98
Davenport, Guy, **Supp. XIV:** 96; **Supp. XXI:** 235
Davenport, Herbert J., **Supp. I Part 2:** 642
Davenport, James, **I:** 546
Daves, E. G., **Supp. I Part 1:** 369
Davey, Frank, **Supp. XIII:** 33
"David" (Garrett), **Supp. VII:** 109–110
"David" (Gordon), **Supp. IV Part 1:** 298–299
David, Gray, **Supp. XX: 260**
"David and Agnes, a Romance" (Keillor), **Supp. XVI:** 175
David Blaize (Benson), **Supp. XX: 234**
David Copperfield (Dickens), **I:** 458; **II:** 290; **Retro. Supp. I:** 33; **Supp. XVI:** 65, 72; **Supp. XX: 234**
"David Crockett's Other Life" (Nye), **Supp. XIII:** 282
Davideis (Cowley), **IV:** 158
David Harum (Westcott), **I:** 216
David Huddle Reader, A: Selected Prose and Poetry (Huddle), **Supp. XXVI:** 160
"David Lynch Keeps His Head" (Wallace), **Supp. X:** 314
David Show, The (Gurney), **Supp. V:** 97
"David's Lamentation for Saul and Jonathan" (Bradstreet), **Retro. Supp. III:** 4
Davidson, Cathy, **Supp. XV:** 238
Davidson, Donald, **I:** 294; **III:** 495, 496; **IV:** 121, 122, 124, 125, 236; **Supp. II Part 1:** 139; **Supp. XIV:** 2; **Supp. XX: 164**
Davidson, James West, **Supp. XXII:** 218
Davidson, Jo, **Supp. XXI:** 7
Davidson, John, **Retro. Supp. I:** 55
Davidson, Michael, **Supp. VIII:** 290, 293, 294, 302–303; **Supp. XXVI:** 224
Davidson, Phebe, **Supp. XXIII:** 252
Davidson, Sara, **Supp. IV Part 1:** 196, 198, 203
Davidson, Sue, **Supp. XIX:** 260
Davidsz de Heem, Jan, **Supp. XI:** 133
Davie, Donald, **III:** 478; **Supp. IV Part 2:** 474; **Supp. V:** 331; **Supp. X:** 55, 59; **Supp. XVII:** 111, 112, 121
Davies, Arthur, **III:** 273
Davies, Sir John, **III:** 541
Davies, Marion, **Supp. XVI:** 186
Da Vinci, Leonardo, **I:** 274; **II:** 536; **III:** 210
Da Vinci Code, The (Brown), **Supp. XXVII:** 5
Davis, Allen F., **Supp. I Part 1:** 1, 7
Davis, Allison, **Supp. I Part 1:** 327
Davis, Angela, **Retro. Supp. III:** 184; **Supp. I Part 1:** 66; **Supp. X:** 249; **Supp. XXVI:** 50
Davis, Arthur B., **Supp. XVIII:** 119
Davis, Bette, **I:** 78; **Supp. I Part 1:** 67
Davis, Bill, **Supp. XIII:** 267
Davis, Christina, **Supp. XV:** 264
Davis, Cynthia, **Supp. XVIII:** 281, 286
Davis, Donald, **Supp. XIII:** 93
Davis, Elizabeth Gould, **Supp. I Part 2:** 567
Davis, George, **II:** 586
Davis, Glover, **Supp. V:** 180, 182, 186
Davis, Jefferson, **II:** 206; **IV:** 122, 125, 126
Davis, Jordan, **Supp. XV:** 178, 181, 186, 188
Davis, Katie, **Supp. VIII:** 83
Davis, L. J., **Supp. XI:** 234
Davis, Lydia, **Supp. XII:** 24; **Supp. XVII:** 21
Davis, Marcia, **Supp. XVIII:** 91, 100
Davis, Mary H., **Supp. XVIII:** 77
Davis, Miles, **Supp. XV:** 346; **Supp. XXII:** 172
Davis, Ossie, Jr., **Supp. IV Part 1:** 362; **Supp. XVI:** 144
Davis, Rebecca Harding, **Supp. I Part 1:** 45; **Supp. XIII:** 292, 295, 305; **Supp. XVI: 79–96**
Davis, Richard Harding, **III:** 328; **Supp. II Part 1:** 393; **Supp. XVI:** 85
Davis, Robert Gorham, **II:** 51; **IV:** 108
Davis, Stuart, **IV:** 409; **Supp. XV:** 295; **Supp. XXI:** 6
Davis, Thadious, **Supp. XVIII:** 120, 121, 123, 127, 129
Davis, Thulani, **Supp. XI:** 179; **Supp. XIII:** 233, 234, 239
Davis, William Virgil, **Supp. IV Part 1:** 63, 64, 68, 69, 70; **Supp. XXI: 83–96**
Davison, Jane, **Supp. XXVI:** 64, 65
Davison, Peter, **Supp. XXI:** 91; **Supp. XXVI: 61–80**
Davy's Lake (M. Finch), **Supp. XVII:** 69
Dawn (Dreiser), **I:** 498, 499, 503, 509, 515, 519
Dawn (O. Butler), **Supp. XIII:** 63, **64**
"Dawnbreaker" (Hayden), **Supp. II Part 1:** 370
Dawn in Russia (W. Frank), **Supp. XX: 76**
Dawn Patrol, The (film), **Supp. XIV:** 81
"Dawn Patrol: A Review of the Literature of the Negro for 1948" (Locke), **Supp. XIV:** 211
Dawson, Edward, **IV:** 151
Dawson, Emma, **I:** 199
Dawson, Melanie, **Supp. XXIV:** 25, 31
Dawson, Ruth, **Supp. XI:** 120
Day, Dorothy, **II:** 215; **Supp. I Part 2:** 524; **Supp. X:** 142; **Supp. XXV:** 19, 30
Day, Douglas, **Retro. Supp. III:** 77
Day, Fred Holland, **Supp. XX: 114, 115**
Day, Georgiana, **Supp. I Part 2:** 585
Day, Richard, **Supp. XVIII:** 251
"Day After Day of the Dead" (Mackey), **Supp. XXVII:** 156
Dayan, Joan, **Retro. Supp. II:** 270
"Day and Night" (Teasdale), **Supp. XXVII:** 293
"Day Book" (Notley), **Supp. XXII:** 230
Day Book, A (Creeley), **Supp. IV Part 1:** 155
"Daybreak" (Kinnell), **Supp. III Part 1:** 250
"Daybreak Blues" (Kees), **Supp. XV:** 133
"Day-Breakers, The" (Bontemps), **Supp. XXII:** 8
"Daybreak in Alabama" (Hughes), **Retro. Supp. I:** 211; **Supp. I Part 1:** 344
Day by Day (R. Lowell), **Retro. Supp. II:** 184, 186, 191
"Day-Care Field Trip: Aquarium" (Karr), **Supp. XI:** 243
"Day-Dream, A" (Bryant), **Supp. I Part 1:** 160
"Day-Dream of a Grocer, The" (Twain), **Supp. XVIII:** 9
"Day for Poetry and Song, A"

(Douglass), **Supp. III Part 1:** 172
"Day in the Life of Half of Rumpelstiltskin, A" (Brockmeier), **Supp. XXII:** 50, 52, 53
"Day Lady Died, The" (O'Hara), **Supp. XIX:** 85; **Supp. XXIII:** 216, 219
Day Late and a Dollar Short, A (McMillan), **Supp. XIII:** 184, **Supp. XIII:** 185, **191–192**
"Day longs for the evening, The" (Levertov), **Supp. III Part 1:** 274
Daynard, Jodi, **Supp. XVIII:** 97
Day of a Stranger (Merton), **Supp. VIII:** 203
"Day of Days, A" (James), **II:** 322
Day of Doom (Wigglesworth), **IV:** 147, 155, 156
Day of the Body (C. Frost), **Supp. XV:** 93, **98–100,** 106
Day of the Locust, The (West), **I:** 298; **IV:** 288, 299–306; **Retro. Supp. II:** 321, 323, 324, 329, **337–338; Supp. II Part 2:** 626; **Supp. XI:** 296; **Supp. XII:** 173; **Supp. XIII:** 170; **Supp. XIV:** 328; **Supp. XVIII:** 246
"Day of Wrath" (Davison), **Supp. XXVI:** 74
"Day on the Big Branch, A" (Nemerov), **III:** 275–276
"Day on the Connecticut River, A" (Merrill), **Supp. III Part 1:** 336
Day Room, The (DeLillo), **Supp. VI:** 4
"Days" (Emerson), **II:** 19, 20
"Days and Nights" (Koch), **Supp. XV:** 179, 180
"Days and Nights: A Journal" (Price), **Supp. VI:** 265
Days Before, The (Porter), **III:** 433, 453
"Day's Ending (Tucson)" (Teasdale), **Supp. XXVII:** 288, 296
Days in the Yellow Leaf (Hoffman), **Supp. XVIII:** 75
"Days of 1935" (Merrill), **Supp. III Part 1:** 325, 328
"Days of 1941 and '44" (Merrill), **Supp. III Part 1:** 336
"Days of 1964" (Merrill), **Supp. III Part 1:** 328, 352
"Days of 1971" (Merrill), **Supp. III Part 1:** 328
"Days of 1981" (Doty), **Supp. XI:** 123
"Days of Awe: The Birth of Lucy Jane" (Wasserstein), **Supp. XV:** 332
"Days of Edward Hopper" (Haines), **Supp. XII:** 210
"Days of Heaven" (Bass), **Supp. XVI:** 20
Days of Obligation: An Argument with My Mexican Father (Rodriguez), **Supp. XIV:** 298, 300, **302–305,** 307, 310
Days of Our Lives (soap opera), **Supp. XI:** 83
Days of Our Lives Lie in Fragments: New and Old Poems (Garrett), **Supp. VII:** 109–110, 111
Days of the Phoenix (Brooks), **I:** 266
Days of Wine and Roses (J. P. Miller), **Supp. XIII:** 262
Days: Tangier Journal, 1987–1989 (Bowles), **Supp. IV Part 1:** 94
Days to Come (Hellman), **Supp. I Part 1:** 276, 277–278
Days without End (O'Neill), **III:** 385, 391, 397
"Day's Work, A" (Capote), **Supp. III Part 1:** 120
"Day's Work, A" (Porter), **III:** 443, 446
"Day the Presidential Candidate Came to Ciudad Tamaulipas, The" (Caldwell), **I:** 309
"Day the Singer Fell, The" (Swados), **Supp. XIX:** 258
Day the World ended, The (Coover), **Supp. V:** 1
"Day with Conrad Green, A" (Lardner), **II:** 428–429, 430
"Deacon, The" (Huddle), **Supp. XXVI:** 151, 153–154, 158
"Deacon's Masterpiece, The" (Holmes), **Supp. I Part 1:** 302, 307
"Dead, The" (Collins), **Supp. XXI:** 64
"Dead, The" (Joyce), **I:** 285; **III:** 343; **Supp. XXIII:** 71
"Dead, The" (Very), **Supp. XXV:** 249
Dead and the Living, The (Olds), **Supp. X:** 201, **204–206,** 207
"Dead Body, The" (Olds), **Supp. X:** 210
"Dead by the Side of the Road, The" (Snyder), **Supp. VIII:** 301
"Dead Doe" (B. Kelly), **Supp. XVII:** 128–129
Dead End (Kingsley), **Supp. I Part 1:** 277, 281
Dead Father, The (Barthelme), **Supp. IV Part 1:** 43, 47, 50–51
"Dead Fiddler, The" (Singer), **IV:** 20
Dead Fingers Talk (Burroughs), **Supp. III Part 1:** 103
"Dead Hand" series (Sinclair), **Supp. V:** 276, 277, 281
"Dead Language Lessons" (Stallings), **Supp. XXV:** 233
"Dead Languages, The" (Humphrey), **Supp. IX:** 109
Dead Lecturer, The (Baraka), **Supp. II Part 1:** 31, 33, 35–37, 49
Dead Letters Sent (Kenny), **Supp. XXIII:** 143, 145
"Dead Letters Sent (By the Ontario Shores)"(Kenny), **Supp. XXIII:** 145
Deadline at Dawn (Odets), **Supp. II Part 2:** 546
Deadlock (Paretsky), **Supp. XXV:** 173, 176, 178–179
"Dead-Lock and Its Key, A" (E. Stoddard), **Supp. XV:** 286
"Dead Loon, The" (Bynner), **Supp. XV: 44–45**
Deadly Affair, A (Lacy), **Supp. XV:** 205–206
Deadly is the Female (film), **Supp. XVII:** 62
Dead Man's Walk (McMurtry), **Supp. V:** 231, 232
Dead Man's Walk (screenplay; McMurtry and Ossana), **Supp. V:** 231
Dead Man Walking (opera libretto, McNally), **Supp. XIII:** 207
Dead Poets Society (film), **Supp. XXI:** 192, 193, 194, 199
"Dead Reckoning" (Jarman), **Supp. XVII:** 113
"Dead Soldier's Talk, The" (Jin), **Supp. XVIII:** 92
Dead Souls (Gogol), **I:** 296
"Dead Souls on Campus" (Kosinski), **Supp. VII:** 222
"Dead Wingman, The" (Jarrell), **II:** 374
"Dead Wood, Green Wood" (Hadas), **Supp. XXIII:** 120
"Dead Yellow Women" (Hammett), **Supp. IV Part 1:** 345
Dead Zone, The (King), **Supp. V:** 139, 143, 144, 148, 152
Dean, James, **I:** 493
Dean, Man Mountain, **II:** 589
Deane, Silas, **Supp. I Part 2:** 509, 524
"Dean of Men" (Taylor), **Supp. V:** 314, 323
Dean's December, The (Bellow), **Retro. Supp. II:** 30–31
"Dear Adolph" (Benét), **Supp. XI:** 46
"Dear America" (Ortiz), **Supp. IV Part 2:** 503
"Dear Dark Continent" (Notley), **Supp. XXII:** 223
"Dearest M—" (Carruth), **Supp. XVI:** 59
Dear Ghosts (Gallagher), **Supp. XXIV:** 166, 167, 170–171, 176
"Dear Judas" (Jeffers), **Supp. II Part 2:** 431–432, 433
Dear Juliette (Sarton), **Supp. VIII:** 265
Dear Life (Munro), **Supp. XXVII:** 195

Dear Lovely Death (Hughes), **Retro. Supp. I:** 203; **Supp. I Part 1:** 328
"Dear Mr. Walrus" (Boyle), **Supp. XXIV:** 58–59
Dear Rafe (Hinojosa), **Supp. XIX:** 98, **105–106**
"Dear Smoker" (Biss), **Supp. XXVI:** 51
"Dear Villon" (Corso), **Supp. XII:** 135
"Dear World" (Gunn Allen), **Supp. IV Part 1:** 321
Deasy, Philip, **Supp. XX: 42**
Death (Allen), **Supp. XV:** 3
"Death" (Corso), **Supp. XII:** 127
"Death" (Mailer), **III:** 38
"Death" (R. Lowell), **II:** 536
"Death" (W. C. Williams), **Retro. Supp. I:** 422
"Death" (West), **IV:** 286
"Death, Decay and Change" (Very), **Supp. XXV:** 243
"Death and Absence" (Glück), **Supp. V:** 82
Death and Birth of David Markand, The (W. Frank), **Supp. XX: 76–77**
Death and Taxes (Parker), **Supp. IX:** 192
"Death and the Child" (Crane), **I:** 414
"Death as a Society Lady" (Hecht), **Supp. X:** 71–72
Death before Bedtime (Vidal as Box), **Supp. IV Part 2:** 682
"Death Be Not Proud" (Donne), **Supp. XVI:** 158
"Death by Water" (Eliot), **I:** 395, 578
Death Comes for the Archbishop (Cather), **I:** 314, 327, 328–330; **Retro. Supp. I:** 16–18, 21; **Retro. Supp. III:** 24; **Supp. XIII:** 253; **Supp. XXIV:** 253
"Death-Drag" (Faulkner), **Retro. Supp. III:** 84
Death in Paradise (Parker), **Supp. XIX:** 186
Death in the Afternoon (Hemingway), **II:** 253; **IV:** 35; **Retro. Supp. I:** 182; **Supp. VIII:** 182; **Supp. XIX:** 246; **Supp. XVI:** 205; **Supp. XX: 76**
"Death in the Country, A" (Benét), **Supp. XI:** 53–54
"Death in the Desert, A" (Cather), **Retro. Supp. III:** 21, 26
Death in the Family, A (Agee), **I:** 25, 29, 42, 45
Death in the Fifth Position (Vidal as Box), **Supp. IV Part 2:** 682
"Death in the Woods" (Anderson), **I:** 114, 115; **Supp. XXIV:** 136
Death in the Woods and Other Stories (Anderson), **I:** 112, 114, 115
Death in Venice (Mann), **III:** 231; **Supp. IV Part 1:** 392; **Supp. V:** 51
"Death in Viet Nam" (Salinas), **Supp. XIII:** 315
"Death in Winter" (C. Frost), **Supp. XV:** 98
Death Is a Lonely Business (Bradbury), **Supp. IV Part 1:** 102, 103, 111–112, 115
"Death Is Not the End" (Wallace), **Supp. X:** 309
Death Is the Place (Bronk), **Supp. XXI:** 32
Death Kit (Sontag), **Supp. III Part 2:** 451, 468–469
"Deathlight" (Huddle), **Supp. XXVI:** 150
Death Likes It Hot (Vidal as Box), **Supp. IV Part 2:** 682
"Death/Muerta" (Mora), **Supp. XIII:** 228
Death Notebooks, The (Sexton), **Supp. II Part 2:** 691, 694, 695
"Death of a Columnist" (Siddons), **Supp. XXII:** 241–242
Death of Adam, The: Essays on Modern Thought (Robinson), **Supp. XXI:** 212
"Death of a Hired Man" (Frost), **Retro. Supp. III:** 97, 98
"Death of a Jazz Musician" (W. J. Smith), **Supp. XIII:** 334
Death of a Kinsman, The (Taylor), **Supp. V:** 324, 326
"Death of a Lady's Man" (Cohen), **Supp. XXVII:** 58
Death of a Man (Boyle), **Supp. XXIV:** 60
"Death of an Old Seaman" (Hughes), **Retro. Supp. I:** 199
"Death of a Pig" (White), **Supp. I Part 2:** 665–668
Death of a Salesman (A. Miller), **I:** 81; **III:** 148, 149, 150, 153–154, 156, 157, 158, 159, 160, 163, 164, 166; **IV:** 389; **Retro. Supp. III:** 165, 167, 169–170, 171, 172–173; **Supp. IV Part 1:** 359; **Supp. XIV:** 102, 239, 254, 255; **Supp. XV:** 205; **Supp. XX: 27; Supp. XXIII:** 199
"Death of a Soldier, The" (Stevens), **Retro. Supp. I:** 299, 312. see also "Lettres d'un Soldat" (Stevens)
"Death of a Soldier, The" (Wilson), **IV:** 427, 445
"Death of a Toad" (Wilbur), **Supp. III Part 2:** 550
"Death of a Traveling Salesman" (Welty), **IV:** 261; **Retro. Supp. I:** 344
"Death of a Young Son by Drowning" (Atwood), **Supp. XIII:** 33
Death of Bessie Smith, The (Albee), **I:** 76–77, 92
Death of Billy the Kid, The (Vidal), **Supp. IV Part 2:** 683
Death of Cock Robin, The (Snodgrass), **Supp. VI:** 315, **317–319,** 324
Death of Dreams, A (Hoffman), **Supp. XVIII:** 79
"Death of General Wolfe, The" (Paine), **Supp. I Part 2:** 504
"Death of Halpin Frayser, The" (Bierce), **I:** 205
"Death of Justina, The" (Cheever), **Supp. I Part 1:** 184–185
Death of Life, The (Barnes), **Supp. III Part 1:** 34
Death of Malcolm X, The (Baraka), **Supp. II Part 1:** 47
"Death of Marilyn Monroe, The" (Olds), **Supp. X:** 205
"Death of Me, The" (Malamud), **Supp. I Part 2:** 437
"Death of Slavery, The" (Bryant), **Supp. I Part 1:** 168–169
"Death of St. Narcissus, The" (Eliot), **Retro. Supp. I:** 291
"Death of the Ball Turret Gunner, The" (Jarrell), **II:** 369–370, 372, 374, 375, 376, 378
"Death of the Fathers, The" (Sexton), **Supp. II Part 2:** 692
"Death of the Flowers, The" (Bryant), **Supp. I Part 1:** 170
Death of the Fox (Garrett), **Supp. VII:** 99, 101–104, 108
"Death of the Hat, The" (Collins), **Supp. XXI:** 59
"Death of the Hired Man, The" (Frost), **III:** 523; **Retro. Supp. I:** 121, 128; **Supp. IX:** 261
Death of the Kapowsin Tavern (Hugo), **Supp. VI:** 133–135
"Death of the Kapowsin Tavern" (Hugo), **Supp. VI:** 137, 141
"Death of the Lyric, The: The Achievement of Louis Simpson" (Jarman and McDowell), **Supp. IX:** 266, 270, 276
"Death of the Virgin, The (Rembrandt)" (Davison), **Supp. XXVI:** 70
"Death of Venus, The" (Creeley), **Supp. IV Part 1:** 143, 144–145
"Death on All Fronts" (Ginsberg), **Supp. II Part 1:** 326
"Deaths" (Dunn), **Supp. XI:** 147
"Death Sauntering About" (Hecht),

Supp. X: 72
Deaths for the Ladies (and Other Disasters) (Mailer), **Retro. Supp. II:** 203
Death's Jest-Book (Beddoes), **Retro. Supp. I:** 285
Death Song (McGrath), **Supp. X:** 127
"Death the Carnival Barker" (Hecht), **Supp. X:** 72
"Death the Film Director" (Hecht), **Supp. X:** 72
"Death the Judge" (Hecht), **Supp. X:** 72
"Death the Mexican Revolutionary" (Hecht), **Supp. X:** 72
"Death the Oxford Don" (Hecht), **Supp. X:** 72
"Death the Painter" (Hecht), **Supp. X:** 72
Death the Proud Brother (Wolfe), **IV:** 456
"Death to Van Gogh's Ear!" (Ginsberg), **Supp. II Part 1:** 320, 322, 323
"Death Warmed Over!" (Bradbury), **Supp. IV Part 1:** 104–105, 112
Death Wish, The (Holding), **Supp. XXII:** 120, **123,** 134, 135
Deaver, Philip F., **Supp. XXVI:** 151, 160–161
Débâcle, La (Zola), **III:** 316
"Debate with the Rabbi" (Nemerov), **III:** 272
Debeljak, Ale&sacaron;, **Supp. VIII:** 272
De Bellis, Jack, **Supp. I Part 1:** 366, 368, 372
Debo, Annette, **Supp. XXI:** 254
DeBoer-Langworthy, Carol, **Supp. XVII:** 98, 99, 100
DeBold, Kathleen, **Supp. XXV:** 4
De Bosis, Lauro, **IV:** 372
"Debriefing" (Sontag), **Supp. III Part 2:** 468–470
Debs, Eugene, **I:** 483, 493; **III:** 580, 581; **Supp. I Part 2:** 524; **Supp. IX:** 1, 15; **Supp. XXIII:** 161, 162
"Debt" (Teasdale), **Supp. XXVII:** 290
Debt to Pleasure, The (Lanchester), **Retro. Supp. I:** 278
Debussy, Claude, **Retro. Supp. II:** 266; **Supp. XIII:** 44
"Decades" (Sorrentino), **Supp. XXI:** 229
Decameron (Boccaccio), **III:** 283, 411; **Supp. IX:** 215
de Camp, L. Sprague, **Supp. XXVII:** 115, 128
"Deceased" (Hughes), **Retro. Supp. I:** 208
"December" (Oliver), **Supp. VII:** 245
"December 1, 1994" (Stern), **Supp. IX:** 299
December 7 (film, Ford), **Supp. XVIII:** 247
"December 24" (Di Piero), **Supp. XIX:** 39
"December 28: Returning to Chicago" (Di Piero), **Supp. XIX:** 39
"December Dawn" (Skloot), **Supp. XX: 202**
"December Eclogue" (Winters), **Supp. II Part 2:** 794
"Decent Woman, A" (Boulton), **Supp. XXII:** 22–23
De Cenzo, Giorgia, **Supp. XXI:** 256
Deception (P. Roth), **Retro. Supp. II:** 291; **Supp. III Part 2:** 426–427
"Deceptions" (Dobyns), **Supp. XIII:** 77
De Chiara, Ann. See Malamud, Mrs. Bernard (Ann de Chiara)
De Chirico, Giorgio, **Supp. XIII:** 317
"Decided Loss, A" (Poe), **II:** 411
"Decision" (Boyle), **Supp. XXIV:** 54
"Decisions to Disappear" (Dunn), **Supp. XI:** 144
"Decisive Moment, The" (Auster), **Supp. XIV:** 292
Decker, James A., **Supp. III Part 2:** 621
Declaration of Gentlemen and Merchants and Inhabitants of Boston, and the Country Adjacent, A (Mather), **Supp. II Part 2:** 450
"Declaration of Paris, The" (Adams), **I:** 4
Declaration of the Rights of Man and the Citizen, **Supp. I Part 2:** 513, 519
Declaration of Universal Peace and Liberty (Paine), **Supp. I Part 2:** 512
Declension in the Village of Chung Luong (Weigl), **Supp. XIX:** 287, 288
Decline and Fall (Waugh), **Supp. I Part 2:** 607; **Supp. XV:** 142
Decline and Fall of the English System of Finance, The (Paine), **Supp. I Part 2:** 518
Decline and Fall of the Roman Empire, The (Gibbons), **Supp. III Part 2:** 629
"Decline of Book Reviewing, The" (Hardwick), **Supp. III Part 1:** 201–202
Decline of the West, The (Spengler), **I:** 270; **IV:** 125
"Decolonizing the Tongue: Reading Speech and Aphasia in the Work of Michelle Cliff" (Aguiar), **Supp. XXII:** 68
Deconstructing Harry (film; Allen), **Supp. XV:** 12, **13**
"Décor" (X. J. Kennedy), **Supp. XV:** 171
"Decoration Day" (Jewett), **II:** 412; **Retro. Supp. II:** 138
Decoration of Houses, The (Wharton and Codman), **IV:** 308; **Retro. Supp. I:** 362, 363–364, 366; **Retro. Supp. III:** 277, 280
"Decoy" (Ashbery), **Supp. III Part 1:** 13–14
Decter, Midge, **Supp. XX: 248**
Dedalus, Stephen, **Supp. XIX:** 47
"De Daumier-Smith's Blue Period" (Salinger), **III:** 560–561
"Dedication" (Nelson), **Supp. XVIII:** 173, 180
"Dedication and Household Map" (Erdrich), **Supp. IV Part 1:** 272
"Dedication Day" (Agee), **I:** 34
"Dedication for a Book" (Hay), **Supp. XIV:** 125
"Dedication for a Book of Criticism" (Winters), **Supp. II Part 2:** 801
"Dedication in Postscript, A" (Winters), **Supp. II Part 2:** 801
Dedications and Other Darkhorses (Komunyakaa), **Supp. XIII:** 112, **113–114**
"Dedication to Hunger" (Glück), **Supp. V:** 83
"Dedication to My Wife, A" (Eliot), **I:** 583
Dee, Jonathan, **Supp. XXIII:** 302
Dee, Ruby, **Supp. IV Part 1:** 362
Deeck, William, **Supp. XXVI:** 278
Deeds of Utmost Kindness (Gander), **Supp. XV:** 340
Deegan, Thomas, **Supp. XXIII:** 100, 107–108
"Deep Breath at Dawn, A" (Hecht), **Supp. X:** 58
Deep End, The (film), **Supp. XXII:** 120, 131, 133
Deeper into Movies: The Essential Kael Collection from '69 to '72 (Kael), **Supp. IX:** 253
"Deeper Wisdom, The" (Hay), **Supp. XIV:** 129
Deep Green Sea (R. O. Butler), **Supp. XII:** 62, **74**
Deephaven (Jewett), **II:** 398–399, 400, 401, 410, 411; **Retro. Supp. II:** 133, 134, 135, 136, 137, 138, 140, 141, 143, 144
"Deep Sight and Rescue Missions" (Bambara), **Supp. XI:** 18–19

Deep Sightings and Rescue Missions: Fiction, Essays, and Conversations (Bambara), **Supp. XI:** 1, 3, **14–20**
Deep Sleep, The (Morris), **III:** 224–225
"Deep Song" (G. Jones), **Supp. XXIV:** 194
Deep South (Caldwell), **I:** 305, 309, 310
Deepstep Come Shining (Wright), **Supp. XV:** 337, 341, 344, **349–350,** 351, 353
"Deep Water" (Marquand), **III:** 56
"Deep Woods" (Nemerov), **III:** 272–273, 275
"Deer at Providencia, The" (Dillard), **Supp. VI:** 28, 32
Deer Camp: Last Light in the Northeast Kingdom (Ostrum, ed.), **Supp. XXII:** 218
"Deer Dancer" (Harjo), **Supp. XII:** 224–225
"Deer Ghost" (Harjo), **Supp. XII:** 225
Deer Park, The (Mailer), **I:** 292; **III:** 27, 31–33, 35–36, 37, 39, 40, 42, 43, 44; **Retro. Supp. II: 200–202,** 205, 207, 211
Deer Park, The: A Play (Mailer), **Retro. Supp. II:** 205
Deer Pasture, The (Bass), **Supp. XVI:** 15, 16, 23
Deerslayer, The (Cooper), **I:** 341, 349, 350, 355; **Supp. I Part 1:** 251
Deese, Helen, **Supp. XXV:** 251
"Defeat" (Boyle), **Supp. XXIV: 60–61**
Defence, The (Nabokov), **Supp. XXII:** 263
"Defence of General Funston, A" (Twain), **Retro. Supp. III:** 269
"Defence of Poesie, The" (Bronk), **Supp. XXI:** 32
"Defence of Poesy, The" (Sidney), **Supp. V:** 250
"Defence of Poetry" (Longfellow), **II:** 493–494
"Defence of Poetry, A" (Shelley), **Retro. Supp. III:** 41
"Defender of the Faith" (P. Roth), **Retro. Supp. II:** 281; **Supp. III Part 2:** 404, 407, 420
"Defending The Searchers (Scenes in the Life of an Obsession)" (Lethem), **Supp. XVIII:** 136,141
"Defenestration in Prague" (Matthews), **Supp. IX:** 168
Defenestration of Prague (Howe), **Supp. IV Part 2:** 419, 426, 429–430
Defense, The (Nabokov), **III:** 251–252; **Retro. Supp. I:** 266, 268, **270–272**
"Defense of Poetry" (Francis), **Supp. IX:** 83–84
DeFeo, Ronald, **Supp. XXIII:** 106
Defiant Ones, The (film), **Supp. I Part 1:** 67
"Defining the Age" (W. V. Davis), **Supp. IV Part 1:** 64
"Definition" (Ammons), **Supp. VII:** 28
Defoe, Daniel, **I:** 204; **II:** 104, 105, 159, 304–305; **III:** 113, 423; **IV:** 180; **Supp. I Part 2:** 523; **Supp. V:** 127
De Forest, John William, **II:** 275, 280, 288, 289; **IV:** 350
DeFrees, Madeline, **Supp. XVIII:** 293; **Supp. XXVI:** 180
Deganawida, the Peacemaker, **Supp. XXVI: 81–100**
"Deganawidah: The Peacemaker"(Kenny), **Supp. XXIII:** 151
Degas, Brian, **Supp. XI:** 307
Degler, Carl, **Supp. I Part 2:** 496
"Degrees of Fidelity" (Dunn), **Supp. XI:** 148, 156
Deguy, Michel, **Supp. XV:** 178
De Haven, Tom, **Supp. XI:** 39; **Supp. XII:** 338–339
Deitch, Joseph, **Supp. VIII:** 125
"Dejection" (Coleridge), **II:** 97
DeJong, Constance, **Supp. XII:** 4
DeJong, David Cornel, **I:** 35
Dekker,Thomas, **Supp. XVII:** 232
de Kooning, Elaine de, **Supp. XXIII:** 210, 217
de Kooning, Willem, **Supp. XII:** 198; **Supp. XV:** 177, 178
de Kooning, Willem de, **Supp. XXIII:** 208, 210, 211, 217, 220
Delacroix, Henri, **I:** 227
De La Mare, Walter, **III:** 429; **Supp. II Part 1:** 4; **Supp. XVII:** 69
Delamotte, Eugenia C., **Supp. XI:** 279
De Lancey, James, **I:** 338
De Lancey, Mrs. James (Anne Heathcote), **I:** 338
De Lancey, Susan A. See Cooper, Mrs. James Fenimore
De Lancey, William Heathcote, **I:** 338, 353
Delano, Amasa, **III:** 90
De la Paz, Oliver, **Supp. XXVI:** 101, 103, 111
Delattre, Roland A., **I:** 558
De Laurentiis, Dino, **Supp. XI:** 170, 307
De la Valdéne, Guy, **Supp. VIII:** 40, 42
Delbanco, Andrew, **Retro. Supp. III:** 152, 161, 162; **Supp. XXIV:** 69
Delbanco, Nicholas, **Supp. XXII:** 204
Del Cabral, Manuel, **Supp. XXI:** 104
DelCorso's Gallery (Caputo), **Supp. XIX:** 22–23
Delectorskaya, Lydia, **Supp. XXII:** 99
De l'éducation d'un homme sauvage (Itard), **Supp. I Part 2:** 564
Deleuze, Gilles, **Retro. Supp. III:** 159; **Supp. XXV:** 123
"Delft" (Goldbarth), **Supp. XII:** 189
Delft: An Essay-Poem (Goldbarth), **Supp. XII:** 187
Delicate Balance, A (Albee), **I:** 86–89, 91, 93, 94
Delicate Balance, The (Hay), **Supp. XIV:** 121, 122, 124, 129, 133–134
"Delicate Balance, The" (Hay), **Supp. XIV:** 122
"Delicate Prey, The" (Bowles), **Supp. IV Part 1:** 86
Delicate Prey and Other Stories, The (Bowles), **Supp. IV Part 1:** 86–87
Délie (Scève), **Supp. III Part 1:** 11
Delights & Shadows (Kooser), **Supp. XIX:** 115, 116, 117, 121, **127–128**
DeLillo, Don, **Retro. Supp. I:** 278; **Retro. Supp. II:** 279; **Supp. IX:** 212; **Supp. VI: 1–18; Supp. XI:** 68; **Supp. XII:** 21, 152; **Supp. XIX:** 54; **Supp. XVII:** 183; **Supp. XVIII:** 136, 140; **Supp. XX: 83, 87, 91; Supp. XXIII:** 109; **Supp. XXVII:** 6
De Lint, Charles, **Supp. XXII:** 59
DeLisle, Anne, **Supp. VIII:** 175
Deliverance (Dickey), **Supp. IV Part 1:** 176, 186–188, 190; **Supp. X:** 30; **Supp. XX: 173–174; Supp. XXIII:** 43, 50
Deliverance, The (Glasgow), **II:** 175, 176, 177–178, 181
"Delivering" (Dubus), **Supp. VII:** 87
Dell, Floyd, **I:** 103, 105; **Supp. I Part 2:** 379; **Supp. XV:** 295; **Supp. XVII:** 96; **Supp. XXI:** 6; **Supp. XXII:** 275; **Supp. XXV:** 18
Della Francesca, Piero, **Supp. XV:** 262
"Della Primavera Trasportata al Morale" (W. C. Williams), **Retro. Supp. I:** 419, 422
DeLoria, Philip J., **Supp. XIV:** 306
Deloria, Vine, Jr., **Supp. IV Part 1:** 323; **Supp. IV Part 2:** 504; **Supp. XXVI:** 98
"Delta" (Rich), **Retro. Supp. III:** 250
"Delta Autumn" (Faulkner), **II:** 71
"Delta Factor, The" (Percy), **Supp. III Part 1:** 386
Delta of Venus: Erotica (Nin), **Supp. X:** 192, 195

Delta Wedding (Welty), **IV:** 261, 268–271, 273, 281; **Retro. Supp. I:** 349–350, 351
Delusions (Berryman), **I:** 170
De Man, Paul, **Retro. Supp. I:** 67; **Supp. XVII:** 70
DeMarinis, Rick, **Supp. XIV:** 22
DeMars, James, **Supp. IV Part 2:** 552
Dembo, L. S., **I:** 386, 391, 396, 397, 398, 402; **III:** 478; **Supp. I Part 1:** 272; **Supp. XIV:** 277, 282, 288, 290; **Supp. XXVI:** 226–227, 235
"Dementia Translucida" (Bierds), **Supp. XVII:** 33
"Demeter"(Crooker), **Supp. XXIII:** 61
"Demeters"(Hadas), **Supp. XXIII:** 113
Demetrakopoulous, Stephanie A., **Supp. IV Part 1:** 12
De Mille, Agnes, **Supp. XXVI:** 66
DeMille, Cecil B., **Supp. IV Part 2:** 520; **Supp. XV:** 42
Demme, Jonathan, **Retro. Supp. III:** 185; **Supp. V:** 14
Democracy (Adams), **I:** 9–10, 20; **Supp. IV Part 1:** 208; **Supp. XIX:** 139
Democracy (Didion), **Supp. IV Part 1:** 198, 208–210
"Democracy" (J. R. Lowell), **Supp. I Part 2:** 419
Democracy and Education (Dewey), **I:** 232
Democracy and Other Addresses (J. R. Lowell), **Supp. I Part 2:** 407
Democracy and Social Ethics (Addams), **Supp. I Part 1:** 8–11
Democracy in America (Tocqueville), **Retro. Supp. I:** 235; **Supp. XIV:** 306
Democratic Vistas (Whitman), **IV:** 333, 336, 348–349, 351, 469; **Retro. Supp. I:** 408; **Retro. Supp. III:** 302; **Supp. I Part 2:** 456
Democritus, **I:** 480–481; **II:** 157; **III:** 606; **Retro. Supp. I:** 247
"Demon Lover, The" (Rich), **Supp. I Part 2:** 556
"Demonstrators, The" (Welty), **IV:** 280; **Retro. Supp. I:** 355
DeMott, Benjamin, **Supp. IV Part 1:** 35; **Supp. V:** 123; **Supp. XIII:** 95; **Supp. XIV: 106; Supp. XXV:** 86
DeMott, Robert, **Supp. VIII:** 40, 41
Demuth, Charles, **IV:** 404; **Retro. Supp. I:** 412, 430; **Supp. XXI:** 6
"Demystified Zone" (Paley), **Supp. VI:** 227
Denby, Edwin, **Supp. XXIV:** 36, 45; **Supp. XXVII:** 23
Denmark Vesey (opera) (Bowles), **Supp. IV Part 1:** 83
Dennett, Daniel, **Supp. XXII:** 265
Denney, Joseph Villiers, **Supp. I Part 2:** 605
Denney, Reuel, **Supp. XII:** 121; **Supp. XXI:** 19
Dennie, Joseph, **II:** 298; **Supp. I Part 1:** 125
Denning, Michael, **Supp. XXVI:** 28
Denniston, Dorothy Hamer, **Supp. XI:** 276, 277
"Den of Lions" (Plath), **Retro. Supp. II:** 242
"Dental Assistant, The" (Simpson), **Supp. IX:** 280
Den Uyl, Douglas, **Supp. IV Part 2:** 528, 530
"Deodand, The" (Hecht), **Supp. X:** 65
"Departing" (Cameron), **Supp. XII:** 81
"Departmental" (Frost), **Retro. Supp. III:** 103
"Departure" (Glück), **Supp. V:** 89
"Departure" (Plath), **Supp. I Part 2:** 537
"Departure, The" (Freneau), **Supp. II Part 1:** 264
"Departure from Hydra, The" (Koch), **Supp. XV:** 180–181
Departures (Justice), **Supp. VII:** 124–127
Departures and Arrivals (Shields), **Supp. VII:** 320, 322
"Depressed by a Book of Bad Poetry, I Walk Toward an Unused Pasture and Invite the Insects to Join Me" (Wright), **Supp. III Part 2:** 600
"Depressed Person, The" (Wallace), **Supp. X:** 309
"Depression Days" (Mora), **Supp. XIII:** 224–225
"Deprived of Unhappiness" (Pickering), **Supp. XXI:** 203
De Puy, John, **Supp. XIII:** 12
De Quincey, Thomas, **Supp. XXVI:** 283
D'Erasmo, Stacey, **Supp. IX:** 121
Derby, J. C., **Supp. XVIII:** 4
De Reilhe, Catherine, **Supp. I Part 1:** 202
De Rerum Natura (Lucretius), **II:** 162
"De Rerum Virtute" (Jeffers), **Supp. II Part 2:** 424
De Rioja, Francisco, **Supp. I Part 1:** 166
"Derivative Sport in Tornado Alley" (Wallace), **Supp. X:** 314
Derleth, August, **Supp. I Part 2:** 465, 472; **Supp. XXV:** 111, 122; **Supp. XXVII:** 117, 119, 128
Deronda, Daniel, **II:** 179
Derricotte, Toi, **Supp. XVIII:** 177
Derrida, Jacques, **Retro. Supp. III:** 237; **Supp. IV Part 1:** 45; **Supp. XV:** 215, 224; **Supp. XVI:** 285, 288
Deruddere, Dominique, **Supp. XI:** 173
Der Wilde Jäger (Bürger), **II:** 306
Derzhavin, Gavrila Romanovich, **Supp. VIII:** 27
Desai, Anita, **Supp. XVI:** 156, 157, 158
Désamère (Notley), **Supp. XXII:** 226
De Santis, Christopher, **Retro. Supp. I:** 194
Descartes, René, **I:** 255; **III:** 618–619; **IV:** 133
"Descendant of Solomon and the Queen of Sheba" (Major), **Supp. XXII:** 182
Descendents, The (Glasgow), **II:** 173, 174–175, 176
Descending Figure (Glück), **Supp. V:** 83–84
"Descending Theology: Christ Human" (Karr), **Supp. XI:** 251
"Descending Theology: The Garden" (Karr), **Supp. XI:** 251
"Descent, The" (W. C. Williams), **Retro. Supp. I:** 428, 429
"Descent from the Cross" (Eliot), **Retro. Supp. I:** 57, 58
"Descent in the Maelström, A" (Poe), **Retro. Supp. II:** 274
"Descent into Proselito" (Knowles), **Supp. XII:** 237
"Descent into the Maelström, A" (Poe), **III:** 411, 414, 416, 424
Descent of Alette, The (Notley), **Supp. XXII:** 223, 224, 226, 227, 233–234
Descent of Man (Boyle), **Supp. VIII:** 1, 12–13; **Supp. XX: 17, 18, 20**
"Descent of Man" (Boyle), **Supp. VIII:** 14; **Supp. XX: 18**
Descent of Man, and Other Stories, The (Wharton), **Retro. Supp. III:** 278
Descent of Man, The (Darwin), **Supp. XIV:** 192
Descent of Man, The (Wharton), **IV:** 311; **Retro. Supp. I:** 367
Descent of Man and Other Stories, The (Wharton), **Retro. Supp. I:** 367
Descent of Winter, The (W. C. Williams), **Retro. Supp. I:** 419, 428
De Schloezer, Doris, **III:** 474
"Describers" (Halliday), **Supp. XIX:** 85
"Description" (Doty), **Supp. XI:** 126
"Description of the great Bones dug up at Clavarack on the Banks of Hudsons River A.D. 1705, The" (Taylor),

IV: 163, 164
"Description without Place" (Stevens), **Retro. Supp. I:** 422
Desdemona (T. Morrison), **Retro. Supp. III:** 185
"Desert" (Hughes), **Retro. Supp. I:** 207
"Deserted Cabin" (Haines), **Supp. XII:** 203
Deserted Village, The (Goldsmith), **II:** 304
Desert Is My Mother, The/El desierto es mi madre (Mora), **Supp. XIII:** 214, 221
Desert Music, The (W. C. Williams), **IV:** 422; **Retro. Supp. I:** 428, 429
"Desert Music, The" (W. C. Williams), **Retro. Supp. I:** 428, 429
"Desert Places" (Frost), **II:** 159; **Retro. Supp. I:** 121, 123, 129, 138, 299; **Retro. Supp. III:** 103; **Supp. XIV:** 229
Desert Rose, The (McMurtry), **Supp. V:** 225, 231
Desert Solitaire (Abbey), **Supp. X:** 30; **Supp. XIII: 7–8,** 12; **Supp. XIV:** 177, 179; **Supp. XXV:** 208
"Design" (Frost), **II:** 158, 163; **Retro. Supp. I:** 121, 126, 138, 139; **Retro. Supp. III:** 103; **Supp. IX:** 81; **Supp. XVII:** 132; **Supp. XVIII:** 298
"Designated National Park, A" (Ortiz), **Supp. IV Part 2:** 509
"Designs on a Point of View" (Everwine), **Supp. XV:** 76
DeSilva, Bruce, **Supp. XXII:** 205, 206, 217
Des Imagistes (Pound), **II:** 513; **Supp. I Part 1:** 257, 261, 262
Desire (album, Dylan), **Supp. XVIII:** 28
"Desire" (Beattie), **Supp. V:** 29
Desire (Bidart), **Supp. XV: 32–34,** 35
"Desire" (Everwine), **Supp. XV:** 85
Desire, Desire, Desire (Durang), **Supp. XXIV:** 113
"Desire and Denial" (Bronk), **Supp. XXI:** 26
"Désirée's Baby" (Chopin), **Retro. Supp. II:** 64, 65; **Supp. I Part 1:** 213–215
"Desire"(Hadas), **Supp. XXIII:** 117
Desire under the Elms (O'Neill), **III:** 387, 390
"Desolate Field, The" (W. C. Williams), **Retro. Supp. I:** 418
"Desolation, A" (Ginsberg), **Supp. II Part 1:** 313
Desolation Angels (Kerouac), **Supp. III Part 1:** 218, 225, 230
"Desolation Is a Delicate Thing" (Wylie), **Supp. I Part 2:** 729
"Desolation Row" (song, Dylan), **Supp. XVIII:** 30
Despair (Nabokov), **Retro. Supp. I:** 270, 274
Desperate Characters (Fox), **Supp. XX: 91**
"Despisals" (Rukeyser), **Supp. VI:** 282
Des Pres, Terrence, **Supp. X:** 113, 120, 124
"Destination Out" (Mackey), **Supp. XXVII:** 152
"Destiny and the Lieutenant" (McCoy), **Supp. XIII:** 171
"Destroyer, The" (Davison), **Supp. XXVI:** 71
"Destruction of Kreshev, The" (Singer), **IV:** 13; **Retro. Supp. II:** 307
Destruction of the European Jews, The (Hilberg), **Supp. V:** 267
"Destruction of the Goetheanum, The" (Salter), **Supp. IX:** 257
"Destruction of the Long Branch, The" (Pinsky), **Supp. VI:** 239, 240, 243–244, 245, 247, 250
Destructive Element, The (Spender), **Retro. Supp. I:** 216
"Detail & Parody for the poem 'Paterson' " (W. C. Williams), **Retro. Supp. I:** 424
Detmold, John, **Supp. I Part 2:** 670
De Tolnay, Charles, **Supp. XXII:** 255
Detour at Night (Endore), **Supp. XVII:** 64
Deuce, The (R. O. Butler), **Supp. XII:** 62, **69–70,** 72
Deus Lo Volt! (Connell), **Supp. XIV:** 80, 81, 95
Deuteronomy (biblical book), **II:** 166
Deutsch, Andre, **Supp. XI:** 297, 301
Deutsch, Babette, **Supp. I Part 1:** 328, 341; **Supp. XV:** 305; **Supp. XXV:** 21; **Supp. XXVII:** 293
Deutsch, Michel, **Supp. IV Part 1:** 104
"Devaluation Blues: Ruminations on Black Families in Crisis" (Coleman), **Supp. XI:** 87
Devane, William, **Supp. XI:** 234
Devasahayam, Madona, **Supp. XXII:** 260
"Development of My Mind and Character, The" (Notley), **Supp. XXII:** 227
"Development of the Literary West" (Chopin), **Retro. Supp. II:** 72
"Development of the Modern English Novel, The" (Lanier), **Supp. I Part 1:** 370–371
DeVeriante (Herbert of Cherbury), **II:** 108
"Devil and Daniel Webster, The" (Benét), **III:** 22; **Supp. XI:** 45–46, 47, 50–51, 52
Devil and Daniel Webster and Other Writings, The (Benét), **Supp. XI:** 48
"Devil and Tom Walker, The" (Irving), **II:** 309–310
Devil At Large, The: Erica Jong on Henry Miller (Jong), **Supp. V:** 115, 131
Devil-Doll, The (film, Browning), **Supp. XVII:** 58–59
Devil Finds Work, The (Baldwin), **Retro. Supp. II:** 14; **Supp. I Part 1:** 48, 52, 66–67
Devil in a Blue Dress (Mosley), **Supp. XIII:** 237, 239
"Devil in Manuscript, The" (Hawthorne), **II:** 226; **Retro. Supp. I:** 150–151
Devil in Paradise, A (H. Miller), **III:** 190
"Devil in the Belfry, The" (Poe), **III:** 425; **Retro. Supp. II:** 273
"Devil Is a Busy Man, The" (Wallace), **Supp. X:** 309
Devil's Dictionary, The (Bierce), **I:** 196, 197, 205, 208, 209, 210
Devil's Stocking, The (Algren), **Supp. IX:** 5, 16
"Devil's Thumb, The" (Krakauer), **Supp. XVIII:** 107
Devil's Tour, The (Karr), **Supp. XI:** 240, **242–244**
Devil Tree, The (Kosinski), **Supp. VII:** 215, 222, 223
"Devising" (Ammons), **Supp. VII:** 28
Devlin, Paul, **Supp. XIX:** 159
De Voe, Edward Thomas, **Supp. XXV:** 23, 29
De Voto, Bernard, **I:** 247, 248; **II:** 446; **Retro. Supp. III:** 84; **Supp. IV Part 2:** 599, 601
"Devout Meditation in Memory of Adolph Eichmann, A" (Merton), **Supp. VIII:** 198, 203
De Vries, Peter, **Supp. I Part 2:** 604
Dewberry, Elizabeth, **Supp. XII:** 62, 72
Dewey, John, **I:** 214, 224, 228, 232, 233, 266, 267; **II:** 20, 27, 34, 229, 361; **III:** 112, 294–295, 296, 303, 309–310, 599, 605; **IV:** 27, 429; **Supp. I Part 1:** 3, 5, 7, 10, 11, 12, 24; **Supp. I Part 2:** 493, 641, 647, 677; **Supp. IX:** 179; **Supp. V:** 290; **Supp. XIV:** 3; **Supp. XV:** 41

Dewey, Joseph, **Supp. IX:** 210
Dewey, Thomas, **IV:** 161
Dewey Defeats Truman (Mallon), **Supp. XIX:** 132, 137, **138**
Dexter, Peter, **Supp. XIV:** 221
De Young, Charles, **I:** 194
Dhairyam, Sagari, **Supp. IV Part 1:** 329, 330
Dharma Bums, The (Kerouac), **Supp. III Part 1:** 230, 231; **Supp. VIII:** 289, 305
"D. H. Lawrence" (Bynner), **Supp. XV:** 46
D. H. Lawrence: An Unprofessional Study (Nin), **Supp. X:** 182–183
D. H. Lawrence: The World of the Major Novels (Sanders), **Supp. XVI:** 267
D'Houdetot, Madame, **Supp. I Part 1:** 250
"Diabetes" (Dickey), **Supp. IV Part 1:** 182
Diaghilev, Sergei, **Supp. I Part 1:** 257
Dial (publication), **I:** 58, 109, 115, 116, 215, 231, 233, 245, 261, 384, 429; **II:** 8, 430; **III:** 194, 470, 471, 485; **IV:** 122, 171, 427; **Retro. Supp. I:** 58; **Retro. Supp. II:** 78; **Supp. I Part 2:** 642, 643, 647; **Supp. II Part 1:** 168, 279, 291; **Supp. II Part 2:** 474; **Supp. III Part 2:** 611
"Dialectical Materialism" (Weigl), **Supp. XIX:** 281
Dialectical Materialism and the Fate of Humanity (C. L. R. James), **Supp. XXI:** 169
"Dialectics of Love, The" (McGrath), **Supp. X:** 116
"Dialogue" (Rich), **Supp. I Part 2:** 560
Dialogue, A (Baldwin and Giovanni), **Supp. I Part 1:** 66
"Dialogue Between Franklin and the Gout" (Franklin), **II:** 121
"Dialogue Between General Wolfe and General Gage in a Wood near Boston, A" (Paine), **Supp. I Part 2:** 504
"Dialogue between Old England and New, A" (Bradstreet), **Retro. Supp. III:** 4, 7; **Supp. I Part 1:** 105–106, 110–111, 116
"Dialogue between the Writer and a Maypole Dresser, A" (Taylor), **IV:** 155
Dialogues (Bush, ed.), **III:** 4
Dialogues in Limbo (Santayana), **III:** 606
"Dialogue: William Harvey; Joan of Arc" (Goldbarth), **Supp. XII:** 178
Dialogue with a Dead Man (J. W. Miller), **Supp. XX: 163, 164, 167**
Diamond, Elin, **Retro. Supp. III:** 137
"Diamond as Big as the Ritz, The" (Fitzgerald), **II:** 88–89
"Diamond Cutters, The" (Rich), **Retro. Supp. III:** 243
Diamond Cutters and Other Poems, The (Rich), **Retro. Supp. III:** 241; **Supp. I Part 2:** 551, 552, 553
"Diamond Guitar, A" (Capote), **Supp. III Part 1:** 124
Diamond Necklace, A (Notley), **Supp. XXII:** 228
"Diamonds in the Mine" (Cohen), **Supp. XXVII:** 51, 60
"Diana and Persis" (Alcott), **Supp. I Part 1:** 32, 41
"Diaper Brigade, The" (Ryan as Quin), **Supp. XVIII:** 230
Diaries (Coward), **Retro. Supp. III:** 171
Diaries of Charlotte Perkins Gilman (Knight, ed.), **Supp. XI:** 201
"Diary–1903" (Boyce), **Supp. XXI:** 8
"Diary Aug. 4–Aug. 5" (Brainard), **Supp. XXVII:** 18
Diary of a Chambermaid, The (film; Renoir), **Supp. XVI:** 193
Diary of Anaïs Nin, The (1931–1974), **Supp. X:** 181, 185–189, 191, 192, 193, 195
Diary of Anne Frank, The, **Supp. XXI:** 245
Diary of a Rapist, The: A Novel (Connell), **Supp. XIV:** 80, 82, 94
Diary of a Young Girl, The (Frank, tr. Mooyart-Doubleday), **Supp. XXVII:** 135, 137
Diary of a Yuppie (Auchincloss), **Supp. IV Part 1:** 31, 32–33
Diary of "Helena Morley", The (Bishop, trans.), **Retro. Supp. II:** 45, 51; **Supp. I Part 1:** 92
Dias, Robert Vas, **Supp. XXII:** 164, 169
Diay of Anne Frank, The (Goodrich and Hackett), **Supp. XXVII:** 136
Díaz, Junot, **Supp. XXIV: 83–95; Supp. XXV:** 49, 61
Díaz del Castillo, Bernál, **III:** 13, 14
Dick, Philip K., **Supp. XVI:** 123; **Supp. XVIII:** 136, 137, 138, 139, 142; **Supp. XXII:** 49
Dickens, Charles, **I:** 152, 198, 505; **II:** 98, 179, 186, 192, 271, 273–274, 288, 290, 297, 301, 307, 316, 322, 559, 561, 563, 577, 582; **III:** 146, 247, 325, 368, 411, 421, 426, 572, 577, 613–614, 616; **IV:** 21, 192, 194, 211, 429; **Retro. Supp. I:** 33, 91, 218; **Retro. Supp. II:** 204; **Retro. Supp. III:** 139; **Supp. I Part 1:** 13, 34, 35, 36, 41, 49; **Supp. I Part 2:** 409, 523, 579, 590, 622, 675; **Supp. IV Part 1:** 293, 300, 341; **Supp. IV Part 2:** 464; **Supp. IX:** 246; **Supp. VIII:** 180; **Supp. XI:** 277; **Supp. XII:** 335, 337; **Supp. XIII:** 233; **Supp. XV:** 62; **Supp. XVI:** 63, 65–66, 72–73, 202; **Supp. XVIII:** 7, 136, 146; **Supp. XX: 21, 87, 195; Supp. XXII:** 206; **Supp. XXIII:** 4, 85, 290; **Supp. XXIV:** 87; **Supp. XXV:** 258; **Supp. XXVII:** 269
Dickerson, Mary Jane, **Retro. Supp. III:** 81
Dickey, James, **I:** 29, 535; **III:** 268; **Retro. Supp. II:** 233; **Supp. III Part 1:** 354; **Supp. III Part 2:** 541, 597; **Supp. IV Part 1: 175–194; Supp. V:** 333; **Supp. X:** 30; **Supp. XI:** 312, 317; **Supp. XIX:** 282; **Supp. XV:** 115, 348; **Supp. XVIII:** 191, 299; **Supp. XXI:** 35; **Supp. XXIII:** 43, 50; **Supp. XXIV:** 42; **Supp. XXVI:** 67
Dick Gibson Show, The (Elkin), **Supp. VI:** 42, **48–49**
Dickie, Margaret, **Retro. Supp. II:** 53, 84
Dickinson, Donald, **Retro. Supp. I:** 206, 212
Dickinson, Edward, **I:** 451–452, 453
Dickinson, Mrs. Edward, **I:** 451, 453
Dickinson, Emily, **I:** 384, 419, 433, **451–473; II:** 272, 276, 277, 530; **III:** 19, 194, 196, 214, 493, 505, 508, 556, 572, 576; **IV:** 134, 135, 331, 444; **Retro. Supp. I: 25–50; Retro. Supp. II:** 39, 40, 43, 45, 50, 76, 134, 155, 170; **Retro. Supp. III:** 248, 251; **Supp. I Part 1:** 29, 79, 188, 372; **Supp. I Part 2:** 375, 546, 609, 682, 691; **Supp. II Part 1:** 4; **Supp. III Part 1:** 63; **Supp. III Part 2:** 600, 622; **Supp. IV Part 1:** 31, 257; **Supp. IV Part 2:** 434, 637, 641, 643; **Supp. IX:** 37, 38, 53, 87, 90; **Supp. V:** 79, 140, 332, 335; **Supp. VIII:** 95, 104, 106, 108, 198, 205, 272; **Supp. XII:** 226; **Supp. XIII:** 153, 339; **Supp. XIV:** 45, 127–128, 133, 261, 284; **Supp. XIX:** 86; **Supp. XV:** 287, 303, 309; **Supp. XVI:** 288; **Supp. XVII:** 71, 73, 74, 75, 132; **Supp. XVIII:** 301; **Supp. XX: 106, 108; Supp. XXI:** 52, 61, 64, 132, 214; **Supp. XXII:** 81, 82, 225, 277–278; **Supp. XXIII:**

19, 165; **Supp. XXVII:** 261, 283, 292
Dickinson, Gilbert, **I:** 469
Dickinson, Goldsworthy Lowes, **Supp. XIV:** 336
Dickinson, Lavinia Norcross, **I:** 451, 453, 462, 470
Dickinson, Stephanie, **Supp. XXIII:** 250
Dickinson, Mrs. William A. (Susan Gilbert), **I:** 452, 453, 456, 469, 470
Dickinson, William Austin, **I:** 451, 453, 469
Dickinson and the Strategies of Reticence (Dobson), **Retro. Supp. I:** 29, 42
Dickson, Helen. See Blackmur, Helen Dickson
Dickstein, Morris, **Supp. XIII:** 106; **Supp. XXIV:** 222, 223
"Dick Whittington and His Cat", **Supp. I Part 2:** 656
"DICTATORSHIP OF THE PROLETARIAT, THE" (Baraka), **Supp. II Part 1:** 54
Dictionary of Afro-American Slang (Major), **Supp. XXII:** 172, 174, 180
Dictionary of American English (Craigie and Hulbert, eds.), **Retro. Supp. III:** 265
Dictionary of Literary Biography (Barron and Meyer, eds.), **Supp. XIX:** 195; **Supp. XVIII:** 173
Dictionary of Literary Biography (Gwynn, ed.), **Supp. XIX:** 121; **Supp. XVIII:** 173
Dictionary of Literary Biography (Kibler, ed.), **Supp. IX:** 94, 109; **Supp. XI:** 297
Dictionary of Literary Biography (Knight, ed.), **Supp. XIV:** 144
Dictionary of Literary Biography (Martine, ed.), **Supp. XXII:** 187
Dictionary of Literary Biography (Sicher, ed.), **Supp. XVII:** 41
Dictionary of Literary Biography (Twentieth-Century American Nature Poets, Bryson and Thompson, eds.), **Supp. XXIII:** 129
Dictionary of Modern English Usage, A (Fowler), **Supp. I Part 2:** 660
Dictionary of the Mohawk Language, A (Pyrlaeus), **Supp. XXVI:** 86
"Dictum: For a Masque of Deluge" (Merwin), **Supp. III Part 1:** 342–343
"Didactic Poem" (Levertov), **Supp. III Part 1:** 280
Diderot, Denis, **II:** 535; **IV:** 440; **Supp. XVI:** 293; **Supp. XVII:** 145
Did I Ever Tell You How Lucky You Are? (Geisel), **Supp. XVI:** 109
Di Dio, François, **Supp. XXVII:** 153
Didion, Joan, **Retro. Supp. I:** 116; **Retro. Supp. II:** 209; **Supp. I Part 1:** 196, 197; **Supp. III Part 1:** 302; **Supp. IV Part 1: 195–216; Supp. XI:** 221; **Supp. XII:** 307; **Supp. XXV:** 208; **Supp. XXVI:** 45, 49, 53
Dido, **I:** 81
Dido, Queen of Hearts (Atherton), **Supp. XXIV:** 26
Di Donato, Peter, **Supp. XX: 34**
Di Donato, Pietro, **Supp. XX: 33–47**
"Did 'Paco's Story' Deserve Its Award" (Kakutani), **Supp. XXII:** 109
"Did You Ever Dream Lucky?" (Ellison), **Supp. II Part 1:** 246
Dieckmann, Katherine, **Supp. XXIII:** 295, 296
"Die-Hard, The" (Benét), **Supp. XI:** 54–55, 56
Diehl, Digby, **Supp. IV Part 1:** 204
Dien Cai Dau (Komunyakaa), **Supp. XIII:** 121, **122–124,** 125, 131, 132
Dies, Martin, **Supp. XVIII:** 229
"Dies Irae" (R. Lowell), **II:** 553
Die Zeit Ohne Beispiel, (Goebbels), **III:** 560
Difference Engine, The (W. Gibson and B. Sterling), **Supp. XVI:** 121, 124, **128–129**
Different Drummer, A (Larkin; film), **Supp. XI:** 20
Different Fleshes (Goldbarth), **Supp. XII:** 181–182, 188
Different Hours (Dunn), **Supp. XI:** 139, 142, 143, 155
"Different Road, A" (Strout), **Supp. XXIII:** 282–283
Different Seasons (King), **Supp. V:** 148, 152
Different Ways to Pray (Nye), **Supp. XIII:** 274, 275, 277, 285, 287
"Different Ways to Pray" (Nye), **Supp. XIII:** 275
"Difficulties of a Statesman" (Eliot), **I:** 580
"Difficulties of Modernism and the Modernism of Difficulty" (Poirier), **Supp. II Part 1:** 136
Diff'rent (O'Neill), **III:** 389; **Supp. XXII:** 22
Di Filippo, Paul, **Supp. XXII:** 260, 261
DiGaetani, John L., **Supp. XIII:** 200
Digges, Deborah, **Supp. XXIII:** 57
"Digging" (Sanders), **Supp. XVI:** 272
"Digging in the Garden of Age I Uncover a Live Root" (Swenson), **Supp. IV Part 2:** 649
Digging Up the Dirt (Moraga), **Supp. XXIII:** 197
Diggins, John P., **Supp. I Part 2:** 650
Digital Barbarism: A Writer's Manifesto (Helprin), **Supp. XXV:** 81, 84, 88–89
"Dignity of Life, The" (C. Bly), **Supp. XVI:** 34, 36–37
Digregorio, Charles, **Supp. XI:** 326
"Digression on Number I, 1948" (O'Hara), **Supp. XXIII:** 214
"Dilemma" (Budbill), **Supp. XIX:** 2
"Dilemma of Determinism, The" (James), **II:** 347–348, 352
"Dilemma of the Negro Writer, The" (speech, C. Himes), **Supp. XVI:** 140
"Dilettante, The" (Wharton), **IV:** 311, 313
"Dilettante, The: A Modern Type" (Dunbar), **Supp. II Part 1:** 199
Dillard, Annie, **Supp. VI: 19–39; Supp. VIII:** 272; **Supp. X:** 31; **Supp. XIII:** 154; **Supp. XXVI:** 31, 37
Dillard, R. H. W., **Supp. XII:** 16
Dillman, Bradford, **III:** 403; **Supp. XII:** 241
Dillon, Brian, **Supp. X:** 209
Dillon, George, **III:** 141; **Supp. III Part 2:** 621
Dillon, Millicent, **Supp. IV Part 1:** 95
Dilsaver, Paul, **Supp. XIII:** 112
Dilthey, Wilhelm, **I:** 58
Dime-Store Alchemy: The Art of Joseph Cornell, **Supp. VIII:** 272
"Diminuendo" (Dunn), **Supp. XI:** 152–153
"Dimout in Harlem" (Hughes), **Supp. I Part 1:** 333
"Dinah's Lament" (Nelson), **Supp. XVIII:** 183
Dinesen, Isak, **IV:** 279; **Supp. VIII:** 171; **Supp. XVI:** 250
Dining Room, The (Gurney), **Supp. V:** 105–106
"Dinner at ------, A" (O. Henry), **Supp. II Part 1:** 402
"Dinner at Sir Nigel's" (Bowles), **Supp. IV Part 1:** 94
Dinner at the Homesick Restaurant (Tyler), **Supp. IV Part 2:** 657, 667–668
"Dinner at Uncle Borris's" (Simic), **Supp. VIII:** 272
Dinner Bridge (Lardner), **II:** 435
Dinosaur Hunter, The (Hickam), **Supp. XXVII:** 111
Dinosaur Tales (Bradbury), **Supp. IV Part 1:** 103

"Diogenes Invents a Game" (Karr), **Supp. XI:** 240–241
"Diogenes Tries to Forget" (Karr), **Supp. XI:** 241
Diomede, Matthew, **Supp. XX: 46**
Dionysis in Doubt (Robinson), **III:** 510
Dionysus in 69 (Schechner), **Supp. XXIV:** 116
Diop, Birago, **Supp. IV Part 1:** 16
Diop, David, **Supp. IV Part 1:** 16
Di Piero, W. S., **Supp. XIX: 33–48; Supp. XVII:** 241
Di Prima, Diane, **Supp. III Part 1:** 30; **Supp. XIV:** 125, 144, 148, 150
Dirda, Michael, **Supp. XXI:** 233
Direction of Poetry, The: An Anthology of Rhymed and Metered Verse Written in the English Language since 1975 (Richman, ed.), **Supp. XV:** 250, 251
Direction of Poetry, The: Rhymed and Metered Verse Written in the English Language since 1975 (Richman), **Supp. XI:** 249
"Directive" (Bishop), **Retro. Supp. II:** 42
"Directive" (Frost), **III:** 287; **Retro. Supp. I:** 140; **Retro. Supp. III:** 105; **Supp. VIII:** 32, 33; **Supp. XXVI:** 77
"Dire Cure" (Matthews), **Supp. IX:** 168
"Dirge" (Dunbar), **Supp. II Part 1:** 199
"Dirge Notes" (Huddle), **Supp. XXVI:** 148, 153
"Dirge without Music" (Millay), **III:** 126
"Dirt" (Salter), **Supp. IX:** 257, 260, 261
"Dirt and Desire: Essay on the Phenomenology of Female Pollution in Antiquity" (Carson), **Supp. XII: 111**
Dirty Bird Blues (Major), **Supp. XXII: 180–181**
Dirty Dingus Magee (film), **Supp. XVII:** 139
"Dirty English Potatoes" (X. J. Kennedy), **Supp. XV:** 165
"Dirty Memories" (Olds), **Supp. X:** 211
Dirty Story (Shanley), **Supp. XIV:** 316, 331
"Dirty Word, The" (Shapiro), **Supp. II Part 2:** 710
Dirty Work (L. Brown), **Supp. XXI:** 37, 39, 40, 42, **45**
"'Disabled Imagination' and the Masculine Metaphor in the Works of Leonard Kriegel, The" (Haugen), **Supp. XXIV:** 215
Disappearance of the Jews, The (Mamet), **Supp. XIV:** 249–250, 250–251, 252, 254
Disappearances (Auster), **Supp. XII:** 23
"Disappearances" (Hogan), **Supp. IV Part 1:** 401
Disappearances (Mosher), **Supp. XXII:** 204, 205, 206, 207, 208, 209, **210**
"Disappeared, The " (C. Baxter), **Supp. XVII:** 19
Disappearing Acts (McMillan), **Supp. XIII:** 182, 183, **188–189,** 192
Disappearing Ink: Poetry at the End of Print Culture (Gioia), **Supp. XV:** 112
"Disappointment, The" (Creeley), **Supp. IV Part 1:** 143
"Disappointment and Desire" (R. Bly), **Supp. IV Part 1:** 71
Disappointment Artist, The (Lethem), **Supp. XVIII:** 135, 141**, 148**
"Discards" (Baker), **Supp. XIII:** 53, 55–56
Discerning the Signs of the Times (Niebuhr), **III:** 300–301, 307–308
Disch, Thomas M., **Supp. XIX:** 1
"Disciple of Bacon, The" (Epstein), **Supp. XII:** 163–164
"Discipline" (L. Brown), **Supp. XXI:** 44
Discomfort, Zone, The: A Personal History (Franzen), **Supp. XX: 83, 84, 95**
"Discordants" (Aiken), **I:** 65
Discourse on Method (Descartes), **I:** 255
"Discourtesies" (Kirsch), **Supp. XV:** 341
"Discovering Theme and Structure in the Novel" (Schuster), **Supp. VIII:** 126
"Discovery" (Freneau), **Supp. II Part 1:** 258
"Discovery of the Madeiras, The" (Frost), **Retro. Supp. I:** 139
"Discovery of What It Means to Be an American, The" (Baldwin), **Supp. I Part 1:** 54–55
Discovery! The Search for Arabian Oil (Stegner), **Supp. IV Part 2:** 599
Discrepant Engagement (Mackey), **Supp. XXVII:** 159, 160, 161
Discrete Series (Oppen), **Supp. XXVI:** 224, 226–227, 230, 235
"Discrete Series" (Zukofsky), **Supp. III Part 2:** 616
"Discretions of Alcibiades" (Pinsky), **Supp. VI:** 241
"Disease, The" (Rukeyser), **Supp. VI:** 279
Disenchanted, The (play, Schulberg and Breit), **Supp. XVIII:** 254
Disenchanted, The (Schulberg), **II:** 98; **Retro. Supp. I:** 113; **Supp. XVIII: 247–250,** 253
Disenchantments: An Anthology of Modern Fairy Tale Poetry (Mieder), **Supp. XIV:** 126
"Dish of Green Pears, A" (Ríos), **Supp. IV Part 2:** 552
"Disillusion and Dogma" (Untermeyer), **Supp. XV:** 306
"Disloyal to Civilization: Feminism, Racism, and Gynephobia" (Rich), **Retro. Supp. III:** 248
Dismantling the Silence (Simic), **Supp. VIII: 273–274,** 275, 276
Disney, Walt, **III:** 275, 426
"Disney of My Mind" (Chabon), **Supp. XI:** 63
Disobedience (Notley), **Supp. XXII:** 235, 236
Dispatches (Herr), **Supp. XI:** 245; **Supp. XIX:** 17
"Displaced Person, The" (O'Connor), **III:** 343–344, 350, 352, 356; **Retro. Supp. II:** 229, 232, 236
"Disposal" (Snodgrass), **Supp. VI:** 314
Dispossessed, The (Berryman), **I:** 170, 172, 173, 174, 175, 176, 178
"Disquieting Muses, The" (Plath), **Supp. I Part 2:** 538
Disraeli, Benjamin, **II:** 127
Dissent (Didion), **Supp. IV Part 1:** 208
"Dissent in Ashcroft's America" (P. N. Warren), **Supp. XX: 273**
"Dissenting Opinion on Kafka, A" (Wilson), **IV:** 437–438
Dissent in Three American Wars (Morison, Merk, and Freidel), **Supp. I Part 2:** 495
Dissertation on Liberty and Necessity, Pleasure and Pain, A (Franklin), **II:** 108
Dissertations on Government; the Affairs of the Bank: and Paper Money (Paine), **Supp. I Part 2:** 510
"Distance" (Carver), **Supp. III Part 1:** 146
"Distance" (Everwine), **Supp. XV:** 85
"Distance" (Paley), **Supp. VI:** 222
"Distance, The" (Karr), **Supp. XI:** 241
"Distance from the Sea, A" (Kees), **Supp. XV:** 147
"Distance Nowhere" (Hughes), **Retro. Supp. I:** 207

"Distance Up Close, The" (Peacock), **Supp. XIX:** 196–197, 198
"Distant Episode, A" (Bowles), **Supp. IV Part 1:** 84–85, 86, 90
Distant Episode, A: The Selected Stories (Bowles), **Supp. IV Part 1:** 79
Distant Rain: A Conversation Between Jakuch[omacron] Setouchi & Tess Gallagher (Setouchi and Gallagher), **Supp. XXIV:** 166, 178
Distinguished Guest, The (Miller), **Supp. XII: 299–301**
Distortions (Beattie), **Supp. V:** 21, 23, 24, 25, 27
"Distrest Shepherdess, The" (Freneau), **Supp. II Part 1:** 258
District of Columbia (Dos Passos), **I:** 478, 489–490, 492
Disturber of the Peace (Manchester), **III:** 103
Disturbing the Peace (Yates), **Supp. XI:** 345, 346
"Diver, The" (Hayden), **Supp. II Part 1:** 368, 372, 373
"Divided Life of Jean Toomer, The" (Toomer), **Supp. III Part 2:** 488
Divided Self, The (Laing), **Supp. XX: 95**
Divina Commedia (Longfellow, trans.), **II:** 490, 492, 493
"Divina Pastora, La" (C. L. R. James), **Supp. XXI:** 160
"Divine, The" (Di Piero), **Supp. XIX:** 41
"Divine Collaborator" (Simic), **Supp. VIII:** 282
Divine Comedies (Merrill), **Supp. III Part 1:** 324, 329–332
Divine Comedy (Dante), **I:** 137, 265, 400, 446; **II:** 215, 335, 490, 492, 493; **III:** 13, 448, 453; **Supp. V:** 283, 331, 338, 345; **Supp. X:** 253; **Supp. XIV:** 6; **Supp. XIX:** 36, 39
Divine Husband, The (Goldman), **Supp. XXV:** 49–50, 55–57
"Divine Image, The" (Blake), **Supp. V:** 257
Divine Pilgrim, The (Aiken), **I:** 50, 55
Divine Right's Trip (Norman), **Supp. XXIII:** 42
Divine Tragedy, The (Longfellow), **II:** 490, 500, 505, 506, 507; **Retro. Supp. II:** 165, 166
Divine Weekes and Workes (Sylvester, trans.), **Supp. I Part 1:** 104
Divine Weeks (Du Bartas), **IV:** 157–158
"Diving into the Wreck" (Rich), **Retro. Supp. III:** 246–247, 252
Diving into the Wreck: Poems 1971–1972 (Rich), **Retro. Supp. III:** 242, 246–247; **Supp. I Part 2:** 550, 559–565, 569; **Supp. XV:** 252
"Diving Past African Violets" (A. Finch), **Supp. XVII:** 72
Diving Rock on the Hudson, A (H. Roth), **Supp. IX:** 236, **237–238**
"Divinity in Its Fraying Fact, A" (Levis), **Supp. XI:** 271
"Divinity School Address" (Emerson), **II:** 12–13
"Divinity School or Trusting the Act of Writing" (Abraham), **Supp. XXIV:** 1, 3–4
"Divisions upon a Ground" (Hecht), **Supp. X:** 58
"Divorce" (Karr), **Supp. XI:** 244
"Divorced Fathers and Pizza Crusts" (Halliday), **Supp. XIX:** 93
Divorced in America: Marriage in an Age of Possibility (Epstein), **Supp. XIV:** 113
"Divorce Dream" (Halliday), **Supp. XIX:** 90
"Divorce in the United States" (Atherton), **Supp. XXIV:** 24
Dix, Douglas Shields, **Supp. XII:** 14
Dixie City Jam (Burke), **Supp. XIV:** 32
Dixon, Ivan, **Supp. IV Part 1:** 362
Dixon, Stephen, **Supp. XII: 139–158**
Dixon, Terrell F., **Supp. XVI:** 21
Dixon, Thomas, Jr., **Supp. II Part 1:** 169, 171, 177
Djbot Baghostus's Run (Mackey), **Supp. XXVII:** 158
Djinn (Robbe-Grillet), **Supp. V:** 48
D'Lugoff, Burt, **Supp. IV Part 1:** 362, 370
Dlugos, Tim, **Supp. XXVII:** 24
Dmytryk, Edward, **Supp. XX: 41**
Do, Lord, Remember Me (Garrett), **Supp. VII:** 98–100, 110
"Doaksology, The" (Wolfe), **IV:** 459
Do Androids Dream of Electric Sheep? (Dick), **Supp. XVIII:** 137
Dobard, Raymond G., **Supp. XXVI:** 200
Dobie, J. Frank, **Supp. V:** 225; **Supp. XIII:** 227
Döblin, Alfred, **Supp. XV:** 137
Dobriansky, Lev, **Supp. I Part 2:** 648, 650
Dobrin, Sidney I., **Supp. XVIII:** 192, 195
Dobson, Joanne, **Retro. Supp. I:** 29, 31, 42; **Supp. XVIII:** 259
Dobyns, Stephen, **Supp. XIII: 73–92**
"Docking at Palermo" (Hugo), **Supp. VI:** 137–138
"Dock Rats" (Moore), **III:** 213
"Dock-Witch, The" (Ozick), **Supp. V:** 262, 264
"Doc Mellhorn and the Pearly Gates" (Benét), **Supp. XI:** 55
"Doctor, The" (Dubus), **Supp. VII:** 80–81
"Doctor and the Doctor's Wife, The" (Hemingway), **II:** 248; **Retro. Supp. I:** 174, 175
Doctor Breen's Practice, a Novel (Howells), **I:** 282
Doctor Faustus (Mann), **III:** 283
Doctor Jazz (Carruth), **Supp. XVI:** 47, 59
"Doctor Jekyll" (Sontag), **Supp. III Part 2:** 469
"Doctor Leavis and the Moral Tradition" (Trilling), **Supp. III Part 2:** 512–513
"Doctor Marino" (Faulkner), **Retro. Supp. III:** 84
Doctor Martino and Other Stories (Faulkner), **II:** 72; **Retro. Supp. I:** 84; **Retro. Supp. III:** 84
"Doctor of the Heart, The" (Sexton), **Supp. II Part 2:** 692
Doctorow, E. L., **Retro. Supp. I:** 97; **Supp. III Part 2:** 590, 591; **Supp. IV Part 1: 217–240; Supp. V:** 45; **Supp. XVI:** 73; **Supp. XVII:** 183; **Supp. XX: 84, 90; Supp. XXI:** 18–19; **Supp. XXII:** 268
Doctor Sax (Kerouac), **Supp. III Part 1:** 220–222, 224–227
Doctor Sleep (Bell), **Supp. X: 9–11**
"Doctors' Row" (Aiken), **I:** 67
Doctor's Son and Other Stories, The (O'Hara), **III:** 361
Doctor Stories, The (W. C. Williams), **Retro. Supp. I:** 424
"Doctor's Wife, The" (Ozick), **Supp. V:** 262, 265
Doctor Zhivago (Pasternak), **IV:** 434, 438, 443
"Documentary" (Simic), **Supp. VIII:** 282
Dodd, Elizabeth, **Supp. V:** 77
Dodd, Susan, **Supp. XXV:** 129
Dodd, Wayne, **Supp. IV Part 2:** 625
Dodge, Mabel, **Supp. XX: 69; Supp. XXI:** 5, 6, 8, 12; **Supp. XXII:** 158, 161. See also Luhan, Mabel Dodge
Dodson, Owen, **Supp. I Part 1:** 54
Dodsworth (Lewis), **II:** 442, 449–450, 453, 456
Doenitz, Karl, **Supp. I Part 2:** 491
Does Civilization Need Religion? (Niebuhr), **III:** 293–294

"Does 'Consciousness' Exist?" (James), **II:** 356
"Does Education Pay?" (Du Bois), **Supp. II Part 1:** 159
"Dog" (B. Kelly), **Supp. XVII:** 126
Dog (Shepard), **Supp. III Part 2:** 434
"Dog Act, The" (Komunyakaa), **Supp. XIII:** 114–115
"Dog and the Playlet, The" (O. Henry), **Supp. II Part 1:** 399
Dog Beneath the Skin, The (Auden), **Supp. II Part 1:** 10
"Dog Creek Mainline" (Wright), **Supp. V:** 340
"Dogdom of the Dead, The" (Stallings), **Supp. XXV:** 228
"Dogfight" (W. Gibson and Swanwick), **Supp. XVI:** 128
Dog in the Manger, The (Vega; Merwin, trans.), **Supp. III Part 1:** 341, 347
Dog of the Marriage, The (Hempel), **Supp. XXI:** 115, 116, 117, 118, **126–127**
"Dog"(P. Benedict), **Supp. XXIII:** 36–37, 39
Dogs Bark, but the Caravan Rolls On (Conroy), **Supp. XVI:** 63, 70, 74, **75–76**
Dogs Bark, The: Public People and Private Places (Capote), **Supp. III Part 1:** 120, 132
"Dog's Eye" (J. W. Miller), **Supp. XX: 167**
"Dogs of Bucharest, The" (Gallagher), **Supp. XXIV:** 171
Dogs of God (Benedict), **Supp. XXIII:** 35, **41–45,** 49–50
Dog Soldiers (Stone), **Supp. V:** 298, 299–301
"Dog's Tale, A" (Twain), **Retro. Supp. III:** 268
Dog Star, The (Di Piero), **Supp. XIX:** 38, **40–41,** 43
"Dog Stories" (Prose), **Supp. XVI:** 256
Dog & the Fever, The (Quevedo), **Retro. Supp. I:** 423
"Dogtown Letters, The" (Jarman and R. McDowell), **Supp. XVII:** 111
"Dogwood, The" (Levertov), **Supp. III Part 1:** 276
"Dogwood Tree, The: A Boyhood" (Updike), **IV:** 218; **Retro. Supp. I:** 318, 319
Doig, Ivan, **Supp. XIV:** 227
"Doing Battle with the Wolf" (Coleman), **Supp. XI:** 87–88
"Doing Jigsaw Puzzles" (Crooker), **Supp. XXIII:** 56
Doing Literary Business: American Women Writers in the Nineteenth Century (Coultrap-McQuin), **Supp. XVI:** 85
Doings and Undoings (Podhoretz), **Supp. VIII: 236–237**
"Do-It-Yourself" (C. Baxter), **Supp. XVII:** 14–15
Dolan, Jill, **Supp. XV:** 327
Dolben, Digby Mackworth, **Supp. XX: 230**
"Dolce Far' Niente" (Humphrey), **Supp. IX:** 106
Dolci, Carlo, **III:** 474–475
Dollars and Cents (A. Warner), **Supp. XVIII:** 264
"Dollhouse, The" (Haines), **Supp. XII:** 204
"Dollhouse, The" (Stallings), **Supp. XXV:** 231, 232
Dollmaker's Ghost, The (Levis), **Supp. XI:** 259, 260, **264–268**
Doll's House, A (Ibsen), **III:** 523; **IV:** 357; **Supp. XVI:** 182
Dolmetsch, Arnold, **III:** 464
Dolores Claiborne (King), **Supp. V:** 138, 141, 147, 148, 149–150, 152
"Dolph Heyliger" (Irving), **II:** 309
Dolphin, The (R. Lowell), **Retro. Supp. II:** 183, 186, 188, **190–191; Supp. XII:** 253–254
"Dolphins" (Francis), **Supp. IX:** 83
Dome of Many-Coloured Class, A (A. Lowell), **II:** 515, 516–517
Domesday Book (Masters), **Supp. I Part 2:** 465, 466–469, 471, 473, 476
"Domestic Economy" (Gilman), **Supp. XI:** 206
"Domestic Manners" (Hardwick), **Supp. III Part 1:** 211
Domestic Work (Trethewey), **Supp. XXI:** 243, 244, **248–251,** 254
"Domestic Work, 1937" (Trethewey), **Supp. XXI:** 248
"Dominant White, The" (McKay), **Supp. X:** 134
Dominguez, Robert, **Supp. VIII:** 83
Domini, John, **Supp. XIX:** 45; **Supp. XXI:** 235
Dominique, Jean. See Closset, Marie
Donahoe, Edward, **Supp. XVIII:** 132
Donahue, Deirdre, **Supp. XXV:** 9
Donahue, Phil, **Supp. IV Part 2:** 526; **Supp. X:** 311
Donaldson, Susan, **Supp. XXII:** 148
Doña Perfecta (Galdós), **II:** 290
Dong, Stella, **Supp. XVI:** 222
Don Juan (Byron), **Supp. XV:** 259
"DON JUAN IN HELL" (Baraka), **Supp. II Part 1:** 33
Donkey of God, The (Untermeyer), **Supp. XV:** 310
"Donna mi Prega" (Cavalcanti), **Supp. III Part 2:** 620, 621, 622
Donn-Byrne, Brian Oswald. See Byrne, Donn
Donne, John, **I:** 358–359, 384, 389, 522, 586; **II:** 254; **III:** 493; **IV:** 83, 88, 135, 141, 144, 145, 151, 156, 165, 331, 333; **Retro. Supp. II:** 76; **Supp. I Part 1:** 80, 364, 367; **Supp. I Part 2:** 421, 424, 467, 725, 726; **Supp. III Part 2:** 614, 619; **Supp. IX:** 44; **Supp. VIII:** 26, 33, 164; **Supp. XII:** 45, 159; **Supp. XIII:** 94, 130; **Supp. XIV:** 122; **Supp. XV:** 92, 251; **Supp. XVI:** 158, 204; **Supp. XVIII:** 35, 39, 50–51, 307; **Supp. XXIV:** 167; **Supp. XXVII:** 220
Donne's Sermons: Selected Passages (L. P. Smith, ed.), **Supp. XIV:** 342
Donoghue, Denis, **I:** 537; **Supp. IV Part 1:** 39; **Supp. VIII:** 105, 189
Donohue, H. E. F., **Supp. IX:** 2, 3, 15, 16
Donoso, José, **Supp. XXIV:** 86
Do Not Deny Me (Thompson), **Supp. XXIII: 300–301**
"Do Not Weep Maiden, For War Is Kind" (Crane), **Supp. XVIII:** 75
Donovan, Josephine, **Retro. Supp. II:** 138, 139, 147
Don Quixote (Cervantes), **I:** 134; **II:** 291, 434; **III:** 113, 614; **Supp. I Part 2:** 422; **Supp. IX:** 94; **Supp. XXIV:** 87
Don Quixote: Which Was a Dream (Acker), **Supp. XII:** 5, **12–14**
Don't Ask (Levine), **Supp. V:** 178
Don't Ask Questions (Marquand), **III:** 58
Don't Bet on the Prince: Contemporary Feminist Fairy Tales in North America and England (Zipes), **Supp. XIV:** 126
Don't Drink the Water (Allen), **Supp. XV:** 3, **14**
Don't Look Back (film, Pennebaker), **Supp. XVIII:** 19
"Don't Miss It" (Stone), **Supp. XXVII:** 260
"Don't Neglect Your Wife" (script, Atherton), **Supp. XXIV:** 25
"Don't Shoot the Warthog" (Corso), **Supp. XII:** 123
Don't Stop the Carnival (Wouk), **Supp. XXV:** 257, 263–264
"Don't Tell Mother" (Wasserstein), **Supp. XV:** 319
"Don't Think Twice, It's All Right"

(song, Dylan), **Supp. XVIII:** 24
Don't Worry About the Kids (Neugeboren), **Supp. XVI:** 226
"Don't Worry About the Kids" (Neugeboren), **Supp. XVI:** 226
Don't You Want to Be Free? (Hughes), **Retro. Supp. I:** 203; **Supp. I Part 1:** 339
"Doodler, The" (Merrill), **Supp. III Part 1:** 321
Doolan, Moira, **Retro. Supp. II:** 247
Doolittle, Hilda (H. D.), **II:** 517, 520–521; **III:** 194, 195–196, 457, 465; **IV:** 404, 406; **Retro. Supp. I:** 288, 412, 413, 414, 415, 417; **Supp. I Part 1: 253–275; Supp. I Part 2:** 707; **Supp. III Part 1:** 48; **Supp. III Part 2:** 610; **Supp. IV Part 1:** 257; **Supp. V:** 79; **Supp. XV:** 43, 249, 301, 302; **Supp. XVII:** 77; **Supp. XXII:** 88; **Supp. XXIV:** 64; **Supp. XXVII:** 160, 261, 287
Doolittle, Thomas, **IV:** 150
"Doomed by Our Blood to Care" (Orfalea), **Supp. XIII:** 278
"Doomsday" (Plath), **Retro. Supp. II:** 242
Doomsters, The (Macdonald), **Supp. IV Part 2:** 462, 463, 472, 473
Doomswoman, The (Atherton), **Supp. XXIV:** 22
Doonesbury (Trudeau), **Supp. XXIV:** 283
"Door, The" (Creeley), **Supp. IV Part 1:** 145, 146, 156–157
Door, The (Rinehart), **Supp. XXV:** 197, 200
"Door, The" (White), **Supp. I Part 2:** 651, 675–676
"Door in the Dark, The" (Frost), **II:** 156
Door in the Hive, A (Levertov), **Supp. III Part 1:** 283, 284
"Door of the Trap, The" (Anderson), **I:** 112
"Doors" (Dybek), **Supp. XXIII:** 69
Doors (Hoffman), **Supp. XVIII:** 86–87
"Doors" (Hoffman), **Supp. XVIII:** 86–87
"Doors, Doors, Doors" (Sexton), **Supp. II Part 2:** 681
Doors, The, **Supp. X:** 186
"Doorways into the Depths" (Sanders), **Supp. XVI:** 272
Doreski, William, **Retro. Supp. II:** 185
Dorfman, Ariel, **Supp. IX:** 131, 138
Dorfman, Joseph, **Supp. I Part 2:** 631, 647, 650
Doris of Dobbs Ferry (Wells), **Supp. XXVI:** 277
Dorman, Jen, **Supp. XI:** 240
Dorn, Edward, **Supp. IV Part 1:** 154; **Supp. XXIV:** 33, 44
Dorn, Sarah, **Supp. XXI:** 243
"Dorothea Dix, Samaritan" (J. Scott), **Supp. XVII:** 189
Dorr, Julia, **Supp. XV:** 286
Dorrance Doings (Wells), **Supp. XXVI:** 277
Dorrance Domain, The (Wells), **Supp. XXVI:** 277
Dorris, Michael, **Supp. IV Part 1:** 260, 272
Dos Passos, John, **I:** 99, 288, 374, 379, **474–496,** 517, 519; **II:** 74, 77, 89, 98; **III:** 2, 28, 29, 70, 172, 382–383; **IV:** 340, 427, 433; **Retro. Supp. I:** 105, 113, 187; **Retro. Supp. II:** 95, 196; **Supp. I Part 2:** 646; **Supp. III Part 1:** 104, 105; **Supp. V:** 277; **Supp. VIII:** 101, 105; **Supp. XIV:** 24; **Supp. XV:** 135, 137, 182; **Supp. XVII:** 105, 107; **Supp. XXI:** 8; **Supp. XXIII:** 68; **Supp. XXVI:** 17, 32, 133, 135
"Dos Passos: Poet Against the World" (Cowley), **Supp. II Part 1:** 143, 145
Dostoesvsky: A Screenplay (Carver and Gallagher), **Supp. XXIV:** 178
Dostoevsky, Fyodor, **I:** 53, 103, 211, 468; **II:** 60, 130, 275, 320, 587; **III:** 37, 61, 155, 174, 176, 188, 189, 267, 272, 283, 286, 354, 357, 358, 359, 467, 571, 572; **IV:** 1, 7, 8, 17, 21, 50, 59, 106, 110, 128, 134, 285, 289, 476, 485, 491; **Retro. Supp. II:** 20, 204, 299; **Supp. I Part 1:** 49; **Supp. I Part 2:** 445, 466; **Supp. IV Part 2:** 519, 525; **Supp. VIII:** 175; **Supp. X:** 4–5; **Supp. XI:** 161; **Supp. XII:** 322; **Supp. XVI:** 63; **Supp. XVII:** 225; **Supp. XVIII:** 278, 280; **Supp. XX: 45; Supp. XXIII:** 4; **Supp. XXIV:** 132
Doty, Mark, **Supp. IX:** 42, 300; **Supp. XI: 119–138; Supp. XXI:** 129, 130, 131, 139, 141; **Supp. XXIII:** 126, 221
Doty, M. R. See Dawson, Ruth; Doty, Mark
Double, The (Dostoevsky), **Supp. IX:** 105
"Double, The" (Levis), **Supp. XI:** 260, **261–263**
Double, The (Rank), **Supp. IX:** 105
Double Agent, The (Blackmur), **Supp. II Part 1:** 90, 108, 146
Double Axe, The (Jeffers), **Supp. II Part 2:** 416, 434
"Double Blind" (Skloot), **Supp. XX: 194, 208**
Doubleday, Frank, **I:** 500, 502, 515, 517; **III:** 327
Doubleday, Mrs. Frank, **I:** 500
Double Deuce (Parker), **Supp. XIX:** 183
Double Down (F. and S. Barthelme), **Supp. XI:** 27, 34, 35, 36–38
Double Dream of Spring, The (Ashbery), **Supp. III Part 1:** 11–13
Double Fold: Libraries and the Assault on Paper (Baker), **Supp. XIII:** 52, 56
Double Game (Calle), **Supp. XII:** 22
"Double Gap, The" (Auchincloss), **Supp. IV Part 1:** 33
"Double-Headed Snake of Newbury, The" (Whittier), **Supp. I Part 2:** 698
Double Honeymoon (Connell), **Supp. XIV:** 80, 87
Double Image, The (Levertov), **Supp. III Part 1:** 274, 276
"Double Image, The" (Sexton), **Supp. II Part 2:** 671, 677–678
Double Indemnity (film), **Supp. IV Part 1:** 130
Double Legacy: Reflections on a Pair of Deaths (Hadas), **Supp. XXIII:** 123, **126–127**
"Double Limbo" (Komunyakaa), **Supp. XIII:** 132
Double Man, The (Auden), **Supp. III Part 1:** 16; **Supp. X:** 118
"Double Ode" (Rukeyser), **Supp. VI:** 282–283, 286
Double Persephone (Atwood), **Supp. XIII:** 19
Double Play (Parker), **Supp. XIX: 189–190**
Doubles in Literary Psychology (Tymms), **Supp. IX:** 105
Double Vision: American Thoughts Abroad (Knowles), **Supp. XII:** 249
"Doubt" (Teasdale), **Supp. XXVII:** 291–292
"Doubt on the Great Divide" (Stafford), **Supp. XI:** 322
Dougherty, Robin, **Supp. XXII:** 205
Dougherty, Steve, **Supp. X:** 262
Douglas, Aaron, **Supp. I Part 1:** 326
Douglas, Alfred, **Supp. X:** 151
Douglas, Ann, **Supp. XII:** 136; **Supp. XVIII:** 258; **Supp. XX: 69**
Douglas, Claire, **III:** 552
Douglas, Ellen, **Supp. XXI:** 38
Douglas, George (pseudonym). See Brown, George Douglas
Douglas, Kirk, **Supp. XIII:** 5–6

Douglas, Lloyd, **IV:** 434
Douglas, Marjory Stoneman, **Supp. XVIII:** 195
Douglas, Melvyn, **Supp. V:** 223
Douglas, Michael, **Supp. XI:** 67
Douglas, Paul, **III:** 294
Douglas, Stephen A., **III:** 577, 588–589; **Supp. I Part 2:** 456, 471
Douglas, William O., **III:** 581
Douglass, Frederick, **Supp. I Part 1:** 51, 345; **Supp. I Part 2:** 591; **Supp. II Part 1:** 157, 195, 196, 292, 378; **Supp. III Part 1: 153–174; Supp. IV Part 1:** 1, 2, 13, 15, 256; **Supp. VIII:** 202; **Supp. XVIII:** 16; **Supp. XX: 109, 281; Supp. XXIII:** 167
Douglass, Thomas E., **Supp. XXIII:** 36
Douglass Pilot, The (Baldwin, ed.), **Supp. I Part 1:** 49
Dove, Belle, **I:** 451
Dove, Rita, **Supp. IV Part 1: 241–258; Supp. XVII:** 71, 110; **Supp. XVIII:** 172, 174; **Supp. XXI:** 243, 246, 247, 249, 251
Dove of the East and Other Stories, A (Helprin), **Supp. XXV:** 79, 83, 84–85
"Dover Beach" (Arnold), **Retro. Supp. I:** 325; **Supp. XIX:** 41
Dow, Lorenzo, **IV:** 265
Dowd, Douglas, **Supp. I Part 2:** 645, 650
"Do We Understand Each Other?" (Ginsberg), **Supp. II Part 1:** 311
Dowie, William, **Supp. V:** 199
Do with Me What You Will (Oates), **Supp. II Part 2:** 506, 515–517
Dowling, Eddie, **IV:** 394
Down and Out (Shanley), **Supp. XIV:** 317
"Down at City Hall" (Didion), **Supp. IV Part 1:** 211
"Down at the Cross" (Baldwin), **Retro. Supp. II:** 1, 2, 7, 12, 13, 15; **Supp. I Part 1:** 60, 61
"Down at the Dinghy" (Salinger), **III:** 559, 563
"Down by the Station, Early in the Morning" (Ashbery), **Supp. III Part 1:** 25
Downers Grove (Hornburg), **Supp. XXVII:** 80
Downey, Sharon D., **Supp. XX: 244**
Downhill Racer (film), **Supp. IX:** 253
"Down Home" (J. W. Miller), **Supp. XX: 169**
"Down in Alabam" (Bierce), **I:** 193
Downing, Ben, **Supp. XII:** 175, 189, 190–191
Downing, Major Jack (pseudonym). See Smith, Seba
Down in My Heart (Stafford), **Supp. XI:** 313, 315
Down Mailer's Way (Solotaroff), **Retro. Supp. II:** 203
"Down the Highway" (song, Dylan), **Supp. XVIII:** 24
Down the Rabbit Hole: Adventures and Misadventures in the Realm of Children's Literature (Lanes), **Supp. XVI:** 104
Down There on a Visit (Isherwood), **Supp. XIV:** 159, 161, 164, **168–169,** 170, 171
Down the River (Abbey), **Supp. XIII:** 12–13
"Down the River with Henry Thoreau" (Abbey), **Supp. XIII:** 12–13
Down These Mean Streets (P. Thomas), **Supp. XIII:** 264
Down the Starry River (Purdy), **Supp. VII:** 278
Down to the River: Portraits of Iowa Musicians (Dyas), **Supp. XIX:** 174
Downtown (Siddons), **Supp. XXII:** 239, 240, 242, **247–249, 251–252,** 253
"Downtrodden Mary's Failed Campaign of Terror" (Saunders), **Supp. XIX:** 226
"Downward Path to Wisdom, The" (Porter), **III:** 442, 443, 446
"Down Where I Am" (Hughes), **Supp. I Part 1:** 344
Down with Starvation Wages in Southeast Missouri (C. L. R. James), **Supp. XXI:** 169
"Dowsing for Joy" (Skloot), **Supp. XX: 203**
Dowson, Ernest C., **I:** 384
Doyle, Arthur Conan, **Retro. Supp. I:** 270; **Retro. Supp. III:** 226; **Supp. IV Part 1:** 128, 341; **Supp. IV Part 2:** 464, 469; **Supp. XI:** 63; **Supp. XXVI:** 282
Doyle, C. W., **I:** 199
Doyno, Victor, **Retro. Supp. III:** 265
"Draba" (Leopold), **Supp. XIV:** 186
Drabble, Margaret, **Supp. IV Part 1:** 297, 299, 305
Drabelle, Dennis, **Supp. XIII:** 13
Drach, Ivan, **Supp. III Part 1:** 268
Dracula (film), **Supp. IV Part 1:** 104; **Supp. XVII:** 57
Dracula (Stoker), **Supp. XXVI:** 58
"Draft Horse, The" (Frost), **Retro. Supp. I:** 141; **Retro. Supp. III:** 107
"Draft Lyrics for Candide" (Agee), **I:** 28
Draft of XVI Cantos, A (Pound), **III:** 472; **Retro. Supp. I:** 292
Draft of XXX Cantos, A (Pound), **III:** 196; **Retro. Supp. I:** 292
Drafts &Fragments (Pound), **Retro. Supp. I:** 293
"Dragon" (Lovecraft), **Supp. XXV:** 111
Dragon Country (T. Williams), **IV:** 383
Dragone, Nichole, **Supp. XXIII:** 157
Dragon Seed (Buck), **Supp. II Part 1:** 124
Dragon's Teeth (Sinclair), **Supp. V:** 290
Dragon Takes a Wife, The (Myers), **Supp. XXVII:** 209
Drake, Benjamin, **Supp. I Part 2:** 584
Drake, Daniel, **Supp. I Part 2:** 584
Drake, Sir Francis, **Supp. I Part 2:** 497
Drake, Robert, **Supp. XX: 274**
Drake, St. Clair, **IV:** 475
Drake, Sylvia, **Supp. XXI:** 155
Drake, William, **Supp. XV:** 295; **Supp. XXVII:** 284, 285, 291, 293, 294, 297
Dramatic Duologues (Masters), **Supp. I Part 2:** 461
"Drapery Factory, Gulfport. Mississippi, 1956" (Trethewey), **Supp. XXI:** 246
Drattel, Deborah, **Supp. XV:** 333
Drat These Brats (X. J. Kennedy), **Supp. XV:** 163
"Draught" (Cowley), **Supp. II Part 1:** 141, 142
Drayton, Michael, **IV:** 135; **Retro. Supp. II:** 76
"Dr. Bergen's Belief" (Schwartz), **Supp. II Part 2:** 650
Dr. Bloodmoney (Dick), **Supp. XVIII:** 138
"Dreadful Has Already Happened, The" (Strand), **Supp. IV Part 2:** 627
Dread Road, The (Le Sueur), **Supp. XXIII:** 168, 169, **169–170,** 173
"Dream, A" (Ginsberg), **Supp. II Part 1:** 312
"Dream, A" (Tate), **IV:** 129
"Dream, The" (Hayden), **Supp. II Part 1:** 368, 377
Dream at the End of the World, The: Paul Bowles and the Literary Renegades in Tangier (Green), **Supp. IV Part 1:** 95
"Dream Avenue" (Simic), **Supp. VIII:** 282
"Dream Boogie" (Hughes), **Retro. Supp. I:** 208; **Supp. I Part 1:** 339–340

"Dreambook Bestiary" (Komunyakaa), **Supp. XIII:** 120
Dreamer (C. Johnson), **Supp. VI:** 186, **196–199**
dreamer examines his pillow, the (Shanley), **Supp. XIV:** 315, **327**
"Dreamer in a Dead Language" (Paley), **Supp. VI:** 217
Dreaming Emmett (Morrison), **Retro. Supp. III:** 184
Dreaming in Cuban (García), **Supp. XI:** 178, **179–185,** 190
"Dreaming of Hair" (L.-Y. Lee), **Supp. XV:** 214
"Dreaming the Breasts" (Sexton), **Supp. II Part 2:** 692
"Dreaming Water" (Espaillat), **Supp. XXI:** 102
"Dream Interpretation" (Hadas), **Supp. XXIII:** 113, 121
"Dream Interpreted, The" (Paine), **Supp. I Part 2:** 505
Dream Jumbo (Longo), **Supp. XVI:** 124
Dream Keeper, The (Hughes), **Supp. I Part 1:** 328, 332, 333, 334
Dream Keeper and Other Poems, The (Hughes), **Retro. Supp. I:** 201, 202
Dreamland (Baker), **Supp. XIV:** 96
"Dream-Land" (Poe), **Retro. Supp. II:** 274
Dream Life of Balso Snell, The (West), **IV:** 286, 287, 288–290, 291, 297; **Retro. Supp. II:** 321, 322, 327, 328, **330–332**
"Dream Machine, The" (Hadas), **Supp. XXIII:** 122–123
Dream Me Home Safely: Writers on Growing up in America (Shreve, ed.), **Supp. XXIII:** 284
Dream of a Common Language, The: Poems, 1974–1977 (Rich), **Retro. Supp. III:** 242, 248–249, 253; **Supp. I Part 2:** 551, 554, 569–576
Dream of Arcadia: American Writers and Artists in Italy (Brooks), **I:** 254
Dream of Governors, A (Simpson), **Supp. IX:** 265, **269–270**
"Dream of Her Grandfather, A" (Zitkala-Ša), **Supp. XXV:** 282, 283
"Dream of Italy, A" (Masters), **Supp. I Part 2:** 458
"Dream of Mourning, The" (Glück), **Supp. V:** 84
"Dream of the Blacksmith's Room, A" (R. Bly), **Supp. IV Part 1:** 73
"Dream of the Cardboard Lover" (Haines), **Supp. XII:** 204
Dream of the Golden Mountains, The (Cowley), **Supp. II Part 1:** 139, 141, 142, 144
"Dream Pang, A" (Frost), **II:** 153
Dream-Quest of Unkown Kadath, The (Lovecraft), **Supp. XXV:** 113–114
"Dreams About Clothes" (Merrill), **Supp. III Part 1:** 328–329
"Dreams"(Dybek), **Supp. XXIII:** 73
Dreams from Bunker Hill (Fante), **Supp. XI:** 160, 166, **172–173**
"Dreams in the Witch House, The" (Lovecraft), **Supp. XXV:** 111, 123
"Dreams"(Kenny), **Supp. XXIII:** 153
"Dreams of Adulthood" (Ashbery), **Supp. III Part 1:** 26
"Dreams of Glory on the Mound" (Plimpton), **Supp. XVI:** 238–239
"Dreams of Math" (Kenyon), **Supp. VII:** 160–161
"Dreams of the Animals" (Atwood), **Supp. XIII:** 33
"Dream Variations" (Hughes), **Retro. Supp. I:** 198; **Supp. I Part 1:** 323
"Dream Vision" (Olsen), **Supp. XIII:** 295–296
"Dream Within a Dream" (Poe), **Retro. Supp. III:** 232
Dream with No Stump Roots in It, A (Huddle), **Supp. XXVI:** 152
"Dream with No Stumps in It, A" (Huddle), **Supp. XXVI:** 152
Dream Work (Oliver), **Supp. VII:** 234–235, 236–238, 240
Dred: A Tale of the Great Dismal Swamp (Stowe), **Supp. I Part 2:** 592
Dreiser, Theodore, **I:** 59, 97, 109, 116, 355, 374, 375, 475, 482, **497–520; II:** 26, 27, 29, 34, 38, 44, 74, 89, 93, 180, 276, 283, 428, 444, 451, 456–457, 467–468; **III:** 40, 103, 106, 251, 314, 319, 327, 335, 453, 576, 582; **IV:** 29, 35, 40, 135, 208, 237, 475, 482, 484; **Retro. Supp. I:** 325, 376; **Retro. Supp. II: 93–110,** 114, 322; **Supp. I Part 1:** 320; **Supp. I Part 2:** 461, 468; **Supp. III Part 2:** 412; **Supp. IV Part 1:** 31, 236, 350; **Supp. IV Part 2:** 689; **Supp. IX:** 1, 14, 15, 308; **Supp. V:** 113, 120; **Supp. VIII:** 98, 101, 102; **Supp. XI:** 207; **Supp. XIV:** 111; **Supp. XVII:** 95, 96–97, 105, 155; **Supp. XVIII:** 1, 6, 76, 226; **Supp. XXI:** 275; **Supp. XXIII:** 161, 164; **Supp. XXV:** 18; **Supp. XXVI:** 133, 273; **Supp. XXVII:** 83, 88
"Drenched in Light" (Hurston), **Retro. Supp. III:** 129; **Supp. VI:** 150–151
Drennen, Eileen M., **Supp. XXII:** 241, 243
Dresser, Paul, **Retro. Supp. II:** 94, 103
Dress Gray (teleplay), **Supp. IV Part 2:** 683
Dress Gray (Truscott), **Supp. IV Part 2:** 683
"Dressing for Dinner" (Ríos), **Supp. IV Part 2:** 548
Dressing Up for the Carnival (Shields), **Supp. VII:** 328
"Dress of One Occasion" (Stallings), **Supp. XXV:** 233
"Dress Rehearsal" (Skloot), **Supp. XX: 204**
Drew, Bettina, **Supp. IX:** 2, 4
Drew, Elizabeth, **Retro. Supp. II:** 242, 243
Drexler, Eric, **Supp. XVI:** 121
Dreyfus, Alfred, **Supp. I Part 2:** 446
"Dr. Hanray's Second Chance" (Richter), **Supp. XVIII:** 218
"Dr. Heidegger's Experiment" (Hawthorne), **Retro. Supp. III:** 114
Drift and Mastery (Lippmann), **I:** 222–223
"Driftwood" (C. Frost), **Supp. XV:** 106–107
"Drinker, The" (R. Lowell), **II:** 535, 550
"Drinking Cold Water" (Everwine), **Supp. XV:** 80–81
"Drinking from a Helmet" (Dickey), **Supp. IV Part 1:** 180
Drinking Gourd, The (Hansberry), **Supp. IV Part 1:** 359, 365–367, 374
Drinks before Dinner (Doctorow), **Supp. IV Part 1:** 231, 234–235
Drinkwater, John, **Retro. Supp. III:** 95
Driscoll, David, **Supp. XIX:** 241, 242
Driskill, Qwo-Li, **Supp. XXIII:** 147, 148, 149
Drive, He Said (Larner), **Supp. XVI:** 220
"Drive Home, The" (Banks), **Supp. V:** 7
"Driver" (Merrill), **Supp. III Part 1:** 331
"Driving Alone in Winter" (W. V. Davis), **Supp. XXI:** 89, 90, 94
"Driving Through Minnesota During the Hanoi Bombings" (R. Bly), **Supp. IV Part 1:** 61; **Supp. XVII:** 243
"Driving through Oregon" (Haines), **Supp. XII:** 207
"Driving to Oregon"(Thompson), **Supp. XXIII:** 291
"Driving toward the Lac Qui Parle River" (R. Bly), **Supp. IV Part 1:** 61

"Dr. Jack-o'-Lantern" (Yates), **Supp. XI:** 340–341
Dr. Jekyll and Mr. Hyde (film), **Supp. XVII:** 57
"Drone" (Coleman), **Supp. XI:** 85–86
Drop City (Boyle), **Supp. XX: 30–31**
Drown (Díaz), **Supp. XXIV:** 83, 84, 85, 86, **88–89,** 90, 93
"Drowned Man, The: Death between Two Rivers" (McGrath), **Supp. X:** 116
"Drowning" (Boyle), **Supp. XX: 18**
"Drowning 1954" (Keillor), **Supp. XVI:** 172
Drowning Pool, The (film), **Supp. IV Part 2:** 474
Drowning Pool, The (Macdonald), **Supp. IV Part 2:** 470, 471
Drowning Season, The (Hoffman), **Supp. X: 82**
Drowning with Others (Dickey), **Supp. IV Part 1:** 176, 178, 179
"Drowsy Day, A" (Dunbar), **Supp. II Part 1:** 198
Dr. Seuss. See Geisel, Theodor Seuss (Dr. Seuss)
Dr. Seuss and Mr. Geisel (J. and N. Morgan), **Supp. XVI:** 103
Dr. Seuss Goes to War: The World War II Editorial Cartoons of Theodor Seuss Geisel (Minear), **Supp. XVI:** 101
Dr. Seuss's ABC (Geisel), **Supp. XVI:** 99
Dr. Strangelove; or, How I Learned to Stop Worrying and Love the Bomb (film), **Supp. XI:** 293, **301–305**
Drugiye Berega (Nabokov), **III:** 247–250, 252
"Drug Shop, The, or Endymion in Edmonstoun" (Benét), **Supp. XI:** 43
"Drug Store" (Shapiro), **Supp. II Part 2:** 705
"Drugstore in Winter, A" (Ozick), **Supp. V:** 272
Drukman, Steven, **Supp. XIII:** 195, 197, 202
"Drum" (Hogan), **Supp. IV Part 1:** 413
"Drum, The" (Alvarez), **Supp. VII:** 7
"Drumlin Woodchuck, A" (Frost), **II:** 159–160; **Retro. Supp. I:** 138
Drummond, William, **Supp. I Part 1:** 369
Drummond de Andrade, Carlos, **Supp. IV Part 2:** 626, 629, 630
Drums at Dusk (Bontemps), **Supp. XXII:** 5, 9–10
Drum-Taps (Whitman), **IV:** 346, 347, 444; **Retro. Supp. I:** 406; **Retro. Supp. III:** 301
"Drunken Fisherman, The" (R. Lowell), **II:** 534, 550
"Drunken Sisters, The" (Wilder), **IV:** 374
Drunk in the Furnace, The (Merwin), **Supp. III Part 1:** 345–346
"Drunk in the Furnace, The" (Merwin), **Supp. III Part 1:** 346
Druten, John van, **Supp. XIV:** 162
"Dr. Williams' Position" (Pound), **Supp. XVII:** 226–227
Dryden, John, **II:** 111, 542, 556; **III:** 15; **IV:** 145; **Retro. Supp. I:** 56; **Supp. I Part 1:** 150; **Supp. I Part 2:** 422; **Supp. IX:** 68; **Supp. XIV:** 5; **Supp. XV:** 258; **Supp. XX: 280; Supp. XXIV:** 158; **Supp. XXV:** 119
Drye, Captain Frank, **Retro. Supp. II:** 115
Dry Salvages, The (T. S. Eliot), **I:** 581
"Dry Salvages, The" (T. S. Eliot), **Retro. Supp. I:** 66; **Retro. Supp. III:** 66, 67–68
"Dry September" (Faulkner), **II:** 72, 73; **Retro. Supp. III:** 82
"Dry Spring"(Thompson), **Supp. XXIII:** 291
Dry Sun, Dry Wind (Wagoner), **Supp. IX:** 323, 324
D'Souza, Dinesh, **Supp. X:** 255
"Dual" (Goldbarth), **Supp. XII:** 188
"Dual Curriculum" (Ozick), **Supp. V:** 270
"Dualism" (Reed), **Supp. X:** 242
Duane's Depressed (McMurtry), **Supp. V:** 233
Du Bartas, Guillaume de Salluste, **Retro. Supp. III:** 3, 5, 8; **Supp. I Part 1:** 98, 104, 111, 118, 119
Dubek, Laura, **Retro. Supp. III:** 138
Duberman, Martin, **Supp. I Part 2:** 408, 409
Dubie, Norman, **Supp. XXIV:** 165
"Dubin's Lives" (Malamud), **Supp. I Part 2:** 451
Dubious Honors (M. F. K. Fisher), **Supp. XVII:** 91
"Dubliners" (J. Joyce), **Supp. XVI:** 41
Dubliners (Joyce), **I:** 130, 480; **III:** 471; **Supp. VIII:** 146
Dublin's Lives (Malamud), **Supp. XIX:** 142
Du Bois, Nina Gomer (Mrs. W. E. B. Du Bois), **Supp. II P art 1:** 158; **Supp. XIV:** 200
Du Bois, Shirley Graham, **Supp. II Part 1:** 186; **Supp. XXI:** 171. See also Graham, Shirley
Du Bois, W. E. B., **I:** 260; **Supp. I Part 1:** 5, 345; **Supp. II Part 1:** 33, 56, 61, **157–189,** 195; **Supp. IV Part 1:** 9, 164, 170, 362; **Supp. X:** 133, 134, 137, 139, 242; **Supp. XIII:** 185, **Supp. XIII:** 186, 233, 238, 243, 244, 247; **Supp. XIV:** 54, 69, 72, 201, 202; **Supp. XIX:** 67, 69, 77; **Supp. XVI:** 135; **Supp. XVIII:** 119, 122, 126, 130; **Supp. XX: 102, 105, 106; Supp. XXI:** 166, 277; **Supp. XXII:** 3; **Supp. XXVI:** 88, 168
DuBose, Martha Hailey, **Supp. XXV:** 192, 199, 200
Dubreuil, Jean, **Supp. IV Part 2:** 425
Dubus, Andre, **Supp. VII: 75–93; Supp. XI:** 347,**Supp. XI:** 349; **Supp. XIV:** 21; **Supp. XXIV:** 97
Dubus, Andre, III, **Supp. XXIV: 97–112**
Duchamp, Marcel, **IV:** 408; **Retro. Supp. I:** 416, 417, 418, 430; **Supp. IV Part 2:** 423, 424; **Supp. XII:** 124; **Supp. XV:** 157; **Supp. XXII:** 162, 163, 168
"Duchess at Prayer, The" (Wharton), **Retro. Supp. I:** 365
Duchess of Malfi, The (Webster), **IV:** 131
"Duckling Girl" (Dubus III), **Supp. XXIV:** 100–101, 105
Duck Soup (film), **Supp. IV Part 1:** 384
Duck Variations, The (Mamet), **Supp. XIV:** 239, 240, 249
Ducornet, Rikki, **Supp. XXII:** 261
Dudley, Anne. See Bradstreet, Anne
Dudley, Joseph, **III:** 52
Dudley, Thomas, **III:** 52; **Retro. Supp. III:** 3; **Supp. I Part 1:** 98, 99, 110, 116
"Duenna"(Schott), **Supp. XXIII:** 249
"Duet, With Muffled Brake Drums" (Updike), **Retro. Supp. I:** 319
Duet for Cannibals (Sontag), **Supp. III Part 2:** 452, 456
Duffey, Bernard, **Supp. I Part 2:** 458, 471
Duffield, Pitts, **Supp. XXI:** 3
Duffus, R. L., **Supp. I Part 2:** 650
Duffy, Martha, **Supp. IV Part 1:** 207; **Supp. XX: 244**
Duffy, William, **Supp. XVI:** 32
Du Fu (Tu Fu), **Supp. XV:** 217
Dufy, Raoul, **I:** 115; **IV:** 80
Dugan, Alan, **Supp. XIII:** 76
Dugan, James, **Supp. XV:** 197
"Dugout"(Kenny), **Supp. XXIII:** 155
Duhamel, Marcel, **Supp. XVI:** 135, 143

Dujardin, Edouard, **I:** 53
"Duke de l'Omelette, The" (Poe), **III:** 411, 425
Duke Herring (Bodenheim), **Supp. XXV:** 27
"Duke in His Domain, The" (Capote), **Supp. III Part 1:** 113, 126
Duke of Deception, The (G. Wolff), **Supp. II Part 1:** 97; **Supp. XI:** 246
"Duke's Child, The" (Maxwell), **Supp. VIII:** 172
"Dulce et Decorum Est" (Owen), **Supp. XVIII:** 92
"Dulham Ladies, The" (Jewett), **II:** 407, 408; **Retro. Supp. II:** 143
"Dulse" (Munro), **Supp. XXVII:** 188
Duluth (Vidal), **Supp. IV Part 2:** 677, 685, 689, 691–692
Dumas, Alexandre, **III:** 386; **Supp. XVII:** 64
Dumas, Henry, **Retro. Supp. III:** 184, 194
"Dumb Oax, The" (Lewis), **Retro. Supp. I:** 170
"Dummy, The" (Sontag), **Supp. III Part 2:** 469
"Dump Ground, The" (Stegner), **Supp. IV Part 2:** 601
Dunant, Sarah, **Supp. XIX:** 186
Dunayevskaya, Raya, **Supp. XXI:** 169
Dunbar, Alice Moore (Mrs. Paul Laurence Dunbar), **Supp. II Part 1:** 195, 200, 217
Dunbar, Paul Laurence, **Supp. I Part 1:** 320; **Supp. II Part 1:** 174, **191–219; Supp. III Part 1:** 73; **Supp. IV Part 1:** 15, 165, 170; **Supp. X:** 136; **Supp. XI:** 277; **Supp. XIII:** 111; **Supp. XXII:** 11; **Supp. XXVII:** 164
Duncan, Harry, **Supp. XV:** 75
Duncan, Isadora, **I:** 483; **Supp. XV:** 42, 50
Duncan, Isla, **Supp. XXVII:** 193
Duncan, Robert, **Retro. Supp. II:** 49; **Supp. III Part 2:** 625, 626, 630, 631; **Supp. VIII:** 304; **Supp. XVI:** 282–283; **Supp. XXIII:** 213; **Supp. XXVII:** 160
Dunciad, The (Pope), **I:** 204
Dunford, Judith, **Supp. VIII:** 107
Dunlap, William, **Supp. I Part 1:** 126, 130, 137, 141, 145
Dunn, Stephen, **Supp. XI: 139–158; Supp. XIX:** 85
Dunne, Finley Peter, **II:** 432
Dunne, John Gregory, **Supp. IV Part 1:** 197, 198, 201, 203, 207
"Dunnet Shepherdess, A" (Jewett), **II:** 392–393; **Retro. Supp. II:** 139
Dunning, Stephen, **Supp. XIV:** 126
Dunning, William Archibald, **Supp. II Part 1:** 170; **Supp. XIV:** 48
Dunnock, Mildred, **III:** 153
Dunster, Henry, **Supp. I Part 2:** 485
"Dunwich Horror, The" (Lovecraft), **Supp. XXV:** 111, 120
"Duo Tried Killing Man with Bacon" (Goldbarth), **Supp. XII:** 176
Dupee, F. W., **I:** 254; **II:** 548; **Supp. IX:** 93, 96; **Supp. VIII:** 231
DuPlessis, Rachel Blau, **Supp. IV Part 2:** 421, 426, 432; **Supp. XVI:** 284; **Supp. XXVI:** 228, 234, 237–238
Duplicate Keys (Smiley), **Supp. VI:** 292, **294–296**
Duplications, The (Koch), **Supp. XV:** 181, 183, 186
Durable Fire, A (Sarton), **Supp. VIII:** 260
Durand, Asher, B., **Supp. I Part 1:** 156, 157
Durand, Régis, **Supp. IV Part 1:** 44
Durang, Christopher, **Supp. XXIV: 113–130,** 263
"Durango Suite" (Gunn Allen), **Supp. IV Part 1:** 326
Durant, Kenneth, **Supp. XXII:** 278, 281
"Durations" (Matthews), **Supp. IX:** 152–153, 154
Dürer, Albrecht, **III:** 212; **Supp. XII:** 44
Durham, David Anthony, **Supp. XVIII:** 100
"During Fever" (R. Lowell), **II:** 547
Durkheim, Émile, **I:** 227; **Retro. Supp. I:** 55, 57; **Supp. I Part 2:** 637, 638
Durrell, Lawrence, **III:** 184, 190; **IV:** 430; **Supp. X:** 108, 187; **Supp. XVI:** 294
Dürrenmatt, Friedrich, **Supp. IV Part 2:** 683
Duse, Eleonora, **II:** 515, 528
Dusk and Other Stories (Salter), **Supp. IX: 260–261**
"Dusk in War Time" (Teasdale), **Supp. XXVII:** 294
Dusk of Dawn: An Essay Toward an Autobiography of a Race Concept (Du Bois), **Supp. II Part 1:** 159, 183, 186
Dusselier, Jane, **Supp. XXVI:** 210
"Dust" (R. Fisher), **Supp. XIX:** 71
"Dusting" (Alvarez), **Supp. VII:** 4
"Dusting" (Dove), **Supp. IV Part 1:** 247, 248
"Dusting" (Schnackenberg), **Supp. XV:** 256
"Dust of Snow" (Frost), **II:** 154; **Retro. Supp. III:** 101, 102
Dust Tracks on a Road (Hurston), **Retro. Supp. III:** 128, 131, 133–134; **Supp. IV Part 1:** 5, 11; **Supp. VI:** 149, 151, 158–159
"Dusty Braces" (Snyder), **Supp. VIII:** 302
Dutchman (Baraka), **Supp. II Part 1:** 38, 40, 42–44, 54, 55
"Dutch Nick Massacre, The" (Twain), **IV:** 195
"Dutch Picture, A" (Longfellow), **Retro. Supp. II:** 171
Dutton, Charles S., **Supp. VIII:** 332, 342
Dutton, Clarence Earl, **Supp. IV Part 2:** 598
Duvall, Robert, **Supp. V:** 227
"Duwamish" (Hugo), **Supp. VI:** 136
"Duwamish, Skagit, Hoh" (Hugo), **Supp. VI:** 136–137
"Duwamish No. 2" (Hugo), **Supp. VI:** 137
Duyckinck, Evert, **III:** 77, 81, 83, 85; **Retro. Supp. I:** 155, 247, 248; **Retro. Supp. III:** 154, 157, 158, 228; **Supp. I Part 1:** 122, 317; **Supp. XXV:** 250
Duyckinck, George, **Supp. I Part 1:** 122; **Supp. XXV:** 250
"Dvonya" (Simpson), **Supp. IX:** 274
Dwelling Places: Poems and Translations (Ferry), **Supp. XXIV: 152–153**
Dwellings: A Spiritual History of the Living World (Hogan), **Supp. IV Part 1:** 397, 410, 415–416, 417
Dwight, Sereno E., **I:** 547
Dwight, Timothy, **Supp. I Part 1:** 124; **Supp. I Part 2:** 516, 580; **Supp. II Part 1:** 65, 69
Dworkin, Andrea, **Supp. XII:** 6
Dwyer, Jim, **Supp. XVI:** 16, 19
Dyas, Sandra, **Supp. XIX:** 174
Dybbuk, A, or Between Two Worlds: Dramatic Legend in Four Acts (Kushner), **Supp. IX:** 138
Dybbuk, The (Ansky), **IV:** 6
Dybek, Stuart, **Supp. XXIII: 67–81**
Dybuk, The (Ansky), **Supp. XXIII:** 8
Dyer, Geoff, **Supp. X:** 169
Dyer, Joyce, **Supp. XX: 166**
Dyer, R. C., **Supp. XIII:** 162
Dyer, Richard, **Supp. XXII:** 261
Dyer's Thistle (Balakian), **Supp. XXIII:** 25
Dying Animal, The (P. Roth), **Retro. Supp. II:** 288
"Dying Elm, The" (Freneau), **Supp. II Part 1:** 258
"Dying Indian, The" (Freneau), **Supp.**

II Part 1: 262
"Dying Man, The" (Roethke), **III:** 540, 542, 543–545
Dykeman, Wilma, **Supp. XX: 163**
Dykes to Watch Out For (Bechdel), **Supp. XXV:** 1, 3–4
Dylan, Bob, **Supp. VIII:** 202; **Supp. XIII:** 114, 119; **Supp. XV:** 349, 350; **Supp. XVIII: 19–34; Supp. XXII:** 83
Dylan's Visions of Sin (Ricks), **Supp. XVIII:** 20
"Dynamics of Heroic Action, The" (lecture, Murray), **Supp. XIX:** 153
Dynamo (O'Neill), **III:** 396
"Dynasties" (Gibran), **Supp. XX: 118**
"Dysfunctional Narratives: Or, 'Mistakes Were Made' " (C. Baxter), **Supp. XVII:** 20
"Dysfunctional Nation" (Karr), **Supp. XI:** 245
Dyson, A. E., **Retro. Supp. II:** 247
Dyson, Freeman, **Supp. XVII:** 42
"Each and All" (Emerson), **II:** 19
Each Happiness Ringer by Lions (Hirshfield), **Supp. XXIII:** 135
Each in His Season (Snodgrass), **Supp. VI:** 324, 327
"Each Like a Leaf" (Swenson), **Supp. IV Part 2:** 644
Eads, Martha Greene, **Supp. XVIII:** 49
Eady, Cornelius, **Supp. XXI:** 246
Eager, Allen, **Supp. XI:** 294
"Eagle, The" (Tate), **IV:** 128
"Eagle and the Mole, The" (Wylie), **Supp. I Part 2:** 710, 711, 713, 714, 729
"Eagle and the Skylark, The" (Gibran), **Supp. XX: 124**
Eagle as Wide as the World, The (X. J. Kennedy), **Supp. XV:** 162, 164
"Eagle Poem" (Harjo), **Supp. XII:** 224, 226
"Eagles" (Dickey), **Supp. IV Part 1:** 186
Eagle's Mile, The (Dickey), **Supp. IV Part 1:** 178, 185–186
"Eagle That Is Forgotten, The" (Lindsay), **Supp. I Part 2:** 382, 387
Eagleton, Terry, **Retro. Supp. I:** 67
Eakin, Paul John, **Supp. VIII:** 167, 168; **Supp. XIII:** 225; **Supp. XVI:** 70
Eakins, Thomas, **Supp. XIV:** 338; **Supp. XXII:** 18–19
Eames, Emma, **Supp. XX: 232, 240**
Eames, Roscoe, **II:** 476
"Earl: My Life with a Louse" (Keillor), **Supp. XVI:** 176
"Earl Painter" (Banks), **Supp. V:** 14–15
"Early Adventures of Ralph Ringwood, The" (Irving), **II:** 314
Early Americana (Richter), **Supp. XVIII:** 208, 210, 211, 220
Early Autumn (Parker), **Supp. XIX:** 184–185
Early Ayn Rand, The: A Selection of Her Unpublished Fiction (Rand), **Supp. IV Part 2:** 520
Early Dark (Price), **Supp. VI:** 262
Early Diary of Anaïs Nin, The, **Supp. X:** 184, 192
Early Elkin (Elkin), **Supp. VI: 42–43,** 45
"Early Evenin' Blues" (Hughes), **Retro. Supp. I:** 205
"Early Evening, Frankfort, Kentucky" (Trethewey), **Supp. XXI:** 243, 250
"Early History of a Seamstress" (Reznikoff), **Supp. XIV:** 277, 289
Early History of a Sewing-Machine Operator (Reznikoff), **Supp. XIV:** 289
"Early History of a Sewing-Machine Operator" (Reznikoff), **Supp. XIV:** 277
"Early History of a Writer" (Reznikoff), **Supp. XIV:** 278, 290
"Early in the Morning" (L.-Y. Lee), **Supp. XV:** 214
Early Lectures of Ralph Waldo Emerson, The (Emerson), **II:** 11
Early Light (Di Piero), **Supp. XIX:** 38, **38–40**
Early Lives of Melville, The (Sealts), **Retro. Supp. I:** 257
"Early Marriage" (Richter), **Supp. XVIII:** 209
Early Martyr and Other Poems, An (W. C. Williams), **Retro. Supp. I:** 423
"Early Morning: Cape Cod" (Swenson), **Supp. IV Part 2:** 641
"Early Rooms"(Hirshfield), **Supp. XXIII:** 130
"Early Spring between Madison and Bellingham" (R. Bly), **Supp. IV Part 1:** 71
Early Writing (O'Hara), **Supp. XXIII:** 220
Earnhardt, Dale, **Supp. XII:** 310
Earnshaw, Doris, **Supp. IV Part 1:** 310
"Earth" (Bryant), **Supp. I Part 1:** 157, 164, 167
"Earth, The" (Sexton), **Supp. II Part 2:** 696
Earth Abides (Stewart), **Supp. XVIII:** 138
"Earth and Fire" (Berry), **Supp. X:** 27
Earth as Air, The: An Ars Poetica (Sobin), **Supp. XVI: 285–286**
"Earth Being" (Toomer), **Supp. IX:** 320
Earth Goat (online), **Supp. XXII:** 61
Earth Gods, The (Gibran), **Supp. XX: 116, 123**
"Earth is parched with heat, The" (Very), **Supp. XXV:** 239
"Earthly Care a Heavenly Discipline" (Stowe), **Supp. I Part 2:** 586
"Earthly City of the Jews, The" (Kazin), **Retro. Supp. II:** 286
Earthly Meditations (Wrigley), **Supp. XVIII:** 304–305
"Earthly Meditations" (Wrigley), **Supp. XVIII:** 304–306
Earthly Possessions (Tyler), **Supp. IV Part 2:** 665–666, 671
Earth Power Coming (Ortiz, ed.), **Supp. IV Part 2:** 502
"Earth's Holocaust" (Hawthorne), **II:** 226, 231, 232, 242; **III:** 82; **Retro. Supp. I:** 152; **Retro. Supp. III:** 119
Earth Without You, The (F. Wright), **Supp. XVII:** 243
Eason, Laura, **Supp. XXIII:** 79
East Coker (T. S. Eliot), **I:** 580, 581, 582, 585, 587
"East Coker" (T. S. Eliot), **Retro. Supp. I:** 66; **Retro. Supp. III:** 66, 67; **Supp. VIII:** 195, 196
"Easter" (Toomer), **Supp. III Part 2:** 486
"Easter, an Ode" (R. Lowell), **II:** 536
"Easter 1916" (Yeats), **Supp. XXI:** 61
"Easter Island: The Statues Speak" (Davison), **Supp. XXVI:** 71
"Easter Morning" (Ammons), **Supp. VII:** 34
"Easter Morning" (Clampitt), **Supp. IX:** 45
"Eastern Standard" (Huddle), **Supp. XXVI:** 149
"Easter Ode, An" (Dunbar), **Supp. II Part 1:** 196
"Easter"(O'Hara), **Supp. XXIII:** 211
Easter Parade, The (Yates), **Supp. XI:** 346, 349
"Easter Sermon, 1866" (Nelson), **Supp. XVIII:** 177
"Easter Service" (Di Piero), **Supp. XIX:** 39–40
"Easter Sunday: Recollection" (Gunn Allen), **Supp. IV Part 1:** 322
"Easter Wings" (Herbert), **Supp. IV Part 2:** 646
"East European Cooking" (Simic), **Supp. VIII:** 277
East Is East (Boyle), **Supp. VIII:** 1–3; **Supp. XX: 23–24, 25, 28**

Edge of the Woods, The: Iroquoia, 1534–1701 (Parmenter), **Supp. XXVI:** 85
Edgers, Geoff, **Supp. XV:** 113
Edgeworth, Maria, **II:** 8; **Supp. XV:** 231; **Supp. XX: 108**
Edible Woman, The (Atwood), **Supp. XIII:** 19, 20, **20–21**
"Edict by the King of Prussia, An" (Franklin), **II:** 120
Edie: An American Biography (Stein), **Supp. XVI:** 245
Edinburgh Days: or, Doing What I Want to Do (Pickering), **Supp. XXI:** 200–201
Edison, Thomas A., **I:** 483; **Supp. I Part 2:** 392
Edith Wharton (Joslin), **Retro. Supp. I:** 376
Edith Wharton: A Biography (Lewis), **Retro. Supp. I:** 362
Edith Wharton: A Woman in Her Time (Auchincloss), **Retro. Supp. I:** 370
Edith Wharton: Matters of Mind and Spirit (Singley), **Retro. Supp. I:** 373
Edith Wharton's Argument with America (Ammons), **Retro. Supp. I:** 364
Edith Wharton's Brave New Politics (Bauer), **Retro. Supp. I:** 381
Edith Wharton's Letters from the Underworld (Waid), **Retro. Supp. I:** 360
Edith Wharton: Traveller in the Land of Letters (Goodwyn), **Retro. Supp. I:** 370
"Editing and Glosses" (Reznikoff), **Supp. XIV:** 283
Editing of Emily Dickinson, The (Franklin), **Retro. Supp. I:** 41
"Editor and the Schoolma'am, The" (Frederic), **II:** 130
"Editor's Easy Chair" (Howells), **II:** 276
"Editor's Study, The" (Howells), **II:** 275, 276, 285
"Editor Whedon" (Masters), **Supp. I Part 2:** 463
Edlin, Mari, **Supp. X:** 266
Edman, Irwin, **III:** 605; **Supp. XXV:** 255, 258
Edmond (Mamet), **Supp. XIV:** 241, 248, 249, 250
Edmonds, Dale, **Supp. XXIII:** 291
Edmondson, Belinda, **Supp. XXII:** 70
Edmundson, Mark, **Retro. Supp. II:** 262
Edmund Wilson (Kriegel), **Supp. XXIV: 216–217**
Edsel (Shapiro), **Supp. II Part 2:** 703, 704, 717–719
Edson, Margaret, **Supp. XVIII: 35–52**
Edson, Russell, **Supp. VIII:** 279
"Educated American Woman, An" (Cheever), **Supp. I Part 1:** 194
"Education, An" (Ozick), **Supp. V:** 267
Education and Living (Bourne), **I:** 252
"Education by Poetry" (Frost), **Retro. Supp. III:** 100; **Supp. XV:** 215
"Education of a Storyteller, The" (Bambara), **Supp. XI:** 20
Education of Black People, The (Du Bois), **Supp. II Part 1:** 186
Education of Harriet Hatfield, The (Sarton), **Supp. VIII: 257–258**
Education of Henry Adams, The (Adams), **I:** 1, 5, 6, 11, 14, 15–18, 19, 20–21, 111; **II:** 276; **III:** 504; **Retro. Supp. I:** 53, 59; **Supp. IX:** 19; **Supp. XIV:** 299
Education of H*y*m*a*n K*a*p*l*a*n, The (Rosten), **Supp. XVII:** 9
"Education of Mingo, The" (C. Johnson), **Supp. VI:** 193, 194
"Education of Norman Podhoretz, The" (Goldberg), **Supp. VIII:** 238
Education of Oscar Fairfax, The (Auchincloss), **Supp. IV Part 1:** 25, 36
"Education of the Poet" (Glück), **Supp. V:** 78, 80
Education sentimentale (Flaubert), **III:** 315
"Education the Imagination" (Koch), **Supp. XV:** 175–176, 177
Edwards, Clifford, **Supp. XVIII:** 220
Edwards, Eli. See McKay, Claude
Edwards, Esther, **I:** 545
Edwards, Harry Stillwell, **Supp. XXII:** 193
Edwards, John, **I:** 478
Edwards, Jonathan, **I: 544–566; II:** 432; **Retro. Supp. II:** 187; **Retro. Supp. III:** 9; **Supp. I Part 1:** 301, 302; **Supp. I Part 2:** 552, 594, 700; **Supp. IV Part 2:** 430; **Supp. VIII:** 205; **Supp. XXIV:** 72
Edwards, Sarah, **I:** 545
Edwards, Thomas, **Supp. XV:** 20
Edwards, Thomas R., **Supp. XVI:** 207
Edwards, Timothy, **I:** 545
Edwards-Yearwood, Grace, **Supp. VIII:** 81; **Supp. XXII:** 213
"Edwin Arlington Robinson" (Cowley), **Supp. II Part 1:** 144
Edwin Arlington Robinson (Winters), **Supp. II Part 2:** 812
Edwin Booth (play), **Supp. IV Part 1:** 89
E. E. Cummings (Marks), **I:** 438
E. E. Cummings: A Miscellany (Cummings), **I:** 429, 441
E. E. Cummings: A Miscellany, Revised (Cummings), **I:** 429
"Effects of Analogy" (Stevens), **Retro. Supp. I:** 297
"Effigy of a Nun" (Teasdale), **Supp. XXVII:** 296
Effluences from the Sacred Caves; More Selected Essays and Reviews (Carruth), **Supp. XVI:** 46
"Effort at Speech between Two People" (Rukeyser), **Supp. VI:** 276, 284
"Efforts of Affection" (Moore), **III:** 214
"Efforts of Affection: A Memoir of Marianne Moore" (Bishop), **Retro. Supp. II:** 52
Egan, Jennifer, **Supp. XIX: 49–63; Supp. XXIII:** 299, 300
Egan, Leona, **Supp. XXI:** 6
"Egg, The" (Anderson), **I:** 113, 114
"Egg, The" (Snyder), **Supp. VIII:** 302
Eggers, David, **Supp. XXIV:** 131, 200
Eggleston, George Cary, **Supp. XVIII:** 15
"Eggplant Epithalamion, The" (Jong), **Supp. V:** 119
"Eggs" (Olds), **Supp. X:** 206
"Eggshell" (Stern), **Supp. IX:** 299
Egoist, The (Meredith), **II:** 186
Egorova, Lubov, **Supp. IX:** 58
"Egotism, or the Bosom Serpent" (Hawthorne), **II:** 227, 239; **Retro. Supp. III:** 114, 116, 120
Egotist, The (Hecht), **Supp. XXVII:** 89
"Egyptian Pulled Glass Bottle in the Shape of a Fish, An" (Moore), **III:** 195, 213
Ehrenfels, Christian von, **Supp. XIV:** 198
Ehrenpreis, Irvin, **Supp. XII:** 128
Ehrenreich, Barbara, **Supp. XVII:** 210
Ehrhart, W. D., **Supp. XIX:** 281
Ehrlich, Gloria C., **Retro. Supp. III:** 278
Ehrlich, Gretel, **Supp. XIV:** 227; **Supp. XVIII:** 189; **Supp. XXVI:** 31, 187
"Ehue! fugaces, Posthume, Posthume, Labuntur anni" (Very), **Supp. XXV:** 243, 247
Eichmann, Adolf, **Supp. XII:** 166
Eichmann in Jerusalem (Arendt), **Retro. Supp. II:** 28; **Supp. VIII:** 243; **Supp. XII:** 166
"Eichmann in New York: The New

York Intellectuals and the Hannah Arendt Controversy" (Rabinbach), **Supp. XII:** 166
"Eidolon" (Warren), **IV:** 239
"Eiger Dreams" (Krakauer), **Supp. XVIII:** 107
Eiger Dreams: Ventures Among Men and Mountains (Krakauer), **Supp. XVIII:** 105, 106, 107
Eight Cousins (Alcott), **Supp. I Part 1:** 29, 38, 42, 43
18 Pine Street series (Myers), **Supp. XXVII:** 211
18 Poems from the Quechua (Strand, trans.), **Supp. IV Part 2:** 630
"18 West 11th Street" (Merrill), **Supp. III Part 1:** 323, 328
1876: A Novel (Vidal), **Supp. IV Part 2:** 677, 684, 688, 689, 691, 692; **Supp. XIX:** 141
"18,000 CDs" (Halliday), **Supp. XIX:** 92
"Eighth Air Force" (Jarrell), **II:** 373–374, 377
Eight Harvard Poets, **I:** 429, 475
"Eighth Avenue Incident" (Halliday), **Supp. XIX:** 89–90
"Eighth Day, The" (Apple), **Supp. XVII:** 6, 50
"Eighth Ditch, The" (Baraka), **Supp. II Part 1:** 40
"'80s Pastoral: Frederick Barthelme's Moon Deluxe Ten Years On" (Peters), **Supp. XI:** 39
Eight Men (Wright), **IV:** 478, 488, 494
80 Flowers (Zukofsky), **Supp. III Part 2:** 631
Eikon Basilike, The, **Supp. IV Part 2:** 435
Eileen (Masters), **Supp. I Part 2:** 460
Eimi (Cummings), **I:** 429, 433, 434, 439–440
"Einstein" (MacLeish), **III:** 5, 8, 10–11, 18–19
Einstein, Albert, **I:** 493; **III:** 8, 10, 21, 161; **IV:** 69, 375, 410, 411, 421; **Retro. Supp. I:** 63; **Supp. I Part 2:** 609, 643; **Supp. III Part 2:** 621; **Supp. V:** 290; **Supp. XII:** 45
Eiseley, Loren, **III:** 227–228
Eisenberg, Deborah, **Supp. XXIII:** 290
Eisenhower, Dwight D., **I:** 136, 376; **II:** 548; **III:** 215; **IV:** 75; **Supp. I Part 1:** 291; **Supp. III Part 2:** 624; **Supp. V:** 45
Eisenstadt, Jill, **Supp. XVIII:** 135
Eisenstein, Sergei, **I:** 481; **Supp. XXI:** 170
Eisinger, Chester E., **I:** 302; **II:** 604; **Supp. IX:** 15
Eisner, Douglas, **Supp. X:** 155
Elam, Angela, **Supp. XI:** 290
Elam, Harry, **Retro. Supp. III:** 314
El Bernardo (Balbuena), **Supp. V:** 11
Elbert, Sarah, **Supp. I Part 1:** 34, 41
Elder, Donald, **II:** 417, 426, 435, 437; **Supp. XV:** 137
Elder, John, **Supp. IX:** 25; **Supp. XXVI:** 38
Elder, Lonne, III, **Supp. IV Part 1:** 362
Elder, Richard, **Supp. XII:** 172
"Elder Sister, The" (Olds), **Supp. X:** 205–206
Elder Statesman, The (T. S. Eliot), **I:** 572, 573, 583; **Retro. Supp. I:** 53, 65; **Retro. Supp. III:** 70
"Eldest Sister to Psyche, The" (Stallings), **Supp. XXV:** 234
E. L. Doctorow (Harter and Thompson), **Supp. IV Part 1:** 217
Eldredge, Kay, **Supp. IX:** 254, 259
Eldridge, Florence, **III:** 154, 403; **IV:** 357
Eleanor of Aquitaine, **III:** 470
Eleanor of Guienne, **I:** 14
Eleanor: or, Slave Catching in the Quaker City (Lippard), **Supp. XXIII:** 180, 185
"Elect, The" (Taylor), **Supp. V:** 323
"Elections, Nicaragua, 1984" (Kingsolver), **Supp. VII:** 208
Elective Affinities (Goethe; Bogan and Mayer, trans.), **Supp. III Part 1:** 63
Electra (Euripides), **III:** 398
Electra (Sophocles), **III:** 398; **IV:** 370; **Supp. IX:** 102
"Electra on Azalea Path" (Plath), **Supp. I Part 2:** 538
"Electrical Storm" (Bishop), **Supp. I Part 1:** 93
"Electrical Storm" (Hayden), **Supp. II Part 1:** 370
"Electric Arrows" (Proulx), **Supp. VII:** 256
"Electric Girl, The"(P. Benedict), **Supp. XXIII:** 40
"Electricity Saviour" (Olds), **Supp. X:** 215
Electric Kool-Aid Acid Test, The (Wolfe), **Supp. III Part 2:** 575–577, 582–584; **Supp. XI:** 239
Electric Lady, The (film), **Supp. XI:** 309
Electronic Book Review, **Supp. XXII:** 256, 257, 261
Elegant Extracts (Knox), **II:** 8
"Elegant Tom Dillar" (Briggs), **Supp. XVIII:** 17
"Elegiac" (Ferry), **Supp. XXIV:** 148–149
Elegiac Feelings American (Corso), **Supp. XII: 131–134**
"Elegiac Fragments" (Everwine), **Supp. XV:** 89
Elegies (Rukeyser), **Supp. VI:** 273
"Elegies" (Rukeyser), **Supp. VI:** 272
"Elegies for Paradise Valley" (Hayden), **Supp. II Part 1:** 363
"Elegy" (Bidart), **Supp. XV:** 25, 29
Elegy (Levis), **Supp. XI:** 257, 259, 261, **271–272**
"Elegy" (Merwin), **Supp. III Part 1:** 351
"Elegy" (Stafford), **Supp. XI:** 322
"Elegy" (Tate), **IV:** 128
"Elegy, for the U.S.N. Dirigible, Macon, An" (Winters), **Supp. II Part 2:** 810
"Elegy Ending in the Sound of a Skipping Rope" (Levis), **Supp. XI:** 271–272
"Elegy for 41 Whales Beached in Florence, Oregon, June 1979" (Bierds), **Supp. XVII:** 27
"Elegy for D. H. Lawrence, An" (W. C. Williams), **Retro. Supp. I:** 421
"Elegy for My Father" (Strand), **Supp. IV Part 2:** 628
"Elegy for My Mother" (Wagoner), **Supp. IX:** 330
"Elegy for Redondo Beach" (Jarman), **Supp. XVII:** 112, 113
Elegy for September, An (Nichols), **Supp. XIII:** 268
"Elegy for Thelonious" (Komunyakaa), **Supp. XIII:** 118
"Elegy for the Lost Umbrella" (Stallings), **Supp. XXIII:** 124; **Supp. XXV:** 231, 232
"Elegy for the Native Guards" (Trethewey), **Supp. XXI:** 255
"Elegy for the U.S.N. Dirigible, Macon, A" (Winters), **Supp. II Part 2:** 810
"Elegy in Dialogue" (Taggard), **Supp. XXII:** 276
"Elegy"(J. Schoolcraft), **Supp. XXIII:** 231
"Elegy of Last Resort" (Nemerov), **III:** 271
"Elegy upon That Honorable and Renowned Knight Sir Philip Sidney, An" (Bradstreet), **Retro. Supp. III:** 7–8
"Elegy with a Thimbleful of Water in the Cage" (Levis), **Supp. XI:** 272
Elegy Written in a Country Churchyard (Gray), **I:** 68

"Elegy Written in a Country Churchyard" (Gray), **Supp. XIV:** 8
"Elementary Scene, The" (Jarrell), **II:** 387, 388, 389
"Elements" (M. Frank), **Supp. X:** 213
Elements of Style, The (Strunk), **Supp. I Part 2:** 670
"Elenita, Cards, Palm, Water" (Cisneros), **Supp. VII:** 64
"Eleonora" (Poe), **III:** 412
Eleothriambos (Lee), **IV:** 158
"Elephant & Ocean" (Notley), **Supp. XXII:** 230
"Elephants" (Moore), **III:** 203
"Elephant's Dance, The" (D. West), **Supp. XVIII:** 281
"Elevator, The" (Dixon), **Supp. XII:** 154
"Elevator Boy" (Hughes), **Retro. Supp. I:** 200; **Supp. I Part 1:** 326
"Eleven" (Cisneros), **Supp. VII:** 69
Eleven Essays in the European Novel (Blackmur), **Supp. II Part 1:** 91, 111
Eleven Heavy Things (installation, July), **Supp. XXIV:** 200
Eleven Kinds of Loneliness (Yates), **Supp. XI: 340–343,** 349
Eleven Poems on the Same Theme (Warren), **IV:** 239–241
"Eleven Times a Poem" (Corso), **Supp. XII:** 132, 133
El Greco (Doménikos Theotokópoulos), **I:** 387; **III:** 212
El-Hage, George N., **Supp. XX: 116**
"El-Hajj Malik El-Shabazz" (Hayden), **Supp. II Part 1:** 379
"Eli, the Fanatic" (P. Roth), **Supp. III Part 2:** 407–408
Elia, Nada, **Supp. XXII:** 73
Eliade, Mircea, **Supp. XVI:** 292
Elie, Paul, **Supp. XXII:** 91–92
Eliot, Charles William, **I:** 5; **II:** 345; **Retro. Supp. I:** 55; **Supp. I Part 2:** 479; **Supp. IX:** 94
Eliot, George, **I:** 375, 458, 459, 461, 467; **II:** 179, 181, 191–192, 275, 319, 324, 338, 577; **IV:** 311, 322; **Retro. Supp. I:** 218, 220, 225; **Supp. I Part 1:** 370; **Supp. I Part 2:** 559, 579; **Supp. IV Part 1:** 31, 297; **Supp. IV Part 2:** 677; **Supp. IX:** 38, 43, 51; **Supp. V:** 258; **Supp. XI:** 68; **Supp. XII:** 335; **Supp. XIV:** 344; **Supp. XX: 108**
Eliot, T. S., **I:** 48, 49, 52, 59, 60, 64, 66, 68, 105, 107, 215–216, 236, 243, 256, 259, 261, 266, 384, 386, 395, 396, 399, 403, 430, 433, 441, 446, 475, 478, 479, 482, 521, 522, 527, **567–591; II:** 65, 96, 158, 168, 316, 371, 376, 386, 529, 530, 532, 537, 542, 545; **III:** 1, 4, 5, 6, 7–8, 9, 10, 11, 14, 17, 20, 21, 23, 26, 34, 174, 194, 195–196, 205–206, 220, 236, 239, 269, 270–271, 277–278, 301, 409, 428, 435, 436, 453, 456–457, 459–460, 461–462, 464, 466, 471, 476, 478, 485, 488, 492, 493, 498, 504, 509, 511, 517, 524, 527, 539, 572, 575, 586, 591, 594, 600, 613; **IV:** 27, 74, 82, 83, 95, 122, 123, 127, 129, 134, 138, 140, 141, 191, 201, 237, 331, 379, 402, 403, 418, 419, 420, 430, 431, 439, 442, 491; **Retro. Supp. I: 51–71,** 74, 80, 89, 91, 171, 198, 210, 283, 289, 290, 292, 296, 298, 299, 311, 324, 359, 411, 413, 414, 416, 417, 420, 428; **Retro. Supp. II:** 79, 178, 189, 262, 326; **Retro. Supp. III:** 46, **57–72,** 74, 101, 103, 251, 255; **Supp. I Part 1:** 257, 264, 268, 270, 274, 299; **Supp. I Part 2:** 387, 423, 455, 536, 554, 624, 659, 721; **Supp. II Part 1:** 1, 4, 8, 20, 30, 91, 98, 103, 136, 314; **Supp. III Part 1:** 9, 10, 26, 31, 37, 41, 43, 44, 48, 62–64, 73, 91, 99–100, 105–106, 273; **Supp. III Part 2:** 541, 611, 612, 617, 624; **Supp. IV Part 1:** 40, 47, 284, 380, 404; **Supp. IV Part 2:** 436; **Supp. IX:** 158–159, 229; **Supp. V:** 79, 97, 101, 338, 343, 344; **Supp. VIII:** 19, 21, 93, 102, 105, 182, 195, 205, 290, 292; **Supp. X:** 59, 115, 119, 124, 187, 324; **Supp. XI:** 242; **Supp. XII:** 45, 159, 198, 308; **Supp. XIII:** 77, 104, 115, 332, 341–342, 344, 346; **Supp. XIV:** 5, 13, 107, 287, 290, 306, 347; **Supp. XIX:** 12; **Supp. XV:** 20, 51, 139, 177, 181, 186, 216, 218, 250, 251, 258, 298, 302, 303, 306, 307; **Supp. XVI:** 158–159, 204, 207, 282; **Supp. XVII:** 36, 71, 75, 111, 240; **Supp. XVIII:** 136; **Supp. XX: 86, 108, 199; Supp. XXIII:** 25, 60, 166; **Supp. XXVI:** 143; **Supp. XXVII:** 153, 284, 287
Eliot's Early Years (Gordon), **Retro. Supp. I:** 55
"Elizabeth" (Longfellow), **I:** 502
"Elizabeth, 1905" (Schnackenberg), **Supp. XV:** 253, 256
Elizabeth Appleton (O'Hara), **III:** 362, 364, 375–377
"Elizabeth Bishop (1911–1979)" (Merrill), **Retro. Supp. II:** 53
"Elizabeth Bishop in Brazil" (Brown), **Supp. I Part 1:** 96
"Elizabeth Bishop's North & South" (R. Lowell), **Retro. Supp. II:** 40–41
"Elizabeth Gone" (Sexton), **Supp. II Part 2:** 674, 681
Elizabeth Rex (Findley), **Supp. XX: 62–63**
Elizabeth Stoddard and the Boundaries of Bourgeois Culture (Mahoney), **Supp. XV:** 270
Elk Heads on the Wall (Ríos), **Supp. IV Part 2:** 540
Elkin, Stanley, **Supp. VI: 41–59**
Elkins, Andrew, **Supp. XXIII:** 131, 135
Elkins, Marilyn, **Supp. XXIV:** 64
"Elk Song" (Hogan), **Supp. IV Part 1:** 406
Ella in Bloom (Hearon), **Supp. VIII: 70–71**
Elledge, Jim, **Supp. XIII:** 88
Ellen Foster: A Novel (Gibbons), **Supp. X:** 41, **42–44,** 46, 47, 49, 50
Ellen Montgomery's Bookshelf (S. and A. Warner), **Supp. XVIII:** 264
Ellen Rogers (Farrell), **II:** 42–43
"Ellen's Dream" (Gioia), **Supp. XV:** 128
"Ellen West" (Bidart), **Supp. XV: 26–27**
Eller, Ernest, **Supp. I Part 2:** 497
Ellerman, Winifred, **Supp. I Part 1:** 258–259. See also McAlmon, Mrs. Robert (Winifred Ellerman)
"El libro de la sexualidad" (Simic), **Supp. VIII:** 283
Ellington, Duke, **Retro. Supp. II:** 115; **Supp. IV Part 1:** 360; **Supp. IX:** 164
Elliot, Charles, **Supp. V:** 161
Elliot, George P., **Supp. XV:** 92
Elliott, George B., **III:** 478
Elliott, J. W. M., **Supp. XXVI:** 87, 88
Ellipse, The: Selected Poems of Leonardo Sinisgalli (Di Piero, trans.), **Supp. XIX:** 34
"Ellipsis" (C. Frost), **Supp. XV:** 107
Ellis, Albert, **Supp. IV Part 2:** 527
Ellis, Anne, **Supp. XVI:** 38
Ellis, Bret Easton, **Supp. X:** 7; **Supp. XII:** 81; **Supp. XVIII:** 135; **Supp. XXVII: 67–81,** 269
Ellis, Charles, **Supp. I Part 1:** 99
Ellis, Havelock, **II:** 276; **Supp. XX: 117, 235; Supp. XXII:** 198
Ellis, John Harvard, **Supp. I Part 1:** 103
Ellis, Katherine, **IV:** 114
Ellis, Kelly, **Supp. XXI:** 249
Ellis, Ron, **Supp. XXII:** 209

Ellis, Thomas Sayers, **Supp. XXI:** 246
"Ellis Island" (Helprin), **Supp. XXV:** 85
Ellis Island and Other Stories (Helprin), **Supp. XXV:** 82, 83, 85
Ellison, Harlan, **Supp. XIII:** 61
Ellison, Ralph, **IV:** 250, 493; **Retro. Supp. II:** 3, **111–130; Retro. Supp. III:** 139; **Supp. II Part 1:** 33, **221–252; Supp. IV, Part 1:** 374; **Supp. IX:** 114, 316; **Supp. VIII:** 105, 245; **Supp. X:** 324; **Supp. XI:** 18, 92, 275; **Supp. XIII:** 186, 233, 305; **Supp. XIV:** 306; **Supp. XIX:** 148, 149, 155; **Supp. XV:** 194; **Supp. XVI:** 135, 139; **Supp. XVIII:** 59, 61, 62, 277, 283
Ellmann, Maud, **Supp. IV Part 1:** 302
Ellmann, Richard, **Supp. VIII:** 105; **Supp. XV:** 74
Ellroy, James, **Supp. XIV:** 26; **Supp. XXI:** 71
Elm, Damas, **Supp. XXVI:** 89
Elman, Richard, **Supp. V:** 40
"Elmer" (Faulkner), **Retro. Supp. I:** 79, 80
Elmer, Jonathan, **Retro. Supp. III:** 237
Elmer Gantry (Lewis), **I:** 26, 364; **II:** 447–449, 450, 455
Elmer the Great (Lardner), **II:** 427
"Elms" (Glück), **Supp. V:** 85
"Elms Dying, The—And My Friend, Lew Stillwell, Dead" (Bronk), **Supp. XXI:** 31
Elmslie, Kenward, **Supp. XXVII:** 19, 23, 26
Eloges (Perse), **Supp. XIII:** 344
"Eloquence of Grief, An" (Crane), **I:** 411
"El Paso Del Norte"(Kenny), **Supp. XXIII:** 150
"El Río Grande" (Mora), **Supp. XIII:** 224
"El Round up" (Alvarez), **Supp. VII:** 11
"El Salvador: Requiem and Invocation" (Levertov), **Supp. III Part 1:** 284
Elsasser, Henry, **I:** 226
"Elsa Wertman" (Masters), **Supp. I Part 2:** 462–463
Elsie John and Joey Martinez: Two Stories (Huncke), **Supp. XIV:** 148
Elsie Venner (Holmes), **Supp. I Part 1:** 243, 315–316
Elton, Charles, **Supp. XIV:** 192
Éluard, Paul, **III:** 528; **Supp. IV Part 1:** 80; **Supp. XVII:** 244
Elvins, Kells, **Supp. III Part 1:** 93, 101
Ely, Richard T., **Supp. I Part 1:** 5; **Supp. I Part 2:** 640, 645
"Emancipation. A Life Fable" (Chopin), **Retro. Supp. II:** 59; **Supp. I Part 1:** 207–208
"Emancipation in the British West Indies" (Emerson), **II:** 13
"Emancipation Proclamation, The" (Emerson), **II:** 13
Emanuel, James, **Supp. I Part 1:** 346
Embargo, The (Bryant), **Supp. I Part 1:** 152–153
"Embarkation for Cythera, The" (Ferry), **Supp. XXIV:** 149
Embarrassments (James), **Retro. Supp. I:** 229
Embezzler, The (Auchincloss), **Supp. IV Part 1:** 24, 30–31
"Embraces" (Davison), **Supp. XXVI:** 72
"Embroidery, The" (C. Frost), **Supp. XV:** 97
"Emerald" (Doty), **Supp. XI:** 131
"Emerald, The" (Merrill), **Supp. III Part 1:** 328
Emerald City (Egan), **Supp. XIX:** 49, **52–53**
"Emerald City" (Egan), **Supp. XIX:** 52
"Emergence of Flight from Aristotle's Mud, The" (Goldbarth), **Supp. XII:** 190
Emergency Exit (Major), **Supp. XXII:** 174, **175,** 182
"Emergency Haying" (Carruth), **Supp. XVI:** 55
"Emergency Room" (Mora), **Supp. XIII:** 218
"Emerging Voices: The Teaching of Writing" (Mora), **Supp. XIII:** 220
Emerson, and Other Essays (Chapman), **Supp. XIV:** 41–44
Emerson, Ellen, **Supp. I Part 1:** 33
Emerson, John, **Supp. XVI:** 185, 186, 190, 192
Emerson, Ralph Waldo, **I:** 98, 217, 220, 222, 224, 228, 239, 246, 251, 252, 253, 257, 260, 261, 283, 386, 397, 402, 424, 433, 444, 447, 455, 458, 460–461, 463, 464, 485, 561; **II: 1–24,** 49, 92, 127–128, 169, 170, 226, 233, 237, 273–274, 275, 278, 289, 295, 301, 313, 315, 336, 338, 344, 402, 491, 503; **III:** 53, 82, 171, 174, 260, 277, 409, 424, 428, 453, 454, 507, 576–577, 606, 614; **IV:** 60, 167, 169, 170, 171, 172, 173–174, 176, 178, 183, 186, 187, 192, 201, 202, 211, 335, 338, 340, 342, 350; **Retro. Supp. I:** 34, 53, 54, 57, 62, 74–75, 76, 125, 148–149, 152–153, 159, 217, 250, 298, 392, 400, 403; **Retro. Supp. II:** 96, 113, 135, 142, 155, 207, 262; **Retro. Supp. III:** 223, 249, 255, 283; **Supp. I Part 1:** 2, 28–29, 31, 33, 188, 299, 308–309, 317, 358, 365, 366, 368; **Supp. I Part 2:** 374, 383, 393, 407, 413, 416, 420, 422, 474, 482, 580, 582, 602, 659, 679; **Supp. II Part 1:** 280, 288; **Supp. III Part 1:** 387; **Supp. IV Part 2:** 439, 597, 619; **Supp. IX:** 38, 90, 175, 176, 181; **Supp. V:** 118; **Supp. VIII:** 42, 105, 106, 108, 198, 201, 204, 205, 292; **Supp. X:** 42, 45, 121, 223; **Supp. XI:** 203; **Supp. XIII:** 141, 145, 233, 246, **Supp. XIII:** 247; **Supp. XIV:** 41–44, 46, 54, 104, 177; **Supp. XV:** 219, 224; **Supp. XVI:** 84; **Supp. XVII:** 42, 236; **Supp. XX: 115, 116; Supp. XXI:** 217; **Supp. XXIII:** 161, 190; **Supp. XXIV:** 4, 67, 74, 77; **Supp. XXV:** 241, 250; **Supp. XXVI:** 37; **Supp. XXVII:** 234
"Emerson and the Essay" (Gass), **Supp. VI:** 88
"Emerson the Lecturer" (J. R. Lowell), **Supp. I Part 2:** 420, 422
Emerson-Thoreau Award, **Retro. Supp. I:** 67
Emery, Amy Fass, **Retro. Supp. III:** 132
Emery, Clark, **III:** 478
Emery, Mary Lou, **Supp. XXII:** 73
E. M. Forster (Trilling), **Supp. III Part 2:** 496, 501, 504
"Emigre in Autumn, An" (Gioia), **Supp. XV:** 120
Emily, Alone (O'Nan), **Supp. XXV:** 145, 149, 150–151
"Emily Dickinson and Class" (Erkkila), **Retro. Supp. I:** 42–43
Emily Dickinson Editorial Collective, **Retro. Supp. I:** 47
Emily Dickinson in Southern California (X. J. Kennedy), **Supp. XV: 164–165**
"Emily Dickinson's Defunct" (Nelson), **Supp. XVIII:** 173
Emily Dickinson: Woman Poet (Bennett), **Retro. Supp. I:** 42
Eminent Victorians (Strachey), **Supp. I Part 2:** 485
Emma (Austen), **Supp. XVIII:** 149
"Emma and Eginhard" (Longfellow), **III:** 505
"Emma Enters a Sentence of Elizabeth Bishop's" (Gass), **Supp. VI:** 93
Emmanuel Appodocca: or, A Blighted

Life (Philip), **Supp. XXI:** 160
"Emmaus" (Di Piero), **Supp. XIX:** 42, 43
Emma Who Saved My Life (Barnhardt), **Supp. XXVII:** 1, 3–5, 7
Emperor Jones, The (O'Neill), **II:** 278; **III:** 391, 392
Emperor of Haiti (Hughes), **Supp. I Part 1:** 339
"Emperor of Ice Cream, The" (Stevens), **IV:** 76, 80–81
"Emperors" (Dunn), **Supp. XI:** 155
"Emperor's New Clothes, The" (Anderson), **I:** 441
"Empire" (Ford), **Supp. V:** 69
Empire: A Novel (Vidal), **Supp. IV Part 2:** 677, 684, 686, 690; **Supp. XIX:** 132
"Empire Builders" (MacLeish), **III:** 14
Empire City, The: or, New York by Night and Day (Lippard), **Supp. XXIII:** 178, 180, 183, 184, 185
Empire Falls (Russo), **Supp. XII: 339–343**
Empire of Summer, The (Doty), **Supp. XI:** 120
Empire of the Senseless (Acker), **Supp. XII:** 5, **6, 14–16**
"Empires" (Simic), **Supp. VIII:** 282
"Emporium" (Shapiro), **Supp. II Part 2:** 705
Empress of the Splendid Season (Hijuelos), **Supp. VIII: 86–89**
Empson, William, **I:** 522, 533; **II:** 536; **III:** 286, 497, 498, 499; **IV:** 136, 431; **Retro. Supp. I:** 263; **Retro. Supp. II:** 253; **Supp. XVI:** 190
Empty Bed, The (Hadas), **Supp. XXIII: 117–118**
Empty Hands, The (Bronk), **Supp. XXI:** 31
"Empty Hills, The" (Winters), **Supp. II Part 2:** 792, 793, 796
"Empty Icon Frame" (Stallings), **Supp. XXV:** 233
Empty Mirror, Early Poems (Ginsberg), **Supp. II Part 1:** 308, 311, 313–314, 319, 329
"Empty Room" (Hughes), **Supp. I Part 1:** 337
"Empty Threat, An" (Frost), **II:** 159
Emshwiller, Ed, **Supp. XVIII:** 145
"Encantadas, The" (Melville), **III:** 89; **Retro. Supp. III:** 158; **Supp. XVIII:** 4
"Enchanted Bluff, The" (Cather), **Retro. Supp. III:** 28, 35
Enchanter, The (Nabokov), **Retro. Supp. I:** 266
"Enclosed Dreams, Highways and Labyrinths: Jonathan Lethem's Amnesia Moon" (Rossi), **Supp. XVIII:** 139
"Encomium Twenty Years Later" (Tate), **I:** 381
"Encounter" (Espaillat), **Supp. XXI:** 107
"Encounter, The" (Pound), **III:** 466
Encounter in April (Sarton), **Supp. VIII:** 259
"Encounter in April" (Sarton), **Supp. VIII:** 259
"Encountering the Sublime" (McClatchy), **Supp. XII:** 261
"Encounter in Vindija Cave, Present-Day Croatia: Late October"(Schott), **Supp. XXIII:** 254
"Encounter on the Seine: Black Meets Brown" (Baldwin), **Retro. Supp. II:** 2
Encounters with Chinese Writers (Dillard), **Supp. VI:** 19, 23, 31
Encounters with the Archdruid (McPhee), **Supp. III Part 1:** 292–294, 301; **Supp. X:** 30
Encyclopedia of Arkansas History and Culture, The (online), **Supp. XXII:** 50
Encyclopedia of Scotland, The (A. Finch), **Supp. XVII: 70–71**
Encyclopedia of World Biography, The, **Supp. XXI:** 74
"End, The" (Olds), **Supp. X:** 205
"Endangered Species" (Mora), **Supp. XIII:** 219–220
Endecott and the Red Cross (R. Lowell), **II:** 545
Endgame (Beckett), **Supp. XIII:** 196; **Supp. XXII:** 263
"Endgame" (Tan), **Supp. X:** 290
"Endicott and the Red Cross" (Hawthorne), **Retro. Supp. II:** 181, 187–188
"End of Books, The" (Coover), **Supp. V:** 53
End of Books, The" (Coover), **Supp. XXII:** 259
End of Dreams, The (Skloot), **Supp. XX: 196, 202–203**
End of Education, The (Postman), **Supp. XI:** 275
"End of FIRPO in the World, The" (Saunders), **Supp. XIX:** 229
End of Me, The (Hayes), **Supp. XXVI:** 142–143
"End of Season" (Warren), **IV:** 239–240
"End of Something, The" (Hemingway), **II:** 248
End of the Affair, The (Greene), **Supp. XI:** 99
End of the Age of Innocence, The (Price), **Retro. Supp. I:** 377
"End of the Line, The" (Helprin), **Supp. XXV:** 81
"End of the Line, The" (Jarrell), **III:** 527
"End of the Rainbow, The" (Jarrell), **II:** 386
End of the Road (film), **Supp. XI:** 309
End of the Road, The (Barth), **I:** 121, 122, 126–131; **Supp. XI:** 309; **Supp. XVIII:** 140, 141
"End of the World, The" (Gioia), **Supp. XV:** 126
"End of the World, The" (MacLeish), **III:** 8
Endor (Nemerov), **III:** 269, 270, 279
Endore, Guy, **Supp. XVII: 53–67**
"Endpapers" (Rich), **Retro. Supp. III:** 252
"Ends" (Dixon), **Supp. XII:** 153
End to Innocence, An: Essays on Culture and Politics (Fiedler), **Supp. XIII: 98–99**
Endure: The Diaries of Charles Walter Stetson (Stetson), **Supp. XI:** 196
"Enduring Chill, The" (O'Connor), **III:** 349, 351, 357; **Retro. Supp. II:** 236; **Retro. Supp. III:** 213
Enduring Vision of Norman Mailer, The (Leeds), **Retro. Supp. II:** 204
Endymion (Keats), **IV:** 405; **Retro. Supp. I:** 412
End Zone (DeLillo), **Supp. VI:** 2, 3, 4, 10, 11, 12
Enemies (Boyce and Hapgood), **Supp. XVII:** 100; **Supp. XXI:** 7, 13
Enemies: A Love Story (Singer), **IV:** 1; **Retro. Supp. II: 310–311**
Enemy, The: Time (T. Williams), **IV:** 391
Enemy of the People, An (adapt. Miller), **III:** 154–156
"Energy Vampire" (Ginsberg), **Supp. II Part 1:** 326
"Enforcement of the Slave Trade Laws, The" (Du Bois), **Supp. II Part 1:** 161
"Engaging the Past" (Bell), **Supp. X:** 17
Engel, Bernard F., **I:** 532
Engels, Friedrich, **IV:** 429, 443–444; **Supp. I Part 1:** 13; **Supp. XXI:** 162
Engels, John, **Supp. XXVI:** 152
Engineer of Beasts, The (Sanders), **Supp. XVI:** 270
Engineer of Moonlight (DeLillo), **Supp. VI:** 4

Engineers and the Price System, The (Veblen), **I:** 475–476; **Supp. I Part 2:** 638, 642, 648
Engines of Creation: the Coming Era of Nanotechnology (Drexler), **Supp. XVI:** 121
"England" (Moore), **III:** 203, 207, 214
Englander, Nathan, **Supp. XX: 177, 179; Supp. XXIV:** 131; **Supp. XXV:** 268
Engle, Paul, **III:** 542; **Retro. Supp. II:** 220, 221; **Supp. V:** 337; **Supp. XI:** 315; **Supp. XIII:** 76; **Supp. XVIII:** 72
English, Parker, **Retro. Supp. III:** 138
English, Zoë, **Supp. XVI:** 293
English Elegy, The: Studies in the Genre from Spenser to Yeats (Sacks), **Supp. IV Part 2:** 450
English Hours (James), **II:** 337; **Retro. Supp. I:** 235
English Language, The (L. P. Smith), **Supp. XIV:** 341
English-Latin Gradus or Verse Dictionary, An (Ainger), **Supp. XX: 230**
"English Lesson"(Strout), **Supp. XXIII:** 273–274, 284
Englishmen of Letters (James), **II:** 327
English Notebooks, The (Hawthorne), **II:** 226, 227–228
English Novel, The (Lanier), **Supp. I Part 1:** 371
English Poets, The: Lessing, Rousseau (J. R. Lowell), **Supp. I Part 2:** 407
English Prosody and Modern Poetry (Shapiro), **Supp. II Part 2:** 710
English Traits (Emerson), **II:** 1, 5, 6–7, 8
"English Writers on America" (Irving), **II:** 308
Engstrand, Stuart, **Supp. I Part 1:** 51
"Enigma Variations" (Nelson), **Supp. XVIII:** 177
"Enoch" (Very), **Supp. XXV:** 246, 247
"Enoch and the Gorilla" (O'Connor), **Retro. Supp. II:** 225
Enormous Changes at the Last Minute (Paley), **Supp. VI:** 218
"Enormous Changes at the Last Minute" (Paley), **Supp. VI:** 226, 232
"Enormous Radio, The" (Cheever), **Supp. I Part 1:** 175–177, 195
Enormous Radio and Other Stories, The (Cheever), **Supp. I Part 1:** 175–177
Enormous Room, The (Cummings), **I:** 429, 434, 440, 445, 477; **Supp. XXI:** 277
"Enough for a Lifetime" (Buck), **Supp. II Part 1:** 127
Enough Rope (Parker), **Supp. IX:** 189, 192
Enquiry Concerning Political Justice (Godwin), **Supp. I Part 1:** 126, 146
"En Route" (Boulton), **Supp. XXII:** 25
Entanglements of Nathaniel Hawthorne, The (Coale), **Retro. Supp. III:** 111
Entered From the Sun (Garrett), **Supp. VII:** 105–106, 107–109
"Entering the Building" (Notley), **Supp. XXII:** 237
"Entering the Kingdom" (Oliver), **Supp. VII:** 234
Entertaining Strangers (Gurney), **Supp. V:** 98, 99
Enter without Desire (Lacy), **Supp. XV:** 201
Entranced, The (Lippard), **Supp. XXIII:** 178, 180, 190
Entrance: Four Chicano Poets, **Supp. XIII:** 316
Entrance to Porlock, The (Buechner), **Supp. XII:** 52
Entries (Berry), **Supp. X:** 23
"Entropy" (Pynchon), **Supp. II Part 2:** 619, 621
"Entry" (Huddle), **Supp. XXVI:** 149
Entry in an Unknown Hand (F. Wright), **Supp. XVII:** 240, 244, 245
Environmental Imagination, The (Buell), **Supp. IX:** 29; **Supp. V:** 209
"Envoy" (Collins), **Supp. XXI:** 57
"Envoys, The" (Merrill), **Supp. III Part 1:** 326
"Envy; or, Yiddish in America" (Ozick), **Supp. V:** 263, 265–266
"Eolian Harp, The" (Coleridge), **I:** 284
"Eolian Harp, The"(Coleridge), **Supp. XXIII:** 231
"Eototo" (Sobin), **Supp. XVI:** 283–284
"Ephemera, The" (Franklin), **II:** 121
Ephesians (biblical book), **Supp. I Part 1:** 117
"Epic Poetry" (Very), **Supp. XXV:** 241
Epictetus, **III:** 566
"Epicurean, The" (Auchincloss), **Supp. IV Part 1:** 25
Epicurus, **I:** 59
Epidemic of Genius, An (Wolfert), **Supp. XXI:** 278
"Epigram" (R. Lowell), **II:** 550
"Epilogue" (R. Lowell), **Retro. Supp. II:** 191
"Epimanes" (Poe), **III:** 411
"Epimetheus" (Longfellow), **II:** 494
"Epiphany" (X. J. Kennedy), **Supp. XV:** 166, 167
"Epipsychidion" (Shelley), **Supp. I Part 2:** 718
"Episode, The" (Huddle), **Supp. XXVI:** 150
Episode in Palmetto (Caldwell), **I:** 297, 307
"Episode in the Life of an Ancestor" (Boyle), **Supp. XXIV:** 56
Episode of the Wandering Knife, The (Rinehart), **Supp. XXV:** 198, 200
"Epistle" (L.-Y. Lee), **Supp. XV:** 212
Epistles (Horace), **Supp. XXIV:** 156
Epistles of Horace, The (Ferry, trans.), **Supp. XXIV: 157–158**
Epistle to a Godson (Auden), **Supp. II Part 1:** 24
"Epistle to Be Left in the Earth" (MacLeish), **III:** 13
"Epistle to George William Curtis" (J. R. Lowell), **Supp. I Part 2:** 416
"Epistle to Léon-Paul Fargue" (MacLeish), **III:** 15
"Epitaph Ending in And, The" (Stafford), **Supp. XI:** 321–322
Epitaph for a Dead Beat (Markson), 139; **Supp. XVII: 136–138,** 141
Epitaph for a Desert Anarchist (Bishop), **Supp. XIII:** 1
Epitaph for a Tramp (Markson), **Supp. XVII:** 136, 137, 139 142
"Epitaph for Fire and Flower" (Plath), **Supp. I Part 2:** 537
"Epitaph for S.P." (Davison), **Supp. XXVI:** 71
"Epitaph for the Race of Man" (Millay), **III:** 127–128
"Epitaph on My Dear and Ever-Honoured Mother Mrs. Dorothy Dudley, An" (Bradstreet), **Retro. Supp. III:** 12
"Epithalamium" (Auden), **Supp. II Part 1:** 15
"Epstein" (P. Roth), **Retro. Supp. II:** 281; **Supp. III Part 2:** 404, 406–407, 412, 422
Epstein, Barbara, **Supp. XIX:** 268
Epstein, Helen, **Supp. XVII:** 47; **Supp. XXII:** 95
Epstein, Jacob, **Supp. XXIII:** 6
Epstein, Jason, **Supp. VIII:** 233
Epstein, Joseph, **Supp. IV Part 2:** 692; **Supp. VIII:** 236, 238; **Supp. XIV: 101–117; Supp. XVI:** 230, 275
Epstein, Leslie, **Supp. XII: 159–174; Supp. XVIII:** 92, 99
Epstein, Philip, **Supp. XII:** 159
"Equal in Paris" (Baldwin), **Retro. Supp. II:** 3; **Supp. I Part 1:** 52
"Equals" (Untermeyer), **Supp. XV:** 304

Equation for Evil (Caputo), **Supp. XIX:** 25–26
"Equations of the Light" (Gioia), **Supp. XV:** 125
"Equilibrists, The" (Ransom), **III:** 490, 494
"Equinox 1980" (Davison), **Supp. XXVI:** 77
"Equinox"(Crooker), **Supp. XXIII:** 55
"Equipment for Pennies" (H. Roth), **Supp. IX:** 233
Erasmus, Desiderius, **Supp. XV:** 258
Erasure (Everett), **Supp. XVIII:** 54, 60**, 61–62**
"Erat Hora" (Pound), **III:** 463; **Retro. Supp. I:** 413
Erdrich, Louise, **Supp. IV Part 1: 259–278,** 333, 404; **Supp. X:** 290; **Supp. XVIII:** 189; **Supp. XXIV:** 245; **Supp. XXVI:** 102
"Erectus" (Karr), **Supp. XI:** 243
"Ere Sleep Comes Down to Soothe the Weary Eyes" (Dunbar), **Supp. II Part 1:** 199, 207–208
"Ergo Non Sum. Est." (Bronk), **Supp. XXI:** 31
"Ergotism"(Schott), **Supp. XXIII:** 245
"Eric Hermannson's Soul" (Cather), **Retro. Supp. III:** 25–26, 28
Erik Dorn (Hecht), **Supp. XXVII:** 83, 87–88, 89
Erikson, Erik, **I:** 58, 214, 218
Erisman, Fred, **Supp. VIII:** 126
Erkkila, Betsy, **Retro. Supp. I:** 42; **Supp. XX: 281, 287, 287–288**
Ernest, John, **Supp. XXI:** 24
"Ernest: or Parent for a Day" (Bourne), **I:** 232
Ernst, Max, **Retro. Supp. II:** 321
Eroding Witness (Mackey), **Supp. XXVII:** 152–153, 154, 157
"Eros" (Komunyakaa), **Supp. XIII:** 130
"Eros and Anteros" (E. Stoddard), **Supp. XV:** 283
Eros and Civilization (Marcuse), **Supp. XII:** 2
"Eros at Temple Stream" (Levertov), **Supp. III Part 1:** 278–279
Eros the Bittersweet (Carson), **Supp. XII:** 97, **98–99**
Eros Trilogy, The (Silver), **Supp. XXIV:** 264, 267
"Eros Turannos" (Robinson), **III:** 510, 512, 513–516, 517, 518
"Eroticism in Women" (Nin), **Supp. X:** 195
"Errand" (Carver), **Supp. III Part 1:** 149
Erskine, Albert, **IV:** 261; **Retro. Supp. II:** 117
Erskine, John, **I:** 223; **Supp. X:** 183; **Supp. XIV:** 120
Erstein, Hap, **Supp. IV Part 2:** 589, 590
"Escape" (MacLeish), **III:** 4
Escape Artist, The (Wagoner), **Supp. IX:** 324, **334–335**
"Escape"(Thompson), **Supp. XXIII:** 301
Escher, M. C., **Supp. XII:** 26; **Supp. XVI:** 102
"Escudilla" (Leopold), **Supp. XIV:** 188
Esenwein, J. Berg, **Supp. XXVI:** 281
Eshleman, Clayton, **Supp. XVI:** 284
"Eskimo Love" (Apple), **Supp. XVII:** 5
Espaillat, Rhina P., **Supp. XXI: 97–114**
Esparza, Laura, **Supp. XXIII:** 197
Especially Maine (Beston), **Supp. XXVI:** 32
Espeland, Pamela, **Supp. XVIII:** 180, 181
Espen, Hal, **Supp. X:** 15
Espey, John, **III:** 463, 468, 478
Esposito, Michael, **Supp. XX: 34, 40**
Esposito, Scott, **Supp. XVII:** 234
Esquibel, Catrióna Rueda, **Supp. XXIII:** 202
Essais (Renouvier), **II:** 344–345
Essay Concerning Human Understanding, An (Locke), **I:** 554; **II:** 8, 348–349
Essay on American Poetry (Brown), **Supp. I Part 1:** 156
"Essay on Aristocracy" (Paine), **Supp. I Part 2:** 515
Essay on Criticism, An (Pope), **Supp. XXVI:** 271, 284
"Essay on Friendship, An" (McClatchy), **Supp. XII:** 258–259
"Essay on Love" (Carruth), **Supp. XVI:** 56
Essay on Man (Pope), **II:** 111; **Supp. I Part 2:** 516
"Essay on Marriage" (Carruth), **Supp. XVI:** 48
Essay on Our Changing Order (Veblen), **Supp. I Part 2:** 629, 642
"Essay on Poetics" (Ammons), **Supp. VII:** 29–31
Essay on Projects (Defoe), **II:** 104
"Essay on Psychiatrists" (Pinsky), **Supp. VI:** 237, 238, 241, 242, 249, 250
Essay on Rime (Shapiro), **I:** 430; **Supp. II Part 2:** 702, 703, 708–711
"Essay on Sanity" (Dunn), **Supp. XI:** 147
"Essay on the Character of Robespierre" (Paine), **Supp. I Part 2:** 515
Essay on the Chinese Written Character (Fenollosa), **III:** 474
"Essay on What I Think About Most" (Carson), **Supp. XII: 111–112**
Essays (Emerson), **II:** 1, 7, 8, 12–13, 15, 21
Essays (Montaigne), **Supp. XXVI:** 39
Essays, Speeches, and Public Letters by William Faulkner (Meriweather, ed.), **Retro. Supp. I:** 77
Essays and Poems (Very), **Supp. XXV:** 247, 249–250
Essays in Anglo-Saxon Law (Adams), **I:** 5
Essays in London (James), **II:** 336
Essays in Radical Empiricism (James), **II:** 355, 356–357
Essays on Norman Mailer (Lucid), **Retro. Supp. II:** 195
Essays on the Nature and Principles of Taste (Alison), **Supp. I Part 1:** 151
Essays to Do Good (Mather), **II:** 104; **Supp. II Part 2:** 461, 467
"Essay: The Love of Old Houses" (Doty), **Supp. XI:** 136
"Essay Toward a Point of View, An" (Brooks), **I:** 244
"Essay Vanishes, The" (Monson), **Supp. XXIV:** 238
"Essence, Absence, and Sobin's Venus Blue" (English), **Supp. XVI:** 293
Essential Dykes to Watch Out For, The (Bechdel), **Supp. XXV:** 2
Essential Haiku, The (Hass), **Supp. VI:** 102
Essential Keats (Levine, ed.), **Supp. V:** 179
"Essential Oils—are wrung" (Dickinson), **I:** 471; **Retro. Supp. I:** 43, 46
"Essentials" (Toomer), **Supp. III Part 2:** 486
Essentials: A Philosophy of Life in Three Hundred Definitions and Aphorisms (Toomer), **Supp. III Part 2:** 486
Essentials: Definitions and Aphorisms (Toomer), **Supp. IX:** 320
"Essentials of Spontaneous Prose" (Kerouac), **Supp. III Part 1:** 227–228
Essential Works of the Founding Fathers, The (Kriegel, ed.), **Supp. XXIV:** 214
Estampas del valle y otras obras (Hinojosa). See Valley, The

(Hinojosa)
Esta puente, mi espalda: Voces de mujeres tercermundistas en los Estados Unidos (Moraga, Castillo, and Alarcón, eds.), **Supp. XXIII:** 194
"Estate Sale" (Nye), **Supp. XIII:** 283
Estess, Sybil, **Supp. IV Part 2:** 449, 452
Esther (Adams), **I:** 9–10, 20
"Esther" (Toomer), **Supp. IX:** 313–314
"Esther Kahn" (Symons), **Supp. XX:** **239**
"Esthétique du Mal" (Stevens), **IV:** 79; **Retro. Supp. I:** 300, 311, 312
"Estoy-eh-muut and the Kunideeyahs (Arrowboy and the Destroyers)" (film), **Supp. IV Part 2:** 560
Estrada, Genaro, **Retro. Supp. II:** 89
Estray, The (Longfellow, ed.), **Retro. Supp. II:** 155
Esty, William, **III:** 358
"Eta Carinae" (Stone), **Supp. XXVII:** 260–261
"Etching, An" (Masters), **Supp. I Part 2:** 458
Eternal Feminine, The (Wells), **Supp. XXVI:** 275
"Eternal Goodness, The" (Whittier), **Supp. I Part 2:** 704
Eternal Spring, The (Boyce), **Supp. XVII:** 100; **Supp. XXI:** 4, 5, 11
"Eternity, An" (W. C. Williams), **Retro. Supp. I:** 423
"Eternity Is Now" (Roethke), **III:** 544–545
"Ethan Brand" (Hawthorne), **II:** 227; **Retro. Supp. III:** 117
Ethan Frome (film, Madden), **Retro. Supp. III:** 290
Ethan Frome (Wharton), **IV:** 316–317, 327; **Retro. Supp. I:** 372–373; **Retro. Supp. III:** 283–284, 287; **Supp. IX:** 108; **Supp. XVIII:** 216; **Supp. XXIII:** 275, 281
"Ethical Turn in Postcolonial Theory and Narrative, The: Michelle Cliff's No Telephone to Heaven" (Moynagh), **Supp. XXII:** 73
Ethics (Spinoza), **IV:** 12; **Retro. Supp. II:** 300
"Ethics of Culture, The" (Locke), **Supp. XIV:** 211
"Ethnics of Frank Costello, The" (Talese), **Supp. XVII:** 202
Etiquette and Vitriol: The Food Chain and Other Plays (Silver), **Supp. XXIV:** 263, 264
"Étiquettes Jaunes, Les"(O'Hara), **Supp. XXIII:** 214
"Etude" (Kooser), **Supp. XIX:** 115
Etulain, Richard, **Supp. IV Part 2:** 597, 601, 604, 606, 607, 608, 610, 611
"Etymology" (Nelson), **Supp. XVIII:** 185
Euclid, **III:** 6, 620
"Euclid Alone Has Looked on Beauty Bare" (Millay), **III:** 133
"Euclidean Spaces: Linear Time" (Bronk), **Supp. XXI:** 31
Eugene, Frank, **Supp. X:** 204
Eugene Onegin (Pushkin), **III:** 246, 263
Eugene Onegin (Pushkin; Nabokov, trans.), **Retro. Supp. I:** 266, 267, 272
Eugenides, Jeffrey, **Supp. XIX:** 138; **Supp. XXI:** 229; **Supp. XXIV:** **131–146**
Eugénie, Empress, **IV:** 309
Eugénie Grandet (Balzac), **II:** 328
"Eugénie Grandet" (Barthelme), **Supp. IV Part 1:** 47
"Eulogy for Richard Hugo (1923–1982)" (Wagoner), **Supp. IX:** 330–331
"Eulogy on the Flapper" (Z. Fitzgerald), **Supp. IX:** 71
Eumenides (Aeschylus), **Retro. Supp. I:** 65
"E Unibus Pluram: Television and U.S. Fiction" (Wallace), **Supp. X:** 315–316
"Euphemisms" (Matthews), **Supp. IX:** **167–168**
Eureka (Poe), **III:** 409, 424, 428–429; **Retro. Supp. III:** 225, 234
Eureka Mill (Rash), **Supp. XXVII:** 217–218
Eurekas (Goldbarth), **Supp. XII:** 181
Euripides, **I:** 325; **II:** 8, 282, 543; **III:** 22, 145, 398; **IV:** 370; **Supp. I Part 1:** 268, 269, 270; **Supp. I Part 2:** 482; **Supp. V:** 277
"Euripides and Professor Murray" (Eliot), **Supp. I Part 1:** 268
"Euripides—A Playwright" (West), **IV:** 286; **Retro. Supp. II:** 326
"Europe" (Ashbery), **Supp. III Part 1:** 7–10, 13, 18
European Discovery of America, The: The Northern Voyages (Morison), **Supp. I Part 2:** 496–497
Europeans, The (H. James), **I:** 452; **II:** 327, 328; **Retro. Supp. I:** 216, 220
Europe Central (Vollmann), **Supp. XVII:** 225, 226, 227, 229, 231, **233–235,** 236
"Europe! Europe!" (Ginsberg), **Supp. II Part 1:** 320, 322
Europe of Trusts, The: Selected Poems (Howe), **Supp. IV Part 2:** 420, 422, 426
Europe without Baedeker (Wilson), **IV:** 429
"Eurydice in Darkness" (Davison), **Supp. XXVI:** 71
Eurydice in the Underworld (Acker), **Supp. XII:** 7
"Eurydice Reveals Her Strength" (Stallings), **Supp. XXV:** 230
"Eurydice's Footnote" (Stallings), **Supp. XXV:** 230
Eustace, Saint, **II:** 215
Eustace Chisholm and the Works (Purdy), **Supp. VII:** 273–274, 279–280
"Euthanasia" (Tate), **IV:** 122
Eva (Levin), **Supp. XXVII:** 135, 143, 145
"Evaluation" (Bronk), **Supp. XXI:** 32
Eva-Mary (McCarriston), **Supp. XIV:** 259, 260, **263–268**
"Evangeline" (Dixon), **Supp. XII:** 153
Evangeline (Longfellow), **II:** 489, 501–502; **Retro. Supp. II:** 155, **156–159,** 162, 164; **Supp. I Part 2:** 586
Evanier, David, **Supp. XVI:** 212
Evans, Alice, **Supp. XVII:** 71, 72
Evans, Mary Ann. See Eliot, George
Evans, Oliver, **Supp. IV Part 1:** 85, 91
Evans, Sandy, **Supp. XIII:** 129
Evans, Walker, **I:** 36, 38, 293; **Retro. Supp. II:** 85
Eva's Man (G. Jones), **Supp. XXIV:** 183, 184, 185, **188–190,** 193
Eve (A. Finch), **Supp. XVII:** **72–74**
"Eve" (W. C. Williams), **Retro. Supp. I:** 423
Even Cowgirls Get the Blues (Robbins), **Supp. X:** 259, 260, 261, 262–263, 264, 266, **269–271,** 272, 274, 277, 284; **Supp. XIII:** 11
"Evening" (Carver), **Supp. III Part 1:** 148
Evening (Minot), **Supp. VI:** 204–205, 208, **213–215**
"Evening at a Country Inn" (Kenyon), **Supp. VII:** 167
"Evening in Advent, An" (W. V. Davis), **Supp. XXI:** 92
"Evening in a Lumber Yard"(Le Sueur), **Supp. XXIII:** 165
"Evening in a Sugar Orchard" (Frost), **Retro. Supp. I:** 133
"Evening in Nuevo Leon, An" (Caldwell), **I:** 309
"Evening in the Sanitarium" (Bogan),

Supp. III Part 1: 61
Evening Light, The (Skloot), **Supp. XX: 196, 201–202**
"Evening Love-of-Self" (Taggard), **Supp. XXII:** 280–281
"Evening of the 4th of July, The" (Kees), **Supp. XV:** 140, 142
"Evening on the Cote d'Azur" (Yates), **Supp. XI:** 349
Evening Performance, An: New and Selected Short Stories (Garrett), **Supp. VII:** 109
"Evenings at Home" (Hardwick), **Supp. III Part 1:** 195–196
"Evening's at Seven, The" (Thurber), **Supp. I Part 2:** 616
"Evening Star" (Bogan), **Supp. III Part 1:** 56
Evening Star, The (McMurtry), **Supp. V:** 230
Evening Star, The (screenplay, McMurtry), **Supp. V:** 232
"Evening Sun" (Kenyon), **Supp. VII:** 168
Evening Sun Turned Crimson, The (Huncke), **Supp. XIV:** 140, 149–150
"Evening Sun Turned Crimson, The" (Huncke), **Supp. XIV:** 137–138, 139
"Evening Wind, The" (Bryant), **Supp. I Part 1:** 164
"Evening without Angels" (Stevens), **Retro. Supp. I:** 302
Evening with Richard Nixon, An (Vidal), **Supp. IV Part 2:** 683
"Even Sea, The" (Swenson), **Supp. IV Part 2:** 641
Even Stephen (Perelman and West), **Retro. Supp. II:** 328
"Event, An" (Wilbur), **Supp. III Part 2:** 547, 554
"Event, The" (Dove), **Supp. IV Part 1:** 242, 247–248
"Even the Vanishing Housed"(Hirshfield), **Supp. XXIII:** 132
"Eventide" (Brooks), **Supp. III Part 1:** 73
"Eventide" (Purdy), **Supp. VII:** 270
"Event Itself, The" (Carruth), **Supp. XVI:** 47
Eve of Saint Agnes, The (Keats), **II:** 82, 531
"Eve of St. Agnes, The" (Clampitt), **Supp. IX:** 40
"Ever a Bridegroom: Reflections on the Failure of Texas Literature" (McMurtry), **Supp. V:** 225
Everett, Alexander Hill, **Supp. I Part 1:** 152
Everett, Percival, **Supp. XVIII: 53–67**
Everlasting Story of Nory, The (Baker), **Supp. XIII:** 52, **Supp. XIII: 53–55**
"Everly Brothers, The" (Skloot), **Supp. XX: 199**
Ever-Present Past, The (Hamilton), **Supp. XVI:** 196
Evers, Medgar, **IV:** 280; **Retro. Supp. II:** 13; **Supp. I Part 1:** 52, 65
Everson, William, **Supp. XXII:** 276
Everwine, Peter, **Supp. V:** 180; **Supp. XIII:** 312; **Supp. XV: 73–90**
"Everybody Knows" (Cohen), **Supp. XXVII:** 52, 62
"Everybody's Protest Novel" (Baldwin), **Retro. Supp. II:** 4; **Supp. I Part 1:** 50, 51
"Everybody's Reading Li Po' Silk-screened on a Purple T-Shirt" (Komunyakaa), **Supp. XIII:** 120
Everybody's Story: Writing by Older Minnesotans (C. Bly, ed.), **Supp. XVI:** 38
"Everybody Was Very Nice" (Benét), **Supp. XI:** 53
"Everyday Alchemy" (Taggard), **Supp. XXII:** 274–275, 276, 279
"Every-Day Girl, A" (Jewett), **Retro. Supp. II:** 132
Everyday People (O'Nan), **Supp. XXV:** 142, 146–147, 150
"Everyday Use" (Walker), **Supp. III Part 2:** 534
"Every-Day Work" (Jewett), **Retro. Supp. II:** 132
Everyman (Ashbery), **Supp. XXIII:** 210
Everyone Says I Love You (film; Allen), **Supp. XV:** 11
Every Pleasure (Goldbarth), **Supp. XII:** 181
Every Soul Is a Circus (Lindsay), **Supp. I Part 2:** 384, 394, 399
"Everything Is a Human Being" (Walker), **Supp. III Part 2:** 527
Everything Is Illuminated (Foer), **Supp. XII:** 169
Everything Is Now (Cliff), **Supp. XXII:** 67, 74, 76
"Everything Stuck to Him" (Carver), **Supp. III Part 1:** 143
Everything That Moves (Schulberg), **Supp. XVIII:** 254
Everything That Rises Must Converge (O'Connor), **III:** 339, 348–349, 350–351; **Retro. Supp. II:** 235, **236–237; Retro. Supp. III:** 208
"Everything That Rises Must Converge" (O'Connor), **III:** 349, 352, 357; **Retro. Supp. II:** 236; **Retro. Supp. III:** 213
Everything You Always Wanted to Know about Sex (film; Allen), **Supp. XV:** 4–5, 13
Eve's Diary (Twain), **IV:** 208–209
"Eve's Diary" (Twain), **Retro. Supp. III:** 269
"Eve Speaks" (Untermeyer), **Supp. XV:** 300
"Eve the Fox" (Gunn Allen), **Supp. IV Part 1:** 331
"Evidence" (Harjo), **Supp. XII:** 219
"Evidence-cum-Witness: Subaltern History, Violence, and the (De)formation of a Nation in Michelle Cliff's No Telephone to Heaven" (Sethuraman), **Supp. XXII:** 73
Evidence of the Senses, The (Kelley), **Supp. IV Part 2:** 529
Evidence of Things Not Seen, The (Baldwin), **Retro. Supp. II:** 15
"Evidences of Revealed Religion, The" (Channing), **Supp. XXIV:** 74
"Evil Seekers, The" (Sexton), **Supp. II Part 2:** 696
"Evolution" (Swenson), **Supp. IV Part 2:** 639
Evolving the Idol: The Poetry of Gustaf Sobin (Crick), **Supp. XVI:** 289
Ewing, Jon, **Supp. X:** 253
Ewings, The (O'Hara), **III:** 383
"Examination at the Womb Door" (Hughes), **Supp. XV:** 347
"Examination of the Hero in a Time of War" (Stevens), **Retro. Supp. I:** 305–306, 308
"Excavation of Troy" (MacLeish), **III:** 18
Excellent Becomes the Permanent, The (Addams), **Supp. I Part 1:** 25
"Excelsior" (Longfellow), **Retro. Supp. II:** 169
"Excerpts from Swan Lake" (Cameron), **Supp. XII:** 80, **84**
"Excerpts from the Epistemology Workshops" (Rand), **Supp. IV Part 2:** 529
"Excess of Charity" (Wylie), **Supp. I Part 2:** 720
"Exchange, The" (Swenson), **Supp. IV Part 2:** 644
"Excitement, The " (Jarman), **Supp. XVII:** 120–121
"Exclusive" (Olds), **Supp. X:** 206
"Excrement Poem, The" (Kumin), **Supp. IV Part 2:** 448
"Excursion" (Garrett), **Supp. VII:** 100
Excursions (Thoreau), **IV:** 188
"Excursion to Canada, An" (Thoreau), **Supp. XVIII:** 4

"Excursus of Reassurance in Begonia Time, An" (Carruth), **Supp. XVI:** 58
Executioner (Weigl), **Supp. XIX:** 277
Executioner's Song, The (Mailer), **Retro. Supp. II:** 108, 209
Exekiel, **Supp. XXI:** 91
Exemplar of Liberty: Native America and the Evolution of Democracy (Grinde and Johansen), **Supp. XXVI:** 98
"Exercise and Abstinence" (Swados), **Supp. XIX:** 265
Exercises in History, Chronology, and Biography, in Question and Answer (Rowson), **Supp. XV:** 245
Ex-Friends: Falling Out with Allen Ginsberg, Lionel and Diana Trilling, Lillian Hellman, Hannah Arendt, and Norman Mailer (Podhoretz), **Supp. VIII:** 239, **242–244**
"Exhausted Bug, The" (R. Bly), **Supp. IV Part 1:** 73
"Exhortation" (Bogan), **Supp. III Part 1:** 58
"Exhortation" (McKay), **Supp. X:** 135
"Ex-husband"(Schott), **Supp. XXIII:** 249
"Exile" (Gass), **Supp. VI:** 92
"Exile" (Oates), **Supp. II Part 2:** 523
Exile, The (Buck), **Supp. II Part 1:** 119, 131
"Exiles, The" (Bradbury), **Supp. IV Part 1:** 113
"Exiles, The" (Whittier), **Supp. I Part 2:** 692–693
Exiles and Fabrications (Scott), **II:** 512
Exile's Daughter, The (Spencer), **Supp. II Part 1:** 121
"Exile's Departure, The" (Whittier), **Supp. I Part 2:** 683
Exiles from Paradise: Zelda and Scott Fitzgerald (Mayfield), **Supp. IX:** 65
"Exile's Letter" (Karr), **Supp. XI:** 241
Exile's Return (Cowley), **Supp. III Part 1:** 136, 138, 140, 141, 144, 147, 148
"Exile's Return, The" (R. Lowell), **II:** 539; **Retro. Supp. II:** 187
Exiles: Three Short Novels (Caputo), **Supp. XIX:** 25, **26–27**
"Existences" (Stafford), **Supp. XI:** 324
Existentialism from Dostoevsky to Sartre (W. Kaufmann), **Supp. XVII:** 137
Exit into History (Hoffman), **Supp. XVI:** 148, 150, **151–153**
Exit to Eden (Rampling), **Supp. VII:** 301–302
Exley (Clarke), **Supp. XXIII:** 109
Exley, Frederick, **Supp. XVI:** 69; **Supp. XVII:** 135; **Supp. XXIII:** 78, **97–110**
Exodus (biblical book), **IV:** 300
Exodus (film), **Supp. XX: 246**
Exodus (Uris), **Supp. IV Part 1:** 379; **Supp. XX: 243–244, 244, 245, 247, 248, 250–251, 257**
Exodus Revisited (Uris), **Supp. XX: 247**
"Exorcism" (Snodgrass), **Supp. VI:** 314
"Exorcism, An" (Malamud), **Supp. I Part 2:** 435
Exorcist, The (film), **Supp. I Part 1:** 66
"Expanded Composition, The" (Major), **Supp. XXII:** 174
"Expanding Rooms" (Notley), **Supp. XXII:** 229
"Expanding the Repertoire" (Mackey), **Supp. XXVII:** 161
"Expanses" (Dickey), **Supp. IV Part 1:** 186
"Ex Parte" (Lardner), **II:** 432
"Expatiation on the Combining of Weathers at Thirty-seventh and Indiana Where the Southern More or Less Crosses the Dog, The" (Carruth), **Supp. XVI:**51–52
"Expectant Father Compares His Wife to a Rabbit, An" (White), **Supp. I Part 2:** 678
"Expedition to the Pole, An" (Dillard), **Supp. VI:** 32, 34
"Expelled" (Cheever), **Supp. I Part 1:** 174, 186
Expense of Greatness, The (Blackmur), **Supp. II Part 1:** 90, 107
Expense of Vision, The (Holland), **Retro. Supp. I:** 216
"Expensive Gifts" (Miller), **Supp. XII:** 294
"Expensive Moment, The" (Paley), **Supp. VI:** 222, **227–228,** 230
Expensive People (Oates), **Supp. II Part 2:** 509, 510–511
"Experience" (Emerson), **Supp. XIV:** 42
"Experience" (Stone), **Supp. XXVII:** 251
"Experience and Fiction" (Jackson), **Supp. IX:** 121
"Experience and the Objects of Knowledge in the Philosophy of F. H. Bradley" (Eliot), **I:** 572; **Retro. Supp. I:** 59
Experience of Literature, The (Trilling), **Supp. III Part 2:** 493
"Experiences and Principles of an Historian" (Morison), **Supp. I Part 2:** 492
Experimental Death Unit # 1 (Baraka), **Supp. II Part 1:** 46
"Experimental Life, The" (Bourne), **I:** 217, 220
"Experiment in Misery, An" (S. Crane), **I:** 411; **Retro. Supp. II:** 97
Experiments and Observations on Electricity (Franklin), **II:** 102, 114–115
Experiments in Survival (Kriegel and Henrich, eds.), **Supp. XXIV:** 214
"Expiation" (Hoffman), **Supp. XVIII:** 86
"Expiation" (Wharton), **Retro. Supp. I:** 367
"Explaining an Affinity for Bats" (Stallings), **Supp. XXV:** 227, 233
"Explaining Evil" (Gordon), **Supp. IV Part 1:** 310
"Explaining Ted Kooser" (Gioia), **Supp. XIX:** 121
"Explanation" (Stevens), **IV:** 79
Explanation of America, An (Pinsky), **Supp. VI:** 237, **241–243**
Exploding Gravy (X. J. Kennedy), **Supp. XV:** 163
"Exploit" (Wharton), **IV:** 324
"Exploration in the Great Tuolumne Cañon" (Muir), **Supp. IX:** 181
"Explorer, The" (Brooks), **Supp. III Part 1:** 79–80
"Exploring the Magalloway" (Parkman), **Supp. II Part 2:** 591
"Exposed Nest, The" (Frost), **Supp. XXVI:** 74
Expositor's Bible, The (G. A. Smith), **III:** 199
Expressions of Sea Level (Ammons), **Supp. VII:** 24, 28, 36
"Exteriority" (Monson), **Supp. XXIV:** 230, 238
"Extinction of Silence, The" (Stallings), **Supp. XXV:** 234
Extract from Captain Stormfeld's Visit to Heaven (Twain), **IV:** 209–210
Extracts from Adam's Diary (Twain), **IV:** 208–209
Extra Indians (Gansworth), **Supp. XXVI:** 104, 107–108
"Extraño, Un" (Gallagher), **Supp. XXIV:** 170
"Exulting, The" (Roethke), **III:** 544
"Eye, The" (Bowles), **Supp. IV Part 1:** 93
Eye, The (Nabokov), **III:** 251
Eye-Beaters, Blood, Victory, Madness, Buckhead and Mercy, The (Dickey), **Supp. IV Part 1:** 178, 182–183

"Eye for an Eye, An" (Humphrey), **Supp. IX:** 108
"Eye in the Rock, The" (Haines), **Supp. XII:** 208, 209
Eye in the Sky (Dick), **Supp. XVIII:** 138
"Eye-Mote, The" (Plath), **Retro. Supp. II:** 246, 247
"Eye of Paris, The" (H. Miller), **III:** 183–184
"Eye of the Outside, The" (Rich), **Retro. Supp. III:** 251
Eye of the Poet, The: Six Views of the Art and Craft of Poetry (Citino, ed.), **Supp. XIII:** 115; **Supp. XXI:** 54
"Eye of the Rock, The" (Haines), **Supp. XII:** 208
"Eye of the Story, The" (Porter), **IV:** 279
Eye of the Story, The: Selected Essays and Reviews (Welty), **Retro. Supp. I:** 339, 342, 344, 345, 346, 351, 354, 355, 356
"Eyes, The" (Wharton), **IV:** 315
"Eyes like They Say the Devil Has" (Ríos), **Supp. IV Part 2:** 543, 544
Eyes of the Dragon, The (King), **Supp. V:** 139, 152
Eyes of the Heart: A Memoir of the Lost and Found (Buechner), **Supp. XII:** 53
"Eyes of Zapata" (Cisneros), **Supp. VII:** 70
"Eyes to See" (Cozzens), **I:** 374
Eye-to-Eye (Nye), **Supp. XIII:** 274
Eysturoy, Annie O., **Supp. IV Part 1:** 321, 322, 323, 328
Ezekiel (biblical book), **II:** 541
"Ezekiel" (R. Fisher), **Supp. XIX:** 71
Ezekiel, Mordecai, **Supp. I Part 2:** 645
"Ezekiel Learns" (R. Fisher), **Supp. XIX:** 71
"Ezra Pound" (Bynner), **Supp. XV:** 49
"Ezra Pound: His Cantos" (Zukofsky), **Supp. III Part 2:** 612, 619, 622
Ezra Pound's Mauberley (Espey), **III:** 463
"Ezra Pound's Very Useful Labors" (Schwartz), **Supp. II Part 2:** 644
Faas, Ekbert, **Supp. VIII:** 292
"Fabbri Tape, The" (Auchincloss), **Supp. IV Part 1:** 21–22
Fabens, Charles, **Supp. XXV:** 283
Faber, Geoffrey, **Retro. Supp. I:** 63
Faber Book of Movie Verse, The (French and Wlaschin, eds.), **Supp. XVI:** 294
"Fable" (Merwin), **Supp. III Part 1:** 343
"Fable" (Wylie), **Supp. I Part 2:** 714
Fable, A (Faulkner), **II:** 55, 73; **Retro. Supp. I:** 74; **Retro. Supp. III:** 87
"Fable, A" (Glück), **Supp. V:** 86
"Fable, The" (Winters), **Supp. II Part 2:** 792, 793, 796
"Fable Containing a Reflection the Size of a Match Head in Its Pupil, A" (Brockmeier), **Supp. XXII:** 59
"Fable Ending in the Sound of a Thousand Parakeets, A" (Brockmeier), **Supp. XXII:** 59
Fable for Critics, A (J. R. Lowell), **Supp. I Part 2:** 406, 407–408, 409, 412–413, 416, 420, 422
"Fable for Critics, A" (J. R. Lowell), **Supp. XVIII:** 3, 8
"Fable of the War, A" (Nemerov), **III:** 272
Fables (Gay), **II:** 111
Fables and Distances: New and Selected Essays (Haines), **Supp. XII:** 197, 199, 207–208, 211
Fables for Our Time (Thurber), **Supp. I Part 2:** 610
Fables of Identity: Studies in Poetic Mythology (Frye), **Supp. X:** 80
Fables of La Fontaine, The (Moore), **III:** 194, 215
"Fables of Representation: Poetry of the New York School" (Hoover), **Supp. XV:** 179
"Fables of the Fallen Guy" (Rosaldo), **Supp. IV Part 2:** 544
"Fables of the Moscow Subway" (Nemerov), **III:** 271
"Fable with a Photograph of a Glass Mobile on the Wall, A" (Brockmeier), **Supp. XXII:** 59
"Fable with Slips of White Paper Spilling from the Pockets, A" (Brockmeier), **Supp. XXII:** 59
Fabulators, The (Scholes), **Supp. V:** 40
Fabulous Small Jews (Epstein), **Supp. XIV:** 112
Face against the Glass, The (Francis), **Supp. IX: 80–81**
Face in the Crowd, A (film, Kazan), **Supp. XVIII:** 252–253
Face in the Crowd, A (O'Nan and King), **Supp. XXV:** 150, 152
Face of Time, The (Farrell), **II:** 28, 34, 35, 39
Faces of Jesus, The (Buechner), **Supp. XII:** 53
Face to the Wind (film), **Supp. XVII:** 141
Face Value (Hwang), **Supp. XXI:** 148, 154, 155
Fachinger, Petra, **Supp. XVI:** 153
"Facing It" (Komunyakaa), **Supp. XIII:** 117, 124, 125
Facing Shadows (Jin), **Supp. XVIII:** 92, **93**
Facing the Music (L. Brown), **Supp. XXI:** 39, 42, **42–44**
"Facing the Music" (L. Brown), **Supp. XXI: 38–39,** 41, 42, 43
"Facing the Music: What's Wrong with All Those Happy Endings" (Neal), **Supp. XXI:** 41
"Facing West from California's Shores" (Jeffers), **Supp. II Part 2:** 437–438
Fact, Fiction, and Representation: Four Novels by Gilbert Sorrentino (Mackey), **Supp. XXI:** 236
"Fact in Fiction, The" (McCarthy), **II:** 562
Fact of a Doorframe, The (Rich), **Retro. Supp. III:** 243
"Fact of Blackness, The" (Fanon), **Supp. XX: 152**
"Facts" (Franzen), **Supp. XX: 85**
"Facts" (Levine), **Supp. V:** 193
"Facts" (Oliver), **Supp. VII:** 231–232
"Facts" (Snyder), **Supp. VIII:** 301
"Facts, The" (Lardner), **II:** 431
Facts, The: A Novelist's Autobiography (P. Roth), **Retro. Supp. II:** 280, 291; **Supp. III Part 2:** 401, 405, 417, 426
"Facts and Traditions Respecting the Existence of Indigenous Intermittent Fever in New England" (Holmes), **Supp. I Part 1:** 303
"Facts Concerning the Recent Carnival of Crime in Connecticut" (Twain), **Retro. Supp. III:** 262
"Facts in the Case of M. Valdemar, The" (Poe), **III:** 416
Fader, Ellen, **Supp. XXVII:** 203–204
Faderman, Lillian, **Retro. Supp. II:** 135; **Supp. XIII:** 313
Fadiman, Clifton, **II:** 430, 431, 443, 591–592; **Supp. IX:** 8; **Supp. XVI:** 100, 106; **Supp. XVII:** 87, 90; **Supp. XXIII:** 2
Fading, My Parmacheene Belle (J. Scott), **Supp. XVII: 184–185,** 188
Fading Smile, The (Davison), **Supp. XXVI:** 61, 66, 68
"Fado" (McClatchy), **Supp. XII:** 265–266
"Fado" (Vaz), **Supp. XXVI:** 261–262
Fado and Other Stories (Vaz), **Supp. XXVI:** 259–264, 268
Faerie Queene, The (Spenser), **III:** 487; **IV:** 253; **Supp. XIV:** 6; **Supp. XV:** 181

Faery, Rebecca Blevins, **Retro. Supp. I:** 374
Fagan, Kathy, **Supp. V:** 180; **Supp. XV:** 73
Fagan, Louise, **Supp. XIX:** 204, 205
Faggen, Robert, **Retro. Supp. III:** 105
Fahrenheit 451 (Bradbury), **Supp. IV Part 1:** 101, 102, 104, 107–109, 110, 113; **Supp. XIII:** 29
"Failure" (Gioia), **Supp. XV:** 125
"Failure" (Zach; Everwine, trans.), **Supp. XV:** 86
"Failure: A Meditation" (Monson), **Supp. XXIV:** 236
"Failure of David Barry, The" (Jewett), **Retro. Supp. II:** 132
Fainlight, Ruth, **Supp. XV:** 261, 264
Faint Perfume (Gale), **Supp. I Part 2:** 613
Fair, Bryan K., **Supp. VIII:** 128
Fairbanks, Douglas, **Supp. XVI:** 185, 186
Fairchild, Frances. See Bryant, Mrs. William Cullen (Frances Fairchild)
Fairchild, Hoxie, **Supp. XIV:** 120
Fairfield, Flora (pseudonym). See Alcott, Louisa May
Fair Gentlemen of Belken County (Hinojosa), **Supp. XIX: 105**
Fairly Conventional Woman, A (Shields), **Supp. VII:** 312, 316, 318
"Fairly Sad Tale, A" (Parker), **Supp. IX:** 192
Fair Warning (R. O. Butler), **Supp. XII:** 62, **75–76**
"Fairy-Tale Logic" (Stallings), **Supp. XXV:** 223, 234
Faith (Goldbarth), **Supp. XII:** 181, **182–183**
Faith and History (Niebuhr), **III:** 308
Faith and the Good Thing (C. Johnson), **Supp. VI:** 187, **188–190,** 191, 193, 194, 196
Faith for Living (Mumford), **Supp. II Part 2:** 479–480
Faithful Narrative of the Surprising Works of God in the Conversion of Many Hundred Souls in Northampton, and the Neighboring Towns and Villages of New-Hampshire in New-England, A (Edwards), **I:** 545, 562
Faithful: Two Diehard Boston Red Sox Fans Chronicle the Historic 2004 Season (O'Nan and King), **Supp. XXV:** 153
"Faith Healer" (Komunyakaa), **Supp. XIII:** 117
Faith Healer of Olive Avenue, The (Muñoz), **Supp. XXV:** 127, 131, 135–137
"Faith in a Tree" (Paley), **Supp. VI:** 217–218, 224, 230
"Faith in Search of Understanding" (Updike), **Retro. Supp. I:** 327
"Faith of an Historian" (Morison), **Supp. I Part 2:** 492
"Faith of Fishermen, The" (J. W. Miller), **Supp. XX: 170**
Faker's Dozen, A (Bukiet), **Supp. XVII:** 47
Falcoff, Mark, **Supp. VIII:** 88
Falcon (Hammett), **Supp. IV Part 1:** 351
Falconer (Cheever), **Supp. I Part 1:** 176, 193–195, 196
Falconer, A. F., **Supp. XIV:** 2
"Falcon of Ser Federigo, The" (Longfellow), **II:** 505
Falcon: Poems on Soviet Themes (Taggard), **Supp. XXII:** 284
Falk, Peter, **Supp. XI:** 174
Falkner, Dean, **II:** 55
Falkner, John, **II:** 55
Falkner, Murray, **II:** 55
Falkner, Murray C., **II:** 55
Falkner, Mrs. Murray C. (Maud Butler), **II:** 55
Falkner, William C., **II:** 55
"Fall" (Francis), **Supp. IX:** 76
"Fall, The" (Bass), **Supp. XVI:** 25
"Fall 1961" (R. Lowell), **II:** 550
Fallen Angels (Myers), **Supp. XXVII:** 204, 207
"Fallen Western Star: The Decline of San Francisco as a Literary Region" (Gioia), **Supp. XV:** 112, **115–116**
"Fallen Western Star" Wars, The: A Debate about Literary California (Foley, ed.), **Supp. XV:** 112, 116
"Fall in Corrales" (Wilbur), **Supp. III Part 2:** 556
Falling (Dickey), **Supp. IV Part 1:** 178, 181–182
"Falling" (Dickey), **Supp. IV Part 1:** 182
"Falling Asleep over the Aeneid" (R. Lowell), **II:** 542; **Retro. Supp. II:** 188
Falling in Place (Beattie), **Supp. V:** 28–29
"Falling into Holes in Our Sentences" (R. Bly), **Supp. IV Part 1:** 71
Falling into Life (Kriegel), **Supp. XXIV: 217–219**
"Falling Water" (Davison), **Supp. XXVI:** 79
"Fall Journey" (Stafford), **Supp. XI:** 322
Fall of a Doll's House, The (J. Davison), **Supp. XXVI:** 65
Fall of America, The: 1965–1971 (Ginsberg), **Retro. Supp. III:** 247; **Supp. II Part 1:** 323, 325, 327; **Supp. XV:** 264
Fall of Eve, The (Loos), **Supp. XVI:** 187
Fall of the City, The: A Verse Play for Radio (MacLeish), **III:** 20
"Fall of the Dolls' House, The" (Davison), **Supp. XXVI:** 73–74
"Fall of the House of Usher, The" (Poe), **III:** 412, 414, 415, 419; **Retro. Supp. II:** 270; **Retro. Supp. III:** 224, 225, 226, 228; **Supp. XXV:** 112
Fall of the Magicians, The (Kees), **Supp. XV:** 144
Fall of the Year, The (Mosher), **Supp. XXII:** 205, 206, 208, 209, **214**
"Fall of Troy, Teh"(Hadas), **Supp. XXIII:** 113
Fallows, James, **Supp. VIII:** 241
Fall Quarter (Kees), **Supp. XV:** 141
Fall & Rise (Dixon), **Supp. XII:** 147–148, 148, 153, 157
Falls, Robert, **Supp. XXI:** 148; **Supp. XXIV:** 270
"Falls, The" (Olds), **Supp. X:** 215
"Falls, The" (Saunders), **Supp. XIX:** 229
"Falls Fight, The" (Howe), **Supp. IV Part 2:** 431–432
Falon, Janet Ruth, **Supp. IV Part 2:** 422
False Coin (Swados), **Supp. XIX: 260–261,** 263
"False Dawn" (Wharton), **Retro. Supp. I:** 381
"False Documents" (Doctorow), **Supp. IV Part 1:** 220, 236
"False Leads" (Komunyakaa), **Supp. XIII:** 116
Falwell, Jerry, **Supp. XX: 273**
Fame and Obscurity: Portraits by Gay Talese (Talese), **Supp. XVII:** 202, 203, 204
Fame & Folly: Essays (Ozick), **Supp. V:** 272
"Familiar Epistle to a Friend, A" (J. R. Lowell), **Supp. I Part 2:** 416
Familiar Territory: Observations on American Life (Epstein), **Supp. XIV: 106**
"Familiar Things" (Pickering), **Supp. XXI:** 204
"Family" (Sanders), **Supp. XVI:** 276
"Family" (Wilson), **IV:** 426
Family, Kinship, and Sympanthy in Nineteenth-Century America (Weinstein), **Supp. XVIII:** 261

"Family, The" (Taggard), **Supp. XXII:** 284
"Family Affair, A" (Chopin), **Retro. Supp. II:** 71
"Family and Socialism, The" (Ryan as Quin), **Supp. XVIII:** 238
Family Arsenal, The (Theroux), **Supp. VIII:** 322
"Family Barcus, The"(Thompson), **Supp. XXIII:** 299
Family Chronicle: An Odyssey from Russia to America (Reznikoff), **Supp. XIV:** 277, 288, 289
Family Devotions (Hwang), **Supp. XXI:** 145, 146
"Family History" (Mora), **Supp. XIII:** 217
"Family History, A" (R. H. Davis), **Supp. XVI:** 82
Family Honor (Parker), **Supp. XIX:** 186
Family Life (Banks), **Supp. V:** 7
Family Markowitz, The (Goodman), **Supp. XXVI:** 119, 121–123
"Family Matters" (Alvarez), **Supp. VII:** 10
Family Moskat, The (Singer), **IV:** 1, 17, 20, 46; **Retro. Supp. II:** 304
"Family of Little Feet, The" (Cisneros), **Supp. VII:** 61
Family Party, A (O'Hara), **III:** 362
Family Pictures (Brooks), **Supp. III Part 1:** 69, 85, 86
Family Pictures (Miller), **Supp. XII:** 291, **295–297,** 299
"Family Portrait" (Trethewey), **Supp. XXI:** 250
"Family Reunion" (J. W. Miller), **Supp. XX: 167**
"Family Reunion" (X. J. Kennedy), **Supp. XV:** 169
Family Reunion, The (T. S. Eliot), **I:** 570–571, 572, 581, 584, 588; **Retro. Supp. I:** 62, 65; **Retro. Supp. III:** 70
"Family Secrets" (Kingsolver), **Supp. VII:** 208
"Family Sideshow, The" (Karr), **Supp. XI:** 245
"Family Story, The" (Skloot), **Supp. XX: 195**
"Family Ties" (Mora), **Supp. XIII:** 215
"Family Tree" (Komunyakaa), **Supp. XIII:** 117–118, 126
"Family Wasserstein, The" (Hoban), **Supp. XV:** 319, 325
Famous American Negroes (Hughes), **Supp. I Part 1:** 345
"Famous Gilson Bequest, The" (Bierce), **I:** 204
Famous Last Words (Findley), **Supp. XX: 49, 55–56**
Famous Negro Athletes (Bontemps), **Supp. XXII:** 6
Famous Negro Music Makers (Hughes), **Supp. I Part 1:** 345
"Famous New York Trials" (Ellison), **Supp. II Part 1:** 230
Fanatic, The (Levin), **Supp. XXVII:** 137, 141, 143, 145, 147
Fanatics, The (Dunbar), **Supp. II Part 1:** 213–214
Fancher, Edwin, **Retro. Supp. II:** 202
Fancher, Lou, **Supp. XVI:** 177
"Fancy and Imagination" (Poe), **III:** 421
Fancy Dancer, The (P. N. Warren), **Supp. XX: 267–268**
"Fancy Flights" (Beattie), **Supp. V:** 25
"Fancy's Show Box" (Hawthorne), **II:** 238
"Fancy Woman, The" (Taylor), **Supp. V:** 316–317, 319, 323
"Fang" (Goldbarth), **Supp. XII:** 190
Fanny: Being the True History of the Adventures of Fanny Hackabout-Jones (Jong), **Supp. V:** 115, 127
Fanny Hill (Cleland), **Supp. V:** 48, 127
Fan of Swords, The (al-Maghut), **Supp. XIII:** 278
Fanon, Frantz, **Retro. Supp. II:** 118; **Retro. Supp. III:** 194; **Supp. X:** 131, 141; **Supp. XX: 152**
"Fan's Further Notes, A"(Exley), **Supp. XXIII:** 108
Fanshawe (Hawthorne), **II:** 223–224; **Retro. Supp. I:** 149, 151; **Retro. Supp. III:** 110, 111
Fan's Notes, A: A Fictional Memoir (Exley), **Supp. XVI:** 69; **Supp. XXIII:** 78, 97, 98, **99–103,** 106, 109
"Fantasia on 'The Nut-Brown Maid' " (Ashbery), **Supp. III Part 1:** 19
"Fantasia on the Relations between Poetry and Photography" (Strand), **Supp. IV Part 2:** 631
"Fantastic Fables" (Bierce), **I:** 209
"Fantasy"(O'Hara), **Supp. XXIII:** 220
Fante, John, **Supp. XI: 159–176**
Fantzius Mallare: A Mysterious Oath (Hecht), **Supp. XXVII:** 88
Faraday, Michael, **I:** 480–481
Far and Away (Jarman), **Supp. XVII:** 110, 115
"Far and Away" (Jarman), **Supp. XVII:** 115
Farber, Jim, **Supp. XXVII:** 45
"Farewell" (Emerson), **II:** 13
"Farewell" (Ryan as Quin), **Supp. XVIII:** 229
Farewell, My Lovely (Chandler), **Supp. IV Part 1:** 122, 125–126, 127, 128, 130
"Farewell, My Lovely!" (White), **Supp. I Part 2:** 661–663, 665
Farewell, The (Gibran), **Supp. XX: 121**
"Farewell Performance" (Merrill), **Supp. III Part 1:** 336–337
Farewell-Sermon Preached at the First Precinct in Northampton, after the People's Publick Rejection of their Minister, A (Edwards), **I:** 548, 562
"Farewell Sweet Dust" (Wylie), **Supp. I Part 2:** 727–728
"Farewell to America, A" (Wheatley), **Supp. XX: 283**
Farewell to Arms, A (Hemingway), **I:** 212, 421, 476, 477; **II:** 68–69, 248–249, 252–253, 254, 255, 262, 265; **Retro. Supp. I:** 171, 178, **180–182,** 187, 189; **Retro. Supp. II:** 108; **Supp. IV Part 1:** 380–381, 381; **Supp. VIII:** 179; **Supp. XII:** 241–242; **Supp. XXI:** 277
"Farewell to Miles" (Berryman), **I:** 173
"Farewell to My Union Brothers" (Ryan as Quin), **Supp. XVIII:** 238
Farewell to Reform (Chamberlain), **Supp. I Part 2:** 647
Farewell to Sport (Gallico), **Supp. XVI:** 238
"Farewell to the Middle Class" (Updike), **Retro. Supp. I:** 321
Far Field, The (Roethke), **III:** 528, 529, 539, 545, 547–548
"Far Field, The" (Roethke), **III:** 537, 540
Far-Flung (Cameron), **Supp. XII:** 81
Far from the Madding Crowd (Hardy), **II:** 291
Fargnoli, Nicholas, **Retro. Supp. III:** 75
Faríd, 'Umar ibn al-, **Supp. XX: 117**
Faris, Athénaíse Charleville, **Supp. I Part 1:** 204
Farley, Abbie, **I:** 458
Farley, Harriet, **Supp. XIII:** 140
"Farm, The" (Creeley), **Supp. IV Part 1:** 155
Farmer (Harrison), **Supp. VIII:** 39, **44–45**
Farmer, Frances, **Supp. XV:** 196–197
Farmer, Richard, **Supp. XIV:** 2
"Farmer and the Fox, The" (Leopold), **Supp. XIV:** 188
Farmer Boy (L. I. Wilder), **Supp. XXII:** 294, 297, 299
"Farmers' Daughters, The" (W. C. Williams), **Retro. Supp. I:** 423
Farmers Hotel, The (O'Hara), **III:** 361

"Farmer's Sorrow, A" (Jewett), **Retro. Supp. II:** 132
"Farmer's Wife, The" (Sexton), **Supp. II Part 2:** 676
"Farmer & Wife" (Davison), **Supp. XXVI:** 79
"Farm Garden" (Nelson), **Supp. XVIII:** 186
"Farm Implements and Rutabagas in a Landscape" (Ashbery), **Supp. III Part 1:** 13
Farming: A Hand Book (Berry), **Supp. X:** 31, 35
"Farmlights in Iowa" (Kooser), **Supp. XIX:** 120
"Farm on the Great Plains, The" (Stafford), **Supp. XI:** 322
Farnol, Jeffrey, **Supp. I Part 2:** 653
Far North (Shepard), **Supp. III Part 2:** 433, 435
"Far Northern Birch, The" (Francis), **Supp. IX:** 90
Farnsworth, Elizabeth, **Supp. XI:** 139
"Farrago" (Kees), **Supp. XV:** 145
Farrand, Max, **II:** 122
Farrar, Geraldine, **Retro. Supp. I:** 10
Farrar, John, **II:** 191; **Supp. XI:** 47
Far Reaches, The (Hickam), **Supp. XXVII:** 111
Farrell, Barry, **Supp. XIV:** 142
Farrell, James Francis, **II:** 25, 26
Farrell, James T., **I:** 97, 288, 475, 508, 517, 519; **II:** **25–53**, 416, 424; **III:** 28, 114, 116, 118, 119, 317, 382; **IV:** 211, 286; **Retro. Supp. II:** 196, 327; **Supp. I Part 2:** 679; **Supp. VIII:** 96, 97; **Supp. XIV:** 3; **Supp. XV:** 141; **Supp. XXVI:** 18; **Supp. XXVII:** 134
Farrell, Mrs. James T. (Dorothy Butler), **II:** 26
Farrell, Mrs. James T. (Hortense Alden), **II:** 26, 27, 45, 48
Farrell, John, **II:** 26
Farrell, John C., **Supp. I Part 1:** 24
Farrell, Kate, **Supp. XV:** 187–188,**Supp. XV:** 190
Farrell, Kevin, **II:** 26
Farrell, Mary, **II:** 25
Farrison, W. Edward, **Retro. Supp. III:** 133
"Far Rockaway" (Schwartz), **Supp. II Part 2:** 649
Farrow, Mia, **Supp. XV:** 8, 10
Far Side of the Dollar, The (Macdonald), **Supp. IV Part 2:** 473
Farther Off from Heaven (Humphrey), **Supp. IX:** 93, 96, 101, **103–104,** 105, 109
Farther Off from Heaven (Inge), **Supp. XXV:** 94, 100
Far Tortuga (Matthiessen), **Supp. V:** 201, 206–207
"Fascinating Fascism" (Sontag), **Supp. III Part 2:** 465
"Fascination of Cities, The" (Hughes), **Supp. I Part 1:** 325
Fashion, Power, Guilt and the Charity of Families (Shields), **Supp. VII:** 323
Fasman, Jonathan, **Supp. V:** 253
Fast, Howard, **Supp. I Part 1:** 295; **Supp. XXI:** 277; **Supp. XXIII:** 165
Fast, Jonathan, **Supp. V:** 115
Fast and Loose (Wharton), **Retro. Supp. I:** 361; **Retro. Supp. III:** 289
"Faster than Light" (Nelson), **Supp. XVIII:** 178–179
"Fastest Runner on Sixty-first Street, The" (Farrell), **II:** 45
Fast Lane on a Dirt Road (Sherman), **Supp. XXII:** 205
Fast Sam, Cool Clyde, and Stuff (Myers), **Supp. XXVII:** 202, 210
Fast Sooner Hound, The (Bontemps and Conroy), **Supp. XXII:** 5, 10–11
"Fat" (Carver), **Supp. III Part 1:** 141
Fatal Interview (Millay), **III:** 128–129, 130
"Fatality" (Bausch), **Supp. VII:** 54
Fatal Lady (film), **Supp. XIII:** 166
"Fate" (Emerson), **II:** 2–3, 4, 16; **Supp. XIV:** 42
"Fate" (Koch), **Supp. XV:** 183
"Fate" (Mailer), **Retro. Supp. II:** 207
"Fate of Pleasure, The" (Trilling), **Supp. III Part 2:** 510
Fate of the Jury, The (Masters), **Supp. I Part 2:** 466, 468, 469
"Fat Girl, The" (Dubus), **Supp. VII:** 84, 85
"Father" (Kooser), **Supp. XIX:** 117, 127
"Father" (Levine), **Supp. V:** 188
"Father" (Sanders), **Supp. XVI:** 277
"Father" (Trethewey), **Supp. XXI:** 253
"Father" (Walker), **Supp. III Part 2:** 522
"Father, The" (Carver), **Supp. III Part 1:** 137, 140
Father, The (Olds), **Supp. X:** **209–211**
"Father (Part I)" (Mullen), **Supp. XXVII:** 167
"Father Abraham" (Faulkner), **Retro. Supp. I:** 81, 82
Fatheralong: A Meditation on Fathers and Sons, Race and Society (Wideman), **Supp. X:** 320, 332–333, 334, 335
"Father and Daughter" (Eberhart), **I:** 539
Father and Glorious Descendant (Lowe), **Supp. X:** 291
"Father and Son" (Eberhart), **I:** 539
Father and Son (Farrell), **II:** 34, 35, 290, 291
Father and Son (Gosse), **Supp. VIII:** 157
"Father and Son" (Hughes), **Retro. Supp. I:** 204; **Supp. I Part 1:** 329, 339
"Father and Son" (Kunitz), **Supp. III Part 1:** 262
Father and Son (L. Brown), **Supp. XXI:** 36, 40, 41, **46–47**
"Father and Son" (Schwartz), **Supp. II Part 2:** 650
Father Bombo's Pilgrimage to Mecca (Freneau), **Supp. II Part 1:** 254
Father Fisheye (Balakian), **Supp. XXIII:** 19
"Father Fisheye"(Balakian), **Supp. XXIII:** 19
"Father Fitzgerald" (Nelson and Espeland), **Supp. XVIII:** 181
"Father Guzman" (Stern), **Supp. IX:** **293,** 296
"Father John Melby and the Ghost of Amy Elizabeth" (Brockmeier), **Supp. XXII:** 60
Father of the Blues (Bontemps as Handy), **Supp. XXII:** 5
"Father out Walking on the Lawn, A" (Dove), **Supp. IV Part 1:** 246
"Fathers" (Creeley), **Supp. IV Part 1:** 157–158
Fathers, The (Tate), **IV:** 120, 127, 130, 131–133, 134, 141; **Supp. X:** 52
Fathers and Crows (Vollmann), **Supp. XVII:** 226, 231–232
"Fathers and Daughters, Mothers and Sons"(Hadas), **Supp. XXIII:** 119
"Fathers and Sons" (Hemingway), **II:** 249, 265–266; **Retro. Supp. I:** 175
"Father's Body, The" (Dickey), **Supp. IV Part 1:** 176
"Father's Day" (Connelly), **Supp. XXI:** 79–80
"Father's Story, A" (Dubus), **Supp. VII:** 88
"Father's Voice" (Stafford), **Supp. XI:** 322
"Fat Lady, The" (Carruth), **Supp. XVI:** 48
"Fat Man, Floating" (Dunn), **Supp. XI:** 144
Fat Men in Skirts (Silver), **Supp. XXIV:** **265–267,** 275
Fatout, Paul, **Retro. Supp. III:** 268

"Fat Tuesday"(P. Benedict), **Supp. XXIII:** 38
Faulkes Chronicle, The (Huddle), **Supp. XXVI:** 148, 158, 159–160
Faulkner, Barry, **Supp. XV:** 41
Faulkner, William, **I:** 54, 97, 99, 105, 106, 115, 117, 118, 123, 190, 204–205, 211, 288, 289, 291, 292, 297, 305, 324, 374, 378, 423, 480, 517; **II:** 28, 51, **54–76,** 131, 174, 194, 217, 223, 228, 230, 259, 301, 306, 431, 458–459, 542, 594, 606; **III:** 45, 70, 108, 164, 218, 220, 222, 236–237, 244, 292, 334, 350, 382, 418, 453, 454, 482, 483; **IV:** 2, 4, 33, 49, 97, 98, 100, 101, 120, 131, 203, 207, 211, 217, 237, 257, 260, 261, 279, 280, 352, 461, 463; **Retro. Supp. I: 73–95,** 215, 339, 347, 356, 379, 382; **Retro. Supp. II:** 19, 221, 326; **Retro. Supp. III: 73–90,** 106, 194; **Supp. I Part 1:** 196, 197, 242, 372; **Supp. I Part 2:** 450, 621; **Supp. III Part 1:** 384–385, 396; **Supp. IV Part 1:** 47, 130, 257, 342; **Supp. IV Part 2:** 434, 463, 468, 502, 677, 682; **Supp. IX:** 20, 95; **Supp. V:** 58, 59, 138, 210, 226, 237, 261, 262, 334–336; **Supp. VIII:** 37, 39, 40, 104, 105, 108, 175, 176, 180, 181, 183, 184, 188, 189, 215; **Supp. X:** 44, 228; **Supp. XI:** 92, 247; **Supp. XII:** 16, 289, 310, 313; **Supp. XIII:** 100, 169; **Supp. XIV:** 1, 12–13, 21, 24, 93, 306; **Supp. XIX:** 97, 154, 166; **Supp. XV:** 92, 135, 338; **Supp. XVI:** 148, 189; **Supp. XVII:** 225; **Supp. XVIII:** 76, 84, 90, 148, 249; **Supp. XX: 137, 162, 185, 195; Supp. XXI:** 36, 38, 256; **Supp. XXII:** 193, 203, 205; **Supp. XXIII:** 166; **Supp. XXIV:** 54, 64, 132, 136, 215; **Supp. XXV:** 49; **Supp. XXVI:** 1, 9, 45, 144, 147; **Supp. XXVII:** 11, 216, 218, 267, 276
Faulkner: A Collection of Critical Essays (Warren), **Retro. Supp. I:** 73
Faulkner at Nagano (Jelliffe, ed.), **I:** 289; **II:** 63, 65
Faulkner-Cowley File, The: Letters and Memories 1944–1962 (Cowley, ed.), **Retro. Supp. I:** 73, 92; **Supp. II Part 1:** 140, 141
"Faultlines"(Hadas), **Supp. XXIII:** 117–118
"Faun" (Plath), **Supp. I Part 2:** 537
"Fauna" (Jeffers), **Supp. II Part 2:** 415
Fauset, Arthur Huff, **Supp. XVIII:** 126
Fauset, Jessie Redmon, **Retro. Supp. III:** 127; **Supp. I Part 1:** 321, 325; **Supp. IV Part 1:** 164; **Supp. XIX:** 69, 78; **Supp. XVIII:** 122,127
Faust (Goethe), **I:** 396; **II:** 489; **III:** 395; **Supp. II Part 1:** 16; **Supp. IX:** 141
Faust, Beatrix Hapgood, **Supp. XXI:** 8
Faust, Clarence H., **II:** 20
Faute de l'Abbé Mouret, La (Zola), **III:** 322
"Favor, The" (Carver and Gallagher), **Supp. XXIV:** 178
Favor Island (Merwin), **Supp. III Part 1:** 346, 347
"Favor of Love, A" (Peacock), **Supp. XIX:** 203
Favourite Game, The (Cohen), **Supp. XXVII:** 51, 54, 56–57, 59
"Favrile" (Doty), **Supp. XI:** 131
"Fawn" (Davison), **Supp. XXVI:** 75
"Fawn, with a Bit of Green" (Swados), **Supp. XIX:** 258
Fay (L. Brown), **Supp. XXI:** 40, 41, 47
Fay, Bernard, **IV:** 41
"Fear, The" (Frost), **Retro. Supp. I:** 128
Fear and Loathing in Las Vegas (Thompson), **Supp. XXIV:** 280, 282, 283, 287, **288–292,** 293
Fear and Loathing on the Campaign Trail '72 (Thompson), **Supp. XXIV:** 279, 281, 282, 289, **292–293**
Fear and Trembling (Kierkegaard), **Supp. XX: 132**
"Fear & Fame" (Levine), **Supp. V:** 192
Fearful Child, The (C. Frost), **Supp. XV:** 96, 97, 106
"Fearful Child, The" (C. Frost), **Supp. XV:** 96
Fearing, Kenneth, **Supp. XV:** 138; **Supp. XXVI:** 134, 143
"Fearless" (Mosley), **Supp. XIII:** 241
Fearless Jones (Mosley), **Supp. XIII: 241–242**
"Fear of Concrete" (Halliday), **Supp. XIX:** 91
Fear of Fifty: A Midlife Memoir (Jong), **Supp. V:** 114, 115, 116, 131
Fear of Flying (Jong), **Supp. V:** 113, 115, 116, 119–123, 124, 129
"Feast, The" (Kinnell), **Supp. III Part 1:** 239, 250
Feast of All Saints, The (Rice), **Supp. VII:** 299–301
Feast of Love, The (C. Baxter), **Supp. XVII:** 13, 21–22
Feast of Love, The (film, R. Benton), **Supp. XVII:** 22
Feast of Snakes, A (Crews), **Supp. XI:** 102, **107–108; Supp. XXI:** 40
"Feast of Stephen, The" (Hecht), **Supp. X:** 63–64
Feast of the Goat, The (Llosa), **Supp. XXIV:** 89
"Featherbed for Critics, A" (Blackmur), **Supp. II Part 1:** 93, 151
Feather Crowns (Mason), **Supp. VIII: 146–147**
"Feathers" (Carver), **Supp. III Part 1:** 145
Feathers (Van Vechten), **Supp. II Part 2:** 736, 749
"Feathers, The" (Hogan), **Supp. IV Part 1:** 416
Feathers Left Around (Wells), **Supp. XXVI:** 282
"February" (Ellison), **Supp. II Part 1:** 229
"February 14th" (Levine), **Supp. V:** 194
February in Sydney (Komunyakaa), **Supp. XIII: 124–125,** 129
"February in Sydney" (Komunyakaa), **Supp. XIII:** 125
"February: Thinking of Flowers" (Kenyon), **Supp. VII:** 171
"Feces" (McClatchy), **Supp. XII:** 266, 267–268
Fechner, Gustav, **II:** 344, 355, 358, 359, 363
Feder, Lillian, **IV:** 136; **Supp. XVI:** 49, 50
Federal Arts Project, **Supp. III Part 2:** 618
Federigo, or, The Power of Love (Nemerov), **III:** 268, 276, 282, 283–284, 285
"Fedge, The" (Halliday), **Supp. XIX:** 93
"Fedora" (Chopin), **Supp. I Part 1:** 220
Fedorko, Kathy A., **Retro. Supp. I:** 361, 374
"Feeling and Precision" (Moore), **III:** 206
Feeling Italian: The Art of Ethnicity in America (Ferraro), **Supp. XX: 43**
"Feeling of Effort, The" (James), **II:** 349
Feeling Very Strange: The Slipstream Anthology (Kelly and Kessel, eds.), **Supp. XIX:** 231
"Feel Like a Bird" (Swenson), **Supp. IV Part 2:** 639
"Feel Me" (Swenson), **Supp. IV Part 2:** 647
Feeney, Mary, **Supp. IX:** 152, 154
Feinsilver, Pamela, **Supp. XX: 135**
Feinstein, Herbert, **Supp. XIX:** 260
Feinstein, Sascha, **Supp. XIII:** 125

Feldman, Charles K., **Supp. XI:** 307
Feldman, Morton, **Supp. XXIII:** 211
Fellini, Federico, **Supp. XII:** 172; **Supp. XV:** 8
"Fellini the Cat" (Peacock), **Supp. XIX:** 206
"Fellow Citizens" (Sandburg), **III:** 553
Fellows, John, **Supp. I Part 2:** 520
Fellow Travelers (Mallon), **Supp. XIX:** 132, **143–144**
"Felo de Se" (Wylie), **Supp. I Part 2:** 727, 729
Felton, Sharon, **Supp. IV Part 1:** 210
"Female Author" (Plath), **Retro. Supp. II:** 243
"Female Frailty" (Freneau), **Supp. II Part 1:** 258
"Female Laughter and Comic Possibilities: Uncommon Women and Others" (Chirico), **Supp. XV:** 323
Female Patriot, The; or, Nature's Rights (Rowson), **Supp. XV:** 237–238
Female Prose Writers of America (Hart), **Supp. XVIII:** 257, 264
"Female Voice in To Kill a Mockingbird, The: Narrative Strategies in Film and Novel" (Shakelford), **Supp. VIII:** 129
" 'Feminine' Epic, The" (Notley), **Supp. XXII:** 232, 234, 236
"Feminine Landscape of Leslie Marmon Silko's Ceremony, The" (Gunn Allen), **Supp. IV Part 1:** 324
Feminine Mystique, The (Friedan), **Retro. Supp. III:** 241
Feminine Note in Fiction, The (Courtney), **Supp. XXIV:** 29
Feminism and the Politics of Literary Reputation: The Example of Erica Jong (Templin), **Supp. V:** 116
"Feminismo" (Robbins), **Supp. X:** 272
"Feminist Criticism in the Wilderness" (Showalter), **Supp. X:** 97
"Feminist Manifesto" (Loy), **Supp. XXII:** 160
Feminization of American Culture, The (Douglas), **Supp. XVIII:** 258
"Fence, The" (Oliver), **Supp. VII:** 232
"Fence Posts" (Snyder), **Supp. VIII:** 304
Fences (film, Washington), **Retro. Supp. III:** 321
Fences (Wilson), **Retro. Supp. III:** 318, 323–325, 325; **Supp. VIII:** 329, 330, 331, **334–337,** 350
Fenick, Elizabeth, **Retro. Supp. II:** 221
"Fenimore Cooper's Literary Offenses" (Twain), **IV:** 204–205; **Retro. Supp. III:** 265
Fennell, Frank L., **Supp. XVII:** 177–178
Fenollosa, Ernest, **III:** 458, 465, 466, 474, 475, 477; **Retro. Supp. I:** 289; **Supp. IV Part 1:** 154
Fenollosa, Mrs. Ernest, **III:** 458
"Fenstad's Mother" (C. Baxter), **Supp. XVII:** 18
Fenton, Charles, **Supp. XI:** 43
Fenton, James, **Supp. XV:** 117
Fenton, William, **Supp. XXVI:** 96
Ferber, Edna, **Retro. Supp. III:** 135
Ferdinand: Including "It Was" (Zukofsky), **Supp. III Part 2:** 630
"Fergus" (Bourne), **I:** 229
Ferguson, James, **Supp. I Part 2:** 503
Ferguson, Otis, **Supp. IX:** 7
Ferguson, SallyAnn H., **Supp. XXVI:** 166
Ferguson, William, **Supp. XII:** 189
Ferguson Affair, The (Macdonald), **Supp. IV Part 2:** 473
Fergusson, Francis, **I:** 265, 440; **Supp. XV:** 20
Ferlinghetti, Lawrence, **Supp. IV Part 1:** 90; **Supp. VIII:** 290, 292; **Supp. XII:** 121, 125; **Supp. XIII:** 275; **Supp. XIX:** 4; **Supp. XXI:** 53; **Supp. XXIII:** 219
Fermata, The (Baker), **Supp. XIII: 49–52,** 54
"Fern" (Toomer), **Supp. III Part 2:** 481; **Supp. IX:** 313
Fern, Fanny, **Retro. Supp. I:** 246; **Supp. V:** 122
Fernández, Enrique, **Supp. VIII:** 73
Fernandez, Ramon, **Retro. Supp. I:** 302, 303; **Supp. XVI:** 214
"Fern-Beds in Hampshire Country" (Wilbur), **Supp. III Part 2:** 558
"Fern Hill" (D. Thomas), **IV:** 93; **Supp. XX: 204**
"Fern-Life" (Larcom), **Supp. XIII:** 143
Ferragammo, Salvatore, **Supp. XVI:** 192
Ferraro, Thomas J., **Supp. XX: 34, 43**
Ferreo, Guglielmo, **Supp. I Part 2:** 481
Ferris, Anthony, **Supp. XX: 124**
Ferris, Beth, **Supp. XXVI:** 183
Ferry, David, **Supp. XXIV: 147–164; Supp. XXV:** 222
"Ferry, The" (Cliff), **Supp. XXII:** 74
Fessenden, Thomas Green, **II:** 300
Fessier, Michael, **Supp. XIII:** 164
"Festival Aspect, The" (Olson), **Supp. II Part 2:** 585
"Festival of Regrets, The" (Wasserstein), **Supp. XV:** 333
Festival of San Joaquin, The (Edgell), **Supp. XXIII:** 84, 85, **90–91,** 94
Fetching the Dead (Sanders), **Supp. XVI:** 269
Fêtes galantes (Verlaine), **IV:** 79
Fetherling, Doug, **Supp. XXVII:** 88, 90, 94
Fetid Itch (Silver), **Supp. XXIV:** 265
"Fetish" (McClatchy), **Supp. XII:** 256
Fetterley, Judith, **Retro. Supp. II:** 139; **Supp. XXIV:** 28
Fetterly, Judith, **Supp. XXV:** 285
"Feud" (Zinberg), **Supp. XV:** 195
"Fever" (Carver), **Supp. III Part 1:** 145
"Fever 103°" (Plath), **Supp. I Part 2:** 541
Fever Pitch (Hornby), **Supp. XII:** 286; **Supp. XXIII:** 109
Fever: Twelve Stories (Wideman), **Supp. X:** 320
"Few Don'ts by an Imagiste, A" (Pound), **III:** 465; **Retro. Supp. I:** 288; **Supp. I Part 1:** 261–262
"Few Kind Words for Anger, A" (Kriegel), **Supp. XXIV:** 220
"Few Stray Comments on the Cultivation of the Lyric, A" (Sobin), **Supp. XVI:** 285
"Few Words of Introduction, A" (McNally), **Supp. XIII:** 198–199
Feydeau, Georges, **Supp. XXIV:** 271
Feynman, Richard, **Supp. XXV:** 267
Fiamengo, Janice, **Supp. XIII:** 35
"Fiat Lux" (H. Johnson), **Supp. XXVI:** 172
Fiber (Bass), **Supp. XVI:** 22
"Fiber: A Post-Pastoral Georgic" (Gifford), **Supp. XVI:** 22
Ficke, Arthur Davison, **Supp. XIII:** 347; **Supp. XV:** 40, 42, 43, 46, 48, 49
"Fiction" (Stafford), **Supp. XI:** 327
"Fiction: A Lens on Life" (Stegner), **Supp. IV Part 2:** 595, 596, 600
Fictional World of William Hoffman, The (Frank, ed.), **Supp. XVIII:** 74, 79, 80, 87
Fiction and the Figures of Life (Gass), **Supp. VI:** 85
Fiction of Joseph Heller, The (Seed), **Supp. IV Part 1:** 391
Fiction of Paule Marshall, The (Denniston), **Supp. XI:** 276
Fiction of the Forties (Eisinger), **I:** 302; **II:** 604
Fictions in Autobiography: Studies in the Art of Self-Invention (Eakin), **Supp. XVI:** 70
"Fiction Writer and His Country, The"

(O'Connor), **III:** 342; **Retro. Supp. II:** 223, 225; **Supp. II Part 1:** 148
Fiddler's Trance, The (Skloot), **Supp. XX: 196, 202**
Fidelity (Glaspell), **Supp. III Part 1:** 177
Fiedler, Leslie A., **II:** 27; **III:** 218; **Retro. Supp. II:** 280, 324; **Supp. II Part 1:** 87; **Supp. IV Part 1:** 42, 86; **Supp. IX:** 3, 227; **Supp. X:** 80; **Supp. XIII: 93–110; Supp. XIV:** 11; **Supp. XIX:** 251; **Supp. XVIII:** 146; **Supp. XXIII:** 42; **Supp. XXV:** 268; **Supp. XXVII:** 133, 262
Fiedler on the Roof: Essays on Literature and Jewish Identity (Fiedler), **Supp. XIII:** 106–107
"Fie! Fie! Fi-Fi!" (Fitzgerald), **Retro. Supp. I:** 100
Field, Eugene, **Supp. II Part 1:** 197
Field, John, **IV:** 179
"Field Events" (Bass), **Supp. XVI:** 19
"Field Full of Black Cats, A" (C. Frost), **Supp. XV:** 101
Field Guide, (Hass), **Supp. VI:** 97–98, **99–101,** 102, 103, 106
Field Guide to Contemporary Poetry and Poetics (Friebert and Young, eds.), **Supp. XI:** 270
"Field Guide to the Western Birds" (Stegner), **Supp. IV Part 2:** 609
Fielding, Henry, **I:** 134; **II:** 302, 304–305; **III:** 61; **Supp. I Part 2:** 421, 422, 656; **Supp. IV Part 2:** 688; **Supp. IX:** 128; **Supp. V:** 127; **Supp. XI:** 277; **Supp. XVIII:** 2, 7; **Supp. XXV:** 258
Fielding, Richard, **Supp. XV:** 232
"Field-larks and Blackbirds" (Lanier), **Supp. I Part 1:** 355
Field of Honor (Hay), **Supp. XIV:** 120–121, 125, 130
"Field of Honor" (Hay), **Supp. XIV:** 120–121, 129–130
Field of Vision, The (Morris), **III:** 226–228, 229, 232, 233, 238
"Field Report" (Corso), **Supp. XII:** 124, **136**
"Fields" (Wright), **Supp. XV:** 342
Fields, Annie Adams, **II:** 401, 402, 403–404, 406, 412; **IV:** 177; **Retro. Supp. II:** 134, 135, 142; **Supp. I Part 1:** 317; **Supp. XVI:** 84, 88
Fields, James T., **II:** 274, 279, 402–403; **Retro. Supp. II:** 135; **Supp. I Part 1:** 317; **Supp. XIII:** 150; **Supp. XVI:** 84, 88
Fields, Mrs. James T., **Supp. XIV:** 44, 46. See Fields, Annie Adams
Fields, Jerry, **Supp. XXVI:** 86
Fields, Joseph, **IV:** 274
Fields, The (Richter), **Supp. XVIII: 213–214,** 220
Fields, W. C., **II:** 427; **IV:** 335
"Fields at Dusk, The" (Salter), **Supp. IX:** 260
Fields of Fire (Webb), **Supp. XXII:** 115
Fields of Praise, The (Nelson), **Supp. XVIII:** 171, 173, **177–178**
Fields of Wonder (Hughes), **Retro. Supp. I:** 206, 207; **Supp. I Part 1:** 333–334
Fierce Invalids Home from Hot Climates (Robbins), **Supp. X:** 267, 276–277, **282–285**
Fiery, Marion, **Supp. XXII:** 293
Fiery Chariot, The (Hurston), **Supp. VI:** 155–156
"Fiesta, 1980" (Díaz), **Supp. XXIV:** 88
15 Poems (Banks), **Supp. V:** 5
"Fifteenth Farewell" (Bogan), **Supp. III Part 1:** 51, 58
"Fifth Avenue, Uptown" (Baldwin), **Supp. I Part 1:** 52
"Fifth Avenue—Spring Afternoon" (Untermeyer), **Supp. XV:** 296
Fifth Book of Peace, The (Kingston), **Supp. V:** 173
Fifth Chinese Daughter (Wong), **Supp. X:** 291
Fifth Column, The (Hemingway), **II:** 254, 258; **Retro. Supp. I:** 184
"Fifth Column of the Fencerow" (Leopold), **Supp. XIV:** 185
Fifth Decad of Cantos, The (Pound), **Retro. Supp. I:** 292
"Fifth Movement: Autobiography" (Zukofsky), **Supp. III Part 2:** 611
Fifth Sunday (Dove), **Supp. IV Part 1:** 251, 252–253
"Fifth Sunday" (Dove), **Supp. IV Part 1:** 252
50 Poems (Cummings), **I:** 430, 440, 442–443, 444–445, 446
Fifty Best American Short Stories (O'Brien), **III:** 56
"Fifty Dollars" (Elkin), **Supp. VI: 43–44**
"55 Miles to the Gas Pump" (Proulx), **Supp. VII:** 264
55 Poems (Zukofsky), **Supp. III Part 2:** 611, 621
"Fifty Grand" (Hemingway), **II:** 250, 424; **Retro. Supp. I:** 177
Fifty Shades of Grey (James), **Supp. XXVII:** 79
Fifty Stories (Boyle), **Supp. XXIV:** 58
"Fifty Suggestions" (Poe), **Retro. Supp. II:** 266
"52 Oswald Street" (Kinnell), **Supp. III Part 1:** 251
Fifty Years Among Authors, Editors, and Publishers (Derby), **Supp. XVIII:** 4
"Fifty Years Among the Black Folk" (Du Bois), **Supp. II Part 1:** 169
"Fifty Years of American Poetry" (Jarrell), **Retro. Supp. I:** 52
Fig Connection, The (Franzen and Siebert), **Supp. XX: 84**
Fight, The (Mailer), **Retro. Supp. II:** 207, 208
Fight Back: For the Sake of the People, For the Sake of the Land (Ortiz), **Supp. IV Part 2:** 497, 498, 499, 503, 510–512, 514
"Fighters, The" (Zinberg), **Supp. XV:** 193
Fight for Freedom (Hughes), **Supp. I Part 1:** 345
Fighting Angel (Buck), **Supp. II Part 1:** 119, 131
Fighting France; From Dunkerque to Belfort (Wharton), **Retro. Supp. I:** 377, 378; **Retro. Supp. III:** 285
Fightin': New and Collected Stories (Ortiz), **Supp. IV Part 2:** 513
"Figlia che Piange, La" (Eliot), **I:** 570, 584; **III:** 9
Figliola, Samantha, **Supp. V:** 143
"Figure a Poem Makes, The" (Frost), **Retro. Supp. I:** 139; **Retro. Supp. III:** 103–104, 105
"Figured Wheel, The" (Pinsky), **Supp. VI:** 243, 244, 245, 246
Figured Wheel, The: New and Collected Poems (Pinsky), **Supp. VI:** 247–248
"Figure in the Carpet, The" (James), **Retro. Supp. I:** 228, 229
"Figure in the Doorway, The" (Frost), **Retro. Supp. I:** 138
Figure of Fulfillment, The (Lerperger; Miller, trans.), **Supp. XX: 165, 167–168**
Figures from the Double World (McGrath), **Supp. X: 118–119**
Figures in Black: Words, Signs, and the "Racial" Self (H. L. Gates), **Supp. XX: 99, 100, 106, 107**
"Figures in the Clock, The" (McCarthy), **II:** 561–562
Figures Made Visible in the Sadness of Time (Everwine), **Supp. XV:** 75, 88
Figures of Time (Hayden), **Supp. II Part 1:** 367
Filbin, Thomas, **Supp. XXIII:** 299
"Filling Out a Blank" (Wagoner),

Supp. IX: 324
Fillmore, Millard, **III:** 101
Film Flam: Essays on Hollywood (McMurtry), **Supp. V:** 228
Films of Ayn Rand, The (Cox), **Supp. IV Part 2:** 524
Filo, John, **Supp. XII:** 211
Filreis, Alan, **Supp. XXI:** 262, 267, 268, 269, 271, 273, 275, 277, 278
Filson, John, **Retro. Supp. I:** 421
Final Beast, The (Buechner), **Supp. XII: 49–51**
"Finale" (Longfellow), **II:** 505, 506–507
"Finale: Presto" (Davison), **Supp. XXVI:** 70
"Final Fear" (Hughes), **Supp. I Part 1:** 338
Final Harvest: Emily Dickinson's Poems (T. H. Johnson, ed.), **I:** 470, 471
"Finally Harriet" (Wolfert), **Supp. XXI: 265–267**
Final Payments (Gordon), **Supp. IV Part 1:** 297, 299, 300–302, 304, 306, 314
"Final Report, A" (Maxwell), **Supp. VIII:** 169
"Final Soliloquy of the Interior Paramour" (Stevens), **Retro. Supp. I:** 312
Final Solution, The (Reitlinger), **Supp. XII:** 161
Financier, The (Dreiser), **I:** 497, 501, 507, 509; **Retro. Supp. II:** 94, 101–102, 105; **Supp. XVIII:** 246
Finch, Annie, **Supp. XVII: 69–79**
Finch, Henry Leroy, **Supp. XVII:** 69
Finch, Margaret Rockwell, **Supp. XVII:** 69
Finch, Robert, **Supp. XIV:** 186–187; **Supp. XXVI:** 38
"Finches, Little Pats of Butter on the Wing"(Crooker), **Supp. XXIII:** 62
Find a Victim (Macdonald), **Supp. IV Part 2:** 467, 472, 473
Fin de Chéri, La (Colette; stage adaptation, Loos), **Supp. XVI:** 194
Finder, Henry, **Supp. XX: 90**
"Fin de Saison Palm Beach" (White), **Supp. I Part 2:** 673
"Finding a Bible in an Abandoned Cabin" (Wrigley), **Supp. XVIII: 293–294,** 296, 297, 300, 301, 303
Finding a Form (Gass), **Supp. VI:** 91–92, 93
Finding a Girl in America (Dubus), **Supp. VII:** 85–88
"Finding a Girl in America" (Dubus), **Supp. VII:** 87
"Finding Amy" (O'Nan), **Supp. XXV:** 143, 150
"Finding Beads" (Hogan), **Supp. IV Part 1:** 400
Finding Losses (Bronk), **Supp. XXI:** 31, 32
"Finding of Zach, The" (Dunbar), **Supp. II Part 1:** 212
Findings and Keepings: Analects for an Autobiography (Mumford), **Supp. II Part 2:** 483
Finding the Center: Narrative Poetry of the Zuni Indians (Tedlock), **Supp. IV Part 2:** 509
Finding the Islands (Merwin), **Supp. III Part 1:** 353, 357
"Finding the Place: A Migrant Childhood" (Stegner), **Supp. IV Part 2:** 597
Findley, Timothy, **Supp. XX: 49–65**
"Find the Woman" (Macdonald, as Millar), **Supp. IV Part 2:** 466
Fine, David, **Supp. XI:** 160
Fine, Richard, **Supp. XVIII:** 248
Fine Clothes to the Jew (Hughes), **Retro. Supp. I:** 200, 201, 203, 205; **Supp. I Part 1:** 326–328
"Fine Old Firm, A" (Jackson), **Supp. IX:** 120
Fine Preserving (Plagemann), **Supp. XVII:** 91
Fine Preserving: M. F. K. Fisher's Annotated Edition of Catherine Plagemann's Cookbook (Plagemann; M. F. K. Fisher, ed.), **Supp. XVII:** 91
Finer Grain, The (James), **II:** 335
Fine Writing (L. P. Smith), **Supp. XIV:** 347
"Fingerprints" (Cohen), **Supp. XXVII:** 56
"Finis" (X. J. Kennedy), **Supp. XV:** 169
"Finished Basement" (Di Piero), **Supp. XIX:** 47
Finished Man, The (Garrett), **Supp. VII:** 96, 97–98
Finishing the Picture (A. Miller), **Retro. Supp. III:** 170, 172, 176
Fink, Jonathan, **Supp. XXI:** 244, 245, 248, 255, 256
Fink, Mike, **IV:** 266
Finkel, Donald, **Supp. XXVII:** 253
Finkelstein, Norman, **Supp. XXI:** 24, 33
Finkle, David, **Supp. XXI:** 47
Finley, John H., **II:** 418
Finn, David, **Supp. VIII:** 106–107
Finn, Mark, **Supp. XXVII:** 128
Finnegan, Robert (pseudonym). See Ryan, Paul William
Finnegans Wake (Joyce), **III:** 7, 12, 14, 261; **IV:** 182, 369–370, 418, 421; **Supp. I Part 2:** 620; **Supp. II Part 1:** 2; **Supp. XIII:** 191; **Supp. XVIII:** 32
Finney, Brian, **Supp. XIV:** 158, 160, 161, 165, 166, 167, 169
"Finnish Rhapsody" (Ashbery), **Supp. III Part 1:** 26
Finster, Howard, **Supp. XV:** 349
Firbank, Ronald, **IV:** 77, 436; **Supp. XXIII:** 209
"Fire" (Hughes), **Supp. I Part 1:** 327
"Fire and Cloud" (Wright), **IV:** 488
"Fire and Ice" (Frost), **II:** 154; **Retro. Supp. I:** 133; **Retro. Supp. III:** 101, 102; **Supp. XIX:** 122
Fire and Ice (Stegner), **Supp. IV Part 2:** 598, 607–608
"Fire and the Cloud, The" (Hurston), **Supp. VI:** 158
"Fire and the Hearth, The" (Faulkner), **II:** 71
Firebird (Doty), **Supp. XI:** 119–120, 121, **132–133,** 134
"Firebombing, The" (Dickey), **Supp. IV Part 1:** 180–181, 187, 189–190
"Fireborn Are at Home in Fire, The" (Sandburg), **III:** 591
"Fire by Night" (R. Fisher), **Supp. XIX:** 70–71
"Fire Chaconne" (Francis), **Supp. IX:** 87
Firecrackers (Van Vechten), **Supp. II Part 2:** 740, 742–744, 749
"Fire Dreams"(Thompson), **Supp. XXIII:** 296
Fire: From "A Journal of Love," the Unexpurgated Diary of Anaïs Nin, 1934–1937, **Supp. X:** 184, 185, 189, 194, 195
"Fire in the House, The" (Davison), **Supp. XXVI:** 71
Firelight Fairy Book, The (Beston), **Supp. XXVI:** 33
"Fireman, The " (Bass), **Supp. XVI:** 24
Fireman's Wife and Other Stories, The (Bausch), **Supp. VII:** 48, 54
Fire Next Time, The (Baldwin), **Retro. Supp. II:** 5, 8, 9; **Supp. I Part 1:** 48, 49, 52, 60–61
"Fire Next Time, The" (Baldwin). See "Down at the Cross" (Baldwin)
"Fire of Driftwood, The" (Longfellow), **II:** 499; **Retro. Supp. II:** 159, 168
"Fire of Life" (McCullers), **II:** 585
Fire on the Mountain (Abbey), **Supp. XIII:** 6

"Fire Poem" (Merrill), **Supp. III Part 1:** 321
"Fires" (Bass), **Supp. XVI:** 20
"Fires" (Carver), **Supp. III Part 1:** 136–139, 147
Fire Sale (Paretsky), **Supp. XXV:** 175–176, 178
Fire Screen, The (Merrill), **Supp. III Part 1:** 319, 325–329
"Fire Season" (Didion), **Supp. IV Part 1:** 199
"Fire Sequence" (Winters), **Supp. II Part 2:** 791, 796, 800
Fire Sermon (Morris), **III:** 238–239
"Fire Sermon, The" (T. S. Eliot), **Retro. Supp. I:** 60–61; **Retro. Supp. III:** 63
Fires: Essays, Poems, Stories (Carver), **Supp. III Part 1:** 136, 140, 142, 146–147
Fireside Travels (J. R. Lowell), **Supp. I Part 2:** 407, 419–420
Firestarter (King), **Supp. IX:** 114; **Supp. V:** 140, 141, 144
"fire the bastards" (Green), **Supp. IV Part 1:** 285
"Fire-Truck, A" (Wilbur), **Supp. III Part 2:** 556
"Fireweed" (Clampitt), **Supp. IX: 44–45**
"Firewood" (Banks), **Supp. V:** 15
"Fireworks" (Ford), **Supp. V:** 69
"Fireworks" (Shapiro), **Supp. II Part 2:** 707
Fireworks: A History and Celebration (Plimpton), **Supp. XVI:** 245
Fir-Flower Tablets (A. Lowell), **II:** 512, 526–527
Firger, Jessica, **Supp. XIX:** 51, 58, 59, 62
Firkins, Oscar W., **II:** 271; **Supp. XV:** 297, 309
"Firmament, The" (Bryant), **Supp. I Part 1:** 162
Firmat, Gustavo Pérez, **Supp. VIII:** 76, 77, 79; **Supp. XI:** 184
"First American, The" (Toomer), **Supp. III Part 2:** 480, 487
"First Birth" (Olds), **Supp. X:** 212
First Book of Africa, The (Hughes), **Supp. I Part 1:** 344–345
First Book of Jazz, The (Hughes), **Supp. I Part 1:** 345
First Book of Negroes, The (Hughes), **Supp. I Part 1:** 345
First Book of Rhythms, The (Hughes), **Supp. I Part 1:** 345
First Book of the West Indies, The (Hughes), **Supp. I Part 1:** 345
Firstborn (Glück), **Supp. V:** 80, 81, 82, 84
"Firstborn" (Wright), **Supp. V:** 340
"First Chaldaic Oracle" (Carson), **Supp. XII: 111**
"First Communion" (Fante), **Supp. XI:** 160
"First Confession" (X. J. Kennedy), **Supp. XV: 154–155**
"First Day of School, The" (Gibbons), **Supp. X:** 41, 42
"First Death in Nova Scotia" (Bishop), **Supp. I Part 1:** 73
"First Formal" (Olds), **Supp. X:** 212
First Four Books of Poems, The (Glück), **Supp. V:** 81, 83
First Four Years, The (L. I. Wilder), **Supp. XXII:** 296, 298, 299–300
"First Grade" (Stafford), **Supp. XI:** 328
First Hand (Bierds), **Supp. XVII:** 32, 34–36
"First Hawaiian Bank" (Nye), **Supp. XIII:** 278
"First Heat" (Taylor), **Supp. V:** 323
First Hour, The (Di Piero), **Supp. XIX:** 36–37, 40
"First Hour of the Night, The" (Bidart), **Supp. XV: 30–32**
"First Hunters and the Last, The" (Sobin), **Supp. XVI:** 292
First Indian on the Moon (Alexie), **Supp. XXVI:** 103
"First Job, The" (Cisneros), **Supp. VII:** 62
"1st Letter on Georges" (Olson), **Supp. II Part 2:** 578
First Light (C. Baxter), **Supp. XVII:** 15, **17–18,** 19, 22
First Light (Preston), **Supp. XVII:** 18
First Light (Wagoner), **Supp. IX:** 330
"Firstling, The" (Davison), **Supp. XXVI:** 69
"First Love" (Welty), **IV:** 264; **Retro. Supp. I:** 347
First Love: A Lyric Sequence (Untermeyer), **Supp. XV:** 295
"First Love: A Quiz" (Stallings), **Supp. XXV:** 221, 233
First Lover and Other Stories, The (Boyle), **Supp. XXIV: 57–58**
First Man, The (O'Neill), **III:** 390
First Manifesto (McGrath), **Supp. X:** 115
"First Meditation" (Roethke), **III:** 545–546
"First Noni Daylight, The" (Harjo), **Supp. XII:** 219
"First Passover" (Longfellow), **II:** 500–501
"First Person Female" (Harrison), **Supp. VIII:** 40, 41, 48
"First Place, The" (Wagoner), **Supp. IX:** 328
First Poems (Buechner), **Supp. XII:** 45
First Poems (Merrill), **Supp. III Part 1:** 318–321, 323
First Poems 1946–1954 (Kinnell), **Supp. III Part 1:** 235, 238–239
"First Praise" (W. C. Williams), **Retro. Supp. I:** 413
First Principles (Spencer), **Supp. I Part 1:** 368
"First Reader" (Collins), **Supp. XXI:** 55–56
"First Ride and First Walk" (Goldbarth), **Supp. XII:** 182–183
"First Seeing the St. Lawrence River"(Kenny), **Supp. XXIII:** 152
"First Seven Years, The" (Malamud), **Supp. I Part 2:** 431
"First Sex" (Olds), **Supp. X:** 208
"First Shift" (Rash), **Supp. XXVII:** 218, 220
"First Snow" (Mosher), **Supp. XXII:** 211
"First Snow in Alsace" (Wilbur), **Supp. III Part 2:** 545, 546, 559
"First Song" (Kinnell), **Supp. III Part 1:** 239
"First Spade in the West, The" (Fiedler), **Supp. XIII:** 103
"First Steps" (McClatchy), **Supp. XII:** 256
First There Is the Need (Reznikoff), **Supp. XIV:** 291
"First Things First" (Auden), **Supp. II Part 1:** 13
"First Thought, Best Thought" (Ginsberg), **Supp. II Part 1:** 327
"First Time I Saw Paris, The" (Fante), **Supp. XI:** 174
"First Travels of Max" (Ransom), **III:** 490–491
"First Tycoon of Teen, The" (Wolfe), **Supp. III Part 2:** 572
"First Views of the Enemy" (Oates), **Supp. II Part 2:** 508
"First Wife, The" (Buck), **Supp. II Part 1:** 127
First Words before Spring (Untermeyer), **Supp. XV:** 310
"First World War" (White), **Supp. I Part 2:** 665
"Fish" (F. Barthelme), **Supp. XI:** 26
"Fish" (Levis), **Supp. XI:** 259–260
Fish, Stanley, **Supp. IV Part 1:** 48; **Supp. XIV:** 14, 15
"Fish, The" (Bishop), **Supp. XV:** 100,

102; **Supp. XXVII:** 228
"Fish, The" (Moore), **III:** 195, 197, 209, 211, 213–214; **Supp. XXI:** 26
"Fish, The" (Oliver), **Supp. VII:** 236
"Fish, The/Lago Chapala" (Everwine), **Supp. XV:** 82–83
"Fish and Shadow" (Pound), **III:** 466
"Fishboy" (Richard), **Supp. XIX:** 212–213
Fishboy: A Ghost's Story (Richard), **Supp. XIX:** 209, **213–220,** 221
Fishburne, Laurence, **Supp. VIII:** 345
"Fish Cannery" (Fante), **Supp. XI:** 167
Fisher, Alexander Metcalf, **Supp. I Part 2:** 582
Fisher, Alfred, **Retro. Supp. II:** 243
Fisher, Barbara, **Supp. XXII:** 206
Fisher, Craig, **Supp. V:** 125
Fisher, Dorothy Canfield, **Retro. Supp. I:** 21, 133; **Supp. II Part 1:** 117. See also Canfield, Dorothy
Fisher, Mary, **Supp. I Part 2:** 455
Fisher, M. F. K., **Supp. XVII: 81–93**
Fisher, Phillip, **Retro. Supp. I:** 39
Fisher, Rudolph, **Retro. Supp. I:** 200; **Supp. I Part 1:** 325; **Supp. X:** 139; **Supp. XIX: 65–80; Supp. XVI:** 143
Fisher, Vardis, **Supp. IV Part 2:** 598
Fisher King, The (Marshall), **Supp. XI:** 275–276, **288–290**
"Fisherman, The" (Merwin), **Supp. II Part 1:** 346
"Fisherman and His Wife, The" (Welty), **IV:** 266
"Fisherman from Chihuahua, The" (Connell), **Supp. XIV:** 86
"Fishing" (Harjo), **Supp. XII:** 227–228
"Fishing Idyll, A" (Mosher), **Supp. XXII:** 209
"Fish in the Stone, The" (Dove), **Supp. IV Part 1:** 245, 257
"Fish in the unruffled lakes" (Auden), **Supp. II Part 1:** 8–9
"Fish R Us" (Doty), **Supp. XI:** 135
Fisk, James, **I:** 4, 474
Fiske, John, **Supp. I Part 1:** 314; **Supp. I Part 2:** 493
Fisketjon, Gary, **Supp. XXIV:** 178
"Fit Against the Country, A" (Wright), **Supp. III Part 2:** 591–592, 601
Fitch, Clyde, **Supp. IV Part 2:** 573
Fitch, Elizabeth. See Taylor, Mrs. Edward (Elizabeth Fitch)
Fitch, James, **IV:** 147
Fitch, Noël Riley, **Supp. X:** 186, 187
"Fits" (Munro), **Supp. XXVII:** 189, 196
"Fitting, The" (Hull), **Supp. XXI:** 134, 135
Fit to Be Tied (Silver), **Supp. XXIV: 271–272**
Fitts, Dudley, **I:** 169, 173; **Supp. I Part 1:** 342, 345; **Supp. XIII:** 346; **Supp. XXII:** 281; **Supp. XXVI:** 65
FitzGerald, Edward, **Supp. I Part 2:** 416; **Supp. III Part 2:** 610
Fitzgerald, Ella, **Supp. XIII:** 132
Fitzgerald, F. Scott, **I:** 107, 117, 118, 123, 188, 221, 288, 289, 358, 367, 374–375, 382, 423, 476, 482, 487, 495, 509, 511; **II: 77–100,** 257, 263, 272, 283, 415, 416, 417–418, 420, 425, 427, 430, 431, 432, 433, 434, 436, 437, 450, 458–459, 482, 560; **III:** 2, 26, 35, 36, 37, 40, 44, 45, 69, 106, 244, 284, 334, 350–351, 453, 454, 471, 551, 552, 572; **IV:** 27, 49, 97, 101, 126, 140, 191, 222, 223, 287, 297, 427, 471; **Retro. Supp. I:** 1, 74, **97–120,** 178, 180, 186, 215, 359, 381; **Retro. Supp. II:** 257, 321, 326, 328; **Supp. I Part 1:** 196, 197; **Supp. I Part 2:** 622; **Supp. III Part 2:** 409, 411, 585; **Supp. IV Part 1:** 123, 197, 200, 203, 341; **Supp. IV Part 2:** 463, 468, 607, 689; **Supp. IX:** 15, 20, 55, 57–63, 199; **Supp. V:** 23, 95, 226, 251, 262, 276, 313; **Supp. VIII:** 101, 103, 106, 137; **Supp. X:** 225; **Supp. XI:** 65, 221, 334; **Supp. XII:** 42, 173, 295; **Supp. XIII:** 170, 263; **Supp. XV:** 135; **Supp. XVI:** 64, 75, 191, 192, 294; **Supp. XVIII:** 148, 246, 248, 251, 254; **Supp. XX: 74; Supp. XXI:** 262; **Supp. XXII:** 82, 92; **Supp. XXIII:** 68, 101, 174
Fitzgerald, Robert, **I:** 27–28; **III:** 338, 348; **Retro. Supp. II:** 179, 221, 222, 223, 228, 229; **Supp. IV Part 2:** 631; **Supp. XV:** 112, 249; **Supp. XXII:** 281; **Supp. XXIII:** 112
Fitzgerald, Zelda (Zelda Sayre), **I:** 482; **II:** 77, 79, 82–85, 88, 90–91, 93, 95; **Supp. IV Part 1:** 310; **Supp. IX: 55–73; Supp. X:** 172. See also Sayre, Zelda
"Fitzgerald's Tragic Sense" (Schorer), **Retro. Supp. I:** 115
"Fitzgerald: The Romance of Money" (Cowley), **Supp. II Part 1:** 143
Fitzpatrick, Catherine, **Supp. XXVII:** 270
5 Detroits (Levine), **Supp. V:** 178
Five Came Back (West), **IV:** 287
Five Corners (screenplay, Shanley), **Supp. XIV:** 316
"Five-Dollar Bill, The" (D. West as Mary Christopher), **Supp. XVIII:** 282
"Five Dollar Guy, The" (W. C. Williams), **Retro. Supp. I:** 423
Five Easy Pieces (film), **Supp. V:** 26
"Five Elephants" (Dove), **Supp. IV Part 1:** 244–245
"Five Fucks" (Lethem), **Supp. XVIII:** 139
Five Groups of Verse (Reznikoff), **Supp. XIV:** 279, 282
Five Hundred Hats of Bartholomew Cubbins, The (Geisel), **Supp. XVI:** 100
Five Hundred Scorpions (Hearon), **Supp. VIII:** 57, 65, **66**
Five Indiscretions (Ríos), **Supp. IV Part 2:** 545–547
Five Men and Pompey (Benét), **Supp. XI:** 43, 44
Five Plays (Hughes), **Retro. Supp. I:** 197, 209
"Five Poems About Poetry" (Oppen), **Supp. XXVI:** 233
"Five Psalms" (Jarman), **Supp. XVII:** 120
Five Temperaments (Kalstone), **Retro. Supp. II:** 40
5,000 Fingers of Dr. T, The (film), **Supp. XVI:** 103
Five Young American Poets, **I:** 170; **II:** 367
Fixer, The (Malamud), **Supp. I Part 2:** 428, 435, 445, 446–448, 450, 451
"Fixin' Road" (Boulton), **Supp. XXII:** 23
"Fix It (Winter)"(Hadas), **Supp. XXIII:** 115
Fjellestad, Danuta Zadworna, **Supp. XVI:** 150
Flaccus, Kimball, **Retro. Supp. I:** 136
Flacius, Matthias, **IV:** 163
"Flagellant's Song" (X. J. Kennedy), **Supp. XV:** 165
Flag for Sunrise, A (Stone), **Supp. V:** 301–304
Flagg, Fannie, **Supp. XXII:** 213–214
Flag Is Born, A (Hecht), **Supp. XXVII:** 94–95
Flag of Childhood, The: Poems from the Middle East (Nye, ed.), **Supp. XIII:** 280
"Flag of Summer" (Swenson), **Supp. IV Part 2:** 645
Flagons and Apples (Jeffers), **Supp. II Part 2:** 413, 414, 417–418
Flags in the Dust (Faulkner), **Retro. Supp. I:** 81, 82, 83, 86, 88; **Retro. Supp. III:** 77
Flame and Shadow (Teasdale), **Supp.**

XXVII: 284, 286, 292–295
Flamel, Nicolas, **Supp. XII:** 178
Flaming Corsage, The (W. Kennedy), **Supp. VII:** 133, 153–156
Flammarion, Camille, **Supp. I Part 1:** 260
Flanagan, John T., **Supp. I Part 2:** 464, 465, 468
Flanner, Janet, **Supp. XVI:** 195
"Flannery O'Connor: Poet to the Outcast" (Sister Rose Alice), **III:** 348
Flappers and Philosophers (Fitzgerald), **II:** 88; **Retro. Supp. I:** 103; **Supp. IX:** 56
"Flappers Were Her Daughters, The: The Liberated, Literary World of Gertrude Atherton" (Richey), **Supp. XXIV:** 30
Flash and Filigree (Southern), **Supp. XI:** 295, **296–297**
"Flashcards" (Dove), **Supp. IV Part 1:** 250
Flash Fiction: Seventy-two Very Short Stories (J. Thomas, ed.), **Supp. XVI:** 268
"Flash in the Pan" (Shaw), **Supp. XIX:** 245
Flats (Wurlitzer), **Supp. XXVI:** 26
"Flat Sky of Summer"(Balakian), **Supp. XXIII:** 25
Flatt, Lester, **Supp. V:** 335
"Flatted Third, The" (Huddle), **Supp. XXVI:** 153
Flaubert, Gustave, **I:** 66, 123, 130, 272, 312, 314, 315, 477, 504, 506, 513, 514; **II:** 182, 185, 194, 198–199, 205, 209, 230, 289, 311, 316, 319, 325, 337, 392, 401, 577, 594; **III:** 196, 207, 251, 315, 461, 467, 511, 564; **IV:** 4, 29, 31, 37, 40, 134, 285, 428; **Retro. Supp. I:** 5, 215, 218, 222, 225, 235, 287; **Retro. Supp. III:** 25; **Supp. III Part 2:** 411, 412; **Supp. XI:** 334; **Supp. XIV:** 87, 336; **Supp. XXIII:** 254; **Supp. XXVII:** 2
"Flavia and Her Artists" (Cather), **Retro. Supp. I:** 5; **Retro. Supp. III:** 21, 26
Flavoring of New England, The (Brooks), **I:** 253, 256
Flavor of Man, The (Toomer), **Supp. III Part 2:** 487
"Flaw, The" (Peacock), **Supp. XIX:** 206
Flawed Texts and Verbal Icons: Literary Authority in American Fiction (Parker), **Retro. Supp. III:** 267
Flaxman, Josiah, **Supp. I Part 2:** 716
"Flea, The" (Donne), **Supp. XVIII:** 307
"Flèche d'Or" (Merrill), **Supp. III Part 1:** 328
Flecker, James Elroy, **Supp. I Part 1:** 257
"Flee on Your Donkey" (Sexton), **Supp. II Part 2:** 683, 685
Fleming, Ian, **Supp. XI:** 307; **Supp. XX: 195; Supp. XXVI:** 126
Fleming, Rene, **Supp. XII:** 321
Fleming, Robert E., **Supp. XVII:** 155; **Supp. XXII:** 184
Flesch, Rudolf, **Supp. XVI:** 105, 106
Flesh and Blood (Cunningham), **Supp. XV: 63–65**
Flesh and Blood (play; Cunnigham and Gaitens), **Supp. XV:** 65
"Flesh and the Spirit, The" (Bradstreet), **Retro. Supp. III:** 9, 11
"Fleshbody" (Ammons), **Supp. VII:** 27
Fletcher, H. D., **II:** 517, 529
Fletcher, John, **Supp. IV Part 2:** 621
Fletcher, John Gould, **I:** 243; **II:** 517, 529; **III:** 458; **Supp. I Part 1:** 263; **Supp. I Part 2:** 422; **Supp. XV:** 298, 302, 306, 307, 308
Fletcher, Phineas, **Supp. I Part 1:** 369
Fletcher, Virginia. See Caldwell, Mrs. Erskine (Virginia Fletcher)
Fleurs du mal, Les (Beaudelaire; Millay and Dillon, trans.), **III:** 141–142
"Flight" (Bierds), **Supp. XVII:** 36
"Flight" (Updike), **IV:** 218, 222, 224; **Retro. Supp. I:** 318
Flight (White), **Supp. XVIII:** 127
"Flight, The" (Haines), **Supp. XII:** 204–205
"Flight, The" (Roethke), **III:** 537–538
Flight 115; or, Pas de Fumer sur la Piste (O'Hara and Berkson), **Supp. XXIII:** 217, 218
Flight among the Tombs (Hecht), **Supp. X:** 58, **71–74**
"Flight for Freedom" (McCoy), **Supp. XIII:** 170
"Flight from Byzantium" (Brodsky), **Supp. VIII:** 30–31
"Flight of Besey Lane, The" (Jewett), **Retro. Supp. II:** 139
Flight of the Rocket, The (Fitzgerald), **II:** 89
Flights of the Harvest-Mare (Bierds), **Supp. XVII:** 26–27
Flight to Canada (Reed), **Supp. X:** 240, **249–252**
Flinn, Mary, **Supp. XVII:** 110
Flint, F. S., **II:** 517; **III:** 459, 464, 465; **Retro. Supp. I:** 127; **Retro. Supp. III:** 95–96; **Supp. I Part 1:** 261, 262
Flint, Helen, **Supp. XXII:** 278
Flint, R. W., **Supp. XVI:** 47, 49, 57
"Flitting Flies" (X. J. Kennedy), **Supp. XV:** 166, **167**
Flivver King, The (Sinclair), **Supp. V:** 290
Floating House, The (Sanders), **Supp. XVI:** 269
Floating Light Bulb, The (Allen), **Supp. XV:** 2, 3, 13
Floating Opera, The (Barth), **I:** 121, 122–126, 127, 129, 130, 131
"Floating Poem, Unnumbered, The" (Rich), **Supp. I Part 2:** 572–573
"Floating Trees" (Wright), **Supp. XV:** 348
Flood (Matthews), **Supp. IX:** 154, **160–161**
Flood (Warren), **IV:** 252, 256–257
"Flood of Years, The" (Bryant), **Supp. I Part 1:** 159, 170, 171; **Supp. I Part 2:** 416
"Floor and the Ceiling, The" (W. J. Smith), **Supp. XIII:** 345, 346
"Floor Plans" (Komunyakaa), **Supp. XIII:** 114
"Floral Conversation" (Peacock), **Supp. XIX:** 200
"Floral Decorations for Bananas" (Stevens), **IV:** 8
Florentine Dagger, The: A Novel for Amateur Detectives (Hecht), **Supp. XXVII:** 89
Florida (Acker), **Supp. XII:** 5
"Florida" (Bishop), **Retro. Supp. II:** 43
"Florida Road Workers" (Hughes), **Retro. Supp. I:** 203
"Florida Sunday, A" (Lanier), **Supp. I Part 1:** 364, 366
Florist's Daughter, The (Hampl), **Supp. XXII:** 84, 85, 94, **95–98**
"Flossie Cabanis" (Masters), **Supp. I Part 2:** 461–462
"Flossy Frills Helps Out" (Wells), **Supp. XXVI:** 276
"Flounder" (Trethewey), **Supp. XXI:** 244, 245, 246, 251
Flow Chart (Ashbery), **Supp. VIII:** 275
"Flowchart" (Ashbery), **Supp. III Part 1:** 26
Flower, Dean, **Supp. XXII:** 205, 212
Flower, Fruit, and Thorn Pieces (Richter), **Supp. XVI:** 182
Flower-de-Luce (Longfellow), **II:** 490
Flower Drum Song (Rodgers and Hammerstein), **Supp. XXI:** 148

Flower Drum Song, The (Lee), **Supp. XXI:** 148
Flower Fables (Alcott), **Supp. I Part 1:** 33
"Flower-Fed Buffaloes, The" (Lindsay), **Supp. I Part 2:** 398
"Flower Garden" (Jackson), **Supp. IX:** 119
"Flower-gathering" (Frost), **II:** 153
Flower Herding on Mount Monadnock (Kinnell), **Supp. III Part 1:** 235, 239, 241–244
"Flower Herding on Mount Monadnock" (Kinnell), **Supp. III Part 1:** 242
"Flowering Death" (Ashbery), **Supp. III Part 1:** 22
"Flowering Dream, The" (McCullers), **II:** 591
"Flowering Judas" (Porter), **III:** 434, 435–436, 438, 441, 445, 446, 450–451
Flowering Judas and Other Stories (Porter), **III:** 433, 434
Flowering of New England, The (Brooks), **IV:** 171–172; **Supp. VIII:** 101
Flowering of the Rod (Doolittle), **Supp. I Part 1:** 272
Flowering Peach, The (Odets), **Supp. II Part 2:** 533, 547, 549–550
"Flowering Plum" (Glück), **Supp. V:** 82
Flowers, The (Gilb), **Supp. XXV:** 138
Flowers for Hitler (Cohen), **Supp. XXVII:** 54
"Flowers for Marjorie" (Welty), **IV:** 262
"Flowers of the Fallow" (Larcom), **Supp. XIII:** 143, 145–146
"Flowers Well if anybody" (Dickinson), **Retro. Supp. I:** 30
"Fluff and Mr. Ripley" (D. West), **Supp. XVIII:** 284
"Fly, The" (Kinnell), **Supp. III Part 1:** 249
"Fly, The" (Shapiro), **Supp. II Part 2:** 705
"Fly, The" (Simic), **Supp. VIII:** 278
Flye, Father James Harold, **I:** 25, 26, 35–36, 37, 42, 46; **IV:** 215
"Fly in Buttermilk, A" (Baldwin), **Retro. Supp. II:** 8
Flying at Night: Poems 1965–1985 (Kooser), **Supp. XIX:** 128
"Flying High" (Levertov), **Supp. III Part 1:** 284
"Flying Home" (Ellison), **Retro. Supp. II:** 117, **125–126; Supp. II Part 1:** 235, 238–239
"Flying Home" (Kinnell), **Supp. III Part 1:** 250
"Flying Home" and Other Stories (Ellison), **Retro. Supp. II:** 119, 124
"Flying Home from Utah" (Swenson), **Supp. IV Part 2:** 645
"Flying over Clouds" (Gioia), **Supp. XV:** 118
Flying Solo (Kriegel), **Supp. XXIV: 219–221**
"Flying to Hanoi" (Rukeyser), **Supp. VI:** 279
Flynn, Elizabeth Gurley, **Supp. XVIII:** 225
Flynn, Richard, **Supp. XVII:** 115; **Supp. XVIII:** 183
Fly-Truffler, The (Sobin), **Supp. XVI: 294–295,** 296
Foata, Anne, **Supp. XI:** 104
FOB (Hwang), **Supp. XXI:** 143, 144, 145, 146, **148–150**
Focillon, Henri, **IV:** 90
Focus (A. Miller), **III:** 150–151, 156; **Retro. Supp. III:** 173, 174–175
Foer, Jonathan Safran, **Supp. XII:** 169; **Supp. XX: 177; Supp. XXIV:** 131; **Supp. XXV:** 268
Foerster, Norman, **I:** 222; **Supp. I Part 2:** 423, 424; **Supp. IV Part 2:** 598
"Fog" (Sandburg), **III:** 586
"Fog Galleon" (Komunyakaa), **Supp. XIII:** 127
"Foggy and dripping" (Kooser), **Supp. XIX:** 125
"Foggy Lane, The" (Simpson), **Supp. IX:** 274
"Fog Man, The" (Boyle), **Supp. XX: 20**
"Fog Patterns" (Hecht), **Supp. XXVII:** 85
Folded Leaf, The (Maxwell), **Supp. III Part 1:** 62; **Supp. VIII: 159–162**
Folding Star, The (Hollinghurst), **Supp. XIII:** 52
Foley, Barbara, **Supp. XXVI:** 28
Foley, Jack, **Supp. X:** 125; **Supp. XV:** 112, 116; **Supp. XVII:** 77
Foley, Martha, **II:** 587; **Supp. XVI:** 225
Folk-Lore in the Old Testament (Frazer), **Supp. XX: 116–117**
Folks, Jeffrey, **Supp. XXVI:** 15
Folks from Dixie (Dunbar), **Supp. II Part 1:** 211–212
Folkways (Sumner), **III:** 102
Follain, Jean, **Supp. IX:** 152, 154
Follett, Wilson, **I:** 405; **Supp. XIII:** 173
Follower of Dusk (Salinas), **Supp. XIII:** 326
"Following the Bones" (W. V. Davis), **Supp. XXI:** 96
Following the Equator (Twain), **II:** 434; **IV:** 208; **Retro. Supp. III:** 255, 267
Follow Me Home (Hoffman), **Supp. XVIII:** 86
Folly (Minot), **Supp. VI:** 205, 208, **210–213**
Folly in the Forest (Wells), **Supp. XXVI:** 276
Folly of Others, The (Boyce), **Supp. XVII:** 100; **Supp. XXI:** 10
Folsom, Charles, **Supp. I Part 1:** 156
Folsom, Ed, **Retro. Supp. I:** 392
Folson, Marcia McClintock, **Retro. Supp. II:** 139
Fonda, Henry, **Supp. I Part 1:** 67; **Supp. IV Part 1:** 236
Fonda, Jane, **III:** 284; **Supp. XI:** 307
Fonda, Peter, **Supp. VIII:** 42; **Supp. XI:** 293, 308
"Fondled Memories" (Molesworth), **Supp. XIX:** 121–122
"Fond Memories of a Black Childhood" (D. West), **Supp. XVIII:** 289
Foner, Eric, **Supp. I Part 2:** 523
Fong and the Indians (Theroux), **Supp. VIII:** 314, 315, **316–317**
Fontanne, Lynn, **III:** 397
Food and Drink (Untermeyer), **Supp. XV:** 310
Food Chain, The (Silver), **Supp. XXIV:** 265, **270–271,** 274
Fool for Love (Shepard), **Supp. III Part 2:** 433, 447, 448
Fooling with Words (PBS special, Moyers), **Supp. XXIII:** 139
"Foolishness" (Pickering), **Supp. XXI:** 197
Fools (Simon), **Supp. IV Part 2:** 584–585
Fools Crow (Welch), **Supp. XXIV:** 257
Fool's Progress, The: An Honest Novel (Abbey), **Supp. XIII:** 4, **13–15**
"Football Rebellion in Backwoods Georgia, A" (Andrews), **Supp. XXVI:** 3, 4
Foot Book, The (Geisel), **Supp. XVI:** 108
Foote, Bud, **Supp. XXVI:** 5
Foote, Horton, **Supp. I Part 1:** 281; **Supp. VIII:** 128, 129
Foote, Mary Hallock, **Retro. Supp. II:** 72; **Supp. IV Part 2:** 611
Foote, Roxanna. See Beecher, Mrs. Lyman (Roxanna Foote)
Foote, Samuel, **Supp. I Part 2:** 584
Foote, Stephanie, **Retro. Supp. II:** 139
"Foot Fault" (pseudonym). See

Thurber, James
Footing on This Earth, A (Hay), **Supp. XIV:** 125, 126, 130
"Footing up a Total" (A. Lowell), **II:** 528
"Footnote to Howl" (Ginsberg), **Supp. II Part 1:** 316–317
"Footnote to Weather Forecasts, A" (Brodsky), **Supp. VIII:** 32
Footprints (Hearon), **Supp. VIII: 69–70**
Footprints (Levertov), **Supp. III Part 1:** 272, 281
"Footsteps of Angels" (Longfellow), **II:** 496
"For A, at Fourteen" (Weigl), **Supp. XIX:** 287
For a Bitter Season: New and Selected Poems (Garrett), **Supp. VII:** 99–100
"For a Dead Kitten" (Hay), **Supp. XIV:** 119–120
"For a Dead Lady" (Robinson), **III:** 508, 513, 517
"For a Ghost Who Once Placed Bets in the Park" (Levis), **Supp. XI:** 265
"Foraging" (H. Johnson), **Supp. XXVI:** 172
"For a Lamb" (Eberhart), **I:** 523, 530, 531
"For All" (Snyder), **Supp. VIII:** 304
"For All Tuesday Travelers" (Cisneros), **Supp. VII:** 67–68
"For a Lost Child" (Stafford), **Supp. XI:** 329
"For a Marriage" (Bogan), **Supp. III Part 1:** 52
"For an Emigrant" (Jarrell), **II:** 371
"For Anna Akmatova" (R. Lowell), **II:** 544
"For Anna Mae Pictou Aquash, Whose Spirit Is Present Here and in the Dappled Stars" (Harjo), **Supp. XII:** 225
"For Anne, at a Little Distance" (Haines), **Supp. XII:** 207
"For Annie" (Poe), **III:** 427; **Retro. Supp. II:** 263
"For an Old Friend Encountered Unexpectedly" (Espaillat), **Supp. XXI:** 111–112
"For a Southern Man" (Cisneros), **Supp. VII:** 67
"For Bailey" (Angelou), **Supp. IV Part 1:** 15
Forbes, Genevieve, **Supp. XXV:** 196
Forbes, Malcolm, **Supp. IV Part 1:** 94
"Forbidden, The" (Glück), **Supp. XIV:** 269
"Forbidden Magic" (Howard), **Supp. XXVII:** 118
"For Bill Nestrick (1940–96)" (Bidart), **Supp. XV:** 35
For Bread Alone (Choukri), **Supp. IV Part 1:** 92
"Force" (Di Piero), **Supp. XIX:** 35–36, 42, 44
Force of Desire, The (Bronk), **Supp. XXI:** 31, 32
Force of Evil (film, Polonsky), **Supp. XXI:** 261, 272, 275
Force of Spirit, The (Sanders), **Supp. XVI:** 277–278
Forché, Carolyn, **Supp. IV Part 1:** 208; **Supp. XIX:** 193
Ford, Arthur, **Supp. IV Part 1:** 140
Ford, Ford Madox, **I:** 288, 405, 409, 417, 421, 423; **II:** 58, 144, 198, 257, 263, 265, 517, 536; **III:** 458, 464–465, 470–471, 472, 476; **IV:** 27, 126, 261; **Retro. Supp. I:** 127, 177, 178, 186, 231, 286–287, 418; **Supp. II Part 1:** 107; **Supp. III Part 2:** 617; **Supp. VIII:** 107; **Supp. XIV:** 3
Ford, Harrison, **Supp. VIII:** 323
Ford, Harry, **Supp. V:** 179; **Supp. XIII:** 76
Ford, Henry, **I:** 295, 480–481; **III:** 292, 293; **Supp. I Part 1:** 21; **Supp. I Part 2:** 644; **Supp. III Part 2:** 612, 613; **Supp. IV Part 1:** 223; **Supp. V:** 290
Ford, John, **Supp. I Part 2:** 422; **Supp. III Part 2:** 619; **Supp. XVIII:** 247
Ford, Mark, **Supp. XXIII:** 220
Ford, Mary K., **Supp. XX: 239**
Ford, Nick Aaron, **Retro. Supp. III:** 140
Ford, Richard, **Supp. IV Part 1:** 342; **Supp. V:** 22, **57–75; Supp. XXIV:** 97
Ford, Webster (pseudonym). See Masters, Edgar Lee
"Fording and Dread" (Harrison), **Supp. VIII:** 41
"Ford Madox Ford" (R. Lowell), **II:** 547; **Retro. Supp. II:** 188
"For Dudley" (Wilbur), **Supp. III Part 2:** 558
Fordyce, David, **II:** 113
For Eager Lovers (Taggard), **Supp. XXII: 274–275**
Foregone Conclusion, A (Howells), **II:** 278–279, 282
"Foreign Affairs" (Kunitz), **Supp. III Part 1:** 265
Foreign Correspondent (screenplay, Hecht), **Supp. XXVII:** 93
"Foreigner, A" (Bynner), **Supp. XV:** 46
"Foreigner, The" (Jewett), **II:** 409–410; **Retro. Supp. II:** 133, 142
"Foreigners" (Jarman), **Supp. XVII:** 113
"Foreign Language, The" (Franzen), **Supp. XX: 84**
"Foreign Shores" (Salter), **Supp. IX:** 260
Forensic and the Navigators (Shepard), **Supp. III Part 2:** 439
Forerunner, The (Boyce), **Supp. XXI:** 2, 4, **10–11**
Forerunner, The: His Parables and Poems (Gibran), **Supp. XX: 115, 118–119, 119**
Foreseeable Future, The (Price), **Supp. VI:** 265
Foreseeable Futures (Matthews), **Supp. IX:** 155, **163,** 169
Foresman, Rebecca, **Supp. XXIV:** 171
"For Esmé with Love and Squalor" (Salinger), **III:** 560
"Forest" (Simic), **Supp. VIII:** 273
Forest, Jean-Claude, **Supp. XI:** 307
Forester's Letters (Paine), **Supp. I Part 2:** 508
"Forest Hymn, A" (Bryant), **Supp. I Part 1:** 156, 162, 163, 164, 165, 170
"Forest in the Seeds, The" (Kingsolver), **Supp. VII:** 203
Forest of the South, The (Gordon), **II:** 197
"Forest of the South, The" (Gordon), **II:** 199, 201
Forest without Leaves (Adams and Haines), **Supp. XII:** 209
"Forever, Said the Duck" (Lethem), **Supp. XVIII:** 139
"Forever and the Earth" (Bradbury), **Supp. IV Part 1:** 102
"Forever in That Year" (Carruth), **Supp. XVI:** 51
"Forever"(Thompson), **Supp. XXIII:** 296
"Forever Young" (Jarman and R. McDowell), **Supp. XVII:** 111
"For Fathers of Girls" (Dunn), **Supp. XI:** 146
For Frank O'Hara's Birthday (Notley), **Supp. XXII:** 224, 227
"For/From Lew" (Snyder), **Supp. VIII:** 303
"For Garrison Keillor, Fantasy Is a Lot More Fun then Reality" (Letofsky), **Supp. XVI:** 167
"For George Santayana" (R. Lowell), **II:** 547
"Forgetfulness" (Collins), **Supp. XXI:** 58

"Forgiveness" (Peacock), **Supp. XIX:** 200
Forgotten Helper, The: A Story for Children (Moore), **Supp. X:** 175
"Forgotten in an Old Notebook" (F. Wright), **Supp. XVII:** 244
Forgotten Village, The (Steinbeck), **IV:** 51
"For Grace, After a party"(O'Hara), **Supp. XXIII:** 214
"For Grizzel McNaught (1709–1792)" (A. Finch), **Supp. XVII:** 72
Forgue, Guy J., **III:** 118, 119
For Her Dark Skin (Everett), **Supp. XVIII:** 56, 60
"FOR HETTIE" (Baraka), **Supp. II Part 1:** 32
"FOR HETTIE IN HER FIFTH MONTH" (Baraka), **Supp. II Part 1:** 32, 38
"For Homer" (Corso), **Supp. XII:** 135
"For I'm the Boy" (Barthelme), **Supp. IV Part 1:** 47
"For James Dean"(O'Hara), **Supp. XXIII:** 214
"For Janice and Kenneth to Voyage"(O'Hara), **Supp. XXIII:** 214
"For Jeff" (Kooser), **Supp. XIX:** 125
"For Jessica, My Daughter" (Strand), **Supp. IV Part 2:** 629
"For John, Who Begs Me not to Enquire Further" (Sexton), **Supp. II Part 2:** 676
"For Johnny Pole on the Forgotten Beach" (Sexton), **Supp. II Part 2:** 675
"For Joy to Leave Upon" (Ortiz), **Supp. IV Part 2:** 508
"For Judy, Whose Husband Is Undergoing Surgery"(Crooker), **Supp. XXIII:** 61
"Fork" (Simic), **Supp. VIII:** 275
"For Karl Shapiro, Having Gone Back to the Sonnet" (Kooser), **Supp. XIX:** 118
"Forked Tongue" (Davison), **Supp. XXVI:** 71
"Forky" (Dubus III), **Supp. XXIV:** 99, 101
"For Lack of a Treaty" (Davison), **Supp. XXVI:** 79
For Lancelot Andrewes (T. S. Eliot), **Retro. Supp. I:** 64; **Retro. Supp. III:** 58
For Lizzie and Harriet (R. Lowell), **Retro. Supp. II:** 183, 186, 190
"Forlorn Hope of Sidney Lanier, The" (Leary), **Supp. I Part 1:** 373
For Love (Creeley), **Supp. IV Part 1:** 139, 140, 142–145, 147–149, 150, 154
"For Love" (Creeley), **Supp. IV Part 1:** 145
For Love (Miller), **Supp. XII: 297–299,** 299
For Love of Imabelle (C. Himes), **Supp. XVI:** 135, 143, 144
Form, Cycle, Infinity: Landscape Imagery in the Poetry of Robert Frost and George Seferis (Hadas), **Supp. XXIII: 121–122**
"Formal Elegy" (Berryman), **I:** 170
Formal Feeling Comes, A (A. Finch, ed.), **Supp. XVII: 71–72**
"Formalist Criticism: Its Principles and Limits" (Burke), **I:** 282
Forman, Henry James, **Supp. XXIV:** 29, 30
Forman, Milos, **Supp. IV Part 1:** 236
"Form and Function of the Novel, The" (Goldbarth), **Supp. XII:** 183
"For Marse Chouchoute" (Chopin), **Retro. Supp. II:** 60
"For Mary Ann Youngren" (Bidart), **Supp. XV:** 29
"Format and Form" (A. Rich), **Supp. XVII:** 74
"Formation of a Separatist, I" (Howe), **Supp. IV Part 2:** 427
"Form Is Emptiness" (Baraka), **Supp. II Part 1:** 51
"For Mr. Death Who Stands with His Door Open" (Sexton), **Supp. II Part 2:** 695
Forms of Discovery (Winters), **Supp. II Part 2:** 812, 813
Forms of Fiction, The (Gardner and Dunlap), **Supp. VI:** 64
"Forms of Love, The" (Oppen), **Supp. XXVI:** 225
"For My Children" (Karr), **Supp. XI:** 254
"For My Daughter" (Kees), **Supp. XV:** 141, 147
"For My Daughter" (Olds), **Supp. X:** 206
"For My Former Wife, Watching TV, in the Past" (Kooser), **Supp. XIX:** 120
"For My Lover, Returning to His Wife" (Sexton), **Supp. II Part 2:** 688
Fornés, Maria Irene, **Supp. XXI:** 144; **Supp. XXIII:** 194, 200
"For Night to Come" (Stern), **Supp. IX:** 292
"For Once, Then, Something" (Frost), **II:** 156–157; **Retro. Supp. I:** 126, 133, 134; **Retro. Supp. III:** 101, 102
"For Peg: A Remnant of Song Still Distantly Sounding" (Carruth), **Supp. XVI:** 54
"For Pot-Boiling" (Hay), **Supp. XIV:** 128
"For Radicals" (Bourne), **I:** 221
"For Rainer Gerhardt" (Creeley), **Supp. IV Part 1:** 142–143, 147
Forrestal, James, **I:** 491; **Supp. I Part 2:** 489
Forrester, Fanny, **Supp. XVIII:** 13
Forrey, Carolyn, **Supp. XXIV:** 30
"For Richard After All" (Kingsolver), **Supp. VII:** 208
"For Sacco and Vanzetti" (Kingsolver), **Supp. VII:** 208
"Forsaken Brother, The"(J. Schoolcraft), **Supp. XXIII:** 235
"Forsaken Merman" (Arnold), **Supp. I Part 2:** 529
"Forsaking the Promised Land" (diss. Collins), **Supp. XXVI:** 12
"For S.F.S. 1875–1962" (J. W. Miller), **Supp. XX: 166**
For Spacious Skies (Buck), **Supp. II Part 1:** 131
Forster, E. M., **I:** 292; **IV:** 201; **Retro. Supp. I:** 59, 232; **Supp. III Part 2:** 503; **Supp. IX:** 128; **Supp. V:** 258; **Supp. VIII:** 155, 171; **Supp. XII:** 79, 81; **Supp. XIV:** 159, 160, 163; **Supp. XV:** 62; **Supp. XVI:** 236; **Supp. XVIII:** 143; **Supp. XX: 229, 235, 239, 240; Supp. XXI:** 233
Forster, John, **II:** 315
Fort, Paul, **II:** 518, 528, 529; **Retro. Supp. I:** 55
"For the Ahkoond" (Bierce), **I:** 209
For the Body (Nelson), **Supp. XVIII:** 173
For the Century's End: Poems 1990–1999 (Haines), **Supp. XII: 211–213**
"For the Chinese New Year and Bill Berkson"(O'Hara), **Supp. XXIII:** 218
"For the Dedication of the New City Library, Boston" (Holmes), **Supp. I Part 1:** 308
"For the Fallen" (Levine), **Supp. V:** 188
For the Health of the Land: Previously Unpublished Essays and Other Writings (Leopold), **Supp. XIV:** 183
"For the Lady in the Black Raincoat Who Slept Through an Entire Poetry Reading" (Espaillat), **Supp. XXI:** 108
"For the Last Wolverine" (Dickey), **Supp. IV Part 1:** 182
"For the Losers of Things" (Stallings),

Supp. XXV: 222
"For the Lovers of the Absolute" (Simic), **Supp. VIII:** 278–279
"For the Man Cutting the Grass" (Oliver), **Supp. VII:** 235
"For the Marriage of Faustus and Helen" (H. Crane), **I:** 395–396, 399, 402; **Retro. Supp. II:** 78–79, 82; **Retro. Supp. III:** 47–48
"For the Meeting of the National Sanitary Association, 1860" (Holmes), **Supp. I Part 1:** 307
For the New Intellectual (Rand), **Supp. IV Part 2:** 521, 526–527, 527, 532
"For the New Railway Station in Rome" (Wilbur), **Supp. III Part 2:** 554
"For the Night" (Kenyon), **Supp. VII:** 163
"For Theodore Roethke: 1908–1963" (R. Lowell), **II:** 554
"For the Poem Patterson" (W. C. Williams), **Retro. Supp. I:** 424
"For the Poets of Chile" (Levine), **Supp. V:** 188
"FOR THE REVOLUTIONARY OUTBURST BY BLACK PEOPLE" (Baraka), **Supp. II Part 1:** 55
"For the Sleepless" (Dunn), **Supp. XI:** 145
For the Time Being (Auden), **Supp. II Part 1:** 2, 17, 18
For the Time Being (Dillard), **Supp. VI:** 23, 27, 29, 32, **34–35**
"For the Twentieth Century" (Bidart), **Supp. XV:** 35
For the Union Dead (R. Lowell), **II:** 543, 550–551, 554, 555; **Retro. Supp. II:** 181, 182, 186, 189; **Supp. X:** 53
"For the Union Dead" (R. Lowell), **II:** 551; **Retro. Supp. II:** 189
"For the Walking Dead" (Komunyakaa), **Supp. XIII:** 121
"For the West" (Snyder), **Supp. VIII:** 299
"For the Word Is Flesh" (Kunitz), **Supp. III Part 1:** 262–264
"Fortress, The" (Glück), **Supp. V:** 82
"Fortress, The" (Sexton), **Supp. II Part 2:** 682
Fortress of Solitude, The (Lethem), **Supp. XVIII:** 135, 136, **145–148,** 150
"Fort Robinson" (Kooser), **Supp. XIX:** 120
"Fortunate Traveler" (Hull), **Supp. XXI:** 140
Fortune, T. Thomas, **Supp. II Part 1:** 159
Fortune's Bones: The Manumission Requiem (Nelson), **Supp. XVIII:** 171, 172–173, 182–183
Fortune's Daughter (Hoffman), **Supp. X:** 77, 85
"Fortune Spill, The" (Nelson), **Supp. XVIII:** 175
45 Mercy Street (Sexton), **Supp. II Part 2:** 694, 695, 697
Forty Poems Touching on Recent American History (Bly, ed.), **Supp. IV Part 1:** 61
42nd Parallel, The (Dos Passos), **I:** 482, 484–485
Forty Stories (Barthelme), **Supp. IV Part 1:** 47, 49, 53, 54
For Whom the Bell Tolls (Hemingway), **II:** 249, 254–255, 261; **III:** 18, 363; **Retro. Supp. I:** 115, 176–177, 178, **184,** 187; **Supp. XVII:** 229; **Supp. XXV:** 146
For Whom the Southern Belle Tolls (Durang), **Supp. XXIV:** 113, 118, 125
Foscolo, Ugo, **II:** 543
Foss, Sam Walter, **Supp. II Part 1:** 197
"Fossils, The" (Kinnell), **Supp. III Part 1:** 244
Foster, Edward, **Supp. IV Part 2:** 431, 434; **Supp. XVI:** 281, 293; **Supp. XXI:** 33
Foster, Edward Halsey, **Supp. XII:** 120, 129, 130, 135; **Supp. XVIII:** 265, 268
Foster, Emily, **II:** 309
Foster, Frances Smith, **Supp. XX: 287**
Foster, Hannah Webster, **Supp. XV:** 234; **Supp. XXV: 35–48**
Foster, John Wilson, **Supp. XIII:** 32–33
Foster, Michael K., **Supp. XXVI:** 83
Foster, Phil, **Supp. IV Part 2:** 574
Foster, Richard, **Supp. XV:** 269
Foster, Stephen, **Supp. I Part 1:** 100–101; **Supp. I Part 2:** 699
Foucault, Michel, **Supp. VIII:** 5; **Supp. XII:** 98; **Supp. XV:** 344; **Supp. XVI:** 285
Foulke, Robert, **Supp. XXV:** 217
"Founder, The" (Stern), **Supp. IX:** 297
Founding of Harvard College, The (Morison), **Supp. I Part 2:** 485
"Foundry Workers" (Bodenheim), **Supp. XXV:** 22
"Fountain, The" (Bryant), **Supp. I Part 1:** 157, 165, 166, 168
Fountain, The (O'Neill), **III:** 391
Fountain and Other Poems, The (Bryant), **Supp. I Part 1:** 157
Fountainhead, The (film), **Supp. IV Part 2:** 524
Fountainhead, The (Rand), **Supp. IV Part 2:** 517, 521–523, 525, 531; **Supp. XXIV:** 281
Fountainhead, The: A Fiftieth Anniversary Celebration (Cox), **Supp. IV Part 2:** 523
"Fountain Piece" (Swenson), **Supp. IV Part 2:** 641
4-H Club (Shepard), **Supp. III Part 2:** 439
"Four Ages of Man, The" (Bradstreet), **Retro. Supp. III:** 1, 6; **Supp. I Part 1:** 111, 115
Four American Indian Literary Masters (Velie), **Supp. IV Part 2:** 486
"Four Angers"(Hadas), **Supp. XXIII:** 115
"Four Beasts in One; the Homo Cameleopard" (Poe), **III:** 425
Four Black Revolutionary Plays (Baraka), **Supp. II Part 1:** 45; **Supp. VIII:** 330
"Four Brothers" (Di Piero), **Supp. XIX:** 37
"Four Brothers, The" (Sandburg), **III:** 585
"Four Dancers at an Irish Wedding" (Gallagher), **Supp. XXIV:** 168, 170
Four Days (screenplay, P. Benedict), **Supp. XXIII:** 35
Four Dogs and a Bone and the Wild Goose (Shanley), **Supp. XIV:** 316, **328–329**
"Four Elements, The" (Bradstreet), **Retro. Supp. III:** 6
"Four Evangelists, The" (Komunyakaa), **Supp. XIII:** 131
"Four for Sir John Davies" (Roethke), **III:** 540, 541
Four for Trane (Mackey), **Supp. XXVII:** 153
"Four Girls, The" (Alvarez), **Supp. VII:** 7
"Four Horse Songs" (Harjo), **Supp. XII:** 220
"Four Humours, The" (Bradstreet), **Retro. Supp. III:** 5, 6
"400-Meter Free Style" (Kumin), **Supp. IV Part 2:** 442
"400-Pound CEO, The" (Saunders), **Supp. XIX:** 225
Fourier, Charles, **II:** 342
"Four in a Family" (Rukeyser), **Supp. VI:** 272
Four in Hand: A Quartet of Novels (Warner), **Supp. VIII:** 164
"Four Lakes' Days" (Eberhart), **I:** 525

"Four Mad Studies" (Di Piero), **Supp. XIX:** 37
"Four Meetings" (James), **II:** 327
Four Million, The (O. Henry), **Supp. II Part 1:** 394, 408
"Four Monarchies, The" (Bradstreet), **Retro. Supp. III:** 4, 6–7; **Supp. I Part 1:** 105, 106, 116
"Four Mountain Wolves" (Silko), **Supp. IV Part 2:** 561
Four of a Kind (Marquand), **III:** 54, 55
"Four of the Horsemen (Hypertense and Stroke, Coronary Occlusion and Cerebral Insult)" (Karr), **Supp. XI:** 250
"Four Poems" (Bishop), **Supp. I Part 1:** 92
"Four Poems at the End of Summer"(Hadas), **Supp. XXIII:** 117
"Four Preludes on Playthings of the Wind" (Sandburg), **III:** 586
Four Quartets (T. S. Eliot), **I:** 570, 576, 580–582, 585, 587; **II:** 537; **III:** 539; **Retro. Supp. I:** 66, 67; **Retro. Supp. III:** 58, 65, 65–68, 69; **Supp. II Part 1:** 1; **Supp. IV Part 1:** 284; **Supp. V:** 343, 344; **Supp. VIII:** 182, 195; **Supp. XIII:** 344; **Supp. XIV:** 167; **Supp. XV:** 216, 260, 266
Four Saints in Three Acts (Stein), **IV:** 30, 31, 33, 43, 44–45
"Four Seasons, The" (Bradstreet), **Retro. Supp. III:** 6, 9, 10, 12; **Supp. I Part 1:** 112–113
Four Seasons of Success, The (Schulberg), **Supp. XVIII:** 254
"Four Sides of One Story" (Updike), **Retro. Supp. I:** 328
"Four Skinny Trees" (Cisneros), **Supp. VII:** 64
"14: In A Dark Wood: Wood Thrushes" (Oliver), **Supp. VII:** 244
"14 Men Stage Head Winter 1624/ 25" (Olson), **Supp. II Part 2:** 574
14 Stories (Dixon), **Supp. XII:** 141, **145–147**
Fourteen Hundred Thousand (Shepard), **Supp. III Part 2:** 439
Fourteen Sisters of Emilio Montez O'Brien, The (Hijuelos), **Supp. VIII: 82–85**
Fourteen Stories (Buck), **Supp. II Part 1:** 126
"Fourteenth Ward, The" (H. Miller), **III:** 175
Fourth Book of Peace, The (Kingston), **Supp. V:** 173
"Fourth Down" (Marquand), **III:** 56
Fourth Group of Verse, A (Reznikoff), **Supp. XIV:** 282, 284
"Fourth of July in Maine" (R. Lowell), **II:** 535, 552–553
Fourth Wall, The (Gurney), **Supp. V:** 109–110
Fowler, Douglas, **Supp. IV Part 1:** 226, 227
Fowler, Gene, **Supp. VIII:** 290
Fowler, Henry Watson, **Supp. I Part 2:** 660
Fowler, Karen Joy, **Supp. XXII:** 49
Fowler, Singrid, **Supp. VIII:** 249, 258
Fowler, Virginia C., **Supp. VIII:** 224
Fox, Alan, **Supp. XIII:** 120
Fox, Dixon Ryan, **I:** 337
Fox, Joe, **Supp. IX:** 259, 261
Fox, John, **Supp. XIII:** 166; **Supp. XXII:** 36
Fox, Linda C., **Supp. XIII:** 217–218
Fox, Paula, **Supp. XX: 91**
Fox, Ruth, **Supp. I Part 2:** 619
"Fox, The" (Levine), **Supp. V:** 181, 189
Fox-Genovese, Elizabeth, **Supp. IV Part 1:** 286; **Supp. XXII:** 190, 192, 200
Fox in Socks (Geisel), **Supp. XVI:** 108, 112
"Fox Night" (Jarman), **Supp. XVII:** 120
Fox of Peapack, The (White), **Supp. I Part 2:** 676, 677–678
"Fox of Peapack, The" (White), **Supp. I Part 2:** 677
Fox: Poems 1998–2000 (Rich), **Retro. Supp. III:** 252
"Fox Point Health Clinic, 1974" (Halliday), **Supp. XIX:** 89, 93
Fox's Earth (Siddons), **Supp. XXII:** 239
Foye, Raymond, **Supp. XIV:** 150
Fradkin, Lori, **Supp. XIX:** 52
Fraenkel, Michael, **III:** 178, 183
"Fragging" (Komunyakaa), **Supp. XIII:** 123
Fragile Beauty, A: John Nichols' Milagro Country: Text and Photographs from His Life and Work (Nichols), **Supp. XIII:** 268
"Fragility" (Shields), **Supp. VII:** 318
"Fragment" (A. Lowell), **II:** 516
"Fragment" (Ashbery), **Supp. III Part 1:** 11, 13, 14, 19, 20
"Fragment" (Ortiz), **Supp. IV Part 2:** 507
"Fragment of a Meditation" (Tate), **IV:** 129
"Fragment of an Agon" (Eliot), **I:** 579–580
"Fragment of a Prologue" (Eliot), **I:** 579–580
"Fragment of New York, 1929" (Eberhart), **I:** 536–537
"Fragments" (Emerson), **II:** 19
"Fragments for Fall" (Salinas), **Supp. XIII:** 320–321
"Fragments of a Hologram Rose" (W. Gibson), **Supp. XVI:** 122, 123, 128
"Fragments of a Liquidation" (Howe), **Supp. IV Part 2:** 426
"Fragments: On Dentistry" (Monson), **Supp. XXIV:** 236
Fragonard, Jean Honoré, **III:** 275; **IV:** 79
Fraiman, Susan, **Supp. IV Part 1:** 324
"Frame" (Rich), **Retro. Supp. III:** 249
"Frame for Poetry, A" (W. J. Smith), **Supp. XIII:** 333
France, Anatole, **IV:** 444; **Supp. I Part 2:** 631; **Supp. XIV:** 79
France and England in North America (Parkman), **Supp. II Part 2:** 596, 600–605, 607, 613–614
Franchere, Hoyt C., **II:** 131
Franchiser, The (Elkin), **Supp. VI: 51–52,** 58
Francini, Antonella, **Supp. XXVI:** 169
Franciosi, Robert, **Supp. XIV:** 283
Francis, Lee, **Supp. IV Part 2:** 499
Francis, Lesley Lee, **Retro. Supp. III:** 95, 107
Francis, Richard, **Supp. XV:** 121
Francis, Robert, **Supp. IX: 75–92**
Francis of Assisi, Saint, **III:** 543; **IV:** 69, 375, 410; **Supp. I Part 2:** 394, 397, 441, 442, 443
Franco, Francisco, **II:** 261
Franco, Harry (pseudonym). See Briggs, Charles Frederick
Franconia (Fraser), **Retro. Supp. I:** 136
"Franconia" tales (Abbott), **Supp. I Part 1:** 38
Frank, Anne, **Supp. X:** 149; **Supp. XVII:** 39
Frank, Frederick S., **Retro. Supp. II:** 273
Frank, Harriet, Jr., **Supp. XXV:** 102
Frank, James M., **Supp. XIV:** 1
Frank, Jerome, **Supp. I Part 2:** 645
Frank, Joseph, **II:** 587
Frank, Mary, **Supp. X:** 213
Frank, Robert, **Supp. XI:** 295; **Supp. XII:** 127; **Supp. XIV:** 150
Frank, Sheldon, **Supp. XXII:** 210
Frank, Waldo, **I:** 106, 109, 117, 229, 236, 245, 259, 400; **Retro. Supp. II:** 77, 79, 83; **Retro. Supp. III:** 47, 49, 50; **Supp. IX:** 308, 309, 311,

320; **Supp. XV:** 298; **Supp. XX: 67–82**
Frank, W. L., Jr., **Supp. XVIII:** 77
Frankel, Charles, **III:** 291
Frankel, Haskel, **Supp. I Part 2:** 448
Frankenberg, Lloyd, **I:** 436, 437, 445, 446; **III:** 194
Frankenheimer, John, **Supp. XI:** 343
Frankenstein (film), **Supp. IV Part 1:** 104; **Supp. XVII:** 57
Frankenstein (Gardner), **Supp. VI:** 72
Frankenstein (Shelley), **Supp. XII:** 79
Frankfurter, Felix, **I:** 489
"Frankie" (Keillor), **Supp. XVI:** 167
Frankie and Johnnie (Levin), **Supp. XXVII:** 134, 139
Frankie and Johnny (film), **Supp. XIII:** 206
Frankie and Johnny in the Clair de Lune (McNally), **Supp. XIII: 200,** 201
Franklin, Benjamin, **II:** 6, 8, 92, **101–125,** 127, 295, 296, 302, 306; **III:** 74, 90; **IV:** 73, 193; **Retro. Supp. III:** 112, 255; **Supp. I Part 1:** 306; **Supp. I Part 2:** 411, 503, 504, 506, 507, 510, 516, 518, 522, 524, 579, 639; **Supp. VIII:** 202, 205; **Supp. XIII:** 150; **Supp. XIV:** 306; **Supp. XVIII:** 12; **Supp. XX: 284; Supp. XXIV:** 224; **Supp. XXVI:** 83, 84
Franklin, Cynthia, **Supp. IV Part 1:** 332
Franklin, Ruth, **Supp. XVI:** 160
Franklin, R. W., **Retro. Supp. I:** 29, 41, 43, 47
Franklin, Sarah, **II:** 122
Franklin, Temple, **II:** 122
Franklin, Walt, **Supp. XXIII:** 54
Franklin, Wayne, **Supp. XXII:** 205
Franklin, William, **II:** 122; **Supp. I Part 2:** 504
Franklin Evans (Whitman), **Retro. Supp. I:** 393; **Retro. Supp. III:** 300
"Frank O'Connor and The New Yorker" (Maxwell), **Supp. VIII:** 172
Frank O'Hara: Poet Among Painters (Perloff), **Supp. XXIII:** 210
Franks, Lucinda, **Supp. XIII:** 12
"Frank Sinatra Has a Cold" (Talese), **Supp. XVII:** 203
"Frank Stanford of the Mulberry Family: An Arkansas Epilogue" (Wright), **Supp. XV:** 339–340
"Franny" (Salinger), **III:** 564, 565–566
Franny and Zooey (Salinger), **III:** 552, 564–567; **IV:** 216; **Supp. XIII:** 263
Franscell, Ron, **Supp. XXII:** 206, 216
Franzen, Jonathan, **Retro. Supp. II:** 279; **Supp. XIX:** 54; **Supp. XX: 83–97; Supp. XXII:** 255; **Supp. XXIV:** 131
Fraser, G. S., **Supp. XII:** 128; **Supp. XIV:** 162
Fraser, Joe, **III:** 46
Fraser, Marjorie Frost, **Retro. Supp. I:** 136
Frayn, Michael, **Supp. IV Part 2:** 582
Frazee, E. S., **Supp. I Part 2:** 381
Frazee, Esther Catherine. See Lindsay, Mrs. Vachel Thomas (Esther Catherine Frazee)
Frazer, Sir James G., **I:** 135; **II:** 204; **III:** 6–7; **IV:** 70; **Retro. Supp. I:** 80; **Supp. I Part 1:** 18; **Supp. I Part 2:** 541; **Supp. XX: 117**
Frazier, Ian, **Supp. VIII:** 272
Frazier, Kathleen, **Supp. XXI:** 22
"Freak Power in the Rockies" (Thompson), **Supp. XXIV:** 286–287, 292, 293
"Freak Show, The" (Sexton), **Supp. II Part 2:** 695
Freaks: Myths and Images of the Secret Self (Fiedler), **Supp. XIII:** 106, 107
Freckles (film), **Supp. XX: 223**
Freckles (Stratton-Porter), **Supp. XX: 211, 218, 218–219, 222**
Fred Allen Show, **Supp. XXV:** 254
Freddy and Fredericka (Helprin), **Supp. XXV:** 81, 84, 87–88
Freddy's Book (Gardner), **Supp. VI: 72**
Frederic, Harold, **I:** 409; **II: 126–149,** 175, 276, 289; **Retro. Supp. I:** 325; **Supp. XXIV:** 30
"Frederick Douglass" (Dunbar), **Supp. II Part 1:** 197, 199
"Frederick Douglass" (Hayden), **Supp. II Part 1:** 363
Frederick Douglass: Slave, Fighter, Freeman (Bontemps), **Supp. XXII:** 13
Frederick the Great, **II:** 103; **Supp. I Part 2:** 433
Fredrickson, George M., **Supp. I Part 2:** 589
"Free" (O'Hara), **III:** 369
Free, and Other Stories (Dreiser), **Retro. Supp. II:** 104
Free Agents (Apple), **Supp. XVII: 5–6**
Free Air (Lewis), **II:** 441
Freeburg, Christopher, **Retro. Supp. III:** 158
Freedman, David, **Supp. XXV:** 255
Freedman, Monroe H., **Supp. VIII:** 127
Freedman, Richard, **Supp. V:** 244
Freedom (Franzen), **Supp. XXII:** 255
"Freedom" (Larsen), **Supp. XVIII:** 124
"Freedom" (White), **Supp. I Part 2:** 659
"Freedom, New Hampshire" (Kinnell), **Supp. III Part 1:** 238, 239, 251
"Freedom and Discipline" (Carruth), **Supp. XVI:** 50
Freedom Business, The (Nelson), **Supp. XVIII: 186**
Freedom Is the Right to Choose: An Inquiry into the Battle for the American Future (MacLeish), **III:** 3
"Freedom's a Hard-Bought Thing" (Benét), **Supp. XI:** 47, 48
"Freedom's Plow" (Hughes), **Supp. I Part 1:** 346
Free Enterprise (Cliff), **Supp. XXII:** 66–67, **77–78**
"Free Everything" (July), **Supp. XXIV:** 210
"Free Fantasia: Tiger Flowers" (Hayden), **Supp. II Part 1:** 363, 366
Freeing of the Dust, The (Levertov), **Supp. III Part 1:** 281–282
"Free Lance, The" (Mencken), **III:** 104, 105
Free-Lance Pallbearers, The (Reed), **Supp. X:** 240, **242–243,** 244
Freeland (Lane), **Supp. XXII:** 297
Free Life, A (Jin), **Supp. XVIII: 101–102**
Freeloaders, The (Lacy), **Supp. XV:** 204
"Freely Espousing" (Schuyler), **Supp. XXVII:** 25
"Free Man" (Hughes), **Supp. I Part 1:** 333
Freeman, Chris, **Supp. XIV:** 157, 159
Freeman, Douglas Southall, **Supp. I Part 2:** 486, 493
Freeman, Jan, **Supp. XXVII:** 257, 262
Freeman, Jesse, **Supp. XXVI:** 11
Freeman, John, **Supp. XVIII:** 90
Freeman, Joseph, **II:** 26; **Supp. I Part 2:** 610; **Supp. XXII:** 274, 277
Freeman, Mary E. Wilkins, **II:** 401; **Retro. Supp. II:** 51, 136, 138; **Supp. IX:** 79
Freeman, Morgan, **Supp. XII:** 317
Freeman, Suzanne, **Supp. X:** 83
Free Man, The (Richter), **Supp. XVIII:** 215
"Free Man's Worship, A" (Russell), **Supp. I Part 2:** 522
Freewheelin' Bob Dylan, The (album, Dylan), **Supp. XVIII:** 20, 24, 29
Free Will & Wanton Lust (Silver), **Supp. XXIV:** 265, **267–268,** 270
Freier, Mary, **Supp. XXV:** 197

Freilicher, Jane, **Supp. XV:** 178; **Supp. XXIII:** 209, 210, 212, 217
Freinman, Dorothy, **Supp. IX:** 94
Frémont, John Charles, **Supp. I Part 2:** 486
Fremont-Smith, Eliot, **Supp. XIII:** 263
Fremstad, Olive, **I:** 319; **Retro. Supp. I:** 10
French, Warren, **Supp. XII:** 118–119
French Chef, The (television program), **Supp. XVII:** 89
French Connection, The (film), **Supp. V:** 226
"French Informal Report, The"(Kenny), **Supp. XXIII:** 152
French Leave (X. J. Kennedy), **Supp. XV:** 165
Frenchman Must Die, A (Boyle), **Supp. XXIV:** 62
French Poets and Novelists (James), **II:** 336; **Retro. Supp. I:** 220
"French Scarecrow, The" (Maxwell), **Supp. VIII:** 169, 170
French Ways and Their Meaning (Wharton), **IV:** 319; **Retro. Supp. I:** 378
Freneau, Eleanor Forman (Mrs. Philip Freneau), **Supp. II Part 1:** 266
Freneau, Philip M., **I:** 335; **II:** 295; **Supp. I Part 1:** 124, 125, 127, 145; **Supp. II Part 1:** 65, **253–277**
Frenzy (Everett), **Supp. XVIII: 59–60**
Frescoes for Mr. Rockefeller's City (MacLeish), **III:** 14–15
"Fresh Air" (Koch), **Supp. XV:** 181, 185
Fresh Air Fiend: Travel Writings, 1985–2000 (Theroux), **Supp. VIII:** 325
Fresh Brats (X. J. Kennedy), **Supp. XV:** 163
"Freshman" (Sanders), **Supp. XVI:** 277
Freud, Sigmund, **I:** 55, 58, 59, 66, 67, 135, 241, 242, 244, 247, 248, 283; **II:** 27, 370, 546–547; **III:** 134, 390, 400, 418, 488; **IV:** 7, 70, 138, 295; **Retro. Supp. I:** 80, 176, 253; **Retro. Supp. II:** 104; **Supp. I Part 1:** 13, 43, 253, 254, 259, 260, 265, 270, 315; **Supp. I Part 2:** 493, 527, 616, 643, 647, 649; **Supp. IV Part 2:** 450; **Supp. IX:** 102, 155, 161, 308; **Supp. VIII:** 103, 196; **Supp. X:** 193, 194; **Supp. XII:** 14–15; **Supp. XIII:** 75; **Supp. XIV:** 83; **Supp. XV:** 219; **Supp. XVI:** 157–158, 161, 292; **Supp. XXII:** 165, 198
"Freud and Literature" (Trilling), **Supp. III Part 2:** 502–503
Freudenberger, Nell, **Supp. XXV:** 149
Freudian Psychology and Veblen's Social Theory, The (Schneider), **Supp. I Part 2:** 650
Freudian Wish and Its Place in Ethics, The (Holt), **I:** 59
"Freud in Turpentine" (Slaughter), **Retro. Supp. III:** 134
"Freud's Room" (Ozick), **Supp. V:** 268
Freud: The Mind of the Moralist (Sontag and Rieff), **Supp. III Part 2:** 455
"Freud: Within and Beyond Culture" (Trilling), **Supp. III Part 2:** 508
Frey, Charles, **Supp. XXII:** 301
Frey, Hillary, **Supp. XIX:** 55; **Supp. XXII:** 53
Frey, James, **Supp. XXII:** 95; **Supp. XXIII:** 109; **Supp. XXIV:** 230, 236
"Friday Morning Trial of Mrs. Solano, The" (Ríos), **Supp. IV Part 2:** 538, 548
Friebert, Stuart, **Supp. XIX:** 276
Frieburger, William, **Supp. XIII:** 239
Friede, Donald, **Supp. XVII:** 85, 86, 87, 90
Friedenberg, Edgar Z., **Supp. VIII:** 240
Friedman, Bruce Jay, **I:** 161; **Supp. IV Part 1:** 379
Friedman, Lawrence S., **Supp. V:** 273
Friedman, Milton, **Supp. I Part 2:** 648
Friedman, Norman, **I:** 431–432, 435, 439
Friedman, Stan, **Supp. XII:** 186
Friedmann, Georges, **Supp. I Part 2:** 645
"Fried Sausage" (Simic), **Supp. VIII:** 270
Friend, Julius, **Retro. Supp. I:** 80
Friend, The (Coleridge), **II:** 10
"Friend Husband's Latest" (Sayre), **Retro. Supp. I:** 104
"Friendly Debate between a Conformist and a Non-Conformist, A" (Wild), **IV:** 155
"Friendly Neighbor" (Keillor), **Supp. XVI:** 172
Friendly Way, The (Brainard), **Supp. XXVII:** 20
Friend of My Youth (Munro), **Supp. XXVII:** 190–191
"Friend of My Youth" (Munro), **Supp. XXVII:** 190
Friend of the Earth, A (Boyle), **Supp. VIII:** 12, 16; **Supp. XX: 29–30**
"Friend of the Fourth Decade, The" (Merrill), **Supp. III Part 1:** 327
"Friends" (Beattie), **Supp. V:** 23, 27
"Friends" (Paley), **Supp. VI:** 219, 226
"Friends" (Sexton), **Supp. II Part 2:** 693
Friend's Delight, The (Bierce), **I:** 195
"Friends from Philadelphia" (Updike), **Retro. Supp. I:** 319
"Friendship" (Emerson), **Supp. II Part 1:** 290; **Supp. XXV:** 250
Friends: More Will and Magna Stories (Dixon), **Supp. XII:** 148, 149
"Friends of Heraclitus, The" (Simic), **Supp. VIII:** 284
"Friends of Kafka, The" (Singer), **Retro. Supp. II:** 308
"Friends of the Family, The" (McCarthy), **II:** 566
"Friend to Alexander, A" (Thurber), **Supp. I Part 2:** 616
"Frigate Pelican, The" (Moore), **III:** 208, 210–211, 215
Frightened Wife, The (Rinehart), **Supp. XXV:** 198, 200
"Frill, The" (Buck), **Supp. XIV:** 274
"Fringe, The" (Bass), **Supp. XVI:** 19
Frings, Ketti, **Supp. XXV:** 95
Frobenius, Leo, **III:** 475; **Supp. III Part 2:** 620
Froebel, Friedrich, **Supp. XIV:** 52–53
Frog (Dixon), **Supp. XII:** 151
"Frog Dances" (Dixon), **Supp. XII:** 151
"Frog Pond, The" (Kinnell), **Supp. III Part 1:** 254
"Frogs" (Nelson), **Supp. XVIII:** 176
"Frog Takes a Swim" (Dixon), **Supp. XII:** 152
Frohock, W. M., **I:** 34, 42
Frolic of His Own, A (Gaddis), **Supp. IV Part 1:** 279, 291, 292–294; **Supp. XX: 91**
From a Broken Bottle Traces of Perfume Still Emanate (Mackey), **Supp. XXVII:** 151, 157–159
"From a Mournful Village" (Jewett), **Retro. Supp. II:** 146
"From an Alabama Farm" (Nelson), **Supp. XVIII:** 182
"From an Old House in America" (Rich), **Supp. I Part 2:** 551, 565–567
From Another World (Untermeyer), **Supp. XV:** 293, 303, 310–311, 313
"From a Phrase of Simone Weil's and Some Words of Hegel's" (Oppen), **Supp. XXVI:** 236
"From a Roadside Motel" (F. Wright), **Supp. XVII:** 245
"From a Survivor" (Rich), **Supp. I Part 2:** 563
From A to Z (musical review; Allen), **Supp. XV:** 3, 13

From a Work in Progress (Notley), **Supp. XXII:** 232
"From a Work in Progress" (Notley), **Supp. XXII:** 232
From a Writer's Notebook (Brooks), **I:** 254
From Bauhaus to Our House (Wolfe), **Supp. III Part 2:** 580, 581, 584
From Bondage (H. Roth), **Supp. IX:** 236, **238–240**
"From Chants to Borders to Communion" (Fox), **Supp. XIII:** 217, 217–218
"From Chicago" (Anderson), **I:** 108–109
From Colony to Nation: Women Activists and the Gendering of Politics in Belize, 1912–1982 (Macpherson), **Supp. XXIII:** 84
From Death to Morning (Wolfe), **IV:** 450, 456, 458
"From Dick to Lethem: The Dickian Legacy, Postmodernism, and Avant-Pop in Jonathan Lethem's Amnesia Moon" (Rossi), **Supp. XVIII:** 137, 138–139
"From Discord, a Wife Makes a Nice New Life—Too Nice" (Linfield), **Supp. XVII:** 177
From Down to the Village (Budbill), **Supp. XIX: 6–7**
"From Feathers to Iron" (Kunitz), **Supp. III Part 1:** 261
"From Fifth Avenue Up" (Barnes), **Supp. III Part 1:** 33, 44
"From Gorbunov and Gorchakov" (Brodsky), **Supp. VIII:** 26
"From Grand Canyon to Burbank" (H. Miller), **III:** 186
"From Hell to Breakfast", **Supp. IX:** 326–327
From Here to Eternity (film), **Supp. XI:** 221
From Here to Eternity (J. Jones), **I:** 477; **Supp. XI:** 215, 216, 217, 218, **219–221,** 223, 224, 226, 229, 230, 231, 232, 234; **Supp. XIX:** 248; **Supp. XX: 248; Supp. XXII:** 140
From Here to Eternity (miniseries), **Supp. XI:** 234
From Jordan's Delight (Blackmur), **Supp. II Part 1:** 91
"From Lumaghi Mine" (Wrigley), **Supp. XVIII:** 295
Fromm, Erich, **I:** 58; **Supp. VIII:** 196
From Morn to Midnight (Kaiser), **I:** 479
"From Native Son to Invisible Man" (Locke), **Supp. IX:** 306
"From Pico, the Women: A Life" (Creeley), **Supp. IV Part 1:** 149
"From Plane to Plane" (Frost), **Retro. Supp. III:** 105
From Plotzk to Boston (Antin), **Supp. XX: 2**
From Ritual to Romance (Weston), **II:** 540; **III:** 12; **Supp. I Part 2:** 439
From Room to Room (Kenyon), **Supp. VII:** 163–165, 166, 167
"From Room to Room" (Kenyon), **Supp. VII:** 159, 163–165
From Sand Creek: Rising in this Heart Which Is Our America (Ortiz), **Supp. IV Part 2:** 512–513
"From Sea Cliff, March" (Swenson), **Supp. IV Part 2:** 649
From Stone Orchard: A Collection of Memories (Findley), **Supp. XX: 57**
"From the Antigone" (Yeats), **III:** 459
From the Ashes: Voices of Watts (Schulberg, ed.), **Supp. XVIII:** 254
From the Barrio: A Chicano Anthology (Salinas and Faderman, eds.), **Supp. XIII:** 313
From the Beginning (Notley), **Supp. XXII:** 226, 235–236
From the Briarpatch File: On Context, Procedure, and American Identity (Murray), **Supp. XIX:** 161
"From the Childhood of Jesus" (Pinsky), **Supp. VI:** 244–245, 247
"From the Corpse Woodpiles, From the Ashes" (Hayden), **Supp. II Part 1:** 370
"From the Country to the City" (Bishop), **Supp. I Part 1:** 85, 86
"From the Cupola" (Merrill), **Supp. III Part 1:** 324–325, 331
"From the Dark Side of the Earth" (Oates), **Supp. II Part 2:** 510
"From the Diary of a New York Lady" (Parker), **Supp. IX:** 201
"From the Diary of One Not Born" (Singer), **IV:** 9
"From the Dreams" (Notley), **Supp. XXII:** 224
"From the East, Light" (Carver), **Supp. III Part 1:** 138
From the First Nine: Poems 1946–1976 (Merrill), **Supp. III Part 1:** 336
"From the Flats" (Lanier), **Supp. I Part 1:** 364
From the Flower Courtyard (Everwine), **Supp. XV:** 75
From the Heart of Europe (Matthiessen), **III:** 310
From the Meadow: Selected and New Poems (Everwine), **Supp. XV:** 75, **88–89**
"From the Memoirs of a Private Detective" (Hammett), **Supp. IV Part 1:** 343
"From the Nursery" (Kenyon), **Supp. VII:** 171
"From the Poets in the Kitchen" (Marshall), **Supp. XI:** 277
"From the Reservation to Dawn of the Dead to James Dickey and Back Again" (Gansworth), **Supp. XXVI:** 113
From the Terrace (O'Hara), **III:** 362
"From the Thirties: Tillie Olsen and the Radical Tradition" (Rosenfelt), **Supp. XIII:** 296, 304
From the Western Door to the Lower West Side (Gansworth and Rogovin), **Supp. XXVI:** 112
"From Trollope's Journal" (Bishop), **Retro. Supp. II:** 47
"Front, A" (Jarrell), **II:** 374
Front, The (film), **Supp. I Part 1:** 295
Frontain, Raymond-Jean, **Supp. XXVI:** 242
"Front and the Back Parts of the House, The" (Maxwell), **Supp. VIII:** 169
Frontier Eden (Bigelow), **Supp. X:** 227
"Frontiers of Culture" (Locke), **Supp. XIV:** 213
"Front Lines" (Snyder), **Supp. VIII:** 301
Front Page, The (Hecht and MacArthur), **Supp. XXVII:** 83, 89–90, 96
Front Porch (Inge), **Supp. XXV:** 94
Front Runner, The (P. N. Warren), **Supp. XX: 259, 262–264**
Frost, A. B., **Retro. Supp. II:** 72
Frost, Carol, **Supp. XV: 91–109**
Frost, Elisabeth, **Supp. XXVII:** 171
Frost, Isabelle Moodie, **II:** 150, 151
Frost, Jeanie, **II:** 151
Frost, Richard, **Supp. XV:** 92
Frost, Robert, **I:** 26, 27, 60, 63, 64, 171, 229, 303, 326, 418; **II:** 55, 58, **150–172,** 276, 289, 388, 391, 471, 523, 527, 529, 535; **III:** 5, 23, 67, 269, 271, 272, 275, 287, 453, 510, 523, 536, 575, 581, 591; **IV:** 140, 190, 415; **Retro. Supp. I:** 67, **121–144,** 276, 287, 292, 298, 299, 311, 413; **Retro. Supp. II:** 40, 47, 50, 146, 178, 181; **Retro. Supp. III: 91–108,** 251; **Supp. I Part 1:** 80, 242, 263, 264; **Supp. I Part 2:** 387, 461, 699; **Supp. II Part 1:** 4, 19, 26, 103; **Supp. III Part 1:** 63, 74–75, 239, 253; **Supp. III Part 2:** 546, 592, 593; **Supp. IV Part 1:** 15; **Supp. IV Part 2:** 439, 445, 447, 448, 599, 601; **Supp. IX:** 41, 42,

75, 76, 80, 87, 90, 266, 308; **Supp. VIII:** 20, 30, 32, 98, 100, 104, 259, 292; **Supp. X:** 64, 65, 66, 74, 120, 172; **Supp. XI:** 43, 123, 150, 153, 312; **Supp. XII:** 130, 241, 303, 307; **Supp. XIII:** 143, 147, 334–335; **Supp. XIV:** 42, 122, 222, 229; **Supp. XIX:** 1, 123; **Supp. XV:** 21, 51, 65, 96, 212, 215, 250, 256, 293, 296, 299, 301, 302, 306, 348; **Supp. XVII:** 36, 110, 115–116; **Supp. XVIII:** 298, 300; **Supp. XX:** **69, 199;** **Supp. XXI:** 19, 28, 51, 99, 104, 107, 205; **Supp. XXII:** 206; **Supp. XXIII:** 79, 145; **Supp. XXIV:** 159; **Supp. XXV:** 222; **Supp. XXVI:** 61, 62, 63, 65, 67, 164; **Supp. XXVII:** 217, 218, 219, 283, 290
Frost, William Prescott, **II:** 150–151
"Frost: A Dissenting Opinion" (Cowley), **Supp. II Part 1:** 143
Frost: A Time to Talk (Francis), **Supp. IX:** 76, **85–86**
"Frost at Midnight" (Coleridge), **Supp. X:** 71
"Frost Flowers" (Kenyon), **Supp. VII:** 168
"Frost: He Is Sometimes a Poet and Sometimes a Stump-Speaker" (News-Week), **Retro. Supp. I:** 137
Frothingham, Nathaniel, **I:** 3
Frothingham, Octavius B., **IV:** 173
"Frozen City, The" (Nemerov), **III:** 270
"Frozen Fields, The" (Bowles), **Supp. IV Part 1:** 80
"Frozen Ship, The" (Very), **Supp. XXV:** 243
Frucht, Abby, **Supp. XXVI:** 156
"Fructifying a Cycle: Homage to Alan Ansen"(Hadas), **Supp. XXIII:** 123
"Fruit Garden Path, The" (A. Lowell), **II:** 516
"Fruit of the Flower" (Cullen), **Supp. IV Part 1:** 167
Fruit of the Tree, The (Wharton), **IV:** 314–315; **Retro. Supp. I:** 367, **370–371,** 373
"Fruit of Travel Long Ago" (Melville), **III:** 93
Fruits and Vegetables (Jong), **Supp. V:** 113, 115, 117, 118, 119
"Fruits of the Sea, The" (Di Piero), **Supp. XIX:** 47
Frumkes, Lewis Burke, **Supp. XII:** 335–336
Fry, Christopher, **Supp. I Part 1:** 270
Fry, Roger, **Supp. XIV:** 336
Fry, Stephen M., **Supp. XIX:** 159
Frye, Joanne, **Supp. XIII:** 292, 296, 298, 302
Frye, Northrop, **Supp. I Part 2:** 530; **Supp. II Part 1:** 101; **Supp. X:** 80; **Supp. XIII:** 19; **Supp. XIV:** 11, 15; **Supp. XVI:** 149, 156; **Supp. XX:** **50;** **Supp. XXIII:** 42
Fryer, Judith, **Retro. Supp. I:** 379
F. Scott Fitzgerald: A Critical Portrait (Piper), **Supp. IX:** 65
"F. S. F., 1896–1996, R.I.P." (Doctorow), **Retro. Supp. I:** 97
Fuchs, Daniel, **Supp. XIII:** 106; **Supp. XXVII:** 134
Fuchs, Miriam, **Supp. IV Part 1:** 284
Fuehrer Bunker, The (Snodgrass), **Supp. VI:** 314, 315–317, 319–321
Fuel (Nye), **Supp. XIII:** 277, **282–284**
"Fuel" (Nye), **Supp. XIII:** 283
Fuertes, Gloria, **Supp. V:** 178
Fugard, Athol, **Retro. Supp. III:** 318; **Supp. VIII:** 330; **Supp. XIII:** 205
Fugitive Group, The (Cowan), **IV:** 120
Fugitive Kind, The (T. Williams), **IV:** 381, 383
Fugitives, The (group), **IV:** 122, 124, 125, 131, 237, 238
Fugitives, The: A Critical Account (Bradbury), **IV:** 130
"Fugitive Slave Law, The" (Emerson), **II:** 13
Fugitive's Return (Glaspell), **Supp. III Part 1:** 182–184
"Fulfillment" (H. Johnson), **Supp. XXVI:** 164, 173
Fuller, B. A. G., **III:** 605
Fuller, Edmund, **Supp. XXII:** 211, 212
Fuller, Hiram, **Supp. XVIII:** 12,14
Fuller, Jesse "Lonecat", **Supp. XV:** 147
Fuller, Margaret, **I:** 261; **II:** 7, 276; **IV:** 172; **Retro. Supp. I:** 155–156, 163; **Retro. Supp. II:** 46; **Retro. Supp. III:** 122; **Supp. I Part 2:** 524; **Supp. II Part 1:** **279–306;** **Supp. IX:** 37; **Supp. XVIII:** 3, 11, 12, 16; **Supp. XXV:** 249
Fuller, Thomas, **II:** 111, 112
Fullerton, Morton, **Retro. Supp. III:** 280, 281–282, 284; **Supp. XX:** **231**
Fullerton Street (Wilson), **Supp. VIII:** 331
"Full Fathom Five" (Plath), **Supp. I Part 2:** 538
Full Measure: Modern Short Stories on Aging (D. Sennett, ed.), **Supp. XVI:** 37
Full Monty, The (musical, McNally), **Supp. XIII:** 207
"Full Moon" (Hayden), **Supp. II Part 1:** 370
Full Moon and Other Plays (Price), **Supp. VI:** 266
"Full Moon and You're Not Here" (Cisneros), **Supp. VII:** 71–72
"Full Moon: New Guinea" (Shapiro), **Supp. II Part 2:** 707
"Fullness of Life, The" (Wharton), **Retro. Supp. I:** 363
Full of Life (Fante), **Supp. XI:** 160
Full of Life (film), **Supp. XI:** 170
Full of Lust and Good Usage (Dunn), **Supp. XI:** **145–147**
Full Speed Ahead: Tales from the Log of a Correspondent with Our Navy (Beston), **Supp. XXVI:** 33
"Full Summer" (Olds), **Supp. X:** 212
Fulton, Ben, **Supp. XXII:** 207
Fulton, Joe B., **Retro. Supp. III:** 266
Fulton, Robert, **Supp. I Part 2:** 519; **Supp. II Part 1:** 73
Fun and Games (Major), **Supp. XXII:** 180
Funaroff, Sol, **Supp. XXVI:** 143
"Functional Poem" (Halliday), **Supp. XIX:** 85
Function of Criticism, The (Winters), **Supp. II Part 2:** 812, 813
"Fundamentalism" (Tate), **IV:** 125
"Fundamental Project of Technology, The" (Kinnell), **Supp. III Part 1:** 253
"Funeral of Bobò, The" (Brodsky), **Supp. VIII:** 27, 28
Fungi from Yuggoth (Lovecraft), **Supp. XXV:** 119–120
Fun Home: A Family Tragicomic (Bechdel), **Supp. XXV:** 1, 4–9
Funiculi-Funicula (Wellman), **Supp. XXV:** 20
Funkhouser, Christopher, **Supp. XXVII:** 151
"Funnel" (Sexton), **Supp. II Part 2:** 675
Fun to Be Free (Hecht and MacArthur), **Supp. XXVII:** 90
"Furious Seasons, The" (Carver), **Supp. III Part 1:** 137
Furious Seasons and Other Stories (Carver), **Supp. III Part 1:** 142, 143, 146
"Furious Versions" (L.-Y. Lee), **Supp. XV:** **215–217,** 218, **220**
Furman, Jan, **Retro. Supp. III:** 187
"Furnished Room, The" (Hayden), **Supp. II Part 1:** 386–387, 394, 397, 399, 406, 408
"Furor Scribendi" (O. Butler), **Supp. XIII:** 70
Furors Die (Hoffman), **Supp. XVIII:** **80–81**

Fur Person, The (Sarton), **Supp. VIII: 264–265**
Further Adventures with You (Wright), **Supp. XV:** 339, 342, **343–345**
Further Fables for Our Time (Thurber), **Supp. I Part 2:** 612
"Further in Summer than the Birds" (Dickinson), **I:** 471
Further Poems of Emily Dickinson (Bianchi and Hampson, ed.), **Retro. Supp. I:** 35
Further Range, A (Frost), **II:** 155; **Retro. Supp. I:** 132, 136, 137, 138, 139; **Retro. Supp. III:** 103, 104
Furthman, Charles, **Supp. XXVII:** 92
"Fury, The (Skloot), **Supp. XX: 197**
"Fury of Aerial Bombardment, The" (Eberhart), **I:** 535–536
"Fury of Flowers and Worms, The" (Sexton), **Supp. II Part 2:** 694
"Fury of Rain Storms, The" (Sexton), **Supp. II Part 2:** 695
Fury of the Jungle (film), **Supp. XIII:** 163
Fussell, Paul, **Supp. V:** 241
Fussell, Paul K., **Supp. XXV:** 253
"Futility" (H. Johnson), **Supp. XXVI:** 167, 172
"Future, if Any, of Comedy, The" (Thurber), **Supp. I Part 2:** 620
Future, The (album, Cohen), **Supp. XXVII:** 54
"Future, The" (Cohen), **Supp. XXVII:** 62
Future, The (film, July), **Supp. XXIV:** 199, 200, 202, **209,** 210
Future in the Present, The (C. L. R. James), **Supp. XXI:** 172
Future is Ours, Comrade, The: Conversations with the Russians (Kosinski), **Supp. VII:** 215
Futureland: Nine Stories of an Imminent World (Mosley), **Supp. XIII: 247–249**
"Future Life, The" (Bryant), **Supp. I Part 1:** 170
Future of Southern Letters, The (J. W. Miller), **Supp. XX: 161**
Future of the Race, The (H. L. Gates), **Supp. XX: 101, 104, 111**
Future Punishment of the Wicked, The (Edwards), **I:** 546
"Gabriel" (Rich), **Supp. I Part 2:** 557
Gabriel, Ralph H., **Supp. I Part 1:** 251
Gabriel, Trip, **Supp. V:** 212
Gabriel Conroy (Harte), **Supp. II Part 1:** 354
"Gabriel's Truth" (Kenyon), **Supp. VII:** 166
Gaddis, William, **Supp. IV Part 1: 279–296; Supp. IV Part 2:** 484; **Supp. IX:** 208; **Supp. V:** 52; **Supp. X:** 301, 302; **Supp. XX: 83, 91; Supp. XXI:** 226; **Supp. XXIII:** 107
Gadiot, Pud, **Supp. XI:** 295
Gaily, Gaily (film), **Supp. XXVII:** 95
Gaily, Gaily (Hecht), **Supp. XXVII:** 95
Gain (Powers), **Supp. IX:** 212, **220–221**
Gaines, Ernest J., **Supp. X:** 24, 250
Gaines, James R., **Supp. IX:** 190
Gainor, J. Ellen, **Supp. XXI:** 6
Gaitens, Peter, **Supp. XV:** 65
Gajarsa, Arthur, **Supp. XXVI:** 83
Galamain, Ivan, **Supp. III Part 2:** 624
Galassi, Jonathan, **Supp. XIX:** 34; **Supp. XVIII:** 92; **Supp. XXII:** 177
Galatea 2.2 (Powers), **Supp. IX:** 212, **219–220**
"Galatea Encore" (Brodsky), **Supp. VIII:** 31
Galbraith, John Kenneth, **Supp. I Part 2:** 645, 650
Galdós, Benito Pérez. See Pérez Galdós, Benito
Gale, Zona, **Supp. I Part 2:** 613; **Supp. VIII:** 155
Galehouse, Maggie, **Supp. XXI:** 215
"Gale in April" (Jeffers), **Supp. II Part 2:** 423
Galignani, Giovanni Antonio, **II:** 315
Galileo Galilei, **I:** 480–481; **Supp. XII:** 180; **Supp. XIII:** 75
Gallagher, Tess, **Supp. XVI:** 36; **Supp. XVII:** 110; **Supp. XXI:** 246; **Supp. XXIV: 165–181**
Gallant, Mavis, **Supp. VIII:** 151
"Gallant Fireman, A" (Twain), **Retro. Supp. III:** 256
Gallatin, Albert, **I:** 5
"Gallery" (Goldbarth), **Supp. XII:** 188
"Gallery of Real Creatures, A" (Thurber), **Supp. I Part 2:** 619
Gallico, Paul, **Supp. XVI:** 238
Gallows Songs (Snodgrass), **Supp. VI:** 317
Gallup, Dick, **Supp. XXIV:** 34, 35, 39, 44; **Supp. XXVII:** 18, 22, 23
Gallup, Donald, **III:** 404, 478
"Galop" (Davison), **Supp. XXVI:** 71
Galsworthy, John, **III:** 70, 153, 382
Galton Case, The (Macdonald), **Supp. IV Part 2:** 463, 473, 474
Galvin, Frances, **Supp. XXI:** 5
"Gal Young 'Un" (Rawlings), **Supp. X:** 228
Gambino, Richard, **Supp. XX: 35**
"Gambler, the Nun, and the Radio, The" (Hemingway), **II:** 250
"Gambler's Wife, The" (Dunbar), **Supp. II Part 1:** 196
Gambone, Philip, **Supp. XII:** 81
"Gambrel Roof, A" (Larcom), **Supp. XIII:** 144
"Game at Salzburg, A" (Jarrell), **II:** 384, 389
Game Management (Leopold), **Supp. XIV:** 182
"Game of Catch, A" (Wilbur), **Supp. III Part 2:** 552
Game Players of Titan, The (Dick), **Supp. XVIII:** 138
"Games in Frank Conroy's Stop-Time" (T. Adams), **Supp. XVI:** 67
"Games Two" (Wilbur), **Supp. III Part 2:** 550
Gammelgaard, Lene, **Supp. XVIII:** 112
"Gamut, The" (Angelou), **Supp. IV Part 1:** 15
Gander, Forrest, **Supp. XV:** 339, 340, 342
Gandhi, Indira, **Supp. X:** 108
Gandhi, Mahatma, **III:** 179, 296–297; **IV:** 170, 185, 367; **Supp. VIII:** 203, 204; **Supp. X:** 27
Gandhi on Non-Violence (Merton, ed.), **Supp. VIII:** 204–205
Gangemi, Merry, **Supp. XXV:** 6
Gang of Five: Leaders at the Center of the Conservative Crusade (Easton), **Supp. XIX:** 137
"Gang of Mirrors, The" (Simic), **Supp. VIII:** 283
Gannett, Ezra Stiles, **Supp. XXIV:** 74
Gansevoort, Guert, **III:** 94
Gansevoort, Peter, **III:** 92
Gansworth, Eric, **Supp. XXVI: 101–116**
"Gap" (Bierds), **Supp. XVII:** 35–36
Garabedian, Michael, **Supp. XIII:** 115
Garbage (Ammons), **Supp. VII:** 24, 35–36
Garbage (Dixon), **Supp. XII:** 147, 148
Garbage Man, The (Dos Passos), **I:** 478, 479, 481, 493
Garber, Frederick, **Supp. IX:** 294–295
Garbo, Greta, **Supp. I Part 2:** 616
García, Cristina, **Supp. VIII:** 74; **Supp. XI: 177–192**
García Lorca, Federico. See Lorca, Federico García
"García Lorca: A Photograph of the Granada Cemetery, 1966" (Levis), **Supp. XI:** 264
García Márquez, Gabriel, **Supp. V:** 244; **Supp. VIII:** 81, 82, 84, 85; **Supp. XII:** 147, 310, 316, 322; **Supp. XIII:** 226; **Supp. XVII:** 45;

Supp. XXIV: 86, 89, 190; **Supp. XXV:** 49, 69
Gard, Claire, **Supp. XXIII:** 94
Gardaphe, Fred, **Supp. XX: 38, 41**
"Garden" (Marvell), **IV:** 161; **Supp. XVI:** 204
"Garden, The" (Glück), **Supp. V:** 83
"Garden, The" (Strand), **Supp. IV Part 2:** 629
"Garden, The" (Very), **Supp. XXV:** 248
"Garden Among Tombs" (B. Kelly), **Supp. XVII:** 126
"Garden by Moonlight, The" (A. Lowell), **II:** 524
"Gardener Delivers a Fawn, The" (C. Frost), **Supp. XV:** 99
Gardener's Son, The (McCarthy), **Supp. VIII:** 187
Garden God, The: A Tale of Two Boys (Reid), **Supp. XX: 235**
"Gardenias" (Doty), **Supp. XI:** 122
"Gardenias" (Monette), **Supp. X:** 159
"Garden Lodge, The" (Cather), **I:** 316, 317; **Retro. Supp. III:** 26
Garden of Adonis, The (Gordon), **II:** 196, 204–205, 209
Garden of Earthly Delights, A (Oates), **Supp. II Part 2:** 504, 507–509
Garden of Earthly Delights, The (Bosch), **Supp. XXII:** 255, 261
"Garden of Eden" (Hemingway), **II:** 259
Garden of Eden, The (Hemingway), **Retro. Supp. I:** 186, **187–188**
"Garden of Flesh, Garden of Stone" (B. Kelly), **Supp. XVII:** 128
Garden of Last Days, The (Dubus III), **Supp. XXIV:** 101**, 107–108**
"Garden of the Moon, The" (Doty), **Supp. XI:** 122
Garden of the Prophet, The (Gibran), **Supp. XX: 119, 122**
"Garden of the Trumpet Tree, The" (B. Kelly), **Supp. XVII:** 131
"Gardens, The" (Oliver), **Supp. VII:** 236
"Gardens of Mont-Saint-Michel, The" (Maxwell), **Supp. VIII:** 169
"Gardens of the Villa D'Este, The" (Hecht), **Supp. X:** 59
"Gardens of Zuñi, The" (Merwin), **Supp. III Part 1:** 351
Garden Thieves, The: Twentieth Century African-American Poetry (Major, ed.), **Supp. XXII:** 172
Gardiner, Judith Kegan, **Supp. IV Part 1:** 205
Gardner, Erle Stanley, **Supp. IV Part 1:** 121, 345
Gardner, Isabella, **IV:** 127
Gardner, John, **Supp. I Part 1:** 193, 195, 196; **Supp. III Part 1:** 136, 142, 146; **Supp. VI: 61–76; Supp. XXV:** 152
Gardner, Thomas, **Supp. XXI:** 214
Gardons, S. S. See Snodgrass, W. D.
"Gare de Lyon" (M. F. K. Fisher), **Supp. XVII:** 91
Garfield, John, **Supp. XII:** 160
Gargoyles (Hecht), **Supp. XXVII:** 88
Garibaldi, Giuseppe, **I:** 4; **II:** 284
Garibay, Angel M., **Supp. XV:** 77
Garland, Hamlin, **I:** 407; **II:** 276, 289; **III:** 576; **Retro. Supp. I:** 133; **Retro. Supp. II:** 72; **Supp. I Part 1:** 217; **Supp. IV Part 2:** 502; **Supp. XVIII:** 6
Garland Companion, The (Zverev), **Retro. Supp. I:** 278
"Garments" (Gibran), **Supp. XX: 124**
Garments the Living Wear (Purdy), **Supp. VII:** 278–279, 280–281
Garner, Dwight, **Supp. X:** 202; **Supp. XVIII:** 89; **Supp. XXV:** 9
Garnett, Edward, **I:** 405, 409, 417; **III:** 27; **Retro. Supp. III:** 98
Garrett, George P., **Supp. I Part 1:** 196; **Supp. VII: 95–113; Supp. X:** 3, 7; **Supp. XI:** 218; **Supp. XVIII:** 74, 75; **Supp. XXVI:** 153, 157
Garrigue, Jean, **Supp. XII:** 260
Garrison, Deborah, **Supp. IX:** 299
Garrison, Fielding, **III:** 105
Garrison, William Lloyd, **Supp. I Part 2:** 524, 588, 683, 685, 686, 687; **Supp. XIV:** 54; **Supp. XXIV:** 77
"Garrison of Cape Ann, The" (Whittier), **Supp. I Part 2:** 691, 694
Garry Moore Show (television show), **Supp. IV Part 2:** 575
"Garter Motif" (White), **Supp. I Part 2:** 673
Gartner, Zsuzsi, **Supp. X:** 276
Garvey, Marcus, **Supp. III Part 1:** 175, 180; **Supp. IV Part 1:** 168; **Supp. X:** 135, 136; **Supp. XXI:** 166, 168; **Supp. XXII:** 7
Garvin, Viola, **Supp. XXVII:** 118
Gas (Kaiser), **I:** 479
Gas-House McGinty (Farrell), **II:** 41–42
Gaskell, Elizabeth, A., **Supp. I Part 2:** 580
Gasoline (Corso), **Supp. XII:** 118, **121–123**, 134
Gasoline Wars, The (Thompson), **Supp. XXIII:** 290
"Gasoline Wars, The"(Thompson), **Supp. XXIII:** 291
Gass, William H., **Supp. IX:** 208; **Supp. V:** 44, 52, 238; **Supp. VI: 77–96; Supp. XII:** 152; **Supp. XIV:** 305; **Supp. XVII:** 183
"Gassire's Lute: Robert Duncan's Vietnam War Poems" (Mackey), **Supp. XXVII:** 160
Gassner, John, **IV:** 381; **Supp. I Part 1:** 284, 292
"Gas Stations" (Apple), **Supp. XVII:** 4
Gastronomical Me, The (M. F. K. Fisher), **Supp. XVII:** 84, 85, 87, 91, 92
Gates, David, **Supp. V:** 24; **Supp. XIII:** 93; **Supp. XVI:** 73, 74; **Supp. XX: 92**
Gates, Elmer, **I:** 515–516
Gates, Henry Louis, Jr., **Retro. Supp. I:** 194, 195, 203; **Retro. Supp. III:** 130; **Supp. X:** 242, 243, 245, 247; **Supp. XIX:** 147, 149; **Supp. XVIII:** 287; **Supp. XX: 99–112, 279, 286; Supp. XXIV:** 192; **Supp. XXVI:** 13
Gates, Lewis E., **III:** 315, 330
Gates, Sondra Smith, **Supp. XVIII:** 267, 269
Gates, The (Rukeyser), **Supp. VI:** 271, 274, 281
"Gates, The" (Rukeyser), **Supp. VI:** 286
Gates, Tudor, **Supp. XI:** 307
Gates of Ivory, the Gates of Horn, The (McGrath), **Supp. X:** 118
Gates of Wrath, The; Rhymed Poems (Ginsberg), **Supp. II Part 1:** 311, 319
"Gathering" (Trethewey), **Supp. XXI:** 249
Gathering Forces, The (C. L. R. James), **Supp. XXI:** 171
"Gathering of Dissidents, A" (Applebaum), **Supp. XVI:** 153
Gathering of Fugitives, A (Trilling), **Supp. III Part 2:** 506, 512
Gathering of Zion, The: The Story of the Mormon Trail (Stegner), **Supp. IV Part 2:** 599, 602–603
Gather Together in My Name (Angelou), **Supp. IV Part 1:** 2, 3, 4–6, 11
Gathorne-Hardy, Robert, **Supp. XIV:** 344, 347, 348, 349
Gaudier-Brzeska, Henri, **III:** 459, 464, 465, 477
Gaughran, Richard, **Supp. XXI:** 47–48
Gauguin, Paul, **I:** 34; **IV:** 290; **Supp. IV Part 1:** 81; **Supp. XII:** 128
"Gauguin in Oregon" (Skloot), **Supp. XX: 203**

"Gauley Bridge" (Rukeyser), **Supp. VI:** 278
Gauss, Christian, **II:** 82; **IV:** 427, 439–440, 444
Gauthier, Jacquie, **Supp. XIX:** 204
Gautier, Théophile, **II:** 543; **III:** 466, 467; **Supp. I Part 1:** 277
Gay, John, **II:** 111; **Supp. I Part 2:** 523; **Supp. XIV:** 337
Gay, Peter, **I:** 560
Gay, Sydney Howard, **Supp. I Part 1:** 158; **Supp. XVIII:** 3
Gay, Walter, **IV:** 317
Gayatri Prayer, The, **III:** 572
Gay Canon, The (Drake), **Supp. XX: 274**
"Gay Chaps at the Bar" (Brooks), **Supp. III Part 1:** 74, 75
" 'Gay Culture': Still of the Wild Frontier" (P. N. Warren), **Supp. XX: 272**
Gaylord, Winfield R., **III:** 579–580
Gay Talese Reader, The: Portraits & Encounters (Talese), **Supp. XVII:** 202, 208
"Gaze, The"(Hadas), **Supp. XXIII:** 120
"Gazebo" (Carver), **Supp. III Part 1:** 138, 144, 145
Gazer's Spirit, The (Hollander), **Supp. XIX:** 121
Gazer Within, The, and Other Essays by Larry Levis, **Supp. XI:** 270
Gazzara, Ben, **Supp. VIII:** 319
Gazzo, Michael V., **III:** 155
"Geas" (Monson), **Supp. XXIV:** 238–239
Geddes, Virgil, **Supp. XXV:** 23
"Geese Flying over Hamilton, New York"(Balakian), **Supp. XXIII:** 24
"Geese Gone Beyond" (Snyder), **Supp. VIII:** 304
Geffen, David, **Supp. XXI:** 154
"Gegenwart" (Goethe), **Supp. II Part 1:** 26
Geisel, Theodor Seuss (Dr. Seuss), **Supp. X:** 56; **Supp. XVI: 97–115**
Geismar, Maxwell, **II:** 178, 431; **III:** 71; **Supp. IX:** 15; **Supp. XI:** 223
Geist, Bill, **Supp. XXIII:** 298
Gelb, Arthur, **IV:** 380; **Supp. XXI:** 12
Gelb, Barbara, **Supp. XXI:** 12
Gelbart, Larry, **Supp. IV Part 2:** 591
Gelder, Robert Van, **Supp. XIII:** 166
Gelfant, Blanche H., **II:** 27, 41; **Supp. XVII:** 161
Gelfman, Jean, **Supp. X:** 3
Gellert, Hugo, **Supp. XXII:** 277
Gellhorn, Martha. See Hemingway, Mrs. Ernest (Martha Gellhorn)
Gelpi, Albert, **Retro. Supp. III:** 242, 250; **Supp. I Part 2:** 552, 554, 560
Gelpi, Barbara, **Supp. I Part 2:** 560
Gemin, Pamela, **Supp. XXI:** 246
Gemini (Innaurato), **Supp. XXIV:** 117
Gemini: an extended autobiographical statement on my first twenty-five years of being a black poet (Giovanni), **Supp. IV Part 1:** 11
Gem of the Ocean (Wilson), **Retro. Supp. III:** 321
"Gen" (Snyder), **Supp. VIII:** 302
"Gender Norms" (Radinovsky), **Supp. XV:** 285
"Gender of Sound, The" (Carson), **Supp. XII: 106**
"Genealogies"(Hadas), **Supp. XXIII:** 116
"Genealogy" (Komunyakaa), **Supp. XIII:** 129
"General Aims and Theories" (Crane), **I:** 389
General Died at Dawn, The (Odets), **Supp. II Part 2:** 546
"General Gage's Confession" (Freneau), **Supp. II Part 1:** 257
"General Gage's Soliloquy" (Freneau), **Supp. II Part 1:** 257
General History of the Robberies and Murders of the Most Notorious Pyrates from Their First Rise and Settlement in the Island of New Providence to the Present Year, A (C. Johnson), **Supp. V:** 128
General in His Labyrinth, The (García Márquez), **Supp. XXIV:** 89
"General Returns from One Place to Another, The"(O'Hara), **Supp. XXIII:** 216–217
"General William Booth Enters into Heaven" (Lindsay), **Supp. I Part 2:** 374, 382, 384, 385–388, 389, 392, 399
General William Booth Enters into Heaven and Other Poems (Lindsay), **Supp. I Part 2:** 379, 381, 382, 387–388, 391
"Generation of the Dispossessed" (P. N. Warren), **Supp. XX: 272**
"Generations"(Kenny), **Supp. XXIII:** 154
"Generations of Men, The" (Frost), **Retro. Supp. I:** 128; **Supp. XIII:** 147
Generation Without Farewell (Boyle), **Supp. XXIV:** 60, 62
"Generation Wuss" (Ellis), **Supp. XXVII:** 78, 79
Generous Man, A (Price), **Supp. VI:** 259, 260, 261
Genesis (biblical book), **I:** 279; **II:** 540; **Retro. Supp. I:** 250, 256; **Supp. XII:** 54
"Genesis" (Stegner), **Supp. IV Part 2:** 604
Genesis: Book One (Schwartz), **Supp. II Part 2:** 640, 651–655
Gene Stratton-Porter (Richards), **Supp. XX: 217–218**
Gene Stratton-Porter, Naturalist and Novelist (Long), **Supp. XX: 212**
"Gene Stratton-Porter: Women's Advocate" (Obuchowski), **Supp. XX: 222**
Genet, Jean, **I:** 71, 82, 83, 84; **Supp. IV Part 1:** 8; **Supp. XI:** 308; **Supp. XII:** 1; **Supp. XIII:** 74; **Supp. XVII:** 95; **Supp. XXIII:** 213; **Supp. XXIV:** 210
"Genetic Coding" (Sorrentino), **Supp. XXI:** 227
"Genetic Expedition" (Dove), **Supp. IV Part 1:** 249, 257
"Genetics of Justice" (Alvarez), **Supp. VII:** 19
"Genial Host, The" (McCarthy), **II:** 564
"Genie in the Bottle, The" (Davison), **Supp. XXVI:** 74
"Genie in the Bottle, The" (Wilbur), **Supp. III Part 2:** 542
"Genius, The" (MacLeish), **III:** 19
Genius and Lust: A Journey through the Major Writings of Henry Miller (Mailer), **Retro. Supp. II:** 208
"Genius Child" (Hughes), **Retro. Supp. I:** 203
"Genius of Bob Dylan, The" (Lethem), **Supp. XVIII:** 146
"Genius," The (Dreiser), **I:** 497, 501, 509–511, 519; **Retro. Supp. II:** 94–95, **102–103,** 104, 105
Genocide of the Mind: New Native America Writing (Moore, ed.), **Supp. XXVI:** 113
Genova, Lisa, **Supp. XXIII:** 127
"Genteel Tradition in American Philosophy, The" (Santayana), **I:** 222
Gent from Bear Creek, A (Howard), **Supp. XXVII:** 117, 126
"Gent from Bear Creek, A" (Howard), **Supp. XXVII:** 127
"Gentle Boys, The" (Hawthorne), **Retro. Supp. III:** 113
"Gentle Communion" (Mora), **Supp. XIII:** 218–219
Gentle Crafter, The (O. Henry), **Supp. II Part 1:** 410
Gentle Furniture-Shop, The (Bodenheim), **Supp. XXV:** 20
"Gentle Lena, The" (Stein), **IV:** 37, 40

Gentleman Caller, The (T. Williams), **IV:** 383
"Gentleman from Cracow, The" (Singer), **IV:** 9
"Gentleman of Bayou Têche, A" (Chopin), **Supp. I Part 1:** 211–212
"Gentleman of Shalott, The" (Bishop), **Supp. I Part 1:** 85, 86
Gentleman's Agreement (Hobson), **III:** 151
"Gentleman's Agreement" (Richard), **Supp. XIX:** 220–221
Gentlemen I Address You Privately (Boyle), **Supp. XXIV: 53–54**
Gentlemen Prefer Blondes (Loos; musical adaptation), **Supp. XVI:** 193
Gentlemen Prefer Blondes: The Illuminating Diary of a Professional Lady (Loos), **Supp. XVI:** 181, 183, 186, **188–189**
Gentlemen Prefer "Books" (J. Yeats), **Supp. XVI:** 190
Gentle People, The: A Brooklyn Fable (Shaw), **Supp. XIX:** 244–245, 249
Gentry, Marshall Bruce, **Supp. IV Part 1:** 236
"Genuine Man, The" (Emerson), **II:** 10
"Genus Narcissus" (Trethewey), **Supp. XXI:** 256
Geo-Bestiary (Harrison), **Supp. VIII:** 53
"Geode" (Frost), **II:** 161
Geographical History of America, The (Stein), **IV:** 31, 45; **Supp. XVIII:** 148
Geography and Plays (Stein), **IV:** 29–30, 32, 43, 44
Geography III (Bishop), **Retro. Supp. II:** 50; **Supp. I Part 1:** 72, 73, 76, 82, 93, 94, 95
Geography of a Horse Dreamer (Shepard), **Supp. III Part 2:** 432
Geography of Home, The: California's Poetry of Place (Bluckey and Young, eds.), **Supp. XIII:** 313
Geography of Lograire, The (Merton), **Supp. VIII:** 208
Geography of the Heart (F. Johnson), **Supp. XI:** 129
"Geometric Poem, The" (Corso), **Supp. XII:** 132, 133–134
George, Diana Hume, **Supp. IV Part 2:** 447, 449, 450
George, Henry, **II:** 276; **Supp. I Part 2:** 518
George, Jan, **Supp. IV Part 1:** 268
George, Lynell, **Supp. XIII:** 234–235, 237, 249
George, Peter, **Supp. XI:** 302, 303, 304
George and the Dragon (Shanley), **Supp. XIV:** 315
George Bernard Shaw: His Plays (Mencken), **III:** 102
George Mills (Elkin), **Supp. VI: 53–54**
George Oppen and the Fate of Modernism (Nicholls), **Supp. XXVI:** 228
George Palmer Putnam: Representative American Publisher (Greenspan), **Supp. XVIII:** 257
"George Robinson: Blues" (Rukeyser), **Supp. VI:** 279
George's Mother (Crane), **I:** 408
"George Thurston" (Bierce), **I:** 202
George Washington Crossing the Delaware (Koch), **Supp. XV:** 186
"George Washington"(Kenny), **Supp. XXIII:** 154
Georgia Boy (Caldwell), **I:** 288, 305–306, 308, 309, 310
"Georgia Dusk" (Toomer), **Supp. IX:** 309
"Georgia: Invisible Empire State" (Du Bois), **Supp. II Part 1:** 179
"Georgia Night" (Toomer), **Supp. III Part 2:** 481
Georgia Scenes (Longstreet), **II:** 70, 313; **Supp. I Part 1:** 352
Georgics (Virgil), **Retro. Supp. I:** 135; **Supp. XVI:** 22; **Supp. XXIV:** 153
Georgics of Virgil, The (Ferry. trans.), **Supp. XXIV: 158–160**
Georgie May (Bodenheim), **Supp. XXV:** 25
Georgoudaki, Ekaterini, **Supp. IV Part 1:** 12
Gerald McBoing-Boing (film), **Supp. XVI:** 102
"Geraldo No Last Name" (Cisneros), **Supp. VII:** 60–61
Gerald's Game (King), **Supp. V:** 141, 148–150, 151, 152
Gerald's Party (Coover), **Supp. V:** 49–50, 51, 52
Gérando, Joseph Marie de, **II:** 10
"Geranium, The" (O'Connor), **Retro. Supp. II:** 221, 236; **Retro. Supp. III:** 208
Gerard, Jeremy, **Supp. XXI:** 147
Gerber, Dan, **Supp. VIII:** 39
Gerber, Lisa, **Supp. XXVI:** 187
Gerhardt, Rainer, **Supp. IV Part 1:** 142
"German Girls! The German Girls!, The" (MacLeish), **III:** 16
"German Refugee, The" (Malamud), **Supp. I Part 2:** 436, 437
"Germany's Reichswehr" (Agee), **I:** 35
Germinal (Zola), **III:** 318, 322
Gernsback, Hugo, **Supp. IV Part 1:** 101
"Gernsback Continuum, The" (W. Gibson), **Supp. XVI:** 123, 128
"Gerontion" (Eliot), **I:** 569, 574, 577, 578, 585, 588; **III:** 9, 435, 436; **Retro. Supp. I:** 290; **Supp. XV:** 341; **Supp. XVI:** 158–159
Gerry, Elbridge, **Supp. I Part 2:** 486
"Gerry's Jazz" (Komunyakaa), **Supp. XIII:** 125
Gershwin, Ira, **Supp. I Part 1:** 281
"Gert" (Monette), **Supp. X:** 158
"Gertrude Atherton and the New Woman" (Forrey), **Supp. XXIV:** 30
Gertrude of Stony Island Avenue (Purdy), **Supp. VII:** 281–282
Gertrude Stein (Sprigge), **IV:** 31
Gertrude Stein: A Biography of Her Work (Sutherland), **IV:** 38
"Gertrude Stein and the Geography of the Sentence" (Gass), **Supp. VI:** 87
Gesell, Silvio, **III:** 473
"Gestalt at Sixty" (Sarton), **Supp. VIII:** 260
"Gesture of a Woman-in-Process" (Trethewey), **Supp. XXI:** 249–250
"Gesture toward an Unfound Renaissance, A" (Stafford), **Supp. XI:** 323
"Get It Again" (Halliday), **Supp. XIX:** 85
Getlin, Josh, **Supp. V:** 22; **Supp. VIII:** 75, 76, 78, 79
"Getting Along" (Larcom), **Supp. XIII:** 144
"Getting Along with Nature" (Berry), **Supp. X:** 31–32
"Getting Away from Already Pretty Much Being Away from It All" (Wallace), **Supp. X:** 314–315
"Getting Born" (Shields), **Supp. VII:** 311
Getting Even (Allen), **Supp. XV:** 3, 14, 15
"Getting Lucky" (L. Michaels), **Supp. XVI:** 205, 209
"Getting Out of Jail on Monday" (Wagoner), **Supp. IX:** 327
"Getting Over Arnette"(P. Benedict), **Supp. XXIII:** 39
"Getting over Robert Frost" (Davison), **Supp. XXVI:** 79
"Getting There" (Plath), **Supp. I Part 2:** 539, 542
"Getting to the Poem" (Corso), **Supp. XII:** 135
Getty, J. Paul, **Supp. X:** 108
Getty, Norris, **Supp. XV:** 136–137, 138, 139, 142, 143, 145, 146
Gettysburg, Manila, Acoma (Masters),

Supp. I Part 2: 471
"Gettysburg: July 1, 1863" (Kenyon), **Supp. VII:** 172
Gevers, Nick, **Supp. XXII:** 59
Geyer, Bernadette, **Supp. XXIII:** 251
Ghachem, Malick, **Supp. X:** 17
Ghazálí, al-, **Supp. XX: 117**
"Ghazals: Homage to Ghalib" (Rich), **Supp. I Part 2:** 557
Ghost, The (Crane), **I:** 409, 421
"Ghost, The" (Peacock), **Supp. XIX:** 199
"Ghost Cat" (Peacock), **Supp. XIX:** 206
"Ghost Chant, et alii" (Komunyakaa), **Supp. XIII:** 114
Ghost Country (Paretsky), **Supp. XXV:** 183
Ghost in the Music, A (Nichols), **Supp. XIII:** 267
"Ghost Jam"(Hadas), **Supp. XXIII:** 119
"Ghostlier Demarcations, Keener Sounds" (Vendler), **Supp. I Part 2:** 565
"Ghostly Father, I Confess" (McCarthy), **II:** 565–566
Ghostly Lover, The (Hardwick), **Supp. III Part 1:** 194–196, 208, 209
Ghost Money (Hull), **Supp. XXI:** 129, **132–135,** 136
"Ghost of a Chance" (Rich), **Retro. Supp. III:** 244
Ghost of Meter, The (A. Finch), **Supp. XVII:** 71, 73
"Ghost of the Buffaloes, The" (Lindsay), **Supp. I Part 2:** 393
Ghost of Tradition, The (Walzer), **Supp. XVIII:** 174
Ghosts (Auster), **Supp. XII:** 22, **24, 26–27**
Ghosts (Ibsen), **III:** 152
Ghosts (Wharton), **IV:** 316, 327
Ghosts of Tsavo: Stalking the Mystery Lions of East Africa (Caputo), **Supp. XIX:** 28
Ghost Town (Coover), **Supp. V:** 52–53
Ghost Trio, The (Bierds), **Supp. XVII:** 29, **30**
Ghost Writer, The (P. Roth), **Retro. Supp. II:** 22, 290, 291; **Supp. III Part 2:** 420–421; **Supp. XVII:** 43
Giachetti, Fosco, **Supp. IV Part 2:** 520
"Giacometti" (Wilbur), **Supp. III Part 2:** 551
Giacometti, Alberto, **Supp. VIII:** 168, 169
Giacomo, Padre, **II:** 278–279
Giant's House, The: A Romance (McCracken), **Supp. X:** 86
"Giant Snail" (Bishop), **Retro. Supp. II:** 49
Giant Weapon, The (Winters), **Supp. II Part 2:** 810
"Giant Woman, The" (Oates), **Supp. II Part 2:** 523
Gibbon, Edward, **I:** 4, 378; **IV:** 126; **Supp. I Part 2:** 503; **Supp. III Part 2:** 629; **Supp. XIII:** 75; **Supp. XIV:** 97
Gibbons, James, **Supp. XVII:** 228
Gibbons, Kaye, **Supp. X: 41–54; Supp. XII:** 311
Gibbons, Reginald, **Supp. X:** 113, 124, 127; **Supp. XIX:** 40, 41–42, 281; **Supp. XV:** 105
Gibbons, Richard, **Supp. I Part 1:** 107
"Gibbs" (Rukeyser), **Supp. VI:** 273
Gibbs, Barbara, **Supp. IV Part 2:** 644
Gibbs, Wolcott, **Supp. I Part 2:** 604, 618; **Supp. VIII:** 151
Gibran, Kahlil, **Supp. XX: 69, 113–129**
"GIBSON" (Baraka), **Supp. II Part 1:** 54
Gibson, Charles Dana, **Supp. X:** 184
Gibson, Graeme, **Supp. XIII:** 20
Gibson, John Arthur, **Supp. XXVI:** 83, 84, 87, 89
Gibson, Simeon, **Supp. XXVI:** 96
Gibson, Wilfrid W., **Retro. Supp. I:** 128; **Retro. Supp. III:** 96
Gibson, William, **Supp. XVI: 117–133; Supp. XXII:** 49
Giddins, Gary, **Supp. XIII:** 245
Gide, André, **I:** 271, 290; **II:** 581; **III:** 210; **IV:** 53, 289; **Retro. Supp. III:** 275; **Supp. I Part 1:** 51; **Supp. IV Part 1:** 80, 284, 347; **Supp. IV Part 2:** 681, 682; **Supp. VIII:** 40; **Supp. X:** 187; **Supp. XIV:** 24, 348; **Supp. XVII:** 242
Gideon Planish (Lewis), **II:** 455
Gielgud, John, **I:** 82; **Supp. XI:** 305
Gierow, Dr. Karl Ragnar, **III:** 404
Gifford, Barry, **Supp. XXV:** 29
Gifford, Bill, **Supp. XI:** 38
Gifford, Terry, **Supp. XVI:** 22
"Gift, The" (Creeley), **Supp. IV Part 1:** 153
"Gift, The" (Doolittle), **Supp. I Part 1:** 267
Gift, The (Hyde), **Supp. XVIII:** 150
"Gift, The" (Jarman), **Supp. XVII:** 116
"Gift, The" (L.-Y. Lee), **Supp. XV:** 213, 214
Gift, The (Nabokov), **III:** 246, 255, 261–263; **Retro. Supp. I:** 264, 266, **268–270,** 273, 274–275, 278
"Gift from the City, A" (Updike), **Retro. Supp. I:** 320
"Gift of God, The" (Robinson), **III:** 512, 517, 518–521, 524
Gift of the Black Folk, The: The Negroes in the Making of America (Du Bois), **Supp. II Part 1:** 179
"Gift of the Magi, The" (O. Henry), **Supp. II Part 1:** 394, 406, 408
"Gift of the Osuo, The" (C. Johnson), **Supp. VI:** 194
"Gift of the Prodigal, The" (Taylor), **Supp. V:** 314, 326
"Gift Outright, The" (Frost), **II:** 152; **Retro. Supp. III:** 91, 106; **Supp. IV Part 1:** 15
"Gifts" (Davison), **Supp. XXVI:** 71
"Gifts of Our Fathers, The" (Gansworth), **Supp. XXVI:** 110
Gigi (Colette; stage adaptation, Loos), **Supp. XVI:** 193
"Gigolo" (Plath), **Retro. Supp. II:** 257
"G.I. Graves in Tuscany" (Hugo), **Supp. VI:** 138
"Gila Bend" (Dickey), **Supp. IV Part 1:** 185–186
Gilb, Dagoberto, **Supp. XXV:** 138
Gilbert, Elizabeth, **Supp. XXII:** 83, 90; **Supp. XXVII:** 258
Gilbert, Jack, **Supp. IX:** 287
Gilbert, Peter, **Supp. IX:** 291, 300
Gilbert, Roger, **Supp. XI:** 124
Gilbert, Sandra M., **Retro. Supp. I:** 42; **Retro. Supp. II:** 324; **Supp. IX:** 66; **Supp. XV:** 270; **Supp. XXIV:** 28; **Supp. XXVII:** 261–262, 263
Gilbert, Susan. See Dickinson, Mrs. William A.
Gilbert and Sullivan, **Supp. IV Part 1:** 389
"Gilbert Stuart Portrait of Washington, The" (Kooser), **Supp. XIX:** 124
Gil Blas (Le Sage), **II:** 290
Gilded Age, The (Twain and Warner), **III:** 504; **IV:** 198; **Retro. Supp. III:** 262
Gilded Lapse of Time, A (Schnackenberg), **Supp. XV:** 258, **260–263**
"Gilded Lapse of Time, A" (Schnackenberg), **Supp. XV:** 257
"Gilded Six-Bits, The" (Hurston), **Retro. Supp. III:** 137, 139; **Supp. VI:** 154–155
Gilder, Richard Watson, **Retro. Supp. II:** 66; **Retro. Supp. III:** 279–280; **Supp. I Part 2:** 418
Gildersleeve, Basil, **Supp. I Part 1:** 369
Gildner, Gary, **Supp. XXVI:** 4
Gilead (Robinson), **Supp. XXI:** 212,

216–220, 223
Giles, H. A., **Retro. Supp. I:** 289
Giles, James R., **Supp. IX:** 11, 15; **Supp. XI:** 219, 223–224, 228, 234
"Giles Corey of the Salem Farms" (Longfellow), **II:** 505, 506; **Retro. Supp. II:** 166, 167
Giles Goat-Boy (Barth), **I:** 121, 122–123, 129, 130, 134, 135–138; **Supp. V:** 39
Gilgamesh: A New Rendering in English Verse (Ferry), **Supp. XXIV:** 147, **150–151**
Gill, Brendan, **Supp. I Part 2:** 659, 660
Gillespie, Nick, **Supp. XIV:** 298, 311
Gillette, Chester, **I:** 512
Gillian, Maria Mazziotti, **Supp. XXIII:** 248
Gilligan, Carol, **Supp. XIII:** 216; **Supp. XXII:** 18
Gillis, Jim, **IV:** 196
Gillis, Steve, **IV:** 195
Gilman, Charlotte Perkins, **Supp. I Part 2:** 637; **Supp. V:** 121, 284, 285; **Supp. XI: 193–211; Supp. XIII:** 295, 306; **Supp. XVI:** 84; **Supp. XXIII:** 26
Gilman, Daniel Coit, **Supp. I Part 1:** 361, 368, 370
Gilman, Owen W., Jr., **Supp. XXVI:** 148
Gilman, Richard, **IV:** 115; **Supp. IV Part 2:** 577; **Supp. XIII:** 100; **Supp. XIX:** 251
Gilmore, Eddy, **Supp. I Part 2:** 618
Gilmore, Leigh, **Supp. XXVI:** 53
Gilmore, Lyman, **Supp. XXI:** 20, 22, 24
Gilmore, Mikal, **Supp. XVI:** 123, 124
Gilpin, Charles, **III:** 392
Gilpin, Dewitt, **Supp. XV:** 197
Gilpin, Laura, **Retro. Supp. I:** 7
Gilpin, Sam, **Supp. V:** 213
Gilpin, William, **Supp. IV Part 2:** 603
"Gil's Furniture Bought & Sold" (Cisneros), **Supp. VII:** 61–62, 64
Gilt Edged Guilt (Wells), **Supp. XXVI:** 281
Gilyard, Keith, **Supp. XXI:** 246
"Gimcrackery" articles (Briggs), **Supp. XVIII:** 8–9
"Gimpel the Fool" (Singer), **IV:** 14; **Retro. Supp. II:** 22, 307
Gimpel the Fool and Other Stories (Singer), **IV:** 1, 7–9, 10, 12
"Gin" (Levine), **Supp. V:** 193
"Gingerbread House, The" (Coover), **Supp. V:** 42–43
Gingerbread Lady, The (Simon), **Supp. IV Part 2:** 580, 583–584, 588
Gingerich, Willard, **Supp. IV Part 2:** 510
Gingertown (McKay), **Supp. X:** 132, 139
Gingold, Hermione, **Supp. XV:** 13
Gingrich, Arnold, **Retro. Supp. I:** 113; **Supp. XVII:** 88; **Supp. XX: 34**
Ginna, Robert, **Supp. IX:** 259
Ginsberg, Allen, **I:** 183; **Retro. Supp. I:** 411, 426, 427; **Retro. Supp. II:** 280; **Retro. Supp. III:** 54; **Supp. II Part 1:** 30, 32, 58, **307–333; Supp. III Part 1:** 2, 91, 96, 98, 100, 222, 226; **Supp. III Part 2:** 541, 627; **Supp. IV Part 1:** 79, 90, 322; **Supp. IV Part 2:** 502; **Supp. IX:** 299; **Supp. V:** 168, 336; **Supp. VIII:** 239, 242–243, 289; **Supp. X:** 120, 204; **Supp. XI:** 135, 297; **Supp. XII:** 118–119, 121–122, 124, 126, 130–131, 136, 182; **Supp. XIV:** 15, 53, 54, 125, 137, 141, 142, 143–144, 148, 150, 269, 280, 283; **Supp. XV:** 134, 177, 263; **Supp. XVI:** 123, 135; **Supp. XVII:** 138, 243; **Supp. XVIII:** 20, 27, 29, 30; **Supp. XXI:** 53; **Supp. XXII:** 172, 225; **Supp. XXIII:** 211, 213, 215; **Supp. XXIV:** 34, 36, 37; **Supp. XXV:** 29; **Supp. XXVI:** 70; **Supp. XXVII:** 18
Gioia, Dana, **Supp. IX:** 279; **Supp. XII:** 209; **Supp. XIII:** 337; **Supp. XIX:** 117, 144; **Supp. XV: 111–131,** 251; **Supp. XVII:** 69, 72, 112; **Supp. XXI:** 99; **Supp. XXIII:** 112; **Supp. XXV:** 222
Giono, Jean, **Supp. XVI:** 135
Giordano, Tony J., **Supp. XXIII:** 125
Giotto di Bondone, **Supp. I Part 2:** 438; **Supp. XI:** 126
Giovani, Regula, **Supp. XV:** 270
Giovanni, Nikki, **Supp. I Part 1:** 66; **Supp. II Part 1:** 54; **Supp. IV Part 1:** 11; **Supp. VIII:** 214; **Supp. XXII:** 11; **Supp. XXVII:** 165, 200, 202
Giovanni's Room (Baldwin), **Retro. Supp. II:** 5, 6, **6–7,** 8, 10; **Supp. I Part 1:** 51, 52, 55–56, 57, 60, 63, 67; **Supp. III Part 1:** 125
Giovannitti, Arturo, **I:** 476; **Supp. XV:** 299, 301, 302, 307
"Giraffe" (Swenson), **Supp. IV Part 2:** 651
Giraldi, Giovanni Battista. See Cinthio
"Girl" (Kincaid), **Supp. VII:** 182–183
Girl, The (Le Sueur), **Supp. XXIII: 172–174**
"Girl, The" (Olds), **Supp. X:** 207
"Girl Friend Poems" (Wright), **Supp. XV:** 349
"Girl from Lynn Bathes Horse!!" (McCarriston), **Supp. XIV:** 266
"Girl from Red Lion, P.A., A" (Mencken), **III:** 111
Girl in Glass, The: Love Poems (W. J. Smith), **Supp. XIII:** 335
Girl in Landscape (Lethem), **Supp. XVIII:** 136, **141–143**
"Girl in the Grave, The" (McCoy), **Supp. XIII:** 170
"Girl in the River, The" (Rash), **Supp. XXVII:** 224
"Girl in the River, The: The Wild and Scenic Chattooga, Ron Rash's Saints at the River, and the Drowning of Rachel Trois" (Lane), **Supp. XXVII:** 216
Girl Like I, A (Loos), **Supp. XVI:** 181, 183, 184, 187, 194, 196
"Girl of the Golden West" (Didion), **Supp. IV Part 1:** 195, 208, 211
Girl of the Golden West, The (Puccini), **III:** 139
Girl of the Limberlost (film), **Supp. XX: 223**
Girl of the Limberlost (Stratton-Porter), **Supp. XX: 211, 221–222**
"Girl on a Scaffold" (C. Frost), **Supp. XV:** 98
"Girl on the Baggage Truck, The" (O'Hara), **III:** 371–372
Girl on the Via Flaminia, The (Hayes), **Supp. XXVI:** 135, 136–137, 144
"Girls" (Gallagher), **Supp. XXIV:** 174–175, 177
Girls at Play (Theroux), **Supp. VIII:** 314, 315, 316, **317**
"Girls at the Sphinx, The" (Farrell), **II:** 45
"Girls in Their Summer Dresses, The" (Shaw), **Supp. XIX:** 246
Girl Sleuth, The: A Feminist Guide (Mason), **Supp. VIII:** 133, 135, **139,** 142
"Girl's Story, A" (Bambara), **Supp. XI:** 10–11
"Girl the Prince Liked, The" (Z. Fitzgerald), **Supp. IX:** 71
Girl Who Had to Die, The (Holding), **Supp. XXII: 126–127**
Girl Who Loved Tom Gordon, The (King), **Supp. V:** 138, 152
"Girl Who Raised Pigeons, The" (E. P. Jones), **Supp. XXII:** 143
Girl with Curious Hair (Wallace), **Supp. X:** 301, **305–308**
"Girl with Curious Hair" (Wallace), **Supp. X:** 306

"Girl with Silver Eyes, The" (Hammett), **Supp. IV Part 1:** 344, 345
"Girl with Talent, The" (Z. Fitzgerald), **Supp. IX:** 71
Girodias, Maurice, **III:** 171; **Supp. XI:** 297
Giroux, Robert, **Retro. Supp. II:** 177, 229, 235; **Supp. IV Part 1:** 280; **Supp. VIII:** 195; **Supp. XV:** 146
Gish, Dorothy, **Retro. Supp. I:** 103
Gish, Lillian, **Supp. XVI:** 184
Gissing, George, **II:** 138, 144
Gitagovinda, **Supp. XXII:** 258
Gita-govínda: Love Songs of Radha and Krishna (Jayadeva; Siegel, trans.), **Supp. XXII:** 258
Gittings, Robert, **II:** 531
Gittleman, Edwin, **Supp. XXV:** 237, 251
"Given" (C. Frost), **Supp. XV:** 96
Given Sugar, Given Salt (Hirshfield), **Supp. XXIII:** 133
"Give Us Back Our Country" (Masters), **Supp. I Part 2:** 472
Give Us This Day (film, Dmytryk), **Supp. XX: 40–41**
"Give Way, Ye Gates" (Roethke), **III:** 536
"Give Your Heart to the Hawks" (Jeffers), **Supp. II Part 2:** 433
"Giving Blood" (Updike), **IV:** 226; **Retro. Supp. I:** 332
Giving Good Weight (McPhee), **Supp. III Part 1:** 307
"Giving in to You" (X. J. Kennedy), **Supp. XV:** 160
"Giving Myself Up" (Strand), **Supp. IV Part 2:** 627
Giving Up America (Abraham), **Supp. XXIV:** 2, 3, **7–9**
Giving Up the Ghost (Moraga), **Supp. XXIII: 197–199**
G. K. the DJ (Keillor), **Supp. XVI:** 171
Glackens, William, **Retro. Supp. II:** 103
Gladden, Washington, **III:** 293; **Supp. I Part 1:** 5
Gladstone, William Ewart, **Supp. I Part 2:** 419
"Gladys Poem, The" (Alvarez), **Supp. VII:** 10
Glamorama (Ellis), **Supp. XXVII:** 68, 71, 75–76, 76, 78
"Glance at German 'Kultur,' A" (Bourne), **I:** 228
Glance Away, A (Wideman), **Supp. X:** 320
"Glance from the Bridge, A" (Wilbur), **Supp. III Part 2:** 551
"Glance in the Mirror, A" (Swados), **Supp. XIX:** 261–262
Glance toward Shakespeare, A (Chapman), **Supp. XIV:** 44
Glancy, Diane, **Supp. XXI:** 246
Glanville-Hicks, Peggy, **Supp. IV Part 1:** 84
Glare (Ammons), **Supp. VII:** 35–36
Glasgow, Cary, **II:** 173, 182
Glasgow, Ellen, **II: 173–195; IV:** 328; **Supp. X:** 228, 234; **Supp. XXIV:** 30; **Supp. XXV:** 201; **Supp. XXVI:** 276
Glasmon, Kubec, **Supp. XIII:** 166
Glaspell, Susan, **Supp. III Part 1: 175–191; Supp. X:** 46; **Supp. XVII:** 99; **Supp. XXI:** 5
"Glass" (Francis), **Supp. IX:** 80
Glass, Irony, and God (Carson), **Supp. XII:** 97, **104–106**
Glass, Philip, **Supp. XXI:** 146, 147
"Glass Ark, The" (Komunyakaa), **Supp. XIII:** 129
Glass Bees, The (Jünger; Bogan and Mayer, trans.), **Supp. III Part 1:** 63
"Glass Blower of Venice" (Malamud), **Supp. I Part 2:** 450
"Glass Essay, The" (Carson), **Supp. XII: 104–105**
"Glass Face in the Rain, A: New Poems" (Stafford), **Supp. XI: 327–328**
Glass Key, The (Hammett), **Supp. IV Part 1:** 351–353
"Glass Meadows" (Bausch), **Supp. VII:** 53–54
Glass Menagerie, The (T. Williams), **I:** 81; **IV:** 378, 379, 380, 382, 383, 385, 386, 387, 388, 389, 390, 391, 392, 393–394, 395, 398; **Supp. IV Part 1:** 84; **Supp. XXV:** 101
"Glass Mountain, The" (Barthelme), **Supp. IV Part 1:** 47
"Glass Tent, The" (Everwine), **Supp. XV:** 76
Glatstein, Jacob, **Supp. X:** 70
Glazer, Nathan, **Supp. VIII:** 93, 243
"Gleaners, The" (Merwin), **Supp. III Part 1:** 346
Gleanings in Europe (Cooper), **I:** 346
Gleason, Ralph J., **Supp. IX:** 16
Glenday, Michael, **Retro. Supp. II:** 210
Glengarry Glen Ross (film), **Supp. XIV:** 242
Glengarry Glen Ross (Mamet), **Supp. XIV:** 239, 240, 242, 245, 246, 250, 254, 255
Glimcher, Arne, **Supp. VIII:** 73
"Glimpses" (Jones), **Supp. XI:** 218
Glimpses of the Moon, The (Wharton), **II:** 189–190; **IV:** 322–323; **Retro. Supp. I:** 381; **Retro. Supp. III:** 288
"Glimpses of Vietnamese Life" (Levertov), **Supp. III Part 1:** 282
Glisson, J. T., **Supp. X:** 234
"Glittering Trout" (Davison), **Supp. XXVI:** 79
Gloria Mundi (Frederic), **II:** 144–145
Gloria Naylor (Fowler), **Supp. VIII:** 224
"Glorious Fourth, The" (Ryan as Quin), **Supp. XVIII:** 229
Glorious Ones, The (Prose), **Supp. XVI:** 251
Glory, The (Wouk), **Supp. XXV:** 254, 257, 265–266
Glory Field, The (Myers), **Supp. XXVII:** 208
Glory of Hera, The (Gordon), **II:** 196–197, 198, 199, 217–220
Glory of the Conquered, The (Glaspell), **Supp. III Part 1:** 176
Glory River (Huddle), **Supp. XXVI:** 151
Gloss, Molly, **Supp. XXIII:** 280
Glossary of Literary Terms (Abrams), **Supp. XVI:** 19
Glotfelty, Cheryll, **Supp. IX:** 25
Glover, Joyce Lee, **Supp. XIX:** 112
Glover, Michael, **Supp. XXIV:** 168
Glow, The (Wrigley), **Supp. XVIII:** 295
"Glow, The" (Wrigley), **Supp. XVIII:** 296–297, 307
Gluck, Christoph Willibald, **II:** 210, 211
Glück, Louise, **Supp. V: 77–94; Supp. VIII:** 272; **Supp. X:** 209; **Supp. XIV:** 269; **Supp. XV:** 19, 252; **Supp. XVII:** 241; **Supp. XXV:** 222
"Glutton, The" (Shapiro), **Supp. II Part 2:** 705
"Glutton for Punishment, A" (Yates), **Supp. XI:** 341
Glyph (Everett), **Supp. XVIII: 60–61**
Gnädiges Fräulein, The (T. Williams), **IV:** 382, 395, 398
Gnomes and Occasions (Nemerov), **III:** 269
Gnomologia (Fuller), **II:** 111
"Gnothis Seauton" (Emerson), **II:** 11, 18–19
Go (Holmes), **Supp. XIV:** 144
"Go Ahead; Goodbye; Good Luck; and Watch Out" (Bronk), **Supp. XXI:** 31
"Goal of Intellectual Men, The" (Eberhart), **I:** 529–530
Go-Between, The (Hartley), **Supp. I**

Part 1: 293
Gobineau, Joseph Arthur de, **Supp. XIV:** 209
God (Allen), **Supp. XV:** 3
God and the American Writer (Kazin), **Supp. VIII: 108–109**
Godard, Jean-Luc, **Supp. I Part 2:** 558
Godbey (Masters), **Supp. I Part 2:** 472
God Bless You, Mr. Rosewater (Vonnegut), **Supp. II Part 2:** 758, 767, 768–769, 771, 772
Goddess Abides, The (Buck), **Supp. II Part 1:** 129, 131–132
Gödel, Kurt, **Supp. IV Part 1:** 43
Godfather (Puzo), **Supp. IV Part 1:** 390
Godfires (Hoffman), **Supp. XVIII: 81–82**
God Help the Child (Morrison), **Retro. Supp. III:** 185, 199–200
God in Ruins, A (Uris), **Supp. XX: 247, 256**
"God in the Doorway" (Dillard), **Supp. VI:** 28
"God is a distant-stately Lover" (Dickinson), **I:** 471
Godkin, E. L., **II:** 274
God Knows (Heller), **Supp. IV Part 1:** 386, 388–389
God Made Alaska for the Indians (Reed), **Supp. X:** 241
God of His Fathers, The (London), **II:** 469
God of Vengeance, The (Asch), **IV:** 11; **Supp. XXIII:** 5, **8–9**
Go Down, Moses (Faulkner), **Retro. Supp. I:** 75, 82, 85, 86, 88, 89, 90, 92; **Retro. Supp. III:** 86, 87; **Supp. XVIII:** 203
"Go Down, Moses" (Faulkner), **II:** 71–72
Go Down, Moses (Hayden), **Supp. II Part 1:** 365
Go Down, Moses and Other Stories (Faulkner), **II:** 71; **Supp. X:** 52
"Go Down Death A Funeral Sermon" (J. W. Johnson), **Supp. IV Part 1:** 7
"God Rest Ye Merry, Gentlemen" (Hemingway), **IV:** 122
Godric (Buechner), **Supp. XII:** 53
Gods, The (Goldbarth), **Supp. XII:** 189, 190
Gods Arrive, The (Wharton), **IV:** 326–327; **Retro. Supp. I:** 382
God Save the Child (Parker), **Supp. XIX:** 183–184
"God Save the Rights of Man" (Freneau), **Supp. II Part 1:** 268
"Godsildren" (Swenson), **Supp. IV Part 2:** 645
"God's Christ Theory" (Carson), **Supp. XII: 106**
God's Country (Everett), **Supp. XVIII: 57–58,** 64, 65
God's Country and My People (Morris), **III:** 238
Gods Determinations touching his Elect: and the Elects Combat in their Conversion, and Coming up to God in Christ together with the Comfortable Effects thereof (Taylor), **IV:** 155–160, 165
God-Seeker, The (Lewis), **II:** 456
God Sends Sunday (Bontemps), **Supp. XXII:** 2, 3, 9
God's Favorite (Simon), **Supp. IV Part 2:** 575, 586, 588, 590
"God's Fool" (Gibran), **Supp. XX: 118**
God's Little Acre (Caldwell), **I:** 288, 289, 290, 297, 298–302, 305–306, 309, 310; **Supp. XXII:** 196
God's Man: A Novel in Wood Cuts (Ward), **I:** 31
Gods of Peg¿na, The (Dunsany), **Supp. XXV:** 113
Gods of Winter, The (Gioia), **Supp. XV:** 112, **121–125**
"Gods of Winter, The" (Gioia), **Supp. XV:** 117
"God's Peace in November" (Jeffers), **Supp. II Part 2:** 420
God's Silence (F. Wright), **Supp. XVII:** 240, 246–247
"God Stiff" (Carson), **Supp. XII: 106**
God's Trombones (J. W. Johnson), **Supp. II Part 1:** 201
"God's Youth" (Untermeyer), **Supp. XV:** 296
"God the Father and the Empty House" (McCarriston), **Supp. XIV:** 273
Godwin, William, **II:** 304; **III:** 415; **Supp. I Part 1:** 126, 146; **Supp. I Part 2:** 512, 513–514, 522, 709, 719
God without Thunder (Ransom), **III:** 495–496, 499
Godwulf Manuscript, The (Parker), **Supp. XIX: 178–182**
Goebbels, Josef, **III:** 560
Goebel, Irma, **Supp. X:** 95
Goen, C. C., **I:** 560
Goethe, Johann Wolfgang von, **I:** 181, 396, 587–588; **II:** 5, 6, 320, 344, 488, 489, 492, 502, 556; **III:** 395, 453, 607, 612, 616; **IV:** 50, 64, 173, 326; **Retro. Supp. I:** 360; **Retro. Supp. II:** 94; **Supp. I Part 2:** 423, 457; **Supp. II Part 1:** 26; **Supp. III Part 1:** 63; **Supp. IX:** 131, 308; **Supp. X:** 60; **Supp. XI:** 169; **Supp. XVIII:** 278; **Supp. XX: 84; Supp. XXIV:** 152
Go for the Body (Lacy), **Supp. XV:** 201, 204
Gogan, Robert, **Supp. XXI:** 24
Gogol, Nikolai, **I:** 296; **IV:** 1, 4; **Retro. Supp. I:** 266, 269; **Retro. Supp. III:** 139; **Supp. VIII:** 14; **Supp. XVII:** 45; **Supp. XVIII:** 102; **Supp. XXII:** 59
Goia, Dana, **Supp. XIX:** 121
Goines, Donald, **Supp. XXIII:** 174
"Going, Going, Gone" (Skloot), **Supp. XX: 207**
Going, William T., **Supp. VIII:** 126
"Going 1960–1970" (Huddle), **Supp. XXVI:** 148
Going After Cacciato (O'Brien), **Supp. V:** 237, 238, 239, 244–246, 248, 249
Going All the Way (Wakefield), **Supp. VIII:** 43
Going Away (Sigal), **Supp. XXVI:** 26
"Going Critical" (Bambara), **Supp. XI:** 14
Going Down (Markson), **Supp. XVII:** 136, 138, **139–140,** 141, 142–143, 144, 145
Going for the Rain (Ortiz), **Supp. IV Part 2:** 499, 505–508, 509, 514
"Going Home by Last Night" (Kinnell), **Supp. III Part 1:** 244
"Going Home in America" (Hardwick), **Supp. III Part 1:** 205
"Going Home"(Kenny), **Supp. XXIII:** 144, 148
Going into the City: Portrait of a Critic as a Young Man (Christgau), **Supp. XXVII:** 33, 39
"Going North" (Salinas), **Supp. XIII:** 316
Going Places (L. Michaels), **Supp. XVI:** 201, **203–206**
"Going Places" (L. Michaels), **Supp. XVI:** 203
"Going South" (J. W. Miller), **Supp. XX: 169**
Going South (Lardner and Buck), **II:** 427
Going To and Fro and Walking Up and Down (Reznikoff), **Supp. XIV:** 280, 282, 284, 285
Going to Meet the Man (Baldwin), **Supp. I Part 1:** 60, 62–63; **Supp. XX: 147**
"Going to Meet the Man" (Baldwin), **Retro. Supp. II:** 8, 9; **Supp. I Part 1:** 62–63
"Going to Naples" (Welty), **IV:** 278; **Retro. Supp. I:** 352, 353
"Going to Shrewsbury" (Jewett), **II:** 393

"Going to the Bakery" (Bishop), **Supp. I Part 1:** 93
Going-to-the-Stars (Lindsay), **Supp. I Part 2:** 398
Going-to-the-Sun (Lindsay), **Supp. I Part 2:** 397–398
Going to the Territory (Ellison), **Retro. Supp. II:** 119, 123–124
"Going towards Pojoaque, A December Full Moon/72" (Harjo), **Supp. XII:** 218
"Going Under" (Dubus), **Supp. VII:** 83
"Gold" (Francis), **Supp. IX:** 82
Gold (O'Neill), **III:** 391
Gold, Arthur, **Supp. XXIV:** 160, 161
Gold, Charles H., **Supp. XXVI:** 6
Gold, Don, **Supp. XXII:** 258
Gold, Michael, **II:** 26; **IV:** 363, 364, 365; **Retro. Supp. II:** 323; **Supp. I Part 1:** 331; **Supp. I Part 2:** 609; **Supp. XIV:** 288; **Supp. XXII:** 277; **Supp. XXVII:** 134
Goldbarth, Albert, **Supp. XII: 175–195**
Goldbarth's Book of Occult Phenomena (Goldbarth), **Supp. XII:** 181
Goldberg, Carole, **Supp. XXII:** 207
Goldberg, Michael, **Supp. XXIII:** 210, 216, 217
Goldberg, S. L., **Supp. VIII:** 238
"Gold Bug, The" (Poe), **III:** 410, 413, 419, 420; **Retro. Supp. III:** 226, 230
Gold Bug Variations, The (Powers), **Supp. IX:** 210, 212, **216–217,** 219
Gold Cell, The (Olds), **Supp. X: 206–209**
Gold Diggers, The (Monette), **Supp. X:** 153
Golde, Miss (Mencken's Secretary), **III:** 104, 107
Golden, Harry, **III:** 579, 581; **Supp. VIII:** 244
Golden, Mike, **Supp. XI:** 294, 295, 297, 299, 303
Golden Age, The (Gurney), **Supp. V:** 101–103
Golden Apples (Rawlings), **Supp. X: 228–229,** 230, 234
Golden Apples, The (Welty), **IV:** 261, 271–274, 281, 293; **Retro. Supp. I:** 341, 342, 343, **350–351,** 352, 355
Golden Apples of the Sun, The (Bradbury), **Supp. IV Part 1:** 102, 103
Golden Book of Springfield, The (Lindsay), **Supp. I Part 2:** 376, 379, 395, 396
Golden Bough, The (Frazer), **II:** 204, 549; **III:** 6–7; **Supp. I Part 1:** 18; **Supp. IX:** 123; **Supp. X:** 124
Golden Bowl, The (James), **II:** 320, 333, 335; **Retro. Supp. I:** 215, 216, 218–219, 232, **234–235,** 374
Golden Boy (Odets), **Supp. II Part 2:** 538, 539, 540–541, 546, 551
Golden Calves, The (Auchincloss), **Supp. IV Part 1:** 35
Golden Child (Hwang), **Supp. XXI:** 147–148
Golden Day, The (Mumford), **Supp. II Part 2:** 471, 475, 477, 483, 484, 488–489, 493
Golden Fleece, The (Gurney), **Supp. V:** 97
Golden Gate (film, Madden), **Supp. XXI:** 147
Golden Gate, The (Seth), **Supp. XVII:** 117
Golden Gate Country (Atherton), **Supp. XXIV:** 27
Golden Grove, The: Selected Passages from the Sermons and Writings of Jeremy Taylor (L. P. Smith), **Supp. XIV:** 345
"Golden Heifer, The" (Wylie), **Supp. I Part 2:** 707
"Golden Honeymoon, The" (Lardner), **II:** 429–430, 431
Golden Journey, The (W. J. Smith and Bogan, comps.), **Supp. XIII:** 347
Golden Ladder series (S. and A. Warner), **Supp. XVIII:** 267
"Golden Lads" (Marquand), **III:** 56
Golden Legend, The (Longfellow), **II:** 489, 490, 495, 505, 506, 507; **Retro. Supp. II:** 159, 165, 166
Golden Mean and Other Poems, The (Tate and Wills), **IV:** 122
Golden Mountain, The (Levin), **Supp. XXVII:** 134, 140
Golden Peacock (Atherton), **Supp. XXIV:** 26
"Golden Retrievals" (Doty), **Supp. XI:** 132
Golden Shakespeare, The: An Anthology (L. P. Smith), **Supp. XIV:** 349
Golden Slippers: An Anthology of Negro Poetry for Young Readers (Bontemps, ed.), **Supp. XXII:** 5, 11
Goldensohn, Lorrie, **Retro. Supp. II:** 51
Golden State (Bidart), **Supp. XV:** 21, **23–25**
"Golden State" (Bidart), **Supp. XV:** 23, 24, 25
Golden States (Cunningham), **Supp. XV:** 55, **56–59,** 63
Golden Treasury of Best Songs and Lyrical Poems in the English Language (Palgrave), **Retro. Supp. I:** 124
Golden Treasury of the Best Songs and Lyrical Poems in the English Language (Palgrave), **Retro. Supp. III:** 91; **Supp. XIV:** 340
Goldenweiser, Alexander Aleksandrovich, **Supp. XXVI:** 89
Golden Whales of California and Other Rhymes in the American Language, The (Lindsay), **Supp. I Part 2:** 394–395, 396
Golden Years, The (A. Miller), **Retro. Supp. III:** 166
Goldfinch, The (Tartt), **Supp. XXVII:** 268, 276–280
"Goldfish Bowl, The" (Francis), **Supp. IX:** 78
Gold Fools (Sorrentino), **Supp. XXI:** 237
Goldin Boys, The (Epstein), **Supp. XIV:** 112
Golding, Arthur, **III:** 467, 468
Golding, William, **Supp. IV Part 1:** 297
Goldini, Carlo, **II:** 274
Goldkorn Tales (Epstein), **Supp. XII: 163–164**
Goldman, Albert, **Supp. XI:** 299
Goldman, Arnold, **Supp. XXI:** 13
Goldman, Emma, **III:** 176, 177; **Supp. I Part 2:** 524; **Supp. XVII:** 96, 103, 104; **Supp. XXIII:** 162
Goldman, Francisco, **Supp. XXV: 49–62**
Goldman, William, **Supp. IV Part 2:** 474
Goldman-Price, Irene, **Retro. Supp. III:** 276, 277, 278
"Gold Mountain Stories" project (Kingston), **Supp. V:** 164
Gold of Chickaree, The (S. and A. Warner), **Supp. XVIII:** 267, 268, 269
Goldring, Douglas, **III:** 458
Goldsmith, Oliver, **II:** 273, 282, 299, 304, 308, 314, 315, 514; **Retro. Supp. I:** 335; **Supp. I Part 1:** 310; **Supp. I Part 2:** 503, 714, 716; **Supp. XVIII:** 12
Gold Standard and the Logic of Naturalism, The (W. B. Michaels), **Retro. Supp. I:** 369
Goldstein, Laurence, **Supp. XXI:** 134
Goldstein, Rebecca, **Supp. XVII:** 44
Goldstein, Richard, **Supp. XXVII:** 43
Goldthwaite, Melissa, **Supp. XXVI:** 56
Goldwater, Barry, **I:** 376; **III:** 38
Goldwyn, Samuel, **Retro. Supp. II:**

199; **Supp. I Part 1:** 281; **Supp. XXIV:** 28; **Supp. XXV:** 195
Golem, The (Leivick), **IV:** 6; **Supp. XXIII:** 8
"Golgotha Is a Mountain" (Bontemps), **Supp. XXII:** 3, 8
"Goliardic Song" (Hecht), **Supp. X:** 63
"Go Like This" (Moore), **Supp. X:** 165
Goll, Ivan, **Supp. III Part 1:** 235, 243–244; **Supp. III Part 2:** 621
Gomes, Albert, **Supp. XXI:** 160
Goncharova, Natalya, **Supp. IX:** 66
Goncourt, Edmond de, **II:** 325, 328; **III:** 315, 317–318, 321; **Retro. Supp. I:** 226
Goncourt, Jules de, **II:** 328; **III:** 315, 317–318, 321
Gone Fishin' (Mosley), **Supp. XIII:** **235–236,** 240
"Gone to Feed the Roses" (Vaz), **Supp. XXVI:** 268
"Gone to War" (E. Stoddard), **Supp. XV:** 282
"Gone West" (Rodriguez), **Supp. XIV:** 308
Gone with the Wind (film), **Retro. Supp. I:** 113; **Supp. XXVII:** 83
Gone with the Wind (Mitchell), **II:** 177; **Retro. Supp. I:** 340; **Supp. XX: 243; Supp. XXII:** 190, 195
Gongora y Argote, Luis de, **II:** 552
Gonzalez, David, **Supp. VIII:** 85
González, Jovita, **Supp. XIX:** 99
Gonzo: The Life of Hunter S. Thompson (Wenner and Seymour), **Supp. XXIV:** 280, 281, 282, 288
Gooch, Brad, **Supp. XII:** 121; **Supp. XXIII:** 218, 220
Good, George, **Supp. XI:** 306
"Good, the Plaid, and the Ugly, The" (Wasserstein), **Supp. XV:** 327
"Good and Not So Good, The" (Dunn), **Supp. XI:** 141
"Good Anna, The" (Stein), **IV:** 37, 40, 43
Good As Gold (Heller), **Supp. IV Part 1:** 386, 388, 394
Good as I Been to You (album, Dylan), **Supp. XVIII:** 28
"Good As Yesterday" (Muñoz), **Supp. XXV:** 134, 135
Good Boys and Dead Girls and Other Essays (Gordon), **Supp. IV Part 1:** 309–310
"Good Brother" (Muñoz), **Supp. XXV:** 135
Good Brother, The (Offutt), **Supp. XIX:** 163, **168–169**
"Good-by and Keep Cold" (Frost), **Retro. Supp. I:** 135
"Goodbye" (Davison), **Supp. XXVI:** 69
"Good-bye" (Emerson), **II:** 19
"Goodbye, Christ" (Hughes), **Retro. Supp. I:** 202, 203
Goodbye, Columbus (P. Roth), **Retro. Supp. II:** 280, 281, 290; **Supp. III Part 2:** 403–406; **Supp. XIV:** 112; **Supp. XX: 177; Supp. XXVI:** 123
"Goodbye, Columbus" (P. Roth), **Supp. III Part 2:** 401, 404, 408–409, 411
Goodbye, Columbus and Five Short Stories (P. Roth), **Retro. Supp. II:** 279
"Goodbye, Goldeneye" (Swenson), **Supp. IV Part 2:** 651
"Goodbye, Mr. Chipstein" (Epstein), **Supp. XIV:** 103, 108
"Goodbye, My Brother" (Cheever), **Supp. I Part 1:** 175, 177, 193
"Goodbye and Good Luck" (Paley), **Supp. VI:** 219, 223
Goodbye Girl, The (film), **Supp. IV Part 2:** 589
Goodbye Girl, The (musical), **Supp. IV Part 2:** 576, 588
Goodbye Girl, The (Simon), **Supp. IV Part 2:** 575
Goodbye Look, The (Macdonald), **Supp. IV Part 2:** 473, 474
"Good-Bye My Fancy" (Whitman), **Retro. Supp. III:** 303
"Good-Bye My Fancy" (Whitman), **IV:** 348
"Goodbye to All That" (Biss), **Supp. XXVI:** 46, 47, 53
"Goodbye to All That" (Didion), **Supp. IV Part 1:** 197
Goodbye to All That (Graves), **I:** 477; **Supp. XXVI:** 53
Goodbye to Berlin (Isherwood), **Supp. XIV:** 159, 161, 162, 169
"Goodbye to My Twinkle Days" (Nguyen), **Supp. XXVI:** 209
"Good-Bye to the Mezzogiorno" (Auden), **Supp. II Part 1:** 19
"Goodbye to the Poetry of Calcium" (Wright), **Supp. III Part 2:** 599
"Good Company" (Matthews), **Supp. IX:** 160
"Good Country People" (O'Connor), **III:** 343, 350, 351, 352, 358; **Retro. Supp. II:** 229, 232; **Retro. Supp. III:** 213, 215, 217–218
Good Day to Die, A (Harrison), **Supp. VIII: 42–44,** 45, 47
Good Day to Die, A (O'Nan as James Coltrane), **Supp. XXV:** 146
Good Doctor, The (Simon), **Supp. IV Part 2:** 575, 585
Good Earth, The (Buck), **Supp. I Part 1:** 49; **Supp. II Part 1:** 115–175, 118, 125, 132
Good European, The (Blackmur), **Supp. II Part 1:** 91
Good Evening Mr. & Mrs. America, and All the Ships at Sea (Bausch), **Supp. VII:** 41, 47, 52
"Good Friday" (Jarman), **Supp. XVII:** 116
"Good Friday, 1613, Riding Westward" (Donne), **Supp. XXVII:** 220
"Good Friday, 1995, Driving Westward" (Rash), **Supp. XXVII:** 219–220
"Good Girl" (Peacock), **Supp. XIX:** 199
Good Gray Poet, The (O'Connor), **Retro. Supp. I:** 407
Good Health and How We Won It (Sinclair), **Supp. V:** 285–286
Good Hearts (Price), **Supp. VI:** 259, 265
"Good Job Gone, A" (Hughes), **Retro. Supp. I:** 204
Good Journey, A (Ortiz), **Supp. IV Part 2:** 497, 499, 503, 505, 509–510, 514
Good Life, The (Nearing and Nearing), **Supp. XXVI:** 35
Good Lord Bird, The (McBride), **Supp. XXVI:** 191, 200, 202–204
Good Luck, Miss Wyckoff (Inge), **Supp. XXV:** 93, 95, 106–107
Good Luck in Cracked Italian (Hugo), **Supp. VI:** 133, 137–138
Goodman, Allegra, **Supp. XII:** 159; **Supp. XVI:** 205; **Supp. XX: 177; Supp. XXVI: 117–132**
Goodman, Ellen, **Supp. XVI:** 103
Goodman, Jack, **Supp. XXI:** 277
Goodman, Jenny, **Supp. XV:** 343, 344
Goodman, Kenneth Sawyer, **Supp. XXVII:** 89
Goodman, Paul, **I:** 218, 261; **III:** 39; **Supp. I Part 2:** 524; **Supp. VIII:** 239–240
Goodman, Philip, **III:** 105, 108
Goodman, Walter, **Supp. IV Part 2:** 532
Good Man Is Hard to Find, A (O'Connor), **III:** 339, 343–345; **Retro. Supp. III:** 208
"Good Man Is Hard to Find, A" (O'Connor), **III:** 339, 344, 353; **Retro. Supp. II:** 230–231; **Retro. Supp. III:** 212
Good Man Is Hard to Find and Other Stories, A (O'Connor), **Retro. Supp.**

II: 229, **230–232**
Good Morning, America (Sandburg), **III:** 592–593
"Good Morning, Major" (Marquand), **III:** 56
Good Morning, Midnight (Rhys), **Supp. III Part 1:** 43
"Good Morning, Revolution" (Hughes), **Retro. Supp. I:** 201, 203
Good Morning Blues: The Autobiography of Count Basie (Murray), **Supp. XIX:** 159
Good Morning Revolution: Uncollected Writings of Social Protest (Hughes), **Retro. Supp. I:** 194, 201, 202, 209
Good Mother, The (Miller), **Supp. XII:** 289, **290–294,** 299, 301
Good News (Abbey), **Supp. XIII: 11–12**
"Good News from New-England" (E. Johnson), **Supp. I Part 1:** 115
Good News of Death and Other Poems (Simpson), **Supp. IX:** 265, **268–269**
"Goodnight, Saigon" (lecture, Caputo), **Supp. XIX:** 17, 30
Good Night, Willie Lee, I'll See You in the Morning (Walker), **Supp. III Part 2:** 520, 531
"Good Oak" (Leopold), **Supp. XIV:** 185, 187, 191
"Good Old Times, The: New York Fifty Years Ago" (Briggs), **Supp. XVIII:** 15
"Good Pine, A" (Offutt), **Supp. XIX:** 174
Goodrich, Chris, **Supp. XXII:** 206, 214
Goodrich, Frances, **Supp. XXVII:** 136
Goodrich, Samuel G., **Supp. I Part 1:** 38
Good Scent from a Strange Mountain, A (R. O. Butler), **Supp. XII:** 62, **70–72**
Good School, A (Yates), **Supp. XI:** 334, **346–347,** 348, 349
"Good Shepherdess, The/La Buena Pastora" (Mora), **Supp. XIII:** 228–229
Good Wife, The (O'Nan), **Supp. XXV:** 145, 149
Good Will (Smiley), **Supp. VI:** 292, **299–300**
Goodwin, K. L., **III:** 478
Goodwin, Stephen, **Supp. V:** 314, 316, 322, 323, 325
"Good Word for Winter, A" (J. R. Lowell), **Supp. I Part 2:** 420
Goodwyn, Janet, **Retro. Supp. I:** 370
Goody, Alex, **Supp. XXII:** 160
"Goophered Grapevine, The" (Chesnutt), **Supp. XIV:** 57, **58–61**
"Goose Fish, The" (Nemerov), **III:** 272, 284
"Goose Pond" (Kunitz), **Supp. III Part 1:** 262
Goose-Step, The (Sinclair), **Supp. V:** 276
Gordimer, Nadine, **Supp. XV:** 251
Gordon, Ambrose, **Supp. XV:** 144
Gordon, A. R., **III:** 199
Gordon, Caroline, **II: 196–222,** 536, 537; **III:** 454, 482; **IV:** 123, 126–127, 139, 282; **Retro. Supp. II:** 177, 222, 229, 233, 235; **Supp. II Part 1:** 139
Gordon, Charles G., **I:** 454
Gordon, Don, **Supp. X:** 119
Gordon, Eugene, **Supp. II Part 1:** 170; **Supp. XVIII:** 280
Gordon, Fran, **Supp. XIII:** 111
Gordon, James Morris, **II:** 197
Gordon, Lois, **Supp. IV Part 1:** 48; **Supp. V:** 46
Gordon, Lyndall, **Retro. Supp. I:** 55
Gordon, Mary, **Supp. IV Part 1: 297–317**
Gordon, Neil, **Supp. XVI:** 156
Gordon, Peter, **Supp. XII:** 3–4, 4–5, 8
Gordon, Ruth, **IV:** 357; **Supp. XX: 50**
Gore, Thomas Pryor, **Supp. IV Part 2:** 679
Gore and Igor (Levin), **Supp. XXVII:** 133
Gores, Joe, **Supp. XXI:** 70
Gorey, Edward, **IV:** 430, 436; **Supp. XXIII:** 209
"Gorge, The" (Huddle), **Supp. XXVI:** 154
Gorilla, My Love (Bambara), **Supp. XI:** 1, **2–7**
"Gorilla, My Love" (Bambara), **Supp. XI:** 2, 3–4
Gorki, Maxim, **I:** 478; **II:** 49; **III:** 402; **IV:** 299; **Supp. I Part 1:** 5, 51; **Supp. XIX:** 241
Gorky, Maxim, **Supp. XXIII:** 1, 4
Gorman, Herbert, **Supp. XXV:** 25
Gorney, Cynthia, **Supp. XVI:** 112
Gorra, Michael, **Supp. V:** 71
Goslings, The (Sinclair), **Supp. V:** 276, 281
Go South to Sorrow (Rowan), **Supp. XIV:** 306
Gospel (Barnhardt), **Supp. XXVII:** 1, 5–7, 8, 11, 13
Gospel According to Joe, The (Gurney), **Supp. V:** 99
"Gospel According to Saint Mark, The" (Gordon), **Supp. IV Part 1:** 310
Gospel according to the Son (Mailer), **Retro. Supp. II:** 213
"Gospel for the Twentieth Century, The" (Locke), **Supp. XIV:** 206
"Gospel of Beauty, The" (Lindsay), **Supp. I Part 2:** 380, 382, 384, 385, 391, 396
Gospels, The (di Donato), **Supp. XX: 45–46**
Gospel Singer, The (Crews), **Supp. XI:** 102, **109**
Gosse, Edmund, **II:** 538; **IV:** 350; **Supp. VIII:** 157
"Gossip" (Conroy), **Supp. XVI:** 71–72
Gossips, Gorgons, and Crones: The Fates of the Earth (Caputi), **Supp. IV Part 1:** 335
Go Tell It on the Mountain (Baldwin), **Retro. Supp. II:** 1, 2, 3, **4–5,** 7, 14; **Supp. I Part 1:** 48, 49, 50, 51, 52, 53–54, 55, 56, 57, 59, 61, 63, 64, 67; **Supp. II Part 1:** 170
Gotera, Vince, **Supp. XIII:** 115, 116, 119, 121, 127
Gothic Revival, The: An Essay on the History of Taste (Clark), **Supp. XIV:** 348
Gothic Writers (Thomson, Voller, and Frank, eds.), **Retro. Supp. II:** 273
"Go to the Devil and Shake Yourself" (song), **Supp. I Part 2:** 580
"Go to the Shine That's on a Tree" (Eberhart), **I:** 523
Go to the Widow-Maker (Jones), **Supp. XI:** 214, **225–226,** 227, 229, 233
"Gots Is What You Got" (Di Piero), **Supp. XIX:** 35, 36, 38, 41, 42, 45–46
Gottfried, Alex, **Supp. XIX:** 260
Gottfried, Martin, **Supp. IV Part 2:** 584
Gotthelf, Allan, **Supp. IV Part 2:** 528
Gottlieb, Adolph, **Supp. XV:** 144
Gottlieb, Edward, **Supp. XX: 250**
Gottlieb, Leopold, **Supp. XXIII:** 6
Gottlieb, Morton, **Supp. XVI:** 196
Gottlieb, Robert, **Supp. IV Part 2:** 474; **Supp. XXVI:** 244, 246, 250
Gottschalk and the Grande Tarantelle (Brooks), **Supp. III Part 1:** 86
"Gottschalk and the Grande Tarantelle" (Brooks), **Supp. III Part 1:** 86–87
Gould (Dixon), **Supp. XII:** 152, **153**
Gould, Edward Sherman, **I:** 346
Gould, Janice, **Supp. IV Part 1:** 322, 327; **Supp. XII:** 229
Gould, Jay, **I:** 4
Gould, Joe, **Supp. XV:** 143

Goulian, Jon-Jon, **Supp. XXVII:** 68
Gourd Dancer, The (Momaday), **Supp. IV Part 2:** 481, 487, 491, 493
Gourmont, Remy de, **I:** 270, 272; **II:** 528, 529; **III:** 457, 467–468, 477; **Retro. Supp. I:** 55
Gouverneurs de la Rosée (Roumain), **Supp. IV Part 1:** 360, 367
Government Girl (film, Nichols), **Supp. XVIII:** 247
"Governors of Wyoming, The" (Proulx), **Supp. VII:** 264
"Gowane"(Kenny), **Supp. XXIII:** 147–148
Goyen, William, **Supp. V:** 220
Grabhorn, Janet, **Supp. XV:** 142
"Grace" (Budbill), **Supp. XIX:** 2
"Grace" (Dubus), **Supp. VII:** 91
"Grace" (Harjo), **Supp. XII:** 224
Grace Notes (Dove), **Supp. IV Part 1:** 248–250, 252
Grace (Eventually): Thoughts on Faith (Lamott), **Supp. XX: 143–145**
Grade, Chaim, **Supp. XVII:** 41
"Grade School" (Stone), **Supp. XXVII:** 252
"Graduation" (Dubus), **Supp. VII:** 84
Grady, Henry W., **Supp. I Part 1:** 370
Graeber, Laurel, **Supp. V:** 15
Graham, Billy, **I:** 308
Graham, David, **Supp. XIX:** 81; **Supp. XV:** 104
Graham, Don, **Supp. XI:** 252, 254
Graham, Jorie, **Supp. IX:** 38, 52; **Supp. X:** 73; **Supp. XII:** 209; **Supp. XIII:** 85; **Supp. XVII:** 110, 111, 133, 240, 241, 242
Graham, Martha, **Supp. XI:** 152
Graham, Maryemma, **Retro. Supp. I:** 201, 204
Graham, Nan, **Supp. XII:** 272
Graham, Sheilah, **II:** 94; **Retro. Supp. I:** 97, 113–114, 115; **Supp. IX:** 63
Graham, Shirley, **Supp. I Part 1:** 51; **Supp. XXI:** 277. See also Du Bois, Shirley Graham
Graham, Stephen, **Supp. I Part 2:** 397
Graham, Tom (pseudonym). See Lewis, Sinclair
"Graham House, April '76"(Balakian), **Supp. XXIII:** 24
Grahn, Judy, **Retro. Supp. III:** 248; **Supp. IV Part 1:** 325, 330; **Supp. XXIII:** 195
"Grain Field" (Crapsey), **Supp. XVII:** 77
Grainger, Percy, **Supp. I Part 2:** 386
Grain of Mustard Seed, A (Sarton), **Supp. VIII: 259–260,** 263
Gramar (Lowth), **II:** 8
"Gramercy Park" (Teasdale), **Supp. XXVII:** 289
Grammar of Motives, A (Burke), **I:** 272, 275, 276–278, 283, 284
Gramsci, Antonio, **Supp. XX: 35–36**
Granados, Gabriel Bernal, **Supp. XV:** 350
Granath, Jack, **Supp. XVIII:** 93
Granberry, Edwin, **I:** 288
Grand Canyon, Inc. (Everett), **Supp. XVIII:** 66
Grand Design, The (Dos Passos), **I:** 489–490
"Grande Malade, The" (Barnes), **Supp. III Part 1:** 36
"Grandfather" (Dunn), **Supp. XI:** 147
"Grandfather and Grandson" (Singer), **Retro. Supp. II:** 307
Grandfathers, The (Richter), **Supp. XVIII: 219–220**
"Grandfather's Blessing" (Alvarez), **Supp. VII:** 2
"Grand Forks" (Bierds), **Supp. XVII:** 34
"Grand Forks" (Simpson), **Supp. IX:** 280–281
"Grand Inquisitor" (Dostoevsky), **IV:** 106
Grandissimes (Cable), **II:** 291
"Grand-Master Nabokov" (Updike), **Retro. Supp. I:** 317
"Grand Miracle, The" (Karr), **Supp. XI:** 251
"Grandmother" (Gunn Allen), **Supp. IV Part 1:** 320, 325
"Grandmother in Heaven" (Levine), **Supp. V:** 186
"Grandmother of the Sun: Ritual Gynocracy in Native America" (Gunn Allen), **Supp. IV Part 1:** 328
Grandmothers of the Light: A Medicine Woman's Sourcebook (Gunn Allen, ed.), **Supp. IV Part 1:** 332, 333–334
"Grandmother Songs, The" (Hogan), **Supp. IV Part 1:** 413
"Grandpa and the Statue" (A. Miller), **III:** 147
"Grandparents" (R. Lowell), **II:** 550
"Grandsire Bells, The" (Bierds), **Supp. XVII:** 28–29
"Grandstand Complex, The" (McCoy), **Supp. XIII:** 166
Grange, Red, **II:** 416
Granger's Index to Poetry (anthology), **Retro. Supp. I:** 37, 39
Granite & Cedar (Miller), **Supp. XXII:** 214
Grant, Gavin, **Supp. XIX:** 175
Grant, Lee, **Supp. XIII:** 295
Grant, Madison, **Supp. II Part 1:** 170
Grant, Richard, **Supp. X:** 282
Grant, Ulysses S., **I:** 4, 15; **II:** 542; **III:** 506, 584; **IV:** 348, 446; **Supp. I Part 2:** 418; **Supp. XXIV:** 224
Grantwood, **Retro. Supp. I:** 416, 417
"Grapes, The" (Hecht), **Supp. X:** 65–66
"Grape Sherbet" (Dove), **Supp. IV Part 1:** 246
Grapes of Wrath, The (Steinbeck), **I:** 301; **III:** 589; **IV:** 51, 53–55, 59, 63, 65, 67, 68, 69; **Supp. V:** 290; **Supp. XI:** 169; **Supp. XIV:** 181; **Supp. XV:** 351; **Supp. XX: 28**
"Grapevine, The" (Ashbery), **Supp. III Part 1:** 4
"Grass" (Sandburg), **III:** 584
Grass, Günter, **Supp. VIII:** 40
Grass County (Kooser), **Supp. XIX:** 119
"Grasse: The Olive Trees" (Wilbur), **Supp. III Part 2:** 550
"Grass Figures" (Hecht), **Supp. XXVII:** 85
Grass Harp, The (Capote), **Supp. III Part 1:** 114–117, 123
Grass Still Grows, The (A. Miller), **III:** 146
"Gratified Desire" (Davison), **Supp. XXVI:** 74
"Grating Parmesan"(Crooker), **Supp. XXIII:** 56
Gratitude to Old Teachers (R. Bly), **Supp. IV Part 1:** 73
Grattan, Bill, **Supp. XXIII:** 273, 274, 275, 276, 279, 280
Graupner, Gottlieb, **Supp. XV:** 240, 244
"Grave, A" (Moore), **III:** 195, 202, 208, 213
Grave, The (Blair), **Supp. I Part 1:** 150
"Grave, The" (Porter), **III:** 433, 443, 445–446
"Grave, The" (Winters), **Supp. II Part 2:** 795, 796
"Graven Image" (O'Hara), **III:** 320
Grave of Light: New and Selected Poems, 1970–2005 (Notley), **Supp. XXII:** 226, 235, 236
Grave of the Right Hand, The (Wright), **Supp. V:** 332, 338, 339
"Grave Piece" (Eberhart), **I:** 533
Graver, Lawrence, **Supp. XXVII:** 136, 137, 140
Graves, Billy, **Supp. I Part 2:** 607
Graves, Jesse, **Supp. XXVII:** 216
Graves, John, **Supp. V:** 220
Graves, Morris, **Supp. X:** 264

Graves, Peter, **Supp. IV Part 2:** 474
Graves, Rean, **Supp. I Part 1:** 326
Graves, Robert, **I:** 437, 477, 523; **Supp. I Part 2:** 541; **Supp. IV Part 1:** 280, 348; **Supp. IV Part 2:** 685; **Supp. XXVI:** 53
"Graveyard, The" (Very), **Supp. XXV:** 249
"Graveyard Blues" (Trethewey), **Supp. XXI:** 245, 255, 256
Graveyard for Lunatics, A (Bradbury), **Supp. IV Part 1:** 102, 114–116
Gravity's Rainbow (Pynchon), **Supp. II Part 2:** 617, 618–619, 621–625, 627, 630, 633–636; **Supp. IV Part 1:** 279; **Supp. V:** 44; **Supp. XIV:** 49; **Supp. XVII:** 236; **Supp. XXII:** 255; **Supp. XXIV:** 140
Gray, Cecil, **Supp. I Part 1:** 258
Gray, Francine Du Plessix, **Supp. V:** 169
Gray, James, **III:** 207; **Supp. I Part 2:** 410
Gray, Jeffrey, **Supp. XV:** 27
Gray, Josie, **Supp. XXIV:** 166, 167, 172, 178
Gray, Paul, **Supp. IV Part 1:** 305; **Supp. IV Part 2:** 639; **Supp. XVI:** 74; **Supp. XVIII:** 94
Gray, Thomas, **I:** 68; **Supp. I Part 1:** 150; **Supp. I Part 2:** 422, 716
Gray, Thomas A., **Supp. I Part 2:** 710
"Gray Heron, The" (Kinnell), **Supp. III Part 1:** 250
"Gray Mills of Farley, The" (Jewett), **Retro. Supp. II:** 132, 144
"Gray Poem" (Everwine), **Supp. XV:** 81
Grayscale: Poems (Huddle), **Supp. XXVI:** 150
Grayson, Charles, **Supp. XIII:** 171
"Gray Squirrel" (Francis), **Supp. IX:** 90
"Gray Wolf's H 'ant, The" (Chesnutt), **Supp. XIV:** 60
Grealy, Lucy, **Supp. XII:** 310
Greasy Lake (Boyle), **Supp. VIII:** **14–15**
"Greasy Lake" (Boyle), **Supp. VIII:** 15; **Supp. XX: 18–19**
Greasy Lake & Other Stories (Boyle), **Supp. XX: 17, 18–19**
Great Action Stories (Kittredge and Krauzer), **Supp. XXVI:** 182
"Great Adventure of Max Breuck, The" (A. Lowell), **II:** 522
Great American Detective, The (Kittredge and Krauzer), **Supp. XXVI:** 182
Great American Novel, The (P. Roth), **Retro. Supp. II:** 283, 288–289; **Supp. III Part 2:** 414–416
Great American Poetry Bake-Off, The (Peters), **Retro. Supp. III:** 245
Great American Short Novels (Phillips, ed.), **Supp. VIII:** 156
Great Battles of the World (Crane), **I:** 415
"Great Carousel, The" (Untermeyer), **Supp. XV:** 296
Great Christian Doctrine of Original Sin Defended, The . . . (Edwards), **I:** 549, 557, 559
Great Circle (Aiken), **I:** 53, 55, 57
"Great Class-Reunion Bazaar, The" (Theroux), **Supp. VIII:** 312
Great Day, The (Hurston), **Retro. Supp. III:** 128, 129, 133, 137; **Supp. VI:** 154
Great Days (Barthelme), **Supp. IV Part 1:** 39
Great Days, The (Dos Passos), **I:** 491
Great Digest (Pound, trans.), **III:** 472
"Great Divider, The" (Saunders), **Supp. XIX:** 235
"Great Elegy for John Donne" (Brodsky), **Supp. VIII:** 21, 23
"Greater Good, A" (Di Piero), **Supp. XIX:** 39
Greater Inclination, The (Wharton), **Retro. Supp. I:** 363, **364–365,** 366; **Retro. Supp. III:** 278, 279
Greater Sea, The (Gibran), **Supp. XX:** **118**
"Greater Self, The" (Gibran), **Supp. XX: 118**
"Greater Torment, The" (Blackmur), **Supp. II Part 1:** 92
Greatest Hits 1969–1996 (Salinas), **Supp. XIII:** 311
"Greatest of These, The" (C. Miller), **Supp. XXII:** 188, 196
"Greatest Thing in the World, The" (Mailer), **Retro. Supp. II:** 196
Great Expectations (Acker), **Supp. XII:** 5, **9–11**
Great Expectations (Dickens), **III:** 247; **Supp. I Part 1:** 35; **Supp. XVI:** 73; **Supp. XVIII:** 146; **Supp. XXVII:** 268
"Great Expectations, No Satisfaction" (D. Gates), **Supp. XVI:** 73
"Great Figure, The" (W. C. Williams), **IV:** 414
"Great Fillmore Street Buffalo Drive, The" (Momaday), **Supp. IV Part 2:** 493
Great Gatsby, The (Fitzgerald), **I:** 107, 375, 514; **II:** 77, 79, 83, 84, 85, 87, 91–93, 94, 96, 98; **III:** 244, 260, 372, 572; **IV:** 124, 297; **Retro. Supp. I:** 98, 105, **105–108,** 110, 114, 115, 335, 359; **Retro. Supp. II:** 107, 201; **Supp. II Part 2:** 626; **Supp. III Part 2:** 585; **Supp. IV Part 2:** 468, 475; **Supp. IX:** 57, 58; **Supp. X:** 175; **Supp. XI:** 65, 69, 334; **Supp. XVI:** 64, 75; **Supp. XVIII:** 76, 148, 165; **Supp. XX: 59, 60, 61, 72; Supp. XXII:** 81, 82, 88; **Supp. XXIII:** 101; **Supp. XXVII:** 9
Great Gatsby, The (Fitzgerald) (Modern Library), **Retro. Supp. I:** 113
Great God Brown, The (O'Neill), **III:** 165, 391, 394–395
Great Goodness of Life: A Coon Show (Baraka), **Supp. II Part 1:** 47
Great Heart: The History of a Labrador Adventure (Davidson and Rugge), **Supp. XXII:** 218
"Great Idea Lives Forever, A: Shouldn't Its Copyright?" (Helprin), **Supp. XXV:** 84, 88
Great Inclination, The (Wharton), **IV:** 310
"Great Infirmities" (Simic), **Supp. VIII:** 277
Great Jones Street (DeLillo), **Supp. VI:** 2, 3, 8–9, 11, 12
"Great Lawsuit, The: Man versus Men: Woman versus Women" (Fuller), **Retro. Supp. I:** 156; **Supp. II Part 1:** 292
Great Ledge, The (Davison), **Supp. XXVI:** 66, 77–78
"Great Ledge, The" (Davison), **Supp. XXVI:** 77, 78
"Great Men and Their Environment" (James), **II:** 347
"Great Mississippi Bubble, The" (Irving), **II:** 314
Great Mistake, The (Rinehart), **Supp. XXV:** 198, 200
"Great Prize Fight, The" (Twain), **Retro. Supp. III:** 259–260
Great Railway Bazaar, The: By Train through Asia (Theroux), **Supp. VIII:** 318, 319, **320–321,** 322
"Great Scott" (Conroy), **Supp. XVI:** 75, 77
Great Shark Hunt, The (Thompson), **Supp. XXIV:** 286
"Great Sleigh-Ride of Brewsterville, The" (Briggs), **Supp. XVIII:** 16
"Great Spirit, The" (Zitkala-Ša), **Supp. XXV:** 276, 282
"Great Stone Face, The" (Hawthorne), **Retro. Supp. III:** 117, 118
Great Stories of Suspense (Millar, ed.),

Supp. IV Part 2: 474
Great Topics of the World (Goldbarth), **Supp. XII:** 187, 189, 191
Great Valley, The (Masters), **Supp. I Part 2:** 465
Great World and Timothy Colt, The (Auchincloss), **Supp. IV Part 1:** 25, 31, 32
Grédy, Jean-Pierre, **Supp. XVI:** 194
"Greek Boy, The" (Bryant), **Supp. I Part 1:** 168
Greek Mind/Jewish Soul: The Conflicted Art of Cynthia Ozick (Strandberg), **Supp. V:** 273
"Greek Partisan, The" (Bryant), **Supp. I Part 1:** 168
"Greeks, The" (McCarriston), **Supp. XIV:** 271
"Greeks, the Chines, or Say the Mayans, The" (Bronk), **Supp. XXI:** 31
Greeley, Horace, **II:** 7; **IV:** 197, 286–287
Green, Anna Katharine, **Supp. XXV:** 199; **Supp. XXVI:** 277, 282
Green, Archie, **Supp. XXVI:** 134
Green, Ashbel, **Supp. IV Part 2:** 474
Green, David Gordon, **Supp. XXV:** 153
Green, Henry, **IV:** 279; **Retro. Supp. I:** 354; **Supp. III Part 1:** 3; **Supp. XI:** 294–295, 296, 297; **Supp. XII:** 315
Green, Jack, **Supp. IV Part 1:** 284–285
Green, Martin, **Supp. I Part 1:** 299
Green, Michelle, **Supp. IV Part 1:** 95
Green, Rose Basile, **Supp. XX: 33, 41**
"Green Automobile, The" (Ginsberg), **Supp. II Part 1:** 322
Greenberg, Clement, **Supp. XV:** 141, 143, 144, 145
Greenberg, Eliezer, **Supp. I Part 2:** 432; **Supp. XXIII:** 7
Greenberg, Hayim, **Supp. XXIII:** 3
Greenberg, Jonathan, **Supp. XII:** 285
Greenberg, Miriam, **Supp. XXII:** 244
Greenberg, Samuel, **I:** 393
Green Bough, A (Faulkner), **Retro. Supp. I:** 84; **Retro. Supp. III:** 84
"Green Canoe" (Halliday), **Supp. XIX:** 88
Green Centuries (Gordon), **II:** 196, 197–207, 209
"Green Crab's Shell, A" (Doty), **Supp. XI:** 126
"Green Door, The" (O. Henry), **Supp. II Part 1:** 395
Greene, A. C., **Supp. V:** 223, 225
Greene, Graham, **I:** 480; **II:** 62, 320; **III:** 57, 556; **Retro. Supp. I:** 215; **Supp. I Part 1:** 280; **Supp. IV Part 1:** 341; **Supp. IX:** 261; **Supp. V:** 298; **Supp. XI:** 99,**Supp. XI:** 104; **Supp. XIII:** 233; **Supp. XIX:** 29–30; **Supp. XVIII:** 79
Greene, Helga, **Supp. IV Part 1:** 134, 135
Greene, J. Lee, **Retro. Supp. II:** 121
Greene, Nathanael, **Supp. I Part 2:** 508
Greene, Richard Tobias, **III:** 76
Greene, Robert, **Supp. XVII:** 232
Green Eggs and Ham (Geisel), **Supp. XVI:** 108, 109
"Greene-ing of the Portables, The" (Cowley), **Supp. II Part 1:** 140
"Greenest Continent, The" (Stevens), **Retro. Supp. I:** 304
Greenfeld, Josh, **III:** 364
Greenfield, Josh, **Supp. XIX:** 269
"Green Hell" (Boyle), **Supp. XX: 18**
Green Hills of Africa (Hemingway), **II:** 253; **Retro. Supp. I:** 182, 186; **Retro. Supp. III:** 255, 264
Greening of America, The (C. Reich), **Supp. XVII:** 3
"Green Lagoons, The" (Leopold), **Supp. XIV:** 188
"Green Lampshade" (Simic), **Supp. VIII:** 283
Greenlanders, The (Smiley), **Supp. VI:** 292, **296–298,** 299, 305, 307
Greenlaw, Edwin A., **IV:** 453
"Greenleaf" (O'Connor), **III:** 350, 351; **Retro. Supp. II:** 233, 237; **Retro. Supp. III:** 208, 213
Greenman, Walter F., **I:** 217, 222
Green Memories (Mumford), **Supp. II Part 2:** 474, 475, 479, 480–481
Green Mountain Ghosts, Ghouls, and Unsolved Mysteries (Citro), **Supp. XXII:** 208, 218
"Green Pasture, The" (Leopold), **Supp. XIV:** 184
Green Pastures, The (Connelly), **Supp. II Part 1:** 223
"Green Red Brown and White" (Swenson), **Supp. IV Part 2:** 639
"Green River" (Bryant), **Supp. I Part 1:** 155, 164
Green Shadows, White Whale (Bradbury), **Supp. IV Part 1:** 102, 103, 116
"Green Shirt, The" (Olds), **Supp. X:** 209
"Greensleeves" (Jarman), **Supp. XVII:** 113
"Greensleeves" (Notley), **Supp. XXII:** 228
Greenslet, Ferris, **I:** 19; **Retro. Supp. I:** 9, 10, 11, 13; **Retro. Supp. II:** 41
Greenspan, Alan, **Supp. IV Part 2:** 526
Greenspan, Ezra, **Supp. XVIII:** 257
Greenstreet, Sydney, **Supp. IV Part 1:** 356
"Green Thought, A" (L. Michaels), **Supp. XVI:** 204
"Green-Thumb Boy" (Nelson), **Supp. XVIII:** 182
Greenwald, Ted, **Supp. IV Part 2:** 423
Green Wall, The (Wright), **Supp. III Part 2:** 591, 593, 595
Green Wave, The (Rukeyser), **Supp. VI:** 273, 280
"Green Ways" (Kunitz), **Supp. III Part 1:** 265
Green with Beasts (Merwin), **Supp. III Part 1:** 340, 344–346
Greenwood, Grace, **Supp. XIII:** 141
"Greeting Card Verse" (Peacock), **Supp. XIX:** 200
Greetings from Ice Country (Muñoz), **Supp. XXV:** 130
Gregerson, Linda, **Supp. IV Part 2:** 651; **Supp. X:** 204–205; **Supp. XI:** 142
"Gregorio Valdes" (Bishop), **Retro. Supp. II:** 51
Gregory, Alyse, **I:** 221, 226, 227, 231
Gregory, Horace, **II:** 512; **Supp. III Part 2:** 614, 615; **Supp. IX:** 229; **Supp. XV:** 143
Gregory, Lady Isabella Augusta, **III:** 458
Gregory, Sinda, **Supp. X:** 260, 268
Grendel (Gardner), **Supp. VI:** 63, **67,** 68, 74
Grenstone Poems (Bynner), **Supp. XV:** 44
"Gretel in Darkness" (Glück), **Supp. V:** 82
Gretta (Caldwell), **I:** 301, 302
Greuze, Jean Baptiste, **Supp. I Part 2:** 714
Grey, Zane, **Supp. XIII:** 5; **Supp. XXVI:** 186
Greyhounding This America (Kenny), **Supp. XXIII: 155**
Gridley Firing (Hayford), **Supp. XXII:** 204
"Grief Has Stamped" (Pedersen; Nelson, trans.), **Supp. XVIII:** 180
Grieg, Michael, **Supp. XV:** 133, 148
Griffin, Bartholomew, **Supp. I Part 1:** 369
Griffin, John Howard, **Supp. VIII:** 208; **Supp. XXI:** 74; **Supp. XXV:** 51
Griffin, Merv, **Supp. IV Part 2:** 526

Griffith, Albert J., **Supp. V:** 325
Griffith, D. W., **I:** 31, 481–482; **Retro. Supp. I:** 103, 325; **Supp. XI:** 45; **Supp. XVI:** 183, 184; **Supp. XXI:** 170
Griffith, Paul, **Supp. XVIII:** 173, 175
Griffiths, Clyde, **I:** 511
Grile, Dod (pseudonym). See Bierce, Ambrose
Grimes, William, **Retro. Supp. III:** 320
Grimm, Herman, **II:** 17
Grimm brothers, **II:** 378; **III:** 101, 491, 492; **IV:** 266; **Supp. I Part 2:** 596, 622; **Supp. X:** 78, 84, 86
Grimshaw, Anna, **Supp. XXI:** 172
Grinde, Donald A., Jr, **Supp. XXVI:** 98
Grinnell, George Bird, **Supp. XVI:** 13
Gris, Juan, **I:** 442; **Retro. Supp. I:** 430
Griswold, Rufus Wilmot, **III:** 409, 429; **Retro. Supp. II:** 261, 262; **Retro. Supp. III:** 225, 236; **Supp. XV:** 277, 278; **Supp. XVI:** 8, 10–11; **Supp. XXV:** 250
"Grizzly" (Kittredge), **Supp. XXVI:** 187
Grogg, Sam, Jr., **Supp. IV Part 2:** 468, 471
Gromer, Crystal, **Supp. XII:** 297
Gronlund, Laurence, **II:** 276
Grooms, Red, **Supp. XV:** 178
Grooves: A Kind of Mystery (Brockmeier), **Supp. XXII:** 55, 56, 59
"Groping for Trouts" (Gass), **Supp. VI:** 87
Grosholz, Emily, **Supp. XII:** 185; **Supp. XIX:** 37–38, 278
Grosman un zun (Grosman and Son) (Asch), **Supp. XXIII:** 7
Gross, Robert A., **Supp. XIX:** 151
Gross, Terry, **Supp. XVI:** 167; **Supp. XXI:** 247, 255
"Grosse Fuge" (Doty), **Supp. XI:** 126–127
Grossman, Allen, **Retro. Supp. II:** 83; **Supp. XIX:** 82, 86, 94; **Supp. XVIII:** 91
Grossman, Lev, **Supp. XXV:** 4, **63–78**
Grosz, George, **III:** 172; **IV:** 438; **Retro. Supp. II:** 321; **Supp. X:** 137; **Supp. XXVII:** 88
"Grotesque in Modern Fiction, The" (E. Hoffman, Ph.D. dissertation), **Supp. XVI:** 147
"Groundhog, The" (Eberhart), **I:** 523, 530–532, 533
"Ground on Which I Stand, The" (Wilson), **Retro. Supp. III:** 319; **Supp. VIII:** 331
"Ground Swell" (Jarman), **Supp. XVII:** 118
Group, The (McCarthy), **II:** 570, 574–578
"Group of Two, A" (Jarrell), **II:** 368
Group Therapy (Hearon), **Supp. VIII:** **64–65**
"Grove" (Goldbarth), **Supp. XII:** 176
Groves of Academe, The (McCarthy), **II:** 568–571
Growing into Love (X. J. Kennedy), **Supp. XV:** 153, **158–160**
Growing Pains (J. S. Untermeyer), **Supp. XV:** 303
"Growing Season, The" (Caldwell), **I:** 309
Growing Up Gay: A Literary Anthology (Singer, ed.), **Supp. IV Part 1:** 330
"Growing Up Good in Maycomb" (Shaffer), **Supp. VIII:** 128
Growing Up Native American (Riley, ed.), **Supp. XXVI:** 104
"Grown-Up" (Jewett), **Retro. Supp. II:** 134
Grown Up All Wrong (Christgau), **Supp. XXVII:** 33, 35–36, 40–41
"Growth" (R. Lowell), **II:** 554
"Growth and Decay in Recent Verse" (Untermeyer), **Supp. XV:** 299
Growth of the American Republic, The (Morison and Commager), **Supp. I Part 2:** 484
"Growtown Buggle, The" (Jewett), **Retro. Supp. II:** 132
Grubin, David, **Supp. XXIII:** 138
Gruenberg, Louis, **III:** 392
Grumbach, Doris, **II:** 560
"Gryphon" (C. Baxter), **Supp. XVII:** 14, 17
"Guacamaja" (Leopold), **Supp. XIV:** 188–189
Guardian Angel (Paretsky), **Supp. XXV:** 178, 179
Guardian Angel, The (Holmes), **Supp. I Part 1:** 315–316
"Guardian of the Law" (R. Fisher), **Supp. XIX:** 71
Guard of Honor (Cozzens), **I:** 370–372, 375, 376–377, 378, 379
Guardsman, The (Molnar), **Supp. XVI:** 187
Guare, John, **Retro. Supp. III:** 318; **Supp. XIII:** 196, 207
Guattari, Félix, **Supp. XXV:** 123
Gubar, Susan, **Retro. Supp. I:** 42; **Retro. Supp. II:** 324; **Supp. IX:** 66; **Supp. XV:** 270; **Supp. XXIV:** 28
"Guenevere" (Teasdale), **Supp. XXVII:** 287
Guerard, Albert, Jr., **Supp. X:** 79; **Supp. XIII:** 172
Guérin, Maurice de, **I:** 241
"Guerrilla Handbook, A" (Baraka), **Supp. II Part 1:** 36
Guess and Spell Coloring Book, The (Swenson), **Supp. IV Part 2:** 648
Guess Who's Coming to Dinner (film), **Supp. I Part 1:** 67
Guest, Barbara, **Supp. XXIII:** 215; **Supp. XXVII:** 23
Guest, Judith, **Supp. XVI:** 36
Guest, Val, **Supp. XI:** 307
Guest Book (Bynner), **Supp. XV:** 51
"Guest Ellen at the Supper for Street People, The" (Ferry), **Supp. XXIV:** 152–153, 162
"Guests of Mrs. Timms, The" (Jewett), **II:** 408; **Retro. Supp. II:** 135
Guevara, Martha, **Supp. VIII:** 74
Guevara, Fray Miguel de, **Supp. XXI:** 104
"Guevara . . .Guevara" (Salinas), **Supp. XIII:** 312–313, 315
Guggenheim, Peggy, **Supp. XXII:** 165
Guided Tours of Hell (Prose), **Supp. XVI:** 257, 261
"Guided Tours of Hell" (Prose), **Supp. XVI:** 257
Guide for the Bedevilled, A (Hecht), **Supp. XXVII:** 94, 95
Guide for the Perplexed (Maimonides), **Supp. XVII:** 46
Guide in the Wilderness, A (Cooper), **I:** 337
"Guidelines" (Espaillat), **Supp. XXI:** 99
"Guide to Dungeness Spit, A" (Wagoner), **Supp. IX:** 325–326, 329
Guide to Ezra Pound's Selected Cantos' (Kearns), **Retro. Supp. I:** 292
Guide to Kulchur (Pound), **III:** 475
Guide to the Ruins (Nemerov), **III:** 269, 270–271, 272
Guillén, Jorge, **Supp. XXIV:** 152
Guillén, Nicolás, **Retro. Supp. I:** 202; **Supp. I Part 1:** 345
Guillevic, Eugene, **Supp. III Part 1:** 283
"Guilt, The" (Peacock), **Supp. XIX:** 200
"Guilt and Incident at Vichy" (A. Miller), **Retro. Supp. III:** 175
"Guilty Man, The" (Kunitz), **Supp. II Part 1:** 263
Guilty of Everything: The Autobiography of Herbert Huncke (Huncke), **Supp. XIV:** 138, 140, 141, 150

Guilty Pleasures (Barthelme), **Supp. IV Part 1:** 44, 45, 53
Guimond, James, **Supp. XXI:** 228
Guinness, Alec, **Retro. Supp. I:** 65; **Supp. XX: 50**
Gulag Archipelago, The (Solzhenitsyn), **Supp. XVII:** 229
"Gulf, The" (Dunn), **Supp. XI:** 149
Gulistan (Saadi), **II:** 19
Gullible's Travels (Lardner), **II:** 426, 427
Gulliver, Adelaide Cromwell, **Supp. XVIII:** 286
"Gulliver Found" (Bronk), **Supp. XXI:** 33
Gulliver's Travels (Swift), **I:** 209, 348, 366; **II:** 301; **Retro. Supp. III:** 154; **Supp. I Part 2:** 656; **Supp. XI:** 209; **Supp. XVI:** 110
"Gulls" (Hayden), **Supp. II Part 1:** 367
"Gulls, The" (Nemerov), **III:** 272
"Gulls on Dumps" (Di Piero), **Supp. XIX:** 41
"Gun, The" (Dobyns), **Supp. XIII:** 88
Gun, with Occasional Music (Lethem), **Supp. XVIII: 137–138**
Günderode: A Translation from the German (Fuller), **Supp. II Part 1:** 293
Gunderson, Gwen, **Supp. XXVI:** 134
Gundy, Jeff, **Supp. XI:** 315; **Supp. XVI:** 46, 265, 275
Gunfight at the O.K. Corral (film), **Supp. XX: 246**
Gunga Din (screenplay, Hecht and MacArthur), **Supp. XXVII:** 83, 90
"Gun Hand, The" (Davison), **Supp. XXVI:** 71
Gun in Cheek (Pronzini), **Supp. XXVI:** 278
Gunman's Rhapsody (Parker), **Supp. XIX:** 187
Gunn, Robin Wright, **Supp. XXI:** 243, 244
Gunn, Thom, **Supp. IX:** 269
Gunn, Thomas, **Supp. V:** 178
Gunn Allen, Paula, **Supp. IV Part 1: 319–340,** 404; **Supp. IV Part 2:** 499, 502, 557, 568; **Supp. XII:** 218
"Gunnar's Sword" (C. Bly), **Supp. XVI:** 34, 35, 37, 42
"Guns as Keys; and the Great Gate Swings" (A. Lowell), **II:** 524
Gurdjieff, Georges, **Supp. IX:** 320; **Supp. V:** 199
Gurganus, Allan, **Supp. XII:** 308–309, 310
Gurko, Leo, **III:** 62
Gurney, A. R., **Supp. IX:** 261; **Supp. V: 95–112**
Gurney, Mary (Molly) Goodyear, **Supp. V:** 95
Gussow, Mel, **Supp. IX:** 93; **Supp. XII:** 325, 328, 341
Gustavus Vassa, the African (Vassa), **Supp. IV Part 1:** 11
Gusto, Thy Name Was Mrs. Hopkins: A Prose Rhapsody (Francis), **Supp. IX:** 89
Guston, Philip, **Supp. XXIII:** 210
Gute Mensch von Sezuan, Der (Brecht), **Supp. IX:** 138
Gutenberg, Johann, **Supp. I Part 2:** 392
Guthrie, A. B., **Supp. X:** 103
Guthrie, Woody, **Supp. XVIII:** 23
Gutman, Herbert, **Supp. I Part 1:** 47
Guttenplan, D. D., **Supp. XI:** 38
"Gutting of Couffignal, The" (Hammett), **Supp. IV Part 1:** 345
Guttman, Allen, **Supp. XXVII:** 134
Guy, David, **Supp. XXVI:** 9
Guy Domville (James), **II:** 331; **Retro. Supp. I:** 228
"Gwendolyn" (Bishop), **Retro. Supp. II:** 51
Gwynn, R. S., **Supp. XVIII:** 184
Gypsy Ballads (Hughes, trans.), **Supp. I Part 1:** 345
Gypsy's Curse, The (Crews), **Supp. XI: 110**
"Gyroscope, The" (Rukeyser), **Supp. VI:** 271
Gysin, Brion, **Supp. XII:** 129
Ha, Quan Manh, **Supp. XXVI:** 213, 214, 215
Haardt, Sara. See Mencken, Mrs. H. L. (Sara Haardt)
Haas, Robert, **Supp. XXII:** 177
Habakkuk (biblical book), **III:** 200, 347
Habibi (Nye), **Supp. XIII:** 273, **279**
"Habit" (James), **II:** 351
Habitations of the Word (Gass), **Supp. VI:** 88
Habit of Being, The (O'Connor; Fitzgerald, ed.), **Retro. Supp. III:** 208
"Hack, The" (Swados), **Supp. XIX:** 267
"Hackberry"(P. Benedict), **Supp. XXIII:** 37–38, 39
Hacker, Marilyn, **Supp. XV:** 250; **Supp. XVII:** 71, 76, 112; **Supp. XVIII:** 177, 178
Hacker, Randi, **Supp. XXVI:** 121
Hacket, Albert, **Supp. XXVII:** 136
Hackett, David, **Supp. XII:** 236
Hadas, Rachel, **Supp. XXIII: 111–128; Supp. XXIV:** 157
Hadda, Janet, **Retro. Supp. II:** 317
Haddād, 'Abd al-Masīh, **Supp. XX: 116**
"Hades Welcomes His Bride" (Stallings), **Supp. XXV:** 229–230
Haeckel, Ernst Heinrich, **II:** 480
Haegert, John, **Supp. XVI:** 69
Hafen, P. Jane, **Supp. XXV:** 280
Hafif, Marcia, **Supp. IV Part 2:** 423
Hagar's Daughter (P. Hopkins), **Supp. XVI:** 143
Hagedorn, Jessica, **Supp. X:** 292
Hagen, Beulah, **Supp. I Part 2:** 679
Hager, Kelly, **Supp. XVIII:** 183
Hagestadt, Emma, **Supp. XXVI:** 212
Haggard, Rider, **III:** 189
Haggas, Carol, **Supp. XXVI:** 159, 160
Hagoromo (play), **III:** 466
Hagstrum, Jean, **Supp. XV:** 74
"Hail Mary" (Fante), **Supp. XI:** 160, 164
Haines, George, IV, **I:** 444
Haines, John, **Supp. XII: 197–214**
"Hair" (Corso), **Supp. XII:** 117, 126, 127
"Hair, The" (Carver), **Supp. III Part 1:** 137
"Haircut" (Lardner), **II:** 430, 436
"Hair Dressing" (Untermeyer), **Supp. XV:** 304, 305
Hairpiece: A Film for Nappy-Headed People (Chenzira; film), **Supp. XI:** 19–20
"Hairs" (Cisneros), **Supp. VII:** 59
Hairs/Pelitos (Cisneros), **Supp. VII:** 58
Hairy Ape, The (O'Neill), **III:** 391, 392, 393
"Haïta the Shepherd" (Bierce), **I:** 203
Haj, The (Uris), **Supp. XX: 244, 245, 247, 255–256**
Hajdu, David, **Supp. XXVII:** 153
Haldeman, Anna, **Supp. I Part 1:** 2
Hale, Edward Everett, **Supp. I Part 2:** 584; **Supp. XI:** 193, 200
Hale, John Parker, **Supp. I Part 2:** 685
Hale, Nancy, **Supp. VIII:** 151, 171
Hale, Sarah Josepha, **Retro. Supp. III:** 231
Haley, Alex, **Supp. I Part 1:** 47, 66
Haley, J. Evetts, **Supp. V:** 226
"Half a Century Gone" (R. Lowell), **II:** 554
"Half a Grapefruit" (Munro), **Supp. XXVII:** 186–187
Half-a-Hundred: Tales by Great American Writers (Grayson, ed.), **Supp. XIII:** 171
Half and Half:Writers on Growing Up

Biracial and Bicultural (Hearn, ed.), **Supp. XXV:** 51
Half Asleep in Frog Pajamas (Robbins), **Supp. X:** 259, **279–282**
Half Breed, The (film), **Supp. XVI:** 185
Half-Century of Conflict, A (Parkman), **Supp. II Part 2:** 600, 607, 610
"Half Deity" (Moore), **III:** 210, 214, 215
"Half Hour of August" (Ríos), **Supp. IV Part 2:** 552
"Half-Life of Cardio-Pulmonary Function, A" (Gansworth), **Supp. XXVI:** 111
Half-Life of Cardio-Pulmonary Function, A: Poems and Paintings (Gansworth), **Supp. XXVI:** 110–111
Half-Lives (Jong), **Supp. V:** 115, 119
Half Moon Street: Two Short Novels (Theroux), **Supp. VIII:** 322, 323
Half of Paradise (Burke), **Supp. XIV:** 22, 24
Half-Past Nation Time (C. Johnson), **Supp. VI:** 187
Half Remembered (Davison), **Supp. XXVI:** 61, 63, 65, 66–67, 70, 71
"Half-Skinned Steer, The" (Proulx), **Supp. VII:** 261–262
"Half Sonnets" (Jarman), **Supp. XVII:** 115
Half Sun Half Sleep (Swenson), **Supp. IV Part 2:** 645–646
Halfway (Kumin), **Supp. IV Part 2:** 441–442
"Halfway" (Rich), **Supp. I Part 2:** 553
Halfway Down the Hall: New and Selected Poems (Hadas), **Supp. XXIII: 118–119**
Halfway Home (Monette), **Supp. X:** 154
Halfway to Silence (Sarton), **Supp. VIII:** 261
Half You Don't Know, The: Selected Stories (Cameron), **Supp. XII:** 79, 80, 81
Haliburton, Thomas Chandler, **II:** 301; **IV:** 193; **Supp. I Part 2:** 411
Halifax, Lord, **II:** 111
Hall, Daniel, **Supp. XII:** 258
Hall, Donald, **I:** 567; **III:** 194; **Supp. IV Part 1:** 63, 72; **Supp. IV Part 2:** 621; **Supp. IX:** 269; **Supp. XIV:** 82, 126; **Supp. XV:** 21, 153, 176; **Supp. XVI:** 39, 230, 235; **Supp. XX: 194; Supp. XXI:** 86; **Supp. XXIII:** 209; **Supp. XXVI:** 68
Hall, Hazel, **Supp. XXII:** 275
Hall, James, **II:** 313; **Supp. I Part 2:** 584, 585
Hall, James Baker, **Supp. X:** 24
Hall, John, **Supp. XXVII:** 253
Hall, Louisa, **Retro. Supp. III:** 8
Hall, Rachel, **Supp. XXIII:** 301
Hall, Timothy L., **Supp. VIII:** 127, 128
Halleck, Fitz-Greene, **Supp. I Part 1:** 156, 158
"Hallelujah" (Cohen), **Supp. XXVII:** 52, 56, 61–62
"Hallelujah: A Sestina" (Francis), **Supp. IX:** 82
"Hallelujah on the Bum" (Abbey), **Supp. XIII:** 2
"Haller's Second Home" (Maxwell), **Supp. VIII:** 169
Halliday, Mark, **Supp. XIX: 81–95; Supp. XV:** 19, 20, 21, 23, 25, 27, 30
Hallock, Rev. Moses, **Supp. I Part 1:** 153
"Hall of Fantasy, The" (Hawthorne), **Retro. Supp. III:** 115
Hall of Mirrors, A (Stone), **Supp. V:** 295, 296–299, 300, 301
"Hallowe'en" (Huncke), **Supp. XIV:** 145
"Halloween Party, The" (Chabon), **Supp. XI:** 72
Halloween Tree, The (Bradbury), **Supp. IV Part 1:** 102, 112–113
"Halls, The" (Halliday), **Supp. XIX:** 90
Hallwas, John E., **Supp. I Part 2:** 454
Halpern, Daniel, **Supp. IV Part 1:** 94–95, 95
Halpern, Paul, **Supp. XXV:** 123
Halpern, Sue, **Supp. XXVI:** 128
Halsey, Theresa, **Supp. IV Part 1:** 330, 331
"Halt in the Desert, A" (Brodsky), **Supp. VIII:** 24
"Halves" (Dunn), **Supp. XI:** 149
Hamburg, Victoria, **Supp. XVI:** 126
Hamerik, Asger, **Supp. I Part 1:** 356
Hamill, Pete, **Supp. XX: 244, 255**
Hamill, Sam, **Supp. X:** 112, 125, 126, 127
Hamilton, Alexander, **I:** 485; **Supp. I Part 2:** 456, 483, 509
Hamilton, Alice, **Supp. I Part 1:** 5
Hamilton, David, **Supp. IX:** 296
Hamilton, Edith, **Supp. XVI:** 196
Hamilton, Lady Emma, **II:** 524
Hamilton, Hamish, **Supp. I Part 2:** 617
Hamilton, Walton, **Supp. I Part 2:** 632
Hamilton Stark (Banks), **Supp. V:** 8, 9–10, 11
"Hamlen Brook" (Wilbur), **Supp. III Part 2:** 564
"Hamlet" (Laforgue), **I:** 573; **III:** 11
Hamlet (Miller and Fraenkel), **III:** 178, 183
Hamlet (Shakespeare), **I:** 53, 183, 205, 377, 586–587; **II:** 158, 531; **III:** 7, 11, 12, 183; **IV:** 116, 131, 227; **Supp. I Part 1:** 369; **Supp. I Part 2:** 422, 457, 471; **Supp. IV Part 2:** 612; **Supp. IX:** 14
Hamlet, The (Faulkner), **II:** 69–71, 73, 74; **IV:** 131; **Retro. Supp. I:** 82, 91, 92; **Retro. Supp. III:** 85, 86; **Supp. IX:** 103; **Supp. VIII:** 178; **Supp. XI:** 247
"Hamlet and His Problems" (Eliot), **I:** 586–587
Hamlet of A. MacLeish, The (MacLeish), **III:** 11–12, 14, 15, 18
Hamlin, Eva, **Retro. Supp. II:** 115
"Hammer" (Bidart), **Supp. XV:** 35
Hammer, Adam, **Supp. XIII:** 112
Hammer, Langdon, **Retro. Supp. II:** 45, 53; **Supp. X:** 65
"Hammer Man, The" (Bambara), **Supp. XI:** 4–5
Hammett, Dashiell, **IV:** 286; **Retro. Supp. II:** 327; **Supp. I Part 1:** 286, 289, 291, 292, 293, 294, 295; **Supp. III Part 1:** 91; **Supp. IV Part 1:** 120, 121, **341–357; Supp. IV Part 2:** 461, 464, 468, 469, 472, 473; **Supp. IX:** 200; **Supp. XI:** 228; **Supp. XIII:** 159; **Supp. XIV:** 21; **Supp. XIX:** 178; **Supp. XVII:** 137; **Supp. XXI:** 68; **Supp. XXVI:** 277, 282
Hammon, Jupiter, **Supp. XXII:** 11
Hammond, John, **Supp. XVIII:** 24
Hammond, Karla, **Supp. IV Part 2:** 439, 442, 448, 637, 640, 644, 648
Hampl, Patricia, **Supp. IX:** 291; **Supp. XI:** 126; **Supp. XVII:** 21; **Supp. XXII: 81–101**
Hampson, Alfred Leete, **Retro. Supp. I:** 35–36, 38
"Hamrick's Polar Bear" (Caldwell), **I:** 309–310
Hamsun, Knut, **Supp. VIII:** 40; **Supp. XI:** 161, 167; **Supp. XII:** 21, 128
Hancock, John, **Supp. I Part 2:** 524; **Supp. XX: 282**
Hancock, Wade, **Supp. XVI:** 34
"Handbill Distributed in Buncombe County, North Carolina: 1915" (Rash), **Supp. XXVII:** 218
Handbook of North American Indians (Sando), **Supp. IV Part 2:** 510
Handcarved Coffins: A Nonfiction Account of an American Crime (Capote), **Supp. III Part 1:** 131

Handel, Georg Friedrich, **III:** 210; **IV:** 369
"Handfasting" (Wright), **Supp. XV:** 343
"Handfuls" (Sandburg), **III:** 584
"Handle with Care" (Fitzgerald), **Retro. Supp. I:** 114
Handley, William R., **Supp. XVIII:** 58
Handmaid's Tale, The (Atwood), **Supp. XIII:** 19, 20, **27–29**
"Hand of Casino, 1954, A" (Skloot), **Supp. XX: 194, 202**
"Hand of Emmagene, The" (Taylor), **Supp. V:** 314, 325–326
Hand of the Potter, The: A Tragedy in Four Acts (Dreiser), **Retro. Supp. II:** 104; **Supp. XVII:** 96
"Hands" (Anderson), **I:** 106, 107
"Hands" (Mora), **Supp. XIII:** 215
Hands of Orlac, The (M. Renard; Crewe-Jones, trans.), **Supp. XVII:** 58
Hand to Mouth (Auster), **Supp. XII:** 21
"Hand to Mouth" (Auster), **Supp. XII:** 31
Handy, Lowney, **Supp. XI:** 217, 220, 221, 225
Handy, W. C., **Supp. VIII:** 337
Handy Guide for Beggars, A (Lindsay), **Supp. I Part 2:** 376–378, 380, 382, 399
Haney, David, **Supp. XXI:** 253
"Hanged Man, A" (Cliff), **Supp. XXII:** 74
"Hanging Burley" (J. W. Miller), **Supp. XX: 167**
Hanging Garden, The (Wagoner), **Supp. IX: 338–339**
"Hanging Gardens of Tyburn, The" (Hecht), **Supp. X:** 58
"Hanging Man, The" (Davison), **Supp. XXVI:** 74
"Hanging of the Crane, The" (Longfellow), **Retro. Supp. II:** 169, 171
Hanging On (Conroy), **Supp. XVI:** 69
"Hanging Pictures in Nanny's Room" (Kenyon), **Supp. VII:** 164
"Hanging the Wash" (Alvarez), **Supp. VII:** 4
"Hangman, The" (Sexton), **Supp. II Part 2:** 680, 691
Hangover Mass (X. J. Kennedy), **Supp. XV:** 165
Hangsaman (Jackson), **Supp. IX:** 116, 123, **124**
Hanh, Thich Nhat, **Supp. V:** 199
Hanks, Lucy, **III:** 587
Hanks, Nancy. See Lincoln, Mrs. Thomas (Nancy Hanks)
Hanley, Lynne T., **Supp. IV Part 1:** 208
"Hanlon Mountain in Mist" (J. W. Miller), **Supp. XX: 164, 166–167**
Hanna, Mark, **Supp. I Part 2:** 395
Hannah, Barry, **Supp. X:** 285; **Supp. XIX:** 209; **Supp. XXI:** 38, 118; **Supp. XXVII:** 269
Hannah and Her Sisters (film; Allen), **Supp. XV:** 9, **10–11**
"Hannah Armstrong" (Masters), **Supp. I Part 2:** 461
"Hannah Binding Shoes" (Larcom), **Supp. XIII:** 141, 143
"Hannah Byde" (D. West), **Supp. XVIII:** 280
Hannah's House (Hearon), **Supp. VIII:** 58, **60–61**
Hanneman, Audre, **II:** 259
Hannibal Lecter, My Father (Acker), **Supp. XII:** 6
Hanoi (McCarthy), **II:** 579
"Hanoi Drifting, January 2003" (Weigl), **Supp. XIX:** 288
Hansberry, Lorraine, **Supp. IV Part 1: 359–377; Supp. VIII:** 329
Hanscom, Leslie, **Supp. XI:** 229
"Hansel and Gretel" (Prose), **Supp. XVI:** 256, 258
Hansen, Erik, **Supp. V:** 241
Hansen, Harry, **IV:** 366; **Supp. XXII:** 194, 277; **Supp. XXVII:** 85, 96
Han-shan, **Supp. VIII:** 292
Hanson, Curtis, **Supp. XI:** 67
Hanson, Elizabeth, **Supp. XXIV:** 220
Hanson, William F., **Supp. XXV:** 279, 280
Han Suyin, **Supp. X:** 291
Hanzlicek, C. G., **Supp. XV:** 73
Hapax (Stallings), **Supp. XXV:** 221, 222, 224, 231–233
Hapgood, Charles H., II, **Supp. XXI:** 6
Hapgood, Hutchins, **Supp. XVII: 95–108; Supp. XXI:** 1, 3, 9, 10
Hapgood, Norman, **Supp. XXI:** 2
Hapgoods, The: Three Earnest Brothers (Marcaccio), **Supp. XVII:** 106
"Happenings: An Art of Radical Juxtaposition" (Sontag), **Supp. III Part 2:** 456
"Happenstance" (Komunyakaa), **Supp. XIII:** 130
Happenstance (Shields), **Supp. VII:** 315–318, 320, 323, 324, 326
Happersberger, Lucien, **Supp. I Part 1:** 51
"Happiest Girl in the Whole U.S.A., The" (Muñoz), **Supp. XXV:** 131, 132
"Happiest I've Been, The" (Updike), **IV:** 219
Happily Ever After (Quindlen), **Supp. XVII:** 167
"Happiness" (Oliver), **Supp. VII:** 236
"Happiness" (Sandburg), **III:** 582–583
"Happiness" (Stone), **Supp. XXVII:** 254–255
"Happiness"(Hadas), **Supp. XXIII:** 117
Happiness of Getting It Down Right, The (Steinman, ed.), **Supp. VIII:** 172
"Happiness of the Garden Variety" (Richard), **Supp. XIX:** 212
"Happy Birthday" (Bambara), **Supp. XI:** 4
Happy Birthday (Loos), **Supp. XVI:** 193
Happy Birthday, Wanda June (Vonnegut), **Supp. II Part 2:** 759, 776–777
Happy Birthday of Death, The (Corso), **Supp. XII: 127–129**
Happy Childhood, A (Matthews), **Supp. IX:** 155, 160, **161–163**
Happy Days (Beckett), **Retro. Supp. I:** 206; **Supp. XXIV:** 123
Happy Days, 1880–1892 (Mencken), **III:** 100, 111, 120
"Happy End" (Simic), **Supp. VIII:** 276–277
"Happy Failure, The" (Melville), **III:** 90
Happy Families Are All Alike (Taylor), **Supp. V:** 322–323, 325
Happy Isles of Oceania, The: Paddling the Pacific (Theroux), **Supp. VIII:** 324
"Happy Journey to Trenton and Camden, The" (Wilder), **IV:** 366
"Happy Man, The" (Lethem), **Supp. XVIII:** 139
"Happy Marriage, The" (MacLeish), **III:** 15–16
Happy Marriage and Other Poems, The (MacLeish), **III:** 4
Happy to Be Here (Keillor), **Supp. XVI:** 165, 171
"Happy To Be Here" (Keillor), **Supp. XVI:** 168
"Hapworth 16, 1924" (Salinger), **III:** 552, 571–572
Haram, Karen, **Supp. XXIII:** 276
"Harbor Dawn, The" (H. Crane), **Supp. XXI:** 132, 136
"Harbor Lights" (Doty), **Supp. XI:** 122
Harcourt, Alfred, **II:** 191, 451–452; **III:**

587; **Retro. Supp. I:** 131; **Retro. Supp. III:** 101; **Supp. XV:** 308
Harcourt, Lewis, **Supp. XX: 232–233**
Harcourt, T. A., **I:** 196
Hardball (Paretsky), **Supp. XXV:** 177, 182, 184
Hard Candy, a Book of Stories (T. Williams), **IV:** 383
"Hardcastle Crags" (Plath), **Supp. I Part 2:** 537
"Hard Daddy" (Hughes), **Retro. Supp. I:** 200
"Hard Drive" (Huddle), **Supp. XXVI:** 151
"Hardened Criminals, The" (Lethem), **Supp. XVIII:** 139
Harder They Fall, The (Schulberg), **Supp. XV:** 194, 201
"Hardest Thing, The" (Huddle), **Supp. XXVI:** 151
Hard Facts (Baraka), **Supp. II Part 1:** 54, 55, 58
Hard Freight (Wright), **Supp. V:** 332, 339–340
Hard Hours, The (Hecht), **Supp. X:** 57, **59–62,** 63, 64
Hardie, Kier, **Supp. I Part 1:** 5
Hardin, Michael, **Supp. XXVI:** 242
Harding, Walter, **IV:** 177, 178
Harding, Warren G., **I:** 486; **II:** 253, 433; **Supp. I Part 1:** 24
"Hard Kind of Courage, The" (Baldwin), **Supp. I Part 1:** 52
Hard Laughter (Lamott), **Supp. XX: 132–133**
Hard Maple (S. and A. Warner), **Supp. XVIII:** 264
"Hard Rain's A-Gonna Fall, A" (song, Dylan), **Supp. XVIII:** 26, 29
Hard Time (Paretsky), **Supp. XXV:** 176, 177, 179, 182, 183
"Hard Time Keeping Up, A" (Ellison), **Retro. Supp. II:** 124
Hard Times (Dickens), **Supp. I Part 2:** 675
"Hard Times in Elfland, The" (Lanier), **Supp. I Part 1:** 365
"Hard Traveling: Fay's Deep South Landscape of Violence" (Beuka), **Supp. XXI:** 47
Hard Way Around, The: The Passages of Joshua Slocum (Wolff), **Supp. XXV:** 217
Hardwick, Elizabeth, **II:** 543, 554, 566; **Retro. Supp. II:** 179, 180, 183, 184, 190, 221, 228–229, 245; **Supp. I Part 1:** 196; **Supp. III Part 1: 193–215; Supp. IV Part 1:** 299; **Supp. V,** 319; **Supp. X,** 171; **Supp. XII:** 209; **Supp. XIV:** 89
"Hard Work 1956" (Dunn), **Supp. XI:** 147
Hardy, Barbara, **Supp. I Part 2:** 527
Hardy, Deborah, **Supp. XXVI:** 241, 242, 246
Hardy, Oliver, **Supp. I Part 2:** 607; **Supp. IV Part 2:** 574
Hardy, René, **Supp. III Part 1:** 235
Hardy, Thomas, **I:** 59, 103, 292, 317, 377; **II:** 181, 184–185, 186, 191–192, 271, 275, 372, 523, 542; **III:** 32, 453, 485, 508, 524; **IV:** 83, 135, 136; **Retro. Supp. I:** 141, 377–378; **Supp. I Part 1:** 217; **Supp. I Part 2:** 429, 512; **Supp. II Part 1:** 4, 26; **Supp. IX:** 40, 78, 85, 108, 211; **Supp. VIII:** 32; **Supp. X:** 228; **Supp. XI:** 311; **Supp. XIII:** 294, **Supp. XIII:** 130; **Supp. XIV:** 24; **Supp. XIX:** 86, 87; **Supp. XV:** 170; **Supp. XVIII:** 74; **Supp. XX: 195; Supp. XXI:** 109; **Supp. XXVI:** 67, 78; **Supp. XXVII:** 218
Hardy and the Poetry of Truth-Seeking (Halliday), **Supp. XIX:** 82
Harjo, Joy, **Supp. IV Part 1:** 325, 404; **Supp. IV Part 2:** 499, 507; **Supp. XII: 215–234; Supp. XVIII:** 189
Harlan's Race (P. N. Warren), **Supp. XX: 264–265**
"Harlem" (Hughes), **Retro. Supp. I:** 194, 204; **Supp. I Part 1:** 340; **Supp. VIII:** 213
Harlem (Myers), **Supp. XXVII:** 211
Harlem, Mecca of the New Negro (Locke), **Supp. XIV:** 201
"Harlem Dancer, The" (McKay), **Supp. X:** 134
Harlem Gallery (Tolson), **Retro. Supp. I:** 208, 209, 210
Harlem Glory: A Fragment of Aframerican Life (McKay), **Supp. X:** 132, **141–142**
Harlem Hellfighters, The: When Pride Met Courage (Myers), **Supp. XXVII:** 208
Harlem: Negro Metropolis (McKay), **Supp. X:** 132, 141, 142
Harlem Renaissance Remembered, The (Bontemps, ed.), **Supp. XXII:** 7
"Harlem Runs Wild" (McKay), **Supp. X:** 140
Harlem Shadows (McKay), **Supp. X:** 131–132, 136
Harlem Underground (Lacy), **Supp. XV:** 206
"Harlequin of Dreams, The" (Lanier), **Supp. I Part 1:** 365
Harlot's Ghost (Mailer), **Retro. Supp. II:** 211–212
Harlow, Jean, **IV:** 256; **Retro. Supp. I:** 110
"Harm" (C. Frost), **Supp. XV:** 101
Harmon, William, **Retro. Supp. I:** 37; **Supp. XI:** 248
"Harmonic" (F. Barthelme), **Supp. XI:** 26
Harmonium (Stevens), **III:** 196; **IV:** 76, 77, 78, 82, 87, 89, 92; **Retro. Supp. I:** 296, 297, 299, **300–302,** 301, 302
"Harmony of the Gospels" (Taylor), **IV:** 149
Harmony of the World (C. Baxter), **Supp. XVII:** 16–17
"Harmony of the World" (C. Baxter), **Supp. XVII:** 16
Harnett, Vincent, **Supp. XV:** 198
"Harp, The" (Weigl), **Supp. XIX:** 278
Harper (film), **Supp. IV Part 2:** 473
Harper, Donna, **Retro. Supp. I:** 194, 195, 209
Harper, Frances E. Watkins, **Supp. II Part 1:** 201–202; **Supp. XVIII:** 284; **Supp. XXII:** 11
Harper, Gordon Lloyd, **Retro. Supp. II:** 23
Harper, Michael S., **Retro. Supp. II:** 116, 123; **Supp. XV:** 74; **Supp. XXIV:** 184; **Supp. XXVII:** 152
Harper, William Rainey, **Supp. I Part 2:** 631
Harper's Anthology of 20th Century Native American Poetry (Niatum, ed.), **Supp. IV Part 1:** 331
"Harriet" (R. Lowell), **II:** 554
Harrigan, Edward, **II:** 276; **III:** 14
Harriman, Margaret, **Supp. XXIV:** 19
Harrington, Michael, **I:** 306
Harrington, Ollie, **Supp. XVI:** 142–143
Harris, Celia, **Retro. Supp. I:** 9
Harris, Corra, **Supp. XXII:** 190, 193, 196
Harris, George, **II:** 70
Harris, George Washington, **Supp. XXII:** 193
Harris, Joel Chandler, **III:** 338; **Supp. I Part 1:** 352; **Supp. II Part 1:** 192, 201; **Supp. XIV:** 61; **Supp. XX: 103**
Harris, Judith, **Supp. XIV:** 269
Harris, Julie, **II:** 587, 601; **Supp. IX:** 125
Harris, Leonard, **Supp. XIV:** 196, 211–212
Harris, MacDonald, **Supp. XI:** 65
Harris, Marie, **Supp. IX:** 153
Harris, Peter, **Supp. X:** 206, 207
Harris, Susan K., **Supp. XV:** 269
Harris, Thomas, **Supp. XIV:** 26; **Supp.**

XXI: 67, 78
Harris, Trudier, **Supp. XXVI:** 13–14
Harris, Victoria Frenkel, **Supp. IV Part 1:** 68, 69
Harris, Violet J., **Supp. XXII:** 10, 13
Harris, William E., **Supp. XXIV:** 26
Harris, Wilson, **Supp. XXI:** 170; **Supp. XXVII:** 160, 161
Harrison, Colin, **Supp. XIV:** 26
Harrison, Hazel, **Retro. Supp. II:** 115
Harrison, Jim, **Supp. VIII: 37–56; Supp. XIX:** 125, 126
Harrison, Judy, **Supp. XXIII:** 278
Harrison, Kathryn, **Supp. X:** 191
Harrison, Ken, **Supp. IX:** 101
Harrison, Oliver (pseudonym). See Smith, Harrison
Harrod, Lois Marie, **Supp. XXIII:** 131–132
Harron, Mary, **Supp. XXVII:** 68
Harry: A Portrait (Boyce), **Supp. XVII:** 104; **Supp. XXI: 7, 13–14**
Harryhausen, Ray, **Supp. IV Part 1:** 115
Harryman, Carla, **Supp. XV:** 344
"Harry of Nothingham" (Hugo), **Supp. VI:** 146–147
"Harry's Death" (Carver), **Supp. III Part 1:** 146
"Harsh Judgment, The" (Kunitz), **Supp. III Part 1:** 264
Hart, Albert Bushnell, **Supp. I Part 2:** 479, 480, 481
Hart, Bernard, **I:** 241, 242, 248–250, 256
Hart, Henry, **Retro. Supp. II:** 187; **Supp. XIV:** 97
Hart, James D., **Supp. XVIII:** 257
Hart, John Seely, **Supp. XVIII:** 257, 258, 264
Hart, Lorenz, **III:** 361
Hart, Moss, **Supp. IV Part 2:** 574; **Supp. XV:** 329
Hart, Pearl, **Supp. X:** 103
"Hart Crane" (Tate), **I:** 381
"Hart Crane and Poetry: A Consideration of Crane's Intense Poetics with Reference to 'The Return' " (Grossman), **Retro. Supp. II:** 83
Harte, Anna Griswold, **Supp. II Part 1:** 341
Harte, Bret, **I:** 193, 195, 203; **II:** 289; **IV:** 196; **Retro. Supp. II:** 72; **Supp. II Part 1: 335–359,** 399; **Supp. XV:** 115
Harte, Walter Blackburn, **I:** 199
Harter, Carol C., **Supp. IV Part 1:** 217
Hartigan, Grace, **Supp. XXIII:** 210, 212, 217
Hartley, David, **III:** 77
Hartley, Lois, **Supp. I Part 2:** 459, 464–465
Hartley, L. P., **Supp. I Part 1:** 293
Hartley, Marsden, **IV:** 409, 413; **Retro. Supp. I:** 430; **Supp. X:** 137; **Supp. XV:** 298
Hartman, Geoffrey, **Supp. IV Part 1:** 119; **Supp. XII:** 130, 253
Hartman, Saidiya, **Supp. XX: 154**
Harum, David, **II:** 102
"Harvard" (R. Lowell), **II:** 554
Harvard College in the Seventeenth Century (Morison), **Supp. I Part 2:** 485
"Harvest" (E. P. Jones), **Supp. XXII:** 141
"Harvest, The" (Hempel), **Supp. XXI:** 115, **122–123**
Harvest, The (Levin), **Supp. XXVII:** 143, 146
Harvester, The (Stratton-Porter), **Supp. XX: 211, 212, 218, 221**
"Harvester, The: The Natural Bounty of Gene Stratton-Porter" (Birkelo), **Supp. XX: 220–221**
"Harvesters of Night and Water" (Hogan), **Supp. IV Part 1:** 412
"Harvest Song" (Toomer), **Supp. III Part 2:** 483
Harvill Book of 20th Century Poetry in English, **Supp. X:** 55
Harvin, Emily, **Supp. XXIII:** 174
"Harv Is Plowing Now" (Updike), **Retro. Supp. I:** 318
Harwood, Lee, **Supp. XXVII:** 22
Haselden, Elizabeth Lee, **Supp. VIII:** 125
"Hasidic Noir" (Abraham), **Supp. XXIV: 14–15**
Haskell, Mary, **Supp. XX: 115, 117**
"Haskell's Mill" (Davison), **Supp. XXVI:** 73, 75, 76
Hass, Robert, **Supp. VI: 97–111; Supp. VIII:** 24, 28; **Supp. XI:** 142, 270; **Supp. XIV:** 83, 84; **Supp. XXI:** 60; **Supp. XXVI:** 61, 68
Hassam, Childe, **Retro. Supp. II:** 136
Hassan, Ihab, **IV:** 99–100, 115; **Supp. XI:** 221
Hasse, Henry, **Supp. IV Part 1:** 102
Hasty-Pudding, The (Barlow), **Supp. II Part 1:** 74, 77–80
"Hater of Mediocrity, The" (Boulton), **Supp. XXII:** 23
Hateship, Friendship, Courtship, Loveship, Marriage (Munro), **Supp. XXVII:** 190, 192–193
Hate That Hate Produced, The (CBS documentary), **Supp. XX: 102**
Hatful of Rain, A (film), **Supp. XXVI:** 134
Hatful of Rain, A (Gazzo), **III:** 155
Hatlen, Burton, **Supp. V:** 138, 139–140; **Supp. XXI:** 24
"Hatred"(O'Hara), **Supp. XXIII:** 212
"Hattie Bloom" (Oliver), **Supp. VII:** 232
Haugen, Hayley Mitchell, **Supp. XXIV:** 215
Haunch, Paunch, and Jowl (Ornitz), **Supp. IX:** 227
Haunted Lady, The (Rinehart), **Supp. XXV:** 198, 200
"Haunted Landscape" (Ashbery), **Supp. III Part 1:** 22
Haunted Merchant, The (Briggs), **Supp. XVIII:** 2, 8
"Haunted Mind" (Simic), **Supp. VIII:** 282
"Haunted Mind, The" (Hawthorne), **II:** 230–231
"Haunted Oak, The" (Dunbar), **Supp. II Part 1:** 207, 208
"Haunted Palace, The" (Poe), **III:** 421
"Haunted Quack, The" (Hawthorne), **Retro. Supp. III:** 114
"Haunted Valley, The" (Bierce), **I:** 200
Haunting, The (film), **Supp. IX:** 125
Haunting of Hill House, The (Jackson), **Supp. IX:** 117, 121, 126
Hauptmann, Gerhart, **III:** 472
Haussmann, Sonja, **Supp. XIII:** 331, **Supp. XIII:** 347
"Havanna vanities come to dust in Miami" (Didion), **Supp. IV Part 1:** 210
Havel, Hippolyte, **Supp. XXI:** 4, 6
Haven, Cynthia, **Supp. XV:** 252, 264; **Supp. XXIII:** 134, 138, 139
Haven's End (Marquand), **III:** 55, 56, 63, 68
"Have You Ever Faked an Orgasm" (Peacock), **Supp. XIX:** 199
"Have You Ever Tried to Enter the Long Black Branches" (Oliver), **Supp. VII:** 247
"Having a Coke with You"(O'Hara), **Supp. XXIII:** 219
"Having Been Interstellar" (Ammons), **Supp. VII:** 25
"Having It Out With Melancholy" (Kenyon), **Supp. VII:** 171
"Having Lost My Sons, I Confront the Wreckage of the Moon: Christmas, 1960" (Wright), **Supp. III Part 2:** 600
"Having Saints" (Davison), **Supp. XXVI:** 71
"Having Snow" (Schwartz), **Supp. II**

Part 2: 652
"Having Words"(Thompson), **Supp. XXIII:** 293–294
"Hawaii, Washington, Vermont: A Frame for the Verse" (Taggard), **Supp. XXII:** 281–282
Hawaiian Hilltop (Taggard), **Supp. XXII:** 275
Hawai'i One Summer (Kingston), **Supp. V:** 157, 160, 166, 169–170
Haweis, Stephen, **Supp. XXII:** 157, 158, 159, 161, 163, 165
"Hawk, The" (Francis), **Supp. IX:** 81
Hawke, David Freeman, **Supp. I Part 2:** 511, 516
Hawkes, John, **I:** 113; **Retro. Supp. II:** 234; **Supp. III Part 1:** 2; **Supp. IX:** 212; **Supp. V:** 40; **Supp. XVII:** 183; **Supp. XXI:** 210
Hawkins, Gary, **Supp. XXI:** 35, 39
Hawkins, William, **II:** 587
Hawk in the Rain, The (Hughes), **Retro. Supp. II:** 244; **Supp. I Part 2:** 537, 540
Hawk Is Dying, The (Crews), **Supp. XI: 111**
Hawk Moon (Shepard), **Supp. III Part 2:** 445
Hawks, Howard, **Supp. IV Part 1:** 130; **Supp. XVIII:** 148
"Hawk's Cry in Autumn, The" (Brodsky), **Supp. VIII:** 29
"Hawks of Outremer" (Howard), **Supp. XXVII:** 120
"Hawk's Shadow" (Glück), **Supp. V:** 85
Hawk's Well, The (Yeats), **III:** 459–460
Hawley, Adelaide, **Supp. XIV:** 207
Hawley, Joseph, **I:** 546
Hawthorne (James), **II:** 372–378; **Retro. Supp. I:** 220, **223–224**
"Hawthorne" (Longfellow), **Retro. Supp. II:** 169
"Hawthorne" (R. Lowell), **II:** 550
Hawthorne, Julian, **II:** 225; **Supp. I Part 1:** 38; **Supp. XV:** 274
Hawthorne, Nathaniel, **I:** 106, 204, 211, 340, 355, 363, 384, 413, 458, 561–562; **II:** 7, 8, 40, 60, 63, 74, 89, 127–128, 138, 142, 198, **223–246,** 255, 259, 264, 267, 272, 274, 277, 281, 282, 295, 307, 309, 311, 313, 322, 324, 326, 402, 408, 446, 501, 545; **III:** 51, 81–82, 83, 84, 85, 87, 88, 91, 92, 113, 316, 359, 412, 415, 421, 438, 453, 454, 507, 565, 572; **IV:** 2, 4, 167, 172, 179, 194, 333, 345, 453; **Retro. Supp. I:** 1, 53, 59, 62, 63, 91, **145–167,** 215, 218, 220, 223, 248–249, 252, 257, 258, 330, 331, 365; **Retro. Supp. II:** 136, 142, 153, 156–157, 158, 159, 187, 221; **Retro. Supp. III:** 44, **109–124,** 155, 157, 194, 223, 225, 233; **Supp. I Part 1:** 38, 188, 197, 317, 372; **Supp. I Part 2:** 420, 421, 545, 579, 580, 582, 587, 595, 596; **Supp. III Part 2:** 501; **Supp. IV Part 1:** 80, 127, 297; **Supp. IV Part 2:** 463, 596; **Supp. IX:** 114; **Supp. V:** 152; **Supp. VIII:** 103, 105, 108, 153, 201; **Supp. X:** 78; **Supp. XI:** 51, 78; **Supp. XII:** 26; **Supp. XIII:** 102; **Supp. XIV:** 48; **Supp. XV:** 269, 272, 282; **Supp. XVI:** 83, 84, 157; **Supp. XVII:** 42; **Supp. XVIII:** 258, 260; **Supp. XXI:** 201; **Supp. XXIII:** 161, 190, 290; **Supp. XXV:** 242, 249
Hawthorne, Mrs. Nathaniel (Sophia Peabody), **II:** 224, 244; **III:** 75, 86
Hawthorne, Rose, **II:** 225
Hawthorne, Una, **II:** 225
"Hawthorne and His Mosses" (Melville), **Retro. Supp. I:** 254; **Supp. XIV:** 48
"Hawthorne Aspect [of Henry James], The" (Eliot), **Retro. Supp. I:** 63
"Hawthorne in Solitude" (Cowley), **Supp. II Part 1:** 143
Hay, John, **I:** 1, 10, 12, 14–15; **Supp. I Part 1:** 352
Hay, Mrs. John, **I:** 14
Hay, Sara Henderson, **Supp. XIV: 119–135**
Hayakawa, S. I., **I:** 448; **Supp. I Part 1:** 315; **Supp. XV:** 176
Haycroft, Howard, **Supp. XXV:** 199; **Supp. XXVI:** 277
Hayden, Robert, **Supp. II Part 1: 361–383; Supp. IV Part 1:** 169; **Supp. XIII:** 115, 127; **Supp. XIV:** 119, 123
Hayden, Sterling, **Supp. XI:** 304
Hayden, William R., **Supp. XXV:** 38
Haydn, Hiram, **IV:** 100, 358
Hayduke Lives! (Abbey), **Supp. XIII: 16**
Hayek, Friedrich A. von, **Supp. IV Part 2:** 524
Hayes, Alfred, **Supp. XXVI: 133–146**
Hayes, Helen, **Supp. XVI:** 193, 195
Hayes, Ira, **Supp. IV Part 1:** 326
Hayes, Kevin, **Retro. Supp. III:** 237
Hayes, Richard, **Supp. V:** 320
Hayes, Rutherford B., **Supp. I Part 2:** 419
Hayford, James, **Supp. XXII:** 204, 218
Haygood, Wil, **Supp. VIII:** 79
"Haying While the Sun Shines" (L. I. Wilder), **Supp. XXII:** 290
Hayne, Paul Hamilton, **Supp. I Part 1:** 352, 354, 355, 360, 372
Haynes, Todd, **Supp. XVIII:** 23
Haynes-Smith, William, **Supp. XX: 231, 232, 233**
Hayward, Florence, **Retro. Supp. II:** 65
Hayward, John, **Retro. Supp. I:** 67
Hayward, Leland, **Supp. XIX:** 250
Haywood, "Big" Bill, **I:** 483; **Supp. V:** 286; **Supp. XXIII:** 162
Hazan, Joe, **Supp. XXIII:** 212
Hazard, Grace, **II:** 530
Hazard of Fortunes, A (Howells), **Retro. Supp. II:** 288
Hazard of New Fortunes, A (Howells), **II:** 275, 276, 286–297, 290
Hazel, Robert, **Supp. VIII:** 137, 138
Hazen, General W. B., **I:** 192, 193
Hazlitt, Henry, **Supp. IV Part 2:** 524
Hazlitt, William, **I:** 58, 378; **II:** 315; **Supp. XXI:** 205
Hazmat (McClatchy), **Supp. XII: 265–270**
Hazo, Samuel, **I:** 386; **Supp. XIV:** 123, 124
Hazzard, Shirley, **Supp. VIII:** 151
H.D. See Doolittle, Hilda
"He" (Porter), **III:** 434, 435
"Head and Shoulders" (Fitzgerald), **Retro. Supp. I:** 101
Headhunter (Findley), **Supp. XX: 57–59, 60, 61**
"Head-Hunter, The" (O. Henry), **Supp. II Part 1:** 403
"Headless Hawk, The" (Capote), **Supp. III Part 1:** 124
Headlines (T. Williams), **IV:** 381
Headlong Hall (Peacock), **Supp. I Part 1:** 307
Headmaster, The (McPhee), **Supp. III Part 1:** 291, 294, 298
"Head of Joaquín Murrieta, The" (Rodriguez), **Supp. XIV:** 303
Headsman, The (Cooper), **I:** 345–346
Heads of Grain (al-Sanábil) (Gibran), **Supp. XX: 124**
"Headwaters" (Momaday), **Supp. IV Part 2:** 486
"Head Wound" (Halliday), **Supp. XIX:** 92
Healing, The (G. Jones), **Supp. XXIV:** 183, 185, **190–192,** 195
Healy, Eloise Klein, **Supp. XI:** 121, 124, 126, 127, 129, 137
Healy, Tim, **II:** 129, 137
Heaney, Sally, **Supp. XVII:** 241
Heaney, Seamus, **Retro. Supp. II:** 245;

Supp. IX: 41, 42; **Supp. X:** 67, 122; **Supp. XI:** 249; **Supp. XV:** 256; **Supp. XXI:** 54, 243
"Heard through the Walls of the Racetrack Glen Motel" (X. J. Kennedy), **Supp. XV:** 170
"Hearing, The" (Huddle), **Supp. XXVI:** 155
Hearn, Lafcadio, **I:** 211; **II:** 311
Hearon, Shelby, **Supp. VIII: 57–72**
Hearst, Patty, **Supp. IV Part 1:** 195
Hearst, William Randolph, **I:** 198, 207, 208; **IV:** 298
Heart and Perimeter (Bierds), **Supp. XVII: 28–29**
"Heart and the Lyre, The" (Bogan), **Supp. III Part 1:** 65
"Heart as Origami, The (Hirshfield), **Supp. XXIII:** 132
"Heartbeat" (Harjo), **Supp. XII:** 221–222
Heartbreak Hotel (Siddons), **Supp. XXII:** 239, 241, 242
Heartbreak Kid, The (film), **Supp. IV Part 2:** 575, 589
"Heart Failure"(Schott), **Supp. XXIII:** 252
"Heart Finds Its Own Conclusion, The" (Muñoz), **Supp. XXV:** 136
Heart for the Gods of Mexico, A (Aiken), **I:** 54
"Hearth" (Rash), **Supp. XXVII:** 222
"Hear the Nightingale Sing" (Gordon), **II:** 200
Hear the Wind Blow (Sanders), **Supp. XVI:** 268
Heart is a Lonely Hunter, The (McCullers), **II:** 586, 588–593, 604, 605
Heartland (film), **Supp. XXVI:** 183–184
Heart of a Woman, The (Angelou), **Supp. IV Part 1:** 2, 5, 7–9, 9, 14, 17
Heart of Darkness (Conrad), **Retro. Supp. II:** 292; **Supp. V:** 249, 311; **Supp. VIII:** 4, 316; **Supp. XIX:** 28; **Supp. XX: 18, 57–58; Supp. XXIV:** 286
"Heart of Darkness" (Conrad), **I:** 575, 578; **II:** 595; **Supp. XVI:** 212
Heart of Darkness (Didion), **Supp. IV Part 1:** 207
Heart of Dixie (film), **Supp. XXII:** 239, 241
Heart of Haiku, The (Hirshfield), **Supp. XXIII:** 137–138
Heart of Happy Hollow, The (Dunbar), **Supp. II Part 1:** 214
Heart of Knowledge, The: American Indians on the Bomb (Gunn Allen and Caputi, eds.), **Supp. IV Part 1:** 334–335
"Heart of Knowledge, The: Nuclear Themes in Native American Thought and Literature" (Caputi), **Supp. IV Part 1:** 335
Heart of the Earth (Moraga), **Supp. XXIII:** 196
"Heart of the Park, The " (O'Connor), **Retro. Supp. II:** 225
Heart of the West (O. Henry), **Supp. II Part 1:** 410
"Hearts, The" (Pinsky), **Supp. VI:** 245–247, 248
"'Hearts and Flowers' " (MacLeish), **III:** 8
"Hearts and Heads" (Ransom), **Supp. I Part 1:** 373
"Heart's Graveyard Shift, The" (Komunyakaa), **Supp. XIII:** 120
Heart-Shape in the Dust (Hayden), **Supp. II Part 1:** 365, 366
Heart's Needle (Snodgrass), **I:** 400
"Heart's Needle" (Snodgrass), **Supp. VI: 311–313,** 320
"Hearts of Oak" (Rowson), **Supp. XV:** 243
"Heart Songs" (Proulx), **Supp. VII:** 254
Heart Songs and Other Stories (Proulx), **Supp. VII:** 252–256, 261
Heart to Artemis, The (Bryher), **Supp. I Part 1:** 259
"Heart to Heart" (Zitkala-Ša), **Supp. XXV:** 284
Heartwood (Burke), **Supp. XIV:** 35
Heath, Shirley, **Supp. XX: 90**
Heath Anthology of American Literature, The, **Supp. IX:** 4; **Supp. XV:** 270, 313
Heathcote, Anne. See De Lancey, Mrs. James
"Heathen Chinee, The" (Harte), **Supp. II Part 1:** 350–351, 352
Heathen Days, 1890–1936 (Mencken), **III:** 100, 111
Heath-Stubbs, John, **Supp. XV:** 153
Heaton, David, **Supp. XXVI:** 7
Heat's On, The (C. Himes), **Supp. XVI:** 143, 144
"Heaven" (Dunn), **Supp. XI:** 154
"Heaven" (Levine), **Supp. V:** 182
"Heaven" (Patchett), **Supp. XII:** 309
Heaven and Earth: A Cosmology (Goldbarth), **Supp. XII: 187**
"Heaven and Earth in Jest" (Dillard), **Supp. VI:** 24, 28
"Heaven as Anus" (Kumin), **Supp. IV Part 2:** 448
Heavenly Conversation, The (Mather), **Supp. II Part 2:** 460
"Heavenly Feast, The" (Schnackenberg), **Supp. XV:** 257, 259
Heavens (Untermeyer), **Supp. XV:** 306
Heavens and Earth (Benét), **Supp. XI:** 44
Heaven's Coast (Doty), **Supp. XI:** 119, 121, **129–130,** 134; **Supp. XXIII:** 126
Heaven's Prisoners (Burke), **Supp. XIV:** 23, 29
"Heavy Angel, The" (Everwine), **Supp. XV:** 80
"Heavy Bear Who Goes with Me, The" (Schwartz), **Supp. II Part 2:** 646
"Heavy Trash" (Halliday), **Supp. XIX:** 92, 93
Hebert, Ernest, **Supp. XXII:** 207
Heble, Ajay, **Supp. XXVII:** 183
"He Came Also Still" (Zukofsky), **Supp. III Part 2:** 612
Hecht, Anthony, **IV:** 138; **Supp. III Part 2:** 541, 561; **Supp. X: 55–75; Supp. XII:** 269–270; **Supp. XV:** 251, 256; **Supp. XXVII:** 218
Hecht, Ben, **I:** 103; **II:** 42; **Supp. I Part 2:** 646; **Supp. XI:** 307; **Supp. XIII:** 106; **Supp. XXV:** 18, 19, 22, 27, 29; **Supp. XXVII: 83–98,** 139
Hecht, S. Theodore, **Supp. III Part 2:** 614
Heckewelder, John, **II:** 503
"Hedge Island" (A. Lowell), **II:** 524
"Hedgerows in England, The" (Stone), **Supp. XXVII:** 258, 259–260
Hedges, William I., **II:** 311–312
"He 'Digesteth Harde Yron' " (Moore), **Supp. IV Part 2:** 454
Hedin, Robert, **Supp. XII:** 200, 202
Hedley, Jane, **Retro. Supp. III:** 249
Hedylus (Doolittle), **Supp. I Part 1:** 259, 270
"Heel & Toe To the End" (W. C. Williams), **Retro. Supp. I:** 430
Heffernan, Michael, **Supp. XII:** 177
"HEGEL" (Baraka), **Supp. II Part 1:** 53
Hegel, Georg Wilhelm Friedrich, **I:** 265; **II:** 358; **III:** 262, 308–309, 480, 481, 487, 607; **IV:** 86, 333, 453; **Supp. I Part 2:** 633, 635, 640, 645; **Supp. XVI:** 289; **Supp. XXVI:** 234
"Hegemony of Race, The" (Du Bois), **Supp. II Part 1:** 181
Hegger, Grace Livingston. See Lewis, Mrs. Sinclair (Grace Livingston Hegger)

"He Had Spent His Youth Dreaming" (Dobyns), **Supp. XIII:** 90

Heidegger, Martin, **II:** 362, 363; **III:** 292; **IV:** 491; **Retro. Supp. II:** 87; **Supp. V:** 267; **Supp. VIII:** 9; **Supp. XVI:** 283, 288; **Supp. XXVI:** 234

Heidenmauer, The (Cooper), **I:** 345–346

Heidi Chronicles, The (Wasserstein), **Supp. IV Part 1:** 309; **Supp. XV:** 319, **325–327**

"Height of the Ridiculous, The" (Holmes), **Supp. I Part 1:** 302

Heilbroner, Robert, **Supp. I Part 2:** 644, 648, 650

Heilbrun, Carolyn G., **Supp. IX:** 66; **Supp. XI:** 208; **Supp. XIV:** 161, 163; **Supp. XX: 108**

Heilman, Robert Bechtold, **Supp. XIV:** 11, 12

Heilpern, John, **Supp. XIV:** 242

Heim, Michael, **Supp. V:** 209

Heine, Heinrich, **II:** 272, 273, 277, 281, 282, 387, 544; **IV:** 5; **Supp. XV:** 293, 299; **Supp. XVI:** 188

Heineman, Frank, **Supp. III Part 2:** 619

Heinemann, Larry, **Supp. XXII: 103–117**

Heinlein, Robert, **Supp. IV Part 1:** 102; **Supp. XVI:** 122; **Supp. XVIII:** 149

Heinz, Helen. See Tate, Mrs. Allen (Helen Heinz)

Heiress, The (film), **Retro. Supp. I:** 222

"Heirs" (Nye), **Supp. XIII:** 284

"He Is Not Worth the Trouble" (Rowson), **Supp. XV:** 240

"He Knew" (C. Himes), **Supp. XVI:** 137

"Helas" (Creeley), **Supp. IV Part 1:** 150, 158

Helburn, Theresa, **IV:** 381

Heldreth, Leonard, **Supp. V:** 151

"Helen" (R. Lowell), **II:** 544

"Helen, Thy Beauty Is to Me" (Fante), **Supp. XI:** 169

"Helen: A Courtship" (Faulkner), **Retro. Supp. I:** 81

"Helen I Love You" (Farrell), **II:** 28, 45

Helen in Egypt (Doolittle), **Supp. I Part 1:** 260, 272, 273, 274; **Supp. XV:** 264

Helen in Egypt (H.D.), **Retro. Supp. III:** 51

Helen Keller: Sketch for a Portrait (Brooks), **I:** 254

Helen of Troy and Other Poems (Teasdale), **Supp. XXVII:** 283, 285–286, 288–289

"Helen of Tyre" (Longfellow), **II:** 496

Heliodora (Doolittle), **Supp. I Part 1:** 266

Helium-3 series (Hickam), **Supp. XXVII:** 111

"He Lives On the Landing" (Espaillat), **Supp. XXI:** 108

"Helix" (Sobin), **Supp. XVI:** 283

Hellbox (O'Hara), **III:** 361

Helle, Anita, **Supp. XXIII:** 117

Heller, Joseph, **III:** 2, 258; **IV:** 98; **Retro. Supp. II:** 324; **Supp. I Part 1:** 196; **Supp. IV Part 1: 379–396;** **Supp. V:** 244; **Supp. VIII:** 245; **Supp. XI:** 307; **Supp. XII:** 167–168; **Supp. XV:** 322; **Supp. XVII:** 139; **Supp. XXIII:** 100

"Hell-Heaven" (Lahiri), **Supp. XXI: 181–183,** 183, 184–186, 188

Hellman, Lillian, **I:** 28; **III:** 28; **Supp. I Part 1: 276–298; Supp. IV Part 1:** 1, 12, 83, 353, 355, 356; **Supp. IX:** 196, 198, 200–201, 204; **Supp. VIII:** 243; **Supp. XXVII:** 133, 136

Hellmann, Lillian, **Retro. Supp. II:** 327

Hello (Creeley), **Supp. IV Part 1:** 155, 157

"Hello, Hello Henry" (Kumin), **Supp. IV Part 2:** 446

"Hello, Stranger" (Capote), **Supp. III Part 1:** 120

Hello Dolly! (musical play), **IV:** 357

Hell's Angels: A Strange and Terrible Saga (Thompson), **Supp. XXIV:** 282, 283, 288, 290–291

Hellyer, John, **Supp. I Part 2:** 468

Helm, Bob, **Supp. XV:** 147

Helm, Levon, **Supp. XVIII:** 26

Helmets (Dickey), **Supp. IV Part 1:** 175, 178, 180

"Helmsman, The" (Doolittle), **Supp. I Part 1:** 266

"Help" (Barth), **I:** 139

"Help Her to Believe" (Olsen). See "I Stand There Ironing" (Olsen)

Helprin, Mark, **Supp. XIX:** 142; **Supp. XXV: 79–91**

Helsel, Philip Browning, **Supp. XXVI:** 53

"Helsinki Window" (Creeley), **Supp. IV Part 1:** 158

"Hema and Kaushik" (Lahiri), **Supp. XXI:** 183, 188

Hemenway, Robert E., **Retro. Supp. III:** 131, 137; **Supp. IV Part 1:** 6

Hemingway, Dr. Clarence Edwards, **II:** 248, 259

Hemingway, Ernest, **I:** 28, 64, 97, 99, 105, 107, 117, 150, 162, 190, 211, 221, 288, 289, 295, 367, 374, 378, 421, 423, 445, 476, 477, 478, 482, 484–485, 487, 488, 489, 491, 495, 504, 517; **II:** 27, 44, 51, 58, 68–69, 78, 90, 97, 127, 206, **247–270,** 289, 424, 431, 456, 457, 458–459, 482, 560, 600; **III:** 2, 18, 20, 35, 36, 37, 40, 61, 108, 220, 334, 363, 364, 382, 453, 454, 471–472, 476, 551, 575, 576, 584; **IV:** 27, 28, 33, 34, 35, 42, 49, 97, 108, 122, 126, 138, 190, 191, 201, 216, 217, 257, 297, 363, 404, 427, 433, 451; **Retro. Supp. I:** 74, 98, 108, 111, 112, 113, 115, **169–191,** 215, 292, 359, 418; **Retro. Supp. II:** 19, 24, 30, 68, 115, 123; **Retro. Supp. III:** 36, 194, 255, 264; **Supp. I Part 2:** 621, 658, 678; **Supp. II Part 1:** 221; **Supp. III Part 1:** 146; **Supp. III Part 2:** 617; **Supp. IV Part 1:** 48, 102, 123, 197, 236, 342, 343, 344, 348, 350, 352, 380–381, 383; **Supp. IV Part 2:** 463, 468, 502, 607, 679, 680, 681, 689, 692; **Supp. IX:** 16, 57, 58, 94, 106, 260, 262; **Supp. V:** 237, 240, 244, 250, 336; **Supp. VIII:** 40, 101, 105, 179, 182, 183, 188, 189, 196; **Supp. X:** 137, 167, 223, 225; **Supp. XI:** 214, 221; **Supp. XIII:** 96, 255, 270; **Supp. XIV:** 24, 83; **Supp. XIX:** 131, 154, 157, 246; **Supp. XV:** 69, 135; **Supp. XVI:** 203, 205–206, 208, 210, 233, 236–237, 281–282; **Supp. XVII:** 4, 105, 107, 137, 228, 229; **Supp. XVIII:** 74, 90, 102; **Supp. XX: 45, 74, 76; Supp. XXI:** 7, 8, 36, 262; **Supp. XXIII:** 4, 68, 166, 174, 275, 299; **Supp. XXIV:** 54, 64, 97, 284; **Supp. XXVI:** 17, 32, 135, 147, 180; **Supp. XXVII:** 134, 141

Hemingway, Mrs. Ernest (Hadley Richardson), **II:** 257, 260, 263

Hemingway, Mrs. Ernest (Martha Gellhorn), **II:** 260

Hemingway, Mrs. Ernest (Mary Welsh), **II:** 257, 260

Hemingway, Mrs. Ernest (Pauline Pfeiffer), **II:** 260

Hemingway, Mrs. Ernest (Martha Gellhorn), **Supp. XXVII:** 141

"Hemingway in Paris" (Cowley), **Supp. II Part 1:** 144

"Hemingway Story, A" (Dubus), **Supp. VII:** 91

"Hemingway: The Old Lion" (Cowley), **Supp. II Part 1:** 143

"Hemp, The" (Benét), **Supp. XI:** 44
Hempel, Amy, **Supp. XIX:** 209; **Supp. XXI: 115–128**
"Henchman, The" (Whittier), **Supp. I Part 2:** 696
Henderson, Alice Corbin, **Supp. I Part 2:** 387; **Supp. XV:** 302–303
Henderson, Darwin L., **Supp. XIII:** 213, 221–222
Henderson, Jane, **Supp. VIII:** 87; **Supp. XX: 84**
Henderson, Katherine, **Supp. IV Part 1:** 203, 207
Henderson, Linda. See Hogan, Linda
Henderson, Robert W., **Supp. VIII:** 124
Henderson, Stephen, **Supp. IV Part 1:** 365
Henderson, the Rain King (Bellow), **I:** 144, 147, 148, 152, 153, 154, 155, 158, 160, 161, 162–163; **Retro. Supp. II:** 19, **24–25,** 30
"Hen Flower, The" (Kinnell), **Supp. III Part 1:** 247–248
Henie, Sonja, **Supp. XII:** 165
Henkin, Joshua, **Supp. XXII:** 216
Henle, James, **II:** 26, 30, 38, 41; **Supp. IX:** 2
Henley, Beth, **Supp. XXI:** 145
Hennesy, Dale, **Supp. XV:** 5
Henning, Barbara, **Supp. XXVII:** 174
Henninger, Katherine, **Supp. XXI:** 253
Henri, Robert, **IV:** 411; **Supp. I Part 2:** 376
Henrich, Edith, **Supp. XXIV:** 214
Henry, Arthur, **I:** 515; **Retro. Supp. II:** 97
Henry, DeWitt, **Supp. XI:** 342
Henry, O., **I:** 201; **III:** 5; **Supp. I Part 2:** 390, 462; **Supp. II Part 1: 385–412; Supp. XV:** 40
Henry, Robert, **Retro. Supp. II:** 103
Henry, William A., III, **Supp. IV Part 2:** 574
Henry and Clara (Mallon), **Supp. XIX:** 132**, 136–137,** 139, 141
Henry and June (film), **Supp. X:** 186
Henry and June: From the Unexpurgated Diary of Anaïs Nin, **Supp. X:** 184, 185, 187, 194
Henry Holt and Company, **Retro. Supp. I:** 121, 131, 133, 136
Henry IV (Shakespeare), **III:** 166; **Supp. VIII:** 164
"Henry James, Jr." (Howells), **II:** 289; **Retro. Supp. I:** 220
"Henry James and the Art of Teaching" (Rowe), **Retro. Supp. I:** 216
"Henry Lagoon" (Huddle), **Supp. XXVI:** 155
"Henry Manley, Living Alone, Keeps Time" (Kumin), **Supp. IV Part 2:** 451
"Henry Manley Looks Back" (Kumin), **Supp. IV Part 2:** 451
"Henry Manley" poems (Kumin), **Supp. IV Part 2:** 446
Henry Miller Reader, The (Durrell, ed.), **III:** 175, 190
"Henry's Confession" (Berryman), **I:** 186
Henry VIII (Shakespeare), **Supp. IX:** 235
Henslee, **Supp. IV Part 1:** 217
Henson, Josiah, **Supp. I Part 2:** 589
Hentoff, Margot, **Supp. IV Part 1:** 205
Henton, Alice, **Retro. Supp. III:** 8
Hentz, Caroline Lee, **Supp. I Part 2:** 584
Henze, Hans Werner, **Supp. II Part 1:** 24
"He of the Assembly" (Bowles), **Supp. IV Part 1:** 90
Hepburn, Katharine, **Supp. IX:** 189; **Supp. XI:** 17
Heraclitus, **II:** 1, 163; **IV:** 86
Herakles: A Play in Verse (MacLeish), **III:** 21, 22
Herald of the Autochthonic Spirit (Corso), **Supp. XII:** 134–136
He Ran All the Way (film), **Supp. XVII:** 63
Herberg, Will, **III:** 291
Herbert, Edward, **II:** 11
Herbert, Francis (pseudonym). See Bryant, William Cullen
Herbert, George, **II:** 12; **IV:** 141, 145, 146, 151, 153, 156, 165; **Retro. Supp. II:** 40; **Supp. I Part 1:** 80, 107, 108, 122; **Supp. IV Part 2:** 646; **Supp. XV:** 92, 212, 251; **Supp. XXI:** 109
Herbert, Zbigniew, **Supp. VIII:** 20
Herbert Huncke Reader, The (Schafer, ed.), **Supp. XIV:** 137, 138, 139, 140, 145, 147, 150, 151–152
Herbert of Cherbury, Lord, **II:** 108
"Herbert West—Reanimator" (Lovecraft), **Supp. XXV:** 112
"Herbert White" (Bidart), **Supp. XV:** 24, 27
Herbs and the Earth (Beston), **Supp. XXVI:** 35–36
Herbst, Josephine, **Retro. Supp. II:** 325, 328; **Supp. XIII:** 295; **Supp. XXVI:** 18, 26, 28
"Her Choice" (Larcom), **Supp. XIII:** 144
"Her Dead Brother" (R. Lowell), **Retro. Supp. II:** 188
"Her Dream Is of the Sea" (Ríos), **Supp. IV Part 2:** 546
"Here" (Kenyon), **Supp. VII:** 164
Here and Beyond (Wharton), **Retro. Supp. I:** 382
Here and Now (Levertov), **Supp. III Part 1:** 275, 276
"Here and There" (Wallace), **Supp. X:** 305–306
Here Comes the Mystery Man (Sanders), **Supp. XVI:** 269
"Here Comes Winston, Full of the Holy Spirit" (Eugenides), **Supp. XXIV:** 133
Heredia, Juanita, **Supp. XI:** 185, 190
Heredity and Variation (Lock), **Retro. Supp. I:** 375
Heredity: A Psychological Study of Its Phenomena, Laws, Causes, and Consequences (Ribot), **Supp. XX: 238**
"Here Follows Some Verses upon the Burning of Our House, July 10th, 1666" (Bradstreet), **Retro. Supp. III:** 9, 11
Here in Harlem: Poems in Many Voices (Myers), **Supp. XXVII:** 211
"Here Inside My Forehead" (Rasmussen; Nelson and Espeland, trans.), **Supp. XVIII:** 180
Here is Your War (Pyle), **Supp. XVII:** 61
Here Let Us Feast (M. F. K. Fisher), **Supp. XVII:** 86, 87
Here Lies (Parker), **Supp. IX:** 192
Herendeen, Anne, **Supp. XXII:** 275
Here on Earth (Hoffman), **Supp. X:** 77, 89
Heresy and the Ideal: On Contemporary Poetry (Baker), **Supp. XI:** 142
"Here to Learn" (Bowles), **Supp. IV Part 1:** 93
"Here to Yonder" (Hughes), **Retro. Supp. I:** 205
"Her Father's Letters" (Milburn), **Supp. XI:** 242
"Her Favorite Story" (Richard), **Supp. XIX:** 211, 212
Herford, Beatrice, **Supp. XXVI:** 275
Herford, Oliver, **Supp. XXVI:** 275
Herford, Reverend Brooke, **I:** 471
Herford, Will, **Supp. XXII:** 275
"Her Game" (Skloot), **Supp. XX: 196, 202**
Hergesheimer, Joseph, **Supp. I Part 2:** 620; **Supp. XVI:** 187
"Heritage" (Cullen), **Supp. IV Part 1:** 164–165, 168, 170, 171
"Heritage" (Hogan), **Supp. IV Part 1:** 413

"Her Kind" (Sexton), **Supp. II Part 2:** 687
Herland (Gilman), **Supp. XI:** 208–209
Herman, Florence. See Williams, Mrs. William Carlos (Florence Herman)
Herman, Jan, **Supp. XIV:** 150–151
Herman, William (pseudonym). See Bierce, Ambrose
"Her Management" (Swenson), **Supp. IV Part 2:** 642
"Herman Melville" (Auden), **Supp. II Part 1:** 14
Herman Melville (Mumford), **Supp. II Part 2:** 471, 476, 489–491
"Hermes of the Ways" (Doolittle), **Supp. I Part 1:** 266
"Hermes: Port Authority: His Song" (Di Piero), **Supp. XIX:** 47
Hermetic Definition (Doolittle), **Supp. I Part 1:** 271, 272, 273, 274
Hermia Suydam (Atherton), **Supp. XXIV:** 21, 28
"Hermitage, The" (Haines), **Supp. XII:** 205–206
Hermit and the Wild Woman, The (Wharton), **IV:** 315; **Retro. Supp. I:** 371
"Hermit and the Wild Woman, The" (Wharton), **Retro. Supp. I:** 372
"Hermit Meets the Skunk, The" (Kumin), **Supp. IV Part 2:** 447
Hermit of 69th Street, The: The Working Papers or Norbert Kosky (Kosinski), **Supp. VII:** 215, 216, 223, 226–227
"Hermit of Saba, The" (Freneau), **Supp. II Part 1:** 259
"Hermit Picks Berries, The" (Kumin), **Supp. IV Part 2:** 447
Hermit's Story, The (Bass), **Supp. XVI:** 23–24
"Hermit Thrush, A" (Clampitt), **Supp. IX:** 40
Hermit-Woman, The (G. Jones), **Supp. XXIV:** 185, 194
Hernández, Miguel, **Supp. V:** 194; **Supp. XIII:** 315, 323; **Supp. XXI:** 104
Herne, James A., **II:** 276; **Supp. II Part 1:** 198
Hernton, Calvin, **Supp. X:** 240
"Hero, The" (Moore), **III:** 200, 211, 212
Hero, The: A Study in Tradition, Myth, and Drama (Raglan), **I:** 135; **Supp. XIX:** 147
Hero and the Blues, The (Murray), **Supp. XIX:** 153, 154
Hérodiade (Mallarmé), **I:** 66
Herodotus, **Supp. I Part 2:** 405
Heroes, The (Ashbery), **Supp. III Part 1:** 3
Heroes and Saints (Moraga), **Supp. XXIII:** 195, 196, 197, **203–204**
Heroes and Saints and Other Plays (Moraga), **Supp. XXIII:** 197
Hero in America, The (Van Doren), **II:** 103
"Heroines of Nature: Four Women Respond to the American Landscape" (Norwood), **Supp. IX:** 24
"Heron, The" (Roethke), **III:** 540–541
"Her One Bad Eye" (Karr), **Supp. XI:** 244
"Her Own People" (Warren), **IV:** 253
Her Place in These Designs (Espaillat), **Supp. XXI:** 99, 104
"Her Quaint Honour" (Gordon), **II:** 196, 199, 200
Herr, Michael, **Supp. XI:** 245; **Supp. XIX:** 17
Herreshoff, David, **Supp. XIX:** 265
Herrick, Robert, **II:** 11, 18, 444; **III:** 463, 592; **IV:** 453; **Retro. Supp. I:** 319; **Retro. Supp. II:** 101; **Supp. I Part 2:** 646; **Supp. XIII:** 334; **Supp. XIV:** 8, 9; **Supp. XV:** 155; **Supp. XXI:** 14
Herrmann, John, **Retro. Supp. II:** 328; **Supp. XXII:** 277
Herron, Don, **Supp. XXVII:** 128
Herron, George, **Supp. I Part 1:** 7
"Hers" (column, Prose), **Supp. XVI:** 254
Herschdorfer, Helen, **Supp. XXI:** 262
Herschel, Sir John, **Supp. I Part 1:** 314
"Her Sense of Timing" (Elkin), **Supp. VI:** 56, 58
Hersey, John, **IV:** 4; **Supp. I Part 1:** 196; **Supp. XVI:** 105–106; **Supp. XX: 251**
"Her Sweet turn to leave the Homestead" (Dickinson), **Retro. Supp. I:** 44
"Her Untold Story"(Thompson), **Supp. XXIII:** 301
Herzog (Bellow), **I:** 144, 147, 149, 150, 152, 153, 154, 155, 156, 157, 158, 159–160; **Retro. Supp. II:** 19, **26–27; Supp. IV Part 1:** 30; **Supp. XIX:** 157
Herzog, Tobey C., **Supp. XXII:** 116
"He's About 22. I'm 63" (H. Johnson), **Supp. XXVI:** 174
Heschel, Abraham, **Supp. XXI:** 110, 112
Hesford, Walter A., **Supp. XV:** 215, 217, 218
"He/She" (Dunn), **Supp. XI:** 149
"Hesitation Blues" (Hughes), **Retro. Supp. I:** 211
He Sleeps (McKnight), **Supp. XX: 151, 152–155, 158**
"He Sleeps" (McKnight), **Supp. XX: 152, 155**
Hesse, Hermann, **Supp. V:** 208
Hester, Carolyn, **Supp. XVIII:** 24
"Hetch Hetchy Valley" (Muir), **Supp. IX:** 185
He Who Gets Slapped (Andreyev), **II:** 425
"He Who Spits at the Sky" (Stegner), **Supp. IV Part 2:** 605
"He Will Not Leave a Note" (Ríos), **Supp. IV Part 2:** 548
Hewitt, James, **Supp. XV:** 240
Hewitt, J. N. B., **Supp. XXVI:** 81, 89, 90, 96, 97
Hewlett, Maurice, **I:** 359
Heyen, William, **Supp. XIII:** 285, 344; **Supp. XV:** 212
"Hey! Hey!" (Hughes), **Supp. I Part 1:** 327–328
Heyman, Stanley, **Supp. XXV:** 253
Hey Rub-a-Dub-Dub (Dreiser), **I:** 515; **II:** 26; **Retro. Supp. II:** 104, 105, 108
"Hey Sailor, What Ship?" (Olsen), **Supp. XIII:** 293, 294, 298, **299**
Heyward, DuBose, **Supp. XIX:** 78; **Supp. XVIII:** 281
Hiawatha, **Supp. XXVI:** 81, 82, 83, 86
Hiawatha (Longfellow), **Supp. I Part 1:** 79; **Supp. III Part 2:** 609, 610; **Supp. XXI:** 53
"Hibernaculum" (Ammons), **Supp. VII:** 26–27
Hichborn, Philip, **Supp. I Part 2:** 707, 708
Hichborn, Mrs. Philip. See Wylie, Elinor
"Hic Jacet" (W. C. Williams), **Retro. Supp. I:** 414
Hickam, Homer, **Supp. XXVII: 99–113**
Hickok, Guy, **Supp. XXI:** 7
Hickok, James Butler ("Wild Bill"), **Supp. V:** 229, 230
Hicks, Granville, **I:** 254, 259, 374; **II:** 26; **III:** 342, 355, 452; **Supp. I Part 1:** 361; **Supp. I Part 2:** 609; **Supp. IV Part 1:** 22; **Supp. IV Part 2:** 526; **Supp. VIII:** 96, 124; **Supp. XII:** 250; **Supp. XIII:** 263; **Supp. XXI:** 276; **Supp. XXII:** 279; **Supp. XXVI:** 144; **Supp. XXVII:** 134
Hicks, Sally, **Supp. XXI:** 255
Hicok, Bethany, **Retro. Supp. II:** 39
"Hidden" (Nye), **Supp. XIII:** 283

"Hidden Gardens" (Capote), **Supp. III Part 1:** 125
Hidden in Plain View (Tobin and Dobard), **Supp. XXVI:** 200
Hidden Law, The (Hecht), **Supp. X:** 58
"Hidden Name and Complex Fate" (Ellison), **Supp. II Part 1:** 245
Hiddenness, Uncertainty, Surprise: Three Generative Energies of Poetry (Hirshfield), **Supp. XXIII:** 137
Hidden Wound, The (Berry), **Supp. X:** 23, 25, 26–27, 29, 34, 35
"Hide-and-Seek" (Francis), **Supp. IX:** 81
"Hiding" (Minot), **Supp. VI:** 203, 206
Hiding Place (Wideman), **Supp. X:** 320, 321, 327, 329, 331–332, 333
"Hidin' Out in Honky Heaven: On Race Relations in Vermont" (Budbill), **Supp. XIX:** 5
Hienger, Jorg, **Supp. IV Part 1:** 106
Hieronymus Bosch (De Tolnay), **Supp. XXII:** 255
Higgins, George, **Supp. IV Part 1:** 356
Higginson, Thomas Wentworth, **I:** 451–452, 453, 454, 456, 458, 459, 463, 464, 465, 470; **Retro. Supp. I:** 26, 31, 33, 35, 39, 40; **Supp. I Part 1:** 307, 371; **Supp. IV Part 2:** 430
Higgs, Robert, **Supp. XX: 166**
"High Bridge above the Tagus River at Toledo, The" (W. C. Williams), **Retro. Supp. I:** 429
"High Dive: A Variant" (Kumin), **Supp. IV Part 2:** 442
"High Diver" (Francis), **Supp. IX:** 82
"Higher Keys, The" (Merrill), **Supp. III Part 1:** 335–336
Higher Learning in America, The (Veblen), **Supp. I Part 2:** 630, 631, 641, 642
Highet, Gilbert, **Supp. I Part 1:** 268
"High Heav'd my breast"(J. Schoolcraft), **Supp. XXIII:** 235
High Noon (film), **Supp. V:** 46
"High on Sadness" (Komunyakaa), **Supp. XIII:** 114
"High School Senior" (Olds), **Supp. X:** 212
Highsmith, Patricia, **Supp. IV Part 1:** 79, 94, 132; **Supp. XXII:** 136
"High Spirits, The" (Huddle), **Supp. XXVI:** 154
High Spirits, The: Stories of Men and Women (Huddle), **Supp. XXVI:** 153–154
"High Tide" (Marquand), **III:** 56
High Tide in Tucson: Essays from Now or Never (Kingsolver), **Supp. VII:** 198, 201, 209
"High-Toned Old Christian Woman, A" (Stevens), **Retro. Supp. I:** 301
"High Water" (Mosher), **Supp. XXII:** 205, 211
"Highway, The" (Merwin), **Supp. III Part 1:** 346
Highway 61 Revisited (album, Dylan), **Supp. XVIII:** 20, 27, 30, 32
"Highway 61 Revisited" (song, Dylan), **Supp. XVIII:** 30
"Highway 99E from Chico" (Carver), **Supp. III Part 1:** 136
"Highway Apple Trees" (Espaillat), **Supp. XXI: 100–102**
High Window, The (Chandler), **Supp. IV Part 1:** 127–129, 130, 131
"High Yaller" (R. Fisher), **Supp. XIX:** 72
Hijuelos, Oscar, **Supp. IV Part 1:** 54; **Supp. VIII: 73–91**
Hike and the Aeroplane (Lewis), **II:** 440–441
Hilberg, Raul, **Supp. V:** 267
Hildebrand, Al, **III:** 118
Hiler, Hilaire, **Retro. Supp. II:** 327; **Supp. III Part 2:** 617
"Hill, A" (Hecht), **Supp. X:** 59–60, 63
Hill, Abram, **Supp. XV:** 194
Hill, Anita, **Supp. XX: 110**
Hill, Geoffrey, **Supp. XXVI:** 67
Hill, Hamlin, **Retro. Supp. II:** 286; **Retro. Supp. III:** 260
Hill, James J., **Supp. I Part 2:** 644
Hill, Joe, **I:** 493; **Supp. XVIII:** 224; **Supp. XXIII:** 162
Hill, Josiah, **Supp. XXVI:** 87, 88
Hill, Lee, **Supp. XI:** 293, 294, 297, 299, 301, 305, 307
Hill, Pamela Smith, **Supp. XXII:** 295
Hill, Patti, **I:** 289
Hill, Peggy, **Supp. XIII:** 163
"Hill, The" (Strand), **Supp. IV Part 2:** 627
"Hill, The" (Toomer), **Supp. III Part 2:** 486
Hill, Vernon, **Supp. I Part 2:** 397
"Hillcrest" (Robinson), **III:** 504
Hill-Lubin, Mildred A., **Supp. IV Part 1:** 13
Hillman, Sidney, **Supp. I Part 1:** 5
Hillringhouse, Mark, **Supp. IX:** 286, 288, 299
Hills Beyond, The (Wolfe), **IV:** 450, 451, 460, 461
"Hills Beyond, The" (Wolfe), **IV:** 460
Hillside and Seaside in Poetry (Larcom, ed.), **Supp. XIII:** 142
"Hillside Thaw, A" (Frost), **Retro. Supp. I:** 133
"Hills Like White Elephants" (Hemingway), **Retro. Supp. I:** 170
Hills of the Shatemuc, The (S. Warner), **Supp. XVIII:** 266
"Hill-Top View, A" (Jeffers), **Supp. II Part 2:** 417
Hill Towns (Siddons), **Supp. XXII:** 239, 253
"Hill Wife, The" (Frost), **II:** 154; **Retro. Supp. I:** 131; **Retro. Supp. III:** 99
Hillyer, Catherine, **Supp. XV:** 244
Hillyer, Robert, **I:** 475; **Supp. IX:** 75; **Supp. XIV:** 11
Hilton, James, **Supp. XIII:** 166
"Hiltons' Holiday, The" (Jewett), **II:** 391; **Retro. Supp. II:** 134
Him (Cummings), **I:** 429, 434–435
Himes, Chester Bomar, **Retro. Supp. II:** 117; **Supp. I Part 1:** 51, 325; **Supp. XIII:** 233; **Supp. XVI: 135–146**
Himes, Norman, **Supp. V:** 128
"Him on a Bicycle" (Weigl), **Supp. XIX:** 276
"Him with His Foot in His Mouth" (Bellow), **Retro. Supp. II:** 34
Him with His Foot in His Mouth and Other Stories (Bellow), **Retro. Supp. II:** 31
Hinchman, Sandra K., **Supp. IV Part 1:** 210
Hinckley, David, **Supp. XXII:** 215
Hindemith, Paul, **IV:** 357; **Supp. IV Part 1:** 81
Hindsell, Oliver, **Supp. XIII:** 162
Hindus, Milton, **Supp. XIV:** 288, 291, 292, 293; **Supp. XXIII:** 16
Hines, Suzanne, **Supp. XIV:** 151
Hinge Picture (Howe), **Supp. IV Part 2:** 423–424
Hinojosa, Rolando, **Supp. XIX: 97–114**
"Hinterlands" (W. Gibson), **Supp. XVI:** 123, 128
"Hippies: Slouching towards Bethlehem" (Didion), **Supp. IV Part 1:** 200
Hippolytus (Euripides), **II:** 543; **Supp. I Part 1:** 270
Hippolytus Temporizes (Doolittle), **Supp. I Part 1:** 270
"Hips" (Cisneros), **Supp. VII:** 61, 62
"Hipster's Hipster" (Ginsberg), **Supp. XIV:** 141
"Hired Girl" (Munro), **Supp. XXVII:** 194
Hirsch, Edward D., **Supp. IX:** 262; **Supp. V:** 177; **Supp. XIV:** 15; **Supp. XIX:** 202; **Supp. XV:** 78,

225; **Supp. XVII:** 23; **Supp. XXIII:** 124
Hirsch, Sidney, **Supp. XIV:** 1. See Mttron-Hirsch, Sidney
Hirschfeld, Jane, **Supp. XVII:** 241
Hirschorn, Clive, **Supp. IV Part 2:** 577, 579
Hirshfield, Jane, **Supp. XXIII: 129–141**
Hirson, Roger, **Supp. XI:** 343
"His Bride of the Tomb" (Dunbar), **Supp. II Part 1:** 196
"His Chest of Drawers" (Anderson), **I:** 113, 114
"His Daily Journal"(Kenny), **Supp. XXIII:** 153
"His Father's Whistle" (Wrigley), **Supp. XVIII:** 299
His First, Best Country (J. W. Miller), **Supp. XX: 163, 166, 172–175**
His Fortunate Grace (Atherton), **Supp. XXIV:** 22
His Girl Friday (film), **Supp. XXVII:** 83
His Human Majesty (Boyle), **Supp. XXIV:** 62
"His Last Day" (C. Himes), **Supp. XVI:** 137
"His Lover" (Dubus), **Supp. VII:** 86
"His Music" (Dunn), **Supp. XI:** 149
"His Own Key" (Ríos), **Supp. IV Part 2:** 543
His Picture in the Papers (film; Emerson), **Supp. XVI:** 185
His Religion and Hers (Gilman), **Supp. XI:** 209
Hiss, Alger, **Supp. XV:** 143
"Hiss, Chambers, and the Age of Innocence" (Fiedler), **Supp. XIII:** 99
"His Shield" (Moore), **III:** 211
"His Story" (Cisneros), **Supp. VII:** 67
His Thought Made Pockets & the Plane Buckt (Berryman), **I:** 170
"His Three Women" (Gioia), **Supp. XV:** 119–120
Histoire comparée des systèmes de philosophie (Gérando), **II:** 10
Histoire de la brume, L' (Dybek; trans. Beget), **Supp. XXIII:** 74
Historical and Moral View of the Origin and Progress of the French Revolution (Wollstonecraft), **Supp. I Part 1:** 126
"Historical Conceptualization" (Huizinga), **I:** 255
Historical Evidence and the Reading of Seventeenth-Century Poetry (Brooks), **Supp. XIV:** 11
"Historical Interpretation of Literature, The" (Wilson), **IV:** 431, 433, 445
Historical Jesus, The: The Life of a Mediterranean Jewish Peasant (Crossan), **Supp. V:** 251
Historical Life of Jesus, The (Pettis), **Supp. XXIII:** 189
"Historical Value of Crèvecoeur's Voyage . . .," (Adams), **Supp. I Part 1:** 251
"History" (Emerson), **II:** 13, 15
"History" (Hughes), **Supp. I Part 1:** 344
History (R. Lowell), **Retro. Supp. II:** 183, 190
"History" (Simic), **Supp. VIII:** 279
"History, Myth, and the Western Writer" (Stegner), **Supp. IV Part 2:** 596, 601
"History among the Rocks" (Warren), **IV:** 252
History as a Literary Art (Morison), **Supp. I Part 2:** 493
"History as Fate in E. L. Doctorow's Tale of a Western Town" (Arnold), **Supp. IV Part 1:** 220
"History Is the Memory of Time" (Olson), **Supp. II Part 2:** 574
"History Lesson" (Trethewey), **Supp. XXI:** 248, 249
"History Lessons" (Komunyakaa), **Supp. XIII:** 126
History Man, The (Bradbury), **Supp. XVIII:** 140
"History of a Literary Movement" (Nemerov), **III:** 270
"History of a Literary Radical, The" (Bourne), **I:** 215, 235, 236
History of a Radical: Essays by Randolph Bourne (Brooks), **I:** 245
"History of Armenia, The"(Balakian), **Supp. XXIII:** 23, 24
"History of Buttons, The" (Goldbarth), **Supp. XII:** 187
History of English Literature (Taine), **III:** 323
History of English Prosody (Saintsbury), **Supp. XV:** 181
History of Fortus, The (Emerson), **II:** 8
History of Henry Esmond, The (Thackeray), **II:** 91, 130
History of Modern Poetry, A (Perkins), **Supp. I Part 2:** 475; **Supp. XV:** 185
History of My Heart (Pinsky), **Supp. VI:** 243, 244, 245
History of New York, from the Beginning of the World to the End of the Dutch Dynasty, A (Irving), **II:** 300–303, 304, 310
History of Pendennis, The (Thackeray), **II:** 291
"History of Red, The" (Hogan), **Supp. IV Part 1:** 411
"History of Rodney, The" (Bass), **Supp. XVI:** 20
History of Roxbury Town (Ellis), **Supp. I Part 1:** 99
History of Southern Literature, The (Rubin), **Supp. XX: 161**
History of the African-American People (Proposed) by Strom Thurmond, The (Everett and Kincaid), **Supp. XVIII:** 62, **63–64**
History of the American Film, A (Durang), **Supp. XXIV:** 113, 117, **118–119**
"History of the Blues, A" (Biss), **Supp. XXVI:** 50
History of the Conquest of Mexico (Prescott), **Retro. Supp. I:** 123
History of the Conquest of Peru (Morison, ed.), **Supp. I Part 2:** 494
History of the Dividing Line betwixt Virginia and North Carolina (Byrd), **Supp. IV Part 2:** 425
History of the French Revolution (Carlyle), **Retro. Supp. III:** 266
History of the Life and Voyages of Christopher Columbus, A (Irving), **II:** 310, 314
History of the Navy of the United States of America (Cooper), **I:** 347
History of the Rise and Fall of the Slavepower in America (Wilson), **Supp. XIV:** 48, 49
History of the Russian Revolution, A (Trotsky), **Supp. XXI:** 161
History of the United States (Bancroft), **Supp. XXII:** 33
History of the United States of America during the Administrations of Thomas Jefferson and James Madison (Adams), **I:** 6–9, 10, 20, 21
History of the Work of Redemption, A (Edwards), **I:** 560
History of the World (Raleigh), **Retro. Supp. III:** 4, 6
History of United States Naval Operations in World War II (Morison), **Supp. I Part 2:** 490–492
History of Womankind in Western Europe, The, **Supp. XI:** 197
"History Teacher, The" (Collins), **Supp. XXI:** 57
"History Through a Beard" (Morison), **Supp. I Part 2:** 490
His Toy, His Dream, His Rest (Berryman), **I:** 169, 170, 183, 184–186
"His Words" (Roethke), **III:** 544
Hitchcock, Ada. See MacLeish, Mrs.

Archibald (Ada Hitchcock)
Hitchcock, Alfred, **IV:** 357; **Supp. IV Part 1:** 132; **Supp. VIII:** 177; **Supp. XX: 253; Supp. XXII:** 119
Hitchcock, George, **Supp. X:** 127; **Supp. XVII:** 110
"Hitch Haiku" (Snyder), **Supp. VIII:** 297
"Hitch-Hikers, The" (Welty), **IV:** 262
"Hitchhiking Is Illegal in Nevada" (Lethem), **Supp. XVIII:** 136
Hitchins, Christopher, **Supp. VIII:** 241
Hitler, Adolf, **I:** 261, 290, 492; **II:** 146, 454, 561, 565, 592; **III:** 2, 3, 110, 115, 140, 156, 246, 298, 446; **IV:** 5, 17, 18, 298, 372; **Supp. I Part 2:** 431, 436, 446, 664; **Supp. V:** 290
Hitler, Wendy, **III:** 404
Hitler Lives ? (film), **Supp. XVI:** 102
Hix, H. L., **Supp. XV:** 114
H. L. Mencken, a Portrait from Memory (Angoff), **III:** 107
"H. L. Mencken Meets a Poet in the West Side Y.M.C.A." (White), **Supp. I Part 2:** 677
H. L. Mencken: The American Scene (Cairns), **III:** 119
H. M. Pulham, Esquire (Marquand), **II:** 482–483; **III:** 58, 59, 65, 68–69
Hnizdovsky, Jacques, **Supp. XIII:** 346
"Hoadley's Test Case in Indiana" (Neugeboren), **Supp. XVI:** 219
Hoagland, Edward, **Supp. XIV:** 80; **Supp. XVI:** 277; **Supp. XXII:** 204, 206
Hoagland, Tony, **Supp. XIX:** 81, 89
"Hoarder, The" (Sexton), **Supp. II Part 2:** 692
"Hoarfrost" (C. Baxter), **Supp. XVII:** 15
Hoban, Phoebe, **Supp. XV:** 319, 325
Hoban, Russell, **Supp. XXIII:** 42
Hobb, Gormley, **I:** 203
Hobbes, Thomas, **I:** 277; **II:** 9, 10, 540; **III:** 306; **IV:** 88; **Supp. XII:** 33; **Supp. XIV:** 5, 7
Hobbit, The (Tolkien), **Supp. XXVII:** 124
Hobson, Geary, **Supp. IV Part 1:** 321; **Supp. IV Part 2:** 502
Hobson, J. A., **I:** 232
Hobson, John A., **Supp. I Part 2:** 650
Hobson, Laura Z., **III:** 151
Hocking, Agnes, **Supp. VIII:** 251
Hocking, William Ernest, **III:** 303
Hodge, Merle, **Supp. XXIII:** 94
Hodges, Campbell B., **Supp. XIV:** 8
Hodgson, Captain Joseph, **III:** 328
Hoffa, Jimmy, **I:** 493
Hoffenberg, Mason, **Supp. XI:** 294, 297, 299, 305
Hoffer, Eric, **Supp. VIII:** 188; **Supp. XIX:** 264
Hoffman, Abbie, **Supp. XIV:** 150
Hoffman, Alice, **Supp. X: 77–94; Supp. XIII:** 13
Hoffman, Allen, **Supp. XVII:** 42, 44
Hoffman, Daniel, **Retro. Supp. II:** 265
Hoffman, Daniel G., **I:** 405; **II:** 307; **Supp. XI:** 152
Hoffman, Dustin, **Supp. IV Part 1:** 236
Hoffman, E. T. A., **Supp. XVI:** 157
Hoffman, Eva, **Supp. XVI: 147–164**
Hoffman, Frederick J., **I:** 60, 67; **II:** 443; **IV:** 113
Hoffman, Josiah Ogden, **II:** 297, 300
Hoffman, Matilda, **II:** 300, 314
Hoffman, Paul, **Supp. XV:** 141–142
Hoffman, Roy, **Supp. XX: 177**
Hoffman, Todd, **Supp. XVIII:** 101
Hoffman, Tyler, **Retro. Supp. III:** 103
Hoffman, William, **Supp. XVIII: 69–88**
Hoffman, William M., **Supp. X:** 153
Hoffman-Jeep, Lynda, **Retro. Supp. III:** 127
Hoffmann, E. T. A., **III:** 415
Hofmann, Hans, **Supp. XV:** 144
Hofmeister, Tim, **Supp. XIX:** 115
Ho for a Hat (W. J. Smith), **Supp. XIII:** 346
Hofstadter, Richard, **Supp. VIII:** 98, 99, 108
Hogan, Linda, **Supp. IV Part 1:** 324, 325, **397–418; Supp. XVIII:** 189
Hogan, Randolph, **Supp. XVI:** 252–253
Hogan, Ron, **Supp. XVIII:** 138, 139
Hogarth, William, **Supp. XII:** 44
Hogg, James, **I:** 53; **Supp. I Part 1:** 349; **Supp. IX:** 275
Hoggart, Richard, **Supp. XIV:** 299
"Hog-Nosed Snake, The" (Kooser), **Supp. XIX:** 128
Hogue, W. Lawrence, **Supp. XXII:** 175–176
Hohne, Karen, **Supp. V:** 147
Hojoki (Chomei), **IV:** 170
Holbrook, David, **Supp. I Part 2:** 526–527, 546
Holcroft, Thomas, **Supp. I Part 2:** 514
Holden, Jonathan, **Supp. XI:** 143
Holden, Raymond, **Supp. XIV:** 121–122
Holden, Stephen, **Retro. Supp. III:** 290
Holden, William, **Supp. XI:** 307
Hölderlin, Friedrich, **Supp. XVI:** 48; **Supp. XXIV:** 152
Holding, Elisabeth Sanxay, **Supp. XXII: 119–137**
"Holding On" (Levine), **Supp. V:** 184
Holding the Line: Women in the Great Arizona Mine Strike of 1983 (Kingsolver), **Supp. VII:** 197, 201–202, 204
"Holding the Mirror Up to Nature" (Nemerov), **III:** 275, 276
"Hold Me" (Levine), **Supp. V:** 186
Holdt, Jacob, **Supp. XXVI:** 26
Hold the Press (film), **Supp. XIII:** 163
Hold with the Hares (Zinberg), **Supp. XV:** 197–198,**Supp. XV:** 203
Hole in Texas, A (Wouk), **Supp. XXV:** 257, 266–267
"Hole in the Floor, A" (Wilbur), **Supp. III Part 2:** 556–557
Hole in the Sky: A Memoir (Kittredge), **Supp. XXVI:** 177, 179, 180–181, 182, 184–185
Holiday (Barry), **Retro. Supp. I:** 104
"Holiday" (Porter), **III:** 454
Holiday (W. Frank), **Supp. XX: 72–73**
Holiday, Billie, **Supp. I Part 1:** 80; **Supp. IV Part 1:** 2, 7; **Supp. XIX:** 147
Holiday Song for Four-Part Chorus of Mixed Voices with Piano Accompaniment (Taggard and Schuman), **Supp. XXII:** 283
Holinshed, Raphael, **IV:** 370
Holladay, Polly, **Supp. XXI:** 6
Holland, Josiah, **Supp. I Part 2:** 420
Holland, Laurence Bedwell, **Retro. Supp. I:** 216
Holland, Theodore, **I:** 453
Holland, Mrs. Theodore, **I:** 453, 455, 465
Holland, William, **IV:** 381
Hollander, John, **Supp. III Part 2:** 541; **Supp. IV Part 2:** 642; **Supp. IX:** 50, 153, 155; **Supp. XII:** 254, 255, 260; **Supp. XIX:** 121; **Supp. XV:** 256; **Supp. XVII:** 112; **Supp. XXIII:** 112
Hollenberg, Donna, **Supp. XXIV:** 64
Holley, Marietta, **Supp. XIII:** 152
Holliday, Billie, **Supp. XXI:** 131
Hollinghurst, Alan, **Supp. XIII:** 52
Hollins Critic (Nelson), **Supp. XIX:** 3
Hollis, Thomas Brand, **Supp. I Part 2:** 514
Holloway, Karla F. C., **Retro. Supp. III:** 183
Hollow Men, The (T. S. Eliot), **I:** 574, 575, 578–579, 580, 585; **III:** 586; **Retro. Supp. I:** 63, 64
"Hollow Men, The" (T. S. Eliot), **Retro. Supp. III:** 65

"Hollow Tree, A" (R. Bly), **Supp. IV Part 1:** 64, 66
Hollyberrys at the Shore, The, **Supp. X:** 42
"Hollywood!" (Vidal), **Supp. IV Part 2:** 688
Hollywood: American Movie-City (Rand, unauthorized), **Supp. IV Part 2:** 519
Hollywood: A Novel of America in the 1920s (Vidal), **Supp. IV Part 2:** 677, 684, 686, 688, 690, 691
Hollywood Ending (film; Allen), **Supp. XV:** 11
Hollywood on Trial (film), **Supp. I Part 1:** 295
Holmes, Abiel, **Supp. I Part 1:** 300, 301, 302, 310
Holmes, Mrs. Abiel (Sarah Wendell), **Supp. I Part 1:** 300
Holmes, John, **I:** 169; **Supp. II Part 1:** 87; **Supp. IV Part 2:** 440–441; **Supp. XIV:** 119; **Supp. XXVI:** 68
Holmes, John Clellon, **Supp. XII:** 118; **Supp. XIV:** 144, 150
Holmes, Martha Stoddard, **Supp. XX: 205, 207**
Holmes, Oliver Wendell, **I:** 487; **II:** 225, 273–274, 402, 403; **III:** 81–82, 590, 591–592; **IV:** 429, 436; **Retro. Supp. II:** 155; **Supp. I Part 1:** 103, 243, 254, **299–319; Supp. I Part 2:** 405, 414, 415, 420, 593, 704, 705; **Supp. XI:** 194; **Supp. XXIV:** 77
Holmes, Oliver Wendell, Jr., **I:** 3, 19; **Supp. IV Part 2:** 422
Holmes, Mrs. Oliver Wendell (Amelia Jackson), **Supp. I Part 1:** 303
Holmes, Steven J., **Supp. IX:** 172, 177
Holmes, Ted, **Supp. V:** 180
Holmes, William Henry, **Supp. IV Part 2:** 603–604
Holmquist, Kathryn, **Supp. XXVII:** 268
Holocaust (Reznikoff), **Supp. XIV:** 281, **291–293**
Holocaust in American Life, The (Novick), **Supp. XVI:** 154
Holt, Edwin E., **I:** 59
Holt, Felix, **II:** 179
Holt, Henry, **II:** 348; **III:** 587; **Retro. Supp. III:** 98
Holt, Patricia, **Supp. XIV:** 89
Holtby, Winifred, **Supp. I Part 2:** 720
Holy Ghostly, The (Shepard), **Supp. III Part 2:** 437–438, 447
"Holy Innocents, The" (R. Lowell), **II:** 539
Holy Sonnets (Donne), **IV:** 145; **Supp. I Part 1:** 367; **Supp. III Part 2:** 619; **Supp. XIII:** 130–131; **Supp. XVIII:** 50–51
"Holy Terror, A" (Bierce), **I:** 203
"Holy Terror, The" (Maxwell), **Supp. VIII:** 169
Holy the Firm (Dillard), **Supp. VI:** 23, **29,** 30, 31, 32
Holy War, The (Bunyan), **IV:** 156
"Holy Week"(Thompson), **Supp. XXIII:** 300
Holz, Patricia, **Supp. XXVII:** 267
"Homage to Arthur Rimbaud" (Wright), **Supp. V:** 339
Homage to Baudelaire (Duncan, ed.), **Supp. XV:** 75
Homage to Catalonia (Orwell), **Supp. XVII:** 229
"Homage to Che Guevara" (Banks), **Supp. V:** 5
Homage to Clio (Auden), **Supp. II Part 1:** 24
"Homage to Elizabeth Bishop" (Ivask, ed.), **Supp. I Part 1:** 96
"Homage to Ezra Pound" (Wright), **Supp. V:** 339
Homage to Frank O'Hara (Ashbery), **Supp. III Part 1:** 2–3
"Homage to Franz Joseph Haydn" (Hecht), **Supp. X:** 69
"Homage to Hemingway" (Bishop), **IV:** 35
Homage to Mistress Bradstreet (Berryman), **I:** 168, 169, 170–171, 172, 174, 175, 178–183, 184, 186
"Homage to Mistress Bradstreet" (Berryman), **Retro. Supp. III:** 14
"Homage to Paul Cézanne" (Wright), **Supp. V:** 341–342
Homage to Sextus Propertius (Pound), **Retro. Supp. I:** 290
"Homage to Sextus Propertius" (Pound), **III:** 462, 476; **Supp. III Part 2:** 622
"Homage to Shakespeare" (Cheever), **Supp. I Part 1:** 180
"Homage to the Empress of the Blues" (Hayden), **Supp. II Part 1:** 379
"Homage to the Memory of Wallace Stevens" (Justice), **Supp. VII:** 126
Homage to Theodore Dreiser (Warren), **I:** 517
Homans, Margaret, **Supp. X:** 229
"Home" (Hughes), **Supp. I Part 1:** 329, 330
"Home" (Mora), **Supp. XIII:** 217
Home (Morrison), **Retro. Supp. III:** 185, 198–199
Home (Robinson), **Supp. XXI:** 212, **220–223**
Home (Updike), **Retro. Supp. I:** 320
"Home" (Weigl), **Supp. XIX:** 287
"Home, Home on the Strange" (J. D. Reed), **Supp. XVI:** 174
"Home, Sweet Home" (Fante), **Supp. XI:** 164, 165
Home, The (Gilman), **Supp. XI: 206–207**
"Home, The" (Jarman), **Supp. XVII:** 116
"Home Address" (Bronk), **Supp. XXI:** 27
"Home after Three Months Away" (R. Lowell), **II:** 547
Home and Colonial Library (Murray), **Retro. Supp. I:** 246
"Home and the Open Road: The Nonfiction of Larry Brown" (Barrier), **Supp. XXI:** 48–49
Home as Found (Cooper), **I:** 348, 349, 350, 351
Home at the End of the World, A (Cunningham), **Supp. XV: 59–62,** 63
"Home Away from Home, A" (Humphrey), **Supp. IX:** 101
Home Book of Shakespeare Quotations (Stevenson), **Supp. XIV:** 120
"Home Burial" (Frost), **Retro. Supp. I:** 124, 125, 128, **129–130; Retro. Supp. III:** 97, 98; **Supp. VIII:** 31; **Supp. XIX:** 9; **Supp. XV:** 159
Homecoming (Alvarez), **Supp. VII:** 1, 3–5, 9
"Homecoming" (Carruth), **Supp. XVI:** 55
"Homecoming" (McGrath), **Supp. X:** 116
"Homecoming, The" (Gioia), **Supp. XV:** 123, 124
Homecoming, The (Wilson), **Supp. VIII:** 330
Homecoming Game, The (Nemerov), **III:** 268, 282, 284–285
"Home during a Tropical Snowstorm I Feed My Father Lunch" (Karr), **Supp. XI:** 241–242, 248
Home Economics (Berry), **Supp. X:** 28, 31–32, 35, 36, 37
"Home Economics for Halfbacks" (Skloot), **Supp. XX: 195, 207**
Home Fires and Reservation Roads (Gansworth), **Supp. XXVI:** 114
Home from the Hill (film), **Supp. IX:** 95
Home from the Hill (Humphrey), **Supp. IX:** 93, 95, **96–98,** 104, 106, 109
"Home Grown" (Vital), **Supp. XVI:** 160

"Homeland" (Merwin), **Supp. III Part 1:** 351
Homeland and Other Stories (Kingsolver), **Supp. VII:** 199, 202–204, 207
Homely Girl (A. Miller), **Retro. Supp. III:** 176
Home on the Range (Baraka), **Supp. II Part 1:** 47
Homeplace (Siddons), **Supp. XXII:** 253
Home Place, The (Morris), **III:** 221, 222, 232
Homeplace, The (Nelson), **Supp. XVIII: 174–175**
Homer, **I:** 312, 433; **II:** 6, 8, 133, 302, 543, 544, 552; **III:** 14, 21, 278, 453, 457, 473, 567; **IV:** 54, 371; **Retro. Supp. I:** 59; **Supp. I Part 1:** 158, 283; **Supp. I Part 2:** 494; **Supp. X:** 36, 120, 122; **Supp. XIV:** 21; **Supp. XVII:** 70, 227
Homer, Louise, **Retro. Supp. I:** 10
Homer, Winslow, **Supp. XXI:** 243
"Home Range" (Leopold), **Supp. XIV:** 184, 185
"Home Repairs" (Skloot), **Supp. XX: 204**
Homer's Art (Notley), **Supp. XXII:** 232
"Homer's Art" (Notley), **Supp. XXII:** 232–233
"Homesick Blues" (Hughes), **Supp. I Part 1:** 327
Home: Social Essays (Baraka), **Supp. II Part 1:** 45, 61
"Homesteading on the Extraterrestrial Frontier" (Abbott), **Supp. XVIII:** 142
Home to Harlem (McKay), **Supp. X:** 132, 137–138, **138–139; Supp. XVIII:** 127
"Home Videos" (Brockmeier), **Supp. XXII:** 60
Homeward Bound (Cooper), **I:** 348
"Homeward Star, The" (Palmer), **Supp. XV:** 81–82
Homewood trilogy (Wideman), **Supp. X:** 319
"Homework" (Cameron), **Supp. XII:** 80, **83,** 84
"Homily" (Tate), **IV:** 121–122
Homing with the Birds (Stratton-Porter), **Supp. XX: 212, 216, 222**
"Homme Moyen Sensuel, L' " (Pound), **III:** 462
Homme révolté, L' (Camus), **III:** 306
"Homoeopathy and Its Kindred Delusions" (Holmes), **Supp. I Part 1:** 303–304, 305
Homo Ludens (Huizinga), **II:** 416–417, 425
"Homosexuality: Is It Disgusting, or Is It Delightful?" (Durang), **Supp. XXIV:** 114
"Homosexuality"(O'Hara), **Supp. XXIII:** 212
"Homosexual Villain, The" (Mailer), **III:** 36
"Homo Will Not Inherit" (Doty), **Supp. XI:** 128
"Homunculus, The: A Novel in One Chapter" (McKnight), **Supp. XX: 152**
Hone and Strong Diaries of Old Manhattan, The (Auchincloss, ed.), **Supp. IV Part 1:** 23
"Honey" (Beattie), **Supp. V:** 33
"Honey" (Wright), **Supp. III Part 2:** 589
Honey, Maureen, **Supp. XXVI:** 166
"Honey, We'll Be Brave" (Farrell), **II:** 45
Honey and Salt (Sandburg), **III:** 594–596
"Honey and Salt" (Sandburg), **III:** 594
"Honey Babe" (Hughes), **Supp. I Part 1:** 334
"Honey Tree, The" (Oliver), **Supp. VII:** 236
Hong, Maxine. See Kingston, Maxine Hong
Hong, Terry, **Supp. XXVI:** 216
Hongo, Garrett, **Supp. X:** 292; **Supp. XIII:** 114; **Supp. XVII:** 112
"Honkytonk" (Shapiro), **Supp. II Part 2:** 705
"Honky Tonk in Cleveland, Ohio" (Sandburg), **III:** 585
Honorable Men (Auchincloss), **Supp. IV Part 1:** 23
Honor Thy Father (Talese), **Supp. XVII:** 204–205, 210
Hood, Mary, **Supp. XXVI:** 15
Hood, Tom, **I:** 195
"Hoodoo in America" (Hurston), **Supp. VI:** 153–154
"Hook" (Wright), **Supp. III Part 2:** 604
Hook, Sidney, **I:** 265; **Supp. IV Part 2:** 527; **Supp. VIII:** 96, 100; **Supp. XIV:** 3
Hooker, Adelaide. See Marquand, Mrs. John P. (Adelaide Hooker)
Hooker, Isabella Beecher, **Supp. XI:** 193
Hooker, Samuel, **IV:** 162, 165
Hooker, Thomas, **II:** 15–16; **IV:** 162
Hooper, Marian. See Adams, Mrs. Henry (Marian Hooper)
Hoops (Myers), **Supp. XXVII:** 201, 204, 205–206
Hoosier Holiday, A (Dreiser), **Retro. Supp. II:** 104
Hoover, Herbert, **Supp. I Part 2:** 638
Hoover, J. Edgar, **Supp. XIII:** 170
Hoover, Paul, **Supp. XV:** 179
"Hope" (Bontemps), **Supp. XXII:** 2
"Hope" (Jarrell), **II:** 389
"Hope" (Matthews), **Supp. IX:** 163
Hope, A. D., **Supp. XIII:** 347
Hope, Lynn, **Supp. II Part 1:** 38
Hope, The (Wouk), **Supp. XXV:** 254, 257, 265–266
"Hope Atherton's Wanderings" (Howe), **Supp. IV Part 2:** 432
"Hopeless Kill, The"(Kenny), **Supp. XXIII:** 145
Hope of Heaven (O'Hara), **III:** 361
"Hopes Rise" (Boyle), **Supp. XX: 20**
"Hop-Frog; or, The Eight Chained Ourang-Outangs" (Poe), **Retro. Supp. II:** 264, 268, 269; **Retro. Supp. III:** 230
"Hop-Frog; or The Eight Chained Ourang-Outangs" (Poe), **Supp. XXV:** 112
Hopkin, Pauline, **Supp. XVI:** 143
Hopkins, Anne Yale, **Retro. Supp. III:** 3; **Supp. I Part 1:** 100, 102, 113
Hopkins, Gerard Manley, **I:** 171, 179, 397, 401, 522, 525, 533; **II:** 537; **III:** 197, 209, 523; **IV:** 129, 135, 141, 421; **Retro. Supp. II:** 40; **Supp. I Part 1:** 79, 81, 94; **Supp. III Part 2:** 551; **Supp. IV Part 1:** 178; **Supp. IV Part 2:** 637, 638, 639, 641, 643; **Supp. IX:** 39, 42; **Supp. V:** 337; **Supp. X:** 61, 115; **Supp. XIII:** 294; **Supp. XIV:** 83; **Supp. XV:** 250, 347; **Supp. XVI:** 282; **Supp. XVII:** 241; **Supp. XVIII:** 78, 79; **Supp. XX: 230; Supp. XXIII:** 121; **Supp. XXVII:** 222
Hopkins, Gerard Walter Sturgis, **Supp. XX: 229, 233, 240**
Hopkins, L. A., **I:** 502
Hopkins, Lemuel, **Supp. II Part 1:** 70
Hopkins, Miriam, **IV:** 381; **Supp. I Part 1:** 281
Hopkins, Pauline, **Supp. XVIII:** 284
Hopkins, Samuel, **I:** 547, 549; **Supp. XXIV:** 68
Hopkins, Vivian, **II:** 20
Hopkinson, Francis, **Supp. I Part 2:** 504
Hopler, Jay, **Supp. XXIII:** 132
Hopper (Strand), **Supp. IV Part 2:** 632
Hopper, Dennis, **Supp. XI:** 293, 308;

Supp. XXVI: 26
Hopper, Edward, **IV:** 411, 413; **Supp. IV Part 2:** 619, 623, 631, 634; **Supp. XIX:** 117
Hopwood, Avery, **Supp. IV Part 2:** 573; **Supp. XXV:** 195
Horace, **II:** 8, 154, 169, 543, 552, 568; **III:** 15; **IV:** 89; **Retro. Supp. III:** 101; **Supp. I Part 2:** 423; **Supp. IX:** 152; **Supp. X:** 65; **Supp. XII:** 258, 260, 262
Horae Canonicae (Auden), **Supp. II Part 1:** 21
"Horatian Ode" (Marvell), **IV:** 135
"Horatian Ode upon Cromwell's Return from Ireland" (Marvell), **Supp. XIV:** 10
Horgan, Paul, **Supp. XV:** 46, 49, 52
Horkheimer, Max, **Supp. I Part 2:** 645; **Supp. IV Part 1:** 301
Horn, Dara, **Supp. XVII:** 50; **Supp. XX: 177**
Horn, Mother, **Supp. I Part 1:** 49, 54
Hornburg, Michael, **Supp. XXVII:** 80
Hornby, Nick, **Supp. XII:** 286; **Supp. XXIII:** 109
Horn of Africa (Caputo), **Supp. XIX:** 21–23
Horn of Life, The (Atherton), **Supp. XXIV:** 26, 27
"Horn of Plenty" (Hughes), **Retro. Supp. I:** 210; **Supp. I Part 1:** 342
Horovitz, Israel, **Supp. XV:** 321
Horowitz, James. See Salter, James
Horowitz, Mark, **Supp. V:** 219, 231
"Horrible" (Halliday), **Supp. XIX:** 91
"Horror at Martin's Beach, The" (Lovecraft and Greene), **Supp. XXV:** 122
"Horror at Red Hook, The" (Lovecraft), **Supp. XXV:** 110
"Horse, The" (Levine), **Supp. V:** 182
"Horse, The" (Wright), **Supp. III Part 2:** 592, 601
"Horse, The"(Le Sueur), **Supp. XXIII:** 168
Horse Eats Hay (play), **Supp. IV Part 1:** 82
Horse Feathers (film), **Supp. IV Part 1:** 384
"Horseflies" (Wrigley), **Supp. XVIII:** 307
Horse Has Six Legs, The (Simic), **Supp. VIII:** 272
"Horselaugh on Dibber Lannon" (Fante), **Supp. XI:** 164
Horseman, Pass By (McMurtry), **Supp. V:** 220–221, 224
"Horses" (Doty), **Supp. XI:** 122
Horses and Men (Anderson), **I:** 112–113, 114
"Horses and Men in Rain" (Sandburg), **III:** 584
"Horse Show, The" (W. C. Williams), **Retro. Supp. I:** 423
Horses Make a Landscape More Beautiful (Walker), **Supp. III Part 2:** 521, 533
"Horse Thief" (Caldwell), **I:** 310
"Horseweed" (Offutt), **Supp. XIX:** 166, 167
Horse With a Green Vinyl Mane (P. N. Warren), **Supp. XX: 261**
"Horsie" (Parker), **Supp. IX:** 193
Horstmann, Steffen, **Supp. XXV:** 226
Horton, George Moses, **Supp. XXII:** 11
Horton, Philip, **I:** 383, 386, 387, 393, 441; **Supp. XV:** 138
Horton Hatches the Egg (Geisel), **Supp. XVI:** 100, 112
Horton Hears a Who! (Geisel), **Supp. XVI:** 102
"Horton's Ape"(P. Benedict), **Supp. XXIII:** 41
Horwitz, Tony, **Supp. XVIII:** 195–196
Hosea (biblical book), **II:** 166
Hospers, John, **Supp. IV Part 2:** 528
"Hospice" (Hull), **Supp. XXI:** 138
Hospital, Janette Turner, **Supp. IV Part 1:** 311–302
Hospital Sketches (Alcott), **Supp. I Part 1:** 34, 35
Hostages to Fortune (Humphrey), **Supp. IX:** 96, **104–106,** 109
Hostess to Murder (Holding), **Supp. XXII:** 126**, 127**
Hostetler, Ann, **Retro. Supp. III:** 193
"Hot Combs" (Trethewey), **Supp. XXI:** 249
"Hot Cross Bum" (Loy), **Supp. XXII:** 168
"Hot Dog" (Stern), **Supp. IX: 298–299**
"Hotel, The"(Hadas), **Supp. XXIII:** 121
"Hotel Bar" (McClatchy), **Supp. XII:** 269
Hotel Dwellers, The (Lacy), **Supp. XV:** 205
Hotel Insomnia (Simic), **Supp. VIII:** 280, **281–282**
Hotel Lambosa and Other Stories (Koch), **Supp. XV:** 186
Hotel New Hampshire, The (Irving), **Supp. VI:** 163, 164, **172–173,** 177, 179; **Supp. XIX:** 164
"Hot-Foot Hannibal" (Chesnutt), **Supp. XIV:** 60
"Hot Ice"(Dybek), **Supp. XXIII:** 72–73
"Hot Night on Water Street" (Simpson), **Supp. IX:** 269, 270
"Hot Time, A" (Gunn Allen), **Supp. IV Part 1:** 333
Houdini, Harry, **IV:** 437; **Supp. XXV:** 121
"Hound of Heaven" (Thompson), **Retro. Supp. I:** 55
"Hourglass, The" (Kees), **Supp. XV:** 147
"Hour in Chartres, An" (Bourne), **I:** 228
"Hour of Peonies, The"(Crooker), **Supp. XXIII:** 58
Hour of the Dragon, The (Howard), **Supp. XXVII:** 126
Hours, The (Cunningham), **Supp. XII:** 80; **Supp. XV: 65–68**
"Hours before Eternity" (Caldwell), **I:** 291
House, Bridge, Fountain, Gate (Kumin), **Supp. IV Part 2:** 448, 449, 451, 454
House, Edward, **Supp. I Part 2:** 643
"House, The" (Merrill), **Supp. III Part 1:** 323
House at Pooh Corner, The (Milne), **Supp. IX:** 189
"House at the End of the World, The" (Brockmeier), **Supp. XXII:** 52, 53
House Behind the Cedars, The (Chesnutt), **Supp. XIV: 69–71**
Houseboat Days (Ashbery), **Supp. III Part 1:** 18–20
Housebreaker of Shady Hill and Other Stories, The (Cheever), **Supp. I Part 1:** 184
"House by the Sea, The" (E. Stoddard), **Supp. XV:** 277
House by the Sea, The (Sarton), **Supp. VIII:** 264
House Divided, A (Buck), **Supp. II Part 1:** 118
"House Divided, The/La Casa Divida" (Kingsolver), **Supp. VII:** 207
"House Guest" (Bishop), **Retro. Supp. II:** 49; **Supp. I Part 1:** 93
"House Holding" (Davison), **Supp. XXVI:** 73, 74
Household Saints (film), **Supp. XVI:** 256
Household Saints (Prose), **Supp. XVI:** 252–253, 254, 261
"House in Athens, The" (Merrill), **Supp. III Part 1:** 323
House in the Uplands, A (Caldwell), **I:** 297, 301, 306
"House in Turk Street, The"

(Hammett), **Supp. IV Part 1:** 344
"House in Winter, The" (Sarton), **Supp. VIII:** 259
"House in Winter, The"(Hirshfield), **Supp. XXIII:** 132
House Is Made of Poetry, The (Baker and Gilbert, eds.), **Supp. XXVII:** 263
"Housekeeping" (Alvarez), **Supp. VII:** 3–5, 10
Housekeeping (Robinson), **Supp. XXI:** 210–211, **212–216,** 218, 223
"Housekeeping" (Trethewey), **Supp. XXI:** 249
"Housekeeping for Men" (Bourne), **I:** 231
House Made of Dawn (Momaday), **Supp. IV Part 1:** 274, 323, 326; **Supp. IV Part 2:** 479, 480, 481–484, 485, 486, 504, 562
Houseman, John, **Supp. IV Part 1:** 173
House Next Door, The (Siddons), **Supp. XXII:** 239
House Next Door, The (television movie), **Supp. XXII:** 239
"House of Caesar, The" (Garvin), **Supp. XXVII:** 118
House of Dust, The: A Symphony (Aiken), **I:** 50
House of Earth trilogy (Buck), **Supp. II Part 1:** 118, 123
House of Five Talents, The (Auchincloss), **Supp. IV Part 1:** 21, 25–27
"House of Flowers" (Capote), **Supp. III Part 1:** 123
House of Games (Mamet), **Supp. XIV:** 243
House of Houses (Mora), **Supp. XIII:** 213, 215, 218, 219, 223–224, **225–227,** 228, 229
House of Incest (Nin), **Supp. III Part 1:** 43; **Supp. X:** 187, 190, 193
House of Lee, The (Atherton), **Supp. XXIV:** 26–27
House of Life, The: Rachel Carson at Work (Brooks), **Supp. IX:** 26
House of Light (Oliver), **Supp. VII:** 238–240
House of Mirth, The (film, Davies), **Retro. Supp. III:** 290
House of Mirth, The (Wharton), **II:** 180, 193; **IV:** 311–313, 314, 316, 318, 323, 327; **Retro. Supp. I:** 360, 366, 367, **367–370,** 373, 380; **Retro. Supp. III:** 280–281, 288; **Supp. XX: 239, 240**
"House of Mist, The" (Rand), **Supp. IV Part 2:** 524
"House of My Own, A" (Cisneros), **Supp. VII:** 64
"House of Night, The" (Freneau), **Supp. II Part 1:** 259, 260
"House of Representatives and Me, The" (Conroy), **Supp. XVI:** 75
House of Sand and Fog (Dubus III), **Supp. XXIV:** 97, **104–107**
House of Sleeping Beauties, The (Hwang), **Supp. XXI:** 146
House of the Far and Lost, The (Wolfe), **IV:** 456
"House of the Injured, The" (Haines), **Supp. XII:** 203
"House of the One Father" (Antin), **Supp. XX: 3, 13**
House of the Prophet, The (Auchincloss), **Supp. IV Part 1:** 31
House of the Seven Gables (Hawthorne), **I:** 106; **II:** 60, 224, 225, 231, 237, 239, 240–241, 243, 244; **Retro. Supp. I:** 63, 149, **160–162,** 163, 164; **Retro. Supp. III:** 118–119; **Supp. I Part 2:** 579
House of the Solitary Maggot, The (Purdy), **Supp. VII:** 274–275
"House on 15th S.W., The" (Hugo), **Supp. VI:** 140
"House on Main Street, The" (B. Kelly), **Supp. XVII:** 127
House on Mango Street, The (Cisneros), **Supp. VII:** 58, 59–64, 65, 66, 67, 68, 72; **Supp. XXV:** 133
"House on Mango Street, The" (Cisneros), **Supp. VII:** 59
House on Marshland, The (Glück), **Supp. V:** 81–83, 84
"House on Moscow Street, The" (Nelson), **Supp. XVIII:** 174
"House on the Heights, A" (Capote), **Supp. III Part 1:** 120
"House on the Hill, The" (Robinson), **III:** 505, 524
"House Raising" (Offutt), **Supp. XIX:** 166
"Houses" (Hogan), **Supp. IV Part 1:** 402
"Houses, The" (Merwin), **Supp. III Part 1:** 354
"Houses of Dreams" (Teasdale), **Supp. XXVII:** 292
"Houses of the Spirit" (Karr), **Supp. XI:** 250
"House Sparrows" (Hecht), **Supp. X: 68**
"House That Doesn't House, The" (Bronk), **Supp. XXI:** 34
House That Tai Maing Built, The (Lee), **Supp. X:** 291
"House Unroofed by the Gale" (Tu Fu), **II:** 526
"House Where Mark Twain Was Born, The" (Masters), **Supp. I Part 2:** 472
"Housewife" (Hempel), **Supp. XXI:** 124
"Housewife" (Sexton), **Supp. II Part 2:** 682
"Housewife's Paradise, The" (Davison), **Supp. XXVI:** 76
" 'Housing the Deliberations': New York, War, and Frank O'Hara"(Ward), **Supp. XXIII:** 218
Housman, A. E., **III:** 15, 136, 606; **Retro. Supp. III:** 27, 74; **Supp. II Part 1:** 4; **Supp. IV Part 1:** 165; **Supp. XV:** 40–41
Houston, Robert, **Supp. XXV:** 54
Houston Trilogy (McMurtry), **Supp. V:** 223–225
How" (Ginsberg), **Supp. XIV:** 142, 143
"How" (Moore), **Supp. X:** 167
"How About This?" (Carver), **Supp. III Part 1:** 141
"How America Came to the Mountains" (J. W. Miller), **Supp. XX: 169**
"How Annandale Went Out" (Robinson), **III:** 513
Howard, Arliss, **Supp. XXI:** 39
Howard, Ben, **Supp. XVI:** 54
Howard, Gerald, **Supp. XII:** 21
Howard, Jane, **Retro. Supp. I:** 334
Howard, June, **Retro. Supp. II:** 139
Howard, Leon, **Supp. I Part 2:** 408, 422, 423
Howard, Maureen, **Supp. XII:** 285; **Supp. XVII:** 183
Howard, Richard, **Retro. Supp. II:** 43; **Supp. IV Part 2:** 624, 626, 640; **Supp. IX:** 324, 326; **Supp. VIII:** 273; **Supp. X:** 152; **Supp. XI:** 317; **Supp. XII:** 254; **Supp. XIII:** 76; **Supp. XV:** 23, 24; **Supp. XXIV:** 155
Howard, Robert E., **Supp. XXV:** 122; **Supp. XXVII: 115–131**
Howard, Vilma, **Retro. Supp. II:** 111, 112
Howards, J. Z., **Supp. VIII:** 178
Howards End (Forster), **Supp. XII:** 87
Howarth, Cora, **I:** 408, 409
Howbah Indians (Ortiz), **Supp. IV Part 2:** 513
"How Black Sees Green and Red" (McKay), **Supp. X:** 136
How Britain Rules Africa (Padmore), **Supp. XXI:** 166
"How David Did Not Care" (R. Bly), **Supp. IV Part 1:** 73
"How Did I Love Him?" (Nelson),

Supp. XVIII: 176
"How Do I Love Thee?" (Browning), **Supp. XVIII:** 176
Howe, Daniel Walker, **Supp. XXIV:** 79
Howe, Darcus, **Supp. XXI:** 170
Howe, E.W., **I:** 106
Howe, Florence, **Supp. XIII:** 295, 306
Howe, Harriet, **Supp. XI:** 200, 201
Howe, Irving, **IV:** 10; **Retro. Supp. I:** 369; **Retro. Supp. II:** 112, 286; **Retro. Supp. III:** 85; **Supp. I Part 2:** 432; **Supp. II Part 1:** 99; **Supp. IX:** 227; **Supp. VI: 113–129; Supp. VIII:** 93, 232; **Supp. X:** 203, 245; **Supp. XII:** 160; **Supp. XIII:** 98; **Supp. XIV:** 103–104, 104; **Supp. XIX:** 257, 265; **Supp. XVII:** 50; **Supp. XXIII:** 3, 7; **Supp. XXIV:** 220–221, 222
Howe, James Wong, **Supp. I Part 1:** 281; **Supp. V:** 223
Howe, Julia Ward, **III:** 505; **Retro. Supp. II:** 135
Howe, LeAnne, **Supp. XXVI:** 84, 98
Howe, M. A. DeWolfe, **I:** 258; **II:** 406; **Supp. XIV:** 54
Howe, Mary Manning, **Supp. IV Part 2:** 422
Howe, Samuel, **Supp. I Part 1:** 153
Howe, Susan, **Retro. Supp. I:** 33, 43; **Supp. IV Part 2: 419–438; Supp. XVI:** 284
Howell, Chris, **Supp. XIII:** 112
Howell, James, **II:** 111
Howells, Margaret, **II:** 271
Howells, William C., **II:** 273
Howells, William Dean, **I:** 109, 192, 204, 210, 211, 254, 355, 407, 411, 418, 459, 469; **II:** 127–128, 130, 131, 136, 137, 138, 140, **271–294,** 322, 331–332, 338, 397–398, 400, 415, 444, 451, 556; **III:** 51, 118, 314, 327–328, 461, 576, 607; **IV:** 192, 202, 342, 349; **Retro. Supp. I:** 220, 334, 362, 378; **Retro. Supp. II:** 93, 101, 135, 288; **Retro. Supp. III:** 258, 259, 262, 264, 268; **Supp. I Part 1:** 306, 318, 357, 360, 368; **Supp. I Part 2:** 414, 420, 645–646; **Supp. II Part 1:** 198, 352; **Supp. IV Part 2:** 678; **Supp. VIII:** 98, 101, 102; **Supp. XI:** 198, 200; **Supp. XIV:** 45–46; **Supp. XV:** 269, 274, 285, 287; **Supp. XVIII:** 6; **Supp. XXIV:** 24
Howells, Mrs. William Dean (Elinor Mead), **II:** 273
Howells, Winifred, **II:** 271
"Howells as Anti-Novelist" (Updike), **Retro. Supp. I:** 334
Howells: His Life and World (Brooks), **I:** 254
Hower, Edward, **Supp. XII:** 330, 343
Howes, Barbara, **Supp. XIII:** 331
How Good Is David Mamet, Anyway? (Heilpern), **Supp. XIV:** 242
"How Hard It Is to Keep from Being King When It's in You and in the Situation" (Frost), **Retro. Supp. III:** 107
"How I Became a Shadow" (Purdy), **Supp. VII:** 269
"How I Came to Vedanta" (Isherwood), **Supp. XIV:** 164
"How I Come to You" (Peacock), **Supp. XIX:** 198
"How I Learned to Sweep" (Alvarez), **Supp. VII:** 4
"How I Spent My Forties" (Wasserstein), **Supp. XV:** 325, 330, 332
"How It Began" (Stafford), **Supp. XI:** 327
"How It Feels to Be Colored Me" (Hurston), **Supp. VI:** 152
"How It Is" (Budbill), **Supp. XIX:** 10
"How It Is" (Everwine), **Supp. XV:** 79, 86
"How I Told My Child About Race" (Brooks), **Supp. III Part 1:** 78
"How I Went to the Mines" (Harte), **Supp. II Part 1:** 336
"How I Write" (Franzen), **Supp. XX: 84**
"How I Write" (Welty), **IV:** 279, 280
"How I Wrote The Promised Land" (Antin), **Supp. XX: 3**
"How Jonah Did Not Care" (R. Bly), **Supp. IV Part 1:** 73
Howl (Ginsberg), **Retro. Supp. I:** 426; **Supp. III Part 1:** 92; **Supp. IV Part 1:** 90; **Supp. V:** 336; **Supp. VIII:** 290; **Supp. XIV:** 15, 126, 157; **Supp. XVIII:** 20, 29
"How Laddie and the Princess Spelled Down at the Christmas Bee" (Stratton-Porter), **Supp. XX: 216**
Howl and Other Poems (Ginsberg), **Supp. II Part 1:** 308, 317–318, 319; **Supp. X:** 123
Howlett, William, **Retro. Supp. I:** 17
Howl: Original Draft Facsimile, Transcript and Variant Versions (Gimsberg), **Supp. XIV:** 142
"How Many Midnights" (Bowles), **Supp. IV Part 1:** 86–87
"How Many Nights" (Kinnell), **Supp. III Part 1:** 245–246
How Much? (Blechman), **Supp. I Part 1:** 290
"How Much Are You Worth" (Salinas), **Supp. XIII:** 325–326
"How Much Earth" (Levine), **Supp. V:** 184
How Much Earth: The Fresno Poets (Buckley, Oliveira, and Williams, eds.), **Supp. XIII:** 313
"How Not to Forget" (Bartov), **Supp. XVI:** 153–154
"How Poetry Comes to Me" (Corso), **Supp. XII:** 122
"How Poetry Comes to Me" (Snyder), **Supp. VIII:** 305
How Reading Changed My Life (Quindlen), **Supp. XVII:** 167, 179–180
"How She Came By Her Name: An Interview with Louis Massiah" (Bambara), **Supp. XI:** 20
"How Soon Hath Time" (Ransom), **IV:** 123
How Spring Comes (Notley), **Supp. XXII:** 226, 229
How Stella Got Her Groove Back (McMillan), **Supp. XIII:** 185, **190–191**
How the Alligator Missed Breakfast (Kinney), **Supp. III Part 1:** 235, 253
"How the Devil Came Down Division Street" (Algren), **Supp. IX:** 3
How the García Girls Lost Their Accents (Alvarez), **Supp. VII:** 3, 5–9, 11, 15, 17, 18
How the Grinch Stole Christmas! (Geisel), **Supp. XVI:** 102
How the Other Half Lives (Riis), **I:** 293
"How the Saint Did Not Care" (R. Bly), **Supp. IV Part 1:** 73
"How the Women Went from Dover" (Whittier), **Supp. I Part 2:** 694, 696, 697
"How They Got Her to Quiet Down" (Stone), **Supp. XXVII:** 263
"How This Magazine Wronged Herman Wouk" (Lewis), **Supp. XXV:** 253
"How To" (Carruth), **Supp. XVI:** 51
"How-To" (Monson), **Supp. XXIV:** 237
How To Be Alone: Essays (Franzen), **Supp. XX: 83, 90, 93–94**
"How to Be an Other Woman" (Moore), **Supp. X:** 165, 167, 168
"How to Become a Writer" (Moore), **Supp. X:** 167, 168
"How to Be Happy: Another Memo to

Myself" (Dunn), **Supp. XI:** 145
"How to Catch Aunt Harriet" (Stone), **Supp. XXVII:** 251
How To Cook a Wolf (M. F. K. Fisher), **Supp. XVII:** 84–85, 87
"How to Date a Browngirl, Blackgirl, Whitegirl, or Halfie" (Díaz), **Supp. XXIV:** 88
How to Develop Your Personality (Shellow), **Supp. I Part 2:** 608
"How to Grow Orchids Without Grounds: A Manual" (Vaz), **Supp. XXVI:** 263
How to Know God: The Yoga Aphorisms of Patanjali (Isherwood and Prabhavananda)), **Supp. XIV:** 164
"How To Like It" (Dobyns), **Supp. XIII: 85–86**
"How to Live on $36,000 a Year" (Fitzgerald), **Retro. Supp. I:** 105
"How to Live. What to Do" (Stevens), **Retro. Supp. I:** 302
"How to Love a Bicycle" (Biss), **Supp. XXVI:** 48
"How Tom is Doin' " (Kees), **Supp. XV:** 143
How to Read (Pound), **Supp. VIII:** 291
How to Read a Novel (Gordon), **II:** 198
How to Read a Poem and Fall in Love with Poetry (Hirsch), **Supp. XIX:** 202
How to Read a Poem: And Fall in Love with Poetry (Hirsch), **Supp. XXIII:** 124
How to Read a Poem . . . and Start a Poetry Circle (Peacock), **Supp. XIX:** 194, 202–203, 205
How to Save Your Own Life (Jong), **Supp. V:** 115, 123–125, 130
"How to Study Poetry" (Pound), **III:** 474
"How to Talk to Your Mother" (Moore), **Supp. X:** 167, 172
"How to Tell a Story" (Twain), **Retro. Supp. III:** 262, 265
"How to Tell Stories to Children" (July), **Supp. XXIV:** 206–207
How to Win Friends and Influence People (Carnegie), **Supp. I Part 2:** 608
How to Worry Successfully (Seabury), **Supp. I Part 2:** 608
How to Write (Stein), **IV:** 32, 34, 35
"How to Write a Blackwood Article" (Poe), **III:** 425; **Retro. Supp. II:** 273
"How to Write a Memoir Like This" (Oates), **Supp. III Part 2:** 509
"How to Write Like Somebody Else" (Roethke), **III:** 540
How to Write Short Stories (Lardner), **II:** 430, 431
"How Vincentine Did Not Care" (R. Bly), **Supp. IV Part 1:** 73
How We Became Human: New and Selected Poems (Harjo), **Supp. XII: 230–232**
"How We Danced" (Sexton), **Supp. II Part 2:** 692
How We Got Insipid (Lethem), **Supp. XVIII:** 149
"How We Got in Town and Out Again" (Lethem), **Supp. XVIII:** 149
"How You Sound??" (Baraka), **Supp. II Part 1:** 30
Hoy, Philip, **Supp. X:** 56, 58
Hoyer, Linda Grace (pseudonym). See Updike, Mrs. Wesley
Hoyt, Constance, **Supp. I Part 2:** 707
Hoyt, Elinor Morton. See Wylie, Elinor
Hoyt, Helen, **Supp. XXII:** 275
Hoyt, Henry (father), **Supp. I Part 2:** 707
Hoyt, Henry (son), **Supp. I Part 2:** 708
Hoyt, Henry Martyn, **Supp. I Part 2:** 707
H. P. Lovecraft (Canan), **Supp. XXV:** 123
Hsu, Kai-yu, **Supp. X:** 292
Hsu, Ruth Y., **Supp. XV:** 212
Hubba City (Reed), **Supp. X:** 241
Hubbard, Elbert, **I:** 98, 383
Hubbell, Jay B., **Supp. I Part 1:** 372
"Hubbub, The" (Ammons), **Supp. VII:** 35
Huber, François, **II:** 6
Huckins, Olga, **Supp. IX:** 32
Huckleberry Finn (Twain). See Adventures of Huckleberry Finn, The (Twain)
Hucksters, The (Wakeman), **Supp. XXV:** 258
Hud (film), **Supp. V:** 223, 226
Huddle, David, **Supp. XXVI: 147–162**
Hudgins, Andrew, **Supp. X:** 206; **Supp. XVII:** 111, 112; **Supp. XVIII:** 176
Hudson, Henry, **I:** 230; **Supp. XXVI:** 86
"Hudsonian Curlew, The" (Snyder), **Supp. VIII:** 302
Hudson River Bracketed (Wharton), **IV:** 326–327; **Retro. Supp. I:** 382
Huebsch, B. W., **III:** 110
Hueffer, Ford Madox, **Supp. I Part 1:** 257, 262. See also Ford, Ford Madox
Huene-Greenberg, Dorothee von, **Supp. XX: 46**
Huff (television series), **Supp. XIX:** 222
"Hug, The" (Gallagher), **Supp. XXIV:** 168
Hug Dancing (Hearon), **Supp. VIII: 67–68**
Huge Season, The (Morris), **III:** 225–226, 227, 230, 232, 233, 238
Hugging the Jukebox (Nye), **Supp. XIII: 275–276,** 277
"Hugging the Jukebox" (Nye), **Supp. XIII:** 276
Hughes, Brigid, **Supp. XVI:** 247
Hughes, Carolyn, **Supp. XII:** 272, 285
Hughes, Frieda, **Supp. I Part 2:** 540, 541
Hughes, Glenn, **Supp. I Part 1:** 255
Hughes, H. Stuart, **Supp. VIII:** 240
Hughes, James Nathaniel, **Supp. I Part 1:** 321, 332
Hughes, John, **Supp. XXVII:** 5
Hughes, Ken, **Supp. XI:** 307
Hughes, Langston, **Retro. Supp. I: 193–214; Retro. Supp. II:** 114, 115, 117, 120; **Retro. Supp. III:** 125, 127, 128, 137; **Supp. I Part 1: 320–348; Supp. II Part 1:** 31, 33, 61, 170, 173, 181, 227, 228, 233, 361; **Supp. III Part 1:** 72–77; **Supp. IV Part 1:** 15, 16, 164, 168, 169, 173, 243, 368; **Supp. IX:** 306, 316; **Supp. VIII:** 213; **Supp. X:** 131, 136, 139, 324; **Supp. XI:** 1; **Supp. XIII:** 75, 111, 132, 233; **Supp. XIX:** 72, 75, 77; **Supp. XVI:** 135, 138; **Supp. XVIII:** 90, 277, 279, 280, 281, 282; **Supp. XXI:** 243; **Supp. XXII:** 3, 4, 5, 6, 8, 13–14; **Supp. XXIV:** 183; **Supp. XXVI:** 166; **Supp. XXVII:** 164
Hughes, Nicholas, **Supp. I Part 2:** 541
Hughes, Robert, **Supp. X:** 73
Hughes, Ted, **IV:** 3; **Retro. Supp. II:** 244, 245, 247, 257; **Supp. I Part 2:** 536, 537, 538, 539, 540, 541; **Supp. XV:** 117, 347, 348; **Supp. XXII:** 30
Hughes, Thomas, **Supp. I Part 2:** 406
"Hugh Harper" (Bowles), **Supp. IV Part 1:** 94
Hughie (O'Neill), **III:** 385, 401, 405
Hugh Selwyn Mauberley (Pound), **I:** 66, 476; **III:** 9, 462–463, 465, 468; **Retro. Supp. I: 289–290,** 291, 299; **Supp. XIV:** 272
Hugo, Richard, **Supp. IX:** 296, 323, 324, 330; **Supp. VI: 131–148; Supp. XI:** 315, 317; **Supp. XII:** 178; **Supp. XIII:** 112, 113, 133; **Supp. XVIII:** 293, 299; **Supp. XXI:**

243; **Supp. XXVI:** 180, 187
Hugo, Victor, **II:** 290, 490, 543; **Supp. IV Part 2:** 518; **Supp. IX:** 308
Hui-neng, **III:** 567
Huis Clos (Sartre), **Supp. IV Part 1:** 84
Huizinga, Johan, **I:** 225; **II:** 416–417, 418, 425
Hulbert, Ann, **Supp. XI:** 38–39
Hulbert, James R., **Retro. Supp. III:** 265
Hull, Lynda, **Supp. XI:** 131; **Supp. XXI: 129–142**
Hull, Thomas, **Supp. XXV:** 123
Hulme, Thomas E., **I:** 68, 69, 475; **III:** 196, 209, 463–464, 465; **IV:** 122; **Supp. I Part 1:** 261, 262; **Supp. XV:** 43
Human, All Too Human (Nietzsche), **Supp. X:** 48
"Human Culture" (Emerson), **II:** 11–12
Human Desire (film), **Supp. XXVI:** 134
Human Factor, The (Greene), **Supp. V:** 298
"Human Figures" (Doty), **Supp. XI:** 123–124
"Human Fly, The" (Boyle), **Supp. XX: 19**
"Human Geography" (Jarman), **Supp. XVII:** 116
"Human Immortality" (James), **II:** 353–354
"Human Life" (Emerson), **II:** 11–12
"Human Pig" (Jin), **Supp. XVIII:** 99
Human Rights, Human Wrongs: The Oxford Amnesty Lectures, 2001, **Supp. XVI:** 155
"Human Soul as a Rube Goldberg Device, The: A Choose-Your-Own-Adventure-Story" (Brockmeier), **Supp. XXII:** 60–61
Human Stain, The (P. Roth), **Retro. Supp. II:** 279, 289, 294–295
"Human Things" (Nemerov), **III:** 279
Human Universe (Olson), **Supp. II Part 2:** 571
"Human Universe" (Olson), **Supp. II Part 2:** 565, 567
Human Vibration (Richter), **Supp. XVIII:** 209
Human Wishes (Hass), **Supp. VI:** 105–106, 107
Human Work (Gilman), **Supp. XI:** 206
Humbert, Humbert, **Supp. X:** 283
Humble Inquiry into the Rules of the Word of God, An, Concerning the Qualifications Requisite to a Complete Standing and Full Communion in the Visible Christian Church (Edwards), **I:** 548
Humboldt, Alexander von, **III:** 428
Humboldt's Gift (Bellow), **Retro. Supp. II:** 19, 28–29, 34; **Supp. XIII:** 320
Hume, David, **I:** 125; **II:** 349, 357, 480; **III:** 618
Humes, Harold, **Supp. V:** 201; **Supp. XIV:** 82
Humes, Harry, **Supp. XIX:** 281; **Supp. XXIII:** 54
Humes, H. L. "Doc", **Supp. XI:** 294
"Humility" (Hoffman), **Supp. XVIII:** 86
Hummer, T. R., **Supp. XIX:** 278; **Supp. XXI:** 91
"Hummingbirds, The" (Welty), **IV:** 273
Humors and/or Not So Humorous (Kenny), **Supp. XXIII:** 155
Humphrey, William, **Supp. IX: 93–112; Supp. XV:** 353
Humphreys, Christmas, **Supp. V:** 267
Humphreys, David, **Supp. II Part 1:** 65, 69, 70, 268
Humphreys, Josephine, **Supp. XII:** 311
Humphries, Rolfe, **III:** 124; **Retro. Supp. I:** 137
Humpty Dumpty (Hecht), **Supp. XXVII:** 88
Hunchback of Notre Dame, The (film), **Supp. IV Part 1:** 101
Hunches in Bunches (Geisel), **Supp. XVI:** 111
Huncke, Herbert, **Supp. XII:** 118; **Supp. XIV: 137–153**
Huncke's Journal (Huncke), **Supp. XIV:** 139, 144, 145, 146
Hundred Camels in the Courtyard, A (Bowles), **Supp. IV Part 1:** 90
"Hundred Collars, A" (Frost), **Retro. Supp. I:** 128; **Supp. XIII:** 147
Hundred Secret Senses, The (Tan), **Supp. X:** 289, 293, 295, 297, 298, 299
Hundreds of Hens and Other Poems for Children by Halfdan Rasmussen (Nelson and Espeland, trans.), **Supp. XVIII:** 180
Hundred White Daffodils, A: Essays, Interviews, Newspaper Columns, and One Poem (Kenyon), **Supp. VII:** 160–162, 165, 166, 167, 174
Huneker, James, **III:** 102
"Hunger" (Davison), **Supp. XXVI:** 69
Hunger (Hamsun), **Supp. XI:** 167
"Hunger" (Hogan), **Supp. IV Part 1:** 411
"Hunger . . ." (Rich), **Supp. I Part 2:** 571
"Hunger" (Rich), **Retro. Supp. III:** 249
"Hungerfield" (Jeffers), **Supp. II Part 2:** 416–417, 436
Hungerfield and Other Poems (Jeffers), **Supp. II Part 2:** 422
Hunger of Memory: The Education of Richard Rodriguez (Rodriguez), **Supp. XIV:** 297, 298, **298–302,** 310
Hungry Ghosts, The (Oates), **Supp. II Part 2:** 504, 510
Hungry Hearts (Prose), **Supp. XVI:** 253
"Hungry Intellectual, A"(Le Sueur), **Supp. XXIII:** 164
Hungry Woman, The: A Mexican Medea (Moraga), **Supp. XXIII:** 196
Hunnewell, Susannah, **Supp. VIII:** 83
Hunt, Erica, **Supp. XXVII:** 163
Hunt, Harriot K., **Retro. Supp. II:** 146
Hunt, Leigh, **II:** 515–516; **Supp. XV:** 175
Hunt, Richard Morris, **IV:** 312
Hunt, Robert, **Supp. XV:** 42, 49, 52
Hunt, William, **II:** 343
"Hunter" (Bierds), **Supp. XVII:** 30
Hunter, Dianna, **Supp. XVI:** 38
Hunter, Dr. Joseph, **II:** 217
Hunter, J. Paul, **Supp. IV Part 1:** 332
Hunter, Kim, **Supp. I Part 1:** 286
"Hunter of Doves" (Herbst), **Retro. Supp. II:** 325
"Hunter of the West, The" (Bryant), **Supp. I Part 1:** 155
Hunters, The (film), **Supp. IX:** 250
Hunters, The (Salter), **Supp. IX:** 246, **249–250**
Hunters and Gatherers (Prose), **Supp. XVI:** 257
"Hunters in the Snow" (Brueghel), **I:** 174; **Retro. Supp. I:** 430
"Hunters in the Snow" (Wolff), **Supp. VII:** 339–340
"Hunter's Moon—Eating the Bear" (Oliver), **Supp. VII:** 234
"Hunter's Vision, The" (Bryant), **Supp. I Part 1:** 160
Hunting for Hope: A Father's Journey (Sanders), **Supp. XVI:** 276–277, 278
"Hunting Is Not Those Heads on the Wall" (Baraka), **Supp. II Part 1:** 45
Huntington, Collis P., **I:** 198, 207
"Hunt in the Black Forest, The" (Jarrell), **II:** 379–380
Huntley, Jobe, **Supp. I Part 1:** 339
"Hurrah, Hurrah" (Nelson), **Supp. XVIII:** 175
Hurray Home (Wideman), **Supp. X:** 320

Hurricane (radio play, Boyce), **Supp. XXI:** 13
"Hurricane, The" (Crane), **I:** 401
"Hurricane, The" (Freneau), **Supp. II Part 1:** 262
"Hurricane Belle" (Notley), **Supp. XXII:** 228
"Hurry Kane" (Lardner), **II:** 425, 426, 427
"Hurry up Please It's Time" (Sexton), **Supp. II Part 2:** 694, 695
Hurst, Fannie, **Retro. Supp. III:** 127, 135, 137; **Supp. XVIII:** 278, 279
Hurston, Zora Neale, **Retro. Supp. I:** 194, 198, 200, 201, 203; **Retro. Supp. III: 125–146**; **Supp. I Part 1:** 325, 326, 332; **Supp. II Part 1:** 33; **Supp. IV Part 1:** 5, 11, 12, 164, 257; **Supp. VI: 149–161; Supp. VIII:** 214; **Supp. X:** 131, 139, 232, 242; **Supp. XI:** 85; **Supp. XIII:** 185, 233, 236, 295, 306; **Supp. XIX:** 72, 75; **Supp. XVIII:** 122, 279, 280, 282; **Supp. XX: 107; Supp. XXII:** 12; **Supp. XXVI:** 1, 12, 164, 167
Hurt, John, **Supp. XIII:** 132
"Hurt Hawks"(Jeffers), **Supp. XXIII:** 145
Hurwitt, Robert, **Supp. XXIII:** 281
Husbands and Wives (film; Allen), **Supp. XV: 12**
"Husband's Song, The" (Di Piero), **Supp. XIX:** 39
Husband's Story, The (Shields), **Supp. VII:** 316. See also "Happenstance" (Shields)
"Husband's Tale, The" (Huddle), **Supp. XXVI:** 151
Husserl, Edmund, **II:** 362, 363; **IV:** 491; **Supp. IV Part 1:** 42, 43
Hussey, Jo Ella, **Supp. XII:** 201
Hustler, The (film), **Supp. XI:** 306
Huston, John, **I:** 30, 31, 33, 35; **II:** 588; **III:** 161; **Retro. Supp. III:** 170; **Supp. IV Part 1:** 102, 116, 355; **Supp. XI:** 307; **Supp. XIII:** 174
Hustvedt, Siri, **Supp. XXVII:** 26
"Huswifery" (Taylor), **IV:** 161; **Supp. I Part 2:** 386
"Hut, The" (Sobin), **Supp. XVI:** 284–285
Hutchens, John K., **Supp. IX:** 276
Hutcheson, Francis, **I:** 559
Hutchins, Patricia, **III:** 478
Hutchinson, Abigail, **I:** 562
Hutchinson, Anne, **Supp. I Part 1:** 100, 101, 113; **Supp. IV Part 2:** 434; **Supp. VIII:** 202, 205
Hutchinson, George, **Supp. XVIII:** 119–120, 121, 132
Hutchinson, Lucy, **Supp. XXV:** 224
Hutchinson, Paul E., **Supp. XXVI:** 156
Hutchinson, Percy, **Retro. Supp. III:** 133
Hutchinson, Thomas, **Supp. XX: 282**
Hutton, James, **Supp. IX:** 180
Huwayyik, Yusuf, **Supp. XX: 115**
Huxley, Aldous, **II:** 454; **III:** 281, 428, 429–430; **IV:** 77, 435; **Supp. I Part 2:** 714; **Supp. XIV:** 3, 164; **Supp. XVI:** 189, 192; **Supp. XVIII:** 137; **Supp. XXIII:** 85–86; **Supp. XXIV:** 281
Huxley, Julian, **Supp. VIII:** 251; **Supp. X:** 108
Huxley, Juliette, **Supp. VIII:** 251, 265
Huxley, Thomas, **III:** 102, 108, 113, 281; **Retro. Supp. II:** 60, 65, 93; **Supp. XXVII:** 126
Huxley, Thomas Henry, **Supp. I Part 1:** 368
Huysmans, Joris Karl (Charles Marie Georges), **I:** 66; **III:** 315; **IV:** 286; **Retro. Supp. II:** 326; **Supp. XX: 239; Supp. XXVII:** 88
"Hwame, Koshkalaka, and the Rest: Lesbians in American Indian Cultures" (Gunn Allen), **Supp. IV Part 1:** 330
Hwang, David Henry, **Retro. Supp. III:** 318; **Supp. X:** 292; **Supp. XXI: 143–157**
"Hyacinth Drift" (Rawlings), **Supp. X: 226–227**
Hyde, Lewis, **Supp. XVIII:** 150
"Hydrangeas" (C. Frost), **Supp. XV:** 106
"Hydras, The" (Merwin), **Supp. III Part 1:** 349
Hydriotaphia, The; or, Death of Dr. Browne: An Epic Farce about Death and Primitive Capital Accumulation (Kushner), **Supp. IX:** 133, **136–138**
"Hydriotaphia; or, Urne-Buriall" (Browne), **Supp. IX:** 136–137
Hyman, Stanley Edgar, **I:** 129, 264, 363, 377, 379; **Retro. Supp. II:** 118; **Supp. IX:** 113, 114, 117, 118, 121, 122, 128
Hymen (Doolittle), **Supp. I Part 1:** 266
"Hymie's Bull" (Ellison), **Retro. Supp. II:** 124; **Supp. II Part 1:** 229
"Hymn Books" (Emerson), **II:** 10
"HYMN FOR LANIE POO" (Baraka), **Supp. II Part 1:** 31, 37
"Hymn from a Watermelon Pavilion" (Stevens), **IV:** 81
"Hymn of the Sea, A" (Bryant), **Supp. I Part 1:** 157, 163, 165
Hymns of St. Bridget and Other Writings (O'Hara and Berkson), **Supp. XXIII:** 220
"Hymns of St. Bridget"(O'Hara and Berkson), **Supp. XXIII:** 218
"Hymns of the Marshes" (Lanier), **Supp. I Part 1:** 364
"Hymn to Death" (Bryant), **Supp. I Part 1:** 169, 170
"Hymn to Earth" (Wylie), **Supp. I Part 2:** 727–729
"Hymn to the Night" (Longfellow), **Supp. I Part 2:** 409
Hynes, Jennifer, **Supp. XV:** 207
Hynes, Samuel, **Supp. XIV:** 159
Hyperion (Longfellow), **II:** 488, 489, 491–492, 496; **Retro. Supp. II:** 58, 155–156
"Hypocrite Auteur" (MacLeish), **III:** 19
"Hypocrite Swift" (Bogan), **Supp. III Part 1:** 55
"Hysteria" (Eliot), **I:** 570
I (Dixon), **Supp. XII:** 141, 155, **156–157**
I, etcetera (Sontag), **Supp. III Part 2:** 451–452, 469
I, Governor of California and How I Ended Poverty (Sinclair), **Supp. V:** 289
I, the Jury (Spillane), **Supp. XVIII:** 236
"I, Too" (Hughes), **Retro. Supp. I:** 193, 199; **Supp. I Part 1:** 320
I Accuse! (film), **Supp. IV Part 2:** 683
"I Actually Thought We Would Revolutionize the Industry" (Myers), **Supp. XXVII:** 200
"I Almost Remember" (Angelou), **Supp. IV Part 1:** 15
"'I Always Wanted You to Admire My Fasting'; or, Looking at Kafka"(P. Roth), **Retro. Supp. II:** 282
I am a Camera (Druten), **Supp. XIV:** 162
"I am a cowboy in the boat of Ra" (Reed), **Supp. X:** 242
"I Am a Dangerous Woman" (Harjo), **Supp. XII:** 216, 219
"I Am Alive" (Momaday), **Supp. IV Part 2:** 489
I Am a Sonnet (Goldbarth), **Supp. XII:** 181
"I Am a Writer of Truth" (Fante), **Supp. XI:** 167
"'I Am Cherry Alive,' the Little Girl Sang" (Schwartz), **Supp. II Part 2:** 663

"I Am Dying, Meester?" (Burroughs), **Supp. III Part 1:** 98
I Am Elijah Thrush (Purdy), **Supp. VII:** 274
"I Am in Love" (Stern), **Supp. IX:** 295
I Am Legend (Matheson), **Supp. XXV:** 141
"I Am Not Flattered" (Francis), **Supp. IX:** 78
I Am Providence: The Life and Times of H. P. Lovecraft (Joshi), **Supp. XXV:** 123
I Am! Says the Lamb (Roethke), **III:** 545
I Am the Sun (Kenny), **Supp. XXIII:** 148
"I Am the Sun"(Kenny), **Supp. XXIII:** 146–147, 149
"I Am the Way" (Very), **Supp. XXV:** 248
"I Am You Again" (Nelson), **Supp. XVIII:** 173
"I and My Chimney" (Melville), **III:** 91
I and Thou (Buber), **III:** 308
"I Apologize" (Komunyakaa), **Supp. XIII:** 120, **Supp. XIII:** 121
I Apologize for the Eyes in My Head (Komunyakaa), **Supp. XIII: 119–121,** 126
"I Believe I Shall Die an Impenetrable Secret": The Writings of Elizabeth Barstow Stoddard (Giovani), **Supp. XV:** 270
Ibn Rushd (Averroes), **Supp. XX: 117**
Ibn Síná (Avicenna), **Supp. XX: 117**
Ibsen, Henrik, **II:** 27, 276, 280, 291–292; **III:** 118, 145, 148, 149, 150, 151, 152, 154–155, 156, 161, 162, 165, 511, 523; **IV:** 397; **Retro. Supp. I:** 228; **Retro. Supp. II:** 94; **Supp. IV Part 2:** 522; **Supp. XIV:** 89; **Supp. XIX:** 241; **Supp. XVII:** 100
"I Came Out of the Mother Naked" (R. Bly), **Supp. IV Part 1:** 62–63, 68
I Can Get It for You Wholesale (Weidman), **Supp. XXVII:** 142
I Can Lick 30 Tigers Today! and Other Stories (Geisel), **Supp. XVI:** 108
"I Cannot Forget with What Fervid Devotion" (Bryant), **Supp. I Part 1:** 154
I Can Read with My Eyes Shut! (Geisel), **Supp. XVI:** 111
"I Can Speak!tm" (Saunders), **Supp. XIX:** 231
"I Can't Stand Your Books: A Writer Goes Home" (Gordon), **Supp. IV Part 1:** 314
"Icarium Mare" (Wilbur), **Supp. III Part 2:** 563
"Icarus in Winter" (C. Frost), **Supp. XV:** 94
Icarus's Mother (Shepard), **Supp. III Part 2:** 446
"Ice" (Bambara), **Supp. XI:** 16
"Ice Age" (Taggard), **Supp. XXII:** 276
Ice at the Bottom of the World, The (Richard), **Supp. XIX:** 209, **210–213,** 218, 220
"Iceberg, The" (Merwin), **Supp. III Part 1:** 345
Ice-Cream Headache, The, and Other Stories (Jones), **Supp. XI:** 215, 227
Ice Fire Water: A Leib Goldkorn Cocktail (Epstein), **Supp. XII: 164–166**
"Ice Fisherman, The" (C. Baxter), **Supp. XVII:** 15
"Ice House, The" (Gordon), **II:** 201
"Ice Man, The" (Di Piero), **Supp. XIX:** 40
Iceman Cometh, The (O'Neill), **I:** 81; **III:** 151, 385, 386, 401, 402–403; **Supp. VIII:** 345; **Supp. XVI:** 193; **Supp. XVII:** 103; **Supp. XXII:** 28
"Ice Palace, The" (Fitzgerald), **II:** 83, 88; **Retro. Supp. I:** 103
Ice-Shirt, The (Vollmann), **Supp. XVII:** 226, 231, 232, 233
"Ice Storm, The" (Ashbery), **Supp. III Part 1:** 26
"Ice-Storm, The" (Pinsky), **Supp. VI:** 247–248
"Ichabod" (Whittier), **Supp. I Part 2:** 687, 689–690; **Supp. XI:** 50
"I Chop Some Parsley While Listening to Art Blakey's Version of 'Three Blind Mice' " (Collins), **Supp. XXI:** 60
"Icicles" (Francis), **Supp. IX:** 83
"Icicles" (Gass), **Supp. VI:** 83
Ickes, Harold, **Supp. I Part 1:** 5
Iconographs (Swenson), **Supp. IV Part 2:** 638, 646–648, 651
"Icosaphere, The" (Moore), **III:** 213
"I Could Believe" (Levine), **Supp. V:** 189
"I Could Take" (Carruth), **Supp. XVI:** 56
I Could Tell You Stories: Sojourns in the Land of Memory (Hampl), **Supp. XXII:** 84, **92–94**
"I Cry, Love! Love!" (Roethke), **III:** 539–540
Ida (Stein), **IV:** 43, 45
"Ida y Vuelta" (Muñoz), **Supp. XXV:** 136
"Idea, The" (Carver), **Supp. III Part 1:** 143
"Idea, The" (Strand), **Supp. IV Part 2:** 631
Ideal Husband (Wilde), **II:** 515
Idea of Florida in the American Literary Imagination, The (Rowe), **Supp. X:** 223
"Idea of Form at Spruce Creek, The" (Weigl), **Supp. XIX:** 283–284
"Idea of Ice, The" (C. Baxter), **Supp. XVII:** 15
"Idea of Order, An" (Wiman), **Supp. XVIII:** 173
"Idea of Order at Key West, The" (Stevens), **IV:** 89–90; **Retro. Supp. I:** 302, 303, 313
Ideas of Order (Stevens), **Retro. Supp. I:** 296, 298, **302–303,** 303, 305
Idema, James, **Supp. XXVII:** 7
"Identification Pleas" (Gansworth), **Supp. XXVI:** 114
"Identity Theft: True Memory, False Memory, and the Holocaust" (R. Franklin), **Supp. XVI:** 160
Ideograms in China (Michaux; Sobin, trans.), **Supp. XVI:** 288
"Ideographs" (Olds), **Supp. X:** 205
Ides of March, The (Wilder), **IV:** 357, 372
"I Did Not Learn Their Names" (Ellison), **Retro. Supp. II:** 124
"I Died with the First Blow & Was Reborn Wrong" (Coleman), **Supp. XI:** 91
"Idiom of a Self, The" (Pinsky), **Supp. VI:** 240
"Idiot, The" (Crane), **I:** 401
Idiot, The (Dostoevsky), **I:** 468
"Idiots First" (Malamud), **Supp. I Part 2:** 434–435, 437, 440–441
Idiots Karamazov, The (Durand and Innaurato), **Supp. XXIV:** 113, 116
"Idiot Wind" (song, Dylan), **Supp. XVIII:** 30
Idle Idylls (Wells), **Supp. XXVI:** 275
I Don't Need You Any More (A. Miller), **III:** 165
Idoru (W. Gibson), **Supp. XVI:** 119, 124, **129–130**
"I Dream I'm the Death of Orpheus" (Rich), **Supp. I Part 2:** 557–558
I Dreamt I Became a Nymphomaniac! Imagining (Acker), **Supp. XII:** 4, 6, **8,** 11
"I Dreamt You Young" (Espaillat), **Supp. XXI:** 107
"Idyll" (Shaw), **Supp. XIX:** 241
Idylls of the King (Tennyson), **III:** 487; **Retro. Supp. III:** 266; **Supp. I Part 2:** 410; **Supp. XIII:** 146
Idyl of Work, An (Larcom), **Supp.**

XIII: 139, 142, 146–147, 150
"If" (Creeley), **Supp. IV Part 1:** 158
If Beale Street Could Talk (Baldwin), **Retro. Supp. II:** 13–14; **Supp. I Part 1:** 48, 59–60, 67
"If Biblical Law Ruled Modern Society . . . " (P. N. Warren), **Supp. XX: 272**
If Blessing Comes (Bambara), **Supp. XI:** 1
"If Death Is Kind" (Teasdale), **Supp. XXVII:** 294
I Feel a Little Jumpy around You (Nye and Janeczko, eds.), **Supp. XIII:** 280
"I felt a Funeral, in my Brain" (Dickinson), **Retro. Supp. I:** 38
"If Grown-Ups Were Smart" (Nelson and Espeland), **Supp. XVIII:** 181
If He Hollers Let Him Go (C. Himes), **Supp. XVI:** 135, 138–139, 142
"If I Could Be Like Wallace Stevens" (Stafford), **Supp. XI:** 327
"If I Could Do Whatever I Wanted" (Nelson and Espeland), **Supp. XVIII:** 181
"If I Could Only Live at the Pitch That Is Near Madness" (Eberhart), **I:** 523, 526–527
If I Could Write This in Fire (Cliff), **Supp. XXII:** 67, 69
"If I Could Write This in Fire, I Would Write This in Fire" (Cliff), **Supp. XXII:** 65–66, 68–69
If I Die in a Combat Zone (O'Brien), **Supp. V:** 238, 239, 240, 245
If I Ever Get Out of Here (Gansworth), **Supp. XXVI:** 102, 108–109
If I Forget Thee, Jerusalem (Faulkner), **Retro. Supp. III:** 85
"If I Had My Way" (Creeley), **Supp. IV Part 1:** 157
"If I Might Be" (Chopin), **Retro. Supp. II:** 61
"I Find the Real American Tragedy" (Dreiser), **Retro. Supp. II:** 105
If I Ran the Circus (Geisel), **Supp. XVI:** 105
If I Ran the Zoo (Geisel), **Supp. XVI:** 104–105
If It Die (Gide), **I:** 290
"If It Were Not for You" (Carruth), **Supp. XVI:** 57
"If I Were a Man" (Gilman), **Supp. XI:** 207
"If I Were the Wind" (Leopold), **Supp. XIV:** 184
If Morning Ever Comes (Tyler), **Supp. IV Part 2:** 658–659
If Mountains Die: A New Mexico Memoir (Nichols), **Supp. XIII:** 255, 257, 267
"If Nancy Was a Boy" (Brainard), **Supp. XXVII:** 21
"If Nancy Was an Ashtray" (Brainard), **Supp. XXVII:** 21
I Forgot to Go to Spain (Harrison), **Supp. VIII:** 39, **52–53**
"If Poetry Were Not a Morality" (Gallagher), **Supp. XXIV:** 170
If the River Was Whiskey (Boyle), **Supp. VIII: 15–16; Supp. XX: 17, 19**
"If They Knew Yvonne" (Dubus), **Supp. VII:** 81
"If We Had Bacon" (H. Roth), **Supp. IX:** 232, 234
"If We Had Known" (Francis), **Supp. IX:** 78
"If We Must Die" (McKay), **Supp. IV Part 1:** 3; **Supp. X:** 132, 134
"If We Take All Gold" (Bogan), **Supp. III Part 1:** 52
If You Call This a Cry Song (Carruth), **Supp. XVI:** 56
If You Want to Write (Ueland), **Supp. XVII:** 13
I Gaspiri (Lardner), **II:** 435
"I Gather the Limbs of Osiris" (Pound), **Retro. Supp. I:** 287
I Get on the Bus (McKnight), **Supp. XX: 148–150, 152**
"I Give You Back" (Harjo), **Supp. XII:** 223
Ignatius of Loyola, **IV:** 151; **Supp. XI:** 162
Ignatius Rising (Nevils and Hardy), **Supp. XXVI:** 241
Ignatow, David, **Supp. XIII:** 275
"Ignis Fatuus" (Tate), **IV:** 128
"Ignorant Lust after Knowledge, The" (Bronk), **Supp. XXI:** 31
"I Go Back to May 1937" (Olds), **Supp. X:** 207
I Go Dreaming Serenades (Salinas), **Supp. XIII:** 316
"I Got a Guy Once" (Gallagher), **Supp. XXIV:** 176
"I Got My Job on the New York Times!" (Schuyler and Brainard), **Supp. XXVII:** 23
I Got the Blues (Odets), **Supp. II Part 2:** 530
Iguana Killer, The (Ríos), **Supp. IV Part 2:** 542–544
"I Had Eight Birds Hatcht in One Nest" (Bradstreet), **Supp. I Part 1:** 102, 115, 117, 119
"I had no time to Hate" (Dickinson), **Retro. Supp. I:** 44–45, 46
I Had Trouble in Getting to Solla Sollew (Geisel), **Supp. XVI:** 108, 109
I Hate Miranda July (blog), **Supp. XXIV:** 200
"I Have a Rendezvous with Life" (Cullen), **Supp. IV Part 1:** 168
"I Have Been Thinking About Snow" (Monson), **Supp. XXIV:** 235
"I Have Increased Power" (Ginsberg), **Supp. II Part 1:** 313
"I Have Moved West" (Taggard), **Supp. XXII:** 274
"I Have Seen Black Hands" (Wright), **Supp. II Part 1:** 228
"I Hear an Army" (Joyce), **Supp. I Part 1:** 262
"I heard a Fly buzz when I died" (Dickinson), **Retro. Supp. I:** 38
"I Heard Immanuel Singing" (Lindsay), **Supp. I Part 2:** 379
I Heard It Through the Grapevine (Turner), **Supp. XX: 110**
"I Hear It Was Charged against Me" (Whitman), **IV:** 343
I Hear Men Talking (Le Sueur), **Supp. XXIII:** 162, 167, **171–172**
"I Held a Shelley Manuscript" (Corso), **Supp. XII:** 128
"I Held His Name" (Ríos), **Supp. IV Part 2:** 547
"Ike and Nina" (Boyle), **Supp. XX: 19**
"I Kiss a Door" (July), **Supp. XXIV:** 204
I Knew a Phoenix (Sarton), **Supp. VIII:** 249, 251–252
"I Know a Man" (Creeley), **Supp. IV Part 1:** 147–148, 149
I Know Some Things: Stories about Childhood by Contemporary Writers (Moore, ed.), **Supp. X:** 175
"I Know the Stars" (Teasdale), **Supp. XXVII:** 293
"I Know Why the Caged Bird Cannot Read" (Prose), **Supp. XVI:** 259
I Know Why the Caged Bird Sings (Angelou), **Supp. IV Part 1:** 2–4, 5, 7, 11, 12, 13, 14, 15, 17; **Supp. XVI:** 259
"Ikon: The Harrowing of Hell" (Levertov), **Supp. III Part 1:** 284
"Iktomi and the Ducks" (Zitkala-Ša), **Supp. XXV:** 275–276
Ile (O'Neill), **III:** 388; **Supp. XXV:** 20
"I Led Three Lives" (television program), **Supp. XX: 195**
"I Let Him Take Me" (Cisneros), **Supp. VII:** 71
Iliad (Bryant, trans.), **Supp. I Part 1:** 158

Iliad (Chapman, trans.), **Supp. XXV:** 226
Iliad (Homer), **II:** 470; **Supp. IV Part 2:** 631; **Supp. IX:** 211; **Supp. X:** 114; **Supp. XVII:** 117; **Supp. XXI:** 36
Iliad (Pope, trans.), **Supp. I Part 1:** 152
"I Like" (Brainard), **Supp. XXVII:** 25
"I like to see it lap the Miles" (Dickinson), **Retro. Supp. I:** 37
"I Live Up Here" (Merwin), **Supp. III Part 1:** 349
"I'll Be Doing More of Same" (Franzen), **Supp. XX: 89**
"Illegal Alien" (Mora), **Supp. XIII:** 215
"Illegal Days, The" (Paley), **Supp. VI:** 222
Illegals, The (film), **Supp. XXVII:** 133, 140, 143
"Illegibility" (F. Wright), **Supp. XVII:** 244
Illig, Joyce, **Retro. Supp. II:** 20
"Illinois" (Masters), **Supp. I Part 2:** 458
"Illinois Bus Ride" (Leopold), **Supp. XIV:** 189
Illinois Poems (Masters), **Supp. I Part 2:** 472
"Illinois Village, The" (Lindsay), **Supp. I Part 2:** 381
"Ill-Lit" (F. Wright), **Supp. XVII:** 245
Ill-Lit: Selected & New Poems (F. Wright), **Supp. XVII:** 245
Illness as Metaphor (Sontag), **Supp. III Part 2:** 452, 461, 466
I'll Take My Stand ("Twelve Southerners"), **II:** 196; **III:** 496; **IV:** 125, 237; **Supp. X:** 25, 52–53; **Supp. XIV:** 3
"I'll Take You to Tennessee" (Connell), **Supp. XIV:** 82
Illumination (Frederic), **II:** 141
Illumination, The (Brockmeier), **Supp. XXII:** 61
Illumination Night (Hoffman), **Supp. X:** 85, **86,** 88, 89
Illuminations (Rimbaud), **Supp. XXI:** 233
"Illusion, An" (Wells), **Supp. XXVI:** 275
Illusion and Reality (Caudwell), **Supp. XXII:** 284
Illusion comique, L' (Corneille), **Supp. IX:** 138
"Illusion of Eternity, The" (Eberhart), **I:** 541
"Illusion of Fiction in Frank Conroy's Stop-Time, The" (R. Ramsey), **Supp. XVI:** 69
Illusions (Dash; film), **Supp. XI:** 20
"Illusions" (Emerson), **II:** 2, 5, 14, 16
Illustrated Man, The (Bradbury), **Supp. IV Part 1:** 102, 103, 113
Illustrations of China and Its People (Thompson), **Supp. XXI:** 151
Illustrations of Political Economy (Martineau), **Supp. II Part 1:** 288
"I Look at My Hand" (Swenson), **Supp. IV Part 2:** 638, 647
I Love Gootie: My Grandmother's Story (Apple), **Supp. XVII: 9–10**
I Love Myself When I Am Laughing . . . : A Zora Neale Hurston Reader (Walker), **Supp. III Part 2:** 531, 532
"I Love the Way It Goes"(O'Hara), **Supp. XXIII:** 220
"I'm a Fool" (Anderson), **I:** 113, 114, 116; **Supp. I Part 2:** 430
Image and Idea (Rahv), **Supp. II Part 1:** 146
Image and the Law, The (Nemerov), **III:** 268, 269–271, 272
"Image in the Mirror, The" (Swados), **Supp. XIX:** 265
"Images" (Hass), **Supp. VI:** 103
"Images and 'Images' " (Simic), **Supp. VIII:** 274
"Images for Godard" (Rich), **Supp. I Part 2:** 558
"Images of Walt Whitman" (Fiedler), **IV:** 352
"Imaginary Dialogue, An" (Espaillat), **Supp. XXI:** 103
"Imaginary Friendships of Tom McGrath, The" (Cohen), **Supp. X:** 112
"Imaginary Iceberg, The" (Bishop), **Retro. Supp. II:** 42; **Supp. I Part 1:** 86, 88
"Imaginary Jew, The" (Berryman), **I:** 174–175
Imaginary Letters (Pound), **III:** 473–474
Imaginary Paintings (C. Baxter), **Supp. XVII:** 18–19
"Imaginary Prisons" (Schnackenberg), **Supp. XV:** 257, 258
Imagination and Fancy; or, Selections from the English Poets, illustrative of those first requisites of their art; with markings of the best passages, critical notices of the writers, and an essay in answer to the question'What is Poetry?' (Hunt), **II:** 515–516
"Imagination as Value" (Stevens), **Retro. Supp. I:** 298
"Imagination of Disaster, The" (Gordon), **Supp. IV Part 1:** 306
Imaginative Qualities of Actual Things (Sorrentino), **Supp. XXI:** 226, 230, 231–232, 234
"Imagine a Day at the End of Your Life" (Beattie), **Supp. V:** 33
Imagined London: A Tour of the World's Greatest Fictional City (Quindlen), **Supp. XVII:** 167, 180
Imagineering Atlanta (Rutheiser), **Supp. XXII:** 244
"Imagine Kissing Pete" (O'Hara), **III:** 372; **Supp. VIII:** 156
Imaging Robert: My Brother, Madness, and Survival (Neugeboren), **Supp. XVI:** 225, **226–229**
"Imagining How It Would Be to Be Dead" (Eberhart), **I:** 533
Imagining Los Angeles: A City in Fiction (Fine), **Supp. XI:** 160
"Imagining Their Own Hymns" (B. Kelly), **Supp. XVII:** 126–127
"Imagining the Midwest" (Sanders), **Supp. XVI:** 275–276
Imagining the Worst: Stephen King and the Representations of Women (Lant and Thompson), **Supp. V:** 141
"Imagisme" (Pound), **Retro. Supp. I:** 288
Imagistes, Des: An Anthology of the Imagists (Pound, ed.), **III:** 465, 471; **Retro. Supp. I:** 288
Imago (O. Butler), **Supp. XIII:** 63, **65–66**
"Imago" (Stevens), **IV:** 74, 89
Imagoes (Coleman), **Supp. XI:** 89–90
I Married a Communist (P. Roth), **Retro. Supp. II:** 289, 293–294
I Married an Angel (film), **Supp. XVI:** 193
"I May, I Might, I Must" (Moore), **III:** 215
Imbusch, Kevin, **Supp. XXIII:** 125
"I'm Crazy" (Salinger), **III:** 553
"I'm Here" (Roethke), **III:** 547
Imitations (R . Lowell), **II:** 550
Imitations (R. Lowell), **II:** 543, 544–545, 555; **Retro. Supp. II:** 181, 187
"Imitations of Drowning" (Sexton), **Supp. II Part 2:** 684, 686
"Immaculate Man" (Gordon), **Supp. IV Part 1:** 311
"Immanence of Dostoevsky, The" (Bourne), **I:** 235
"Immigrants" (Mora), **Supp. XIII:** 216
Immigrant Saint: The Life of Mother Cabrini (di Donato), **Supp. XX: 44**
"Immigrant Story, The" (Paley), **Supp. VI:** 230

Immobile Wind, The (Winters), **Supp. II Part 2:** 786
"Immobile Wind, The" (Winters), **Supp. II Part 2:** 788, 811
"Immolatus" (Komunyakaa), **Supp. XIII:** 126
"Immoral Proposition, The" (Creeley), **Supp. IV Part 1:** 144
"Immortal Autumn" (MacLeish), **III:** 13
"Immortality Ode" (Nemerov), **III:** 87
Immortality Ode (Wordsworth), **II:** 17; **Supp. I Part 2:** 673
Immortal Marriage, The (Atherton), **Supp. XXIV:** 26
"Immortal Woman, The" (Tate), **IV:** 130, 131, 137
"I'm Not Ready to Die Yet" (Harjo), **Supp. XII:** 231
I'm Not There (film, Haynes), **Supp. XVIII:** 23
"I'm on My Way" (Salinas), **Supp. XIII:** 320
"Impasse" (Hughes), **Supp. I Part 1:** 343
"Impatient Mary" (Taggard), **Supp. XXII:** 278
Imperative Duty, An, a Novel (Howells), **II:** 286
Imperial Bedrooms (Ellis), **Supp. XXVII:** 77–78
Imperial Eyes: Travel Writing and Transculturation (Pratt), **Retro. Supp. II:** 48
Imperial Germany and the Industrial Revolution (Veblen), **Supp. I Part 2:** 642, 643
Imperial Way, The: By Rail from Peshawar to Chittagong (Theroux), **Supp. VIII:** 323
"Implements from the 'Tomb of the Poet' " (Stallings), **Supp. XXV:** 232
"Implosions" (Rich), **Supp. I Part 2:** 556
"Imp of the Perverse, The" (Poe), **III:** 414–415; **Retro. Supp. II:** 267
Impolite Interviews, **Supp. XI:** 293
"Importance of Artists' Biographies, The" (Goldbarth), **Supp. XII:** 183, 184, 191
Importance of Being Earnest, The (Wilde), **Supp. XIV:** 324, 339
Importance of Gaining and Preserving the Friendship of the Indians to the British Interest Considered (Kennedy and Parker), **Supp. XXVI:** 84
"Important Houses, The" (Gordon), **Supp. IV Part 1:** 315
"Impossible Indispensability of the Ars Poetica, The" (Carruth), **Supp. XVI:** 57
"Impossible to Tell" (Pinsky), **Supp. VI:** 247, 248
"Imposter, The" (West), **Retro. Supp. II:** 322, 327
"Impressionism and Symbolism in Heart of Darkness" (Watt), **Supp. VIII:** 4
"Impressionism"(Crooker), **Supp. XXIII:** 57
"Impressions of a European Tour" (Bourne), **I:** 225
"Impressions of an Indian Childhood" (Zitkala-Ša), **Supp. XXV:** 272
"Impressions of a Plumber" (H. Roth), **Supp. IX:** 228, 234
"Impressions of Europe, 1913–1914" (Bourne), **I:** 225
"I Must Have Called and So He Comes" (Notley), **Supp. XXII:** 224
"I'm Walking behind the Spanish" (Salinas), **Supp. XIII:** 323–324
I'm Your Man (album, Cohen), **Supp. XXVII:** 54
"I'm Your Man" (Cohen), **Supp. XXVII:** 52, 61
"I/Myself" (Shields), **Supp. VII:** 311
"In a (Low) Bar" (Ferry), **Supp. XXIV:** 153
"In Absence" (Lanier), **Supp. I Part 1:** 364
"In Absentia" (Bowles), **Supp. IV Part 1:** 94
"In a Cab" (Untermeyer), **Supp. XV:** 296
"In a Coffee Pot" (Hayes), **Supp. XXVI:** 133–134, 144
"In a Country Cemetery" (Kooser), **Supp. XIX:** 120
Inada, Lawson Fusao, **Supp. V:** 180
"In a Dark Room, Furniture" (Nye), **Supp. XIII:** 274
"In a Dark Time" (Roethke), **III:** 539, 547, 548
In a Different Voice (Gilligan), **Supp. XXII:** 18
"In a Disused Graveyard" (Frost), **Retro. Supp. I:** 126, 133
In a Dusty Light (Haines), **Supp. XII:** 207
"In a Garden" (A. Lowell), **II:** 513
"In a Hard Intellectual Light" (Eberhart), **I:** 523
"In a Hollow of the Hills" (Harte), **Supp. II Part 1:** 354
In America (Sontag), **Supp. XIV:** 95–96
"In Amicitia" (Ransom), **IV:** 141
In a Narrow Grave: Essays on Texas (McMurtry), **Supp. V:** 220, 223
In an Iridescent Time, Poems, 1953–58 (Stone), **Supp. XXVII:** 250–251, 253, 262
"Inanna" (A. Finch), **Supp. XVII:** 72
"In Another Country" (Hemingway), **I:** 484–485; **II:** 249
In April Once (Percy), **Retro. Supp. I:** 341
"In a Prominent Bar in Secaucus One Day" (X. J. Kennedy), **Supp. XV:** 154, 155–156
"In Armenia, 1987"(Balakian), **Supp. XXIII:** 25
In A Shallow Grave (Purdy), **Supp. VII:** 272
In a shlekhter tsayt (In a bad time) (Asch), **Supp. XXIII:** 4
"In a Stadium" (A. Lowell), **Supp. XXVII:** 295
"In a Station of the Metro" (Pound), **Retro. Supp. I:** 288; **Supp. I Part 1:** 265; **Supp. XIV:** 284–285
"In a Strange Town" (Anderson), **I:** 114, 115
"In Athens Once" (Rodriguez), **Supp. XIV:** 303
"In a Tub" (Hempel), **Supp. XXI:** 119
In Battle for Peace: The Story of My 83rd Birthday (Du Bois), **Supp. II Part 1:** 185
In Bed One Night & Other Brief Encounters (Coover), **Supp. V:** 49, 50
"In Bertram's Garden" (Justice), **Supp. VII:** 117
"In Blackwater Woods" (Oliver), **Supp. VII:** 244, 246
In Black & Whitey (Lacy), **Supp. XV:** 206–207
"In Broad Daylight" (Jin), **Supp. XVIII:** 94
In Broken Country (Wagoner), **Supp. IX:** 330
"In California" (Simpson), **Supp. IX:** 271
"In Camp" (Stafford), **Supp. XI:** 329
"Incant against Suicide" (Karr), **Supp. XI:** 249
"In Celebration of My Uterus" (Sexton), **Supp. II Part 2:** 689
"Incendiary, The" (Rowson), **Supp. XV:** 234
"In Certain Places and Certain Times There Can Be More of You" (Dunn), **Supp. XI:** 144
Incest: From "A Journal of Love," the Unexpurgated Diary of Anaïs Nin, 1932–1934 (Nin), **Supp. X:** 182, 184, 185, 187, 191

"In Chandler Country" (Gioia), **Supp. XV:** 119
Inchbald, Elizabeth, **II:** 8
"In Cheever Country" (Gioia), **Supp. XV:** 119
Inchiquin, the Jesuit's Letters (Ingersoll), **I:** 344
"Incident" (Cullen), **Supp. IV Part 1:** 165, 166
Incidental Numbers (Wylie), **Supp. I Part 2:** 708
Incidentals (Sandburg), **III:** 579
Incidentals in the Day World (Notley), **Supp. XXII:** 223, 226, 227
Incident at Vichy (A. Miller), **III:** 165, 166; **Retro. Supp. III:** 173, 175–176
Incidents in the Life of a Slave Girl (Brent), **Supp. IV Part 1:** 13
Incidents in the Life of a Slavegirl (Jacobs), **Supp. XVI:** 85
"Incipience" (Rich), **Supp. I Part 2:** 559
"In Clare" (McCarriston), **Supp. XIV:** 270–271
Including Horace (Untermeyer), **Supp. XV:** 301, 303–304
In Cold Blood: A True Account of a Multiple Murder and Its Consequences (Capote), **Retro. Supp. II:** 107–108; **Supp. I Part 1:** 292; **Supp. III Part 1:** 111, 117, 119, 122, 123, 125–131; **Supp. III Part 2:** 574; **Supp. IV Part 1:** 220; **Supp. XIV:** 162; **Supp. XXV:** 57
In Cold Hell, in Thicket (Olson), **Supp. II Part 2:** 571
"In Cold Hell, in Thicket" (Olson), **Supp. II Part 2:** 558, 563–564, 566, 572, 580
"Incoming Tide"(Strout), **Supp. XXIII:** 282, 285
"Incomparable Light, The" (Eberhart), **I:** 541
Incorporative Consciousness of Robert Bly, The (Harris), **Supp. IV Part 1:** 68
In Country (Mason), **Supp. VIII:** 133, **142–143,** 146
"In Country of Conscience" (J. W. Miller), **Supp. XX: 165**
" 'Incredible Eloquence': How Ron Rash's Novels Keep the Celtic Literary Tradition Alive" (K. Baldwin), **Supp. XXVII:** 216
"Incredible Survival of Coyote, The" (Snyder), **Supp. VIII:** 297
"Increment" (Ammons), **Supp. VII:** 28
In Defense of Ignorance (Shapiro), **Supp. II Part 2:** 703, 704, 713–714
In Defense of Reason (Winters), **Supp. I Part 1:** 268
In Defense of Women (Mencken), **III:** 109
Indelible (Hadas), **Supp. XXIII: 119**
Indelible Alison Bechdel, The (Bechdel), **Supp. XXV:** 4
Indemnity Only (Paretsky), **Supp. XXV:** 172–173, 176, 178
Independence Day (film), **Supp. X:** 80
Independence Day (Ford), **Supp. V:** 57, 62–63, 67–68
"Independent Candidate, The, a Story of Today" (Howells), **II:** 277
"Indestructible Mr. Gore, The" (Vidal), **Supp. IV Part 2:** 679
Index of American Design, **Supp. III Part 2:** 618
"India" (Rodriguez), **Supp. XIV:** 302
"Indian at the Burial-Place of His Fathers, An" (Bryant), **Supp. I Part 1:** 155–156, 167–168
"Indian Burying Ground, The" (Freneau), **Supp. II Part 1:** 264, 266
"Indian Camp" (Hemingway), **II:** 247–248, 263; **Retro. Supp. I:** 174–175, 176, 177, 181; **Supp. XVI:** 208
Indian Country (Caputo), **Supp. XIX:** 22–25
Indian Country (Matthiessen), **Supp. V:** 211
"Indian Country" (McCarriston), **Supp. XIV:** 271
"Indian Country" (Simpson), **Supp. IX:** 274
Indian Earth (Bynner), **Supp. XV:** 46
"Indian Gifts to Civilized Man" (Zitkala-Ša), **Supp. XXV:** 281
"Indian Girls" (McCarriston), **Supp. XIV:** 272–273
"Indian Manifesto" (Deloria), **Supp. IV Part 1:** 323
"Indian Names" (Sigourney), **Retro. Supp. II:** 47
"Indian's Awakening, The" (Zitkala-Ša), **Supp. XXV:** 281
"Indian Student, The" (Freneau), **Supp. II Part 1:** 264
"Indian Student, The" (Simpson), **Supp. IX:** 280
Indian Summer (Howells), **II:** 275, 279–281, 282
Indian Summer (Knowles), **Supp. XII:** 249, 250
Indian Summer: Musings on the Gift of Life (Pickering), **Supp. XXI:** 204
Indian Summers (Gansworth), **Supp. XXVI:** 104
"Indian Teacher Among Indians, An" (Zitkala-Ša), **Supp. XXV:** 272
"Indian Uprising, The" (Barthelme), **Supp. IV Part 1:** 44
"Indian Wooing" (C. Miller), **Supp. XXII:** 197–198
Indifferent Children, The (Auchincloss), **Supp. IV Part 1:** 25
Indirections (Cox), **Supp. XXI:** 21
Indiscretions (Pound), **Retro. Supp. I:** 284
"Indispensability of the Eyes, The" (Olds), **Supp. X:** 202
"In Distrust of Merits" (Moore), **III:** 201, 214
"Individual and the State, The" (Emerson), **II:** 10
Individualism, Old and New (Dewey), **Supp. I Part 2:** 677
"Indolence" (Pickering), **Supp. XXI:** 203
In Dreams Begin Responsibilities (Schwartz), **Supp. II Part 2:** 642, 645–650
"In Dreams Begin Responsibilities" (Schwartz), **Supp. II Part 2:** 641, 649, 654
In Dubious Battle (Steinbeck), **IV:** 51, 55–56, 59, 63
"In Durance" (Pound), **Retro. Supp. I:** 285
"Industry of Hard Kissing, The" (Ríos), **Supp. IV Part 2:** 547
"In Duty Bound" (Gilman), **Supp. XI:** 196–197
"I Need, I Need" (Roethke), **III:** 535–536
"I Need Help" (Stern), **Supp. IX:** 290
"Ineffectual Marriage" (Loy), **Supp. XXII:** 165
"Inés in the Kitchen" (García), **Supp. XI:** 190
"I never saw a Moor" (Dickinson), **Retro. Supp. I:** 37
I Never Told Anybody: Teaching Poetry Writing in a Nursing Home (Koch), **Supp. XV:** 190
"I Never Will Be Married, I'd Rather Be Excus'd" (Rowson), **Supp. XV:** 240
Inevitable Exiles (Kielsky), **Supp. V:** 273
"Inevitable Trial, The" (Holmes), **Supp. I Part 1:** 318
"Inexhaustible Hat, The" (Wagoner), **Supp. IX:** 327
"In Extremis" (Berry), **Supp. X:** 23
Inez, Colette, **Supp. XXIII:** 54, 245
"Infancy" (Wilder), **IV:** 375
"Infant Boy at Midcentury" (Warren), **IV:** 244–245, 252

Infante, Guillermo Cabrera, **Retro. Supp. I:** 278
"Infant Sea Turtles" (F. Wright), **Supp. XVII:** 245
Infants of the Spring (Thurman), **Supp. XIX:** 73; **Supp. XVIII:** 281
Inferno (Dante), **IV:** 139; **Supp. V:** 338; **Supp. VIII:** 219–221
Inferno of Dante, The (Pinsky), **Supp. VI:** 235, 248
Infidel (Ali), **Supp. XXIV:** 15
"Infidelity" (Komunyakaa), **Supp. XIII:** 130
Infidels (album, Dylan), **Supp. XVIII:** 28
"Infiltration of the Universe" (MacLeish), **III:** 19
Infinite Jest: A Novel (Wallace), **Supp. X:** 301, **310–314; Supp. XX: 91; Supp. XXVII:** 6
"Infinite Reason, The" (MacLeish), **III:** 19
"Infirmity" (R. Lowell), **II:** 554
"Infirmity" (Roethke), **III:** 548
In Five Years Time (Haines), **Supp. XII:** 206
"In Flower" (Snodgrass), **Supp. VI:** 325
"Influence of Landscape upon the Poet, The" (Eliot), **Retro. Supp. I:** 67
"In Football Season" (Updike), **IV:** 219
Informer, The (film), **Supp. III Part 2:** 619
Informers, The (Ellis), **Supp. XXVII:** 74–75
Informers, The (screenplay, Ellis and Jarecki), **Supp. XXVII:** 68, 79
Inge, William, **Supp. XXV: 93–108**
Ingersoll, Charles J., **I:** 344
Ingersoll, Robert Green, **Supp. II Part 1:** 198
Ingmundson, Kris, **Supp. XXIV:** 230, 234
Ingraham, Lloyd, **Supp. XVI:** 184
"Ingrained Reflexes" (Huddle), **Supp. XXVI:** 154
Ingster, Boris, **Retro. Supp. II:** 330
"In Guatemala, All Is Forgotten" (Goldman), **Supp. XXV:** 58
Inhabitants, The (Morris), **III:** 221–222
"Inheritance and Invention in Li-Young Lee's Poetry" (Xiaojing), **Supp. XV:** 214
"Inheritance"(Kenny), **Supp. XXIII:** 154
"Inheritance of Tools, The" (Sanders), **Supp. XVI:** 273
Inheritors (Glaspell), **Supp. III Part 1:** 175, 179–181, 186, 189
"In him we live, & move, & have our being" (Very), **Supp. XXV:** 246
"In Hollywood with the Zuni God of War" (Major), **Supp. XXII:** 180
"In Honor of David Anderson Brooks, My Father" (Brooks), **Supp. III Part 1:** 79
"In Honor of That High and Mighty Princess Queen Elizabeth of Happy Memory" (Bradstreet), **Retro. Supp. III:** 8–9
"Inhumanist, The" (Jeffers), **Supp. II Part 2:** 423, 426
"In Illo Tempore" (Karr), **Supp. XI:** 242
"In Interims: Outlyer" (Harrison), **Supp. VIII:** 38
"Initial" (F. Wright), **Supp. XVII:** 243
"Injudicious Gardening" (Moore), **III:** 198
"Injustice" (Paley), **Supp. VI:** 220
Injustice Collectors, The (Auchincloss), **Supp. IV Part 1:** 25
Ink, Blood, Semen (Goldbarth), **Supp. XII:** 181, 183
Ink Dark Moon, The: Love Poems by Ono no Komachi and Izumi Shikibu (Aratani and Hirshfield, trans.), **Supp. XXIII:** 136
Ink Truck, The (W. Kennedy), **Supp. VII:** 132, 133–138, 140, 141, 149, 152
In Life Sentences: Literary Essays (Epstein), **Supp. XIV:** 112
"In Limbo" (Wilbur), **Supp. III Part 2:** 544, 561
In Limestone Country (Sanders), **Supp. XVI:** 272
"In Line" (Major), **Supp. XXII:** 185
In Love (Hayes), **Supp. XXVI:** 133, 139, 140–141
In Love and Trouble: Stories of Black Women (Walker), **Supp. III Part 2:** 520, 521, 530, 531, 532
In Mad Love and War (Harjo), **Supp. XII: 224–226**
"In Memoriam" (Emerson), **II:** 13
"In Memoriam" (Hay), **Supp. XIV:** 122, 127
"In Memoriam" (Tennyson), **Retro. Supp. I:** 325; **Supp. I Part 2:** 416
In Memoriam: 1933 (Reznikoff), **Supp. XIV:** 280, 285
In Memoriam to Identity (Acker), **Supp. XII:** 5, **16–18**
"In Memory of Arthur Winslow" (R. Lowell), **II:** 541, 547, 550; **Retro. Supp. II:** 187
"In Memory of Congresswoman Barbara Jordan" (Pinsky), **Supp. VI:** 250
"In Memory of Joe Brainard" (Bidart), **Supp. XV:** 33
"In Memory of My Dear Grandchild Elizabeth Bradstreet" (Bradstreet), **Retro. Supp. III:** 13
"In Memory of My Feelings" (O'Hara), **Supp. XV:** 215–216
In Memory of My Feelings (O'Hara; Berkson, ed.), **Supp. XXIII:** 220
"In Memory of My Feelings"(O'Hara), **Supp. XXIII:** 208, 215–216
"In Memory of Vachel Lindsay" (Teasdale), **Supp. XXVII:** 297
"In Memory of W. B. Yeats" (Auden), **Supp. VIII:** 19, 30; **Supp. XI:** 243, 244; **Supp. XIX:** 85
"In Memory of W. H. Auden" (Stern), **Supp. IX:** 288
"In Memory"(Schott), **Supp. XXIII:** 254
"In Mercy on Broadway" (Doty), **Supp. XI:** 132
In Morocco (Wharton), **Retro. Supp. I:** 380; **Supp. IV Part 1:** 81
Inmost Leaf, The: A Selection of Essays (Kazin), **Supp. VIII:** 102, 103
In Motley (Bierce), **I:** 209
In My Father's Court (Singer), **IV:** 16–17; **Retro. Supp. II: 301–302**
"In My Life" (Dubus), **Supp. VII:** 81
"In My Other Life" (Huddle), **Supp. XXVI:** 151
Innaurato, Albert, **Supp. XXIV:** 113, 116, 117
"In Navaho Country" (Bronk), **Supp. XXI:** 30
Inner Circle, The (Boyle), **Supp. XX: 24, 26**
Inner Landscape (Sarton), **Supp. VIII:** 259
Inner Room, The (Merrill), **Supp. III Part 1:** 336
"In Nine Sleep Valley" (Merrill), **Supp. III Part 1:** 328
Innocent Mrs. Duff, The (Holding), **Supp. XXII:** 119, 120, 123, **130–131,** 135, 136
Innocents, The: A Story for Lovers (Lewis), **II:** 441
Innocents Abroad, The (Twain), **Retro. Supp. III:** 257–258, 260–261, 267
Innocents Abroad, The; or, The New Pilgrim's Progress (Twain), **II:** 275, 434; **IV:** 191, 196, 197–198
Innocents at Cedro, The: A Memoir of Thorstein Veblen and Some Others (Duffus), **Supp. I Part 2:** 650
"In Off the Cliffs of Moher"

(McCarriston), **Supp. XIV:** 270
In Old Plantation Days (Dunbar), **Supp. II Part 1:** 214
In Ole Virginia (Page), **Supp. II Part 1:** 201
In Orbit (Morris), **III:** 236
In Other Words (Swenson), **Supp. IV Part 2:** 650–652
In Other Words: Literature by Latinas of the United States (Fernandez, ed.), **Supp. XXI:** 104
In Our Terribleness (Some elements and meaning in black style) (Baraka), **Supp. II Part 1:** 52, 53
In Our Time (Hemingway), **I:** 117; **II:** 68, 247, 252, 263; **IV:** 42; **Retro. Supp. I:** 170, 173, 174, 178, 180; **Supp. IX:** 106
"In Our Time" (Wolfe), **Supp. III Part 2:** 584
"Inpatient" (Kenyon), **Supp. VII:** 169
In Persuasion Nation (Saunders), **Supp. XIX: 231–234**
"In Persuasion Nation" (Saunders), **Supp. XIX:** 233–234
In Pharaoh's Army: Memories of the Lost War (Wolff), **Supp. VII:** 331–334, 335, 338
"In Plaster" (Plath), **Supp. I Part 2:** 540
"In Prague, in Montmartre" (Bierds), **Supp. XVII:** 27
"In Praise of Johnny Appleseed" (Lindsay), **Supp. I Part 2:** 397
"In Praise of Limestone" (Auden), **Supp. II Part 1:** 20–21; **Supp. VIII:** 23
In Pursuit of a Vanishing Star (Sobin), **Supp. XVI: 294**
"In Quercy, 1993" (Davison), **Supp. XXVI:** 78
In Quest of the Ordinary (Cavell), **Retro. Supp. I:** 307
Inquiry into the Moral and Religious Character of the American Government, An (H. Warner), **Supp. XVIII:** 259
Inquiry into the Nature of Peace, An (Veblen), **Supp. I Part 2:** 642
Inquisitor, The (Rowson), **Supp. XV: 232,** 238
In Radical Pursuit (Snodgrass), **Supp. VI:** 312, 316, 318
In Reckless Ecstasy (Sandburg), **III:** 579
In Recognition of William Gaddis (Kuehl and Moore), **Supp. IV Part 1:** 279
"In Reference to Her Children, 23 June 1659" (Bradstreet), **Retro. Supp. III:** 3, 13
"In Retirement" (Malamud), **Supp. I Part 2:** 437
"In Retrospect" (Angelou), **Supp. IV Part 1:** 15
"In Right" (Wolfert), **Supp. XXI:** 263, 264, 272
"Inroads of Time, The" (D. West), **Supp. XVIII:** 286–287
In Russia (A. Miller), **III:** 165
"In Sabine" (Chopin), **Supp. I Part 1:** 213
"In School-Days" (Whittier), **Supp. I Part 2:** 699–700
"Inscription for the Entrance to a Wood" (Bryant), **Supp. I Part 1:** 154, 155, 161–162
Inscriptions, 1944–1956 (Reznikoff), **Supp. XIV:** 281
In Search (Levin), **Supp. XXVII:** 133, 134, 138, 142, 143, 146–147
In Search of America: The Image of the United States in Travel Writing of the 1980s and 1990s (Rutkowska), **Supp. XXII:** 208
"In Search of a Motif for Expressive Female Figuration" (Major), **Supp. XXII:** 184
In Search of Bisco (Caldwell), **I:** 296
In Search of Lost Time (Proust), **Supp. XXV:** 71
In Search of Nella Larsen: A Biography of the Color Line (Hutchinson), **Supp. XVIII:** 120
"In Search of Our Mothers' Gardens" (Walker), **Supp. III Part 2:** 520–532, 524, 525, 527, 529, 532–533, 535, 536; **Supp. IX:** 306; **Supp. XVIII:** 200, 283
"In Search of Thomas Merton" (Griffin), **Supp. VIII:** 208
"In Search of Yage" (Burroughs), **Supp. III Part 1:** 98
"Insect Life in Florida" (Hull), **Supp. XXI:** 133
Insel (Loy), **Supp. XXII:** 167
"Insertion of Self into a Space of Borderless Possibilities, The" (Fjellestad), **Supp. XVI:** 150
"In Shadow" (Crane), **I:** 386
"In Shadow" (H. Crane), **Retro. Supp. III:** 45
"In Sickness and in Health" (Auden), **Supp. II Part 1:** 15
"In Sickness and in Health" (Humphrey), **Supp. IX:** 94
Inside, Outside (Wouk), **Supp. XXV:** 254, 255, 257, 265
Inside Diameter: The France Poems (Major), **Supp. XXII:** 182
Inside His Mind (A. Miller), **III:** 154
Inside Memory (Findley), **Supp. XX: 51, 63**
"Inside Norman Mailer" (Apple), **Supp. XVII:** 3, 4
"Insider Baseball" (Didion), **Supp. IV Part 1:** 211
Inside Sports magazine, **Supp. V:** 58, 61
"Insipid Profession of Jonathan Horneboom, The" (Lethem), **Supp. XVIII:** 149
"In So Many Dark Rooms" (Hogan), **Supp. IV Part 1:** 400
"Insomnia" (Bishop), **Supp. I Part 1:** 92
"Insomniac" (Plath), **Supp. I Part 2:** 539
"In Spain, Throwing Carnations" (P. N. Warren), **Supp. XX: 272**
"Inspiration for Greatness" (Caldwell), **I:** 291
"Instability of Race Types, The" (Boas), **Supp. XIV:** 209
"Installation #6" (Beattie), **Supp. V:** 33
"Instead of Dying" (Gallagher), **Supp. XXIV:** 171
"Insterstices" (Berrigan), **Supp. XXIV:** 36
Instinct of Workmanship and the State of the Industrial Arts, The (Veblen), **Supp. I Part 2:** 642
Instincts of the Herd in Peace and War, The (Trotter), **I:** 249
Institute (Calvin), **IV:** 158, 160
"Instruction Manual, The" (Ashbery), **Supp. III Part 1:** 6–7, 10, 12
Instructions, The (Levin), **Supp. XXII:** 268
"Instructions for the Afternoon" (Gioia), **Supp. XV:** 120
Instructions to the Double (Gallagher), **Supp. XXIV:** 165, 167, 168, 169, 174
"Instructions to the Double" (Gallagher), **Supp. XXIV:** 168
"Instruction to Myself" (Brooks), **Supp. III Part 1:** 87
Instrument, The (O'Hara), **III:** 362, 364
"In Such Times, Ties Must Bind" (Nye), **Supp. XIII:** 286
In Sunlight and in Shadow (Helprin), **Supp. XXV:** 81, 88
"Insurance and Social Change" (Stevens), **Retro. Supp. I:** 297
Insurgent Mexico (Reed), **I:** 476
In Suspect Terrain (McPhee), **Supp. III Part 1:** 309, 310

"In Tall Grass" (Sandburg), **III:** 585
"Integer Vitae" (Horace), **Supp. XV:** 304
"Integrity" (Rich), **Retro. Supp. III:** 249
Intellectual History, An (Senghor), **Supp. X:** 139
"Intellectual Pre-Eminence of Jews in Modern Europe, The" (Veblen), **Supp. I Part 2:** 643–644
Intellectual Things (Kunitz), **Supp. III Part 1:** 260, 262–264
Intellectual versus the City, The (White), **I:** 258
"In Temporary Pain" (Bynner), **Supp. XV:** 41–42
Intensive Care (Myers), **Supp. XXVII:** 211
Intentions (Wilde), **Retro. Supp. I:** 56
"Interest in Life, An" (Paley), **Supp. VI:** 222, 224–225
Interest of Great Britain Considered, with Regard to Her Colonies and the Acquisition of Canada and Guadeloupe, The (Franklin), **II:** 119
"Interior" (H. Crane), **Retro. Supp. III:** 45
Interior Landscapes (Vizenor), **Supp. IV Part 1:** 262
Interiors (film; Allen), **Supp. IV Part 1:** 205; **Supp. XV: 1, 7,** 10
Interlocking Lives (Koch), **Supp. XV:** 185
"Interlude" (A. Lowell), **Retro. Supp. II:** 46
Interlunar (Atwood), **Supp. XIII:** 35
"Intermezzo" (Schnackenberg), **Supp. XV:** 254
"In Terms of the Toenail: Fiction and the Figures of Life" (Gass), **Supp. VI:** 85
"International Episode, An" (James), **II:** 327
International Workers Order, **Retro. Supp. I:** 202
Interpretation of Christian Ethics, An (Niebuhr), **III:** 298–300, 301, 302
"Interpretation of Dreams, The" (Matthews), **Supp. IX:** 162–163
Interpretation of Music of the XVIIth and XVIIIth Centuries, The (Dolmetsch), **III:** 464
Interpretations and Forecasts: 1922–1972 (Mumford), **Supp. II Part 2:** 481
Interpretations of Poetry and Religion (Santayana), **III:** 611
Interpreter of Maladies (Lahiri), **Supp. XXI:** 175–176, **177–180,** 183
"Interpreter of Maladies" (Lahiri), **Supp. XXI:** 183, 184
Interpreters and Interpretations (Van Vechten), **Supp. II Part 2:** 729, 733–734
"Interrogate the Stones" (MacLeish), **III:** 9
"Interrogation of the Prisoner Bung By Mister Hawkins and Sergeant Tree, The" (Huddle), **Supp. XXVI:** 147, 149, 152
Interrogations at Noon (Gioia), **Supp. XV:** 112, **125–127,** 128, 129
"Interrupted Conversation, An" (Van Vechten), **Supp. II Part 2:** 735
"Interrupted Elegy" (Peacock), **Supp. XIX:** 200
Intersect: Poems (Shields), **Supp. VII:** 310–311
Intersexes, The (Prime-Stevenson as Mayne), **Supp. XX: 235**
Interstate (Dixon), **Supp. XII:** 140, 152–153, 153, 156
"Interview" (Hay), **Supp. XIV:** 132
"Interview, The" (Thurber), **Supp. I Part 2:** 616
"Interview With a Lemming" (Thurber), **Supp. I Part 2:** 603
"Interview with Larry Rivers, An"(O'Hara), **Supp. XXIII:** 214
"Interview with Peter Everwine, An" (Veinberg and Buckley), **Supp. XV:** 76–77
"Interview with the Crab" (Lethem), **Supp. XVIII:** 148
Interview with the Vampire (Rice), **Supp. VII:** 287, 288–291, 297–298, 303
"Interview with the Vampire" (Rice), **Supp. VII:** 288
Interzone (Burroughs), **Supp. IV Part 1:** 90
"In the Absence of Bliss" (Kumin), **Supp. IV Part 2:** 453
"In the Afternoon" (Dunn), **Supp. XI:** 146
"In the Alley" (Elkin), **Supp. VI: 46–47**
In the American Grain (W. C. Williams), **Retro. Supp. I:** 420–421
In the American Jungle (W. Frank), **Supp. XX: 76**
In the American Tree (Silliman), **Supp. IV Part 2:** 426
"In the Arboretum" (Stone), **Supp. XXVII:** 260
In the Bank of Beautiful Sins (Wrigley), **Supp. XVIII: 300–302**
In the Bar of a Tokyo Hotel (T. Williams), **IV:** 382, 386, 387, 391, 393
In the Beauty of the Lilies (Updike), **Retro. Supp. I:** 322, 325, 326, 327, 333
"In the Beeyard" (Bierds), **Supp. XVII:** 29
"In the Beginning" (Quindlen), **Supp. XVII:** 166
"In the Beginning . . ." (Simic), **Supp. VIII:** 270, 271
In the Belly of the Beast: Letters from Prison (Abbott), **Retro. Supp. II:** 210
"In the Black Morning" (Wolfert), **Supp. XXI:** 265
"In the Black Museum" (Nemerov), **III:** 275
"In the Blink of God's Eye" (E. P. Jones), **Supp. XXII:** 150
"In the Bodies of Words" (Swenson), **Supp. IV Part 2:** 651
"In the Boston Children's Hospital" (Huddle), **Supp. XXVI:** 151
"In the Box"(Kenny), **Supp. XXIII:** 155
"In the Cage" (Gass), **Supp. VI:** 85
In the Cage (James), **Retro. Supp. I:** 229
"In the Cage" (James), **II:** 332; **Retro. Supp. I:** 231
"In the Cage" (R. Lowell), **Retro. Supp. II:** 187
"In the Cave at Lone Tree Meadow" (Haines), **Supp. XII:** 212
"In the Cemetery Where Al Jolson Is Buried" (Hempel), **Supp. XXI:** 115, **121–122**
"In the City Ringed with Giants" (Kingsolver), **Supp. VII:** 209
"In the Clearing" (Brodsky), **Supp. VIII:** 32
In the Clearing (Frost), **II:** 153, 155, 164; **Retro. Supp. I:** 121, 122, 141; **Retro. Supp. III:** 107
"In the Closet of the Soul" (Walker), **Supp. III Part 2:** 526
"In the Cold Air Register" (W. V. Davis), **Supp. XXI:** 94
"In the Confidence of a Story-Writer" (Chopin), **Retro. Supp. II:** 66–67; **Supp. I Part 1:** 217
In the Country of Last Things (Auster), **Supp. XII:** 23, **29–30,** 31, 32
"In the Courtyard of the Isleta Missions" (R. Bly), **Supp. IV Part 1:** 71
"In the Dark" (Levine), **Supp. V:** 194
In the Dark (Stone), **Supp. XXVII:** 257
"In the Dark New England Days" (Jewett), **Retro. Supp. II:** 139

"In the Days of Prismatic Colour" (Moore), **III:** 205, 213
In the Days of the Comet (Wells), **Supp. XX: 233, 240**
In the Electric Mist with Confederate Dead (Burke), **Supp. XIV:** 30, 31–32
"In the Field" (Wilbur), **Supp. III Part 2:** 558
"In the 51st State" (Berrigan), **Supp. XXIV:** 35
"In the First Stanza" (C. Kizer), **Supp. XVII:** 75
"In the Fleeting Hand of Time" (Corso), **Supp. XII:** 122–123
"In the Footsteps of Gutenberg" (Mencken), **III:** 101
"In the Forest" (Simpson), **Supp. IX:** 270
"In the Forest of the Laughing Elephant" (Caputo), **Supp. XIX:** 27
"In the Forties" (R. Lowell), **II:** 554
"In the Garden" (Ferry), **Supp. XXIV:** 153
In the Garden of the North American Martyrs (Wolff), **Supp. VII:** 341–342
In the Garret (Van Vechten), **Supp. II Part 2:** 735
"In the Grove: The Poet at Ten" (Kenyon), **Supp. VII:** 160
"In the Hall of Mirrors" (Merrill), **Supp. III Part 1:** 322
In the Harbor (Longfellow), **II:** 491
In the Heart of the Heart of the Country (Gass), **Supp. VI: 82–83,** 84, 85, 93
In the Heat of the Night (Ball), **Supp. XV:** 202
In the Heat of the Night (film), **Supp. I Part 1:** 67
In the Hollow of His Hand (Purdy), **Supp. VII:** 278–280
In the House of Light (Everwine, trans.), **Supp. XV:** 73, 75, **76–78,** 82
"In the Laboratory of Kisses" (Gallagher), **Supp. XXIV:** 170
In the Lake of the Woods (O'Brien), **Supp. V:** 240, 243, 250–252
In the Land of the White Death: A Epic Story of Survival in the Siberian Arctic (Albanov), **Supp. XVIII:** 114
"In the Last Days" (Everwine), **Supp. XV:** 88, 89
"In the Late Summer Garden"(Crooker), **Supp. XXIII:** 55
In the Loyal Mountains (Bass), **Supp. XVI: 19–20**
"In the Loyal Mountains" (Bass), **Supp. XVI:** 20
"In the Mean Mud Season" (Huddle), **Supp. XXVI:** 154
In the Mecca (Brooks), **Supp. III Part 1:** 74
"In the Mecca" (Brooks), **Supp. III Part 1:** 70, 83–84
"In the Metropolitan Museum" (Teasdale), **Supp. XXVII:** 289
In the Midst of Life (Bierce), **I:** 200–203, 204, 206, 208, 212
"In the Miro District" (Taylor), **Supp. V:** 323
In the Miro District and Other Stories (Taylor), **Supp. V:** 325–326
In the Money (W. C. Williams), **Retro. Supp. I:** 423
"In the Motel" (X. J. Kennedy), **Supp. XV:** 163
"In the Naked Bed, in Plato's Cave" (Schwartz), **Supp. II Part 2:** 646–649
In the Name of the Neither (Sobin), **Supp. XVI:** 291
In the Next Galaxy (Stone), **Supp. XXVII:** 257, 262
"In the Next Galaxy" (Stone), **Supp. XXVII:** 253
"In the Night" (Kincaid), **Supp. VII:** 183
In the Night Season: A Novel (Bausch), **Supp. VII:** 52–53
"In the Old Neighborhood" (Dove), **Supp. IV Part 1:** 241, 257
"In the Old World" (Oates), **Supp. II Part 2:** 503, 504
"In the Park" (Biss), **Supp. XXVI:** 48
"In the Park" (Huncke), **Supp. XIV:** 139
In the Pines (Notley), **Supp. XXII:** 236–237
"In the Pit" (Proulx), **Supp. VII:** 255, 261
In the Pond (Jin), **Supp. XVIII: 95–96**
In the Presence of the Sun (Momaday), **Supp. IV Part 2:** 489, 490, 491–493, 493
"In the Quiet Night" (Li Po), **Supp. XV:** 47
"In the Realm of the Fisher King" (Didion), **Supp. IV Part 1:** 211
"In the Red Room" (Bowles), **Supp. IV Part 1:** 93
"In the Region of Ice" (Oates), **Supp. II Part 2:** 520
In the Room We Share (Simpson), **Supp. IX:** 279
"In These Dissenting Times" (Walker), **Supp. III Part 2:** 522
"In the Shadow of Gabriel, A.D.1550" (Frederic), **II:** 139
In the Shadow of Memory (Skloot), **Supp. XX: 193, 196, 205, 205–206**
"In the Shadow of Memory" (Skloot), **Supp. XX: 206**
In the Shadow of the Morning: Essays on Wild Lands, Wild Waters, and a Few Untamed People (Caputo), **Supp. XIX:** 28–29
In the Spirit of Crazy Horse (Matthiessen), **Supp. V:** 211
"In the Subway" (Untermeyer), **Supp. XV:** 296
In the Summer House (Jane Bowles), **Supp. IV Part 1:** 83, 89
"In the Syntax: Rewriting Joan Didion's 'Goodbye to All That' " (Biss), **Supp. XXVI:** 54
In the Tennessee Country (Taylor), **Supp. V:** 328
"In the Thick of Darkness" (Salinas), **Supp. XIII:** 325
In the Time of Butterflies (Alvarez), **Supp. XXIV:** 89
"In the Time of the Blossoms" (Mervin), **Supp. III Part 1:** 352
In the Time of the Butterflies (Alvarez), **Supp. VII:** 1, 12–15, 18
In the Time of the Present (Kenny), **Supp. XXIII:** 146, **156**
"In the Tube" (Jarman), **Supp. XVII:** 121
"In the Tunnel Bone of Cambridge" (Corso), **Supp. XII:** 120–121
"In the Upper Pastures" (Kumin), **Supp. IV Part 2:** 453
In the Valley (Frederic), **II:** 133–134, 136, 137
"In the Village" (Bishop), **Retro. Supp. II:** 38; **Supp. I Part 1:** 73, 74–75, 76, 77, 78, 88
"In the Waiting Room" (Bishop), **Retro. Supp. II:** 50; **Supp. I Part 1:** 81, 94, 95; **Supp. IV Part 1:** 249
In the Walled City (O'Nan), **Supp. XXV:** 142
"In the Ward: The Sacred Wood" (Jarrell), **II:** 376, 377
In the Western Night: Collected Poems 1965–90 (Bidart), **Supp. XV:** 19, **30–32**
"In the White Night" (Beattie), **Supp. V:** 30–31
"In the Wind My Rescue Is" (Ammons), **Supp. VII:** 25
"In the Winter Dark" (Peacock), **Supp. XIX:** 206
In the Winter of Cities (T. Williams), **IV:** 383
"In the X-Ray of the Sarcophagus of

Ta-pero" (Goldbarth), **Supp. XII:** 191
"In the Yard" (Swenson), **Supp. IV Part 2:** 647
In the Zone (O'Neill), **III:** 388
In This, Our Life (film), **Supp. I Part 1:** 67
"In This Country, but in Another Language, My Aunt Refuses to Marry the Men Everyone Wants Her To" (Paley), **Supp. VI:** 225
"In This Dream" (J. W. Miller), **Supp. XX: 170**
In This Hung-up Age (Corso), **Supp. XII: 119–120,** 129
In This Our Life (Glasgow), **II:** 175, 178, 189
In This Our World (Gilman), **Supp. XI:** 196, 200, 202
"In Those Days" (Jarrell), **II:** 387–388
"Intimately Connected to the Zeitgeist" (Franzen), **Supp. XX: 94**
Intimates (Huddle), **Supp. XXVI:** 155–156
"In Time of War" (Auden), **Supp. II Part 1:** 8, 13
In Times Like These (Edgell), **Supp. XXIII:** 84, **89–90,** 94
"Into Egypt" (Benét), **Supp. XI:** 56, 57–58
Intolerance (film; Griffith), **Supp. XVI:** 184
"Into My Own" (Frost), **II:** 153; **Retro. Supp. I:** 127; **Retro. Supp. III:** 94–95
Into My Own: The English Years of Robert Frost (Walsh), **Retro. Supp. III:** 95
"Into Night" (McKnight), **Supp. XX: 151–152**
"Into the Gorge" (Rash), **Supp. XXVII:** 228
Into the Interior (Cliff), **Supp. XXII:** 67, 78–79
"Into the Night Life . . ." (H. Miller), **III:** 180, 184
"Into the Nowhere" (Rawlings), **Supp. X:** 220
Into the Stone (Dickey), **Supp. IV Part 1:** 178
"Into the Stone" (Dickey), **Supp. IV Part 1:** 179
Into the Stone and Other Poems (Dickey), **Supp. IV Part 1:** 176
"Into the Streets May First" (Hayes), **Supp. XXVI:** 134, 144
Into the Wild (Krakauer), **Supp. XVIII:** 106, **107–108,** 116, 117
Into Thin Air: A Personal Account of the Mount Everest Disaster (Krakauer), **Supp. XVII:** 210; **Supp. XVIII:** 105, **109–113,** 117
In Touch: The Letters of Paul Bowles (J. Miller, ed.), **Supp. IV Part 1:** 95
"Intoxicated, The" (Jackson), **Supp. IX:** 116
"Intrigue" (Crane), **I:** 419
Introducing Irony: A Book of Poetic Short Stories and Poems (Bodenheim), **Supp. XXV:** 22–23
"Introducing the Fathers" (Kumin), **Supp. IV Part 2:** 452
Introductio ad Prudentiam (Fuller), **II:** 111
"Introduction"(Strout; Ploughshares spring 2010), **Supp. XXIII:** 284
"Introduction to a Haggadah" (Paley), **Supp. VI:** 219
Introduction to Objectivist Epistemology (Rand), **Supp. IV Part 2:** 527, 528–529
Introduction to Objectivist Epistemology 2nd ed. (Rand), **Supp. IV Part 2:** 529
"Introduction to Poetry" (Collins), **Supp. XXI:** 57
Introduction to Poetry, An (Gioia and X. J. Kennedy), **Supp. XV:** 113, 153
"Introduction to Some Poems, An" (Stafford), **Supp. XI:** 311, 324
Introduction to the Geography of Iowa, The (Doty), **Supp. XI:** 120
"Introduction to the Hoh" (Hugo), **Supp. VI:** 136–137
"Introduction to The New Writing in the USA" (Creeley), **Supp. IV Part 1:** 153–154
"Introduction to William Blake, An" (Kazin), **Supp. VIII:** 103
Introitus (Longfellow), **II:** 505, 506–507
"Intruder, The" (Dubus), **Supp. VII:** 76–78, 91
Intruder, The (Maeterlinck), **I:** 91
Intruder in the Dust (Faulkner), **II:** 71, 72; **Retro. Supp. III:** 86, 87; **Supp. XVI:** 148
Intuition (Goodman), **Supp. XXVI:** 128–130
"Invaders, The" (Haines), **Supp. XII:** 205
Invaders, The (W. Frank), **Supp. XX: 79–80**
Invasion (Myers), **Supp. XXVII:** 207
Invasion of Privacy: The Cross Creek Trial of Marjorie Kinnan Rawlings (Acton), **Supp. X:** 233
Inventing Memory: A Novel of Mothers and Daughters (Jong), **Supp. V:** 115, 129
Inventing the Abbotts (Miller), **Supp. XII: 294–295**
"Invention of Autobiography. The" (Hampl), **Supp. XXII:** 93–94
"Invention of God in a Mouthful of Milk, The" (Karr), **Supp. XI:** 250
Invention of Solitude, The (Auster), **Supp. XII:** 21–22
"Inventions of the March Hare" (Eliot), **Retro. Supp. I:** 55
Inventions of the March Hare (T. S. Eliot), **Retro. Supp. I:** 55–56, 58; **Retro. Supp. III:** 59
"Inventory" (Parker), **Supp. IX:** 192
Inverness, Amy Beth, **Supp. XXVII:** 103
"Inverted Forest, The" (Salinger), **III:** 552, 572
"Investigation" (Ryan as Quin), **Supp. XVIII:** 227–228
"Investigations of a Dog" (Kafka), **IV:** 438
"Investiture, The" (Banks), **Supp. V:** 7
"Investiture at Cecconi's" (Merrill), **Supp. III Part 1:** 336
"Invicibility"(O'Hara), **Supp. XXIII:** 214
"Invisible" (Pickering), **Supp. XXI:** 201
Invisible Circus, The (Egan), **Supp. XIX:** 49, **50–52**
Invisible Company, The (Sanders), **Supp. XVI:** 270–271
Invisible Man (Ellison), **IV:** 493; **Retro. Supp. II:** 3, 12, 111, 112, 113, 117, 119, **120–123,** 125; **Supp. II Part 1:** 40, 170, 221, 224, 226, 227, 230, 231–232, 235, 236, 241–245; **Supp. IX:** 306; **Supp. X:** 242; **Supp. XI:** 18, 92; **Supp. XIX:** 154, 155; **Supp. XVIII:** 59; **Supp. XXVI:** 215
Invisible: Poems (Nye), **Supp. XIII:** 277
Invisible Spectator, An (Sawyer-Lauçanno), **Supp. IV Part 1:** 95
Invisible Swords (Farrell), **II:** 27, 46, 48–49
Invisible Worm, The (Millar), **Supp. IV Part 2:** 465
Invitation to a Beheading (Nabokov), **III:** 252–253, 254, 257–258; **Retro. Supp. I:** 265, 270, 273
"Invitation to the Country, An" (Bryant), **Supp. I Part 1:** 160
"Invocation" (H. Johnson), **Supp. XXVI:** 166, 174
"Invocation" (McKay), **Supp. X:** 134
Invocation (Rash), **Supp. XXVII:** 217

"Invocation" (Untermeyer), **Supp. XV:** 296
"Invocation to Kali" (Sarton), **Supp. VIII:** 260
"Invocation: To my Maternal Grandfather on hearing his descent from Chippewa ancestors misrepresented"(J. Schoolcraft), **Supp. XXIII:** 232
"Invocation to the Social Muse" (MacLeish), **III:** 15
"In Weather" (Hass), **Supp. VI: 102–103**
In Writing Huck Finn: Mark Twain's Creative Process (Doyno), **Retro. Supp. III:** 265
"In Your Fugitive Dream" (Hugo), **Supp. VI:** 143
"In Your Good Dream" (Hugo), **Supp. VI:** 143–144
"Iola, Kansas" (Clampitt), **Supp. IX: 45–46**
Iola Leroy (Harper), **Supp. XVIII:** 284
Ion (Doolittle, trans.), **Supp. I Part 1:** 269, 274
Ion (Plato), **I:** 523
"Ione" (Dunbar), **Supp. II Part 1:** 199
Ionesco, Eugène, **I:** 71, 74, 75, 84, 295; **II:** 435; **Supp. VIII:** 201; **Supp. XIX:** 131; **Supp. XXIV:** 113
Ionica (Cory), **Supp. XX: 230**
Ionica II (Cory), **Supp. XX: 230**
"I Only Am Escaped Alone to Tell Thee" (Nemerov), **III:** 272, 273–274
"I Opened All the Portals Wide" (Chopin), **Retro. Supp. II:** 71
I Ought to Be in Pictures (Simon), **Supp. IV Part 2:** 584
Iphigenia (Notley), **Supp. XXII:** 226, 235
Iphigenia in Tauris (Euripedes), **Supp. XV:** 42, 50
I Promessi Sposi (Manzoni), **II:** 291
"I Put My Hand on My Son's Head" (Kooser), **Supp. XIX:** 120
Iram, Dhát al-'Imád (Gibran), **Supp. XX: 116**
"Iraq Drifting, July 2003" (Weigl), **Supp. XIX:** 288
"Irascibles, The" (Kees), **Supp. XV:** 145–146
Ireland: A Terrible Beauty (Uris), **Supp. XX: 244, 245–246, 246, 254**
I Remember (Brainard), **Supp. XXVII:** 17, 18, 26, 29
I Remember (collected edition, Brainard), **Supp. XXVII:** 19
"I Remember" (Sexton), **Supp. II Part 2:** 680
I Remember Christmas (Brainard), **Supp. XXVII:** 19
I Remember More (Brainard), **Supp. XXVII:** 19
"Irene" (Poe), **Retro. Supp. III:** 231
"Irenicon" (Shapiro), **Supp. II Part 2:** 704
Irigaray, Luce, **Supp. XII:** 6
Iris (Jarman), **Supp. XVII:** 110, **116–117**
"Iris by Night" (Frost), **Retro. Supp. I:** 132
"Irises" (L.-Y. Lee), **Supp. XV:** 214–215
Irish in America, The (Coffey, ed.), **Supp. XIX:** 133
Irish Stories of Sarah Orne Jewett, The (Jewett), **Retro. Supp. II:** 142
Irish Triangle, An (Barnes), **Supp. III Part 1:** 34
"Iron Characters, The" (Nemerov), **III:** 279, 282
"Iron Hans" (Sexton), **Supp. II Part 2:** 691
Iron Heel, The (London), **II:** 466, 480
Iron John: A Book about Men (R. Bly), **Supp. IV Part 1:** 59, 67; **Supp. XVI:** 177
"Iron Table, The" (Jane Bowles), **Supp. IV Part 1:** 82–83
"Iron Throat, The" (Olsen), **Supp. XIII:** 292, 297, 299
Ironweed (W. Kennedy), **Supp. VII:** 132, 133, 134, 135, 142, 144, 145–147, 148, 150, 153
"Irony as Art: The Short Fiction of William Humphrey" (Tebeaux), **Supp. IX:** 109
"Irony Is Not Enough: Essay on My Life as Catherine Deneuve" (Carson), **Supp. XII: 112–113**
Irony of American History, The (Niebuhr), **III:** 292, 306–307, 308
"Irrational Element in Poetry, The" (Stevens), **Retro. Supp. I:** 298, 301
"Irrevocable Diameter, An" (Paley), **Supp. VI:** 231–232
Irvine, Lorna, **Supp. XIII:** 26
Irving, Ebenezer, **II:** 296
Irving, Sir Henry, **IV:** 350
Irving, John, **Supp. VI: 163–183; Supp. X:** 77, 85
Irving, John Treat, **II:** 296
Irving, Peter, **II:** 296, 297, 298, 299, 300, 303
Irving, Washington, **I:** 211, 335, 336, 339, 343; **II: 295–318,** 488, 495; **III:** 113; **IV:** 309; **Retro. Supp. I:** 246; **Supp. I Part 1:** 155, 157, 158, 317; **Supp. I Part 2:** 377, 487, 585; **Supp. II Part 1:** 335; **Supp. IV Part 1:** 380; **Supp. XVIII:** 12; **Supp. XXIII:** 178
Irving, William, **II:** 296
Irving, William, Jr., **II:** 296, 297, 298, 299, 303
Irwin, Mark, **Supp. XII:** 21, 22, 24, 29
Irwin, Robert, **Supp. XX: 120**
Irwin, William Henry, **Supp. II Part 1:** 192
Is 5 (Cummings), **I:** 429, 430, 434, 435, 440, 445, 446, 447
"Isaac and Abraham" (Brodsky), **Supp. VIII:** 21
"Isaac and Archibald" (Robinson), **III:** 511, 521, 523
Isaacs, Neil D., **Supp. XIX:** 255
"Isabelle" (Saunders), **Supp. XIX:** 225
"Isabel Sparrow" (Oliver), **Supp. VII:** 232
Isaiah (biblical book), **Supp. I Part 1:** 236; **Supp. I Part 2:** 516; **Supp. XXI:** 107
"Isaiah Beethoven" (Masters), **Supp. I Part 2:** 461
I Sailed with Magellan (Dybek), **Supp. XXIII: 75–78,** 79
"I Saw in Louisiana a Live-Oak Growing" (Whitman), **I:** 220
"I Shall Be Released" (Dylan), **Supp. XV:** 349
"I Shall Live to Be Old" (Teasdale), **Supp. XXVII:** 296
I Shall Spit on Your Graves (film), **Supp. I Part 1:** 67
Isháq, Adib, **Supp. XX: 117**
Isherwood, Christopher, **II:** 586; **Supp. II Part 1:** 10, 11, 13; **Supp. IV Part 1:** 79, 82, 102; **Supp. XI:** 305; **Supp. XIV: 155–175; Supp. XVI:** 194
Isherwood Century, The (Berg and Freeman), **Supp. XIV:** 157, 159
Isherwood's Fiction (Schwerdt), **Supp. XIV:** 155
Ishiguro, Kazuo, **Supp. VIII:** 15
Ishi Means Man (Merton), **Supp. VIII:** 208
"Ishmael's Dream" (Stern), **Supp. IX:** 287
I Should Have Stayed Home (McCoy), **Supp. XIII:** 167, **168–170,** 171
"I Should Worry" (Kees), **Supp. XV:** 140
"I Sigh in the Afternoon" (Salinas), **Supp. XIII:** 318
"I Sing the Body Electric" (Whitman), **Retro. Supp. I:** 394, 395; **Retro. Supp. III:** 305
"Isis: Dorothy Eady, 1924" (Doty),

Supp. XI: 122
"Is It O.K. to Be a Luddite?" (Pynchon), **Supp. XVI:** 128
"Is It True?" (Hughes), **Supp. I Part 1:** 342
I: Six Nonlectures (Cummings), **I:** 430, 433, 434
"Island" (Hughes), **Supp. I Part 1:** 340
"Island Fever" (Vaz), **Supp. XXVI:** 261
Island Garden, An (Thaxter), **Retro. Supp. II:** 136; **Supp. XIII:** 152
Island Holiday, An (Henry), **I:** 515
Island in the Atlantic (W. Frank), **Supp. XX: 79**
Island in the Sun (film), **Supp. XXVI:** 134
"Island of the Fay, The" (Poe), **III:** 412, 417
Islands (Siddons), **Supp. XXII:** 239
"Islands, The" (Hayden), **Supp. II Part 1:** 373
"Island Sheaf, An" (Doty), **Supp. XI:** 136
Islands in the Stream (Hemingway), **II:** 258; **Retro. Supp. I:** 186
Isn't It Romantic (Wasserstein), **Supp. XV: 323–325,** 327
Is Objectivism a Religion? (Ellis), **Supp. IV Part 2:** 527
"Isolation of Modern Poetry, The" (Schwartz), **Supp. II Part 2:** 644
"Israel" (Reznikoff), **Supp. XIV:** 283
Israel Potter: His Fifty Years of Exile (Melville), **III:** 90; **Retro. Supp. III:** 158–159; **Supp. XVIII:** 4
"Israfel" (Poe), **III:** 411
Is Sex Necessary? (Thurber and White), **Supp. I Part 2:** 607, 612, 614, 653
"Issues, The" (Olds), **Supp. X:** 205
"Istanbul" (Collins), **Supp. XXI:** 60
"I Stand Here Ironing" (Olsen), **Supp. XIII:** 292, 294, 296, 298, 300, 305
I Stole a Million (West), **IV:** 287
"Is Verse a Dying Technique?" (Wilson), **IV:** 431
It (Creeley), **Supp. IV Part 1:** 157, 158
IT (King), **Supp. V:** 139, 140, 141, 146–147, 151, 152
"It" (Olds), **Supp. X:** 208
It Ain't All for Nothin' (Myers), **Supp. XXVII:** 202–203
Italian American Reconciliation: A Folktale (Shanley), **Supp. XIV:** 315, **324–326,** 328, 330
Italian Backgrounds (Wharton), **Retro. Supp. I:** 370; **Retro. Supp. III:** 279
Italian Hours (James), **I:** 12; **II:** 337; **Retro. Supp. I:** 235
Italian Journeys (Howells), **II:** 274
"Italian Morning" (Bogan), **Supp. III Part 1:** 58
Italian Villas and Their Gardens (Wharton), **IV:** 308; **Retro. Supp. I:** 361, 367; **Retro. Supp. III:** 279–280
Italie, Hillel, **Supp. XV:** 128
It All Adds Up: From the Dim Past to the Uncertain Future (Bellow), **Retro. Supp. II:** 32
"It Always Breaks Out" (Ellison), **Retro. Supp. II:** 126; **Supp. II Part 1:** 248
Itard, Jean-Marc Gaspard, **Supp. I Part 2:** 564
"I taste a liquor never brewed" (Dickinson), **Retro. Supp. I:** 30, 37
It Came from Outer Space (film), **Supp. IV Part 1:** 102
It Can't Happen Here (Lewis), **II:** 454
It Chooses You (July), **Supp. XXIV:** 199, 209, 210
"It Don't Mean a Thing If It Ain't Got That Swing" (Matthews), **Supp. IX: 164–165**
I Tell You Now (Ortiz), **Supp. IV Part 2:** 500
"It Follows" (Stone), **Supp. XXVII:** 257
"It Goes Something Like This" (Gansworth), **Supp. XXVI:** 110
"Ithaca" (Glück), **Supp. V:** 89
It Happened One Night (Capra), **Supp. XV:** 197
It Has Come to Pass (Farrell), **II:** 26
"I think to live May be a Bliss" (Dickinson), **Retro. Supp. I:** 44
"I Thought It Was Harry" (Bronk), **Supp. XXI:** 31
I Thought of Daisy (Wilson), **IV:** 428, 434, 435
"It If Be Your Will" (Cohen), **Supp. XXVII:** 60
"Itinerary of an Obsession" (Kumin), **Supp. IV Part 2:** 450
"It Is a Strange Country" (Ellison), **Supp. II Part 1:** 238
"It Is Dangerous to Read Newspapers" (Atwood), **Supp. XIII:** 33
"It Is the Lesbian in Us ..." (Rich), **Retro. Supp. III:** 248
"It Must Be Abstract" (Stevens), **IV:** 95; **Retro. Supp. I:** 307
"It Must Change" (Stevens), **Retro. Supp. I:** 300, 307, 308
"It Must Give Pleasure" (Stevens), **Retro. Supp. I:** 307, 308, 309
"'It Out-Herods Herod. Pray You, Avoid It' " (Hecht), **Supp. X:** 62, 64
"It's All Over Now, Baby Blue" (song, Dylan), **Supp. XVIII:** 30
It's Loaded, Mr. Bauer (Marquand), **III:** 59
It's Nation Time (Baraka), **Supp. II Part 1:** 52, 53
"It's Nation Time" (Baraka), **Supp. II Part 1:** 53
It's Only a Play (McNally), **Supp. XIII:** 198
"It's Tartt—But Is It Art?" (Vanity Fair), **Supp. XXVII:** 277
It Was (Zukofsky), **Supp. III Part 2:** 630
"It Was Romance" (July), **Supp. XXIV:** 202–203
It Was the Nightingale (Ford), **III:** 470–471
"It Was When" (Snyder), **Supp. VIII:** 300
Ivanhoe (Scott), **I:** 216; **Supp. I Part 2:** 410
Ivens, Bryna, **Supp. XV:** 311, 312
Ivens, Joris, **I:** 488; **Retro. Supp. I:** 184
"Iverson Boy, The" (Simpson), **Supp. IX:** 280
"Ives" (Rukeyser), **Supp. VI:** 273, 283
Ives, George H., **Supp. I Part 1:** 153
I've Seen the Promised Land (Myers), **Supp. XXVII:** 209
Ivory Grin, The (Macdonald), **Supp. IV Part 2:** 471, 472
"Ivory Novel, The" (Halliday), **Supp. XIX:** 90
Ivory Tower, The (James), **II:** 337–338
"Ivory Tower, The: Louis Untermeyer as Critic" (Aiken), **Supp. XV:** 298
Ivry, Sara, **Supp. XX: 179**
"Ivy Winding" (Ammons), **Supp. VII:** 33
Iwamatsu, Mako, **Supp. XXI:** 150
"I Wandered Lonely as a Cloud" (Wordsworth), **Retro. Supp. I:** 121–122; **Supp. X:** 73; **Supp. XIV:** 184
"I want, I want" (Plath), **Retro. Supp. II:** 246
"I Wanted to Be There When My Father Died" (Olds), **Supp. X:** 210
"I Want to Be a Father Like the Men" (Cisneros), **Supp. VII:** 71
"I Want to Be Miss America" (Alvarez), **Supp. VII:** 18
"I Want to Know Why" (Anderson), **I:** 114, 115, 116; **II:** 263
"I Want You Women Up North To Know" (Olsen), **Supp. XIII:** 292, 297

"I Was Born in Lucerne" (Levine), **Supp. V:** 181, 189
"I Was Marching"(Le Sueur), **Supp. XXIII:** 167
"I Was Really Very Hungry" (M. F. K. Fisher), **Supp. XVII:** 91
"I Went into the Maverick Bar" (Snyder), **Supp. VIII:** 301
"I Will Lie Down" (Swenson), **Supp. IV Part 2:** 640
I Will Say Beauty (C. Frost), **Supp. XV:** 96, **105–107**
I Wonder As I Wander (Hughes), **Retro. Supp. I:** 196, 203; **Supp. I Part 1:** 329, 332–333
I Would Have Saved Them If I Could (L. Michaels), **Supp. XVI:** 203, 205, **206–210**
"I Would Live in Your Love" (Teasdale), **Supp. XXVII:** 292
"Iya, the Camp-Eater" (Zitkala-Ša), **Supp. XXV:** 276
"Iyani: It goes this Way" (Gunn Allen), **Supp. IV Part 1:** 321
"I years had been from home" (Dickinson), **I:** 471
Iyer, Pico, **Supp. V:** 215
Izzo, David Garrett, **Supp. XIV:** 155, 156, 159, 160, 161, 163, 169, 171
Jab (Halliday), **Supp. XIX: 91–94**
"Jachid and Jechidah" (Singer), **IV:** 15
Jack and Jill (Alcott), **Supp. I Part 1:** 42
"Jack and the Beanstalk" (Hay), **Supp. XIV:** 124
"Jack in the Pot" (D. West), **Supp. XVIII:** 283
Jack Kelso (Masters), **Supp. I Part 2:** 456, 471–472
Jacklight (Erdrich), **Supp. IV Part 1:** 259, 270
Jack London, Hemingway, and the Constitution (Doctorow), **Supp. IV Part 1:** 220, 222, 224, 232, 235
Jackman, Harold, **Supp. XVIII:** 131
Jackpot (Caldwell), **I:** 304
"Jack Schmidt, Arts Administrator" (Keillor), **Supp. XVI:** 171
"Jack Schmidt on the Burning Sands" (Keillor), **Supp. XVI:** 171
Jackson, Amelia. See Holmes, Mrs. Oliver Wendell (Amelia Jackson)
Jackson, Andrew, **I:** 7, 20; **III:** 473; **IV:** 192, 248, 298, 334, 348; **Supp. I Part 2:** 456, 461, 473, 474, 493, 695
Jackson, Blyden, **Supp. I Part 1:** 337
Jackson, Charles, **Supp. I Part 1:** 303
Jackson, David Kelly, **Retro. Supp. III:** 237
Jackson, George, **Supp. I Part 1:** 66
Jackson, Helen Hunt, **I:** 459, 470; **Retro. Supp. I:** 26, 27, 30–31, 32, 33
Jackson, James, **Supp. I Part 1:** 302, 303
Jackson, J. O., **III:** 213
Jackson, Joe, **Supp. I Part 2:** 441
Jackson, Katherine Gauss, **Supp. VIII:** 124
Jackson, Lawrence, **Retro. Supp. II:** 113, 115
Jackson, Lawrence P., **Supp. XXII:** 140
Jackson, Melanie, **Supp. X:** 166
Jackson, Michael, **Supp. VIII:** 146
Jackson, Richard, **II:** 119; **Supp. IX:** 165
Jackson, Shelley, **Supp. XVIII:** 136
Jackson, Shirley, **Supp. IX: 113–130**
Jackson, Thomas J. ("Stonewall"), **IV:** 125, 126
"Jackson Hotel" (Hull), **Supp. XXI:** 134, 135
Jackson Pollock (O'Hara), **Supp. XXIII:** 214–215
"Jackson Square" (Levertov), **Supp. III Part 1:** 276
Jackstraws (Simic), **Supp. VIII:** 280, 282–283
"Jackstraws" (Simic), **Supp. VIII: 283**
Jack Tier (Cooper), **I:** 354, 355
"Jacob" (Garrett), **Supp. VII:** 109–110
"Jacob" (Schwartz), **Supp. II Part 2:** 663
Jacob, Max, **Supp. XV:** 178, 182
"Jacob and the Indians" (Benét), **Supp. XI:** 47–48
"Jacob Bayer and the Telephone" (Helprin), **Supp. XXV:** 81
Jacobs, Catherine Haydon, **Supp. XXI:** 98
Jacobs, Harriet, **Supp. XVI:** 85
Jacobs, Jill Suzanne, **Supp. XX: 178, 186**
Jacobs, Rita D., **Supp. XII:** 339
Jacobsen, Jens Peter, **Retro. Supp. III:** 140
Jacobsen, Josephine, **Supp. XIII:** 346; **Supp. XIV:** 260
"Jacob's Ladder" (Rawlings), **Supp. X:** 224, 228
Jacob's Ladder, The (Levertov), **Supp. III Part 1:** 272, 276–278, 281
"Jacob's Ladder, The" (Levertov), **Supp. III Part 1:** 278
Jacobson, Dale, **Supp. X:** 112
Jacobson, Kristin, **Supp. XVIII:** 113
Jacobson, Leslie, **Supp. XV:** 323
Jacoby, Russell, **Supp. IV Part 2:** 692
"Jacquerie, The" (Lanier), **Supp. I Part 1:** 355, 356, 360, 364, 370
Jacques le fataliste (D. Diderot), **Supp. XVII:** 145
Jade Mountain, The: A Chinese Anthology, Being Three Hundred Poems of the T'ang Dynasty (Bynner, trans.), **II:** 527; **Supp. XV:** 46, 47, 48
Jafsie and John Henry: Essays on Hollywood, Bad Boys, and Six Hours of Perfect Poker (Mamet), **Supp. XIV:** 252
Jaggi, Maya, **Supp. XXV:** 50, 56, 57
Jaguar Totem (LaBastille), **Supp. X:** 99, 106, **107–109**
Jailbird (Vonnegut), **Supp. II Part 2:** 760, 779–780
Jaimes, M. Annette, **Supp. IV Part 1:** 330, 331
Jain, Manju, **Retro. Supp. I:** 53, 58
"Jake Flower, The" (Major), **Supp. XXII:** 182
Jake's Women (Simon), **Supp. IV Part 2:** 576, 588
"Jakie's Mother" (Fante), **Supp. XI:** 164
Jakobson, Roman, **Supp. IV Part 1:** 155
Jamaica 1968 (Brainard), **Supp. XXVII:** 27
"Jamaica Kincaid's New York" (Kincaid), **Supp. VII:** 181
James, Alice, **I:** 454; **Retro. Supp. I:** 228, 235
James, A. Lloyd, **Supp. XIV:** 343
James, Caryn, **Supp. X:** 302, 303
James, C. L. R., **Retro. Supp. III:** 162
James, C. L. R. (Cyril Lionel Robert), **Supp. XXI: 159–173**
James, Etta, **Supp. X:** 242
James, Henry, **I:** 4, 5, 9, 10, 12, 15, 16, 20, 52, 93, 109, 211, 226, 228, 244, 246, 251, 255, 258, 259, 336, 363, 374, 375, 379, 384, 409, 429, 436, 439, 452, 454, 459, 461–462, 463, 464, 485, 500, 504, 513, 514, 517–518, 571; **II:** 38, 58, 60, 73, 74, 95, 138, 140, 144, 147, 196, 198, 199, 228, 230, 234, 243, 259, 267, 271, 272, 275, 276, 278, 281, 282, 283, 284, 285, 286, 287, 288, 290, 306, 309, 316, **319–341,** 398, 404, 410, 415, 427, 444, 542, 544, 547–548, 556, 600; **III:** 44, 51, 136, 194–195, 199, 206, 208, 218, 228–229, 237, 281, 319, 325, 326, 334, 409, 453, 454, 457, 460, 461, 464, 511, 522, 576, 607; **IV:** 8, 27, 34, 37, 40, 53, 58, 73, 74, 134, 168, 172, 182, 198, 202, 285, 308, 309, 310,

311, 314, 316, 317, 318, 319, 321, 322, 323, 324, 328, 347, 352, 359, 433, 439, 476; **Retro. Supp. I:** 1, 8, 53, 56, 59, 108, 112, **215–242,** 272, 283, 284, 362, 366, 367, 368, 371, 373, 374, 375, 376, 377, 378, 379; **Retro. Supp. II:** 93, 135, 136, 203, 223; **Retro. Supp. III:** 20, 22, 26, 60, 275, 279, 281; **Supp. I Part 1:** 35, 38, 43; **Supp. I Part 2:** 414, 454, 608, 609, 612–613, 618, 620, 646; **Supp. II Part 1:** 94–95; **Supp. III Part 1:** 14, 200; **Supp. III Part 2:** 410, 412; **Supp. IV Part 1:** 31, 35, 80, 127, 197, 349, 353; **Supp. IV Part 2:** 613, 677, 678, 682, 689, 693; **Supp. IX:** 121; **Supp. V:** 97, 101, 103, 258, 261, 263, 313; **Supp. VIII:** 98, 102, 156, 166, 168; **Supp. XI:** 153; **Supp. XIII:** 102; **Supp. XIV:** 40, 110, 112, 335, 336, 348, 349; **Supp. XV:** 41; **Supp. XVII:** 5, 47; **Supp. XVIII:** 160, 258; **Supp. XX: 227, 228, 232, 233, 238, 240; Supp. XXI:** 225; **Supp. XXII:** 89; **Supp. XXIV:** 132, 224; **Supp. XXVI:** 141, 145; **Supp. XXVII:** 268
James, Henry (father), **II:** 7, 275, 321, 337, 342–344, 364; **IV:** 174; **Supp. I Part 1:** 300
James, Henry (nephew), **II:** 360
James, Horace, **Supp. XIV:** 57
James, P. D., **Supp. XIX:** 131
James, William, **I:** 104, 220, 224, 227, 228, 255, 454; **II:** 20, 27, 165, 166, 276, 321, 337, **342–366,** 411; **III:** 303, 309, 509, 599, 600, 605, 606, 612; **IV:** 26, 27, 28–29, 31, 32, 34, 36, 37, 43, 46, 291, 486; **Retro. Supp. I:** 57, 216, 227, 228, 235, 295, 300, 306; **Retro. Supp. III:** 99; **Supp. I Part 1:** 3, 7, 11, 20; **Supp. XIV:** 40, 50, 197, 199, 212, 335; **Supp. XVII:** 97; **Supp. XXVII:** 33, 34
James, William (grandfather), **II:** 342
James Baldwin: The Legacy (Troupe, ed.), **Retro. Supp. II:** 15
James Baldwin—The Price of the Ticket (film), **Retro. Supp. II:** 2
James Dickey and the Politics of Canon (Suarez), **Supp. IV Part 1:** 175
"James Dickey on Yeats: An Interview" (Dickey), **Supp. IV Part 1:** 177
James Hogg: A Critical Study (Simpson), **Supp. IX:** 269, 276
"James Is a Girl" (Egan), **Supp. XIX:** 61
James Jones: A Friendship (Morris), **Supp. XI:** 234
James Jones: An American Literary Orientalist Master (Carter), **Supp. XI:** 220
"James Jones and Jack Kerouac: Novelists of Disjunction" (Stevenson), **Supp. XI:** 230
James Jones: Reveille to Taps (television documentary), **Supp. XI:** 234
Jameson, Anna Brownell, **Supp. XXIII:** 225, 226, 232, 235
Jameson, F. R., **Supp. IV Part 1:** 119
Jameson, Sir Leander Starr, **III:** 327
James Shore's Daughter (Benét), **Supp. XI:** 48
"James Thurber" (Pollard), **Supp. I Part 2:** 468
"James Whitcomb Riley (From a Westerner's Point of View)" (Dunbar), **Supp. II Part 1:** 198
Jammes, Francis, **II:** 528; **Retro. Supp. I:** 55
"Jan, the Son of Thomas" (Sandburg), **III:** 593–594
Jan. 31 (Goldbarth), **Supp. XII:** 177, **178–179,** 180
"Jane Awake"(O'Hara), **Supp. XXIII:** 210
Janeczko, Paul, **Supp. XIII:** 280
Jane Eyre (Brontë), **Supp. XVI:** 158; **Supp. XXII:** 120
"Jane Lampton Clemens" (Twain), **Retro. Supp. III:** 256
Janet, Pierre, **I:** 248, 249, 252; **Retro. Supp. I:** 55, 57
Jane Talbot: A Novel (Brown), **Supp. I Part 1:** 145–146
"Janet Waking" (Ransom), **III:** 490, 491
"Janice" (Jackson), **Supp. IX:** 117
Janowitz, Tama, **Supp. X:** 7; **Supp. XXVII:** 68, 269
Jantz, Harold S., **Supp. I Part 1:** 112
"January" (Barthelme), **Supp. IV Part 1:** 54
"January" (W. V. Davis), **Supp. XXI:** 89, 90
January Man, The (screenplay, Shanley), **Supp. XIV:** 316
"January Thaw" (Leopold), **Supp. XIV:** 183–184
"Janus" (Beattie), **Supp. V:** 31
Janzen, Jean, **Supp. V:** 180
"Japan" (Collins), **Supp. XXI:** 56
Japanese Americans: The Formation and Transformations of an Ethnic Group (Spickard), **Supp. XXI:** 149
"Japanese Beetles" (X. J. Kennedy), **Supp. XV:** 161, 165
Japanese by Spring (Reed), **Supp. X:** 241, **253–255**
Japanese Cooking: A Simple Art (Tsuji), **Supp. XVII:** 90
"Japan's Young Dreams" (Geisel), **Supp. XVI:** 102
Jara, Victor, **Supp. IV Part 2:** 549
Jarecki, Dave, **Supp. XXIII:** 239
Jarecki, Nicholas, **Supp. XXVII:** 68
Jarman, Mark, **Supp. IV Part 1:** 68; **Supp. IX:** 266, 270, 276; **Supp. XII:** 209; **Supp. XV:** 251; **Supp. XVIII:** 178; **Supp. XXV:** 221–222
Jarmon, Mark, **Supp. XVII: 109–122**
Jarrell, Randall, **I:** 167, 169, 173, 180; **II: 367–390,** 539–540; **III:** 134, 194, 213, 268, 527; **IV:** 352, 411, 422; **Retro. Supp. I:** 52, 121, 135, 140; **Retro. Supp. II:** 44, 177, 178, 182; **Supp. I Part 1:** 89; **Supp. I Part 2:** 552; **Supp. II Part 1:** 109, 135; **Supp. III Part 1:** 64; **Supp. III Part 2:** 541, 550; **Supp. IV Part 2:** 440; **Supp. IX:** 94, 268; **Supp. V:** 315, 318, 323; **Supp. VIII:** 31, 100, 271; **Supp. XI:** 311, 315; **Supp. XII:** 121, 260, 297; **Supp. XV:** 93, 153; **Supp. XVII:** 111; **Supp. XXVI:** 67
Jarrell, Mrs. Randall (Mary von Schrader), **II:** 368, 385
Jarry, Alfred, **Retro. Supp. II:** 326; **Supp. XV:** 177–178, 182, 188
Jarvis, John Wesley, **Supp. I Part 2:** 501, 520
Jaskoski, Helen, **Supp. IV Part 1:** 325; **Supp. XXII:** 166
"Jasmine" (Komunyakaa), **Supp. XIII:** 132
"Jason" (Hecht), **Supp. X:** 62
"Jason" (MacLeish), **III:** 4
Jason and Medeia (Gardner), **Supp. VI:** 63, **68–69**
"Jasper Notes" (G. Jones), **Supp. XXIV:** 194
Jaspers, Karl, **III:** 292; **IV:** 491
Jauss, David, **Supp. XXI:** 129, 132, 133, 134, 139
Jay, William, **I:** 338
Jayber Crow (Berry), **Supp. X:** 28, 34
"Jaz Fantasia" (Sandburg), **III:** 585
Jazz (Morrison), **Retro. Supp. III:** 184, 193, 194, 195
Jazz (Myers), **Supp. XXVII:** 211
"Jazz Age Clerk, A" (Farrell), **II:** 45
Jazz Country: Ralph Ellison in America (Porter), **Retro. Supp. II:** 127
"Jazzonia" (Hughes), **Supp. I Part 1:** 324

Jazz Poetry Anthology, The (Komunyakaa and Feinstein, eds.), **Supp. XIII:** 125
"Jazztet Muted" (Hughes), **Supp. I Part 1:** 342
J. B.: A Play in Verse (MacLeish), **II:** 163, 228; **III:** 3, 21–22, 23; **Supp. IV Part 2:** 586
"Jealous" (Ford), **Supp. V:** 71
Jealous Gods, The (Atherton), **Supp. XXIV:** 26
Jealousies, The: A Faery Tale, by Lucy Vaughan Lloyd of China Walk, Lambeth (Keats), **Supp. XII:** 113
Jean-Christophe (Rolland), **Supp. XX: 70**
"Jean Harlow's Wedding Night" (Wasserstein), **Supp. XV:** 328
Jean Huguenot (Benét), **Supp. XI:** 44
"Jeff Briggs's Love Story" (Harte), **Supp. II Part 1:** 355
Jeffers, Robinson, **I:** 66; **III:** 134; **Retro. Supp. I:** 202; **Retro. Supp. III:** 250; **Supp. II Part 2: 413–440; Supp. IX:** 77; **Supp. VIII:** 33, 292; **Supp. X:** 112; **Supp. XI:** 312; **Supp. XV:** 113, 114, 115; **Supp. XVII:** 111, 112, 117; **Supp. XXI:** 87; **Supp. XXIII:** 145
Jeffers, Una Call Kuster (Mrs. Robinson Jeffers), **Supp. II Part 2:** 414
Jefferson, Blind Lemon, **Supp. VIII:** 349
Jefferson, Margo, **Supp. XX: 87; Supp. XXIV:** 271
Jefferson, Thomas, **I:** 1, 2, 5, 6–8, 14, 485; **II:** 5, 6, 34, 217, 300, 301, 437; **III:** 3, 17, 18, 294–295, 306, 310, 473, 608; **IV:** 133, 243, 249, 334, 348; **Retro. Supp. III:** 148; **Supp. I Part 1:** 146, 152, 153, 229, 230, 234, 235; **Supp. I Part 2:** 389, 399, 456, 474, 475, 482, 507, 509, 510, 511, 516, 518–519, 520, 522; **Supp. X:** 26; **Supp. XIV:** 191; **Supp. XX: 285; Supp. XXIV:** 85, 281
Jefferson and/or Mussolini (Pound), **Retro. Supp. I:** 292
"Jefferson Davis as a Representative American" (Du Bois), **Supp. II Part 1:** 161
J-E-L-L-O (Baraka), **Supp. II Part 1:** 47
"Jelly-Bean, The" (Fitzgerald), **II:** 88
"Jellyfish, A" (Moore), **III:** 215
Jemie, Onwuchekwa, **Supp. I Part 1:** 343
Jenkins, Jerry B., **Supp. XXVII:** 5
Jenkins, J. L., **I:** 456
Jenkins, Joe, **Supp. XX: 117, 120, 122**
Jenkins, Kathleen, **III:** 403
Jenkins, Susan, **IV:** 123
Jenks, Deneen, **Supp. IV Part 2:** 550, 554
Jenks, Tom, **Supp. XIX:** 51
Jenkyns, Richard, **Supp. XXV:** 223
Jennie Gerhardt (Dreiser), **I:** 497, 499, 500, 501, 504–505, 506, 507, 519; **Retro. Supp. II:** 94, **99–101**
"Jennie M'Grew" (Masters), **Supp. I Part 2:** 468
Jennifer Lorn (Wylie), **Supp. I Part 2:** 709, 714–717, 718, 721, 724
Jennison, Peter S., **Supp. XIX:** 268
"Jenny Garrow's Lover" (Jewett), **II:** 397
"Jerboa, The" (Moore), **III:** 203, 207, 209, 211–212
Jeremiah, **Supp. X:** 35
Jeremy's Version (Purdy), **Supp. VII:** 274
"Je Reviens"(Dybek), **Supp. XXIII:** 78
"Jericho" (R. Lowell), **II:** 536
Jerome, Judson, **Supp. XXIII:** 54
"Jerry's Garage" (Budbill), **Supp. XIX:** 7
"Jersey City Gendarmerie, Je T'aime" (Lardner), **II:** 433
Jersey Rain (Pinsky), **Supp. VI:** 235, **247–250**
"Jerusalem" (Nye), **Supp. XIII:** 287
Jerusalem: Song of Songs (Uris), **Supp. XX: 244–245, 246, 255**
Jerusalem the Golden (Reznikoff), **Supp. XIV:** 280, 285, 286
"Jessie and Jesus" (Andrews), **Supp. XXVI:** 11
Jessie and Jesus and Cousin Claire (Andrews), **Supp. XXVI:** 2, 10, 11–12
Jessup, Richard, **Supp. XI:** 306
"Je Suis Perdu" (Taylor), **Supp. V:** 314, 321–322
Jesuits in North America in the Seventeenth Century, The (Parkman), **Supp. II Part 2:** 597, 603–605
Jesus, **I:** 27, 34, 68, 89, 136, 552, 560; **II:** 1, 16, 197, 198, 214, 215, 216, 218, 219, 239, 373, 377, 379, 537, 538, 539, 549, 569, 585, 591, 592; **III:** 39, 173, 179, 270, 291, 296–297, 300, 303, 305, 307, 311, 339, 340, 341, 342, 344, 345, 346, 347, 348, 352, 353, 354, 355, 436, 451, 489, 534, 564, 566, 567, 582; **IV:** 51, 69, 86, 107, 109, 117, 137, 138, 141, 144, 147, 149, 150, 151, 152, 155, 156, 157, 158, 159, 163, 164, 232, 241, 289, 293, 294, 296, 331, 364, 392, 396, 418, 430; **Supp. I Part 1:** 2, 54, 104, 107, 108, 109, 121, 267, 371; **Supp. I Part 2:** 379, 386, 458, 515, 580, 582, 583, 587, 588, 683; **Supp. V:** 280
Jesus, the Son of Man (Gibran), **Supp. XX: 115–116, 117, 122–123**
"Jesus Asleep" (Sexton), **Supp. II Part 2:** 693
"Jesus of Nazareth, Then and Now" (Price), **Supp. VI:** 268
"Jesus Papers, The" (Sexton), **Supp. II Part 2:** 693
"Jesus Raises Up the Harlot" (Sexton), **Supp. II Part 2:** 693
"Jesus Shaves" (Davison), **Supp. XXVI:** 74
"Jesus Stories, The" (Brockmeier), **Supp. XXII:** 52
Jetée, La (film), **Supp. IV Part 2:** 436
"Jeune Parque, La" (Valéry), **IV:** 92
"Jew as Writer/The Writer as Jew, The: Reflections on Literature and Identity" (Apple), **Supp. XVII:** 1, 9
"Jewbird, The" (Malamud), **Supp. I Part 2:** 435
"Jewboy, The" (P. Roth), **Supp. III Part 2:** 412
"Jewels" (Teasdale), **Supp. XXVII:** 290, 291
Jewett, Caroline, **II:** 396
Jewett, Katharine, **Retro. Supp. II:** 46
Jewett, Mary, **II:** 396, 403
Jewett, Rutger, **Retro. Supp. I:** 381
Jewett, Sarah Orne, **I:** 313; **II: 391–414; Retro. Supp. I:** 6, 7, 19; **Retro. Supp. II:** 51, 52, **131–151,** 156; **Retro. Supp. III:** 22, 26, 37; **Supp. I Part 2:** 495; **Supp. IX:** 79; **Supp. VIII:** 126; **Supp. XIII:** 153; **Supp. XXIII:** 275, 278
Jewett, Theodore Furber, **II:** 395
Jewett, Dr. Theodore Herman, **II:** 396–397, 402
"Jew for Export, The" (Mamet), **Supp. XIV:** 251–252
Jew in Love, A (Hecht), **Supp. XXVII:** 94
Jew in Our Day, The (W. Frank), **Supp. XX: 79**
Jew in the American Novel, The (Fiedler), **Supp. XIII:** 106
"Jewish Graveyards, Italy" (Levine), **Supp. V:** 190
"Jewish Hunter, The" (Moore), **Supp. X:** 163, 165, **174**
Jewison, Norman, **Supp. XI:** 306; **Supp. XIV:** 316
"Jew of Persia, A" (Helprin), **Supp. XXV:** 80, 85

Jews of Shklov (Schneour), **IV:** 11
Jews without Money (Gold), **Supp. XIV:** 288–289
JFK (film), **Supp. XIV:** 48
Jig of Forslin, The: A Symphony (Aiken), **I:** 50, 51, 57, 62, 66
Jigonsaseh, **Supp. XXVI:** 81, 82, 83, 86
"Jig Tune: Not for Love" (McGrath), **Supp. X:** 116
"Jihad" (McClatchy), **Supp. XII:** 266
"Jilting of Granny Weatherall, The" (Porter), **III:** 434, 435, 438
"Jim Baker's Blue-Jay Yarn" (Twain), **Retro. Supp. III:** 255, 268
Jim Crow's Last Stand (Hughes), **Retro. Supp. I:** 205
Jiménez, Juan Ramón, **Supp. XIII:** 315, 323
Jimmie Higgins (Sinclair), **Supp. V:** 288
"Jimmy Harlow" (X. J. Kennedy), **Supp. XV:** 170
Jimmy's Blues (Baldwin), **Retro. Supp. II:** 8, 9, 15
Jim's Book: A Collection of Poems and Short Stories (Merrill), **Supp. III Part 1:** 319
"Jim Smiley and His Jumping Frog" (Twain), **Retro. Supp. III:** 255, 257, 260
Jin, Ha, **Supp. XVIII: 89–104**
Jitney (Wilson), **Retro. Supp. III:** 318, 321; **Supp. VIII:** 330, 331, 351
Jitterbug Perfume (Robbins), **Supp. X:** 273, **274–276,** 279
Joachim, Harold, **Retro. Supp. I:** 58
Joan, Pope, **IV:** 165
Joanna and Ulysses (Sarton), **Supp. VIII: 254–255**
Joan of Arc, **IV:** 241; **Supp. I Part 1:** 286–288; **Supp. I Part 2:** 469
"Joan of Arc" (Cohen), **Supp. XXVII:** 59
Joans, Ted, **Supp. IV Part 1:** 169
Job (biblical book), **II:** 165, 166–167, 168; **III:** 21, 199, 512; **IV:** 13, 158; **Supp. I Part 1:** 125
Job, The (Burroughs and Odier), **Supp. III Part 1:** 97, 103
Job, The: An American Novel (Lewis), **II:** 441
"Job History" (Proulx), **Supp. VII:** 262
Jobim, Antonio Carlos, **Supp. IV Part 2:** 549
Jobim, Antônio Carlos, **Supp. XXI:** 100
"Job of the Plains, A" (Humphrey), **Supp. IX:** 101
Jocks, Christopher, **Supp. XXVI:** 97
"Jody Rolled the Bones" (Yates), **Supp. XI:** 335, 341
"Joe" (Alvarez), **Supp. VII:** 7–8
Joe (Brown), **Supp. XVIII:** 195
Joe (L. Brown), **Supp. XXI:** 41, **45–46,** 47
"Joe, the Vanishing American" (Swados), **Supp. XIX:** 258–259
Joe: A Memoir of Joe Brainard (Padgett), **Supp. XXVII:** 18
"Joe Hill" (Hayes), **Supp. XXVI:** 134
Joe Hill: A Biographical Novel (Stegner), **Supp. IV Part 2:** 599
Joe Jones (Lamott), **Supp. XX: 134–135**
"Joe Louis: The King as a Middle-Aged Man" (Talese), **Supp. XVII:** 202
"Joe Messenger Is Dreaming"(P. Benedict), **Supp. XXIII:** 47
"Joe's Jitters" (Bronk), **Supp. XXI:** 27
Joe Turner's Come and Gone (Wilson), **Retro. Supp. III:** 318, 325–326; **Supp. VIII:** 334, **337–342,** 345
Joe versus the Volcano (screenplay, Shanley), **Supp. XIV:** 316
"Joey Martiney" (Huncke), **Supp. XIV:** 149
Johannes in Eremo (Mather), **Supp. II Part 2:** 453
Johansen, Bruce E., **Supp. XXVI:** 98
John XXIII, Pope, **Supp. I Part 2:** 492
John (biblical book), **I:** 68; **Supp. XV:** 222, 224
"John" (Shields), **Supp. VII:** 310–311
John, Augustus, **Supp. XXII:** 157
John, Elton, **Supp. XXI:** 148
"John, John Chinaman" (Buck), **Supp. II Part 1:** 128
John, Orrick, **Supp. XXVI:** 134
John Addington Symonds: A Biographical Study (Brooks), **I:** 240, 241
John-a Dreams: A Tale (J. Sturgis), **Supp. XX: 233**
"John Archer's Nose" (R. Fisher), **Supp. XIX:** 71–72, 78
John Barleycorn (London), **II:** 467, 481
John Brown (Du Bois), **Supp. II Part 1:** 171–172
"John Brown" (Emerson), **II:** 13
"John Brown" (Lindsay), **Supp. I Part 2:** 393
John Brown's Body (Benét), **II:** 177; **Supp. XI:** 45, 46, 47, **56–57**
John Brown: The Making of a Martyr (Warren), **IV:** 236
John Bull in America; or, The New Munchausen (Paulding), **I:** 344
"John Burke" (Olson), **Supp. II Part 2:** 579, 580
"John Burns of Gettysburg" (Harte), **Supp. II Part 1:** 343
"John Carter" (Agee), **I:** 27
John Chancellor Makes Me Cry (Siddons), **Supp. XXII:** 245
"John Coltrane: Where Does Art Come From?" (Baraka), **Supp. II Part 1:** 60
John Deth: A Metaphysical Legend and Other Poems (Aiken), **I:** 61
"John Endicott" (Longfellow), **II:** 505, 506; **Retro. Supp. II:** 165–166, 167
"John Evereldown" (Robinson), **III:** 524
John Fante Reader, The (Cooper, ed.), **Supp. XI:** 174
John Fante: Selected Letters, 1932–1981 (Cooney, ed.), **Supp. XI:** 170
"John Gardner: The Writer As Teacher" (Carver), **Supp. III Part 1:** 136, 146–147
John Gaunt (R. H. Davis), **Supp. XVI:** 89
John Jay Chapman and His Letters (Howe), **Supp. XIV:** 54
John Keats (A. Lowell), **II:** 530–531
John Kennedy Toole: The Omega Point (film, Sandord), **Supp. XXVI:** 240, 241, 243, 246, 253
"John Kinsella's Lament for Mrs. Mary Moore" (Yeats), **Supp. XVII:** 144
"John Lamar" (R. H. Davis), **Supp. XVI:** 89–90
John Lane, **Retro. Supp. I:** 59
"John L. Sullivan" (Lindsay), **Supp. I Part 2:** 394, 395
"John Marr" (Melville), **III:** 93
John Marr and Other Sailors (Melville), **III:** 93; **Retro. Supp. I:** 257; **Retro. Supp. III:** 161
John Muir: A Reading Bibliography (Kimes and Kimes), **Supp. IX:** 178
Johnny Appleseed and Other Poems (Lindsay), **Supp. I Part 2:** 397
"Johnny Bear" (Steinbeck), **IV:** 67
Johnny Got His Gun (Trumbo), **Supp. XXI:** 45
"Johnny Mnemonic" (W. Gibson), **Supp. XVI:** 122, 123–125, 128, 131
"Johnny Panic and the Bible of Dreams" (Plath), **Retro. Supp. II:** 245
"Johnny Ray" (Ríos), **Supp. IV Part 2:** 543
Johnny Tremain (Forbes), **Supp. XIX:** 235
John of the Cross (Saint), **I:** 585; **Supp. IV Part 1:** 284; **Supp. XV:** 223; **Supp. XVII:** 112

John Paul Jones: A Sailor's Biography (Morison), **Supp. I Part 2:** 494–495
"John Redding Goes to Sea" (Hurston), **Retro. Supp. III:** 127; **Supp. VI:** 150
Johns, George Sibley, **Retro. Supp. II:** 65
Johns, Jasper, **Supp. XXIII:** 217
Johns, Orrick, **Retro. Supp. II:** 71; **Supp. XXVII:** 285
John Sloan: A Painter's Life (Brooks), **I:** 254
"John Smith Liberator" (Bierce), **I:** 209
Johnson, Alexandra, **Supp. X:** 86
Johnson, Alvin, **I:** 236; **Supp. XV:** 304
Johnson, Ben, **Retro. Supp. I:** 56
Johnson, Buffie, **Supp. IV Part 1:** 94
Johnson, Caitlin, **Supp. XXIII:** 281
Johnson, Carol Siri, **Supp. XXIII:** 257, 258, 264, 269
Johnson, Charles, **Supp. I Part 1:** 325; **Supp. V:** 128; **Supp. VI: 185–201;** **Supp. X:** 239; **Supp. XIII:** 182; **Supp. XIX:** 160
Johnson, Charles S., **Supp. IX:** 309; **Supp. XXII:** 6, 7
Johnson, Claudia Durst, **Supp. VIII:** 126–127
Johnson, Clifton, **Supp. XXI:** 248, 250
Johnson, Denis, **Supp. XIX:** 209; **Supp. XXI:** 118, 131
Johnson, Diane, **Retro. Supp. I:** 196; **Supp. XIII:** 127
Johnson, Eastman, **IV:** 321
Johnson, Edward, **IV:** 157; **Supp. I Part 1:** 110, 115
Johnson, Fenton, **Supp. XI:** 129
Johnson, Georgia Douglas, **Supp. IV Part 1:** 164
Johnson, Helene, **Supp. XVIII:** 282; **Supp. XXVI: 163–176**
Johnson, James Weldon, **Retro. Supp. II:** 114; **Retro. Supp. III:** 127; **Supp. I Part 1:** 324, 325; **Supp. II Part 1:** 33, 194, 200, 202–203, 206–207; **Supp. III Part 1:** 73; **Supp. IV Part 1:** 7, 11, 15, 16, 164, 165, 166, 169; **Supp. X:** 42, 136, **246;** **Supp. XIX:** 73; **Supp. XVIII:** 122, 127, 282
Johnson, Jeff, **Supp. XXV:** 98
Johnson, Joyce, **Supp. XIV:** 150
Johnson, Kent, **Supp. XV:** 347
Johnson, Lady Bird, **Supp. IV Part 1:** 22
Johnson, Laura K., **Retro. Supp. III:** 288
Johnson, Lyndon B., **I:** 254; **II:** 553, 582; **Retro. Supp. II:** 27
Johnson, Marguerite. See Angelou, Maya
Johnson, Mat, **Retro. Supp. III:** 236
Johnson, Maurice, **Supp. XV:** 136, 137, 138
Johnson, Michael K., **Supp. XVIII:** 59, 64
Johnson, Mordecai, **Supp. XIV:** 202
Johnson, Nunnally, **Supp. IV Part 1:** 355
Johnson, Pamela Hansford, **IV:** 469
Johnson, Rafer, **Supp. I Part 1:** 271
Johnson, Reed, **Supp. IV Part 2:** 589
Johnson, Richard, **Supp. XIII:** 132
Johnson, Robert, **Supp. IV Part 1:** 146; **Supp. VIII:** 15, 134
Johnson, Robert K., **Supp. IV Part 2:** 573, 584
Johnson, Robert Underwood, **Supp. IX:** 182, 184, 185
Johnson, Samuel, **II:** 295; **III:** 491, 503; **IV:** 452; **Retro. Supp. I:** 56, 65; **Supp. I Part 1:** 33; **Supp. I Part 2:** 422, 498, 503, 523, 656; **Supp. IV Part 1:** 34, 124; **Supp. XI:** 209; **Supp. XII:** 159; **Supp. XIII:** 55, 347; **Supp. XVI:** 204; **Supp. XVII:** 1; **Supp. XXIV:** 152
Johnson, Samuel, Jr., **Supp. XXV:** 241, 250
Johnson, Sarah Anne, **Supp. XIX:** 49, 50, 52, 54, 55, 56, 58, 59, 60, 61; **Supp. XVIII:** 145
Johnson, Steve, **Supp. XVI:** 177
Johnson, Thomas H., **I:** 470–471; **IV:** 144, 158; **Retro. Supp. I:** 26, 28, 36, 39, 40, 41, 43
Johnson, Walter, **II:** 422
Johnson, Willard "Spud", **Supp. XV:** 42, 46
"Johnson Girls, The" (Bambara), **Supp. XI:** 7
Johnsrud, Harold, **II:** 562
Johnston, Basil, **Supp. IV Part 1:** 269
Johnston, Jill, **Supp. XXV:** 5
Johnston, Mary, **II:** 194
Johnston, Robert M., **Supp. I Part 1:** 369
"John Sutter" (Winters), **Supp. II Part 2:** 810
John's Wife (Coover), **Supp. V:** 51–52
John the Baptist, **I:** 389; **II:** 537, 591
John Wesley Harding (album, Dylan), **Supp. XVIII:** 27
Jolas, Eugène, **Retro. Supp. II:** 85, 328; **Supp. IV Part 1:** 80
Jolie Blon's Bounce (Burke), **Supp. XIV:** 26, 33–34
Jolly (Mamet), **Supp. XIV:** 240, 254
"Jolly Corner, The" (James), **I:** 571; **Retro. Supp. I:** 235
Jolly Plays for Holidays (Wells), **Supp. XXVI:** 275
"Jon" (Saunders), **Supp. XIX:** 232, 234
"Jonah" (R. Lowell), **II:** 536
Jonah's Gourd Vine (Hurston), **Retro. Supp. III:** 126, 128–129, 132, 139; **Supp. VI:** 149, 155
"Jonathan Edwards" (Holmes), **Supp. I Part 1:** 302, 315
"Jonathan Edwards in Western Massachusetts" (R. Lowell), **II:** 550
Jonathan Franzen at the End of Postmodernism (Burns), **Supp. XX: 85**
Jonathan Troy (Abbey), **Supp. XIII:** 4, 13
Jones, Anne, **Supp. X:** 8
Jones, Anne Goodwyn, **Supp. XXII:** 252
Jones, Carolyn M., **Supp. VIII:** 128; **Supp. XIX:** 160
Jones, Chuck, **Supp. XVI:** 102
Jones, David, **Supp. XVII:** 241
Jones, Dennis, **Supp. XXIII:** 228, 233
Jones, Derek Anson, **Supp. XVIII:** 38, 39
Jones, Edith Newbold. See Wharton, Edith
Jones, Edward P., **Supp. XXI:** 247; **Supp. XXII: 139–153**
Jones, E. Stanley, **III:** 297
Jones, Everett LeRoi. See Baraka, Imamu Amiri
Jones, Gayl, **Retro. Supp. III:** 184, 194; **Supp. XXIV: 183–197**
Jones, George Frederic, **IV:** 309
Jones, Grover, **Supp. XIII:** 166
Jones, Harry, **Supp. I Part 1:** 337
Jones, Harry L., **Supp. XXV:** 251
Jones, Howard Mumford, **I:** 353; **Supp. IV Part 2:** 606; **Supp. XIV:** 11; **Supp. XXVI:** 63
Jones, James, **III:** 40; **IV:** 98; **Supp. XI: 213–237;** **Supp. XIX:** 248, 252; **Supp. XX: 248;** **Supp. XXV:** 145
Jones, James Earl, **Supp. VIII:** 334; **Supp. XI:** 309
Jones, Jennifer, **Supp. IV Part 2:** 524
Jones, John Paul, **II:** 405–406; **Supp. I Part 2:** 479, 480, 494–495
Jones, Kirkland C., **Supp. XVIII:** 173, 174, 175; **Supp. XXII:** 9
Jones, LeRoi. See Baraka, Imamu Amiri
Jones, Louis B., **Supp. XVI:** 41
Jones, Loyal, **Supp. XX: 170**
Jones, Lucretia Stevens Rhinelander, **IV:** 309
Jones, Madison, **Retro. Supp. II:** 235;

Supp. X: 1
Jones, Major (pseudonym). See Thompson, William T.
Jones, Malcolm, **Supp. V:** 219; **Supp. XX: 93, 138**
Jones, Mildred, **Supp. XVIII:** 281
Jones, Robert Edmond, **III:** 387, 391, 394, 399; **Supp. XXI:** 6, 12
Jones, Rodney, **Supp. XXVI:** 66
Jones, Sharon L., **Supp. XVIII:** 280, 285, 286
Jones, Tommy Lee, **Supp. V:** 227
Jones, Will Owen, **Retro. Supp. III:** 21
"Jones's Private Argyment" (Lanier), **Supp. I Part 1:** 352
"Jones's The Thin Red Line: The End of Innocence" (Michel-Michot), **Supp. XI:** 224–225
Jong, Allan, **Supp. V:** 115
Jong, Erica, **Supp. V: 113–135**
Jong-Fast, Molly Miranda, **Supp. V:** 115
Jonson, Ben, **I:** 58, 358; **II:** 11, 16, 17, 18, 436, 556; **III:** 3, 463, 575–576; **IV:** 395, 453; **Retro. Supp. II:** 76; **Supp. I Part 2:** 423; **Supp. IV Part 2:** 585; **Supp. XX: 197; Supp. XXIV:** 159
Jonsson, Thorsten, **Retro. Supp. I:** 73
Joplin, Janis, **Supp. IV Part 1:** 206; **Supp. XI:** 239
Joplin, Scott, **Supp. IV Part 1:** 223
Jordan, A. Van, **Supp. XVIII:** 172
Jordan, Barbara, **Supp. VIII:** 63; **Supp. XI:** 249
Jordan, David, **Supp. XIX:** 141
Jordan, Denise, **Supp. XXVII:** 209
Jordan, June, **Retro. Supp. III:** 184; **Supp. XII:** 217; **Supp. XXII:** 172; **Supp. XXIV:** 188
Jordan, Marie, **Supp. XV:** 224
Jo's Boys (Alcott), **Supp. I Part 1:** 32, 35, 40–41, 42
Joseph Heller (Ruderman), **Supp. IV Part 1:** 380
"Josephine Has Her Day" (Thurber), **Supp. I Part 2:** 606
Josephine Stories, The (Fitzgerald), **Retro. Supp. I:** 109
"Joseph Martinez" (Huncke), **Supp. XIV:** 149
"Joseph Pockets" (Stern), **Supp. IX:** 292
Josephson, Matthew, **I:** 259
"José's Country" (Winters), **Supp. II Part 2:** 789, 790
Joshi, S. T., **Supp. XXIV:** 23; **Supp. XXV:** 111, 118, 123; **Supp. XXVII:** 128
Josh Thurlow series (Hickam), **Supp. XXVII:** 111
Joshua (biblical book), **Supp. I Part 2:** 515
"Joshua Clark"(Kenny), **Supp. XXIII:** 154
Joslin, Katherine, **Retro. Supp. I:** 376
Journal (Emerson), **Supp. I Part 1:** 309
"Journal" (L. Michaels), **Supp. XVI:** 213
Journal (Thoreau), **IV:** 175
Journal (Woolman), **Supp. VIII:** 202
"Journal for My Daughter" (Kunitz), **Supp. III Part 1:** 268
"Journal of an Airman" (Auden), **Supp. XIX:** 151
Journal of Arthur Stirling, The (Sinclair), **Supp. V:** 280
"Journal of a Solitary Man, The" (Hawthorne), **II:** 226
Journal of a Solitude (Sarton), **Supp. VIII:** 256, 262–263
Journal of My Other Self (Rilke), **Retro. Supp. II:** 20
Journal of the Fictive Life (Nemerov), **III:** 267, 268, 269, 272, 273, 274, 280–281, 284–285, 286, 287
Journal of the Plague Year, A (Defoe), **III:** 423
"Journal of the Year of the Ox, A" (Wright), **Supp. V:** 343
Journals (Thoreau), **Supp. I Part 1:** 299
Journals and Other Documents on the Life and Voyages of Christopher Columbus (Morison, ed.), **Supp. I Part 2:** 494
Journals of Ralph Waldo Emerson, The (Emerson), **II:** 8, 17, 21
Journals of Susanna Moodie, The: Poems (Atwood), **Supp. XIII:** 33
"Journey, A" (Wharton), **Retro. Supp. I:** 364
"Journey, The" (Winters), **Supp. II Part 2:** 795
"Journey, The" (Wright), **Supp. III Part 2:** 605–606
"Journey, the Arrival and the Dream, The" (Gioia), **Supp. XV:** 120
"Journey, The: For Jane at Thirteen" (Kumin), **Supp. IV Part 2:** 442
Journey and Other Poems, The (Winters), **Supp. II Part 2:** 786, 794, 795, 796, 799, 800, 801
Journey Around My Room: The Autobiography of Louise Bogan—A Mosaic (Bogan), **Supp. III Part 1:** 47, 48, 52, 53
Journey Down, The (Bernstein), **IV:** 455
Journey Home, The (Abbey), **Supp. XIII:** 2, 12
"Journey into Speech, A" (Cliff), **Supp. XXII:** 69
Journeyman (Caldwell), **I:** 297, 302–304, 307, 309; **Supp. XXVI:** 134
Journeyman: Travels of a Writer (Findley), **Supp. XX: 50**
"Journey of an Eyeball, The" (Vaz), **Supp. XXVI:** 261
Journey of Tai-me, The (Momaday), **Supp. IV Part 2:** 485
"Journey of the Magi" (Eliot), **Retro. Supp. I:** 64
Journey to a War (Auden and Isherwood), **Supp. II Part 1:** 13; **Supp. XIV:** 156, 158, 162
Journey to Love (W. C. Williams), **IV:** 422; **Retro. Supp. I:** 429
Journey to My Father; Isaac Bashevis Singer (Zamir), **Retro. Supp. II:** 317
"Journey to Nine Miles" (Walker), **Supp. III Part 2:** 527
"Journey to the Interior" (W. J. Smith), **Supp. XIII:** 339, 340
Journey with Genius: Recollections and Reflections Concerning the D. H. Lawrences (Bynner), **Supp. XV:** 46
Jowett, Benjamin, **Supp. XIV:** 335
"Joy" (Moore), **Supp. X:** 174
"Joy" (Singer), **IV:** 9; **Retro. Supp. II:** 307
Joyce, Cynthia, **Supp. X:** 194, 195, 196
Joyce, James, **I:** 53, 105, 108, 130, 174, 256, 285, 377, 395, 475–476, 478, 480, 483, 576; **II:** 27, 42, 58, 73, 74, 198, 209, 264, 320, 569; **III:** 7, 16, 26–27, 45, 174, 181, 184, 261, 273, 277, 343, 396, 398, 465, 471, 474; **IV:** 32, 73, 85, 95, 103, 171, 182, 211, 286, 370, 412, 418, 419, 428, 434, 456; **Retro. Supp. I:** 59, 63, 75, 80, 89, 91, 108, 109, 127, 287, 290, 292, 334, 335, 420; **Retro. Supp. II:** 221, 326; **Supp. I Part 1:** 257, 262, 270; **Supp. I Part 2:** 437, 546, 613, 620; **Supp. II Part 1:** 136; **Supp. III Part 1:** 35, 36, 65, 225, 229; **Supp. III Part 2:** 611, 617, 618; **Supp. IV Part 1:** 40, 47, 80, 227, 300, 310; **Supp. IV Part 2:** 424, 677; **Supp. IX:** 211, 229, 235, 308; **Supp. V:** 261, 331; **Supp. VIII:** 14, 40, 103; **Supp. X:** 115, 137, 194, 324; **Supp. XI:** 66; **Supp.**

XII: 139, 151, 165, 191, 289; **Supp. XIV:** 83; **Supp. XIX:** 151, 172; **Supp. XVI:** 41, 189, 282; **Supp. XVII:** 44; **Supp. XXI:** 7; **Supp. XXII:** 141, 143–144; **Supp. XXIII:** 162; **Supp. XXVI:** 17, 135
Joy Comes in the Morning (J. Rosen), **Supp. XVII:** 50
Joy in the Morning (B. Smith), **Supp. XXIII:** 257, 258, **269–270**
Joy Luck Club, The (Tan), **Supp. X:** 289, 291, 293, 294, 296, 297, 298, 299
"Joy of Sales Resistance, The" (Berry), **Supp. X:** 36
J R (Gaddis), **Supp. IV Part 1:** 279, 280, 285–289, 291, 294; **Supp. IV Part 2:** 484; **Supp. XXI:** 226
Juana Inés de la Cruz, Sor, **Supp. XXI:** 94, 104
Juan de la Cruz (John of the Cross), **Supp. XXI:** 99, 104
"Juan's Song" (Bogan), **Supp. III Part 1:** 50
Juba! (Myers), **Supp. XXVII:** 201, 202, 211
Juba to Jive: A Dictionary of African-American Slang (Major), **Supp. XXII:** 172, 180
Jubilate Agno (Smart), **Supp. IV Part 2:** 626
Judah, Hettie, **Supp. XIII:** 246
Judah the Pious (Prose), **Supp. XVI:** 249, 250, 262
"Judas Maccabaeus" (Longfellow), **II:** 506; **Retro. Supp. II:** 165, 167
Judd, Sylvester, **II:** 290; **Supp. I Part 2:** 420
Judd Rankin's Daughter (Glaspell), **Supp. III Part 1:** 186–188
Jude the Obscure (Hardy), **Supp. I Part 1:** 217
Judevine (Budbill), **Supp. XIX:** 4, **8–9,** 12
Judevine: A Play in Three Acts/Two Acts (Budbill), **Supp. XIX: 12–13**
Judge, Jane, **Supp. XXII:** 191
"Judgement Day" (O'Connor), **III:** 349, 350; **Retro. Supp. II:** 236; **Retro. Supp. III:** 214
Judgment Day (Farrell), **II:** 29, 31, 32, 34, 39
"Judgment of Paris, The" (Merwin), **Supp. III Part 1:** 350
Judgment of Paris, The (Vidal), **Supp. IV Part 2:** 680, 682
"Judgment of the Sage, The" (Crane), **I:** 420
Judith (Farrell), **II:** 46, 48
"Judith" (Garrett), **Supp. VII:** 109–110
"Juggernaut" (Bass), **Supp. XVI:** 16–17
"Jug of Sirup, A" (Bierce), **I:** 206
"Jugurtha" (Longfellow), **II:** 499
"Juice or Gravy" (P. Roth), **Retro. Supp. II:** 279
"Juke Box Love Song" (Hughes), **Retro. Supp. I:** 209
"Julia" (Hellman), **Supp. I Part 1:** 280, 293
Julia France and Her Times (Atherton), **Supp. XXIV:** 24, 27
"Julia Miller" (Masters), **Supp. I Part 2:** 461
Julian (Vidal), **Supp. IV Part 2:** 677, 684–685, 685, 689
Julian, Norman, **Supp. XXVII:** 101
Julian the Apostate, **Retro. Supp. I:** 247
"Julian Vreden" (Bowles), **Supp. IV Part 1:** 94
Julie and Romeo (Ray), **Supp. XII:** 308, 310
Julien, Isaac, **Supp. XI:** 19
Julie; ou, La nouvelle Héloïse (Rousseau), **Supp. XVI:** 184
Julier, Laura, **Supp. IV Part 1:** 211
Julip (Harrison), **Supp. VIII: 51**
Julius Caesar (Shakespeare), **I:** 284; **Supp. XXVI:** 40
July, Miranda, **Supp. XXIV: 199–211**
"July Midnight" (A. Lowell), **II:** 521
"July 1949" (Rash), **Supp. XXVII:** 218
Jumbo (Hecht and MacArthur), **Supp. XXVII:** 90
Jumel, Madame, **Supp. I Part 2:** 461
Jump at the Sun: Zora Neale Hurston's Cosmic Comedy (Lowe), **Retro. Supp. III:** 140
Jumping Out of Bed (R. Bly), **Supp. IV Part 1:** 71
"Jump-Up Day" (Kingsolver), **Supp. VII:** 203
"Junctions" (Lamott), **Supp. XX: 143**
"June 1940" (Kees), **Supp. XV:** 141
"June Light" (Wilbur), **Supp. III Part 2:** 545
June Moon (Lardner and Kaufman), **II:** 427
"June Recital" (Welty), **IV:** 272–273
Juneteenth (Ellison), **Retro. Supp. II:** 119, 124, **126–128**
"Juneteenth" (Ellison), **Retro. Supp. II:** 119, 126; **Supp. II Part 1:** 248
"June the Third" (Gander), **Supp. XV:** 340
June-Tree: New and Selected Poems, 1974–2000 (Balakian), **Supp. XXIII:** 19, **24–25,** 32
Jung, Carl, **I:** 58, 135, 241, 248, 252, 402; **III:** 400, 534, 543; **Supp. I Part 2:** 439; **Supp. IV Part 1:** 68, 69; **Supp. VIII:** 45; **Supp. X:** 193; **Supp. XV:** 214; **Supp. XX: 63, 117**
Junger, Ernst, **Supp. III Part 1:** 63
Jungle, The (Sinclair), **III:** 580; **Supp. V:** 281–284, 285, 289
Jungle Lovers (Theroux), **Supp. VIII:** 314, 315, 316, **317**
"Junior Addict" (Hughes), **Supp. I Part 1:** 343
"Juniper" (Francis), **Supp. IX:** 79
"Junk" (Wilbur), **Supp. III Part 2:** 556
Junker, Howard, **Supp. XV:** 116
Junkie: Confessions of an Unredeemed Drug Addict (Burroughs), **Supp. III Part 1:** 92, 94–96, 101
Junky (Burroughs), **Supp. XIV:** 143
Juno and the Paycock (O'Casey), **Supp. IV Part 1:** 361
"Jupiter Doke, Brigadier General" (Bierce), **I:** 204
Jupiter Laughs (A. Cronin), **Supp. XVII:** 59
Jurgen (Cabell), **III:** 394; **IV:** 286; **Retro. Supp. I:** 80; **Supp. I Part 2:** 718
Jury of Her Peers, A: American Women Writers from Anne Bradstreet to Annie Proulx (Showalter), **Supp. XX: 274**
Jusserand, Jules, **II:** 338
Just above My Head (Baldwin), **Retro. Supp. II:** 14–15
"Just a Little One" (Parker), **Supp. IX:** 191
Just and the Unjust, The (Cozzens), **I:** 367–370, 372, 375, 377, 378, 379
Just an Ordinary Day (Jackson), **Supp. IX:** 120
Just Before Dark: Collected Nonfiction (Harrison), **Supp. VIII:** 41, 45, 46, 53
Just Before the Divorce (Hayes), **Supp. XXVI:** 144
"Just Before the War with the Eskimos" (Salinger), **III:** 559
"Just Boys" (Farrell), **II:** 45
"Just for the Thrill: An Essay on the Difference Between Women and Men" (Carson), **Supp. XII: 103–104**
"Justice" (Hughes), **Supp. I Part 1:** 331
"Justice, A" (Faulkner), **Retro. Supp. I:** 83
Justice, Donald, **Retro. Supp. I:** 313; **Supp. III Part 2:** 541; **Supp. V:** 180, 337, 338, 341; **Supp. VII: 115–**

130; Supp. XI: 141, 315; **Supp. XIII:** 76, 312; **Supp. XV:** 74, 93, 118, 119, 134; **Supp. XVII:** 110, 120, 246; **Supp. XX: 199; Supp. XXIV:** 165
Justice and Expediency (Whitter), **Supp. I Part 2:** 686
"Justice Denied in Massachusetts" (Millay), **III:** 140
Justice for Salcido (Endore), **Supp. XVII:** 63
Justice of Gold in the Damnation of Sinners, The (Edwards), **I:** 559
"Justice to Feminism" (Ozick), **Supp. V:** 272
"Just Introduced" (Taggard), **Supp. XXII:** 274
Just Kids (Smith), **Supp. XXII:** 94
"Just Like a Woman" (Dylan), **Supp. XV:** 350
"Just Like Job" (Angelou), **Supp. IV Part 1:** 15
"Just One of the Boys" (Swados), **Supp. XIX:** 259
Just Whistle: A Valentine (Wright), **Supp. XV: 346–348**
Just Wild About Harry (H. Miller), **III:** 190
Just Write! Here's How (Myers), **Supp. XXVII:** 209–210
Juvenal, **II:** 8, 169, 552
K (Rinehart), **Supp. XXV:** 193–194, 200
"K, The" (Olson), **Supp. II Part 2:** 558, 563, 569
Kaaterskill Falls (Goodman), **Supp. XXVI:** 123–125
Kabir, **Supp. IV Part 1:** 74
"Kabnis" (Toomer), **Supp. III Part 2:** 481, 484; **Supp. IX:** 309, 310, **319–320**
Kachel, Elsie. See Stevens, Mrs. Wallace (Elsie Kachel)
"Kaddish" (Ginsberg), **Supp. II Part 1:** 319, 327
Kaddish and Other Poems, 1958–1960 (Ginsberg), **Supp. II Part 1:** 309, 319–320; **Supp. XIV:** 269
Kael, Pauline, **Supp. IX:** 253; **Supp. XV:** 147, 148
Kafka, Franz, **II:** 244, 565, 569; **III:** 51, 253, 418, 566, 572; **IV:** 2, 113, 218, 437–439, 442; **Retro. Supp. II:** 20, 221, 282; **Supp. I Part 1:** 197; **Supp. III Part 1:** 105; **Supp. III Part 2:** 413; **Supp. IV Part 1:** 379; **Supp. IV Part 2:** 623; **Supp. VIII:** 14, 15, 103; **Supp. XII:** 21, 37, 98, 168; **Supp. XIII:** 305; **Supp. XVI:** 17, 201, 206, 209; **Supp. XVII:** 244; **Supp. XX: 18, 21, 85, 87; Supp. XXII:** 89, 90, 94; **Supp. XXIII:** 68
Kafka Americana (Lethem and Scholtz), **Supp. XVIII:** 144–145
Kaganoff, Penny, **Supp. XI:** 122
Kagan's Superfecta (A. Hoffman), **Supp. XVII:** 42
Kahane, Jack, **III:** 171, 178
Kahn, Otto, **I:** 385; **IV:** 123; **Retro. Supp. II:** 81, 84, 85; **Supp. XX: 75**
Kahn, R. T., **Supp. XI:** 216
Kahn, Sholom Jacob, **Retro. Supp. III:** 107
"Kai, Today" (Snyder), **Supp. VIII:** 300
Kaiser, Georg, **I:** 479
Kaiser, Henry, **Supp. I Part 2:** 644
Kakutani, Michiko, **Supp. IV Part 1:** 196, 201, 205, 211, 212; **Supp. V:** 63; **Supp. VIII:** 81, 84, 86, 88, 141; **Supp. X:** 171, 301, 302, 310, 314; **Supp. XI:** 38, 179; **Supp. XII:** 165, 171, 172, 299; **Supp. XIX:** 142; **Supp. XVI:** 71; **Supp. XVII:** 6; **Supp. XX: 92, 94; Supp. XXII:** 109; **Supp. XXVI:** 246; **Supp. XXVII:** 274
Kalem, T. E., **Supp. IV Part 2:** 585
Kalevala (Finnish epic), **II:** 503, 504; **Retro. Supp. II:** 155
Kalevala (Lönnrot), **Retro. Supp. II:** 159, 160
Kalfus, Ken, **Supp. XVII:** 50
Kalki: A Novel (Vidal), **Supp. IV Part 2:** 677, 682, 685, 691, 692
Kallan, Richard A., **Supp. XX: 244**
Kallen, Horace, **I:** 229; **Supp. I Part 2:** 643; **Supp. XIV:** 195, 197, 198
Kallman, Chester, **II:** 586; **Supp. II Part 1:** 15, 17, 24, 26
"Kallundborg Church" (Whittier), **Supp. I Part 2:** 696
Kalstone, David, **Retro. Supp. II:** 40
Kamel, Rose, **Supp. XIII:** 306
Kamenev, Lev, **Supp. XXI:** 167
Kamera Obskura (Nabokov), **III:** 255
Kamhi, Michelle Moarder, **Supp. IV Part 2:** 529, 530
Kaminsky, Wally, **Supp. XVIII:** 72
Kamp, David, **Supp. XVIII:** 150
Kandy-Kolored Tangerine-Flake Streamline Baby, The (Wolfe), **Supp. III Part 2:** 569, 573–576, 580, 581
Kane, Daniel, **Supp. XXIV:** 37
Kane, Julie, **Supp. XVII:** 78
Kane, Lesley, **Supp. XIV:** 250
Kanellos, Nicolás, **Supp. VIII:** 82; **Supp. XIII:** 213
Kanin, Garson, **Supp. IV Part 2:** 574
"Kansas City Coyote" (Harjo), **Supp. XII:** 219, 222
"Kansas Emigrants, The" (Whittier), **Supp. I Part 2:** 687
Kant, Immanuel, **I:** 61, 277, 278; **II:** 10–11, 362, 480, 580–581, 582, 583; **III:** 300, 480, 481, 488, 612; **IV:** 90; **Supp. I Part 2:** 640; **Supp. IV Part 2:** 527; **Supp. XIV:** 198, 199; **Supp. XVI:** 184
Kanter, Hal, **IV:** 383
Kapital, Das (Marx), **III:** 580; **Supp. XXI:** 161, 162, 163
Kaplan, Abraham, **I:** 277
Kaplan, Carla, **Retro. Supp. III:** 138
Kaplan, Justin, **I:** 247–248; **Retro. Supp. I:** 392; **Retro. Supp. III:** 261
Kaplan, Mary Jo, **Supp. XIX:** 266
Kaplan, Steven, **Supp. V:** 238, 241, 243, 248
Karate Is a Thing of the Spirit (Crews), **Supp. XI: 112–113**
Karbo, Karen, **Supp. X:** 259, 262
"Karintha" (Toomer), **Supp. IX:** 311
Karl, Frederick R., **Supp. IV Part 1:** 384; **Supp. XXI:** 234
Karloff, Boris, **Supp. XXVII:** 119
"Karloff and the Rock" (Di Piero), **Supp. XIX:** 44
Karl Shapiro's America (film), **Supp. II Part 2:** 703
Karmi, T., **Supp. XV:** 78, 88
Karr, Mary, **Supp. XI: 239–256; Supp. XIII:** 285; **Supp. XV:** 223; **Supp. XVI:** 63, 70, 77; **Supp. XVII:** 242
Karsner, David, **Supp. XXVII:** 83
Karyotakis, Konstantine, **Supp. XXIII:** 125
Kasabian, Linda, **Supp. IV Part 1:** 206
Kasper, Catherine, **Supp. XVI:** 294–295
Kate Chopin (Toth), **Retro. Supp. II:** 71
Kate Chopin: A Critical Biography (Seyersted), **Retro. Supp. II:** 65; **Supp. I Part 1:** 225
Kate Chopin and Edith Wharton: An Annotated Bibliographical Guide to Secondary Sources (Springer), **Supp. I Part 1:** 225
Kate Chopin and Her Creole Stories (Rankin), **Retro. Supp. II:** 57; **Supp. I Part 1:** 200, 225
"Kate Chopin's The Awakening in the Perspective of Her Literary Career" (Arms), **Supp. I Part 1:** 225
Kate Vaiden (Price), **Supp. VI:** 264, 265
"Käthe Kollwitz" (Rukeyser), **Supp.**

VI: 283, 284
Katherine and Jean (Rice), **Supp. VII:** 288
"Kathleen" (Whittier), **Supp. I Part 2:** 693
Kathleen and Frank: The Autobiography of a Family (Isherwood), **Supp. XIV:** 158, 171
Kathy Goes to Haiti (Acker), **Supp. XII:** 5
Katz, Alan, **Supp. XXII:** 177
Katz, Alex, **Supp. XV:** 185; **Supp. XXVII:** 21, 22
Katz, Jonathan, **Supp. XII:** 179
Katz, Steve, **Supp. V:** 44
Katz, Steven T., **Supp. XVI:** 154
Katzenberg, Jffrey, **Supp. XXI:** 154
Kauffman, Carol, **Supp. XI:** 295
Kauffmann, Stanley, **III:** 452; **Supp. I Part 2:** 391; **Supp. XVI:** 74
Kaufman, Boris, **Supp. XVIII:** 251
Kaufman, Charlie, **Supp. XV:** 16
Kaufman, Ellen, **Supp. XXIII:** 132, 133
Kaufman, George S., **II:** 427, 435, 437; **III:** 62, 71–72, 394; **Retro. Supp. II:** 327; **Retro. Supp. III:** 177; **Supp. IV Part 2:** 574; **Supp. IX:** 190; **Supp. XV:** 329
Kaufmann, James, **Supp. XI:** 39
Kaufmann, Walter, **Supp. XVII:** 137
Kauvar, Elaine M., **Supp. V:** 273
Kavanaugh (Longfellow), **I:** 458; **II:** 489, 491; **Retro. Supp. II:** 156; **Supp. I Part 2:** 420
Kaveney, Roz, **Supp. XI:** 39
Kawabata, Yasunari, **Supp. XV:** 186; **Supp. XXI:** 146
Kawin, Bruce, **Retro. Supp. III:** 75
Kay, Terry, **Supp. XXVII:** 104
Kay Boyle: Artist and Activist (Spanier), **Supp. XXIV:** 64
Kay Boyle: Author of Herself (Mellen), **Supp. XXIV:** 64
Kay Boyle for the Twenty-First Century (Austenfeld, ed.), **Supp. XXIV:** 64
Kaye-Smith, Sheila, **Supp. XVIII:** 130–131
Kazan, Elia, **III:** 153, 163; **IV:** 383; **Retro. Supp. III:** 166, 171; **Supp. I Part 1:** 66, 295; **Supp. XVI:** 193; **Supp. XVIII:** 250–251, 252; **Supp. XXV:** 95, 102
Kazin, Alfred, **I:** 248, 417, 419, 517; **II:** 177, 459; **IV:** 236; **Retro. Supp. II:** 206, 243, 246, 286; **Supp. I Part 1:** 195, 196, 294, 295, 296; **Supp. I Part 2:** 536, 631, 647, 650, 678, 679, 719; **Supp. II Part 1:** 143; **Supp. IV Part 1:** 200, 382; **Supp. IX:** 3, 227; **Supp. V:** 122; **Supp. VIII: 93–111; Supp. XIII:** 98, 106; **Supp. XIV:** 11; **Supp. XV:** 142; **Supp. XXIII:** 2, 106; **Supp. XXIV:** 222; **Supp. XXVII:** 134
Keach, Stacey, **Supp. XI:** 309
Kean, Danuta, **Supp. XXI:** 80
Keane, Sarah, **Supp. I Part 1:** 100
Kearns, Cleo McNelly, **Retro. Supp. I:** 57
Kearns, George, **Retro. Supp. I:** 292
Keating, AnnLouise, **Supp. IV Part 1:** 330
Keaton, Buster, **I:** 31; **Supp. I Part 2:** 607; **Supp. IV Part 2:** 574
Keaton, Diane, **Supp. XV:** 5
Keats, John, **I:** 34, 103, 284, 314, 317–318, 385, 401, 448; **II:** 82, 88, 97, 214, 368, 512, 516, 530–531, 540, 593; **III:** 4, 10, 45, 122, 133–134, 179, 214, 237, 272, 275, 469, 485, 523; **IV:** 360, 405, 416; **Retro. Supp. I:** 91, 301, 313, 360, 395, 412; **Retro. Supp. III:** 74; **Supp. I Part 1:** 82, 183, 266, 267, 312, 349, 362, 363, 365; **Supp. I Part 2:** 410, 422, 424, 539, 552, 675, 719, 720; **Supp. III Part 1:** 73; **Supp. IV Part 1:** 123, 168, 325; **Supp. IV Part 2:** 455; **Supp. IX:** 38, 39, 45; **Supp. VIII:** 41, 273; **Supp. XI:** 43, 320; **Supp. XII:** 9, 113, 255; **Supp. XIII:** 131, 281; **Supp. XIV:** 274; **Supp. XIX:** 33, 276; **Supp. XV:** 92; **Supp. XVII:** 76, 112; **Supp. XX: 115, 116; Supp. XXI:** 131; **Supp. XXIV:** 159
Keats, John (other), **Supp. IX:** 190, 195, 200
Keegan, Abigail, **Supp. XXIII:** 129, 130, 136
"Keela, the Outcast Indian Maiden" (Welty), **IV:** 263
Keeley, Mary Paxton, **Supp. XV:** 136
"Keen Scalpel on Racial Ills" (Bruell), **Supp. VIII:** 126
Keep, The (Egan), **Supp. XIX:** 49, **56–61**
"Keep A-Inchin' Along" (Van Vechten), **Supp. III Part 2:** 744
Keeper's Son, The (Hickam), **Supp. XXVII:** 111–112
Keeping (Goldbarth), **Supp. XII:** 179–180, 180
"Keeping Accounts" (Davison), **Supp. XXVI:** 77
"Keeping Informed in D.C." (Nemerov), **III:** 287
Keeping Slug Woman Alive: A Holistic Approach to American Indian Texts (Sarris), **Supp. IV Part 1:** 329
"'Keeping Their World Large' " (Moore), **III:** 201–202
Keeping the Night (Everwine), **Supp. XV:** 75, **81–85,** 86
"Keeping Things Whole" (Strand), **Supp. IV Part 2:** 624
Keep It Simple: A Defense of the Earth (Nichols), **Supp. XIII:** 268
"Keep the Saving Habit" (L. I. Wilder), **Supp. XXII:** 290
"Keep Your Pity" (Boyle), **Supp. XXIV:** 58, 59
Kees, Weldon, **Supp. X:** 118; **Supp. XII:** 198; **Supp. XV:** 113, 114, 115, **133–149**
Kehe, Marjorie, **Supp. XXVI:** 209
Keillor, Garrison, **Supp. XII:** 343; **Supp. XIII:** 274; **Supp. XVI: 165–179; Supp. XXI:** 53, 62; **Supp. XXII:** 83; **Supp. XXIII:** 57, 58, 138
Keillor, Gary Edward. See Keiller, Garrison
Keith, Brian, **Supp. IV Part 2:** 474
Keith, Minor C., **I:** 483
Kelleghan, Fiona, **Supp. XVIII:** 136, 139, 140
Keller, A. G., **III:** 108
Keller, Christopher J., **Supp. XVIII:** 192, 195
Keller, Helen, **I:** 254, 258; **Supp. XXIII:** 161
Keller, Lynn, **Supp. IV Part 2:** 423; **Supp. V:** 78, 80
Kelley, David, **Supp. IV Part 2:** 528, 529
Kelley, Florence, **Supp. I Part 1:** 5, 7
Kelley, Mary, **Supp. XVIII:** 257, 260
Kelley, Robin, **Supp. XVIII:** 231
Kellogg, Reverend Edwin H., **III:** 200
Kellogg, Paul U., **Supp. I Part 1:** 5, 7, 12
Kelly, **II:** 464
Kelly, Brigit Pegeen, **Supp. XVII: 123–134; Supp. XXIII:** 54
Kelly, Emmett, **Supp. XI:** 99, 106
Kelly, Gene, **Supp. XXI:** 148
Kelly, James Patrick, **Supp. XIX:** 231; **Supp. XVIII:** 145
Kelly, Walt, **Supp. XI:** 105
Kelly, William, **Supp. XV:** 75, 88
Kelsey, Penelope Myrtle, **Supp. XXIII:** 143, 153–164
Kelsh, Nick, **Supp. XVII:** 167, 179
Kemble, Fanny, **Retro. Supp. I:** 228
Kemble, Gouverneur, **II:** 298
Kemble, Peter, **II:** 298
Kempf, Andrea, **Supp. XXVI:** 212
Kempton, Murray, **Supp. VIII:** 104

Kempton-Wace Letters, The (London and Strunsky), **II:** 465
Kendall, Elaine, **Supp. XXVI:** 121
Kennan, George F., **Supp. VIII:** 241
Kennedy, Albert J., **Supp. I Part 1:** 19
Kennedy, Archibald, **Supp. XXVI:** 84
Kennedy, Arthur, **III:** 153
Kennedy, Burt, **Supp. IV Part 1:** 236
Kennedy, Jeffery, **Supp. XXI:** 6; **Supp. XXV:** 20
Kennedy, J. Gerald, **Retro. Supp. II:** 271; **Retro. Supp. III:** 237
Kennedy, John F., **I:** 136, 170; **II:** 49, 152–153; **III:** 38, 41, 42, 234, 411, 415, 581; **IV:** 229; **Supp. I Part 1:** 291; **Supp. I Part 2:** 496; **Supp. VIII:** 98, 104, 203; **Supp. XII:** 132; **Supp. XXVI:** 43
Kennedy, Mrs. John F., **I:** 136
Kennedy, John Pendleton, **II:** 313; **Retro. Supp. III:** 224; **Supp. XXII:** 193
Kennedy, Robert, **Supp. V:** 291
Kennedy, Robert F., **I:** 294; **Supp. I Part 1:** 52; **Supp. XI:** 343
Kennedy, Sarah, **Supp. XVIII:** 293, 299, 301
Kennedy, William, **Supp. VII: 131–157; Supp. XIX:** 141; **Supp. XVII:** 135; **Supp. XX: 90; Supp. XXIV:** 281, 282, 283
Kennedy, X. J., **Supp. V:** 178, 182; **Supp. XV:** 113, **151–173**
Kenner, Hugh, **III:** 475, 478; **IV:** 412; **Supp. I Part 1:** 255; **Supp. IV Part 2:** 474; **Supp. XV:** 147; **Supp. XXI:** 235; **Supp. XXVI:** 228
Kenneth Koch, a Tragedy (O'Hara and Rivers), **Supp. XXIII:** 217
"Kenneth Koch's 'Serious Moment' " (Spurr), **Supp. XV:** 183
Kenneth Millar/Ross Macdonald: A Checklist (Bruccoli), **Supp. IV Part 2:** 464, 469, 471
Kenney, Michael, **Supp. XIX:** 51, 52–53
Kenney, Susan, **Supp. XVIII:** 288, 289
Kenny, Maurice, **Supp. IV Part 2:** 502; **Supp. XXIII: 143–159**
Kent, George, **Supp. IV Part 1:** 11
Kent, Rockwell, **Supp. XV:** 41; **Supp. XXII:** 281
Kenton, Edna, **Supp. XXI:** 6; **Supp. XXV:** 21
Kenton, Maxwell. See Burnett, David; Hoffenberg, Mason; Southern, Terry
"Kent State, May 1970" (Haines), **Supp. XII:** 211
"Kentucky Derby Is Decadent and Depraved, The" (Thompson), **Supp. XXIV:** 282, **287–288**
Kentucky Straight (Offutt), **Supp. XIX: 163–167,** 171, 172
Kenya, the Land of Conflict (Kenyatta), **Supp. XXI:** 166
Kenyatta, Jomo, **Supp. X:** 135; **Supp. XXI:** 166
Kenyon, Jane, **Supp. VII: 159–177; Supp. VIII:** 272
Keogh, Tom, **Supp. XVI:** 230
Kepler, Johannes, **III:** 484; **IV:** 18
Keplinger, David, **Supp. XIX:** 273
Keppel, Frederick P., **I:** 214
"Kéramos" (Longfellow), **II:** 494; **Retro. Supp. II:** 167, 169
Kéramos and Other Poems (Longfellow), **II:** 490
Kerber, Linda K., **Supp. XXV:** 44
Kercheval, Jesse Lee, **Supp. XIX:** 51
Kerim, Ussin, **Supp. IX:** 152
Kermode, Frank, **IV:** 133; **Retro. Supp. I:** 301
Kern, Jerome, **II:** 427
Kerouac, Jack, **III:** 174; **Retro. Supp. I:** 102; **Supp. II Part 1:** 31, 307, 309, 318, 328; **Supp. III Part 1:** 91–94, 96, 100, **217–234; Supp. IV Part 1:** 90, 146; **Supp. IX:** 246; **Supp. V:** 336; **Supp. VIII:** 42, 138, 289, 305; **Supp. XII:** 118, 121, 122, 123, 126, 131, 132; **Supp. XIII:** 275, 284; **Supp. XIV:** 137, 138, 141, 142, 143–144; **Supp. XV:** 134, 221; **Supp. XVI:** 123; **Supp. XVII:** 135, 138; **Supp. XX: 17; Supp. XXIII:** 100, 213; **Supp. XXIV:** 34, 44; **Supp. XXV:** 29; **Supp. XXVI:** 252; **Supp. XXVII:** 18
Kerr, Deborah, **Supp. XI:** 307
Kerr, Orpheus C. (pseudonym). See Newell, Henry
Kerr, Walter, **Supp. IV Part 2:** 575, 579
Kerridge, Richard, **Supp. XVI:** 26
Kesey, Ken, **III:** 558; **Supp. III Part 1:** 217; **Supp. V:** 220, 295; **Supp. X:** 24, 265; **Supp. XI:** 104; **Supp. XXIII:** 100
Kessel, John, **Supp. XIX:** 231; **Supp. XVIII:** 145
Kessler, Milton, **Supp. XIX:** 195
Kessler, Rod, **Supp. XXVI:** 156
Kesten, Stephen, **Supp. XI:** 309
Ketchum, Liza, **Supp. XIX:** 266
Ketchup (Shanley), **Supp. XIV:** 315
Kevane, Bridget, **Supp. XI:** 185, 190
"Key, The" (Welty), **IV:** 262
"Keys" (Nye), **Supp. XIII:** 281
"Key to the Highway" (Halliday), **Supp. XIX:** 84
Key to Uncle Tom's Cabin, A (Stowe), **Supp. I Part 2:** 580
Key West (H. Crane), **Retro. Supp. II:** 84
"Key West" (H. Crane), **I:** 400
Key West: An Island Sheaf (Crane), **I:** 385, 399–402
"Khalil the Heretic" (Gibran), **Supp. XX: 124**
Khrushchev, Nikita, **I:** 136
Kiang Kang-hu, **Supp. XV:** 45, 47
Kick (Myers and Workman), **Supp. XXVII:** 206
Kick for a Bite, A (Cobbett), **Supp. XV:** 237
"Kicking the Candles Out" (Jarman), **Supp. XVII:** 113
Kid, The (Aiken), **I:** 61
Kid, The (Chaplin), **I:** 386
Kidder, Tracy, **Supp. III Part 1:** 302; **Supp. XVIII:** 106, 114
Kiddush Ha-Shem: An Epic of 1648 (Asch), **Supp. XXIII:** 3, 6, **10,** 11, 12, 16
Kidesh ha-Shem (Sanctification of the name) (Asch), **Supp. XXIII:** 6
Kidman, Nicole, **Supp. X:** 80
"Kidnaper" (Gallagher), **Supp. XXIV:** 168, 174
"Kidnapping in the Family, A" (Fante), **Supp. XI:** 164
"Kid's Guide to Divorce, The" (Moore), **Supp. X:** 167, 172
Kidwell, Clara Sue, **Supp. IV Part 1:** 333
Kielsky, Vera Emuma, **Supp. V:** 273
Kiely, Brendan, **Supp. XVII:** 75
Kieran, John, **II:** 417
Kierkegaard, Søren Aabye, **II:** 229; **III:** 292, 305, 309, 572; **IV:** 438, 491; **Retro. Supp. I:** 326; **Retro. Supp. II:** 222; **Supp. V:** 9; **Supp. VIII:** 7–8; **Supp. XX: 132**
Kiernan, Robert F., **Supp. IV Part 2:** 684
Kieseritsky, L., **III:** 252
Kilcup, Karen, **Retro. Supp. III:** 101
Kilgo, Jim, **Supp. XVIII:** 192
"Kilim" (McClatchy), **Supp. XII:** 258
Kilina, Patricia (pseudonym). See Warren, Patricia Nell
"Killed at Resaca" (Bierce), **I:** 202
"Killed at the Ford" (Longfellow), **Retro. Supp. II:** 170–171
Killens, John Oliver, **Supp. IV Part 1:** 8, 369; **Supp. XXVII:** 202
"Killer in the Rain" (Chandler), **Supp. IV Part 1:** 122
"Killers, The" (Hemingway), **II:** 249; **Retro. Supp. I:** 188, 189

Killers, The: A Narrative of Real Life in Philadelphia (Lippard), **Supp. XXIII:** 178, 184
Killing Mister Watson (Matthiessen), **Supp. V:** 212, 214
"Killing of a State Cop, The" (Ortiz), **Supp. IV Part 2:** 499
Killing of Sister George, The (Marcus), **Supp. I Part 1:** 277
Killing Orders (Paretsky), **Supp. XXV:** 176, 177, 179, 182–813
"Killings" (Dubus), **Supp. VII:** 85–86
"Killing the Ghost of Ripton" (Carruth), **Supp. XIX:** 1
"Killing the Plants" (Kenyon), **Supp. VII:** 167, 168
Kilmer, Joyce, **Supp. I Part 2:** 387; **Supp. XV:** 294
Kilpatrick, James K., **Supp. X:** 145
Kilvert, Francis, **Supp. VIII:** 172
Kim (Kipling), **Supp. X:** 230
Kim, Alfred, **Supp. XI:** 140
Kim, Sharon, **Supp. XVIII:** 267
Kimball, Frederic, **Supp. XXI:** 146
Kimball, J. Golden, **Supp. IV Part 2:** 602
Kimbrough, Mary Craig. See Sinclair, Mary Craig (Mary Craig Kimbrough)
Kimes, Maymie B., **Supp. IX:** 178
Kimes, William F., **Supp. IX:** 178
Kimmelman, Bert, **Supp. XXI:** 24
Kimura, Takeshi, **Supp. XXVI:** 88
"Kin" (Welty), **IV:** 277; **Retro. Supp. I:** 353
Kinard, Agnes Dodds, **Supp. XIV:** 122, 123, 127
Kincaid, Jamaica, **Supp. VII: 179–196**
Kincaid, James, **Supp. XVIII:** 62, 63
"Kindness" (Dunn), **Supp. XI:** 149, 150
"Kindness" (Nye), **Supp. XIII:** 285
"Kindness" (Plath), **Retro. Supp. II:** 256
Kind of Light that Shines on Texas, The (McKnight), **Supp. XX: 151–152**
"Kind of Light that Shines on Texas, The" (McKnight), **Supp. XX: 151**
Kind of Order, A Kind of Folly, A: Essays and Conversations (Kunitz), **Supp. III Part 1:** 262, 268
Kindred (O. Butler), **Supp. XIII: 59–60,** 69
"Kind Sir: These Woods" (Sexton), **Supp. II Part 2:** 673
Kinds of Love (Sarton), **Supp. VIII: 253–254,** 256
Kinfolk (Buck), **Supp. II Part 1:** 126
King, Alexander, **IV:** 287
King, Carole, **Supp. XII:** 308
King, Clarence, **I:** 1
King, Ernest, **Supp. I Part 2:** 491
King, Fisher, **II:** 425
King, Francis, **Supp. XIV:** 155, 156, 166, 169
King, Grace, **Retro. Supp. II:** 136
King, Martin Luther, Jr., **Retro. Supp. II:** 12, 13; **Supp. XVIII:** 24; **Supp. XX: 281**
King, Michael, **Supp. XII:** 182
King, Queen, Knave (Nabokov), **III:** 251; **Retro. Supp. I:** 270
King, Starr, **Supp. II Part 1:** 341, 342
King, Stephen, **Supp. IV Part 1:** 102, 104; **Supp. IV Part 2:** 467; **Supp. IX:** 114; **Supp. V: 137–155; Supp. XIII:** 53; **Supp. XXIII:** 290; **Supp. XXV:** 123, 152, 153; **Supp. XXVII:** 276
King, Tabitha (Mrs. Stephen King), **Supp. V:** 137
King, The (Barthelme), **Supp. IV Part 1:** 47, 52
"King, The" (Gibran), **Supp. XX: 123–124**
King Coffin (Aiken), **I:** 53–54, 57
"King David" (Benét), **Supp. XI:** 44
"King David" (Reznikoff), **Supp. XIV:** 283
Kingdom and the Power, The (Talese), **Supp. XVII:** 202, 203, 204, 210
Kingdom by the Sea, The: A Journey around Great Britain (Theroux), **Supp. VIII:** 323
"Kingdom County Come" (Mosher), **Supp. XXII:** 211–212
Kingdom Far and Clear, A: The Complete Swan Lake Trilogy (Helprin), **Supp. XXV:** 87
Kingdom of Earth (T. Williams), **IV:** 382, 386, 387, 388, 391, 393, 398
"Kingdom of Earth, The" (T. Williams), **IV:** 384
Kingdom of Fear (Thompson), **Supp. XXIV:** 283
"Kingdom of God Is Within You, The" (Very), **Supp. XXV:** 249
Kingfisher, The (Clampitt), **Supp. IX:** 38
"Kingfishers, The" (Olson), **Supp. II Part 2:** 557, 558–563, 582
King Jasper (Robinson), **III:** 523
King Kong (film), **Supp. IV Part 1:** 104; **Supp. XVII:** 58
King Lear (Shakespeare), **I:** 538; **II:** 540, 551; **Retro. Supp. I:** 248; **Supp. IV Part 1:** 31, 36; **Supp. IX:** 14; **Supp. XI:** 172; **Supp. XV:** 349
King Leopold's Soliloquy (Twain), **IV:** 208
"King Leopold's Soliloquy: A Defense of His Congo Rule" (Twain), **Retro. Supp. III:** 269
King My Father's Wreck, The (Simpson), **Supp. IX:** 266, 267, 270, 275, 276
King of Babylon Shall Not Come Against You, The (Garrett), **Supp. VII:** 110–111; **Supp. X:** 3
"King of Beasts" (P. N. Warren), **Supp. XX: 272**
"King of Folly Island, The" (Jewett), **II:** 394; **Retro. Supp. II:** 132, 133
King of Kings (film), **Supp. IV Part 2:** 520
King of Paris (Endore), **Supp. XVII:** 64
King of Spain, The (Bodenheim), **Supp. XXV:** 26
"King of the Bingo Game" (Ellison), **Retro. Supp. II:** 117, 125; **Supp. II Part 1:** 235, 238, 240–241
"King of the Cats, The" (Benét), **Supp. XI:** 49–50
"King of the Clock Tower" (Yeats), **III:** 473
"King of the Desert, The" (O'Hara), **III:** 369
King of the Fields, The (Singer), **Retro. Supp. II:** 317
King of the Jews (Epstein), **Supp. XII:** 161, **166–170,** 172
King of the Mountain (Garrett), **Supp. VII:** 96, 97
"King of the River" (Kunitz), **Supp. III Part 1:** 263, 267–268
"King of the Sea" (Marquand), **III:** 60
"King over the Water" (Blackmur), **Supp. II Part 1:** 107
"King Pandar" (Blackmur), **Supp. II Part 1:** 92, 102
"King Pest" (Poe), **Retro. Supp. II:** 273
Kingsblood Royal (Lewis), **II:** 456
Kingsbury, John, **Supp. I Part 1:** 8
"King's Daughters, Home for Unwed Mothers, 1948" (Stanford), **Supp. XV:** 345
King's Henchman, The (Millay), **III:** 138–139
Kingsley, Sidney, **Supp. I Part 1:** 277, 281
King's Mare, The (Canolle; Loos, trans.), **Supp. XVI:** 194
"King's Missive, The" (Whittier), **Supp. I Part 2:** 694
Kingsolver, Barbara, **Supp. VII: 197–**

214; Supp. XIII: 16; **Supp. XVIII:** 189
King's Stilts, The (Geisel), **Supp. XVI:** 100, 104
Kingston, Earll, **Supp. V:** 160
Kingston, Maxine Hong, **Supp. IV Part 1:** 1, 12; **Supp. V: 157–175,** 250; **Supp. X:** 291–292; **Supp. XI:** 18, 245; **Supp. XV:** 220, 223
"King Volmer and Elsie" (Whittier), **Supp. I Part 2:** 696
Kinkaid, Jamaica, **Supp. XXII:** 65
Kinmont, Alexander, **Supp. I Part 2:** 588–589
Kinnaird, John, **Retro. Supp. I:** 399
Kinnell, Galway, **Supp. III Part 1: 235–256; Supp. III Part 2:** 541; **Supp. IV Part 2:** 623; **Supp. V:** 332; **Supp. VIII:** 39; **Supp. XI:** 139; **Supp. XII:** 241; **Supp. XV:** 212; **Supp. XVI:** 53; **Supp. XXII:** 83; **Supp. XXVI:** 67
Kinsella, Thomas, **Supp. XX: 195–196, 197, 207**
Kinsey, Alfred, **IV:** 230; **Supp. XIV:** 140
Kinzie, Mary, **Supp. XII:** 181; **Supp. XXIII:** 124
"Kipling" (Trilling), **Supp. III Part 2:** 495
Kipling, Rudyard, **I:** 421, 587–588; **II:** 271, 338, 404, 439; **III:** 55, 328, 508, 511, 521, 524, 579; **IV:** 429; **Supp. IV Part 2:** 603; **Supp. X:** 255; **Supp. XX: 23**
Kirby, David, **Supp. XIII:** 89; **Supp. XIX:** 81
Kirk, Connie, **Retro. Supp. III:** 210
Kirkland, Caroline, **Supp. XVIII:** 258
Kirkland, David, **Supp. XVI:** 186
Kirkland, Jack, **I:** 297
Kirkland, John, **Supp. XXIV:** 70
Kirkpatrick, Jeane, **Supp. VIII:** 241
Kirkus, Virginia, **Supp. XV:** 198
Kirkwood, Cynthia A., **Supp. XI:** 177, 178, 179
Kirp, David L., **Supp. XI:** 129
Kirsch, Adam, **Supp. XV:** 251, 260, 264, 266, 341, 347, 350–351; **Supp. XXV:** 222, 233, 253, 262, 268; **Supp. XXVII:** 144
Kirsch, Robert, **Supp. XXVII:** 134
Kirstein, Lincoln, **Supp. II Part 1:** 90, 97; **Supp. IV Part 1:** 82, 83; **Supp. XXII:** 281
Kishef-makherin fun Kastilye, Di (The witch of Castle) (Asch), **Supp. XXIII:** 6
"Kiss, The" (Di Piero), **Supp. XIX:** 45, 47
Kiss, The (Harrison), **Supp. X:** 191
"Kiss, The" (Sexton), **Supp. II Part 2:** 687
"Kiss, The" (Teasdale), **Supp. XXVII:** 291
"Kiss Away" (C. Baxter), **Supp. XVII:** 20
Kissel, Howard, **Supp. IV Part 2:** 580
Kiss Hollywood Good-by (Loos), **Supp. XVI:** 190, 195
Kissinger, Henry, **Supp. IV Part 1:** 388; **Supp. XII:** 9, 14; **Supp. XXV:** 264
Kiss of the Spider Woman, the Musical (McNally), **Supp. XIII:** 207, **Supp. XIII:** 208
Kiss Tomorrow Good-bye (McCoy), **Supp. XIII:** 170, **172–173,** 174
"Kit and Caboodle" (Komunyakaa), **Supp. XIII:** 115
Kit Brandon: A Portrait (Anderson), **I:** 111
Kitchen, Judith, **Supp. IV Part 1:** 242, 245, 252; **Supp. IX:** 163; **Supp. XI:** 312, 313, 315, 317, 319, 320, 326, 329; **Supp. XV:** 215, 219; **Supp. XXVI:** 154–155
"Kitchenette" (Brooks), **Retro. Supp. I:** 208
Kitchen God's Wife, The (Tan), **Supp. X:** 289, 292, 293, 294–295, 296–297, 298–299
"Kitchen Terrarium: 1983" (McCarriston), **Supp. XIV:** 270
Kit O'Brien (Masters), **Supp. I Part 2:** 471
Kittel, Frederick August. See Wilson, August
Kittredge, Charmian. See London, Mrs. Jack (Charmian Kittredge)
Kittredge, William, **Supp. VIII:** 39; **Supp. XI:** 316; **Supp. XII:** 209; **Supp. XIII:** 16; **Supp. XXVI: 177–190**
"Kitty Hawk" (Frost), **II:** 164; **Retro. Supp. I:** 124, 141; **Retro. Supp. III:** 107
Kizer, Carolyn, **Supp. XVII:** 71, 72, 73, 74
Klaidman, Stephen, **Supp. XIX:** 269
Klail City (Hinojosa), **Supp. XIX:** 97, **101–103**
Klail City Death Trip (Hinojosa). See Ask a Policeman (Hinojosa); Becky and Her Friends (Hinojosa); Dear Rafe (Hinojosa); Fair Gentlemen of Belken County (Hinojosa); Klail City (Hinojosa); Korean Love Songs from Klail City Death Trip (Hinojosa); Partners in Crime: A Rafe Buenrostro Mystery (Hinojosa); Rites and Witnesses: A Comedy (Hinojosa); Useless Servants, The (Hinojosa); Valley, The (Hinojosa)
"Klassikal Lymnaeryx" (Stallings), **Supp. XXV:** 233
Klein, Joe, **Supp. XII:** 67–68
Klein, Marcus, **Supp. I Part 2:** 432; **Supp. XI:** 233
Kleist, Heinrich von, **Supp. IV Part 1:** 224
Kline, Franz, **Supp. XII:** 198; **Supp. XXIII:** 210, 211, 217
Kline, George, **Supp. VIII:** 22, 28
Klinghoffer, David, **Supp. XVI:** 74
Klinkowitz, Jerome, **Supp. IV Part 1:** 40; **Supp. X:** 263; **Supp. XI:** 347; **Supp. XXI:** 233
Klise, James, **Supp. XXII:** 53
Kloefkorn, Bill, **Supp. XIX:** 119
Knapp, Adeline, **Supp. XI:** 200
Knapp, Friedrich, **III:** 100
Knapp, Samuel, **I:** 336
Knapp, Samuel Lorenzo, **Supp. XV:** 246
"Kneeling Down to Look into a Culvert" (R. Bly), **Supp. XXI:** 88
Kneel to the Rising Sun (Caldwell), **I:** 304, 309
"Knees/Dura-Europos" (Goldbarth), **Supp. XII:** 185
"Knife" (Simic), **Supp. VIII:** 275
"Knife Longs for the Ruby, The" (Vaz), **Supp. XXVI:** 266–267
Knight, Arthur, **Supp. XIV:** 144
Knight, Etheridge, **Supp. XI:** 239; **Supp. XXIII:** 174
Knight, Lania, **Supp. XXIII:** 273, 274, 275, 276, 279, 280
"Knight, The" (Rich), **Retro. Supp. III:** 244
"Knight in Disguise, The" (Lindsay), **Supp. I Part 2:** 390
Knightly Quest, The (T. Williams), **IV:** 383
Knight's Gambit (Faulkner), **II:** 72
Knish, Anne. See Ficke, Arthur Davison
"Knit One, Purl Two" (K. Snodgrass), **Supp. XVI:** 42
"Knock" (Dickey), **Supp. IV Part 1:** 182
Knocked Out Loaded (album, Dylan), **Supp. XVIII:** 28
"Knocking Around" (Ashbery), **Supp. III Part 1:** 22
"Knocking on Heaven's Door" (Lamott), **Supp. XX: 140–141**
"Knocking on Three, Winston"

(Epstein), **Supp. XIV:** 109
Knock on Any Door (film, Ray), **Supp. XVII:** 150
Knock on Any Door (W. Motley), 158; **Supp. XVII: 150–155,** 159, 160
Knockout Artist, The (Crews), **Supp. XI: 113–114**
Knoll, Robert E., **Supp. XV:** 118
Knopf, Alfred A., **III:** 99, 105, 106, 107; **Retro. Supp. I:** 13, 19, 317; **Supp. I Part 1:** 324, 325, 327; **Supp. IV Part 1:** 125, 354; **Supp. XIII:** 172
Knopf, Blanche, **Supp. I Part 1:** 324, 325, 327, 328, 332, 341; **Supp. IV Part 1:** 128, 346, 348; **Supp. XIII:** 169
"Knot, The" (Rich), **Supp. I Part 2:** 555
Knot-Holes (Bodenheim and Saphier), **Supp. XXV:** 20
Knotts, Kristina, **Supp. XIII:** 238
"Knowing, The" (Olds), **Supp. X:** 215
"Knowledge Forwards and Backwards" (Stern), **Supp. IX:** 296
"Knowledge of Plates" (Bronk), **Supp. XXI:** 33
Knowles, John, **Supp. IV Part 2:** 679; **Supp. XII: 235–250; Supp. XX: 84**
Known World, The (E. P. Jones), **Supp. XXII:** 139, 140, 142**, 146–150,** 150
Knox, Bernard, **Supp. XXIV:** 153
Knox, Frank, **Supp. I Part 2:** 488, 489
Knox, Israel, **Supp. X:** 70
Knox, Vicesimus, **II:** 8
Knoxville: Summer of 1915 (Agee), **I:** 42–46
Knudson, R. Rozanne, **Supp. IV Part 2:** 648
Kober, Arthur, **Supp. I Part 1:** 292
Koch, Frederick, **IV:** 453
Koch, John, **Supp. VIII:** 88
Koch, Kenneth, **Supp. XIX:** 81; **Supp. XV: 175–192; Supp. XXIII:** 124, 207, 209, 210, 211, 215, 217, 220; **Supp. XXIV:** 33, 36, 42, 44; **Supp. XXVII:** 23, 26
Koch, Vivienne, **III:** 194; **IV:** 136, 140; **Retro. Supp. I:** 428, 430
"Kochinnenako in Academe: Three Approaches to Interpreting a Keres Indian Tale" (Gunn Allen), **Supp. IV Part 1:** 329
"Kodachromes of the Island" (Hayden), **Supp. II Part 1:** 367, 380
Koestler, Arthur, **I:** 258; **Supp. I Part 2:** 671; **Supp. XXIII:** 1
Kokkinen, Eila, **Supp. XIV:** 146, 148
"Kola Street"(Asch), **Supp. XXIII:** 7
Kolba, Ellen D., **Supp. XVIII:** 257
Kolbenheyer, Dr. Frederick, **Supp. I Part 1:** 207
Kolodny, Annette, **Supp. X:** 97, 103, 229
Komisarjevsky, W. P., **Supp. XXIII:** 5
"Komodo" (C. Frost), **Supp. XV:** 95
Komunyakaa, Yusef, **Supp. XIII: 111–136; Supp. XXI:** 129, 139; **Supp. XXIII:** 254; **Supp. XXVII:** 166
Konigsberg, Allan Stewart. See Allen, Woody
Kon-Tiki (Heyerdahl), **II:** 477
Koopman, Harry Lyman, **Retro. Supp. I:** 40
Ko; or, A Season on Earth (Koch), **Supp. XV:** 175, 180, 181, 183, 186
Kooser, Ted, **Supp. XIX: 115–130; Supp. XV:** 113, 115; **Supp. XXI:** 243
Kootz, Samuel, **Supp. XV:** 144
Kora and Ka (Doolittle), **Supp. I Part 1:** 270
Kora in Hell (W. C. Williams), **Retro. Supp. I:** 416, **417–418,** 419, 430, 431; **Supp. XXI:** 232
Korb, Rena, **Supp. XI:** 2
Korczak, Janosz, **Supp. X:** 70
Korean Love Songs from Klail City Death Trip (Hinojosa), **Supp. XIX:** 98, **103–104**
Kornblatt, Joyce Reiser, **Supp. XV:** 62
Kornfield, Jack, **Supp. XX: 142; Supp. XXIII:** 138
Korrektur (Bernhard), **Supp. XX: 91**
Kort, Amy, **Supp. XIII:** 148
Korwin, Yala, **Supp. XXI:** 99
Kosinski, Jerzy, **Supp. VII: 215–228; Supp. XII:** 21
"Kostas Tympakianakis" (Merrill), **Supp. III Part 1:** 326
Kostelanetz, Richard, **Supp. XXVII:** 166
Koteliansky, S. S., **Supp. VIII:** 251, 265
Kouidis, Virginia M., **Supp. XXII:** 161, 162, 166, 167, 169
Kovic, Ron, **Supp. XIX:** 17; **Supp. XXII:** 104
Kowloon Tong (Theroux), **Supp. VIII:** 325
Kozlenko, William, **IV:** 378, 381
Krabbenhoft, Ken, **Supp. XVII:** 112
Kraft, James, **Supp. XV:** 40, 41, 42, 43, 52
Krakauer, Jon, **Supp. XVII:** 210; **Supp. XVIII: 105–118**
Kramer, Dale, **Supp. I Part 2:** 669
Kramer, Glenn Philip, **Supp. XXIII:** 125
Kramer, Hilton, **III:** 537; **Supp. I Part 1:** 295, 296; **Supp. VIII:** 239; **Supp. XIX:** 269; **Supp. XV:** 113; **Supp. XXVII:** 23
Kramer, Lawrence, **Supp. IV Part 1:** 61, 65, 66; **Supp. IX:** 291
Kramer, Peter D., **Supp. XVI:** 229
Kramer, Robert, **Supp. XXVI:** 26
Kramer, Stanley, **II:** 421, 587
Krapp's Last Tape (Beckett), **I:** 71; **III:** 387; **Retro. Supp. I:** 206
Krassner, Paul, **Supp. IV Part 1:** 385; **Supp. XI:** 293
Kraus, Karl, **Supp. XX: 84**
Krauth, Leland, **Supp. XVIII:** 58
Krauzer, Steven M., **Supp. XXVI:** 181, 182, 188
Kreisler, Harry, **Supp. XVI:** 155
Kreitman, Esther, **IV:** 2
Krementz, Jill, **Supp. XXV:** 263
"Kremlin of Smoke" (Schnackenberg), **Supp. XV:** 257–258
Kreyling, Michael, **Supp. XXVI:** 14
Kreymborg, Alfred, **II:** 530; **III:** 465; **IV:** 76; **Retro. Supp. I:** 417; **Supp. XV:** 301, 306; **Supp. XXII:** 161–162; **Supp. XXV:** 18, 19, 21
Kriegel, Leonard, **Supp. XXIV: 213–228**
Krim, Seymour, **Supp. XV:** 338; **Supp. XVI:** 217; **Supp. XVIII:** 285
Krisak, Len, **Supp. XXI:** 99, 104
Kristeva, Julia, **Supp. XII:** 6
Kristofferson, Kris, **Supp. XIII:** 119
Kristol, Irving, **Supp. VIII:** 93, 244; **Supp. XIII:** 98
Kristwald, Elfriede, **Supp. XXVI:** 4, 7
Krivak, Andrew, **Supp. XVII:** 242
Kroll, Jack, **Supp. IV Part 2:** 590; **Supp. XXIII:** 103
Kroll, Judith, **Supp. I Part 2:** 541–543, 544, 546
Kroll Ring, Frances. See Ring, Frances Kroll
Krondorfer, Björn, **Supp. XVI:** 160
Kronenberger, Louis, **Supp. XXII:** 191, 192
Krook, Dorothea, **Retro. Supp. II:** 243
Kropotkin, Peter, **I:** 493; **Supp. I Part 1:** 5; **Supp. IV Part 2:** 521
Krueger, Bill, **Supp. XXVII:** 13
Kruif, Paul de, **II:** 446
Krupat, Arnold, **Supp. IV Part 2:** 500
Krupnick, Mark, **Supp. XVI:** 153
Krutch, Joseph Wood, **II:** 459; **III:** 425; **IV:** 70, 175
Krutikov, Mikhail, **Supp. XXIII:** 11
Kubach, David, **Supp. XXVI:** 243, 245, 246, 248
Kublai Khan, **III:** 395
"Kubla Khan" (Coleridge), **Supp.**

XIII: 131, 283
Kubrick, Stanley, **Supp. IV Part 1:** 392; **Supp. XI:** 293,**Supp. XI:** 301, 302–303
"Kubuku Rides (This Is It) " (L. Brown), **Supp. XXI:** 39, 42–43
Kuehl, John, **Supp. IV Part 1:** 279, 284, 285, 287
Kuehl, Linda, **Supp. IV Part 1:** 199
"Kugelmass Episode, The" (Allen), **Supp. XV:** 15, 16
Kukachin, Princess, **III:** 395
"Ku Klux" (Hughes), **Retro. Supp. I:** 205
Kulshrestha, Chirantan, **Retro. Supp. II:** 21
Kumin, Maxine, **Supp. IV Part 2: 439–457; Supp. XIII:** 294; **Supp. XVII:** 71, 75–76; **Supp. XX: 164; Supp. XXVI:** 68; **Supp. XXVII:** 256
Kundera, Milan, **Retro. Supp. III:** 320; **Supp. VIII:** 241
Kunerth, Jeff, **Supp. XXI:** 47
Kunitz, Stanley, **I:** 179, 180, 181, 182, 521; **II:** 545; **Supp. III Part 1: 257–270; Supp. V:** 79; **Supp. XI:** 259; **Supp. XIII:** 341; **Supp. XXVI:** 64, 67, 68
Kuo, Helena, **Supp. X:** 291
Kuropatkin, General Aleksei Nikolaevich, **III:** 247–248
Kurth, Peter, **Supp. XVIII:** 145
Kurzy of the Sea (Barnes), **Supp. III Part 1:** 34
Kushner, Tony, **Retro. Supp. III:** 165; **Supp. IX: 131–149; Supp. XX: 177; Supp. XXI:** 145; **Supp. XXIV:** 263
Kussy, Bella, **IV:** 468
Kutnik, Jerzy, **Supp. XXII:** 177
Kuttner, Henry, **Supp. IV Part 1:** 102
Kuzma, Greg, **Supp. XV:** 118
Kyger, Joanne, **Supp. XXIV:** 37
LaBastille, Anne, **Supp. X: 95–110; Supp. XXVI:** 34
"Labor Day Dinner" (Munro), **Supp. XXVII:** 188
"Labor's Cultural Degradation" (Swados), **Supp. XIX:** 264–265
"Labours of Hercules, The" (Moore), **III:** 201
La Bruyère, Jean de, **I:** 58
La Bufera e Altro (Montale), **Supp. V:** 337
LaBute, Neil, **Supp. XXI:** 147
Labyrinth of Love (Untermeyer), **Supp. XV:** 312
Labyrinth of Solitude, The (Paz), **Supp. XIII:** 223
Lacan, Jacques, **Retro. Supp. III:** 237; **Supp. IV Part 1:** 45; **Supp. VIII:** 5; **Supp. XII:** 98
La Casa en Mango Street (Cisneros), **Supp. VII:** 58–59
Lacayo, Richard, **Supp. XXV:** 4
Lachaise, Gaston, **I:** 434
"Lackawanna" (Merwin), **Supp. III Part 1:** 350
Lackawanna Elegy (Goll; Kinnell, trans.), **Supp. III Part 1:** 235, 243–244
Laclède, Pierre, **Supp. I Part 1:** 205
"Lacquer Prints" (A. Lowell), **II:** 524–525
Lacy, Ed, **Supp. XV: 193–210**
Ladder, The (Rasmussen; Nelson, trans.), **Supp. XVIII:** 180–181
Ladder of Years (Tyler), **Supp. IV Part 2:** 657, 671–672
Ladders to Fire (Nin), **Supp. X:** 185
Laddie (Stratton-Porter), **Supp. XX: 211, 213**
"Laddie, the Princess and the Pie" (Stratton-Porter), **Supp. XX: 216**
"Ladies" (Coleman), **Supp. XI:** 93
Ladies Almanack (Barnes), **Supp. III Part 1:** 37–39, 42; **Supp. XXII:** 167
Ladies and Gentlemen (Hecht and MacArthur), **Supp. XXVII:** 90
Ladies Auxiliary, The (Mirvis), **Supp. XX: 177, 179–185**
"Ladies in Spring" (Welty), **IV:** 276–277; **Retro. Supp. I:** 353
Lady, The (Richter), **Supp. XVIII: 211–212,** 220
Lady Audley's Secret (Braddon), **Supp. I Part 1:** 35, 36
"Lady Barberina" (James), **Retro. Supp. I:** 227
"Lady Bates" (Jarrell), **II:** 380–381
Lady Chatterley's Lover (Lawrence), **III:** 170; **IV:** 434; **Retro. Supp. III:** 25; **Supp. XVI:** 267
Ladye Annabel (Lippard), **Supp. XXIII:** 178
Lady from Louisiana (film, Vorhaus), **Supp. XVII:** 59
"Lady from Redhorse, A" (Bierce), **I:** 203
Lady in Kicking Horse Reservoir, The (Hugo), **Supp. VI:** 134, **138–139**
Lady in the Lake, The (Chandler), **Supp. IV Part 1:** 127, 129–130
"Lady in the Lake, The" (Chandler), **Supp. IV Part 1:** 129
Lady in the Lake, The (film), **Supp. IV Part 1:** 130
"Lady in the Pink Mustang, The" (Erdrich), **Supp. IV Part 1:** 270
"Lady Is Civilized, The" (Taylor), **Supp. V:** 315
Lady Is Cold, The (White), **Supp. I Part 2:** 653
Lady Killer (Holding), **Supp. XXII:** 126, **127,** 130
"Lady Lazarus" (Plath), **Retro. Supp. II:** 250, 251, 255; **Supp. I Part 2:** 529, 535, 542, 545
Lady of Aroostook, The (Howells), **II:** 280
"Lady of Bayou St. John, A" (Chopin), **Retro. Supp. II:** 58
"Lady of the Lake, The" (Malamud), **Supp. I Part 2:** 437
Lady Oracle (Atwood), **Supp. XIII:** 21, **23–24**
"Lady Poverty" (Notley), **Supp. XXII:** 234–235
Lady Sings the Blues (film), **Supp. I Part 1:** 67
"Lady's Maid's Bell, The" (Wharton), **IV:** 316
"Lady Wentworth" (Longfellow), **II:** 505
"Lady with a Lamp" (Parker), **Supp. IX:** 193
"Lady with the Heron, The" (Merwin), **Supp. III Part 1:** 343
"Lady with the Pet Dog, The" (Chekov), **Supp. XXII:** 60
"Lady with the Pet Tribble, The" (Brockmeier), **Supp. XXII:** 60
La Farge, John, **I:** 1, 2, 20; **II:** 322, 338; **Retro. Supp. I:** 217
La Farge, Oliver, **Supp. IV Part 2:** 503
Lafayette, Marquis de, **I:** 344, 345; **II:** 405–406; **Supp. I Part 2:** 510, 511, 683
"La Figlia Che Piange" (T. S. Eliot), **Retro. Supp. I:** 63; **Retro. Supp. III:** 60
La Follette, Robert, **I:** 483, 485, 492; **III:** 580
La Fontaine, Jean de, **II:** 154; **III:** 194; **IV:** 80
Laforgue, Jules, **I:** 386, 569, 570, 572–573, 575, 576; **II:** 528; **III:** 8, 11, 466; **IV:** 37, 79, 80, 122; **Retro. Supp. I:** 55, 56; **Retro. Supp. III:** 57, 59; **Supp. XIII:** 332, 335, 346; **Supp. XV:** 165
La Gallienne, Eva, **Supp. VIII:** 251
"Lager Beer" (Dunbar), **Supp. II Part 1:** 193
"La Gringuita: On Losing a Native Language" (Alvarez), **Supp. VII:** 18
Laguna Woman (Silko), **Supp. IV Part 2:** 557, 560–561
LaHaye, Tim, **Supp. XXVII:** 5

Lahiri, Jhumpa, **Supp. XXI: 175–189; Supp. XXIII:** 289
Lahr, John, **Supp. XXI:** 18
Laing, R. D., **Supp. I Part 2:** 527; **Supp. XX: 94**
La kabbale pratique (Ambelain), **Supp. I Part 1:** 273
"Lake, The" (Bradbury), **Supp. IV Part 1:** 101
Lake, The (play), **Supp. IX:** 189
"Lake, The" (Poe), **Retro. Supp. III:** 231
Lakeboat (Mamet), **Supp. XIV:** 240–241
"Lake Chelan" (Stafford), **Supp. XI:** 321
Lake Effect Country (Ammons), **Supp. VII:** 34, 35
"Lake Isle of Innisfree, The" (Yeats), **Retro. Supp. I:** 413; **Supp. XIX:** 92
"Lake Return" (Wright), **Supp. XV:** 345
Lake Wobegon Days (Keillor), **Supp. XVI:** 165, 166, **173–174**
Lake Wobegon Summer 1956 (Keillor), **Supp. XVI:** 178
Lalic, Ivan V., **Supp. VIII:** 272
Lamantia, Philip, **Supp. VIII:** 289
Lamb, Brian, **Supp. XIX:** 156; **Supp. XX: 101**
Lamb, Charles, **III:** 111, 207; **Supp. VIII:** 125
Lamb, Wendy, **Supp. IV Part 2:** 658
Lambardi, Marilyn May, **Retro. Supp. II:** 45–46
Lamb in His Bosom (C. Miller), **Supp. XXII:** 187, **189–191,** 193–194, 195, 197, 198, 199, 200
"Lambkill" (Davison), **Supp. XXVI:** 75
"Lame Feet of Salvation, The" (W. V. Davis), **Supp. XXI:** 87–88
"Lament" (Wilbur), **Supp. III Part 2:** 550
Lament and Chastisement (O'Hara), **Supp. XXIII:** 209
"Lamentation in Winter"(Schott), **Supp. XXIII:** 243
"Lamentations" (Glück), **Supp. V:** 83, 84
"Lament for Dark Peoples" (Hughes), **Retro. Supp. I:** 199
"Lament for Saul and Jonathan" (Bradstreet), **Supp. I Part 1:** 111
"Lament-Heaven" (Doty), **Supp. XI:** 125
"Lament of a New England Mother, The" (Eberhart), **I:** 539
Laments for the Living (Parker), **Supp. IX:** 192
"Lame Shall Enter First, The" (O'Connor), **III:** 348, 351, 352, 355, 356–357, 358; **Retro. Supp. II:** 237; **Retro. Supp. III:** 215
"Lamia" (Davison), **Supp. XXVI:** 74
Lamia (Keats), **II:** 512; **III:** 523
Lamming, George, **Supp. XXI:** 170
Lamott, Anne, **Supp. XX: 131–146**
La Motte-Fouqué, Friedrich Heinrich Karl, **III:** 77, 78
L'Amour, Louis, **Supp. XIII:** 5; **Supp. XXVI:** 186
Lamp for Nightfall, A (Caldwell), **I:** 297
Lamplit Answer, The (Schnackenberg), **Supp. XV:** 251, 254, **256–260**
"Lana Turner Has Collapsed!"(O'Hara), **Supp. XXIII:** 220
"Lance" (Nabokov), **Retro. Supp. I:** 266
Lancelot (Percy), **Supp. III Part 1:** 384, 395–396
Lancelot (Robinson), **III:** 513, 522
Lanchester, John, **Retro. Supp. I:** 278
"Land" (Emerson), **II:** 6
"Land Aesthetic, The" (Callicott), **Supp. XIV:** 184
Land and Freedom (film, Loach), **Supp. XXIII:** 163
"Land and Language" (J. W. Miller), **Supp. XX: 170**
Landau, Deborah, **Supp. XI:** 122, 123
"Land beyond the Blow, The" (Bierce), **I:** 209
"Land Ethic, The" (Leopold), **Supp. XIV:** 179, 180, 183, 191, 192
Landfall (Wagoner), **Supp. IX:** 330
"Landing in Luck" (Faulkner), **Retro. Supp. I:** 85
"Landing on the Moon" (Swenson), **Supp. IV Part 2:** 643
"Landings" (Hoffman), **Supp. XVIII:** 86
"Landing Under Water, I See Roots" (A. Finch), **Supp. XVII:** 76
"Land"(Kenny), **Supp. XXIII:** 147
Landlord at Lion's Head, The (Howells), **II:** 276, 287–288
Landmarks of Healing: A Study of House Made of Dawn (Scarberry-García), **Supp. IV Part 2:** 486
Land of Little Rain, The (Dillard), **Supp. VI: 27–28**
Land of Look Behind, The (Cliff), **Supp. XXII:** 65–66, 68–69
Land of the Free U.S.A. (MacLeish), **I:** 293; **III:** 16–17
Land of Unlikeness (R. Lowell), **II:** 537–538, 539, 547; **Retro. Supp. II:** 177, 178, **184–185**
Landor, Walter Savage, **III:** 15, 469; **Supp. I Part 2:** 422
"Landscape" (Sarton), **Supp. VIII:** 259
"Landscape #11" (Halliday), **Supp. XIX:** 93
Landscape and Journey (W. V. Davis), **Supp. XXI:** 83, 88, 90, **92–93,** 95
"Landscape as a Nude" (MacLeish), **III:** 14
Landscape at the End of the Century (Dunn), **Supp. XI:** 139, 143, **150–151**
"Landscape Chamber, The" (Jewett), **II:** 408–409
"Landscape for the Disappeared" (Komunyakaa), **Supp. XIII:** 120, 126
Landscape in American Poetry (Larcom), **Supp. XIII:** 142
"Landscape Painter, A" (James), **II:** 322; **Retro. Supp. I:** 219
"Landscape Symbolism in Kate Chopin's At Fault" (Arner), **Retro. Supp. II:** 62
"Landscape: The Eastern Shore" (Barth), **I:** 122
"Landscape with Boat" (Stevens), **Retro. Supp. I:** 306
"Landscape with Bottles"(Schott), **Supp. XXIII:** 242
"Landscape with the Fall of Icarus" (Brueghel), **Retro. Supp. I:** 430
Land's End: A Walk through Provincetown (Cunningham), **Supp. XV:** 69
Land That Drank the Rain, The (Hoffman), **Supp. XVIII:** 76, 80, 81, 82
"Land Where There Is No Death, The" (Benét), **Supp. XI:** 56
Lane, Ann, **Supp. XI:** 195, 208
Lane, Cornelia. See Anderson, Mrs. Sherwood
Lane, Homer, **Supp. II Part 1:** 6; **Supp. XIV:** 160
Lane, John, **Supp. XXIV:** 22; **Supp. XXVII:** 216
Lane, Nathan, **Supp. XIII:** 207
Lane, Rose Wilder, **Supp. IV Part 2:** 524; **Supp. XXII:** 293–294, 295, 296, 297, 301
Lanes, Selma G., **Supp. XVI:** 104, 107
Lang, Andrew, **Retro. Supp. I:** 127; **Supp. XXVI:** 33
Lang, John, **Supp. XXVII:** 215, 221, 227, 229
Lang, Violet, **Supp. XII:** 119

Lang, V. R. "Bunny", **Supp. XXIII:** 209
Langdon, Olivia. See Clemens, Mrs. Samuel Langhorne (Olivia Langdon)
Lange, Carl Georg, **II:** 350
Lange, Dorothea, **I:** 293; **Supp. XIV:** 181
Langland, Joseph, **III:** 542
Langston Hughes, American Poet (Walker), **Supp. III Part 2:** 530–531
Langston Hughes and the "Chicago Defender": Essays on Race, Politics, and Culture (De Santis, ed.), **Retro. Supp. I:** 194
Langston Hughes: Modern Critical Views (Bloom, ed.), **Retro. Supp. I:** 193
Langston Hughes Reader, The (Hughes), **Retro. Supp. I:** 202; **Supp. I Part 1:** 345
Langston Hughes: The Poet and His Critics (Barksdale), **Retro. Supp. I:** 202
"Language, Visualization and the Inner Library" (Shepard), **Supp. III Part 2:** 436, 438, 449
Language and Imagery of the Bible, The (Caird), **Supp. XXI:** 91–92
"Language and the Writer" (Bambara), **Supp. XI:** 18
Language As Gesture (Blackmur), **Supp. II Part 1:** 108
Language as Symbolic Action (Burke), **I:** 275, 282, 285
Language Book, The (Andrews and Bernstein), **Supp. IV Part 2:** 426
"Language Divine!"(J. Schoolcraft), **Supp. XXIII:** 225
Language God Talks, The: On Science and Religion (Wouk), **Supp. XXV:** 257, 267
Language in Thought and Action (Hayakawa), **I:** 448
"Language of Being and Dying, The" (Gass), **Supp. VI:** 91
"Language of Home, The" (Wideman), **Supp. X:** 320, 323–324
Language of Life, The (Moyers, television series), **Supp. XIII:** 274, 276
Language of the American South, The (Brooks), **Supp. XIV:** 14
"Language of the Brag, The" (Olds), **Supp. X:** 204
"Language We Know, The" (Ortiz), **Supp. IV Part 2:** 500
Lanier, Clifford, **Supp. I Part 1:** 349, 350, 353, 355, 356, 371
Lanier, James F. D., **Supp. I Part 1:** 350
Lanier, Lyle H., **Supp. X:** 25
Lanier, Robert Sampson, **Supp. I Part 1:** 349, 351, 355, 356, 361
Lanier, Mrs. Robert Sampson (Mary Jane Anderson), **Supp. I Part 1:** 349
Lanier, Sidney, **IV:** 444; **Supp. I Part 1: 349–373; Supp. I Part 2:** 416; **Supp. IV Part 1:** 165
Lanier, Mrs. Sidney (Mary Day), **Supp. I Part 1:** 351, 355, 357, 361, 362, 364, 370, 371
"Lanier as Poet" (Parks), **Supp. I Part 1:** 373
"Lanier's Reading" (P. Graham), **Supp. I Part 1:** 373
"Lanier's Use of Science for Poetic Imagery" (Beaver), **Supp. I Part 1:** 373
Lankes, J. J., **Supp. XXII:** 275
Lannegan, Helen. See Caldwell, Mrs. Erskine
Lannin, Paul, **II:** 427
Lanny Budd novels (Sinclair), **Supp. V:** 290
Lansdale, Joe R., **Supp. XXV:** 145
Lant, Kathleen Margaret, **Supp. V:** 141
Lanterns on the Levee (Percy), **Supp. XXII:** 193
Lanthenas, François, **Supp. I Part 2:** 515
"Lanyard, The" (Collins), **Supp. XXI:** 56, **62–64**
Laotzu, **III:** 173, 189, 567; **Supp. XV:** 39, 46, 48
Lapine, James, **Supp. XXI:** 147–148
"Lapis Lazuli" (Yeats), **I:** 532; **III:** 40
Laplace, Pierre Simon de, **III:** 428
Lapouge, M. G., **Supp. I Part 2:** 633
Lappa, Katherine, **Supp. XV:** 176
Lapsing to Grace (Espaillat), **Supp. XXI:** 99, 100
Lapsley, Gaillard, **Retro. Supp. III:** 289; **Supp. XX: 231**
Laqueur, Thomas, **Supp. XVI:** 154
Larbaud, Valery, **IV:** 404; **Supp. XIII:** 332; **Supp. XIV:** 338
Larcom, Lucy, **Retro. Supp. II:** 145; **Supp. XIII: 137–157**
Larcom's Poetical Works (Larcom), **Supp. XIII:** 142
Lardner, James, **Supp. XXVII:** 141
Lardner, John, **II:** 437
Lardner, Ring, **I:** 487; **II:** 44, 91, 259, 263, **415–438; III:** 566, 572; **IV:** 433; **Retro. Supp. I:** 105; **Retro. Supp. II:** 222; **Supp. I Part 2:** 609; **Supp. IX:** 200; **Supp. XVI:** 189
Lardner, Ring, Jr., **Supp. XI:** 306
"Lardner, Shakespeare and Chekhov" (Matthews), **II:** 430
"Large Bad Picture" (Bishop), **Retro. Supp. II:** 43; **Supp. I Part 1:** 73, 80–82, 85, 86, 89, 90
"Large Coffee" (Lardner), **II:** 437
Large Glass, or The Bride Stripped Bare by Her Bachelors, Even (Duchamp), **Supp. IV Part 2:** 423, 424
Largo (Handel), **IV:** 369
"Lark" (Taggard), **Supp. XXII:** 280
Lark, The (Hellman), **Supp. I Part 1:** 286–288, 297
Lark: Four-Part Chorus for Mixed Voices (A Capella) with Baritone Solo (Taggard and Copland), **Supp. XXII:** 283
Larkin, Philip, **Supp. I Part 2:** 536; **Supp. XI:** 243, 249; **Supp. XIII:** 76, 85; **Supp. XV:** 117, 251; **Supp. XVII:** 110; **Supp. XVIII:** 173; **Supp. XX: 199; Supp. XXI:** 84, 93; **Supp. XXVI:** 67
Larkin, Sharon Alile, **Supp. XI:** 20
Larmore, Phoebe, **Supp. X:** 266
Larner, Jeremy, **Supp. XVI:** 220
La Rochefoucauld, François de, **I:** 279; **II:** 111; **Supp. XIV:** 130
"La Rose des Vents" (Wilbur), **Supp. III Part 2:** 550
"Larry Brown's Dirty Work: A Study of Man's Responsibility for Suffering" (Prevost), **Supp. XXI:** 45
"Larry"(O'Hara), **Supp. XXIII:** 212
Larry's Party (Shields), **Supp. VII:** 324, 326–327
Larsen, Nella, **Retro. Supp. III:** 140; **Supp. I Part 1:** 325, 326; **Supp. IV Part 1:** 164; **Supp. XVIII: 119–134**
Larson, Charles, **Supp. IV Part 1:** 331
Larson, Clinton, **Supp. XI:** 328
Larson, Kelli, **Supp. XVIII:** 131
LaRue, Dorie, **Supp. XXI:** 43
"Larval Stage of a Bookworm" (Mencken), **III:** 101
La Salle and the Discovery of the Great West (Parkman), **Supp. II Part 2:** 595, 598, 605–607; **Supp. XVIII:** 114
Las Casas, Bartolomé de, **Supp. XXIV:** 87
Lasch, Christopher, **I:** 259
Lasdun, James, **Supp. XXIV:** 154
Lasher (Rice), **Supp. VII:** 299–300
Lask, Thomas, **III:** 576; **Supp. XVI:** 250
Laski, Harold, **Supp. I Part 2:** 632, 643
Lass, Abraham H., **Supp. XXIV:** 214
Lassalle, Ferdinand, **IV:** 429
Lasser, Louise, **Supp. XV:** 4

"Last Acts" (Olds), **Supp. X:** 210
Last Adam, The (Cozzens), **I:** 362–363, 364, 368, 375, 377, 378, 379
Last Analysis, The (Bellow), **I:** 152, 160, 161; **Retro. Supp. II:** 26
Last and Lost Poems of Delmore Schwartz (Phillips, ed.), **Supp. II Part 2:** 661, 665
Last Avant-Garde, The: The Making of the New York School of Poets (Lehman), **Supp. XV:** 178–179, 187
Last Beautiful Days of Autumn, The (Nichols), **Supp. XIII:** 254, 255, 267, 269
Last Best Place, The: A Montana Anthology (Kittredge and Smith, eds.), **Supp. XXVI:** 188
Last Blue (Stern), **Supp. IX: 299–300**
Last Book, The (Pickering), **Supp. XXI:** 203–204
Last Carousel, The (Algren), **Supp. IX:** 16
Last Centennial, The (P. N. Warren as Kilina), **Supp. XX: 261–262**
"Last Child" (X. J. Kennedy), **Supp. XV:** 162, 165
"Last Class with Roethke" (Gallagher), **Supp. XXIV:** 171
Last Clean Shirt, The (film, Leslie and O'Hara), **Supp. XXIII:** 217
Last Coyote, The (Connelly), **Supp. XXI: 71**
"Last Dance" (Dubus III), **Supp. XXIV:** 100
"Last Day in the Field, The" (Gordon), **II:** 200
"Last Day of the Last Furlough" (Salinger), **III:** 552–553
"Last Days of Alice" (Tate), **IV:** 129
"Last Days of August, The" (Nye), **Supp. XIII:** 284
"Last Days of John Brown, The" (Thoreau), **IV:** 185
Last Days of Louisiana Red, The (Reed), **Supp. X:** 240, **248–249**
Last Decade, The (Trilling), **Supp. III Part 2:** 493, 499
"Last Demon, The" (Singer), **IV:** 15, 21
Last Detective, The (Crais), **Supp. XXI:** 70
Last Exit to Brooklyn (Selby), **Supp. III Part 1:** 125; **Supp. XXI:** 227, 231
Last Flower, The (Thurber), **Supp. I Part 2:** 610
"Last Frontier" (McCarriston), **Supp. XIV:** 272
Last Generation, The (Moraga), **Supp. XXIII:** 201
Last Gentleman, The (Percy), **Supp. III Part 1:** 383–388, 392–393
"Last Good Country, The" (Hemingway), **II:** 258–259
Last Good Time, The (Bausch), **Supp. VII:** 45–46
"Last Great Saloon, The"(Exley), **Supp. XXIII:** 103
"Last Hiding Places of Snow, The" (Kinnell), **Supp. III Part 1:** 252
"Last Hours, The" (Dunn), **Supp. XI:** 141
Last House: Reflections, Dreams, and Observations, 1943–1991 (M. F. K. Fisher), **Supp. XVII:** 92
Last Husband and Other Stories, The (Humphrey), **Supp. IX:** 94
"Last Interview" (Rash), **Supp. XXVII:** 218
Last Jew in America, The (Fiedler), **Supp. XIII:** 103
"Last Jew in America, The" (Fiedler), **Supp. XIII:** 103
Last Laugh, Mr. Moto (Marquand), **III:** 57
"Last Leaf, The" (Holmes), **Supp. I Part 1:** 302, 309
"Last Leaf, The" (Porter), **III:** 444
"Last Lie, The" (Weigl), **Supp. XIX:** 279
"Last Light" (Major), **Supp. XXII:** 185
"Last Look at the Lilacs" (Stevens), **IV:** 74
Last Man, The (Kees), **Supp. XV:** 142, 143, 145
"Last May" (Dixon), **Supp. XII: 143**
"Last Mermother, The" (A. Finch), **Supp. XVII:** 72
"Last Mohican, The" (Malamud), **Supp. I Part 2:** 437–438, 450, 451
"Lastness" (Kinnell), **Supp. III Part 1:** 248–249
"Last Night" (Olds), **Supp. X:** 212
Last Night at the Lobster (O'Nan), **Supp. XXV:** 149–150, 151
"Last Night at Tía's" (Alvarez), **Supp. VII:** 5
Last Night of Summer, The (Caldwell), **I:** 292–293
Last Notes from Home (Exley), **Supp. XXIII:** 97, 98, **106–108**
Last of Mr. Norris, The (Isherwood), **Supp. XIV:** 161
"Last of the Brooding Miserables, The" (Karr), **Supp. XI:** 250
"Last of the Caddoes, The" (Humphrey), **Supp. IX:** 101
Last of the Crazy People, The (Findley), **Supp. XX: 51–52**
"Last of the Gold Star Mothers, The" (C. Bly), **Supp. XVI:** 34, 35, 36
"Last of the Legions, The" (Benét), **Supp. XI:** 56, 57
Last of the Mohicans, The (Cooper), **I:** 341, 342, 349
Last of the Red Hot Lovers (Simon), **Supp. IV Part 2:** 575, 583, 589
"Last of the Valerii, The" (James), **II:** 327; **Retro. Supp. I:** 218
"Last One, The" (Merwin), **Supp. III Part 1:** 355
Last Picture Show, The (film), **Supp. V:** 223, 226
Last Picture Show, The (McMurtry), **Supp. V:** 220, 222–223, 233
Last Place on Earth, The: Scott and Amundsen's Race to the South Pole (Huntford), **Supp. XVIII:** 114
Last Puritan, The (Santayana), **III:** 64, 600, 604, 607, 612, 615–617
Last Radio Baby, The (Andrews), **Supp. XXVI:** 2–3, 7, 10
"Last Ride Together, The" (Browning), **I:** 468
"Last River, The" (Kinnell), **Supp. III Part 1:** 236
Last Song, The (Harjo), **Supp. XII:** 218
"Last Song for the Mend-It Shop" (Nye), **Supp. XIII:** 283
"Last Tango in Fresno" (Salinas), **Supp. XIII:** 318
"Last Trip to Greece"(Hadas), **Supp. XXIII:** 118–119
Last Tycoon, The: An Unfinished Novel (Fitzgerald), **II:** 84, 98; **Retro. Supp. I:** 109, 114, **114–115; Retro. Supp. II:** 337; **Supp. IV Part 1:** 203; **Supp. IX:** 63; **Supp. XII:** 173; **Supp. XIII:** 170; **Supp. XVIII:** 248, 250
"Last WASP in the World, The" (Fiedler), **Supp. XIII:** 103
"Last Watch, The" (Gibran), **Supp. XX: 119**
Last Watch of the Night: Essays Too Personal and Otherwise (Monette), **Supp. X:** 147, 148, 153, **157–159**
"Last Will" (Stallings), **Supp. XXV:** 232
"Last Word, The" (column, Quindlen), **Supp. XVII:** 165, 167, 170
Last Word, The: Letters between Marcia Nardi and William Carlos Williams (O'Neil, ed.), **Retro. Supp. I:** 427
"Last Words" (Levine), **Supp. V:** 190
"Last Words" (Olds), **Supp. X:** 210
Last Worthless Evening, The (Dubus), **Supp. VII:** 87–88

Last Yankee, The (A. Miller), **Retro. Supp. III:** 170, 172
"Las Vegas (What?) Las Vegas (Can't Hear You! Too Noisy) Las Vegas! ! ! !" (Wolfe), **Supp. III Part 2:** 572
"Late" (Bogan), **Supp. III Part 1:** 53
"Late Air" (Bishop), **Supp. I Part 1:** 89
"Late Autumn" (Sarton), **Supp. VIII:** 261
"Late Bronze, Early Iron: A Journey Book" (Sobin), **Supp. XVI:** 290
Late Child, The (McMurtry), **Supp. V:** 231
"Late Conversation" (Doty), **Supp. XI:** 122
"Late Elegy for John Berryman, A" (W. V. Davis), **Supp. XXI:** 91
"Late Encounter with the Enemy, A" (O'Connor), **III:** 345; **Retro. Supp. II:** 232
Late Fire, Late Snow (Francis), **Supp. IX: 89–90**
"Late Fragment" (Gallagher), **Supp. XXIV:** 172
Late George Apley, The (Marquand), **II:** 482–483; **III:** 50, 51, 52, 56–57, 58, 62–64, 65, 66
Late George Apley, The (Marquand and Kaufman), **III:** 62
"Late Hour" (Everwine), **Supp. XV:** 85
Late Hour, The (Strand), **Supp. IV Part 2:** 620, 629–630
"Lately, at Night" (Kumin), **Supp. IV Part 2:** 442
"Late Moon" (Levine), **Supp. V:** 186
"Late Night Ode" (McClatchy), **Supp. XII:** 262–263
Later (Creeley), **Supp. IV Part 1:** 153, 156, 157
Later Life (Gurney), **Supp. V:** 103, 105
La Terre (Zola), **III:** 316, 322
Later the Same Day (Paley), **Supp. VI:** 218
"Late September in Nebraska" (Kooser), **Supp. XIX:** 120
Late Settings (Merrill), **Supp. III Part 1:** 336
"Late Sidney Lanier, The" (Stedman), **Supp. I Part 1:** 373
"Late Snow & Lumber Strike of the Summer of Fifty-Four, The" (Snyder), **Supp. VIII:** 294
"Late Start, A" (L. Brown), **Supp. XXI:** 40–41
"Latest Freed Man, The" (Stevens), **Retro. Supp. I:** 306
"Latest Injury, The" (Olds), **Supp. X:** 209
Latest Literary Essays and Addresses (J. R. Lowell), **Supp. I Part 2:** 407
"Late Subterfuge" (Warren), **IV:** 257
"Late Summer Lilies" (Weigl), **Supp. XIX:** 288
"Late Summer Love Song" (Davison), **Supp. XXVI:** 69
"Late Supper, A" (Jewett), **Retro. Supp. II:** 137
"Late Victorians" (Rodriguez), **Supp. XIV:** 303–304
"Late Walk, A" (Frost), **II:** 153; **Retro. Supp. I:** 127
Latham, Edyth, **I:** 289
Lathrop, George Parsons, **Supp. I Part 1:** 365
Lathrop, H. B., **Supp. III Part 2:** 612
Lathrop, Julia, **Supp. I Part 1:** 5
Latière de Trianon, La (Wekerlin), **II:** 515
"La Tigresse" (Van Vechten), **Supp. II Part 2:** 735, 738
Latimer, Hugh, **II:** 15
Latimer, Margery, **Supp. IX:** 320
La Tour Dreams of the Wolf Girl (Huddle), **Supp. XXVI:** 148, 151, 158, 159
La Traviata (Verdi), **III:** 139
"Latter-Day Warnings" (Holmes), **Supp. I Part 1:** 307
"Latter Rain, The" (Very), **Supp. XXV:** 249
"Lattice Work: Formal Tendencies in the Poetry of Robert Morgan and Ron Rash" (Graves), **Supp. XXVII:** 216
La Turista (Shepard), **Supp. III Part 2:** 440
Lauber, John, **Supp. XIII:** 21
Laud, Archbishop, **II:** 158
"Lauds" (Auden), **Supp. II Part 1:** 23
"Laughing Man, The" (Salinger), **III:** 559
Laughing Matters (Siegel), **Supp. XXII:** 260
Laughing to Keep From Crying (Hughes), **Supp. I Part 1:** 329–330
Laughing Wild (Durang), **Supp. XXIV:** 114, **124**
"Laughing with One Eye" (Schnackenberg), **Supp. XV:** 253
Laughlin, James, **III:** 171; **Retro. Supp. I:** 423, 424, 428, 430, 431; **Supp. VIII:** 195; **Supp. XV:** 140; **Supp. XVI:** 284; **Supp. XXI:** 29
Laughlin, Jay, **Supp. II Part 1:** 94
Laughlin, J. Laurence, **Supp. I Part 2:** 641
Laughter in the Dark (Nabokov), **III:** 255–258; **Retro. Supp. I:** 270
"Laughter of Women, The" (Davison), **Supp. XXVI:** 75
Laughter on the 23rd Floor (Simon), **Supp. IV Part 2:** 575, 576, 588, 591–592
"Launcelot" (Lewis), **II:** 439–440
"Laura Dailey's Story" (Bogan), **Supp. III Part 1:** 52
Laurel, Stan, **Supp. I Part 2:** 607; **Supp. IV Part 2:** 574
Laurel and Hardy Go to Heaven (Auster), **Supp. XII:** 21
Laurence, Alexander, **Supp. XVIII:** 138
Laurence, Dan H., **II:** 338–339
Laurens, John, **Supp. I Part 2:** 509
Lauter, Paul, **Supp. XV:** 313
Lautréamont, Comte de, **III:** 174
Lavender Locker Room, The (P. N. Warren), **Supp. XX: 261, 273–274**
Law, John, **Supp. XI:** 307
Law and Order (television), **Supp. XVII:** 153
Law and the Testimony, The (S. and A. Warner), **Supp. XVIII:** 264
Lawd Today (Wright), **IV:** 478, 492
Law for the Lion, A (Auchincloss), **Supp. IV Part 1:** 25
Lawgiver, The (Wouk), **Supp. XXV:** 253, 256, 257, 267–268
"Law Lane" (Jewett), **II:** 407
"Lawns of June, The" (Peacock), **Supp. XIX:** 196
"Law of Nature and the Dream of Man, The: Ruminations of the Art of Fiction" (Stegner), **Supp. IV Part 2:** 604
Lawrence, D. H., **I:** 291, 336, 377, 522, 523; **II:** 78, 84, 98, 102, 264, 517, 523, 532, 594, 595; **III:** 27, 33, 40, 44, 46, 172, 173, 174, 178, 184, 229, 261, 423, 429, 458, 546–547; **IV:** 138, 339, 342, 351, 380; **Retro. Supp. I:** 7, 18, 203, 204, 421; **Retro. Supp. II:** 68; **Retro. Supp. III:** 25, 147; **Supp. I Part 1:** 227, 230, 243, 255, 257, 258, 263, 329; **Supp. I Part 2:** 546, 613, 728; **Supp. II Part 1:** 1, 9, 20, 89; **Supp. IV Part 1:** 81; **Supp. VIII:** 237; **Supp. X:** 137, 193, 194; **Supp. XII:** 172; **Supp. XIV:** 310; **Supp. XV:** 45, 46, 158, 254; **Supp. XVI:** 267; **Supp. XX: 69; Supp. XXII:** 198; **Supp. XXIII:** 166, 275; **Supp. XXIV:** 51, 52, 57, 58, 64; **Supp. XXVI:** 144
Lawrence, Elizabeth, **Supp. XXIII:** 259, 264
Lawrence, Frieda, **Supp. XV:** 46

Lawrence, Rhoda, **Supp. I Part 1:** 45
Lawrence, Seymour, **Supp. IX:** 107; **Supp. XI:** 335, 346, 348
Lawrence, T. E., **Supp. XIV:** 159
Lawrence of Arabia (Aldington), **Supp. I Part 1:** 259
Lawrence of Arabia (film), **Supp. I Part 1:** 67
Laws (Hadas), **Supp. XXIII: 119–120,** 124
Laws (Plato), **Supp. IV Part 1:** 391
Laws of Ice, The (Price), **Supp. VI:** 264
Laws of Our Fathers, The (Turow), **Supp. XVII: 218–219**
Lawson, John Howard, **I:** 479, 482
Lawton Girl, The (Frederic), **II:** 132–133, 144
Layachi, Larbi (Driss ben Hamed Charhadi), **Supp. IV Part 1:** 92, 93
Layard, John, **Supp. XIV:** 160
Lay Down My Sword and Shield (Burke), **Supp. XIV:** 22, 25, 34
"Layers, The" (Kunitz), **Supp. III Part 1:** 260, 266–267
"Layers, The: Some Notes on 'The Abduction' " (Kunitz), **Supp. III Part 1:** 266
"Lay-mans Lamentation, The" (Taylor), **IV:** 162–163
Lay of the Land, The: Metaphor as Experience and History in American Life and Letters (Kolodny), **Supp. X:** 97
"Layover" (Hass), **Supp. VI:** 109
"Lay Preacher" (Dennie), **Supp. I Part 1:** 125
Layton, Irving, **Supp. XII:** 121
Lazar, Irving "Swifty", **Supp. XIX:** 250
Lazarillo de Tormes (Mendoza), **III:** 182
Lazar Malkin Enters Heaven (S. Stern), **Supp. XVII:** 42; **Supp. XX: 178**
Lazarus Laughed (O'Neill), **III:** 391, 395–396
Lazer, Hank, **Supp. IX:** 265
Lea, Luke, **IV:** 248
Leachman, Cloris, **Supp. XXI:** 146
Leacock, Stephen, **Supp. IV Part 2:** 464
"LEADBELLY GIVES AN AUTOGRAPH" (Baraka), **Supp. II Part 1:** 49
Leaflets: Poems, 1965–1968 (Rich), **Retro. Supp. III:** 242, 244; **Supp. I Part 2:** 551, 556–557
"League of American Writers, The: Communist Organizational Activity among American Writers 1929–1942" (Wolfe), **Supp. III Part 2:** 568
League of Brightened Philistines and Other Papers, The (Farrell), **II:** 49
Leahy, Anna, **Supp. XXI:** 246
"Leakage" (Skloot), **Supp. XX: 202**
Leal, Luis, **Supp. XIX:** 98, 112
"Leaning" (Webb), **Supp. XX: 56**
Leaning Forward (Paley), **Supp. VI:** 221
"Leaning Tower, The" (Porter), **III:** 442, 443, 446–447
Leaning Tower and Other Stories, The (Porter), **III:** 433, 442, 443–447
"Leap, The" (Dickey), **Supp. IV Part 1:** 182
"Leaping Up into Political Poetry" (R. Bly), **Supp. IV Part 1:** 61, 63
Leap Year (Cameron), **Supp. XII:** 79–80, 81, **85–86,** 88
Lear, Bernadette, **Retro. Supp. III:** 264
Lear, Edward, **III:** 428, 536; **Supp. XVI:** 103; **Supp. XXVI:** 274
Lear, Linda, **Supp. IX:** 19, 22, 25, 26
Learned Ladies, The (Molière; Wilbur, trans.), **Supp. III Part 2:** 560
"Learning a Dead Language" (Merwin), **Supp. III Part 1:** 345
Learning a Trade: A Craftsman's Notebooks, 1955–1997 (Price), **Supp. VI:** 254, 255, 267
"Learning Bones" (Espaillat), **Supp. XXI:** 107
Learning to Live in This World (Schott), **Supp. XXIII:** 248
Learning to Love: Exploring Solitude and Freedom (Merton), **Supp. VIII:** 200
Learning to Love You More (website), **Supp. XXIV:** 200
"Learning to Read" (Harper), **Supp. II Part 1:** 201–202
"Learning to Speak" (Everwine), **Supp. XV:** 79
"Learning to Speak" (Gansworth), **Supp. XXVI:** 111
"Learning to Think" (Kittredge), **Supp. XXVI:** 181
"Learning to Work Together" (L. I. Wilder), **Supp. XXII:** 290
Learning Tree, The (Park), **Supp. XIX:** 154
Leary, Lewis, **III:** 478
Leary, Paris, **Supp. IV Part 1:** 176
Leary, Timothy, **Supp. X:** 265; **Supp. XIV:** 150
Lease, Joseph, **Supp. XXI:** 246
Least Heat Moon, William, **Supp. V:** 169
Leather-Stocking Tales, The (Cooper), **I:** 335
Leatherwood God, The (Howells), **II:** 276, 277, 288
Leave It to Beaver (television show), **Supp. XX: 103**
"Leave Me Alone a Little" (Taggard), **Supp. XXII:** 274
"Leaves" (Updike), **Retro. Supp. I:** 323, 329, 335
Leaves and Ashes (Haines), **Supp. XII:** 206
Leaves from the Notebook of a Tamed Cynic (Niebuhr), **III:** 293
Leaves of Grass (Whitman), **II:** 8; **IV:** 331, 332, 333, 334, 335, 336, 340, 341–342, 348, 350, 405, 464; **Retro. Supp. I:** 387, 388, 389, 390, **392–395,** 406, 407, 408; **Retro. Supp. II:** 93; **Retro. Supp. III:** 298, 300, 302, 303–304, 310; **Supp. I Part 1:** 365; **Supp. I Part 2:** 416, 579; **Supp. III Part 1:** 156; **Supp. IX:** 265; **Supp. V:** 170; **Supp. VIII:** 275; **Supp. X:** 120; **Supp. XIV:** 334; **Supp. XIX:** 276; **Supp. XV:** 218; **Supp. XVIII:** 4; **Supp. XXI:** 205; **Supp. XXII:** 92; **Supp. XXIII:** 165; **Supp. XXIV:** 85
"Leaves of Grass" (Whitman), **IV:** 463
Leaves of Grass (1856) (Whitman), **Retro. Supp. I:** 399–402
Leaves of Grass (1860) (Whitman), **Retro. Supp. I:** 402–405
Leaves of the Tree, The (Masters), **Supp. I Part 2:** 460
"Leaving" (Hogan), **Supp. IV Part 1:** 400
"Leaving" (Wilbur), **Supp. III Part 2:** 563
"Leaving, The" (B. Kelly), **Supp. XVII:** 127, 132
Leaving a Doll's House: A Memoir (C. Bloom), **Retro. Supp. II:** 281
Leaving Another Kingdom: Selected Poems (Stern), **Supp. IX:** 296
"Leaving Bartram's Garden in Southwest Philadelphia" (Di Piero), **Supp. XIX:** 46
"Leaving Brooklyn" (Neugeboren), **Supp. XVI:** 226
Leaving Cheyenne (McMurtry), **Supp. V:** 220, 221–222, 224, 229
Leaving Home (Keillor), **Supp. XVI:** 175
"Leaving One, The" (Offutt), **Supp. XIX:** 165–166
"Leaving the Island" (Olds), **Supp. X:** 214
"Leaving the Yellow House" (Bellow),

Retro. Supp. II: 27, 32
"Leaving Town" (Kenyon), **Supp. VII:** 163
Leavis, F. R., **I:** 522; **III:** 462–463, 475, 478; **Retro. Supp. I:** 67; **Retro. Supp. II:** 243; **Supp. I Part 2:** 536; **Supp. VIII:** 234, 236, 245
Leavis, Queenie, **Supp. XX: 232**
"Leavis-Snow Controversy, The" (Trilling), **Supp. III Part 2:** 512
Leavitt, Caroline, **Supp. XX: 186**
Leavitt, David, **Supp. VIII:** 88
Lebanon (C. Miller), **Supp. XXII:** 198–199
Le Braz, Anatole, **Supp. XIII:** 253
Le Carre, John, **Supp. XX: 195**
Lecker, Robert, **Supp. XIII:** 21
LeClair, Thomas (Tom), **Supp. IV Part 1:** 286; **Supp. V:** 53; **Supp. XII:** 152; **Supp. XX: 93; Supp. XXII:** 206, 210, 261, 264
Le Conte, Joseph, **II:** 479; **III:** 227–228
"Lecture, The" (Singer), **IV:** 21
"LECTURE PAST DEAD CATS" (Baraka), **Supp. II Part 1:** 52
Lectures in America (Stein), **IV:** 27, 32, 33, 35, 36, 41, 42
"Lectures on Poetry" (Bryant), **Supp. I Part 1:** 159, 161
Lectures on Rhetoric (Blair), **II:** 8
"Leda and the Swan" (Yeats), **III:** 347; **Supp. IX:** 52
Ledger (Fitzgerald), **Retro. Supp. I:** 109, 110
Lee (Masters), **Supp. I Part 2:** 471
Lee, Baayork, **Supp. XXI:** 148
Lee, C. Y., **Supp. XXI:** 148
Lee, Don, **Supp. XII:** 295; **Supp. XVII:** 13, 14, 15, 16
Lee, Don L. See Madhubuti, Haki R.
Lee, Gypsy Rose, **II:** 586; **III:** 161; **Supp. IV Part 1:** 84
Lee, Harper, **Supp. VIII: 113–131; Supp. XXVII:** 276
Lee, Harriett, **Supp. XV:** 230
Lee, Hermione, **Retro. Supp. III:** 277, 279, 283, 284, 287
Lee, James Kyun-Jin, **Supp. XV:** 213
Lee, James W., **Supp. IX:** 94, 97, 109
Lee, James Ward, **Supp. VIII:** 57
Lee, Lawrence, **Supp. XXV:** 29
Lee, Li Lin, **Supp. XV:** 211, 212
Lee, Li-Young, **Supp. XV: 211–228; Supp. XVII:** 241
Lee, Richard E., **Supp. XIX:** 226, 227
Lee, Robert E., **II:** 150, 206; **IV:** 126; **Supp. I Part 2:** 471, 486
Lee, Robert N., **Supp. XXVII:** 92
Lee, Samuel, **IV:** 158
Lee, Spike, **Retro. Supp. II:** 12; **Supp. XI:** 19; **Supp. XIII:** 179, 186; **Supp. XVI:** 144; **Supp. XX: 110; Supp. XXVI:** 199
Lee, Virginia Chin-lan, **Supp. X:** 291
Leeds, Barry, **Retro. Supp. II:** 204
Leeds, Daniel, **II:** 110
Leeds, Titan, **II:** 110, 111
Leeming, David, **Retro. Supp. II:** 4, 10
"Lees of Happiness, The" (Fitzgerald), **II:** 88
"Le Filme" (Weigl), **Supp. XIX:** 288
Left Behind series (LaHaye and Jenkins), **Supp. XXVII:** 5
Left Hand of God, The (film), **Supp. XXVI:** 134
Left Out in the Rain: New Poems 1947–1985 (Snyder), **Supp. VIII:** 305
Leftovers, The (Perrota), **Supp. XXVII:** 6
"Legacy" (Dunn), **Supp. XI:** 148
"Legacy" (Komunyakaa), **Supp. XIII:** 132
"Legacy" (W. V. Davis), **Supp. XXI:** 93–94
"Legacy of Aldo Leopold, The" (Stegner), **Supp. XIV:** 193
"Legacy of Channing, The" (Robinson), **Supp. XXIV:** 79
Legacy of Fear, A (Farrell), **II:** 39
"Legacy of the Ancestral Arts, The" (Locke), **Supp. XIV:** 201
Legacy of the Civil War, The: Meditations on the Centennial (Warren), **IV:** 236
"Legal Alien" (Mora), **Supp. XIII:** 215
"Legal Tender Act, The" (Adams), **I:** 5
"Legend" (H. Crane), **Retro. Supp. III:** 45
Légende de la mort, La (Le Braz), **Supp. XIII:** 253
"Legend of Duluoz, The" (Kerouac), **Supp. III Part 1:** 218, 226, 227, 229
"Legend of Lillian Hellman, The" (Kazin), **Supp. I Part 1:** 297
"Legend of Monte del Diablo, The" (Harte), **Supp. II Part 1:** 339
"Legend of Paper Plates, The" (Haines), **Supp. XII:** 204
"Legend of Sammtstadt, A" (Harte), **Supp. II Part 1:** 355
"Legend of Sleepy Hollow, The" (Irving), **II:** 306–308
Legends (A. Lowell), **II:** 525–526
Legends and Dreams (P. N. Warren), **Supp. XX: 261**
Legends of Mexico (Lippard), **Supp. XXIII:** 178, 186
Legends of New England (Whittier), **Supp. I Part 2:** 684, 692
Legends of the Fall (Harrison), **Supp. VIII:** 38, 39, **45–46,** 48
"Legends of the Revolution"(series, Lippard), **Supp. XXIII:** 178
Legends of the West (Hall), **II:** 313
Léger, Fernand, **Retro. Supp. I:** 292
Legge, James, **III:** 472
Leggett, William, **Supp. I Part 1:** 157
"Legion, The" (Karr), **Supp. XI:** 243
"Legs" (Halliday), **Supp. XIX:** 90
Legs (W. Kennedy), **Supp. VII:** 133, 134, 138–142, 143, 151
Le Guin, Ursula K., **Supp. IV Part 1:** 333; **Supp. XXII:** 49
Lehan, Richard, **Retro. Supp. II:** 104
Lehman, David, **Supp. IX:** 161; **Supp. XIII:** 130; **Supp. XV:** 178–179, 180, 187, 190; **Supp. XXI:** 246; **Supp. XXVI:** 50
Lehmann, John, **Retro. Supp. II:** 243; **Supp. XIV:** 158, 159
Lehmann, Paul, **III:** 311
Lehmann-Haupt, Christopher, **Retro. Supp. II:** 291; **Supp. IV Part 1:** 205, 209, 306; **Supp. IX:** 95, 103; **Supp. XVI:** 73, 210, 294, 295; **Supp. XXII:** 205, 213; **Supp. XXIII:** 103
Lehrer, Jim, **Supp. XVIII:** 39
Leiber, Fritz, **Supp. XVI:** 123
Leibling, A. J., **Supp. XIV:** 112
Leibniz, Gottfried Wilhelm von, **II:** 103; **III:** 428
Leibowitz, Herbert A., **I:** 386; **Supp. XV:** 78
Leich, Roland, **Supp. XIV:** 123
Leichum, Laura, **Supp. XIX:** 197
Leider, Emily Wortis, **Supp. XXIV:** 19, 20, 22, 26, 27, 30
Leiding, Reba, **Supp. XXVI:** 159
Leighton, Betty, **Supp. XXI:** 42
Leimbach, Laura, **Supp. XXIII:** 54
Leithauser, Brad, **Retro. Supp. I:** 133; **Supp. XV:** 250; **Supp. XVII:** 112; **Supp. XXII:** 207
Leitz, Robert, **Supp. XIV:** 62
Leivick, H., **IV:** 6
Lekachman, Robert, **Supp. I Part 2:** 648
Leland, Charles, **Supp. II Part 1:** 193
Leland, Charles Godfrey, **I:** 257
Leland, John, **Supp. XIX:** 157; **Supp. XV:** 69
Lem, Stanislaw, **Supp. IV Part 1:** 103
"Le marais du cygne" (Whittier), **Supp. I Part 2:** 687
Lemay, Harding, **Supp. IX:** 98; **Supp.**

VIII: 125
Lemercier, Eugène, **Retro. Supp. I:** 299
Lemkin, Raphael, **Supp. XXIII:** 31
"Lemorne versus Huell" (E. Stoddard), **Supp. XV:** 270, 273, 283
Le Morte D'Arthur Notes (Gardner), **Supp. VI:** 65, 66
Lenhard, Elizabeth, **Supp. XXVII:** 267
Lenin, V. I., **I:** 366, 439, 440; **III:** 14–15, 262, 475; **IV:** 429, 436, 443–444; **Supp. I Part 2:** 647; **Supp. XXI:** 164
Lennertz, Carl, **Supp. XXVII:** 267
Lennon, J. Robert, **Supp. XXV:** 151
"Lenny Dying, Pacific Standard Time"(Thompson), **Supp. XXIII:** 294
"Lenore" (Poe), **III:** 411
"Lenox Avenue: Midnight" (Hughes), **Retro. Supp. I:** 198
"Lens of Poetry, The" (Bronk). See Attendant, The (Bronk)
Leonard, Elmore, **Supp. IV Part 1:** 356; **Supp. X:** 5; **Supp. XIV:** 26
Leonard, John, **Supp. IV Part 1:** 24; **Supp. IV Part 2:** 474; **Supp. V:** 164, 223–224; **Supp. XI:** 13; **Supp. XIX:** 269; **Supp. XVIII:** 147, 148; **Supp. XXI:** 233, 239
Leonardo da Vinci, **Supp. XII:** 44; **Supp. XXII:** 171
León-Portilla, Miguel, **Supp. XV:** 77
Leontiev, Constantine, **Supp. XIV:** 98
Leopard, The (Lampedusa), **Supp. XII:** 13–14
Leopardi, Giacomo, **II:** 543; **Supp. XIX:** 33, 43
"Leopard Man's Story, The" (London), **II:** 475
Leopard's Mouth Is Dry and Cold Inside, The (Levis), **Supp. XI:** 258
Leopold, Aldo, **Supp. V:** 202; **Supp. X:** 108; **Supp. XIV: 177–194; Supp. XXI:** 203; **Supp. XXVI:** 31
"Leper's Bell, the" (Komunyakaa), **Supp. XIII:** 118
Lerman, Leo, **Supp. X:** 188; **Supp. XVI:** 194
Lerner, Ben, **Supp. XXIV:** 45
Lerner, Max, **III:** 60; **Supp. I Part 2:** 629, 630, 631, 647, 650, 654; **Supp. XXVII:** 134
Lerperger, Emil, **Supp. XX: 165, 167**
Lesbian Nation: The Feminist Solution (Johnston), **Supp. XXV:** 5
"Lesbos" (Plath), **Retro. Supp. II:** 254
Lesesne, Teri, **Supp. XIII:** 277
LeSieg, Theo (pseudonym). See Geisel, Theodor Seuss (Dr. Seuss)
Leskov, Nikolai, **IV:** 299
Leslie, Alfred, **Supp. XII:** 127; **Supp. XXIII:** 217
"Less and Less Human, O Savage Spirit" (W. Stevens), **Supp. XVI:** 64
Lesser, Wendy, **Supp. IV Part 2:** 453; **Supp. XII:** 297; **Supp. XVI:** 201
Lessing, Gotthold, **Supp. I Part 2:** 422
"Lesson, The" (Bambara), **Supp. XI:** 5–6
"Lesson, The" (Dunbar), **Supp. II Part 1:** 199
"Lesson, The" (Olsen), **Supp. XIII:** 297
"Lesson, The"(Schott), **Supp. XXIII:** 254
"Lesson for the Ill Clothed and Ill Fed, A" (Ryan as Quin), **Supp. XVIII:** 230–231
Lesson of the Master, The (James), **Supp. XVIII:** 248
"Lesson of the Master, The" (James), **Retro. Supp. I:** 227
Lesson of the Masters: An Anthology of the Novel from Cervantes to Hemingway (Cowley-Hugo, ed.), **Supp. II Part 1:** 140
"Lesson on Concealment, A" (Brown), **Supp. I Part 1:** 133
"Lessons" (Epstein), **Supp. XII:** 163
"Lessons from an Older Man"(Thompson), **Supp. XXIII:** 293
"Lessons of the Body" (Simpson), **Supp. IX:** 267
Less than One (Brodsky), **Supp. VIII:** 22, 29–31
Less Than Zero (Ellis), **Supp. XXVII:** 67, 69–70, 71, 74, 75, 77, 78, 269
Less Than Zero (film), **Supp. XXVII:** 68, 77
Lester, Jerry, **Supp. IV Part 2:** 574
Lester, Ketty, **Supp. XV:** 133, 147
Le Style Apollinaire (Zukofsky), **Supp. III Part 2:** 616
Le Sueur, Arthur, **Supp. XXIII:** 161, 162
LeSueur, Joe, **Supp. XXIII:** 212, 216, 218, 220
Le Sueur, Meridel, **Supp. V:** 113, 130; **Supp. XII:** 217; **Supp. XXIII: 161–176; Supp. XXVI:** 28
Lesy, Michael, **Supp. XXV:** 146
"Let America Be America Again" (Hughes), **Retro. Supp. I:** 202; **Supp. I Part 1:** 331
Let Evening Come (Kenyon), **Supp. VII:** 160, 169–171
Lethem, Jonathan, **Supp. IX:** 122; **Supp. XVIII: 135–153; Supp. XXII:** 49; **Supp. XXVII:** 67
Let It Come Down (Bowles), **Supp. IV Part 1:** 87
Let It Ride (Pickering), **Supp. XXI:** 198–199
"Let Me Be" (Levine), **Supp. V:** 181, 189
"Let Me Begin Again" (Levine), **Supp. V:** 181, 189
"Let No Charitable Hope" (Wylie), **Supp. I Part 2:** 713–714, 729
Let No Man Write My Epitaph (film, Leacock), **Supp. XVII:** 150, 158
Let No Man Write My Epitaph (W. Motley), **Supp. XVII:** 150, **158–160**
Let Noon Be Fair (W. Motley), **Supp. XVII: 161**
Letofsky, Irv, **Supp. XVI:** 167
"Let one Eye his watches keep/While the Other Eye doth sleep" (Fletcher), **Supp. IV Part 2:** 621
Let's Balance the Books (radio show; Untermeyer), **Supp. XV:** 311
"Letter . . ." (Whittier), **Supp. I Part 2:** 687
"Letter, A" (Bogan), **Supp. III Part 1:** 54
"Letter, May 2, 1959" (Olson), **Supp. II Part 2:** 579, 580
"Letter, Much Too Late" (Stegner), **Supp. IV Part 2:** 613
"Letter, The" (Boulton), **Supp. XXII:** 22
"Letter, The" (Gioia), **Supp. XV:** 120
"Letter, The" (Malamud), **Supp. I Part 2:** 435–436
"Letter about Money, Love, or Other Comfort, If Any, The" (Warren), **IV:** 245
Letter Addressed to the People of Piedmont, on the Advantages of the French Revolution, and the Necessity of Adopting Its Principles in Italy, A (Barlow), **Supp. II Part 1:** 80, 81
"Letter for Marion, A" (McGrath), **Supp. X:** 116
"Letter from Aldermaston" (Merwin), **Supp. III Part 1:** 347
"Letter from a London Attic" (Pickering), **Supp. XXI:** 194
"Letter from a Region in My Mind" (Baldwin). See "Down at the Cross"
"Letter from Aunt Belle, A" (Kooser), **Supp. XIX:** 117
"Letter from Carson City" (Twain), **Retro. Supp. III:** 259
Letter from Li Po, A (Aiken), **I:** 68
"Letter from 'Manhattan' " (Didion),

Supp. IV Part 1: 205
"Letter from the Country" (column, C. Bly), **Supp. XVI:** 33
Letter from the End of the Twentieth Century (Harjo), **Supp. XII:** 223
"Letter from the End of the Twentieth Century" (Harjo), **Supp. XII:** 227
"Letter Home" (Trethewey), **Supp. XXI:** 254
"Letter on Céline" (Kerouac), **Supp. III Part 1:** 232
Letters (Cato), **II:** 114
Letters (Landor), **Supp. I Part 2:** 422
Letters (White), **Supp. I Part 2:** 651, 653, 675, 680
Letters (Wolfe), **IV:** 462
"Letters, The" (Swados), **Supp. XIX:** 261, 262
Letters and Leadership (Brooks), **I:** 228, 240, 245, 246
"Letters for the Dead" (Levine), **Supp. V:** 186
Letters from an American Farmer (Crèvecoeur), **Supp. I Part 1:** 227–251
Letters from Bohemia (Hecht), **Supp. XXVII:** 95
Letters from Maine (Sarton), **Supp. VIII: 261**
"Letters from Maine" (Sarton), **Supp. VIII:** 261
"Letters from My Father" (R. O. Butler), **Supp. XII:** 71
Letters from the Country (C. Bly), **Supp. XVI: 33–34,** 35, 37
Letters from the Earth (Twain), **IV:** 209
Letters from the East (Bryant), **Supp. I Part 1:** 158
"Letters from the Ming Dynasty" (Brodsky), **Supp. VIII:** 28
"Letters from the Samantha" (Helprin), **Supp. XXV:** 85
Letters of Angelicus and Fidelio Fobb (O'Hara and Berkson), **Supp. XXIII:** 218
Letters of a Traveller (Bryant), **Supp. I Part 1:** 158
Letters of a Traveller, Second Series (Bryant), **Supp. I Part 1:** 158
Letters of a Woman Homesteader (Stewart), **Supp. XXVI:** 183
Letters of Emily Dickinson, The (T. H. Johnson and Ward, eds.), **I:** 470; **Retro. Supp. I:** 28
Letters of William James (Henry James, ed.), **II:** 362
Letters on Various Interesting and Important Subjects . . . (Freneau), **Supp. II Part 1:** 272
Letters to a Niece (Adams), **I:** 22
Letters to a Teacher (Pickering), **Supp. XXI:** 195, 201–202
Letters to a Young Poet (Rilke), **Supp. XIII:** 74; **Supp. XV:** 93
"Letters to Dead Imagists" (Sandburg), **I:** 421
"Letters Written on a Ferry While Crossing Long Island Sound" (Sexton), **Supp. II Part 2:** 683
"Letter to Abbé Raynal" (Paine), **Supp. I Part 2:** 510
"Letter to a Kiss That Died for Us" (Gallagher), **Supp. XXIV:** 170
Letter to a Man in the Fire: Does God Exist or Does He Care? (Price), **Supp. VI:** 267–268
"Letter to American Teachers of History, A" (Adams), **I:** 19
Letter to an Imaginary Friend (McGrath), **Supp. X:** 111, 112–113, 116, **119–125**
"Letter to a Reader" (Sanders), **Supp. XVI:** 266, 267, 268, 269, 275
"Letter to a Young Author" (P. N. Warren), **Supp. XX: 272**
"Letter to a Young Contributor" (Higginson), **Retro. Supp. I:** 31
"Letter to a Young Writer" (Price), **Supp. VI:** 267
"Letter to Bell from Missoula" (Hugo), **Supp. VI:** 142–143
"Letter to E. Franklin Frazier" (Baraka), **Supp. II Part 1:** 49
"Letter to Elaine Feinstein" (Olson), **Supp. II Part 2:** 561
"Letter to Francis Picabia, A" (Boyle), **Supp. XXIV:** 63
"Letter to Freddy" (music) (Bowles), **Supp. IV Part 1:** 82
"Letter to Garber from Skye" (Hugo), **Supp. VI:** 146
"Letter to George Washington" (Paine), **Supp. I Part 2:** 517
"Letter to Her Husband, Absent upon Public Employment, A" (Bradstreet), **Retro. Supp. III:** 12
"Letter to His Brother" (Berryman), **I:** 172, 173
Letter to His Countrymen, A (Cooper), **I:** 346, 347, 349
"Letter to Kizer from Seattle" (Hugo), **Supp. VI:** 142
Letter to Lord Byron (Auden), **Supp. II Part 1:** 11
"Letter to Lord Byron" (Mumford), **Supp. II Part 2:** 494
"Letter to Matthews from Barton Street Flats" (Hugo), **Supp. VI:** 133
"Letter to Mexico" (Biss), **Supp. XXVI:** 48
"Letter to Minnesota" (Dunn), **Supp. XI:** 146
"Letter to Mr." (Poe), **III:** 411
"Letter Too Late to Vallejo" (Salinas), **Supp. XIII:** 313, 324
"Letter to Sister Madeline from Iowa City" (Hugo), **Supp. VI:** 142–143
"Letter to Soto" (Salinas), **Supp. XIII:** 325
"Letter to the Lady of the House" (Bausch), **Supp. VII:** 48
"Letter to the Rising Generation, A" (Comer), **I:** 214
"Letter to Walt Whitman" (Doty), **Supp. XI:** 135–136
"Letter to Wendell Berry, A" (Stegner), **Supp. IV Part 2:** 600
"Letter Writer, The" (Singer), **IV:** 20–21
"Let the Air Circulate" (Clampitt), **Supp. IX:** 45
Let the Hurricane Roar (Lane), **Supp. XXII:** 297
"Letting Down of the Hair, The" (Sexton), **Supp. II Part 2:** 692
Letting Go (P. Roth), **Retro. Supp. II:** 282, 283; **Supp. III Part 2:** 403, 404, 409–412
"Letting the Puma Go" (Dunn), **Supp. XI:** 149
"Lettres d'un Soldat" (Stevens), **Retro. Supp. I:** 299
Let Us Compare Mythologies (Cohen), **Supp. XXVII:** 53
Let Us Go into the Starry Night (Shanley), **Supp. XIV:** 317
Let Us Highly Resolve (Stratton-Porter), **Supp. XX: 223**
Let Us Now Praise Famous Men (Agee and Evans), **I:** 25, 27, 35, 36–39, 42, 45, 293
Let Your Mind Alone! (Thurber), **Supp. I Part 2:** 608
Leutze, Emanuel, **Supp. X:** 307
Levels of the Game (McPhee), **Supp. III Part 1:** 292, 294, 301
Levertov, Denise, **Retro. Supp. I:** 411; **Supp. III Part 1: 271–287; Supp. III Part 2:** 541; **Supp. IV Part 1:** 325; **Supp. VIII:** 38, 39; **Supp. XIX:** 282; **Supp. XVI:** 39, 40; **Supp. XXI:** 228; **Supp. XXII:** 83, 168, 177
Levi, Primo, **Supp. X:** 149; **Supp. XVII:** 48
Leviathan (Auster), **Supp. XII:** 27, **33–34**
"Leviathan" (Merwin), **Supp. III Part 1:** 345
"Leviathan" (R. Lowell), **II:** 537, 538

Levin, Adam, **Supp. XXII:** 268
Levin, Harry, **Supp. I Part 2:** 647
Levin, Jennifer, **Supp. X:** 305
Levin, Jonathan, **Retro. Supp. III:** 99
Levin, Meyer, **Supp. XX: 34; Supp. XXVII: 133–149**
Lévinas, Emmanuel, **Supp. XVI:** 290, 291
Levine, Ellen, **Supp. V:** 4; **Supp. XI:** 178
Levine, Paul, **Supp. IV Part 1:** 221, 224
Levine, Philip, **Supp. III Part 2:** 541; **Supp. IX:** 293; **Supp. V: 177–197,** 337; **Supp. XI:** 123, 257, 259, 267, 271, 315; **Supp. XIII:** 312; **Supp. XIX:** 45; **Supp. XV:** 73, 74, 212
Levine, Rosalind, **Supp. XII:** 123
Levine, Sherry, **Supp. XII:** 4
Levis, Larry, **Supp. IX:** 299; **Supp. V:** 180; **Supp. XI: 257–274; Supp. XIII:** 312; **Supp. XV:** 73; **Supp. XVII:** 110
Lévi-Strauss, Claude, **Supp. I Part 2:** 636; **Supp. IV Part 1:** 45; **Supp. IV Part 2:** 490; **Supp. XVIII:** 190
Levitation: Five Fictions (Ozick), **Supp. V:** 268–270
"Levitation with Baby" (Nelson), **Supp. XVIII:** 173
Levitt, Saul, **Supp. XV:** 197
Levy, Alan, **Supp. IV Part 2:** 574, 589
Levy, D. A., **Supp. XXIII:** 174
Levy, G. Rachel, **Supp. I Part 2:** 567
Levy, Julien, **Supp. XXII:** 167, 168
Lévy-Bruhl, Lucien, **Retro. Supp. I:** 57
Levy Mayer and the New Industrial Era (Masters), **Supp. I Part 2:** 473
Lewallen, Constance M., **Supp. XXVII:** 20, 21
Lewes, George Henry, **II:** 569
Lewin, Albert, **Supp. XIV:** 279, 293
Lewis, C. Day, **III:** 527
Lewis, Dr. Claude, **II:** 442
Lewis, C. S., **Supp. XXV:** 73
Lewis, David Levering, **Supp. XIX:** 74, 75; **Supp. XVIII:** 127; **Supp. XXII:** 13
Lewis, Edith, **I:** 313; **Retro. Supp. I:** 19, 21, 22; **Retro. Supp. III:** 24, 37
Lewis, Edwin, J., **II:** 439, 442
Lewis, Jerry, **Supp. IV Part 2:** 575; **Supp. X:** 172
Lewis, John L., **I:** 493
Lewis, Lilburn, **IV:** 243
Lewis, Lorene, **Supp. IV Part 2:** 596, 597
Lewis, Lucy, **IV:** 243
Lewis, Maggie, **Supp. V:** 23
Lewis, Meriwether, **II:** 217; **III:** 14; **IV:** 179, 243, 283
Lewis, Merrill, **Supp. IV Part 2:** 596, 597
Lewis, Michael, **II:** 451, 452; **Supp. XVII:** 210
Lewis, Michael J., **Supp. XXV:** 253
Lewis, Nancy, **Retro. Supp. III:** 282
Lewis, Robert Q., **Supp. IV Part 2:** 574
Lewis, R. W. B., **I:** 386, 561; **II:** 457–458; **Retro. Supp. I:** 362, 367; **Retro. Supp. III:** 282; **Supp. I Part 1:** 233; **Supp. XIII:** 93; **Supp. XXIII:** 42
Lewis, Sinclair, **I:** 116, 212, 348, 355, 362, 374, 378, 487, 495; **II:** 27, 34, 74, 79, 271, 277, 306, **439–461,** 474; **III:** 28, 40, 51, 60, 61, 63–64, 66, 70, 71, 106, 394, 462, 572, 606; **IV:** 53, 326, 366, 455, 468, 475, 482; **Retro. Supp. I:** 332; **Retro. Supp. II:** 95, 108, 197, 322; **Supp. I Part 2:** 378, 613, 709; **Supp. IV Part 2:** 678; **Supp. IX:** 308; **Supp. V:** 278; **Supp. X:** 137; **Supp. XVII:** 41; **Supp. XVIII:** 278; **Supp. XXII:** 190; **Supp. XXIII:** 165, 166; **Supp. XXIV:** 29
Lewis, Mrs. Sinclair (Dorothy Thompson), **II:** 449–450, 451, 453
Lewis, Mrs. Sinclair (Grace Livingston Hegger), **II:** 441
Lewis, Wyndham, **III:** 458, 462, 465, 470; **Retro. Supp. I:** 59, 170, 292; **Supp. III Part 2:** 617; **Supp. XXVI:** 144
Lewisohn, Ludwig, **Supp. XXIII:** 1
Lexicon Tetraglotton (Howell), **II:** 111
"Lexington Avenue Musedog" (Peacock), **Supp. XIX:** 204
"Leyenda" (Mora), **Supp. XIII:** 214
Leyner, Mark, **Supp. XIX:** 223
Leyte (Morison), **Supp. I Part 2:** 491
"Liar, The" (Baraka), **Supp. II Part 1:** 36
"Liars, The" (Sandburg), **III:** 586
Liars' Club, The: A Memoir (Karr), **Supp. XI:** 239, 240, 241, 242, **244–248,** 252, 254; **Supp. XVI:** 70
Liar's Dice (C. Frost), **Supp. XV:** 93, 96
"Liar's Dice" (C. Frost), **Supp. XV:** 94, 107
Liars in Love (Yates), **Supp. XI:** 348, 349
Libation Bearers, The (Aeschylus), **III:** 398; **Supp. IX:** 103
Li Bay. See Li Po
Libby, Anthony, **Supp. XIII:** 87
Libera, Padre, **II:** 278
Liberal Imagination, The (Trilling), **III:** 308; **Retro. Supp. I:** 97, 216; **Supp. II Part 1:** 146; **Supp. III Part 2:** 495, 498, 501–504
Liberating Voices: Oral Tradition in African American Literature (G. Jones), **Supp. XXIV:** 185
Liberation (J. Scott), **Supp. XVII:** 192, **194–196**
"Liberation" (Winters), **Supp. II Part 2:** 791
Liber Brunenesis (yearbook), **IV:** 286
Liberties, The (Howe), **Supp. IV Part 2:** 426–428, 430, 432
Liberties of America, The (H. Warner), **Supp. XVIII:** 259
Liberty Jones (play), **Supp. IV Part 1:** 83
"Liberty Tree" (Paine), **Supp. I Part 2:** 505
Libra (DeLillo), **Supp. VI:** 2, **4, 5,** 6, **7,** 9, 10, 12, 13, 14, 16
Library for Juana, A (Mora), **Supp. XIII:** 218
Library of America, **Retro. Supp. I:** 2
"Library of Babel, The" (J. Borges), **Supp. XVII:** 47
"Library of Law, A" (MacLeish), **III:** 4
"Library of Moloch, The" (Bukiet), **Supp. XVII:** 47, 49
"Librettos for Eros" (Gander), **Supp. XV:** 340
Lice, The (Merwin), **Supp. III Part 1:** 339, 341–342, 346, 348, 349, 355
"License Plate, The" (Ferry), **Supp. XXIV:** 157
Lichtenberg, Georg Christoph, **Supp. XIV:** 339
Lichtenstein, Roy, **Supp. I Part 2:** 665; **Supp. XV:** 186; **Supp. XXVII:** 21
"Liddy's Orange" (Olds), **Supp. X:** 209
"Lie, The" (Antin), **Supp. XX: 7, 9–10**
Lieberman, Herman (Chaim), **Supp. XXIII:** 3, 7
Lieberman, Laurence, **Supp. XI:** 323–324
Liebestod (Wagner), **I:** 284, 395
Liebling, A. J., **IV:** 290; **Supp. VIII:** 151; **Supp. XVI:** 167; **Supp. XXVII:** 46–47
Lie Down in Darkness (Styron), **IV:** 98, 99, 100–104, 105, 111; **Supp. XI:** 343
"Lie Down with the Lamb" (Gallagher), **Supp. XXIV:** 171
Lie of the Mind, A (Shepard), **Supp.**

III Part 2: 433, 435, 441, 447–449
"Lies" (Haines), **Supp. XII:** 204
Lies (Hoffman), **Supp. XVIII: 78–79**
"Lies and Consequences" (Pickering), **Supp. XXI:** 204
Lies Like Truth (Clurman), **IV:** 385
Lieutenant, The (Dubus), **Supp. VII:** 78
"Life" (Hecht), **Supp. XXVII:** 86
Life (Richards), **Supp. XXVII:** 40
"Life" (Wharton), **Retro. Supp. I:** 372
Life along the Passaic River (W. C. Williams), **Retro. Supp. I:** 423
Life Among the Savages (Jackson), **Supp. IX:** 115, **125**
Life and Adventures of Charles Anderson Chester, The (Lippard), **Supp. XXIII:** 184
"Life and Death Kisses, The" (Grossman), **Supp. XIX:** 87
Life and Gabriella (Glasgow), **II:** 175, 176, 182–183, 184, 189
Life and I (Wharton), **Retro. Supp. I:** 360, 361, 362; **Retro. Supp. III:** 276
"Life and Letters" (Epstein), **Supp. XIV:** 104–105
"Life and Letters in New England" (Emerson), **Supp. XXIV:** 67
Life and Letters of Harrison Gray Otis, Federalist, 1765–1848, The (Morison), **Supp. I Part 2:** 480–481
Life and Letters of Sir Henry Wotton (L. P. Smith), **Supp. XIV:** 340–341
Life and Mind of Emily Dickinson, The (Taggard), **Supp. XXII:** 279
Life and Times of Frederick Douglass, Written by Himself, The (Douglass), **Supp. III Part 1:** 155, 159–163
Life and Writings of Horace McCoy, The (Wolfson), **Supp. XIII:** 172, 174
"Life Apart, The: L'Ame Close" (Wharton), **Retro. Supp. III:** 281–282
"Life as a Visionary Spirit" (Eberhart), **I:** 540, 541
"Life at Angelo's, A" (Benét), **Supp. XI:** 53
Life at Happy Knoll (Marquand), **III:** 50, 61
Life Before Man (Atwood), **Supp. XIII: 24–25**
Lifeboat (screenplay, Hecht), **Supp. XXVII:** 93
"Life Cycle of Common Man" (Nemerov), **III:** 278
"Lifecycle Stairmaster" (Karr), **Supp. XI:** 250
Life Estates (Hearon), **Supp. VIII: 68–69**
Life for Life's Sake (Aldington), **Supp. I Part 1:** 256
Life Full of Holes, A (Layachi), **Supp. IV Part 1:** 92
"Lifeguard" (Updike), **IV:** 226; **Retro. Supp. I:** 325
"Lifeguard, The" (Dickey), **Supp. IV Part 1:** 179–180
"Life in the 30s" (column, Quindlen), **Supp. XVII:** 165, 167–169
Life in the Clearings (Shields), **Supp. VII:** 313
"Life in the Country: A City Friend Asks, 'Is It Boring?' " (Paley), **Supp. VI:** 231
Life in the Forest (Levertov), **Supp. III Part 1:** 282–283
Life in the Iron Mills (R. H. Davis), **Supp. XIII:** 292, 295, 299, 305; **Supp. XVI:** 79–82, **85–88,** 91
Life in the Iron Mills and Other Stories (T. Olson, ed.), **Supp. XVI:** 83
Life in the Theatre, A (Mamet), **Supp. XIV:** 241, 255
Life in the War Zone (Atherton), **Supp. XXIV:** 24
Life Is a Miracle: An Essay Against Modern Superstition (Berry), **Supp. X:** 35
"Life Is Fine" (Hughes), **Supp. I Part 1:** 334, 338
"Life Is Motion" (Stevens), **IV:** 74
Life & Letters of Gene Stratton-Porter (Meehan), **Supp. XX: 213**
Life of Albert Gallatin, The (Adams), **I:** 6, 14
"Life of a Man of the World, The"(Lippard), **Supp. XXIII:** 189
Life of an Ordinary Woman, The: Anne Ellis (A. Ellis), **Supp. XVI:** 38
Life of Captain Cipriani, The: An Account of British Government in the West Indies (C. L. R. James), **Supp. XXI:** 161
Life of Dryden (S. Johnson), **Retro. Supp. II:** 223
Life of Emily Dickinson, The (Sewall), **Retro. Supp. I:** 25
Life of Forms, The (Focillon), **IV:** 90
Life of Franklin Pierce (Hawthorne), **Retro. Supp. I:** 163
Life of George Cabot Lodge, The (Adams), **I:** 21
Life of George Washington (Irving), **II:** 314, 315–316
Life of Henry James (Edel), **Retro. Supp. I:** 224
"Life of Irony, The" (Bourne), **I:** 219
Life of Jesus (Renan), **Supp. XX: 122**
"Life of Lincoln West, The" (Brooks), **Supp. III Part 1:** 86
Life of Mary, The (Rilke; F. Wright, trans.), **Supp. XVII:** 244
Life of Michelangelo (Grimm), **II:** 17
"Life of Nancy, The" (Jewett), **Retro. Supp. II:** 133, 144
Life of Oliver Goldsmith, The, with Selections from His Writings (Irving), **II:** 315
Life of Phips (Mather), **Supp. II Part 2:** 451, 452, 459
Life of Poetry, The (Rukeyser), **Supp. VI:** 271, 273, 275–276, 282, 283, 286
Life of Samuel Johnson (Boswell), **Supp. I Part 2:** 656
Life of Savage (S. Johnson), **Supp. I Part 2:** 523
Life of the Drama, The (Bentley), **IV:** 396
"Life of the Mind, The" (Kees), **Supp. XV:** 140
Life of the Right Reverend Joseph P. Machebeuf, The (Howlett), **Retro. Supp. I:** 17
Life of Thomas Paine, author of Rights of Men, With a Defence of his Writings (Chalmers), **Supp. I Part 2:** 514
Life of Thomas Paine, The (Cobbett), **Supp. I Part 2:** 517
"Life of Towne, The" (Carson), **Supp. XII: 102**
Life of William Ellery Channing (W. H. Channing), **Supp. XXIV:** 68
"Life on Beekman Place, A" (Naylor), **Supp. VIII:** 214
"Life on the Black List" (Endore), **Supp. XVII:** 63
Life on the Hyphen: The Cuban-American Way (Firmat), **Supp. VIII:** 76; **Supp. XI:** 184
Life on the Mississippi (Twain), **I:** 209; **IV:** 198, 199; **Retro. Supp. III:** 256, 264, 267; **Supp. I Part 2:** 440
"Life on the Rocks: The Galápagos" (Dillard), **Supp. VI:** 32
"Life Stories, East and West" (E. Hoffman), **Supp. XVI:** 157
Life Story (Baker), **II:** 259
Life Studies (R. Lowell), **I:** 400; **II:** 384, 386, 543, 546–550, 551, 555; **Retro. Supp. II:** 180, 185, 186, 188, 189, 191; **Retro. Supp. III:** 41; **Supp. I Part 2:** 543; **Supp. XI:** 240, 244, 250, 317; **Supp. XII:** 255; **Supp. XIV:** 15; **Supp. XV:** 252
"Life Studies" (R. Lowell), **Retro.**

Supp. II: 188
"Life Styles in the Golden Land" (Didion), **Supp. IV Part 1:** 200
Life Supports: New and Collected Poems (Bronk), **Supp. XXI:** 19, 31, 32
"Life That Is, The" (Bryant), **Supp. I Part 1:** 169
"Life Work" (Stafford), **Supp. XI:** 329–330
"Life You Save May Be Your Own, The" (O'Connor), **III:** 344, 350, 354; **Retro. Supp. II:** 229, 230, 233; **Retro. Supp. III:** 208, 215, 219
Lifshin, Lyn, **Supp. XVI:** 37
"Lifting, The" (Olds), **Supp. X:** 210
"Ligeia" (Poe), **III:** 412, 414; **Retro. Supp. II:** 261, 270, 271, 275; **Retro. Supp. III:** 228–229
Liggett, Walter W., **Supp. XIII:** 168
Light, James F., **IV:** 290; **Retro. Supp. II:** 325
Light, Kate, **Supp. XVII:** 109
Light and Dark (Bronk), **Supp. XXI:** **27–29,** 31
"Light and the Sufferer" (Lethem), **Supp. XVIII:** 139–140
Light around the Body, The (R. Bly), **Supp. IV Part 1:** 61–62, 62; **Supp. XVII:** 243; **Supp. XXI:** 84–85
"Light Comes Brighter, The" (Roethke), **III:** 529–530
"Lighter than Air" (Stone), **Supp. XXVII:** 251
"Light from Above" (Eberhart), **I:** 541
Light in August (Faulkner), **II:** 63–64, 65, 74; **IV:** 207; **Retro. Supp. I:** 82, 84, 85, 86, 89, 92; **Retro. Supp. III:** 74, 80, 82–83; **Supp. XIV:** 12
Light in the Forest, The (Richter), **Supp. XVIII: 216–217**
Light in the Morning (Baker), **Supp. XVIII:** 263, 269
"Light in the Piazza, The" (Spencer), **Supp. XXVII:** 13
Light in the Window, A (Rinehart), **Supp. XXV:** 198–199, 202
"Light Man, A" (James), **II:** 322; **Retro. Supp. I:** 219
"Lightning" (Barthelme), **Supp. IV Part 1:** 53
"Lightning" (Bynner), **Supp. XV:** 44
"Lightning" (Oliver), **Supp. VII:** 235
"Lightning, The" (Swenson), **Supp. IV Part 2:** 645
"Lightning Flash, The" (Gibran), **Supp. XX: 123**
"Lightning Rod Man, The" (Melville), **III:** 90; **Supp. XVIII:** 4
"Light of the Body, The" (Davison), **Supp. XXVI:** 71
"Light of the World, The" (Hemingway), **II:** 249
"Lights"(Dybek), **Supp. XXIII:** 72
Lights in the Valley (Bodenheim), **Supp. XXV:** 29
"Lights in the Windows" (Nye), **Supp. XIII:** 280
"Lights Must Never Go Out, The"(Hadas), **Supp. XXIII:** 125
"Light Through the Window, The" (Brockmeier), **Supp. XXII:** 52, 59
Light Verse and Satires (Bynner), **Supp. XV:** 52
Light Years (Salter), **Supp. IX: 257–259**
"LIKE, THIS IS WHAT I MEANT!" (Baraka), **Supp. II Part 1:** 59
"Like All the Other Nations" (Paley), **Supp. VI:** 220
"Like a Rolling Stone" (song, Dylan), **Supp. XVIII:** 20, 30
"Like Decorations in a Nigger Cemetery" (Stevens), **IV:** 74, 79; **Retro. Supp. I:** 305
Like Ghosts of Eagles (Francis), **Supp. IX:** 86
"Like Life" (Moore), **Supp. X:** 163, 165, **172–173**
Like Life: Stories (Moore), **Supp. X:** 163, **171–175,** 177, 178
"Likeness to God" (Channing), **Supp. XXIV: 75–76,** 77, 78
"Like Talk" (Mills), **Supp. XI:** 311
"Like the New Moon I Will Live My Life" (R. Bly), **Supp. IV Part 1:** 71
Li'l Abner (Capp), **IV:** 198
"Lilacs" (A. Lowell), **II:** 527
"Lilacs, The" (Wilbur), **Supp. III Part 2:** 557–558
"Lilacs for Ginsberg" (Stern), **Supp. IX:** 299
Liliom (Molnar), **Supp. XVI:** 187
Lilith's Brood (O. Butler), **Supp. XIII:** 63
Lillabulero Press, **Supp. V:** 4, 5
Lillian Hellman (Adler), **Supp. I Part 1:** 297
Lillian Hellman (Falk), **Supp. I Part 1:** 297
Lillian Hellman: Playwright (Moody), **Supp. I Part 1:** 280
Lillo, George, **II:** 111, 112
"Lily Daw and the Three Ladies" (Welty), **IV:** 262
Lily for My Love, A (Berrigan), **Supp. XXIV:** 35
Lima, Agnes de, **I:** 231, 232
Lima, Frank, **Supp. XXIII:** 217, 221; **Supp. XXVII:** 23
Lima, Maria Helena, **Supp. XXII:** 73
Lima Beans (Kreymborg), **Supp. XXII:** 163
"Limbo: Altered States" (Karr), **Supp. XI:** 249–250
"Limen" (Trethewey), **Supp. XXI:** 250
Lime Orchard Woman, The (Ríos), **Supp. IV Part 2:** 538, 547–550, 553
"Lime Orchard Woman, The" (Ríos), **Supp. IV Part 2:** 548
Limitations (Turow), **Supp. XVII: 222–223**
"Limits" (Emerson), **II:** 19
Limits of Mortality, The: An Essay on Wordsworth's Major Poems (Ferry), **Supp. XXIV:** 147, 148
Lincoln, Abraham, **I:** 1, 4, 30; **II:** 8, 13, 135, 273, 555, 576; **III:** 576, 577, 580, 584, 587–590, 591; **IV:** 192, 195, 298, 347, 350, 444; **Supp. I Part 1:** 2, 8, 26, 309, 321; **Supp. I Part 2:** 379, 380, 382, 385, 390, 397, 399, 418, 424, 454, 456, 471, 472, 473, 474, 483, 579, 687; **Supp. IX:** 15; **Supp. VIII:** 108; **Supp. XIV:** 73
Lincoln, Kenneth, **Supp. IV Part 1:** 329; **Supp. IV Part 2:** 507
Lincoln, Thomas, **III:** 587
Lincoln, Mrs. Thomas (Nancy Hanks), **III:** 587
Lincoln: A Novel (Vidal), **Supp. IV Part 2:** 677, 684, 685, 688, 689–690, 691, 692
"Lincolnites" (Rash), **Supp. XXVII:** 229
Lincoln Lawyer, The (Connelly), **Supp. XXI: 77,** 78
Lincoln on Race and Slavery (H. L. Gates), **Supp. XX: 108–109**
"Lincoln Relics, The" (Kunitz), **Supp. III Part 1:** 269
Lincoln: The Man (Masters), **Supp. I Part 2:** 471, 473–474
Lindbergh, Charles A., **I:** 482
"Linden Branch, The" (MacLeish), **III:** 19, 20
Linden Hills (Naylor), **Supp. VIII:** 214, 218, **219–223**
Linderman, Lawrence, **Supp. IV Part 2:** 579, 583, 585, 589
Lindner, April, **Supp. XV:** 111, 119
"Lindo y Querido" (Muñoz), **Supp. XXV:** 135
Lindsay, Howard, **III:** 284
Lindsay, John, **Supp. I Part 2:** 374
Lindsay, Olive, **Supp. I Part 2:** 374, 375, 392
Lindsay, Vachel, **I:** 384; **II:** 263, 276,

530; **III:** 5, 505; **Retro. Supp. I:** 133; **Retro. Supp. III:** 101; **Supp. I Part 1:** 324; **Supp. I Part 2: 374–403,** 454, 473, 474; **Supp. III Part 1:** 63, 71; **Supp. XV:** 293, 297, 299, 301, 306; **Supp. XVI:** 184–185; **Supp. XXV:** 18; **Supp. XXVII:** 286, 294, 297
Lindsay, Mrs. Vachel (Elizabeth Connors), **Supp. I Part 2:** 398, 399, 473
Lindsay, Vachel Thomas, **Supp. I Part 2:** 374, 375
Lindsay, Mrs. Vachel Thomas (Esther Catherine Frazee), **Supp. I Part 2:** 374, 375, 384–385, 398
Lindsey, David, **Supp. XIV:** 26
"Line, The" (Olds), **Supp. X:** 206
Lineage of Ragpickers, Songpluckers, Elegiasts, and Jewelers, A (Goldbarth), **Supp. XII:** 191
"Line"(Crooker), **Supp. XXIII:** 58
Line Dance (Crooker), **Supp. XXIII:** 56, **58–60**
"Line Dance"(Crooker), **Supp. XXIII:** 59
"Line of Least Resistance, The" (Wharton), **Retro. Supp. I:** 366
Line Out for a Walk, A: Familiar Essays (Epstein), **Supp. XIV: 107**
"Liner Notes for the Poetically Unhep" (Hughes), **Retro. Supp. I:** 210
"Lines, Written on Reading Stuart's Account of the Treatment of Slaves in Charleston" (Very), **Supp. XXV:** 239
"Lines After Rereading T. S. Eliot" (Wright), **Supp. V:** 343
"Lines Composed a Few Miles Above Tintern Abbey" (Wordsworth), **Supp. III Part 1:** 12
"Lines Composed Over Three Thousand Miles from Tintern Abbey" (Collins), **Supp. XXI:** 57–58
"Lines for an Interment" (MacLeish), **III:** 15
"Lines for My Father" (Cullen), **Supp. IV Part 1:** 167
"Lines from Israel" (R. Lowell), **II:** 554
"Lines from Pietro Longhi" (Sobin), **Supp. XVI:** 289
"Lines on Revisiting the Country" (Bryant), **Supp. I Part 1:** 164
"Lines Suggested by a Tennessee Song" (Agee), **I:** 28
"Lines to a Friend Asleep"(J. Schoolcraft), **Supp. XXIII:** 228, 230
"Line-Storm Song, A" (Frost), **Retro. Supp. I:** 127
"Lines written at Castle Island, Lake Superior"(J. Schoolcraft), **Supp. XXIII:** 229, 232, 233
"Lines Written at Port Royal" (Freneau), **Supp. II Part 1:** 264
"Lines Written in an Asylum" (Carruth), **Supp. XVI:** 48
"Lines Written in Manassas", **Supp. XV:** 99–100
Lineup, The (Connelly), **Supp. XXI:** 67, 68–69
"Line Written in the Dark Illegible Next Day" (F. Wright), **Supp. XVII:** 242
Linfield, Susie, **Supp. XVII:** 169, 177
Lingeman, Richard, **Supp. X:** 82; **Supp. XXII:** 104
"Linguistics 101" (Huddle), **Supp. XXVI:** 152
Linn, Elizabeth. See Brown, Mrs. Charles Brockden (Elizabeth Linn)
Linn, John Blair, **Supp. I Part 1:** 145
Linnaeus, Carolus, **II:** 6; **Supp. I Part 1:** 245
"Linnets" (Levis), **Supp. XI:** 260, 261
"Linoleum" (Gallagher), **Supp. XXIV:** 170
"Linoleum Roses" (Cisneros), **Supp. VII:** 63, 66
Linotte: 1914–1920 (Nin), **Supp. X:** 193, 196, 197
Linschoten, Hans, **II:** 362, 363, 364
"Lion" (B. Kelly), **Supp. XVII:** 133
"Lion and Honeycomb" (Nemerov), **III:** 275, 278, 280
Lion and the Archer, The (Hayden), **Supp. II Part 1:** 366, 367
Lion and the Honeycomb, The (Blackmur), **Supp. II Part 1:** 91
Lion Country (Buechner), **Supp. XII:** 52, 53
Lionel Lincoln (Cooper), **I:** 339, 342
"Lion for Real, The" (Ginsberg), **Supp. II Part 1:** 320
Lionhearted, The: A Story about the Jews of Medieval England (Reznikoff), **Supp. XIV:** 280, 289
Lion in the Garden (Meriweather and Millgate), **Retro. Supp. I:** 91
"Lionizing" (Poe), **III:** 411, 425
"Lions, Harts, and Leaping Does" (Powers), **III:** 356
Lions and Shadows: An Education in the Twenties (Isherwood), **Supp. XIV:** 158, 159, 160, 162
"Lions in Sweden" (Stevens), **IV:** 79–80
Lipman, William R., **Supp. XIII:** 170
Li Po, **Supp. XI:** 241; **Supp. XII:** 218; **Supp. XV:** 47, 217
Lippard, George, **Supp. XXIII: 177–192**
Lippard, Lucy, **Supp. XXVII:** 39
Lippmann, Walter, **I:** 48, 222–223, 225; **III:** 291, 600; **IV:** 429; **Supp. I Part 2:** 609, 643; **Supp. VIII:** 104
Lipschitz, Moryce, **Supp. XXIII:** 6
Lips Together, Teeth Apart (McNally), **Supp. XIII: 201–202,** 208, 209
Lipsyte, Robert, **Supp. XVI:** 220
Lipton, James, **Supp. IV Part 2:** 576, 577, 579, 583, 586, 588
Lipton, Lawrence, **Supp. IX:** 3
"Lisbon Story" (Vaz), **Supp. XXVI:** 267–268
Lisbon Traviata, The (McNally), **Supp. XIII:** 198, **199–200,** 201, 204, 208
Lish, Gordon, **Supp. XIX:** 209; **Supp. XXI:** 115, 121; **Supp. XXIII:** 274; **Supp. XXIV:** 166, 177
Lisicky,Paul, **Supp. XI:** 120, 131, 135
Lisk, Thomas, **Supp. XXI:** 24
"Lisp, The" (Olds), **Supp. X:** 211
Listen, Ruben Fontanez (Neugeboren), **Supp. XVI: 220–221**
"Listeners, The" (de la Mare), **Supp. XVII:** 69
"Listeners and Readers: The Unforgetting of Vachel Lindsay" (Trombly), **Supp. I Part 2:** 403
"Listening" (J. W. Miller), **Supp. XX: 167**
"Listening" (Paley), **Supp. VI:** 218, 231, 232
"Listening" (Stafford), **Supp. XI:** 321, 322
Listening to Prozac (P. Kramer), **Supp. XVI:** 229
"Listening to the Desert" (Henderson), **Supp. XIII:** 221–222
"Listening to the Mockingbird" (Woodard), **Supp. VIII:** 128
Listening to Your Life: Daily Meditations with Frederick Buechner (Buechner), **Supp. XII:** 53
Listen to the Desert/Oye al desierto (Mora), **Supp. XIII:** 221
"Listen to the People" (Benét), **Supp. XI:** 51–52
Liston, Sonny, **III:** 38, 42
Li T'ai-po, **II:** 526
"Litany" (Ashbery), **Supp. III Part 1:** 21–22, 25, 26
"Litany" (Collins), **Supp. XXI:** 56–57
"Litany" (Sandburg), **III:** 593
"Litany, The" (Gioia), **Supp. XV:** 125, 126
"Litany for Dictatorships" (Benét), **Supp. XI:** 46, 58

"Litany for Survival, A" (Lorde), **Supp. XII:** 220
"Litany of the Dark People, The" (Cullen), **Supp. IV Part 1:** 170, 171
"Litany of the Heroes" (Lindsay), **Supp. I Part 2:** 397
"Litany of Washington Street, The" (Lindsay), **Supp. I Part 2:** 376, 398–399
"Literary Achievement of Meyer Levin, The" (Bossin), **Supp. XXVII:** 133
Literary Anthropology (Trumpener and Nyce), **Retro. Supp. I:** 380
Literary Art and Activism of Rick Bass, The (Weltzien), **Supp. XVI:** 20–21
"Literary Blacks and Jews" (Ozick), **Supp. V:** 272
"Literary Career of Elizabeth Barstow Stoddard, The" (Matlack), **Supp. XV:** 269
Literary Criticism: A Short History (Brooks and Wimsatt), **Supp. XIV:** 12
"Literary Criticism of Georg Lukács, The" (Sontag), **Supp. III Part 2:** 453
"Literary Development or California, The" (Atherton), **Supp. XXIV:** 22
Literary Disruptions (Klinkowitz), **Supp. XXI:** 233
Literary Essays of Thomas Merton, The, **Supp. VIII:** 207
"Literary Folk As They Came and Went with Ourselves" (E. Stoddard), **Supp. XV:** 274
Literary Friends and Acquaintance (Howells), **Supp. I Part 1:** 318; **Supp. XV:** 287
"Literary Heritage of Tennyson, The" (Locke), **Supp. XIV:** 197
Literary History of the United States (Spiller et al., ed.), **Supp. I Part 1:** 104; **Supp. II Part 1:** 95
"Literary Importation" (Freneau), **Supp. II Part 1:** 264
"Literary Life of America, The" (Brooks), **I:** 245
"Literary London" (Atherton), **Supp. XXIV:** 24
Literary Outlaw: The Life and Times of William S. Burroughs (Morgan), **Supp. XIV:** 141
Literary Situation, The (Cowley), **Supp. II Part 1:** 135, 140, 144, 146, 147, 148
"Literary Worker's Polonius, The" (Wilson), **IV:** 431, 432
"Literature" (Emerson), **II:** 6
Literature (X. J. Kennedy), **Supp. XV:** 153
Literature and American Life (Boynton), **Supp. I Part 2:** 415
Literature and Insurgency: Ten Studies in Racial Evolution (Underwood), **Supp. XXIV:** 29
Literature and Life (Howells), **Supp. XIV:** 45–46
Literature and Morality (Farrell), **II:** 49
"Literature and Place: Varieties of Regional Experience" (Erisman), **Supp. VIII:** 126
"Literature and War" (Faulkner), **Retro. Supp. III:** 76
"Literature as a Symptom" (Warren), **IV:** 237
"Literature in Low Life" (Hapgood), **Supp. XVII:** 103
"Literature of Exhaustion, The" (Barth), **Supp. IV Part 1:** 48
"Lithuanian Nocturne" (Brodsky), **Supp. VIII:** 29
"Lit Instructor" (Stafford), **Supp. XI:** 321
Littauer, Kenneth, **Retro. Supp. I:** 114
Little Acts of Kindness (Budbill), **Supp. XIX: 3, 14–15**
"Little Annie's Ramble" (Hawthorne), **Retro. Supp. III:** 113
"Little Bernhardt" (Shaw), **Supp. XIX:** 246
Little Big Man (Berger), **Supp. XII:** 171
Little Big Man (film), **Supp. X:** 124
Littlebird, Harold, **Supp. IV Part 2:** 499
Littlebird, Larry, **Supp. IV Part 2:** 499, 505
Little Birds: Erotica (Nin), **Supp. X:** 192, 195
"Little Brown Baby" (Dunbar), **Supp. II Part 1:** 206
"Little Brown Jug" (Baraka), **Supp. II Part 1:** 51
"Little Burst, A"(Strout), **Supp. XXIII:** 282
"Little by Little"(Hadas), **Supp. XXIII:** 115
Little Casino (Sorrentino), **Supp. XXI:** 237, 238
"Little Clown, My Heart" (Cisneros), **Supp. VII:** 71
"Little Cosmic Dust Poem" (Haines), **Supp. XII:** 209–210
"Little Country Girl, A" (Chopin), **Retro. Supp. II:** 71
"Little Curtis" (Parker), **Supp. IX:** 193
Little Disturbances of Man, The (Paley), **Supp. VI:** 218
"Little Dog" (Hughes), **Supp. I Part 1:** 329
Little Dorrit (Dickens), **Supp. I Part 1:** 35
"Little Edward" (Stowe), **Supp. I Part 2:** 587
"Little Elegy" (X. J. Kennedy), **Supp. XV:** 155
"Little Elegy for Antonio Machado"(O'Hara), **Supp. XXIII:** 220
Little Essays Drawn from the Writings of George Santayana (L. P. Smith), **Supp. XIV:** 342
"Little Expressionless Animals" (Wallace), **Supp. X:** 305
"Little Fable" (Hay), **Supp. XIV:** 131
Little Face and Other Stories (Thompson), **Supp. XXIII: 293–294**
"Little Face"(Thompson), **Supp. XXIII:** 293
Littlefield, Catherine, **Supp. IX:** 58
Little Fling, A (Pickering), **Supp. XXI:** 203
Little Foxes, The (Hellman), **Supp. I Part 1:** 276, 278–279, 281, 283, 297
"Little Fred, the Canal Boy" (Stowe), **Supp. I Part 2:** 587
"Little French Mary" (Jewett), **II:** 400
Little Friend, Little Friend (Jarrell), **II:** 367, 372, 375–376
Little Friend, The (Tartt), **Supp. XXVII:** 267, 269, 270, 274–276
"Little Gidding" (T. S. Eliot), **I:** 582, 588; **II:** 539; **Retro. Supp. I:** 66; **Retro. Supp. III:** 68
"Little Girl, My Stringbean, My Lovely Woman" (Sexton), **Supp. II Part 2:** 686
"Little Girl, The" (Paley), **Supp. VI:** 222, **228–229**
"Little Girl Tells a Story to a Lady, A" (Barnes), **Supp. III Part 1:** 36
"Little Goose Girl, The" (Grimm), **IV:** 266
Little Ham (Hughes), **Retro. Supp. I:** 203; **Supp. I Part 1:** 328, 339
Little House in the Big Woods (L. I. Wilder), **Supp. XXII:** 294, 295, 296, 297, 298–299, 300
Little House on the Prairie (L. I. Wilder), **Supp. XXII:** 294, 295–296, 297, 299, 301
Little House on the Prairie (television series), **Supp. XXII:** 289
"Little House" series (L. A. Wilder), **Supp. XXII:** 289
"Little House" series (L. I. Wilder),

Supp. XXVI: 217–218
Little House Traveler, A (L. I. Wilder), **Supp. XXII:** 301
Little Ignorance, A (Schott), **Supp. XXIII:** 239, 241
Little King, The (Bynner), **Supp. XV:** 42, 50
Little Lady of the Big House, The (London), **II:** 481–482
Little Liar, The (film; Ingraham), **Supp. XVI:** 184–185
"Little Lion Face" (Swenson), **Supp. IV Part 2:** 651
"Little Lobelia's Song" (Bogan), **Supp. III Part 1:** 66
"Little Local Color, A" (Henry), **Supp. II Part 1:** 399
Little Lord Fauntleroy (Burnett), **Retro. Supp. I:** 188; **Supp. XVI:** 182
"Little Love, The" (H. Johnson), **Supp. XXVI:** 173
"Little Lyric" (Hughes), **Supp. I Part 1:** 334
Little Man, Little Man (Baldwin), **Supp. I Part 1:** 67
"Little Man at Chehaw Station, The" (Ellison), **Retro. Supp. II:** 123
Little Me (musical), **Supp. IV Part 2:** 575
Little Men (Alcott), **Supp. I Part 1:** 32, 39, 40
"Little Morning Music, A" (Schwartz), **Supp. II Part 2:** 662–663
Little Ocean (Shepard), **Supp. III Part 2:** 447
"Little Old Girl, A" (Larcom), **Supp. XIII:** 144
"Little Old Spy" (Hughes), **Supp. I Part 1:** 329
Little Orphan Annie (film), **Supp. XVIII:** 244
"Little Owl Who Lives in the Orchard" (Oliver), **Supp. VII:** 239
"Little Peasant, The" (Sexton), **Supp. II Part 2:** 690
"Little People"(Kenny), **Supp. XXIII:** 151
"Little Rapids, The" (Swenson), **Supp. IV Part 2:** 645
Little Red Song Book (Hill), **Supp. XVIII:** 224
Little Regiment and Other Episodes of the American Civil War, The (Crane), **I:** 408
Little River: New and Selected Poems (McCarriston), **Supp. XIV: 269–272**
"Little Road not made of Man , A" (Dickinson), **Retro. Supp. I:** 44
"Little Sawtooth" (Huddle), **Supp. XXVI:** 154, 155
Little Sister, The (Chandler), **Supp. IV Part 1:** 122, 130, 131–132
"Little Sleep's-Head Sprouting Hair in the Moonlight" (Kinnell), **Supp. III Part 1:** 247
"Little Snow White" (Grimm), **IV:** 266
"Little Spirit, or Boy-Man, The: An Odjibwa Tale"(J. Schoolcraft), **Supp. XXIII:** 234
Little Star (Halliday), **Supp. XIX:** 82, **84–85,** 87
"Little Star" (Halliday), **Supp. XIX:** 83, 84, 93
"Little Testament of Bernard Martin, Aet. 30" (Mumford), **Supp. II Part 2:** 472, 473, 474
"Little Things" (Olds), **Supp. X:** 208
Little Tour in France (James), **II:** 337
Little Town, The (Asch), **Supp. XXIII:** 4, 5, **7–8**
"Little Travel Diary, A"(O'Hara), **Supp. XXIII:** 220
Little Women (Alcott), **Supp. I Part 1:** 28, 29, 32, 35, 37, 38, 39–40, 41, 43, 44; **Supp. IX:** 128
Little Yellow Dog, A (Mosley), **Supp. XIII:** 237, 241
"Liturgy and Spiritual Personalism" (Merton), **Supp. VIII:** 199
Litz, A. Walton, **Retro. Supp. I:** 306
"Liu Ch'e" (Pound), **III:** 466
"Live" (Sexton), **Supp. II Part 2:** 684, 686
Live from Baghdad (screenplay, Shanley), **Supp. XIV:** 316
Live from Golgotha (Vidal), **Supp. IV Part 2:** 677, 682, 691, 692
Live Now and Pay Later (Garrett), **Supp. VII:** 111
"Live-Oak with Moss" (Whitman), **Retro. Supp. I:** 403
Live or Die (Sexton), **Supp. II Part 2:** 670, 683–687
Liveright, Horace, **Retro. Supp. I:** 80, 81, 83; **Supp. I Part 2:** 464; **Supp. XX: 71, 75; Supp. XXII:** 25; **Supp. XXIV:** 28; **Supp. XXV:** 24
Livermore, Elizabeth, **Supp. XXII:** 70
Lives (Plutarch), **II:** 5, 104
Lives of a Cell, The (L. Thomas), **Retro. Supp. I:** 322, 323
Lives of Distinguished American Naval Officers (Cooper), **I:** 347
Lives of Girls and Women (Munro), **Supp. XXVII:** 181, 182, 184
"Lives of Gulls and Children, The" (Nemerov), **III:** 271, 272
Lives of the Animals (Wrigley), **Supp. XVIII: 306–308**
Lives of the Artists (Vasari), **Supp. I Part 2:** 450
"Lives of the Bohemians" (Lethem), **Supp. XVIII:** 135
Lives of the Heart, The (Hirshfield), **Supp. XXIII:** 132–133, 135
Lives of the Muses, The: Nine Women and the Artists They Inspired (Prose), **Supp. XVI:** 250, 260
"Lives of the Philosophers, The" (Brockmeier), **Supp. XXII:** 59, 61
Lives of the Poets (Doctorow), **Supp. IV Part 1:** 234
"Lives of the Poets" (Doctorow), **Supp. IV Part 1:** 234
"Lives of the—Wha'?, The" (Goldbarth), **Supp. XII:** 191
"Living" (Wright), **Supp. XV:** 345
Living, The (Dillard), **Supp. VI:** 23
"Living at Home" (Gordon), **Supp. IV Part 1:** 311
Living by Fiction (Dillard), **Supp. VI:** 23, 31, **32,** 33
Living by the Word (Walker), **Supp. III Part 2:** 521, 522, 526, 527, 535
Living End, The (Elkin), **Supp. VI: 54,** 58
Living Instead (Bronk), **Supp. XXI:** 32
"Living in the Cult of Likability" (Ellis), **Supp. XXVII:** 79
"Living in the Flatlands" (Carruth), **Supp. XVI:** 54
Living in Time (Hadas), **Supp. XXIII:** 120, **122–123**
Living Is Easy, The (D. West), **Supp. XVIII:** 277, 280, **284–286,** 287
"Living Like Weasels" (Dillard), **Supp. VI:** 26, 33
Living Novel, The (Hicks), **III:** 342
Living of Charlotte Perkins Gilman, The (Gilman), **Supp. XI:** 193, 209
Living off the Country: Essays on Poetry and Place (Haines), **Supp. XII:** 199, 203, 207
"Living on a Giant" (X. J. Kennedy), **Supp. XV:** 163
Living Out Loud (Quindlen), **Supp. XVII:** 166, **167–169**
Living Present, The (Atherton), **Supp. XXIV:** 24
Living Reed, The (Buck), **Supp. II Part 1:** 129–130
Livingston, Myra Cohn, **Supp. XV:** 153, 162
Living Theater, **Retro. Supp. I:** 424
"Living There" (Dickey), **Supp. IV Part 1:** 182–183
Living the Spirit: A Gay American Indian Anthology (Roscoe, ed.),

Supp. IV Part 1: 330
"Living Together: A Letter" (Biss), **Supp. XXVI:** 51
Living to Prowl (Pickering), **Supp. XXI:** 203
"Living with a Peacock" (O'Connor), **III:** 350
"Living Words and Cartoon Translations" (Jocks), **Supp. XXVI:** 97
"Livvie" (Welty), **IV:** 265; **Retro. Supp. I:** 348–349
"Livvie Is Back" (Welty), **Retro. Supp. I:** 351
Livy, **II:** 8
"Lizards in Jamshyd's Courtyard" (Faulkner), **Retro. Supp. III:** 85
Lizzie (film), **Supp. IX:** 125
"Llantos de La Llorona: Warnings from the Wailer" (Mora), **Supp. XIII:** 217, 224
"L'Lapse" (Barthelme), **Supp. IV Part 1:** 45–47, 48
Llosa, Mario Vargas, **Supp. XIX:** 131; **Supp. XXIV:** 89
Lloyd, Fabien. See Cravan, Arthur
Lloyd, Henry Demarest, **Supp. I Part 1:** 5
Lloyd George, Harold, **I:** 490
"LMFBR" (Snyder), **Supp. VIII:** 302
Loach, Ken, **Supp. XXIII:** 163
"Loaded Inflections" (Halliday), **Supp. XIX:** 90, 91
"Loam" (Sandburg), **III:** 584–585
"Loan, The" (Malamud), **Supp. I Part 2:** 427, 428, 431, 437
Loberer, Eric, **Supp. XV:** 339
"Local" (McCarriston), **Supp. XIV:** 270
Local Color (Capote), **Supp. III Part 1:** 120
"Local Color" (London), **II:** 475
"Local Family Keeps Son Happy" (Keillor), **Supp. XVI:** 168, 169
Local Girls (Hoffman), **Supp. X:** 77, **90–91,** 92
"Local Girls" (Hoffman), **Supp. X:** 90
Local Habitation & A Name, A (Kooser), **Supp. XIX:** 116, 118, **119–120**
Local Men (Whitehead), **Supp. XV:** 339
"Local Metaphysics" (Huddle), **Supp. XXVI:** 149
Local Time (Dunn), **Supp. XI:** 143, **148–149**
Local Wonders: Seasons in the Bohemian Alps (Kooser), **Supp. XIX:** 115**, 126**
"Location" (Halliday), **Supp. XIX:** 87
Lock, Helen, **Supp. XIII:** 233, 237–238
Lock, Robert H., **IV:** 319; **Retro. Supp. I:** 375
Lockdown (Myers), **Supp. XXVII:** 204, 205
Locke, Alain, **Retro. Supp. II:** 115; **Retro. Supp. III:** 127, 128, 131, 140; **Supp. I Part 1:** 323, 325, 341; **Supp. II Part 1:** 53, 176, 182, 228, 247; **Supp. IV Part 1:** 170; **Supp. IX:** 306, 309; **Supp. X:** 134, 137, 139; **Supp. XIV: 195–219; Supp. XIX:** 69, 75; **Supp. XVIII:** 122; **Supp. XXII:** 7, 13
Locke, Duane, **Supp. IX:** 273
Locke, Jane Ermine, **Supp. XXV:** 38
Locke, John, **I:** 554–555, 557; **II:** 15–16, 113–114, 348–349, 480; **III:** 294–295; **IV:** 149; **Supp. I Part 1:** 130, 229, 230; **Supp. I Part 2:** 523
Locke, Sondra, **II:** 588
"Locked House, A" (Snodgrass), **Supp. VI:** 323
Locked Room, The (Auster), **Supp. XII:** 22, 24, **27–28**
Locket, The (Masters), **Supp. I Part 2:** 460
Lockridge, Ross, Jr., **Supp. XIX:** 263
"Locksley Hall" (Tennyson), **Supp. IX:** 19
Lockwood Concern, The (O'Hara), **III:** 362, 364, 377–382
"Locus" (Ammons), **Supp. VII:** 28
"Locus" (Hayden), **Supp. II Part 1:** 361–362, 381
"Locusts, the Plaza, the Room, The" (Kees), **Supp. XV:** 141
Loden, Barbara, **III:** 163
Lodge, Henry Cabot, **I:** 11–12, 21
Lodge, Mrs. Henry Cabot, **I:** 11–12, 19
Lodge, Thomas, **IV:** 370
Loeb, Gerald, **Supp. IV Part 2:** 523
Loeb, Harold, **Supp. XXIV:** 49
Loeb, Jacques, **I:** 513; **Retro. Supp. II:** 104; **Supp. I Part 2:** 641
Loeffler, Jack, **Supp. XIII:** 1, 3, 12, 14, 16
Loft, William D., **Supp. XXVI:** 96
Loftus, Mary J., **Supp. XXI:** 245
Lofty Dogmas (A. Finch, M. Kumin and D. Brown, eds.), **Supp. XVII:** 75–76
"Log" (Merrlll), **Supp. III Part 1:** 328
Logan, Joshua, **Supp. XXV:** 95
Logan, Rayford W., **Supp. II Part 1:** 171, 194; **Supp. XIV:** 73
Logan, William, **Supp. X:** 201, 213; **Supp. XI:** 131, 132; **Supp. XII:** 98, 107, 113, 184; **Supp. XV:** 212, 226, 251, 257, 260–261, 262,**Supp. XV:** 263, 266
Log Book of "The Loved One," The, **Supp. XI:** 306
Logenbach, James, **Supp. XVII:** 183
"Logging and Pimping and 'Your Pal, Jim' " (Maclean), **Supp. XIV:** 229
"Logos" (W. Stone), **Supp. XXVII:** 255
Logue, Christopher, **Supp. XIV:** 82
Lohengrin (Wagner), **I:** 216
Lohrfinck, Rosalind, **III:** 107, 117
Lolita (Nabokov), **III:** 246, 247, 255, 258–261; **Retro. Supp. I:** 263, 264, 265, 266, 269, 270, **272–274,** 275; **Supp. V:** 127, 252; **Supp. VIII:** 133; **Supp. XVI:** 294; **Supp. XXII:** 260
"Lolita" (Parker), **Supp. IX:** 193
Lolly Dinks' Doings (E. Stoddard), **Supp. XV:** 273,**Supp. XV:** 286
Lombard, Kandace, **Supp. XXVII:** 262
Lombardi, Marilyn May, **Retro. Supp. II:** 40
Lomokome Papers, The (Wouk), **Supp. XXV:** 256, 262
London, Eliza, **II:** 465
London, Jack, **I:** 209; **II:** 264, 440, 444, 451, **462–485; III:** 314, 580; **Supp. IV Part 1:** 236; **Supp. IX:** 1, 14; **Supp. V:** 281; **Supp. XIII:** 312; **Supp. XIV:** 227; **Supp. XV:** 115; **Supp. XVI:** 181; **Supp. XVIII:** 90; **Supp. XXII:** 203; **Supp. XXVII:** 126
London, Mrs. Jack (Bessie Maddern), **II:** 465, 466, 473, 478
London, Mrs. Jack (Charmian Kittredge), **II:** 466, 468, 473, 476, 478, 481
London, John, **II:** 464, 465
London, Scott, **Supp. XIV:** 301, 307, 311
"London 1972: Silent Zone" (Davison), **Supp. XXVI:** 72
London Embassy, The (Theroux), **Supp. VIII:** 323
London Fields (Amis), **Retro. Supp. I:** 278
"London Letter" (column; Eliot), **Supp. XV:** 306
London Magazine (Plath), **Supp. I Part 2:** 541
London Snow: A Christmas Story (Theroux), **Supp. VIII:** 322
London Suite (Simon), **Supp. IV Part 2:** 576, 581, 582, 588
London: The Biography (Ackroyd), **Supp. XVII:** 180

Loneliness of the Long Distance Runner, The (Sillitoe), **Supp. XX: 195**
Lonely Are the Brave (film), **Supp. XIII:** 6
"Lonely Coast, A" (Proulx), **Supp. VII:** 264
Lonely Crusade (C. Himes), **Supp. XVI:** 135, 139–140
Lonely for the Future (Farrell), **II:** 46, 47
"Lonely Gay Teen Seeking Same" (Egan), **Supp. XIX:** 61
Lonely Impulse of Delight, A (Shanley), **Supp. XIV:** 317–318
"Lonely Street, The" (W. C. Williams), **IV:** 413
"Lonely Worker, A" (Jewett), **Retro. Supp. II:** 132
Lonergan, Wayne, **Supp. I Part 1:** 51
Lonesome Boy (Bontemps), **Supp. XXII:** 6, 13–14
Lonesome Dove (McMurtry), **Supp. V:** 226–228, 231, 232, 233
Lonesome Traveler (Kerouac), **Supp. III Part 1:** 219, 225
"Lonesome Whistle Blowing" (Skow), **Supp. XVI:** 174
"Lone Striker, A" (Frost), **Retro. Supp. I:** 136, 137
Long, Ada, **Supp. V:** 178
Long, Frank Belknap, **Supp. XXV:** 111, 122; **Supp. XXVII:** 117
Long, Haniel, **Supp. XV:** 46, 49
Long, Huey, **I:** 489; **II:** 454; **IV:** 249; **Supp. IV Part 2:** 679; **Supp. XIV:** 14
Long, John Luther, **Supp. XXI:** 150
Long, Judith Reick, **Supp. XX: 212, 215, 217, 223**
Long, Ray, **II:** 430; **III:** 54
Long after Midnight (Bradbury), **Supp. IV Part 1:** 102
Long Ago in France: The Years in Dijon (M. F. K. Fisher), **Supp. XVII:** 91
Long and Happy Life, A (Price), **Supp. VI:** 258, **259–260,** 262, 264, 265
Long Approach, The (Kumin), **Supp. IV Part 2:** 452–453, 453
Longbottom, Robert, **Supp. XXI:** 148
Long Christmas Dinner, The (Wilder), **IV:** 357, 365; **Supp. V:** 105
Long Christmas Dinner and Other Plays (Wilder), **IV:** 365–366
Long Day's Dying, A (Buechner), **Supp. XII: 45–47**
Long Day's Journey into Night (O'Neill), **III:** 385, 401, 403–404; **Supp. IV Part 1:** 359; **Supp. XIV:** 327; **Supp. XXI:** 13; **Supp. XXII:** 27, 29, 30
Long Desire, A (Connell), **Supp. XIV:** 79, 80, 97
"Long Distance" (Stafford), **Supp. XI:** 329
"Long-Distance Runner, The" (Paley), **Supp. VI:** 221–222, 228, 230
Long Dream, The (Wright), **IV:** 478, 488, 494
"Long Embrace, The" (Levine), **Supp. V:** 187
"Long Enough" (Rukeyser), **Supp. VI:** 274
"Longest Night of My Life, The " (Nichols), **Supp. XIII:** 269
Longfellow, Henry Wadsworth, **I:** 458, 471; **II:** 274, 277, 295–296, 310, 313, 402, **486–510; III:** 269, 412, 421, 422, 577; **IV:** 309, 371; **Retro. Supp. I:** 54, 123, 150, 155, 362; **Retro. Supp. II: 153–174; Retro. Supp. III:** 106, 109, 113, 116, 225, 233, 255; **Supp. I Part 1:** 158, 299, 306, 317, 362, 368; **Supp. I Part 2:** 405, 406, 408, 409, 414, 416, 420, 586, 587, 602, 699, 704; **Supp. II Part 1:** 291, 353; **Supp. III Part 2:** 609; **Supp. IV Part 1:** 165; **Supp. IV Part 2:** 503; **Supp. XII:** 260; **Supp. XIII:** 141; **Supp. XIV:** 120; **Supp. XVIII:** 4; **Supp. XXI:** 51; **Supp. XXIII:** 223
"Long Feud" (Untermeyer), **Supp. XV:** 309
Long Feud: Selected Poems (Untermeyer), **Supp. XV:** 312
"Long Fourth, A" (Taylor), **Supp. V:** 313
Long Fourth and Other Stories, A (Taylor), **Supp. V:** 318–319
Long Gay Book, A (Stein), **IV:** 42
Long Goodbye, The (Chandler), **Supp. IV Part 1:** 120, 122, 132–134, 135
Long Goodbye, The (T. Williams), **IV:** 381
"Long Hair" (Snyder), **Supp. VIII:** 300
Longing for Home, The: Recollections and Reflections (Buechner), **Supp. XII:** 53
Longinus, Dionysius Cassius, **I:** 279
"Long-Legged House, The" (Berry), **Supp. X:** 21, 24–25, 27, 31
Long Live Man (Corso), **Supp. XII:** 129–130, 132
Long Love, The (Sedges), **Supp. II Part 1:** 125
Long Made Short (Dixon), **Supp. XII:** 152
Long March, The (Styron), **IV:** 97, 99, 104–107, 111, 113, 117
"Long Night, The" (Bambara), **Supp. XI:** 9
Long Night of White Chickens, The (Goldman), **Supp. XXV:** 49, 51–53
"Long Novel, A" (Ashbery), **Supp. III Part 1:** 6
Longo, Robert, **Supp. XVI:** 124
Long Patrol, The (Mailer), **III:** 46
"Long Peace Among Iroquois Nations, The" (Crawford), **Supp. XXVI:** 85
"Long Point Light" (Doty), **Supp. XI:** 127
Long Road of Woman's Memory, The (Addams), **Supp. I Part 1:** 17–18
"Long Run, The" (Wharton), **IV:** 314
Long Season, The (Brosnan), **II:** 424, 425; **Supp. XX: 195**
"Long Shadow of Lincoln, The: A Litany" (Sandburg), **III:** 591, 593
Longshot O'Leary (McGrath), **Supp. X:** 117
"Long Shower, The" (Francis), **Supp. IX:** 90
"Long Stemmed Roses" (Jarman), **Supp. XVII:** 115
Long Story Short (Gingher, ed.), **Supp. XXVII:** 12
Longstreet, Augustus B., **II:** 70, 313; **Supp. I Part 1:** 352; **Supp. V:** 44; **Supp. X:** 227
Longstreet, Augustus Baldwin, **Retro. Supp. III:** 259
"Long Summer" (R. Lowell), **II:** 553–554
"Long Term" (Dunn), **Supp. XI:** 149
"Long Thoughts, The"(Dybek), **Supp. XXIII:** 71
Longtime Companion (film), **Supp. X:** 146, 152
Long Valley, The (Steinbeck), **IV:** 51
Long View (Taggard), **Supp. XXII: 283–284**
Long Voyage Home, The (O'Neill), **III:** 388
"Long Wail, A" (Crews), **Supp. XI:** 101
"Long Walk, The" (Bogan), **Supp. III Part 1:** 61
Long Walk Home, The (Kriegel), **Supp. XXIV:** 214–216
Long Walks and Intimate Talks (Paley), **Supp. VI:** 221
Long Way from Home, A (McKay), **Supp. X:** 132, 140
Long Winter, The (L. I. Wilder), **Supp. XXII:** 291, 294, 295
Lönnrot, Elias, **Retro. Supp. II:** 159
Looby, Christopher, **Supp. XIII:** 96
Look, Dan, **Supp. XXV:** 123

Look, Stranger! (Auden), **Supp. II Part 1:** 11
"Look, The" (Olds), **Supp. X:** 210
Look at Me (Egan), **Supp. XIX:** 49, **53–56,** 60, 61
Look at the Harlequins (Nabokov), **Retro. Supp. I:** 266, 270
Lookaway, Lookaway (Barnhardt), **Supp. XXVII:** 1, 9–11, 13
"Look for My White Self" (Ammons), **Supp. VII:** 25
"Look Fred, You're a Doctor, My Problem Is Something Like This" (Berrigan), **Supp. XXIV:** 37
Look Homeward, Angel (Wolfe), **II:** 457; **IV:** 450, 452, 453, 454, 455–456, 461, 462, 463, 464, 468, 471; **Supp. XI:** 216
"Looking" (Sanders), **Supp. XVI:** 277
"Looking a Mad Dog Dead in the Eyes" (Komunyakaa), **Supp. XIII:** 114
"Looking at Each Other" (Rukeyser), **Supp. VI:** 280, 285–286
"Looking at Kafka" (P. Roth), **Supp. III Part 2:** 402
"Looking at Women" (Sanders), **Supp. XVI:** 274
"Looking Back" (Harjo), **Supp. XII:** 218
"Looking Back" (Merwin), **Supp. III Part 1:** 352
"Looking Back at Girlhood" (Jewett), **Retro. Supp. II:** 131, 133
Looking Backward (Bellamy), **II:** 276; **Supp. I Part 2:** 641; **Supp. XI:** 200
"Looking for a Ship" (McPhee), **Supp. III Part 1:** 312–313
"Looking for Dragon Smoke" (R. Bly), **Supp. IV Part 1:** 60
Looking for Holes in the Ceiling (Dunn), **Supp. XI:** 139, **143–145**
Looking for Langston (Julien; film), **Supp. XI:** 19, 20
Looking for Lincoln (television production), **Supp. XX: 99**
Looking for Luck (Kumin), **Supp. IV Part 2:** 453, 454–455
"Looking for Mr. Green" (Bellow), **Retro. Supp. II:** 27
"Looking for the Buckhead Boys" (Dickey), **Supp. IV Part 1:** 182, 183
"Looking Forward to Age" (Harrison), **Supp. VIII:** 49
"Looking from Inside My Body" (R. Bly), **Supp. IV Part 1:** 71
"Looking Glass, The" (Wharton), **Retro. Supp. I:** 382
"Lookout's Journal" (Snyder), **Supp. VIII:** 291
"Looks Like They'll Never Learn" (McCoy), **Supp. XIII:** 166
"Look to the Woods" (P. N. Warren), **Supp. XX: 272**
"Look to Thy Heart . . ." (Hay), **Supp. XIV:** 130
Loon, Hendrik Willem van, **Supp. XVI:** 185
Loon Lake (Doctorow), **Supp. IV Part 1:** 219, 222, 224–227, 230, 231, 232, 233
"Loon Point" (O'Brien), **Supp. V:** 237
Loos, Adolf, **Supp. XVI:** 187
Loos, Anita, **Supp. XVI: 181–199**
Loos, Mary Anita, **Supp. XVI:** 196
Loose Canons (H. L. Gates), **Supp. XX: 101, 108, 109–110, 111**
Loosestrife (Dunn), **Supp. XI: 152–154**
"Loosestrife" (Dunn), **Supp. XI:** 154
"Loose Woman" (X. J. Kennedy), **Supp. XV:** 159
Loose Woman: Poems (Cisneros), **Supp. VII:** 58, 71–72
Lopate, Edward, **Supp. XVI:** 266
Lopate, Philip, **Supp. XII:** 184; **Supp. XIII:** 280–281; **Supp. XVI:** 230
Lopatnikoff, Nikolai, **Supp. XIV:** 123
Lopez, Barry, **Supp. IV Part 1:** 416; **Supp. V:** 211; **Supp. X:** 29, 31; **Supp. XIII:** 16; **Supp. XIV:** 227
Lopez, Rafael, **Supp. IV Part 2:** 602
Lorax, The (Geisel), **Supp. XVI:** 109–110
Lorca, Federico García, **IV:** 380; **Supp. I Part 1:** 345; **Supp. IV Part 1:** 83; **Supp. VIII:** 38, 39; **Supp. XIII:** 315, 323, 324; **Supp. XV:** 186; **Supp. XXI:** 100; **Supp. XXVII:** 53, 151, 155, 160
Lorch, Fred, **Retro. Supp. III:** 268
Lord, Audre, **Retro. Supp. III:** 247
Lord, Judge Otis P., **I:** 454, 457, 458, 470
Lorde, Audre, **Supp. I Part 2:** 550, 571; **Supp. IV Part 1:** 325; **Supp. XI:** 20; **Supp. XII:** 217, 220; **Supp. XIII:** 295; **Supp. XVII:** 71; **Supp. XXIII:** 194
Lord Jim (Conrad), **I:** 422; **II:** 26; **Retro. Supp. II:** 292; **Supp. I Part 2:** 623; **Supp. IV Part 2:** 680; **Supp. V:** 251
"Lord of Hosts" (Pinsky), **Supp. VI:** 244
Lord of the Flies (W. Golding), **Supp. XVI:** 65
Lord of the Rings (Tolkien), **Supp. V:** 140; **Supp. XXVII:** 128
Lords of Misrule, The (X. J. Kennedy), **Supp. XV:** 154, **170–171**
Lords of the Housetops (Van Vechten), **Supp. II Part 2:** 736
Lord's Prayer, **I:** 579
Lord Timothy Dexter of Newburyport, Mass. (Marquand), **III:** 55
Lord Weary's Castle (R. Lowell), **II:** 538, 542–551; **Retro. Supp. II:** 178, **186–187,** 188; **Supp. XV:** 252
"Lorelei" (Plath), **Retro. Supp. II:** 246; **Supp. I Part 2:** 538
Lorentzen, Christian, **Supp. XXVII:** 195–196
"Lorenzo" (Bynner), **Supp. XV:** 46, 50
Lorimer, George Horace, **II:** 430; **Retro. Supp. I:** 101, 113
Lori-Parks, Suzan, **Retro. Supp. III:** 319
Lorre, Peter, **Supp. IV Part 1:** 356
"Los Alamos" (Momaday), **Supp. IV Part 2:** 482
Los Amigos de Becky (Hinojosa). See Becky and Her Friends (Hinojosa)
"Los Angeles, 1980" (Gunn Allen), **Supp. IV Part 1:** 325
"Los Angeles Days" (Didion), **Supp. IV Part 1:** 211
Los Cerritos (Atherton), **Supp. XXIV:** 22
"Lo! School in Poetry, The" (Taggard), **Supp. XXII:** 276
"Loser, The" (Talese), **Supp. XVII:** 202, 208
Loser and Still Champion: Muhammad Ali (Schulberg), **Supp. XVIII:** 254
Losey, Joseph, **IV:** 383
Lose Your Mother: A Journey Along the Atlantic Slave Route (Hartman), **Supp. XX: 154**
"Losing a Language" (Merwin), **Supp. III Part 1:** 356
Losing Battles (Welty), **IV:** 261, 281–282; **Retro. Supp. I:** 341, 352, **353–354**
"Losing the Marbles" (Merrill), **Supp. III Part 1:** 337
"Losing Track of Language" (Clampitt), **Supp. IX:** 38, 40
Losses (Jarrell), **II:** 367, 372, 373–375, 376, 377, 380–381
"Losses" (Jarrell), **II:** 375–376
Lossky, N. O., **Supp. IV Part 2:** 519
"Loss of Breath" (Poe), **III:** 425–426
"Loss of My Arms and Legs, The" (Kingsolver), **Supp. VII:** 208
Loss of Roses, A (Inge), **Supp. XXV:** 95, 103–104, 106
"Loss of the Creature, The" (Percy), **Supp. III Part 1:** 387

"Lost" (Wagoner), **Supp. IX:** 328
"Lost, The" (Boyle), **Supp. XXIV:** 59
"Lost, The/Los Perdidos" (Kingsolver), **Supp. VII:** 208
"Lost and Found" (Levine), **Supp. V:** 188
"Lost and Found" (Nelson), **Supp. XVIII:** 176
"Lost Bodies" (Wright), **Supp. V:** 342
"Lost Boy, The" (Wolfe), **IV:** 451, 460, 466–467
"Lost Children, The"(Crooker), **Supp. XXIII:** 54
"Lost Decade, The" (Fitzgerald), **II:** 98
"Lost Dogs of Phnom Penh, The" (Boyle), **Supp. XXIV:** 64
Lost Ecstasy (Rinehart), **Supp. XXV:** 196
Lost Father, The (Simpson), **Supp. XXVII:** 237–239
"Lost Fugue for Chet" (Hull), **Supp. XXI:** 137–138, 141
Lost Galleon and Other Tales, The (Harte), **Supp. II Part 1:** 344
Lost Get-Back Boogie, The (Burke), **Supp. XIV:** 22, 25
"Lost Girls, The" (Hogan), **Supp. IV Part 1:** 406–407
Lost Grizzlies, The: A Search for Survivors in the Wilderness of Colorado (Bass), **Supp. XVI:** 25, 26
Lost Highway (film), **Supp. X:** 314
Lost Illusions (Balzac), **I:** 500
"Lost in Nostalgia: The Autobiographies of Eva Hoffman and Richard Rodriguez" (Fachinger), **Supp. XVI:** 153
Lost in the Bonewheel Factory (Komunyakaa), **Supp. XIII: 114–115,** 116
Lost in the City (E. P. Jones), **Supp. XXII:** 140, 142, **143–146,** 148, 149
Lost in the Cosmos: The Last Self-Help Book (Percy), **Supp. III Part 1:** 397
Lost in the Funhouse (Barth), **I:** 122, 135, 139; **Supp. X:** 307
"Lost in the Whichy Thicket" (Wolfe), **Supp. III Part 2:** 573, 574
Lost in Translation (E. Hoffman), **Supp. XVI:** 147, **148–151,** 153, 154, 159
"Lost in Translation" (Hass), **Supp. VIII:** 28
"Lost in Translation" (Merrill), **Supp. III Part 1:** 324, 329–330
Lost in Yonkers (film), **Supp. IV Part 2:** 588
Lost in Yonkers (Simon), **Supp. IV Part 2:** 576, 577, 584, 587–588, 590–591
"Lost Jerusalem" (Untermeyer), **Supp. XV:** 307
"Lost Keys of Glory, The" (Hurston), **Retro. Supp. III:** 139
Lost Lady, A (Cather), **I:** 323–325, 327; **Retro. Supp. I: 15–16,** 20, 21, 382; **Retro. Supp. III:** 24, 33–34, 36
Lost Light (Connelly), **Supp. XXI:** 72, **75–76**
"Lost Lives" (Sorrentino), **Supp. XXI:** 226
"Lost Lover, A" (Jewett), **II:** 400–401, 402; **Retro. Supp. II:** 137
"Lost Loves" (Kinnell), **Supp. III Part 1:** 237, 245
Lost Man's River (Matthiessen), **Supp. V:** 212, 213, 214, 215
"Lost on September Trail, 1967" (Ríos), **Supp. IV Part 2:** 540
Lost Puritan (Mariani), **Retro. Supp. II:** 189
Lost Roads Project, The: A Walk-In Book of Arkansas (exhibition; Wright and Luster), **Supp. XV:** 337, 348
"Lost Sailor, The" (Freneau), **Supp. II Part 1:** 264
Lost Son, The (Roethke), **III:** 529, 530–532, 533
"Lost Son, The" (Roethke), **III:** 536, 537–539, 542
"Lost Sons" (Salter), **Supp. IX:** 260
Lost Souls (Singer). See Meshugah (Singer)
"Lost"(Thompson), **Supp. XXIII:** 299, 300
"Lost Treaties of the California Indians" (Zitkala-Ša), **Supp. XXV:** 284
Lost Weekend, The (Jackson), **Supp. XIII:** 262
"Lost World, A" (Ashbery), **Supp. III Part 1:** 9
"Lost World, The" (Chabon), **Supp. XI:** 72–73
Lost World, The (Jarrell), **II:** 367, 368, 371, 379–380, 386, 387
"Lost World, The" cycle (Chabon), **Supp. XI: 71–73**
"Lost World of Richard Yates, The: How the Great Writer of the Age of Anxiety Disappeared from Print" (O'Nan), **Supp. XI:** 348
"Lost Young Intellectual, The" (Howe), **Supp. VI:** 113, **115–116**
Lost Zoo, The: (A Rhyme for the Young, But Not Too Young) (Cullen), **Supp. IV Part 1:** 173
Loti, Pierre, **II:** 311, 325; **Supp. IV Part 1:** 81
"Lot of People Bathing in a Stream, A" (Stevens), **IV:** 93
Lotringer, Sylvère, **Supp. XII:** 4
"Lot's Wife" (Nemerov), **III:** 270
"Lottery, The" (Jackson), **Supp. IX:** 113, 114, 118, 120, **122–123**
Lottery, The; or, The Adventures of James Harris (Jackson), **Supp. IX:** 113, 115, 116, 124, 125
Lotze, Hermann, **III:** 600
Loud and Clear (Quindlen), **Supp. XVII:** 167, **170–172**
"Loud Like Love" (video, Ellis), **Supp. XXVII:** 80
Louganis, Greg, **Supp. XX: 264**
"Louie, His Cousin & His Other Cousin" (Cisneros), **Supp. VII:** 60
Louinet, Patrice, **Supp. XXVII:** 128
Louis, Joe, **II:** 589; **Supp. IV Part 1:** 360
Louis, Pierre Charles Alexandre, **Supp. I Part 1:** 302, 303
"Louisa, Please Come Home" (Jackson), **Supp. IX:** 122
Louis Lambert (Balzac), **I:** 499
"Louis Simpson and Walt Whitman: Destroying the Teacher" (Lazer), **Supp. IX:** 265
"Louis Zukofsky: All: The Collected Short Poems, 1923–1958" (Creeley), **Supp. IV Part 1:** 154
"Lounge" (Francis), **Supp. IX:** 83
Lounsberry, Barbara, **Supp. XVII:** 208
Lounsbury, Floyd G., **Supp. XXVI:** 89
Lounsbury, Thomas R., **I:** 335
Louter, Jan, **Supp. XI:** 173
"Love" (Collins), **Supp. XXI:** 61
"Love," (Gibran), **Supp. XX: 119**
Love (Morrison), **Retro. Supp. III:** 185, 196–197
"Love" (Olson), **Supp. II Part 2:** 571
"Love" (Paley), **Supp. VI:** 219, 222, 230
Love, Deborah, **Supp. V:** 208, 210
Love Alone: 18 Elegies for Rog (Monette), **Supp. X:** 146, 154
Love Always (Beattie), **Supp. V:** 29, 30, 35
Love among the Cannibals (Morris), **III:** 228, 230–231
"Love Among the Ruins" (Mosley), **Supp. XIII:** 247
"Love and Art" (Huddle), **Supp. XXVI:** 150
Love and Death (film; Allen), **Supp. XV:** 2, **5–6,** 7, 11
Love and Death in the American Novel

(Fiedler), **Supp. XIII:** 93, 96, **99–101,** 104
Love and Exile (Singer), **Retro. Supp. II: 302–304,** 315
Love and Fame (Berryman), **I:** 170
Love and Friendship (Bloom), **Retro. Supp. II:** 31, 33–34
Love and Glory (Parker), **Supp. XIX:** 189
"Love and How to Cure It" (Wilder), **IV:** 365
Love and Other Games of Chance (Siegel), **Supp. XXII:** 255, 256, **261–265,** 266, 267
Love and Scorn: New and Selected Poems (C. Frost), **Supp. XV:** 95, 96, 100, 103–105, 106
Love and Theft (album, Dylan), **Supp. XVIII:** 28, 31
"Love and the Hate, The" (Jeffers), **Supp. II Part 2:** 434–435
Love and the Incredibly Old Man (Siegel), **Supp. XXII: 267–268**
Love and Will (Dixon), **Supp. XII:** 148, 149
Love and Work (Price), **Supp. VI:** 261
"Love as a Great Power" (Bronk), **Supp. XXI:** 31
"Love Calls Us to the Things of This World" (Wilbur), **Supp. III Part 2:** 544, 552–553
Love Course, The (Gurney), **Supp. V:** 98
Lovecraft, H. P., **Retro. Supp. III:** 235; **Supp. XXII:** 49; **Supp. XXV: 109–126; Supp. XXVII:** 115, 117, 119, 128
Lovecraft and Influence (R. H. Waugh, ed.), **Supp. XXV:** 123
Loved One, The (film), **Supp. XI: 305–306,** 307
Loved One, The (Waugh), **Supp. XI:** 305
Love Expert, The (film; Kirkland), **Supp. XVI:** 186
Love Feast (Buechner), **Supp. XII:** 52
Love for Love (Congreve), **Supp. XVIII:** 12
"Love Fossil" (Olds), **Supp. X:** 203
"Love"(Hadas), **Supp. XXIII:** 117
Love in a Dead Language (Siegel), **Supp. XXII:** 255, **258–261,** 265–266, 267
Love in Buffalo (Gurney), **Supp. V:** 96
Love in Chartres (Asch), **Supp. XXVI:** 18, 19, 20–21, 25
"Love—In Other Words" (Lee), **Supp. VIII:** 113
"Love in the Air" (Jin), **Supp. XVIII:** 93–94
"Love in the Morning" (Dubus), **Supp. VII:** 91
Love in the Ruins: The Adventures of a Bad Catholic at a Time near the End of the World (Percy), **Supp. III Part 1:** 385, 387, 393–394, 397–398
Love in the Western World (de Rougemont), **Retro. Supp. I:** 328
"Love Is a Deep and a Dark and a Lonely" (Sandburg), **III:** 595
"Love Is a Fire" (Cohen), **Supp. XXVII:** 60
"Love Itself" (Cohen), **Supp. XXVII:** 61
Lovejoy, Elijah P., **Supp. I Part 2:** 588; **Supp. XXIV:** 78
Lovejoy, Owen R., **Supp. I Part 1:** 8
Lovejoy, Thomas, **Supp. X:** 108
"Lovejoy Street" (Stallings), **Supp. XXV:** 224
Lovelace, Richard, **II:** 590
"Love Letter (Schnackenberg), **Supp. XV:** 258–259
Love Letters (film), **Supp. IV Part 2:** 524
Love Letters (Gurney), **Supp. V:** 105, 108–109
Love Letters, The (Massie), **Supp. IV Part 2:** 524
Love Letters and Two Other Plays: The Golden Age and What I Did Last Summer (Gurney), **Supp. V:** 100
"Love Lies Sleeping" (Bishop), **Retro. Supp. II:** 42
Love Life (Mason), **Supp. VIII:** 145–146
"Love Life" (Mason), **Supp. VIII: 145–146**
Lovell, Julia, **Supp. XVIII:** 101
Lovely Bones, The (Sebold), **Supp. XXII:** 55
Lovely Lady, The (Lawrence), **Retro. Supp. I:** 203
"Lovely Lady, The" (Lawrence), **Supp. I Part 1:** 329
Love Me (Keillor), **Supp. XVI:** 178
Love Medicine (Erdrich), **Supp. IV Part 1:** 259, 260, 261, 263, 265, 266, 267–268, 270, 271, 274–275; **Supp. X:** 290
Love Medicine (expanded version) (Erdrich), **Supp. IV Part 1:** 263, 273, 274, 275
"Love Minus Zero/No Limit" (song, Dylan), **Supp. XVIII:** 31
"Love Nest, The" (Lardner), **II:** 427, 429
Love Nest, The, and Other Stories (Lardner), **II:** 430–431, 436
Lovenheim, Barbara, **Supp. X:** 169
Love of a Good Woman, The (Munro), **Supp. XXVII:** 190, 192
"Love of a Good Woman, The" (Munro), **Supp. XXVII:** 192
"Love of Annunziata, The" (di Donato), **Supp. XX: 40**
"Love of Elsie Barton: A Chronicle, The" (Warren), **IV:** 253
Love of Landry, The (Dunbar), **Supp. II Part 1:** 212
"Love of Morning, The" (Levertov), **Supp. III Part 1:** 284
Love of the Last Tycoon, The: A Western. See Last Tycoon, The
"Love on the Bon Dieu" (Chopin), **Supp. I Part 1:** 213
Love on the Hoof (O'Hara and Lima), **Supp. XXIII:** 217
Love Poems (Sexton), **Supp. II Part 2:** 687–689
Love Poems (Tentative Title) (O'Hara), **Supp. XXIII:** 219
Love Poems of May Swenson, The (Swenson), **Supp. IV Part 2:** 652, 653
"Love Poet" (Agee), **I:** 28
"Lover" (Hoffman), **Supp. XVIII:** 87
"Love Ritual" (Mora), **Supp. XIII:** 215
Lover of Horses, The (Gallagher), **Supp. XXIV:** 166, 172, 173–174, 176
"Lover of Horses, The" (Gallagher), **Supp. XXIV:** 173–174, 176
Loveroot (Jong), **Supp. V:** 115, 130
"Lovers, The" (Berryman), **I:** 174
"Lovers, The" (Buck), **Supp. II Part 1:** 128
"Lover's Garden, A" (Ginsberg), **Supp. II Part 1:** 311
"Lovers of the Poor, The" (Brooks), **Supp. III Part 1:** 81, 85
Lovers Should Marry (Martin), **Supp. IV Part 1:** 351
"Lover's Song" (Yeats), **Supp. I Part 1:** 80
"Love Rushes By" (Salinas), **Supp. XIII:** 326–327
"Love's Ghost" (Nelson), **Supp. XVIII:** 176
Lovesick (Stern), **Supp. IX: 295–296**
Love's Labour's Lost (Shakespeare), **III:** 263
Love's Old Sweet Song (Saroyan), **Supp. IV Part 1:** 83
"Love Song During Riot with Many Voices" (Hull), **Supp. XXI:** 136
"Love Song of J. Alfred Prufrock, The" (T. S. Eliot), **I:** 52, 66, 569–570; **III:** 460; **Retro. Supp. I:** 55, 56, 57, 60; **Retro. Supp. III:** 61–62, 66; **Supp.**

II Part 1: 5; **Supp. XIII:** 346; **Supp. XVI:** 150; **Supp. XXV:** 22; **Supp. XXVI:** 237
"Love Song of St. Sebastian" (Eliot), **Retro. Supp. I:** 57
"Love Songs" (Loy), **Supp. XXII:** 161
Love Songs (Teasdale), **Supp. XXVII:** 283, 289, 290–291
"Love Songs to Joannes" (Loy), **Supp. XXII:** 161, 163
Love's Pilgrimage (Sinclair), **Supp. V:** 286
"Love's Relative" (Stone), **Supp. XXVII:** 251
"Love the Wild Swan" (Jeffers), **Supp. VIII:** 33
Love to Mamá: A Tribute to Mothers (Mora, ed.), **Supp. XIII:** 221
Lovett, Robert Morss, **II:** 43
Lovett-Graff, Bennett, **Supp. XXV:** 123
"Love-Unknown" (Herbert), **Supp. I Part 1:** 80
Love! Valor! Compassion! (film), **Supp. XIII:** 206
Love! Valour! Compassion! (McNally), **Supp. XIII:** 199, **203–204,** 208, 209
"Love versus Law" (Stowe), **Supp. I Part 2:** 585–586
"Love Wall" (Peacock), **Supp. XIX:** 200
Love with a Few Hairs (Mrabet), **Supp. IV Part 1:** 92
Loving a Woman in Two Worlds (R. Bly), **Supp. IV Part 1:** 66, 67, 68–69, 71, 72
Loving in the War Years: Lo que nunca pasó por sus labios (Moraga), **Supp. XXIII:** 194, 195
"Loving on Borrowed Time" (J. W. Miller), **Supp. XX: 164**
"Loving Shepherdess, The" (Jeffers), **Supp. II Part 2:** 432
"Loving the Killer" (Sexton), **Supp. II Part 2:** 688
"Loving Wife" (C. Miller), **Supp. XXII:** 196–197, 199
Lovin' Molly (film), **Supp. V:** 223, 226
Low Country (Siddons), **Supp. XXII:** 239
Lowe, John, **Retro. Supp. III:** 133, 134, 138, 140; **Supp. XIII:** 238
Lowe, Pardee, **Supp. X:** 291
Lowell, Abbott Lawrence, **I:** 487; **II:** 513; **Supp. I Part 2:** 483
Lowell, Amy, **I:** 231, 384, 405, 475, 487; **II:** 174, **511–533,** 534; **III:** 465, 581, 586; **Retro. Supp. I:** 131, 133, 288; **Retro. Supp. II:** 46, 175; **Retro. Supp. III:** 98, 101; **Supp. I Part 1:** 257–259, 261–263, 265, 266; **Supp. I Part 2:** 465, 466, 707, 714, 729; **Supp. XIV:** 128; **Supp. XV:** 43, 293, 295, 297, 298, 299, 300, 301, 303, 306; **Supp. XX: 69; Supp. XXII:** 161; **Supp. XXVII:** 288, 295
Lowell, Blanche, **Supp. I Part 2:** 409
Lowell, Harriet, **II:** 553, 554
Lowell, James Russell, **I:** 216, 458; **II:** 273, 274, 289, 302, 320, 402, 529, 530, 532, 534, 551; **III:** 409; **IV:** 129, 171, 175, 180, 182–183, 186; **Retro. Supp. I:** 228; **Retro. Supp. II:** 155, 175, 326; **Retro. Supp. III:** 106, 223, 232, 233, 236; **Supp. I Part 1:** 168, 299, 300, 303, 306, 311, 312, 317, 318, 362; **Supp. I Part 2: 404–426; Supp. II Part 1:** 197, 291, 352; **Supp. XV:** 278, 279; **Supp. XVI:** 84; **Supp. XVIII:** 2–3, 4, 8, 12
Lowell, Mrs. James Russell (Maria White), **Supp. I Part 2:** 405, 406, 414, 424
Lowell, Percival, **II:** 513, 525, 534
Lowell, Robert, **I:** 172, 381, 382, 400, 442, 521, 544–545, 550; **II:** 371, 376, 377, 384, 386–387, 532, **534–557; III:** 39, 44, 142, 508, 527, 528–529, 606; **IV:** 120, 138, 402, 430; **Retro. Supp. I:** 67, 140, 411; **Retro. Supp. II:** 27, 40, 44, 46, 48, 50, **175–193,** 221, 228–229, 235, 245; **Retro. Supp. III:** 41, 54, 243, 245; **Supp. I Part 1:** 89; **Supp. I Part 2:** 538, 543, 554; **Supp. III Part 1:** 6, 64, 84, 138, 147, 193, 194, 197–202, 205–208; **Supp. III Part 2:** 541, 543, 555, 561, 599; **Supp. IV Part 2:** 439, 620, 637; **Supp. IX:** 325; **Supp. V:** 81, 179, 180, 315–316, 337, 344; **Supp. VIII:** 27, 100, 271; **Supp. X:** 53, 58; **Supp. XI:** 146, 240, 244, 250, 317; **Supp. XII:** 253–254, 255; **Supp. XIII:** 76; **Supp. XIV:** 15, 126, 269; **Supp. XIX:** 197; **Supp. XV:** 20, 22, 93, 184, 249, 251, 253, 340; **Supp. XVII:** 239; **Supp. XX: 199, 203; Supp. XXI:** 131; **Supp. XXIII:** 211, 220; **Supp. XXIV:** 153; **Supp. XXVI:** 67, 68
Lowell, Rose, **Supp. I Part 2:** 409
"Lowell in the Classrom" (Vendler), **Retro. Supp. II:** 191
Lowenthal, Michael, **Supp. XII:** 82
Lower Depths, The (Gorki), **III:** 402
"Lower the Standard" (Shapiro), **Supp. II Part 2:** 715
Lowes, John Livingston, **II:** 512, 516, 532; **IV:** 453, 455
Lowin, Joseph, **Supp. V:** 273
"Low Lands" (Davison), **Supp. XXVI:** 76
"Low-Lands" (Pynchon), **Supp. II Part 2:** 620, 624
Lowle, Percival, **Supp. I Part 2:** 404
Lownsbrough, John, **Supp. IV Part 1:** 209, 211
Lowry, Beverly, **Supp. XXI:** 48
Lowry, Malcolm, **Supp. XVII:** 135, 136; **Supp. XXVI:** 28
Lowth, Richard, **II:** 8
Loy, Mina, **III:** 194; **Supp. XXII: 155–170**
Loy, Myrna, **Supp. IV Part 1:** 355
"Loyal Woman's No, A" (Larcom), **Supp. XIII:** 142, 143–144
"Luani of the Jungle" (Hughes), **Supp. I Part 1:** 328
Lubbock, Percy, **I:** 504; **II:** 337; **IV:** 308, 314, 319, 322; **Retro. Supp. I:** 366, 367, 373; **Supp. VIII:** 165; **Supp. XX: 231**
Lubin, Isidor, **Supp. I Part 2:** 632
Lubow, Arthur, **Supp. VIII:** 310
Lucas, Craig, **Supp. XXIV:** 263
Lucas, Victoria (pseudonym). See Plath, Sylvia
Luce, Dianne C., **Supp. VIII:** 189
Lucid, Robert F., **Retro. Supp. II:** 195, 204
"Lucid Eye in Silver Town, The" (Updike), **IV:** 218
"Lucid Walking" (A. Finch), **Supp. XVII:** 72
"Lucinda Matlock" (Masters), **Supp. I Part 2:** 461, 465
"Luck" (Dunn), **Supp. XI:** 149
Luck, Jessica Lewis, **Supp. XXVII:** 173
Luck of Barry Lyndon, The (Thackeray), **II:** 290
"Luck of Roaring Camp, The" (Harte), **Supp. II Part 1:** 335, 344, 345–347
"Luck of the Bogans, The" (Jewett), **Retro. Supp. II:** 142
Lucky Life (Stern), **Supp. IX: 290–291**
"Lucky Lucy's Daily Dream Book" (Di Piero), **Supp. XIX:** 38–39
"Lucretia Smith's Soldier" (Twain), **Retro. Supp. III:** 260
Lucretius, **I:** 59; **II:** 162, 163; **III:** 600, 610–611, 612; **Supp. I Part 1:** 363
Lucy (Kincaid), **Supp. VII:** 180, 185, 186, 187–188, 194
Lucy, Saint, **II:** 211
Lucy Crown (Shaw), **Supp. XIX:** 251

Lucy Gayheart (Cather), **I:** 331; **Retro. Supp. I:** 19
"Lucy Tavish's Journey" (E. Stoddard), **Supp. XV:** 286
Lucy Temple (Rowson). See Charlotte's Daughter; or, The Three Orphans
Ludlow, Andrea, **Supp. XVIII:** 90
Ludvigson, Susan, **Supp. IV Part 2:** 442, 446, 447, 448, 451
Lueders, Edward, **Supp. XVI:** 265
"Luggage" (Bidart), **Supp. XV:** 35
Luhan, Mabel Dodge, **Retro. Supp. I:** 7; **Supp. XV:** 46, 50; **Supp. XXIV:** 30. See also Dodge, Mabel
Lu Ji, **Supp. VIII:** 303
Lukas, Michael, **Supp. XXVI:** 56
Luke (biblical book), **III:** 606
"Luke Havergal" (E. A. Robinson), **Supp. XVII:** 69
"Luke Havergal" (Robinson), **III:** 524
Lukeman, Gary, **Supp. XV:** 221
Luks, George, **IV:** 411; **Retro. Supp. II:** 103
"Lullaby" (Auden), **Supp. II Part 1:** 9
"Lullaby" (Bishop), **Supp. I Part 1:** 85
"Lullaby" (Everwine), **Supp. XV:** 89
"Lullaby" (Silko), **Supp. IV Part 2:** 560, 568–569
"Lullaby for Amy" (Jarman), **Supp. XVII:** 113, 121
"Lullaby of Cape Cod" (Brodsky), **Supp. VIII:** 27–28
Lullaby Raft (Nye), **Supp. XIII:** 278
Lullaby Raft (Nye, album), **Supp. XIII:** 274
Lullaby: The Comforting of Cock Robin (Snodgrass), **Supp. VI:** 324
"Lulls" (Walker), **Supp. III Part 2:** 525
"Lulu" (Wedekind), **Supp. XII:** 14
Lulu on the Bridge (film), **Supp. XII:** 21
Lulu's Library (Alcott), **Supp. I Part 1:** 43
"Lumber" (Baker), **Supp. XIII:** 55, 56
"Lumens, The" (Olds), **Supp. X:** 209
Lume Spento, A (Pound), **III:** 470
Lumet, Sidney, **Supp. IV Part 1:** 236; **Supp. IX:** 253
Luminous Debris: Reflecting on Vestige in Provence and Languedoc (Sobin), **Supp. XVI: 291–293,** 293–294
Luminous Face, The (Wells), **Supp. XXVI:** 280
"Lumumba's Grave" (Hughes), **Supp. I Part 1:** 344
"Luna, Luna" (Mora), **Supp. XIII:** 217
Lunar Baedecker (Loy), **Supp. XXII:** 165,**Supp. XXII:** 167, 166, 168
Lunar Baedecker and Time-Tables (Loy), **Supp. XXII:** 168
Lunar Follies (Sorrentino), **Supp. XXI:** 226, 237, 238–239
Lunar Park (Ellis), **Supp. XXVII:** 68, 71, 76–77
"Lunatic" (Hecht), **Supp. XXVII:** 95
Lunch Poems (O'Hara), **Supp. XXIII:** 219–220, 220
Lunsford, Bascom Lamar, **Supp. XX: 163**
Lupercal (Hughes), **Retro. Supp. II:** 245; **Supp. I Part 2:** 540
Lupton, Mary Jane, **Supp. IV Part 1:** 7
Lure of the Labrador Wild, The (Wallace), **Supp. XXII:** 218
Luria, Isaac, **IV:** 7
Lurie, Alison, **Supp. X:** 166; **Supp. XVI:** 103, 111–112
Lusitania Songspiel, Das (Durang), **Supp. XXIV:** 113, 116
Lust and Other Stories (Minot), **Supp. VI:** 205
Luster, Deborah, **Supp. XV:** 337,**Supp. XV:** 353, 348, 349, 350
Lustgarten, Edith, **III:** 107
Lustra (Pound), **Retro. Supp. I:** 289, 290
"Luther" (Huddle), **Supp. XXVI:** 152
Luther, Martin, **II:** 11–12, 506; **III:** 306, 607; **IV:** 490
"Luther on Sweet Auburn" (Bambara), **Supp. XI:** 16–17
Lux, Thomas, **Supp. XI:** 270; **Supp. XIX:** 276
Luxury Girl, The (McCoy), **Supp. XIII:** 163
Lyall, Sarah, **Supp. XIII:** 247
Lycidas (Milton), **II:** 540; **IV:** 347; **Retro. Supp. I:** 60; **Retro. Supp. II:** 186; **Supp. I Part 1:** 370; **Supp. IX:** 41
Lycographia (Paullini), **Supp. XVII:** 55
"Lydia and Marian" (Rowson), **Supp. XV:** 234
Lydon, Meghan, **Supp. XXVI:** 14–15
Lydon, Susan, **Supp. XII:** 170
Lyell, Charles, **Supp. IX:** 180
Lyell, Frank H., **Supp. VIII:** 125
Lyford, Harry, **Supp. I Part 2:** 679
"Lying" (Wilbur), **Supp. III Part 2:** 547, 562
"Lying and Looking" (Swenson), **Supp. IV Part 2:** 652
"Lying in a Hammock at William Duffy's Farm in Pine Island, Minnesota" (Wright), **Supp. III Part 2:** 589, 599, 600
"Lying in the Pollen and Water" (C. Frost), **Supp. XV:** 96
Lying Ladies, The (Ryan as Finnegan), **Supp. XVIII: 233–235,** 237
"Lying Next to the Knife" (McElwee), **Supp. XXIV:** 167, 173
Lyles, Lois F., **Supp. XI:** 7, 8
Lyly, John, **III:** 536; **Supp. I Part 1:** 369
Lynch, Anne, **Supp. XV:** 273
Lynch, Doris, **Supp. XVI:** 294
Lynchburg (Gander), **Supp. XV:** 340
"Lynched Man, The" (Karr), **Supp. XI:** 241
Lynchers, The (Wideman), **Supp. X:** 320
"Lynching, The" (McKay), **Supp. I Part 1:** 63
"Lynching of Jube Benson, The" (Dunbar), **Supp. II Part 1:** 214
"Lynching Song" (Hughes), **Supp. I Part 1:** 331
Lynd, Staughton, **Supp. VIII:** 240
Lynda Hull: Collected Poems (Hull), **Supp. XXI:** 129
Lynes, Katherine R., **Supp. XXVI:** 166, 170, 171, 175
Lynn, Kenneth S., **Retro. Supp. III:** 259; **Supp. XIII:** 96–97; **Supp. XIV:** 103
Lynn, Vera, **Supp. XI:** 304
Lyon, George Ella, **Supp. XX: 161–162**
Lyon, Kate, **I:** 409; **II:** 138, 143, 144
Lyon, Thomas, **Supp. IX:** 175
"Lyonnesse" (Plath), **Supp. I Part 2:** 541
Lyons, Bonnie, **Supp. V:** 58; **Supp. VIII:** 138
Lyons, Donald, **Supp. XXIV:** 274
Lyons, Nathan, **Supp. XXV:** 251
Lyons, The (Silver), **Supp. XXIV:** 263, **276**
Lyotard, Jean-François, **Supp. IV Part 1:** 54
Lyrical Ballads (Wordsworth), **III:** 583; **IV:** 120; **Supp. IX:** 274; **Supp. XI:** 243; **Supp. XIX:** 1; **Supp. XV:** 21
Lyrics of Love and Laughter (Dunbar), **Supp. II Part 1:** 207
Lyrics of Lowly Life (Dunbar), **Supp. II Part 1:** 197, 199, 200, 207
Lyrics of the Hearthside (Dunbar), **Supp. II Part 1:** 206
Lytal, Tammy, **Supp. XI:** 102
Lytle, Andrew, **IV:** 125; **Retro. Supp. II:** 220, 221, 235; **Supp. II Part 1:**

139; **Supp. X:** 1, 25; **Supp. XI:** 101
Lyttelton, Alfred, **Supp. XX: 230**
Lytton of Knebworth. See Bulwer-Lytton, Edward George
Mabbott, Thomas, **Retro. Supp. III:** 231, 232, 237
Mabie, Hamilton W., **Supp. XVIII:** 257
MCabe, Susan, **Supp. XXII:** 234
MacAdams, William, **Supp. XXVII:** 84, 91, 93, 96
McAlexander, Hubert H., **Supp. V:** 314, 319, 320, 323
McAlmon, Robert, **IV:** 404; **Retro. Supp. I:** 418, 419, 420; **Retro. Supp. II:** 328; **Supp. I Part 1:** 259; **Supp. III Part 2:** 614; **Supp. XXII:** 166, 215; **Supp. XXIV:** 62, 63
McAlmon, Mrs. Robert (Winifred Ellerman), **III:** 194. See also Ellerman, Winifred
McAlpine, Erica, **Supp. XXV:** 222, 233, 234
McAninch, Jerry, **Supp. XI:** 297, 298
MacArthur, Charles, **Supp. XXVII:** 83, 89
Macaulay, Catherine, **Supp. I Part 2:** 522
Macaulay, Rose, **Supp. XII:** 88; **Supp. XIV:** 348
Macaulay, Thomas, **II:** 15–16; **III:** 113, 591–592
Macauley, Robie, **Retro. Supp. II:** 228; **Supp. X:** 56
Macbeth (Shakespeare), **I:** 271; **IV:** 227; **Retro. Supp. I:** 131; **Supp. I Part 1:** 67; **Supp. I Part 2:** 457; **Supp. IV Part 1:** 87; **Supp. XIV:** 8; **Supp. XXVII:** 225
Macbeth (silent film), **Supp. XVI:** 184
MacBeth, George, **Retro. Supp. II:** 250
McBride, James, **Supp. XXVI: 191–205**
MacBride, Roger, **Supp. XXII:** 297, 301
McCabe, Tracy, **Supp. XXVI:** 166
McCafferty, Larry, **Supp. XVII:** 227
McCaffery, Larry, **Supp. IV Part 1:** 217, 227, 234; **Supp. V:** 53, 238; **Supp. VIII:** 13, 14; **Supp. X:** 260, 268, 301, 303, 307; **Supp. XVI:** 117; **Supp. XXII:** 177
McCann, Janet, **Supp. XXIII:** 51, 53, 54, 64
McCann, Jannet, **Supp. XXI:** 92
McCarriston, Linda, **Supp. X:** 204; **Supp. XIV: 259–275**
McCarthy, Charles Joseph, Jr. See McCarthy, Cormac
McCarthy, Cormac, **Supp. VIII: 175–192; Supp. XII:** 310; **Supp. XVII:** 185; **Supp. XXI:** 38, 40; **Supp. XXII:** 49; **Supp. XXIII:** 42, 44
McCarthy, Eugene, **Retro. Supp. II:** 182
McCarthy, Joseph, **I:** 31, 492; **II:** 562, 568; **Supp. I Part 1:** 294, 295; **Supp. I Part 2:** 444, 611, 612, 620; **Supp. XV:** 198, 311–312; **Supp. XXIII:** 7
McCarthy, Mary, **II: 558–584; Supp. I Part 1:** 84; **Supp. IV Part 1:** 209, 297, 310; **Supp. VIII:** 96, 99, 100; **Supp. X:** 177; **Supp. XI:** 246; **Supp. XIV:** 3; **Supp. XV:** 142; **Supp. XVI:** 64, 70; **Supp. XVII:** 43; **Supp. XXVII:** 89
McCay, Maura, **Supp. XII:** 271, 276
McClanahan, Ed, **Supp. X:** 24
McClanahan, Thomas, **Supp. XII:** 125–126
McClatchy, J. D., **Supp. XII: 253–270; Supp. XV:** 185, 257, 258
McClaurin, Irma, **Supp. XXIII:** 84, 86, 93, 94
McClellan, John L., **I:** 493
McClung, Isabelle, **Retro. Supp. I:** 5; **Retro. Supp. III:** 20, 22, 34, 37
McClure, Charlotte, **Supp. XXIV:** 29
McClure, H. H., **Retro. Supp. III:** 21
McClure, John, **Retro. Supp. I:** 80
McClure, Michael, **Supp. II Part 1:** 32; **Supp. VIII:** 289; **Supp. XVI:** 283
McClure, S. S., **I:** 313; **II:** 465; **III:** 327; **Retro. Supp. I:** 5, 6, 9; **Retro. Supp. III:** 21; **Supp. XV:** 40
McCluskey, John, Jr., **Supp. XIX:** 65, 68, 71, 72, 78
McCombs, Judith, **Supp. XIII:** 33
McConagha, Alan, **Supp. XVI:** 166
McConnell, Frank, **Supp. X:** 260, 274
McCorkle, Jill, **Supp. X:** 6; **Supp. XVIII:** 195; **Supp. XXV:** 129, 130
McCourt, Frank, **Supp. XII: 271–287**
McCoy, Horace, **Supp. XIII: 159–177; Supp. XXV:** 26
McCracken, Elizabeth, **Supp. X:** 86; **Supp. XII:** 310, 315–316, 321
McCrae, Fiona, **Supp. XVIII:** 60, 62
McCullers, Carson, **I:** 113, 190, 211; **II: 585–608; IV:** 282, 384, 385, 386; **Retro. Supp. II:** 324; **Supp. II Part 1:** 17; **Supp. IV Part 1:** 31, 84; **Supp. IV Part 2:** 502; **Supp. VIII:** 124; **Supp. XII:** 309; **Supp. XIV:** 120; **Supp. XV:** 338
McCullers, Reeves, **III:** 585, 586, 587
McCulloch, Jeanne, **Supp. XXVII:** 180
McDavid, Raven I., **III:** 120; **Supp. XIV:** 14
McDermott, Alice, **Supp. XII:** 311; **Supp. XVIII: 155–169**
McDermott, John J., **II:** 364
MacDiarmid, Hugh, **Supp. X:** 112
Macdonald, C. G., **Supp. XVII:** 73–74
MacDonald, Dwight, **Supp. XXV:** 268
Macdonald, Dwight, **I:** 233, 372, 379; **III:** 39; **Supp. V:** 265; **Supp. XIV:** 340; **Supp. XV:** 140
McDonald, E. J., **Supp. I Part 2:** 670
Macdonald, George, **Supp. XIII:** 75
MacDonald, Jeanette, **II:** 589
Macdonald, Ross, **Supp. IV Part 1:** 116, 136; **Supp. IV Part 2: 459–477; Supp. XIII:** 233; **Supp. XVIII:** 137,136; **Supp. XXI:** 67
MacDonald, Ruth K., **Supp. XVI:** 102
McDonnell, Thomas P., **Supp. XX: 45**
MacDougall, Ruth Doan, **Supp. XV:** 58; **Supp. XVI:** 174
MacDowell, Edward, **I:** 228; **III:** 504, 508, 524
McDowell, Frederick P. W., **II:** 194
McDowell, Mary, **Supp. I Part 1:** 5
McDowell, Robert, **Supp. IX:** 266, 270, 276, 279
MacDowell, Robert, **Supp. XI:** 249
McDowell, Robert, **Supp. XVII:** 109, 110, 111
McDowell. Deborah, **Supp. XVIII:** 125, 129
McElderry, Margaret K., **Supp. XV:** 162
McElligot's Pool (Geisel), **Supp. XVI:** 104
McElrath, Joseph, **Supp. XIV:** 62
McElroy, Joseph, **Supp. IV Part 1:** 279, 285
McElwee, Caroline, **Supp. XXIV:** 167, 173
McEuen, Kathryn, **II:** 20
McEwen, Arthur, **I:** 206
McFarland, Ron, **Supp. IX:** 323, 327, 328, 333
McGann, Jerome, **Retro. Supp. I:** 47
McGill, Meredith, **Supp. XVIII:** 17
McGillis, Ian, **Supp. XVIII:** 150
MacGillivray, William, **Supp. XVI:** 8
McGinity, Keren, **Supp. XX: 9**
McGovern, Edythe M., **Supp. IV Part 2:** 573, 582, 585
McGovern, George, **III:** 46
MacGowan, Christopher, **Retro. Supp. I:** 430
MacGowan, Kenneth, **III:** 387, 391

McGrath, Abigail, **Supp. XXVI:** 164, 165, 172
McGrath, Douglas, **Supp. XV:** 12
McGrath, Joseph, **Supp. XI:** 307, 309
McGrath, Patrick, **Supp. IX:** 113; **Supp. XXII:** 58
McGrath, Thomas, **Supp. X: 111–130**
"McGrath on McGrath" (McGrath), **Supp. X:** 119, 120
McGuane, Thomas, **Supp. V:** 53, 220; **Supp. VIII:** 39, 40, 42, 43
MacGuffin, The (Elkin), **Supp. VI: 55–56**
McGuiness, Daniel, **Supp. XV:** 261
McGuinniss, Joe, **Supp. XXVII:** 67
McGuirk, Kevin, **Retro. Supp. III:** 248
Machado y Ruiz, Antonio, **Supp. XIII:** 315, 323
Machan, Tibor, **Supp. IV Part 2:** 528
McHaney, Pearl, **Supp. XXI:** 244, 255, 256, 257
McHaney, Thomas, **Supp. XVIII:** 199,203
Machen, Arthur, **IV:** 286
McHenry, Tim, **Supp. XXV:** 161
Machiavelli, Niccolò, **I:** 485; **Supp. XIX:** 34
"Machine-Gun, The" (Jarrell), **II:** 371
"Machines Mourn the Passing of People, The" (Stallings), **Supp. XXV:** 228
"Machine Song" (Anderson), **I:** 114
McHugh, Heather, **Supp. XIX:** 84; **Supp. XXIV:** 154
McHugh, Vincent, **Supp. XV:** 147
McInerney, Jay, **Supp. X:** 7, 166; **Supp. XI:** 65; **Supp. XII:** 81; **Supp. XVIII:** 148; **Supp. XXVII:** 68, 269
"Mac in Love" (Dixon), **Supp. XII: 142**
McIntire, Holly, **Supp. V:** 338
McIntosh, Maria, **Retro. Supp. I:** 246
Macintyre, Ben, **Supp. XXVII:** 270
Mack, Maynard, **Supp. XIV:** 12
Mackail, John William, **Supp. I Part 1:** 268; **Supp. I Part 2:** 461
McKay, Claude, **Supp. I Part 1:** 63; **Supp. III Part 1:** 75, 76; **Supp. IV Part 1:** 3, 79, 164; **Supp. IX:** 306; **Supp. X: 131–144; Supp. XI:** 91; **Supp. XIX:** 73; **Supp. XVII:** 74; **Supp. XVIII:** 122, 127, 280, 282; **Supp. XX: 69; Supp. XXII:** 275
McKay, Donald, **Supp. I Part 2:** 482
McKay, Nellie, **Retro. Supp. III:** 189
McKay, Nellie Y., **Supp. XX: 105**
McKee, Elizabeth, **Retro. Supp. II:** 221, 222
McKee, Ellen, **Retro. Supp. II:** 67
McKeen, William, **Supp. XXIV:** 279, 280, 281, 282, 288
McKeithan, Daniel Morley, **Retro. Supp. III:** 261
McKenney, Eileen, **IV:** 288; **Retro. Supp. II:** 321, 330
McKenney, Ruth, **IV:** 288; **Retro. Supp. II:** 321; **Supp. XVIII:** 238
MacKenzie, Agnes, **I:** 199
Mackenzie, Captain Alexander, **III:** 94
McKenzie, Cameron, **Retro. Supp. III:** 22
Mackenzie, Compton, **II:** 82; **Retro. Supp. I:** 100, 102
McKenzie, Geraldine, **Supp. XII:** 107
MacKenzie, Margaret, **I:** 199
Mackey, Louis, **Supp. XXI:** 236, 237
Mackey, Nathaniel, **Supp. XXVII: 151–162,** 163, 168
McKibben, Bill, **Supp. XVIII:** 192
McKinley, William, **I:** 474; **III:** 506; **Supp. I Part 2:** 395–396, 707
MacKinnon, Catharine, **Supp. XII:** 6
McKnight, Reginald, **Supp. XX: 147–159**
MacLachlan, Suzanne L., **Supp. XII:** 300,**Supp. XII:** 299
MacLauchlin, Cory, **Supp. XXVI:** 240, 241, 242, 243, 244, 246, 252
McLaverty, Michael, **Supp. X:** 67
McLay, Catherine, **Supp. XIII:** 21
Maclean, Alasdair, **Supp. V:** 244
McLean, Carolyn (pseudonym). See Bly, Carol
Maclean, Norman, **Supp. XIV: 221–237; Supp. XVI:** 98; **Supp. XXVI:** 184
MacLeish, Archibald, **I:** 283, 293, 429; **II:** 165, 228; **III: 1–25,** 427; **Supp. I Part 1:** 261; **Supp. I Part 2:** 654; **Supp. IV Part 1:** 359; **Supp. IV Part 2:** 586; **Supp. X:** 120; **Supp. XIV:** 11
MacLeish, Mrs. Archibald (Ada Hitchcock), **III:** 1
MacLeish, Kenneth, **III:** 1
McLellan, Dennis, **Supp. XXVII:** 5
McLellan, Joseph, **Supp. XXIV:** 226
McLennan, Gordon Lawson, **Supp. IX:** 89
McLeod, A. W., **Supp. I Part 1:** 257
MacLeod, Charlotte, **Supp. XXV:** 192
McLuhan, Marshall, **Supp. IV Part 2:** 474
McLure, Michael, **Supp. XIV:** 150
Macmahon, Arthur, **I:** 226
McMahon, Helen, **Supp. IV Part 2:** 579
McMichael, Barbara Lloyd, **Supp. XXII:** 206, 207, 215, 216
McMichael, George, **Supp. VIII:** 124
McMichael, Morton, **Supp. I Part 2:** 707
McMichaels, James, **Supp. XIII:** 114
McMillan, James B., **Supp. VIII:** 124
McMillan, Terry, **Supp. XIII: 179–193**
McMullan, Jim, **Supp. XIV:** 124
McMurtry, Josephine, **Supp. V:** 220
McMurtry, Larry, **Supp. V: 219–235; Supp. X:** 24; **Supp. XI:** 172
McNally, Terrence, **Supp. XIII: 195–211**
McNally, T. M., **Supp. XX: 92**
McNamee, Thomas, **Supp. XXII:** 218
McNamer, Deirdre, **Supp. XI:** 190
Macnaughton, William, **Retro. Supp. III:** 258
McNeese, Gretchen, **Supp. V:** 123
MacNeice, Louis, **II:** 586; **III:** 527; **Supp. II Part 1:** 17, 24; **Supp. IV Part 2:** 440; **Supp. X:** 116; **Supp. XIII:** 347
McNeil, Claudia, **Supp. IV Part 1:** 360, 362
M-a-c-n-o-l-i-a (Jordan), **Supp. XVIII:** 172
McPhee, John, **Supp. III Part 1: 289–316; Supp. X:** 29, 30; **Supp. XVIII:** 106–107, 114
MacPherson, Aimee Semple, **Supp. V:** 278
Macpherson, Anne, **Supp. XXIII:** 84
McPherson, Dolly, **Supp. IV Part 1:** 2, 3, 4, 6, 8, 11, 12
McPherson, James Alan, **Supp. XXII:** 141
McPherson, James Allen, **Retro. Supp. II:** 126
Macpherson, Jay, **Supp. XIII:** 19
MacPherson, Jennifer, **Supp. XXIII:** 248
MacPherson, Kenneth, **Supp. I Part 1:** 259
McPherson, Sandra, **Supp. XXIII:** 57
McPhillips, Robert, **Supp. XV:** 119, 250, 251, 252, 264, 266; **Supp. XXIII:** 111, 112, 114, 127
McQuade, Molly, **Supp. IX:** 151, 163; **Supp. VIII:** 277, 281; **Supp. XX: 90**
McQueen, Steve, **Supp. XI:** 306
Macrae, John, **I:** 252–253
McRobbie, Angela, **Supp. IV Part 2:** 691
MacShane, Frank, **Supp. IV Part 2:** 557; **Supp. XI:** 214, 216
"MacSwiggen" (Freneau), **Supp. II Part 1:** 259
McTaggart, John, **I:** 59
McTeague (Norris), **III:** 314, 315,

316–320, 322, 325, 327–328, 330, 331, 333, 335; **Retro. Supp. II:** 96; **Supp. IX:** 332
McWhorter, Dianne, **Supp. XXIII:** 38
McWilliams, Carey, **Supp. XI:** 169; **Supp. XXIV:** 282
Madama Butterfly (opera, Puccini), **III:** 139; **Supp. XXI:** 150, 155
"Madam and the Minister" (Hughes), **Supp. I Part 1:** 335
"Madam and the Wrong Visitor" (Hughes), **Supp. I Part 1:** 335
"Madame and Ahmad" (Bowles), **Supp. IV Part 1:** 93
"Madame Bai and the Taking of Stone Mountain" (Bambara), **Supp. XI:** 14–15
Madame Bovary (Flaubert), **II:** 185; **Retro. Supp. I:** 225; **Retro. Supp. II:** 70; **Supp. XI:** 334; **Supp. XX: 58**
"Madame Célestin's Divorce" (Chopin), **Supp. I Part 1:** 213
Madame Curie (film), **Retro. Supp. I:** 113
"Madame de Mauves" (James), **II:** 327; **Retro. Supp. I:** 218, 220
Madame de Treymes (Wharton), **IV:** 314, 323; **Retro. Supp. I:** 376; **Retro. Supp. III:** 281
"Madame Rose Hanie" (Gibran), **Supp. XX: 124**
"Madame Swann at Home"(Hadas), **Supp. XXIII:** 113
"Madam's Calling Cards" (Hughes), **Retro. Supp. I:** 206
Madden, David, **Supp. IV Part 1:** 285
Maddern, Bessie. See London, Mrs. Jack (Bessie Maddern)
Mad Dog Black Lady (Coleman), **Supp. XI: 85–89,** 90
Mad Dog Blues (Shepard), **Supp. III Part 2:** 437, 438, 441
Maddox, Lucy, **Supp. IV Part 1:** 323, 325
Mad Ducks and Bears: Football Revisited (Plimpton), **Supp. XVI:** 243
Mademoiselle Coeur-Brisé (Sibon, trans.), **IV:** 288
Mademoiselle de Maupin (Gautier), **Supp. I Part 1:** 277
"Mad Farmer, Flying the Flag of Rough Branch, Secedes from the Union, The" (Berry), **Supp. X:** 35
"Mad Farmer Manifesto, The: The First Amendment" (Berry), **Supp. X:** 35
"Mad Farmer's Love Song, The" (Berry), **Supp. X:** 35
Madheart (Baraka), **Supp. II Part 1:** 47
Madhouse, The (Farrell), **II:** 41
Madhubuti, Haki R. (Don L. Lee), **Supp. II Part 1:** 34, 247; **Supp. IV Part 1:** 244; **Supp. XXVII:** 165
Madison, Charles, **Supp. XXIII:** 6, 13
Madison, Dolley, **II:** 303
Madison, James, **I:** 1, 2, 6–9; **II:** 301; **Supp. I Part 2:** 509, 524
"Madison Smartt Bell: The Year of Silence" (Garrett), **Supp. X:** 7
Mad Love (film, Freund), **Supp. XVII:** 58
"Madman, A" (Updike), **Retro. Supp. I:** 320
Madman, The: His Parables and Poems (Gibran), **Supp. XX: 115, 118, 125**
"Madman's Song" (Wylie), **Supp. I Part 2:** 711, 729
Madonick, Michael, **Supp. XVII:** 123
"Madonna" (R. Lowell), **II:** 535–536
"Madonna of the Evening Flowers" (A. Lowell), **II:** 524
"Madonna of the Future, The" (James), **Retro. Supp. I:** 219
"Mad Song" (Gioia), **Supp. XV:** 128
Madwoman in the Attic, The (Gilbert and Gubar), **Retro. Supp. I:** 42; **Supp. IX:** 66
"Maelzel's Chess-Player" (Poe), **III:** 419, 420
"Maestria" (Nemerov), **III:** 275, 278–279
Maeterlinck, Maurice, **I:** 91, 220; **Supp. XX: 115, 116**
"Magalu" (H. Johnson). See "Magula" (H. Johnson)
"Magazine-Writing Peter Snook" (Poe), **III:** 421
Magdeburg Centuries (Flacius), **IV:** 163
Magellan, Ferdinand, **Supp. I Part 2:** 497
Maggie: A Girl of the Streets (S. Crane), **I:** 407, 408, 410–411, 416; **IV:** 208; **Retro. Supp. II:** 97, 107; **Supp. XVII:** 228; **Supp. XXIII:** 165
Maggie Cassidy (Kerouac), **Supp. III Part 1:** 220–221, 225, 227, 229, 232
Maggie-Now (B. Smith), **Supp. XXIII:** 258, **267–269**
"Maggie of the Green Bottles" (Bambara), **Supp. XI:** 2–3
"Maggie's Farm" (song, Dylan), **Supp. XVIII:** 25, 26
"Magi" (Plath), **Supp. I Part 2:** 544–545
"Magi, The" (Garrett), **Supp. VII:** 97
"Magic" (Pickering), **Supp. XXI:** 202
"Magic" (Porter), **III:** 434, 435
"Magical Thinking" (Hull), **Supp. XXI:** 137, 139
Magic Barrel, The (Malamud), **Supp. I Part 2:** 427, 428, 430–434
"Magic Barrel, The" (Malamud), **Supp. I Part 2:** 427, 428, 431, 432–433
Magic Christian, The (film), **Supp. XI:** 309
Magic Christian, The (Southern), **Supp. XI:** 297, **299–301,** 309
Magic City (Komunyakaa), **Supp. XIII: 125–127,** 128, 131
"Magic Flute, The" (Epstein), **Supp. XII:** 165
Magic Flute, The (Mozart), **III:** 164
Magician King, The (Grossman), **Supp. XXV:** 74–77
Magician of Lublin, The (Singer), **IV:** 6, 9–10; **Retro. Supp. II: 308–309**
Magicians, The (Grossman), **Supp. XXV:** 64, 68–74
Magician's Assistant, The (Patchett), **Supp. XII:** 307, 310, **317–320,** 322
Magician's Land, The (Grossman), **Supp. XXV:** 77
"Magician's Wife, The" (Gordon), **Supp. IV Part 1:** 306
Magic Journey, The (Nichols), **Supp. XIII:** 266–267
Magic Keys, The (Murray), **Supp. XIX: 157–158**
Magic Kingdom, The (Elkin), **Supp. VI:** 42, **54–55,** 56, 58
"Magic Mirror, The: A Study of the Double in Two of Doestoevsky's Novels" (Plath), **Supp. I Part 2:** 536
Magic Mountain, The (Mann), **III:** 281–282; **Supp. IV Part 2:** 522; **Supp. XII:** 321; **Supp. XVII:** 137
Magic Tower, The (Willams), **IV:** 380
Magnaghi, Ambrogio, **Supp. XVI:** 286
Magnalia Christi Americana (Mather), **II:** 302; **Retro. Supp. III:** 4; **Supp. I Part 1:** 102; **Supp. I Part 2:** 584; **Supp. II Part 2:** 441, 442, 452–455, 460, 467, 468; **Supp. IV Part 2:** 434
Magnes, Judah, **Supp. XXIII:** 6
Magnificat (Nelson), **Supp. XVIII: 176–177**
"Magnificent Little Gift" (Salinas), **Supp. XIII:** 318
"Magnifying Mirror" (Karr), **Supp. XI:** 240
Magpie, The (Baldwin, ed.), **Supp. I Part 1:** 49
"Magpie Exhorts"(Schott), **Supp. XXIII:** 250
Magpie's Shadow, The (Winters),

Supp. II Part 2: 786, 788
"Magpie's Song" (Snyder), **Supp. VIII:** 302
Magritte, René, **Supp. IV Part 2:** 623
Maguire, Roberta S., **Supp. XIX:** 160–161
"Magula" (H. Johnson), **Supp. XXVI:** 164, 166, 170–172, 174
Magus, The (Fowles), **Supp. XIX:** 58
Mahan, Albert Thayer, **Supp. I Part 2:** 491
Mahan, David C., **Supp. XXI:** 86
"Mahatma Joe" (Bass), **Supp. XVI:** 19
Mahin, John Lee, **Supp. XXVII:** 93
Mahlis, Kristen, **Supp. XXIII:** 90, 94
"Mahogany Tree, The" (M. F. K. Fisher), **Supp. XVII:** 88
Mahomet and His Successors (Irving), **II:** 314
Mahoney, Jeremiah, **IV:** 285
Mahoney, Lynn, **Supp. XV:** 270
"Maiden, Maiden" (Boyle), **Supp. XXIV:** 58
"Maiden in a Tower" (Stegner), **Supp. IV Part 2:** 613
Maiden's Prayer, The (Silver), **Supp. XXIV:** 275–276
"Maiden Without Hands" (Sexton), **Supp. II Part 2:** 691
"Maid of St. Philippe, The" (Chopin), **Retro. Supp. II:** 63
"Maid's Shoes, The" (Malamud), **Supp. I Part 2:** 437
Mailer, Fanny, **III:** 28
Mailer, Isaac, **III:** 28
Mailer, Norman, **I:** 261, 292, 477; **III:** **26–49,** 174; **IV:** 98, 216; **Retro. Supp. II:** 182, **195–217,** 279; **Supp. I Part 1:** 291, 294; **Supp. III Part 1:** 302; **Supp. IV Part 1:** 90, 198, 207, 236, 284, 381; **Supp. IV Part 2:** 689; **Supp. VIII:** 236; **Supp. XI:** 104, 218, 222, 229; **Supp. XIV:** 49, 53, 54, 111, 162; **Supp. XVII:** 225, 228, 236; **Supp. XVIII:** 19–20; **Supp. XX:** **90;** **Supp. XXIII:** 105, 106; **Supp. XXIV:** 281; **Supp. XXV:** 145
"Maimed Man, The" (Tate), **IV:** 136
Maimonides, Moses, **Supp. XVII:** 46–47
Main Currents in American Thought: The Colonial Mind, 1625–1800 (Parrington), **I:** 517; **Supp. I Part 2:** 484
"Maine Roustabout, A" (Eberhart), **I:** 539
"Maine Speech" (White), **Supp. I Part 2:** 669–670
Maine Woods, The (Thoreau), **IV:** 188
Mains d'Orlac, Les (M. Renard), **Supp. XVII:** 58
Main Street (Lewis), **I:** 362; **II:** 271, 440, 441–442, 447, 449, 453; **III:** 394; **Supp. XIX:** 142; **Supp. XXII:** 282
"Maintenance" (Pickering), **Supp. XXI:** 204
Mainwaring, Marion, **Retro. Supp. III:** 289–290
Maitland, Margaret Todd, **Supp. XVI:** 292
Majdoubeh, Ahmad, **Supp. XX:** **116**
"Majesty" (July), **Supp. XXIV:** 201–202, 203
Major, Clarence, **Supp. XXII:** **171–186**
"Majorat, Das" (Hoffman), **III:** 415
Major Barbara (Shaw), **III:** 69
"Major Chord, The" (Bourne), **I:** 221
Majors and Minors (Dunbar), **Supp. II Part 1:** 197, 198
"Major's Tale, The" (Bierce), **I:** 205
Make Believe (J. Scott), **Supp. XVII:** **191–192,** 193, 194, 195
Make-Believe Town: Essays and Remembrances (Mamet), **Supp. XIV:** 240, 251
Make It New (Pound), **III:** 470
Makers and Finders (Brooks), **I:** 253, 254, 255, 257, 258
Makers of the Modern World (Untermeyer), **Supp. XV:** 312
"Making a Change" (Gilman), **Supp. XI:** 207
"Making a Living" (Sexton), **Supp. II Part 2:** 695
"Making Changes" (L. Michaels), **Supp. XVI:** 204
"Making Do" (Hogan), **Supp. IV Part 1:** 406
Making Face, Making Soul: Haciendo Caras, Creative and Critical Perspectives by Feminists of Color (Anzaldúa, ed.), **Supp. IV Part 1:** 330
Making It (Podhoretz), **Supp. VIII:** 231, 232, 233, **237–238,** 239, 244
"Making Light of Auntie" (X. J. Kennedy), **Supp. XV:** 163
"Making Love in 2003" (July), **Supp. XXIV:** 204–205, 210
"Making Marks" (Davison), **Supp. XXVI:** 72
"Making Much of Orioles" (Davison), **Supp. XXVI:** 74, 75
"Making of a Marginal Farm, The" (Berry), **Supp. X:** 22
Making of Americans, The (Stein), **IV:** 35, 37, 40–42, 45, 46; **Supp. III Part 1:** 37
"Making of Ashenden, The" (Elkin), **Supp. VI:** 49, 50
"Making of a Soldier USA, The" (Simpson), **Supp. IX:** 270
"Making of Garrison Keillor, The" (McConagha), **Supp. XVI:** 166"
Making of Modern Atlanta, The (documentary), **Supp. XXII:** 251
"Making of Paths, The" (Stegner), **Supp. IV Part 2:** 614
"Making of Poems, The" (W. J. Smith), **Supp. XIII:** 348
Making of the Modern Mind (Randall), **III:** 605
Making the Light Come: The Poetry of Gerald Stern (Somerville), **Supp. IX:** 296–297
"Making Up Stories" (Didion), **Supp. IV Part 1:** 196, 203, 205
Making Your Own Days: The Pleasures of Reading and Writing Poetry (Koch), **Supp. XV:** 188; **Supp. XXIII:** 124
Maladies de la volonté, Les (Ribot), **Supp. XX:** **238**
Malady of the Ideal, The: Oberman, Maurice de Guérin, and Amiel (Brooks), **I:** 240, 241, 242
Malamud, Bernard, **I:** 144, 375; **II:** 424, 425; **III:** 40, 272; **IV:** 216; **Retro. Supp. II:** 22, 279, 281; **Supp. I Part 2:** **427–453;** **Supp. IV Part 1:** 297, 382; **Supp. IX:** 114, 227; **Supp. V:** 257, 266; **Supp. XIII:** 106, 264, 265, 294; **Supp. XVI:** 220; **Supp. XXVI:** 180
Malamud, Mrs. Bernard (Ann de Chiara), **Supp. I Part 2:** 451
Malandrinos, Cheryl C., **Supp. XXVI:** 219
Malanga, Gerard, **Supp. III Part 2:** 629; **Supp. XXIII:** 221
Malaquais, Jean, **Retro. Supp. II:** 199
Malatesta, Sigismondo de, **III:** 472, 473
Malcolm (Purdy), **Supp. VII:** 270–273, 277
"Malcolm Cowley and the American Writer" (Simpson), **Supp. II Part 1:** 147
Malcolm Lowry's "Volcano": Myth Symbol Meaning (Markson), **Supp. XVII:** 142, 144
"MALCOLM REMEMBERED (FEB. 77)" (Baraka), **Supp. II Part 1:** 60
Malcolm X, **Retro. Supp. II:** 12, 13; **Supp. I Part 1:** 52, 63, 65, 66; **Supp. IV Part 1:** 2, 10; **Supp. VIII:**

330, 345; **Supp. X:** 240; **Supp. XIV:** 306
Malcolm X (film), **Retro. Supp. II:** 12
Malcolm X: A Fire Burning Bright (Myers), **Supp. XXVII:** 209
Malcolm X: By Any Means Necessary (Myers), **Supp. XXVII:** 209
"Maldrove" (Jeffers), **Supp. II Part 2:** 418
Male, Roy, **II:** 239
Male Animal, The (Thurber), **Supp. I Part 2:** 605, 606, 610–611
"Malediction upon Myself" (Wylie), **Supp. I Part 2:** 722
Malefactors, The (Gordon), **II:** 186, 199, 213–216; **IV:** 139
"Malest Cornifici Tuo Catullo" (Ginsberg), **Supp. II Part 1:** 315
Malick, Terrence, **Supp. XI:** 234; **Supp. XV:** 351
Malin, Irving, **I:** 147; **Supp. XVI:** 71–72
"Malinche's Tips: Pique from Mexico's Mother" (Mora), **Supp. XIII:** 223
"Malinke's Atonement" (Antin), **Supp. XX: 10**
"Mallard" (C. Frost), **Supp. XV:** 98, 99
Mallarmé, Stéphane, **I:** 66, 569; **II:** 529, 543; **III:** 8, 409, 428; **IV:** 80, 86; **Retro. Supp. I:** 56; **Retro. Supp. III:** 57; **Supp. I Part 1:** 261; **Supp. II Part 1:** 1; **Supp. III Part 1:** 319–320; **Supp. III Part 2:** 630; **Supp. XIII:** 114; **Supp. XV:** 158; **Supp. XVI:** 282, 285
Malle, Louis, **Supp. XXIII:** 122
Mallia, Joseph, **Supp. XII:** 26, 29, 37
Mallon, Anne-Marie, **Supp. XXI:** 215
Mallon, Thomas, **Supp. IV Part 1:** 200, 209; **Supp. XIX: 131–145**
Maloff, Saul, **Supp. VIII:** 238
Malory, Thomas, **II:** 302; **III:** 486; **IV:** 50, 61; **Supp. IV Part 1:** 47
"Mal Paso Bridge" (Jeffers), **Supp. II Part 2:** 415, 420
Malraux, André, **I:** 33–34, 127, 509; **II:** 57, 376; **III:** 35, 310; **IV:** 236, 247, 434; **Retro. Supp. I:** 73; **Retro. Supp. II:** 115–116, 119; **Supp. II Part 1:** 221, 232; **Supp. XIX:** 157
Maltese Falcon, The (film), **Supp. IV Part 1:** 342, 353, 355
Maltese Falcon, The (Hammett), **IV:** 286; **Supp. IV Part 1:** 345, 348–351
Mama (McMillan), **Supp. XIII:** 182, **187–188**
"Mama and Daughter" (Hughes), **Supp. I Part 1:** 334
Mama Day (Naylor), **Supp. VIII: 223–226,** 230
"Mama I Remember" (Nelson), **Supp. XVIII:** 173
Mama Poc: An Ecologist's Account of the Extinction of a Species (LaBastille), **Supp. X:** 99, **104–105,** 106
Mama Poems, The (Kenny), **Supp. XXIII:** 143, **154**
Mama's Bank Account (K. Forbes), **Supp. XVII:** 9
Mama's Promises (Nelson), **Supp. XVIII: 173–174**
"Mama Still Loves You" (Naylor), **Supp. VIII:** 214
Mambo Hips and Make Believe (Coleman), **Supp. XI: 94–96**
Mambo Kings, The (film), **Supp. VIII:** 73, 74
Mambo Kings Play Songs of Love, The (Hijuelos), **Supp. VIII:** 73–74, **79–82**
"Ma'me Pélagie" (Chopin), **Retro. Supp. II:** 64
Mamet, David, **Retro. Supp. III:** 165, 172; **Supp. XIV: 239–258,** 315
"Mamie" (Sandburg), **III:** 582
Mammedaty, Novarro Scott. See Momaday, N. Scott
"Mammon and the Archer" (O. Henry), **Supp. II Part 1:** 394, 408
Mammonart (Sinclair), **Supp. V:** 276–277
"Mammy" (D. West), **Supp. XVIII:** 283
"Mamouche" (Chopin), **Retro. Supp. II:** 66
Mamoulian, Rouben, **Supp. XVIII:** 281
"Man" (Corso), **Supp. XII:** 130
"Man" (Herbert), **II:** 12
"Man Against the Sky, The" (Robinson), **III:** 509, 523
"Man and a Woman Sit Near Each Other, A" (R. Bly), **Supp. IV Part 1:** 71
Man and Boy (Morris), **III:** 223, 224, 225
"Man and the Snake, The" (Bierce), **I:** 203
"Man and Woman" (Caldwell), **I:** 310
Manassas (Sinclair), **Supp. V:** 280, 281, 285
"Man Bring This Up Road" (T. Williams), **IV:** 383–384
"Man Carrying Thing" (Stevens), **IV:** 90
Manchester, William, **III:** 103
"Man Child, The" (Baldwin), **Supp. I Part 1:** 63
Man Could Stand Up, A (Ford), **I:** 423
"Mandarin's Jade" (Chandler), **Supp. IV Part 1:** 125
Mandel, Charlotte, **Supp. XVI:** 57
Mandelbaum, Maurice, **I:** 61
Mandelbaum, Michael, **Supp. XXV:** 264
Mandelstam, Osip, **Retro. Supp. I:** 278; **Supp. III Part 1:** 268; **Supp. VIII:** 21, 22, 23, 27; **Supp. XIII:** 77; **Supp. XV:** 254, 261, 263
"Mandelstam: The Poem as Event" (Dobyns), **Supp. XIII:** 78
"Mandolin" (Dove), **Supp. IV Part 1:** 247
"Mandoline" (Verlaine), **IV:** 79
"Mandrin Question, The" (Vaz), **Supp. XXVI:** 267
"Man Eating" (Kenyon), **Supp. VII:** 173
"Manet in Late Summer" (Skloot), **Supp. XX: 201**
"Man Feeding Pigeons" (Clampitt), **Supp. IX: 49–50,** 52
Manfred, Frederick, **Supp. X:** 126
Man from Kinvara, The (Gallagher), **Supp. XXIV:** 166, 172, 173
Man From Limbo, The (Endore), **Supp. XVII:** 55
Man fun natseres, Der (Asch), **Supp. XXIII:** 6
Mangione, Jerre, **Supp. XXV:** 28
"Mango Says Goodbye Sometimes" (Cisneros), **Supp. VII:** 64
Manhattan (film; Allen), **Supp. IV Part 1:** 205; **Supp. XV:** 5, **7–8,** 13
"Manhattan Dawn" (Justice), **Supp. VII:** 117
"Manhattan: Luminism" (Doty), **Supp. XI:** 135
Manhattan Murder Mystery (film; Allen), **Supp. XV:** 5, 11
Manhattan Transfer (Dos Passos), **I:** 26, 475, 478, 479, 480, 481, 482–484, 487; **II:** 286; **Supp. I Part 1:** 57; **Supp. XXVI:** 18
"Mania" (R. Lowell), **II:** 554
"Manic in the Moon, The" (Thurber), **Supp. I Part 2:** 620
Manifest; and Furthermore (Bronk), **Supp. XXI:** 32
"Manifesto: A Press Release from PRKA" (Saunders), **Supp. XIX:** 235
Manikin, The (J. Scott), **Supp. XVII: 189–191,** 192, 194
"Man in Black" (Plath), **Supp. I Part 2:** 538
Man in Lower Ten, The (Rinehart),

Supp. XXV: 192, 200
Man in Prehistory (Chard), **Supp. XII:** 177–178
Man in the Black Coat Turns, The (R. Bly), **Supp. IV Part 1:** 66–68, 71, 73
"Man in the Brooks Brothers Shirt, The" (McCarthy), **II:** 563–564
"Man in the Drawer, The" (Malamud), **Supp. I Part 2:** 437
Man in the Flying Lawn Chair and Other Excursions and Observations, The (Plimpton), **Supp. XVI:** 234
Man in the Gray Flannel Suit, The (Wilson), **Supp. IV Part 1:** 387
Man in the High Castle, The (Dick), **Supp. XVIII:** 138
Man in the Middle, The (Wagoner), **Supp. IX:** 324, **332–333**
"Man in the Rain, The" (Ryan as Quin), **Supp. XVIII:** 226
"Man in the Toolhouse, The" (Swados), **Supp. XIX:** 263
Mankiewicz, Frank, **Supp. XXIV:** 279
Mankiewicz, Herman J., **Supp. XVI:** 189; **Supp. XXVII:** 91
Mankiewicz, Joseph, **Retro. Supp. I:** 113
Mankowitz, Wolf, **Supp. XI:** 307
"Man Made of Words, The" (Momaday), **Supp. IV Part 2:** 481, 484–485, 486, 487, 488
Man-Made World, The (Gilman), **Supp. XI:** 207
"Man-Moth, The" (Bishop), **Retro. Supp. II:** 42; **Supp. I Part 1:** 85–87, 88
Mann, Barbara Alice, **Supp. XXVI:** 81, 85, 86, 88, 90, 92, 95
Mann, Charles, **Retro. Supp. II:** 40
Mann, Erika, **Supp. II Part 1:** 11
Mann, Seymour (Samuel Weisman), **Supp. V:** 113
Mann, Thomas, **I:** 271, 490; **II:** 42, 539; **III:** 231, 281–282, 283; **IV:** 70, 73, 85; **Supp. IV Part 1:** 392; **Supp. IV Part 2:** 522; **Supp. IX:** 21; **Supp. V:** 51; **Supp. XI:** 275; **Supp. XII:** 173, 310, 321; **Supp. XIV:** 87; **Supp. XIX:** 147, 151, 157; **Supp. XVII:** 137; **Supp. XX: 85; Supp. XXIII:** 4
Mannequins' Demise: A Play in Eight Scenes (Budbill), **Supp. XIX: 12**
Mannerhouse (Wolfe), **IV:** 460
Manner Music, The (Reznikoff), **Supp. XIV: 293–295**
"Manners" (Bishop), **Supp. I Part 1:** 73
"Manners" (Emerson), **II:** 4, 6
"Manners, Morals, and the Novel" (Trilling), **Supp. III Part 2:** 502, 503
Mannheim, Karl, **I:** 279; **Supp. I Part 2:** 644
Manning, Ambrose, **Supp. XX: 166**
Manning, Frederic, **III:** 459
Manning, Robert, **Supp. IX:** 236
Mannix, Daniel P., **Supp. II Part 1:** 140
Man Nobody Knows, The (B. Barton), **Retro. Supp. I:** 179
Mano, D. Keith, **Supp. XVI:** 250
Mano, Guy Levis, **Supp. XVI:** 282
"Man of Indeterminate Age on a Subway Grate, A" (DI Piero), **Supp. XIX:** 47
"Man of Letters" (Pickering), **Supp. XXI:** 192, 195–196
"Man of Letters as a Man of Business, The" (Howells), **Supp. XIV:** 45–46
"Man of No Account, The" (Harte), **Supp. II Part 1:** 339
"Man of Property to His Muse, The" (W. Stone), **Supp. XXVII:** 255
"Man of the Crowd, The" (Poe), **III:** 412, 417; **Retro. Supp. I:** 154; **Retro. Supp. III:** 226
Man on Spikes (Asinof), **II:** 424
Man on Stage (Dixon), **Supp. XII:** 141, **154–155**
"Man on the Dump, The" (Stevens), **IV:** 74; **Retro. Supp. I:** 306
"Man on the Stairs, The" (July), **Supp. XXIV:** 202
"Man on the Train, The" (Percy), **Supp. III Part 1:** 387
Manor, The (Singer), **IV:** 6, 17–19
Manrique, Jorge, **Retro. Supp. II:** 154
Mansart Builds a School (Du Bois), **Supp. II Part 1:** 185–186
Man's Fate (Malraux), **I:** 127; **Retro. Supp. II:** 121
"Man's Fate A Film Treatment of the Malraux Novel" (Agee), **I:** 33–34
Mansfield, June, **Supp. X:** 183, 194
Mansfield, Katherine, **III:** 362, 453
Mansfield, Stephanie, **Supp. IV Part 1:** 227
Man's Hope (Malraux), **IV:** 247
Mansion, The (Faulkner), **II:** 73; **Retro. Supp. I:** 74, 82; **Retro. Supp. III:** 86
Man's Nature and His Communities (Niebuhr), **III:** 308
Manson, Charles, **Supp. IV Part 1:** 205
"Man Splitting Wood in the Daybreak, The" (Kinnell), **Supp. III Part 1:** 254
"Man's Pride" (Jeffers), **Supp. II Part 2:** 417
"Man's Story, The" (Anderson), **I:** 114
Man's Woman, A (Norris), **III:** 314, 322, 328, 329, 330, 332, 333
Man That Corrupted Hadleyburg, The (Twain), **I:** 204; **IV:** 208
"Man That Corrupted Hadleyburg, The" (Twain), **Retro. Supp. III:** 269
"Man That Was Used Up, The" (Poe), **III:** 412, 425
"Mantis" (Zukofsky), **Supp. III Part 2:** 617
"'Mantis': An Interpretation" (Zukofsky), **Supp. III Part 2:** 617–618
"Man to Know in the Restaurants, The" (Siddons), **Supp. XXII:** 244
Man to Send Rain Clouds, The (Rosen, ed.), **Supp. IV Part 2:** 499, 505, 513
"Man to Send Rain Clouds, The" (Silko), **Supp. IV Part 2:** 559
Mantrap (Lewis), **II:** 447
Manuductio Ad Ministerium (Mather), **Supp. II Part 2:** 465–467
"Manuelzinho" (Bishop), **Retro. Supp. II:** 47–48
Manuscript Books of Emily Dickinson, The (Franklin, ed.), **Retro. Supp. I:** 29, 41
"Manuscript Found in a Bottle, The" (Poe), **Retro. Supp. III:** 224
"Man Waiting for It to Stop, A" (Dunn), **Supp. XI:** 144
"Man Who Became a Woman, The" (Anderson), **I:** 114
"Man Who Carries the Desert Around Inside Himself, The: For Wally" (Komunyakaa), **Supp. XIII:** 125
"Man Who Closed Shop, The" (Dunn), **Supp. XI:** 149
Man Who Gave Up His Name, The (Harrison), **Supp. VIII:** 45, 52
Man Who Had All the Luck, The (A. Miller), **III:** 148, 149, 164, 166; **Retro. Supp. III:** 166
"Man Who Knew Belle Star, The" (Bausch), **Supp. VII:** 46
"Man Who Knew Coolidge, The" (Lewis), **II:** 449
Man Who Knew Coolidge, The: Being the Soul of Lowell Schmaltz, Constructive and Nordic Citizen (Lewis), **II:** 450
Man Who Lived Underground, The (Wright), **Supp. II Part 1:** 40
"Man Who Lived Underground, The" (Wright), **IV:** 479, 485–487, 492; **Retro. Supp. II:** 121

"Man Who Made Me Love Him, The" (Weigl), **Supp. XIX:** 278
"Man Who Makes Brooms, The" (Nye), **Supp. XIII:** 276
"Man Who Studied Yoga, The" (Mailer), **III:** 35–36; **Retro. Supp. II:** 200
"Man Who Wanted to Win, The" (McCoy), **Supp. XIII:** 161
"Man Who Was Made of Netting, The" (Vaz), **Supp. XXVI:** 266
Man Who Was There, The (Morris), **III:** 220–221
"Man Who Was Used Up, The" (Poe), **Retro. Supp. III:** 225
"Man Who Writes Ants, The" (Merwin), **Supp. III Part 1:** 348
"Man with a Family" (Humphrey), **Supp. IX:** 94
Man without a Country, The (Hale), **I:** 488
"Man with the Blue Guitar, The" (Stevens), **I:** 266; **IV:** 85–87; **Retro. Supp. I: 303–305,** 306, 307, 309
Man with the Blue Guitar and Other Poems, The (Stevens), **IV:** 76; **Retro. Supp. I:** 303, 422
Man with the Golden Arm, The (Algren), **Supp. IX:** 1, 3, **9–11,** 14, 15; **Supp. V:** 4
Man with the Golden Arm, The (film), **Supp. IX:** 3
"Man with the Golden Beef, The" (Podhoretz), **Supp. IX:** 3
"Man with the Hoe, The" (Markham), **Supp. XV:** 115
Man with the Mask, The (Lippard), **Supp. XXIII:** 178, 183–184, 188
Many a Monster (Ryan as Finnegan), **Supp. XVIII:** 233, **236–238**
Manyan Letters (Olson), **Supp. II Part 2:** 571
Many Circles (Goldbarth), **Supp. XII:** 193
"Many Handles" (Sandburg), **III:** 594
"Many Happy Returns" (Auden), **Supp. II Part 1:** 15
Many Happy Returns (Berrigan), **Supp. XXII:** 224; **Supp. XXIV:** 37, 41
Many Loves (W. C. Williams), **Retro. Supp. I:** 424
"Many Mansions" (H. Roth), **Supp. IX:** 233, 234
Many Marriages (Anderson), **I:** 104, 111, 113
"Many of Our Waters: Variations on a Poem by a Black Child" (Wright), **Supp. III Part 2:** 602
"Many Swans" (A. Lowell), **II:** 526
"Many Thousands Gone" (Baldwin), **Retro. Supp. II:** 4; **Supp. I Part 1:** 51
"Many Wagons Ago" (Ashbery), **Supp. III Part 1:** 22
Many-Windowed House, A (Cowley), **Supp. II Part 1:** 141, 143
"Many-Windowed House, A" (Cowley), **Supp. II Part 1:** 137
Mao II (DeLillo), **Supp. VI:** 2, 4, **5,** 6, **7,** 8, 9, 14, 16
"Map, The" (Bishop), **Retro. Supp. II:** 41; **Supp. I Part 1:** 72, 82, 85–88, 93
"Map, The" (Strand), **Supp. IV Part 2:** 623–624
"Maple Leaf, The" (Joplin), **Supp. IV Part 1:** 223
"Maple Tree, The" (D. West), **Supp. XVIII:** 284
Map of Another Town: A Memoir of Provence (M. F. K. Fisher), **Supp. XVII:** 88, 89, 92
"Map of Montana in Italy, A" (Hugo), **Supp. VI:** 139
Mapp and Lucia (Benson), **Supp. XX: 229**
Mapping American Culture (Franklin and Steiner), **Supp. XXII:** 205
"Maps" (Hass), **Supp. VI:** 103–104
Mapson, Jo-Ann, **Supp. IV Part 2:** 440, 454
Map to the Next World, A: Poems and Tales (Harjo), **Supp. XII: 228–230**
"Maquillage" (Hull), **Supp. XXI:** 133
"Mara" (Jeffers), **Supp. II Part 2:** 434
Ma Rainey's Black Bottom (Wilson), **Retro. Supp. III:** 314–315, 318, 321–323, 325; **Supp. VIII:** 331, **332–334,** 346, 349, 350
Maranen (Asch), **Supp. XXIII:** 10
Marat, Jean Paul, **IV:** 117; **Supp. I Part 2:** 514, 515, 521
"Marathon" (Glück), **Supp. V:** 85
Marble Faun, The (Faulkner), **II:** 55, 56; **Retro. Supp. I:** 79; **Retro. Supp. III:** 74–75, 122–123
Marble Faun, The; or, The Romance of Monte Beni (Hawthorne), **II:** 225, 239, 242–243, 290, 324; **IV:** 167; **Retro. Supp. I:** 63, 149, 163, **164–165; Supp. I Part 1:** 38; **Supp. I Part 2:** 421, 596; **Supp. XIII:** 102
Marbles (Brodsky), **Supp. VIII:** 26–27
Marburg, Anita, **Supp. XXII:** 281
Marcaccio, Michael, **Supp. XVII:** 97, 106
Marcel, Kelly, **Supp. XXVII:** 79
"March" (W. C. Williams), **Retro. Supp. I:** 418
March, Alan, **Supp. XVI:** 242
March, Fredric, **III:** 154, 403; **IV:** 357; **Supp. X:** 220
"March, March on Down the Field" (Shaw), **Supp. XIX:** 246
Marchalonis, Shirley, **Supp. XIII:** 138, 140, 141, 143, 147–148
Marchand, Philip, **Supp. XXVII:** 196
"Marché aux Oiseaux" (Wilbur), **Supp. III Part 2:** 550
"Märchen, The" (Jarrell), **II:** 378–379
March Hares (Frederic), **II:** 143–144
Marching Men (Anderson), **I:** 99, 101, 103–105, 111
"Marching Music" (Simic), **Supp. VIII:** 281
"Marcia" (R. H. Davis), **Supp. XVI:** 91–92
Marcks, Greg, **Supp. XVIII:** 150
Marckwardt, Albert H., **Supp. XXIV:** 255
Marco Millions (O'Neill), **III:** 391, 395
Marcosson, Isaac, **III:** 322
Marcus, Greil, **Supp. XVIII:** 30, 53; **Supp. XXVI:** 142
Marcus, Steven, **Retro. Supp. II:** 196, 200
Marcus Aurelius, **II:** 1; **III:** 566; **Supp. XVIII:** 304
Marcuse, Herbert, **Supp. I Part 2:** 645; **Supp. VIII:** 196; **Supp. XII:** 2
Mardi and a Voyage Thither (Melville), **I:** 384; **II:** 281; **III:** 77–79, 84, 87, 89; **Retro. Supp. I:** 247, 254, 256; **Retro. Supp. III:** 147, 154, 157
Margaret (Judd), **II:** 290
Margaret & Dusty (Notley), **Supp. XXII:** 231
"Margaret Fuller, 1847" (Clampitt), **Supp. IX:** 43
"Marginalia" (Wilbur), **Supp. III Part 2:** 544
Margin of Hope, A: An Intellectual Autobiography (Howe), **Supp. VI:** 113–114, 117, 125, 128
"Margins of Maycomb, The: A Rereading of To Kill a Mockingbird" (Phelps), **Supp. VIII:** 128
Margoshes, Samuel, **Supp. X:** 70
"Margrave" (Jeffers), **Supp. II Part 2:** 426
Margret Howth (R. H. Davis), **Supp. XVI:** 81, 83, 84, **88–89**
Margret Howth: A Story of Today (J. Yellin, ed.), **Supp. XVI:** 88
Margulies, Donald, **Supp. XXI:** 145
"Maria Concepción" (Porter), **III:** 434–435, 451
Mariana (Vaz), **Supp. XXVI:** 258–259, 263

Mariani, Paul L., **Retro. Supp. I:** 412, 419; **Retro. Supp. II:** 189
Marianne Moore Reader, (Moore), **III:** 199
Marie Antoinette (film), **Retro. Supp. I:** 113
Marie Blythe (Mosher), **Supp. XXII:** 206, 209, **212**
Marie Grubbe (Jacobsen), **Retro. Supp. III:** 140
Marie Laveau (Prose), **Supp. XVI:** 251
Mariella Gable, Sister, **III:** 339, 355
"Marijuana and a Pistol" (C. Himes), **Supp. XVI:** 137
"Marijuana Notation" (Ginsberg), **Supp. II Part 1:** 313
Maril, Herman, **Supp. XXI:** 22, 23
Marilyn: A Biography (Mailer), **Retro. Supp. II:** 208
"Marin" (Cisneros), **Supp. VII:** 60, 61
Marin, Jay, **Retro. Supp. II:** 325
"Marina" (Eliot), **I:** 584, 585; **Retro. Supp. I:** 64
Mariners, Renegades, and Castaways (C. L. R. James), **Supp. XXI:** 159, 169–170
"Marine Surface, Low Overcast" (Clampitt), **Supp. IX: 47–48**
Marinetti, F. T., **Supp. XXII:** 159, 160, 161, 163
Marinetti, Tommaso, **Retro. Supp. I:** 59
Marionettes, The (Faulkner), **Retro. Supp. I:** 79
"Mari Sandoz's Slogum House: Greed as a Woman" (Riley), **Supp. XXIV:** 252
Maritain, Jacques, **I:** 402; **Supp. XXVI:** 231, 232
Maritime Compact (Paine), **Supp. I Part 2:** 519
Maritime History of Massachusetts, 1783–1860, The (Morison), **Supp. I Part 2:** 481–483
Marjolin, Jean-Nicolas, **Supp. I Part 1:** 302
Marjorie Kinnan Rawlings: Sojourner at Cross Creek (Silverthorne), **Supp. X:** 220, 234
Marjorie Morningstar (film), **Supp. XXV:** 262
Marjorie Morningstar (Wouk), **Supp. XXV:** 253, 254, 256, 258, 261–262, 268
"Mark, The" (Bogan), **Supp. III Part 1:** 52
Marker, Chris, **Supp. IV Part 2:** 434, 436
"Market" (Hayden), **Supp. II Part 1:** 368, 369
Marketplace, The (Frederic), **II:** 145–146
Markham, Edwin, **I:** 199, 207; **Supp. XV:** 115
Markings (Hammarskjold), **Supp. II Part 1:** 26
Mark of the Vampire (film, Browning), **Supp. XVII:** 58
Markopoulos, Gregory, **Supp. XII:** 2
Markowick-Olczakova, Hanna, **Supp. X:** 70
Marks, Alison, **Supp. I Part 2:** 660
Marks, Barry A., **I:** 435, 438, 442, 446
Markson, David, **Supp. XVII: 135–147**
Mark Twain and Southwestern Humor (Lynn), **Retro. Supp. III:** 259
Mark Twain as a Literary Comedian (Sloane), **Retro. Supp. III:** 259
Mark Twain in Eruption (Twain), **IV:** 209
Mark Twain in the Margins (Fulton), **Retro. Supp. III:** 266
Mark Twain's America (De Voto), **I:** 248
Mark Twain's Autobiography (Twain), **IV:** 209
Mark Twain Speaking (Fatout), **Retro. Supp. III:** 268
Mark Twain: The Complete Interviews (Scharnhorst), **Retro. Supp. III:** 268
Marley, Bob, **Supp. IX:** 152
Marlowe, Christopher, **I:** 68, 368, 384; **II:** 590; **III:** 259, 491; **Retro. Supp. I:** 127; **Retro. Supp. II:** 76; **Supp. I Part 2:** 422; **Supp. XXI:** 227
Marlowe, Kimberly B., **Supp. XXII:** 214
"Marlowe Takes on the Syndicate" (Chandler), **Supp. IV Part 1:** 135
Marne, The (Wharton), **IV:** 319, 320; **Retro. Supp. I:** 378; **Retro. Supp. III:** 286
Marquand, John, **Supp. XI:** 301
Marquand, Mrs. John P. (Adelaide Hooker), **III:** 57, 61
Marquand, Mrs. John P. (Christina Sedgwick), **III:** 54, 57
Marquand, J. P., **I:** 362, 375; **II:** 459, 482–483; **III: 50–73,** 383; **Supp. I Part 1:** 196; **Supp. IV Part 1:** 31; **Supp. V:** 95
Marquand, Philip, **III:** 52
Marquis, Don, **Supp. I Part 2:** 668
Marra, Anthony, **Supp. XXVI:** 216
Marrásh, Francis al-, **Supp. XX: 117**
"Marriage" (Corso), **Supp. XII:** 117, 124, **127–128**
Marriage (Moore), **III:** 194
"Marriage" (Moore), **III:** 198–199, 213
"Marriage, A" (Untermeyer), **Supp. XV:** 305
Marriage A-la-Mode (Dryden), **Supp. IX:** 68
Marriage and Other Science Fiction (Goldbarth), **Supp. XII:** 189, 190
"Marriage in the Sixties, A" (Rich), **Retro. Supp. III:** 244; **Supp. I Part 2:** 554
Marriage of Bette and Boo, The (Durang), **Supp. XXIV:** 114, 121, **122–123**
Marriage of Heaven and Hell (Blake), **Supp. XXII:** 257
"Marriage of Heaven and Hell, The" (Blake), **III:** 544–545; **Supp. VIII:** 99
"Marriage of Phaedra, The" (Cather), **Retro. Supp. I:** 5; **Retro. Supp. III:** 26
Marriage Plot, The (Eugenides), **Supp. XXIV:** 135, **143–145**
"Marriage Rhapsody"(Hadas), **Supp. XXIII:** 114
Married (Strindberg), **Supp. XXII:** 23
"Married" (Taggard), **Supp. XXII:** 274
Married Men (Wolfert), **Supp. XXI:** 277
Married People (Rinehart), **Supp. XXV:** 201
Marrow of Tradition, The (Chesnutt), **Supp. XIV:** 63, **71–75,** 76
Marryat, Captain Frederick, **III:** 423
"Marrying Absurd" (Didion), **Supp. IV Part 1:** 200
"Marrying Iseult?" (Updike), **Retro. Supp. I:** 329
Marrying Man (Simon), **Supp. IV Part 2:** 588
"Marrying the Hangman" (Atwood), **Supp. XIII:** 34
Marry Me: A Romance (Updike), **Retro. Supp. I:** 329, 330, 332
"Mars and Hymen" (Freneau), **Supp. II Part 1:** 258
Marsden, Dora, **III:** 471; **Retro. Supp. I:** 416
Marsena (Frederic), **II:** 135, 136–137
Marsh, Edward, **Retro. Supp. III:** 96; **Supp. I Part 1:** 257, 263
Marsh, Frederick T., **Supp. XX: 39, 46**
Marsh, Fred T., **Supp. IX:** 232
Marsh, John R., **Supp. XIX:** 187
Marsh, Mae, **Supp. I Part 2:** 391
Marshall, George, **III:** 3
Marshall, John, **Supp. I Part 2:** 455; **Supp. XIX:** 62; **Supp. XVI:** 117; **Supp. XXIII:** 275, 276
Marshall, Paule, **Supp. IV Part 1:** 8,

14, 369; **Supp. XI:** 18, **275–292; Supp. XIII:** 295; **Supp. XX: 154**
Marshall, Tod, **Supp. XV:** 224; **Supp. XVII:** 25, 26, 29, 32
"Marshall Carpenter" (Masters), **Supp. I Part 2:** 463
"Marshes of Glynn, The" (Lanier), **Supp. I Part 1:** 364, 365–368, 370, 373
"'Marshes of Glynn, The': A Study in Symbolic Obscurity" (Ross), **Supp. I Part 1:** 373
Marsh Island, A (Jewett), **II:** 405; **Retro. Supp. II:** 134
"Marshland Elegy" (Leopold), **Supp. XIV:** 187, 189
"Mars Is Heaven!" (Bradbury), **Supp. IV Part 1:** 103, 106
Mars-Jones, Adam, **Supp. XXI:** 116
Marsman, Henrik, **Supp. IV Part 1:** 183
Marston, Ed, **Supp. IV Part 2:** 492
Marston, Elsa, **Supp. XXIII:** 241
Marta y Maria (Valdes), **II:** 290
"Martha's Lady" (Jewett), **Retro. Supp. II:** 140, 143
Marthe, Saint, **II:** 213
Martial, **II:** 1, 169; **Supp. IX:** 152
Martian Chronicles, The (Bradbury), **Supp. IV Part 1:** 102, 103, 106–107
Martian Time-Slip (Dick), **Supp. XVIII:** 142
Martin, Benjamin, **Supp. I Part 2:** 503
Martin, Charles, **Supp. XVII:** 112
Martin, Dick, **Supp. XII:** 44
Martin, Jay, **I:** 55, 58, 60, 61, 67; **III:** 307; **Retro. Supp. II:** 326, 327, 329; **Supp. XI:** 162
Martin, John, **Supp. XI:** 172
Martin, Judith, **Supp. V:** 128
Martin, Nell, **Supp. IV Part 1:** 351, 353
Martin, Reginald, **Supp. X:** 247, 249
Martin, Robert, **Retro. Supp. III:** 173; **Supp. XX: 165**
Martin, Stephen-Paul, **Supp. IV Part 2:** 430
Martin, Tom, **Supp. X:** 79
Martin du Gard, Roger, **Supp. I Part 1:** 51
Martineau, Harriet, **Supp. II Part 1:** 282, 288, 294; **Supp. XVIII:** 7; **Supp. XXIV:** 78
Martin Eden (London), **II:** 466, 477–481
Martinelli, Sheri, **Supp. IV Part 1:** 280
Martínez, Guillermo, **Supp. XIII:** 313
Martinez-Avila, Raul, **Supp. XXIII:** 125
Martini, Adrienne, **Supp. XVIII:** 35
Martín-Lucas, Belén, **Supp. XXVI:** 218
Mart'nez, Rafael, **Retro. Supp. I:** 423
Martone, John, **Supp. V:** 179
Marty (Chayefsky), **Supp. XV:** 205
"Martyr, The" (Porter), **III:** 454
Martz, Louis L., **IV:** 151, 156, 165; **Supp. I Part 1:** 107; **Supp. XIV:** 12; **Supp. XXI:** 85
Marvell, Andrew, **IV:** 135, 151, 156, 161, 253; **Retro. Supp. I:** 62, 127; **Retro. Supp. II:** 186, 189; **Supp. I Part 1:** 80; **Supp. XII:** 159; **Supp. XIV:** 10; **Supp. XVI:** 204; **Supp. XXI:** 227; **Supp. XXIII:** 62
"Marvella, for Borrowing" (Ríos), **Supp. IV Part 2:** 551
"Marvelous Sauce, The", **Supp. XVII:** 189
Marvels and Masterpieces (al-Badá'i' wa'l-Tará'if) (Gibran), **Supp. XX: 116, 124**
Marx, Eleanor, **Supp. XVI:** 85
Marx, Karl, **I:** 60, 267, 279, 283, 588; **II:** 376, 462, 463, 483, 577; **IV:** 429, 436, 443–444, 469; **Retro. Supp. I:** 254; **Supp. I Part 2:** 518, 628, 632, 633, 634, 635, 639, 643, 645, 646; **Supp. III Part 2:** 619; **Supp. IV Part 1:** 355; **Supp. IX:** 133; **Supp. VIII:** 196; **Supp. X:** 119, 134; **Supp. XIII:** 75; **Supp. XXI:** 162, 263
Marx, Leo, **Supp. I Part 1:** 233
"Marxism and Monastic Perpectives" (Merton), **Supp. VIII:** 196
Mary (Asch), **Supp. XXIII:** 2, 7, **14**
Mary (Nabokov), **Retro. Supp. I: 267–268,** 270, 277
"Mary" (Trethewey), **Supp. XXI:** 246
"Mary in Old Age" (Ferry), **Supp. XXIV:** 162
"Mary Karr, Mary Karr, Mary Karr, Mary Karr" (Harmon), **Supp. XI:** 248
Maryles, Daisy, **Supp. XII:** 271
Mary Magdalene, **I:** 303
"Mary Magdalene at Easter" (Davison), **Supp. XXVI:** 71
Mary; or, The Test of Honour (Rowson), **Supp. XV: 233,** 236
"Mary O'Reilly" (Anderson), **II:** 44
"Mary Osaka , I Love You" (Fante), **Supp. XI:** 169
Mary Roberts Rinehart Crime Book, The (Rinehart), **Supp. XXV:** 199
"Mary Snorak the Cook, Skermo the Gardener, and Jack the Parts Man Provide Dinner for a Wandering Stranger" (Grossman), **Supp. XIX:** 87
"Mary's Song" (Plath), **Supp. I Part 2:** 541
"Mary Winslow" (R. Lowell), **Retro. Supp. II:** 187
Marzynski, Marian, **Supp. XVI:** 153
"Masculinities and Murder: George Pemberton in Ron Rash's Serena" (Willis), **Supp. XXVII:** 216
Masefield, John, **II:** 552; **III:** 523
Masked and Anonymous (film, Dylan and Charles), **Supp. XVIII:** 21, 28
Mask for Janus, A (Merwin), **Supp. III Part 1:** 339, 341, 342
Maslin, Janet, **Supp. XVI:** 213; **Supp. XXI:** 79
Maslow, Abraham, **Supp. I Part 2:** 540
Maso, Carole, **Supp. XXII:** 261
Mason, Bobbie Ann, **Supp. VIII: 133–149; Supp. XI:** 26; **Supp. XII:** 294, 298, 311; **Supp. XX: 162; Supp. XXV:** 153
Mason, Charlotte Osgood, **Retro. Supp. III:** 127–128, 139; **Supp. XIV:** 201
Mason, David, **Supp. V:** 344; **Supp. XV:** 116, 251; **Supp. XVII:** 109, 110, 112, 121; **Supp. XVIII:** 182, 183
Mason, Jennifer, **Supp. XVIII:** 263
Mason, Lowell, **I:** 458
Mason, Margaret, **Supp. XXIII:** 209
Mason, Marsha, **Supp. IV Part 2:** 575, 586
Mason, Otis Tufton, **Supp. I Part 1:** 18
Mason, Walt, **Supp. XV:** 298
Mason & Dixon (Pynchon), **Supp. XVII:** 232
"Mason Jars by the Window" (Ríos), **Supp. IV Part 2:** 548
"Masque in Green and Black"(Hadas), **Supp. XXIII:** 121
Masque of Mercy, A (Frost), **II:** 155, 165, 167–168; **Retro. Supp. I:** 131, 140; **Retro. Supp. III:** 104, 105
"Masque of Mummers, The" (MacLeish), **III:** 18
"Masque of Pandora, The" (Longfellow), **Retro. Supp. II:** 167
Masque of Pandora, The, and Other Poems (Longfellow), **II:** 490, 494, 506; **Retro. Supp. II:** 169
Masque of Poets, A (Lathrop, ed.), **Retro. Supp. I:** 31; **Supp. I Part 1:** 365, 368
Masque of Reason, A (Frost), **II:** 155, 162, 165–167; **Retro. Supp. I:** 131,

140; **Retro. Supp. II:** 42; **Retro. Supp. III:** 104, 105
"Masque of the Red Death, The" (Poe), **III:** 412, 419, 424; **Retro. Supp. II:** 262, 268–269; **Retro. Supp. III:** 225
"Masquerade" (Banks), **Supp. V:** 7
Massachusetts, Its Historians and Its History (Adams), **Supp. I Part 2:** 484
"Massachusetts 1932" (Bowles), **Supp. IV Part 1:** 94
"Massachusetts to Virginia" (Whittier), **Supp. I Part 2:** 688–689
"Massacre and the Mastermind, The" (Bausch), **Supp. VII:** 49
"Massacre at Scio, The" (Bryant), **Supp. I Part 1:** 168
"Massacre of the Innocents, The" (Davison), **Supp. XXVI:** 70
"Massacre of the Innocents, The" (Simic), **Supp. VIII:** 282
Masses and Man (Toller), **I:** 479
"Masseur de Ma Soeur, Le" (Hecht), **Supp. X:** 58
Massey, Raymond, **Supp. IV Part 2:** 524
"Mass Eye and Ear: The Ward" (Karr), **Supp. XI:** 244
"Mass for the Day of St. Thomas Didymus" (Levertov), **Supp. III Part 1:** 283
Massie, Chris, **Supp. IV Part 2:** 524
Massing, Michael, **Supp. IV Part 1:** 208
Massinger, Philip, **Supp. I Part 2:** 422; **Supp. XV:** 238
Master Builder, The (Ibsen), **Supp. IV Part 2:** 522
Master Class (McNally), **Supp. XIII:** **204–205,** 208
"Masterful" (Matthews), **Supp. IX:** **161–162**
Mastering the Art of French Cooking (Child), **Supp. XVII:** 89
"Master Misery" (Capote), **Supp. III Part 1:** 117
Master of Dreams: A Memoir of Isaac Bashevis Singer (Telushkin), **Retro. Supp. II:** 317
"Master of Secret Revenges, The" (Gass), **Supp. VI:** 93
Master of the Crossroads (Bell), **Supp. X:** **16–17**
"'Masterpiece of Filth, A': Portrait of Knoxville Forgets to Be Fair" (Howards), **Supp. VIII:** 178
Masterpieces of American Fiction, **Supp. XI:** 198
"Master Player, The" (Dunbar), **Supp. II Part 1:** 200
Masters, Edgar Lee, **I:** 106, 384, 475, 480, 518; **II:** 276, 529; **III:** 505, 576, 579; **IV:** 352; **Retro. Supp. I:** 131; **Supp. I Part 2:** 378, 386, 387, **454–478; Supp. III Part 1:** 63, 71, 73, 75; **Supp. IV Part 2:** 502; **Supp. IX:** 308; **Supp. XIV:** 282–283; **Supp. XV:** 256, 293, 297, 301, 306; **Supp. XXV:** 18; **Supp. XXVII:** 283, 290
Masters, Hardin W., **Supp. I Part 2:** 468
Masters, Hilary, **Supp. IX:** 96
Masters of Sociological Thought (Coser), **Supp. I Part 2:** 650
Masters of the Dew (Roumain), **Supp. IV Part 1:** 367
Masters of the Short Story (Kriegel and Lass, eds.), **Supp. XXIV:** 214
"Masters of War" (song, Dylan), **Supp. XVIII:** 24
"Master's Pieces, The" (H. L. Gates), **Supp. XX: 109**
Matchmaker, The (Wilder), **IV:** 357, 369, 370, 374; **Supp. XX: 50**
Mate of the Daylight, The, and Friends Ashore (Jewett), **II:** 404; **Retro. Supp. II:** 146–147
Materassi, Mario, **Supp. IX:** 233
"Material" (Munro), **Supp. XXVII:** 185
Materials, The (Oppen), **Supp. XXVI:** 229–232
"Math Bending unto Angels" (Vaz), **Supp. XXVI:** 260
Mather, Cotton, **II:** 10, 104, 302, 506, 536; **III:** 442; **IV:** 144, 152–153, 157; **Retro. Supp. III:** 4; **Supp. I Part 1:** 102, 117, 174, 271; **Supp. I Part 2:** 584, 599, 698; **Supp. II Part 2: 441–470; Supp. IV Part 2:** 430, 434
Mather, Increase, **II:** 10; **IV:** 147, 157; **Supp. I Part 1:** 100
Mathews, Cornelius, **III:** 81; **Supp. I Part 1:** 317
Mathews, Shailer, **III:** 293
"Matinees" (Merrill), **Supp. III Part 1:** 319, 327
"Matins" (C. Frost), **Supp. XV:** 105
"Matins" (Glück), **Supp. V:** 88
"Matins" (Nelson), **Supp. XVIII:** 177
Matisse, Henri, **III:** 180; **IV:** 90, 407; **Supp. I Part 2:** 619; **Supp. IX:** 66; **Supp. VIII:** 168; **Supp. X:** 73, 74; **Supp. XXII:** 98, 99; **Supp. XXVI:** 259
"Matisse: Blue Interior with Two Girls–1947" (Hecht), **Supp. X: 73–74**
"Matisse: The Red Studio" (Snodgrass), **Supp. VI:** 316–317
Matlack, James, **Supp. XV:** 269, 271, 286
Matlock, Lucinda, **Supp. I Part 2:** 462
Matos, Juan, **Supp. XXI:** 104
Matrimaniac, The (film), **Supp. XVI:** 185, 186
Matrix Trilogy, The (film), **Supp. XVI:** 271
Matson, Harold, **Supp. XIII:** 164, 166, 167, 169, 172
Matson, Peter, **Supp. IV Part 1:** 299
Matson, Suzanne, **Supp. VIII:** 281
"Matter of Hannibal" (Twain), **Retro. Supp. III:** 258
"Matter of the River" (Twain), **Retro. Supp. III:** 258
Matters of Fact and Fiction: Essays 1973–1976 (Vidal), **Supp. IV Part 2:** 687
Matters of Life and Death: New American Stories (Wolff, ed.), **Supp. XXIII:** 289
Matthew (biblical book), **IV:** 164; **Supp. XV:** 222
Matthew Arnold (Trilling), **Supp. III Part 2:** 500–501
Matthews, Brander, **Retro. Supp. III:** 264
Matthews, Jackson, **Supp. XVI:** 282
Matthews, T. S., **II:** 430; **Supp. XV:** 142
Matthews, William, **Supp. IX: 151–170; Supp. V:** 4, 5; **Supp. XIII:** 112; **Supp. XXI:** 87; **Supp. XXVI:** 66
Matthiessen, F. O., **I:** 254, 259–260, 517; **II:** 41, 554; **III:** 310, 453; **IV:** 181; **Retro. Supp. I:** 40, 217; **Retro. Supp. II:** 137; **Supp. IV Part 2:** 422; **Supp. XIII:** 93; **Supp. XIV:** 3; **Supp. XXI:** 277; **Supp. XXV:** 251
Matthiessen, Peter, **Supp. V: 199–217,** 332; **Supp. XI:** 231, 294; **Supp. XIV:** 82; **Supp. XIX:** 268; **Supp. XVI:** 230
Mattingly, Garrett, **Supp. IV Part 2:** 601
Mattos, Anita, **Supp. XXIII:** 197
Mattu, Ravi, **Supp. XVI:** 124
"Maud Island" (Caldwell), **I:** 310
Maud Martha (Brooks), **Supp. III Part 1:** 74, 78–79, 87; **Supp. XI:** 278
"Maud Muller" (Whittier), **Supp. I Part 2:** 698
Maugham, W. Somerset, **III:** 57, 64; **Supp. IV Part 1:** 209; **Supp. X:** 58; **Supp. XIV:** 161
Maule's Curse: Seven Studies in the

History of American Obscurantism (Winters), **Supp. II Part 2:** 807–808, 812
"Mau-mauing the Flak Catchers" (Wolfe), **Supp. III Part 2:** 577
Maupassant, Guy de, **I:** 309, 421; **II:** 191–192, 291, 325, 591; **IV:** 17; **Retro. Supp. II:** 65, 66, 67, 299; **Supp. I Part 1:** 207, 217, 223, 320; **Supp. XIV:** 336
"Maurice Barrès and the Youth of France" (Bourne), **I:** 228
Maurice Kenny: Celebrations of a Mohawk Writer (Kelsey, ed.), **Supp. XXIII:** 143
Maurier, George du, **II:** 338
Maurras, Charles, **Retro. Supp. I:** 55
Maus II: And Here My Troubles Began (A. Speigelman), **Supp. XVII:** 48
Mauve Gloves & Madmen, Clutter & Vine (Wolfe), **Supp. III Part 2:** 581
Maverick, Augustus, **Supp. XVIII:** 4
Maverick in Mauve (Auchincloss), **Supp. IV Part 1:** 26
"Mavericks, The" (play) (Auchincloss), **Supp. IV Part 1:** 34
"Mavericks, The" (story) (Auchincloss), **Supp. IV Part 1:** 32
"Max" (H. Miller), **III:** 183
Max, D. T., **Supp. XXI:** 117
Max and the White Phagocytes (H. Miller), **III:** 178, 183–184
Maximilian (emperor of Mexico), **Supp. I Part 2:** 457–458
Maximilian: A Play in Five Acts (Masters), **Supp. I Part 2:** 456, 457–458
"Maximus, to Gloucester" (Olson), **Supp. II Part 2:** 574
"Maximus, to himself" (Olson), **Supp. II Part 2:** 565, 566, 567, 569, 570, 572
Maximus Poems, The (Olson), **Retro. Supp. I:** 209; **Supp. II Part 2:** 555, 556, 563, 564–580, 584; **Supp. VIII:** 305; **Supp. XV:** 170, 264, 349; **Supp. XVI:** 287
Maximus Poems 1–10, The (Olson), **Supp. II Part 2:** 571
Maximus Poems IV, V, VI (Olson), **Supp. II Part 2:** 555, 580, 582–584
Maximus Poems Volume Three, The (Olson), **Supp. II Part 2:** 555, 582, 584–585
"Maximus to Gloucester, Letter 19 (A Pastoral Letter)" (Olson), **Supp. II Part 2:** 567
"Maximus to Gloucester, Sunday July 19" (Olson), **Supp. II Part 2:** 580
"Maximus to himself June 1964" (Olson), **Supp. II Part 2:** 584
Maxwell, Glyn, **Supp. XV:** 252, 253, 260, 261, 263, 264
Maxwell, William, **Supp. I Part 1:** 175; **Supp. III Part 1:** 62; **Supp. VIII: 151–174; Supp. XVII:** 23
May, Abigail (Abba). See Alcott, Mrs. Amos Bronson (Abigail May)
May, Charles, **Supp. XXVII:** 189, 196
May, Elaine Tyler, **Supp. XXII:** 81, 95
May, Jill, **Supp. VIII:** 126
"May 24, 1980" (Brodsky), **Supp. VIII:** 28
"May 1968" (Olds), **Supp. X:** 211–212
Mayakovsky, Vladimir, **Supp. XXIII:** 207; **Supp. XXVI:** 144
"Mayakovsky"(O'Hara), **Supp. XXIII:** 212, 214
"Mayan Glyphs Unread, The" (Bronk), **Supp. XXI:** 31
"Mayan Warning" (Mora), **Supp. XIII:** 214
Maybe (Hellman), **Supp. IV Part 1:** 12
"Maybe" (Oliver), **Supp. VII:** 239
"Maybe, Someday" (Ritsos), **Supp. XIII:** 78
May Blossom (Belasco), **Supp. XVI:** 182
"Mayday" (Faulkner), **Retro. Supp. I:** 80
"May Day" (Fitzgerald), **II:** 88–89; **Retro. Supp. I:** 103
"May Day Dancing, The" (Nemerov), **III:** 275
May Days (Pickering), **Supp. XXI:** 197–198
May Days: An Anthology of Verse from Masses-Liberator (Taggard, ed.), **Supp. XXII:** 275–276
"May Day Sermon to the Women of Gilmer County, Georgia, by a Woman Preacher Leaving the Baptist Church" (Dickey), **Supp. IV Part 1:** 182
Mayer, Bernadette, **Supp. XXIV:** 41
Mayer, Elizabeth, **Supp. II Part 1:** 16; **Supp. III Part 1:** 63
Mayer, John, **Retro. Supp. I:** 58
Mayer, Louis B., **Supp. XII:** 160; **Supp. XVIII:** 250
Mayes, Wendell, **Supp. IX:** 250
Mayfield, Sara, **Supp. IX:** 65
"May First" (Hayes), **Supp. XXVI:** 144
Mayflower, The (Stowe), **Supp. I Part 2:** 585, 586
Mayle, Peter, **Supp. XVI:** 295
Maynard, Joyce, **Supp. V:** 23
Maynard, Tony, **Supp. I Part 1:** 65
Mayne, Xavier. See Prime-Stevenson, Edward Irenaeus
Mayo, Robert, **III:** 478
Mayor (Allen), **Supp. XXII:** 245
Mayorga, Margaret, **IV:** 381
"Mayor of Glory River, The" (Huddle), **Supp. XXVI:** 151
"May-Pole of Merry Mount, The" (Hawthorne), **II:** 229; **Retro. Supp. III:** 113; **Supp. XXII:** 44
"May Queen" (Di Piero), **Supp. XIX:** 41
May Sarton: Selected Letters 1916–1954, **Supp. VIII:** 265
"May Sun Sheds an Amber Light, The" (Bryant), **Supp. I Part 1:** 170
"May Swenson: The Art of Perceiving" (Stanford), **Supp. IV Part 2:** 637
May the Generations Die in the Right Order (Schott), **Supp. XXIII: 248–250**
"Maze" (Eberhart), **I:** 523, 525–526, 527
Mazel (R. Goldstein), **Supp. XVII:** 44
Mazower, David, **Supp. XXIII:** 4, 5
Mazur, Gail, **Supp. XVIII:** 92
Mazurkiewicz, Margaret, **Supp. XI:** 2
Mazzeno, Laurence W., **Supp. XXV:** 253, 256, 258, 259, 263
Mazzini, Giuseppe, **Supp. I Part 1:** 2, 8; **Supp. II Part 1:** 299
M. Butterfly (Hwang), **Supp. X:** 292; **Supp. XXI:** 143, 147, **150–154**
Mc. Names starting with Mc are alphabetized as if spelled Mac.
"M. Degas Teaches Art & Science at Durfee Intermediate School, Detroit, 1942" (Levine), **Supp. V:** 181, 193
"Me, Boy Scout" (Lardner), **II:** 433
Me, Mop, and the Moondance Kid (Myers), **Supp. XXVII:** 206
Me, Vashya! (T. Williams), **IV:** 381
Mead, Elinor. See Howells, Mrs. William Dean (Elinor Mead)
Mead, George Herbert, **II:** 27, 34; **Supp. I Part 1:** 5; **Supp. I Part 2:** 641
Mead, Margaret, **Retro. Supp. III:** 133; **Supp. I Part 1:** 49, 52, 66; **Supp. IX:** 229
Mead, Taylor, **Supp. XV:** 187
Meade, Frank, **Retro. Supp. II:** 114
Meade, Marion, **Supp. IX:** 191, 193, 194, 195
Meadow, Lynne, **Supp. XIII:** 198
"Meadow House" (Carruth), **Supp. XVI:** 48
Meadowlands (Glück), **Supp. V:** 88–90
"Mean, Mrs." (Gass), **Supp. VI:** 83

"Me and the Mule" (Hughes), **Supp. I Part 1:** 334
Me and You and Everyone We Know (film, July), **Supp. XXIV:** 199, 200, 201, 203, 206**, 207–209**
Mean Free Path (Lerner), **Supp. XXIV:** 45
Meaning a Life (M. Oppen), **Supp. XXVI:** 225, 228
"Meaningless Institution, A" (Ginsberg), **Supp. II Part 1:** 313
"Meaning of a Literary Idea, The" (Trilling), **Supp. III Part 2:** 498
"Meaning of Birds, The" (C. Smith), **Supp. X:** 177
"Meaning of Death, The, An After Dinner Speech" (Tate), **IV:** 128, 129
"Meaning of Life, The" (Tate), **IV:** 137
"Meaning of Simplicity, The" (Ritsos), **Supp. XIII:** 78
"Mean Mud Season, The" (Huddle), **Supp. XXVI:** 149
Means of Escape (Caputo), **Supp. XIX:** 18, 21, 25
Mean Spirit (Hogan), **Supp. IV Part 1:** 397, 404, 407–410, 415, 416–417
Means to Freedom, A: The Letters of H. P. Lovecraft and Robert Howard (Burke, Joshi, and Schultz eds.), **Supp. XXVII:** 128
Meantime, The (Bronk), **Supp. XXI:** 31
Mearns, Hughes, **III:** 220
"Measure" (Hass), **Supp. VI: 99–100,** 101
Measure for Measure (Shakespeare), **Supp. XXVI:** 78
"Measuring My Blood" (Vizenor), **Supp. IV Part 1:** 262
Meatyard, Gene, **Supp. X:** 30
Me: By Jimmy (Big Boy) Valente (Keillor), **Supp. XVI:** 177
Mechan, Dennis B., **Supp. XVI:** 267–268
Mechanic, The (Bynner and DeMille), **Supp. XV:** 42, 50
"Mechanism" (Ammons), **Supp. VII:** 28
"Mechanism in Thought and Morals" (Holmes), **Supp. I Part 1:** 314
Mecom, Mrs. Jane, **II:** 122
"Meddlesome Jack" (Caldwell), **I:** 309
Medea (Jeffers), **Supp. II Part 2:** 435
Medea and Some Poems, The (Cullen), **Supp. IV Part 1:** 169, 173
"Me Decade and the Third Great Awakening, The" (Wolfe), **Supp. III Part 2:** 581
"Médecin Malgré Lui, Le" (W. C. Williams), **IV:** 407–408
"Medfield" (Bryant), **Supp. I Part 1:** 157
Medical History of Contraception, A (Himes), **Supp. V:** 128
"Medicine Song" (Gunn Allen), **Supp. IV Part 1:** 326
Médicis, Marie de, **II:** 548
Medina (McCarthy), **II:** 579
"Meditation, A" (Eberhart), **I:** 533–535
"Meditation 1.6" (Taylor), **IV:** 165
"Meditation 1.20" (Taylor), **IV:** 165
"Meditation 2.68A" (Taylor), **IV:** 165
"Meditation 2.102" (Taylor), **IV:** 150
"Meditation 2.112" (Taylor), **IV:** 165
"Meditation 20" (Taylor), **IV:** 154–155
"Meditation 40" (Second Series) (Taylor), **IV:** 147
"Meditation at Lagunitas" (Hass), **Supp. VI:** 104–105; **Supp. XXI:** 60; **Supp. XXVI:** 61
"Meditation at Oyster River" (Roethke), **III:** 537, 549
Meditations (Descartes), **III:** 618
Meditations (Marcus Aurelius), **Supp. XVIII:** 304
"Meditations for a Savage Child" (Rich), **Supp. I Part 2:** 564–565
Meditations from a Movable Chair (Dubus), **Supp. VII:** 91
Meditations in an Emergency (O'Hara), **Supp. XXIII: 213–214,** 219, 220
"Meditations in an Emergency"(O'Hara), **Supp. XXIII:** 212, 214
"Meditations in a Swine Yard" (Komunyakaa), **Supp. XIII:** 131
"Meditations of an Old Woman" (Roethke), **III:** 529, 540, 542, 543, 545–547, 548
"Meditations on Grass"(Crooker), **Supp. XXIII:** 55
Meditations on the Insatiable Soul (R. Bly), **Supp. IV Part 1:** 72–73
Meditative Poems, The (Martz), **IV:** 151
"Mediterranean, The" (Tate), **IV:** 129
"Medium of Fiction, The" (Gass), **Supp. VI:** 85–86
"Medley" (Bambara), **Supp. XI:** 9
"Medusa" (Bogan), **Supp. III Part 1:** 50, 51
Meehan, Jeannette Porter, **Supp. XX: 213, 214, 217, 220, 224**
Meehan, Thomas, **Supp. IV Part 2:** 577–578, 586, 590
Meek, Martha, **Supp. IV Part 2:** 439, 440, 441, 442, 445, 447, 448
Meeker, Richard K., **II:** 190
Meese, Elizabeth, **Supp. XIII:** 297
"Meeting" (J. W. Miller), **Supp. XX: 167**
"Meeting, The" (F. Wright), **Supp. XVII:** 245
"Meeting and Greeting Area, The" (Cameron), **Supp. XII: 84–85**
Meeting by the River, A (Isherwood), **Supp. XIV:** 164, **170–171,** 172
"Meeting-House Hill" (A. Lowell), **II:** 522, 527
"Meeting in the Kitchen, The" (Schnackenberg), **Supp. XV:** 256
"Meeting of the Tisdale Fellows, The" (Huddle), **Supp. XXVI:** 155
"Meeting South, A" (Anderson), **I:** 115
"Meeting the Mountains" (Snyder), **Supp. VIII:** 300
Meeting Trees (Sanders), **Supp. XVI:** 269
Meet Me at the Morgue (Macdonald), **Supp. IV Part 2:** 472
Mehta, Sonny, **Supp. XI:** 178
Mehta, Ved, **Supp. XX: 87**
Meine, Curt, **Supp. XIV:** 179
Meiners, R. K., **IV:** 136, 137, 138, 140
Meinong, Alexius, **Supp. XIV:** 198, 199
Meisner, Sanford, **Supp. XIV:** 240, 242
Meister, Charles W., **II:** 112
Mejia, Jaime, **Supp. XIX:** 97
"Melancholia" (Dunbar), **Supp. II Part 1:** 194
Melancholy Baby (Parker), **Supp. XIX:** 186
"Melanctha" (Stein), **IV:** 30, 34, 35, 37, 38–40, 45
"Melancthon" (Moore), **III:** 212, 215
Melbourne House (S. and A. Warner), **Supp. XVIII:** 268
Meliboeus Hipponax (Lowell). See Bigelow Papers, The (Lowell)
Melinda and Melinda (Allen), **Supp. XV:** 16
Mellaart, James, **Supp. I Part 2:** 567
Mellard, James, **Supp. IV Part 1:** 387
Mellen, Joan, **Supp. XXIV:** 51, 52, 56, 64
Mellon, Andrew, **III:** 14
Mellor, W. M., **Supp. XX: 56**
Melnick, Jeffrey, **Supp. X:** 252
Melnick, Ralph, **Supp. XXVII:** 137–138
Melnyczuk, Askold, **Supp. IV Part 1:** 70
Melodrama Play (Shepard), **Supp. III Part 2:** 440–441, 443, 445
Melodramatists, The (Nemerov), **III:** 268, 281–283, 284
Melopoeia (Espaillat and Tavano),

Supp. XXI: 99–100
Melting-Pot, The (Zangwill), **I:** 229
"Melungeons" (Offutt), **Supp. XIX:** 171
Melville, Allan, **III:** 74, 77
Melville, Gansevoort, **III:** 76
Melville, Herman, **I:** 104, 106, 211, 288, 340, 343, 348, 354, 355, 561–562; **II:** 27, 74, 224–225, 228, 230, 232, 236, 255, 259, 271, 272, 277, 281, 295, 307, 311, 319, 320, 321, 418, 477, 497, 539–540, 545; **III:** 29, 45, 70, **74–98,** 359, 438, 453, 454, 507, 562–563, 572, 576; **IV:** 57, 105, 194, 199, 202, 250, 309, 333, 345, 350, 380, 444, 453; **Retro. Supp. I:** 54, 91, 160, 215, 220, **243–262; Retro. Supp. II:** 76; **Retro. Supp. III: 147–164,** 194, 223; **Supp. I Part 1:** 147, 238, 242, 249, 309, 317, 372; **Supp. I Part 2:** 383, 495, 579, 580, 582, 602; **Supp. IV Part 2:** 463, 613; **Supp. V:** 279, 281, 298, 308; **Supp. VIII:** 48, 103, 104, 105, 106, 108, 156, 175, 181, 188; **Supp. XI:** 83; **Supp. XII:** 282; **Supp. XIII:** 294, 305; **Supp. XIV:** 48, 227; **Supp. XV:** 287; **Supp. XVII:** 42, 185; **Supp. XVIII:** 1, 4, 6, 7, 9; **Supp. XXI:** 169; **Supp. XXII:** 174, 262; **Supp. XXIII:** 164, 165, 174, 190; **Supp. XXIV:** 88
Melville, Mrs. Herman (Elizabeth Shaw), **III:** 77, 91, 92
Melville, Maria Gansevoort, **III:** 74, 77, 85
Melville, Thomas, **III:** 77, 79, 92; **Supp. I Part 1:** 309
Melville, Whyte, **IV:** 309
Melville Goodwin, USA (Marquand), **III:** 60, 65–66
Melville's Marginalia (Cowen), **Supp. IV Part 2:** 435
"Melville's Marginalia" (Howe), **Supp. IV Part 2:** 435
Member of the Wedding, The (McCullers), **II:** 587, 592, 600–604, 605, 606; **Supp. VIII:** 124
"Meme Ortiz" (Cisneros), **Supp. VII:** 60
Memmon (song cycle) (Bowles), **Supp. IV Part 1:** 82
Memmott, Carol, **Supp. XXVI:** 209
Memnoch the Devil (Rice), **Supp. VII:** 289, 290, 294, 296–299
"Memoir" (Hempel), **Supp. XXI:** 118
"Memoir" (Untermeyer), **II:** 516–517
"Memoir, A" (Koch), **Supp. XV:** 184
Memoir from Antproof Case (Helprin), **Supp. XXV:** 84, 87
"Memoirist's Apology, A" (Karr), **Supp. XI:** 245, 246
Memoir of Mary Ann, A (O'Connor), **III:** 357
Memoir of Thomas McGrath, A (Beeching), **Supp. X:** 114, 118
Memoirs (W. Frank), **Supp. XX: 67, 69, 70, 81**
Memoirs of a Preacher, a Revelation of the Church and the Home, The (Lippard), **Supp. XXIII:** 178, 183–184, 188, 190
Memoirs of Arii Taimai (Adams), **I:** 2–3
"Memoirs of Carwin, the Biloquist" (Brown), **Supp. I Part 1:** 132
Memoirs of Hecate County (Wilson), **IV:** 429
Memoirs of Margaret Fuller Ossoli (Fuller), **Supp. II Part 1:** 280, 283, 285
"Memoirs of Stephen Calvert" (Brown), **Supp. I Part 1:** 133, 144
Memorabilia (Xenophon), **II:** 105
Memorable Providences (Mather), **Supp. II Part 2:** 458
Memorial, The: Portrait of a Family (Isherwood), **Supp. XIV:** 156, 159, 160–161
"Memorial Day" (Cameron), **Supp. XII:** 80, **82–83**
"Memorial for the City" (Auden), **Supp. II Part 1:** 20
"Memorial Rain" (MacLeish), **III:** 15
"Memorial to Ed Bland" (Brooks), **Supp. III Part 1:** 77
"Memorial Tribute" (Wilbur), **Supp. IV Part 2:** 642
"Memories" (Whittier), **Supp. I Part 2:** 699
Memories of a Catholic Girlhood (McCarthy), **II:** 560–561, 566; **Supp. XI:** 246; **Supp. XVI:** 64, 70
"Memories of East Texas" (Karr), **Supp. XI:** 239
"Memories of Uncle Neddy" (Bishop), **Retro. Supp. II:** 38; **Supp. I Part 1:** 73, 93
"Memories of West Street and Lepke" (R. Lowell), **II:** 550
"Memory" (Epstein), **Supp. XII:** 163
"Memory" (Everwine), **Supp. XV:** 82
"Memory, A" (Welty), **IV:** 261–262; **Retro. Supp. I:** 344–345
"Memory, Narrative, and the Discourses of Identity in Abeng and No Telephone to Heaven" (Smith), **Supp. XXII:** 70
"Memory, The" (Gioia), **Supp. XV:** 119
Memory and Enthusiasm: Essays, 1975–1985 (Di Piero), **Supp. XIX:** 34, 41, 42
"Memory and Imagination" (Hampl), **Supp. XXII:** 94
Memory Gardens (Creeley), **Supp. IV Part 1:** 141, 157
"Memory Harbor" (Skloot), **Supp. XX: 201**
Memory of Murder, A (Bradbury), **Supp. IV Part 1:** 103
Memory of Old Jack, The (Berry), **Supp. X:** 34
Memory of Two Mondays, A (A. Miller), **III:** 153, 156, 158–159, 160, 166
"Memory's Power" (Huddle), **Supp. XXVI:** 160
"Memo to Non-White Peoples" (Hughes), **Retro. Supp. I:** 209
"Men" (Boyle), **Supp. XXIV:** 61
Men, Women and Ghosts (A. Lowell), **II:** 523–524
"Menace of the Peyote, The" (Zitkala-Ša), **Supp. XXV:** 281
Menaker, Charlotte, **Supp. XIX:** 266
Menaker, Daniel, **Supp. VIII:** 151; **Supp. XXIII:** 276
Menand, Louis, **Supp. XIV:** 40, 197; **Supp. XVI:** 106, 107; **Supp. XXIII:** 104–105
Men and Angels (Gordon), **Supp. IV Part 1:** 304–305, 306, 308
Men and Brethen (Cozzens), **I:** 363–365, 368, 375, 378, 379
Men and Cartoons (Lethem), **Supp. XVIII:** 145, **148**
"Men and Women" (R. Bly), **Supp. IV Part 1:** 72
"Men at Forty" (Justice), **Supp. VII:** 126–127
Mencius (Meng-tzu), **IV:** 183
Mencken, August, **III:** 100, 108
Mencken, August, Jr., **III:** 99, 109, 118–119
Mencken, Mrs. August (Anna Abhau), **III:** 100, 109
Mencken, Burkhardt, **III:** 100, 108
Mencken, Charles, **III:** 99
Mencken, Gertrude, **III:** 99
Mencken, H. L., **I:** 199, 210, 212, 235, 245, 261, 405, 514, 515, 517; **II:** 25, 27, 42, 89, 90, 91, 271, 289, 430, 443, 449; **III: 99–121,** 394, 482; **IV:** 76, 432, 440, 475, 482; **Retro. Supp. I:** 1, 101; **Retro. Supp. II:** 97, 98, 102, 265; **Supp. I Part 2:** 484, 629–630, 631, 647, 651, 653, 659, 673; **Supp. II Part 1:** 136; **Supp. IV Part 1:** 201, 314, 343;

Supp. IV Part 2: 521, 692, 693; **Supp. XI:** 163–164, 166; **Supp. XIII:** 161; **Supp. XIV:** 111; **Supp. XV:** 297, 301, 303; **Supp. XVI:** 187–188, 189; **Supp. XVII:** 106; **Supp. XXII:** 23, 187, 277; **Supp. XXIV:** 26, 281; **Supp. XXVII:** 86
Mencken, Mrs. H. L. (Sara Haardt), **III:** 109, 111
"Men Deified Because of Their Cruelty" (Simic), **Supp. VIII:** 282
Mendelbaum, Paul, **Supp. V:** 159
Mendele, **IV:** 3, 10
Mendelief, Dmitri Ivanovich, **IV:** 421
Mendelsohn, Daniel, **Supp. X:** 153, 154; **Supp. XV:** 257, 258, 261, 266
Mendelsohn, Jack, **Supp. XXIV:** 72, 77
Mendelsohn, Jane, **Supp. XXVI:** 158
Mendelssohn, Moses, **Supp. XXIII:** 4
Mendes, Alfred, **Supp. XXI:** 160
Mending Skins (Gansworth), **Supp. XXVI:** 103, 104, 106
"Mending Wall" (Frost), **II:** 153–154; **Retro. Supp. I:** 128, 130; **Retro. Supp. III:** 97, 98; **Supp. X:** 64
"Meneseteung" (Munro), **Supp. XXVII:** 190–191
Men from the Boys, The (Lacy), **Supp. XV:** 202, 205
"Menielle" (Stallings), **Supp. XXV:** 223
Men in the Off Hours (Carson), **Supp. XII: 111–113**
"Men in the Storm, The" (Crane), **I:** 411
"Men Loved Wholly Beyond Wisdom" (Bogan), **Supp. III Part 1:** 50
"Men Made Out of Words" (Stevens), **IV:** 88
Men Must Act (Mumford), **Supp. II Part 2:** 479
Mennes, John, **II:** 111
Mennoti, Gian Carlo, **Supp. IV Part 1:** 84
Men of Brewster Place, The (Naylor), **Supp. VIII:** 213, **228–230**
"Men of Color, to Arms!" (Douglass), **Supp. III Part 1:** 171
Men of Good Hope: A Story of American Progressives (Aaron), **Supp. I Part 2:** 650
Mens' Club, The (film), **Supp. XVI:** 212–213
Men's Club, The (L. Michaels), **Supp. XVI:** 206, **210–212**
"Men's Sauna" (Huddle), **Supp. XXVI:** 150
"Menstruation at Forty" (Sexton), **Supp. II Part 2:** 686
"Mental Hospital Garden, The" (W. C. Williams), **Retro. Supp. I:** 428
Mental Radio (Sinclair), **Supp. V:** 289
Mentoria; or, The Young Lady's Friend (Rowson), **Supp. XV: 233–234,** 238
"Men We Carry in Our Minds, The" (Sanders), **Supp. XVI:** 273
Men Who Made the Nation, The (Dos Passos), **I:** 485
"Men Who Raised the Dead, The" (Rash), **Supp. XXVII:** 220
Men Without Women (Hemingway), **II:** 249; **Retro. Supp. I:** 170, 176; **Supp. IX:** 202
"Merced" (Rich), **Supp. I Part 2:** 563
"Mercedes" (E. Stoddard), **Supp. XV:** 278
"Mercedes Hospital" (Bishop), **Retro. Supp. II:** 51
"Mercenary, A" (Ozick), **Supp. V:** 267
Mercer, Johnny, **Supp. XXII:** 6
Merchandising (Hwang), **Supp. XXI:** 147
Merchant of Venice, The (Shakespeare), **IV:** 227; **Supp. XIV:** 325
Mercury Theatre, **Retro. Supp. I:** 65
Mercy, A (Morrison), **Retro. Supp. III:** 185, 197–198
Mercy, Pity, Peace, and Love (Ozick), **Supp. V:** 257, 258
Mercy, The (Levine), **Supp. V:** 194–195
Mercy of a Rude Stream (H. Roth), **Supp. IX:** 231, 234, **235–242**
"Mercy"(P. Benedict), **Supp. XXIII:** 49
Mercy Philbrick's Choice (Jackson), **Retro. Supp. I:** 26, 27, 33
Mercy Street (Sexton), **Supp. II Part 2:** 683, 689
"Mercy"(Thompson), **Supp. XXIII:** 295, 296
Meredith, George, **II:** 175, 186; **Supp. IV Part 1:** 300
Meredith, Mary. See Webb, Mary
Meredith, William, **II:** 545; **Retro. Supp. II:** 181
"Merely by Wilderness" (Peacock), **Supp. XIX:** 199
"Merely to Know" (Rich), **Supp. I Part 2:** 554
"Mère Pochette" (Jewett), **II:** 400
"Merger II, The" (Auchincloss), **Supp. IV Part 1:** 34
Meri (Asch), **Supp. XXIII:** 5, 11
"Mericans" (Cisneros), **Supp. VII:** 69
"Merida, 1969" (Matthews), **Supp. IX:** 151
"Meridian" (Clampitt), **Supp. IX: 48–49**
Meridian (Walker), **Supp. III Part 2:** 520, 524, 527, 528, 531–537
Mérimée, Prosper, **II:** 322
Meriwether, James B., **Retro Supp. I:** 77, 91
"Meriwether Connection, The" (Cowley), **Supp. II Part 1:** 142
Merker, Kim K., **Supp. XI:** 261; **Supp. XV:** 75, 77
"Merlin" (Emerson), **II:** 19, 20
Merlin (Robinson), **III:** 522
"Merlin Enthralled" (Wilbur), **Supp. III Part 2:** 544, 554
"Mermother" (A. Finch), **Supp. XVII:** 72
Merril, Judith, **Supp. XVI:** 123
Merrill, Cavafy, Poems, and Dreams (Hadas), **Supp. XXIII: 123–124**
Merrill, Christopher, **Supp. XI:** 329
Merrill, Flora, **Retro. Supp. III:** 33
Merrill, James, **Retro. Supp. I:** 296; **Retro. Supp. II:** 53; **Supp. III Part 1: 317–338; Supp. III Part 2:** 541, 561; **Supp. IX:** 40, 42, 48, 52; **Supp. X:** 73; **Supp. XI:** 123, 131, 249; **Supp. XII:** 44, 254, 255, 256, 261–262, 269–270; **Supp. XIII:** 76, 85; **Supp. XV:** 249, 250, 253; **Supp. XVII:** 123; **Supp. XXIII:** 112, 122, 123; **Supp. XXV:** 222, 227–228; **Supp. XXVI:** 67
Merrill, Mark (pseudonym). See Markson, David
Merrill, Robert, **Retro. Supp. II:** 201
Merrill, Ronald, **Supp. IV Part 2:** 521
Merritt, A., **Supp. XXV:** 122
Merritt, Abraham, **Supp. XVII:** 58
Merritt, Theresa, **Supp. VIII:** 332
Merritt, Vernon, **Supp. XXII:** 245
"Merry-Go-Round" (Hughes), **Retro. Supp. I:** 194, 205; **Supp. I Part 1:** 333
Merry-Go-Round, The (Van Vechten), **Supp. II Part 2:** 734, 735
Merry Month of May, The (Jones), **Supp. XI: 227–228**
Merry Widow, The (Lehar), **III:** 183
Merton, Thomas, **III:** 357; **Supp. VIII: 193–212; Supp. XXII:** 83, 90; **Supp. XXIV:** 133
Merwin, W. S., **Supp. III Part 1: 339–360; Supp. III Part 2:** 541; **Supp. IV Part 2:** 620, 623, 626; **Supp. IX:** 152, 155, 290; **Supp. V:** 332; **Supp. XIII:** 274, 277; **Supp. XIX:** 82; **Supp. XV:** 222, 342; **Supp. XXI:** 95; **Supp. XXVI:** 67, 68

Meryman, Richard, **Supp. IV Part 2:** 579, 583
Meshiekhs tsaytn (Times of the Messiah) (Asch), **Supp. XXIII:** 5
Meshugah (Singer), **Retro. Supp. II: 315–316**
Mesic, Michael, **Supp. IV Part 1:** 175
Mesic, Penelope, **Supp. X:** 15
Message in the Bottle, The (Percy), **Supp. III Part 1:** 387–388, 393, 397
"Message in the Bottle, The" (Percy), **Supp. III Part 1:** 388
"Message of Flowers and Fire and Flowers, The" (Brooks), **Supp. III Part 1:** 69
Messengers Will Come No More, The (Fiedler), **Supp. XIII:** 103
Messerli, Douglas, **Supp. XVI:** 293
Messiah (Vidal), **Supp. IV Part 2:** 677, 680, 681–682, 685, 691, 692
"Messiah, The" (Wasserstein), **Supp. XV:** 328
Messiah of Stockholm, The (Ozick), **Supp. V:** 270–271; **Supp. XVII:** 42
Messud, Claire, **Supp. XVIII:** 98
Metamorphic Tradition in Modern Poetry (Quinn), **IV:** 421
Metamorphoses (Golding, trans.), **Supp. XXV:** 226
Metamorphoses (Ovid), **II:** 542–543; **III:** 467, 468; **Supp. XV:** 33; **Supp. XVI:** 20; **Supp. XX: 280; Supp. XXIV:** 132
Metamorphoses (Pound, trans.), **III:** 468–469
"Metamorphosis" (Huddle), **Supp. XXVI:** 151
Metamorphosis, The (Kafka), **IV:** 438; **Retro. Supp. II:** 287–288; **Supp. VIII:** 3; **Supp. XXI:** 89
"Metamorphosis and Survival" (Woodcock), **Supp. XIII:** 33
"Metaphor as Mistake" (Percy), **Supp. III Part 1:** 387–388
"Metaphor for Guatemala, A: The Long Night of White Chickens" (Perera), **Supp. XXV:** 50
Metaphor & Memory: Essays (Ozick), **Supp. V:** 272
Metaphor of Trees and Last Poems (Bronk), **Supp. XXI:** 32
"Metaphors of a Magnifico" (Stevens), **IV:** 92
Metaphysical Club, The (Menand), **Supp. XIV:** 40, 197
"Metaphysical Poets, The" (Eliot), **I:** 527, 586
"Metaphysics" (Ginsberg), **Supp. II Part 1:** 313
Metcalf, Paul, **Supp. XIV:** 96; **Supp. XXIII:** 163, 174
"Meteor, The" (Bradbury), **Supp. IV Part 1:** 102
Methinks the Lady...(Endore), **Supp. XVII:** 61–62
"Metonymy as an Approach to the Real World" (Bronk), **Supp. XXI:** 30
Metress, Christopher P., **Supp. V:** 314
Metrical History of Christianity, The (Taylor), **IV:** 163
"Metrical Regularity" (Lovecraft), **Supp. XXV:** 120
Metropolis, The (Sinclair), **Supp. V:** 285
"Metropolitan Tower, The" (Teasdale), **Supp. XXVII:** 286, 289
"Metterling Lists, The" (Allen), **Supp. XV:** 15
"Metzengerstein" (Poe), **III:** 411, 417
Mew, Charlotte, **Retro. Supp. II:** 247
Mewshaw, Michael, **Supp. V:** 57; **Supp. X:** 82
"Mexican Hands" (Ryan as Quin), **Supp. XVIII:** 227
"Mexico" (R. Lowell), **II:** 553, 554
"Mexico, Age Four" (Salinas), **Supp. XIII:** 315
Mexico City Blues (Kerouac), **Supp. III Part 1:** 225, 229
"Mexico Is a Foreign Country: Five Studies in Naturalism" (Warren), **IV:** 241, 252
"Mexico's Children" (Rodriguez), **Supp. XIV:** 302
Meyer, Carolyn, **Supp. XIX:** 194–195, 197
Meyer, Donald B., **III:** 298
Meyer, Ellen Hope, **Supp. V:** 123
Meyer, Robert, **Supp. XXI:** 23
Meyers, Jeffrey, **Retro. Supp. I:** 124, 138; **Retro. Supp. II:** 191
Meynell, Alice, **Supp. I Part 1:** 220
Mezey, Robert, **Supp. IV Part 1:** 60; **Supp. V:** 180; **Supp. XIII:** 312; **Supp. XV:** 74
Mezzanine, The (Baker), **Supp. XIII: 41–43,** 44, 45, 48, 55
"Mezzo Cammin" (Longfellow), **II:** 490
"Mi Abuelo" (Ríos), **Supp. IV Part 2:** 541
Miami (Didion), **Supp. IV Part 1:** 199, 210
Miami and the Siege of Chicago (Mailer), **Retro. Supp. II:** 206
Miasma (Holding), **Supp. XXII: 121–122**
"Michael" (Wordsworth), **III:** 523
Michael, Magali Cornier, **Supp. XIII:** 32
"Michael Angelo: A Fragment" (Longfellow), **II:** 490, 494, 495, 506; **Retro. Supp. II:** 167
"Michael Egerton" (Price), **Supp. VI:** 257–258, 260
Michael Kohlhaas (Kleist), **Supp. IV Part 1:** 224
Michael O'Halloran (Stratton-Porter), **Supp. XX: 222**
Michaels, Leonard, **Supp. XVI: 201–215**
Michaels, Walter Benn, **Retro. Supp. I:** 115, 369, 379
Michael Scarlett (Cozens), **I:** 358–359, 378
"Michael's Veterans Remember" (Espaillat), **Supp. XXI:** 110
Michaux, Henri, **Supp. XVI:** 288
Michelangelo, **I:** 18; **II:** 11–12; **III:** 124; **Supp. I Part 1:** 363; **Supp. XVII:** 112
Michel-Michot, Paulette, **Supp. XI:** 224–225
Michelson, Albert, **IV:** 27
"Michigan Avenue" (Hecht), **Supp. XXVII:** 85
Mickelsson's Ghosts (Gardner), **Supp. VI:** 63, **73–74**
Mickiewicz, Adam, **Supp. II Part 1:** 299
"Microscope" (Trethewey), **Supp. XXI:** 251
Midair (Conroy), **Supp. XVI:** 63, **71–72**
"Mid-Air" (Conroy), **Supp. XVI:** 69, 71
Mid-American Chants (Anderson), **I:** 109, 114
"Midas" (Winters), **Supp. II Part 2:** 801
"Mid-August at Sourdough Mountain Lookout" (Snyder), **Supp. VIII:** 292–293
Midcentury (Dos Passos), **I:** 474, 475, 478, 490, 492–494; **Supp. I Part 2:** 646
Mid-Century American Poets, **III:** 532
"Mid-Day" (Doolittle), **Supp. I Part 1:** 266–267
"Middle Age" (R. Lowell), **II:** 550
"Middle-Aged, Middle-Class Woman at Midnight, A" (Taggard), **Supp. XXII:** 282–283
"Middleaged Man, The" (Simpson), **Supp. IX:** 274–275
Middle Ages, The (Gurney), **Supp. V:** 96, 105, 108
Middlebrook, Diane Wood, **Supp. IV**

Part 2: 444, 451; **Supp. XXVI:** 66
"Middle Daughter, The" (Kingsolver), **Supp. VII:** 209
Middlemarch (G. Eliot), **I:** 457, 459; **II:** 290, 291; **Retro. Supp. I:** 225; **Supp. I Part 1:** 174; **Supp. IX:** 43; **Supp. XI:** 68; **Supp. XII:** 335
Middle of My Tether, The: Familiar Essays (Epstein), **Supp. XIV: 106–107**
"Middle of Nowhere, The" (Wagoner), **Supp. IX:** 327–328
Middle of the Journey, The (Trilling), **Supp. III Part 2:** 495, 504–506
"Middle of the Way" (Kinnell), **Supp. III Part 1:** 242
Middle Passage (C. Johnson), **Supp. VI: 194–196,** 198, 199; **Supp. XIII:** 182
"Middle Passage" (Hayden), **Supp. II Part 1:** 363, 375–376
Middlesex (Eugenides), **Supp. XXIV:** 131, 134–135, **138–142**
"Middle Toe of the Right Foot, The" (Bierce), **I:** 203
Middleton, Thomas, **Retro. Supp. I:** 62
"Middle Way, The"(Hadas), **Supp. XXIII:** 121
Middle Years, The (James), **II:** 337–338; **Retro. Supp. I:** 235
"Middle Years, The" (James), **Retro. Supp. I:** 228, 272
"Midnight" (Dunn), **Supp. XI:** 147
"Midnight Consultations, The" (Freneau), **Supp. II Part 1:** 257
Midnight Cry, A (Mather), **Supp. II Part 2:** 460
"Midnight Gladness" (Levertov), **Supp. III Part 1:** 284–285
Midnight Lantern (Gallagher), **Supp. XXIV:** 167, 171
"Midnight Lantern" (Gallagher), **Supp. XXIV:** 171
"Midnight Magic" (Mason), **Supp. VIII:** 146
Midnight Magic: Selected Stories of Bobbie Ann Mason (Mason), **Supp. VIII:** 148
Midnight Mass (Bowles), **Supp. IV Part 1:** 93
"Midnight Postscript" (F. Wright), **Supp. XVII:** 245, 246
Midnight Queen, The (Lippard), **Supp. XXIII:** 180
"Midnight Salvage" (Rich), **Retro. Supp. III:** 252
Midnight Salvage: Poems 1995–1998 (Rich), **Retro. Supp. III:** 252
"Midnight Show" (Shapiro), **Supp. II Part 2:** 705
"Midpoint" (Updike), **Retro. Supp. I:** 321, 323, 327, 330, 335
Midpoint and Other Poems (Updike), **IV:** 214
"Midrash on Happiness" (Paley), **Supp. VI:** 217
"Midsummer" (Bronk), **Supp. XXI:** 30
"Midsummer in the Blueberry Barrens" (Clampitt), **Supp. IX:** 40–41
"Midsummer Letter" (Carruth), **Supp. XVI:** 47
Midsummer Night's Dream, A (Shakespeare), **Supp. I Part 1:** 369–370; **Supp. X:** 69
Midsummer Night's Sex Comedy, A (film; Allen), **Supp. XV:** 8
"Midwest" (Stafford), **Supp. XI:** 317
"Midwest Poetics" (C. Baxter), **Supp. XVII:** 18
Mieder, Wolfgang, **Supp. XIV:** 126
Mies van der Rohe, Ludwig, **Supp. IV Part 1:** 40
Mighty Aphrodite (film; Allen), **Supp. XV:** 11
"Mighty Fortress, A" (Leopold), **Supp. XIV:** 185
"Mighty Lord, The (Rowson), **Supp. XV:** 243
"Migration, The" (Tate), **IV:** 130
Mihailovitch, Bata, **Supp. VIII:** 272
Mikado, The (Gilbert and Sullivan), **Supp. XXI:** 151
Miklitsch, Robert, **Supp. IV Part 2:** 628, 629
Mikolowski, Ken and Ann, **Supp. XXIV:** 43
Mila 18 (Uris), **Supp. IV Part 1:** 379; **Supp. XX: 244, 247, 248, 251–252, 253**
Milagro Beanfield War, The (film), **Supp. XIII:** 267
Milagro Beanfield War, The (Nichols), **Supp. XIII:** 253, **265–266**
Milburn, Michael, **Supp. XI:** 239, 242
Milch, David, **Supp. XI:** 348
Mild Day, The (Bronk), **Supp. XXI:** 32
Miles, Barry, **Supp. XII:** 123
Miles, Diana, **Retro. Supp. III:** 139
Miles, Jack, **Supp. VIII:** 86
Miles, Josephine, **Supp. XIII:** 275
Miles, Julie, **I:** 199
Miles, Kitty, **I:** 199
"Miles of Night, The" (Halliday), **Supp. XIX:** 91
Milestone, Lewis, **Supp. I Part 1:** 281
Milestones (Kramer), **Supp. XXVI:** 26
Miles Wallingford (Cooper). See Afloat and Ashore (Cooper)
Milford, Kate, **Supp. XVIII:** 150
Milford, Nancy, **II:** 83; **Supp. IX:** 60
Milhaud, Darius, **Supp. IV Part 1:** 81
Miligate, Michael, **IV:** 123, 130, 132
"Militant Nudes" (Hardwick), **Supp. III Part 1:** 210–211
"Military Parachuting Exercise" (Huddle), **Supp. XXVI:** 150, 153
Milk (film), **Supp. XX: 269**
"Milk Bottles" (Anderson), **I:** 114
"Milk Prose" (Weigl), **Supp. XIX:** 278
Milk Train Doesn't Stop Here Anymore, The (T. Williams), **IV:** 382, 383, 384, 386, 390, 391, 392, 393, 394, 395, 398
Mill, James, **II:** 357
Mill, John Stuart, **III:** 294–295; **Supp. XI:** 196; **Supp. XIV:** 22
Millar, Kenneth. See Macdonald, Ross
Millar, Margaret (Margaret Sturm), **Supp. IV Part 2:** 464, 465
Millay, Cora, **III:** 123, 133–134, 135–136
Millay, Edna St. Vincent, **I:** 482; **II:** 530; **III: 122–144; IV:** 433, 436; **Retro. Supp. II:** 48; **Supp. I Part 2:** 707, 714, 726; **Supp. IV Part 1:** 168; **Supp. IV Part 2:** 607; **Supp. IX:** 20; **Supp. V:** 113; **Supp. XIV:** 120, 121, 122, 127; **Supp. XV:** 42, 46, 51, 250, 293, 307; **Supp. XVII:** 69, 75, 96; **Supp. XXII:** 273; **Supp. XXIII:** 164; **Supp. XXVI:** 170, 171; **Supp. XXVII:** 261, 283, 284
Millennium Approaches (Kushner), **Supp. IX:** 141, 142, 145
Miller, Arthur, **I:** 81, 94; **III: 145–169; Retro. Supp. III: 165–181,** 313; **Supp. IV Part 1:** 359; **Supp. IV Part 2:** 574; **Supp. VIII:** 334; **Supp. XIII:** 127; **Supp. XIV:** 102, 239; **Supp. XVI:** 194
Miller, Mrs. Arthur (Ingeborg Morath), **III:** 162–163
Miller, Mrs. Arthur (Marilyn Monroe), **III:** 161, 162–163
Miller, Mrs. Arthur (Mary Grace Slattery), **III:** 146, 161
Miller, Brown, **Supp. IV Part 1:** 67
Miller, Carol, **Supp. IV Part 1:** 400, 405, 409, 410, 411
Miller, Caroline, **Supp. XXII: 187–201**
Miller, Henry, **I:** 97, 157; **III:** 40, **170–192; IV:** 138; **Retro. Supp. II:** 327; **Supp. I Part 2:** 546; **Supp. V:** 119, 131; **Supp. X:** 183, 185, 187, 194, 195; **Supp. XIII:** 1, 17; **Supp. XXII:** 88, 256, 257, 258; **Supp. XXIII:** 100; **Supp. XXIV:** 52, 281

Miller, Henry (actor), **Supp. XVI:** 182
Miller, Herman, **Supp. I Part 2:** 614, 617
Miller, James E., Jr., **IV:** 352
Miller, Jean Baker, **Supp. XXII:** 18
Miller, Jeffrey, **Supp. IV Part 1:** 95
Miller, J. Hillis, **Supp. IV Part 1:** 387
Miller, Jim Wayne, **Supp. XX: 161–176; Supp. XXIII:** 39
Miller, Joaquin, **I:** 193, 195, 459; **Supp. II Part 1:** 351
Miller, John Duncan, **Supp. I Part 2:** 604
Miller, John E., **Supp. XXII:** 295
Miller, John M., **Supp. XXII:** 214, 218
Miller, Jonathan, **Retro. Supp. II:** 181
Miller, Laura, **Supp. XIII:** 48; **Supp. XIX:** 53, 54, 56; **Supp. XXII:** 239; **Supp. XXV:** 12, 13
Miller, Marilyn, **Supp. XVI:** 187
Miller, Matt, **Supp. XV:** 211
Miller, Matthew, **Supp. XVI:** 47, 51
Miller, Orilla, **Supp. I Part 1:** 48
Miller, Perry, **I:** 546, 547, 549, 550, 560; **IV:** 186; **Supp. I Part 1:** 31, 104; **Supp. I Part 2:** 484; **Supp. IV Part 2:** 422; **Supp. VIII:** 101; **Supp. XXV:** 251
Miller, R. Baxter, **Retro. Supp. I:** 195, 207
Miller, Rebecca, **Retro. Supp. III:** 177
Miller, Robert Ellis, **II:** 588
Miller, Ruth, **Supp. X:** 324
Miller, Stuart, **Supp. XVI:** 242
Miller, Sue, **Supp. X:** 77, 85; **Supp. XI:** 190; **Supp. XII: 289–305**
Miller of Old Church, The (Glasgow), **II:** 175, 181
"Miller's Tale" (Chaucer), **III:** 283
Miller Williams and the Poetry of the Particular (Burns), **Supp. XV:** 339
Millett, Kate, **Supp. X:** 193, 196
Millgate, Michael, **Retro. Supp. I:** 91
Mill Hand's Lunch Bucket (Bearden), **Supp. VIII:** 337
Millhauser, Steven, **Supp. XXII:** 49
Millier, Brett C., **Retro. Supp. II:** 39
Milligan, Bryce, **Supp. XIII:** 274, 275, 277
Million Little Pieces, A (Frey), **Supp. XXII:** 95; **Supp. XXIII:** 109; **Supp. XXIV:** 230, 236
Millions of Strange Shadows (Hecht), **Supp. X:** 57, **62–65**
"Million Young Workmen, 1915, A" (Sandburg), **III:** 585
Millroy the Magician (Theroux), **Supp. VIII:** 325
Mills, Alice, **Supp. XIII:** 233
Mills, Benjamin Fay, **III:** 176
Mills, C. Wright, **Supp. I Part 2:** 648, 650
Mills, Florence, **Supp. I Part 1:** 322
Mills, Ralph J., Jr., **III:** 530; **Supp. IV Part 1:** 64; **Supp. XI:** 311
Mills, Tedi López, **Supp. XVI:** 281
Mills of the Kavanaughs, The (R. Lowell), **II:** 542–543, 546, 550; **III:** 508; **Retro. Supp. II:** 178, 179, 188; **Supp. XXIII:** 211
"Mills of the Kavanaughs, The" (R. Lowell), **II:** 542–543
Milne, A. A., **Supp. IX:** 189; **Supp. XXIV:** 132, 133
Milne, A. J. M., **I:** 278
Milosz, Czeslaw, **Supp. III Part 2:** 630; **Supp. VIII:** 20, 22; **Supp. XI:** 267, 312; **Supp. XVII:** 241; **Supp. XX: 165; Supp. XXI:** 132; **Supp. XXII:** 92; **Supp. XXIII:** 134, 140
Miltner, Robert, **Supp. XI:** 142
Milton, Edith, **Supp. VIII:** 79; **Supp. X:** 82
Milton, John, **I:** 6, 138, 273, 587–588; **II:** 11, 15, 113, 130, 411, 540, 542; **III:** 40, 124, 201, 225, 274, 468, 471, 486, 487, 503, 511; **IV:** 50, 82, 126, 137, 155, 157, 241, 279, 347, 422, 461, 494; **Retro. Supp. I:** 60, 67, 127, 360; **Retro. Supp. II:** 161, 295; **Retro. Supp. III:** 104; **Supp. I Part 1:** 124, 150, 370; **Supp. I Part 2:** 412, 422, 491, 501, 522, 622, 722, 724; **Supp. IV Part 2:** 430, 634; **Supp. VIII:** 294; **Supp. X:** 22, 23, 36; **Supp. XII:** 180; **Supp. XIV:** 5, 7; **Supp. XX: 108; Supp. XXIII:** 122; **Supp. XXIV:** 159
Milton, John R., **Supp. IV Part 2:** 503
Milton and His Modern Critics (L. P. Smith), **Supp. XIV:** 347
"Milton by Firelight" (Snyder), **Supp. II Part 1:** 314; **Supp. VIII:** 294
"Miltonic Sonnet, A" (Wilbur), **Supp. III Part 2:** 558
Mimesis (Auerbach), **III:** 453
"Mimnermos and the Motions of Hedonism" (Carson), **Supp. XII: 99–100**
"Mimnermos Interviews, The" (Carson), **Supp. XII: 100–101**
Mims, Edwin, **Supp. I Part 1:** 362, 364, 365, 371
"Mind" (Wilbur), **Supp. III Part 2:** 554
"Mind, The" (Kinnell), **Supp. III Part 1:** 245
Mind Breaths: Poems 1972–1977 (Ginsberg), **Supp. II Part 1:** 326
Mindfield: New and Selected Poems (Corso), **Supp. XII: 136**
"Mind in the Modern World" (Trilling), **Supp. III Part 2:** 512
"Mind Is Shapely, Art Is Shapely" (Ginsberg), **Supp. II Part 1:** 327
Mindlin, Henrique, **Supp. I Part 1:** 92
Mind of My Mind (O. Butler), **Supp. XIII:** 62, 63
Mind of Primitive Man, The (Boas), **Supp. XIV:** 209
Mind-Reader, The (Wilbur), **Supp. III Part 2:** 560–562
"Mind-Reader, The" (Wilbur), **Supp. III Part 2:** 561–562
"Mind's Landscape on an Early Winter Day, The" (Bronk), **Supp. XXI:** 28
"Mind's Own Place, The" (Oppen), **Supp. XXVI:** 227
Mindwheel (Pinsky), **Supp. VI:** 235
Minear, Richard H., **Supp. XVI:** 101, 102
"Mined Country" (Wilbur), **Supp. III Part 2:** 546–548
"Minefields" (Espaillat), **Supp. XXI:** 106
"Mine Own John Berryman" (Levine), **Supp. V:** 179–180
Miner, Bob, **Supp. V:** 23
Miner, Earl, **III:** 466, 479
Miner, Madonne, **Supp. XIII:** 29
Miner, Valerie, **Supp. XXIII:** 295, 296
"Minerva Writes Poems" (Cisneros), **Supp. VII:** 63–64, 66
Mingus, Charles, **Supp. IX:** 152
"Mingus in Diaspora" (Matthews), **Supp. IX:** 166
"Mingus in Shadow" (Matthews), **Supp. IX:** 168–169
Ming Yellow (Marquand), **III:** 56
"Minimal, The" (Roethke), **III:** 531–532
Minimus Poems, The (X. J. Kennedy), **Supp. XV:** 169–170
"Mini-novela: Rosa y sus espinas" (Mora), **Supp. XIII:** 218
"Minions of Midas, The" (London), **II:** 474–475
Minister's Charge, The, or The Apprenticeship of Lemuel Barber (Howells), **II:** 285–286, 287
Minister's Wooing, The (Stowe), **II:** 541
"Minister's Wooing, The" (Stowe), **Supp. I Part 2:** 592–595
"Ministration of Our Departed Friends, The" (Stowe), **Supp. I Part 2:** 586–587
Minna and Myself (Bodenheim), **Supp. XXV:** 21
"Minneapolis Poem, The" (Wright), **Supp. III Part 2:** 601–602

Minnesota Grain Show, The (radio, Keillor), **Supp. XVI:** 170
"Minnesota Transcendentalist" (Peseroff), **Supp. IV Part 1:** 71
Minnie, Temple, **II:** 344
Minock, Daniel, **Supp. XXVI:** 187
Minority Report: H. L. Mencken's Notebooks (Mencken), **III:** 112
Minor Pleasures of Life, The (Macaulay), **Supp. XIV:** 348
"Minor Poems" (Eliot), **I:** 579
"Minor Poet" (Hay), **Supp. XIV:** 127
"Minor Topics" (Howells), **II:** 274
Minot, Stephen, **Supp. XXIII:** 290
Minot, Susan, **Supp. VI: 203–215**
"Minotaur Loves His Labyrinth, The" (Simic), **Supp. VIII:** 270, 279, 281
"Minstrel Man" (Hughes), **Supp. I Part 1:** 325
Mint (Nye), **Supp. XIII:** 277
"Minting Time" (Sarton), **Supp. VIII:** 259
Mint Snowball (Nye), **Supp. XIII:** 277–278, **284–285**
"Mint Snowball" (Nye), **Supp. XIII:** 278, 284
"Mint Snowball II" (Nye), **Supp. XIII:** 284, 285
Minty Alley (C. L. R. James), **Supp. XXI:** 159, 161
Mintz, Susannah B., **Supp. XXVI:** 52
Mintzlaff, Dorothy, **Supp. XV:** 153
Minus, Marian, **Supp. XVIII:** 282
Minutes to Go (Corso, Gysin, Beiles and Burroughs), **Supp. XII:** 129
Mi querido Rafa (Hinojosa). See Dear Rafe (Hinojosa)
Mirabai: Ecstatic Poems (Hirshfield and Bly, trans.), **Supp. XXIII:** 136
Mirabell: Books of Number (Merrill), **Supp. III Part 1:** 332–334
"Miracle" (Carver), **Supp. III Part 1:** 139–140
Miracle at St. Anna (film, Lee), **Supp. XXVI:** 199
Miracle at St. Anna (McBride), **Supp. XXVI:** 194–199
Miracle at Verdun (Chlumberg), **Supp. XIX:** 242
Miracle Boy and Other Stories (P. Benedict), **Supp. XXIII:** 35, **45–50**
"Miracle Boy"(P. Benedict), **Supp. XXIII:** 45–46, 50
"Miracle for Breakfast, A" (Bishop), **Retro. Supp. II:** 43
Miracle of Catfish, A (L. Brown), **Supp. XXI:** 39–40, 47, **48**
"Miracle of Lava Canyon, The" (Henry), **Supp. II Part 1:** 389, 390
Miracle of Mindfulness, The: A Manual on Meditation (Thich Nhat Hanh), **Supp. V:** 199–200
Mirage (Masters), **Supp. I Part 2:** 459, 470, 471
"Mirages, The" (Hayden), **Supp. II Part 1:** 373
"Miranda" (Buck), **Supp. II Part 1:** 128
Miranda, Carmen, **Supp. XII:** 165
Miranda, Francisco de, **Supp. I Part 2:** 522
"Miranda Over the Valley" (Dubus), **Supp. VII:** 81–83
"Miriam" (Capote), **Supp. III Part 1:** 117, 120, 122
"Miriam" (Whittier), **Supp. I Part 2:** 691, 703
"Miriam Tazewell" (Ransom), **Supp. X:** 58
"Mirror" (Merrill), **Supp. III Part 1:** 322
"Mirror" (Plath), **Retro. Supp. II:** 248–249, 257
"Mirror" (Rash), **Supp. XXVII:** 222
"Mirror, The" (Glück), **Supp. V:** 83
"Mirror, The"(Hadas), **Supp. XXIII:** 116
"Mirroring Evil: Nazi Images/Recent Art" (Epstein), **Supp. XII:** 166
"Mirror of Leopold Leopoldovitch Siegelevsky, The" (Siegel), **Supp. XXII:** 257–258
Mirrors (Creeley), **Supp. IV Part 1:** 156
Mirrors and Windows (Nemerov), **III:** 269, 275–277
Mirrors of Astonishment (Hadas), **Supp. XXIII: 115–116**
"Mirrors of Chartres Street" (Faulkner), **II:** 56
"Mirrors of Tuzun Thune, The" (Howard), **Supp. XXVII:** 123
Mirsky, Norman, **Supp. XX: 244**
Mirvis, Tova, **Supp. XX: 177–191**
Misanthrope, The (Molière; Wilbur, trans.), **Supp. III Part 2:** 552, 560
Miscellaneous Poems (Rowson), **Supp. XV:** 243
Miscellaneous Works of Mr. Philip Freneau, Containing His Essays and Additional Poems (Freneau), **Supp. II Part 1:** 263, 264, 266
Miscellany of American Poetry, A (Untermeyer, ed.), **Supp. XV:** 305, 310
Misérables, Les (Hugo), **II:** 179; **Supp. I Part 1:** 280
Misery (King), **Supp. V:** 140, 141, 142, 147–148, 151, 152
Mises, Ludwig von, **Supp. IV Part 2:** 524
Misfits, The (A. Miller), **III:** 147, 149, 156, 161–162, 163; **Retro. Supp. III:** 170, 172
Misfit: The Strange Life of Frederick Exley (Yardley), **Supp. XXIII:** 97
Mish, Jeanetta Calhoun, **Supp. XXVI:** 112
"Mishösha, or the Magician and his daughters: A Chippewa Tale"(J. Schoolcraft), **Supp. XXIII:** 234, 235
"Misogamist, The" (Dubus), **Supp. VII:** 86–87
Misread City, The: New Literary Los Angeles (Gioia and Timberg, eds.), **Supp. XV:** 116
Misrepresentations Corrected, and Truth Vindicated, in a Reply to the Rev. Mr. Solomon Williams's Book (Edwards), **I:** 549
Miss Crandall's School for Young Ladies & Little Misses of Color (Nelson and Alexander), **Supp. XVIII:** 171, 175, 181, **185–186**
"Miss Cynthie" (R. Fisher), **Supp. XIX:** 65, 69
Miss Doll, Go Home (Markson), **Supp. XVII:** 138
"Miss Ella" (Z. Fitzgerald), **Supp. IX:** 57, 59, **71–72**
"Miss Emily and the Bibliographer" (Tate), **Supp. II Part 1:** 103
"Miss Furr and Miss Skeene" (Stein), **IV:** 29–30
"Missing Child" (Simic), **Supp. VIII:** 282
"Missing in Action" (Komunyakaa), **Supp. XIII:** 123, 124
Missing/Kissing: Missing Marisa, Kissing Christine (Shanley), **Supp. XIV:** 316
Missing Link (X. J. Kennedy), **Supp. XV:** 165
Missing Link, The (Wells), **Supp. XXVI:** 281
"Missing Poem, The" (Halliday), **Supp. XIX:** 93–94
"Missionary Brings a Young Native to America, A" (H. Johnson), **Supp. XXVI:** 167, 173, 174
"Mission of Jane, The" (Wharton), **Retro. Supp. I:** 367
"Missions, The" (Rodriguez), **Supp. XIV:** 303
Mission to Moscow (film), **Supp. I Part 1:** 281
"Mississippi" (Bass), **Supp. XVI:** 17

"Mississippi" (Faulkner), **Retro. Supp. I:** 77
"Mississippi" (Simpson), **Supp. IX:** 271
"Missive Missile, A" (Frost), **Retro. Supp. III:** 104
"Miss Kate in H-1" (Twain), **IV:** 193
Miss Kelly (Holding), **Supp. XXII: 133–134**
Miss Leonora When Last Seen (Taylor), **Supp. V:** 323
Miss Lonelyhearts (West), **I:** 107; **II:** 436; **III:** 357; **IV:** 287, 288, 290–297, 300, 301, 305, 306; **Retro. Supp. II:** 321, 322, 325, 328, **332–335**
"Miss Lora" (Díaz), **Supp. XXIV:** 86
Miss Mamma Aimee (Caldwell), **I:** 308, 309, 310
"Miss Mary Pask" (Wharton), **IV:** 316; **Retro. Supp. I:** 382
"Miss McEnders" (Chopin), **Retro. Supp. II:** 67
Miss Morissa: Doctor of the Gold Trail (Sandoz), **Supp. XXIV:** 244, **255–256**
"Missoula Softball Tournament" (Hugo), **Supp. VI:** 132
Miss Pinkerton (Rinehart), **Supp. XXV:** 197
Miss Ravenel's Conversion from Secession to Loyalty (De Forest), **IV:** 350
Miss Saigon (musical), **Supp. XXI:** 155
"Miss Tempy's Watchers" (Jewett), **II:** 401; **Retro. Supp. II:** 139
"Miss Terriberry to Wed in Suburbs" (Updike), **Retro. Supp. I:** 335
"Miss Urquhart's Tiara" (Jarman), **Supp. XVII:** 116
Miss Witherspoon (Durang), **Supp. XXIV:** 113, **126**
"Mist, The" (King), **Supp. V:** 144
"Mistaken Charity, A" (Freeman), **Retro. Supp. II:** 138
"Mister Brother" (Cunningham), **Supp. XV:** 68
Misterioso (Sorrentino), **Supp. XXI:** 236, 237
"Mister Toussan" (Ellison), **Retro. Supp. II:** 124–125; **Supp. II Part 1:** 238
"Mistress of Sydenham Plantation, The" (Jewett), **Retro. Supp. II:** 141
Mitcham, Matthew, **Supp. XX: 264**
Mitchell, Burroughs, **Supp. XI:** 218, 222, 227
Mitchell, David, **Supp. XXIV:** 86
Mitchell, Don, **Supp. XXII:** 207, 211, 212
Mitchell, Joan, **Supp. XXIII:** 210
Mitchell, Margaret, **II:** 177; **Supp. XX: 243; Supp. XXII:** 195
Mitchell, Pat, **Supp. XXIV:** 35, 42; **Supp. XXVII:** 18, 24
Mitchell, Roger, **Supp. IV Part 1:** 70; **Supp. XV:** 213, 215
Mitchell, Dr. S. Weir, **IV:** 310
Mitchell, Tennessee. See Anderson, Mrs. Sherwood (Tennessee Mitchell)
Mitchell, Verner, **Supp. XVIII:** 281, 286
Mitchell, Werner, **Supp. XXVI:** 165, 170, 171–172, 174
Mitchell, Wesley C., **Supp. I Part 2:** 632, 643
"Mitchie-Gawa" (Taggard), **Supp. XXII:** 272
Mitch Miller (Masters), **Supp. I Part 2:** 456, 466, 469–471, 474, 475, 476
Mitchum, Robert, **Supp. IX:** 95, 250
Mitgang, Herbert, **Supp. IV Part 1:** 220, 226, 307; **Supp. VIII:** 124; **Supp. XIX:** 251; **Supp. XX: 243**
Mitla Pass (Uris), **Supp. XX: 244, 247, 248, 256**
Mixed Company: Collected Short Stories (Shaw), **Supp. XIX:** 251
"Mixed Sequence" (Roethke), **III:** 547
Miyazawa Kenji, **Supp. VIII:** 292
Mizener, Arthur, **II:** 77, 81, 84, 94; **IV:** 132; **Supp. XVIII:** 249
Mizner, Addison, **Supp. XVI:** 191
Mizner, Wilson, **Supp. XVI:** 191, 195
Mladenoff, Nancy, **Supp. X:** 176
"M'liss: An Idyl of Red Mountain" (Harte), **Supp. II Part 1:** 339
"Mnemonic Devices" (Goldbarth), **Supp. XII:** 183
"Mnemosyne" (Hölderlin), **Supp. XXIV:** 152
"Mobile in Back of the Smithsonian, The" (Swenson), **Supp. IV Part 2:** 646
Mobilio, Albert, **Supp. VIII:** 3; **Supp. XIX:** 45; **Supp. XVIII:** 144
Moby Dick (film), **Supp. IV Part 1:** 102, 116
Moby Dick; or, The Whale (Melville), **I:** 106, 354; **II:** 33, 224–225, 236, 539–540; **III:** 28–29, 74, 75, 77, 81, 82, 83–86, 87, 89, 90, 91, 93, 94, 95, 359, 453, 556; **IV:** 57, 199, 201, 202; **Retro. Supp. I:** 160, 220, 243, 244, 248, **249–253**, 254, 256, 257, 335; **Retro. Supp. II:** 121, 186, 275; **Retro. Supp. III:** 147, 148–149, 150, 151, 155, 156–157, 160, 161; **Supp. I Part 1:** 249; **Supp. I Part 2:** 579; **Supp. IV Part 2:** 613; **Supp. V:** 281; **Supp. VIII:** 106, 188, 198; **Supp. XXI:** 159; **Supp. XXII:** 81, 268; **Supp. XXIV:** 88
Mock, John, **Supp. XIII:** 174
"Mocking-Bird, The" (Bierce), **I:** 202
"Mock Orange" (Glück), **Supp. V:** 84–85
Modarressi, Mitra, **Supp. IV Part 2:** 657
"Model Father" (Huddle), **Supp. XXVI:** 150
"Model of Christian Charity, A" (Winthrop), **Retro. Supp. III:** 2
Models of Misrepresentation: On the Fiction of E. L. Doctorow (Morris), **Supp. IV Part 1:** 231
Model World and Other Stories, A (Chabon), **Supp. XI:** 66
Modern American and British Poetry (Untermeyer, ed.), **Supp. XV:** 306
Modern American Poetry (Untermeyer, ed.), **Retro. Supp. III:** 100; **Supp. XV:** 293, 303, 306, 312
Modern American Poets (Aiken, ed.), **Supp. XXVI:** 225
Modern American Verse (Untermeyer, ed.), **Supp. XV:** 301
Modern Brazilian Architecture (Bishop, trans.), **Supp. I Part 1:** 92
Modern British Poetry (Untermeyer, ed.), **Supp. XV:** 305, 308, 312
Modern Fiction Studies, **Supp. V:** 238
Modern Fiction Studies (Haegert), **Supp. XVI:** 69
"Modern Greek for 'Nightmare' Is Ephialtes, The" (Stallings), **Supp. XXV:** 233
Modern Instance a Novel, A (Howells), **II:** 275, 279, 282–283, 285
Modern Library, The, **Retro. Supp. I:** 112, 113
Modern Mephistopheles, A (Alcott), **Supp. I Part 1:** 37–38
Modern Poetic Sequence, The (Rosenthal), **Supp. V:** 333
"Modern Poetry" (Crane), **I:** 390
Modern Poetry and the Tradition (Brooks), **Supp. XIV: 5–7**
"Modern Primer: Helpful Hints to Tell Appearances from Truth" (Taubman), **Supp. XXV:** 106
"Modern Race Creeds and Their Fallacies" (Locke), **Supp. XIV:** 210
Modern Rhetoric, with Readings (Brooks and Warren), **Supp. XIV:** 11
"Modern Sorcery" (Simic), **Supp. VIII:** 283

Modern Times (album, Dylan), **Supp. XVIII:** 28, 31, 33
"Modern Times" (Zukofsky), **Supp. III Part 2:** 624
Modern Writer, The (Anderson), **I:** 117
Modersohn, Otto, **Supp. I Part 2:** 573
Modersohn, Mrs. Otto (Paula Becker), **Supp. I Part 2:** 573–574
"Modes of Being" (Levertov), **Supp. III Part 1:** 282
Modest Enquiry into the Nature and Necessity of a Paper-Currency, A (Franklin), **II:** 108–109
"Modest Proposal, A" (Swift), **I:** 295; **Retro. Supp. II:** 287
"Modest Proposal with Feline Feeling, A" (Neugeboren), **Supp. XVI:** 219
"Modest Self-Tribute, A" (Wilson), **IV:** 431, 432
Modigliani, Amedeo, **Supp. XXVI:** 259
Moeller, Philip, **III:** 398, 399
"Moench von Berchtesgaden, Der" (Voss), **I:** 199–200
Moers, Ellen, **Retro. Supp. II:** 99
Moe's Villa and Other Stories (Purdy), **Supp. VII:** 270, 280
Moffat, Juan, **Supp. XX: 52**
Moffet, Penelope, **Supp. XXIV:** 165, 167
Mogen, David, **Supp. IV Part 1:** 106
Mohammed, **I:** 480; **II:** 1
Mohawk (Russo), **Supp. XII: 326–328**
Moir, William Wilmerding, **Supp. V:** 279
Mojo Hand (Phillips), **Supp. XXIII:** 174
Moldaw, Carol, **Supp. XV:** 264; **Supp. XVII:** 127, 130
"Moles" (Oliver), **Supp. VII:** 235
Molesworth, Charles, **Supp. IV Part 1:** 39; **Supp. VIII:** 292, 306; **Supp. XIX:** 121–122
Molière (Jean-Baptiste Poquelin), **III:** 113; **Supp. I Part 2:** 406; **Supp. III Part 2:** 552, 560; **Supp. IV Part 2:** 585; **Supp. V:** 101
"Molino Rojo, El" (Ríos), **Supp. IV Part 2:** 544
Moll Flanders (Defoe), **Supp. V:** 127; **Supp. XIII:** 43
"Molloch in State Street" (Whittier), **Supp. I Part 2:** 687
"Moll Pitcher" (Whittier), **Supp. I Part 2:** 684
"Molly Brant, Iroquois Matron" (Gunn Allen), **Supp. IV Part 1:** 331
"Molly Brant to Willie"(Kenny), **Supp. XXIII:** 153
Molnar, Ferenc, **Supp. XVI:** 187
"Moloch" (H. Miller), **III:** 177
Momaday, N. Scott, **Supp. IV Part 1:** 274, 323, 324, 404; **Supp. IV Part 2: 479–496,** 504, 557, 562; **Supp. XII:** 209; **Supp. XVIII:** 58
" 'Momentary Stay against Confusion,' A: Frank Conroy's Stop-Time" (T. Adams), **Supp. XVI:** 69
Moment of Untruth (Lacy), **Supp. XV:** 206, 207
Moments of the Italian Summer (Wright), **Supp. III Part 2:** 602
Moment to Moment: Poems of a Mountain Recluse (Budbill), **Supp. XIX:** 2, 7, **9–10**
"Momus" (Robinson), **III:** 508
Monaghan, Charles, **Supp. XIX:** 155
Monaghan, Pat, **Supp. XI:** 121
Monaghan, Patricia, **Supp. XVII:** 76, 123, 127, 129
Mona Lisa Overdrive (W. Gibson), **Supp. XVI:** 119, 120, **127–128**
"Mon Ami" (Bourne), **I:** 227
Monday Night (Boyle), **Supp. XXIV:** 54
Monet, Claude, **Retro. Supp. I:** 378
"Monet's 'Waterlilies' " (Hayden), **Supp. II Part 1:** 361–362
Monette, Paul, **Supp. X: 145–161**
Money (Amis), **Retro. Supp. I:** 278
"Money" (Matthews), **Supp. IX:** 166
"Money" (Nemerov), **III:** 287
Money, Money, Money (Wagoner), **Supp. IX:** 324, **333–334**
Moneyball: The Art of Winning an Unfair Game (M. Lewis), **Supp. XVII:** 210
Moneychangers, The (Sinclair), **Supp. V:** 285
Money Writes! (Sinclair), **Supp. V:** 277
Monica, Saint, **IV:** 140
Monikins, The (Cooper), **I:** 348, 354
Monk, Craig, **Supp. XXIV:** 64
Monk, Thelonious, **Supp. XVIII:** 62
Monk and the Hangman's Daughter, The (Bierce), **I:** 199–200, 209
"Monkey" (Weigl), **Supp. XIX:** 278
Monkey Business (screenplay, Hecht), **Supp. XXVII:** 91, 94
"Monkey Garden, The" (Cisneros), **Supp. VII:** 63
"Monkey Junk: A Satire on Modern Divorce" (Hurston), **Retro. Supp. III:** 127
"Monkey Puzzle, The" (Moore), **III:** 194, 207, 211
Monkeys (Minot), **Supp. VI:** 203–205, **206–210**
"Monkeys, The" (Moore), **III:** 201, 202
Monkey Wars, The (Weigl), **Supp. XIX:** 276, 278–280
Monkey Wrench Gang, The (Abbey), **Supp. VIII:** 42; **Supp. XIII: 9–11,** 16
"Monk of Casal-Maggiore, The" (Longfellow), **II:** 505
"Monocle de Mon Oncle, Le" (Stevens), **IV:** 78, 84; **Retro. Supp. I:** 301; **Supp. III Part 1:** 20; **Supp. X:** 58
"Monody to the Sound of Zithers" (Boyle), **Supp. XXIV:** 63
"Monolog from a Mattress" (Untermeyer), **Supp. XV:** 307
"Monologue for Mothers" (Taggard), **Supp. XXII:** 279
"Mon Plaisir" (July), **Supp. XXIV:** 205–206
Monro, Harold, **III:** 465; **Retro. Supp. I:** 127; **Supp. XV:** 296
Monroe, Harriet, **I:** 235, 384, 390, 393; **III:** 458, 581, 586; **IV:** 74; **Retro. Supp. I:** 58, 131; **Retro. Supp. II:** 82, 83; **Supp. I Part 1:** 256, 257, 258, 262, 263, 267; **Supp. I Part 2:** 374, 387, 388, 464, 610, 611, 613, 614, 615, 616; **Supp. XIV:** 286; **Supp. XV:** 43, 299, 302; **Supp. XXV:** 18; **Supp. XXVII:** 283, 286, 289–290, 297
Monroe, James, **Supp. I Part 2:** 515, 517
Monroe, Lucy, **Retro. Supp. II:** 70
Monroe, Marilyn, **III:** 161, 162–163; **Supp. XXVII:** 95
Monroe's Embassy; or, the Conduct of the Government in Relation to Our Claims to the Navigation of the Mississippi (Brown), **Supp. I Part 1:** 146
Monson, Ander, **Supp. XXIV: 229–242**
"Monsoon Season" (Komunyakaa), **Supp. XIII:** 122
Monsour, Leslie, **Supp. XV:** 125
Monster (graphic novel, Myers), **Supp. XXVII:** 199, 202, 203, 204, 205
"Monster, The" (Crane), **I:** 418
Monster, The, and Other Stories (Crane), **I:** 409
"Monstro" (Díaz), **Supp. XXIV:** 86
Montage of a Dream Deferred (Hughes), **Retro. Supp. I:** 194, **208–209; Supp. I Part 1:** 333, 339–341
Montagu, Ashley, **Supp. I Part 1:** 314
"Montaigne" (Emerson), **II:** 6
Montaigne, Michel de, **II:** 1, 5, 6, 8,

14–15, 16, 535; **III:** 600; **Retro. Supp. I:** 247; **Supp. XIV:** 105; **Supp. XXI:** 111, 205; **Supp. XXVI:** 39
Montale, Eugenio, **Supp. III Part 1:** 320; **Supp. V:** 337–338; **Supp. VIII:** 30; **Supp. XV:** 112
Montalembert, Hughes de, **Supp. XV:** 349
"Montana Memory" (Maclean), **Supp. XIV:** 221
"Montana; or the End of Jean-Jacques Rousseau" (Fiedler), **Supp. XIII: 97–98**
"Montana Ranch Abandoned" (Hugo), **Supp. VI:** 139
"Mont Blanc" (Shelley), **Supp. IX:** 52
Montcalm, Louis Joseph de, **Supp. I Part 2:** 498
Montcalm and Wolfe (Parkman), **Supp. II Part 2:** 596, 609, 610, 611–613
Montemarano, Nicholas, **Supp. XVI:** 227
Montgomery, Benilde, **Supp. XIII:** 202
Montgomery, George, **Supp. XXIII:** 209
Montgomery, Robert, **Supp. I Part 2:** 611; **Supp. IV Part 1:** 130
Month of Sundays, A (Updike), **Retro. Supp. I:** 325, 327, 329, 330, 331, 333, 335
Monti, Luigi, **II:** 504
Montoya, José, **Supp. IV Part 2:** 545
"Montrachet-le-Jardin" (Stevens), **IV:** 82
Mont-Saint-Michel and Chartres (Adams), **I:** 1, 9, 12–14, 18, 19, 21; **Supp. I Part 2:** 417
Montserrat (Hellman), **Supp. I Part 1:** 283–285
Montserrat (Robles), **Supp. I Part 1:** 283–285
"Monument, The" (Bishop), **Supp. I Part 1:** 89
Monument, The (Strand), **Supp. IV Part 2:** 629, 630
"Monument in Utopia, A" (Schnackenberg), **Supp. XV:** 261, 263
"Monument Mountain" (Bryant), **Supp. I Part 1:** 156, 162
"Monument to After-Thought Unveiled, A" (Frost), **Retro. Supp. I:** 124
Moo (Smiley), **Supp. VI:** 292, **303–305**
Moods (Alcott), **Supp. I Part 1:** 33, 34–35, 43
Moody, Anne, **Supp. IV Part 1:** 11
Moody, Richard, **Supp. I Part 1:** 280
Moody, Rick, **Supp. XXI:** 117; **Supp. XXIV:** 131
Moody, Ron, **Supp. XXII:** 49
Moody, William Vaughn, **III:** 507; **IV:** 26
Moody, Mrs. William Vaughn, **I:** 384; **Supp. I Part 2:** 394
Moody-Freeman, Julie, **Supp. XXIII:** 91, 94, 95
"Moon" (A. Finch), **Supp. XVII:** 77
Moon, Henry Lee, **Supp. XVIII:** 281, 285
"Moon and the Night and the Men, The" (Berryman), **I:** 172
"Moon and the Yew Tree, The" (Plath), **Supp. XXVII:** 296
Moon Crossing Bridge (Gallagher), **Supp. XXIV:** 166, 170
"Moon Deluxe" (F. Barthelme), **Supp. XI:** 26, 27, 33, 36
Mooney, Tom, **I:** 505
"Moon-Face" (London), **II:** 475
Moon-Face and Other Stories (London), **II:** 483
"Moon Flock" (Dickey), **Supp. IV Part 1:** 186
Moon for the Misbegotten, A (O'Neill), **III:** 385, 401, 403, 404
Moon in a Mason Jar (Wrigley), **Supp. XVIII: 295–298**
Moon in Its Flight, The (Sorrentino), **Supp. XXI:** 226
"Moon in Its Flight, The" (Sorrentino), **Supp. XXI:** 229
Moon Is a Gong, The (Dos Passos). See Garbage Man, The (Dos Passos)
Moon Is Down, The (Steinbeck), **IV:** 51
Moon Lady, The (Tan), **Supp. X:** 289
"Moonlight Alert" (Winters), **Supp. II Part 2:** 801, 811, 815
"Moonlight: Chickens on a Road" (Wrigley), **Supp. XVIII:** 295–296, 297
"Moonlit Night" (Reznikoff), **Supp. XIV:** 285–286
Moon of the Caribbees, The (O'Neill), **III:** 388
Moon Palace (Auster), **Supp. XII:** 22, 27, **30–32**
"Moonshine" (Komunyakaa), **Supp. XIII:** 127, 128
Moons of Jupiter, The (Munro), **Supp. XXVII:** 182, 187–189
"Moons of Jupiter, The" (Munro), **Supp. XXVII:** 188–189
"Moon Solo" (Laforgue), **Supp. XIII:** 346
Moonstone, The (Collins), **Supp. XX: 236**
Moonstruck (screenplay, Shanley), **Supp. XIV:** 315, 316, **321–324**
"Moon upon her fluent Route, The" (Dickinson), **I:** 471
Moony's Kid Don't Cry (T. Williams), **IV:** 381
Moore, Arthur, **Supp. I Part 1:** 49
Moore, C. L., **Supp. XXV:** 122
Moore, Deborah Dash, **Supp. XX: 246**
Moore, Dennis, **Supp. XXVII:** 275
Moore, George, **I:** 103
Moore, Hannah, **Supp. XV:** 231
Moore, Jack B., **Supp. XXV:** 24, 26, 27
Moore, John Milton, **III:** 193
Moore, Julie L., **Supp. XXIII:** 252
Moore, Lorrie, **Supp. VIII:** 145; **Supp. X: 163–180; Supp. XXV:** 142
Moore, Marianne, **I:** 58, 285, 401, 428; **III: 193–217,** 514, 592–593; **IV:** 74, 75, 76, 91, 402; **Retro. Supp. I:** 416, 417; **Retro. Supp. II:** 39, 44, 48, 50, 82, 178, 179, 243, 244; **Supp. I Part 1:** 84, 89, 255, 257; **Supp. I Part 2:** 707; **Supp. II Part 1:** 21; **Supp. III Part 1:** 58, 60, 63; **Supp. III Part 2:** 612, 626, 627; **Supp. IV Part 1:** 242, 246, 257; **Supp. IV Part 2:** 454, 640, 641; **Supp. XIV:** 124, 130; **Supp. XV:** 306, 307; **Supp. XVII:** 131; **Supp. XXI:** 98; **Supp. XXII:** 273–274
Moore, Marie Lorena. See Moore, Lorrie
Moore, MariJo, **Supp. XXVI:** 113
Moore, Mary Tyler, **Supp. V:** 107
Moore, Mary Warner, **III:** 193
Moore, Dr. Merrill, **III:** 506
Moore, Steven, **Supp. IV Part 1:** 279, 283, 284, 285, 287; **Supp. XII:** 151; **Supp. XVII:** 230, 231, 232; **Supp. XXII:** 261, 265
Moore, Sturge, **III:** 459
Moore, Thomas, **II:** 296, 299, 303; **Supp. IX:** 104; **Supp. X:** 114; **Supp. XXIII:** 138
Moore, Virginia, **Supp. XV:** 308
Moorehead, Caroline, **Supp. XIV:** 337
Moorepack, Howard, **Supp. XV:** 199
"Moorings" (Hoffman), **Supp. XVIII:** 87
Moos, Malcolm, **III:** 116, 119
"Moose, The" (Bishop), **Retro. Supp. II:** 50; **Supp. I Part 1:** 73, 93, 94, 95; **Supp. IX:** 45, 46
"Moose Wallow, The" (Hayden), **Supp. II Part 1:** 367
"Moowis, The Indian Coquette"(J.

Schoolcraft), **Supp. XXIII:** 234
Mooyart-Doubleday, B. M., **Supp. XXVII:** 135
Mop, Moondance, and the Nagasaki Knights (Myers), **Supp. XXVII:** 206
"Moquihuitzin's Answer" (Everwine), **Supp. XV:** 78
Mora, Pat, **Supp. XIII: 213–232**
Moraga, Cherríe, **Supp. XXIII: 193–206**
"Moral Argument Against Calvinism, The" (Channing), **Supp. XXIV: 73–74,** 75
"Moral Bully, The" (Holmes), **Supp. I Part 1:** 302
"Moral Character, the Practice of Law, and Legal Education" (Hall), **Supp. VIII:** 127
"Moral Equivalent for Military Service, A" (Bourne), **I:** 230
"Moral Equivalent of War, The" (James), **II:** 361; **Supp. I Part 1:** 20
"Moral Imperatives for World Order" (Locke), **Supp. XIV:** 207, 213
Moralités Légendaires (Laforgue), **I:** 573
"Morality and Mercy in Vienna" (Pynchon), **Supp. II Part 2:** 620, 624
"Morality of Indian Hating, The" (Momaday), **Supp. IV Part 2:** 484
"Morality of Poetry, The" (Wright), **Supp. III Part 2:** 596–597, 599
Moral Man and Immoral Society (Niebuhr), **III:** 292, 295–297
"Morals Is Her Middle Name" (Hughes), **Supp. I Part 1:** 338
"Morals of Chess, The" (Franklin), **II:** 121
"Moral Substitute for War, A" (Addams), **Supp. I Part 1:** 20
"Moral Theology of Atticus Finch, The" (Shaffer), **Supp. VIII:** 127
"Moral Thought, A" (Freneau), **Supp. II Part 1:** 262
Moran, Thomas, **Supp. IV Part 2:** 603–604
Moran, William L., **Supp. XXIV:** 150–151, 152
Moran of the Lady Letty (Norris), **II:** 264; **III:** 314, 322, 327, 328, 329, 330, 331, 332, 333
Morath, Ingeborg. See Miller, Mrs. Arthur (Ingeborg Morath)
Moravec, Paul, **Supp. XIX:** 123
Moravia, Alberto, **I:** 301
More (Crooker), **Supp. XXIII: 60–62**
Moré, Gonzalo, **Supp. X:** 185
More, Henry, **I:** 132
More, Paul Elmer, **I:** 223–224, 247; **Supp. I Part 2:** 423
Moreau, Gustave, **I:** 66
"More Blues and the Abstract Truth" (Wright), **Supp. XV:** 345
More Boners (Abingdon), **Supp. XVI:** 99
More Conversations with Eudora Welty (Prenshaw, ed.), **Retro. Supp. I:** 340, 341, 342, 343, 344, 352, 353, 354
More Dangerous Thoughts (Ryan as Quin), **Supp. XVIII:** 226, **229–230,** 231, 238
More Die of Heartbreak (Bellow), **Retro. Supp. II:** 31, 33, 34
"More Girl Than Boy" (Komunyakaa), **Supp. XIII:** 117
More I Remember More (Brainard), **Supp. XXVII:** 19
"More Light! More Light! (Hecht), **Supp. X:** 60
"More Like an Extension of the Spirit: Clothing in Lyric Poems"(Hadas), **Supp. XXIII:** 124
"Morella" (Poe), **III:** 412; **Retro. Supp. II:** 270
"More Love in the Western World" (Updike), **Retro. Supp. I:** 327–328, 329
"Morels" (W. J. Smith), **Supp. XIII: 336–339**
Moreno, Gary, **Supp. XV:** 5
"More Observations Now" (Conroy), **Supp. XVI:** 75
"More of a Corpse Than a Woman" (Rukeyser), **Supp. VI:** 280
"More Pleasant Adventures" (Ashbery), **Supp. III Part 1:** 1
More Poems to Solve (Swenson), **Supp. IV Part 2:** 640, 642, 648
More Stately Mansions (O'Neill), **III:** 385, 401, 404–405
"More Than Human" (Chabon), **Supp. XI:** 71–72
More Things Change The More They Stay the Same, The (J. W. Miller), **Supp. XX: 164**
More Tish (Rinehart), **Supp. XXV:** 194
More Triva (L. P. Smith), **Supp. XIV:** 339
Morgan, Edmund S., **IV:** 149; **Supp. I Part 1:** 101, 102; **Supp. I Part 2:** 484
Morgan, Edwin, **Supp. IV Part 2:** 688
Morgan, Emanuel. See Bynner, Witter
Morgan, Henry, **II:** 432; **IV:** 63; **Supp. XXV:** 255
Morgan, Jack, **Retro. Supp. II:** 142
Morgan, J. P., **I:** 494; **III:** 14, 15
Morgan, Judith, **Supp. XVI:** 103
Morgan, Neil, **Supp. XVI:** 103
Morgan, Robert, **Supp. V:** 5; **Supp. XX: 161, 162**
Morgan, Robin, **Supp. I Part 2:** 569
Morgan, Ted, **Supp. XIV:** 141
Morgan's Passing (Tyler), **Supp. IV Part 2:** 666–667, 668, 669
Morgenstern, Dan, **Supp. XIX:** 159
Morgenthau, Hans, **III:** 291, 309
Morgenthau, Henry, Sr., **Supp. XXIII:** 21, 22, 26, 30
Morgesons, The (E. Stoddard), **Supp. XV:** 270, 273, 274, 278, **279–282,** 283
Morgesons and Other Writings, Published and Unpublished, The (Buell and Zagarell), **Supp. XV:** 269
Moricand, Conrad, **III:** 190
Morison, Samuel Eliot, **Supp. I Part 2: 479–500; Supp. XXII:** 35
Morison, Mrs. Samuel Eliot (Elizabeth Shaw Greene), **Supp. I Part 2:** 483
Morison, Mrs. Samuel Eliot (Priscilla Barton), **Supp. I Part 2:** 493, 496, 497
Morita, Pat, **Supp. XXI:** 146
"Morituri Salutamus" (Longfellow), **II:** 499, 500; **Retro. Supp. II:** 169; **Supp. I Part 2:** 416
"Moriturus" (Millay), **III:** 126, 131–132
Morley, Christopher, **III:** 481, 483, 484; **Supp. I Part 2:** 653; **Supp. IX:** 124
Morley, Edward, **IV:** 27
Morley, Lord John, **I:** 7
Mormon Country (Stegner), **Supp. IV Part 2:** 598, 601–602
"Morning, The" (Updike), **Retro. Supp. I:** 329
"Morning after My Death, The" (Levis), **Supp. XI:** 260, 263–264
"Morning Arrives" (F. Wright), **Supp. XVII:** 244
Morning Face (Stratton-Porter), **Supp. XX: 223**
Morning for Flamingos, A (Burke), **Supp. XIV:** 30, 31, 32
"Morning Glory" (Merrill), **Supp. III Part 1:** 337
Morning Glory, The (R. Bly), **Supp. IV Part 1:** 63–65, 66, 71
"Morning Imagination of Russia, A" (W. C. Williams), **Retro. Supp. I:** 428
Morning in Antibes (Knowles), **Supp. XII:** 249
Morning in the Burned House

(Atwood), **Supp. XIII:** 20, 35
Morning Is Near Us, The (Glaspell), **Supp. III Part 1:** 184–185
Morning Noon and Night (Cozzens), **I:** 374, 375, 376, 377, 379, 380
"Morning of the Day They Did It, The" (White), **Supp. I Part 2:** 663
"Morning Prayers" (Harjo), **Supp. XII:** 231
"Morning Roll Call" (Anderson), **I:** 116
"Morning Roudup" (Sorrentino), **Supp. XXI:** 228
"Mornings, I Walk Past the First Cemetery of Athens" (Stallings), **Supp. XXV:** 225
"Morning Shadows" (Skloot), **Supp. XX: 199**
"Mornings in a New House" (Merrill), **Supp. III Part 1:** 327
"Mornings in Ormos"(Hadas), **Supp. XXIII:** 112, 113, 123
Mornings Like This (Dillard), **Supp. VI:** 23, 34
"Morning Song" (Plath), **Retro. Supp. II:** 252; **Supp. XXIII:** 115
Morning Watch, The (Agee), **I:** 25, 39–42
"Morning with Broken Window" (Hogan), **Supp. IV Part 1:** 405
"Moro Like Me" (Goldman), **Supp. XXV:** 51
Morrell, Ottoline, **Retro. Supp. I:** 60
Morris, Bernard E., **Supp. XV:** 154, 169
Morris, Christopher D., **Supp. IV Part 1:** 231, 236
Morris, Gary, **Supp. XXII:** 262
Morris, George Sylvester, **Supp. I Part 2:** 640
Morris, Gouverneur, **Supp. I Part 2:** 512, 517, 518
Morris, Lloyd, **III:** 458
Morris, Robert, **Supp. I Part 2:** 510
Morris, Timothy, **Retro. Supp. I:** 40
Morris, William, **II:** 323, 338, 523; **IV:** 349; **Supp. I Part 1:** 260, 356; **Supp. XI:** 202
Morris, Willie, **Supp. XI:** 216, 231, 234; **Supp. XIX:** 151, 252; **Supp. XXVII:** 269
Morris, Wright, **I:** 305; **III: 218–243,** 558, 572; **IV:** 211
Morrison, Charles Clayton, **III:** 297
Morrison, Jim, **Supp. IV Part 1:** 206
Morrison, Kay, **Retro. Supp. III:** 104
Morrison, Toni, **Retro. Supp. II:** 15, 118; **Retro. Supp. III: 183–205; Supp. III Part 1: 361–381; Supp. IV Part 1:** 2, 13, 14, 250, 253, 257; **Supp. V:** 169, 259; **Supp. VIII:** 213, 214; **Supp. X:** 85, 239, 250, 325; **Supp. XI:** 4, 14, 20, 91; **Supp. XII:** 289, 310; **Supp. XIII:** 60, 185; **Supp. XVI:** 143; **Supp. XVII:** 183; **Supp. XX: 108; Supp. XXI:** 172, 243; **Supp. XXII:** 65, 78; **Supp. XXIV:** 183, 184, 185; **Supp. XXV:** 142; **Supp. XXVI:** 14
"Morro Bay" (Jeffers), **Supp. II Part 2:** 422
Morrow, Christopher, **Supp. XXVII:** 216, 225
Morrow, W. C., **I:** 199
Morse, Jedidiah, **Supp. XV:** 243
Morse, Robert, **Supp. XI:** 305
Morse, Samuel F. B., **Supp. I Part 1:** 156
Morse, Samuel French, **Supp. XXI:** 17, 19, 23, 27
Mortal Acts, Mortal Words (Kinnell), **Supp. III Part 1:** 235, 236, 237, 249–254
Mortal Antipathy, A (Holmes), **Supp. I Part 1:** 315–316
"Mortal Enemies" (Humphrey), **Supp. IX:** 109
"Mortal Eternal" (Olds), **Supp. X:** 214
Mortal No, The (Hoffman), **IV:** 113
Mortal Stakes (Parker), **Supp. XIX:** 183–184
Morte D'Arthur, Le (Malory), **Supp. IV Part 1:** 47
Mortmere Stories, The (Isherwood and Upward), **Supp. XIV:** 159
Morton, David, **Supp. IX:** 76
Morton, Jelly Roll, **Supp. X:** 242
Morton, Thomas, **Supp. XXII:** 44, 45, 46
"Mosaic of the Nativity: Serbia, Winter 1993" (Kenyon), **Supp. VII:** 173
Mosby's Memoirs and Other Stories (Bellow), **Retro. Supp. II:** 27
"Moscow, Idaho" (Offutt), **Supp. XIX:** 170
Moscow under Fire (Caldwell), **I:** 296
Moser, Barry, **Supp. XIV:** 223
Moses (Asch), **Supp. XXIII:** 7
Moses (Untermeyer), **Retro. Supp. III:** 133; **Supp. XV: 309**
Moses, Man of the Mountain (Hurston), **Retro. Supp. III:** 130, 132–133, 139; **Supp. VI:** 149, 158, 160
"Moses on Sinai" (Untermeyer), **Supp. XV:** 300
Mosher, Howard Frank, **Supp. XXII: 203–221**
Moskowitz, Alfred, **Supp. XXI:** 98, 106
Mosle, Sara, **Supp. XI:** 254
Mosley, Walter, **Supp. XIII: 233–252; Supp. XVI:** 143
Mosquito (G. Jones), **Supp. XXIV:** 183, 184, 185, 190, **192–194,** 195
Mosquito Coast, The (film), **Supp. VIII:** 323
Mosquito Coast, The (Theroux), **Supp. VIII:** 321, **322–323**
Mosquitoes (Faulkner), **II:** 56; **Retro. Supp. I:** 79, 81; **Retro. Supp. III:** 77
Moss, Howard, **III:** 452; **Supp. IV Part 2:** 642; **Supp. IX:** 39; **Supp. XIII:** 114; **Supp. XV:** 143, 152
Moss, Stanley, **Supp. XI:** 321
Moss, Thylias, **Supp. XI:** 248
Mosses from an Old Manse (Hawthorne), **I:** 562; **II:** 224; **III:** 82, 83; **Retro. Supp. I:** 157, 248; **Retro. Supp. III:** 114–116, 122, 156
Moss Mystery, The (Wells), **Supp. XXVI:** 278
"Moss of His Skin" (Sexton), **Supp. II Part 2:** 676
Most, Doug, **Supp. XVIII:** 101
"Most Extraordinary Case, A" (James), **II:** 322; **Retro. Supp. I:** 218
"Most Girl Part of You, The" (Hempel), **Supp. XXI:** 116
Most Likely to Succeed (Dos Passos), **I:** 491
"Most of It, The" (Frost), **Retro. Supp. I:** 121, 125, 129, 139; **Retro. Supp. III:** 104; **Supp. XVIII:** 300
"Most Popular Novels in America, The" (Mabie), **Supp. XVIII:** 257
Motel Chronicles (Shepard), **Supp. III Part 2:** 445
"Mother" (Kooser), **Supp. XIX:** 117, 126, 127
"Mother" (Paley), **Supp. VI: 222–223**
Mother (Schjeldahl), **Supp. XXIV:** 44
"Mother" (Snyder), **Supp. VIII:** 298
Mother (Whistler), **IV:** 369
Mother, The (Buck), **Supp. II Part 1:** 118–119
"Mother and Child #3" (Davison), **Supp. XXVI:** 77
"Mother and Jack and the Rain" (Sexton), **Supp. II Part 2:** 686
"Mother and Son" (Tate), **IV:** 128, 137–138
Mother Country: Britain, the Welfare State and Nuclear Pollution (Robinson), **Supp. XXI:** 211
Mother Courage and Her Children (Brecht), **III:** 160; **Supp. IX:** 140; **Supp. XII:** 249

"Mother Earth: Her Whales" (Snyder), **Supp. VIII:** 302
"Motherhood" (Swenson), **Supp. IV Part 2:** 645
Mother Hubbard (Reed), **Supp. X:** 241
Motherless Brooklyn (Lethem), **Supp. XXII:** 49
Motherless in Brooklyn (Lethem), **Supp. XVIII:** 135, **143–144**
Mother Love (Dove), **Supp. IV Part 1:** 250–251, 254
"Mother Marie Therese" (R. Lowell), **Retro. Supp. II:** 188
Mother Night (Vonnegut), **Supp. II Part 2:** 757, 758, 767, 770, 771
"Mother-Right" (Rich), **Retro. Supp. III:** 249
"Mother Rosarine" (Kumin), **Supp. IV Part 2:** 442
"Mothers and Daughters in the Fiction of the New Republic" (Davidson), **Supp. XV:** 238
"Mother's lament for the absence of a child, A"(J. Schoolcraft), **Supp. XXIII:** 236
"Mother Song" (Huddle), **Supp. XXVI:** 151
Mother's Recompense, The (Wharton), **IV:** 321, 324; **Retro. Supp. I:** 382; **Retro. Supp. III:** 288–289
"Mother's Tale, A" (Agee), **I:** 29–30
"Mother's Things" (Creeley), **Supp. IV Part 1:** 141
"Mother Suite, The"(Crooker), **Supp. XXIII:** 61
"Mother's Voice" (Creeley), **Supp. IV Part 1:** 156
Mother to Daughter, Daughter to Mother (Olsen, ed.), **Supp. XIII:** 295
"Mother Tongue" (Simic), **Supp. VIII:** 283
"Mother to Son" (Hughes), **Retro. Supp. I:** 199, 203; **Supp. I Part 1:** 321–322, 323
Motherwell, Robert, **Supp. XV:** 145; **Supp. XXI:** 125
"Mother Writes to the Murderer, The: A Letter" (Nye), **Supp. XIII:** 276
Moths of the Limberlost (Stratton-Porter), **Supp. XX: 218**
"Motion, The" (Olson), **Supp. II Part 2:** 571
Motion of History, The (Baraka), **Supp. II Part 1:** 55, 56
"Motive for Metaphor, The" (Stevens), **IV:** 89; **Retro. Supp. I:** 310
Motiveless Malignity (Auchincloss), **Supp. IV Part 1:** 31
Motke ganef (Asch), **Supp. XXIII:** 5
Motley, John Lothrop, **Supp. I Part 1:** 299; **Supp. I Part 2:** 479; **Supp. XX: 228, 231**
Motley, Willard, **Supp. XVII: 149–163; Supp. XXIII:** 145
"Motor Car, The" (White), **Supp. I Part 2:** 661
Motor-Flight Through France (Wharton), **I:** 12; **Retro. Supp. I:** 372
Motown and Didi (Myers), **Supp. XXVII:** 204, 211
Mott, Michael, **Supp. VIII:** 204, 208
Motta, Gustavo, **Supp. XXIII:** 125
Mottetti: Poems of Love: The Motets of Eugenio Montale (Montale; Gioia, trans.), **Supp. XV:** 112, **127–128**
Mottke, the Thief (Asch), **Supp. XXIII: 9,** 12
Mottke, the Thief (Asch; tr. Willa and Edwin Muir), **Supp. XXIII:** 5
Mouawad, Nelly, **Supp. XX: 126**
"Mound, The" (Lovecraft and Bishop), **Supp. XXV:** 122
"Mountain, The" (Frost), **Retro. Supp. I:** 121
"Mountain Hermitage, The: Pages from a Japanese Notebook" (Passin), **Supp. XIII:** 337
Mountain Interval (Frost), **II:** 154; **Retro. Supp. I:** 131, 132, 133; **Retro. Supp. III:** 99–100
"Mountain Lion" (Hogan), **Supp. IV Part 1:** 412
"Mountain Music" essays (Sanders), **Supp. XVI:** 276–277
Mountain on the Desert, The (Richter), **Supp. XVIII:** 216, 219
Mountainous Journey, A (Tuqan), **Supp. XIII:** 278
"Mountains" (Dubus III), **Supp. XXIV:** 101
Mountains, The (Wolfe), **IV:** 461
Mountains and Rivers without End (Snyder), **Supp. VIII:** 295, **305–306**
"Mountains grow unnoticed, The" (Dickinson), **Retro. Supp. I:** 46
Mountains Have Come Closer, The (J. W. Miller), **Supp. XX: 165, 168, 169–170**
Mountains Look Down, The: A History of Chichester, a Company Town in the Catskills (Bennett), **Supp. XXII:** 218
Mountains of California, The (Muir), **Supp. IX:** 183
"Mountain Whippoorwill, The" (Benét), **Supp. XI:** 44–45, 46, 47
"Mount-Joy: or Some Passages Out of the Life of a Castle-Builder" (Irving), **II:** 314
"Mount Venus" (Wright), **Supp. XV:** 346
"Mourners" (Kooser), **Supp. XIX:** 127
"Mourners, The" (Malamud), **Supp. I Part 2:** 431, 435, 436–437
Mourners Below (Purdy), **Supp. VII:** 274, 280
"Mourning and Melancholia" (Freud), **Supp. IV Part 2:** 450; **Supp. XVI:** 161
Mourning Becomes Electra (O'Neill), **III:** 391, 394, 398–400
"Mourning Doves" (Pedersen; Nelson, trans.), **Supp. XVIII:** 180
"Mourning Poem for the Queen of Sunday" (Hayden), **Supp. II Part 1:** 379–380
"Mouse Elegy" (Olds), **Supp. X:** 209
Mouse Is Born, A (Loos), **Supp. XVI:** 193
"Mouse Roulette Wheel, The" (C. Bly), **Supp. XVI:** 34
Moustapha's Eclipse (McKnight), **Supp. XX: 147, 150**
"Mouth of Brass" (Humphrey), **Supp. IX:** 101
Moveable Feast, A (Hemingway), **II:** 257; **Retro. Supp. I:** 108, 171, **186–187**
Movement, The: Documentary of a Struggle for Equality (Student Nonviolent Coordinating Committee), **Supp. IV Part 1:** 369
"Move over Macho, Here Comes Feminismo" (Robbins), **Supp. X:** 272
Movers and Shakers (Sochen), **Supp. XXI:** 1
"Moves, The" (July), **Supp. XXIV:** 205
"Move to California, The" (Stafford), **Supp. XI:** 318, 321
"Movie" (Shapiro), **Supp. II Part 2:** 707
Movie at the End of the World, The (McGrath), **Supp. X:** 127
Moviegoer, The (Percy), **Supp. III Part 1:** 383–385, 387, 389–392, 394, 397
"Movie Magazine, The: A Low 'Slick' " (Percy), **Supp. III Part 1:** 385
Movies (Dixon), **Supp. XII:** 147
Movies About the Movies (Ames), **Supp. XVIII:** 242–243
"Movie Star Peter at the Supper for Street People" (Ferry), **Supp. XXIV:** 153
"Moving Around" (Matthews), **Supp. IX:** 155

"Moving Finger, The" (Wharton), **Retro. Supp. I:** 365
"Moving Inward at Last" (Bly), **Supp. XXI:** 84–85
Moving On (McMurtry), **Supp. V:** 223–224
"Moving On" (Pickering), **Supp. XXI:** 197
Moving Pictures: Memoirs of a Hollywood Prince (Schulberg), **Supp. XVIII:** 242, 243, 254
"Moving Sale" (Stallings), **Supp. XXV:** 228
Moving Target, The (Macdonald), **Supp. IV Part 2:** 462, 463, 467, 470, 471, 473, 474
Moving Target, The (Merwin), **Supp. III Part 1:** 346, 347–348, 352, 357
Mowat, Farley, **Supp. XXVI:** 61
"Mowbray Family, The" (Farrell and Alden), **II:** 45
"Mowing" (Frost), **II:** 169–170; **Retro. Supp. I:** 127, 128; **Retro. Supp. III:** 96
"Moxan's Master" (Bierce), **I:** 206
Moxley, Jennifer, **Supp. XVII:** 70
Moyers, Bill, **Supp. IV Part 1:** 267; **Supp. VIII:** 331; **Supp. XI:** 126, 132; **Supp. XII:** 217; **Supp. XIII:** 274, 276; **Supp. XV:** 212; **Supp. XXIII:** 129, 130, 131, 139
Moylan, Virginia Lynn, **Retro. Supp. III:** 136
Moynagh, Maureen, **Supp. XXII:** 73
Moynihan, Daniel Patrick, **Retro. Supp. II:** 123; **Supp. VIII:** 241; **Supp. XIX:** 150–151
"Moyshele"(Asch), **Supp. XXIII:** 4
"Mozart" (C. Frost), **Supp. XV:** 94
Mozart, Wolfgang Amadeus, **I:** 479, 588; **IV:** 74, 358; **Supp. IV Part 1:** 284
"Mozart and the Gray Steward" (Wilder), **IV:** 358
Mrabet, Mohammed, **Supp. IV Part 1:** 92, 93
Mr. and Mrs. Baby and Other Stories (Strand), **Supp. IV Part 2:** 631
"Mr. and Mrs. Fix-It" (Lardner), **II:** 431
Mr. Arcularis (Aiken), **I:** 54, 56
"Mr. Big" (Allen), **Supp. XV:** 15
Mr. Bridge (Connell), **Supp. XIV:** 80, 82, 93; **Supp. XXIII:** 302
Mr. Brown Can Moo! Can You? (Geisel), **Supp. XVI:** 104
"Mr. Bruce" (Jewett), **II:** 397; **Retro. Supp. II:** 134, 143
"Mr. Burnshaw and the Statue" (Stevens), **Retro. Supp. I:** 298, 303
"Mr. Carson Death on His Nights Out" (McGrath), **Supp. X:** 118
Mr. Clemens and Mark Twain (Kaplan), **I:** 247–248
"Mr. Coffee and Mr. Fixit" (Carver), **Supp. III Part 1:** 145
"Mr. Cornelius Johnson, Office-Seeker" (Dunbar), **Supp. II Part 1:** 211, 213
"Mr. Costyve Duditch" (Toomer), **Supp. III Part 2:** 486
"Mr. Dajani, Calling from Jericho" (Nye), **Supp. XIII:** 286–287
"Mr. Edwards and the Spider" (R. Lowell), **I:** 544; **II:** 550; **Retro. Supp. II:** 187
Mr. Field's Daughter (Bausch), **Supp. VII:** 47–48, 51–52
"Mr. Flood's Party" (Robinson), **III:** 512
"Mr. Forster's Pageant" (Maxwell), **Supp. VIII:** 172
"Mr. Frost's Chickens" (Oliver), **Supp. VII:** 232–233
"Mr. Higginbotham's Catastrophe" (Hawthorne), **Retro. Supp. III:** 113
Mr. Hodge and Mr. Hazard (Wylie), **Supp. I Part 2:** 708, 709, 714, 721–724
"Mr. Hueffer and the Prose Tradition" (Pound), **III:** 465
Mr. Ives' Christmas (Hijuelos), **Supp. VIII: 85–86**
Mr. Kelso's Lion (Bontemps), **Supp. XXII:** 7
"Mr. Longfellow and His Boy" (Sandburg), **III:** 591
"Mr. Luna and History" (Ríos), **Supp. IV Part 2:** 551
"Mr. Mitochondria" (Stollman), **Supp. XVII:** 50
Mr. Moto Is So Sorry (Marquand), **III:** 57, 58
Mr. Norris Changes Trains (Isherwood), **Supp. XIV:** 161
Mr Peters' Connections (A. Miller), **Retro. Supp. III:** 170, 172, 176
"Mr. Preble Gets Rid of His Wife" (Thurber), **Supp. I Part 2:** 615
"Mr. Rat"(Thompson), **Supp. XXIII:** 301–302
"Mr. Rolfe" (Wilson), **IV:** 436
Mr. Rutherford's Children (S. and A. Warner), **Supp. XVIII:** 264
"Mrs. Adis" (Kaye-Smith), **Supp. XVIII:** 130–131
Mrs. Albert Grundy: Observations in Philistia (Frederic), **II:** 138–139
Mr. Sammler's Planet (Bellow), **I:** 144, 147, 150, 151, 152, 158; **Retro. Supp. II:** 19, 28, 30
Mrs. Balfame (Atherton), **Supp. XXIV:** 20
"Mrs. Bilingsby's Wine" (Taylor), **Supp. V:** 323
Mrs. Bob Cratchit's Wild Christmas Binge (Durang), **Supp. XXIV:** 113, 125
Mrs. Bridge: A Novel (Connell), **Supp. XIV:** 79, 80, 81, 82, **89–94,** 95; **Supp. XXIII:** 302
"Mrs. Cassidy's Last Year" (Gordon), **Supp. IV Part 1:** 306
"Mrs. Cross and Mrs. Kidd" (Munro), **Supp. XXVII:** 188
Mrs. Dalloway (Woolf), **Supp. IV Part 1:** 299; **Supp. VIII:** 5; **Supp. XV:** 55, 65–66
"Mrs. Dimbleby" (Barnhardt), **Supp. XXVII:** 12
"Mrs. Green" (Huddle), **Supp. XXVI:** 148
"Mr. Shelley Speaking" (Wylie), **Supp. I Part 2:** 719
"Mrs. Jellison" (Hay), **Supp. XIV:** 123
"Mrs. Krikorian" (Olds), **Supp. X:** 211
"Mrs. Maecenas" (Burke), **I:** 271
"Mrs. Mandrill" (Nemerov), **III:** 278
"Mrs. Manstey's View" (Wharton), **Retro. Supp. I:** 362, 363
"Mrs. Mobry's Reason" (Chopin), **Retro. Supp. II:** 61
Mr. Spaceman (R. O. Butler), **Supp. XII:** 62, **74–75**
Mrs. Reynolds (Stein), **IV:** 43
"Mrs. Sen's" (Lahiri), **Supp. XXI: 177–178,** 180–181
Mrs. Stevens Hears the Mermaids Singing (Sarton), **Supp. VIII:** 252–253, **256–257**
Mrs. Ted Bliss (Elkin), **Supp. VI: 56,** 58
"Mrs. Turner Cutting the Grass" (Shields), **Supp. VII:** 319–320
"Mrs. Walpurga" (Rukeyser), **Supp. VI:** 273
"Mr. Thompson's Prodigal" (Harte), **Supp. II Part 1:** 354
"Mr. Trumm's Eyes"(Schott), **Supp. XXIII:** 243
Mr. Vertigo (Auster), **Supp. XII: 34–35,** 36
"Mr. Vonnegut in Sumatra" (Saunders), **Supp. XIX:** 235
"Mr. Whittier" (Scott), **Supp. I Part 2:** 705
Mr. Wilson's War (Dos Passos), **I:** 485
"Mr. Woodriff's Neckties" (Gallagher), **Supp. XXIV:** 175–176
"MS. Found in a Bottle" (Poe), **III:** 411, 416; **Retro. Supp. II:** 274

"Ms. Lot" (Rukeyser), **Supp. VI:** 281
Ms. Magazine, **Supp. V:** 259
Mttron-Hirsch, Sidney, **III:** 484–485
Mu (album, Do Cherry), **Supp. XXVII:** 154
"mu" (Mackey), **Supp. XXVII:** 155, 156
"Muchas Gracias Por Todo" (Nye), **Supp. XIII:** 282–283
"Much Madness is divinest Sense" (Dickinson), **Retro. Supp. I:** 37–38
"Muck-A-Muck" (Harte), **Supp. II Part 1:** 342
"Mud Below, The" (Proulx), **Supp. VII:** 262
Mudge, Alden, **Supp. XIV:** 35
"Mudman"(P. Benedict), **Supp. XXIII:** 47
Mudrick, Marvin, **Retro. Supp. II:** 289
"Mud Season" (Kenyon), **Supp. VII:** 167–168
Mueller, Lisel, **Supp. I Part 1:** 83, 88; **Supp. XIV:** 268
Muggli, Mark, **Supp. IV Part 1:** 207
Muhammad, Elijah, **Supp. I Part 1:** 60
Muir, Edwin, **I:** 527; **II:** 368; **III:** 20; **Supp. XXII:** 166; **Supp. XXIII:** 1; **Supp. XXVI:** 67
Muir, John, **Supp. IX:** 33, **171–188; Supp. VIII:** 296; **Supp. X:** 29; **Supp. XIV:** 177, 178, 181; **Supp. XXVI:** 34, 37, 43
Muir, Willa, **Supp. XXIII:** 1
Muirhead, Deborah, **Supp. XVIII:** 186
Mujica, Barbara, **Supp. VIII:** 89
Mulas, Franco, **Supp. XX: 38**
Mulatto (Hughes), **Retro. Supp. I:** 197, 203; **Supp. I Part 1:** 328, 339
Mulching of America, The (Crews), **Supp. XI:** 107
Muldoon, William, **I:** 500–501
Mule Bone (Hughes and Hurston), **Retro. Supp. I:** 194, 203; **Supp. VI:** 154
Mule Bone (Hurston), **Retro. Supp. III:** 128
Mules and Men (Hurston), **Retro. Supp. III:** 128, 130, 132, 137, 138; **Supp. VI:** 149, 153, 154, 160
Mulford, Prentice, **I:** 193
Mullen, Harryette, **Supp. XXVII: 163–177**
Mullennix, Joel, **Supp. XXIII:** 281
Muller, Kathryn, **Supp. XXVI:** 95
Mulligan, Robert, **Supp. VIII:** 128, 129
Mulligan Stew (Sorrentino), **Supp. XII:** 139; **Supp. XXI:** 233
Mullins, Eustace, **III:** 479
Mullins, Priscilla, **II:** 502–503
"Multiplication of Wool, The" (Sanders), **Supp. XVI:** 268
Multitudes, Multitudes (Clampitt), **Supp. IX:** 39
Mumbo Jumbo (Reed), **Supp. X:** 240, 242, **245–248,** 251
Mumford, Lewis, **I:** 245, 250, 251, 252, 259, 261; **II:** 271, 473–474; **Supp. I Part 2:** 632, 638; **Supp. II Part 2: 471–501**
Mumford, Sophia Wittenberg (Mrs. Lewis Mumford), **Supp. II Part 2:** 474, 475
"Mummers, The" (Di Piero), **Supp. XIX:** 44
Mummy, The (film), **Supp. IV Part 1:** 104; **Supp. XVII:** 57
Mundo y Palabra (Espaillat), **Supp. XXI:** 104
"Mundus et Infans" (Auden), **Supp. II Part 1:** 15
Mundy, Talbot, **Supp. XXVII:** 121
"Munich, 1938" (R. Lowell), **II:** 554
"Munich Mannequins, The" (Plath), **Retro. Supp. II:** 256
"Municipal Report, A" (Henry), **Supp. II Part 1:** 406–407
Muñoz, Manuel, **Supp. XXV: 127–139**
Munro, Alice, **Supp. IX:** 212; **Supp. X:** 290; **Supp. XII:** 289–290, 310; **Supp. XXIII:** 289, 296; **Supp. XXVII: 179–198**
Munsey, Frank, **I:** 501; **Supp. XXVII:** 120
Munson, Gorham, **I:** 252, 388, 432; **Retro. Supp. II:** 77, 78, 79, 82, 83; **Retro. Supp. III:** 45, 48; **Supp. I Part 2:** 454; **Supp. XX: 70, 74**
Münsterberg, Hugo, **Supp. XIV:** 197
Murakami, Haruki, **Supp. XVI:** 124
"Muralist, The" (Rich), **Retro. Supp. III:** 241
"Murano" (Doty), **Supp. XI:** 131
Murasaki, Lady, **II:** 577
Muratori, Fred, **Supp. XVI:** 281
Muray, Nicholas, **Supp. I Part 2:** 708
Murchison, Ginger, **Supp. XXV:** 222, 223, 226
Murder, My Sweet (film), **Supp. IV Part 1:** 130
"Murder Comes for the Bishop" (Goldman), **Supp. XXV:** 57
"Murderer Guest, The" (Gordon), **Supp. IV Part 1:** 306
"Murderers" (L. Michaels), **Supp. XVI:** 207–208
"Murderer's Grog" (Howard), **Supp. XXVII:** 121
Murder in Mount Holly (Theroux), **Supp. VIII:** 315–316
Murder in the Cathedral (T. S. Eliot), **I:** 571, 573, 580, 581; **II:** 20; **Retro. Supp. I:** 65; **Retro. Supp. II:** 222; **Retro. Supp. III:** 66, 69–70
Murder of Lidice, The (Millay), **III:** 140
"Murders in the Rue Morgue, The" (Poe), **III:** 412, 416, 419–420; **Retro. Supp. II:** 271, 272; **Retro. Supp. III:** 225–226, 226–227; **Supp. XIX:** 77
Murdoch, Iris, **Supp. VIII:** 167; **Supp. XVIII:** 136,149
Murnau, F. W., **Supp. XV:** 128
Murphy, Brenda, **Supp. XXI:** 6
Murphy, Cullen, **Supp. XXVI:** 61
Murphy, Jacqueline Shea, **Retro. Supp. II:** 143
Murphy, Patrick, **Supp. XIII:** 214
Murphy, Richard, **Retro. Supp. II:** 250; **Supp. XXIII:** 75
Murray, Albert, **Retro. Supp. II:** 119, 120; **Supp. XIX: 147–162**
Murray, Bill, **Supp. XXI:** 51
Murray, Edward, **I:** 229
Murray, G. E., **Supp. X:** 201; **Supp. XI:** 143, 155
Murray, Gilbert, **III:** 468–469
Murray, Jan, **Supp. IV Part 2:** 574
Murray, John, **II:** 304; **III:** 76, 79; **Retro. Supp. I:** 246
Murray, Judith Sargent, **Supp. XV:** 236–237
Murray, Les, **Supp. XIX:** 131
Murray, Margaret A., **Supp. V:** 128
Murrell, John A., **IV:** 265
Mursell, James L., **Supp. I Part 2:** 608
"Muse" (Ammons), **Supp. VII:** 29
"Muse, Postmodern and Homeless, The" (Ozick), **Supp. V:** 272
Muse & Drudge (Mullen), **Supp. XXVII:** 171–172, 176
"Musée des Beaux Arts" (Auden), **Retro. Supp. I:** 430; **Supp. II Part 1:** 14
"Musée des Beaux Arts Revisited" (Collins), **Supp. XXI:** 60
"Muse of Aboutness, The" (Baker), **Supp. XVI:** 288
Muses Are Heard, The (Capote), **Supp. III Part 1:** 126
"Muses of Terrence McNally, The" (Zinman), **Supp. XIII:** 207–208
"Muse's Tragedy, The" (Wharton), **Retro. Supp. I:** 364; **Retro. Supp. III:** 279
Museum (Dove), **Supp. IV Part 1:** 245–247, 248
"Museum" (Hass), **Supp. VI:** 107

Museums and Women (Updike), **Retro. Supp. I:** 321
"Museum Vase" (Francis), **Supp. IX:** 83
"Mushrooms" (Plath), **Retro. Supp. II:** 246; **Supp. I Part 2:** 539
"Music" (Huddle), **Supp. XXVI:** 150
"Music" (Oliver), **Supp. VII:** 236
Music (al-Músíqá) (Gibran), **Supp. XX: 115, 124**
Music After the Great War (Van Vechten), **Supp. II Part 2:** 732
Music and Bad Manners (Van Vechten), **Supp. II Part 2:** 733
Music Appreciation (Skloot), **Supp. XX: 196, 197–201**
"Music for a Farce" (Bowles), **Supp. IV Part 1:** 83
Music for Chameleons (Capote), **Supp. III Part 1:** 120, 125–127, 131, 132
"Music for Museums?" (Van Vechten), **Supp. II Part 2:** 732
"Music for the Movies" (Van Vechten), **Supp. II Part 2:** 733
"Music from Spain" (Welty), **IV:** 272
Music Like Dirt (Bidart), **Supp. XV:** 35
"Music Like Dirt" (Bidart), **Supp. XV:** 35
Music of Chance, The (Auster), **Supp. XII:** 21, 23, **32–33**
"Music of My Own Kind Too, The" (Budbill), **Supp. XIX:** 10
"Music of Prose, The" (Gass), **Supp. VI:** 92
Music of Spain, The (Van Vechten), **Supp. II Part 2:** 734, 735
"Music of the Spheres" (Epstein), **Supp. XII:** 165
"Music School" (B. Kelly), **Supp. XVII:** 124
Music School, The (Updike), **IV:** 214, 215, 219, 226, 227; **Retro. Supp. I:** 320, 328, 329, 330
"Music School, The" (Updike), **Retro. Supp. I:** 326, 329, 335
"Music Swims Back to Me" (Sexton), **Supp. II Part 2:** 673
Muske, Carol, **Supp. IV Part 2:** 453–454
"Mussel Hunter at Rock Harbor" (Plath), **Supp. I Part 2:** 529, 537
Musset, Alfred de, **I:** 474; **II:** 543
Mussolini, Benito, **III:** 115, 473, 608; **IV:** 372, 373; **Supp. I Part 1:** 281, 282; **Supp. I Part 2:** 618; **Supp. V:** 290; **Supp. XVI:** 191
"Mustafa Ferrari" (X. J. Kennedy), **Supp. XV:** 170–171
Mustich, James, **Supp. XXI:** 52
"Must the Novelist Crusade?" (Welty), **IV:** 280
"Mutability of Literature, The" (Irving), **II:** 308
"Mutation of the Spirit" (Corso), **Supp. XII:** 132, 133
Mute, The (McCullers), **II:** 586
Mutilated, The (T. Williams), **IV:** 382, 386, 393
Mutiny of the Elsinore, The (London), **II:** 467
"Muttsy" (Hurston), **Supp. XVIII:** 279; **Supp. XXVI:** 164
Muyumba, Walton, **Supp. XIX:** 158
"My Adventures as a Social Poet" (Hughes), **Retro. Supp. I:** 194, 207
"My Alba" (Ginsberg), **Supp. II Part 1:** 320, 321
My Alexandria (Doty), **Supp. XI:** 119, 120, 121, **123–125,** 130
"My Amendment" (Saunders), **Supp. XIX:** 232
My Amputations (Major), **Supp. XXII:** 174, **175–176**
My Ántonia (Cather), **I:** 321–322; **Retro. Supp. I:** 1, 3, 4, **11–13,** 14, 17, 18, 22; **Retro. Supp. III:** 18, 20, 23, 30–32, 36; **Supp. IV Part 2:** 608; **Supp. XVI:** 226
"My Appearance" (Wallace), **Supp. X:** 306–307
My Argument with the Gestapo: A Macaronic Journal (Merton), **Supp. VIII:** 207; **Supp. XV:** 344
"My Arkansas" (Angelou), **Supp. IV Part 1:** 15
"My Aunt" (Holmes), **Supp. I Part 1:** 302, 310
"My Beginnings" (Simpson), **Supp. IX:** 273
"My Bird Problem" (Franzen), **Supp. XX: 94**
My Black Horse (Gallagher), **Supp. XXIV:** 170
"My Bodyguard" (Notley), **Supp. XXII:** 230
My Bondage and My Freedom (Douglass), **Supp. III Part 1:** 155, 173
"My Bones Here Are Waiting for Yours" (Vaz), **Supp. XXVI:** 265–266
My Brother (Kincaid), **Supp. VII:** 191–193
"My Brother Paul" (Dreiser), **Retro. Supp. II:** 94
"My Brothers the Silent" (Merwin), **Supp. III Part 1:** 349–350
"My Brother's Work" (Dunn), **Supp. XI:** 147
"My Brother Takes a Hammer to the Mirror" (F. Wright), **Supp. XVII:** 244
"My Butterfly" (Frost), **II:** 151; **Retro. Supp. I:** 124; **Retro. Supp. III:** 91–92, 94
"My Children, and a Prayer for Us" (Ortiz), **Supp. IV Part 2:** 507
My Children! My Africa! (Fugard), **Supp. XXIV:** 267
"My College Sex Group" (Peacock), **Supp. XIX:** 199
"My Coney Island Uncle" (Swados), **Supp. XIX:** 267–268
"My Confession" (McCarthy), **II:** 562
"My Confessional Sestina" (Gioia), **Supp. XV:** 123
"My Corner" (Major), **Supp. XXII:** 184
My Country and My People (Yutang), **Supp. X:** 291
"My Country Tish of Thee" (Rinehart), **Supp. XXV:** 194
"My Country 'Tis of Thee" (Reznikoff), **Supp. III Part 2:** 616
"My Daughter Considers Her Body" (Skloot), **Supp. XX: 197–198, 200**
My Days of Anger (Farrell), **II:** 34, 35–36, 43
"My Dear Niece" (Boyce), **Supp. XXI:** 10
"My Dear Republican Mother" (C. Bly), **Supp. XVI:** 31–32
My Death My Life by Pier Paolo Pasolini (Acker), **Supp. XII:** 7
My Dog Stupid (Fante), **Supp. XI:** 160, **170–171**
My Dog Tulip (Ackerley), **Supp. XX: 237**
"My Ear-Rings"(J. Schoolcraft), **Supp. XXIII:** 226
My Emily Dickinson (Howe), **Retro. Supp. I:** 33, 43; **Supp. IV Part 2:** 430–431
"My English" (Alvarez), **Supp. VII:** 2
Myers, Christopher, **Supp. XXVII:** 211
Myers, John Bernard, **Supp. XXIII:** 210, 219
Myers, Linda A., **Supp. IV Part 1:** 10
Myers, Walter Dean, **Supp. XXVII: 199–214**
Myerson, Julie, **Supp. XXVII:** 278
"My Extended Family" (Theroux), **Supp. VIII:** 311
My Face for the World to See (Hayes), **Supp. XXVI:** 139, 141–142
"My Father" (Biss), **Supp. XXVI:** 47
"My Father" (Budbill), **Supp. XIX:** 5
"My Father" (L. Michaels), **Supp.**

XVI: 214
"My Father" (Sterne), **IV:** 466
"My Father at Eighty-Five" (R. Bly), **Supp. IV Part 1:** 73
"My Father Is a Simple Man" (Salinas), **Supp. XIII:** 324
"My Father Is with Me" (Budbill), **Supp. XIX:** 15
"My Father: October 1942" (Stafford), **Supp. XI:** 323
My Father Photographed with Friends (Bronk), **Supp. XXI:** 26–27,**Supp. XXI:** 31
"My Father Photographed with Friends" (Bronk), **Supp. XXI:** 23, 27
"My Fathers Came From Kentucky" (Lindsay), **Supp. I Part 2:** 395
"My Father's Employment"(Schott), **Supp. XXIII:** 247
"My Father's Friends" (Maxwell), **Supp. VIII:** 171
"My Father's Ghost" (Wagoner), **Supp. IX:** 330
"My Father's God" (Fante), **Supp. XI:** 160, 174
My Father's House (film), **Supp. XXVII:** 141
"My Father's House" (L.-Y. Lee), **Supp. XV:** 225
"My Father's Love Letters" (Gallagher), **Supp. XXIV:** 171–172
"My Father's Love Letters" (Komunyakaa), **Supp. XIII:** 127
"My Father Speaks to me from the Dead" (Olds), **Supp. X:** 210
"My Father's Telescope" (Dove), **Supp. IV Part 1:** 246, 248
"My Father with Cigarette Twelve Years Before the Nazis Could Break His Heart" (Levine), **Supp. V:** 194
"My Favorite Murder" (Bierce), **I:** 205
My Favorite Plant: Writers and Gardeners on the Plants They Love (Kincaid), **Supp. VII:** 193–194
My Favorites in Suspense (Hitchcock, ed.), **Supp. XXII:** 119
"My Fifty-Plus Years Celebrate Spring" (Salinas), **Supp. XIII:** 327
"My First Book" (Harte), **Supp. II Part 1:** 343
My First Summer in the Sierra (Muir), **Supp. IX:** 172, 173, **178–181,** 183, 185; **Supp. XIV:** 177
"My Flamboyant Grandson" (Saunders), **Supp. XIX:** 231–232
"My Fountain Pen" (McClatchy), **Supp. XII:** 254, 260
My Friend, Henry Miller (Perlès), **III:** 189
My Friend, Julia Lathrop (Addams), **Supp. I Part 1:** 25
"My Friend, Walt Whitman" (Oliver), **Supp. VII:** 245
"My Garden Acquaintance" (J. R. Lowell), **Supp. I Part 2:** 420
My Garden [Book]: (Kincaid), **Supp. VII:** 193–194
"My Good-bye" (Weigl), **Supp. XIX:** 288
"My Good Man" (Gansworth), **Supp. XXVI:** 114
"My Grandfather" (R. Lowell), **II:** 554
"My Grandmother's Love Letters" (H. Crane), **Retro. Supp. II:** 78; **Retro. Supp. III:** 46
My Grandparents Were Married for Sixty-five Years (Schott), **Supp. XXIII:** 240–241
"My Grandson, Home at Last" (Angelou), **Supp. IV Part 1:** 13
My Green Hills of Jamaica (McKay), **Supp. X:** 132, 142
"My Gun" (Gallagher), **Supp. XXIV:** 175
My Guru and His Disciple (Isherwood), **Supp. XIV:** 157, 164, 172
"My Heart" (Collins), **Supp. XXI:** 58
My Heart's in the Highlands (Saroyan), **Supp. IV Part 1:** 83
"My High School Reunion" (Kingston), **Supp. V:** 169
My Hollywood (Simpson), **Supp. XXVII:** 242–244
"My House New-Painted" (Bronk), **Supp. XXI:** 30
"My Hunt for King Sebastião" (Vaz), **Supp. XXVI:** 260
"My Ideal Home" (Stratton-Porter), **Supp. XX: 222**
"My Indigo" (L.-Y. Lee), **Supp. XV:** 214
My Kind of Place: Travel Stories from a Woman Who's Been Everywhere (Orlean), **Supp. XXV:** 160, 164–165
"My Kinsman, Major Molineux" (Hawthorne), **II:** 228, 229, 237–239, 243; **Retro. Supp. I:** 153–154, 158, 160, 161; **Retro. Supp. II:** 181, 187; **Retro. Supp. III:** 110, 112; **Supp. XVI:** 157
My Kinsman, Major Molineux (R. Lowell), **II:** 545–546
"My Last Afternoon with Uncle Devereux Winslow" (R. Lowell), **II:** 547–548; **Retro. Supp. II:** 189
"My Last Drive" (Hardy), **Supp. VIII:** 32
"My Last Duchess" (R. Browning), **Supp. XV:** 121; **Supp. XXV:** 229; **Supp. XXVII:** 218
Myles, Eileen, **Supp. XXIV:** 45
"My Life" (Strand), **Supp. IV Part 2:** 627
My Life, Starring Dara Falcon (Beattie), **Supp. V:** 31, 34–35
My Life a Loaded Gun: Dickinson, Plath, Rich, and Female Creativity (Bennett), **Retro. Supp. I:** 29
My Life and Hard Times (Thurber), **Supp. I Part 2:** 607, 609
My Life and Loves in Greenwich Village (attr. Bodenheim), **Supp. XXV:** 30
My Life as a Man (P. Roth), **Retro. Supp. II:** 281, 286, 289; **Supp. III Part 2:** 401, 404, 405, 417–418
"My Life as a P.I.G., or the True Adventures of Smokey the Cop" (Abbey), **Supp. XIII:** 3
"My life closed twice before its close" (Dickinson), **Retro. Supp. I:** 38
"My Life had stood a Loaded Gun" (Dickinson), **Retro. Supp. I:** 42, 43, 45, 46; **Supp. IV Part 2:** 430
My Life of Absurdity (C. Himes), **Supp. XVI:** 145
"My Life with Medicine" (Nye), **Supp. XIII:** 282
"My Life with Playboy" (Plimpton), **Supp. XVI:** 246
"My Life with R. H. Macy" (Jackson), **Supp. IX:** 118
"My Little Utopia" (Simic), **Supp. VIII:** 283
My Lives and How I Lost Them (Cullen), **Supp. IV Part 1:** 173
"My Lord Bag of Rice" (C. Bly), **Supp. XVI:** 40
My Lord Bag of Rice: New and Selected Stories (C. Bly), **Supp. XVI:** 41
"My Lost City" (Fitzgerald), **Retro. Supp. I:** 102
"My Lost Youth" (Longfellow), **II:** 487, 499; **Retro. Supp. II:** 168
My Love Affair with America: The Cautionary Tale of a Cheerful Conservative (Podhoretz), **Supp. VIII:** 232, 233, 237, **244–246**
"My Lover Has Dirty Fingernails" (Updike), **Retro. Supp. I:** 332, 333
"My lover is tall and handsome"(J. Schoolcraft), **Supp. XXIII:** 235
"My Lucy Friend Who Smells Like Corn" (Cisneros), **Supp. VII:** 68–69
"My Mammogram" (McClatchy), **Supp. XII:** 263–264
"My Man Bovanne" (Bambara), **Supp. XI:** 2

"My Mariner" (Larcom), **Supp. XIII:** 147
My Mark Twain (Howells), **II:** 276; **Retro. Supp. III:** 262
"My Metamorphosis" (Harte), **Supp. II Part 1:** 339
My Mistress's Sparrow Is Dead (Eugenides, ed.), **Supp. XXIV:** 135
"My Moby Dick" (Humphrey), **Supp. IX:** 95
"My Monkey" (Nelson), **Supp. XVIII:** 178
"My Moral Life" (Halliday), **Supp. XIX:** 89
My Mortal Enemy (Cather), **I:** 327–328; **Retro. Supp. I:** 16–17; **Supp. I Part 2:** 719
"My Mother" (Biss), **Supp. XXVI:** 47
My Mother, My Father and Me (Hellman), **Supp. I Part 1:** 290–291
"My Mother and My Sisters" (Ortiz), **Supp. IV Part 2:** 499
My Mother: Demonology (Acker), **Supp. XII:** 6
"My Mother Is Speaking from the Desert" (Gordon), **Supp. IV Part 1:** 309, 314
"My Mother Remembers That She Was Beautiful" (Gallagher), **Supp. XXIV:** 169
"My Mother's Goofy Song" (Fante), **Supp. XI:** 164
"My Mother's Memoirs, My Father's Lie, and Other True Stories" (Banks), **Supp. V:** 15
"My Mother's Nipples" (Hass), **Supp. VI:** 109
"My Mother's Story" (Kunitz), **Supp. III Part 1:** 259
"My Mother's Voice" (Very), **Supp. XXV:** 244
"My Mother"(Taylor), **Supp. XXIII:** 231
"My Mother Then and Now" (Wasserstein), **Supp. XV:** 327
"My Mother with Purse the Summer They Murdered the Spanish Poet" (Levine), **Supp. V:** 194
My Movie Business: A Memoir (Irving), **Supp. VI:** 164
"My Name" (Cisneros), **Supp. VII:** 60
"My Negro Problem—And Ours" (Podhoretz), **Supp. VIII: 234–236**
"My Neighborhood"(Dybek), **Supp. XXIII:** 69
"My New Diet" (Karr), **Supp. XI:** 241
My Next Bride (Boyle), **Supp. XXIV: 53,** 59
"My November Guest" (Frost), **Retro. Supp. III:** 96
"My Number" (Collins), **Supp. XXI:** 64
"My Old Man" (Hemingway), **II:** 263
My Other Life (Theroux), **Supp. VIII:** 310, 324
"My Own Story" (E. Stoddard), **Supp. XV:** 273, 279, 283
My Own True Name: New and Selected Poems for Young Adults, 1984–1999 (Mora), **Supp. XIII:** 222
"My Papa's Waltz" (Roehke), **Supp. XXVII:** 250
"My Parents Have Come Home Laughing" (Jarman), **Supp. XVII:** 113
"My Passion for Ferries" (Whitman), **IV:** 350
"My People" (Hughes), **Retro. Supp. I:** 197; **Supp. I Part 1:** 321–322, 323
"My Philosophy" (Allen), **Supp. XV:** 15
"My Playmate" (Whittier), **Supp. I Part 2:** 699–700
"My Priests" (Monette), **Supp. X:** 159
"My Public" (Rinehart), **Supp. XXV:** 201
Myra Breckinridge (Vidal), **Supp. IV Part 2:** 677, 685–686, 689, 691
"My Race" (H. Johnson), **Supp. XXVI:** 163
"My Raptor" (A. Finch), **Supp. XVII:** 72
"My Recollections of S. B. Fairchild" (Jackson), **Supp. IX:** 118–119
"My Religion" (Carson), **Supp. XII: 105–106**
Myrer, Anton, **Supp. XXV:** 145
"My Road to Hell Was Paved" (Patchett), **Supp. XII:** 310–311
Myron (Vidal), **Supp. IV Part 2:** 677, 685, 686, 691
"My Roomy" (Lardner), **II:** 420, 421, 428, 430
"My Sad Self" (Ginsberg), **Supp. II Part 1:** 320
My San Francisco (Atherton), **Supp. XXIV:** 27
My Secret History (Theroux), **Supp. VIII:** 310, 324
"Myself" (Audubon), **Supp. XVI:** 1–2, 5, 12
Myself Painting (Major), **Supp. XXII: 184–185**
"My Shoes" (Simic), **Supp. VIII:** 275
"My Side of the Matter" (Capote), **Supp. III Part 1:** 114, 115
My Silk Purse and Yours: The Publishing Scene and American Literary Art (Garrett), **Supp. VII:** 111; **Supp. X:** 7
My Sister Eileen (McKenney), **IV:** 288; **Retro. Supp. II:** 321
My Sister's Hand in Mine: The Collected Works of Jane Bowles, **Supp. IV Part 1:** 82–83
"My Son" (Strand), **Supp. IV Part 2:** 629
My Son, John (film), **Supp. I Part 1:** 67
"My Son, the Murderer" (Malamud), **Supp. I Part 2:** 437
My Son Is a Splendid Driver (Inge), **Supp. XXV:** 93, 95, 107
"My Son the Man" (Olds), **Supp. X:** 212
"My Speech to the Graduates" (Allen), **Supp. XV:** 16
"Mysteries of Caesar, The" (Hecht), **Supp. X:** 73
"Mysteries of Eleusis, The" (Hardwick), **Supp. III Part 1:** 195
Mysteries of Paris, The (Sue), **Supp. XXIII:** 182
Mysteries of Pittsburgh, The (Chabon), **Supp. XI:** 65, 68, **69–71; Supp. XIX:** 135
Mysteries of Small Houses (Notley), **Supp. XXII:** 223, 224, 226, 234–235
"Mysterious Case of R, The" (Conroy), **Supp. XVI:** 72
Mysterious Stranger, The (Twain), **IV:** 190–191, 210; **Retro. Supp. III:** 269
Mystery, A (Shields). See Swann (Shields)
"Mystery, The" (Dunbar), **Supp. II Part 1:** 199, 210
"Mystery, The" (Glück), **Supp. V:** 91
"Mystery, The" (Teasdale), **Supp. XXVII:** 293
Mystery and Manners (O'Connor), **Retro. Supp. II:** 230; **Retro. Supp. III:** 208
"'Mystery Boy' Looks for Kin in Nashville" (Hayden), **Supp. II Part 1:** 366, 372
"Mystery of Coincidence, The" (Conroy), **Supp. XVI:** 74
"Mystery of Heroism, A" (Crane), **I:** 414
"Mystery of Marie Rogêt, The" (Poe), **III:** 413, 419; **Retro. Supp. II:** 271
"Mystic" (Plath), **Retro. Supp. II:** 257; **Supp. I Part 2:** 539, 541
"Mystical Poet, A" (Bogan), **Retro. Supp. I:** 36
"Mystic of Sex, The—A First Look at D. H. Lawrence" (Nin), **Supp. X:** 188

"Mystic Vision in 'The Marshes of Glynn' " (Warfel), **Supp. I Part 1:** 366, 373
"Mystification" (Poe), **III:** 425
"My Story" (Monroe), **Supp. XXVII:** 95
"My Strange New Poetry" (Halliday), **Supp. XIX:** 88, 94
My Study Windows (J. R. Lowell), **Supp. I Part 2:** 407
"My Teacher" (Conroy), **Supp. XVI:** 75
"Myth" (Rukeyser), **Supp. VI:** 281–282
"Myth" (Trethewey), **Supp. XXI:** 245, 255, 256
"Myth"(Hadas), **Supp. XXIII:** 119
"Mythmaker" (Trethewey), **Supp. XXI:** 243
Myth of American Manhood, The (Kriegel, ed.), **Supp. XXIV:** 214
Myth of Sisyphus, The (Camus), **I:** 294; **Supp. XIII:** 165
"Myth of the Happy Worker, The" (Swados), **Supp. XIX:** 265
"Myth of the Isolated Artist, The" (Oates), **Supp. II Part 2:** 520
Myth of the Machine, The (Mumford), **Supp. II Part 2:** 476, 478, 482, 483, 493, 497
"Myth of the Powerful Worker, The" (Swados), **Supp. XIX:** 265
Mythology and the Romantic Tradition in English Poetry (Bush), **Supp. I Part 1:** 268
Myths and Texts (Snyder), **Supp. VIII:** **295–296**
"Myths of Bears, The" (Bass), **Supp. XVI:** 19, 20
"My Tocaya" (Cisneros), **Supp. VII:** 69
My Uncle Dudley (Morris), **I:** 305; **III:** 219–220
"My Uncle's Favorite Coffee Shop" (Nye), **Supp. XIII:** 283
"My Unopened Life" (Gallagher), **Supp. XXIV:** 171
"My Weariness of Epic Proportions" (Simic), **Supp. VIII:** 276
My Wicked Wicked Ways (Cisneros), **Supp. VII:** 58, 64–68, 71
"My Wicked Wicked Ways" (Cisneros), **Supp. VII:** 58, 64–66
My Wisdom (Thompson), **Supp. XXIII: 291–293**
"My Word-house" (Mora), **Supp. XIII:** 219, 225
My Works and Days (Mumford), **Supp. II Part 2:** 475, 477, 481
"My World and My Critics" (Stratton-Porter), **Supp. XX: 220**
My World and Welcome to It (Thurber), **Supp. I Part 2:** 610
Nabokov, Peter, **Supp. IV Part 2:** 490
Nabokov, Véra, **Retro. Supp. I:** 266, 270
Nabokov, Vladimir, **I:** 135; **III: 244–266,** 283, 286; **Retro. Supp. I: 263–281,** 317, 335; **Supp. I Part 1:** 196; **Supp. II Part 1:** 2; **Supp. IV Part 1:** 135; **Supp. IX:** 152, 212, 261; **Supp. V:** 127, 237, 251, 252, 253; **Supp. VIII:** 105, 133, 138; **Supp. X:** 283; **Supp. XI:** 66; **Supp. XII:** 310; **Supp. XIII:** 46, 52; **Supp. XVI:** 148, 294; **Supp. XVIII:** 98, 102; **Supp. XXII:** 263; **Supp. XXIV:** 133
Nabokov's Dozen (Nabokov), **Retro. Supp. I:** 266
Nabokov's Garden: A Guide to Ada (Mason), **Supp. VIII:** 138
Naca, Kristin, **Supp. XIII:** 133
Nadeau, Robert, **Supp. X:** 261, 270
Nadel, Alan, **Supp. IV Part 1:** 209
Naimy, Mikhail, **Supp. XX: 116, 119, 120**
Naipaul, V. S., **Supp. IV Part 1:** 297; **Supp. VIII:** 314; **Supp. X:** 131; **Supp. XIV:** 111; **Supp. XX: 87; Supp. XXI:** 170; **Supp. XXII:** 240, 241, 242, 246, 253
Naison, Mark, **Supp. XVIII:** 231
Naked and the Dead, The (Mailer), **I:** 477; **III:** 26, 27, 28–30, 31, 33, 35, 36, 44; **Retro. Supp. II: 197–199; Supp. IV Part 1:** 381; **Supp. XI:** 218; **Supp. XIX:** 248; **Supp. XX: 248; Supp. XXI:** 277
Naked Author (di Donato), **Supp. XX: 45**
Naked Babies (Quindlen and Kelsh), **Supp. XVII:** 167, 179
Naked in Garden Hills (Crews), **Supp. XI:** 102, **110**
Naked Lunch (Burroughs), **Supp. III Part 1:** 92–95, 97–105; **Supp. IV Part 1:** 90
"Naked Nude" (Malamud), **Supp. I Part 2:** 450
Naked on Roller Skates (Bodenheim), **Supp. XXV:** 27
Naked Poetry (Berg and Mezey, eds.), **Supp. IV Part 1:** 60
Naked Poetry (Levine), **Supp. V:** 180
Naked Revenge (film), **Supp. XVII:** 141
Nall, Gus, **Supp. XXII:** 172, 184
Namedropping: Mostly Literary Memoirs (Coover), **Supp. V:** 40
"Name in the Papers" (Hughes), **Supp. I Part 1:** 330
Name Is Archer, The (Macdonald, under Millar), **Supp. IV Part 2:** 466
"Name Is Burroughs, The" (Burroughs), **Supp. III Part 1:** 93
Name Is Fogarty, The: Private Papers on Public Matters (Farrell), **II:** 49
"Names" (Carruth), **Supp. XVI:** 54, 56
"Names, The" (Collins), **Supp. XXI:** 54, 61–62
Names, The (DeLillo), **Supp. VI:** 3, 10, 13, 14
Names, The (Momaday), **Supp. IV Part 2:** 479, 480, 483, 486, 487, 488, 489
Namesake, The (Lahiri), **Supp. XXI:** 176, 184**, 186–188**
Names and Faces of Heroes, The (Price), **Supp. VI:** 258, 260
Names of the Dead, The (O'Nan), **Supp. XXV:** 142, 143–144, 149, 151
Names of the Lost, The (Levine), **Supp. V:** 177–178, 179, 187–188
"Naming for Love" (Carruth), **Supp. XVI:** 48
"Naming Myself" (Kingsolver), **Supp. VII:** 208
"Naming of Names, The" (Sanders), **Supp. XVI:** 268
Naming of the Beasts, The (Stern). See Rejoicings: Selected Poems, 1966–1972 (Stern)
Naming the Unseen (Ray), **Supp. XVIII:** 192**, 193–195**
"Naming the Unseen" (Ray), **Supp. XVIII:** 203
Nana (Zola), **III:** 321
Nance, Kevin, **Supp. XXVI:** 58; **Supp. XXVII:** 268
"Nancy Culpepper" (Mason), **Supp. VIII:** 141
Nancy Drew stories, **Supp. VIII:** 133, 135, 137, 142
"Nancy Knapp" (Masters), **Supp. I Part 2:** 461
"Naola Beauty Academy, New Orleans, 1943" (Trethewey), **Supp. XXI:** 246
"Naomi Counting Time"(Thompson), **Supp. XXIII:** 293
"Naomi Shihab Nye: U.S. Mideast-History a Harbinger of 9-11?" (Nye), **Supp. XIII:** 286
"Naomi Trimmer" (X. J. Kennedy), **Supp. XV:** 170
"Nap, The" (Banks), **Supp. V:** 7
"Napoleon" (Emerson), **II:** 6
Napoleon I, **I:** 6, 7, 8, 474; **II:** 5, 309,

315, 321, 523; **Supp. I Part 1:** 153; **Supp. I Part 2:** 518, 519
Napolitano, Louise, **Supp. XX: 35, 45, 46–47**
Narcissa and Other Fables (Auchincloss), **Supp. IV Part 1:** 21, 34
"Narcissus as Narcissus" (Tate), **IV:** 124
"Narcissus Leaves the Pool" (Epstein), **Supp. XIV:** 110
Narcissus Leaves the Pool: Familiar Essays (Epstein), **Supp. XIV:** 110
Nardal, Paulette, **Supp. X:** 139
Nardi, Marcia, **Retro. Supp. I:** 426, 427
"Narragansett Boulevard" (Halliday), **Supp. XIX:** 91
Narration (Stein), **IV:** 27, 30, 32, 33, 36
Narrative of a Four Months' Residence among the Natives of a Valley of the Marquesas Islands (Melville), **III:** 76
Narrative of Arthur Gordon Pym, The (Poe), **III:** 412, 416; **Retro. Supp. II:** 265, **273–275; Retro. Supp. III:** 224, 234, 235–236; **Supp. XI:** 293; **Supp. XXII:** 58
Narrative of the Life of Frederick Douglass, an American Slave, Written by Himself (Douglass), **Supp. III Part 1:** 154–159, 162, 165; **Supp. IV Part 1:** 13; **Supp. VIII:** 202
"Narrativity Scenes" (Wright), **Supp. XV:** 345
Narrenschiff, Das (Brant), **III:** 447
"Narrow Fellow in the Grass, A" (Dickinson), **Retro. Supp. I:** 30, 37
Narrow Heart, A: Portrait of a Woman (Gordon), **II:** 197, 217
Narrow Rooms (Purdy), **Supp. VII:** 274
Narrows, The (Connelly), **Supp. XXI:** 71, **76**
Nasby, Petroleum, **Supp. XVIII:** 1
Nash, Noreen, **Supp. XXII:** 256
Nash, Ogden, **Supp. XXI:** 51; **Supp. XXIV:** 45
Nash, Roderick, **Supp. IX:** 185; **Supp. XIV:** 191–192
Nash, Susan Smith, **Supp. XVI:** 274
Nash, Thomas, **Supp. III Part 1:** 387–388
Nashe, Thomas, **I:** 358; **Supp. XVII:** 232
Nashville (film), **Supp. IX:** 143
"Nashville Gone to Ashes" (Hempel), **Supp. XXI:** 115, 118, **120–121**
Nashville Skyline (album, Dylan), **Supp. XVIII:** 27
Nason, Elias, **Supp. XV:** 242
Nasser, Gamal Abdel, **IV:** 490
Nasty Bits (Silver), **Supp. XXIV:** 265
Natalie Mann (Toomer), **Supp. III Part 2:** 484–486
Nathan, Amy, **Supp. XXVII:** 200
Nathan, George Jean, **II:** 91; **III:** 103, 104, 106, 107; **IV:** 432; **Supp. IV Part 1:** 343; **Supp. IX:** 56–57; **Supp. XIII:** 161; **Supp. XXII:** 23; **Supp. XXVII:** 86
"Nathanael West" (Herbst), **Retro. Supp. II:** 325
Nathanael West: The Art of His Life (Martin), **Retro. Supp. II:** 325
Nathan Coulter (Berry), **Supp. X:** 24, 33
National Dream, The: Building the Impossible Railway (Findley and Whitehead), **Supp. XX: 51**
"Nationalist, The" (Anderson), **I:** 115
"Nation Is Like Ourselves, The" (Baraka), **Supp. II Part 1:** 53
"Native, The" (Olds), **Supp. X:** 215
"Native American Attitudes to the Environment" (Momaday), **Supp. IV Part 2:** 481, 491
Native American Renaissance (Lincoln), **Supp. IV Part 2:** 507
Native American Testimony (Nabokov, ed.), **Supp. IV Part 2:** 490
"Native Blessing" (Ray), **Supp. XVIII:** 202
Native Guard (Trethewey), **Supp. XXI:** 243, 244, 247, **254–257**
"Native Guard" (Trethewey), **Supp. XXI:** 256
"Native Hill, A" (Berry), **Supp. X:** 21
Native in a Strange Land: Trials & Tremors (Coleman), **Supp. XI: 84–85,** 87
Native of Winby and Other Tales, A (Jewett), **II:** 396; **Retro. Supp. II:** 138
"Natives Don't Cry" (Boyle), **Supp. XXIV:** 57–58
Native Son (Wright), **IV:** 476, 477, 478, 479, 481, 482–484, 485, 487, 488, 491, 495; **Retro. Supp. II:** 107, 116; **Supp. I Part 1:** 51, 64, 67, 337; **Supp. II Part 1:** 170, 235–236; **Supp. IX:** 306; **Supp. XIV:** 73; **Supp. XVII:** 155; **Supp. XVIII:** 283, 286; **Supp. XXI:** 169
"Native Trees" (Merwin), **Supp. III Part 1:** 355
Natorp, Paul, **Supp. XIV:** 198
Natural, The (Malamud), **II:** 424, 425; **Retro. Supp. II:** 288; **Supp. I Part 2:** 438–441, 443; **Supp. XXVI:** 180
"Natural, The: Malamud's World Ceres" (Wasserman), **Supp. I Part 2:** 439
Natural Affection (Inge), **Supp. XXV:** 95, 103, 104–105, 106
"Natural History" (Olds), **Supp. X:** 210
"Natural History Note" (Hay), **Supp. XIV:** 124, 130
"Natural History of Some Poems, A" (Harrison), **Supp. VIII:** 53
"Natural History of the Dead" (Hemingway), **II:** 206; **Retro. Supp. I:** 176
Natural Laws of Good Luck, The (Graf), **Supp. XXVI:** 46
"Naturally Superior School, A" (Knowles), **Supp. XII:** 235, 240–241
"Natural Method of Mental Philosophy" (Emerson), **II:** 14
"Natural Resources" (Rich), **Retro. Supp. III:** 249; **Supp. I Part 2:** 575
Natural Selection (F. Barthelme), **Supp. XI:** 2, 28, 32, 33
Nature (Emerson), **I:** 463; **II:** 1, 8, 12, 16; **IV:** 171, 172–173; **Supp. XXIV:** 75, 79; **Supp. XXV:** 241
"Nature" (Emerson), **Retro. Supp. I:** 250; **Supp. I Part 2:** 383; **Supp. III Part 1:** 387; **Supp. IX:** 178
"Nature" (Very), **Supp. XXV:** 242
"Nature, Inc." (Lewis), **II:** 441
Nature and Destiny of Man, The (Niebuhr), **III:** 292, 303–306, 310
"Nature and Life" (Emerson), **II:** 19
"Nature and New America Painting"(O'Hara), **Supp. XXIII:** 212
"Nature and Nurture: When It Comes to Twins, Sometimes It's Hard to Tell the Two Apart" (Bausch), **Supp. VII:** 40
Nature and Purpose of the Universe, The (Durang), **Supp. XXIV: 115–116**
"Nature-Metaphors" (Lanier), **Supp. I Part 1:** 352
Nature Morte (Brodsky), **Supp. VIII:** 25
Nature of Evil, The (James), **II:** 343
Nature of Generosity, The (Kittredge), **Supp. XXVI:** 186, 187–188, 189
Nature of Peace, The (Veblen), **Supp. I Part 2:** 642
Nature of Things, The (Lucretius; Stallings, trans.), **Supp. XXV:** 221, 226–227

Nature of Things, The (television show), **Supp. XX: 51**
Nature of True Virtue, The (Edwards), **I:** 549, 557–558, 559
Nature of Yearning, The (Huddle), **Supp. XXVI:** 149–150
Nature: Poems Old and New (Swenson), **Supp. IV Part 2:** 652
Nature's Economy: A History of Ecological Ideas (Worster), **Supp. IX:** 19
Nature's Way (Wouk), **Supp. XXV:** 253
Naumburg, Margaret, **Supp. XX: 68, 74–75**
Nausea (Sartre), **Supp. VIII:** 7
"Navajo Blanket, A" (Swenson), **Supp. IV Part 2:** 649
Navarette, Don Martín de, **II:** 310
Navarro, Ramon, **Supp. IV Part 1:** 206
Navigator, The (film), **I:** 31
Navratilova, Martina, **Supp. XX: 264**
Naylor, Gloria, **Supp. VIII: 213–230; Supp. XX: 108**
Naylor, Paul Kenneth, **Supp. IV Part 2:** 420
Nazarene, The (Asch), **Supp. XXIII:** 2, 3, 4, 6, 9, **12–13,** 14, 15, 16
Nazarene, The: or, The Last of the Washingtons (Lippard), **Supp. XXIII:** 183, 184, 187, 190
Nazimova, **III:** 399
Neal, Darlin', **Supp. XXI:** 41
Neal, Larry, **Retro. Supp. II:** 112, 128; **Retro. Supp. III:** 316; **Supp. X:** 324, 328
Neal, Lawrence P., **Supp. II Part 1:** 53
Neal, Patricia, **Supp. I Part 1:** 286; **Supp. IV Part 2:** 524; **Supp. V:** 223
Neale, Walter, **I:** 192, 208
"Near Damascus" (Di Piero), **Supp. XIX:** 43
Nearer the Moon: From "A Journal of Love," the Unexpurgated Diary of Anaïs Nin, 1937–1939, **Supp. X:** 184, 185
Nearing, Helen and Scott, **Supp. XXVI:** 35
Near-Johannesburg Boy and Other Poems, The (Brooks), **Supp. III Part 1:** 86
Near Klamath (Carver), **Supp. III Part 1:** 137
"Near Perigord" (Pound), **Retro. Supp. I:** 289, 290
"Near Spring" (Pickering), **Supp. XXI:** 198
Near the Ocean (R. Lowell), **II:** 543, 550, 551–553, 554, 555; **Retro. Supp. II:** 182, 186, 189–190
"Near View of the High Sierra, A" (Muir), **Supp. IX:** 183
Nebeker, Helen, **Supp. IX:** 122
"Nebraska Blizzard" (F. Wright), **Supp. XVII:** 247
Necessary Angel, The (Stevens), **IV:** 76, 79, 89, 90
"Necessities of Life" (Rich), **Retro. Supp. III:** 244
Necessities of Life: Poems, 1962–1965 (Rich), **Retro. Supp. III:** 242, 244; **Supp. I Part 2:** 553, 555
"Necessity of Blacks' Writing Fiction About the South, The" (Andrews), **Supp. XXVI:** 1, 13
"Necessity of Lemons, The"(Schott), **Supp. XXIII:** 247, 248
Nechayev, Sergey, **Supp. XXI:** 164
Neck Deep and Other Predicaments (Monson), **Supp. XXIV:** 230, **234–236,** 241
"Necrological" (Ransom), **III:** 486–489, 490, 492
Ned Christie's War (Conley), **Supp. V:** 232
"Need for a Cultural Base to Civil Rites & Bpower Mooments, The" (Baraka), **Supp. II Part 1:** 48
"Need for Christian Preaching, The" (Buechner), **Supp. XII:** 49
Needful Things (King), **Supp. V:** 139, 146
"Needle" (Simic), **Supp. VIII:** 275
"Needle Trade" (Reznikoff), **Supp. XIV:** 277, 289
"Need of Being Versed in Country Things, The" (Frost), **II:** 154; **Retro. Supp. I:** 133, 135
"Need to Say It, The" (Hampl), **Supp. XXII:** 94
Neel, Philippe, **Supp. XIV:** 338
Neelakantappa, Tara, **Supp. XV:** 104–105
Neeley, Barbara, **Supp. XVI:** 143
"Negative Capability" (Komunyakaa), **Supp. XIII:** 131
Negligible Tales (Bierce), **I:** 209
"Negotiating the Darkness, Fortified by Poets' Strength" (Karr), **Supp. XI:** 254; **Supp. XIII:** 285
Negotiating with the Dead (Atwood), **Supp. XIII:** 20, 35
Negritude movement, **Supp. X:** 131, 139
"Negro" (Hughes), **Supp. I Part 1:** 321–322
Negro, The (Du Bois), **Supp. II Part 1:** 178, 179, 185
Negro, The: The Southerner's Problem (Page), **Supp. II Part 1:** 168
Negro: An Anthology (Cunard, ed.), **Retro. Supp. III:** 129
Negro and His Music, The (Locke), **Supp. XIV:** 202
"Negro-Art Hokum, The" (Schuyler), **Supp. XXVI:** 167
"Negro Artisan, The" (Du Bois), **Supp. II Part 1:** 166
"Negro Artist and the Racial Mountain, The" (Hughes), **Retro. Supp. I:** 200, 207; **Supp. I Part 1:** 323, 325; **Supp. IV Part 1:** 169
Negro Art: Past and Present (Locke), **Supp. XIV:** 202
"Negro Assays the Negro Mood, A" (Baldwin), **Supp. I Part 1:** 52
"Negro Citizen, The" (Du Bois), **Supp. II Part 1:** 179
"Negro Dancers" (Hughes), **Retro. Supp. I:** 199; **Supp. I Part 1:** 324
"Negroes" (Bodenheim), **Supp. XXV:** 22
Negroes in America, The (McKay), **Supp. X:** 132, 136
"Negroes of Farmville, Virginia, The: A Social Study" (Du Bois), **Supp. II Part 1:** 166
Negro Family, The: The Case for National Action (Moynihan), **Retro. Supp. II:** 123
"Negro Farmer, The" (Du Bois), **Supp. II Part 1:** 167
"Negro Fight, The" (column, C. L. R. James), **Supp. XXI:** 169
"Negro Ghetto" (Hughes), **Supp. I Part 1:** 331
Negro in America, The (Locke), **Supp. XIV:** 208
Negro in American Civilization, The (Du Bois), **Supp. II Part 1:** 179
Negro in American Culture, The (Locke and Butcher), **Supp. XIV:** 202–203
Negro in Art, The: A Pictorial Record of the Negro Artist and of the Negro Theme in Art (Locke), **Supp. XIV:** 202
"Negro in Large Cities, The" (Du Bois), **Supp. II Part 1:** 169
"Negro in Literature and Art, The" (Du Bois), **Supp. II Part 1:** 174
Negro in New York, The (Ellison), **Supp. II Part 1:** 230
"Negro in the Black Belt, The: Some Social Sketches" (Du Bois), **Supp. II Part 1:** 166
Negro in the Caribbean, The (Williams), **Supp. XXI:** 166

"Negro in the Three Americas, The" (Locke), **Supp. XIV:** 211
"Negro in the Well, The" (Caldwell), **I:** 309
"Negro Love Song, A" (Dunbar), **Supp. II Part 1:** 204
"Negro Martyrs Are Needed" (C. Himes), **Supp. XVI:** 138
Negro Mother, The (Hughes), **Supp. I Part 1:** 328
Negro Mother and Other Dramatic Recitations, The (Hughes), **Retro. Supp. I:** 203
Negro Novel in America, The (Bone), **Supp. IX:** 318–319; **Supp. XVIII:** 285
Negro Publication Society of America, **Retro. Supp. I:** 205
"Negro Renaissance, The: Jean Toomer and the Harlem of the 1920s" (Bontemps), **Supp. IX:** 306
"Negro Schoolmaster in the New South, A" (Du Bois), **Supp. II Part 1:** 168
"Negro's Contribution to American Culture, The" (Locke), **Supp. XIV:** 210, 211
"Negro Sermon, A: Simon Legree" (Lindsay), **Supp. I Part 2:** 393
"Negro Sings of Rivers, The" (Hughes), **Supp. IV Part 1:** 16
"Negro Speaks of Rivers, The" (Hughes), **Retro. Supp. I:** 199; **Supp. I Part 1:** 321
"Negro Spirituals, The (Locke), **Supp. XIV:** 201
"Negro Takes Stock, The" (Du Bois), **Supp. II Part 1:** 180
"Negro Theatre, The" (Van Vechten), **Supp. II Part 2:** 735
"Negro Voter Sizes Up Taft, A" (Hurston), **Supp. VI:** 160
"Negro Writer and His Roots, The: Toward a New Romanticism" (Hansberry), **Supp. IV Part 1:** 364
"Negro Youth Speaks" (Locke), **Supp. XIV:** 201
"Nehemias Americanus" (Mather), **Supp. II Part 2:** 453
Nehru, Jawaharlal, **IV:** 490
"Neighbor" (Hugo), **Supp. VI:** 135–136
"Neighborhood Drunk"(Dybek), **Supp. XXIII:** 71
"Neighbors" (Carver), **Supp. III Part 1:** 135, 139, 141; **Supp. XI:** 153
"Neighbors" (Hogan), **Supp. IV Part 1:** 405
"Neighbors, The" (Hay), **Supp. XIV:** 126
"Neighbour Rosicky" (Cather), **I:** 331–332
Neil Simon (R. K. Johnson), **Supp. IV Part 2:** 573
"Neil Simon's Jewish-Style Comedies" (Walden), **Supp. IV Part 2:** 584, 591
"Neil Simon: Toward Act III?" (Walden), **Supp. IV Part 2:** 591
Neilson, Heather, **Supp. IV Part 2:** 681
Neiman, Gilbert, **Supp. XV:** 140
"Neither Out Far nor In Deep" (Frost), **I:** 303; **Retro. Supp. I:** 121, 138; **Retro. Supp. III:** 103
"Nellie Clark" (Masters), **Supp. I Part 2:** 461
Nelson, Alice Dunbar, **Supp. XVII:** 75
Nelson, Cary, **Supp. XVIII:** 226, 227, 230, 231; **Supp. XXII:** 271
Nelson, Ernest, **I:** 388
Nelson, Howard, **Supp. IV Part 1:** 66, 68; **Supp. XIX:** 3; **Supp. XXI:** 95
Nelson, Lord Horatio, **II:** 524
Nelson, Lynn (pseudonym). See Nelson, Marilyn
Nelson, Marilyn, **Supp. XVII:** 74, 112; **Supp. XVIII: 171–188**
Nelson, Shirley, **Supp. XII:** 293
Nelson, Steve, **Supp. XVIII:** 226
Nelson Algren (Cox and Chatterton), **Supp. IX:** 11–12
Nelson Algren: A Life on the Wild Side (Drew), **Supp. IX:** 2
Nemerov, David, **II:** 268
Nemerov, Howard, **III: 267–289; IV:** 137, 140; **Supp. III Part 2:** 541; **Supp. IV Part 2:** 455, 650; **Supp. IX:** 114
"Nemesis" (Lovecraft), **Supp. XXV:** 119
Nemesis (P. Roth), **Supp. XXIV:** 214
Nemiroff, Robert Barron, **Supp. IV Part 1:** 360, 361, 365, 369, 370, 374
Neoconservative Criticism: Norman Podhoretz, Kenneth S. Lynn, and Joseph Epstein (Winchell), **Supp. VIII:** 241; **Supp. XIV:** 103
"Neo-Formalism: A Dangerous Nostalgia" (Sadoff), **Supp. XXI:** 100
"Neo-Hoodoo Manifesto, The" (Reed), **Supp. X:** 242
Neon Bible, The (Toole), **Supp. XXVI:** 239, 241, 242, 246–250, 253
Neon Rain, The (Burke), **Supp. XIV:** 22, 24, 26–27, 28–29, 30
Neon Vernacular (Komunyakaa), **Supp. XIII:** 121, **127–128,** 131
Neon Wilderness, The (Algren), **Supp. IX:** 3, 4
Neo-Slave Narratives (Rushdy), **Supp. X:** 250
Nepantla: Essays from the Land in the Middle (Mora), **Supp. XIII:** 213, **219–221,** 227
Nephew, The (Purdy), **Supp. VII:** 271, 273, 282
"Nereids of Seriphos, The" (Clampitt), **Supp. IX:** 41
Nericcio, William, **Supp. XIV:** 304–305
Neruda, Pablo, **Supp. I Part 1:** 89; **Supp. IV Part 2:** 537; **Supp. IX:** 157, 271; **Supp. V:** 332; **Supp. VIII:** 272, 274; **Supp. X:** 112; **Supp. XI:** 191; **Supp. XII:** 217; **Supp. XIII:** 114, 315, 323; **Supp. XXI:** 61, 100; **Supp. XXIV:** 170
"Nerves" (Huddle), **Supp. XXVI:** 149
Nesbit, Edith, **Supp. VIII:** 171
Nesbit, Lynn, **Supp. XXIII:** 100
Nesbitt, Robin, **Supp. VIII:** 89
Nessmuk (George Washington Sears), **Supp. XIX:** 10
Nesting Ground, The (Wagoner), **Supp. IX:** 324, **325–326**
Nest of Ninnies, A (Ashbery and Schuyler), **Supp. III Part 1:** 3; **Supp. XV:** 178
"Nests"(Le Sueur), **Supp. XXIII:** 165
Net of Cobwebs (Holding), **Supp. XXII:** 126, **129–130,** 134
Net of Magic: Wonders and Deceptions in India (Siegel), **Supp. XXII:** 262
Nets to Catch the Wind (Wylie), **Supp. I Part 2:** 709, 710–712, 714
Nettleton, Asahel, **I:** 458
"Net to Snare the Moonlight, A" (Lindsay), **Supp. I Part 2:** 387
Neubauer, Carol E., **Supp. IV Part 1:** 9
Neugeboren, Jacob Mordecai. See Neugeboren, Jay
Neugeboren, Jay, **Supp. XVI: 217–231**
Neugroschel, Joachim, **Supp. IX:** 138
Neuhaus, Richard John, **Supp. VIII:** 245; **Supp. XIX:** 144
Neumann, Erich, **Supp. I Part 2:** 567; **Supp. IV Part 1:** 68, 69
Neuromancer (W. Gibson), **Supp. XII:** 15; **Supp. XVI:** 117, 119–120, 122, 124, **125–126,** 127, 129, 131
Neurotica: Jewish Writers on Sex (Bukiet, ed.), **Supp. XVII:** 48
"Neurotic America and the Sex Impulse" (Dreiser), **Retro. Supp. II:** 105
Neutra, Richard, **Supp. XVI:** 192
"Never Again Would Birds' Song Be

the Same" (Frost), **Retro. Supp. III:** 104
"Never Been" (Huddle), **Supp. XXVI:** 150
"Never Bet the Devil Your Head" (Poe), **III:** 425; **Retro. Supp. II:** 273
Never Come Morning (Algren), **Supp. IX:** 3, **7–9**
Never in a Hurry: Essays on People and Places (Nye), **Supp. XIII:** 273, **280–282,** 286
"Never Marry a Mexican" (Cisneros), **Supp. VII:** 70
"Never Room with a Couple" (Hughes), **Supp. I Part 1:** 330
"Nevertheless" (Moore), **III:** 214
Nevils, René Pol, **Supp. XXVI:** 241, 242, 246
Nevins, Allan, **I:** 253; **Supp. I Part 2:** 486, 493
"Nevsky Prospekt" (Olds), **Supp. X:** 205
New Adam, The (Untermeyer), **Supp. XV:** 304, 305
New Addresses (Koch), **Supp. XV:** 177, 184
"New Age of the Rhetoricians, The" (Cowley), **Supp. II Part 1:** 135
New American Cyclopedia, **Supp. XVIII:** 4
New American Literature, The (Pattee), **II:** 456
New American Novel of Manners, The (Klinkowitz), **Supp. XI:** 347
"New American Ode, The" (Wright), **Supp. XV:** 346
New American Poetry (Allen, ed.), **Supp. XXVI:** 223
New American Poetry, 1945–1960, The (Allen, ed.), **Supp. VIII:** 291, 292; **Supp. XIII:** 112; **Supp. XXIII:** 215–216
New American Poetry, The (Allen, ed.), **Supp. XXVII:** 25
"New American Writer, A" (W. C. Williams), **Retro. Supp. II:** 335
New and Collected Poems (Reed), **Supp. X:** 241
New and Collected Poems (Wilbur), **Supp. III Part 2:** 562–564
New and Selected Poems (Nemerov), **III:** 269, 275, 277–279
New and Selected Poems (Oliver), **Supp. VII:** 240–241, 245
New and Selected Poems (W. J. Smith), **Supp. XIII:** 332
New and Selected Poems (Wagoner), **Supp. IX: 326–327**
New and Selected Poems, 1958–1998 (Sorrentino), **Supp. XXI:** 229
New and Selected Poems: 1974–1994 (Dunn), **Supp. XI: 151–152**
New and Selected Things Taking Place (Swenson), **Supp. IV Part 2:** 648–650, 651
"New Aristocracy, The" (Atherton), **Supp. XXIV:** 24
"New Art Gallery Society, The" (Wolfe), **Supp. III Part 2:** 580
Newberger, Julee, **Supp. XVIII:** 168
"New Birth, The" (Very), **Supp. XXV:** 246, 247, 248
New Black Poetry, The (Major, ed.), **Supp. XXII:** 172, 174, 176, 180
New Bridge, The (Levin), **Supp. XXVII:** 133
"New Capitalist Tool, The" (Wasserstein), **Supp. XV:** 328
New Collected Poems (Oppen), **Supp. XXVI:** 224
Newcomb, Ralph, **Supp. XIII:** 12
Newcomb, Robert, **II:** 111
New Conscience and an Ancient Evil, A (Addams), **Supp. I Part 1:** 14–15, 16
"New Conservatism in American Poetry, The" (Wakoski), **Supp. XVII:** 112
"New Conservatives, The: Intellectuals in Retreat" (Epstein), **Supp. XIV:** 103
New Critical Essays on H. P. Lovecraft (Simmons, ed.), **Supp. XXV:** 123
New Criticism, The (Ransom), **III:** 497–498, 499, 501
"New Day, A" (Levine), **Supp. V:** 182
Newdick, Robert Spangler, **Retro. Supp. I:** 138
Newdick's Season of Frost (Newdick), **Retro. Supp. I:** 138
New Dictionary of Quotations, A (Mencken), **III:** 111
New Directions Anthology in Prose and Poetry (Laughlin, ed.), **Supp. XVI:** 284
"New Directions in Poetry" (D. Locke), **Supp. IX:** 273
"New Dog, The: Variations on a Text by Jules Laforgue" (C. Frost), **Supp. XV:** 98
Newell, Henry, **IV:** 193
"New England" (R. Lowell), **II:** 536
"New England" (Robinson), **III:** 510, 524
"New England Bachelor, A" (Eberhart), **I:** 539
"New Englander, The" (Anderson), **I:** 114
New England Girlhood, A (Larcom), **Supp. XIII:** 137, 142, 143, 144, **147–154**
New England Gothic Literature (Ringel), **Supp. XXII:** 205
New England: Indian Summer (Brooks), **I:** 253, 256
New England Local Color Literature (Donovan), **Retro. Supp. II:** 138
"New England Sabbath-Day Chace, The" (Freneau), **Supp. II Part 1:** 273
New-England Tale, A (Sedgwick), **I:** 341
New England Tragedies, The (Longfellow), **II:** 490, 505, 506; **Retro. Supp. II:** 165, 167
New English Canaan (Morton), **Supp. XXII:** 45
New Era in American Poetry, The (Untermeyer, ed.), **Supp. XV:** 301, 303, 306
Newer Ideals of Peace (Addams), **Supp. I Part 1:** 11–12, 15, 16–17, 19, 20–21
"New Experience in Millinery, A" (Stratton-Porter), **Supp. XX: 216**
New Feminist Criticism, The: Essays on Women, Literature, and Theory (Showalter), **Supp. X:** 97
New Fire: To Put Things Right Again (Moraga), **Supp. XXIII:** 197
"New Folsom Prison" (Matthews), **Supp. IX:** 165
New Formalism, The: A Critical Introduction (McPhillips), **Supp. XV:** 250, 251, 252, 264
Newfound (J. W. Miller), **Supp. XX: 163, 166, 170–172**
New Found Land: Fourteen Poems (MacLeish), **III:** 12–13
New Hampshire (Frost), **II:** 154–155; **Retro. Supp. I:** 132, 133, 135; **Retro. Supp. III:** 101–102, 105
"New Hampshire" (Frost), **Retro. Supp. III:** 101, 102; **Supp. XXVI:** 78
"New Hampshire, February" (Eberhart), **I:** 536
New Hard-Boiled Writers (Panek), **Supp. XIV:** 27
"New Home" (Richter), **Supp. XVIII:** 209
Newhouse, Seth, **Supp. XXVI:** 87, 89, 90
New Industrial State, The (Galbraith), **Supp. I Part 2:** 648
"New Journalism, The" (Wolfe), **Supp. III Part 2:** 571
New Journalism, The (Wolfe and E. W. Johnson, eds.), **Supp. III Part 2:**

570, 579–581, 583, 586; **Supp. XXIV:** 282; **Supp. XXVII:** 38
New Left, The: The Anti-Industrial Revolution (Rand), **Supp. IV Part 2:** 527
"New Letters from Thomas Jefferson" (Stafford), **Supp. XI:** 324
New Letters on the Air: Contemporary Writers on Radio, **Supp. X:** 165, 169, 173
"New Life" (Glück), **Supp. V:** 90
New Life, A (Malamud), **Supp. I Part 2:** 429–466
"New Life, The" (Bynner), **Supp. XV:** 44
"New Life, The"(Schott), **Supp. XXIII:** 242
"New Life at Kyerefaso" (Sutherland), **Supp. IV Part 1:** 9
"New Light on Veblen" (Dorfman), **Supp. I Part 2:** 650
"New Man, A" (E. P. Jones), **Supp. XXII:** 144
Newman, Charles, **Supp. I Part 2:** 527, 546–548
Newman, Edwin, **Supp. IV Part 2:** 526
Newman, Frances, **Supp. XXII:** 198
Newman, Judie, **Supp. IV Part 1:** 304, 305
Newman, Paul, **Supp. IV Part 2:** 473, 474
New Man, The (Merton), **Supp. VIII:** 208
"New Mecca, The" (Saunders), **Supp. XIX:** 235, 236
"New Medea, The" (Howells), **II:** 282
New Mexico trilogy (Nichols), **Supp. XIII:** 269
New Morning (album, Dylan), **Supp. XVIII:** 27, 33
"New Mother" (Olds), **Supp. X:** 206
"New Mothers, The" (Shields), **Supp. VII:** 310
New Music (Price), **Supp. VI:** 264, 265
"New Mutants, The" (Fiedler), **Supp. XIII:** 104
"New Name for Some Old Ways of Thinking, A" (James), **II:** 353
New Native American Novel, The: Works in Progress (Bartlett), **Supp. IV Part 1:** 335
"New Natural History, A" (Thurber), **Supp. I Part 2:** 619
New Negro, The (Locke), **Supp. XIX:** 69
"New Negro, The" (Locke), **Supp. XIV:** 201
New Negro, The (Locke, ed.), **Supp. II Part 1:** 176; **Supp. IX:** 309; **Supp. X:** 137; **Supp. XXII:** 8
New Negro, The: An Interpretation (Locke, ed.), **Retro. Supp. I:** 199; **Supp. IV Part 1:** 170; **Supp. XIV:** 195, 201–202
New Negro for a New Century, A (Washington, Wood, and Williams), **Supp. XIV:** 201
New New Journalism, The (R. Boynton), **Supp. XVII:** 209
"New Nomads, The" (E. Hoffman), **Supp. XVI:** 161
"New Orleans" (Carruth), **Supp. XVI:** 50
New Orleans Sketches (Faulkner), **Retro. Supp. I:** 80
New Path to the Waterfall, A (Carver), **Supp. III Part 1:** 138–140, 147, 149; **Supp. XXIV:** 172
"New Patricians, The" (Untermeyer), **Retro. Supp. III:** 47
"New Poem, The" (Wright), **Supp. V:** 339, 340
"New Poems" (MacLeish), **III:** 19
"New Poems" (Oliver), **Supp. VII:** 240
New Poems 1960 (Bynner), **Supp. XV:** 51
New Poems: 1980–88 (Haines), **Supp. XII: 209–210**
New Poetry, The (Monroe and Henderson, eds.), **Supp. I Part 2:** 387
"New Poetry Handbook, The" (Strand), **Supp. IV Part 2:** 626
New Poetry of Mexico (Strand, trans.), **Supp. IV Part 2:** 630
New Poets of England and America (Hall, Pack, and Simpson, eds.), **Supp. IV Part 2:** 621
"Newport of Anchuria" (Henry), **Supp. II Part 1:** 409
New Princeton Encyclopedia of Poetry and Poetics (Preminger and Brogan, eds.), **Supp. XV:** 250
"New Republic Moves Uptown, The" (Cowley), **Supp. II Part 1:** 142
"New Rose Hotel" (W. Gibson), **Supp. XVI:** 120, 122, 124
"News, The" (McClatchy), **Supp. XII:** 269
News Crew (Cruisers) series (Myers), **Supp. XXVII:** 212
"New Season" (Levine), **Supp. V:** 188
New Seeds of Contemplation (Merton), **Supp. VIII:** 200, 208
News from the Glacier: Selected Poems 1960–1980 (Haines), **Supp. XII:** 207, 208–209
"News Item" (Parker), **Supp. IX:** 190
News of a Kidnapping (García Márquez), **Supp. XXV:** 57
New Song, A (Hughes), **Retro. Supp. I:** 202; **Supp. I Part 1:** 328, 331–332
"New Song"(Kenny), **Supp. XXIII:** 156
Newson-Horst, Adele, **Supp. XXIII:** 95
"New South, The" (Lanier), **Supp. I Part 1:** 352, 354, 370
New Southern Girl, The: Female Adolescence in the Works of 12 Women Authors (Town), **Supp. XVIII:** 195
Newspaper Days, 1899–1906 (Mencken), **III:** 100, 102, 120
"New Spirit, The" (Ashbery), **Supp. III Part 1:** 14, 15
New Spoon River, The (Masters), **Supp. I Part 2:** 461–465, 473
New Star Chamber and Other Essays, The (Masters), **Supp. I Part 2:** 455–456, 459
New Tales of the Vampires (Rice), **Supp. VII:** 290
New Tenant, The (Ionesco), **Supp. XXIV:** 113
New Testament, **I:** 303, 457, 458; **II:** 167; **III:** 305; **IV:** 114, 134, 152; **Retro. Supp. I:** 58, 140, 360; **Supp. I Part 1:** 104, 106; **Supp. I Part 2:** 516; **Supp. XVII:** 155; **Supp. XXIII:** 13. See also names of New Testament books
New Testament, A (Anderson), **I:** 101, 114
"New Theory of Thorstein Veblen, A" (Galbraith), **Supp. I Part 2:** 650
Newton, Benjamin Franklin, **I:** 454
Newton, Huey P., **Supp. I Part 1:** 66; **Supp. IV Part 1:** 206; **Supp. XXVII:** 168
Newton, Isaac, **I:** 132, 557; **II:** 6, 103, 348–349; **III:** 428; **IV:** 18, 149
Newton, Maud, **Supp. XXIII:** 290
Newton, Sarah Emily, **Supp. XV:** 234
"New-Wave Format, A" (Mason), **Supp. VIII:** 141, 143, 147
New West of Edward Abbey, The (Ronald), **Supp. XIII:** 4
"New Wife" (Halliday), **Supp. XIX:** 89
New Wolves, The: The Return of the Mexican Wolf to the American Southwest (Bass), **Supp. XVI:** 26–27
New Woman's Survival Sourcebook, The (Rennie and Grimstead, eds.), **Supp. I Part 2:** 569
New World, The (Bronk), **Supp. XXI:**

25–26, 31
New World, The (Bynner), **Supp. XV:** 41, 42
"New World, The" (Very), **Supp. XXV:** 248
New World, The: Tales (Banks), **Supp. V:** 8, 9, 10
New World Naked, A (Mariani), **Retro. Supp. I:** 419
New Worlds of Literature (Beaty and Hunter, eds.), **Supp. IV Part 1:** 331
New World Writing (Updike), **IV:** 217
"New Year, The" (Very), **Supp. XXV:** 240, 244
New Year Letter (Auden), **Supp. II Part 1:** 14, 16
"New Year's Day" (Wharton), **Retro. Supp. I:** 381
"New Year's Eve" (Schwartz), **Supp. II Part 2:** 640, 656–657
New Year's Eve/1929 (Farrell), **II:** 43
"New Year's Eve 1968" (R. Lowell), **II:** 554
New Year's Eve: A Play (W. Frank), **Supp. XX: 75**
"New Year's Gift, The" (Stowe), **Supp. I Part 2:** 587
"New Year Two Thousand, The" (Weigl), **Supp. XIX:** 287–288
"New York" (Capote), **Supp. III Part 1:** 122
"New York" (Moore), **III:** 196, 198, 202, 206
"New York 1965" (Bowles), **Supp. IV Part 1:** 94
New York: A Serendipiter's Journey (Talese), **Supp. XVII:** 202, 203
"New York Breeze" (Halliday), **Supp. XIX:** 85
New York City Arts Project, **Supp. III Part 2:** 618
"New York City in 1979"(Acker), **Supp. XII:** 5
New York Edition, **Retro. Supp. I:** 235
"New York Edition" (James), **II:** 336, 337
"New York Gold Conspiracy, The" (Adams), **I:** 4
New York Hat, The (film; Griffith), **Supp. XVI:** 183
New York Intellectuals, **Supp. VIII:** 93
"New York Intellectuals, The" (Howe), **Supp. VI:** 120
"New York Is a City of Things Unnoticed" (Talese), **Supp. XVII:** 202, 209
New York: Its Upper Ten and Lower Million (Lippard), **Supp. XXIII:** 180, 183, 184
New York Jew (Kazin), **Supp. VIII:** 95, **97–100**
New York Madness (Bodenheim), **Supp. XXV:** 28
"New York Theater: Isn't It Romantic" (Wasserstein), **Supp. XV:** 320
New York Trilogy, The (Auster), **Supp. XII:** 21, **24–28**
Next (McNally), **Supp. XIII:** 197
"Next in Line, The" (Bradbury), **Supp. IV Part 1:** 102
"Next Rodeo, The" (Kittredge), **Supp. XXVI:** 185–186
Next Rodeo, The: New and Selected Essays (Kittredge), **Supp. XXVI:** 185–186
Next Room of the Dream, The (Nemerov), **III:** 269, 275, 278, 279–280, 284
"Next Time I Crossed the Line into Oklahoma, The" (Wright), **Supp. XV:** 345
Next-to-Last Things: New Poems and Essays (Kunitz), **Supp. III Part 1:** 257–259, 261, 262, 265, 266, 268
"'Next to Reading Matter' " (Henry), **Supp. II Part 1:** 399
Nexus (H. Miller), **III:** 170, 187, 188, 189
Nguyen, Bich Minh, **Supp. XXVI: 207–222**
Niatum, Duane, **Supp. IV Part 1:** 331; **Supp. IV Part 2:** 505
Nice and Noir (Schwartz), **Supp. XIV:** 23
"Nice Girl" (Nelson), **Supp. XVIII:** 178
Nice Jewish Boy, The (P. Roth), **Supp. III Part 2:** 412
"Nice Part f Town, A" (Hayes), **Supp. XXVI:** 144
Nicholas II, Tsar, **Supp. I Part 2:** 447
"Nicholas in the Park" (Halliday), **Supp. XIX:** 88
Nicholls, Peter, **Supp. XIX:** 232; **Supp. XXVI:** 228, 232
Nichols, Charles, **Retro. Supp. I:** 194
Nichols, Dudley, **Supp. XVIII:** 247
Nichols, John Treadwell, **Supp. XIII: 253–272**
Nichols, Luther, **Supp. X:** 265
Nichols, Mike, **Supp. IV Part 1:** 234; **Supp. IV Part 2:** 577
Nicholson, Colin, **Supp. VIII:** 129
Nicholson, Harold, **Supp. XIV:** 163
Nicholson, Jack, **Supp. V:** 26; **Supp. VIII:** 45; **Supp. XI:** 308
Nicholson, John, **Supp. XVI:** 293
Nick Adams Stories, The (Hemingway), **II:** 258; **Retro. Supp. I:** 174
"Nick and the Candlestick" (Plath), **Supp. I Part 2:** 544
Nickel and Dimed: On (Not) Getting By in America (Ehrenreich), **Supp. XVII:** 210
Nickel Eclipse: Iroquois Moon (Gansworth), **Supp. XXVI:** 110
Nickel Mountain: A Pastoral Novel (Gardner), **Supp. VI:** 63, 64, 68, **69**
Nickerson, Catherine Ross, **Supp. XXV:** 192, 200, 202
"Nicodemus" (Keillor), **Supp. XVI:** 167
Nicoll, Allardyce, **III:** 400
Nicoloff, Philip, **II:** 7
Niebuhr, Gustav, **III:** 292
Niebuhr, H. Richard, **I:** 494
Niebuhr, Lydia, **III:** 292
Niebuhr, Reinhold, **III: 290–313; Supp. I Part 2:** 654; **Supp. XX: 79**
Niedecker, Lorine, **Supp. III Part 2:** 616, 623; **Supp. XIV:** 287; **Supp. XXIII:** 174
Nielsen, Ed, **Supp. IX:** 254
Nielson, Dorothy, **Supp. I Part 2:** 659
Nietzsche, Friedrich Wilhelm, **I:** 227, 283, 383, 389, 396, 397, 402, 509; **II:** 7, 20, 27, 42, 90, 145, 262, 462, 463, 577, 583, 585; **III:** 102–103, 113, 156, 176; **IV:** 286, 491; **Supp. I Part 1:** 254, 299, 320; **Supp. I Part 2:** 646; **Supp. IV Part 1:** 104, 105–106, 107, 110, 284; **Supp. IV Part 2:** 519; **Supp. V:** 277, 280; **Supp. VIII:** 11, 181, 189; **Supp. X:** 48; **Supp. XII:** 98; **Supp. XIV:** 339; **Supp. XX: 117; Supp. XXVII:** 34
Nieves, Felipe, **Supp. XVIII:** 90
Niflis, N. Michael, **Supp. IV Part 1:** 175
Niger, S. See Charney, Samuel
Nigger Heaven (Van Vechten), **Supp. II Part 2:** 739, 744–746; **Supp. XIX:** 76; **Supp. XVIII:** 123, 127
"Nigger Jeff" (Dreiser), **Retro. Supp. II:** 97
Nigger of the "Narcissus," The (Conrad), **II:** 91; **Retro. Supp. I:** 106; **Supp. XVIII:** 224; **Supp. XXIV:** 286
"NIGGY THE HO" (Baraka), **Supp. II Part 1:** 54
"Night" (H. Johnson), **Supp. XXVI:** 173
"Night" (Huddle), **Supp. XXVI:** 155
"Night, Death, Mississippi" (Hayden), **Supp. II Part 1:** 369

'Night, Mother (Norman), **Supp. VIII:** 141
"Night above the Avenue" (Merwin), **Supp. III Part 1:** 355
"Night among the Horses, A" (Barnes), **Supp. III Part 1:** 33–34, 39, 44
"Night and the Madman" (Gibran), **Supp. XX: 118**
Night at the Movies, A, or, You Must Remember This: Fictions (Coover), **Supp. V:** 50–51
"Night at the Opera, A" (Matthews), **Supp. IX:** 167
"Night before the Sentence Is Carried Out, The" (Wright), **Supp. XV:** 341
"Nightbird" (Komunyakaa), **Supp. XIII:** 132
Night-Blooming Cereus, The (Hayden), **Supp. II Part 1:** 367, 373
"Night-Blooming Cereus, The" (Hayden), **Supp. II Part 1:** 367
Night-Born, The (London), **II:** 467
"Nightbreak" (Rich), **Retro. Supp. III:** 244; **Supp. I Part 2:** 556
"Nightclub" (Collins), **Supp. XXI:** 60
Night Country, The (O'Nan), **Supp. XXV:** 141, 148–149, 150
Night Dance (Price), **Supp. VI:** 264
"Night Dances, The" (Plath), **Supp. I Part 2:** 544
"Night Dream, The" (MacLeish), **III:** 15
"Nightfall" (Teasdale), **Supp. XXVII:** 293
"Night Ferry" (Doty), **Supp. XI:** 124
"Nightfishing" (Schnackenberg), **Supp. XV:** 254
"Nighthawks"(Dybek), **Supp. XXIII:** 73, 74
"Night I Met Little Floyd, The" (Wright), **Supp. XV:** 345–346
Night in Acadie, A (Chopin), **Retro. Supp. II: 66–67,** 73; **Supp. I Part 1:** 200, 219, 220, 224
"Night in Acadie, A" (Chopin), **Retro. Supp. II:** 66
"Night in June, A" (W. C. Williams), **Retro. Supp. I:** 424
"Night in New Arabia, A" (Henry), **Supp. II Part 1:** 402
Night in Question, The: Stories (Wolff), **Supp. VII:** 342–344
"Night Journey" (Roethke), **Supp. III Part 1:** 260
"Night Letter to the Reader" (Collins), **Supp. XXI:** 55
Night Light (Justice), **Supp. VII:** 126–127
"Nightmare" (Kumin), **Supp. IV Part 2:** 442
Nightmare Factory, The (Kumin), **Supp. IV Part 2:** 444–447, 451
"Nightmare Factory, The" (Kumin), **Supp. IV Part 2:** 445, 453
Nightmare on Main Street (Poe), **Retro. Supp. II:** 262
"Nightmare" poems (Benét), **Supp. XI:** 46, 58
"Night Mirror" (L.-Y. Lee), **Supp. XV:** 225
Night Music (Odets), **Supp. II Part 2:** 541, 543, 544
"Night of First Snow" (R. Bly), **Supp. IV Part 1:** 71
Night of January 16th (Rand), **Supp. IV Part 2:** 527
Night of the Iguana, The (T. Williams), **IV:** 382, 383, 384, 385, 386, 387, 388, 391, 392, 393, 394, 395, 397, 398
"Night of the Iguana, The" (T. Williams), **IV:** 384
"Night of the Living Beanfield: How an Unsuccessful Cult Novel Became an Unsuccessful Cult Film in Only Fourteen Years, Eleven Nervous Breakdowns, and $20 Million" (Nichols), **Supp. XIII:** 267
Night Passage (Parker), **Supp. XIX:** 185–186
Night Rider (Warren), **IV:** 243, 246–247
Nights (Doolittle), **Supp. I Part 1:** 270, 271
Nights and Days (Merrill), **Supp. III Part 1:** 319, 320, 322–325
"Nights and Days" (Rich), **Supp. I Part 2:** 574
"Night's for Cryin,' The" (C. Himes), **Supp. XVI:** 137
"Night Shift" (Plath), **Supp. I Part 2:** 538
"Nightshine Beyond Memory, A: Ten More Years with Ray" (Gallagher), **Supp. XXIV:** 167, 172
Night-Side (Oates), **Supp. II Part 2:** 522
"Night-Side" (Oates), **Supp. II Part 2:** 523
Night-Side, The (Skloot), **Supp. XX: 193, 196, 205, 208**
Nights in the Gardens of Brooklyn (Swados), **Supp. XIX: 261–264**
"Nights in the Gardens of Brooklyn" (Swados), **Supp. XIX:** 261
"Night Sketches: Beneath an Umbrella" (Hawthorne), **II:** 235–237, 238, 239, 242; **Supp. XXI:** 201
"Night Sport" (Hoffman), **Supp. XVIII:** 86, 87
"Night-Sweat" (R. Lowell), **II:** 554
"Night-Talk" (Ellison), **Retro. Supp. II:** 126; **Supp. II Part 1:** 248
Night the New Jesus Fell to Earth, The (Rash), **Supp. XXVII:** 216–217, 227
Night Thoughts (Young), **III:** 415
"Night-Time River Road, A" (Ferry), **Supp. XXIV:** 150
Night Traveler, The (Oliver), **Supp. VII:** 233
"Night Watch" (Gioia), **Supp. XV:** 117
"Night Watch, The" (Wright), **Supp. V:** 339
"Night We All Had Grippe, The" (Jackson), **Supp. IX:** 118
Nightwood (Barnes), **Supp. III Part 1:** 31, 32, 35–37, 39–43
Night World and the Word Night, The (F. Wright), **Supp. XVII:** 240, 244–245
"Nihilist as Hero, The" (R. Lowell), **II:** 554; **Retro. Supp. II:** 190
Nijinsky, Vaslav, **Supp. XV:** 28–29
Nikolai Gogol (Nabokov), **Retro. Supp. I:** 266
"Nilda" (Díaz), **Supp. XXIV:** 92
Niles, Thomas, **Retro. Supp. I:** 35
Niles, Thomas, Jr., **Supp. I Part 1:** 39
Nilsson, Christine, **Supp. I Part 1:** 355
Nilsson, Harry, **Supp. XI:** 309
Nilsson, Jenny Lind, **Supp. XVI:** 177
Nimitz, Chester, **Supp. I Part 2:** 491
"Nimram" (Gardner), **Supp. VI:** 73
Nims, John Frederick, **III:** 527; **Supp. XVII:** 112
Nin, Anaïs, **III:** 182, 184, 190; **Supp. III Part 1:** 43; **Supp. IV Part 2:** 680; **Supp. X: 181–200; Supp. XIX:** 134
"9" (Oliver), **Supp. VII:** 244
"9 Failures of the Imagination" (Lethem), **Supp. XVIII:** 148
"Nine-Ball" (Offutt), **Supp. XIX:** 166, 167
Nine Dragons (Connelly), **Supp. XXI:** 74, **79–80**
"Nine from Eight" (Lanier), **Supp. I Part 1:** 352–354
Nine Gates: Entering the Mind of Poetry (Hirshfield), **Supp. XXIII:** 136, 137
Nine Headed Dragon River: Zen Journals 1969–1982 (Matthiessen), **Supp. V:** 199
Nine Horses (Collins), **Supp. XXI:** 55, 60, 61, 62, 65
"Nine Horses" (Collins), **Supp. XXI:** 61
Ninemile Wolves,The (Bass), **Supp.**

XVI: 24–25, 26
"Nine Nectarines" (Moore), **III:** 203, 209, 215
Nine Plays (Reznikoff), **Supp. XIV:** 288
"Nine Poems for the Unborn Child" (Rukeyser), **Supp. VI:** 280–281, 284
Nine Stories (Nabokov), **Retro. Supp. I:** 266
Nine Stories (Salinger), **III:** 552, 558–564
"19 Hadley Street" (Schnackenberg), **Supp. XV:** 253
19 Necromancers from Now (Reed), **Supp. X:** 240
19 Varieties of Gazelle (Nye), **Supp. XIII:** 275, **286–288**
"19 Varieties of Gazelle" (Nye), **Supp. XIII:** 286
1984 (Orwell), **Supp. XIII:** 29; **Supp. XVIII:** 137, 138
"1953 Dodge Coronet" (Huddle), **Supp. XXVI:** 151
"1940" (Stafford), **Supp. XI:** 328–329
"1945–1985: Poem for the Anniversary" (Oliver), **Supp. VII:** 237
"1941" (Stone), **Supp. XXVII:** 253
1919 (Dos Passos), **I:** 482, 485–486, 487, 489, 490, 492
"1975" (Wright), **Supp. V:** 341
"1973"(Hirshfield), **Supp. XXIII:** 130
"1910" (Mora), **Supp. XIII:** 215
Nineteenth-Century Minor Poets (Auden), **Supp. XXV:** 237
"1938" (Komunyakaa), **Supp. XIII:** 114
1939 (Boyle), **Supp. XXIV:** 62
"1939" (Taylor), **Supp. V:** 316
1933 (Levine), **Supp. V:** 185–187
"1933" (Levine), **Supp. V:** 188
"Nineteenth New York, The" (Doctorow), **Supp. IV Part 1:** 232
"1929" (Auden), **Supp. II Part 1:** 6
"1926" (Kees), **Supp. XV:** 135
"93990" (Saunders), **Supp. XIX:** 233
"90 North" (Jarrell), **II:** 370, 371
90 Trees (Zukofsky), **Supp. III Part 2:** 631
95 Poems (Cummings), **I:** 430, 433, 435, 439, 446, 447
"91 Revere Street" (R. Lowell), **II:** 547; **Retro. Supp. II:** 188; **Supp. XI:** 240
Ninety Percent of Everything (Lethem, Kelly and Kessel), **Supp. XVIII:** 145
"92 Days" (L. Brown), **Supp. XXI:** 44–45
"Nine Years Later" (Brodsky), **Supp. VIII:** 32
Ninth Avenue (Bodenheim), **Supp. XXV:** 24–25
"Nirvana" (Lanier), **Supp. I Part 1:** 352
Nirvana Blues, The (Nichols), **Supp. XIII:** 266, 267
Nishikigi (play), **III:** 466
Niven, David, **Supp. XI:** 307
Nixon (film), **Supp. XIV:** 48
Nixon, Richard M., **I:** 376; **III:** 38, 46; **Supp. I Part 1:** 294, 295; **Supp. V:** 45, 46, 51; **Supp. XII:** 14; **Supp. XIV:** 306
"NJ Transit" (Komunyakaa), **Supp. XIII:** 132
Nketia, J. H., **Supp. IV Part 1:** 10
Nketsia, Nana, **Supp. IV Part 1:** 2, 10
Nkize, Julius, **Supp. IV Part 1:** 361
Nkrumah, Kwame, **I:** 490, 494; **Supp. IV Part 1:** 361; **Supp. X:** 135
Nkrumah and the Ghana Revolution (C. L. R. James), **Supp. XXI:** 159, 171–172
NO (Major), **Supp. XXII:** 174
"Noah" (Biss), **Supp. XXVI:** 48
Noailles, Anna de, **IV:** 328
Noa Noa (Gauguin), **I:** 34
Nobel Lecture (Singer), **Retro. Supp. II:** 300
"No Better Than a 'Withered Daffodil' " (Moore), **III:** 216
Noble, David W., **Supp. I Part 2:** 650
Noble, Marianne, **Supp. XVIII:** 267
"Noble Rider and the Sound of Words, The" (Stevens), **Retro. Supp. I:** 299
Noble Savage, The (Coover), **Supp. V:** 40
"No Bobolink reverse His Singing" (Dickinson), **Retro. Supp. I:** 45
Nobodaddy (MacLeish), **III:** 5–6, 8, 10, 11, 18, 19, 20
"Nobodaddy" (W. Blake), **Supp. XVII:** 245
"Nobody in Hollywood" (Bausch), **Supp. VII:** 54
Nobody Knows My Name (Baldwin), **Supp. XIII:** 111
"Nobody Knows My Name" (Baldwin), **Retro. Supp. II:** 8; **Supp. I Part 1:** 52
Nobody Knows My Name: More Notes of a Native Son (Baldwin), **Retro. Supp. II:** 6, 8; **Supp. I Part 1:** 47, 52, 55
"Nobody knows this little Rose" (Dickinson), **Retro. Supp. I:** 30
"Nobody Said Anything" (Carver), **Supp. III Part 1:** 141
"Nobody's Business" (Lahiri), **Supp. XXI:** 183
Nobody's Fool (Russo), **Supp. XII:** 326, **331–335,** 340
"No Change of Place" (Auden), **Supp. II Part 1:** 5
"Noche Triste, La" (Frost), **Retro. Supp. I:** 123
Nock, Albert Jay, **I:** 245; **Supp. IV Part 2:** 521, 524
"No Coward Soul Is Mine" (Brontë), **I:** 458
"No Crime in the Mountains" (Chandler), **Supp. IV Part 1:** 129
"Nocturne" (Komunyakaa), **Supp. XIII:** 126
"Nocturne" (MacLeish), **III:** 8
"Nocturne at Bethesda" (Bontemps), **Supp. XXII:** 3, 8
"Nocturne in a Deserted Brickyard" (Sandburg), **III:** 586
Nocturne of Remembered Spring (Aiken), **I:** 50
Nod House (Mackey), **Supp. XXVII:** 156
No Direction Home (documentary film, Scorsese), **Supp. XVIII:** 22, 23, 29
No Direction Home (Shelton), **Supp. XVIII:** 21
No Door (Wolfe), **IV:** 451–452, 456
"No Door" (Wolfe), **IV:** 456
"No End" (Huddle), **Supp. XXVI:** 151
"No Epitaph" (Carson), **Supp. XII: 111**
No Exit (Sartre), **I:** 82, 130; **Supp. XIV:** 320
No Exit (Sartre; Bowles, trans.), **Supp. IV Part 1:** 84
No Gifts from Chance (Benstock), **Retro. Supp. I:** 361
"No-Good Blues" (Komunyakaa), **Supp. XIII:** 130
No Hero (Marquand), **III:** 57
No Heroes: A Memoir of Coming Home (Offutt), **Supp. XIX:** 163, **172–174,** 175
No! In Thunder (Fiedler), **Supp. XIII:** 101
"Noir" (Stallings), **Supp. XXV:** 232
"Noiseless Patient Spider" (Whitman), **III:** 555; **IV:** 348; **Supp. IV Part 1:** 325
Noises Off (Frayn), **Supp. IV Part 2:** 582
Noi vivi. See We the Living (film)
"No Jury Would Convict" (Shaw), **Supp. XIX:** 245
"No Lamp Has Ever Shown Us Where to Look" (MacLeish), **III:** 9
Nolan, Sidney, **Retro. Supp. II:** 189
No Laughing Matter (Heller and

Vogel), **Supp. IV Part 1:** 384, 389
No Love Lost, a Romance of Travel (Howells), **II:** 277
Nomad (Ali), **Supp. XXIV:** 15
Nomad's Land (Rinehart), **Supp. XXV:** 195
No Man Is an Island (Merton), **Supp. VIII:** 207
"No Man's Land" (Biss), **Supp. XXVI:** 47, 56
"No More This Home" (Taggard), **Supp. XXII:** 277, 280
No Mother to Guide Her (Loos), **Supp. XVI:** 194
No Name in the Street (Baldwin), **Retro. Supp. II:** 13, 14; **Supp. I Part 1:** 47, 48, 52, 65–66, 67
No Nature: New and Selected Poems (Snyder), **Supp. VIII: 305**
Nonconformist's Memorial, The (Howe), **Supp. IV Part 2:** 434, 435–436
Nonconformity (Algren), **Supp. IX:** 15
None but the Lonely Heart (film), **Supp. II Part 2:** 546
Nones (Auden), **Supp. II Part 1:** 21
"Nones" (Auden), **Supp. II Part 1:** 22–23
None Shall Look Back (Gordon), **II:** 205–207, 208
"No No, Bad Daddy" (Nelson), **Supp. XVIII:** 177, 178
"Non-Tenured" (Halliday), **Supp. XIX:** 90, 91
Nonverbal Communication: Notes on the Visual Perception of Human Relations (Kees and Ruesch), **Supp. XV:** 147
"Noon" (Bryant), **Supp. I Part 1:** 157
No One Belongs Here More Than You (July), **Supp. XXIV:** 199, **200–207**
"No One Remembers" (Levine), **Supp. V:** 187
"Noon Walk on the Asylum Lawn" (Sexton), **Supp. II Part 2:** 673
"Noon Wine" (Porter), **III:** 436, 437–438, 442, 446
"No Pain Whatsoever" (Yates), **Supp. XI:** 341
"No Place for You, My Love" (Welty), **IV:** 278, 279; **Retro. Supp. I:** 353
No Plays of Japan, The (Waley), **III:** 466
No Pockets in a Shroud (McCoy), **Supp. XIII: 166–168,** 171, 172, 173, 174
"No Poem So Fine" (Francis), **Supp. IX:** 83
Norcross, Frances, **I:** 456, 462
Norcross, Louise, **I:** 456, 462
Nordfeldt, B. J. O., **Supp. XXI:** 6
Nordfeldt, Margaret, **Supp. XXI:** 6
Nordyke, Lewis, **Supp. XIII:** 5
No Relief (Dixon), **Supp. XII:** 139, **142–143**
No Resting Place (Humphrey), **Supp. IX:** 94, **106–108**
Norfolk Poems, The (Carruth), **Supp. XVI:** 47, 48
Norma (Bellini), **IV:** 309
Norma Ashe (Glaspell), **Supp. III Part 1:** 175, 186–187
"Normal Life, A"(Thompson), **Supp. XXIII:** 300
"Normal Motor Adjustments" (Stein and Solomons), **IV:** 26
Norman, Charles, **III:** 479
Norman, Gurney, **Supp. X:** 24; **Supp. XXIII:** 42
Norman, Jessye, **Supp. XX: 110**
Norman, Marsha, **Supp. VIII:** 141; **Supp. XXI:** 145; **Supp. XXIV:** 124
Norman Mailer (Poirier), **Retro. Supp. II:** 207–208
Norman Mailer: Modern Critical Views (Bloom), **Retro. Supp. II:** 205
Norman Mailer Revisited (Merrill), **Retro. Supp. II:** 201
Norna; or, The Witch's Curse (Alcott), **Supp. I Part 1:** 33
Norris, Charles, **III:** 320; **Retro. Supp. I:** 100; **Supp. XVIII:** 226
Norris, Frank, **I:** 211, 355, 500, 506, 517, 518, 519; **II:** 89, 264, 276, 289, 307; **III:** 227, **314–336,** 596; **IV:** 29; **Retro. Supp. I:** 100, 325; **Retro. Supp. II:** 96, 101; **Supp. III Part 2:** 412; **Supp. IX:** 14, 15; **Supp. VIII:** 101, 102; **Supp. XV:** 115
"North" (Budbill), **Supp. XIX:** 7–8
"North" (Hugo), **Supp. VI:** 135
North, Milou (pseudonym), **Supp. IV Part 1:** 260. See also Dorris, Michael; Erdrich, Louise
North, Sir Thomas, **IV:** 370
"North American Sequence" (Roethke), **I:** 171–172, 183; **III:** 529, 545, 547, 548
"North American Time" (Rich), **Retro. Supp. III:** 250
"North Beach" (Snyder), **Supp. VIII:** 289
North Country: A Personal Journey Through the Borderland (Mosher), **Supp. XXII: 203–204,** 206, 212, **217–218**
"North Country Sketches" (McClatchy), **Supp. XII:** 256
"Northeast Playground" (Paley), **Supp. VI:** 226–227, 229
Northern Borders (Mosher), **Supp. XXII:** 203, 204, 206, 207, 208, 209, **213–214**
Northern Lights (O'Brien), **Supp. V:** 237, 239, 241–244, 250
"Northern Motive" (Levine), **Supp. V:** 195
Northfield Poems (Ammons), **Supp. VII:** 29
"Northhanger Ridge" (Wright), **Supp. V:** 335, 340
"North Haven" (Bishop), **Retro. Supp. II:** 50
"North Labrador" (H. Crane), **I:** 386; **Retro. Supp. III:** 45
North of Boston (Frost), **II:** 152, 153–154, 527; **Retro. Supp. I:** 121, 125, 127, **128–130,** 131; **Retro. Supp. III:** 97–98; **Supp. I Part 1:** 263; **Supp. XIII:** 146
North of Jamaica (Simpson), **Supp. IV Part 2:** 448; **Supp. IX:** 275, 276
North of the Danube (Caldwell), **I:** 288, 290, 293, 294, 309, 310
North: Poems of Home (Kenny), **Supp. XXIII: 147–148**
Northrup, Cyrus, **Supp. I Part 1:** 350
North Sea (Jarman), **Supp. XVII:** 110, 113
"North Sea Undertaker's Complaint, The" (R. Lowell), **II:** 550
North & South (Bishop), **Retro. Supp. II: 41–43; Supp. I Part 1:** 72, 84, 85, 89
North Star, The (Hellman), **Supp. I Part 1:** 281
Northup, Solomon, **Supp. XIV:** 32
"Northwest Writers at Work" (Baker), **Supp. XXIV:** 178
"North Winter" (Carruth), **Supp. XVI:** 53
Norton, Charles Eliot, **I:** 223, 568; **II:** 279, 322–323, 338; **Retro. Supp. I:** 371; **Retro. Supp. II:** 135; **Supp. I Part 1:** 103; **Supp. I Part 2:** 406, 479
Norton, Jody, **Supp. VIII:** 297
Norton, John, **Supp. I Part 1:** 99, 110, 112, 114
Norton Anthology of African American Literature, The (H. L. Gates and McKay, eds.), **Supp. X:** 325; **Supp. XX: 105**
Norton Anthology of American Literature, **Supp. X:** 325; **Supp. XV:** 270
Norton Anthology of Literature by Women (Gilbert and Gubar, eds.), **Supp. XV:** 270
Norton Anthology of Modern Poetry, The, **Supp. XI:** 259; **Supp. XV:**

258; **Supp. XXIV:** 35, 39
Norton Anthology of Poetry, The, **Supp. XVIII:** 20
Norton Anthology of Short Fiction, The, **Supp. IX:** 4
Norton Book of Personal Essays, The, **Supp. XIV:** 105
Norton Lectures, **Retro. Supp. I:** 65
Norwood, Vera, **Supp. IX:** 24
No Safe Harbour (Porter), **III:** 447
Nosferatu: An Opera Libretto (Gioia), **Supp. XV:** 112, **128**
"Nosferatu's Serenade" (Gioia), **Supp. XV:** 128
No Siege Is Absolute (Char; version of F. Wright), **Supp. XVII:** 244
"No Snake" (A. Finch), **Supp. XVII:** 72
"No Speak English" (Cisneros), **Supp. VII:** 63
"Nostalgia" (Collins), **Supp. XXI:** 57
"Nostalgia" (Saunders), **Supp. XIX:** 235
Nostalgia for 70 (J. W. Miller), **Supp. XX: 165**
"Nostalgia of the Lakefronts" (Justice), **Supp. VII:** 118, 119, 120
"Nostalgic Mood" (Farrell), **II:** 45
No Star Is Lost (Farrell), **II:** 34, 35, 44
Nostrandt, Jeanne, **Supp. XVIII:** 80–81
Nostromo (Conrad), **II:** 600; **IV:** 245
"Nosty Fright, A" (Swenson), **Supp. IV Part 2:** 651
"Not" (Huddle), **Supp. XXVI:** 157
Not about Nightingales (T. Williams), **IV:** 381
"Not a Sparrow" (Gallagher), **Supp. XXIV:** 171
Not: A Trio (Huddle), **Supp. XXVI:** 150, 156–157
"Not a Womb in the House" (Quindlen), **Supp. XVII:** 166, 171
"(Not) Born in he U.S.A." (Gansworth), **Supp. XXVI:** 111
Not Coming to Be Barked At (Kooser), **Supp. XIX:** 116, **120**
Not Dancing (Dunn), **Supp. XI:** 143, **148**
"Note about Iconographs, A" (Swenson), **Supp. IV Part 2:** 646
Notebook (R. Lowell), **Retro. Supp. II:** 186, 190; **Supp. V:** 343
Notebook 1967–68 (R. Lowell), **II:** 553–555; **Retro. Supp. II:** 182, 186, 190
Notebook of Malte Laurids Brigge, The (Rilke), **III:** 571
Notebooks (Fitzgerald), **Retro. Supp. I:** 110
Notebooks of Captain George, The (Renoir), **Supp. XXII:** 257
"Notebooks on Poetry and Politics" (Rich), **Retro. Supp. III:** 251
No Telephone to Heaven (Cliff), **Supp. XXII:** 66, 69, 71–72
"Note on Abraham Lincoln" (Vidal), **Supp. IV Part 2:** 688
"Note on Commercial Theatre" (Hughes), **Retro. Supp. I:** 207
"Note on Ezra Pound, A" (Eliot), **Retro. Supp. I:** 290
"Note on Lanier's Music, A" (P. Graham), **Supp. I Part 1:** 373
Note on Literary Criticism, A (Farrell), **II:** 26, 49
"Note on Poetry, A" (Doolittle), **Supp. I Part 1:** 254, 267–268
"Note on Realism, A" (Anderson), **I:** 110
"Note on the Limits of 'History' and the Limits of 'Criticism,' A" (Brooks), **Supp. XIV:** 11
"Note on the Poetry of Love, A" (Untermeyer), **Supp. XV:** 304
"Note on the Truth of the Tales, A" (Vollmann), **Supp. XVII:** 230
"Notes" (Dove), **Supp. IV Part 1:** 246
"Notes for a Moving Picture: The House" (Agee), **I:** 33, 34
"Notes for an Autobiography" (Van Vechten), **Supp. II Part 2:** 749
"Notes for a Novel About the End of the World" (Percy), **Supp. III Part 1:** 393
"Notes for a Preface" (Sandburg), **III:** 591, 596–597
"NOTES FOR A SPEECH" (Baraka), **Supp. II Part 1:** 33
Notes for the Green Box (Duchamp), **Supp. IV Part 2:** 423
Notes for the Two-Dollar Window: Portraits from an American Neighborhood (Kriegel), **Supp. XXIV: 223–224**
Notes from a Bottle Found on the Beach at Carmel (Connell), **Supp. XIV:** 80, 87, 96, 97
Notes from a Sea Diary: Hemingway All the Way (Algren), **Supp. IX:** 16
Notes from No Man's Land (Biss), **Supp. XXVI:** 45, 46, 47, 48, 50, 53, 55–57
"Notes from the Childhood and Girlhood" (Brooks), **Supp. III Part 1:** 77
"Notes from the River" (Stern), **Supp. IX:** 285, 287, 294, 295
Notes from Underground (Dostoevsky), **III:** 571; **IV:** 485; **Retro. Supp. II:** 121
Notes Left Behind: Last and Selected Poems (Hayford), **Supp. XXII:** 218
"Notes of a Faculty Wife" (Jackson), **Supp. IX:** 126
"Notes of a Native Daughter" (Didion), **Supp. IV Part 1:** 196, 197, 200, 201
Notes of a Native Son (Baldwin), **Retro. Supp. II:** 1, 2, 3, 5, 6; **Supp. I Part 1:** 50, 52, 54; **Supp. IV Part 1:** 163
"Notes of a Native Son" (Baldwin), **Supp. I Part 1:** 50, 54
Notes of a Son and Brother (James), **II:** 337; **Retro. Supp. I:** 235
"Notes on a Departure" (Trilling), **Supp. III Part 2:** 498
"Notes on Babbitt and More" (Wilson), **IV:** 435
"Notes on 'Camp' " (Sontag), **Supp. III Part 2:** 455–456; **Supp. XIV:** 167
Notes on Democracy (Mencken), **III:** 104, 107–108, 109, 116, 119
Notes on Dialectics (C. L. R. James), **Supp. XXI:** 169
"Notes on Free Verse" (Dobyns), **Supp. XIII:** 77
"Notes on 'Layover' " (Hass), **Supp. VI:** 109
"Notes on Memory and Enthusiasm" (Di Piero), **Supp. XIX:** 42
Notes on Novelists (James), **II:** 336, 337; **Retro. Supp. I:** 235
"Notes on Nukes, Nookie, and Neo-Romanticism" (Robbins), **Supp. X:** 272
"Notes on Poetry" (Eberhart), **I:** 524, 527–528, 529
"Notes on Teaching"(Hadas), **Supp. XXIII:** 122
"Notes on the Craft of Poetry" (Strand), **Supp. IV Part 2:** 626
"Notes on the Decline of Outrage" (Dickey), **Supp. IV Part 1:** 181
"Notes on the New Formalism" (Gioia), **Supp. XV:** 113, 114–115
"Notes on the Novel-as-Autobiography" (P. Bailey), **Supp. XVI:** 69
"Notes on 'The Poetry of Everday Life' " (Notley), **Supp. XXII:** 232
Notes on the State of Virginia (1781–1782) (Jefferson), **Supp. XIV:** 191
"Notes on Writing Weird Fiction" (Lovecraft), **Supp. XXV:** 120–121
"Notes to Be Left in a Cornerstone" (Benét), **Supp. XI:** 46, 58

"Notes Toward a Politics of Location" (Rich), **Retro. Supp. III:** 251
"Notes toward a Supreme Fiction" (Stevens), **IV:** 87–89; **Retro. Supp. I:** 300, 306, **306–309,** 311; **Retro. Supp. III:** 51; **Supp. I Part 1:** 80
"Notes towards a Poem That Can Never Be Written" (Atwood), **Supp. XIII:** 34–35
"Not Exactly for Talia" (Halliday), **Supp. XIX:** 94
"Not Forgotten" (Davison), **Supp. XXVI:** 70
No Thanks (Cummings), **I:** 430, 431, 432, 436, 437, 441, 443, 446
Not Heaven: A Novel in the Form of Prelude, Variations, and Theme (W. Frank), **Supp. XX: 80**
"Nothing" (C. Frost), **Supp. XV:** 94
"Nothing Big" (Komunyakaa), **Supp. XIII:** 121
Nothing Can Make Me Do This (Huddle), **Supp. XXVI:** 147, 151–152, 158–159
Nothing Ever Breaks Except the Heart (Boyle), **Supp. XXIV:** 59
Nothing for Tigers (Carruth), **Supp. XVI:** 47, 48, 50
"Nothing Gold Can Stay" (Frost), **Retro. Supp. I:** 133; **Retro. Supp. III:** 102
Nothing Gold Can Stay (Rash), **Supp. XXVII:** 215, 224, 229–230
"Nothing in Heaven Functions as It Ought" (X. J. Kennedy), **Supp. XV:** 158–159
Nothing Makes You Free: Writings by Descendants of Jewish Holocaust Survivors (Bukiet, ed.), **Supp. XVII: 39–40,** 48–49
"Nothing Missing" (O'Hara), **III:** 369
Nothing Personal (Baldwin), **Supp. I Part 1:** 58, 60
Nothing Sacred (film), **Supp. XVIII:** 243
Nothing Sacred (screenplay, Hecht), **Supp. XXVII:** 83, 91, 93
"Nothing Song, The" (Snodgrass), **Supp. VI:** 326
"Nothing Stays Put" (Clampitt), **Supp. IX:** 42
"Nothing Sudden" (Davison), **Supp. XXVI:** 76
Nothing to Write Home About (Brainard), **Supp. XXVII:** 20, 28
"Nothing Will Yield" (Nemerov), **III:** 279
No Third Path (Kosinski), **Supp. VII:** 215
"Not Ideas About the Thing but the Thing Itself" (Stevens), **IV:** 87
"No Time" (Collins), **Supp. XXI:** 61
Notions of the Americans: Picked up by a Travelling Bachelor (Cooper), **I:** 343–345, 346
"Not-Knowing" (Barthelme), **Supp. IV Part 1:** 48
"Not Leaving the House" (Snyder), **Supp. VIII:** 300
Notley, Alice, **Supp. XXII: 223–238; Supp. XXIII:** 221; **Supp. XXIV:** 35, 37, 39, 41, 43, 45
"'Not Marble nor the Gilded Monument' " (MacLeish), **III:** 12
Not Mine to Finish: Poems, 1928–1934 (Taggard), **Supp. XXII:** 280
"Not My Bones" (Nelson), **Supp. XVIII:** 183
Not Now But Now (M. F. K. Fisher), **Supp. XVII:** 86, 90
Notorious (screenplay, Hecht), **Supp. XXVII:** 83, 91, 93
"Not Quite Social" (Frost), **II:** 156
"Not Sappho, Sacco" (Rukeyser), **Supp. VI:** 277
"Not Sixteen" (Anderson), **I:** 114
"Not Slightly" (Stein), **IV:** 44
Not So Deep as a Well (Parker), **Supp. IX:** 192
"Not Somewhere Else, but Here" (Rich), **Supp. I Part 2:** 552, 573
Not-So-Simple Neil Simon (McGovern), **Supp. IV Part 2:** 573
Not So Simple: The "Simple" Stories by Langston Hughes (Harper), **Retro. Supp. I:** 194, 209
"Not the Point" (Cameron), **Supp. XII: 83**
"Not They Who Soar" (Dunbar), **Supp. II Part 1:** 199
Not This Pig (Levine), **Supp. V:** 178, 181, 182–183
"Not to Be Satan nor to Deal with Him" (Bronk), **Supp. XXI:** 32
Not to Eat; Not for Love (Weller), **III:** 322
Not Under Forty (Cather), **Retro. Supp. III:** 17, 24, 36
Not Wanted on the Voyage (Findley), **Supp. XX: 50, 56–57, 59**
Not Without Laughter (Hughes), **Retro. Supp. I:** 197, 198, 201; **Supp. I Part 1:** 328, 332; **Supp. XIX:** 73, 154
Nouvelle Héloïse, La (Rousseau), **Supp. XV:** 232
Nova Express (Burroughs), **Supp. III Part 1:** 93, 103, 104; **Supp. XVIII:** 137
Novel, The (Bulwer), **Retro. Supp. II:** 58
Novel, The: An Alternative History (Moore), **Supp. XXII:** 261
"Novel as a Function of American Democracy, The" (Ellison), **Retro. Supp. II:** 124
"Novel Démeublé, The" (Cather), **Retro. Supp. I:** 15; **Retro. Supp. III:** 17, 24
Novel History: Historians and Novelists Confront America's Past (and Each Other) (Carnes), **Supp. X:** 14
"Novelist and Believer" (O'Connor), **Retro. Supp. III:** 209
"Novelists of 2007" (Halliday), **Supp. XIX:** 90
Novella (Goethe; Bogan and Mayer, trans.), **Supp. III Part 1:** 63
Novellas and Other Writings (Wharton), **Retro. Supp. I:** 360
"Novel of the Thirties, A" (Trilling), **Supp. III Part 2:** 499
Novels and Other Writings (Bercovitch), **Retro. Supp. II:** 325
Novels and Tales of Henry James, The (James), **Retro. Supp. I:** 232
"Novel-Writing and Novel-Reading" (Howells), **II:** 276, 290
"November" (Larcom), **Supp. XIII:** 143
"November Cotton Flower" (Toomer), **Supp. IX:** 312
November Twenty Six Nineteen Sixty Three (Berry), **Supp. X:** 24
"Novices" (Moore), **III:** 200–201, 202, 213
Novick, Peter, **Supp. XVI:** 154–155
"Novogodnee" ("New Year's Greetings") (Tsvetayeva), **Supp. VIII:** 30
"Novotny's Pain" (P. Roth), **Supp. III Part 2:** 403
"No Voyage" (Oliver), **Supp. VII:** 231
No Voyage and Other Poems (Oliver), **Supp. VII:** 230–231, 232
Now and Another Time (Hearon), **Supp. VIII:** 58, **61–62**
Now and Then (Buechner), **Supp. XII:** 49, 53
"Now and Then, America" (Mora), **Supp. XIII:** 217
"Nowhere" (J. Scott), **Supp. XVII:** 189
Nowhere Is a Place: Travels in Patagonia (Theroux and Chatwin), **Supp. VIII:** 322
"Now I Am Married" (Gordon), **Supp. IV Part 1:** 299
"Now I Lay Me" (Hemingway), **II:**

249; **Retro. Supp. I:** 175
"Now I Lay Me" (Olds), **Supp. X:** 208
"Now Is the Air Made of Chiming Balls" (Eberhart), **I:** 523
Now Is Your Time! The African American Struggle for Freedom (Myers), **Supp. XXVII:** 209
"No Word" (Kunitz), **Supp. III Part 1:** 263
"No Worst" (Nelson), **Supp. XVIII:** 177, 178
Now Sheba Sings the Song (Angelou), **Supp. IV Part 1:** 16
"Now That We Live" (Kenyon), **Supp. VII:** 165
"Now the Servant's Name Was Malchus" (Wilder), **IV:** 358
"Now We Know" (O'Hara), **III:** 368–369
NOW with Bill Moyers (television), **Supp. XIII:** 286
Noyes, Alfred, **IV:** 434
Nuamah, Grace, **Supp. IV Part 1:** 10
"Nuances of a Theme by Williams" (Stevens), **Retro. Supp. I:** 422
Nuclear Age, The (O'Brien), **Supp. V:** 238, 243, 244, 246–248, 249, 251
"Nuclear Arms and Morality" (Sanders), **Supp. XVI:** 266
"Nude at a Dressing Table" (Peacock), **Supp. XIX:** 204
Nude Croquet (Fiedler), **Supp. XIII:** 103
"Nude Descendig a Staircase" (X. J. Kennedy), **Supp. XV:** 168
Nude Descending a Staircase (Duchamp), **IV:** 408; **Retro. Supp. I:** 416; **Supp. XXII:** 162
Nude Descending a Staircase (X. J. Kennedy), **Supp. XV:** 153, **154–157**
Nugent, Bruce, **Retro. Supp. I:** 200
Nugent, Elliot, **Supp. I Part 2:** 606, 611, 613
Nuggets and Dust (Bierce), **I:** 195
"Nullipara" (Olds), **Supp. X:** 209
Number One (Dos Passos), **I:** 489
"Numbers" (Skloot), **Supp. XX: 196, 207**
"Numbers, Letters" (Baraka), **Supp. II Part 1:** 50
"Numbers Trouble" (Stallings), **Supp. XXV:** 224
Nunc Dimittis (Brodsky), **Supp. VIII:** 25–26, 28
"Nun No More, A" (Fante), **Supp. XI:** 160
"Nun's Priest's Tale" (Chaucer), **III:** 492
Nunzio, Nanzia, **IV:** 89
Nuptial Flight, The (Masters), **Supp. I Part 2:** 460, 471
"Nuptials" (Tate), **IV:** 122
Nursery Rhymes from Mother Stone (Stone), **Supp. XXVII:** 257
"Nurse Whitman" (Olds), **Supp. X:** 203
Nurture (Kumin), **Supp. IV Part 2:** 453–454, 455
Nussbaum, Emily, **Supp. XI:** 143
Nussbaum, Felicity A., **Supp. X:** 189
Nutcracker, The (Tchaikovsky), **Retro. Supp. I:** 196
"Nux Postcoenatica" (Holmes), **Supp. I Part 1:** 303
Nyberg, Björn, **Supp. XXVII:** 128
Nyce, James M., **Retro. Supp. I:** 380
Nye, Naomi Shihab, **Supp. XI:** 316; **Supp. XIII: 273–290; Supp. XXIII:** 253; **Supp. XXVII:** 166
Nyerere, Julius, **Supp. X:** 135
"Nympholepsy" (Faulkner), **Retro. Supp. I:** 81
Nymphs of the Valley ('Ará'is al-Murúj) (Gibran), **Supp. XX: 115, 124, 125**
"Ö" (Dove), **Supp. IV Part 1:** 245
Oak and Ivy (Dunbar), **Supp. II Part 1:** 98
"Oak Bluffs" column (D. West), **Supp. XVIII:** 286
Oak Openings, The (Cooper), **I:** 354, 355
Oandasan, Bill, **Supp. IV Part 2:** 499
Oasis, The (McCarthy), **II:** 566–568
Oates, Joyce Carol, **Supp. II Part 2: 503–527; Supp. IV Part 1:** 205; **Supp. IV Part 2:** 447, 689; **Supp. V:** 323; **Supp. XI:** 239; **Supp. XII:** 343; **Supp. XIII:** 306; **Supp. XIV:** 26, 109; **Supp. XXIII:** 35; **Supp. XXV:** 86, 123; **Supp. XXVI:** 126
Oates, Stephen B., **Retro. Supp. III:** 75, 77
"Oath, The" (Tate), **IV:** 127
Obbligati (Hecht), **Supp. X:** 57
Ober, Harold, **Retro. Supp. I:** 101, 103, 105, 110, 113
Oberndorf, Clarence P., **Supp. I Part 1:** 315
Obey, André, **IV:** 356, 375
"Obit" (R. Lowell), **II:** 554
"Obituaries" (Collins), **Supp. XXI:** 65
"Obituary Writer, The" (Davison), **Supp. XXVI:** 72
"Objective Value of a Social Settlement, The" (Addams), **Supp. I Part 1:** 4
"Objective Woman, The" (Jong), **Supp. V:** 119
Objectivist Anthology, An, **Supp. XIV:** 287
"Objectivist Ethics, The" (Rand), **Supp. IV Part 2:** 530–532
"Objectivists" Anthology, An (Zukofsky), **Supp. III Part 2:** 613, 615
Objectivist's Anthology, An (Zukofsky, ed.), **Supp. XXVI:** 226
Object Lessons (Quindlen), **Supp. XVII: 173–174**
"Objects" (Wilbur), **Supp. III Part 2:** 545–547
Oblique Prayers (Levertov), **Supp. III Part 1:** 283
"Oblivion" (Justice), **Supp. VII:** 121
Oblivion Seekers, The (Eberhardt), **Supp. IV Part 1:** 92
"Oblong Box, The" (Poe), **III:** 416
"Obnoxious Truth, The" (Notley), **Supp. XXII:** 234
Obregon, Maurice, **Supp. I Part 2:** 488
O'Briant, Don, **Supp. X:** 8
O'Brien, Edward, **Supp. XV:** 140
O'Brien, Edward J., **I:** 289; **III:** 56; **Supp. XIX:** 256; **Supp. XVIII:** 227; **Supp. XX: 34**
O'Brien, Edwin, **Supp. XVIII:** 208
O'Brien, Fitzjames, **I:** 211
O'Brien, Geoffrey, **Supp. IV Part 2:** 471, 473
O'Brien, Joe, **Supp. XXI:** 5, 6
O'Brien, John, **Supp. V:** 48, 49; **Supp. X:** 239, 244; **Supp. XXI:** 228, 229, 233
O'Brien, Sharon, **Retro. Supp. III:** 19, 25, 37
O'Brien, Tim, **Retro. Supp. III:** 104; **Supp. V: 237–255; Supp. XI:** 234; **Supp. XVII:** 14; **Supp. XXI:** 122; **Supp. XXV:** 142, 143, 153
"Obscene Poem, An" (Creeley), **Supp. IV Part 1:** 150
Obscure Destinies (Cather), **I:** 331–332; **Retro. Supp. I:** 19
"Observation Relative to the Intentions of the Original Founders of the Academy in Philadelphia" (Franklin), **II:** 114
"Observations" (Dillard), **Supp. VI:** 34
Observations (Moore), **III:** 194, 195–196, 197, 199, 203, 205, 215
"Observations Now" (Conroy), **Supp. XVI:** 75
Observations: Photographs by Richard Avedon: Comments by Truman Capote, **Supp. III Part 1:** 125–126
Obsession, The (Levin), **Supp. XXVII:**

133, 136, 138, 143, 147
Obsession with Anne Frank, An: Meyer Levin and the Diary (Graver), **Supp. XXVII:** 136, 137
Obuchowski, Mary DeJong, **Supp. XX: 222**
O Canada: An American's Notes on Canadian Culture (Wilson), **IV:** 429–430
"O Captain! My Captain" (Whitman), **Retro. Supp. III:** 297
"O Carib Isle!" (H. Crane), **I:** 400–401; **Retro. Supp. III:** 43–44
O'Casey, Sean, **III:** 145; **Supp. IV Part 1:** 359, 361, 364
"Occidentals" (Ford), **Supp. V:** 71–72
Occom, Samuel, **Supp. XX: 288**
"Occultation of Orion, The" (Longfellow), **Retro. Supp. II:** 168
"Occurrence at Owl Creek Bridge, An" (Bierce), **I:** 200–201; **II:** 264; **Supp. XXV:** 26
"Ocean 1212-W" (Plath), **Supp. I Part 2:** 528
"Ocean of Words" (Jin), **Supp. XVIII:** 94
Ocean of Words: Army Stories (Jin), **Supp. XVIII:** 89, 92, **93–94**
O'Connell, Nicholas, **Supp. IX:** 323, 325, 334
O'Connell, Shaun, **Supp. XXI:** 231
O'Connor, Edward F., Jr., **III:** 337
O'Connor, Flannery, **I:** 113, 190, 211, 298; **II:** 606; **III: 337–360; IV:** 4, 217, 282; **Retro. Supp. II:** 179, **219–239,** 272, 324; **Retro. Supp. III: 207–221**; **Supp. I Part 1:** 290; **Supp. III Part 1:** 146; **Supp. V:** 59, 337; **Supp. VIII:** 13, 14, 158; **Supp. X:** 1, 26, 69, 228, 290; **Supp. XI:** 104; **Supp. XIII:** 294; **Supp. XIV:** 93; **Supp. XIX:** 166, 209, 223; **Supp. XV:** 338; **Supp. XVI:** 219; **Supp. XVII:** 43, 114; **Supp. XVIII:** 156, 161, 194; **Supp. XXI:** 197; **Supp. XXIII:** 289; **Supp. XXV:** 142; **Supp. XXVI:** 152, 252; **Supp. XXVII:** 11, 216, 218, 230, 267, 276
O'Connor, Frank, **III:** 158; **Retro. Supp. II:** 242; **Supp. I Part 2:** 531; **Supp. VIII:** 151, 157, 165, 167, 171; **Supp. XV:** 74
O'Connor, Philip F., **Supp. XXIII:** 290
O'Connor, Richard, **II:** 467
O'Connor, T. P., **II:** 129
O'Connor, William, **IV:** 346; **Retro. Supp. I:** 392, 407
O'Connor, William Van, **III:** 479; **Supp. I Part 1:** 195
O'Crowley, Peggy, **Supp. XXVII:** 201
"Octascope" (Beattie), **Supp. V:** 27, 28
"Octaves" (Robinson), **Supp. III Part 2:** 593
"Octet" (Wallace), **Supp. X:** 309
"October" (Frost), **Retro. Supp. III:** 96
October (Isherwood), **Supp. XIV:** 157, 164
"October" (Oliver), **Supp. VII:** 241
"October" (Swenson), **Supp. IV Part 2:** 649
"October, 1866" (Bryant), **Supp. I Part 1:** 169
"October 1913" (McCarriston), **Supp. XIV:** 266
"October and November" (R. Lowell), **II:** 554
"October in the Railroad Earth" (Kerouac), **Supp. III Part 1:** 225, 227, 229
October Light (Gardner), **Supp. VI:** 63, **69–71,** 72
"October Maples, Portland" (Wilbur), **Supp. III Part 2:** 556
October Palace, The (Hirshfield), **Supp. XXIII:** 131
October Sky (film), **Supp. XXVII:** 101, 103, 106
"October: With Rain" (W. V. Davis), **Supp. XXI:** 94
"Octopus, An" (Moore), **III:** 202, 207–208, 214
"Octopus, The" (Merrill), **Supp. III Part 1:** 321
Octopus, The (Norris), **I:** 518; **III:** 314, 316, 322–326, 327, 331–333, 334, 335
"O Daedalus, Fly Away Home" (Hayden), **Supp. II Part 1:** 377–378
"OD and Hepatitis Railroad or Bust, The" (Boyle), **Supp. VIII:** 1
Odd Couple, The (1985 version, Simon), **Supp. IV Part 2:** 580
Odd Couple, The (film), **Supp. IV Part 2:** 589
Odd Couple, The (Simon), **Supp. IV Part 2:** 575, 579–580, 585, 586; **Supp. XVII:** 8
Odd Jobs (Updike), **Retro. Supp. I:** 334
Odd Mercy (Stern), **Supp. IX: 298–299**
Odd Number (Sorrentino), **Supp. XXI:** 236
"Odds, The" (Hecht), **Supp. X:** 64–65
Odds, The (O'Nan), **Supp. XXV:** 150, 151–152
"Odds, The" (Salinas), **Supp. XIII:** 321
"Ode" (Emerson), **II:** 13
"Ode" (Sobin), **Supp. XVI:** 284–285
"Ode" (X. J. Kennedy), **Supp. XV:** 160
"Ode (Intimations of Immortality)" (Matthews), **Supp. IX:** 162
"Ode for Memorial Day" (Dunbar), **Supp. II Part 1:** 199
"Ode for the American Dead in Asia" (McGrath), **Supp. X:** 119
"Ode: For the Budding of Islands" (Sobin), **Supp. XVI:** 287
"Ode Inscribed to W. H. Channing" (Emerson), **Supp. XIV:** 46
"Ode: Intimations of Immortality" (Wordsworth), **Supp. I Part 2:** 729; **Supp. III Part 1:** 12; **Supp. XIV:** 8
"Ode in Time of Crisis" (Taggard), **Supp. XXII:** 271
Odell, Margeretta Matilda, **Supp. XX: 278, 284, 288**
"Ode: My 24th Year" (Ginsberg), **Supp. II Part 1:** 312
"Ode on a Grecian Urn" (Keats), **I:** 284; **III:** 472; **Supp. XII:** 113; **Supp. XIV:** 8, 9–10; **Supp. XV:** 100; **Supp. XXI:** 64
"Ode on Human Destinies" (Jeffers), **Supp. II Part 2:** 419
"Ode on Indolence" (Keats), **Supp. XII:** 113
"Ode on Melancholy" (Keats), **Retro. Supp. I:** 301
Ode Recited at the Harvard Commemoration (J. R. Lowell), **Supp. I Part 2:** 416–418, 424
"Ode Recited at the Harvard Commemoration" (R. Lowell), **II:** 551
Odes (Horace), **Supp. XXIV:** 153
Odes (O'Hara), **Supp. XXIII:** 216
"Ode: Salute to the French Negro Poets"(O'Hara), **Supp. XXIII:** 216
"Ode Secrète" (Valéry), **III:** 609
"Odes of Estrangement" (Sobin), **Supp. XVI:** 289
Odes of Horace, The (Ferry, trans.), **Supp. XXIV: 153–156**
"Odes to Natural Processes" (Updike), **Retro. Supp. I:** 323
"Ode: The Capris" (Halliday), **Supp. XIX:** 88
"Ode to a Nightingale" (Keats), **II:** 368; **Retro. Supp. II:** 261; **Supp. IX:** 52
"Ode to Autumn" (Masters), **Supp. I Part 2:** 458
"Ode to Cervantes" (Salinas), **Supp. XIII:** 324
"Ode to Coit Tower" (Corso), **Supp. XII:** 122
"Ode to Ethiopia" (Dunbar), **Supp. II Part 1:** 199, 207, 208, 209

"Ode to Fear" (Tate), **IV:** 128
Ode to Harvard and Other Poems, An (Bynner), **Supp. XV:** 41, 44
"Ode to Joy"(O'Hara), **Supp. XXIII:** 208, 216
"Ode to Meaning" (Pinsky), **Supp. VI:** **249–250,** 251
"Ode to Michael Goldberg ('s Birth and Other Births)"(O'Hara), **Supp. XXIII:** 209, 216, 218
"Ode to Night" (Masters), **Supp. I Part 2:** 458
"Ode to Our Young Pro-Consuls of the Air" (Tate), **IV:** 135
"Ode to the Austrian Socialists" (Benét), **Supp. XI:** 46, 58
"Ode to the Confederate Dead" (Tate), **II:** 551; **IV:** 124, 133, 137; **Supp. X:** 52
"Ode to the Johns Hopkins University" (Lanier), **Supp. I Part 1:** 370
"Ode to the Maggot" (Komunyakaa), **Supp. XIII:** 130
"Ode to the Mexican Experience" (Salinas), **Supp. XIII:** 316–317
"Ode to the Virginian Voyage" (Drayton), **IV:** 135
"Ode to the West Wind" (Shelley), **Retro. Supp. I:** 308; **Supp. I Part 2:** 728; **Supp. IX:** 52; **Supp. XII:** 117; **Supp. XIV:** 271–272; **Supp. XV:** 221
"Ode to Walt Whitman" (Benét), **Supp. XI:** 52
"Ode to Willem de Kooning"(O'Hara), **Supp. XXIII:** 208, 216
Odets, Clifford, **Supp. I Part 1:** 277, 295; **Supp. I Part 2:** 679; **Supp. II Part 2: 529–554; Supp. IV Part 2:** 587; **Supp. V:** 109; **Supp. VIII:** 96; **Supp. XVIII:** 238; **Supp. XX: 34; Supp. XXVII:** 134
Odier, Daniel, **Supp. III Part 1:** 97
"Odi et Amo" (Catullus), **Supp. XV:** 27, 32, 35
"Odom"(P. Benedict), **Supp. XXIII:** 41
O'Donnell, George Marion, **II:** 67
O'Donnell, Mary King, **Supp. XVIII:** 232
O'Donnell, Thomas F., **II:** 131
"Odor of Verbena, An" (Faulkner), **II:** 66; **Retro. Supp. III:** 85
O'Doul, Lefty, **II:** 425
Odysseus (Homer), **Supp. XXVI:** 79
"Odysseus to Telemachus" (Brodsky), **Supp. VIII:** 25
Odyssey (Bryant, trans.), **Supp. I Part 1:** 158
Odyssey (Homer), **III:** 14, 470; **Retro. Supp. I:** 286, 290; **Retro. Supp. II:** 121; **Supp. I Part 1:** 185; **Supp. IV Part 2:** 631; **Supp. IX:** 211; **Supp. X:** 114; **Supp. XIV:** 191; **Supp. XVII:** 117; **Supp. XXI:** 36
"Odyssey of a Wop, The" (Fante), **Supp. XI:** 164, 165
Oedipus at Colonus (Sophocles), **Retro. Supp. III:** 70
Oedipus Rex (Sophocles), **I:** 137; **III:** 145, 151, 152, 332; **Supp. I Part 2:** 428
Oedipus Tyrannus (Sophocles), **II:** 203; **Supp. XV:** 265
Oehlschlaeger, Fritz, **Supp. IX:** 123
Oelze, Richard, **Supp. XXII:** 167
"Of Alexander Crummell" (Du Bois), **Supp. II Part 1:** 170
O'Faoláin, Seán, **Supp. II Part 1:** 101
Of a World That Is No More (Singer), **IV:** 16
Of Being Numerous (Oppen), **Supp. XXVI:** 223, 230, 233–234, 237
"Of Being Numerous" (Oppen), **Supp. XXVI:** 232, 233–234, 236
"Of Booker T. Washington and Others" (Du Bois), **Supp. II Part 1:** 168
"Of Bright & Blue Birds & the Gala Sun" (Stevens), **IV:** 93
"Of Christian Heroism" (Ozick), **Supp. V:** 272
"Of Dying Beauty" (Zukofsky), **Supp. III Part 2:** 610
"Of Epiphanies and Poets" (Phillips), **Supp. XX: 221**
"Of 'Father and Son' " (Kunitz), **Supp. III Part 1:** 262
Offenbach, Jacques, **II:** 427
"Offering for Mr. Bluehart, An" (Wright), **Supp. III Part 2:** 596, 601
"Offerings" (Mason), **Supp. VIII:** 141
"Offertory" (Hempel), **Supp. XXI:** **126–127**
Office, The (Asch), **Supp. XXVI:** 18–20, 21, 25
"Office, The" (Munro), **Supp. XXVII:** 183–184
Official Entry Blank (Kooser), **Supp. XIX:** 116, **117–118**
"Official Entry Form" (Kooser), **Supp. XIX:** 117
"Official Piety" (Whittier), **Supp. I Part 2:** 687
Off Keck Road (Simpson), **Supp. XXVII:** 240–242
"Offloading for Mrs. Schwartz" (Saunders), **Supp. XIX:** 225–226
"Of Freemasons, Kings, and Constitutions" (P. N. Warren), **Supp. XX: 273**
"Off-Shore Pirates, The" (Fitzgerald), **II:** 88
Off the Beaten Path (Proulx), **Supp. VII:** 261
Off the Beaten Path: Stories of Place, **Supp. XVI:** 22
"Off the Cuff" (Simpson), **Supp. IX:** 278
"Off the Highway" (Wolfert), **Supp. XXI:** 265
Off the Map (Levine), **Supp. V:** 178
Offut, Chris, **Supp. XIX: 163–176**
Offutt, Chris, **Supp. XXVII:** 217
Of Gravity and Angels (Hirshfield), **Supp. XXIII:** 131
O'Flaherty, George, **Supp. I Part 1:** 202, 205–206
O'Flaherty, Kate. See Chopin, Kate
O'Flaherty, Thomas, **Supp. I Part 1:** 202, 203–204, 205
O'Flaherty, Thomas, Jr., **Supp. I Part 1:** 202
"Of Maids and Other Muses" (Alvarez), **Supp. VII:** 11
"Of Margaret" (Ransom), **III:** 491
Of Mice and Men (Steinbeck), **IV:** 51, 57–58
"Of Modern Poetry" (Stevens), **IV:** 92
Of No Country I Know: New and Selected Poems and Translations (Ferry), **Supp. XXIV: 157**
Of Plymouth Plantation (Bradford), **Retro. Supp. II:** 161, 162; **Retro. Supp. III:** 9; **Supp. XXII:** 33, **35–47**
Of Plymouth Plantation (Morison, ed.), **Supp. I Part 2:** 494
"Ofrenda for Lobo" (Mora), **Supp. XIII:** 224
"Often" (Kenyon), **Supp. VII:** 171
"Often, in Dreams, He Moved through a City" (Dobyns), **Supp. XIII:** 90
"Of the Coming of John" (Du Bois), **Supp. II Part 1:** 170
"Of the Culture of White Folk" (Du Bois), **Supp. II Part 1:** 175
Of the Farm (Updike), **IV:** 214, 217, 223–225, 233; **Retro. Supp. I:** 318, 329, 332
"Of the Four-Winged Cherubim as Signature" (Sobin), **Supp. XVI:** 287
"Of 'The Frill' " (McCarriston), **Supp. XIV:** 274
"Of the Passing of the First-Born" (Du Bois), **Supp. II Part 1:** 170
"Of the Sorrow Songs" (Du Bois), **Supp. II Part 1:** 170
"Of the Vanity of All Worldly Creature"

(Bradstreet), **Retro. Supp. III:** 4
"Of the Wings of Atlanta" (Du Bois), **Supp. II Part 1:** 170
Of This Time, Of This Place (Trilling), **Supp. III Part 2:** 498, 504
Of Time and the River (Wolfe), **IV:** 450, 451, 452, 455, 456, 457, 458, 459, 462, 464–465, 467, 468, 469
Of Woman Born: Motherhood as Experience and Institution (Rich), **Retro. Supp. III:** 242, 246; **Supp. I Part 2:** 554, 567–569
Of Women and Their Elegance (Mailer), **Retro. Supp. II:** 209
Ogden, Archie, **Supp. XIII:** 174
Ogden, Henry, **II:** 298
Ogden, Uzal, **Supp. I Part 2:** 516
Ogle, Connie, **Supp. XXIII:** 300, 301
"Oh, Atonement" (Weigl), **Supp. XIX:** 287
"Oh, Fairest of the Rural Maids" (Bryant), **Supp. I Part 1:** 169
"Oh, Immobility, Death's Vast Associate" (Dobyns), **Supp. XIII:** 89
"Oh, Joseph, I'm So Tired" (Yates), **Supp. XI:** 348
Oh, the Places You'll Go! (Geisel), **Supp. XVI:** 111
Oh, the Thinks You can Think! (Geisel), **Supp. XVI:** 111
"O'Halloran's Luck" (Benét), **Supp. XI:** 47
O'Hara, Frank, **Supp. XII:** 121; **Supp. XIX:** 81, 85; **Supp. XV:** 93, 176, 177, 178, 179–180, 182, 186, 187, 215–216; **Supp. XXII:** 226, 236; **Supp. XXIII: 207–222; Supp. XXIV:** 33, 34, 36, 42, 43, 44; **Supp. XXVII:** 19, 22, 23
O'Hara, J. D., **Supp. IV Part 1:** 43; **Supp. V:** 22; **Supp. XVI:** 221; **Supp. XXI:** 228
O'Hara, John, **I:** 375, 495; **II:** 444, 459; **III:** 66, **361–384; IV:** 59; **Retro. Supp. I:** 99, 112; **Supp. I Part 1:** 196; **Supp. II Part 1:** 109; **Supp. IV Part 1:** 31, 383; **Supp. IV Part 2:** 678; **Supp. IX:** 208; **Supp. V:** 95; **Supp. VIII:** 151, 156; **Supp. XIX:** 209
O'Hara, John Myers, **Supp. XXVII:** 285, 289
O'Hara's Choice (Uris), **Supp. XX: 247, 256–257**
"O Heaven born muse! inspire my humble lay" (Very), **Supp. XXV:** 239
O'Hehir, Andrew, **Supp. XII:** 280
O. Henry Biography (C. A. Smith), **Supp. II Part 1:** 395
"Ohio Pagan, An" (Anderson), **I:** 112, 113
Ohio trilogy (Richter), **Supp. XVIII:** 212–215
Oh Mercy (album, Dylan), **Supp. XVIII:** 28, 33
Oh Say Can You Say? (Geisel), **Supp. XVI:** 111
Oil! (Sinclair), **Supp. V:** 276, 277–279, 282, 288, 289
Oil Notes (Bass), **Supp. XVI:** 17
"Oil Painting of the Artist as the Artist" (MacLeish), **III:** 14
"O-jib-way Maid, The"(J. Schoolcraft), **Supp. XXIII:** 235
O'Keeffe, Georgia, **Supp. IX:** 62, 66; **Supp. XX: 75**
"Oklahoma" (Levis), **Supp. XI:** 267
Oklahoma's Poor Rich Indians: An Orgy of Graft and Exploitation of the Five Civilized Tribes—Legalized Robbery (Zitkala-Ša, Sniffen, and Fabens), **Supp. XXV:** 283
Oktenberg, Adrian, **Supp. XVII:** 76; **Supp. XXI:** 253; **Supp. XXIII:** 133
"Old, Old, Old, Old Andrew Jackson" (Lindsay), **Supp. I Part 2:** 398
"Old Amusement Park, An" (Moore), **III:** 216
"Old Angel Midnight" (Kerouac), **Supp. III Part 1:** 229–230
"Old Apple Dealer, The" (Hawthorne), **II:** 227, 233–235, 237, 238
"Old Apple-Tree, The" (Dunbar), **Supp. II Part 1:** 198
"Old Army Game, The" (Garrett), **Supp. VII:** 100–101
"Old Aunt Peggy" (Chopin), **Retro. Supp. II:** 64
"Old Barn at the Bottom of the Fogs, The" (Frost), **Retro. Supp. I:** 138
Old Battle-Ax, The (Holding), **Supp. XXII: 128–129**
Old Beauty and Others, The (Cather), **I:** 331
"Old Boys, Old Girls" (E. P. Jones), **Supp. XXII:** 151
Old Bruin: Commodore Matthew C. Perry, 1794–1858 (Morison), **Supp. I Part 2:** 494–495
Old Bunch, The (Levin), **Supp. XXVII:** 134, 139, 143
"Old Cracked Tune, An" (Kunitz), **Supp. III Part 1:** 264
Old Curiosity Shop, The (Dickens), **I:** 458; **Supp. I Part 2:** 409
"Old Enemy, The" (Teasdale), **Supp. XXVII:** 296
Oldest Killed Lake in North America, The (Carruth), **Supp. XVI:** 51
"Oldest Man, The" (M. F. K. Fisher), **Supp. XVII:** 91
"Old Farmer, The" (Jeffers), **Supp. II Part 2:** 418
Old-Fashioned Girl, An (Alcott), **Supp. I Part 1:** 29, 41, 42
"Old Father Morris" (Stowe), **Supp. I Part 2:** 586
Old Favorites and New Fancies for 1909 (Wells), **Supp. XXVI:** 275
"Old Flame, The" (R. Lowell), **II:** 550
"Old Florist" (Roethke), **III:** 531
"Old Folsom Prison" (Matthews), **Supp. IX:** 165
Old Forest, The (Taylor), **Supp. V:** 320, 321, 326, 327
"Old Forest, The" (Taylor), **Supp. V:** 313, 321, 323, 326
Old Forest and Other Stories (Taylor), **Supp. V:** 326
Old Friends and New (Jewett), **II:** 402; **Retro. Supp. II:** 137, 140
Old Glory, The (R. Lowell), **II:** 543, 545–546, 555; **Retro. Supp. II:** 188
Old Helmet, The (S. and A. Warner), **Supp. XVIII:** 267
"Old Homestead, The" (Dunbar), **Supp. II Part 1:** 198
"Old House" (Espaillat), **Supp. XXI:** 112, 113
Old Indian Legends (Zitkala-Ša), **Supp. XXV:** 275, 278, 285
"Old Iron" (Nye), **Supp. XIII:** 276
"Old Ironsides" (Holmes), **Supp. I Part 1:** 302
Old Jules (Sandoz), **Supp. XXIV:** 243, 244, **245–246,** 249, 251, 255, 257
"Old Lady We Saw, An" (Shields), **Supp. VII:** 310–311
"Old Love" (Singer), **Retro. Supp. II:** 307
"Old McGrath Place, The" (McGrath), **Supp. X:** 114
"Old Maid, The" (Wharton), **Retro. Supp. I:** 381, 382
"Old Man, The" (Faulkner), **II:** 68, 69; **Retro. Supp. III:** 85
Old Man and the Sea, The (Hemingway), **II:** 250, 256–257, 258, 265; **III:** 40; **Retro. Supp. I:** 180, **185,** 186
"Old Man Drunk" (Wright), **Supp. III Part 2:** 595
"Old Man Feeding Hens" (Francis), **Supp. IX:** 78
"Old Man on the Hospital Porch" (Ríos), **Supp. IV Part 2:** 546–547
Old Man Rubbing His Eyes (R. Bly), **Supp. IV Part 1:** 65

"Old Manse, The" (Hawthorne), **II:** 224
"Old Man's Winter Night, An" (Frost), **Retro. Supp. I:** 126, 131
Old Man Who Love Cheese, The (Keillor), **Supp. XVI:** 177
"Old Man with a Dog" (Wright), **Supp. XV:** 346
Old Marriage and New (Kooser), **Supp. XIX: 120–121**
"Old Meeting House, The" (Stowe), **Supp. I Part 2:** 586
"Old Memory, An" (Dunbar), **Supp. II Part 1:** 198
"Old Men, Old Horses" (P. N. Warren as Kilina), **Supp. XX: 262**
"Old Men, The" (McCarthy), **II:** 566
"Old Men Pitching Horseshoes" (X. J. Kennedy), **Supp. XV:** 166
Old Money (Wasserstein), **Supp. XV: 333–334**
"Old Morgue, The" (Prose), **Supp. XVI:** 250
Old Morning Program, The (radio show, Keillor). See Prairie Home Companion, A (radio show, Keillor)
"Old Mortality" (Porter), **III:** 436, 438–441, 442, 445, 446
"Old Mrs. Harris" (Cather), **I:** 332; **Retro. Supp. I:** 19
Old Neighborhood, The (Mamet), **Supp. XIV:** 240, 241, 242, 249–250, 251, 252, 254
"Old News" (Hawthorne), **Retro. Supp. III:** 111
Old New York (Wharton), **IV:** 322; **Retro. Supp. I:** 381; **Retro. Supp. III:** 288
"Ol' Doc Hyar" (Campbell), **Supp. II Part 1:** 202
"Old of the Moon" (Offutt), **Supp. XIX:** 165, 166
Old One-Two, The (Gurney), **Supp. V:** 98
"Old Order, The" (Porter), **III:** 443, 444–445, 451
"Old Osawatomie" (Sandburg), **III:** 584
Old Patagonia Express, The: By Train through the Americas (Theroux), **Supp. VIII:** 322
"Old People" (Ferry), **Supp. XXIV:** 162
"Old People, The" (Faulkner), **II:** 71–72
"Old Photograph" (Davison), **Supp. XXVI:** 72
"Old Photograph, An" (Kooser), **Supp. XIX:** 121
"Old Poet Moves to a New Apartment 14 Times, The" (Zukofsky), **Supp. III Part 2:** 628
Old Possum's Book of Practical Cats (T. S. Eliot), **Supp. XIII:** 228, 344
"Old Red" (Gordon), **II:** 199, 200, 203
Old Red and Other Stories (Gordon), **II:** 157
Old Régime in Canada, The (Parkman), **Supp. II Part 2:** 600, 607, 608–609, 612
Old Religion, The (Mamet), **Supp. XIV:** 253
Olds, Sharon, **Supp. X: 201–217; Supp. XI:** 139, 142, 244; **Supp. XII:** 229; **Supp. XIV:** 265; **Supp. XVII:** 114, 240; **Supp. XXI:** 249
"Old Saws" (Garrett), **Supp. VII:** 96–97
Old South, The: "A Summer Tragedy" and Other Stories (Bontemps), **Supp. XXII:** 7
"Old Stories" (Skloot), **Supp. XX: 200**
Old Testament, **I:** 109, 181, 300, 328, 401, 410, 419, 431, 457, 458; **II:** 166, 167, 219; **III:** 270, 272, 348, 390, 396; **IV:** 41, 114, 152, 309; **Retro. Supp. I:** 122, 140, 249, 311, 360; **Retro. Supp. II:** 299; **Supp. I Part 1:** 60, 104, 106, 151; **Supp. I Part 2:** 427, 515, 516; **Supp. IX:** 14. See also names of Old Testament books
"Old Things, The" (James), **Retro. Supp. I:** 229
"Old Times on the Mississippi" (Twain), **IV:** 199; **Retro. Supp. III:** 256, 264
Oldtown Folks (Stowe), **Supp. I Part 2:** 587, 596–598
"Old Town of Berwick, The" (Jewett), **Retro. Supp. II:** 132
"Old Trails" (Robinson), **III:** 513, 517
"Old Tyrannies" (Bourne), **I:** 233
"Old West" (Bausch), **Supp. VII:** 48
"Old Whorehouse, An" (Oliver), **Supp. VII:** 235
"Old Woman" (Pinsky), **Supp. VI:** 238
"Old Woman of Beare, The" (X. J. Kennedy), **Supp. XV:** 156
"Old Woman's Tale, An" (Hawthorne), **Retro. Supp. III:** 111
"Old Word, The" (Simic), **Supp. VIII:** 282
"Old-World Landowners" (Gogol), **Supp. XV:** 262
Oldys, Francis. See Chalmers, George
Oleanna (Mamet), **Supp. XIV:** 239, 241, 245, 248, 250
Olendorf, Donna, **Supp. IV Part 1:** 196
"Olga Poems, The" (Levertov), **Supp. III Part 1:** 279–281
"Olive Groves of Thasos, The" (Clampitt), **Supp. IX: 51–52**
Olive Kitteridge (Strout), **Supp. XXIII:** 273, 275, **280–284,** 285
Oliver, Bill, **Supp. VIII:** 138
Oliver, Douglas, **Supp. XXII:** 225, 226, 233, 235
Oliver, Mary, **Supp. VII: 229–248; Supp. X:** 31; **Supp. XVI:** 39; **Supp. XVII:** 111, 240; **Supp. XXIII:** 51
Oliver, Sydney, **I:** 409
Oliver Goldsmith: A Biography (Irving), **II:** 315
Oliver Twist (Dickens), **I:** 354; **Supp. IV Part 2:** 464
Olives (Stallings), **Supp. XXV:** 221, 223, 224, 233–234
"Olivia" (Salinas), **Supp. XIII:** 316
"Olivier Bergmann" (Halliday), **Supp. XIX:** 93–94
Olivieri, David (pseudonym), **Retro. Supp. I:** 361. See also Wharton, Edith
Ollive, Samuel, **Supp. I Part 2:** 503
Olmsted, Frederick Law, **Supp. I Part 1:** 355
Olor de la memoria, El/The Scent of Memory (Espaillat), **Supp. XXI:** 104
Olsen, Lance, **Supp. IV Part 1:** 54; **Supp. IV Part 2:** 623
Olsen, Tillie, **Supp. V:** 114, 220; **Supp. XIII: 291–309; Supp. XVI:** 83, 90
Olshan, Joseph, **Supp. XIX:** 52
Olson, Charles, **Retro. Supp. I:** 209; **Retro. Supp. III:** 245; **Supp. II Part 1:** 30, 328; **Supp. II Part 2: 555–587; Supp. III Part 1:** 9, 271; **Supp. III Part 2:** 542, 624; **Supp. IV Part 1:** 139, 144, 146, 153, 154, 322; **Supp. IV Part 2:** 420, 421, 423, 426; **Supp. VIII:** 290, 291; **Supp. XII:** 2, 198; **Supp. XIII:** 104; **Supp. XIV:** 96; **Supp. XV:** 177; **Supp. XXI:** 19, 21, 23; **Supp. XXIV:** 42; **Supp. XXVII:** 160
Olson, Clarence, **Supp. XX: 84, 85, 86**
Olson, Ray, **Supp. XVII:** 111, 112, 119
Olson, Tillie, **Supp. XXVII:** 256
"Ol' Tunes, The" (Dunbar), **Supp. II Part 1:** 197
"O Lull Me, Lull Me" (Roethke), **III:** 536–537
O'Malley, Anne, **Supp. XXII:** 56
Omar Khayyam, **Supp. I Part 1:** 363
O'Meally, Robert, **Retro. Supp. II:** 112
Omega the Unknown (comic book

series), **Supp. XVIII:** 149
"Omen" (Komunyakaa), **Supp. XIII:** 126, 127
Omensetter's Luck (Gass), **Supp. VI:** **80–82,** 87
Omeros (Walcott), **Supp. XV:** 264
"Ominous Baby, An" (Crane), **I:** 411
Ommateum, with Doxology (Ammons), **Supp. VII:** 24–26, 27, 28, 36
Omni-Americans, The: New Perspectives on Black Experience and American Culture (Murray), **Supp. XIX:** 147, **149–151,** 154
"Omnibus Jaunts and Drivers" (Whitman), **IV:** 350
Omoo (Melville), **III:** 76–77, 79, 84; **Retro. Supp. I:** 247; **Retro. Supp. III:** 147, 152, 153, 154, 155
O My Land, My Friends (H. Crane), **Retro. Supp. II:** 76
"On Abrigador Hill" (Nelson), **Supp. XVIII:** 183
"On a Certain Condescension in Foreigners" (J. R. Lowell), **Supp. I Part 2:** 419
"On a Certain Engagement South of Seoul" (Carruth), **Supp. XVI:** 47
"On a Child Who Lived One Minute" (X. J. Kennedy), **Supp. XV:** 152, 155
"On Acquiring Riches" (Banks), **Supp. V:** 5
On a Darkling Plain (Stegner), **Supp. IV Part 2:** 598, 607
On a Fire on the Moon (Mailer), **Retro. Supp. II:** 206
"On a Hill Far Away" (Dillard), **Supp. VI:** 28
"On a Honey Bee, Drinking from a Glass and Drowned Therein" (Freneau), **Supp. II Part 1:** 273
"On a Monument to a Pigeon" (Leopold), **Supp. XIV:** 187–188
"On a Mountainside" (Wagoner), **Supp. IX:** 332
O'Nan, Stewart, **Supp. XI:** 348; **Supp. XXV: 141–155**
"On a New Novel" (Ellis), **Supp. XXVII:** 78
"On an Old Photograph of My Son" (Carver), **Supp. III Part 1:** 140
"Onan's Soliloquy" (X. J. Kennedy), **Supp. XV:** 165
"On Antiphon Island" (Mackey), **Supp. XXVII:** 156
"On a Proposed Trip South" (W. C. Williams), **Retro. Supp. I:** 413
"On a Scale of 1 to 10: Life Writing and Lyrical Pain" (Mintz), **Supp. XXVI:** 52–53
Onassis, Jacqueline Kennedy, **Supp. XVIII:** 287
"On a Tree Fallen across the Road" (Frost), **Retro. Supp. I:** 134
"On a View of Pasadena from the Hills" (Winters), **Supp. II Part 2:** 795, 796–799, 814
"On a Visit to a Halfway House after a Long Absence" (Salinas), **Supp. XIII:** 325
"On a Windy Night" (Dixon), **Supp. XII:** 155
On Becoming a Novelist (Gardner), **Supp. VI:** 64
"On Being an American" (Toomer), **Supp. III Part 2:** 479
"On Being Asked to Write a Poem against the War in Vietnam" (Carruth), **Supp. XVI:** 55–56
"On Being a Woman" (Parker), **Supp. IX:** 201
On Being Blue (Gass), **Supp. VI:** 77, 78, 86, 94; **Supp. XIV:** 305
"On Being Brought from Africa to America" (Wheatley), **Supp. XX: 280–281, 286–287**
"On Being Too Inhibited" (Hay), **Supp. XIV:** 130
"On Being Unable to Read" (Cornell), **Supp. XX: 94–95**
On Beyond Zebra! (Geisel), **Supp. XVI:** 105
"On Burroughs' Work" (Ginsberg), **Supp. II Part 1:** 320
Once (Walker), **Supp. III Part 2:** 519, 522, 530
Once at Antietam (Gaddis), **Supp. IV Part 1:** 285
"Once by the Pacific" (Frost), **II:** 155; **Retro. Supp. I:** 122, 137; **Retro. Supp. III:** 102
Once in a Blue Moon (film), **Supp. XXVII:** 90
"Once More, the Round" (Roethke), **III:** 529
Once More around the Block: Familiar Essays (Epstein), **Supp. XIV: 107**
"Once More to the Lake" (White), **Supp. I Part 2:** 658, 668, 673–675
"On Certain Political Measures Proposed to Their Consideration" (Barlow), **Supp. II Part 1:** 82
"Once There Was Light" (Kenyon), **Supp. VII:** 171–172
Once Upon a Time in Atlanta (Andrews), **Supp. XXVI:** 3, 11
"On Credo Ut Intelligam" (Bronk), **Supp. XXI:** 31
Ondaatje, Michael, **Supp. IV Part 1:** 252
"On Dining Alone" (M. F. K. Fisher), **Supp. XVII:** 83
On Distant Ground (R. O. Butler), **Supp. XII:** 62, **66–68,** 69, 74
"On Divers Geometries" (Bronk), **Supp. XXI:** 31
"On Dreams"(Hadas), **Supp. XXIII:** 117
"One, The" (Weigl), **Supp. XIX:** 282–283
"1 January 1965" (Brodsky), **Supp. VIII:** 23–24
O'Neale, Sondra, **Supp. IV Part 1:** 2
"One A.M. with Voices" (X. J. Kennedy), **Supp. XV:** 157
"One Arm" (T. Williams), **IV:** 383
One Arm, and Other Stories (T. Williams), **IV:** 383
"One Art" (Bell), **Supp. X:** 2
One Art (Bishop), **Retro. Supp. II:** 51
"One Art" (Bishop), **Retro. Supp. II:** 50; **Supp. I Part 1:** 72, 73, 82, 93, 94–95, 96; **Supp. XV:** 126; **Supp. XXI:** 58; **Supp. XXIII:** 117; **Supp. XXV:** 222
"One Art: The Poetry of Elizabeth Bishop, 1971–1976" (Schwartz), **Supp. I Part 1:** 81
One Big Self: Prisoners of Louisiana (Wright and Luster), **Supp. XV:** 337, 344, 350, **351–353**
"One Blessing had I than the rest" (Dickinson), **Retro. Supp. I:** 45
"One Body" (Hass), **Supp. VI:** 106
One Boy's Boston, 1887–1901 (Morison), **Supp. I Part 2:** 494
"One Coat of Paint" (Ashbery), **Supp. III Part 1:** 26
"One Dash-Horses" (Crane), **I:** 416
One Day (Morris), **III:** 233–236
One Day, When I Was Lost (Baldwin), **Retro. Supp. II:** 13; **Supp. I Part 1:** 48, 66, 67
"One Dead Friend" (Kumin), **Supp. IV Part 2:** 441
One Destiny: An Epistle to the Christians (Asch), **Supp. XXIII:** 2, 7
"One Down" (Goodman), **Supp. XXVI:** 122–123
One Fish Two Fish Red Fish Blue Fish (Geisel), **Supp. XVI:** 108
One Flesh (Major), **Supp. XXII: 183–184**
One Flew Over the Cuckoo's Nest (Kesey), **III:** 558
One Flew Over the Cuckoo's Nest (Kesey), **Supp. XXIII:** 100
One Foot in Eden (Rash), **Supp.**

XXVII: 222–223, 226
"One for the Road" (Swados), **Supp. XIX:** 259
One for the Rose (Levine), **Supp. V:** 178, 179, 181, 187, 189–191
"One for the Rose" (Levine), **Supp. V:** 181, 190
"One Friday Morning" (Hughes), **Supp. I Part 1:** 330
"One Holy Night" (Cisneros), **Supp. VII:** 69–70
"One Home" (Stafford), **Supp. XI:** 321
100 Faces of Death, The, Part IV (Boyle), **Supp. VIII:** 16
100 Great Poets of the English Language (Gioia, ed.), **Supp. XXI:** 99
100 Years of Negro Freedom (Bontemps), **Supp. XXII:** 6
145 Street: Short Stories (Myers), **Supp. XXVII:** 210, 211
$106,000 Blood Money (Hammett), **Supp. IV Part 1:** 345
"$106,000 Blood Money" (Hammett), **Supp. IV Part 1:** 345, 346
One Hundred Days in Europe (Holmes), **Supp. I Part 1:** 317
180 More: Extraordinary Poems for Every Day (Collins, ed.), **Supp. XXI:** 54
158-Pound Marriage, The (Irving), **Supp. VI:** 163, 164, **167–170**
O'Neil, Elizabeth Murrie, **Retro. Supp. I:** 427
O'Neill, Brendan, **Supp. XII:** 286
O'Neill, Eugene, **I:** 66, 71, 81, 94, 393, 445; **II:** 278, 391, 427, 585; **III:** 151, 165, **385–408; IV:** 61, 383; **Retro. Supp. II:** 82, 104; **Retro. Supp. III:** 48, 165, 174, 177, 313; **Supp. III Part 1:** 177–180, 189; **Supp. IV Part 1:** 359; **Supp. IV Part 2:** 587, 607; **Supp. V:** 277; **Supp. VIII:** 332, 334; **Supp. XIV:** 239, 320, 328; **Supp. XVI:** 193; **Supp. XVII:** 96, 99–100, 103, 105, 107; **Supp. XX: 69; Supp. XXI:** 6, 13; **Supp. XXII:** 17, 18, 22, 28; **Supp. XXV:** 19
O'Neill, Oona, **Supp. XXII:** 25, 26
"One Is a Wanderer" (Thurber), **Supp. I Part 2:** 616
One Is the Sun (P. N. Warren), **Supp. XX: 269–270**
One L (Turow), **Supp. XVII: 214,** 215, 217
"One Last Look at the Adige: Verona in the Rain" (Wright), **Supp. III Part 2:** 603
One Life (Rukeyser), **Supp. VI:** 273, 281, 283
One Life at a Time, Please (Abbey), **Supp. XIII:** 13
One Man in His Time (Glasgow), **II:** 178, 184
"One Man's Fortunes" (Dunbar), **Supp. II Part 1:** 211, 212–213
One Man's Initiation (Dos Passos), **I:** 476–477, 479, 488
One Man's Meat (White), **Supp. I Part 2:** 654, 669, 676
"One Man's Meat" (White), **Supp. I Part 2:** 655
One Matchless Time: A Life of William Faulkner (Parini), **Retro. Supp. III:** 73; **Supp. XXII:** 205
"One Moment on Top of the Earth" (Nye), **Supp. XIII:** 282
One More July: A Football Dialogue with Bill Curry (Plimpton), **Supp. XVI:** 243
"One More"(Kenny), **Supp. XXIII:** 156
"One More Song" (Lindsay), **Supp. I Part 2:** 400–401
"One More Thing" (Carver), **Supp. III Part 1:** 138, 144
"One More Time" (Gordon), **II:** 200
One Nation (Stegner), **Supp. IV Part 2:** 599, 608
"One-Night Homecoming" (X. J. Kennedy), **Supp. XV:** 167
"ONE NIGHT STAND" (Baraka), **Supp. II Part 1:** 32
"One of Our Conquerors" (Bourne), **I:** 223
One of Ours (Cather), **I:** 322–323; **Retro. Supp. I:** 1, 3, **13–15,** 20; **Retro. Supp. III:** 23, 36
One of the Dangerous Trades (Davison), **Supp. XXVI:** 61, 67–68
"One of the Missing" (Bierce), **I:** 201–202
"One of the Rooming Houses of Heaven" (Doty), **Supp. XI:** 131
"One of the Smallest" (Stern), **Supp. IX:** 299–300
"One of Us" (Fante), **Supp. XI:** 165
Oneóta: or, The Red Race of America (H. Schoolcraft), **Supp. XXIII:** 232
"One Out of Twelve: Writers Who Are Women in Our Century" (Olsen), **Supp. XIII:** 294
"One Part Humor, 2 Parts Whining" (Kakutani), **Supp. XI:** 38
"One Person" (Wylie), **Supp. I Part 2:** 709, 724–727
"One Reel Tragedy" (Stone), **Supp. XXVII:** 254
"One Sister have I in our house" (Dickinson), **Retro. Supp. I:** 34
165 Meeting House Lane (Notley), **Supp. XXII:** 224, 225, 226
"One Song, The" (Strand), **Supp. IV Part 2:** 619
"One Summer in Spain" (Coover), **Supp. V:** 40
One That Got Away, The (Everett), **Supp. XVIII:** 54
1000 Airplanes on the Roof (Glass, Hwang, and Sirlin), **Supp. XXI:** 147
1001 Afternoons in Chicago (Hecht), **Supp. XXVII:** 83, 85, 88
One Thousand Avant-Garde Plays (Koch), **Supp. XV:** 187
"One Thousandth, The" (Weigl), **Supp. XIX:** 288
One Time, One Place: Mississippi in the Depression, a Snapshot Album (Welty), **Retro. Supp. I:** 339, 343, 344
1 x 1 (One Times One) (Cummings), **I:** 430, 436, 438–439, 441, 446, 447, 448
"One Touch of Nature" (McCarthy), **II:** 580
One Train (Koch), **Supp. XV:** 177, 184
"One Trip Abroad" (Fitzgerald), **II:** 95
One True Thing (film), **Supp. XVII:** 176
One True Thing (Quindlen), **Supp. XVII:** 166, **174–176**
"One Way" (Creeley), **Supp. IV Part 1:** 150–151
One Way or Another (Cameron), **Supp. XII:** 81
One-Way Ticket (Hughes), **Retro. Supp. I:** 206, 207, 208; **Supp. I Part 1:** 333–334
One Way to Heaven (Cullen), **Supp. IV Part 1:** 170, 172
One Way to Reconstruct the Scene (W. V. Davis), **Supp. XXI:** 83, **88–91**
"One Way to Reconstruct the Scene" (W. V. Davis), **Supp. XXI: 88–89,** 90, 91, 92, 93
One Way to Spell Man (Stegner), **Supp. IV Part 2:** 595, 598, 601, 609
"One Way to Spell Man" (Stegner), **Supp. IV Part 2:** 601
One Whose Eyes Open When You Close Your Eyes, The (F. Wright), **Supp. XVII:** 240, 243
"One Who Skins Cats, The" (Gunn Allen), **Supp. IV Part 1:** 331
One Who Walked Alone (Price), **Supp. XXVII:** 117
"One Who Went Forth to Feel Fear" (Grimms), **Supp. X:** 86
"One Winter I Devise a Plan of My

Own" (Ríos), **Supp. IV Part 2:** 549
One Winter Night in August (X. J. Kennedy), **Supp. XV:** 154, 162
One World at a Time (Kooser), **Supp. XIX:** 116, **122–123**
One Writer's Beginnings (Welty), **Retro. Supp. I:** 339, 340, 341, 343, 344, 355–356
"One Year" (Olds), **Supp. X:** 210
On Fire (L. Brown), **Supp. XXI:** 41, **48–49**
On Fire (Silver), **Supp. XXIV:** 264
"On First Looking Into Chapman's Homer" (Keats), **Supp. XXI:** 64; **Supp. XXV:** 226
"On First Looking Out through Juan de la Cosa's Eyes" (Olson), **Supp. II Part 2:** 565, 566, 570, 579
"On First Opening The Lyric Year" (W. C. Williams), **Retro. Supp. I:** 414
"On Freedom's Ground" (Wilbur), **Supp. III Part 2:** 562
On Glory's Course (Purdy), **Supp. VII:** 275–276, 279, 280
On Grief and Reason (Brodsky), **Supp. VIII: 31–32**
"On Hearing a Symphony of Beethoven" (Millay), **III:** 132–133
"On Hearing the Airlines Will Use a Psychological Profile to Catch Potential Skyjackers" (Dunn), **Supp. XI:** 144–145
On Human Finery (Bell), **Supp. I Part 2:** 636
"On Imagerie: Esther Williams, 1944" (Sobin), **Supp. XVI:** 294
"On Imagination" (Wheatley), **Supp. XX: 281**
"On Imminence: An Essay" (Sobin), **Supp. XVI:** 291
On Immunity: An Inoculation (Biss), **Supp. XXVI:** 45, 57–58, 59
"Onionskin" (Goodman), **Supp. XXVI:** 121, 125
"On Ithaka" (Davison), **Supp. XXVI:** 79
On Kingdom Mountain (Mosher), **Supp. XXII:** 203, 205, 206, 207, 208, 209, 212, 214, **216**
Onkl Mozes (Uncle Moses) (Asch), **Supp. XXIII:** 5
"On leaving my children John and Jane at School, in the Atlantic states, and preparing to return to the interior"(J. Schoolcraft), **Supp. XXIII:** 227, 228, 232, 233, 235, 236
On Liberty (Mill), **Supp. XI:** 196
On Lies, Secrets, and Silence: Selected Prose 1966–1978 (Rich), **Retro. Supp. III:** 242, 246, 247–248
"On Looking Alone at a Place" (M. F. K. Fisher), **Supp. XVII:** 91
"On Looking at a Copy of Alice Meynell's Poems, Given Me, Years Ago, by a Friend" (A. Lowell), **II:** 527–528
"On Lookout Mountain" (Hayden), **Supp. II Part 1:** 380
Only a Few of Us Left (Marquand), **III:** 55
"Only Animal, The" (F. Wright), **Supp. XVII:** 245
"Only a Pawn in Their Game" (song, Dylan), **Supp. XVIII:** 24
Only as Far as Brooklyn (Kenny), **Supp. XXIII: 148–151,** 152
"Only Bar in Dixon, The" (Hugo), **Supp. VI:** 140, 141
Only Dangerous Thing, The (Di Piero), **Supp. XIX: 37–38**
Only Dark Spot in the Sky, The (Dove), **Supp. IV Part 1:** 244
"Only Good Indian, The" (Humphrey), **Supp. IX:** 101
"Only Goodness" (Lahiri), **Supp. XXI:** 186, 188
Only in America (Golden), **Supp. VIII:** 244
"Only in the Dream" (Eberhart), **I:** 523
"Only Path to Tomorrow, The" (Rand), **Supp. IV Part 2:** 524
"Only Professional Player of the Toy Piano, Margaret Leng Tan, The" (Biss), **Supp. XXVI:** 51
"Only Rose, The" (Jewett), **II:** 408
"Only Son of the Doctor, The" (Gordon), **Supp. IV Part 1:** 305, 306
"Only the Cat Escapes", **Supp. XII:** 150–151
"Only the Dead Know Brooklyn" (Wolfe), **IV:** 451
Only the Little Bone (Huddle), **Supp. XXVI:** 152–153
"Only the Little Bone" (Huddle), **Supp. XXVI:** 151, 153
"Only When I Am Quiet and Do Not Speak"(Hirshfield), **Supp. XXIII:** 133
Only When I Laugh (Simon), **Supp. IV Part 2:** 575
Only World, The (Hull), **Supp. XXI:** 129, **138–141**
On Man and Manhood (Kriegel), **Supp. XXIV: 224–225**
"On Manhood, Disease, and the Authentic Self" (Kriegel), **Supp. XXIV:** 215
"On Meditation"(J. Schoolcraft), **Supp. XXIII:** 229
"On Meeting My Father in a Bar for the First Time" (Gansworth), **Supp. XXVI:** 110
"On Messrs. Hussey and Coffin" (Wheatley), **Supp. XX: 280**
On Moral Fiction (Gardner), **Supp. VI:** 61, **71,** 72, 73
"On Morality" (Didion), **Supp. IV Part 1:** 196
"On Mt. Philo in November" (Di Piero), **Supp. XIX:** 37, 39
"On Murder Considered as One of the Fine Arts" (De Quincey), **Supp. XXVI:** 283
"On My Own" (Levine), **Supp. V:** 181, 189–190
"On My Own Work" (Wilbur), **Supp. III Part 2:** 541–542
On Native Grounds: An Interpretation of Modern American Prose Literature (Kazin), **I:** 517; **Supp. I Part 2:** 650; **Supp. VIII:** 93, 96–97, 98, **100–102**
"On Not Being a Dove" (Updike), **Retro. Supp. I:** 323
"On Open Form" (Merwin), **Supp. III Part 1:** 347–348, 353
On Photography (Sontag), **Supp. III Part 2:** 451, 458, 462–465
"On Poetry"(Hadas), **Supp. XXIII:** 115, 116
"On Political Poetry" (R. Bly), **Supp. IV Part 1:** 61
On Politics: A Carnival of Buncombe (Moos, ed.), **III:** 116
"On Pretentiousness" (Kushner), **Supp. IX:** 131–132
"On Quitting a Little College" (Stafford), **Supp. XI:** 321
"On Reading Eckerman's Conversations with Goethe" (Masters), **Supp. I Part 2:** 458
On Reading Shakespeare (L. P. Smith), **Supp. XIV:** 345–346
"On Reading to Oneself" (Gass), **Supp. VI:** 88, 89
"On Recollection" (Wheatley), **Supp. XX: 287**
On Revolution (Arendt), **Retro. Supp. I:** 87
On Second Thought (Kenny), **Supp. XXIII:** 144
"On Seeing Larry Rivers's Washington Crossing the Delaware at the Museum of Modern Art" (O'Hara), **Supp. XV:** 186; **Supp. XXIII:** 208, 214
"On Seeing Red" (Walker), **Supp. III Part 2:** 527
"On Social Plays" (A. Miller), **III:**

147, 148, 159
Onstad, Katrina, **Supp. XXIV:** 209
"On Steinbeck's Story 'Flight' " (Stegner), **Supp. IV Part 2:** 596
"On Style" (Sontag), **Supp. III Part 2:** 456–459, 465–466
"On Suicide" (Hay), **Supp. XIV:** 130, 132
"On Teaching the Young Laurel to Shoot" (Bynner), **Supp. XV:** 50
"On the Antler" (Proulx), **Supp. VII:** 252–253
"On the Avenue" (Espaillat), **Supp. XXI:** 112
On the Banks of Plum Creek (L. I. Wilder), **Supp. XXII:** 294, 299
"On the Banks of the Wabash" (Paul Dresser), **Retro. Supp. II:** 94
"On the Beach, at Night" (Whitman), **IV:** 348
"On the Bosom of This Grave and Wasted Land I Will Lay My Head" (Ray), **Supp. XVIII:** 189
On the Boundary (Tillich), **Retro. Supp. I:** 326
"On the Building of Springfield" (Lindsay), **Supp. I Part 2:** 381
"On the Coast of Maine" (Hayden), **Supp. II Part 1:** 381
On the Contrary: Articles of Belief (McCarthy), **II:** 559, 562
"On the Death of a Friend's Child" (J. R. Lowell), **Supp. I Part 2:** 409
"On the Death of Cardinal Tisserant" (Bronk), **Supp. XXI:** 32
"On the Death of General Wooster" (Wheatley), **Supp. XX: 287**
"On the Death of Rev. Mr. George Whitefield—1770" (Wheatley), **Supp. XX: 280,Supp. XX: 282–283**
"On the Death of Senator Thomas J. Walsh" (Winters), **Supp. II Part 2:** 802, 806
"On the Death of Yeats" (Bogan), **Supp. III Part 1:** 59
"On the Death of Zhukov" (Brodsky), **Supp. VIII:** 27
"On the Disadvantages of Central Heating" (Clampitt), **Supp. IX:** 41, 47, 52
"On the Doric Rock, Lake Superior"(J. Schoolcraft), **Supp. XXIII:** 232
On the Drumhead: A Selection from the Writing of Mike Quin (Carlisle, ed.), **Supp. XVIII:** 223, 226
"On the Edge" (Levine), **Supp. V:** 181–182
On the Edge and Over (Levine), **Supp. V:** 178, 180–182, 186
On the Edge of the Great Rift: Three Novels of Africa (Theroux), **Supp. VIII:** 316
"On the Edge of Visible Light"(Schott), **Supp. XXIII:** 242
"On the Eve of the Feast of the Immaculate Conception, 1942" (R. Lowell), **II:** 538; **Retro. Supp. II:** 185
"On the Eyes of an SS Officer" (Wilbur), **Supp. III Part 2:** 548
"On the Failure of Meaning in the Absence of Objective Analogs" (Bronk), **Supp. XXI:** 31
"On the Fall of General Earl Cornwallis" (Freneau), **Supp. II Part 1:** 261
"On the Folly of Writing Poetry" (Freneau), **Supp. II Part 1:** 263
"On the Four Parts of the World" (Dudley), **Retro. Supp. III:** 3
On the Frontier (Auden and Isherwood), **Supp. II Part 1:** 13; **Supp. XIV:** 163
On the Great Atlantic Rainway: Selected Poems, 1950–1988 (Koch), **Supp. XV:** 177
"On the History of Poetry" (Halliday), **Supp. XIX:** 88, 89
"On the Hysterical Playground" (Watman), **Supp. XX: 93**
"On the Island" (Stern), **Supp. IX:** 290
"On the Late Eclipse" (Bryant), **Supp. I Part 1:** 152
On the Laws of the Poetic Art (Hecht), **Supp. X:** 58
On the Line (Swados), **Supp. XIX: 258–260**
"On the Line" (Swados), **Supp. XIX:** 259
"On the Marginal Way" (Wilbur), **Supp. III Part 2:** 558, 559
On the Mesa (Nichols), **Supp. XIII:** 268
"On the Moon and Matriarchal Consciousness" (Neumann), **Supp. IV Part 1:** 68
"On the Morning after the Sixties" (Didion), **Supp. IV Part 1:** 205, 206
On the Motion and Immobility of Douve (Bonnefoy; Kinnell, trans.), **Supp. III Part 1:** 235
"On the Mullica"(Schott), **Supp. XXIII:** 253
"On the Murder of Lieutenant José del Castillo by the Falangist Bravo Martinez, July 12, 1936" (Levine), **Supp. V:** 187
"On the Night of a Friend's Wedding" (Robinson), **III:** 524
"On the Occasion of a Poem: Richard Hugo" (Wright), **Supp. III Part 2:** 596
On the Occasion of My Last Afternoon (Gibbons), **Supp. X:** 46, **50–53**
On the Origin of Species (Darwin), **Supp. XIV:** 192
"On the Parapet" (Tanner), **Retro. Supp. II:** 205
"On the Platform" (Nemerov), **III:** 287
On the Poetry of Philip Levine: Stranger to Nothing (Levis), **Supp. XI:** 257
"On the Pottlecombe Cornice" (Sturgis), **Supp. XX: 233, 240**
"On the Powers of the Human Understanding" (Freneau), **Supp. II Part 1:** 274
On the Prejudices, Predilections, and Firm Beliefs of William Faulkner (Brooks), **Supp. XIV:** 13
"On the Pulse of Morning" (Angelou), **Supp. IV Part 1:** 15–17
"On the Railway Platform" (Jarrell), **II:** 370
"On the Rainy River" (O'Brien), **Supp. V:** 250
On the Rebound: A Story and Nine Poems (Purdy), **Supp. VII:** 276–277
"On the Religion of Nature" (Freneau), **Supp. II Part 1:** 275
"On the River" (Dunbar), **Supp. II Part 1:** 193
"On the River" (Levine), **Supp. V:** 193
On the River Styx and Other Stories (Matthiessen), **Supp. V:** 212
On the Road (Kerouac), **Retro. Supp. I:** 102; **Supp. III Part 1:** 92, 218, 222–224, 226, 230–231; **Supp. V:** 336; **Supp. X:** 269; **Supp. XIII:** 275; **Supp. XIV:** 138, 150; **Supp. XV:** 221; **Supp. XVIII:** 20, 138; **Supp. XXI:** 53; **Supp. XXIV:** 281; **Supp. XXVI:** 26, 252
"On the Road Home" (Stevens), **Retro. Supp. I:** 306
On the Road with the Archangel (Buechner), **Supp. XII:** 54
"On the Rope" (Richard), **Supp. XIX:** 211–212
"On the Run" (Boyle), **Supp. XXIV:** 52
On These I Stand: An Anthology of the Best Poems of Countee Cullen (Cullen), **Supp. IV Part 1:** 173
"On the Skeleton of a Hound" (Wright), **Supp. III Part 2:** 593
"On the Staten Island Ferry"(Kenny), **Supp. XXIII:** 154
"On the Street" (Peacock), **Supp. XIX:** 199

"On the Street: Monument" (Gunn Allen), **Supp. IV Part 1:** 326
"On the Subway" (Olds), **Supp. X:** 207
"On the System of Policy Hitherto Pursued by Their Government" (Barlow), **Supp. II Part 1:** 82
"On the Teaching of Modern Literature" (Trilling), **Supp. III Part 2:** 509–510
"On the Uniformity and Perfection of Nature" (Freneau), **Supp. II Part 1:** 275
"On the Universality and Other Attributes of the God of Nature" (Freneau), **Supp. II Part 1:** 275
"On the Use of Trisyllabic Feet in Iambic Verse" (Bryant), **Supp. I Part 1:** 156
On the Verge: Emerging Poets (Ellis and Lease, eds.), **Supp. XXI:** 246
On the Waterfront (film, Kazan), **Supp. XVIII: 250–251,** 252, 253
"On the Way" (Stone), **Supp. XXVII:** 251, 253
"On the Way Home" (L. I. Wilder), **Supp. XXII:** 292
On the Way to the Island (Ferry), **Supp. XXIV:** 147, **148–149,** 150
"On the Way to the San Remo"(O'Hara), **Supp. XXIII:** 212, 219
On the Way toward a Phenomenological Psychology: The Psychology of William James (Linschoten), **II:** 362
"On the Way to Work" (Dunn), **Supp. XI:** 149–150
"On the Wide Heath" (Millay), **III:** 130
"On the Writing of Novels" (Buck), **Supp. II Part 1:** 121
On the Yard (Braly), **Supp. XVIII:** 147
On This Island (Auden), **Supp. II Part 1:** 11
On This Side of the River (Ferry), **Supp. XXIV: 161–162**
"On Time" (O'Hara), **III:** 369–370
"Ontological Episode of the Asylum" (Carruth), **Supp. XVI:** 48, 50
"Ontology of the Sentence, The" (Gass), **Supp. VI:** 77
"On Top" (Leopold), **Supp. XIV:** 188
"On Top" (Snyder), **Supp. VIII:** 304
"On Translating Akhmatova" (Kunitz), **Supp. III Part 1:** 268
"On Turning Ten" (Collins), **Supp. XXI:** 64
"On Visiting a Borrowed Country House in Arcadia" (Stallings), **Supp. XXV:** 233–234
"On Waking to Old Debts" (Keillor), **Supp. XVI:** 167
On William Stafford: The Worth of Local Things (Andrews, ed.), **Supp. XI:** 311, 312, 317, 321, 324, 326
On Writers and Writing (O'Nan, ed.), **Supp. XXV:** 152–153
"On Writing" (Carver), **Supp. III Part 1:** 142–143
"On Writing" (Nin), **Supp. X:** 182
On Your Own (Gallagher), **Supp. XXIV:** 166
Opatoshu, Joseph, **IV:** 9
"Open Boat, The" (Crane), **I:** 408, 415, 416–417, 423; **Retro. Supp. I:** 325; **Supp. XIV:** 51
Open Boat and Other Stories (Crane), **I:** 408
Open Door, The (Skloot), **Supp. XX: 194, 196, 208**
Open Heart: A Patient's Story of Life-Saving Medicine and Life-Giving Friendship (Neugeboren), **Supp. XVI:** 217, **229–230**
Open House (Roethke), **III:** 529–530, 540
"Open House" (Roethke), **III:** 529
"Opening, An" (Swenson), **Supp. IV Part 2:** 639
Opening of the Field, The (Duncan), **Supp. III Part 2:** 625
Opening the Hand (Merwin), **Supp. III Part 1:** 341, 353, 355
"Open Letter" (Roethke), **III:** 532, 534
"Open Letter to Surrealists Everywhere, An" (H. Miller), **III:** 184
Open Meeting, The (Gurney), **Supp. V:** 98
Open Net (Plimpton), **Supp. XVI:** 241
"Open Road, The" (Dreiser), **II:** 44
Open Sea, The (Masters), **Supp. I Part 2:** 471
Open Season: Sporting Adventures (Humphrey), **Supp. IX:** 95
"Open Secret" (Nelson), **Supp. XVIII:** 185
Open Secrets (Munro), **Supp. XXVII:** 190, 191–192
"Open Secrets" (Munro), **Supp. XXVII:** 191–192
"Open the Gates" (Kunitz), **Supp. III Part 1:** 264–265, 267
"Opera, The" (Whitman), **Retro. Supp. III:** 309–310
"Opera Company, The" (Merrill), **Supp. III Part 1:** 326
Operating Instructions: A Journal of My Son's First Year (Lamott), **Supp. XX: 136–137, 142**
"Operation, The" (Sanders), **Supp. XVI:** 266
"Operation, The" (Sexton), **Supp. II Part 2:** 675, 679
Operation Shylock: A Confession (P. Roth), **Retro. Supp. II:** 279, 280, 291
Operation Sidewinder (Shepard), **Supp. III Part 2:** 434–435, 439, 446–447
Operations in North African Waters (Morison), **Supp. I Part 2:** 490
Operation Wandering Soul (Powers), **Supp. IX:** 212, **217–219**
Opffer, Emil, **Retro. Supp. II:** 80; **Retro. Supp. III:** 46, 48
"Opinion" (Du Bois), **Supp. II Part 1:** 173
Opinionator, The (Bierce), **I:** 209
Opinions of Oliver Allston (Brooks), **I:** 254, 255, 256
O Pioneers! (Cather), **I:** 314, 317–319, 320; **Retro. Supp. I:** 1, 5, 6, **7–9,** 10, 13, 20; **Retro. Supp. II:** 136; **Retro. Supp. III:** 18, 20, 22, 23, 28–30, 36
Oppen, George, **IV:** 415; **Supp. III Part 2:** 614, 615, 616, 626, 628; **Supp. XIV:** 285, 286, 287; **Supp. XVI:** 282, 283; **Supp. XVII:** 243; **Supp. XXI:** 19,**Supp. XXI:** 29, 23; **Supp. XXIII:** 165–166, 168; **Supp. XXVI: 223–238**
Oppen, Mary, **Supp. XXVI:** 225
Oppenheim, James, **I:** 106, 109, 239, 245; **Supp. XV:** 294, 296, 298, 299, 301, 302, 307, 313; **Supp. XX: 68**
Oppenheimer, J. Robert, **I:** 137, 492
Oppenheimer, Judy, **Supp. IX:** 115, 116, 118, 120, 126
"Opportunity for American Fiction, An" (Howells), **Supp. I Part 2:** 645–646
Opposing Self, The (Trilling), **Supp. III Part 2:** 506–507
"Opposition" (Lanier), **Supp. I Part 1:** 368, 373
Oprah's Roots: An African American Lives Special (television production), **Supp. XX: 99**
Opticks: A Poem in Seven Sections (Goldbarth), **Supp. XII:** 177, **178**
Optimist's Daughter, The (Welty), **IV:** 261, 280; **Retro. Supp. I:** 339, 355
"Optimist's Daughter, The" (Welty), **IV:** 280–281
Options (O. Henry), **Supp. II Part 1:** 410
Opus Posthumous (Stevens), **IV:** 76, 78
Opus Posthumous (W. Stevens), **Supp. XVII:** 241
Oracle at Stoneleigh Court, The

(Taylor), **Supp. V:** 328
Orage, Alfred, **III:** 473
"O/Rain-in-the-Face"(Kenny), **Supp. XXIII:** 156
"Oral History" (Goodman), **Supp. XXVI:** 118, 119
Orange, Max (pseudonym). See Heller, Joseph
Orange Fish, The (Shields), **Supp. VII:** 318, 320, 323, 328
Orangery, The (Sorrentino), **Supp. XXI:** 228
Oranges (exhibition, Hartigan), **Supp. XXIII:** 210
Oranges (McPhee), **Supp. III Part 1:** 298–299, 301, 309
Oranges: 12 Pastorals (O'Hara), **Supp. XXIII:** 210
"Oranging of America, The" (Apple), **Supp. XVII:** 3–4, 6
Oranging of America and Other Short Stories, The (Apple), **Supp. XVII:** 1–2, **3–4,** 7, 8
Oration Delivered at Washington, July Fourth, 1809 (Barlow), **Supp. II Part 1:** 80, 83
Orations and Addresses (Bryant), **Supp. I Part 1:** 158
Orators, The (Auden), **Supp. II Part 1:** 6, 7, 11, 18–19
Orbach, Jerry, **Supp. XXIII:** 103
Orb Weaver, The (Francis), **Supp. IX: 81–82**
"Orchard" (Doolittle), **Supp. I Part 1:** 263–264, 265, 266
"Orchard" (Eberhart), **I:** 539
Orchard, The (B. Kelly), **Supp. XVII:** 123, 127**, 130–133**
"Orchard, The" (B. Kelly), **Supp. XVII:** 133
Orchard Keeper, The (McCarthy), **Supp. VIII: 175–176**
Orchestra (Davies), **III:** 541
"Orchid Fever" (Orlean), **Supp. XXV:** 160
"Orchids" (Roethke), **III:** 530–531
Orchid Thief, The: A True Story of Beauty and Obsession (Orlean), **Supp. XXV:** 160, 161–162
"Or Consider Prometheus" (Clampitt), **Supp. IX:** 44
Ordeal of Mansart, The (Du Bois), **Supp. II Part 1:** 185–186
Ordeal of Mark Twain, The (Brooks), **I:** 240, 247, 248; **II:** 482
Ordering the Façade: Photography and Contemporary Southern Women's Writing (Henninger), **Supp. XXI:** 253
"Order of Insects" (Gass), **Supp. VI:** 83
Order Out of Chaos (McPherson), **Supp. IV Part 1:** 2, 12
"Orders" (Duncan), **Supp. XXVII:** 160
"Ordinary Afternoon in Charlottesville, An" (Wright), **Supp. V:** 344
"Ordinary Days" (Dunn), **Supp. XI:** 151
"Ordinary Evening in New Haven, An" (Stevens), **IV:** 91–92; **Retro. Supp. I:** 297, 300, 311, 312
Ordinary Heroes (Turow), **Supp. XVII: 221–222,** 223
Ordinary Life (Crooker), **Supp. XXIII: 56**
Ordinary Love (Smiley), **Supp. VI:** 292, **299–300**
Ordinary Love; and Good Will: Two Novellas (Smiley), **Supp. VI:** 292, **299–300**
Ordinary Miracles (Jong), **Supp. V:** 115, 130–131
Ordinary Seaman, The (Goldman), **Supp. XXV:** 49, 50, 53–54
"Ordinary Time: Virginia Woolf and Thucydides on War" (Carson), **Supp. XII: 111**
"Ordinary Women, The" (Stevens), **IV:** 81
Ordinary Words (Stone), **Supp. XXVII:** 257, 262
Ordways, The (Humphrey), **Supp. IX:** 95, **98–100,** 109; **Supp. XV:** 353
"Oread" (Doolittle), **II:** 520–521; **Supp. I Part 1:** 265–266
Oregon Message, An (Stafford), **Supp. XI: 328–329**
Oregon Trail, The (Parkman), **II:** 312; **Supp. II Part 2:** 592, 595–596, 598, 606
Oresteia (Aeschylus), **Supp. IX:** 103
"Orestes at Tauris" (Jarrell), **II:** 376, 377
Orfalea, Gregory, **Supp. XIII:** 278
Orfeo ed Euridice (Gluck), **II:** 210, 211
Orff, Carl, **Supp. X:** 63
"Organizer's Wife, The" (Bambara), **Supp. XI:** 8–9
"Organmeister: Hasse After Marienkirche" (Bierds), **Supp. XVII:** 34
"Orgy" (Rukeyser), **Supp. VI:** 280
Orgy, The (Rukeyser), **Supp. VI:** 274, 283
"Orgy of Southerness, An" (Pickering), **Supp. XXI:** 203
"Oriental Rug"(Balakian), **Supp. XXIII:** 23, 24–25
"Orientation of Hope, The" (Locke), **Supp. XIV:** 212–213
Orient Express (Dos Passos), **I:** 480
"Orient Express, The" (Jarrell), **II:** 382, 383–384
Origen, Adamantius, **IV:** 153
"Origin" (Harjo), **Supp. XII:** 219
Original Child Bomb: Points for Meditation to Be Scratched on the Walls of a Cave (Merton), **Supp. VIII:** 203
Original Essays on the Poetry of Anne Sexton (George), **Supp. IV Part 2:** 450
"Original Follies Girl, The" (Z. Fitzgerald), **Supp. IX:** 71
Original Light (Goldbarth), **Supp. XII:** 181, **183–184,** 188
Original Love (Peacock), **Supp. XIX: 199–201,** 206
Original of Laura, The (Nabokov), **Retro. Supp. I:** 266
"Original Sin" (Jeffers), **Supp. II Part 2:** 426
"Original Sin" (Vaz), **Supp. XXVI:** 259–260
"Original Sin" (Warren), **IV:** 245
"Original Story" (Gansworth), **Supp. XXVI:** 114
Origin: Hawaii (Taggard), **Supp. XXII:** 272, 284
"Origin of Extermination in the Imagination, The" (Gass), **Supp. VI:** 89
Origin of Species (Darwin), **Supp. XXVII:** 34
Origin of Species, The (Darwin), **II:** 173, 462; **Supp. XVI:** 13
Origin of the Brunists, The (Coover), **Supp. V:** 39, 41, 52
"Origin of the Miscodeed, or the Maid of Taquimenon"(J. Schoolcraft), **Supp. XXIII:** 235
"Origin of the Robin, The"(J. Schoolcraft), **Supp. XXIII:** 234, 235
"Origins and History of Consciousness" (Rich), **Retro. Supp. III:** 249; **Supp. I Part 2:** 570
"Origins of a Nonfiction Writer" (Talese), **Supp. XVII:** 208
"Origins of a Poem" (Levertov), **Supp. III Part 1:** 273
"Origins of the Beat Generation, The" (Kerouac), **Supp. III Part 1:** 231
Origo, Iris, **IV:** 328
"O'Riley's Late-Bloomed Little Son" (X. J. Kennedy), **Supp. XV:** 159
"Orion" (Rich), **Retro. Supp. III:** 244, 245; **Supp. I Part 2:** 557
O'Riordan, Conal Holmes O'Connell, **III:** 465
Orlacs Hände (film, Weine), **Supp.**

XVII: 58
Orlando (V. Woolf), **Supp. XVII:** 86
Orlando (Woolf), **Supp. I Part 2:** 718; **Supp. VIII:** 263; **Supp. XII:** 9
Orlando Furioso (Ariosto), **Supp. XV:** 175
Orlean, Susan, **Supp. XXV: 157–167**
Orlik, Emil, **Supp. XXIII:** 6
Orloff, Chana, **Supp. XXIII:** 6
Orlovsky, Peter, **Supp. XII:** 121, 126; **Supp. XIV:** 150; **Supp. XVIII:** 27
Ormonde, Czenzi, **Supp. IV Part 1:** 132
Ormond; or, The Secret Witness (Brown), **Supp. I Part 1:** 133–137
Ornament and Crime (Loos), **Supp. XVI:** 187
Orne, Sarah. See Jewett, Sarah Orne
Ornithological Biography; or, An Account of the Habits of the Birds of the United States of America, and Interspersed with Delineations of American Scenery and Manners (Audubon), **7–10; Supp. XVI:**13
"Ornithology" (Hull), **Supp. XXI:** 138–139
Ornitz, Samuel, **Supp. IX:** 227; **Supp. XIII:** 166
Ornstein, Leo, **Supp. XX: 75**
O'Rourke, Meghan, **Supp. XXV:** 10
O'Rourke, William, **Supp. XXII:** 213
Orphan Angel, The (Wylie), **Supp. I Part 2:** 707, 709, 714, 717, 719–721, 722, 724
Orphan's Tale, An (Neugeboren), **Supp. XVI:** 222, 223
Orpheus (film), **Supp. XXVII:** 80
Orpheus (Rukeyser), **Supp. VI:** 273
"Orpheus" (Winters), **Supp. II Part 2:** 801
"Orpheus, Eurydice, Hermes" (Rilke), **Supp. VIII:** 31, 32
"Orpheus (1)" (Atwood), **Supp. XIII:** 35
"Orpheus (2)" (Atwood), **Supp. XIII:** 35
"Orpheus Alone" (Strand), **Supp. IV Part 2:** 632
Orpheus Descending (T. Williams), **IV:** 380, 381, 382, 385, 386, 387, 389, 391–392, 395, 396, 398
Orr, David, **Retro. Supp. III:** 99; **Supp. XXI:** 62
Orr, Peter, **Supp. I Part 2:** 538, 540, 543
Orse, Brian, **Supp. XX: 264**
Ortega y Gasset, José, **I:** 218, 222; **Supp. IV Part 2:** 521; **Supp. XXIII:** 165
Ortiz, Simon J., **Supp. IV Part 1:** 319, 404; **Supp. IV Part 2: 497–515,** 557; **Supp. XII:** 217, 218
"Ortlieb's Uptown Taproom" (Di Piero), **Supp. XIX:** 46, 47
Orton, Joe, **Supp. XXIV:** 113, 126, 263
O'Ruddy, The (Crane), **I:** 409, 424
Orwell, George, **I:** 489; **II:** 454, 580; **Supp. I Part 2:** 523, 620; **Supp. II Part 1:** 143; **Supp. IV Part 1:** 236; **Supp. V:** 250; **Supp. VIII:** 241; **Supp. XIV:** 112, 158; **Supp. XVII:** 228, 229; **Supp. XVIII:** 137, 138; **Supp. XX: 86**
Osborn, Dwight, **III:** 218–219, 223
"Osborn Look, The" (Morris), **III:** 221
Osgood, Frances, **Supp. XVII:** 75
Osgood, J. R., **II:** 283
O'Shea, Kitty, **II:** 137
O'Shea, Milo, **Supp. XI:** 308
"Oshkikwe's Baby" (traditional Chippewa story), **Supp. IV Part 1:** 333
Oshogay, Delia, **Supp. IV Part 1:** 333
Ossana, Diana, **Supp. V:** 230–231, 232
Ossian, **Supp. I Part 2:** 491
Ossip, Kathleen, **Supp. X:** 201
"Osso Bucco" (Collins), **Supp. XXI:** 60
Ostanovka v Pustyne (A halt in the wilderness) (Brodsky), **Supp. VIII:** 21
Oster, Judith, **Supp. XVI:** 151
Ostriker, Alicia, **Supp. I Part 2:** 540; **Supp. IV Part 2:** 439, 447, 449; **Supp. X:** 207, 208; **Supp. XI:** 143; **Supp. XV:** 251; **Supp. XXVII:** 261
Ostrom, Hans, **Retro. Supp. I:** 195
Oswald, Lee Harvey, **III:** 234, 235
Oswald II (DeLillo), **Supp. VI:** 16
Oswald's Tale (Mailer), **Retro. Supp. II:** 212–213
"Otagamiad, The"(J. Schoolcraft), **Supp. XXIII:** 223
O Taste and See (Levertov), **Supp. III Part 1:** 278–279, 281
Othello (Shakespeare), **I:** 284–285
"Other, The" (Sexton), **Supp. II Part 2:** 692
Other America, The (Harrington), **I:** 306
"Other American Renaissance, The" (Tompkins), **Supp. XVIII:** 258
Other Destinies: Understanding the American Indian Novel (Owens), **Supp. IV Part 1:** 404
otherelectricities.com, **Supp. XXIV:** 240–241
Other Electricities: Stories (Monson), **Supp. XXIV:** 230, **231–234,** 235–236, 238, 241
"Other Frost, The" (Jarrell), **Retro. Supp. I:** 121
"Other Gods, The" (Lovecraft), **Supp. XXV:** 114
Other Gods: An American Legend (Buck), **Supp. II Part 1:** 123, 130–131
Other House, The (James), **Retro. Supp. I:** 229
"Other League of Nations, The" (Ríos), **Supp. IV Part 2:** 552
"Other Margaret, The" (Trilling), **Supp. III Part 2:** 504–505
"Other Miller, The" (Wolff), **Supp. VII:** 343–344
"Other Mothers" (Paley), **Supp. VI:** 225
"Other Night at Columbia, The" (Trilling), **Supp. XII:** 126
"Other People's Secrets" (Hampl), **Supp. XXII:** 94
"Other Robert Frost, The" (Jarrell), **Retro. Supp. I:** 135
Others (Shields), **Supp. VII:** 310
Other Side, The (Gordon), **Supp. IV Part 1:** 299, 306, 307–309, 310–311
Other Side, The/El Otro Lado (Alvarez), **Supp. VII:** 9–12
"Other Side, The"(Hadas), **Supp. XXIII:** 120
Other Side of the River, The (Wright), **Supp. V:** 332–333, 342
"Other Side of the River, The" (Wright), **Supp. V:** 335
"Other Tradition, The" (Ashbery), **Supp. III Part 1:** 15, 18
"Other Two, The" (Wharton), **Retro. Supp. I:** 367
Other Voices, Other Rooms (Capote), **Supp. III Part 1:** 113–118, 121, 123–124
"Other Wanderer, The" (Gibran), **Supp. XX: 124**
"Other War, The" (Cowley), **Supp. II Part 1:** 144
"Otherwise" (Kenyon), **Supp. VII:** 172, 174
Otherwise: New and Selected Poems (Kenyon), **Supp. VII:** 167, 172–174
Otherwise Than Being; or, Beyond Essence (Lévinas), **Supp. XVI:** 290, 291
"Other Woman, The" (Anderson), **I:** 114
"Other World, The" (Wrigley), **Supp. XVIII:** 307
Other Worlds Than This (Hadas), **Supp. XXIII:** 118, **124–125**
Otho the Great: A Tragedy in Five Acts (Keats), **Supp. XII:** 113
Otis, Harrison Gray, **Supp. I Part 2:**

479–481, 483, 486, 488
Otis, James, **III:** 577; **Supp. I Part 2:** 486; **Supp. XV:** 229
O to Be a Dragon (Moore), **III:** 215
"Otravida, Otravez" (Díaz), **Supp. XXIV:** 93
Ott, Bill, **Supp. XXVI:** 187
"Ottawa Valley, The" (Munro), **Supp. XXVII:** 185–186
Otter, Samuel, **Retro. Supp. III:** 157
Otto, Rudolf, **Supp. XVII:** 243
"Ouija" (McClatchy), **Supp. XII:** 269–270
Oupensky, Peter, **Supp. XIV:** 188
Our America (Michaels), **Retro. Supp. I:** 379
Our America (W. Frank), **I:** 229; **Supp. IX:** 308; **Supp. XX: 69–70, 75**
Our American Humorists (Masson), **Supp. XXVI:** 275
Our Aperture (Monson), **Supp. XXIV:** 230, 239
"Our Assistant's Column" (Twain), **IV:** 193
"Our Bourgeois Literature" (Sinclair), **Supp. V:** 281
Our Brains and What Ails Them (Gilman), **Supp. XI:** 207
Our Century (Wilder), **IV:** 374
"Our Christmas Party" (E. Stoddard), **Supp. XV:** 273, 278
Our Country (Strong), **Supp. XIV:** 64
"Our Countrymen in Chains!" (Whittier), **Supp. I Part 2:** 688
"Our Cultural Humility" (Bourne), **I:** 223, 228
Our Depleted Society (Seymour), **Supp. XIII:** 264
"Our Dust" (Wright), **Supp. XV:** 345, 346
"Our Eyes" (Davison), **Supp. XXVI:** 78
"Our Father Who Drowns the Birds" (Kingsolver), **Supp. VII:** 208–209
"Our Fellow Savages of the Sandwich Islands" (Twain), **Retro. Supp. III:** 268
"Our First House" (Kingston), **Supp. V:** 169
Our Gang (P. Roth), **Retro. Supp. II:** 287; **Supp. III Part 2:** 414; **Supp. IV Part 1:** 388
"Our Good Day" (Cisneros), **Supp. VII:** 60
Our Ground Time Here Will Be Brief (Kumin), **Supp. IV Part 2:** 450–452
Our House in the Last World (Hijuelos), **Supp. VIII:** 73, **76–79**, 87, 88
"Our Lady" (A. Finch), **Supp. XVII:** 77
"Our Lady of the Annunciation/Nuestra Señora de Anunciación" (Mora), **Supp. XIII:** 217, 224, 228
"Our Lady of the Artichokes" (Vaz), **Supp. XXVI:** 265
Our Lady of the Artichokes and Other Portuguese-American Stories (Vaz), **Supp. XXVI:** 264–268
"Our Lady of Troy" (MacLeish), **III:** 3, 20
"Our Limitations" (Holmes), **Supp. I Part 1:** 314
"Our Martyred Soldiers" (Dunbar), **Supp. II Part 1:** 193
"Our Master" (Whittier), **Supp. I Part 2:** 704
"Our Mother Pocahontas" (Lindsay), **Supp. I Part 2:** 393
Our Mr. Wrenn: The Romantic Adventures of a Gentle Man (Lewis), **II:** 441
Our National Parks (Muir), **Supp. IX:** 181, 184
Our New York: A Personal Vision in Words and Photographs (Kazin), **Supp. VIII: 106–107**
Our Nig (Wilson), **Supp. XX: 105**
"Our Old Aunt Who Is Now in a Retirement Home" (Shields), **Supp. VII:** 310
Our Old Home (Hawthorne), **II:** 225; **Retro. Supp. I:** 163; **Retro. Supp. III:** 122
"Our Own Movie Queen" (Z. Fitzgerald), **Supp. IX:** 71
"Our River Now" (L.-Y. Lee), **Supp. XV:** 224, 225
Our Selves (Bronk), **Supp. XXI:** 32
Ourselves to Know (O'Hara), **III:** 362, 365
Our Sister Killjoy: or, Reflections from a Black-Eyed Squint (Aidoo), **Supp. XXII:** 68
"Our Story Begins" (Wolff), **Supp. VII:** 345
"Our Sweating Selves" (Di Piero), **Supp. XIX:** 36
Our Town (Wilder), **IV:** 357, 364, 365, 366, 368–369
"Our Unplanned Cities" (Bourne), **I:** 229, 230
Our Wonder World, **Retro. Supp. I:** 341
Ouspensky, P. D., **I:** 383; **Supp. XX: 116**
"Out" (Harjo), **Supp. XII:** 219
" 'Out, Out—' " (Frost), **Retro. Supp. I:** 131; **Retro. Supp. III:** 99
"Outcast" (McKay), **Supp. X:** 135
"Outcasts of Poker Flats, The" (Harte), **Supp. II Part 1:** 345, 347–348
Outcroppings (Harte), **Supp. II Part 1:** 343
Out Cry (T. Williams), **IV:** 383, 393
Outcry, The (James), **Retro. Supp. I:** 235
"Outdoor Shower" (Olds), **Supp. X:** 214
Outer Banks (Siddons), **Supp. XXII:** 239
Outerbridge Reach (Stone), **Supp. V:** 306–308
Outer Dark (McCarthy), **Supp. VIII: 176–177**
Outermost Dream, The: Essays and Reviews (Maxwell), **Supp. VIII: 171–172**
Outermost House, The (Beston), **Supp. XXVI:** 31, 34, 37–43
"Outing, The" (Baldwin), **Supp. I Part 1:** 63
"Outlantish" (Mackey), **Supp. XXVII:** 154–155
Outlaw Journalist (McKeen), **Supp. XXIV:** 279, 288
"Out Like a Lamb" (Dubus), **Supp. VII:** 91
"Outline of an Autobiography" (Toomer), **Supp. III Part 2:** 478
"Outline Toward a Theory of the Mine Versus the Mind and the Harvard Outline" (Monson), **Supp. XXIV:** 235
Outlyer and Ghazals (Harrison), **Supp. VIII:** 41
"Out of Business" (Mora), **Supp. XIII:** 217
Out of Eden: Essays on Modern Art (Di Piero), **Supp. XIX:** 41, 42
"Out of My Deeper Heart" (Gibran), **Supp. XX: 118**
Out of My League (Plimpton), **Supp. XVI:** 233, 239
"Out of Nowhere into Nothing" (Anderson), **I:** 113
"Out of Season" (Hemingway), **II:** 263
"Out of the Cradle Endlessly Rocking" (Whitman), **IV:** 342, 343–345, 346, 351; **Retro. Supp. I:** 404, 406; **Retro. Supp. III:** 304, 306–308
"Out of the Deeps" (E. Stoddard), **Supp. XV:** 286
"Out of the Hospital and Under the Bar" (Ellison), **Retro. Supp. II:** 118–119; **Supp. II Part 1:** 246
"Out of the Rainbow End" (Sandburg), **III:** 594–595
"Out of the Sea, Early" (Swenson),

Supp. IV Part 2: 645
"Out of the Snow" (Dubus), **Supp. VII:** 91
Out of the Stars (Purdy), **Supp. VII:** 281–282
"Out of the Woods" (Offutt), **Supp. XIX:** 169–170
Out of the Woods: Stories (Offutt), **Supp. XIX:** 163, 167, **169–172,** 175
"Out of Your Nakedness, Out of My Nakedness"(Hadas), **Supp. XXIII:** 125
"Outrageous" (Pickering), **Supp. XXI:** 202
Outre-Mer: A Pilgrimage beyond the Sea (Longfellow), **II:** 313, 491; **Retro. Supp. II:** 155, 165
"Outside" (Stafford), **Supp. XI:** 318
Outside, The (Glaspell), **Supp. III Part 1:** 179, 187
"Outside In" (Pickering), **Supp. XXI:** 197
Outsider, The (Wright), **IV:** 478, 481, 488, 491–494, 495
Outside Shot, The (Myers), **Supp. XXVII:** 205, 206
Outside World, The (Mirvis), **Supp. XX: 177, 178, 185–190**
Out Went the Candle (Swados), **Supp. XIX: 257**
Out West (Shanley), **Supp. XIV:** 317
"Out with the Old" (Yates), **Supp. XI:** 342
"Ouzo for Robin" (Merrill), **Supp. III Part 1:** 326
"Oval Portrait, The" (Poe), **III:** 412, 415; **Retro. Supp. II:** 270
"Oven Bird, The" (Frost), **Retro. Supp. I:** 131; **Retro. Supp. III:** 99; **Supp. XI:** 153; **Supp. XIX:** 15
"Over 2,000 Illustrations and a Complete Concordance" (Bishop), **Retro. Supp. II:** 45; **Supp. I Part 1:** 90–91
"Over by the River" (Maxwell), **Supp. VIII:** 169, 170
"Overcoat, The" (Gogol), **Supp. XXII:** 59
"Overgrown Pasture, The" (A. Lowell), **II:** 523
"Overheard through the Walls of the Invisible City" (Bidart), **Supp. XV:** 32
"Over Kansas" (Ginsberg), **Supp. II Part 1:** 320
Overland to the Islands (Levertov), **Supp. III Part 1:** 275, 276
Overlook, The (Connelly), **Supp. XXI: 78**
"Overlooking Lake Champlain" (Di Piero), **Supp. XIX:** 47
"Overnight Pass" (X. J. Kennedy), **Supp. XV:** 168
Overreachers, The (Talese), **Supp. XVII:** 202
"Over-Soul, The" (Emerson), **II:** 7
Over the Blue Mountain (Richter), **Supp. XVIII:** 220
"Over the Edge"(Hadas), **Supp. XXIII:** 115
"Over the Hill" (Dubus), **Supp. VII:** 76, 79–80
Overtime (Gurney), **Supp. V:** 104
Overton, Grant, **Supp. XXV:** 200
"Overwhelming Question, An" (Taylor), **Supp. V:** 323
Ovid, **I:** 62; **II:** 542–543; **III:** 457, 467, 468, 470; **Retro. Supp. I:** 63; **Supp. IV Part 2:** 634; **Supp. XII:** 264
"Ovid in Exile" (Di Piero), **Supp. XIX:** 44
"Ovid's Farewell" (McClatchy), **Supp. XII:** 257–258
Owen, David, **II:** 34
Owen, Maureen, **Supp. IV Part 2:** 423
Owen, Wilfred, **II:** 367, 372; **III:** 524; **Supp. X:** 146; **Supp. XIX:** 17; **Supp. XVII:** 245; **Supp. XVIII:** 92; **Supp. XXVII:** 295
Owens, Hamilton, **III:** 99, 109
Owens, Louis, **Supp. IV Part 1:** 404
"O Where Are You Going?" (Auden), **Supp. X:** 116
"Owl, The" (Wrigley), **Supp. XVIII:** 297–298, 301
Owl in the Attic, The (Thurber), **Supp. I Part 2:** 614
Owl in the Mask of the Dreamer, The: Collected Poems (Haines), **Supp. XII:** 211
"Owl in the Sarcophagus, The" (Stevens), **Retro. Supp. I:** 300
Owl's Clover (Stevens), **Retro. Supp. I:** 298, **303–304**
"Owl's Clover" (Stevens), **IV:** 75
Owl's Insomnia, Poems by Rafael Alberti, The (Strand, trans.), **Supp. IV Part 2:** 630
Owl Spirit Dwelling (Gallagher), **Supp. XXIV:** 170
Owlstone Crown, The (X. J. Kennedy), **Supp. XV:** 162, **164**
"Owl Who Was God, The" (Thurber), **Supp. I Part 2:** 610
Owning It All (Kittredge), **Supp. XXVI:** 184, 187
Owning Jolene (Hearon), **Supp. VIII: 66–67**
"Owning the Masters" (Nelson), **Supp. XVIII:** 171
Oxford Anthology of American Literature, The, **III:** 197; **Supp. I Part 1:** 254
Oxford Book of American Verse (Matthiessen, ed.), **Retro. Supp. I:** 40
Oxford Book of Children's Verse in America, The (Hall, ed.), **Supp. XIV:** 126
Oxford Companion to African American Literature, The (Andrews et al., eds), **Supp. XXVI:** 166
Oxford Companion to Twentieth-Century Poetry (Hamilton, ed.), **Supp. XVII:** 243
Oxford History of the American People, The (Morison), **Supp. I Part 2:** 495–496
Oxford History of the United States, 1783–1917, The (Morison), **Supp. I Part 2:** 483–484
"Oxford Town" (song, Dylan), **Supp. XVIII:** 24
Oxherding Tale (C. Johnson), **Supp. VI: 190–192,** 193, 194, 196
Oxley, William, **Supp. XV:** 125
"O Yes" (Olsen), **Supp. XIII:** 294, 298, **299–300,** 301
"O Youth and Beauty!" (Cheever), **Retro. Supp. I:** 335
"Oysters" (Sexton), **Supp. II Part 2:** 692
"Ozark Odes" (Wright), **Supp. XV:** 346
Ozick, Cynthia, **Supp. V: 257–274; Supp. VIII:** 141; **Supp. X:** 192; **Supp. XVII:** 42, 43, 49, 50
O-Zone (Theroux), **Supp. VIII:** 323–324
Pace, Patricia, **Supp. XI:** 245
Pacernik, Gary, **Supp. IX:** 287, 291
Pacific and Other Stories, The (Helprin), **Supp. XXV:** 84, 85
"Pacific Distances" (Didion), **Supp. IV Part 1:** 211
"Pacific Village" (M. F. K. Fisher), **Supp. XVII:** 83
"Pacifist War Song" (Lovecraft), **Supp. XXV:** 119
Pack, Robert, **Supp. IV Part 2:** 621
"Packed Dirt, Churchgoing, a Dying Cat, a Traded Cat" (Updike), **IV:** 219
Packer, Nancy Huddleston, **Supp. XXIII:** 290
"Packing Mother's Things" (C. Frost), **Supp. XV:** 97
Pack of Lies (Sorrentino), **Supp. XXI:** 236, 237
Paco's Story (Heinemann), **Supp. XXII:** 103, **109–114,** 115

Paddock, Joe, **Supp. XVI:** 36
Paddock, Nancy, **Supp. XVI:** 36
Padel, Ruth, **Supp. XII:** 107
Padgett, Ron, **Supp. XV:** 190; **Supp. XXIII:** 218, 221; **Supp. XXIV:** 33, 34, 35, 37, 38, 39, 41, 42, 43, 44; **Supp. XXVII:** 18, 19, 20, 22, 24, 26, 28, 29
Padmore, Dorothy, **Supp. XXI:** 166
Padmore, George, **Supp. XXI:** 166
"Paesano with a Trowel" (Time), **Supp. XX: 46**
Pafko at the Wall (DeLillo), **Supp. VI:** 4
"Paganini and the Powers of Darkness" (Skloot), **Supp. XX: 201**
"Pagan Prayer" (Cullen), **Supp. IV Part 1:** 170
"Pagan Rabbi, The" (Ozick), **Supp. V:** 262, 264, 265; **Supp. XVII:** 43
Pagan Rabbi and Other Stories, The (Ozick), **Supp. V:** 260, 261, 263–265
Pagan Spain (Wright), **IV:** 478, 488, 495
Page, Geraldine, **Supp. XV:** 7
Page, Kirby, **III:** 297
Page, Myra, **Supp. XXIII:** 166
"Page, The" (Huddle), **Supp. XXVI:** 155
Page, Thomas Nelson, **II:** 174, 176, 194; **Supp. XIV:** 61; **Supp. XXII:** 193
Page, Walter Hines, **II:** 174, 175; **Supp. I Part 1:** 370
Page, William, **Supp. XVIII:** 2, 11
Pages from a Cold Island (Exley), **Supp. XXIII:** 97, **103–106,** 108
"Pages from Cold Point" (Bowles), **Supp. IV Part 1:** 85, 86, 87
Paid on Both Sides: A Charade (Auden), **Supp. II Part 1:** 6, 18–19
Paige, Satchel, **Supp. I Part 1:** 234
Paige, T. D. D., **III:** 475
"Pail, The" (R. Bly), **Supp. XXI:** 85
Pain, Joseph, **Supp. I Part 2:** 502
Paine, Albert Bigelow, **I:** 249; **Retro. Supp. III:** 269
Paine, Thomas, **I:** 490; **II:** 117, 302; **III:** 17, 148, 219; **Retro. Supp. I:** 390; **Supp. I Part 1:** 231; **Supp. I Part 2: 501–525; Supp. XI:** 55
"Pain has an Element of Blank" (Dickinson), **Retro. Supp. I:** 44
"Pain Scale, The" (Biss), **Supp. XXVI:** 51–53
"Painstaking Historian, The" (Skloot), **Supp. XX: 205–206**
"Paint and Powder" (Z. Fitzgerald), **Supp. IX:** 71
Painted Bird, The (Kosinski), **Supp. VII:** 215–217, 219–221, 222, 227
Painted Desert (F. Barthelme), **Supp. XI:** 28–29, 32
Painted Dresses (Hearon), **Supp. VIII: 63**
"Painted Head" (Ransom), **III:** 491, 494; **Supp. II Part 1:** 103, 314
Painted Turtle: Woman with Guitar (Major), **Supp. XXII: 178–180,** 182
Painted Word, The (Wolfe), **Supp. III Part 2:** 580–581, 584; **Supp. XV:** 143
Painter, Pamela, **Supp. XXIII:** 295
"Painter, The" (Ashbery), **Supp. III Part 1:** 5–6, 13
Painter Dreaming in the Scholar's House, The (Nemerov), **III:** 269
"Painters" (Rukeyser), **Supp. VI:** 281
"Painting a Mountain Stream" (Nemerov), **III:** 275
"Pair a Spurs" (Proulx), **Supp. VII:** 263–264
"Pair of Bright Blue Eyes, A" (Taylor), **Supp. V:** 321
"Pair of Glasses, A" (Gallagher), **Supp. XXIV:** 174, 176
Paisan (film, Rossellini), **Supp. XXVI:** 134
"Pajamas" (Olds), **Supp. X:** 206
Pakula, Alan, **Supp. XIII:** 264
Palace at 4 A.M. (Giacometti), **Supp. VIII:** 169
Palahniuk, Chuck, **Supp. XXI:** 116
"Palantine, The" (Whittier), **Supp. I Part 2:** 694, 696
Palatella, John, **Retro. Supp. II:** 48; **Supp. XXIV:** 39
"Palatski Man, The"(Dybek), **Supp. XXIII:** 70
Pale Fire (Nabokov), **III:** 244, 246, 252, 263–265; **Retro. Supp. I:** 264, 265, 266, 270, 271, 272, 276, 278, 335; **Supp. V:** 251, 253; **Supp. XXII:** 260
"Pale Horse, Pale Rider" (Porter), **III:** 436, 437, 441–442, 445, 446, 449
Pale Horse, Pale Rider: Three Short Novels (Porter), **III:** 433, 436–442; **Supp. VIII:** 157
"Pale Pink Roast, The" (Paley), **Supp. VI:** 217
"Pale Rider" (B. Kelly), **Supp. XVII:** 132–133
Paley, Grace, **Supp. IX:** 212; **Supp. VI: 217–233; Supp. X:** 79, 164; **Supp. XII:** 309; **Supp. XXI:** 118; **Supp. XXII:** 172
Paley, William, **II:** 9
Palgrave, Francis Turner, **Retro. Supp. I:** 124; **Retro. Supp. III:** 91; **Supp. XIV:** 340
Palgrave's Golden Treasury (Palgrave), **IV:** 405
Palimpsest (Doolittle), **Supp. I Part 1:** 259, 268, 269, 270–271
Palimpsest (Vidal), **Supp. X:** 186
"Palingenesis" (Longfellow), **II:** 498
Pal Joey (O'Hara), **III:** 361, 367–368
"Pal Joey" stories (O'Hara), **III:** 361
Pallbearers Envying the One Who Rides (Dobyns), **Supp. XIII:** 89
Palm, Edward Frederick, **Supp. XXII:** 103
"Palm, The" (Merwin), **Supp. III Part 1:** 355
Palmer, Charles, **II:** 111
Palmer, Elihu, **Supp. I Part 2:** 520
Palmer, George Herbert, **Supp. XIV:** 197
Palmer, Michael, **Supp. IV Part 2:** 421; **Supp. XVI:** 284; **Supp. XVII:** 240
Palmer, Samuel, **Supp. XV:** 81
Palmerston, Lord, **I:** 15
Palm-of-the-Hand-Stories (Kawabata), **Supp. XV:** 186
"Palm Wine" (McKnight), **Supp. XX: 155**
"Palo Alto: The Marshes" (Hass), **Supp. VI:** 100
Palpable God, A: Thirty Stories Translated from the Bible with an Essay on the Origins and Life of Narrative (Price), **Supp. VI:** 262, 267
Palubinskas, Helen, **Supp. X:** 292
Palumbo, Carmine, **Supp. XXVI:** 241
Pamela (Richardson), **Supp. V:** 127; **Supp. XX: 236; Supp. XXII:** 120
Pamela's First Musical (Wasserstein), **Supp. XV:** 333
Panache de bouquets (Komunyakaa; Cadieux, trans.), **Supp. XIII:** 127
Pan-African movement, **Supp. II Part 1:** 172, 175
Pancake, Breece D'J, **Supp. XXIII:** 35
Pandaemonium (Epstein), **Supp. XII:** 161, **172–173**
"Pandora" (Adams), **I:** 5
Pandora: New Tales of Vampires (Rice), **Supp. VII:** 295
Panek, LeRoy, **Supp. XIV:** 27
"Pangolin, The" (Moore), **III:** 210
Panic: A Play in Verse (MacLeish), **III:** 2, 20
Panic in Needle Park (film), **Supp. IV Part 1:** 198
Pankey, Eric, **Supp. XIX:** 44
Pantagruel (Rabelais), **II:** 112

"Pantaloon in Black" (Faulkner), **II:** 71
"Panther, The: A Bedtime Story"(P. Benedict), **Supp. XXIII:** 40
Panther and the Lash, The (Hughes), **Retro. Supp. I:** 204, 211; **Supp. I Part 1:** 342–344, 345–346
"Panthers, The" (Southern), **Supp. XI:** 295
"Panties and the Buddha" (Peacock), **Supp. XIX:** 199
"Pan versus Moses" (Ozick), **Supp. V:** 262
"Paolo Castelnuovo" (Everwine), **Supp. XV:** 83–84
"Papa and Mama Dance, The" (Sexton), **Supp. II Part 2:** 688
"Papago II"(Kenny), **Supp. XXIII:** 149–150
"Papago I"(Kenny), **Supp. XXIII:** 149–150
"Papa Who Wakes Up Tired in the Dark" (Cisneros), **Supp. VII:** 62
Pape, Greg, **Supp. V:** 180; **Supp. XIII:** 312; **Supp. XV:** 73
Paper Boy (Huddle), **Supp. XXVI:** 148, 150, 151
"Paper Covers Rock"(Thompson), **Supp. XXIII:** 291
Paper Doll (Parker), **Supp. XIX:** 184
"Paper Dolls Cut Out of a Newspaper" (Simic), **Supp. VIII:** 282
"Paper House, The" (Mailer), **III:** 42–43
Paper Lion (film, March), **Supp. XVI:** 242
Paper Lion: Confessions of a Last-String Quarterback (Plimpton), **Supp. XVI: 242–243**
Papernick, Jon, **Supp. XVII:** 50
Papers on Literature and Art (Fuller), **Supp. II Part 1:** 292, 299
Papini, Giovanni, **Supp. XVI:** 195; **Supp. XXII:** 159, 161, 163
Papp, Joseph, **Supp. IV Part 1:** 234; **Supp. XXI:** 145
"Paprika Johnson" (Barnes), **Supp. III Part 1:** 33
"Par" (Bausch), **Supp. VII:** 54
"Parable from a Christian" (Notley), **Supp. XXII:** 235
"Parable in the Later Novels of Henry James" (Ozick), **Supp. V:** 257
"Parable of the Gift" (Glück), **Supp. V:** 89
"Parable of the Hostages" (Glück), **Supp. V:** 89
"Parable of the King" (Glück), **Supp. V:** 89
Parable of the Sower (O. Butler), **Supp. XIII: 66–67,** 69
Parable of the Talents (O. Butler), **Supp. XIII:** 61,**Supp. XIII:** 66, **67–69**
"Parable of the Trellis" (Glück), **Supp. V:** 89
Parachutes & Kisses (Jong), **Supp. V:** 115, 123, 125–126, 129
Paracritical Hinge: Essays, Talks, Notes, Interviews (Mackey), **Supp. XXVII:** 159, 160–161
"Paradelle for Susan" (Collins), **Supp. XXI:** 58
"Parade of Painters" (Swenson), **Supp. IV Part 2:** 645
"Paradigm, The" (Tate), **IV:** 128
Paradine Case, The (screenplay, Hecht), **Supp. XXVII:** 93
Paradise (Barthelme), **Supp. IV Part 1:** 52
"Paradise" (Caputo), **Supp. XIX:** 26–27
"Paradise" (Doty), **Supp. XI:** 123
Paradise (Morrison), **Retro. Supp. III:** 184, 194–195
Paradise, Piece by Piece (Peacock), **Supp. XIX:** 193, 194–195, 195–196, **201–202**
Paradise Lost (Milton), **I:** 137; **II:** 168, 549; **IV:** 126; **Retro. Supp. III:** 139; **Supp. XII:** 173, 297; **Supp. XV:** 181; **Supp. XX: 280**
Paradise Lost (Odets), **Supp. II Part 2:** 530, 531, 538–539, 550
Paradise Now (Living Theater), **Supp. XXIV:** 116
"Paradise of Bachelors and the Tartarus of Maids, The" (Melville), **III:** 91; **Retro. Supp. III:** 159
Paradise of Bombs, The (Sanders), **Supp. XVI:** 265, 272–273
Paradise Park (Goodman), **Supp. XXVI:** 126–128
Paradise Poems (Stern), **Supp. IX: 293–294,** 295
Paradiso (Dante), **Supp. IX:** 50
"Paradoxes and Oxymorons" (Ashbery), **Supp. III Part 1:** 23–24
Paradox of Progressive Thought, The (Noble), **Supp. I Part 2:** 650
Paragon, The (Knowles), **Supp. XII:** 249
"Paragraphs" (Carruth), **Supp. XVI:** 52–53
"Parameters" (Dunn), **Supp. XI:** 154
"Para Mi Tataranieto El Astropionero" (Espaillat), **Supp. XXI:** 104
"Paraphrase" (Crane), **I:** 391–392, 393
"Pardon, The" (Wilbur), **Supp. III Part 2:** 544, 550
Paredes, Américo, **Supp. XIII:** 225; **Supp. XIX:** 97, 98, 100
Paredes, Raymund A., **Supp. XIII:** 320, 321
"Parentage" (Stafford), **Supp. XI:** 321, 322
Parentheses: An Autobiographical Journey (Neugeboren), **Supp. XVI:** 217, 218, 219, 221, 226
"Parents" (F. Barthelme), **Supp. XI:** 34
"Parents Taking Shape" (Karr), **Supp. XI:** 243
"Parents' Weekend: Camp Kenwood" (Kenyon), **Supp. VII:** 169
Pareto, Vilfredo, **II:** 577
Paretsky, Sara, **Supp. IV Part 2:** 462; **Supp. XIV:** 26; **Supp. XXV: 169–187**
Parini, Jay, **Retro. Supp. III:** 73, 75, 88, 91, 105; **Supp. X:** 17; **Supp. XIX:** 120, 129; **Supp. XX: 243; Supp. XXI:** 192; **Supp. XXII:** 205; **Supp. XXV:** 251
"Paris" (Collins), **Supp. XXI:** 60
"Paris" (Stern), **Supp. IX:** 300
"Paris, 7 A.M." (Bishop), **Retro. Supp. II:** 41, 42; **Supp. I Part 1:** 85, 89
Paris, Bob, **Supp. XX: 264**
Paris, Paris (Shaw), **Supp. XIX:** 240
Paris France (Stein), **IV:** 45
Park, Ed, **Supp. XXII:** 255
Park, Robert, **IV:** 475
"Park Bench" (Hughes), **Supp. I Part 1:** 331–332
Park City (Beattie), **Supp. V:** 24, 35–36
"Park City" (Beattie), **Supp. V:** 35
Parker, Arthur C., **Supp. XXVI:** 87, 88
Parker, Charlie, **Supp. I Part 1:** 59; **Supp. X:** 240, 242, 246; **Supp. XIII:** 129
Parker, Dorothy, **Retro. Supp. II:** 327; **Supp. IV Part 1:** 353; **Supp. IX:** 62, 114, **189–206; Supp. X:** 164; **Supp. XI:** 28; **Supp. XVIII:** 242, 246, 252; **Supp. XXVI:** 275; **Supp. XXVII:** 283, 284
Parker, Emily, **Supp. XVIII:** 102
Parker, Hershel, **Retro. Supp. III:** 152, 267
Parker, Idella, **Supp. X:** 232, 234–235
Parker, James, **Supp. XXVI:** 84
Parker, Joan, **Supp. XIX:** 187
Parker, Lonnae O'Neal, **Supp. XXIII:** 276
Parker, Muriel, **Supp. IX:** 232
Parker, Patricia, **Supp. XV:** 242
Parker, Robert B., **Supp. IV Part 1:**

135, 136; **Supp. XIX: 177–192**
Parker, Robert Dale, **Supp. XXIII:** 223, 228, 229
Parker, Theodore, **Supp. I Part 1:** 38; **Supp. I Part 2:** 518; **Supp. XXIV:** 70
Parker, Thomas, **Supp. I Part 1:** 102
"Parker's Back" (O'Connor), **III:** 348, 352, 358; **Retro. Supp. III:** 213, 216–217
"Parkersburg" (Halliday), **Supp. XIX:** 92
Parkes, Henry Bamford, **Supp. I Part 2:** 617
Park-Fuller, Linda, **Supp. XIII:** 297
Parkman, Francis, **II:** 278, 310, 312; **IV:** 179, 309; **Supp. I Part 2:** 420, 479, 481–482, 486, 487, 493, 498; **Supp. II Part 2: 589–616**
Parkman Reader, The (Morison, ed.), **Supp. I Part 2:** 494
Parks, Gordon, Sr., **Supp. XI:** 17
Parks, Larry, **Supp. I Part 1:** 295
Parks, Rosa, **Supp. I Part 1:** 342
"Park Street Cemetery, The" (R. Lowell), **II:** 537, 538
Par le Détroit (cantata) (Bowles), **Supp. IV Part 1:** 82
Parliament of Fowls, The (Chaucer), **III:** 492
Parmenides (Plato), **II:** 10
Parmenter, Jon, **Supp. XXVI:** 85
Parnassus (Emerson), **II:** 8, 18
Parnell, Charles Stewart, **II:** 129, 137
Parole (film), **Supp. XIII:** 166
Parole Fixer (film), **Supp. XIII:** 170
Parrington, Vernon Louis, **I:** 254, 517, 561; **III:** 335, 606; **IV:** 173; **Supp. I Part 2:** 484, 640
Parrish, Dillwyn, **Supp. XVII:** 83–84, 90
Parrish, Robert, **Supp. XI:** 307
"Parrot, The" (Merrill), **Supp. III Part 1:** 320
"Parsley" (Dove), **Supp. IV Part 1:** 245, 246
Parson, Annie, **Supp. I Part 2:** 655
Parsons, Elsie Clews, **I:** 231, 235
Parsons, Ian, **Supp. IX:** 95
Parsons, Louella, **Supp. XII:** 173
Parsons, Talcott, **Supp. I Part 2:** 648
Parsons, Theophilus, **II:** 396, 504; **Retro. Supp. II:** 134; **Supp. I Part 1:** 155
"Parthian Shot, The" (Hammett), **Supp. IV Part 1:** 343
Partial Glossary, A (Bronk), **Supp. XXI:** 26
Partial Payments: Essays on Writers and Their Lives (Epstein), **Supp. XIV:** 111
Partial Portraits (James), **II:** 336
"Partial Relief" (Halliday), **Supp. XIX:** 91
Partial Truth (Nelson), **Supp. XVIII: 175–176,** 178
"Particulars" (Pickering), **Supp. XXI:** 197
Parties (Van Vechten), **Supp. II Part 2:** 739, 747–749
"Parting" (Kunitz), **Supp. III Part 1:** 263
"Parting Gift" (Wylie), **Supp. I Part 2:** 714
"Parting Glass, The" (Freneau), **Supp. II Part 1:** 273
"Partings" (Hogan), **Supp. IV Part 1:** 413
Partington, Blanche, **I:** 199
Partisans (Matthiessen), **Supp. V:** 201
"Partner, The" (Roethke), **III:** 541–542
Partners, The (Auchincloss), **Supp. IV Part 1:** 31, 34
Partners in Crime: A Rafe Buenrostro Mystery (Hinojosa), **Supp. XIX: 107–108**
"Part of a Letter" (Wilbur), **Supp. III Part 2:** 551
Part of a Long Story: Eugene O'Neill as a Young Man in Love (Boulton), **Supp. XXII:** 18, 21, 27–30
Part of Speech, A (Brodsky), **Supp. VIII:** 22
"Part of the Bee's Body Embedded in the Flesh, The" (C. Frost), **Supp. XV:** 105, 107
"Part of the Story" (Dobyns), **Supp. XIII:** 79
Part of Vermont, A (Taggard), **Supp. XXII:** 284
Parton, Sara, **Retro. Supp. I:** 246
Partridge, Jeffrey F., **Supp. XV:** 219
Partridge, John, **II:** 110, 111
"Parts of a Journal" (Gordon), **Supp. IV Part 1:** 310
Parts of a World (Stevens), **Retro. Supp. I: 305–306,** 307, 309, 313
"Parturition" (Loy), **Supp. XXII:** 159, 160–161
"Party, The" (Dunbar), **Supp. II Part 1:** 198, 205–206
"Party, The" (Taylor), **Supp. V:** 315
Party at Jack's, The (Wolfe), **IV:** 451–452, 469
"Party Down at the Square, A" (Ellison), **Retro. Supp. II:** 124
Party of Five (television series), **Supp. XIX:** 222
"Party Poem" (Huddle), **Supp. XXVI:** 149
Pascal, Blaise, **II:** 8, 159; **III:** 292, 301, 304, 428; **Retro. Supp. I:** 326, 330
"Paskudnyak" (Pilcer), **Supp. XVII:** 50
"Pass, The" (Neugeboren), **Supp. XVI:** 225
"Passage" (Crane), **I:** 391
"Passage in the Life of Mr. John Oakhurst, A" (Harte), **Supp. II Part 1:** 353–354
Passage in the Night, A (Asch), **Supp. XXIII:** 7
"Passages" (Duncan), **Supp. XVI:** 287
"Passages for Puritans" (Davison), **Supp. XXVI:** 62
"Passages from a Relinquished Work" (Hawthorne), **Retro. Supp. I:** 150
Passages toward the Dark (McGrath), **Supp. X:** 126, 127
"Passage to India" (Whitman), **IV:** 348; **Retro. Supp. III:** 308
Passage to India, A (Forster), **II:** 600; **Supp. XVIII:** 143
Passaro, Vince, **Supp. X:** 167, 302, 309, 310
"Passenger, The" (Brockmeier), **Supp. XXII:** 52
"Passenger Pigeons" (Jeffers), **Supp. II Part 2:** 437
Passin, Herbert, **Supp. XIII:** 337
Passing (Larsen), **Supp. XVIII:** 119, 123**, 127–130**
"Passing Beauty" (C. Frost), **Supp. XV:** 97
"Passing of Grandison, The" (Chesnutt), **Supp. XIV:** 62, **66–69**
"Passing of Sister Barsett, The" (Jewett), **Retro. Supp. II:** 138–139, 143
"Passing Ports and Crossing Walks" (Gansworth), **Supp. XXVI:** 114
"Passing Show, The" (Bierce), **I:** 208
"Passing Through" (Kunitz), **Supp. III Part 1:** 265
"Passion, The" (Barnes), **Supp. III Part 1:** 36
"Passion, The" (Merwin), **Supp. III Part 1:** 343
Passionate, Accurate Story, The: Making Your Heart's Truth into Literature (C. Bly), **Supp. XVI: 41–42**
Passionate Pilgrim, A (James), **II:** 324; **Retro. Supp. I:** 219
"Passionate Pilgrim, A" (James), **II:** 322, 323–324; **Retro. Supp. I:** 218
Passion Play (Kosinski), **Supp. VII:** 215, 225–226
Passions of Uxport, The (Kumin), **Supp. IV Part 2:** 444

Pass It On (Hadas), **Supp. XXIII: 115,** 123
"Pass It On, I"(Hadas), **Supp. XXIII:** 115
"Pass It On, II"(Hadas), **Supp. XXIII:** 115
"Passive Resistance" (McKay), **Supp. X:** 133
Passport to the War (Kunitz), **Supp. III Part 1:** 261–264
Passwords (Stafford), **Supp. XI: 329–330**
"Past, The" (Bryant), **Supp. I Part 1:** 157, 170
Past, The (Kinnell), **Supp. III Part 1:** 235, 253–254
"Past, The" (Kinnell), **Supp. III Part 1:** 254
Past and Present (Carlyle), **Supp. I Part 2:** 410
Pasternak, Boris, **II:** 544; **Supp. XXIII:** 209
"Pastiches et Pistaches" (Van Vechten), **Supp. II Part 2:** 732
"Past Is the Present, The" (Moore), **III:** 199–200
"Pastoral" (Carver), **Supp. III Part 1:** 137, 146
"Pastoral" (Dove), **Supp. IV Part 1:** 249
"Pastoral" (Trethewey), **Supp. XXI:** 257
"Pastoral Hat, A" (Stevens), **IV:** 91
Pastoralia (Saunders), **Supp. XIX: 227–229**
"Pastoralia" (Saunders), **Supp. XIX:** 227, 229
"Pastor Dowe at Tacaté" (Bowles), **Supp. IV Part 1:** 87
Pastorela (ballet) (Kirstein), **Supp. IV Part 1:** 83
Pastorius, Francis Daniel, **Supp. I Part 2:** 700
"Pasture, The" (Frost), **Retro. Supp. III:** 97
"Pasture Poems" (Kumin), **Supp. IV Part 2:** 446
Pastures of Heaven, The (Steinbeck), **IV:** 51
Patch, Jerry, **Supp. XVIII:** 38
Patchen, Kenneth, **Supp. III Part 2:** 625
Patchett, Ann, **Supp. XII: 307–324**
Patchwork Planet (Lethem), **Supp. XVIII:** 150
Pater, Walter, **I:** 51, 272, 476; **II:** 27, 338; **III:** 604; **IV:** 74; **Retro. Supp. I:** 56, 79; **Retro. Supp. II:** 326; **Supp. I Part 2:** 552; **Supp. IX:** 66
Paterna (Mather), **Supp. II Part 2:** 451
Paternostro, Silvana, **Supp. XXV:** 55, 58
"Paterson" (Ginsberg), **Supp. II Part 1:** 314–315, 321, 329
Paterson (W. C. Williams), **I:** 62, 446; **IV:** 418–423; **Retro. Supp. I:** 209, 284, 413, 419, 421, **424–428,** 428, 429, 430; **Retro. Supp. II:** 321, 328; **Retro. Supp. III:** 50; **Supp. II Part 2:** 557, 564, 625; **Supp. VIII:** 275, 305; **Supp. XIV:** 96; **Supp. XV:** 264, 349
Paterson, Book Five (W. C. Williams), **IV:** 422–423
Paterson, Book One (W. C. Williams), **IV:** 421–422
Paterson, Isabel, **Supp. IV Part 2:** 524
Paterson, Part Three (W. C. Williams), **IV:** 420–421
Pat Garrett and Billy the Kid (film, Peckinpah), **Supp. XVIII:** 27
"Path, The" (Bryant), **Supp. I Part 1:** 169
Pathfinder, The (Cooper), **I:** 349, 350, 355
Pat Hobby Stories, The (Fitzgerald), **Retro. Supp. I:** 114
"Pathos of Low Life, The" (Hapgood), **Supp. XVII:** 103
"Patience of a Saint, The" (Humphrey), **Supp. IX:** 106
Patience Sparhawk and Her Times (Atherton), **Supp. XXIV:** 18, 20, 22, 27
Patient 002 (Skloot), **Supp. XX: 194, 208**
Patinkin, Mandy, **Supp. IV Part 1:** 236
Paton, Alan, **Supp. VIII:** 126
Paton, Priscilla, **Retro. Supp. III:** 95
Patria Mia (Pound), **III:** 460–461; **Retro. Supp. I:** 284
"Patria Mia" (Pound), **Retro. Supp. I:** 284
"Patriarch, The" (Alvares), **Supp. V:** 11
"Patrick Kavanagh at First Light" (Skloot), **Supp. XX: 204**
Patrimony: A True Story (P. Roth), **Retro. Supp. II:** 279, 280, 291; **Supp. III Part 2:** 427
Patriot, The (Buck), **Supp. II Part 1:** 122–123
Patriot, The (Connell), **Supp. XIV:** 94–95
Patriot Act (Gansworth), **Supp. XXVI:** 114
Patriotic Gore: Studies in the Literature of the American Civil War (Wilson), **III:** 588; **IV:** 430, 438, 443, 445–445, 446; **Supp. VIII:** 100
"Patriotic Thing, The" (Ryan as Quin), **Supp. XVIII:** 229
"Patriots, The/Los Patriotas" (Kingsolver), **Supp. VII:** 209
Patrol (Myers), **Supp. XXVII:** 208
Patron Saint of Liars, The (Patchett), **Supp. XII:** 307, 310, **311–314,** 317
Pattee, Fred L., **II:** 456
Patten, Gilbert, **II:** 423
Patten, Simon, **Supp. I Part 2:** 640
Patternmaster (O. Butler), **Supp. XIII:** 61, 62, 63
Patternmaster Series (O. Butler), **Supp. XIII: 62–63**
Pattern Recognition (W. Gibson), **Supp. XVI:** 124, **130–131**
"Patterns" (A. Lowell), **II:** 524
Patterson, Floyd, **III:** 38
Patterson, Margot, **Supp. XXII:** 85
Patterson, William M., **Supp. I Part 1:** 265
Patton, General George, **III:** 575; **Supp. I Part 2:** 664
Patton, Venetra K., **Supp. XXVI:** 166
"Patty-Cake, Patty-Cake...A Memoir" (Apple), **Supp. XVII:** 7
Patty Fairfield series (Wells), **Supp. XXVI:** 276
Paul, Saint, **I:** 365; **II:** 15, 494; **IV:** 122, 154, 164, 335; **Retro. Supp. I:** 247; **Supp. I Part 1:** 188
Paul, Sherman, **I:** 244; **IV:** 179
"Paula Becker to Clara Westhoff" (Rich), **Retro. Supp. III:** 249; **Supp. I Part 2:** 573–574
"Paula Gunn Allen" (Ruppert), **Supp. IV Part 1:** 321
Paul Ardenheim, the Monk of Wissahikon (Lippard), **Supp. XXIII:** 178, 186, 187, 189, 190
Paul Bowles: Romantic Savage (Caponi), **Supp. IV Part 1:** 95
Paulding, James Kirke, **I:** 344; **II:** 298, 299, 303; **Supp. I Part 1:** 157
Pauley, Jane, **Supp. XXI:** 39
Paul Jones (Hapgood), **Supp. XVII:** 100–101
Paul Marchand, F.M.C. (Chesnutt), **Supp. XIV:** 76
"Paul Monette: The Brink of Summer's End" (film), **Supp. X:** 152
"Paul Revere" (Longfellow), **II:** 489, 501
"Paul Revere's Ride" (Longfellow), **Retro. Supp. II:** 163
"Paul's Case" (Cather), **I:** 314–315; **Retro. Supp. I:** 3, 5; **Retro. Supp. III:** 20, 27
Paulsen, Friedrich, **III:** 600
"Pauper Witch of Grafton, The" (Frost),

Retro. Supp. II: 42
"Pause by the Water, A" (Merwin), **Supp. III Part 1:** 354
"Pavane for the Nursery, A" (W. J. Smith), **Supp. XIII:** 335
"Pavement, The" (Olson), **Supp. II Part 2:** 571
Pavese, Cesare, **Supp. XXI:** 132
Pavic, Milorad, **Supp. XXII:** 265
Pavilion of Women (Buck), **Supp. II Part 1:** 125–126
"Pawnbroker, The" (Kumin), **Supp. IV Part 2:** 442, 443–444, 451
Pawnbroker, The (Wallant), **Supp. XVI:** 220
Pay Day (Asch), **Supp. XXVI:** 19, 21–23
"Paying Dues" (Bass), **Supp. XVI:** 16
Payne, Daniel, **Supp. V:** 202; **Supp. XXVI:** 33, 35, 37, 40
Payne, John Howard, **II:** 309
Payne Tom, **Supp. XXII:** 266
Paz, Octavio, **Supp. III Part 2:** 630; **Supp. VIII:** 272; **Supp. XI:** 191; **Supp. XIII:** 223
P. D. Kimerakov (Epstein), **Supp. XII:** 160, **162**
Peabody, Elizabeth Palmer, **Retro. Supp. I:** 155–156, 225; **Supp. XXIV:** 75; **Supp. XXV:** 242, 246, 250
Peabody, Francis G., **III:** 293; **Supp. I Part 1:** 5
Peabody, Josephine Preston, **III:** 507; **Supp. XX: 115**
Peaceable Kingdom, The (Prose), **Supp. XVI:** 256–257
Peace and Bread in Time of War (Addams), **Supp. I Part 1:** 21, 22–23
"Peace Between Black and White in the United States" (Locke), **Supp. XIV:** 205
Peace Breaks Out (Knowles), **Supp. XII:** 249
"Peacemaker"(Kenny), **Supp. XXIII:** 151
"Peace March, The" (Simpson), **Supp. IX:** 279
"Peace of Cities, The" (Wilbur), **Supp. III Part 2:** 545
"Peace of Mind" (Boyle), **Supp. XX: 19**
"Peaches" (Davison), **Supp. XXVI:** 77
"Peaches—Six in a Tin Box, Sarajevo" (Cisneros), **Supp. VII:** 67
Peachtree Road (Siddons), **Supp. XXII:** 239, 240, 242, **246–247, 248–251,** 252
Peaco, Ed, **Supp. XXIV:** 221
Peacock, Doug, **Supp. VIII:** 38; **Supp. XIII:** 12
Peacock, Gibson, **Supp. I Part 1:** 360
Peacock, Molly, **Supp. XIX: 193–207; Supp. XVII:** 74
"Peacock, The" (Merrill), **Supp. III Part 1:** 320
"Peacock, The" (Mosher), **Supp. XXII:** 211
Peacock, Thomas Love, **Supp. I Part 1:** 307; **Supp. VIII:** 125
"Peacock Room, The" (Hayden), **Supp. II Part 1:** 374–375
"Peacocks of Avignon, The" (Swados), **Supp. XIX:** 263
Pearce, Richard, **Supp. IX:** 254
Pearce, Roy Harvey, **II:** 244; **Supp. I Part 1:** 111, 114; **Supp. I Part 2:** 475
"Pearl" (Kooser), **Supp. XIX:** 127–128
Pearl, The (Steinbeck), **IV:** 51, 62–63
Pearlman, Daniel, **III:** 479
Pearlman, Mickey, **Supp. XIII:** 293, 306
Pearl of Orr's Island, The (Stowe), **Supp. I Part 2:** 592–593, 595
"Pearls" (A. Finch), **Supp. XVII:** 72
Pears, Peter, **II:** 586; **Supp. IV Part 1:** 84
Pearson, Drew, **Supp. XIV:** 126
Pearson, Norman Holmes, **Supp. I Part 1:** 259, 260, 273
Pearson, Tom, **Supp. XXVI:** 113
"Pear Tree" (C. Frost), **Supp. XV:** 105
"Peasants' Way O' Thinkin' " (McKay), **Supp. X:** 133
Pease, Donald E., **Supp. IV Part 2:** 687
"Peboan and Seegwun (Winter and Spring): A Chippewa Allegory"(J. Schoolcraft), **Supp. XXIII:** 235
Peck, Gregory, **Supp. VIII:** 128, 129; **Supp. XII:** 160, 173
Peckinpah, Sam, **Supp. XI:** 306; **Supp. XVIII:** 27
"Peck of Gold, A" (Frost), **II:** 155
Peculiar Treasures: A Biblical Who's Who (Buechner), **Supp. XII:** 53
Pedagogy of the Oppressed (Freire), **Supp. XXV:** 133
"Pedal Point" (Francis), **Supp. IX:** 87
Pedersen, Inge, **Supp. XVIII:** 179
"Pedersen Kid, The" (Gass), **Supp. VI:** 83
"Pedigree, The" (Creeley), **Supp. IV Part 1:** 150
Peebles, Melvin Van, **Supp. XI:** 17; **Supp. XVI:** 144
"Peed Onk" (Moore). See "People Like That Are the Only People Here: Canonical Babbling in Peed Onk" (Moore)
"Peeler, The" (O'Connor), **Retro. Supp. II:** 225
"Peeper, The" (Davison), **Supp. XXVI:** 69
Peich, Michael, **Supp. XV:** 113, 117; **Supp. XXV:** 222
Peikoff, Leonard, **Supp. IV Part 2:** 520, 526, 529
Peirce, Charles Sanders, **II:** 20, 352–353; **III:** 599; **Supp. I Part 2:** 640; **Supp. III Part 2:** 626
Pelagius, **III:** 295
"Pelican, The" (Merrill), **Supp. III Part 1:** 320
"Pelican, The" (Wharton), **IV:** 310; **Retro. Supp. I:** 364
Pellacchia, Michael, **Supp. XIII:** 16
Pelley, Denise, **Supp. XIX:** 205
Pelonero, Michael, **Supp. XXIII:** 125
Peltier, Leonard, **Supp. V:** 212
"Pemberton's Bride" (Rash), **Supp. XXVII:** 225
"Penance"(Dybek), **Supp. XXIII:** 69
"Pen and Paper and a Breath of Air" (Oliver), **Supp. VII:** 245
Pence, Amy, **Supp. XV:** 211, 223
"Pencil, The" (Chandler), **Supp. IV Part 1:** 135
Pencillings by the Way (Willis), **II:** 313; **Supp. XVIII:** 12
"Pencils" (Sandburg), **III:** 592
Pendleton, Devon, **Supp. XVIII:** 151
"Pendulum" (Bradbury and Hasse), **Supp. IV Part 1:** 102
"Penelope's Song" (Glück), **Supp. V:** 89
Penelope: The Story of the Half-Scalped Woman (Schott), **Supp. XXIII:** 240, **244–245**
Penhally (Gordon), **II:** 197, 199, 201–203, 204
"Penis" (McClatchy), **Supp. XII:** 266–267
Penitent, The (di Donato), **Supp. XX: 44, 45**
Penitent, The (Singer), **Retro. Supp. II: 309–310,** 313
Penland, Nell Bates, **Supp. XXII:** 188
Penn, Robert, **I:** 489
Penn, Sean, **Supp. XI:** 107
Penn, Thomas, **II:** 118
Penn, William, **Supp. I Part 2:** 683
Penna, Sandro, **Supp. XIX:** 34
Pennebaker, D. A., **Supp. XVIII:** 19, 26
Penney, Rob, **Retro. Supp. III:** 317
"Pennsylvania Pilgrim, The" (Whittier), **Supp. I Part 2:** 700

"Pennsylvania Planter, The" (Freneau), **Supp. II Part 1:** 268
"Pennsylvania Station" (Faulkner), **Retro. Supp. III:** 84
Penny, Rob, **Supp. VIII:** 330
"Penny, The" (D. West), **Supp. XVIII:** 283–284
Penrod (Tarkington), **III:** 223
"Penseroso, Il" (Milton), **Supp. XIV:** 8
Pensieri (Leopardi; Di Piero, trans.), **Supp. XIX:** 34
"Pensive Hours"(J. Schoolcraft), **Supp. XXIII:** 230–231
Pentagon of Power, The (Mumford), **Supp. II Part 2:** 498
Pentimento (Hellman), **Supp. I Part 1:** 280, 292–294, 296; **Supp. IV Part 1:** 12; **Supp. VIII:** 243; **Supp. XXVII:** 137
"Peonies at Dusk" (Kenyon), **Supp. VII:** 171
People, The (Glaspell), **Supp. III Part 1:** 179
People, Yes, The (Sandburg), **III:** 575, 589, 590, 591
"PEOPLE BURNING, THE" (Baraka), **Supp. II Part 1:** 49
"People in Hell Just Want a Drink of Water" (Proulx), **Supp. VII:** 263
"People Like That Are the Only People Here: Canonical Babbling in Peed Onk" (Moore), **Supp. X:** 168, **178–179**
People Live Here: Selected Poems 1949–1983 (Simpson), **Supp. IX:** 269, 277
"People Next Door, The" (Simpson), **Supp. IX:** 279
People of the Abyss, The (London), **II:** 465–466
"People on the Roller Coaster, The" (Hardwick), **Supp. III Part 1:** 196
People Shall Continue, The (Ortiz), **Supp. IV Part 2:** 510
People's History of the United States, A (Zinn), **Supp. XXIV:** 87
"People's Surroundings" (Moore), **III:** 201, 202, 203
"People v. Abe Lathan, Colored, The" (Caldwell), **I:** 309
"Peppermint Lounge Revisited, The" (Wolfe), **Supp. III Part 2:** 571
Peppis, Paul, **Supp. XXII:** 160
Pepys, Samuel, **Supp. I Part 2:** 653
"Perchance to Dream" (Franzen), **Supp. XX: 90, 93**
Perchance to Dream: Robert B. Parker's Sequel to Raymond Chandler's "Big Sleep" (Parker), **Supp. XIX:** 189
"Perch'io non spero di tornar giammai" (Cavalcanti), **Supp. III Part 2:** 623
Perch of the Devil (Atherton), **Supp. XXIV:** 24, 29
Percy, Thomas, **Supp. XIV:** 2
Percy, Walker, **Supp. III Part 1: 383–400; Supp. IV Part 1:** 297; **Supp. V:** 334; **Supp. X:** 42; **Supp. XIV:** 21; **Supp. XIX:** 209; **Supp. XXVI:** 253
Percy, William, **Supp. V:** 334
Percy, William Alexander, **Retro. Supp. I:** 341; **Supp. XXII:** 193
Peregrin, Tony, **Supp. XV:** 69
"Peregrine" (Wylie), **Supp. I Part 2:** 712–713, 714
Perelman, Bob, **Supp. XII:** 23
Perelman, S. J., **IV:** 286; **Retro. Supp. I:** 342; **Retro. Supp. II:** 321, 322, 325, 326, 327, 336; **Supp. IV Part 1:** 353; **Supp. XI:** 66
Perera, Victor, **Supp. XXV:** 50, 52
Perestroika (Kushner), **Supp. IX:** 141, 142, 145
Péret, Benjamin, **Supp. VIII:** 272
Peretz, Isaac Leib, **IV:** 1, 3; **Retro. Supp. II:** 299; **Supp. XXIII:** 4, 7, 8–9
Pérez Galdós, Benito, **II:** 275
Perfect Analysis Given by a Parrot, A (T. Williams), **IV:** 395
"Perfect Couple, The" (Nelson), **Supp. XVIII:** 173
"Perfect Day for Bananafish, A" (Salinger), **III:** 563–564, 571
Perfect Fiction, The (Sorrentino), **Supp. XXI:** 228
Perfect Ganesh, A (McNally), **Supp. XIII: 202–203,** 208, 209
"Perfect Gerbil, The: Reading Barthelme's 'The School' " (Saunders), **Supp. XIX:** 235
"Perfection" (Helprin), **Supp. XXV:** 80
"Perfect Knight, The" (Chandler), **Supp. IV Part 1:** 120
Perfect Mother, The (Schott), **Supp. XXIII: 241–242**
Perfect Party, The (Gurney), **Supp. V:** 100, 105, 106–107
"Perfect Things" (F. Barthelme), **Supp. XI:** 30, 33–34
Perfidy (Hecht), **Supp. XXVII:** 95
"Performance, The" (Dickey), **Supp. IV Part 1:** 178–179, 181
"Perfume" (Mora), **Supp. XIII:** 218
"Perhaps the World Ends Here" (Harjo), **Supp. XII:** 228, 231
Perhaps Women (Anderson), **I:** 114
Pericles (Shakespeare), **I:** 585; **Supp. III Part 2:** 624, 627, 629
Perillo, Lucia, **Supp. XXVI:** 68
"Period Metaphor" (Bronk), **Supp. XXI:** 33
Period of Adjustment (T. Williams), **IV:** 382, 386, 387, 388, 389, 390, 392, 393, 394, 397
"Period Pieces from the Mid-Thirties" (Agee), **I:** 28
"Peripheral Vision" (Davison), **Supp. XXVI:** 69–70
"Periphery" (Ammons), **Supp. VII:** 28
Perkins, David, **Supp. I Part 2:** 459, 475; **Supp. XV:** 185
Perkins, Maxwell, **I:** 252, 289, 290; **II:** 87, 93, 95, 252; **IV:** 452, 455, 457, 458, 461, 462, 463, 469; **Retro. Supp. I:** 101, 105, 108, 109, 110, 113, 114, 178; **Supp. IX:** 57, 58, 60, 232; **Supp. X:** 219, 224, 225, 229, 230, 233; **Supp. XI:** 218, 227
Perlès, Alfred, **III:** 177, 183, 187, 189
Perloff, Marjorie, **Supp. I Part 2:** 539, 542; **Supp. IV Part 1:** 68; **Supp. IV Part 2:** 420, 424, 432; **Supp. XXII:** 161, 271; **Supp. XXIII:** 210, 220
Permanence and Change (Burke), **I:** 274
Permanent Errors (Price), **Supp. VI:** 261
"Permanent Traits of the English National Genius" (Emerson), **II:** 18
Permit Me Voyage (Agee), **I:** 25, 27
"Perosa Canavese" (Everwine), **Supp. XV:** 84
Perrault, Charles, **IV:** 266; **Supp. I Part 2:** 622
Perrin, Noel, **Supp. XVI:** 34; **Supp. XXII:** 205, 207, 211, 218
Perrins, Carol. See Frost, Carol
Perrota, Tom, **Supp. XXVII:** 5
Perry, Anne, **Supp. V:** 335
Perry, Bliss, **I:** 243
Perry, Donna, **Supp. IV Part 1:** 322, 327, 335
Perry, Edgar A., **III:** 410
Perry, Keith Ronald, **Supp. XXI:** 42
Perry, Lincoln, **Supp. V:** 24, 33
Perry, Matthew C., **Supp. I Part 2:** 494–495
Perry, Pam, **Supp. XXVI:** 12
Perry, Patsy Brewington, **Supp. I Part 1:** 66
Perry, Phyllis Alesia, **Supp. XVIII:** 96
Perry, Ralph Barton, **I:** 224; **II:** 356, 362, 364; **Supp. XIV:** 197
Perry, Dr. William, **II:** 395, 396
Perse, St.-John, **III:** 12, 13, 14, 17; **Supp. III Part 1:** 14; **Supp. IV**

Part 1: 82; Supp. XIII: 344; Supp. XV: 178
"Persephone in Hell" (Dove), Supp. IV Part 1: 250, 251
"Persephone"(Le Sueur), Supp. XXIII: 162, 165, 170–171
"Persephone to Psyche" (Stallings), Supp. XXV: 234
"Persephone Writes a Letter to Her Mother" (Stallings), Supp. XXV: 228
"Persimmons" (L.-Y. Lee), Supp. XV: 211, 213
"Persistence of Desire, The" (Updike), IV: 222–223, 228
"Persistence of Poetry, The" (Bynner), Supp. XV: 49
"Persistences" (Hecht), Supp. X: 68–69
Person, Place, and Thing (Shapiro), Supp. II Part 2: 702, 705
Personae of Ezra Pound (Pound), III: 458
Personae: The Collected Poems (Pound), Retro. Supp. I: 285, 286; Supp. I Part 1: 255; Supp. XVII: 32
"Personal" (Stern), Supp. IX: 299
"Personal and Occasional Pieces" (Welty), Retro. Supp. I: 355
"Personal and the Individual, The" (L. Michaels), Supp. XVI: 201
Personal Injuries (Turow), Supp. XVII: 219–220, 221, 223
"Personalities" (column, Briggs), Supp. XVIII: 15
"Personal Narrative" (Edward), Retro. Supp. III: 9
Personal Narrative (Edwards), I: 545, 552, 553, 561, 562; Supp. I Part 2: 700
"Personal Poem #9" (Berrigan), Supp. XXIV: 34, 35
"Personal Poem"(O'Hara), Supp. XXIII: 219
Personal Recollection of Joan of Arc (Twain), IV: 208
Personals (Bontemps), Supp. XXII: 7, 8
"Personals" (Didion), Supp. IV Part 1: 200
"Personism" (O'Hara), Supp. XV: 181
"Personism: A Manifesto" (O'Hara), Supp. XXIII: 212, 215; Supp. XXIV: 43
Persons and Places (Santayana), III: 615
Persons in Hiding (film), Supp. XIII: 170
Persons in Hiding (Hoover), Supp. XIII: 170
Person Sitting in Darkness, A (Twain), IV: 208
"Persons Who Interest Us" (Harper's Bazaar), Supp. XXV: 277–278
"Perspective" (Francis), Supp. IX: 78
"Perspective: Anniversary D-Day" (Karr), Supp. XI: 241
Perspectives by Incongruity (Burke), I: 284–285
"Perspectives: Is It Out of Control?" (Gleason), Supp. IX: 16
Perspectives on Cormac McCarthy (Arnold and Luce, eds.), Supp. VIII: 189
Persse, Dudley Jocelyn, Supp. XX: 232
Pertes et Fracas (McCoy), Supp. XIII: 175
"Peruvian Child" (Mora), Supp. XIII: 218
Peseroff, Joyce, Supp. IV Part 1: 71
Pesetsky, Bette, Supp. XXIV: 173
"Pestilence" (Nelson), Supp. XVIII: 186
Pest Maiden, The (Schott), Supp. XXIII: 245–246
"Peter" (Cather), Retro. Supp. I: 4
"Peter" (Moore), III: 210, 212
Peter, Saint, III: 341, 346; IV: 86, 294
"Peter Goldthwaite's Treasure" (Hawthorne), Retro. Supp. III: 113
Peterkin, Julia, Supp. I Part 1: 328; Supp. XXII: 12, 189
"Peter Klaus" (German tale), II: 306
Peter Pan (Barrie), Supp. XV: 319
"Peter Parley" works (Goodrich), Supp. I Part 1: 38
"Peter Pendulum" (Poe), III: 425
"Peter Quince at the Clavier" (Stevens), IV: 81, 82
Peter Rabbit tales, Retro. Supp. I: 335
Peters, Cora, Supp. I Part 2: 468
Peters, Jacqueline, Supp. XII: 225
Peters, Margot, Supp. VIII: 252
Peters, Robert, Retro. Supp. III: 245; Supp. XIII: 114
Peters, S. H. (pseudonym). See Henry, O.
Peters, Timothy, Supp. XI: 39
"Peter's Avocado" (Rodriguez), Supp. XIV: 308–309
Petersen, David, Supp. XIII: 2
Petersen, Donald, Supp. V: 180; Supp. XV: 74, 92
Peterson, Dorothy, Supp. XVIII: 131, 132
Peterson, George, Supp. XXII: 250
Peterson, Houston, I: 60
Peterson, Roger Tory, Supp. V: 202
Peterson, Virgilia, Supp. IV Part 1: 30
Peter Whiffle: His Life and Works (Van Vechten), Supp. II Part 2: 728–729, 731, 735, 738–741, 749
"Petey and Yotsee and Mario" (H. Roth), Supp. IX: 234
"Petition, A" (Winters), Supp. II Part 2: 785
"Pet Milk"(Dybek), Supp. XXIII: 74
"'Pet Negro' System, The" (Hurston), Supp. VI: 159
"Petra and Its Surroundings" (Frost), Retro. Supp. I: 124
Petrarch, I: 176; II: 590; III: 4
"Petrarch, Shakespeare, and the Blues" (C. Frost), Supp. XV: 92, 104, 105
"Petrified Man" (Welty), IV: 262; Retro. Supp. I: 345, 351
"Petrified Man, The" (Twain), IV: 195; Retro. Supp. III: 257
"Petrified Woman, The" (Gordon), II: 199
Petronius, III: 174, 179
Petry, Ann, Supp. VIII: 214; Supp. XI: 6, 85; Supp. XVIII: 286
Pet Sematary (King), Supp. V: 138, 143, 152
Pettengill, Claire C., Supp. XXV: 40
Pettengill, Richard, Supp. VIII: 341, 345, 348
Pettingell, Phoebe, Supp. XV: 251, 256–257, 262
Pettis, Joyce, Supp. XI: 276, 277, 278, 281
Pettis, Olive G., Supp. XXIII: 189
Petty, Jill, Supp. XXI: 244, 248, 249, 250
Pfaelzer, Jean, Supp. XVI: 88, 90
Pfaff, Timothy, Supp. V: 166
Pfeil, Fred, Supp. XIV: 36
Pfister, Karin, IV: 467, 475
Phaedo (Plato), II: 10
Phaedra (Lowell and Barzun, trans.), II: 543–544
"Phantasia for Elvira Shatayev, The" (Rich), Retro. Supp. III: 249; Supp. I Part 2: 570
Phantasms of War (A. Lowell), II: 512
"Phantom of the Movie Palace, The" (Coover), Supp. V: 50–51
Phantom Ship, The (Marryat), Supp. XVII: 55
"Pharaoh, The" (Kenyon), Supp. VII: 172
"Pharmacy"(Strout), Supp. XXIII: 281
Pharr, Mary, Supp. V: 147
"Phases" (E. Stoddard), Supp. XV: 273
"Phases" (Stevens), Retro. Supp. I: 299

Phases of an Inferior Planet (Glasgow), **II:** 174–175
"Pheasant, The" (Carver), **Supp. III Part 1:** 146
Phelan, Alice, **Supp. XXII:** 193
Pheloung, Grant, **Supp. XI:** 39
Phelps, Donald, **Supp. XXIII:** 174
Phelps, Elizabeth Stuart, **Retro. Supp. II:** 146; **Supp. XIII:** 141; **Supp. XVI:** 80
Phelps, Teresa Godwin, **Supp. VIII:** 128
Phelps, William Lyon "Billy", **Supp. XX: 68, 75, 220**
"Phenomena and Laws of Race Contacts, The" (Locke), **Supp. XIV:** 210
Phenomenal Fauna, A (Wells), **Supp. XXVI:** 275
"Phenomenology of Anger, The" (Rich), **Retro. Supp. III:** 247; **Supp. I Part 2:** 562–563, 571
Phenomenology of Moral Experience, The (Mandelbaum), **I:** 61
"Phenomenology of On Moral Fiction" (C. Johnson), **Supp. VI:** 188
Phidias, **Supp. I Part 2:** 482
Philadelphia Fire (Wideman), **Supp. X:** 320, 334
Philadelphia Negro, The (Du Bois), **Supp. II Part 1:** 158, 163–164, 166
Philbrick, Thomas, **I:** 343
"Philemon and Baucis"(Hadas), **Supp. XXIII:** 114
"Phil in the Marketplace" (Lethem), **Supp. XVIII:** 148
Philip, Jim, **Supp. XII:** 136
Philip, Maxwell, **Supp. XXI:** 160
Philip, Prince, **Supp. X:** 108
"Philip of Pokanoket" (Irving), **II:** 303
Philippians (biblical book), **IV:** 154
"Philippine Conquest, The" (Masters), **Supp. I Part 2:** 456
"Philip Roth Reconsidered" (Howe), **Retro. Supp. II:** 286
"Philistinism and the Negro Writer" (Baraka), **Supp. II Part 1:** 39, 44
Phillips, Adam, **Supp. XII:** 97–98
Phillips, Anne K., **Supp. XX: 221**
Phillips, Carl, **Supp. XXI:** 246
Phillips, David Graham, **II:** 444; **Retro. Supp. II:** 101
Phillips, Gene D., **Supp. XI:** 306
Phillips, Jayne Anne, **Supp. XIV:** 21
Phillips, J. J., **Supp. XXIII:** 174
Phillips, J. O. C., **Supp. I Part 1:** 19
Phillips, Robert, **Supp. XIII:** 335, 344
Phillips, Wendell, **Supp. I Part 1:** 103; **Supp. I Part 2:** 524
Phillips, Willard, **Supp. I Part 1:** 154, 155
Phillips, William, **Supp. VIII:** 156
Phillips, William L., **I:** 106
"Philly Babylon" (Di Piero), **Supp. XIX:** 46
"Philoctetes"(Hadas), **Supp. XXIII:** 115
"Philoctetes: The Wound and the Bow" (Wilson), **Supp. XXIV:** 217
"Philosopher, The" (Farrell), **II:** 45
Philosopher of the Forest (pseudonym). See Freneau, Philip
Philosophes classiques, Les (Taine), **III:** 323
"Philosophical Cobbler, The" (Sanders), **Supp. XVI:** 268
"Philosophical Concepts and Practical Results" (James), **II:** 352
"Philosophical Investigation of Metaphor, A" (Gass), **Supp. VI:** 79
Philosophical Transactions (Watson), **II:** 114
"Philosophy, Or Something Like That" (P. Roth), **Supp. III Part 2:** 403
"Philosophy and Its Critics" (James), **II:** 360
"Philosophy and the Form of Fiction" (Gass), **Supp. VI:** 85
"Philosophy for People" (Emerson), **II:** 14
"Philosophy in Warm Weather" (Kenyon), **Supp. VII:** 168
"Philosophy Lesson" (Levine), **Supp. V:** 195
Philosophy of Alain Locke, The: Harlem Renaissance and Beyond (Harris, ed.), **Supp. XIV:** 196, 211–212
"Philosophy of Composition, The" (Poe), **III:** 416, 421; **Retro. Supp. II:** 266, 267, 271; **Retro. Supp. III:** 233–234; **Supp. XXV:** 120, 121
Philosophy of Friedrich Nietzsche, The (Mencken), **III:** 102–103
"Philosophy of Handicap, A" (Bourne), **I:** 216, 218
"Philosophy of History" (Emerson), **II:** 11–12
Philosophy of Literary Form, The (Burke), **I:** 275, 281, 283, 291
Philosophy of the Human Mind, The (Stewart), **II:** 8
Philosophy: Who Needs It (Rand), **Supp. IV Part 2:** 517, 518, 527, 533
Philoxenes, **Supp. VIII:** 201
"Phineas" (Knowles), **Supp. XII:** 238–240
Phineas: Six Stories (Knowles), **Supp. XII:** 249
"Phocion" (R. Lowell), **II:** 536
Phoebe Light (Notley), **Supp. XXII:** 227
Phoenix and the Turtle, The (Shakespeare), **I:** 284
"Phoenix Lyrics" (Schwartz), **Supp. II Part 2:** 665
"Phoenix on the Sword, The" (Howard), **Supp. XXVII:** 117, 124–125
"Phone Booths, The" (Jarman), **Supp. XVII:** 112–113
"Phony War Films" (Jones), **Supp. XI:** 217, 232
"Photograph: Carlisle Indian School (1879–1918)"(Kenny), **Supp. XXIII:** 156
"Photograph: Migrant Worker, Parlier, California, 1967" (Levis), **Supp. XI:** 272
"Photograph of a Bawd Drinking Raleigh Rye" (Trethewey), **Supp. XXI:** 254
"Photograph of a Child on a Vermont Hillside" (Kenyon), **Supp. VII:** 168
"Photograph of My Mother as a Young Girl" (Gioia), **Supp. XV:** 119
"Photograph of the Girl" (Olds), **Supp. X:** 205
"Photograph of the Unmade Bed" (Rich), **Supp. I Part 2:** 558
Photographs (Welty), **Retro. Supp. I:** 343
"Photographs, The" (Barthelme), **Supp. IV Part 1:** 53
"Photography" (Levine), **Supp. V:** 194
Phyrrho, **Retro. Supp. I:** 247
"Physical Universe" (Simpson), **Supp. IX:** 278
"Physicist We Know, A" (Shields), **Supp. VII:** 310
"Physics and Cosmology in the Fiction of Tom Robbins" (Nadeau), **Supp. X:** 270
Physiologie du goût (Brillat-Savarin), **Supp. XVII:** 82, 86
Physiology of Taste, The; or, Meditations on Transcendent Gastronomy (Brillat-Savarin; M. F. K. Fisher, trans.), **Supp. XVII:** 86, 87, 91
"Physiology of Versification, The: Harmonies of Organic and Animal Life" (Holmes), **Supp. I Part 1:** 311
Physique de l'Amour (Gourmont), **III:** 467–468
Piaf, Edith, **Supp. IV Part 2:** 549
Piaget, Jean, **Supp. XIII:** 75
"Piano" (Lawrence), **Supp. XV:** 254
"Piano Fingers" (Mason), **Supp. VIII:** 146
Piano Lesson, The (Bearden), **Supp.**

VIII: 342
Piano Lesson, The (television film), **Retro. Supp. III:** 326
Piano Lesson, The (Wilson), **Retro. Supp. III:** 318, 325, 326–328; **Supp. VIII: 342–345**
Piano Man's Daughter, The (Findley), **Supp. XX: 59–61**
"Piano Player, The"(Strout), **Supp. XXIII:** 283, 285
Piatt, James, **Supp. I Part 2:** 420
Piatt, John J., **II:** 273
Piazza, Ben, **Supp. XIII:** 163
Piazza, Paul, **Supp. XIV:** 157, 160, 171
"Piazza de Spagna, Early Morning" (Wilbur), **Supp. III Part 2:** 553
Piazza Tales, The (Melville), **III:** 91; **Retro. Supp. III:** 158
Picabia, Francis, **Retro. Supp. I:** 416; **Retro. Supp. II:** 331; **Supp. XXII:** 162
Picasso (Stein), **IV:** 28, 32, 45
Picasso, Pablo, **I:** 429, 432, 440, 442, 445; **II:** 602; **III:** 197, 201, 470; **IV:** 26, 31, 32, 46, 87, 407, 436; **Retro. Supp. I:** 55, 63; **Supp. IV Part 1:** 81; **Supp. IX:** 66
Piccione, Anthony, **Supp. XV:** 212
"Piccola Comedia" (Wilbur), **Supp. III Part 2:** 561
Pickard, Samuel T., **Supp. I Part 2:** 682
Picked-Up Pieces (Updike), **Retro. Supp. I:** 320, 322, 323, 335
Picker, Lauren, **Supp. VIII:** 78, 83
Picker, Tobias, **Supp. XII:** 253
Pickering, Sam, **Supp. XXI: 191–207**
Pickford, Mary, **Retro. Supp. I:** 325; **Supp. I Part 2:** 391
"Picking and Choosing" (Moore), **III:** 205
"Pickman's Model" (Lovecraft), **Supp. XXV:** 113, 114
Picnic (film), **Supp. XXV:** 95
Picnic (Inge), **Supp. XXV:** 93, 95, 97–99
"Picnic" (Peacock), **Supp. XIX:** 206
Picnic, Lightning (Collins), **Supp. XXI:** 54, 60
"Picnic, Lightning" (Collins), **Supp. XXI:** 64–65
Picnic Cantata (music) (Bowles), **Supp. IV Part 1:** 89
"Picnic Remembered" (Warren), **IV:** 240
Pictorial History of the Negro in America, A (Hughes), **Supp. I Part 1:** 345
"Picture" (Huddle), **Supp. XXVI:** 150
"Picture, The" (Olson), **Supp. II Part 2:** 574
Picture Bride (Son), **Supp. X:** 292
"Picture I Want, The" (Olds), **Supp. X:** 209
Picture of Dorian Gray, The (Wilde), **Supp. IX:** 105
"Picture of Little J. A. in a Prospect of Flowers, A" (Ashbery), **Supp. III Part 1:** 3
Picture Palace (Theroux), **Supp. VIII:** 322
"Pictures" (Pickering), **Supp. XXI:** 197
"Pictures at an Extermination" (Epstein), **Supp. XII:** 161
"Pictures from an Expedition" (Duffy), **Supp. IV Part 1:** 207
Pictures from an Institution (Jarrell), **II:** 367, 385
Pictures from Brueghel (W. C. Williams), **Retro. Supp. I:** 429–431
"Pictures from Brueghel" (W. C. Williams), **Retro. Supp. I:** 419
"Pictures of Columbus, the Genoese, The" (Freneau), **Supp. II Part 1:** 258
Pictures of Fidelman: An Exhibition (Malamud), **Supp. I Part 2:** 450–451
"Pictures of the Artist" (Malamud), **Supp. I Part 2:** 450
Pictures of the Floating World (A. Lowell), **II:** 521, 524–525; **Supp. XXVII:** 295
Pictures of Travel (Heine), **II:** 281
Picturesque America; or, the Land We Live In (Bryant, ed.), **Supp. I Part 1:** 158
"Picturesque Ghetto, The" (Hapgood), **Supp. XVII:** 101
"Picturesque: San Cristóbal de las Casas" (Mora), **Supp. XIII:** 218
Picture This (Heller), **Supp. IV Part 1:** 386, 388, 390–391
Picturing Will (Beattie), **Supp. V:** 29, 31–32, 34
"Pie" (X. J. Kennedy), **Supp. XV:** 170
"Piece, A" (Creeley), **Supp. IV Part 1:** 155, 156
"Piece of Moon, A" (Hogan), **Supp. IV Part 1:** 407
Piece of My Heart, A (Ford), **Supp. V:** 57, 58–61, 62
Piece of My Mind, A: Reflections at Sixty (Wilson), **IV:** 426, 430, 438, 441
"Piece of News, A" (Welty), **IV:** 263; **Retro. Supp. I:** 345, 346
Pieces (Creeley), **Supp. IV Part 1:** 155
Pieces and Pontifications (Mailer), **Retro. Supp. II:** 209–210
Pieces of the Frame (McPhee), **Supp. III Part 1:** 293
"Pie of the Month"(Thompson), **Supp. XXIII:** 300
Pierce, Franklin, **II:** 225, 226, 227; **III:** 88; **Retro. Supp. I:** 150, 163, 164, 165
Pierce, Frederick, **Retro. Supp. I:** 136
Piercy, Josephine, **Retro. Supp. III:** 9
Piercy, Josephine K., **Supp. I Part 1:** 103
"Pierian Handsprings" (column, Untermeyer), **Supp. XV:** 294
Pierpont, Claudia Roth, **Supp. X:** 192, 193, 196
Pierre et Jean (Maupassant), **I:** 421
Pierre: or The Ambiguities (Melville), **III:** 86–88, 89; **IV:** 194; **Retro. Supp. I:** 249, 253–254, 256; **Retro. Supp. III:** 147, 149, 150, 157–158; **Supp. I Part 2:** 579
Pierrepont, Sarah. See Edwards, Sarah
Pierrot qui pleure et Pierrot qui rit (Rostand), **II:** 515
Pierson, George W, **Supp. XXII:** 289
Pig Cookies (Ríos), **Supp. IV Part 2:** 537, 550, 552–554
Pigeon Feathers (Updike), **IV:** 214, 218, 219, 221–223, 226
"Pigeon Feathers" (Updike), **Retro. Supp. I:** 318, 322, 323
"Pigeons" (Rilke), **II:** 544
"Pigeons, The" (Espaillat), **Supp. XXI:** 98
"Pigeons from Hell" (Howard), **Supp. XXVII:** 116, 119–120
"Pigeon Woman" (Swenson), **Supp. IV Part 2:** 644
"Pig Helmet and the Wall of Life"(P. Benedict), **Supp. XXIII: 48–49**
Pigs in Heaven (Kingsolver), **Supp. VII:** 197, 199, 209–210
Pike County Ballads, The (Hay), **Supp. I Part 1:** 352
Piket, Vincent, **Supp. IV Part 1:** 24
Pilar San-Mallafre, Maria del, **Supp. V:** 40
Pilcer, Sonya, **Supp. XVII:** 50
Pilgrim (Findley), **Supp. XX: 61–62**
"Pilgrim" (Freneau), **Supp. I Part 1:** 125
"Pilgrimage" (Ray), **Supp. XVIII:** 193
"Pilgrimage" (Sontag), **Supp. III Part 2:** 454–455
"Pilgrimage" (Trethewey), **Supp. XXI:** 255
"Pilgrimage, The" (Maxwell), **Supp. VIII:** 169, 171

Pilgrimage of Festus, The (Aiken), **I:** 50, 55, 57
Pilgrimage of Henry James, The (Brooks), **I:** 240, 248, 250; **IV:** 433
Pilgrim at Tinker Creek (Dillard), **Supp. VI:** 22, **23–26,** 28, 29, **30–31,** 34; **Supp. XVIII:** 189
"Pilgrim Makers" (R. Lowell), **II:** 541
Pilgrim's Harbor (Skloot), **Supp. XX: 196, 207**
Pilgrim's Progress (Bunyan), **I:** 92; **II:** 15, 168, 572; **Supp. I Part 1:** 32, 38; **Supp. I Part 2:** 599
Pili's Wall (Levine), **Supp. V:** 178, 183–184
"Pillar of Fire" (Bradbury), **Supp. IV Part 1:** 113–114
Pillars of Hercules, The: A Grand Tour of the Mediterranean (Theroux), **Supp. VIII:** 325
"Pillow" (L.-Y. Lee), **Supp. XV:** 224
Pilot, The (Cooper), **I:** 335, 337, 339, 342–343, 350
"Pilot from the Carrier, A" (Jarrell), **II:** 374
"Pilots, Man Your Planes" (Jarrell), **II:** 374–375
"Pilots, The" (Levertov), **Supp. III Part 1:** 282
Pilsudski, Joseph, **Supp. XXIII:** 6
"Pimp's Revenge, A" (Malamud), **Supp. I Part 2:** 435, 450, 451
Pinball (Kosinski), **Supp. VII:** 215, 226
Pinchot, Gifford, **Supp. IX:** 184; **Supp. XIV:** 178
Pindar, **I:** 381; **II:** 543; **III:** 610
"Pine" (Dickey), **Supp. IV Part 1:** 183
Pine Barrens, The (McPhee), **Supp. III Part 1:** 298–301, 309
"Pineys, The" (Stern), **Supp. IX:** 288, 296
Pinget, Robert, **Supp. V:** 39
Pinhook: Finding Wholeness in a Fragmented Land (Ray), **Supp. XVIII:** 189, 192, 202–204
"Pink Dog" (Bishop), **Retro. Supp. II:** 48
"Pink Dress, The" (Boulton), **Supp. XXII:** 19
Pinker, James B., **I:** 409; **Retro. Supp. I:** 231
Pinkerton, Jan, **Supp. V:** 323–324
"Pink Moon—The Pond" (Oliver), **Supp. VII:** 234
Pinktoes (C. Himes), **Supp. XVI: 142**
Pinocchio in Venice (Coover), **Supp. V:** 40, 51
Pinsker, Sanford, **Retro. Supp. II:** 23; **Supp. IX:** 293, 327; **Supp. V:** 272; **Supp. XI:** 251, 254, 317
Pinsky, Robert, **Retro. Supp. II:** 50; **Supp. IX:** 155, 158; **Supp. VI: 235–251; Supp. XIII:** 277, 285; **Supp. XXI:** 243; **Supp. XXIII:** 111, 124
Pinter, Harold, **I:** 71; **Supp. XIII:** 20, 196; **Supp. XIV:** 239; **Supp. XVI:** 207
Pinto, Ferdinand Mendes (pseudonym). See Briggs, Charles Frederick
Pinto and Sons (Epstein), **Supp. XII:** 170, **171–172**
Pinto letters (Briggs), **Supp. XVIII:** 3, **12–13**
"Pinup" (Collins), **Supp. XXI:** 59
"Pioneer Girl" (L. I. Wilder), **Supp. XXII:** 290, 293, 294, 295
Pioneer Girl (Nguyen), **Supp. XXVI:** 216–220
Pioneers, The (Cooper), **I:** 336, 337, 339, 340–341, 342, 348; **II:** 313
Pioneers of France in the New World (Parkman), **Supp. III Part 2:** 599, 602
"Pioneers! O Pioneers!" (Whitman), **Retro. Supp. I:** 8
"Pioneer's Vision, The" (Larcom), **Supp. XIII:** 140
Pious and Secular America (Niebuhr), **III:** 308
Pipe Night (O'Hara), **III:** 361, 368
Piper, Dan, **Supp. IX:** 65
Pipers at the Gates of Dawn: The Wisdom of Children's Literature (Cott), **Supp. XVI:** 104
"Piper's Rocks" (Olson), **Supp. IV Part 1:** 153
"Pipistrelles" (B. Kelly), **Supp. XVII:** 129–130
Pipkin, Charles W., **Supp. XIV:** 3
Pippa Passes (Browning), **IV:** 128
Piquion, René, **Supp. I Part 1:** 346
Pirandello, Luigi, **Supp. IV Part 2:** 576, 588
Piranesi, Giovanni Battista, **Supp. XV:** 258
Pirate, The (Robbins), **Supp. XII:** 6
Pirate, The (Scott), **I:** 339
Pirates of Penzance, The (Gilbert and Sullivan), **IV:** 386
Pisan Cantos, The (Pound), **III:** 476; **Retro. Supp. I:** 140, 283, 285, 293; **Supp. III Part 1:** 63; **Supp. V:** 331, 337; **Supp. XIV:** 11; **Supp. XV:** 351
Pisarev, Dimitri, **Supp. XXI:** 164
Piscator, Erwin, **IV:** 394
"Pissaro: Tropical Impressions"(Kenny), **Supp. XXIII:** 146
Pissarro, Camille, **I:** 478
"Pissing off the Back of the Boat into the Nevernais Canal" (Matthews), **Supp. IX:** 160–161
Pistol, The (Jones), **Supp. XI:** 219, **223–224,** 227, 234
"Pistol Politics" (Howard), **Supp. XXVII:** 128
Pit, The (Norris), **III:** 314, 322, 326–327, 333, 334
"Pit, The" (Roethke), **III:** 538
"Pit and the Pendulum, The" (Poe), **III:** 413, 416; **Retro. Supp. II:** 264, 269–270, 273
"Pitcher" (Francis), **Supp. IX:** 82
"Pitcher, The" (Dubus), **Supp. VII:** 87
Pitchford, Nicola, **Supp. XII:** 13
"Pits, The" (D. Graham), **Supp. XI:** 252, 254
Pitt, William, **Supp. I Part 2:** 510, 518
Pitts, Rebecca, **Supp. XXII:** 280, 281
"Pittsburgh" (Carruth), **Supp. XVI:** 58
Pittsburgh Cycle (Wilson). See Century Cycle (Wilson)
"Pity" (Huddle), **Supp. XXVI:** 151
"Pity Me" (Wylie), **Supp. I Part 2:** 729
Pity the Monsters (Williamson), **Retro. Supp. II:** 185
Pius II, Pope, **III:** 472
Pius IX, Pope, **II:** 79
"Piute Creek" (Snyder), **Supp. VIII:** 293
Pixley, Frank, **I:** 196
Pizer, Donald, **III:** 321; **Retro. Supp. II:** 100, 199
"Place" (Hoffman), **Supp. XVIII:** 86
"Place at the Outskirts" (Simic), **Supp. VIII:** 282
Place Called Estherville, A (Caldwell), **I:** 297, 307
Place Called Freedom, A (Sanders), **Supp. XVI:** 269
Place for My Head, A (Hoffman), **Supp. XVIII:** 76
"Place in Fiction" (Welty), **IV:** 260, 279
Place of Dead Roads, The (Burroughs), **Supp. III Part 1:** 196
Place of Love, The (Shapiro), **Supp. II Part 2:** 702, 706
"Place of Poetry, The" (Stevens), **Retro. Supp. I:** 304
Place of Science in Modern Civilization and Other Essays, The (Veblen), **Supp. I Part 2:** 629, 642
"Place of Trumpets, The" (B. Kelly), **Supp. XVII:** 127
Place on Earth, A (Berry), **Supp. X:** 33–34, 36
Places Left Unfinished at the Time of

Creation (Santos), **Supp. XIII:** 274
"Places to Look for Your Mind" (Moore), **Supp. X:** 174–175
"Place They'd Never Seen, A: The Theater" (Wasserstein), **Supp. XV:** 332
"Place to Live, A" (Levertov), **Supp. III Part 1:** 281
"Place to Stand, A" (Price), **Supp. VI:** 258
Place to Stand, A (Wagoner), **Supp. IX:** 324
"Place (Any Place) to Transcend All Places, A" (W. C. Williams), **Retro. Supp. I:** 422
"Place Where My Poems Are Coming From, The"(Crooker), **Supp. XXIII:** 64
Placi, Carlo, **IV:** 328
Plagemann, Catherine, **Supp. XVII:** 91
"Plagiarist, The" (Singer), **IV:** 19
Plagued by the Nightingale (Boyle), **Supp. XXIV: 51–52,** 53, 56
Plague of Dreamers, A (Stern), **Supp. XX: 178**
Plainest Narrative, The (Bronk), **Supp. XXI:** 31
"Plain Language from Truthful James" (Harte). See "Heathen Chinee, The"
"Plain Sense of Things, The" (Stevens), **Retro. Supp. I:** 298, 299, 307, 312
"Plain Song" (Carruth), **Supp. XVI:** 54
Plain Song (Harrison), **Supp. VIII: 38–39**
"Plain Song" (Kooser), **Supp. XIX:** 120
"Plain Song for Comadre, A" (Wilbur), **Supp. III Part 2:** 554
"Plain Talk". See Common Sense (Paine)
Plaint of a Rose, The (Sandburg), **III:** 579
Plain Truth: Or, Serious Considerations on the Present State of the City of Philadelphia, and Province of Pennsylvania (Franklin), **II:** 117–119
Plainwater: Essays and Poetry (Carson), **Supp. XII:** 97, **99–104**
Plan B (C. Himes), **Supp. XVI:** 143, 144
Plan B: Further Thoughts on Faith (Lamott), **Supp. XX: 142–143**
"Planchette" (London), **II:** 475–476
"Planetarium" (Rich), **Retro. Supp. III:** 245; **Supp. I Part 2:** 557
Planet News: 1961–1967 (Ginsberg), **Supp. II Part 1:** 321
Planet Waves (album, Dylan), **Supp. XVIII:** 27
"Plantation a beginning, a" (Olson), **Supp. II Part 2:** 573
Plant Dreaming Deep (Sarton), **Supp. VIII:** 250, 263
Plante, David, **Supp. IV Part 1:** 310
Planting a Sequoia (Gioia), **Supp. XV:** 117
"Planting a Sequoia" (Gioia), **Supp. XV:** 111, 112, 117, **121–122**
"Plants Fed On By Fawns" (B. Kelly), **Supp. XVII:** 133
Plarr, Victor, **III:** 459, 477
Plath, James, **Retro. Supp. I:** 334; **Supp. XXIII:** 73, 74, 80
Plath, Sylvia, **Retro. Supp. II:** 181, **241–260; Retro. Supp. III:** 243; **Supp. I Part 2: 526–549,** 554, 571; **Supp. III Part 2:** 543, 561; **Supp. IV Part 2:** 439; **Supp. V:** 79, 81, 113, 117, 118, 119, 344; **Supp. X:** 201, 202, **203,** 215; **Supp. XI:** 146, 240, 241, 317; **Supp. XII:** 217, 308; **Supp. XIII:** 35, 76, 312; **Supp. XIV:** 269; **Supp. XV:** 123, 148, 184, 252, 253, 340; **Supp. XVII:** 239; **Supp. XXI:** 58; **Supp. XXII:** 30, 92, 93; **Supp. XXIII:** 63, 64, 112, 113, 254; **Supp. XXV:** 222; **Supp. XXVI:** 45, 64, 67, 68, 77; **Supp. XXVII:** 261, 296
Plath, Warren, **Supp. I Part 2:** 528
Plato, **I:** 224, 279, 383, 389, 485, 523; **II:** 5, 8, 10, 15, 233, 346, 391–392, 591; **III:** 115, 480, 600, 606, 609, 619–620; **IV:** 74, 140, 333, 363, 364; **Retro. Supp. I:** 247; **Retro. Supp. II:** 31; **Supp. I Part 2:** 595, 631; **Supp. IV Part 1:** 391; **Supp. IV Part 2:** 526; **Supp. X:** 78
"Plato" (Emerson), **II:** 6
"Platonic Relationship, A" (Beattie), **Supp. V:** 22
Platonic Scripts (Justice), **Supp. VII:** 115
Platonov, Dmitri, **Supp. VIII:** 30
Platt, Anthony M., **Supp. I Part 1:** 13–14
Platt, Edward, **Supp. XXIII:** 97
Platte River (Bass), **Supp. XVI:** 19
"Platte River" (Bass), **Supp. XVI:** 20
"Plausible Man" (Davison), **Supp. XXVI:** 71
Plausible Prejudices: Essays on American Writing (Epstein), **Supp. XIV:** 111
Plautus, Titus Maccius, **IV:** 155; **Supp. III Part 2:** 630
"Play, A" (Brainard), **Supp. XXVII:** 18
Play and Other Stories, The (Dixon), **Supp. XII:** 148, 149
Playback (Chandler), **Supp. IV Part 1:** 134–135; **Supp. XVIII:** 138
Playback (script) (Chandler), **Supp. IV Part 1:** 131
"Play Ball!" (Francis), **Supp. IX:** 89
Playboy of the Western World, The (Synge), **Supp. III Part 1:** 34
Play Days (Jewett), **Retro. Supp. II:** 135
Play Days: A Book of Stories for Children (Jewett), **II:** 401–402
Player Piano (Vonnegut), **Supp. II Part 2:** 756, 757, 760–765
Players (DeLillo), **Supp. VI:** 3, 6, 8, 14
"Players, The" (W. J. Smith), **Supp. XIII:** 340, 343
"Playground, The" (Bradbury), **Supp. IV Part 1:** 104
"Playing" (Huddle), **Supp. XXVI:** 151, 154
Playing at Stillness (Espaillat), **Supp. XXI:** 112
Playing for Time (A. Miller), **Retro. Supp. III:** 174
Playing in the Dark (Morrison), **Retro. Supp. II:** 118; **Retro. Supp. III:** 184, 194; **Supp. XIII:** 185–186
"Playing the Bawd at Twenty" (Skloot), **Supp. XX: 204–205**
Play in Poetry (Untermeyer), **Supp. XV:** 310
"Playin with Punjab" (Bambara), **Supp. XI:** 6
Play It Again Sam (Allen), **Supp. XV:** 2, 3, 14
Play It as It Lays (Didion), **Supp. IV Part 1:** 198, 201–203, 203, 211
Play It as It Lays (film), **Supp. IV Part 1:** 198
"Plays and Operas Too" (Whitman), **IV:** 350
Plays of Negro Life: A Source-Book of Native American Drama (Locke and Gregory), **Supp. XIV:** 202
Plays: Six (A. Miller), **Retro. Supp. III:** 176
Plays: Winesburg and Others (Anderson), **I:** 113
"Playthings" (Komunyakaa), **Supp. XIII:** 126
"Playtime: Danish Fun" (Larsen), **Supp. XVIII:** 120, 122–123
"Playtime: Three Scandinavian Stories" (Larsen), **Supp. XVIII:** 122–123
Playwright's Voice, The (Savran), **Supp. XIII:** 209; **Supp. XV:** 321; **Supp. XXIV:** 263

Plaza Suite (Simon), **Supp. IV Part 2:** 575, 581–582, 583, 589
"Pleaders, The" (Davison), **Supp. XXVI:** 71
Pleading Guilty (Turow), **Supp. XVII: 218,** 219
"Plea for Captain Brown, A" (Thoreau), **IV:** 185
"Plea of a Plebeian" (H. Johnson), **Supp. XXVI:** 173
"Please" (Komunyakaa), **Supp. XIII:** 122
"Please Don't Kill Anything" (A. Miller), **III:** 161
"Please Don't Take My Sunshine Away" (Conroy), **Supp. XVI:** 69
Please Louise (Morrison and S. Morrison), **Retro. Supp. III:** 185
"Pleasure" (Very), **Supp. XXV:** 242, 244
Pleasure Dome (Frankenberg), **I:** 436
Pleasure Dome (Komunyakaa), **Supp. XIII:** 113, 121, **131–133**
Pleasure of Hope, The (Emerson), **II:** 8
"Pleasure of Ruins, The" (McClatchy), **Supp. XII:** 256
"Pleasures of Formal Poetry, The" (Bogan), **Supp. III Part 1:** 51
"Pleasures of Peace, The" (Koch), **Supp. XV:** 180
"Plea to the Protestant Churches, A" (Brooks), **Supp. XIV:** 4
Plimpton, George, **Retro. Supp. III:** 88; **Supp. IV Part 1:** 386; **Supp. IX:** 256; **Supp. V:** 201; **Supp. VIII:** 82, 157; **Supp. XI:** 294; **Supp. XIV:** 82; **Supp. XVI: 233–248**
Pliny the Elder, **Supp. XVI:** 292
Pliny the Younger, **II:** 113
"Ploesti Isn't Long Island" (Zinberg), **Supp. XV:** 195
"Plot against the Giant, The" (Stevens), **IV:** 81
Plotinus, **Supp. XV:** 33; **Supp. XVI:** 291
Plough and the Stars, The (O'Casey), **III:** 159
"Ploughing on Sunday" (Stevens), **IV:** 74
Plowing the Dark (Powers), **Supp. IX:** 212–213, **221–224**
Plum Bun (Fauset), **Supp. XIX:** 73; **Supp. XVIII:** 127
Plumed Serpent, The (Lawrence), **Supp. XV:** 46
"Plumet Basilisk, The" (Moore), **III:** 203, 208, 215
Plumly, Stanley, **Supp. IV Part 2:** 625
Plummer, Amanda, **Supp. IV Part 1:** 236
Plunder (serial movie), **Supp. IV Part 2:** 464
Plunket, Robert, **Supp. XV:** 68
Plunkett, Edward (Lord Dunsany), **Supp. XXV:** 113
"Plunkville Patriot" (O'Henry), **Supp. II Part 1:** 389
"Pluralism and Ideological Peace" (Locke), **Supp. XIV:** 202, 212
"Pluralism and Intellectual Democracy" (Locke), **Supp. XIV:** 202, 208, 212
Pluralistic Universe, A (James), **II:** 342, 348, 357–358
Plutarch, **II:** 5, 8, 16, 555; **Retro. Supp. I:** 360; **Supp. XVI:** 292
Plymell, Charles, **Supp. XIV:** 149
Plymell, Pam, **Supp. XIV:** 149
Pnin (Nabokov), **III:** 246; **Retro. Supp. I:** 263, 265, 266, 275, 335
"Po' Boy Blues" (Hughes), **Supp. I Part 1:** 327
Pocahontas, **I:** 4; **II:** 296; **III:** 584
"Pocahontas to Her English Husband, John Rolfe" (Gunn Allen), **Supp. IV Part 1:** 331
"Pocketbook and Sauerkraut" (Di Piero), **Supp. XIX:** 35, 36, 41, 42, 45
"Pocketknives" (Rash), **Supp. XXVII:** 222
"Pocket Poem" (Kooser), **Supp. XIX:** 128
Podhoretz, Norman, **IV:** 441; **Retro. Supp. II:** 323; **Supp. IV Part 1:** 382; **Supp. IX:** 3; **Supp. VIII:** 93, **231–247; Supp. XIV:** 103; **Supp. XXV:** 253, 268
Podnieks, Elizabeth, **Supp. X:** 189, 190, 191, 192
"Pod of the Milkweed" (Frost), **Retro. Supp. I:** 141
Podulka, Fran, **Supp. XXVI:** 6
Poe (screenplay, O'Nan), **Supp. XXV:** 154
Poe, Edgar Allan, **I:** 48, 53, 103, 190, 194, 200, 210, 211, 261, 340, 459; **II:** 74, 77, 194, 255, 273, 295, 308, 311, 313, 421, 475, 482, 530, 595; **III:** 259, **409–432,** 485, 507, 593; **IV:** 123, 129, 133, 141, 187, 261, 345, 350, 432, 438, 439, 453; **Retro. Supp. I:** 41, 273, 365, 421; **Retro. Supp. II:** 102, 104, 160, 164, 220, **261–277,** 322; **Retro. Supp. III:** 44, 194, **223–239**; **Supp. I Part 1:** 36, 309; **Supp. I Part 2:** 376, 384, 385, 388, 393, 405, 413, 421, 474, 682; **Supp. II Part 1:** 385, 410; **Supp. III Part 2:** 544, 549–550; **Supp. IV Part 1:** 80, 81, 101, 128, 341, 349; **Supp. IV Part 2:** 464, 469; **Supp. IX:** 115; **Supp. VIII:** 105; **Supp. X:** 42, 78; **Supp. XI:** 85, 293; **Supp. XIII:** 100, 111; **Supp. XV:** 275; **Supp. XVI:** 294; **Supp. XVIII:** 3, 11; **Supp. XX: 74; Supp. XXI:** 51; **Supp. XXIII:** 161, 164, 169, 177, 178; **Supp. XXIV:** 54; **Supp. XXV:** 111, 119; **Supp. XXVI:** 282; **Supp. XXVII:** 84
Poe Abroad: Influence, Reputation, Affinities (Vines), **Retro. Supp. II:** 261
"Poe-et's Nightmare, The" (Lovecraft), **Supp. XXV:** 119
Poe Log, The: A Documentary Life, 1809–1849 (Thomas and Jackson), **Retro. Supp. III:** 237
"Poem" (Bishop), **Retro. Supp. II:** 40; **Supp. I Part 1:** 73, 76–79, 82, 95
"Poem" (Harrison), **Supp. VIII:** 38
"Poem" (Justice), **Supp. VII:** 125
"Poem" (Kunitz), **Supp. III Part 1:** 263
"Poem" (Notley), **Supp. XXII:** 228–229
"Poem" (O'Hara), **Supp. XIX:** 85
"Poem" (Wright), **Supp. III Part 2:** 590
"Poem, the Snow, Jane Goodall, the Vase of Daffodils, The" (Huddle), **Supp. XXVI:** 150
"Poem About Black Power, A" (Boyle), **Supp. XXIV:** 64
"Poem About George Doty in the Death House, A" (Wright), **Supp. III Part 2:** 594–595, 597–598
"Poem about People" (Pinsky), **Supp. VI: 240–241,** 244, 248
"Poem as Mask, The" (Rukeyser), **Supp. VI:** 281, 285
"Poem as Time Machine, The" (Gallagher), **Supp. XXIV:** 172
"Poem Beginning 'The' " (Zukofsky), **Supp. III Part 2:** 610, 611, 614
"Poem Catching Up with an Idea" (Carruth), **Supp. XVI:** 56
"Poem for a Birthday" (Plath), **Supp. I Part 2:** 539
"POEM FOR ANNA RUSS AND FANNY JONES, A" (Baraka), **Supp. II Part 1:** 58
"Poem for Black Hearts, A" (Baraka), **Supp. II Part 1:** 50
"POEM FOR DEEP THINKERS, A" (Baraka), **Supp. II Part 1:** 55
"Poem for D. H. Lawrence" (Creeley),

Supp. IV Part 1: 141
"Poem for Don Cherry" (Mackey), **Supp. XXVII:** 154
"Poem for Dorothy, A" (Merwin), **Supp. III Part 1:** 342
"Poem for Hemingway and W. C. Williams" (Carver), **Supp. III Part 1:** 147
"Poem for my Son" (Kumin), **Supp. IV Part 2:** 442
"Poem for People Who Are Understandably Too Busy to Read Poetry" (Dunn), **Supp. XI:** 147
"Poem for Someone Killed in Spain, A" (Jarrell), **II:** 371
"Poem for the Blue Heron, A" (Oliver), **Supp. VII:** 235–236
"Poem for Two Voices" (Everwine), **Supp. XV:** 89
"Poem For Willie Best, A" (Baraka), **Supp. II Part 1:** 36
"Poem in Prose" (Bogan), **Supp. III Part 1:** 58
"Poem in the Park, The" (Davison), **Supp. XXVI:** 74
"Poem in Which I Refuse Contemplation" (Dove), **Supp. IV Part 1:** 249
"Poem Is a Walk, A" (Ammons), **Supp. VII:** 36
"Poem Like a Grenade, A" (Haines), **Supp. XII:** 204
"Poem of Flight, The" (Levine), **Supp. V:** 189
"Poem of Liberation, The" (Stern), **Supp. IX:** 292
Poem of the Cid (Merwin, trans.), **Supp. III Part 1:** 347
"Poem of the Forgotten" (Haines), **Supp. XII:** 202–203
"Poem (V (F) W)"(O'Hara), **Supp. XXIII:** 219
"Poem on a Line by Anne Sexton, 'We Are All Writing God's Poem' "(Crooker), **Supp. XXIII:** 59
"Poem on the Memorable Victory Obtained by the Gallant Captain Paul Jones" (Freneau), **Supp. II Part 1:** 261
"Poem out of Childhood" (Rukeyser), **Supp. VI:** 272, 277
Poem-Paintings (O'Hara and Bluhm), **Supp. XXIII:** 217
"Poem Read at the Dinner Given to the Author by the Medical Profession" (Holmes), **Supp. I Part 1:** 310–311
Poems (Auden), **Supp. II Part 1:** 6
Poems (Berryman), **I:** 170
Poems (Bryant), **II:** 311; **Supp. I Part 1:** 155, 157
Poems (Cummings), **I:** 430, 447
Poems (E. Stoddard), **Supp. XV:** 274
Poems (Eliot), **I:** 580, 588; **IV:** 122; **Retro. Supp. I:** 59, 291
Poems (Emerson), **II:** 7, 8, 12–13, 17
Poems (Holmes), **Supp. I Part 1:** 303
Poems (J. R. Lowell), **Supp. I Part 2:** 405
Poems (Koch), **Supp. XV:** 179
Poems (Moore), **III:** 194, 205, 215
Poems (Poe), **III:** 411; **Retro. Supp. III:** 224, 231
Poems (Reznikoff), **Supp. XIV:** 282, 283, 284, 285
Poems (Tate), **IV:** 121
Poems (W. C. Williams), **Retro. Supp. I:** 412–413, 416, 424
Poems (W. J. Smith), **Supp. XIII:** 332
Poems (Williams), **Supp. XXIV:** 35
Poems (Winters), **Supp. II Part 2:** 809, 810
Poems (Wordsworth), **I:** 468
Poems, 1909–1925 (Eliot), **Retro. Supp. I:** 64
Poems, 1924–1933 (MacLeish), **III:** 7, 15
Poems, 1943–1956 (Wilbur), **Supp. III Part 2:** 554
Poems, 1953–58 (W. Stone), **Supp. XXVII:** 254
Poems, The (Freneau), **Supp. II Part 1:** 263
Poems 1918–1975 : The Complete Poems of Charles Reznikoff (Cooney, ed.), **Supp. XIV:** 289
Poems 1940–1953 (Shapiro), **Supp. II Part 2:** 703, 711
Poems 1947–1954 (Kees), **Supp. XV:** 147
Poems: 1947–1957 (W. J. Smith), **Supp. XIII:** 333
Poems 1957–1967 (Dickey), **Supp. IV Part 1:** 178, 181
Poems about God (Ransom), **III:** 484, 486, 491; **IV:** 121
"Poems about Painting" (Snodgrass), **Supp. VI:** 316
Poems and Essays (Ransom), **III:** 486, 490, 492
Poems and New Poems (Bogan), **Supp. III Part 1:** 60–62
"Poems and Places" (Haines), **Supp. XII:** 203
Poems and Poetry of Europe, The (Longfellow, ed.), **Retro. Supp. II:** 155
Poems by Emily Dickinson (Todd and Higginson, eds.), **I:** 469, 470; **Retro. Supp. I:** 35, 39
Poems by Emily Dickinson, Second Series (Todd and Higginson, eds.), **I:** 454; **Retro. Supp. I:** 35
Poems by Emily Dickinson, The (Bianchi and Hampson, eds.), **Retro. Supp. I:** 35
Poems by Emily Dickinson, Third Series (Todd, ed.), **Retro. Supp. I:** 35
Poems by James Russell Lowell, Second Series (J. R. Lowell), **Supp. I Part 2:** 406, 409
Poems by Sidney Lanier, (Lanier), **Supp. I Part 1:** 364
Poems from Black Africa (Hughes, ed.), **Supp. I Part 1:** 344
"Poems I Have Lost, The" (Ortiz), **Supp. IV Part 2:** 507
Poems: North & South–A Cold Spring, (Bishop), **Supp. I Part 1:** 83, 89
Poems of a Jew (Shapiro), **Supp. II Part 2:** 703, 712–713
"Poems of a Mountain Recluse" (Budbill), **Supp. XIX:** 9, 10
Poems of Anna Akhmatova, The (Kunitz and Hayward, trans.), **Supp. III Part 1:** 269
Poems of Emily Dickinson, The (Bianchi and Hampson, eds.), **Retro. Supp. I:** 35
Poems of Emily Dickinson, The (T. H. Johnson, ed.), **I:** 470
Poems of François Villon (Kinnell, trans.), **Supp. III Part 1:** 235, 243, 249
"Poems of Our Climate, The" (Stevens), **Retro. Supp. I:** 313
Poems of Peter Davison, The (Davison), **Supp. XXVI:** 66, 78
Poems of Philip Freneau, Written Chiefly during the Late War (Freneau), **Supp. II Part 1:** 261
Poems of Places (Longfellow, ed.), **II:** 490; **Retro. Supp. II:** 155; **Supp. I Part 1:** 368
Poems of Stanley Kunitz, The (Kunitz), **Supp. III Part 1:** 258, 263, 264, 266, 268
"Poems of These States" (Ginsberg), **Supp. II Part 1:** 323, 325
Poems of Two Friends (Howells and Piatt), **II:** 273, 277
"POEM SOME PEOPLE WILL HAVE TO UNDERSTAND, A" (Baraka), **Supp. II Part 1:** 49
Poems on Slavery (Longfellow), **II:** 489; **Retro. Supp. II:** 157, 168; **Supp. I Part 2:** 406
Poems on Various Subjects (Rowson), **Supp. XV:** 232
Poems on Various Subjects, Religious

and Moral (Wheatley), **Supp. XX: 277, 282, 284, 285, 289**
Poem Spoken at the Public Commencement at Yale College, in New Haven; September 1, 1781, A (Barlow), **Supp. II Part 1:** 67–68, 74, 75
Poems Retrieved (O'Hara), **Supp. XXIII:** 220
Poems: Selected and New, 1950–1974 (Rich), **Retro. Supp. III:** 247
Poems to Solve (Swenson), **Supp. IV Part 2:** 642
Poems Written and Published during the American Revolutionary War (Freneau), **Supp. II Part 1:** 273, 274
Poems Written between the Years 1768 and 1794 (Freneau), **Supp. II Part 1:** 269
"Poem That Took the Place of a Mountain" (Olson), **Supp. II Part 2:** 582
"Poem to My First Lover" (Olds), **Supp. X:** 206
"Poem to the Reader" (Olds), **Supp. X:** 213
"Poem with No Ending, A" (Levine), **Supp. V:** 186, 190
"Poem You Asked For, The" (Levis), **Supp. XI:** 259–260
Poe Poe Poe Poe Poe Poe Poe (Hoffman), **Retro. Supp. II:** 265
Poesía Náhuatl, **Supp. XV:** 77
Poésies 1917–1920 (Cocteau), **Retro. Supp. I:** 82
"Poesis: A Conceit" (Sobin), **Supp. XVI:** 288
"Poet" (Taggard), **Supp. XXII:** 284
Poet, The (Connelly), **Supp. XXI: 71,** 78
"Poet, The" (Dunbar), **Supp. II Part 1:** 207, 209–210
"Poet, The" (Emerson), **II:** 13, 19, 20, 170; **Retro. Supp. III:** 301
"Poet, The" (Ortiz), **Supp. IV Part 2:** 505
"Poet and His Book, The" (Millay), **III:** 126, 138
"Poet and His Public, The" (Jarrell), **Supp. I Part 1:** 96
"Poet and His Song, The" (Dunbar), **Supp. II Part 1:** 199
"Poet and the Person, The" (Kinard), **Supp. XIV:** 127
"Poet and the Queen, The" (Shaw), **Supp. XIX:** 241
"Poet and the World, The" (Cowley), **Supp. II Part 1:** 145
"Poet as Anti-Specialist, The" (Swenson), **Supp. IV Part 2:** 638, 643
"Poet as Curandera" (Mora), **Supp. XIII:** 214, 220
"Poet as Hero, The: Keats in His Letters" (Trilling), **Supp. III Part 2:** 506–507
"Poet as Religious Moralist, The" (Larson), **Supp. XI:** 328
"Poet at Seven, The" (Rimbaud), **II:** 545
Poet at the Breakfast-Table, The (Holmes), **Supp. I Part 1:** 313–314
"Poète contumace, Le" (Corbiere), **II:** 384–385
"Poet for President, A" (Mora), **Supp. XIII:** 220–221
Poetic Achievement of Ezra Pound, The (Alexander), **Retro. Supp. I:** 293
Poetic Diction: A Study in Meaning (Barfield), **III:** 274, 279
"Poetic Principle, The" (Poe), **III:** 421, 426; **Retro. Supp. II:** 266; **Retro. Supp. III:** 225, 234
"Poetics" (Ammons), **Supp. VII:** 29–30
Poetics (Aristotle), **III:** 422; **Supp. XI:** 249; **Supp. XIII:** 75; **Supp. XIV:** 243; **Supp. XV:** 265
Poetics of Space, The (Bachelard), **Supp. XIII:** 225; **Supp. XVI:** 292
"Poetics of the Periphery: Literary Experimentalism in Kathy Acker's In Memoriam to Identity" (Acker), **Supp. XII:** 17
"Poetics of the Physical World, The" (Kinnell), **Supp. III Part 1:** 239
"Poetics of Tourette Syndrome, The: Language, Neurobiology, and Poetry" (Schleifer), **Supp. XVIII:** 144
Poet in the World, The (Levertov), **Supp. III Part 1:** 271, 273, 278, 282
"Poet or the Growth of a Lit'ry Figure" (White), **Supp. I Part 2:** 676
Poetry (Barber), **Supp. IV Part 2:** 550
"Poetry" (Moore), **III:** 204–205, 215
"Poetry" (Nye), **Supp. XIII:** 282
"Poetry" (Wrigley), **Supp. XVIII:** 301–302
"Poetry, Community and Climax" (Snyder), **Supp. VIII:** 290
"Poetry, Pleasure, and the Hedonist Reader" (Collins), **Supp. XXI:** 54
"Poetry: A Metrical Essay" (Holmes), **Supp. I Part 1:** 310
"Poetry and Belief in Thomas Hardy" (Schwartz), **Supp. II Part 2:** 666
Poetry and Criticism (Nemerov, ed.), **III:** 269
"Poetry and Drama" (Eliot), **I:** 588
Poetry and Fiction: Essays (Nemerov), **III:** 269, 281
"Poetry and Place" (Berry), **Supp. X:** 22, 28, 31, 32
Poetry and Poets (A. Lowell), **II:** 512
"Poetry and Religion" (Jarman), **Supp. XVII:** 111
Poetry and the Age (Jarrell), **IV:** 352; **Retro. Supp. I:** 121; **Supp. II Part 1:** 135
"Poetry and the Primitive: Notes on Poetry as an Ecological Survival Technique" (Snyder), **Supp. VIII:** 291, 292, 299, 300
"Poetry and the Public World" (MacLeish), **III:** 11
Poetry and the World (Pinsky), **Supp. VI:** 236, 239, 244, 247
Poetry and Truth (Olson), **Supp. II Part 2:** 583
"Poetry and Uncertainty"(Hirshfield), **Supp. XXIII:** 137
"Poetry As a Way of Life" (Bishop interview), **Retro. Supp. II:** 53
"Poetry as Survival" (Harrison), **Supp. VIII:** 45
"Poetry Baron, The" (Gallagher), **Supp. XXIV:** 166, 177
"Poetry Failure" (Halliday), **Supp. XIX:** 92
Poetry for Students (Taibl), **Supp. XV:** 255
"Poetry for the Advanced" (Baraka), **Supp. II Part 1:** 58
"Poetry Friendship on Earth" (Halliday), **Supp. XIX:** 90, 91
Poetry Handbook, A (Oliver), **Supp. VII:** 229, 245
Poetry Home Repair Manual, The (Kooser), **Supp. XIX:** 116, 128
Poetry in Motion (film), **Supp. XXIV:** 33
Poetry in Motion: 100 Poems from the Subways and Buses (Peacock, ed.), **Supp. XIX:** 195
"Poetry in Translation: Literary Imperialism or, Defending the Musk Ox" (Gallagher), **Supp. XXIV:** 172
"Poetry of Barbarism, The" (Santayana), **IV:** 353
Poetry of Chaucer, The (Gardner), **Supp. VI: 63**
Poetry of Meditation, The (Martz), **IV:** 151; **Supp. I Part 1:** 107
Poetry of Mourning: The Modern Elegy from Hardy to Heaney (Ramazani), **Supp. IV Part 2:** 450
Poetry of Stephen Crane, The (Hoffman), **I:** 405
Poetry of the Negro, 1746–1949, The

(Hughes and Bontemps), **Supp. I Part 1:** 345; **Supp. XXII:** 11
Poetry 180: A Turning Back to Poetry (Collins, ed.), **Supp. XXI:** 54
Poetry Reading against the Vietnam War, A (Bly and Ray, eds.), **Supp. IV Part 1:** 61, 63
"Poetry Workshop, The" (column, Kumin), **Supp. XX: 164**
"Poetry Wreck, The" (Shapiro), **Supp. II Part 2:** 717
Poetry Wreck, The: Selected Essays (Shapiro), **Supp. II Part 2:** 703, 704, 717
"Poets" (X. J. Kennedy), **Supp. XV:** 158
Poet's Alphabet, A: Reflections on the Literary Art and Vocation (Bogan), **Supp. III Part 1:** 55, 64
Poets and Poetry of America (Griswold), **Supp. XV:** 277; **Supp. XXV:** 250
Poets and Poetry of America, The (Griswold), **Retro. Supp. III:** 236
Poet's Choice (Engle and Langland, eds.), **III:** 277, 542
Poet's Guide to Poetry, A (Kinzie), **Supp. XXIII:** 124
"Poet's Husband Engages in Gourmet Cooking, The" (Espaillat), **Supp. XXI:** 99
Poets of the Old Testament, The (Gordon), **III:** 199
Poets of Today (Hall, ed.), **Supp. XXVII:** 253, 256
Poets of Today (Wheelock, ed.), **Supp. IV Part 2:** 639
Poets on Poetry (Nemerov, ed.), **III:** 269
"Poet's Tact, and a Necessary Tactlessness, The" (C. Frost), **Supp. XV:** 94–95
"Poet's View, A" (Levertov), **Supp. III Part 1:** 284
"Poet's Voice, The" (Oliver), **Supp. VII:** 245
"Poets with History and Poets Without History"(Tsvetaeva), **Supp. XXIII:** 168
"Poet Turns on Himself, The" (Dickey), **Supp. IV Part 1:** 177, 181, 185
Poganuc People (Stowe), **Supp. I Part 2:** 581, 596, 599–600
Pogo (comic strip), **Supp. XI:** 105
Pohl, R. D., **Supp. XXVI:** 102
Pohrt, Tom, **Supp. XIX:** 123
Poincaré, Raymond, **IV:** 320
"Point, The" (Hayden), **Supp. II Part 1:** 373
"Point at Issue!, A" (Chopin), **Retro. Supp. II:** 61; **Supp. I Part 1:** 208
"Point of Age, A" (Berryman), **I:** 173
Point of No Return (Marquand), **III:** 56, 59–60, 65, 67, 69
Point Reyes Poems (R. Bly), **Supp. IV Part 1:** 71
"Points" (Hoffman), **Supp. XVIII:** 86
Points for a Compass Rose (Connell), **Supp. XIV:** 79, 80, 96
"Point Shirley" (Plath), **Supp. I Part 2:** 529, 538
Points in Time (Bowles), **Supp. IV Part 1:** 93
"Points West" (column), **Supp. IV Part 1:** 198
Poirier, Richard, **I:** 136, 239; **III:** 34; **Retro. Supp. I:** 134; **Retro. Supp. II:** 207–208; **Retro. Supp. III:** 102; **Supp. I Part 2:** 660, 665; **Supp. IV Part 2:** 690
"Poison Oak" (Huddle), **Supp. XXVI:** 148, 152
Poison Pen (Garrett), **Supp. VII:** 111
Poisonwood Bible, The (Kingsolver), **Supp. VII:** 197–198, 202, 210–213
Poitier, Sidney, **Supp. IV Part 1:** 360, 362
Pokerface (Collins), **Supp. XXI:** 53
"Polack Reverie" (Halliday), **Supp. XIX:** 88
Polanco, Richard, **Supp. XX: 260**
"Polar Bear" (Heller), **Supp. IV Part 1:** 383
"Polar Bears and Others" (Boyle), **Supp. XXIV:** 57
"Polar Seas and Sir John Franklin, The" (Briggs), **Supp. XVIII:** 14
Pole, Rupert, **Supp. X:** 185
"Pole Star" (MacLeish), **III:** 16
Po Li, **Supp. I Part 1:** 262
Police (Baraka), **Supp. II Part 1:** 47
"Police" (Corso), **Supp. XII:** 117, 127
"Police Court Saturday Morning" (X. J. Kennedy), **Supp. XV:** 170
"Police Dreams" (Bausch), **Supp. VII:** 47
Politian (Poe), **III:** 412; **Retro. Supp. III:** 234
"Political and Practical Conceptions of Race, The" (Locke), **Supp. XIV:** 209–210
Political Essays (J. R. Lowell), **Supp. I Part 2:** 407
Political Fable, A (Coover), **Supp. V:** 44, 46, 47, 49, 51
"Political Fables" (Mather), **Supp. II Part 2:** 450
"Political Interests" (Stevens), **Retro. Supp. I:** 295
"Political Litany, A" (Freneau), **Supp. II Part 1:** 257
"Political Migrations: A Family Story" (Mallon), **Supp. XIX:** 141–142
"Political Pastoral" (Frost), **Retro. Supp. I:** 139
"Political Poem" (Baraka), **Supp. II Part 1:** 36
Politics (Acker), **Supp. XII:** 3, 4
Politics (Macdonald), **I:** 233–234
"Politics" (Paley), **Supp. VI:** 217
"Politics, Structure, and Poetic Development" (McCombs), **Supp. XIII:** 33
"Politics and the English Language" (Orwell), **Retro. Supp. II:** 287; **Supp. I Part 2:** 620
Politics and the Novel (Howe), **Supp. VI:** 113
"Politics and the Personal Lyric in the Poetry of Joy Harjo and C. D. Wright" (Goodman), **Supp. XV:** 344
"Politics of Ethnic Authorship, The: Li-Young Lee, Emerson, and Whitman at the Banquet Table" (Partridge), **Supp. XV:** 219
"Politics of Silence, The" (Monette), **Supp. X:** 148
Polito, Robert, **Supp. XVIII:** 33; **Supp. XXIV:** 234; **Supp. XXVI:** 55
Politt, Katha, **Supp. XII:** 159
Poliziano (Angelo Ambrogini), **Supp. XXIV:** 152
Polk, James, **Supp. XIII:** 20
Polk, James K., **I:** 17; **II:** 433–434
Pollack, Sydney, **Supp. XIII:** 159
"Pollen" (Nye), **Supp. XIII:** 284
Pollitt, Katha, **Supp. X:** 186, 191, 193; **Supp. XVI:** 39
Pollock, Jackson, **IV:** 411, 420; **Supp. XIX:** 33; **Supp. XV:** 145, 177, 178; **Supp. XXIII:** 208, 210, 211
"Polly" (Chopin), **Retro. Supp. II:** 72
Polo, Marco, **III:** 395
Polonsky, Abraham, **Supp. XXI:** 261, 275
Polybius, **Supp. I Part 2:** 491
"Polydore" (Chopin), **Retro. Supp. II:** 66
"Pomegranate" (Glück), **Supp. V:** 82
"Pomegranate Seed" (Wharton), **IV:** 316; **Retro. Supp. I:** 382
Ponce de Leon, Luis, **III:** 391
"Pond, The" (Nemerov), **III:** 272
"Pond at Dusk, The" (Kenyon), **Supp. VII:** 168
Ponder Heart, The (Welty), **IV:** 261, 274–275, 281; **Retro. Supp. I:** 351–352
"Ponderosa Pine" (Huncke), **Supp.**

XIV: 146
Ponsot, Margaret, **Supp. XVII:** 241
"Pony" (Sanders), **Supp. XVI:** 277
"Pony Car"(P. Benedict), **Supp. XXIII:** 47
Poodle Springs (Parker and Chandler), **Supp. IV Part 1:** 135; **Supp. XIX:** 189
Poodle Springs Story, The (Chandler), **Supp. IV Part 1:** 135
"Pool, The" (Doolittle), **Supp. I Part 1:** 264–265
Poole, Ernest, **II:** 444
"Pool Lights" (F. Barthelme), **Supp. XI:** 25, 26–27, 36
"Pool Room in the Lions Club" (Merwin), **Supp. III Part 1:** 346
"Poolside" (Skloot), **Supp. XX: 202–203**
"Poor Black Fellow" (Hughes), **Retro. Supp. I:** 204
"Poor Bustard, The" (Corso), **Supp. XII:** 134
"Poor but Happy" (Mamet), **Supp. XIV:** 252, 253
"Poor Dead Feet of My First Husband, The"(Schott), **Supp. XXIII:** 241
Poore, Charles, **III:** 364; **Supp. XIX:** 257, 264; **Supp. XX: 38**
Poor Fool (Caldwell), **I:** 291, 292, 308
Poorhouse Fair, The (Updike), **IV:** 214, 228–229, 232; **Retro. Supp. I:** 317, 320
"Poor Joanna" (Jewett), **II:** 394
"Poor Man's Pudding and Rich Man's Crumbs" (Melville), **III:** 89–90
"Poor Richard" (James), **II:** 322
Poor Richard's Almanac for 1733 (Franklin), **II:** 108, 110
Poor Richard's Almanac for 1739 (Franklin), **II:** 112
Poor Richard's Almanac for 1758 (Franklin), **II:** 101
Poor Richard's Almanac (undated) (Franklin), **II:** 112
Poor White (Anderson), **I:** 110–111
"Poor Working Girl" (Z. Fitzgerald), **Supp. IX:** 71
Popa, Vasko, **Supp. VIII:** 272
Pope, Alexander, **I:** 198, 204; **II:** 17, 114; **III:** 263, 267, 288, 517; **IV:** 145; **Retro. Supp. I:** 335; **Supp. I Part 1:** 150, 152, 310; **Supp. I Part 2:** 407, 422, 516, 714; **Supp. II Part 1:** 70, 71; **Supp. X:** 32, 36; **Supp. XII:** 260; **Supp. XV:** 258; **Supp. XX: 280; Supp. XXV:** 119; **Supp. XXVI:** 284
Pope, James, **Supp. XXII:** 196
Pope-Hennessy, James, **Supp. XIV:** 348
"Pope's Penis, The" (Olds), **Supp. X:** 207
"Poplar, Sycamore" (Wilbur), **Supp. III Part 2:** 549
Popo and Fifina: Children of Haiti (Hughes and Bontemps), **Retro. Supp. I:** 203; **Supp. XXII:** 4, 10, 12
"Poppies" (Oliver), **Supp. VII:** 240
"Poppies in July" (Plath), **Supp. I Part 2:** 544
"Poppies in July"(Crooker), **Supp. XXIII:** 61
"Poppies in October" (Plath), **Supp. I Part 2:** 544
"Poppycock" (Francis), **Supp. IX:** 87
"Poppy Juice" (Taggard), **Supp. XXII:** 276
"Poppy Seed" (A. Lowell), **II:** 523
"Popular Art and the Cultural Tradition" (C. L. R. James), **Supp. XXI:** 170
Popular Book, The: A History of America's Literary Taste (Hart), **Supp. XVIII:** 257, 258
Popular Culture (Goldbarth), **Supp. XII: 186**
Popular History of the United States (Gay), **Supp. I Part 1:** 158
Popular Problems (album, Cohen), **Supp. XXVII:** 63
"Popular Songs" (Ashbery), **Supp. III Part 1:** 6
"Populist Manifesto" (Ferlinghetti), **Supp. VIII:** 290
"Porcelain Bowl" (Glück), **Supp. V:** 83
Porcher, Frances, **Retro. Supp. II:** 71
Porco, Mike, **Supp. XVIII:** 24
"Porcupine, The" (Kinnell), **Supp. III Part 1:** 244
Porcupine's Kiss, The (Dobyns), **Supp. XIII: 89–90**
"Por esas coases que pasan" (Hinojosa), **Supp. XIX:** 101
Porgy and Bess (film), **Supp. I Part 1:** 66
Porgy and Bess (play), **Supp. IV Part 1:** 6
"Porn Bought my Football" (Offutt), **Supp. XIX:** 163
"Porphyria's Lover" (Browning), **II:** 522
Portable Beat Reader, The (Charters, ed.), **Supp. XIV:** 152
Portable Blake, The (Kazin, ed.), **Supp. VIII:** 103
Portable Faulkner, The (Cowley, ed.), **II:** 57, 59; **Retro. Supp. I:** 73
Portable Kisses: Love Poems (Gallagher), **Supp. XXIV:** 170
Portable Paul and Jane Bowles, The (Dillon), **Supp. IV Part 1:** 95
Portable Veblen, The (Veblen), **Supp. I Part 2:** 630, 650
"Porte-Cochere" (Taylor), **Supp. V:** 320
"Porter" (Hughes), **Supp. I Part 1:** 327
"Porter" (Nelson), **Supp. XVIII:** 175
Porter, Bern, **III:** 171
Porter, Cole, **Supp. IX:** 189
Porter, Eliot, **Supp. IV Part 2:** 599
Porter, Fairfield, **Supp. XV:** 178; **Supp. XXIII:** 209, 211, 212; **Supp. XXIV:** 41; **Supp. XXVII:** 21
Porter, Herman W., **Supp. I Part 1:** 49
Porter, Horace, **Retro. Supp. II:** 4, 127
Porter, Jacob, **Supp. I Part 1:** 153
Porter, Katherine Anne, **I:** 97, 385; **II:** 194, 606; **III: 433–455,** 482; **IV:** 26, 138, 246, 261, 279, 280, 282; **Retro. Supp. I:** 354; **Retro. Supp. II:** 233, 235; **Retro. Supp. III:** 36, 37, 53; **Supp. IV Part 1:** 31, 310; **Supp. IX:** 93, 94, 95, 98, 128; **Supp. V:** 225; **Supp. VIII:** 156, 157; **Supp. X:** 50; **Supp. XIII:** 294; **Supp. XIV:** 3; **Supp. XV:** 338; **Supp. XXIV:** 52; **Supp. XXVI:** 23
Porter, Nicodemus, **Supp. XXVI:** 87
Porter, Noah, **Supp. I Part 2:** 640
Porter, William Sydney. See Henry, O.
"Porter Paints a Picture"(O'Hara), **Supp. XXIII:** 212
Porteus, Beilby, **Supp. I Part 1:** 150
Portis, Rowe, **Supp. XXVI:** 147
"Portland Going Out, The" (Merwin), **Supp. III Part 1:** 345
Portnoy's Complaint (P. Roth), **Retro. Supp. II: 282–286,** 291; **Supp. III Part 2:** 401, 404, 405, 407, 412–414, 426; **Supp. V:** 119, 122; **Supp. XI:** 140; **Supp. XVII:** 8, 43; **Supp. XX: 177; Supp. XXVII:** 142
Port of Saints (Burroughs), **Supp. III Part 1:** 106
"Portrait" (Dixon), **Supp. XII:** 154
"Portrait, A" (Parker), **Supp. IX:** 192–193
"Portrait, The" (Kunitz), **Supp. III Part 1:** 263
"Portrait, The" (Wharton), **Retro. Supp. I:** 364
"Portrait d'une Femme" (Pound), **Retro. Supp. I:** 288
Portrait in Brownstone (Auchincloss), **Supp. IV Part 1:** 21, 23, 27, 31

"Portrait in Georgia" (Toomer), **Supp. IX:** 314
"Portrait in Greys, A" (W. C. Williams), **Retro. Supp. I:** 416
"Portrait of a Girl in Glass" (T. Williams), **IV:** 383
"Portrait of a Jewelry Drummer" (Untermeyer), **Supp. XV:** 299–300
"Portrait of a Lady" (T. S. Eliot), **I:** 569, 570, 571, 584; **III:** 4; **Retro. Supp. I:** 55, 56, 62; **Retro. Supp. III:** 60–61
Portrait of a Lady, The (James), **I:** 10, 258, 461–462, 464; **II:** 323, 325, 327, 328–329, 334; **Retro. Supp. I:** 215, 216, 217, 219, 220, 223, **224–225,** 232, 233, 381
"Portrait of an Artist" (P. Roth), **Supp. III Part 2:** 412
Portrait of an Eye: Three Novels (Acker), **Supp. XII:** 6, **7–9**
"Portrait of an Invisible Man" (Auster), **Supp. XII:** 21
"Portrait of a Supreme Court Judge" (Untermeyer), **Supp. XV:** 299
Portrait of Bascom Hawkes, A (Wolfe), **IV:** 451–452, 456
Portrait of Edith Wharton (Lubbock), **Retro. Supp. I:** 366
Portrait of Logan Pearsall Smith, Drawn from His Letters and Diaries, A (Russell, ed.), **Supp. XIV:** 349
Portrait of Picasso as a Young Man (Mailer), **Retro. Supp. II:** 213
"Portrait of the Artist as an Old Man, A" (Humphrey), **Supp. IX:** 109
Portrait of the Artist as a Young Man, A (Joyce), **I:** 475–476; **III:** 471, 561; **Retro. Supp. I:** 127; **Retro. Supp. II:** 4, 331; **Supp. IX:** 236; **Supp. XIII:** 53, 95
"Portrait of the Artist with Hart Crane" (Wright), **Supp. V:** 342
"Portrait of the Great White Hunter Foxhunting in the Absence of Big Game" (Major), **Supp. XXII:** 183
"Portrait of the Intellectual as a Yale Man" (McCarthy), **II:** 563, 564–565
"Portrait of the Reader with a Bowl of Cereal, A" (Collins), **Supp. XXI:** 55
"Portrait of the Self . . . , A" (Sobin), **Supp. XVI:** 288
Portraits and Elegies (Schnackenberg), **Supp. XV:** 249, **253–256**
"Portraits of Grief" (New York Times), **Supp. XIX:** 142
"Port Town" (Hughes), **Retro. Supp. I:** 199
Portuguese Voyages to America in the Fifteenth Century (Morison), **Supp. I Part 2:** 488
"Po' Sandy" (Chesnutt), **Supp. XIV:** 60
Poseidon Adventure, The (film), **Supp. XII:** 321
Poseidon Adventure, The (Gallico), **Supp. XVI:** 238
"Poseidon and Company" (Carver), **Supp. III Part 1:** 137
"Positive Obsession" (O. Butler), **Supp. XIII:** 70
Poss, Stanley, **Supp. XIV:** 166
Possession (Byatt), **Supp. XXI:** 147
"Possessions" (H. Crane), **I:** 392–393; **Retro. Supp. II:** 78
Possible World, A (Koch), **Supp. XV:** 184
Postal Inspector (film), **Supp. XIII:** 166
"Postcard from Greece" (Stallings), **Supp. XXV:** 229, 231
Postcards (Proulx), **Supp. VII:** 249, 256–258, 262
"Postcard to Send to Sumer, A" (Bronk), **Supp. XXI:** 31
"Postcolonialism and Autobiography" (Skinner and Waller), **Supp. XXII:** 78
"Postcolonial Tale, A" (Harjo), **Supp. XII:** 227
"Posthumous Letter to Gilbert White" (Auden), **Supp. II Part 1:** 26
"Post-Larkin Triste" (Karr), **Supp. XI:** 242–243
Postlethwaite, Diana, **Supp. XII:** 317–318; **Supp. XVI:** 176
"Postlude" (W. C. Williams), **Retro. Supp. I:** 415
Post-Luria, Sheila, **Retro. Supp. III:** 158, 160
Postman, Neil, **Supp. XI:** 275
Postman Always Rings Twice, The (Cain), **Supp. XIII:** 165–166
Postman Always Rings Twice, The (film), **Supp. XIV:** 241
"Postmaster and the Clerk, The" (Budbill), **Supp. XIX:** 9
"Postmortem Guide, A" (Dunn), **Supp. XI:** 155
Post Oaks and Sand Roughs (Howard), **Supp. XXVII:** 116
Postrel, Virginia, **Supp. XIV:** 298, 311
"Postscript" (Du Bois), **Supp. II Part 1:** 173
"Postscript" (Nye), **Supp. XIII:** 287
Postsouthern Sense of Place, The (Bone), **Supp. XXII:** 247
"Potato" (Wilbur), **Supp. III Part 2:** 545
"Potatoes' Dance, The" (Lindsay), **Supp. I Part 2:** 394
Pot of Earth, The (MacLeish), **III:** 5, 6–8, 10, 12, 18
Potok, Chaim, **Supp. XXVI:** 124
"Pot Roast" (Strand), **Supp. IV Part 2:** 629
Potshot (Parker), **Supp. XIX:** 185
Pot Shots at Poetry (Francis), **Supp. IX: 83–84**
Potter, Beatrix, **Supp. I Part 2:** 656; **Supp. XVI:** 100
Potter, Stephen, **IV:** 430
Potter's House, The (Stegner), **Supp. IV Part 2:** 598, 606
Poulenc, Francis, **Supp. IV Part 1:** 81
Poulin, Al, Jr., **Supp. IX:** 272; **Supp. XI:** 259
Pound, Ezra, **I:** 49, 58, 60, 66, 68, 69, 105, 236, 243, 256, 384, 403, 428, 429, 475, 476, 482, 487, 521, 578; **II:** 26, 55, 168, 263, 316, 371, 376, 513, 517, 520, 526, 528, 529, 530; **III:** 2, 5, 8, 9, 13–14, 17, 174, 194, 196, 278, 430, 453, **456–479,** 492, 504, 511, 523, 524, 527, 575–576, 586, 590; **IV:** 27, 28, 407, 415, 416, 433, 446; **Retro. Supp. I:** 51, 52, 55, 58, 59, 63, 82, 89, 127, 140, 171, 177, 178, 198, 216, **283–294,** 298, 299, 359, 411, 412, 413, 414, 417, 418, 419, 420, 423, 426, 427, 430, 431; **Retro. Supp. II:** 178, 183, 189, 326; **Retro. Supp. III:** 58, 59, 74, 96; **Supp. I Part 1:** 253, 255–258, 261–268, 272, 274; **Supp. I Part 2:** 387, 721; **Supp. II Part 1:** 1, 8, 20, 30, 91, 136; **Supp. III Part 1:** 48, 63, 64, 73, 105, 146, 225, 271; **Supp. III Part 2:** 542, **609–617,** 619, 620, 622, 625, 626, 628, 631; **Supp. IV Part 1:** 153, 314; **Supp. IX:** 291; **Supp. V:** 331, 338, 340, 343, 345; **Supp. VIII:** 39, 105, 195, 205, 271, 290, 291, 292, 303; **Supp. X:** 24, 36, 112, 120, 122; **Supp. XII:** 97; **Supp. XIV:** 11, 55, 83, 272, 284, 286, 287, 347; **Supp. XIX:** 42; **Supp. XV:** 20, 42, 43, 51, 93, 161, 181, 297, 298, 299, 301, 302, 306; **Supp. XVI:** 47, 282; **Supp. XVII:** 111, 226–227; **Supp. XXI:** 33; **Supp. XXII:** 165; **Supp. XXIII:** 26, 166, 174; **Supp. XXIV:** 37; **Supp. XXVI:** 143, 144, 224, 226; **Supp. XXVII:** 261, 284, 287, 288
Pound, Louise, **Retro. Supp. I:** 4; **Supp. XV:** 137
Pound, T. S., **I:** 428
"Pound Reweighed" (Cowley), **Supp.**

II Part 1: 143
Powell, Anthony, **Supp. XIX:** 131; **Supp. XVIII:** 136, 146
Powell, Betty, **Retro. Supp. II:** 140
Powell, D. A., **Supp. XXIII:** 221
Powell, Dawn, **Supp. IV Part 2:** 678, 682; **Supp. XIX:** 143
Powell, Dick, **Supp. IX:** 250
Powell, John Wesley, **Supp. IV Part 2:** 598, 604, 611
Powell, Lawrence Clark, **III:** 189
Powell, Margaret K., **Supp. XXIV:** 170
Powell, William, **Supp. IV Part 1:** 355
"Power" (Corso), **Supp. XII:** 117, 126, 127, **128**
"Power" (Emerson), **II:** 2, 3
"Power" (Rich), **Retro. Supp. III:** 249; **Supp. I Part 2:** 569
Power, Samantha, **Supp. XXIII:** 25, 26, 27
"Power and Danger: Works of a Common Woman" (Rich), **Retro. Supp. III:** 248
"Power and Light" (Dickey), **Supp. IV Part 1:** 182
Power and the Glory, The (Greene), **III:** 556
"Powerhouse" (Welty), **Retro. Supp. I:** 343, 346
"Power Never Dominion" (Rukeyser), **Supp. VI:** 281
"Power of Fancy, The" (Freneau), **Supp. II Part 1:** 255
Power of Myth, The (Campbell), **Supp. IX:** 245
"Power of Prayer, The" (Lanier), **Supp. I Part 1:** 357
"Power of Stories, The" (Sanders), **Supp. XVI:** 278
"Power of Suggestion" (Auchincloss), **Supp. IV Part 1:** 33
Power of Sympathy, The (W. H. Brown), **Supp. II Part 1:** 74; **Supp. XXV:** 38
Power Politics (Atwood), **Supp. XIII:** 20, 33–34, 35
Powers, Catherine A., **Supp. XXII:** 217
Powers, J. F., **Supp. V:** 319; **Supp. XVII:** 43
Powers, Kim, **Supp. VIII:** 329, 340
Powers, Richard, **Supp. IX: 207–225; Supp. XVII:** 183; **Supp. XX: 93; Supp. XXII:** 49; **Supp. XXIV:** 131
Powers of Attorney (Auchincloss), **Supp. IV Part 1:** 31, 32, 33
"Powers of Darkness" (Wharton), **Retro. Supp. I:** 379
"Powers of Recuperation" (Rich), **Retro. Supp. III:** 252
Powless, Peter, **Supp. XXVI:** 87
Powys, John Cowper, **Supp. I Part 2:** 454, 476; **Supp. IX:** 135
Poynton, Jerome, **Supp. XIV:** 147, 150
Pozorski, Aimee L., **Supp. XXII:** 160, 166
Practical Agitation (Chapman), **Supp. XIV:** 41
"Practical Application in This Life, by Men as Social and Intellectual Beings, of the Certainty of a Future State, The" (Very), **Supp. XXV:** 240
Practical Criticism: A Study of Literary Judgment (Richards), **Supp. XIV:** 3, 16
Practical Magic (film), **Supp. X:** 80
Practical Magic (Hoffman), **Supp. X:** 78, 82, **88–89**
"Practical Methods of Meditation, The" (Dawson), **IV:** 151
Practical Navigator, The (Bowditch), **Supp. I Part 2:** 482
Practice of Perspective, The (Dubreuil), **Supp. IV Part 2:** 425
Practice of Reading, The (Donoghue), **Supp. VIII:** 189
Pragmatism (W. James), **Supp. XXVII:** 33
Pragmatism: A New Name for Some Old Ways of Thinking (James), **II:** 352
"Pragmatism's Conception of Truth" (James), **Supp. XIV:** 40
Prague Orgy, The (P. Roth), **Retro. Supp. II:** 280
"Praire, The" (Clampitt), **Supp. IX:** 42
"Prairie" (Sandburg), **III:** 583, 584
Prairie, The (Cooper), **I:** 339, 342
"Prairie Birthday" (Leopold), **Supp. XIV:** 185
Prairie Home Companion, A (Keillor, radio program), **Supp. XIII:** 274; **Supp. XVI:** 169–171, 173–178
Prairie Home Morning Show, A (Keillor, radio program), **Supp. XVI:** 171
"Prairie Life, A Citizen Speaks" (Dunn), **Supp. XI:** 145
"Prairies, The" (Bryant), **Supp. I Part 1:** 157, 162, 163, 166
"Prairie Spring" (Cather), **Retro. Supp. III:** 23
Praise (Hass), **Supp. VI:** 104–105, 106
"Praise for an Urn" (Crane), **I:** 388
"Praise for Sick Women" (Snyder), **Supp. VIII:** 294
"Praise in Summer" (Wilbur), **Supp. III Part 2:** 546–548, 560, 562
"Praise of a Palmtree" (Levertov), **Supp. III Part 1:** 284
"Praise of the Committee" (Rukeyser), **Supp. VI:** 278
"Praises, The" (Goldbarth), **Supp. XII:** 185
"Praises, The" (Olson), **Supp. II Part 2:** 558, 560, 563, 564
Praises and Dispraises (Des Pres), **Supp. X:** 120
Praisesong for the Widow (Marshall), **Supp. IV Part 1:** 14; **Supp. XI:** 18, 276, 278, **284–286,** 287; **Supp. XX: 154**
"Praise to the End!" (Roethke), **III:** 529, 532, 539
Prajadhipok, King of Siam, **I:** 522
Prater Violet (Isherwood), **Supp. XIV: 164–166,** 169–170, 171
Pratt, Anna (Anna Alcott), **Supp. I Part 1:** 33
Pratt, Louis H., **Retro. Supp. II:** 6
Pratt, Mary Louise, **Retro. Supp. II:** 48
Pratt, Parley, **Supp. IV Part 2:** 603
"Prattler" (newspaper column), **I:** 207
"Prattler, The" (Bierce), **I:** 196
"Prayer" (Gioia), **Supp. XV:** 117
"Prayer" (Olds), **Supp. X:** 204
"Prayer" (Peacock), **Supp. XIX:** 198, 199, 200
"Prayer" (Toomer), **Supp. IX:** 318
"Prayer, A" (Kushner), **Supp. IX: 134**
"Prayer for Columbus" (Whitman), **IV:** 348
"Prayer for My Daughter" (Yeats), **II:** 598
"Prayer for My Grandfather to Our Lady, A" (R. Lowell), **II:** 541–542
"Prayer for my Son" (C. Frost), **Supp. XV:** 98–99
"Prayer for Our Daughters" (Jarman), **Supp. XVII:** 120
Prayer for Owen Meany, A (Irving), **Supp. VI:** 164, 165, 166, **175–176**
"PRAYER FOR SAVING" (Baraka), **Supp. II Part 1:** 52–53
Prayer for the Dying, A (O'Nan), **Supp. XXV:** 141, 142, 144, 145–146, 148
"Prayer in Spring, A" (Frost), **II:** 153, 164
"Prayer Meeting" (Di Piero), **Supp. XIX:** 46, 47
"Prayer on All Saint's Day" (Cowley), **Supp. II Part 1:** 138, 153
Prayers for Dark People (Du Bois), **Supp. II Part 1:** 186
"Prayer to Hermes" (Creeley), **Supp. IV Part 1:** 156, 157
"Prayer to Masks" (Senghor), **Supp. IV Part 1:** 16
"Prayer to the Child of Prague"

(Salinas), **Supp. XIII:** 327
"Prayer to the Good Poet" (Wright), **Supp. III Part 2:** 603
"Prayer to the Pacific" (Silko), **Supp. IV Part 2:** 560
"Prayer to the Verb" (Davison), **Supp. XXVI:** 79
Praying Wrong (Davison), **Supp. XXVI:** 66, 76–77
"Pray without Ceasing" (Emerson), **II:** 9–10
Praz, Mario, **IV:** 430
"Preacher, The" (Whittier), **Supp. I Part 2:** 698–699
Preacher and the Slave, The (Stegner), **Supp. IV Part 2:** 599, 608, 609
"Preacher Is Called to Testify for the Accused, The" (Rash), **Supp. XXVII:** 219
"Preacher Who Takes Up Serpents Laments the Presence of Skeptics in His Church, A" (Rash), **Supp. XXVII:** 219
Precaution (Cooper), **I:** 337, 339
"Precautions"(Karyotakis, trans. Hadas), **Supp. XXIII:** 125
"Preconceptions of Economic Science, The" (Veblen), **Supp. I Part 2:** 634
Predecessors, Et Cetera (Clampitt), **Supp. IX:** 37
"Predicament, A" (Poe), **Retro. Supp. II:** 273
Predilections (Moore), **III:** 194
Prefaces and Prejudices (Mencken), **III:** 99, 104, 106, 119
Preface to a Twenty Volume Suicide Note. . . . (Baraka), **Supp. II Part 1:** 31, 33–34, 51, 61
"Preference" (Wylie), **Supp. I Part 2:** 713
"Prejudice against the Past, The" (Moore), **IV:** 91
Prejudices (Mencken), **Supp. I Part 2:** 630
Prejudices: A Selection (Farrell, ed.), **III:** 116
Prejudices: First Series (Mencken), **III:** 105
"Preliminary Remarks on the Poetry in the First Person" (Wright), **Supp. XV:** 339
Prell (exhibition, Brainard), **Supp. XXVII:** 21
Prelude, A: Landscapes, Characters and Conversations from the Earlier Years of My Life (Wilson), **IV:** 426, 427, 430, 434, 445
Prelude, The (Wordsworth), **III:** 528; **IV:** 331, 343; **Supp. I Part 2:** 416, 676; **Supp. XI:** 248
Prelude and Liebestod (McNally), **Supp. XIII:** 201
"Preludes" (T. S. Eliot), **I:** 573, 576, 577; **Retro. Supp. I:** 55; **Retro. Supp. III:** 60; **Supp. IV Part 2:** 436
Preludes for Memnon (Aiken), **I:** 59, 65
Preludes from Memnon (Aiken), **Supp. X:** 50
"Prelude to an Evening" (Ransom), **III:** 491, 492–493
Prelude to Darkness (Salinas), **Supp. XIII:** 311, **318–319,** 320
"Prelude to the Present" (Mumford), **Supp. II Part 2:** 471
"Premature Burial, The" (Poe), **III:** 415, 416, 418; **Retro. Supp. II:** 270
"Premeditations"(Schott), **Supp. XXIII:** 247
Preminger, Otto, **Supp. IX:** 3, 9; **Supp. XX: 246–247**
"Premonition" (Hay), **Supp. XIV:** 122
"Premonitions of the Bread Line" (Komunyakaa), **Supp. XIII:** 114, 115
Prenshaw, Peggy Whitman, **Supp. X:** 229
"Preparations" (Silko), **Supp. IV Part 2:** 560
Preparatory Meditations (Taylor), **IV:** 145, 148, 149, 150, 152, 153, 154–155, 164, 165
"Prepare" (Carruth), **Supp. XVI:** 59
Prepositions: The Collected Critical Essays of Louis Zukofsky (Zukofsky), **Supp. III Part 2:** 630
Prescott, Anne, **Supp. IV Part 1:** 299
Prescott, Orville, **Supp. IV Part 2:** 680; **Supp. XI:** 340; **Supp. XXIII:** 13
Prescott, Peter, **Supp. X:** 83
Prescott, Peter S., **Supp. XVI:** 212
Prescott, William, **Retro. Supp. I:** 123
Prescott, William Hickling, **II:** 9, 310, 313–314; **IV:** 309; **Supp. I Part 2:** 414, 479, 493, 494
"Prescription of Painful Ends" (Jeffers), **Supp. II Part 2:** 424
"Presence, The" (Gordon), **II:** 199, 200
"Presence, The" (Kumin), **Supp. IV Part 2:** 445, 455
Presence and Desire: Essays on Gender, Sexuality, Performance (Dolan), **Supp. XV:** 327
"Presence of Others, The" (Kenyon), **Supp. VII:** 164
Presences (Taylor), **Supp. V:** 325
"Present Age, The" (Emerson), **II:** 11–12
Present Danger, The: Do We Have the Will to Reverse the Decline of American Power? (Podhoretz), **Supp. VIII:** 241
"Present for the Boy, A" (Swados), **Supp. XIX:** 259
Present for Young Ladies, A (Rowson), **Supp. XV:** 245
"Present Hour" (Sandburg), **III:** 593–594
Presenting Walter Dean Myers (Bishop), **Supp. XXVII:** 203
Present Philosophical Tendencies (Perry), **I:** 224
"Present State of Ethical Philosophy, The" (Emerson), **II:** 9
"Present State of Poetry, The" (Schwartz), **Supp. II Part 2:** 666
"Preservation of Innocence" (Baldwin), **Supp. I Part 1:** 51
"Preserving Wildness" (Berry), **Supp. X:** 28, 29, 32
"President and Other Intellectuals, The" (Kazin), **Supp. VIII:** 104
Presidential Papers, The (Mailer), **III:** 35, 37–38, 42, 45; **Retro. Supp. II:** 203, 204, 206
"Presidents" (Merwin), **Supp. III Part 1:** 351
Presnell, Robert, Sr., **Supp. XIII:** 166
Pressley, Nelson, **Supp. XVIII:** 37–38
"PRES SPOKE IN A LANGUAGE" (Baraka), **Supp. II Part 1:** 60
"Presto Manifesto" (Stallings), **Supp. XXV:** 227
Presumed Innocent (Turow), 217; **Supp. XVII:** 214–216, 223
Pretending to Be Asleep (Davison), **Supp. XXVI:** 65, 71–72
"Pretext, The" (Wharton), **Retro. Supp. I:** 371
Pretty Baby (film), **Supp. XXI:** 252
Pretty Boy Floyd (McMurtry), **Supp. V:** 231
"Pretty Girl, The" (Dubus), **Supp. VII:** 87–88
"Pretty Mouth and Green My Eyes" (Salinger), **III:** 560
"Previous Condition" (Baldwin), **Supp. I Part 1:** 51, 55, 63
"Previous Tenant, The" (Simpson), **Supp. IX:** 278–279
Prevost, Verbie Lovorn, **Supp. XXI:** 45
Priaulx, Allan, **Supp. XI:** 228
Price, Alan, **Retro. Supp. I:** 377
Price, E. Hoffman, **Supp. XXV:** 114
Price, Novalyne, **Supp. XXVII:** 117
Price, Reynolds, **Supp. IX:** 256, 257; **Supp. VI: 253–270**

Price, Richard, **II:** 9; **Supp. I Part 2:** 522; **Supp. XX: 85**
Price, The (A. Miller), **III:** 165–166; **Retro. Supp. III:** 172, 173–174
"Price, The: The Power of the Past" (A. Miller), **Retro. Supp. III:** 174
"Price Is Right, The" (Skloot), **Supp. XX: 198–199**
"Price of Poetry, The" (Biss), **Supp. XXVI:** 48
"Price of the Harness, The" (Crane), **I:** 414
Pricksongs & Descants; Fictions (Coover), **Supp. V:** 39, 42, 43, 49, 50
"Pride" (Hughes), **Supp. I Part 1:** 331
Pride and Prejudice (Austen), **II:** 290; **Supp. XXVI:** 117–118
Prideaux, Tom, **Supp. IV Part 2:** 574, 590
"Priesthood, The" (Winters), **Supp. II Part 2:** 786
Priestly, Joseph, **Supp. I Part 2:** 522
Primary Colors, The (A. Theroux), **Supp. VIII:** 312
"Primary Ground, A" (Rich), **Supp. I Part 2:** 563
"Prime" (Auden), **Supp. II Part 1:** 22
"Primer Class" (Bishop), **Retro. Supp. II:** 38, 51
Primer for Blacks (Brooks), **Supp. III Part 1:** 85
Primer for Combat (Boyle), **Supp. XXIV:** 62
"Primer for the Nuclear Age" (Dove), **Supp. IV Part 1:** 246
Primer mensaje a la América Hispana (W. Frank), **Supp. XX: 76**
Primer of Ignorance, A (Blackmur), **Supp. II Part 1:** 91
Prime-Stevenson, Edward Irenaeus, **Supp. XX: 235**
Primitive (Oppen), **Supp. XXVI:** 237
Primitive, The (C. Himes), **Supp. XVI:** 139, **141–142**
"Primitive Black Man, The" (Du Bois), **Supp. II Part 1:** 176
"Primitive Like an Orb, A" (Stevens), **IV:** 89; **Retro. Supp. I:** 309
Primitive People (Prose), **Supp. XVI:** 255, 256, 257
"Primitive Singing" (Lindsay), **Supp. I Part 2:** 389–390
Primitivism and Decadence (Winters), **Supp. II Part 2:** 786, 803–807, 812
Primrose, Archibald Philip, **Supp. XX: 230**
Prince, F. T., **Supp. XXIV:** 45
Prince, Richard, **Supp. XII:** 4
"Prince, The" (Jarrell), **II:** 379
"Prince, The" (Winters), **Supp. II Part 2:** 802
Prince and the Pauper, The (Twain), **IV:** 200–201, 206; **Retro. Supp. III:** 255, 262, 264
Prince Hagen (Sinclair), **Supp. V:** 280
Prince of a Fellow, A (Hearon), **Supp. VIII:** 58, **62–63**
Princess, The (Tennyson), **Supp. I Part 2:** 410
Princess and the Goblins, The (Macdonald), **Supp. XIII:** 75
Princess Casamassima, The (James), **II:** 276, 291; **IV:** 202; **Retro. Supp. I:** 216, 221, 222, 225, **226–227**
"Princess Casamassima, The" (Trilling), **Supp. III Part 2:** 502, 503
Princess of Arcady, A (Henry), **Retro. Supp. II:** 97
"Principles" (Du Bois), **Supp. II Part 1:** 172
Principles of Literary Criticism (Richards), **I:** 274; **Supp. I Part 1:** 264; **Supp. XIV:** 3
Principles of Psychology, The (James), **II:** 321, 350–352, 353, 354, 357, 362, 363–364; **IV:** 28, 29, 32, 37
Principles of Psychology, The (W. James), **Supp. XVII:** 97
Principles of Zoölogy (Agassiz), **Supp. I Part 1:** 312
Prior, Sir James, **II:** 315
Prior, Matthew, **II:** 111; **III:** 521
"Prison, The" (Malamud), **Supp. I Part 2:** 431, 437
"Prisoned Love" (Boyce), **Supp. XXI:** 9
"Prisoner of Ours, The" (Weigl), **Supp. XIX:** 288
Prisoner of Second Avenue, The (Simon), **Supp. IV Part 2:** 583, 584
Prisoner of Sex, The (Mailer), **III:** 46; **Retro. Supp. II:** 206
Prisoner of Zenda, The (film), **Supp. I Part 2:** 615
Prisoner's Dilemma (Powers), **Supp. IX:** 212, **214–216,** 221
Prison Memoirs of an Anarchist (A. Berkman), **Supp. XVII:** 103–104
Pritchard, William H., **Retro. Supp. I:** 131, 141; **Retro. Supp. III:** 104, 105; **Supp. IV Part 1:** 285; **Supp. IV Part 2:** 642; **Supp. XI:** 326; **Supp. XVI:** 71
Pritchett, V. S., **II:** 587; **Supp. II Part 1:** 143; **Supp. VIII:** 171; **Supp. XIII:** 168
Pritikin, Renny, **Supp. XXIV:** 40
"Privatation and Publication" (Cowley), **Supp. II Part 1:** 149
Private Contentment (Price), **Supp. VI:** 263
"Private History of a Campaign That Failed, The" (Twain), **IV:** 195; **Retro. Supp. III:** 256
Private I, The: Privacy in a Public World (Peacock, ed.), **Supp. XIX:** 193, 203
Private Life of Axie Reed, The (Knowles), **Supp. XII:** 249
Private Line (Major), **Supp. XXII:** 174
"Private Man Confronts His Vulgarities at Dawn, A" (Dunn), **Supp. XI:** 146
Private Memoirs and Confessions of a Justified Sinner, The (Hogg), **Supp. IX:** 276
"Private Property and the Common Wealth" (Berry), **Supp. X:** 25
Private Snafu series (Geisel), **Supp. XVI:** 102
"Private Theatricals" (Howells), **II:** 280
Private Women, Public Stage: Literary Domesticity in Nineteenth-Century America (Kelley), **Supp. XVIII:** 257
"Privilege" (Munro), **Supp. XXVII:** 186, 187
Privilege, The (Kumin), **Supp. IV Part 2:** 442–444, 451
Prize Stories 1918 : The O. Henry Awards, **Supp. XVI:** 16
"Probe" (Ryan as Quin), **Supp. XVIII:** 229
"Probing the Dark" (Komunyakaa), **Supp. XIII:** 131
"Problem from Hell, A": America and the Age of Genocide (Power), **Supp. XXIII:** 25, 27–28
"Problem from Milton, A" (Wilbur), **Supp. III Part 2:** 550
"Problem of Anxiety, The" (Koch), **Supp. XV:** 183
"Problem of Being, The" (James), **II:** 360
Problem of Classification in the Theory of Value, The (Locke), **Supp. XIV:** 199
"Problem of Evil into Cocoon" (Taggard), **Supp. XXII:** 284
"Problem of Housing the Negro, The" (Du Bois), **Supp. II Part 1:** 168
"Problem of the Religious Novel, The" (Isherwood), **Supp. XIV:** 172
Problems and Other Stories (Updike), **Retro. Supp. I:** 322, 329
Problems of Dostoevsky's Poetics (Bakhtin), **Supp. XXII:** 259

"Problem Solving" (Goldbarth), **Supp. XII:** 185
Procedures for Underground (Atwood), **Supp. XIII:** 33
"Procedures for Underground" (Atwood), **Supp. XIII:** 33
Process (Boyle), **Supp. XXIV:** 51
Procession, The (al-Mawákib) (Gibran), **Supp. XX: 116, 124**
Processional (Lawson), **I:** 479
"Procession at Candlemas, A" (Clampitt), **Supp. IX:** 41
"Proclamation" (Saunders), **Supp. XIX:** 235
Proclus, **Retro. Supp. I:** 247
"Prodigal" (Ammons), **Supp. VII:** 29
"Prodigal" (Hoffman), **Supp. XVIII:** 86
"Prodigal, The" (Bishop), **Supp. I Part 1:** 90, 92
Prodigal Parents, The (Lewis), **II:** 454–455
"Prodigy" (Simic), **Supp. VIII:** 278
Producers, The (film, M. Brooks), **Supp. XVII:** 45
"Proem" (Crane), **I:** 397
"Proem, The: By the Carpenter" (O. Henry), **Supp. II Part 1:** 409
"Professions for Women" (Woolf), **Supp. XIII:** 305
"Professor" (Hughes), **Supp. I Part 1:** 330
"Professor, The" (Bourne), **I:** 223
Professor at the Breakfast Table, The (Holmes), **Supp. I Part 1:** 313, 316
"Professor Clark's Economics" (Veblen), **Supp. I Part 2:** 634
Professor of Desire, The (P. Roth), **Retro. Supp. II:** 288; **Supp. III Part 2:** 403, 418–420
Professor's House, The (Cather), **I:** 325–336; **Retro. Supp. I:** 16; **Retro. Supp. III:** 24, 32–33, 34–35
"Professor Veblen" (Mencken), **Supp. I Part 2:** 630
Proffer, Carl R., **Supp. VIII:** 22
Profile Makers, The (Bierds), **Supp. XVII:** 29, **30–32,** 33
"Profile of the Tenderloin Street Prostitute, A" (Vollmann), **Supp. XVII:** 230
Profits of Religion, The (Sinclair), **Supp. V:** 276
"Prognosis" (Warren), **IV:** 245
"Progress" (F. Wright), **Supp. XVII:** 247
Progress of Love, The (Munro), **Supp. XXVII:** 189
"Progress of Love, The" (Munro), **Supp. XXVII:** 189
"Progress Report" (Simic), **Supp. VIII:** 278
"Project for a Trip to China" (Sontag), **Supp. II Part 2:** 454, 469
"Project for The Ambassadors" (James), **Retro. Supp. I:** 229
"Projection" (Nemerov), **III:** 275
"Projective Verse" (Olson), **Supp. III Part 1:** 30; **Supp. III Part 2:** 555, 556, 557, 624; **Supp. IV Part 1:** 139, 153; **Supp. VIII:** 290
"Projector, The" (Baker), **Supp. XIII:** 53, 55
Prokofiev, Sergey Sergeyevich, **Supp. IV Part 1:** 81
"Prolegomena, Section 1" (Pound), **Supp. III Part 2:** 615–616
"Prolegomena, Section 2" (Pound), **Supp. III Part 2:** 616
"Prolegomenon to a Biography of Mailer" (Lucid), **Retro. Supp. II:** 195
Proletarian Literature in the United States (Hicks), **Supp. I Part 2: 609–610; Supp. XXVI:** 134
"Prologue" (MacLeish), **III:** 8, 14
Prologue, for Full Chorus of Mixed Voices and Orchestra (Taggard and Schuman), **Supp. XXII:** 283
"Prologue, The" (Bradstreet), **Retro. Supp. III:** 1, 4, 5, 7, 8, 10
"Prologue to a Life" (D. West), **Supp. XVIII:** 280
"Prologue to Our Time" (Mumford), **Supp. III Part 2:** 473
"Prometheus" (Longfellow), **II:** 494
Prometheus Bound (R. Lowell), **II:** 543, 544, 545, 555
Promise, The (Buck), **Supp. II Part 1:** 124
"Promise, The" (Olds), **Supp. X:** 213
"Promise and Fulfillment" (D. West), **Supp. XVIII:** 278
Promised Land (Parker), **Supp. XIX:** 183, 184, 190
Promised Land, The (M. Antin), **Supp. IX:** 227; **Supp. XVI:** 148, 149; **Supp. XX:** 1, 2, 3, **4–9,** 11
Promised Land, The (Porter), **III:** 447
"Promised Land, The" (R. Fisher), **Supp. XIX:** 72
Promised Lands (Sontag), **Supp. III Part 2:** 452
Promise of American Life, The (Croly), **I:** 229
"Promise of Blue Horses, The" (Harjo), **Supp. XII:** 228
Promise of Rest, The (Price), **Supp. VI:** 262, 266
Promises (Warren), **Supp. XIV:** 15
Promises, Promises (musical), **Supp. IV Part 2:** 575
Promises: Poems 1954–1956 (Warren), **IV:** 244–245, 249, 252
"Promise This When You Be Dying" (Dickinson), **Retro. Supp. I:** 44, 46
"Pronoun Variations"(Hadas), **Supp. XXIII:** 120
Pronzini, Bill, **Supp. XXVI:** 277, 278, 282
Proof, The (Winters), **Supp. II Part 2:** 786, 791, 792–794
"Proofreader, The" (Huddle), **Supp. XXVI:** 151, 152
Proofs and Theories: Essays on Poetry (Glück), **Supp. V:** 77, 79, 92; **Supp. XIV:** 269
"Propaganda of History, The" (Du Bois), **Supp. II Part 1:** 182
Propertius, Sextus, **III:** 467; **Retro. Supp. II:** 187; **Supp. XII:** 2
Property Of: A Novel (Hoffman), **Supp. X:** 77, 79, **80–82**
"Property of Loss" (W. V. Davis), **Supp. XXI:** 95
"Prophecy of Samuel Sewall, The" (Whittier), **Supp. I Part 2:** 699
Prophet, The (Asch), **Supp. XXIII:** 7
Prophet, The (Gibran), **Supp. XX: 113, 115, 119–121, 126**
"Prophet, The" (Notley), **Supp. XXII:** 229
"Prophet, The" (Very), **Supp. XXV:** 248–249
"Prophet and the Child, The" (Gibran), **Supp. XX: 123**
Propheteers, The (Apple), **Supp. XVII: 6–7**
"Prophetic Pictures, The" (Hawthorne), **II:** 227
"Proportion" (A. Lowell), **Retro, Supp. II:** 525
"Proposal" (Carver), **Supp. III Part 1:** 149
Proposals Relating to the Education of Youth in Pensilvania (Franklin), **II:** 113
"Proposed New Version of the Bible" (Franklin), **II:** 110
Prose, Francine, **Supp. XII:** 333; **Supp. XIX:** 209; **Supp. XVI: 249–264; Supp. XXIII:** 300; **Supp. XXVI:** 121, 130
"Prose for Departure" (Merrill), **Supp. III Part 1:** 336
Prose Pieces (Bynner), **Supp. XV:** 52
"Prose Poem as an Evolving Form, The" (R. Bly), **Supp. IV Part 1:** 64
"Proserpina and the Devil" (Wilder), **IV:** 358

"Prosody" (Espaillat), **Supp. XXI:** 102
"Prosody" (Shapiro), **Supp. II Part 2:** 710
Prospect before Us, The (Dos Passos), **I:** 491
"Prospective Immigrants Please Note" (Rich), **Supp. I Part 2:** 555
Prospect of Peace, The (Barlow), **Supp. II Part 1:** 67, 68, 75
Prospects of Literature, The (L. P. Smith), **Supp. XIV:** 343
Prospects on the Rubicon (Paine), **Supp. I Part 2:** 510–511
Prospectus of a National Institution, to Be Established in the United States (Barlow), **Supp. II Part 1:** 80, 82
Prospice (Browning), **IV:** 366
"Protestant Easter" (Sexton), **Supp. II Part 2:** 684
"Prothalamion" (Schwartz), **Supp. II Part 2:** 649, 652
"Prothalamion" (Spenser), **Retro. Supp. I:** 62
Proud, Robert, **Supp. I Part 1:** 125
"Proud Farmer, The" (Lindsay), **Supp. I Part 2:** 381
Proud Flesh (Humphrey), **Supp. IX:** 94, 95, 96, **102–103,** 104, 105, 109
"Proud Flesh" (Warren), **IV:** 243
Proud Highway, The (Thompson), **Supp. XXIV:** 283
Proud Lady (Boyce), **Supp. XXI:** 7, 12
"Proud Lady" (Wylie), **Supp. I Part 2:** 711–712
"Proud Music of the Storms" (Whitman), **Retro. Supp. III:** 305
Proulx, Annie, **Supp. VII: 249–267; Supp. XXIV:** 245, 251; **Supp. XXVI:** 186
Proust, Marcel, **I:** 89, 319, 327, 377, 461; **II:** 377, 514, 606; **III:** 174, 181, 184, 244–245, 259, 471; **IV:** 32, 201, 237, 301, 312, 328, 359, 428, 431, 434, 439, 443, 466, 467; **Retro. Supp. I:** 75, 89, 169, 335; **Supp. III Part 1:** 10, 12, 14, 15; **Supp. IV Part 2:** 600; **Supp. IX:** 211; **Supp. VIII:** 103; **Supp. X:** 193, 194; **Supp. XII:** 289; **Supp. XIV:** 24, 83, 95; **Supp. XVI:** 295; **Supp. XXI:** 231; **Supp. XXIII:** 122
Proverbs, **Supp. X:** 45
"Proverbs" (Jarman), **Supp. XVII:** 118
"Providence" (Komunyakaa), **Supp. XIII:** 132
"Provident Woman, A" (Boyce), **Supp. XXI:** 10
"Provincetown Postcards" (F. Wright), **Supp. XVII:** 244
"Provincia deserta" (Pound), **Retro. Supp. I:** 289
"Provisional Remarks on Being / A Poet / of Arkansas" (Wright), **Supp. XV:** 337
"Prue" (Munro), **Supp. XXVII:** 188
Pruette, Lorine, **Supp. IV Part 2:** 522
Prufrock and Other Observations (T. S. Eliot), **I:** 569–570, 571, 573, 574, 576–577, 583, 584, 585; **Retro. Supp. I:** 59, 62; **Retro. Supp. III:** 58, 59–60
"Prufrock's Perivigilium" (T. S. Eliot), **Retro. Supp. I:** 57
Pryor, Richard, **Supp. XIII:** 343
Pryse, Marjorie, **Retro. Supp. II:** 139, 146; **Supp. XXV:** 285
"Psalm" (Ginsberg), **Supp. II Part 1:** 312
"Psalm" (Oppen), **Supp. XXVI:** 232–233, 235
"Psalm" (Simic), **Supp. VIII:** 282
"Psalm, A, or Supplication for mercy, and confession of Sin, addressed to the Author of Life, in the Odjibway-Alqonquin tongue"(J. Schoolcraft), **Supp. XXIII:** 232
"Psalm and Lament" (Justice), **Supp. VII:** 116, 117–118, 120–122, 124
"Psalm for Pinhook" (Ray), **Supp. XVIII:** 202
"Psalm Jew, The"(Asch). See Salvation (Asch)
"Psalm of Life, A" (Longfellow), **II:** 489, 496; **Retro. Supp. II:** 164, 168, 169; **Supp. I Part 2:** 409
"Psalm of the West" (Lanier), **Supp. I Part 1:** 362, 364
"Psalm: Our Fathers" (Merwin), **Supp. III Part 1:** 350
Psalms (biblical book), **I:** 83; **II:** 168, 232; **Retro. Supp. I:** 62; **Supp. I Part 1:** 125
Psalms, Hymns, and Spiritual Songs of the Rev. Isaac Watts, The (Worcester, ed.), **I:** 458
Psychiatric Novels of Oliver Wendell Holmes, The (Oberndorf), **Supp. I Part 1:** 315
"Psychology and Form" (Burke), **I:** 270
Psychology: Briefer Course (James), **II:** 351–352
Psychology of Art (Malraux), **IV:** 434
Psychology of Insanity, The (Hart), **I:** 241–242, 248–250
Psychopathia Sexualis (Shanley), **Supp. XIV:** 316, **329**
Psychophysiks (Fechner), **II:** 358
Pterodactyls (Silver), **Supp. XXIV: 268–270**
Ptomaine Street (Wells), **Supp. XXVI:** 275
"Pu-239" (Kalfus), **Supp. XVII:** 50
"Publication is the Auction" (Dickinson), **Retro. Supp. I:** 31
"Public Bath, The" (Snyder), **Supp. VIII:** 298
Public Burning, The (Coover), **Supp. IV Part 1:** 388; **Supp. V:** 44, 45, 46–47, 48, 51, 52; **Supp. XVII:** 6
"Public Burning of Julius and Ethel Rosenberg, The: An Historical Romance" (Coover), **Supp. V:** 44
"Public Figure" (Hay), **Supp. XIV:** 124
"Public Garden, The" (R. Lowell), **II:** 550
Public Good (Paine), **Supp. I Part 2:** 509–510
Public Poetry of Robert Lowell, The (Cosgrave), **Retro. Supp. II:** 185
"Public & Private" (column, Quindlen), **Supp. XVII:** 165, 167, 169–170
Public Speech: Poems (MacLeish), **III:** 15–16
Public Spirit (Savage), **II:** 111
"Public Woman, A" (Cliff), **Supp. XXII:** 76
Puccini, Giacomo, **Supp. XXI:** 150, 151
"Puck" (Monette), **Supp. X:** 157–158
Pudd'nhead Wilson (Twain), **I:** 197; **Retro. Supp. III:** 267
"Pudd'nhead Wilson's Calendar" (Twain), **I:** 197
"Pueblo Revolt, The" (Sando), **Supp. IV Part 2:** 510
Puella (Dickey), **Supp. IV Part 1:** 178, 185
Pulitzer, Alfred, **Retro. Supp. I:** 257
Pull Down Vanity (Fiedler), **Supp. XIII:** 103
Pullman, George, **Supp. I Part 1:** 9
"Pullman Car Hiawatha" (Wilder), **IV:** 365–366
Pull My Daisy (film), **Supp. XII:** 126–127
"Pulp Cutters' Nativity, A" (Budbill), **Supp. XIX:** 9
"Pulpit and the Pew, The" (Holmes), **Supp. I Part 1:** 302
"Pulse-Beats and Pen-Strokes" (Sandburg), **III:** 579
"Pump, The" (Humphrey), **Supp. IX:** 101
Pump House Gang, The (Wolfe), **Supp. III Part 2:** 575, 578, 580, 581
Punch, Brothers, Punch and Other

Sketches (Twain), **IV:** 200
Punch: The Immortal Liar, Documents in His History (Aiken), **I:** 57, 61
Punishment Without Vengeance (Vega; Merwin, trans.), **Supp. III Part 1:** 341, 347
"Pupil" (F. Barthelme), **Supp. XI:** 26
"Pupil, The" (H. James), **Supp. XX: 233**
"Pupil, The" (James), **II:** 331; **Retro. Supp. I:** 217, 219, 228
"Purchase" (Banks), **Supp. V:** 6
"Purchase of Some Golf Clubs, A" (O'Hara), **III:** 369
"Purdah" (Plath), **Supp. I Part 2:** 602
Purdy, Charles, **Supp. VIII:** 330
Purdy, James, **Supp. VII: 269–285**
Purdy, John Lloyd, **Supp. XXVI:** 101, 103, 105, 111
Purdy, Theodore, **Supp. VIII:** 153
Pure (C. Frost), **Supp. XV:** 93, **101–102,** 104, 106
"Pure" (C. Frost), **Supp. XV:** 101–102
"Pure and the Good, The: On Baseball and Backpaking" (Maclean), **Supp. XIV:** 222
"Pure Good of Theory, The" (Stevens), **Retro. Supp. I:** 310
Purgatorio (Dante), **III:** 182; **Retro. Supp. III:** 65
"Purim Parade" (Espaillat), **Supp. XXI:** 108
Puritan Family (Morgan), **Supp. I Part 1:** 101
"Puritanical Pleasures" (Hardwick), **Supp. III Part 1:** 213–214
Puritan Origins of the American Self, The (Bercovitch), **Supp. I Part 1:** 99
Puritan Pronaos, The: Studies in the Intellectual Life of New England in the Seventeenth Century (Morison), **Supp. I Part 2:** 485
"Puritan Realism: The Wide, Wide World and Robinson Crusoe" (Kim), **Supp. XVIII:** 267
Puritans, The (P. Miller), **Supp. VIII:** 101
"Puritan's Ballad, The" (Wylie), **Supp. I Part 2:** 723
"Purloined Letter, The" (Poe), **Retro. Supp. II:** 271, 272; **Retro. Supp. III:** 225, 227
Purple Cane Road (Burke), **Supp. XIV:** 32, 33
Purple Decades, The (Wolfe), **Supp. III Part 2:** 584
"Purple Hat, The" (Welty), **IV:** 264
Purple Rose of Cairo, The (film; Allen), **Supp. XV:** 1, **9–10,** 12, 14
Purser, John T., **Supp. XIV:** 4
"Pursuit of Happiness" (Simpson), **Supp. IX:** 279
"Pursuit of Happiness, The" (Ashbery), **Supp. III Part 1:** 23
Pursuit of the Prodigal, The (Auchincloss), **Supp. IV Part 1:** 25
Pushcart at the Curb, A (Dos Passos), **I:** 478, 479
"Pushcart Man" (Hughes), **Supp. I Part 1:** 330
Pushcart Prize, XIII, The (Ford), **Supp. V:** 58
Pushcart Prize VII, The (Hendeson, ed.), **Supp. XVII:** 16
Pushcart Prize XIV, The (Henderson, ed.), **Supp. XVII:** 18
Pushcart Prize XX, The (Henderson, ed.), **Supp. XVII:** 20
"Pushing 100" (Mora), **Supp. XIII:** 215
Pushkin, Aleksander, **III:** 246, 261, 262; **Retro. Supp. I:** 266, 269; **Supp. XVI:** 188
Pussy, King of the Pirates (Acker), **Supp. XII:** 6–7
"Pussycat and the Expert Plumber Who Was a Man, The" (A. Miller), **III:** 146–147
Pussycat Fever (Acker), **Supp. XII:** 6
Putnam, George Haven, **Supp. XVIII:** 257, 260
Putnam, George P., **II:** 314; **Supp. XVIII:** 3–4, 14, 260
Putnam, Phelps, **I:** 288
Putnam, Samuel, **II:** 26; **III:** 479; **Supp. III Part 2:** 615
"Put Off the Wedding Five Times and Nobody Comes to It" (Sandburg), **III:** 586–587
Puttenham, George, **Supp. I Part 1:** 113
Puttermesser Papers, The (Ozick), **Supp. V:** 269
"Putting a Burden Down" (Peacock), **Supp. XIX:** 199
Putting It Together (Sondheim), **Supp. XXIV:** 124
"Putting on Visit to a Small Planet" (Vidal), **Supp. IV Part 2:** 683
Put Yourself in My Shoes (Carver), **Supp. III Part 1:** 139
"Put Yourself in My Shoes" (Carver), **Supp. III Part 1:** 139, 141
Putzi, Jennifer, **Supp. XV:** 284
Puzo, Mario, **Supp. IV Part 1:** 390
"Puzzle of Modern Society, The" (Kazin), **Supp. VIII:** 103
Pygmalion (Shaw), **Supp. XII:** 14
Pyle, Ernie, **III:** 148; **Supp. V:** 240; **Supp. XVII:** 61
Pylon (Faulkner), **II:** 64–65, 73; **Retro. Supp. I:** 84, 85; **Retro. Supp. III:** 77, 83
Pym (M. Johnson), **Retro. Supp. III:** 236
Pynchon, Thomas, **III:** 258; **Retro. Supp. I:** 278; **Retro. Supp. II:** 279, 324; **Supp. II Part 2:** 557, **617–638; Supp. III Part 1:** 217; **Supp. IV Part 1:** 53, 279; **Supp. IV Part 2:** 570; **Supp. IX:** 207, 208, 212; **Supp. V:** 40, 44, 52; **Supp. VIII:** 14; **Supp. X:** 260, 301, 302; **Supp. XI:** 103; **Supp. XII:** 289; **Supp. XIV:** 49, 53, 54, 96; **Supp. XIX:** 223; **Supp. XVI:** 123, 128; **Supp. XVII:** 183, 225, 232, 236; **Supp. XX: 21, 83, 87; Supp. XXIII:** 42, 101; **Supp. XXVII:** 183
Pyne, John, **Supp. XXI:** 7
Pyne, Mary, **Supp. XXI:** 7
Pyrah, Gill, **Supp. V:** 126
"Pyramid Club, The" (Doctorow), **Supp. IV Part 1:** 234
Pyrlaeus, Johann Christopher, **Supp. XXVI:** 86
"Pyrography" (Ashbery), **Supp. III Part 1:** 18
Pythagoras, **I:** 332
Pythagorean Silence (Howe), **Supp. IV Part 2:** 426, 428–429
QBVII (television movie), **Supp. XX: 247**
QBVII (Uris), **Supp. XX: 244, 247, 248, 251, 253–254**
"Qebehseneuf" (Goldbarth), **Supp. XII:** 186
"Quadroons, The" (Child), **Supp. XVIII:** 124
"Quai d'Orléans" (Bishop), **Supp. I Part 1:** 89
"Quail for Mr. Forester" (Humphrey), **Supp. IX:** 94
"Quail in Autumn" (W. J. Smith), **Supp. XIII:** 334–335, 339
Quaker City, The: or, The Monks of Monk Hall (Lippard), **Supp. XXIII:** 177, 178–179, **180–183,** 184, 187, 188–189, 190
"Quaker Graveyard in Nantucket, The" (R. Lowell), **II:** 54, 550; **Retro. Supp. II:** 178, 186–187
"Quake Theory" (Olds), **Supp. X:** 203
Qualey, Carlton C., **Supp. I Part 2:** 650
Quality of Hurt, The (C. Himes), **Supp. XVI:** 137, 145
"Quality of Wine" (Carruth), **Supp. XVI:** 59

"Quality Time" (Kingsolver), **Supp. VII:** 203
"Quandary" (F. Wright), **Supp. XVII:** 244
Quang-Ngau-chè, **III:** 473
Quarles, Francis, **I:** 178, 179
"Quarrel" (Taggard), **Supp. XXII:** 276
Quarry, The (Chesnutt), **Supp. XIV:** 76
"Quarry, The" (Nemerov), **III:** 272
Quarry, The: New Poems (Eberhart), **I:** 532, 539
Quartermain, Peter, **Supp. IV Part 2:** 423, 434
Quatermain, Peter, **Supp. XXII:** 163
"Quaternions, The" (Bradstreet), **Supp. I Part 1:** 104–106, 114, 122
"Quatrains for Ishi" (Komunyakaa), **Supp. XIII:** 129
Quatuor pour la fin du temps (Messiaen), **Supp. XXVII:** 152
Queechy (S. Warner as Wetherell), **Supp. XVIII:** 257, **264–266**
Queen Christmas (Wells), **Supp. XXVI:** 275
"Queen Elizabeth and the Blind Girl or Music for the Dead Children" (B. Kelly), **Supp. XVII:** 124, 125
Queen of Outer Space (film), **Supp. XXVII:** 94
"Queen of the Black Coast" (Howard), **Supp. XXVII:** 125
"Queen of the Blues" (Brooks), **Supp. III Part 1:** 75
Queen of the Damned, The (Rice), **Supp. VII:** 290, 292–293, 297, 299
Queen of the Mob (film), **Supp. XIII:** 170
"Queens of France" (Wilder), **IV:** 365
"Queen's Twin, The" (Jewett), **Retro. Supp. II:** 138
Queen's Twin, The, and Other Stories (Jewett), **Retro. Supp. II:** 140
Queen Victoria (Strachey), **Supp. I Part 2:** 485, 494; **Supp. XIV:** 342
Queer (Burroughs), **Supp. III Part 1:** 93–102
"Queer Aztlán"(Moraga), **Supp. XXIII:** 201
"Queer Beer" (Hansberry), **Supp. IV Part 1:** 374
"Quelques considérations sur la méthode subjective" (James), **II:** 345–346
"Quest, The" (Gibran), **Supp. XX: 124**
"Question" (Swenson), **Supp. IV Part 2:** 640
"Question and Answer" (Hughes), **Retro. Supp. I:** 211
"Questioning Faces" (Frost), **Retro. Supp. I:** 141
"Question Mark in the Circle, The" (Stegner), **Supp. IV Part 2:** 597
"Questionnaire, The" (Snodgrass), **Supp. VI:** 318
"Question of Fidelity, A" (Beauvoir), **Supp. IX:** 4
"Question of Loneliness, A" (Swados), **Supp. XIX:** 262
"Question of Our Speech, The" (Ozick), **Supp. V:** 272
"Question of Simone de Beauvoir, The" (Algren), **Supp. IX:** 4
Questions About Angels (Collins), **Supp. XXI:** 54, 58, 59, 60, 64
Questions for Ecclesiastes (Jarman), **Supp. XVII:** 109, 110, **118–119**
"Questions of Geography" (Hollander), **Supp. I Part 1:** 96
"Questions of Swimming, 1935" (Davison), **Supp. XXVI:** 76
Questions of Travel (Bishop), **Retro. Supp. II: 46–48; Supp. I Part 1:** 72, 83, 92, 94
"Questions of Travel" (Bishop), **Retro. Supp. II:** 47
"Questions to Tourists Stopped by a Pineapple Field" (Merwin), **Supp. III Part 1:** 355
"Questions without Answers" (T. Williams), **IV:** 384
"Quest of the Purple-Fringed, The" (Frost), **Retro. Supp. I:** 139; **Retro. Supp. III:** 104
Quest of the Silver Fleece, The (Du Bois), **Supp. II Part 1:** 176–178
Quevedo y Villegas, Francisco Gómez, **Retro. Supp. I:** 423
Quickly: A Column for Slow Readers (Mailer), **Retro. Supp. II:** 202
Quicksand (Larsen), **Supp. XVIII:** 119, 121, 122, **124–127**
Quicksand and Passing (Larsen; Mc-Dowell, ed.), **Supp. XVIII:** 125
"Quies," (Pound), **Retro. Supp. I:** 413
Quiet American, The (Greene), **Supp. XIX:** 29
"Quiet and clear" (Kooser), **Supp. XIX:** 125
Quiet City (Shaw), **Supp. XIX:** 244
Quiet Days in Clichy (H. Miller), **III:** 170, 178, 183–184, 187
"Quiet Desperation" (Simpson), **Supp. IX:** 277–278
"Quiet Hour" (Huddle), **Supp. XXVI:** 149–150
"Quiet Light, A" (Skloot), **Supp. XX: 203**
"Quiet of the Mind" (Nye), **Supp. XIII:** 284
"Quiet Woman, The" (Taggard), **Supp. XXII:** 274
"QUILLA" (Trethewey), **Supp. XXI:** 246
"Quilting" (D. West), **Supp. XVIII:** 283
Quin, Mike (pseudonym). See Ryan, Paul William
Quincy, Edmund, **Supp. XVIII:** 4
Quindlen, Anna, **Supp. XVI:** 108; **Supp. XVII: 165–181**
Quinlan, Kathleen, **Supp. X:** 80
Quinn, Anthony, **Supp. XXI:** 46
Quinn, Arthur Hobson, **Retro. Supp. III:** 236
Quinn, John, **III:** 471
Quinn, Paul, **Supp. V:** 71
Quinn, Sister M. Bernetta, **III:** 479; **IV:** 421
Quinn, Vincent, **I:** 386, 401, 402; **Supp. I Part 1:** 270
"Quinnapoxet" (Kunitz), **Supp. III Part 1:** 263
Quinn's Book (W. Kennedy), **Supp. VII:** 133, 148–150, 153
Quintero, José, **III:** 403
Quintilian, **IV:** 123
Quinzaine for This Yule, A (Pound), **Retro. Supp. I:** 285
Quite Contrary: The Mary and Newt Story (Dixon), **Supp. XII: 144,** 153
Quitting Time (Kriegel), **Supp. XXIV: 225–227**
Quod Erat Demonstrandum (Stein), **IV:** 34
Quo Vadis? (Sienkiewicz), **Supp. IV Part 2:** 518; **Supp. XVI:** 182
Raab, Max, **Supp. XI:** 309
Raban, Jonathan, **Supp. XXV:** 208, 217
"Rabbi, The" (Hayden), **Supp. II Part 1:** 363, 369
Rabbit, Run (Updike), **IV:** 214, 223, 230–234; **Retro. Supp. I:** 320, 325, 326, 327, 331, 333, 335; **Supp. XI:** 140; **Supp. XII:** 298; **Supp. XVI:** 220
"Rabbit, The" (Barnes), **Supp. III Part 1:** 34
Rabbit at Rest (Updike), **Retro. Supp. I:** 334
Rabbit Dance (Gansworth), **Supp. XXVI:** 114
Rabbit Factory, The (L. Brown), **Supp. XXI:** 40, **47–48**
"Rabbit Factory, The: Escaping the Isolation of the Cage" (Gaughran), **Supp. XXI:** 47–48
Rabbit Is Rich (Updike), **Retro. Supp. I:** 334; **Supp. XXVI:** 142

Rabbit novels (Updike), **Supp. V:** 269
Rabbit Redux (Updike), **IV:** 214; **Retro. Supp. I:** 332, 333
Rabbit's Umbrella, The (Plimpton), **Supp. XVI:** 244
"Rabbits Who Caused All the Trouble, The" (Thurber), **Supp. I Part 2:** 610
Rabe, David, **Supp. XXIV:** 117; **Supp. XXV:** 153
Rabelais, and His World (Bakhtin), **Retro. Supp. II:** 273
Rabelais, François, **I:** 130; **II:** 111, 112, 302, 535; **III:** 77, 78, 174, 182; **IV:** 68; **Supp. I Part 2:** 461
Rabelais and His World (Bakhtin), **Supp. X:** 120
Rabinbach, Anson, **Supp. XII:** 166
Rabinowitz, Dorothy, **Supp. XXVII:** 134
Rabinowitz, Paula, **Supp. V:** 161
"Race" (Emerson), **II:** 6
"Race, Privilege, and the Politics of (Re)Writing History: An Analysis of the Novels of Michelle Cliff" (Edmondson), **Supp. XXII:** 70
"Race Cannot Become Great Until It Recognizes Its Talent" (Hurston), **Retro. Supp. III:** 129
Race Contacts and Interracial Relations: Lectures on the Theory and Practice of Race (Locke), **Supp. XIV:** 196, 199, 209, **209–210,** 211
"'RACE LINE' IS A PRODUCT OF CAPITALISM, THE" (Baraka), **Supp. II Part 1:** 61
"Race of Life, The" (Thurber), **Supp. I Part 2:** 614
"Race Problems and Modern Society" (Toomer), **Supp. III Part 2:** 486
Race Questions, Provincialism, and Other American Problems (Royce), **Supp. XIV:** 199
"Race Riot, Tulsa, 1921" (Olds), **Supp. X:** 205
Race Rock (Matthiessen), **Supp. V:** 201
"Races, The" (R. Lowell), **II:** 554
"Rachel" (D. West), **Supp. XVIII:** 289
Rachel Carson: Witness for Nature (Lear), **Supp. IX:** 19
Rachel River (film, Smolan), **Supp. XVI:** 36
"Racial Progress and Race Adjustment" (Locke), **Supp. XIV:** 210
Racine, Jean Baptiste, **II:** 543, 573; **III:** 145, 151, 152, 160; **IV:** 317, 368, 370; **Supp. I Part 2:** 716
Radcliffe, Ann, **Supp. XX: 108**
Radiance (Crooker), **Supp. XXIII: 57–58**
"Radical" (Moore), **III:** 211
"Radical Chic" (Wolfe), **Supp. III Part 2:** 577–578, 584, 585
Radical Chic & Mau-mauing the Flak Catchers (Wolfe), **Supp. III Part 2:** 577–578
Radical Empiricism of William James, The (Wild), **II:** 362, 363–364
Radicalism in America, The (Lasch), **I:** 259
"Radical Jewish Humanism: The Vision of E. L. Doctorow" (Clayton), **Supp. IV Part 1:** 238
"Radically Condensed History of Postindustrial Life, A" (Wallace), **Supp. X:** 309
Radical's America, A (Swados), **Supp. XIX: 264–265**
Radinovsky, Lisa, **Supp. XV:** 284, 285
"Radio" (O'Hara), **III:** 369
Radio Days (film; Allen), **Supp. XV:** 9
Radio Golf (Wilson), **Retro. Supp. III:** 321
"Radio Pope" (Goldbarth), **Supp. XII:** 188, 192
Raditzer (Matthiessen), **Supp. V:** 201
Radkin, Paul, **Supp. I Part 2:** 539
"Rafaela Who Drinks Coconut & Papaya Juice on Tuesdays" (Cisneros), **Supp. VII:** 63
Rafelson, Bob, **Supp. XIV:** 241
Raffalovich, Marc-André, **Supp. XIV:** 335
Rafferty, Terence, **Supp. XX: 87, 92**
"Raft, The" (Lindsay), **Supp. I Part 2:** 393
Rag and Bone Shop of the Heart, The: Poems for Men (Bly, Hillman, and Meade, eds.), **Supp. IV Part 1:** 67
Rage in Harlem (C. Himes). See For Love of Imabelle (C. Himes)
Rage to Live, A (O'Hara), **III:** 361
Raglan, Lord, **I:** 135
Rago, Henry, **Supp. III Part 2:** 624, 628, 629
"Rag Rug"(Hadas), **Supp. XXIII:** 118
Ragtime (Doctorow), **Retro. Supp. II:** 108; **Supp. IV Part 1:** 217, 222–224, 231, 232, 233, 234, 237, 238; **Supp. V:** 45; **Supp. XXIV:** 227
"Ragtime" (Doctorow), **Supp. IV Part 1:** 234
Ragtime (film), **Supp. IV Part 1:** 236
Ragtime (musical, McNally), **Supp. XIII:** 207
Rahab (W. Frank), **Supp. XX: 71–72, 76**
Rahaim, Liz, **Supp. XVII:** 2
Rahv, Philip, **Retro. Supp. I:** 112; **Supp. II Part 1:** 136; **Supp. IX:** 8; **Supp. VIII:** 96; **Supp. XIV:** 3; **Supp. XV:** 140; **Supp. XXVII:** 134
"Raid" (Hughes), **Retro. Supp. I:** 208
Raids on the Unspeakable (Merton), **Supp. VIII:** 201, 208
Raikin, Judith, **Supp. XXII:** 66
Rail, DeWayne, **Supp. XIII:** 312
"Rain, the Rez, and Other Things, The" (Gansworth), **Supp. XXVI:** 111
Rain and Other Fictions (Kenny), **Supp. XXIII:** 157
"Rain and the Rhinoceros" (Merton), **Supp. VIII:** 201
Rainbow, The (Lawrence), **III:** 27
"Rainbows" (Marquand), **III:** 56
Rainbow Stories, The (Vollmann), **Supp. XVII:** 226, 227, 230, 231, 233
Rainbow Tulip, The (Mora), **Supp. XIII:** 221
"Rain Country" (Haines), **Supp. XII:** 210
"Rain-Dream, A" (Bryant), **Supp. I Part 1:** 164
Raine, Kathleen, **I:** 522, 527
"Rain Falling Now, The" (Dunn), **Supp. XI:** 147
"Rain Flooding Your Campfire" (Gallagher), **Supp. XXIV:** 177
"Rain in the Heart" (Taylor), **Supp. V:** 317, 319
Rain in the Trees, The (Merwin), **Supp. III Part 1:** 340, 342, 345, 349, 354–356
"Rainmaker, The" (Humphrey), **Supp. IX:** 101
Raintree County (Lockridge), **Supp. XIX:** 263
Rainwater, Catherine, **Supp. V:** 272
"Rainy Day" (Longfellow), **II:** 498
"Rainy Day, The" (Buck), **Supp. II Part 1:** 127
"Rainy Mountain Cemetery" (Momaday), **Supp. IV Part 2:** 486
Rainy Mountain Christmas Doll (painting) (Momaday), **Supp. IV Part 2:** 493
"Rainy Season: Sub-Tropics" (Bishop), **Supp. I Part 1:** 93
"Rainy Sunday" (Espaillat), **Supp. XXI:** 106
Raised in Captivity (Silver), **Supp. XXIV: 271**
"Raise High the Roof Beam, Carpenters" (Salinger), **III:** 567–569, 571
Raise High the Roof Beam, Carpenters; and Seymour: An Introduction (Salinger), **III:** 552, 567–571, 572
Raise Race Rays Raze: Essays Since

1965 (Baraka), **Supp. II Part 1:** 47, 52, 55
Raisin (musical), **Supp. IV Part 1:** 374
Raising Demons (Jackson), **Supp. IX: 125–126**
Raising the Dead (Rash), **Supp. XXVII:** 220–221, 222
Raisin in the Sun, A (film: Columbia Pictures), **Supp. IV Part 1:** 360, 367
Raisin in the Sun, A (Hansberry), **Supp. IV Part 1:** 359, 360, 361, 362–364; **Supp. VIII:** 343
Raisin in the Sun, A (television film: American Playhouse), **Supp. IV Part 1:** 367, 374
Raisin in the Sun, A (unproduced screenplay) (Hansberry), **Supp. IV Part 1:** 360
Rajan, R., **I:** 390
"Rake, The" (Mamet), **Supp. XIV:** 240
Rake's Progress, The (opera), **Supp. II Part 1:** 24
Rakosi, Carl, **Supp. III Part 2:** 614, 615, 616, 617, 618, 621, 629; **Supp. XIV:** 286, 287
Ralegh, Sir Walter, **Supp. I Part 1:** 98
Raleigh, John Henry, **IV:** 366
Raleigh, Walter, **Retro. Supp. III:** 4, 6
Ralph, Brett, **Supp. XVII:** 245
Ramakrishna, Sri, **III:** 567
Ramakrishna and His Disciples (Isherwood), **Supp. XIV:** 164
Ramazani, Jahan, **Supp. IV Part 2:** 450
"Ramble of Aphasia, A" (O. Henry), **Supp. II Part 1:** 410
Ramey, Phillip, **Supp. IV Part 1:** 94
Ramírez, Juan, **Supp. XXIII:** 203
Ramona (Jackson), **Supp. XXIV:** 27
Rampersad, Arnold, **Retro. Supp. I:** 196, 200, 201, 204; **Supp. IV Part 1:** 244, 250
Rampling, Anne, **Supp. VII:** 201. See also Rice, Anne
Rampling, Charlotte, **Supp. IX:** 253
Ramsey, Priscilla R., **Supp. IV Part 1:** 15
Ramsey, Roger, **Supp. XVI:** 69
Ramsey, William, **Supp. XVIII:** 66
Ramus, Petrus, **Supp. I Part 1:** 104
Rancière, Jacques, **Supp. XXVI:** 18, 135, 136, 141
Rand, Ayn, **Supp. I Part 1:** 294; **Supp. IV Part 2: 517–535**
Randall, Jarrell, 1914–1965 (Lowell, Taylor, and Warren, eds.), **II:** 368, 385
Randall, John H., **III:** 605
Randolph, John, **I:** 5–6
Randolph, Ladette, **Supp. XXIII:** 274
"Randolphs of the Redwoods, The" (Atherton), **Supp. XXIV:** 18
"Range-Finding" (Frost), **Retro. Supp. I:** 131
Range of the Possible (T. Marshall), **Supp. XVII:** 36
Rangoon (F. Barthelme), **Supp. XI:** 25
Rangus, Eric, **Supp. XXI:** 244, 254
Rank, Otto, **I:** 135; **Supp. IX:** 105; **Supp. X:** 183, 185, 193
Ranke, Leopold von, **Supp. I Part 2:** 492
Rankin, Daniel, **Retro. Supp. II:** 57, 72; **Supp. I Part 1:** 200, 203, 225
Rankin, Tom, **Supp. XXI:** 36
Rankine, Annette, **Supp. XX: 69**
Ranlett, William H., **Supp. XVIII:** 3
Ransohoff, Martin, **Supp. XI:** 305, 306
Ransom, John Crowe, **I:** 265, 301; **II:** 34, 367, 385, 389, 536–537, 542; **III:** 454, **480–502,** 549; **IV:** 121, 122, 123, 124, 125, 127, 134, 140, 141, 236, 237, 433; **Retro. Supp. I:** 90; **Retro. Supp. II:** 176, 177, 178, 183, 220, 228, 246; **Supp. I Part 1:** 80, 361; **Supp. I Part 2:** 423; **Supp. II Part 1:** 90, 91, 136, 137, 139, 318; **Supp. II Part 2:** 639; **Supp. III Part 1:** 318; **Supp. III Part 2:** 542, 591; **Supp. IV Part 1:** 217; **Supp. V:** 315, 331, 337; **Supp. X:** 25, 56, 58; **Supp. XIV:** 1; **Supp. XIX:** 123; **Supp. XXIII:** 145
Ransome, Arthur, **Supp. XXV:** 205
"Rape" (Coleman), **Supp. XI:** 89–90
"Rape" (Rich), **Retro. Supp. III:** 247
"Rape, The" (Baraka), **Supp. II Part 1:** 40
Rape of Bunny Stuntz, The (Gurney), **Supp. V:** 109
"Rape of Philomel, The" (Shapiro), **Supp. II Part 2:** 720
"Rape of the Lock, The" (Pope), **Supp. XIV:** 8
Rapf, Joanna, **Supp. XVIII:** 251
Raphael, **I:** 15; **III:** 505, 521, 524; **Supp. I Part 1:** 363
"Rapist" (Dunn), **Supp. XI:** 144
Rap on Race, A (Baldwin and Mead), **Supp. I Part 1:** 66
Rapoport, Nessa, **Supp. XXVI:** 124
"Rappaccini's Daughter" (Hawthorne), **II:** 229; **Retro. Supp. III:** 115, 117
"Rapture of the Deep" (Hempel), **Supp. XXI: 123**
"Rapunzel" (Sexton), **Supp. II Part 2:** 691
Rare & Endangered Species: A Novella & Short Stories (Bausch), **Supp. VII:** 51, 54
"Raree Show" (MacLeish), **III:** 9
Rascoe, Burton, **III:** 106, 115
Rash, Ron, **Supp. XXVII: 215–231**
Raskin, Jonah, **Supp. XV:** 116
Raskin, Saul, **Supp. XXIII:** 6
"Raskolnikov" (Simic), **Supp. VIII:** 282
Rasmussen, Douglas, **Supp. IV Part 2:** 528, 530
Rasmussen, Halfdan, **Supp. XVIII:** 180
"Raspberries" (Rash), **Supp. XXVII:** 222
Rasporich, Beverly, **Supp. XXVII:** 180, 182
Rasselas (S. Johnson), **Supp. XI:** 209
Rathmann, Andrew, **Supp. XV:** 34
Ratiner, Steven, **Supp. XXIII:** 134
"Rat in the Engine" (Espaillat), **Supp. XXI:** 106
"Ration" (Baraka), **Supp. II Part 1:** 50
"Rationale of Verse, The" (Poe), **III:** 427–428; **Retro. Supp. II:** 266
Ratner, Rochelle, **Supp. XV:** 105; **Supp. XXIV:** 168; **Supp. XXVI:** 160
Ratner's Star (DeLillo), **Supp. VI:** 1, 2, 3, 4, 10, 12, 14; **Supp. XVIII:** 140
"Rat of Faith, The" (Levine), **Supp. V:** 192
"Rats in the Walls, The" (Lovecraft), **Supp. XXV:** 109, 112
Rattigan, Terence, **III:** 152
Raugh, Joseph, **Supp. I Part 1:** 286
Rauh, Ida, **Supp. XXI:** 6
Rauschenberg, Robert, **Supp. XV:** 187
Rauschenbusch, Walter, **III:** 293; **Supp. I Part 1:** 7
Ravelstein (Bellow), **Retro. Supp. II:** 19, **33–34**
Raven, Simon, **Supp. XII:** 241
Raven, The (film, Friedlander), **Supp. XVII:** 58
"Raven, The" (Poe), **III:** 413, 421–422, 426; **Retro. Supp. II:** 265, 266–267; **Retro. Supp. III:** 225, 232, 234, 237; **Supp. XVII:** 58
Raven, The, and Other Poems (Poe), **III:** 413
Ravenal, Shannon, **Supp. IV Part 1:** 93
"Raven Days, The" (Lanier), **Supp. I Part 1:** 351
Ravenel, Shannon, **Supp. XXI:** 39
Ravenna, Michael. See Welty, Eudora
"Ravens at Deer Creek" (Wrigley), **Supp. XVIII:** 299–300, 306

Raven's Road (Gunn Allen), **Supp. IV Part 1:** 330, 335
Raver, Anne, **Supp. XVIII:** 191
Ravetch, Irving, **Supp. XXV:** 102
"Ravine, The" (Carruth), **Supp. XVI:** 53
Ravits, Martha, **Supp. XXI:** 215
Raw Heaven (Peacock), **Supp. XIX: 196–197**
Rawlings, Marjorie Kinnan, **Retro. Supp. III:** 134, 135; **Supp. X: 219–237; Supp. XVIII:** 194–195
Rawlins, C. L., **Supp. XVII:** 72, 73
Ray, David, **Supp. IV Part 1:** 61
Ray, Janisse, **Supp. XVIII: 189–206**
Ray, Jeanne Wilkinson, **Supp. XII:** 308, 310
Ray, John, **II:** 111, 112
Ray, Man, **IV:** 404; **Retro. Supp. I:** 416; **Supp. XII:** 124; **Supp. XXIII:** 6
Ray, Nicholas, **Supp. XVIII:** 253
Ray Bradbury Theatre, The (television show), **Supp. IV Part 1:** 103
Raymond, Henry J., **Supp. XVIII:** 4
"Raymond and Ann" (Budbill), **Supp. XIX:** 9
"Raymond Andrews as Griot" (Collins), **Supp. XXVI:** 13
Raymond Carver: A Writer's Life (Sklenicka), **Supp. XXIV:** 166
"Raymond Carver: The Kindest Cut" (Wood), **Supp. XXIV:** 166
"Razor's Edge, The" (Wasserstein), **Supp. XV:** 328
Reactionary Essays on Poetry and Ideas (Tate), **Supp. II Part 1:** 106, 146
Read, Deborah, **II:** 122
Read, Forrest, **III:** 478
Read, Herbert, **I:** 523; **II:** 372–373, 377–378; **Retro. Supp. I:** 54; **Supp. III Part 1:** 273; **Supp. III Part 2:** 624, 626
Read, William A., **Supp. XIV:** 4
Reade, Charles, **Supp. I Part 2:** 580
Reader, Constant. See Parker, Dorothy
Reader, Dennis J., **Supp. I Part 2:** 454
"Reader, The" (F. Wright), **Supp. XVII:** 246
Reader's Block (Markson), **Supp. XVII: 143–145,** 146
Reader's Encyclopedia, The: An Encyclopedia of World Literature and the Arts (W. Benét), **Supp. XI:** 44
Reader's Guide to William Gaddis's The Recognitions, A (Moore), **Supp. IV Part 1:** 283
Reader's Map of Arkansas (Wright), **Supp. XV:** 348
"Reader's Tale, A" (Doty), **Supp. XI:** 119, 120, 128, 129
"Reading" (Auden), **Supp. VIII:** 155
"Reading, The" (Di Piero), **Supp. XIX:** 41
"Reading, Writing, Region" (J. W. Miller), **Supp. XX: 165**
"Reading an Anthology of Chinese Poems of the Sung Dynasty, I Pause to Admire the Length and Clarity of Their Titles" (Collins), **Supp. XXI:** 56
"Reading at Forty" (Pickering), **Supp. XXI:** 196
Reading at the Social Limit (Elmer), **Retro. Supp. III:** 237
"Reading Group Guide", **Supp. XI:** 244–245
"Reading Lao Tzu Again in the New Year" (Wright), **Supp. V:** 343
"Reading Late of the Death of Keats" (Kenyon), **Supp. VII:** 169
"Reading Myself" (R. Lowell), **II:** 555
Reading Myself and Others (P. Roth), **Retro. Supp. II:** 282; **Supp. V:** 45
"Reading Ode to the West Wind 25 Years Later" (McCarriston), **Supp. XIV:** 271–272
"Reading of the Psalm, The" (Francis), **Supp. IX:** 79
"Reading Ovid" (Di Piero), **Supp. XIX:** 44
"Reading Philosophy at Night" (Simic), **Supp. VIII:** 272
Reading Rilke: Reflections on the Problems of Translation (Gass), **Supp. VI:** 92, **93–94**
"Reading Rorty and Paul Celan One Morning in Early June" (Wright), **Supp. V:** 343
"Reading Sarcophagi: An Essay" (Sobin), **Supp. XVI:** 290
"Readings of History" (Rich), **Supp. I Part 2:** 554
"Reading the Russians" (Stone), **Supp. XXVII:** 251–252
"Reading the Signs, Empowering the Eye" (Bambara), **Supp. XI:** 17–18
Reading the Spirit (Eberhart), **I:** 525, 527, 530
Ready, Richard M., **Supp. XIX:** 154
"Ready Or Not" (Baraka), **Supp. II Part 1:** 50
Reagan, Ronald, **Supp. IV Part 1:** 224–225
"Real Bowery, The" (Hapgood), **Supp. XVII:** 103
"Real Class" (Vidal), **Supp. IV Part 1:** 35
Real Cool Killers, The (C. Himes), **Supp. XVI:** 143
Real Dope, The (Lardner), **II:** 422–423
"Real Estate" (Moore), **Supp. X:** 178
"Real Gone Guy, A" (McGrath), **Supp. X:** 117
"Real Horatio Alger Story, The" (Cowley), **Supp. II Part 1:** 143
"Realities" (MacLeish), **III:** 4
"Reality in America" (Trilling), **Supp. III Part 2:** 495, 502
"Reality! Reality! What Is It?" (Eberhart), **I:** 536
Reality Sandwiches, 1953–60 (Ginsberg), **Supp. II Part 1:** 315, 320
"Reality U.S.A." (Halliday), **Supp. XIX:** 89
Real Life of Sebastian Knight, The (Nabokov), **III:** 246; **Retro. Supp. I:** 266, 269, 270, 274
"Really Good Jazz Piano, A" (Yates), **Supp. XI:** 342
"Real Movie, with Stars, The" (Hull), **Supp. XXI:** 136
Real Presence: A Novel (Bausch), **Supp. VII:** 42–43, 50
"Real Revolution Is Love, The" (Harjo), **Supp. XII:** 224, 225–226
"Real Surrounding, The: On Canaletto's Venice" (Bronk), **Supp. XXI:** 32
"Real Thing, The" (H. James), **Retro. Supp. I:** 228; **Retro. Supp. II:** 223
"Real Two-Party System" (Vidal), **Supp. IV Part 2:** 679
Real West Marginal Way, The (Hugo), **Supp. VI:** 132, 134; **Supp. XVIII:** 299
"Real World around Us, The" (Carson), **Supp. IX:** 21
Reaper Essays, The (Jarman and McDowell), **Supp. IX:** 270; **Supp. XVII:** 110–111
"Reaper Interviews Jean Doh and Sean Dough, The" (Jarman and McDowell), **Supp. XVII:** 110
"Reapers" (Toomer), **Supp. III Part 2:** 481; **Supp. IX:** 312
Reason and Other Women (Notley), **Supp. XXII:** 224, 227, 235, 236, 237
"Reason and Race: A Review of the Literature of the Negro for 1946" (Locke), **Supp. XIV:** 206
"Reason for Moving, A" (Strand), **Supp. IV Part 2:** 624
"Reason for Stories, The: Toward a Moral Fiction" (Stone), **Supp. V:** 298, 300
Reasons for Moving (Strand), **Supp.**

IV Part 2: 624–626, 626
"Reasons for Music" (MacLeish), **III:** 19
"Reasons of the Body" (Sanders), **Supp. XVI:** 274
Reasons to Live (Hempel), **Supp. XXI:** 115, 117, 118, **119–122**
Rebecca (du Maurier), **Supp. XIX:** 57–58; **Supp. XXII:** 120
Rebecca, or, The Fille de Chambre (Rowson), **Supp. XV:** 229, **235–236,** 238
Rebecca Harding Davis Reader, A (Pfaelzer, ed.), **Supp. XVI:** 88, 90
Rebel Angels: Twenty-five Poets of the New Formalism (Jarman and Mason, eds.), **Supp. XV:** 251; **Supp. XVII:** 109, 110, 112, 121
"Rebellion" (R. Lowell), **Retro. Supp. II:** 187
Rebel Powers (Bausch), **Supp. VII:** 41, 45–46, 49–51
Rebel without a Cause (film), **Supp. XII:** 9
"Rebirth" (McKnight), **Supp. XX: 147, 157**
"Rebirth of God and the Death of Man, The " (Fiedler), **Supp. XIII:** 108
Rebolledo, Tey Diana, **Supp. XIII:** 214
Reb Shloyme nogid: A poeme fun yidishn leben (Shloyme the wealthy: A poem of Jewish life)(Asch), **Supp. XXIII:** 4, 5
Recapitulation (Stegner), **Supp. IV Part 2:** 598, 600, 612–613
"Recapitulation, The" (Eberhart), **I:** 522
"Recapitulations" (Shapiro), **Supp. II Part 2:** 701, 702, 708, 710–711
"Receding Horizons" (Lethem and Scholtz), **Supp. XVIII:** 145
"Recencies in Poetry" (Zukofsky), **Supp. III Part 2:** 615
Recent Killing, A (Baraka), **Supp. II Part 1:** 55
"Recent Negro Fiction" (Ellison), **Supp. II Part 1:** 233, 235
"Recessional" (A. Finch), **Supp. XVII:** 70–71
"Recital, The" (Ashbery), **Supp. III Part 1:** 14
"Recitative" (H. Crane), **I:** 390; **Retro. Supp. II:** 78
Reckless Eyeballing (Reed), **Supp. X:** 241
Reckless Moment, The (film), **Supp. XXII:** 120, 131, 132
Recognition of Robert Frost: Twenty-Fifth Anniversary (Thornton, ed.), **Retro. Supp. III:** 103
Recognitions, The (Gaddis), **Supp. IV Part 1:** 279, 280–285, 286, 287, 288, 289, 291, 292, 294; **Supp. XX: 91; Supp. XXIV:** 140
"Recollection and Perhaps a Tribute, A" (Espaillat), **Supp. XXI:** 103–104
Recollections (R. H. Stoddard), **Supp. XV:** 271
Recollections of Logan Pearsall Smith: The Story of a Friendship (Gathorne-Hardy), **Supp. XIV:** 344
"Reconciliation" (Whitman), **IV:** 347
"Reconstructed but Unregenerate" (Ransom), **III:** 496
"Reconstruction and Its Benefits" (Du Bois), **Supp. II Part 1:** 171
Recovering (Sarton), **Supp. VIII:** 264
Recovering the U.S. Hispanic Literary Heritage (Paredes), **Supp. XIII:** 320
"Recovery" (Dove), **Supp. IV Part 1:** 248
Re-Creation Story (Gansworth), **Supp. XXVI:** 113–114
Rector of Justin, The (Auchincloss), **Supp. IV Part 1:** 21, 23, 27–30, 36
"Recurrent Dream" (Nelson), **Supp. XVIII:** 176
Recyclopedia: Trimmings, S*PeRM**K*T, and Muse & Drudge (Mullen), **Supp. XXVII:** 171, 174–175
"RED AUTUMN" (Baraka), **Supp. II Part 1:** 55
Red Badge of Courage, The (S. Crane), **I:** 201, 207, 212, 405, 406, 407, 408, 412–416, 419, 421, 422, 423, 477, 506; **II:** 264; **III:** 317; **IV:** 350; **Retro. Supp. II:** 108; **Supp. IV Part 1:** 380; **Supp. XIV:** 51; **Supp. XVII:** 228; **Supp. XVIII:** 75; **Supp. XXI:** 277; **Supp. XXVII:** 207
"Redbirds" (C. Frost), **Supp. XV:** 99
"Red Bow, The" (Saunders), **Supp. XIX:** 232–233, 234
"Redbreast in Tampa" (Lanier), **Supp. I Part 1:** 364
"Red Brocade" (Nye), **Supp. XIII:** 288
Redburn: His First Voyage (Melville), **III:** 79–80, 84; **Retro. Supp. I:** 245, 247–248, 249; **Retro. Supp. III:** 147, 148, 150–151, 152, 154–155; **Supp. XVIII:** 6
Red Calico (Miller and Bowden), **Supp. XXII:** 188
"Red Carpet for Shelley, A" (Wylie), **Supp. I Part 2:** 724
Red Channels (Harnett), **Supp. XV:** 198
"Red Clowns" (Cisneros), **Supp. VII:** 63
Red Coal, The (Stern), **Supp. IX: 291–292**
Red Coat, The (Shanley), **Supp. XIV:** 316–317
"Red Cords" (Lamott), **Supp. XX: 142**
"Red"(Crooker), **Supp. XXIII:** 63
"Red Cross" (Hughes), **Retro. Supp. I:** 205
Red Cross (Shepard), **Supp. III Part 2:** 440, 446
Red Death, A (Mosley), **Supp. XIII:** 237, 239, 240
"Red Deer" (C. Frost), **Supp. XV:** 101
Redding, Josephine, **Supp. XXI:** 2
Redding, Saunders, **Supp. I Part 1:** 332, 333
Reddings, J. Saunders, **Supp. IV Part 1:** 164
Red Dust (Levine), **Supp. V:** 178, 183–184, 188
"Red Dust" (Levine), **Supp. V:** 184
"Redemption" (Gardner), **Supp. VI:** 72
Redemption (Uris), **Supp. XX: 244, 246, 247, 248, 254, 255**
"Red Ensign, The" (Gallagher), **Supp. XXIV:** 175, 176
"Redeployment" (Nemerov), **III:** 267, 272
Redfield, Robert, **IV:** 475
Redford, Robert, **Supp. IX:** 253, 259; **Supp. XIII:** 267; **Supp. XIV:** 223
Redgrave, Lynn, **Supp. V:** 107
Red Harvest (Hammett), **Supp. IV Part 1:** 346–348, 348; **Supp. IV Part 2:** 468; **Supp. XXI:** 272
"Red Hat, The"(Hadas), **Supp. XXIII:** 111, 113, 118, 119, 124, 128
Red-Headed Woman (film), **Retro. Supp. I:** 110; **Supp. XVI:** 191
Red Helmet (Hickam), **Supp. XXVII:** 110–111
"Red Horse Wind over Albuquerque" (Harjo), **Supp. XII:** 219
Red Hot Vacuum, The (Solotaroff), **Retro. Supp. II:** 281
Rediscovery of America, The (W. Frank), **Supp. XX: 75**
Rediscovery of Man, The (W. Frank), **Supp. XX: 67–68, 80**
"Red Leaves" (Faulkner), **II:** 72
"Red Meat: What Difference Did Stesichoros Make?" (Carson), **Supp. XII:** 107
"Red Nails" (Howard), **Supp. XXVII:** 126
"Red Pawn" (Rand), **Supp. IV Part 2:** 520
Red Pony, The (Steinbeck), **IV:** 50, 51, 58, 70

Redrawing the Boundaries (Fisher), **Retro. Supp. I:** 39
Red Robins, The (Koch), **Supp. XV:** 185–186, 187
Red Roses for Bronze (Doolittle), **Supp. I Part 1:** 253, 268, 271
Red Rover, The (Cooper), **I:** 342–343, 355
Red Ryder (comic books), **Supp. XXVII:** 23
"Red Rydler and His Dog" (O'Hara and Brainard), **Supp. XXVII:** 23
Reds (Beatty), **Supp. XXIV:** 227
"Red Shadows" (Howard), **Supp. XXVII:** 122
"Red Shift" (Berrigan), **Supp. XXIV:** 46
"Red Silk Stockings" (Hughes), **Retro. Supp. I:** 200
Redskins, The (Cooper), **I:** 351, 353
Red Sox and Bluefish: And Other Things That Make New England New England (Orlean), **Supp. XXV:** 159
"Red Sox Nation, North" (Mosher), **Supp. XXII:** 209
"Red Star, Winter Orbit" (W. Gibson and B. Sterling), **Supp. XVI:** 123
Red Suitcase (Nye), **Supp. XIII:** 277, 278, 287
Red the Fiend (Sorrentino), **Supp. XXI:** 227, 231, 237
Red Wallflower, A (S. Warner), **Supp. XVIII:** 260
"Red Wheelbarrow, The" (W. C. Williams), **IV:** 411–412; **Retro. Supp. I:** 419, 430
"Red Wind" (Chandler), **Supp. IV Part 1:** 122
"Red Wing Church, The" (Kooser), **Supp. XIX:** 119
"Redwings" (Wright), **Supp. III Part 2:** 603
Reed, Edward Bliss, **Supp. XV:** 297, 298, 300
Reed, Ishmael, **Retro. Supp. II:** 111, 324–325; **Supp. II Part 1:** 34; **Supp. X: 239–257,** 331; **Supp. XIII:** 181, 182; **Supp. XVI:** 143; **Supp. XX: 107; Supp. XXII:** 172; **Supp. XXVII:** 167
Reed, J. D., **Supp. XVI:** 174
Reed, John, **I:** 48, 476, 483; **Supp. X:** 136; **Supp. XV:** 295, 299; **Supp. XVII:** 96, 99, 100; **Supp. XVIII:** 225; **Supp. XXI:** 6, 12; **Supp. XXII:** 274, 275; **Supp. XXIII:** 161, 162
Reed, Lou, **Retro. Supp. II:** 266
"Reedbeds of the Hackensack, The" (Clampitt), **Supp. IX:** 41
"Reed of Pan, A" (McCullers), **II:** 585
Reedy, Billy, **Retro. Supp. II:** 65, 67, 71, 73
Reedy, William Marion, **Supp. I Part 2:** 456, 461, 465; **Supp. XXVII:** 287
Reef, The (Wharton), **IV:** 317–318, 322; **Retro. Supp. I:** 372, **373–374; Retro. Supp. III:** 284, 285
Reena and Other Stories (Marshall), **Supp. XI:** 275, 277, 278
Reese, Debbie, **Supp. XXVI:** 108–109
"Reese in Evening Shadow" (Skloot), **Supp. XX: 204**
Reeve, F. D., **Retro. Supp. III:** 107; **Supp. XV:** 344, 349
Reeve's Tale (Chaucer), **I:** 131
"Refiguring the Postcolonial Imagination: Tropes of Visuality in Writing by Rhys, Kincaid, and Cliff" (Emery), **Supp. XXII:** 73
Refiner's Fire: The Life and Adventures of Marshall Pearl, a Foundling (Helprin), **Supp. XXV:** 83, 85–86
"Reflection from Anita Loos" (Empson), **Supp. XVI:** 190
"Reflections" (Carruth), **Supp. XVI:** 54
"Reflections" (Komunyakaa), **Supp. XIII:** 117
Reflections at Fifty and Other Essays (Farrell), **II:** 49
"Reflections by a Fire" (Sarton), **Supp. VIII:** 259
Reflections in a Golden Eye (McCullers), **II:** 586, 588, 593–596, 604; **IV:** 384, 396
Reflections of a Jacobite (Auchincloss), **Supp. IV Part 1:** 31
Reflections on a Gift of Watermelon Pickle (Dunning), **Supp. XIV:** 126
Reflections on Poetry and Poetics (Nemerov), **III:** 269
"Reflections on the Constitution of Nature" (Freneau), **Supp. II Part 1:** 274
"Reflections on the Death of the Reader" (Morris), **III:** 237
Reflections on the End of an Era (Niebuhr), **III:** 297–298
"Reflections on the Life and Death of Lord Clive" (Paine), **Supp. I Part 2:** 505
Reflections on the Revolution in France (Burke), **Supp. I Part 2:** 511, 512
Reflections: Thinking Part I (Arendt), **Supp. I Part 2:** 570
"Reflex Action and Theism" (James), **II:** 345, 363
Reflex and Bone Structure (Major), **Supp. XXII: 174–175**
"Refrains/Remains/Reminders" (Goldbarth), **Supp. XII:** 180–181, 181
"Refuge" (Kingsolver), **Supp. VII:** 208
"Refuge" (Teasdale), **Supp. XXVII:** 291
"Refuge, A" (Goldbarth), **Supp. XII:** 190
Refugee Children: Theory, Research, and Services (Ahearn and Athey, eds.), **Supp. XI:** 184
"Refugees, The" (Jarrell), **II:** 371
"Refusal" (C. Frost), **Supp. XV:** 102
"Refusal to Publish Fifth Book" (Halliday), **Supp. XIX:** 94
"Regalia" (H. Johnson), **Supp. XXVI:** 172
Regarding Wave (Snyder), **Supp. VIII: 299–300**
Regina (Epstein), **Supp. XII: 170–171**
"Regional Literature of the South" (Rawlings), **Supp. X:** 228
"Regional Writer, The" (O'Connor), **Retro. Supp. II:** 223, 225
Régnier, Henri de, **II:** 528–529
Regular Guy, A (Simpson), **Supp. XXVII:** 239–240
Regulators, The (King), **Supp. V:** 141
Rehder, Robert, **Supp. IV Part 1:** 69
Rehearsing Absence (Espaillat), **Supp. XXI:** 99
Reich, Tova, **Supp. XVI:** 158
Reichel, Hans, **III:** 183
Reichl, Ruth, **Supp. X:** 79, 85
Reid, B. L., **II:** 41, 47
Reid, Forrest, **Supp. XX: 235**
Reid, Thomas, **II:** 9; **Supp. I Part 1:** 151
Reign of Snakes (Wrigley), **Supp. XVIII:** 293, **302–306**
"Reign of Snakes" (Wrigley), **Supp. XVIII:** 302–304
Reign of Wonder, The (Tanner), **I:** 260
Rein, Yevgeny, **Supp. VIII:** 22
Reinagle, Alexander, **Supp. XV:** 238, 240
"Reincarnation" (Dickey), **Supp. IV Part 1:** 181–182
Reine des pommes, La (C. Himes). See For Love of Imabelle (C. Himes)
Reiner, Carl, **Supp. IV Part 2:** 591
Reinfeld, Linda, **Supp. IV Part 2:** 421
Reinhardt, Max, **Supp. XV:** 307
Reinventing the Enemy's Language: Contemporary Native Women's Writing of North America (Bird and Harjo, eds.), **Supp. XII:** 216, 217
Reisman, Jerry, **Supp. III Part 2:** 618

Reiter, Amy, **Supp. XIX:** 54, 56
Reitlinger, Gerald, **Supp. XII:** 161
Reivers, The: A Reminiscence (Faulkner), **I:** 305; **II:** 57, 73; **Retro. Supp. I:** 74, 82, 91; **Retro. Supp. III:** 87–88
"Rejoicings" (Stern), **Supp. IX:** 289–290
Rejoicings: Selected Poems, 1966–1972 (Stern), **Supp. IX: 289–290**
Relation of My Imprisonment, The (Banks), **Supp. V:** 8, 12–13
"Relations" (Biss), **Supp. XXVI:** 56
"Relations between Poetry and Painting, The" (Stevens), **Retro. Supp. I:** 312
Relations of the Alabama-Georgia Dialect to the Provincial Dialects of Great Britain, The (Brooks), **Supp. XIV:** 3
Relative Stranger, A (C. Baxter), **Supp. XVII:** 19, 22
"Relativity of Beauty, The" (Rawlings), **Supp. X:** 226
Relearning the Alphabet (Levertov), **Supp. III Part 1:** 280, 281
"Release" (C. Baxter), **Supp. XVII:** 15
"Release, The" (MacLeish), **III:** 16
Reles, Abe ("Kid Twist"), **Supp. IV Part 1:** 382
"Relevance of an Impossible Ethical Ideal, The" (Niebuhr), **III:** 298
"Religion" (Dunbar), **Supp. II Part 1:** 199
"Religion" (Emerson), **II:** 6
Religion of Nature Delineated, The (Wollaston), **II:** 108
"Religious Instruction" (Peacock), **Supp. XIX:** 200, 201
Religious Rebel, A: The Letters of "H. W. S." (Mrs. Pearsall Smith) (L. P. Smith), **Supp. XIV:** 349
"Reluctance" (Frost), **II:** 153; **Retro. Supp. III:** 96
Reluctantly: Autobiographical Essays (Carruth), **Supp. XVI:** 45–46, 50
Remains (Snodgrass), **Supp. VI:** 311, **313–314**
"Remains, The" (Strand), **Supp. IV Part 2:** 627
"Remains of Princess Kaiulani's Garden, The" (Vaz), **Supp. XXVI:** 262–263
"Remarks on Color" (Wright), **Supp. XV:** 346
"Remarks on National Literature" (Channing), **Supp. XXIV: 76–77**
"Remarks on Spencer's Definition of Mind as Correspondence" (James), **II:** 345
Remarque, Erich Maria, **Retro. Supp. I:** 113; **Supp. IV Part 1:** 380
Rembrandt, **II:** 536; **IV:** 310; **Supp. IV Part 1:** 390, 391
"Rembrandt, The" (Wharton), **IV:** 310
"Rembrandt's Hat" (Malamud), **Supp. I Part 2:** 435, 437
Rembrandt Takes a Walk (Strand), **Supp. IV Part 2:** 631
"Rembrandt to Rembrandt" (Robinson), **III:** 521–522
Remembered Earth, The: An Anthology of Contemporary Native American Literature (Hobson, ed.), **Supp. IV Part 1:** 321
Remembered Yesterdays (R. U. Johnson), **Supp. IX:** 184
"Remembering" (Angelou), **Supp. IV Part 1:** 15
"Remembering Allen Tate" (Cowley), **Supp. II Part 1:** 153
"Remembering Barthes" (Sontag), **Supp. III Part 2:** 451, 471
"Remembering Guston" (Kunitz), **Supp. III Part 1:** 257
"Remembering James Laughlin" (Karr), **Supp. XI:** 242
Remembering Laughter (Stegner), **Supp. IV Part 2:** 598, 606, 607, 608, 611, 614
"Remembering Lobo" (Mora), **Supp. XIII:** 220, 227
"Remembering My Father" (Berry), **Supp. X:** 23
"Remembering My Parents Remembering the Books They Read" (Espaillat), **Supp. XXI:** 107
"Remembering that Island" (McGrath), **Supp. X:** 116
"Remembering the Children of Auschwitz" (McGrath), **Supp. X:** 127
"Remembering the Lost World" (Jarrell), **II:** 388
"Remembering the Sixties" (Simpson), **Supp. IX:** 279
Remember Me to Tom (T. Williams), **IV:** 379–380
"Remember Not" (H. Johnson), **Supp. XXVI:** 166
"Remember the Moon Survives" (Kingsolver), **Supp. VII:** 209
Remember to Remember (H. Miller), **III:** 186
"Remembrance, A" (Gioia), **Supp. XV:** 112
Remembrance of Things Past (Proust), **Supp. IV Part 2:** 600; **Supp. XII:** 9; **Supp. XIII:** 44
Remembrance Rock (Sandburg), **III:** 590
Reminiscence, A (Ashbery), **Supp. III Part 1:** 2
Remnick, David, **Supp. XVI:** 246
"Remora" (Merrill), **Supp. III Part 1:** 326
"Removal" (White), **Supp. I Part 2:** 664–665
"Removal, The" (Merwin), **Supp. III Part 1:** 350, 351
"Removal Service Request" (Halliday), **Supp. XIX:** 90
Removed from Time (Matthews and Feeney), **Supp. IX:** 154
Remsen, Ira, **Supp. I Part 1:** 369
"Rémy de Gourmont, A Distinction" (Pound), **III:** 467
"Renaissance" (Carruth), **Supp. XVI:** 56
Renaissance in the South (Bradbury), **I:** 288–289
Renaldo and Clara (film, Dylan and Shepard), **Supp. XVIII:** 21, 28, 31
"Renaming the Kings" (Levine), **Supp. V:** 184
Renan, Ernest, **Supp. XX: 122**
Renan, Joseph Ernest, **II:** 86; **IV:** 440, 444
Renard, Jules, **IV:** 79
"Renascence" (Millay), **III:** 123, 125–126, 128; **Supp. XV:** 42
Renault, Mary, **Supp. IV Part 2:** 685
"Rendezvous, The" (Kumin), **Supp. IV Part 2:** 455
René, Norman, **Supp. X:** 146, 152
Renée (anonymous author), **Supp. XVI:** 64, 66
"Renegade, The" (Jackson), **Supp. IX:** 120
Renewal of Life series (Mumford), **Supp. II Part 2:** 476, 479, 481, 482, 485, 495, 497
"Reno Hill ... Little Bighorn"(Kenny), **Supp. XXIII:** 155
Renoir, Jean, **Supp. XII:** 259; **Supp. XXII:** 256
Renouvrier, Charles, **II:** 344–345, 346
"Renunciation" (Banks), **Supp. V:** 10
Renza, Louis A., **Retro. Supp. II:** 142
"Repair" (Peacock), **Supp. XIX:** 204
"Repeating Dream" (Gander), **Supp. XV:** 340
Repent in Haste (Marquand), **III:** 59
Reperusals and Re-Collections (L. P. Smith), **Supp. XIV:** 346–347
"Repetitive Heart, The: Eleven Poems in Imitation of the Fugue Form"

(Schwartz), **Supp. II Part 2:** 645–646
"Replacing Regionalism" (Murphy), **Retro. Supp. II:** 143
Replansky, Naomi, **Supp. X:** 119
Replenishing Jessica (Bodenheim), **Supp. XXV:** 24, 25
"Reply to Mr. Wordsworth" (MacLeish), **III:** 19
"Reply to the Editor of 'The Art of Authorship' " (Twain), **Retro. Supp. III:** 265
"Report, A" (Jin), **Supp. XVIII:** 93
Reporter, The (Levin), **Supp. XXVII:** 139
"Report from a Forest Logged by the Weyhaeuser Company" (Wagoner), **Supp. IX:** 328
"Report from North Vietnam" (Paley), **Supp. VI:** 227
Report from Part One (Brooks), **Supp. III Part 1:** 70, 72, 80, 82–85
Report from Part Two (Brooks), **Supp. III Part 1:** 87
Report on a Game Survey of the North Central States (Leopold), **Supp. XIV:** 182
"Report on the Barnhouse Effect" (Vonnegut), **Supp. II Part 2:** 756
"Report to an Academy, A" (Kafka), **Supp. XX: 18**
"Report to Crazy Horse" (Stafford), **Supp. XI: 324–325**
"Repose of Rivers" (H. Crane), **I:** 393; **Retro. Supp. II:** 78, 81
"Repossession of a Heritage, The" (Zagarell), **Supp. XV:** 270, 281
Repp, John, **Supp. XXIII:** 302
"Representation and the War for Reality" (Gass), **Supp. VI:** 88
"Representative Indian, The" (Outlook), **Supp. XXV:** 277, 278
Representative Men (Emerson), **II:** 1, 5–6, 8
"Representing Far Places" (Stafford), **Supp. XI:** 321
Repression and Recovery (Nelson), **Supp. XVIII:** 226
"REPRISE OF ONE OF A. G.'S BEST POEMS" (Baraka), **Supp. II Part 1:** 59
"RepRoach" (Stallings), **Supp. XXV:** 230–231
"Reproducing Ourselves Is All Very Well" (E. Hoffman), **Supp. XVI:** 155
Republic (Plato), **I:** 485; **Retro. Supp. III:** 94
"Republican Manifesto, A" (Paine), **Supp. I Part 2:** 511
"Republican Mother, The: Woman and the Enlightenment—An American Perspective" (Kerber), **Supp. XXV:** 44
Republic of Love, The (Shields), **Supp. VII:** 323–324, 326, 327
"Requa" (Olsen), **Supp. XIII:** 294, **302–303,** 304
Requa, Kenneth A., **Supp. I Part 1:** 107
"Requa I" (Olsen). See "Requa" (Olsen)
"Request for Offering" (Eberhart), **I:** 526
"Requiem" (Akhmatova), **Supp. VIII:** 20
"Requiem" (LaBastille), **Supp. X:** 105
Requiem for a Nun (Faulkner), **II:** 57, 72–73; **Retro. Supp. III:** 73, 86, 87
Requiem for Harlem (H. Roth), **Supp. IX:** 235, 236, **240–242**
"Rescue, The" (Updike), **IV:** 214
Rescued Year, The (Stafford), **Supp. XI: 321–322**
"Rescued Year, The" (Stafford), **Supp. XI:** 322, 323
"Rescue with Yul Brynner" (Moore), **III:** 215
"Rescuing Moon"(P. Benedict), **Supp. XXIII:** 40
"Resemblance" (Bishop), **Supp. I Part 1:** 86
"Resemblance" (Ferry), **Supp. XXIV:** 161
"Resemblance between a Violin Case and a Coffin, A" (T. Williams), **IV:** 378–379
"Reservations" (Taylor), **Supp. V:** 323
"Reserved Memorials" (Mather), **Supp. II Part 2:** 446, 449
"Resignaci6n" (Espaillat), **Supp. XXI:** 104
"Resignation"(J. Schoolcraft), **Supp. XXIII:** 228, 229–230
"Resistance to Civil Government" (Thoreau), **Supp. X:** 27, 28
Resist Much, Obey Little (Berry), **Supp. XIII:** 2
Resolution (Parker), **Supp. XIX:** 187
"Resolution" (Rash), **Supp. XXVII:** 221
"Resolution and Independence" (Wordsworth), **Supp. XV:** 346
"Resonance" (Stone), **Supp. XXVII:** 253
"Resort" (Hampl), **Supp. XXII:** 86–87
Resort and Other Poems (Hampl), **Supp. XXII:** 83, 86–87
Resources of Hope (R. Williams), **Supp. IX:** 146
"Respectable Place, A" (O'Hara), **III:** 369
"Respectable Woman, A" (Chopin), **Retro. Supp. II:** 66
"Respite" (Pedersen; Nelson, trans.), **Supp. XVIII:** 180
Responses (Wilbur), **Supp. III Part 2:** 541
"Response to a Rumor that the Oldest Whorehouse in Wheeling, West Virginia, Has Been Condemned" (Wright), **Supp. III Part 2:** 602
"Rest Cure" (Boyle), **Supp. XXIV:** 57
Restif de La Bretonne, Nicolas, **III:** 175
"Rest of Life, The" (Gordon), **Supp. IV Part 1:** 311
Rest of Life, The: Three Novellas (Gordon), **Supp. IV Part 1:** 310–312
Rest of My Life, The (Wells), **Supp. XXVI:** 271, 283
Rest of the Way, The (McClatchy), **Supp. XII:** 255, **258–259**
Restoration comedy, **Supp. I Part 2:** 617
Restorers, The (Di Piero), **Supp. XIX:** 42–43, 44
"Restorers, The" (Di Piero), **Supp. XIX:** 43
"Restraint" (F. Barthelme), **Supp. XI:** 26
"Result" (Emerson), **II:** 6
"Résumé" (Parker), **Supp. IX:** 189
"Resurrecting Methuselah" (E. P. Jones), **Supp. XXII:** 151
Resurrection (Della Francesca), **Supp. XV:** 262
"Resurrection" (Harjo), **Supp. XII:** 224
"Resurrection" (Jin), **Supp. XVIII:** 94–95
Resurrection, The (Gardner), **Supp. VI:** 61, 63, **64–65,** 68, 69, 73, 74
"Resurrection, The" (Very), **Supp. XXV:** 247–248
Resurrection Blues (A. Miller), **Retro. Supp. III:** 176–177
"Retort" (Hay), **Supp. XIV:** 133
Retour amont (Char; Sobin, trans.), **Supp. XVI:** 282
Retrieval System, The (Kumin), **Supp. IV Part 2:** 449, 451, 452
"Retrievers in Translation" (Doty), **Supp. XI:** 132
"Retroduction to American History" (Tate), **IV:** 129
"Retrospects and Prospects" (Lanier), **Supp. I Part 1:** 352
"Return" (Corso), **Supp. XII:** 135

"Return" (Creeley), **Supp. IV Part 1:** 141, 145
"Return" (MacLeish), **III:** 12
"Return" (Oppen), **Supp. XXVI:** 231
"Return, The" (Bidart), **Supp. XV:** 32–33
"Return, The" (Bontemps), **Supp. XXII:** 3, 8
"Return, The" (Pound), **Retro. Supp. I:** 288
"Return, The" (Ray), **Supp. XVIII:** 194
"Return, The" (Roethke), **III:** 533
"Return, The: Orihuela, 1965" (Levine), **Supp. V:** 194
"Return: An Elegy, The" (Warren), **IV:** 239
"Return: Buffalo" (Hogan), **Supp. IV Part 1:** 411
"Returning" (Komunyakaa), **Supp. XIII:** 122
"Returning a Lost Child" (Glück), **Supp. V:** 81
"Returning from the Enemy" (Harjo), **Supp. XII:** 229–230
"Returning the Borrowed Road" (Komunyakaa), **Supp. XIII:** 113, 133
"Return of Alcibiade, The" (Chopin), **Retro. Supp. II:** 58, 64
Return of Ansel Gibbs, The (Buechner), **III:** 310; **Supp. XII: 48**
"Return of Eros to Academe, The" (Bukiet), **Supp. XVII:** 47
"Return of Spring" (Winters), **Supp. II Part 2:** 791
Return of the Native, The (Hardy), **II:** 184–185, 186
Return of the Vanishing American, The (Fiedler), **Supp. XIII:** 103
Return to a Place Lit by a Glass of Milk (Simic), **Supp. VIII:** 274, 276, 283
"Return to Lavinia" (Caldwell), **I:** 310
"Return to Thin Air: The Everest Disaster Ten Years Later" (Outside), **Supp. XVIII:** 113
Return to Zion, The (Asch), **Supp. XXIII:** 5
Reuben (Wideman), **Supp. X:** 320
Reuben and Rachel; or, Tales of Old Times (Rowson), **Supp. XV: 240–241**
Reunion (Mamet), **Supp. XIV:** 240, 247, 254
"Reunion in Brooklyn" (H. Miller), **III:** 175, 184
"Reunion Joke, The" (Huddle), **Supp. XXVI:** 156
Reuther brothers, **I:** 493
"Reveille" (Kingsolver), **Supp. VII:** 208
"Reveille" (Untermeyer), **Supp. XV:** 300
"Reveille, The" (Harte), **Supp. II Part 1:** 342–343
Revelation (biblical book), **II:** 541; **IV:** 104, 153, 154; **Supp. I Part 1:** 105, 273
"Revelation" (O'Connor), **III:** 349, 353–354; **Retro. Supp. II:** 237; **Retro. Supp. III:** 208, 212–213
"Revelation" (Warren), **III:** 490
Revelations of Divine Love (Julian of Norwich), **Retro. Supp. III:** 68
Revenge (Harrison), **Supp. VIII:** 39, 45
"Revenge of Hamish, The" (Lanier), **Supp. I Part 1:** 365
"Revenge of Hannah Kemhuff, The" (Walker), **Supp. III Part 2:** 521
"Revenge of Rain-in-the-Face, The" (Longfellow), **Retro. Supp. II:** 170
"Reverberation"(Kenny), **Supp. XXIII:** 155
Reverberator, The (James), **Retro. Supp. I:** 227
"Reverdure" (Berry), **Supp. X:** 22
Reverdy, Pierre, **Supp. XV:** 178, 182; **Supp. XXIII:** 208
"Reverend Father Gilhooley" (Farrell), **II:** 45
Reverse Transcription (Kushner), **Supp. IX:** 138
Reversible Errors (Turow), **Supp. XVII: 220–221**
"Rev. Freemont Deadman" (Masters), **Supp. I Part 2:** 463
Reviewer's ABC, A (Aiken), **I:** 58
Review of Contemporary Fiction, 1990 (Tabbi, ed.), **Supp. XVII:** 143
"Revolt, against the Crepuscular Spirit in Modern Poetry" (Pound), **Retro. Supp. I:** 286
"Revolution" (C. L. R. James), **Supp. XXI:** 160
"Revolution" (Taggard), **Supp. XXII:** 275
"Revolutionary Answer to the Negro Problem in the USA, The" (statement, C. L. R. James), **Supp. XXI:** 169
Revolutionary Petunias (Walker), **Supp. III Part 2:** 520, 522, 530
Revolutionary Road (Yates), **Supp. XI:** 334, **335–340**
"Revolutionary Symbolism in America" (Burke), **I:** 272
"Revolutionary Theatre, The" (Baraka), **Supp. II Part 1:** 42
Revolution in Taste, A: Studies of Dylan Thomas, Allen Ginsberg, Sylvia Plath, and Robert Lowell (Simpson), **Supp. IX:** 276
"Revolution in the Revolution in the Revolution" (Snyder), **Supp. VIII:** 300
Revon, Marcel, **II:** 525
"Rewaking, The" (W. C. Williams), **Retro. Supp. I:** 430
"Rewrite" (Dunn), **Supp. XI:** 147
"Rewriting Tradition in the Digital Era: The Vision of Eric Gansworth" (Purdy), **Supp. XXVI:** 105
Rexroth, Kenneth, **II:** 526; **Supp. II Part 1:** 307; **Supp. II Part 2:** 436; **Supp. III Part 2:** 625, 626; **Supp. IV Part 1:** 145–146; **Supp. VIII:** 289; **Supp. XIII:** 75; **Supp. XIV:** 287; **Supp. XV:** 140, 141, 146; **Supp. XXII:** 168
Reynolds, Ann (pseudonym). See Bly, Carol
Reynolds, Clay, **Supp. XI:** 254
Reynolds, David, **Supp. XV:** 269; **Supp. XXIII:** 187
Reynolds, Sir Joshua, **Supp. I Part 2:** 716
Reynolds, Quentin, **IV:** 286
Reza, Yasmina, **Supp. XXI:** 148
Rezanov (Atherton), **Supp. XXIV:** 23
Reznikoff, Charles, **IV:** 415; **Retro. Supp. I:** 422; **Supp. III Part 2:** 615, 616, 617, 628; **Supp. XIV: 277–296; Supp. XXIII:** 174; **Supp. XXIV:** 36, 45; **Supp. XXVI:** 226
"Rhapsodist, The" (Brown), **Supp. I Part 1:** 125–126
"Rhapsody on a Windy Night" (T. S. Eliot), **Retro. Supp. I:** 55; **Retro. Supp. III:** 60
Rhetoric of Motives, A (Burke), **I:** 272, 275, 278, 279
Rhetoric of Religion, The (Burke), **I:** 275, 279
"Rhobert" (Toomer), **Supp. IX:** 316–317
"Rhode Show" (Mallon), **Supp. XIX:** 137–138
"Rhododendrons" (Levis), **Supp. XI:** 260, 263
Rhubarb Show, The (radio, Keillor), **Supp. XVI:** 178
"Rhyme of Sir Christopher, The" (Longfellow), **II:** 501
Rhymes to Be Traded for Bread (Lindsay), **Supp. I Part 2:** 380, 381–382
Rhys, Ernest, **III:** 458
Rhys, Jean, **Supp. III Part 1:** 42, 43;

Supp. XVIII: 131
"Rhythm" (Stone), **Supp. XXVII:** 249–250
"Rhythm & Blues" (Baraka), **Supp. II Part 1:** 37–38
Rhythms (Reznikoff), **Supp. XIV:** 279, 282, 283
Rhythms II (Reznikoff), **Supp. XIV:** 282, 283, 284
Ribalow, Harold, **Supp. IX:** 236; **Supp. XXVII:** 133
Ribbentrop, Joachim von, **IV:** 249
Ribicoff, Abraham, **Supp. IX:** 33
Ribot, Théodule Armand, **Supp. XX: 238**
Ricardo, David, **Supp. I Part 2:** 628, 634
Rice, Allen Thorndike, **Retro. Supp. I:** 362
Rice, Anne, **Supp. VII: 287–306**
Rice, Elmer, **I:** 479; **III:** 145, 160–161
Rice, Mrs. Grantland, **II:** 435
Rice, Philip Blair, **IV:** 141
Rice, Stan, **Supp. XII:** 2
Rice, Tim, **Supp. XXI:** 148
Rice, Tom, **Supp. XIV:** 125
Rich, Adrienne, **Retro. Supp. I:** 8, 36, 42, 47, 404; **Retro. Supp. II:** 43, 191, 245; **Retro. Supp. III:** 1, 12, 14, **241–254**; **Supp. I Part 2:** 546–547, **550–578; Supp. III Part 1:** 84, 354; **Supp. III Part 2:** 541, 599; **Supp. IV Part 1:** 257, 325; **Supp. V:** 82; **Supp. VIII:** 272; **Supp. XII:** 217, 229, 255; **Supp. XIII:** 294; **Supp. XIV:** 126, 129; **Supp. XIX:** 83, 193; **Supp. XV:** 176, 252; **Supp. XVII:** 32, 74; **Supp. XXII:** 65, 66; **Supp. XXV:** 3; **Supp. XXVI:** 45, 68; **Supp. XXVII:** 165
Rich, Arnold, **Supp. I Part 2:** 552
Rich, Frank, **Supp. IV Part 2:** 585, 586; **Supp. V:** 106; **Supp. XXI:** 146; **Supp. XXIV:** 121, 124
Richard, Mark, **Supp. XIX: 209–222**
Richard Cory (Gurney), **Supp. V:** 99–100, 105
"Richard Hunt's 'Arachne' " (Hayden), **Supp. II Part 1:** 374
Richard II (Shakespeare), **Supp. XVII:** 244
Richard III (Shakespeare), **Supp. I Part 2:** 422
Richards, Bertrand F., **Supp. XX: 217–218**
Richards, Constance S., **Supp. XXII:** 73
Richards, David, **Supp. IV Part 2:** 576; **Supp. XXIV:** 266, 269
Richards, Grant, **I:** 515
Richards, I. A., **I:** 26, 273–274, 279, 522; **III:** 498; **IV:** 92; **Supp. I Part 1:** 264, 265; **Supp. I Part 2:** 647; **Supp. XXVI:** 63
Richards, Ivor Armonstrong, **Supp. XIV:** 2–3, 16
Richards, Keith, **Supp. XXVII:** 40, 41, 45
Richards, Laura E., **II:** 396; **III:** 505–506, 507
Richards, Leonard, **Supp. XIV:** 48
Richards, Lloyd, **Retro. Supp. III:** 315, 318, 323; **Supp. IV Part 1:** 362; **Supp. VIII:** 331
Richards, Rosalind, **III:** 506
Richards, Tad, **Supp. XVII:** 77
Richardson, Alan, **III:** 295
Richardson, Charles F., **Retro. Supp. III:** 261; **Supp. XVIII:** 14, 15
Richardson, Dorothy, **I:** 53; **II:** 320; **Supp. III Part 1:** 65
Richardson, Helen Patges, **Retro. Supp. II:** 95
Richardson, Henry Hobson, **I:** 3, 10
Richardson, Maurice, **Supp. XII:** 241
Richardson, Samuel, **I:** 134; **II:** 104, 111, 322; **Supp. IX:** 128; **Supp. V:** 127; **Supp. XV:** 232; **Supp. XX: 236**
Richardson, Tony, **Supp. XI:** 305, 306
"Richard Wright and Recent Negro Fiction" (Ellison), **Retro. Supp. II:** 116
"Richard Wright's Blues" (Ellison), **Retro. Supp. II:** 117, 124
"Richard Yates: A Requiem" (Lawrence), **Supp. XI:** 335
"Rich Boy, The" (Fitzgerald), **II:** 94; **Retro. Supp. I:** 98, 108
Richer, the Poorer, The: Sketches and Reminiscences (D. West), **Supp. XVIII:** 277, 289
"Riches" (Bausch), **Supp. VII:** 54
"Riches" (Teasdale), **Supp. XXVII:** 290
Richey, Elinor, **Supp. XXIV:** 30
Richler, Mordecai, **Supp. XI:** 294, 297
Rich Man, Poor Man (miniseries), **Supp. XIX:** 252
Rich Man, Poor Man (Shaw), **Supp. XIX:** 251–252
Richman, Robert, **Supp. XI:** 249; **Supp. XV:** 120–121, 251
Richman, Shira, **Supp. XXIV:** 167
Richmond (Masters), **Supp. I Part 2:** 471
Richmond, M. A., **Supp. XX: 277, 279, 282, 286, 289, 290**
Rich Relations (Hwang), **Supp. XXI:** 146–147
Richter, Conrad, **Supp. X:** 103; **Supp. XVIII: 207–222**
Richter, Jean Paul, **II:** 489, 492; **Supp. XVI:** 182
Rick Bass (Weltzien), **Supp. XVI:** 20
Rickman, Clio, **Supp. I Part 2:** 519
Ricks, Christopher, **Retro. Supp. I:** 56; **Supp. XVIII:** 20, 30, 32
Riddel, Joseph N., **IV:** 95
"Riddle, The" (Hay), **Supp. XIV:** 130
Ride down Mt Morgan, The (A. Miller), **Retro. Supp. III:** 173
"Ride in an Omnibus, A" (Briggs), **Supp. XVIII:** 9, 16
Rideout, Walter B., **Supp. XXVI:** 28
"Riders to the Blood-Red Wrath" (Brooks), **Supp. III Part 1:** 82–83
Riders to the Sea (Synge), **III:** 157
Ridge, Lola, **Supp. IX:** 308; **Supp. XV:** 307; **Supp. XXIV:** 49, 52; **Supp. XXVI:** 23
Riding, Alan, **Supp. XVI:** 294
Riding, Laura, **I:** 437
"Riding Out at Evening" (McCarriston), **Supp. XIV:** 262–263
Riding the Iron Rooster: By Train through China (Theroux), **Supp. VIII:** 324
Ridley, Clifford, **Supp. XXIV:** 282
Riesenberg, Felix, **I:** 360, 361
Riesman, David, **Supp. I Part 2:** 649, 650
"Rif, to Music, The" (Bowles), **Supp. IV Part 1:** 89
Riffs & Reciprocities (Dunn), **Supp. XI: 154–155**
Rifkin, Libby, **Supp. XXIV:** 39, 44
Rifles, The (Vollmann), **Supp. XVII:** 226, 233
Riggs, Marlon, **Supp. XI:** 19
Right Distance, The (Pickering), **Supp. XXI:** 196–197
Right Madness on Skye, The (Hugo), **Supp. VI:** 145–147
Rights of Man (Paine), **Supp. I Part 2:** 508, 511, 512–514, 516, 519, 523
"Rights of Woman" (Rowson), **Supp. XV:** 243
"Rights of Women, The" (Brown). See Alcuin: A Dialogue (Brown)
Right Stuff, The (Wolfe), **Supp. III Part 2:** 581–584
Right Thoughts in Sad Hours (Mather), **IV:** 144
Rigney, Barbara Hill, **Supp. VIII:** 215
"Rigorists" (Moore), **III:** 198
Rihani, Ameen, **Supp. XX: 115**
Rihoku, **Supp. XXII:** 228
Riis, Jacob A., **I:** 293; **Supp. I Part 1:** 13; **Supp. XVII:** 101, 106

Riley, Glenda, **Supp. XXIV:** 252
Riley, James Whitcomb, **I:** 205; **Supp. II Part 1:** 192, 193, 196, 197
Rilke, Rainer Maria, **I:** 445, 523; **II:** 367, 381, 382–383, 389, 543, 544; **III:** 552, 558, 563, 571, 572; **IV:** 380, 443; **Retro. Supp. II:** 20, 187; **Supp. I Part 1:** 264; **Supp. I Part 2:** 573; **Supp. III Part 1:** 239, 242, 246, 283, 319–320; **Supp. IV Part 1:** 284; **Supp. V:** 208, 343; **Supp. VIII:** 30, 40; **Supp. X:** 164; **Supp. XI:** 126; **Supp. XIII:** 74, 88; **Supp. XV:** 93, 212, 222,**Supp. XV:** 223, 225; **Supp. XVI:** 292; **Supp. XVII:** 244; **Supp. XXII:** 89, 90, 94; **Supp. XXIII:** 207; **Supp. XXIV:** 37, 38, 152, 162; **Supp. XXVI:** 259
Rilke on Love and Other Difficulties (Rilke), **Supp. X:** 164
"Rilke's Growth as a Poet" (Dobyns), **Supp. XIII:** 77
"Rimbaud" (Kerouac), **Supp. III Part 1:** 232
Rimbaud, Arthur, **I:** 381, 383, 389, 391, 526; **II:** 528, 543, 545; **III:** 23, 174, 189; **IV:** 286, 380, 443; **Retro. Supp. I:** 56; **Retro. Supp. II:** 187, 326; **Supp. III Part 1:** 14, 195; **Supp. IV Part 2:** 624; **Supp. VIII:** 39, 40; **Supp. XII:** 1, 16, 128, 255; **Supp. XIII:** 284; **Supp. XIV:** 338; **Supp. XVIII:** 23, 33; **Supp. XXI:** 225, 233; **Supp. XXIII:** 207; **Supp. XXIV:** 39, 40
Rindge, Debora, **Supp. XXI:** 246
Rinehart, Mary Roberts, **Supp. XXV: 189–203; Supp. XXVI:** 276, 281, 282
Rinehart, Stanley, **III:** 36
Ring, Frances Kroll, **Supp. IX:** 63, 64
Ring and the Book, The (Browning), **Supp. I Part 2:** 416, 468
Ring cycle (Wagner), **Supp. IV Part 1:** 392
Ringe, Donald, **I:** 339, 343; **Retro. Supp. II:** 270
Ringel, Faye, **Supp. XXII:** 205, 207
"Ringing" (Bierds), **Supp. XVII:** 28
"Ringing the Bells" (Sexton), **Supp. II Part 2:** 672, 687
Ringle, Ken, **Supp. X:** 15
Ring of Heaven: Poems (Hongo), **Supp. X:** 292
Rink, The (musical, McNally), **Supp. XIII:** 207
Rin Tin Tin: The Life and the Legend (Orlean), **Supp. XXV:** 160, 165–166
Rio Lobo (film), **Supp. XVI:** 246
Ríos, Alberto Alvaro, **Supp. IV Part 2: 537–556**
"Riot" (Brooks), **Supp. III Part 1:** 71, 84–85
Riot (Myers), **Supp. XXVII:** 208
Ripening (Le Sueur), **Supp. XXIII:** 165
Ripley, Ezra, **II:** 8; **IV:** 172
Rip-off Red, Girl Detective (Acker), **Supp. XII:** 3–4
Ripostes (Pound), **Retro. Supp. I:** 287–288, 413
Ripostes of Ezra Pound, The, Whereunto Are Appended the Complete Poetical Works of T. E. Hulme, with Prefatory Note (Pound), **III:** 458, 464, 465
Riprap (Snyder), **Supp. VIII: 292–294,** 295
"Riprap" (Snyder), **Supp. VIII:** 293–294
"Rip Van Winkle" (Irving), **II:** 304–306; **Supp. I Part 1:** 185
Rischin, Moses, **Supp. XVII:** 101, 103, 106
Risco-Lozado, Eliezar, **Supp. XIII:** 313
Rise and Shine (Quindlen), **Supp. XVII:** 179
Rise of David Levinsky, The (Cahan), **Supp. IX:** 227; **Supp. XIII:** 106; **Supp. XXVI:** 123
Rise of Silas Lapham, The (Howells), **II:** 275, 279, 283–285; **IV:** 202; **Retro. Supp. II:** 93, 101
"Rise of the Middle Class" (Banks), **Supp. V:** 10
Rising and Falling (Matthews), **Supp. IX:** 154, **160**
"Rising Daughter, The" (Olds), **Supp. X:** 204
Rising from the Plains (McPhee), **Supp. III Part 1:** 309–310
Rising Glory of America, The (Brackenridge and Freneau), **Supp. I Part 1:** 124; **Supp. II Part 1:** 67, 253, 256, 263
"Rising of the Storm, The" (Dunbar), **Supp. II Part 1:** 199
Rising Sun in the Pacific, The (Morison), **Supp. I Part 2:** 490
Rising Up and Rising Down (Vollmann), **Supp. XVII:** 225, 226, **229–230,** 232, 233, 235–236
Risk Pool, The (Russo), **Supp. XII: 328–331**
Ristovic, Aleksandar, **Supp. VIII:** 272
"Rita Dove: Identity Markers" (Vendler), **Supp. IV Part 1:** 247, 257
Ritchey, John, **Supp. XIV:** 122
Ritchie, Anne Thackeray, **Supp. XX: 231, 233**
"Rite of Passage" (Olds), **Supp. X:** 206
"Rites and Ceremonies" (Hecht), **Supp. X:** 61
Rites and Witnesses: A Comedy (Hinojosa), **Supp. XIX: 106–107**
"Rites of Spring, The" (Morris), **III:** 223
Ritivoi, Andreea Deciu, **Supp. XVI:** 148
Ritschl, Albrecht, **III:** 309, 604
Ritsos, Yannis, **Supp. X:** 112
"Ritsos and the Metaphysical Moment" (Dobyns), **Supp. XIII:** 78
Rittenhouse, David, **Supp. I Part 2:** 507
Rittenhouse, Jessie, **Supp. XV:** 295; **Supp. XXVII:** 286, 288, 289, 297
"Ritual, The" (Jarman), **Supp. XVII:** 114
"Ritual and Renewal: Keres Traditions in the Short Fiction of Leslie Silko" (Ruoff), **Supp. IV Part 2:** 559
Ritz, The (film), **Supp. XIII:** 206
Ritz, The (McNally), **Supp. XIII:** 198
"Rival, The" (Plath), **Retro. Supp. II:** 254
Riven Rock (Boyle), **Supp. VIII:** 5–6; **Supp. XX: 25–26**
"River" (Ammons), **Supp. VII:** 28
"River, The" (O'Connor), **III:** 344, 352, 353, 354, 356; **Retro. Supp. II:** 229, 231–232; **Retro. Supp. III:** 213
Rivera, Tomás, **Supp. XIII:** 216, 221; **Supp. XIX:** 97, 102
Riverbed (Wagoner), **Supp. IX: 327–328**
"River Driftwood" (Jewett), **Retro. Supp. II:** 132, 133, 147
"River Jordan, The" (DeLillo), **Supp. VI:** 3, 4
River King, The (Hoffman), **Supp. X:** 78, 85, 90, **91–92**
"River Merchant's Wife: A Letter, The" (Pound), **III:** 463
"River Now, The" (Hugo), **Supp. VI:** 144
River of Forgetfulness, The (Hadas), **Supp. XXIII: 120**
"River of Rivers in Connecticut, The" (Stevens), **Retro. Supp. I:** 313
River of the Mother of God and Other Essays by Aldo Leopold, The (Leopold), **Supp. XIV:** 180
"River"(O'Hara), **Supp. XXIII:** 212
"River Profile" (Auden), **Supp. II Part 1:** 26

"River Road" (Kunitz), **Supp. III Part 1:** 260
River Runs Through It, A (film), **Supp. XXVI:** 184
"River Runs Through It, A" (Maclean), **Supp. XIV:** 222–223, **223–229,** 233, 234, 235; **Supp. XVI:** 98
River Runs Through It and Other Stories, A (Maclean), **Supp. XIV:** 221, 223
Rivers, Allison, **Supp. XXIII:** 51
Rivers, Larry, **Supp. III Part 1:** 3; **Supp. XV:** 177, 178, 186; **Supp. XXIII:** 209, 210, 211, 212, 215, 216, 217, 220
Rivers and Mountains (Ashbery), **Supp. III Part 1:** 10, 26
Riverside Drive (Simpson), **Supp. IX: 275–276**
Riverside Poetry (Auden, Moore, and Shapiro, eds.), **Supp. XXI:** 98
Rivers to the Sea (Teasdale), **Supp. XV:** 295; **Supp. XXVII:** 283, 286, 289, 290, 294
"River"(Strout), **Supp. XXIII:** 283
River Styx, Ohio, and Other Poems, The (Oliver), **Supp. VII:** 231, 232
"River That Is East, The" (Kinnell), **Supp. III Part 1:** 241–242
"River"(theater performance, Strout), **Supp. XXIII:** 281
"River Towns" (Masters), **Supp. I Part 2:** 473
Rives, Amélie, **II:** 194
Rivière, Jacques, **Retro. Supp. I:** 63
"Rivington's Last Will and Testament" (Freneau), **Supp. II Part 1:** 261
"Rivulet, The" (Bryant), **Supp. I Part 1:** 155, 162
Rix, Alice, **I:** 199
RL's Dream (Mosley), **Supp. XIII:** 234, **244–245,** 249
Roach, Max, **Supp. X:** 239
"Road, Roadsides, and the Disparate Frames of a Sequence" (Sobin), **Supp. XVI:** 288
"Road, The" (H. Johnson), **Supp. XXVI:** 164
Road, The (McCarthy), **Supp. XXII:** 49
Road, The: In Search of America (Asch), **Supp. XXVI:** 17, 21, 23, 25, 26–28
Road Between, The (Farrell), **II:** 29, 38, 39–40
"Road Between Here and There, The" (Kinnell), **Supp. III Part 1:** 254
"Road Home, The" (Hammett), **Supp. IV Part 1:** 343
Road Home, The (Harrison), **Supp. VIII:** 37, 45, 48, **49–50,** 53
Road Is Before Us, The (Boulton), **Supp. XXII:** 17, 25–26
Roadless Yaak, The: Reflections and Observations about One of Our Last Great Wild Places (Bass, ed.), **Supp. XVI:** 23
"Road Not Taken, The" (Frost), **II:** 154; **Retro. Supp. I:** 131; **Retro. Supp. III:** 99; **Supp. XI:** 150; **Supp. XV:** 127
Road Not Taken, The: Finding America in the Poem Everyone Loves and Almost Everyone Gets Wrong (Orr), **Retro. Supp. III:** 99
"Roadside Flowers" (Collins), **Supp. XXI:** 61
Roadside Poems for Summer Travellers (Larcom, ed.), **Supp. XIII:** 142
"Roadside Resurrection, A" (L. Brown), **Supp. XXI:** 40, 42
Roads of Destiny (O. Henry), **Supp. II Part 1:** 410
Road through the Wall, The (Jackson), **Supp. IX:** 115, 118, 120, 123–124
"Road to Avignon, The" (A. Lowell), **II:** 516
"Road to Hell, The" (Fante), **Supp. XI:** 160
Road to Los Angeles, The (Fante), **Supp. XI:** 160, 166, 167, **168,** 172
Road to Many a Wonder, The (Wagoner), **Supp. IX:** 327, **336**
Road to the Temple, The (Glaspell), **Supp. III Part 1:** 175, 182, 186; **Supp. XXI:** 6
Road to Wellville, The (Boyle), **Supp. VIII:** 6–8; **Supp. XX: 24–25, 26, 28**
Road to Xanadu, The (Lowes), **IV:** 453
"Road Warrior" (Pickering), **Supp. XXI:** 204
"Roan Stallion" (Jeffers), **Supp. II Part 2:** 428–429
"Roast-beef" (Stein), **IV:** 43
Roast Leviatham (Untermeyer), **Supp. XV:** 307
"Roast Possum" (Dove), **Supp. IV Part 1:** 247, 248
Robards, Jason, Jr., **III:** 163, 403
Robb, Christina, **Supp. XV:** 251
Robbe-Grillet, Alain, **I:** 123; **IV:** 95; **Supp. IV Part 1:** 42; **Supp. V:** 47, 48; **Supp. XXIII:** 213
Robber Bride, The (Atwood), **Supp. XIII: 30–31**
Robber Bridegroom, The (Welty), **IV:** 261, 266–268, 271, 274; **Retro. Supp. I:** 347
Robbins, Amy Moorman, **Supp. XXVII:** 170
Robbins, Harold, **Supp. XII:** 6
Robbins, Henry, **Supp. IV Part 1:** 198, 201, 210, 211
Robbins, Katherine Robinson, **Supp. X:** 264
Robbins, Thomas, **Supp. XV:** 271
Robbins, Tom, **Supp. IV Part 1:** 227; **Supp. VIII:** 14; **Supp. X: 259–288; Supp. XIII:** 11
"Robe, The" (Douglas), **IV:** 434
Robert Bly (Sugg), **Supp. IV Part 1:** 68
"Robert Bly" (W. V. Davis), **Supp. IV Part 1:** 70
"Robert Bly and the Trouble with America" (Mitchell), **Supp. IV Part 1:** 70
Robert Bly: An Introduction to the Poetry (Nelson), **Supp. IV Part 1:** 66
Robert Bly: The Poet and His Critics (W. V. Davis), **Supp. IV Part 1:** 63; **Supp. XXI:** 84, **85–86,** 87, 95
Robert Coover: The Universal Fictionmaking Process (Gordon), **Supp. V:** 46
Robert Creeley (Ford), **Supp. IV Part 1:** 140
Robert Creeley and the Genius of the American Common Place (Clark), **Supp. IV Part 1:** 140
Robert Creeley's Poetry: A Critical Introduction (Edelberg), **Supp. IV Part 1:** 155
Robert E. Howard: Selected Poems (Coffman, ed.), **Supp. XXVII:** 118
Robert Frost (Meyers), **Retro. Supp. I:** 138
Robert Lowell (Meyers), **Retro. Supp. II:** 191
Robert Lowell and the Sublime (Hart), **Retro. Supp. II:** 187
Robert Lowell's Shifting Colors (Doreski), **Retro. Supp. II:** 185
Robert Lowell: The First Twenty years (Staples), **Retro. Supp. II:** 187
Roberts, Carol, **Supp. XX: 53**
Roberts, David, **Supp. XVIII:** 106
Roberts, Diane, **Supp. X:** 15; **Supp. XXVII:** 2
Roberts, J. M., **IV:** 454
Roberts, Leo, **II:** 449
Roberts, Margaret, **II:** 449; **IV:** 453, 454
Roberts, Matthew, **Retro. Supp. II:** 324
Roberts, Meade, **IV:** 383
Roberts, Michael, **I:** 527, 536
Roberts, Richard, **III:** 297

Roberts, Victoria, **Supp. XIX:** 205
Roberts, Wally, **Supp. XI:** 119, 120, 126
Roberts, William, **Supp. XI:** 343
Roberts Brothers, **Retro. Supp. I:** 31, 35
Robertson, David, **Supp. VIII:** 305
Robertson, D. B., **III:** 311
Robertson, Lisa, **Supp. XXII:** 155
Robertson, Nan, **Supp. IV Part 1:** 300
Robertson, William, **II:** 8
Robert the Devil (Merwin, trans.), **Supp. III Part 1:** 341, 346
Robeson, Paul, **III:** 392; **Supp. IV Part 1:** 360, 361; **Supp. X:** 137; **Supp. XIX:** 66; **Supp. XXI:** 167
Robeson, Susan L., **Supp. XVIII:** 268
Robespierre, Maximilien, **Supp. I Part 2:** 514, 515, 517
"Robinson" (Kees), **Supp. XV:** 143–144
Robinson, Christopher L., **Supp. XII:** 13, 14
Robinson, David, **Supp. XXIV:** 70, 71, 78–79
Robinson, Dean, **III:** 506
Robinson, Edward, **III:** 505
Robinson, Edward G., **Supp. XI:** 306
Robinson, Edwin Arlington, **I:** 480; **II:** 388, 391, 529, 542; **III:** 5, **503–526,** 576; **Retro. Supp. III:** 104; **Supp. I Part 2:** 699; **Supp. II Part 1:** 191; **Supp. III Part 1:** 63, 75; **Supp. III Part 2:** 592, 593; **Supp. IX:** 77, 266, 276, 308; **Supp. XIX:** 123; **Supp. XV:** 256, 299, 300, 301, 306; **Supp. XVII:** 69; **Supp. XXVII:** 283
Robinson, Forrest G., **Supp. IV Part 2:** 597, 601, 604
Robinson, Herman, **III:** 506–507
Robinson, H. M., **IV:** 369, 370
Robinson, Jackie, **Supp. I Part 1:** 338
Robinson, James Harvey, **I:** 214; **Supp. I Part 2:** 492
Robinson, James K., **Supp. IX:** 328
Robinson, Margaret G., **Supp. IV Part 2:** 597, 601, 604
Robinson, Marilynne, **Supp. XXI: 209–224; Supp. XXII:** 50; **Supp. XXVI:** 45, 187
Robinson, Mary, **Supp. XI:** 26
Robinson, Rowland E., **Supp. XIX:** 6
Robinson, Roxana, **Supp. XXV:** 60
Robinson, Sugar Ray, **Supp. IV Part 1:** 167
Robinson, Ted, **Supp. XIII:** 166
Robinson Crusoe (Defoe), **II:** 159; **III:** 113, 423; **IV:** 369; **Retro. Supp. II:** 274; **Supp. I Part 2:** 714; **Supp. IV Part 2:** 502
Robison, Mary, **Supp. V:** 22; **Supp. XXI:** 115, 116, 118
Roblès, Emmanuel, **Supp. I Part 1:** 283
"Robstown" (Salinas), **Supp. XIII:** 315
Rochefort, Christina, **Supp. XVI:** 143
Rochefoucauld, Louis Alexandre, **Supp. I Part 2:** 510
Rochman, Hazel, **Supp. XXVII:** 204
"Rock" (Nye), **Supp. XIII:** 287
Rock (Wagoner), **Supp. IX:** 324, **334,** 335
Rock, Catherine, **Supp. XII:** 17
Rock, The (Stevens), **Retro. Supp. I:** 309, 312
"Rock, The" (Stevens), **Retro. Supp. I:** 312
Rock, The (T. S. Eliot), **Retro. Supp. I:** 65; **Retro. Supp. III:** 69, 70
Rockaway (Shanley), **Supp. XIV:** 315
"Rock Climbers, The" (Francis), **Supp. IX:** 82
Rock-Drill (Pound), **Retro. Supp. I:** 293
Rockefeller, John D., **I:** 273; **III:** 580; **Supp. I Part 2:** 486; **Supp. V:** 286; **Supp. XXIII:** 26
Rockefeller, Nelson, **III:** 14, 15
Rocket Boys (Hickam), **Supp. XXVII:** 101, 103–106
Rocket Boys (musical), **Supp. XXVII:** 103
Rockets and Rodeos and Other American Spectacles (Mallon), **Supp. XIX:** 137
Rocket to the Moon (Odets), **Supp. II Part 2:** 541–543, 544
Rock Garden, The (Shepard), **Supp. III Part 2:** 432, 447
"Rocking Horse Winner, The" (Lawrence), **Supp. I Part 1:** 329
Rocking the Boat (Vidal), **Supp. IV Part 2:** 683
"Rockpile, The" (Baldwin), **Supp. I Part 1:** 63
Rock Springs (Ford), **Supp. V:** 57, 58–59, 68–69
Rockwell, John, **Supp. XXVII:** 45, 46
Rocky Mountains, The: or, Scenes, Incidents, and Adventures in the Far West; Digested from the Journal of Captain E. L. E Bonneville, of the Army of the United States, and Illustrated from Various Other Sources (Irving), **II:** 312
Rodden, John, **Supp. XVI:** 63, 69, 72
Roddenberry, Gene, **Supp. XXII:** 60
Rodefer, Stephen, **Supp. XXIV:** 38
Roderick, David, **Supp. XV:** 223
Roderick Hudson (James), **II:** 284, 290, 324, 326, 328; **Retro. Supp. I:** 219, **220–221,** 221, 226; **Supp. IX:** 142
Rodgers, Richard, **III:** 361
Rodgers, Ronald, **Supp. IV Part 2:** 503
Rodker, John, **III:** 470
Rodman, Selden, **Supp. I Part 1:** 83; **Supp. X:** 115
Rodney, Walter, **Supp. XXI:** 171
"Rodrigo Returns to the Land and Linen Celebrates" (Cisneros), **Supp. VII:** 68
Rodríguez, Diane, **Supp. XXIII:** 203
Rodriguez, Randy A., **Supp. XIV:** 312
Rodriguez, Richard, **Supp. XIV: 297–313**
Roethke, Charles, **III:** 531
Roethke, Theodore, **I:** 167, 171–172, 183, 254, 285, 521; **III:** 273, **527–550; IV:** 138, 402; **Retro. Supp. II:** 178, 181, 246; **Supp. I Part 2:** 539; **Supp. III Part 1:** 47, 54, 56, 239, 253, 260–261, 350; **Supp. IV Part 2:** 626; **Supp. IX:** 323; **Supp. XV:** 140, 145, 212; **Supp. XVIII:** 90; **Supp. XX: 199; Supp. XXIII:** 19; **Supp. XXIV:** 165, 171; **Supp. XXVII:** 250
"Roger Malvin's Burial" (Hawthorne), **II:** 243; **Retro. Supp. I:** 153
Rogers, Michael, **Supp. X:** 265, 266
Rogers, Pattiann, **Supp. XVIII:** 189
Rogers, Samuel, **II:** 303; **Supp. I Part 1:** 157
Rogers, Will, **I:** 261; **IV:** 388
Roger's Version (Updike), **Retro. Supp. I:** 325, 327, 330
Roget, Peter Mark, **Supp. I Part 1:** 312
Rogin, Michael Paul, **Retro. Supp. III:** 150
"Rogue River Jet-Board Trip, Gold Beach, Oregon, July 4, 1977" (Carver), **Supp. III Part 1:** 140
"Rogue's Gallery" (McCarthy), **II:** 563
Rohr, Richard, **Supp. XX: 143**
Roiphe, Katie, **Supp. XXV:** 10
Roland de La Platière, Jean Marie, **II:** 554
Rolando Hinojosa and the American Dream (Glover), **Supp. XIX:** 112
Rolando Hinojosa: A Reader's Guide (Zilles), **Supp. XIX:** 112
Rolando Hinojosa Reader, The (Saldívar, ed.), **Supp. XIX:** 112
Rôle du Nègre dans la culture des Amériques, La (Locke), **Supp. XIV:** 202

"Role of a Lifetime, The" (Skloot), **Supp. XX: 203**
"Role of Society in the Artist, The" (Ammons), **Supp. VII:** 34
Rolfe, Alfred, **IV:** 427
Rolfe, Frederick, **Supp. XX: 235**
"Roll, Jordan, Roll" (spiritual), **Supp. IV Part 1:** 16
Rolland, Romain, **Supp. XX: 70**
"Roll Call" (Hoffman), **Supp. XVIII:** 86
"Roll Call" (Komunyakaa), **Supp. XIII:** 123
Rolle, Esther, **Supp. IV Part 1:** 367
Rollin, Charles, **II:** 113
Rolling Stones (O. Henry), **Supp. II Part 1:** 410
Rolling Thunder Logbook (Shepard), **Supp. III Part 2:** 433
Rolling Thunder Logbook, The (Shepard), **Supp. XVIII:** 31
"Rolling Up" (Simpson), **Supp. IX:** 265, 274, 280
Rollins, Howard E., Jr., **Supp. IV Part 1:** 236
Rollins, Hyder E., **Supp. IV Part 1:** 168
Rollins, Sonny, **Supp. V:** 195
"Rollo" tales (Abbott), **Supp. I Part 1:** 38
"Roma I" (Wright), **Supp. V:** 338
"Roma II" (Wright), **Supp. V:** 338
Romains, Jules, **I:** 227
Román, David, **Supp. XIII:** 208
Romance, A (Weigl), **Supp. XIX: 277–278**
"Romance, A" (Weigl), **Supp. XIX:** 278
"Romance and a Reading List" (Fitzgerald), **Retro. Supp. I:** 101
Romance of a Plain Man, The (Glasgow), **II:** 175, 180–181
"Romance of Certain Old Clothes, The" (James), **II:** 322; **Retro. Supp. I:** 218
Romance Reader, The (Abraham), **Supp. XXIV:** 1–2, 3, **4–7**
Romancing the Shadow: Poe and Race (Kennedy and Weissberg, eds.), **Retro. Supp. III:** 237
"Roman Elegies" (Brodsky), **Supp. VIII:** 29
"Roman Fever" (Wharton), **Retro. Supp. I:** 382
"Roman Fountain" (Bogan), **Supp. III Part 1:** 56
"Romanitas of Gore Vidal, The" (Tatum), **Supp. IV Part 2:** 684
Romaniuk, Zbigniew, **Supp. XVI:** 154
Romano, John, **Supp. XV:** 253
"Roman Sarcophagus, A" (R. Lowell), **II:** 544
Roman Spring of Mrs. Stone, The (T. Williams), **IV:** 383, 385
"Romantic, The" (Bogan), **Supp. III Part 1:** 50
Romantic Comedians, The (Glasgow), **II:** 175, 186, 190, 194
Romantic Education, A (Hampl), **Supp. XXII:** 82, 83, **87–90,** 91
Romantic Egoists, The (Auchincloss), **Supp. IV Part 1:** 25
Romantic Egotist, The (Fitzgerald), **II:** 82
"Romantic Egotist, The" (Fitzgerald), **Retro. Supp. I:** 100
"Romanticism and Classicism" (Hulme), **III:** 196
"Romanticism Comes Home" (Shapiro), **Supp. II Part 2:** 713
Romantic Manifesto, The: A Philosophy of Literature (Rand), **Supp. IV Part 2:** 521, 523, 527, 529–530
"Romantic Regionalism of Harper Lee, The" (Erisman), **Supp. VIII:** 126
Romantics, The (Rinehart), **Supp. XXV:** 196
"Rome" (W. C. Williams), **Retro. Supp. I:** 420
Rome Brothers, **Retro. Supp. I:** 393
Romeo and Juliet (Shakespeare), **Supp. V:** 252; **Supp. VIII:** 223
Romola (G. Eliot), **II:** 291; **IV:** 311
Romulus: A New Comedy (Vidal), **Supp. IV Part 2:** 683
Romulus der Grosse (Dürrenmatt), **Supp. IV Part 2:** 683
Ronald, Ann, **Supp. XIII:** 4, 5, 6, 7, 9, 11
"Rondel for a September Day" (White), **Supp. I Part 2:** 676
"Ron Narrative Reconstructions, The" (Coleman), **Supp. XI:** 83
"Ron Padgett's Visual Imagination" (Notley), **Supp. XXII:** 224
Ron Rash Reader, The (Rash; Wilhelm, ed.), **Supp. XXVII:** 215
Ronsard, Pierre de, **Supp. X:** 65; **Supp. XV:** 165
Rood, John, **IV:** 261
"Roof, the Steeple, and the People, The" (Ellison), **Retro. Supp. II:** 118, 126; **Supp. II Part 1:** 248
"Room" (Levertov), **Supp. III Part 1:** 282
Roomates (film, P. Yates), **Supp. XVII:** 8, 9
Roomates: My Grandfather's Story (Apple), **Supp. XVII: 2, 7–9**
"Room at the Heart of Things, A" (Merrill), **Supp. III Part 1:** 337
Room Called Remember, A: Uncollected Pieces (Buechner), **Supp. XII:** 53
"Roomful of Hovings, A" (McPhee), **Supp. III Part 1:** 291, 294
Room of One's Own, A (Woolf), **Supp. IX:** 19; **Supp. V:** 127; **Supp. XIII:** 305
Room Rented by a Single Woman (Wright), **Supp. XV:** 340–341
"Rooms" (Collins), **Supp. XXI:** 61
Room Temperature (Baker), **Supp. XIII:** 41, **43–45,** 48, 50
Room to Swing (Lacy), **Supp. XV:** 202, 203, 205, 207
"Room Upstairs, The" (Gioia), **Supp. XV:** 120–121, 124
Roosevelt, Eleanor, **IV:** 371; **Supp. IV Part 2:** 679; **Supp. XXVII:** 137
Roosevelt, Franklin, **Supp. V:** 290
Roosevelt, Franklin Delano, **I:** 482, 485, 490; **II:** 553, 575; **III:** 2, 18, 69, 110, 297, 321, 376, 476, 580, 581; **Supp. I Part 2:** 488, 489, 490, 491, 645, 654, 655
Roosevelt, Kermit, **III:** 508
Roosevelt, Theodore, **I:** 14, 62; **II:** 130; **III:** 508; **IV:** 321; **Retro. Supp. I:** 377; **Supp. I Part 1:** 1, 21; **Supp. I Part 2:** 455, 456, 502, 707; **Supp. IX:** 184; **Supp. V:** 280, 282; **Supp. XIX:** 29; **Supp. XX: 221; Supp. XXIII:** 26
Roosevelt After Inauguration And Other Atrocities (Burroughs), **Supp. III Part 1:** 98
"Roosevelt Chair, The" (Skloot), **Supp. XX: 205**
"Roosters" (Bishop), **Retro. Supp. II:** 39, 43, 250; **Supp. I Part 1:** 89
Root, Abiah, **I:** 456
Root, Elihu, **Supp. IV Part 1:** 33
Root, Simeon, **I:** 548
Root, Timothy, **I:** 548
Rootabaga Stories (Sandburg), **III:** 583, 587
"Rootedness: The Ancestor as Foundation" (Morrison), **Supp. III Part 1:** 361
"Roots" (Halliday), **Supp. XIX:** 88
Roots in the Soil (film), **Supp. IV Part 1:** 83
"Rope" (Porter), **III:** 451
Rope (screenplay, Hecht), **Supp. XXVII:** 93
Rope, The (O'Neill), **III:** 388
Ropemakers of Plymouth, The (Morison), **Supp. I Part 2:** 494
"Ropes" (Nye), **Supp. XIII:** 276

"Rope's End, The" (Nemerov), **III:** 282
Roquelaure, A. N., **Supp. VII:** 301. See also Rice, Anne
Rorem, Ned, **Supp. IV Part 1:** 79, 84; **Supp. XXIII:** 217
Rorschach Test (F. Wright), **Supp. XVII:** 240, 245
Rorty, James, **Supp. XXII:** 276, 277
"Rosa" (Ozick), **Supp. V:** 271
Rosa, Rodrigo Rey, **Supp. IV Part 1:** 92
Rosaldo, Renato, **Supp. IV Part 2:** 544
"Rosalia" (Simic), **Supp. VIII:** 278
Roscoe, Will, **Supp. IV Part 1:** 330
"Roscoe in Hell" (McKnight), **Supp. XX: 151**
"Rose" (Dubus), **Supp. VII:** 88
Rose (L.-Y. Lee), **Supp. XV:** 211, **212–215,** 218
Rose, Alice, Sister, **III:** 348
Rose, Charlie, **Supp. XIX:** 26, 30; **Supp. XXVII:** 270
Rose, Lloyd, **Supp. XXIV:** 267
Rose, Mickey, **Supp. XV:** 3
Rose, Philip, **Supp. IV Part 1:** 362
"Rose, The" (Roethke), **III:** 537
"Rose, The" (W. C. Williams), **Retro. Supp. I:** 419
Rose, Where Did You Get That Red?: Teaching Great Poetry to Children (Koch), **Supp. XV:** 189
"Rose for Emily, A" (Faulkner), **II:** 72; **Retro. Supp. III:** 82, 84; **Supp. IX:** 96; **Supp. XX: 179; Supp. XXIV:** 136
Rose-Hued Cities (P. N. Warren), **Supp. XX: 261**
Rose in Bloom (Alcott), **Supp. I Part 1:** 42
"Rose-Johnny" (Kingsolver), **Supp. VII:** 203
Rose Madder (King), **Supp. V:** 141, 148, 150, 152
"Rose-Morals" (Lanier), **Supp. I Part 1:** 364
Rosen, Jody, **Supp. XXVII:** 46
Rosen, Jonathan, **Supp. XVII:** 50; **Supp. XX: 179**
Rosen, Kenneth, **Supp. IV Part 2:** 499, 505, 513
Rosen, Norma, **Supp. XVII:** 49, 50
Rosenbaum, Alissa Zinovievna. See Rand, Ayn
Rosenbaum, Thane, **Supp. XVII:** 48
Rosenberg, Bernard, **Supp. I Part 2:** 650
Rosenberg, Harold, **Supp. XIX:** 159; **Supp. XV:** 143; **Supp. XXIII:** 211
Rosenberg, Isaac, **Supp. XXVII:** 295
Rosenberg, Julia, **Supp. XVIII:** 136
Rosenberg, Julius and Ethel, **Supp. I Part 1:** 295; **Supp. I Part 2:** 532; **Supp. V:** 45
Rosenberg, Liz, **Supp. XV:** 251
Rosenberg, Shlomo, **Supp. XXIII:** 6
Rosenbloom, Joel, **Supp. IV Part 2:** 527
Rosenblum, Martin, **Supp. XXVI:** 236
Rosenfeld, Alvin H., **Supp. I Part 1:** 120
Rosenfeld, Isaac, **Supp. XII:** 160
Rosenfeld, Paul, **I:** 116, 117, 231, 245
Rosenfelt, Deborah, **Supp. XIII:** 296, 304
Rosenfield, Isaac, **IV:** 3
Rosengarten, Theodore, **Supp. XVIII:** 183
Rosenthal, Ira, **Supp. XIV:** 146–147
Rosenthal, Lois, **Supp. VIII:** 258
Rosenthal, M. L., **II:** 550; **III:** 276, 479; **Supp. V:** 333
Rosenthal, Peggy, **Supp. XVII:** 119
Rose of Wissahikon, The (Lippard), **Supp. XXIII:** 178
"Rose Pogonias" (Frost), **Retro. Supp. I:** 127
"Rose Red and Snow White" (Grimms), **Supp. X:** 82
"Rose Room" (Sorrentino), **Supp. XXI:** 228
"Roses" (Conroy), **Supp. XVI:** 72
"Roses" (Dove), **Supp. IV Part 1:** 246
"Roses and Skulls" (Goldbarth), **Supp. XII:** 192
"Roses for Lubbock" (Nye), **Supp. XIII:** 281
"Roses Only" (Moore), **III:** 195, 198, 200, 202, 215
Rose Tattoo, The (T. Williams), **IV:** 382, 383, 387, 388, 389, 392–393, 394, 397, 398
Rose Theatre (Sorrentino), **Supp. XXI:** 236
"Rosewood, Ohio" (Matthews), **Supp. IX:** 160
Rosie (Lamott), **Supp. XX: 133–134**
"Rosie Baby" (Huddle), **Supp. XXVI:** 147, 152
Rosiebelle Lee Wildcat Tennessee (Andrews), **Supp. XXVI:** 6–7
Rosinante to the Road Again (Dos Passos), **I:** 478
Roskies, David, **Supp. XVII:** 39, 44, 49–50
Roskolenko, Harry, **Supp. XV:** 179
Rosmersholm (Ibsen), **III:** 152
Rosmond, Babette, **II:** 432
Ross, Eleanor. See Taylor, Eleanor Ross
Ross, Harold, **Supp. I Part 1:** 174; **Supp. I Part 2:** 607, 617, 653, 654, 655, 660; **Supp. IX:** 190; **Supp. VIII:** 151, 170
Ross, Herbert, **Supp. XV:** 2
Ross, Jean, **Supp. XXI:** 144, 146
Ross, John F., **II:** 110
Ross, Lillilan, **Retro. Supp. II:** 198
Ross, Mary, **Supp. XXII:** 195
Ross, Mitchell S., **Supp. IV Part 2:** 692; **Supp. X:** 260
Ross, Robert, **Supp. XXIV:** 167
Rossen, Robert, **Supp. XI:** 306
Rosset, Barney, **III:** 171
Rossetti, Christina, **Supp. XIV:** 128; **Supp. XXVII:** 284
Rossetti, Dante Gabriel, **I:** 433; **II:** 323; **Retro. Supp. I:** 128, 286; **Supp. I Part 2:** 552; **Supp. XXII:** 156
Rossetti, William Michael, **Retro. Supp. I:** 407
Rossi, Umberto, **Supp. XVIII:** 137, 138–139
Rossini, Clare, **Supp. XVII:** 111
Rosskam, Edwin, **IV:** 477
Ross Macdonald (Bruccoli), **Supp. IV Part 2:** 468, 470
Rostand, Edmond, **II:** 515; **Supp. IV Part 2:** 518
Rosten, Leo, **Supp. XVII:** 9
Rosy Crucifixion, The (H. Miller), **III:** 170, 187, 188–189, 190
Rote Walker, The (Jarman), **Supp. XVII:** 110, **113–115**
Roth, Henry, **Supp. IV Part 1:** 314; **Supp. IX: 227–243; Supp. VIII:** 233; **Supp. XIII:** 106; **Supp. XXVII:** 134
Roth, Philip, **I:** 144, 161; **II:** 591; **Retro. Supp. II:** 22, **279–297; Supp. I Part 1:** 186, 192; **Supp. I Part 2:** 431, 441, 443; **Supp. II Part 1:** 99; **Supp. III Part 2: 401–429; Supp. IV Part 1:** 236, 379, 388; **Supp. IX:** 227; **Supp. V:** 45, 119, 122, 257, 258; **Supp. VIII:** 88, 236, 245; **Supp. XI:** 64, 68, 99, 140; **Supp. XII:** 190, 310; **Supp. XIV:** 79, 93, 111, 112; **Supp. XVI:** 206; **Supp. XVII:** 43, 48, 183; **Supp. XVIII:** 89; **Supp. XXI:** 234; **Supp. XXII:** 268; **Supp. XXVI:** 119, 123; **Supp. XXVII:** 142
Roth, Rita, **Supp. XVI:** 112
Roth, William, **Supp. XV:** 142
Rothenberg, Jerome, **Supp. VIII:** 292; **Supp. XII:** 3; **Supp. XXIV:** 37
Rothermere, Lady Mary, **Retro. Supp. I:** 63

Rothko, Mark, **Supp. XV:** 144
Rothstein, Mervyn, **Supp. VIII:** 142
"Rouen, France"(Kenny), **Supp. XXIII:** 152
"Rouge High" (Hughes), **Supp. I Part 1:** 330
Rougemont, Denis de, **II:** 586; **IV:** 216; **Retro. Supp. I:** 328, 329, 330, 331
Rough Edges (Skloot), **Supp. XX: 196**
Roughing It (Twain), **II:** 312; **IV:** 195, 197, 198; **Retro. Supp. III:** 258, 261, 267
Roughing It in the Bush (Shields), **Supp. VII:** 313
"Rough Outline" (Simic), **Supp. VIII:** 276
"Rough-Skinned Newt, The"(Schott), **Supp. XXIII:** 253–254
Rough South of Larry Brown, The (film, Hawkins), **Supp. XXI:** 39
Rougon-Macquart, Les (Zola), **II:** 175–176
Roumain, Jacques, **Retro. Supp. I:** 202; **Supp. IV Part 1:** 360, 367
"Round, The" (Kunitz), **Supp. III Part 1:** 268
"Roundelay Between Two Shepherdesses, A" (Notley), **Supp. XXII:** 229
"Round Trip" (Dunn), **Supp. XI:** 148–149
Round Up (Lardner), **II:** 426, 430, 431
Rountree, Owen (pseud.). See Kittredge, William; Krauzer, Steven M.
Rourke, Constance, **I:** 258; **IV:** 339, 352
Rourke, Milton, **Retro. Supp. II:** 89
Rousseau, Jean-Jacques, **I:** 226; **II:** 8, 343; **III:** 170, 178, 259; **IV:** 80, 173, 440; **Retro. Supp. III:** 109; **Supp. I Part 1:** 126; **Supp. I Part 2:** 637, 659; **Supp. IV Part 1:** 171; **Supp. XI:** 245; **Supp. XVI:** 292; **Supp. XXI:** 83; **Supp. XXVI:** 38–39
Roussel, Raymond, **Supp. III Part 1:** 6, 7, 10, 15, 16, 21; **Supp. XV:** 182
"Route 302" (Halliday), **Supp. XIX:** 93
"Routes" (Everwine), **Supp. XV:** 82
"Route Six" (Kunitz), **Supp. III Part 1:** 258
Route Two (Erdrich and Dorris), **Supp. IV Part 1:** 260
"Routine Things Around the House, The" (Dunn), **Supp. XI:** 148
Rover Boys (Winfield), **III:** 146
Rovit, Earl, **IV:** 102
Rowan, Carl T., **Supp. XIV:** 306
Rowe, Anne E., **Supp. X:** 223
Rowe, John Carlos, **Retro. Supp. I:** 216
Rowe, Kenneth Thorpe, **Supp. XXIII:** 258
Rowell, Charles, **Supp. XXI:** 250, 254, 255; **Supp. XXIV:** 184
"Rowing" (Sexton), **Supp. II Part 2:** 696
"Rowing Endeth, The" (Sexton), **Supp. II Part 2:** 696
Rowlandson, Mary, **Supp. IV Part 2:** 430, 431
Rowling, J. K., **Supp. XXV:** 70
"Rows of Cold Trees, The" (Winters), **Supp. II Part 2:** 790–791, 800
Rowson, Susanna, **Supp. I Part 1:** 128; **Supp. XV: 229–248**
Roxanna Slade (Price), **Supp. VI:** 267
Roxie Hart (Watkins), **Supp. XVI:** 188
Royal Family, The (Vollmann), **Supp. XVII:** 226, 230, 233
"Royal Palm" (Crane), **I:** 401
Royce, Josiah, **I:** 443; **III:** 303, 600; **IV:** 26; **Retro. Supp. I:** 57; **Supp. XIV:** 197, 199; **Supp. XVII:** 97
"Roy McInnes" (Budbill), **Supp. XIX:** 6–7
"Roy Spivey" (July), **Supp. XXIV:** 210
Royster, Sarah Elmira, **III:** 410, 429
Royte, Elizabeth, **Supp. XV:** 59
Rózewicz, Tadeusz, **Supp. X:** 60
R. S. Thomas: Poetry and Theology (W. V. Davis), **Supp. XXI: 86–87**
Ruas, Charles, **Supp. IV Part 1:** 383
Ruback, Max, **Supp. XXIII:** 290
Rubáiyát (Khayyám), **I:** 568
Rubáiyát of Omar Khayyam (Fitzgerald), **Supp. I Part 2:** 416; **Supp. III Part 2:** 610; **Supp. XV:** 156; **Supp. XXVII:** 262
"Rubber Life" (Prose), **Supp. XVI:** 256
Rubel, Nora L., **Supp. XXIV:** 7
Rub from Snub, A (Swanwick), **Supp. XV:** 237
"Rubicon" (Cliff), **Supp. XXII:** 76
Rubin, Louis, **Supp. I Part 2:** 672, 673, 679; **Supp. X:** 42
Rubin, Louis D., Jr., **IV:** 116, 462–463
Rubin, Stan, **Supp. XIV:** 307, 310
Rubin, Stan Sanvel, **Supp. IV Part 1:** 242, 245, 252
Rubins, Josh, **Supp. XX: 89**
"Ruby Brown" (Hughes), **Supp. I Part 1:** 327
"Ruby Daggett" (Eberhart), **I:** 539
Rucker, Rudy, **Supp. X:** 302
Rudd, Hughes, **Supp. XII:** 141
"Rude Awakening, A" (Chopin), **Retro. Supp. II:** 64
Rudens (Plautus), **Supp. III Part 2:** 630
Ruderman, Judith, **Supp. IV Part 1:** 380
Rudge, Olga, **Supp. V:** 338
Rudikoff, Sonya, **Supp. XIV:** 113
Rudman, Mark, **Supp. XXIII:** 124; **Supp. XXIV:** 153
Rueckert, William, **I:** 264
Ruesch, Jurgen, **Supp. XV:** 147
Rugby Chapel (Arnold), **Supp. I Part 2:** 416
"Rugby Road" (Garrett), **Supp. VII:** 100
Rugge, John, **Supp. XXII:** 218
Ruining the New Road (Matthews), **Supp. IX:** 154, **155–157**
"Ruins of Italica, The" (Bryant, trans.), **Supp. I Part 1:** 166
Rukeyser, Muriel, **Retro. Supp. II:** 48; **Retro. Supp. III:** 251; **Supp. VI: 271–289; Supp. XV:** 349; **Supp. XVII:** 74
"Rule of Phase Applied to History, The" (Adams), **I:** 19
Rule of the Bone (Banks), **Supp. V:** 16
Rulers of Kings (Atherton), **Supp. XXIV:** 23
"Rules by Which a Great Empire May Be Reduced to a Small One" (Franklin), **II:** 120
Rules For the Dance: A Handbook for Reading and Writing Metrical Verse (Oliver), **Supp. VII:** 229, 247
Rules of Attraction, The (Ellis), **Supp. XXVII:** 68, 70–71, 74, 76
Rules of the Game, The (film), **Supp. XII:** 259
Rulfo, Juan, **Supp. IV Part 2:** 549
Rumba (film, Gering), **Supp. XVII:** 57
Rumbaut, Rubén, **Supp. XI:** 184
Rum Diary, The (Thompson), **Supp. XXIV:** 281, **283–286,** 293
Rümelin-Oesterlen, Natalie, **Supp. XX: 235**
Rumens, Carol, **Supp. XI:** 14; **Supp. XVI:** 212
Rumi, **Supp. XX: 117**
"Rumination of Rivers, The" (Bronk), **Supp. XXI:** 32
Rumkowski, Chaim, **Supp. XII:** 168
Rummel, Mary Kay, **Supp. XIII:** 280
"Rumor and a Ladder" (Bowles), **Supp. IV Part 1:** 93
Rumor of War, A (Caputo), **Supp. XIX: 17–21,** 25, 30
Rumors (Simon), **Supp. IV Part 2:** 582–583, 591

Rumpelstiltskin (Gardner), **Supp. VI:** 72
"Rumpelstiltskin" (Grimm), **IV:** 266
"Rumpelstiltskin" (Sexton), **Supp. II Part 2:** 690
Run, Sheep, Run (Bodenheim), **Supp. XXV:** 27
"Runagate Runagate" (Hayden), **Supp. II Part 1:** 377
Runaway (Munro), **Supp. XXVII:** 190, 193–194
"Runes" (Nemerov), **III:** 267, 277–278
Run Man Run (C. Himes), **Supp. XVI:** 142, 143
"Runner, The" (Grossman), **Supp. XIX:** 83
"Running" (Wilbur), **Supp. III Part 2:** 558–559
"RUNNING-AWAY"(Strout), **Supp. XXIII:** 274
Running Dog (DeLillo), **Supp. VI:** 3, 6, 8, 14
"Running in Church" (A. Finch), **Supp. XVII:** 72
"Running the Table" Conroy), **Supp. XVI:** 75
"Run of Bad Luck, A" (Proulx), **Supp. VII:** 253–254
Run of Jacks, A (Hugo), **Supp. VI:** 131, 133, 134, 135, 136
Run River (Didion), **Supp. IV Part 1:** 197, 199–200, 201
Ruoff, A. LaVonne Brown, **Supp. IV Part 1:** 324, 327; **Supp. IV Part 2:** 559
Rupert, Jim, **Supp. XII:** 215
Ruppert, James, **Supp. IV Part 1:** 321
Rural Hours (Cooper), **Supp. XIII:** 152
"Rural Route" (Wright), **Supp. V:** 340
"Rural South, The" (Du Bois), **Supp. II Part 1:** 174
Rush, Benjamin, **Supp. I Part 2:** 505, 507
Rushdie, Salman, **Supp. IV Part 1:** 234, 297
Rushdy, Ashraf, **Supp. X:** 250
Rushing, Jimmy, **Retro. Supp. II:** 113
Rusk, Dean, **II:** 579
Ruskin, John, **II:** 323, 338; **IV:** 349; **Retro. Supp. I:** 56, 360; **Supp. I Part 1:** 2, 10, 87, 349; **Supp. I Part 2:** 410
Rusnak, Karl, **Supp. XVIII:** 149
Russ, Joanna, **Retro. Supp. III:** 36, 37
Russell, Ada Dwyer, **II:** 513, 527
Russell, Bertrand, **II:** 27; **III:** 605, 606; **Retro. Supp. I:** 57, 58, 59, 60; **Supp. I Part 2:** 522; **Supp. V:** 290; **Supp. XII:** 45; **Supp. XIV:** 337
Russell, Diarmuid, **Retro. Supp. I:** 342, 345, 346–347, 349–350
Russell, George, **Retro. Supp. I:** 342
Russell, Herb, **Supp. I Part 2:** 465–466
Russell, John, **Supp. XIV:** 344, 347, 348; **Supp. XXVII:** 22
Russell, Peter, **III:** 479
Russell, Richard, **Supp. XI:** 102
Russell, Robert, **Supp. XX: 195**
Russell, Sue, **Supp. IV Part 2:** 653
Russello, Gerald, **Supp. XXIV:** 159
Russert, Margaret, **Supp. XVIII:** 62
Russert, Tim, **Supp. XII:** 272
Russia at War (Caldwell), **I:** 296
"Russia Between Myth and Reality: From Meri to Three Cities"(Krutikov), **Supp. XXIII:** 11
Russian Journal, A (Steinbeck), **IV:** 52, 63
Russo, Richard, **Supp. XI:** 349; **Supp. XII: 325–344; Supp. XXIII:** 302
"Rusty Autumn" (Swenson), **Supp. IV Part 2:** 640
Rutabaga-Roo: I've Got a Song and It's for You (Nye, album), **Supp. XIII:** 274
Ruth (biblical book), **Supp. I Part 2:** 516
Ruth, George Herman ("Babe"), **II:** 423; **Supp. I Part 2:** 438, 440
Rutheiser, Charles, **Supp. XXII:** 244
Ruth Hall (Fern), **Supp. V:** 122
Ruthven, K. K., **Supp. XXII:** 261
Rutkowska, Malgorzata, **Supp. XXII:** 208
Rutledge, Ann, **III:** 588; **Supp. I Part 2:** 471
Ruwe, Donelle R., **Supp. XII:** 215
Ryan, Alan, **Supp. XXVI:** 5
Ryan, Katy, **Supp. XXI:** 215
Ryan, Kay, **Supp. XXI:** 20; **Supp. XXV:** 222
Ryan, Maureen, **Supp. XXI:** 215
Ryan, Paul William, **Supp. XVIII: 223–239; Supp. XXI:** 264–265
Ryder (Barnes), **Supp. III Part 1:** 31, 36–38, 42, 43
"Ryder" (Rukeyser), **Supp. VI:** 273, 283
"Ry¿kan Says" (Budbill), **Supp. XIX:** 11
Ryle, Herbert Edward, **Supp. XX: 230**
Rymer, Thomas, **IV:** 122
S. (Updike), **Retro. Supp. I:** 330, 331, 332, 333
S-1 (Baraka), **Supp. II Part 1:** 55, 57
Saadi, **II:** 19
Saar, Doreen Alvarez, **Supp. XV:** 237
Sabbatai Zevi (Asch), **Supp. XXIII:** 12
"Sabbath, The" (Stowe), **Supp. I Part 2:** 587
"Sabbath Mom" (White), **Supp. I Part 2:** 671–672
Sabbaths (Berry), **Supp. X:** 31
Sabbath's Theater (P. Roth), **Retro. Supp. II:** 279, 288
"Sabbatical, The" (Stallings), **Supp. XXV:** 234
"Sabbioneta to Parma" (Di Piero), **Supp. XIX:** 36–37
Sabines, Jaime, **Supp. V:** 178
Sabol, Cathy, **Supp. XXVI:** 160
"Sabotage" (Baraka), **Supp. II Part 1:** 49, 53
"Saboteur" (Jin), **Supp. XVIII:** 97
Sacco, Nicola, **I:** 482, 486, 490, 494; **II:** 38–39, 426; **III:** 139–140; **Supp. I Part 2:** 446; **Supp. IX:** 199; **Supp. V:** 288–289; **Supp. XXII:** 277
Sachs, Hanns, **Supp. I Part 1:** 259; **Supp. X:** 186
Sack Full of Old Quarrels, A (Weigl), **Supp. XIX:** 277
"Sacks" (Carver), **Supp. III Part 1:** 143–144
Sacks, Oliver, **Supp. XVIII:** 143
Sacks, Peter, **Supp. IV Part 2:** 450
Sackville-West, Vita, **Supp. VIII:** 263
"Sacrament of Divorce, The" (Patchett), **Supp. XII:** 309
"Sacrament of Self: Catholic Roots of Contemporary Memoir" (lecture, Hampl), **Supp. XXII:** 81
"Sacraments" (Dubus), **Supp. VII:** 91
Sacred and Profane Memories (Van Vechten), **Supp. II Part 2:** 735, 749
"Sacred Chant for the Return of Black Spirit and Power" (Baraka), **Supp. II Part 1:** 51
"Sacred Factory, The" (Toomer), **Supp. IX:** 320
Sacred Fount, The (James), **II:** 332–333; **Retro. Supp. I:** 219, 228, 232
"Sacred Heart" (Egan), **Supp. XIX:** 52
"Sacred Hoop, The: A Contemporary Perspective" (Gunn Allen), **Supp. IV Part 1:** 324
Sacred Hoop, The: Recovering the Feminine in American Indian Traditions (Gunn Allen), **Supp. IV Part 1:** 319, 320, 322, 324, 325, 328–330, 331, 333, 334
Sacred Journey, The (Buechner), **Supp. XII:** 42, 53
"Sacred Thing, The" (Ryan as Quin), **Supp. XVIII:** 227
Sacred Wood, The (T. S. Eliot), **IV:**

431; **Retro. Supp. I:** 59, 60; **Retro. Supp. III:** 66; **Supp. I Part 1:** 268; **Supp. II Part 1:** 136, 146
Sacrifice, The (Bidart), **Supp. XV:** 22, **27–30,** 35
"Sacrifice, The" (Bidart), **Supp. XV:** 29
"Sacrifice, The" (Oates), **Supp. II Part 2:** 523
Sacrilege of Alan Kent, The (Caldwell), **I:** 291–292
"Sad Brazil" (Hardwick), **Supp. III Part 1:** 210
Sad Days of Light (Balakian), **Supp. XXIII:** 20
"Sad Dust Glories" (Ginsberg), **Supp. II Part 1:** 376
Sad Dust Glories: Poems Written Work Summer in Sierra Woods (Ginsberg), **Supp. II Part 1:** 326
Sade, Marquis de, **III:** 259; **IV:** 437, 442; **Supp. XII:** 1, 14–15
Sad-Faced Boy (Bontemps), **Supp. XXII:** 5, 12
Sad Flower in the Sand, A (film), **Supp. XI:** 173
Sad Heart at the Supermarket, A (Jarrell), **II:** 386
"Sadie" (Matthiessen), **Supp. V:** 201
"Sadie and Maud" (Brooks), **Supp. XVIII:** 175
Sadness and Happiness (Pinsky), **Supp. VI:** 235, **237–241**
"Sadness of Brothers, The" (Kinnell), **Supp. III Part 1:** 237, 251
"Sadness of Days, The" (Salinas), **Supp. XIII:** 325
Sadness of Days, The: Selected and New Poems (Salinas), **Supp. XIII:** 311, **324–326**
"Sadness of Lemons, The" (Levine), **Supp. V:** 184
Sadoff, Ira, **Supp. XVII:** 241; **Supp. XXI:** 100
"Sad Rite" (Karr), **Supp. XI:** 243
"Sad Strains of a Gay Waltz" (Stevens), **Retro. Supp. I:** 302
"Safe" (Gordon), **Supp. IV Part 1:** 299, 306
"Safe in their Alabaster Chambers" (Dickinson), **Retro. Supp. I:** 30
Safer, Morley, **Supp. XIX:** 25
"Safe Subjects" (Komunyakaa), **Supp. XIII:** 118
Safety Features (Monson), **Supp. XXIV:** 230
"Safeway" (F. Barthelme), **Supp. XI:** 26, 27, 36
Saffin, John, **Supp. I Part 1:** 115
Saffy, Edna, **Supp. X:** 227
Sagan, Miriam, **Supp. XXIII:** 133
"Saga of an American Ranch" (P. N. Warren), **Supp. XX: 261**
"Saga of Arturo Bandini" (Fante), **Supp. XI:** 159, **166–169**
"Saga of King Olaf, The" (Longfellow), **II:** 489, 505; **Retro. Supp. II:** 154, 155, 164
"Sage of Stupidity and Wonder, The" (Goldbarth), **Supp. XII:** 191
Sahl, Mort, **II:** 435–436
"Sah Sin" (Gallagher), **Supp. XXIV:** 171
"Said" (Dixon), **Supp. XII:** 149–150
Said, Edward, **Retro. Supp. III:** 194; **Supp. XXI:** 153
"Sailing after Lunch" (Stevens), **IV:** 73
Sailing Alone Around the Room: New and Selected Poems (Collins), **Supp. XXI:** 54, 56, 62
Sailing Alone Around the World (Slocum), **Supp. XXV:** 205, 206, 208, 213–216, 218
"Sailing Home from Rapallo" (R. Lowell), **Retro. Supp. II:** 189
Sailing through China (Theroux), **Supp. VIII:** 323
"Sailing to Byzantium" (Yeats), **III:** 263; **Supp. VIII:** 30; **Supp. X:** 74; **Supp. XI:** 281
"Sail Made of Rags, The" (Nye), **Supp. XIII:** 277
"Sailor off the Bremen" (Shaw), **Supp. XIX:** 247
"Sailor's Grudge" (Howard), **Supp. XXVII:** 124
"Sailors Lost at Sea" (Shields), **Supp. VII:** 318
"St Anne/Santa Ana" (Mora), **Supp. XIII:** 229
"Saint Anthony of Padua/San Antonio de Padua" (Mora), **Supp. XIII:** 228
"St. Augustine and the Bullfights" (Porter), **III:** 454
Sainte-Beuve, Charles Augustin, **IV:** 432
St. Elmo (Wilson), **Retro. Supp. I:** 351–352
"Saint Emmanuel the Good, Martyr" (Unamuno; Everwine, trans.), **Supp. XV:** 79
Sainte Vierge, La (Picabia), **Retro. Supp. II:** 331
Saint-Exupéry, Antoine de, **Supp. IX:** 247
"St. Francis Einstein of the Daffodils" (W. C. Williams), **IV:** 409–411
Saint-Gaudens, Augustus, **I:** 18, 228; **II:** 551
Saint-Gaudens, Homer, **Supp. XV:** 41
"St. George, the Dragon, and the Virgin" (R. Bly), **Supp. IV Part 1:** 73
St. George and the Godfather (Mailer), **III:** 46; **Retro. Supp. II:** 206, 208
Saint Jack (Theroux), **Supp. VIII:** 319
St. John, David, **Supp. V:** 180; **Supp. XI:** 270, 272; **Supp. XIII:** 312
St. John, Edward B., **Supp. IV Part 2:** 490
St. John, James Hector. See Crèvecoeur, Michel-Guillaume Jean de
"Saint John and the Back-Ache" (Stevens), **Retro. Supp. I:** 310
Saint Judas (Wright), **Supp. III Part 2: 595–599**
"Saint Judas" (Wright), **Supp. III Part 2:** 598–599
St. Louis Woman (Bontemps and Cullen), **Supp. IV Part 1:** 170
St. Mawr (Lawrence), **II:** 595
Saint Maybe (Tyler), **Supp. IV Part 2:** 670–671
"Saint Nicholas" (Moore), **III:** 215
"Saint"(O'Hara), **Supp. XXIII:** 219
St. Petersburg (Biely), **Supp. XII:** 13
Saint-Phalle, Niki de, **Supp. XV:** 187
"St. Roach" (Rukeyser), **Supp. VI:** 286
"Saint Robert" (Dacey), **Supp. IV Part 1:** 70
Saints at the River (Rash), **Supp. XXVII:** 222, 223–224, 226
Saintsbury, George, **IV:** 440; **Supp. XV:** 181
Saints' Everlasting Rest, The (Baxter), **III:** 199; **IV:** 151, 153
Saint-Simon, Claude Henri, **Supp. I Part 2:** 648
"St. Thomas Aquinas" (Simic), **Supp. VIII:** 281
Saks, Gene, **Supp. IV Part 2:** 577, 588
Salamun, Tomaz, **Supp. VIII:** 272
Salazar, Dixie, **Supp. V:** 180; **Supp. XV:** 73
Saldívar, José David, **Supp. IV Part 2:** 544, 545; **Supp. XIX:** 110, 112–113
Sale, Richard, **Supp. IV Part 1:** 379
Sale, Roger, **Supp. V:** 244
Saleh, Dennis, **Supp. V:** 182, 186
"Salem" (R. Lowell), **II:** 550
Salemi, Joseph, **Supp. IV Part 1:** 284
Salem's Lot (King), **Supp. V:** 139, 144, 146, 151
"Sale of the Hessians, The" (Franklin), **II: 120**
"Salesman at Fifty" (A. Miller), **Retro. Supp. III:** 173
Salick, Roydan, **Supp. XXIII:** 93, 94
Salinas, Luis Omar, **Supp. IV Part 2:** 545; **Supp. V:** 180; **Supp. XIII:**

311–330; Supp. XV: 73
"Salinas Is on His Way" (Salinas), **Supp. XIII:** 317
"Salinas Sends Messengers to the Stars" (Salinas), **Supp. XIII:** 317
"Salinas Summering at the Caspian and Thinking of Hamlet" (Salinas), **Supp. XIII:** 320
"Salinas Wakes Early and Goes to the Park to Lecture Sparrows" (Salinas), **Supp. XIII:** 320
Salinger, Doris, **III:** 551
Salinger, J. D., **II:** 255; **III: 551–574; IV:** 190, 216, 217; **Retro. Supp. I:** 102, 116, 335; **Supp. IV Part 2:** 502; **Supp. V:** 23, 119; **Supp. VIII:** 151; **Supp. XI:** 2, 66; **Supp. XIV:** 93; **Supp. XXIII:** 100; **Supp. XXVI:** 119
Salisbury, Harrison, **Supp. I Part 2:** 664
Salle, David, **Supp. XII:** 4
Salley, Columbus, **Supp. XIV:** 195
"Sally" (Cisneros), **Supp. VII:** 63
"Sally's Choice" (E. Stoddard), **Supp. XV:** 282
Salmagundi; or, The Whim-Whams and Opinions of Launcelot Langstaff Esq., and Others (Irving), **II:** 299, 300, 304
Salmon, Edward G., **Supp. XVIII:** 258
Salome (Strauss), **IV:** 316
Salon (online magazine), **Supp. VIII:** 310; **Supp. X:** 202
"Salt"(Crooker), **Supp. XXIII:** 62
Salt Eaters, The (Bambara), **Supp. XI:** 1, **12–14**
Salt Ecstasies, The (White), **Supp. XI:** 123
Salter, James, **Supp. IX: 245–263; Supp. XIX:** 252; **Supp. XVI:** 237, 247
Salter, Mary Jo, **Supp. IV Part 2:** 653; **Supp. IX:** 37, 292; **Supp. XV:** 251, 253; **Supp. XVII:** 112; **Supp. XXIII:** 112
Salter, Sarah, **Supp. XXVI:** 57
Salt Garden, The (Nemerov), **III:** 269, 272–275, 277
"Salt Garden, The" (Nemerov), **III:** 267–268
Salting the Ocean (Nye, ed.), **Supp. XIII:** 280
Salt Lesson, The (C. Frost), **Supp. XV:** 92, 96
"Salt Lesson, The" (C. Frost), **Supp. XV:** 99
"Salts and Oils" (Levine), **Supp. V:** 190
Salt to the Devil (film, Dmytryk), **Supp. XX: 41**
Saltzman, Arthur, **Supp. XIII:** 48
Saltzman, Harry, **Supp. XI:** 307
"Salut au Monde!" (Whitman), **Retro. Supp. I:** 387, 396, 400
"Salute" (MacLeish), **III:** 13
Salute (Shaw), **Supp. XIX:** 244
"Salute to Mister Yates, A" (Dubus), **Supp. XI:** 347, 349
Salute to Spring (Le Sueur), **Supp. XXIII:** 164, 165, 166, 172
Salvador (Didion), **Supp. IV Part 1:** 198, 207–208, 210
"Salvage" (Clampitt), **Supp. IX:** 41
"Salvage" (Rinehart), **Supp. XXV:** 194
Salvation (Asch), **Supp. XXIII:** 3, 4, **12,** 13, 15
Salvos: An Informal Book About Books and Plays (W. Frank), **Supp. XX: 75**
Samain, Albert, **II:** 528
Same Door, The (Updike), **IV:** 214, 219, 226; **Retro. Supp. I:** 320
"Same in Blues" (Hughes), **Retro. Supp. I:** 208
"Same Kiss After Many Years, The" (Gallagher), **Supp. XXIV:** 169
Same River Twice, The (Offutt), **Supp. XIX:** 163, 164**, 167–168,** 175
"Samhain" (A. Finch), **Supp. XVII:** 72
Sam Lawson's Oldtown Fireside Stories (Stowe), **Supp. I Part 2:** 587, 596, 598–599
Sam Patch, the High, Wide & Handsome Jumper (Bontemps and Conroy), **Supp. XXII:** 5, 11
"Sa'm Pèdi" (Bell), **Supp. X:** 17
"Sampler, A" (MacLeish), **III:** 4
Sampoli, Maria, **Supp. V:** 338
Sampson, Edward, **Supp. I Part 2:** 664, 673
Sampson, Martin, **Supp. I Part 2:** 652
"Sam's Dad" (Lamott), **Supp. XX: 142–143**
Sam's Legacy (Neugeboren), **Supp. XVI:** 221, 222
Samson, John, **Retro. Supp. III:** 152
Samson Agonistes (Milton), **III:** 274
"Samson and Delilah" (Masters), **Supp. I Part 2:** 459
Samuel, Maurice, **Supp. XXIII:** 1, 7
Samuel de Champlain: Father of New France (Morison), **Supp. I Part 2:** 496–497
Samuels, Charles Thomas, **Retro. Supp. I:** 334
"Samuel Sewall" (Hecht), **Supp. X:** 58
"Samwheel" (Lamott), **Supp. XX: 144–145**
Sanborn, Franklin B., **IV:** 171, 172, 178
Sanborn, Geoffrey, **Retro. Supp. III:** 152
Sanborn, Kate, **Supp. XIII:** 152
Sanborn, Sara, **Supp. XIV:** 113
Sanchez, Carol Anne, **Supp. IV Part 1:** 335
Sanchez, Carol Lee, **Supp. IV Part 2:** 499, 557
Sanchez, Sonia, **Retro. Supp. III:** 316; **Supp. II Part 1:** 34; **Supp. XXVII:** 167
Sánchez Beras, César, **Supp. XXI:** 100, 104
Sanctified Church, The (Hurston), **Supp. VI:** 150
"Sanctified Church, The" (Hurston), **Retro. Supp. III:** 133
"Sanction of the Victims, The" (Rand), **Supp. IV Part 2:** 528
Sanctuary (Faulkner), **II:** 57, 61–63, 72, 73, 74, 174; **Retro. Supp. I:** 73, 84, 86–87, 87; **Retro. Supp. III:** 81–82, 87; **Supp. I Part 2:** 614; **Supp. XII:** 16
"Sanctuary" (Larsen), **Supp. XVIII:** 119, 130–131
Sanctuary (Wharton), **IV:** 311; **Retro. Supp. III:** 278
"Sanctuary" (Wylie), **Supp. I Part 2:** 711
"Sanctuary, The" (Nemerov), **III:** 272, 274
"Sanctuary, The" (Teasdale), **Supp. XXVII:** 294
Sanctuary V (Schulberg), **Supp. XVIII:** 254
"Sanctus" (Nelson), **Supp. XVIII:** 183
Sand, George, **II:** 322; **Retro. Supp. I:** 235, 372; **Supp. XV:** 275
"Sandalphon" (Longfellow), **II:** 498
Sand and Foam: A Book of Aphorisms (Gibran), **Supp. XX: 115, 121–122**
Sandbox, The (Albee), **I:** 74–75, 89
Sandburg, Carl, **I:** 103, 109, 384, 421; **II:** 529; **III:** 3, 20, **575–598; Retro. Supp. I:** 133, 194; **Supp. I Part 1:** 257, 320; **Supp. I Part 2:** 387, 389, 454, 461, 653; **Supp. III Part 1:** 63, 71, 73, 75; **Supp. IV Part 1:** 169; **Supp. IV Part 2:** 502; **Supp. IX:** 1, 15, 308; **Supp. XIII:** 274, 277; **Supp. XV:** 293, 299, 300, 301, 302, 306; **Supp. XXII:** 275; **Supp. XXIII:** 161, 165; **Supp. XXV:** 18; **Supp. XXVII:** 83
Sandburg, Mrs. Carl (Lillian Steichen), **III:** 580
Sandburg, Helga, **III:** 583

Sandburg, Janet, **III:** 583, 584
Sandburg, Margaret, **III:** 583, 584
Sand County Almanac and Sketches Here and There, A (Leopold), **Supp. XIV:** 177, 178, **182–192**
"Sand Creek, Colorado"(Kenny), **Supp. XXIII:** 155
"Sand Dabs" (Oliver), **Supp. VII:** 245
"Sand Dunes" (Frost), **Retro. Supp. I:** 137; **Retro. Supp. II:** 41
Sander, August, **Supp. IX:** 211
Sanders, Mark, **Supp. XIX:** 119, 121
Sanders, Scott Russell, **Supp. XVI: 265–280**
Sandlin, Tim, **Supp. XXII:** 114
"Sandman, The" (Barthelme), **Supp. IV Part 1:** 47
Sandman's Dust (Bukiet), **Supp. XVII:** 40, 41
Sando, Joe S., **Supp. IV Part 2:** 510
Sandoe, James, **Supp. IV Part 1:** 131; **Supp. IV Part 2:** 470
Sandoval, Chela, **Supp. XXIII:** 204
Sandoz, Mari, **Supp. XV:** 141; **Supp. XXIII:** 146; **Supp. XXIV: 243–261**
Sandperl, Ira, **Supp. VIII:** 200
"Sand-Quarry and Moving Figures" (Rukeyser), **Supp. VI:** 271, 278
Sand Rivers (Matthiessen), **Supp. V:** 203
"Sand Roses, The" (Hogan), **Supp. IV Part 1:** 401
Sands, Diana, **Supp. IV Part 1:** 362
Sands, Robert, **Supp. I Part 1:** 156, 157
"Sands at Seventy" (Whitman), **IV:** 348
"Sandstone Farmhouse, A" (Updike), **Retro. Supp. I:** 318
Sandy Bottom Orchestra,The (Keillor and Nilsson), **Supp. XVI:** 177
Sanford, John, **IV:** 286, 287
San Francisco (film), **Supp. XVI:** 181, 192
"San Francisco" (Hempel), **Supp. XXI:** 118
"San Francisco Blues" (Kerouac), **Supp. III Part 1:** 225
Sangamon County Peace Advocate, The (Lindsay), **Supp. I Part 2:** 379
Sanger, Margaret, **Supp. I Part 1:** 19; **Supp. XXI:** 6; **Supp. XXIII:** 161
Sankofa (film), **Supp. XX: 154**
Sansom, William, **IV:** 279
Sans Soleil (film), **Supp. IV Part 2:** 436
"Santa" (Sexton), **Supp. II Part 2:** 693
Santa Claus: A Morality (Cummings), **I:** 430, 441
"Santa Fe, New Mexico"(Kenny), **Supp. XXIII:** 150
"Santa Fé Trail, The" (Lindsay), **Supp. I Part 2:** 389
"Santa Lucia" (Hass), **Supp. VI:** 105–106
"Santa Lucia II" (Hass), **Supp. VI:** 105–106
Santayana, George, **I:** 222, 224, 236, 243, 253, 460; **II:** 20, 542; **III:** 64, **599–622; IV:** 26, 339, 351, 353, 441; **Retro. Supp. I:** 55, 57, 67, 295; **Retro. Supp. II:** 179; **Supp. I Part 2:** 428; **Supp. II Part 1:** 107; **Supp. X:** 58; **Supp. XIV:** 199, 335, 340, 342; **Supp. XVI:** 189; **Supp. XVII:** 97, 106; **Supp. XX: 228, 229, 231**
Santiago, Esmeralda, **Supp. XI:** 177
"Santorini: Stopping the Leak" (Merrill), **Supp. III Part 1:** 336
Santos, John Phillip, **Supp. XIII:** 274
Santos, Sherod, **Supp. VIII:** 270
Saphier, William, **Supp. XXV:** 19, 20
Sapir, Edward, **Supp. VIII:** 295; **Supp. XVI:** 283
"Sapphics for Patience" (A. Finch), **Supp. XVII:** 72
Sapphira and the Slave Girl (Cather), **I:** 331; **Retro. Supp. I:** 2, **19–20; Retro. Supp. III:** 18.**Retro. Supp. III:** 33, 24
Sappho, **II:** 544; **III:** 142; **Retro. Supp. III:** 19; **Supp. I Part 1:** 261, 269; **Supp. I Part 2:** 458; **Supp. XII:** 98, 99; **Supp. XVII:** 74; **Supp. XXV:** 222; **Supp. XXVII:** 171, 283, 288
"Sappho" (Wright), **Supp. III Part 2:** 595, 604
"Sappho, Keats"(Hadas), **Supp. XXIII:** 113
"Sara" (song, Dylan), **Supp. XVIII:** 28
"Sarah" (Schwartz), **Supp. II Part 2:** 663
Sarah; or, The Exemplary Wife (Rowson), **Supp. XV:** 242
"Saratoga" mysteries (Dobyns), **Supp. XIII:** 79–80
Sardonic Arm, The (Bodenheim), **Supp. XXV:** 22, 23
Sargent, John Singer, **II:** 337, 338; **Supp. XX: 231**
Sarlós, Robert K., **Supp. XXI:** 7, 12, 13
Saroyan, Aram, **Supp. XV:** 182
Saroyan, William, **III:** 146–147; **IV:** 393; **Supp. I Part 2:** 679; **Supp. IV Part 1:** 83; **Supp. IV Part 2:** 502; **Supp. XIII:** 280; **Supp. XXIII:** 20; **Supp. XXV:** 29
Sarris, Greg, **Supp. IV Part 1:** 329, 330
Sarton, George, **Supp. VIII:** 249
Sarton, May, **Supp. III Part 1:** 62, 63; **Supp. VIII: 249–268; Supp. XIII:** 296; **Supp. XVII:** 71
Sartoris (Faulkner), **II:** 55, 56–57, 58, 62; **Retro. Supp. I:** 77, 81, 82, 83, 88; **Retro. Supp. III:** 74, 77–78
Sartor Resartus (Carlyle), **II:** 26; **III:** 82
Sartre, Jean-Paul, **I:** 82, 494; **II:** 57, 244; **III:** 51, 204, 292, 453, 619; **IV:** 6, 223, 236, 477, 487, 493; **Retro. Supp. I:** 73; **Supp. I Part 1:** 51; **Supp. IV Part 1:** 42, 84; **Supp. IX:** 4; **Supp. VIII:** 11; **Supp. XIII:** 74, 171; **Supp. XIV:** 24; **Supp. XVII:** 137; **Supp. XXIV:** 281
Sassone, Ralph, **Supp. X:** 171
Sassoon, Siegfried, **II:** 367; **Supp. XIX:** 18; **Supp. XV:** 308; **Supp. XXVII:** 295
Satan in Goray (Singer), **IV:** 1, 6–7, 12; **Retro. Supp. II:** 303, **304–305**
Satan Says (Olds), **Supp. X:** 201, 202, **202–204,** 215
"Satan Says" (Olds), **Supp. X:** 202; **Supp. XVII:** 114
Satanstoe (Cooper), **I:** 351–352, 355
"Sather Gate Illumination" (Ginsberg), **Supp. II Part 1:** 329
"Satire as a Way of Seeing" (Dos Passos), **III:** 172
Satires of Persius, The (Merwin, trans.), **Supp. III Part 1:** 347
Satirical Rogue on Poetry, The (Francis). See Pot Shots at Poetry (Francis)
Satori in Paris (Kerouac), **Supp. III Part 1:** 231
"Saturday" (Salinas), **Supp. XIII:** 315
"Saturday Matinee" (Trethewey), **Supp. XXI:** 251
Saturday Night (Orlean), **Supp. XXV:** 159, 161
Saturday Night at the War (Shanley), **Supp. XIV:** 315
"Saturday Rain" (Kees), **Supp. XV:** 136
"Saturday Route, The" (Wolfe), **Supp. III Part 2:** 580
Satyagraha (Gandhi), **IV:** 185
"Satyr's Heart, The" (B. Kelly), **Supp. XVII:** 132
Saucedo, José Guadalupe, **Supp. XXIII:** 197
Saudade (Vaz), **Supp. XXVI:** 256–258, 263

Saul and Patsy (C. Baxter), **Supp. XVII:** 22–23
"Saul and Patsy" (C. Baxter), **Supp. XVII:** 17
"Saul and Patsy Are Getting Comfortable in Michigan" (C. Baxter), **Supp. XVII:** 22
"Saul and Patsy Are in Labor" (C. Baxter), **Supp. XVII:** 20, 22
"Saul and Patsy Are Pregnant" (C. Baxter), **Supp. XVII:** 22
Saunders, George, **Supp. XIX: 223–237; Supp. XXII:** 49; **Supp. XXIV:** 199
Saunders, Richard, **II:** 110
Savage, Augusta, **Retro. Supp. II:** 115
Savage, James, **II:** 111
Savage, Tom, **Supp. XXIV:** 45
Savage Holiday (Wright), **IV:** 478, 488
Savage in Limbo: A Concert Play (Shanley), **Supp. XIV:** 315, **319–321,** 323, 324
Savage Love (Shepard and Chaikin), **Supp. III Part 2:** 433
Savage Place, A (Parker), **Supp. XIX:** 185
Savage Sword of Conan, The (comic), **Supp. XXVII:** 129
Savage Wilds (Reed), **Supp. X:** 241
Save Me, Joe Louis (Bell), **Supp. X:** 7, 10, **11–12**
Save Me the Waltz (Z. Fitzgerald), **II:** 95; **Retro. Supp. I:** 110; **Supp. IX:** 58, 59, 65, **66–68**
"Save One for Mainz" (Huddle), **Supp. XXVI:** 150, 153
Savers, Michael, **Supp. XI:** 307
Saving Lives (Goldbarth), **Supp. XII:** 192
Saving Private Ryan (film), **Supp. V:** 249; **Supp. XI:** 234
Savings (Hogan), **Supp. IV Part 1:** 397, 404, 405, 406, 410
Saving Sebastian (Taylor), **Supp. XXIII:** 57
Savo, Jimmy, **I:** 440
Savran, David, **Supp. IX:** 145; **Supp. XIII:** 209; **Supp. XV:** 321; **Supp. XXIV:** 263, 264
"Sawdust" (Offutt), **Supp. XIX:** 164
Sawyer-Lauçanno, Christopher, **Supp. IV Part 1:** 95
Saxon, Lyle, **Retro. Supp. I:** 80
"Saxophone" (Di Piero), **Supp. XIX:** 38
"Sax's and Selves" (Halliday), **Supp. XIX:** 88
"Say All" (Ray), **Supp. XVIII:** 193
Say and Seal (S. and A. Warner), **Supp. XVIII:** 258, 266
Saye and Sele, Lord, **Supp. I Part 1:** 98
Sayer, Mandy, **Supp. XIII:** 118
Sayers, Dorothy, **Supp. IV Part 1:** 341; **Supp. IV Part 2:** 464
Sayers, Valerie, **Supp. XI:** 253; **Supp. XVIII:** 99
"Say Good-bye" (Weigl), **Supp. XIX:** 288
Say Her Name (Goldman), **Supp. XXV:** 50, 59–62
"Sayings/For Luck" (Goldbarth), **Supp. XII:** 176
"Saying What Needs To Be Said" (Skloot), **Supp. XX: 201**
Say! Is This the U.S.A.? (Caldwell), **I:** 293, 294–295, 304, 309, 310
Saylor, Bruce, **Supp. XII:** 253
Sayre, Joel, **Supp. XIII:** 166
Sayre, Nora, **Supp. XII:** 119
Sayre, Zelda, **Retro. Supp. I:** 101, 102–103, 104, 105, 108, 109, 110, 113, 114. See also Fitzgerald, Zelda (Zelda Sayre)
"Say Yes" (Wolff), **Supp. VII:** 344
"Say You Love Me" (Peacock), **Supp. XIX:** 198
Scafe, Suzanne, **Supp. XXIII:** 94, 95
"Scale" (Halliday), **Supp. XIX:** 92
"Scales of the Eyes, The" (Nemerov), **III:** 272, 273, 277
Scalpel (McCoy), **Supp. XIII: 174–175**
Scalpel (screen treatment, McCoy), **Supp. XIII:** 174
Scandalabra (Zelda Fitzgerald), **Supp. IX:** 60, 61, 65, 67, **68–70**
"Scandal Detectives, The" (Fitzgerald), **II:** 80–81; **Retro. Supp. I:** 99
Scarberry-García, Susan, **Supp. IV Part 2:** 486
Scarborough, Dorothy, **Supp. XVIII:** 279–280
Scarecrow, The (Connelly), **Supp. XXI:** 71, 74, 78, **79**
"Scarecrow, The" (Farrell), **II:** 45
"Scarf, A" (Shields), **Supp. VII:** 328
Scarface (screenplay, Hecht), **Supp. XXVII:** 83, 91, 92–93
Scarlet Cabinet, The (Notley), **Supp. XXII:** 233
"Scarlet Citadel, The" (Howard), **Supp. XXVII:** 125, 126
Scarlet Letter, The (Hawthorne), **II:** 63, 223, 224, 231, 233, 239–240, 241, 243, 244, 255, 264, 286, 290, 291, 550; **Retro. Supp. I:** 63, 145, 147, 152, **157–159,** 160, 163, 165, 220, 248, 330, 335; **Retro. Supp. II:** 100; **Retro. Supp. III:** 116–117; **Supp. I Part 1:** 38; **Supp. II Part 1:** 386; **Supp. VIII:** 108, 198; **Supp. XII:** 11; **Supp. XVII:** 143; **Supp. XX: 178, 183; Supp. XXII:** 147
"Scarlet Letter Aleph, The" (Mirvis), **Supp. XX: 183**
Scarlet Plague, The (London), **II:** 467
Scarlet Sister Mary (Peterkin), **Supp. XXII:** 189
Scar Lover (Crews), **Supp. XI:** 103, 107, **114–115**
"Scarred Girl, The" (Dickey), **Supp. IV Part 1:** 180
Scates, Maxine, **Supp. XIV:** 264, 265, 274
"Scenario" (H. Miller), **III:** 184
"Scene" (Howells), **II:** 274
"Scene in Jerusalem, A" (Stowe), **Supp. I Part 2:** 587
"Scenes" (Shields), **Supp. VII:** 318
Scènes d'Anabase (chamber music) (Bowles), **Supp. IV Part 1:** 82
"Scenes from a Documentary History of Mississippi" (Trethewey), **Supp. XXI:** 255–256
Scenes from American Life (Gurney), **Supp. V:** 95, 96, 105, 108
Scenes from Another Life (McClatchy), **Supp. XII: 255–256**
"Scenes from Childhood" (W. V. Davis), **Supp. XXI:** 95
"Scenes of Childhood" (Merrill), **Supp. III Part 1:** 322, 323, 327
"Scented Herbage of My Breast" (Whitman), **IV:** 342–343
"Scent of a Woman's Ink" (Prose), **Supp. XVI:** 259
"Scent of Unbought Flowers, The" (Ríos), **Supp. IV Part 2:** 547
Scepticisms (Aiken), **I:** 58
Scève, Maurice, **Supp. III Part 1:** 11
Schad, Christian, **Supp. IV Part 1:** 247
Schafer, Benjamin G., **Supp. XIV:** 144
Schafer, William, **Supp. XIX:** 164, 172
Schaller, George, **Supp. V:** 208, 210–211
Schapiro, Meyer, **II:** 30
Scharmann, Hermann Balthazar, **Supp. XII:** 41
Scharnhort, Gary, **Retro. Supp. III:** 268
Scharper, Alice, **Supp. XXII:** 175
Scharper, Diane, **Supp. XXIII:** 134
Schary, Dore, **Supp. IV Part 1:** 365; **Supp. XIII:** 163
Schatz, Tom, **Supp. XVIII:** 242
Schaum, Melita, **Supp. XXII:** 166
Schaumbergh, Count de, **II:** 120
Schechner, Richard, **Supp. XXIV:** 116
Scheele, Roy, **Supp. XVI:** 54; **Supp.**

XXI: 103
Scheeman, George, Supp. XXII: 230
Scheffauer, G. H., I: 199
"Scheherazade" (Ashbery), Supp. III Part 1: 18
"Scheherazade Is Nailed and Mailed in Five Days" (Stone), Supp. XXVII: 257
Scheick, William, Supp. V: 272
Schelberg, Budd, Supp. XVIII: 241–256
Scheler, Max, I: 58
Schelling, Friedrich, Supp. I Part 2: 422
Schenck, Joseph, Supp. XVI: 186
Schenk, Margaret, I: 199
Scheponik, Peter, Supp. X: 210
Scherer, Loline, Supp. XIII: 161
"Scherzo"(Hadas), Supp. XXIII: 113
Schevill, James, I: 116
Schickel, Richard, Supp. XV: 1
Schifano, Mario, Supp. XXIII: 217
Schifino, Martin, Supp. XXVI: 145
Schilder, Paul, Supp. I Part 2: 622
Schildkraut, Rudolph, Supp. XXIII: 8
Schiller, Andrew, II: 20
Schiller, Frederick, Supp. V: 290
Schiller, Johann Christoph Friedrich von, I: 224; Supp. IV Part 2: 519; Supp. XVI: 292
Schiller, Lawrence, Retro. Supp. II: 208, 212, 214
Schimmel, Harold, Supp. V: 336
"Schizoid Nature of the Implied Author in Twentieth-Century American Ethnic Novels, The" (Nelson), Supp. XVIII: 172
Schjeldahl, Peter, Supp. XXIV: 44; Supp. XXVII: 23
Schlegel, Augustus Wilhelm, III: 422, 424
Schlegell, David von, Supp. IV Part 2: 423
Schleiermacher, Friedrich, III: 290–291, 309
Schleifer, Ronald, Supp. XVIII: 144
Schlepping Through the Alps (S. Apple), Supp. XVII: 8
Schlesinger, Arthur, Jr., III: 291, 297–298, 309
Schleuning, Neala, Supp. XXIII: 165
Schmidt, Jon Zlotnik, Supp. IV Part 1: 2
Schmidt, Kaspar. See Stirner, Max
Schmidt, Michael, Supp. X: 55
Schmitt, Carl, I: 386–387
Schmitz, Neil, Supp. X: 243
Schnackenberg, Gjertrud, Supp. XV: 249–268
Schneeman, George, Supp. XXIV: 41
Schneider, Alan, I: 87
Schneider, Dean, Supp. XXVII: 208
Schneider, Louis, Supp. I Part 2: 650
Schneider, Romy, Supp. IV Part 2: 549
Schneider, Steven, Supp. IX: 271, 274
Schnellock, Emil, III: 177
Schneour, Zalman, IV: 11
"Schnetzer Day" (Halliday), Supp. XIX: 93
Schnitzler, Arthur, Supp. XV: 307; Supp. XVI: 187
Schoen, Carol, Supp. XXVII: 297
Schoerke, Meg, Supp. XVII: 110
"Scholar Gypsy, The" (Arnold), II: 541
"Scholastic and Bedside Teaching" (Holmes), Supp. I Part 1: 305
Schöler, Bo, Supp. IV Part 1: 399, 400, 403, 407, 409; Supp. IV Part 2: 499
Scholes, Robert, Supp. V: 40, 42
Scholtz, Carter, Supp. XVIII: 144
Schomburg, Arthur, Supp. X: 134; Supp. XXII: 6
Schomburg Library of Nineteenth-Century Black Women Writers (H. L. Gates, ed.), Supp. XX: 105
Schönberg, Claude-Michel, Supp. XXI: 155
"School Among the Ruins, The" (Rich), Retro. Supp. III: 252
School Among the Ruins, The: Poems 2000–2004 (Rich), Retro. Supp. III: 252
Schoolboy Howlers (Abingdon), Supp. XVI: 99
Schoolcraft, Henry Rowe, II: 503; Retro. Supp. II: 160; Supp. XXIII: 223, 227, 228, 232, 233–234
Schoolcraft, Jane Johnston (Bamewawagezhikaquay), Supp. XXIII: 223–238
"School Days of an Indian Girl, The" (Zitkala-Ša), Supp. XXV: 272
"School Daze" (Bambara), Supp. XI: 19
School Daze (film), Supp. XI: 19, 20
"Schoolhouse" (Levis), Supp. XI: 258
"School of Giorgione, The" (Pater), I: 51
School of Udhra (Mackey), Supp. XXVII: 154–155
"School Play, The" (Merrill), Supp. III Part 1: 336
"Schooner Fairchild's Class" (Benét), Supp. XI: 55
Schopenhauer, Arthur, III: 600, 604; IV: 7; Retro. Supp. I: 256; Retro. Supp. II: 94; Supp. I Part 1: 320; Supp. I Part 2: 457; Supp. X: 187; Supp. XVI: 184
Schorer, Mark, II: 28; III: 71; Retro. Supp. I: 115; Supp. IV Part 1: 197, 203, 211; Supp. XVI: 206
Schott, Penelope Scambly, Supp. XXIII: 239–256
Schott, Webster, Supp. IX: 257
Schøtt-Khristensen, Lene, Supp. XXVI: 124, 125
Schotts, Jeffrey, Supp. XII: 193
Schrader, Mary von. See Jarrell, Mrs. Randall (Mary von Schrader)
Schreiber, Jan, Supp. XXI: 105, 111
Schreiner, Olive, I: 419; Supp. XI: 203
"Schreuderspitze, The" (Helprin), Supp. XXV: 85
Schroeder, Eric James, Supp. V: 238, 244
Schubert, Bernard L., Supp. XVII: 58
Schubert, David, Supp. XXIV: 45
Schubert, Franz Peter, Supp. I Part 1: 363
Schubnell, Matthias, Supp. IV Part 2: 486
Schudel, Matt, Supp. XXII: 205, 214
Schuessler, Jennifer, Supp. XXVI: 126
Schulberg, Budd, II: 98; Retro. Supp. I: 113; Supp. XIII: 170; Supp. XV: 194; Supp. XXVII: 142
Schulberg, Stuart, Supp. XVIII: 254
Schulman, Grace, Supp. XXIII: 58
Schulman, Tom, Supp. XXI: 193, 194
Schultz, David E., Supp. XXVII: 128
Schulz, Bruno, Supp. IV Part 2: 623; Supp. XVII: 41
Schuman, William, Supp. XII: 253; Supp. XXII: 283
Schumann, Dr. Alanson Tucker, III: 505
Schuster, Edgar H., Supp. VIII: 126
Schuyler, George S., III: 110; Supp. XIX: 78; Supp. XVI: 142; Supp. XXVI: 167
Schuyler, James, Supp. XV: 177, 178; Supp. XXIII: 207, 212, 215, 217; Supp. XXIV: 33; Supp. XXVII: 21, 23, 24, 26, 28
Schuyler, William, Supp. I Part 1: 211
"Schuylkill, The" (Halliday), Supp. XIX: 92
Schwartz, Delmore, I: 67, 168, 188, 288; IV: 128, 129, 437; Retro. Supp. II: 29, 178; Supp. II Part 1: 102, 109; Supp. II Part 2: 639–668; Supp. IX: 299; Supp. VIII: 98; Supp. XIII: 320; Supp. XIV: 3; Supp. XIX: 257; Supp. XV: 184
Schwartz, Leonard, Supp. XVI: 289
Schwartz, Lloyd, Supp. I Part 1: 81;

Supp. XXIV: 160
Schwartz, Marilyn, **Supp. XII:** 126, 128, 130, 132
Schwartz, Meryl F., **Supp. XXII:** 65, 66
Schwartz, Richard B., **Supp. XIV:** 23, 27
Schwarz, A. B. Christa, **Supp. XIX:** 77, 79
Schwed, Peter, **Supp. XXII:** 119
Schweitzer, Albert, **Supp. IV Part 1:** 373
Schweitzer, Harold, **Supp. X:** 210
Schwerdt, Lisa M., **Supp. XIV:** 155, 171
Schwind, Jean, **Retro. Supp. III:** 36
Schwitters, Kurt, **III:** 197; **Retro. Supp. II:** 322, 331, 336; **Supp. IV Part 1:** 79
"Science" (Jeffers), **Supp. II Part 2:** 426
Science and Health with Key to the Scriptures (Eddy), **I:** 383
"Science Favorable to Virtue" (Freneau), **Supp. II Part 1:** 274
Science of English Verse, The (Lanier), **Supp. I Part 1:** 368, 369
"Science of the Night, The" (Kunitz), **Supp. III Part 1:** 258, 265
"Sci-Fi Floater Genius" (Halliday), **Supp. XIX:** 91
Sciolino, Martina, **Supp. XII:** 9
"Scissors" (C. Baxter), **Supp. XVII:** 19
Scofield, Sandra, **Supp. XXI:** 119
Scooter tetralogy (Murray). See Magic Keys, The (Murray); Seven League Boots, The (Murray); Spyglass Tree, The (Murray); Train Whistle Guitar (Murray)
Scopes, John T., **III:** 105, 495
"Scorched Face, The" (Hammett), **Supp. IV Part 1:** 344
"Scorn" (C. Frost), **Supp. XV:** 105
"Scorpion, The" (Bowles), **Supp. IV Part 1:** 84, 86
Scorpions (Myers), **Supp. XXVII:** 203, 204, 205
Scorsese, Martin, **Supp. IV Part 1:** 356; **Supp. XVIII:** 22
"Scotland" (Huddle), **Supp. XXVI:** 155
Scott, Anne Firor, **Supp. I Part 1:** 19
Scott, A. O., **Supp. X:** 301, 302; **Supp. XII:** 343
Scott, Duncan C., **Supp. XXVI:** 87
Scott, Evelyn, **Retro. Supp. I:** 73; **Supp. XXII:** 198
Scott, Gavin, **Supp. XXII:** 218
Scott, George C., **III:** 165–166; **Supp. XI:** 304
Scott, George Lewis, **Supp. I Part 2:** 503, 504
Scott, Hazel, **Supp. XXII:** 12
Scott, Herbert, **Supp. V:** 180
Scott, Howard, **Supp. I Part 2:** 645
Scott, Joanna, **Supp. XVII: 183–197**
Scott, Lizabeth, **Supp. IV Part 2:** 524
Scott, Lynn Orilla, **Retro. Supp. II:** 12
Scott, Mark, **Retro. Supp. I:** 127
Scott, Mary Ellen, **Supp. XXVI:** 235
Scott, Nathan A., Jr., **II:** 27
Scott, Paul, **Supp. IV Part 2:** 690
Scott, Ridley, **Supp. XIII:** 268
Scott, Walter, **Supp. XVI:** 7, 13
Scott, Sir Walter, **I:** 204, 339, 341, 343, 354; **II:** 8, 17, 18, 217, 296, 301, 303, 304, 308; **III:** 415, 482; **IV:** 204, 453; **Retro. Supp. I:** 99; **Supp. I Part 2:** 579, 580, 685, 692; **Supp. IV Part 2:** 690; **Supp. IX:** 175; **Supp. X:** 51, 114
Scott, Whitney, **Supp. XXVI:** 49
Scott, Winfield Townley, **II:** 512; **Supp. I Part 2:** 705; **Supp. XV:** 51
Scottsboro boys, **I:** 505; **Supp. I Part 1:** 330
Scottsboro Limited (Hughes), **Retro. Supp. I:** 203; **Supp. I Part 1:** 328, 330–331, 332
Scoundrel, The (film), **Supp. XXVII:** 90
Scoundrel Time (Hellman), **Supp. I Part 1:** 294–297; **Supp. IV Part 1:** 12; **Supp. VIII:** 243
Scrambled Eggs Super! (Geisel), **Supp. XVI:** 105
Scrambled Eggs & Whiskey: Poems, 1991–1995 (Carruth), **Supp. XVI:** 47
Scratch (MacLeish), **III:** 22–23
"Scratch Music" (Wright), **Supp. XV:** 343
"Scream, The" (R . Lowell), **II:** 550
"Screamer, The" (Coleman), **Supp. XI: 92–93**
"Screamers, The" (Baraka), **Supp. II Part 1:** 38
"Screech Owl" (Huddle), **Supp. XXVI:** 151
"Screen Guide for Americans" (Rand), **Supp. IV Part 2:** 524
"Screen Memory" (Cliff), **Supp. XXII:** 75
"Screeno" (Schwartz), **Supp. II Part 2:** 660
Screens, The (Genet), **Supp. XII:** 12
Screen Sirens Scream! (Parla and Mitchell), **Supp. XXII:** 256
Scribblers on the Roof: Contemporary American Jewish Fiction (Bukiet and Roskies, eds.), **Supp. XVII:** 39, 49–50
Scripts for the Pageant (Merrill), **Supp. III Part 1:** 332, 333, 335
Scrolls from the Dead Sea, The (Wilson), **IV:** 429
Scruggs, Earl, **Supp. V:** 335
Scudder, Horace Elisha, **II:** 400, 401; **Retro. Supp. II:** 67; **Supp. I Part 1:** 220; **Supp. I Part 2:** 410, 414
Scully, James, **Supp. XII:** 131
"Sculpting the Whistle" (Ríos), **Supp. IV Part 2:** 549
"Sculptor" (Plath), **Supp. I Part 2:** 538
"Sculptor's Funeral, The" (Cather), **I:** 315–316; **Retro. Supp. I:** 5, 6; **Retro. Supp. III:** 20, 26; **Supp. XV:** 40
Scum (Singer), **Retro. Supp. II:** 316–317
Scupoli, Lorenzo, **IV:** 156
"Scythe Song" (Lang), **Retro. Supp. I:** 128
Sea and the Mirror, The: A Commentary on Shakespeare's "The Tempest" (Auden), **Supp. II Part 1:** 2, 18
Sea around Us, The (Carson), **Supp. IX:** 19, **23–25**
Sea around Us, The (film), **Supp. IX:** 25
Sea Birds Are Still Alive, The (Bambara), **Supp. XI:** 1, 4, **7–12**
"Sea Birds Are Still Alive, The" (Bambara), **Supp. XI:** 8
"Sea-Blue and Blood-Red" (A. Lowell), **II:** 524
Seabrook, John, **Supp. VIII:** 157
"Sea Burial from the Cruiser Reve" (Eberhart), **I:** 532–533
Seabury, David, **Supp. I Part 2:** 608
"Sea Calm" (Hughes), **Retro. Supp. I:** 199
"Sea Chanty" (Corso), **Supp. XII:** 118
"Sea Dream, A" (Whitter), **Supp. I Part 2:** 699
"Seafarer, The" (Pound, trans.), **Retro. Supp. I:** 287
Seagall, Harry, **Supp. XIII:** 166
Sea Garden (Doolittle), **Supp. I Part 1:** 257, 259, 266, 269, 272; **Supp. XXVII:** 288
Seager, Allan, **IV:** 305
Seagull on the Step, The (Boyle), **Supp. XXIV:** 60, 62
"Seagulls and Children" (C. Frost), **Supp. XV:** 95

Sea Lady, The (Boyce), **Supp. XXI:** 8, 13
"Sea Lily" (Doolittle), **Supp. I Part 1:** 266
Sea Lions, The (Cooper), **I:** 354, 355
Sealts, Merton M., Jr., **Retro. Supp. I:** 257
Seaman, Benjamin, **Supp. XXIII:** 69–70, 72
Seaman, Donna, **Supp. VIII:** 86; **Supp. X:** 1, 4, 12, 16, 213; **Supp. XIX:** 53, 55, 57, 58, 59, 60, 61; **Supp. XV:** 65; **Supp. XVIII:** 102; **Supp. XXI:** 236; **Supp. XXII:** 266; **Supp. XXIII:** 71, 74, 134, 135, 298; **Supp. XXIV:** 167, 171; **Supp. XXVI:** 150–151, 158
"Seamy Side, The"(Hadas), **Supp. XXIII:** 119
"Séance, The" (Singer), **IV:** 20
Séance and Other Stories, The (Singer), **IV:** 19–21
"Sea Oak" (Saunders), **Supp. XIX:** 228, 229, 231
Sea of Cortez (Steinbeck), **IV:** 52, 54, 62, 69
Sea of Grass, The (film), **Supp. XVIII:** 211
Sea of Grass, The (Richter), **Supp. XVIII: 210–211,** 215–216, 217, 220
"Sea Pieces" (Melville), **III:** 93
Searchers, The (film, Ford), **Supp. XVIII:** 57, 58, 135–136, 141
Searches and Seizures (Elkin), **Supp. VI: 49**
"Search for Southern Identity, The" (Woodward), **Retro. Supp. I:** 75; **Supp. XXII:** 194
Search for the King, A: A Twelfth-Century Legend (Vidal), **Supp. IV Part 2:** 681
Searching for Caleb (Tyler), **Supp. IV Part 2:** 663–665, 671
"Searching for Poetry: Real vs. Fake" (B. Miller), **Supp. IV Part 1:** 67
Searching for Survivors (Banks), **Supp. V:** 7
"Searching for Survivors (I)" (Banks), **Supp. V:** 8
"Searching for Survivors (II)" (Banks), **Supp. V:** 7, 8
Searching for the Ox (Simpson), **Supp. IX:** 266, **274–275**
"Searching for the Ox" (Simpson), **Supp. IX:** 275, 280
"Searching in the Britannia Tavern" (Wagoner), **Supp. IX:** 327
Searching Wing, The, (Hellman), **Supp. I Part 1:** 277, 278, 281–282, 283, 292, 297
Search-Light. See Frank, Waldo
"Search Party, The" (Matthews), **Supp. IX: 156**
Searle, Ronald, **Supp. I Part 2:** 604, 605
Sea Road to the Indies (Hart), **Supp. XIV:** 97
"Seascape" (Bishop), **Retro. Supp. II:** 42–43
Seascape: Needle's Eye (Oppen), **Supp. XXVI:** 236–237
"Sea's Green Sameness, The" (Updike), **IV:** 217
Seaside and the Fireside, The (Longfellow), **II:** 489; **Retro. Supp. II:** 159, 168
"Season, The" (Stone), **Supp. XXVII:** 250–251
Season in Hell, A (Rimbaud), **III:** 189
Seasons, The (Thomson), **II:** 304; **Supp. I Part 1:** 151
Seasons' Difference, The (Buechner), **Supp. XII: 47**
Seasons of Celebration (Merton), **Supp. VIII:** 199, 208
Seasons of the Heart: In Quest of Faith (Kinard, comp.), **Supp. XIV:** 127
"Seasons of the Soul" (Tate), **IV:** 136–140
Seasons on Earth (Koch), **Supp. XV: 183–184**
"Sea Surface Full of Clouds" (Stevens), **IV:** 82
"Sea Tides" (Hoffman), **Supp. XVIII:** 87
"Sea Treader" (Hoffman), **Supp. XVIII:** 87
"Sea Unicorns and Land Unicorns" (Moore), **III:** 202–203
Seaver, Edwin, **Supp. XXV:** 28
Seaver, Richard, **Supp. XI:** 301
"Seaweed" (Longfellow), **II:** 498
Sea-Wolf, The (London), **II:** 264, 466, 472–473
Sebald, W. G., **Supp. XIV:** 96; **Supp. XXI:** 92
Sebold, Alice, **Supp. XXII:** 55
Seckler, David, **Supp. I Part 2:** 650
"2nd Air Force" (Jarrell), **II:** 375
Second American Revolution and Other Essays (1976–1982), The (Vidal), **Supp. IV Part 2:** 679, 687, 688
Secondary Colors, The (A. Theroux), **Supp. VIII:** 312
Second Avenue (O'Hara), **Supp. XXIII:** 216
"Second Avenue"(O'Hara), **Supp. XXIII:** 208, 211, 218
Second Blush, The (Peacock), **Supp. XIX:** 197, **205–206**
Second Chance (Auchincloss), **Supp. IV Part 1:** 33
"Second Chances" (Hugo), **Supp. VI:** 144, 145
Second Coming, The (Percy), **Supp. III Part 1:** 383, 384, 387, 388, 396–397
"Second Coming, The" (Yeats), **III:** 294; **Retro. Supp. I:** 290, 311; **Supp. VIII:** 24; **Supp. XIX:** 85; **Supp. XVI:** 159
Second Decade, The. See Stephen King, The Second Decade: "Danse Macabre" to "The Dark Half" (Magistrale)
Second Dune, The (Hearon), **Supp. VIII:** 58, **59–60**
Second Flowering, A: Works and Days of the Lost Generation (Cowley), **Retro. Supp. II:** 77; **Supp. II Part 1:** 135, 141, 143, 144, 147, 149
Second Growth (Stegner), **Supp. IV Part 2:** 599, 608
Second-Hand Coat: Poems New and Selected (Stone), **Supp. XXVII:** 250, 257, 262
"Second Hour of the Night, The" (Bidart), **Supp. XV:** 32, **33–34**
Second Marriage (F. Barthelme), **Supp. XI:** 32, 33
"Second Marriage" (McCarriston), **Supp. XIV:** 262
"Second Mortgage" (Shaw), **Supp. XIX:** 245–246
Second Nature (Hoffman), **Supp. X:** 88, 89
"Second Nesting" (Davison), **Supp. XXVI:** 77
Seconds, The (Bierds), **Supp. XVII: 33–34**
Second Set, The (Komunyakaa and Feinstein, eds.), **Supp. XIII:** 125
Second Sex, The (Beauvoir), **Retro. Supp. III:** 243; **Supp. IV Part 1:** 360
"Second Sight" (Mosher), **Supp. XXII:** 214
Second Stone, The (Fiedler), **Supp. XIII:** 102
"Second Swimming, The" (Boyle), **Supp. VIII:** 13, 14
Second Tree from the Corner (White), **Supp. I Part 2:** 654
"Second Tree from the Corner" (White), **Supp. I Part 2:** 651
Second Twenty Years at Hull-House, The: September 1909 to September 1929, with a Record of a Growing World Consciousness (Addams), **Supp. I Part 1:** 24–25

Second Voyage of Columbus, The (Morison), **Supp. I Part 2:** 488
Second Words, (Atwood), **Supp. XIII:** 35
Second World, The (Blackmur), **Supp. II Part 1:** 91
Secret, The (E. Hoffman), **Supp. XVI:** 151, **155–158,** 161
"Secret, The" (Levine), **Supp. V:** 195
Secret Agent, The (Conrad), **Supp. IV Part 1:** 341
Secret Agent X-9 (Hammett), **Supp. IV Part 1:** 355
"Secret Courts of Men's Hearts, The: Code and Law in Harper Lee's To Kill a Mockingbird" (C. D. Johnson), **Supp. VIII:** 126
"Secret Dog, The" (Cameron), **Supp. XII: 83–84**
Secret Garden, The (Burnett), **Supp. I Part 1:** 44
"Secret Garden, The" (Hoffman), **Supp. XVIII:** 86
"Secret Gladness, A" (C. Frost), **Supp. XV:** 91
Secret Historie (J. Smith), **I:** 131
Secret History, The (Tartt), **Supp. XXVII:** 267, 268, 269, 270–273
Secret History of the Dividing Line (Howe), **Supp. IV Part 2:** 424, 425–426
"Secret Integration, The" (Pynchon), **Supp. II Part 2:** 624
"Secret Life of Musical Instruments, The" (Wright), **Supp. XV:** 343
"Secret Life of Walter Mitty, The" (Thurber), **Supp. I Part 2:** 623; **Supp. XVI:** 233
"Secret Lion, The" (Ríos), **Supp. IV Part 2:** 543, 544
"Secret Nature of the Mechanical Rabbit, The"(P. Benedict), **Supp. XXIII:** 49
"Secret Ocean, The" (Jarman), **Supp. XVII:** 120
Secret of Poetry, The: Essays (Jarman), **Supp. XVII:** 110, 111, 120
"Secret of the Russian Ballet, The" (Van Vechten), **Supp. II Part 2:** 732
"Secret Profession, The" (Stone), **Supp. XXVII:** 258–259
"Secret Prune" (Ríos), **Supp. IV Part 2:** 549
Secret River, The (Rawlings), **Supp. X:** 233
Secrets and Surprises (Beattie), **Supp. V:** 23, 27, 29
Secrets from the Center of the World (Harjo), **Supp. XII: 223–224**
"Secret Sharer, The" (J. Conrad), **Supp. IX:** 105; **Supp. XVI:** 158; **Supp. XXV:** 217
"Secret Society, A" (Nemerov), **III:** 282
Secrets of the Heart (Gibran), **Supp. XX: 116**
"Secrets of the Summer, The" (Ellis), **Supp. XXVII:** 75
Secrets of the Universe: Scenes from the Journey Home (Sanders), **Supp. XVI:** 273–274
"Secular" (Trethewey), **Supp. XXI:** 249
Secular Journal of Thomas Merton, The, **Supp. VIII:** 206
"Security" (Boyle), **Supp. XXIV:** 58
"Security" (Stafford), **Supp. XI:** 329
"Security"(Strout), **Supp. XXIII:** 283
Sedaris, David, **Supp. XXIII:** 289
Sedges, John (pseudonym). See Buck, Pearl S.
Sedgwick, Catherine Maria, **I:** 341; **Supp. I Part 1:** 155, 157
Sedgwick, Christina. See Marquand, Mrs. John P. (Christina Sedgwick)
Sedgwick, Ellery, **I:** 217, 229, 231; **III:** 54–55
Sedgwick, Eve, **Supp. XX: 267**
Sedgwick, Henry, **Supp. I Part 1:** 156
Sedgwick, Robert, **Supp. I Part 1:** 156
Sedore, Timothy, **Supp. XIV:** 312
"Seduction and Betrayal" (Hardwick), **Supp. III Part 1:** 207
Seduction and Betrayal: Women and Literature (Hardwick), **Supp. III Part 1:** 194, 204, 206–208, 212, 213; **Supp. XIV:** 89
See, Carolyn, **Supp. XXII:** 206, 217
Seed, David, **Supp. IV Part 1:** 391
"Seed Eaters, The" (Francis), **Supp. IX:** 82
"Seed Leaves" (Wilbur), **Supp. III Part 2:** 558
"Seeds" (Anderson), **I:** 106, 114
Seeds of Contemplation (Merton), **Supp. VIII:** 199, 200, 207, 208
Seeds of Destruction (Merton), **Supp. VIII:** 202, 203, 204, 208
"Seeing Red" (column, Ryan as Quin), **Supp. XVIII:** 226
Seeing through the Sun (Hogan), **Supp. IV Part 1:** 397, 400, 401–402, 402, 413
"See in the Midst of Fair Leaves" (Moore), **III:** 215
"Seekers, The" (McGrath), **Supp. X:** 117
"Seeking a Vision of Truth, Guided by a Higher Power" (Burke), **Supp. XIV:** 21, 23
"See(k)ing the Self: Mirrors and Mirroring in Bicultural Texts" (Oster), **Supp. XVI:** 151
"Seele im Raum" (Jarrell), **II:** 382–383
"Seele im Raum" (Rilke), **II:** 382–383
"See Naples and Die" (Hecht), **Supp. X:** 69, 70
"Seen from the 'L' " (Barnes), **Supp. III Part 1:** 33
"See the Moon?" (Barthelme), **Supp. IV Part 1:** 42, 49–50, 50
Sefarim, Mendele Mokher, **Supp. XXIII:** 4
Seferis, George, **Supp. XXV:** 225
Segal, D. (pseudonym). See Singer, Isaac Bashevis
Segal, George, **Supp. XI:** 343
Segal, Lore, **Supp. XVI:** 203
Segregation: The Inner Conflict in the South (Warren), **IV:** 237, 238, 246, 252
"*Se: Hegel's Absolute and Heidegger's Ereignis" (Agamben), **Supp. XVI:** 289
Seidel, Frederick, **I:** 185
Seidman, Hugh, **Supp. XXI:** 228
Seize the Day (Bellow), **I:** 144, 147, 148, 150, 151, 152, 153, 155, 158, 162; **Retro. Supp. II:** 19, **23–24,** 27, 32, 34; **Supp. I Part 2:** 428
Selby, Hubert, **Supp. III Part 1:** 125
Selby, Hubert, Jr., **Supp. XXI:** 227
Selby, John, **Retro. Supp. II:** 221, 222
Selden, John, **Supp. XIV:** 344
Seldes, Gilbert, **II:** 437, 445; **Retro. Supp. I:** 108
Selected Criticism: Prose, Poetry (Bogan), **Supp. III Part 1:** 64
Selected Essays (Eliot), **I:** 572
Selected Essays and Reviews (Carruth), **Supp. XVI:** 46
Selected Journals and Other Writings (Audubon), **Supp. XVI:** 10, 12, 13
Selected Letters (Bynner), **Supp. XV:** 52
Selected Letters (Oppen), **Supp. XXVI:** 228
Selected Letters (W. C. Williams), **Retro. Supp. I:** 430
Selected Letters, 1940–1956 (Kerouac), **Supp. XIV:** 137, 144
Selected Letters of Robert Frost (Thompson, ed.), **Retro. Supp. I:** 125
Selected Letters of Willa Cather, The, **Retro. Supp. III:** 37
Selected Levis, The (Levis), **Supp. XI:** 257, 272

Selected Plays (O'Hara), **Supp. XXIII:** 216
Selected Poems (A. Lowell), **II:** 512, 516
Selected Poems (Aiken), **I:** 69
Selected Poems (Ashbery), **Supp. III Part 1:** 25–26
Selected Poems (Berrigan), **Supp. XXIV:** 37
Selected Poems (Bodenheim), **Supp. XXV:** 29
Selected Poems (Brodsky), **Supp. VIII:** 22
Selected Poems (Brooks), **Supp. III Part 1:** 82–83
Selected Poems (Bynner), **Supp. XV:** 51, 52
Selected Poems (Corso), **Supp. XII:** 129
Selected Poems (Dove), **Supp. IV Part 1:** 241, 243, 250
Selected Poems (Frost), **Retro. Supp. I:** 133, 136; **Retro. Supp. III:** 102, 103
Selected Poems (Guillevic; Levertov, trans.), **Supp. III Part 1:** 283
Selected Poems (Hayden), **Supp. II Part 1:** 363, 364, 367
Selected Poems (Hughes), **Retro. Supp. I:** 202; **Supp. I Part 1:** 341, 345, 346
Selected Poems (Hugo), **Supp. VI:** 143
Selected Poems (Jarrell), **II:** 367, 370, 371, 374, 377, 379, 380, 381, 382, 384
Selected Poems (Justice), **Supp. VII:** 115
Selected Poems (Kinnell), **Supp. III Part 1:** 235, 253
Selected Poems (Levine, 1984), **Supp. V:** 178, 179
Selected Poems (Merton), **Supp. VIII:** 207, 208
Selected Poems (Moore), **III:** 193, 194, 205–206, 208, 215
Selected Poems (Notley), **Supp. XXII:** 234
Selected Poems (O'Hara; Allen, ed.), **Supp. XXIII:** 220
Selected Poems (O'Hara; Ford, ed.), **Supp. XXIII:** 220
Selected Poems (Pound), **Retro. Supp. I:** 289, 291
Selected Poems (R. Bly), **Supp. IV Part 1:** 60, 62, 65, 66, 68, 69–71
Selected Poems (R. Lowell), **Retro. Supp. II:** 184, 186, 188, 190
Selected Poems (Ransom), **III:** 490, 492
Selected Poems (Reznikoff), **Supp. XIV:** 288
Selected Poems (Rukeyser), **Supp. VI:** 274
Selected Poems (Sexton), **Supp. IV Part 2:** 449
Selected Poems (Sorrentino), **Supp. XXI:** 226
Selected Poems (Strand), **Supp. IV Part 2:** 630
Selected Poems, 1923–1943 (Warren), **IV:** 241–242, 243
Selected Poems, 1928–1958 (Kunitz), **Supp. III Part 1:** 261, 263–265
Selected Poems, 1938–1988 (McGrath), **Supp. X:** 127
Selected Poems, 1958–1980 (Sorrentino), **Supp. XXI:** 228
Selected Poems, 1963–1983 (Simic), **Supp. VIII:** 275
Selected Poems 1936–1965 (Eberhart), **I:** 541
Selected Poems: 1957–1987 (Snodgrass), **Supp. VI:** 314–315, 323, 324
Selected Poems 1965–1975 (Atwood), **Supp. XIII: 32–34**
Selected Poems: 1975–2005 (Skloot), **Supp. XX: 196**
Selected Poems II: Poems Selected and New, 1976–1986 (Atwood), **Supp. XIII:** 20, **34–35**
Selected Poems of Ezra Pound (Pound), **Supp. V:** 336
Selected Poems of Gabriela Mistral (Hughes, trans.), **Supp. I Part 1:** 345
Selected Poems of Stanley Kunitz, The, **Supp. XXVI:** 64
Selected Poetry of Amiri Baraka/LeRoi Jones (Baraka), **Supp. II Part 1:** 58
Selected Poetry of Hayden Carruth, The (Carruth), **Supp. XVI:** 53
Selected Stories (Dubus), **Supp. VII:** 88–89
Selected Stories of Richard Bausch, The (Bausch), **Supp. VII:** 42
Selected Translations (Snodgrass), **Supp. VI:** 318, 324, **325–326**
Selected Verse of Margaret Haskins Durber, The (Keillor), **Supp. XVI:** 171
Selected Witter Bynner, The, **Supp. XV:** 52
Selected Works of Djuna Barnes, The (Barnes), **Supp. III Part 1:** 44
Selected Writings (Brainard), **Supp. XXVII:** 20
Selected Writings 1950–1990 (Howe), **Supp. VI:** 116–117, 118, 120
Selected Writings of Edgar Allan Poe: Authoritative Texts, Backgrounds and Contexts, Criticism (Thompson, ed.), **Retro. Supp. III:** 237
Selected Writings of John Jay Chapman, The (Barzun), **Supp. XIV:** 54
Select Epigrams from the Greek Anthology (Mackail), **Supp. I Part 2:** 461
"Selecting a Reader" (Kooser), **Supp. XIX:** 119–120
"Selene Afterwards" (MacLeish), **III:** 8
"Self" (James), **II:** 351
Self, William, **Supp. XXII:** 172
Self and the Dramas of History, The (Niebuhr), **III:** 308
"Self-Appraisal" (Davison), **Supp. XXVI:** 68
Self-Consciousness (Updike), **Retro. Supp. I:** 318, 319, 320, 322, 323, 324
"Self-Culture" (Channing), **Supp. XXIV: 78–79**
"Self-Exposed, The" (X. J. Kennedy), **Supp. XV:** 159
Self-Help: Stories (Moore), **Supp. X:** 163, 166, **167–169,** 174, 175
"Self-Importance" (Halliday), **Supp. XIX:** 90
Self-Interviews (Dickey), **Supp. IV Part 1:** 179
"Self-Made Man, A" (Crane), **I:** 420
"Self Pity" (C. Frost), **Supp. XV:** 93, 94, 101, 102, 104
Self Portrait (album, Dylan), **Supp. XVIII:** 27
Self-Portrait (Brainard and Waldman), **Supp. XXVII:** 23–24
"Self-Portrait" (Creeley), **Supp. IV Part 1:** 156
"Self-Portrait" (Davison), **Supp. XXVI:** 68
"Self-Portrait" (Mumford), **Supp. II Part 2:** 471
"(Self) Portrait" (Trethewey), **Supp. XXI:** 253
"Self-Portrait" (Wylie), **Supp. I Part 2:** 729
"Self Portrait at Fifty-three" (Weigl), **Supp. XIX:** 288
Self-Portrait: Ceaselessly into the Past (Millar, ed. Sipper), **Supp. IV Part 2:** 464, 469, 472, 475
"Self-Portrait in a Convex Mirror" (Ashbery), **Supp. III Part 1:** 5, 7, 9, 16–19, 22, 24, 26
"Self-Portrait on a Christmas Night" (Brainard), **Supp. XXVII:** 24–25
"Self-Portrait with 1911 NY Yankees Cap" (Skloot), **Supp. XX: 202**

"Self-Reliance" (Emerson), **II:** 7, 15, 17; **Retro. Supp. I:** 159; **Retro. Supp. II:** 155; **Supp. X:** 42, 45
Selfwolf (Halliday), **Supp. XIX:** 81, **89–91,** 93
Sélincourt, Ernest de, **Supp. I Part 2:** 676
Selinger, Eric, **Supp. XVI:** 47
Selinger, Eric Murphy, **Supp. XI:** 248
Sell, Henry, **Supp. XVI:** 188
Sellers, Isaiah, **IV:** 194–195
Sellers, Peter, **Supp. XI:** 301, 304, 306, 307, 309
Sellers, William, **IV:** 208
Seltzer, Mark, **Retro. Supp. I:** 227
Selznick, David O., **Retro. Supp. I:** 105, 113; **Supp. IV Part 1:** 353; **Supp. XVIII:** 242; **Supp. XXII:** 195
Semi, Allen (pseudonym). See Larsen, Nella
"Semi-Lunatics of Kilmuir, The" (Hugo), **Supp. VI:** 145
"Semiotics/The Doctor's Doll" (Goldbarth), **Supp. XII:** 183–184
Semmelweiss, Ignaz, **Supp. I Part 1:** 304
Senancour, Étienne Divert de, **I:** 241
Senator North (Atherton), **Supp. XXIV:** 22
Sendak, Maurice, **Supp. IX:** 207, 208, 213, 214; **Supp. XVI:** 110
Seneca, **II:** 14–15; **III:** 77
Senghor, Leopold Sédar, **Supp. IV Part 1:** 16; **Supp. X:** 132, 139
Senier, Siobhan, **Supp. IV Part 1:** 330
"Senility" (Anderson), **I:** 114
Senior, Olive, **Supp. XXIII:** 94
"Senior Partner's Ethics, The" (Auchincloss), **Supp. IV Part 1:** 33
Senlin: A Biography (Aiken), **I:** 48, 49, 50, 52, 56, 57, 64
Sennett, Dorothy, **Supp. XVI:** 43
Sennett, Mack, **III:** 442
"Señora X No More" (Mora), **Supp. XIII:** 218
"Señor Ong and Señor Ha" (Bowles), **Supp. IV Part 1:** 87
Señor Presidente, El (Asturias), **Supp. XXIV:** 89
"Señor X" (Muñoz), **Supp. XXV:** 135
Sensational Designs: The Cultural Work of American Fiction, 1790–1860 (Tompkins), **Supp. XVIII:** 258–259
Sense and Sensibility (Austen), **Supp. XXVI:** 130, 212
Sense of Beauty, The (Santayana), **III:** 600
Sense of Life in the Modern Novel, The (Mizener), **IV:** 132
"Sense of Shelter, A" (Updike), **Retro. Supp. I:** 318
"Sense of the Meeting, The" (Conroy), **Supp. XVI:** 72
Sense of the Past, The (James), **II:** 337–338
"Sense of the Past, The" (Trilling), **Supp. III Part 2:** 503
"Sense of the Present, The" (Hardwick), **Supp. III Part 1:** 210
"Sense of the Sleight-of-Hand Man, The" (Stevens), **IV:** 93
"Sense of Where You Are, A" (McPhee), **Supp. III Part 1:** 291, 296–298
"Sensibility! O La!" (Roethke), **III:** 536
"Sensible Emptiness, A" (Kramer), **Supp. IV Part 1:** 61, 66
Sensualists, The (Hecht), **Supp. XXVII:** 96
"Sensuality Plunging Barefoot Into Thorns" (Cisneros), **Supp. VII:** 68
"Sentence" (Barthelme), **Supp. IV Part 1:** 47
Sent for You Yesterday (Wideman), **Supp. X:** 320, 321
Sentimental Education (Flaubert), **Supp. XXVII:** 2
"Sentimental Education, A" (Banks), **Supp. V:** 10
"Sentimental Journey" (Oates), **Supp. II Part 2:** 522, 523
"Sentimental Journey, A" (Anderson), **I:** 114
Sentimental Journey, A (Sterne), **Supp. I Part 2:** 714
"Sentimental Journeys" (Didion), **Supp. IV Part 1:** 211
Sentimental Journey through France and Italy, A (Sterne), **Supp. XV:** 232
"Sentiment of Rationality, The" (James), **II:** 346–347
"Separated Father" (Halliday), **Supp. XIX:** 92, 93
Separate Flights (Dubus), **Supp. VII:** 78–83
"Separate Flights" (Dubus), **Supp. VII:** 83
Separate Peace, A (Knowles), **Supp. IV Part 2:** 679; **Supp. XII:** **241–249**
Separate Way (Reznikoff), **Supp. XIV:** 280
"Separating" (Updike), **Retro. Supp. I:** 321
"Separation, The" (Kunitz), **Supp. III Part 1:** 263
"Sepia High Stepper" (Hayden), **Supp. II Part 1:** 379
Septagon (Levin), **Supp. XXVII:** 139
September (film; Allen), **Supp. XV:** 11
"September" (Komunyakaa), **Supp. XIII:** 130
"September" (Pickering), **Supp. XXI:** 198
"September 1, 1939" (Auden), **Supp. II Part 1:** 13; **Supp. IV Part 1:** 225; **Supp. VIII:** 30, 32; **Supp. XV:** 117–118
September 11, 2001: American Writers Respond (Heyen), **Supp. XIII:** 285
"September's Book" (Notley), **Supp. XXII:** 229
September Song (Humphrey), **Supp. IX:** 101, 102, **108–109**
"September Twelfth, 2001" (X. J. Kennedy), **Supp. XV:** 171
Septet for the End of Time (Mackey), **Supp. XXVII:** 152
"Sept Vieillards, Les" (Millay, trans.), **III:** 142
Sequel to Drum-Taps (Whitman), **Retro. Supp. I:** 406
"Sequence, Sometimes Metaphysical" (Roethke), **III:** 547, 548
Sequence of Seven Plays with a Drawing by Ron Slaughter, A (Nemerov), **III:** 269
Sequoya, Jana, **Supp. IV Part 1:** 334
Seraglio, The (Merrill), **Supp. III Part 1:** 331
Seraphita (Balzac), **I:** 499
Seraph on the Suwanee (Hurston), **Retro. Supp. III:** 134–135; **Supp. VI:** 149, 159–160
Serena (film), **Supp. XXVII:** 222
Serena (Rash), **Supp. XXVII:** 222, 224–225, 226
Serenissima: A Novel of Venice (Jong). See Shylock's Daughter: A Novel of Love in Venice (Serenissima) (Jong)
Sergeant, Elizabeth Shepley, **I:** 231, 236, 312, 319, 323, 328; **Retro. Supp. III:** 18, 21, 22, 23, 24, 29, 30, 36
Sergeant Bilko (television show), **Supp. IV Part 2:** 575
Sergi, Paula, **Supp. XXI:** 246
"Serious Talk, A" (Carver), **Supp. III Part 1:** 138, 144
Serly, Tibor, **Supp. III Part 2:** 617, 619
"Sermon, Now Encrypted" (Monson), **Supp. XXIV:** 239–240
"Sermon by Doctor Pep" (Bellow), **I:** 151
Sermones (Horace), **II:** 154
"Sermon for Our Maturity" (Baraka),

Supp. II Part 1: 53
"Sermon in the Cotton Field" (Nelson), **Supp. XVIII:** 177
"Sermon in the Depths, The" (Hecht), **Supp. XXVII:** 86
Sermons and Soda Water (O'Hara), **III:** 362, 364, 371–373, 382
"Sermons on the Warpland" (Brooks), **Supp. III Part 1:** 84
"Serpent in the Wilderness, The" (Masters), **Supp. I Part 2:** 458
"Servant of History, A" (Rash), **Supp. XXVII:** 229
Servant of the Bones (Rice), **Supp. VII:** 298, 302
"Servant to Servants, A" (Frost), **Retro. Supp. I:** 125, 128; **Supp. X:** 66
Serve It Forth (M. F. K. Fisher), **Supp. XVII:** 83, 86, 87, 89, 92
Service, Robert W., **Supp. XXI:** 51; **Supp. XXII:** 203
Seshachari, Neila, **Supp. V:** 22
"Session, The" (Adams), **I:** 5
"Sestina" (Bishop), **Supp. I Part 1:** 73, 88
Set-angya, **Supp. IV Part 2:** 493
Seth, Vikram, **Supp. XVII:** 117
Seth's Brother's Wife (Frederic), **II:** 131–132, 137, 144
Sethuraman, Ramchandran, **Supp. XXII:** 73
Setouchi, Jakuch[omacron], **Supp. XXIV:** 166
Set This House on Fire (Styron), **IV:** 98, 99, 105, 107–113, 114, 115, 117
Setting Free the Bears (Irving), **Supp. VI:** 163, **166–167,** 169–170
Setting the Tone (Rorem), **Supp. IV Part 1:** 79
Settle, Mary Lee, **Supp. IX:** 96
Settlement Horizon, The: A National Estimate (Woods and Kennedy), **Supp. I Part 1:** 19
Settlers, The (Levin), **Supp. XXVII:** 134, 143, 146
"Settling the Colonel's Hash" (McCarthy), **II:** 559, 562
Setzer, Helen, **Supp. IV Part 1:** 217
"Seurat's Sunday Afternoon along the Seine" (Schwartz), **Supp. II Part 2:** 663–665
Sevag, Aris, **Supp. XXIII:** 28, 29
7 Years from Somehwere (Levine), **Supp. V:** 178, 181, 188–189
Seven against Thebes (Aeschylus; Bacon and Hecht, trans.), **Supp. X:** 57
Seven Ages of Man, The (Wilder), **IV:** 357, 374–375
Seven Deadly Sins, The (Wilder), **IV:** 357, 374–375
Seven Descents of Myrtle, The (T. Williams), **IV:** 382
"Seven Fat Brides, The" (P. Abraham), **Supp. XVII:** 50
Seven Guitars (Wilson), **Retro. Supp. III:** 318; **Supp. VIII:** 331, **348–351**
Seven Lady Godivas, The (Geisel), **Supp. XVI:** 100, 103
Seven League Boots, The (Murray), **Supp. XIX: 156–157**
Seven-League Crutches, The (Jarrell), **II:** 367, 372, 381, 382, 383–384, 389
Seven Mountains of Thomas Merton, The (Mott), **Supp. VIII:** 208
Seven-Ounce Man, The (Harrison), **Supp. VIII:** 51
"Seven Places of the Mind" (Didion), **Supp. IV Part 1:** 200, 210
Seven Plays (Shepard), **Supp. III Part 2:** 434
"Seven Selves, The" (Gibran), **Supp. XX: 118**
"Seven Sentences"(Dybek), **Supp. XXIII:** 74
"Seven Stanzas at Easter" (Updike), **IV:** 215
Seven Storey Mountain, The (Merton), **Supp. VIII:** 193, 195, 198, 200, 207, 208
Seventeen (Berrigan and Padgett), **Supp. XXIV:** 41
Seventh Beggar, The (Abraham), **Supp. XXIV:** 2, 3, **9–12,** 13, 14
Seventh Heaven (Hoffman), **Supp. X:** 87, 89
"Seventh of March" (Webster), **Supp. I Part 2:** 687
"7000 Romaine, Los Angeles 38" (Didion), **Supp. IV Part 1:** 200
"Seventh Street" (Toomer), **Supp. IX:** 316
Seven Types of Ambiguity (Empson), **II:** 536; **IV:** 431
77 Dream Songs (Berryman), **I:** 168, 169, 170, 171, 174, 175, 183–188
73 Poems (Cummings), **I:** 430, 431, 446, 447, 448
Seven Valleys and the Four Valleys, The (Bahá'u'lláh), **Supp. XX: 121**
"Several Short Questions About Crumbs"(Schott), **Supp. XXIII:** 249
Sevier, Jack, **IV:** 378
Sévigné, Madame de, **IV:** 361
Sewall, Richard, **Retro. Supp. I:** 25
Sewall, Samuel, **IV:** 145, 146, 147, 149, 154, 164; **Supp. I Part 1:** 100, 110
Sewell, Elizabeth, **Supp. XIII:** 344
"Sex" (Carruth), **Supp. XVI:** 58
Sex, Economy, Freedom and Community (Berry), **Supp. X:** 30, 36
"Sex Camp" (Mamet), **Supp. XIV:** 240
Sex Castle, The (Lacy), **Supp. XV:** 206
Sex & Character (Weininger), **Retro. Supp. I:** 416
"Sext" (Auden), **Supp. II Part 1:** 22
Sexton, Anne, **Retro. Supp. II:** 245; **Supp. I Part 2:** 538, 543, 546; **Supp. II Part 2: 669–700; Supp. III Part 2:** 599; **Supp. IV Part 1:** 245; **Supp. IV Part 2:** 439, 440–441, 442, 444, 447, 449, 451, 620; **Supp. V:** 113, 118, 124; **Supp. X:** 201, 202, 213; **Supp. XI:** 146, 240, 317; **Supp. XII:** 217, 253, 254, 256, 260, 261; **Supp. XIII:** 35, 76, 294, 312; **Supp. XIV:** 125, 126, 132, 269; **Supp. XIX:** 82, 203; **Supp. XV:** 123, 252, 340; **Supp. XVII:** 239; **Supp. XX: 199; Supp. XXVI:** 68; **Supp. XXVII:** 261
Sexual Behavior in the American Male (Kinsey), **Supp. XIII:** 96–97
Sexual Perversity in Chicago (Mamet), **Supp. XIV:** 239, 240, 246–247, 249
"Sexual Revolution, The" (Dunn), **Supp. XI:** 142
Sexus (H. Miller), **III:** 170, 171, 184, 187, 188
"Sex Without Love" (Olds), **Supp. X:** 206
"Sexy" (Lahiri), **Supp. XXI:** 183–184
Seyersted, Per E., **Retro. Supp. II:** 65; **Supp. I Part 1:** 201, 204, 211, 216, 225; **Supp. IV Part 2:** 558
Seyfried, Robin, **Supp. IX:** 324
Seymour, Corey, **Supp. XXIV:** 280
Seymour, Miranda, **Supp. VIII:** 167
"Seymour: An Introduction" (Salinger), **III:** 569–571, 572
Sgt. Pepper column (Christgau), **Supp. XXVII:** 42–44
"Shack" (L. Brown), **Supp. XXI:** 49
Shacochis, Bob, **Supp. VIII:** 80
"Shadow" (Creeley), **Supp. IV Part 1:** 158
"Shadow, The" (A. Lowell), **II:** 522
Shadow and Act (Ellison), **Retro. Supp. II:** 119; **Supp. II Part 1:** 245–246
"Shadow and Shade" (Tate), **IV:** 128
"Shadow and the Flesh, The" (London), **II:** 475
"Shadow A Parable" (Poe), **III:** 417–418
Shadow Country (Gunn Allen), **Supp. IV Part 1:** 322, 324, 325–326
"Shadow Kingdom, The" (Howard),

Supp. XXVII: 122–123, 127
Shadow-Line, The (Conrad), **Supp. XXV:** 217
Shadow Man, The (Gordon), **Supp. IV Part 1:** 297, 298, 299, 312–314, 315
Shadow of a Dream, The, a Story (Howells), **II:** 285, 286, 290
Shadow of a Man (Moraga), **Supp. XXIII:** 195, 197, **199–203**
Shadow of Heaven (Hayes), **Supp. XXVI:** 137–139
"Shadow of the Crime, The: A Word from the Author" (Mailer), **Retro. Supp. II:** 214
"Shadow of the Vulture, The" (Howard), **Supp. XXVII:** 120–121
Shadow on the Dial, The (Bierce), **I:** 208, 209
"Shadow out of Time, The" (Lovecraft), **Supp. XXV:** 111
Shadow over Innsmouth, The (Lovecraft), **Supp. XXV:** 111, 117–118, 120, 121
"Shadow Passing" (Merwin), **Supp. III Part 1:** 355
Shadowplay (C. Baxter), **Supp. XVII:** 15, 19–20
Shadows (Gardner), **Supp. VI:** 74
Shadows and Fog (film; Allen), **Supp. XV:** 11
Shadows Burning (Di Piero), **Supp. XIX:** 42, 43–44
Shadows by the Hudson (Singer), **IV:** 1
Shadows of Africa (Matthiessen), **Supp. V:** 203
"Shadows of Zamboula" (Howard), **Supp. XXVII:** 125–126
Shadows on the Hudson (Singer), **Retro. Supp. II: 311–313**
Shadows on the Rock (Cather), **I:** 314, 330–331, 332; **Retro. Supp. I:** 18; **Retro. Supp. III:** 24
"Shadows over Lovecraft: Reactionary Fantasy and Immigrant Eugenics" (Lovett-Graff), **Supp. XXV:** 123
Shadow Train (Ashbery), **Supp. III Part 1:** 23–24, 26
"Shad-Time" (Wilbur), **Supp. III Part 2:** 563
Shaffer, Thomas L., **Supp. VIII:** 127, 128
Shaft (Parks; film), **Supp. XI:** 17
Shaftesbury, Earl of, **I:** 559
Shahid, Irfan, **Supp. XX: 113, 127**
Shahn, Ben, **Supp. X:** 24
Shakedown for Murder (Lacy), **Supp. XV:** 203
Shakelford, Dean, **Supp. VIII:** 129
Shaker, Why Don't You Sing? (Angelou), **Supp. IV Part 1:** 16
Shakespear, Mrs. Olivia, **III:** 457; **Supp. I Part 1:** 257
"Shakespeare" (Emerson), **II:** 6
"Shakespeare" (Very), **Supp. XXV:** 244
Shakespeare, William, **I:** 103, 271, 272, 284–285, 358, 378, 433, 441, 458, 461, 573, 585, 586; **II:** 5, 8, 11, 18, 72, 273, 297, 302, 309, 320, 411, 494, 577, 590; **III:** 3, 11, 12, 82, 83, 91, 124, 130, 134, 145, 153, 159, 183, 210, 263, 286, 468, 473, 492, 503, 511, 567, 575–576, 577, 610, 612, 613, 615; **IV:** 11, 50, 66, 127, 132, 156, 309, 313, 362, 368, 370, 373, 453; **Retro. Supp. I:** 43, 64, 91, 248; **Retro. Supp. II:** 114, 299; **Retro. Supp. III:** 156; **Supp. I Part 1:** 79, 150, 262, 310, 356, 363, 365, 368, 369, 370; **Supp. I Part 2:** 397, 421, 422, 470, 494, 622, 716, 720; **Supp. II Part 2:** 624, 626; **Supp. IV Part 1:** 31, 83, 87, 243; **Supp. IV Part 2:** 430, 463, 519, 688; **Supp. IX:** 14, 133; **Supp. V:** 252, 280, 303; **Supp. VIII:** 160, 164; **Supp. X:** 42, 62, 65, 78; **Supp. XII:** 54–57, 277, 281; **Supp. XIII:** 111, 115, 233; **Supp. XIV:** 97, 120, 225, 245, 306; **Supp. XV:** 92; **Supp. XVIII:** 278; **Supp. XXII:** 206; **Supp. XXIV:** 33, 34, 40, 87, 159
Shakespeare and His Forerunners (Lanier), **Supp. I Part 1:** 369
Shakespeare in Harlem (Hughes), **Retro. Supp. I:** 194, 202, 205, 206, 207, 208; **Supp. I Part 1:** 333, 334, 345
Shalit, Gene, **Supp. VIII:** 73
Shalit, Wendy, **Supp. XX: 179, 182, 186**
Shall We Gather at the River (Wright), **Supp. III Part 2:** 601–602; **Supp. XVII:** 241
"Shame" (Oates), **Supp. II Part 2:** 520
"Shame" (Wilbur), **Supp. III Part 2:** 556
"Shame and Forgetting in the Information Age" (C. Baxter), **Supp. XVII:** 21
"Shameful Affair, A" (Chopin), **Retro. Supp. II:** 61
Shamela (Fielding), **Supp. V:** 127
"Shampoo, The" (Bishop), **Retro. Supp. II:** 46; **Supp. I Part 1:** 92
Shange, Ntozake, **Supp. VIII:** 214; **Supp. XVII:** 70; **Supp. XVIII:** 172; **Supp. XXI:** 172
Shank, Randy, **Supp. X:** 252
Shankaracharya, **III:** 567
Shanley, John Patrick, **Retro. Supp. III:** 318; **Supp. XIV: 315–332**
Shannon, Sandra, **Supp. VIII:** 333, 348
"Shape of Flesh and Bone, The" (MacLeish), **III:** 18–19
Shape of Me and Other Stuff, The (Geisel), **Supp. XVI:** 111
Shape of the Journey, The (Harrison), **Supp. VIII:** 53
Shapes of Clay (Bierce), **I:** 208, 209
Shaping Joy, A: Studies in the Writer's Craft (Brooks), **Supp. XIV:** 13
Shapiro, Alan, **Supp. XXIV:** 157
Shapiro, Charles, **Supp. XIX:** 257, 259–260
Shapiro, David, **Supp. XII:** 175, 185; **Supp. XXIV:** 34
Shapiro, Dorothy, **IV:** 380
Shapiro, Edward S., **Supp. XXV:** 253
Shapiro, Karl, **I:** 430, 521; **II:** 350; **III:** 527; **Supp. II Part 2: 701–724; Supp. III Part 2:** 623; **Supp. IV Part 2:** 645; **Supp. X:** 116; **Supp. XI:** 315; **Supp. XIX:** 117, 118, 119; **Supp. XXI:** 98; **Supp. XXV:** 30
Shapiro, Laura, **Supp. IX:** 120; **Supp. XX: 87, 89**
Share, Don, **Supp. XXVII:** 152
"Sharecropping in the Golden Ladn" (Kawin), **Retro. Supp. III:** 75
"Shared Patio, The" (July), **Supp. XXIV:** 201, 202
Sharif, Omar, **Supp. IX:** 253
"Sharing" (Huddle), **Supp. XXVI:** 153
"Shark Meat" (Snyder), **Supp. VIII:** 300
Shatayev, Elvira, **Supp. I Part 2:** 570
Shaviro, Steven, **Supp. VIII:** 189
Shaw, Bernard, **Retro. Supp. III:** 165
Shaw, Chris, **Supp. XXIII:** 155–156
Shaw, Colonel Robert Gould, **II:** 551
Shaw, Elizabeth. See Melville, Mrs. Herman (Elizabeth Shaw)
Shaw, George Bernard, **I:** 226; **II:** 82, 271, 276, 581; **III:** 69, 102, 113, 145, 155, 161, 162, 163, 373, 409; **IV:** 27, 64, 397, 432, 440; **Retro. Supp. I:** 100, 228; **Supp. IV Part 1:** 36; **Supp. IV Part 2:** 585, 683; **Supp. IX:** 68, 308; **Supp. V:** 243–244, 290; **Supp. XI:** 202; **Supp. XII:** 94; **Supp. XIV:** 343; **Supp. XVII:** 100; **Supp. XXIV:** 33, 34
Shaw, Irwin, **IV:** 381; **Supp. IV Part 1:** 383; **Supp. IX:** 251; **Supp. XI:** 221, 229, 231; **Supp. XIX: 239–254**
Shaw, Joseph Thompson ("Cap"), **Supp. IV Part 1:** 121, 345, 351;

Supp. XIII: 161
Shaw, Judge Lemuel, **III:** 77, 88, 91
Shaw, Lytle, **Supp. XXIII:** 208; **Supp. XXIV:** 44
Shaw, Peter, **Supp. XVI:** 70
Shaw, Robert B., **Supp. XXIII:** 112
Shaw, Sarah Bryant, **Supp. I Part 1:** 169
Shaw, Wilbur, Jr., **Supp. XIII:** 162
Shawl, The (Mamet), **Supp. XIV:** 245
Shawl, The (Ozick), **Supp. V:** 257, 260, 271
"Shawl, The" (Ozick), **Supp. V:** 271–272
Shawl and Prarie du Chien, The: Two Plays (Mamet), **Supp. XIV:** 243–244
Shawn, William, **Supp. VIII:** 151, 170
"Shawshank Redemption, The" (King), **Supp. V:** 148
She (Haggard), **III:** 189
Shea, Renee, **Supp. XXIII:** 85, 86, 90, 95
Sheaffer, Louis, **Supp. XXI:** 6
Shearer, Flora, **I:** 199
"Sheaves, The" (Robinson), **III:** 510, 524
"She Came and Went" (J. R. Lowell), **Supp. I Part 2:** 409
"She Devil" (Howard), **Supp. XXVII:** 121
"She-Devil" (Nelson), **Supp. XVIII:** 178
She-Devil Circus (Nelson), **Supp. XVIII:** 176, **178**
Sheed, Wilfrid, **IV:** 230; **Supp. XI:** 233; **Supp. XXI:** 233
Sheeler, Charles, **IV:** 409; **Retro. Supp. I:** 430
"Sheep Child" (B. Kelly), **Supp. XVII:** 131–132
"Sheep Child, The" (Dickey), **Supp. XVII:** 131–132
Sheeper (Rosenthal), **Supp. XIV:** 147
"Shee-Show" (Rash), **Supp. XXVII:** 220
Sheffer, Jonathan, **Supp. IV Part 1:** 95
She Had Some Horses (Harjo), **Supp. XII: 220–223,** 231
"She Had Some Horses" (Harjo), **Supp. XII:** 215, 222
"Shell, The" (Humphrey), **Supp. IX:** 94
Shelley, Mary, **Supp. XX: 108**
Shelley, Percy Bysshe, **I:** 18, 68, 381, 476, 522, 577; **II:** 331, 516, 535, 540; **III:** 412, 426, 469; **IV:** 139; **Retro. Supp. I:** 308, 360; **Retro. Supp. III:** 44; **Supp. I Part 1:** 79, 311, 349; **Supp. I Part 2:** 709, 718, 719, 720, 721, 722, 724, 728; **Supp. IV Part 1:** 235; **Supp. IX:** 51; **Supp. V:** 258, 280; **Supp. XII:** 117, 132, 136–137, 263; **Supp. XIV:** 271–272; **Supp. XV:** 92, 175, 182; **Supp. XX: 115; Supp. XXI:** 131
Shellow, Sadie Myers, **Supp. I Part 2:** 608
Shelnut, Blevin, **Supp. XXV:** 36
"Shelter" (C. Baxter), **Supp. XVII:** 19
"Shelter" (Doty), **Supp. XI:** 132
Sheltered Life, The (Glasgow), **II:** 174, 175, 179, 186, 187–188
Sheltering Sky, The (Bowles), **Supp. IV Part 1:** 82, 84, 85–86, 87
Sheltering Sky, The (film), **Supp. IV Part 1:** 94, 95
Shelton, Frank, **Supp. IV Part 2:** 658
Shelton, Richard, **Supp. XI:** 133; **Supp. XIII:** 7
Shelton, Robert, **Supp. XVIII:** 20, 21, 22, 23, 24, 25, 26
Shelton, Mrs. Sarah. See Royster, Sarah Elmira
"Shelton Laurel" (Rash), **Supp. XXVII:** 221
Shenandoah (Schwartz), **Supp. II Part 2:** 640, 651–652
"Shenandoah" (Shapiro), **Supp. II Part 2:** 704
Shepard, Alice, **IV:** 287
Shepard, Gregory, **Supp. XXII:** 119
Shepard, Harvey, **Supp. XVII:** 240
Shepard, Jim, **Supp. XXI:** 115
Shepard, Odell, **II:** 508; **Supp. I Part 2:** 418
Shepard, Richard F., **Supp. XXIV:** 216
Shepard, Sam, **Supp. III Part 2: 431–450; Supp. XVIII:** 21, 28, 31; **Supp. XXI:** 144, 145
Shepard, Thomas, **I:** 554; **IV:** 158
"Shepherd of Resumed Desire, The" (Wright), **Supp. XV:** 349
Sheppard Lee (Bird), **III:** 423
"She Remembers the Future" (Harjo), **Supp. XII:** 222
Sheridan, Richard Brinsley, **Retro. Supp. I:** 127
Sherlock, William, **IV:** 152
Sherman, Joe, **Supp. XXII:** 205
Sherman, Sarah Way, **Retro. Supp. II:** 145
Sherman, Stuart Pratt, **I:** 222, 246–247; **Supp. I Part 2:** 423
Sherman, Susan, **Supp. VIII:** 265
Sherman, Tom, **IV:** 446
Sherman, William T., **IV:** 445, 446
"She Rock" (Hurston), **Retro. Supp. III:** 127
Sherry, Denver William, **Supp. XXII:** 190
Sherwood, Robert, **II:** 435; **Supp. IX:** 190
Sherwood Anderson & Other Famous Creoles (Faulkner), **I:** 117; **II:** 56
Sherwood Anderson Reader, The (Anderson), **I:** 114, 116
Sherwood Anderson's Memoirs (Anderson), **I:** 98, 101, 102, 103, 108, 112, 116
Sherwood Anderson's Notebook (Anderson), **I:** 108, 115, 117
She's Having a Baby (film, Hughes), **Supp. XXVII:** 5
"She Sings" (Taggard), **Supp. XXII:** 272
She Stoops to Conquer (Goldsmith), **II:** 514
Shestov, Lev, **Supp. VIII:** 20, 24
Shetley, Vernon, **Supp. IX:** 292; **Supp. XI:** 123
"She Wept, She Railed" (Kunitz), **Supp. III Part 1:** 265
"Shiddah and Kuziba" (Singer), **IV:** 13, 15
Shidyak, Paris al-, **Supp. XX: 117**
Shield of Achilles, The (Auden), **Supp. II Part 1:** 21
"Shield of Achilles, The" (Auden), **Supp. II Part 1:** 21, 25
Shields, Carol, **Supp. VII: 307–330**
Shields, John C., **Supp. XX: 279, 280, 281, 286**
Shifting Landscape: A Composite, 1925–1987 (H. Roth), **Supp. IX: 233–235**
Shifts of Being (Eberhart), **I:** 525
Shigematsu, Soiko, **Supp. III Part 1:** 353
Shihab, Aziz, **Supp. XIII:** 273
Shih-hsiang Chen, **Supp. VIII:** 303
Shiksa Goddess; or, How I Spent My Forties (Wasserstein), **Supp. XV:** 319, 320, 325, 332, 333
Shilling, Jane, **Supp. XXVII:** 276
"Shiloh" (Mason), **Supp. VIII:** 140
Shiloh and Other Stories (Mason), **Supp. VIII:** 133, **139–141,** 143, 145
Shilts, Randy, **Supp. X:** 145
Shimmering Verge, The (one-woman show, Peacock), **Supp. XIX:** 194, **204–205**
Shining, The (King), **Supp. V:** 139, 140, 141, 143–144, 146, 149, 151, 152
"Shining Ones, The" (P. N. Warren), **Supp. XX: 272**
Shining Victory (film, Rapper), **Supp. XVII:** 60

Shinn, Everett, **Retro. Supp. II:** 103
Shi Pei Pu, **Supp. XXI:** 152, 153, 154
"Ship in a Bottle"(Strout), **Supp. XXIII:** 283
"Ship of Death" (Lawrence), **Supp. I Part 2:** 728
Ship of Fools (Porter), **III:** 433, 447, 453, 454; **IV:** 138
Shipping News, The (Proulx), **Supp. VII:** 249, 258–259
"Ships" (O. Henry), **Supp. II Part 1:** 409
Ships Going into the Blue: Essays and Notes on Poetry (Simpson), **Supp. IX:** 275
Ship to America, A (Singer), **IV:** 1
"Shipwreck, The" (Merwin), **Supp. III Part 1:** 346
Shirley, John, **Supp. XVI:** 123, 128
"Shirt" (Pinsky), **Supp. VI: 236–237,** 239, 240, 241, 245, 247
"Shirt Poem, The" (Stern), **Supp. IX:** 292
"Shirts, The" (Gallagher), **Supp. XXIV:** 169
"Shirts of a Single Color" (Ryan), **Supp. XVIII:** 227
"Shiva and Parvati Hiding in the Rain" (Pinsky), **Supp. VI:** 244
Shively, Charley, **Retro. Supp. I:** 391; **Supp. XII:** 181, 182
Shnayerson, Michael, **Supp. XIX:** 248
Shneidman, Edwin, **Supp. XXVI:** 246
"Shock of Good Poetry, The"(Hirshfield), **Supp. XXIII:** 136
Shock of Recognition, The (Wilson), **II:** 530
Shock of the New, The (Hughes), **Supp. X:** 73
Shoe Bird, The (Welty), **IV:** 261; **Retro. Supp. I:** 353
Shoemaker of Dreams (Ferragammo), **Supp. XVI:** 192
"Shoes" (O. Henry), **Supp. II Part 1:** 409
"Shoes of Wandering, The" (Kinnell), **Supp. III Part 1:** 248
Sholem Asch: Zayn levn un zayne verk (Sholem Asch: His life and his work), **Supp. XXIII:** 6
Sholl, Betsy, **Supp. XXI:** 129, 131
Shooter (Myers), **Supp. XXVII:** 203, 204
"Shooters, Inc." (Didion), **Supp. IV Part 1:** 207, 211
"Shooting, The" (Dubus), **Supp. VII:** 84, 85
"Shooting Niagara; and After?" (Carlyle), **Retro. Supp. I:** 408
"Shooting of the Red Eagle" (Zitkala-Ša), **Supp. XXV:** 275
"Shooting Script" (Rich), **Retro. Supp. III:** 245; **Supp. I Part 2:** 558; **Supp. IV Part 1:** 257
Shooting Star, A (Stegner), **Supp. IV Part 2:** 599, 608–609
"Shooting the Works" (Di Piero), **Supp. XIX:** 41–42
Shooting the Works: On Poetry and Pictures (Di Piero), **Supp. XIX: 41–42**
"Shooting Whales" (Strand), **Supp. IV Part 2:** 630
"Shopgirls" (F. Barthelme), **Supp. XI:** 26, 27, 33, 36
Shopping for Joe (O'Hara and Steven Rivers), **Supp. XXIII:** 217
"Shopping with Bob Berwick" (Halliday), **Supp. XIX:** 88
Shop Talk (P. Roth), **Retro. Supp. II:** 282
Shoptaw, John, **Supp. IV Part 1:** 247
Shore Acres (Herne), **Supp. II Part 1:** 198
Shorebirds of North America, The (Matthiessen), **Supp. V:** 204
"Shore House, The" (Jewett), **II:** 397
Shore Leave (Wakeman), **Supp. IX:** 247
"Shoreline Horses" (Ríos), **Supp. IV Part 2:** 553
"Shoreline Life" (Skloot), **Supp. XX: 201**
Shores of Light, The: A Literary Chronicle of the Twenties and Thirties (Wilson), **IV:** 432, 433
Shorey, Paul, **III:** 606
Short Account of the Destruction of the Indies, A (Las Casas), **Supp. XXIV:** 87
Short and the Long of It, The (Kenny), **Supp. XXIII:** 155–156
Short Cuts (film, Altman), **Supp. IX:** 143; **Supp. XXIV:** 166, 172, 178
"Short End, The" (Hecht), **Supp. X:** 65
"Shorter View, The" (X. J. Kennedy), **Supp. XV:** 160, 168
Short Fiction of Norman Mailer, The (Mailer), **Retro. Supp. II:** 205
"Short Flight, The" (Huddle), **Supp. XXVI:** 156
Short Friday and Other Stories (Singer), **IV:** 14–16
Short Girls (Nguyen), **Supp. XXVI:** 212–216
Short Guide to a Happy Life, A (Quindlen), **Supp. XVII:** 167, 179
"Short Happy Life of Francis Macomber, The" (Hemingway), **II:** 250, 263–264; **Retro. Supp. I:** 182; **Supp. IV Part 1:** 48; **Supp. IX:** 106
Short Night, The (Turner), **Supp. XV:** 201
Short Novels of Thomas Wolfe, The (Wolfe), **IV:** 456
Short Poems (Berryman), **I:** 170
"SHORT SPEECH TO MY FRIENDS" (Baraka), **Supp. II Part 1:** 35
Short Stories (Rawlings), **Supp. X:** 224
Short Stories: Five Decades (Shaw), **Supp. XIX:** 252–253
"Short Story, The" (Welty), **IV:** 279
Short Story Masterpieces, **Supp. IX:** 4
Short Studies of American Authors (Higginson), **I:** 455
"Short-timer's Calendar" (Komunyakaa), **Supp. XIII:** 125
"Short Weight" (Davison), **Supp. XXVI:** 75
Shosha (Singer), **Retro. Supp. II: 313–314**
Shostak, Debra, **Supp. XXIV:** 136
Shostakovich, Dimitri, **IV:** 75; **Supp. VIII:** 21
"Shotgun Wedding" (Stone), **Supp. XXVII:** 253
Shot of Love (album, Dylan), **Supp. XVIII:** 28
"Shots" (Ozick), **Supp. V:** 268
Shotts, Jeffrey, **Supp. XV:** 103, 104
"Should Wizard Hit Mommy?" (Updike), **IV:** 221, 222, 224; **Retro. Supp. I:** 335
Shoup, Barbara, **Supp. XV:** 55, 59, 62, 69
"Shoveling Snow with Buddha" (Collins), **Supp. XXI:** 60
"Shovel Man, The" (Sandburg), **III:** 553
Showalter, Elaine, **Retro. Supp. I:** 368; **Supp. IV Part 2:** 440, 441, 444; **Supp. X:** 97; **Supp. XVI:** 80, 92; **Supp. XX: 274; Supp. XXIV:** 28
"Shower of Gold" (Welty), **IV:** 271–272
Show World (Barnhardt), **Supp. XXVII:** 1, 7–9
Shreve, Porter, **Supp. XXVI:** 209
Shribman, David M., **Supp. XXII:** 205, 218
"Shrike and the Chipmunks, The" (Thurber), **Supp. I Part 2:** 617
Shrimp Girl (Hogarth), **Supp. XII:** 44
"Shrine and the Burning Wheel, The" (Jarman), **Supp. XVII:** 116
"Shrine with Flowers" (Di Piero), **Supp. XIX:** 43, 44
"Shriveled Meditation" (X. J.

Kennedy), **Supp. XV:** 170
Shropshire Lad, A (Housman), **Supp. XV:** 41
"Shrouded Stranger, The" (Ginsberg), **Supp. II Part 1:** 312
"Shroud of Color, The" (Cullen), **Supp. IV Part 1:** 166, 168, 170, 171
Shrunken Head of Pancho Villa, The (Valdez), **Supp. XXIII:** 203
Shtetl (film; Marzynski), **Supp. XVI:** 153
Shtetl: The Life and Death of a Small Town and the World of Polish Jews (E. Hoffman), **Supp. XVI:** 152, **153–155**
Shue, Elizabeth, **Supp. XXIII:** 276
Shuffle (L. Michaels), **Supp. XVI:** 202, 203, 213
Shuffle Along (musical), **Supp. I Part 1:** 322; **Supp. X:** 136
Shulman, Polly, **Supp. XXVI:** 158
Shultz, George, **Supp. IV Part 1:** 234
Shuman, R. Baird, **Supp. XXV:** 96
Shurr, William, **Retro. Supp. I:** 43
Shuster, Joel, **Supp. XI:** 67
Shusterman, Richard, **Retro. Supp. I:** 53
"Shut a Final Door" (Capote), **Supp. III Part 1:** 117, 120, 124
Shut Up, He Explained (Lardner), **II:** 432
Shylock's Daughter: A Novel of Love in Venice (Serenissima) (Jong), **Supp. V:** 115, 127, 128–129
Siamanto (Atom Yarjanian), **Supp. XXIII:** 28
"Siasconset: How It Arose and What It Is" (Briggs), **Supp. XVIII:** 9
Siberian Village, The (Dove), **Supp. IV Part 1:** 255, 256
Sibley, Celestine, **Supp. XXII:** 194, 199
Sibley, Mulford Q., **Supp. I Part 2:** 524
"Sibling Mysteries" (Rich), **Supp. I Part 2:** 574
Siblings (Quindlen and Kelsh), **Supp. XVII:** 167, 179
Siblings in Paradise (or Moscow when It Sizzles) (Silver), **Supp. XXIV:** 265
Sibon, Marcelle, **IV:** 288
"Sicilian Emigrant's Song" (W. C. Williams), **Retro. Supp. I:** 413
Sicilian Miniatures (Sobin), **Supp. XVI:** 288
"Sick Wife, The" (Kenyon), **Supp. VII:** 173, 174
"'Sic transit gloria mundi' " (Dickinson), **Retro. Supp. I:** 30
Sid Caesar Show (television show), **Supp. IV Part 2:** 575
Siddons, Anne Rivers, **Supp. XXII: 239–254**
Siddons, Sarah, **II:** 298
Side Effects (Allen), **Supp. XV:** 3, 14, **15–16**
"Side Effects of Lucille, The" (Huddle), **Supp. XXVI:** 155–156
Side of Paradise, This (Fitgerald), **Supp. IX:** 56
"Sidewalk, The" (Biss), **Supp. XXVI:** 48
Sidnee Poet Heroical, The (Baraka), **Supp. II Part 1:** 55
Sidney, Algernon, **II:** 114
Sidney, Mary, **Supp. I Part 1:** 98
Sidney, Philip, **II:** 470; **Retro. Supp. III:** 3, 7; **Supp. I Part 1:** 98, 111, 117–118, 122; **Supp. I Part 2:** 658; **Supp. II Part 1:** 104–105; **Supp. V:** 250; **Supp. XII:** 264; **Supp. XIV:** 128
Sidney, Sylvia, **Supp. I Part 1:** 67
Sidney Lanier: A Bibliographical and Critical Study (Starke), **Supp. I Part 1:** 371
Sidney Lanier: A Biographical and Critical Study (Starke), **Supp. I Part 1:** 371
Siebert, Kathy, **Supp. XX: 84**
Siege (Shaw), **Supp. XIX:** 244
Siegel, Barry, **Supp. XIV:** 82
Siegel, Ben, **Supp. XXIII:** 3, 4, 10, 11, 12, 14, 16
Siegel, Catherine, **Supp. XII:** 126
Siegel, Jerry, **Supp. XI:** 67
Siegel, Lee, **Supp. XXII: 255–269; Supp. XXV:** 56
"Siege of London, The" (James), **Retro. Supp. I:** 227
Siegle, Robert, **Supp. XII:** 8
Sienkiewicz, Henryk, **Supp. IV Part 2:** 518; **Supp. XVI:** 182
"Sierra Kid" (Levine), **Supp. V:** 180–181
Sigal, Clancy, **Supp. XXI:** 44; **Supp. XXIII:** 166; **Supp. XXVI:** 26
Sigg, Eric, **Retro. Supp. I:** 53
"Sight" (Merwin), **Supp. III Part 1:** 356
Sighted Singer, The (Halliday), **Supp. XIX:** 82, **86–87**
"Sight in Camp in the Daybreak Gray and Dim, A" (Whitman), **II:** 373
Sights and Spectacles (McCarthy), **II:** 562
"Sights from a Steeple" (Hawthorne), **Retro. Supp. I:** 62; **Retro. Supp. III:** 113, 120; **Supp. XXI:** 201
Sights Unseen (Gibbons), **Supp. X: 49–50**
Sight Unseen and the Confession (Rinehart), **Supp. XXV:** 195, 200
"Signals" (Carver), **Supp. III Part 1:** 143
"Signature for Tempo" (MacLeish), **III:** 8–9
"Signed Confession of Crimes against the State" (Merton), **Supp. VIII:** 201
Signifying Monkey, The (Hughes), **Retro. Supp. I:** 195
Signifying Monkey, The: A Theory of Afro-American Literary Criticism (H. L. Gates), **Supp. X:** 243; **Supp. XX: 99, 106–107**
"Signing, The (Dixon), **Supp. XII: 146**
Sign in Sidney Brustein's Window, The (Hansberry), **Supp. IV Part 1:** 359, 365, 369, 370–372
"Sign in the Sky, A: Dating the League of the Haudenosaunee" (Mann and Fields), **Supp. XXVI:** 86
Sign of Jonas, The (Merton), **Supp. VIII:** 194–195, 195, 197, 200, 206, 207
"Sign of Saturn, The" (Olds), **Supp. X:** 206
"Signs" (Rash), **Supp. XXVII:** 219
"Signs, Oakvale, Mississippi, 1941" (Trethewey), **Supp. XXI:** 248–249
Signs and Wonders (Bukiet), **Supp. XVII: 45–46**
Sigourney, Lydia, **Supp. I Part 2:** 684
Sikora, Malgorzata, **Retro. Supp. II:** 324
Silas Marner (G. Eliot), **II:** 26
Silberg, Richard, **Supp. XV:** 116
Silberman, James, **Supp. XXIV:** 288
"Silence" (Moore), **III:** 212
"Silence" (Munro), **Supp. XXVII:** 193–194
"Silence" (Poe), **III:** 416
"Silence" (Sanders), **Supp. XVI:** 278
"Silence, A" (Clampitt), **Supp. IX:** 53
"Silence—A Fable" (Poe), **III:** 416
Silence and Metaphor (Bronk), **Supp. XXI:** 31, 32
"Silence Before Harvest, The" (Merwin), **Supp. III Part 1:** 352
Silence Dogood Papers, The (Franklin), **II:** 106–107
Silence in the Snowy Fields (R. Bly), **Supp. IV Part 1:** 60–61, 62, 63, 65, 66, 72; **Supp. XXI:** 84, 85
Silence of History, The (Farrell), **II:** 46–47
Silence of the Lambs, The (T. Harris), **Supp. XXI:** 78

Silence Opens, A (Clampitt), **Supp. IX: 53**
Silences (Olsen), **Supp. XIII:** 293, 294, 295, 296, **304–306**
"Silences: When Writers Don't Write" (Olsen), **Supp. XIII:** 294
Silencing the Past: Power and the Production of History (Trouillot), **Supp. X:** 14
"Silent in America" (Levine), **Supp. V:** 183
Silent Life, The (Merton), **Supp. VIII:** 208
Silent Partner, The (Odets), **Supp. II Part 2:** 539
"Silent Piano, The" (Davison), **Supp. XXVI:** 78
"Silent Poem" (Francis), **Supp. IX:** 86
"Silent Season of a Hero, The" (Talese), **Supp. XVII:** 203–204
"Silent Slain, The" (MacLeish), **III:** 9
"Silent Snow, Secret Snow" (Aiken), **I:** 52
Silent Spring (Carson), **Supp. IX:** 19, 24, **31–34; Supp. V:** 202; **Supp. XIV:** 177; **Supp. XVI:** 36; **Supp. XVIII:** 189
Silhouettes of American Life (R. H. Davis), **Supp. XVI:** 85
"Silken Tent, The" (Frost), **Retro. Supp. I:** 138–139; **Retro. Supp. III:** 104; **Supp. IV Part 2:** 448
Silko, Leslie Marmon, **Supp. IV Part 1:** 274, 319, 325, 333–334, 335, 404; **Supp. IV Part 2:** 499, 505, **557–572; Supp. V:** 169; **Supp. XI:** 18; **Supp. XII:** 217; **Supp. XVIII:** 58; **Supp. XXVI:** 102
Silliman, Ron, **Supp. IV Part 2:** 426; **Supp. XV:** 344; **Supp. XVII:** 70, 77
Silliman's Blog (R. Silliman), **Supp. XVII:** 70
Silman, Roberta, **Supp. X:** 6
Silver, Nicky, **Supp. XXIV:** 128, **263–277**
Silver, Sam, **Supp. XXVII:** 36
Silverblatt, Michael, **Supp. XV:** 224
"Silver Crown, The" (Malamud), **Supp. I Part 2:** 434–435, 437; **Supp. V:** 266
"Silver Dish, The" (Bellow), **Retro. Supp. II:** 30
"Silver Filigree" (Wylie), **Supp. I Part 2:** 707
"Silver Key, The" (Lovecraft), **Supp. XXV:** 114
"Silver Lake" (B. Kelly), **Supp. XVII:** 130
Silverman, Joseph, **Supp. XXIII:** 8
Silvers, Phil, **Supp. IV Part 2:** 574
Silverthorne, Elizabeth, **Supp. X:** 220, 221, 222, 226, 234
"Silver To Have and to Hurl" (Didion), **Supp. IV Part 1:** 197
Simic, Charles, **Supp. V:** 5, 332; **Supp. VIII:** 39, **269–287; Supp. XI:** 317; **Supp. XIX:** 277, 282; **Supp. XV:** 179, 185
"Similar Cases" (Gilman), **Supp. XI:** 200, 202
Similitudes, from the Ocean and Prairie (Larcom), **Supp. XIII:** 141
Simmel, Georg, **Supp. I Part 2:** 644; **Supp. XVII:** 98
Simmons, Charles, **Supp. XI:** 230
Simmons, David, **Supp. XXV:** 123
Simmons, Maggie, **Retro. Supp. II:** 21
Simms, Michael, **Supp. XII:** 184
Simms, William Gilmore, **I:** 211
Simon, Greg, **Supp. XXIV:** 166
Simon, John, **Supp. IV Part 2:** 691
Simon, Neil, **Supp. IV Part 2: 573–594; Supp. XVII:** 8
Simone, Nina, **Supp. XXI:** 243
"Simone Weil's Passion Mysticism: The Paradox of Chronic Pain and the Transformation of the Cross" (Helsel), **Supp. XXVI:** 53
"Simon Gerty" (Wylie), **Supp. I Part 2:** 713
Simonides, **Supp. XII:** 110–111
"Simon Ortiz" (Gingerich), **Supp. IV Part 2:** 510
Simon Ortiz (Wiget), **Supp. IV Part 2:** 509
Simonson, Lee, **III:** 396; **Supp. XXI:** 6
"Simple" (Peacock), **Supp. XIX:** 200
"Simple Art of Murder, The" (Chandler), **Supp. IV Part 1:** 121, 341
"Simple Autumnal" (Bogan), **Supp. III Part 1:** 52–53
Simple Heart (Flaubert), **I:** 504
Simple Honorable Man, A (Richter), **Supp. XVIII:** 208, 218, **219,** 220
"Simple Purchase, A" (Peacock), **Supp. XIX:** 199
Simple Speaks his Mind (Hughes), **Retro. Supp. I:** 209; **Supp. I Part 1:** 337
Simple Stakes a Claim (Hughes), **Retro. Supp. I:** 209; **Supp. I Part 1:** 337
Simple's Uncle Sam (Hughes), **Retro. Supp. I:** 209; **Supp. I Part 1:** 337
Simple Takes a Wife (Hughes), **Retro. Supp. I:** 209; **Supp. I Part 1:** 337
Simple Truth, The (Hardwick), **Supp. III Part 1:** 199, 200, 208
Simple Truth, The (Levine), **Supp. V:** 178, 179, 193–194
"Simple Widsom, The" (Skloot), **Supp. XX: 207**
"Simplicity" (Sanders), **Supp. XVI:** 276
Simplicity (Stone), **Supp. XXVII:** 257, 262
Simply, Trixi, **Supp. XXV:** 2
Simply Heavenly (Hughes), **Retro. Supp. I:** 209; **Supp. I Part 1:** 338, 339
Simpson, Louis, **Supp. III Part 2:** 541; **Supp. IV Part 2:** 448, 621; **Supp. IX: 265–283,** 290; **Supp. VIII:** 39, 279; **Supp. XI:** 317; **Supp. XII:** 130; **Supp. XIII:** 337
Simpson, Mona, **Supp. XVI:** 206; **Supp. XXVII:** 180, **233–237**
"Sin" (C. Frost), **Supp. XV:** 96
Sinatra, Frank, **Supp. IX:** 3; **Supp. X:** 119; **Supp. XI:** 213
"Since Death Brushed Past Me" (Teasdale), **Supp. XXVII:** 297
Sincere Convert, The (Shepard), **IV:** 158
Sincerely, Willis Wayde (Marquand), **III:** 61, 63, 66, 67–68, 69
Sincerity (Rowson), **Supp. XV:** 242
Sincerity and Authenticity (Trilling), **Supp. III Part 2:** 510–512
"Sincerity and Objectification: With Special Reference to the Work of Charles Reznikoff" (Zukofsky), **Supp. XIV:** 286
Sinclair, Mary Craig (Mary Craig Kimbrough), **Supp. V:** 275, 286, 287
Sinclair, Upton, **II:** 34, 440, 444, 451; **III:** 580; **Retro. Supp. II:** 95; **Supp. V: 275–293; Supp. VIII:** 11
Sinclair Lewis: An American Life (Schorer), **II:** 459
"Sine Qua Non" (Stallings), **Supp. XXV:** 232
"Singapore" (Oliver), **Supp. VII:** 239, 240
Singer, Bennett L., **Supp. IV Part 1:** 330
Singer, Beth, **Supp. XIV:** 203
Singer, Isaac Bashevis, **I:** 144; **IV: 1–24; Retro. Supp. II:** 22, **299–320; Supp. IX:** 114; **Supp. XVIII:** 215, 220; **Supp. XXI:** 106; **Supp. XXII:** 258
Singer, Israel Joshua, **IV:** 2, 16, 17; **Retro. Supp. II:** 302; **Supp. XVII:** 41

Singer, Joshua, **IV:** 4
Singer, Rabbi Pinchos Menachem, **IV:** 16
Singin' and Swingin' and Gettin' Merry Like Christmas (Angelou), **Supp. IV Part 1:** 2, 5, 6–7, 9, 13, 14
"Singing & Doubling Together" (Ammons), **Supp. VII:** 34–35
Singing Jailbirds (Sinclair), **Supp. V:** 277
"Singing the Black Mother" (Lupton), **Supp. IV Part 1:** 7
Single Hound, The (Sarton), **Supp. VIII:** 251, 265
Single Hound, The: Poems of a Lifetime (Dickinson; Bianchi, ed.), **Retro. Supp. I:** 35
Single Man, A (Isherwood), **Supp. XIV:** 157, 164, **169–170,** 171
"Single Sonnet" (Bogan), **Supp. III Part 1:** 56–58
Singley, Carol, **Retro. Supp. I:** 373
Singular Family, A: Rosacoke and Her Kin (Price), **Supp. VI: 258–259,** 260
"Singular First Person, The" (Sanders), **Supp. XVI:** 274
Singularities (Howe), **Supp. IV Part 2:** 431
Sin in Their Blood (Lacy), **Supp. XV:** 200
"Sinister Adolescents, The" (Dos Passos), **I:** 493
Sinister Street (Mackenzie), **II:** 82
Sinking of Clay City, The (Wrigley), **Supp. XVIII: 294–295**
Sinners in the Hands of an Angry God (Edwards), **I:** 546, 552–553, 559, 562; **Supp. XXIV:** 72
Sinning with Annie, and Other Stories (Theroux), **Supp. VIII:** 318
"Sins of Kalamazoo, The" (Sandburg), **III:** 586
Sintram and His Companions (La Motte-Fouqué), **III:** 78
"Siope" (Poe), **III:** 411
"Sioux Woman's Love for Her Grandchild, A" (Zitkala-Ša), **Supp. XXV:** 281
"Sipapu: A Cultural Perspective" (Gunn Allen), **Supp. IV Part 1:** 323
Sipchen, Bob, **Supp. X:** 145
Sipper, Ralph B., **Supp. IV Part 2:** 475
"Sire" (Cisneros), **Supp. VII:** 62–63, 64
"Siren and Signal" (Zukofsky), **Supp. III Part 2:** 611, 612
Sirens of Titan, The (Vonnegut), **Supp. II Part 2:** 757, 758, 760, 765–767
"Sir Galahad" (Tennyson), **Supp. I Part 2:** 410
Sirin, V. (pseudonym), **Retro. Supp. I:** 266. See also Nabokov, Vladimir
Sirlin, Jerome, **Supp. XXI:** 147
Sir Vadia's Shadow: A Friendship across Five Continents (Theroux), **Supp. VIII:** 309, 314, 321, 325
"Sir William's Reply to Molly"(Kenny), **Supp. XXIII:** 153
"Sis" (F. Barthelme), **Supp. XI:** 26
"S is for Sad" (M. F. K. Fisher), **Supp. XVII:** 86
Sisley, Alfred, **I:** 478
Sissman, L. E., **Supp. X:** 69; **Supp. XXVI:** 68, 74
"Sister" (Hughes), **Retro. Supp. I:** 208
"Sister" (Lamott), **Supp. XX: 142**
"Sister, The" (July), **Supp. XXIV:** 202
Sister Age (M. F. K. Fisher), **Supp. XVII:** 88, 91
Sister Carrie (Dreiser), **I:** 482, 497, 499, 500, 501–502, 503–504, 505, 506, 515, 519; **III:** 327; **IV:** 208; **Retro. Supp. I:** 376; **Retro. Supp. II:** 93, **96–99; Supp. XVIII:** 76, 243; **Supp. XXIII:** 165; **Supp. XXV:** 129
Sister Mary Ignatius Explains It All for You (Durang), **Supp. XXIV:** 114, **119–120**
"Sister of the Minotaur" (Stevens), **IV:** 89; **Supp. IX:** 332
"Sisters" (Boulton), **Supp. XXII:** 20
"Sisters" (Nelson), **Supp. XVIII:** 176
"Sisters, The" (Whittier), **Supp. I Part 2:** 696
Sister's Choice (Showalter), **Retro. Supp. I:** 368
Sisters-in-Law, The (Atherton), **Supp. XXIV:** 25
Sisters of the Earth: Women's Prose and Poetry About Nature (Anderson, ed.), **Supp. XVIII:** 189
Sisters Rosensweig, The (Wasserstein), **Supp. XV:** 320, **328–330**
"Sisyphus" (Kumin), **Supp. IV Part 2:** 443, 444, 451
"Sitalkas" (Doolittle), **Supp. I Part 1:** 266
"Site of Memory, The" (Morrison), **Retro. Supp. III:** 191, 194
"Sites of Memory" (Cliff), **Supp. XXII:** 69, 74
Sitney, P. Adams, **Supp. XII:** 2
Sitting Bull, **Supp. IV Part 2:** 492
"Sitting in a Rocking Chair Going Blind" (Komunyakaa), **Supp. XIII:** 114
Sitting In: Selected Writings on Jazz, Blues, and Related Topics (Carruth), **Supp. XVI:** 46
"Sitting Up Late with My Father, 1977" (F. Wright), **Supp. XVII:** 247
Sitti's Secrets (Nye), **Supp. XIII:** 278
Situation Normal (A. Miller), **III:** 148, 149, 156, 164
Situation of Poetry, The: Contemporary Poetry and Its Traditions (Pinsky), **Supp. VI: 237–238,** 239, 241, 242
Sitwell, Edith, **IV:** 77; **Supp. I Part 1:** 271
6 A.M. (Bodenheim), **Supp. XXV:** 27
"Six Brothers" (Cisneros), **Supp. VII:** 67
Six Characters in Search of an Author (Pirandello), **Supp. IV Part 2:** 576
"Six Days: Some Rememberings" (Paley), **Supp. VI:** 226
"65290" (Leopold), **Supp. XIV:** 184–185
Six French Poets (A. Lowell), **II:** 528–529
"Six in All" (Bierds), **Supp. XVII:** 31
Six Lips (Schott), **Supp. XXIII: 251–252**
"Six Persons" (Baraka), **Supp. II Part 1:** 53
Six Sections from Mountains and Rivers without End (Snyder), **Supp. VIII:** 305
"Sixteen Months" (Sandburg), **III:** 584
1601, or Conversation as It Was by the Fireside in the Time of the Tudors (Twain), **IV:** 201
"Sixth-Month Song in the Foothills" (Snyder), **Supp. VIII:** 297
Sixties, The (magazine) (R. Bly), **Supp. IV Part 1:** 60; **Supp. IX:** 271
"Sixty" (Dunn), **Supp. XI:** 155
"Sixty Acres" (Carver), **Supp. III Part 1:** 141
"64 Elmgrove" (Halliday), **Supp. XIX:** 88
"69 Hidebound Opinions, Propositions, and Several Asides from a Manila Folder concerning the Stuff of Poetry" (Wright), **Supp. XV:** 344–345
Sixty Seconds (Bodenheim), **Supp. XXV:** 26
Sixty Stories (Barthelme), **Supp. IV Part 1:** 41, 42, 44, 47, 49, 50
63: Dream Palace (Purdy), **Supp. VII:** 270–271
"Six Variations" (Levertov), **Supp. III Part 1:** 277–278
"Six-Year-Old Boy" (Olds), **Supp. X:** 206
"Six Years Later" (Brodsky), **Supp. VIII:** 26, 28

"Size and Sheer Will" (Olds), **Supp. X:** 206
Size of Thoughts, The: Essays and Other Lumber (Baker), **Supp. XIII: 52–53,** 55, 56
Sizwe Bansi Is Dead (Fugard), **Supp. VIII:** 330
Sjöwall, Maj, **Supp. XX: 87**
"Skagway" (Haines), **Supp. XII:** 206
"Skaters, The" (Ashbery), **Supp. III Part 1:** 10, 12, 13, 18, 25
"Skaters, The" (Jarrell), **II:** 368–369
Skau, Michael, **Supp. XII:** 129, 130, 132, 134
Skeeters Kirby (Masters), **Supp. I Part 2:** 459, 470, 471
Skeleton at the Feast, The (Wells), **Supp. XXVI:** 278, 282
Skeleton Crew (King), **Supp. V:** 144
"Skeleton in Armor, The" (Longfellow), **Retro. Supp. II:** 168
"Skeleton's Cave, The" (Bryant), **Supp. I Part 1:** 157
Skelton, John, **III:** 521
Skepticisms (Aiken), **Supp. XV:** 298, 302
Sketch Book of Geoffrey Crayon, Gent., The (Irving), **II:** 295, 303, 304–308, 309, 311, 491; **Supp. I Part 1:** 155
Sketches of Art (Jameson), **Retro. Supp. II:** 58
Sketches of Eighteenth Century America (Crèvecoeur), **Supp. I Part 1:** 233, 240–241, 250, 251
"Sketches of Female Biography" (Rowson), **Supp. XV:** 245
Sketches of Switzerland (Cooper), **I:** 346
Sketches Old and New (Twain), **IV:** 198
"Sketch for a Job-Application Blank" (Harrison), **Supp. VIII:** 38
"Sketch"(Kenny), **Supp. XXIII:** 155
Sketch of Old England, by a New England Man (Paulding), **I:** 344
Skibell, Joseph, **Supp. XVII:** 48
"Skier and the Mountain, The" (Eberhart), **I:** 528–529
"Skiing by Moonlight" (Davison), **Supp. XXVI:** 74
"Skin-Boats: 1830, The" (Bierds), **Supp. XVII:** 28
Skinker, Mary Scott, **Supp. IX:** 20
Skinner, Ewart, **Supp. XXII:** 78
Skinny Island (Auchincloss), **Supp. IV Part 1:** 33
Skinny Legs and All (Robbins), **Supp. X:** 267, 273, **276–279**
Skin of Our Teeth, The (Wilder), **IV:** 357, 358, 369–372; **Supp. IV Part 2:** 586; **Supp. XX: 50**
"Skins" (Wright), **Supp. V:** 340
Skins and Bones: Poems 1979–1987 (Gunn Allen), **Supp. IV Part 1:** 321, 331
"Skipper Ireson's Ride" (Whittier), **Supp. I Part 2:** 691, 693–694
"Skirmish at Sartoris" (Faulkner), **II:** 67
"Skirt" (Halliday), **Supp. XIX:** 90
Skirts and Slacks (Di Piero), **Supp. XIX:** 35, 36, 38, 45–47
Sklenicka, Carol, **Supp. XXIV:** 166
Skloot, Floyd, **Supp. XX: 193–209**
Skotheim, Robert Allen, **Supp. XVII:** 104
Skow, John, **Supp. V:** 213; **Supp. XVI:** 174
Skube, Michael, **Supp. XVIII:** 96
"Skunk Cabbage" (Bronk), **Supp. XXI:** 31
"Skunk Cabbage" (Oliver), **Supp. VII:** 235, 236
"Skunk Hour" (R. Lowell), **II:** 548–550; **Retro. Supp. II:** 188, 189; **Supp. XIV:** 269; **Supp. XX: 203**
Skurnick, Lizzie, **Supp. XXVI:** 49
Sky, The Stars, The Wilderness, The (Bass), **Supp. XVI:** 19, 20
Sky Changes, The (Sorrentino), **Supp. XXI:** 228, 230, 231; **Supp. XXVI:** 26
"Sky Dance" (Leopold), **Supp. XIV:** 186
"Sky Line" (Taylor), **Supp. V:** 316
"Sky Line, The" (Mumford), **Supp. II Part 2:** 475
Sky of Stone (Hickam), **Supp. XXVII:** 101, 106, 108–110
"Skyscraper" (Sandburg), **III:** 581–582
Sky's the Limit, The: A Defense of the Earth (Nichols), **Supp. XIII:** 268
"Sky Valley Rider" (Wright), **Supp. V:** 335, 340
Sky-Walk; or the Man Unknown to Himself (Brown), **Supp. I Part 1:** 127–128
Slam! (Myers), **Supp. XXVII:** 201, 202, 206
"Slang in America" (Whitman), **IV:** 348
Slappy Hooper, the Wonderful Sign Painter (Bontemps and Conroy), **Supp. XXII:** 5, 11
Slapstick (Vonnegut), **Supp. II Part 2:** 753, 754, 778
Slapstick Tragedy (T. Williams), **IV:** 382, 393
Slate, Lane, **Supp. IX:** 251, 253
Slater Brown, William, **Retro. Supp. III:** 48
Slattery, Mary Grace. See Miller, Mrs. Arthur (Mary Grace Slattery)
Slattery's Hurricane (Wouk), **Supp. XXV:** 257, 262–263
Slaughter, Frank G., **Retro. Supp. III:** 134
"Slaughterer, The" (Singer), **IV:** 19
Slaughterhouse-Five (Vonnegut), **Supp. II Part 2:** 755, 758–759, 760, 770, 772–776; **Supp. V:** 41, 244; **Supp. XIX:** 235
Slaughter Rule, The (film; Alex and Andrew Smith), **Supp. XIX:** 174
Slave, The (Baraka), **Supp. II Part 1:** 42, 44, 56
Slave, The: A Novel (Singer), **IV:** 13; **Retro. Supp. II: 305–307**
"Slave Canal" (Ray), **Supp. XVIII:** 193
"Slave Coffle" (Angelou), **Supp. IV Part 1:** 16
"Slave of the Sky" (P. N. Warren), **Supp. XX: 261**
"Slave on the Block" (Hughes), **Supp. I Part 1:** 329
Slave Power, The: The Free North and Southern Domination, 1780–1860 (Richards), **Supp. XIV:** 48
"Slave Quarters" (Dickey), **Supp. IV Part 1:** 181
Slavery (Channing), **Supp. XXIV:** 77–78
"Slave's Dream, The" (Longfellow), **Supp. I Part 2:** 409
Slave Ship: A Historical Pageant (Baraka), **Supp. II Part 1:** 47–49, 53, 56–57
"Slave-Ships, The" (Whittier), **Supp. I Part 2:** 687–688
Slaves in Algiers; or, A Struggle for Freedom (Rowson), **Supp. XV: 236–237**
"Slave Trade, The: View from the Middle Passage" (Major), **Supp. XXII:** 182
Slavs! Thinking about the Longstanding Problems of Virtue and Happiness (Kushner), **Supp. IX: 146**
Sledge, Eugene, **Supp. V:** 250
Sleek for the Long Flight (Matthews), **Supp. IX:** 154, 155, **157–158**
Sleep (Dixon), **Supp. XII:** 154
"Sleep, The" (Strand), **Supp. IV Part 2:** 627
Sleeper (film; Allen), **Supp. XV:** 5
"Sleeper, The" (Poe), **III:** 411; **Retro. Supp. III:** 231–232

"Sleeper 1, The" (Hay), **Supp. XIV:** 132–133
"Sleeper 2, The" (Hay), **Supp. XIV:** 132–133
"Sleepers, The" (Whitman), **IV:** 336; **Retro. Supp. III:** 308
"Sleepers in Jaipur" (Kenyon), **Supp. VII:** 172
Sleepers in Moon-Crowned Valleys (Purdy), **Supp. VII:** 274, 275
Sleepers Joining Hands (R. Bly), **Supp. XXI:** 85
"Sleepers Joining Hands" (R. Bly), **Supp. IV Part 1:** 63, 73
Sleeping Beauty (Macdonald), **Supp. IV Part 2:** 474, 475
Sleeping Beauty, The (Carruth), **Supp. XVI:** 53, 57–58
"Sleeping Beauty IV" (Stone), **Supp. XXVII:** 263
"Sleeping Beauty Syndrome, The: The New Agony of Single Men" (Wasserstein), **Supp. XV:** 328
Sleeping Dogs (Wells), **Supp. XXVI:** 280–281
Sleeping Fires (Atherton), **Supp. XXIV:** 25
"Sleeping Fury, The" (Bogan), **Supp. III Part 1:** 58
Sleeping Fury, The: Poems (Bogan), **Supp. III Part 1:** 55–58
Sleeping Gypsy and Other Poems, The (Garrett), **Supp. VII:** 96–98
Sleeping in the Forest (Oliver), **Supp. VII:** 233
"Sleeping in the Forest" (Oliver), **Supp. VII:** 233–234
Sleeping in the Woods (Wagoner), **Supp. IX: 328**
Sleeping on Fists (Ríos), **Supp. IV Part 2:** 540
Sleeping on the Wing: An Anthology of Modern Poetry (Koch and Farrell, eds.), **Supp. XV:** 187–188
"Sleeping on the Wing"(O'Hara), **Supp. XXIII:** 214
"Sleeping Standing Up" (Bishop), **Supp. I Part 1:** 85, 89, 93
"Sleeping with Animals" (Kumin), **Supp. IV Part 2:** 454
Sleeping with One Eye Open (Strand), **Supp. IV Part 2:** 621–624, 623, 628
Sleeping with the Dictionary (Mullen), **Supp. XXVII:** 173–174, 176
Sleep in Thunder (Lacy), **Supp. XV:** 206
"Sleepless, The" (L.-Y. Lee), **Supp. XV:** 224
"Sleepless at Crown Point" (Wilbur), **Supp. III Part 2:** 561
Sleepless Nights (Hardwick), **Supp. III Part 1:** 193, 208–211
"Sleepless Nights" (Nelson), **Supp. XVIII:** 174
"Sleep-Walkers, The" (Gibran), **Supp. XX: 118**
Sleepy Lagoon Mystery, The (Endore), **Supp. XVII:** 60
"Sleepy People" (Lethem), **Supp. XVIII:** 140
Sleigh, Tom, **Supp. XIX:** 38, 40
Sleight, Ken, **Supp. XIII:** 12
Slick, Sam (pseudonym). See Haliburton, Thomas Chandler
"Slick Gonna Learn" (Ellison), **Retro. Supp. II:** 116; **Supp. II Part 1:** 237–238
"Slight Rebellion off Madison" (Salinger), **III:** 553
"Slight Sound at Evening, A" (White), **Supp. I Part 2:** 672
"Slim Graves Show, The" (Keillor), **Supp. XVI:** 172
"Slim Greer" series (Hayden), **Supp. II Part 1:** 369
"Slim in Hell" (Hayden), **Supp. II Part 1:** 369
"Slim Man Canyon" (Silko), **Supp. IV Part 2:** 560
"Slip, Shift, and Speed Up: The Influence of Robinson Jeffers's Narrative Syntax" (Jarman), **Supp. XVII:** 111, 112
"Slippery Fingers" (Hammett), **Supp. IV Part 1:** 343
Slipping-Down Life, A (Tyler), **Supp. IV Part 2:** 660–661
Sloan, Jacob, **IV:** 3, 6
Sloan, John, **I:** 254; **IV:** 411; **Retro. Supp. II:** 103; **Supp. XXII:** 277
Sloane, David E. E., **Retro. Supp. III:** 259
Sloane, John, **Supp. XV:** 295
"Slob" (Farrell), **II:** 25, 28, 31
Slocum, Joshua, **Supp. I Part 2:** 497; **Supp. XXV: 205–219**
Slogum House (Sandoz), **Supp. XXIV:** 244, **251–252,** 255
Slomovitz, Philip, **Retro. Supp. III:** 133
Slonim, Véra. See Nabokov, Véra
Slopen, Beverly, **Supp. XX: 59**
Slouching towards Bethlehem (Didion), **Supp. IV Part 1:** 196, 197, 200–201, 202, 206, 210
Slovic, Scott, **Supp. XVI:** 277
"Slow Child with a Book of Birds" (Levis), **Supp. XI:** 268
"Slow Dance with Icarus" (Monson), **Supp. XXIV:** 240
Slow Dancing Through Ether: A Fine Binding Project (Monson and Ingmundson), **Supp. XXIV:** 230, 234
"Slow Down for Poetry" (Strand), **Supp. IV Part 2:** 620
Slow Music (Taggard), **Supp. XXII:** 284
"Slow Pacific Swell, The" (Winters), **Supp. II Part 2:** 790, 793, 795, 796, 799
Slow Parade (Kees), **Supp. XV:** 137
Slow Train Coming (album, Dylan), **Supp. XVIII:** 28
Slow Transparency (Hadas), **Supp. XXIII: 113–114**
Slow Vision (Bodenheim), **Supp. XXV:** 28
"Slum Church" (Espaillat), **Supp. XXI:** 110–111
"Slumgullions" (Olsen), **Supp. IV Part 1:** 54
Slumgullion Stew: An Edward Abbey Reader (Abbey), **Supp. XIII:** 4
Slung, Michelle, **Supp. XX: 87**
"S & M" (Komunyakaa), **Supp. XIII:** 114
"Small" (C. Frost), **Supp. XV:** 102
Small, Albion, **Supp. I Part 1:** 5
"Small, Good Thing, A" (Carver), **Supp. III Part 1:** 145, 147
Small, Miriam Rossiter, **Supp. I Part 1:** 319
Small Boy and Others, A (James), **II:** 337, 547; **Retro. Supp. I:** 235
"Small but Urgent Request to the Unknowable" (Karr), **Supp. XI:** 243
Small Ceremonies (Shields), **Supp. VII:** 312–315, 320
Small Craft Warnings (T. Williams), **IV:** 382, 383, 384, 385, 386, 387, 392, 393, 396, 398
"Small Degrees" (Brockmeier), **Supp. XXII:** 52, 59
"Small Fry" (Peacock), **Supp. XIX:** 206
Small Place, A (Kincaid), **Supp. VII:** 186–187, 188, 191
"Small Rain, The" (Pynchon), **Supp. II Part 2:** 620
Small Room, The (Sarton), **Supp. VIII:** 252, **255–256**
Smalls, Bob, **II:** 128
"Small Song for Andrew" (Weigl), **Supp. XIX:** 280
Small Time Crooks (film; Allen), **Supp. XV:** 11
Small Town, A (Hearon), **Supp. VIII: 65–66**
"Small Vases from Hebron, The"

(Nye), **Supp. XIII:** 283
"Small Vision, The" (Goldbarth), **Supp. XII:** 180
"Small Voice from the Wings" (Everwine), **Supp. XV:** 76
"Small Wire" (Sexton), **Supp. II Part 2:** 696
Small Worlds (A. Hoffman), **Supp. XVII:** 44
Smardz, Zofia, **Supp. XVI:** 155
Smart, Christopher, **III:** 534; **Supp. I Part 2:** 539; **Supp. IV Part 2:** 626
Smart, Joyce H., **Supp. XI:** 169
"Smart Cookie, A" (Cisneros), **Supp. VII:** 64
"Smash"(Thompson), **Supp. XXIII:** 301, 302
"Smashup" (Thurber), **Supp. I Part 2:** 616
Smedly, Agnes, **Supp. XIII:** 295
"Smell of a God, The" (Peacock), **Supp. XIX:** 199
"Smelt Fishing" (Hayden), **Supp. II Part 1:** 367
"Smile of the Bathers, The" (Kees), **Supp. XV:** 145
"Smile on the Face of a Kouros, The" (Bronk), **Supp. XXI:** 31
"Smiles" (Dunn), **Supp. XI:** 151
Smiles, Samuel, **Supp. X:** 167
Smiley, Jane, **Supp. VI: 291–309; Supp. XII:** 73, 297; **Supp. XIII:** 127; **Supp. XIX:** 54
Smith, Adam, **II:** 9; **Supp. I Part 2:** 633, 634, 639; **Supp. XVII:** 235
Smith, Amanda, **Supp. XXVII:** 211
Smith, Annick, **Supp. XIV:** 223; **Supp. XXVI:** 183, 186, 188
Smith, Barbara, **Supp. XXIII:** 194
Smith, Benjamin, **IV:** 148
Smith, Bernard, **I:** 260
Smith, Bessie, **Retro. Supp. I:** 343; **Retro. Supp. III:** 314; **Supp. VIII:** 330; **Supp. XIX:** 147
Smith, Betty, **Supp. XXIII: 257–271**
Smith, Charlie, **Supp. X:** 177
Smith, Clark Ashton, **Supp. XXV:** 111; **Supp. XXVII:** 117
Smith, Dale, **Supp. XV:** 136, 138, 139
Smith, Dave, **Supp. V:** 333; **Supp. XI:** 152; **Supp. XII:** 178, 198; **Supp. XIX:** 277, 282
Smith, David, **Supp. XIII:** 246, 247
Smith, David Nichol, **Supp. XIV:** 2
Smith, Dinitia, **Supp. VIII:** 74, 82, 83; **Supp. XVIII:** 162; **Supp. XXIV:** 2–3
Smith, Elihu Hubbard, **Supp. I Part 1:** 126, 127, 130
Smith, Ernest J., **Supp. XXIII:** 111, 113, 117
Smith, George Adam, **III:** 199
Smith, Hannah Whitall, **Supp. XIV:** 333, 334, 338
Smith, Harriet, **Retro. Supp. III:** 261
Smith, Harrison, **II:** 61
Smith, Henry Justin, **Supp. XXVII:** 85
Smith, Henry Nash, **IV:** 210; **Retro. Supp. III:** 78, 266; **Supp. I Part 1:** 233
Smith, Herbert F., **Supp. I Part 2:** 423
Smith, Iain Crichton, **Supp. XVIII:** 196
Smith, James, **II:** 111
Smith, Jedediah Strong, **Supp. IV Part 2:** 602
Smith, Jerome, **Supp. IV Part 1:** 369
Smith, Joe, **Supp. IV Part 2:** 584
Smith, John, **I:** 4, 131; **II:** 296
Smith, John Allyn, **I:** 168
Smith, Johnston (pseudonym). See Crane, Stephen
Smith, Katherine Capshaw, **Supp. XXII:** 10, 13–14
Smith, Kellogg, **Supp. I Part 2:** 660
Smith, Lamar, **II:** 585
Smith, Mrs. Lamar (Marguerite Walters), **II:** 585, 587
Smith, Lane, **Supp. XIX:** 231
Smith, Larry David, **Supp. XVIII:** 22
Smith, Lee, **Supp. XII:** 311; **Supp. XVIII:** 195; **Supp. XXII:** 206, 213
Smith, Lillian, **Supp. XXII:** 67
Smith, Logan Pearsall, **Supp. XIV: 333–351**
Smith, Lula Carson. See McCullers, Carson
Smith, Mark, **Supp. XVIII:** 155
Smith, Martha Nell, **Retro. Supp. I:** 33, 43, 46, 47
Smith, Mary Rozet, **Supp. I Part 1:** 5, 22
Smith, Oliver, **II:** 586
Smith, Patricia Clark, **Supp. IV Part 1:** 397, 398, 402, 406, 408, 410; **Supp. IV Part 2:** 509; **Supp. XII:** 218
Smith, Patrick, **Supp. VIII:** 40, 41
Smith, Patti, **Supp. XII:** 136; **Supp. XIV:** 151
Smith, Porter, **III:** 572
Smith, Red, **II:** 417, 424
Smith, Robert McClure, **Supp. XV:** 270
Smith, Robert Pearsall, **Supp. XIV:** 333
Smith, Sarah A., **Supp. XVIII:** 99
Smith, Seba, **Supp. I Part 2:** 411
Smith, Sidonie, **Supp. IV Part 1:** 11; **Supp. XXII:** 70
Smith, Stevie, **Supp. V:** 84
Smith, Sydney, **II:** 295; **Supp. XIV:** 112
Smith, Thorne, **Supp. IX:** 194
Smith, Valerie, **Supp. XXII:** 146
Smith, Wallace, **Supp. XXVII:** 88
Smith, Wendy, **Supp. XII:** 330, 335; **Supp. XVIII:** 89, 92
Smith, Wilford Bascom "Pitchfork", **Supp. XIII:** 168
Smith, William, **II:** 114
Smith, William Gardner, **Supp. XVI:** 142–143
Smith, William Jay, **Supp. XIII: 331–350**
Smitherman, Geneva, **Supp. XXVI:** 13
"Smoke" (Di Piero), **Supp. XIX:** 38
Smoke (film), **Supp. XII:** 21
"Smoke" (Huddle), **Supp. XXVI:** 149
Smoke and Steel (Sandburg), **III:** 585–587, 592
Smoke Dancing (Gansworth), **Supp. XXVI:** 104–105
"Smokehouse" (Offutt), **Supp. XIX:** 166, 167
"Smokers" (Wolff), **Supp. VII:** 340–341
Smokey Bites the Dust (film, C. Griffith), **Supp. XVII:** 9
Smoking Mountain, The: Stories of Postwar Germany (Boyle), **Supp. XXIV:** 61
"Smoking My Prayers" (Ortiz), **Supp. IV Part 2:** 503
"Smoking Room, The" (Jackson), **Supp. IX:** 116
"Smoky Gold" (Leopold), **Supp. XIV:** 186
Smolan, Sandy, **Supp. XVI:** 36
Smollett, Tobias G., **I:** 134, 339, 343; **II:** 304–305; **III:** 61; **Supp. XVIII:** 7; **Supp. XXV:** 258
Smooding, Robert, **Supp. XXIII:** 294
Smuggler's Bible, A (McElroy), **Supp. IV Part 1:** 285
Smuggler's Handbook, The (Goldbarth), **Supp. XII:** 181, 183
Smugglers of Lost Soul's Rock, The (Gardner), **Supp. VI: 70**
Smyth, Albert Henry, **II:** 123
Smyth, Jacqui, **Supp. XXI:** 215
"Snack Firm Maps New Chip Push" (Keillor), **Supp. XVI:** 168, 169
"Snail, The" (Hay), **Supp. XIV:** 124
"Snake, The" (Berry), **Supp. X:** 31
"Snake, The" (Crane), **I:** 420
"Snakecharmer" (Plath), **Supp. I Part 2:** 538

"Snakes, Mongooses" (Moore), **III:** 207
"Snakeskin" (Kooser), **Supp. XIX:** 123
"Snakes of September, The" (Kunitz), **Supp. III Part 1:** 258
"Snapshot of 15th S.W., A" (Hugo), **Supp. VI:** 141
"Snapshot Rediscovered, A" (X. J. Kennedy), **Supp. XV:** 170
"Snapshots in an Album" (Espaillat), **Supp. XXI:** 111
"Snapshots of a Daughter-in-Law" (Rich), **Retro. Supp. III:** 243; **Supp. I Part 2:** 553–554
Snapshots of a Daughter-in-Law: Poems, 1954–1962 (Rich), **Retro. Supp. III:** 241, 243–244; **Supp. I Part 2:** 550–551, 553–554; **Supp. XII:** 255
Snaring the Flightless Birds (Bierds), **Supp. XVII:** 26
Sneetches and Other Stories, The (Geisel), **Supp. XVI:** 109
"Sneeze, The" (Chekhov), **Supp. IV Part 2:** 585
Snell, Ebenezer, **Supp. I Part 1:** 151
Snell, Thomas, **Supp. I Part 1:** 153
Sniffen, Matthew, **Supp. XXV:** 283
"Snob, The" (Boulton), **Supp. XXII:** 23
"Snob, The" (Shapiro), **Supp. II Part 2:** 705
Snobbery: The America Version (Epstein), **Supp. XIV:** 102, 114–115
Snodgrass, Kathleen, **Supp. XVI:** 42
Snodgrass, W. D., **I:** 400; **Retro. Supp. II:** 179; **Supp. III Part 2:** 541; **Supp. V:** 337; **Supp. VI: 311–328; Supp. XI:** 141, 315; **Supp. XIII:** 312; **Supp. XV:** 92, 153; **Supp. XVII:** 239
"Snow" (C. Baxter), **Supp. XVII:** 19
"Snow" (Frost), **Retro. Supp. I:** 133
"Snow" (Haines), **Supp. XII:** 212
"Snow" (Sexton), **Supp. II Part 2:** 696
"Snow" (W. V. Davis), **Supp. XXI:** 89, 90, 93
Snow, C. P., **Supp. I Part 2:** 536
Snow, Dean, **Supp. XXVI:** 86
Snow, Hank, **Supp. V:** 335
Snow Angels (film), **Supp. XXV:** 153–154
Snow Angels (O'Nan), **Supp. XXV:** 142, 143, 150
Snow Ball, The (Gurney), **Supp. V:** 99
"Snow-Bound" (Whittier), **Supp. I Part 2:** 700–703
"Snow Bound at Eagle's" (Harte), **Supp. II Part 1:** 356
"Snowflakes" (Longfellow), **II:** 498
"Snow Goose, The" (Gallico), **Supp. XVI:** 238
Snow-Image, The (Hawthorne), **Retro. Supp. III:** 110, 117–118
"Snow-Image, The" (Hawthorne), **Retro. Supp. III:** 117–118
Snow-Image and Other Twice Told Tales, The (Hawthorne), **II:** 237; **Retro. Supp. I:** 160
"Snowing in Greenwich Village" (Updike), **IV:** 226; **Retro. Supp. I:** 321
"Snow in New York" (Swenson), **Supp. IV Part 2:** 644
Snow Leopard, The (Matthiessen), **Supp. V:** 199, 207–211
"Snow Man, The" (Stevens), **IV:** 82–83; **Retro. Supp. I:** 299, 300, 302, 306, 307, 312; **Supp. XXI:** 60
"Snowmass Cycle, The" (Dunn), **Supp. XI:** 152
Snow: Meditations of a Cautious Man in Winter (Banks), **Supp. V:** 6
Snow Poems, The (Ammons), **Supp. VII:** 32–34
Snowshoe Trek to Otter River (Budbill), **Supp. XIX:** 11
Snow's Music, The (Skloot), **Supp. XX: 196, 204–205**
"Snows of Kilimanjaro, The" (Hemingway), **II:** 78, 257, 263, 264; **Retro. Supp. I:** 98, 182; **Supp. XII:** 249
"Snows of Studiofiftyfour, The" (Plimpton), **Supp. XVI:** 245
"Snow Songs" (Snodgrass), **Supp. VI:** 324
"Snowstorm, The" (Oates), **Supp. II Part 2:** 523
"Snowstorm as It Affects the American Farmer, A" (Crèvecoeur), **Supp. I Part 1:** 251
Snow White (Barthelme), **Supp. IV Part 1:** 40, 47, 48–49, 50, 52; **Supp. V:** 39
"Snowy Egret" (Weigl), **Supp. XIX:** 280–281
"Snowy Mountain Song, A" (Ortiz), **Supp. IV Part 2:** 506
Snyder, Gary, **Supp. III Part 1:** 350; **Supp. IV Part 2:** 502; **Supp. V:** 168–169; **Supp. VIII:** 39, **289–307; Supp. XVI:** 283; **Supp. XXII:** 276
Snyder, Mike, **Supp. XIV:** 36
Snyder, Phillip A., **Retro. Supp. III:** 134
Soak the Rich (film), **Supp. XXVII:** 90
"So-and-So Reclining on Her Couch" (Stevens), **IV:** 90
"Soapland" (Thurber), **Supp. I Part 2:** 619
Soares, Lota de Macedo, **Retro. Supp. II:** 44; **Supp. I Part 1:** 89, 94
"Sobbin' Women, The" (Benét), **Supp. XI:** 47
Sobin, Gustaf, **Supp. XVI: 281–298**
Sochen, June, **Supp. XXI:** 1
Social Ethics (Gilman), **Supp. XI:** 207
"Social Function of the Story Teller, The" (lecture, Murray), **Supp. XIX:** 153
"Socialism and the Negro" (McKay), **Supp. X:** 135
"Socialism of the Skin, A (Liberation, Honey!)" (Kushner), **Supp. IX:** 135
Social Thought in America: The Revolt against Formalism (White), **Supp. I Part 2:** 648, 650
"Society, Morality, and the Novel" (Ellison), **Retro. Supp. II:** 118, 123–124
"Society of Eros" (Kittredge), **Supp. XXVI:** 178, 184
"Sociological Habit Patterns in Linguistic Transmogrification" (Cowley), **Supp. II Part 1:** 143
"Sociological Poet, A" (Bourne), **I:** 228
Socrates, **I:** 136, 265; **II:** 8–9, 105, 106; **III:** 281, 419, 606; **Supp. I Part 2:** 458; **Supp. XII:** 98
Socrates Fortlow stories (Mosley), **Supp. XIII: 242–243**
So Forth (Brodsky), **Supp. VIII:** 32–33
"So Forth" (Brodsky), **Supp. VIII:** 33
"Soft Flame" (Skloot), **Supp. XX: 203**
"Soft-Hearted Sioux, The" (Zitkala-Ša), **Supp. XXV:** 274, 282
Soft Machine, The (Burroughs), **Supp. III Part 1:** 93, 103, 104
"Soft Mask" (Karr), **Supp. XI:** 243
Soft Side, The (James), **II:** 335; **Retro. Supp. I:** 229
"Soft Spring Night in Shillington, A" (Updike), **Retro. Supp. I:** 318, 319
"Soft Wood" (R. Lowell), **II:** 550–551
"So Help Me" (Algren), **Supp. IX:** 2
Soil and Survival: Land Stewardship and the Future of American Agriculture (C. Bly, J. Paddock and N. Paddock), **Supp. XVI:** 36–37
"Soirée in Hollywood" (H. Miller), **III:** 186
Sojourner, The (Rawlings), **Supp. X:** 233–234
"Sojourn in a Whale" (Moore), **III:** 211, 213
"Sojourns" (Didion), **Supp. IV Part 1:** 205

Sokolow, Jayme, **Supp. XIX:** 134
Solanus, Jane, **Supp. XVI:** 293
Solar Lottery (Dick), **Supp. XVIII:** 138
Solar Storms (Hogan), **Supp. IV Part 1:** 397, 410, 414–415
"Soldier, The" (Frost), **II:** 155
"Soldier Asleep at the Tomb" (Schnackenberg), **Supp. XV:** 262–263
Soldier Blue (film), **Supp. X:** 124
"Soldier of Fortune" (Wright), **Supp. XV:** 341
Soldier of the Great War, A (Helprin), **Supp. XXV:** 83–84, 86–87
"Soldier's Home" (Hemingway), **Retro. Supp. I:** 189
Soldier's Joy (Bell), **Supp. X:** 7, **7–8,** 10, 11; **Supp. XXIII:** 43
Soldiers of the Storm (film), **Supp. XIII:** 163
Soldiers' Pay (Faulkner), **I:** 117; **II:** 56, 68; **Retro. Supp. I:** 80, 81; **Retro. Supp. III:** 76–77
"Soldier's Testament, The" (Mumford), **Supp. II Part 2:** 473
"Soliloquy: Man Talking to a Mirror" (Komunyakaa), **Supp. XIII:** 116–117
"Solipsism" (Monson), **Supp. XXIV:** 230
"Solitary, The" (Teasdale), **Supp. XXVII:** 296
"Solitary Confinement" (X. J. Kennedy), **Supp. XV:** 157
"Solitary Pond, The" (Updike), **Retro. Supp. I:** 323
So Little Time (Marquand), **III:** 55, 59, 65, 67, 69
"Solitude" (Maupassant), **Supp. I Part 1:** 223
Solnit, Rebecca, **Supp. XXVI:** 45
Solo Faces (Salter), **Supp. IX: 259–260**
Solomon, Andy, **Supp. X:** 11
Solomon, Carl, **Supp. XIV:** 143, 150
Solomon, Charles, **Supp. VIII:** 82
Solomon, Deborah, **Supp. XXI:** 245
Solomon, Henry, Jr., **Supp. I Part 2:** 490
Solomons, Leon, **IV:** 26
"So Long, Marianne" (Cohen), **Supp. XXVII:** 51, 60
So Long, See You Tomorrow (Maxwell), **Supp. VIII:** 156, 160, 162, **167–169; Supp. XVII:** 23
"So Long Ago" (Bausch), **Supp. VII:** 41–42
Solotaroff, Robert, **Retro. Supp. II:** 203
Solotaroff, Theodore, **III:** 452–453; **Retro. Supp. II:** 281; **Supp. I Part 2:** 440, 445; **Supp. X:** 79; **Supp. XI:** 340; **Supp. XII:** 291; **Supp. XIX:** 268; **Supp. XXVI:** 118
Solstice (Di Piero), **Supp. XIX:** 36
"Solstice" (Jeffers), **Supp. II Part 2:** 433, 435
"Solstice, The" (Merwin), **Supp. III Part 1:** 356
"Solus Rex" (Nabokov), **Retro. Supp. I:** 274
Solution, The (Stone), **Supp. XXVII:** 257
"Solutions" (McCarthy), **II:** 578
"Solving the Puzzle" (Dunn), **Supp. XI:** 152
Solzhenitsyn, Alexandr, **Retro. Supp. I:** 278; **Supp. VIII:** 241
"Some Afternoon" (Creeley), **Supp. IV Part 1:** 150–151
Some American People (Caldwell), **I:** 292, 294, 295, 296, 304, 309
"Some Ashes Drifting above Piedra, California" (Levis), **Supp. XI:** 264–265
"Some Aspects of the Grotesque in Southern Fiction" (O'Connor), **Retro. Supp. II:** 223, 224
"Some Birds on a Dun Field" (Bronk), **Supp. XXI:** 27
"Somebody Always Grabs the Purple" (H. Roth), **Supp. IX:** 234
Somebody Else, Somewhere Else: The Raymond Andrews Story (film, Freeman), **Supp. XXVI:** 11
Somebody in Boots (Algren), **Supp. IX:** 3, **5–7,** 12
Somebody's Darling (McMurtry), **Supp. V:** 225
Some Came Running (film), **Supp. XI:** 213
Some Came Running (Jones), **Supp. XI:** 214, 215, 220, **222–223,** 226, 227, 232
Some Can Whistle (McMurtry), **Supp. V:** 229
"Some Children of the Goddess" (Mailer), **Retro. Supp. II:** 204
Someday, Maybe (Stafford), **Supp. XI: 323–325; Supp. XIII:** 281
Some Drawings and Some Notes to Myself (Brainard), **Supp. XXVII:** 20
"Some Dreamers of the Golden Dream" (Didion), **Supp. IV Part 1:** 200
"Some Esoteric Aspects of the League of the Iroquois" (Hewitt), **Supp. XXVI:** 96
Some Faces in the Crowd (Schulberg), **Supp. XVIII:** 252
"Some Foreign Letters" (Sexton), **Supp. II Part 2:** 674
"Some General Instructions" (Koch), **Supp. XV:** 182
"Some Good News" (Olson), **Supp. II Part 2:** 575, 576, 577
"Some Grass along a Ditch Bank" (Levis), **Supp. XI:** 266
"Some Greek Writings" (Corso), **Supp. XII:** 130
Some Honorable Men: Political Conventions, 1960–1972 (Mailer), **Retro. Supp. II:** 208
Some Imagist Poets (A. Lowell), **III:** 511, 518, 520; **Supp. I Part 1:** 257, 261
"Some keep the Sabbath going to Church" (Dickinson), **Retro. Supp. I:** 30; **Supp. XVIII:** 301
"Some Laughed" (L. Michaels), **Supp. XVI:** 207
"Some Like Indians Endure" (Gunn Allen), **Supp. IV Part 1:** 330
"Some Like Them Cold" (Lardner), **II:** 427–428, 430, 431; **Supp. IX:** 202
"Some Lines from Whitman" (Jarrell), **IV:** 352
"Some Matters Concerning the Occupant" (Keillor), **Supp. XVI:** 167
"Some Musicians Play Chamber Music for Us" (Bronk), **Supp. XXI:** 27–28
"Some Negatives: X. at the Chateau" (Merrill), **Supp. III Part 1:** 322
"Some Neglected Points in the Theory of Socialism" (Veblen), **Supp. I Part 2:** 635
"Some Notes for an Autobiographical Lecture" (Trilling), **Supp. III Part 2:** 493, 497, 500
"Some Notes on French Poetry" (R. Bly), **Supp. IV Part 1:** 61
"Some Notes on Miss L." (West), **IV:** 290–291, 295; **Retro. Supp. II:** 322
"Some Notes on Organic Form" (Levertov), **Supp. III Part 1:** 272, 279
"Some Notes on Teaching: Probably Spoken" (Paley), **Supp. VI:** 225
"Some Notes on the Gazer Within" (Levis), **Supp. XI:** 270
"Some Notes on Violence" (West), **IV:** 304; **Retro. Supp. II:** 322, 323
"Some Observations Now" (Conroy), **Supp. XVI:** 75
Some Observations of a Stranger at Zuni in the Later Part of the Century (Major), **Supp. XXII:** 179–180
"Some Observations of a Stranger at

Zuni in the Later Part of the Century" (Major), **Supp. XXII:** 179
Some of the Dharma (Kerouac), **Supp. III Part 1:** 225
"Some of Us Have Fewer" (Monson), **Supp. XXIV:** 240
"Someone Is Buried" (Salinas), **Supp. XIII:** 324
"Someone Is Writing a Poem" (Rich), **Retro. Supp. III:** 251
"Someone Puts a Pineapple Together" (Stevens), **IV:** 90–91
"Someone's Blood" (Dove), **Supp. IV Part 1:** 245
"Someone Talking" (Harjo), **Supp. XII:** 219–220
"Someone Talking to Himself" (Wilbur), **Supp. III Part 2:** 557
"Someone to Watch Over Me" (Stern), **Supp. IX:** 300
Someone to Watch Over Me: Stories (Bausch), **Supp. VII:** 53
Some People, Places, & Things That Will Not Appear in My Next Novel (Cheever), **Supp. I Part 1:** 184–185
"Some Poets' Criticism and the Age" (Yenser), **Supp. XV:** 113–114
Some Problems of Philosophy: A Beginning of an Introduction to Philosophy (James), **II:** 360–361
"Some Questions You Might Ask" (Oliver), **Supp. VII:** 238–239
"Some Remarks on Humor" (White), **Supp. I Part 2:** 672
"Some Remarks on Rhythm" (Roethke), **III:** 548–549
Somers, Fred, **I:** 196
Somerville, Jane, **Supp. IX:** 289, 296–297
"Some Secrets" (Stern), **Supp. IX:** 286, 287, 288, 289, 295
Some Sort of Epic Grandeur (Bruccoli), **Retro. Supp. I:** 115, 359
"Something" (Oliver), **Supp. VII:** 236
"Something Broken" (Rich), **Retro. Supp. III:** 244
Something Happened (Heller), **Supp. IV Part 1:** 383, 386–388, 389, 392
"Something Happened: The Imaginary, the Symbolic, and the Discourse of the Family" (Mellard), **Supp. IV Part 1:** 387
Something in Common (Hughes), **Supp. I Part 1:** 329–330
Something Inside: Conversations with Gay Fiction Writers (Gambone), **Supp. XII:** 81
Something I've Been Meaning to Tell You (Munro), **Supp. XXVII:** 182, 184–185
"Something Matters but We Don't " (Bronk), **Supp. XXI:** 32
"Something Might Be Gaining" (Mosher), **Supp. XXII:** 209
"Something New" (Stern), **Supp. IX:** 290
"Something Rich and Strange" (Rash), **Supp. XXVII:** 223–224
Some Things (Berrigan, Padgett, and Brainard), **Supp. XXIV:** 41
Something Said (Sorrentino), **Supp. XXI:** 226, 227, 229, 235
"Something's Going to Happen" (Zinberg), **Supp. XV:** 196
"Something Spurious from the Mindinao Deep" (Stegner), **Supp. IV Part 2:** 605
"Something That Needs Nothing" (July), **Supp. XXIV:** 203
"Something to Believe In" (Pitts), **Supp. XXII:** 280
Something to Declare (Alvarez), **Supp. VII:** 1, 2, 11, 17–19
Something to Remember Me By (Bellow), **Retro. Supp. II:** 32
"Something to Remember Me By (Bellow), **Retro. Supp. II:** 32
"Something Wicked" (O'Nan), **Supp. XXV:** 148
Something Wicked This Way Comes (Bradbury), **Supp. IV Part 1:** 101, 110–111; **Supp. XXV:** 148
"Something Wild . . ." (T. Williams), **IV:** 381
"Some Thoughts" (McNally), **Supp. XIII:** 207
"Some Thoughts on the Line" (Oliver), **Supp. VII:** 238
"Some Thoughts on the Science of Onanism" (Twain), **Retro. Supp. III:** 262
"Sometimes, Reading" (Stafford), **Supp. XI:** 314
"Sometimes It Just Happens That Way, That's All" (Hinojosa), **Supp. XIX:** 101
"Sometimes I Wonder" (Hughes), **Supp. I Part 1:** 337
Sometimes Mysteriously (Salinas), **Supp. XIII:** 311, **326–328**
"Sometimes Mysteriously" (Salinas), **Supp. XIII:** 328
Some Trees (Ashbery), **Supp. III Part 1:** 3–7, 12
"Some Trees" (Ashbery), **Supp. III Part 1:** 2
"Some Truths About American Readers" (Atherton), **Supp. XXIV:** 24, 27
"Some Views on the Reading and Writing of Short Stories" (Welty), **Retro. Supp. I:** 351
"Somewhere" (Nemerov), **III:** 279–280
"Somewhere Else" (Paley), **Supp. VI:** 227
"Somewhere in Africa" (Sexton), **Supp. II Part 2:** 684–685
Somewhere in the Darkness (Myers), **Supp. XXVII:** 203–204
"Somewhere Is Such a Kingdom" (Ransom), **III:** 492
"Somewhere near Phu Bai: (Komunyakaa), **Supp. XIII:** 123–124
Some Words (Bronk), **Supp. XXI:** 32
"Some Words with a Mummy" (Poe), **III:** 425
"Some Yips and Barks in the Dark" (Snyder), **Supp. VIII:** 291
Sommers, Michael, **Supp. IV Part 2:** 581
Sommers, William, **I:** 387, 388
"Somnambulism" (Brown), **Retro. Supp. III:** 226
"Somnambulisma" (Stevens), **Retro. Supp. I:** 310
"So Much Summer" (Dickinson), **Retro. Supp. I:** 26, 44, 45
"So Much the Worse for Boston" (Lindsay), **Supp. I Part 2:** 398
"So Much Water So Close to Home" (Carver), **Supp. III Part 1:** 143, 146
Son, Cathy, **Supp. X:** 292
"Son, The" (Dove), **Supp. IV Part 1:** 245
"Son and Father" (Pickering), **Supp. XXI:** 197
"Sonata" (Schnackenberg), **Supp. XV:** 259
"Sonata for the Invisible" (Harjo), **Supp. XII:** 228
Sonata for Two Pianos (Bowles), **Supp. IV Part 1:** 83
Son at the Front, A (Wharton), **II:** 183; **IV:** 320; **Retro. Supp. I:** 378; **Retro. Supp. III:** 286
Sondheim, Stephen, **Supp. XII:** 260; **Supp. XVI:** 194
Son Excellence Eugène Rougon (Zola), **III:** 322
Son from Sleep, A (Hadas), **Supp. XXIII: 114–115**
Song (B. Kelly), **Supp. XVII:** 123, **127–130**
"Song" (B. Kelly), **Supp. XVII:** 127
"Song" (Bogan), **Supp. III Part 1:** 57
"Song" (Bryant). See "Hunter of the West, The"
"Song" (Dunbar), **Supp. II Part 1:** 199

"Song" (Espaillat), **Supp. XXI:** 106–107
"Song" (Ginsberg), **Supp. II Part 1:** 317
"Song" (Kenyon), **Supp. VII:** 169
"Song" (Rich), **Supp. I Part 2:** 560
"Song" (Wylie), **Supp. I Part 2:** 729
"Song, A" (Creeley), **Supp. IV Part 1:** 145
"Song, The" (Gioia), **Supp. XV:** 117
"Song, The" (Very), **Supp. XXV:** 242
Song and Idea (Eberhart), **I:** 526, 529, 533, 539
"Song: Enlightenment" (X. J. Kennedy), **Supp. XV:** 169
"Song for a Lover Killed in Battle"(J. Schoolcraft), **Supp. XXIII:** 235
Song for Anninho (G. Jones), **Supp. XXIV:** 185, 195
Song for My Father, A: A Play in Two Acts (Budbill), **Supp. XIX:** 3, **15–16**
"Song for Myself and the Deer to Return On" (Harjo), **Supp. XII:** 225
"Song for My Sixtieth Year" (Carruth), **Supp. XVI:** 54
"Song for Occupations, A" (Whitman), **Retro. Supp. I:** 394; **Retro. Supp. III:** 305
"Song for Simeon, A" (Eliot), **Retro. Supp. I:** 64
"Song for the Coming of Smallpox" (Wagoner), **Supp. IX:** 329, 330
"Song for the End of Time" (Gioia), **Supp. XV:** 126–127
"Song for the First People" (Wagoner), **Supp. IX:** 328
"Song for the Last Act" (Bogan), **Supp. III Part 1:** 64
"Song for the Middle of the Night, A" (Wright), **Supp. III Part 2:** 594
"Song for the Rainy Season" (Bishop), **Supp. I Part 1:** 93–94, 96
"Song for the Romeos, A" (Stern), **Supp. IX:** 296
"Song for Woody" (song, Dylan), **Supp. XVIII:** 24
"Song from a Courtyard Window" (Gioia), **Supp. XV:** 119
"Song III" (Taggard), **Supp. XXII:** 284
"Song in the Front Yard, A" (Brooks), **Supp. XVIII:** 181
"Songline of Dawn" (Harjo), **Supp. XII:** 229
"Song: Love in Whose Rich Honor" (Rukeyser), **Supp. VI:** 285
"Song: Now That She Is Here" (Carruth), **Supp. XVI:** 59
"Song of Absinthe Granny, The" (Stone), **Supp. XXVII:** 263
"Song of Advent, A" (Winters), **Supp. II Part 2:** 789
"Song of a Man Who Rushed at the Enemy" (Wagoner), **Supp. IX:** 329, 330
"Song of Courage, A" (Masters), **Supp. I Part 2:** 458
Song of God, The: Bhagavad-Gita (Isherwood and Prabhavananda, trans.), **Supp. XIV:** 156, 157, 164
Song of Hiawatha, The (Longfellow), **II:** 501, 503–504; **Retro. Supp. II:** 155, **159–161,** 162, 163; **Supp. XXIII:** 223, 234–235
"Song of Innocence, A" (Ellison), **Retro. Supp. II:** 126; **Supp. II Part 1:** 248
"Song of My Fiftieth Birthday, The" (Lindsay), **Supp. I Part 2:** 399
"Song of Myself" (Whitman), **II:** 544; **III:** 572, 584, 595; **IV:** 333, 334, 337–339, 340, 341, 342, 344, 348, 349, 351, 405; **Retro. Supp. I:** 388, 389, 395–399, 400; **Retro. Supp. III:** 299, 305, 308; **Supp. IX:** 131, 136, 143, 328, 331; **Supp. V:** 122; **Supp. XIV:** 139; **Supp. XVIII:** 194, 304; **Supp. XXII:** 81
Song of Napalm (Weigl), **Supp. XIX:** 278–282
"Song of Napalm" (Weigl), **Supp. XIX:** 276–277
Song of Russia (film), **Supp. I Part 1:** 281, 294; **Supp. XVII:** 60–61
"Song of Self" (Huncke), **Supp. XIV:** 138–139, 145
Song of Solomon (biblical book), **III:** 118; **IV:** 150
Song of Solomon (Morrison), **Retro. Supp. III:** 184, 189–190; **Supp. III Part 1:** 364, 368, 369, 372, 379; **Supp. XVIII:** 55
Song of Songs (biblical book), **II:** 538; **IV:** 153–154; **Supp. XV:** 221
"Song of the Adoumboulou: 3" (Mackey), **Supp. XXVII:** 157
"Song of the Adoumboulou: 6" (Mackey), **Supp. XXVII:** 157
"Song of the Adoumboulou: 7" (Mackey), **Supp. XXVII:** 157
"Song of the Andoumboulou" (Mackey), **Supp. XXVII:** 153–154, 155, 156
"Song of the Andoumboulou: 1" (Mackey), **Supp. XXVII:** 153–154
"Song of the Andoumboulou: 8" (Mackey), **Supp. XXVII:** 154
"Song of the Andoumboulou: 16" (Mackey), **Supp. XXVII:** 155
"Song of the Andoumboulou: 26" (Mackey), **Supp. XXVII:** 155
"Song of the Answerer" (Whitman), **Retro. Supp. I:** 393, 399
Song of the Cardinal, The (Stratton-Porter), **Supp. XX: 217, 218, 219**
"Song of the Chattahoochee, The" (Lanier), **Supp. I Part 1:** 365, 368
"Song of the Degrees, A" (Pound), **III:** 466
"Song of the Drunkard" (Ferry), **Supp. XXIV:** 153, 162
"Song of the Dryads" (Taggard), **Supp. XXII:** 272
"Song of the Exposition" (Whitman), **IV:** 332
"Song of the Gavilan" (Leopold), **Supp. XIV:** 189
"Song of the Gourd" (Wright), **Supp. XV:** 348–349
"Song of the Greek Amazon" (Bryant), **Supp. I Part 1:** 168
Song of the Lark, The (Cather), **I:** 312, 319–321, 323; **Retro. Supp. I:** 1, 3, 7, **9–11,** 13, 19, 20; **Retro. Supp. III:** 18, 23, 30
"Song of the Okogis, or Frog in Spring"(J. Schoolcraft), **Supp. XXIII:** 232, 233, 235
"Song of the Open Road" (McGrath), **Supp. X:** 127
"Song of the Open Road" (Whitman), **IV:** 340–341; **Retro. Supp. I:** 400; **Retro. Supp. III:** 305; **Supp. IX:** 265
"Song of the Redwood Tree" (Whitman), **IV:** 348
"Song of the Scullery" (McCarriston), **Supp. XIV:** 272
"Song of the Sky Loom" (traditional Tewa poem), **Supp. IV Part 1:** 325
"Song of the Son" (Toomer), **Supp. III Part 2:** 482–483; **Supp. IX:** 313
"Song of the Sower, The" (Bryant), **Supp. I Part 1:** 169
"Song of the Stars" (Bryant), **Supp. I Part 1:** 163
"Song of the Swamp-Robin, The" (Frederic), **II:** 138
"Song of the Vermonters, The" (Whittier), **Supp. I Part 2:** 692
"Song of Three Smiles" (Merwin), **Supp. III Part 1:** 344
"Song of Wandering Aengus, The" (Yeats), **IV:** 271; **Retro. Supp. I:** 342, 350
"Song of Welcome" (Brodsky), **Supp. VIII:** 32
"Song on Captain Barney's Victory" (Freneau), **Supp. II Part 1:** 261
"Song/Poetry and Language-Expression and Perception" (Ortiz),

Supp. IV Part 2: 500, 508
"Song Rehearsal, The" (Stallings), **Supp. XXV:** 233
"Song: 'Rough Winds Do Shake the Darling Buds of May' " (Simpson), **Supp. IX:** 268
Songs (Boyce), **Supp. XXI:** 9
Songs and Satires (Masters), **Supp. I Part 2:** 465–466
Songs and Sonnets (L. P. Smith), **Supp. XIV:** 341
Songs and Sonnets (Masters), **Supp. I Part 2:** 455, 459, 461, 466
"Songs for a Colored Singer" (Bishop), **Supp. I Part 1:** 80, 85
Songs for a Summer's Day (A Sonnet Cycle) (MacLeish), **III:** 3
Songs for Eve (MacLeish), **III:** 3, 19
"Songs for Eve" (MacLeish), **III:** 19
"Songs for My Father" (Komunyakaa), **Supp. XIII:** 128
Songs for the Missing (O'Nan), **Supp. XXV:** 143, 148, 150
Songs for the Unborn Second Baby (Notley), **Supp. XXII:** 228
"Songs for Two Seasons" (C. Frost), **Supp. XV:** 95–96
Songs from a Room (album, Cohen), **Supp. XXVII:** 54
Songs from This Earth on Turtle's Back: Contemporary American Indian Poetry (Bruchac, ed.), **Supp. IV Part 1:** 320, 328
"Songs of a Housewife" (Rawlings), **Supp. X:** 221–222
"Songs of Billy Bathgate, The" (Doctorow), **Supp. IV Part 1:** 230
Songs of Innocence (Blake), **Supp. I Part 2:** 708
Songs of Jamaica (McKay), **Supp. X:** 131, 133
Songs of Leonard Cohen (album, Cohen), **Supp. XXVII:** 54, 59
Songs of Love and Hate (album, Cohen), **Supp. XXVII:** 54
"Songs of Maximus, The" (Olson), **Supp. II Part 2:** 567
"Songs of Parting" (Whitman), **IV:** 348
Songs of the Doomed (Thompson), **Supp. XXIV:** 283
Songs of the North: A Sigurd Olson Reader (Mosher, ed.), **Supp. XXII:** 218
Songs of the Sierras (J. Miller), **I:** 459
Songs of Three Centuries (Whittier and Larcom, eds.), **Supp. XIII:** 142
"Song to David" (Smart), **III:** 534
"Song to No Music, A" (Brodsky), **Supp. VIII:** 26
"Song V" (Taggard), **Supp. XXII:** 284
Song Yet Sung (McBride), **Supp. XXVI:** 194, 199–201, 204
Soniat, Katherine, **Supp. XXI:** 245
Sonneschein, Rosa, **Retro. Supp. II:** 65
"Sonnet" (Rukeyser), **Supp. VI:** 284
"Sonnet, A" (Very), **Supp. XXV:** 242
"Sonnet Crown for Two Voices" (Bierds), **Supp. XVII:** 35
"Sonnet"(J. Schoolcraft), **Supp. XXIII:** 229
"Sonnet of Good Cheer, A" (Howard), **Supp. XXVII:** 118–119
"Sonnets" (Carruth), **Supp. XVI:** 56
Sonnets, The (Berrigan), **Supp. XXII:** 224; **Supp. XXIV:** 33, 34, 35, 37, 38–41, 45
"Sonnets at Christmas" (Tate), **IV:** 135
Sonnets to Duse and Other Poems (Teasdale), **Supp. XXVII:** 287
Sonnets to Orpheus (Rilke), **Supp. XV:** 222; **Supp. XXIV:** 38
"Sonnet to a Negro in Harlem" (H. Johnson), **Supp. XXVI:** 166, 167–170
"Sonnet—To Science" (Poe), **Retro. Supp. III:** 231
"Sonnet-To Zante" (Poe), **III:** 421
"Sonnet XV" (Berrigan), **Supp. XXIV:** 38–39, 44
"Sonny's Blues" (Baldwin), **Retro. Supp. II:** 7, 8, 10, 14; **Supp. I Part 1:** 58–59, 63, 67; **Supp. XI:** 288; **Supp. XXVII:** 201
Son of Laughter, The: A Novel (Buechner), **Supp. XII:** 54
Son of Perdition, The (Cozzens), **I:** 359–360, 377, 378, 379
Son of the Circus, A (Irving), **Supp. VI:** 165, 166, **176–179**
Son of the Gamblin' Man: The Youth of an Artist (Sandoz), **Supp. XXIV:** 244, **256–257**
"Son of the Gods, A" (Bierce), **I:** 202
Son of the Morning (Oates), **Supp. II Part 2:** 518, 519, 520–522
Son of the Morning Star: Custer and the Little Bighorn (Connell), **Supp. XIV:** 80, 82, 97
"Son of the Romanovs, A" (Simpson), **Supp. IX:** 273–274
"Son of the White Wolf" (Howard), **Supp. XXVII:** 121
Son of the Wolf, The (London), **II:** 465, 469
"Son of the Wolfman" (Chabon), **Supp. XI:** 76
"Sonrisas" (Mora), **Supp. XIII:** 216, 219
Sons (Buck), **Supp. II Part 1:** 117–118
"Sons" (Teasdale), **Supp. XXVII:** 295
Sons and Lovers (Lawrence), **III:** 27
Sons of Kai, The: The Story the Indian Told (Beston), **Supp. XXVI:** 33
Sontag, Kate, **Supp. XV:** 104
Sontag, Susan, **IV:** 13, 14; **Retro. Supp. II:** 279; **Supp. I Part 2:** 423; **Supp. III Part 2: 451–473; Supp. VIII:** 75; **Supp. XIV:** 14, 15, 95–96, 167; **Supp. XVI:** 201, 204, 206; **Supp. XX: 205; Supp. XXI:** 243; **Supp. XXVI:** 45
"Soon" (Munro), **Supp. XXVII:** 193, 194
"Soonest Mended" (Ashbery), **Supp. III Part 1:** 1, 13
"Sootfall and Fallout" (White), **Supp. I Part 2:** 671
Sophisticates, The (Atherton), **Supp. XXIV:** 20, 25
Sophocles, **I:** 274; **II:** 291, 385, 577; **III:** 145, 151, 152, 153, 159, 398, 476, 478, 609, 613; **IV:** 291, 363, 368, 370; **Supp. I Part 1:** 153, 284; **Supp. I Part 2:** 491; **Supp. V:** 97; **Supp. VIII:** 332; **Supp. XV:** 265, 266
"Sophronsiba" (Bourne), **I:** 221
Sorayam, Aram, **Supp. XXII:** 25
Sorby, Angela, **Supp. XXIII:** 132
Sorcerer's Apprentice, The: Tales and Conjurations (C. Johnson), **Supp. VI: 192–193,** 194
"Sorcerer's Eye, The" (Nemerov), **III:** 283
Sordello (Browning), **III:** 467, 469, 470
"Sordid? Good God!" (Williams), **Retro. Supp. II:** 334
So Red the Rose (Young), **Supp. XXII:** 190, 193
"Sorghum" (Mason), **Supp. VIII:** 146
Sorkin, Adam, **Supp. XXIV:** 178
Sorokin, Pitirim, **Supp. I Part 2:** 679
Sorrentino, Christopher, **Supp. XVIII:** 148
Sorrentino, Gilbert, **Retro. Supp. I:** 426; **Supp. IV Part 1:** 286; **Supp. XII:** 139; **Supp. XXI: 225–241; Supp. XXII:** 261; **Supp. XXVI:** 26; **Supp. XXVII:** 18
Sorrento (Notley), **Supp. XXII:** 231
"Sorrow" (Komunyakaa), **Supp. XIII:** 119
Sorrow Dance, The (Levertov), **Supp. III Part 1:** 279–280, 283
"Sorrowful Guest, A" (Jewett), **Retro. Supp. II:** 137

Sorrows of Fat City, The: A Selection of Literary Essays and Reviews (Garrett), **Supp. VII:** 111
Sorrows of Young Werther, The (Goethe), **Supp. XI:** 169; **Supp. XX: 234, 236**
Sorrows of Young Werther, The (Goethe; Bogan and Mayer, trans.), **Supp. III Part 1:** 63
"Sorry Fugu" (Boyle), **Supp. XX: 19**
"Sorting Facts; or, Nineteen Ways of Looking at Marker" (Howe), **Supp. IV Part 2:** 434, 436
"Sort of Song, A" (W. C. Williams), **Supp. XVII:** 243
"S O S" (Baraka), **Supp. II Part 1:** 50
"So Sassafras" (Olson), **Supp. II Part 2:** 574
"So There" (Creeley), **Supp. IV Part 1:** 157
"So This Is Nebraska" (Kooser), **Supp. XIX:** 120
Sotirov, Vasil, **Supp. IX:** 152
Soto, Gary, **Supp. IV Part 2:** 545; **Supp. V:** 180; **Supp. XI:** 270; **Supp. XIII:** 313, 315, 316, 320, 323; **Supp. XV:** 73; **Supp. XXV:** 130
"Soto Thinking of the Ocean" (Salinas), **Supp. XIII:** 321
"Sotto Voce" (Kunitz), **Supp. III Part 1:** 265
Sot-Weed Factor, The (Barth), **I:** 122, 123, 125, 129, 130, 131–134, 135; **Supp. XXII:** 259
"Soul" (Ferry), **Supp. XXIV:** 162
Soul, The (Brooks), **I:** 244
Soul and Body of John Brown, The (Rukeyser), **Supp. VI:** 273
Soul Barnacles: Ten More Years with Ray (Gallagher; Simon, ed.), **Supp. XXIV:** 166, 167, 171, 172
Soul Clap Hands and Sing (Marshall), **Supp. XI:** 276, 278, **280–282**
Soul Expeditions (Singer). See Shosha (Singer)
Soul Gone Home (Hughes), **Retro. Supp. I:** 203; **Supp. I Part 1:** 328
"Soul inside the Sentence, The" (Gass), **Supp. VI:** 88
Soul Is Here for Its Own Joy, The (Bly, ed.), **Supp. IV Part 1:** 74
Soul of Man under Socialism, The (Wilde), **Supp. IX:** 134–135
"Soul of Spain, The [In the manner of Gertrude Stein]" (Hemingway), **Supp. XX: 74**
Soul of the Far East, The (P. Lowell), **II:** 513
"Soul on Bench" (Halliday), **Supp. XIX:** 91
Soul on Ice (Cleaver), **Retro. Supp. II:** 12, 13
"Souls Belated" (Wharton), **Retro. Supp. I:** 364; **Retro. Supp. III:** 278–279, 287
"Soul selects her own Society, The" (Dickinson), **Retro. Supp. I:** 37
Souls of Black Folk, The (Du Bois), **Supp. II Part 1:** 33, 40, 160, 168–170, 176, 183; **Supp. IV Part 1:** 164; **Supp. IX:** 305, 306; **Supp. X:** 133; **Supp. XIII:** 185, 238, 243
Souls of Black Folk. The (Du Bois), **Supp. XX: 102**
"Sound, The" (Olds), **Supp. X:** 214
Sound and Beauty (Hwang), **Supp. XXI:** 146
"Sound and Fury" (O. Henry), **Supp. II Part 1:** 402
Sound and the Fury, The (Faulkner), **I:** 480; **II:** 55, 57, 58–60, 73; **III:** 237; **IV:** 100, 101, 104; **Retro. Supp. I:** 73, 75, 77, 82, **83–84,** 86, 88, 89, 90, 91, 92; **Retro. Supp. III:** 74, 78–80, 82, 84; **Supp. IX:** 103; **Supp. VIII:** 215; **Supp. X:** 44; **Supp. XII:** 33; **Supp. XIV:** 12; **Supp. XVII:** 138; **Supp. XVIII:** 84; **Supp. XXVII:** 11
"Sound Bites" (Alvarez), **Supp. VII:** 11
Sound I Listened For, The (Francis), **Supp. IX: 78–79,** 87
"Soundless Trumpet, The" (Antin), **Supp. XX: 12**
"Sound Mind, Sound Body" (R. Lowell), **II:** 554
Sound of a Voice, The (Hwang), **Supp. XXI:** 146
"Sound of Distant Thunder, A" (Elkin), **Supp. VI: 42–43,** 44
"Sound of Light, The" (Merwin), **Supp. III Part 1:** 356
Sound of Mountain Water, The (Stegner), **Supp. IV Part 2:** 595, 596, 598, 600, 608
"Sound of Talking" (Purdy), **Supp. VII:** 270
Sounds of Poetry (television special, Moyers), **Supp. XXIII:** 139
Sounds of Poetry, The (Pinsky), **Supp. VI:** 236, 247, 248; **Supp. XXIII:** 124
Sound the Stars Make Rushing Through the Sky, The: The Writings of Jane Johnston Schoolcraft (Parker, ed.), **Supp. XXIII:** 223–224, 227, 228
Soupault, Philippe, **IV:** 288, 404; **Retro. Supp. II:** 85, 321, 324
Source (Doty), **Supp. XI:** 121, **134–137**
"Source" (Doty), **Supp. XI:** 136
"Source, The" (Olds), **Supp. X:** 211
"Source, The" (Porter), **III:** 443
Source of Light, The (Price), **Supp. VI: 262,** 266
"Sources" (Rich), **Retro. Supp. III:** 250
"Sources of Soviet Conduct, The" (Kennan), **Supp. VIII:** 241
Sour Grapes (W. C. Williams), **Retro. Supp. I:** 418
"Sour Grapes"(Moraga), **Supp. XXIII:** 202
"Sourwood Nocturne" (Skloot), **Supp. XX: 202**
"South" (Levis), **Supp. XI:** 266
"South" (Trethewey), **Supp. XXI:** 247, 256
"South, The" (Hughes), **Supp. I Part 1:** 321
South American Journey (W. Frank), **Supp. XX: 79**
"Southampton Variations"(O'Hara), **Supp. XXIII:** 212
"Southbound on the Freeway" (Swenson), **Supp. IV Part 2:** 643
South Dakota Guidebook, The (C. Baxter), **Supp. XVII:** 15
Southern, Terry, **Supp. IV Part 1:** 379; **Supp. V:** 40, 201; **Supp. XI: 293–310; Supp. XVI:** 230
Southern Cross, The (Wright), **Supp. V:** 332, 342
"Southern Cross, The" (Wright), **Supp. V:** 338
"Southerner's Problem, The" (Du Bois), **Supp. II Part 1:** 168
"Southern Girl" (Zelda Fitzgerald), **Supp. IX:** 71
"Southern Gothic" (Trethewey), **Supp. XXI:** 256
"Southern History" (Trethewey), **Supp. XXI:** 256, 257
"Southern Mode of the Imagination, A" (Tate), **IV:** 120
"Southern Road, A" (H. Johnson), **Supp. XXVI:** 165, 167, 172, 174
"Southern Romantic, A" (Tate), **Supp. I Part 1:** 373
"Southern Sojourn, A" (Hoffman), **Supp. XVIII:** 87
Southern Terry, **Supp. XIV:** 82
Southern Writers: A New Biographical Dictionary (Flora, Vogel, and Giemza, eds.), **Supp. XXVI:** 148
Southey, Robert, **II:** 304, 502; **Supp. I Part 1:** 154; **Supp. XXIV:** 74
"South Lingers On, The" (R. Fisher),

Supp. XIX: 69–70
South Moon Under (Rawlings), **Supp. X: 225–226,** 229, 233
South Pacific Affair (Lacy), **Supp. XV:** 206
Southpaw, The (Harris), **II:** 424–425
"South Sangamon" (Cisneros), **Supp. VII:** 66
"South State Street: Chicago" (Bodenheim), **Supp. XXV:** 22
South to a Very Old Place (Murray), **Supp. XIX: 151–153**
Southwell, Robert, **IV:** 151
Southwestern Homelands (Kittredge), **Supp. XXVI:** 188
Southwick, Marcia, **Supp. XI:** 259
Southworth, E. D. E. N, **Retro. Supp. I:** 246
Souvenir of the Ancient World, Selected Poems of Carlos Drummond de Andrade (Strand, trans.), **Supp. IV Part 2:** 630
Sovereign Bones: New Native American Writing (Gansworth, ed.), **Supp. XXVI:** 113
"Sow" (Plath), **Supp. I Part 2:** 537
"Sowing and Reaping in Furors Die" (Nostrandt), **Supp. XVIII:** 80–81
Soyinka, Wole, **Supp. XX: 100**
"Space" (Brockmeier), **Supp. XXII:** 51
Space between Our Footsteps, The: Poems and Paintings from the Middle East (Nye, ed.), **Supp. XIII:** 280
"Space Quale, The" (James), **II:** 349
"Spaces Between, The" (Kingsolver), **Supp. VII:** 209
"Spaceships Have Landed" (Munro), **Supp. XXVII:** 191
"Space Where Sex Should Be, The: Toward a Definition of the Black Literary Tradition" (Nelson), **Supp. XVIII:** 172
Spack, Ruth, **Supp. XXV:** 278
Spackman, Peter, **Supp. XVI:** 221
Spacks, Patricia, **Supp. XVI:** 251
"Spain" (Auden), **Supp. II Part 1:** 12–13, 14
"Spain in Fifty-Ninth Street" (White), **Supp. I Part 2:** 677
Spanier, Sandra, **Supp. XXIV:** 51, 64
"Spanish-American War Play" (Crane), **I:** 422
Spanish Ballads (Merwin, trans.), **Supp. III Part 1:** 347
Spanish Bayonet (Benét), **Supp. XI:** 45, 47
Spanish Earth, The (film), **Retro. Supp. I:** 184
Spanish Love (Rinehart), **Supp. XXV:** 195
Spanish Papers and Other Miscellanies (Irving), **II:** 314
"Spanish Revolution, The" (Bryant), **Supp. I Part 1:** 153, 168
Spanish Student, The (Longfellow), **II:** 489, 506; **Retro. Supp. II:** 165
"Spanish Winter" (Egan), **Supp. XIX:** 52
Spanking the Maid (Coover), **Supp. V:** 47, 48, 49, 52
Spare Change (Parker), **Supp. XIX:** 186–187
Spargo, John, **Supp. I Part 1:** 13
"Spark, The" (Wharton), **Retro. Supp. I:** 381
"Sparkles from the Wheel" (Whitman), **IV:** 348
Sparks, Debra, **Supp. X:** 177
Sparks, Jared, **Supp. I Part 1:** 156; **Supp. XXIV:** 71
"Sparrow" (Berry), **Supp. X:** 31
Sparrow, Henry, **III:** 587
Sparrow, Mrs. Henry, **III:** 587
"Sparrow's Gate, The" (B. Kelly), **Supp. XVII:** 133
Spaulding, William, **Supp. XVI:** 106
"Spawning Run, The" (Humphrey), **Supp. IX:** 95
"Speak, Gay Memory" (Kirp), **Supp. XI:** 129
"Speak, Hoyt-Schermerhorn" (Lethem), **Supp. XVIII:** 148
Speak, Memory (Nabokov), **III:** 247–250, 252; **Retro. Supp. I:** 264, 265, 266, 267, 268, 277; **Supp. XVI:** 148
Speak, Memory (V. Nabakov), **Supp. XVII:** 47
Speaking and Language (Shapiro), **Supp. II Part 2:** 721
Speaking for Nature: How Literary Naturalists from Henry Thoreau to Rachel Carson Have Shaped America (Brooks), **Supp. IX:** 31
Speaking for Ourselves: American Ethnic Writing (Faderman and Bradshaw, eds.), **Supp. XIII:** 313
Speaking of Accidents (Everwine), **Supp. XV:** 75, 88
"Speaking of Accidents" (Everwine), **Supp. XV:** 88–89
"Speaking of Counterweights" (White), **Supp. I Part 2:** 669
Speaking of Literature and Society (Trilling), **Supp. III Part 2:** 494, 496, 499
"Speaking of Love" (Gioia), **Supp. XV:** 124–125
Speaking of Race, Speaking of Sex: Hate Speech, Civil Rights, and Civil Liberties (H. L. Gates, Griffin, Lively, and Strossen), **Supp. XX: 111**
Speaking on Stage (Kolin and Kullman, eds.), **Supp. IX:** 145
Speaking on Stage: Interviews with Contemporary American Playwrights (Balakian), **Supp. XV:** 327
"Speaking Passions" (Kitchen), **Supp. XV:** 215
Speak of the Devil (Holding), **Supp. XXII: 127**
Speak What We Feel (Not What We Ought to Say): Reflections on Literature and Faith (Buechner), **Supp. XII:** 57
Spear, Roberta, **Supp. V:** 180; **Supp. XV:** 73
"Spear and Fang" (Howard), **Supp. XXVII:** 116
"Special Kind of Fantasy, A: James Dickey on the Razor's Edge" (Niflis), **Supp. IV Part 1:** 175
"Special Pleading" (Lanier), **Supp. I Part 1:** 364
"Special Problems in Teaching Leslie Marmon Silko's Ceremony" (Gunn Allen), **Supp. IV Part 1:** 333
Special Providence, A (Yates), **Supp. XI:** 342, **344–345**
"Special Time, a Special School, A" (Knowles), **Supp. XII:** 236
Special View of History, The (Olson), **Supp. II Part 2:** 566, 569, 572
Specimen Days (Whitman), **IV:** 338, 347, 348, 350; **Retro. Supp. I:** 408
Specimens of the American Poets, **Supp. I Part 1:** 155
"Speckled Trout" (Rash), **Supp. XXVII:** 222
"Spectacles, The" (Poe), **III:** 425
Spectator Bird, The (Stegner), **Supp. IV Part 2:** 599, 604, 606, 611–612
Spector, Herman, **Supp. XXV:** 26; **Supp. XXVI:** 143
Spector, Robert, **Supp. XIII:** 87
Spectra: A Book of Poetic Experiments (Bynner and Ficke), **Supp. XV:** 43
"Spectre Bridegroom, The" (Irving), **II:** 304
"Spectre Pig, The" (Holmes), **Supp. I Part 1:** 302
"Speculating Woman" (X. J. Kennedy), **Supp. XV:** 168
"Speech Sounds" (O. Butler), **Supp. XIII:** 61, **70**
"Speech to a Crowd" (MacLeish), **III:** 16

"Speech to the Detractors" (MacLeish), **III:** 16
"Speech to the Young" (Brooks), **Supp. III Part 1:** 79, 86
"Speech to Those Who Say Comrade" (MacLeish), **III:** 16
Speedboat (Adler), **Supp. X:** 171
Speed of Darkness, The (Rukeyser), **Supp. VI:** 274, 281
Speed Queen, The (O'Nan), **Supp. XXV:** 142, 144
Speed-the-Plow (Mamet), **Supp. XIV:** 241, 246, 249, 250, 251
"Speedy Gonzales Was the Fastest Mouse in Mexico" (P. N. Warren as Kilina), **Supp. XX: 262**
Speilberg, Steven, **Supp. XI:** 234
Speirs, Logan, **Supp. XIX:** 282
"Spell" (Francis), **Supp. IX:** 87
"Spell, The" (Peacock), **Supp. XIX:** 198, 200
Spellbound (screenplay, Hecht), **Supp. XXVII:** 93
"Spell for the Manufacture & Use of a Magic Carpet" (Hull), **Supp. XXI:** 132–133, 139, 141
Spelling Dictionary, A (Rowson), **Supp. XV:** 244
Spence, Thomas, **Supp. I Part 2:** 518
Spence + Lila (Mason), **Supp. VIII:** 133, **143–145**
Spencer, Edward, **Supp. I Part 1:** 357, 360
Spencer, Elizabeth, **Supp. XXVII:** 13
Spencer, Herbert, **I:** 515; **II:** 345, 462–463, 480, 483, 536; **III:** 102, 315; **IV:** 135; **Retro. Supp. II:** 60, 65, 93, 98; **Supp. I Part 1:** 368; **Supp. I Part 2:** 635; **Supp. XXVII:** 126
Spencer, Sharon, **Supp. X:** 185, 186, 195, 196
Spencer, Theodore, **I:** 433; **Supp. III Part 1:** 2
Spender, Natasha, **Supp. IV Part 1:** 119, 127, 134
Spender, Stephen, **II:** 371; **III:** 504, 527; **Retro. Supp. I:** 216; **Retro. Supp. II:** 243, 244; **Supp. I Part 2:** 536; **Supp. II Part 1:** 11; **Supp. IV Part 1:** 82, 134; **Supp. IV Part 2:** 440; **Supp. X:** 116
Spengler, Oswald, **I:** 255, 270; **II:** 7, 577; **III:** 172, 176; **Retro. Supp. II:** 324; **Supp. I Part 2:** 647
Spens, Sir Patrick, **Supp. I Part 2:** 404
Spenser, Edmund, **I:** 62; **III:** 77, 78, 89; **IV:** 155, 453; **Retro. Supp. I:** 62; **Supp. I Part 1:** 98, 152, 369; **Supp. I Part 2:** 422, 719; **Supp. XXIV:** 159
"Spenser's Ireland" (Moore), **III:** 211, 212
"Spermaceti Papers"(Lippard), **Supp. XXIII:** 178
S*PeRM**K*T (Mullen), **Supp. XXVII:** 169, 170–171
Sperry, Margaret, **Supp. IV Part 1:** 169
Spheres of Existence (C. L. R. James), **Supp. XXI:** 172
Sphere: The Form of a Motion (Ammons), **Supp. VII:** 24, 32, 33, 35, 36
"Sphinx" (Hayden), **Supp. II Part 1:** 373
Spice-Box of Earth, The (Cohen), **Supp. XXVII:** 54
"Spiced Plums" (Ríos), **Supp. IV Part 2:** 553
Spickard, Paul, **Supp. XXI:** 149
"Spider and the Ghost of the Fly, The" (Lindsay), **Supp. I Part 2:** 375
Spider Bay (Van Vechten), **Supp. II Part 2:** 746
"Spider Heart, The" (Peacock), **Supp. XIX:** 200
"Spiders" (Schwartz), **Supp. II Part 2:** 665
Spider's House, The (Bowles), **Supp. IV Part 1:** 87–89, 90, 91
Spider Woman's Granddaughters: Traditional Tales and Contemporary Writing by Native American Women (Gunn Allen, ed.), **Supp. IV Part 1:** 320, 326, 332–333; **Supp. IV Part 2:** 567
Spiegel, Sam, **Supp. XVIII:** 251, 252
Spiegelman, Art, **Supp. XVII:** 48
Spiegelman, Willard, **Supp. XI:** 126
Spielberg, Steven, **Supp. XXI:** 154
Spillane, Mickey, **Supp. IV Part 2:** 469, 472; **Supp. XV:** 200; **Supp. XVIII:** 236, 237
"Spillcorn" (Rash), **Supp. XXVII:** 222
Spiller, Robert E., **I:** 241; **Supp. I Part 1:** 104
Spillers, Hortense, **Supp. XX: 109**
"Spillikins: Gregor Mendel at the Table" (Bierds), **Supp. XVII:** 34–35
Spillville (Hampl), **Supp. XXII:** 98
Spillway (Barnes), **Supp. III Part 1:** 44
Spingarn, Amy, **Supp. I Part 1:** 325, 326
Spingarn, Joel, **I:** 266; **Supp. I Part 1:** 325
Spinoza, Baruch, **I:** 493; **II:** 590, 593; **III:** 600; **IV:** 5, 7, 11, 12, 17; **Retro. Supp. II:** 300; **Supp. I Part 1:** 274; **Supp. I Part 2:** 643; **Supp. XVI:** 184
"Spinoza of Market Street, The" (Singer), **IV:** 12–13; **Retro. Supp. II:** 307
"Spinster" (Plath), **Supp. I Part 2:** 536
"Spinster's Tale, A" (Taylor), **Supp. V:** 314–315, 316–317, 319, 323
Spiral of Memory, The: Interviews (Coltelli, ed.), **Supp. XII:** 215
Spires, Elizabeth, **Supp. X:** 8
"Spire Song" (Bowles), **Supp. IV Part 1:** 80
Spirit and Flame: An Anthology of African American Poetry (Gilyard, ed.), **Supp. XXI:** 246
Spirit and the Flesh, The: Sexual Diversity in American Indian Culture (W. L. Williams), **Supp. IV Part 1:** 330
"Spirit Birth" (Cullen), **Supp. IV Part 1:** 168
Spirit Brides (Gibran). See Nymphs in the Valley
Spirit in Man, The (Jung), **Supp. IV Part 1:** 68
"Spirit in Me, The" (Hoffman), **Supp. XVIII:** 87
"Spirit Made Visible" (art exhibit), **Supp. XXII:** 180
Spirit of Culver (West), **IV:** 287
Spirit of Labor, The (Hapgood), **Supp. XVII:** 96, 99, 101–102; **Supp. XXI:** 4
Spirit of Romance, The (Pound), **III:** 470; **Retro. Supp. I:** 286
Spirit of the Ghetto, The: Studies of the Jewish Quarter of New York (Hapgood), **Supp. XVII:** 96, 101, 103, 106
Spirit of Youth and the City Streets, The (Addams), **Supp. I Part 1:** 6–7, 12–13, 16, 17, 19
"Spirits" (Bausch), **Supp. VII:** 46–47
Spirits, and Other Stories (Bausch), **Supp. VII:** 46–47, 54
"Spirit Says, You Are Nothing, The" (Levis), **Supp. XI:** 265–266
Spirits Rebellious (al-Arwá&hudot; al-Mutamarrida) (Gibran), **Supp. XX: 115, 124, 125**
Spiritual Adventures (Symons), **Supp. XX: 239**
Spiritual Conflict, The (Scupoli), **IV:** 156
Spiritual Exercises, The (Loyola), **IV:** 151; **Supp. XI:** 162
"Spiritual Manifestation, A" (Whittier), **Supp. I Part 2:** 699
"Spirituals and Neo-Spirituals"

(Hurston), **Supp. VI:** 152–153
"Spirituals and Non-Spirituals" (Hurston), **Retro. Supp. III:** 129
Spits, Ellen Handler, **Supp. XII:** 166
"Spitzbergen Tales" (Crane), **I:** 409, 415, 423
Spitzer, Philip, **Supp. XIV:** 21
Splay Anthem (Mackey), **Supp. XXVII:** 152, 155–156, 159
"Spleen" (Eliot), **I:** 569, 573–574
Spleen de Paris, Le (Baudelaire), **Supp. XIV:** 337
Splendid Drunken Twenties, The (Van Vechten), **Supp. II Part 2:** 739–744
Splendide-Hôtel (Sorrentino), **Supp. XXI:** 233
Splendid Table, The (radio show), **Supp. XXIII:** 138
Splendor in the Grass (screenplay, Inge), **Supp. XXV:** 93, 95, 102–103, 104
"Splinters" (Bukiet), **Supp. XVII:** 47
"Split at the Root: An Essay on Jewish Identity" (Rich), **Retro. Supp. III:** 241, 251
"Split Infinitive" (Pickering), **Supp. XXI:** 204
"Splitting an Order" (Kooser), **Supp. XIX:** 128–129
"Splittings" (Rich), **Retro. Supp. III:** 249; **Supp. I Part 2:** 570–571
"Splitting Wood at Six Above" (Kumin), **Supp. IV Part 2:** 449
Spofford, Harriet Prescott, **Supp. XIII:** 143
Spoils of Poynton, The (James), **I:** 463; **Retro. Supp. I:** 229–230
Spoken Page, The (Nye), **Supp. XIII:** 274
"Spokes" (Auster), **Supp. XII:** 23
Spokesmen (Whipple), **II:** 456
Spook Sonata, The (Strindberg), **III:** 387, 392
Spooky Art, The: A Book about Writing (Mailer), **Retro. Supp. II:** 214
"Spoon, The" (Simic), **Supp. VIII:** 275
Spoon River Anthology (Masters), **I:** 106; **III:** 579; **Supp. I Part 2:** 454, 455, 456, 460–465, 466, 467, 471, 472, 473, 476; **Supp. IX:** 306; **Supp. XIV:** 282–283; **Supp. XIX:** 121; **Supp. XXII:** 282; **Supp. XXVII:** 211, 290
Sport and a Pastime, A (Salter), **Supp. IX: 254–257; Supp. XVI:** 237
Sporting Club, The (McGuane), **Supp. VIII:** 43
Sport of the Gods, The (Dunbar), **Supp. II Part 1:** 193, 200, 207, 214–217
Sports Illustrated Training with Weights (Parker and Marsh), **Supp. XIX:** 187
"Sportsman Born and Bred, A" (Plimpton), **Supp. XVI:** 241
Sportsman's Sketches, A (Turgenev), **I:** 106; **IV:** 277
Sportswriter, The (Ford), **Supp. V:** 57, 58, 62–67
"Spotted Horses" (Faulkner), **IV:** 260; **Retro. Supp. III:** 85
Sprague, Morteza, **Retro. Supp. II:** 115
Spratling, William, **II:** 56; **Retro. Supp. I:** 80
Sprawl trilogy (W. Gibson), **Supp. XVI:** 117, 122, 124
"Spray, The" (Lethem), **Supp. XVIII:** 148
"Spray Paint King, The" (Dove), **Supp. IV Part 1:** 252–253
Spreading Fires (Knowles), **Supp. XII:** 249
Sprigge, Elizabeth, **IV:** 31
"Spring" (Kooser), **Supp. XIX:** 126
"Spring" (Millay), **III:** 126
"Spring" (Mora), **Supp. XIII:** 217
"Spring 1967" (Carruth), **Supp. XVI:** 55
Spring and All (W. C. Williams), **Retro. Supp. I:** 412, 418, **418–420,** 427, 430, 431
"Spring and All" (W. C. Williams), **Retro. Supp. I:** 419
Spring Awakening (Wedeking, trans. Franzen), **Supp. XX: 85**
"Spring Break-Up" (Carruth), **Supp. XVI:** 56
"Spring Bulletin" (Allen), **Supp. XV:** 15
Springer's Progress (Markson), **Supp. XVII: 141–142,** 143, 146
"Spring Evening" (Farrell), **II:** 45
"Spring Evening" (Kenyon), **Supp. VII:** 173
"Springfield Magical" (Lindsay), **Supp. I Part 2:** 379
Spring in New Hampshire and Other Poems (McKay), **Supp. X:** 131, 135
"Spring in the Naugatuck Valley" (Teasdale), **Supp. XXVII:** 294
"Spring Lizards" (Rash), **Supp. XXVII:** 219
"Spring Notes from Robin Hill" (Carruth), **Supp. XVI:** 48
"Spring Pastoral" (Wylie), **Supp. I Part 2:** 707
"Spring Pools" (Frost), **II:** 155; **Retro. Supp. I:** 137
"Spring Snow" (Matthews), **Supp. IX:** 160
"SPRING SONG" (Baraka), **Supp. II Part 1:** 60
Springsteen, Bruce, **Supp. VIII:** 143
"Spring Strains" (W. C. Williams), **Retro. Supp. I:** 416
Spring Tides (Morison), **Supp. I Part 2:** 494
Springtime and Harvest (Sinclair), **Supp. V:** 280
"Springtime for You" (Halliday), **Supp. XIX:** 87
"Spring Torrents" (Teasdale), **Supp. XXVII:** 293
Spruance, Raymond, **Supp. I Part 2:** 479, 491
"Spruce Has No Taproot, The" (Clampitt), **Supp. IX:** 41–42
"Spunk" (Hurston), **Retro. Supp. III:** 127, 139; **Supp. VI:** 150, 151–152
Spunk: The Selected Stories (Hurston), **Supp. VI:** 150
Spurr, David, **Supp. XV:** 183
Spy, The (Cooper), **I:** 335, 336, 337, 339, 340; **Supp. I Part 1:** 155
"Spy, The" (Francis), **Supp. IX:** 81
Spy, The (Freneau), **Supp. II Part 1:** 260
Spyglass Tree, The (Murray), **Supp. XIX: 155–156**
Spy in the House of Love, A (Nin), **Supp. X:** 186
Squanto, **Supp. I Part 2:** 486
"Square Business" (Baraka), **Supp. II Part 1:** 49
Square Root of Wonderful, The (McCullers), **II:** 587–588
"Squash in Blossom" (Francis), **Supp. IX:** 81
"Squatter on Company Land, The" (Hugo), **Supp. VI:** 133
"Squatter's Children" (Bishop), **Retro. Supp. II:** 47
"Squeak, Memory" (Bukiet), **Supp. XVII:** 47
Squeeze Play (Auster), **Supp. XII:** 21
Squires, Radcliffe, **IV:** 127; **Supp. XV:** 118
Squirrels (Mamet), **Supp. XIV:** 240
S.S. Gliencairn (O'Neill), **III:** 387, 388, 405
S.S. San Pedro (Cozzens), **I:** 360–362, 370, 378, 379
"Ssshh" (Olds), **Supp. X:** 215
"Stacking the Straw" (Clampitt), **Supp. IX:** 41
Stade, George, **Supp. IV Part 1:** 286
Staël, Madame de, **II:** 298

"Staff of Life, The" (H. Miller), **III:** 187
Stafford, Jean, **II:** 537; **Retro. Supp. II:** 177; **Supp. V:** 316
Stafford, William, **Supp. IV Part 1:** 72; **Supp. IV Part 2:** 642; **Supp. IX:** 273; **Supp. XI: 311–332; Supp. XIII:** 76, 274, 276, 277, 281, 283; **Supp. XIV:** 119, 123; **Supp. XX: 161; Supp. XXI:** 246
"Stage All Blood, The" (MacLeish), **III:** 18
"Staggerlee Wonders" (Baldwin), **Retro. Supp. II:** 15
Stained White Radiance, A (Burke), **Supp. XIV:** 28, 31
Stalin, Joseph, **I:** 261, 490; **II:** 39, 40, 49, 564; **III:** 30, 298; **IV:** 372; **Supp. V:** 290; **Supp. XXI:** 164, 165, 167
"Stalking" (J. W. Miller), **Supp. XX: 167**
"Stalking the Billion-Footed Beast: A Literary Manifesto for the New Social Novel" (Wolfe), **Supp. III Part 2:** 586
Stallings, A. E., **Supp. XXIII:** 111, 124; **Supp. XXV: 221–236**
Stallings, H. A., **Supp. XXII:** 194
Stallman, R. W., **I:** 405
Stamberg, Susan, **Supp. IV Part 1:** 201; **Supp. XII:** 193
Stamford, Anne Marie, **Supp. XII:** 162
Stanard, Mrs. Jane, **III:** 410, 413
Stand, The (King), **Supp. V:** 139, 140–141, 144–146, 148, 152
"Standard of Liberty, The" (Rowson), **Supp. XV:** 243
"Standard of Living, The" (Parker), **Supp. IX: 198–199**
Stander, Lionel, **Supp. I Part 1:** 289
"Standing and the Waiting, The" (M. F. K. Fisher), **Supp. XVII:** 83
Standing by Words (Berry), **Supp. X:** 22, 27, 28, 31, 32, 33, 35
Standing Fast (Swados), **Supp. XIX: 268–269**
"Standing Fast: Fox into Hedgehog" (Davison), **Supp. XXVI:** 72
"Standing Halfway Home" (Wagoner), **Supp. IX:** 324
"Standing Humbly Before Nature" (Gerber), **Supp. XXVI:** 187
"Standing In" (Caputo), **Supp. XIX:** 26
Standing Still and Walking in New York (O'Hara), **Supp. XXIII:** 220
Stand in the Mountains, A (Taylor), **Supp. V:** 324
Standish, Burt L. (pseudonym). See Patten, Gilbert
Standish, Miles, **I:** 471; **II:** 502–503
Standley, Fred L., **Retro. Supp. II:** 6
Stand Still Like the Hummingbird (H. Miller), **III:** 184
"Stand Up" (Salinas), **Supp. XIII:** 315
Stand with Me Here (Francis), **Supp. IX:** 76
Stanford, Ann, **Retro. Supp. I:** 41; **Retro. Supp. III:** 1, 9; **Supp. I Part 1:** 99, 100, 102, 103, 106, 108, 109, 113, 117; **Supp. IV Part 2:** 637
Stanford, Charles Villiers, **Supp. XX: 228**
Stanford, Donald E., **II:** 217
Stanford, Frank, **Supp. XV:** 338, 339, 341, 342–343, 343, 345, 348, 350
Stanford, Ginny (Crouch), **Supp. XV:** 339
Stanford, Leland, **I:** 196, 198
Stanislavsky, Konstantin, **Supp. XIV:** 240, 243
Stanley, Jodee, **Supp. XIX:** 52
Stanley, Marion Cummings, **Supp. XXVII:** 288
"Stanley Kunitz" (Oliver), **Supp. VII:** 237
Stansell, Christine, **Supp. XVII:** 106; **Supp. XXI:** 4
Stanton, Frank L., **Supp. II Part 1:** 192
Stanton, Robert J., **Supp. IV Part 2:** 681
"Stanzas, Written in 1815 before going to hear my Father read religious services"(J. Schoolcraft), **Supp. XXIII:** 229
"Stanzas from the Grande Chartreuse" (Arnold), **Supp. I Part 2:** 417
Stanzas in Meditation (Stein), **Supp. III Part 1:** 13
Staples, Hugh, **Retro. Supp. II:** 187
Star, Alexander, **Supp. X:** 310
Starbuck, George, **Retro. Supp. II:** 53, 245; **Supp. I Part 2:** 538; **Supp. IV Part 2:** 440; **Supp. XIII:** 76; **Supp. XXVI:** 68
Star Child (Gunn Allen), **Supp. IV Part 1:** 324
"Star Dust" (Wrigley), **Supp. XVIII:** 296
Stardust Lounge, The (Digges), **Supp. XXIII:** 57
Stardust Memories (film; Allen), **Supp. XV:** 1, 4, **8,** 9, 13
"Stare, The" (Updike), **Retro. Supp. I:** 329
"Starfish, The" (R. Bly), **Supp. IV Part 1:** 72
"Star in a Stoneboat" (Frost), **Retro. Supp. III:** 101
"Staring at the Sea on the Day of the Death of Another" (Swenson), **Supp. IV Part 2:** 652
Star Is Born, A (film), **Supp. IV Part 1:** 198; **Supp. IX:** 198; **Supp. XVIII:** 242, 243
Stark, David, **Supp. XII:** 202
Stark, Heidi, **Supp. XXIII:** 228, 233
"Stark Boughs on the Family Tree" (Oliver), **Supp. VII:** 232
Starke, Aubrey Harrison, **Supp. I Part 1:** 350, 352, 356, 360, 362, 365, 370, 371
Starkey, David, **Supp. XII:** 180, 181
Star Ledger (Hull), **Supp. XXI:** 129, **136–138**
"Star Ledger" (Hull), **Supp. XXI:** 136
"Starlight" (Levine), **Supp. V:** 188
"Starlight Scope Myopia" (Komunyakaa), **Supp. XIII:** 123, 124
Starlight Wonder Book, The (Beston), **Supp. XXVI:** 33
Starna, William A., **Supp. XXVI:** 85, 86
Starnino, Carmine, **Supp. XVII:** 74
"Star of the Nativity" (Brodsky), **Supp. VIII:** 33
Starr, Ellen Gates, **Supp. I Part 1:** 4, 5, 11
Starr, Jean. See Untermeyer, Jean Starr
Starr, Kevin, **Supp. XXIV:** 17, 22
Starr, Ringo, **Supp. XI:** 309
Star Rover, The (London), **II:** 467
"Starry Night, The" (Sexton), **Supp. II Part 2:** 681
"Stars" (Frost), **II:** 153
Stars, the Snow, the Fire, The: Twenty-five Years in the Northern Wilderness (Haines), **Supp. XII: 199–201,** 206, 209
Star Shines over Mt. Morris Park, A (H. Roth), **Supp. IX:** 227, 236, **236–237**
"Stars of the Summer Night" (Longfellow), **II:** 493
"Stars over Harlem" (Hughes), **Retro. Supp. I:** 207
"Star-Spangled" (García), **Supp. XI:** 177, 178
Star-Spangled Girl, The (Simon), **Supp. IV Part 2:** 579
"Star-Splitter, The" (Frost), **Retro. Supp. I:** 123, 133
Stars Principal (McClatchy), **Supp. XII: 256–258**
"Start Again Somewhere" (Gallagher), **Supp. XXIV:** 169
"Star That Would Not Shine, The" (C.

225; **Supp. IV Part 2:** 502; **Supp. IX:** 33, 171; **Supp. V:** 290, 291; **Supp. VIII:** 10; **Supp. XI:** 169; **Supp. XIII:** 1, 17; **Supp. XIV:** 21, 181; **Supp. XIX:** 3; **Supp. XVII:** 228; **Supp. XVIII:** 90, 102, 254
Steinbeck, Olive Hamilton, **IV:** 51
Steinberg, Saul, **Supp. VIII:** 272
Steinberg, Sybil, **Supp. XVII:** 165, 166; **Supp. XXIII:** 241; **Supp. XXVI:** 258
Steinem, Gloria, **Supp. IV Part 1:** 203; **Supp. XXIII:** 104, 105, 106
Steiner, George, **Retro. Supp. I:** 327; **Supp. IV Part 1:** 286; **Supp. XVI:** 230
Steiner, Michael, **Supp. XXII:** 205
Steiner, Nancy, **Supp. I Part 2:** 529
Steiner, Stan, **Supp. IV Part 2:** 505
Steinfels, Margaret, **Supp. XVII:** 170
Steinhoff, Eirik, **Supp. XVI:** 290
Steinman, Michael, **Supp. VIII:** 172
Steinmetz, Charles P., **Supp. XXIII:** 161
Steinmetz, Charles Proteus, **I:** 483
Steinway Quintet Plus Four, The (Epstein), **Supp. XII:** 159, **162–166**
Stekel, Wilhelm, **III:** 554
Stella (Goethe), **Supp. IX:** 133, 138
Stella (Kushner), **Supp. IX:** 133
Stella, Joseph, **I:** 387
"Stellaria" (Francis), **Supp. IX:** 83
Stelligery and Other Essays (Wendell), **Supp. I Part 2:** 414
St. Elmo (Evans), **Supp. XXII:** 120
Sten, Christopher, **Retro. Supp. III:** 153
Stendhal, **I:** 316; **III:** 465, 467; **Supp. I Part 1:** 293; **Supp. I Part 2:** 445
Stepanchev, Stephen, **Supp. XI:** 312
Stephen, Leslie, **IV:** 440
Stephen, Sir Leslie, **IV:** 440; **Supp. I Part 1:** 306
Stephen, Saint, **II:** 539; **IV:** 228
Stephen Crane (Berryman), **I:** 169–170, 405
Stephen King, The Second Decade: "Danse Macabre" to "The Dark Half" (Magistrale), **Supp. V:** 138, 146, 151
Stephen King: The Art of Darkness (Winter), **Supp. V:** 144
Stephens, Jack, **Supp. X:** 11, 14, 15, 17
Stephens, James, **Supp. XIX:** 204
Stephens, Uriah, **Supp. XXIII:** 187
Stephenson, Gregory, **Supp. XII:** 120, 123
Stephenson, Neal, **Supp. XXII:** 49
"Stepping Out" (Dunn), **Supp. XI:** 140, 141
Stepping Outside (Gallagher), **Supp. XXIV:** 165, 167
Steps (Kosinski), **Supp. VII:** 215, 221–222, 225
"Steps" (Nye), **Supp. XIII:** 288
Steps to the Temple (Crashaw), **IV:** 145
"Steps Toward Poverty and Death" (R. Bly), **Supp. IV Part 1:** 60
Stepto, Robert B., **Retro. Supp. II:** 116, 120, 123
Sterile Cuckoo, The (Nichols), **Supp. XIII:** 258, **259–263,** 264
Sterling, Bruce, **Supp. XVI:** 118, 121, 123, 124, 128–129
Sterling, George, **I:** 199, 207, 208, 209; **II:** 440; **Supp. V:** 286; **Supp. XXII:** 276, 277
Sterling, Phillip, **Supp. XXIII:** 102
Stern, Bernhard J., **Supp. XIV:** 202, 213
Stern, Daniel, **Supp. VIII:** 238
Stern, Frederick C., **Supp. X:** 114, 115, 117
Stern, Gerald, **Supp. IX: 285–303; Supp. XI:** 139, 267; **Supp. XV:** 211, 212
Stern, Madeleine B., **Supp. I Part 1:** 35
Stern, Maurice, **IV:** 285
Stern, Philip Van Doren, **Supp. XIII:** 164
Stern, Richard, **Retro. Supp. II:** 291
Stern, Richard G., **Retro. Supp. II:** 204
Stern, Steven, **Supp. XVII:** 42, 48, 49; **Supp. XX: 178**
"Sterne" (Schwartz), **Supp. II Part 2:** 663
Sterne, Laurence, **II:** 302, 304–305, 308; **III:** 454; **IV:** 68, 211, 465; **Supp. I Part 2:** 714; **Supp. IV Part 1:** 299; **Supp. V:** 127; **Supp. X:** 324; **Supp. XV:** 232
Sterritt, David, **Supp. IV Part 2:** 574
Stetson, Caleb, **IV:** 178
Stetson, Charles Walter, **Supp. XI:** 195, 196, 197, 202, 204, 209
Steve Nelson, American Radical (Nelson), **Supp. XVIII:** 226
Stevens, Frances Simpson, **Supp. XXII:** 159, 162
Stevens, Hampton, **Supp. XXVII:** 45
Stevens, James, **Supp. XXIII:** 152
Stevens, Wallace, **I:** 60, 61, 266, 273, 462, 521, 528, 540–541; **II:** 56, 57, 530, 552, 556; **III:** 19, 23, 194, 216, 270–271, 272, 278, 279, 281, 453, 463, 493, 509, 521, 523, 600, 605, 613, 614; **IV: 73–96,** 140, 141, 332, 402, 415; **Retro. Supp. I:** 67, 89, 193, 284, 288, **295–315,** 335, 403, 411, 416, 417, 422; **Retro. Supp. II:** 40, 44, 326; **Retro. Supp. III:** 251; **Supp. I Part 1:** 80, 82, 257; **Supp. II Part 1:** 9, 18; **Supp. III Part 1:** 2, 3, 12, 20, 48, 239, 318, 319, 344; **Supp. III Part 2:** 611; **Supp. IV Part 1:** 72, 393; **Supp. IV Part 2:** 619, 620, 621, 634; **Supp. IX:** 41; **Supp. V:** 337; **Supp. VIII:** 21, 102, 195, 271, 292; **Supp. X:** 58; **Supp. XI:** 123, 191, 312; **Supp. XIII:** 44, 45; **Supp. XIX:** 7, 40, 86, 87; **Supp. XV:** 39, 41, 92, 115, 250, 261, 298, 302, 306, 307; **Supp. XVI:** 64, 158, 202, 210, 288; **Supp. XVII:** 36, 42, 110, 129, 130, 240, 241; **Supp. XXI:** 19, 28, 60, 133; **Supp. XXII:** 162; **Supp. XXIII:** 53, 57, 65; **Supp. XXIV:** 41, 45; **Supp. XXVI:** 67; **Supp. XXVII:** 261
Stevens, Mrs. Wallace (Elsie Kachel), **IV:** 75
"Stevens and the Idea of the Hero" (Bromwich), **Retro. Supp. I:** 305
Stevens and the Interpersonal (Halliday), **Supp. XIX: 85–86**
Stevenson, Adlai, **II:** 49; **III:** 581
Stevenson, Anne, **Supp. XV:** 121; **Supp. XVII:** 74; **Supp. XXVI:** 66
Stevenson, Burton E., **Supp. XIV:** 120
Stevenson, David, **Supp. XI:** 230
Stevenson, David L., **Retro. Supp. III:** 86
Stevenson, Ellen Borden, **Supp. XXV:** 30
Stevenson, Robert Louis, **I:** 2, 53; **II:** 283, 290, 311, 338; **III:** 328; **IV:** 183–184, 186, 187; **Retro. Supp. I:** 224, 228; **Supp. I Part 1:** 49; **Supp. II Part 1:** 404–405; **Supp. IV Part 1:** 298, 314; **Supp. VIII:** 125; **Supp. XIII:** 75; **Supp. XIV:** 40; **Supp. XVII:** 69; **Supp. XXI:** 204
Stevick, Robert D., **III:** 509
Stewart, Dugald, **II:** 8, 9; **Supp. I Part 1:** 151, 159; **Supp. I Part 2:** 422
Stewart, Elinore Pruitt, **Supp. XXVI:** 183
Stewart, George, **Supp. XVIII:** 138
Stewart, Jeffrey C., **Supp. XIV:** 196, 209, 210
Stewart, Randall, **II:** 244; **Supp. XX: 164**
Stewart, Robert E., **Supp. XI:** 216
"St. Francis of Assisi" (Di Piero), **Supp. XIX:** 43

Stickeen (Muir), **Supp. IX:** 182
Sticks and Bones (Rabe), **Supp. XXIV:** 117
"Sticks and Stones" (L. Michaels), **Supp. XVI:** 205
Sticks and Stones (Mumford), **Supp. II Part 2:** 475, 483, 487–488
Sticks & Stones (Matthews), **Supp. IX:** 154, 155, 157, 158
Stieglitz, Alfred, **Retro. Supp. I:** 416; **Retro. Supp. II:** 103; **Supp. VIII:** 98; **Supp. XVII:** 96; **Supp. XX: 74, 75**
"Stigmata" (Oates), **Supp. II Part 2:** 520
Stiles, Ezra, **II:** 108, 122; **IV:** 144, 146, 148; **Supp. XXIV:** 68
Still, James, **Supp. XX: 163; Supp. XXVII:** 217
Still, William Grant, **Retro. Supp. I:** 203
Still Alice (Genova), **Supp. XXIII:** 127
"Stillborn" (Plath), **Supp. I Part 2:** 544
"Still Here" (Hughes), **Retro. Supp. I:** 211
"Still Just Writing" (Tyler), **Supp. IV Part 2:** 658
"Still Life" (Hecht), **Supp. X:** 68
"Still Life" (Malamud), **Supp. I Part 2:** 450
Still Life (Pickering), **Supp. XXI:** 198
"Still Life" (Pickering), **Supp. XXI:** 198
"Still Life" (Sandburg), **III:** 584
"Still Life" (Vaz), **Supp. XXVI:** 261
"Still Life: Moonlight Striking up on a Chess-Board" (A. Lowell), **II:** 528
"Still Life Or" (Creeley), **Supp. IV Part 1:** 141, 150, 158
Still Life with Oysters and Lemon (Doty), **Supp. XI:** 119, 121, **133–134**
Still Life with Woodpecker (Robbins), **Supp. X:** 260, **271–274,** 282
"Still Moment, A" (Welty), **IV:** 265; **Retro. Supp. I:** 347
Stillness (Gardner), **Supp. VI:** 74
"Stillness in the Air" (Dickinson), **Supp. XV:** 261
Stillness of Dancing, The (Bierds), **Supp. XVII: 27–28**
"Still Small Voices, The" (Fante), **Supp. XI:** 164
Still Such (Salter), **Supp. IX:** 246
"Still the Place Where Creation Does Some Work on Itself" (W. V. Davis), **Supp. IV Part 1:** 68
Stimpson, Catharine R., **Supp. IV Part 2:** 686
Stimson, Eleanor Kenyon. See Brooks, Mrs. Van Wyck
"Stimulants, Poultices, Goads" (Wright), **Supp. XV:** 349
"Stings" (Plath), **Retro. Supp. II:** 255; **Supp. I Part 2:** 541
"Stirling Street September" (Baraka), **Supp. II Part 1:** 51
Stirner, Max, **II:** 27
"Stirrup-Cup, The" (Lanier), **Supp. I Part 1:** 364
Stitt, Peter, **Supp. IV Part 1:** 68; **Supp. IV Part 2:** 628; **Supp. IX:** 152, 163, 291, 299; **Supp. XI:** 311, 317; **Supp. XIII:** 87; **Supp. XIX:** 121; **Supp. XV:** 98, 99
Stivers, Valerie, **Supp. X:** 311
St. John, David, **Supp. XV:** 73, 253
St. Louis Woman (Bontemps and Cullen), **Supp. XXII:** 6
St. Mark, Tyler, **Supp. XX: 260**
Stock, Noel, **III:** 479
Stockbroker, the Bitter Young Man, and the Beautiful Girl, The (Hayes), **Supp. XXVI:** 143
Stockton, Frank R., **I:** 201
Stoddard, Charles Warren, **I:** 193, 195, 196; **Supp. II Part 1:** 192, 341, 351
Stoddard, Elizabeth, **II:** 275; **Supp. XV: 269–291**
Stoddard, Richard, **Supp. I Part 1:** 372
Stoddard, Richard Henry, **Supp. XV:** 269, 271, 272, 273, 274, 278, 279, 286
Stoddard, Solomon, **I:** 545, 548; **IV:** 145, 148
Stoffman, Judy, **Supp. XVIII:** 97
Stoic, The (Dreiser), **I:** 497, 502, 508, 516; **Retro. Supp. II:** 95, 96, 101, 108
Stoker, Bram, **Supp. XXVI:** 58
Stokes, Geoffrey, **Supp. XV:** 256
Stokes, Olivia Egleston Phelps, **Supp. XVIII:** 261
"Stolen Calf, The" (Dunbar), **Supp. II Part 1:** 196
Stolen Jew, The (Neugeboren), **Supp. XVI: 222–224,** 225
Stolen Legacy of Anne Frank, The: Meyer Levin, Lillian Hellman, and the Staging of the Diary (Melnick), **Supp. XXVII:** 137–138
Stolen Past, A (Knowles), **Supp. XII:** 249
Stolen Words: Forays into the Origins and Ravages of Plagiarism (Mallon), **Supp. XIX: 134–135**
Stollman, Aryeh Lev, **Supp. XVII:** 49; **Supp. XXIV:** 2, 8, 10–11
Stolmar, Thomas, **Supp. XVIII:** 138
"Stoma" (Barnhardt), **Supp. XXVII:** 12
Stomping the Blues (Murray), **Supp. XIX: 158–159**
"Stone" (Ozick), **Supp. XVII:** 50
Stone, Edward, **III:** 479
Stone, Herbert S., **Supp. XXI:** 2
Stone, I. F., **Supp. XIV:** 3
Stone, Irving, **II:** 463, 466, 467
Stone, Oliver, **Supp. XIV:** 48, 316
Stone, Phil, **II:** 55; **Retro. Supp. III:** 74
Stone, Richard, **Supp. XIV:** 54
Stone, Robert, **Supp. V: 295–312; Supp. X:** 1; **Supp. XIX:** 54
Stone, Rosetta (pseudonym). See Geisel, Theodor Seuss (Dr. Seuss)
Stone, Ruth, **Supp. XXVII: 249–265**
Stone, Wilmer, **Supp. I Part 1:** 49
Stone and the Shell, The (Hay), **Supp. XIV:** 122, 123, 127, 130
"Stone Bear, The" (Haines), **Supp. XII:** 206–207, 212
"Stone City" (Proulx), **Supp. VII:** 251–253
Stone Country (Sanders), **Supp. XVI:** 271–272
Stone Diaries, The (Shields), **Supp. VII:** 307, 315, 324–326, 327
"Stone Dreams" (Kingsolver), **Supp. VII:** 203
Stone Harp, The (Haines), **Supp. XII: 204,** 205, 206, 207
Stonemason, The (McCarthy), **Supp. VIII:** 175, 187
"Stones" (Hoffman), **Supp. XVIII:** 86
"Stones" (Kumin), **Supp. IV Part 2:** 447
Stones (lithograph series, O'Hara and Rivers), **Supp. XXIII:** 217
"Stones, The" (Plath), **Supp. I Part 2:** 535, 539
"Stones in My Passway, Hellhounds on My Trail" (Boyle), **Supp. VIII:** 15
Stones of Florence, The (McCarthy), **II:** 562
"Stonewall Jackson" (Melville), **Retro. Supp. III:** 161
"Stone Walls" (Sarton), **Supp. VIII:** 259
"Stop" (Wilbur), **Supp. III Part 2:** 556
Stop-Loss (screenplay, Richard), **Supp. XIX:** 222
"Stop Me If You've Heard This One" (Lardner), **II:** 433
Stopover: Tokyo (Marquand), **III:** 53, 57, 61, 70

Stoppard, Tom, **Retro. Supp. I:** 189
Stopping by Home (Huddle), **Supp. XXVI:** 149
"Stopping by Woods on a Snowy Evening" (Frost), **II:** 154; **Retro. Supp. I:** 129, 133, 134, 135, 139; **Retro. Supp. III:** 95, 102
"Stopping the Bullies" (Myers and Carillo), **Supp. XXVII:** 204
Stopping Westward (Richards), **II:** 396
"Stop Player. Joke No. 4" (Gaddis), **Supp. IV Part 1:** 280
Stop-Time (Conroy), **Supp. XVI: 63–71,** 72, 75, 76–77
"Store, The" (E. P. Jones), **Supp. XXII:** 144–145
Store, The (Stribling), **Supp. VIII:** 126; **Supp. XXII:** 195
"Store and Mockingbird: Two Pulitzer Novels about Alabama" (Going), **Supp. VIII:** 126
Store of a Million Items, The (Cliff), **Supp. XXII:** 67, 74, 75
"Store of a Million Items, The" (Cliff), **Supp. XXII:** 75
Storer, Edward, **Supp. I Part 1:** 261, 262
Stories, Fables and Other Diversions (Nemerov), **III:** 268–269, 285
Stories: Elizabeth Stoddard, **Supp. XV:** 270
"Stories for Sale" (Kolba), **Supp. XVIII:** 257
Stories for the Sixties (Yates, ed.), **Supp. XI:** 343
Stories from Our Living Past (Prose), **Supp. XVI:** 251
Stories from the Italian Poets (Hunt), **Supp. XV:** 175
Stories from the Old Testament Retold (L. P. Smith), **Supp. XIV:** 342
Stories from World Literature, **Supp. IX:** 4
"Stories in the Snow" (Leopold), **Supp. XIV:** 183
Stories into Film (Kittredge and Krauzer), **Supp. XXVI:** 182
Stories of an Imaginary Childhood (Bukiet), **Supp. XVII: 41–44,** 45
Stories of F. Scott Fitzgerald, The (Cowley, ed.), **Retro. Supp. I:** 115
Stories of F. Scott Fitzgerald, The (Fitzgerald), **II:** 94
Stories of Modern America, **Supp. IX:** 4
Stories of Stephen Dixon, The (Dixon), **Supp. XII:** 152
Stories of the American Experience (Kriegel and Lass, eds.), **Supp. XXIV:** 214
Stories of the Spanish Civil War (Hemingway), **II:** 258
Stories Revived (James), **II:** 322
Stories that Could Be True (Stafford), **Supp. XI: 325–327**
Stories Toto Told Me (Rolfe), **Supp. XX: 235**
Storm, The (Buechner), **Supp. XII: 54–57**
"Storm, The" (Chopin), **Retro. Supp. II:** 60, 68; **Supp. I Part 1:** 218, 224
Storm, The (al-'Awásif) (Gibran), **Supp. XX: 116, 124, 125**
"Storm Fear" (Frost), **II:** 153; **Retro. Supp. I:** 127
"Storm Ship, The" (Irving), **II:** 309
"Storm Warning" (Rich), **Retro. Supp. III:** 242
"Storm Warnings" (Kingsolver), **Supp. VII:** 207–208
"Stormy Weather" (Ellison), **Supp. II Part 1:** 233
"Story" (Everwine), **Supp. XV:** 89
"Story, A" (Jarrell), **II:** 371
Story, Julian, **Supp. XX: 232**
Story, Richard David, **Supp. IV Part 2:** 575, 588
Story, William Wetmore, **Supp. XX: 228**
"Story about Chicken Soup, A" (Simpson), **Supp. IX: 272–273**
"Story about the Anteater, The" (Benét), **Supp. XI:** 53
"Story About the Body, A" (Hass), **Supp. VI: 107–108**
Story Behind the Story, The (Turchi and Barrett, eds.), **Supp. XXVII:** 1, 12
"Story for Teddy, A" (Swados), **Supp. XIX:** 266–267
Story for Teddy, A—and Others (Swados), **Supp. XIX: 266–268**
"Story Hearer, The" (Paley), **Supp. VI:** 230, 231
"Story Hour" (Hay), **Supp. XIV:** 124
"Story Hour" (Jarman), **Supp. XVII:** 116
Story Hour: A Second Look at Cinderella, Bluebeard, and Company (Hay), **Supp. XIV:** 119, 124, 125, 132, 133
Story of a Country Town, The (Howe), **I:** 106
Story of a Lover, The (Hapgood), **Supp. XVII:** 99, 100, 104; **Supp. XXI:** 3, 5, 7
"Story of America, The: A Tribalography" (Howe), **Supp. XXVI:** 84
Story of a Million Years, The (Huddle), **Supp. XXVI:** 147, 152, 157–158
Story of an American Family, The: Letters of the Hapgood Family, 1648–1917 (Boyce), **Supp. XVII:** 97; **Supp. XXI:** 9, 14
"Story of an Hour, The" (Chopin), **Retro. Supp. II:** 72; **Supp. I Part 1:** 212–213, 216
Story of a Novel, The (Wolfe), **IV:** 456, 458
"Story of a Proverb, The" (Lanier), **Supp. I Part 1:** 365
"Story of a Proverb, The: A Fairy Tale for Grown People" (Lanier), **Supp. I Part 1:** 365
Story of a Story and Other Stories, The: A Novel (Dixon), **Supp. XII:** 155
Story of a Wonder Man, The (Lardner), **II:** 433–434
"Story of a Year, The" (James), **Retro. Supp. I:** 218
Story of George Washington Carver, The (Bontemps), **Supp. XXII:** 13
Story of G.I. Joe, The (film, Wellman), **Supp. XVII:** 61, 62
"Story of Gus, The" (A. Miller), **III:** 147–148
"Story of How a Wall Stands, A" (Ortiz), **Supp. IV Part 2:** 499, 507
Story of Mist, The (Dybek), **Supp. XXIII: 74–75,** 78
"Story of Mist, The"(Dybek), **Supp. XXIII:** 74–75
Story of Mount Desert Island, Maine, The (Morison), **Supp. I Part 2:** 494
Story of My Boyhood and Youth, The (Muir), **Supp. IX: 172–174,** 176
Story of My Father, The: A Memoir (Miller), **Supp. XII:** 301
Story of O, The (Réage), **Supp. XII:** 9, 10
Story of Our Lives, The (Strand), **Supp. IV Part 2:** 620, 628–629, 629
"Story of Poppy Van Buster, The" (Briggs), **Supp. XVIII:** 8
"Story of the Bad Little Boy That Bore a Charmed Life, The" (Twain), **Retro. Supp. III:** 263
"Story of the Good Little Boy Who Did Not Prosper, The" (Twain), **Retro. Supp. III:** 263
Story of the Negro (Bontemps), **Supp. XXII:** 6, 12–13
Story of the Normans, The, Told Chiefly in Relation to Their Conquest of England (Jewett), **II:** 406
Story of the Telegraph, The (Briggs, and Maverick), **Supp. XVIII:** 4
"Story of Toby, The" (Melville), **III:** 76

"Story of To-day, A" (Davis). See also Margret Howth
"Story of To-day, A" (R. H. Davis), **Supp. XVI:** 88, 89
Story of Utopias, The (Mumford), **Supp. II Part 2:** 475, 483–486, 495
Story of Wine in California, The (M. F. K. Fisher), **Supp. XVII:** 88
Story on Page One, The (Odets), **Supp. II Part 2:** 546
Storyteller (Silko), **Supp. IV Part 2:** 558, 559, 560, 561, **566–570**
"Storyteller" (Silko), **Supp. IV Part 2:** 569
"Storyteller: Grandmother Spider's Web" (Danielson), **Supp. IV Part 2:** 569
"Storyteller's Notebook, A" (Carver), **Supp. III Part 1:** 142–143
Story Teller's Story, A: The Tale of an American Writer's Journey through His Own Imaginative World and through the World of Facts . . . (Anderson), **I:** 98, 101, 114, 117
"Story That Could Be True, A" (Stafford), **Supp. XI:** 326
Stothard, Peter, **Supp. XXV:** 221
"Stout Gentleman, The" (Irving), **II:** 309
Stover at Yale (Johnson), **III:** 321
Stowe, Calvin, **IV:** 445; **Supp. I Part 2:** 587, 588, 590, 596, 597
Stowe, Charles, **Supp. I Part 2:** 581, 582
Stowe, Eliza, **Supp. I Part 2:** 587
Stowe, Harriet Beecher, **II:** 274, 399, 403, 541; **Retro. Supp. I:** 34, 246; **Retro. Supp. II:** 4, 138, 156; **Supp. I Part 1:** 30, 206, 301; **Supp. I Part 2: 579–601; Supp. III Part 1:** 154, 168, 171; **Supp. IX:** 33; **Supp. X:** 223, 246, 249, 250; **Supp. XI:** 193; **Supp. XIII:** 141, 295; **Supp. XV:** 278; **Supp. XVI:** 82, 85
Stowe, Samuel Charles, **Supp. I Part 2:** 587
Stowe, William, **Supp. IV Part 1:** 129
Strachey, Lytton, **I:** 5; **IV:** 436; **Retro. Supp. I:** 59; **Supp. I Part 2:** 485, 494; **Supp. XIV:** 342; **Supp. XVI:** 191
"Stradivari" (Bierds), **Supp. XVII:** 28
Straight Cut (Bell), **Supp. X:** 5, **6–7,** 10
Straight Man (Russo), **Supp. XII: 335–339,** 340
Straits: Poems (Koch), **Supp. XV:** 184
Strand, Mark, **Supp. IV Part 2: 619–636; Supp. IX:** 155; **Supp. V:** 92, 332, 337, 338, 343; **Supp. XI:** 139, 145; **Supp. XII:** 254; **Supp. XIII:** 76; **Supp. XV:** 74; **Supp. XXIV:** 165
Strand, Paul, **Supp. VIII:** 272
Strandberg, Victor, **Supp. V:** 273
Strange, Sharan, **Supp. XXI:** 246
"Strange Beautiful Woman, A" (Nelson), **Supp. XVIII:** 173
Strange Bedfellows (Woods), **Supp. XXI:** 70
Strange Case of Dr. Jekyll and Mr. Hyde, The (Stevenson), **II:** 290
Strange Children, The (Gordon), **II:** 196, 197, 199, 211–213
Strange Commonplace, A (Sorrentino), **Supp. XXI:** 232, 237, 238
Strange Crime in Bermuda, The (Holding), **Supp. XXII: 124–125,** 127**,** 129
Strange Fire (Bukiet), **Supp. XVII: 46**
"Strange Fruit" (Harjo), **Supp. XII:** 224, 225
"Strange Fruit" (song), **Supp. I Part 1:** 80; **Supp. XVIII:** 228
Strange Interlude (O'Neill), **III:** 391, 397–398; **IV:** 61; **Supp. XXII:** 24
Stranger, The (Camus), **I:** 53, 292; **Supp. VIII:** 11; **Supp. XV:** 352
"Stranger, The" (Rich), **Supp. I Part 2:** 555, 560
"Stranger, The" (Salinger), **III:** 552–553
Strange Relation (Hadas), **Supp. XXIII:** 111, 113, 120**, 127**
"Stranger in My Own Life, A: Alienation in American Indian Poetry and Prose" (Gunn Allen), **Supp. IV Part 1:** 322
Stranger in the Kingdom, A (Mosher), **Supp. XXII:** 204, 205, 206, 207, 208, 209, **212–213**
"Stranger in the Village" (Baldwin), **Retro. Supp. II:** 3; **Supp. I Part 1:** 54; **Supp. IV Part 1:** 10
"Stranger in Town" (Hughes), **Supp. I Part 1:** 334
Stranger Music (Cohen), **Supp. XXVII:** 54
"Strangers" (Howe), **Supp. VI:** 120
Strangers: A Book of Poems (Ferry), **Supp. XXIV: 149–150**
Strangers and Wayfarers (Jewett), **Retro. Supp. II:** 138
"Strangers from the Horizon" (Merwin), **Supp. III Part 1:** 356
"Stranger's Gift, The" (Very), **Supp. XXV:** 242
Strangers on a Train (Highsmith), **Supp. IV Part 1:** 132
Strangers on a Train (screenplay, Hecht), **Supp. XXVII:** 93
"Strange Story, A" (Taylor), **Supp. V:** 323
"Strange Story, A" (Wylie), **Supp. I Part 2:** 723
Strange Things (Atwood), **Supp. XIII:** 35
Strange Victory (Teasdale), **Supp. XXVII:** 284, 296–297
"Strato in Plaster" (Merrill), **Supp. III Part 1:** 328
Stratton-Porter, Gene, **Supp. XX: 211–225**
Straub, Peter, **Supp. XXV:** 145
Straus, Ralph, **Supp. XIII:** 168
Straus, Roger, **Supp. VIII:** 82; **Supp. XV:** 59
Strauss, Harold, **Supp. XV:** 137
Strauss, Helen, **Supp. XXIII:** 258
Strauss, Johann, **I:** 66
Strauss, Richard, **IV:** 316
Strauss, Robert, **Supp. XI:** 141, 142
Stravinsky (De Schloezer), **III:** 474
Stravinsky, Igor, **Retro. Supp. I:** 378; **Supp. IV Part 1:** 81; **Supp. XI:** 133; **Supp. XV:** 265
"Stravinsky's Three Pieces 'Grotesques,' for String Quartet" (A. Lowell), **II:** 523
Straw, The (O'Neill), **III:** 390
"Strawberry Milkshake" (Halliday), **Supp. XIX:** 92, 94
"Stray Document, A" (Pound), **II:** 517
"Strays" (Richard), **Supp. XIX:** 210–211, 220
Streaks of the Tulip, The: Selected Criticism (W. J. Smith), **Supp. XIII:** 333, 334, 344, **347–348**
Streamline Your Mind (Mursell), **Supp. I Part 2:** 608
Strecker, Trey, **Supp. XXI:** 238
"Street, Cloud" (Ríos), **Supp. IV Part 2:** 549
Street, The (Petry), **Supp. XVIII:** 286
Streetcar Named Desire, A (T. Williams), **IV:** 382, 383, 385, 386, 387, 389–390, 395, 398; **Supp. IV Part 1:** 359
Street in Bronzeville, A (Brooks), **Retro. Supp. I:** 208; **Supp. III Part 1:** 74–78
"Street Moths" (X. J. Kennedy), **Supp. XV:** 170
"Street Musicians" (Ashbery), **Supp. III Part 1:** 18
"Street of Crocodiles" (Hull), **Supp. XXI:** 130
"Street off Sunset, A" (Jarrell), **II:** 387
Street of Seven Stars, The (Rinehart), **Supp. XXV:** 193

"Streets" (Dixon), **Supp. XII: 145–146**
Streets in Their Own Ink (Dybek), **Supp. XXIII:** 78
Streets in the Moon (MacLeish), **III:** 5, 8–11, 15, 19
Streets of Laredo (McMurtry), **Supp. V:** 230
"Streets of Laredo" (screenplay) (McMurtry and Ossana), **Supp. V:** 226, 230
Streets of Night (Dos Passos), **I:** 478, 479–480, 481, 488
Streitfield, David, **Supp. XIII:** 234; **Supp. XVI:** 63
Strength of Fields, The (Dickey), **Supp. IV Part 1:** 178
"Strength of Fields, The" (Dickey), **Supp. IV Part 1:** 176, 184–185
"Strength of Gideon, The" (Dunbar), **Supp. II Part 1:** 212
Strength of Gideon and Other Stories, The (Dunbar), **Supp. II Part 1:** 211, 212
"Strenuous Artistry" (Zagarell), **Supp. XV:** 281
Strether, Lambert, **II:** 313
"Stretto" (Davison), **Supp. XXVI:** 77
Stribling, T. S., **Supp. VIII:** 126
Strickland, Barbara, **Supp. XIX:** 102
Strickland, Joe (pseudonym). See Arnold, George W.
"Strictly Bucolic" (Simic), **Supp. VIII:** 278
Strictly Business (O. Henry), **Supp. II Part 1:** 410
"Strike, The" (Olsen), **Supp. XIII:** 292, 297
Strike at Shane's, The (Skloot), **Supp. XX: 216**
"Strikers" (Untermeyer), **Supp. XV:** 296
Strindberg, August, **I:** 78; **III:** 145, 165, 387, 390, 391, 392, 393; **IV:** 17; **Supp. XVII:** 100; **Supp. XXII:** 23
"String, The" (Dickey), **Supp. IV Part 1:** 179
String Light (Wright), **Supp. XV: 345–346**
"String Quartet, The" (Weigl), **Supp. XIX:** 278
"Strivings of the Negro People" (Du Bois), **Supp. II Part 1:** 167
Stroby, W. C., **Supp. XIV:** 26
Strohbach, Hermann, **Supp. XI:** 242
"Stroke of Good Fortune, A" (O'Connor), **III:** 344; **Retro. Supp. II:** 229, 232
Strom, Stephen, **Supp. XII:** 223
Strong, Anna Louise, **Supp. XVIII:** 238; **Supp. XXIII:** 166
Strong, George Templeton, **IV:** 321
Strong, Josiah, **Supp. XIV:** 64
"Strong Draughts of Their Refreshing Minds" (Dickinson), **Retro. Supp. I:** 46
Stronghold, The (Levin), **Supp. XXVII:** 143, 145–146
Strong Motion (Franzen), **Supp. XX: 85, 88–89, 92, 95**
Strong Opinions (Nabokov), **Retro. Supp. I:** 263, 266, 270, 276
"Strong Room of the House, The" (Bronk), **Supp. XXI:** 32
"Strong Women" (Dorman), **Supp. XI:** 240
Strout, Elizabeth, **Supp. X:** 86; **Supp. XXIII: 273–287**
Structure of Nations and Empires, The (Niebuhr), **III:** 292, 308
"Structure of Rime, The" (Duncan), **Supp. XVI:** 287
Structuring the Void (Klinkowitz), **Supp. XXI:** 233
Struggle, The (film; Griffith), **Supp. XVI:** 191
"Strumpet Song" (Plath), **Retro. Supp. II:** 246; **Supp. I Part 2:** 536
Strunk, William, **Supp. I Part 2:** 652, 662, 670, 671, 672
Strunsky, Anna, **II:** 465
"Strut for Roethke, A" (Berryman), **I:** 188
Strychacz, Thomas F., **Supp. XVI:** 69–70
Stuart, Dabney, **Supp. XVIII:** 79
Stuart, Gilbert, **I:** 16
Stuart, J. E. B., **III:** 56
Stuart, Jesse, **Supp. XX: 162–163, 165**
Stuart, Michael, **Supp. XV:** 140
Stuart Little (White), **Supp. I Part 2:** 655–658
"Stubborn Kisses" (Gallagher), **Supp. XXIV:** 170
Stuckey, W. J., **Supp. XXII:** 191–192
"Student, The" (Moore), **III:** 212, 215
"Student of Clouds" (Collins), **Supp. XXI:** 60
"Student of Salmanaca, The" (Irving), **II:** 309
"Student's Wife, The" (Carver), **Supp. III Part 1:** 141
Studies in American Indian Literature: Critical Essays and Course Designs (Gunn Allen), **Supp. IV Part 1:** 324, 333
Studies in Classic American Literature (Lawrence), **II:** 102; **III:** 33; **IV:** 333; **Retro. Supp. I:** 421
Studies in Short Fiction (Edmonds), **Supp. XXIII:** 291
Studies in Short Fiction (Malin), **Supp. XVI:** 71
Studies in the Psychology of Sex (Ellis), **Supp. XX: 235**
"Studs" (Farrell), **II:** 25, 28, 31
Studs Lonigan: A Trilogy (Farrell), **II:** 25, 26, 27, 31–34, 37, 38, 41–42
"Study in Orange and White" (Collins), **Supp. XXI:** 60
"Study of Images" (Stevens), **IV:** 79
"Study of Lanier's Poems, A" (Kent), **Supp. I Part 1:** 373
Study of Milton's Prosody (Bridges), **II:** 537
"Study of the Negro Problems, The" (Du Bois), **Supp. II Part 1:** 165
Stuewe, Paul, **Supp. IV Part 1:** 68
Stuhlmann, Gunther, **Supp. X:** 182, 184, 185, 187
Stull, William L., **Supp. XXIV:** 177
Stultifera Navis (Brant), **III:** 447
"Stumps" (Davison), **Supp. XXVI:** 72
Sturak, John Thomas, **Supp. XIII:** 162, 163, 165, 168
Sturgeon, Theodore, **Supp. XVIII:** 145
Sturgis, George, **III:** 600
Sturgis, Howard, **IV:** 319; **Retro. Supp. I:** 367, 373
Sturgis, Howard Overing, **Supp. XX: 227–242**
Sturgis, Julian Russell, **Supp. XX: 228, 233, 238**
Sturgis, Susan, **III:** 600
Sturm, Margaret. See Millar, Margaret
Stuttaford, Genevieve, **Supp. IX:** 279
Stuyvesant, Peter, **II:** 301
"Style" (Nemerov), **III:** 275
Styles of Radical Will (Sontag), **Supp. III Part 2:** 451, 459, 460–463
"Stylist, The" (Egan), **Supp. XIX:** 51, 52
Styne, Jule, **Supp. XVI:** 193
Styron, William, **III:** 40; **IV:** 4, **97–119**, 216; **Supp. IX:** 208; **Supp. V:** 201; **Supp. X:** 15–16, 250; **Supp. XI:** 229, 231, 343; **Supp. XIV:** 82; **Supp. XVI:** 235–236; **Supp. XXIII:** 107, 109
Suares, J. C., **Supp. IV Part 1:** 234
Suarez, Ernest, **Supp. IV Part 1:** 175; **Supp. V:** 180
Suarez, Ray, **Supp. XXI:** 243
"Sub, The" (Dixon), **Supp. XII:** 146
Subjection of Women, The (Mill), **Supp. XI:** 196, 203
"Subjective Necessity for Social Settlements" (Addams), **Supp. I Part 1:** 4
"Subject of Childhood, A" (Paley),

Supp. VI: 221; **Supp. XXI:** 118
"Submarginalia" (Howe), **Supp. IV Part 2:** 422
Substance and Shadow (James), **II:** 344
"Subterranean Homesick Blues" (song, Dylan), **Supp. XVIII:** 25
Subterraneans, The (Kerouac), **Supp. III Part 1:** 225, 227–231
"Subtitle" (Kees), **Supp. XV:** 139
Subtreasury of American Humor, A (White and White), **Supp. I Part 2:** 668
"Suburban Culture, Imaginative Wonder: The Fiction of Frederick Barthelme" (Brinkmeyer), **Supp. XI:** 38
Suburban Sketches (Howells), **II:** 274, 277
"Subversive Element, The" (Ryan as Quin), **Supp. XVIII:** 230
"Subverted Flower, The" (Frost), **Retro. Supp. I:** 139
"Subway, The" (Tate), **IV:** 128
"Subway Singer, The" (Clampitt), **Supp. IX:** 45
"Success" (Mora), **Supp. XIII:** 217
Successful Love and Other Stories (Schwartz), **Supp. II Part 2:** 661, 665
Successful Women (Taves), **Supp. XXV:** 198
Succession, The: A Novel of Elizabeth and James (Garrett), **Supp. VII:** 104–107, 108
"Success is counted sweetest" (Dickinson), **Retro. Supp. I:** 30, 31–32, 38; **Supp. XV:** 126
Success Stories (Banks), **Supp. V:** 14–15
"Success Story" (Banks), **Supp. V:** 15
"Such Counsels You Gave to Me" (Jeffers), **Supp. II Part 2:** 433
Such Silence (Milburn), **Supp. XI:** 242
"Such Things Happen Only in Books" (Wilder), **IV:** 365
Such Was the Season (Major), **Supp. XXII: 177–178,** 179, 182
"Sudden Journey" (Gallagher), **Supp. XXIV:** 169
Suddenly, Last Summer (film) (Vidal), **Supp. IV Part 2:** 683
Suddenly Last Summer (T. Williams), **I:** 73; **IV:** 382, 383, 385, 386, 387, 389, 390, 391, 392, 395–396, 397, 398
Suder (Everett), **Supp. XVIII: 54–55**
Sudermann, Hermann, **I:** 66
Sue, Eugène, **Supp. XXIII:** 182
Sugg, Richard P., **Supp. IV Part 1:** 68
"Suggestion from a Friend" (Kenyon), **Supp. VII:** 171
"Suicide" (Barnes), **Supp. III Part 1:** 33
"Suicide off Egg Rock" (Plath), **Supp. I Part 2:** 529, 538
Suicides and Jazzers (Carruth), **Supp. XVI:** 46
"Suicide's Note" (Hughes), **Retro. Supp. I:** 199
"Suitable Surroundings, The" (Bierce), **I:** 203
"Suitcase, The" (Ozick), **Supp. V:** 262, 264
"Suite for Augustus, A" (Dove), **Supp. IV Part 1:** 245
"Suite for Emily" (Hull), **Supp. XXI:** 139–140
"Suite for Lord Timothy Dexter" (Rukeyser), **Supp. VI:** 283, 285
"Suite from the Firebird" (Stravinsky), **Supp. XI:** 133
"Suitor, The" (Kenyon), **Supp. VII:** 164–165
Sukarno, **IV:** 490
Sukenick, Ronald, **Supp. V:** 39, 44, 46; **Supp. XII:** 139
Sula (Morrison), **Retro. Supp. III:** 184, 187–189; **Supp. III Part 1:** 362, 364, 367, 368, 379; **Supp. VIII:** 219
Sullivan, Andrew, **Supp. IX:** 135
Sullivan, Arthur, **Supp. XX: 228**
Sullivan, Frank, **Supp. IX:** 201
Sullivan, Harry Stack, **I:** 59
Sullivan, Jack, **Supp. X:** 86; **Supp. XII:** 331
Sullivan, Noel, **Retro. Supp. I:** 202; **Supp. I Part 1:** 329, 333
Sullivan, Patrick, **Supp. XXVI:** 158
Sullivan, Richard, **Supp. VIII:** 124
Sullivan, Walter, **Supp. VIII:** 168
"Sullivan County Sketches" (Crane), **I:** 407, 421
"Sumach and Goldenrod: An American Idyll" (Mumford), **Supp. II Part 2:** 475
Suma Genji (Play), **III:** 466
Sumerian Vistas (Ammons), **Supp. VII:** 34, 35
"Summa Lyrica" (Grossman), **Supp. XIX:** 86
"Summer" (Emerson), **II:** 10
Summer (Gioia), **Supp. XV:** 117
"Summer" (R. Lowell), **II:** 554
Summer (Wharton), **IV:** 317; **Retro. Supp. I:** 360, 367, 374, **378–379,** 382; **Retro. Supp. III:** 286–287; **Supp. XXIII:** 275, 281
Summer, Bob, **Supp. X:** 1, 5, 6, 42
Summer and Smoke (T. Williams), **IV:** 382, 384, 385, 386, 387, 395, 397, 398; **Supp. IV Part 1:** 84
Summer Anniversaries, The (Justice), **Supp. VII:** 115, 117
Summer Blue (Skloot), **Supp. XX: 196, 207–208**
Summer Brave (Inge), **Supp. XXV:** 99
"Summer Commentary, A" (Winters), **Supp. II Part 2:** 808
"Summer Day" (O'Hara), **III:** 369
"Summer Days, The" (Oliver), **Supp. VII:** 239
"Summer Evening" (Boyle), **Supp. XXIV:** 61
"Summer Lake" (Huddle), **Supp. XXVI:** 150
Summer Lake: New and Selected Poems (Huddle), **Supp. XXVI:** 150
"Summer Love Overheated" (Díaz), **Supp. XXIV:** 89
"Summer Matures" (H. Johnson), **Supp. XXVI:** 174
Summer Never Ends (W. Frank), **Supp. XX: 78**
"Summer Night" (Hughes), **Supp. I Part 1:** 325
"Summer Night, A" (Auden), **Supp. II Part 1:** 8
"Summer Night—Broadway" (Untermeyer), **Supp. XV:** 296
"Summer Noon: 1941" (Winters), **Supp. II Part 2:** 811
"Summer of '82" (Merwin), **Supp. III Part 1:** 355–356
Summer on the Lakes in 1843 (Fuller), **Supp. II Part 1:** 279, 295–296
"Summer People" (Hemingway), **II:** 258–259
"Summer People, The" (Jackson), **Supp. IX:** 120
"Summer People, The" (Merrill), **Supp. III Part 1:** 325–326
"Summer Perdu" (Halliday), **Supp. XIX:** 89
"Summer Planning" (Halliday), **Supp. XIX:** 92
"Summer Ramble, A" (Bryant), **Supp. I Part 1:** 162, 164
Summers, Claude J., **Supp. IV Part 2:** 680–681; **Supp. XIV:** 161, 169
Summers, Robert, **Supp. IX:** 289
"Summer School" (Davison), **Supp. XXVI:** 69
"Summer Solstice, New York City" (Olds), **Supp. X:** 207
"Summer's Reading, A" (Malamud), **Supp. I Part 2:** 430–431, 442
"Summer Storm" (Gioia), **Supp. XV:** 127

"Summer Storm" (Simpson), **Supp. IX:** 268
"'Summertime and the Living . . .' " (Hayden), **Supp. II Part 1:** 363, 366
Summertime Island (Caldwell), **I:** 307–308
"Summer Tragedy" (Bontemps), **Supp. XXII:** 9
"Summer: West Side" (Updike), **Retro. Supp. I:** 320
"Summer with Tu Fu, A" (Carruth), **Supp. XVI:** 55, 58
"Summit Beach, 1921" (Dove), **Supp. IV Part 1:** 249
Summoning of Stones, A (Hecht), **Supp. X:** 57, 58, **58–59**
"Summons" (Gansworth), **Supp. XXVI:** 114
"Summons" (Untermeyer), **Supp. XV:** 296
Summons to Memphis, A (Taylor), **Supp. V:** 313, 314, 327
Summons to the Free, A (Benét), **Supp. XI:** 47
Sumner, Charles, **I:** 3, 15; **Supp. I Part 2:** 685, 687
Sumner, John, **Retro. Supp. II:** 95
Sumner, John B., **I:** 511
Sumner, William Graham, **III:** 102, 108; **Supp. I Part 2:** 640
"Sumptuous Destination" (Wilbur), **Supp. III Part 2:** 553
"Sun" (Moore), **III:** 215
"Sun" (Swenson), **Supp. IV Part 2:** 640
"Sun, Sea, and Sand" (Marquand), **III:** 60
Sun Also Rises, The (Hemingway), **I:** 107; **II:** 68, 90, 249, 251–252, 260, 600; **III:** 36; **IV:** 35, 297; **Retro. Supp. I:** 171, **177–180,** 181, 189; **Supp. I Part 2:** 614; **Supp. XIII:** 263; **Supp. XVIII:** 74; **Supp. XXVII:** 87
"Sun and Moon" (Kenyon), **Supp. VII:** 168
"Sun and the Still-born Stars, The" (Southern), **Supp. XI:** 295
Sun at Midnight (Soseki; Merwin and Shigematsu, trans.), **Supp. III Part 1:** 353
"Sun Crosses Heaven from West to East Bringing Samson Back to the Womb, The" (R. Bly), **Supp. IV Part 1:** 73
Sun Dance Land (Hanson), **Supp. XXV:** 280
Sun Dance Opera, The (Zitkala-Ša and Hanson), **Supp. XXV:** 279–280
"Sun Dance Shield" (Momaday), **Supp. IV Part 2:** 491
Sunday, Billy, **II:** 449
"Sunday Afternoon" (Munro), **Supp. XXVII:** 194
"Sunday Afternoons" (Komunyakaa), **Supp. XIII:** 127
Sunday after the War (H. Miller), **III:** 184
"Sunday at Home" (Hawthorne), **II:** 231–232; **Retro. Supp. III:** 113
"Sunday Evening at Middlefork Creek Pentecostal Church" (Rash), **Supp. XXVII:** 219
"Sunday Following Mother's Day. The" (E. P. Jones), **Supp. XXII:** 145
"Sunday Morning" (Stevens), **II:** 552; **III:** 278, 463, 509; **IV:** 92–93; **Retro. Supp. I:** 296, 300, 301, 304, 307, 313; **Supp. XIX:** 40; **Supp. XV:** 120; **Supp. XVI:** 210; **Supp. XVII:** 42; **Supp. XXI:** 28, 133; **Supp. XXIII:** 57
"Sunday Morning Apples" (Crane), **I:** 387
"Sunday Morning Prophecy" (Hughes), **Supp. I Part 1:** 334
"Sunday Morning with the Sensational Nightingales" (Collins), **Supp. XXI:** 60
"Sundays" (B. Kelly), **Supp. XVII:** 124–125
"Sundays" (Salter), **Supp. IX:** 257
"Sundays, They Sleep Late" (Rukeyser), **Supp. VI:** 278
"Sundays of Satin-Legs Smith, The" (Brooks), **Supp. III Part 1:** 74, 75
"Sundays Visiting" (Ríos), **Supp. IV Part 2:** 541
Sundial, The (Jackson), **Supp. IX: 126–127**
Sundog (Harrison), **Supp. VIII: 46–48**
Sun Dogs (R. O. Butler), **Supp. XII: 64–65**
Sun Do Move, The (Hughes), **Supp. I Part 1:** 339
Sundquist, Eric, **Supp. XIV:** 66, 71
"Sunfish" (C. Frost), **Supp. XV:** 100–101, 102
"Sunflower Sutra" (Ginsberg), **Supp. II Part 1:** 317, 321; **Supp. XV:** 215
Sung Sex (Elmslie), **Supp. XXVII:** 20
Sunlight Dialogues, The (Gardner), **Supp. VI:** 63, **68,** 69, 70
"Sunlight Is Imagination" (Wilbur), **Supp. III Part 2:** 549
"Sunny Ridge, The" (Halliday), **Supp. XIX:** 92
Sun Out: Selected Poems, 1952–1954 (Koch), **Supp. XV:** 179
"Sunrise" (Lanier), **Supp. I Part 1:** 370
"Sunrise and the Bomb" (Halliday), **Supp. XIX:** 84, 85, 92
Sunrise over Fallujah (Myers), **Supp. XXVII:** 207
"Sunrise runs for Both, The" (Dickinson), **Retro. Supp. I:** 45
Sunrise with Seamonsters: Travels and Discoveries, 1964–1984 (Theroux), **Supp. VIII:** 311, 313, 323, 325
"Sun Rising" (Donne), **Supp. VIII:** 164
"Sunset" (Ransom), **III:** 484
"Sunset from Omaha Hotel Window" (Sandburg), **III:** 584
Sunset Gun (Parker), **Supp. IX:** 192
Sunset Limited (Burke), **Supp. XIV:** 32, 33
Sunset Limited (Harrison), **Supp. VIII:** 51
"Sunset Maker, The" (Justice), **Supp. VII:** 123
Sunset Maker, The: Poems, Stories, a Memoir (Justice), **Supp. VII:** 116, 118, 119, 123–124
Sunshine Boys, The (film), **Supp. IV Part 2:** 589
Sunshine Boys, The (Simon), **Supp. IV Part 2:** 575, 584–585
"Sunthin' in the Pastoral Line" (J. R. Lowell), **Supp. I Part 2:** 415–416
Sun to Sun (Hurston), **Supp. VI:** 154
Sun Tracks (Ortiz), **Supp. IV Part 2:** 499, 500
Sun Under Wood (Hass), **Supp. VI:** 103, 108–109
"Superb Lily, The" (Pinsky), **Supp. VI:** 250
"Super Goat Man" (Lethem), **Supp. XVIII:** 148
"Superman Comes to the Supermarket" (Mailer), **Retro. Supp. II:** 204
"Supermarket in California, A" (Ginsberg), **Retro. Supp. III:** 54; **Supp. XI:** 135
"Supernatural Horror in Literature" (Lovecraft), **Supp. XXV:** 120
"Supernatural Love" (Schnackenberg), **Supp. XV:** 257, 259–260
Supernatural Love: Poems 1976–1992 (Schnackenberg), **Supp. XV:** 253, 256, 260, 263
Suplee, Curt, **Supp. XVI:** 202
"Supper After the Last, The" (Kinnell), **Supp. III Part 1:** 239
"Supposedly Fun Thing I'll Never Do Again, A" (Wallace), **Supp. X:** 315
Supposedly Fun Thing I'll Never Do Again, A: Essays and Arguments

(Wallace), **Supp. X: 314–316**
Suppressed Desires (Glaspell and Cook), **Supp. III Part 1:** 178; **Supp. XXI:** 6
Suppression of the African Slave Trade to the United States of America, 1638–1870 (Du Bois), **Supp. II Part 1:** 157, 162
Supreme Fiction, The (Stevens), **Supp. XVI:** 158
"Supremes, The" (Jarman), **Supp. XVII:** 115
Sure Hand of God, The (Caldwell), **I:** 297, 302
Sure Signs: New and Selected Poems (Kooser), **Supp. XIX:** 116, 117, **121–122**
"Surety and Fidelity Claims" (Stevens), **Retro. Supp. I:** 296, 309
Surface of Earth, The (Price), **Supp. VI:** 261–262
"Surfaces" (Ammons), **Supp. VII:** 36
Surfaces and Masks (Major), **Supp. XXII:** 180
Surfacing (Atwood), **Supp. XIII:** 20, 21, **22–23,** 24, 33, 35
"Surgeon at 2 A.M." (Plath), **Supp. I Part 2:** 545
Surmmer Knowledge (Schwartz), **Supp. II Part 2:** 662, 665
"Surprise" (Kenyon), **Supp. VII:** 173
Surprised by Sin: The Reader in Paradise Lost (Fish), **Supp. XIV:** 15
Surreal South (eds. P. Benedict and L. Benedict), **Supp. XXIII:** 35
"Surround, The Imagining Herself as the Environment,/She Speaks to James Wright at Sundow" (Dickey), **Supp. IV Part 1:** 185
"Surrounded by Weasels" (Gray and Gallagher), **Supp. XXIV:** 178
"Survey of Literature" (Ransom), **III:** 480
"Survey of the Literature, A" (Saunders), **Supp. XIX:** 235
"Surveyor, The" (H. Roth), **Supp. IX:** 233, 234
Survival (Atwood), **Supp. XIII:** 20, 22, 35
"Survival, Infantry" (Oppen), **Supp. XXVI:** 232
"Survival as Tao, Beginning at 5:00 A.M." (Carruth), **Supp. XVI:** 56
Survival of the Bark Canoe, The (McPhee), **Supp. III Part 1:** 301, 302, 308, 313
Survival This Way: Interviews with American Indian Poets (Bruchac), **Supp. IV Part 2:** 506
"Surviving Love" (Berryman), **I:** 173
Survivor (O. Butler), **Supp. XIII:** 62, 63
Susan and Anna Warner (Foster), **Supp. XVIII:** 265
Susan and God (film; Cukor), **Supp. XVI:** 192
Susanna Moodie: Voice and Vision (Shields), **Supp. VII:** 313
Susan Warner ("Elizabeth Wetherell") (A. Warner), **Supp. XVIII:** 259, 260
Suspect in Poetry, The (Dickey), **Supp. IV Part 1:** 177
"Sustained by Fiction" (Hoffman), **Supp. X:** 90, 92
"Susto" (Ríos), **Supp. IV Part 2:** 553
Sutherland, Donald, **IV:** 38, 44; **Supp. IX:** 254
Sutherland, Efua, **Supp. IV Part 1:** 9, 16
Sutherland, Zena, **Supp. XXVII:** 202
Sutherland-Smith, James, **Supp. X:** 211, 212
Sut Lovingood (Harris), **II:** 70; **Supp. XXII:** 193
Sutton, Roger, **Supp. X:** 266; **Supp. XXVII:** 212
Sutton, Walter, **III:** 479
"Sutton Pie Safe, The"(P. Benedict), **Supp. XXIII:** 36
Suttree (McCarthy), **Supp. VIII: 178–180,** 189
Suvero, Mark di, **Supp. IX:** 251
"Suzanne" (Cohen), **Supp. XXVII:** 51, 54, 59
Svevo, Italo, **Supp. XIV:** 112
Swados, Harvey, **Supp. XI:** 222; **Supp. XIX: 255–271**
Swales, Martin, **Supp. XIX:** 183
Swallow, Alan, **Supp. X:** 112, 115, 116, 120, 123
Swallow Barn (J. P. Kennedy), **II:** 313
Swallow Barn (Kennedy), **Supp. XXII:** 193
Swallow the Lake (Major), **Supp. XXII:** 174
"Swamp Boy" (Bass), **Supp. XVI:** 20
Swan, Barbara, **Supp. IV Part 2:** 447
Swan, Jon, **Supp. IV Part 1:** 176
Swan Lake (Helprin), **Supp. XXV:** 83, 87
Swan Lake (Tchaikovsky), **Supp. IX:** 51
Swan Lake Trilogy (Helprin), **Supp. XXV:** 81, 84, 87
"Swan Legs" (Stern), **Supp. IX:** 299
Swann (Shields), **Supp. VII:** 315, 318–323, 326
Swann, Brian, **Supp. IV Part 2:** 500
Swanson, Gloria, **II:** 429
Swanson, Stevenson, **Supp. XIV:** 111
Swan Song (Hecht and MacArthur), **Supp. XXVII:** 90
Swanton, John Reed, **Supp. VIII:** 295
Swan Watch (Schulberg), **Supp. XVIII:** 254
Swanwick, John, **Supp. XV:** 237
Swanwick, Michael, **Supp. XVI:** 128
"Swarm, The" (Plath), **Retro. Supp. II:** 255
"Sway" (Simpson), **Supp. IX:** 276
Sweat (Hurston), **Supp. VI:** 152
"Sweat" (Hurston), **Retro. Supp. III:** 139
Swedenborg, Emanuel, **II:** 5, 10, 321, 342, 343–344, 396
Sweeney Agonistes (T. S. Eliot), **I:** 580; **Retro. Supp. I:** 64, 65; **Retro. Supp. II:** 247; **Retro. Supp. III:** 58, 69
"Sweeney Among the Nightingales" (Eliot), **III:** 4
"Sweeper, The" (Kooser), **Supp. XIX:** 125
Sweet, Blanche, **Supp. I Part 2:** 391
Sweet, Timothy, **Supp. IV Part 1:** 330
Sweet and Lowdown (film; Allen), **Supp. XV:** 11
Sweet and Sour (O'Hara), **III:** 361
"Sweet Armageddon" (Hoffman), **Supp. XVIII:** 85, 86
Sweet Bird of Youth (T. Williams), **IV:** 382, 383, 385, 386, 387, 388, 389, 390, 391, 392, 395, 396, 398; **Supp. IV Part 1:** 84, 89
Sweet Charity (musical), **Supp. IV Part 2:** 575
Sweet Flypaper of Life, The (Hughes), **Supp. I Part 1:** 335–336
"Sweetgrass"(Kenny), **Supp. XXIII:** 148
"Sweetheart" (Notley), **Supp. XXII:** 231
"Sweetheart of the Song Tra Bong, The" (O'Brien), **Supp. V:** 243, 249
"Sweethearts" (Ford), **Supp. V:** 69
Sweet Hereafter, The (Banks), **Supp. V:** 15–16
Sweet Illusions (Myers), **Supp. XXVII:** 208–209
Sweet Lorain (Weigl), **Supp. XIX:** 282
Sweet Machine (Doty), **Supp. XI:** 121, **131–132,** 135
Sweet Science, The (Liebling), **Supp. XXVII:** 46–47
Sweet Sue (Gurney), **Supp. V:** 105, 107–108
Sweet Sweetback's Baadasss Song (Peebles; film), **Supp. XI:** 17
Sweet Thursday (Steinbeck), **IV:** 50, 52, 64–65

Sweet Will (Levine), **Supp. V:** 178, 187, 189, 190
"Sweet Will" (Levine), **Supp. V:** 190
"Sweet Willy"(J. Schoolcraft), **Supp. XXIII:** 226, 231
"Sweet Words on Race" (Hughes), **Retro. Supp. I:** 211
Sweezy, Paul, **Supp. I Part 2:** 645
"Swell-Looking Girl, A" (Caldwell), **I:** 310
Swenson, May, **Retro. Supp. II:** 44; **Supp. IV Part 2: 637–655; Supp. XIX:** 123; **Supp. XXVI:** 66, 67
Swetman, Glenn R., **Supp. XXI:** 91
"Swift" (Schwartz), **Supp. II Part 2:** 663
Swift, Jonathan, **I:** 125, 194, 209, 441; **II:** 110, 302, 304–305, 577; **III:** 113; **IV:** 68; **Retro. Supp. I:** 66; **Retro. Supp. III:** 109, 139; **Supp. I Part 2:** 406, 523, 603, 656, 665, 708, 714; **Supp. IV Part 1:** 51; **Supp. IV Part 2:** 692; **Supp. XI:** 105, 209; **Supp. XII:** 276; **Supp. XV:** 258; **Supp. XVI:** 110; **Supp. XVIII:** 2, 12; **Supp. XXV:** 87
"Swimmer" (Francis), **Supp. IX:** 82
"Swimmer" (Skloot), **Supp. XX: 199, 200**
"Swimmer, The" (Cheever), **Supp. I Part 1:** 185, 187
"Swimmer, The" (Glück), **Supp. V:** 82
"Swimmers" (Untermeyer), **Supp. XV:** 300
"Swimmers, The" (Fitzgerald), **Retro. Supp. I:** 110, 111
"Swimmers, The" (Tate), **IV:** 136
"Swimming" (Harjo), **Supp. XII:** 218
Swimming Pool, The (Rinehart), **Supp. XXV:** 189, 198, 200, 202
"Swimming Pool, The"(Strout), **Supp. XXIII:** 284
"Swim Team, The" (July), **Supp. XXIV:** 201
Swinburne, Algernon C., **I:** 50, 384, 568; **II:** 3, 4, 129, 400, 524; **IV:** 135; **Retro. Supp. I:** 100; **Retro. Supp. III:** 44, 60, 74; **Supp. I Part 1:** 79; **Supp. I Part 2:** 422, 552; **Supp. XIV:** 120, 344
"Swinburne as Poet" (Eliot), **I:** 576
Swinger of Birches, A: A Portrait of Robert Frost (Cox), **Retro. Supp. I:** 132
"Swinging an Arc Before Him As He Goes" (Espaillat), **Supp. XXI:** 108
"Swinging on a Birch-Tree" (Larcom), **Supp. XIII:** 147
Swiss, Tom, **Supp. XIX:** 40
Switch, The (Dixon), **Supp. XII:** 141
Swope, D. B., **Supp. IX:** 95
Sword Blades and Poppy Seed (A. Lowell), **II:** 518, 520, 522, 532
Sword of God, The: Jeanne D'Arc (Endore), **Supp. XVII:** 55
Sybil (Auchincloss), **Supp. IV Part 1:** 25
Sybil and Chryssa (S. and A. Warner), **Supp. XVIII:** 264
"Sycamore" (Frost), **Retro. Supp. III:** 104
"Sycamore" (Stern), **Supp. IX:** 294
"Sycamore, The" (Moore), **III:** 216
"Sycamores, The" (Whittier), **Supp. I Part 2:** 699
Sylvester, Johnny, **Supp. I Part 2:** 438
Sylvester, Joshua, **I:** 178, 179; **II:** 18; **III:** 157; **Supp. I Part 1:** 98, 104, 114, 116
Sylvia (Gurney), **Supp. V:** 105
"Sylvia" (L. Michaels), **Supp. XVI:** 202, 213
"Sylvia" (Larcom), **Supp. XIII:** 144
"Sylvia" (Stern), **Supp. IX:** 297
Sylvia: A Fictional Memoir (L. Michaels), **Supp. XVI:** 202, 213
Sylvia Plath: Method and Madness (Butscher), **Supp. I Part 2:** 526
Sylvia Plath: Poetry and Existence (Holbrook), **Supp. I Part 2:** 526–527
"Sylvia's Death" (Sexton), **Supp. II Part 2:** 671, 684, 685
"Symbol and Image in the Shorter Poems of Herman Melville" (Dickey), **Supp. IV Part 1:** 176
Symbolist Movement in Literature, The (Symons), **I:** 50, 569; **Retro. Supp. I:** 55; **Retro. Supp. III:** 57
Symonds, John Addington, **I:** 241, 242, 251, 259; **IV:** 334; **Supp. XIV:** 329, 335; **Supp. XX: 230**
Symons, Arthur, **I:** 50, 569; **Retro. Supp. I:** 55; **Retro. Supp. III:** 57; **Supp. XX: 239; Supp. XXVII:** 287
Symons, Julian, **Supp. IV Part 1:** 343, 351
"Sympathy" (Dunbar), **Supp. IV Part 1:** 15
Sympathy of Souls, A (Goldbarth), **Supp. XII:** 175, 176, **186–187**
"Symphony, The" (Lanier), **Supp. I Part 1:** 352, 360–361, 364; **Supp. I Part 2:** 416
Symposium (Plato), **Retro. Supp. II:** 31; **Supp. IV Part 1:** 391
Symposium: To Kill a Mockingbird (Alabama Law Review), **Supp. VIII:** 127, 128
Symptoms and Madness (Major), **Supp. XXII:** 174
Symptoms of Being 35 (Lardner), **II:** 434
Synanon (Endore), **Supp. XVII:** 65
Synanon (film, Quine), **Supp. XVII:** 65
Synanon City (Endore), **Supp. XVII:** 65
Syncopated Cakewalk, The (Major), **Supp. XXII:** 174
Synge, John Millington, **I:** 434; **III:** 591–592; **Supp. III Part 1:** 34; **Supp. VIII:** 155
Synthetic Philosophy (Spencer), **II:** 462–463
"Syringa" (Ashbery), **Supp. III Part 1:** 19–21, 25
"Syrinx" (Clampitt), **Supp. IX:** 53
"Syrinx" (Merrill), **Supp. III Part 1:** 328
Syrkin, Marie, **Supp. XIV:** 279, 288, 291; **Supp. XXVII:** 133–134
"System, The" (Ashbery), **Supp. III Part 1:** 14, 15, 18, 21–22
System of Dante's Hell, The (Baraka), **Supp. II Part 1:** 39–41, 55
"System of Dante's Inferno, The" (Baraka), **Supp. II Part 1:** 40
"System of Doctor Tarr and Professor Fether, The" (Poe), **III:** 419, 425
System of General Geography, A (Brown), **Supp. I Part 1:** 146
Szaylay, Michael, **Supp. XXI:** 267
Sze, Mai-mai, **Supp. X:** 291
Szentgyorgyi, Tom, **Supp. IX:** 135, 136, 140, 141–142
Szilagyi, Anca, **Supp. XXVI:** 218
Szukalski, Stanislaus, **Supp. XXV:** 19, 23
Szulc, Tad, **Supp. XVI:** 154
Szumskyj, Benjamin, **Supp. XXVII:** 128
Szwarc, Marek, **Supp. XXVII:** 140
Szymborka, Wislawa, **Supp. XI:** 267
Szymborska, Wislawa, **Supp. XVIII:** 29
"T-2 Tanker Blues" (Snyder), **Supp. VIII:** 294
Tabios, Eileen, **Supp. XV:** 214, 225, 226
"Table of Delectable Contents, The" (Simic), **Supp. VIII:** 276
Tabloid Dreams (R. O. Butler), **Supp. XII: 70–72,** 74
Tacey Cromwell (Richter), **Supp. XVIII: 211,** 215, 217
Tacitus, Cornelius, **I:** 485; **II:** 113
Tadic, Novica, **Supp. VIII:** 272
Taft (Patchett), **Supp. XII:** 307, 312, **314–317**

"Tag" (Hughes), **Supp. I Part 1:** 341
Taggard, Genevieve, **IV:** 436; **Supp. XXII: 271–287; Supp. XXVI:** 144
Taggart, John, **Supp. IV Part 2:** 421
Tagore, Rabindranath, **I:** 383; **Supp. XX: 117**
"Taibele and Her Demon" (Singer), **Retro. Supp. II:** 307
Taibl, Erika, **Supp. XV:** 255
"Tailor Shop, The" (H. Miller), **III:** 175
"Tails" (Dixon), **Supp. XII:** 154
Taine, Hippolyte, **I:** 503; **II:** 271; **III:** 323; **IV:** 440, 444
"Tain't So" (Hughes), **Supp. I Part 1:** 330
"Taipei Tangle" (Halliday), **Supp. XIX:** 91
Takasago (play), **III:** 466
Takazauckas, Albert, **Supp. XXIII:** 203
Take Away the Darkness (Bynner), **Supp. XV:** 51
Take Heart (Peacock), **Supp. XIX: 197–199,** 206
Take Me Back: A Novel (Bausch), **Supp. VII:** 41, 43–45, 46, 49
"Take My Saddle from the Wall: A Valediction" (McMurtry), **Supp. V:** 219
"'Take No for an Answer' " (Didion), **Supp. IV Part 1:** 203
"Take Pity" (Malamud), **Supp. I Part 2:** 427, 428, 435, 436, 437
"Takers, The" (Olds), **Supp. X:** 205
"Take the I Out" (Olds), **Supp. X:** 213
Take the Money and Run (film; Allen), **Supp. XV: 3–4,** 6
"Taking a Stitch in a Dead Man's Arm" (Vaz), **Supp. XXVI:** 264
"Taking Away the Name of a Nephew" (Ríos), **Supp. IV Part 2:** 545–546
Taking Care of Mrs. Carroll (Monette), **Supp. X:** 153
Taking Care: Thoughts on Storytelling and Belief (Kittredge), **Supp. XXVI:** 181, 182, 183, 185
"Taking of Captain Ball, The" (Jewett), **Retro. Supp. II:** 134
"Taking Off Emily Dickinson's Clothes" (Collins), **Supp. XXI:** 59, 60
"Taking Out the Lawn Chairs" (Karr), **Supp. XI:** 241
"Taking the Bypass" (J. Epstein), **Supp. XIV:** 110; **Supp. XVI:** 230
"Taking the Forest" (Howe), **Supp. IV Part 2:** 433
"Taking the Lambs to Market" (Kumin), **Supp. IV Part 2:** 455
Talbot, Daniel, **Supp. XIX:** 264
"Tale, A" (Bogan), **Supp. III Part 1:** 50, 51
Taleb-Khyar, Mohamed, **Supp. IV Part 1:** 242, 243, 244, 247, 257
Talented Mr. Ripley, The (Highsmith), **Supp. XXII:** 119
"Tale of Jerusalem, A" (Poe), **III:** 411
Tale of Possessors Self-Dispossessed, A (O'Neill), **III:** 404
Tale of the Body Thief, The (Rice), **Supp. VII:** 290, 293–294, 297
"Tale of the White Pyramid, The" (Cather), **Retro. Supp. III:** 25
Tale of Two Cities, A (film), **Supp. I Part 1:** 67
"Tale of Two Liars, A" (Singer), **IV:** 12
Tales (Baraka), **Supp. II Part 1:** 39, 55
Tales (Poe), **III:** 413; **Retro. Supp. III:** 225
Tales and Stories for Black Folks (Bambara, ed.), **Supp. XI:** 1
Tales before Midnight (Benét), **Supp. XI:** 46, 53, 57
Talese, Gay, **Supp. XVI:** 273; **Supp. XVII: 199–211; Supp. XXIV:** 282
Tales of a Traveller (Irving), **II:** 309–310
Tales of a Wayside Inn (Longfellow), **II:** 489, 490, 501, 502, 504–505; **Retro. Supp. II:** 154, **162–165**
Tales of Glauber-Spa (Bryant, ed.), **Supp. I Part 1:** 157
Tales of H. P. Lovecraft (Oates, ed.), **Supp. XXV:** 123
Tales of Manhattan (Auchincloss), **Supp. IV Part 1:** 23
Tales of Men and Ghosts (Wharton), **IV:** 315; **Retro. Supp. I:** 372
Tales of My People (Asch), **Supp. XXIII:** 7
Tales of Rhoda, The (Rice), **Supp. VII:** 288
Tales of Soldiers and Civilians (Bierce), **I:** 200–203, 204, 206, 208, 212
Tales of the Argonauts (Harte), **Supp. II Part 1:** 337, 348, 351
Tales of the Fish Patrol (London), **II:** 465
Tales of the Grotesque and Arabesque (Poe), **II:** 273; **III:** 412, 415; **Retro. Supp. II:** 270; **Retro. Supp. III:** 225, 228
Tales of the Jazz Age (Fitzgerald), **II:** 88; **Retro. Supp. I:** 105; **Supp. IX:** 57
Tales You Won't Believe (Stratton-Porter), **Supp. XX: 217**
Taliaferro, Frances, **Supp. XXII:** 210
"Talisman, A" (Moore), **III:** 195–196
Talisman, The (King), **Supp. V:** 140, 144, 152
"Talkin Bout Sonny" (Bambara), **Supp. XI:** 6–7
"Talking" (Merwin), **Supp. III Part 1:** 354
Talking All Morning (R. Bly), **Supp. IV Part 1:** 59, 60, 61, 62, 64, 65
Talking Dirty to the Gods (Komunyakaa), **Supp. XIII: 130–131**
Talking History (television program), **Supp. XXI:** 172
"Talking Horse" (Malamud), **Supp. I Part 2:** 435
Talking Soft Dutch (McCarriston), **Supp. XIV: 260–263,** 266, 270, 271
"Talking to Barr Creek" (Wagoner), **Supp. IX:** 328
"Talking to Sheep" (Sexton), **Supp. II Part 2:** 695
Talking to the Sun: An Illustrated Anthology of Poems for Young People (Koch and Farrell, eds.), **Supp. XV:** 188
"Talking Water" (Taggard), **Supp. XXII:** 276
"Talk of Heroes" (C. Bly), **Supp. XVI:** 34
"Talk of the Town" (The New Yorker column), **IV:** 215; **Supp. IV Part 1:** 53, 54
"Talk on Guadalcanal" (Wolfert), **Supp. XXI:** 264
Talk Talk (Boyle), **Supp. XX: 24**
"Talk with the Yellow Kid, A" (Bellow), **I:** 151
Tallent, Elizabeth, **Supp. IV Part 2:** 570
Tallman, Warren, **Supp. IV Part 1:** 154
TallMountain, Mary, **Supp. IV Part 1:** 324–325
Talma, Louise, **IV:** 357
Talmadge, Constance, **Supp. XVI:** 186, 187, 196
Talmadge, Norma, **Supp. XVI:** 186, 187, 196
Talmadge Girls, The (Loos), **Supp. XVI:** 186, 196
Talmey, Allene, **Supp. IV Part 1:** 197; **Supp. XIII:** 172
Talmud, **IV:** 8, 17
Taltos: Lives of the Mayfair Witches (Rice), **Supp. VII:** 299–300
"Tamar" (Jeffers), **Supp. II Part 2:** 427–428, 436

Tamar and Other Poems (Jeffers), **Supp. II Part 2:** 416, 419
"Tambourine Life" (Berrigan), **Supp. XXIV:** 42
Tambourines to Glory (Hughes), **Supp. I Part 1:** 338–339
"Tame Indians" (Jewett), **Retro. Supp. II:** 141
"Tamerlane" (Poe), **III:** 426
Tamerlane and Other Poems (Poe), **III:** 410; **Retro. Supp. III:** 224, 231
"Tammany Man, The" (Hapgood), **Supp. XVII:** 103
"Tam O'Shanter" (Burns), **II:** 306
Tamsen Donner: A Woman's Journey (Whitman), **Supp. XXI:** 246
Tan, Amy, **Supp. X: 289–300**
Tangential Views (Bierce), **I:** 209
"Tangier 1975" (Bowles), **Supp. IV Part 1:** 94
Tanguay, Pablo, **Supp. XXIII:** 299
"Tankas" (McClatchy), **Supp. XII:** 266
Tanner, Laura E., **Supp. X:** 209; **Supp. XXI:** 217
Tanner, Obour, **Supp. XX: 281, 288**
Tanner, Tony, **I:** 260, 261; **Retro. Supp. II:** 205; **Supp. IV Part 1:** 285; **Supp. XVI:** 65, 69
Tannhäuser (Wagner), **I:** 315
"Tan Ta Ra, Cries Mars...," (Wagoner), **Supp. IX:** 325
Tao of Physics, The (Capra), **Supp. X:** 261
Tao Teh Ching (Bynner, trans.), **Supp. XV:** 46, 47
Tapahonso, Luci, **Supp. IV Part 1:** 404; **Supp. IV Part 2:** 499, 508
Tape for the Turn of the Year (Ammons), **Supp. VII:** 31–33, 35
"Tapestry" (Ashbery), **Supp. III Part 1:** 22–23
"Tapestry" (E. P. Jones), **Supp. XXII:** 152
Tapestry Room Murder, The (Wells), **Supp. XXVI:** 282
"Tapiama" (Bowles), **Supp. IV Part 1:** 89–90
"Tapiola" (W. C. Williams), **Retro. Supp. I:** 429
Tappan, Arthur, **Supp. I Part 2:** 588
Tapping the White Cane of Solitude (F. Wright), **Supp. XVII:** 243
Taps at Reveille (Fitzgerald), **II:** 94, 96; **Retro. Supp. I:** 113
Taradash, Daniel, **Supp. XXV:** 95
Tar: A Midwest Childhood (Anderson), **I:** 98, 115; **II:** 27
Tarantino, Quentin, **Supp. IV Part 1:** 356
Tarantula (Dylan), **Supp. XVIII:** 21, 29, **31–32**
Tar Baby (Morrison), **Retro. Supp. III:** 190–191; **Supp. III Part 1:** 364, 369–372, 379; **Supp. IV Part 1:** 13
Tarbell, Ida, **III:** 322, 580; **Retro. Supp. II:** 101
"Target Practice" (Offutt), **Supp. XIX:** 171
"Target Study" (Baraka), **Supp. II Part 1:** 49–50, 54
Tarkington, Booth, **II:** 444; **III:** 70; **Retro. Supp. I:** 100; **Supp. XV:** 41
Tarnawsky, Yuriy (George) Orest, **Supp. XX: 259**
Tarpon (film), **Supp. VIII:** 42
Tarr, Rodger L., **Supp. X:** 222, 224, 226
Tárrega, Francisco, **Supp. XXI:** 100
Tartt, Donna, **Supp. XVIII:** 135; **Supp. XXVII:** 67, **267–281**
Tartuffe (Molière; Wilbur, trans.), **Supp. III Part 2:** 560
Tarumba, Selected Poems of Jaime Sabines (Levine and Trejo, trans.), **Supp. V:** 178
Tarzan Finds a Son (film, Weismuller), **Supp. XX: 18**
"Tarzan Is an Expatriate" (Theroux), **Supp. VIII:** 313
Tasis, Juan de, **Supp. XXI:** 104
Task, The (Cowper), **II:** 304
Tasker Street (Halliday), **Supp. XIX:** 82, **87–89**
Tasso, Torquato, **I:** 276
Taste of Palestine, A: Menus and Memories (Shihab), **Supp. XIII:** 273
Tate, Alan, **Supp. XV:** 141
Tate, Allen, **I:** 48, 49, 50, 67, 69, 381, 382, 386, 390, 396, 397, 399, 402, 441, 468; **II:** 197–198, 367, 536, 537, 542, 551, 554; **III:** 424, 428, 454, 482, 483, 485, 493, 495, 496, 497, 499, 500, 517; **IV: 120–143,** 236, 237, 433; **Retro. Supp. I:** 37, 41, 90; **Retro. Supp. II:** 77, 79, 82, 83, 89, 176, 178, 179; **Retro. Supp. III:** 48, 49, 50; **Supp. I Part 1:** 364, 371; **Supp. I Part 2:** 423; **Supp. II Part 1:** 90–91, 96, 98, 103–104, 136, 139, 144, 150, 151, 318; **Supp. II Part 2:** 643; **Supp. III Part 2:** 542; **Supp. V:** 315, 331; **Supp. X:** 1, 52; **Supp. XIV:** 2; **Supp. XXI:** 256; **Supp. XXII:** 277
Tate, Mrs. Allen (Caroline Gordon). See Gordon, Caroline
Tate, Mrs. Allen (Helen Heinz), **IV:** 127
Tate, Mrs. Allen (Isabella Gardner), **IV:** 127
Tate, Benjamin Lewis Bogan, **IV:** 127
Tate, Greg, **Supp. XIII:** 233, 237
Tate, James, **Supp. V:** 92, 338; **Supp. VIII:** 39, 279; **Supp. XV:** 250; **Supp. XVII:** 242
Tate, John Allen, **IV:** 127
Tate, Michael Paul, **IV:** 127
Tate, Nancy, **II:** 197
Tatonetti, Lisa, **Supp. XXIII:** 149–150
Tattooed Countess, The (Van Vechten), **I:** 295; **Supp. II Part 2:** 726–728, 738, 742
Tattooed Feet (Nye), **Supp. XIII:** 274
"Tattoos" (McClatchy), **Supp. XII:** 266–267, 268
"Tattoos" (Wright), **Supp. V:** 335, 340
Tatum, Anna, **I:** 516
Tatum, James, **Supp. IV Part 2:** 684
Taubman, Howard, **Supp. XXV:** 106
Taupin, René, **II:** 528, 529; **Supp. III Part 2:** 614, 615, 617, 621
Tavano, John, **Supp. XXI:** 99
Taves, Isabella, **Supp. XXV:** 198
Tawney, Richard Henry, **Supp. I Part 2:** 481
Taylor, Ann, **Supp. XXIII:** 231
Taylor, Bayard, **II:** 275; **Supp. I Part 1:** 350, 361, 362, 365, 366, 372; **Supp. XV:** 269
Taylor, Chuck, **Supp. XXIII:** 57
Taylor, Cora. See Howarth, Cora
Taylor, Deems, **III:** 138
Taylor, Edward, **III:** 493; **IV: 144–166; Retro. Supp. III:** 3; **Supp. I Part 1:** 98; **Supp. I Part 2:** 375, 386, 546
Taylor, Mrs. Edward (Elizabeth Fitch), **IV:** 147, 165
Taylor, Mrs. Edward (Ruth Wyllys), **IV:** 148
Taylor, Eleanor Ross, **Supp. V:** 317, 318
Taylor, Elizabeth, **II:** 588
Taylor, Frank, **III:** 81
Taylor, Frederick Winslow, **Supp. I Part 2:** 644
Taylor, Graham, **Supp. I Part 1:** 5
Taylor, Henry, **Retro. Supp. I:** 212; **Supp. XI:** 317; **Supp. XIII:** 333
Taylor, Henry W., **IV:** 144
Taylor, Jeremy, **II:** 11; **III:** 487; **Supp. I Part 1:** 349; **Supp. XII:** 45; **Supp. XIV:** 344, 345
Taylor, John, **IV:** 149
Taylor, Katherine, **Supp. VIII:** 251
Taylor, Kezia, **IV:** 148
Taylor, Nathaniel W., **Supp. I Part 2:** 580
Taylor, Paul, **I:** 293

Taylor, Peter, **Retro. Supp. II:** 179; **Supp. V: 313–329; Supp. XIV:** 3
Taylor, Raynor, **Supp. XV:** 238
Taylor, Richard, **IV:** 146
Taylor, Robert, **Supp. I Part 1:** 294; **Supp. XV:** 135, 138; **Supp. XVI:** 277
Taylor, Samuel A., **Supp. XX: 253**
Taylor, Stephan, **Supp. XVI:** 203
Taylor, Thomas, **II:** 10
Taylor, William, **IV:** 145–146
Taylor, Zachary, **I:** 3; **II:** 433–434
Tchelitchew, Peter, **II:** 586
Tea and Sympathy (Anderson), **Supp. I Part 1:** 277; **Supp. V:** 108
"Tea at the Palaz of Hoon" (Stevens), **Retro. Supp. I:** 300, 302, 306
"Teacher's Pet" (Thurber), **Supp. I Part 2:** 605–606
"Teaching and Story Telling" (Maclean), **Supp. XIV:** 234
Teaching a Stone to Talk: Expeditions and Encounters (Dillard), **Supp. VI:** 23, 26, 28, 32, 33, 34–35
"Teaching Emily Dickenson"(Hadas), **Supp. XXIII:** 115
"Teaching Hanh the Blues" (Weigl), **Supp. XIX:** 287
Teachings of Don B., The (Barthelme), **Supp. IV Part 1:** 53
Teachout, Terry, **Supp. XIX:** 137
Teale, Edwin Way, **Supp. XIII:** 7
Teall, Dorothy, **I:** 221
"Team Blue/Team Square: Revisiting the Lyric and the Narrative" (Biss and Zapruder), **Supp. XXVI:** 54–55
"Team Players" (Biss), **Supp. XXVI:** 46
Team Team Team (film), **Supp. IX:** 251
"Tea on the Mountain" (Bowles), **Supp. IV Part 1:** 90
"Tea Party, The" (MacLeish), **III:** 11
Tear and a Smile, A (Dam'a wa Ibtisáma) (Gibran), **Supp. XX: 116, 118, 124**
Teare, Brian, **Supp. XXII:** 236
"Tears, Idle Tears" (Lord Tennyson), **Supp. XIV:** 8
"Tears of the Pilgrims, The" (McClatchy), **Supp. XII:** 256
Teasdale, Sara, **Retro. Supp. I:** 133; **Supp. I Part 2:** 393, 707; **Supp. XIV:** 127; **Supp. XV:** 295, 297, 301, 305, 307, 308; **Supp. XVII:** 69, 75; **Supp. XXVII: 283–298**
"Tease" (Swados), **Supp. XIX:** 267
Tebeaux, Elizabeth, **Supp. IX:** 109
"Technical Manifesto of Futurist Literature" (Marinetti), **Supp. XXII:** 161
Technics and Civilization (Mumford), **Supp. I Part 2:** 638; **Supp. II Part 2:** 479, 493, 497
Technics and Human Development (Mumford), **Supp. I Part 2:** 638; **Supp. II Part 2:** 497
Technique of the Mystery Story, The (Wells), **Supp. XXVI:** 277, 280, 281–282
"Technology, The" (Egan), **Supp. XIX:** 61
"Teddy" (Salinger), **III:** 561–563, 571
"Te Deum" (Reznikoff), **Supp. XIV:** 281
Tedlock, Dennis, **Supp. IV Part 2:** 509
"Teeth Mother Naked at Last, The" (R. Bly), **Supp. IV Part 1:** 63, 68, 73
Teggart, Richard, **Supp. I Part 2:** 650
Tegnér, Esaias, **Retro. Supp. II:** 155
Teilhard de Chardin, Pierre, **Supp. I Part 1:** 314
Tekonwatonti/Molly Brant (Kenny), **Supp. XXIII:** 143, 147, 151, **152–153,** 154
"Telegraphs from a Distracted Sibyl" (Mullen), **Supp. XXVII:** 166, 176
Telephone, The (film), **Supp. XI:** 309
"Telephone Call, A" (Parker), **Supp. IX: 202–203**
"Telephone Number of the Muse, The" (Justice), **Supp. VII:** 124–125
Telephone Poles and Other Poems (Updike), **IV:** 214, 215
"Television" (Beattie), **Supp. V:** 33
Teller, Edward, **I:** 137
"Tell Him About Brother John" (Muñoz), **Supp. XXV:** 136
"Telling" (Ortiz), **Supp. IV Part 2:** 509
"Telling It in Black and White: The Importance of the Africanist Presence in To Kill a Mockingbird" (Baecker), **Supp. VIII:** 128
Telling Secrets (Buechner), **Supp. XII:** 53–54
Telling Stories (Didion), **Supp. IV Part 1:** 197
"Telling Stories" (Didion), **Supp. IV Part 1:** 197
"Telling the Bees" (Whittier), **Supp. I Part 2:** 694–695
Telling the Little Secrets (J. Burstein), **Supp. XVII:** 44
Telling the Truth: The Gospel as Tragedy, Comedy, and Fairy Tale (Buechner), **Supp. XII:** 53
"Tell Me" (Hughes), **Supp. VIII:** 213
"Tell Me, Sir, ... What Is 'Black' Literature?" (H. L. Gates), **Supp. XX: 108**
Tell Me, Tell Me (Moore), **III:** 215
Tell Me Again (Notley), **Supp. XXII:** 224, 230–231
Tell Me Again How the White Heron Rises and Flies across the Nacreous River at Twilight toward the Distant Islands (Carruth), **Supp. XVI:**56
Tell Me a Riddle (film), **Supp. XIII:** 295
Tell Me a Riddle (Olsen), **Supp. XIII:** 294, 296, **298–302,** 303, 305
"Tell Me a Riddle" (Olsen), **Supp. XIII:** 294, 297, 298, **300–302,** 305
"Tell Me a Story" (McDermott), **Supp. XVIII:** 177
Tell Me How Long the Train's Been Gone (Baldwin), **Retro. Supp. II:** 9, **11–12,** 14; **Supp. I Part 1:** 48, 52, 63–65, 67
"Tell Me My Fortune" (Epstein), **Supp. XII:** 163
Tell Me True: Memoir, History, and Writing a Life (Hampl and May, eds.), **Supp. XXII:** 81–82, 84, **94–95**
Tell Me Your Answer True (Sexton), **Supp. II Part 2:** 683
Tell My Horse (Hurston), **Retro. Supp. III:** 130, 131–132; **Supp. VI:** 149, 156, 158
"Tell-Tale Heart, The" (Poe), **III:** 413, 414–415, 416; **Retro. Supp. II:** 267, 269, 270; **Retro. Supp. III:** 227; **Supp. XXV:** 112
"Tell the Women We're Going" (Carver), **Supp. III Part 1:** 138, 144
"Telluride Blues—A Hatchet Job" (Abbey), **Supp. XIII:** 10
Telushkin, Dvorah, **Retro. Supp. II:** 317
Temblor (Howe), **Supp. IV Part 2:** 431
Temperamental People (Rinehart), **Supp. XXV:** 196
Tempering of Eugene O'Neill, The (D. Alexander), **Supp. XVII:** 99
"Temper of Steel, The" (Jones), **Supp. XI:** 218
Tempers, The (W. C. Williams), **Retro. Supp. I: 413–414,** 415, 416, 424
Tempest, The (Shakespeare), **I:** 394; **II:** 12; **III:** 40, 61, 263; **Retro. Supp. I:** 61; **Retro. Supp. III:** 190–191; **Supp. IV Part 2:** 463; **Supp. V:** 302–303; **Supp. XII:** 54–57; **Supp. XV:** 255, 256
Temple, Minnie, **II:** 323
Temple, The (Herbert), **IV:** 145, 153

Temple, William, **III:** 303
Temple House (E. Stoddard), **Supp. XV:** 273, **284–286**
Temple of My Familiar, The (Walker), **Supp. III Part 2:** 521, 527, 529, 535, 537; **Supp. IV Part 1:** 14
"Temple of the Holy Ghost, A" (O'Connor), **III:** 344, 352; **Retro. Supp. II:** 232; **Retro. Supp. III:** 215–216
Templin, Charlotte, **Supp. V:** 116
Temporary Shelter (Gordon), **Supp. IV Part 1:** 299, 305–307
"Temporary Shelter" (Gordon), **Supp. IV Part 1:** 306
Temptation Game, The (Gardner), **Supp. VI:** 72
Temptation of Don Volpi, The (Hayes), **Supp. XXVI:** 135, 137
"Temptation of St. Anthony, The" (Barthelme), **Supp. IV Part 1:** 47
Temptations, The, **Supp. X:** 242
"10 Best Weathers of 1983, The" (Notley), **Supp. XXII:** 224
"10 Things I Do Every Day" (Berrigan), **Supp. XXII:** 224; **Supp. XXIV:** 41
"Tenancy, A" (Merrill), **Supp. III Part 1:** 322, 323
"Tenant" (Hoffman), **Supp. XVIII:** 86
Tenants, The (Malamud), **Supp. I Part 2:** 448–450
"Ten Best Issues of Comic Books, The" (Notley), **Supp. XXII:** 224
Ten Commandments (McClatchy), **Supp. XII: 262–265**
Ten Days That Shook the World (Reed), **II:** 577; **Supp. X:** 136; **Supp. XVIII:** 225
Tendencies in Modern American Poetry (A. Lowell), **II:** 529; **Retro. Supp. III:** 100
"Tender, Hilarious Reminiscences of Life in Mythical Lake Wobegon" (MacDougall), **Supp. XVI:** 174
Tender Buttons (G. Stein), **I:** 103, 105; **IV:** 27, 42–43; **Retro. Supp. II:** 331; **Supp. XV:** 347; **Supp. XXVII:** 169
"Tenderfoot" (Haines), **Supp. XII:** 209
Tender Is the Night (Fitzgerald), **I:** 375; **II:** 79, 84, 91, 95–96, 97, 98, 420; **Retro. Supp. I:** 105, 108, 109, **110–112,** 114; **Supp. IX:** 59, 60, 61; **Supp. XV:** 197; **Supp. XXI:** 11
"Tenderloin" (Crane), **I:** 408
"Tenderly" (Dobyns), **Supp. XIII:** 86–87
'Tender Man, A" (Bambara), **Supp. XI:** 9–10
"Tenderness" (Dunn), **Supp. XI:** 149, 150
"Tender Offer, The" (Auchincloss), **Supp. IV Part 1:** 34
"Tender Organizations, The" (C. Bly), **Supp. XVI:** 40, 42
"Tenebrae" (Komunyakaa), **Supp. XIII:** 132
Tenenbaum, Joseph, **Supp. XX: 253**
"Ten Forty-Four" (Kingsolver), **Supp. VII:** 208
Ten Indians (Bell), **Supp. X:** 7, **12**
Ten Introductions: A Collection of Modern Verse (Taggard and Fitts, ed.), **Supp. XXII:** 281
Tennant, Agnieszka, **Supp. XX: 140**
"Ten Neglected American Writers Who Deserve to Be Better Known" (Cantor), **Supp. IV Part 1:** 285
Tennent, Gilbert, **I:** 546
Tennessee Day in St. Louis (Taylor), **Supp. V:** 324
"Tennessee's Partner" (Harte), **Supp. II Part 1:** 345, 348–350
"Tennis" (Pinsky), **Supp. VI:** 241, 242
Tennis Court Oath, The (Ashbery), **Supp. III Part 1:** 7, 9, 12, 14, 26
Ten North Frederick (O'Hara), **III:** 361
Tennyson, Alfred, Lord, **I:** 587–588; **II:** 18, 82, 273, 338, 404, 439, 604; **III:** 5, 409, 469, 485, 511, 521, 523; **Retro. Supp. I:** 100, 325; **Retro. Supp. II:** 135; **Retro. Supp. III:** 60, 266; **Supp. I Part 1:** 349, 356; **Supp. I Part 2:** 410, 416, 552; **Supp. IX:** 19; **Supp. X:** 157; **Supp. XIII:** 111; **Supp. XIV:** 40, 120; **Supp. XV:** 275; **Supp. XVIII:** 78; **Supp. XXVII:** 261
"Tenochtitlan" (Bronk), **Supp. XXI:** 31
"Ten O'Clock News" (Ortiz), **Supp. IV Part 2:** 503–504
"Te-Non-An-At-Che"(Kenny), **Supp. XXIII:** 151
Tenorman (Huddle), **Supp. XXVI:** 150, 151, 153, 156, 159
Ten Poems (Dove), **Supp. IV Part 1:** 244
Ten Poems of Francis Ponge Translated by Robert Bly and Ten Poems of Robert Bly Inspired by the Poems by Francis Ponge (R. Bly), **Supp. IV Part 1:** 71
"Tension in Poetry" (Tate), **IV:** 128, 129, 135
Tenth Muse, The (Bradstreet), **Retro. Supp. III:** 1, 4–14; **Supp. I Part 1:** 102, 103, 114
10,000 Days of Thunder: A History of the Vietnam War (Caputo), **Supp. XIX:** 29
Tenting Tonight (Rinehart), **Supp. XXV:** 195
"Tent on the Beach, The" (Whittier), **Supp. I Part 2:** 703
"Ten True Things" (July), **Supp. XXIV:** 205
"Teodoro Luna Confesses after Years to His Brother, Anselmo the Priest, Who Is Required to Understand, But Who Understands Anyway, More Than People Think" (Ríos), **Supp. IV Part 2:** 552
Teodoro Luna's Two Kisses (Ríos), **Supp. IV Part 2:** 550–552, 553
"Tepeyac" (Cisneros), **Supp. VII:** 69
"Terce" (Auden), **Supp. II Part 1:** 22
Terence, **IV:** 155, 363; **Supp. I Part 2:** 405
Terkel, Studs, **Supp. IV Part 1:** 364
"Term" (Merwin), **Supp. III Part 1:** 356–357
"Terminal Days at Beverly Farms" (R. Lowell), **Retro. Supp. II:** 189
Terminating, or Sonnet LXXV, or "Lass Meine Schmerzen nicht verloren sein, or Ambivalence" (Kushner), **Supp. IX:** 132
Terminations (James), **Retro. Supp. I:** 229
"Terminus" (Emerson), **II:** 13, 19
"Terminus" (Wharton), **Retro. Supp. I:** 371; **Retro. Supp. III:** 283
"Terms in Which I Think of Reality, The" (Ginsberg), **Supp. II Part 1:** 311
Terms of Endearment (film), **Supp. V:** 226
Terms of Endearment (McMurtry), **Supp. V:** 224–225
"Terrace, The" (Wilbur), **Supp. III Part 2:** 550
Terrarium (Sanders), **Supp. XVI:** 270
"Terrence McNally" (Bryer), **Supp. XIII:** 200
"Terrence McNally" (Di Gaetani), **Supp. XIII:** 200
Terrence McNally: A Casebook (Zinman), **Supp. XIII:** 209
"Terrestrial Cuckoo"(O'Hara), **Supp. XXIII:** 210
"Terrible Peacock, The" (Barnes), **Supp. III Part 1:** 33
Terrible Threes, The (Reed), **Supp. X:** 241, 253
Terrible Twos, The (Reed), **Supp. X:** 241, **252–253**
"Terrific Mother" (Moore), **Supp. X:** 178

Territory Ahead, The (Morris), **III:** 228–229, 236
Terrorism (Wright), **Supp. XV:** 341, 342
"Terrorism" (Wright), **Supp. XV:** 341
"Terrors of the Amazon" (Grossman), **Supp. XXV:** 66
Terry, Edward A., **II:** 128, 129
Terry, Rose, **Supp. I Part 2:** 420
Tertium Organum (Ouspensky), **I:** 383; **Supp. XX: 116**
"Terza Rima" (Rich), **Retro. Supp. III:** 252
Terzian, Peter, **Supp. XXV:** 12, 13
Tess of the d'Ubervilles (Hardy), **II:** 181; **Retro. Supp. II:** 100
"Testament" (Berry), **Supp. X:** 36
"Testament" (Carruth), **Supp. XVI:** 59
"Testament (Or, Homage to Walt Whitman)" (Jong), **Supp. V:** 130
"Testament of Flood" (Warren), **IV:** 253
Testament of François Villon, The (Pound, opera), **Retro. Supp. I:** 287
"Testament: Vermeer in December" (Bierds), **Supp. XVII:** 33
"Testimonia on the Question of Stesichoros' Blinding by Helen" (Carson), **Supp. XII:** 107
"Testimonies of a Roasted Chicken" (Jarman), **Supp. XVII:** 120
"Testimony" (Komunyakaa), **Supp. XIII:** 129
"Testimony of James Apthorp, The" (Kees), **Supp. XV:** 146
Testimony: The United States (1885–1890): Recitative (Reznikoff), **Supp. XIV:** 279, 280, 281, 285, **289–291**
Testimony: The United States (1891–1900): Recitative (Reznikoff), **Supp. XIV:** 291
Testing-Tree, The (Kunitz), **Supp. III Part 1:** 260, 263, 264, 267, 268
"Testing-Tree, The" (Kunitz), **Supp. III Part 1:** 269
Test of Poetry, A (Zukofsky), **Supp. III Part 2:** 618, 622
Teuton, Christopher, **Supp. XXVI:** 102, 110, 111
"Teutonic Scholar" (X. J. Kennedy), **Supp. XV:** 161
"Texas Moon, and Elsewhere, The" (McMurtry), **Supp. V:** 225
Texas Poets in Concert: A Quartet (Gwynn, ed.), **Supp. XIII:** 277
Texas Summer (Southern), **Supp. XI:** 309
Texasville (McMurtry), **Supp. V:** 228, 233
Thacher, Molly Day, **IV:** 381
Thacker, Robert, **Supp. XXVII:** 180, 182
Thackeray, William Makepeace, **I:** 194, 354; **II:** 182, 271, 282, 288, 316, 321, 322; **III:** 64, 70; **IV:** 326; **Retro. Supp. I:** 218; **Supp. I Part 1:** 307; **Supp. I Part 2:** 421, 495, 579; **Supp. IV Part 1:** 297; **Supp. IX:** 200; **Supp. XI:** 277; **Supp. XIV:** 306; **Supp. XX: 228**
Thaddeus, Janice Farrar, **Supp. IV Part 1:** 299
"Thailand" (Barthelme), **Supp. IV Part 1:** 41
Thalberg, Irving, **Retro. Supp. I:** 109, 110, 114; **Supp. XVI:** 191, 192
Thales, **I:** 480–481
Thalia Trilogy (McMurtry), **Supp. V:** 220–223, 234
Tham, Claire, **Supp. VIII:** 79
"Thanatopsis" (Bryant), **Supp. I Part 1:** 150, 154, 155, 170
Thanatos Syndrome, The (Percy), **Supp. III Part 1:** 385, 397–399
"Thanks Can Be Named to Death" (Peacock), **Supp. XIX:** 199
"Thanksgiving" (Davison), **Supp. XXVI:** 74
"Thanksgiving" (Glück), **Supp. V:** 83
"Thanksgiving, A" (Auden), **Supp. II Part 1:** 26
"Thanksgiving for a Habitat" (Auden), **Supp. II Part 1:** 24
Thanksgivings (Traherne), **Supp. XVI:** 288
"Thanksgiving Spirit" (Farrell), **II:** 45
Thanksgiving Visitor, The (Capote), **Supp. III Part 1:** 116, 118, 119
"Thank You, Esther Forbes" (Saunders), **Supp. XIX:** 235
Thank You, Fog (Auden), **Supp. II Part 1:** 24
"Thank You, Lord" (Angelou), **Supp. IV Part 1:** 15
Thank You, Mr. Moto (Marquand), **III:** 57, 58
Thank You and Other Poems (Koch), **Supp. XV:** 180–181
"Thank You in Arabic" (Nye), **Supp. XIII:** 273, 281
"Thar's More in the Man Than Thar Is in the Land" (Lanier), **Supp. I Part 1:** 352–353, 359–360
That Affair Next Door (Green), **Supp. XXVI:** 277
"That Evening Sun" (Faulkner), **II:** 72; **Retro. Supp. I:** 75, 83; **Retro. Supp. III:** 82
That Horse (Hogan), **Supp. IV Part 1:** 397, 404, 405
"That House, This Room" (W. V. Davis), **Supp. XXI:** 90
"That I Had the Wings" (Ellison), **Supp. II Part 1:** 238
That Night (McDermott), **Supp. XVIII:** 155, **158–160,** 162, 163, 166
"That's the Place Indians Talk About" (Ortiz), **Supp. IV Part 2:** 511
That Tantalus (Bronk), **Supp. XXI:** 31
"That the Soul May Wax Plump" (Swenson), **Supp. IV Part 2:** 650
"That the Universe Is Chrysalid" (Sobin), **Supp. XVI:** 284
"That Tree" (Porter), **III:** 434–435, 446, 451
That Was the Week That Was (television program), **Supp. XIV:** 125
"That Winter" (Stone), **Supp. XXVII:** 253
"That Year" (Olds), **Supp. X:** 203
"Thaw" (C. Frost), **Supp. XV:** 93, 104, 105
Thaxter, Celia, **Retro. Supp. II:** 136, 147; **Supp. XIII:** 143, 153
Thayer, Abbott, **I:** 231
Thayer, Scofield, **I:** 231; **Retro. Supp. I:** 58
Thayer and Eldridge, **Retro. Supp. I:** 403
"Theater" (Toomer), **Supp. IX:** 309, 317–318
"Theater Chronicle" (McCarthy), **II:** 562
"Theater Problems? Call Dr. Chekhov" (Wasserstein), **Supp. XV:** 320
Theatricals (James), **Retro. Supp. I:** 228
The Blacker the Berry: A Novel of Negro Life (Thurman), **Supp. XIX:** 73; **Supp. XVIII:** 281
"Theft" (Porter), **III:** 434, 435
Theft, A (Bellow), **Retro. Supp. II:** 31–32, 34
The Harder They Fall (Schulberg), **Supp. XVIII: 247,** 253
The Harder They Fall: Celebrities Tell Their Real-Life Stories of Addiction and Recovery (F. Wright), **Supp. XVII:** 240
"Their Ancient, Glittering Eyes" (Rash), **Supp. XXVII:** 227–228
Their Dogs Came with Them (Viramontes), **Supp. XXV:** 130, 138
Their Eyes Were Watching God (Hurston), **Retro. Supp. III:** 130–131, 132, 135, 137, 138, 139, 140; **Supp. VI:** 149, 152, 156–157; **Supp. XX: 107**
Their Heads Are Green and Their

Hands Are Blue: Scenes from the Non-Christian World (Bowles), **Supp. IV Part 1:** 89
"Their Losses" (Taylor), **Supp. V:** 320
"Their Name is Macaroni" (Boyle), **Supp. XXIV:** 61
"Their Sleep" (W. V. Davis), **Supp. XXI:** 93
Their Wedding Journey (Howells), **II:** 277–278; **Retro. Supp. I:** 334
them (Oates), **Supp. II Part 2:** 503, 511–514
Theme Is Freedom, The (Dos Passos), **I:** 488–489, 492, 494
Theme Time Radio Hour (radio show, Dylan), **Supp. XVIII:** 28
"Theme with Variations" (Agee), **I:** 27
"Then" (Barthelme), **Supp. IV Part 1:** 48
"Then as Now" (Cliff), **Supp. XXII:** 76
"The Night Rhonda Ferguson Was Killed" (E. P. Jones), **Supp. XXII:** 144
"Then It All Came Down" (Capote), **Supp. III Part 1:** 125, 131
Theocritus, **II:** 169; **Retro. Supp. I:** 286; **Supp. XXIV:** 156
Theodore Roethke's Far Fields: The Evolution of His Poetry (Balakian), **Supp. XXIII:** 19
"Theodore the Poet" (Masters), **Supp. I Part 2:** 461
Theological Position, A (Coover), **Supp. V:** 44
Theophrastus, **I:** 58
"Theoretical and Scientific Conceptions of Race, The" (Locke), **Supp. XIV:** 209
"Theoretical Subject(s) of This Bridge Called My Back, The"(Alarcón), **Supp. XXIII:** 204–205
"Theories of Time and Space" (Trethewey), **Supp. XXI:** 255
"Theory" (Huddle), **Supp. XXVI:** 149
Theory and Practice of Rivers and Other Poems, The (Harrison), **Supp. VIII:** 47, 49
Theory of Business Enterprise, The (Veblen), **Supp. I Part 2:** 638, 641, 644
Theory of Flight (Rukeyser), **Supp. VI:** 272, 275, **277–278,** 284
"Theory of Flight" (Rukeyser), **Supp. VI:** 277–278
Theory of Moral Sentiments, The (A. Smith), **Supp. I Part 2:** 634
Theory of the Leisure Class, The (Veblen), **I:** 475–476; **Supp. I Part 2:** 629, 633, 641, 645; **Supp. IV Part 1:** 22
"There" (Taylor), **Supp. V:** 323
"There Are No Such Trees in Alpine California" (Haines), **Supp. XII:** 207
"There Goes (Varoom! Varoom!) That Kandy-Kolored Tangerine-Flake Streamline Baby" (Wolfe), **Supp. III Part 2:** 569–571
"There Have Been Changes" (Pickering), **Supp. XXI:** 202–203
"There Is a Lesson" (Olsen), **Supp. XIII:** 292, 297
"There is a Man" (Espaillat), **Supp. XXI:** 108–109
"There Is Only One of Everything" (Atwood), **Supp. XIII:** 34
There Is Something Out There (McNally). See And Things That Go Bump in the Night (McNally)
"There Must Be" (Peacock), **Supp. XIX:** 199
"There's a certain Slant of light" (Dickinson), **Retro. Supp. I:** 38
There's a Wocket in My Pocket! (Geisel), **Supp. XVI:** 111
Thérèse de Lisieux, Saint, **Supp. VIII:** 195
"There She Is She Is Taking Her Bath" (Anderson), **I:** 113, 114
"There Was a Child Went Forth" (Whitman), **IV:** 348; **Retro. Supp. III:** 304–306; **Supp. XXVI:** 230
"There Was a Man, There Was a Woman" (Cisneros), **Supp. VII:** 70
"There Was an Old Woman She Had So Many Children She Didn't Know What to Do" (Cisneros), **Supp. VII:** 60
"There Was a Youth Whose Name Was Thomas Granger" (Olson), **Supp. II Part 2:** 558, 560, 563
There Were Giants in the Land (Benét), **Supp. XI:** 50
"There Will Come Soft Rains" (Teasdale), **Supp. XXVII:** 295
There You Are (Simpson), **Supp. IX:** **279–280**
"There You Are" (Simpson), **Supp. IX:** 279
"Thermopylae" (Clampitt), **Supp. IX:** 43
Theroux, Alexander, **Supp. VIII:** 312
Theroux, Marcel, **Supp. VIII:** 325
Theroux, Paul, **Supp. V:** 122; **Supp. VIII:** **309–327**
"These Are My People" (Hayden), **Supp. II Part 1:** 365
These Are My Same Hands (Schott), **Supp. XXIII:** 241, 242
"These are the days when Birds come back" (Dickinson), **Retro. Supp. I:** 30
"These Days" (Davison), **Supp. XXVI:** 79
"These Days" (Olds), **Supp. X:** 215
"These Flames and Generosities of the Heart: Emily Dickinson and the Illogic of Sumptuary Values" (Howe), **Supp. IV Part 2:** 431
"These Hands" (Brockmeier), **Supp. XXII:** 51, 52, 53
These Happy Golden Years (L. I. Wilder), **Supp. XXII:** 294, 297, 299
These Low Grounds (Turpin), **Supp. XVIII:** 283
"These Nerves" (Biss), **Supp. XXVI:** 50–51
"These saw Visions" (Dickinson), **Retro. Supp. I:** 46
These 13 (Faulkner), **II:** 72; **Retro. Supp. III:** 82
These Three (film), **Supp. I Part 1:** 281
These Times (Untermeyer), **Supp. XV:** **299–300,** 303
"These Times" (Untermeyer), **Supp. XV:** 300
"Thessalonica: A Roman Story" (Brown), **Supp. I Part 1:** 133
Thévenaz, Paul, **Supp. XV:** 42
Thew, Harvey, **Supp. XIII:** 166
"They Ain't the Men They Used To Be" (Farrell), **II:** 45
"They Burned the Books" (Benét), **Supp. XI:** 46
They Came Like Swallows (Maxwell), **Supp. VIII:** **155–159,** 168, 169
"They Can't Turn Back" (Baldwin), **Supp. I Part 1:** 52
They Do Not: The Letters of a Non-Professional Lady Arranged for Public Consumption (Clements), **Supp. XVI:** 190
They Feed They Lion (Levine), **Supp. V:** 178, 179, 181, 184–185, 186
"They Feed They Lion" (Levine), **Supp. V:** 188
"They Lion Grow" (Levine), **Supp. V:** 184–185
"They're Not Your Husband" (Carver), **Supp. III Part 1:** 141, 143
They're Playing Our Song (musical), **Supp. IV Part 2:** 589
They Seek a City (Bontemps and Conroy), **Supp. XXII:** 5, 11
They Shall Inherit the Laughter (Jones), **Supp. XI:** 217, 218, 232
"They Shall Not Die" (Ryan as Quin), **Supp. XVIII:** 228–229

They Shoot Horses (film), **Supp. XIII:** 159
They Shoot Horses, Don't They? (McCoy), **Supp. XIII:** 159, **164–166,** 168, 171, 172, 174; **Supp. XXV:** 26
"They Sing, They Sing" (Roethke), **III:** 544
They Stooped to Folly (Glasgow), **II:** 175, 186–187
They Were Expendable (film), **Supp. XVIII:** 247
"They Weren't Going to Die" (Boyle), **Supp. XXIV:** 61
They Whisper (R. O. Butler), **Supp. XII: 72–73**
They Who Knock at Our Gates: A Complete Gospel of Immigration (Antin), **Supp. XX: 2–3, 10–11, 12**
"Thick and Thin"(Hadas), **Supp. XXIII:** 119
Thidwick the Big-Hearted Moose (Geisel), **Supp. XVI:** 104
Thief's Journal, The (Genet), **Supp. XXIV:** 210
"Thief's Philosophy of Life, The" (Hapgood), **Supp. XVII:** 103
"Thief's Wife, The" (B. Kelly), **Supp. XVII:** 125–126
"Thieves" (Yates), **Supp. XI:** 349
Thieves of Paradise (Komunyakaa), **Supp. XIII:** 113, **128–130,** 132
"Thimble, The" (Kenyon), **Supp. VII:** 164
"Thing and Its Relations, The" (James), **II:** 357
" 'Thing Not Named, The': Willa Cather as a Lesbian Writer" (O'Brien), **Retro. Supp. III:** 37
"Things" (Haines), **Supp. XII:** 207
"Things" (Kenyon), **Supp. VII:** 169
"Things, The" (Kinnell), **Supp. III Part 1:** 246
Things As They Are (Stein), **IV:** 34, 37, 40
"Things Can Be Named to Death" (Peacock), **Supp. XIX:** 199
"Things Don't Stop" (Nye), **Supp. XIII:** 287
Things Gone and Things Still Here (Bowles), **Supp. IV Part 1:** 91
"Things of August" (Stevens), **Retro. Supp. I:** 309
Things of This World (Wilbur), **Supp. III Part 2:** 552–555
Things That Fall from the Sky (Brockmeier), **Supp. XXII: 50–53**
"Things That Fall from the Sky" (Brockmeier), **Supp. XXII:** 51, 53
Things Themselves: Essays and Scenes (Price), **Supp. VI:** 261
Things They Carried, The (T. O'Brien), **Supp. V:** 238, 239, 240, 243, 248–250; **Supp. XVII:** 14; **Supp. XXI:** 122
"Things to Do in New York City" (Berrigan), **Supp. XXII:** 224
Things We Don't Understand and Definitely Are Not Going to Talk About (performance piece, July), **Supp. XXIV:** 200
"Thing That Killed My Father Off, The" (Carver), **Supp. III Part 1:** 143
Thingy World!: or, How We Got to Where We Are: A Satire in One Act (Budbill), **Supp. XIX: 13–14**
"Think about It" (Conroy), **Supp. XVI:** 75
Think Back on Us . . . (Cowley), **Supp. II Part 1:** 139, 140, 142
Think Fast, Mr. Moto (Marquand), **III:** 57, 58
"Thinking about Barbara Deming" (Paley), **Supp. VI:** 227
"Thinking about Being Called Simple by a Critic" (Stafford), **Supp. XI:** 328
Thinking about the Longstanding Problems of Virtue and Happiness: Essays, a Play, Two Poems, and a Prayer (Kushner), **Supp. IX:** 131, 134, 135
"Thinking about the Past" (Justice), **Supp. VII:** 123–124
"Thinking about Western Thinking" (Didion), **Supp. IV Part 1:** 204, 206
"'Thinking against Oneself': Reflections on Cioran" (Sontag), **Supp. III Part 2:** 459–460
"Thinking Back Through Our Mothers: Traditions in Canadian Women's Writing" (Shields), **Supp. VII:** 307–308
"Thinking for Berky" (Stafford), **Supp. XI:** 320
"Thinking in Subversion" (Gansworth), **Supp. XXVI:** 114
"Thinking like a Mountain" (Leopold), **Supp. XIV:** 188, 189
"Thinking of the Lost World" (Jarrell), **II:** 338–389
Thinking Out Loud (Quindlen), **Supp. XVII:** 167, **169–170**
Thin Man, The (film), **Supp. IV Part 1:** 342, 355
Thin Man, The (Hammett), **Supp. IV Part 1:** 354–355
"Thinnest Shadow, The" (Ashbery), **Supp. III Part 1:** 5
"Thin People, The" (Plath), **Supp. I Part 2:** 538, 547
Thin Red Line, The (film; Malick), **Supp. V:** 249; **Supp. XV:** 351
Thin Red Line, The (Jones), **Supp. XI:** 219, **224–225,** 229, 231, 232, 233, 234
"Thin Strips" (Sandburg), **III:** 587
"Third and Final Continent, The" (Lahiri), **Supp. XXI: 178–180**
"Third Avenue in Sunlight" (Hecht), **Supp. X:** 61
"Third Body, A" (R. Bly), **Supp. IV Part 1:** 71
Third Circle, The (Norris), **III:** 327
"Third Expedition, The" (Bradbury), **Supp. IV Part 1:** 103, 106
Third Generation, The (C. Himes), **Supp. XVI:** 135, **140–141**
Third Life of Grange Copeland, The (Walker), **Supp. III Part 2:** 520, 527–536
Third Mind, The (Burroughs), **Supp. XII:** 3
"Third Myth, The" (Muñoz), **Supp. XXV:** 134
Third Rose, The (Brinnin), **IV:** 26
"Third Sermon on the Warpland, The" (Brooks), **Supp. III Part 1:** 85
"Third Thing That Killed My Father Off, The" (Carver), **Supp. III Part 1:** 144
Third Violet, The (Crane), **I:** 408, 417–418
Thirlwall, John C., **Retro. Supp. I:** 430
"Thirst: Introduction to Kinds of Water" (Carson), **Supp. XII: 103**
"13, 1977, 21" (Lethem), **Supp. XVIII:** 148
13 by Shanley (Shanley), **Supp. XIV:** 316
13 Seconds: A Look Back at the Kent State Shootings (Caputo), **Supp. XIX:** 29
Thirteen Hands: A Play in Two Acts (Shields), **Supp. VII:** 322–323
Thirteen O'Clock (Benét), **Supp. XI:** 46
Thirteen Other Stories (Purdy), **Supp. VII:** 278
Thirteen Stories and Thirteen Epitaphs (Vollmann), **Supp. XVII:** 226
"Thirteenth and Pennsylvania" (Stafford), **Supp. XI:** 324
Thirteenth Month, The (Pedersen; Nelson, trans.), **Supp. XVIII:** 179–180
"Thirteen Ways of Looking at a Blackbird" (Stevens), **IV:** 94; **Supp. IX:**

47; **Supp. XVII:** 130; **Supp. XXIII:** 253
"Thirteen Ways of Looking at a Blackbird" (W. Stevens), **Supp. XX: 110**
Thirteen Ways of Looking at a Black Man (H. L. Gates), **Supp. XX: 102, 110**
30/6 (poetry chapbook), **Supp. V:** 5, 6
"30. Meditation. 2. Cor. 5.17. He Is a New Creature" (Taylor), **IV:** 144
30: Pieces of a Novel (Dixon), **Supp. XII:** 152, **153–154**
"Thirty Bob a Week" (Davidson), **Retro. Supp. I:** 55
"Thirty Delft Tiles" (Doty), **Supp. XI:** 131
"35/10" (Olds), **Supp. X:** 206
"35,000 Feet—The Lanterns" (Goldbarth), **Supp. XII:** 182
31 Letters and 13 Dreams (Hugo), **Supp. VI:** 141–144
Thirty Poems (Bryant), **Supp. I Part 1:** 157, 158
Thirty-Six Poems (Warren), **IV:** 236, 239, 240
"33" (Alvarez), **Supp. VII:** 4
"3275" (Monette), **Supp. X:** 148, 159
Thirty Years (Marquand), **III:** 56, 60–61
Thirty Years of Treason (Bentley), **Supp. I Part 1:** 297
This, My Letter (Hay), **Supp. XIV:** 121, 122, 129, 131
"This, That & the Other" (Nemerov), **III:** 269
This Body Is Made of Camphor and Gopherwood (R. Bly), **Supp. IV Part 1:** 63–65, 66, 71; **Supp. XXI:** 85
This Boy's Life: A Memoir (T. Wolff), **Supp. VII:** 334–339, 340, 343; **Supp. XI:** 246, 247; **Supp. XXV:** 208
This Bridge Called My Back: Writings by Radical Women of Color (Moraga and Anzaldúa, eds.), **Supp. XXIII:** 193, 194, 196, **204–205**
"This Bright Dream" (Benét), **Supp. XI:** 55
This Coffin Has No Handles (McGrath), **Supp. X:** 117
"This Configuration" (Ashbery), **Supp. III Part 1:** 22
"This Corruptible" (Wylie), **Supp. I Part 2:** 727, 729
"This Crazy Wickedness, Little Nests of Light" (Notley), **Supp. XXII:** 228
"This Crutch That I Love" (Nye), **Supp. XIII:** 288
"This Gentile World" (H. Miller), **III:** 177
"This Hand" (Wylie), **Supp. I Part 2:** 713
"This Hour" (Olds), **Supp. X:** 212
"This House I Cannot Leave" (Kingsolver), **Supp. VII:** 208
This Hunger (Nin), **Supp. X:** 185
This in Which (Oppen), **Supp. XXVI:** 225, 230, 232–233, 234
"This Is a Photograph of Me" (Atwood), **Supp. XIII:** 33
"This Is a Poem, Good Afternoon" (Keillor), **Supp. XVI:** 167
"This Is a Young World" (Howard), **Supp. XXVII:** 118
"This Is for You" (Cohen), **Supp. XXVII:** 60
This Is How You Lose Her (Díaz), **Supp. XXIV:** 83, 84, 86, 88, **92–93**
"This Is It" (Stern), **Supp. IX:** 290
"This Is Just to Say" (W. C. Williams), **Supp. XI:** 328
This Is My God: The Jewish Way of Life (Wouk), **Supp. XXV:** 253, 255–256, 263, 268
"This Is My Heart" (Harjo), **Supp. XII:** 230
This Is Not a Novel (Markson), **Supp. XVII:** 145–146
"This Is Not Who We Are" (Nye), **Supp. XIII:** 285, 286
This Is Our Time: Secular Cantata No. 1, Mixed Voice Chorus and Orchestra (Taggard, Schuman and Weissleder), **Supp. XXII:** 283
"This Is Us, Excellent" (Richard), **Supp. XIX:** 212
"This Is What I Said" (Salinas), **Supp. XIII:** 322
This Journey (Wright), **Supp. III Part 2:** 605–606
"This Lime-Tree Bower My Prison" (Coleridge), **Supp. XXI:** 52, 55
This Man and This Woman (Farrell), **II:** 42
"This Monkey, My Back" (Boyle), **Supp. XX: 17**
"This Morning" (Huddle), **Supp. XXVI:** 151
"This Morning" (Kenyon), **Supp. VII:** 164
"This Morning, This Evening, So Soon" (Baldwin), **Supp. I Part 1:** 63
"This Morning Again It Was in the Dusty Pines" (Oliver), **Supp. VII:** 240
This Music Crept by Me upon the Waters (MacLeish), **III:** 21
"This New England: Newport, Vermont" (Mosher), **Supp. XXII:** 209
This Old House (J. Davison), **Supp. XXVI:** 65
This People Israel: The Meaning of Jewish Existence (Baeck), **Supp. V:** 260
"This Person" (July), **Supp. XXIV:** 202
"This Personal Maze Is Not the Prize" (Selinger), **Supp. XI:** 248
"This Place in the Ways" (Rukeyser), **Supp. VI:** 273–274
This Property Is Condemned (T. Williams), **IV:** 378
This Proud Heart (Buck), **Supp. II Part 1:** 119–120
This Same Sky: A Collection of Poems from around the World (Nye, ed.), **Supp. XIII:** 280
"This Sandwich Has No Mayonnaise" (Salinger), **III:** 552–553
This Shape We're In (Lethem), **Supp. XVIII:** 145
"This Shape We're In" (Lethem), **Supp. XVIII:** 148
This Side of Paradise (Fitzgerald), **I:** 358; **II:** 77, 80, 81, 82–83, 84, 85–87, 88; **Retro. Supp. I:** 99–100, **101–102,** 103, 105, 106, 110, 111; **Supp. XVIII:** 248
This Singing World: An Anthology of Modern Poetry for Young People (Untermeyer, ed.), **Supp. XV:** 306
This Strange Joy: Selected Poems of Sandro Penna (Di Perio, trans.), **Supp. XIX:** 34
This Stubborn Self: Texas Autobiographies (Almon), **Supp. XIII:** 288
"This They Took with Them" (Boyle), **Supp. XXIV:** 61
This Thing Don't Lead to Heaven (Crews), **Supp. XI: 112**
This Time: New and Selected Poems (Stern), **Supp. IX:** 290–291, **299**
"Thistle Seed in the Wind" (Francis), **Supp. IX:** 81
"Thistles in Sweden, The" (Maxwell), **Supp. VIII:** 169
"This Tokyo" (Snyder), **Supp. VIII:** 298
This Tree Will Be Here for a Thousand Years (R. Bly), **Supp. IV Part 1:** 65–66, 71, 72
This Tree Will Be Here for a Thousand Years (revised edition) (R. Bly), **Supp. IV Part 1:** 66
This Very Earth (Caldwell), **I:** 297, 302
This Waiting for Love (Mitchell, ed.), **Supp. XXVI:** 165, 173

This Wheel's on Fire: Levon Helm and the Story of the Band (Helm), **Supp. XVIII:** 26
This Woman (di Donato), **Supp. XX: 33, 41–42, 46**
Thoens, Karen, **Supp. V:** 147
Thomas, Brandon, **II:** 138
Thomas, Dave, **Supp. XXVI:** 18
Thomas, Debra, **Supp. XIII:** 114
Thomas, D. M., **Supp. VIII:** 5
Thomas, Dwight, **Retro. Supp. III:** 237
Thomas, Dylan, **I:** 49, 64, 382, 432, 526, 533; **III:** 21, 521, 528, 532, 534; **IV:** 89, 93, 136; **Supp. I Part 1:** 263; **Supp. III Part 1:** 42, 47; **Supp. IX:** 114; **Supp. V:** 344; **Supp. VIII:** 21; **Supp. X:** 115; **Supp. XV:** 74; **Supp. XVII:** 135; **Supp. XX: 199, 204; Supp. XXIV:** 54; **Supp. XXVII:** 222
Thomas, Edna Lewis, **Supp. XVIII:** 281
Thomas, Edward, **II:** 154; **Retro. Supp. I:** 127, 131, 132; **Retro. Supp. III:** 98; **Supp. I Part 1:** 263; **Supp. II Part 1:** 4
Thomas, Jacob ("Jake"), **Supp. XXVI:** 83
Thomas, James, **Supp. XVI:** 268
Thomas, Joseph, **Supp. XVIII:** 183
Thomas, J. Parnell, **Supp. I Part 1:** 286; **Supp. XV:** 198
Thomas, June, **Supp. XXV:** 2, 3
Thomas, Lewis, **Retro. Supp. I:** 323
Thomas, Lorenzo, **Supp. XXIV:** 37; **Supp. XXVII:** 166, 167
Thomas, Louisa, **Supp. XXIII:** 280, 283
Thomas, Rob, **Supp. XVIII:** 100, 101
Thomas, R. S., **Supp. XXI:** 83, 86–87, 93, 95, 96
Thomas, William I., **Supp. I Part 2:** 641
Thomas-a-Kempis, **Retro. Supp. I:** 247
Thomas and Beulah (Dove), **Supp. IV Part 1:** 242, 247–248, 249; **Supp. XVIII:** 174; **Supp. XXI:** 249
Thomas Aquinas (Saint), **I:** 13, 14, 265, 267; **III:** 270; **Retro. Supp. II:** 222; **Supp. IV Part 2:** 526
"Thomas at the Wheel" (Dove), **Supp. IV Part 1:** 248
"Thomas Eakins and the Photograph of a Man in Motion" (Major), **Supp. XXII:** 183
"Thomas Eakins' Delaware River Paintings" (Major), **Supp. XXII:** 183
"Thomas McGrath: Words for a Vanished Age" (Vinz), **Supp. X:** 117
Thomas Merton on Peace, **Supp. VIII:** 208
Thomas Merton Studies Center, The, **Supp. VIII:** 208
Thompson, Barbara, **Supp. V:** 322
Thompson, Caroline, **Supp. XXIII:** 291
Thompson, Cy, **I:** 538
Thompson, Daniel, **Supp. XXIII:** 174
Thompson, Dorothy, **II:** 449–450, 451, 453; **Supp. XV:** 307
Thompson, Edward, **Supp. XXI:** 172
Thompson, E. P., **Supp. X:** 112, 117
Thompson, Francis, **Retro. Supp. I:** 55
Thompson, Frank, **II:** 20
Thompson, George, **Supp. I Part 2:** 686; **Supp. XXIII:** 182
Thompson, Hunter S., **Supp. VIII:** 42; **Supp. XI:** 105; **Supp. XIII:** 1, 17; **Supp. XVII:** 95, 102, 228; **Supp. XXIV: 279–294**
Thompson, James R., **Supp. IV Part 1:** 217
Thompson, Jean, **Supp. XXIII: 289–305**
Thompson, John, **Supp. V:** 323; **Supp. XXI:** 151
Thompson, Juliet, **Supp. XX: 117**
Thompson, Lawrance Roger, **II:** 508; **Retro. Supp. I:** 138, 141; **Retro. Supp. III:** 102
Thompson, Lisa B., **Supp. XXIII:** 202
Thompson, Morton, **Supp. XIII:** 170
Thompson, Theresa, **Supp. V:** 141
Thompson, William T., **Supp. I Part 2:** 411
Thomson, James, **II:** 304; **Supp. I Part 1:** 150, 151; **Supp. XXIV:** 159
Thomson, Virgil, **IV:** 45; **Supp. IV Part 1:** 81, 83, 84, 173; **Supp. XVI:** 195
"Thoreau" (J. R. Lowell), **Supp. I Part 2:** 420, 422
Thoreau, Henry David, **I:** 98, 104, 228, 236, 257, 258, 261, 305, 433; **II:** 7, 8, 13, 17, 101, 159, 224, 273–274, 295, 312–313, 321, 457–458, 540, 546–547; **III:** 171, 174, 186–187, 189, 208, 214–215, 453, 454, 507, 577; **IV: 167–189,** 191, 341; **Retro. Supp. I:** 51, 62, 122; **Retro. Supp. II:** 13, 96, 142, 158; **Retro. Supp. III:** 249; **Supp. I Part 1:** 29, 34, 116, 188, 299, 358; **Supp. I Part 2:** 383, 400, 420, 421, 507, 540, 579, 580, 655, 659, 660, 664, 678; **Supp. III Part 1:** 340, 353; **Supp. IV Part 1:** 236, 392, 416; **Supp. IV Part 2:** 420, 430, 433, 439, 447; **Supp. IX:** 25, 90, 171; **Supp. V:** 200, 208; **Supp. VIII:** 40, 42, 103, 105, 198, 201, 204, 205, 292, 303; **Supp. X:** 21, 27, 28–29, 101, 102; **Supp. XI:** 155; **Supp. XIII:** 1, 17; **Supp. XIV:** 40, 54, 106, 177, 181; **Supp. XVIII:** 4; **Supp. XX: 116, 221; Supp. XXI:** 203, 217; **Supp. XXII:** 206; **Supp. XXIII:** 174; **Supp. XXVI:** 31, 34, 37
Thoreau, John, **IV:** 171, 182
Thoreau, Mrs. John, **IV:** 172
"Thoreau's Hound: On Hiddenness"(Hirshfield), **Supp. XXIII:** 137
"Thorn, The" (Gordon), **Supp. IV Part 1:** 314
Thorne, Francis, **Supp. XII:** 253
"Thorn Merchant, The" (Komunyakaa), **Supp. XIII:** 119–120
Thornton, Billy Bob, **Supp. VIII:** 175
Thornton, Lionel, **III:** 291
Thornton, Richard, **Retro. Supp. III:** 103
"Thorofare" (Minot), **Supp. VI: 209–210**
"Thorow" (Howe), **Supp. IV Part 2:** 419, 420, 421, 431, 433–434
Thorp, Willard, **Supp. XIII:** 101
Thorpe, Thomas Bangs, **Retro. Supp. III:** 259
Thorslev, Peter L., Jr., **I:** 524
Thorstein Veblen (Dowd), **Supp. I Part 2:** 650
Thorstein Veblen (Qualey, ed.), **Supp. I Part 2:** 650
Thorstein Veblen: A Chapter in American Economic Thought (Teggart), **Supp. I Part 2:** 650
Thorstein Veblen: A Critical Interpretation (Riesman), **Supp. I Part 2:** 649, 650
Thorstein Veblen: A Critical Reappraisal (Dowd, ed.), **Supp. I Part 2:** 650
Thorstein Veblen and His America (Dorfman), **Supp. I Part 2:** 631, 650
Thorstein Veblen and the Institutionalists: A Study in the Social Philosophy of Economics (Seckler), **Supp. I Part 2:** 650
"Those before Us" (R . Lowell), **II:** 550
"Those Being Eaten by America" (R. Bly), **Supp. IV Part 1:** 62
Those Bones Are Not My Child (Bambara), **Supp. XI:** 1, 14, **20–22**

Those Extraordinary Twins (Twain), **IV:** 205–206; **Retro. Supp. III:** 267
"Those Graves in Rome" (Levis), **Supp. XI:** 266
"Those of Us Who Think We Know" (Dunn), **Supp. XI:** 146
Those That Be in Bondage (Webber), **Supp. XXI:** 160
"Those Times . . ." (Sexton), **Supp. II Part 2:** 670, 684
"Those Various Scalpels" (Moore), **III:** 202
"Those Were the Days" (Levine), **Supp. V:** 190
"Those Who Don't" (Cisneros), **Supp. VII:** 60
"Those Who Love" (Teasdale), **Supp. XXVII:** 296
"Those Who Thunder" (Hogan), **Supp. IV Part 1:** 406
"Thought, A" (Sarton), **Supp. VIII:** 262
Thought and Character of William James (Perry), **II:** 362
Thoughtbook of Francis Scott Key Fitzgerald (Fitzgerald), **Retro. Supp. I:** 99
"Thought Experiment" (Saunders), **Supp. XIX:** 235
"Thoughtful Roisterer Declines the Gambit, The" (Hecht), **Supp. X:** 63
"Thought of Heaven, The" (Stern), **Supp. IX:** 297
"Thoughts after Lambeth" (Eliot), **I:** 587; **Retro. Supp. I:** 324
Thoughts and Reflections (Lord Halifax), **II:** 111
Thoughts in Solitude (Merton), **Supp. VIII:** 207
"Thoughts on Being Bibliographed" (Wilson), **IV:** 435
"Thoughts on the Establishment of a Mint in the United States" (Paine), **Supp. I Part 2:** 512
"Thoughts on the Gifts of Art" (Kenyon), **Supp. VII:** 167
Thousand Acres, A (Smiley), **Supp. VI:** 292, **301–303**
"Thousand and Second Night, The" (Merrill), **Supp. III Part 1:** 324
"Thousand Dollar Vagrant, The" (Olsen), **Supp. XIII:** 292, 297
"Thousand Faces of Danny Torrance, The" (Figliola), **Supp. V:** 143
"Thousand Genuflections, A" (McCarriston), **Supp. XIV:** 266
Thousand-Mile Walk to the Gulf, A (Muir), **Supp. IX: 177–178**
Thousand Plateaus, A (Deleuze and Guattari), **Supp. XXV:** 123
"Thou Shalt Not Steal" (McClatchy), **Supp. XII:** 264
"Thread, The" (Merwin), **Supp. III Part 1:** 351
Three (film), **Supp. IX:** 253
3-3-8 (Marquand), **III:** 58
"3 A.M. Kitchen: My Father Talking" (Gallagher), **Supp. XXIV:** 169
"Three Academic Pieces" (Stevens), **IV:** 90
"Three Agee Wards, The" (Morris), **III:** 220–221
"Three American Singers" (Cather), **Retro. Supp. I:** 10
"Three Around the Old Gentleman" (Berryman), **I:** 188
"Three Avilas, The" (Jeffers), **Supp. II Part 2:** 418
"Three Black Women Writers" (C. L. R. James), **Supp. XXI:** 172
Three Books of Song (Longfellow), **II:** 490
"Three Bushes" (Yeats), **Supp. I Part 1:** 80
Three Cantos (Pound), **Retro. Supp. I:** 290
Three Centuries of Harvard (Morison), **Supp. I Part 2:** 485
Three Changes (Silver), **Supp. XXIV:** 275
Three Circles of Light (di Donato), **Supp. XX: 33, 42–43, 44, 46**
Three Cities: A Trilogy (Asch), **Supp. XXIII:** 1, 5, **10–12**
Three Comrades (Remarque), **Retro. Supp. I:** 113
"Three Corollaries of Cultural Relativism" (Locke), **Supp. XIV:** 202
"Three-Day Blow, The" (Hemingway), **II:** 248
Three Essays on America (Brooks), **I:** 246
Three Farmers on Their Way to a Dance (Powers), **Supp. IX:** 211–212, **213–214,** 222
"Three Fates, The" (Benét), **Supp. XI:** 48–49, 50
"Three Generations of Secrets" (A. Finch), **Supp. XVII:** 73
"Three Gifts, The" (Gibran), **Supp. XX: 124**
Three Gospels (Price), **Supp. VI:** 267
365 Days (Boyle), **Supp. XXIV:** 50, 60
"Three Kings, The: Hemingway, Faulkner, and Fitzgerald" (Ford), **Supp. V:** 59
Three Lives (Auchincloss), **Supp. IV Part 1:** 25
Three Lives (Stein), **I:** 103; **IV:** 26, 27, 31, 35, 37–41, 42, 45, 46; **Supp. IX:** 306; **Supp. XXIII:** 166
"THREE MOVEMENTS AND A CODA" (Baraka), **Supp. II Part 1:** 50
Three One Act Plays (Riverside Drive, Old Saybrook, and Central Park West) (Allen), **Supp. XV:** 3
Three on the Tower: The Lives and Works of Ezra Pound, T. S. Eliot, and William Carlos Williams (Simpson), **Supp. IX:** 276
Three Papers on Fiction (Welty), **IV:** 261
Three-Penny Opera (Brecht), **I:** 301; **Supp. XIV:** 162
"Three Percent Own All the Wealth" (Ryan as Quin), **Supp. XVIII:** 231–232
Three Philosophical Poets (Santayana), **III:** 610–612
"Three Pigs in Five Days" (Prose), **Supp. XVI:** 257, 258
"Three Players of a Summer Game" (T. Williams), **IV:** 383
Three Poems (Ashbery), **Supp. III Part 1:** 2, 3, 14, 15, 18, 24–26
"Three Poems for my Daughter" (Di Piero), **Supp. XIX:** 40
"Three Pokes of a Thistle" (Nye), **Supp. XIII:** 281
Three Prophets of Religious Liberalism (Wright), **Supp. XXIV:** 71
Three Roads, The (Macdonald, under Millar), **Supp. IV Part 2:** 466, 467
Three Short Plays with Long Titles (Silver and Ann), **Supp. XXIV:** 264
"Three Silences of Molinos, The" (Longfellow), **Retro. Supp. II:** 169
Three Sisters, The (Chekhov), **Supp. XV:** 323
"Three Sisters, The" (Cisneros), **Supp. VII:** 64
Three Soldiers (Dos Passos), **I:** 477–478, 480, 482, 488, 493–494; **Supp. XXI:** 277
"Three Songs at the End of Summer" (Kenyon), **Supp. VII:** 169–170
"Three Steps to the Graveyard" (Wright), **Supp. III Part 2:** 593, 596
Three Stories and Ten Poems (Hemingway), **II:** 68, 263; **Supp. XVII:** 105
Three Tall Women (Albee), **Supp. XXIV:** 270
Three Taverns, The (Robinson), **III:** 510
"Three Taverns, The" (Robinson), **III:** 521, 522

Three Tenant Families (Agee), **I:** 37–38
Three Tenors, One Vehicle: A Book of Songs (X. J. Kennedy, Camp, and Waldrop), **Supp. XV:** 165
"Three Types of Poetry" (Tate), **IV:** 131
"Three Vagabonds of Trinidad" (Harte), **Supp. II Part 1:** 338
"Three Waterfalls, The" (Lanier), **Supp. I Part 1:** 350
"Three-Way Mirror" (Brooks), **Supp. III Part 1:** 69–70
Three Weeks in Spring (Parker and Parker), **Supp. XIX:** 187
"Three Women" (Plath), **Supp. I Part 2:** 539, 541, 544, 545, 546
Three Young Poets (Swallow, ed.), **Supp. X:** 116
Threnody (Emerson), **Supp. I Part 2:** 416
"Threnody" (Emerson), **II:** 7
"Threnody for a Brown Girl" (Cullen), **Supp. IV Part 1:** 166
"Threshing-Floor, The" (Baldwin), **Supp. I Part 1:** 50
"Threshing Wheat" (Huddle), **Supp. XXVI:** 148
Threshold (film), **Supp. IX:** 254
"Threshold" (Goldbarth), **Supp. XII:** 175
Threshold (Jackson), **Supp. IX:** 117
Thriller (television show), **Supp. XXVII:** 119
"Throat" (Goldbarth), **Supp. XII:** 177–178
Throne of Labdacus, The (Schnackenberg), **Supp. XV:** 260, **263–266**
Thrones (Pound), **Retro. Supp. I:** 293
Through Dooms of Love (Kumin), **Supp. IV Part 2:** 444
Through Glacier Park in 1915 (Rinehart), **Supp. XXV:** 195
"Through the Black Curtain" (Kingston), **Supp. V:** 169
Through the Forest: New and Selected Poems, 1977–1987 (Wagoner), **Supp. IX: 330–331**
"Through the Gates of the Silver Key" (Lovecraft and Price), **Supp. XXV:** 114, 123
"Through the Hills of Spain" (Salinas), **Supp. XIII:** 315
"Through the Hole in the Mundane Millstone" (West), **Retro. Supp. II:** 321, 322
Through the Ivory Gate (Dove), **Supp. IV Part 1:** 242, 243, 251, 252, 253–254, 254
"Through the Kitchen Window, Chiapas" (Nye), **Supp. XIII:** 277
Through the Safety Net (C. Baxter), **Supp. XVII:** 17, 22
"Through the Smoke Hole" (Snyder), **Supp. VIII:** 299
Throw Like a Girl (Thompson), **Supp. XXIII: 299–300**
"Throw Like a Girl"(Thompson), **Supp. XXIII:** 299, 300
"Thrush Relinquished, The" (Grossman), **Supp. XIX:** 83
Thucydides, **II:** 418; **IV:** 50; **Supp. I Part 2:** 488, 489, 492; **Supp. IV Part 1:** 391; **Supp. XIII:** 233
Thunderbolt and Lightfoot (film), **Supp. X:** 126
"Thunder from a Cloudless Sky" (Mosher), **Supp. XXII:** 209
"Thunderhead" (MacLeish), **III:** 19
Thurber, James, **I:** 487; **II:** 432; **IV:** 396; **Supp. I Part 2: 602–627,** 653, 654, 668, 672, 673, 679; **Supp. II Part 1:** 143; **Supp. IV Part 1:** 349; **Supp. IX:** 118; **Supp. XIV:** 104; **Supp. XVI:** 167; **Supp. XVII:** 4
Thurber, Mrs. James (Althea Adams), **Supp. I Part 2:** 613, 615, 617
Thurber, Mrs. James (Helen Muriel Wismer), **Supp. I Part 2:** 613, 617, 618
Thurber, Robert, **Supp. I Part 2:** 613, 617
Thurber, Rosemary, **Supp. I Part 2:** 616
Thurber, William, **Supp. I Part 2:** 602
Thurber Album, The (Thurber), **Supp. I Part 2:** 611, 619
Thurber Carnival, The (Thurber), **Supp. I Part 2:** 620; **Supp. XIV:** 104
Thurman, Judith, **Supp. IV Part 1:** 309; **Supp. XXV:** 2
Thurman, Wallace, **Retro. Supp. I:** 200; **Retro. Supp. III:** 127, 137; **Supp. I Part 1:** 325, 326, 328, 332; **Supp. IV Part 1:** 164; **Supp. X:** 136, 139; **Supp. XIX:** 78; **Supp. XVI:** 135; **Supp. XVIII:** 279, 281; **Supp. XXII:** 2
"Thursday" (Millay), **III:** 129
"Thurso's Landing" (Jeffers), **Supp. II Part 2:** 433
"Thus Do I Refute Gioia" (Junker), **Supp. XV:** 116
"Thus Far by Faith" (Nelson), **Supp. XVIII:** 177
Thus Spake Zarathustra (Nietzsche), **II:** 463; **Supp. IV Part 1:** 110; **Supp. IV Part 2:** 519
Thwaite, Lady Alicia. See Rawlings, Marjorie Kinnan
"Thyme" (Stallings), **Supp. XXV:** 232–233
Thy Neighbor's Wife (Talese), **Supp. XVII:** 204, 205–206, 207, 208, 210
"Tiara" (Doty), **Supp. XI:** 122
"Tibetan Time" (Prose), **Supp. XVI:** 255
Ticket for a Seamstitch, A (Harris), **II:** 424–425
Tickets for a Prayer Wheel (Dillard), **Supp. VI:** 22, 34
Ticket That Exploded, The (Burroughs), **Supp. III Part 1:** 93, 103, 104
Tickless Time (Glaspell), **Supp. III Part 1:** 179
Ticknor, George, **II:** 488; **Supp. I Part 1:** 313
Ticknor, William, **Supp. XVIII:** 258
"Ti Démon" (Chopin), **Supp. I Part 1:** 225
Tide of Time, The (Masters), **Supp. I Part 2:** 471
"Tide of Voices" (Hull), **Supp. XXI:** 132, 133–134, 136
"Tide Rises, the Tide Falls, The" (Longfellow), **I:** 498
"Tides" (Hoffman), **Supp. XVIII:** 86
Tidewater Blood (Hoffman), **Supp. XVIII: 82–83**
Tidyman, Ernest, **Supp. V:** 226
Tietjens, Eunice, **Supp. XV:** 47, 297; **Supp. XXVII:** 286
"Tiger" (Blake), **Supp. I Part 1:** 80; **Supp. VIII:** 26
Tiger (Bynner), **Supp. XV:** 42, 50
"Tiger, The" (Buechner), **Supp. XII:** 48
Tiger in the House, The (Van Vechten), **Supp. II Part 2:** 736
Tiger Joy (Benét), **Supp. XI:** 45
Tiger-Lilies (Lanier), **Supp. I Part 1:** 350–351, 357, 360, 371
Tiger Who Wore White Gloves, The: or, What You Are, You Are (Brooks), **Supp. III Part 1:** 86
Till, Emmett, **Supp. I Part 1:** 61
Till, Eric, **Supp. XXIII:** 103
Tillich, Paul, **II:** 244; **III:** 291, 292, 303, 309; **IV:** 226; **Retro. Supp. I:** 325, 326, 327; **Supp. V:** 267; **Supp. XIII:** 74, 91
Tillie Olsen: A Study of the Short Fiction (Frye), **Supp. XIII:** 292, 296, 298, 299, 302
Tillman, Lynne, **Supp. XII:** 4
Tillotson, John, **II:** 114
Tillotson, Kristen, **Supp. XVII:** 23
Tillstrom, Burr, **Supp. XIV:** 125

Till the Day I Die (Odets), **Supp. II Part 2:** 530, 533–536, 552
Tilton, Eleanor, **Supp. I Part 1:** 317
Tilton, Theodore, **Supp. XVIII:** 4
Timaeus (Plato), **II:** 10; **III:** 609
Tim: A Story of School Life (Sturgis), **Supp. XX: 227, 230, 232, 233–235**
Timber (Jonson), **II:** 16
Timberg, Scott, **Supp. XV:** 116
"Timberwolf" (Halliday), **Supp. XIX:** 91
Timbuktu (Auster), **Supp. XII:** 34, **35–36**
"Time" (Matthews), **Supp. IX: 165–166**
"Time" (Merrill), **Supp. III Part 1:** 325
"Time" (Very), **Supp. XXV:** 249
"Time and Again" (Sanders), **Supp. XVI:** 269
Time and a Place, A (Humphrey), **Supp. IX:** 95, 98, **100–102**
"Time and Distance Overcome" (Biss), **Supp. XXVI:** 55–56
"Time and the Garden" (Winters), **Supp. II Part 2:** 801, 809
"Time and the Liturgy" (Merton), **Supp. VIII:** 199
Time and the River (Edgell), **Supp. XXIII:** 84, 85, **91–93**
Time and Tide: A Walk through Nantucket (Conroy), **Supp. XVI:** 63, 71, **76–77**
Timebends (A. Miller), **Retro. Supp. III:** 172
"Time Exposure" (C. Baxter), **Supp. XVII:** 20–21
Time Exposures, by Search-Light (W. Frank), **Supp. XX: 75**
Time in the Rock (Aiken), **I:** 65
Time Is Noon, The (Buck), **Supp. II Part 1:** 129, 130–131
Time & Money (Matthews), **Supp. IX:** 155, **165–167**
"Time of Death, A" (Munro), **Supp. XXVII:** 180
"Time of Friendship, The" (Bowles), **Supp. IV Part 1:** 90–91
"Time of Her Time, The" (Mailer), **III:** 37, 45; **Retro. Supp. II:** 200
Time of Our Time, The (Mailer), **Retro. Supp. II:** 213–214
Time of the Assassins, The: A Study of Rimbaud (H. Miller), **III:** 189
"Time of the Missile" (Oppen), **Supp. XXVI:** 232
Time Out of Mind (album, Dylan), **Supp. XVIII:** 28
"Time Past" (Morris), **III:** 232
"Time Present" (Morris), **III:** 232
"Times" (Beattie), **Supp. V:** 31
"Times, The" (Emerson), **II:** 11–12
Times Are Never So Bad, The (Dubus), **Supp. VII:** 87–88
Time's Arrow (Amis), **Retro. Supp. I:** 278
"Time Shall Not Die" (Chandler), **Supp. IV Part 1:** 120
Times of Melville and Whitman, The (Brooks), **I:** 257
Time's Power: Poems 1985–1988 (Rich), **Retro. Supp. III:** 250
Times They Are A-Changin', The (album, Dylan), **Supp. XVIII:** 20, 25
"Times They Are A-Changin,' The" (song, Dylan), **Supp. XVIII:** 30
"Timesweep" (Sandburg), **III:** 595–596
Time to Act, A (MacLeish), **III:** 3
Time to Be Born, A (Powell), **Supp. XIX:** 143
Time to Go (Dixon), **Supp. XII:** 147
Time to Kill (film), **Supp. IV Part 1:** 130
Time to Speak, A (MacLeish), **III:** 3
Time Will Darken It (Maxwell), **Supp. VIII:** 159, **162–164,** 169
"Timing of Sin, The" (Dubus), **Supp. VII:** 91
Tim O'Brien (Herzog), **Supp. V:** 239
Timoleon (Melville), **III:** 93; **Retro. Supp. I:** 257; **Retro. Supp. III:** 161
Timothy Dexter Revisited (Marquand), **III:** 55, 62, 63
Timothy Findley: Stories from a Life (Roberts), **Supp. XX: 53**
Timrod, Henry, **Supp. XVIII:** 31, 33
Tin Can, The (W. J. Smith), **Supp. XIII:** 334, **Supp. XIII:** 336, 337
"Tin Can, The" (W. J. Smith), **Supp. XIII: 337–339**
Tin Can Tree, The (Tyler), **Supp. IV Part 2:** 659–660
Tinguely, Jean, **Supp. XV:** 187
Tinker, Chauncey Brewster, **Supp. XIV:** 12
"Tinseled Bucks: A Historical Study of Indian Homosexuality"(Kenny), **Supp. XXIII:** 149
Tintern Abbey (Wordsworth), **Supp. I Part 2:** 673, 675
Tiny Alice (Albee), **I:** 81–86, 87, 88, 94
"Tiny Closet, The" (Inge), **Supp. XXV:** 105–106
"Tiny Mummies! The True Story of the Ruler of 43rd Street's Land of the Walking Dead" (Wolfe), **Supp. III Part 2:** 573, 574
Tip on a Dead Jockey and Other Stories (Shaw), **Supp. XIX:** 251
"Tip-Top Club, The" (Keillor), **Supp. XVI:** 172
"Tired" (Hughes), **Supp. I Part 1:** 331
"Tired and Unhappy, You Think of Houses" (Schwartz), **Supp. II Part 2:** 649
"Tiresias" (Garrett), **Supp. VII:** 96–97
'Tis (McCourt), **Supp. XII:** 271, **279–286**
Tisch (Dixon), **Supp. XII:** 141, **155–156**
" 'Tis Finished" (Very), **Supp. XXV:** 249
Tish (Rinehart), **Supp. XXV:** 194
Tish Marches On (Rinehart), **Supp. XXV:** 194
Tish Plays the Game (Rinehart), **Supp. XXV:** 194
Titan, The (Dreiser), **I:** 497, 501, 507–508, 509, 510; **Retro. Supp. II:** 94, 101, 102
Titanic Operas (Dickinson Electronic Archives), **Supp. XXVII:** 261
Titian, **Supp. I Part 2:** 397, 714
"Tito's Goodbye" (García), **Supp. XI:** 190
"To a Bird, Seen Under My Window in the Garden"(J. Schoolcraft), **Supp. XXIII:** 230
To a Blossoming Pear Tree (Wright), **Supp. III Part 2:** 602–605
"To a Blossoming Pear Tree" (Wright), **Supp. III Part 2:** 604
"To Abolish Children" (Shapiro), **Supp. II Part 2:** 717
To Abolish Children and Other Essays (Shapiro), **Supp. II Part 2:** 703
"To a Calvinist in Bali" (Millay), **Supp. XXVI:** 170
"To a Caty-Did, the Precursor of Winter" (Freneau), **Supp. II Part 1:** 274–275
"To a Chameleon" (Moore), **III:** 195, 196, 215
"To a Conscript of 1940" (Read), **II:** 372–373, 377–378
"To a Contemporary Bunk Shooter" (Sandburg), **III:** 582
"To a Cough in the Street at Midnight" (Wylie), **Supp. I Part 2:** 727, 729–730
"To a Defeated Savior" (Wright), **Supp. III Part 2:** 593–594, 596
"To a Face in the Crowd" (Warren), **IV:** 239
"To a Fish Head Found on the Beach near Malaga" (Levine), **Supp. V:** 185
"To a Friend" (Nemerov), **III:** 272

"To a Friend"(O'Hara), **Supp. XXIII:** 212
"To a Friend Whose Work Has Come to Triumph" (Sexton), **Supp. II Part 2:** 683
To a God Unknown (Steinbeck), **I:** 107; **IV:** 51, 59–60, 67
"To a Greek Marble" (Aldington), **Supp. I Part 1:** 257
"To a Locomotive in Winter" (Whitman), **IV:** 348
"To a Mad Friend" (Davison), **Supp. XXVI:** 69
"To a Military Rifle" (Winters), **Supp. II Part 2:** 810, 811, 815
"To a Mouse" (Burns), **Supp. IX:** 173
"To an American Workman Dying of Starvation" (Taggard), **Supp. XXII:** 282
"To an Athlete Dying Young" (Houseman), **Supp. XVII:** 121
"To a Negro Jazz Band in a Parisian Cabaret" (Hughes), **Supp. I Part 1:** 325
"To an Old Philosopher in Rome" (Stevens), **III:** 605; **Retro. Supp. I:** 312
"To an Old Poet in Peru" (Ginsberg), **Supp. II Part 1:** 322
"To a Now-Type Poet" (X. J. Kennedy), **Supp. XV:** 161
"To Answer Your Question" (Jarman), **Supp. XVII:** 114–115
"To Any Would-Be Terrorists" (Nye), **Supp. XIII:** 285, 286
"To a Picture of Eleonora Duse" (Teasdale), **Supp. XXVII:** 287
"To a Poet" (Rich), **Supp. I Part 2:** 571; **Supp. XIX:** 83
"To a Prize Bird" (Moore), **III:** 215
"To a Republican, with Mr. Paine's Rights of Man" (Freneau), **Supp. II Part 1:** 267
"To a Revolutionary Girl" (Bodenheim), **Supp. XXV:** 28
"To a Shade" (Yeats), **III:** 18
"To a Skylark" (Shelley), **Supp. I Part 2:** 720; **Supp. X:** 31
"Toast to Harlem, A" (Hughes), **Supp. I Part 1:** 338
"To Aunt Rose" (Ginsberg), **Supp. II Part 1:** 320
"To Autumn" (Keats), **Supp. IX:** 50
"To a Waterfowl" (Bryant), **Supp. I Part 1:** 154, 155, 162, 171
"To a Young Poet" (X. J. Kennedy), **Supp. XV:** 161
"To a Young Writer" (Stegner), **Supp. X:** 24
"Tobacco" (Rash), **Supp. XXVII:** 218
Tobacco Road (Caldwell), **I:** 288, 289, 290, 295–296, 297, 298, 302, 307, 309, 310; **IV:** 198; **Supp. XXII:** 196
"To Be a Monstrous Clever Fellow" (Fante), **Supp. XI:** 167
"To Become Music or Break" (Jauss), **Supp. XXI:** 133
To Bedlam and Part Way Back (Sexton), **Retro. Supp. II:** 245; **Supp. II Part 2:** 672–678; **Supp. IV Part 2:** 441; **Supp. XI:** 317
"To Beethoven" (Lanier), **Supp. I Part 1:** 364
To Begin Again: Stories and Memoirs, 1908–1929 (M. F. K. Fisher), **Supp. XVII:** 92
Tobey, Mark, **Supp. X:** 264
To Be Young, Gifted, and Black: Lorraine Hansberry in Her Own Words (Nemiroff), **Supp. IV Part 1:** 372, 374
"To Big Mary from an Ex-Catholic" (Mora), **Supp. XIII:** 217, 224, 228
Tobin, Jacqueline L., **Supp. XXVI:** 200
"Tobin's Palm" (O. Henry), **Supp. II Part 1:** 408; **Supp. XV:** 40
Tobit (apocryphal book), **I:** 89
"To Brooklyn Bridge" (H. Crane), **Retro. Supp. III:** 51
"To Build a Fire" (London), **II:** 468
Toby Tyler: or, Ten Weeks with a Circus (Otis), **III:** 577
"To Change in a Good Way" (Ortiz), **Supp. IV Part 2:** 511
"To Charlotte Cushman" (Lanier), **Supp. I Part 1:** 364
"To Cole, the Painter, Departing for Europe" (Bryant), **Supp. I Part 1:** 157, 161
Tocqueville, Alexis de, **III:** 261; **IV:** 349; **Retro. Supp. I:** 235; **Supp. I Part 1:** 137; **Supp. I Part 2:** 659, 660; **Supp. II Part 1:** 281, 282, 284; **Supp. XIV:** 306, 312
"To Crispin O'Conner" (Freneau), **Supp. II Part 1:** 268
"To Da-Duh, In Memoriam" (Marshall), **Supp. XI:** 276
"TODAY" (Baraka), **Supp. II Part 1:** 55
"Today" (Ginsberg), **Supp. II Part 1:** 328
"Today Is a Good Day To Die" (Bell), **Supp. X:** 7
"Today"(O'Hara), **Supp. XXIII:** 210–211
Today We Live (film), **Retro. Supp. III:** 84
"Today Will Be a Quiet Day" (Hempel), **Supp. XXI:** 117,**Supp. XXI:** 118
Todd, Mabel Loomis, **I:** 454, 470; **Retro. Supp. I:** 33, 34, 35, 39, 47
"To Death" (Levertov), **Supp. III Part 1:** 274
"To Delmore Schwartz" (R. Lowell), **II:** 547; **Retro. Supp. II:** 188
"to disembark" (Brooks), **Supp. III Part 1:** 86
"To Dorothy on Her Exclusion from The Guinness Book of Records" (X. J. Kennedy), **Supp. XV:** 166
"To Dream of Bears" (Gallagher), **Supp. XXIV:** 176
"To Dr. Thomas Shearer" (Lanier), **Supp. I Part 1:** 370
"To Earthward" (Frost), **II:** 154
"To Edward John Moreton Drax Plunkett, Eighteenth Baron Dunsany" (Lovecraft), **Supp. XXV:** 113
"To Edwin V. McKenzie" (Winters), **Supp. II Part 2:** 801
"To Eleonora Duse" (A. Lowell), **II:** 528
"To Elizabeth Ward Perkins" (A. Lowell), **II:** 516
"To Elsie" (W. C. Williams), **Retro. Supp. I:** 419
"To Emily Dickinson" (H. Crane), **Retro. Supp. II:** 76
"To E. T." (Frost), **Retro. Supp. I:** 132
To Feel These Things (L. Michaels), **Supp. XVI:** 205, **213–214**
"To Feel These Things" (L. Michaels), **Supp. XVI:** 214
Toffler, Alvin, **Supp. IV Part 2:** 517
"To Fill" (Moore), **Supp. X:** 168, 169
"To Gabriela, a Young Writer" (Mora), **Supp. XIII:** 220
"To George May" (Bodenheim), **Supp. XXV:** 25
To Have and Have Not (film), **Retro. Supp. III:** 85; **Supp. XV:** 347
To Have and Have Not (Hemingway), **I:** 31; **II:** 253–254, 264; **Retro. Supp. I:** 182, **183,** 187
"To Helen" (Poe), **III:** 410, 411, 427; **Retro. Supp. II:** 102; **Retro. Supp. III:** 224, 232
"To Hell With Dying" (Walker), **Supp. III Part 2:** 523
"To Her Father with Some Verses" (Bradstreet), **Retro. Supp. III:** 2, 12
"To His Coy Mistress"(Marvell), **Supp. XXIII:** 62
"To His Excellency General Washington" (Wheatley), **Supp. XX: 289**
"To His Father" (Jeffers), **Supp. II**

Part 2: 415
Toilet, The (Baraka), **Supp. II Part 1:** 37, 40–42
"To James Russell Lowell" (Holmes), **Supp. I Part 1:** 311
To Jerusalem and Back (Bellow), **Retro. Supp. II:** 29
"To Jesus on His Birthday" (Millay), **III:** 136–137
"To John Keats" (A. Lowell), **II:** 516
"To Judge Faolain, Dead Long Enough: A Summons" (McCarriston), **Supp. XIV:** 264–265
"To Justify My Singing" (Wright), **Supp. III Part 2:** 590
"To Kill a Deer" (C. Frost), **Supp. XV:** 102
To Kill a Mockingbird (film), **Supp. VIII:** 128–129
To Kill a Mockingbird (Lee), **Supp. VIII: 113–129; Supp. XIX:** 142; **Supp. XVI:** 259; **Supp. XXVII:** 13
"To Kill a Mockingbird: Harper Lee's Tragic Vision" (Dave), **Supp. VIII:** 126
To Kill a Mockingbird: Threatening Boundaries (C. D. Johnson), **Supp. VIII:** 126
Toklas, Alice B., **IV:** 27; **Supp. IV Part 1:** 81, 91; **Supp. XVI:** 187
"Tokyo Story" (Wasserstein), **Supp. XV:** 328
"To Larry Rivers"(O'Hara), **Supp. XXIII:** 212
"To Light" (Hogan), **Supp. IV Part 1:** 402
"To Ligurinus" (Horace; Ferry, trans.), **Supp. XXIV:** 155
"To Ligurinus" (Horace; Howard, trans.), **Supp. XXIV:** 155
"To Live and Diet" (Wasserstein), **Supp. XV:** 328
Tolkien, J. R. R., **Supp. V:** 140
Tolkin, Michael, **Supp. XI:** 160
Toller, Ernst, **I:** 479
"To Lose the Earth" (Sexton), **Supp. II Part 2:** 684, 685
Tolson, Melvin, **Retro. Supp. I:** 208, 209, 210
Tolstoy, Leo, **I:** 6, 7, 58, 103, 312, 376; **II:** 191–192, 205, 271, 272, 275, 276, 281, 285, 286, 320, 407, 542, 559, 570, 579, 606; **III:** 37, 45, 61, 323, 467, 572; **IV:** 17, 21, 170, 285; **Retro. Supp. I:** 91, 225; **Retro. Supp. II:** 299; **Supp. I Part 1:** 2, 3, 6, 20; **Supp. IV Part 1:** 392; **Supp. IX:** 246; **Supp. V:** 277, 323; **Supp. XI:** 68; **Supp. XII:** 310, 322; **Supp. XIV:** 87, 97, 98; **Supp. XIX:** 241; **Supp. XXIII:** 4, 11, 275; **Supp. XXIV:** 132; **Supp. XXV:** 142
"To Lu Chi" (Nemerov), **III:** 275
"To Lydia" (Horace; Ferry, trans.), **Supp. XXIV:** 154
"To Lydia" (Horace; McHugh, trans.), **Supp. XXIV:** 154
Tom (Cummings), **I:** 430
"Tom" (Oliver), **Supp. VII:** 232
"To M." (Teasdale), **Supp. XXVII:** 297
"Tom, Tom, the Piper's Son" (Ransom), **Supp. X:** 58
"To M, with a Rose" (Lanier), **Supp. I Part 1:** 364
To Make a Prairie (Kumin), **Supp. IV Part 2:** 440, 441
"To Make Words Disappear" (Simpson), **Supp. IX:** 265–266
Tomás and the Library Lady (Mora), **Supp. XIII:** 216, 221
"Tomatoes" (Francis), **Supp. IX:** 82
"Tom Ball's Barn" (Kooser), **Supp. XIX:** 119
"Tom Brown at Fisk" (Du Bois), **Supp. II Part 1:** 160
Tom Brown's School Days (Hughes), **Supp. I Part 2:** 406
"Tomb Stone" (Dickey), **Supp. IV Part 1:** 185
"Tombstone Blues" (song, Dylan), **Supp. XVIII:** 30
Tomcat in Love (O'Brien), **Supp. V:** 238, 240, 243, 252–254
"Tomcat's Wife, The" (C. Bly), **Supp. XVI:** 40
Tomcat's Wife and Other Stories, The (C. Bly), **Supp. XVI:** 40–41
"Tom Fool at Jamaica" (Moore), **III:** 215
To Mix with Time (Swenson), **Supp. IV Part 2:** 637, 643–645, 645
Tom Jones (Fielding), **I:** 131; **Supp. V:** 127
Tomlinson, Charles, **Supp. XVI:** 284
Tommy Gallagher's Crusade (Farrell), **II:** 44
Tommyknockers, The (King), **Supp. V:** 139, 144
"Tommy's Burglar" (Henry), **Supp. II Part 1:** 399, 401
"Tommy Stames" (Budbill), **Supp. XIX:** 8
Tomo Cheeki (pseudonym). See Freneau, Philip
Tomorrow Is Another Day (E. P. Jones), **Supp. XXII:** 252
Tomorrow is Another Day (film, Feist), **Supp. XVII:** 62
"Tomorrow the Moon" (Dos Passos), **I:** 493
Tomorrow Will Be Better (B. Smith), **Supp. XXIII:** 258, **264–267**
"Tom Outland's Story" (Cather), **I:** 325–326
Tompkins, Jane, **Supp. XVI:** 89; **Supp. XVIII:** 258, 259, 263
Tompson, Benjamin, **Supp. I Part 1:** 110, 111
"Tom-Rock Through Eels" (Hempel), **Supp. XXI:** 116, 118, **123–124**
Tom Sawyer (Twain). See Adventures of Tom Sawyer, The (Twain)
Tom Sawyer Abroad (Twain), **II:** 482; **IV:** 19, 204
Tom Sawyer Detective (Twain), **IV:** 204
Tom Sawyer (musical) (Gurney), **Supp. V:** 96
"Tom's Husband" (Jewett), **Retro. Supp. II:** 132, 141
Tom Swift (Stratemeyer), **III:** 146
Tom-Walker, The (Sandoz), **Supp. XXIV:** 244, **253–255**
"Tom Wolfe's Guide to Etiquette" (Wolfe), **Supp. III Part 2:** 578
"To My Brother Killed: Haumont Wood: October, 1918" (Bogan), **Supp. III Part 1:** 58
"To My Class, on Certain Fruits and Flowers Sent Me in Sickness" (Lanier), **Supp. I Part 1:** 370
"To My Dear and Loving Husband" (Bradstreet), **Retro. Supp. III:** 12
"To My Dear Children" (Bradstreet), **Retro. Supp. III:** 13
"To my ever beloved & lamented son William Henry"(J. Schoolcraft), **Supp. XXIII:** 226, 231
"To My Father's Ghost" (Everwine), **Supp. XV:** 76
"To My Ghost Reflected in the Auxvasse River" (Levis), **Supp. XI:** 265
"To My Greek" (Merrill), **Supp. III Part 1:** 326
"To My Missionary Critics" (Twain), **Retro. Supp. III:** 268–269
"To My Mother" (Berry), **Supp. X:** 23
"To My Sister—Ernestine Kealoha Taggard, 1900–1943" (Taggard), **Supp. XXII:** 284
"To My Small Son, at the Photographer's" (Hay), **Supp. XIV:** 121
"To My Small Son, on Certain Occasions" (Hay), **Supp. XIV:** 121
"To My Students" (Taggard), **Supp. XXII:** 280
"To Name is to Possess" (Kincaid),

Supp. VII: 194
Tone, Aileen, **I:** 21–22
"Tongue Is, The" (Komunyakaa), **Supp. XIII:** 113
"Tongue of the Jews" (Bukiet), **Supp. XVII:** 47
Tongues (Shepard and Chaikin), **Supp. III Part 2:** 433
Tongues of Angels, The (Price), **Supp. VI:** 265
Tongues Untied (Riggs; film), **Supp. XI:** 19, 20
"Tonight" (R. Lowell), **II:** 538
"Tonight Is Part of the Struggle"(Le Sueur), **Supp. XXIII: 172**
Tonight Is the Night of the Prom (Jarman), **Supp. XVII:** 110, **112–113**
"Tonight Is the Night of the Prom" (Jarman), **Supp. XVII:** 113
Tonight No Poetry Will Serve: Poems 2007–2010 (Rich), **Retro. Supp. III:** 252
Tonkin, Boyd, **Supp. XXVII:** 270
Tony Kushner in Conversation (Vorlicky, ed.), **Supp. IX:** 132
"Too Anxious for Rivers" (Frost), **II:** 162
"Too Blue" (Hughes), **Retro. Supp. I:** 207
"Too Damn Close: Thresholds and Their Maintenance in Rick Bass's Work" (Kerridge), **Supp. XVI:** 26
"Too Early" (Leopold), **Supp. XIV:** 186
"Too Early Spring" (Benét), **Supp. XI:** 53
"Too Far from Home" (Bowles), **Supp. IV Part 1:** 94–95
Too Far from Home: Selected Writings of Paul Bowles (Halpern, ed.), **Supp. IV Part 1:** 94, 95
Too Far to Go: The Maples Stories (Updike), **Retro. Supp. I:** 321
"Too Good To Be True": The Life and Art of Leslie Fiedler (Winchell), **Supp. XIII:** 94, 98, 99, 101
Toohey, John Peter, **Supp. IX:** 190
Toolan, David, **Supp. IV Part 1:** 308
Too Late (Dixon), **Supp. XII: 143–144**
"Too Late" (Pickering), **Supp. XXI:** 197
"Too-Late Born, The" (Hemingway), **III:** 9
Toole, John Kennedy, **Supp. XIV:** 21; **Supp. XXVI: 239–254**
"Toolless" (Pickering), **Supp. XXI:** 204
Too Many Bottles (Holding), **Supp. XXII:** 126, **134–135**
"Too Many Friends" (video, Ellis), **Supp. XXVII:** 80
Toomer, Jean, **Retro. Supp. II:** 79; **Retro. Supp. III:** 48; **Supp. I Part 1:** 325, 332; **Supp. III Part 2: 475–491; Supp. IV Part 1:** 16, 164, 168; **Supp. IX: 305–322; Supp. XIII:** 305; **Supp. XVIII:** 122; **Supp. XX: 73; Supp. XXII:** 6
Toomer, Nathan Eugene Pinchback. See Toomer, Jean
Too Much Happiness (Munro), **Supp. XXVII:** 195
"Too Much Happiness" (Munro), **Supp. XXVII:** 195
Too Much Johnson (film), **Supp. IV Part 1:** 83
"To One Who Said Me Nay" (Cullen), **Supp. IV Part 1:** 166
"Tooth, The" (Jackson), **Supp. IX:** 122
Tooth and Claw (Boyle), **Supp. XX: 20**
Tooth of Crime, The (Shepard), **Supp. III Part 2:** 432, 441–445, 447
"Too Young" (O'Hara), **III:** 369
Topaz (film), **Supp. XX: 253**
Topaz (Uris), **Supp. XX: 247, 248, 253**
"Top Israeli Official Hints at 'Shared' Jerusalem" (Nye), **Supp. XIII:** 287
"To P. L., 1916–1937" (Levine), **Supp. V:** 185
"To Please a Shadow" (Brodsky), **Supp. VIII:** 30
"Top of the Food Chain" (Boyle), **Supp. XX: 20**
"Top of the Hill" (Jewett), **II:** 406
"Topography" (Olds), **Supp. X:** 208
Topography and Other Poems (Stone), **Supp. XXVII:** 256, 262
Topper (T. Smith), **Supp. IX:** 194
To Praise the Music (Bronk), **Supp. XXI:** 31, 32
To Quito and Back (Hecht), **Supp. XXVII:** 89
Torah, **IV:** 19
"Torch Songs" (Wrigley), **Supp. XVIII:** 296
Torday, Daniel, **Supp. XXII:** 151
"To Reach Japan" (Munro), **Supp. XXVII:** 195
"Toronto, More or Less, in Fifteen Years" (Gansworth), **Supp. XXVI:** 110
Torpedo 8: The Story of Swede Larsen's Bomber Squadron (Wolfert), **Supp. XXI:** 267
Torpedo Junction (Hickam), **Supp. XXVII:** 103, 111
"Torquemada" (Bukiet), **Supp. XVII:** 44
"Torquemada" (Longfellow), **II:** 505; **Retro. Supp. II:** 164
Torrence, Ridgely, **III:** 507
Torrent and the Night Before, The (Robinson), **III:** 504
Torrents of Spring, The (Hemingway), **I:** 117; **II:** 250–251
Torres, Ben Fong, **Supp. XXVI:** 209
Torres, Héctor A., **Supp. XIII:** 225
Torres, Louis, **Supp. IV Part 2:** 529, 530
Torres-Saillant, Silvio, **Supp. XXI:** 104, 105, 108, 109
Torsney, Cheryl, **Retro. Supp. I:** 224
Tortilla Curtain, The (Boyle), **Supp. VIII: 9–10; Supp. XX: 28–29**
Tortilla Flat (Steinbeck), **IV:** 50, 51, 61, 64
Tortilla Flats (Steinbeck), **Supp. XX: 28**
Tortured Skins, and Other Fictions (Kenny), **Supp. XXIII:** 150, 156, 157
Tory Lover, The (Jewett), **II:** 406; **Retro. Supp. II:** 144–145
"Toscana" (Dixon), **Supp. XII:** 154
"To Sestius" (Horace; Ferry, trans.), **Supp. XXIV:** 155
"To Sestius" (Horace; Lasdun, trans.), **Supp. XXIV:** 154
"To Sir Toby" (Freneau), **Supp. II Part 1:** 269
"To Sophy, Expectant" (Mumford), **Supp. II Part 2:** 475
"To Speak of Woe That Is in Marriage" (R. Lowell), **II:** 550
"To Statecraft Embalmed" (Moore), **III:** 197
To Stay Alive (Levertov), **Supp. III Part 1:** 280–282
"Total Eclipse" (Dillard), **Supp. VI:** 28
"Total Eclipse of the Moon"(Crooker), **Supp. XXIII:** 55
Total Immersion (Goodman), **Supp. XXVI:** 118–121, 125
"Total Immersion" (Goodman), **Supp. XXVI:** 120
Total Recall (Paretsky), **Supp. XXV:** 172, 180, 181, 183–184
Toth, Emily, **Retro. Supp. II:** 71
Toth, Susan Allan, **Retro. Supp. II:** 138
"To the Americans of the United States" (Freneau), **Supp. II Part 1:** 271
"To the Apennines" (Bryant), **Supp. I Part 1:** 157, 164
"To the Bleeding Hearts Association of

American Novelists" (Nemerov), **III:** 281
"To the Botequim & Back" (Bishop), **Retro. Supp. II:** 51
To the Bright and Shining Sun (Burke), **Supp. XIV:** 22, 25
"To the Citizens of the United States" (Paine), **Supp. I Part 2:** 519–520
"To the Dandelion" (J. R. Lowell), **Supp. I Part 2:** 424
"To the End" (Haines), **Supp. XII:** 212–213
To the Ends of the Earth: The Selected Travels of Paul Theroux, **Supp. VIII:** 324
"To the Fabulous Constellation" (Ferry), **Supp. XXIV:** 148–149
"To the Film Industry in Crisis"(O'Hara), **Supp. XXIII:** 214
To the Finland Station: A Study in the Writing and Acting of History (Wilson), **IV:** 429, 436, 443–444, 446
"To the Governor & Legislature of Massachusetts" (Nemerov), **III:** 287
To the Green Man (Jarman), **Supp. XVII:** 110, 120–121
"To the Harbormaster" (O'Hara), **Supp. XXIII:** 208, 212, 214; **Supp. XXIV:** 42
To the Holy Spirit (Winters), **Supp. II Part 2:** 810
"To the Keeper of the King's Water Works" (Freneau), **Supp. II Part 1:** 269
"To the Lacedemonians" (Tate), **IV:** 134
"To the Laodiceans" (Jarrell), **Retro. Supp. I:** 121, 140
To the Lighthouse (Woolf), **I:** 309; **II:** 600; **Retro. Supp. II:** 337; **Retro. Supp. III:** 128; **Supp. VIII:** 155
"To the Man on Trail" (London), **II:** 466
"To the Memory of My Dear and Ever Honoured Father Thomas Dudley" (Bradstreet), **Retro. Supp. III:** 12
"To the Memory of the Brave Americans Under General Greene" (Freneau), **Supp. II Part 1:** 262, 274
"To the Miscodeed"(J. Schoolcraft), **Supp. XXIII:** 230
"To the Muse" (Wright), **Supp. III Part 2:** 601
"To the Natural World: at 37" (Taggard), **Supp. XXII:** 279–280
"To the Nazi Leaders" (Hay), **Supp. XIV:** 121
"To the New World" (Jarrell), **II:** 371
"To the One of Fictive Music" (Stevens), **IV:** 89; **Retro. Supp. I:** 297, 300
"To the One Upstairs" (Simic), **Supp. VIII:** 283
"To the Peoples of the World" (Du Bois), **Supp. II Part 1:** 172
"To the Person Sitting in Darkness" (Twain), **Retro. Supp. III:** 268
"To the Pine Tree on first seeing it on returning from Europe"(J. Schoolcraft), **Supp. XXIII:** 225, 228, 232–233
To the Place of Trumpets (B. Kelly), 132; **Supp. XVII: 123–127**
"To the Pliocene Skull" (Harte), **Supp. II Part 1:** 343–344
"To the Powers of Darkness" (Taggard), **Supp. XXII:** 279, 280
"To the Powers of Desolation" (Taggard), **Supp. XXII:** 280
"To the pure all things are pure" (Very), **Supp. XXV:** 242, 248
"To the Queen of Heaven" (Taggard), **Supp. XXII:** 280
"To the Reader" (Baudelaire), **II:** 544–545
"To The Reader" (Jarman), **Supp. XVII:** 115
"To the Reader" (Levertov), **Supp. III Part 1:** 277
"To the Republic" (Horace; Ferry, trans.), **Supp. XXIV:** 154
"To the Right Honourable William, Earl of Dartmouth" (Wheatley), **Supp. XX: 278, 284, 287–288**
"To the River Arve" (Bryant), **Supp. I Part 1:** 163
"To the Snake" (Levertov), **Supp. III Part 1:** 277
"To the Stone-Cutters" (Jeffers), **Supp. II Part 2:** 420
"To the Unseeable Animal" (Berry), **Supp. X:** 31
"To the Western World" (Simpson), **Supp. IX:** 269, 270
To the White Sea (Dickey), **Supp. IV Part 1:** 186, 190–191
"To the Young Who Want to Die" (Brooks), **Supp. III Part 1:** 85–86
"To Tlaoc of the Rain" (Everwine), **Supp. XV:** 77
"To Train a Writer" (Bierce), **I:** 199
"Touch, The" (Sexton), **Supp. II Part 2:** 687
Touch and Go (M. F. K. Fisher and D. Parrish), **Supp. XVII:** 84
"Touching the Tree" (Merwin), **Supp. III Part 1:** 355
Touching the World (Eakin), **Supp. VIII:** 167
Touch of Danger, A (Jones), **Supp. XI:** 226, **228–229**
Touch of the Poet, A (O'Neill), **III:** 385, 401, 404
Touchstone, The (Wharton), **Retro. Supp. I:** 365; **Retro. Supp. III:** 278, 279
Touchstone Anthology of Contemporary Nonfiction, The: Work from 1970 to the Present (Williford and Martone, eds.), **Supp. XXVI:** 53
"Touch-up Man" (Komunyakaa), **Supp. XIII:** 119
Tough Guys Don't Dance (Mailer), **Retro. Supp. II:** 211
"Tough People" (Offutt), **Supp. XIX:** 170–171
Toulet, Paul Jean, **IV:** 79
Tour (McNally), **Supp. XIII:** 197
"Tour 5" (Hayden), **Supp. II Part 1:** 381
To Urania (Brodsky), **Supp. VIII:** 22, 28–29
Tourgée, Albion W., **Supp. XIV:** 63
"Tour Guide" (Komunyakaa), **Supp. XIII:** 114
"Tourist Death" (MacLeish), **III:** 12
Tourmaline (J. Scott), **Supp. XVII: 192–194,** 195
Tour of Duty (Dos Passos), **I:** 489
"Tour of the Labyrinth" (Stallings), **Supp. XXV:** 229
Touron the Prairies, A (Irving), **II:** 312–313
Toussaint L'Ouverture, **Supp. XXI:** 166
Toussaint L'Ouverture (C. L. R. James), **Supp. XXI:** 167
Tovey, Donald Francis, **Supp. XIV:** 336
"To Virgil" (Horace; Ferry, trans.), **Supp. XXIV:** 155
"To Virgil" (Horace; Wright, trans.), **Supp. XXIV:** 155
To Walk a Crooked Mile (McGrath), **Supp. X:** 117
Toward a New Synthesis (Begiebing), **Retro. Supp. II:** 210
"Toward an Understanding of the Public Life" (Davison), **Supp. XXVI:** 73
"Toward a Woman-Centered University" (Rich), **Retro. Supp. III:** 248
"Toward Nightfall" (Simic), **Supp. VIII:** 277
Towards a Better Life (Burke), **I:** 270
"Towards a Chicano Poetics: The Making of the Chicano Subject, 1969–

1982" (Saldívar), **Supp. IV Part 2:** 544
Towards an Enduring Peace (Bourne), **I:** 232
"Towards Morning" (Pedersen; Nelson, trans.), **Supp. XVIII:** 180
Toward the Blanched Alphabets (Sobin), **Supp. XVI:** 290
Toward the Gulf (Masters), **Supp. I Part 2:** 465–466
"Toward the Solstice" (Rich), **Supp. I Part 2:** 575–576
Toward Wholeness in Paule Marshall's Fiction (Pettis), **Supp. XI:** 276
"Tower" (Merwin), **Supp. III Part 1:** 343
"Tower Beyond Tragedy, The" (Jeffers), **Supp. II Part 2:** 429–430
Tower of Ivory (Atherton), **Supp. XXIV:** 21, 23
Tower of Ivory (MacLeish), **III:** 3–4
"Tower of Song" (Cohen), **Supp. XXVII:** 52
"Tower of the Elephant, The" (Howard), **Supp. XXVII:** 117, 125
Towers, Robert, **Supp. IX:** 259; **Supp. XVI:** 211; **Supp. XXV:** 86
"To What Red Hell" (C. Himes), **Supp. XVI:** 137
"To Whistler, American" (Pound), **III:** 465–466
"To Wine" (Bogan), **Supp. III Part 1:** 57, 58
Towle, Tony, **Supp. XXIII:** 221; **Supp. XXVII:** 23
Town, Caren J., **Supp. XVIII:** 195, 199
Town, The (Faulkner), **II:** 57, 73; **Retro. Supp. I:** 74, 82; **Retro. Supp. III:** 86
Town, The (Richter), **Supp. XVIII:** 207, **214–215,** 217
Town and the City, The (Kerouac), **Supp. III Part 1:** 222–224; **Supp. XIV:** 143
"Town Crier" (Bierce), **I:** 193, 194, 195, 196
"Town Crier Exclusive, Confessions of a Princess Manqué: 'How Royals Found Me "Unsuitable" to Marry Their Larry' " (Elkin), **Supp. VI:** 56
Town Down the River, The (Robinson), **III:** 508
"Town Dump, The" (Nemerov), **III:** 272, 275, 281
Towne, Robert, **Supp. XI:** 159, 172, 174
"Townhouse Interior with Cat" (Clampitt), **Supp. IX:** 40
Townie (Dubus III), **Supp. XXIV:** 98, **108–111**
"Townies" (Dubus), **Supp. VII:** 86
Town in the Forest, The: Life Story of Richmond, New Hampshire (Boyce; Faust, ed.), **Supp. XXI:** 8
"Town of the Sound of a Twig Breaking" (Carson), **Supp. XII: 102**
"Town Poor, The" (Jewett), **Retro. Supp. II:** 138, 139, 143
Townsend, Alison, **Supp. XIII:** 222; **Supp. XXIII:** 132, 139
Townsend, Ann, **Supp. V:** 77
Townsend, Jim, **Supp. XXII:** 243
"Towns in Colour" (A. Lowell), **II:** 523–524
Townsman, The (Sedges), **Supp. II Part 1:** 124–125
Town Smokes (P. Benedict), **Supp. XXIII: 35–39**
"Town Smokes"(P. Benedict), **Supp. XXIII:** 37
"To World War Two" (Koch), **Supp. XV:** 184
Toys in a Field (Komunyakaa), **Supp. XIII: 121–122**
"Toys in a Field" (Komunyakaa), **Supp. XIII:** 122
Toys in the Attic (Hellman), **Supp. I Part 1:** 289–290
Toyter mentsh, Der (The dead man) (Asch), **Supp. XXIII:** 9
Tracer (F. Barthelme), **Supp. XI:** 31–32, 33
Traces of Thomas Hariot, The (Rukeyser), **Supp. VI:** 273, 274, 283
"Tracing Life with a Finger" (Caldwell), **I:** 291
Tracker (Wagoner), **Supp. IX:** 329, **336–337**
"Tracking" (Wagoner), **Supp. IX:** 329
"Track Meet, The" (Schwartz), **Supp. II Part 2:** 665
Tracks (Erdrich), **Supp. IV Part 1:** 259, 262–263, 269, 272, 273–274, 274, 275
"Track-Workers" (Bodenheim), **Supp. XXV:** 22
"Tract" (W. C. Williams), **Retro. Supp. I:** 414
"Tract against Communism, A" (Twelve Southerners), **IV:** 125, 237
Tractatus (Wittgenstein), **Supp. XVII:** 143
Tracy, Benjamin, **Supp. XVIII:** 4
Tracy, D. H., **Supp. XVIII:** 178
Tracy, Lee, **IV:** 287, 288
Tracy, Steven, **Retro. Supp. I:** 195
"Trade, The" (Levine), **Supp. V:** 193
Trading Twelves (Callahan and Murray, eds.), **Retro. Supp. II:** 119
Trading Twelves: The Selected Letters of Ralph Ellison and Albert Murray (Murray and Callahan, eds.), **Supp. XIX:** 148, 158
Traditional History of the Confederacy of the Six Nations (Scott), **Supp. XXVI:** 87
" 'Traditional' Marriage: A Secular Affair" (P. N. Warren), **Supp. XX: 273**
"Tradition and Industrialization" (Wright), **IV:** 489–490
"Tradition and Mythology: Signatures of Landscape in Chicana Poetry" (Rebolledo), **Supp. XIII:** 214
"Tradition and the Individual Talent" (Eliot), **I:** 441, 574, 585; **Retro. Supp. I:** 59, 286
"Tradition and the Individual Talent" (T. S. Eliot), **Retro. Supp. III:** 66
Tragedies, Life and Letters of James Gates Percival (Swinburne), **Supp. I Part 2:** 422
Tragedy of Bees, A (P. N. Warren), **Supp. XX: 261**
"Tragedy of Bees, A" (P. N. Warren), **Supp. XX: 272**
Tragedy of Don Ippolito, The (Howells), **II:** 279
"Tragedy of Error, A" (James), **II:** 322; **Retro. Supp. I:** 218
Tragedy of Pudd'nhead Wilson, The (Twain), **IV:** 206–207
Tragic America (Dreiser), **Retro. Supp. II:** 95
"Tragic Dialogue" (Wylie), **Supp. I Part 2:** 724
Tragic Ground (Caldwell), **I:** 297, 306
Tragic Muse, The (James), **Retro. Supp. I:** 227
Traherne, Thomas, **IV:** 151; **Supp. III Part 1:** 14; **Supp. V:** 208; **Supp. XV:** 212; **Supp. XVI:** 282, 288, 295
"Trail, The" (W. J. Smith), **Supp. XIII:** 342
Trailerpark (Banks), **Supp. V:** 12
"Trailing Arbutus, The" (Whittier), **Supp. I Part 2:** 691
Trail of the Lonesome Pine, The (Fox), **Supp. XIII:** 166
"Train, The" (O'Connor), **Retro. Supp. II:** 225
"Train Dreams" (Berrigan), **Supp. XXIV:** 45
"Train Ride" (Berrigan), **Supp. XXIV:** 42, 43–44
"Train Rising Out of the Sea" (Ashbery), **Supp. III Part 1:** 22
"Trains" (Banks), **Supp. V:** 8

"Train Tune" (Bogan), **Supp. III Part 1:** 64
Train Whistle Guitar (Murray), **Supp. XIX: 153–155,** 157
Traitor, The (Wouk), **Supp. XXV:** 256, 259
"Traits of Indian Character" (Irving), **II:** 303
Trakl, Georg, **Supp. XVII:** 241
Tramp Abroad, A (Twain), **IV:** 200; **Retro. Supp. III:** 267, 268
Tramping With a Poet in the Rockies (S. Graham), **Supp. I Part 2:** 397
Tramp's Excuse, The (Lindsay), **Supp. I Part 2:** 379, 380, 382
Tran, Sharon, **Supp. XXVI:** 216, 218
"Trance, The" (Taggard), **Supp. XXII:** 280
"Transaction" (Cliff), **Supp. XXII:** 75
"Transatlantic" (Toomer), **Supp. III Part 2:** 486
Transatlantic Sketches (James), **II:** 324; **Retro. Supp. I:** 219
"Transcendental Etude" (Rich), **Retro. Supp. III:** 249; **Supp. I Part 2:** 576
"Transcontinental Highway" (Cowley), **Supp. II Part 1:** 141
"Transducer" (Ammons), **Supp. VII:** 28
"Transfiguration" (Jarman), **Supp. XVII:** 118, 119
"Transfigured Bird" (Merrill), **Supp. III Part 1:** 320–321
"Transformations" (Harjo), **Supp. XII:** 226
Transformations (Sexton), **Supp. II Part 2:** 689–691; **Supp. IV Part 2:** 447; **Supp. XIV:** 125
Transforming Madness: New Lives for People Living with Mental Illness (Neugeboren), **Supp. XVI:** 229
"Transit" (Conroy), **Supp. XVI:** 72
Transit to Narcissus, A (Mailer), **Retro. Supp. II:** 196
"Translation" (Espaillat), **Supp. XXI:** 107
"Translation and Transposition" (Carne-Ross), **Supp. I Part 1:** 268–269
"Translation of a Fragment of Simonides" (Bryant), **Supp. I Part 1:** 153, 155
"Translations" (Rich), **Supp. I Part 2:** 563
Translations of Ezra Pound, The (Kenner, ed.), **III:** 463
Translations of the Gospel Back into Tongues (Wright), **Supp. XV: 342–343,** 346
"Translator's Task, The"(Benjamin), **Supp. XXIII:** 28
"Trans-National America" (Bourne), **I:** 229, 230
"Transparency" (X. J. Kennedy), **Supp. XV:** 159–160
"Transparent Itineraries: 1983" (Sobin), **Supp. XVI:** 287
"Transparent Itineraries: 1984" (Sobin), **Supp. XVI:** 287
"Transparent Itineraries: 1992" (Sobin), **Supp. XVI:** 289
"Transparent Itineraries" poems (Sobin), **Supp. XVI:** 290
Transparent Man, The (Hecht), **Supp. X:** 57, **69–71**
"Transparent Man, The" (Hecht), **Supp. X: 69–70**
Transparent Things (Nabokov), **Retro. Supp. I:** 266, 270, 277
"Transport" (Simic), **Supp. VIII:** 282
Transport to Summer (Stevens), **IV:** 76, 93; **Retro. Supp. I:** 309–312
Tranströmer, Thomas, **Supp. IV Part 2:** 648
"Traps for the Unwary" (Bourne), **I:** 235
Trash Trilogy (McMurtry), **Supp. V:** 225–226, 231
Traub, James, **Supp. XXIV:** 221, 222
Traubel, Horace, **IV:** 350
"Travel: After a Death" (Kenyon), **Supp. VII:** 169
Travel Alarm (Nye), **Supp. XIII:** 277
"Traveled World, The" (Pickering), **Supp. XXI:** 203
"Traveler, The" (Haines), **Supp. XII:** 203–204, 210
"Traveler, The" (Stegner), **Supp. IV Part 2:** 605
Traveler at Forty, A (Dreiser), **I:** 515
Traveler from Altruria, a Romance A, (Howells), **II:** 285, 287
Traveler's Tree, The: New and Selected Poems (W. J. Smith), **Supp. XIII:** 332, 347
"Traveling" (Paley), **Supp. VI:** 230
"Traveling Light" (Wagoner), **Supp. IX:** 329
Traveling Mercies: Some Thoughts on Faith (Lamott), **Supp. XX: 132, 140–142**
"Traveling Onion, The" (Nye), **Supp. XIII:** 276
Traveling through the Dark (Stafford), **Supp. XI:** 311, 316, **318–321**
"Traveling through the Dark" (Stafford), **Supp. XI:** 318–320, 321, 323, 329
Traveling with the Innocents Abroad (McKeithan), **Retro. Supp. III:** 261
Travelling in Amherst: A Poet's Journal, 1931–1954, **Supp. IX: 88–89**
Travelling Standing Still: Poems, 1918–1928 (Taggard), **Supp. XXII:** 278
Travelling Thirds, The (Atherton), **Supp. XXIV:** 23
Travels in Alaska (Muir), **Supp. IX:** 182, 185–186
"Travels in Georgia" (McPhee), **Supp. III Part 1:** 293–294
"Travels in North America" (Kees), **Supp. XV:** 133–134
Travels in the Congo (Gide), **III:** 210
"Travels in the South" (Ortiz), **Supp. IV Part 2:** 506
Travels with Charley (Steinbeck), **IV:** 52
"Travel Writing: Why I Bother" (Theroux), **Supp. VIII:** 310
Travis, Merle, **Supp. V:** 335
Travisano, Thomas, **Retro. Supp. II:** 40
Treadway, Jessica, **Supp. XXIII:** 280
Treasure Hunt (Buechner), **Supp. XII:** 52
Treasure Island (Stevenson), **Retro. Supp. III:** 88; **Supp. X:** 230
Treasure of the Humble, The (Maeterlinck), **Supp. XX: 116**
"Treasure of the Redwoods, A" (Harte), **Supp. II Part 1:** 337
Treasury of Art Masterpieces, A: From the Renaissance to the Present Day (Craven), **Supp. XII:** 44
Treasury of English Aphorisms, A (L. P. Smith), **Supp. XIV:** 344
Treasury of English Prose, A (L. P. Smith, ed.), **Supp. XIV:** 341
Treasury of the Theatre, A (Gassner), **Supp. I Part 1:** 292
Treasury of Yiddish Stories, A (Howe and Greenberg, eds.), **Supp. I Part 2:** 432; **Supp. XXIII:** 7
Treat 'Em Rough (Lardner), **II:** 422–423
Treatise Concerning Religious Affections (Edwards), **I:** 547, 552, 554, 555, 557, 558, 560, 562
Treatise Concerning the Lord's Supper (Doolittle), **IV:** 150
"Treatise on Poetry" (Milosz), **Supp. VIII:** 20
Treatise on Right and Wrong, A (Mencken), **III:** 110, 119
"Treatise on Tales of Horror, A" (Wilson), **IV:** 438
Treatise on the Gods, A (Mencken), **III:** 108–109, 119
"Treatment" (Wright), **Supp. XV:** 343

Trece poetas del mundo azteca (León-Portilla), **Supp. XV:** 77
Tre Croce (Tozzi), **Supp. III Part 2:** 616
"Tree, a Rock, a Cloud, A" (McCullers), **II:** 587
"Tree, The" (Pound), **Retro. Supp. I:** 286; **Supp. I Part 1:** 255
"Tree, The" (Stone), **Supp. XXVII:** 250
"Tree, the Bird, The" (Roethke), **III:** 548
"Tree at My Window" (Frost), **II:** 155
Tree Grows in Brooklyn, A (B. Smith), **Supp. XVII:** 9; **Supp. XXIII:** 257, **259–264,** 265, 271
Tree Grows in Brooklyn, A (film; Kazan), **Supp. XVI:** 193
"Tree House at Night, The" (Dickey), **Supp. IV Part 1:** 179
"Tree House"(Thompson), **Supp. XXIII:** 301
Tree Is Older Than You Are, The (Nye, ed.), **Supp. XIII:** 280
"Tree of Laughing Bells, The" (Lindsay), **Supp. I Part 2:** 376
"Tree of Life, The" (Swados), **Supp. XIX:** 268
"Tree of Night, A" (Capote), **Supp. III Part 1:** 114, 120
Tree of Night and Other Stories, A (Capote), **Supp. III Part 1:** 114
"Trees, The" (Rich), **Supp. I Part 2:** 555
Trees, The (Richter), **Supp. XVIII: 212–213,** 220
"Trees at Night" (H. Johnson), **Supp. XXVI:** 174
"Trees Listening to Bach" (Merrill), **Supp. III Part 1:** 336
Tree Tall Woman (Mullen), **Supp. XXVII:** 166–167, 169, 170, 172, 174, 176
Tree That Came to Stay, The (Quindlen), **Supp. XVII:** 167
Tree Where Man Was Born, The (Matthiessen), **Supp. V:** 199, 203, 204
Trejo, Ernesto, **Supp. V:** 178, 180; **Supp. XIII:** 313, 316; **Supp. XV:** 73
Trelawny, Edward John, **Supp. I Part 2:** 721
"Trellis for R., A" (Swenson), **Supp. IV Part 2:** 647
Tremblay, Bill, **Supp. XIII:** 112
Tremble (Wright), **Supp. XV: 348–349**
"Trespass" (Frost), **Retro. Supp. I:** 139
Trespassing (Pickering), **Supp. XXI:** 202
"Trespassing" (Pickering), **Supp. XXI:** 202
Trethewey, Eric, **Supp. XXI:** 243, 244
Trethewey, Natasha, **Supp. XXI: 243–259**
"Tretitoli, Where the Bomb Group Was" (Hugo), **Supp. VI:** 138
Trevelyan, Robert C., **Supp. XIV:** 334
Trevor-Roper, Hugh, **Supp. XIV:** 348
Trial, The (Kafka), **IV:** 113; **Retro. Supp. II:** 20
"Trial, The" (Rukeyser), **Supp. VI:** 278
"Trial by Existence, The" (Frost), **II:** 166; **Retro. Supp. III:** 94
"Trial for Arson, The"(Hadas), **Supp. XXIII:** 114
Trial of a Poet, The (Shapiro), **Supp. II Part 2:** 710
Trial of the Hawk, The: A Comedy of the Seriousness of Life (Lewis), **II:** 441
"Trial path, The" (Zitkala-Ša), **Supp. XXV:** 274–275, 282
Trials of the Human Heart (Rowson), **Supp. XV:** 237, 239
Tribal Secrets: Recovering American Indian Intellectual Traditions (Warrior), **Supp. IV Part 1:** 329
"Tribute" (A. Finch), **Supp. XVII:** 72, 73–74
"Tribute, A" (Easton), **Supp. IV Part 2:** 461
"Tribute, The" (Doolittle), **Supp. I Part 1:** 267
"Tribute (To My Mother)" (Cullen), **Supp. IV Part 1:** 166
Tribute to Freud (Doolittle), **Supp. I Part 1:** 253, 254, 258, 259, 260, 268
Tribute to the Angels (Doolittle), **Supp. I Part 1:** 272
"Trick on the World, A" (Ríos), **Supp. IV Part 2:** 553
"Tricks" (Olds), **Supp. X:** 203–204
"Trick Scenery" (F. Barthelme), **Supp. XI:** 26
Trifler, The (Masters), **Supp. I Part 2:** 459–460
Trifles (Glaspell), **Supp. III Part 1:** 175, 178, 179, 182, 186, 187; **Supp. X:** 46; **Supp. XXI:** 12
Trifonov, Iurii V., **Retro. Supp. I:** 278
Triggering Town, The: Lectures and Essays on Poetry and Writing (Hugo), **Supp. VI:** 133, 140
Trilling, Diana, **II:** 587, 600; **Supp. I Part 1:** 297; **Supp. XII:** 126; **Supp. XXI:** 271, 275
Trilling, Lionel, **I:** 48; **II:** 579; **III:** 308, 310, 319, 327; **IV:** 201, 211; **Retro. Supp. I:** 19, 97, 121, 216, 227; **Retro. Supp. III:** 78, 106; **Supp. III Part 2: 493–515; Supp. IX:** 266, 287; **Supp. V:** 259; **Supp. VIII:** 93, 98, 190, 231, 236, 243; **Supp. XIII:** 100–101; **Supp. XIV:** 280, 288–289; **Supp. XV:** 20, 140, 152
Trilogy (Doolittle), **Supp. I Part 1:** 271, 272
Trilogy of Desire (Dreiser), **I:** 497, 508; **Retro. Supp. II:** 94, 96, **101–102**
Trimberger, Ellen Kay, **Supp. XVII:** 96, 106; **Supp. XXI:** 12
Trimmed Lamp, The (O. Henry), **Supp. II Part 1:** 410
Trimmings (Mullen), **Supp. XXVII:** 169–170, 171
"Trinc" (McGrath), **Supp. X:** 127
Trinity (Uris), **Supp. XX: 243, 244, 245, 246, 247, 248, 253, 254–255**
Trio (Baker), **Supp. I Part 1:** 277
Trio (Saroyan), **Supp. XXII:** 25
"Triolets for Triolet" (Nelson), **Supp. XVIII:** 179
"Trip" (F. Barthelme), **Supp. XI:** 26
Triple Thinkers, The: Ten Essays on Literature (Wilson), **IV:** 428, 431; **Supp. II Part 1:** 146
"Triplex" (Doolittle), **Supp. I Part 1:** 271
Tripmaster Monkey: His Fake Book (Kingston), **Supp. V:** 157, 158, 169, 170–173
Trippings in Authorland (Forrester), **Supp. XVIII:** 13
Trippings of Tom Pepper, The (Briggs), **Supp. XVIII:** 3, **13–14**
"Trip to Hanoi" (Sontag), **Supp. III Part 2:** 460–462
Trip to Parnassus, A; or, The Judgement of Apollo on Dramatic Authors and Performers (Rowson), **Supp. XV: 232–233**
"Triptych" (Eberhart), **I:** 522, 539
Tristam Shandy (Sterne), **Supp. XXII:** 267
Tristan and Iseult, **Retro. Supp. I:** 328, 329, 330, 331
Tristessa (Kerouac), **Supp. III Part 1:** 225, 227, 229
Tristram (Robinson), **III:** 521, 522, 523
Tristram Shandy (Sterne), **I:** 299; **IV:** 465–466; **Supp. V:** 127; **Supp. XVIII:** 60
"Triumph" (C. L. R. James), **Supp. XXI:** 160

"Triumphal March" (Eliot), **I:** 580; **III:** 17; **Retro. Supp. I:** 64
Triumph of Achilles, The (Glück), **Supp. V:** 79, 84–86, 92
"Triumph of a Modern, The, or, Send for the Lawyer" (Anderson), **I:** 113, 114
"Triumph of the Egg, The" (Anderson), **I:** 113
Triumph of the Egg, The: A Book of Impressions from American Life in Tales and Poems (Anderson), **I:** 112, 114
Triumph of the Spider Monkey, The (Oates), **Supp. II Part 2:** 522
Triumphs of the Reformed Religion in America (Mather), **Supp. II Part 2:** 453
Trivial Breath (Wylie), **Supp. I Part 2:** 709, 722–724
Trivia; or, the Art of Walking the Streets of London (Gay), **Supp. XIV:** 337
Trivia: Printed from the Papers of Anthony Woodhouse, Esq. (L. P. Smith), **Supp. XIV:** 336, **337–340**
"Trivia Tea" (Skloot), **Supp. XX: 205**
Trocchi, Alexander, **Supp. XI:** 294, 295, 301
Troilus and Criseyde (Chaucer), **Retro. Supp. I:** 426
Trois contes (Flaubert), **IV:** 31, 37
Trojan Horse, The: A Play (MacLeish), **III:** 21
"Trojan Women, The" (Maxwell), **Supp. VIII:** 169
Troll Garden, The (Cather), **I:** 313, 314–316, 322; **Retro. Supp. I:** 5, 6, 8, 14; **Retro. Supp. III:** 20, 21, 22, 26–28, 36
"Trolling for Blues" (Wilbur), **Supp. III Part 2:** 563–564
Trollope, Anthony, **I:** 10, 375; **II:** 192, 237; **III:** 51, 70, 281, 382; **Retro. Supp. I:** 361
Trombly, Albert Edmund, **Supp. I Part 2:** 403
Trombold, John, **Supp. XVIII:** 111
"Trompe L'Oeil" (Collins), **Supp. XXI:** 60
"Troop Train" (Shapiro), **Supp. II Part 2:** 707
"Tropes of the Text" (Gass), **Supp. VI:** 88
Tropic of Cancer (H. Miller), **III:** 170, 171, 174, 177, 178–180, 181, 182, 183, 187, 190; **Supp. V:** 119; **Supp. X:** 187; **Supp. XXII:** 230, 257
Tropic of Capricorn (H. Miller), **III:** 170, 176–177, 178, 182, 183, 184, 187, 188–189, 190
"Tropic of Cuba" (di Donato), **Supp. XX: 45**
Trotsky, Leon, **I:** 366; **II:** 562, 564; **IV:** 429; **Supp. XXI:** 161, 164, 165, 167, 168
Trotter, W., **I:** 249
"Trouble at the Home Office" (Huddle), **Supp. XXVI:** 156
Troubled Air, The (Shaw), **Supp. XIX: 249–250**
Troubled Island (opera; Hughes and Still), **Retro. Supp. I:** 203
Troubled Lovers in History (Goldbarth), **Supp. XII:** 176, **192–193**
Trouble Follows Me (Macdonald, under Millar), **Supp. IV Part 2:** 466
Trouble in July (Caldwell), **I:** 297, 304–305, 306, 309
Trouble Island (Hughes), **Supp. I Part 1:** 328
"Trouble of Marcie Flint, The" (Cheever), **Supp. I Part 1:** 186
Trouble with Francis, The: An Autobiography (Francis), **Supp. IX:** 76, 77, 82, **84–85**
Trouble with God, The (Francis), **Supp. IX:** 88
"Trouble with Poetry, The" (Collins), **Supp. XXI:** 57
Trouble with Poetry and Other Poems, The (Collins), **Supp. XXI:** 55, 57, 62
"Trouble with the Stars and Stripes" (Nye), **Supp. XIII:** 277
Trouillot, Michel-Rolphe, **Supp. X:** 14–15
Troupe, Quincy, **Retro. Supp. II:** 15, 111; **Supp. X:** 242
"Trout" (Hugo), **Supp. VI:** 135
Trout Fishing in America (Brautigan), **Supp. VIII:** 43
"Trouvée" (Bishop), **Retro. Supp. II:** 49
Trowbridge, John Townsend, **Retro. Supp. III:** 303
Troy (film), **Supp. XX: 273**
"Truce" (Taggard), **Supp. XXII:** 276–277
"Truce of the Bishop, The" (Frederic), **II:** 139–140
"Truck Stop: Minnesota" (Dunn), **Supp. XI:** 145–146
Trudeau, Garry, **Supp. XXIV:** 283
True Account, The: A Novel of the Lewis & Clark & Kinneson Expeditions (Mosher), **Supp. XXII:** 206, 207, 208, **214–215**
True and False: Heresy and Common Sense for the Actor (Mamet), **Supp. XIV:** 241, 243
True Blood (television series), **Supp. XIX:** 174
Trueblood, Valerie, **Supp. XIII:** 306
True Confessions (Dunne), **Supp. IV Part 1:** 198
True Confessions (film), **Supp. IV Part 1:** 198
"True Crime" (Gansworth), **Supp. XXVI:** 114
"True Feeling Leaves No Memory" (Davison), **Supp. XXVI:** 69
Trueheart, Charles, **Supp. XXI:** 238
True History of the Conquest of New Spain, The (Castillo), **III:** 13
True Intellectual System of the Universe, The (Cuddleworth), **II:** 10
"True Love" (Olds), **Supp. X:** 212
Trueman, Matthew (pseudonym). See Lowell, James Russell
"True Morality" (Bell), **Supp. X:** 13
"True Romance" (Everett), **Supp. XVIII:** 65
Truesdale, C. W., **Supp. XXI:** 246
True Stories (Atwood), **Supp. XIII:** 34–35
"True Stories" (Atwood), **Supp. XIII:** 34
"True Stories of Bitches" (Mamet), **Supp. XIV:** 246, 252
True Stories of History and Biography (Hawthorne), **Retro. Supp. III:** 121
"True Story, A" (Twain), **Retro. Supp. III:** 262
"Truest Sport, The: Jousting with Sam and Charlie" (Wolfe), **Supp. III Part 2:** 581–582
"True Vine" (Wylie), **Supp. I Part 2:** 723
True West (Shepard), **Supp. III Part 2:** 433, 441, 445, 447, 448
Truman, Harry, **III:** 3
Truman Capote: In Which Various Friends, Enemies, Acquaintances, and Detractors Recall His Turbulent Career (Plimpton), **Supp. XVI:**245
Truman Show, The (film), **Supp. XVI:** 271
Trumbo, Dalton, **Supp. I Part 1:** 295; **Supp. XIII:** 6; **Supp. XVII:** 63; **Supp. XX: 246; Supp. XXI:** 45
Trumbull, John, **Supp. II Part 1:** 65, 69, 70, 268
Trump, Donald, **Supp. IV Part 1:** 393
Trumpener, Katie, **Retro. Supp. I:** 380
"Trumpet Player" (Hughes), **Supp. I Part 1:** 333
"Trumpet Player, 1963" (Halliday), **Supp. XIX:** 92

Trumpet Shall Sound, The (Wilder), **IV:** 356
Trumpet Unblown, The (Hoffman), **Supp. XVIII:** 71, **74–75**
Trunk Music (Connelly), **Supp. XXI: 72,** 75
"Truro Bear, The" (Oliver), **Supp. VII:** 234
Truscott, Lucian K., **Supp. IV Part 2:** 683
Trust (Ozick), **Supp. V:** 257–258, 259, 260–263, 270, 272
Trust Me (Updike), **Retro. Supp. I:** 322
"Trusty, The" (Rash), **Supp. XXVII:** 229–230
"Trust Yourself" (Emerson), **II:** 10
"Truth" (Emerson), **II:** 6
"Truth, The" (Halliday), **Supp. XIX:** 87, 88, 94
"Truth, The" (Jarrell), **II:** 381–382
Truth About Celia, The (Brockmeier), **Supp. XXII: 53–55**
"Truth about God, The" (Carson), **Supp. XII: 105–106**
"Truth be told" (Trethewey), **Supp. XXI:** 255, 256
"Truthful James" (Harte), **IV:** 196
"Truth Is, The" (Hogan), **Supp. IV Part 1:** 401–402
"Truth Is Forced, The" (Swenson), **Supp. IV Part 2:** 652
"Truth of the Matter, The" (Nemerov), **III:** 270
Truth Serum (Cooper), **Supp. XI:** 129
"Truth the Dead Know, The" (Sexton), **Supp. II Part 2:** 681
"Trying to Evangelize a Cut Flower" (Peacock), **Supp. XIX:** 199
Trying to Find Chinatown (Hwang), **Supp. XXI:** 147
Trying to Save Piggy Sneed (Irving), **Supp. VI: 19–165**
"Trying to Talk with a Man" (Rich), **Retro. Supp. III:** 247; **Supp. I Part 2:** 559
"Tryptich I" (Bell), **Supp. X:** 7
"Tryst, The" (Wharton), **Retro. Supp. I:** 378
"Try the Girl" (Chandler), **Supp. IV Part 1:** 125
Try! Try! (O'Hara), **Supp. XXIII:** 209, 210, 216
"Ts'ai Chih" (Pound), **III:** 466
T. S. Eliot and American Philosophy (Jain), **Retro. Supp. I:** 58
T. S. Eliot's Silent Voices (Mayer), **Retro. Supp. I:** 58
Tsuji, Shizuo, **Supp. XVII:** 90
Tsurikgekumen (The return) (Asch), **Supp. XXIII:** 5
Tsvetaeva, Marina, **Supp. VIII:** 30; **Supp. XXIII:** 168
"Tuberoses" (E. Stoddard), **Supp. XV:** 282
Tubert, Susana, **Supp. XXIII:** 203
Tuck, James A., **Supp. XXVI:** 83
Tucker, Benjamin R., **Supp. XXI:** 9
Tuckerman, Frederick Goddard, **IV:** 144; **Supp. XXV:** 241
Tucker's People (Wolfert), **Supp. XXI:** 261, 262, 263, 267, **267–275,** 278
"Tuesday, November 5th, 1940" (Benét), **Supp. XI:** 46, 52
"Tuesday April 25th 1966" (Olson), **Supp. II Part 2:** 585
"Tuesday Night at the Savoy Ballroom" (Komunyakaa), **Supp. XIII:** 132
Tuffield, Aviva, **Supp. XVI:** 147, 148
"Tuft of Flowers, The" (Frost), **II:** 153; **Retro. Supp. I:** 126, 127; **Retro. Supp. III:** 94, 95, 99
Tufts, James Hayden, **Supp. I Part 2:** 632
Tu Fu, **II:** 526; **Supp. XV:** 47
Tu Fu (Ayscough), **II:** 527
Tugwell, Rexford Guy, **Supp. I Part 2:** 645
"Tulip" (Hammett), **Supp. IV Part 1:** 356
"Tulip Man, The" (McCarriston), **Supp. XIV:** 261
"Tulips" (Nye), **Supp. XIII:** 281
"Tulips" (Plath), **Retro. Supp. II:** 252–253; **Supp. I Part 2:** 540, 542, 544
"Tulips" (Snodgrass), **Supp. VI:** 325
Tulips and Chimneys (Cummings), **I:** 436, 437, 440, 445, 447
"Tulips"(Strout), **Supp. XXIII:** 283, 285
"Tulips"(theater performance, Strout), **Supp. XXIII:** 281
Tully, Jim, **III:** 103, 109
Tumble Home (Hempel), **Supp. XXI:** 115, **124–125**
"Tumble Home" (Hempel), **Supp. XXI:** 115, 116, **124–125,** 126
Tumble Tower (Modarressi and Tyler), **Supp. IV Part 2:** 657
"Tuned in Late One Night" (Stafford), **Supp. XI:** 327–328
Tunnel, The (Gass), **Supp. V:** 44; **Supp. VI: 89–91,** 94
"Tunnel, The" (Strand), **Supp. IV Part 2:** 622
"Tunnels" (Komunyakaa), **Supp. XIII:** 123
Tunnel Vision (Paretsky), **Supp. XXV:** 173–174, 177, 178, 181
Tuon, Bunkong, **Supp. XXVI:** 211, 220
Tuqan, Fadwa, **Supp. XIII:** 278
Tura, Cosimo, **III:** 474–475
Turandot and Other Poems (Ashbery), **Supp. III Part 1:** 3
Turco, Lewis, **Supp. XV:** 118
Turgenev, Ivan Sergeevich, **I:** 106; **II:** 263, 271, 275, 280, 281, 288, 319, 320, 324–325, 338, 407; **III:** 461; **IV:** 17, 277; **Retro. Supp. I:** 215, 222; **Supp. VIII:** 167
Turgot, Anne Robert Jacques, **II:** 103; **Supp. I Part 1:** 250
"Turkey and Bones and Eating and We Liked It" (Stein), **IV:** 44
"Turkey Season, The" (Munro), **Supp. XXVII:** 188
Turman, Glynn, **Supp. IV Part 1:** 362
"Turnabout" (Faulkner), **Retro. Supp. III:** 84
Turnbull, Dr. George, **II:** 113
Turnbull, Lawrence, **Supp. I Part 1:** 352
"Turned" (Gilman), **Supp. XI:** 207
Turner, Addie, **IV:** 123
Turner, Darwin, **Supp. I Part 1:** 339; **Supp. IV Part 1:** 165
Turner, Frederick Jackson, **Supp. I Part 2:** 480, 481, 632, 640; **Supp. IV Part 2:** 596
Turner, Guinevere, **Supp. XXVII:** 68
Turner, Nat, **IV:** 113–114, 115, 116, 117
Turner, Patricia A., **Supp. XIII:** 237; **Supp. XX: 110**
Turner, Russell. See Lacy, Ed
Turner, Victor, **Supp. IV Part 1:** 304
"Turning Away Variations on Estrangement" (Dickey), **Supp. IV Part 1:** 183
Turning Point, The (McCoy), **Supp. XIII:** 175
"Turning Thirty, I Contemplate Students Bicycling Home" (Dove), **Supp. IV Part 1:** 250
Turning Wind, A (Rukeyser), **Supp. VI:** 272–273, 279–280
Turn in the South, A (Naipaul), **Supp. XXII:** 240
Turn of the Screw, The (H. James), **Retro. Supp. I:** 219, 231; **Supp. IV Part 2:** 682
"Turn of the Screw, The" (H. James), **II:** 331–332; **Retro. Supp. I:** 228, 229, 231, 232; **Supp. XVII:** 143
Turns and Movies and Other Tales in Verse (Aiken), **I:** 65
"Turn with the Sun, A" (Knowles), **Supp. XII:** 237–238

"Turn Your Radio On" (J. W. Miller), **Supp. XX: 169**
Turow, Scott, **Supp. V:** 220; **Supp. XVII: 213–224**
"Turpentine" (Gallagher), **Supp. XXIV:** 174, 175, 176
Turpin, E. Walters, **Supp. XVIII:** 283
Turrinus, Lucius Mamilius, **IV:** 373
"Turtle" (Hogan), **Supp. IV Part 1:** 401
Turtle, Swan (Doty), **Supp. XI: 121–122**
"Turtle, Swan" (Doty), **Supp. XI:** 121–122
Turtle Island (Snyder), **Supp. VIII: 300–303**
Turtle Moon (Hoffman), **Supp. X:** 77, **87–88,** 89
"Turtle Shrine near Chittagong, The" (Nye), **Supp. XIII:** 277
Turtotte, James, **Supp. XXIII:** 125
Turturro, John, **Supp. XI:** 174
Tuscan Cities (Howells), **II:** 280
Tuskegee movement, **Supp. II Part 1:** 169, 172
Tuten, Frederic, **Supp. VIII:** 75, 76; **Supp. XIII:** 237, 249
Tuten, James, **Supp. XVIII:** 195
Tuthill, Louisa Cavolne, **Supp. I Part 2:** 684
"Tutored Child, The" (Kunitz), **Supp. III Part 1:** 264
Tuttleton, James W., **Supp. IV Part 1:** 166, 168
"T.V.A." (Agee), **I:** 35
Tvedten, Brother Benet, **Supp. IV Part 2:** 505
"TV Men" (Carson), **Supp. XII: 105, 112**
Twain, Mark, **I:** 57, 103, 107, 109, 190, 192, 193, 195, 197, 203, 209, 245, 246, 247–250, 255, 256, 257, 260, 261, 292, 342, 418, 469, 485; **II:** 70, 140, 259, 262, 266–268, 271, 272, 274–275, 276, 277, 280, 285–286, 287, 288, 289, 301, 304, 306, 307, 312, 415, 432, 434, 436, 446, 457, 467, 475, 476, 482; **III:** 65, 101, 102, 112–113, 114, 220, 347, 357, 409, 453, 454, 504, 507, 554, 558, 572, 575, 576; **IV: 190–213,** 333, 349, 451; **Retro. Supp. I:** 169, 194, 195; **Retro. Supp. II:** 123; **Retro. Supp. III: 255–273**; **Supp. I Part 1:** 37, 39, 44, 247, 251, 313, 317; **Supp. I Part 2:** 377, 385, 393, 410, 455, 456, 457, 473, 475, 579, 602, 604, 618, 629, 651, 660; **Supp. II Part 1:** 193, 344, 354, 385; **Supp. IV Part 1:** 386, 388; **Supp. IV Part 2:** 463, 468, 603, 607, 693; **Supp. IX:** 14, 171; **Supp. V:** 44, 113, 131; **Supp. VIII:** 40, 189; **Supp. X:** 51, 227; **Supp. XII:** 343; **Supp. XIII:** 1, 17; **Supp. XV:** 41; **Supp. XVI:** 66, 208; **Supp. XVIII:** 1, 9, 13; **Supp. XXI:** 205; **Supp. XXII:** 89, 203, 205, 206; **Supp. XXIII:** 85; **Supp. XXVII:** 84, 218
"Twa Sisters, The" (ballad), **Supp. I Part 2:** 696
Twelfth Night (Shakespeare), **Supp. IV Part 1:** 83; **Supp. IX:** 14; **Supp. XXII:** 229
Twelve (Blok), **Supp. XXVI:** 144
"12 O'Clock News" (Bishop), **Retro. Supp. II:** 48
Twelve Men (Dreiser), **Retro. Supp. II:** 94, 104
Twelve Moons (Oliver), **Supp. VII:** 231, 233–236, 238, 240
Twelve Southerners, **IV:** 125; **Supp. X:** 25
Twelve Years a Slave (Northup), **Supp. XIV:** 32
Twentieth Century (Hecht and MacArthur), **Supp. XXVII:** 90
Twentieth Century Authors, **I:** 376, 527
"Twentieth Century Fiction and the Black Mask of Humanity" (Ellison), **Retro. Supp. II:** 118
Twentieth Century Pleasures (Hass), **Supp. VI:** 103, 106, 109
Twenty Drawings (Gibran), **Supp. XX: 116**
"28" (Levine), **Supp. V:** 187, 191
"Twenty-Four Poems" (Schwartz), **Supp. II Part 2:** 646, 649
"2433 Agnes, First Home, Last House in Missoula" (Hugo), **Supp. VI:** 139–140
"Twenty Hill Hollow" (Muir), **Supp. IX:** 178
Twenty Love Poems and a Song of Despair (Neruda), **Supp. XXIV:** 170
"Twenty Minutes" (Salter), **Supp. IX:** 260
29 Mini-Essays (Brainard), **Supp. XXVII:** 28
Twenty-One Love Poems (Rich), **Retro. Supp. III:** 242, 248; **Supp. I Part 2:** 572–573
"Twenty-One Poems" (MacLeish), **III:** 19
Twenty Poems (Haines), **Supp. XII:** 204, **205–206**
Twenty Poems of Anna Akhmatova (Kenyon), **Supp. VII:** 165–166
Twenty Questions: (Posed by Poems) (McClatchy), **Supp. XII:** 254, **259–262**
27 Views of Raleigh (Barnhardt, ed.), **Supp. XXVII:** 12
27 Wagons Full of Cotton and Other One-Act Plays (T. Williams), **IV:** 381, 383
Twenty-seventh City, The (Franzen), **Supp. XX: 83–84, 84, 85, 86–88, 88, 89, 91, 92, 95**
Twentysomething Essays by Twenty-something Writers (Kellogg and Quint, eds.), **Supp. XXVI:** 53
Twenty Thousand Leagues under the Sea (Verne), **I:** 480; **Supp. XI:** 63
"Twenty Years Ago" (Lindsay), **Supp. I Part 2:** 384, 399
Twenty Years at Hull-House (Addams), **Supp. I Part 1:** 3, 4, 11, 16
Twersky, David, **Supp. XX: 244**
Twice over Lightly: New York Ten and Now (Hayes and Loos), **Supp. XVI:** 195
Twice-Told Tales (Hawthorne), **I:** 354; **II:** 224; **III:** 412, 421; **Retro. Supp. I:** 154–155, 160; **Retro. Supp. III:** 109, 110, 113–114, 225, 233, 234
Twichell, Chase, **Supp. V:** 16; **Supp. XVII:** 110, 112
Twilight (Frost), **II:** 151
"Twilight's Last Gleaming" (Burroughs and Elvins), **Supp. III Part 1:** 93, 94, 101
Twilight Sleep (Wharton), **IV:** 320–322, 324–325, 327, 328; **Retro. Supp. I:** 381
"Twin, The" (Olds), **Supp. X:** 207
"Twin Beds in Rome" (Updike), **Retro. Supp. I:** 332
"Twins of Table Mountain, The" (Harte), **Supp. II Part 1:** 355
"Twist, The" (Olson), **Supp. II Part 2:** 570
Twitch and Shout (film), **Supp. XVIII:** 143
Twitchell-Waas, Jeffrey, **Supp. XVIII:** 99; **Supp. XXII:** 163
"Two" (Huddle), **Supp. XXVI:** 150
Two Admirals, The (Cooper), **I:** 350
Two against One (F. Barthelme), **Supp. XI:** 32, 33, 36
"Two and One"(Hadas), **Supp. XXIII:** 114–115
"Two Boys" (Moore), **Supp. X:** 173
"Two Brothers, The" (Jewett), **Retro. Supp. II:** 132
Two-Character Play, The (T. Williams), **IV:** 382, 386, 393, 398
Two Citizens (Wright), **Supp. III Part 2:** 602–604

"Two Deer" (Bass), **Supp. XVI:** 24
"Two Domains, The" (Goldbarth), **Supp. XII:** 192
"Two-Eleven All Around" (Offutt), **Supp. XIX:** 170
"Two Environments, The" (Trilling), **Supp. III Part 2:** 510
"Two-Fisted Self Pity" (Broyard), **Supp. XI:** 348
Two for Texas (Burke), **Supp. XIV:** 25, 34
"Two Friends" (Cather), **I:** 332
"Two Gardens in Linndale" (Robinson), **III:** 508
Two Gentlemen in Bonds (Ransom), **III:** 491–492
Two: Gertrude Stein and Her Brother (Stein), **IV:** 43
"Two Ghosts" (Francis), **Supp. IX:** 87
Two-Gun Bob (Szumskyj), **Supp. XXVII:** 128
"Two Hangovers" (Wright), **Supp. III Part 2:** 596
Two-Headed Poems (Atwood), **Supp. XIII:** 34
Two Hot to Handle (Lacy), **Supp. XV:** 206
Two Hours to Doom (Bryant), **Supp. XI:** 302
"Two Hundred Years in an Hour" (Boyce), **Supp. XXI:** 8
"Two Kitchens in Provence" (M. F. K. Fisher), **Supp. XVII:** 88, 91
"Two Ladies in Retirement" (Taylor), **Supp. V:** 320
Two Letters to the Citizens of the United States, and One to General Washington (Barlow), **Supp. II Part 1:** 80
Two Little Women on a Holiday (Wells), **Supp. XXVI:** 277
"Two Lives, The" (Hogan), **Supp. IV Part 1:** 400, 402, 403, 406, 411
Two Long Poems (Stern), **Supp. IX:** 296
"Two Look at Two" (Frost), **Supp. XXI:** 26
"Two Lovers and a Beachcomber by the Real Sea" (Plath), **Supp. I Part 2:** 536
"Two Men" (McClatchy)", **Supp. XII:** 269
Two Men (E. Stoddard), **Supp. XV:** 272, 273, **283–284**
Two Men of Sandy Bar (Harte), **Supp. II Part 1:** 354
Twomey, Jay, **Supp. XVII:** 111
"Two Moods of Love" (Cullen), **Supp. IV Part 1:** 166
Two Moons (Mallon), **Supp. XIX:** 132, **138–141**
"Two Morning Monologues" (Bellow), **I:** 150; **Retro. Supp. II:** 20
"Two Nations of Black America, The" (Frontline), **Supp. XX: 99**
Two-Ocean War, The (Morison), **Supp. I Part 2:** 491
"Two of Hearts" (Hogan), **Supp. IV Part 1:** 410
"Two on a Party" (T. Williams), **IV:** 388
"Two or Three Things I Dunno About John Cassavetes" (Lethem), **Supp. XVIII:** 148
"Two Pendants: For the Ears" (W. C. Williams), **Retro. Supp. I:** 423
"Two Poems of Going Home" (Dickey), **Supp. IV Part 1:** 182–183
"Two Portraits" (Chopin), **Supp. I Part 1:** 218
"Two Presences, The" (R. Bly), **Supp. IV Part 1:** 65
"Two Rivers" (Stegner), **Supp. IV Part 2:** 605
Tworkov, Jack, **Supp. XII:** 198
"Two Scenes" (Ashbery), **Supp. III Part 1:** 4
Two Serious Ladies (Jane Bowles), **Supp. IV Part 1:** 82
"Two Silences" (Carruth), **Supp. XVI:** 55
"Two Sisters" (Farrell), **II:** 45
Two Sisters: A Memoir in the Form of a Novel (Vidal), **Supp. IV Part 2:** 679
"Two Sisters of Persephone" (Plath), **Retro. Supp. II:** 246
"Two Songs on the Economy of Abundance" (Agee), **I:** 28
Two Sons, The (Boyce), **Supp. XXI:** 7, 13
"Two Tales of Clumsy" (Schnackenberg), **Supp. XV:** 258
"Two Temples, The" (Melville), **III:** 89–90
Two Thousand Seasons (Armah), **Supp. IV Part 1:** 373
Two Towns in Provence (M. F. K. Fisher), **Supp. XVII:** 91
Two Trains Running (Wilson), **Supp. VIII: 345–348**
"Two Tramps in Mudtime" (Frost), **II:** 164; **Retro. Supp. I:** 137; **Supp. IX:** 261
"Two Trams in Mudtime" (Frost), **Retro. Supp. III:** 103
"Two Twilights for William Carlos Williams" (Boyle), **Supp. XXIV:** 63
"Two Views of a Cadaver Room" (Plath), **Supp. I Part 2:** 538
"Two Villages" (Paley), **Supp. VI:** 227
"Two Voices in a Meadow" (Wilbur), **Supp. III Part 2:** 555
Two Weeks in Another Town (Shaw), **Supp. XIX:** 251
"Two Witches" (Frost), **Retro. Supp. I:** 135
"Two Words" (Francis), **Supp. IX:** 81
Two Worlds Walking: A Mixed-Blood Anthology (Glancy and Truesdale, eds.), **Supp. XXI:** 246
Two Years Before the Mast (Dana), **I:** 351; **Retro. Supp. III:** 150; **Supp. XXV:** 208
"Tyger, The" (Blake), **Supp. XVII:** 128
Tyler, Anne, **Supp. IV Part 2: 657–675; Supp. V:** 227, 326; **Supp. VIII:** 141; **Supp. X:** 1, 77, 83, 85; **Supp. XII:** 307; **Supp. XVI:** 37; **Supp. XVIII:** 157, 195; **Supp. XXIII:** 298
Tyler, Royall, **I:** 344; **Retro. Supp. I:** 377
Tymms, Ralph, **Supp. IX:** 105
Tyndale, William, **II:** 15
Tyndall, John, **Retro. Supp. II:** 93
Typee: A Peep at Polynesian Life (Melville), **III:** 75–77, 79, 84; **Retro. Supp. I:** 245–246, 249, 252, 256; **Retro. Supp. III:** 147, 149, 151, 152–153
Types From City Streets (Hapgood), **Supp. XVII:** 103
"Typewriter, The" (D. West), **Supp. XVIII:** 279; **Supp. XXVI:** 164
Typewriter Town (W. J. Smith), **Supp. XIII:** 332
"Typhus" (Simpson), **Supp. IX:** 277
Tyranny of the Normal (Fiedler), **Supp. XIII: 107–108**
"Tyranny of the Normal" (Fiedler), **Supp. XIII:** 107–108
"Tyrant of Syracuse" (MacLeish), **III:** 20
"Tyrian Businesses" (Olson), **Supp. II Part 2:** 567, 568, 569
Tytell, John, **Supp. XIV:** 140
Tzara, Tristan, **Supp. III Part 1:** 104, 105
U and I (Baker), **Supp. XIII: 45–47,** 48, 52, 55
Überdie Seelenfrage (Fechner), **II:** 358
Ubik (Dick), **Supp. XVIII:** 136
"Ubi Sunt Lament for the Eccentric Museums of My Childhood" (Stallings), **Supp. XXV:** 232
Ubu Roi (Jarry), **Supp. XV:** 178, 186

Ueland, Brenda, **Supp. XVII:** 13
Uhry, Alfred, **Supp. XX: 177**
ukanhavyrfuckinciti back (Phillips), **Supp. XXIII:** 174
Ukrainian Dumy (P. N. Warren as Kilina and Tarnawsky, trans.), **Supp. XX: 261**
"Ulalume" (Poe), **III:** 427; **Retro. Supp. II:** 264, 266
Ulin, David, **Supp. XIII:** 244; **Supp. XVI:** 74
Ullman, Leslie, **Supp. IV Part 2:** 550; **Supp. XVIII:** 175
Ultimate Good Luck, The (Ford), **Supp. V:** 57, 61–62
Ultimate Punishment: A Lawyer's Reflections on Dealing with the Death Penalty (Turow), **Supp. XVII:** 220–221
Ultima Thule (Longfellow), **II:** 490; **Retro. Supp. II:** 169
"Ultima Thule" (Nabokov), **Retro. Supp. I:** 274
Ultramarine (Carver), **Supp. III Part 1:** 137, 138, 147, 148
"Ultrasound" (Stallings), **Supp. XXV:** 225, 233, 234
Ulysses (Joyce), **I:** 395, 475–476, 478, 479, 481; **II:** 42, 264, 542; **III:** 170, 398; **IV:** 103, 418, 428, 455; **Retro. Supp. I:** 59, 63, 290, 291; **Retro. Supp. II:** 121; **Supp. I Part 1:** 57; **Supp. III Part 2:** 618, 619; **Supp. IV Part 1:** 285; **Supp. IV Part 2:** 424; **Supp. IX:** 102; **Supp. V:** 261; **Supp. X:** 114; **Supp. XIII:** 43, 191; **Supp. XV:** 305; **Supp. XVII:** 140, 227; **Supp. XXV:** 65; **Supp. XXVII:** 6, 70
"Ulysses, Order and Myth" (Eliot), **Retro. Supp. I:** 63
"Ulysses, Order and Myth" (T. S. Eliot), **Retro. Supp. III:** 63
"Umbrella, The" (Peacock), **Supp. XIX:** 203–204
Unaccountable Worth of the World, The (Price), **Supp. VI:** 267
Unaccustomed Earth (Lahiri), **Supp. XXI:** 176, **181–183,** 183, 188
"Unaccustomed Earth" (Lahiri), **Supp. XXI:** 186
Unamuno y Jugo, Miguel de, **III:** 310; **Supp. XV:** 79
"Unattached Smile, The" (Crews), **Supp. XI:** 101
"Unbelievable Thing Usually Goes to the Heart of the Story, The: Magic Realism in the Fiction of Rick Bass" (Dwyer), **Supp. XVI:** 16
"Unbeliever, The" (Bishop), **Retro. Supp. II:** 43
"Unborn Song" (Rukeyser), **Supp. VI:** 274
Unbought Spirit: A John Jay Chapman Reader (Stone, ed.), **Supp. XIV:** 54
Uncalled, The (Dunbar), **Supp. II Part 1:** 200, 211, 212
Uncentering the Earth: Copernicus and The Revolutions of the Heavenly Spheres (Vollmann), **Supp. XVII:** 226
Uncertain Certainty, The: Interviews, Essays, and Notes on Poetry (Simic), **Supp. VIII:** 270, 273, 274
Uncertainty and Plenitude: Five Contemporary Poets (Stitt), **Supp. IX:** 299
"Uncle" (Levine), **Supp. V:** 186
"Uncle Adler" (Kooser), **Supp. XIX:** 120
"Uncle Christmas" (Ríos), **Supp. IV Part 2:** 552
"Uncle Jim's Baptist Revival Hymn" (Lanier and Lanier), **Supp. I Part 1:** 353
"Uncle Lot" (Stowe), **Supp. I Part 2:** 585–586
Uncle Moses (Asch), **Supp. XXIII:** 14
"Uncle Moustapha's Eclipse" (McKnight), **Supp. XX: 148**
Uncle Remus Tales (Harris), **Supp. II Part 1:** 201
"Uncle Tomitudes" (Briggs), **Supp. XVIII:** 14
Uncle Tom's Cabin (Stowe), **II:** 291; **Supp. I Part 1:** 49; **Supp. I Part 2:** 410, 579, 582, 589–592; **Supp. II Part 1:** 170; **Supp. III Part 1:** 154, 171; **Supp. IX:** 19; **Supp. X:** 246, 249, 250; **Supp. XIII:** 95; **Supp. XVI:** 82, 85, 88; **Supp. XVIII:** 14
Uncle Tom's Children (Wright), **IV:** 476, 478, 488; **Retro. Supp. III:** 131; **Supp. II Part 1:** 228, 235; **Supp. XVIII:** 283
"Uncle Wiggily in Connecticut" (Salinger), **III:** 559–560, 563
"Unclouded Day, The" (Proulx), **Supp. VII:** 254–255
"Uncommon Visage" (Brodsky), **Supp. VIII:** 31
"Uncommon Woman: An Interview with Wendy Wasserstein" (Cohen), **Supp. XV:** 323
Uncommon Women and Others (Wasserstein), **Supp. XV:** 320–321, **322–323; Supp. XXIV:** 117
Uncompromising Fictions of Cynthia Ozick (Pinsker), **Supp. V:** 272
"Unconscious Came a Beauty" (Swenson), **Supp. IV Part 2:** 646
"Uncreation, The" (Pinsky), **Supp. VI:** 245
"Undead, The" (Wilbur), **Supp. III Part 2:** 556
"Undefeated, The" (Hemingway), **II:** 250; **Retro. Supp. I:** 180
Under a Glass Bell (Nin), **Supp. X:** 186
"Under Ben Bulben" (Yeats), **Supp. V:** 220
Undercliff: Poems 1946–1953 (Eberhart), **I:** 528, 536–537
Under Cover (Goldbarth), **Supp. XII:** 177, 180, 193
Undercover Doctor (film), **Supp. XIII:** 170
"Under Cygnus" (Wilbur), **Supp. III Part 2:** 558
"Under Forty" (Trilling), **Supp. III Part 2:** 494
"Underground" (Hayes), **Supp. XXVI:** 144
Underground, The Story of a People (Tenenbaum), **Supp. XX: 253**
Underground Man, The (film), **Supp. IV Part 2:** 474
Underground Man, The (Macdonald), **Supp. IV Part 2:** 474, 475
Underground Woman, The (Boyle), **Supp. XXIV:** 62
"Under Libra: Weights and Measures" (Merrill), **Supp. III Part 1:** 328
Under Milk Wood (D. Thomas), **III:** 21
"Undersea" (Carson), **Supp. IX:** 21
Understanding Cynthia Ozick (Friedman), **Supp. V:** 273
Understanding Drama (Brooks and Heilman), **Supp. XIV:** 12
Understanding E. L. Doctorow (Fowler), **Supp. IV Part 1:** 226
Understanding Fiction (Brooks and Warren), **IV:** 279; **Supp. XIV:** 11
Understanding Fiction (Brooks and Warren, eds.), **Supp. XIX:** 246
Understanding Flannery O'Connor (Whitt), **Retro. Supp. II:** 226
Understanding Nicholson Baker (Saltzman), **Supp. XIII:** 48
Understanding Poetry: An Anthology for College Students (Brooks and Warren), **IV:** 236; **Retro. Supp. I:** 40, 41; **Supp. XIV:** 4–5
Understanding Robert Bly (W. V. Davis), **Supp. XXI: 84–85,** 88
Understanding Ron Rash (Lang), **Supp. XXVII:** 215–216
"Understandings of Food as Culture" (Dusselier), **Supp. XXVI:** 210

Understanding Tim O'Brien (Kaplan), **Supp. V:** 241
Understanding To Kill a Mockingbird: A Student Casebook to Issues, Sources, and Documents (C. D. Johnson), **Supp. VIII:** 127
Under Stars (Gallagher), **Supp. XXIV:** 166, 167, 168–169, 170
Undertaker's Garland, The (Wilson and Bishop), **IV:** 427
Under Taos Mountain: The Terrible Quarrel of Magpie and Tía (Schott), **Supp. XXIII: 250–251**
Under the Banner of Heaven: A Story of Violent Faith (Krakauer), **Supp. XVIII:** 105, **114–116,** 117
"Under the Cedarcroft Chestnut" (Lanier), **Supp. I Part 1:** 364
Under the Feet of Jesus (Viramontes), **Supp. XXV:** 130
"Under the Harbour Bridge" (Komunyakaa), **Supp. XIII:** 125
"Under the Influence" (Sanders), **Supp. XVI:** 274, 277
"Under the Language Sea" (Davison), **Supp. XXVI:** 79
Under the Lilacs (Alcott), **Supp. I Part 1:** 42–43, 44
"Under the Maud Moon" (Kinnell), **Supp. III Part 1:** 246–247
Under the Mountain Wall: A Chronicle of Two Seasons in the Stone Age (Matthiessen), **Supp. V:** 202
Under the Red Flag (Jin), **Supp. XVIII:** 89, **94–95**
"Under the Roof of Memory" (Davison), **Supp. XXVI:** 78
"Under the Rose" (Pynchon), **Supp. II Part 2:** 620
"Under the Seal of My Widowhood" (Lombard), **Supp. XXVII:** 262
Under the Sea-Wind: A Naturalist's Picture of Ocean Life (Carson), **Supp. IX:** 19, **22–23**
Under the Shadow (Sorrentino), **Supp. XXI:** 236–237
Under the Sign of Saturn (Sontag), **Supp. III Part 2:** 451, 452, 458, 470–471
"Under the Sign of Saturn" (Sontag), **Supp. III Part 2:** 470
"Under the Sky" (Bowles), **Supp. IV Part 1:** 87
"Under the Sun"(Schott), **Supp. XXIII:** 247, 248
" 'Under the Umbrella of Black Civilization': A Conversation with Reginald McKnight" (Ashe), **Supp. XX: 154**
Under the Volcano (M. Lowry), **Supp. XVII:** 135, 139, 140; **Supp. XXVI:** 28
"Under the Willows" (J. R. Lowell), **Supp. I Part 2:** 416
Under the Willows and Other Poems (J. R. Lowell), **Supp. I Part 2:** 424
"Undertow" (Boyce), **Supp. XXI:** 10
"Underwater Spring" (Huddle), **Supp. XXVI:** 153
Underwood, John Curtis, **Supp. XXIV:** 29
Underwood, Wilbur, **Retro. Supp. II:** 79; **Retro. Supp. III:** 46
Underworld (DeLillo), **Supp. VI:** 2, 4–5, 6–7, 8, 9, 10, 11, **13–15; Supp. XI:** 68; **Supp. XX: 91; Supp. XXVII:** 6
Underworld (screenplay, Hecht), **Supp. XXVII:** 83, 90, 91
Underworld, The (Wolfert). See Tucker's World (Wolfert)
"Undesirable, The" (Huddle), **Supp. XXVI:** 148, 153
Undine (La Motte-Fouqué), **II:** 212; **III:** 78
Undiscovered Country, The (Howells), **II:** 282
"Undressing, The" (C. Frost), **Supp. XV:** 98
"Undressing the Vanity Dolls" (Vaz), **Supp. XXVI:** 260–261
Undset, Sigrid, **Retro. Supp. III:** 24
Uneasy Chair, The (Stegner), **Supp. IV Part 2:** 599
"Unemployed, Disabled, and Insane, The" (Haines), **Supp. XII:** 211–212
Unending Blues (Simic), **Supp. VIII: 278–279**
Unending Dialogue: Voices from an AIDS Poetry Workshop (Hadas, Barber, et al), **Supp. XXIII:** 118, **125–126**
"Unexpected Freedom" (Peacock), **Supp. XIX:** 199
"Unexpressed" (Dunbar), **Supp. II Part 1:** 199
"Unfinished Bronx, The" (Paley), **Supp. VI:** 228
Unfinished Crime, The (Holding), **Supp. XXII:** 120, **123–124,** 135, 136
"Unfinished Poems" (Eliot), **I:** 579
"Unfinished Song" (C. Frost), **Supp. XV:** 97
Unfinished Woman, An (Hellman), **Supp. I Part 1:** 292, 293, 294; **Supp. IV Part 1:** 12, 353–354; **Supp. IX:** 196, 200–201
Unforeseen Wilderness, The: An Essay on Kentucky's Red River Gorge (Berry), **Supp. X:** 28, 29, 30, 36
Unforgotten Years (L. P. Smith), **Supp. XIV:** 333, 334, 335, 336, 347
"Unfortunate Coincidence" (Parker), **Supp. IX:** 190
Unframed Originals (Merwin), **Supp. III Part 1:** 341
Ungar, Sanford, **Supp. XI:** 228
Ungaretti, Giuseppe, **Supp. V:** 337
Unguided Tour (Sontag), **Supp. III Part 2:** 452
"Unheimliche, Das" (The Uncanny) (Freud), **Supp. XVI:** 157–158
Unholy Garden (screenplay, Hech and MacArthur), **Supp. XXVII:** 90
Unholy Sonnets (Jarman), **Supp. XVII:** 109, 110, **119–120; Supp. XVIII:** 178
"Unholy Sonnets" (Jarman), **Supp. XVII:** 118, 119–120
"Unidentified Flying Object" (Hayden), **Supp. II Part 1:** 368
"Unifying Principle, The" (Ammons), **Supp. VII:** 28
"Unimportant Man, An" (D. West), **Supp. XVIII:** 280
"Union" (Hughes), **Supp. I Part 1:** 331
"Union" (Stone), **Supp. XXVII:** 254
"Union Square" (Teasdale), **Supp. XXVII:** 286, 289
"Union Street: San Francisco, Summer 1975" (Carver), **Supp. III Part 1:** 138
"Unitarian Christianity" (Channing), **Supp. XXIV: 71–73,** 77
Unitarians and the Universalists, The (Robinson), **Supp. XXIV:** 70
"United"(Kenny), **Supp. XXIII:** 149
United States Army in World War II (Morison), **Supp. I Part 2:** 490
United States Constitution, **I:** 6, 283
United States Essays, 1951–1991 (Vidal), **Supp. IV Part 2:** 678, 687
"United States of Huck, The: Introduction to Adventures of Huckleberry Finn" (Saunders), **Supp. XIX:** 235
"United States of Lyncherdom, The" (Twain), **Retro. Supp. III:** 268
United States of Poetry, The (television series), **Supp. XIII:** 274
"Unity through Diversity" (Locke), **Supp. XIV:** 212, 213
Universal Baseball Asociation, Inc., J. Henry Waugh, Prop., The (Coover), **Supp. V:** 39, 41–42, 44, 46
Universal Passion (Young), **III:** 111
"Universe of Death, The" (H. Miller), **III:** 184
Universe of Time, A (Anderson), **II:**

27, 28, 45, 46, 48, 49
"Universities" (Emerson), **II:** 6
"Universities: A Mirage? " (Mora), **Supp. XIII:** 219
"University" (Shapiro), **Supp. II Part 2:** 704–705, 717
"University Avenue" (Mora), **Supp. XIII:** 216
"University Days" (Thurber), **Supp. I Part 2:** 605
"University Hospital, Boston" (Oliver), **Supp. VII:** 235
"University's Peril, The" (Taggard), **Supp. XXII:** 273
"Unknowable, The" (Levine), **Supp. V:** 195
"Unknown Girl in the Maternity Ward" (Sexton), **Supp. II Part 2:** 676
"Unknown Love, The" (Chandler), **Supp. IV Part 1:** 120
Unknown Messages (Stone), **Supp. XXVII:** 257
Unknown Rilke, The (Rilke; F. Wright, trans.), **Supp. XVII:** 244
"Unknown War, The" (Sandburg), **III:** 594
Unkown Constellations, The (Swados), **Supp. XIX:** 256
Unleashed (anthology), **Supp. XI:** 132
Unleashed: Poems by Writers' Dogs (Hempel and Shepard, eds.), **Supp. XXI:** 115
"Unlighted Lamps" (Anderson), **I:** 112
Unlit Lamp, The (Holding), **Supp. XXII: 121,** 130
Unloved Wife, The (Alcott), **Supp. I Part 1:** 33
Unmarried Woman, An (film), **Supp. IV Part 1:** 303
"Unnatural Mother, The" (Gilman), **Supp. XI:** 207
"Unnatural State of the Unicorn" (Komunyakaa), **Supp. XIII:** 119
"Unparalleled Adventure of One Hans Pfaall, The" (Poe), **III:** 424
"Unpleasant Profession of Jonathan Hoag, The" (Heinlein), **Supp. XVIII:** 149
Unprecedented Era, The (Goebbels), **III:** 560
"Unprofitable Servant, The" (O. Henry), **Supp. II Part 1:** 403
Unpublished Poems of Emily Dickinson (Bianchi and Hampson, ed.), **Retro. Supp. I:** 35
Unpunished (Gilman), **Supp. XI:** 208
Unraveling Strangeness, The (Weigl), **Supp. XIX: 287–288**
"Unreal City" (Eliot), **Supp. XV:** 218
"Unreality of Modern Realism, The" (Rinehart), **Supp. XXV:** 201
"Unreasoning Heart" (Untermeyer), **Supp. XV:** 309
"Unsaid (Gioia), **Supp. XV:** 129
"Unseen, The" (Pinsky), **Supp. VI:** 243–244
"Unseen, The" (Singer), **Retro. Supp. II:** 307
Unseen Hand, The (Shepard), **Supp. III Part 2:** 439, 445–446
Unselected Poems (Levine), **Supp. V:** 179
Unsettling of America, The: Culture and Agriculture (Berry), **Supp. X:** 22, 26, 29, 32, 33, 35; **Supp. XIV:** 177, 179
Unspeakable Gentleman, The (Marquand), **III:** 53–54, 60, 63
Unspeakable Practices, Unnatural Acts (Barthelme), **Supp. IV Part 1:** 39
"Unspeakable Things Unspoken: The Afro-American Presence in American Literature" (Morrison), **Retro. Supp. III:** 194; **Supp. III Part 1:** 375, 377–379
Unspoken and Other Poems, The (Bremer), **Supp. XXII:** 277
"Untelling, The" (Strand), **Supp. IV Part 2:** 629
Unterecker, John, **I:** 386
Untermeyer, Jean Starr, **II:** 530; **Supp. XV:** 294, 295, 303, 307, 308, 310; **Supp. XXVII:** 286
Untermeyer, Louis, **II:** 516–517, 530, 532; **III:** 268; **Retro. Supp. I:** 124, 133, 136; **Retro. Supp. III:** 47, 100, 133; **Supp. III Part 1:** 2; **Supp. IX:** 76; **Supp. XIV:** 119, 123; **Supp. XV: 293–318; Supp. XXI:** 277; **Supp. XXV:** 21, 23; **Supp. XXVII:** 252, 286, 289
Untimely Papers (Bourne), **I:** 218, 233
"Untitled" (C. Frost), **Supp. XV:** 103
"Untitled Blues" (Komunyakaa), **Supp. XIII:** 117
Unto the Sons (Talese), **Supp. XVII:** 199–200, **206–207,** 208, 209, 210
"Untrustworthy Speaker, The" (Glück), **Supp. V:** 86
"Unused" (Anderson), **I:** 112, 113
Unvanquished, The (Faulkner), **II:** 55, 67–68, 71; **Retro. Supp. I:** 84; **Retro. Supp. III:** 85; **Supp. I Part 2:** 450
"Unvexed Isles, The" (Warren), **IV:** 253
"Unwedded" (Larcom), **Supp. XIII:** 144
"Unweepables, The" (Karr), **Supp. XI:** 243
"Unwelcome Guest, An" (Papernick), **Supp. XVII:** 50
Unwelcome Man, The (W. Frank), **Supp. XX: 70, 76**
Unwelcome Words (Bowles), **Supp. IV Part 1:** 93, 94
"Unwelcome Words" (Bowles), **Supp. IV Part 1:** 94, 95
Unwin, T. Fisher, **Supp. XI:** 202
"Unwithered Garland, The" (Kunitz), **Supp. III Part 1:** 265
Unwobbling Pivot, The (Pound, trans.), **III:** 472
"Unwritten, The" (Merwin), **Supp. III Part 1:** 352
"Unwritten Law" (Glück), **Supp. V:** 91
Up (Sukenick), **Supp. V:** 39
Up Above the World (Bowles), **Supp. IV Part 1:** 82, 91, 92
"Up and Down" (Merrill), **Supp. III Part 1:** 328
Upanishads, **IV:** 183
Up Country: Poems of New England (Kumin), **Supp. IV Part 2:** 446, 447–448, 453
"Update" (Dunn), **Supp. XI:** 150–151
Updike, John, **I:** 54; **III:** 572; **IV: 214–235; Retro. Supp. I:** 116, **317–338; Retro. Supp. II:** 213, 279, 280; **Supp. I Part 1:** 186, 196; **Supp. IV Part 2:** 657; **Supp. IX:** 208; **Supp. V:** 23, 43, 95, 119; **Supp. VIII:** 151, 167, 236; **Supp. XI:** 65, 66, 99, 140; **Supp. XII:** 140, 296, 298, 310; **Supp. XIII:** 45–46, 47, 52; **Supp. XIV:** 79, 93, 111; **Supp. XVI:** 205, 207, 220; **Supp. XX: 17; Supp. XXI:** 116, 226; **Supp. XXIII:** 109
Updike, Mrs. Wesley, **IV:** 218, 220
Up from Slavery (Washington), **Supp. II Part 1:** 169; **Supp. IX:** 19
Upham, Thomas Goggswell, **II:** 487
"Upholsterers, The" (Lardner), **II:** 435
"Up in Michigan" (Hemingway), **II:** 263; **Supp. XIX:** 241
Upjohn, Richard, **IV:** 312
"Upon a Fit of Sickness, Anno 1632" (Bradstreet), **Retro. Supp. III:** 13
"Upon a Spider Catching a Fly" (Taylor), **IV:** 161
"Upon a Wasp Child with Cold" (Taylor), **IV:** 161
"Upon Meeting Don L. Lee, in a Dream" (Dove), **Supp. IV Part 1:** 244
"Upon My Dear and Loving Husband His Going into England, Jan. 16, 1661" (Bradstreet), **Supp. I Part 1:** 110
"Upon My Mother's Death"(Hadas),

Supp. XXIII: 118
"Upon Returning to the Country Road" (Lindsay), **Supp. I Part 2:** 382
"Upon Some Distemper of Body" (Bradstreet), **Retro. Supp. III:** 2
"Upon the Burning of Our House, July 10th, 1666" (Bradstreet), **Supp. I Part 1:** 107–108, 122
"Upon the Sweeping Flood" (Taylor), **IV:** 161
"Upon Wedlock, and Death of Children" (Taylor), **IV:** 144, 147, 161
"Upon Westminster Bridge" (Wordsworth), **Supp. XXIV:** 148
"Upset, An" (Merrill), **Supp. III Part 1:** 336
Upstairs and Downstairs (Vonnegut), **Supp. II Part 2:** 757
Upstate (Wilson), **IV:** 447
Upton, Lee, **Supp. X:** 209
"Upturned Face" (Crane), **I:** 423
Upward, Allen, **Supp. I Part 1:** 262
Upward, Edward, **Supp. XIV:** 159, 160
"Upward Moon and the Downward Moon, The" (R. Bly), **Supp. IV Part 1:** 71
Urama, Kelechi, **Supp. XXVII:** 202
Urania: A Rhymed Lesson (Holmes), **Supp. I Part 1:** 300
"Urban Convalescence, An" (Merrill), **Supp. III Part 1:** 322–324
"Urban Renewal" (Komunyakaa), **Supp. XIII:** 113
Urban Tumbleweed: Notes from a Tanka Diary (Mullen), **Supp. XXVII:** 175–176
Urdang, Constance, **Supp. XV:** 74
"Urganda and Fatima" (Rowson), **Supp. XV:** 234
Urial Accosta: A Play (Reznikoff), **Supp. XIV:** 282, 288
Urich, Robert, **Supp. V:** 228
"Uriel" (Emerson), **II:** 19
Uris, Leon, **Supp. IV Part 1:** 285, 379; **Supp. XX: 243–258; Supp. XXVII:** 147
Uroff, Margaret D., **Supp. I Part 2:** 542
Ursu, Liliana, **Supp. XXIV:** 178
"Us" (Sexton), **Supp. II Part 2:** 687
U.S. 1 (Rukeyser), **Supp. VI:** 272, 278, 283, 285
U.S.A. (Dos Passos), **I:** 379, 475, 478, 482–488, 489, 490, 491, 492, 493, 494, 495; **Retro. Supp. II:** 197; **Supp. I Part 2:** 646; **Supp. III Part 1:** 104, 105; **Supp. XIV:** 24; **Supp. XXVI:** 23
"U.S.A. School of Writing, The" (Bishop), **Retro. Supp. II:** 43
USA the Movie (film), **Supp. XXVII:** 263
"U.S. Commercial Orchid, The" (Agee), **I:** 35
"Used-Boy Raisers, The" (Paley), **Supp. VI:** 218, 228
"Used Cars on Oahu" (Nye), **Supp. XIII:** 282
"Used Side of the Sofa, The" (Ríos), **Supp. IV Part 2:** 551
Useless Servants, The (Hinojosa), **Supp. XIX:** 98, 103, 104**, 109–110**
Use of Fire, The (Price), **Supp. VI:** 265
"Use of Force, The" (W. C. Williams), **Retro. Supp. I:** 424
Use of Poetry and the Use of Criticism, The (Eliot), **Retro. Supp. I:** 65
Uses of Enchantment, The: The Meaning and Importance of Fairy Tales (Bettelheim), **Supp. X:** 77; **Supp. XIV:** 126
"Uses of Hell, The" (E. Hoffman), **Supp. XVI:** 154
"Uses of Hell, The: An Exchange"(Novick, Katz, and Szulc), **Supp. XVI:** 154
Uses of Literacy, The (Hoggart), **Supp. XIV:** 299
Uses of Literature, The (Calvino), **Supp. XXII:** 263
"Uses of Poetry, The" (W. C. Williams), **Retro. Supp. I:** 412
"Uses of the Blues, The" (Baldwin), **Retro. Supp. II:** 8
"Use-Unuse of Us, The" (Bronk), **Supp. XXI:** 32
"USFS 1919: The Ranger, the Cook, and a Hole in the Sky" (Maclean), **Supp. XIV:** 230, 234
Ushant: An Essay (Aiken), **I:** 49, 54, 55, 56, 57
"Usher 11" (Bradbury), **Supp. I Part 2:** 622
U.S.I. (Kramer), **Supp. XXVI:** 26
"Using Parrots to Kill Mockingbirds: Yet Another Racial Prosecution and Wrongful Conviction in Maycomb" (Fair), **Supp. VIII:** 128
USS Constellation: Pride of the American Navy (Myers), **Supp. XXVII:** 208
Ustedes y Nosotros: Nuevo Mensaje a Ibero-América (W. Frank), **Supp. XX: 79**
"Usual Objects"(Schott), **Supp. XXIII:** 248
Usual Star, The (Doolittle), **Supp. I Part 1:** 270
"Usurpation (Other People's Stories)" (Ozick), **Supp. V:** 268, 271
Utopia 14 (Vonnegut), **Supp. II Part 2:** 757
V. (Pynchon), **Supp. II Part 2:** 618, 620–622, 627–630; **Supp. IV Part 1:** 279
"Vacation" (Stafford), **Supp. XI:** 321, 322
Vacationland (Monson), **Supp. XXIV:** 230, 231, 234
"Vacation Trip" (Stafford), **Supp. XI:** 322
Vachel Lindsay: A Poet in America (Masters), **Supp. I Part 2:** 473, 474
"Vachel Lindsay: The Midwest as Utopia" (Whitney), **Supp. I Part 2:** 403
"Vachel Lindsay Writes to Floyd Dell" (Tanselle), **Supp. I Part 2:** 403
"Vacillation" (Yeats), **Supp. XV:** 253
Vadim, Roger, **Supp. XI:** 293, 307
"Vag" (Dos Passos), **I:** 487–488
Vagina Monologues, The (Ensler), **Supp. XIX:** 204–205
Vail, Laurence, **Supp. XXIV:** 50
Valdez, Luis, **Supp. XXIII:** 203
"Vale" (Stallings), **Supp. XXV:** 230, 231
Valediction (Parker), **Supp. XIX:** 185
"Valediction Forbidding Mourning, A" (Rich), **Retro. Supp. III:** 245–246
Valentine, Jean, **Supp. V:** 92
Valentine, Saint, **IV:** 396
Valentines (Kooser), **Supp. XIX:** 116, 123**, 128–129**
Valentino, Rudolph, **I:** 483
Valéry, Paul, **II:** 543, 544; **III:** 279, 409, 428, 609; **IV:** 79, 91, 92, 428, 443; **Retro. Supp. II:** 187
"Valhalla" (Francis), **Supp. IX:** 77
Valhalla and Other Poems (Francis), **Supp. IX:** 76
Valiant Runaways, The (Atherton), **Supp. XXIV:** 22
Validity in Interpretation (Hirsch), **Supp. XIV:** 15
Valitsky, Ken, **Supp. XII:** 7
Vallejo, César, **Supp. IX:** 271; **Supp. V:** 332; **Supp. XIII:** 114, 315, 323; **Supp. XXI:** 132
Valley, The (Asch), **Supp. XXVI:** 17, 21, 23–26
"Valley, The" (Bass), **Supp. XVI:** 20, 22
Valley, The (Hinojosa), **Supp. XIX:** 97, 99**, 100–101**
"Valley Between, The" (Marshall), **Supp. XI:** 278
Valley of Decision, The (Wharton), **IV:** 311, 315; **Retro. Supp. I:** 365–367;

Retro. Supp. III: 279
"Valley of the Monsters, The" (Peacock), **Supp. XIX:** 198
Valley of the Moon, The (London), **II:** 467, 481
"Valley of Unrest, The" (Poe), **III:** 411
Valli, Alida, **Supp. IV Part 2:** 520
"Valor" (Bausch), **Supp. VII:** 54
Valparaiso (DeLillo), **Supp. VI:** 4, 12
"Value of a Place, The" (Bass), **Supp. XVI:** 18
"Values and Fictions" (Toomer), **Supp. III Part 2:** 485–486
"Values and Imperatives" (Locke), **Supp. XIV:** 199, 202, 212
Values of Veblen, The: A Critical Appraisal (Rosenberg), **Supp. I Part 2:** 650
"Vampire" (Karr), **Supp. XI:** 241
Vampire Armand, The (Rice), **Supp. VII:** 290, 294–295
Vampire Chronicles, The (Rice), **Supp. VII:** 290
Vampire Lestat, The (Rice), **Supp. VII:** 290–292, 298, 299
Van Aalst, Mariska, **Supp. XIX:** 50, 51
Van Arsdale, Sarah, **Supp. XXV:** 4
Van Buren, Floyd, **Retro. Supp. III:** 82
Van Buren, Martin, **II:** 134, 312; **III:** 473
"Vandals" (Munro), **Supp. XXVII:** 192
Vande Kieft, Ruth M., **IV:** 260
Vanderbilt, Cornelius, **III:** 14
VanDerWerff, Todd, **Supp. XXV:** 75
Van Dine, S. S., **Supp. IV Part 1:** 341; **Supp. XXVI:** 283
Van Doren, Carl, **I:** 252–253, 423; **II:** 103, 111, 112; **Supp. I Part 2:** 474, 486, 707, 709, 717, 718, 727; **Supp. II Part 1:** 395; **Supp. VIII:** 96–97
Van Doren, Mark, **I:** 168; **III:** 4, 23, 589; **Supp. I Part 2:** 604; **Supp. III Part 2:** 626; **Supp. IX:** 266, 268; **Supp. VIII:** 231; **Supp. XV:** 152, 305, 307; **Supp. XXII:** 275
Vandover and the Brute (Norris), **III:** 314, 315, 316, 320–322, 328, 333, 334
Van Duyn, Mona, **Supp. IX:** 269
Van Dyke, Annette, **Supp. IV Part 1:** 327
Van Dyke, Henry, **I:** 223; **II:** 456
Van Engen, Abram, **Retro. Supp. III:** 12
Van Gogh, Vincent, **I:** 27; **IV:** 290; **Supp. I Part 2:** 451; **Supp. IV Part 1:** 284; **Supp. XXII:** 171–172
Van Gogh Field and Other Stories, The (Kittredge), **Supp. XXVI:** 181, 182, 184
Van Gogh's Room at Arles (Elkin), **Supp. VI: 56**
"Vanilla Dunk" (Lethem), **Supp. XVIII:** 139
"Vanisher, The" (Whittier), **Supp. I Part 2:** 691
Vanishing of Betty Varian, The (Wells), **Supp. XXVI:** 278
Vanishing Point (Markson), **Supp. XVII:** 135, 137, 138, 145–146
"Vanishing Point, The" (Davison), **Supp. XXVI:** 76
"Vanishing Point: Former City" (Monson), **Supp. XXIV:** 238
"Vanishing Point for Solo Voice" (Monson), **Supp. XXIV:** 239
Vanishing Point: Not a Memoir (Monson), **Supp. XXIV:** 230, **236–239,** 241–242
"Vanishing Point: Panera" (Monson), **Supp. XXIV:** 238
"Vanishing Red, The" (Frost), **Retro. Supp. II:** 47; **Retro. Supp. III:** 99
"Vanity" (B. Diop), **Supp. IV Part 1:** 16
Vanity Fair (Thackeray), **I:** 354; **II:** 91; **III:** 70; **Supp. IX:** 200
"Vanity of All Worldly Things, The" (Bradstreet), **Retro. Supp. III:** 11; **Supp. I Part 1:** 102, 119
Vanity of Duluoz (Kerouac), **Supp. III Part 1:** 221, 222
"Vanity of Existence, The" (Freneau), **Supp. II Part 1:** 262
Van Matre, Lynn, **Supp. V:** 126
Vann, Barbara, **Supp. XV:** 187
Vanquished, The (Faulkner), **I:** 205
"Vanquished, The" (Rash), **Supp. XXVII:** 220
Van Rensselaer, Stephen, **I:** 351
Van Vechten, Carl, **I:** 295; **IV:** 76; **Retro. Supp. I:** 199; **Retro. Supp. III:** 127, 134, 137; **Supp. I Part 1:** 324, 327, 332; **Supp. I Part 2:** 715; **Supp. II Part 2: 725–751; Supp. X:** 247; **Supp. XIX:** 76; **Supp. XVI:** 135; **Supp. XVII:** 96, 97, 101, 104; **Supp. XVIII:** 123, 131, 132, 279, 280; **Supp. XX: 69; Supp. XXI:** 5, 8; **Supp. XXII:** 5, 158, 160
Van Vliet, Don, **Supp. XXIII:** 174
Vanya and Sonia and Masha and Spike (Durang), **Supp. XXIV: 127–128**
Vanzetti, Bartolomeo, **I:** 482, 486, 490, 494; **II:** 38–39, 426; **III:** 139–140; **Supp. I Part 2:** 446, 610, 611; **Supp. IX:** 199; **Supp. V:** 288–289; **Supp. XXII:** 277
"Vapor Trail Reflected in the Frog Pond" (Kinnell), **Supp. III Part 1:** 242–243
"Vapor Trails" (Snyder), **Supp. VIII:** 298
"Variant Text" (Goodman), **Supp. XXVI:** 118
"Variation: Ode to Fear" (Warren), **IV:** 241
"Variation on a Sentence" (Bogan), **Supp. III Part 1:** 60
"Variation on Gaining a Son" (Dove), **Supp. IV Part 1:** 248
"Variation on Pain" (Dove), **Supp. IV Part 1:** 248
"Variations: The air is sweetest that a thistle guards" (Merrill), **Supp. III Part 1:** 321
"Variations: White Stag, Black Bear" (Merrill), **Supp. III Part 1:** 321
"Varick Street" (Bishop), **Supp. I Part 1:** 90, 92
Varieties of Metaphysical Poetry, The (Eliot), **Retro. Supp. I:** 65
Varieties of Religious Experience, The (William James), **II:** 344, 353, 354, 359–360, 362; **IV:** 28, 291; **Supp. IX:** 19
Variety (film), **Supp. XII:** 7
Variorum (Whitman), **Retro. Supp. I:** 406
Various Antidotes (J. Scott), **Supp. XVII: 188–189**
Various Miracles (Shields), **Supp. VII:** 318–320, 323, 324
"Various Miracles" (Shields), **Supp. VII:** 318–319, 324
Various Poems (Zach), **Supp. XV:** 86
Various Positions (album, Coen), **Supp. XXVII:** 54
"Various Tourists" (Connell), **Supp. XIV:** 79
"Varmint Question, The" (Leopold), **Supp. XIV:** 180–181
Varno, David, **Supp. XIX:** 205
Vasari, Giorgio, **Supp. I Part 2:** 450; **Supp. III Part 1:** 5
Vasquez, Robert, **Supp. V:** 180
Vassall Morton (Parkman), **Supp. II Part 2:** 595, 597–598
Vasse, W. W., **III:** 478
Vaudeville for a Princess (Schwartz), **Supp. II Part 2:** 661–662
"Vaudeville Moment" (Bodenheim), **Supp. XXV:** 22
Vaughan, Henry, **IV:** 151; **Supp. XV:** 251
Vaughn, Robert, **Supp. XI:** 343
Vaughn, Stephanie, **Supp. XXV:** 142

"Vaunting Oak" (Ransom), **III:** 490
Vaz, Katherine, **Supp. XXVI: 255–269**
Vazirani, Reetika, **Supp. XIII:** 133
Veblen (Hobson), **Supp. I Part 2:** 650
Veblen, Andrew, **Supp. I Part 2:** 640
Veblen, Oswald, **Supp. I Part 2:** 640
Veblen, Thorstein, **I:** 104, 283, 475–476, 483, 498, 511; **II:** 27, 272, 276, 287; **Supp. I Part 2: 628–650; Supp. IV Part 1:** 22
Veblen, Mrs. Thorstein (Ellen Rolfe), **Supp. I Part 2:** 641
Veblenism: A New Critique (Dobriansky), **Supp. I Part 2:** 648, 650
"Veblen's Attack on Culture" (Adorno), **Supp. I Part 2:** 650
Vecsey, Christopher, **Supp. XXVI:** 90
Vectors and Smoothable Curves (Bronk), **Supp. XXI: 24–26,** 32
Vedanta for Modern Man (Isherwood, ed.), **Supp. XIV:** 164
Vedanta for the Western World (Isherwood, ed.), **Supp. XIV:** 164
Vedas, **IV:** 183
Vega, Janine Pommy, **Supp. XIV:** 148
Vega, Lope de, **Retro. Supp. I:** 285; **Supp. III Part 1:** 341, 347
Vegetable, The (Fitzgerald), **Retro. Supp. I:** 105; **Supp. IX:** 57
Vegetable, The, or From President to Postman (Fitzgerald), **II:** 91
"Vegetable Love" (Apple), **Supp. XVII:** 4
"Vegetable Love"(Crooker), **Supp. XXIII:** 62
"Vegetable Wisdom" (Halliday), **Supp. XIX:** 88
Veg tsu zikh, Der (The road to one's self) (Asch), **Supp. XXIII:** 5, 11
Veil of Snows, A (Helprin), **Supp. XXV:** 84, 87
Veinberg, Jon, **Supp. V:** 180; **Supp. XIII:** 313; **Supp. XV:** 76–77, 86
Vein of Iron (Glasgow), **II:** 175, 186, 188–189, 191, 192, 194
Vein of Riches, A (Knowles), **Supp. XII:** 249
Vein of Words (J. W. Miller), **Supp. XX: 165**
Velie, Alan R., **Supp. IV Part 2:** 486
Velocities: New and Selected Poems, 1966–1992 (Dobyns), **Supp. XIII:** 86–87, 87, 88
"Velocity" (Collins), **Supp. XXI:** 61
"Velorio" (Cisneros), **Supp. VII:** 66
"Velvet Gentleman, The (Skloot), **Supp. XX: 201**
"Velvet Shoes" (Wylie), **Supp. I Part 2:** 711, 714
Venant, Elizabeth, **Supp. XI:** 343
Vencloca, Thomas, **Supp. VIII:** 29
Vendler, Helen H., **Retro. Supp. I:** 297; **Retro. Supp. II:** 184, 191; **Supp. I Part 1:** 77, 78, 92, 95; **Supp. I Part 2:** 565; **Supp. IV Part 1:** 245, 247, 249, 254, 257; **Supp. IV Part 2:** 448; **Supp. V:** 78, 82, 189, 343; **Supp. XII:** 187, 189; **Supp. XV:** 20, 184
"Venetian Blind, The" (Jarrell), **II:** 382–383
Venetian Glass Nephew, The (Wylie), **Supp. I Part 2:** 707, 709, 714, 717–719, 721, 724
Venetian Life (Howells), **II:** 274, 277, 279
Venetian Vespers, The (Hecht), **Supp. X:** 57, **65–69**
"Venetian Vespers, The" (Hecht), **Supp. X:** 65, **66–67**
Venice Observed (McCarthy), **II:** 562
Ventadorn, Bernard de, **Supp. IV Part 1:** 146
"Ventriloquists' Conversations" (Gentry), **Supp. IV Part 1:** 236
Venturesome Voyages of Captain Voss, The (Voss), **Supp. XXV:** 217
"Venus, Cupid, Folly and Time" (Taylor), **Supp. V:** 322–323
Venus and Adonis (film), **Supp. IV Part 1:** 82
Venus and Don Juan (C. Frost), **Supp. XV:** 93, **102–103,** 104, 107
"Venus and Don Juan" (C. Frost), **Supp. XV:** 103
Venus Blue (Sobin), **Supp. XVI: 293–294,** 294
Venus in Sparta (Auchincloss), **Supp. IV Part 1:** 25
"Venus Pandemos" (Halliday), **Supp. XIX:** 85, 89, 90, 93
"Venus's-flytraps" (Komunyakaa), **Supp. XIII:** 126, 127
"Veracruz" (Hayden), **Supp. II Part 1:** 371, 373
Verducci, Tom, **Supp. XXII:** 209
"Verdun" (Beston), **Supp. XXVI:** 32
Verga, Giovanni, **II:** 271, 275
Verghese, Abraham, **Supp. X:** 160
Verhaeren, Emile, **I:** 476; **II:** 528, 529
Verlaine, Paul, **II:** 529, 543; **III:** 466; **IV:** 79, 80, 86, 286; **Retro. Supp. I:** 56, 62; **Retro. Supp. II:** 326
"Vermeer" (Nemerov), **III:** 275, 278, 280
Vermeer, Jan, **Retro. Supp. I:** 335
"Vermont" (Carruth), **Supp. XVI:** 54
"Vermont" (Huddle), **Supp. XXVI:** 161
Vermont Journal: 1971 (Brainard), **Supp. XXVII:** 27
Vermont Notebook, The (Ashbery), **Supp. III Part 1:** 1
"Vermont Tale, A" (Helprin), **Supp. XXV:** 85
Vermont Writers: A State of Mind (Daley), **Supp. XXII:** 216
"Vernal Ague, The" (Freneau), **Supp. II Part 1:** 258
Verne, Jules, **I:** 480; **Retro. Supp. I:** 270; **Retro. Supp. III:** 235; **Supp. XI:** 63
Vernon, John, **Supp. X:** 15
Verplanck, Gulian C., **Supp. I Part 1:** 155, 156, 157, 158
Verrazano, Giovanni da, **Supp. I Part 2:** 496, 497
Verse (Zawacki), **Supp. VIII:** 272
"Verse for Urania" (Merrill), **Supp. III Part 1:** 329, 330
Verses (Wharton), **Retro. Supp. I:** 362; **Retro. Supp. III:** 276
Verses, Printed for Her Friends (Jewett), **II:** 406
"Verses for Children" (A. Lowell), **II:** 516
"Verses Made at Sea in a Heavy Gale" (Freneau), **Supp. II Part 1:** 262
"Verses on the Death of T. S. Eliot" (Brodsky), **Supp. VIII:** 19
"Version of a Fragment of Simonides" (Bryant), **Supp. I Part 1:** 153, 155
"Vers Libre Epidemic, The" (Lovecraft), **Supp. XXV:** 120
Verulam, Baron. See Bacon, Francis
Very, Jones, **III:** 507; **Supp. XXV: 237–252**
"Very Hot Sun in Bermuda, The" (Jackson), **Supp. IX:** 126
Very Old Bones (W. Kennedy), **Supp. VII:** 133, 148, 150–153
"Very Old Man with Enormous Wings, A" (García Márquez), **Supp. XXIV:** 190
Very Persistent Gappers of Frip, The (Saunders), **Supp. XIX: 229–230**
"Very Proper Gander, The" (Thurber), **Supp. I Part 2:** 610
"Very Short Story, A" (Hemingway), **II:** 252; **Retro. Supp. I:** 173
"Vesalius in Zante" (Wharton), **Retro. Supp. I:** 372
Vesey, Denmark, **Supp. I Part 2:** 592
Vesey, Desmond, **Supp. XIV:** 162
"Vespers" (Auden), **Supp. II Part 1:** 23
"Vespers" (Glück), **Supp. V:** 88
"Vespers"(Dybek), **Supp. XXIII:** 78
Vestal Lady on Brattle, The (Corso),

Supp. XII: 119, **120–121,** 134
Vested Interests and the Common Man, The (Veblen), **Supp. I Part 2:** 642
"Vesuvius at Home" (Rich), **Retro. Supp. I:** 42; **Retro. Supp. III:** 248
"Veteran, The" (Crane), **I:** 413
"Veterans' Cemetery" (Gioia), **Supp. XV:** 117
"Veteran Sirens" (Robinson), **III:** 512, 524
"Veterinarian" (X. J. Kennedy), **Supp. XV:** 168
"Vetiver" (Ashbery), **Supp. III Part 1:** 26
Vetter, Lara, **Supp. XXII:** 166
"Via Dieppe-Newhaven" (H. Miller), **III:** 183
"Via Negativa" (Salter), **Supp. IX:** 257
Vicar of Wakefeld, The (Goldsmith), **I:** 216
Vicious Circle, The (film, Wilder), **Supp. XVII:** 62
"Vicissitudes of the Avant-Garde, The" (Gass), **Supp. VI:** 91
Vicky Van (Wells), **Supp. XXVI:** 280
Vico, Giambattista, **Supp. XX: 38**
Victim, The (Bellow), **I:** 144, 145, 147, 149, 150, 151, 152, 153, 155, 156, 158, 159, 164; **IV:** 19; **Retro. Supp. II:** 21, 22, 34
"Victor" (Mumford), **Supp. II Part 2:** 476
Victoria (Rowson), **Supp. XV:** 231
Victorian in the Modern World, A (Hapgood), **Supp. XVII:** 95, 97, 100, 101, 103, 105, 106; **Supp. XXI:** 8
"Victoria's Secret" (Collins), **Supp. XXI:** 58–59
"Victories" (Untermeyer), **Supp. XV:** 300
"Victory at Sea" (television series), **Supp. I Part 2:** 490
"Victory comes late" (Dickinson), **Retro. Supp. I:** 45
"Victory of the Moon, The" (Crane), **I:** 420
Vida, Vendela, **Supp. XIX:** 49, 50, 53, 57, 58, 59, 61, 62
Vidal, Gore, **II:** 587; **IV:** 383; **Supp. IV Part 1:** 22, 35, 92, 95, 198; **Supp. IV Part 2: 677–696; Supp. IX:** 96; **Supp. X:** 186, 195; **Supp. XIV:** 156, 170, 338; **Supp. XIX:** 131, 132
Video Poems (Collins), **Supp. XXI:** 53
Viebahn, Fred, **Supp. IV Part 1:** 248
Viera, Joseph M., **Supp. XI:** 178, 186
Viereck, Peter, **Supp. I Part 2:** 403
Viertel, Berthold, **Supp. XIV:** 165
Viertel, Salka, **Supp. XVI:** 192
Viet Journal (Jones), **Supp. XI: 230–231**
Vietnam (McCarthy), **II:** 578–579
"Vietnam in Me, The" (O'Brien), **Supp. V:** 241, 252
Vietnamization of New Jersey, The (Durang), **Supp. XXIV:** 113, **117–118**
Vietnam Reader, The: The Definitive Collection of Fiction and Nonfiction on the War (O'Nan, ed.), **Supp. XXV:** 153
Vie unanime, La (Romains), **I:** 227
"View, The" (Roussel), **Supp. III Part 1:** 15, 16, 21
View from 80, The (Cowley), **Supp. II Part 1:** 141, 144, 153
"View from an Institution" (F. Wright), **Supp. XVII:** 244
View from Castle Rock, The (Munro), **Supp. XXVII:** 194–195
"View from the Backyard" (W. V. Davis), **Supp. XXI:** 96
View from the Bridge, A (A. Miller), **III:** 147, 148, 156, 158, 159–160; **Retro. Supp. III:** 165, 167, 168–169, 173; **Supp. XXV:** 93
View from the Seventh Layer, The (Brockmeier), **Supp. XXII: 59–61**
"View from the Seventh Layer, The" (Brockmeier), **Supp. XXII:** 61
View of My Own, A: Essays in Literature and Society (Hardwick), **Supp. III Part 1:** 194, 200
"View of the Capital from the Library of Congress" (Bishop), **Retro. Supp. II:** 45
View of the Soil and Climate of the United States, A (Brown, trans.), **Supp. I Part 1:** 146
"View of the Woods, A" (O'Connor), **III:** 349, 351, 358; **Retro. Supp. II:** 237
"Viewpoint" (column, Siddons), **Supp. XXII:** 240, 245
"Views of the Mysterious Hill: The Appearance of Parnassus in American Poetry" (Strand), **Supp. IV Part 2:** 631
"Vigil" (Karr), **Supp. XI:** 241
"Vigil, The" (Dante), **III:** 542
"Vigil at Heiligenkreuz" (W. V. Davis), **Supp. XXI:** 93
"Vigil"(Dybek), **Supp. XXIII:** 78
"Vignette" (Trethewey), **Supp. XXI:** 253, 254
Vigny, Alfred Victor de, **II:** 543
Vildrac, Charles, **Supp. XV:** 50
Vile Bodies (Waugh), **Supp. I Part 2:** 607
Villa, Pancho, **I:** 210; **III:** 584
"Villa dei Pini" (Davison), **Supp. XXVI:** 79
"Village, The" (Huddle), **Supp. XXVI:** 156
"Village Blacksmith, The" (Longfellow), **Retro. Supp. II:** 167, 168; **Supp. I Part 2:** 409
Village Hymns, a Supplement to Dr. Watts's Psalms and Hymns (Nettleton), **I:** 458
"Village Improvement Parade, The" (Lindsay), **Supp. I Part 2:** 388, 389
Village Magazine, The (Lindsay), **Supp. I Part 2:** 379–380, 382
Village Virus, The (Lewis), **II:** 440
"Villanelle at Sundown" (Justice), **Supp. VII:** 119, 122–123
"Villanelle of Change" (Robinson), **III:** 524
Villard, Oswald, **Supp. I Part 1:** 332
"Villa Selene" (Simpson), **Supp. IX:** 279
Villon, François, **II:** 544; **III:** 9, 174, 592; **Retro. Supp. I:** 286; **Supp. I Part 1:** 261; **Supp. III Part 1:** 235, 243, 249, 253; **Supp. III Part 2:** 560; **Supp. IX:** 116
"Villonaud for This Yule" (Pound), **Retro. Supp. I:** 286
Vincent, Steven, **Supp. XXV:** 201
"Vincenzo Tailor" (Di Piero), **Supp. XIX:** 38
Vindication of the Rights of Woman (Wollstonecraft), **Supp. I Part 1:** 126; **Supp. XI:** 203
Viner, Katherine, **Supp. XXVII:** 276
Vines, Lois Davis, **Retro. Supp. II:** 261
"Vineyard of Red Wine, The" (Beston), **Supp. XXVI:** 32
Vintage Book of Amnesia, The (Lethem, ed.), **Supp. XVIII:** 138
"Vintage Thunderbird, A" (Beattie), **Supp. V:** 27
Vinz, Mark, **Supp. X:** 117
Viol de Lucrèce, Le (Obey), **IV:** 356
Violence (Bausch), **Supp. VII:** 48–49, 54
Violent Bear It Away, The (O'Connor), **III:** 339, 345–348, 350, 351, 354, 355, 356, 357; **Retro. Supp. II:** 233, **234–236; Retro. Supp. III:** 208, 210–211, 213, 215
Violent Hero, Wilderness Heritage and Urban Reality, The: A Study of the Private Eye in the Novels of Dashiell Hammett, Raymond Chandler and

Ross Macdonald (Parker), **Supp. XIX:** 177
"Violent Vet, The" (O'Brien), **Supp. V:** 238
Violin (Rice), **Supp. VII:** 302
Viorst, Judith, **Supp. X:** 153
Viper Run (Karr), **Supp. XI: 248–251**
Viramontes, Helene María, **Supp. XXV:** 130, 133, 138
Virgil, **I:** 312, 322, 587; **II:** 133, 542; **IV:** 137, 359; **Retro. Supp. I:** 135; **Supp. I Part 1:** 153; **Supp. I Part 2:** 494; **Supp. IV Part 2:** 631
"Virgin and Child with Music and Numbers" (Bronk), **Supp. XXI:** 30
"Virgin and the Dynamo" (Adams), **III:** 396
"Virgin Carrying a Lantern, The" (Stevens), **IV:** 80
Virgin Huntress, The (Holding), **Supp. XXII:** 119, 124, **135–136**
Virginia (Glasgow), **II:** 175, 178, 181–182, 193, 194
"Virginia" (Lindsay), **Supp. I Part 2:** 398
"Virginia Britannia" (Moore), **III:** 198, 208–209
"Virginians Are Coming Again, The" (Lindsay), **Supp. I Part 2:** 399
Virginia Reels (Hoffman), **Supp. XVIII:** 79, 86
Virgin Spain (W. Frank), **Supp. XX: 76**
"Virgins Plus Curtains Minus Dots" (Loy), **Supp. XXII:** 161
Virgin Suicides, The (Eugenides), **Supp. XXIV:** 134, **136–138,** 141, 142
Virgin Time: In Search of the Contemplative Life (Hampl), **Supp. XXII:** 82, 83–84, **90–92**
"Virgin Violeta" (Porter), **III:** 454
"Virility" (Ozick), **Supp. V:** 262, 265
Virtual Light (W. Gibson), **Supp. XVI:** 124, **129,** 130
Virtue of Selfishness, The: A New Concept of Egoism (Rand), **Supp. IV Part 2:** 527, 530–532
"Virtuoso" (Francis), **Supp. IX:** 82
Virtuous Girl, A (Bodenheim), **Supp. XXV:** 27
Virtuous Woman, A (Gibbons), **Supp. X: 44–45,** 46, 50
Visconti, Luchino, **Supp. V:** 51
Viscusi, Robert, **Supp. XX: 46**
Visible Saints: The History of a Puritan Idea (Morgan), **IV:** 149
"Vision, A" (Olds), **Supp. X:** 214
"Vision, A" (Winters), **Supp. II Part 2:** 785, 795
"Vision and Prayer" (D. Thomas), **I:** 432
"Visionary, The" (Poe), **III:** 411
Visionary Farms, The (Eberhart), **I:** 537–539
Visioning, The (Glaspell), **Supp. III Part 1:** 175–177, 180, 187, 188
Vision in Spring (Faulkner), **Retro. Supp. I:** 79
Vision of Columbus (Barlow), **Supp. I Part 1:** 124; **Supp. II Part 1:** 67, 68, 70–75, 77, 79
Vision of Sir Launfal, The (J. R. Lowell), **Supp. I Part 1:** 311; **Supp. I Part 2:** 406, 409, 410
"Vision of the World, A" (Cheever), **Supp. I Part 1:** 182, 192
"Visions and Voices" (Davison), **Supp. XXVI:** 71
"Visions of Budhardin"(Dybek), **Supp. XXIII:** 70–71
Visions of Cody (Kerouac), **Supp. III Part 1:** 225–227
Visions of Gerard (Kerouac), **Supp. III Part 1:** 219–222, 225, 227, 229
"Visions of the Daughters of Albion" (Blake), **III:** 540
"Visit" (Ammons), **Supp. VII:** 28–29
"Visit, The" (Kenyon), **Supp. VII:** 169
"Visitant, The" (Dunn), **Supp. XI:** 147
"Visitation, The/La Visitación" (Mora), **Supp. XIII:** 217, 224, 228
"Visitation"(Kenny), **Supp. XXIII:** 157
"Visit Home, A" (Stafford), **Supp. XI:** 318
Visit in 2001, The (musical, McNally), **Supp. XIII:** 207
"Visiting My Own House in Iowa City" (Stern), **Supp. IX:** 300
Visiting Villain, The (Wells), **Supp. XXVI:** 278, 280
"Visit of Charity, A" (Welty), **IV:** 262
"Visit of the Hawk" (Huddle), **Supp. XXVI:** 149
"Visitors" (J. W. Miller), **Supp. XX: 167**
"Visitors" (Salinas), **Supp. XIII:** 318
"Visitors, The/Los Visitantes" (Kingsolver), **Supp. VII:** 208
"Visits to St. Elizabeths" (Bishop), **Retro. Supp. II:** 47
Visit to a Small Planet: A Comedy Akin to Vaudeville (Vidal), **Supp. IV Part 2:** 682–683
"Visit to a Small Planet" (teleplay) (Vidal), **Supp. IV Part 2:** 682
"Visit to Avoyelles, A" (Chopin), **Supp. I Part 1:** 213
"Visit to Manafon, A" (W. V. Davis), **Supp. XXI:** 96
"Vissi d'Arte" (Moore), **Supp. X: 173–174**
Vistas of History (Morison), **Supp. I Part 2:** 492
"Vita" (Stafford), **Supp. XI:** 330
"Vita Brevis" (Hull), **Supp. XXI:** 138
Vital, David, **Supp. XVI:** 160
Vital Provisions (Price), **Supp. VI:** 262–263
"Vitamins" (Carver), **Supp. III Part 1:** 138
Vita Nova (Glück), **Supp. V:** 90–92
Vita Nuova, La (Dante), **Retro. Supp. III:** 65
Vitruvius, **Supp. XVI:** 292
Vittorio, the Vampire (Rice), **Supp. VII:** 295–296
Viudas (Dorfman), **Supp. IX:** 138
"Vivaldi"(Dybek), **Supp. XXIII:** 68
"Viva Vargas!" (Allen), **Supp. XV:** 15
Viva Villa! (screenplay, Hecht), **Supp. XXVII:** 93
Viviparous Quadrupeds of North America, The (Audubon and Bachman), **Supp. XVI:** 10
Vivisections (Siegel), **Supp. XXII:** 257
Vizenor, Gerald, **Supp. IV Part 1:** 260, 262, 329, 404; **Supp. IV Part 2:** 502
Vladimir Nabokov: The American Years (Nabokov), **Retro. Supp. I:** 275
Vlag, Piet, **Supp. XV:** 295
"Vlemk, the Box Painter" (Gardner), **Supp. VI:** 73
"V-Letter" (Shapiro), **Supp. II Part 2:** 707
V-Letter and Other Poems (Shapiro), **Supp. II Part 2:** 702, 706
"Vocabulary of Dearness" (Nye), **Supp. XIII:** 284
"Vocation" (Stafford), **Supp. XI:** 312, 321
Vocation and a Voice, A (Chopin), **Retro. Supp. II:** 67, 72
"Vocation and a Voice, A" (Chopin), **Retro. Supp. II:** 72; **Supp. I Part 1:** 200, 220, 224, 225
Vogel, David, **Supp. XV:** 88
Vogel, Speed, **Supp. IV Part 1:** 390
"Vogue Vista" (Peacock), **Supp. XIX:** 200
"Voice" (F. Wright), **Supp. XVII:** 245
"Voice" (Notley), **Supp. XXII:** 230
"Voice, The" (Dunn), **Supp. XI:** 152
Voice at the Back Door, The (Spencer), **Supp. XXVII:** 13
Voiced Connections of James Dickey, The (Dickey), **Supp. IV Part 1:** 177

"Voice from the Wilderness" (Ray), **Supp. XVIII:** 202
"Voice from the Woods, A" (Humphrey), **Supp. IX:** 101
"Voice from Under the Table, A" (Wilbur), **Supp. III Part 2:** 553, 554
Voice in the Mountain, A (Davison), **Supp. XXVI:** 65, 73–75, 77
"Voice of God, The" (Very), **Supp. XXV:** 243
Voice of Reason, The: Essays in Objectivist Thought (Rand), **Supp. IV Part 2:** 527, 528, 532
"Voice of Rock, The" (Ginsberg), **Supp. II Part 1:** 313
Voice of the Butterfly, The (Nichols), **Supp. XIII:** 270
Voice of the City, The (O. Henry), **Supp. II Part 1:** 410
"Voice of the Mountain, The" (Crane), **I:** 420
Voice of the Negro (Barber), **Supp. II Part 1:** 168
"Voice of the Past, The" (Skloot), **Supp. XX: 207**
Voice of the People, The (Glasgow), **II:** 175, 176
Voice of the Turtle: American Indian Literature 1900–1970 (Gunn Allen, ed.), **Supp. IV Part 1:** 332, 334
Voices from the Moon (Dubus), **Supp. VII:** 88–89
"Voices from the Other World" (Merrill), **Supp. III Part 1:** 331
Voices in the House (Sedges), **Supp. II Part 1:** 125
Voices of a Summer Day (Shaw), **Supp. XIX:** 251
Voices of the Night (Longfellow), **II:** 489, 493; **Retro. Supp. II:** 154, 157, 168
"Voices of Village Square, The" (Wolfe), **Supp. III Part 2:** 571–572
Voice That Is Great within Us, The (Caruth, ed.), **Supp. XIII:** 112
Void Moon (Connelly), **Supp. XXI: 73,** 74
Voigt, Ellen Bryan, **Supp. XIII:** 76
"Voir Dire" (Monson), **Supp. XXIV:** 237
Voix humaine, La (Cocteau), **Supp. XX: 236**
Volkening, Henry, **Retro. Supp. II:** 117; **Supp. XV:** 142
Vollmann, William T., **Supp. XIV:** 96; **Supp. XVII: 225–237; Supp. XX: 93**
Volney, Constantin François de Chasseboeuf, **Supp. I Part 1:** 146
Voltaire, **I:** 194; **II:** 86, 103, 449; **III:** 420; **IV:** 18; **Retro. Supp. II:** 94; **Retro. Supp. III:** 109; **Supp. I Part 1:** 288–289; **Supp. I Part 2:** 669, 717; **Supp. XV:** 258; **Supp. XX: 285**
Voltaire! Voltaire! (Endore), **Supp. XVII:** 65
Volunteer Poilu, A (Beston), **Supp. XXVI:** 32
Volunteers, The (Rowson and Reinagle), **Supp. XV:** 238
Volynsky, Akim (Chaim Flekser), **Supp. XXIII:** 11
Vonnegut, Kurt, **Retro. Supp. I:** 170; **Supp. II Part 2:** 557, 689, **753–784; Supp. IV Part 1:** 227, 392; **Supp. V:** 40, 42, 237, 244, 296; **Supp. X:** 260; **Supp. XI:** 104; **Supp. XII:** 139, 141; **Supp. XVIII:** 242, 252; **Supp. XXI:** 226; **Supp. XXIII:** 42, 101, 109
Vonnegut, Kurt, Jr., **Supp. XIX:** 223; **Supp. XVII:** 41, 135
"Voracities and Verities" (Moore), **III:** 214
Vore, Nellie, **I:** 199
Vorlicky, Robert, **Supp. IX:** 132, 135, 136, 141, 144, 147
Vorse, Mary Heaton, **Supp. XVII:** 99; **Supp. XX: 76; Supp. XXI:** 5, 6, 9, 13
Vortex, The (Coward), **Supp. XXIV:** 267
"Vorticism" (Pound), **Retro. Supp. I:** 288
Vosjoli, Philippe de, **Supp. XX: 253**
Voss, J. C., **Supp. XXV:** 217
Voss, Ralph E., **Supp. XXV:** 93
Voss, Richard, **I:** 199–200
"Vow, The" (Hecht), **Supp. X:** 64
"Vowels 2" (Baraka), **Supp. II Part 1:** 51
Vow of Conversation, A: Journal, 1964–1965 (Merton), **Supp. VIII:** 206
Vox (Baker), **Supp. XIII: 47–49,** 50, 52, 53
"Voyage" (MacLeish), **III:** 15
Voyage, The (Caputo), **Supp. XIX:** 25, 27–28
"Voyage, The" (Irving), **II:** 304
Voyage, The, and Other Versions of Poems by Baudelaire (R. Lowell), **Retro. Supp. II:** 187
Voyage dans la Haute Pennsylvanie et dans l'état de New-York (Crèvecoeur), **Supp. I Part 1:** 250–251
Voyage of the Beagle (Darwin), **Supp. IX:** 211
Voyage of the Dawn Treader (C. S. Lewis), **Supp. XXV:** 74
Voyage of the Destroyer from New York to Brazil, The (Slocum), **Supp. XXV:** 208, 212–213
Voyage of the Liberdade, The (Slocum), **Supp. XXV:** 208, 210–212
Voyage Out, The (Woolf), **Supp. XV:** 65
"Voyager, The" (Everwine), **Supp. XV:** 75
"Voyages" (H. Crane), **I:** 393–395; **Retro. Supp. II:** 78, 80, 81; **Retro. Supp. III:** 46, 49
"Voyages" (Levine), **Supp. V:** 190
Voyages and Discoveries of the Companions of Columbus (Irving), **II:** 310
Voyage to Pagany, A (W. C. Williams), **IV:** 404; **Retro. Supp. I:** 418–419, **420–421,** 423
Voyaging Portraits (Sobin), **Supp. XVI:** 282, 287
"Voyeur, The" (Gioia), **Supp. XV:** 125
"Voz de America" (column, W. Frank), **Supp. XX: 80**
Voznesensky, Andrei, **II:** 553; **Supp. III Part 1:** 268; **Supp. III Part 2:** 560
Vrbovska, Anca, **Supp. IV Part 2:** 639
V. S. Naipaul: An Introduction to His Work (Theroux), **Supp. VIII:** 314, 318
"V. S. Pritchett's Apprenticeship" (Maxwell), **Supp. VIII:** 172
Vukelich, James, **Supp. XXIII:** 228, 233
"Vulgarity in Literature" (Huxley), **III:** 429–430
"Vultures" (Oliver), **Supp. VII:** 235
"Vultures of Wahpeton" (Howard), **Supp. XXVII:** 126–127
"V. V." (Alcott), **Supp. I Part 1:** 37
W (Viva) (Cummings), **I:** 429, 433, 434, 436, 443, 444, 447
Wabash (R. O. Butler), **Supp. XII:** 61, **68–69**
Wade, Grace, **I:** 216
"Wading at Wellfleet" (Bishop), **Retro. Supp. II:** 42, 43; **Supp. I Part 1:** 80, 85, 86
Wadsworth, Charles, **I:** 454, 470; **Retro. Supp. I:** 32, 33
Wage, William, **Supp. XXVI:** 87
Wagenknecht, Edward, **II:** 508; **Supp. I Part 2:** 408, 584; **Supp. IV Part 2:** 681

"Wages of Poetry, The" (Wright), **Supp. XV:** 337
Wagner, Erica, **Supp. XXI:** 117
Wagner, Jean, **Supp. I Part 1:** 341, 346; **Supp. IV Part 1:** 165, 167, 171
Wagner, Karl, **Supp. XXVII:** 128
Wagner, Richard, **I:** 284, 395; **II:** 425; **III:** 396, 507; **Supp. IV Part 1:** 392
Wagner, Robert, **Supp. IX:** 250
"Wagnerians, The" (Auchincloss), **Supp. IV Part 1:** 23
"Wagner Matinée, A" (Cather), **I:** 315–316; **Retro. Supp. I:** 5, 8; **Retro. Supp. III:** 21, 25, 27–28
Wagoner, David, **Supp. IX: 323–340; Supp. XII:** 178; **Supp. XX: 200**
Wahlöö, Per, **Supp. XX: 87**
Waid, Candace, **Retro. Supp. I:** 360, 372, 373
Waif, The (Longfellow, ed.), **Retro. Supp. II:** 155
"Waif of the Plains, A" (Harte), **Supp. II Part 1:** 354
Wain, John, **Supp. XIV:** 166
"Wait" (Kinnell), **Supp. III Part 1:** 250
"Waiter in a California Vietnamese Restaurant" (Major), **Supp. XXII:** 182
"Waiting" (Dubus), **Supp. VII:** 87
Waiting (Jin), **Supp. XVIII:** 89, **96–97,** 99
"Waiting" (W. C. Williams), **Retro. Supp. I:** 418
"Waiting, The" (L.-Y. Lee), **Supp. XV:** 218
"Waiting, The" (Olds), **Supp. X:** 209
"Waiting between the Trees" (Tan), **Supp. X:** 290
"Waiting by the Gate" (Bryant), **Supp. I Part 1:** 171
Waiting for God (Weil), **I:** 298
Waiting for Godot (Beckett), **I:** 78, 91, 298; **Supp. IV Part 1:** 368–369; **Supp. XXIII:** 213
Waiting for Lefty (Odets), **Supp. I Part 1:** 277; **Supp. II Part 2:** 529, 530–533, 540; **Supp. V:** 109; **Supp. XIX:** 242
Waiting for Sweet Betty (Major), **Supp. XXII: 183**
Waiting for Teddy Williams (Mosher), **Supp. XXII:** 205, 206, 207, 208, 209, **215–216**
Waiting for the End of the World (Bell), **Supp. X: 4–5,** 11
"Waiting for the Ladies" (L. Brown), **Supp. XXI:** 44
Waiting for the Verdict (R. H. Davis), **Supp. XVI:** 85, 89, 90
"Waiting in a Rain Forest" (Wagoner), **Supp. IX:** 329
Waiting in the Wings (Loraga), **Supp. XXIII:** 195
Waiting Room, The (Kees), **Supp. XV:** 133, 148
Waiting to Exhale (McMillan), **Supp. XIII:** 184, 185, **189–190,** 191
"Waiting to Freeze" (Banks), **Supp. V:** 5, 6
Waiting to Freeze: Poems (Banks), **Supp. V:** 6, 8
Waits, Tom, **Supp. VIII:** 12
Wait until Spring, Bandini (Fante), **Supp. XI:** 160, 161, 164, 165, **166–167**
Wait until Spring, Bandini (film), **Supp. XI:** 173
"Wake, The" (Dove), **Supp. IV Part 1:** 250
"Wakefield" (Hawthorne), **Retro. Supp. I:** 154, 159; **Retro. Supp. III:** 118, 120
Wakefield, Dan, **Supp. VIII:** 43; **Supp. XIX:** 257, 258; **Supp. XVI:** 220
Wakefield, Richard, **Supp. IX:** 323
"Wake Island" (Rukeyser), **Supp. VI:** 273
"Wake"(Kenny), **Supp. XXIII:** 155
Wakeman, Frederic, **Supp. IX:** 247
Wake Up and Live! (Brande), **Supp. I Part 2:** 608
"Waking" (C. Frost), **Supp. XV:** 93
Waking (Rash), **Supp. XXVII:** 220, 221–222, 224
Waking, The (Roethke), **III:** 541
"Waking Early Sunday Morning" (R. Lowell), **II:** 552
"Waking Early Sunday Morning" (R. Lowell), **Retro. Supp. II:** 190
"Waking in the Blue" (R. Lowell), **II:** 547; **Retro. Supp. II:** 180
"Waking in the Dark" (Rich), **Supp. I Part 2:** 559
"Waking Up the Rake" (Hogan), **Supp. IV Part 1:** 415–416, 416
Wakoski, Diane, **Supp. V:** 79; **Supp. XII:** 184; **Supp. XV:** 252; **Supp. XVII:** 112; **Supp. XXIII:** 52; **Supp. XXIV:** 37
Walbridge, John, **Supp. XX: 125**
Walcott, Charles C., **II:** 49
Walcott, Derek, **Supp. VIII:** 28; **Supp. X:** 122, 131; **Supp. XV:** 256; **Supp. XXIV:** 86
Walcott, Jersey Joe, **Supp. V:** 182
Wald, Alan, **Supp. XV:** 202; **Supp. XVIII:** 223; **Supp. XXI:** 261, 262, 271, 275–276, 277, 278
Wald, Lillian, **Supp. I Part 1:** 12
Walden (Thoreau), **Supp. XIV:** 177, 227; **Supp. XV:** 275; **Supp. XVIII:** 14, 80, 189; **Supp. XXIV:** 73; **Supp. XXVI:** 34, 41, 43
Walden, Daniel, **Supp. IV Part 2:** 584, 591; **Supp. V:** 272
Walden; or, Life in the Woods (Thoreau), **I:** 219, 305; **II:** 8, 142, 159, 312–313, 458; **IV:** 168, 169, 170, 176, 177–178, 179–182, 183, 187; **Retro. Supp. I:** 62; **Supp. I Part 2:** 579, 655, 664, 672; **Supp. VIII:** 296; **Supp. X:** 27, 101; **Supp. XIII:** 152
Waldman, Anne, **Supp. XIV:** 150; **Supp. XXIII:** 221; **Supp. XXIV:** 33, 41, 45; **Supp. XXVII:** 22, 23, 26
Waldmeir, Joseph, **III:** 45
Waldmeir, Joseph J., **Supp. I Part 2:** 476
Waldo (Theroux), **Supp. VIII:** 313, 314, **314–315**
Waldo Frank: A Study (Munson), **Supp. XX: 74**
Waldron, Jeremy, **Supp. XVII:** 235
Waldron, Nan Turner, **Supp. XXVI:** 37
Waldrop, Keith, **Supp. XV:** 153, 165
Waley, Arthur, **II:** 526; **III:** 466; **Supp. V:** 340
"Walk, A" (Snyder), **Supp. VIII:** 297
Walkabout Year: Twelve Months in Australia (Pickering), **Supp. XXI:** 199, 200
"Walk at Sunset, A" (Bryant), **Supp. I Part 1:** 155
"Walk before Mass, A" (Agee), **I:** 28–29
Walker, Alice, **Retro. Supp. I:** 215; **Retro. Supp. III:** 136, 137, 184, 247; **Supp. I Part 2:** 550; **Supp. III Part 2:** 488, **517–540; Supp. IV Part 1:** 14; **Supp. IX:** 306, 311; **Supp. VIII:** 141, 214; **Supp. X:** 85, 228, 252, 325, 330; **Supp. XIII:** 179, 185, 291, 295; **Supp. XVI:** 39; **Supp. XVIII:** 200, 283; **Supp. XX: 84, 107, 108; Supp. XXI:** 172; **Supp. XXII:** 172
Walker, Cheryl, **Supp. XI:** 145; **Supp. XXVII:** 284, 296
Walker, David, **Supp. V:** 189; **Supp. XVII:** 246
Walker, Franklin D., **III:** 321
Walker, Gue, **Supp. XII:** 207
Walker, Margaret, **Supp. XVIII:** 282; **Supp. XX: 106**
Walker, Marianne, **Supp. VIII:** 139

Walker, Obadiah, **II:** 113
Walker, Scott, **Supp. XV:** 92
Walker in the City, A (Kazin), **Supp. VIII: 93–95,** 99
Walk Hard (Blum and Hill), **Supp. XV:** 194
Walk Hard-Talk Loud (Zinberg), **Supp. XV:** 194, 202
"Walking" (Hogan), **Supp. IV Part 1:** 416
"Walking" (Thoreau), **Supp. IV Part 1:** 416; **Supp. IX:** 178
"Walking Along in Winter" (Kenyon), **Supp. VII:** 167
"Walking around the Block with a Three-Year-Old" (Wagoner), **Supp. IX:** 331–332
"Walking at Noon Near the Burlington Depot in Lincoln, Nebraska" (Kooser), **Supp. XIX:** 122
"Walking Backwards into the Future" (R. Williams), **Supp. IX:** 146
Walking Down the Stairs: Selections from Interviews (Kinnell), **Supp. III Part 1:** 235, 249
"Walking Home" (Schnackenberg). See "Laughing with One Eye" (Schnackenberg)
"Walking Home at Night" (Ginsberg), **Supp. II Part 1:** 313
"Walking Is Almost Falling" (Peacock), **Supp. XIX:** 196, 197
Walking Light (Dunn), **Supp. XI:** 140, 141, 153
"Walking Man of Rodin, The" (Sandburg), **III:** 583
"Walking Sticks and Paperweights and Water Marks" (Moore), **III:** 215
Walking Tall (Dunn), **Supp. XI:** 140
Walking the Black Cat (Simic), **Supp. VIII:** 280, **282–284**
Walking the Boundaries (Davison), **Supp. XXVI:** 65, 72–73, 74
"Walking the Boundaries" (Davison), **Supp. XXVI:** 73
Walking to Gatlinburg (Mosher), **Supp. XXII:** 204, 205, 206, 207, 208, 209, 215, **216–217**
Walking to Martha's Vineyard (F. Wright), **Supp. XVII:** 240, 241, 245, 246
Walking to Sleep (Wilbur), **Supp. III Part 2:** 557–560
"Walking to Sleep" (Wilbur), **Supp. III Part 2:** 544, 557, 559, 561, 562
"Walking Wounded" (Shaw), **Supp. XIX:** 248
Walkin' the Dog (Mosley), **Supp. XIII:** 242
"Walk in the Moonlight, A" (Anderson), **I:** 114
Walk Me to the Distance (Everett), **Supp. XVIII: 55–56,** 57
Walk on the Wild Side, A (Algren), **Supp. IX:** 3, **12–13,** 14; **Supp. V:** 4
"Walks in Rome" (Merrill), **Supp. III Part 1:** 337
Walk to the River, A (Hoffman), **Supp. XVIII: 77–78**
Walk with Tom Jefferson, A (Levine), **Supp. V:** 179, 187, 190–191
Wall, Cheryl, **Supp. XXVI:** 165, 166
"Wall, The" (Bronk), **Supp. XXI:** 31
"Wall, The" (Brooks), **Supp. III Part 1:** 70, 71, 84
Wall, The (Hersey), **IV:** 4; **Supp. XX: 251**
Wall, The (Rinehart), **Supp. XXV:** 197–198, 200
"Wall, The" (Roethke), **III:** 544
"Wall, The" (Sexton), **Supp. II Part 2:** 696
Wallace, Daniel, **Supp. XXII:** 49
Wallace, David, **Supp. XXI:** 277
Wallace, David Foster, **Retro. Supp. II:** 279; **Supp. X: 301–318; Supp. XIX:** 223; **Supp. XVII:** 226; **Supp. XX: 91, 93; Supp. XXII:** 260, 261; **Supp. XXVII:** 6, 79
Wallace, Henry, **I:** 489; **III:** 111, 475; **Supp. I Part 1:** 286; **Supp. I Part 2:** 645
Wallace, Jim, **Supp. XX: 143**
Wallace, Mike, **Supp. IV Part 1:** 364; **Supp. IV Part 2:** 526; **Supp. XX: 102**
Wallace, Paul, **Supp. XXVI:** 90, 96–97
Wallace, Richard, **Supp. XVIII:** 101–102
Wallace Stevens (Kermode), **Retro. Supp. I:** 301
Wallace Stevens: The Poems of our Climate (Bloom), **Retro. Supp. I:** 299
Wallace Stevens: Words Chosen out of Desire (Stevens), **Retro. Supp. I:** 297
Wallach, Eli, **III:** 161
Wallant, Edward Lewis, **Supp. XVI:** 220
Wallas, Graham, **Supp. I Part 2:** 643
"Walled City" (Oates), **Supp. II Part 2:** 524
Wallenstein, Anna. See Weinstein, Mrs. Max (Anna Wallenstein)
Waller, Edmund, **III:** 463
Waller, Fats, **IV:** 263
Waller, Nicole, **Supp. XXII:** 78
"Wallet, The" (Rash), **Supp. XXVII:** 222
Walling, William English, **Supp. I Part 2:** 645; **Supp. XV:** 295
"Wall of Paintings, The" (Notley), **Supp. XXII:** 230
Wall of the Sky, the Wall of the Eye, The (Lethem), **Supp. XVIII:** 139
Walls Do Not Fall, The (Doolittle), **Supp. I Part 1:** 271, 272
Walls of Jericho, The (R. Fisher), **Supp. XIX:** 65, 67, 70, **72–77,** 78
"Wall Songs" (Hogan), **Supp. IV Part 1:** 413
Wall Writing (Auster), **Supp. XII:** 23–24
Walpole, Horace, **I:** 203; **Supp. I Part 2:** 410, 714
Walpole, Hugh, **Retro. Supp. I:** 231; **Supp. XX: 232**
Walpole, Robert, **IV:** 145
Walsh, David M., **Supp. XV:** 5
Walsh, Ed, **II:** 424
Walsh, Ernest, **Supp. XXIV:** 50
Walsh, George, **Supp. IV Part 2:** 528
Walsh, John Evangelist, **Retro. Supp. III:** 95, 98
Walsh, Keenan, **Supp. XXVI:** 152
Walsh, Raoul, **Supp. XIII:** 174
Walsh, Richard J., **Supp. II Part 1:** 119, 130
Walsh, William, **Supp. IV Part 1:** 242, 243, 246, 248, 252, 254, 257; **Supp. XXVI:** 4, 9
"Walt, the Wounded" (Di Piero), **Supp. XIX:** 37
"Walt and Will" (Apple), **Supp. XVII:** 6
Walter, Eugene, **Supp. XVI:** 230
Walter, Joyce, **Supp. XV:** 121
Walter, Natasha, **Supp. XXVII:** 275
Walter Benjamin at the Dairy Queen: Reflections at Sixty and Beyond (McMurtry), **Supp. V:** 232
Walters, Barbara, **Supp. XIV:** 125
Walters, Marguerite. See Smith, Mrs. Lamar (Marguerite Walters)
"Walter T. Carriman" (O'Hara), **III:** 368
Walton, Izaak, **Supp. I Part 2:** 422
"Walt Whitman" (Kooser), **Supp. XIX:** 118
"Walt Whitman" (Masters), **Supp. I Part 2:** 458
"Walt Whitman at Bear Mountain" (Simpson), **Supp. IX:** 265
Walt Whitman Bathing (Wagoner), **Supp. IX: 331–332**
Walt Whitman Handbook (Allen), **IV:** 352
Walt Whitman Reconsidered (Chase), **IV:** 352

"Waltz, The" (Parker), **Supp. IX:** 204
"Waltzer in the House, The" (Kunitz), **Supp. III Part 1:** 258
Waltzing Matilda (Notley), **Supp. XXII:** 229–230
"Waltzing Matilda" (Notley), **Supp. XXII:** 230
Waltzing the Magpies: A Year in Australia (Pickering), **Supp. XXI:** 199, 200
Walzer, Kevin, **Supp. XII:** 202; **Supp. XV:** 118; **Supp. XVIII:** 174
Wambaugh, Joseph, **Supp. X:** 5; **Supp. XXI:** 67
Wampeters, Foma, & Granfalloons (Vonnegut), **Supp. II Part 2:** 758, 759–760, 776, 779
Wand, David Hsin-fu, **Supp. X:** 292
"Wanderer, The" (W. C. Williams), **Retro. Supp. I:** 414, 421
Wanderer, The: His Parables and His Sayings (Gibran), **Supp. XX: 116, 123–124**
"Wanderers, The" (Welty), **IV:** 273–274
"Wandering Jew, The" (Robinson), **III:** 505, 516–517
Wanderings of Oisin (Yeats), **Supp. I Part 1:** 79
Wang, Dorothy, **Supp. X:** 289
Wang Wei, **Supp. XV:** 47
Waniek, Marilyn Nelson, **Supp. IV Part 1:** 244. See also Nelson, Marilyn
Wanking 'Tards (Silver), **Supp. XXIV:** 265
"Wan Lee, the Pagan" (Harte), **Supp. II Part 1:** 351
"Want, The" (Olds), **Supp. X:** 210
Want Bone, The (Pinsky), **Supp. VI:** 236–237, 244–245, 247
"Wanted: An Ontological Critic" (Ransom), **III:** 498
"Wanting to Die" (Sexton), **Supp. II Part 2:** 684, 686; **Supp. XIV:** 132
"Wants" (Paley), **Supp. VI:** 219
Waples, Dorothy, **I:** 348
Wapshot Chronicle, The (Cheever), **Supp. I Part 1:** 174, 177–180, 181, 196
Wapshot Scandal, The (Cheever), **Supp. I Part 1:** 180–184, 187, 191, 196
"War" (Findley), **Supp. XX: 49**
"War" (H. Johnson), **Supp. XXVI:** 173
"War" (Jin), **Supp. XVIII:** 93
"War" (Kingston), **Supp. V:** 169
"War" (Simic), **Supp. VIII:** 282
"War, Response, and Contradiction" (Burke), **I:** 283
"War and Peace" (Sanders), **Supp. XVI:** 277
War and Peace (Tolstoy), **I:** 6, 7; **II:** 191, 205, 291; **IV:** 446; **Supp. V:** 277; **Supp. XI:** 68; **Supp. XIV:** 97; **Supp. XXIII:** 11
War and Remembrance (miniseries), **Supp. XXV:** 265
War and Remembrance (Wouk), **Supp. XX: 243; Supp. XXV:** 253, 254, 257, 258, 264–265
"War and the Small Nations" (Gibran), **Supp. XX: 127**
War and War (F. Barthelme), **Supp. XI:** 25
"War Between Men and Women, The" (Thurber), **Supp. I Part 2:** 615
War Bulletins (Lindsay), **Supp. I Part 2:** 378–379
Ward, Aileen, **II:** 531
Ward, Artemus (pseudonym). See Browne, Charles Farrar
Ward, Cynthia, **Retro. Supp. III:** 138
Ward, Douglas Turner, **Supp. IV Part 1:** 362
Ward, Geoff, **Supp. XXIII:** 218
Ward, Henry, **Supp. I Part 2:** 588
Ward, Mrs. Humphry, **II:** 338
Ward, Leo R., **Supp. VIII:** 124
Ward, Lester F., **Supp. I Part 2:** 640; **Supp. XI:** 202, 203
Ward, Lynn, **I:** 31
Ward, Nathaniel, **Retro. Supp. III:** 4; **Supp. I Part 1:** 99, 102, 111, 116
Ward, Susan, **Supp. XXIII:** 146
Ward, Theodora, **I:** 470; **Retro. Supp. I:** 28
Ward, William Hayes, **Supp. I Part 1:** 371
"War Debt, A" (Jewett), **Retro. Supp. II:** 138, 141
"War Diary" (Boyce), **Supp. XVII:** 104; **Supp. XXI:** 6
"War Diary, A" (Bourne), **I:** 229
War Dispatches of Stephen Crane, The (Crane), **I:** 422
"Ward Line, The" (Morris), **III:** 220
Ware, Amy, **Supp. XXVI:** 113
Warfel, Harry R., **Supp. I Part 1:** 366
War Games (Morris), **III:** 238
War Goes On, The (Asch), **Supp. XXIII:** 6
"Warhol / Blue Jackie"(Balakian), **Supp. XXIII:** 32
War in Heaven, The (Shepard and Chaikin), **Supp. III Part 2:** 433
War Is Kind (S. Crane), **I:** 409; **III:** 585
"War Is Kind" (S. Crane), **I:** 419; **Supp. XXVI:** 173
Warlock (Harrison), **Supp. VIII:** 45, **46**
Warm as Wool (Sanders), **Supp. XVI:** 269
"Warming" (Trethewey), **Supp. XXI:** 245
Warner, Anna, **Supp. XVIII:** 258–275
Warner, Charles Dudley, **II:** 405; **IV:** 198; **Retro. Supp. III:** 262
Warner, Jack, **Supp. XII:** 160–161; **Supp. XVIII:** 249; **Supp. XXVII:** 92
Warner, John R., **III:** 193
Warner, Oliver, **I:** 548
Warner, Susan, **Retro. Supp. I:** 246; **Supp. XV:** 275; **Supp. XVIII: 257–275**
Warner, Sylvia Townsend, **Supp. VIII:** 151, 155, 164, 171
Warner, W. Lloyd, **III:** 60
Warner Family and the Warner Books, The (Baker), **Supp. XVIII:** 259, 267
"Warning" (Hughes), **Supp. I Part 1:** 343
"Warning" (Pound), **III:** 474
"Warning, A" (Howard), **Supp. XXVII:** 118
"Warning, The" (Creeley), **Supp. IV Part 1:** 150
"Warning, The" (Longfellow), **II:** 498
Warning Hill (Marquand), **III:** 55–56, 60, 68
"War of Eyes, A" (Coleman), **Supp. XI:** 93–94
War of Eyes and Other Stories, A (Coleman), **Supp. XI: 91–92**
War of the Classes (London), **II:** 466
"War of the Wall, The" (Bambara), **Supp. XI:** 15–16
"War of Vaslav Nijinsky, The" (Bidart), **Supp. XV:** 21–22, **27–29**
Warp (Grossman), **Supp. XXV:** 64, 65–66
"War Poems" (Sandburg), **III:** 581
Warren, Austin, **I:** 265, 268, 271; **Supp. I Part 2:** 423
Warren, David, **Supp. XXIV:** 269
Warren, Earl, **III:** 581
Warren, Gabriel, **IV:** 244
Warren, Mercy Otis, **Supp. XV:** 230
Warren, Patricia Nell, **Supp. XX: 259–276**
Warren, Robert Penn, **I:** 190, 211, 517; **II:** 57, 217, 228, 253; **III:** 134, 310, 382–383, 454, 482, 485, 490, 496, 497; **IV:** 121, 122, 123, 125, 126, **236–259,** 261, 262, 279, 340–341, 458; **Retro. Supp. I:** 40, 41, 73, 90; **Retro. Supp. II:** 220, 235; **Supp. I Part 1:** 359, 371; **Supp. I Part 2:**

386, 423; **Supp. II Part 1:** 139; **Supp. III Part 2:** 542; **Supp. IX:** 257; **Supp. V:** 261, 316, 318, 319, 333; **Supp. VIII:** 126, 176; **Supp. X:** 1, 25, 26; **Supp. XI:** 315; **Supp. XII:** 254, 255; **Supp. XIV:** 1, 2, 3, 4, 11, 14, 15; **Supp. XIX:** 246; **Supp. XVIII:** 77, 78–79; **Supp. XXI:** 256; **Supp. XXVI:** 63, 67, 78
Warren, Mrs. Robert Penn (Eleanor Clark), **IV:** 244
Warren, Rosanna, **IV:** 244; **Supp. XIX:** 34; **Supp. XV:** 251, 261, 262, 263
Warren, Vincent, **Supp. XXIII:** 218, 219
Warrington Poems, The (Ríos), **Supp. IV Part 2:** 540
Warrior, Robert Allen, **Supp. IV Part 1:** 329
"Warrior, The" (Gunn Allen), **Supp. IV Part 1:** 326
"Warrior: 5th Grade" (Olds), **Supp. X:** 214
"Warrior Road" (Harjo), **Supp. XII:** 217
"Warrior's Daughter, A" (Zitkala-Ša), **Supp. XXV:** 274, 275, 282
Wars, The (Findley), **Supp. XX: 53–54**
Warsh, Lewis, **Supp. XXIV:** 41
Warshavsky, Isaac (pseudonym). See Singer, Isaac Bashevis
Warshow, Robert, **Supp. I Part 1:** 51
Wars I Have Seen (Stein), **IV:** 27, 36, 477
Wartime (Fussell), **Supp. V:** 241
War Trash (Jin), **Supp. XVIII:** 89, **100–101**
"War Widow, The" (Frederic), **II:** 135–136
"Was" (Creeley), **Supp. IV Part 1:** 155
"Was" (Faulkner), **II:** 71
"Wash" (Faulkner), **II:** 72; **Retro. Supp. III:** 84
Wash, Richard, **Supp. XII:** 14
"Washboard Wizard" (Nelson), **Supp. XVIII:** 182
Washburn, Keith, **Supp. XXVI:** 148–149
"Washed in the Rain" (Fante), **Supp. XI:** 165
"Washing of Hands, A" (Kooser), **Supp. XIX:** 115
Washington, Booker T., **Supp. I Part 2:** 393; **Supp. II Part 1:** 157, 160, 167, 168, 171, 225; **Supp. XIV:** 198, 199, 201; **Supp. XVIII:** 121–122
Washington, D.C. (Vidal), **Supp. IV Part 2:** 677, 684, 686–687, 690
"Washington, D.C. Journal" (Brainard), **Supp. XXVII:** 27
Washington, George, **I:** 453; **II:** 313–314; **Supp. I Part 2:** 399, 485, 508, 509, 511, 513, 517, 518, 520, 599
Washington, Mary Helen, **Supp. XVIII:** 119, 284
Washington, Teresa, **Retro. Supp. III:** 130
Washington and His Generals (Lippard), **Supp. XXIII:** 178, **185–186,** 187
Washington Crossing the Delaware (Rivers), **Supp. XV:** 186
Washington Post Book World (Lesser), **Supp. IV Part 2:** 453; **Supp. VIII:** 80, 84, 241; **Supp. X:** 282
Washington Square (James), **II:** 327, 328; **Retro. Supp. I:** 215, 220, **222–223**
"Washington Square, 1946" (Ozick), **Supp. V:** 272
Washington Square Ensemble, The (Bell), **Supp. X:** 1, **3–4**
"Washman"(P. Benedict), **Supp. XXIII:** 40
"Was Lowell an Historical Critic?" (Altick), **Supp. I Part 2:** 423
Wasserman, Earl R., **Supp. I Part 2:** 439, 440
Wasserman, Jakob, **Supp. I Part 2:** 669
Wasserstein, Wendy, **Retro. Supp. III:** 318; **Supp. IV Part 1:** 309; **Supp. XV: 319–336; Supp. XXIV:** 116, 117, 119, 128
Wasson, Ben, **Retro. Supp. I:** 79, 83
"Waste Carpet, The" (Matthews), **Supp. IX: 158–159**
Waste Land, The (T. S. Eliot), **I:** 107, 266, 298, 395, 396, 482, 570–571, 572, 574–575, 577–578, 580, 581, 584, 585, 586, 587; **III:** 6–8, 12, 196, 277–278, 453, 471, 492, 586; **IV:** 122, 123, 124, 140, 418, 419, 420; **Retro. Supp. I:** 51, 60, **60–62,** 63, 64, 66, 210, 290, 291, 299, 311, 420, 427; **Retro. Supp. II:** 85, 121, 190; **Retro. Supp. III:** 47, 50–51, 58, 59, 62–65, 66, 67, 101; **Supp. I Part 1:** 272; **Supp. I Part 2:** 439, 455, 614; **Supp. II Part 1:** 4, 5, 11, 96; **Supp. III Part 1:** 9, 10, 41, 63, 105; **Supp. IV Part 1:** 47, 284; **Supp. IX:** 158, 305; **Supp. V:** 338; **Supp. X:** 125; **Supp. XIII:** 341–342, 344, 346; **Supp. XIV:** 6, 284; **Supp. XIX:** 288; **Supp. XV:** 21, 181, 261, 306; **Supp. XVI:** 204; **Supp. XVII:** 140–141, 144, 227; **Supp. XVIII:** 78, 79–80; **Supp. XXIII:** 23, 25, 79, 165; **Supp. XXIV:** 140; **Supp. XXVII:** 287
"Waste Land, The": A Facsimile and Transcript of the Original Drafts Including the Annotations of Ezra Pound (Eliot, ed.), **Retro. Supp. I:** 58
Waste Land and Other Poems, The (T. S. Eliot), **Supp. XV:** 305
Wat, Alexander, **Supp. XVI:** 155, 161
Watch, The (Bass), **Supp. XVI: 16–17**
"Watch, The, —" (Bass), **Supp. XVI:** 17
Watch and Ward (James), **II:** 323; **Retro. Supp. I:** 218, **219,** 220
"Watcher" (Trethewey), **Supp. XXI:** 247
"Watcher, The" (R. Bly), **Supp. IV Part 1:** 71
"Watcher by the Dead, A" (Bierce), **I:** 203
Watchfires (Auchincloss), **Supp. IV Part 1:** 23
"Watching Crow, Looking toward the Manzano Mountains" (Harjo), **Supp. XII:** 219
"Watching the Oregon Whale" (A. Finch), **Supp. XVII:** 77
"Watching the Sunset" (Coleman), **Supp. XI:** 92
"Watching the Vulture at the Road Kill" (Stallings), **Supp. XXV:** 230
Watch on the Rhine (Hellman), **Supp. I Part 1:** 276, 278, 279–281, 283–284; **Supp. IV Part 1:** 83
"Watch Out for Landmines" (Biss), **Supp. XXVI:** 47, 51, 56
"Water" (Emerson), **II:** 19
"Water" (Komunyakaa), **Supp. XIII:** 132
"Water" (R. Lowell), **II:** 550
"Waterbird" (Swenson), **Supp. IV Part 2:** 651
"Water Borders" (Dillard), **Supp. VI:** 27
"Water Buffalo" (Komunyakaa), **Supp. XIII:** 122
"Watercolor of Grantchester Meadows" (Plath), **Supp. I Part 2:** 537
Water Cure, The (Everett), **Supp. XVIII: 64–66**
"Water Drum"(Kenny), **Supp. XXIII:** 144
"Waterfall, The" (Clampitt), **Supp. IX:** 44
Waterfront (Schulberg), **Supp. XVIII: 251–252**
"Water Hose Is on Fire, The" (Simic), **Supp. XV:** 185
Waterhouse, Keith, **Supp. VIII:** 124

"Waterlily Fire" (Rukeyser), **Supp. VI:** 285, 286
Waterlily Fire: Poems 1935–1962 (Rukeyser), **Supp. VI:** 274, 283, 285
Watermark (Brodsky), **Supp. VIII:** 29
Water-Method Man, The (Irving), **Supp. VI:** 163, **167–179,** 180
Water Music (Boyle), **Supp. VIII:** 1, 3–5, 8, 14; **Supp. XX: 20–22**
"Water Music for the Progress of Love in a Life-Raft Down the Sammamish Slough" (Wagoner), **Supp. IX:** 326
"Water People" (Burke), **Supp. XIV:** 21
"Water Picture" (Swenson), **Supp. IV Part 2:** 641
"Water Quilt" (Rash), **Supp. XXVII:** 222
"Water Rising" (Hogan), **Supp. IV Part 1:** 400
Waters, Ethel, **II:** 587
Waters, Frank, **Supp. X:** 124
Waters, Muddy, **Supp. VIII:** 345
Watershed (Everett), **Supp. XVIII: 58–59,** 64
"Watershed" (Kingsolver), **Supp. VII:** 208
"Watershed" (Warren), **IV:** 239
"Watershed, The" (Auden), **Supp. II Part 1:** 5
Waters of Kronos, The (Richter), **Supp. XVIII:** 207, 208, **218–219,** 220
Waters of Siloe, The (Merton), **Supp. VIII:** 196, 208
Waterston, Sam, **Supp. IX:** 253
Water Street (Merrill), **Supp. III Part 1:** 321–323
"Water Walker" (Wilbur), **Supp. III Part 2:** 548, 560
Water-Witch, The (Cooper), **I:** 342–343
"Water Witch"(P. Benedict), **Supp. XXIII:** 38
Waterworks, The (Doctorow), **Supp. IV Part 1:** 218, 222, 223, 231–233, 234
"Water Works, The" (Doctorow), **Supp. IV Part 1:** 234
Watkin, E. I., **Retro. Supp. II:** 187
Watkins, Floyd C., **IV:** 452
Watkins, James T., **I:** 193, 194
Watkins, Maureen, **Supp. XVI:** 188
Watkins, Mel, **Supp. X:** 330; **Supp. XIII:** 246
Watman, Max, **Supp. XX: 92**
Watrous, Peter, **Supp. VIII:** 79
Watson, Brook, **Supp. XX: 284**
Watson, Burton, **Supp. XV:** 47
Watson, James Sibley, Jr., **I:** 261
Watson, Jay, **Supp. XVIII:** 195; **Supp. XXI:** 46
Watson, J. B., **II:** 361
Watson, Julia, **Supp. XXV:** 8
Watson, Richard, **Supp. I Part 2:** 516, 517
Watson, William, **II:** 114
Watsonville: Some Place Not Here (Moraga), **Supp. XXIII:** 195, 196, 202, 203
Watt, Ian, **Supp. VIII:** 4
Watteau, Jean Antoine, **III:** 275; **IV:** 79
Watts, Emily Stipes, **Supp. I Part 1:** 115
Waugh, Arthur, **Supp. XXIV:** 30
Waugh, Evelyn, **I:** 480; **III:** 281; **Supp. I Part 2:** 607; **Supp. IV Part 2:** 688; **Supp. XI:** 305, 306; **Supp. XIX:** 131; **Supp. XXV:** 70
Waugh, Robert H., **Supp. XXV:** 123
"Wave" (Snyder), **Supp. VIII:** 299
Wave, A (Ashbery), **Supp. III Part 1:** 1, 4, 24–26
"Wave, A" (Ashbery), **Supp. III Part 1:** 9, 19, 24–25
"Wave, The" (MacLeish), **III:** 19
"Wave, The" (Untermeyer), **Supp. XV:** 300
Wave Amplitude in the Mona Passage (Schott), **Supp. XXIII: 242–243**
"Wavemaker Falters, The" (Saunders), **Supp. XIX:** 225
"Waxwings" (Francis), **Supp. IX:** 82
Way, The (Steiner and Witt, eds.), **Supp. IV Part 2:** 505
"Way Down, The" (Kunitz), **Supp. III Part 1:** 263
"Way It Is, The" (Ellison), **Supp. II Part 1:** 245
"Way It Is, The" (Jones), **Supp. XI:** 229
Way It Is, The (Stafford), **Supp. XIII:** 274
"Way It Is, The" (Strand), **Supp. IV Part 2:** 627
"Wayland" (Sanders), **Supp. XVI:** 275
Wayne, John, **Supp. IV Part 1:** 200
Way of Chuang-Tzu, The (Merton), **Supp. VIII:** 208
"Way of Exchange in James Dickey's Poetry, The" (Weatherby), **Supp. IV Part 1:** 175
Way of Life According to Laotzu, The (Bynner), **Supp. XV:** 46, 48
Way Out, A (Frost), **Retro. Supp. I:** 133; **Retro. Supp. III:** 100
Wayside Motor Inn, The (Gurney), **Supp. V:** 96, 105, 109
"Ways of Breaking: Lynda Hull's 'Ornithology' " (Jauss), **Supp. XXI:** 139
"Ways of Talking" (Jin), **Supp. XVIII:** 93
Ways of the Hour, The (Cooper), **I:** 354
Ways of White Folks, The (Hughes), **Retro. Supp. I:** 203, 204; **Supp. I Part 1:** 329, 330, 332
Way Some People Die, The (Macdonald), **Supp. IV Part 2:** 470, 471, 472, 474
Way Some People Live, The (Cheever), **Supp. I Part 1:** 175
"Way the Cards Fall, The" (Komunyakaa), **Supp. XIII:** 117
"Way the Luck Runs, The" (Wolfert), **Supp. XXI:** 265
"Way Things Are, The" (Turow, unpub.), **Supp. XVII:** 215, 218
Way to Rainy Mountain, The (Momaday), **Supp. IV Part 2:** 485–486, 487–489, 491, 493
Way to Wealth, The (Franklin), **II:** 101–102, 110; **Supp. XX: 27**
Wayward and the Seeking, The: A Collection of Writings by Jean Toomer (Toomer), **Supp. III Part 2:** 478–481, 484, 487
Wayward Bus, The (Steinbeck), **IV:** 51, 64–65
"Way We Live Now, The" (Sontag), **Supp. III Part 2:** 467–468
"Way You'll Never Be, A" (Hemingway), **II:** 249
"W. D. Sees Himself Animated" (Snodgrass), **Supp. VI:** 327
"W. D. Sits in Kafka's Chair and Is Interrogated Concerning the Assumed Death of Cock Robin" (Snodgrass), **Supp. VI:** 319
"W. D. Tries to Warn Cock Robin" (Snodgrass), **Supp. VI:** 319
"We" (Alexander), **Supp. XVIII:** 185
Weaks, Mary Louise, **Supp. X:** 5
Weales, Gerald, **II:** 602
"Wealth," from Conduct of Life, The (Emerson), **II:** 2, 3–4
"Wealth," from English Traits (Emerson), **II:** 6
Wealth of Nations, The (A. Smith), **II:** 109
"We Are Looking at You, Agnes" (Caldwell), **I:** 309
We Are Not Afraid (Hickam), **Supp. XXVII:** 99, 100
We Are Not in This Together (Kittredge), **Supp. XXVI:** 182, 183, 184
We Are Still Married: Stories and Letters (Keillor), **Supp. XVI:** 176, 177

"We Are the Crazy Lady and Other Feisty Feminist Fables" (Ozick), **Supp. V:** 259
Weary Blues, The (Hughes), **Retro. Supp. I:** 195, 197, 198, 199, 200, 203, 205; **Supp. I Part 1:** 325
"Weary Blues, The" (Hughes), **Retro. Supp. I:** 198, 199; **Supp. I Part 1:** 324, 325
"Weary Kingdom" (Irving), **Supp. VI:** 163
Weasels and Wisemen: Ethics and Ethnicity in the Work of David Mamet (Kane), **Supp. XIV:** 250
Weather and the Women Treat Me Fair, The (Everett), **Supp. XVIII:** 66
Weatherby, H. L., **Supp. IV Part 1:** 175
Weather Central (Kooser), **Supp. XIX:** 116, **123–125**
"Weathering Out" (Dove), **Supp. IV Part 1:** 248
"Weather Report" (Huddle), **Supp. XXVI:** 152
Weathers. Glenda, **Retro. Supp. III:** 139–140
"Weather Within, The" (M. F. K. Fisher), **Supp. XVII:** 88, 91
Weaver, Harriet, **III:** 471
Weaver, James, **Supp. XVIII:** 72
Weaver, Michael, **Supp. XVIII:** 176, 177
Weaver, Mike, **Retro. Supp. I:** 430
Weaver, Raymond, **Retro. Supp. III:** 162
Weaver, Robert, **Supp. XXVII:** 181
Weaver, Will, **Supp. XVI:** 39
"Weaving" (Larcom), **Supp. XIII:** 142, **Supp. XIII:** 144–145, 150, 151
"Web" (Oliver), **Supp. VII:** 236
Web and the Rock, The (Wolfe), **IV:** 451, 455, 457, 459–460, 462, 464, 467, 468
Webb, Beatrice, **Supp. I Part 1:** 5
Webb, Mary, **I:** 226
Webb, Phyllis, **Supp. XX: 56**
Webb, Sidney, **Supp. I Part 1:** 5
Webb, W. P., **Supp. V:** 225
Webber, A. R. F., **Supp. XXI:** 160
Weber, Brom, **I:** 383, 386
Weber, Carl, **Supp. IX:** 133, 138, 141
Weber, Max, **I:** 498; **Supp. I Part 2:** 637, 648
Weber, Sarah, **Supp. I Part 1:** 2
Weberman, A. J., **Supp. XVIII:** 27
Web of Earth, The (Wolfe), **IV:** 451–452, 456, 458, 464, 465
Web of Iniquity, The (Nickerson), **Supp. XXV:** 200
"Web of Life, The" (Nemerov), **III:** 282
Webster, Brenda, **Supp. XVI:** 157, 161
Webster, Daniel, **II:** 5, 9; **Supp. I Part 2:** 659, 687, 689, 690
Webster, John, **I:** 384; **Supp. I Part 2:** 422
Webster, Noah, **Supp. I Part 2:** 660; **Supp. II Part 1:** 77
Wector, Dixon, **II:** 103
Wedding, The (D. West), **Supp. XVIII:** 277, **287–289; Supp. XXVI:** 174
"Wedding, The" (Everwine), **Supp. XV:** 83
"Wedding, The" (Major), **Supp. XXII:** 185
Wedding, The (television miniseries), **Supp. XVIII:** 277, 289
"Wedding Cake" (Nye), **Supp. XIII:** 283
"Wedding Dance, The" (Di Piero), **Supp. XIX:** 47
"Wedding Day" (Boyle), **Supp. XXIV:** 56–57
Wedding Day and Other Stories (Boyle), **Supp. XXIV: 56–57**
"Wedding in Brownsville, A" (Singer), **IV:** 15
Wedding in Hell, A (Simic), **Supp. VIII:** 280, **282**
"Wedding of Henry Markowitz, The" (Goodman), **Supp. XXVI:** 121–122
"Wedding of the Rose and Lotus, The" (Lindsay), **Supp. I Part 2:** 387
"Wedding Supper, The" (Rowson), **Supp. XV:** 243
"Wedding Toast, A" (Wilbur), **Supp. III Part 2:** 561
Wedekind, Frank, **III:** 398; **Supp. XX: 85; Supp. XXII:** 23
Wedge, The (W. C. Williams), **Retro. Supp. I:** 424
"We Didn't"(Dybek), **Supp. XXIII:** 77–78
"Wednesday at the Waldorf" (Swenson), **Supp. IV Part 2:** 647
We Don't Live Here Anymore (Dubus), **Supp. XXIV:** 97
"We Don't Live Here Anymore" (Dubus), **Supp. VII:** 78–79, 85
"Weed" (McCarriston), **Supp. XIV:** 259, 273
"Weed, The" (Bishop), **Supp. I Part 1:** 80, 88–89
"Weed, The" (Taggard), **Supp. XXII:** 284
"Weeds, The" (McCarthy), **II:** 566
"Weekend" (Beattie), **Supp. V:** 27
"Weekend" (Hempel), **Supp. XXI:** 124
Weekend, The (Cameron), **Supp. XII:** 80, 81, **86–88**
"Weekend at Ellerslie, A" (Wilson), **IV:** 431
Weekend Edition (National Public Radio), **Supp. IX:** 299; **Supp. XVII:** 240, 242
Weekend in Dinlock (Sigal), **Supp. XXIII:** 166
"Week in the Word, A" (Hampl), **Supp. XXII:** 85
Week on the Concord and Merrimack Rivers, A (Thoreau), **IV:** 168, 169, 177, 182–183; **Supp. I Part 2:** 420; **Supp. XIV:** 227
Weeks, Edward, **III:** 64
Weeks, Jerome, **Supp. VIII:** 76
"Weeping Burgher" (Stevens), **IV:** 77
"Weeping Women" (Levertov), **Supp. III Part 1:** 282
We Fished All Night (W. Motley), **Supp. XVII: 155–158,** 159, **160**
We Fly Away (Francis), **Supp. IX: 79–80,** 84
" ' We Had Some Good Times Anyway' " (Gansworth), **Supp. XXVI:** 114
We Happy Few (Hinojosa), **Supp. XIX:** 99, **111–112**
We Have Always Lived in the Castle (Jackson), **Supp. IX:** 121, 126, **127–128**
"We Have Our Arts So We Won't Die of Truth" (Bradbury), **Supp. IV Part 1:** 105
We Have Tomorrow (Bontemps), **Supp. XXII:** 6, 12
Weich, Dave, **Supp. XII:** 321; **Supp. XVIII:** 91
Weidman, Jerome, **Supp. XXVII:** 142
"Weighing In" (Espaillat), **Supp. XXI:** 111
"Weight" (Wideman), **Supp. X:** 321
"Weights" (C. Baxter), **Supp. XVII:** 16
Weigl, Bruce, **Supp. VIII:** 269, 274; **Supp. XIX: 273–290; Supp. XV:** 342
Weik, Alexa, **Supp. XXIV:** 64
Weil, Dorothy, **Supp. XV:** 231
Weil, James L., **Supp. XXI:** 23, 31
Weil, Robert, **Supp. IX:** 236
Weil, Simone, **I:** 298; **Supp. XV:** 259; **Supp. XXII:** 93; **Supp. XXVI:** 234
Weiland (C. B. Brown), **Supp. XIII:** 100
Weinauer, Ellen, **Supp. XV:** 270, 284
Weinberger, Eliot, **Supp. IV Part 1:** 66; **Supp. VIII:** 290, 292; **Supp. XVI:** 284
Weinberger, Eric, **Supp. XXII:** 264

Weinfield, Henry, **Supp. XXI:** 24, 28, 33
Weininger, Otto, **Retro. Supp. I:** 416
Weinraub, Judith, **Supp. XXI:** 39
Weinreb, Mindy, **Supp. X:** 24
Weinreich, Regina, **Supp. XIV:** 22
Weinstein, Cindy, **Supp. XVIII:** 261
Weinstein, Hinda, **IV:** 285
Weinstein, Max, **IV:** 285
Weinstein, Mrs. Max (Anna Wallenstein), **IV:** 285, 287
Weinstein, Nathan. See West, Nathanael
Weinstein, Selma, **Supp. XXI:** 170
Weir, Sybil, **Supp. XXIV:** 20
Weisheit, Rabbi, **IV:** 76
Weismuller, Johnny, **Supp. X:** 264; **Supp. XX: 18**
Weiss, David, **Supp. XVI:** 55
Weiss, Jane, **Supp. XVIII:** 267, 269
Weiss, Peter, **IV:** 117
Weiss, Theodore, **Supp. IV Part 2:** 440; **Supp. IX:** 96
Weissberg, Liliane, **Retro. Supp. III:** 237
Weissleder, Paul, **Supp. XXII:** 283
Weist, Dianne, **Supp. X:** 80
Weithas, Art, **Supp. XI:** 231
Welch, Dave, **Supp. XXI:** 118
Welch, Don, **Supp. XIX:** 119
Welch, James, **Supp. IV Part 1:** 404; **Supp. IV Part 2:** 503, 513, 557, 562; **Supp. XXIV:** 257; **Supp. XXVI:** 186, 188
Welch, Lew, **Supp. V:** 170; **Supp. VIII:** 303; **Supp. XXII:** 276
"Welcome from War" (Rukeyser), **Supp. VI:** 286
"Welcome Morning" (Sexton), **Supp. II Part 2:** 696
"Welcome the Wrath" (Kunitz), **Supp. III Part 1:** 261
Welcome to Hard Times (Doctorow), **Supp. IV Part 1:** 218, 219–220, 222, 224, 230, 238
Welcome to Hard Times (film), **Supp. IV Part 1:** 236
"Welcome to New Dork" (Leonard), **Supp. XVIII:** 148
Welcome to Our City (Wolfe), **IV:** 461
Welcome to the Castle (Hayes), **Supp. XXVI:** 144
Welcome to the Monkey House (Vonnegut), **Supp. II Part 2:** 758
Welcome to the Moon (Shanley), **Supp. XIV:** 318
Welcome to the Moon and Other Plays (Shanley), **Supp. XIV:** 315, **316–319**
Weld, Theodore, **Supp. I Part 2:** 587, 588
Weld, Tuesday, **Supp. XI:** 306
Welded (O'Neill), **III:** 390; **Supp. XXII:** 24
"Welfare Worker, Disenchanted, Contemplates Friday Afternoon, The" (Trethewey), **Supp. XXI:** 246
"Well, The" (Momaday), **Supp. IV Part 2:** 483
"Well Dressed Man with a Beard, The" (Stevens), **Retro. Supp. I:** 297
Wellek, René, **I:** 253, 261, 282; **II:** 320; **Supp. XIV:** 12, 14
Weller, George, **III:** 322
Welles, Gideon, **Supp. I Part 2:** 484
Welles, Orson, **IV:** 476; **Supp. I Part 1:** 67; **Supp. IV Part 1:** 82, 83; **Supp. V:** 251; **Supp. VIII:** 46; **Supp. XI:** 169, 307
"Wellfleet Whale, The" (Kunitz), **Supp. III Part 1:** 263, 269
Wellfleet Whale and Companion Poems, The (Kunitz), **Supp. III Part 1:** 263
Wellink, Yvonne, **Supp. XVIII:** 257
Wellman, Flora, **II:** 463–464, 465
Wellman, Rita, **Supp. XXV:** 20
"Well Rising, The" (Stafford), **Supp. XI:** 318
Wells, Carolyn, **Supp. XXVI: 271–287**
Wells, H. G., **I:** 103, 226, 241, 243, 253, 405, 409, 415; **II:** 82, 144, 276, 337, 338, 458; **III:** 456; **IV:** 340, 455; **Retro. Supp. I:** 100, 228, 231; **Supp. XVI:** 190; **Supp. XXI:** 8
Wellspring, The (Olds), **Supp. X: 211–212**
Well Wrought Urn, The: Studies in the Structure of Poetry (Brooks), **Supp. XIV:** 1, **8–9**, 14, 15, 16
Welsh, Mary, **Supp. XIX:** 248. See also Hemingway, Mrs. Ernest (Mary Welsh)
Welty, Eudora, **II:** 194, 217, 606; **IV: 260–284; Retro. Supp. I:** 339–358; **Retro. Supp. II:** 235; **Retro. Supp. III:** 36; **Supp. IV Part 2:** 474; **Supp. V:** 59, 315, 336; **Supp. VIII:** 94, 151, 171; **Supp. X:** 42, 290; **Supp. XII:** 310, 322; **Supp. XIV:** 3; **Supp. XV:** 338; **Supp. XXIV:** 223; **Supp. XXVI:** 152; **Supp. XXVII:** 216, 218, 267
Welty, Eurora, **Supp. XIX:** 151
Weltzien, O. Alan, **Supp. XVI:** 20–21, 28
"We miss Her, not because We see—" (Dickinson), **Retro. Supp. I:** 46
We Must Dance My Darlings (Trilling), **Supp. I Part 1:** 297
Wendell, Barrett, **III:** 507; **Supp. I Part 2:** 414; **Supp. XIV:** 197
Wendell, Sarah. See Holmes, Mrs. Abiel (Sarah Wendell)
Wendy Wasserstein: A Casebook (Barnett), **Supp. XV:** 323, 330
"Wendy Wasserstein's Three Sisters: Squandered Privilege" (Brewer), **Supp. XV:** 330
Wenner, Jann S., **Supp. XXIV:** 280, 283
Wept of Wish-ton-Wish, The (Cooper), **I:** 339, 342, 350
Werbe, Peter, **Supp. XIII:** 236
"We Real Cool" (Brooks), **Supp. III Part 1:** 80
"We're All Pharaohs When We Die" (Gallagher), **Supp. XXIV:** 170
We're Back! A Dinosaur's Story (screenplay, Shanley), **Supp. XIV:** 316
"We're Friends Again" (O'Hara), **III:** 372–373
"Were the Whole Realm of Nature Mine" (Watts), **I:** 458
Werewolf (M. Sommers), **Supp. XVII:** 55
Were-Wolf, The (C. Housman), **Supp. XVII:** 55
Werewolf of Paris, The (Endore), **Supp. XVII:** 55–56
Werewolves in Their Youth (Chabon), **Supp. XI:** 66, **76–77**
Werlock, Abby, **Supp. XIII:** 293
Werthman, Michael, **Supp. V:** 115
"Wer-Trout, The" (Proulx), **Supp. VII:** 255–256
Wescott, Glenway, **I:** 288; **II:** 85; **III:** 448, 454; **Supp. VIII:** 156; **Supp. XIV:** 342; **Supp. XVI:** 195
"We Shall All Be Born Again But We Shall Not All Be Saved" (Matthews), **Supp. IX:** 162
West, Anthony, **Supp. IV Part 1:** 284
West, Benjamin, **Supp. I Part 2:** 511
West, Dorothy, **Retro. Supp. III:** 127; **Supp. XIII:** 295; **Supp. XIX:** 72; **Supp. XVIII: 277–291; Supp. XXVI:** 164, 173, 174
West, James, **II:** 562
West, M. Genevieve, **Retro. Supp. III:** 127
West, Nathanael, **I:** 97, 107, 190, 211, 298; **II:** 436; **III:** 357, 425; **IV: 285–307; Retro. Supp. II: 321–341; Supp. IV Part 1:** 203; **Supp. VIII:** 97; **Supp. XI:** 85, 105, 159, 296; **Supp. XII:** 173, 310; **Supp. XIII:** 106, 170; **Supp. XIX:** 223;

Supp. XVIII: 251, 253, 254
West, Ray, **Supp. XV:** 142
West, Rebecca, **II:** 412, 445; **Supp. XVI:** 152, 153
Westall, Julia Elizabeth. See Wolfe, Mrs. William Oliver (Julia Elizabeth Westall)
"We Stand United" (Benét), **Supp. XI:** 46
"West Authentic, The: Willa Cather" (Stegner), **Supp. IV Part 2:** 608
"West Coast, The: Region with a View" (Stegner), **Supp. IV Part 2:** 608–609
"West Coast Waterfront: End of an Era" (Swados), **Supp. XIX:** 264
Westcott, Edward N., **II:** 102
"Western Association of Writers" (Chopin), **Supp. I Part 1:** 217
"Western Ballad, A" (Ginsberg), **Supp. II Part 1:** 311
Western Borders, The (Howe), **Supp. IV Part 2:** 424–425
Western Canon (Bloom), **Supp. XXV:** 251
Western Canon: The Books and Schools of the Ages (Bloom), **Supp. IX:** 146
Western Lands, The (Burroughs), **Supp. III Part 1:** 106
"Western North Carolina" (Halliday), **Supp. XIX:** 85
Western Star (Benét), **Supp. XI:** 46, 47, 57
"Westland" (C. Baxter), **Supp. XVII:** 18, 19
"West Marginal Way" (Hugo), **Supp. VI:** 131, 135
West of Eden: Writers in Hollywood, 1928–1940 (Fine), **Supp. XVIII:** 248
West of Yesterday, East of Summer: New and Selected Poems, 1973–1993 (Monette), **Supp. X:** 159
West of Your City (Stafford), **Supp. XI:** 316, **317–318,** 321, 322
Weston, Jessie L., **II:** 540; **III:** 12; **Supp. I Part 2:** 438
"West Real" (Ríos), **Supp. IV Part 2:** 539, 540
West-running Brook (Frost), **II:** 155; **Retro. Supp. I:** 136, 137; **Retro. Supp. III:** 102
"West-running Brook" (Frost), **II:** 150, 162–164; **Retro. Supp. III:** 102
"West Wall" (Merwin), **Supp. III Part 1:** 355
"Westward Beach, A" (Jeffers), **Supp. II Part 2:** 418
Westward Ho (Harrison), **Supp. VIII:** 51, **52**
Westward the Course of Empire (Leutze), **Supp. X:** 307
"Westward the Course of Empire Takes Its Way" (Wallace), **Supp. X: 307–308; Supp. XXII:** 260
"West Wind" (Oliver), **Supp. VII:** 246
"West Wind, The" (Bryant), **Supp. I Part 1:** 155
West Wind: Poems and Prose Poems (Oliver), **Supp. VII:** 243, 246–248
"Wet Casements" (Ashbery), **Supp. III Part 1:** 18–20
We the Living (film), **Supp. IV Part 2:** 520
We the Living (Rand), **Supp. IV Part 2:** 520–521
Wetherell, Elizabeth (pseudonym). See Warner, Susan
Wet Parade (Sinclair), **Supp. V:** 289
Wetzsteon, Ross, **Supp. XXI:** 12
"We've Adjusted Too Well" (O'Brien), **Supp. V:** 247
Wevill, David, **Retro. Supp. II:** 247, 249
"We Wear the Mask" (Dunbar), **Supp. II Part 1:** 199, 207, 209–210
We Were Heroes: The Journal of Scott Pendleton Collins, a World War II Soldier, Normandy, France, 1944 (Myers), **Supp. XXVII:** 208
We Will Be Citizens: New Essays on Gay and Lesbian Theatre (Fischer, ed.), **Supp. XXIV:** 263
We Will Never Die (Hecht), **Supp. XXVII:** 94
Weybright, Victor, **Supp. XIII:** 172
Weyden, Rogier van der, **Supp. IV Part 1:** 284
Whalen, Marcella, **Supp. I Part 1:** 49
Whalen, Philip, **Supp. VIII:** 289; **Supp. XXII:** 226
Whalen, Terence, **Retro. Supp. III:** 237
Whalen-Bridge, John, **Retro. Supp. II:** 211–212
"Whales off Wales, The" (X. J. Kennedy), **Supp. XV:** 163
"Whales Weep" (Boyle), **Supp. XX: 19**
"Whales Weep Not!" (D. H. Lawrence), **Supp. XVII:** 77
Wharton, Edith, **I:** 12, 375; **II:** 96, 180, 183, 186, 189–190, 193, 283, 338, 444, 451; **III:** 69, 175, 576; **IV:** 8, 53, 58, **308–330; Retro. Supp. I:** 108, 232, **359–385; Retro. Supp. III: 275–293**; **Supp. IV Part 1:** 23, 31, 35, 36, 80, 81, 310; **Supp. IX:** 57; **Supp. XII:** 308; **Supp. XIV:** 337, 347; **Supp. XVI:** 189; **Supp. XVIII:** 278; **Supp. XX: 227, 229, 232, 239, 240; Supp. XXIII:** 275; **Supp. XXIV:** 29, 64; **Supp. XXV:** 201; **Supp. XXVI:** 145, 276; **Supp. XXVII:** 4
Wharton, Edward Robbins, **IV:** 310, 313–314, 319
"What" (Dunn), **Supp. XI:** 144
What a Kingdom It Was (Kinnell), **Supp. III Part 1:** 235, 238, 239
"What America Would Be Like without Blacks" (Ellison), **Retro. Supp. II:** 123
What Are Masterpieces (Stein), **IV:** 30–31
What Are Years (Moore), **III:** 208–209, 210, 215
"What Are Years?" (Moore), **III:** 211, 213
What a Way to Go (Morris), **III:** 230–232
"What a Wonder among the Instruments Is the Walloping Trombone!" (Carruth), **Supp. XVI:** 51
"What Became of the Flappers?" (Zelda Fitzgerald), **Supp. IX:** 71
"What Can I Tell My Bones?" (Roethke), **III:** 546, 549
What Century? (O'Hara), **Supp. XXIII:** 216
"What Child Is This?" (Jarman), **Supp. XVII:** 113–114, 115
"What Do I Care?" (Teasdale), **Supp. XXVII:** 284
"What Do I Care for Morning" (H. Johnson), **Supp. XXVI:** 173
"What Do We Have Here" (Carson), **Supp. XII: 101**
"What Do We See" (Rukeyser), **Supp. VI:** 282
What Do Women Want? Bread Roses Sex Power (Jong), **Supp. V:** 115, 117, 129, 130
"What Do You Do in San Francisco?" (Carver), **Supp. III Part 1:** 143
What Dreams My Come (Atherton as Frank Lin), **Supp. XXIV:** 28
What D'Ya Know for Sure (Zinberg), **Supp. XV:** 196
Whatever Happened to Gloomy Gus of the Chicago Bears? (Coover), **Supp. V:** 51, 52
Whatever Happened to Jacy Farrow? (Cleveland), **Supp. V:** 222
"What Every Boy Should Know" (Maxwell), **Supp. VIII:** 169
"What Feels Like the World" (Bausch), **Supp. VII:** 46

"What Fort Sumter Did for Me" (E. Stoddard), **Supp. XV:** 282
"What Girls Read" (Salmon), **Supp. XVIII:** 258
"What God Is Like to Him I Serve" (Bradstreet), **Supp. I Part 1:** 106–107
"What Happened Here Before" (Snyder), **Supp. VIII:** 302
"What Happened to Georgia" (Ray), **Supp. XVIII:** 194
What Happens (Herrmann), **Supp. XXII:** 277
What Have I Ever Lost by Dying? (R. Bly), **Supp. IV Part 1:** 71–72
What Have You Lost? (Nye, ed.), **Supp. XIII:** 280
What I Believe (Asch), **Supp. XXIII:** 2
"What I Believe" (Mumford), **Supp. II Part 2:** 479
"What I Call What They Call Onanism" (Goldbarth), **Supp. XII:** 175
What I Did Last Summer (Gurney), **Supp. V:** 96, 100, 107, 108
"What if God" (Olds), **Supp. X:** 208
What I Have Done with Birds: Character Studies of Native American Birds (Stratton-Porter), **Supp. XX: 218**
"What I Have to Defend, What I Can't Bear Losing" (Stern), **Supp. IX:** 286, 287, 288, 298
"What I Knew" (Nelson), **Supp. XVIII:** 178
"What I Know about Being a Playwright" (McNally), **Supp. XIII:** 195, 207
"What I Mean" (Ortiz), **Supp. IV Part 2:** 497
"What Is an Emotion" (James), **II:** 350
What Is Art? (Tolstoy), **I:** 58
"What Is Civilization? Africa's Answer" (Du Bois), **Supp. II Part 1:** 176
"What Is College For?" (Bourne), **I:** 216
"What Is Exploitation?" (Bourne), **I:** 216
What Is Found There: Notebooks on Poetry and Politics (Rich), **Retro. Supp. III:** 241, 251; **Supp. XVII:** 74
"What Is It?" (Carver), **Supp. III Part 1:** 139
What Is Man? (Twain), **II:** 434; **IV:** 209
"What Is Man" (Twain), **Retro. Supp. III:** 269
"What Is Poetry" (Ashbery), **Supp. III Part 1:** 19
"What Is Seized" (Moore), **Supp. X:** 164, 168, 169, 172, 175
"What Is the Earth?" (Olds), **Supp. X:** 213
"What Is This Poet" (Stern), **Supp. IX:** 295
What Is To Be Done? (Lenin), **Supp. XXI:** 164
"What I Think" (Hogan), **Supp. IV Part 1:** 406
What Love Comes To: New & Selected Poems (Stone), **Supp. XXVII:** 249, 257, 262
What Maisie Knew (H. James), **II:** 332; **Retro. Supp. I:** 229, **230; Supp. XVIII:** 160
What Makes Sammy Run? (NBC broadcast, Schulberg and Schulberg), **Supp. XVIII:** 254
What Makes Sammy Run (Schulberg), **Supp. XXVII:** 142
What Makes Sammy Run? (Schulberg), **Supp. XIII:** 170; **Supp. XVIII:** 241, **244–247,** 248, 249, 253
"What Makes Sammy Run?" (Schulberg), **Supp. XVIII:** 241
What Moon Drove Me to This? (Harjo), **Supp. XII: 218–220**
"What Must" (MacLeish), **III:** 18
What My Father Believed (Wrigley), **Supp. XVIII:** 298–300
"What My Father Believed" (Wrigley), **Supp. XVIII: 298–299**
What Price Hollywood? (film), **Supp. XVIII:** 243
Whatsaid Serif (Mackey), **Supp. XXVII:** 155, 156
"What Sally Said" (Cisneros), **Supp. VII:** 63
What Saves Us (Weigl), **Supp. XIX:** 282
"What's Happening in America" (Sontag), **Supp. III Part 2:** 460–461
"What She Couldn't Tell" (Hampl), **Supp. XXII:** 92
"What's in Alaska?" (Carver), **Supp. III Part 1:** 141, 143
"What's in a Name" (H. L. Gates), **Supp. XX: 101**
What's New, Pussycat? (film; Allen), **Supp. XI:** 307; **Supp. XV:** 1, 2, 14
"What's New in American and Canadian Poetry" (R. Bly), **Supp. IV Part 1:** 67
What's O'Clock (A. Lowell), **II:** 511, 527, 528
What's Up, Tiger Lily? (film; Allen), **Supp. XV: 2, 3**
"What the Arts Need Now" (Baraka), **Supp. II Part 1:** 47
"What the Bed Knows"(Schott), **Supp. XXIII:** 249
"What the Body Can Say" (Trethewey), **Supp. XXI:** 255
"What the Brand New Freeway Won't Go By" (Hugo), **Supp. VI:** 132–133
"What the Gypsies Told My Grandmother While She Was Still a Young Girl" (Simic), **Supp. VIII:** 283
"What the Prose Poem Carries with It" (R. Bly), **Supp. IV Part 1:** 64
"What the Stone Says" (Huddle), **Supp. XXVI:** 151
What They Found: Love on 145th Street (Myers), **Supp. XXVII:** 210–211
"What They Wanted" (Dunn), **Supp. XI:** 151
What Thou Lovest Well (Hugo), **Supp. VI:** 140, 141
"What Thou Lovest Well Remains American" (Hugo), **Supp. VI:** 140, 141
What Time Collects (Farrell), **II:** 46, 47–48
What to Do? (Chernyshevsky), **Retro. Supp. I:** 269
"What to Keep, What to Discard" (Taggard), **Supp. XXII:** 280
"What to the Slave is Your Fourth of July?"(Douglass), **Supp. XXIII:** 167
What Use Are Flowers? (Hansberry), **Supp. IV Part 1:** 359, 368–369, 374
What Was Literature? (Fiedler), **Supp. XIII:** 96–97, **105–106**
What Was Mine (Beattie), **Supp. V:** 33, 35
What Was the Relationship of the Lone Ranger to the Means of Production? (Baraka), **Supp. II Part 1:** 58
"What We Came Through" (Goldbarth), **Supp. XII:** 179–180
"What Were the White Things?" (Hempel), **Supp. XXI:** 126
What We Talk About When We Talk About Love (Carver), **Supp. III Part 1:** 142–146; **Supp. XII:** 139; **Supp. XXIV:** 177
"What Why When How Who" (Pinsky), **Supp. VI:** 244
What Will Suffice: Contemporary American Poets on the Art of Poetry (Buckley and Young, eds.), **Supp. XIII:** 313
What Work Is (Levine), **Supp. V:** 181, 187, 192–193
"What You Hear from Em" (Taylor), **Supp. V:** 314, 320, 324

"What You Live For" (Huddle), **Supp. XXVI:** 150
What You See in the Dark (Muñoz), **Supp. XXV:** 127, 137–139
"What You Want" (O. Henry), **Supp. II Part 1:** 402
"What You Would Do" (Weigl), **Supp. XIX:** 288
Wheatley, Phillis, **Supp. XIII:** 111; **Supp. XVII:** 74–75; **Supp. XX:** **106, 277–291**
Whedon, Tony, **Supp. XXI:** 131, 132
"Wheelchairs" (Kriegel), **Supp. XXIV:** 220
Wheeler, David, **Supp. XVI:** 277
Wheeler, John, **II:** 433
Wheeler, Monroe, **Supp. XV:** 295
Wheelock, John Hall, **IV:** 461; **Supp. IX:** 268; **Supp. XIV:** 120; **Supp. XV:** 301; **Supp. XXVII:** 286, 291, 293, 294, 297
Wheel of Life, The (Glasgow), **II:** 176, 178, 179, 183
Wheelwright, Philip, **Supp. XV:** 20
"When" (Olds), **Supp. X:** 207
When Boyhood Dreams Come True (Farrell), **II:** 45
"When Death Came April Twelve 1945" (Sandburg), **III:** 591, 593
"When Death Comes" (Oliver), **Supp. VII:** 241
"When De Co'n Pone's Hot" (Dunbar), **Supp. II Part 1:** 202–203
"When God First Said" (Zach; Everwine trans.), **Supp. XV:** 87
"When Grandma Died—1942" (Shields), **Supp. VII:** 311
"When Howitzers Began" (Carruth), **Supp. XVI:** 55
"When I Buy Pictures" (Moore), **III:** 205
"When I Came from Colchis" (Merwin), **Supp. III Part 1:** 343
"When I Have Fears I May Cease to Be" (Keats), **Supp. XIX:** 92
"When I Left Business for Literature" (Anderson), **I:** 101
"When I Love You" (Peacock), **Supp. XIX:** 199
"When in Rome—Apologia" (Komunyakaa), **Supp. XIII:** 120
"When It Comes" (Olds), **Supp. X:** 213
"When It's Clear and Hot" (Trethewey), **Supp. XXI:** 246
When I Was Alive (Notley), **Supp. XXII:** 228
"When I Was Alive" (Notley), **Supp. XXII:** 229
"When I Was Seventeen" (Kincaid), **Supp. VII:** 181
"When I Was Thirty-Five, You Took My Photograph" (Stone), **Supp. XXVII:** 254
"When I Was Twenty-five" (Talese), **Supp. XVII:** 202
When Knighthood Was in Flower (Major), **III:** 320
"[When] Let by rain" (Taylor), **IV:** 160–161
"When Lilacs Last in the Dooryard Bloom'd" (Whitman), **IV:** 347–348, 351; **Retro. Supp. I:** 406; **Supp. IV Part 1:** 16; **Supp. XV:** 215
"When Malindy Sings" (Dunbar), **Supp. II Part 1:** 200, 204–205
When Peoples Meet: A Study of Race and Culture (Locke and Stern), **Supp. XIV:** 202, 213
When She Was Good (P. Roth), **Retro. Supp. II:** 282, 283, 284; **Supp. III Part 2:** 403, 405, 410–413
"When Sue Wears Red" (Hughes), **Retro. Supp. I:** 195, 204
"When the Acacia Blooms"(Crooker), **Supp. XXIII:** 60
"When the Dead Ask My Father about Me" (Olds), **Supp. X:** 210
"When the Frost Is on the Punkin" (Riley), **Supp. II Part 1:** 202
When the Jack Hollers (Hughes), **Retro. Supp. I:** 203; **Supp. I Part 1:** 328
"When the Last Riders" (Zach; Everwine, trans.), **Supp. XV:** 75, 86
"When the Light Gets Green" (Warren), **IV:** 252
"When the Model Does Not Show" (Major), **Supp. XXII:** 184
"When the Peace Corps Was Young" (Theroux), **Supp. VIII:** 314
When the Sun Tries to Go On (Koch), **Supp. XV:** 185
"When the Sun Tries to Go On" (Koch), **Supp. XV:** 179, 180
"When the World Ended as We Knew It" (Harjo), **Supp. XII:** 231
When Time Was Born (Farrell), **II:** 46, 47
"When We Dead Awaken" (Rich), **Retro. Supp. III:** 246
"When We Dead Awaken: Writing as Re-Vision" (Rich), **Retro. Supp. III:** 246; **Supp. I Part 2:** 552–553, 560
"When We Gonna Rise" (Baraka), **Supp. II Part 1:** 48
"When We Have To" (Salinas), **Supp. XIII:** 322–323
"WHEN WE'LL WORSHIP JESUS" (Baraka), **Supp. II Part 1:** 54
"When We Sold the Tent" (Espaillat), **Supp. XXI:** 102
"When we speak of God, is it God we speak of?" (J. Logan), **Supp. XVII:** 113
"When Women Throw Down Bundles: Strong Women Make Strong Nations" (Gunn Allen), **Supp. IV Part 1:** 328
"When You Come into Your Kingdom" (Muñoz), **Supp. XXV:** 136
"'When You Finally See Them': The Unconquered Eye in To Kill a Mockingbird" (Champion), **Supp. VIII:** 128
"When You Lie Down, the Sea Stands Up" (Swenson), **Supp. IV Part 2:** 643
"Where Are the People of Color?" (Myers), **Supp. XXVII:** 199
"Where Blue Is Blue" (Richard), **Supp. XIX:** 221
Where Does One Go When There's No Place Left to Go? (Crews), **Supp. XI:** 103
Where Does the Day Go? (Myers), **Supp. XXVII:** 199, 200, 202
"Where Go the Boats" (R. Stevenson), **Supp. XVII:** 69
Where Horizons Go (Espaillat), **Supp. XXI:** 99, 103, 104
"Where I Come from Is Like This" (Gunn Allen), **Supp. IV Part 1:** 319
"Where I'm Calling From" (Carver), **Supp. III Part 1:** 145
Where I'm Calling From: New and Selected Stories (Carver), **Supp. III Part 1:** 138, 148; **Supp. XXIV:** 178
"Where I Ought to Be" (Erdrich), **Supp. IV Part 1:** 265
Where Is My Wandering Boy Tonight? (Wagoner), **Supp. IX: 335–336**
"Where Is the Island?" (Francis), **Supp. IX:** 78
"Where Is the Voice Coming From?" (Welty), **IV:** 280; **Retro. Supp. I:** 355
Where Joy Resides (Isherwood), **Supp. XIV:** 156
"Where Knock Is Open Wide" (Roethke), **III:** 533–535
"Where My Sympathy Lies" (H. Roth), **Supp. IX:** 234
Where's Daddy? (Inge), **Supp. XXV:** 95, 105, 106
Where's My Money? (Shanley), **Supp. XIV:** 316, 328, **330–331**
Where the Bluebird Sings to the Lemonade Springs (Stegner), **Supp. IV**

Part 2: 596, 597, 598, 600, 604, 606, 613; **Supp. XXII:** 205
"Where the Bones Move" (W. V. Davis), **Supp. XXI:** 92
Where the Cross Is Made (O'Neill), **III:** 388, 391
Where There's a Will (Rinehart), **Supp. XXV:** 193
Where the Rivers Flow North (Mosher), **Supp. XXII:** 205, 207, 208, **210–212**
"Where the Rivers Flow North" (Mosher), **Supp. XXII:** 204, 206, 207, 208, 209, **210–211**
Where the Sea Used to Be (Bass), **Supp. XVI:** 21
"Where the Sea Used to Be" (Bass), **Supp. XVI:** 20, 21
"Where the Sea Used to Be: Rick Bass and the Novel of Ecological Education" (Dixon), **Supp. XVI:** 21
"Where the Soft Air Lives" (Nye), **Supp. XIII:** 275
Where the Twilight Never Ends (Haines), **Supp. XII:** 211
Where the Wild Grape Grows: Selected Writings, 1930–1950 (D. West; Mitchell and Davis, eds.), **Supp. XVIII:** 283, 286
Where the Wild Things Are (Sendak), **Supp. IX:** 207
"Wherever Home Is" (Wright), **Supp. III Part 2:** 605, 606
"Wherever I Am Not" (Huddle), **Supp. XXVI:** 156–157
Where Water Comes Together With Other Water (Carver), **Supp. III Part 1:** 147, 148
"Where We Crashed" (Hugo), **Supp. VI:** 138
"Where We Must Look for Help" (R. Bly), **Supp. XXI:** 84
"Where You Are" (Doty), **Supp. XI:** 131
Where You'll Find Me, and Other Stories (Beattie), **Supp. V:** 30–31
Whicher, Stephen, **II:** 20
"Which Is More Than I Can Say for Some People" (Moore), **Supp. X:** 177, 178
Which Ones Are the Enemy? (Garrett), **Supp. VII:** 98
"Which Theatre Is the Absurd One?" (Albee), **I:** 71
"Which Way to the Future?" (Rehder), **Supp. IV Part 1:** 69
"While Hendrix Played a Solo: 'Burning of the Midnight Lamp' " (Gansworth), **Supp. XXVI:** 112
While I Was Gone (Miller), **Supp. XII:** 290, **301–303**
"While Seated in a Plane" (Swenson), **Supp. IV Part 2:** 645
While the Messiah Tarries (Bukiet), **Supp. XVII:** 43, **46–47**
While We've Still Got Feet (Budbill), **Supp. XIX:** 5, 7, **10–11,** 15
Whilomville Stories (Crane), **I:** 414
"Whip, The" (Robinson), **III:** 513
Whipple, Thomas K., **II:** 456, 458; **IV:** 427
"Whippoorwill, The" (Francis), **Supp. IX:** 90
"Whip-poor-will, The" (Thurber), **Supp. I Part 2:** 616
Whirl Asunder, A (Atherton), **Supp. XXIV:** 22
Whirlpool (film, Preminger), **Supp. XVII:** 62
"Whisperer in Darkness, The" (Lovecraft), **Supp. XXV:** 114
"Whispering Gallery, The" (Komunyakaa), **Supp. XIII:** 132
"Whispering Leaves" (Glasgow), **II:** 190
Whispering to Fool the Wind (Ríos), **Supp. IV Part 2:** 540–541, 544, 545
"Whispers in the Next Room" (Simic), **Supp. VIII:** 278
"Whispers of Heavenly Death" (Whitman), **IV:** 348
"Whispers of Immortality" (Eliot), **Supp. XI:** 242
Whistle (Jones), **Supp. XI:** 219, 224, **231–234**
"Whistle, The" (Franklin), **II:** 121
"Whistle, The" (Komunyakaa), **Supp. XIII:** 111, 126
"Whistle, The" (Welty), **IV:** 262
Whistler, James, **I:** 484; **III:** 461, 465, 466; **IV:** 77, 369
Whistler, James Abbott McNeill, **Supp. XIV:** 335–336
"Whistling Dick's Christmas Stocking" (O. Henry), **Supp. II Part 1:** 390, 392
Whistling in the Dark (Garrett), **Supp. VII:** 111
Whistling in the Dark: True Stories and Other Fables (Garrett), **Supp. VII:** 95
Whitcher, Frances Miriam Berry, **Supp. XIII:** 152
"White" (Simic), **Supp. VIII: 275–276**
White, Barbara, **Retro. Supp. I:** 379
White, Dana, **Supp. XXII:** 251
White, E. B., **Retro. Supp. I:** 335; **Supp. I Part 2:** 602, 607, 608, 612, 619, 620, **651–681; Supp. II Part 1:** 143; **Supp. IX:** 20, 32; **Supp. VIII:** 171; **Supp. XVI:** 167
White, Elizabeth Wade, **Retro. Supp. III:** 3; **Supp. I Part 1:** 100, 103, 111
White, Henry Kirke, **Supp. I Part 1:** 150
White, James L., **Supp. XI:** 123
White, Joel, **Supp. I Part 2:** 654, 678
White, Katharine. (Katharine Sergeant Angell), **Supp. I Part 2:** 610, 653, 655, 656, 669; **Supp. VIII:** 151, 171
White, Lillian, **Supp. I Part 2:** 651
White, Lucia, **I:** 258
White, Maria. See Lowell, Mrs. James Russell (Maria White)
White, Morton, **I:** 258; **Supp. I Part 2:** 647, 648, 650
White, Roberta, **Supp. XII:** 293
White, Stanford, **Supp. IV Part 1:** 223
White, Stanley, **Supp. I Part 2:** 651, 655
White, T. H., **III:** 522
White, T. W., **III:** 411, 415
White, Walter, **Supp. I Part 1:** 345; **Supp. XIX:** 73; **Supp. XVIII:** 123, 127
White, William, **Retro. Supp. II:** 326
White, William A., **I:** 252
White Album, The (Didion), **Supp. IV Part 1:** 198, 202, 205–207, 210
"White Album, The" (Didion), **Supp. IV Part 1:** 205, 206
"White Angel" (Cunningham), **Supp. XV:** 59
"White Apache" (Markson), **Supp. XVII:** 136
"White as Snow" (Boyle), **Supp. XXIV:** 58, 59
White Boys (McKnight), **Supp. XX: 155–157**
"White Boys, The" (McKnight), **Supp. XX: 155–157**
White Buildings (H. Crane), **I:** 385, 386, 390–395, 400; **Retro. Supp. II:** 77–78, **80–81,** 82, 83, 85; **Retro. Supp. III:** 49, 50
White Butterfly (Mosley), **Supp. XIII:** 237, 238, 240
White Center (Hugo), **Supp. VI:** 144–145
"White Center" (Hugo), **Supp. VI:** 144, 146
Whited, Stephen, **Supp. XI:** 135
White Deer, The (Thurber), **Supp. I Part 2:** 606
White Doves at Morning (Burke), **Supp. XIV:** 22–23, 32, 35–36
"White Eagle, The" (Chopin), **Retro. Supp. II:** 72

White Fang (London), **II:** 471–472, 481
Whitefield, George, **I:** 546; **Supp. XX: 280**
White-Footed Deer and Other Poems (Bryant), **Supp. I Part 1:** 157
White Goddess, The (Graves), **Supp. IV Part 1:** 280
White-Haired Lover (Shapiro), **Supp. II Part 2:** 703, 717
Whitehead, Alfred North, **III:** 605, 619, 620; **IV:** 88; **Supp. I Part 2:** 554, 647
Whitehead, Mrs. Catherine, **IV:** 116
Whitehead, Colson, **Supp. XIII:** 233, 241
Whitehead, James, **Supp. XV:** 339
Whitehead, Margaret, **IV:** 114, 115, 116
Whitehead, William, **Supp. XX: 50–51, 53**
White Heat (Walsh), **Supp. XIII:** 174
"White Heron, A" (Jewett), **II:** 409; **Retro. Supp. II:** 17
White Heron and Other Stories, A (Jewett), **II:** 396
White Horses (Hoffman), **Supp. X: 83–85,** 90, 92
"White Horses of Vienna, The" (Boyle), **Supp. XXIV: 59–60**
White Horses of Vienna, The, and Other Stories (Boyle), **Supp. XXIV:** 57, **58–59**
White House Diary, A (Lady Bird Johnson), **Supp. IV Part 1:** 22
White-Jacket (Melville), **III:** 80, 81, 84, 94; **Retro Supp. I:** 248, 249, 254; **Retro. Supp. III:** 147, 152, 154, 155, 156; **Supp. XVIII:** 7, 9
White Lantern, The (Connell), **Supp. XIV:** 97
"White Lies" (Trethewey), **Supp. XXI:** 244, 246, 251
"White Lights, The" (Robinson), **III:** 524
"White Lilies, The" (Glück), **Supp. V:** 88
White Man, Listen! (Wright), **IV:** 478, 488, 489, 494
White Morning, The (Atherton), **Supp. XXIV:** 24, 29
"White Mulberry Tree, The" (Cather), **I:** 319; **Retro. Supp. I:** 7, 9, 17
White Mule (W. C. Williams), **Retro. Supp. I:** 423
"White Negro, The" (Mailer), **III:** 36–37; **Retro. Supp. II:** 202
"Whiteness of the Whale, The" (Melville), **III:** 84, 86
"White Night" (Oliver), **Supp. VII:** 236
"White Nights" (Auster), **Supp. XII:** 23–24
White Noise (DeLillo), **Supp. VI:** 1, 3–4, 5–7, 10, 11–12, 16; **Supp. XVIII:** 140; **Supp. XX: 91**
White Oxen and Other Stories, The (Burke), **I:** 269, 271
White Paper on Contemporary American Poetry (McClatchy), **Supp. XII:** 253, **259–260**
"White Phosphorous" (Notley), **Supp. XXII:** 232, 233
"White Pine" (Oliver), **Supp. VII:** 244
White Pine: Poems and Prose Poems (Oliver), **Supp. VII:** 243–246
White Poems, The (Crooker), **Supp. XXIII: 54–55**
White Rat (G. Jones), **Supp. XXIV:** 185
White Roots of Peace (Wallace), **Supp. XXVI:** 90, 96–97
White Sail (Sorrentino), **Supp. XXI:** 228
"White Ship, The" (Lovecraft), **Supp. XXV:** 113
"White Silence, The" (London), **II:** 468
"White Silk" (Nye), **Supp. XIII:** 275
"White Snake, The" (Sexton), **Supp. II Part 2:** 691
"White Spot" (Anderson), **I:** 116
"White-Tailed Hornet, The" (Frost), **Retro. Supp. I:** 138
"White Trash Cowboys of Father and Son, The" (Bjerre), **Supp. XXI:** 41
"White Trees, Hammer Moon" (Dubus III), **Supp. XXIV:** 101, 104
Whitfield, Raoul, **Supp. IV Part 1:** 345
Whitfield, Stephen J., **Supp. XX: 243, 244**
Whitlock, Brand, **II:** 276
Whitman (Masters), **Supp. I Part 2:** 473, 475, 476
Whitman, George, **IV:** 346, 350
Whitman, Ruth, **Supp. XXI:** 246
Whitman, Sarah Helen, **Retro. Supp. III:** 225, 236
Whitman, Sarah Wyman, **Retro. Supp. II:** 136
Whitman, Walt, **I:** 61, 68, 98, 103, 104, 109, 219, 220, 227, 228, 242, 246, 250, 251, 260, 261, 285, 381, 384, 386, 396, 397, 398, 402, 419, 430, 459, 460, 483, 485, 486, 577; **II:** 7, 8, 18, 127, 140, 273–274, 275, 289, 295, 301, 320, 321, 373, 445, 446, 451, 457, 494, 529, 530, 552; **III:** 171, 175, 177, 181–182, 189, 203, 234, 260, 426, 430, 453, 454, 461, 505, 507–508, 511, 528, 548, 552, 555, 559, 567, 572, 576, 577, 579, 584, 585, 595, 606, 609; **IV:** 74, 169, 191, 192, 202, **331–354,** 405, 409, 416, 444, 450–451, 457, 463, 464, 469, 470, 471; **Retro. Supp. I:** 8, 52, 194, 254, 283, 284, 333, **387–410,** 412, 417, 427; **Retro. Supp. II:** 40, 76, 93, 99, 155, 156, 158, 170, 262; **Retro. Supp. III:** 41, 44, 49, 244, 245, 251, 283, **295–311**; **Supp. I Part 1:** 6, 79, 167, 311, 314, 325, 365, 368, 372; **Supp. I Part 2:** 374, 384, 385, 387, 389, 391, 393, 399, 416, 436, 455, 456, 458, 473, 474, 475, 525, 540, 579, 580, 582, 682, 691; **Supp. III Part 1:** 6, 20, 156, 239–241, 253, 340; **Supp. III Part 2:** 596; **Supp. IV Part 1:** 16, 169, 325; **Supp. IV Part 2:** 597, 625; **Supp. IX:** 8, 9, 15, 38, 41, 44, 48, 53, 131, 292, 298, 299, 308, 320; **Supp. V:** 113, 118, 122, 130, 170, 178, 183, 277, 279, 332; **Supp. VIII:** 42, 95, 105, 126, 198, 202, 269; **Supp. X:** 36, 112, 203, 204; **Supp. XI:** 83, 123, 132, 135, 203, 321; **Supp. XII:** 132, 185, 190, 256; **Supp. XIII:** 1, 77, 115, 153, 221, 304, 335; **Supp. XIV:** 89, 312, 334, 335, 338; **Supp. XIX:** 118, 276; **Supp. XV:** 41, 93, 181, 183, 212, 213, 218, 250, 275, 301, 302, 303, 309, 352; **Supp. XVI:** 209; **Supp. XVII:** 42, 71, 112, 133; **Supp. XVIII:** 4, 194, 196, 304; **Supp. XX: 69, 115, 116, 221; Supp. XXI:** 169, 217, 227, 256; **Supp. XXII:** 81, 82, 86, 92; **Supp. XXIII:** 19, 109, 166, 207; **Supp. XXVI:** 227, 230, 233, 234; **Supp. XXVII:** 160
"Whitman Pinch Hits, 1861" (Skloot), **Supp. XX: 203**
"Whitman: The Poet and the Mask" (Cowley), **Supp. II Part 1:** 143
Whitmarsh, Jason, **Supp. VIII:** 283
Whitmer, Peter, **Supp. X:** 264, 265
Whitney, Blair, **Supp. I Part 2:** 403
Whitney, Josiah, **Supp. IX:** 180, 181
Whitt, Margaret Earley, **Retro. Supp. II:** 226
Whittemore, Reed, **III:** 268; **Supp. XI:** 315
Whittier, Elizabeth, **Supp. I Part 2:** 700, 701, 703; **Supp. XIII:** 141, 142
Whittier, John Greenleaf, **I:** 216; **II:** 275; **III:** 52; **Retro. Supp. I:** 54;

Retro. Supp. II: 155, 163, 169; **Supp. I Part 1:** 168, 299, 313, 317, 372; **Supp. I Part 2:** 420, 602, **682–707; Supp. VIII:** 202, 204; **Supp. XI:** 50; **Supp. XIII:** 140, 145; **Supp. XV:** 246; **Supp. XXIII:** 156
Whittier, Mary, **Supp. I Part 2:** 683
"Whittier Birthday Speech" (Twain), **Retro. Supp. III:** 262, 268; **Supp. I Part 1:** 313
"Who" (Kenyon), **Supp. VII:** 174
"Who" (Sobin), **Supp. XVI:** 284–285
"Who Am I—Who I Am" (Corso), **Supp. XII:** 134
"Who Be Kind To" (Ginsberg), **Supp. II Part 1:** 323
Who Do You Love (Thompson), **Supp. XXIII:** 289, **295–296**
Who Do You Think You Are? (Munro), **Supp. XXVII:** 181, 182, 184, 186–187, 194
"Whoever Was Using This Bed" (Carver), **Supp. III Part 1:** 148
"Whoever You Are Holding Me Now in Hand" (Whitman), **IV:** 342; **Retro. Supp. I:** 52
Who Gathered and Whispered behind Me (Goldbarth), **Supp. XII:** 181, 182
"Who in One Lifetime" (Rukeyser), **Supp. VI:** 276, 279
Who Is the Widow's Muse? (Stone), **Supp. XXVII:** 257, 262
Who Is Witter Bynner? (Kraft), **Supp. XV:** 40, 52
"Who Is Your Mother? Red Roots of White Feminism" (Gunn Allen), **Supp. IV Part 1:** 329
Whole Hog (Wagoner), **Supp. IX: 337–338**
"Whole Mess...Almost, The" (Corso), **Supp. XII:** 135
"Whole Moisty Night, The" (R. Bly), **Supp. IV Part 1:** 69
Whole New Life, A (Price), **Supp. VI:** 265, **266,** 267
"Whole Self, The" (Nye), **Supp. XIII:** 275
"Whole Soul, The" (Levine), **Supp. V:** 192
"Whole Story, The" (Strand), **Supp. IV Part 2:** 622
Whole Town's Talking, The (Loos), **Supp. XVI:** 187
Whole Wide World, The (film), **Supp. XXVII:** 117
"Whole World Knows, The" (Welty), **IV:** 272; **Retro. Supp. I:** 343
Who'll Stop the Rain (film), **Supp. V:** 301
Who Lost an American? (Algren), **Supp. IX: 15–16**
Who Owns America? (symposium), **Supp. XIV:** 4
Who Owns the West? (Kittredge), **Supp. XXVI:** 185
"Who Puts Together" (Hogan), **Supp. IV Part 1:** 403, 405, 412–413
"Whore of Mensa, The" (Allen), **Supp. XV:** 15
Whores for Gloria (Vollmann), **Supp. XVII:** 226, 230
Whorf, Benjamin Lee, **Supp. XVI:** 283
Who's Afraid? (Holding), **Supp. XXII:** 120, **125–126**
Who's Afraid of Virginia Woolf? (Albee), **I:** 71, 77–81, 83, 85, 86, 87, 94; **IV:** 230
Who Shall Be the Sun? Poems Based on the Lore, Legends, and Myths of the Northwest Coast and Plateau Indians (Wagoner), **Supp. IX:** 328, **329–330,** 337
"Whosis Kid, The" (Hammett), **Supp. IV Part 1:** 344
"Who Sit Watch in Daylight" (Wright), **Supp. XV:** 342
"Who's Passing for Who?" (Hughes), **Supp. I Part 1:** 330
"Who Speak on the Page?" (Sanders), **Supp. XVI:** 278
Who We Are: On Being (and Not Being) a Jewish American Writer (Rubin, ed.), **Supp. XXIV:** 3
Who Will Run the Frog Hospital?: A Novel (Moore), **Supp. X:** 163, 165, 169, **175–177**
Who Wrote the Book of Love? (Siegel), **Supp. XXII: 265–267,** 267
Why Are We in Vietnam? (Mailer), **III:** 27, 29, 30, 33, 34–35, 39, 42, 44; **Retro. Supp. II:** 205–206
"Why Bother?" (Franzen). See "Perchance to Dream" (Franzen)
"Why China?" (Egan), **Supp. XIX:** 51, 52
"Why Did the Balinese Chicken Cross the Road?" (Walker), **Supp. III Part 2:** 527
"Why Do the Heathens Rage?" (O'Connor), **III:** 351
"Why Do They Prate?" (H. Johnson), **Supp. XXVI:** 174
"Why Do You Write About Russia?" (Simpson), **Supp. IX:** 277
"Why Have We Not More Great Novelists?" (Atherton), **Supp. XXIV:** 24
"Why I Am a Danger to the Public" (Kingsolver), **Supp. VII:** 204
"Why I Am a Pagan" (Zitkala-Ša), **Supp. XXV:** 276–277
Why I Am Not a Christian (Russell), **Supp. I Part 2:** 522
"Why I Am Not a Painter"(O'Hara), **Supp. XXIII:** 208
Why I Came to Judevine (Budbill), **Supp. XIX:** 2, **7–8,** 15
"Why I Do Not Wish to Float in Space"(Schott), **Supp. XXIII:** 251
"Why I Entered the Gurdjieff Work" (Toomer), **Supp. III Part 2:** 481
"Why I Like Laurel" (Patchett), **Supp. XII:** 309
"Why I Live at the P.O." (Welty), **IV:** 262; **Retro. Supp. I:** 345
"Why I Make Sam Go to Church" (Lamott), **Supp. XX: 141**
"Why Is American Literature Bourgeois?" (Atherton), **Supp. XXIV:** 24, 28
"Why Is Economics Not an Evolutionary Science?" (Veblen), **Supp. I Part 2:** 634
"Why I Write" (Didion), **Supp. IV Part 1:** 201, 203
"Why I Wrote Phil: An Exclusive Essay for Amazon.com" (Saunders), **Supp. XIX:** 230–231
Why Johnny Can't Read: And What You Can Do About It (Flesch), **Supp. XVI:** 105
"Why Negro Women Leave Home" (Brooks), **Supp. III Part 1:** 75
Why Poetry Matters (Parini), **Supp. XIX:** 120, 129
"Why Resign from the Human Race?" (Swados), **Supp. XIX:** 265
"Why the Little Frenchman Wears His Hand in a Sling" (Poe), **III:** 425
Why Torture Is Wrong, and the People Who Love Them (Durang), **Supp. XXIV: 126–127**
"Why We Are Forgiven" (Weigl), **Supp. XIX:** 282–283
Why We Behave Like Microbe Hunters (Thurber), **Supp. I Part 2:** 606
Why We Were in Vietnam (Podhoretz), **Supp. VIII:** 241
"Why Write?" (Updike), **Retro. Supp. I:** 317
"Wichita Vortex Sutra" (Ginsberg), **Supp. II Part 1:** 319, 321, 323–325, 327
Wickenden, Dorothy, **Supp. XXIII:** 291
Wickes, George, **Supp. XIV:** 165
Wickford Point (Marquand), **III:** 50, 58, 64–65, 69
Wicks, Robert Russell, **Supp. XII:** 49
Wide, Wide World, The (S. Warner as

Wetherell), **Supp. XV:** 275; **Supp. XVIII:** 257, 260, **262–264,** 265
Wide Blue Yonder (Thompson), **Supp. XXIII:** 289, **296–298**
"Wide Empty Landscape with a Death in the Foreground" (Momaday), **Supp. IV Part 2:** 492
Wideman, Edgar, **Supp. XXV:** 146, 147
Wideman, John Edgar, **Retro. Supp. II:** 123; **Supp. X:** 239, 250, **319–336; Supp. XI:** 245; **Supp. XIII:** 247; **Supp. XVIII:** 89; **Supp. XXI:** 246; **Supp. XXIV:** 183
Widener, Jeff, **Supp. XVIII:** 91
"Wideness" (Pickering), **Supp. XXI:** 203
"Wide Net, The" (Welty), **IV:** 266
Wide Net and Other Stories, The (Welty), **IV:** 261, 264–266, 271; **Retro. Supp. I: 347–349,** 352, 355
Widening Spell of the Leaves, The (Levis), **Supp. XI:** 258, 259, 261, **268–269,** 271
"Wide Prospect, The" (Jarrell), **II:** 376–377
Wide Sargasso Sea (Rhys), **Supp. XVIII:** 131
"Widespread Enigma Concerning Blue-Star Woman" (Zitkala-Ša), **Supp. XXV:** 282–283
"Widow" (Peacock), **Supp. XIX:** 206
"Widower" (Robison), **Supp. XXI:** 118
Widow for One Year, A (Irving), **Supp. VI:** 165, **179–181**
Widow's Mite (Holding), **Supp. XXII: 136**
Widows of Thornton, The (Taylor), **Supp. V:** 320, 321
Widow's Story, A (Oates), **Supp. XXV:** 60
"Widow's Wish, The" (Briggs), **Supp. XVIII:** 15
Wieland; or, The Transformation (Brown), **Retro. Supp. III:** 226; **Supp. I Part 1:** 128–132, 133, 137, 140
Wiene, Robert, **Retro. Supp. I:** 268
Wiener, John, **Supp. IV Part 1:** 153
Wieners, John, **Supp. II Part 1:** 32; **Supp. XXIII:** 215
Wiesel, Elie, **Supp. XVII:** 47, 48, 49
Wiest, Dianne, **Supp. XV:** 12
"Wife, Forty-five, Remembers Love, A" (Shields), **Supp. VII:** 310
"Wifebeater, The" (Sexton), **Supp. II Part 2:** 693
"Wife for Dino Rossi, A" (Fante), **Supp. XI:** 165
"Wife of His Youth, The" (Chesnutt), **Supp. XIV: 63–66**
Wife of His Youth and Other Stories of the Color Line, The (Chesnutt), **Supp. XIV:** 62, 63
"Wife of Jesus Speaks, The" (Karr), **Supp. XI:** 250–251
"Wife of Nashville, A" (Taylor), **Supp. V:** 320
"Wife's Story, The" (R. H. Davis), **Supp. XVI:** 85, 91, 92–93
Wife's Story, The (Shields), **Supp. VII:** 316. See also Happenstance
"Wife-Wooing" (Updike), **IV:** 226
Wigan, Gareth, **Supp. XI:** 306
Wiget, Andrew, **Supp. IV Part 2:** 509
Wigglesworth, Michael, **IV:** 147, 156; **Supp. I Part 1:** 110, 111
Wilbur, Richard, **III:** 527; **Retro. Supp. II:** 50; **Supp. III Part 1:** 64; **Supp. III Part 2: 541–565; Supp. IV Part 2:** 626, 634, 642; **Supp. V:** 337; **Supp. VIII:** 28; **Supp. X:** 58, 120; **Supp. XII:** 258; **Supp. XIII:** 76, 336; **Supp. XV:** 51, 251, 256; **Supp. XVII:** 26; **Supp. XVIII:** 178; **Supp. XX: 199; Supp. XXI:** 247; **Supp. XXIV:** 36, 45; **Supp. XXVI:** 64, 68
Wilcocks, Alexander, **Supp. I Part 1:** 125
Wilcox, Ella Wheeler, **Supp. II Part 1:** 197
Wilcox, Kirstin, **Supp. XX: 283, 284, 285**
Wild, John, **II:** 362, 363–364
Wild, Peter, **Supp. V:** 5
Wild, Robert, **IV:** 155
"Wild, The" (Berry), **Supp. X:** 30
Wild 90 (film) (Mailer), **Retro. Supp. II:** 205
Wild and Woolly (film), **Supp. XVI:** 185
"Wild Boar in These Woods: The Influence of Seamus Heaney on the Poetry of Ron Rash" (Boyelston), **Supp. XXVII:** 216
Wild Boy of Aveyron, The (Itard). See De l'éducation d'un homme sauvage
Wild Boys, The: A Book of the Dead (Burroughs), **Supp. III Part 1:** 106–107
Wild Card Quilt: Taking A chance on Home (Ray), **Supp. XVIII:** 189, 192, 193, 196, 198, **200–202,** 204
Wilde, Oscar, **I:** 50, 66, 381, 384; **II:** 515; **IV:** 77, 350; **Retro. Supp. I:** 56, 102, 227; **Retro. Supp. II:** 76, 326; **Retro. Supp. III:** 44; **Supp. IV Part 2:** 578, 679, 683; **Supp. IX:** 65, 66, 68, 189, 192; **Supp. V:** 106, 283; **Supp. X:** 148, 151, 188–189; **Supp. XIV:** 324, 334; **Supp. XV:** 350; **Supp. XXIV:** 263
Wilder, Alec, **Supp. XXVII:** 42
Wilder, Amos Parker, **IV:** 356
Wilder, Mrs. Amos Parker (Isabella Thornton Niven), **IV:** 356
Wilder, Billy, **Supp. IV Part 1:** 130; **Supp. XI:** 307
Wilder, Isabel, **IV:** 357, 366, 375
Wilder, Laura Ingalls, **Supp. XXI:** 2; **Supp. XXII: 289–303; Supp. XXVI:** 217
Wilder, Thornton, **I:** 360, 482; **IV: 355–377,** 431; **Retro. Supp. I:** 109, 359; **Supp. I Part 2:** 609; **Supp. IV Part 2:** 586; **Supp. IX:** 140; **Supp. V:** 105; **Supp. XII:** 236–237; **Supp. XX: 50**
"Wilderness" (Leopold), **Supp. XIV:** 190
Wilderness (Parker), **Supp. XIX:** 177, **188–189**
"Wilderness" (Sandburg), **III:** 584, 595
Wilderness (Warren), **IV:** 256
"Wilderness, The" (Merwin), **Supp. III Part 1:** 340, 345
"Wilderness, The" (Robinson), **III:** 524
Wilderness of Vision, The: On the Poetry of John Haines (Bezner and Walzer, eds.), **Supp. XII:** 202
Wilderness Plots: Tales about the Settlement of the American Land (Sanders), **Supp. XVI:** 267–268, 269
"Wilderness Station, A" (Munro), **Supp. XXVII:** 191
"Wilderness"(Thompson), **Supp. XXIII:** 301
Wilderness World of Anne LaBastille, The (LaBastille), **Supp. X: 105,** 106
Wild Flag, The (White), **Supp. I Part 2:** 654
"Wildflower, The" (W. C. Williams), **Retro. Supp. I:** 420
"Wild Flowers" (Caldwell), **I:** 310
"Wildflowers" (Minot), **Supp. VI:** 208
"Wild Geese" (Oliver), **Supp. VII:** 237
"Wild Honey Suckle, The" (Freneau), **Supp. II Part 1:** 253, 264, 266
Wild in the Country (Odets), **Supp. II Part 2:** 546
"Wild in the Woods" (Skloot), **Supp. XX: 206**
Wild Iris, The (Glück), **Supp. V:** 79, 87–89, 91
Wildlife (Ford), **Supp. V:** 57, 69–71
Wildlife in America (Matthiessen), **Supp. V:** 199, 201, 204
"Wildlife in American Culture"

(Leopold), **Supp. XIV:** 190, 191
"Wild Light" (Skloot), **Supp. XX: 200**
Wild Man, The (P. N. Warren), **Supp. XX: 260, 270–272**
"Wildness" (Sanders), **Supp. XVI:** 276
Wild Old Wicked Man, The (MacLeish), **III:** 3, 20
Wild Palms, The (Faulkner), **II:** 68–69; **Retro. Supp. I:** 85. See also If I Forget Thee, Jerusalem (Faulkner)
"Wild Palms, The" (Faulkner), **II:** 68; **Retro. Supp. III:** 85
Wild Patience Has Taken Me This Far, A: Poems 1978–1981 (Rich), **Retro. Supp. III:** 249
"Wild Peaches" (Wylie), **Supp. I Part 2:** 707, 712
Wild Roses of Cape Ann and Other Poems (Larcom), **Supp. XIII:** 142, 147
Wild Seed (O. Butler), **Supp. XIII:** 62, 63
"Wild Swans at Coole, The " (W. B. Yeats), **Supp. XVI:** 48
"Wild Swans at Norfolk, The" (Carruth), **Supp. XVI:** 48
"Wild Thing" (L. Brown), **Supp. XXI:** 44
Wild Thorn (Hoffman), **Supp. XVIII: 84–85**
Wild to the Heart (Bass), **Supp. XVI:** 16
"Wild Turkeys: Dignity of the Damned" (B. Kelly), **Supp. XVII:** 129
"Wildwest" (MacLeish), **III:** 14
Wiley, Catherine, **Supp. XXIII:** 199
Wiley, Craig, **Supp. VIII:** 313
Wilhelm, Randall, **Supp. XXVII:** 215, 224
Wilhelm Meister (Goethe), **II:** 291
Wilkes, John, **Supp. I Part 2:** 503, 519, 522
Wilkie, Curtis, **Supp. V:** 11
Wilkins, Roy, **Supp. I Part 1:** 345
Wilkinson, Alec, **Supp. VIII:** 164, 168, 171
Wilkinson, Marguerite, **Supp. XXVII:** 292–293
Wilkinson, Max, **Supp. IX:** 251
Will, The (Swados), **Supp. XIX: 265–266**
Willa Cather: The Emerging Voice (O'Brien), **Retro. Supp. III:** 19, 37
Willard, Nancy, **Supp. XIX:** 138
Willard, Samuel, **IV:** 150
Willard Gibbs (Rukeyser), **Supp. VI:** 273, 283, 284
Willcutts, Tim, **Supp. XVII:** 239, 241, 246
Willett, Ralph, **Supp. XIV:** 27
Willey, Basil, **Retro. Supp. II:** 243
"William Butler Yeats Among the Ghosts" (Skloot), **Supp. XX: 204–205**
William Carlos Williams (Koch), **Retro. Supp. I:** 428
William Carlos Williams: An American Artist (Breslin), **Retro. Supp. I:** 430
William Carlos Williams and Alterity (Ahearn), **Retro. Supp. I:** 415
William Carlos Williams and the Meanings of Measure (Cushman), **Retro. Supp. I:** 430
William Carlos Williams: The American Background (Weaver), **Retro. Supp. I:** 430
William Ellery Channing: An Intellectual Portrait (Edgell), **Supp. XXIV:** 71
William Ellery Channing: Selected Writings (Robinson, ed.), **Supp. XXIV:** 71
William Faulkner: A Critical Study (Howe), **Supp. VI:** 119–120, 125
William Faulkner: A Literary Companion (Fargnoli), **Retro. Supp. III:** 75
William Faulkner: Early Prose and Poetry (Faulkner), **Retro. Supp. I:** 80
William Faulkner: First Encounters (Brooks), **Supp. XIV:** 13
"William Faulkner's Legend of the South" (Cowley), **Supp. II Part 1:** 143
"William Faulkner: The Stillness of Light in August" (Kazin), **Supp. VIII:** 104
William Faulkner: The Yoknapatawpha Country (Brooks), **Supp. XIV: 12–13,** 16
William Faulkner: Toward Yoknapatawpha and Beyond (Brooks), **Supp. XIV:** 13
"William Humphrey, 73, Writer of Novels about Rural Texas" (Gussow), **Supp. IX:** 93
William Humphrey, Destroyer of Myths (Almon), **Supp. IX:** 93
William Humphrey. Boise State University Western Writers Series (Winchell), **Supp. IX:** 109
"William Humphrey Remembered" (Masters), **Supp. IX:** 96
William Humphrey. Southwestern Series (Lee), **Supp. IX:** 109
William Inge and the Subversion of Gender (J. Johnson), **Supp. XXV:** 98
"William Ireland's Confession" (A. Miller), **III:** 147–148
William James and Phenomenology: A Study of the "Principles of Psychology" (Wilshire), **II:** 362
William Lloyd Garrison (Chapman), **Supp. XIV:** 46–51, 52, 53, 55
William Maxwell Portrait, A: Memories and Appreciations (C. Baxter, Collier, and Hirsch, eds.), **Supp. XVII:** 23
Williams, Annie Laurie, **Supp. IX:** 93
Williams, Blanch Colton, **Supp. XVIII:** 279
Williams, Cecil, **II:** 508
Williams, Charles, **Supp. II Part 1:** 15, 16
Williams, C. K., **Supp. XIII:** 114; **Supp. XVII:** 112
Williams, Cratis, **Supp. XX: 163**
Williams, Dakin, **IV:** 379
Williams, David Reichard, **Supp. XIII:** 162
Williams, Edward, **IV:** 404
Williams, Edwina Dakin, **IV:** 379
Williams, Eric, **Supp. XXI:** 166, 170, 171
Williams, Esther, **Supp. XII:** 165
Williams, Fannie Barrier, **Supp. XIV:** 201
Williams, Garth, **Supp. XXII:** 301
Williams, George, **Supp. V:** 220
Williams, Henry Sylvester, **Supp. XXI:** 166
Williams, Horace, **IV:** 453
Williams, Joan, **Supp. IX:** 95
Williams, John A., **Supp. XVI:** 143
Williams, John Alexander, **Supp. XXIII:** 39
Williams, John Sharp, **IV:** 378
Williams, Jonathan, **Supp. XXII:** 168
Williams, Kenny J., **Supp. XX: 281, 286**
Williams, Lyle, **Supp. XIV:** 22
Williams, Michael, **Supp. V:** 286
Williams, Miller, **Supp. XIV:** 126; **Supp. XV:** 339; **Supp. XVIII:** 177
Williams, Paul, **IV:** 404
Williams, Raymond, **Supp. IX:** 146
Williams, Roger, **Supp. I Part 2:** 699; **Supp. XXIII:** 15
Williams, Rose, **IV:** 379
Williams, Sherley Anne, **Supp. V:** 180
Williams, Solomon, **I:** 549
Williams, Stanley T., **II:** 301, 316; **Supp. I Part 1:** 251
Williams, Stephen, **IV:** 148
Williams, Ted, **IV:** 216; **Supp. IX:** 162
Williams, Ted. C., **Supp. XXVI:** 102
Williams, Tennessee, **I:** 73, 81, 113, 211; **II:** 190, 194; **III:** 145, 147; **IV:**

4, **378–401; Retro. Supp. III:** 165, 177, 313; **Supp. I Part 1:** 290, 291; **Supp. IV Part 1:** 79, 83, 84, 359; **Supp. IV Part 2:** 574, 682; **Supp. IX:** 133; **Supp. XI:** 103; **Supp. XIII:** 331; **Supp. XIV:** 250, 315; **Supp. XVI:** 194; **Supp. XXIV:** 113; **Supp. XXV:** 94, 96, 97
Williams, Terry Tempest, **Supp. XIII:** 16; **Supp. XVIII:** 189
Williams, Walter L., **Supp. IV Part 1:** 330, 331
Williams, William, **IV:** 404, 405
Williams, William Carlos, **I:** 61, 62, 229, 255, 256, 261, 285, 428, 438, 446, 539; **II:** 133, 536, 542, 543, 544, 545; **III:** 194, 196, 198, 214, 269, 409, 453, 457, 458, 464, 465, 591; **IV:** 30, 74, 75, 76, 94, 95, 286, 287, **402–425; Retro. Supp. I:** 51, 52, 62, 209, 284, 285, 288, 296, 298, **411–433; Retro. Supp. II:** 178, 181, 189, 250, 321, 322, 326, 327, 328, 334, 335; **Retro. Supp. III:** 47, 52, 245, 251; **Supp. I Part 1:** 254, 255, 259, 266; **Supp. II Part 1:** 9, 30, 308, 318; **Supp. II Part 2:** 421, 443; **Supp. III Part 1:** 9, 147, 239, 271, 275, 276, 278, 350; **Supp. III Part 2:** 542, 610, 613, 614, 615, 616, 617, 621, 622, 626, 628; **Supp. IV Part 1:** 151, 153, 246, 325; **Supp. IX:** 38, 268, 291; **Supp. V:** 180, 337; **Supp. VIII:** 195, 269, 272, 277, 292; **Supp. X:** 112, 120, 204; **Supp. XI:** 311, 328; **Supp. XII:** 198; **Supp. XIII:** 77, 90, 335; **Supp. XIV:** 280, 284, 285, 293; **Supp. XIX:** 1, 42, 117, 119, 121; **Supp. XV:** 42, 51, 182, 250, 306, 307; **Supp. XVI:** 48, 282; **Supp. XVII:** 36, 113, 227, 243; **Supp. XXI:** 226, 227, 230, 233; **Supp. XXII:** 162, 165, 168, 226, 227, 228; **Supp. XXIII:** 164, 207, 211; **Supp. XXIV:** 39, 41, 52, 63; **Supp. XXV:** 19; **Supp. XXVI:** 78, 143, 224, 226; **Supp. XXVII:** 284
Williams, Mrs. William Carlos (Florence Herman), **IV:** 404
Williams, Wirt, **Supp. XIV:** 24
Williamson, Alan, **Retro. Supp. II:** 185; **Supp. XIX:** 91
Williamson, J. W., **Supp. XX: 164**
William Styron's Nat Turner: Ten Black Writers Respond (Clarke, ed.), **IV:** 115
Williams-Walsh, Mary Ellen, **Supp. IV Part 2:** 611
William the Conqueror, **Supp. I Part 2:** 507
William Wetmore Story and His Friends (James), **Retro. Supp. I:** 235; **Supp. XX: 228**
William Wilson (Gardner), **Supp. VI:** 72
"William Wilson" (Poe), **II:** 475; **III:** 410, 412; **Retro. Supp. II:** 269; **Retro. Supp. III:** 224, 225; **Supp. IX:** 105
"Willie" (Angelou), **Supp. IV Part 1:** 15
Willie Masters' Lonesome Wife (Gass), **Supp. VI:** 77, **84–85, 86–87**
"Willing" (Moore), **Supp. X:** 178
Willingly (Gallagher), **Supp. XXIV:** 166, 168, 169, 170, 176
Willis, Bruce, **Supp. IV Part 1:** 236
Willis, Dail, **Supp. XXIII:** 298
Willis, Gordon, **Supp. XV:** 7
Willis, Mary Hard, **Supp. V:** 290–291
Willis, Meredith, **Supp. XXVI:** 153
Willis, Nathaniel Parker, **II:** 313; **Retro. Supp. III:** 232, 236; **Supp. I Part 2:** 405; **Supp. XVIII:** 12
Willis, Rachel, **Supp. XXVII:** 216
Williwaw (Vidal), **Supp. IV Part 2:** 677, 680, 681
Willow Field, The (Kittredge), **Supp. XXVI:** 184
"Willow Woman" (Francis), **Supp. IX:** 78
Wills, Garry, **Supp. I Part 1:** 294; **Supp. IV Part 1:** 355
Wills, Ridley, **IV:** 122
Wills, Ross B., **Supp. XI:** 169
"Will to Believe, The" (James), **II:** 352; **Supp. XIV:** 50
Will to Believe, The, and Other Essays in Popular Philosophy (James), **II:** 356; **IV:** 28
Will to Change, The: Poems, 1968–1970 (Rich), **Retro. Supp. III:** 242, 244, 245; **Supp. I Part 2:** 551, 557–559
Will to Live On, The: This Is Our Heritage (Wouk), **Supp. XXV:** 257, 266
"Will We Plug Chips into Our Brains?" (W. Gibson), **Supp. XVI:** 117–118
Will You Please Be Quiet, Please? (Carver), **Supp. III Part 1:** 138, 140, 144
"Will You Please Be Quiet, Please?" (Carver), **Supp. III Part 1:** 137, 141
"Will You Tell Me?" (Barthelme), **Supp. IV Part 1:** 42, 47
Wilsdorf, Anne, **Supp. XVI:** 177
Wilsey, Sean, **Supp. XXV:** 1, 8
Wilshire, Bruce, **II:** 362, 364
Wilshire, Gaylord, **Supp. V:** 280
Wilson, Adrian, **Supp. XV:** 147
Wilson, Alexander, **Supp. XVI:** 4, 6
Wilson, Angust, **IV:** 430, 435
Wilson, August, **Retro. Supp. III: 313–329**; **Supp. VIII: 329–353; Supp. XIX:** 132
Wilson, Augusta Jane Evans, **Retro. Supp. I:** 351
Wilson, Earl, **Supp. X:** 264
Wilson, Edmund, **I:** 67, 185, 236, 247, 260, 434, 482; **II:** 79, 80, 81, 86, 87, 91, 97, 98, 146, 276, 430, 530, 562, 587; **III:** 588; **IV:** 308, 310, **426–449; Retro. Supp. I:** 1, 97, 100, 101, 103, 104, 105, 115, 274; **Retro. Supp. II:** 321, 327, 329; **Supp. I Part 1:** 372; **Supp. I Part 2:** 407, 646, 678, 709; **Supp. II Part 1:** 19, 90, 106, 136, 137, 143; **Supp. III Part 2:** 612; **Supp. IV Part 2:** 693; **Supp. IX:** 55, 65, 190; **Supp. VIII:** 93, 95, 96, 97, 98–99, 100, 101, 103, 105, 162; **Supp. X:** 186; **Supp. XI:** 160; **Supp. XIII:** 170; **Supp. XIV:** 338; **Supp. XV:** 142, 308; **Supp. XVI:** 194; **Supp. XX: 76, 81; Supp. XXII:** 278; **Supp. XXIII:** 104–105, 106; **Supp. XXIV:** 62, 217, 222, 281
Wilson, Edmund (father), **IV:** 441
Wilson, E. O., **Supp. X:** 35
Wilson, Harriet, **Supp. XX: 105**
Wilson, Henry, **Supp. XIV:** 48
Wilson, Reuel, **II:** 562
Wilson, Robert, **Supp. XI:** 144
Wilson, Robley, **Supp. XXIII:** 290
Wilson, Sloan, **Supp. IV Part 1:** 387
Wilson, Thomas, **IV:** 153
Wilson, Tracy, **Supp. XVIII:** 101
Wilson, Victoria, **Supp. X:** 166
Wilson, Woodrow, **I:** 245, 246, 490; **II:** 183, 253; **III:** 105, 581; **Supp. I Part 1:** 21; **Supp. I Part 2:** 474, 643; **Supp. V:** 288
Wilton, David, **IV:** 147
Wiman, Christian, **Supp. XV:** 251, 253, 264; **Supp. XVII:** 74; **Supp. XVIII:** 173, 174
Wimberly, Lowry, **Supp. XV:** 136, 137
"Wimp, The" (Gallagher), **Supp. XXIV:** 174
Wimsatt, William K., **Supp. XIV:** 12
Winch, Terence, **Supp. XXIII:** 291
Winchell, Mark, **Supp. VIII:** 176, 189
Winchell, Mark Royden, **Supp. IX:** 97, 98, 109; **Supp. VIII:** 241; **Supp. XIII:** 94, 98, 99, 101; **Supp. XIV:** 103, 106, 111

Winchell, Walter, **Supp. XXV:** 29
Winckelmann, Johann Joachim, **Supp. XII:** 178
Wind, Sand, and Stars (Saint-Exupéry), **Supp. IX:** 247
Wind Across the Everglades (film, Ray), **Supp. XVIII:** 253
Wind Chrysalid's Rattle (Sobin), **Supp. XVI:** 283
"Windfall" (B. Kelly), **Supp. XVII:** 132
Windflower Home Almanac of Poetry, The (Kooser, ed.), **Supp. XIX:** 119
Windham, Donald, **IV:** 382
"Windhover" (Hopkins), **I:** 397; **II:** 539; **Supp. IX:** 43
Winding Stair and Other Poems, The (Yeats), **Supp. XV:** 253
"Winding Street, The" (Petry), **Supp. XI:** 6
"Window" (Pinsky), **Supp. VI:** 237, 247
"Window, The" (Hull), **Supp. XXI:** 140–141
Window at the White Cat, The (Rinehart), **Supp. XXV:** 192
Windows (Creeley), **Supp. IV Part 1:** 157, 158
"Windows" (Jarrell), **II:** 388, 389
"Window Seat, A" (Goldbarth), **Supp. XII:** 185
Wind Remains, The (opera) (Bowles), **Supp. IV Part 1:** 83
"Winds, The" (Welty), **IV:** 265; **Retro. Supp. I:** 348, 350
"Winds and Clouds over a Funeral" (Jin), **Supp. XVIII:** 94
Winds of War, The (miniseries), **Supp. XXV:** 265
Winds of War, The (Wouk), **Supp. XX: 243; Supp. XXV:** 254, 257, 258
"Wind up Sushi" (Goldbarth), **Supp. XII:** 186–187
Windy City Blues (Paretsky), **Supp. XXV:** 171
"Windy Day at the Reservoir, A" (Beattie), **Supp. V:** 33
Windy McPherson's Son (Anderson), **I:** 101, 102–103, 105, 111
"Wine" (Carver), **Supp. III Part 1:** 138
"Wine Menagerie, The" (H. Crane), **I:** 389, 391; **Retro. Supp. II:** 82
Wine of the Puritans, The: A Study of Present-Day America (Brooks), **I:** 240
"Wine of Wizardry, A" (Sterling), **I:** 208
Winer, Linda, **Supp. IV Part 2:** 580; **Supp. XV:** 332
Winesburg, Ohio (Anderson), **I:** 97, 102, 103, 104, 105–108; **III:** 112, 113, 114, 116, 224, 579; **Retro. Supp. III:** 76; **Supp. IX:** 306, 308; **Supp. V:** 12; **Supp. XI:** 164; **Supp. XVI:** 17; **Supp. XXII:** 282; **Supp. XXIV:** 281
Winfrey, Oprah, **Retro. Supp. III:** 183; **Supp. XIX:** 194, 204; **Supp. XX: 83, 93**
Wing-and-Wing, The (Cooper), **I:** 350, 355
Winged Seed, The: A Remembrance (L.-Y. Lee), **Supp. XV:** 211, **220–223**
Winged Words: American Indian Writers Speak (Coltelli), **Supp. IV Part 2:** 493, 497
"Wingfield" (Wolff), **Supp. VII:** 341–342
"Wings, The" (Doty), **Supp. XI:** 124
"Wings in the Night" (Howard), **Supp. XXVII:** 122
Wings of the Dove, The (James), **I:** 436; **II:** 320, 323, 333, 334–335; **Retro. Supp. I:** 215, 216, 217, 232, **233–234; Supp. II Part 1:** 94–95; **Supp. IV Part 1:** 349
Winik, Marion, **Supp. XXVI:** 212
Winkelberg (Hecht), **Supp. XXVII:** 95
"Wink of the Zenith, The" (Skloot), **Supp. XX: 207**
Wink of the Zenith, The: The Shaping of a Writer's Life (Skloot), **Supp. XX: 195, 196, 207**
"Winkte"(Kenny), **Supp. XXIII:** 148–149
"Winky" (Saunders), **Supp. XIX:** 228–229, 229
"Winner, The" (Davison), **Supp. XXVI:** 64
Winner Names the Age, The: A Collection of Works by Lillian Smith (Cliff, ed.), **Supp. XXII:** 67
Winners, Viola Hopkins, **Retro. Supp. III:** 289
Winner Take Nothing (Hemingway), **II:** 249; **Retro. Supp. I:** 170, 175, 176, 181
"Winnie" (Brooks), **Supp. III Part 1:** 86
Winokur, Maxine. See Kumin, Maxine
Winslow, Art, **Supp. XVIII:** 102
Winslow, Devereux, **II:** 547
Winslow, Harriet, **II:** 552–553
Winslow, Ola Elizabeth, **I:** 547
Winslow, Warren, **II:** 540
Winston, Andrew, **Supp. XII:** 189
Winston, Michael R., **Supp. XIV:** 197
Winter, Douglas, **Supp. V:** 144
Winter, Johnny and Edgar, **Supp. V:** 334
Winter, Kate, **Supp. X:** 104
"Winter Branch, A" (Irving), **Supp. VI:** 163
"Winter Burial, A" (Clampitt), **Supp. IX:** 48
Winter Carnival (film), **Retro. Supp. I:** 113
"Winter Concert"(Strout), **Supp. XXIII:** 283
"Winter Daybreak at Vence, A" (Wright), **Supp. III Part 1:** 249–250
Winter Diary, A (Van Doren), **I:** 168
"Winter Dreams" (Fitzgerald), **II:** 80, 94; **Retro. Supp. I:** 108
"Winter Drive, A" (Jewett), **Retro. Supp. II:** 147
"Winter Eden, A" (Frost), **Retro. Supp. I:** 137
"Winter Father, The" (Dubus), **Supp. VII:** 83, 87
Winter Hours: Prose, Prose Poems, and Poems (Oliver), **Supp. VII:** 230, 247
"Winter in Dunbarton" (R. Lowell), **II:** 547; **Retro. Supp. II:** 187
"Wintering" (Plath), **Retro. Supp. II:** 255
"Wintering Over" (Davison), **Supp. XXVI:** 76
Winter Insomnia (Carver), **Supp. III Part 1:** 138
Winter in the Blood (Welch), **Supp. IV Part 2:** 562
"Winter Landscape" (Berryman), **I:** 174; **Retro. Supp. I:** 430
Winter Light (W. V. Davis), **Supp. XXI: 92,** 93
"Winter Light" (W. V. Davis), **Supp. XXI:** 90, 92
Winter Lightning (Nemerov), **III:** 269
Winter Morning Walks: One Hundred Postcards to Jim Harrison (Kooser), **Supp. XIX:** 116, **125–126**
Winter News (Haines), **Supp. XII:** 199, **201–204,** 207–208, 208
"Winter Night, A" (Teasdale), **Supp. XXVII:** 289
Winternitz, Mary. See Cheever, Mrs. John (Mary Winternitz)
Winter: Notes from Montana (Bass), **Supp. XVI:** 17–18
Winter of Our Discontent, The (Steinbeck), **IV:** 52, 65–66, 68
"Winter on Earth" (Toomer), **Supp. III Part 2:** 486
"Winter Piece, A" (Bryant), **Supp. I Part 1:** 150, 155

"Winter Rains, Cataluña" (Levine), **Supp. V:** 182
"Winter Remembered" (Ransom), **III:** 492–493
"Winter Roses" (W. V. Davis), **Supp. XXI:** 94
Winterrowd, Prudence, **I:** 217, 224
Winters, Ivor, **Retro. Supp. III:** 50
Winters, Jonathan, **Supp. XI:** 305
Winters, Yvor, **I:** 59, 63, 386, 393, 397, 398, 402, 471; **III:** 194, 498; **IV:** 153; **Retro. Supp. II:** 76, 77, 78, 82, 83, 85, 89; **Supp. I Part 1:** 268; **Supp. II Part 2:** 416, 666, **785–816; Supp. IV Part 2:** 480; **Supp. V:** 180, 191–192; **Supp. XIV:** 287; **Supp. XV:** 74, 341; **Supp. XXV:** 250
"Winter Sacrament" (Bronk), **Supp. XXI:** 33
"Winter Scenes" (Bryant). See "Winter Piece, A"
Winterset (Anderson), **III:** 159
"Winter Shrub, A" (Bronk), **Supp. XXI:** 28
"Winter Skyline Late" (F. Wright), **Supp. XVII:** 245
"Winter Sleep" (Wylie), **Supp. I Part 2:** 711, 729
Winter's Night (Boyce), **Supp. XXI:** 7, **12–13**
Winter's Tale (film, Goldsman), **Supp. XXV:** 86
Winter's Tale (Helprin), **Supp. XXV:** 79–80, 81, 82, 83, 86
Winter's Tale, The (Shakespeare), **Supp. XIII:** 219
Winter Stars (Levis), **Supp. XI:** 259, **266–268**
"Winter Stars" (Levis), **Supp. XI:** 267–268
"Winter Stars" (Teasdale), **Supp. XXVII:** 295
Winter Stop-Over (Everwine), **Supp. XV:** 74, 76
"Winter Stop-Over" (Everwine), **Supp. XV:** 76
Winter Studies and Summer Rambles in Canada (Jameson), **Supp. XXIII:** 225, 226
"Winter Sunrise" (Davison), **Supp. XXVI:** 69
"Winter Swan" (Bogan), **Supp. III Part 1:** 52
"Winter Thunder" (Sandoz), **Supp. XXIV:** 255
Winter Thunder (X. J. Kennedy), **Supp. XV:** 167
"Winter Thunder" (X. J. Kennedy), **Supp. XV:** 169
"Winter Trees" (Pedersen; Nelson, trans.), **Supp. XVIII:** 180
Winter Trees (Plath), **Retro. Supp. II:** 257; **Supp. I Part 2:** 526, 539, 541; **Supp. XXVII:** 296
"Winter Walk" (W. V. Davis), **Supp. XXI:** 92
"Winter Weather Advisory" (Ashbery), **Supp. III Part 1:** 26
"Winter Wheat" (Hoffman), **Supp. XVIII:** 86, 87
"Winter Wind" (Munro), **Supp. XXVII:** 185
"Winter without Snow, The" (C. Frost), **Supp. XV:** 96, 105–106
"Winter Words" (Levine), **Supp. V:** 192
Winthrop, John, **Retro. Supp. III:** 3; **Supp. I Part 1:** 99, 100, 101, 102, 105; **Supp. I Part 2:** 484, 485
Winthrop Covenant, The (Auchincloss), **Supp. IV Part 1:** 23
"Wires of the Night, The" (Collins), **Supp. XXI:** 64
Wirt, William, **I:** 232
Wirth, Louis, **IV:** 475
Wisconsin Death Trip (Lesy), **Supp. XXV:** 146
Wisconsin Death Trip (Levy), **Supp. XIX:** 102
"Wisdom" (Teasdale), **Supp. XXVII:** 291
"Wisdom Cometh with the Years" (Cullen), **Supp. IV Part 1:** 166
Wisdom of the African World (McKnight, ed.), **Supp. XX: 157–158**
Wisdom of the Desert, The: Sayings from the Desert Fathers of the Fourth Century (Merton), **Supp. VIII:** 201
Wisdom of the Heart, The (H. Miller), **III:** 178, 184
Wise Blood (O'Connor), **III:** 337, 338, 339–343, 344, 345, 346, 350, 354, 356, 357; **Retro. Supp. II:** 219, 221, 222, 223, **225–228; Retro. Supp. III:** 208, 209–210, 213, 215
Wise Men, The (Price), **Supp. VI:** 254
"Wiser Than a God" (Chopin), **Retro. Supp. II:** 61; **Supp. I Part 1:** 208
Wishes, Lies, and Dreams: Teaching Children to Write Poetry (Koch), **Supp. XV:** 176, 189; **Supp. XXVII:** 26
"Wish for a Young Wife" (Roethke), **III:** 548
Wishful Thinking: A Theological ABC (Buechner), **Supp. XII:** 53
Wishing Tree, The: Christopher Isherwood on Mystical Religion (Adjemian, ed.), **Supp. XIV:** 164, 173
"Wish List" (Goodman), **Supp. XXVI:** 119–120
Wish You Were Here (O'Nan), **Supp. XXV:** 142, 147–148, 150, 152
Wismer, Helen Muriel. See Thurber, Mrs. James (Helen Muriel Wismer)
Wisse, Ruth, **Supp. XII:** 167, 168
Wister, Owen, **I:** 62; **Retro. Supp. II:** 72; **Supp. XIV:** 39
Wit (Edson), **Supp. XVIII:** 35–36, 37, **38–51**
"Witchbird" (Bambara), **Supp. XI:** 11
"Witch Burning" (Plath), **Supp. I Part 2:** 539
Witchcraft of Salem Village, The (Jackson), **Supp. IX:** 121
"Witch Doctor" (Hayden), **Supp. II Part 1:** 368, 380
Witches of Eastwick, The (Updike), **Retro. Supp. I:** 330, 331
Witch from Castile, The (Asch), **Supp. XXIII:** 6, 10
Witching Hour, The (Rice), **Supp. VII:** 299–300
"Witch of Coös, The" (Frost), **II:** 154–155; **Retro. Supp. I:** 135; **Retro. Supp. II:** 42
"Witch of Owl Mountain Springs, The: An Account of Her Remarkable Powers" (Taylor), **Supp. V:** 328
"Witch of Wenham, The" (Whittier), **Supp. I Part 2:** 694, 696
Witek, Terri, **Supp. XVII:** 117
"With a Little Help from My Friends" (Kushner), **Supp. IX:** 131
With Bold Knife and Fork (M. F. K. Fisher), **Supp. XVII:** 89, 91
"With Che at Kitty Hawk" (Banks), **Supp. V:** 6
"With Che at the Plaza" (Banks), **Supp. V:** 7
"With Che in New Hampshire" (Banks), **Supp. V:** 6
"With Child" (Taggard), **Supp. XXII:** 276, 278
"Withdrawal Symptoms" (Mora), **Supp. XIII:** 216
"Withered Leaf, A—Seen on a Poet's Table" (Very), **Supp. XXV:** 243
"Withered Skins of Berries" (Toomer), **Supp. III Part 2:** 485; **Supp. IX:** 320
Withers, Harry Clay, **Supp. XIII:** 161
Witherspoon, John, **Supp. I Part 2:** 504
With Eyes at the Back of Our Heads

(Levertov), **Supp. III Part 1:** 276–277
With Her in Ourland (Gilman), **Supp. XI:** 208–209
With His Pistol in His Hand (Paredes), **Supp. XIII:** 225; **Supp. XIX:** 98
"Within the Words: An Apprenticeship" (Haines), **Supp. XII:** 197
"With Kit, Age 7, at the Beach" (Stafford), **Supp. XI:** 323
With Love to Lesbia (Kenny), **Supp. XXIII:** 145
"With Mercy for the Greedy" (Sexton), **Supp. II Part 2:** 680
With My Trousers Rolled (Epstein), **Supp. XIV:** 101, 105
Without a Hero (Boyle), **Supp. VIII:** 16; **Supp. XX: 20**
Without Feathers (Allen), **Supp. XV:** 3, 14, 15
Without Stopping (Bowles), **Supp. IV Part 1:** 79, 81, 85, 90, 91, 92
"Without Tradition and within Reason: Judge Horton and Atticus Finch in Court" (C. D. Johnson), **Supp. VIII:** 127
With Shuddering Fall (Oates), **Supp. II Part 2:** 504–506
"With the Dog at Sunrise" (Kenyon), **Supp. VII:** 170
With the Empress Dowager of China (Carl), **III:** 475
"With the Horse in the Winter Pasture" (McCarriston), **Supp. XIV:** 262
With the Old Breed: At Peleliu and Okinawa (Sledge), **Supp. V:** 249–250
"With the Violin" (Chopin), **Retro. Supp. II:** 61
"Witness" (Clampitt), **Supp. IX:** 42–43, 45, 46
"Witness" (Dubus), **Supp. VII:** 89
"Witness" (Harjo), **Supp. XII:** 227–228
Witness (McNally), **Supp. XIII:** 197
"Witness" (Nelson), **Supp. XVIII:** 186
"Witness, The" (Porter), **III:** 443–444
"Witness for Poetry, A" (Stafford), **Supp. XI:** 324
"Witness for the Defense" (Hay), **Supp. XIV:** 124
"Witnessing My Father's Will" (Karr), **Supp. XI:** 241
"Witnessing to a Shared World" (Sanders), **Supp. XVI:** 278
Witness to the Times! (McGrath), **Supp. X:** 118
Witness Tree, A (Frost), **II:** 155; **Retro. Supp. I:** 122, 137, 139; **Retro. Supp. III:** 104
Wit's End: Days and Nights of the Algonquin Round Table (Gaines), **Supp. IX:** 190
Wits Recreations (Mennes and Smith), **II:** 111
Witt, Shirley Hill, **Supp. IV Part 2:** 505
Witte, John, **Supp. XX: 200**
Wittels, Anne F., **Supp. XV:** 59
Wittenberg, Judith Bryant, **Retro. Supp. II:** 146
Wittgenstein, Ludwig, **Retro. Supp. I:** 53; **Supp. III Part 2:** 626–627; **Supp. X:** 304; **Supp. XII:** 21; **Supp. XV:** 344, 346
Wittgensteins' Mistress (Markson), **Supp. XVII:** 135, 142, 143, 145
Wittliff, William, **Supp. V:** 227
"Witty War, A" (Simpson), **Supp. IX:** 268
Witz (Cohen), **Supp. XXII:** 268
"Wives and Mistresses" (Hardwick), **Supp. III Part 1:** 211–212
"Wives of the Dead, The" (Hawthorne), **Retro. Supp. III:** 110–111
Wizard of Loneliness, The (Nichols), **Supp. XIII:** 259, 263, 264
Wizard of Oz, The (Baum), **Supp. IV Part 1:** 113
Wizard of Oz, The (film), **Supp. X:** 172, 214
Wizard's Tide, The: A Story (Buechner), **Supp. XII:** 54
"WLT (The Edgar Era)" (Keillor), **Supp. XVI:** 172
WLT: A Radio Romance (Keillor), **Supp. XVI:** 176
Wobegon Boy (Keillor), **Supp. XVI:** 177
Wodehouse, P. G., **Supp. IX:** 195; **Supp. XXI:** 204–205
Woiwode, Larry, **Supp. VIII:** 151; **Supp. XVI:** 206
Wojahn, David, **Supp. IX:** 161, 292, 293; **Supp. XXI:** 130, 131, 132, 138, 139, 141
Wolcott, Derek, **Retro. Supp. III:** 318
Wolcott, James, **Supp. IX:** 259
Wolf, Christa, **Supp. IV Part 1:** 310, 314
Wolf, Daniel, **Retro. Supp. II:** 202
Wolf, Robert L., **Supp. XXII:** 274, 277, 279, 280
Wolf: A False Memoir (Harrison), **Supp. VIII:** 40, **41–42,** 45
Wolfe, Ben, **IV:** 454
Wolfe, Gregory, **Supp. XIV:** 307
Wolfe, James, **Supp. I Part 2:** 498
Wolfe, Linnie, **Supp. IX:** 176
Wolfe, Mabel, **IV:** 454
Wolfe, Thomas, **I:** 288, 289, 374, 478, 495; **II:** 457; **III:** 40, 108, 278, 334, 482; **IV:** 52, 97, 357, **450–473; Retro. Supp. I:** 382; **Supp. I Part 1:** 29; **Supp. IV Part 1:** 101; **Supp. IX:** 229; **Supp. X:** 225; **Supp. XI:** 213, 216, 217, 218; **Supp. XIII:** 17; **Supp. XIV:** 122; **Supp. XVIII:** 78; **Supp. XX: 163; Supp. XXVII:** 38
Wolfe, Tom, **Supp. III Part 2: 567–588; Supp. IV Part 1:** 35, 198; **Supp. V:** 296; **Supp. X:** 264; **Supp. XI:** 239; **Supp. XV:** 143; **Supp. XVII:** 202; **Supp. XVIII:** 72, 117; **Supp. XXIV:** 282, 283
Wolfe, William Oliver, **IV:** 454
Wolfe, Mrs. William Oliver (Julia Elizabeth Westall), **IV:** 454
"Wolfe Homo Scribens" (Cowley), **Supp. II Part 1:** 144
Wolfert, Ira, **Supp. XXI: 261–279**
Wolfert's Roost (Irving), **II:** 314
Wolff, Cynthia Griffin, **Retro. Supp. I:** 379; **Supp. IV Part 1:** 203
Wolff, Donald, **Supp. XIII:** 316, 317, 326
Wolff, Geoffrey, **Supp. II Part 1:** 97; **Supp. XI:** 239, 245, 246; **Supp. XXII:** 206, 211; **Supp. XXV:** 217
Wolff, Tobias, **Retro. Supp. I:** 190; **Supp. V:** 22; **Supp. VII: 331–346; Supp. X:** 1; **Supp. XI:** 26, 239, 245, 246, 247; **Supp. XV:** 223; **Supp. XVI:** 39, 41, 63, 70, 77; **Supp. XXIII:** 289; **Supp. XXV:** 142, 208
"Wolf in the Bed, The"(Hadas), **Supp. XXIII:** 118
Wolfreys, Julian, **Supp. XVIII:** 61
"Wolfshead" (Howard), **Supp. XXVII:** 116, 119
Wolfson, P. J., **Supp. XIII:** 172
"Wolf Town" (Carson), **Supp. XII: 102**
Wolf Willow: A History, a Story, and a Memory of the Last Plains Frontier (Stegner), **Supp. IV Part 2:** 595, 596, 597, 598, 599, 600, 601, 604, 606, 611, 613, 614
Wolitzer, Hilma, **Supp. XV:** 55; **Supp. XXIII:** 108
Wolitzer, Meg, **Supp. XV:** 65
Wolkomir, Richard, **Supp. XXII:** 218
Wollaston, William, **II:** 108
Wollstonecraft, Mary, **Supp. I Part 1:** 126; **Supp. I Part 2:** 512, 554
"Wolves in the Asheville Zoo, The" (Rash), **Supp. XXVII:** 220
"Wolves in the Marsh" (Dubus III), **Supp. XXIV:** 99–100
Womack, Craig, **Supp. XXIII:** 147, 153, 154–155

"Woman" (Bogan), **Supp. X:** 102
"Woman, I Got the Blues" (Komunyakaa), **Supp. XIII:** 117
"Woman, Why Are You Weeping?" (Kenyon), **Supp. VII:** 174–175
"Woman, Young and Old, A" (Paley), **Supp. VI:** 222, 225
Woman Aroused, The (Lacy), **Supp. XV:** 199–200
"Woman at the Pond, The" (Rash), **Supp. XXVII:** 215, 230
Woman at the Washington Zoo, The (Jarrell), **II:** 367, 386, 387, 389
Woman Before an Aquarium (Hampl), **Supp. XXII:** 83, 86, 98
"Woman Before an Aquarium" (Hampl), **Supp. XXII:** 85, 98
"Womand and the Woman's Movement" (Briggs), **Supp. XVIII:** 14
"Woman Dead in Her Forties, A" (Rich), **Retro. Supp. III:** 249; **Supp. I Part 2:** 574–575
Woman Driver, The (Thompson), **Supp. XXIII:** 291, **294–295**
"Woman Enough" (Gallagher), **Supp. XXIV:** 169
"Woman Hanging from the Thirteenth Floor Window, The" (Harjo), **Supp. XII:** 216, 221
"Woman Hollering Creek" (Cisneros), **Supp. VII:** 70
Woman Hollering Creek and Other Stories (Cisneros), **Supp. VII:** 58, 68–70
"Womanhood" (Brooks), **Supp. III Part 1:** 77
"Woman in Rain" (X. J. Kennedy), **Supp. XV:** 168
Woman in the Dark (Hammett), **Supp. IV Part 1:** 343
"Woman in the House, A" (Caldwell), **I:** 310
Woman in the Nineteenth Century (Fuller), **Retro. Supp. I:** 156; **Supp. II Part 1:** 279, 292, 294–296; **Supp. XI:** 197, 203; **Supp. XVIII:** 3, 11
"Woman in the Shoe, The" (Ryan as Quin), **Supp. XVIII:** 231
Woman in White, The (Collins), **Supp. I Part 1:** 35, 36
"Woman Is Talking to Death, A"(Grahn), **Supp. XXIII:** 195
"Womanizer, The" (Ford), **Supp. V:** 71, 72
"Woman Like Yourself, A" (C. Frost), **Supp. XV:** 107
Woman Lit by Fireflies, The (Harrison), **Supp. VIII: 50–51**
"Woman Loses Cookie Bake-Off, Sets Self on Fire" (R. O. Butler), **Supp. XII:** 72
Woman of Andros, The (Wilder), **IV:** 356, 363–364, 367, 368, 374
Woman of Means, A (Taylor), **Supp. V:** 319–320
"Woman of Tomorrow, The" (Atherton), **Supp. XXIV:** 29
Woman on the Edge of Time (Piercy), **Supp. XIII:** 29
Woman on the Porch, The (Gordon), **II:** 199, 209–211
"Woman on the Stair, The" (MacLeish), **III:** 15–16
"Woman's Dream, A" (E. Stoddard), **Supp. XV:** 278
Woman's Fiction: A Guide to Novels By and About Women in America, 1820–1870 (Baym), **Supp. XVIII:** 258
"Woman's Heartlessness" (Thaxter), **Retro. Supp. II:** 147
Woman's Honor (Glaspell), **Supp. III Part 1:** 179
"Woman Singing" (Ortiz), **Supp. IV Part 2:** 513
Woman's Place, A (C. L. R. James and Weinstein), **Supp. XXI:** 170
Woman's Share in Primitive Culture (Mason), **Supp. I Part 1:** 18
"Woman Struck by Car Turns into Nymphomaniac" (R. O. Butler), **Supp. XII:** 72
"Woman's Work" (Alvarez), **Supp. VII:** 4
"Woman Taken in Adultery, A"(Thompson), **Supp. XXIII:** 300
"Woman Uses Glass Eye to Spy on Philandering Husband" (R. O. Butler), **Supp. XII:** 70, 72
Woman Warrior (Kingston), **Supp. IV Part 1:** 12; **Supp. V:** 157, 158, 159, 160–164, 166, 169; **Supp. X:** 291–292; **Supp. XIV:** 162
Woman Warrior, The (Kingston), **Supp. XV:** 220
"Woman Who Believed in Jaguars, The" (Rash), **Supp. XXVII:** 228
Woman Who Fell from the Sky, The (Harjo), **Supp. XII: 226–228**
"Woman Who Fell From the Sky, The" (Iroquois creation story), **Supp. IV Part 1:** 327
Woman Who Owned the Shadows, The (Gunn Allen), **Supp. IV Part 1:** 320, 322, 326, 327–328
"Woman Who Plays Trumpet Is Deported, A" (Cliff), **Supp. XXII:** 74
"Woman Who Prayed, The" (Gallagher), **Supp. XXIV:** 175
"Woman Who Raised Goats, The" (Gallagher), **Supp. XXIV:** 168
"Woman Who Went Backwards, The"(Schott), **Supp. XXIII:** 241
Woman Within, The (Glasgow), **II:** 183, 190–191
"Womanwork" (Gunn Allen), **Supp. IV Part 1:** 326
Women (Bukowski), **Supp. XI:** 172
"Women" (Didion), **Supp. IV Part 1:** 205
"Women" (Swenson), **Supp. IV Part 2:** 647
Women, The (Boyle), **Supp. XX: 24, 26–27**
Women, The (film), **Retro. Supp. I:** 113
Women, The (film; Cukor), **Supp. XVI:** 181, 192
Women, Violence, and Testimony in the Works of Zora Neale Hurston (Miles), **Retro. Supp. III:** 139
"Women and Children First" (Prose), **Supp. XVI:** 254
Women and Children First: Stories (Prose), **Supp. XVI:** 254
Women and Economics (Gilman), **Supp. I Part 2:** 637; **Supp. V:** 284; **Supp. XI:** 200, **203–204,** 206
"Women and Honor: Some Notes on Lying" (Rich), **Retro. Supp. III:** 247–248
"Women and Poetry" (Notley), **Supp. XXII:** 236
Women and Thomas Harrow (Marquand), **III:** 50, 61, 62, 66, 68, 69–70, 71
Women and Vodka (Markson as Merrill, ed.), **Supp. XVII:** 136
Women and Wilderness (LaBastille), **Supp. X:** 97, **102–104**
"Women as They Are" (Rowson), **Supp. XV:** 243
Women at Point Sur, The (Jeffers), **Supp. II Part 2:** 430–431
Women Authors of Our Day in Their Homes (Halsey), **Supp. XXIV:** 20
Women in Love (Lawrence), **III:** 27, 34; **Supp. XXIV:** 58
Women in Praise of the Sacred: 43 Centuries of Spiritual Poetry by Women (Hirshfield, ed.), **Supp. XXIII:** 136, 137
"Women of Auschwitz, The" (Gallagher), **Supp. XXIV:** 171
Women of Belize: Gender and Change in Central America (McClaurin), **Supp. XXIII:** 84
Women of Brewster Place, The: A Novel in Seven Stories (Naylor),

Supp. VIII: 213, **214–218**
Women of Manhattan: An Upper West Side Story (Shanley), **Supp. XIV:** 315, **326–327**
"Women of My Color" (Coleman), **Supp. XI:** 88–89
Women of Mystery: The Lives and Works of Notable Women Crime Novelists (DuBose), **Supp. XXV:** 199
Women of Trachis (Pound, trans.), **III:** 476
"Women on the Breadlines"(Le Sueur), **Supp. XXIII:** 166, 167
Women on the Wall, The (Stegner), **Supp. IV Part 2:** 599, 605, 606
Women Poets in English (Stanford, ed.), **Retro. Supp. I:** 41
"Women Reformers and American Culture, 1870–1930" (Conway), **Supp. I Part 1:** 19
Women's Barracks (T. Levin), **Supp. XXVII:** 140
"Women's Movement, The" (Didion), **Supp. IV Part 1:** 206
"Women Waiting" (Shields), **Supp. VII:** 320
"Women We Love Whom We Never See Again" (R. Bly), **Supp. IV Part 1:** 66
"Women We Never See Again" (R. Bly), **Supp. IV Part 1:** 66
Women Who Make Our Novels, The (Overton), **Supp. XXV:** 200
Women with Men (Ford), **Supp. V:** 57, 71–72
"Wonder" (Olds), **Supp. X:** 210
Wonder-Book for Girls and Boys, A (Hawthorne), **Retro. Supp. III:** 121
Wonder Boys (Chabon), **Supp. XI:** 67, **73–75,Supp. XI:** 78; **Supp. XVI:** 259
Wonder Boys (film), **Supp. XI:** 67
Wonderful O, The (Thurber), **Supp. I Part 2:** 612
"Wonderful Old Gentleman, The" (Parker), **Supp. IX:** 197
"Wonderful Pen, The" (Swenson), **Supp. IV Part 2:** 650
Wonderful Wizard of Oz, The (Baum), **Supp. XXV:** 129
Wonderful Words, Silent Truth: Essays on Poetry and a Memoir (Simic), **Supp. VIII:** 270
Wonder Hat and Other One-Act Plays, The (Hecht and Goodman), **Supp. XXVII:** 89
Wonderland (Oates), **Supp. II Part 2:** 511, 512, 514–515
Wonders Hidden (Sanders), **Supp. XVI:** 269
Wonders of the African World (television series), **Supp. XX: 99**
Wonders of the Invisible World, The (Mather), **Supp. II Part 2:** 456–459, 460, 467
Wonder-Working Providence (E. Johnson), **IV:** 157
Wong, Hertha, **Supp. IV Part 1:** 275
Wong, Jade Snow, **Supp. X:** 291
Wong, Nellie, **Supp. XVII:** 72
Wong, Shawn, **Supp. XV:** 221
Wong, Timothy, **Supp. XVIII:** 94
"Wood" (Nye), **Supp. XIII:** 276
Wood, Audrey, **IV:** 381
Wood, Charles Erskine Scott, **Supp. XV:** 301
Wood, Clement, **Supp. XV:** 298
Wood, Clement Biddle, **Supp. XI:** 307
Wood, Gaby, **Supp. XXIV:** 166
Wood, Harrison, **Supp. XXII:** 283
Wood, Mrs. Henry, **Supp. I Part 1:** 35
Wood, James, **Supp. XIV:** 95–96; **Supp. XIX:** 138
Wood, Mabel, **I:** 199
Wood, Michael, **Supp. IV Part 2:** 691
Wood, Norman Barton, **Supp. XIV:** 201
Wood, Susan, **Supp. XVI:** 123
Woodard, Calvin, **Supp. VIII:** 128
Woodard, Charles L., **Supp. IV Part 2:** 484, 493
Woodard, Deborah, **Supp. XIII:** 114
Woodberry, George Edward, **III:** 508
Woodbridge, Frederick, **I:** 217, 224
Woodbridge, John, **Retro. Supp. III:** 3, 4; **Supp. I Part 1:** 101, 102, 114
Woodbury, Hanni, **Supp. XXVI:** 8, 82, 87, 90, 95
"Wood-Choppers, The" (Chopin), **Retro. Supp. II:** 72
Woodcock, George, **Supp. XIII:** 33
Woodcome, Beth, **Supp. XVII:** 240
"Wood Dove at Sandy Spring, The" (MacLeish), **III:** 19
"Wooden Spring" (Rukeyser), **Supp. VI:** 285
"Wooden Umbrella, The" (Porter), **IV:** 26
Woodhull, Victoria, **Supp. XVIII:** 4
"Woodnotes" (Emerson), **II:** 7, 19
"Wood-Pile, The" (Frost), **Retro. Supp. I:** 128; **Retro. Supp. III:** 97; **Supp. IV Part 2:** 445
Woodress, James, **Retro. Supp. III:** 21
Woodrow, James, **Supp. I Part 1:** 349, 366
"Woods, Books, and Truant Officers, The" (Maclean), **Supp. XIV:** 221, 225
Woods, James, **Supp. XXVII:** 277
"Woods, New York, The" (Bronk), **Supp. XXI:** 27
Woods, Paula L., **Supp. XXI:** 70
Woods, Robert A., **Supp. I Part 1:** 19
Woods, The (Mamet), **Supp. XIV:** 241, 254–255
Woodson, Jon, **Retro. Supp. III:** 140
Woodswoman (LaBastille), **Supp. X:** 95, **96–99,** 108
Woodswoman III: Book Three of the Woodswoman's Adventures (LaBastille), **Supp. X:** 95, **106–107**
"Wood Thrush" (Kenyon), **Supp. VII:** 172
Woodward, C. Vann, **IV:** 114, 470–471; **Retro. Supp. I:** 75, 76; **Supp. XIX:** 152; **Supp. XXII:** 194
"Woof: A Plea of Sorts" (Saunders), **Supp. XIX:** 235
"Woofing" (Hurston), **Retro. Supp. III:** 137
"Wooing the Inanimate" (Brodsky), **Supp. VIII:** 32
Woolcott, Alexander, **Supp. IX:** 197
Wooley, Bryan, **Supp. V:** 225
Woolf, Douglas, **Supp. XXIII:** 174
Woolf, Leonard, **Supp. IX:** 95
Woolf, Virginia, **I:** 53, 79, 112, 309; **II:** 320, 415; **IV:** 59; **Retro. Supp. I:** 59, 75, 170, 215, 291, 359; **Supp. I Part 2:** 553, 714, 718; **Supp. IV Part 1:** 299; **Supp. IX:** 66, 109; **Supp. V:** 127; **Supp. VIII:** 5, 155, 251, 252, 263, 265; **Supp. XI:** 134, 193; **Supp. XII:** 81, 98, 289; **Supp. XIII:** 305; **Supp. XIV:** 341–342, 342, 343, 346, 348; **Supp. XIX:** 134; **Supp. XV:** 55, 65; **Supp. XXIII:** 275; **Supp. XXVII:** 183
Woollcott, Alexander, **IV:** 432; **Retro. Supp. II:** 327; **Supp. I Part 2:** 664; **Supp. IX:** 190, 194
Woolley, Leonard, **Supp. XXIII:** 33
Woollstonecraft, Mary, **Supp. XVI:** 184
"Woolly Mammoth" (X. J. Kennedy), **Supp. XV:** 163–164
Woolman, John, **Supp. VIII:** 202, 204, 205
Woolson, Constance Fenimore, **Retro. Supp. I:** 224, 228
Woolverton, Linda, **Supp. XXI:** 148
Wooster, David, **Supp. XX: 288**
Worcester, Samuel, **I:** 458
Word and Idioms: Studies in the English Language (L. P. Smith), **Supp. XIV:** 343

"Word by Word" (column, Lamott), **Supp. XX: 140**
"Word from the Outer Dark, A" (Howard), **Supp. XXVII:** 118
"Wordless Winter" (Davison), **Supp. XXVI:** 75–76
Word of God and the Word of Man, The (Barth), **Retro. Supp. I:** 327
"Word out of the Sea, A" (Whitman), **IV:** 344
Words (Creeley), **Supp. IV Part 1:** 139, 150–153, 154, 155, 158
"Words" (Creeley), **Supp. IV Part 1:** 152
"Words" (Gioia), **Supp. XV:** 125
"Words" (Merwin), **Supp. III Part 1:** 352
"Words" (Plath), **Supp. I Part 2:** 547
"Words" (Shields), **Supp. VII:** 323
"Words, The" (Wagoner), **Supp. IX:** 326
"Words above a Narrow Entrance" (Wagoner), **Supp. IX:** 325
"Words for a Bike-Racing, Osprey-Chasing Wine-Drunk Squaw Man" (Gunn Allen), **Supp. IV Part 1:** 325
Words for Dr. Y (Sexton), **Supp. II Part 2:** 698
"Words for Hart Crane" (R. Lowell), **I:** 381; **II:** 547; **Retro. Supp. II:** 188; **Retro. Supp. III:** 41, 54
"Words for Love" (Berrigan), **Supp. XXIV:** 35
"Words for Maria" (Merrill), **Supp. III Part 1:** 327
"Words for My Father" (Davison), **Supp. XXVI:** 72
"Words for My Grandmother"(Balakian), **Supp. XXIII:** 19, 20
Words for the Chisel (Taggard), **Supp. XXII: 276–277**
"Words for the Unknown Makers" (Kunitz), **Supp. III Part 1:** 264
Words for the Wind (Roethke), **III:** 529, 533, 541, 543, 545
"Words for the Wind" (Roethke), **III:** 542–543
Words in the Mourning Time (Hayden), **Supp. II Part 1:** 361, 366, 367
"Words in the Mourning Time" (Hayden), **Supp. II Part 1:** 370–371
"Words into Fiction" (Welty), **IV:** 279
"Words into Worlds Won't Go" (Major), **Supp. XXII:** 174
"Words Like Freedom" (Hughes), **Retro. Supp. I:** 207
"Words of a Young Girl" (R. Lowell), **II:** 554
"Words of Prey" (Stallings), **Supp. XXV:** 230
Words under the Words: Selected Poems (Nye), **Supp. XIII:** 277
Wordsworth, Dorothy, **Supp. IX:** 38
Wordsworth, William, **I:** 283, 522, 524, 525, 588; **II:** 7, 11, 17, 18, 97, 169, 273, 303, 304, 532, 549, 552; **III:** 219, 263, 277, 278, 511, 521, 523, 528, 583; **IV:** 120, 331, 343, 453, 465; **Retro. Supp. I:** 121, 196; **Supp. I Part 1:** 150, 151, 154, 161, 163, 312, 313, 349, 365; **Supp. I Part 2:** 375, 409, 416, 422, 607, 621, 622, 673, 674, 675, 676, 677, 710–711, 729; **Supp. II Part 1:** 4; **Supp. III Part 1:** 12, 15, 73, 279; **Supp. IV Part 2:** 597, 601; **Supp. IX:** 38, 41, 265, 274; **Supp. V:** 258; **Supp. VIII:** 273; **Supp. X:** 22, 23, 65, 120; **Supp. XI:** 248, 251, 312; **Supp. XIII:** 214; **Supp. XIV:** 184; **Supp. XIX:** 1; **Supp. XV:** 93, 250; **Supp. XX: 108, 116; Supp. XXI:** 131; **Supp. XXIV:** 74, 159
" 'Word Which Made All Clear, The': The Silent Close of The House of Mirth" (Benstock), **Supp. XX: 240**
Work (Alcott), **Supp. I Part 1:** 32–33, 42
Work (Dixon), **Supp. XII:** 141, **143**
"Work" (Halliday), **Supp. XIX:** 85
"Work" (Huddle), **Supp. XXVI:** 149
"Work" (Oliver), **Supp. VII:** 243
Work and Love (Dunn), **Supp. XI: 147–148**
"Worker" (Coleman), **Supp. XI:** 89
Worker Writers (Le Sueur), **Supp. XXIII:** 165
Working a Passage; or, Life on a Liner (Briggs), **Supp. XVIII:** 2, **9–10**
Working Class Movement in America, The (E. Marx and E. Aveling), **Supp. XVI:** 85
Working Papers: Selected Essays and Reviews (Carruth), **Supp. XVI:** 46
"Working Roots: A Collection of Poetry and Prose" (Trethewey), **Supp. XXI:** 245
"Working the Landscape" (Dunn), **Supp. XI:** 151
Working Through: A Teacher's Journey in the Urban University (Kriegel), **Supp. XXIV: 222–223**
Workin' on the Chain Gang: Shaking Off the Dead Hand of History (Mosley), **Supp. XIII:** 247, 248
Workman, Ross, **Supp. XXVII:** 206, 209–210
"Work Notes '66" (Baraka), **Supp. II Part 1:** 47
Work of Art (Lewis), **II:** 453–454
"Work of Shading, The" (Simic), **Supp. VIII:** 277–278
Work of Stephen Crane, The (Follett, ed.), **I:** 405
"Work on Red Mountain, The" (Harte), **Supp. II Part 1:** 339
Works and Days (Erga Kai H¿merai) (Hesiod; Stallings, trans.), **Supp. XXV:** 221
"Workshop" (Espaillat), **Supp. XXI:** 105
Works of Love, The (Morris), **III:** 223–224, 225, 233
Works of the Late Edgar Allan Poe: With Notices of His Life and Genius (Griswold, Parker, and Lowell, eds.), **Retro. Supp. III:** 236
Works of Witter Bynner, The (Kraft, ed.), **Supp. XV:** 52
"World, The" (Bronk), **Supp. XXI:** 32
"World, The" (Simic), **Supp. VIII:** 282
"World, the Flesh, and the Devil, The"(P. Benedict), **Supp. XXIII:** 48
World, the Worldless, The (Bronk), **Supp. XXI: 29–31**
"World, World—" (Oppen), **Supp. XXVI:** 233
World According to Garp, The (Irving), **Supp. VI:** 163, 164, **170–173,** 181
World and Africa, The: An Inquiry into the Part Which Africa Has Played in World History (Du Bois), **Supp. II Part 1:** 184–185
"World and All Its Teeth, The" (Nye), **Supp. XIII:** 282
"World and the Door, The" (O. Henry), **Supp. II Part 1:** 402
"World and the Jug, The" (Ellison), **Retro. Supp. II:** 112, 119, 123
"World as We Know It, The" (Barresi), **Supp. XV:** 100
World Authors 1950–1970, **Supp. XIII:** 102
World Away, A (O'Nan), **Supp. XXV:** 141, 144–145, 149
World Below, The (Miller), **Supp. XII: 303–304**
World Below the Window, The: Poems 1937–1997 (W. J. Smith), **Supp. XIII:** 332, 340, 345
World Doesn't End, The (Simic), **Supp. VIII:** 272, **279–280**
World Elsewhere, A: The Place of Style in American Literature (Poirier), **I:** 239
"World Ends Here, The" (Harjo), **Supp. XII:** 227–228
World Enough and Time (Warren), **IV:** 243, 253–254

World Gone Wrong (album, Dylan), **Supp. XVIII:** 28
"World I Live In, The" (T. Williams), **IV:** 388
World I Never Made, A (Farrell), **II:** 34, 35, 424
World in the Attic, The (Morris), **III:** 222–223, 224
World in the Evening, The (Isherwood), **Supp. XIV:** 157, 164, 165, **166–167,** 170
World Is a Wedding, The (Schwartz), **Supp. II Part 2:** 643, 654–660
"World Is a Wedding, The" (Schwartz), **Supp. II Part 2:** 655–656, 657
"World Is Too Much with Us, The" (Wordsworth), **Supp. I Part 1:** 312
Worldly Hopes (Ammons), **Supp. VII:** 34
Worldly Philosophers, The (Heilbroner), **Supp. I Part 2:** 644, 650
World Made Straight, The (film), **Supp. XXVII:** 222
World Made Straight, The (Rash), **Supp. XXVII:** 222, 224, 228, 229
World of Apples, The (Cheever), **Supp. I Part 1:** 191, 193
World of David Wagoner, The (McFarland), **Supp. IX:** 323
"World of Easy Rawlins, The" (Mosley), **Supp. XIII:** 234, 236
World of Gwendolyn Brooks, The (Brooks), **Supp. III Part 1:** 83, 84
World of H. G. Wells, The (Brooks), **I:** 240, 241, 242
World of Light, A (Skloot), **Supp. XX: 196, 205, 206–207**
"World of Light, A" (Skloot), **Supp. XX: 194, 207**
World of Light, A: Portraits and Celebrations (Sarton), **Supp. III Part 1:** 62; **Supp. VIII:** 249, 253, 262
World of Our Fathers: The Journey of the Eastern European Jews to America and the Life They Found and Made (Howe), **Supp. VI:** 113, 114, 116, 118, 119, **120–125; Supp. XIV:**104; **Supp. XXIII:** 3; **Supp. XXIV:** 220–221
"World of Pure Experience, A" (James), **II:** 356–357
World of Raymond Chandler, The (Spender), **Supp. IV Part 1:** 119
World of Sex, The (H. Miller), **III:** 170, 178, 187
"World of the Perfect Tear, The" (McGrath), **Supp. X:** 116, 118
World of the Ten Thousand Things, The: Selected Poems (Wright), **Supp. V:** 333
"World of Tomorrow, The" (White), **Supp. I Part 2:** 663
World of Washington Irving, The (Brooks), **I:** 256–257
World of Willa Cather, The (Bannet), **Retro. Supp. III:** 18
World Over, The (Wharton), **Retro. Supp. I:** 382
World Revolution (C. L. R. James), **Supp. XXI:** 167
"Worlds" (Goldbarth), **Supp. XII:** 183, 189
World's Body, The (Ransom), **III:** 497, 499; **Supp. II Part 1:** 146
World's End (Boyle), **Supp. VIII: 11–12; Supp. XX: 22–23**
World's End and Other Stories (Theroux), **Supp. VIII:** 322
"World's Fair" (Berryman), **I:** 173
World's Fair (Doctorow), **Supp. IV Part 1:** 217, 224, 227–229, 234, 236–237
World's Fair, The (Fitzgerald), **II:** 93
Worlds of Color (Du Bois), **Supp. II Part 1:** 185–186
"Worlds of Color" (Du Bois), **Supp. II Part 1:** 175
World So Wide (Lewis), **II:** 456
"World's Worst Boyfriends, The" (Wasserstein), **Supp. XV:** 328
"World-Telegram" (Berryman), **I:** 173
World to Come, The (D. Horn), **Supp. XVII:** 50
"World Trade Center / Mail runner / '73"(Balakian), **Supp. XXIII:** 32–33
World View on Race and Democracy: A Study Guide in Human Group Relations (Locke), **Supp. XIV:** 205, 206
World within the Word, The (Gass), **Supp. VI:** 77
"World Without Objects Is a Sensible Place, A" (Wilbur), **Supp. III Part 2:** 550
"World Without Rodrigo, The" (Cisneros), **Supp. VII:** 68
"Worm Moon" (Oliver), **Supp. VII:** 234
Wormser, Baron, **Supp. XXIII:** 57
"Worms of the Earth" (Howard), **Supp. XXVII:** 123–124
"Worn Path, A" (Welty), **IV:** 262; **Retro. Supp. I:** 345–346
"Worsening Situation" (Ashbery), **Supp. III Part 1:** 17–18
"Worship" (Emerson), **II:** 2, 4–5
"Worship" (H. Johnson), **Supp. XXVI:** 172
"Worship and Church Bells" (Paine), **Supp. I Part 2:** 521
Worster, Donald, **Supp. IX:** 19
Worthington, Marjorie, **Supp. XII:** 13
Wouk, Herman, **Supp. XX: 243; Supp. XXV: 253–270; Supp. XXVII:** 134, 147
Wouldn't Take Nothing for My Journey Now (Angelou), **Supp. IV Part 1:** 10, 12, 14, 15, 16
"Wound" (Pedersen; Nelson, trans.), **Supp. XVIII:** 180
Wound and the Bow, The: Seven Studies in Literature (Wilson), **IV:** 429; **Supp. XXIV:** 217
Wounded (Everett), **Supp. XVIII:** 54, **64,** 65
Wounds in the Rain (Crane), **I:** 409, 414, 423
Woven Stone (Ortiz), **Supp. IV Part 2:** 501, 514
Woven Stories (Ortiz), **Supp. IV Part 2:** 503
"Wraith, The" (Roethke), **III:** 542
"Wrath of God, The" (Fante), **Supp. XI:** 160, 164
"Wreath for a Bridal" (Plath), **Supp. I Part 2:** 537
"Wreath for Emmet Till, A" (Nelson), **Supp. XVIII:** 177
Wreath for Emmett Till, A (Nelson), **Supp. XVIII:** 171, 173, 175, 181, **183–185**
Wreath for Garibaldi and Other Stories, A (Garrett), **Supp. VII:** 99–101
"Wreath of Women" (Rukeyser), **Supp. VI:** 280
Wreckage (Jin), **Supp. XVIII: 98–99**
Wreckage of Agathon, The (Gardner), **Supp. VI:** 63, **65–66**
Wrecking Crew (Levis), **Supp. XI: 259–260**
Wrecking Yard, The (Benedict), **Supp. XXIII:** 35, **39–41**
"Wrecking Yard, The (P. Benedict), **Supp. XXIII:** 39–40
"Wreck of Rivermouth, The" (Whittier), **Supp. I Part 2:** 694, 696–697
"Wreck of the Deutschland" (Hopkins), **Supp. X:** 61
"Wreck of the Hesperus, The" (Longfellow), **Retro. Supp. II:** 168, 169
Wrestler's Cruel Study, The (Dobyns), **Supp. XIII: 82–83**
"Wrestler with Sharks, A" (Yates), **Supp. XI:** 341
"Wrestling with Augie March" (Kriegel), **Supp. XXIV:** 220

Wright, Bernie, **I:** 191, 193
Wright, C. D. (Carolyn Doris), **Supp. XV: 337–355**
Wright, Charles, **Supp. V:** 92, **331–346; Supp. VIII:** 272; **Supp. XIII:** 114; **Supp. XVII:** 71; **Supp. XXI:** 95, 255; **Supp. XXIV:** 155
Wright, Chauncey, **II:** 344
Wright, Conrad, **Supp. XXIV:** 71, 72
Wright, Farnworth, **Supp. XXVII:** 120, 125
Wright, Frank Lloyd, **I:** 104, 483
Wright, Franz, **Supp. XVII: 239–249**
Wright, George, **III:** 479
Wright, Harold Bell, **II:** 467–468
Wright, Holly, **Supp. VIII:** 272
Wright, James, **I:** 291; **Supp. III Part 1:** 249; **Supp. III Part 2:** 541, **589–607; Supp. IV Part 1:** 60, 72; **Supp. IV Part 2:** 557, 558, 561, 566, 571, 623; **Supp. IX:** 152, 155, 159, 265, 271, 290, 293, 296; **Supp. V:** 332; **Supp. X:** 69, 127; **Supp. XI:** 150; **Supp. XII:** 217; **Supp. XIII:** 76; **Supp. XIX:** 122, 273; **Supp. XV:** 79, 93, 212; **Supp. XVII:** 239, 241, 243, 244; **Supp. XXVI:** 68
Wright, Nathalia, **IV:** 155
Wright, Philip Green, **III:** 578, 579, 580
Wright, Richard, **II:** 586; **IV:** 40, **474–497; Retro. Supp. II:** 4, 111, 116, 120; **Retro. Supp. III:** 131, 140; **Supp. I Part 1:** 51, 52, 64, 332, 337; **Supp. II Part 1:** 17, 40, 221, 228, 235, 250; **Supp. IV Part 1:** 1, 11, 84, 374; **Supp. IX:** 316; **Supp. VIII:** 88; **Supp. X:** 131, 245, 254; **Supp. XI:** 85; **Supp. XII:** 316; **Supp. XIII:** 46, 233; **Supp. XIV:** 73; **Supp. XVI:** 135, 139, 141, 143; **Supp. XVIII:** 277, 282, 286; **Supp. XXI:** 169; **Supp. XXIII:** 166
Wright, Mrs. Richard (Ellen Poplar), **IV:** 476
Wright, Sarah, **Supp. IV Part 1:** 8; **Supp. XIII:** 295
Wright, William, **Retro. Supp. II:** 76, 77; **Retro. Supp. III:** 45
Wrigley, Robert, **Supp. XVIII: 293–308**
"Writer" (Sanders), **Supp. XVI:** 277
"Writer, The" (Wilbur), **Supp. III Part 2:** 561, 562
"Writer and the Jewish Community, The" (Levin), **Supp. XXVII:** 134
"Writer as Alaskan, The" (Haines), **Supp. XII:** 199
Writer in America, The (Brooks), **I:** 253, 254, 257
Writer in America, The (Stegner), **Supp. IV Part 2:** 597, 599, 607
"Writers" (R. Lowell), **II:** 554
Writer's Almanac, The (Keillor, radio program), **Supp. XIII:** 274; **Supp. XVI:** 178; **Supp. XXIII:** 138
Writer's America, A: Landscape in Literature (Kazin), **Supp. VIII:** 106
Writers and Their Craft (Delbanco, ed.), **Supp. XXII:** 204
"Writer's Bed, A" (Mirvis), **Supp. XX: 179**
Writer's Capital, A (Auchincloss), **Supp. IV Part 1:** 21, 23, 24, 31
"Writer's Credo, A" (Abbey), **Supp. XIII:** 1, 17
Writer's Eye, A: Collected Book Reviews (Welty), **Retro. Supp. I:** 339, 354, 356
Writers in America (Schulberg), **Supp. XVIII:** 242, 243, 250, 254
Writers in Revolt (Southern, Seaver, and Trocchi, eds.), **Supp. XI:** 301
Writer's Life, A (Talese), **Supp. XVII:** 208–209, 210
Writer's Notebook, A (Maugham), **Supp. X:** 58
Writers on America (U.S. Department of State, ed.), **Supp. XIII:** 288
Writers on the Left (Aaron), **IV:** 429; **Supp. II Part 1:** 137
Writers on Writing (Prose), **Supp. XVI:** 259
"Writer's Prologue to a Play in Verse" (W. C. Williams), **Retro. Supp. I:** 424
"Writer's Quest for a Parnassus, A" (T. Williams), **IV:** 392
Writers' Workshop (University of Iowa), **Supp. V:** 42
"Writers Workshop, The" (Conroy), **Supp. XVI:** 76
"Writing" (Nemerov), **III:** 275
"Writing About the Universe" (Mosley), **Supp. XIII:** 247
"Writing American Fiction" (P. Roth), **Retro. Supp. II:** 279; **Supp. I Part 1:** 192; **Supp. I Part 2:** 431; **Supp. III Part 2:** 414, 420, 421; **Supp. V:** 45
"Writing and a Life Lived Well" (Patchett), **Supp. XII:** 308
"Writing and Writers: Disjecta Membra" (Sorrentino), **Supp. XXI:** 235
Writing a Woman's Life (Heilbrun), **Supp. IX:** 66
"Writing Between Worlds" (Mirvis), **Supp. XX: 177, 178, 179**
Writing Brave and Free: Encouraging Words for People Who Want to Start Writing (Kooser and Cox), **Supp. XIX:** 116, 128
Writing Chicago: Modernism, Ethnography, and the Novel (Cappetti), **Supp. IX:** 4, 8
Writing Creative Nonfiction: The Literature of Reality (Talese and Lounsberry, eds.), **Supp. XVII:** 208
Writing Dylan: The Songs of a Lonesome Traveler (Smith), **Supp. XVIII:** 22
Writing from the Center (Sanders), **Supp. XVI:** 266, 275–276
"Writing from the Inside Out: Style Is Not the Frosting; It's the Cake" (Robbins), **Supp. X:** 266
Writing Habit, The (Huddle), **Supp. XXVI:** 152, 160
"Writing Habit, The" (Huddle), **Supp. XXVI:** 160
"Writing here last autumn of my hopes of seeing a hoopoe" (Updike), **Retro. Supp. I:** 335
Writing Home (Crooker), **Supp. XXIII:** 54
Writing in an Age of Silence (Paretsky), **Supp. XXV:** 169, 181
Writing in Restaurants (Mamet), **Supp. XIV:** 246
"Writing Is Work" (Rinehart), **Supp. XXV:** 198
"Writing Lesson, The" (Gordon), **Supp. IV Part 1:** 306
Writing Life, The (Dillard), **Supp. VI:** 23, 31
"Writing of Apollinaire, The" (Zukofsky), **Supp. III Part 2:** 616, 617
"Writing of Fearless Jones, The" (Mosley), **Supp. XIII:** 242
Writing on the Wall, The, and Literary Essays (McCarthy), **II:** 579
Writings to an Unfinished Accompaniment (Merwin), **Supp. III Part 1:** 352
"Writing the Rez: Popular Obsessions in the Works of Eric Gansworth" (de la Paz and Purdy), **Supp. XXVI:** 102, 111
"Writing the Universe-Mind" (Tabios), **Supp. XV:** 225
Writing the World (Stafford), **Supp. XI:** 314
"Writing to Save Our Lives" (Milligan), **Supp. XIII:** 274
Writing Vietnam, Writing Life: Caputo, Heinemann, O'Brien, Butler (Herzog), **Supp. XXII:** 116
Writin' Is Fightin' (Reed), **Supp. X:** 241

"Writ on the Eve of My 32nd Birthday" (Corso), **Supp. XII:** 129–130
"Written History as an Act of Faith" (Beard), **Supp. I Part 2:** 492
"Written on the Land" (J. W. Miller), **Supp. XX: 170**
"Wrong Man, The" (Larsen), **Supp. XVIII:** 124
"Wrong Notes" (S. Kauffmann), **Supp. XVI:** 74
"Wrought Figure" (McCarriston), **Supp. XIV:** 272
Wrozynski, Henryk, **Supp. XXIII:** 64
"Wunderkind" (McCullers), **II:** 585
Wunderlich, Mark, **Supp. XI:** 119, 132
Wundt, Wilhelm, **II:** 345
Wurlitzer, Rudolph, **Supp. XXVI:** 26
Wurster, William Wilson, **Supp. IV Part 1:** 197
WUSA (film), **Supp. V:** 301
Wuthering Heights (E. Brontë), **Supp. V:** 305; **Supp. X:** 89
Wuthering Heights (screenplay, Hecht and MacArthur), **Supp. XXVII:** 90
WWII (Jones), **Supp. XI:** 219, 231
Wyandotté (Cooper), **I:** 350, 355
Wyatt, Robert B., **Supp. V:** 14
Wyatt, Thomas, **Supp. I Part 1:** 369
Wyce, Marion, **Supp. XXVI:** 57
Wycherly Woman, The (Macdonald), **Supp. IV Part 2:** 473
Wych Hazel (S. and A. Warner), **Supp. XVIII:** 267, **268–269**
Wydra, Ewa. See Hoffman, Eva
Wyeth, Andrew, **Supp. XIX:** 117
Wyler, William, **Supp. XV:** 195
Wylie, Elinor, **IV:** 436; **Supp. I Part 2: 707–730; Supp. III Part 1:** 2, 63, 318–319; **Supp. XI:** 44; **Supp. XIV:** 127; **Supp. XV:** 307; **Supp. XXVII:** 283, 284
Wylie, Horace, **Supp. I Part 2:** 708, 709
Wylie, Philip, **III:** 223
Wyllys, Ruth. See Taylor, Mrs. Edward (Ruth Wyllys)
"Wyoming Valley Tales" (Crane), **I:** 409
Wyzewa, Théodore de, **Supp. XIV:** 336
Xaipe (Cummings), **I:** 430, 432–433, 447
Xarque and Other Poems (G. Jones), **Supp. XXIV:** 194
Xenogenesis trilogy (O. Butler), **Supp. XIII: 63–66,** 69
Xenophon, **II:** 105
X Factor, The: A Quest for Excellence" (Plimpton), **Supp. XVI:** 241
X Files (television series), **Supp. XVI:** 125
Xiaojing, Zhou, **Supp. XV:** 214
Xicana Codex of Changing Consciousness, A: Writings, 2000–2010 (Moraga), **Supp. XXIII:** 197
Xingu and Other Stories (Wharton), **IV:** 314, 320; **Retro. Supp. I:** 378
Xionia (Wright), **Supp. V:** 333
XLI Poems (Cummings), **I:** 429, 432, 440, 443
Xu, Wenying, **Supp. XXVI:** 212
"Xuthal of the Dusk" (Howard), **Supp. XXVII:** 126
Yabroff, Jennie, **Supp. XIX:** 50, 58, 61
Yacoubi, Ahmed, **Supp. IV Part 1:** 88, 92, 93
Yage Letters, The (Burroughs), **Supp. III Part 1:** 94, 98, 100
Yagoda, Ben, **Supp. VIII:** 151
Yamamoto, Isoroku, **Supp. I Part 2:** 491
Yancey's War (Hoffman), **Supp. XVIII:** 71, **75–76**
Yankee City (Warner), **III:** 60
Yankee Clipper (ballet) (Kirstein), **Supp. IV Part 1:** 82
Yankee in Canada, A (Thoreau), **IV:** 188
Yankey in London (Tyler), **I:** 344
"Yánnina" (Merrill), **Supp. III Part 1:** 329
"Yanosz Korczak's Last Walk" (Markowick-Olczakova), **Supp. X:** 70
Yarboro, Chelsea Quinn, **Supp. V:** 147
Yarbro-Bejarano, Yvonne, **Supp. XXIII:** 196, 201
Yardley, Jonathan, **Supp. V:** 326; **Supp. XI:** 67; **Supp. XXIII:** 97, 99, 103, 104, 107, 108, 109
"Yard Sale" (Kenyon), **Supp. VII:** 169
Yates, Richard, **Supp. XI: 333–350; Supp. XXIII:** 289; **Supp. XXIV:** 97; **Supp. XXV:** 154
"Year, The" (Sandburg), **III:** 584
Year at the Races, A (Parker and Parker), **Supp. XIX:** 187
Year Before Last (Boyle), **Supp. XXIV: 52–53**
"Year Between, The" (Neugeboren), **Supp. XVI:** 226
Year in Provence, A (Mayle), **Supp. XVI:** 295
Yearling, The (Rawlings), **Supp. X:** 219, **230–231,** 233, 234; **Supp. XXII:** 195
"Year of Grace" (Swados), **Supp. XIX:** 262–263
Year of Happy, A (Goldbarth), **Supp. XII:** 180
Year of Magical Thinking, The (Didion), **Supp. XXV:** 60, 208
"Year of Mourning, The" (Jeffers), **Supp. II Part 2:** 415
Year of Silence, The (Bell), **Supp. X:** 1, **5–6,** 7
"Year of Silence, The" (Brockmeier), **Supp. XXII:** 59
"Year of the Double Spring, The" (Swenson), **Supp. IV Part 2:** 647
Year's Best Fantasy and Horror, 2004, **Supp. XXII:** 55
Year's Best Science Fiction, The (Merril, ed.), **Supp. XVI:** 123
Year's Life, A (J. R. Lowell), **Supp. I Part 2:** 405
"Years of Birth" (Cowley), **Supp. II Part 1:** 149
Years of Conscience: The Muckrakers: An Anthology of Reform Journalism (Swados, ed.), **Supp. XIX:** 264
Years of My Youth (Howells), **II:** 276
"Years of Wonder" (White), **Supp. I Part 2:** 652, 653
"Years Without Understanding, The" (Weigl), **Supp. XIX:** 282–283
Years With Ross, The (Thurber), **Supp. I Part 2:** 619
Year the Lights Came On, The (Kay), **Supp. XXVII:** 104
Year We Left Home, The (Thompson), **Supp. XXIII:** 301, **302–303**
Yeats, Jack, **Supp. XVI:** 190
Yeats, Jack B., **Supp. XX: 201**
Yeats, John Butler, **III:** 458; **Supp. XX: 69**
Yeats, William Butler, **I:** 69, 172, 384, 389, 403, 434, 478, 494, 532; **II:** 168–169, 566, 598; **III:** 4, 5, 8, 18, 19, 20, 23, 29, 40, 205, 249, 269, 270–271, 272, 278, 279, 294, 347, 409, 457, 458–460, 472, 473, 476–477, 521, 523, 524, 527, 528, 533, 540, 541, 542, 543–544, 591–592; **IV:** 89, 93, 121, 126, 136, 140, 271, 394, 404; **Retro. Supp. I:** 59, 66, 127, 141, 270, 283, 285, 286, 288, 290, 311, 342, 350, 378, 413; **Retro. Supp. II:** 185, 331; **Retro. Supp. III:** 74; **Supp. I Part 1:** 79, 80, 254, 257, 262; **Supp. I Part 2:** 388, 389; **Supp. II Part 1:** 1, 4, 9, 20, 26, 361; **Supp. III Part 1:** 59, 63, 236, 238, 253; **Supp. IV Part 1:** 81; **Supp. IV Part 2:** 634; **Supp. IX:** 43, 119; **Supp. V:** 220; **Supp. VIII:** 19, 21, 30, 155, 156, 190, 239, 262, 292; **Supp. X:** 35, 58, 119, 120;

Supp. XI: 140; **Supp. XII:** 132, 198, 217, 266; **Supp. XIII:** 77, **Supp. XIII:** 87; **Supp. XIV:** 7; **Supp. XV:** 36, 41, 181, 186; **Supp. XVI:** 47–48, 159; **Supp. XVII:** 36; **Supp. XXI:** 61; **Supp. XXVII:** 227, 228
Yee, Amy, **Supp. XVIII:** 93, 94
"Ye Have Your Closes" (Davison), **Supp. XXVI:** 78
Yehuda (Levin), **Supp. XXVII:** 139, 146
Yellin, Jean Fagan, **Supp. XVI:** 88, 89
Yellow Back Radio Broke-Down (Reed), **Supp. X:** 240, 242, **243–245**
"Yellow Dog Café" (Komunyakaa), **Supp. XIII:** 126
Yellow Face (Hwang), **Supp. XXI:** 143, 148**, 154–156**
"Yellow Girl" (Caldwell), **I:** 310
Yellow Glove (Nye), **Supp. XIII:** 275, **276–277**
"Yellow Glove" (Nye), **Supp. XIII:** 276
"Yellow Gown, The" (Anderson), **I:** 114
Yellow House on the Corner, The (Dove), **Supp. IV Part 1:** 244, 245, 246, 254
"Yellow Raft, The" (Connell), **Supp. XIV: 85–86**
"Yellow River" (Tate), **IV:** 141
Yellow Room, The (Rinehart), **Supp. XXV:** 198, 200
"Yellowstone, The"(Kenny), **Supp. XXIII:** 155
"Yellow Violet, The" (Bryant), **Supp. I Part 1:** 154, 155
"Yellow Wallpaper, The" (Gilman), **Supp. XI: 198–199,** 207; **Supp. XVI:** 84
"Yellow Woman" (Keres stories), **Supp. IV Part 1:** 327
"Yellow Woman" (Silko), **Supp. IV Part 2:** 567–568
Yelverton, Theresa, **Supp. IX:** 181
Yenser, Stephen, **Supp. X:** 207, 208; **Supp. XV:** 113–114
"Yentl the Yeshiva Boy" (Singer), **IV:** 15, 20
Yerkes, Charles E., **I:** 507, 512
Yerma (opera) (Bowles), **Supp. IV Part 1:** 89
Yertle the Turtle and Other Stories (Geisel), **Supp. XVI:** 109
"Yes" (Stafford), **Supp. XI:** 329
Yes, Mrs. Williams (W. C. Williams), **Retro. Supp. I:** 423
Yes, Yes, No, No (Kushner), **Supp. IX:** 133
"Yes and It's Hopeless" (Ginsberg), **Supp. II Part 1:** 326
"Yes"(Crooker), **Supp. XXIII:** 62
Yesenin, Sergey, **Supp. VIII:** 40
"Yes: I Mean So OK–Love" (Bronk), **Supp. XXI:** 31
"Yes! No!" (Oliver), **Supp. VII:** 243–244
Yesterday and Today: A Comparative Anthology of Poetry (Untermeyer, ed.), **Supp. XV:** 309
Yesterday's Self: Nostalgia and the Immigrant Identity (Ritivoi), **Supp. XVI:** 148
Yesterday Will Make You Cry (C. Himes), **Supp. XVI:** 137
"Yet Another Example of the Porousness of Certain Borders" (Wallace), **Supp. X:** 309
"Yet Do I Marvel" (Cullen), **Supp. IV Part 1:** 165, 169
Yet Other Waters (Farrell), **II:** 29, 38, 39, 40
"Yevtushenko" (Kooser), **Supp. XIX:** 124
Yevtushenko, Yevgeny, **Supp. III Part 1:** 268
Yezzi, David, **Supp. XII:** 193
Yiddish Policemen's Union, The (Chabon), **Supp. XXII:** 49
Yizkor Book, **Supp. XVI:** 154
...y no se lo tragó la tierra (Rivera), **Supp. XIX:** 99, 101
Y no se lo trago la tierra (And the Earth Did Not Cover Him) (Rivera), **Supp. XIII:** 216
¡Yo! (Alvarez), **Supp. VII:** 1, 15–17
"Yogurt of Vasirin Kefirovsky, The" (Apple), **Supp. XVII:** 3, 4
Yohannan, J. D., **II:** 20
"Yoke, The" (Bidart), **Supp. XV:** 33
"Yom Kippur 1984" (Rich), **Retro. Supp. III:** 250–251
Yonge, Charlotte, **II:** 174
"Yonnondio" (Whitman), **Supp. XIII:** 304
Yonnondio: From the Thirties (Olsen), **Supp. XIII:** 295, 295, **Supp. XIII:** 292, 296, **303–304,** 305
"Yore" (Nemerov), **III:** 283
York, Jake Adam, **Supp. XXI:** 257
York, Lorraine, **Supp. XX: 51**
"York Beach" (Toomer), **Supp. III Part 2:** 486
Yorke, Dorothy, **Supp. I Part 1:** 258
Yorke, Henry Vincent. See Green, Henry
"York Garrison, 1640" (Jewett), **Retro. Supp. II:** 141
Yosemite, The (Muir), **Supp. IX:** 185
"Yosemite Glaciers: Ice Streams of the Great Valley" (Muir), **Supp. IX:** 181
Yoshe Kalb (Singer), **IV:** 2
"You, Andrew Marvell" (MacLeish), **III:** 12–13
"You, Dr. Martin" (Sexton), **Supp. II Part 2:** 673
You, Emperors, and Others: Poems 1957–1960 (Warren), **IV:** 245
"You, Genoese Mariner" (Merwin), **Supp. III Part 1:** 343
"You, Reader" (Collins), **Supp. XXI:** 55
"You, Too, Will Have This Printed Word (World) of Your Own" (Gansworth), **Supp. XXVI:** 114
"You All Know the Story of the Other Woman" (Sexton), **Supp. II Part 2:** 688
"You Are Gorgeous and I'm Coming"(O'Hara), **Supp. XXIII:** 219
You Are Happy (Atwood), **Supp. XIII:** 34
"You Are Happy" (Atwood), **Supp. XIII:** 34
"You Are in Bear Country" (Kumin), **Supp. IV Part 2:** 453, 455
"You Are Not I" (Bowles), **Supp. IV Part 1:** 87
"You Begin" (Atwood), **Supp. XIII:** 34
You Bright and Risen Angels (Vollmann), **Supp. XVII:** 225, 226
"You Bring Out the Mexican in Me" (Cisneros), **Supp. VII:** 71
You Came Along (film), **Supp. IV Part 2:** 524
"You Can Go Home Again" (TallMountain), **Supp. IV Part 1:** 324–325
"You Can Have It" (Levine), **Supp. V:** 188–189
You Can't Go Home Again (Wolfe), **IV:** 450, 451, 454, 456, 460, 462, 468, 469, 470
You Can't Keep a Good Woman Down (Walker), **Supp. III Part 2:** 520, 525, 531
You Can't Pet a Possom (Bontemps), **Supp. XXII:** 4, 12
You Can't Take It with You (Kaufman and Hart), **Supp. XIV:** 327
"You Can't Tell a Man by the Song He Sings" (P. Roth), **Supp. III Part 2:** 406
"You Don't Know Us Negroes" (Hurston), **Retro. Supp. III:** 129
"You Don't Know What Love Is" (Carver), **Supp. III Part 1:** 147

You Don't Love Me Yet (Lethem), **Supp. XVIII: 149–150**
"You Have Left Your Lotus Pods on the Bus" (Bowles), **Supp. IV Part 1:** 91
You Have Seen Their Faces (Caldwell), **I:** 290, 293–294, 295, 304, 309
You Know Me, Al: A Busher's Letters (Lardner), **Supp. XVI:** 189
You Know Me Al (comic strip), **II:** 423
You Know Me Al (Lardner), **II:** 26, 415, 419, 422, 431
"You Know More Than You Think You Do"(Hadas), **Supp. XXIII:** 124
"You Know What" (Beattie), **Supp. V:** 33
"You Know Who You Are" (Nye), **Supp. XIII:** 275
"You Live Like a God" (Cohen), **Supp. XXVII:** 60
You Might As Well Live: The Life and Times of Dorothy Parker (Keats), **Supp. IX:** 190
"You Must Relax!" (J. Scott), **Supp. XVII:** 189
You Must Revise Your Life (Stafford), **Supp. XI:** 312–313, 313–314, 315
"Young" (Sexton), **Supp. II Part 2:** 680
Young, Al, **Supp. X:** 240; **Supp. XXVI:** 12
Young, Art, **IV:** 436
Young, Barbara, **Supp. XX: 119, 123**
Young, Brigham, **Supp. IV Part 2:** 603
Young, Courtland, **Supp. XXII:** 21
Young, David, **Supp. XIX:** 276
Young, Dianne, **Supp. XXII:** 252
Young, Edward, **II:** 111; **III:** 415, 503
Young, Gary, **Supp. XV:** 88
Young, Hershini Bhana, **Supp. XXIV:** 189
Young, Mary, **Supp. XIII:** 236, 238, 239, 240
Young, Philip, **II:** 306; **Retro. Supp. I:** 172
Young, Stark, **Retro. Supp. III:** 74; **Supp. XXII:** 193
Young Adventure (Benét), **Supp. XI:** 44
"Young America" (Brooks), **Supp. XV:** 298
Youngblood Hawke (film), **Supp. XXV:** 263
Youngblood Hawke (Wouk), **Supp. XXV:** 256, 257, 258, 259, 263
"Young Child and His Pregnant Mother, A" (Schwartz), **Supp. II Part 2:** 650
Young Christian, The (Abbott), **Supp. I Part 1:** 38
"Young Dr. Gosse" (Chopin), **Supp. I Part 1:** 211, 216
Younger Choir, The (anthology), **Supp. XV:** 294
Younger Quire, The (Untermeyer), **Supp. XV:** 294, 297
"Young Folks, The" (Salinger), **III:** 551
Young Folk's Cyclopaedia of Persons and Places (Champlin), **III:** 577
"Young Girl's Lament, A" (Jin), **Supp. XVIII:** 99
"Young Goodman Brown" (Hawthorne), **II:** 229; **Retro. Supp. I:** 151–152, 153, 154; **Retro. Supp. III:** 110, 111–112; **Supp. XI:** 51; **Supp. XIV:** 48, 50
Young Harvard: First Poems of Witter Bynner (Bynner), **Supp. XV:** 41
Young Hearts Crying (Yates), **Supp. XI:** 348
"Young Housewife, The" (W. C. Williams), **Retro. Supp. I:** 415
Young Immigrants, The (Lardner), **II:** 426
"Young Lady's Friend, The: Verses, Addressed to a Young Lady, on Her Leaving School" (Rowson), **Supp. XV:** 234
Young Landlords (Myers), **Supp. XXVII:** 204
"Young Lions" (E. P. Jones), **Supp. XXII:** 145
Young Lions, The (Shaw), **Supp. XIX: 248–249**
Young Lonigan: A Boyhood in Chicago Streets (Farrell), **II:** 31, 41
Young Manhood of Studs Lonigan, The (Farrell), **II:** 31, 34
"Young Man on the Go" (column, Siddons), **Supp. XXII:** 244
Young Martin's Promise (Myers), **Supp. XXVII:** 209
Young Men and Fire (Maclean), **Supp. XIV:** 221, **231–233**
Young People's Pride (Benét), **Supp. XI:** 44
Young Poet's Primer (Brooks), **Supp. III Part 1:** 86
Youngren, J. Alan, **Supp. XVI:** 174
"Young Sammy's First Wild Oats" (Santayana), **III:** 607, 615
"Young Sor Juana, The" (Mora), **Supp. XIII:** 218
"Your Arkansas Traveler" (Schulberg), **Supp. XVIII:** 252
"Your Dailiness" (Notley), **Supp. XXII:** 227
"Your Death" (Dove), **Supp. IV Part 1:** 250
"You're History" (Hampl), **Supp. XXII:** 84, 95
You're Only Old Once! (Geisel), **Supp. XVI:** 111
"You're Ugly, Too" (Moore), **Supp. X:** 171
"Your Face on the Dog's Neck" (Sexton), **Supp. II Part 2:** 686
"Your Hand, Your Hand" (Hoffman), **Supp. XVIII:** 79
Your Job in Germany (film, Capra), **Supp. XVI:** 102
Your Job in Japan (film, Capra), **Supp. XVI:** 102
"Your Life" (Stafford), **Supp. XI:** 329
"Your Mother's Eyes" (Kingsolver), **Supp. VII:** 209
Your Native Land, Your Life: Poems (Rich), **Retro. Supp. III:** 250–251
"You Take a Train through a Foreign Country" (Dobyns), **Supp. XIII:** 90
"Youth" (Hughes), **Supp. I Part 1:** 321; **Supp. XXII:** 12
"Youth" (Huncke), **Supp. XIV:** 145
Youth and Life (Bourne), **I:** 217–222, 232
Youth and the Bright Medusa (Cather), **I:** 322; **Retro. Supp. I:** 14
"Youthful Religious Experiences" (Corso), **Supp. XII:** 117
Youth of Parnassus, and Other Stories, The (L. P. Smith), **Supp. XIV:** 336
Youth's First Steps in Geography (Rowson), **Supp. XV:** 243
You Touched Me! (Williams and Windham), **IV:** 382, 385, 387, 390, 392–393
"You Touch Me" (X. J. Kennedy), **Supp. XV:** 166
You Went Away (Findley), **Supp. XX: 49**
"You Who Sleep Soundly Through Our Bleakest Hour" (Espaillat), **Supp. XXI:** 110
Yurchenco, Henrietta, **Supp. XVIII:** 20
Yurka, Blanche, **Supp. I Part 1:** 67
Yutang, Adet, **Supp. X:** 291
Yutang, Anor, **Supp. X:** 291
Yutang, Lin, **Supp. X:** 291; **Supp. XVI:** 190
Yutang, Mei-mei, **Supp. X:** 291
Yvernelle: A Legend of Feudal France (Norris), **III:** 314
Y & X (Olson), **Supp. II Part 2:** 556
Zabel, Morton Dauwen, **II:** 431; **III:** 194, 215; **Supp. I Part 2:** 721
Zach, Natan, **Supp. XV:** 75, 82, 85

Zaehner, R. C., **Supp. XXII:** 258
Zagajewski, Adam, **Supp. XVII:** 241
Zagarell, Sandra, **Supp. XV:** 269, 270, 278, 281, 282
Zagarell, Sandra A., **Retro. Supp. II:** 140, 143
"Zagrowsky Tells" (Paley), **Supp. VI:** 229
Zaino, Nick, **Supp. XXII:** 207
Zakrzewska, Marie, **Retro. Supp. II:** 146
Zaleski, Jeff, **Supp. XI:** 143; **Supp. XIX:** 54; **Supp. XXVI:** 158
Zall, Paul, **Supp. XIV:** 156
Zaltzberg, Charlotte, **Supp. IV Part 1:** 374
"Zambesi and Ranee" (Swenson), **Supp. IV Part 2:** 647
Zamir, Israel, **Retro. Supp. II:** 303, 317
Zamora, Bernice, **Supp. IV Part 2:** 545
Zamoyski, Adam, **Supp. XV:** 257
Zangwill, Israel, **I:** 229; **Supp. XX: 2**
Zanita: A Tale of the Yosemite (Yelverton), **Supp. IX:** 181
Zanuck, Darryl F., **Supp. XI:** 170; **Supp. XII:** 165
Zapata, Emiliano, **Supp. XIII:** 324
"Zapatos" (Boyle), **Supp. VIII:** 15
Zapruder, Matthew, **Supp. XVI:** 55; **Supp. XXVI:** 54
Zarathustra, **III:** 602
Zawacki, Andrew, **Supp. VIII:** 272
"Zaydee" (Levine), **Supp. V:** 186
Zebra-Striped Hearse, The (Macdonald), **Supp. IV Part 2:** 473
Zechariah (biblical book), **IV:** 152
Zeidner, Lisa, **Supp. IV Part 2:** 453; **Supp. XXIII:** 297
"Zeitl and Rickel" (Singer), **IV:** 20
Zeke and Ned (McMurtry and Ossana), **Supp. V:** 232
Zeke Proctor, Cherokee Outlaw (Conley), **Supp. V:** 232
Zelazny, Roger, **Supp. XXV:** 73
Zelazo, Suzanne, **Supp. XXII:** 158, 167
Zelda: A Biography (Milford), **Supp. IX:** 60
"Zelda and Scott: The Beautiful and Damned" (National Portrait Gallery exhibit), **Supp. IX:** 65
Zelig (film; Allen), **Supp. XV:** 4, 6, **8–9**
Zeller, Maya Jewell, **Supp. XXIV:** 167
Zen and the Birds of Appetite (Merton), **Supp. VIII:** 205–206, 208
Zend-Avesta (Fechner), **II:** 358
"Zenith: Walker Creek" (Davison), **Supp. XXVI:** 74
Zeno, **Retro. Supp. I:** 247
Zero db and Other Stories (Bell), **Supp. X:** 1, 5, 6
"Zeus over Redeye" (Hayden), **Supp. II Part 1:** 380
Zevi, Sabbatai, **IV:** 6
Ziegfeld, Florenz, **II:** 427–428
Ziegler, Cyd, **Supp. XX: 273**
Ziegler, Heidi, **Supp. XXII:** 260
Ziggurat (Balakian), **Supp. XXIII:** 19, **32–33**
Zigrosser, Carl, **I:** 226, 228, 231
Zigzagger (Muñoz), **Supp. XXV:** 127, 132, 133, 134
"Zigzagger" (Muñoz), **Supp. XXV:** 134
Zilles, Klaus, **Supp. XIX:** 112
Zimmerman, Paul D., **Supp. IV Part 2:** 583, 589, 590
Zimmerman, Robert. See Dylan, Bob
Zimmerman, Robert Allen. See Dylan, Bob
Zinberg, Leonard S. See Lacy, Ed
Zinman, Toby Silverman, **Supp. XIII:** 207–208, 209
Zinn, Howard, **Supp. V:** 289; **Supp. XXIV:** 87
Zinovyev, Grigory, **Supp. XXI:** 167
Zinsser, Hans, **I:** 251, 385
Zip: A Novel of the Left and Right (Apple), **Supp. XVII: 4–5**
Zipes, Jack, **Supp. XIV:** 126
"Zipper, The" (L. Michaels), **Supp. XVI:** 214
Zitkala-Ša (Gertrude Simmons Bonnin), **Supp. XXV: 271–287**
"Zizi's Lament" (Corso), **Supp. XII:** 123
Zodiac, The (Dickey), **Supp. IV Part 1:** 178, 183–184, 185
"Zog-19: A Scientific Romance"(P. Benedict), **Supp. XXIII:** 49
Zola, Émile, **I:** 211, 411, 474, 500, 502, 518; **II:** 174, 175–176, 182, 194, 275, 276, 281, 282, 319, 325, 337, 338; **III:** 315, 316, 317–318, 319–320, 321, 322, 323, 393, 511, 583; **IV:** 326; **Retro. Supp. I:** 226, 235; **Retro. Supp. II:** 93; **Supp. I Part 1:** 207; **Supp. II Part 1:** 117
Zolotow, Maurice, **III:** 161
"Zone" (Bogan), **Supp. III Part 1:** 60–61
Zone Journals (Wright), **Supp. V:** 332–333, 342–343
"Zooey" (Salinger), **III:** 564–565, 566, 567, 569, 572
"Zoo Revisited" (White), **Supp. I Part 2:** 654
Zoo Story, The (Albee), **I:** 71, 72–74, 75, 77, 84, 93, 94; **III:** 281
Zorach, William, **I:** 260
"Zora Neale Hurston's Dust Tracks: Autobiography and Artist Novel" (Snyder), **Retro. Supp. III:** 134
Zu-Bolton, Ahmos, **Supp. XXVII:** 166, 168
Zuccotti, Susan, **Supp. XVI:** 154
Zuckerman Bound: A Trilogy and Epilogue (P. Roth), **Supp. III Part 2:** 423
Zuckerman Unbound (P. Roth), **Retro. Supp. II:** 283; **Supp. III Part 2:** 421–422
Zueblin, Charles, **Supp. I Part 1:** 5
Zuger, Abigail, **Supp. X:** 160
Zukofsky, Celia (Mrs. Louis), **Supp. III Part 2:** 619–621, 623, 625, 626–629, 631
Zukofsky, Louis, **IV:** 415; **Retro. Supp. I:** 422; **Supp. III Part 2: 619–636; Supp. IV Part 1:** 154; **Supp. XIV:** 279, 282, 285, 286–287; **Supp. XXVI:** 224, 226, 227, 229
Zukofsky, Paul, **Supp. III Part 2:** 622, 623–626, 627, 628
Zuleika Dobson (Beerbohm), **Supp. I Part 2:** 714
Zulus (Everett), **Supp. XVIII:** 54, **56–57**
"Zuni Potter: Drawing the Heartline" (Bierds), **Supp. XVII:** 26
Zverev, Aleksei, **Retro. Supp. I:** 278
Zwinger, Ann, **Supp. X:** 29
Zyda, Joan, **Retro. Supp. II:** 52